WHITAKER'S
2021

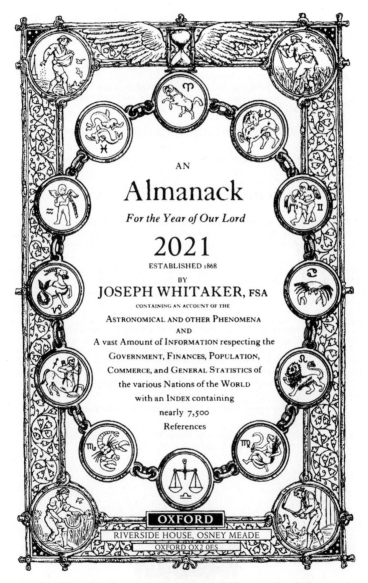

AN

Almanack

For the Year of Our Lord

2021

ESTABLISHED 1868

BY

JOSEPH WHITAKER, FSA

CONTAINING AN ACCOUNT OF THE

ASTRONOMICAL AND OTHER PHENOMENA

AND

A vast Amount of INFORMATION respecting the
GOVERNMENT, FINANCES, POPULATION,
COMMERCE, and GENERAL STATISTICS of
the various Nations of the WORLD
with an INDEX containing
nearly 7,500
References

OXFORD

RIVERSIDE HOUSE, OSNEY MEADE
OXFORD OX2 0ES

The traditional design of the title page for Whitaker's Almanack which has appeared in each edition since 1868

Published 2021 by Rebellion Publishing Ltd
Riverside House, Osney Mead, Oxford, OX2 0ES, UK

ISBN: 978-1-7810-8978-1 CONCISE EDITION: 978-1-7810-8979-8

REBELLION, WHITAKER'S, and the Whitaker's logo are trademarks of Rebellion Publishing Ltd

Published annually since 1868
153rd edition © Rebellion Publishing Ltd, 2021

A CIP catalogue record for this book is available from the British Library

Typeset by DLxml, a division of RefineCatch Limited, Bungay, Suffolk
Printed and bound in Italy by L.E.G.O. S.p.A.

To find out more about our publications visit www.rebellionpublishing.com

CONTENTS

THE WORLD

THE YEAR 2019–20

TIME AND SPACE

Lists and data underpin our modern information-driven society more than ever. It is refreshing to know that a positive, mild obsession with collecting facts is an ancient phenomenon, and the rise of the printed Almanack, in all its glorious forms before the digital revolution, is an expression of that human drive.

When we first heard that *Whitaker's* was going to cease publication, I was both sad, and intrigued that it was still even going. I had bought copies on many occasions over the years because I felt the contents might come in useful sometime. They have always done so for me, usually when I least expect it, and often to solve a dinner table discussion.

The idea of actually acquiring the book came a few days later when I realised that this beloved tome of things was valuable for its content, but also an important cultural icon. I felt that keeping it in print would be worth the investment of time, money and editorial effort.

At the time of going to press on *Whitaker's 2021*, the UK was once again in lockdown due to COVID-19, with the now-steady rollout of vaccines providing hope for tens of millions of people across the country, and indeed the world. Acquiring and producing a new edition of this wonderful tome presented its own unique challenges over the last year, from building a new team of editors, learning new processes and catching up on time lost between publishers. It would, perhaps, have been easy to miss this year, but the continuity of such a legendary resource in these difficult times, beset as we are by the rise of fake news, 'alternative facts' and conspiracy theories, has never been more vital. While there are sections of the book that are, regretfully, not updated this year, and a few that are missing due to the pressures of the pandemic, we are delighted that a huge amount of the book has been updated as usual. In particular, I would like to mention The Year 2019–20 section, and the many excellent articles on our arts, culture and heritage, as well as politics.

I hope those that buy it and flick through the pages occasionally find it valuable, as might future historians doggedly researching for details in a world whose digital databases have somehow been erased or are now inaccessible.

Jason Kingsley OBE
CEO, Rebellion
www.rebellionpublishing.com

COVER PHOTOGRAPHS

Main image: The Queen confers the honour of knighthood on Captain Sir Thomas Moore at Windsor Castle, on 17 July 2020 © Getty Images

Top, from left to right:
1. Jordan Henderson holds the Premier League Trophy aloft as Liverpool FC celebrate winning the league following their Premier League match against Chelsea FC at Anfield, Liverpool on 22 July 2020 © Getty Images
2. UK in lockdown due to the COVID-19 pandemic at Chessington, England on 30 March 2020 © Getty Images
3. Boris Johnson leaves Downing Street for Prime Minister's Questions a day after announcing new coronavirus restrictions, on 23 September 2020 © Getty Images
4. Artist's depiction of the COVID-19 coronavirus, by Radoslav Zilinsky © Getty Images

SOURCES

Whitaker's was compiled with the assistance of HM Revenue and Customs; The Met Office; Oxford Cartographers; Press Association; UK Hydrographic Office; and The World Bank.

Material was reproduced from (in addition to that indicated): *Abolitionist and Retentionist Countries 2019* © 2020 Amnesty International (**W** www.amnesty.org); *CIA World Factbook 2020; Corruption Perceptions Index 2019* © Transparency International licensed under CC-BY-ND 4.0 (**W** www.transparency.org); *Human Development Indicators* published by the UN Development Programme and *UN Statistics* published by UN data; *World Press Freedom Score 2020* © Reporters Without Borders; Stockholm International Peace Research Institute (SIPRI) 2019; *World Development Indicators* published by The World Bank; *World Economic Outlook Database 2019* © International Monetary Fund; UNESCO Institute for Statistics (UIS) 2020 (**W** www.uis.unesco.org/datacentre); Crown copyright material is reproduced with the permission of the Controller of Her Majesty's Stationery Office.

Government cabinet lists are sourced from *People in Power* © Cambridge International Reference on Current Affairs Ltd (**W** www.circaworld.com). People in Power provides a constantly updated service at www.peopleinpower.com

EDITORIAL STAFF
Chief Executive Officer: Jason Kingsley OBE
Chief Technical Officer: Chris Kingsley OBE
Head of Publishing: Ben Smith
Publishing Manager: Beth Lewis
Senior Commissioning Editor: Michael Rowley
Editors and Contributors: Kristen Mankosa; Dr Adam McKie
In-House Designer: Sam Gratton

Thanks to David Francis, Bridette Ledgerwood, Bryce Payton, Donna Scott, Paul Simpson and Kate Townshend. Thanks also to Ruth Northey.

CONTRIBUTORS (where not listed)
Sheridan Williams FRAS, Dr John Savage, John Flannery (Astronomy); Stephen Kershaw (Peerage); Anthea Lipsett (Education); Graham Bartram (Flags); Clive Longhurst (Insurance); Chris Priestley, John Huxley (Legal Notes, England & Wales); Richard McMeeken (Legal Notes, Scotland); Sarah Perkins (Taxation) and Sean Clarke (Weather)

Geomagnetism and Space Weather data supplied by Dr Susan Macmillan of the British Geological Survey.

THE YEAR 2021

THE YEAR 2021

CHRONOLOGICAL CYCLES AND ERAS

Dominical Letter	C
Epact	16
Golden Number (Lunar Cycle)	VIII
Julian Period	6734
Roman Indiction	14
Solar Cycle	14

	Beginning
*Muslim year AH 1442	19/20 Aug 2020
Japanese year Reiwa 3	1 Jan
Roman year 2774 AUC	14 Jan
Regnal year 70	6 Feb
Chinese year of the Ox	12 Feb
Sikh new year	14 Mar
Indian (Saka) year 1943	22 Mar
Hindu new year (Chaitra)	12 Apr
*Jewish year AM 5782	7 Sep

* Year begins at sunset on the previous day

RELIGIOUS CALENDARS

CHRISTIAN

Epiphany	6 Jan
Presentation of Christ in the Temple	2 Feb
Ash Wednesday	17 Feb
The Annunciation	25 Mar
Palm Sunday	28 Mar
Maundy Thursday	1 Apr
Good Friday	2 Apr
Easter Day (western churches)	4 Apr
Easter Day (Eastern Orthodox)	2 May
Rogation Sunday	9 May
Ascension Day	13 May
Pentecost (Whit Sunday)	23 May
Trinity Sunday	30 May
Corpus Christi	3 Jun
All Saints' Day	1 Nov
Advent Sunday	28 Nov
Christmas Day	25 Dec

HINDU

Makar Sankranti	14 Jan
Vasant Panchami (Sarasvati Puja)	16 Feb
Shivaratri	11 Mar
Holi	29 Mar
Chaitra (Spring new year)	12 Apr
Rama Navami	21 Apr
Raksha Bandhan	22 Aug
Krishna Janmashtami	30 Aug
Ganesh Chaturthi, first day	10 Sep
Navratri festival (Durga Puja), first day	7 Oct
Dussehra	14 Oct
Diwali (New Year festival of lights), first day	4 Nov

JEWISH

Purim	26 Feb
Pesach (Passover), first day	28 Mar
Shavuot (Feast of Weeks), first day	17 May
Rosh Hashanah (Jewish new year)	7 Sep
Yom Kippur (Day of Atonement)	16 Sep
Sukkot (Feast of Tabernacles), first day	21 Sep
Hanukkah (Festival of Lights), first day	28 Nov

MUSLIM†

Al-Hijra (Muslim new year)	20 Aug 2020
Ashura	29 Aug 2020
Ramadan, first day	13 April
Eid-ul-Fitr	13 May
Hajj, first day	17 Jul
Eid-ul-Adha	20 Jul

SIKH

Birthday of Guru Gobind Singh Ji	5 Jan
1 Chet (Sikh new year)	14 Mar
‡Hola Mohalla	29 Mar
Vaisakhi	14 Apr
Martyrdom of Guru Arjan Dev Ji	16 Jun
‡Birthday of Guru Nanak Dev Ji	19 Nov
Martyrdom of Guru Tegh Bahadur Ji	24 Nov

† The Islamic calendar is lunar so religious dates may vary by one or two days locally and according to when the new Moon is first seen
‡ Currently celebrated according to the lunar, rather than Nanakshahi, calendar, so the date varies annually

CIVIL CALENDAR

Duchess of Cambridge's birthday	9 Jan
Countess of Wessex's birthday	20 Jan
Accession of the Queen	6 Feb
Duke of York's birthday	19 Feb
St David's Day	1 Mar
Commonwealth Day	8 Mar
Earl of Wessex's birthday	10 Mar
St Patrick's Day	17 Mar
Birthday of the Queen	21 Apr
St George's Day	23 Apr
Coronation Day	2 Jun
Duke of Edinburgh's birthday	10 Jun
The Queen's Official Birthday	12 Jun
Duke of Cambridge's birthday	21 Jun
Duchess of Cornwall's birthday	17 Jul
Princess Royal's birthday	15 Aug
Lord Mayor's Day	13 Nov
Remembrance Sunday	14 Nov
Prince of Wales' birthday	14 Nov
Wedding Day of the Queen	20 Nov
St Andrew's Day	30 Nov

LEGAL CALENDAR

LAW TERMS

Hilary Term	11 Jan to 31 Mar
Easter Term	13 Apr to 28 May
Trinity Term	8 Jun to 30 Jul
Michaelmas Term	1 Oct to 21 Dec

QUARTER DAYS
(England, Wales & Northern Ireland)

Lady – 25 Mar	
Midsummer – 24 Jun	
Michaelmas – 29 Sep	
Christmas – 25 Dec	

TERM DAYS *(Scotland)*

Candlemas – 28 Feb	
Whitsunday – 28 May	
Lammas – 28 Aug	
Martinmas – 28 Nov	

2021

JANUARY
Sunday		3 10 17 24 31
Monday		4 11 18 25
Tuesday		5 12 19 26
Wednesday		6 13 20 27
Thursday		7 14 21 28
Friday	1	8 15 22 29
Saturday	2	9 16 23 30

FEBRUARY
Sunday		7 14 21 28
Monday	1	8 15 22
Tuesday	2	9 16 23
Wednesday	3	10 17 24
Thursday	4	11 18 25
Friday	5	12 19 26
Saturday	6	13 20 27

MARCH
Sunday		7 14 21 28
Monday	1	8 15 22 29
Tuesday	2	9 16 23 30
Wednesday	3	10 17 24 31
Thursday	4	11 18 25
Friday	5	12 19 26
Saturday	6	13 20 27

APRIL
Sunday		4 11 18 25
Monday		5 12 19 26
Tuesday		6 13 20 27
Wednesday		7 14 21 28
Thursday	1	8 15 22 29
Friday	2	9 16 23 30
Saturday	3	10 17 24

MAY
Sunday		2 9 16 23 30
Monday		3 10 17 24 31
Tuesday		4 11 18 25
Wednesday		5 12 19 26
Thursday		6 13 20 27
Friday		7 14 21 28
Saturday	1	8 15 22 29

JUNE
Sunday		6 13 20 27
Monday		7 14 21 28
Tuesday	1	8 15 22 29
Wednesday	2	9 16 23 30
Thursday	3	10 17 24
Friday	4	11 18 25
Saturday	5	12 19 26

JULY
Sunday		4 11 18 25
Monday		5 12 19 26
Tuesday		6 13 20 27
Wednesday		7 14 21 28
Thursday	1	8 15 22 29
Friday	2	9 16 23 30
Saturday	3	10 17 24 31

AUGUST
Sunday	1	8 15 22 29
Monday	2	9 16 23 30
Tuesday	3	10 17 24 31
Wednesday	4	11 18 25
Thursday	5	12 19 26
Friday	6	13 20 27
Saturday	7	14 21 28

SEPTEMBER
Sunday		5 12 19 26
Monday		6 13 20 27
Tuesday		7 14 21 28
Wednesday	1	8 15 22 29
Thursday	2	9 16 23 30
Friday	3	10 17 24
Saturday	4	11 18 25

OCTOBER
Sunday		3 10 17 24 31
Monday		4 11 18 25
Tuesday		5 12 19 26
Wednesday		6 13 20 27
Thursday		7 14 21 28
Friday	1	8 15 22 29
Saturday	2	9 16 23 30

NOVEMBER
Sunday		7 14 21 28
Monday	1	8 15 22 29
Tuesday	2	9 16 23 30
Wednesday	3	10 17 24
Thursday	4	11 18 25
Friday	5	12 19 26
Saturday	6	13 20 27

DECEMBER
Sunday		5 12 19 26
Monday		6 13 20 27
Tuesday		7 14 21 28
Wednesday	1	8 15 22 29
Thursday	2	9 16 23 30
Friday	3	10 17 24 31
Saturday	4	11 18 25

PUBLIC HOLIDAYS

	England and Wales	Scotland	Northern Ireland
New Year	1 January†	1, 4† January	1 January†
St Patrick's Day	—	—	17 March
*Good Friday	2 April	2 April	2 April
Easter Monday	5 April	—	5 April
Early May	3 May†	3 May	3 May†
Spring	31 May	31 May†	31 May
Battle of the Boyne	—	—	12 July‡
Summer	30 August	2 August	30 August
St Andrew's Day	—	30 November§	—
*Christmas	27, 28 December	27†, 28 December	27, 28 December

* In England, Wales and Northern Ireland, Christmas Day and Good Friday are common law holidays
† Subject to royal proclamation
‡ Subject to proclamation by the Secretary of State for Northern Ireland
§ The St Andrew's Day Holiday (Scotland) Bill was approved by parliament on 29 November 2006; it does not oblige employers to change their existing pattern of holidays but provides the legal framework in which the St Andrew's Day bank holiday could be substituted for an existing local holiday from another date in the year
Note: In the Channel Islands, Liberation Day is a bank and public holiday

2022

JANUARY							FEBRUARY						MARCH					
Sunday		2	9	16	25	30	Sunday		6	13	20	27	Sunday		6	13	20	27
Monday		3	10	17	26	31	Monday		7	14	21	28	Monday		7	14	21	28
Tuesday		4	11	18	27		Tuesday	1	8	15	22		Tuesday	1	8	15	22	29
Wednesday		5	12	19	26		Wednesday	2	9	16	23		Wednesday	2	9	16	23	30
Thursday		6	13	20	27		Thursday	3	10	17	24		Thursday	3	10	17	24	31
Friday		7	14	21	28		Friday	4	11	18	25		Friday	4	11	18	25	
Saturday	1	8	15	22	29		Saturday	5	12	19	26		Saturday	5	12	19	26	

APRIL							MAY							JUNE					
Sunday		3	10	17	24		Sunday	1	8	15	22	29		Sunday		5	12	19	26
Monday		4	11	18	25		Monday	2	9	16	23	30		Monday		6	13	20	27
Tuesday		5	12	19	26		Tuesday	3	10	17	24	31		Tuesday		7	14	21	28
Wednesday		6	13	20	27		Wednesday	4	11	18	25			Wednesday	1	8	15	22	29
Thursday		7	14	21	28		Thursday	5	12	19	26			Thursday	2	9	16	23	30
Friday	1	8	15	22	29		Friday	6	13	20	27			Friday	3	10	17	24	
Saturday	2	9	16	23	30		Saturday	7	14	21	28			Saturday	4	11	18	25	

JULY							AUGUST						SEPTEMBER					
Sunday		3	10	17	25		Sunday		7	14	21	28	Sunday		4	11	18	25
Monday		4	11	18	26		Monday	1	8	15	22	29	Monday		5	12	19	26
Tuesday		5	12	19	27		Tuesday	2	9	16	23	30	Tuesday		6	13	20	27
Wednesday		6	13	20	28		Wednesday	3	10	17	24	31	Wednesday		7	14	21	28
Thursday		7	14	21	29		Thursday	4	11	18	25		Thursday	1	8	15	22	29
Friday	1	8	15	23	30		Friday	5	12	19	26		Friday	2	9	16	23	30
Saturday	2	9	16	24	31		Saturday	6	13	20	27		Saturday	3	10	17	24	

OCTOBER							NOVEMBER						DECEMBER					
Sunday		2	9	16	23	30	Sunday		6	13	20	27	Sunday		4	11	18	25
Monday		3	10	17	24	31	Monday		7	14	21	28	Monday		5	12	19	26
Tuesday		4	11	18	25		Tuesday	1	8	15	22	29	Tuesday		6	13	20	27
Wednesday		5	12	19	26		Wednesday	2	9	16	23	30	Wednesday		7	14	21	28
Thursday		6	13	20	27		Thursday	3	10	17	24		Thursday	1	8	15	22	29
Friday		7	14	21	28		Friday	4	11	18	25		Friday	2	9	16	23	30
Saturday	1	8	15	22	29		Saturday	5	12	19	26		Saturday	3	10	17	24	31

PUBLIC HOLIDAYS

	England and Wales	Scotland	Northern Ireland
New Year	1 January†	1, 4† January	1 January†
St Patrick's Day	—	—	17 March
*Good Friday	15 April	15 April	15 April
Easter Monday	18 April	—	18 April
Early May	2 May†	2 May	2 May†
Spring	2 June	2 June†	2 June
Battle of the Boyne	—	—	12 July‡
Summer	30 August	2 August	30 August
St Andrew's Day	—	30 November§	—
*Christmas	26, 27 December	26†, 27 December	26, 27 December

* In England, Wales and Northern Ireland, Christmas Day and Good Friday are common law holidays
† Subject to royal proclamation
‡ Subject to proclamation by the Secretary of State for Northern Ireland
§ The St Andrew's Day Holiday (Scotland) Bill was approved by parliament on 29 November 2006; it does not oblige employers to change their existing pattern of holidays but provides the legal framework in which the St Andrew's Day bank holiday could be substituted for an existing local holiday from another date in the year
Note: In the Channel Islands, Liberation Day is a bank and public holiday

FORTHCOMING EVENTS

Due to the impact of the coronavirus pandemic, the format and
dates of many of these events may change.

JANUARY 2021
14–24	London Short Film Festival (online)
15–2 Feb	Celtic Connections Music Festival (online only)
20–31	London Art Fair, Business Design Centre (online only)
29–31	RSPB Big Garden Birdwatch

FEBRUARY
2	World Wetlands Day
3– 21	Leicester Comedy Festival (online)

MARCH
3	World Wildlife Day
4	World Book Day
5–14	Belfast Children's Festival
8	International Women's Day
21	World Poetry Day
26–11 Apr	Ideal Home Show, Olympia, London

APRIL
11	British Academy Film Awards, Royal Opera House, London
22	Earth Day
25	Academy Awards, Los Angeles

MAY
8–16	Stratford-upon-Avon Literary Festival
18–23	RHS Chelsea Flower Show, Royal Hospital, London
20–29 August	Glyndebourne Festival
27–6 June	Hay Festival of Literature and the Arts, Hay-on-Wye
29–30	Bath Festival

JUNE
12	Trooping the Colour, Horse Guards Parade, London
17–20	Isle of Wight Festival
17–20	Royal Highland Show, Edinburgh
Late June	Glastonbury Festival of Contemporary Performing Arts, Somerset
26	Pride Parade, London
29–1 July	London Book Fair, Olympia, London

JULY
2–9	Cheltenham Music Festival
6–11	RHS Hampton Court Palace Flower Show, Surrey
15–18	Crufts Dog Show, NEC, Birmingham
16–18	Tolpuddle Martyrs Festival, Dorset
17–24	The Welsh Proms, St David's Hall, Cardiff
Mid Jul–11 Sep	BBC Promenade Concerts, Royal Albert Hall, London
21–25	RHS Flower Show, Tatton Park, Cheshire
22–25	WOMAD Festival, Charlton Park, Wiltshire
24–31	Three Choirs Festival, Worcester
29–1 Aug	Cambridge Folk Festival
31–7 Aug	National Eisteddfod of Wales, Ceredigion County

AUGUST
6–28	Edinburgh Military Tattoo, Edinburgh Castle
6–29	Edinburgh International Festival
7–8	Brighton Pride, Brighton and Hove
29–30	Notting Hill Carnival, London

SEPTEMBER
3–7 Nov	Blackpool Illuminations, Blackpool Promenade
4	Braemar Royal Highland Gathering, Aberdeenshire
8	International Literacy Day
12–15	TUC Annual Congress
Mid–Late Sept	Liberal Democrat Party Conference
25–29	Labour Party Conference
Sep–Oct	Conservative Party Conference

OCTOBER
13–17	Frieze Art Fair, Regent's Park, London
Mid Oct	Booker Prize Awards
Mid Oct	BFI London Film Festival

NOVEMBER
13	Lord Mayor's Procession and Show, City of London
Mid Nov	CBI Annual Conference

SPORTS EVENTS

JANUARY 2021

9–24	Bowls: World Indoor Bowls Championships, Hopton-on-Sea
10–17	Snooker: Masters, Marshall Arena, Milton Keynes
14–26	Cricket: England tour Sri Lanka, two-Test series

FEBRUARY

6–20 Mar	Rugby Union: Six Nations Championship, Europe
5–8 March	Cricket: England tour India, four-Test series
7	American Football: Super Bowl 55, Tampa, Florida, USA
10–22	Tennis: Australian Open, Melbourne

MARCH

16–19	Horse Racing: Cheltenham Festival
27	Gymnastics: World Cup, Birmingham

APRIL

1–3 Oct	Baseball: Major League Baseball Season
4	Rowing: The Boat Race, Putney to Mortlake, London
8–10	Horse Racing: Grand National, Aintree, Liverpool
10–11	Golf: Masters, Augusta, Georgia, USA
17–3 May	Snooker: World Championship, Crucible Theatre, Sheffield
25	Football: EFL Cup final, Wembley Stadium, London
30–1 May	Horse Racing: Kentucky Derby, Louisville, Kentucky, USA

MAY

5–9	Equestrian: Badminton Horse Trials, Badminton
8	Football: Scottish Cup Final, Hampden Park, Glasgow
10–23	Aquatics: European Championships, Budapest, Hungary
12–16	Equestrian: Royal Windsor Horse Show, Home Park, Windsor
15	Football: FA Cup Final, Wembley Stadium, London
16	Football: Women's Champions League Final, Gamla Ullevi, Gothenburg, Sweden
20–23	Formula 1: Monaco Grand Prix, Monte Carlo
20–23	Golf: US PGA Championship, Ocean Course, Kiawah Island, South Carolina
22	Football: Women's FA Cup Final, Wembley Stadium, London
22	Rugby Union: European Challenge Cup Final & European Champions Cup Final, Stade de Marseille, France
23–6 Jun	Tennis: French Open, Paris
26	Football: UEFA Europa League Final, Stadion Miejski, Gdansk, Poland
28	Motor Racing: Indianapolis 500, Indiana, USA
29	Football: UEFA Champions League Final, Atatürk Olympic Stadium, Istanbul, Turkey

JUNE

4–5	Horse Racing: The Derby, Epsom Downs, Surrey
11–11 Jul	Football: UEFA Euro 2020
15–19	Horse Racing: Royal Ascot, Berkshire
17–20	Golf: US Open, Torrey Pines Golf Course, San Diego, California
26–18 Jul	Cycling: Tour de France
28–11 Jul	Tennis: Wimbledon Championships, All England Lawn Tennis Club, London
29–4 Jul	Rowing: Henley Royal Regatta, Henley-on-Thames

JULY

13	Athletics: Diamond League Anniversary Games, London Stadium
15–18	Golf: Open Championship, Royal St Georges, Kent
17	Rugby League: Challenge Cup Final, Wembley Stadium, London
18	Formula 1: British Grand Prix, Silverstone, Northamptonshire
23–8 Aug	XXXII Summer Olympic Games, Tokyo, Japan
Late Jul–Aug	Cricket: The Hundred, England

AUGUST

4–14 Sep	Cricket: India tour England, five-Test series
19–22	Golf: Women's British Open, Carnoustie, Angus, Scotland
24–5 Sep	Athletics: Summer Paralympic Games, Tokyo, Japan
30–12 Sep	Tennis: US Open, New York

SEPTEMBER

Early Sep–Late Dec	American Football: NFL Season
2–5	Equestrian: Burghley Horse Trials, Stamford, Lincolnshire
12	Athletics: Great North Run, Newcastle
18–16 Oct	Rugby Union: Women's Rugby World Cup, New Zealand
24–26	Golf: 43rd Ryder Cup, Whistling Straits, Wisconsen, USA
27–1 Oct	Cricket: Bob Willis Trophy Final, Lord's, London

OCTOBER

3	Athletics: London Marathon
9	Rugby League: Super League Grand Final, Old Trafford, Manchester
13–17	Cycling: UCI Track Cycling World Championships, Ashgabat, Turkmenistan
18–15 Nov	Cricket: ICC T20 Men's World Cup, India
23–27 Nov	Rugby League: Rugby League World Cup, England
Late Oct–Early Nov	Baseball: World Series

NOVEMBER

1	Athletics: New York City Marathon, New York, USA
14–21	Tennis: ATP World Tour Finals, Pala Alpitour, Turin
22–28	Tennis: Davis Cup Finals, Madrid, Spain
23–5 Dec	Snooker: UK Championship, Barbican Centre, York
Late Nov–Jan 2022	Cricket: The Ashes, Australia, five-Test series

14

CENTENARIES

2020

1520
7 Jun   A summit between England and France began in the Field of the Cloth of Gold
30 Sep   Suleiman the Magnificent succeeded his father Selim I as Ottoman Sultan
21 Oct   The islands of St Pierre and Miquelon were discovered by explorer Joao Alvares Fagundes
28 Nov   Ferdinand Magellan and his fleet became the first Europeans to sail into the Pacific Ocean

1620
16 May   William Adams, navigator, died
7 Aug   Johannes Kepler's mother was arrested for witchcraft
8 Nov   Catholic forces were victorious in the Battle of White Mountain (Thirty Years' War 1618–48)
11 Nov   The *Mayflower* anchored at Cape Cod
31 Oct   John Evelyn, writer, born

1720
10 Feb   Edmond Halley was appointed the second Astronomer Royal at the Greenwich Observatory
17 Feb   The War of the Quadruple Alliance ended with the Treaty of The Hague
6 Mar   Pieter van Bloemen, Flemish painter, died
6 Apr   The South Sea bill was passed in the House of Lords
25 May   The ship *Grand-Saint-Antoine* arrived in Marseille, bringing Europe's last major plague outbreak, which killed around 100,000
15 Nov   Female pirates Anne Bonny and Mary Read are captured in Jamaica along with Captain 'Calico Jack' Rackham and his crew
29 Dec   Theatre Royal Haymarket, then called the 'Hay Market', opens with the play *La Fille à la Mode*

1820
17 Jan   Anne Brontë, novelist and poet, born
29 Jan   King George IV ascended to the throne on the death of his father George III, ending the English Regency
30 Jan   Captain Edward Bransfield became the first person to sight the Antarctic mainland
10 Mar   The Royal Astronomical Society was founded in London
15 Mar   Maine became the 23rd state of the Union, following the Missouri Compromise
11 May   HMS *Beagle,* the ship that carried Charles Darwin on his scientific voyage, was launched
12 May   Florence Nightingale, social reformer and statistician, born
26 Jul   Union Bridge, crossing the River Tweed between England and Scotland, opened
1 Aug   The second half of the Regent's Canal in London, from Camden to Limehouse, was completed
28 Nov   Friedrich Engels, German political philosopher, born

1920
2 Jan   Isaac Asimov, American writer and biochemist, born
10 Jan   The Covenant of the League of Nations came into force
16 Jan   Alcohol Prohibition came into effect nationwide in the USA

23 Jan   Queen Wilhelmina of the Netherlands refused to extradite former German Kaiser Wilhelm II
2 Feb   Soviet Russia recognised the independence of the Republic of Estonia in the Treaty of Tartu
16 May   Joan of Arc (Jeanne d'Arc) was canonised by Pope Benedict XV
21 May   Mexican President Venustiano Carranza was executed by army generals
4 Jun   The Allied Powers defined the borders of the Kingdom of Hungary at the Treaty of Trianon
12 Jul   Soviet Russia recognised the sovereignty of Lithuania
10 Aug   The Treaty of Sèvres abolished the Ottoman Empire
11 Aug   Soviet Russia recognised Latvia's independence in the Treaty of Riga
14 Aug   The Games of the VII Olympiad opened in Antwerp, Belgium
16 Aug   Charles Bukowski, American writer, born
18 Aug   The 19th Amendment to the US Constitution was ratified, granting American women the right to vote
1 Sep   Greater Lebanon was declared a state under the French Mandate for Syria and the Lebanon
29 Sep   Peter D. Mitchell, Nobel Prize winning biochemist, born
2 Nov   Warren G. Harding was elected President of the USA
10 Dec   The Nobel Peace Prize was awarded to US president Woodrow Wilson

2021

1521
3 Jan   Pope Leo X excommunicated the German priest Martin Luther from the Roman Catholic church
28 Jan   Charles V, Holy Roman Emperor, opened the Diet of Worms
17 Mar   Portuguese navigator Ferdinand Magellan reached the Philippines
20 Apr   Zhengde, 11th Emperor of the Ming dynasty, died
23 Apr   Royalists defeated the *comuneros* at the Battle at Villalar
27 Apr   Portuguese navigator Ferdinand Magellan killed by Filipino natives
25 May   The Edict of Worms, outlawing Martin Luther, was issued
13 Aug   The Battle of Tenochtitlan ended with the capture of Cuauhtemoc, last Aztec Emperor
1 Dec   Takeda Shingen, Japanese warlord, born
13 Dec   King Manuel I of Portugal, died

1621
28 Jan   Pope Paul V, persecutor of Galileo, died
9 Feb   Alessandro Ludovisi was elected as Pope Gregory XV
31 Mar   King Philip of Spain (III) and Portugal (II), died
5 Apr   The *Mayflower* set sail from Plymouth, USA on its return voyage to England
3 May   Francis Bacon was accused of bribery
8 Jun   Anne de Xainctonge, founder of the first non-cloistered women's religious community, died
9 Oct   The Ottoman Empire and the Polish-Lithuanian Commonwealth signed the Treaty of Khotyn

1721

19 Mar	Pope Clement XI, died
3 Apr	Robert Walpole was appointed First Lord of the Treasury; *de facto* first prime minister of Great Britain
8 May	Michelangelo dei Conti was elected Pope Innocent XIII
30 Aug	Russia and Sweden signed the Treaty of Nystad, ending the Great Northern War
2 Nov	Tsar Peter I declared Emperor of All Russia
29 Dec	Madame De Pompadour, mistress of King Louis XV of France, born

1821

23 Feb	John Keats, English Romantic poet, died
5 May	Napoleon Bonaparte, military leader and Emperor of France, died
19 Jul	George IV was crowned king of the United Kingdom of Great Britain and Ireland
5 Aug	Bellingshausen's Russian Antarctic expedition, arrived back in Kronstadt
24 Aug	The Treaty of Córdoba was signed by Mexican and Spanish officials
15 Sep	Guatemala enacted the Act of Independence of Central America

1921

4 Feb	Betty Friedan, American feminist and author of *The Feminine Mystique,* born
17 Mar	Dr Marie Stopes opened Britain's first birth control clinic in London
19 Mar	Tommy Cooper, British comedian, born
7 June	The Parliament of Northern Ireland sat for the first time
23 Jul	The Communist Party of China was founded
29 Jul	Adolf Hitler assumed the leadership of the National Socialist German Workers' Party
31 Oct	The Fédération Sportive Féminine Internationale was formed
9 Nov	Benito Mussolini formed the National Fascist Party in Italy
23 Nov	US president Warren G. Harding signed the Willis-Campbell Act, prohibiting the medical prescription of beer or liquor
6 Dec	Anglo-Irish Treaty was signed, marking the end of the Irish War of Independence

2022

1322

14 Oct	King Edward II of England was defeated by Robert the Bruce of Scotland at the Battle of Old Byland

1422

31 Aug	King Henry V died while in France. Henry VI became King of England, aged nine months

1522

6 Sep	Spanish carrack *Nao Victoria* became the first ship to circumnavigate the world
21 Sep	Martin Luther published a translation of the New Testament in German
22 Oct	An earthquake destroyed the original capital of Vila Franca do Campo on Sao Miguel Island

1622

20 May	Osman II, Sultan of the Ottoman Empire, was murdered by his Janissaries
6 Sep	A fleet of Spanish treasure ships sank off the Florida Keys; discovered in 1985, it was later declared the most valuable shipwreck in the world

1722

10 Feb	Notorious pirate Bartholomew 'Black Bart' Roberts was killed off the coast of West Africa
5 Apr	Dutch explorer Jacob Roggeveen became the first European to discover Easter Island, subsequently naming it
27 Sep	Samuel Adams, Founding Father of the United States, born
20 Dec	Kangxi, Emperor of the Qing dynasty, died after a 61-year reign

1822

1 Jan	The Greek Constitution was adopted by the First National Assembly at Epidaurus during the Greek War of Independence
16 Feb	Sir Francis Galton, English polymath, born
25 Apr	Monrovia in Liberia was founded by the American Colonization Society with the aim of sending black American slaves 'back to Africa'
27 Apr	Ulysses S. Grant, 18th US President, born
8 Jul	Percy Shelley, English Romantic poet, died
20 Jul	Gregor Mendel, Czech geneticist, born
7 Sep	Brazil declared its independence from Portugal
27 Sep	French scholar Jean-François Champollion announced he had deciphered Egyptian hieroglyphs using the Rosetta Stone
1 Dec	Pedro I was crowned the first Emperor of Brazil
27 Dec	Louis Pasteur, French microbiologist and chemist, born

1922

5 Jan	Sir Ernest Shackleton, Anglo-Irish explorer, died
2 Feb	*Ulysses* by Irish author James Joyce was published
15 Feb	The inaugural session of the Permanent Court of International Justice was held at The Hague
28 Feb	Britain ended its protectorate over Egypt through a Unilateral Declaration of Independence, nominally granting independence
18 Mar	Mahatma Gandhi was sentenced to six years in prison for sedition in British India
3 Apr	Joseph Stalin was appointed General Secretary of the Communist Party of the Soviet Union
24 Jun	Walther Rathenau, German Foreign Minister and architect of the Treaty of Rapallo, was assassinated by right-wing militants
20 Jul	The German protectorate of Togoland was formally divided into French Togoland and British Togoland
18 Oct	The BBC was formed, and began broadcasting on 14 November
31 Oct	King Victor Emmanuel III appointed Benito Mussolini, leader of the National Fascist Party, as Prime Minister of Italy following the March on Rome
1 Nov	The Ottoman Empire was dissolved, and the sultanate was abolished
4 Nov	British archaeologist Howard Carter's crew discovered the entrance to Pharaoh Tutankhamun's tomb in the Valley of the Kings
18 Nov	Marcel Proust, French author, died
6 Dec	The Irish Free State officially came into existence
30 Dec	The Union of Soviet Socialist Republics was formed

THE UNITED KINGDOM

THE UK IN FIGURES

The United Kingdom comprises Great Britain (England, Wales and Scotland) and Northern Ireland. The Isle of Man and the Channel Islands are Crown dependencies with their own legislative systems and are not part of the UK.

ABBREVIATIONS
ONS — Office for National Statistics
NISRA — Northern Ireland Statistics and Research Agency

All data is for the UK unless otherwise stated.

AREA OF THE UNITED KINGDOM

	Sq. km	Sq. miles
United Kingdom	243,122	93,870
England	130,280	50,301
Wales	20,733	8,005
Scotland	77,958	30,100
Northern Ireland	14,150	5,463

Source: ONS (Crown copyright)

POPULATION

The first official census of population in England, Wales and Scotland was taken in 1801 and a census has been taken every ten years since, except in 1941 when there was no census because of the Second World War. The last official census in the UK was taken on 27 March 2011.

The first official census of population in Ireland was taken in 1841. However, all figures given below refer only to the area which is now Northern Ireland. Figures for Northern Ireland in 1921 and 1931 are estimates based on the censuses taken in 1926 and 1937 respectively.

Estimates of the population of England before 1801, calculated from the number of baptisms, burials and marriages, are:

1570	4,160,221	1670	5,773,646
1600	4,811,718	1700	6,045,008
1630	5,600,517	1750	6,517,035

Further details are available on the ONS website (**W** www.ons.gov.uk).

CENSUS RESULTS (THOUSANDS)

	United Kingdom			England and Wales			Scotland			Northern Ireland		
	Total	Male	Female	Total	Male	Female	Total	Male	Female	Total	Male	Female
1801	–	–	–	8,893	4,255	4,638	1,608	739	869	–	–	–
1811	13,368	6,368	7,000	10,165	4,874	5,291	1,806	826	980	–	–	–
1821	15,472	7,498	7,974	12,000	5,850	6,150	2,092	983	1,109	–	–	–
1831	17,835	8,647	9,188	13,897	6,771	7,126	2,364	1,114	1,250	–	–	–
1841	20,183	9,819	10,364	15,914	7,778	8,137	2,620	1,242	1,378	1,649	800	849
1851	22,259	10,855	11,404	17,928	8,781	9,146	2,889	1,376	1,513	1,443	698	745
1861	24,525	11,894	12,631	20,066	9,776	10,290	3,062	1,450	1,612	1,396	668	728
1871	27,431	13,309	14,122	22,712	11,059	11,653	3,360	1,603	1,757	1,359	647	712
1881	31,015	15,060	15,955	25,974	12,640	13,335	3,736	1,799	1,936	1,305	621	684
1891	34,264	16,593	17,671	29,003	14,060	14,942	4,026	1,943	2,083	1,236	590	646
1901	38,237	18,492	19,745	32,528	15,729	16,799	4,472	2,174	2,298	1,237	590	647
1911	42,082	20,357	21,725	36,070	17,446	18,625	4,761	2,309	2,452	1,251	603	648
1921	44,027	21,033	22,994	37,887	18,075	19,811	4,882	2,348	2,535	1,258	610	648
1931	46,038	22,060	23,978	39,952	19,133	20,819	4,843	2,326	2,517	1,243	601	642
1951	50,225	24,118	26,107	43,758	21,016	22,742	5,096	2,434	2,662	1,371	668	703
1961	52,709	25,481	27,228	46,105	22,304	23,801	5,179	2,483	2,697	1,425	694	731
1971	55,515	26,952	28,562	48,750	23,683	25,067	5,229	2,515	2,714	1,536	755	781
1981	55,848	27,104	28,742	49,155	23,873	25,281	5,131	2,466	2,664	*1,533	750	783
1991	56,467	27,344	29,123	49,890	24,182	25,707	4,999	2,392	2,607	1,578	769	809
2001	58,789	28,581	30,208	52,042	25,327	26,715	5,062	2,432	2,630	1,685	821	864
2011	63,182	31,028	32,153	56,076	27,574	28,502	5,295	2,567	2,728	1,810	887	923

* Figure includes 44,500 non-enumerated persons

ISLANDS

	Isle of Man			Jersey			Guernsey		
	Total	Male	Female	Total	Male	Female	Total	Male	Female
1901	54,752	25,496	29,256	52,576	23,940	28,636	40,446	19,652	20,794
1921	60,284	27,329	32,955	49,701	22,438	27,263	38,315	18,246	20,069
1951	55,123	25,749	29,464	57,296	27,282	30,014	43,652	21,221	22,431
1971	56,289	26,461	29,828	72,532	35,423	37,109	51,458	24,792	26,666
1991	69,788	33,693	36,095	84,082	40,862	43,220	58,867	28,297	30,570
2001	76,315	37,372	38,943	87,186	42,485	44,701	59,807	29,138	30,669
2006	80,058	39,523	40,535	–	–	–	–	–	–
2011	84,497	41,971	42,526	97,857	48,296	49,561	62,915	31,025	31,890

Source: Guernsey Annual Publication Bulletin, Isle of Man Government, States of Jersey Statistics Unit

RESIDENT POPULATION

ACTUAL AND PROJECTED BY COUNTRY
people, thousands

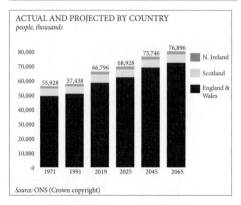

Source: ONS (Crown copyright)

PROJECTED AGE DISTRIBUTION, 2019 AND 2065
percentage

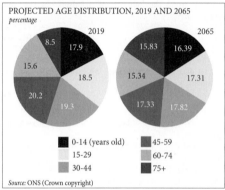

Source: ONS (Crown copyright)

NON-UK BORN RESIDENTS BY COUNTRY OF BIRTH
thousands

	2004	2019
India	94	863
Poland	505	813
Pakistan	285	546
Romania	–	427
Republic of Ireland	453	359
Germany	276	290
Bangladesh	–	260
South Africa	181	251
Italy	228	234
China	152	217

Source: ONS (Crown Copyright)

BY AGE AND SEX (UK), 2018
people, thousands

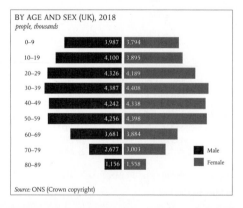

Source: ONS (Crown copyright)

ASYLUM

NATIONALITIES APPLYING FOR UK ASYLUM
in the year ending June

Top 5 Nationalities	2019	2020
1) Iran	4,900	5,169
2) Albania	3,559	3,630
3) Iraq	4,198	3,478
4) Pakistan	2,520	2,172
5) Eritrea	2,294	1,850

Source: Home Office, National Statistics: Asylum

BIRTHS

	Live births 2018	Birth rate 2018*
United Kingdom	731,213	11.0
England and Wales	657,076	11.1
Scotland	51,308	9.4
Northern Ireland	22,829	12.1

* Live births per 1,000 population
Source: ONS (Crown copyright)

FERTILITY RATES
Total fertility rate is the average number of children which would be born to a woman if she experienced the age-specific fertility rates of the period in question throughout her child-bearing life span. The figures for the years 1960–2 are estimates.

	1960–2	2000	2018
United Kingdom	3.07	1.62	1.68
England and Wales	2.77	1.65	1.70
Scotland	2.98	1.48	1.42
Northern Ireland	3.47	1.75	1.85

Source: General Register Office for Scotland, NISRA, ONS (Crown copyright)

MATERNITY RATES FOR ENGLAND AND WALES 2019

	All maternities*	Singleton	All multiple	Twins	Triplets
All ages	633,086	623,430	9,656†	9,513	137
>20	17,683	17,568	115	115	0
20–24	86,260	85,405	855	849	5
25–29	172,301	170,033	2,268	2,242	25
30–34	207,331	204,033	3,298	3,259	39
35–39	120,559	118,216	2,298	2,258	38
40-44	26,700	26,042	658	641	16
45+	2,228	2,065	163	148	14

* Includes stillbirths
† Total includes live maternities of quads and above
Source: ONS (Crown copyright)

TOP TEN BABY NAMES (ENGLAND AND WALES)

	1904 Girls	1904 Boys	2019 Girls	2019 Boys
1	Mary	William	Olivia	Oliver
2	Florence	John	Amelia	George
3	Doris	George	Ilsa	Noah
4	Edith	Thomas	Ava	Arthur
5	Dorothy	Arthur	Mia	Harry
6	Anne	James	Isabella	Leo
7	Margaret	Charles	Sophia	Muhammad
8	Alice	Frederick	Grace	Jack
9	Elizabeth	Albert	Lily	Charlie
10	Elsie	Ernest	Freya	Oscar

Source: ONS (Crown copyright)

LIVE BIRTHS (ENGLAND AND WALES)
by age of mother

Year	under 20	20-29	30-39	40+	All ages
1949	31,850	446,198	224,759	27,711	730,518
1959	46,067	462,643	220,736	19,055	748,501
1969	81,659	527,393	173,238	15,248	797,538
1979	59,143	415,311	157,058	6,516	638,028
1989	55,543	428,061	194,785	9,336	687,725
1999	48,375	292,653	266,592	14,252	621,872
2009	43,243	330,141	305,888	26,976	706,248
2019	17,720	260,700	332,314	29,618	640,370

Source: ONS (Crown copyright)

MARRIAGE AND DIVORCE

	Marriages 2016–17	Divorces 2016–17
England and Wales	249,793	101,669
Scotland	28,440	7,938
Northern Ireland	8,306	2,089

Source: NISRA, ONS (Crown copyright), Scottish Government

LEGAL ABORTIONS

	2005	2018
England and Wales	186,416	200,608
Scotland	12,665	13,286

Source: Department of Health, NHS Scotland

DEATHS

INFANT MORTALITY RATE 2017*

United Kingdom	3.9
England and Wales	3.9
Scotland	3.2
Northern Ireland	4.2

* Deaths of infants under one year of age per 1,000 live births
Source: NISRA, ONS (Crown copyright), Scottish Government

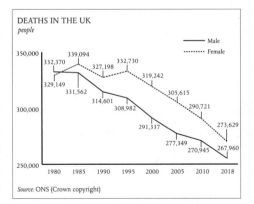

DEATHS IN THE UK
people

Source: ONS (Crown copyright)

EMPLOYMENT

MEDIAN FULL-TIME GROSS ANNUAL EARNINGS BY REGION (£)

Region	2005	2018
UK	22,888	29,574
England	23,280	29,005
North East	20,263	26,297
North West	21,777	27,315
Yorkshire and the Humber	21,506	26,894
East Midlands	21,494	26,749
West Midlands	21,447	27,716
East	22,883	29,128
London	29,882	38,826
South East	24,229	30,826
South West	21,279	27,969
Wales	20,634	26,346
Scotland	21,312	29,274
Northern Ireland	20,060	27,006

Source: ONS (Crown Copyright)

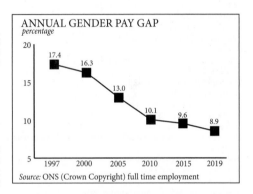

ANNUAL GENDER PAY GAP
percentage

Source: ONS (Crown Copyright) full time employment

OVERSEAS VISITS TO THE UK

Year	Visits (thousands)	Spending (£m)
1980	12,419	2,961
1985	14,450	5,442
1990	18,017	7,748
1995	23,538	11,762
2000	25,207	12,806
2005	29,970	14,247
2010	29,804	16,714
2011	30,798	17,998
2012	31,085	18,640
2013	32,689	21,259
2014	34,380	21,851
2015	36,115	22,072
2016	37,610	22,544
2017	39,214	24.507
2018	37,905	22,897
2019	40,900	28,400

DEATHS BY CAUSE, 2017

	England and Wales	Scotland	N. Ireland
Total deaths	533,253	57,883	16,036
Deaths from natural causes	512,027	54,731	15,757
Certain infectious and parasitic diseases	5,368	686	212
Intestinal infectious diseases	1,259	128	24
Respiratory and other tuberculosis	153	10	3
Meningococcal infection	49	1	2
Viral hepatitis	179	28	3
Human immunodeficiency virus (HIV)	162	6	3
Neoplasms	149,652	16,558	4,581
Malignant neoplasms	146,269	16,207	4,960
Malignant neoplasm of trachea, bronchus and lung	30,131	4,069	1,058
Malignant melanoma of skin	2,106	185	71
Malignant neoplasm of breast	10,219	954	317
Malignant neoplasm of cervix uteri	730	105	19
Malignant neoplasm of prostate	10,755	986	301
Leukaemia	4,315	387	319
Diseases of the blood and blood-forming organs and certain disorders involving the immune mechanism	1,099	98	40
Endocrine, nutritional and metabolic diseases	8,435	1,330	345
Diabetes mellitus	6,046	1,016	230
Mental and behavioural disorders	50,765	4,591	1,457
Vascular and unspecified dementia	49,657	4,161	1,317
Diseases of the nervous system	33,051	3,976	1,063
Meningitis (excluding meningococcal)	154	19	3
Alzheimer's disease	17,984	2,388	583
Diseases of the circulatory system	133,511	15,114	3,780
Ischaemic heart diseases	57,923	6,727	1,825
Cerebrovascular diseases	31,713	3,927	988
Diseases of the respiratory system	73,455	136	1,973
Influenza and Pneumonia	27,635	3,535	742
Bronchitis, emphysema and other chronic obstructive pulmonary diseases	28,597	3,449	1,845
Asthma	1,320	106	38
Diseases of the digestive system	25,627	3,134	800
Gastric and duodenal ulcer	1,866	121	31
Diseases of the liver	8,450	1,063	186
Diseases of the skin and subcutaneous tissue	2,132	188	25
Diseases of the musculo-skeletal system and connective tissue	3,751	388	122
Osteoporosis	810	70	13
Diseases of the genitourinary system	9,106	957	282
Complications of pregnancy, childbirth and the puerperium	26	5	–
Certain conditions originating in the perinatal period	188	98	35
Congenital malformations, deformations and chromosomal abnormalities*	1,414	192	81
Symptoms, signs and abnormal findings not classified elsewhere	12,448	587	127
Senility	7,666	227	42
Sudden infant death syndrome	78	15	–
Deaths from external causes	21,226	3,152	773
Suicide and intentional self-harm	3,930	587	311
Assault	†269	56	20

* Excludes neonatal deaths (those at age under 28 days): for England and Wales neonatal deaths are included in the total number of deaths but excluded from the cause figures
† This will not be a true figure as registration of homicide and assault deaths in England and Wales is often delayed by adjourned inquests
Source: General Register Office for Scotland, NISRA, ONS (Crown copyright)

THE NATIONAL FLAG

The national flag of the United Kingdom is the Union Flag, generally known as the Union Jack.

The Union Flag is a combination of the cross of St George, patron saint of England, the cross of St Andrew, patron saint of Scotland and the cross of St Patrick, patron saint of Ireland.

Cross of St George: cross Gules in a field Argent (red cross on a white ground)

Cross of St Andrew: saltire Argent in a field Azure (white diagonal cross on a blue ground)

Cross of St Patrick: saltire Gules in a field Argent (red diagonal cross on a white ground)

A flag combining the cross of St George and the cross of St Andrew was first introduced by royal decree in 1606 following the conjoining of the English and Scottish crowns in 1603. In 1707 this flag became the flag of Great Britain after the parliaments of the two kingdoms were united. The cross of St Patrick was added in 1801 after the union of Great Britain and Ireland.

FLYING THE UNION FLAG

The correct orientation of the Union Flag when flying is with the broader diagonal band of white uppermost in the hoist (ie near the pole) and the narrower diagonal band of white uppermost in the fly (ie furthest from the pole).

The flying of the Union Flag on government buildings is decided by the Department for Digital Culture, Media and Sport (DCMS) at the Queen's command. There is no formal definition of a government building but it is generally accepted to mean a building owned or used by the Crown and/or predominantly occupied or used by civil servants or the Armed Forces.

The Scottish or Welsh governments are responsible for drawing up their own flag-flying guidance for their buildings. In Northern Ireland, the flying of flags is constrained by The Flags Regulations (Northern Ireland) 2000 and the Police Emblems and Flag Regulations (Northern Ireland) 2002. Individuals, local authorities and other organisations may fly the Union Flag whenever they wish, subject to compliance with any local planning requirement.

FLAGS AT HALF-MAST

Flags are flown at half-mast (ie two-thirds up between the top and bottom of the flagstaff) on the following occasions:

- from the announcement of the death of the sovereign until the funeral
- the death or funeral of a member of the royal family*
- the funerals of foreign rulers*
- the funerals of prime ministers and ex-prime ministers of the UK*
- the funerals of first ministers and ex-first ministers of Scotland, Wales and Northern Ireland (unless otherwise commanded by the sovereign, this only applies to flags in their respective countries)*
- other occasions by special command from the Queen

* By special command from the Queen in each case

DAYS FOR FLYING FLAGS

On 25 March 2008 the DCMS announced that UK government departments in England, Scotland and Wales may fly the Union Flag on their buildings whenever they choose and not just on the designated days listed below. In addition, on the patron saints' days of Scotland and Wales, the appropriate national flag may be flown alongside the Union Flag on UK government buildings in the wider Whitehall area. When flying on designated days flags are hoisted from 8am to sunset.

Duchess of Cambridge's birthday	9 Jan
Countess of Wessex's birthday	20 Jan
Accession of the Queen	6 Feb
Duke of York's birthday	19 Feb
St David's Day (in Wales only)*	1 Mar
Earl of Wessex's birthday	10 Mar
Commonwealth Day (2021)	8 Mar
St Patrick's Day (in Northern Ireland only)†	17 Mar
The Queen's birthday	21 Apr
St George's Day (in England only)*	23 Apr
Europe Day†	9 May
Coronation Day	2 Jun
The Queen's official birthday (2021)	21 Jun
Duke of Edinburgh's birthday	10 Jun
Duke of Cambridge's birthday	21 Jun
Duchess of Cornwall's birthday	17 Jul
Princess Royal's birthday	15 Aug
Remembrance Day (2021)	7 Nov
Prince of Wales' birthday	14 Nov
Wedding Day of the Queen	20 Nov
St Andrew's Day (in Scotland only)*	30 Nov

Opening of parliament by the Queen‡
Prorogation of parliament by the Queen‡

* The appropriate national flag, or the European flag, may be flown in addition to the Union Flag (where there are two or more flagpoles), but not in a superior position
† Only the Union Flag should be flown
‡ Only in the Greater London area, whether or not the Queen performs the ceremony in person

THE ROYAL STANDARD

The Royal Standard comprises four quarterings – two for England (three lions passant), one for Scotland* (a lion rampant) and one for Ireland (a harp).

The Royal Standard is flown when the Queen is in residence at a royal palace, on transport being used by the Queen for official journeys and from Victoria Tower when the Queen attends parliament. It may also be flown on any building (excluding ecclesiastical buildings) during a visit by the Queen. If the Queen is to be present in a building, advice on flag flying can be obtained from the DCMS.

The Royal Standard is never flown at half-mast, even after the death of the sovereign, as the new monarch immediately succeeds to the throne.

* In Scotland a version with two Scottish quarterings is used

THE ROYAL FAMILY

THE SOVEREIGN

ELIZABETH II, by the Grace of God, of the United Kingdom of Great Britain and Northern Ireland and of her other Realms and Territories Queen, Head of the Commonwealth, Defender of the Faith
Her Majesty Elizabeth Alexandra Mary of Windsor, elder daughter of King George VI and of HM Queen Elizabeth the Queen Mother
Born 21 April 1926, at 17 Bruton Street, London W1
Ascended the throne 6 February 1952
Crowned 2 June 1953, at Westminster Abbey
Married 20 November 1947, in Westminster Abbey, HRH the Prince Philip, Duke of Edinburgh
Official residences Buckingham Palace, London SW1A 1AA; Windsor Castle, Berks; Palace of Holyroodhouse, Edinburgh
Private residences Sandringham, Norfolk; Balmoral Castle, Aberdeenshire

HUSBAND OF THE QUEEN

HRH THE PRINCE PHILIP, DUKE OF EDINBURGH, KG, KT, OM, GCVO, GBE, Royal Victorian Chain, AK, QSO, PC, Ranger of Windsor Park
Born 10 June 1921, son of Prince and Princess Andrew of Greece and Denmark, naturalised a British subject 1947, created Duke of Edinburgh, Earl of Merioneth and Baron Greenwich 1947

CHILDREN OF THE QUEEN

HRH THE PRINCE OF WALES (Prince Charles Philip Arthur George), KG, KT, GCB, OM and Great Master of the Order of the Bath, AK, QSO, PC, ADC(P)
Born 14 November 1948, created Prince of Wales and Earl of Chester 1958, succeeded as Duke of Cornwall, Duke of Rothesay, Earl of Carrick and Baron Renfrew, Lord of the Isles and Great Steward of Scotland 1952
Married (1) 29 July 1981 Lady Diana Frances Spencer (Diana, Princess of Wales (1961–97), youngest daughter of the 8th Earl Spencer and the Hon. Mrs Shand Kydd), marriage dissolved 1996; (2) 9 April 2005 Mrs Camilla Rosemary Parker Bowles, now HRH the Duchess of Cornwall, GCVO, PC (*born* 17 July 1947, daughter of Major Bruce Shand and the Hon. Mrs Rosalind Shand)
Residences Clarence House, London SW1A 1BA; Highgrove, Doughton, Tetbury, Glos GL8 8TN; Birkhall, Ballater, Aberdeenshire
Issue
1. HRH the Duke of Cambridge (Prince William Arthur Philip Louis), KG, KT, PC *born* 21 June 1982, *created* Duke of Cambridge, Earl of Strathearn and Baron Carrickfergus 2011 *married* 29 April 2011 Catherine Elizabeth Middleton, now HRH the Duchess of Cambridge, GCVO (*born* 9 January 1982, elder daughter of Michael and Carole Middleton), and has issue, HRH Prince George of Cambridge (Prince George Alexander Louis), *born* 22 July 2013; HRH Princess Charlotte of Cambridge (Princess Charlotte Elizabeth Diana), *born* 2 May 2015; HRH Prince

Louis of Cambridge (Prince Louis Arthur Charles), *born* 23 April 2018 *Residences* Kensington Palace, London W8 4PU; Anmer Hall, Norfolk PE31 6RW
2. HRH the Duke of Sussex (Prince Henry Charles Albert David), KCVO *born* 15 September 1984, *created* Duke of Sussex, Earl of Dumbarton and Baron Kilkeel 2018 *married* 19 May 2018 (Rachel) Meghan Markle, now HRH the Duchess of Sussex (*born* 4 August 1981, daughter of Thomas Markle and Doria Ragland), and has issue, Archie Harrison Mountbatten-Windsor, *born* 6 May 2019 *Residence* Frogmore Cottage, Home Park, Windsor, Berks SL4 2JG

HRH THE PRINCESS ROYAL (Princess Anne Elizabeth Alice Louise), KG, KT, GCVO
Born 15 August 1950, declared the Princess Royal 1987
Married (1) 14 November 1973 Captain Mark Anthony Peter Phillips, CVO (*born* 22 September 1948); marriage dissolved 1992; (2) 12 December 1992 Vice-Adm. Sir Timothy James Hamilton Laurence, KCVO, CB, ADC (P) (*born* 1 March 1955)
Residence Gatcombe Park, Minchinhampton, Glos GL6 9AT
Issue
1. Peter Mark Andrew Phillips, *born* 15 November 1977, *married* 17 May 2008 Autumn Patricia Kelly, and has issue, Savannah Phillips, *born* 29 December 2010; Isla Elizabeth Phillips, *born* 29 March 2012
2. Zara Anne Elizabeth Tindall, MBE, *born* 15 May 1981, *married* 30 July 2011 Michael James Tindall, MBE, and has issue, Mia Grace Tindall, *born* 17 January 2014; Lena Elizabeth Tindall, *born* 18 June 2018

HRH THE DUKE OF YORK (Prince Andrew Albert Christian Edward), KG, GCVO, ADC(P)
Born 19 February 1960, created Duke of York, Earl of Inverness and Baron Killyleagh 1986
Married 23 July 1986 Sarah Margaret Ferguson, now Sarah, Duchess of York (*born* 15 October 1959, younger daughter of Major Ronald Ferguson and Mrs Hector Barrantes), marriage dissolved 1996
Residence Royal Lodge, Windsor Great Park, Berks
Issue
1. HRH Princess Beatrice of York (Princess Beatrice Elizabeth Mary), *born* 8 August 1988
2. HRH Princess Eugenie, Mrs Jack Brooksbank (Princess Eugenie Victoria Helena), *born* 23 March 1990, *married* 12 October 2018 Jack Christopher Stamp Brooksbank

HRH THE EARL OF WESSEX (Prince Edward Antony Richard Louis), KG, GCVO, ADC(P)
Born 10 March 1964, created Earl of Wessex, Viscount Severn 1999 and Earl of Forfar 2019
Married 19 June 1999 Sophie Helen Rhys-Jones, now HRH the Countess of Wessex, GCVO (*born* 20 January 1965, daughter of Mr and Mrs Christopher Rhys-Jones)
Residence Bagshot Park, Bagshot, Surrey GU19 5HS
Issue
1. Lady Louise Mountbatten-Windsor (Louise Alice Elizabeth Mary Mountbatten-Windsor), *born* 8 November 2003
2. Viscount Severn (James Alexander Philip Theo Mountbatten-Windsor), *born* 17 December 2007

NEPHEW AND NIECE OF THE QUEEN

Children of HRH the Princess Margaret, Countess of Snowdon and the Earl of Snowdon (*see* House of Windsor):
EARL OF SNOWDON (DAVID ALBERT CHARLES ARMSTRONG-JONES), *born* 3 November 1961, *married* 8 October 1993 Hon. Serena Alleyne Stanhope, and has issue, Viscount Linley (Charles Patrick Inigo Armstrong-Jones), *born* 1 July 1999; Lady Margarita Armstrong-Jones (Margarita Elizabeth Alleyne Armstrong-Jones), *born* 14 May 2002
LADY SARAH CHATTO (Sarah Frances Elizabeth), *born* 1 May 1964, *married* 14 July 1994 Daniel Chatto, and has issue, Samuel David Benedict Chatto, *born* 28 July 1996; Arthur Robert Nathaniel Chatto, *born* 5 February 1999

COUSINS OF THE QUEEN

Child of HRH the Duke of Gloucester and HRH Princess Alice, Duchess of Gloucester (*see* House of Windsor):
HRH THE DUKE OF GLOUCESTER (Prince Richard Alexander Walter George), KG, GCVO, Grand Prior of the Order of St John of Jerusalem
Born 26 August 1944
Married 8 July 1972 Birgitte Eva van Deurs, now HRH the Duchess of Gloucester, GCVO (*born* 20 June 1946, daughter of Asger Henriksen and Vivian van Deurs)
Residence Kensington Palace, London W8 4PU
Issue
1. Earl of Ulster (Alexander Patrick Gregers Richard), *born* 24 October 1974 *married* 22 June 2002 Dr Claire Alexandra Booth, and has issue, Lord Culloden (Xan Richard Anders), *born* 12 March 2007; Lady Cosima Windsor (Cosima Rose Alexandra), *born* 20 May 2010
2. Lady Davina Windsor (Davina Elizabeth Alice Benedikte), *born* 19 November 1977 *married* 31 July 2004 Gary Christie Lewis (marriage dissolved 2018), and has issue, Senna Kowhai Lewis, *born* 22 June 2010; Tane Mahuta Lewis, *born* 25 May 2012
3. Lady Rose Gilman (Rose Victoria Birgitte Louise), *born* 1 March 1980 *married* 19 July 2008 George Edward Gilman, and has issue, Lyla Beatrix Christabel Gilman, *born* 30 May 2010; Rufus Gilman, *born* 2 November 2012

Children of HRH the Duke of Kent and Princess Marina, Duchess of Kent (*see* House of Windsor):
HRH THE DUKE OF KENT (Prince Edward George Nicholas Paul Patrick), KG, GCMG, GCVO, ADC(P)
Born 9 October 1935
Married 8 June 1961 Katharine Lucy Mary Worsley, now HRH the Duchess of Kent, GCVO (*born* 22 February 1933, daughter of Sir William Worsley, Bt.)
Residence Wren House, Palace Green, London W8 4PY
Issue
1. Earl of St Andrews (George Philip Nicholas), *born* 26 June 1962, *married* 9 January 1988 Sylvana Tomaselli, and has

issue, Lord Downpatrick (Edward Edmund Maximilian George), *born* 2 December 1988; Lady Marina-Charlotte Windsor (Marina-Charlotte Alexandra Katharine Helen), *born* 30 September 1992; Lady Amelia Windsor (Amelia Sophia Theodora Mary Margaret), *born* 24 August 1995
2. Lady Helen Taylor (Helen Marina Lucy), *born* 28 April 1964, *married* 18 July 1992 Timothy Verner Taylor, and has issue, Columbus George Donald Taylor, *born* 6 August 1994; Cassius Edward Taylor, *born* 26 December 1996; Eloise Olivia Katharine Taylor, *born* 3 March 2003; Estella Olga Elizabeth Taylor, *born* 21 December 2004
3. Lord Nicholas Windsor (Nicholas Charles Edward Jonathan), *born* 25 July 1970, *married* 4 November 2006 Princess Paola Doimi de Lupis Frankopan Subic Zrinski, and has issue, Albert Louis Philip Edward Windsor, *born* 22 September 2007; Leopold Ernest Augustus Guelph Windsor, *born* 8 September 2009; Louis Arthur Nicholas Felix Windsor, *born* 27 May 2014

HRH PRINCESS ALEXANDRA, THE HON. LADY OGILVY (Princess Alexandra Helen Elizabeth Olga Christabel), KG, GCVO
Born 25 December 1936
Married 24 April 1963 the Rt. Hon. Sir Angus Ogilvy, KCVO (1928–2004), second son of 12th Earl of Airlie
Residence Thatched House Lodge, Richmond Park, Surrey TW10 5HP
Issue
1. James Robert Bruce Ogilvy, *born* 29 February 1964, *married* 30 July 1988 Julia Rawlinson, and has issue, Flora Alexandra Ogilvy, *born* 15 December 1994; Alexander Charles Ogilvy, *born* 12 November 1996
2. Marina Victoria Alexandra Ogilvy, *born* 31 July 1966, *married* 2 February 1990 Paul Julian Mowatt (marriage dissolved 1997), and has issue, Zenouska May Mowatt, *born* 26 May 1990; Christian Alexander Mowatt, *born* 4 June 1993

HRH PRINCE MICHAEL OF KENT (Prince Michael George Charles Franklin), GCVO
Born 4 July 1942
Married 30 June 1978 Baroness Marie-Christine Agnes Hedwig Ida von Reibnitz, now HRH Princess Michael of Kent (*born* 15 January 1945, daughter of Baron Gunther von Reibnitz)
Residence Kensington Palace, London W8 4PU
Issue
1. Lord Frederick Windsor (Frederick Michael George David Louis), *born* 6 April 1979, *married* 12 September 2009 Sophie Winkleman, and has issue, Maud Elizabeth Daphne Marina Windsor, *born* 15 August 2013; Isabella Alexandra May Windsor, *born* 16 January 2016
2. Lady Gabriella Kingston (Gabriella Marina Alexandra Ophelia), *born* 23 April 1981, *married* 18 May 2019 Thomas Kingston

ORDER OF SUCCESSION

The Succession to the Crown Act 2013 received royal assent on 25 April 2013 and made provision for the order of succession to the Crown not to be dependent on gender and for those members of the royal family married to a Roman Catholic to retain the right of succession to the throne. The provisions of the Act came into force on 26 March 2015, following its ratification by all 16 Realms of the Commonwealth.

On the Act's commencement HRH Prince Michael of Kent and the Earl of St Andrews were restored to the succession. In addition, all male members of the royal family born after 28 October 2011 no longer precede any elder female siblings; and their place in the order of succession changed accordingly.

The following list includes all living descendants of the sons of King George V eligible to succeed to the Crown under the current legislation. Lord Nicholas Windsor, Lord Downpatrick and Lady Marina-Charlotte Windsor renounced their rights to the throne on converting to Roman Catholicism in 2001, 2003 and 2008 respectively. Their children remain in succession provided that they are in communion with the Church of England.

1	HRH the Prince of Wales	31	Lady Davina Windsor
2	HRH the Duke of Cambridge	32	Senna Lewis
3	HRH Prince George of Cambridge	33	Tane Lewis
4	HRH Princess Charlotte of Cambridge	34	Lady Rose Gilman
5	HRH Prince Louis of Cambridge	35	Lyla Gilman
6	HRH the Duke of Sussex	36	Rufus Gilman
7	Archie Mountbatten-Windsor	37	HRH the Duke of Kent
8	HRH the Duke of York	38	Earl of St Andrews
9	HRH Princess Beatrice of York, Mrs Edoardo Mapelli	39	Lady Amelia Windsor
10	HRH Princess Eugenie, Mrs Jack Brooksbank	40	Albert Windsor
11	HRH the Earl of Wessex	41	Leopold Windsor
12	Viscount Severn	42	Louis Windsor
13	Lady Louise Mountbatten-Windsor	43	Lady Helen Taylor
14	HRH the Princess Royal	44	Columbus Taylor
15	Peter Phillips	45	Cassius Taylor
16	Savannah Phillips	46	Eloise Taylor
17	Isla Phillips	47	Estella Taylor
18	Zara Tindall	48	HRH Prince Michael of Kent
19	Mia Tindall	49	Lord Frederick Windsor
20	Lena Tindall	50	Maud Windsor
21	Earl of Snowdon	51	Isabella Windsor
22	Viscount Linley	52	Lady Gabriella Kingston
23	Lady Margarita Armstrong-Jones	53	HRH Princess Alexandra, the Hon. Lady Ogilvy
24	Lady Sarah Chatto	54	James Ogilvy
25	Samuel Chatto	55	Alexander Ogilvy
26	Arthur Chatto	56	Flora Vesterberg
27	HRH the Duke of Gloucester	57	Marina Ogilvy
28	Earl of Ulster	58	Christian Mowatt
29	Lord Culloden	59	Zenouska Mowatt
30	Lady Cosima Windsor		

THE ROYAL HOUSEHOLD

The PRIVATE SECRETARY is responsible for:
- informing and advising the Queen on constitutional, governmental and political matters in the UK, her other Realms and the wider Commonwealth, including communications with the prime minister and government departments
- organising the Queen's domestic and overseas official programme
- the Queen's speeches, messages, patronage, photographs, portraits and official presents
- communications in connection with the role of the royal family
- dealing with correspondence to the Queen from members of the public
- royal travel policy
- coordinating and initiating research to support engagements by members of the royal family

The DIRECTOR OF ROYAL COMMUNICATIONS is in charge of Buckingham Palace's communications office and reports to the Private Secretary. The director is responsible for:
- developing communications strategies to enhance the public understanding of the role of the monarchy
- briefing the British and international media on the role and duties of the Queen and issues relating to the royal family
- responding to media enquiries
- arranging media facilities in the UK and overseas to support royal functions and engagements
- the management of the royal website

The Private Secretary is keeper of the royal archives and is responsible for the care of the records of the sovereign and the royal household from previous reigns, preserved in the royal archives at Windsor. As keeper, it is the Private Secretary's responsibility to ensure the proper management of the records of the present reign with a view to their transfer to the archives as and when appropriate. The Private Secretary is an *ex officio* trustee of the Royal Collection Trust.

The KEEPER OF THE PRIVY PURSE AND TREASURER TO THE QUEEN is responsible for:
- the Sovereign Grant, which is the money paid from the government's Consolidated Fund to meet official expenditure relating to the Queen's duties as Head of State and Head of the Commonwealth and is provided by the government in return for the net surplus from the Crown Estate and other hereditary revenues (*see also* Royal Finances)
- through the Director of Human Resources, the planning and management of personnel policy across the royal household, the allocation of employee and pensioner housing and the administration of all its pension schemes and private estates employees
- information systems and telecommunications
- property services at occupied royal palaces in England, comprising Buckingham Palace, St James's Palace, Clarence House, Marlborough House Mews, the residential and office areas of Kensington Palace, Windsor Castle and buildings in the Home and Great Parks of Windsor and Hampton Court Mews and Paddocks
- delivery of all official and approved travel operations
- audit services
- health and safety; insurance matters
- the Privy Purse, which is mainly financed by the net income of the Duchy of Lancaster, and meets both official and private expenditure incurred by the Queen
- liaison with other members of the royal family and their households on financial matters
- the Queen's private estates at Sandringham and Balmoral, the Queen's Racing Establishment and the Royal Studs and liaison with the Ascot Authority
- the Home Park at Windsor and liaison with the Crown Estate Commissioners concerning the Home Park and the Great Park at Windsor
- the Royal Philatelic Collection
- administrative aspects of the Military Knights of Windsor
- administration of the Royal Victorian Order, of which the Keeper of the Privy Purse is secretary, Long and Faithful Service Medals, and the Queen's cups, medals and prizes, and policy on commemorative medals

The Keeper of the Privy Purse is also responsible for the Royal Mews, assisted by the CROWN EQUERRY, who has day-to-day responsibility for:
- the provision of carriage processions for the state opening of parliament, state visits, Trooping of the Colour, Royal Ascot, the Garter Ceremony, the Thistle Service, the presentation of credentials to the Queen by incoming foreign ambassadors and high commissioners, and other state and ceremonial occasions
- the provision of chauffeur-driven cars
- coordinating travel arrangements by road in respect of the royal household
- supervision and administration of the Royal Mews at Buckingham Palace, Windsor Castle, Hampton Court and the Palace of Holyroodhouse

The Keeper of the Privy Purse is one of three royal trustees (in respect of his responsibilities for the Sovereign Grant) and is Receiver-General of the Duchy of Lancaster and a member of the Duchy's Council.

The Keeper of the Privy Purse has overall responsibility for the DIRECTOR OF OPERATIONS, ROYAL TRAVEL, who is responsible for the provision of travel arrangements by air and rail and is also an *ex officio* trustee of the Royal Collection Trust.

The DIRECTOR OF THE PROPERTY SECTION has day-to-day responsibility for the royal household's property section:
- fire and health and safety
- repairs and refurbishment of buildings and new building work
- utilities and telecommunications
- putting up stages, tents and other work in connection with ceremonial occasions, garden parties and other official functions

The property section is also responsible, on a sub-contract basis from the DCMS, for the maintenance of Marlborough House (which is occupied by the Commonwealth Secretariat).

The MASTER OF THE HOUSEHOLD is responsible for:
- delivering the majority of the official and private entertaining in the Queen's annual programme across all the occupied palaces and residences in the UK when required
- periodic support for entertaining by all other members of the royal family
- furnishings and internal decorative refurbishment of all the occupied palaces in the UK in conjunction with the Director, Royal Collection Trust
- all operational, domestic and kitchen staff in the royal household

The COMPTROLLER, LORD CHAMBERLAIN'S OFFICE is responsible for:

- the organisation of all ceremonial engagements, including state visits to the Queen in the UK, royal weddings and funerals, the state opening of parliament, Guards of Honour at Buckingham Palace, investitures, and the Garter and Thistle ceremonies
- garden parties at Buckingham Palace and the Palace of Holyroodhouse
- the Crown Jewels, which are part of the Royal Collection, when they are in use on state occasions
- coordination of the arrangements for the Queen to be represented at funerals and memorial services and at the arrival and departure of visiting heads of state
- advising on matters of precedence, style and titles, dress, flying of flags, gun salutes, mourning and other ceremonial issues
- supervising the applications for Royal Warrants of Appointment
- advising on the commercial use of royal emblems and contemporary royal photographs
- the ecclesiastical household, the medical household, the bodyguards and certain ceremonial appointments such as Gentlemen Ushers and Pages of Honour
- the Lords in Waiting, who represent the Queen on various occasions and escort visiting heads of state during incoming state visits
- the Queen's bargemaster and watermen and the Queen's swans
- the Royal Almonry and Royal Maundy Service

The Comptroller also has overall responsibility for the MARSHAL OF THE DIPLOMATIC CORPS, who is responsible for the relationship between the royal household and the Diplomatic Heads of Mission in London; and the SECRETARY OF THE CENTRAL CHANCERY OF THE ORDERS OF KNIGHTHOOD, who administers the Orders of Chivalry, makes arrangements for investitures and the distribution of insignia, and ensures the proper public notification of awards through *The London Gazette*.

The DIRECTOR, ROYAL COLLECTION TRUST is responsible for:

- the administration and custodial control of the Royal Collection in all royal residences
- the care, display, conservation and restoration of items in the collection
- initiating and assisting research into the collection and publishing catalogues and books on the collection
- making the collection accessible to the public and educating and informing the public about the collection

The Royal Collection, which contains a large number of works of art, is held by the Queen as sovereign in trust for her successors and the nation and is not owned by her as an individual. The administration, conservation and presentation of the Royal Collection are funded by the Royal Collection Trust solely from income from visitors to Windsor Castle, Buckingham Palace and the Palace of Holyroodhouse. The Royal Collection Trust is chaired by the Prince of Wales. The Lord Chamberlain, the Private Secretary and the Keeper of the Privy Purse are *ex officio* trustees and there are three external trustees appointed by the Queen.

The Director, Royal Collection Trust is also at present the SURVEYOR OF THE QUEEN'S WORKS OF ART, responsible for paintings, miniatures and works of art on paper, including the watercolours, prints and drawings in the Print Room at Windsor Castle, and for the books, manuscripts, coins, medals and insignia in the Royal Library.

Royal Collection Enterprises Limited is the trading subsidiary of the Royal Collection Trust. The company, whose chair is the Keeper of the Privy Purse, is responsible for:

- managing access by the public to Windsor Castle (including Frogmore House), Buckingham Palace (including the Royal Mews and the Queen's Gallery) and the Palace of Holyroodhouse (including the Queen's Gallery)
- running shops at each location
- managing the images and intellectual property rights of the Royal Collection

The Director, Royal Collection Trust is also an *ex officio* trustee of Historic Royal Palaces.

PRIVATE SECRETARIES

THE QUEEN
Office: Buckingham Palace, London SW1A 1AA **T** 020-7930 4832
Private Secretary to The Queen, Rt. Hon. Sir Edward Young, KCVO

PRINCE PHILIP, THE DUKE OF EDINBURGH
Office: Buckingham Palace, London SW1A 1AA **T** 020-7930 4832
Private Secretary, Brig. Archie Miller-Bakewell

THE PRINCE OF WALES AND THE DUCHESS OF CORNWALL
Office: Clarence House, London SW1A 1BA **T** 020-7930 4832
Principal Private Secretary, Clive Alderton, CVO

THE DUKE AND DUCHESS OF CAMBRIDGE
Office: Kensington Palace, Palace Green, London W8 4PU
T 020-7930 4832
Private Secretary to the Duke of Cambridge, Simon Case, CVO
Private Secretary to the Duchess of Cambridge, Catherine Quinn

THE DUKE AND DUCHESS OF SUSSEX
Office, Kensington Palace, Palace Green, London W8 4PU
T 020-7930 4832
Private Secretary to the Duke and Duchess of Sussex, Fiona Mcilwham

THE DUKE OF YORK
Office: Buckingham Palace, London SW1A 1AA **T** 020-7024 4227
Private Secretary, Amanda Thirsk, LVO

THE EARL AND COUNTESS OF WESSEX
Office: Bagshot Park, Surrey GU19 5PL **T** 01276-707040
Private Secretary, Capt. Andy Aspden, RN

THE PRINCESS ROYAL
Office: Buckingham Palace, London SW1A 1AA **T** 020-7024 4199
Private Secretary, Charles Davies, MVO

THE DUKE AND DUCHESS OF GLOUCESTER
Office: Kensington Palace, London W8 4PU **T** 020-7368 1000
Private Secretary, Lt.-Col. Alastair Todd

THE DUKE OF KENT
Office: York House, St James's Palace, London SW1A 1BQ
T 020-7930 4872
Private Secretary, Nicholas Turnbull, MBE, QGM

PRINCE AND PRINCESS MICHAEL OF KENT
Office: Kensington Palace, London W8 4PU
W www.princemichael.org.uk
Private Secretary, Camilla Rogers

PRINCESS ALEXANDRA, THE HON. LADY OGILVY
Office: Buckingham Palace, London SW1A 1AA
T 020-7024 4270
Private Secretary, Diane Duke, LVO

SENIOR MANAGEMENT OF THE ROYAL HOUSEHOLD

Lord Chamberlain, Earl Peel, GCVO, PC

HEADS OF DEPARTMENT
Private Secretary to The Queen, Rt. Hon. Edward Young, CVO
Keeper of the Privy Purse, Sir Michael Stevens, KCVO
Master of the Household, Vice-Adm. Tony Johnstone-Burt, CB, OBE
Comptroller, Lord Chamberlain's Office, Lt.-Col. Michael Vernon
Director of the Royal Collection, Tim Knox

NON-EXECUTIVE MEMBERS
Private Secretary to the Duke of Edinburgh, Brig. Archie Miller-Bakewell
Principal Private Secretary to the Prince of Wales and the Duchess of Cornwall, Clive Alderton, LVO

ASTRONOMER ROYAL

The post of Astronomer Royal dates back to 1675, when astronomy had many practical applications in navigation. Today the post is largely honorary, although the Astronomer Royal is expected to be available for consultation on scientific matters for as long as the holder remains a professional astronomer. The Astronomer Royal receives a stipend of £100 a year and is a member of the royal household.

Astronomer Royal, Lord Rees of Ludlow, OM, *apptd* 1995

MASTER OF THE QUEEN'S MUSIC

The office of Master of the Queen's Music is an honour conferred on a musician of great distinction. The office was first created in 1626, when the master was responsible for the court musicians. Since the reign of King George V, the position has had no fixed duties, although the Master may choose to produce compositions to mark royal or state occasions. The Master of the Queen's Music is paid an annual stipend of £15,000. In 2004 the length of appointment was changed from life tenure to a ten-year term.

Master of the Queen's Music, Judith Weir, CBE, *apptd* 2014

POET LAUREATE

The post of Poet Laureate was officially established when John Dryden was appointed by royal warrant as Poet Laureate and Historiographer Royal in 1668. The post is attached to the royal household and was originally conferred on the holder for life; in 1999 the length of appointment was changed to a ten-year term. It is customary for the Poet Laureate to write verse to mark events of national importance. The postholder currently receives an honorarium of £5,750 a year.

The Poet Laureate, Simon Armitage, *apptd* 2019

ROYAL FINANCES

Dating back to the late 17th century the Civil List was originally used by the sovereign to supplement hereditary revenues for paying the salaries of judges, ambassadors and other government officers as well as the expenses of the royal household. In 1760, on the accession of George III, it was decided that the Civil List would be provided by parliament to cover all relevant expenditure in return for the king surrendering the hereditary revenues of the Crown. At that time parliament undertook to pay the salaries of judges, ambassadors etc. In 1831 parliament agreed also to meet the costs of the royal palaces in return for a reduction in the Civil List.

Until 1 April 2012 the Civil List met the central staff costs and running expenses of the Queen's official household. Annual grants-in-aid provided for the maintenance of the occupied royal palaces (*see* Royal Household for a list of occupied palaces) and royal travel.

THE SOVEREIGN GRANT
Under the Sovereign Grant Act 2011, which came into force on 1 April 2012, the funding previously provided by the Civil List and the grants-in-aid was consolidated in the Sovereign Grant. It is provided by HM Treasury from public funds in exchange for the surrender by the Queen of the revenue of the Crown Estate.

For 2016–17 the Sovereign Grant was calculated based on 15 per cent of the income account net surplus of the Crown Estate for the financial year two years previous. From 2017–18 this increased to 25 per cent, providing for a Sovereign Grant of £82.2m in 2018–19. The additional grant generated (£32.9m in 2018–19) will be used to fund the reservicing of Buckingham Palace over a ten-year period.

Official core expenditure met by the Sovereign Grant in 2018–19 amounted to £49.6m. Royal travel accounted for £4.6m of the expenditure and property maintenance for £23.7m. The excess of core expenditure over core Sovereign Grant of £0.3m was transferred from the Sovereign Grant reserve.

The legislative requirement is for Sovereign Grant accounts to be audited by the Comptroller and Auditor-General, scrutinised by the National Audit Office, and submitted to parliament annually. They are subjected to the same scrutiny as for any other government department. The annual report for the year to 31 March 2019 was published in June 2019.

£m	2017–18	2018–19
Sovereign Grant	76.1	82.2
Core	45.7	49.3
Buckingham Palace	30.4	32.9
Transfer (to)/ from the reserve	(28.7)	(15.2)
Core	(2.4)	0.3
Buckingham Palace	(26.3)	(15.5)
Net Expenditure	47.4	67.0

PARLIAMENTARY ANNUITIES
The Civil List acts provided for other members of the royal family to receive annuities from government funds to meet the expenses of carrying out their official duties. Since 1993 these annuities the Queen reimbursed HM Treasury for all of them except those paid to the late Queen Elizabeth the Queen Mother and the Duke of Edinburgh. The Sovereign Grant Act 2011 repealed all parliamentary annuities paid to the royal family, with the exception of that paid to the Duke of Edinburgh (£359,000 in 2018–19). This is now paid directly from the Consolidated Fund.

THE PRIVY PURSE
The funds received by the Privy Purse pay for official expenses incurred by the Queen as head of state and for some of the Queen's private expenditure. The revenues of the Duchy of Lancaster are the principal source of income for the privy purse. The revenues of the Duchy were retained by George III in 1760 when the hereditary revenues were surrendered. The Duchy Council reports to the Chancellor of the Duchy of Lancaster, who is accountable directly to the sovereign rather than to parliament. However the chancellor does answer parliamentary questions on matters relating to the Duchy's responsibilities.

THE DUCHY OF LANCASTER, 1 Lancaster Place, London · WC2E 7ED **W** www.duchyoflancaster.co.uk
Chancellor of the Duchy of Lancaster, Rt. Hon. Michael Gove, MP, *apptd* 2019
Chair of the Council, Sir Alan Reid, GCVO
Chief Executive and Clerk, Nathan Thompson
Receiver-General, Sir Michael Stevens, KCVO
Attorney-General, Robert Miles, QC

PERSONAL INCOME
The Queen's personal income derives mostly from investments, and is used to meet private expenditure.

PRINCE OF WALES' FUNDING
The Duchy Estate was created in 1337 by Edward III for his son Prince Edward (the Black Prince) who became the Duke of Cornwall. The Duchy's primary function is to provide an income from its assets for the Prince of Wales. Under a 1337 charter, confirmed by subsequent legislation, the Prince of Wales is not entitled to the proceeds or profit on the sale of Duchy assets but only to the annual income which is generated. The Duchy is responsible for the sustainable and commercial management of its properties, investment portfolio and 55,120 hectares of land, based mostly in the south-west of England. The Prince of Wales also uses a proportion of his Duchy income to meet the cost of his official public duties and the public, charitable and private activities of the Duchess of Cornwall, the Duke and Duchess of Cambridge and the Duke and Duchess of Sussex.

THE DUCHY OF CORNWALL, 10 Buckingham Gate, London SW1E 6LA **T** 020-7834 7346 **W** www.duchyofcornwall.org
Lord Warden of the Stannaries, Sir Nicholas Bacon, Bt., OBE
Receiver-General, Hon. Sir James Leigh-Pemberton, CVO
Attorney-General, Jonathan Crow, QC
Secretary and Keeper of the Records, Alastair Martin

TAXATION
The sovereign is not legally liable to pay income tax or capital gains tax, but since 6 April 1993 has paid both on a voluntary basis. The main provisions for the Queen and the Prince of Wales to pay tax are set out in a Memorandum of Understanding on Royal Taxation presented to parliament on 11 February 1993. The Queen pays income and capital gains tax in respect of her private income and assets, and on the proportion of the income and capital gains of the Privy Purse used for private purposes. Inheritance tax will be paid on the Queen's assets, except for those which pass to the next sovereign, whether automatically or by gift or bequest. The Prince of Wales pays income tax on income from the Duchy of Cornwall used for private purposes.

ROYAL SALUTES

ENGLAND

The basic royal salute is 21 rounds with an extra 20 rounds fired at Hyde Park because it is a royal park. At the Tower of London 62 rounds are fired on royal anniversaries (21 plus a further 20 because the Tower is a royal palace and a further 21 'for the City of London') and 41 on other occasions. When the Queen's official birthday coincides with the Duke of Edinburgh's birthday, 124 rounds are fired from the Tower (62 rounds for each birthday). Gun salutes occur on the following royal anniversaries:

- Accession Day
- The Queen's birthday
- Coronation Day
- Duke of Edinburgh's birthday
- The Queen's Official Birthday
- The Prince of Wales' birthday
- State opening of parliament

Gun salutes also occur when parliament is prorogued by the sovereign, on royal births and when a visiting head of state meets the sovereign in London, Windsor or Edinburgh.

In London, salutes are fired at Hyde Park and the Tower of London although on some occasions (state visits, state opening of parliament and the Queen's birthday parade) Green Park is used instead of Hyde Park. Other military saluting stations in England are at Colchester, Dover, Plymouth, Woolwich and York.

Constable of the Royal Palace and Fortress of London, Gen. Lord Houghton of Richmond, GCB, CBE

Lieutenant of the Tower of London, Lt.-Gen. Sir Simon Mayall, KBE, CB

Master Gunner within The Tower, Col. Hon. Mark Vincent, MBE

Resident Governor and Keeper of the Jewel House, Col. Richard Harrold, CVO, OBE

Master Gunner of St James's Park, Lt.-Gen. Sir Andrew Gregory, KBE, CB

MILITARY RANKS AND TITLES

THE QUEEN

ARMY
Colonel-in-Chief
The Life Guards; The Blues and Royals (Royal Horse Guards and 1st Dragoons); The Royal Scots Dragoon Guards (Carabiniers and Greys); The Royal Lancers (Queen Elizabeths' Own); The Royal Tank Regiment; Corps of Royal Engineers; Grenadier Guards; Coldstream Guards; Scots Guards; Irish Guards; Welsh Guards; The Royal Regiment of Scotland; The Duke of Lancaster's Regiment (King's, Lancashire and Border); The Royal Welsh; Adjutant General's Corps; The Governor General's Horse Guards (of Canada); The King's Own Calgary Regiment (Royal Canadian Armoured Corps); Canadian Forces Military Engineering Branch; Le Royal 22e Regiment; The Governor General's Foot Guards; The Canadian Grenadier Guards; The Stormont, Dundas and Glengarry Highlanders; Le Régiment de la Chaudière; The Royal New Brunswick Regiment; The North Shore (New Brunswick) Regiment; 48th Highlanders of Canada; The Argyll and Sutherland Highlanders of Canada (Princess Louise's); The Calgary Highlanders; Royal Australian Engineers; Royal Australian Infantry Corps; Royal Australian Army Ordnance Corps; Royal Australian Army Nursing Corps; The Corps of Royal New Zealand Engineers; Royal New Zealand Infantry Regiment
Affiliated Colonel-in-Chief
The Queen's Gurkha Engineers
Captain-General
Royal Regiment of Artillery; The Honourable Artillery Company; Combined Cadet Force; Royal Regiment of Canadian Artillery; Royal Regiment of Australian Artillery; Royal Regiment of New Zealand Artillery; Royal New Zealand Armoured Corps
Royal Colonel
Balaklava Company, 5th Battalion The Royal Regiment of Scotland
Patron
Royal Army Chaplains' Department

ROYAL AIR FORCE
Air Commodore-in-Chief
Royal Auxiliary Air Force; Royal Air Force Regiment; Air Reserve (of Canada); Royal Australian Air Force Reserve; Territorial Air Force (of New Zealand)
Commandant-in-Chief
RAF College, Cranwell
Royal Honorary Air Commodore
RAF Marham; 603 (City of Edinburgh) Squadron Royal Auxiliary Air Force

TRI-SERVICE
Colonel-in-Chief
The Canadian Armed Forces Legal Branch

PRINCE PHILIP, DUKE OF EDINBURGH

ROYAL NAVY
Lord High Admiral of the United Kingdom
Admiral of the Fleet
Admiral of the Fleet, Royal Australian Navy
Admiral of the Fleet, Royal New Zealand Navy
Admiral, Royal Canadian Navy
Admiral, Royal Canadian Sea Cadets

ARMY
Field Marshal
Field Marshal, Australian Military Forces
Field Marshal, New Zealand Army
General, Royal Canadian Army
Colonel-in-Chief
The Queen's Royal Hussars (Queen's Own and Royal Irish); The Rifles; Corps of Royal Electrical and Mechanical Engineers; Intelligence Corps; Army Cadet Force Association; The Royal Canadian Regiment; The Royal Hamilton Light Infantry (Wentworth Regiment of Canada); The Cameron Highlanders of Ottawa; The Queen's Own Cameron Highlanders of Canada; The Seaforth Highlanders of Canada; The Royal Canadian Army Cadets; The Royal Australian Corps of Electrical and Mechanical Engineers; The Australian Army Cadet Corps
Royal Colonel
The Highlanders, 4th Battalion The Royal Regiment of Scotland
Honorary Colonel
The Trinidad and Tobago Regiment
Member
Honourable Artillery Company

ROYAL AIR FORCE
Marshal of the Royal Air Force
Marshal of the Royal Australian Air Force
Marshal of the Royal New Zealand Air Force
General, Royal Canadian Air Force
Air Commodore-in-Chief
Royal Canadian Air Cadets
Honorary Air Commodore
RAF Northolt

THE PRINCE OF WALES

ROYAL NAVY
Admiral of the Fleet
Admiral of the Fleet, Royal New Zealand Navy
Vice-Admiral
Royal Canadian Navy
Commodore-in-Chief
HM Naval Base Plymouth; Fleet Atlantic, Royal Canadian Navy
Honorary Commodore-in-Chief
Aircraft Carriers

ARMY
Field Marshal
Field Marshal, New Zealand Army
Lieutenant-General
Canadian Army
Colonel-in-Chief
The Royal Dragoon Guards; The Parachute Regiment; The Royal Gurkha Rifles; Army Air Corps; The Royal Canadian Dragoons; Lord Strathcona's Horse (Royal Canadians); The Royal Regiment of Canada; Royal Winnipeg Rifles; Royal Australian Armoured Corps; The Royal Pacific Islands Regiment; 1st The Queen's Dragoon Guards; The Black Watch (Royal Highland Regiment) of Canada; The Toronto Scottish Regiment (Queen Elizabeth The Queen Mother's Own); The Mercian Regiment; 2nd Battalion The Irish Regiment of Canada
Royal Colonel
The Black Watch, 3rd Battalion The Royal Regiment of Scotland; 51st Highland, 7th Battalion The Royal Regiment of Scotland

Colonel
    The Welsh Guards
Royal Honorary Colonel
    The Queen's Own Yeomanry

ROYAL AIR FORCE
Marshal of the RAF
Marshal of the Royal New Zealand Air Force
Lieutenant-General
    Royal Canadian Air Force
Honorary Air Commodore
    RAF Valley
Colonel-in-Chief
    Air Reserve Canada

THE DUCHESS OF CORNWALL

ROYAL NAVY
Commodore-in-Chief
    Royal Naval Medical Services; Naval Chaplaincy Services
Lady Sponsor
    HMS *Astute;* HMS *Prince of Wales*

ARMY
Colonel-in-Chief
    Queen's Own Rifles of Canada; Royal Australian Corps of
    Military Police
Royal Colonel
    4th Battalion The Rifles

ROYAL AIR FORCE
Honorary Air Commodore
    RAF Halton; RAF Leeming

THE DUKE OF CAMBRIDGE

ROYAL NAVY
Lieutenant Commander
Commodore-in-Chief
    Scotland Command; Submarines Command

ARMY
Colonel
    Irish Guards
Major
    The Blues and Royals (Royal Horse Guards and 1st
    Dragoons)

ROYAL AIR FORCE
Squadron Leader
Honorary Air Commandant
    RAF Coningsby

THE DUCHESS OF CAMBRIDGE

ROYAL AIR FORCE
Honorary Air Commandant
    Air Cadets

THE DUKE OF SUSSEX

ROYAL NAVY
Lieutenant-Commander
Commodore-in-Chief
    Small Ships and Diving Command

ROYAL MARINES
Captain-General

ARMY
Major
    The Blues and Royals (Royal Horse Guards and 1st
    Dragoons)

ROYAL AIR FORCE
Squadron Leader
Honorary Air Commandant
    RAF Honington

THE DUKE OF YORK

ROYAL NAVY
Vice-Admiral
Commodore-in-Chief
    Fleet Air Arm
Admiral of the Sea Cadets Corps

ARMY
Colonel-in-Chief
    The Royal Irish Regiment (27th (Inniskilling), 83rd, 87th
    and The Ulster Defence Regiment); The Yorkshire
    Regiment (14th/15th, 19th and 33rd/76th Foot); Small
    Arms School Corps; The Queen's York Rangers (First
    Americans); Royal New Zealand Army Logistics Regiment;
    The Royal Highland Fusiliers of Canada; The Princess
    Louise Fusiliers (Canada)
Deputy Colonel-in-Chief
    The Royal Lancers (Queen Elizabeths' Own)
Colonel
    Grenadier Guards
Royal Colonel
    The Royal Highland Fusiliers, 2nd Battalion The Royal
    Regiment of Scotland

ROYAL AIR FORCE
Honorary Air Commodore
    RAF Lossiemouth

THE EARL OF WESSEX

ROYAL NAVY
Commodore-in-Chief
    Royal Fleet Auxiliary
Patron
    Royal Fleet Auxiliary Association

ARMY
Colonel-in-Chief
    Hastings and Prince Edward Regiment; Saskatchewan
    Dragoons; Prince Edward Island Regiment
Royal Colonel
    2nd Battalion, The Rifles
Royal Honorary Colonel
    Royal Wessex Yeomanry; The London Regiment

ROYAL AIR FORCE
Honorary Air Commodore
    RAF Waddington

THE COUNTESS OF WESSEX

ARMY
Colonel-in-Chief
    Corps of Army Music; Queen Alexandra's Royal Army
    Nursing Corps; The Lincoln and Welland Regiment; South
    Alberta Light Horse Regiment
Royal Colonel
    5th Battalion, The Rifles
Patron
    Queen Alexandra's Royal Army Nursing Corps Association

ROYAL AIR FORCE
Honorary Air Commodore
    RAF Wittering

ROYAL NAVY
Sponsor
HMS *Daring*

THE PRINCESS ROYAL

ROYAL NAVY
Admiral (Chief Commandant for Women in the Royal Navy)
Commodore-in-Chief
HM Naval Base Portsmouth; Fleet Pacific Royal Canadian Navy

ARMY
Colonel-in-Chief
The King's Royal Hussars; Royal Corps of Signals; Royal Logistic Corps; The Royal Army Veterinary Corps; 8th Canadian Hussars (Princess Louise's); Royal Newfoundland Regiment; Canadian Forces Communications and Electronics Branch; The Grey and Simcoe Foresters; The Royal Regina Rifles; Royal Canadian Medical Service; Royal Canadian Hussars; Royal Australian Corps of Signals; Royal Australian Corps of Transport; Royal New Zealand Corps of Signals; Royal New Zealand Nursing Corps
Affiliated Colonel-in-Chief
The Queen's Gurkha Signals; The Queen's Own Gurkha Transport Regiment
Royal Colonel
1st Battalion (Royal Scots Borderers), The Royal Regiment of Scotland; 6th Battalion (52nd Lowland Volunteers), The Royal Regiment of Scotland
Colonel
The Blues and Royals (Royal Horse Guards and 1st Dragoons)
Honorary Colonel
University of London Officers' Training Corps; City of Edinburgh Universities Officers' Training Corps
Commandant-in-Chief
First Aid Nursing Yeomanry (Princess Royal's Volunteer Corps)

ROYAL AIR FORCE
Honorary Air Commodore
RAF Brize Norton; University of London Air Squadron

THE DUKE OF GLOUCESTER

ARMY
Colonel-in-Chief
The Royal Anglian Regiment; Royal Army Medical Corps; Royal New Zealand Army Medical Corps
Deputy Colonel-in-Chief
The Royal Logistic Corps
Royal Colonel
6th Battalion, The Rifles
Royal Honorary Colonel
Royal Monmouthshire Royal Engineers (Militia)

ROYAL AIR FORCE
Honorary Air Marshal
Honorary Air Commodore
RAF Odiham; No. 501 (County of Gloucester) Logistic Support Squadron

THE DUCHESS OF GLOUCESTER

ARMY
Colonel-in-Chief
Royal Army Dental Corps; Royal Australian Army Educational Corps; Royal New Zealand Army Educational Corps; Royal Canadian Dental Corps; The Royal Bermuda Regiment

Deputy Colonel-in-Chief
Adjutant General's Corps
Royal Colonel
7th Battalion, The Rifles
Vice-Patron
Adjutant General's Corps Regimental Association
Patron
Royal Army Educational Corps Association; Army Families Federation

THE DUKE OF KENT

ARMY
Field Marshal
Colonel-in-Chief
The Royal Regiment of Fusiliers; Lorne Scots (Peel, Dufferin and Hamilton Regiment)
Deputy Colonel-in-Chief
The Royal Scots Dragoon Guards (Carabiniers and Greys)
Royal Colonel
1st Battalion The Rifles
Colonel
Scots Guards

ROYAL AIR FORCE
Honorary Air Chief Marshal

THE DUCHESS OF KENT

ARMY
Honorary Major-General
Deputy Colonel-in-Chief
The Royal Dragoon Guards; Adjutant General's Corps; The Royal Logistic Corps

PRINCE MICHAEL OF KENT

ROYAL NAVY
Honorary Vice-Admiral of the Royal Naval Reserves
Commodore-in-Chief of the Maritime Reserves

ARMY
Colonel-in-Chief
Essex and Kent Scottish Regiment (Ontario)
Royal Honorary Colonel
Honourable Artillery Company
Senior Colonel
King's Royal Hussars

ROYAL AIR FORCE
Honorary Air Marshal
RAF Benson

PRINCESS ALEXANDRA, THE HON. LADY OGILVY

ROYAL NAVY
Patron
Queen Alexandra's Royal Naval Nursing Service

ARMY
Colonel-in-Chief
The Canadian Scottish Regiment (Princess Mary's)
Deputy Colonel-in-Chief
The Royal Lancers
Royal Colonel
3rd Battalion The Rifles
Royal Honorary Colonel
The Royal Yeomanry

ROYAL AIR FORCE
Patron and Air Chief Commandant
Princess Mary's RAF Nursing Service

KINGS AND QUEENS

ENGLISH KINGS AND QUEENS 927–1603

HOUSES OF CERDIC AND DENMARK

927–939   ÆTHELSTAN
Son of Edward the Elder, by Ecgwynn, and grandson of Alfred *acceded* to Wessex and Mercia *c.*924, established direct rule over Northumbria 927, effectively creating the Kingdom of England *reigned* 15 years

939–946   EDMUND I
born 921, son of Edward the Elder, by Eadgifu *married* (1) Ælfgifu (2) Æthelflæd *killed* aged 25 *reigned* 6 years

946–955   EADRED
Son of Edward the Elder, by Eadgifu *reigned* 9 years

955–959   EADWIG
born before 943, son of Edmund and Ælfgifu *married* Ælfgifu *reigned* 3 years

959–975   EDGAR I
born 943, son of Edmund and Ælfgifu *married* (1) Æthelflæd (2) Wulfthryth (3) Ælfthryth *died* aged 32 *reigned* 15 years

975–978   EDWARD I (the Martyr)
born c.962, son of Edgar and Æthelflæd *assassinated* aged *c.*16 *reigned* 2 years

978–1016   ÆTHELRED (the Unready)
born 968/969, son of Edgar and Ælfthryth *married* (1) Ælfgifu (2) Emma, daughter of Richard I, Count of Normandy, 1013–14 dispossessed of kingdom by Swegn Forkbeard (King of Denmark 987–1014) *died* aged *c.*47, *reigned* 38 years

1016   EDMUND II (Ironside)
(Apr–Nov)   *born* before 993, son of Æthelred and Ælfgifu *married* Ealdgyth *died* aged over 23 *reigned* 7 months

1016–1035   CNUT (Canute)
born c.995, son of Swegn Forkbeard, King of Denmark, and Gunhild *married* (1) Ælfgifu (2) Emma, widow of Æthelred the Unready. Gained submission of West Saxons 1015, Northumbrians 1016, Mercia 1016, King of all England after Edmund's death, King of Denmark 1019–35, King of Norway 1028–35 *died* aged *c.*40 *reigned* 19 years

1035–1040   HAROLD I (Harefoot)
born 1016/17, son of Cnut and Ælfgifu *married* Ælfgifu 1035 recognised as regent for himself and his brother Harthacnut; 1037 recognised as king *died* aged *c.*23 *reigned* 4 years

1040–1042   HARTHACNUT (Harthacanute)
born c.1018, son of Cnut and Emma. Titular king of Denmark from 1028, acknowledged King of England 1035–7 with Harold I as regent; effective king after Harold's death *died* aged *c.*24 *reigned* 2 years

1042–1066   EDWARD III (the Confessor)
born between 1002 and 1005, son of Æthelred the Unready and Emma *married* Eadgyth, daughter of Godwine, Earl of Wessex *died* aged over 60 *reigned* 23 years

1066   HAROLD II (Godwinesson)
(Jan–Oct)   *born* c.1020, son of Godwine, Earl of Wessex, and Gytha *married* (1) Eadgyth (2) Ealdgyth *killed* in battle aged *c.*46 *reigned* 10 months

THE HOUSE OF NORMANDY

1066–1087   WILLIAM I (the Conqueror)
born 1027/8, son of Robert I, Duke of Normandy; obtained the Crown by conquest *married* Matilda, daughter of Baldwin, Count of Flanders *died* aged *c.*60, *reigned* 20 years

1087–1100   WILLIAM II (Rufus)
born between 1056 and 1060, third son of William I; succeeded his father in England only *killed* aged *c.*40 *reigned* 12 years

1100–1135   HENRY I (Beauclerk)
born 1068, fourth son of William I *married* (1) Edith or Matilda, daughter of Malcolm III of Scotland (2) Adela, daughter of Godfrey, Count of Louvain *died* aged 67 *reigned* 35 years

1135–1154   STEPHEN
born not later than 1100, third son of Adela, daughter of William I, and Stephen, Count of Blois *married* Matilda, daughter of Eustace, Count of Boulogne. Feb–Nov 1141 held captive by adherents of Matilda, daughter of Henry I, who contested the Crown until 1153 *died* aged over 53 *reigned* 18 years

THE HOUSE OF ANJOU (PLANTAGENETS)

1154–1189   HENRY II (Curtmantle)
born 1133, son of Matilda, daughter of Henry I, and Geoffrey, Count of Anjou *married* Eleanor, daughter of William, Duke of Aquitaine, and divorced queen of Louis VII of France *died* aged 56 *reigned* 34 years

1189–1199   RICHARD I (Coeur de Lion)
born 1157, third son of Henry II *married* Berengaria, daughter of Sancho VI, King of Navarre *died* aged 42 *reigned* 9 years

1199–1216   JOHN (Lackland)
born 1167, fifth son of Henry II *married* (1) Isabella or Avisa, daughter of William, Earl of Gloucester (divorced) (2) Isabella, daughter of Aymer, Count of Angoulême *died* aged 48 *reigned* 17 years

1216–1272   HENRY III
born 1207, son of John and Isabella of Angoulême *married* Eleanor, daughter of Raymond, Count of Provence *died* aged 65 *reigned* 56 years

1272–1307   EDWARD I (Longshanks)
born 1239, eldest son of Henry III *married* (1) Eleanor, daughter of Ferdinand III, King of Castile (2) Margaret, daughter of Philip III of France *died* aged 68 *reigned* 34 years

1307–1327   EDWARD II
born 1284, eldest surviving son of Edward I and Eleanor *married* Isabella, daughter of Philip IV of France *deposed* Jan 1327 *killed* Sep 1327 aged 43 *reigned* 19 years

1327–1377   EDWARD III
born 1312, eldest son of Edward II *married* Philippa, daughter of William, Count of Hainault *died* aged 64 *reigned* 50 years

1377–1399   RICHARD II
born 1367, son of Edward (the Black Prince), eldest son of Edward III *married* (1) Anne, daughter of Emperor Charles IV (2) Isabelle, daughter of Charles VI of France *deposed* Sep 1399 *killed* Feb 1400 aged 33 *reigned* 22 years

THE HOUSE OF LANCASTER

1399–1413   HENRY IV
born 1366, son of John of Gaunt, fourth son of Edward III, and Blanche, daughter of Henry, Duke of Lancaster married (1) Mary, daughter of Humphrey, Earl of Hereford (2) Joan, daughter of Charles, King of Navarre, and widow of John, Duke of Brittany died aged c.47 reigned 13 years

1413–1422   HENRY V
born 1387, eldest surviving son of Henry IV and Mary married Catherine, daughter of Charles VI of France died aged 34 reigned 9 years

1422–1471   HENRY VI
born 1421, son of Henry V married Margaret, daughter of René, Duke of Anjou and Count of Provence deposed Mar 1461 restored Oct 1470 deposed Apr 1471 killed May 1471 aged 49 reigned 39 years

THE HOUSE OF YORK

1461–1483   EDWARD IV
born 1442, eldest son of Richard of York (grandson of Edmund, fifth son of Edward III; and son of Anne, great-granddaughter of Lionel, third son of Edward III) married Elizabeth Woodville, daughter of Richard, Lord Rivers, and widow of Sir John Grey acceded Mar 1461 deposed Oct 1470 restored Apr 1471 died aged 40 reigned 21 years

1483   EDWARD V
(Apr–Jun)   born 1470, eldest son of Edward IV deposed Jun 1483, died probably Jul–Sep 1483, aged 12 reigned 2 months

1483–1485   RICHARD III
born 1452, fourth son of Richard of York married Anne Neville, daughter of Richard, Earl of Warwick, and widow of Edward, Prince of Wales, son of Henry VI killed in battle aged 32 reigned 2 years

THE HOUSE OF TUDOR

1485–1509   HENRY VII
born 1457, son of Margaret Beaufort (great-granddaughter of John of Gaunt, fourth son of Edward III) and Edmund Tudor, Earl of Richmond married Elizabeth, daughter of Edward IV died aged 52 reigned 23 years

1509–1547   HENRY VIII
born 1491, second son of Henry VII married (1) Catherine, daughter of Ferdinand II, King of Aragon, and widow of his elder brother Arthur (divorced) (2) Anne, daughter of Sir Thomas Boleyn (executed) (3) Jane, daughter of Sir John Seymour (died in childbirth) (4) Anne, daughter of John, Duke of Cleves (divorced) (5) Catherine Howard, niece of the Duke of Norfolk (executed) (6) Catherine, daughter of Sir Thomas Parr and widow of Lord Latimer died aged 55 reigned 37 years

1547–1553   EDWARD VI
born 1537, son of Henry VIII and Jane Seymour died aged 15 reigned 6 years

1553   JANE
***(6/10–   born 1537, daughter of Frances (daughter of
19 Jul)**   Mary Tudor, the younger daughter of Henry VII) and Henry Grey, Duke of Suffolk married Lord Guildford Dudley, son of the Duke of Northumberland deposed Jul 1553 executed Feb 1554 aged 16 reigned 13/9 days

1553–1558   MARY I
born 1516, daughter of Henry VIII and Catherine of Aragon married Philip II of Spain died aged 42 reigned 5 years

1558–1603   ELIZABETH I
born 1533, daughter of Henry VIII and Anne Boleyn died aged 69 reigned 44 years

* Depending on whether the date of her predecessor's death (6 July) or that of her official proclamation as Queen (10 July) is taken as the beginning of her reign

BRITISH KINGS AND QUEENS SINCE 1603

THE HOUSE OF STUART

1603–1625   JAMES I (VI OF SCOTLAND)
born 1566, son of Mary, Queen of Scots (granddaughter of Margaret Tudor, elder daughter of Henry VII), and Henry Stewart, Lord Darnley married Anne, daughter of Frederick II of Denmark died aged 58 reigned 22 years

1625–1649   CHARLES I
born 1600, second son of James I married Henrietta Maria, daughter of Henry IV of France executed 1649 aged 48 reigned 23 years

INTERREGNUM 1649–1660

1649–1653   Government by a council of state
1653–1658   Oliver Cromwell, Lord Protector
1658–1659   Richard Cromwell, Lord Protector

1660–1685   CHARLES II
born 1630, eldest son of Charles I married Catherine, daughter of John of Portugal died aged 54 reigned 24 years

1685–1688   JAMES II (VII OF SCOTLAND)
born 1633, second son of Charles I married (1) Lady Anne Hyde, daughter of Edward, Earl of Clarendon (2) Mary, daughter of Alphonso, Duke of Modena. Reign ended with flight from kingdom Dec 1688 died 1701 aged 67 reigned 3 years

INTERREGNUM 11 Dec 1688 to 12 Feb 1689

1689–1702   WILLIAM III
born 1650, son of William II, Prince of Orange, and Mary Stuart, daughter of Charles I married Mary, elder daughter of James II died aged 51 reigned 13 years

and

1689–1694   MARY II
born 1662, elder daughter of James II and Anne died aged 32 reigned 5 years

1702–1714   ANNE
born 1665, younger daughter of James II and Anne married Prince George of Denmark, son of Frederick III of Denmark died aged 49 reigned 12 years

THE HOUSE OF HANOVER

1714–1727   GEORGE I (Elector of Hanover)
born 1660, son of Sophia (daughter of Frederick, Elector Palatine, and Elizabeth Stuart, daughter of James I) and Ernest Augustus, Elector of Hanover *married* Sophia Dorothea, daughter of George William, Duke of Lüneburg-Celle *died* aged 67 *reigned* 12 years

1727–1760   GEORGE II
born 1683, son of George I *married* Caroline, daughter of John Frederick, Margrave of Brandenburg-Anspach *died* aged 76 *reigned* 33 years

1760–1820   GEORGE III
born 1738, son of Frederick, eldest son of George II *married* Charlotte, daughter of Charles Louis, Duke of Mecklenburg-Strelitz *died* aged 81 *reigned* 59 years

REGENCY 1811–1820
Prince of Wales regent owing to the insanity of George III

1820–1830   GEORGE IV
born 1762, eldest son of George III *married* Caroline, daughter of Charles, Duke of Brunswick-Wolfenbüttel *died* aged 67 *reigned* 10 years

1830–1837   WILLIAM IV
born 1765, third son of George III *married* Adelaide, daughter of George, Duke of Saxe-Meiningen *died* aged 71 *reigned* 7 years

1837–1901   VICTORIA
born 1819, daughter of Edward, fourth son of George III *married* Prince Albert of Saxe-Coburg and Gotha *died* aged 81 *reigned* 63 years

THE HOUSE OF SAXE-COBURG AND GOTHA

1901–1910   EDWARD VII
born 1841, eldest son of Victoria and Albert *married* Alexandra, daughter of Christian IX of Denmark *died* aged 68 *reigned* 9 years

THE HOUSE OF WINDSOR

1910–1936   GEORGE V
born 1865, second son of Edward VII *married* Victoria Mary, daughter of Francis, Duke of Teck *died* aged 70 *reigned* 25 years

1936 (20 Jan–11 Dec)   EDWARD VIII
born 1894, eldest son of George V *married* (1937) Mrs Wallis Simpson *abdicated* 1936 *died* 1972 aged 77 *reigned* 10 months

1936–1952   GEORGE VI
born 1895, second son of George V *married* Lady Elizabeth Bowes-Lyon, daughter of 14th Earl of Strathmore and Kinghorne *died* aged 56 *reigned* 15 years

1952–   ELIZABETH II
born 1926, elder daughter of George VI *married* Philip, son of Prince Andrew of Greece

KINGS AND QUEENS OF SCOTS 1016–1603

1016–1034   MALCOLM II
born c.954, son of Kenneth II *acceded* to Alba 1005, secured Lothian c.1016, obtained Strathclyde for his grandson Duncan c.1016, thus reigning over an area approximately the same as that governed by later rulers of Scotland *died* aged c.80 *reigned* 18 years

THE HOUSE OF ATHOLL

1034–1040   DUNCAN I
son of Bethoc, daughter of Malcolm II, and Crinan, Mormaer of Atholl *married* a cousin of Siward, Earl of Northumbria *reigned* 5 years

1040–1057   MACBETH
born c.1005, son of a daughter of Malcolm II and Finlaec, Mormaer of Moray *married* Gruoch, granddaughter of Kenneth III *killed* aged c.52 *reigned* 17 years

1057–1058 (Aug–Mar)   LULACH
born c.1032, son of Gillacomgan, Mormaer of Moray, and Gruoch (and stepson of Macbeth) *died* aged c.26 *reigned* 7 months

1058–1093   MALCOLM III (Canmore)
born c.1031, elder son of Duncan I *married* (1) Ingibiorg (2) Margaret (St Margaret), granddaughter of Edmund II of England *killed* in battle aged c.62 *reigned* 35 years

1093–1097   DONALD III BÁN
born c.1033, second son of Duncan I *deposed* May 1094 *restored* Nov 1094 *deposed* Oct 1097 *reigned* 3 years

1094 (May–Nov)   DUNCAN II
born c.1060, elder son of Malcolm III and Ingibiorg *married* Octreda of Dunbar *killed* aged c.34 *reigned* 6 months

1097–1107   EDGAR
born c.1074, second son of Malcolm III and Margaret *died* aged c.32 *reigned* 9 years

1107–1124   ALEXANDER I (the Fierce)
born c.1077, fifth son of Malcolm III and Margaret *married* Sybilla, illegitimate daughter of Henry I of England *died* aged c.47 *reigned* 17 years

1124–1153   DAVID I (the Saint)
born c.1085, sixth son of Malcolm III and Margaret *married* Matilda, daughter of Waltheof, Earl of Huntingdon *died* aged c.68 *reigned* 29 years

1153–1165   MALCOLM IV (the Maiden)
born c.1141, son of Henry, Earl of Huntingdon, second son of David I *died* aged c.24 *reigned* 12 years

1165–1214   WILLIAM I (the Lion)
born c.1142, brother of Malcolm IV *married* Ermengarde, daughter of Richard, Viscount of Beaumont *died* aged c.72 *reigned* 49 years

1214–1249   ALEXANDER II
born 1198, son of William I *married* (1) Joan, daughter of John, King of England (2) Marie, daughter of Ingelram de Coucy *died* aged 50 *reigned* 34 years

1249–1286   ALEXANDER III
born 1241, son of Alexander II and Marie *married* (1) Margaret, daughter of Henry III of England (2) Yolande, daughter of the Count of Dreux *killed* accidentally aged 44 *reigned* 36 years

1286–1290   MARGARET (the Maid of Norway)
born 1283, daughter of Margaret (daughter of Alexander III) and Eric II of Norway *died* aged 7 *reigned* 4 years

FIRST INTERREGNUM 1290–1292
Throne disputed by 13 competitors. Crown awarded to John Balliol by adjudication of Edward I of England

THE HOUSE OF BALLIOL

1292–1296   **JOHN (Balliol)**
born c.1250, son of Dervorguilla, great-great-granddaughter of David I, and John de Balliol married Isabella, daughter of John, Earl of Surrey abdicated 1296 died 1313 aged c.63 reigned 3 years

SECOND INTERREGNUM 1296–1306
Edward I of England declared John Balliol to have forfeited the throne for contumacy in 1296 and took the government of Scotland into his own hands

THE HOUSE OF BRUCE

1306–1329   **ROBERT I (Bruce)**
born 1274, son of Robert Bruce and Marjorie, Countess of Carrick, and great-grandson of the second daughter of David, Earl of Huntingdon, brother of William I married (1) Isabella, daughter of Donald, Earl of Mar (2) Elizabeth, daughter of Richard, Earl of Ulster died aged 54 reigned 23 years

1329–1371   **DAVID II**
born 1324, son of Robert I and Elizabeth married (1) Joanna, daughter of Edward II of England (2) Margaret Drummond, widow of Sir John Logie (divorced) died aged 46 reigned 41 years

1332   Edward Balliol, son of John Balliol
(Sep–Dec)

1333–1336   Edward Balliol

THE HOUSE OF STEWART

1371–1390   **ROBERT II (Stewart)**
born 1316, son of Marjorie (daughter of Robert I) and Walter, High Steward of Scotland married (1) Elizabeth, daughter of Sir Robert Mure of Rowallan (2) Euphemia, daughter of Hugh, Earl of Ross died aged 74 reigned 19 years

1390–1406   **ROBERT III**
born c.1337, son of Robert II and Elizabeth married Annabella, daughter of Sir John Drummond of Stobhall died aged c.69 reigned 16 years

1406–1437   **JAMES I**
born 1394, son of Robert III married Joan Beaufort, daughter of John, Earl of Somerset assassinated aged 42 reigned 30 years

1437–1460   **JAMES II**
born 1430, son of James I married Mary, daughter of Arnold, Duke of Gueldres killed accidentally aged 29 reigned 23 years

1460–1488   **JAMES III**
born 1452, son of James II married Margaret, daughter of Christian I of Denmark assassinated aged 36 reigned 27 years

1488–1513   **JAMES IV**
born 1473, son of James III married Margaret Tudor, daughter of Henry VII of England killed in battle aged 40 reigned 25 years

1513–1542   **JAMES V**
born 1512, son of James IV married (1) Madeleine, daughter of Francis I of France (2) Mary of Lorraine, daughter of the Duc de Guise died aged 30 reigned 29 years

1542–1567   **MARY**
born 1542, daughter of James V and Mary married (1) the Dauphin, afterwards Francis II of France (2) Henry Stewart, Lord Darnley (3) James Hepburn, Earl of Bothwell abdicated 1567, prisoner in England from 1568, executed 1587 reigned 24 years

1567–1625   **JAMES VI (and I of England)**
born 1566, son of Mary, Queen of Scots, and Henry, Lord Darnley acceded 1567 to the Scottish throne reigned 58 years succeeded 1603 to the English throne, so joining the English and Scottish crowns in one person. The two kingdoms remained distinct until 1707 when the parliaments of the kingdoms became conjoined

WELSH SOVEREIGNS AND PRINCES

Wales was ruled by sovereign princes from the earliest times until the death of Llywelyn in 1282. The first English Prince of Wales was the son of Edward I, who was born in Caernarvon town on 25 April 1284. According to a discredited legend, he was presented to the Welsh chieftains as their prince, in fulfilment of a promise that they should have a prince who 'could not speak a word of English' and should be native born. This son, who afterwards became Edward II, was created 'Prince of Wales and Earl of Chester' at the Lincoln Parliament on 7 February 1301.

The title Prince of Wales is borne after individual conferment and is not inherited at birth, though some Princes have been declared and styled Prince of Wales but never formally so created (s.). The title was conferred on Prince Charles by the Queen on 26 July 1958. He was invested at Caernarvon on 1 July 1969.

INDEPENDENT PRINCES AD 844 TO 1282

844–878	Rhodri the Great
878–916	Anarawd, son of Rhodri
916–950	Hywel Dda, the Good
950–979	Iago ab Idwal (or Ieuaf)
979–985	Hywel ab Ieuaf, the Bad
985–986	Cadwallon, his brother
986–999	Maredudd ab Owain ap Hywel Dda
999–1005	Cynan ap Hywel ab Ieuaf
1005–1018	Aeddan ap Blegywyrd
1018–1023	Llywelyn ap Seisyll
1023–1039	Iago ab Idwal ap Meurig
1039–1063	Gruffydd ap Llywelyn ap Seisyll
1063–1075	Bleddyn ap Cynfyn
1075–1081	Trahaern ap Caradog
1081–1137	Gruffydd ap Cynan ab Iago
1137–1170	Owain Gwynedd
1170–1194	Dafydd ab Owain Gwynedd
1194–1240	Llywelyn Fawr, the Great
1240–1246	Dafydd ap Llywelyn
1246–1282	Llywelyn ap Gruffydd ap Llywelyn

ENGLISH PRINCES SINCE 1301

1301	Edward (Edward II)
1343	Edward the Black Prince, son of Edward III
1376	Richard (Richard II), son of the Black Prince
1399	Henry of Monmouth (Henry V)
1454	Edward of Westminster, son of Henry VI
1471	Edward of Westminster (Edward V)
1483	Edward, son of Richard III (d. 1484)
1489	Arthur Tudor, son of Henry VII
1504	Henry Tudor (Henry VIII)
1610	Henry Stuart, son of James I (d. 1612)
1616	Charles Stuart (Charles I)
c.1638 (s.)	Charles Stuart (Charles II)
1688 (s.)	James Francis Edward Stuart (The Old Pretender), son of James II (d. 1766)
1714	George Augustus (George II)
1729	Frederick Lewis, son of George II (d. 1751)
1751	George William Frederick (George III)
1762	George Augustus Frederick (George IV)
1841	Albert Edward (Edward VII)
1901	George (George V)
1910	Edward (Edward VIII)
1958	Charles, son of Elizabeth II

PRINCESSES ROYAL

The style Princess Royal is conferred at the sovereign's discretion on his or her eldest daughter. It is an honorary title, held for life, and cannot be inherited or passed on. It was first conferred on Princess Mary, daughter of Charles I, in approximately 1642.

c.1642	Princess Mary (1631–60), daughter of Charles I
1727	Princess Anne (1709–59), daughter of George II
1766	Princess Charlotte (1766–1828), daughter of George III
1840	Princess Victoria (1840–1901), daughter of Victoria
1905	Princess Louise (1867–1931), daughter of Edward VII
1932	Princess Mary (1897–1965), daughter of George V
1987	Princess Anne (b. 1950), daughter of Elizabeth II

DESCENDANTS OF QUEEN VICTORIA

I. HRH Princess Victoria Adelaide Mary Louisa, Princess Royal (1840–1901) *m* Friedrich III (1831–88), later German Emperor

II. HRH Prince Albert Edward (HM KING EDWARD VII) (1841–1910) *succeeded* 22 Jan 1901 *m* HRH Princess Alexandra of Denmark (1844–1925)

III. HRH Princess Alice Maud Mary (1843–78) *m* Prince Ludwig (1837–92), later Grand Duke of Hesse

IV. HRH Prince Alfred Ernest Albert, Duke of Edinburgh (1844–1900) *succeeded* as Duke of Saxe-Coburg and Gotha 1893 *m* Grand Duchess Marie Alexandrovna of Russia (1853–1920)

Column I

1. HIM Wilhelm II (1859–1941), later German Emperor *m* (1) Princess Augusta Victoria of Schleswig-Holstein-Sonderburg-Augustenburg (1858–1921) (2) Princess Hermine of Reuss (1887–1947). *Issue* Wilhelm (1882–1951); Eitel-Friedrich (1883–1942); Adalbert (1884–1948); August Wilhelm (1887–1949); Oskar (1888–1958); Joachim (1890–1920); Viktoria Luise (1892–1980)

2. Charlotte (1860–1919) *m* Bernhard, Duke of Saxe-Meiningen (1851–1928). *Issue* Feodora (1879–1945)

3. Heinrich (1862–1929) *m* Princess Irene of Hesse (*see* III.3). *Issue* Waldemar (1889–1945); Sigismund (1896–1978); Heinrich (1900–4)

4. Sigismund (1864–6)

5. Victoria (1866–1929) *m* (1) Prince Adolf of Schaumburg-Lippe (1859–1916) (2) Alexander Zubkov (1900–36)

6. Waldemar (1868–79)

7. Sophie (1870–1932) *m* Constantine I (1868–1923), later King of the Hellenes. *Issue* George II (1890–1947); Alexander I (1893–1920); Helena (1896–1982); Paul I (1901–64); Irene (1904–74); Katherine (1913–2007)

8. Margarethe (1872–1954) *m* Prince Friedrich Karl of Hesse (1868–1940). *Issue* Friedrich Wilhelm (1893–1916); Maximilian (1894–1914); Philipp (1896–1980); Wolfgang (1896–1989); Richard (1901–69); Christoph (1901–43)

Column II

1. Albert Victor, Duke of Clarence and Avondale (1864–92)

2. George (HM KING GEORGE V) (1865–1936) (*see* House of Windsor)

3. Louise (1867–1931), later Princess Royal *m* 1st Duke of Fife (1849–1912). *Issue* Alexandra (1891–1959); Maud (1893–1945)

4. Victoria (1868–1935)

5. Maud (1869–1938) *m* Prince Carl of Denmark (1872–1957), later King Haakon VII of Norway. *Issue* Olav V (1903–91)

6. Alexander (6–7 Apr 1871)

Column III

1. Victoria (1863–1950) *m* Prince Louis of Battenberg (1854–1921), later 1st Marquess of Milford Haven. *Issue* Alice (1885–1969); Louise (1889–1965); George (1892–1938); Louis (1900–79)

2. Elizabeth (1864–1918) *m* Grand Duke Sergius of Russia (1857–1905)

3. Irene (1866–1953) *m* Prince Heinrich of Prussia (*see* I.3)

4. Ernst Ludwig (1868–1937), Grand Duke of Hesse, *m* (1) Princess Victoria Melita of Saxe-Coburg (see IV.3) (2) Princess Eleonore of Solms-Hohensolms-Lich (1871–1937). *Issue* Elizabeth (1895–1903); George (1906–37); Ludwig (1908–68)

5. Frederick William (1870–3)

6. Alix (Tsaritsa of Russia) (1872–1918) *m* Nicholas II, Tsar of All the Russias (1868–1918). *Issue* Olga (1895–1918); Tatiana (1897–1918); Marie (1899–1918); Anastasia (1901–18); Alexis (1904–18)

7. Marie (1874–8)

QUEEN VICTORIA (Alexandrina Victoria) (1819–1901) *succeeded* 20 Jun 1837 *m* (Francis) Albert Augustus Charles Emmanuel, Duke of Saxony, Prince of Saxe-Coburg and Gotha (HRH Albert, Prince Consort) (1819–61)

VI. HRH Princess Louise Caroline Alberta (1848–1939) *m* Marquess of Lorne (1845–1914), later 9th Duke of Argyll

VII. HRH Prince Arthur William Patrick Albert, Duke of Connaught (1850–1942) *m* Princess Louisa of Prussia (1860–1917)

VIII. HRH Prince Leopold George Duncan Albert, Duke of Albany (1853–84) *m* Princess Helena of Waldeck (1861–1922)

IX. HRH Princess Beatrice Mary Victoria Feodore (1857–1944) *m* Prince Henry of Battenberg (1858–96)

1. Alfred, Prince of Saxe-Coburg (1874–99)

2. Marie (1875–1938) *m* Ferdinand (1865–1927), later King of Roumania. *Issue* Carol II (1893–1953); Elisabeth (1894–1956); Marie (1900–61); Nicolas (1903–78); Ileana (1909–91); Mircea (1913–16)

3. Victoria Melita (1876–1936) *m* (1) Grand Duke Ernst Ludwig of Hesse (*see* III.4) (2) Grand Duke Kirill of Russia (1876–1938). *Issue* Marie (1907–51); Kira (1909–67); Vladimir (1917–92)

4. Alexandra (1878–1942) *m* Ernst, Prince of Hohenlohe Langenburg (1863–1950). *Issue* Gottfried (1897–1960); Maria (1899–1967); Alexandra (1901–63); Irma (1902–86)

5. Beatrice (1884–1966) *m* Alfonso of Orleans, Infante of Spain (1886–1975). *Issue* Alvaro (1910–97); Alonso (1912–36); Ataulfo (1913–74)

1. Margaret (1882–1920) *m* Crown Prince Gustaf Adolf (1882–1973), later King of Sweden. *Issue* Gustaf Adolf (1906–47); Sigvard (1907–2002); Ingrid (1910–2000); Bertil (1912–97); Count Carl Bernadotte (1916–2012)

2. Arthur (1883–1938) *m* HH Duchess of Fife (1891–1959). *Issue* Alastair Arthur (1914–43)

3. (Victoria) Patricia (1886–1974) *m* Adm. Hon. Sir Alexander Ramsay (1881–1972). *Issue* Alexander (1919–2000)

1. Alice (1883–1981) *m* Prince Alexander of Teck (1874–1957), later 1st Earl of Athlone. *Issue* May (1906–94); Rupert (1907–28); Maurice (Mar–Sep 1910)

2. Charles Edward (1884–1954), Duke of Albany until title suspended 1917, Duke of Saxe-Coburg-Gotha *m* Princess Victoria Adelheid of Schleswig-Holstein-Sonderburg-Glücksburg (1885–1970). *Issue* Johann Leopold (1906–72); Sibylla (1908–72); Dietmar Hubertus (1909–43); Caroline (1912–83); Friedrich Josias (1918–98)

1. Alexander, 1st Marquess of Carisbrooke (1886–1960) *m* Lady Irene Denison (1890–1956). *Issue* Iris (1920–82)

2. Victoria Eugénie (1887–1969) *m* Alfonso XIII, King of Spain (1886–1941). *Issue* Alfonso (1907–38); Jaime (1908–75); Beatriz (1909–2002); Maria (1911–96); Juan (1913–93); Gonzalo (1914–34)

3. Maj. Lord Leopold Mountbatten (1889–1922)

4. Maurice (1891–1914)

V. HRH Princess Helena Augusta Victoria (1846–1923) *m* Prince Christian of Schleswig-Holstein-Sonderburg-Augustenburg (1831–1917)

1. Christian Victor (1867–1900)

2. Albert (1869–1931), later Duke of Schleswig-Holstein

3. Helena (1870–1948)

4. Marie Louise (1872–1956), *m* Prince Aribert of Anhalt (1864–1933)

5. Harold (12–20 May 1876)

THE HOUSE OF WINDSOR

King George V assumed by royal proclamation (17 July 1917) for his House and family, as well as for all descendants in the male line of Queen Victoria who are subjects of these realms, the name of Windsor.

KING GEORGE V
(George Frederick Ernest Albert), second son of King Edward VII *born* 3 June 1865 *married* 6 July 1893 HSH Princess Victoria Mary Augusta Louise Olga Pauline Claudine Agnes of Teck (Queen Mary *born* 26 May 1867 *died* 24 March 1953) *succeeded* to the throne 6 May 1910 *died* 20 January 1936. *Issue*

1. HRH PRINCE EDWARD Albert Christian George Andrew Patrick David *born* 23 June 1894 *succeeded* to the throne as King Edward VIII, 20 January 1936 *abdicated* 11 December 1936 *created* Duke of Windsor 1937 *married* 3 June 1937 Mrs Wallis Simpson (Her Grace The Duchess of Windsor *born* 19 June 1896 *died* 24 April 1986) *died* 28 May 1972

2. HRH PRINCE ALBERT Frederick Arthur George *born* 14 December 1895 *created* Duke of York 1920 *married* 26 April 1923 Lady Elizabeth Bowes-Lyon, youngest daughter of the 14th Earl of Strathmore and Kinghorne (HM Queen Elizabeth the Queen Mother *born* 4 August 1900 *died* 30 March 2002) *succeeded* to the throne as King George VI, 11 December 1936 *died* 6 February 1952. *Issue*
(1) HRH Princess Elizabeth Alexandra Mary *succeeded* to the throne as Queen Elizabeth II, 6 February 1952 (*see* Royal Family)
(2) HRH Princess Margaret Rose (later HRH The Princess Margaret, Countess of Snowdon) *born* 21 August 1930 *married* 6 May 1960 Antony Charles Robert Armstrong-Jones, GCVO *created* Earl of Snowdon 1961 (1930–2017), *marriage dissolved* 1978, *died* 9 February 2002, having had issue (*see* Royal Family)

3. HRH PRINCESS (Victoria Alexandra Alice) MARY *born* 25 April 1897 *created* Princess Royal 1932 *married* 28 February 1922 Viscount Lascelles, later the 6th Earl of Harewood (1882–1947) *died* 28 March 1965. *Issue:*

(1) George Henry Hubert Lascelles, 7th Earl of Harewood, KBE *born* 7 February 1923 *died* 11 July 2011 *married* (1) 1949 Maria (Marion) Stein (marriage dissolved 1967) *issue (a)* David Henry George, 8th Earl of Harewood *born* 1950 *(b)* James Edward *born* 1953 *(c)* (Robert) Jeremy Hugh *born* 1955 (2) 1967 Patricia Tuckwell *issue (d)* Mark Hubert *born* 1964
(2) Gerald David Lascelles *born* 21 August 1924 *died* 27 February 1998 *married* (1) 1952 Angela Dowding (marriage dissolved 1978) *issue (a)* Henry Ulick *born* 1953 (2) 1978 Elizabeth Collingwood (Elizabeth Colvin) *issue (b)* Martin David *born* 1962

4. HRH PRINCE HENRY William Frederick Albert *born* 31 March 1900 *created* Duke of Gloucester, Earl of Ulster and Baron Culloden 1928 *married* 6 November 1935 Lady Alice Christabel Montagu-Douglas-Scott, daughter of the 7th Duke of Buccleuch and Queensberry (HRH Princess Alice, Duchess of Gloucester *born* 25 December 1901 *died* 29 October 2004) *died* 10 June 1974. *Issue*
(1) HRH Prince William Henry Andrew Frederick *born* 18 December 1941 accidentally *killed* 28 August 1972
(2) HRH Prince Richard Alexander Walter George (HRH The Duke of Gloucester, *see* Royal Family)

5. HRH PRINCE GEORGE Edward Alexander Edmund *born* 20 December 1902 *created* Duke of Kent, Earl of St Andrews and Baron Downpatrick 1934 *married* 29 November 1934 HRH Princess Marina of Greece and Denmark (*born* 30 November 1906 *died* 27 August 1968) *killed* on active service 25 August 1942. *Issue*
(1) HRH Prince Edward George Nicholas Paul Patrick (HRH The Duke of Kent, *see* Royal Family)
(2) HRH Princess Alexandra Helen Elizabeth Olga Christabel (HRH Princess Alexandra, the Hon. Lady Ogilvy, *see* Royal Family)
(3) HRH Prince Michael George Charles Franklin (HRH Prince Michael of Kent, *see* Royal Family)

6. HRH PRINCE JOHN Charles Francis *born* 12 July 1905 *died* 18 January 1919

PRECEDENCE

ENGLAND AND WALES

The Sovereign
The Prince Philip, Duke of Edinburgh
The Prince of Wales
The Sovereign's younger sons
The Sovereign's grandsons
The Sovereign's cousins
Archbishop of Canterbury
Lord High Chancellor
Archbishop of York
The Prime Minister
Lord President of the Council
Speaker of the House of Commons
Speaker of the House of Lords
President of the Supreme Court
Lord Chief Justice of England and
  Wales
Lord Privy Seal
Ambassadors and High Commissioners
Lord Great Chamberlain
Earl Marshal
Lord Steward of the Household
Lord Chamberlain of the Household
Master of the Horse
Dukes, according to their patent of
  creation:
  1. of England
  2. of Scotland
  3. of Great Britain
  4. of Ireland
  5. those created since the Union
Eldest sons of Dukes of the Blood
  Royal
Ministers, Envoys, and other important
  overseas visitors
Marquesses, according to their patent
  of creation:
  1. of England
  2. of Scotland
  3. of Great Britain
  4. of Ireland
  5. those created since the Union
Dukes' eldest sons
Earls, according to their patent of
  creation:
  1. of England
  2. of Scotland
  3. of Great Britain
  4. of Ireland
  5. those created since the Union
Younger sons of Dukes of Blood
  Royal

Marquesses' eldest sons
Dukes' younger sons
Viscounts, according to their patent of
  creation:
  1. of England
  2. of Scotland
  3. of Great Britain
  4. of Ireland
  5. those created since the Union
Earls' eldest sons
Marquesses' younger sons
Bishop of London
Bishop of Durham
Bishop of Winchester
Other English Diocesan Bishops,
  according to seniority of
  consecration
Retired Church of England Diocesan
  Bishops, according to seniority of
  consecration
Suffragan Bishops, according to
  seniority of consecration
Secretaries of State, if of the degree of
  a Baron
Barons, according to their patent of
  creation:
  1. of England
  2. of Scotland (Lords of Parliament)
  3. of Great Britain
  4. of Ireland
  5. those created since the Union,
    including Life Barons
Master of the Rolls
Deputy President of the Supreme
  Court
Justices of the Supreme Court,
  according to seniority of
  appointment
Treasurer of the Household
Comptroller of the Household
Vice-Chamberlain of the Household
Secretaries of State under the degree of
  Baron
Viscounts' eldest sons
Earls' younger sons
Barons' eldest sons
Knights of the Garter
Privy Counsellors
Chancellor of the Order of the Garter
Chancellor of the Exchequer
Chancellor of the Duchy of Lancaster
President of the Queen's Bench
  Division
President of the Family Division

Chancellor of the High Court
Lord Justices of Appeal, according to
  seniority of appointment
Judges of the High Court, according to
  seniority of appointment
Viscounts' younger sons
Barons' younger sons
Sons of Life Peers
Baronets, according to date of patent
Knights of the Thistle
Knights Grand Cross of the Bath
Knights Grand Cross of St Michael
  and St George
Knights Grand Cross of the Royal
  Victorian Order
Knights Grand Cross of the British
  Empire
Knights Commanders of the Bath
Knights Commanders of St Michael
  and St George
Knights Commanders of the Royal
  Victorian Order
Knights Commanders of the British
  Empire
Knights Bachelor
Circuit Judges, according to priority
  and order of their respective
  appointments
Master of the Court of Protection
Companions of the Bath
Companions of St Michael and St
  George
Commanders of the Royal Victorian
  Order
Commanders of the British Empire
Companions of the Distinguished
  Service Order
Lieutenants of the Royal Victorian
  Order
Officers of the British Empire
Companions of the Imperial Service
  Order
Eldest sons of younger sons of peers
Baronets' eldest sons
Eldest sons of knights, in the same
  order as their fathers
Members of the Royal Victorian Order
Members of the British Empire
Baronets' younger sons
Knights' younger sons, in the same
  order as their fathers
Esquires
Gentlemen

WOMEN

Women take the same rank as their husbands or as their brothers; but the daughter of a peer marrying a commoner retains her title as Lady or Honourable. Daughters of peers rank next immediately after the wives of their elder brothers, and before their younger brothers' wives. Daughters of peers marrying peers of a lower degree take the same order of precedence as that of their husbands; thus the daughter of a

Duke marrying a Baron becomes of the rank of Baroness only, while her sisters married to commoners retain their rank and take precedence over the Baroness. Merely official rank on the husband's part does not give any similar precedence to the wife.
  Peeresses in their own right take the same precedence as peers of the same rank, ie from their date of creation.

SCOTLAND

The Sovereign
The Prince Philip, Duke of Edinburgh
The Lord High Commissioner to the
  General Assembly of the Church of
  Scotland (while that assembly is
  sitting)
The Duke of Rothesay (eldest son of
  the Sovereign)
The Sovereign's younger sons
The Sovereign's grandsons
The Sovereign's nephews
Lord-Lieutenants
Lord Provosts, during their term of
  office*
Sheriffs Principal, during their term of
  office and within the bounds of
  their respective sheriffdoms
Lord Chancellor of Great Britain
Moderator of the General Assembly of
  the Church of Scotland
Keeper of the Great Seal of Scotland
  (the First Minister)
Presiding Officer
The Secretary of State for Scotland
Hereditary High Constable of Scotland
Hereditary Master of the Household in
  Scotland
Dukes, as in England
Eldest sons of Dukes of the Blood
  Royal

Marquesses, as in England
Dukes' eldest sons
Earls, as in England
Younger sons of Dukes of Blood
  Royal
Marquesses' eldest sons
Dukes' younger sons
Lord Justice General
Lord Clerk Register
Lord Advocate
The Advocate General
Lord Justice Clerk
Viscounts, as in England
Earls' eldest sons
Marquesses' younger sons
Lords of Parliament or Barons, as in
  England
Eldest sons of Viscounts
Earls' younger sons
Eldest sons of Lords of Parliament or
  Barons
Knights and Ladies of the Garter
Knights and Ladies of the Thistle
Privy Counsellors
Senators of the College of Justice
  (Lords of Session)
Viscounts' younger sons
Younger sons of Lords of Parliament
  or Barons
Baronets
Knights and Dames Grand Cross of
  orders, as in England

Knights and Dames Commanders of
  orders, as in England
Solicitor-General for Scotland
Lord Lyon King of Arms
Sheriffs Principal, when not within
  own county
Knights Bachelor
Sheriffs
Companions of Orders, as in England
Commanders of the Royal Victorian
  Order
Commanders of the British Empire
Lieutenants of the Royal Victorian
  Order
Companions of the Distinguished
  Service Order
Officers of the British Empire
Companions of the Imperial Service
  Order
Eldest sons of younger sons of peers
Eldest sons of baronets
Eldest sons of knights, as in England
Members of the Royal Victorian Order
Members of the British Empire
Baronets' younger sons
Knights' younger sons
Queen's Counsel
Esquires
Gentlemen

* The Lord Provosts of Aberdeen, Dundee,
Edinburgh and Glasgow are Lord-Lieutenants
for these cities *ex officio* and take precedence as
such

THE PEERAGE

ABBREVIATIONS AND SYMBOLS

S.	Scottish title
I.	Irish title
**	hereditary peer remaining in the House of Lords
°	there is no 'of' in the title
b.	born
s.	succeeded
m.	married
c.p.	civil partnership
w.	widower or widow
M.	minor
cr.	created

§	life peer disqualified from sitting in the House of Lords as a member of the judiciary
ℂ	life peer who has resigned permanently from the House of Lords
E.	life peer expelled for absenteeism under section 2 of the House of Lords Reform Act 2014 (see below)
F_	represents forename
S_	represents surname
†	heir not ascertained at time of going to press
‡	title not ascertained at time of going to press

A full entry in italic type indicates that the recipient of a life peerage died within a year of it being conferred. The name is included in our list for one year for purposes of record.

The rules which govern the creation and succession of peerages are extremely complicated. There are, technically, five separate peerages, the Peerage of England, of Scotland, of Ireland, of Great Britain, and of the United Kingdom. The Peerage of Great Britain dates from 1707 when an Act of Union combined the two kingdoms of England and Scotland and separate peerages were discontinued. The Peerage of the United Kingdom dates from 1801 when Great Britain and Ireland were combined under an Act of Union. Some Scottish peers have received additional peerages of Great Britain or of the UK since 1707, and some Irish peers additional peerages of the UK since 1801.

The Peerage of Ireland was not entirely discontinued from 1801 but holders of Irish peerages, whether pre-dating or created subsequent to the Union of 1801, were not entitled to sit in the House of Lords if they had no additional English, Scottish, Great Britain or UK peerage. However, they were eligible for election to the House of Commons and to vote in parliamentary elections. An Irish peer holding a peerage of a lower grade which enabled him to sit in the House of Lords was introduced there by the title which enabled him to sit, though for all other purposes he was known by his higher title.

In the Peerage of Scotland there is no rank of Baron; the equivalent rank is Lord of Parliament, abbreviated to 'Lord' (the female equivalent is 'Lady').

All peers of England, Scotland, Great Britain or the UK who were 21 years or over, and of British, Irish or Commonwealth nationality were entitled to sit in the House of Lords until the House of Lords Act 1999, when hereditary peers lost the right to sit. However, section two of the act provided an exception for 90 hereditary peers plus the holders of the office of Earl Marshal and Lord Great Chamberlain to remain as members of the House of Lords for their lifetime or pending further reform. Of the 90 hereditary peers, 75 were elected by the hereditary peers in their political party, or Crossbench grouping, and the remaining 15 by the whole house. Until 7 November 2002 any vacancy arising due to the death of one of the 90 excepted hereditary peers was filled by the runner-up to the original election. From 7 November 2002 any vacancy due to a death – or, from 2014, a permanent retirement – has been filled by holding a by-election. By-elections are conducted in accordance with arrangements made by the Clerk of the Parliaments and have to take place within three months of a vacancy occurring. If the vacancy is among the 75, only the excepted hereditary peers in the relevant party or Crossbench grouping are entitled to vote. If the vacancy is among the other 15, the whole house is entitled to vote.

In the list below, peers currently holding one of the 92 hereditary places in the House of Lords are indicated by **.

HEREDITARY WOMEN PEERS
Most hereditary peerages pass on death to the nearest male heir, but there are exceptions, and several are held by women.

A woman peer in her own right retains her title after marriage, and if her husband's rank is the superior she is designated by the two titles jointly, the inferior one second. Her hereditary claim still holds good in spite of any marriage whether higher or lower. No rank held by a woman can confer any title or even precedence upon her husband but the rank of a hereditary woman peer in her own right is inherited by her eldest son (or in some cases daughter).

After the Peerage Act 1963, hereditary women peers in their own right were entitled to sit in the House of Lords, subject to the same qualifications as men, until the House of Lords Act 1999.

LIFE PEERS
From 1876 to 2009 non-hereditary or life peerages were conferred on certain eminent judges to enable the judicial functions of the House of Lords to be carried out. These lords were known as Lords of Appeal in Ordinary or law lords. The judicial role of the House of Lords as the highest appeal court in the UK ended on 30 July 2009 and since 1 October 2009, under the Constitutional Reform Act 2005, any peer who holds a senior judicial office is disqualified from sitting in the House of Lords until they retire from that office. In the list of life peerages which follows, members of the judiciary who are currently disqualified from sitting and voting in the House of Lords until retirement, are marked by a '§'.

Under the Constitutional Reform and Governance Act 2010, five peers permanently resigned from the House of Lords.

Since 1958 life peerages have been conferred upon distinguished men and women from all walks of life, giving them seats in the House of Lords in the degree of Baron or Baroness. They are addressed in the same way as hereditary lords and barons, and their children have similar courtesy titles.

HOUSE OF LORDS REFORM ACT 2014
The House of Lords Reform Act 2014 makes provision for a member of the House of Lords who is a peer to retire or resign by giving notice in writing to the Clerk of Parliaments. Resignations may not be rescinded. A number of life peers and elected hereditary peers have already retired permanently

under this provision. The Act also makes provision for the expulsion of peers who do not attend the House of Lords for an entire parliamentary session which is longer than six months (indicated by an 'E.' in the following list). Peers on leave of absence or subject to a suspension or disqualification which results in absenteeism for an entire session will not be expelled. The House can also resolve that a peer should not be expelled by reason of special circumstances.

All life peers who have resigned permanently from the House of Lords are indicated by a '℃' in the following list.

PEERAGES EXTINCT SINCE SEPTEMBER 2020
BARONY: Greenhill (cr. 1950)
LIFE PEERAGES: Armstrong of Ilminster (cr. 1988); Bramall (cr. 1987); Chalfont (cr. 1964); Eden of Winton (cr. 1983); Feldman (cr. 1996); Garel-Jones (cr. 1997); Gordon of Strathblane (cr. 1997); Graham of Edmonton (cr. 1983); Hutton (cr. 1997); Lester of Herne Hill (cr. 1993); Maclennan of Rogart (cr. 2001); Maddock (cr. Mawhinney (cr. 2005); May of Oxford (cr. 2001); Nicholls of Birkenhead (cr. 1994); O'Neill of Clackmannan (cr. 2005); Renton of Mount Harry (cr. 1997); Sheldon (cr. 2001); Tombs (cr. 1990); Williams of Elvel (cr. 1985); Wright of Richmond (cr. 1994)

DISCLAIMER OF PEERAGES
The Peerage Act 1963 enables peers to disclaim their peerages for life. Peers alive in 1963 could disclaim within twelve months after the passing of the act (31 July 1963); a person subsequently succeeding to a peerage may disclaim within 12 months (one month if an MP) after the date of succession, or of reaching 21, if later. The disclaimer is irrevocable but does not affect the descent of the peerage after the disclaimant's death, and children of a disclaimed peer may, if they wish, retain their precedence and any courtesy titles and styles borne as children of a peer. The disclaimer

permitted the disclaimant to sit in the House of Commons if elected as an MP. As the House of Lords Act 1999 removed the automatic right of hereditary peers to sit in the House of Lords, they are now entitled to sit in the House of Commons without having to disclaim their titles.

The following peerages are currently disclaimed:
EARLDOM: Selkirk (1994)
BARONIES: Sanderson of Ayot (1971); Silkin (2002)
PEERS WHO ARE MINORS (ie under 21 years of age)
EARLDOM: St Germans (b. 2004)

FORMS OF ADDRESS
Forms of address are given under the style for each individual rank of the peerage. Both formal and social forms of address are given where usage differs; nowadays, the social form is generally preferred to the formal, which increasingly is used only for official documents and on very formal occasions.

ROLL OF THE PEERAGE

Crown Office, House of Lords, London SW1A 0PW
T 020-7219 4687 E hereditary.claims@gmail.com

The Roll of the Peerage is kept at the Crown Office and maintained by the Registrar and Assistant Registrar of the Peerage in accordance with the terms of a 2004 royal warrant. The roll records the names of all living life peers and hereditary peers who have proved their succession to the satisfaction of the Lord Chancellor. The Roll of the Peerage is maintained in addition to the Clerk of the Parliaments' register of hereditary peers eligible to stand for election in House of Lords' by-elections.

A person whose name is not entered on the Roll of the Peerage can not be addressed or mentioned by the title of a peer in any official document.

Registrar, Mrs Ceri King

HEREDITARY PEERS

PEERS OF THE BLOOD ROYAL

Style, His Royal Highness the Duke of _/His Royal Highness the Earl of_/His Royal Highness the Lord_
Style of address (formal) May it please your Royal Highness; *(informal)* Sir

Created	Title, order of succession, name, etc	Heir
	Dukes	
1947	*Edinburgh (1st),* HRH the Prince Philip, Duke of Edinburgh	The Prince of Wales *
1337	*Cornwall,* HRH the Prince of Wales, *s.* 1952	‡
1398 S.	*Rothesay,* HRH the Prince of Wales, *s.* 1952	‡
2011	*Cambridge (1st),* HRH Prince William of Wales	HRH Prince George of Cambridge
2018	*Sussex (1st),* HRH Prince Henry of Wales	Archie Mountbatten-Windsor
1986	*York (1st),* Prince Andrew, HRH the Duke of York	None
1928	*Gloucester (2nd),* Prince Richard, HRH the Duke of Gloucester, *s.* 1974	Earl of Ulster
1934	*Kent (2nd),* Prince Edward, HRH the Duke of Kent, *s.* 1942	Earl of St Andrews
	Earl	
1999	*Wessex (1st) and Forfar (1st) (2019),* Prince Edward, HRH the Earl of Wessex	Viscount Severn

* In June 1999 Buckingham Palace announced that the current Earl of Wessex will be granted the Dukedom of Edinburgh when the title reverts to the Crown. The title will only revert to the Crown on both the death of the current Duke of Edinburgh and the Prince of Wales' succession as king
‡ The title is held by the sovereign's eldest son from the moment of his birth or the sovereign's accession

DUKES

Coronet, Eight strawberry leaves

Style, His Grace the Duke of _
Envelope (formal), His Grace the Duke of _; *(social)*, The Duke of _. *Letter (formal)*, My Lord Duke; *(social)*, Dear Duke. *Spoken (formal)*, Your Grace; *(social)*, Duke
Wife's style, Her Grace the Duchess of _
Envelope (formal), Her Grace the Duchess of _; *(social)*, The Duchess of _. *Letter (formal)*, Dear Madam; *(social)*, Dear Duchess. *Spoken*, Duchess
Eldest son's style, Takes his father's second title as a courtesy title (*see* Courtesy Titles)
Younger sons' style, 'Lord' before forename (F_) and surname (S_)
Envelope, Lord F_ S_. *Letter (formal)*, My Lord; *(social)*, Dear Lord F_. *Spoken (formal)*, My Lord; *(social)*, Lord F_
Daughters' style, 'Lady' before forename (F_) and surname (S_)
Envelope, Lady F_ S_. *Letter (formal)*, Dear Madam; *(social)*, Dear Lady F_. *Spoken*, Lady F_

Created	Title, order of succession, name, etc	Heir
1868 I.	*Abercorn (5th)*, James Hamilton, KG, *b.* 1934, *s.* 1979, *w.*	Marquess of Hamilton, *b.* 1969
1701 S.	*Argyll (13th)*, Torquhil Ian Campbell, *b.* 1968, *s.* 2001, *m.*	Marquess of Lorne, *b.* 2004
1703 S.	*Atholl (12th)*, Bruce George Ronald Murray, *b.* 1960, *s.* 2012, *m.*	Marquis of Tullibardine, *b.* 1985
1682	*Beaufort (12th)*, Henry John Fitzroy Somerset, *b.* 1952, *s.* 2017, *m.*	Marquess of Worcester, *b.* 1989
1694	*Bedford (15th)*, Andrew Ian Henry Russell, *b.* 1962, *s.* 2003, *m.*	Marquess of Tavistock, *b.* 2005
1663 S.	*Buccleuch (10th) and Queensberry (12th) (S. 1684)*, Richard Walter John Montagu Douglas Scott, KT, KBE, *b.* 1954, *s.* 2007, *m.*	Earl of Dalkeith, *b.* 1984
1694	*Devonshire (12th)*, Peregrine Andrew Morny Cavendish, KCVO, CBE, *b.* 1944, *s.* 2004, *m.*	Earl of Burlington, *b.* 1969
1900	*Fife (4th)*, David Charles Carnegie, *b.* 1961, *s.* 2015, *m.*	Earl of Southesk, *b.* 1989
1675	*Grafton (12th)*, Henry Oliver Charles FitzRoy, *b.* 1978, *s.* 2011, *m.*	Earl of Euston, *b.* 2012
1643 S.	*Hamilton (16th) and Brandon (13th) (1711)*, Alexander Douglas Douglas-Hamilton, *b.* 1978, *s.* 2010, *m. Premier Peer of Scotland*	Marquess of Douglas and Clydesdale, *b.* 2012
1766 I.	*Leinster (9th)*, Maurice FitzGerald, *b.* 1948, *s.* 2004, *m. Premier Duke, Marquess and Earl of Ireland*	Edward F., *b.* 1988
1719	*Manchester (13th)*, Alexander Charles David Drogo Montagu, *b.* 1962, *s.* 2002, *m.*	Lord Kimble W. D. M., *b.* 1964
1702	*Marlborough (12th)*, Charles James Spencer-Churchill, *b.* 1955, *s.* 2014, *m.*	Marquess of Blandford, *b.* 1992
1707 S. **	*Montrose (8th)*, James Graham, *b.* 1935, *s.* 1992, *w.*	Marquis of Graham, *b.* 1973
1483 **	*Norfolk (18th)*, Edward William Fitzalan-Howard, *b.* 1956, *s.* 2002, *m. Premier Duke and Earl Marshal*	Earl of Arundel and Surrey, *b.* 1987
1766	*Northumberland (12th)*, Ralph George Algernon Percy, *b.* 1956, *s.* 1995, *m.*	Earl Percy, *b.* 1984
1675	*Richmond (11th), Gordon (6th) (1876) and Lennox (11th) (S. 1675)*, Charles Henry Gordon Lennox, *b.* 1955, *s.* 2017, *m.*	Earl of March and Kinrara, *b.* 1994
1707 S.	*Roxburghe (11th)*, Charles Robert George Innes-Ker, *b.* 1981, *s.* 2019 *Premier Baronet of Scotland*	Lord Edward A. G. I.-K., *b.* 1984
1703	*Rutland (11th)*, David Charles Robert Manners, *b.* 1959, *s.* 1999, *m.*	Marquess of Granby, *b.* 1999
1684	*St Albans (14th)*, Murray de Vere Beauclerk, *b.* 1939, *s.* 1988, *m.*	Earl of Burford, *b.* 1965
1547 **	*Somerset (19th)*, John Michael Edward Seymour, *b.* 1952, *s.* 1984, *m.*	Lord Seymour, *b.* 1982
1833	*Sutherland (7th)*, Francis Ronald Egerton, *b.* 1940, *s.* 2000, *m.*	Marquess of Stafford, *b.* 1975
1814 **	*Wellington (9th)*, Arthur Charles Valerian Wellesley, OBE, *b.* 1945, *s.* 2014, *m.*	Earl of Mornington, *b.* 1978
1874	*Westminster (7th) and 9th Marquess of Westminster (1831)*, Hugh Richard Louis Grosvenor, *b.* 1991, *s.* 2016	To Marquessate only, Earl of Wilton (*see* that title)

MARQUESSES

Coronet, Four strawberry leaves alternating with four silver balls

Style, The Most Hon. the Marquess (of) _ . In Scotland the spelling 'Marquis' is preferred for pre-Union creations
Envelope (formal), The Most Hon. the Marquess of _; *(social)*, The Marquess of _. *Letter (formal)*, My Lord; *(social)*, Dear Lord _.
Spoken (formal), My Lord; *(social)*, Lord _
Wife's style, The Most Hon. the Marchioness (of) _
Envelope (formal), The Most Hon. the Marchioness of _; *(social)*, The Marchioness of _. *Letter (formal)*, Madam; *(social)*, Dear
Lady _. *Spoken*, Lady _
Eldest son's style, Takes his father's second title as a courtesy title (*see* Courtesy Titles)
Younger sons' style, 'Lord' before forename and surname, as for Duke's younger sons
Daughters' style, 'Lady' before forename and surname, as for Duke's daughter

Created	Title, order of succession, name, etc	Heir
1915	*Aberdeen and Temair (8th)*, George Ian Alastair Gordon, *b.* 1983, *s.* 2020, *m.*	Earl of Haddo, *b.* 2012
1876	*Abergavenny (6th) and 10th Earl of Abergavenny (1784)*, Christopher George Charles Nevill, *b.* 1955, *s.* 2000, *m.*	To Earldom only, David M. R. N., *b.* 1941
1821	*Ailesbury (8th)*, Michael Sidney Cedric Brudenell-Bruce, *b.* 1926, *s.* 1974	Earl of Cardigan, *b.* 1952
1831	*Ailsa (9th)*, David Thomas Kennedy, *b.* 1958, *s.* 2015, *m.*	Earl of Cassilis, *b.* 1995
1815	*Anglesey (8th)*, Charles Alexander Vaughan Paget, *b.* 1950, *s.* 2013, *m.*	Earl of Uxbridge, *b.* 1986
1789	*Bath (8th)*, Ceawlin Henry Laszlo Thynn, *b.* 1974, *s.* 2020, *m.*	Viscount Weymouth, *b.* 2014
1826	*Bristol (8th)*, Frederick William Augustus Hervey, *b.* 1979, *s.* 1999, *m.*	Timothy H. H., *b.* 1960
1796	*Bute (7th)*, John Colum Crichton-Stuart, *b.* 1958, *s.* 1993, *m.*	Earl of Dumfries, *b.* 1989
1812 °	*Camden (6th)*, David George Edward Henry Pratt, *b.* 1930, *s.* 1983	Earl of Brecknock, *b.* 1965
1815 **	*Cholmondeley (7th)*, David George Philip Cholmondeley, KCVO, *b.* 1960, *s.* 1990, *m. Lord Great Chamberlain*	Earl of Rocksavage, *b.* 2009
1816 I. °	*Conyngham (8th)*, Henry Vivian Pierpoint Conyngham, *b.* 1951, *s.* 2009, *m.*	Earl of Mount Charles, *b.* 1975
1791 I.	*Donegall (8th)*, Arthur Patrick Chichester, *b.* 1952, *s.* 2007, *m.*	Earl of Belfast, *b.* 1990
1789 I.	*Downshire (9th)*, (Arthur Francis) Nicholas Wills Hill, *b.* 1959, *s.* 2003, *m.*	Earl of Hillsborough, *b.* 1996
1801 I.	*Ely (9th)*, Charles John Tottenham, *b.* 1943, *s.* 2006, *m.*	Lord Timothy C. T., *b.* 1948
1801	*Exeter (8th)*, (William) Michael Anthony Cecil, *b.* 1935, *s.* 1988, *m.*	Lord Burghley, *b.* 1970
1800 I.	*Headfort (7th)*, Thomas Michael Ronald Christopher Taylour, *b.* 1959, *s.* 2005, *w.*	Earl of Bective, *b.* 1989
1793	*Hertford (9th)*, Henry Jocelyn Seymour, *b.* 1958, *s.* 1997, *m.*	Earl of Yarmouth, *b.* 1993
1599 S.	*Huntly (13th)*, Granville Charles Gomer Gordon, *b.* 1944, *s.* 1987, *m.* *Premier Marquess of Scotland*	Earl of Aboyne, *b.* 1973
1784	*Lansdowne (9th)*, Charles Maurice Mercer Nairne Petty-Fitzmaurice, LVO, *b.* 1941, *s.* 1999, *m.*	Earl of Kerry, *b.* 1970
1902	*Linlithgow (4th)*, Adrian John Charles Hope, *b.* 1946, *s.* 1987	Earl of Hopetoun, *b.* 1969
1816 I.	*Londonderry (10th)*, Frederick Aubrey Vane-Tempest-Stewart, *b.* 1972, *s.* 2012	Lord Reginald A. V.-T.-S., *b.* 1977
1701 S.	*Lothian (13th) and Baron Kerr of Monteviot (life peerage, 2010)*, Michael Andrew Foster Jude Kerr (Michael Ancram), PC, QC, *b.* 1945, *s.* 2004, *m.*	Lord Ralph W. F. J. K., *b.* 1957
1917	*Milford Haven (4th)*, George Ivar Louis Mountbatten, *b.* 1961, *s.* 1970, *m.*	Earl of Medina, *b.* 1991
1838	*Normanby (5th)*, Constantine Edmund Walter Phipps, *b.* 1954, *s.* 1994, *m.*	Earl of Mulgrave, *b.* 1994
1812	*Northampton (7th)*, Spencer Douglas David Compton, *b.* 1946, *s.* 1978, *m.*	Earl Compton, *b.* 1973
1682 S.	*Queensberry (12th)*, David Harrington Angus Douglas, *b.* 1929, *s.* 1954, *m.*	Viscount Drumlanrig, *b.* 1967
1926	*Reading (4th)*, Simon Charles Henry Rufus Isaacs, *b.* 1942, *s.* 1980, *m.*	Viscount Erleigh, *b.* 1986
1789	*Salisbury (7th) and Baron Gascoyne-Cecil (life peerage, 1999)*, Robert Michael James Gascoyne-Cecil, KG, KCVO, PC, *b.* 1946, *s.* 2003, *m.*	Viscount Cranborne, *b.* 1970
1800 I.	*Sligo (12th)*, Sebastian Ulick Browne, *b.* 1964, *s.* 2014, *m.*	Earl of Altamont, *b.* 1988
1787 °	*Townshend (8th)*, Charles George Townshend, *b.* 1945, *s.* 2010, *m.*	Viscount Raynham, *b.* 1977
1694 S.	*Tweeddale (14th)*, Charles David Montagu Hay, *b.* 1947, *s.* 2005	(Lord) Alistair J. M. H., *b.* 1955
1789 I.	*Waterford (9th)*, Henry Nicholas de la Poer Beresford, *b.* 1958, *s.* 2015, *m.*	Earl of Tyrone, *b.* 1987
1551	*Winchester (18th)*, Nigel George Paulet, *b.* 1941, *s.* 1968, *m. Premier Marquess of England*	Earl of Wiltshire, *b.* 1969
1892	*Zetland (4th)*, Lawrence Mark Dundas, *b.* 1937, *s.* 1989, *m.*	Earl of Ronaldshay, *b.* 1965

EARLS

Coronet, Eight silver balls on stalks alternating with eight gold strawberry leaves

Style, The Rt. Hon. the Earl (of) _

Envelope (formal), The Rt. Hon. the Earl (of) _; *(social)*, The Earl (of) _. *Letter (formal)*, My Lord; *(social)*, Dear Lord _. *Spoken (formal)*, My Lord; *(social)*, Lord _.

Wife's style, The Rt. Hon. the Countess (of) _

Envelope (formal), The Rt. Hon. the Countess (of) _; *(social)*, The Countess (of) _. *Letter (formal)*, Madam; *(social)*, Lady _. *Spoken (formal)*, Madam; *(social)*, Lady _.

Eldest son's style, Takes his father's second title as a courtesy title (*see* Courtesy Titles)

Younger sons' style, 'The Hon.' before forename and surname, as for Baron's children

Daughters' style, 'Lady' before forename and surname, as for Duke's daughter

Created	Title, order of succession, name, etc	Heir
1639 S.	*Airlie (13th)*, David George Coke Patrick Ogilvy, KT, GCVO, PC, Royal Victorian Chain, *b.* 1926, *s.* 1968, *m.*	Lord Ogilvy, *b.* 1958
1696	*Albemarle (10th)*, Rufus Arnold Alexis Keppel, *b.* 1965, *s.* 1979	Viscount Bury, *b.* 2003
1952 °	*Alexander of Tunis (2nd)*, Shane William Desmond Alexander, *b.* 1935, *s.* 1969, *m.*	Hon. Brian J. A., CMG, *b.* 1939
1662 S.	*Annandale and Hartfell (11th)*, Patrick Andrew Wentworth Hope Johnstone, *b.* 1941, *s.* 1983, *m.* claim established 1985	Lord Johnstone, *b.* 1971
1789 I. °	*Annesley (12th)*, Michael Robert Annesley, *b.* 1933, *s.* 2011, *w.*	Viscount Glerawly, *b.* 1957
1785 I.	*Antrim (9th)*, Alexander Randal Mark McDonnell, *b.* 1935, *s.* 1977, *m.*	Viscount Dunluce, *b.* 1967
1762 I. **	*Arran (9th) and 5th UK Baron Sudley (1884)*, Arthur Desmond Colquhoun Gore, *b.* 1938, *s.* 1983, *m.*	To Earldom only, William H. G., *b.* 1950
1955 ° **	*Attlee (3rd)*, John Richard Attlee, *b.* 1956, *s.* 1991, *m.*	None
1714	*Aylesford (12th)*, Charles Heneage Finch-Knightley, *b.* 1947, *s.* 2008, *m.*	Lord Guernsey, *b.* 1985
1937 °	*Baldwin of Bewdley (4th)*, Edward Alfred Alexander Baldwin, *b.* 1938, *s.* 1976, *w.*	Viscount Corvedale, *b.* 1973
1922	*Balfour (5th)*, Roderick Francis Arthur Balfour, *b.* 1948, *s.* 2003, *m.*	Charles G. Y. B., *b.* 1951
1772 °	*Bathurst (9th)*, Allen Christopher Bertram Bathurst, *b.* 1961, *s.* 2011, *m.*	Lord Apsley, *b.* 1990
1919 °	*Beatty (3rd)*, David Beatty, *b.* 1946, *s.* 1972	Viscount Borodale, *b.* 1973
1797 I.	*Belmore (8th)*, John Armar Lowry-Corry, *b.* 1951, *s.* 1960, *m.*	Viscount Corry, *b.* 1985
1739 I.	*Bessborough (12th)*, Myles Fitzhugh Longfield Ponsonby, *b.* 1941, *s.* 2002, *m.*	Viscount Duncannon, *b.* 1974
1815	*Bradford (7th)*, Richard Thomas Orlando Bridgeman, *b.* 1947, *s.* 1981, *m.*	Viscount Newport, *b.* 1980
1469 S.	*Buchan (17th)*, Malcolm Harry Erskine, *b.* 1930, *s.* 1984, *m.*	Lord Cardross, *b.* 1960
1746	*Buckinghamshire (10th)*, (George) Miles Hobart-Hampden, *b.* 1944, *s.* 1983, *m.*	Sir John V. Hobart, Bt., *b.* 1945
1800 °	*Cadogan (8th)*, Charles Gerald John Cadogan, KBE, *b.* 1937, *s.* 1997, *m.*	Viscount Chelsea, *b.* 1966
1878 °	*Cairns (6th)*, Simon Dallas Cairns, CVO, CBE, *b.* 1939, *s.* 1989, *m.*	Viscount Garmoyle, *b.* 1965
1455 S. **	*Caithness (20th)*, Malcolm Ian Sinclair, PC, *b.* 1948, *s.* 1965	Lord Berriedale, *b.* 1981
1800 I.	*Caledon (7th)*, Nicholas James Alexander, KCVO, *b.* 1955, *s.* 1980, *m.*	Viscount Alexander, *b.* 1990
1661	*Carlisle (13th)*, George William Beaumont Howard, *b.* 1949, *s.* 1994	Hon. Philip C. W. H., *b.* 1963
1793	*Carnarvon (8th)*, George Reginald Oliver Molyneux Herbert, *b.* 1956, *s.* 2001, *m.*	Lord Porchester, *b.* 1992
1748 I.	*Carrick (11th)*, Arion Thomas Piers Hamilton Butler, *b.* 1975, *s.* 2008, *m.*	Hon. Piers E. T. L. B., *b.* 1979
1800 I.°	*Castle Stewart (8th)*, Arthur Patrick Avondale Stuart, *b.* 1928, *s.* 1961, *m.*	Viscount Stuart, *b.* 1953
1814 ° **	*Cathcart (7th)*, Charles Alan Andrew Cathcart, *b.* 1952, *s.* 1999, *m.*	Lord Greenock, *b.* 1986
1647 I.	*Cavan (13th)*, Roger Cavan Lambart, *b.* 1944, *s.* 1988 (claim to the peerage not yet established)	Cavan C. E. L., *b.* 1957
1827 °	*Cawdor (7th)*, Colin Robert Vaughan Campbell, *b.* 1962, *s.* 1993, *m.*	Viscount Emlyn, *b.* 1998
1801	*Chichester (9th)*, John Nicholas Pelham, *b.* 1944, *s.* 1944, *m.*	Richard A. H. P., *b.* 1952
1803 I. **	*Clancarty (9th)*, Nicholas Power Richard Le Poer Trench, *b.* 1952, *s.* 1995, *m.*	None
1776 I.	*Clanwilliam (8th)*, Patrick James Meade, *b.* 1960, *s.* 2009, *m.*	Lord Gillford, *b.* 1998
1776	*Clarendon (8th)*, George Edward Laurence Villiers, *b.* 1976, *s.* 2009, *m.*	Lord Hyde, *b.* 2008
1620 I. **	*Cork and Orrery (15th)*, John Richard Boyle, *b.* 1945, *s.* 2003, *m.*	Viscount Dungarvan, *b.* 1978
1850	*Cottenham (9th)*, Mark John Henry Pepys, *b.* 1983, *s.* 2000, *m.*	Viscount Crowhurst, *b.* 2020
1762 I. **	*Courtown (9th)*, James Patrick Montagu Burgoyne Winthrop Stopford, *b.* 1954, *s.* 1975, *m.*	Viscount Stopford, *b.* 1988
1697	*Coventry (13th)*, George William Coventry, *b.* 1939, *s.* 2004, *m.*	David D. S. C., *b.* 1973

1857 °	*Cowley (8th),* Garret Graham Wellesley, *b.* 1965, *s.* 2016, *m.*	Viscount Dangan, *b.* 1991
1892	*Cranbrook (5th),* Gathorne Gathorne-Hardy, *b.* 1933, *s.* 1978, *m.*	Lord Medway, *b.* 1968
1801	*Craven (9th),* Benjamin Robert Joseph Craven, *b.* 1989, *s.* 1990	Rupert J. E. C., *b.* 1926
1398 S.	*Crawford (29th) and Balcarres (12th) (S. 1651) and Baron Balniel (life peerage, 1974),* Robert Alexander Lindsay, KT, GCVO, PC, *b.* 1927, *s.* 1975, *m.* Premier Earl on Union Roll	Lord Balniel, *b.* 1958
1861	*Cromartie (5th),* John Ruaridh Blunt Grant Mackenzie, *b.* 1948, *s.* 1989, *m.*	Viscount Tarbat, *b.* 1987
1901	*Cromer (4th),* Evelyn Rowland Esmond Baring, *b.* 1946, *s.* 1991, *m.*	Viscount Errington, *b.* 1994
1633 S.	*Dalhousie (17th),* James Hubert Ramsay, *b.* 1948, *s.* 1999, *m. Lord Steward*	Lord Ramsay, *b.* 1981
1725 I.	*Darnley (12th),* Ivo Donald Stuart Bligh, *b.* 1968, *s.* 2017, *m.*	Lord Clifton, *b.* 1999
1711	*Dartmouth (10th),* William Legge, *b.* 1949, *s.* 1997, *m.*	Hon. Rupert L., *b.* 1951
1761 °	*De La Warr (11th),* William Herbrand Sackville, *b.* 1948, *s.* 1988, *m.*	Lord Buckhurst, *b.* 1979
1622	*Denbigh (12th) and Desmond (11th) (I. 1622),* Alexander Stephen Rudolph Feilding, *b.* 1970, *s.* 1995, *m.*	Viscount Feilding, *b.* 2005
1485	*Derby (19th),* Edward Richard William Stanley, *b.* 1962, *s.* 1994, *m.*	Lord Stanley, *b.* 1998
1553 **	*Devon (19th),* Charles Peregrine Courtenay, *b.* 1975, *s.* 2015, *m.*	Lord Courtenay, *b.* 2009
1800 I.	*Donoughmore (8th),* Richard Michael John Hely-Hutchinson, *b.* 1927, *s.* 1981, *m.*	Viscount Suirdale, *b.* 1952
1661 I.	*Drogheda (12th),* Henry Dermot Ponsonby Moore, *b.* 1937, *s.* 1989, *m.*	Viscount Moore, *b.* 1983
1837	*Ducie (7th),* David Leslie Moreton, *b.* 1951, *s.* 1991, *m.*	Lord Moreton, *b.* 1981
1860	*Dudley (5th),* William Humble David Jeremy Ward, *b.* 1947, *s.* 2013	Hon. Leander G. D. W., *b.* 1971
1660 S. **	*Dundee (12th),* Alexander Henry Scrymgeour, *b.* 1949, *s.* 1983, *w.*	Lord Scrymgeour, *b.* 1982
1669 S.	*Dundonald (15th),* Iain Alexander Douglas Blair Cochrane, *b.* 1961, *s.* 1986	Lord Cochrane, *b.* 1991
1686 S.	*Dunmore (12th),* Malcolm Kenneth Murray, *b.* 1946, *s.* 1995, *w.*	Hon. Geoffrey C. M., *b.* 1949
1833	*Durham (7th),* Edward Richard Lambton, *b.* 1961, *s.* 2006, *m.*	Viscount Lambton, *b.* 1985
1643 S.	*Dysart (13th),* John Peter Grant of Rothiemurchus, *b.* 1946, *s.* 2011, *m.*	Lord Huntingtower, *b.* 1977
1837	*Effingham (7th),* David Mowbray Algernon Howard, *b.* 1939, *s.* 1996, *m.*	Lord Howard of Effingham, *b.* 1971
1507 S.	*Eglinton (19th) and Winton (10th) (S. 1600),* Hugh Archibald William Montgomerie, *b.* 1966, *s.* 2018, *m.*	Lord Montgomerie, *b.* 2007
1821	*Eldon (6th),* John Francis Thomas Marie Joseph Columba Fidelis Scott, *b.* 1962, *s.* 2017, *m.*	Viscount Encombe, *b.* 1996
1633 S.	*Elgin (11th) and Kincardine (15th) (S. 1647),* Andrew Douglas Alexander Thomas Bruce, KT, *b.* 1924, *s.* 1968, *m.*	Lord Bruce, *b.* 1961
1789 I.	*Enniskillen (7th),* Andrew John Galbraith Cole, *b.* 1942, *s.* 1989, *m.*	Berkeley A. C., *b.* 1949
1789 I.	*Erne (7th),* John Henry Michael Ninian Crichton, *b.* 1971, *s.* 2016, *m.*	Charles D. B. C., *b.* 1953
1452 S. **	*Erroll (24th),* Merlin Sereld Victor Gilbert Hay, *b.* 1948, *s.* 1978, *w.* Hereditary Lord High Constable and Knight Marischal of Scotland	Lord Hay, *b.* 1984
1661	*Essex (11th),* Frederick Paul de Vere Capell, *b.* 1944, *s.* 2005	William J. C., *b.* 1952
1711 °	*Ferrers (14th),* Robert William Saswalo Shirley, *b.* 1952, *s.* 2012, *m.*	Viscount Tamworth, *b.* 1984
1789 °	*Fortescue (8th),* Charles Hugh Richard Fortescue, *b.* 1951, *s.* 1993, *m.*	John A. F. F., *b.* 1955
1841	*Gainsborough (6th),* Anthony Baptist Noel, *b.* 1950, *s.* 2009, *m.*	Viscount Campden, *b.* 1977
1623 S.	*Galloway (14th),* Andrew Clyde Stewart, *b.* 1949, *s.* 2020, *m.*	Lord Garlies, *b.* 1980
1703 S.**	*Glasgow (10th),* Patrick Robin Archibald Boyle, *b.* 1939, *s.* 1984, *m.*	Viscount of Kelburn, *b.* 1978
1806 I.	*Gosford (7th),* Charles David Nicholas Alexander John Sparrow Acheson, *b.* 1942, *s.* 1966, *m.*	Nicholas H. C. A., *b.* 1947
1945	*Gowrie (2nd),* Alexander Patrick Greysteil Hore Ruthven, PC, *b.* 1939, *s.* 1955, *m.*	Viscount Ruthven of Canberra, *b.* 1964
1684 I.	*Granard (10th),* Peter Arthur Edward Hastings Forbes, *b.* 1957, *s.* 1992, *m.*	Viscount Forbes, *b.* 1981
1833 °	*Granville (6th),* Granville George Fergus Leveson-Gower, *b.* 1959, *s.* 1996, *m.*	Lord Leveson, *b.* 1999
1806 °	*Grey (7th),* Philip Kent Grey, *b.* 1940, *s.* 2013, *m.*	Viscount Howick, *b.* 1968
1752	*Guilford (10th),* Piers Edward Brownlow North, *b.* 1971, *s.* 1999, *m.*	Lord North, *b.* 2002
1619 S.	*Haddington (14th),* George Edmund Baldred Baillie-Hamilton, *b.* 1985, *s.* 2016	Thomas R. Hamilton-Baillie, *b.* 1948
1919 °	*Haig (3rd),* Alexander Douglas Derrick Haig, *b.* 1961, *s.* 2009, *m.*	None
1944	*Halifax (3rd),* Charles Edward Peter Neil Wood, *b.* 1944, *s.* 1980, *m.*	Lord Irwin, *b.* 1977
1754	*Hardwicke (10th),* Joseph Philip Sebastian Yorke, *b.* 1971, *s.* 1974, *m.*	Viscount Royston, *b.* 2009
1812	*Harewood (8th),* David Henry George Lascelles, *b.* 1950, *s.* 2011, *m.*	Viscount Lascelles, *b.* 1980
1742	*Harrington (12th),* Charles Henry Leicester Stanhope, *b.* 1945, *s.* 2009, *m.*	Viscount Petersham, *b.* 1967
1809	*Harrowby (8th),* Dudley Adrian Conroy Ryder, *b.* 1951, *s.* 2007, *m.*	Viscount Sandon, *b.* 1981
1605 S. **	*Home (15th),* David Alexander Cospatrick Douglas-Home, KT, CVO, CBE, *b.* 1943, *s.* 1995, *m.*	Lord Dunglass, *b.* 1987
1821 ° **	*Howe (7th),* Frederick Richard Penn Curzon, PC, *b.* 1951, *s.* 1984, *m.*	Viscount Curzon, *b.* 1994
1529	*Huntingdon (17th),* William Edward Robin Hood Hastings-Bass, LVO, *b.* 1948, *s.* 1990	Hon. John P. R. H. H.-B., *b.* 1954
1885	*Iddesleigh (5th),* John Stafford Northcote, *b.* 1957, *s.* 2004, *m.*	Viscount St Cyres, *b.* 1985
1756	*Ilchester (10th),* Robin Maurice Fox-Strangways, *b.* 1942, *s.* 2006, *m.*	Paul A. F-S., *b.* 1950
1929	*Inchcape (4th),* (Kenneth) Peter (Lyle) Mackay, *b.* 1943, *s.* 1994, *m.*	Viscount Glenapp, *b.* 1979
1919	*Iveagh (4th),* Arthur Edward Rory Guinness, *b.* 1969, *s.* 1992, *m.*	Viscount Elveden, *b.* 2003
1925 °	*Jellicoe (3rd),* Patrick John Bernard Jellicoe, *b.* 1950, *s.* 2007	Hon. Nicholas C. J., *b.* 1953

1697	*Jersey (10th),* George Francis William Child Villiers, *b.* 1976, *s.* 1998, *m.*	Viscount Villiers, *b.* 2015
1822 I.	*Kilmorey (6th),* Sir Richard Francis Needham, PC, *b.* 1942, *s.* 1977, *m.* (Does not use title)	Viscount Newry and Mourne, *b.* 1966
1866	*Kimberley (5th),* John Armine Wodehouse, *b.* 1951, *s.* 2002, *m.*	Lord Wodehouse, *b.* 1978
1768 I.	*Kingston (12th),* Robert Charles Henry King-Tenison, *b.* 1969, *s.* 2002	Viscount Kingsborough, *b.* 2000
1633 S. **	*Kinnoull (16th),* Charles William Harley Hay, *b.* 1962, *s.* 2013, *m.*	Viscount Dupplin, *b.* 2011
1677 S.	*Kintore (14th),* James William Falconer Keith, *b.* 1976, *s.* 2004, *m.*	Lord Inverurie, *b.* 2010
1624 S.	*Lauderdale (18th),* Ian Maitland, *b.* 1937, *s.* 2008, *w.*	Viscount Maitland, *b.* 1965
1837	*Leicester (8th),* Thomas Edward Coke, *b.* 1965, *s.* 2015, *m.*	Viscount Coke, *b.* 2003
1641 S.	*Leven (15th) and Melville (14th) (S. 1690),* Alexander Ian Leslie Melville, *b.* 1984, *s.* 2012	Hon. Archibald R. L. M., *b.* 1957
1831	*Lichfield (6th),* Thomas William Robert Hugh Anson, *b.* 1978, *s.* 2005, *m.*	Viscount Anson, *b.* 2011
1803 I.	*Limerick (7th),* Edmund Christopher Pery, *b.* 1963, *s.* 2003, *m.*	Viscount Pery, *b.* 1991
1572	*Lincoln (19th),* Robert Edward Fiennes-Clinton, *b.* 1972, *s.* 2001	Hon. William J. Howson, *b.* 1980
1633 S. **	*Lindsay (16th),* James Randolph Lindesay-Bethune, *b.* 1955, *s.* 1989, *m.*	Viscount Garnock, *b.* 1990
1626	*Lindsey (14th) and Abingdon (9th) (1682),* Richard Henry Rupert Bertie, *b.* 1931, *s.* 1963, *m.*	Lord Norreys, *b.* 1958
1776 I.	*Lisburne (9th),* David John Francis Malet Vaughan, *b.* 1945, *s.* 2014, *m.*	Hon. Michael J. W. M. V., *b.* 1948
1822 I.**	*Listowel (6th),* Francis Michael Hare, *b.* 1964, *s.* 1997	Hon. Timothy P. H., *b.* 1966
1905 **	*Liverpool (5th),* Edward Peter Bertram Savile Foljambe, *b.* 1944, *s.* 1969, *m.*	Viscount Hawkesbury, *b.* 1972
1945 °	*Lloyd George of Dwyfor (4th),* David Richard Owen Lloyd George, *b.* 1951, *s.* 2010, *m.*	Viscount Gwynedd, *b.* 1986
1785 I.	*Longford (8th),* Thomas Frank Dermot Pakenham, *b.* 1933, *s.* 2001, *m.* (Does not use title)	Edward M. P., *b.* 1970
1807	*Lonsdale (8th),* Hugh Clayton Lowther, *b.* 1949, *s.* 2006, *m.*	Hon. William J. L., *b.* 1957
1633 S.	*Loudoun (15th),* Simon Michael Abney-Hastings, *b.* 1974, *s.* 2012	Hon. Marcus W. A.-H., *b.* 1981
1795 I.	*Lucan (8th),* George Charles Bingham, *b.* 1967, *s.* 2016, *m.*	Lord Bingham, *b.* 2019
1880 **	*Lytton (5th),* John Peter Michael Scawen Lytton, *b.* 1950, *s.* 1985, *m.*	Viscount Knebworth, *b.* 1989
1721	*Macclesfield (9th),* Richard Timothy George Mansfield Parker, *b.* 1943, *s.* 1992, *m.*	Hon. J. David G. P., *b.* 1945
1800	*Malmesbury (7th),* James Carleton Harris, *b.* 1946, *s.* 2000, *m.*	Viscount FitzHarris, *b.* 1970
1776	*Mansfield (8th) and Mansfield (9th) (1792),* Alexander David Mungo Murray, *b.* 1956, *s.* 2015, *m.*	Viscount Stormont, *b.* 1988
1565 S.	*Mar (14th) and Kellie (16th) (S. 1616) and Baron Erskine of Alloa Tower (life peerage, 2000),* James Thorne Erskine, *b.* 1949, *s.* 1994, *m.*	Hon. Alexander D. E., *b.* 1952
1785 I.	*Mayo (11th),* Charles Diarmuidh John Bourke, *b.* 1953, *s.* 2006, *m.*	Lord Naas, *b.* 1985
1627 I.	*Meath (15th),* John Anthony Brabazon, *b.* 1941, *s.* 1998, *m.*	Lord Ardee, *b.* 1977
1766 I.	*Mexborough (8th),* John Christopher George Savile, *b.* 1931, *s.* 1980, *m.*	Viscount Pollington, *b.* 1959
1813	*Minto (7th),* Gilbert Timothy George Lariston Elliot-Murray-Kynynmound, *b.* 1953, *s.* 2005, *m.*	Viscount Melgund, *b.* 1984
1562 S.	*Moray (21st),* John Douglas Stuart, *b.* 1966, *s.* 2011, *m.*	Lord Doune, *b.* 2002
1815	*Morley (7th),* Mark Lionel Parker, *b.* 1956, *s.* 2015, *m.*	Edward G. P., *b.* 1967
1458 S.	*Morton (22nd),* John Stewart Sholto Douglas, *b.* 1952, *s.* 2016, *m.*	Lord Aberdour, *b.* 1986
1789	*Mount Edgcumbe (8th),* Robert Charles Edgcumbe, *b.* 1939, *s.* 1982, *m.*	Piers V. E., *b.* 1946
1947 °	*Mountbatten of Burma (3rd),* Norton Louis Philip Knatchbull, *b.* 1947, *s.* 2017, *m.*	Lord Brabourne, *b.* 1981
1805 °	*Nelson (10th),* Simon John Horatio Nelson, *b.* 1971, *s.* 2009, *m.*	Viscount Merton, *b.* 2010
1660 S.	*Newburgh (12th),* Don Filippo Giambattista Camillo Francesco Aldo Maria Rospigliosi, *b.* 1942, *s.* 1986, *m.*	Princess Donna Benedetta F. M. R., *b.* 1974
1827 I.	*Norbury (7th),* Richard James Graham-Toler, *b.* 1967, *s.* 2000	None
1806 I.	*Normanton (7th),* James Shaun Christian Welbore Ellis Agar, *b.* 1982, *s.* 2019, *m.*	Viscount Somerton, *b.* 2016
1647 S.	*Northesk (15th),* Patrick Charles Carnegy, *b.* 1940, *s.* 2010, *m.*	Hon. Colin D. C., *b.* 1942
1801	*Onslow (8th),* Rupert Charles William Bullard Onslow, *b.* 1967, *s.* 2011, *m.*	Anthony E. E. O., *b.* 1955
1696 S.	*Orkney (9th),* (Oliver) Peter St John, *b.* 1938, *s.* 1998, *m.*	Viscount Kirkwall, *b.* 1969
1328 I.	*Ormonde and Ossory (I. 1527),* The 25th/18th Earl (7th Marquess) died in 1988	†Viscount Mountgarret *b.* 1961 (*see* that title)
1925 **	*Oxford and Asquith (3rd),* Raymond Benedict Bartholomew Michael Asquith, OBE, *b.* 1952, *s.* 2011, *m.*	Viscount Asquith, *b.* 1979
1929 ° **	*Peel (3rd),* William James Robert Peel, GCVO, PC, *b.* 1947, *s.* 1969, *m.* Lord Chamberlain	Viscount Clanfield, *b.* 1976
1551	*Pembroke (18th) and Montgomery (15th) (1605),* William Alexander Sidney Herbert, *b.* 1978, *s.* 2003, *m.*	Lord Herbert, *b.* 2012
1605 S.	*Perth (18th),* John Eric Drummond, *b.* 1935, *s.* 2002, *m.*	Viscount Strathallan, *b.* 1965
1905	*Plymouth (4th),* Ivor Edward Other Windsor-Clive, *b.* 1951, *s.* 2018, *m.*	Viscount Windsor, *b.* 1981
1785 I.	*Portarlington (7th),* George Lionel Yuill Seymour Dawson-Damer, *b.* 1938, *s.* 1959, *m.*	Viscount Carlow, *b.* 1965
1689	*Portland (12th),* Count Timothy Charles Robert Noel Bentinck, MBE, *b.* 1953, *s.* 1997, *m.*	Viscount Woodstock, *b.* 1984
1743	*Portsmouth (10th),* Quentin Gerard Carew Wallop, *b.* 1954, *s.* 1984, *m.*	Viscount Lymington, *b.* 1981
1804	*Powis (8th),* John George Herbert, *b.* 1952, *s.* 1993, *m.*	Viscount Clive, *b.* 1979

1765	*Radnor (9th),* William Pleydell-Bouverie, *b.* 1955, *s.* 2008, *m.*	Viscount Folkestone, *b.* 1999
1831 I.	*Ranfurly (8th),* Edward John Knox, *b.* 1957, *s.* 2018, *m.*	Viscount Northland, *b.* 1994
1771 I.	*Roden (10th),* Robert John Jocelyn, *b.* 1938, *s.* 1993, *m.*	Viscount Jocelyn, *b.* 1989
1801	*Romney (8th),* Julian Charles Marsham, *b.* 1948, *s.* 2004, *m.*	Viscount Marsham, *b.* 1977
1703 S.	*Rosebery (7th),* Neil Archibald Primrose, *b.* 1929, *s.* 1974, *m.*	Lord Dalmeny, *b.* 1967
1806 I.	*Rosse (7th),* William Brendan Parsons, *b.* 1936, *s.* 1979, *m.*	Lord Oxmantown, *b.* 1969
1801 **	*Rosslyn (7th),* Peter St Clair-Erskine, CVO, QPM, *b.* 1958, *s.* 1977, *m.*	Lord Loughborough, *b.* 1986
1457 S.	*Rothes (22nd),* James Malcolm David Leslie, *b.* 1958, *s.* 2005	Hon. Alexander J. L., *b.* 1962
1861 °	*Russell (7th),* John Francis Russell, *b.* 1971, *s.* 2014, *m.*	None
1915 °	*St Aldwyn (3rd),* Michael Henry Hicks Beach, *b.* 1950, *s.* 1992, *m.*	Hon. David S. H. B., *b.* 1955
1815 M.	*St Germans (11th),* Albert Charger Eliot, *b.* 2004, *s.* 2016	Hon. Louis R. E., *b.* 1968
1660 **	*Sandwich (11th),* John Edward Hollister Montagu, *b.* 1943, *s.* 1995, *m.*	Viscount Hinchingbrooke, *b.* 1969
1690	*Scarbrough (13th),* Richard Osbert Lumley, *b.* 1973, *s.* 2004, *m.*	Hon. Thomas H. L., *b.* 1980
1701 S.	*Seafield (13th),* Ian Derek Francis Ogilvie-Grant, *b.* 1939, *s.* 1969, *m.*	Viscount Reidhaven, *b.* 1963
1882	*Selborne (4th),* John Roundell Palmer, GBE, *b.* 1940, *s.* 1971, *m.*	Viscount Wolmer, *b.* 1971
1646 S.	*Selkirk (11th),* Disclaimed for life 1994 (*see* Lord Selkirk of Douglas, Life Peers)	Master of Selkirk, *b.* 1978
1672	*Shaftesbury (12th),* Nicholas Edmund Anthony Ashley-Cooper, *b.* 1979, *s.* 2005, *m.*	Lord Ashley, *b.* 2011
1756 I.	*Shannon (10th),* Richard Henry John Boyle, *b.* 1960, *s.* 2013	Robert F. B., *b.* 1930
1442 **	*Shrewsbury and Waterford (22nd) (I. 1446),* Charles Henry John Benedict Crofton Chetwynd Chetwynd-Talbot, *b.* 1952, *s.* 1980, *m. Premier Earl of England and Ireland*	Viscount Ingestre, *b.* 1978
1961	*Snowdon (2nd),* David Albert Charles Armstrong-Jones, *b.* 1961, *s.* 2017	Viscount Linley, *b.* 1999
1765 °	*Spencer (9th),* Charles Edward Maurice Spencer, *b.* 1964, *s.* 1992, *m.*	Viscount Althorp, *b.* 1994
1703 S.**	*Stair (14th),* John David James Dalrymple, *b.* 1961, *s.* 1996, *m.*	Viscount Dalrymple, *b.* 2008
1984	*Stockton (2nd),* Alexander Daniel Alan Macmillan, *b.* 1943, *s.* 1986	Viscount Macmillan of Ovenden, *b.* 1974
1821	*Stradbroke (6th),* Robert Keith Rous, *b.* 1937, *s.* 1983, *m.*	Viscount Dunwich, *b.* 1961
1847	*Strafford (9th),* William Robert Byng, *b.* 1964, *s.* 2016, *m.*	Viscount Enfield, *b.* 1998
1606 S.	*Strathmore and Kinghorne (19th) (S. 1677),* Simon Patrick Bowes Lyon, *b.* 1986, *s.* 2016	Hon. John F. B. L., *b.* 1988
1603	*Suffolk (21st) and Berkshire (14th) (1626),* Michael John James George Robert Howard, *b.* 1935, *s.* 1941, *m.*	Viscount Andover, *b.* 1974
1235	*Sutherland (25th),* Alastair Charles St Clair Sutherland, *b.* 1947, *s.* 2019, *m.*	Lord Strathnaver, *b.* 1981
1955	*Swinton (3rd),* Nicholas John Cunliffe-Lister, *b.* 1939, *s.* 2006, *m.*	Lord Masham, *b.* 1970
1714	*Tankerville (10th),* Peter Grey Bennet, *b.* 1956, *s.* 1980	Adrian G. B., *b.* 1958
1822 °	*Temple of Stowe (9th),* James Grenville Temple-Gore-Langton, *b.* 1955, *s.* 2013, *m.*	Hon. Robert C. T.-G.-L., *b.* 1957
1815	*Verulam (7th),* John Duncan Grimston, *b.* 1951, *s.* 1973, *m.*	Viscount Grimston, *b.* 1978
1729 °	*Waldegrave (13th),* James Sherbrooke Waldegrave, *b.* 1940, *s.* 1995	Viscount Chewton, *b.* 1986
1759	*Warwick (9th) and Brooke (9th) (1746),* Guy David Greville, *b.* 1957, *s.* 1996, *m.*	Lord Brooke, *b.* 1982
1633 S.	*Wemyss (13th) and March (9th) (S. 1697),* James Donald Charteris, *b.* 1948, *s.* 2008, *m.*	Lord Elcho, *b.* 1984
1621 I.	*Westmeath (13th),* William Anthony Nugent, *b.* 1928, *s.* 1971, *m.*	Sean C. W. N., *b.* 1965
1624	*Westmorland (16th),* Anthony David Francis Henry Fane, *b.* 1951, *s.* 1993, *m.*	Hon. Harry St C. F., *b.* 1953
1876	*Wharncliffe (5th),* Richard Alan Montagu Stuart Wortley, *b.* 1953, *s.* 1987, *m.*	Viscount Carlton, *b.* 1980
1801	*Wilton (8th),* Francis Egerton Grosvenor, *b.* 1934, *s.* 1999, *w.*	Viscount Grey de Wilton, *b.* 1959
1628	*Winchilsea (17th) and Nottingham (12th) (1681),* Daniel James Hatfield Finch Hatton, *b.* 1967, *s.* 1999, *m.*	Viscount Maidstone, *b.* 1998
1766 I. °	*Winterton (8th),* (Donald) David Turnour, *b.* 1943, *s.* 1991, *m.*	Robert C. T., *b.* 1950
1956	*Woolton (3rd),* Simon Frederick Marquis, *b.* 1958, *s.* 1969, *m.*	None
1837	*Yarborough (8th),* Charles John Pelham, *b.* 1963, *s.* 1991, *m.*	Lord Worsley, *b.* 1990

COUNTESSES IN THEIR OWN RIGHT

Style, The Rt. Hon. the Countess (of) _
Envelope (formal), The Rt. Hon. the Countess (of) _; *(social),* The Countess (of) _. *Letter (formal),* Madam; *(social),* Lady _. *Spoken (formal),* Madam; *(social),* Lady _.
Husband, Untitled
Children's style, As for children of an Earl
In Scotland, the heir to a Countess may be styled 'The Master/Mistress of _ (title of peer)'

Created	Title, order of succession, name, etc	Heir
c.1115 S.	*Mar (31st),* Margaret of Mar, *b.* 1940, *s.* 1975, *m.* Premier Earldom of Scotland	Mistress of Mar, *b.* 1963

VISCOUNTS

Coronet, Sixteen silver balls

Style, The Rt. Hon. the Viscount _
Envelope (formal), The Rt. Hon. the Viscount _; *(social),* The Viscount _. *Letter (formal),* My Lord; *(social),* Dear Lord _. *Spoken,* Lord _.
Wife's style, The Rt. Hon. the Viscountess _
Envelope (formal), The Rt. Hon. the Viscountess _; *(social),* The Viscountess _. *Letter (formal),* Madam; *(social),* Dear Lady _. *Spoken,* Lady _.
Children's style, 'The Hon.' before forename and surname, as for Baron's children
In Scotland, the heir to a Viscount may be styled 'The Master/Mistress of _ (title of peer)'

Created	Title, order of succession, name, etc	Heir
1945	*Addison (4th),* William Matthew Wand Addison, *b.* 1945, *s.* 1992, *m.*	Hon. Paul W. A., *b.* 1973
1919	*Allenby (4th),* Henry Jaffray Hynman Allenby, *b.* 1968, *s.* 2014, *m.*	Hon. Harry M. E. A., *b.* 2000
1911	*Allendale (4th),* Wentworth Peter Ismay Beaumont, *b.* 1948, *s.* 2002, *m.*	Hon. Wentworth A. I. B., *b.* 1979
1642 S.	*of Arbuthnott (17th),* John Keith Oxley Arbuthnott, *b.* 1950, *s.* 2012, *m.*	Master of Arbuthnott, *b.* 1977
1751 I.	*Ashbrook (11th),* Michael Llowarch Warburton Flower, *b.* 1935, *s.* 1995, *m.*	Hon. Rowland F. W. F., *b.* 1975
1917 **	*Astor (4th),* William Waldorf Astor, *b.* 1951, *s.* 1966, *m.*	Hon. William W. A., *b.* 1979
1781 I.	*Bangor (8th),* William Maxwell David Ward, *b.* 1948, *s.* 1993, *m.*	Hon. E. Nicholas W., *b.* 1953
1925	*Bearsted (5th),* Nicholas Alan Samuel, *b.* 1950, *s.* 1996, *m.*	Hon. Harry R. S., *b.* 1988
1963	*Blakenham (3rd),* Caspar John Hare, *b.* 1972, *s.* 2018, *m.*	Hon. Inigo H., *b. c.*2006
1935	*Bledisloe (4th),* Rupert Edward Ludlow Bathurst, *b.* 1964, *s.* 2009, *m.*	Hon. Benjamin R. L. B., *b.* 2004
1712	*Bolingbroke (9th) and St John (10th) (1716),* Nicholas Alexander Mowbray St John, *b.* 1974, *s.* 2011, *m.*	German A. St J., *b.* 1980
1960	*Boyd of Merton (2nd),* Simon Donald Rupert Neville Lennox-Boyd, *b.* 1939, *s.* 1983, *m.*	Hon. Benjamin A. L.-B., *b.* 1964
1717 I.	*Boyne (11th),* Gustavus Michael Stucley Hamilton-Russell, *b.* 1965, *s.* 1995, *m.*	Hon. Gustavus A. E. H.-R., *b.* 1999
1929	*Brentford (4th),* Crispin William Joynson-Hicks, *b.* 1933, *s.* 1983, *m.*	Hon. Paul W. J.-H., MBE, *b.* 1971
1929 **	*Bridgeman (3rd),* Robin John Orlando Bridgeman, *b.* 1930, *s.* 1982, *m.*	Hon. Luke R. O. B., *b.* 1971
1868	*Bridport (4th) and 7th Duke, Bronte in Sicily, 1799,* Alexander Nelson Hood, *b.* 1948, *s.* 1969	Hon. Peregrine A. N. H., *b.* 1974
1952 **	*Brookeborough (3rd),* Alan Henry Brooke, KG, *b.* 1952, *s.* 1987, *m.*	Hon. Christopher A. B., *b.* 1954
1933	*Buckmaster (4th),* Adrian Charles Buckmaster, *b.* 1949, *s.* 2007, *m.*	Hon. Andrew N. B., *b.* 1980
1939	*Caldecote (3rd),* Piers James Hampden Inskip, *b.* 1947, *s.* 1999, *m.*	Hon. Thomas J. H. I., *b.* 1985
1941	*Camrose (5th),* Jonathan William Berry, *b.* 1970, *s.* 2016, *m.*	Hon. Hugo W. B., *b.* 2000
1954	*Chandos (3rd) and Baron Lyttelton of Aldershot (life peerage, 2000),* Thomas Orlando Lyttelton, *b.* 1953, *s.* 1980, *m.*	Hon. Oliver A. L., *b.* 1986
1665 I.	*Charlemont (15th),* John Dodd Caulfeild, *b.* 1966, *s.* 2001, *m.*	Hon. Shane A. C., *b.* 1996

1921	*Chelmsford (4th)*, Frederic Corin Piers Thesiger, *b.* 1962, *s.* 1999, *m.*	Hon. Frederic T., *b.* 2006
1717 I.	*Chetwynd (11th)*, Adam Douglas Chetwynd, *b.* 1969, *s.* 2015, *m.*	Hon. Connor A. C., *b.* 2001
1911	*Chilston (4th)*, Alastair George Akers-Douglas, *b.* 1946, *s.* 1982, *m.*	Hon. Oliver I. A.-D., *b.* 1973
1718	*Cobham (12th)*, Christopher Charles Lyttelton, *b.* 1947, *s.* 2006, *m.*	Hon. Oliver C. L., *b.* 1976
1902 **	*Colville of Culross (5th)*, Charles Mark Townshend Colville, *b.* 1959, *s.* 2010	Master of Colville, *b.* 1961
1826	*Combermere (6th)*, Thomas Robert Wellington Stapleton-Cotton, *b.* 1969, *s.* 2000, *m.*	Hon. Laszlo M. W. S.-C., *b.* 2010
1917	*Cowdray (4th)*, Michael Orlando Weetman Pearson, *b.* 1944, *s.* 1995, *m.*	Hon. Peregrine J. D. P., *b.* 1994
1927 **	*Craigavon (3rd)*, Janric Fraser Craig, *b.* 1944, *s.* 1974	None
1943	*Daventry (4th)*, James Edward FitzRoy Newdegate, *b.* 1960, *s.* 2000, *m.*	Hon. Humphrey J. F. N., *b.* 1995
1937	*Davidson (4th)*, John Nicolas Alexander Davidson, *b.* 1971, *s.* 2020, *m..*	None
1956	*De L'Isle (2nd)*, Philip John Algernon Sidney, CVO, MBE, *b.* 1945, *s.* 1991, *m.*	Hon. Philip W. E. S., *b.* 1985
1776 I.	*de Vesci (7th)*, Thomas Eustace Vesey, *b.* 1955, *s.* 1983	Hon. Oliver I. V., *b.* 1991
1917	*Devonport (3rd)*, Terence Kearley, *b.* 1944, *s.* 1973, *m.*	Chester D. H. K., *b.* 1932
1964	*Dilhorne (2nd)*, John Mervyn Manningham-Buller, *b.* 1932, *s.* 1980, *m.*	Hon. James E. M.-B., *b.* 1956
1622 I.	*Dillon (22nd)*, Henry Benedict Charles Dillon, *b.* 1973, *s.* 1982, *m.*	Hon. Francis C. R. D., *b.* 2013
1785 I.	*Doneraile (10th)*, Richard Allen St Leger, *b.* 1946, *s.* 1983, *m.*	Hon. Nathaniel W. R. St J. St L., *b.* 1971
1680 I.	*Downe (12th)*, Richard Henry Dawnay, *b.* 1967, *s.* 2002	Thomas P. D., *b.* 1978
1959	*Dunrossil (3rd)*, Andrew William Reginald Morrison, *b.* 1953, *s.* 2000, *m.*	Hon. Callum A. B. M., *b.* 1994
1964 **	*Eccles (2nd)*, John Dawson Eccles, CBE, *b.* 1931, *s.* 1999, *m.*	Hon. William D. E., *b.* 1960
1897	*Esher (5th)*, Christopher Lionel Baliol Brett, *b.* 1936, *s.* 2004, *m.*	Hon. Matthew C. A. B., *b.* 1963
1816	*Exmouth (10th)*, Paul Edward Pellew, *b.* 1940, *s.* 1970	Hon. Edward F. P., *b.* 1978
1620 S.**	*of Falkland (15th)*, Lucius Edward William Plantagenet Cary, *b.* 1935, *s.* 1984, *m. Premier Scottish Viscount on the Roll*	Master of Falkland, *b.* 1963
1720	*Falmouth (9th)*, George Hugh Boscawen, *b.* 1919, *s.* 1962, *w.*	Hon. Evelyn A. H. B., *b.* 1955
1720 I.	*Gage (8th)*, (Henry) Nicolas Gage, *b.* 1934, *s.* 1993, *m.*	Hon. Henry W. G., *b.* 1975
1727 I.	*Galway (13th)*, John Philip Monckton, *b.* 1952, *s.* 2017, *m.*	Alan S. M., *b.* 1934
1478 I.	*Gormanston (17th)*, Jenico Nicholas Dudley Preston, *b.* 1939, *s.* 1940, *m. Premier Viscount of Ireland*	Hon. Jenico F. T. P., *b.* 1974
1816 I.	*Gort (9th)*, Foley Robert Standish Prendergast Vereker, *b.* 1951, *s.* 1995, *m.*	Hon. Robert F. P. V., *b.* 1993
1900 **	*Goschen (4th)*, Giles John Harry Goschen, *b.* 1965, *s.* 1977, *m.*	Hon. Alexander J. E. G., *b.* 2001
1849	*Gough (5th)*, Shane Hugh Maryon Gough, *b.* 1941, *s.* 1951	None
1929	*Hailsham (3rd) and Baron Hailsham of Kettlethorpe (life peerage, 2015)*, Douglas Martin Hogg, PC, QC, *b.* 1945, *s.* 2001, *m.*	Hon. Quintin J. N. M. H., *b.* 1973
1891	*Hambleden (5th)*, William Henry Bernard Smith, *b.* 1955, *s.* 2012, *m.*	Hon. Bernardo J. S., *b.* 1957
1884	*Hampden (7th)*, Francis Anthony Brand, *b.* 1970, *s.* 2008, *m.*	Hon. Lucian A. B., *b.* 2005
1936 **	*Hanworth (3rd)*, David Stephen Geoffrey Pollock, *b.* 1946, *s.* 1996, *m.*	Harold W. C. P., *b.* 1988
1791 I.	*Harberton (11th)*, Henry Robert Pomeroy, *b.* 1958, *s.* 2004, *m.*	Hon. Patrick C. P., *b.* 1995
1846	*Hardinge (8th)*, Thomas Henry de Montarville Hardinge, *b.* 1993, *s.* 2014	Hon. Jamie A. D. H., *b.* 1996
1791 I.	*Hawarden (9th)*, (Robert) Connan Wyndham Leslie Maude, *b.* 1961, *s.* 1991, *m.*	Hon. Varian J. C. E. M., *b.* 1997
1960	*Head (2nd)*, Richard Antony Head, *b.* 1937, *s.* 1983, *m.*	Hon. Henry J. H., *b.* 1980
1550	*Hereford (19th)*, Charles Robin de Bohun Devereux, *b.* 1975, *s.* 2004, *m. Premier Viscount of England*	Hon. Henry W. de B. D., *b.* 2015
1842	*Hill (9th)*, Peter David Raymond Charles Clegg-Hill, *b.* 1945, *s.* 2003, *m.*	Hon. Michael C. D. C.-H., *b.* 1988
1796	*Hood (8th)*, Henry Lyttelton Alexander Hood, *b.* 1958, *s.* 1999, *m.*	Hon. Archibald L. S. H., *b.* 1993
1945	*Kemsley (3rd)*, Richard Gomer Berry, *b.* 1951, *s.* 1999, *m.*	Hon. Luke G. B., *b.* 1998
1911	*Knollys (3rd)*, David Francis Dudley Knollys, *b.* 1931, *s.* 1966, *m.*	Hon. Patrick N. M. K., *b.* 1962
1895	*Knutsford (6th)*, Michael Holland-Hibbert, *b.* 1926, *s.* 1986, *w.*	Hon. Henry T. H.-H., *b.* 1959
1954	*Leathers (3rd)*, Christopher Graeme Leathers, *b.* 1941, *s.* 1996, *m.*	Hon. James F. L., *b.* 1969
1781 I.	*Lifford (9th)*, (Edward) James Wingfield Hewitt, *b.* 1949, *s.* 1987, *m.*	Hon. James T. W. H., *b.* 1979
1921	*Long (5th)*, James Richard Long, *b.* 1960, *s.* 2017	None
1957	*Mackintosh of Halifax (3rd)*, (John) Clive Mackintosh, *b.* 1958, *s.* 1980, *m.*	Hon. Thomas H. G. M., *b.* 1985
1955	*Malvern (3rd)*, Ashley Kevin Godfrey Huggins, *b.* 1949, *s.* 1978	Hon. M. James H., *b.* 1928
1945	*Marchwood (3rd)*, David George Staveley Penny, *b.* 1936, *s.* 1979, *m.*	Hon. Peter G. W. P., *b.* 1965
1942	*Margesson (3rd)*, Richard Francis David Margesson, *b.* 1960, *s.* 2014, *m.*	None
1660 I.	*Massereene (14th) and Ferrard (7th) (I. 1797)*, John David Clotworthy Whyte-Melville Foster Skeffington, *b.* 1940, *s.* 1992, *m.*	Hon. Charles J. C. W.-M. F. S., *b.* 1973
1802	*Melville (10th)*, Robert Henry Kirkpatrick Dundas, *b.* 1984, *s.* 2011, *m.*	Hon. Max D. H. M. D., *b.* 2018
1916	*Mersey (5th) and 14th Lord Nairne (S. 1681)*, Edward John Hallam Bigham, *b.* 1966, *s.* 2006, *m.*	Hon. David E. H. B., *b.* 1938 (to Viscountcy); Mistress of Nairne, *b.* 2003 (to Lordship of Nairne)
1717 I.	*Midleton (12th)*, Alan Henry Brodrick, *b.* 1949, *s.* 1988, *m.*	Hon. Ashley R. B., *b.* 1980
1962	*Mills (3rd)*, Christopher Philip Roger Mills, *b.* 1956, *s.* 1988, *m.*	None
1716 I.	*Molesworth (12th)*, Robert Bysse Kelham Molesworth, *b.* 1959, *s.* 1997	Hon. William J. C. M., *b.* 1960
1801 I.	*Monck (7th)*, Charles Stanley Monck, *b.* 1953, *s.* 1982 (Does not use title)	Hon. George S. M., *b.* 1957

1957	*Monckton of Brenchley (3rd)*, Christopher Walter Monckton, *b.* 1952, *s.* 2006, *m.*	Hon. Timothy D. R. M., *b.* 1955
1946	*Montgomery of Alamein (3rd)*, Henry David Montgomery, *b.* 1954, *s.* 2020, *w.*	None
1550 I.	*Mountgarret (18th)*, Piers James Richard Butler, *b.* 1961, *s.* 2004, *m.*	Hon. Theo O. S. B., *b.* 2015
1952	*Norwich (3rd)*, Jason Charles Duff Bede Cooper, *b.* 1959, *s.* 2018	None
1651 S.	*of Oxfuird (14th)*, Ian Arthur Alexander Makgill, *b.* 1969, *s.* 2003, *m.*	Master of Oxfuird, *b.* 2012
1873	*Portman (10th)*, Christopher Edward Berkeley Portman, *b.* 1958, *s.* 1999, *m.*	Hon. Luke O. B. P., *b.* 1984
1743 I.	*Powerscourt (11th) and 5th UK Baron Powerscourt (1885)*, Mervyn Anthony Wingfield, *b.* 1963, *s.* 2015, *m.*	To Viscountcy only, Richard D. N. W., *b.* 1966
1900 **	*Ridley (5th)*, Matthew White Ridley, *b.* 1958, *s.* 2012, *m.*	Hon. Matthew W. R., *b.* 1993
1960	*Rochdale (3rd)*, Jonathan Hugo Durival Kemp, *b.* 1961, *s.* 2015, *m.*	George T. K., *b.* 2001
1919	*Rothermere (4th)*, (Harold) Jonathan Esmond Vere Harmsworth, *b.* 1967, *s.* 1998, *m.*	Hon. Vere R. J. H. H., *b.* 1994
1937	*Runciman of Doxford (3rd)*, Walter Garrison (Garry) Runciman, CBE, *b.* 1934, *s.* 1989, *m.*	Hon. David W. R., *b.* 1967
1918	*St Davids (4th)*, Rhodri Colwyn Philipps, *b.* 1966, *s.* 2009, *m.*	Hon. Roland A. J. E. P., *b.* 1970
1801	*St Vincent (8th)*, Edward Robert James Jervis, *b.* 1951, *s.* 2006, *m.*	Hon. James R. A. J., *b.* 1982
1937	*Samuel (5th)*, Jonathan Herbert Samuel, *b.* 1965, *s.* 2014, *m.*	Hon. Benjamin A. S., *b.* 1983
1911	*Scarsdale (4th)*, Peter Ghislain Nathaniel Curzon, *b.* 1949, *s.* 2000, *m.*	Hon. David J. N. C., *b.* 1958
1905	*Selby (6th)*, Christopher Rolf Thomas Gully, *b.* 1993, *s.* 2001	Hon. (James) Edward H. G. G., *b.* 1945
1805	*Sidmouth (8th)*, Jeremy Francis Addington, *b.* 1947, *s.* 2005, *w.*	Hon. John A., *b.* 1990
1940 **	*Simon (3rd)*, Jan David Simon, *b.* 1940, *s.* 1993, *m.*	None
1960	*Slim (3rd)*, Mark William Rawdon Slim, *b.* 1960, *s.* 2019, *m.*	Hon. Rufus W. R. S., *b.* 1995
1954	*Soulbury (4th)*, Oliver Peter Ramsbotham, *b.* 1943, *s.* 2010, *m.*	Hon. Edward H. R., *b.* 1966
1776 I.	*Southwell (8th)*, Richard Andrew Pyers Southwell, *b.* 1956, *s.* 2020, *m.*	Hon. Charles A. J. S., *b.* 1962
1942	*Stansgate (3rd)*, Stephen Michael Wedgwood Benn, *b.* 1951, *s.* 2014, *m.*	Hon. Daniel J. W. B., *b.* 1991
1959	*Stuart of Findhorn (3rd)*, Dominic Stuart, *b.* 1948, *s.* 1999	Hon. Andrew M. S., *b.* 1957
1957	*Tenby (3rd)*, William Lloyd George, *b.* 1927, *s.* 1983, *m.*	Hon. Timothy H. G. L. G., *b.* 1962
1952 **	*Thurso (3rd)*, John Archibald Sinclair, PC, *b.* 1953, *s.* 1995, *m.*	Hon. James A. R. S., *b.* 1984
1721	*Torrington (11th)*, Timothy Howard St George Byng, *b.* 1943, *s.* 1961, *m.*	Colin H. Cranmer-Byng, *b.* 1960
1936 **	*Trenchard (3rd)*, Hugh Trenchard, *b.* 1951, *s.* 1987, *m.*	Hon. Alexander T. T., *b.* 1978
1921 **	*Ullswater (2nd)*, Nicholas James Christopher Lowther, LVO, PC, *b.* 1942, *s.* 1949, *m.*	Hon. Benjamin J. L., *b.* 1975
1642 I.	*Valentia (16th)*, Francis William Dighton Annesley, *b.* 1959, *s.* 2005, *m.*	Hon. Peter J. A., *b.* 1967
1952 **	*Waverley (3rd)*, John Desmond Forbes Anderson, *b.* 1949, *s.* 1990, *m.*	Hon. Forbes A. R. A., *b.* 1996
1938	*Weir (3rd)*, William Kenneth James Weir, *b.* 1933, *s.* 1975, *m.*	Hon. James W. H. W., *b.* 1965
1918	*Wimborne (4th)*, Ivor Mervyn Vigors Guest, *b.* 1968, *s.* 1993, *m.*	Hon. Ivor N. G. I. G., *b.* 2016
1923 **	*Younger of Leckie (5th)*, James Edward George Younger, *b.* 1955, *s.* 2003, *m.*	Hon. Alexander W. G. Y., *b.* 1993

BARONS/LORDS

Coronet, Six silver balls

Style, The Rt. Hon. the Lord _
  Envelope (formal), The Rt. Hon. Lord _; *(social)*, The Lord _. *Letter (formal)*, My Lord; *(social)*, Dear Lord _. *Spoken*, Lord _.
In the Peerage of Scotland there is no rank of Baron; the equivalent rank is Lord of Parliament and Scottish peers should always be styled 'Lord', never 'Baron'.

Wife's style, The Rt. Hon. the Lady _
Envelope (formal), The Rt. Hon. Lady _; *(social)*, The Lady _. *Letter (formal)*, My Lady; *(social)*, Dear Lady _. *Spoken*, Lady _
Children's style, 'The Hon.' before forename (F_) and surname (S_)
Envelope, The Hon. F_ S_. *Letter*, Dear Mr/Miss/Mrs S_. *Spoken*, Mr/Miss/Mrs S_
In Scotland, the heir to a Lord may be styled 'The Master/Mistress of _ (title of peer)'

Created	*Title, order of succession, name, etc*	*Heir*
1911	*Aberconway (4th)*, (Henry) Charles McLaren, *b.* 1948, *s.* 2003, *m.*	Hon. Charles S. M., *b.* 1984
1873 **	*Aberdare (5th)*, Alastair John Lyndhurst Bruce, *b.* 1947, *s.* 2005, *m.*	Hon. Hector M. N. B., *b.* 1974
1835	*Abinger (9th)*, James Harry Scarlett, *b.* 1959, *s.* 2002, *m.*	Hon. Peter R. S., *b.* 1961

1869	*Acton (5th),* John Charles Ferdinand Harold Lyon-Dalberg-Acton, *b.* 1966, *s.* 2010, *m.*	Hon. Robert P. L.-D.-A., *b.* 1946
1887 **	*Addington (6th),* Dominic Bryce Hubbard, *b.* 1963, *s.* 1982, *m.*	Hon. Michael W. L. H., *b.* 1965
1896	*Aldenham (6th) and Hunsdon of Hunsdon (4th) (1923),* Vicary Tyser Gibbs, *b.* 1948, *s.* 1986, *m.*	Hon. Humphrey W. F. G., *b.* 1989
1962	*Aldington (2nd),* Charles Harold Stuart Low, *b.* 1948, *s.* 2000, *m.*	Hon. Philip T. A. L., *b.* 1990
1945	*Altrincham (4th),* (Edward) Sebastian Grigg, *b.* 1965, *s.* 2020, *m.*	Hon. Edward L. D. de M. G., *b.* 1995
1929	*Alvingham (3rd),* Robert Richard Guy Yerburgh, *b.* 1956, *s.* 1956, *m.*	Hon. Robert W. G. Y., *b.* 1971
1892	*Amherst of Hackney (5th),* Hugh William Amherst Cecil, *b.* 1968, *s.* 2009, *m.*	Hon. Jack W. A. C., *b.* 2001
1881	*Ampthill (5th),* David Whitney Erskine Russell, *b.* 1947, *s.* 2011, *m.*	Hon. Anthony J. M. R., *b.* 1952
1947	*Amwell (3rd),* Keith Norman Montague, *b.* 1943, *s.* 1990, *m.*	Hon. Ian K. M., *b.* 1973
1863	*Annaly (6th),* Luke Richard White, *b.* 1954, *s.* 1990	Hon. Luke H. W., *b.* 1990
1885	*Ashbourne (5th),* Edward Charles d'Olier Gibson, *b.* 1967, *s.* 2020	Hon. Edward A. G., *b.* 2002
1835	*Ashburton (8th),* Mark Francis Robert Baring, *b.* 1958, *s.* 2020, *m.*	Hon. Frederick C. F. B., *b.* 1990
1892	*Ashcombe (5th),* Mark Edward Cubitt, *b.* 1964, *s.* 2013, *m.*	Hon. Richard R. A. C., *b.* 1995
1911 **	*Ashton of Hyde (4th),* Thomas Henry Ashton, PC, *b.* 1958, *s.* 2008, *m.*	Hon. John E. A., *b.* 1966
1800 I.	*Ashtown (8th),* Roderick Nigel Godolphin Trench, *b.* 1944, *s.* 2010, *m.*	Hon. Timothy R. H. T., *b.* 1968
1956 **	*Astor of Hever (3rd),* John Jacob Astor, PC, *b.* 1946, *s.* 1984, *m.*	Hon. Charles G. J. A., *b.* 1990
1789 I.	*Auckland (10th) and Auckland (10th) (1793),* Robert Ian Burnard Eden, *b.* 1962, *s.* 1997, *m.*	Henry V. E., *b.* 1958
1313	*Audley,* Barony in abeyance between three co-heiresses since 1997	
1900	*Avebury (5th),* Lyulph Ambrose Lubbock, *b.* 1954, *s.* 2016, *m.*	Hon. Alexander L. R. L., *b.* 1985
1718 I.	*Aylmer (14th),* (Anthony) Julian Aylmer, *b.* 1951, *s.* 2006, *m.*	Hon. Michael H. A., *b.* 1991
1929	*Baden-Powell (4th),* David Michael Baden-Powell, *b.* 1940, *s.* 2019, *m.*	Hon. David R. B.-P., *b.* 1971
1780	*Bagot (10th),* (Charles Hugh) Shaun Bagot, *b.* 1944, *s.* 2001, *m.*	Julian W. D'A. B., *b.* 1943
1953	*Baillieu (3rd),* James William Latham Baillieu, *b.* 1950, *s.* 1973, *m.*	Hon. Robert L. B., *b.* 1979
1924	*Banbury of Southam (3rd),* Charles William Banbury, *b.* 1953, *s.* 1981, *m.*	None
1698	*Barnard (12th),* Henry Francis Cecil Vane, *b.* 1959, *s.* 2016, *m.*	Hon. William H. C. V., *b.* 2005
1887	*Basing (6th),* Stuart Anthony Whitfield Sclater-Booth, *b.* 1969, *s.* 2007	Hon. Luke W. S.-B., *b.* 2000
1917	*Beaverbrook (3rd),* Maxwell William Humphrey Aitken, *b.* 1951, *s.* 1985, *m.*	Hon. Maxwell F. A., *b.* 1977
1647 S.	*Belhaven and Stenton (13th),* Robert Anthony Carmichael Hamilton, *b.* 1927, *s.* 1961, *m.*	Master of Belhaven, *b.* 1953
1848 I.	*Bellew (8th),* Bryan Edward Bellew, *b.* 1943, *s.* 2010, *m.*	Hon. Anthony R. B. B., *b.* 1972
1856	*Belper (5th),* Richard Henry Strutt, *b.* 1941, *s.* 1999, *w.*	Hon. Michael H. S., *b.* 1969
1421	*Berkeley (18th) and Gueterbock (life peerage, 2000),* Anthony Fitzhardinge Gueterbock, OBE, *b.* 1939, *s.* 1992, *m.*	Hon. Thomas F. G., *b.* 1969
1922 **	*Bethell (5th),* James Nicholas Bethell, *b.* 1967, *s.* 2007, *m.*	Hon. Jacob N. D. B., *b.* 2006
1938	*Bicester (5th),* Charles James Vivian Smith, *b.* 1963, *s.* 2016, *m.*	Hon. Milo L. V. S., *b.* 2007
1903	*Biddulph (5th),* (Anthony) Nicholas Colin Maitland Biddulph, *b.* 1959, *s.* 1988	Hon. Robert J. M. B., *b.* 1994
1958	*Birkett (3rd),* Thomas Birkett, *b.* 1982, *s.* 2015, *m.*	None
1907	*Blyth (5th),* James Audley Ian Blyth, *b.* 1970, *s.* 2009, *m.*	Hon. Hugo A. J. B., *b.* 2006
1797	*Bolton (8th),* Harry Algar Nigel Orde-Powlett, *b.* 1954, *s.* 2001, *w.*	Hon. Thomas P. A. O.-P., MC, *b.* 1979
1452 S.	*Borthwick (24th),* John Hugh Borthwick, *b.* 1940, *s.* 1996, *m.*	Hon. James H. A. B. of Glengelt, *b.* 1940
1922 **	*Borwick (5th),* (Geoffrey Robert) James Borwick, *b.* 1955, *s.* 2007, *m.*	Hon. Edwin D. W. B., *b.* 1984
1761	*Boston (11th),* George William Eustace Boteler Irby, *b.* 1971, *s.* 2007, *m.*	Hon. Thomas W. G. B. I., *b.* 1999
1942 **	*Brabazon of Tara (3rd),* Ivon Anthony Moore-Brabazon, PC, *b.* 1946, *s.* 1974, *m.*	Hon. Benjamin R. M.-B., *b.* 1983
1925	*Bradbury (3rd),* John Bradbury, *b.* 1940, *s.* 1994, *m.*	Hon. John T. B., *b.* 1973
1962	*Brain (3rd),* Michael Cottrell Brain, *b.* 1928, *s.* 2014, *m.*	Hon. Thomas R. B., *b.* 1965
1938	*Brassey of Apethorpe (4th),* Edward Brassey, *b.* 1964, *s.* 2015, *m.*	Hon. Christian B., *b.* 2003
1788	*Braybrooke (11th),* Richard Ralph Neville, *b.* 1977, *s.* 2017, *m.*	Hon. Edward A. N., *b.* 2015
1957	*Bridges (3rd),* Mark Thomas Bridges, KCVO, *b.* 1954, *s.* 2017, *m.*	Hon. Nicholas E. B., *b.* 1956
1945	*Broadbridge (5th),* Air Vice-Marshal Richard John Martin Broadbridge, CB, *b.* 1959, *s.* 2020, *m.*	Hon. Mark A. B., *b.* 1983
1933	*Brocket (3rd),* Charles Ronald George Nall-Cain, *b.* 1952, *s.* 1967, *m.*	Hon. Alexander C. C. N.-C., *b.* 1984
1860 **	*Brougham and Vaux (5th),* Michael John Brougham, CBE, *b.* 1938, *s.* 1967	Hon. Charles W. B., *b.* 1971
1776	*Brownlow (7th),* Edward John Peregrine Cust, *b.* 1936, *s.* 1978, *m.*	Hon. Peregrine E. Q. C., *b.* 1974
1942	*Bruntisfield (3rd),* Michael John Victor Warrender, *b.* 1949, *s.* 2007, *m.*	Hon. John M. P. C. W., *b.* 1996
1950	*Burden (4th),* Fraser William Elsworth Burden, *b.* 1964, *s.* 2000	Hon. Ian S. B., *b.* 1967
1529	*Burgh (8th),* (Alexander) Gregory Disney Leith, *b.* 1958, *s.* 2001, *m.*	Hon. Alexander J. S. L., *b.* 1986
1903	*Burnham (7th),* Harry Frederick Alan Lawson, *b.* 1968, *s.* 2005	None
1897	*Burton (4th),* Evan Michael Ronald Baillie, *b.* 1949, *s.* 2013, *m.*	Hon. James E. B., *b.* 1975
1643	*Byron (13th),* Robert James Byron, *b.* 1950, *s.* 1989, *m.*	Hon. Charles R. G. B., *b.* 1990
1937	*Cadman (3rd),* John Anthony Cadman, *b.* 1938, *s.* 1966, *m.*	Hon. Nicholas A. J. C., *b.* 1977
1945	*Calverley (3rd),* Charles Rodney Muff, *b.* 1946, *s.* 1971, *m.*	Hon. Jonathan E. Brown, *b.* 1975

1383	*Camoys (7th)*, (Ralph) Thomas Campion George Sherman Stonor, GCVO, PC, *b.* 1940, *s.* 1976, *m.*	Hon. R. William R. T. S., *b.* 1974
1715 I.	*Carbery (12th)*, Michael Peter Evans-Freke, *b.* 1942, *s.* 2012, *m.*	Hon. Dominic R. C. E.-F., *b.* 1969
1834 I.	*Carew (7th) and Carew (7th) (1838)*, Patrick Thomas Conolly-Carew, *b.* 1938, *s.* 1994, *m.*	Hon. William P. C.-C., *b.* 1973
1916	*Carnock (5th)*, Adam Nicolson, *b.* 1957, *s.* 2008, *m.*	Hon. Thomas N., *b.* 1984
1796 I.**	*Carrington (7th) and Carrington (7th) (1797)*, Rupert Francis John Carington, *b.* 1948, *s.* 2018, *m.*	Hon. Robert C., *b.* 1990
1812 I.	*Castlemaine (8th)*, Roland Thomas John Handcock, MBE, *b.* 1943, *s.* 1973, *m.*	Hon. Ronan M. E. H., *b.* 1989
1936	*Catto (3rd)*, Innes Gordon Catto, *b.* 1950, *s.* 2001, *m.*	Hon. Alexander G. C., *b.* 1952
1918	*Cawley (4th)*, John Francis Cawley, *b.* 1946, *s.* 2001, *m.*	Hon. William R. H. C., *b.* 1981
1858	*Chesham (7th)*, Charles Gray Compton Cavendish, *b.* 1974, *s.* 2009, *m.*	Hon. Oliver N. B. C., *b.* 2007
1945	*Chetwode (2nd)*, Philip Chetwode, *b.* 1937, *s.* 1950, *m.*	Hon. Roger C., *b.* 1968
1945	*Chorley (3rd)*, Nicholas Rupert Debenham Chorley, *b.* 1966, *s.* 2016, *m.*	Hon. Patrick A. C. C., *b.* 2000
1815	*Churchill (7th)*, Michael Richard de Charriere Spencer, *b.* 1960, *s.* 2020, *m.*	Hon. David A. de C. S., *b.* 1970
1858	*Churston (5th)*, John Francis Yarde-Buller, *b.* 1934, *s.* 1991, *m.*	Hon. Benjamin F. A. Y.-B., *b.* 1974
1800 I.	*Clanmorris (8th)*, Simon John Ward Bingham, *b.* 1937, *s.* 1988, *m.*	Robert D. de B. B., *b.* 1942
1672	*Clifford of Chudleigh (14th)*, Thomas Hugh Clifford, *b.* 1948, *s.* 1988, *m.*	Hon. Alexander T. H. C., *b.* 1985
1299	*Clinton (22nd)*, Gerard Nevile Mark Fane Trefusis, *b.* 1934, *s.* 1965, *m.*	Hon. Charles P. R. F. T., *b.* 1962
1955	*Clitheroe (2nd)*, Ralph John Assheton, *b.* 1929, *s.* 1984, *m.*	Hon. Ralph C. A., *b.* 1962
1919	*Clwyd (4th)*, (John) Murray Roberts, *b.* 1971, *s.* 2006, *m.*	Hon. John D. R., *b.* 2006
1948	*Clydesmuir (3rd)*, David Ronald Colville, *b.* 1949, *s.* 1996, *m.*	Hon. Richard C., *b.* 1980
1960	*Cobbold (2nd)*, David Antony Fromanteel Lytton Cobbold, *b.* 1937, *s.* 1987, *m.*	Hon. Henry F. L. C., *b.* 1962
1919	*Cochrane of Cults (5th)*, Thomas Hunter Vere Cochrane, *b.* 1957, *s.* 2017, *m.*	Hon. Michael C. N. C., OBE, *b.* 1959
1954	*Coleraine (3rd)*, James Peter Bonar Law, *b.* 1975, *s.* 2020	Hon. Andrew B. L., *b.* 1933
1873	*Coleridge (5th)*, William Duke Coleridge, *b.* 1937, *s.* 1984, *w.*	Hon. James D. C., *b.* 1967
1946 **	*Colgrain (4th)*, Alastair Colin Leckie Campbell, *b.* 1951, *s.* 2008, *m.*	Hon. Thomas C. D. C., *b.* 1984
1917 **	*Colwyn (3rd)*, (Ian) Anthony Hamilton-Smith, CBE, *b.* 1942, *s.* 1966, *m.*	Hon. Craig P. H.-S., *b.* 1968
1956	*Colyton (2nd)*, Alisdair John Munro Hopkinson, *b.* 1958, *s.* 1996, *m.*	Hon. James P. M. H., *b.* 1983
1841	*Congleton (9th)*, John Patrick Christian Parnell, *b.* 1959, *s.* 2015, *m.*	Hon. Christopher J. E. P., *b.* 1987
1927	*Cornwallis (4th)*, Fiennes Wykeham Jeremy Cornwallis, *b.* 1946, *s.* 2010, *m.*	Hon. Fiennes A. W. M. C., *b.* 1987
1874	*Cottesloe (6th)*, Thomas Francis Henry Fremantle, *b.* 1966, *s.* 2018	Hon. Edward W. F., *b.* 1961
1929	*Craigmyle (4th)*, Thomas Columba Shaw, *b.* 1960, *s.* 1998, *m.*	Hon. Alexander F. S., *b.* 1988
1899	*Cranworth (3rd)*, Philip Bertram Gurdon, *b.* 1940, *s.* 1964, *m.*	Hon. Sacha W. R. G., *b.* 1970
1959 **	*Crathorne (2nd)*, Charles James Dugdale, KCVO, *b.* 1939, *s.* 1977, *w.*	Hon. Thomas A. J. D., *b.* 1977
1892	*Crawshaw (5th)*, David Gerald Brooks, *b.* 1934, *s.* 1997, *m.*	Hon. John P. B., *b.* 1938
1940	*Croft (3rd)*, Bernard William Henry Page Croft, *b.* 1949, *s.* 1997, *m.*	None
1797 I.	*Crofton (8th)*, Edward Harry Piers Crofton, *b.* 1988, *s.* 2007	Hon. Charles M. G. C., *b.* 1988
1375 **	*Cromwell (7th)*, Godfrey John Bewicke-Copley, *b.* 1960, *s.* 1982, *m.*	Hon. David G. B.-C., *b.* 1997
1947	*Crook (3rd)*, Robert Douglas Edwin Crook, *b.* 1955, *s.* 2001, *m.*	Hon. Matthew R. C., *b.* 1990
1920	*Cullen of Ashbourne (4th)*, Michael John Cokayne, *b.* 1950, *s.* 2016, *m.*	None
1914	*Cunliffe (3rd)*, Roger Cunliffe, *b.* 1932, *s.* 1963, *m.*	Hon. Henry C., *b.* 1962
1332	*Darcy de Knayth (19th)*, Caspar David Ingrams, *b.* 1962, *s.* 2008	Hon. Thomas R. I., *b.* 1999
1927	*Daresbury (4th)*, Peter Gilbert Greenall, *b.* 1953, *s.* 1996, *m.*	Hon. Thomas E. G., *b.* 1984
1924	*Darling (3rd)*, (Robert) Julian Henry Darling, *b.* 1944, *s.* 2003, *m.*	Hon. Robert J. C. D., *b.* 1972
1946	*Darwen (4th)*, David Paul Cedric Davies, *b.* 1962, *s.* 2011, *m.*	Hon. Oscar K. D., *b.* 1996
1932	*Davies (3rd)*, David Davies, *b.* 1940, *s.* 1944, *w.*	Hon. David D. D., *b.* 1975
1812 I.	*Decies (7th)*, Marcus Hugh Tristram de la Poer Beresford, *b.* 1948, *s.* 1992, *m.*	Hon. Robert M. D. de la P. B., *b.* 1988
1299	*de Clifford (28th)*, Miles Edward Southwell Russell, *b.* 1966, *s.* 2018, *m.*	Hon. Edward S. R., *b.* 1998
1851	*De Freyne (8th)*, Fulke Charles Arthur John French, *b.* 1957, *s.* 2009, *m.*	Hon. Alexander J. C. F., *b.* 1988
1821	*Delamere (5th)*, Hugh George Cholmondeley, *b.* 1934, *s.* 1979, *m.*	Hugh D. C., *b.* 1998
1838 **	*de Mauley (7th)*, Rupert Charles Ponsonby, TD, *b.* 1957, *s.* 2002, *m.*	Ashley G. P., *b.* 1959
1937 **	*Denham (2nd)*, Bertram Stanley Mitford Bowyer, KBE, PC, *b.* 1927, *s.* 1948, *m.*	Hon. Richard G. G. B., *b.* 1959
1834	*Denman (6th)*, Richard Thomas Stewart Denman, *b.* 1946, *s.* 2012, *m.*	Hon. Robert J. D., *b.* 1995
1887	*De Ramsey (4th)*, John Ailwyn Fellowes, *b.* 1942, *s.* 1993, *m.*	Hon. Freddie J. F., *b.* 1978
1264	*de Ros (28th)*, Peter Trevor Maxwell, *b.* 1958, *s.* 1983, *m. Premier Baron of England*	Hon. Finbar J. M., *b.* 1988
1881	*Derwent (5th)*, Robin Evelyn Leo Vanden-Bempde-Johnstone, LVO, *b.* 1930, *s.* 1986, *m.*	Hon. Francis P. H. V.-B.-J., *b.* 1965
1831	*de Saumarez (7th)*, Eric Douglas Saumarez, *b.* 1956, *s.* 1991, *m.*	Hon. Victor T. S., *b.* 1956
1910	*de Villiers (4th)*, Alexander Charles de Villiers, *b.* 1940, *s.* 2001, *m.*	None
1930	*Dickinson (3rd)*, Martin Hyett Dickinson, *b.* 1961, *s.* 2019, *m.*	Hon. Andrew D., *b.* 1963
1620 I.	*Digby (13th) and Digby (6th) (1765)*, Henry Noel Kenelm Digby, *b.* 1954, *s.* 2018, *m.*	Hon. Edward St V. K. D., *b.* 1985
1615	*Dormer (18th)*, William Robert Dormer, *b.* 1960, *s.* 2016, *m.*	Hon. Hugo E. G. D., *b.* 1995

1943	*Dowding (3rd)*, Piers Hugh Tremenheere Dowding, *b.* 1948, *s.* 1992, *m.*	Hon. Mark D. J. D., *b.* 1949
1439	*Dudley (15th)*, Jim Anthony Hill Wallace, *b.* 1930, *s.* 2002, *m.*	Hon. Jeremy W. G. W., *b.* 1964
1800 I.	*Dufferin and Clandeboye (11th)*, John Francis Blackwood, *b.* 1944, *s.* 1991, *m.* (claim to the peerage not yet established)	Hon. Francis S. B., *b.* 1979
1929	*Dulverton (3rd)*, (Gilbert) Michael Hamilton Wills, *b.* 1944, *s.* 1992, *m.*	Hon. Robert A. H. W., *b.* 1983
1800 I.	*Dunalley (7th)*, Henry Francis Cornelius Prittie, *b.* 1948, *s.* 1992, *m.*	Hon. Joel H. P., *b.* 1981
1324 I.	*Dunboyne (30th)*, Richard Pierce Theobald Butler, *b.* 1983, *s.* 2013, *m.*	Hon. Caspian F. B., *b.* 2020
1892	*Dunleath (6th)*, Brian Henry Mulholland, *b.* 1950, *s.* 1997, *m.*	Hon. Andrew H. M., *b.* 1981
1439 I.	*Dunsany (21st)*, Randal Plunkett, *b.* 1983, *s.* 2011	Hon. Oliver P., *b.* 1985
1780	*Dynevor (10th)*, Hugo Griffith Uryan Rhys, *b.* 1966, *s.* 2008	Robert D. A. R., *b.* 1963
1963	*Egremont (2nd) and Leconfield (7th) (1859)*, John Max Henry Scawen Wyndham, *b.* 1948, *s.* 1972, *m.*	Hon. George R. V. W., *b.* 1983
1643 S.	*Elibank (15th)*, Robert Francis Alan Erskine-Murray, *b.* 1964, *s.* 2017, *m.*	Hon. Timothy A. E. E.-M., *b.* 1967
1802	*Ellenborough (9th)*, Rupert Edward Henry Law, *b.* 1955, *s.* 2013, *m.*	Hon. James R. T. L., *b.* 1983
1509 S.	*Elphinstone (19th) and Elphinstone (5th) (1885)*, Alexander Mountstuart Elphinstone, *b.* 1980, *s.* 1994, *m.*	Master of Elphinstone, *b.* 2011
1934 **	*Elton (2nd)*, Rodney Elton, TD, *b.* 1930, *s.* 1973, *m.*	Hon. Edward P. E., *b.* 1966
1627 S. **	*Fairfax of Cameron (14th)*, Nicholas John Albert Fairfax, *b.* 1956, *s.* 1964, *m.*	Hon. Edward N. T. F., *b.* 1984
1961	*Fairhaven (3rd)*, Ailwyn Henry George Broughton, *b.* 1936, *s.* 1973, *m.*	Maj. Hon. James H. A. B., *b.* 1963
1916	*Faringdon (3rd)*, Charles Michael Henderson, KCVO, *b.* 1937, *s.* 1977, *m.*	Hon. James H. H., *b.* 1961
1756 I.	*Farnham (13th)*, Simon Kenlis Maxwell, *b.* 1933, *s.* 2001, *w.*	Hon. Robin S. M., *b.* 1965
1856 I.	*Fermoy (6th)*, Maurice Burke Roche, *b.* 1967, *s.* 1984, *m.*	Hon. E. Hugh B. R., *b.* 1972
1826	*Feversham (7th)*, Jasper Orlando Slingsby Duncombe, *b.* 1968, *s.* 2009, *m.*	Hon. Orlando B. D., *b.* 2009
1798 I.	*ffrench (8th)*, Robuck John Peter Charles Mario ffrench, *b.* 1956, *s.* 1986, *m.*	None
1909	*Fisher (4th)*, Patrick Vavasseur Fisher, *b.* 1953, *s.* 2012, *m.*	Hon. Benjamin C. V. F., *b.* 1986
1295	*Fitzwalter (22nd)*, Julian Brook Plumptre, *b.* 1952, *s.* 2004, *m.*	Hon. Edward B. P., *b.* 1989
1776	*Foley (9th)*, Thomas Henry Foley, *b.* 1961, *s.* 2012	Rupert T. F., *b.* 1970
1445 S.	*Forbes (23rd)*, Malcolm Nigel Forbes, *b.* 1946, *s.* 2013, *m. Premier Lord of Scotland*	Master of Forbes, *b.* 2010
1821	*Forester (9th)*, Charles Richard George Weld-Forester, *b.* 1975, *s.* 2004, *m.*	Hon. Brook G. P. W.-F., *b.* 2014
1922	*Forres (4th)*, Alastair Stephen Grant Williamson, *b.* 1946, *s.* 1978, *m.*	Hon. George A. M. W., *b.* 1972
1917	*Forteviot (4th)*, John James Evelyn Dewar, *b.* 1938, *s.* 1993, *w.*	Hon. Alexander J. E. D., *b.* 1971
1951 **	*Freyberg (3rd)*, Valerian Bernard Freyberg, *b.* 1970, *s.* 1993, *m.*	Hon. Joseph J. F., *b.* 2007
1917	*Gainford (4th)*, George Pease, *b.* 1926, *s.* 2013, *w.*	Hon. Adrian C. P., *b.* 1960
1818 I.	*Garvagh (6th)*, Spencer George Stratford de Redcliffe Canning, *b.* 1953, *s.* 2013, *m.*	Hon. Stratford G. E. de R. C., *b.* 1990
1942 **	*Geddes (3rd)*, Euan Michael Ross Geddes, *b.* 1937, *s.* 1975, *m.*	Hon. James G. N. G., *b.* 1969
1876	*Gerard (5th)*, Anthony Robert Hugo Gerard, *b.* 1949, *s.* 1992	Hon. Rupert B. C. G., *b.* 1981
1824	*Gifford (6th)*, Anthony Maurice Gifford, QC, *b.* 1940, *s.* 1961, *m.*	Hon. Thomas A. G., *b.* 1967
1917	*Gisborough (3rd)*, Thomas Richard John Long Chaloner, *b.* 1927, *s.* 1951, *m.*	Hon. T. Peregrine L. C., *b.* 1961
1899	*Glanusk (5th)*, Christopher Russell Bailey, TD, *b.* 1942, *s.* 1997, *m.*	Hon. Charles H. B., *b.* 1976
1918 **	*Glenarthur (4th)*, Simon Mark Arthur, *b.* 1944, *s.* 1976, *m.*	Hon. Edward A. A., *b.* 1973
1911	*Glenconner (4th)*, Cody Charles Edward Tennant, *b.* 1994, *s.* 2010	Euan L. T., *b.* 1983
1964	*Glendevon (3rd)*, Jonathan Charles Hope, *b.* 1952, *s.* 2009	None
1922	*Glendyne (4th)*, John Nivison, *b.* 1960, *s.* 2008	None
1939	*Glentoran (3rd)*, (Thomas) Robin (Valerian) Dixon, CBE, *b.* 1935, *s.* 1995, *m.*	Hon. Daniel G. D., *b.* 1959
1909	*Gorell (5th)*, John Picton Gorell Barnes, *b.* 1959, *s.* 2007, *m.*	Hon. Oliver G. B., *b.* 1993
1953 **	*Grantchester (3rd)*, Christopher John Suenson-Taylor, *b.* 1951, *s.* 1995, *m.*	Hon. Jesse D. S.-T., *b.* 1977
1782	*Grantley (8th)*, Richard William Brinsley Norton, *b.* 1956, *s.* 1995	Hon. Francis J. H. N., *b.* 1960
1794 I.	*Graves (10th)*, Timothy Evelyn Graves, *b.* 1960, *s.* 2002, *m.*	None
1445 S.	*Gray (23rd)*, Andrew Godfrey Diarmid Stuart Campbell-Gray, *b.* 1964, *s.* 2003, *m.*	Master of Gray, *b.* 1996
1927 **	*Greenway (4th)*, Ambrose Charles Drexel Greenway, *b.* 1941, *s.* 1975, *m.*	Nicholas W. P. G., *b.* 1988
1902	*Grenfell (3rd) and Grenfell of Kilvey (life peerage, 2000)*, Julian Pascoe Francis St Leger Grenfell, *b.* 1935, *s.* 1976, *m.*	Richard A. St L. G., *b.* 1966
1944	*Gretton (4th)*, John Lysander Gretton, *b.* 1975, *s.* 1989, *m.*	Hon. John F. B. G., *b.* 2008
1397	*Grey of Codnor (6th)*, Richard Henry Cornwall-Legh, *b.* 1936, *s.* 1996, *m.*	Hon. Richard S. C. C.-L., *b.* 1976
1955	*Gridley (3rd)*, Richard David Arnold Gridley, *b.* 1956, *s.* 1996, *m.*	Peter A. C. G., *b.* 1940
1964	*Grimston of Westbury (3rd)*, Robert John Sylvester Grimston, *b.* 1951, *s.* 2003, *m.*	Hon. Gerald C. W. G., *b.* 1953
1886	*Grimthorpe (5th)*, Edward John Beckett, *b.* 1954, *s.* 2003, *m.*	Hon. Harry M. B., *b.* 1993
1945	*Hacking (3rd)*, Douglas David Hacking, *b.* 1938, *s.* 1971, *m.*	Hon. Douglas F. H., *b.* 1968
1950	*Haden-Guest (5th)*, Christopher Haden-Guest, *b.* 1948, *s.* 1996, *m.*	Hon. Nicholas H.-G., *b.* 1951
1886	*Hamilton of Dalzell (5th)*, Gavin Goulburn Hamilton, *b.* 1968, *s.* 2006, *m.*	Hon. Francis A. J. G. H., *b.* 2009
1874	*Hampton (7th)*, John Humphrey Arnott Pakington, *b.* 1964, *s.* 2003, *m.*	Hon. Charles R. C. P., *b.* 2005
1939	*Hankey (3rd)*, Donald Robin Alers Hankey, *b.* 1938, *s.* 1996, *m.*	Hon. Alexander M. A. H., *b.* 1947

1958   *Harding of Petherton (3rd)*, William Allan John Harding, *b.* 1969, *s.* 2016, *m.* — Hon. Angus J. E. H., *b.* 2001

1910   *Hardinge of Penshurst (4th)*, Julian Alexander Hardinge, *b.* 1945, *s.* 1997, *m.* — Hon. Hugh F. H., *b.* 1948

1876   *Harlech (7th)*, Jasset David Cody Ormsby-Gore, *b.* 1986, *s.* 2016 — None

1939   *Harmsworth (3rd)*, Thomas Harold Raymond Harmsworth, *b.* 1939, *s.* 1990, *m.* — Hon. Dominic M. E. H., *b.* 1973

1815   *Harris (8th)*, Anthony Harris, *b.* 1942, *s.* 1996, *w.* — Rear-Adm. Michael G. T. H., *b.* 1941

1954   *Harvey of Tasburgh (3rd)*, Charles John Giuseppe Harvey, *b.* 1951, *s.* 2010, *m.* — Hon. John C. G. H., *b.* 1993

1295   *Hastings (23rd)*, Delaval Thomas Harold Astley, *b.* 1960, *s.* 2007, *m.* — Hon. Jacob A. A., *b.* 1991

1835   *Hatherton (8th)*, Edward Charles Littleton, *b.* 1950, *s.* 1985, *m.* — Hon. Thomas E. L., *b.* 1977

1776   *Hawke (12th)*, William Martin Theodore Hawke, *b.* 1995, *s.* 2009 — None

1927   *Hayter (4th)*, George William Michael Chubb, *b.* 1943, *s.* 2003, *m.* — Hon. Thomas F. F. C., *b.* 1986

1945   *Hazlerigg (3rd)*, Arthur Grey Hazlerigg, *b.* 1951, *s.* 2002, *m.* — Hon. Arthur W. G. H., *b.* 1987

1943   *Hemingford (3rd)*, (Dennis) Nicholas Herbert, *b.* 1934, *s.* 1982, *w.* — Hon. Christopher D. C. H., *b.* 1973

1906   *Hemphill (6th)*, Charles Andrew Martyn Martyn-Hemphill, *b.* 1954, *s.* 2012, *m.* — Hon. Richard P. L. M.-H., *b.* 1990

1799 I. **   *Henley (8th) and Northington (6th) (1885)*, Oliver Michael Robert Eden, PC, *b.* 1953, *s.* 1977, *m.* — Hon. John W. O. E., *b.* 1988

1800 I.   *Henniker (9th) and Hartismere (6th) (1866)*, Mark Ian Philip Chandos Henniker-Major, *b.* 1947, *s.* 2004 — Hon. Edward G. M. H.-M., *b.* 1985

1461   *Herbert (19th)*, David John Seyfried Herbert, *b.* 1952, *s.* 2002, *m.* Title called out of abeyance 2002 — Hon. Oliver R. S. H., *b.* 1976

1935   *Hesketh (3rd)*, Thomas Alexander Fermor-Hesketh, KBE, PC, *b.* 1950, *s.* 1955, *m.* — Hon. Frederick H. F.-H., *b.* 1988

1828   *Heytesbury (7th)*, James William Holmes à Court, *b.* 1967, *s.* 2004, *w.* — Peter M. H. H. à. C., *b.* 1968

1886   *Hindlip (6th)*, Charles Henry Allsopp, *b.* 1940, *s.* 1993, *w.* — Hon. Henry W. A., *b.* 1973

1950   *Hives (3rd)*, Matthew Peter Hives, *b.* 1971, *s.* 1997, *m.* — Robert G. H., *b.* 1953

1912   *Hollenden (4th)*, Ian Hampden Hope-Morley, *b.* 1946, *s.* 1999, *m.* — Hon. Edward H.-M., *b.* 1981

1897   *Holm Patrick (4th)*, Hans James David Hamilton, *b.* 1955, *s.* 1991, *m.* — Hon. Ion H. J. H., *b.* 1956

1797 I.   *Hotham (8th)*, Henry Durand Hotham, *b.* 1940, *s.* 1967, *m.* — Hon. William B. H., *b.* 1972

1881   *Hothfield (6th)*, Anthony Charles Sackville Tufton, *b.* 1939, *s.* 1991, *m.* — Hon. William S. T., *b.* 1977

1930   *Howard of Penrith (3rd)*, Philip Esme Howard, *b.* 1945, *s.* 1999, *m.* — Hon. Thomas P. H., *b.* 1974

1960   *Howick of Glendale (2nd)*, Charles Evelyn Baring, *b.* 1937, *s.* 1973, *m.* — Hon. David E. C. B., *b.* 1975

1796 I.   *Huntingfield (7th)*, Joshua Charles Vanneck, *b.* 1954, *s.* 1994, *w.* — Hon. Gerard C. A. V., *b.* 1985

1866 **   *Hylton (5th)*, Raymond Hervey Jolliffe, *b.* 1932, *s.* 1967, *m.* — Hon. William H. M. J., *b.* 1967

1933   *Iliffe (3rd)*, Robert Peter Richard Iliffe, *b.* 1944, *s.* 1996, *m.* — Hon. Edward R. I., *b.* 1968

1543 I.   *Inchiquin (18th)*, Conor Myles John O'Brien, *b.* 1943, *s.* 1982, *m.* — Conor J. A. O'B., *b.* 1952

1962   *Inchyra (3rd)*, Christian James Charles Hoyer Millar, *b.* 1962, *s.* 2011, *m.* — Hon. Jake C. R. M., *b.* 1996

1964 **   *Inglewood (2nd)*, (William) Richard Fletcher-Vane, *b.* 1951, *s.* 1989, *m.* — Hon. Henry W. F. F.-V., *b.* 1990

1919   *Inverforth (4th)*, Andrew Peter Weir, *b.* 1966, *s.* 1982, *m.* — Hon. Benjamin A. W., *b.* 1997

1941   *Ironside (3rd)*, Charles Edmund Grenville Ironside, *b.* 1956, *s.* 2020, *m.* — Hon. Frederick T. G. I., *b.* 1991

1952   *Jeffreys (3rd)*, Christopher Henry Mark Jeffreys, *b.* 1957, *s.* 1986, *m.* — Hon. Arthur M. H. J., *b.* 1989

1906   *Joicey (5th)*, James Michael Joicey, *b.* 1953, *s.* 1993, *m.* — Hon. William J. J., *b.* 1990

1937   *Kenilworth (4th)*, (John) Randle Siddeley, *b.* 1954, *s.* 1981, *m.* — Hon. William R. J. S., *b.* 1992

1935   *Kennet (3rd)*, William Aldus Thoby Young, *b.* 1957, *s.* 2009 — Hon. Archibald W. K. Y., *b.* 1992

1776 I.   *Kensington (9th) and Kensington (6th) (1886)*, William Owen Edwardes, *b.* 1964, *s.* 2018, *m.* — Hon. William F. I. E., *b.* 1993

1951   *Kenswood (3rd)*, Michael Christopher Whitfield, *b.* 1955, *s.* 2016, *m.* — Hon. Anthony J. W., *b.* 1957

1788   *Kenyon (7th)*, Lloyd Nicholas Tyrell-Kenyon, *b.* 1972, *s.* 2019 — Hon. Alexander S. T.-K., *b.* 1975

1947   *Kershaw (4th)*, Edward John Kershaw, *b.* 1936, *s.* 1962, *m.* — Hon. John C. E. K., *b.* 1971

1943   *Keyes (3rd)*, Charles William Packe Keyes, *b.* 1951, *s.* 2005, *m.* — Hon. (Leopold R.) J. K., *b.* 1956

1909   *Kilbracken (4th)*, Christopher John Godley, *b.* 1945, *s.* 2006, *m.* — Hon. James J. G., *b.* 1972

1900   *Killanin (4th)*, (George) Redmond Fitzpatrick Morris, *b.* 1947, *s.* 1999, *m.* — Hon. Luke M. G. M., *b.* 1975

1943   *Killearn (3rd)*, Victor Miles George Aldous Lampson, *b.* 1941, *s.* 1996, *m.* — Hon. Miles H. M. L., *b.* 1977

1789 I.   *Kilmaine (8th)*, John Francis Sandford Browne, *b.* 1983, *s.* 2013 — Mark Caulfield-Browne, *b.* 1966

1831   *Kilmarnock (8th)*, Dr Robin Jordan Boyd, *b.* 1941, *s.* 2009, *m.* — Hon. Simon J. B., *b.* 1978

1941   *Kindersley (4th)*, Rupert John Molesworth Kindersley, *b.* 1955, *s.* 2013, *m.* — Hon. Frederick H. M. K., *b.* 1987

1223 I.   *Kingsale (36th)*, Nevinson Mark de Courcy, *b.* 1958, *s.* 2005 *Premier Baron of Ireland* — Joseph K. C. de C., *b.* 1955

1902   *Kinross (5th)*, Christopher Patrick Balfour, *b.* 1949, *s.* 1985, *m.* — Hon. Alan I. B., *b.* 1978

1951   *Kirkwood (3rd)*, David Harvie Kirkwood, PHD, *b.* 1931, *s.* 1970, *m.* — Hon. James S. K., *b.* 1937

1800 I.   *Langford (10th)*, Owain Grenville Rowley-Conwy, *b.* 1958, *s.* 2017, *m.* — Hon. Thomas A. R.-C., *b.* 1987

1942   *Latham (2nd)*, Dominic Charles Latham, *b.* 1954, *s.* 1970 — Anthony M. L., *b.* 1954

1431   *Latymer (9th)*, Crispin James Alan Nevill Money-Coutts, *b.* 1955, *s.* 2003, *m.* — Hon. Drummond W. T. M.-C., *b.* 1986

1869   *Lawrence (5th)*, David John Downer Lawrence, *b.* 1937, *s.* 1968 — None

1947   *Layton (4th)*, Jonathan Francis Layton, *b.* 1942, *s.* 2018, *m.* — Hon. Jeremy S. L., *b.* 1978

1839   *Leigh (6th)*, Christopher Dudley Piers Leigh, *b.* 1960, *s.* 2003 — Hon. Rupert D. L., *b.* 1994

1962	*Leighton of St Mellons (3rd)*, Robert William Henry Leighton Seager, *b.* 1955, *s.* 1998, *m.*	Hon. Simon J. L. S., *b.* 1957
1797	*Lilford (8th)*, Mark Vernon Powys, *b.* 1975, *s.* 2005, *m.*	Michael J. P., *b.* 1934
1945	*Lindsay of Birker (3rd)*, James Francis Lindsay, *b.* 1945, *s.* 1994, *m.*	Alexander S. L., *b.* 1940
1758 I.	*Lisle (9th)*, (John) Nicholas Geoffrey Lysaght, *b.* 1960, *s.* 2003	Hon. David J. L., *b.* 1963
1850	*Londesborough (9th)*, Richard John Denison, *b.* 1959, *s.* 1968, *m.*	Hon. James F. D., *b.* 1990
1541 I.	*Louth (17th)*, Jonathan Oliver Plunkett, *b.* 1952, *s.* 2013	Hon. Matthew O. P., *b.* 1982
1458 S.	*Lovat (16th) and Lovat (5th) (1837)*, Simon Christopher Joseph Fraser, *b.* 1977, *s.* 1995, *m.*	Hon. Jack H. F., *b.* 1984
1946	*Lucas of Chilworth (3rd)*, Simon William Lucas, *b.* 1957, *s.* 2001, *m.*	Hon. John R. M. L., *b.* 1995
1663 **	*Lucas (11th) and Dingwall (8th) (S. 1609)*, Ralph Matthew Palmer, *b.* 1951, *s.* 1991, *m.*	Hon. Lewis E. P., *b.* 1987
1929	*Luke (4th)*, Ian James St John Lawson Johnston, *b.* 1963, *s.* 2016, *m.*	Hon. Samuel A. J. St J. L. J., *b.* 2000
1859	*Lyveden (8th)*, Colin Ronald Vernon, *b.* 1967, *s.* 2017, *m.*	Hon. Robert H. V., *b.* 1942
1959	*MacAndrew (3rd)*, Christopher Anthony Colin MacAndrew, *b.* 1945, *s.* 1989	Hon. Oliver C. J. M., *b.* 1983
1776 I.	*Macdonald (8th)*, Godfrey James Macdonald of Macdonald, *b.* 1947, *s.* 1970, *m.*	Hon. Godfrey E. H. T. M., *b.* 1982
1937	*McGowan (4th)*, Harry John Charles McGowan, *b.* 1971, *s.* 2003, *m.*	Hon. Dominic J. W. M., *b.* 1951
1922	*Maclay (3rd)*, Joseph Paton Maclay, *b.* 1942, *s.* 1969, *m.*	Hon. Joseph P. M., *b.* 1977
1955	*McNair (3rd)*, Duncan James McNair, *b.* 1947, *s.* 1989, *m.*	Hon. William S. A. M., *b.* 1958
1951	*Macpherson of Drumochter (3rd)*, James Anthony Macpherson, *b.* 1979, *s.* 2008, *m.*	Hon. Daniel T. M., *b.* 2013
1937 **	*Mancroft (3rd)*, Benjamin Lloyd Stormont Mancroft, *b.* 1957, *s.* 1987, *m.*	Hon. Arthur L. S. M., *b.* 1995
1807	*Manners (6th)*, John Hugh Robert Manners, *b.* 1956, *s.* 2008, *m.*	Hon. John A. D. M., *b.* 2011
1922	*Manton (4th)*, Miles Ronald Marcus Watson, *b.* 1958, *s.* 2003, *m.*	Hon. Thomas N. C. D. W., *b.* 1985
1908	*Marchamley (4th)*, William Francis Whiteley, *b.* 1968, *s.* 1994, *m.*	Hon. Leon W., *b.* 2004
1965	*Margadale (3rd)*, Alastair John Morrison, *b.* 1958, *s.* 2003, *m.*	Hon. Declan J. M., *b.* 1993
1961	*Marks of Broughton (3rd)*, Simon Richard Marks, *b.* 1950, *s.* 1998, *m.*	Hon. Michael M., *b.* 1989
1964	*Martonmere (2nd)*, John Stephen Robinson, *b.* 1963, *s.* 1989, *m.*	Hon. James I. R., *b.* 2003
1776 I.	*Massy (10th)*, David Hamon Somerset Massy, *b.* 1947, *s.* 1995	Hon. John H. S. M., *b.* 1950
1935	*May (4th)*, Jasper Bertram St John May, *b.* 1965, *s.* 2006, *m.*	None
1925	*Merrivale (4th)*, Derek John Philip Duke, *b.* 1948, *s.* 2007, *m.*	Hon. Thomas D., *b.* 1980
1911	*Merthyr (5th)*, David Trevor Lewis, *b.* 1977, *s.* 2015, *m.*	Hon. Peter H. L., *b.* 1937
1919	*Meston (3rd)*, James Meston, QC, *b.* 1950, *s.* 1984, *m.*	Hon. Thomas J. D. M., *b.* 1977
1838	*Methuen (8th)*, James Paul Archibald Methuen-Campbell, *b.* 1952, *s.* 2014	Thomas R. M. M.-C., *b.* 1977
1711	*Middleton (13th)*, Michael Charles James Willoughby, *b.* 1948, *s.* 2011, *m.*	Hon. James W. M. W., *b.* 1976
1939	*Milford (4th)*, Guy Wogan Philipps, QC, *b.* 1961, *s.* 1999, *m.*	Hon. Archie S. P., *b.* 1997
1933	*Milne (3rd)*, George Alexander Milne, *b.* 1941, *s.* 2005	Hon. Iain C. L. M., *b.* 1949
1951	*Milner of Leeds (3rd)*, Richard James Milner, *b.* 1959, *s.* 2003, *m.*	None
1947	*Milverton (2nd)*, Revd Fraser Arthur Richard Richards, *b.* 1930, *s.* 1978, *w.*	Hon. Michael H. R., *b.* 1936
1873	*Moncreiff (6th)*, Rhoderick Harry Wellwood Moncreiff, *b.* 1954, *s.* 2002, *m.*	Hon. Harry J. W. M., *b.* 1986
1884	*Monk Bretton (3rd)*, John Charles Dodson, *b.* 1924, *s.* 1933, *m.*	Hon. Christopher M. D., *b.* 1958
1885	*Monkswell (6th)*, James Adrian Collier, *b.* 1977, *s.* 2020	Hon. Robert W. G. C., *b.* 1979
1728	*Monson (12th)*, Nicholas John Monson, *b.* 1955, *s.* 2011, *m.*	Hon. Andrew A. J. M., *b.* 1959
1885	*Montagu of Beaulieu (4th)*, Ralph Douglas-Scott-Montagu, *b.* 1961, *s.* 2015, *m.*	Hon. Jonathan D. D.-S.-M., *b.* 1975
1839	*Monteagle of Brandon (7th)*, Charles James Spring Rice, *b.* 1953, *s.* 2013, *m.*	Hon. Michael S. R., *b.* 1935
1943	*Moran (3rd)*, James McMoran Wilson, *b.* 1952, *s.* 2014, *m.*	Hon. David A. M. W., *b.* 1990
1918	*Morris (4th)*, Thomas Anthony Salmon Morris, *b.* 1982, *s.* 2011	Hon. John M. M., *b.* 1983
1950	*Morris of Kenwood (3rd)*, Jonathan David Morris, *b.* 1968, *s.* 2004, *m.*	Hon. Benjamin J. M., *b.* 1998
1831	*Mostyn (7th)*, Gregory Philip Roger Lloyd-Mostyn, *b.* 1984, *s.* 2011	Roger H. L.-M., *b.* 1941
1933	*Mottistone (6th)*, Christopher David Peter Seely, *b.* 1974, *s.* 2013	Hon. Richard W. A. S., *b.* 1988
1945 **	*Mountevans (4th)*, Jeffrey Richard de Corban Evans, *b.* 1948, *s.* 2014, *m.*	Hon. Alexander R. A. E., *b.* 1975
1283	*Mowbray (27th), Segrave (28th) (1295) and Stourton (24th) (1448)*, Edward William Stephen Stourton, *b.* 1953, *s.* 2006, *m.*	Hon. James C. P. S., *b.* 1991
1932	*Moyne (3rd)*, Jonathan Bryan Guinness, *b.* 1930, *s.* 1992, *m.*	Hon. Valentine G. B. G., *b.* 1959
1929 **	*Moynihan (4th)*, Colin Berkeley Moynihan, *b.* 1955, *s.* 1997	Hon. Nicholas E. B. M., *b.* 1994
1781 I.	*Muskerry (9th)*, Robert Fitzmaurice Deane, *b.* 1948, *s.* 1988, *m.*	Hon. Jonathan F. D., *b.* 1986
1627 S.	*Napier (15th) and Ettrick (6th) (1872)*, Francis David Charles Napier, *b.* 1962, *s.* 2012, *m.*	Master of Napier, *b.* 1996
1868	*Napier of Magdala (6th)*, Robert Alan Napier, *b.* 1940, *s.* 1987, *m.*	Hon. James R. N., *b.* 1966
1940	*Nathan (3rd)*, Rupert Harry Bernard Nathan, *b.* 1957, *s.* 2007, *m.*	Hon. Alasdair H. St J. N., *b.* 1999
1960	*Nelson of Stafford (4th)*, Alistair William Henry Nelson, *b.* 1973, *s.* 2006, *m.*	Hon. James J. N., *b.* 1947
1959	*Netherthorpe (3rd)*, James Frederick Turner, *b.* 1964, *s.* 1982, *m.*	Hon. Andrew J. E. T., *b.* 1993
1946	*Newall (2nd)*, Francis Storer Eaton Newall, *b.* 1930, *s.* 1963, *m.*	Hon. Richard H. E. N., *b.* 1961
1776 I.	*Newborough (8th)*, Robert Vaughan Wynn, *b.* 1949, *s.* 1998, *m.*	Antony C. V. W., *b.* 1949
1892	*Newton (5th)*, Richard Thomas Legh, *b.* 1950, *s.* 1992, *m.*	Hon. Piers R. L., *b.* 1979

1930	*Noel-Buxton (4th),* Charles Connal Noel-Buxton, *b.* 1975, *s.* 2013	Hon. Simon C. N.-B., *b.* 1943
1957	*Norrie (2nd),* (George) Willoughby Moke Norrie, *b.* 1936, *s.* 1977, *m.*	Hon. Mark W. J. N., *b.* 1972
1884	*Northbourne (6th),* Charles Walter Henri James, *b.* 1960, *s.* 2019, *m.*	Hon. Christopher W. J., *b.* 1988
1866 **	*Northbrook (6th),* Francis Thomas Baring, *b.* 1954, *s.* 1990, *m.*	To the Baronetcy, Peter B., *b.* 1939
1878	*Norton (8th),* James Nigel Arden Adderley, *b.* 1947, *s.* 1993, *m.*	Hon. Edward J. A. A., *b.* 1982
1906	*Nunburnholme (6th),* Stephen Charles Yanath Wilson, *b.* 1973, *s.* 2000, *m.*	Hon. Charles T. C. W., *b.* 2002
1950	*Ogmore (4th),* Tudor David Rees-Williams, *b.* 1991, *s.* 2004,	Hon. Dylane R.-W., *b.* 1994
1870	*O'Hagan (4th),* Charles Towneley Strachey, *b.* 1945, *s.* 1961, *m.*	Hon. Richard T. S., *b.* 1950
1868	*O'Neill (4th),* Raymond Arthur Clanaboy O'Neill, KCVO, TD, *b.* 1933, *s.* 1944, *w.*	Hon. Shane S. C. O'N., *b.* 1965
1836 I.	*Oranmore and Browne (5th) and Mereworth (3rd) (1926),* Dominick Geoffrey Thomas Browne, *b.* 1929, *s.* 2002	Shaun D. B., *b.* 1964
1933 **	*Palmer (4th),* Adrian Bailie Nottage Palmer, *b.* 1951, *s.* 1990	Hon. Hugo B. R. P., *b.* 1980
1914	*Parmoor (5th),* Michael Leonard Seddon Cripps, *b.* 1942, *s.* 2008, *m.*	Hon. Henry W. A. C., *b.* 1976
1937	*Pender (4th),* Henry John Richard Denison-Pender, *b.* 1968, *s.* 2016, *m.*	Hon. Miles J. C. D.-P., *b.* 2000
1866	*Penrhyn (7th),* Simon Douglas-Pennant, *b.* 1938, *s.* 2003, *m.*	Hon. Edward S. D.-P., *b.* 1966
1603	*Petre (18th),* John Patrick Lionel Petre, KCVO, *b.* 1942, *s.* 1989, *m.*	Hon. Dominic W. P., *b.* 1966
1918	*Phillimore (5th),* Francis Stephen Phillimore, *b.* 1944, *s.* 1994, *m.*	Hon. Tristan A. S. P., *b.* 1977
1945	*Piercy (3rd),* James William Piercy, *b.* 1946, *s.* 1981	Hon. Mark E. P. P., *b.* 1953
1827	*Plunket (9th),* Tyrone Shaun Terence Plunket, *b.* 1966, *s.* 2013, *m.*	Hon. Rory P. R. P., *b.* 2001
1831	*Poltimore (7th),* Mark Coplestone Bampfylde, *b.* 1957, *s.* 1978, *m.*	Hon. Henry A. W. B., *b.* 1985
1690 S.	*Polwarth (11th),* Andrew Walter Hepburne-Scott, *b.* 1947, *s.* 2005, *m.*	Master of Polwarth, *b.* 1973
1930	*Ponsonby of Shulbrede (4th) and Ponsonby of Roehampton (life peerage, 2000),* Frederick Matthew Thomas Ponsonby, *b.* 1958, *s.* 1990, *m.*	Hon. Cameron J. J. P., *b.* 1995
1958	*Poole (2nd),* David Charles Poole, *b.* 1945, *s.* 1993, *m.*	Hon. Oliver J. P., *b.* 1972
1852	*Raglan (6th),* Geoffrey Somerset, *b.* 1932, *s.* 2010, *w.*	Inigo A. F. S., *b.* 2004
1932	*Rankeillour (5th),* Michael Richard Hope, *b.* 1940, *s.* 2005, *w.*	Hon. James F. H., *b.* 1968
1953	*Rathcavan (3rd),* Hugh Detmar Torrens O'Neill, *b.* 1939, *s.* 1994, *m.*	Hon. François H. N. O'N., *b.* 1984
1916	*Rathcreedan (3rd),* Christopher John Norton, *b.* 1949, *s.* 1990, *m.*	Hon. Adam G. N., *b.* 1952
1868 I.	*Rathdonnell (5th),* Thomas Benjamin McClintock-Bunbury, *b.* 1938, *s.* 1959, *m.*	Hon. William L. M.-B., *b.* 1966
1911**	*Ravensdale (4th),* Daniel Nicholas Mosley, *b.* 1982, *s.* 2017, *m.*	Hon. Alexander L. M., *b.* 2012
1821	*Ravensworth (9th),* Thomas Arthur Hamish Liddell, *b.* 1954, *s.* 2004, *m.*	Hon. Henry A. T. L., *b.* 1987
1821	*Rayleigh (6th),* John Gerald Strutt, *b.* 1960, *s.* 1988, *m.*	Hon. John F. S., *b.* 1993
1937	*Rea (4th),* Matthew James Rea, *b.* 1956, *s.* 1981, *m.*	Hon. Daniel W. R., *b.* 1958
1628 S.**	*Reay (15th),* Aeneas Simon Mackay, *b.* 1965, *s.* 2013, *m.*	Master of Reay, *b.* 2010
1902	*Redesdale (6th) and Mitford (life peerage, 2000),* Rupert Bertram Mitford, *b.* 1967, *s.* 1991, *m.*	Hon. Bertram D. M., *b.* 2000
1940	*Reith (3rd),* James Harry John Reith, *b.* 1971, *s.* 2016, *m.*	Hon. Harry J. J. R., *b.* 2006
1928	*Remnant (3rd),* James Wogan Remnant, CVO, *b.* 1930, *s.* 1967, *m.*	Hon. Philip J. R., CBE, *b.* 1954
1806 I.	*Rendlesham (9th),* Charles William Brooke Thellusson, *b.* 1954, *s.* 1999, *m.*	James H. T., *b.* 1961
1933	*Rennell (4th),* James Roderick David Tremayne Rodd, *b.* 1978, *s.* 2006	None
1964	*Renwick (3rd),* Robert James Renwick, *b.* 1966, *s.* 2020	Hon. Michael D. R., *b.* 1968
1885	*Revelstoke (7th),* Alexander Rupert Baring, *b.* 1970, *s.* 2012	Hon. Thomas J. B., *b.* 1971
1905	*Ritchie of Dundee (6th),* Charles Rupert Rendall Ritchie, *b.* 1958, *s.* 2008, *m.*	Hon. Sebastian R., *b.* 2004
1935	*Riverdale (3rd),* Anthony Robert Balfour, *b.* 1960, *s.* 1998	Arthur M. B., *b.* 1938
1961	*Robertson of Oakridge (3rd),* William Brian Elworthy Robertson, *b.* 1975, *s.* 2009	None
1938	*Roborough (4th),* Massey John Henry Lopes, *b.* 1969, *s.* 2015, *m.*	Hon. Henry M. P. L., *b.* 1997
1931	*Rochester (3rd),* David Charles Lamb, *b.* 1944, *s.* 2017, *m.*	Hon. Daniel L., *b.* 1971
1934	*Rockley (4th),* Anthony Robert Cecil, *b.* 1961, *s.* 2011, *m.*	Hon. William E. C., *b.* 1996
1782	*Rodney (11th),* John George Brydges Rodney, *b.* 1999, *s.* 2011	Nicholas S. H. R., *b.* 1947
1651 S.	*Rollo (14th) and Dunning (5th) (1869),* David Eric Howard Rollo, *b.* 1943, *s.* 1997, *m.*	Master of Rollo, *b.* 1972
1959	*Rootes (3rd),* Nicholas Geoffrey Rootes, *b.* 1951, *s.* 1992, *m.*	William B. R., *b.* 1944
1796 I.	*Rossmore (7th) and Rossmore (6th) (1838),* William Warner Westenra, *b.* 1931, *s.* 1958, *m.*	Hon. Benedict W. W., *b.* 1983
1939 **	*Rotherwick (3rd),* (Herbert) Robin Cayzer, *b.* 1954, *s.* 1996, *m.*	Hon. H. Robin C., *b.* 1989
1885	*Rothschild (4th),* (Nathaniel Charles) Jacob Rothschild, OM, GBE, CVO, *b.* 1936, *s.* 1990, *w.*	Hon. Nathaniel P. V. J. R., *b.* 1971
1911	*Rowallan (4th),* John Polson Cameron Corbett, *b.* 1947, *s.* 1993, *m.*	Hon. Jason W. P. C. C., *b.* 1972
1947	*Rugby (3rd),* Robert Charles Maffey, *b.* 1951, *s.* 1990, *m.*	Hon. Timothy J. H. M., *b.* 1975
1919 **	*Russell of Liverpool (3rd),* Simon Gordon Jared Russell, *b.* 1952, *s.* 1981, *m.*	Hon. Edward C. S. R., *b.* 1985
1876	*Sackville (7th),* Robert Bertrand Sackville-West, *b.* 1958, *s.* 2004, *m.*	Hon. Arthur G. S.-W., *b.* 2000
1964	*St Helens (2nd),* Richard Francis Hughes-Young, *b.* 1945, *s.* 1980, *w.*	Hon. Henry T. H.-Y., *b.* 1986
1559 **	*St John of Bletso (21st),* Anthony Tudor St John, *b.* 1957, *s.* 1978, *m.*	Hon. Oliver B. St J., *b.* 1995
1887	*St Levan (5th),* James Piers Southwell St Aubyn, *b.* 1950, *s.* 2013, *m.*	Hon. Hugh J. St A., *b.* 1983
1885	*St Oswald (6th),* Charles Rowland Andrew Winn, *b.* 1959, *s.* 1999, *m.*	Hon. Rowland C. S. H. W., *b.* 1986

1960	*Sanderson of Ayot (2nd)*, Alan Lindsay Sanderson, *b.* 1931, *s.* 1971, *m.* Disclaimed for life 1971.	Hon. Michael S., *b.* 1959
1945	*Sandford (3rd)*, James John Mowbray Edmondson, *b.* 1949, *s.* 2009, *w.*	Hon. Devon J. E., *b.* 1986
1871	*Sandhurst (6th)*, Guy Rhys John Mansfield, QC, *b.* 1949, *s.* 2002, *m.*	Hon. Edward J. M., *b.* 1982
1888	*Savile (4th)*, John Anthony Thornhill Lumley-Savile, *b.* 1947, *s.* 2008, *m.*	Hon. James G. A. L.-S., *b.* 1975
1447	*Saye and Sele (21st)*, Nathaniel Thomas Allen Fiennes, *b.* 1920, *s.* 1968, *m.*	Hon. Martin G. F., *b.* 1961
1826	*Seaford (6th)*, Colin Humphrey Felton Ellis, *b.* 1946, *s.* 1999, *m.*	Hon. Benjamin F. T. Ellis-Goodbody, *b.* 1976
1932 **	*Selsdon (3rd)*, Malcolm McEacharn Mitchell-Thomson, *b.* 1937, *s.* 1963, *m.*	Hon. Callum M. M. M.-T., *b.* 1969
1489 S.	*Sempill (21st)*, James William Stuart Whitemore Sempill, *b.* 1949, *s.* 1995, *m.*	Master of Sempill, *b.* 1979
1916	*Shaughnessy (5th)*, Charles George Patrick Shaughnessy, *b.* 1955, *s.* 2007, *m.*	David J. B. S., *b.* 1957
1946	*Shepherd (3rd)*, Graeme George Shepherd, *b.* 1949, *s.* 2001, *m.*	Hon. Patrick M. S., *b.* 1980
1964	*Sherfield (3rd)*, Dwight William Makins, *b.* 1951, *s.* 2006, *m.*	None
1902	*Shuttleworth (5th)*, Charles Geoffrey Nicholas Kay-Shuttleworth, KG, KCVO, *b.* 1948, *s.* 1975, *m.*	Hon. Thomas E. K.-S., *b.* 1976
1950	*Silkin (3rd)*, Christopher Lewis Silkin, *b.* 1947, *s.* 2001. Disclaimed for life 2002.	Rory L. S., *b.* 1954
1963	*Silsoe (3rd)*, Simon Rupert Trustram Eve, *b.* 1966, *s.* 2005	Hon. Peter N. T. E., OBE, *b.* 1930
1947	*Simon of Wythenshawe (3rd)*, Matthew Simon, *b.* 1955, *s.* 2002, *w.* In dormancy since 2016 when the 3rd baron officially reassigned his gender.	Michael B. S., *b.* 1970
1449 S.	*Sinclair (18th)*, Matthew Murray Kennedy St Clair, *b.* 1968, *s.* 2004, *m.*	Master of Sinclair, *b.* 2007
1957	*Sinclair of Cleeve (3rd)*, John Lawrence Robert Sinclair, *b.* 1953, *s.* 1985, *m.*	None
1919	*Sinha (6th)*, Arup Kumar Sinha, *b.* 1966, *s.* 1999, *m.*	Hon. Dilip K. S., *b.* 1967
1828	*Skelmersdale (8th)*, Andrew Bootle-Wilbraham, *b.* 1977, *s.* 2018, *m.*	Hon. Daniel P. B.-W., *b.* 2007
1916	*Somerleyton (4th)*, Hugh Francis Saville Crossley, *b.* 1971, *s.* 2012, *m.*	Hon. John de B. T. S. C., *b.* 2010
1784	*Somers (9th)*, Philip Sebastian Somers Cocks, *b.* 1948, *s.* 1995	Jonathan B. C., *b.* 1985
1780	*Southampton (7th)*, Edward Charles FitzRoy, *b.* 1955, *s.* 2015, *m.*	Hon. Charles E. M. F., *b.* 1983
1959	*Spens (4th)*, Patrick Nathaniel George Spens, *b.* 1968, *s.* 2001	Hon. Peter L. S., *b.* 2000
1640	*Stafford (15th)*, Francis Melfort William Fitzherbert, *b.* 1954, *s.* 1986, *m.*	Hon. Benjamin J. B. F., *b.* 1983
1938	*Stamp (4th)*, Trevor Charles Bosworth Stamp, MD, *b.* 1935, *s.* 1987	Hon. Nicholas C. T. S., *b.* 1978
1839	*Stanley of Alderley (9th)*, Sheffield (9th) (I. 1738) and Eddisbury (8th) (1848), Richard Oliver Stanley, *b.* 1956, *s.* 2013, *m.*	Hon. Charles E. S., *b.* 1960
1318	*Strabolgi (12th)*, Andrew David Whitley Kenworthy, *b.* 1967, *s.* 2010, *m.*	Hon. Joel B. K., *b.* 2004
1628	*Strange (17th)*, Adam Humphrey Drummond of Megginch, *b.* 1953, *s.* 2005, *m.*	Hon. John A. H. D. of M., *b.* 1992
1955	*Strathalmond (3rd)*, William Roberton Fraser, *b.* 1947, *s.* 1976, *m.*	Hon. William G. F., *b.* 1976
1936	*Strathcarron (3rd)*, Ian David Patrick Macpherson, *b.* 1949, *s.* 2006, *m.*	Hon. Rory D. A. M., *b.* 1982
1955 **	*Strathclyde (2nd)*, Thomas Galloway Dunlop du Roy de Blicquy Galbraith, CH, PC, *b.* 1960, *s.* 1985, *m.*	Hon. Charles W. du R. de B. G., *b.* 1962
1900	*Strathcona and Mount Royal (5th)*, Donald Alexander Smith Howard, *b.* 1961, *s.* 2018, *m.*	Hon. Donald A. R. H., *b.* 1994
1836	*Stratheden (7th) and Campbell (7th) (1841)*, David Anthony Campbell, *b.* 1963, *s.* 2011, *m.*	None
1884	*Strathspey (6th)*, James Patrick Trevor Grant of Grant, *b.* 1943, *s.* 1992	Hon. Michael P. F. G., *b.* 1953
1838	*Sudeley (7th)*, Merlin Charles Sainthill Hanbury-Tracy, *b.* 1939, *s.* 1941, *m.*	Nicholas E. J. H.-T., *b.* 1959
1786	*Suffield (13th)*, John Edward Richard Harbord-Hamond, *b.* 1956, *s.* 2016, *m.*	Hon. Sam C. A. H.-H., *b.* 1989
1893	*Swansea (5th)*, Richard Anthony Hussey Vivian, *b.* 1957, *s.* 2005, *m.*	Hon. James H. H. V., *b.* 1999
1907	*Swaythling (5th)*, Charles Edgar Samuel Montagu, *b.* 1954, *s.* 1998, *m.*	Rupert A. S. M., *b.* 1965
1919 **	*Swinfen (3rd)*, Roger Mynors Swinfen Eady, MBE, *b.* 1938, *s.* 1977, *m.*	Hon. Charles R. P. S. E., *b.* 1971
1831 I.	*Talbot of Malahide (11th)*, Richard John Tennant Arundell, *b.* 1957, *s.* 2016, *m.*	Hon. John R. A., *b.* 1998
1946	*Tedder (3rd)*, Robin John Tedder, *b.* 1955, *s.* 1994, *m.*	Hon. Benjamin J. T., *b.* 1985
1884	*Tennyson (6th)*, David Harold Alexander Tennyson, *b.* 1960, *s.* 2006	Alan J. D. T., *b.* 1965
1918	*Terrington (6th)*, Christopher Richard James Woodhouse, MB, *b.* 1946, *s.* 2001, *m.*	Hon. Jack H. L. W., *b.* 1978
1940	*Teviot (2nd)*, Charles John Kerr, *b.* 1934, *s.* 1968, *m.*	Hon. Charles R. K., *b.* 1971
1616	*Teynham (20th)*, John Christopher Ingham Roper-Curzon, *b.* 1928, *s.* 1972, *m.*	Hon. David J. H. I. R.-C., *b.* 1965
1964	*Thomson of Fleet (3rd)*, David Kenneth Roy Thomson, *b.* 1957, *s.* 2006	Hon. Benjamin J. L. T., *b.* 2006
1792 **	*Thurlow (9th)*, Roualeyn Robert Hovell-Thurlow-Cumming-Bruce, *b.* 1952, *s.* 2013, *m.*	Hon. Nicholas E. H.-T.-C.-B., *b.* 1986
1876	*Tollemache (5th)*, Timothy John Edward Tollemache, KCVO, *b.* 1939, *s.* 1975, *m.*	Hon. Edward J. H. T., *b.* 1976
1564 S.	*Torphichen (15th)*, James Andrew Douglas Sandilands, *b.* 1946, *s.* 1975, *m.*	Robert P. S., *b.* 1950
1947 **	*Trefgarne (2nd)*, David Garro Trefgarne, PC, *b.* 1941, *s.* 1960, *m.*	Hon. George G. T., *b.* 1970
1921 **	*Trevethin (5th) and Oaksey (3rd) (1947)*, Patrick John Tristram Lawrence, QC, *b.* 1960, *s.* 2012, *m.*	Hon. Oliver J. T. L., *b.* 1990
1880	*Trevor (5th)*, Marke Charles Hill-Trevor, *b.* 1970, *s.* 1997	Hon. Iain R. H.-T., *b.* 1971
1461 I.	*Trimlestown (21st)*, Raymond Charles Barnewall, *b.* 1930, *s.* 1997	None

1940	*Tryon (4th)*, Charles George Barrington Tryon, *b.* 1976, *s.* 2018, *m.*	Hon. Guy A. G. T., *b.* 2015
1935	*Tweedsmuir (4th)*, John William de l'Aigle (Toby) Buchan, *b.* 1950, *s.* 2008, *m.*	Hon. John A. G. B., *b.* 1986
1523 **	*Vaux of Harrowden (12th)*, Richard Hubert Gordon Gilbey, *b.* 1965, *s.* 2014, *m.*	Hon. Alexander J. C. G., *b.* 2000
1800 I.	*Ventry (8th)*, Andrew Wesley Daubeny de Moleyns, *b.* 1943, *s.* 1987, *m.*	Hon. Francis W. D. de M., *b.* 1965
1762	*Vernon (11th)*, Anthony William Vernon-Harcourt, *b.* 1939, *s.* 2000, *m.*	Hon. Simon A. V.-H., *b.* 1969
1922	*Vestey (3rd)*, Samuel George Armstrong Vestey, GCVO, *b.* 1941, *s.* 1954, *m.*	Hon. William G. V., *b.* 1983
1841	*Vivian (7th)*, Charles Crespigny Hussey Vivian, *b.* 1966, *s.* 2004	Thomas C. B. V., *b.* 1971
1934	*Wakehurst (3rd)*, (John) Christopher Loder, *b.* 1925, *s.* 1970, *m.*	Hon. Timothy W. L., *b.* 1958
1723	*Walpole (10th) and Walpole of Wolterton (8th) (1756)*, Robert Horatio Walpole, *b.* 1938, *s.* 1989, *m.*	Hon. Jonathan R. H. W., *b.* 1967
1780	*Walsingham (9th)*, John de Grey, MC, *b.* 1925, *s.* 1965, *w.*	Hon. Robert de G., *b.* 1969
1792 I.	*Waterpark (8th)*, Roderick Alexander Cavendish, *b.* 1959, *s.* 2013, *m.*	Hon. Luke F. C., *b.* 1990
1942	*Wedgwood (5th)*, Antony John Wedgwood, *b.* 1944, *s.* 2014, *m.*	Hon. Josiah T. A. W., *b.* 1978
1861	*Westbury (6th)*, Richard Nicholas Bethell, MBE, *b.* 1950, *s.* 2001, *m.*	Hon. Richard A. D. B., *b.* 1986
1944	*Westwood (4th)*, (William) Fergus Westwood, *b.* 1972, *s.* 2019	Hon. Alistair C. W., *b.* 1974
1544/5	*Wharton (12th)*, Myles Christopher David Robertson, *b.* 1964, *s.* 2000, *m.*	Hon. Meghan Z. M. R., *b.* 2006
1935	*Wigram (3rd)*, Andrew Francis Clive Wigram, MVO, *b.* 1949, *s.* 2017, *m.*	Hon. Harry R. C. W., *b.* 1977
1491 **	*Willoughby de Broke (21st)*, Leopold David Verney, *b.* 1938, *s.* 1986, *m.*	Hon. Rupert G. V., *b.* 1966
1937	*Windlesham (4th)*, James Rupert Hennessy, *b.* 1968, *s.* 2010, *m.*	Hon. George R. J. H., *b.* 2006
1951	*Wise (3rd)*, Christopher John Clayton Wise, *b.* 1949, *s.* 2012, *m.*	Hon. Thomas C. C. W., *b.* 1989
1869	*Wolverton (8th)*, Miles John Glyn, *b.* 1966, *s.* 2011	Jonathan C. G., *b.* 1990
1928	*Wraxall (4th)*, Antony Hubert Gibbs, *b.* 1958, *s.* 2017, *m.*	Hon. Orlando H. G., *b.* 1995
1915	*Wrenbury (4th)*, William Edward Buckley, *b.* 1966, *s.* 2014, *m.*	Arthur B. B., *b.* 1967
1838	*Wrottesley (6th)*, Clifton Hugh Lancelot de Verdon Wrottesley, *b.* 1968, *s.* 1977, *m.*	Hon. Victor E. F. de V. W., *b.* 2004
1829	*Wynford (9th)*, John Philip Robert Best, *b.* 1950, *s.* 2002, *m.*	Hon. Harry R. F. B., *b.* 1987
1308	*Zouche (18th)*, James Assheton Frankland, *b.* 1943, *s.* 1965, *m.*	Hon. William T. A. F., *b.* 1984

BARONESSES/LADIES IN THEIR OWN RIGHT

Style, The Rt. Hon. the Lady _ , *or* The Rt. Hon. the Baroness _ , according to her preference. Either style may be used, except in the case of Scottish titles (indicated by S.), which are not baronies and whose holders are always addressed as Lady.

Envelope, may be addressed in same way as a Baron's wife or, if she prefers *(formal)*, The Rt. Hon. the Baroness _; *(social)*, The Baroness _. Otherwise as for a Baron's wife

Husband, Untitled

Children's style, As for children of a Baron

In Scotland, the heir to a Lady may be styled 'The Master/Mistress of _ (title of peer)'

Created	Title, order of succession, name, etc	Heir
1664	*Arlington (11th)*, Jennifer Jane Forwood, *b.* 1939, *s.* 1999, *w.* Title called out of abeyance 1999	Hon. Patrick J. D. F., *b.* 1967
1607	*Balfour of Burleigh (9th)*, Victoria Bruce, *b.* 1973, *s.* 2019, *m.*	Hon. Laetitia B., *b.* 2007
1455	*Berners (16th)*, Pamela Vivien Kirkham, *b.* 1929, *s.* 1995, *w.* Title called out of abeyance 1995	Hon. Rupert W. T. K., *b.* 1953
1529	*Braye (8th)*, Mary Penelope Aubrey-Fletcher, *b.* 1941, *s.* 1985, *m.*	Linda K. C. Fothergill, *b.* 1930
1321	*Dacre (29th)*, Emily Beamish, *b.* 1983, *s.* 2014, *m.*	Three co-heiresses
1283	*Fauconberg (10th) and Conyers (16th) (1509)*, Baronies in abeyance between two co-heiresses since 2013	
1490 S.	*Herries of Terregles (16th)*, (Theresa) Jane Kerr, Marchioness of Lothian, *b.* 1945, *s.* 2017, *m.*	Lady Clare T. Hurd, *b.* 1979
1597	*Howard de Walden (10th)*, Mary Hazel Caridwen Czernin, *b.* 1935, *s.* 2004, *w.* Title called out of abeyance 2004	Hon. Peter J. J. C., *b.* 1966
1602 S.	*Kinloss (13th)*, Teresa Mary Nugent Freeman-Grenville, *b.* 1957, *s.* 2012	Mistress of Kinloss, *b.* 1960
1445 S.	*Saltoun (20th)*, Flora Marjory Fraser, *b.* 1930, *s.* 1979, *w.*	Hon. Katharine I. M. I. F., *b.* 1957
1313	*Willoughby de Eresby (27th)*, (Nancy) Jane Marie Heathcote-Drummond-Willoughby, *b.* 1934, *s.* 1983	Two co-heirs

LIFE PEERS

Veronica Judith Colleton Wadley, CBE; James Stephen Wharton; Deborah Ann Wilcox; John Zak Woodcock; Anthony J. Woodley; Sir Simon Andrew Woolley

Style, The Rt. Hon. the Lord _ /The Rt. Hon. the Lady _ , *or* The Rt. Hon. the Baroness _ , according to her preference *Envelope (formal),* The Rt. Hon. Lord _/Lady_/Baroness_; *(social),* The Lord _/Lady_/Baroness_ *Letter (formal),* My Lord/Lady; *(social),* Dear Lord/Lady _. *Spoken,* Lord/Lady _

Wife's style, The Rt. Hon. the Lady _
Husband, Untitled
Children's style, 'The Hon.' before forename (F_) and surname (S_)
Envelope, The Hon. F_ S_. *Letter,* Dear Mr/Miss/Mrs S_.
Spoken, Mr/Miss/Mrs S_

KEY
* Hereditary peer who has been granted a life peerage. For further details, please refer to the Hereditary Peers section. For example, life peer *Balniel* can be found under his hereditary title *Earl of Crawford and Balcarres*
§ Members of the Judiciary currently disqualified from sitting or voting in the House of Lords until they retire from that office. For further information *see* Law Courts and Offices
‡ Title not confirmed at time of going to press
❦ Peer who has permanently resigned from the House of Lords
E. Peer who has been expelled for absenteeism, under section 2 of the House of Lords Reform Act 2014, for failing to attend a sitting of the House during a session lasting six months or longer *see* The Peerage, introduction

A full entry in italic type indicates that the recipient of a life peerage died within a year of it being conferred. The name is included in our list for one year for purposes of record.

NEW LIFE PEERAGES
Since December 2020

Ian Christopher Austin; Rt. Hon. Gavin Laurence Barwell; Sir Henry Campbell Bellingham; Natalie Louise Bennett; Christine Blower; Sir Ian Terence Botham, OBE; David Ellis Brownlow, CVO; Harold Mark Carter, CB; Dame Louise Casey, DBE, CB; Zameer Mohammed Choudrey, CBE; Kathryn Sloan Clark; Rt. Hon. Kenneth Harry Clarke, CH, QC; Sir (Nigel) Kim Darroch, KCMG; Brinley Howard Davies; (Henry) Byron Davies; Rt. Hon. Ruth Elizabeth Davidson, MSP; Rt. Hon. Nigel Alexander Dodds, OBE; Rt. Hon. Frank Field; Claire Regina Fox; David George Hamilton Frost, CMG; Lorraine Fullbrook; Rt. Hon. (Frank) Zac(harias) Robin Goldsmith; Stephen John Greenhalgh; Sir Gerald Edgar Grimstone, CVO; Rt. Hon. Dame Heather Carol Hallett, DBE; Rt. Hon. Philip Hammond; Susan Mary Hayman; John Hendy, QC; Rt. Hon. Nicholas Le Quesne Herbert, CBE; Catharine Letitia Hoey; Ruth Elizabeth Hunt; Rt. Hon. Joseph Edmund Johnson; Rt. Hon. (John) Mark Lancaster, TD, VR; Evgeny Alexandrovich Lebedev; Rt. Hon. Sir Patrick Alan McLoughlin, CH; John Mann; Neil Francis Jeremy Mendoza; Rt. Hon. Nicola Ann Morgan; Charles Hilary Moore; Dame Helena Louise Morrissey, DBE; Daniel Michael Gerald Moylan; Stephen Graeme Parkinson; Joanna Carolyn Penn; Raminder Singh Ranger, CBE; Margaret Mary Ritchie; Elizabeth Jenny Rosemary Sanderson Aamer Ahmad Sarfraz; Sir Mark Philip Sedwill, KCMG; Andrew Michael Gordon Sharpe, OBE; Dame Nemat (Minouche) Talaat Shafik, DBE; Prem Nath Sikka; Michael Alan Spencer; Keith Douglas Stewart, QC; Rt. Hon. Gisela Stuart; Sir Edward Julian Udny-Lister; Rt. Hon. Edward Henry Butler Vaizey;

CREATED UNDER THE APPELLATE JURISDICTION ACT 1876 (AS AMENDED)

BARONS
Created
2004   *Brown of Eaton-under-Heywood,* Simon Denis Brown, PC, *b.* 1937, *m.*
2004   ❦*Carswell,* Robert Douglas Carswell, PC, *b.* 1934, *m.*
2009   *Collins of Mapesbury,* Lawrence Antony Collins, PC, *b.* 1941, *m.*
1995   *Hoffmann,* Leonard Hubert Hoffmann, PC, *b.* 1934, *m.*
2009   *Kerr of Tonaghmore,* Brian Francis Kerr, PC, *b.* 1948, *m.*
1993   ❦*Lloyd of Berwick,* Anthony John Leslie Lloyd, PC, *b.,* 1929, *m.*
2005   *Mance,* Jonathan Hugh Mance, PC, *b.* 1943, *m.*
1998   ❦*Millett,* Peter Julian Millett, PC, *b.* 1932, *m.*
2007   *Neuberger of Abbotsbury,* David Edmond Neuberger, PC, *b.* 1948, *m.*
1999   *Phillips of Worth Matravers,* Nicholas Addison Phillips, KG, PC, *b.* 1938, *m.*
1997   *Saville of Newdigate,* Mark Oliver Saville, PC, *b.* 1936, *m.*
2000   ❦*Scott of Foscote,* Richard Rashleigh Folliott Scott, PC, *b.* 1934, *m.*
2003   *Walker of Gestingthorpe,* Robert Walker, PC, *b.* 1938, *m.*
1992   *Woolf,* Harry Kenneth Woolf, CH, PC, *b.* 1933, *m.*

BARONESSES
2004   *Hale of Richmond,* Brenda Marjorie Hale, DBE, PC, *b.* 1945, *w.*

CREATED UNDER THE LIFE PEERAGES ACT 1958

BARONS
Created
2001   *Adebowale,* Victor Olufemi Adebowale, CBE, *b.* 1962
2005   *Adonis,* Andrew Adonis, PC, *b.* 1963, *m.*
2017   *Agnew of Oulton,* Theodore Thomas More Agnew, *b.* 1961, *m.*
2011   *Ahmad of Wimbledon,* Tariq Mahmood Ahmad, *b.* 1968, *m.*
1998   *Ahmed,* Nazir Ahmed, *b.* 1957, *m.*
1996   *Alderdice,* John Thomas Alderdice, *b.* 1955, *m.*
2010   *Allan of Hallam,* Richard Beecroft Allan, *b.* 1966
2013   *Allen of Kensington,* Charles Lamb Allen, CBE, *b.* 1957
1998   *Alli,* Waheed Alli, *b.* 1964
2004   *Alliance,* David Alliance, CBE, *b.* 1932
1997   *Alton of Liverpool,* David Patrick Paul Alton, *b.* 1951, *m.*
2018   *Anderson of Ipswich,* David William Kinloch Anderson, KBE, QC, *b.* 1961, *m.*
2005   *Anderson of Swansea,* Donald Anderson, PC, *b.* 1939, *m.*
2015   *Arbuthnot of Edrom,* James Norwich Arbuthnot, PC, *b.* 1952, *m.*
1992   *Archer of Weston-super-Mare,* Jeffrey Howard Archer, *b.* 1940, *m.*
2000   ❦*Ashcroft,* Michael Anthony Ashcroft, KCMG, PC, *b.* 1946, *m.*
2020   *Austin,* Ian Christopher Austin, *b.* 1965
1998   *Bach,* William Stephen Goulden Bach, *b.* 1946, *m.*
1997   *Baker of Dorking,* Kenneth Wilfred Baker, CH, PC, *b.* 1934, *m.*

2013 *Balfe,* Richard Andrew Balfe, *b.* 1944, *m.*
1974 ❲*Balniel,* The Earl of Crawford and Balcarres, KT, GCVO, PC, *b.* 1927, *m. (see* Hereditary Peers)
2013 *Bamford,* Anthony Paul Bamford, *b.* 1945, *m.*
2015 *Barker of Battle,* Gregory Leonard George Barker, PC, *b.* 1966
2019 *Barwell,* Gavin Laurence Barwell, PC, *b.* 1972, *m.*
1997 *Bassam of Brighton,* (John) Steven Bassam, PC, *b.* 1953
2008 *Bates,* Michael Walton Bates, PC, *b.* 1961, *m.*
2010 *Beecham,* Jeremy Hugh Beecham, *b.* 1944, *m.*
2015 *Beith,* Alan James Beith, PC, *b.* 1943, *w.*
2020 ‡*Bellingham,* Henry Campbell Bellingham, *b.* 1955, *m.*
2013 *Berkeley of Knighton,* Michael Fitzhardinge Berkeley, CBE, *b.* 1948, *m.*
2001 *Best,* Richard Stuart Best, OBE, *b.* 1945, *m.*
2007 *Bew,* Prof. Paul Anthony Elliott Bew, *b.* 1950, *m.*
2001 *Bhatia,* Amirali Alibhai Bhatia, OBE, *b.* 1932, *m.*
2010 *Bichard,* Michael George Bichard, KCB, *b.* 1947, *m.*
2006 *Bilimoria,* Karan Faridoon Bilimoria, CBE, *b.* 1961, *m.*
2015 *Bird,* John Anthony Bird, MBE, *b.* 1946, *m.*
2000 *Birt,* John Francis Hodgess Birt, *b.* 1944, *m.*
2010 *Black of Brentwood,* Guy Vaughan Black, *b.* 1964, *m.*
2001 *Black of Crossharbour,* Conrad Moffat Black, *b.* 1944, *m.*
1997 *Blackwell,* Norman Roy Blackwell, *b.* 1952, *m.*
2010 *Blair of Boughton,* Ian Warwick Blair, QPM, *b.* 1953, *m.*
2011 *Blencathra,* David John Maclean, PC, *b.* 1953
2015 *Blunkett,* David Blunkett, PC, *b.* 1947, *m.*
1995 ❲*Blyth of Rowington,* James Blyth, *b.* 1940, *m.*
2010 *Boateng,* Paul Yaw Boateng, PC, *b.* 1951, *m.*
2010 *Boswell of Aynho,* Timothy Eric Boswell, *b.* 1942, *m.*
2020 *Botham,* Ian Terence Botham, OBE, *b.* 1955, *m.*
2013 *Bourne of Aberystwyth,* Nicholas Henry Bourne, *b.* 1952
1996 *Bowness,* Peter Spencer Bowness, CBE, *b.* 1943, *m.*
2003 *Boyce,* Michael Boyce, KG, GCB, OBE, *b.* 1943, *w.*
2006 §*Boyd of Duncansby,* Colin David Boyd, PC, *b.* 1953, *m.*
2006 *Bradley,* Keith John Charles Bradley, PC, *b.* 1950, *m.*
1999 *Bradshaw,* William Peter Bradshaw, *b.* 1936, *m.*
1998 *Bragg,* Melvyn Bragg, CH, *b.* 1939, *m.*
2000 *Brennan,* Daniel Joseph Brennan, QC, *b.* 1942, *m.*
2015 *Bridges of Headley,* James George Robert Bridges, MBE, *b.* 1970, *m.*
2004 *Broers,* Prof. Alec (Nigel) Broers, *b.* 1938, *m.*
1997 *Brooke of Alverthorpe,* Clive Brooke, *b.* 1942, *m.*
2001 ❲*Brooke of Sutton Mandeville,* Peter Leonard Brooke, CH, PC, *b.* 1934, *m.*
1998 ❲*Brookman,* David Keith Brookman, *b.* 1937, *m.*
2006 *Browne of Belmont,* Wallace Hamilton Browne, *b.* 1947
2010 *Browne of Ladyton,* Desmond Henry Browne, PC, *b.* 1952
2001 *Browne of Madingley,* Edmund John Phillip Browne, *b.* 1948
2019 *Brownlow of Shurlock Row,* David Ellis Brownlow, CVO, *b.* 1963
2015 *Bruce of Bennachie,* Malcolm Gray Bruce, PC, *b.* 1944, *m.*
2006 *Burnett,* John Patrick Aubone Burnett, *b.* 1945, *m.*
2017 §*Burnett of Maldon,* Ian Duncan Burnett, PC, *b.* 1958, *m. Lord Chief Justice of England and Wales*
1998 *Burns,* Terence Burns, GCB, *b.* 1944, *m.*
1998 *Butler of Brockwell,* (Frederick Edward) Robin Butler, KG, GCB, CVO, PC, *b.* 1938, *m.*
2016 *Caine,* Jonathan Michael Caine, *b.* 1966
2014 *Callanan,* Martin John Callanan, *b.* 1961, *m.*
2004 *Cameron of Dillington,* Ewen (James Hanning) Cameron, *b.* 1949, *m.*
1984 ❲*Cameron of Lochbroom,* Kenneth John Cameron, PC, *b.* 1931, *m.*

2015 *Campbell of Pittenweem,* (Walter) Menzies Campbell, CH, CBE, PC, QC, *b.* 1941, *m.*
2001 *Campbell-Savours,* Dale Norman Campbell-Savours, *b.* 1943, *m.*
2002 *Carey of Clifton,* Rt. Revd George Leonard Carey, PC, Royal Victorian Chain, *b.* 1935, *m.*
1999 *Carlile of Berriew,* Alexander Charles Carlile, CBE, QC, *b.* 1948, *m.*
2013 *Carrington of Fulham,* Matthew Hadrian Marshall Carrington, *b.* 1947, *m.*
2008 *Carter of Barnes,* Stephen Andrew Carter, CBE, *b.* 1964, *m.*
2004 *Carter of Coles,* Patrick Robert Carter, *b.* 1946, *m.*
2019 *Carter of Haslemere,* Harold Mark Carter, CB
2014 *Cashman,* Michael Maurice Cashman, CBE, *b.* 1950
1990 *Cavendish of Furness,* (Richard) Hugh Cavendish, *b.* 1941, *m.*
1996 *Chadlington,* Peter Selwyn Gummer, *b.* 1942, *m.*
2017 *Chartres,* Rt. Revd Richard John Carew Chartres, GCVO, PC, *b.* 1947, *m.*
2005 *Chidgey,* David William George Chidgey, *b.* 1942, *m.*
2019 *Choudrey,* Zameer Mohammed Choudrey, CBE, *b.* 1958, *m.*
1998 *Christopher,* Anthony Martin Grosvenor Christopher, CBE, *b.* 1925, *m.*
2001 *Clark of Windermere,* David George Clark, PC, PHD, *b.* 1939, *m.*
1998 *Clarke of Hampstead,* Anthony James Clarke, CBE, *b.* 1932, *m.*
2020 *Clarke of Nottingham,* Kenneth Harry Clarke, CH, PC, QC, *b.* 1940, *w.*
2009 ❲*Clarke of Stone-Cum-Ebony,* Anthony Peter Clarke, PC, *b.* 1943, *m.*
1998 *Clement-Jones,* Timothy Francis Clement-Jones, CBE, *b.* 1949, *m.*
1990 ❲*Clinton-Davis,* Stanley Clinton Clinton-Davis, PC, *b.* 1928, *m.*
2000 *Coe,* Sebastian Newbold Coe, CH, KBE, *b.* 1956, *m.*
2011 *Collins of Highbury,* Raymond Edward Harry Collins, *b.* 1954, *m.*
2001 ❲*Condon,* Paul Leslie Condon, QPM, *b.* 1947, *m.*
2014 *Cooper of Windrush,* Andrew Timothy Cooper, *b.* 1963, *m.*
1997 ❲*Cope of Berkeley,* John Ambrose Cope, PC, *b.* 1937, *m.*
2010 *Cormack,* Patrick Thomas Cormack, *b.* 1939, *m.*
2006 *Cotter,* Brian Joseph Michael Cotter, *b.* 1938, *m.*
1991 *Craig of Radley,* David Brownrigg Craig, GCB, OBE, *b.* 1929, *w.*
2006 *Crisp,* (Edmund) Nigel (Ramsay) Crisp, KCB, *b.* 1952, *m.*
2003 ❲*Cullen of Whitekirk,* William Douglas Cullen, KT, PC, *b.* 1935, *m.*
2005 *Cunningham of Felling,* John Anderson Cunningham, PC, *b.* 1939, *m.*
1996 *Currie of Marylebone,* David Anthony Currie, *b.* 1946, *m.*
2011 *Curry of Kirkharle,* Donald Thomas Younger Curry, CBE, *b.* 1944, *m.*
2011 *Dannatt,* (Francis) Richard Dannatt, GCB, CBE, MC, *b.* 1950, *m.*
2015 ❲*Darling of Roulanish,* Alistair Maclean Darling, PC, *b.* 1953, *m.*
2019 ‡*Darroch of Kew,* (Nigel) Kim Darroch, KCMG, *b.* 1954, *m.*
2007 *Darzi of Denham,* Ara Warkes Darzi, OM, KBE, PC, *b.* 1960, *m.*
2006 *Davidson of Glen Clova,* Neil Forbes Davidson, QC, *b.* 1950, *m.*
2009 *Davies of Abersoch,* Evan Mervyn Davies, CBE, *b.* 1952, *m.*

2020   *Davies of Brixton,* Brinley Howard Davies, *b.* 1944
2019   *Davies of Gower,* (Henry) Byron Davies, *b.* 1952
1997   *Davies of Oldham,* Bryan Davies, PC, *b.* 1939, *m.*
2010   *Davies of Stamford,* John Quentin Davies, *b.* 1944, *m.*
2006   *Dear,* Geoffrey (James) Dear, QPM, *b.* 1937, *m.*
2010   *Deben,* John Selwyn Gummer, PC, *b.* 1939, *m.*
2012   *Deighton,* Paul Clive Deighton, KBE, *b.* 1956, *m.*
1991   *Desai,* Prof. Meghnad Jagdishchandra Desai, PHD, *b.* 1940, *m.*
1997   *Dholakia,* Navnit Dholakia, OBE, PC, *b.* 1937, *m.*
1993   *Dixon-Smith,* Robert William Dixon-Smith, *b.* 1934, *m.*
2010   *Dobbs,* Michael John Dobbs, *b.* 1948, *m.*
2020   *Dodds,* Nigel Alexander Dodds, OBE, PC, *b.* 1958, *m.*
1985   *Donoughue,* Bernard Donoughue, DPHIL, *b.* 1934, *m.*
2004   *Drayson,* Paul Rudd Drayson, PC, *b.* 1960, *m.*
1994   *Dubs,* Alfred Dubs, *b.* 1932, *m.*
2017   *Duncan of Springbank,* Ian James Duncan, *b.* 1973, *c.p.*
2015   *Dunlop,* Andrew James Dunlop, *b.* 1959, *m.*
2004   *Dykes,* Hugh John Maxwell Dykes, *b.* 1939
1995   *Eames,* Rt. Revd Robert Henry Alexander Eames, OM, PHD, *b.* 1937, *m.*
1992   *Eatwell,* John Leonard Eatwell, PHD, *b.* 1945, *m.*
2011   ℂ*Edmiston,* Robert Norman Edmiston, *b.* 1946, *m.*
1999   *Elder,* Thomas Murray Elder, *b.* 1950
1992   *Elis-Thomas,* Dafydd Elis Elis-Thomas, PC, *b.* 1946, *m.*

1981   ℂ*Elystan-Morgan,* Dafydd Elystan Elystan-Morgan, *b.* 1932, *w.*
2011   *Empey,* Reginald Norman Morgan Empey, OBE, *b.* 1947, *m.*
2000   ℂ*Erskine of Alloa Tower,* Earl of Mar and Kellie, *b.* 1949, *m. (see* Hereditary Peers)
1998   *Evans of Watford,* David Charles Evans, *b.* 1942, *m.*
2014   *Evans of Weardale,* Jonathan Douglas Evans, KCB, *b.* 1958
1997   *Falconer of Thoroton,* Charles Leslie Falconer, PC, QC, *b.* 1951, *m.*
2014   *Farmer,* Michael Stahel Farmer, *b.* 1944, *m.*
1999   *Faulkner of Worcester,* Richard Oliver Faulkner, *b.* 1946, *m.*
2010   *Faulks,* Edward Peter Lawless Faulks, QC, *b.* 1950, *m.*
2001   ℂ*Fearn,* Ronald Cyril Fearn, OBE, *b.* 1931, *m.*
2010   *Feldman of Elstree,* Andrew Simon Feldman, PC, *b.* 1966, *m.*
1999   *Fellowes,* Robert Fellowes, GCB, GCVO, PC, *b.* 1941, *m.*
2011   *Fellowes of West Stafford,* Julian Alexander Fellowes, *b.* 1949, *m.*
2020   *Field of Birkenhead,* Frank Field, PC, *b.* 1942
1999   *Filkin,* David Geoffrey Nigel Filkin, CBE, *b.* 1944, *m.*
2011   *Fink,* Stanley Fink, *b.* 1957, *m.*
2013   *Finkelstein,* Daniel William Finkelstein, OBE, *b.* 1962, *m.*
2011   *Flight,* Howard Emerson Flight, *b.* 1948, *m.*
1999   *Forsyth of Drumlean,* Michael Bruce Forsyth, PC, *b.* 1954, *m.*
2015   *Foster of Bath,* Donald Michael Ellison Foster, PC, *b.* 1947, *m.*
1999   ℂ*Foster of Thames Bank,* Norman Robert Foster, OM, *b.* 1935, *m.*
2005   *Foulkes of Cumnock,* George Foulkes, PC, *b.* 1942, *m.*
2001   *Fowler,* (Peter) Norman Fowler, PC, *b.* 1938, *m. Lord Speaker*
2014   *Fox,* Christopher Francis Fox, *b.* 1957, *m.*
2011   *Framlingham,* Michael Nicholson Lord, *b.* 1938, *m.*
2016   *Fraser of Corriegarth,* (Alexander) Andrew (Macdonell) Fraser, *b.* 1946, *m.*
1997   ℂ*Freeman,* Roger Norman Freeman, PC, *b.* 1942, *m.*
2020   *Frost,* David George Hamilton Frost, CMG, *b.* 1965
2009   *Freud,* David Anthony Freud, PC, *b.* 1950, *m.*
2016   *Gadhia,* Jitesh Kishorekumar Gadhia, *b.* 1970, *m.*

2010   *Gardiner of Kimble,* John Gardiner, *b.* 1956, *m.*
2018   *Garnier,* Edward Henry Garnier, PC, QC, *b.* 1952, *m.*
1999   ℂ*Gascoyne-Cecil,* The Marquess of Salisbury, KG, KCVO, PC, *b.* 1946, *m. (see* Hereditary Peers)
2017   *Geidt,* Christopher Edward Wollaston MacKenzie Geidt, GCB, GCVO, OBE, PC, *b.* 1961, *m.*
2010   *German,* Michael James German, OBE, *b.* 1945, *m.*
2004   *Giddens,* Prof. Anthony Giddens, *b.* 1938, *m.*
2015   *Gilbert of Panteg,* Stephen Gilbert, *b.* 1963
2011   *Glasman,* Maurice Mark Glasman, *b.* 1961, *m.*
2011   *Glendonbrook,* Michael David Bishop, CBE, *b.* 1942
2014   *Goddard of Stockport,* David Goddard, *b.* 1952
2011   *Gold,* David Laurence Gold, *b.* 1951, *m.*
1999   *Goldsmith,* Peter Henry Goldsmith, PC, QC, *b.* 1950, *m.*
2020   *Goldsmith of Richmond Park,* (Frank) Zac(harias) Robin Goldsmith, PC, *b.* 1975, *m.*
2005   *Goodlad,* Alastair Robertson Goodlad, KCMG, PC, *b.* 1943, *m.*
1999   *Grabiner,* Anthony Stephen Grabiner, QC, *b.* 1945, *m.*
2011   *Grade of Yarmouth,* Michael Ian Grade, CBE, *b.* 1943, *m.*
2000   *Greaves,* Anthony Robert Greaves, *b.* 1942, *m.*
2014   *Green of Deddington,* Andrew Fleming Green, KCMG, *b.* 1941, *m.*
2010   *Green of Hurstpierpoint,* Stephen Keith Green, *b.* 1948, *m.*
2020   *Greenhalgh,* Stephen John Greenghalgh, *b.* 1967, *m.*
2000   ℂ*Grenfell of Kilvey,* Lord Grenfell, *b.* 1935, *m. (see* Hereditary Peers)
2004   *Griffiths of Burry Port,* Revd Dr Leslie John Griffiths, *b.* 1942, *m.*
1991   *Griffiths of Fforestfach,* Brian Griffiths, *b.* 1941, *m.*
2020   *Grimstone of Boscobel,* Gerald Edgar Grimstone, CVO, *b.* 1949
2001   *Grocott,* Bruce Joseph Grocott, PC, *b.* 1940, *m.*
2000   *Gueterbock,* Lord Berkeley, OBE, *b.* 1939, *m. (see* Hereditary Peers)
2000   ℂ*Guthrie of Craigiebank,* Charles Ronald Llewelyn Guthrie, GCB, GCVO, OBE, *b.* 1938, *m.*
2015   *Hague of Richmond,* William Jefferson Hague, PC, *b.* 1961, *m.*
2015   *Hailsham of Kettlethorpe,* Viscount Hailsham, PC, QC, *b.* 1945, *m. (see* Hereditary Peers)
2015   *Hain,* Peter Gerald Hain, PC, *b.* 1950, *m.*
2010   *Hall of Birkenhead,* Anthony William Hall, CBE, *b.* 1951, *m.*
2007   *Hameed,* Dr Khalid Hameed, CBE, *b.* 1941, *m.*
2005   *Hamilton of Epsom,* Archibald Gavin Hamilton, PC, *b.* 1941, *m.*
2020   *Hammond,* Philip Hammond, PC, *b.* 1955, *m.*
2001   *Hannay of Chiswick,* David Hugh Alexander Hannay, GCMG, CH, *b.* 1935, *w.*
1998   *Hanningfield,* Paul Edward Winston White, *b.* 1940
1997   ℂ*Hardie,* Andrew Rutherford Hardie, PC, QC, *b.* 1946, *m.*
2006   *Harries of Pentregarth,* Rt. Revd Richard Douglas Harries, *b.* 1936, *m.*
1998   *Harris of Haringey,* (Jonathan) Toby Harris, *b.* 1953, *m.*
1996   *Harris of Peckham,* Philip Charles Harris, *b.* 1942, *m.*
1999   *Harrison,* Lyndon Henry Arthur Harrison, *b.* 1947, *m.*
2018   *Haselhurst,* Alan Gordon Barraclough Haselhurst, PC, *b.* 1937, *m.*
1993   *Haskel,* Simon Haskel, *b.* 1934, *m.*
1998   *Haskins,* Christopher Robin Haskins, *b.* 1937, *m.*
2005   *Hastings of Scarisbrick,* Michael John Hastings, CBE, *b.* 1958, *m.*

1997 ℂ*Hattersley,* Roy Sidney George Hattersley, PC, *b.* 1932, *m.*
2013 *Haughey,* William Haughey, OBE, *b.* 1956, *m.*
2004 *Haworth,* Alan Robert Haworth, *b.* 1948, *m.*
2014 *Hay of Ballyore,* William Alexander Hay, *b.* 1950, *m.*
2015 *Hayward,* Robert Antony Hayward, OBE, *b.* 1949
2019 *Hendy,* John Hendy, QC, *b.* 1948
2010 *Hennessy of Nympsfield,* Prof. Peter John Hennessy, *b.* 1947, *m.*
2020 *Herbert of South Downs,* Nicholas Le Quesne Herbert, CBE, PC, *b.* 1963, cp.
2001 *Heseltine,* Michael Ray Dibdin Heseltine, CH, PC, *b.* 1933, *m.*
2018 *Heywood of Whitehall, Jeremy John Heywood,* GCB, CVO, *b.* 1961, m., *d.* 2018
1997 ℂ*Higgins,* Terence Langley Higgins, KBE, PC, *b.* 1928, *m.*
2010 *Hill of Oareford,* Jonathan Hopkin Hill, CBE, PC, *b.* 1960, *m.*
2000 *Hodgson of Astley Abbotts,* Robin Granville Hodgson, CBE, *b.* 1942, *m.*
2017 *Hogan-Howe,* Bernard Hogan-Howe, QPM, *b.* 1957, *m.*
1991 *Hollick,* Clive Richard Hollick, *b.* 1945, *m.*
2013 *Holmes of Richmond,* Christopher Holmes, MBE, *b.* 1971
1995 *Hope of Craighead,* (James Arthur) David Hope, KT, PC, *b.* 1938, *m.*
2005 ℂ*Hope of Thornes,* Rt. Revd David Michael Hope, KCVO, PC, *b.* 1940
2013 *Horam,* John Rhodes Horam, *b.* 1939, *m.*
2017 *Houghton of Richmond,* John Nicholas Reynolds Houghton, GCB, CBE, *b.* 1954, *m.*
2010 *Howard of Lympne,* Michael Howard, CH, PC, QC, *b.* 1941, *m.*
2004 *Howard of Rising,* Greville Patrick Charles Howard, *b.* 1941, *m.*
2005 *Howarth of Newport,* Alan Thomas Howarth, CBE, PC, *b.* 1944
1997 *Howell of Guildford,* David Arthur Russell Howell, PC, *b.* 1936, *m.*
1997 *Hoyle,* (Eric) Douglas Harvey Hoyle, *b.* 1930, *w.*
1997 *Hughes of Woodside,* Robert Hughes, *b.* 1932, *m.*
2000 *Hunt of Chesterton,* Julian Charles Roland Hunt, CB, *b.* 1941, *m.*
1997 *Hunt of Kings Heath,* Philip Alexander Hunt, OBE, PC, *b.* 1949, *m.*
1997 *Hunt of Wirral,* David James Fletcher Hunt, MBE, PC, *b.* 1942, *m.*
1997 ℂ*Hurd of Westwell,* Douglas Richard Hurd, CH, CBE, PC, *b.* 1930, *w.*
2011 *Hussain,* Qurban Hussain, *b.* 1956, *m.*
2010 *Hutton of Furness,* John Matthew Patrick Hutton, PC, *b.* 1955, *m.*
1997 ℂ*Inge,* Peter Anthony Inge, KG, GCB, PC, *b.* 1935, *w.*
1987 *Irvine of Lairg,* Alexander Andrew Mackay Irvine, PC, QC, *b.* 1940, *m.*
2006 *James of Blackheath,* David Noel James, CBE, *b.* 1937, *m.*
2007 *Janvrin,* Robin Berry Janvrin, GCB, GCVO, PC, *b.* 1946, *m.*
2006 *Jay of Ewelme,* Michael (Hastings) Jay, GCMG, *b.* 1946, *m.*
2020 *Johnson of Marylebone,* Joseph Edmund Johnson, PC, *b.* 1971, *m.*
2001 *Jones,* (Stephen) Barry Jones, PC, *b.* 1937, *m.*
2007 ℂ*Jones of Birmingham,* Digby Marritt Jones, *b.* 1955, *m.*
2005 *Jones of Cheltenham,* Nigel David Jones, *b.* 1948, *m.*
1997 *Jopling,* (Thomas) Michael Jopling, PC, *b.* 1930, *m.*
2000 *Jordan,* William Brian Jordan, CBE, *b.* 1936, *m.*

1991 *Judd,* Frank Ashcroft Judd, *b.* 1935, *m.*
2008 *Judge,* Igor Judge, PC, *b.* 1941, *m.*
2010 *Kakkar,* Prof. Ajay Kumar Kakkar, PC, *b.* 1964, *m.*
2004 *Kalms,* Harold Stanley Kalms, *b.* 1931, *m.*
2015 *Keen of Elie,* Richard Sanderson Keen, PC, QC, *b.* 1954, *m.*
2010 *Kennedy of Southwark,* Roy Francis Kennedy, *b.* 1962, *m.*
2004 *Kerr of Kinlochard,* John (Olav) Kerr, GCMG, *b.* 1942, *m.*
2010 **Kerr of Monteviot,* Marquess of Lothian (Michael Ancram), PC, QC, *b.* 1945, *m.* (*see* Hereditary Peers)
2015 *Kerslake,* Robert Walter Kerslake, *b.* 1955, *m.*
2011 *Kestenbaum,* Jonathan Andrew Kestenbaum, *b.* 1959, *m.*
2001 *Kilclooney,* John David Taylor, PC (NI), *b.* 1937, *m.*
2001 *King of Bridgwater,* Thomas Jeremy King, CH, PC, *b.* 1933, *m.*
2013 *King of Lothbury,* Mervyn Allister King, KG, GBE, *b.* 1948
2005 *Kinnock,* Neil Gordon Kinnock, PC, *b.* 1942, *m.*
1999 *Kirkham,* Graham Kirkham, *b.* 1944, *m.*
1975 ℂ*Kirkhill,* John Farquharson Smith, *b.* 1930, *m.*
2016 *Kirkhope of Harrogate,* Timothy John Robert Kirkhope, *b.* 1945, *m.*
2005 ℂ*Kirkwood of Kirkhope,* Archibald Johnstone Kirkwood, *b.* 1946, *m.*
2010 *Knight of Weymouth,* James Philip Knight, PC, *b.* 1965, *m.*
2007 *Krebs,* Prof. John (Richard) Krebs, FRS, *b.* 1945, *m.*
2004 ℂ*Laidlaw,* Irvine Alan Stewart Laidlaw, *b.* 1942, *m.*
1998 *Laming,* (William) Herbert Laming, CBE, PC, *b.* 1936, *w.*
1998 *Lamont of Lerwick,* Norman Stewart Hughson Lamont, PC, *b.* 1942
2020 *Lancaster of Kimbolton,* (John) Mark Lancaster, TD, VR, PC, *b.* 1970, *m.*
1997 *Lang of Monkton,* Ian Bruce Lang, PC, *b.* 1940, *m.*
2015 *Lansley,* Andrew David Lansley, CBE, PC, *b.* 1956, *m.*
1992 *Lawson of Blaby,* Nigel Lawson, PC, *b.* 1932
2000 *Layard,* Peter Richard Grenville Layard, *b.* 1934, *m.*
1999 *Lea of Crondall,* David Edward Lea, OBE, *b.* 1937
2020 ‡*Lebedev,* Evgeny Alexandrovich Lebedev, *b.* 1980
2006 *Lee of Trafford,* John Robert Louis Lee, *b.* 1942, *m.*
2013 *Leigh of Hurley,* Howard Darryl Leigh, *b.* 1959, *m.*
2004 *Leitch,* Alexander Park Leitch, *b.* 1947, *m.*
2014 *Lennie,* Christopher John Lennie, *b.* 1953, *m.*
1997 *Levene of Portsoken,* Peter Keith Levene, KBE, *b.* 1941, *m.*
1997 *Levy,* Michael Abraham Levy, *b.* 1944, *m.*
2010 *Lexden,* Alistair Basil Cooke, OBE, *b.* 1945
2010 *Liddle,* Roger John Liddle, *b.* 1947, *m.*
2018 *Lilley,* Peter Bruce Lilley, PC, *b.* 1943, *m.*
2010 *Lingfield,* Robert George Alexander Balchin, *b.* 1942, *m.*
1999 *Lipsey,* David Lawrence Lipsey, *b.* 1948, *m.*
2020 ‡*Lister,* Edward Julian Udny-Lister, *b.* 1949, *m.*
2014 *Lisvane,* Robert James Rogers, KCB, *b.* 1950, *m.*
2015 *Livermore,* Spencer Elliot Livermore, *b.* 1975
2013 *Livingston of Parkhead,* Ian Paul Livingston, *b.* 1964, *m.*
2016 *Llewellyn of Steep,* Edward David Gerard Llewellyn, OBE, PC, *b.* 1965, *m.*
1997 ℂ*Lloyd-Webber,* Andrew Lloyd Webber, *b.* 1948, *m.*
2011 *Loomba,* Rajinder Paul Loomba, CBE, *b.* 1943, *m.*
2006 *Low of Dalston,* Prof. Colin MacKenzie Low, CBE, *b.* 1942, *m.*
2000 ℂ*Luce,* Richard Napier Luce, KG, GCVO, PC, *b.* 1936, *m.*
2015 *Lupton,* James Roger Crompton Lupton, CBE, *b.* 1955, *m.*
2000 **Lyttelton of Aldershot,* The Viscount Chandos, *b.* 1953, *m.* (*see* Hereditary Peers)

2010   *McAvoy,* Thomas McLaughlin McAvoy, PC, *b.* 1943, *m.*

1989   *McColl of Dulwich,* Ian McColl, CBE, FRCS, FRCSE, *b.* 1933, *w.*

2010   *McConnell of Glenscorrodale,* Dr Jack Wilson McConnell, PC, *b.* 1960, *m.*

2018   *McCrea of Magherafelt and Cookstown,* Revd Dr (Robert Thomas) William McCrea, *b.* 1948, *m.*

2020   *McLoughlin,* Patrick Alan McLoughlin, CH, PC, *b.* 1957, *m.*

2010   *Macdonald of River Glaven,* Kenneth Donald John Macdonald, QC, *b.* 1953, *m.*

1998   ❮*Macdonald of Tradeston,* Angus John Macdonald, CBE, PC, *b.* 1940, *m.*

2010   *McFall of Alcluith,* John Francis McFall, PC, *b.* 1944, *m.*

1991   ❮*Macfarlane of Bearsden,* Norman Somerville Macfarlane, KT, FRSE, *b.* 1926, *m.*

2001   ❮*MacGregor of Pulham Market,* John Roddick Russell MacGregor, CBE, PC, *b.* 1937, *m.*

2016   *McInnes of Kilwinning,* Mark McInnes, CBE, *b.* 1976

1979   *Mackay of Clashfern,* James Peter Hymers Mackay, KT, PC, FRSE, *b.* 1927, *m.*

1999   *MacKenzie of Culkein,* Hector Uisdean MacKenzie, *b.* 1940

1998   *Mackenzie of Framwellgate,* Brian Mackenzie, OBE, *b.* 1943, *m.*

2004   *McKenzie of Luton,* William David McKenzie, *b.* 1946, *m.*

1996   ❮*MacLaurin of Knebworth,* Ian Charter MacLaurin, *b.* 1937, *m.*

1995   *McNally,* Tom McNally, PC, *b.* 1943, *m.*

2018   *McNicol of West Kilbride,* Iain Mackenzie McNicol, *b.* 1969, *m.*

2016   *Macpherson of Earl's Court,* Nicholas Ian Macpherson, GCB, *b.* 1959, *m.*

2011   *Magan of Castletown,* George Morgan Magan, *b.* 1945, *m.*

2001   *Maginnis of Drumglass,* Kenneth Wiggins Maginnis, *b.* 1938, *m.*

2015   *Mair,* Prof. Robert James Mair, CBE, PHD, FRS, *b.* 1950, *m.*

2007   *Malloch-Brown,* George Mark Malloch Brown, KCMG, PC, *b.* 1953, *m.*

2008   *Mandelson,* Peter Benjamin Mandelson, PC, *b.* 1953

2019   *Mann,* John Mann, *b.* 1960, *m.*

2011   *Marks of Henley-on-Thames,* Jonathan Clive Marks, QC, *b.* 1952, *m.*

2006   *Marland,* Jonathan Peter Marland, *b.* 1956

1991   *Marlesford,* Mark Shuldham Schreiber, *b.* 1931, *m.*

2015   *Maude of Horsham,* Francis Anthony Aylmer Maude, TD, PC, *b.* 1953, *m.*

2007   *Mawson,* Revd Andrew Mawson, OBE, *b.* 1954, *m.*

2004   *Maxton,* John Alston Maxton, *b.* 1936, *m.*

2013   *Mendelsohn,* Jonathan Neil Mendelsohn, *b.* 1966, *m.*

2020   *Mendoza,* Neil Francis Jeremy Mendoza, *b.* 1959, *m.*

2000   *Mitchell,* Parry Andrew Mitchell, *b.* 1943, *m.*

2000   *⋆Mitford,* Lord Redesdale, *b.* 1967, *m.* (*see* Hereditary Peers)

2008   ❮*Mogg,* John (Frederick) Mogg, KCMG, *b.* 1943, *m.*

2010   *Monks,* John Stephen Monks, *b.* 1945, *m.*

2005   *Moonie,* Dr Lewis George Moonie, *b.* 1947, *m.*

2020   *Moore of Etchingham,* Charles Hilary Moore, *b.* 1956, *m.*

2000   *Morgan,* Kenneth Owen Morgan, *b.* 1934, *m.*

2001   *Morris of Aberavon,* John Morris, KG, PC, QC, *b.* 1931, *m.*

2006   ❮*Morris of Handsworth,* William Manuel Morris, *b.* 1938, *w.*

2006   *Morrow,* Maurice George Morrow, *b.* 1948, *m.*

2020   *Moylan,* Daniel Michael Gerald Moylan, *b.* 1956

2015   *Murphy of Torfaen,* Paul Peter Murphy, PC, *b.* 1948

2008   *Myners,* Paul Myners, CBE, *b.* 1948, *m.*

1997   *Naseby,* Michael Wolfgang Laurence Morris, PC, *b.* 1936, *m.*

2013   *Nash,* John Alfred Stoddard Nash, *b.* 1949, *m.*

1997   *Newby,* Richard Mark Newby, OBE, PC, *b.* 1953, *m.*

1994   ❮*Nickson,* David Wigley Nickson, KBE, FRSE, *b.* 1929, *m.*

1998   *Norton of Louth,* Philip Norton, *b.* 1951

2000   *Oakeshott of Seagrove Bay,* Matthew Alan Oakeshott, *b.* 1947, *m.*

2015   *Oates,* Jonathan Oates, *b.* 1969, *c.p.*

2012   *O'Donnell,* Augustine Thomas (Gus) O'Donnell, GCB, *b.* 1952, *m.*

2015   *O'Neill of Gatley,* Terence James O'Neill, *b.* 1957, *m.*

2015   *O'Shaughnessy,* James Richard O'Shaughnessy, *b.* 1976, *m.*

2001   ❮*Ouseley,* Herman George Ouseley, *b.* 1945, *m.*

1992   *Owen,* David Anthony Llewellyn Owen, CH, PC, *b.* 1938, *m.*

1999   *Oxburgh,* Ernest Ronald Oxburgh, KBE, FRS, PHD, *b.* 1934, *m.*

2013   *Paddick,* Brian Leonard Paddick, *b.* 1958, *m.*

2011   *Palmer of Childs Hill,* Monroe Edward Palmer, OBE, *b.* 1938, *m.*

1991   ❮*Palumbo,* Peter Garth Palumbo, *b.* 1935, *m.*

2013   *Palumbo of Southwark,* James Rudolph Palumbo, *b.* 1963

2008   *Pannick,* David Philip Pannick, QC, *b.* 1956, *m.*

2000   *Parekh,* Bhikhu Chhotalal Parekh, *b.* 1935, *m.*

2019   *Parkinson of Whitley Bay,* Stephen Graeme Parkinson, *b.* 1983

1999   *Patel,* Narendra Babubhai Patel, KT, *b.* 1938, *m.*

2006   *Patel of Bradford,* Prof. Kamlesh Kumar Patel, OBE, *b.* 1960, *m.*

1997   *Patten,* John Haggitt Charles Patten, PC, *b.* 1945, *m.*

2005   *Patten of Barnes,* Christopher Francis Patten, CH, PC, *b.* 1944, *m.*

1996   *Paul,* Swraj Paul, PC, *b.* 1931, *m.*

1990   *Pearson of Rannoch,* Malcolm Everard MacLaren Pearson, *b.* 1942, *m.*

2001   *Pendry,* Thomas Pendry, PC, *b.* 1934, *m.*

1998   ❮*Phillips of Sudbury,* Andrew Wyndham Phillips, OBE, *b.* 1939, *m.*

2018   *Pickles,* Eric (Jack) Pickles, PC, *b.* 1952, *m.*

1992   *Plant of Highfield,* Prof. Raymond Plant, PHD, *b.* 1945, *m.*

1987   ❮*Plumb,* (Charles) Henry Plumb, *b.* 1925, *w.*

2015   *Polak,* Stuart Polak, CBE, *b.* 1961

2000   *⋆Ponsonby of Roehampton,* Lord Ponsonby of Shulbrede, *b.* 1958, *m.* (*see* Hereditary Peers)

2010   *Popat,* Dolar Amarshi Popat, *b.* 1953, *m.*

2015   *Porter of Spalding,* Gary Andrew Porter, CBE, *b.* 1960, *m.*

2000   *Powell of Bayswater,* Charles David Powell, KCMG, *b.* 1941, *m.*

2010   *Prescott,* John Leslie Prescott, *b.* 1938, *m.*

2016   *Price,* Mark Ian Price, CVO, *b.* 1961, *m.*

2015   *Prior of Brampton,* David Gifford Leathes Prior, *b.* 1954, *m.*

2013   *Purvis of Tweed,* Jeremy Purvis, *b.* 1974

1997   *Puttnam,* David Terence Puttnam, CBE, *b.* 1941, *m.*

2001   *Radice,* Giles Heneage Radice, PC, *b.* 1936, *m.*

2005   *Ramsbotham,* David John Ramsbotham, GCB, CBE, *b.* 1934, *m.*

2004   *Rana,* Dr Diljit Singh Rana, MBE, *b.* 1938

2018   *Randall of Uxbridge,* (Alexander) John Randall, PC, *b.* 1955, *m.*

2019   *Ranger,* Raminder Singh Ranger, CBE, *b.* 1947

1997   *Razzall,* (Edward) Timothy Razzall, CBE, *b.* 1943

2019	§*Reed,* Robert John Reed, PC, *b.* 1956, *m.* President of the Supreme Court
2005	*Rees of Ludlow,* Prof. Martin John Rees, OM, *b.* 1942, *m.*
2010	*Reid of Cardowan,* Dr John Reid, PC, *b.* 1947, *m.*
1991	*Renfrew of Kaimsthorn,* (Andrew) Colin Renfrew, FBA, *b.* 1937, *m.*
1999	*Rennard,* Christopher John Rennard, MBE, *b.* 1960, *m.*
1997	ℭ*Renwick of Clifton,* Robin William Renwick, KCMG, *b.* 1937, *m.*
2010	*Ribeiro,* Bernard Francisco Ribeiro, CBE, *b.* 1944, *m.*
2014	*Richards of Herstmonceux,* David Julian Richards, GCB, CBE, DSO, *b.* 1952, *m.*
2016	*Ricketts,* Peter (Forbes) Ricketts, GCMG, GCVO, *b.* 1952, *m.*
2010	*Risby,* Richard John Grenville Spring, *b.* 1946
2015	*Robathan,* Andrew Robathan, PC, *b.* 1951, *m.*
2004	*Roberts of Llandudno,* Revd John Roger Roberts, *b.* 1935, *w.*
1999	*Robertson of Port Ellen,* George Islay MacNeill Robertson, KT, GCMG, PC, *b.* 1946, *m.*
1992	*Rodgers of Quarry Bank,* William Thomas Rodgers, PC, *b.* 1928, *w.*
1999	*Rogan,* Dennis Robert David Rogan, *b.* 1942, *m.*
1996	*Rogers of Riverside,* Richard George Rogers, CH, RA, RIBA, *b.* 1933, *m.*
2001	*Rooker,* Jeffrey William Rooker, PC, *b.* 1941, *m.*
2014	*Rose of Monewden,* Stuart Alan Ransom Rose, *b.* 1949
2004	*Rosser,* Richard Andrew Rosser, *b.* 1944, *m.*
2006	*Rowe-Beddoe,* David (Sydney) Rowe-Beddoe, *b.* 1937, *m.*
2004	*Rowlands,* Edward Rowlands, CBE, *b.* 1940, *w.*
1997	*Ryder of Wensum,* Richard Andrew Ryder, OBE, PC, *b.* 1949, *m.*
1996	*Saatchi,* Maurice Saatchi, *b.* 1946, *w.*
2009	*Sacks,* Chief Rabbi Dr Jonathan Henry Sacks, *b.* 1948, *m.*
1989	*Sainsbury of Preston Candover,* John Davan Sainsbury, KG, *b.* 1927, *m.*
1997	*Sainsbury of Turville,* David John Sainsbury, *b.* 1940, *m.*
1985	ℭ*Sanderson of Bowden,* Charles Russell Sanderson, *b.* 1933, *m.*
2020	*Sarfraz,* Aamer Ahmad Sarfraz, *b.* 1982
2010	*Sassoon,* James Meyer Sassoon, *b.* 1955, *m.*
1998	*Sawyer,* Lawrence (Tom) Sawyer, *b.* 1943
2014	*Scriven,* Paul James Scriven, *b.* 1966
2020	*Sedwill,* Mark Philip Sedwill, KCMG, *b.* 1964, *m.*
1997	*Selkirk of Douglas,* James Alexander Douglas-Hamilton, PC, QC, *b.* 1942, *m.*
1996	ℭ*Sewel,* John Buttifant Sewel, CBE, *b.* 1946
2010	*Sharkey,* John Kevin Sharkey, *b.* 1947, *m.*
1999	ℭ*Sharman,* Colin Morven Sharman, OBE, *b.* 1943, *m.*
1994	ℭ*Shaw of Northstead,* Michael Norman Shaw, *b.* 1920, *m.*
2006	*Sheikh,* Mohamed Iltaf Sheikh, *b.* 1941, *m.*
2013	*Sherbourne of Didsbury,* Stephen Ashley Sherbourne, CBE, *b.* 1945
2015	*Shinkwin,* Kevin Joseph Maximilian Shinkwin, *b.* 1971
2010	*Shipley,* John Warren Shipley, OBE, *b.* 1946, *m.*
2020	*Sharpe of Epsom,* Andrew Michael Gordon Sharpe, OBE, *b.* 1962
2000	*Shutt of Greetland,* David Trevor Shutt, OBE, PC, *b.* 1942, *m.*
2020	*Sikka,* Prem Nath Sikka, *b.* 1951, *m.*
1997	ℭ*Simon of Highbury,* David Alec Gwyn Simon, CBE, *b.* 1939, *m.*
1997	ℭ*Simpson of Dunkeld,* George Simpson, *b.* 1942, *m.*
2011	*Singh of Wimbledon,* Indarjit Singh, CBE, *b.* 1932, *m.*
1991	*Skidelsky,* Robert Jacob Alexander Skidelsky, DPHIL, *b.* 1939, *m.*

1997	ℭ*Smith of Clifton,* Trevor Arthur Smith, *b.* 1937, *m.*
2005	*Smith of Finsbury,* Christopher Robert Smith, PC, *b.* 1951
2015	*Smith of Hindhead,* Philip Roland Smith, CBE, *b.* 1966
2008	*Smith of Kelvin,* Robert (Haldane) Smith, KT, CH, *b.* 1944, *m.*
1999	*Smith of Leigh,* Peter Richard Charles Smith, *b.* 1945, *m.*
2004	*Snape,* Peter Charles Snape, *b.* 1942, *m.*
2005	*Soley,* Clive Stafford Soley, *b.* 1939
2020	*Spencer,* Michael Alan Spencer, *b.* 1955, *m.*
1997	ℭ*Steel of Aikwood,* David Martin Scott Steel, KT, KBE, PC, *b.* 1938, *m.*
2011	*Stephen,* Nicol Ross Stephen, *b.* 1960, *m.*
1991	*Sterling of Plaistow,* Jeffrey Maurice Sterling, GCVO, CBE, *b.* 1934, *m.*
2007	*Stern of Brentford,* Nicholas Herbert Stern, CH, *b.* 1946, *m.*
2005	*Stevens of Kirkwhelpington,* John Arthur Stevens, QPM, *b.* 1942, *m.*
1987	*Stevens of Ludgate,* David Robert Stevens, *b.* 1936, *m.*
2010	*Stevenson of Balmacara,* Robert Wilfrid Stevenson, *b.* 1947, *m.*
1999	*Stevenson of Coddenham,* Henry Dennistoun Stevenson, CBE, *b.* 1945, *m.*
2020	‡*Stewart,* Keith Douglas Stewart, QC, *b.* 1964, *m.*
2011	*Stirrup,* Graham Eric Stirrup, KG, GCB, AFC, *b.* 1949, *m.*
1983	*Stoddart of Swindon,* David Leonard Stoddart, *b.* 1926, *m.*
1997	*Stone of Blackheath,* Andrew Zelig Stone, *b.* 1942, *m.*
2011	*Stoneham of Droxford,* Benjamin Russell Mackintosh Stoneham, *b.* 1948, *m.*
2011	*Storey,* Michael John Storey, CBE, *b.* 1949, *m.*
2011	*Strasburger,* Paul Cline Strasburger, *b.* 1946, *m.*
2015	*Stunell,* Robert Andrew Stunell, OBE, PC, *b.* 1942, *m.*
2009	*Sugar,* Alan Michael Sugar, *b.* 1947, *m.*
2014	*Suri,* Ranbir Singh Suri, *b.* 1935
1971	ℭ*Tanlaw,* Simon Brooke Mackay, *b.* 1934, *m.*
1996	*Taverne,* Dick Taverne, QC, *b.* 1928, *m.*
2010	*Taylor of Goss Moor,* Matthew Owen John Taylor, *b.* 1963, *m.*
2006	*Taylor of Holbeach,* John Derek Taylor, CBE, PC, *b.* 1943, *m.*
1996	*Taylor of Warwick,* John David Beckett Taylor, *b.* 1952, *m.*
1992	*Tebbit,* Norman Beresford Tebbit, CH, PC, *b.* 1931, *m.*
2006	*Teverson,* Robin Teverson, *b.* 1952, *m.*
2013	*Thomas of Cwmgiedd,* Roger John Laugharne Thomas, PC, *b.* 1947, *m.*
1996	*Thomas of Gresford,* Donald Martin Thomas, OBE, QC, *b.* 1937, *m.*
1998	*Tomlinson,* John Edward Tomlinson, *b.* 1939, *m.*
1994	*Tope,* Graham Norman Tope, CBE, *b.* 1943, *m.*
2010	*Touhig,* James Donnelly Touhig, PC, *b.* 1947, *m.*
2012	*Trees,* Alexander John Trees, PHD, *b.* 1946, *m.*
2004	*Triesman,* David Maxim Triesman, *b.* 1943, *m.*
2006	*Trimble,* William David Trimble, PC, *b.* 1944, *m.*
2010	*True,* Nicholas Edward True, CBE, *b.* 1951, *m.*
2004	*Truscott,* Dr Peter Derek Truscott, *b.* 1959, *m.*
1993	*Tugendhat,* Christopher Samuel Tugendhat, *b.* 1937, *m.*
2004	*Tunnicliffe,* Denis Tunnicliffe, CBE, *b.* 1943, *m.*
2000	*Turnberg,* Leslie Arnold Turnberg, MD, *b.* 1934, *m.*
2005	*Turnbull,* Andrew Turnbull, KCB, CVO, PC, *b.* 1945, *m.*
2005	*Turner of Ecchinswell,* (Jonathan) Adair Turner, *b.* 1955, *m.*
2005	*Tyler,* Paul Archer Tyler, CBE, PC, *b.* 1941, *m.*
2018	*Tyrie,* Andrew Guy Tyrie, PC, *b.* 1957

2020   *Vaizey of Didcot,* Edward Henry Butler Vaizey, PC, *b.* 1968, *m.*

2004   *Vallance of Tummel,* Iain (David Thomas) Vallance, *b.* 1943, *w.*

2013   *Verjee,* Rumi Verjee, CBE, *b.* 1957

1985   *Vinson,* Nigel Vinson, LVO, *b.* 1931, *m.*

1992   *Wakeham,* John Wakeham, PC, *b.* 1932, *m.*

1999   *Waldegrave of North Hill,* William Arthur Waldegrave, PC, *b.* 1946, *m.*

2007   *Walker of Aldringham,* Michael John Dawson Walker, GCB, CMG, CBE, *b.* 1944, *m.*

1995   *Wallace of Saltaire,* William John Lawrence Wallace, PC, PHD, *b.* 1941, *m.*

2007   *Wallace of Tankerness,* James Robert Wallace, PC, QC, *b.* 1954, *m.*

2020   *Woodcock,* John Zak Woodcock, *b.* 1978

1998   *Warner,* Norman Reginald Warner, PC, *b.* 1940, *m.*

2011   *Wasserman,* Gordon Joshua Wasserman, *b.* 1938 *m.*

1997   *Watson of Invergowrie,* Michael Goodall Watson, *b.* 1949, *m.*

1999   *Watson of Richmond,* Alan John Watson, CBE, *b.* 1941, *m.*

2015   *Watts,* David Leonard Watts, *b.* 1951, *m.*

2010   *Wei,* Nathanael Ming-Yan Wei, *b.* 1977, *m.*

2007   *West of Spithead,* Alan William John West, GCB, DSC, PC, *b.* 1948, *m.*

2020   *Wharton of Yarm,* James Stephen Wharton, *b.* 1984

2013   *Whitby,* Michael John Whitby, *b.* 1948, *m.*

1996   *Whitty,* John Lawrence (Larry) Whitty, PC, *b.* 1943, *m.*

2011   *Wigley,* Dafydd Wynne Wigley, PC, *b.* 1943, *m.*

2015   *Willetts,* David Lindsay Willetts, PC, *b.* 1956, *m.*

2013   ℭ*Williams of Oystermouth,* Rt. Revd Rowan Douglas Williams, PC, Royal Victorian Chain, DPHIL, *b.* 1950, *m.*

2010   *Willis of Knaresborough,* George Philip Willis, *b.* 1941, *m.*

2010   *Wills,* Michael David Wills, PC, *b.* 1952, *m.*

2002   *Wilson of Dinton,* Richard Thomas James Wilson, GCB, *b.* 1942, *m.*

1992   *Wilson of Tillyorn,* David Clive Wilson, KT, GCMG, PHD, *b.* 1935, *m.*

1995   *Winston,* Robert Maurice Lipson Winston, FRCOG, *b.* 1940, *m.*

2010   *Wolfson of Aspley Guise,* Simon Adam Wolfson, *b.* 1967, *m.*

1991   E. *Wolfson of Sunningdale,* David Wolfson, *b.* 1935, *m.*

2011   *Wood of Anfield,* Stewart Martin Wood, *b.* 1968, *m.*

2020   ‡*Woodley,* Anthony J. Woodley, *b.* 1948, *m.*

2019   *Woolley of Woodford,* Simon Andrew Woolley, *b.* 1962

1999   ℭ*Woolmer of Leeds,* Kenneth John Woolmer, *b.* 1940, *m.*

2013   *Wrigglesworth,* Ian William Wrigglesworth, *b.* 1939, *m.*

2015   *Young of Cookham,* George Samuel Knatchbull Young, CH, PC, *b.* 1941, *m.*

1984   *Young of Graffham,* David Ivor Young, CH, PC, *b.* 1932, *m.*

2004   *Young of Norwood Green,* Anthony (Ian) Young, *b.* 1942, *m.*

BARONESSES
Created

2005   *Adams of Craigielea,* Katherine Patricia Irene Adams, *b.* 1947, *w.*

2007   *Afshar,* Prof. Haleh Afshar, OBE, *b.* 1944, *m.*

2015   *Altmann,* Dr Rosalind Miriam Altmann, CBE, *b.* 1956, *m.*

1997   *Amos,* Valerie Ann Amos, CH, PC, *b.* 1954

2000   *Andrews,* Elizabeth Kay Andrews, OBE, *b.* 1943

1996   *Anelay of St Johns,* Joyce Anne Anelay, DBE, PC, *b.* 1947, *m.*

2010   *Armstrong of Hill Top,* Hilary Jane Armstrong, PC, *b.* 1945, *m.*

1999   *Ashton of Upholland,* Catherine Margaret Ashton, GCMG, PC, *b.* 1956, *m.*

2011   *Bakewell,* Joan Dawson Bakewell, DBE, *b.* 1933

2013   *Bakewell of Hardington Mandeville,* Catherine Mary Bakewell, MBE, *b.* 1949, *m.*

1999   *Barker,* Elizabeth Jean Barker, *b.* 1961, *m.*

2018   *Barran,* Diana Francesca Caroline Barran, MBE, *b.* 1959, *m.*

2010   *Benjamin,* Floella Karen Yunies Benjamin, DBE, *b.* 1949, *m.*

2019   *Bennett of Manor Castle,* Natalie Louise Bennett, *b.*1966

2011   *Berridge,* Elizabeth Rose Berridge, *b.* 1972

2016   *Bertin,* Gabrielle Louise Bertin, *b.* 1978, *m.*

2000   *Billingham,* Angela Theodora Billingham, DPHIL, *b.* 1939, *w.*

1987   *Blackstone,* Tessa Ann Vosper Blackstone, PC, PHD, *b.* 1942

2019   *Blackwood of North Oxford,* Nicola Claire Blackwood, *b.* 1979, *m.*

1999   ℭ*Blood,* May Blood, MBE, *b.* 1938

2016   *Bloomfield of Hinton Waldrist,* Olivia Caroline Bloomfield, *b.* 1960, *m.*

2019   *Blower,* Christine Blower, *b.* 1951

2004   *Bonham-Carter of Yarnbury,* Jane Bonham Carter, *b.* 1957, *w.*

2000   *Boothroyd,* Betty Boothroyd, OM, PC, *b.* 1929

2005   *Bottomley of Nettlestone,* Virginia Hilda Brunette Maxwell Bottomley, PC, *b.* 1948, *m.*

2015   *Bowles of Berkhamsted,* Sharon Margaret Bowles, *b.* 1953, *m.*

2018   *Boycott,* Rosel Marie Boycott, MBE, *b.* 1951, *m.*

2014   *Brady,* Karren Rita Brady, CBE, *b.* 1969, *m.*

2011   *Brinton,* Sarah Virginia Brinton, *b.* 1955, *m.*

2015   *Brown of Cambridge,* Prof. Julia Elizabeth King, DBE, PHD, FRENG, *b.* 1954, *m.*

2010   *Browning,* Angela Frances Browning, *b.* 1946, *m.*

2018   *Bryan of Partick,* Pauline Christina Bryan, *b.* 1950

2018   *Bull,* Deborah Clare Bull, CBE, *b.* 1963

2015   *Burt of Solihull,* Lorely Jane Burt, *b.* 1954, *m.*

1998   *Buscombe,* Peta Jane Buscombe, *b.* 1954, *m.*

2006   *Butler-Sloss,* (Ann) Elizabeth (Oldfield) Butler-Sloss, GBE, PC, *b.* 1933, *m.*

1996   ℭ*Byford,* Hazel Byford, DBE, *b.* 1941, *w.*

2008   *Campbell of Loughborough,* Susan Catherine Campbell, DBE, *b.* 1948

2007   *Campbell of Surbiton,* Jane Susan Campbell, DBE, *b.* 1959, *m.*

2020   ‡*Casey,* Louise Casey, DBE, CB, *b.* 1965

2016   *Cavendish of Little Venice,* Hilary Camilla Cavendish, *b.* 1968, *m.*

2016   *Chakrabarti,* Sharmishta Chakrabarti, PC, CBE, *b.* 1969

1992   *Chalker of Wallasey,* Lynda Chalker, PC, *b.* 1942

2014   *Chisholm of Owlpen,* Caroline Elizabeth (Carlyn) Chisholm, *b.* 1951, *m.*

2005   *Clark of Calton,* Dr Lynda Margaret Clark, PC, *b.* 1949

2020   *Clark,* Kathryn Sloan Clark, *b.* 1967

2000   *Cohen of Pimlico,* Janet Cohen, *b.* 1940, *m.*

2005   *Corston,* Jean Ann Corston, PC, *b.* 1942, *w.*

2007   *Coussins,* Jean Coussins, *b.* 1950, *m.*

2016   *Couttie,* Philippa Marion Roe, *b.* 1962, *m.*

1982   *Cox,* Caroline Anne Cox, *b.* 1937, *w.*

1998   *Crawley,* Christine Mary Crawley, *b.* 1950, *m.*

1990   *Cumberlege,* Julia Frances Cumberlege, CBE, *b.* 1943, *m.*

2020   ‡*Davidson,* Ruth Elizabeth Davidson, PC, MSP, *b.* 1978, *m.*

2005	*Deech,* Ruth Lynn Deech, DBE, *b.* 1943, *m.*
2010	*Donaghy,* Rita Margaret Donaghy, CBE, *b.* 1944, *m.*
2010	*Doocey,* Elizabeth Deirdre Doocey, OBE, *b.* 1948, *m.*
2010	*Drake,* Jean Lesley Patricia Drake, CBE, *b.* 1948, *m.*
2004	*D'Souza,* Dr Frances Gertrude Claire D'Souza, CMG, PC, *b.* 1944, *m.*
1990	ℂ*Dunn,* Lydia Selina Dunn, DBE, *b.* 1940, *m.*
2010	*Eaton,* Ellen Margaret Eaton, DBE, *b.* 1942, *m.*
1990	*Eccles of Moulton,* Diana Catherine Eccles, *b.* 1933, *m.*
1997	ℂ*Emerton,* Audrey Caroline Emerton, DBE, *b.* 1935
2014	*Evans of Bowes Park,* Natalie Jessica Evans, PC, *b.* 1975, *m.*
2017	*Fairhead,* Rona Alison Fairhead, CBE, *b.* 1961, *m.*
2004	*Falkner of Margravine,* Kishwer Falkner, *b.* 1955, *m.*
2015	*Fall,* Catherine Susan Fall, *b.* 1967, *m.*
2015	*Featherstone,* Lynne Choona Featherstone, PC, *b.* 1951
2001	*Finlay of Llandaff,* Ilora Gillian Finlay, *b.* 1949, *m.*
2015	*Finn,* Simone Jari Finn, *b.* 1968, *m.*
1990	*Flather,* Shreela Flather, *b.* 1934, *w.*
2020	*Fleet,* Veronica Judith Colleton Wadley, CBE, *b.* 1952, *m.*
1997	*Fookes,* Janet Evelyn Fookes, DBE, *b.* 1936
2006	*Ford,* Margaret Anne Ford, OBE, *b.* 1957, *m.*
2020	*Fox of Buckley,* Claire Regina Fox, *b.* 1960
2005	*Fritchie,* Irene Tordoff Fritchie, DBE, *b.* 1942, *w.*
2020	*Fullbrook,* Lorraine Fullbrook, *b.* 1959, *m.*
1999	*Gale,* Anita Gale, *b.* 1940
2007	*Garden of Frognal,* Susan Elizabeth Garden, PC, *b.* 1944, *w.*
1981	*Gardner of Parkes,* (Rachel) Trixie (Anne) Gardner, *b.* 1927, *w.*
2013	*Goldie,* Annabel MacNicholl Goldie, *b.* 1950
2001	*Golding,* Llinos Golding, *b.* 1933, *w.*
1998	*Goudie,* Mary Teresa Goudie, *b.* 1946, *m.*
1993	ℂ*Gould of Potternewton,* Joyce Brenda Gould, *b.* 1932, *m.*
2001	*Greenfield,* Susan Adele Greenfield, CBE, *b.* 1950
2000	*Greengross,* Sally Ralea Greengross, OBE, *b.* 1935, *w.*
2013	*Grender,* Rosalind Mary Grender, MBE, *b.* 1962, *m.*
2010	*Grey-Thompson,* Tanni Carys Davina Grey-Thompson, DBE, *b.* 1969, *m.*
2019	*Hallett,* Heather Carol Hallett, DBE, PC, *b.* 1949, *m.*
1991	*Hamwee,* Sally Rachel Hamwee, *b.* 1947
1999	ℂ*Hanham,* Joan Brownlow Hanham, CBE, *b.* 1939, *m.*
2014	*Harding of Winscombe,* Diana Mary (Dido) Harding, *b.* 1967, *m.*
1999	*Harris of Richmond,* Angela Felicity Harris, *b.* 1944, *m.*
1996	*Hayman,* Helene Valerie Hayman, GBE, PC, *b.* 1949, *m.*
2020	*Hayman of Ullock,* Susan Mary Hayman, *b.* 1962, *m.*
2010	*Hayter of Kentish Town,* Dr Dianne Hayter, *b.* 1949, *m.*
2010	*Healy of Primrose Hill,* Anna Healy, *b.* 1955, *m.*
2014	*Helic,* Arminka Helic, *b.* 1968
2004	*Henig,* Ruth Beatrice Henig, CBE, *b.* 1943, *m.*
1991	*Hilton of Eggardon,* Jennifer Hilton, QPM, *b.* 1936
2013	*Hodgson of Abinger,* Fiona Ferelith Hodgson, CBE, *b.* 1954, *m.*
2020	*Hoey,* Catharine Letitia Hoey, *b.* 1946
1995	*Hogg,* Sarah Elizabeth Mary Hogg, *b.* 1946, *m.*
2010	*Hollins,* Prof. Sheila Clare Hollins, *b.* 1946, *m.*
1985	*Hooper,* Gloria Dorothy Hooper, CMG, *b.* 1939
2001	*Howarth of Breckland,* Valerie Georgina Howarth, OBE, *b.* 1940
2001	ℂ*Howe of Idlicote,* Elspeth Rosamond Morton Howe, CBE, *b.* 1932, *w.*
1999	ℂ*Howells of St Davids,* Rosalind Patricia-Anne Howells, OBE, *b.* 1931, *m.*
2010	*Hughes of Stretford,* Beverley Hughes, PC, *b.* 1950, *m.*
2013	*Humphreys,* Christine Mary Humphreys, *b.* 1947
2019	*Hunt of Bethnal Green,* Ruth Elizabeth Hunt, *b.*1980
2010	*Hussein-Ece,* Meral Hussein Ece, OBE, *b.* 1953
2014	*Janke,* Barbara Lilian Janke, *b.* 1947, *m.*
1992	*Jay of Paddington,* Margaret Ann Jay, PC, *b.* 1939, *m.*
2011	*Jenkin of Kennington,* Anne Caroline Jenkin, *b.* 1955, *m.*
2010	*Jolly,* Judith Anne Jolly, *b.* 1951, *m.*
2013	*Jones of Moulsecoomb,* Jennifer Helen Jones, *b.* 1949
2006	*Jones of Whitchurch,* Margaret Beryl Jones, *b.* 1955
2013	*Kennedy of Cradley,* Alicia Pamela Kennedy, *b.* 1969, *m.*
1997	*Kennedy of the Shaws,* Helena Ann Kennedy, QC, *b.* 1950, *m.*
2012	*Kidron,* Beeban Tania Kidron, OBE, *b.* 1961, *m.*
2011	*King of Bow,* Oona Tamsyn King, *b.* 1967, *m.*
2006	*Kingsmill,* Denise Patricia Byrne Kingsmill, CBE, *b.* 1947, *m.*
2009	*Kinnock of Holyhead,* Glenys Elizabeth Kinnock, *b.* 1944, *m.*
1997	ℂ*Knight of Collingtree,* (Joan Christabel) Jill Knight, DBE, *b.* 1927, *w.*
2010	*Kramer,* Susan Veronica Kramer, PC, *b.* 1950, *w.*
2013	*Lane-Fox of Soho,* Martha Lane Fox, CBE, *b.* 1973
2013	*Lawrence of Clarendon,* Doreen Delceita Lawrence, OBE, *b.* 1952
2010	*Liddell of Coatdyke,* Helen Lawrie Liddell, PC, *b.* 1950, *m.*
1997	ℂ*Linklater of Butterstone,* Veronica Linklater, *b.* 1943, *m.*
2011	*Lister of Burtersett,* Margot Ruth Aline Lister, CBE, *b.* 1949
1997	*Ludford,* Sarah Ann Ludford, *b.* 1951, *m.*
2004	*McDonagh,* Margaret Josephine McDonagh, *b.* 1961
2015	*McGregor-Smith,* Ruby McGregor-Smith, CBE, *b.* 1963, *m.*
1999	*McIntosh of Hudnall,* Genista Mary McIntosh, *b.* 1946
2015	*McIntosh of Pickering,* Anne Caroline Ballingall McIntosh, *b.* 1954, *m.*
1991	*Mallalieu,* Ann Mallalieu, QC, *b.* 1945
2008	*Manningham-Buller,* Elizabeth (Lydia) Manningham-Buller, LG, DCB, *b.* 1948, *m.*
2013	*Manzoor,* Zahida Parveen Manzoor, CBE, *b.* 1958, *m.*
1970	*Masham of Ilton,* Susan Lilian Primrose Cunliffe-Lister, *b.* 1935, *w.*
1999	*Massey of Darwen,* Doreen Elizabeth Massey, *b.* 1938, *m.*
2006	*Meacher,* Molly Christine Meacher, *b.* 1940, *m.*
2018	*Meyer,* Catherine Irene Jacqueline Meyer, CBE, *b.* 1953, *m.*
1998	*Miller of Chilthorne Domer,* Susan Elizabeth Miller, *b.* 1954, *m.*
2014	*Mobarik,* Nosheena Shaheen Mobarik, CBE, MEP, *b.* 1957, *m.*
2015	*Mone,* Michelle Georgina Mone, OBE, *b.* 1971
2020	*Morgan of Cotes,* Nicola Ann Morgan, PC, *b.* 1972, *m.*
2004	*Morgan of Drefelin,* Delyth Jane Morgan, *b.* 1961, *m.*
2011	*Morgan of Ely,* Mair Eluned Morgan, *b.* 1967, *m.*
2001	*Morgan of Huyton,* Sally Morgan, *b.* 1959, *m.*
2004	*Morris of Bolton,* Patricia Morris, OBE, *b.* 1953, *m.*
2005	*Morris of Yardley,* Estelle Morris, PC, *b.* 1952
2020	*Morrissey,* Helena Louise Morrissey, DBE, *b.* 1966, *m.*
2004	*Murphy,* Elaine Murphy, *b.* 1947, *m.*
2004	*Neuberger,* Rabbi Julia (Babette Sarah) Neuberger, DBE, *b.* 1950, *m.*
2007	*Neville-Jones,* (Lilian) Pauline Neville-Jones, DCMG, PC, *b.* 1939
2013	*Neville-Rolfe,* Lucy Jeanne Neville-Rolfe, DBE, CMG, *b.* 1953, *m.*
2010	*Newlove,* Helen Margaret Newlove, *b.* 1961, *w.*
1997	*Nicholson of Winterbourne,* Emma Harriet Nicholson, *b.* 1941, *w.*
2000	*Noakes,* Sheila Valerie Masters, DBE, *b.* 1949, *m.*
2000	*Northover,* Lindsay Patricia Granshaw, PC, *b.* 1954
2010	*Nye,* Susan Nye, *b.* 1955, *m.*
1991	*O'Cathain,* Detta O'Cathain, OBE, *b.* 1938, *w.*

2009	*O'Loan,* Nuala Patricia O'Loan, DBE, *b.* 1951, *m.*
1999	*O'Neill of Bengarve,* Onora Sylvia O'Neill, CH, CBE, FRS, FBA, *b.* 1941
1989	ℭ*Oppenheim-Barnes,* Sally Oppenheim-Barnes, PC, *b.* 1930, *w.*
2018	*Osamor,* Martha Otito Osamor, *b.* 1940, *w.*
2006	ℭ*Paisley of St George's,* Eileen Emily Paisley, *b.* 1931, *w.*
2010	*Parminter,* Kathryn Jane Parminter, *b.* 1964, *m.*
2019	*Penn,* Joanna Carolyn Penn, *b.* 1985
1991	ℭ*Perry of Southwark,* Pauline Perry, *b.* 1931, *w.*
2015	*Pidding,* Emma Samantha Pidding, CBE, *b.* 1966
2014	*Pinnock,* Kathryn Mary Pinnock, *b.* 1946, *m.*
1997	*Pitkeathley,* Jill Elizabeth Pitkeathley, OBE, *b.* 1940, *m.*
1999	*Prashar,* Usha Kumari Prashar, CBE, PC, *b.* 1948, *m.*
2015	*Primarolo,* Dawn Primarolo, DBE, PC, *b.* 1954, *m.*
2004	*Prosser,* Margaret Theresa Prosser, OBE, *b.* 1937
2006	*Quin,* Joyce Gwendoline Quin, PC, *b.* 1944
1996	*Ramsay of Cartvale,* Margaret Mildred (Meta) Ramsay, *b.* 1936
2011	*Randerson,* Jennifer Elizabeth Randerson, *b.* 1948, *m.*
1994	*Rawlings,* Patricia Elizabeth Rawlings, *b.* 1939
2014	*Rebuck,* Gail Ruth Rebuck, DBE, *b.* 1952, *m.*
2015	*Redfern,* Elizabeth Marie Redfern, *b.* 1947, *w.*
1998	ℭ*Richardson of Calow,* Kathleen Margaret Richardson, OBE, *b.* 1938, *m.*
2019	*Ritchie of Downpatrick,* Margaret Mary Ritchie, *b.* 1958
2015	*Rock,* Kate Harriet Alexandra Rock, *b.* 1968, *m.*
2004	*Royall of Blaisdon,* Janet Anne Royall, PC, *b.* 1955, *m.*
2019	*Sanderson of Welton,* Elizabeth Jenny Rosemary Sanderson, *b.*1971
2018	*Sater,* Amanda Jacqueline Sater, *b.* 1960, *m.*
1997	*Scotland of Asthal,* Patricia Janet Scotland, PC, QC, *b.* 1955, *m.*
2015	*Scott of Bybrook,* Jane Antoinette Scott, OBE, *b.* 1947, *m.*
2000	*Scott of Needham Market,* Rosalind Carol Scott, *b.* 1957, *m.*
1991	*Seccombe,* Joan Anna Dalziel Seccombe, DBE, *b.* 1930, *w.*
2010	*Shackleton of Belgravia,* Fiona Sara Shackleton, LVO, *b.* 1956, *m.*
2020	*Shafik,* Nemat (Minouche) Talaat Shafik, DBE, *b.* 1962, *m.*
1998	ℭ*Sharp of Guildford,* Margaret Lucy Sharp, *b.* 1938, *m.*
1973	ℭ*Sharples,* Pamela Sharples, *b.* 1923, *w.*
2015	*Sheehan,* Shaista Ahmad Sheehan, *b.* 1959, *m.*
2005	*Shephard of Northwold,* Gillian Patricia Shephard, PC, *b.* 1940, *m.*
2010	*Sherlock,* Maeve Christina Mary Sherlock, OBE, *b.* 1960
2014	*Shields,* Joanna Shields, OBE, *b.* 1962, *m.*
2010	*Smith of Basildon,* Angela Evans Smith, PC, *b.* 1959, *m.*
1995	*Smith of Gilmorehill,* Elizabeth Margaret Smith, *b.* 1940, *w.*
2014	*Smith of Newnham,* Dr Julie Elizabeth Smith, *b.* 1969
2010	*Stedman-Scott,* Deborah Stedman-Scott, OBE, *b.* 1955, *c.p.*
1999	*Stern,* Vivien Helen Stern, CBE, *b.* 1941
2020	*Stuart of Edgbaston,* Gisela Stuart, PC, *b.* 1955, *w.*
2011	*Stowell of Beeston,* Tina Wendy Stowell, MBE, PC, *b.* 1967
2015	*Stroud,* Philippa Claire Stroud, *b.* 1965, *m.*
2016	*Sugg,* Elizabeth Grace Sugg, CBE, *b.* 1977
2013	*Suttie,* Alison Mary Suttie, *b.* 1968
1996	*Symons of Vernham Dean,* Elizabeth Conway Symons, PC, *b.* 1951, *w.*
2005	*Taylor of Bolton,* Winifred Ann Taylor, PC, *b.* 1947, *m.*
1994	**E.** *Thomas of Walliswood,* Susan Petronella Thomas, OBE, *b.* 1935, *w.*
2006	*Thomas of Winchester,* Celia Marjorie Thomas, MBE, *b.* 1945
2015	*Thornhill,* Dorothy Thornhill, MBE, *b.* 1955, *m.*
1998	*Thornton,* (Dorothea) Glenys Thornton, *b.* 1952, *m.*
2005	*Tonge,* Dr Jennifer Louise Tonge, *b.* 1941, *m.*
2011	*Tyler of Enfield,* Claire Tyler, *b.* 1957
1998	*Uddin,* Manzila Pola Uddin, *b.* 1959, *m.*
2007	*Vadera,* Shriti Vadera, PC, *b.* 1962
2005	*Valentine,* Josephine Clare Valentine, *b.* 1958, *m.*
2016	*Vere of Norbiton,* Charlotte Sarah Emily Vere, *b.* 1969
2006	*Verma,* Sandip Verma, *b.* 1959, *m.*
2000	*Walmsley,* Joan Margaret Walmsley, *b.* 1943, *m.*
2007	*Warsi,* Sayeeda Hussain Warsi, PC, *b.* 1971, *m.*
1999	*Warwick of Undercliffe,* Diana Mary Warwick, *b.* 1945, *m.*
2015	*Watkins of Tavistock,* Mary Jane Watkins, PHD, *b.* 1955, *m.*
2010	*Wheatcroft,* Patience Jane Wheatcroft, *b.* 1951, *m.*
2010	*Wheeler,* Margaret Eileen Joyce Wheeler, MBE, *b.* 1949
1999	*Whitaker,* Janet Alison Whitaker, *b.* 1936, *w.*
1996	*Wilcox,* Judith Ann Wilcox, *b.* 1940, *w.*
2019	*Wilcox of Newport,* Deborah Ann Wilcox, *b.* 1969
1999	ℭ*Wilkins,* Rosalie Catherine Wilkins, *b.* 1946
1993	ℭ*Williams of Crosby,* Shirley Vivien Teresa Brittain Williams, CH, PC, *b.* 1930, *w.*
2013	*Williams of Trafford,* Susan Frances Maria Williams, *b.* 1967, *m.*
2014	*Wolf of Dulwich,* Alison Margaret Wolf, CBE, *b.* 1949, *m.*
2011	*Worthington,* Bryony Katherine Worthington, *b.* 1971, *m.*
2017	*Wyld,* Laura Lee Wyld, *b.* 1978, *m.*
2004	*Young of Hornsey,* Prof. Margaret Omolola Young, OBE, *b.* 1951, *m.*
1997	*Young of Old Scone,* Barbara Scott Young, *b.* 1948

COURTESY TITLES

The heir apparent to a Duke, Marquess or Earl uses the highest of his father's other titles as a courtesy title. For example, the Marquess of Blandford is heir to the Dukedom of Marlborough, and Viscount Amberley to the Earldom of Russell. Titles of second heirs (when in use) are also given, and the courtesy title of the father of a second heir is indicated by * eg Earl of Mornington, eldest son of *Marquess of Douro.

The holder of a courtesy title is not styled 'the Most Hon.' or 'the Rt. Hon.', and in correspondence 'the' is omitted before the title. The heir apparent to a Scottish title may use the title 'Master'.

MARQUESSES

Blandford – *Marlborough, D.*
Douglas and Clydesdale – *Hamilton and Brandon, D.*
Graham – *Montrose, D.*
Granby – *Rutland, D.*
*Hamilton – *Abercorn, D.*
Lorne – *Argyll, D.*
Stafford – *Sutherland, D.*
Tavistock – *Bedford, D.*
Tullibardine – *Atholl, D.*
Worcester – *Beaufort, D.*

EARLS

*Aboyne – *Huntly, M.*
Altamont – *Sligo, M.*
Arundel and Surrey – *Norfolk, D.*
Bective – *Headfort, M.*
Belfast – *Donegall, M.*
Brecknock – *Camden, M.*
*Burford – *St Albans, D.*
*Burlington – *Devonshire, D.*
*Cardigan – *Ailesbury, M.*
Cassilis – *Ailsa, M.*
Compton – *Northampton, M.*
Dalkeith – *Buccleuch and Queensberry, D.*
Dumfries – *Bute, M.*
Euston – *Grafton, D.*
Haddo – *Aberdeen and Temair, M.*
Hillsborough – *Downshire, M.*
*Hopetoun – *Linlithgow, M.*
*Kerry – *Lansdowne, M.*
March and Kinrara – *Richmond, Gordon and Lennox, D.*
Medina – *Milford Haven, M.*
*Mornington – **Wellington, D.*
*Mount Charles – *Conyngham, M.*
Mulgrave – *Normanby, M.*
Percy – *Northumberland, D.*
Rocksavage – *Cholmondeley, M.*
Ronaldshay – *Zetland, M.*
*St Andrews – *Kent, D.*
Southesk – *Fife, D.*
Tyrone – *Waterford, M.*
*Ulster – *Gloucester, D.*
Uxbridge – *Anglesey, M.*
*Wiltshire – *Winchester, M.*
Yarmouth – *Hertford, M.*

VISCOUNTS

Aithrie – **Hopetoun, E.*
Alexander – *Caledon, E.*

Althorp – *Spencer, E.*
Andover – *Suffolk and Berkshire, E.*
Anson – *Lichfield, E.*
Asquith – *Oxford and Asquith, E.*
Borodale – *Beatty, E.*
Bury – *Albemarle, E.*
Calne and Calston – **Kerry, E.*
Campden – *Gainsborough, E.*
Carlow – *Portarlington, E.*
Carlton – *Wharncliffe, E.*
Chelsea – *Cadogan, E.*
Chewton – *Waldegrave, E.*
Clanfield – *Peel, E.*
Clive – *Powis, E.*
Coke – *Leicester, E.*
Corry – *Belmore, E.*
Corvedale – *Baldwin of Bewdley, E.*
Cranborne – *Salisbury, M.*
Crowhurst – *Cottenham, E.*
Curzon – *Howe, E.*
Dalrymple – *Stair, E.*
Dangan – *Cowley, E.*
Drumlanrig – *Queensberry, M.*
Duncannon – *Bessborough, E.*
Dungarvan – *Cork and Orrery, E.*
Dunluce – *Antrim, E.*
Dunwich – *Stradbroke, E.*
Dupplin – *Kinnoull, E.*
Elveden – *Iveagh, E.*
Emlyn – *Cawdor, E.*
Encombe – *Eldon, E.*
Enfield – *Strafford, E.*
Erleigh – *Reading, M.*
Errington – *Cromer, E.*
Feilding – *Denbigh and Desmond, E.*
FitzHarris – *Malmesbury, E.*
Folkestone – *Radnor, E.*
Forbes – *Granard, E.*
Garmoyle – *Cairns, E.*
Garnock – *Lindsay, E.*
Glenapp – *Inchcape, E.*
Glerawly – *Annesley, E.*
Grey de Wilton – *Wilton, E.*
Grimston – *Verulam, E.*
Gwynedd – *Lloyd George of Dwyfor, E.*
Hawkesbury – *Liverpool, E.*
Hinchingbrooke – *Sandwich, E.*
Howick – *Grey, E.*
Ikerrin – *Carrick, E.*
Ingestre – *Shrewsbury and Waterford, E.*
Jocelyn – *Roden, E.*

Kelburn – *Glasgow, E.*
Kingsborough – *Kingston, E.*
Kirkwall – *Orkney, E.*
Knebworth – *Lytton, E.*
Lambton – *Durham, E.*
Lascelles – *Harewood, E.*
Linley – *Snowdon, E.*
Lymington – *Portsmouth, E.*
Macmillan of Ovenden – *Stockton, E.*
Maidstone – *Winchilsea and Nottingham, E.*
Maitland – *Lauderdale, E.*
Marsham – *Romney, E.*
Melgund – *Minto, E.*
Merton – *Nelson, E.*
Moore – *Drogheda, E.*
Newport – *Bradford, E.*
Newry and Mourne – *Kilmorey, E.*
Northland – *Ranfurly, E.*
Pery – *Limerick, E.*
Petersham – *Harrington, E.*
Pollington – *Mexborough, E.*
Raynham – *Townshend, M.*
Reidhaven – *Seafield, E.*
Royston – *Hardwicke, E.*
Ruthven of Canberra – *Gowrie, E.*
St Cyres – *Iddesleigh, E.*
Sandon – *Harrowby, E.*
Savernake – **Cardigan, E.*
Severn – *Wessex, E.*
Slane – **Mount Charles, E.*
Somerton – *Normanton, E.*
Stopford – *Courtown, E.*
Stormont – *Mansfield and Mansfield, E.*
Strabane – **Hamilton, M.*
Strathallan – *Perth, E.*
Stuart – *Castle Stewart, E.*
Suirdale – *Donoughmore, E.*
Tamworth – *Ferrers, E.*
Tarbat – *Cromartie, E.*
Villiers – *Jersey, E.*
Wellesley – **Mornington, E.*
Weymouth – *Bath, M.*
Windsor – *Plymouth, E.*
Wolmer – *Selborne, E.*
Woodstock – *Portland, E.*

BARONS (LORDS)

Aberdour – *Morton, E.*
Apsley – *Bathurst, E.*
Ardee – *Meath, E.*
Ashley – *Shaftesbury, E.*
Balniel – *Crawford and Balcarres, E.*
Berriedale – *Caithness, E.*

Bingham – *Lucan, E.*
Brabourne – *Mountbatten of Burma, E.*
Brooke – *Warwick and Brooke, E.*
Bruce – *Elgin and Kincardine, E.*
Buckhurst – *De La Warr, E.*
Burghley – *Exeter, M.*
Cardross – *Buchan, E.*
Cavendish – **Burlington, E.*
Clifton – *Darnley, E.*
Cochrane – *Dundonald, E.*
Courtenay – *Devon, E.*
Culloden – * *Ulster, E.*
Dalmeny – *Rosebery, E.*
Doune – *Moray, E.*
Downpatrick – **St Andrews, E.*
Dunglass – *Home, E.*
Elcho – *Wemyss and March, E.*
Garlies – *Galloway, E.*
Gillford – *Clanwilliam, E.*
Greenock – *Cathcart, E.*
Guernsey – *Aylesford, E.*
Hay – *Erroll, E.*
Herbert – *Pembroke and Montgomery, E.*
Howard of Effingham – *Effingham, E.*
Huntingtower – *Dysart, E.*
Hyde – *Clarendon, E.*
Inverurie – *Kintore, E.*
Irwin – *Halifax, E.*
Johnstone – *Annandale and Hartfell, E.*
Leveson – *Granville, E.*
Loughborough – *Rosslyn, E.*
Masham – *Swinton, E.*
Medway – *Cranbrook, E.*
Montgomerie – *Eglinton and Winton, E.*
Moreton – *Ducie, E.*
Naas – *Mayo, E.*
Norreys – *Lindsey and Abingdon, E.*
North – *Guilford, E.*
Ogilvy – *Airlie, E.*
Oxmantown – *Rosse, E.*
Porchester – *Carnarvon, E.*
Ramsay – *Dalhousie, E.*
St John – **Wiltshire, E.*
Scrymgeour – *Dundee, E.*
Seymour – *Somerset, D.*
Stanley – *Derby, E.*
Strathavon – **Aboyne, E.*
Strathnaver – *Sutherland, E.*
Vere of Hanworth – **Burford, E.*
Wodehouse – *Kimberley, E.*
Worsley – *Yarborough, E.*

PEERS' SURNAMES

The following symbols indicate the rank of the peer holding each title:

C. Countess
D. Duke
E. Earl
M. Marquess
V. Viscount
* Life Peer

Where no designation is given, the title is that of a hereditary Baron or Baroness.

Abney-Hastings – Loudoun, E.
Acheson – Gosford, E.
Adams – A. of Craigielea*
Adderley – Norton
Addington – Sidmouth, V.
Agar – Normanton, E.
Agnew – A. of Oulton*
Ahmad – A. of Wimbledon*
Aitken – Beaverbrook
Akers-Douglas – Chilston, V.
Alexander – A. of Tunis, E.
Alexander – Caledon, E.
Allan – A. of Hallam*
Allen – A. of Kensington*
Allsopp – Hindlip
Alton – A. of Liverpool*
Anderson – A. of Ipswich*
Anderson – A. of Swansea*
Anderson – Waverley, V.
Anelay – A. of St Johns*
Annesley – Valentia, V.
Anson – Lichfield, E.
Arbuthnot – A. of Edrom*
Archer – A. of Weston-super-Mare*
Armstrong – A. of Hill Top*
Armstrong-Jones – Snowdon, E.
Arthur – Glenarthur
Arundell – Talbot of Malahide
Ashley-Cooper – Shaftesbury, E.
Ashton – A. of Hyde
Ashton – A. of Upholland*
Asquith – Oxford and Asquith, E.
Assheton – Clitheroe
Astley – Hastings
Astor – A. of Hever
Aubrey-Fletcher – Braye
Austin – A. of Dudley*
Bailey – Glanusk
Baillie – Burton
Baillie Hamilton – Haddington, E.
Baker – B. of Dorking*
Bakewell – B. of Hardington Mandeville*
Balchin – Lingfield*
Baldwin – B. of Bewdley, E.
Balfour – Kinross
Balfour – Riverdale
Bampfylde – Poltimore

Banbury – B. of Southam
Baring – Ashburton
Baring – Cromer, E.
Baring – Howick of Glendale
Baring – Northbrook
Baring – Revelstoke
Barker – B. of Battle*
Barnes – Gorell
Barnewall – Trimlestown
Bassam – B. of Brighton*
Bathurst – Bledisloe, V.
Beamish – Dacre
Beauclerk – St Albans, D.
Beaumont – Allendale, V.
Beckett – Grimthorpe
Benn – Stansgate, V.
Bennet – Tankerville, E.
Bennett – B. of Manor Castle*
Bentinck – Portland, E.
Beresford – Decies
Beresford – Waterford, M.
Berkeley – B. of Knighton*
Berry – Camrose, V.
Berry – Kemsley, V.
Bertie – Lindsey and Abingdon, E.
Best – Wynford
Bethell – Westbury
Bewicke-Copley – Cromwell
Bigham – Mersey, V.
Bingham – Clanmorris
Bingham – Lucan, E.
Bishop – Glendonbrook*
Black – B. of Brentwood*
Black – B. of Crossharbour*
Blackwood – B. of North Oxford*
Blackwood – Dufferin and Clandeboye
Blair – B. of Boughton*
Bligh – Darnley, E.
Bloomfield – B. of Hinton Waldrist*
Blyth – B. of Rowington*
Bonham Carter – B.-C. of Yarnbury*
Bootle-Wilbraham – Skelmersdale
Boscawen – Falmouth, V.
Boswell – B. of Aynho*
Bottomley – B. of Nettlestone*
Bourke – Mayo, E.
Bourne – B. of Aberystwyth*
Bowes Lyon – Strathmore and Kinghorne, E.
Bowles – B. of Berkhamsted*
Bowyer – Denham
Boyd – B. of Duncansby*
Boyd – Kilmarnock
Boyle – Cork and Orrery, E.
Boyle – Glasgow, E.
Boyle – Shannon, E.
Brabazon – Meath, E.
Brand – Hampden, V.
Brassey – B. of Apethorpe
Bryan – B. of Partick*

Brett – Esher, V.
Bridgeman – Bradford, E.
Brodrick – Midleton, V.
Brooke – B. of Alverthorpe*
Brooke – B. of Sutton Mandeville*
Brooke – Brookeborough, V.
Brooks – Crawshaw
Brougham – Brougham and Vaux
Broughton – Fairhaven
Brown – B. of Eaton-under-Heywood*
Browne – B. of Belmont*
Browne – B. of Ladyton*
Browne – B. of Madingley*
Browne – Kilmaine
Browne – Oranmore and Browne
Browne – Sligo, M.
Brownlow – B. of Shurlock Row*
Bruce – Aberdare
Bruce – Balfour of Burleigh
Bruce – B. of Bennachie*
Bruce – Elgin and Kincardine, E.
Brudenell-Bruce – Ailesbury, M.
Buchan – Tweedsmuir
Buckley – Wrenbury
Burnett – B. of Maldon*
Burt – B. of Solihull*
Butler – B. of Brockwell*
Butler – Carrick, E.
Butler – Dunboyne
Butler – Mountgarret, V.
Byng – Strafford, E.
Byng – Torrington, V.
Cameron – C. of Dillington*
Cameron – C. of Lochbroom*
Campbell – Argyll, D.
Campbell – C. of Loughborough*
Campbell – C. of Pittenweem*
Campbell – C. of Surbiton*
Campbell – Cawdor, E.
Campbell – Colgrain
Campbell – Stratheden and Campbell
Campbell-Gray – Gray
Canning – Garvagh
Capell – Essex, E.
Carey – C. of Clifton*
Carington – Carrington
Carlisle – C. of Berriew*
Carnegie – Fife, D.
Carnegy – Northesk, E.
Carrington – C. of Fulham*
Carter – C. of Barnes*
Carter – C. of Coles*
Carter – C. of Haslemere*
Cary – Falkland, V.
Caulfeild – Charlemont, V.
Cavendish – C. of Furness*
Cavendish – C. of Little Venice*

Cavendish – Chesham
Cavendish – Devonshire, D.
Cavendish – Waterpark
Cayzer – Rotherwick
Cecil – Amherst of Hackney
Cecil – Exeter, M.
Cecil – Rockley
Chalker – C. of Wallasey*
Chaloner – Gisborough
Charteris – Wemyss and March, E.
Chetwynd-Talbot – Shrewsbury and Waterford, E.
Chichester – Donegall, M.
Child Villiers – Jersey, E.
Chisholm – C. of Owlpen*
Cholmondeley – Delamere
Chubb – Hayter
Clark – C. of Calton*
Clark – C. of Kilwinning*
Clarke – C. of Hampstead*
Clarke – C. of Nottingham*
Clarke – C. of Stone-Cum-Ebony*
Clegg-Hill – Hill, V.
Clifford – C. of Chudleigh
Cochrane – C. of Cults
Cochrane – Dundonald, E.
Cocks – Somers
Cohen – C. of Pimlico*
Cokayne – Cullen of Ashbourne
Coke – Leicester, E.
Cole – Enniskillen, E.
Collier – Monkswell
Collins – C. of Highbury*
Collins – C. of Mapesbury*
Colville – Clydesmuir
Colville – C. of Culross, V.
Compton – Northampton, M.
Conolly-Carew – Carew
Cooke – Lexden*
Cooper – C. of Windrush*
Cooper – Norwich, V.
Cope – C. of Berkeley*
Corbett – Rowallan
Cornwall-Legh – Grey of Codnor
Courtenay – Devon, E.
Craig – C. of Radley*
Craig – Craigavon, V.
Crichton – Erne, E.
Crichton-Stuart – Bute, M.
Cripps – Parmoor
Crossley – Somerleyton
Cubitt – Ashcombe
Cunliffe-Lister – Masham of Ilton*
Cunliffe-Lister – Swinton, E.
Cunningham – C. of Felling*
Currie – C. of Marylebone*
Curry – C. of Kirkharle*
Curzon – Howe, E.
Curzon – Scarsdale, V.
Cust – Brownlow
Czernin – Howard de Walden
Dalrymple – Stair, E.

Darling – *D. of Roulanish*★
Darroch – *D. of Kew*★
Darzi – *D. of Denham*★
Daubeny de Moleyns – *Ventry*
Davidson – *D. of Glen Clova*★
Davies – *D. of Brixton*★
Davies – *Darwen*
Davies – *D. of Abersoch*★
Davies – *D. of Gower*★
Davies – *D. of Oldham*★
Davies – *D. of Stamford*★
Dawnay – *Downe, V.*
Dawson-Damer – *Portarlington, E.*
Deane – *Muskerry*
de Courcy – *Kingsale*
de Grey – *Walsingham*
Denison – *Londesborough*
Denison-Pender – *Pender*
Devereux – *Hereford, V.*
Dewar – *Forteviot*
Dixon – *Glentoran*
Dodds – *D. of Duncairn*★
Dodson – *Monk Bretton*
Douglas – *Morton, E.*
Douglas – *Queensberry, M.*
Douglas-Hamilton – *Hamilton and Brandon, D.*
Douglas-Hamilton – *Selkirk, E.*
Douglas-Hamilton – *Selkirk of Douglas*★
Douglas-Home – *Home, E.*
Douglas-Pennant – *Penrhyn*
Douglas-Scott-Montagu – *Montagu of Beaulieu*
Drummond – *Perth, E.*
Drummond of Megginch – *Strange*
Dugdale – *Crathorne*
Duke – *Merrivale*
Duncan – *D. of Springbank*★
Duncombe – *Feversham*
Dundas – *Melville, V.*
Dundas – *Zetland, M.*
Eady – *Swinfen*
Eccles – *E. of Moulton*★
Ece – *Hussein-Ece*★
Eden – *Auckland*
Eden – *E. of Winton*★
Eden – *Henley*
Edgcumbe – *Mount Edgcumbe, E.*
Edmondson – *Sandford*
Edwardes – *Kensington*
Egerton – *Sutherland, D.*
Eliot – *St Germans, E.*
Elliot-Murray-Kynynmound – *Minto, E.*
Ellis – *Seaford*
Erskine – *Buchan, E.*
Erskine – *Mar and Kellie, E.*
Erskine-Murray – *Elibank*
Evans – *E. of Bowes Park*★
Evans – *E. of Watford*★
Evans – *E. of Weardale*★
Evans – *Mountevans*
Evans-Freke – *Carbery*
Eve – *Silsoe*

Fairfax – *F. of Cameron*
Falconer – *F. of Thoroton*★
Falkner – *F. of Margravine*★
Fane – *Westmorland, E.*
Faulkner – *F. of Worcester*★
Feilding – *Denbigh and Desmond, E.*
Feldman – *F. of Elstree*★
Fellowes – *De Ramsey*
Fellowes – *F. of West Stafford*★
Fermor-Hesketh – *Hesketh*
Field – *F. of Birkenhead*★
Fiennes – *Saye and Sele*
Fiennes-Clinton – *Lincoln, E.*
Finch Hatton – *Winchilsea and Nottingham, E.*
Finch-Knightley – *Aylesford, E.*
Finlay – *F. of Llandaff*★
Fitzalan-Howard – *Norfolk, D.*
FitzGerald – *Leinster, D.*
Fitzherbert – *Stafford*
FitzRoy – *Grafton, D.*
FitzRoy – *Southampton*
FitzRoy Newdegate – *Daventry, V.*
Fletcher-Vane – *Inglewood*
Flower – *Ashbrook, V.*
Foljambe – *Liverpool, E.*
Forbes – *Granard, E.*
Forsyth – *F. of Drumlean*★
Forwood – *Arlington*
Foster – *F. of Bath*★
Foster – *F. of Thames Bank*★
Foulkes – *F. of Cumnock*★
Fox – *F. of Buckley*★
Fox-Strangways – *Ilchester, E.*
Frankland – *Zouche*
Fraser – *F. of Corriegarth*★
Fraser – *Lovat*
Fraser – *Saltoun*
Fraser – *Strathalmond*
Freeman-Grenville – *Kinloss*
Fremantle – *Cottesloe*
French – *De Freyne*
Galbraith – *Strathclyde*
Garden – *G. of Frognal*★
Gardiner – *G. of Kimble*★
Gardner – *G. of Parkes*★
Gascoyne-Cecil – *Salisbury, M.*
Gathorne-Hardy – *Cranbrook, E.*
Gibbs – *Aldenham*
Gibbs – *Wraxall*
Gibson – *Ashbourne*
Gilbert – *G. of Panteg*★
Gilbey – *Vaux of Harrowden*
Glyn – *Wolverton*
Goddard – *G. of Stockport*★
Godley – *Kilbracken*
Golding – *G. of Newcastle-under-Lyme*★
Goldsmith – *G. of Richmond Park*★
Gordon – *Aberdeen and Temair, M.*
Gordon – *Huntly, M.*
Gordon Lennox – *Richmond, Gordon and Lennox, D.*

Gore – *Arran, E.*
Gould – *G. of Potternewton*★
Grade – *G. of Yarmouth*★
Graham – *Montrose, D.*
Graham-Toler – *Norbury, E.*
Granshaw – *Northover*★
Grant of Grant – *Strathspey*
Grant of Rothiemurchus – *Dysart, E.*
Green – *G. of Deddington*★
Green – *G. of Hurstpierpoint*★
Greenall – *Daresbury*
Greville – *Warwick and Brooke, E.*
Griffiths – *G. of Burry Port*★
Griffiths – *G. of Fforestfach*★
Grigg – *Altrincham*
Grimstone – *G. of Boscobel*★
Grimston – *G. of Westbury*
Grimston – *Verulam, E.*
Grosvenor – *Westminster, D.*
Grosvenor – *Wilton, E.*
Guest – *Wimborne, V.*
Gueterbock – *Berkeley*
Guinness – *Iveagh, E.*
Guinness – *Moyne*
Gully – *Selby, V.*
Gummer – *Chadlington*★
Gummer – *Deben*★
Gurdon – *Cranworth*
Guthrie – *G. of Craigiebank*★
Hague – *H. of Richmond*★
Hale – *H. of Richmond*★
Hall – *H. of Birkenhead*★
Hamilton – *Abercorn, D.*
Hamilton – *Belhaven and Stenton*
Hamilton – *H. of Dalzell*
Hamilton – *H. of Epsom*★
Hamilton – *Holm Patrick*
Hamilton-Russell – *Boyne, V.*
Hamilton-Smith – *Colwyn*
Hammond – *H. Runnymede*★
Hanbury-Tracy – *Sudeley*
Handcock – *Castlemaine*
Hannay – *H. of Chiswick*★
Harbord-Hamond – *Suffield*
Harding – *H. of Petherton*
Harding – *H. of Winscombe*★
Hardinge – *H. of Penshurst*
Hare – *Blakenham, V.*
Hare – *Listowel, E.*
Harmsworth – *Rothermere, V.*
Harries – *H. of Pentregarth*★
Harris – *H. of Haringey*★
Harris – *H. of Peckham*★
Harris – *H. of Richmond*★
Harris – *Malmesbury, E.*
Harvey – *H. of Tasburgh*
Hastings – *H. of Scarisbrick*★
Hastings Bass – *Huntingdon, E.*
Hay – *Erroll, E.*
Hay – *H. of Ballyore*★
Hay – *Kinnoull, E.*
Hay – *Tweeddale, M.*
Hayman – *H. of Ullock*★
Hayter – *H. of Kentish Town*★
Healy – *H. of Primrose Hill*★

Heathcote-Drummond-Willoughby – *Willoughby de Eresby*
Hely-Hutchinson – *Donoughmore, E.*
Henderson – *Faringdon*
Hennessy – *H. of Nympsfield*★
Hennessy – *Windlesham*
Henniker-Major – *Henniker*
Hepburne-Scott – *Polwarth*
Herbert – *Carnarvon, E.*
Herbert – *H. of South Downs*★
Herbert – *Hemingford*
Herbert – *Pembroke and Montgomery, E.*
Herbert – *Powis, E.*
Hervey – *Bristol, M.*
Hewitt – *Lifford, V.*
Heywood – *H. of Whitehall*★
Hicks Beach – *St Aldwyn, E.*
Hill – *Downshire, M.*
Hill – *H. of Oareford*★
Hill-Trevor – *Trevor*
Hilton – *H. of Eggardon*★
Hobart-Hampden – *Buckinghamshire, E.*
Hodgson – *H. of Abinger*★
Hodgson – *H. of Astley Abbotts*★
Hogg – *Hailsham, V.*
Holland-Hibbert – *Knutsford, V.*
Holmes – *H. of Richmond*★
Holmes à Court – *Heytesbury*
Hood – *Bridport, V.*
Hope – *Glendevon*
Hope – *H. of Craighead*★
Hope – *H. of Thornes*★
Hope – *Linlithgow, M.*
Hope – *Rankeillour*
Hope Johnstone – *Annandale and Hartfell, E.*
Hope-Morley – *Hollenden*
Hopkinson – *Colyton*
Hore Ruthven – *Gowrie, E.*
Houghton – *H. of Richmond*★
Hovell-Thurlow-Cumming-Bruce – *Thurlow*
Howard – *Carlisle, E.*
Howard – *Effingham, E.*
Howard – *H. of Lympne*★
Howard – *H. of Penrith*
Howard – *H. of Rising*★
Howard – *Strathcona and Mount Royal*
Howard – *Suffolk and Berkshire, E.*
Howarth – *H. of Breckland*★
Howarth – *H. of Newport*★
Howe – *H. of Idlicote*★
Howell – *H. of Guildford*★
Howells – *H. of St. Davids*★
Hubbard – *Addington*
Huggins – *Malvern, V.*
Hughes – *H. of Stretford*★
Hughes – *H. of Woodside*★
Hughes-Young – *St Helens*
Hunt – *H. of Bethnal Green*★
Hunt – *H. of Chesterton*★

Parker – *Macclesfield, E.*
Parker – *Morley, E.*
Parkinson – *P. of Whitley Bay**
Parnell – *Congleton*
Parsons – *Rosse, E.*
Patel – *P. of Bradford**
Patten – *P. of Barnes**
Paulet – *Winchester, M.*
Pearson – *Cowdray, V.*
Pearson – *P. of Rannoch**
Pease – *Gainford*
Pelham – *Chichester, E.*
Pelham – *Yarborough, E.*
Pellew – *Exmouth, V.*
Penny – *Marchwood, V.*
Pepys – *Cottenham, E.*
Percy – *Northumberland, D.*
Perry – *P. of Southwark**
Pery – *Limerick, E.*
Philipps – *Milford*
Philipps – *St Davids, V.*
Phillips – *P. of Sudbury**
Phillips – *P. of Worth
   Matravers**
Phipps – *Normanby, M.*
Plant – *P. of Highfield**
Pleydell-Bouverie – *Radnor, E.*
Plumptre – *Fitzwalter*
Plunkett – *Dunsany*
Plunkett – *Louth*
Pollock – *Hanworth, V.*
Pomeroy – *Harberton, V.*
Ponsonby – *Bessborough, E.*
Ponsonby – *de Mauley*
Ponsonby – *P. of Shulbrede*
Porter – *P. of Spalding**
Powell – *P. of Bayswater**
Powys – *Lilford*
Pratt – *Camden, M.*
Preston – *Gormanston, V.*
Primrose – *Rosebery, E.*
Prittie – *Dunalley*
Purvis – *P. of Tweed**
Ramsay – *Dalhousie, E.*
Ramsay – *R. of Cartvale**
Ramsbotham – *Soulbury, V.*
Randall –*R. of Uxbridge**
Reed – *R. of Allermuir**
Rees – *R. of Ludlow**
Rees-Williams – *Ogmore*
Reid – *R. of Cardowan**
Renfrew – *R. of Kaimsthorn**
Renwick – *R. of Clifton**
Rhys – *Dynevor*
Richards – *Milverton*
Richards – *R. of Herstmonceux**
Richardson – *R. of Calow**
Ritchie – *R. of Downpatrick**
Ritchie – *R. of Dundee*
Roberts – *Clwyd*
Roberts – *R. of Llandudno**
Robertson – *R. of Oakridge*
Robertson – *R. of Port Ellen**
Robertson – *Wharton*
Robinson – *Martonmere*
Roche – *Fermoy*
Rodd – *Rennell*
Rodgers – *R. of Quarry Bank**
Roe – *Couttie**

Rogers – *Lisvane**
Rogers – *R. of Riverside**
Roper-Curzon – *Teynham*
Rose – *R. of Monewden**
Rospigliosi – *Newburgh, E.*
Rous – *Stradbroke, E.*
Rowley-Conwy – *Langford*
Royall – *R. of Blaisdon**
Runciman – *R. of Doxford, V.*
Russell – *Ampthill*
Russell – *Bedford, D.*
Russell – *de Clifford*
Russell – *R. of Liverpool*
Ryder – *Harrowby, E.*
Ryder – *R. of Wensum**
Sackville – *De La Warr, E.*
Sackville-West – *Sackville*
Sainsbury – *S. of Preston
   Candover**
Sainsbury – *S. of Turville**
St Aubyn – *St Levan*
St Clair – *Sinclair*
St Clair-Erskine – *Rosslyn, E.*
St John – *Bolingbroke and St
   John, V.*
St John – *St John of Bletso*
St Leger – *Doneraile, V.*
Samuel – *Bearsted, V.*
Sanderson – *S. of Ayot*
Sanderson – *S. of Bowden**
Sanderson – *S. of Welton**
Sandilands – *Torphichen*
Saumarez – *de Saumarez*
Savile – *Mexborough, E.*
Saville – *S. of Newdigate**
Scarlett – *Abinger*
Schreiber – *Marlesford**
Sclater-Booth – *Basing*
Scotland – *S. of Asthal**
Scott – *Eldon, E.*
Scott – *S. of Bybrook**
Scott – *S. of Foscote**
Scott – *S. of Needham Market**
Scrymgeour – *Dundee, E.*
Seager – *Leighton of St Mellons*
Seely – *Mottistone*
Seymour – *Hertford, M.*
Seymour – *Somerset, D.*
Shackleton – *S. of Belgravia**
Sharp – *S. of Guildford**
Sharpe – *S. of Epsom**
Shaw – *Craigmyle*
Shaw – *S. of Northstead**
Shephard – *S. of Northwold**
Sherbourne – *S. of Didsbury**
Shirley – *Ferrers, E.*
Shutt – *S. of Greetland**
Siddeley – *Kenilworth*
Sidney – *De L'Isle, V.*
Simon – *S. of Highbury**
Simon – *S. of Wythenshawe*
Simpson – *S. of Dunkeld**
Sinclair – *Caithness, E.*
Sinclair – *S. of Cleeve*
Sinclair – *Thurso, V.*
Singh – *S. of Wimbledon**
Skeffington – *Massereene and
   Ferrard, V.*

Smith – *Bicester*
Smith – *Hambleden, V.*
Smith – *Kirkhill**
Smith – *S. of Basildon**
Smith – *S. of Clifton**
Smith – *S. of Finsbury**
Smith – *S. of Gilmorehill**
Smith – *S. of Hindhead**
Smith – *S. of Kelvin**
Smith – *S. of Leigh**
Smith – *S. of Newnham**
Somerset – *Beaufort, D.*
Somerset – *Raglan*
Spencer – *Churchill*
Spencer – *S. of Alresford**
Spencer-Churchill –
   Marlborough, D.
Spring – *Risby**
Spring Rice – *Monteagle of
   Brandon*
Stanhope – *Harrington, E.*
Stanley – *Derby, E.*
Stanley – *S. of Alderley and
   Sheffield*
Stapleton-Cotton –
   Combermere, V.
Steel – *S. of Aikwood**
Sterling – *S. of Plaistow**
Stern – *S. of Brentford**
Stevens – *S. of
   Kirkwhelpington**
Stevens – *S. of Ludgate**
Stevenson – *S. of Balmacara**
Stevenson – *S. of Coddenham**
Stewart – *Galloway, E.*
Stoddart – *S. of Swindon**
Stone – *S. of Blackheath**
Stoneham – *S. of Droxford**
Stonor – *Camoys*
Stopford – *Courtown, E.*
Stourton – *Mowbray, Segrave
   and S.*
Stowell – *S. of Beeston**
Strachey – *O'Hagan*
Strutt – *Belper*
Strutt – *Rayleigh*
Stuart – *Castle Stewart, E.*
Stuart – *S. of Edgbaston**
Stuart – *Moray, E.*
Stuart – *S. of Findhorn, V.*
Suenson-Taylor – *Grantchester*
Symons – *S. of Vernham Dean**
Taylor – *Kilclooney**
Taylor – *T. of Bolton**
Taylor – *T. of Goss Moor**
Taylor – *T. of Holbeach**
Taylor – *T. of Warwick**
Taylour – *Headfort, M.*
Temple-Gore-Langton –
   Temple of Stowe, E.
Tennant – *Glenconner*
Thellusson – *Rendlesham*
Thesiger – *Chelmsford, V.*
Thomas – *T. of Cwmgiedd**
Thomas – *T. of Gresford**
Thomas – *T. of Walliswood**
Thomas – *T. of Winchester**
Thomson – *T. of Fleet*
Thynn – *Bath, M.*

Tottenham – *Ely, M.*
Trefusis – *Clinton*
Trench – *Ashtown*
Tufton – *Hothfield*
Turner – *Netherthorpe*
Turner – *T. of Ecchinswell**
Turnour – *Winterton, E.*
Tyler – *T. of Enfield**
Tyrell-Kenyon – *Kenyon*
Vaizey – *V. of Didcot**
Vallance – *V. of Tummel**
Vanden-Bempde-Johnstone –
   Derwent
Vane – *Barnard*
Vane-Tempest-Stewart –
   Londonderry, M.
Vanneck – *Huntingfield*
Vaughan – *Lisburne, E.*
Vere – *V. of Norbiton**
Vereker – *Gort, V.*
Verney – *Willoughby de Broke*
Vernon – *Lyveden*
Vesey – *de Vesci, V.*
Villiers – *Clarendon, E.*
Vivian – *Swansea*
Wadley – *Fleet**
Waldegrave – *W. of North
   Hill**
Walker – *W. of Aldringham**
Walker – *W. of Gestingthorpe**
Wallace – *Dudley*
Wallace – *W. of Saltaire**
Wallace – *W. of Tankerness**
Wallop – *Portsmouth, E.*
Ward – *Bangor, V.*
Ward – *Dudley, E.*
Warrender – *Bruntisfield*
Warwick – *W. of Undercliffe**
Watkins – *W. of Tavistock**
Watson – *Manton*
Watson – *W. of Invergowrie**
Watson – *W. of Richmond**
Webber – *Lloyd-Webber**
Weir – *Inverforth*
Weld-Forester – *Forester*
Wellesley – *Cowley, E.*
Wellesley – *Wellington, D.*
West – *W. of Spithead**
Westenra – *Rossmore*
Wharton – *W. or Yarm**
White – *Annaly*
White – *Hanningfield**
Whiteley – *Marchamley*
Whitfield – *Kenswood*
Wilcox – *W. of Newport**
Williams – *W. of Crosby**
Williams – *W. of Oystermouth**
Williams – *W. of Trafford**
Williamson – *Forres*
Willis – *W. of Knaresborough**
Willoughby – *Middleton*
Wills – *Dulverton*
Wilson – *Moran*
Wilson – *Nunburnholme*
Wilson – *W. of Dinton**
Wilson – *W. of Tillyorn**
Windsor – *Gloucester, D.*

Windsor – *Kent, D.*
Windsor-Clive – *Plymouth, E.*
Wingfield – *Powerscourt, V.*
Winn – *St Oswald*
Wodehouse – *Kimberley, E.*
Wolf – *W. of Dulwich**
Wolfson – *W. of Aspley Guise**

Wolfson – *W. of Sunningdale**
Wood – *Halifax, E.*
Wood – *W. of Anfield**
Woodcock – *Walney**
Woodhouse – *Terrington*
Woolley – *W. of Woodford**
Woolmer – *W. of Leeds**

Wright – *W. of Richmond**
Wyndham – *Egremont and Leconfield*
Wynn – *Newborough*
Yarde-Buller – *Churston*
Yerburgh – *Alvingham*
Yorke – *Hardwicke, E.*

Young – *Kennet*
Young – *Y. of Cookham**
Young – *Y. of Graffham**
Young – *Y. of Hornsey**
Young – *Y. of Norwood Green**
Young – *Y. of Old Scone**
Younger – *Y. of Leckie, V.*

LORDS SPIRITUAL

The Lords Spiritual are the Archbishops of Canterbury and York and 24 other diocesan bishops of the Church of England. The Bishops of London, Durham and Winchester always have seats in the House of Lords; the other 21 seats were previously filled by the remaining diocesan bishops in order of seniority. However, the Lords Spiritual (Women) Act 2015 provides for vacancies among the remaining 21 places to be filled by any female diocesan bishop in office at the time and, only if there is no female diocesan bishop without a seat, by the longest serving male diocesan bishop. The provision will remain in place for ten years from 2015, equivalent to two fixed-term parliaments. At the end of this period, the provision under the Act will end and the previous arrangements under which vacancies are filled according to length of service as a diocesan bishop will be restored.

The Bishop of Sodor and Man and the Bishop of Gibraltar in Europe are not eligible to sit in the House of Lords.

ARCHBISHOPS

Style, The Most Revd and Rt. Hon. the Lord Archbishop of_
Addressed as Archbishop *or* Your Grace

INTRODUCED TO HOUSE OF LORDS
2012 *Canterbury* (105th), Justin Portal Welby, PC, *b.* 1956, *m., cons.* 2011, *elected* 2011, *trans.* 2013
2006 *York* (98th), Stephen Geoffrey Cottrell, PC, *b.* 1958, *m., cons.* 2004, *elected* 2010, *trans.* 2020

BISHOPS

Style, The Rt. Revd the Lord/Lady Bishop of _
Addressed as Bishop *or* My Lord/Lady
elected date of confirmation as diocesan bishop

INTRODUCED TO HOUSE OF LORDS
as at December 2020
2010 *Birmingham* (9th), David Andrew Urquhart, KCMG, *b.* 1952, *cons.* 2000, *elected* 2006
2012 *Worcester* (113th), John Geoffrey Inge, PHD, *b.* 1955, *m., cons.* 2003, *elected* 2007
2012 *Winchester* (97th), Timothy John Dakin, *b.* 1958, *m., elected* 2011, *cons.* 2012
2013 *Coventry* (9th), Christopher John Cocksworth, PHD, *b.* 1959, *m., cons.* 2008, *elected* 2008
2013 *Oxford* (44th), Stephen John Lindsey Croft, PHD, *b.* 1957, *m., cons.* 2009, *elected* 2009, *trans.* 2016
2013 *Carlisle* (66th), James William Scobie Newcome, *b.* 1953, *m., cons.* 2002, *elected* 2009
2013 *St Albans* (10th), Alan Gregory Clayton Smith, PHD, *b.* 1957, *cons.* 2001, *elected* 2009
2014 *Peterborough* (38th), Donald Spargo Allister, *b.* 1952, *m., cons.* 2010, *elected* 2010
2014 *Portsmouth* (9th), Christopher Richard James Foster, *b.* 1953, *m., cons.* 2001, *elected* 2010
2014 *Chelmsford* (10th), Stephen Geoffrey Cottrell, *b.* 1958, *m., cons.* 2004, *elected* 2010
2014 *Rochester* (107th), James Henry Langstaff, *b.* 1956, *m., cons.* 2004, *elected* 2010

2014 *Ely* (69th), Stephen David Conway, *b.* 1957, *cons.* 2006, *elected* 2010
2014 *Southwark* (10th), Christopher Thomas James Chessun, *b.* 1956, *cons.* 2005, *elected* 2011
2014 *Durham* (74th), Paul Roger Butler, *b.* 1955, *m., cons.* 2004, *elected* 2009, *trans.* 2014
2015 *Leeds* (1st), Nicholas Baines, *b.* 1957, *m., cons.* 2003, *elected* 2011, *trans.* 2014
2015 *Salisbury* (78th), Nicholas Roderick Holtam, *b.* 1954, *m., cons.* 2011, *elected* 2011
2015 *Gloucester* (41st), Rachel Treweek, *b.* 1963, *m., cons.* 2015, *elected* 2015
2016 *Newcastle* (12th), Christine Elizabeth Hardman, *b.* 1951, *m., cons.* 2015, *elected* 2015
2017 *Lincoln* (72nd), Christopher Lowson, *b.* 1953, *m., cons.* 2011, *elected* 2011
2018 *Chichester* (103rd), Martin Clive Warner, PHD, *b.* 1958, *cons.* 2010, *elected* 2012
2018 *Bristol* (56th), Vivienne Frances Faull, *b.* 1955, *m., cons.* 2018, *elected* 2018
2018 *London* (133rd), Dame Sarah Elisabeth Mullally, DBE, PC, *b.* 1952, *m., cons.* 2015, *elected* 2018
2019 *Derby* (8th), Elizabeth Jane Holden Lane, *b.* 1966, *m., cons.* 2015, *elected* 2019
2020 *Blackburn* (9th), Julian Tudor Henderson, *b.* 1954, *m., cons.* 2013, *elected* 2013
2020 *Manchester* (12th), David Stuart Walker, *b.* 1957, *m., cons.* 2000, *elected* 2013

BISHOPS AWAITING SEATS, in order of seniority
as at December 2020
Bath and Wells (79th), Peter Hancock, *b.* 1955, *m., cons.* 2010, *elected* 2014
Exeter (71st), Robert Ronald Atwell, *b.* 1954, *cons.* 2008, *elected* 2014
Liverpool (8th), Paul Bayes, *b.* 1953, *m., cons.* 2010, *elected* 2014
Hereford (106th), Richard Charles Jackson, *b.* 1961, *m., cons.* 2014, *elected* 2019
Guildford (10th), Andrew John Watson, *b.* 1961, *m., cons.* 2008, *elected* 2014
St Edmundsbury and Ipswich (11th), Martin Alan Seeley, *b.* 1954, *m., cons.* 2015, *elected* 2015
Southwell and Nottingham (12th), Paul Gavin Williams, *b.* 1968, *m., cons.* 2009, *elected* 2015
Leicester (7th), Martyn James Snow, *b.* 1968, *m., cons.* 2013, *elected* 2016
Lichfield (99th), Michael Geoffrey Ipgrave, OBE, PHD, *b.* 1958, *m., cons.* 2012, *elected* 2016
Sheffield (8th), Peter Jonathan Wilcox, DPHIL, *b.* 1961, *m., cons.* 2017, *elected* 2017
Truro (16th), Philip Ian Mountstephen, *b.* 1959, *m., cons.* 2018, *elected* 2018
Norwich (72nd), Graham Barham Usher, *b.* 1970, *m., cons.* 2014, *elected* 2019
Chester (41st), Mark Simon Austin Tanner, *b.* 1970, *m., cons.* 2016, *elected* 2020
Chelmsford, vacant

ORDERS OF CHIVALRY

THE MOST NOBLE ORDER OF THE GARTER (1348)

KG
Ribbon, Blue
Motto, Honi soit qui mal y pense (*Shame on him who thinks evil of it*)

The number of Knights and Ladies Companion is limited to 24

SOVEREIGN OF THE ORDER
The Queen

LADIES OF THE ORDER
HRH The Princess Royal, 1994
HRH Princess Alexandra, The Hon. Lady Ogilvy, 2003

ROYAL KNIGHTS
HRH The Prince Philip, Duke of Edinburgh, 1947
HRH The Prince of Wales, 1958
HRH The Duke of Kent, 1985
HRH The Duke of Gloucester, 1997
HRH The Duke of York, 2006
HRH The Earl of Wessex, 2006
HRH The Duke of Cambridge, 2008

EXTRA KNIGHTS COMPANION AND LADIES
HM The Queen of Denmark, 1979
HM The King of Sweden, 1983
HM King Juan Carlos, 1988
HRH Princess Beatrix of the Netherlands, 1989
HIM, Akihito, Emperor Emeritus of Japan, 1998
HM The King of Norway, 2001
HM The King of Spain, 2017
HM The King of the Netherlands, 2018

KNIGHTS AND LADIES COMPANION
Lord Sainsbury of Preston Candover, 1992
Sir Timothy Colman, 1996
Duke of Abercorn, 1999
Lord Inge, 2001
Sir Anthony Acland, 2001
Lord Butler of Brockwell, 2003
Lord Morris of Aberavon, 2003
Sir John Major, 2005

Lord Luce, 2008
Sir Thomas Dunne, 2008
Lord Phillips of Worth Matravers, 2011
Lord Boyce, 2011
Lord Stirrup, 2013
Baroness Manningham-Buller, 2014
Lord King of Lothbury, 2014
Lord Shuttleworth, 2016
Sir David Brewer, 2016
Viscount Brookeborough, 2018
Dame Mary Fagan, 2018
Marquess of Salisbury, 2019
Dame Mary Peters, 2019

Prelate, Bishop of Winchester
Chancellor, Duke of Abercorn, KG
Register, Dean of Windsor, KCVO
Garter King of Arms, Thomas Woodcock, CVO
Lady Usher of the Black Rod, Sarah Clarke, OBE
Secretary, Patric Dickinson, LVO

THE MOST ANCIENT AND MOST NOBLE ORDER OF THE THISTLE (REVIVED 1687)

KT
Ribbon, Green
Motto, Nemo me impune lacessit (*No one provokes me with impunity*)

The number of Knights and Ladies of the Thistle is limited to 16

SOVEREIGN OF THE ORDER
The Queen

ROYAL KNIGHTS
HRH The Prince Philip, Duke of Edinburgh, 1952
HRH The Prince of Wales, Duke of Rothesay, 1977
HRH The Duke of Cambridge, Earl of Strathearn, 2012

ROYAL LADY OF THE ORDER
HRH The Princess Royal, 2000

KNIGHTS AND LADIES
Earl of Elgin and Kincardine, 1981
Earl of Airlie, 1985
Earl of Crawford and Balcarres, 1996
Lord Macfarlane of Bearsden, 1996

Lord Mackay of Clashfern, 1997
Lord Wilson of Tillyorn, 2000
Lord Steel of Aikwood, 2004
Lord Robertson of Port Ellen, 2004
Lord Cullen of Whitekirk, 2007
Lord Hope of Craighead, 2009
Lord Patel, 2009
Earl of Home, 2013
Lord Smith of Kelvin, 2013
Duke of Buccleuch and Queensberry, 2017
Sir Ian Wood, 2018

Chancellor, Earl of Airlie, KT, GCVO, PC
Dean, Very Revd Prof. David Fergusson, OBE
Secretary, Mrs Christopher Roads, LVO
Lord Lyon King of Arms, Dr Joseph Morrow, CBE, QC
Gentleman Usher of the Green Rod, Rear-Adm. Christopher Layman, CB, DSO, LVO

THE MOST HONOURABLE ORDER OF THE BATH (1725)

GCB   GCB *Civil*
Military

GCB   Knight (or Dame) Grand Cross
KCB   Knight Commander
DCB   Dame Commander
CB   Companion

Ribbon, Crimson
Motto, Tria juncta in uno (*Three joined in one*)

Remodelled 1815, and enlarged many times since. The order is divided into civil and military divisions. Women became eligible for the order from 1 January 1971.

THE SOVEREIGN

GREAT MASTER AND FIRST OR PRINCIPAL KNIGHT GRAND CROSS
HRH The Prince of Wales, KG, KT, GCB, OM

Dean of the Order, Dean of Westminster
King of Arms, Air Chief Marshal Sir Stephen Dalton, GCB
Registrar and Secretary, Rear-Adm. Iain Henderson, CB, CBE

Genealogist, Thomas Woodcock, CVO
Gentleman Usher of the Scarlet Rod, Maj.-
Gen. James Gordon, CB, CBE
Deputy Secretary, Secretary of the
Central Chancery of the Orders of
Knighthood
Chancery, Central Chancery of the Orders
of Knighthood, St James's Palace,
London SW1A 1BH

THE ORDER OF MERIT (1902)

OM *Military*   OM *Civil*

OM
Ribbon, Blue and crimson

This order is designed as a special distinction for eminent men and women without conferring a knighthood upon them. The order is limited in numbers to 24, with the addition of foreign honorary members.

THE SOVEREIGN
HRH The Prince Philip, Duke of
Edinburgh, 1968
Lord Foster of Thames Bank, 1997
Prof. Sir Roger Penrose, 2000
Sir Tom Stoppard, 2000
HRH The Prince of Wales, 2002
Lord Rothschild, 2002
Sir David Attenborough, 2005
Baroness Boothroyd, 2005
Sir Timothy Berners-Lee, 2007
Lord Eames, 2007
Lord Rees of Ludlow, 2007
Rt. Hon. Jean Chrétien, QC, 2009
Robert Neil MacGregor, 2010
Hon. John Howard, 2011
David Hockney, 2011
Sir Simon Rattle, 2013
Prof. Sir Magdi Yacoub, 2013
Lord Darzi of Denham, 2016
Prof. Dame Ann Dowling, 2016
Sir James Dyson, 2016

Secretary and Registrar, Lord Fellowes,
GCB, GCVO, PC, QSO
Chancery, Central Chancery of the Orders
of Knighthood, St James's Palace,
London SW1A 1BH

THE MOST DISTINGUISHED ORDER OF ST MICHAEL AND ST GEORGE (1818)

GCMG   KCMG

GCMG   Knight (or Dame) Grand Cross
KCMG   Knight Commander
DCMG   Dame Commander
CMG   Companion

Ribbon, Saxon blue, with scarlet centre
Motto, Auspicium melioris aevi (*Token of a better age*)

THE SOVEREIGN

GRAND MASTER
HRH The Duke of Kent, KG, GCMG,
GCVO, ADC

Prelate, Rt. Revd David Urquhart,
KCMG
Chancellor, Lord Robertson of Port
Ellen, KT, GCMG, PC
Secretary, Permanent Under-Secretary
of State at the Foreign and
Commonwealth Office and Head of
the Diplomatic Service
Registrar, Sir David Manning, GCMG,
KCVO
King of Arms, Baroness Ashton of
Upholland, GCMG, PC
Lady Usher of the Blue Rod, Dame
DeAnne Julius, DCMG, CBE
Dean, Dean of St Paul's
Deputy Secretary, Secretary of the
Central Chancery of the Orders of
Knighthood
Hon. Genealogist, Timothy Duke
Chancery, Central Chancery of the Orders
of Knighthood, St James's Palace,
London SW1A 1BH

THE IMPERIAL ORDER OF THE CROWN OF INDIA (1877) FOR LADIES

CI

Badge, the royal cipher of Queen Victoria in jewels within an oval, surmounted by an heraldic crown and attached to a bow of light blue watered ribbon, edged white

The honour does not confer any rank or title upon the recipient

No conferments have been made since 1947

HM The Queen, 1947

THE ROYAL VICTORIAN ORDER (1896)

GCVO   KCVO

GCVO   Knight or Dame Grand Cross
KCVO   Knight Commander
DCVO   Dame Commander
CVO   Commander
LVO   Lieutenant
MVO   Member

Ribbon, Blue, with red and white edges

Motto, Victoria

THE SOVEREIGN

GRAND MASTER
HRH The Princess Royal, KG, KT,
GCVO, QSO

Chancellor, Lord Chamberlain
Secretary, Keeper of the Privy Purse
Registrar, Secretary of the Central
Chancery of the Orders of
Knighthood
Chaplain, Chaplain of the Queen's
Chapel of the Savoy
Hon. Genealogist, David White

THE MOST EXCELLENT ORDER OF THE BRITISH EMPIRE (1917)

GBE   KBE

The order was divided into military and civil divisions in December 1918

GBE   Knight or Dame Grand Cross
KBE   Knight Commander
DBE   Dame Commander
CBE   Commander
OBE   Officer
MBE   Member

Ribbon, Rose pink edged with pearl grey with vertical pearl stripe in centre (military division); without vertical pearl stripe (civil division)
Motto, For God and the Empire

THE SOVEREIGN

GRAND MASTER
HRH The Prince Philip, Duke of
Edinburgh, KG, KT, OM, GCVO,
GBE, PC

Prelate, Bishop of London
King of Arms, Lt.-Gen. Sir Robert Fulton, KBE
Registrar, Secretary of the Central Chancery of the Orders of Knighthood
Secretary, Secretary of the Cabinet and Head of the Home Civil Service
Dean, Dean of St Paul's
Lady Usher of the Purple Rod, Dame Amelia Fawcett, DBE, CVO

Chancery, Central Chancery of the Orders of Knighthood, St James's Palace, London SW1A 1BH

ORDER OF THE COMPANIONS OF HONOUR (1917)

CH

Ribbon, Carmine, with gold edges

This order consists of one class only and carries with it no title. The number of awards is limited to 65 (excluding honorary members).

Amos, Baroness, 2016
Anthony, John, 1981
Attenborough, Sir David, 1995
Atwood, Margaret, 2018
Baker, Dame Janet, 1993
Baker of Dorking, Lord, 1992
Birtwistle, Sir Harrison, 2000
Bragg, Lord, 2017
Brook, Peter, 1998
Brooke of Sutton Mandeville, Lord, 1992
Campbell of Pittenweem, Lord, 2013
Clarke, of Nottingham, Lord, 2014
Coe, Lord, 2012
De Chastelain, Gen. John, 1998
Dench, Dame Judi, 2005
Elder, Sir Mark, 2017
Elton, Sir John, 2020
Eyre, Sir Richard, 2016
Fraser, Lady Antonia, 2017
Glennie, Dame Evelyn, 2016
Grey, Dame Beryl, 2017
Hannay of Chiswick, Lord, 2003
Henderson, Prof. Richard, 2018
Heseltine, Lord, 1997

Higgs, Prof. Peter, 2012
Hockney, David, 1997
Howard of Lympne, Lord, 2011
Hurd of Westwell, Lord, 1995
Jeffreys, Sir Alec, 2016
King of Bridgwater, Lord, 1992
Lovelock, Prof. James, 2002
McCartney, Sir Paul, 2017
McKellen, Sir Ian Murray, 2007
McKenzie, Prof. Dan Peter, 2003
McLoughlin, Lord, 2019
MacMillan, Prof. Margaret, 2017
Major, Sir John, 1998
O'Neill of Bengarve, Baroness, 2013
Osborne, George, 2016
Owen, Lord, 1994
Patten of Barnes, Lord, 1998
Peters, Dame Mary, 2014
Riley, Bridget, 1998
Rogers of Riverside, Lord, 2008
Rowling, Joanne, 2017
Serota, Sir Nicholas, 2013
Shirley, Dame Stephanie, 2017
Smith, Delia, 2017
Smith, Dame Margaret (Maggie), 2014
Smith of Kelvin, Lord, 2016
Smith, Sir Paul, 2020
Somare, Sir Michael, 1978
Stern of Brentford, Lord, 2017
Strathclyde, Lord, 2013
Strong, Sir Roy, 2015
Te Kanawa, Dame Kiri, 2018
Tebbit, Lord, 1987
Thomas, Sir Keith, 2020
Williams of Crosby, Baroness, 2016
Woolf, Lord, 2015
Young of Cookham, Lord, 2012
Young of Graffham, Lord, 2014
Honorary Members, Bernard Haitink, 2002; Prof. Amartya Sen, 2000; Most Revd Desmond Tutu, 2015
Secretary and Registrar, Secretary of the Central Chancery of the Orders of Knighthood

THE DISTINGUISHED SERVICE ORDER (1886)

DSO

Ribbon, Red, with blue edges

Bestowed in recognition of especial services in action of commissioned officers in the Navy, Army and Royal Air Force and (since 1942) Mercantile Marine. The members are Companions only. A bar may be awarded for any additional act of service.

THE IMPERIAL SERVICE ORDER (1902)

ISO

Ribbon, Crimson, with blue centre

Appointment as companion of this order is open to members of the civil services whose eligibility is determined by the grade they hold. The order consists of the sovereign and companions to a number not exceeding 1,900, of whom 1,300 may belong to the home civil services and 600 to overseas civil services. The then prime minister announced in March 1993 that he would make no further recommendations for appointments to the order.

Secretary, Head of the Home Civil Service
Registrar, Secretary of the Central Chancery of the Orders of Knighthood

THE ROYAL VICTORIAN CHAIN (1902)

It confers no precedence on its holders

HM The Queen

HM The Queen of Denmark, 3501974
HM The King of Sweden, 1975
HRH Princess Beatrix of the Netherlands, 1982
Gen. Antonio Eanes, 1985
HM King Juan Carlos, 1986
HM The King of Norway, 1994
Earl of Airlie, 1997
Rt. Revd and Rt. Hon. Lord Carey of Clifton, 2002
HRH Prince Philip, Duke of Edinburgh, 2007
Rt. Revd and Rt. Hon. Lord Williams of Oystermouth, 2012

BARONETAGE AND KNIGHTAGE

BARONETS

Style, 'Sir' before forename and surname, followed by 'Bt.'
  Envelope, Sir F_ S_, Bt. *Letter (formal)*, Dear Sir; *(social)*, Dear Sir F_. *Spoken*, Sir F_
Wife's style, 'Lady' followed by surname
  Envelope, Lady S_. *Letter (formal)*, Dear Madam; *(social)*, Dear Lady S_. *Spoken*, Lady S_
Style of Baronetess, 'Dame' before forename and surname, followed by 'Btss.' *(see also* Dames)

There are five different creations of baronetcies: Baronets of England (creations dating from 1611); Baronets of Ireland (creations dating from 1619); Baronets of Scotland or Nova Scotia (creations dating from 1625); Baronets of Great Britain (creations after the Act of Union 1707 which combined the kingdoms of England and Scotland); and Baronets of the United Kingdom (creations after the union of Great Britain and Ireland in 1801).

Badge of Baronets of the UK   *Badge of Baronets of Nova Scotia*   *Badge of Ulster*

The patent of creation limits the destination of a baronetcy, usually to male descendants of the first baronet. In some cases, however, special remainders have allowed baronetcies to pass, in the absence of sons, to another relative. In the case of baronetcies of Scotland or Nova Scotia, a special remainder of 'heirs male and of tailzie' allows the baronetcy to descend to heirs general, including women. There are four existing Scottish baronetcies with such a remainder.

The Official Roll of the Baronetage is kept at the Crown Office and maintained by the Registrar and Assistant Registrar of the Baronetage. Anyone who considers that he or she is entitled to be entered on the roll may apply through the Crown Office to prove their succession. Every person succeeding to a baronetcy must exhibit proofs of succession to the Lord Chancellor. A person whose name is not entered on the official roll will not be addressed or mentioned by the title of baronet or baronetess in any official document, nor will he or she be accorded precedence as a baronet or baronetess.

The Standing Council of the Baronetage, established in 1898 as the Honourable Society of the Baronetage, is responsible for maintaining the interests of the Baronetage and for publishing the Official Roll of the Baronetage as established by royal warrant in 1910 (**W** www.baronetage.org/official-roll-of-the-baronets).

OFFICIAL ROLL OF THE BARONETAGE, Crown Office, House of Lords, London SW1A 0PW **T** 020-7219 4687
E hereditary.claims@gmail.com
Registrar, Mrs Ceri King

KNIGHTS

Style, 'Sir' before forename and surname, followed by appropriate post-nominal initials if a Knight Grand Cross or Knight Commander
  Envelope, Sir F_ S_. *Letter (formal)*, Dear Sir; *(social)*, Dear Sir F_. *Spoken*, Sir F_
Wife's style, 'Lady' followed by surname
  Envelope, Lady S_. *Letter (formal)*, Dear Madam; *(social)*, Dear Lady S_. *Spoken*, Lady S_

The prefix 'Sir' is not used by knights who are clerics of the Church of England, who do not receive the accolade. Their wives are entitled to precedence as the wife of a knight but not to the style of 'Lady'.

ORDERS OF KNIGHTHOOD
Knight Grand Cross and Knight Commander are the higher classes of the Orders of Chivalry (*see* Orders of Chivalry). Honorary knighthoods of these orders may be conferred on men who are citizens of countries of which the Queen is not head of state. As a rule, the prefix 'Sir' is not used by honorary knights.

KNIGHTS BACHELOR

The Knights Bachelor do not constitute a royal order, but comprise the surviving representation of the ancient state orders of knighthood. The Register of Knights Bachelor, instituted by James I in the 17th century, lapsed, and in 1908 a voluntary association under the title of the Society of Knights (now the Imperial Society of Knights Bachelor) was formed with the primary objectives of continuing the various registers dating from 1257 and obtaining the uniform registration of every created Knight Bachelor. In 1926 a design for a badge to be worn by Knights Bachelor was approved and adopted; in 1974 a neck badge and miniature were added.

THE IMPERIAL SOCIETY OF KNIGHTS BACHELOR,
Magnesia House, 6 Playhouse Yard, London EC4V 5EX
Knight Principal, Rt. Hon. Sir Gary Hickinbottom
Prelate, Rt. Revd and Rt. Hon. Dame Sarah Mullally, DBE
Registrar, Sir Michael Hirst
Hon. Treasurer, Sir Clive Thompson
Clerk to the Council, Col. Simon Doughty

LIST OF BARONETS AND KNIGHTS

as at 31 December 2020
†   Not registered on the Official Roll of the Baronetage
( )   The date of creation of the baronetcy is given in parentheses
I   Baronet of Ireland
NS   Baronet of Nova Scotia
S   Baronet of Scotland

A full entry in italic type indicates that the recipient of a knighthood died within a year of the honour being conferred. The name is included in our list for one year for purposes of record. Peers are not included in this list.

A-B

Aaronson, Sir Michael John, Kt., CBE
†Abdy, Sir Robert Etienne Eric, Bt. (1850)
Abed, *Dr* Sir Fazle Hasan, KCMG
Abel, Sir Christopher Charles, Kt.
Acher, Sir Gerald, Kt., CBE, LVO
Ackroyd, Sir Timothy Robert Whyte, Bt. (1956)
Acland, Sir Antony Arthur, KG, GCMG, GCVO
Acland, *Lt.-Col.* Sir (Christopher) Guy (Dyke), Bt. (1890), LVO
Acland, Sir Dominic Dyke, Bt. (1678)
Adams, Sir Geoffrey Doyne, KCMG
Adams, Sir William James, KCMG
Adjaye, Sir David Frank, Kt., OBE
Adsetts, Sir William Norman, Kt., OBE
Adye, Sir John Anthony, KCMG
Aga Khan IV, HH Prince Karim, KBE
Agnew, Sir Crispin Hamlyn, Bt. (S. 1629)
Agnew, Sir George Anthony, Bt. (1895)
Agnew, Sir Rudolph Ion Joseph, Kt.
Agnew-Somerville, Sir James Lockett Charles, Bt. (1957)
Ah Koy, Sir James Michael, KBE
Aikens, *Rt. Hon.* Sir Richard John Pearson, Kt.
Ainslie, Sir Charles Benedict, Kt., CBE
†Ainsworth, Sir Anthony Thomas Hugh, Bt. (1917)
Aird, Sir (George) John, Bt. (1901)
Airy, *Maj.-Gen.* Sir Christopher John, KCVO, CBE
Aitchison, Sir Charles Walter de Lancey, Bt. (1938)
Ajegbo, Sir Keith Onyema, Kt., OBE
Akenhead, *Hon.* Sir Robert, Kt.
Akers-Jones, Sir David, KBE, CMG
Alberti, *Prof.* Sir Kurt George Matthew Mayer, Kt.
Albu, Sir George, Bt. (1912)
Alcock, *Air Chief Marshal* Sir (Robert James) Michael, GCB, KBE
Aldridge, Sir Rodney Malcolm, Kt., OBE
Alexander, *Rt. Hon.* Sir Daniel (Grian), Kt.
Alexander, Sir Douglas, Bt. (1921)
Alexander, Sir Edward Samuel, Bt. (1945)
Alghanim, Sir Kutayba Yusuf, KCMG
Allan, *Hon.* Sir Alexander Claud Stuart, KCB

Allen, Sir Errol Newton Fitzrose, KCMG
Allen, *Prof.* Sir Geoffrey, Kt., PHD, FRS
Allen, Sir Mark John Spurgeon, Kt., CMG
Allen, *Hon.* Sir Peter Austin Philip Jermyn, Kt.
Allen, Sir Thomas Boaz, Kt., CBE
Allen, *Hon.* Sir William Clifford, KCMG
Allen, Sir William Guilford, Kt.
Alleyne, Sir George Allanmoore Ogarren, Kt.
Alleyne, *Revd* John Olpherts Campbell, Bt. (1769)
Allinson, Sir (Walter) Leonard, KCVO, CMG
Allison, *Air Chief Marshal* Sir John Shakespeare, KCB, CBE
Alston, Sir Richard John William, Kt.,CBE
Altman, Sir Paul Bernard, Kt.
Amess, Sir David Anthony Andrew, Kt.
Amet, *Hon.* Sir Arnold Karibone, Kt.
Amory, Sir Ian Heathcoat, Bt. (1874)
Anderson, *Dr* Sir James Iain Walker, Kt., CBE
Anderson, Sir John Anthony, KBE
Anderson, Sir Leith Reinsford Steven, Kt., CBE
Anderson, *Prof.* Sir Roy Malcolm, Kt.
Anderson, *Air Marshal* Sir Timothy Michael, KCB, DSO
Anderson, Sir (William) Eric Kinloch, KT
Anderton, Sir (Cyril) James, Kt., CBE, QPM
Andrew, Sir Robert John, KCB
Andrew, Sir Warwick, Kt.
Andrews, Sir Ian Charles Franklin, Kt., CBE, TD
Angest, Sir Henry, Kt.
Annesley, Sir Hugh Norman, Kt., QPM
Anson, Sir John, KCB
Anson, Sir Philip Roland, Bt. (1831)
Anstruther, Sir Sebastian Paten Campbell, Bt. (S. 1694 and S. 1700)
Anstruther-Gough-Calthorpe, Sir Euan Hamilton, Bt. (1929)
Antrobus, Sir Edward Philip, Bt. (1815)

Appleyard, Sir Leonard Vincent, KCMG
Arbib, Sir Martyn, Kt.
Arbuthnot, Sir Keith Robert Charles, Bt. (1823)
Arbuthnot, Sir William Reierson, Bt. (1964)
Arbuthnott, *Prof.* Sir John Peebles, Kt., PHD, FRSE
†Archdale, Sir Nicholas Edward, Bt. (1928)
Arculus, Sir Thomas David Guy, Kt.
Armitage, *Air Chief Marshal* Sir Michael John, KCB, CBE
Armitt, Sir John Alexander, Kt., CBE
Armour, *Prof.* Sir James, Kt., CBE
Armstrong, Sir Christopher John Edmund Stuart, Bt. (1841), MBE
Armstrong, Sir Richard, Kt., CBE
Armytage, Sir John Martin, Bt. (1738)
Arnold, *Hon.* Sir Richard David, Kt.
Arnold, Sir Thomas Richard, Kt.
Arnott, Sir Alexander John Maxwell, Bt. (1896)
†Arthur, Sir Benjamin Nathan, Bt. (1841)
Arthur, *Lt.-Gen.* Sir (John) Norman Stewart, KCB, CVO
Arthur, Sir Michael Anthony, KCMG
Arulkumaran, *Prof.* Sir Sabaratnam, Kt.
Asbridge, Sir Jonathan Elliott, Kt.
Ash, *Prof.* Sir Eric Albert, Kt., CBE, FRS, FRENG
Ashburnham, Sir James Fleetwood, Bt. (1661)
Ashworth, *Dr* Sir John Michael, Kt.
Aske, Sir Robert John Bingham, Bt. (1922)
Askew, Sir Bryan, Kt.
Asquith, *Hon.* Sir Dominic Anthony Gerard, KCMG
Astill, *Hon.* Sir Michael John, Kt.
Astley-Cooper, Sir Alexander Paston, Bt. (1821)
Astwood, *Hon.* Sir James Rufus, KBE
Atha, *Air Marshal* Sir Stuart David, KBE, CB, DSO
Atkins, *Rt. Hon.* Sir Robert James, Kt.
Atkinson, Sir William Samuel, Kt.
Atopare, Sir Sailas, GCMG
Attenborough, Sir David Frederick, Kt., OM, CH, CVO, CBE, FRS
Aubrey-Fletcher, Sir Henry Egerton, Bt. (1782), KCVO
Audland, Sir Christopher John, KCMG
Augier, *Prof.* Sir Fitzroy Richard, Kt.

Auld, *Rt. Hon.* Sir Robin Ernest, Kt.
Austen-Smith, *Air Marshal* Sir Roy David, KBE, CB, CVO, DFC
Austin, Sir Peter John, Bt. (1894)
Austin, *Air Marshal* Sir Roger Mark, KCB, AFC
Avei, Sir Moi, KBE
Ayaz, *Dr* Sir Iftikhar Ahmad, KBE
Ayckbourn, Sir Alan, Kt., CBE
Aykroyd, Sir Henry Robert George, Bt. (1920)
Aykroyd, Sir James Alexander Frederic, Bt. (1929)
Aylmer, Sir Richard John, Bt. (I. 1622)
Aylward, *Prof.* Sir Mansel, Kt., CB
Aynsley-Green, *Prof.* Sir Albert, Kt.
Bacha, Sir Bhinod, Kt., CMG
Backhouse, Sir Alfred James Stott, Bt. (1901)
Bacon, Sir Nicholas Hickman Ponsonby, Bt., OBE (1611 and 1627), *Premier Baronet of England*
Baddeley, Sir John Wolsey Beresford, Bt. (1922)
Badge, Sir Peter Gilmour Noto, Kt.
Bagge, Sir (John) Jeremy Picton, Bt. (1867)
Baggott, Sir Matthew David, Kt., CBE, QPM
Bagnall, *Air Chief Marshal* Sir Anthony, GBE, KCB
Bai, Sir Brown, KBE
Bailey, Sir Alan Marshall, KCB
Bailey, Sir Brian Harry, Kt., OBE
Bailey, Sir John Bilsland, KCB
Bailey, Sir John Richard, Bt. (1919)
Bailhache, Sir Philip Martin, Kt.
Bailhache, Sir William, Kt.
Baillie, Sir Adrian Louis, Bt. (1823)
Bain, *Prof.* Sir George Sayers, Kt.
Baird, Sir Charles William Stuart, Bt. (1809)
Baird, Sir James Andrew Gardiner, Bt. (S. 1695)
Baird, *Air Marshal* Sir John Alexander, KBE
Baird, *Vice-Adm.* Sir Thomas Henry Eustace, KCB
Baker, *Hon.* Sir Andrew William, Kt.
Baker, Sir Bryan William, Kt.
Baker, *Hon.* Sir Jeremy Russell, Kt.
Baker, *Prof.* Sir John Hamilton, Kt., QC
Baker, Sir John William, Kt., CBE
Baker, *Rt. Hon.* Sir Jonathan Leslie, Kt.
Baker, *Rt. Hon.* Sir (Thomas) Scott (Gillespie), Kt.
Balasubramanian, *Prof.* Sir Shankar, Kt.
Baldry, Sir Antony Brian, Kt.
Baldwin, *Prof.* Sir Jack Edward, Kt., FRS
Ball, Sir Christopher John Elinger, Kt.
Ball, *Prof.* Sir John Macleod, Kt.
Ball, Sir Richard Bentley, Bt. (1911)
Ballantyne, *Dr* Sir Frederick Nathaniel, GCMG
Band, *Adm.* Sir Jonathon, GCB
Banham, Sir John Michael Middlecott, Kt.

Bannerman, Sir David Gordon, Bt. (S. 1682), OBE
Barber, Sir Brendan, Kt.
Barber, Sir Michael Bayldon, Kt.
Barber, Sir (Thomas) David, Bt. (1960)
Barclay, Sir David Rowat, Kt.
Barclay, Sir Frederick Hugh, Kt.
Barclay, Sir Robert Colraine, Bt. (S. 1668)
Baring, Sir John Francis, Bt. (1911)
Barker, *Hon.* Sir (Richard) Ian, Kt.
Barling, *Hon.* Sir Gerald Edward, Kt.
Barlow, Sir Christopher Hilaro, Bt. (1803)
Barlow, Sir Frank, Kt., CBE
Barlow, Sir James Alan, Bt. (1902)
Barlow, Sir John Kemp, Bt. (1907)
Barnes, Sir (James) David (Francis), Kt., CBE
Barnett, *Hon.* Sir Michael Lancelot Patrick, Kt.
Barnett, *Prof.* Sir Richard Robert, Kt.
Barnewall, Sir Peter Joseph, Bt. (I. 1623)
†Barran, Sir John Ruthven, Bt. (1895)
Barrett, Sir Stephen Jeremy, KCMG
†Barrett-Lennard, Sir Peter John, Bt. (1801)
†Barrington, Sir Benjamin, Bt. (1831)
Barrington-Ward, *Rt. Revd* Simon, KCMG
Barron, *Rt. Hon.* Sir Kevin, Kt.
Barrons, *Gen.* Sir Richard, KCB, CBE, ADC
Barrow, Sir Anthony John Grenfell, Bt. (1835)
Barrow, Sir Timothy Earle, KCMG, LVO, MBE
Barry, Sir (Lawrence) Edward (Anthony Tress), Bt. (1899)
Barter, Sir Peter Leslie Charles, Kt., OBE
†Bartlett, Sir Andrew Alan, Bt. (1913)
Barttelot, *Col.* Sir Brian Walter de Stopham, Bt. (1875), OBE
Bate, *Prof.* Sir Andrew Jonathan, Kt., CBE
Bates, Sir James Geoffrey, Bt. (1880)
Bates, Sir Richard Dawson Hoult, Bt. (1937)
Batho, Sir Peter Ghislain, Bt. (1928)
Bathurst, *Admiral of the Fleet* Sir (David) Benjamin, GCB
Battishill, Sir Anthony Michael William, GCB
Baulcombe, *Prof.* Sir David Charles, Kt., FRS
Baxendell, Sir Peter Brian, Kt., CBE, FRENG
Bayley, Sir Hugh Nigel Edward, Kt.
Bayne, Sir Nicholas Peter, KCMG
Baynes, Sir Christopher Rory, Bt. (1801)
Bazalgette, Sir Peter Lytton, Kt.
Bazley, Sir Thomas John Sebastian, Bt. (1869)
Beache, *Hon.* Sir Vincent Ian, KCMG
Beale, *Lt.-Gen.* Sir Peter John, KBE, FRCP

Beamish, Sir Adrian John, KCMG
Beamish, Sir David Richard, KCB
Bean, *Dr* Sir Charles Richard, Kt.
Bean, *Rt. Hon.* Sir David Michael, Kt.
Bear, Sir Michael David, Kt.
Beatson, *Rt. Hon.* Sir Jack, Kt.
Beaumont, Sir William Blackledge, Kt., CBE
Beavis, *Air Chief Marshal* Sir Michael Gordon, KCB, CBE, AFC
Beck, Sir Edgar Philip, Kt.
Beckett, Sir Richard Gervase, Bt. (1921), QC
Beckett, *Lt.-Gen.* Sir Thomas Anthony, KCB, CBE
Beckwith, Sir John Lionel, Kt., CBE
Beddington, *Prof.* Sir John Rex, Kt., CMG
†Beecham, Sir Robert Adrian, Bt. (1914)
Beevor, Sir Antony James, Kt.
Beevor, Sir Thomas Hugh Cunliffe, Bt. (1784)
Behan, Sir David, Kt., CBE
Beldam, *Rt. Hon.* Sir (Alexander) Roy (Asplan), Kt.
Belgrave, *HE* Sir Elliott Fitzroy, GCMG
Bell, Sir David Charles Maurice, Kt.
Bell, Sir David Robert, KCB
Bell, *Prof.* Sir John Irving, GBE
Bell, Sir John Lowthian, Bt. (1885)
Bell, *Prof.* Sir Peter Robert Frank, Kt.
Bell, *Hon.* Sir Rodger, Kt.
Bellamy, *Hon.* Sir Christopher William, Kt.
Bellingham, Sir Henry Campbell, Kt.
†Bellingham, Sir William Alexander Noel Henry, Bt. (1796)
Bender, Sir Brian Geoffrey, KCB
Benjamin, Sir George William John, Kt., CBE
Benn, Sir (James) Jonathan, Bt. (1914)
Bennett, *Air Vice-Marshal* Sir Erik Peter, KBE, CB
Bennett, *Hon.* Sir Hugh Peter Derwyn, Kt.
Bennett, *Gen.* Sir Phillip Harvey, KBE, DSO
Bennett, Sir Ronald Wilfrid Murdoch, Bt. (1929)
Benson, Sir Christopher John, Kt.
Benton-Jones, Sir James Peter Martin, Bt. (1919)
Beresford, Sir (Alexander) Paul, Kt.
Beresford-Peirse, Sir Henry Njers de la Poer, Bt. (1814)
Berghuser, *Hon.* Sir Eric, Kt., MBE
Beringer, *Prof.* Sir John Evelyn, Kt., CBE
Berman, Sir Franklin Delow, KCMG
Bernard, Sir Dallas Edmund, Bt. (1954)
Berners-Lee, Sir Timothy John, OM, KBE, FRS
Berney, Sir Julian Reedham Stuart, Bt. (1620)
Bernstein, Sir Howard, Kt.

Berragan, *Lt.-Gen.* Sir Gerald William, KBE, CB

Berridge, *Prof.* Sir Michael John, Kt., FRS

Berriman, Sir David, Kt.

Berry, *Prof.* Sir Colin Leonard, Kt., FRCPATH

Berry, *Prof.* Sir Michael Victor, Kt., FRS

Berthoud, Sir Martin Seymour, KCVO, CMG

Berwick, *Prof.* Sir George Thomas, Kt., CBE

Besley, *Prof.* Sir Timothy John, Kt., CBE

Best-Shaw, Sir Thomas Joshua, Bt. (1665)

Bethel, Sir Baltron Benjamin, KCMG

Bethlehem, Sir Daniel, KCMG

Bett, Sir Michael, Kt., CBE

Bettison, Sir Norman George, Kt., QPM

Bevan, Sir James David, KCMG

Bevan, Sir Martyn Evan Evans, Bt. (1958)

Bevan, Sir Nicolas, Kt., CB

Beverley, *Lt.-Gen.* Sir Henry York La Roche, KCB, OBE, RM

Bhadeshia, *Prof.* Sir Harshad Kumar Dharamshi, Kt., FRS

Bibby, Sir Michael James, Bt. (1959)

Biddulph, Sir Ian D'Olier, Bt. (1664)

Biggam, Sir Robin Adair, Kt.

Bilas, Sir Angmai Simon, Kt., OBE

Bill, *Lt.-Gen.* Sir David Robert, KCB

Billière, *Gen.* Sir Peter Edgar de la Cour de la, KCB, KBE, DSO, MC

Bindman, Sir Geoffrey Lionel, Kt.

Bingham, *Hon.* Sir Eardley Max, Kt.

Birch, Sir John Allan, KCVO, CMG

Birch, Sir Roger, Kt., CBE, QPM

Bird, *Prof.* Sir Adrian Peter, Kt., CBE, FRS, FRSE

Bird, Sir Richard Geoffrey Chapman, Bt. (1922)

Birkett, Sir Peter, Kt.

Birkin, Sir John Christian William, Bt. (1905)

Birkin, Sir (John) Derek, Kt., TD

Birkmyre, Sir James, Bt. (1921)

Birrell, Sir James Drake, Kt.

Birss, *Hon.* Sir Colin Ian, Kt.

Birt, Sir Michael, Kt.

Birtwistle, Sir Harrison, Kt., CH

Bischoff, Sir Winfried Franz Wilhelm, Kt.

Black, *Prof.* Sir Nicholas Andrew, Kt.

Black, Sir Robert David, Bt. (1922)

Blackburn, *Vice-Adm.* Sir David Anthony James, KCVO, CB

Blackburne, *Hon.* Sir William Anthony, Kt.

Blackett, Sir Hugh Francis, Bt. (1673)

Blackham, *Vice-Adm.* Sir Jeremy Joe, KCB

Blackman, Sir Frank Milton, KCVO, OBE

Blair, Sir Patrick David Hunter, Bt. (1786)

Blair, *Hon.* Sir William James Lynton, Kt.

†Blake, Sir Charles Valentine Bruce, Bt. (I. 1622)

Blake, Sir Francis Michael, Bt. (1907)

Blake, *Hon.* Sir Nicholas John Gorrod, Kt.

Blake, Sir Peter Thomas, Kt., CBE

Blake, Sir Quentin Saxby, Kt., CBE

Blakemore, *Prof.* Sir Colin Brian, Kt., FRS

Blaker, Sir John, Bt. (1919)

Blakiston, Sir Ferguson Arthur James, Bt. (1763)

Blanch, Sir Malcolm, KCVO

Bland, *Lt.-Col.* Sir Simon Claud Michael, KCVO

Blank, Sir Maurice Victor, Kt.

Blatchford, Sir Ian Craig, Kt.

Blatherwick, Sir David Elliott Spiby, KCMG, OBE

Blavatnik, Sir Leonard, Kt.

Blennerhassett, Sir (Marmaduke) Adrian Francis William, Bt. (1809)

Blewitt, *Maj.* Sir Shane Gabriel Basil, GCVO

Blofeld, *Hon.* Sir John Christopher Calthorpe, Kt.

Blois, Sir Charles Nicholas Gervase, Bt. (1686)

Blomefield, Sir Thomas Charles Peregrine, Bt. (1807)

Bloom, *Prof.* Sir Stephen Robert, Kt.

Bloomfield, Sir Kenneth Percy, KCB

Blundell, *Prof.* Sir Richard William, Kt., CBE, FBA

Blundell, Sir Thomas Leon, Kt., FRS

†Blunden, Sir Hubert Chisholm, Bt. (I. 1766)

Blunt, Sir David Richard Reginald Harvey, Bt. (1720)

Blyth, Sir Charles (Chay), Kt., CBE, BEM

Boardman, *Prof.* Sir John, Kt., FSA, FBA

Bodey, *Hon.* Sir David Roderick Lessiter, Kt.

Bodmer, Sir Walter Fred, Kt., PHD, FRS

Bogan, Sir Nagora, KBE

Bogle, Sir Nigel, Kt.

Boileau, Sir Nicolas Edmond George, Bt. (1838)

Boleat, Sir Mark John, Kt.

Boles, Sir Richard Fortescue, Bt. (1922)

Bollom, *Air Marshal* Sir Simon John, KBE, CB

Bona, Sir Kina, KBE

Bonallack, Sir Michael Francis, Kt., OBE

Bond, Sir John Reginald Hartnell, Kt.

Bond, *Prof.* Sir Michael Richard, Kt., FRCPSYCH, FRCPGLAS, FRCSE

Bone, *Prof.* Sir (James) Drummond, Kt., FRSE

Bone, Sir Roger Bridgland, KCMG

Bonfield, Sir Peter Leahy, Kt., CBE, FRENG

Bonham, Sir George Martin Antony, Bt. (1852)

Bonington, Sir Christian John Storey, Kt., CVO, CBE

Bonsor, Sir Nicholas Cosmo, Bt. (1925)

Boord, Sir Andrew Richard, Bt. (1896)

Boorman, *Lt.-Gen.* Sir Derek, KCB

Booth, Sir Clive, Kt.

Booth, Sir Douglas Allen, Bt. (1916)

Boothby, Sir Brooke Charles, Bt. (1660)

Bore, Sir Albert, Kt.

Boreel, Sir Stephan Gerard, Bt. (1645)

Borthwick, Sir Antony Thomas, Bt. (1908)

Borysiewicz, *Prof.* Sir Leszek Krzysztof, Kt.

Boseto, *Revd* Leslie Tanaboe, KBE

Bosher, Sir Robin, Kt.

Bossano, *Hon.* Sir Joseph John, KCMG

Bossom, Sir Bruce Charles, Bt. (1953)

Boswell, *Lt.-Gen.* Sir Alexander Crawford Simpson, KCB, CBE

Botham, Sir Ian Terence, Kt., OBE

Bottomley, Sir Peter James, Kt.

Bottoms, *Prof.* Sir Anthony Edward, Kt.

Boughey, Sir John George Fletcher, Bt. (1798)

Boulton, Sir John Gibson, Bt. (1944)

Bouraga, Sir Phillip, KBE

Bourn, Sir John Bryant, KCB

Bourne, Sir Matthew Christopher, Kt., OBE

Bowater, Sir Euan David Vansittart, Bt. (1939)

†Bowater, Sir Michael Patrick, Bt. (1914)

Bowden, Sir Andrew, Kt., MBE

Bowden, Sir Nicholas Richard, Bt. (1915)

Bowen, Sir Barry Manfield, KCMG

Bowen, Sir Geoffrey Fraser, Kt.

Bowen, Sir George Edward Michael, Bt. (1921)

Bowes Lyon, Sir Simon Alexander, KCVO

Bowlby, Sir Richard Peregrine Longstaff, Bt. (1923)

Bowman, Sir Charles Edward Beck, Kt.

Bowman, Sir Edwin Geoffrey, KCB

Bowman, Sir Jeffery Haverstock, Kt.

Bowness, Sir Alan, Kt., CBE

Bowyer-Smyth, Sir Thomas Weyland, Bt. (1661)

Boyce, Sir Graham Hugh, KCMG

Boyce, Sir Robert Charles Leslie, Bt. (1952)

Boycott, Sir Geoffrey, Kt., OBE

Boyd, Sir Alexander Walter, Bt. (1916)

Boyd, *Prof.* Sir Ian Lamont, Kt., FRSE

Boyd, Sir John Dixon Iklé, KCMG

Boyd, Sir Michael, Kt.

Boyd, *Prof.* Sir Robert David Hugh, Kt.

Boyd-Carpenter, Sir (Marsom) Henry, KCVO

Boyd-Carpenter, *Lt.-Gen. Hon.* Sir Thomas Patrick John, KBE

Boyle, *Prof.* Sir Roger Michael, Kt., CBE

Boyle, Sir Simon Hugh Patrick, KCVO

Boyle, Sir Stephen Gurney, Bt. (1904)

Bracewell-Smith, Sir Charles, Bt. (1947)

Bradford, Sir Edward Alexander Slade, Bt. (1902)

Bradshaw, *Lt.-Gen.* Sir Adrian, KCB, OBE

Brady, Sir Graham Stuart, Kt.

Brady, *Prof.* Sir John Michael, Kt., FRS

Brailsford, Sir David John, Kt., CBE

Braithwaite, Sir Rodric Quentin, GCMG

Bramley, *Prof.* Sir Paul Anthony, Kt.

Branagh, Sir Kenneth Charles, Kt.

Branson, Sir Richard Charles Nicholas, Kt.

Bratza, *Hon.* Sir Nicolas Dušan, Kt.

Brazier, Sir Julian William Hendy, Kt., TD

Breckenridge, *Prof.* Sir Alasdair Muir, Kt., CBE

Brennan, *Hon.* Sir (Francis) Gerard, KBE

Brenton, Sir Anthony Russell, KCMG

Brewer, Sir David William, KG, CMG, CVO

Brierley, Sir Ronald Alfred, Kt.

Briggs, *Rt. Hon.* Sir Michael Townley Featherstone, Kt. (Lord Briggs of Westbourne)

Brighouse, *Prof.* Sir Timothy Robert Peter, Kt.

Bright, Sir Graham Frank James, Kt.

Bright, Sir Keith, Kt.

Brigstocke, *Adm.* Sir John Richard, KCB

†Brinckman, Sir Theodore Jonathan, Bt. (1831)

†Brisco, Sir Campbell Howard, Bt. (1782)

Briscoe, Sir Brian Anthony, Kt.

Briscoe, Sir John Geoffrey James, Bt. (1910)

Bristow, Sir Laurence Stanley Charles, KCMG

Brittan, Sir Samuel, Kt.

Britton, Sir Paul John James, Kt., CB

†Broadbent, Sir Andrew George, Bt. (1893)

Broadbent, Sir Richard John, KCB

Brocklebank, Sir Aubrey Thomas, Bt. (1885)

†Brodie, Sir Benjamin David Ross, Bt. (1834)

Bromhead, Sir John Desmond Gonville, Bt. (1806)

†Bromley, Sir Charles Howard, Bt. (1757)

Bromley, Sir Michael Roger, KBE

Bromley-Davenport, Sir William Arthur, KCVO

Brook, *Prof.* Sir Richard John, Kt., OBE

Brooke, Sir Alistair Weston, Bt. (1919)

Brooke, Sir Francis George Windham, Bt. (1903)

Brooke, Sir Richard Christopher, Bt. (1662)

Brooke, Sir Rodney George, Kt., CBE

Brooking, Sir Trevor David, Kt., CBE

Brooksbank, Sir (Edward) Nicholas, Bt. (1919)

†Broughton, Sir David Delves, Bt. (1661)

Broughton, Sir Martin Faulkner, Kt.

Broun, Sir Wayne Hercules, Bt. (S. 1686)

Brown, Sir (Austen) Patrick, KCB

Brown, *Adm.* Sir Brian Thomas, KCB, CBE

Brown, Sir David, Kt.

Brown, Sir Ewan, Kt., CBE

Brown, Sir George Francis Richmond, Bt. (1863)

Brown, Sir Mervyn, KCMG, OBE

Brown, Sir Peter Randolph, Kt.

Brown, *Rt. Hon.* Sir Stephen, GBE

Brown, Sir Stephen David Reid, KCVO

†Brownrigg, Sir Michael (Gawen), Bt. (1816)

Browse, *Prof.* Sir Norman Leslie, Kt., MD, FRCS

Bruce, Sir (Francis) Michael Ian, Bt. (s. 1628)

Bruce-Clifton, Sir Hervey Hamish Peter, Bt. (1804)

Bruce-Gardner, Sir Edmund Thomas Peter, Bt. (1945)

Brunner, Sir Hugo Laurence Joseph, KCVO

Brunner, Sir Nicholas Felix Minturn, Bt. (1895)

†Brunton, Sir James Lauder, Bt. (1908)

Bryan, *Hon.* Sir Simon James, Kt.

Bryant, *Air Chief Marshal* Sir Simon, KCB, CBE, ADC

Brydon, Sir Donald Hood, Kt., CBE

Bubb, Sir Stephen John Limrick, Kt.

Buchan-Hepburn, Sir John Alastair Trant Kidd, Bt. (1815)

Buchanan, Sir Andrew George, Bt. (1878), KCVO

Buchanan-Jardine, Sir John Christopher Rupert, Bt. (1885)

Buckland, Sir Ross, Kt.

Buckley, *Dr* Sir George William, Kt.

Buckley, Sir Michael Sidney, Kt.

Buckley, *Lt.-Cdr.* Sir (Peter) Richard, KCVO

Buckley, *Hon.* Sir Roger John, Kt.

Bucknall, *Lt.-Gen.* Sir James Jeffrey Corfield, KCB, CBE

†Buckworth-Herne-Soame, Sir Richard John, Bt. (1697)

Budd, Sir Alan Peter, GBE

Budd, Sir Colin Richard, KCMG

Buffini, Sir Damon Marcus, Kt.

Bull, Sir George Jeffrey, Kt.

†Bull, Sir Stephen Louis, Bt. (1922)

Bullock, Sir Stephen Michael, Kt.

Bultin, Sir Bato, Kt., MBE

Bunbury, Sir Michael William, Bt. (1681), KCVO

Bunyard, Sir Robert Sidney, Kt., CBE, QPM

†Burbidge, Sir John Peter, Bt. (1916)

Burden, Sir Anthony Thomas, Kt., QPM

Burdett, Sir Crispin Peter, Bt. (1665)

Burgen, Sir Arnold Stanley Vincent, Kt., FRS

Burgess, Sir (Joseph) Stuart, Kt., CBE, PHD, FRSC

Burgess, *Prof.* Sir Robert George, Kt.

Burke, Sir James Stanley Gilbert, Bt. (I. 1797)

Burke, Sir (Thomas) Kerry, Kt.

Burn, *Prof.* Sir John, Kt.

Burnell-Nugent, *Vice-Adm.* Sir James Michael, KCB, CBE, ADC

Burnett, Sir Charles David, Bt. (1913)

Burney, Sir Nigel Dennistoun, Bt. (1921)

Burns, *Dr* Sir Henry, Kt.

Burns, Sir (Robert) Andrew, KCMG

Burns, *Rt. Hon.* Sir Simon Hugh McGuigan, Kt.

Burnton, *Rt. Hon.* Sir Stanley Jeffrey, Kt.

Burrell, Sir Charles Raymond, Bt. (1774)

Burridge, *Air Chief Marshal* Sir Brian Kevin, KCB, CBE, ADC

Burton, *Lt.-Gen.* Sir Edmund Fortescue Gerard, KBE

Burton, Sir Graham Stuart, KCMG

Burton, *Hon.* Sir Michael John, GBE

Burton, Sir Michael St Edmund, KCVO, CMG

Butcher, *Hon.* Sir Christopher John, Kt.

Butler, *Dr* Sir David Edgeworth, Kt., CBE

Butler, Sir Percy James, Kt., CBE

Butler, Sir Reginald Richard Michael, Bt. (1922)

Butler, Sir Richard Pierce, Bt. (I. 1628)

Butterfield, *Hon.* Sir Alexander Neil Logie, Kt.

Butterfill, Sir John Valentine, Kt.

Buxton, Sir Crispin Charles Gerard, Bt. (1840)

Buxton, *Rt. Hon.* Sir Richard Joseph, Kt.

Buzzard, Sir Anthony Farquhar, Bt. (1929)

Byatt, Sir Ian Charles Rayner, Kt.

Byron, *Rt. Hon.* Sir Charles Michael Dennis, Kt.

C-F

Cable, *Rt. Hon.* Sir (John) Vincent, Kt., PHD

†Cable-Alexander, Sir Patrick Desmond William, Bt. (1809)

Cadbury, Sir (Nicholas) Dominic, Kt.

Cadogan, *Prof.* Sir John Ivan George, Kt., CBE, FRS, FRSE

Cahn, Sir Albert Jonas, Bt. (1934)

Cahn, Sir Andrew Thomas, KCMG

Caine, Sir Michael (Maurice Micklewhite), Kt., CBE
Caines, Sir John, KCB
Cairns, *Very Revd* John Ballantyne, KCVO
Caldwell, Sir Edward George, KCB
Callaghan, Sir William Henry, Kt.
Callan, Sir Ivan Roy, KCVO, CMG
Callender, Sir Colin Nigel, Kt., CBE
Callman, *His Hon.* Sir Clive Vernon, Kt.
Calman, *Prof.* Sir Kenneth Charles, KCB, MD, FRCP, FRCS, FRSE
Calne, *Prof.* Sir Roy Yorke, Kt., FRS
Calvert-Smith, Sir David, Kt., QC
Cameron, Sir Hugh Roy Graham, Kt., QPM
Campbell, *Rt. Hon* Sir Alan, Kt.
Campbell, *Prof.* Sir Colin Murray, Kt.
Campbell, Sir Ian Tofts, Kt., CBE, VRD
Campbell, Sir James Alexander Moffat Bain, Bt. (S. 1668)
Campbell, Sir John Park, Kt., OBE
Campbell, Sir Lachlan Philip Kemeys, Bt. (1815)
Campbell, Sir Louis Auchinbreck, Bt. (S. 1628)
Campbell, *Dr* Sir Philip Henry Montgomery, Kt.
Campbell, Sir Roderick Duncan Hamilton, Bt. (1831)
Campbell, *Dr* Sir Simon Fraser, Kt., CBE
Campbell, *Rt. Hon.* Sir William Anthony, Kt.
†Campbell-Orde, Sir John Simon Arthur, Bt. (1790)
Cannadine, *Prof.* Sir David Nicholas, Kt.
Capewell, *Lt.-Gen.* Sir David Andrew, KCB, OBE, RM
Carden, Sir Christopher Robert, Bt. (1887)
†Carden, Sir John Craven, Bt. (I. 1787)
Carew, Sir Rivers Verain, Bt. (1661)
Carey, Sir de Vic Graham, Kt.
Carleton-Smith, *Gen.* Sir Mark Alexander Popham, KCB, CBE, ADC
Carleton-Smith, *Maj.-Gen.* Sir Michael Edward, Kt., CBE
Carlisle, Sir James Beethoven, GCMG
Carlisle, Sir John Michael, Kt.
Carlisle, Sir Kenneth Melville, Kt.
Carnegie, Sir Roderick Howard, Kt.
Carnwath, *Rt. Hon.* Sir Robert John Anderson, Kt., CVO (Lord Carnwath of Notting Hill)
Carr, Sir Roger Martyn, Kt.
Carrick, Sir Roger John, KCMG, LVO
Carrington, Sir Nigel Martyn, Kt.
Carruthers, Sir Ian James, Kt., OBE
Carsberg, *Prof.* Sir Bryan Victor, Kt.
Carter, Sir Andrew Nicholas, Kt., OBE
Carter, Sir David Anthony, Kt.
Carter, *Prof.* Sir David Craig, Kt., FRCSE, FRCSGLAS, FRCPE

Carter, Sir Edward Charles, KCMG
Carter, Sir John Gordon Thomas, Kt.
Carter, *Gen.* Sir Nicholas Patrick, GCB, CBE, DSO, ADC
Cartledge, Sir Bryan George, KCMG
Caruna, *Hon.* Sir Peter Richard, KCMG, QC
†Cary, Sir Nicolas Robert Hugh, Bt. (1955)
Cash, Sir Andrew John, Kt., OBE
Cash, Sir William Nigel Paul, Kt.
Cass, Sir Geoffrey Arthur, Kt.
Cassel, Sir Timothy Felix Harold, Bt. (1920)
Cassidi, *Adm.* Sir (Arthur) Desmond, GCB
Castell, Sir William Martin, Kt.
Catto, *Prof.* Sir Graeme Robertson Dawson, Kt.
Caulfield, *Prof.* Sir Mark Jonathan, Kt.
Cavanagh, *Hon.* Sir John, Kt.
Cave, Sir George Charles, Bt. (1896)
Cave-Browne-Cave, Sir John Robert Charles, Bt. (1641)
Cayley, Sir Digby William David, Bt. (1661)
Cazalet, *Hon.* Sir Edward Stephen, Kt.
Cenac, *HE* Sir (Emmanuel) Neville, GCMG
Chadwick, *Rt. Hon.* Sir John Murray, Kt.
Chadwick, Sir Joshua Kenneth Burton, Bt. (1935)
Chadwyck-Healey, Sir Charles Edward, Bt. (1919)
Chakrabarti, Sir Sumantra, KCB
Chalmers, Sir Iain Geoffrey, Kt.
Chalmers, Sir Neil Robert, Kt.
Chalstrey, Sir (Leonard) John, Kt., MD, FRCS
Chamberlain, *Hon.* Sir Martin Daniel, Kt.
Chan, *Rt. Hon.* Sir Julius, GCMG, KBE
Chan, Sir Thomas Kok, Kt., OBE
Chance, Sir John Sebastian, Bt. (1900)
Chandler, Sir Colin Michael, Kt.
Chantler, *Prof.* Sir Cyril, GBE, MD, FRCP
Chaplin, Sir Malcolm Hilbery, Kt., CBE
Chapman, Sir David Robert Macgowan, Bt. (1958)
Chapman, Sir Frank, Kt.
Chapman, Sir George Alan, Kt.
Chapple, *Field Marshal* Sir John Lyon, GCB, CBE
Charles, *Hon.* Sir Arthur William Hessin, Kt.
Charlton, Sir Robert (Bobby), Kt., CBE
Charnley, Sir (William) John, Kt., CB, FRENG
Chastanet, Sir Michael Thomas, KCMG, OBE
†Chaytor, Sir Bruce Gordon, Bt. (1831)
Checketts, *Sqn. Ldr.* Sir David John, KCVO
Checkland, Sir Michael, Kt.

Cheshire, Sir Ian Michael, Kt.
Cheshire, *Air Chief Marshal* Sir John Anthony, KBE, CB
Chessells, Sir Arthur David (Tim), Kt.
†Chetwynd, Sir Peter James Talbot, Bt. (1795)
Cheyne, Sir Patrick John Lister, Bt. (1908)
Chichester, Sir James Henry Edward, Bt. (1641)
Chilcot, *Rt. Hon.* Sir John Anthony, GCB
Chilcott, Sir Dominick John, KCMG
Child, Sir (Coles John) Jeremy, Bt. (1919)
Chinn, Sir Trevor Edwin, Kt., CVO
†Chinubhai, Sir Prashant, Bt. (1913)
Chipperfield, *Prof.* Sir David Alan, Kt., CBE
Chipperfield, Sir Geoffrey Howes, KCB
Chisholm, Sir John Alexander Raymond, Kt., FRENG
†Chitty, Sir Andrew Edward Willes, Bt. (1924)
Cholmeley, Sir Hugh John Frederick Sebastian, Bt. (1806)
Chope, Sir Christopher Robert, Kt., OBE
Choudhury, *Hon.* Sir Akhlaq Ur-Rahman, Kt.
Chow, Sir Chung Kong, Kt.
Chow, Sir Henry Francis, Kt., OBE
Christopher, Sir Duncan Robin Carmichael, KBE, CMG
Chung, Sir Sze-yuen, GBE, FRENG
Clark, *Prof.* Sir Christopher Munro, Kt.
Clark, Sir Francis Drake, Bt. (1886)
Clark, Sir Jonathan George, Bt. (1917)
Clark, Sir Terence Joseph, KBE, CMG, CVO
Clark, Sir Timothy Charles, KBE
Clarke, Sir Charles Lawrence Somerset, Bt. (1831)
Clarke, *Rt. Hon.* Sir Christopher Simon Courtenay Stephenson, Kt.
Clarke, *Hon.* Sir David Clive, Kt.
Clarke, Sir Jonathan Dennis, Kt.
Clarke, Sir Paul Robert Virgo, KCVO
Clarke, Sir Rupert Grant Alexander, Bt. (1882)
Clary, *Prof.* Sir David Charles, Kt.
Clay, Sir Edward, KCMG
Clay, Sir Richard Henry, Bt. (1841)
Clayton, Sir David Robert, Bt. (1732)
Cleobury, *Dr* Sir Stephen John, Kt., CBE
Cleaver, Sir Anthony Brian, Kt.
Clegg, *Rt. Hon.* Sir Nicholas William Peter, Kt.
Clementi, Sir David Cecil, Kt.
Clerk, Sir Robert Maxwell, Bt. (S. 1679), OBE
Clerke, Sir Francis Ludlow Longueville, Bt. (1660)
Clifford, Sir Roger Joseph, Bt. (1887)
Clifford, Sir Timothy Peter Plint, Kt.
Clifton-Brown, Sir Geoffrey Robert, Kt.

Coates, Sir Anthony Robert Milnes, Bt. (1911)

Coates, Sir David Frederick Charlton, Bt. (1921)

†Coats, Sir Alexander James Stuart, Bt. (1905)

Cobb, *Hon.* Sir Stephen William Scott, Kt.

Cochrane, Sir (Henry) Marc (Sursock), Bt. (1903)

†Cockburn, Sir Charles Christopher, Bt. (S. 1671)

Cockburn-Campbell, Sir Alexander Thomas, Bt. (1821)

Cockell, Sir Merrick, Kt.

Cockshaw, Sir Alan, Kt., FRENG

Codrington, Sir Christopher George Wayne, Bt. (1876)

Codrington, Sir Giles Peter, Bt. (1721)

Codron, Sir Michael Victor, Kt., CBE

Coghill, Sir Patrick Kendal Farley, Bt. (1778)

Coghlin, *Rt. Hon.* Sir Patrick, Kt.

Cohen, Sir Ivor Harold, Kt., CBE, TD

Cohen, *Hon.* Sir Jonathan Lionel, Kt.

Cohen, *Prof.* Sir Philip, Kt., PHD, FRS

Cohen, Sir Robert Paul, Kt., CBE

Cohen, Sir Ronald, Kt.

Cole, Sir (Robert) William, Kt.

Coleman, Sir Robert John, KCMG

Coleridge, *Hon.* Sir Paul James Duke, Kt.

Coles, Sir (Arthur) John, GCMG

Coles, Sir Jonathan Andrew, Kt.

Colfox, Sir Philip John, Bt. (1939)

Collas, Sir Richard John, Kt.

Collett, Sir Ian Seymour, Bt. (1934)

Collier, Sir Paul, Kt., CBE

Collins, Sir Alan Stanley, KCVO, CMG

Collins, *Hon.* Sir Andrew David, Kt.

Collins, Sir Bryan Thomas Alfred, Kt., OBE, QFSM

Collins, *Dr* Sir David John, Kt., CBE

Collins, Sir John Alexander, Kt.

Collins, Sir Kenneth Darlingston, Kt.

Collins, *Dr* Sir Kevan Arthur, Kt.

Collins, *Prof.* Sir Rory Edwards, Kt.

Collyear, Sir John Gowen, Kt.

Colman, Sir Michael Jeremiah, Bt. (1907)

Colman, Sir Timothy, KG

Colquhoun of Luss, Sir Rory Malcolm, Bt. (1786)

Colt, Sir Edward William Dutton, Bt. (1694)

Colthurst, Sir Charles St John, Bt. (I. 1744)

Colton, *Hon.* Sir Adrian George Patrick, Kt.

Conant, Sir John Ernest Michael, Bt. (1954)

Conner, *Rt Revd* David John, KCVO

Connery, Sir Sean, Kt.

Connolly, Sir William (Billy), Kt., CBE

Connor, Sir William Joseph, Kt.

Conran, Sir Terence Orby, Kt., CH

Cons, *Hon.* Sir Derek, Kt.

Constantinou, Sir Kosta George, Kt., OBE

Constantinou, Sir Theophilus George, Kt., CBE

Conway, *Prof.* Sir Gordon Richard, KCMG, FRS

Cook, Sir Alastair Nathan, Kt., CBE

Cook, Sir Andrew, Kt., CBE

Cook, Sir Christopher Wymondham Rayner Herbert, Bt. (1886)

Cook, *Prof.* Sir Peter Frederic Chester, Kt.

Cooke, *Hon.* Sir Jeremy Lionel, Kt.

Cooke, *Prof.* Sir Ronald Urwick, Kt.

Cooke-Yarborough, Sir Anthony Edmund, Bt. (1661)

Cooksey, Sir David James Scott, GBE

Cooper, *Prof.* Sir Cary Lynn, Kt., CBE

Cooper, *Gen.* Sir George Leslie Conroy, GCB, MC

Cooper, Sir Richard Adrian, Bt. (1905)

Cooper, Sir Robert Francis, KCMG, MVO

Cooper, *Maj.-Gen.* Sir Simon Christie, GCVO

Cooper, Sir William Daniel Charles, Bt. (1863)

Coote, Sir Nicholas Patrick, Bt. (I. 1621), *Premier Baronet of Ireland*

Corbett, *Maj.-Gen.* Sir Robert John Swan, KCVO, CB

Corder, *Vice-Adm.* Sir Ian Fergus, KBE, CB

Cordy-Simpson, *Lt.-Gen.* Sir Roderick Alexander, KBE, CB

Corness, Sir Colin Ross, Kt.

Corry, Sir James Michael, Bt. (1885)

Cory, Sir (Clinton Charles) Donald, Bt. (1919)

Cory-Wright, Sir Richard Michael, Bt. (1903)

Cossons, Sir Neil, Kt., OBE

Cotter, Sir Patrick Laurence Delaval, Bt. (I. 1763)

Cotterell, Sir Henry Richard Geers, Bt. (1805), OBE

†Cotts, Sir Richard Crichton Mitchell, Bt. (1921)

Coulson, *Rt. Hon.* Sir Peter David William, Kt.

Couper, Sir James George, Bt. (1841)

Courtenay, Sir Thomas Daniel, Kt.

Cousins, *Air Chief Marshal* Sir David, KCB, AFC

Coville, *Air Marshal* Sir Christopher Charles Cotton, KCB

Cowan, *Gen.* Sir Samuel, KCB, CBE

Coward, *Lt.-Gen.* Sir Gary Robert, KBE, CB, OBE

Coward, *Vice-Adm.* Sir John Francis, KCB, DSO

Cowdery, Sir Clive, Kt.

Cowley, *Prof.* Sir Steven Charles, Kt., FRS, FRENG

Cowper-Coles, Sir Sherard Louis, KCMG, LVO

Cox, Sir Alan George, Kt., CBE

Cox, *Prof.* Sir David Roxbee, Kt.

Cox, Sir George Edwin, Kt.

Craft, *Prof.* Sir Alan William, Kt.

Cragg, *Prof.* Sir Anthony Douglas, Kt., CBE

Cragnolini, Sir Luciano, Kt.

Craig-Cooper, Sir (Frederick Howard) Michael, Kt., CBE, TD

Craig-Martin, Sir Michael, Kt., CBE

Crane, *Prof.* Sir Peter Robert, Kt.

Cranston, *Hon.* Sir Ross Frederick, Kt.

Craufurd, Sir Robert James, Bt. (1781)

Crausby, Sir David Anthony, Kt.

Craven, Sir John Anthony, Kt.

Craven, Sir Philip Lee, Kt., MBE

Crawford, *Prof.* Sir Frederick William, Kt., FRENG

Crawford, Sir Robert William Kenneth, Kt., CBE

Crawley-Boevey, Sir Thomas Michael Blake, Bt. (1784)

Cresswell, *Hon.* Sir Peter John, Kt.

Crew, Sir (Michael) Edward, Kt., QPM

Crewe, *Prof.* Sir Ivor Martin, Kt.

Crisp, Sir John Charles, Bt. (1913)

Critchett, Sir Charles George Montague, Bt. (1908)

Crittin, *Hon.* Sir John Luke, KBE

Croft, Sir Owen Glendower, Bt. (1671)

Croft, Sir Thomas Stephen Hutton, Bt. (1818)

Crofton, Sir Edward Morgan, Bt. (1801)

Crofton, Sir William Robert Malby, Bt. (1838)

Crombie, Sir Alexander, Kt.

Crompton, Sir Dan, Kt., CBE, QPM

Cropper, Sir James Anthony, KCVO

Crosby, Sir Lynton Keith, Kt.

Crossley, Sir Sloan Nicholas, Bt. (1909)

Crowe, Sir Brian Lee, KCMG

Cruickshank, Sir Donald Gordon, Kt.

Cubie, *Dr* Sir Andrew, Kt., CBE

Cubitt, Sir Hugh Guy, Kt., CBE

Cubitt, *Maj.-Gen.* Sir William George, KCVO, CBE

Cullen, Sir (Edward) John, Kt., FRENG

Culme-Seymour, Sir Michael Patrick, Bt. (1809)

Culpin, Sir Robert Paul, Kt.

Cummins, Sir Michael John Austin, Kt.

Cunliffe, *Prof.* Sir Barrington, Kt., CBE

Cunliffe, Sir David Ellis, Bt. (1759)

Cunliffe, Sir Jonathan Stephen, Kt., CB

Cunliffe-Owen, Sir Hugo Dudley, Bt. (1920)

Cunningham, *Lt.-Gen.* Sir Hugh Patrick, KBE

Cunningham, *Prof.* Sir John, KCVO

Cunningham, Sir Roger Keith, Kt., CBE

Cunningham, Sir Thomas Anthony, Kt.

Cunynghame, Sir Andrew David Francis, Bt. (S. 1702)

Curran, *Prof.* Sir Paul James, Kt.

Curtain, Sir Michael, KBE

Curtice, *Prof.* Sir John Kevin, Kt., FBA, FRSE

Curtis, Sir Barry John, Kt.

Curtis, Sir Edward Philip, Bt. (1802)

Curtis, *Hon.* Sir Richard Herbert, Kt.

Cuschieri, *Prof.* Sir Alfred, Kt.

Cyrus, *Dr* Sir Arthur Cecil, KCMG, OBE

Dain, Sir David John Michael, KCVO

Dales, Sir Richard Nigel, KCVO

Dalglish, Sir Kenneth, Kt., MBE

Dalrymple-Hay, Sir Malcolm John Robert, Bt. (1798)

†Dalrymple-White, Sir Jan Hew, Bt. (1926)

Dalton, Sir David Nigel, Kt.

Dalton, *Vice-Adm.* Sir Geoffrey Thomas James Oliver, GCB

Dalton, Sir Richard John, KCMG

Dalton, *Air Chief Marshal* Sir Stephen Gary George, GCB

Dalyell, Sir Gordon Wheatley, Bt. (NS 1685)

Dancer, Sir Eric, KCVO, CBE

Daniel, Sir John Sagar, Kt., DSC

Darell, Sir Guy Jeffrey Adair, Bt. (1795)

Darrington, Sir Michael John, Kt.

Dasgupta, *Prof.* Sir Partha Sarathi, Kt.

Dashwood, *Prof.* Sir (Arthur) Alan, KCMG, CBE, QC

Dashwood, Sir Edward John Francis, Bt. (1707), *Premier Baronet of Great Britain*

Dashwood, Sir Frederick George Mahon, Bt. (1684)

Daunt, Sir Timothy Lewis Achilles, KCMG

Davey, *Rt. Hon.* Sir Edward Jonathan, Kt.

Davidson, Sir Martin Stuart, KCMG

Davies, *Prof.* Sir David Evan Naughton, Kt., CBE, FRS, FRENG

Davies, Sir David John, Kt.

Davies, Sir Frank John, Kt., CBE

Davies, *Prof.* Sir Graeme John, Kt., FRENG

Davies, Sir John Howard, Kt.

Davies, Sir John Michael, KCB

Davies, Sir Raymond Douglas, Kt.

Davies, Sir Rhys Everson, Kt., QC

Davis, Sir Andrew Frank, Kt., CBE

Davis, Sir Crispin Henry Lamert, Kt.

Davis, Sir Ian Edward Lamert, Kt.

†Davis, Sir Richard Charles, Bt. (1946)

Davis, Sir Michael Lawrence, Kt.

Davis, *Rt. Hon.* Sir Nigel Anthony Lamert, Kt.

Davis, Sir Peter John, Kt.

Davis, *Hon.* Sir William Easthope, Kt.

Davis-Goff, Sir Robert (William), Bt. (1905)

Davson, Sir George Trenchard Simon, Bt. (1927)

Dawanincura, Sir John Norbert, Kt., OBE

Dawbarn, Sir Simon Yelverton, KCVO, CMG

Dawson, *Hon.* Sir Daryl Michael, KBE, CB

Dawson, Sir Nicholas Anthony Trevor, Bt. (1920)

Day, Sir Barry Stuart, Kt., OBE

Day, *Air Chief Marshal* Sir John Romney, KCB, OBE, ADC

Day, Sir Jonathan Stephen, Kt., CBE

Day, Sir (Judson) Graham, Kt.

Day, Sir Michael John, Kt., OBE

Day, Sir Simon James, Kt.

Day-Lewis, Sir Daniel Michael Blake, Kt.

Deane, *Hon.* Sir William Patrick, KBE

Dearlove, Sir Richard Billing, KCMG, OBE

Deaton, *Prof.* Sir Angus Stewart, Kt.

†Debenham, Sir Thomas Adam, Bt. (1931)

Deegan, Sir Michael, Kt., CBE

Deeny, *Rt. Hon.* Sir Donnell Justin Patrick, Kt.

De Haan, Sir Roger Michael, Kt., CBE

De Halpert, *Rear-Adm.* Sir Jeremy Michael, KCVO, CB

de Hoghton, Sir (Richard) Bernard (Cuthbert), Bt. (1611)

†de la Rue, Sir Edward Walter Henry, Bt. (1898)

Dellow, Sir John Albert, Kt., CBE

Delves, *Lt.-Gen.* Sir Cedric Norman George, KBE

Denison-Smith, *Lt.-Gen.* Sir Anthony Arthur, KBE

Denny, Sir Charles Alistair Maurice, Bt. (1913)

Denny, Sir Piers Anthony de Waltham, Bt. (I. 1782)

Desmond, Sir Denis Fitzgerald, KCVO, CBE

de Trafford, Sir John Humphrey, Bt. (1841)

Devane, Sir Ciaran Gearoid, Kt.

Deverell, *Lt.-Gen.* Sir Christopher Michael, KCB, MBE

Deverell, *Gen.* Sir John Freegard, KCB, OBE

Devereux, Sir Robert, KCB

De Ville, Sir Harold Godfrey Oscar, Kt., CBE

Devine, *Prof.* Sir Thomas Martin, Kt., OBE, FRSE

Devitt, Sir James Hugh Thomas, Bt. (1916)

Dewey, Sir Rupert Grahame, Bt. (1917)

De Witt, Sir Ronald Wayne, Kt.

Diamond, *Prof.* Sir Ian David, Kt., FRSE

Dick-Lauder, Sir Piers Robert, Bt. (S. 1690)

Dilke, Revd Charles John Wentworth, Bt. (1862)

Dilley, Sir Philip Graham, Kt.

Dillon, Sir Andrew Patrick, Kt., CBE

Dillwyn-Venables-Llewelyn, Sir John Michael, Bt. (1890)

Dilnot, Sir Andrew William, Kt., CBE

Dingemans, *Hon.* Sir James Michael, Kt.

Dion, Sir Leo, KBE

Dixon, Sir Jeremy, Kt.

Dixon, Sir Jonathan Mark, Bt. (1919)

Dixon, *Dr* Sir Michael, Kt.

Dixon, Sir Peter John Bellett, Kt.

Djanogly, Sir Harry Ari Simon, Kt., CBE

Dobson, *Vice-Adm.* Sir David Stuart, KBE

Dollery, Sir Colin Terence, Kt.

Don-Wauchope, Sir Roger (Hamilton), Bt. (S. 1667)

Donaldson, *Rt. Hon.* Sir Jeffrey Mark, Kt.

Donaldson, *Prof.* Sir Liam Joseph, Kt.

Donaldson, *Prof.* Sir Simon Kirwan, Kt.

Donnelly, Sir Joseph Brian, KBE, CMG

Donnelly, Sir Martin Eugene, KCB, CMG

Donnelly, *Prof.* Sir Peter James, Kt.

Donohoe, Sir Brian Harold, Kt.

Dorfman, Sir Lloyd, Kt., CBE

Dorman, Sir Philip Henry Keppel, Bt. (1923)

Douglas, *Prof.* Sir Neil James, Kt.

Douglas, *Hon.* Sir Roger Owen, Kt.

Dove, *Hon.* Sir Ian William, Kt.

Dowell, Sir Anthony James, Kt., CBE

Dowling, Sir Robert, Kt.

Downes, *Prof.* Sir Charles Peter, Kt., OBE, FRSE

Downey, Sir Gordon Stanley, KCB

Doyle, Sir Reginald Derek Henry, Kt., CBE

D'Oyly, Sir Hadley Gregory, Bt. (1663)

Drewry, *Lt.-Gen.* Sir Christopher Francis, KCB, CBE

Dryden, Sir John Stephen Gyles, Bt. (1733 and 1795)

Duberly, Sir Archibald Hugh, KCVO, CBE

Duckworth, Sir James Edward Dyce, Bt. (1909)

du Cros, Sir Julian Claude Arthur Mallet, Bt. (1916)

Dudley-Williams, Sir Alastair Edgcumbe James, Bt. (1964)

Duff, *Prof.* Sir Gordon William, Kt.

Duff-Gordon, Sir Andrew Cosmo Lewis, Bt. (1813)

Duffell, *Lt.-Gen.* Sir Peter Royson, KCB, CBE, MC

Duffy, Sir (Albert) (Edward) Patrick, Kt., PHD

Dugdale, Sir (William) Matthew Stratford, Bt. (1936)

Duggin, Sir Thomas Joseph, Kt.

Dunbar, Sir Edward Horace, Bt. (S. 1700)

Dunbar, Sir James Michael, Bt. (S. 1694)

Dunbar, Sir Robert Drummond Cospatrick, Bt. (S. 1698)

Dunbar of Hempriggs, Sir Richard Francis, Bt. (S. 1706)

Dunbar-Nasmith, *Prof.* Sir James Duncan, Kt., CBE

Duncan, *Rt. Hon.* Sir Alan James Carter, KCMG

Duncan, Sir James Blair, Kt.

Dunford, *Dr* Sir John Ernest, Kt., OBE

Dunlop, Sir Thomas, Bt. (1916)

Dunne, Sir Martin, KCVO

Dunne, Sir Thomas Raymond, KG, KCVO

Dunning, Sir Simon William Patrick, Bt. (1930)

Dunnington-Jefferson, Sir John Alexander, Bt. (1958)

Dunstone, Sir Charles William, Kt., CVO

Dunt, *Vice-Adm.* Sir John Hugh, KCB

†Duntze, Sir Daniel Evans, Bt. (1774)

Dupre, Sir Tumun, Kt., MBE

Durand, Sir Edward Alan Christopher David Percy, Bt. (1892)

Durie, Sir David Robert Campbell, KCMG

Durrant, Sir David Alexander, Bt. (1784)

Duthie, Sir Robert Grieve (Robin), Kt., CBE

Dutton, *Lt.-Gen.* Sir James Benjamin, KCB, CBE

Dwyer, Sir Joseph Anthony, Kt.

†Dyer-Bennet, Sir David, Bt. (1678)

Dyke, Sir David William Hart, Bt. (1677)

Dymock, *Vice-Adm.* Sir Anthony Knox, KBE, CB

Dyson, Sir James, Kt., OM, CBE

Dyson, *Rt. Hon.* Sir John Anthony, Kt. (Lord Dyson)

Eadie, Sir James Raymond, Kt., QC

Eady, *Hon.* Sir David, Kt.

Eardley-Wilmot, Sir Benjamin John Assheton, Bt. (1821)

Earle, Sir (Hardman) George (Algernon), Bt. (1869)

Eastwood, *Prof.* Sir David Stephen, Kt.

Eaton, *Adm.* Sir Kenneth John, GBE, KCB

Ebdon, *Prof.* Sir Leslie Colin, Kt., CBE

Ebrahim, Sir (Mahomed) Currimbhoy, Bt. (1910)

Eddington, Sir Roderick Ian, Kt.

Eden, Hon. Sir Robert Frederick Calvert, Bt. (E 1672 and 1776)

Eder, *Hon.* Sir Henry Bernard, Kt.

Edis, *Hon.* Sir Andrew Jeremy Coulter, Kt.

Edge, *Capt.* Sir (Philip) Malcolm, KCVO

†Edge, Sir William, Bt. (1937)

Edmonstone, Sir Archibald Bruce Charles, Bt. (1774)

Edward, *Rt. Hon.* Sir David Alexander Ogilvy, KCMG

Edwardes, Sir Michael Owen, Kt.

Edwards, Sir Christopher John Churchill, Bt. (1866)

Edwards, *Prof.* Sir Christopher Richard Watkin, Kt.

Edwards, Sir Gareth Owen, Kt., CBE

Edwards, Sir Llewellyn Roy, Kt.

Edwards, *Prof.* Sir Michael, OBE

Edwards, Sir Robert Paul, Kt.

†Edwards-Moss, Sir David John, Bt. (1868)

Edwards-Stuart, *Hon.* Sir Antony James Cobham, Kt.

Egan, Sir John Leopold, Kt.

Egerton, Sir William de Malpas, Bt. (1617)

Ehrman, Sir William Geoffrey, KCMG

Elder, Sir Mark Philip, Kt., CH, CBE

Eldon, Sir Stewart Graham, KCMG, OBE

Elias, *Rt. Hon.* Sir Patrick, Kt.

Eliott of Stobs, Sir Rodney Gilbert Charles, Bt. (S. 1666)

Elliott, Sir David Murray, KCMG, CB

Elliott, Sir Ivo Antony Moritz, Bt. (1917)

Elliott, *Prof.* Sir John Huxtable, Kt., FBA

Ellis, Sir Vernon James, Kt.

Ellwood, Sir Peter Brian, Kt., CBE

Elphinston, Sir Alexander, Bt. (S. 1701)

Elphinstone, Sir John Howard Main, Bt. (1816)

Elton, Sir Arnold, Kt., CBE

Elton, Sir Charles Abraham Grierson, Bt. (1717)

Elvidge, Sir John, KCB

Elwes, *Dr* Sir Henry William, KCVO

Elwes, Sir Jeremy Vernon, Kt., CBE

Elwood, Sir Brian George Conway, Kt., CBE

Elworthy, *Air Cdre Hon.* Sir Timothy Charles, KCVO, CBE

Enderby, *Prof.* Sir John Edwin, Kt. CBE, FRS

English, Sir Terence Alexander Hawthorne, KBE, FRCS

Ennals, Sir Paul Martin, Kt., CBE

Epstein, *Prof.* Sir (Michael) Anthony, Kt., CBE, FRS

Errington, Sir Robin Davenport, Bt. (1963)

Erskine, Sir (Thomas) Peter Neil, Bt. (1821)

Erskine-Hill, Sir Alexander Roger, Bt. (1945)

Esmonde, Sir Thomas Francis Grattan, Bt. (I. 1629)

†Esplen, Sir William John Harry, Bt. (1921)

Esquivel, *Rt. Hon.* Sir Manuel, KCMG

Essenhigh, *Adm.* Sir Nigel Richard, GCB

Etherington, Sir Stuart James, Kt.

Etherton, *Rt. Hon.* Sir Terence Michael Elkan Barnet, Kt.

Evans, *Rt. Hon.* Sir Anthony Howell Meurig, Kt., RD

Evans, *Prof.* Sir Christopher Thomas, Kt., OBE

Evans, *Air Chief Marshal* Sir David George, GCB, CBE

Evans, *Hon.* Sir David Roderick, Kt.

Evans, Sir Harold Matthew, Kt.

Evans, Sir John Stanley, Kt., QPM

Evans, Sir Malcolm David, KCMG, OBE

Evans, *Prof.* Sir Martin John, Kt., FRS

Evans, Sir Richard Harry, Kt., CBE

Evans, *Prof.* Sir Richard John, Kt.

Evans, Sir Robert, Kt., CBE, FRENG

Evans-Lombe, *Hon.* Sir Edward Christopher, Kt.

†Evans-Tipping, Sir David Gwynne, Bt. (1913)

Evennett, *Rt. Hon.* Sir David Anthony, Kt.

Everard, Sir Henry Peter Charles, Bt. (1911)

Everard, *Lt.-Gen.* Sir James Rupert, KCB, CBE

Everington, *Dr* Sir Anthony Herbert, Kt., OBE

Every, Sir Henry John Michael, Bt. (1641)

Ewart, Sir William Michael, Bt. (1887)

Eyre, Sir Richard Charles Hastings, Kt., CH, CBE

†Fagge, Sir John Christopher Frederick, Bt. (1660)

Fahy, Sir Peter, Kt., QPM

Fairbairn, Sir Robert William, Bt. (1869)

Fairlie-Cuninghame, Sir Robert Henry, Bt. (S. 1630)

Fairweather, Sir Patrick Stanislaus, KCMG

Faldo, Sir Nicholas Alexander, Kt., MBE

†Falkiner, Sir Benjamin Simon Patrick, Bt. (I. 1778)

Fall, Sir Brian James Proetel, GCVO, KCMG

Fallon, *Rt. Hon.* Sir Michael Cathel, KCB

Fancourt, *Hon.* Sir Timothy Miles, Kt.

Fang, *Prof.* Sir Harry, Kt., CBE

Farah, Sir Mohamed (Mo) Muktar Jama, Kt., CBE

Fareed, Sir Djamil Sheik, Kt.

Farmer, Sir Thomas, Kt., CVO, CBE

Farquhar, Sir Michael Fitzroy Henry, Bt. (1796)

Farr, Sir Charles Blandford, Kt., CMG, OBE

Farrar, *Prof.* Sir Jeremy James, Kt., OBE

Farrell, Sir Terence, Kt., CBE

Farrer, Sir (Charles) Matthew, GCVO

Farrington, Sir Henry William, Bt. (1818)

Faull, Sir Jonathan Michael Howard, KCMG

Fay, Sir (Humphrey) Michael Gerard, Kt.

Feachem, *Prof.* Sir Richard George Andrew, KBE

Fean, Sir Thomas Vincent, KCVO

Feilden, Sir Henry Rudyard, Bt. (1846)

Feldmann, *Prof.* Sir Marc, Kt.

Fell, Sir David, KCB

Fender, Sir Brian Edward Frederick, Kt., CMG, PHD

Fenwick, Sir Leonard Raymond, Kt., CBE

Fergus, Sir Howard Archibald, KBE

Ferguson, *Prof.* Sir Michael Anthony John, Kt., CBE, FRS

Ferguson-Davie, Sir Michael, Bt. (1847)

Fergusson, *Rt. Hon.* Sir Alexander Charles Onslow, Kt.

Fergusson of Kilkerran, Sir Charles, Bt. (S. 1703)

Fersht, *Prof.* Sir Alan Roy, Kt., FRS

ffolkes, Sir Robert Francis Alexander, Bt. (1774), OBE

Field, Sir Malcolm David, Kt.

Field, *Hon.* Sir Richard Alan, Kt.

Fielding, Sir Leslie, KCMG

Fields, Sir Allan Clifford, KCMG

Fiennes, Sir Ranulph Twisleton-Wykeham, Bt. (1916), OBE

Figgis, Sir Anthony St John Howard, KCVO, CMG

Finlay, Sir David Ronald James Bell, Bt. (1964)

Finlayson, Sir Garet Orlando, KCMG, OBE

Fish, *Prof.* Sir David Royden, Kt.

†Fison, Sir Charles William, Bt. (1905)

Fittall, Sir William Robert, Kt.

FitzGerald, Sir Adrian James Andrew Denis, Bt. (1880)

†Fitzgerald, Sir Andrew Peter, Bt. (1903)

FitzHerbert, Sir Richard Ranulph, Bt. (1784)

Fitzpatrick, *Air Marshal* Sir John Bernard, KBE, CB

Flanagan, Sir Ronald, GBE, QPM

Flaux, *Rt. Hon.* Sir Julian Martin, Kt.

Flint, Sir Douglas Jardine, Kt., CBE

Floud, *Prof.* Sir Roderick Castle, Kt.

Floyd, *Rt. Hon.* Sir Christopher David, Kt.

Floyd, Sir Giles Henry Charles, Bt. (1816)

Foley, *Lt.-Gen.* Sir John Paul, KCB, OBE, MC

Follett, *Prof.* Sir Brian Keith, Kt., FRS

†Forbes of Craigievar, Sir Andrew Iain Ochoncar, Bt. (S. 1630)

Forbes, *Adm.* Sir Ian Andrew, KCB, CBE

Forbes, Sir James Thomas Stewart, Bt. (1823)

Forbes, *Vice-Adm.* Sir John Morrison, KCB

Forbes, *Hon.* Sir Thayne John, Kt.

Forbes Adam, Sir Nigel Colin, Bt. (1917)

Forbes-Leith, Sir George Ian David, Bt. (1923)

Ford, *Lt.-Col.* Sir Andrew Charles, KCVO

Ford, Sir Andrew Russell, Bt. (1929)

Forestier-Walker, Sir Michael Leolin, Bt. (1835)

Forrest, *Prof.* Sir (Andrew) Patrick (McEwen), Kt.

Forte, *Hon.* Sir Rocco John Vincent, Kt.

Forwood, *Hon.* Sir Nicholas James, Kt., QC

Foskett, *Hon.* Sir David Robert, Kt.

Foster, Sir Andrew William, Kt.

Foster, *Prof.* Sir Christopher David, Kt.

Foster, Sir Saxby Gregory, Bt. (1930)

Foulkes, Sir Arthur Alexander, GCMG

Fountain, *Hon.* Sir Cyril Stanley Smith, Kt.

Fowke, Sir David Frederick Gustavus, Bt. (1814)

Fowler, Sir (Edward) Michael Coulson, Kt.

Fox, Sir Ashley, Kt.

Fox, Sir Christopher, Kt., QPM

Fox, Sir Paul Leonard, Kt., CBE

Francis, Sir Horace William Alexander, Kt., CBE, FRENG

Francis, *Hon.* Sir Peter Nicholas, Kt.

Francis, Sir Robert Anthony, Kt., QC

Frank, Sir Robert Andrew, Bt. (1920)

†Fraser, Sir Benjamin James, Bt. (1943)

Fraser, Sir Charles Annand, KCVO

Fraser, Sir James Murdo, KBE

Fraser, *Hon.* Sir Peter Donald, Kt.

Fraser, Sir Simon James, GCMG

Frayling, *Prof.* Sir Christopher John, Kt.

Frederick, Sir Christopher St John, Bt. (1723)

Freedman, *Hon.* Sir (Benjamin) Clive, Kt.

Freedman, *Rt. Hon. Prof.* Sir Lawrence David, KCMG, CBE

†Freeman, Sir James Robin, Bt. (1945)

French, *Air Marshal* Sir Joseph Charles, KCB, CBE

Frere, *Vice-Adm.* Sir Richard Tobias, KCB

Friend, *Prof.* Sir Richard Henry, Kt.

Froggatt, Sir Peter, Kt.

Fry, Sir Graham Holbrook, KCMG

Fry, *Lt.-Gen.* Sir Robert Allan, KCB, CBE

Fry, *Dr* Sir Roger Gordon, Kt., CBE

Fulford, *Rt. Hon.* Sir Adrian Bruce, Kt.

Fuller, Sir James Henry Fleetwood, Bt. (1910)

Fulton, *Lt.-Gen.* Sir Robert Henry Gervase, KBE

Furness, Sir Stephen Roberts, Bt. (1913)

G-I

Gage, *Rt. Hon.* Sir William Marcus, Kt, QC

Gains, Sir John Christopher, Kt.

Gainsford, Sir Ian Derek, Kt.

Gale, *Rt. Hon.* Sir Roger James, Kt.

Galsworthy, Sir Anthony Charles, KCMG

Galway, Sir James, Kt., OBE

Gamble, Sir David Hugh Norman, Bt. (1897)

Gambon, Sir Michael John, Kt., CBE

Gammell, Sir William Benjamin Bowring, Kt.

Gardiner, Sir John Eliot, Kt., CBE

Gardner, *Prof.* Sir Richard Lavenham, Kt.

Gardner, Sir Roy Alan, Kt.

Garland, *Hon.* Sir Patrick Neville, Kt.

Garland, *Hon.* Sir Ransley Victor, KBE

Garland, *Dr* Sir Trevor, KBE

Garnett, *Adm.* Sir Ian David Graham, KCB

Garnham, *Hon.* Sir Neil Stephen, Kt.

Garnier, *Rear-Adm.* Sir John, KCVO, CBE

Garrard, Sir David Eardley, Kt.

Garrett, Sir Anthony Peter, Kt., CBE

Garrick, Sir Ronald, Kt., CBE, FRENG

Garthwaite, Sir (William) Mark (Charles), Bt. (1919)

Garwood, *Air Marshal* Sir Richard Frank, KBE, CB, DFC

Gass, Sir Simon Lawrance, KCMG, CVO

Geim, *Prof.* Sir Andre Konstantin, Kt.

Geno, Sir Makena Viora, KBE

Gent, Sir Christopher Charles, Kt.

George, *Prof.* Sir Charles Frederick, Kt., MD, FRCP

Gerken, *Vice-Adm.* Sir Robert William Frank, KCB, CBE

Gershon, Sir Peter Oliver, Kt., CBE

Gethin, Sir Richard Joseph St Lawrence, Bt. (I. 1665)

Gibb, Sir Barry Alan Crompton, Kt., CBE

Gibb, Sir Robbie Paul, Kt.

Gibbings, Sir Peter Walter, Kt.

Gibbons, Sir William Edward Doran, Bt. (1752)

Gibbs, *Hon.* Sir Richard John Hedley, Kt.

†Gibson, *Revd* Christopher Herbert, Bt. (1931)

Gibson, Sir Ian, Kt., CBE

Gibson, Sir Kenneth Archibald, Kt.

Gibson, *Rt. Hon.* Sir Peter Leslie, Kt.

Gibson-Craig-Carmichael, Sir David Peter William, Bt. (S. 1702 and 1831)

Gieve, Sir Edward John Watson, KCB

Giffard, Sir (Charles) Sydney (Rycroft), KCMG

Gifford, Sir Michael Roger, Kt.

Gilbert, *Air Chief Marshal* Sir Joseph Alfred, KCB, CBE

Gilbey, Sir Walter Gavin, Bt. (1893)

Gill, Sir Robin Denys, KCVO

Gillam, Sir Patrick John, Kt.

Gillen, *Hon.* Sir John de Winter, Kt.

Gillett, Sir Nicholas Danvers Penrose, Bt. (1959)

Gillinson, Sir Clive Daniel, Kt., CBE

Gilmore, *Prof.* Sir Ian Thomas, Kt.

Gilmour, *Hon.* Sir David Robert, Bt. (1926)

Gilmour, Sir John Nicholas, Bt. (1897)

Gina, Sir Lloyd Maepeza, KBE

Giordano, Sir Richard Vincent, KBE

Girolami, Sir Paul, Kt.

Girvan, *Rt. Hon.* Sir (Frederick) Paul, Kt.

Gladstone, Sir Charles Angus, Bt. (1846)

Glean, Sir Carlyle Arnold, GCMG

Globe, *Hon.* Sir Henry Brian, Kt.

Glover, Sir Victor Joseph Patrick, Kt.

Glyn, Sir Richard Lindsay, Bt. (1759 and 1800)

Gobbo, Sir James Augustine, Kt., AC

Godfray, *Prof.* Sir Hugh Charles Jonathan, Kt., CBE

Goldberg, *Prof.* Sir David Paul Brandes, Kt.

Goldring, *Rt. Hon.* Sir John Bernard, Kt.

Gomersall, Sir Stephen John, KCMG

Gonsalves-Sabola, *Hon.* Sir Joaquim Claudino, Kt.

Gooch, Sir Arthur Brian Sherlock Heywood, Bt. (1746)

Gooch, Sir Miles Peter, Bt. (1866)

Good, Sir John James Griffen, Kt., CBE

Goodall, *Air Marshal* Sir Roderick Harvey, KBE, CB, AFC

Goode, *Prof.* Sir Royston Miles, Kt., CBE, QC

Goodenough, Sir Anthony Michael, KCMG

Goodenough, Sir William McLernon, Bt. (1943)

Goodhart, Sir Robert Anthony Gordon, Bt. (1911)

Goodison, Sir Nicholas Proctor, Kt.

Goodson, Sir Alan Reginald, Bt. (1922)

Goodwin, Sir Frederick, KBE

Goold, Sir George William, Bt. (1801)

Goose, *Hon.* Sir Julian Nicholas, Kt.

Gordon, Sir Donald, Kt.

Gordon, Sir Gerald Henry, Kt., CBE, QC

Gordon, Sir Robert James, Bt. (S. 1706)

Gordon-Cumming, Sir Alexander Alastair Penrose, Bt. (1804)

Gore, Sir Hugh Frederick Corbet, Bt. (I. 1622)

Gore-Booth, Sir Josslyn Henry Robert, Bt. (I. 1760)

Goring, Sir William Burton Nigel, Bt. (1678)

Gormley, Sir Antony Mark David, Kt., OBE

Gormley, Sir Paul Brendan, KCMG, MBE

Goschen, Sir (Edward) Alexander, Bt. (1916)

Gosling, Sir (Frederick) Donald, KCVO

Goss, *Hon.* Sir James Richard William, Kt.

Goulden, Sir (Peter) John, GCMG

†Goulding, Sir (William) Lingard Walter, Bt. (1904)

Gourlay, Sir Simon Alexander, Kt.

Gowans, Sir James Learmonth, Kt., CBE, FRCP, FRS

Gowers, *Prof.* Sir William Timothy, Kt.

Gozney, Sir Richard Hugh Turton, KCMG

Graaff, Sir De Villiers, Bt. (1911)

Graham, Sir Alexander Michael, GBE

Graham, Sir Andrew John Noble, Bt. (1906)

Graham, Sir James Bellingham, Bt. (1662)

Graham, Sir James Fergus Surtees, Bt. (1783)

Graham, Sir James Thompson, Kt., CMG

Graham, Sir John Alistair, Kt.

Graham, Sir John Moodie, Bt. (1964)

Graham, Sir Peter, KCB, QC

Graham, *Lt.-Gen.* Sir Peter Walter, KCB, CBE

†Graham, Sir Ralph Stuart, Bt. (1629)

Graham-Moon, Sir Peter Wilfred Giles, Bt. (1855)

Graham-Smith, *Prof.* Sir Francis, Kt.

Grainge, Sir Lucian Charles, Kt., CBE

Grange, Sir Kenneth Henry, Kt., CBE

Grant, Sir Archibald, Bt. (S. 1705)

Grant, *Dr* Sir David, Kt., CBE

Grant, Sir Ian David, Kt., CBE

Grant, Sir John Douglas Kelso, KCMG

Grant, *Prof.* Sir Malcolm John, Kt., CBE

Grant, Sir Mark Justin Lyall, GCMG

Grant, Sir Patrick Alexander Benedict, Bt. (S. 1688)

Grant, Sir Paul Joseph Patrick, Kt.

Grant, *Lt.-Gen.* Sir Scott Carnegie, KCB

Grant-Suttie, Sir James Edward, Bt. (S. 1702)

Granville-Chapman, *Gen.* Sir Timothy John, GBE, KCB, ADC

Grattan-Bellew, Sir Henry Charles, Bt. (1838)

Gray, Sir Bernard Peter, Kt.

Gray, *Hon.* Sir Charles Anthony St John, Kt.

Gray, Sir Charles Ireland, Kt., CBE

Gray, *Prof.* Sir Denis John Pereira, Kt., OBE, FRCGP

Gray, *Dr* Sir John Armstrong Muir, Kt., CBE

Gray, Sir Robert McDowall (Robin), Kt.

Gray, Sir William Hume, Bt. (1917)

Graydon, *Air Chief Marshal* Sir Michael James, GCB, CBE

Grayson, Sir Jeremy Brian Vincent Harrington, Bt. (1922)

Greaves, *Prof.* Sir Melvyn Francis, Kt.

Green, Sir Allan David, KCB, QC

Green, Sir David John Mark, Kt., CB, QC

Green, Sir Edward Patrick Lycett, Bt. (1886)

Green, Sir Gregory David, KCMG

Green, *Hon.* Sir Guy Stephen Montague, KBE

Green, *Prof.* Sir Malcolm, Kt.

Green, *Rt. Hon.* Sir Nicholas Nigel, Kt.

Green, Sir Philip Green, Kt.

Green-Price, Sir Robert John, Bt. (1874)

Greenaway, *Prof.* Sir David, Kt.

Greenaway, Sir Thomas Edward Burdick, Bt. (1933)

Greener, Sir Anthony Armitage, Kt.

Greenstock, Sir Jeremy Quentin, GCMG

Greenwell, Sir Edward Bernard, Bt. (1906)

Greenwood, *Prof.* Sir Brian Mellor, Kt., CBE

Greenwood, *Prof.* Sir Christopher John, GBE, CMG

Gregory, *Lt.-Gen.* Sir Andrew Richard, KBE, CB

Gregory, *Prof.* Sir Michael John, Kt., CBE

Gregson, *Prof.* Sir Peter John Kt., FRENG

Grey, Sir Anthony Dysart, Bt. (1814)

Grice, Sir Paul Edward, Kt.

Griffiths, Sir Michael, Kt.

Grigson, *Hon.* Sir Geoffrey Douglas, Kt.

Grimshaw, Sir Nicholas Thomas, Kt., CBE

Grimstone, Sir Gerald Edgar, Kt.

Grimwade, Sir Andrew Sheppard, Kt., CBE

Grose, *Vice-Adm.* Sir Alan, KBE

Gross, *Rt. Hon.* Sir Peter Henry, Kt.

Grossart, Sir Angus McFarlane McLeod, Kt., CBE

Grotrian, Sir Philip Christian Brent, Bt. (1934)

†Grove, Sir Charles Gerald, Bt. (1874)

Grundy, Sir Mark, Kt.

Guinness, Sir John Ralph Sidney, Kt., CB

Guinness, Sir Kenelm Edward Lee, Bt. (1867)

Guise, Sir Christopher James, Bt. (1783)

Gull, Sir Rupert William Cameron, Bt. (1872)

†Gunning, Sir John Robert, Bt. (1778)

Gunston, Sir John Wellesley, Bt. (1938)

Gurdon, *Prof.* Sir John Bertrand, Kt., DPHIL, FRS

Guthrie, Sir Malcolm Connop, Kt. (1936)

Habgood, Sir Anthony John, Kt.

Haddacks, *Vice-Adm.* Sir Paul Kenneth, KCB

Haddon-Cave, *Rt. Hon.* Sir Charles Anthony, Kt.

Hadlee, Sir Richard John, Kt., MBE

Hagart-Alexander, Sir Claud, Bt. (1886)

Haines, *Prof.* Sir Andrew Paul, Kt.

Haji-Ioannou, Sir Stelios, Kt.

Halberg, Sir Murray Gordon, Kt., MBE

Hall, *Dr* Sir Andrew James, Kt.

Hall, Sir David Bernard, Bt. (1919)

Hall, Sir David Christopher, Bt. (1923)

Hall, *Prof.* Sir David Michael Baldock, Kt.

Hall, Sir Ernest, Kt., OBE

Hall, Sir Geoffrey, Kt.

Hall, Sir Graham Joseph, Kt.

Hall, Sir Iain Robert, Kt.

Hall, Sir John, Kt.

Hall, Sir John Douglas Hoste, Bt. (S. 1687)

Hall, HE *Prof.* Sir Kenneth Octavius, GCMG

Hall, Sir Peter Edward, KBE, CMG

Hall, *Revd* Wesley Winfield, Kt.

Hall, Sir William Joseph, KCVO

Halliday, *Prof.* Sir Alexander Norman, Kt., FRS

Haloute, Sir Assad John, Kt.

Halpern, Sir Ralph Mark, Kt.

Halsey, *Revd* John Walter Brooke, Bt. (1920)

Halstead, Sir Ronald, Kt., CBE

Ham, *Prof.* Sir Christopher John, Kt., CBE

Hamblen, *Rt. Hon.* Sir Nicholas Archibald, Kt.

Hambling, Sir Herbert Peter Hugh, Bt. (1924)

Hamilton, Sir Andrew Caradoc, Bt. (S. 1646)

Hamilton, Sir David, Kt.

Hamilton, Sir George Ernest Craythorne, Kt., QPM

Hamilton, Sir Nigel, KCB

†Hamilton-Dalrymple, Sir Hew Richard, Bt. (S. 1698)

Hamilton-Spencer-Smith, Sir John, Bt. (1804)

Hammick, Sir Jeremy Charles, Bt. (1834)

Hammond, Sir Anthony Hilgrove, KCB, QC

Hampel, Sir Ronald Claus, Kt.

Hampson, Sir Stuart, Kt., CVO

Hampton, Sir (Leslie) Geoffrey, Kt.

Hampton, Sir Philip Roy, Kt.

Hanham, Sir William John Edward, Bt. (1667)

Hankes-Drielsma, Sir Claude Dunbar, KCVO

Hanley, *Rt. Hon.* Sir Jeremy James, KCMG

Hanmer, Sir Wyndham Richard Guy, Bt. (1774)

Hannam, Sir John Gordon, Kt.

Hanson, Sir (Charles) Rupert (Patrick), Bt. (1918)

Harcourt-Smith, *Air Chief Marshal* Sir David, GBE, KCB, DFC

Hardie Boys, *Rt. Hon.* Sir Michael, GCMG

Harding, *Marshal of the Royal Air Force* Sir Peter Robin, GCB

Hardy, Sir David William, Kt.

Hardy, Sir James Gilbert, Kt., OBE

Hare, Sir David, Kt., FRSL

Hare, Sir Nicholas Patrick, Bt. (1818)

Haren, *Dr* Sir Patrick Hugh, Kt.

Harford, Sir Mark John, Bt. (1934)

Harington, Sir David Richard, Bt. (1611)

Harkness, *Very Revd* James, KCVO, CB, OBE

Harley, *Gen.* Sir Alexander George Hamilton, KBE, CB

Harman, *Hon.* Sir Jeremiah LeRoy, Kt.

Harman, Sir John Andrew, Kt.

Harmsworth, Sir Hildebrand Harold, Bt. (1922)

Harper, *Air Marshal* Sir Christopher Nigel, KBE

Harper, Sir Ewan William, Kt., CBE

Harper, *Prof.* Sir Peter Stanley, Kt., CBE

Harris, Sir Christopher John Ashford, Bt. (1932)

Harris, *Air Marshal* Sir John Hulme, KCB, CBE

Harris, *Prof.* Sir Martin Best, Kt., CBE

Harris, Sir Michael Frank, Kt.

Harris, Sir Thomas George, KBE, CMG

Harrison, *Prof.* Sir Brian Howard, Kt.

Harrison, Sir David, Kt., CBE, FRENG

†Harrison, Sir Edwin Michael Harwood, Bt. (1961)

Harrison, *Hon.* Sir Michael Guy Vicat, Kt.

†Harrison, Sir John Wyndham Fowler, Bt. (1922)

Harrop, Sir Peter John, KCB

Hart, *Hon.* Sir Anthony Ronald, Kt.

Hart, Sir Graham Allan, KCB

Hartwell, Sir (Francis) Anthony Charles Peter, Bt. (1805)

Harvey, Sir Charles Richard Musgrave, Bt. (1933)

Harvey, Sir Nicholas Barton, Kt.

Harvie, Sir John Smith, Kt., CBE

Harvie-Watt, Sir James, Bt. (1945)

Harwood, Sir Ronald, Kt., CBE

Haslam, *Prof.* Sir David Antony, Kt., CBE

Hastie, *Cdre* Sir Robert Cameron, KCVO, CBE, RD

Hastings, Sir Max Macdonald, Kt.

Hastings, *Dr* Sir William George, Kt., CBE

Hatter, Sir Maurice, Kt.

Havelock-Allan, Sir (Anthony) Mark David, Bt. (1858), QC

Hawkes, Sir John Garry, Kt., CBE

Hawkhead, Sir Anthony Gerard, Kt., CBE

Hawkins, Sir Richard Caesar, Bt. (1778)

Hawley, Sir James Appleton, KCVO, TD

Haworth, Sir Christopher, Bt. (1911)

†Hay, Sir Ronald Frederick Hamilton, Bt. (S. 1703)

Hayden, *Hon.* Sir Anthony Paul, Kt.

Hayes, Sir Brian, Kt., CBE, QPM

Hayes, Sir Brian David, GCB

Hayes, *Rt. Hon.* Sir John Henry, Kt., CBE

Hayman-Joyce, *Lt.-Gen.* Sir Robert John, KCB, CBE

Hayter, Sir Paul David Grenville, KCB, LVO

Hazlewood, Sir Frederick Asa, KCMG

Head, Sir Patrick, Kt.

Head, Sir Richard Douglas Somerville, Bt. (1838)

Heald, *Rt. Hon.* Sir Oliver, Kt.

Heap, Sir Peter William, KCMG

Heap, *Prof.* Sir Robert Brian, Kt., CBE, FRS

Hearne, Sir Graham James, Kt., CBE

Heathcote, Sir Simon Robert Mark, Bt. (1733), OBE

†Heathcote, Sir Timothy Gilbert, Bt. (1733)

Heaton, Sir Richard, KCB

Heber-Percy, Sir Algernon Eustace Hugh, KCVO

Hedley, *Hon.* Sir Mark, Kt.

Hegarty, Sir John Kevin, Kt.

Heiser, Sir Terence Michael, GCB

Helfgott, Sir Ben, Kt., MBE

Heller, Sir Michael Aron, Kt.

Hempleman-Adams, *Dr* Sir David Kim, KCVO, OBE

Henderson, *Rt Hon.* Sir Launcelot Dinadin James, Kt.

Henderson, *Maj.* Sir Richard Yates, KCVO

Hendrick, Sir Mark, Kt.

Hendry, *Prof.* Sir David Forbes, Kt.

Hendy, Sir Peter Gerard, Kt., CBE

Hennessy, Sir James Patrick Ivan, KBE, CMG

†Henniker, Sir Adrian Chandos, Bt. (1813)

Henniker-Heaton, Sir Yvo Robert, Bt. (1912)

Henriques, *Hon.* Sir Richard Henry Quixano, Kt.

Henry, Sir Lenworth George, Kt., CBE

†Henry, Sir Patrick Denis, Bt. (1923)

Henshaw, Sir David George, Kt.

Herbecq, Sir John Edward, KCB

Heron, Sir Conrad Frederick, KCB, OBE

†Heron-Maxwell, Sir Nigel Mellor, Bt. (S. 1683)

Hervey, Sir Roger Blaise Ramsay, KCVO, CMG

Hervey-Bathurst, Sir Frederick William John, Bt. (1818)

Heseltine, *Rt. Hon.* Sir William Frederick Payne, GCB, GCVO

Hewetson, Sir Christopher Raynor, Kt., TD

Hewett, Sir Richard Mark John, Bt. (1813)

Hewitt, Sir (Cyrus) Lenox (Simson), Kt., OBE

Hewitt, Sir Nicholas Charles Joseph, Bt. (1921)

Heygate, Sir Richard John Gage, Bt. (1831)

Heywood, Sir Peter, Bt. (1838)

Hickey, Sir John Tongri, Kt., CBE

Hickinbottom, *Rt. Hon.* Sir Gary Robert, Kt.

Hickman, Sir (Richard) Glenn, Bt. (1903)
Hicks, Sir Robert, Kt.
Hielscher, Sir Leo Arthur, Kt.
Higgins, Sir David Hartmann, Kt.
Higgins, *Rt. Hon.* Sir Malachy Joseph, Kt.
Hildyard, *Hon.* Sir Robert Henry Thoroton, Kt.
Hill, *Rt. Revd Dr* Christopher John, KCVO
Hill, Sir James Frederick, Bt. (1917), OBE
Hill, Sir John Alfred Rowley, Bt. (I. 1779)
Hill, *Vice-Adm.* Sir Robert Charles Finch, KBE, FRENG
Hill-Norton, *Vice-Adm. Hon.* Sir Nicholas John, KCB
Hill-Wood, Sir Samuel Thomas, Bt. (1921)
Hillhouse, Sir (Robert) Russell, KCB
Hillier, *Air Marshal* Sir Stephen John, KCB, CBE, DFC
Hills, Sir John Robert, Kt., CBE
Hilly, Sir Francis Billy, KCMG
Hine, *Air Chief Marshal* Sir Patrick Bardon, GCB, GBE
Hintze, Sir Michael, Kt.
Hirsch, *Prof.* Sir Peter Bernhard, Kt., PHD, FRS
Hirst, Sir Michael William, Kt.
Hitchens, Sir Timothy Mark, KCVO, CMG
Hoare, *Prof.* Sir Charles Anthony Richard, Kt., FRS
Hoare, Sir Charles James, Bt. (I. 1784)
Hoare, Sir David John, Bt. (1786)
Hobart, Sir John Vere, Bt. (1914)
Hobbs, *Maj.-Gen.* Sir Michael Frederick, KCVO, CBE
Hobhouse, Sir Charles John Spinney, Bt. (1812)
†Hodge, Sir Andrew Rowland, Bt. (1921)
Hodge, Sir James William, KCVO, CMG
Hodgkinson, Sir Michael Stewart, Kt.
Hodson, Sir Michael Robin Adderley, Bt. (I. 1789)
Hogg, Sir Christopher Anthony, Kt.
Hogg, Sir Piers Michael James, Bt. (1846)
Hohn, Sir Christopher, KCMG
Holcroft, Sir Charles Anthony Culcheth, Bt. (1921)
Holden, Sir John David, Bt. (1919)
Holden, Sir Michael Peter, Bt. (1893)
†Holder, Sir Nigel John Charles, Bt. (1898)
Holderness, Sir Martin William, Bt. (1920)
Holdgate, Sir Martin Wyatt, Kt., CB, PHD
Holgate, *Hon.* Sir David John, Kt.
Holland, *Hon.* Sir Christopher John, Kt.
Holland, Sir John Anthony, Kt.

Hollingbery, Sir George Michael Edward, KCMG
Holm, Sir Ian (Holm Cuthbert), Kt., CBE
Holman, *Hon.* Sir Edward James, Kt.
Holman, *Prof.* Sir John Stranger, Kt.
Holmes, Sir John Eaton, GCVO, KBE, CMG
Holroyd, Sir Michael De Courcy Fraser, Kt., CBE
Holroyde, *Rt. Hon.* Sir Timothy Victor, Kt.
Home, Sir William Dundas, Bt. (S. 1671)
Honywood, Sir Filmer Courtenay William, Bt. (1660)
†Hood, Sir John Joseph Harold, Bt. (1922)
Hooper, *Rt. Hon.* Sir Anthony, Kt.
Hope, Sir Alexander Archibald Douglas, Bt. (S. 1628), OBE
Hope-Dunbar, Sir David, Bt. (S. 1664)
Hopkin, *Prof.* Sir Deian Rhys, Kt.
Hopkin, Sir Royston Oliver, KCMG
Hopkins, Sir Anthony Philip, Kt., CBE
Hopkins, Sir Michael John, Kt., CBE, RA, RIBA
Hopwood, *Prof.* Sir David Alan, Kt., FRS
Hordern, *Rt. Hon.* Sir Peter Maudslay, Kt.
Horlick, *Vice-Adm.* Sir Edwin John, KBE, FRENG
Horlick, Sir James Cunliffe William, Bt. (1914)
Horn-Smith, Sir Julian Michael, Kt.
Horne, Sir Alan Gray Antony, Bt. (1929)
Horner, *Hon.* Sir Thomas Mark, Kt.
Horsbrugh-Porter, Sir Andrew Alexander Marshall, Bt. (1902)
Horsfall, Sir Edward John Wright, Bt. (1909)
Hort, Sir Andrew Edwin Fenton, Bt. (1767)
Hosker, Sir Gerald Albery, KCB, QC
Hoskins, *Prof.* Sir Brian John, Kt., CBE, FRS
Hoskyns, Sir Robin Chevallier, Bt. (1676)
Hotung, Sir Joseph Edward, Kt.
Hough, *Prof.* Sir James, Kt., OBE
Houghton, Sir John Theodore, Kt., CBE, FRS
Houghton, Sir Stephen Geoffrey, Kt., CBE
Houldsworth, Sir Richard Thomas Reginald, Bt. (1887)
Hourston, Sir Gordon Minto, Kt.
Housden, Sir Peter James, KCB
House, Sir Stephen, Kt., QPM
Houssemayne du Boulay, Sir Roger William, KCVO, CMG
Houstoun-Boswall, Sir (Thomas) Alford, Bt. (1836)
Howard, Sir David Howarth Seymour, Bt. (1955)
Howard, *Dr* Sir Laurence, KCVO, OBE

Howard, *Prof.* Sir Michael Eliot, Kt., OM, CH, CBE, MC
Howard-Lawson, Sir John Philip, Bt. (1841)
Howarth, *Rt. Hon.* Sir George Edward, Kt.
Howarth, Sir (James) Gerald Douglas, Kt.
Howells, Sir Eric Waldo Benjamin, Kt., CBE
Howes, Sir Christopher Kingston, KCVO, CB
Howlett, *Gen.* Sir Geoffrey Hugh Whitby, KBE, MC
Hoy, Sir Christopher Andrew, Kt., MBE
Hoyle, *Rt. Hon.* Sir Lindsay Harvey, Kt.
Huddleston, *Hon.* Sir Ian William, Kt.
Hudson, Sir Mark, KCVO
Hughes, *Rt. Hon.* Sir Anthony Philip Gilson, Kt. (Lord Hughes of Ombersley)
Hughes, *Rt. Hon.* Sir Simon Henry Ward, Kt.
Hughes, Sir Thomas Collingwood, Bt. (1773), OBE
Hughes-Hallett, Sir Thomas Michael Sydney, Kt.
Hughes-Morgan, Sir (Ian) Parry David, Bt. (1925)
Hull, *Prof.* Sir David, Kt.
Hulme, Sir Philip William, Kt.
Hulse, Sir Edward Jeremy Westrow, Bt. (1739)
Hum, Sir Christopher Owen, KCMG
Humphreys, *Prof.* Sir Colin John, Kt., CBE
Hunt, *Dr* Sir Richard Timothy, Kt.
Hunte, *Hon. Dr* Sir Julian Robert, KCMG, OBE
Hunter, Sir Alistair John, KCMG
Hunter, *Prof.* Sir Laurence Colvin, Kt., CBE, FRSE
Hunter, *Dr* Sir Philip John, Kt., CBE
Hunter, Sir Thomas Blane, Kt.
Huntington-Whiteley, Sir Leopold Maurice, Bt. (1918)
Hurn, Sir (Francis) Roger, Kt.
Hurst, Sir Geoffrey Charles, Kt., MBE
Husbands, *Prof.* Sir Christopher Roy, Kt.
†Hutchison, Sir James Colville, Bt. (1956)
Hutchison, *Rt. Hon.* Sir Michael, Kt.
Hutchison, Sir Robert, Bt. (1939)
Hutt, Sir Dexter Walter, Kt.
Hytner, Sir Nicholas, Kt.
Iacobescu, Sir George, Kt., CBE
Ibbotson, *Vice-Adm.* Sir Richard Jeffrey, KBE, CB, DSC
Ife, *Prof.* Sir Barry William, Kt., CBE
Imbert-Terry, Sir Michael Edward Stanley, Bt. (1917)
Imray, Sir Colin Henry, KBE, CMG
Ingham, Sir Bernard, Kt.
Ingilby, Sir Thomas Colvin William, Bt. (1866)
Inglis, Sir William St Clair, Bt. (S. 1687)

†Inglis of Glencorse, Sir Ian Richard, Bt. (S. 1703)

Ingram, Sir James Herbert Charles, Bt. (1893)

Innes, Sir Alastair Charles Deverell, Bt. (NS 1686)

Innes of Edingight, Sir Malcolm Rognvald, KCVO

Innes, Sir Peter Alexander Berowald, Bt. (S. 1628)

Insall, Sir Donald William, Kt., CBE

Ipatas, *Hon.* Sir Peter, KBE

Irving, *Prof.* Sir Miles Horsfall, Kt., MD, FRCS, FRCSE

Irwin, *Lt.-Gen.* Sir Alistair Stuart Hastings, KCB, CBE

Irwin, *Rt. Hon.* Sir Stephen John, Kt.

Isaacs, Sir Jeremy Israel, Kt.

Isham, Sir Norman Murray Crawford, Bt. (1627), OBE

Ishiguro, Sir Kazuo, Kt., OBE

Italeli, *HE* Sir Iakoba Taeia, GCMG

Ive, Sir Jonathan Paul, KBE

Ivory, Sir Brian Gammell, Kt., CBE

J-L

Jack, Sir Malcolm Roy, KCB

Jack, *Hon.* Sir Raymond Evan, Kt.

Jackling, Sir Roger Tustin, KCB, CBE

Jackson, Sir Barry Trevor, Kt.

Jackson, Sir Kenneth Joseph, Kt.

Jackson, *Gen.* Sir Michael David, GCB, CBE

†Jackson, Sir Neil Keith, Bt. (1815)

Jackson, Sir Nicholas Fane St George, Bt. (1913)

Jackson, *Rt. Hon.* Sir Peter Arthur Brian, Kt.

Jackson, *Rt. Hon.* Sir Rupert Matthew, Kt.

Jackson, Sir Thomas Saint Felix, Bt. (1902)

Jackson, Sir (William) Roland Cedric, Bt. (1869)

Jacob, *Rt. Hon.* Sir Robert Raphael Hayim (Robin), Kt.

Jacobi, Sir Derek George, Kt., CBE

Jacobs, Sir Cecil Albert, Kt., CBE

Jacobs, *Rt. Hon.* Sir Francis Geoffrey, KCMG, QC

Jacobs, *Dr* Sir Michael Graham, Kt.

Jacobs, *Hon.* Sir Richard David, Kt.

Jacomb, Sir Martin Wakefield, Kt.

Jaffray, Sir William Otho, Bt. (1892)

Jagger, Sir Michael Philip, Kt.

James, Sir Jeffrey Russell, KBE

James, Sir John Nigel Courtenay, KCVO, CBE

Jameson, *Brig.* Sir Melville Stewart, KCVO, CBE

Jardine, Sir Andrew Colin Douglas, Bt. (1916)

Jardine of Applegirth, Sir William Murray, Bt. (S. 1672)

Jarman, *Prof.* Sir Brian, Kt., OBE

Jarratt, Sir Alexander Anthony, Kt., CB

Jay, *Hon.* Sir Robert Maurice, Kt.

Jeewoolall, Sir Ramesh, Kt.

Jeffery, Sir Thomas Baird, Kt., CB

Jeffrey, Sir William Alexander, KCB

Jeffreys, *Prof.* Sir Alec John, Kt., CH, FRS

Jeffries, *Hon.* Sir John Francis, Kt.

Jehangir, Sir Cowasji, Bt. (1908)

Jejeebhoy, Sir Jamsetjee, Bt. (1857)

Jenkin, *Hon.* Sir Bernard Christison, Kt.

Jenkins, Sir Brian Garton, GBE

Jenkins, Sir James Christopher, KCB, QC

Jenkins, Sir John, KCMG, LVO

Jenkins, *Dr* Sir Karl William Pamp, Kt., CBE

Jenkins, Sir Michael Nicholas Howard, Kt., OBE

Jenkins, Sir Simon, Kt.

Jenkinson, Sir John Banks, Bt. (1661)

Jenks, Sir (Richard) Peter, Bt. (1932)

Jenner, *Air Marshal* Sir Timothy Ivo, KCB

Jennings, Sir John Southwood, Kt., CBE, FRSE

Jennings, Sir Peter Neville Wake, Kt., CVO

Jephcott, Sir David Welbourn, Bt. (1962)

Jessel, Sir Charles John, Bt. (1883)

Jewkes, Sir Gordon Wesley, KCMG

Jewson, Sir Richard Wilson, KCVO

Job, Sir Peter James Denton, Kt.

John, Sir David Glyndwr, KCMG

John, Sir Elton Hercules (Reginald Kenneth Dwight), Kt., CBE

Johns, *Vice-Adm.* Sir Adrian James, KCB, CBE, ADC

Johns, *Air Chief Marshal* Sir Richard Edward, GCB, KCVO, CBE

Johnson, Sir Colpoys Guy, Bt. (1755)

Johnson, *Gen.* Sir Garry Dene, KCB, OBE, MC

Johnson, *Hon.* Sir Jeremy Charles, Kt.

†Johnson, Sir Patrick Eliot, Bt. (1818)

Johnson, *Hon.* Sir Robert Lionel, Kt.

Johnson-Ferguson, Sir Mark Edward, Bt. (1906)

Johnston, *Lt.-Gen.* Sir Maurice Robert, KCB, CVO, OBE

Johnston, Sir Thomas Alexander, Bt. (S. 1626)

Johnston, Sir William Ian Ridley, Kt., CBE, QPM

Johnstone, *Vice-Adm.* Sir Clive Charles Carruthers, KBE, CB

Johnstone, Sir Geoffrey Adams Dinwiddie, KCMG

Johnstone, Sir (George) Richard Douglas, Bt. (S. 1700)

Johnstone, Sir (John) Raymond, Kt., CBE

Jolliffe, Sir Anthony Stuart, GBE

Jolly, Sir Arthur Richard, KCMG

Jonas, Sir John Peter, Kt., CBE

Jones, Sir Alan Jeffrey, Kt.

Jones, Sir Bryn Terfel, Kt., CBE

Jones, Sir Clive William, KCMG, CBE

Jones, Sir David Charles, Kt., CBE

Jones, Sir Derek William, KCB

Jones, Sir Harry George, Kt., CBE

Jones, *Rt. Revd* James Stuart, KBE

Jones, Sir John Francis, Kt.

Jones, Sir Kenneth Lloyd, Kt., QPM

Jones, Sir Lyndon, Kt.

Jones, Sir Mark Ellis Powell, Kt.

Jones, *Vice-Adm.* Sir Philip Andrew, KCB

Jones, Sir Richard Anthony Lloyd, KCB

Jones, Sir Robert Edward, Kt.

Jones, Sir Roger Spencer, Kt., OBE

†Joseph, *Hon.* Sir James Samuel, Bt. (1943)

Jowell, *Prof.* Sir Jeffrey Lionel, KCMG, QC

Jowitt, *Hon.* Sir Edwin Frank, Kt.

Jugnauth, *Rt. Hon.* Sir Aneerood, KCMG

Jungius, *Vice-Adm.* Sir James George, KBE

Kaberry, *Hon.* Sir Christopher Donald, Bt. (1960)

Kabui, Sir Frank Utu Ofagioro, GCMG, OBE

Kadoorie, *Hon.* Sir Michael David, Kt.

Kakaraya, Sir Pato, KBE

Kamit, Sir Leonard Wilson, Kt., CBE

Kapoor, Sir Anish Mikhail, Kt., CBE

Kaputin, Sir John Rumet, KBE, CMG

Kavali, Sir Thomas, Kt., OBE

Kay, *Rt. Hon.* Sir Maurice Ralph, Kt.

Kay, Sir Nicholas Peter, KCMG

Kaye, Sir Paul Henry Gordon, Bt. (1923)

Keane, Sir John Charles, Bt. (1801)

Kearney, *Hon.* Sir William John Francis, Kt., CBE

Keegan, *Dr* Sir Donal Arthur John, KCVO, OBE

Keehan, *Hon.* Sir Michael Joseph, Kt.

Keene, *Rt. Hon.* Sir David Wolfe, Kt.

Keenlyside, Sir Simon John, Kt., CBE

Keith, *Hon.* Sir Brian Richard, Kt.

Keith, *Rt. Hon.* Sir Kenneth, KBE

†Kellett, Sir Stanley Charles, Bt. (1801)

Kelly, Sir Christopher William, KCB

Kelly, Sir David Robert Corbett, Kt., CBE

Kemakeza, Sir Allan, Kt.

Kemball, *Air Marshal* Sir (Richard) John, KCB, CBE

Kemp-Welch, Sir John, Kt.

Kendall, Sir Peter Ashley, Kt.

Kennaway, Sir John-Michael, Bt. (1791)

†Kennedy, Sir George Matthew Rae, Bt. (1836)

Kennedy, *Hon.* Sir Ian Alexander, Kt.

Kennedy, *Prof.* Sir Ian McColl, Kt.

Kennedy, *Rt. Hon.* Sir Paul Joseph Morrow, Kt.

Kenny, Sir Anthony John Patrick, Kt., DPHIL, DLITT, FBA

Kenny, Sir Paul Stephen, Kt.

Kentridge, Sir Sydney Woolf, KCMG, QC

Kenyon, Sir Nicholas Roger, Kt., CBE

Keogh, *Prof.* Sir Bruce Edward, KBE

Kere, *Dr* Sir Nathan, KCMG

Kerr, *Adm.* Sir John Beverley, GCB

Kerr, Sir Ronald James, Kt., CBE

Kerr, *Hon.* Sir Timothy Julian, Kt.

Kershaw, *Prof.* Sir Ian, Kt.

Keswick, Sir Henry Neville Lindley, Kt.

Keswick, Sir John Chippendale Lindley, Kt.

Kevau, *Prof.* Sir Isi Henao, Kt., CBE

Khaw, *Prof.* Sir Peng Tee, Kt.

Kikau, *Ratu* Sir Jone Latianara, KBE

Kimber, Sir Rupert Edward Watkin, Bt. (1904)

King, *Prof.* Sir David Anthony, Kt., FRS

King, Sir James Henry Rupert, Bt. (1888)

King, Sir Julian Beresford, KCVO, CMG

King, *Hon.* Sir Timothy Roger Alan, Kt.

King, Sir Wayne Alexander, Bt. (1815)

Kingman, *Prof.* Sir John Frank Charles, Kt., FRS

Kingman, Sir John Oliver Frank, KCB

Kingsley, Sir Ben, Kt.

Kinloch, Sir David, Bt. (S. 1686)

Kinloch, Sir David Oliphant, Bt. (1873)

Kipalan, Sir Albert, Kt.

Kirch, Sir David Roderick, KBE

Kirkpatrick, Sir Ivone Elliott, Bt. (S. 1685)

Kiszely, *Lt.-Gen.* Sir John Panton, KCB, MC

Kitchin, *Rt. Hon.* Sir David James Tyson, Kt. (Lord Kitchin)

Kitson, *Gen.* Sir Frank Edward, GBE, KCB, MC

Kleinwort, Sir Richard Drake, Bt. (1909)

Klenerman, *Prof.* Sir David, Kt., FRS

Knight, *Rt. Hon.* Sir Gregory, Kt.

Knight, Sir Kenneth John, Kt., CBE, QFSM

Knight, *Air Chief Marshal* Sir Michael William Patrick, KCB, AFC

Knight, *Prof.* Sir Peter, Kt.

Knill, Sir Thomas John Pugin Bartholomew, Bt. (1893)

Knowles, Sir Charles Francis, Bt. (1765)

Knowles, *Hon.* Sir Julian Bernard, Kt.

Knowles, Sir Nigel Graham, Kt.

Knowles, *Hon.* Sir Robin St John, Kt.

Knox, Sir David Laidlaw, Kt.

Knox-Johnston, Sir William Robert Patrick (Sir Robin), Kt., CBE, RD

Koraea, Sir Thomas, Kt.

Kornberg, *Prof.* Sir Hans Leo, Kt., DSc, SCD, PHD, FRS

Korowi, Sir Wiwa, GCMG

Kulukundis, Sir Elias George (Eddie), Kt., OBE

Kulunga, Sir Toami, Kt., OBE, QPM

Kumar, Sir Harpal Singh, Kt.

Kwok-Po Li, *Dr* Sir David, Kt., OBE

Lachmann, *Prof.* Sir Peter Julius, Kt.

Lacon, Sir Edmund Richard Vere, Bt. (1818)

Lacy, Sir Patrick Brian Finucane, Bt. (1921)

Laing, Sir (John) Martin (Kirby), Kt., CBE

Lake, Sir Edward Geoffrey, Bt. (1711)

Lakin, Sir Richard Anthony, Bt. (1909)

Lamb, Sir Albert Thomas, KBE, CMG, DFC

Lamb, *Lt.-Gen.* Sir Graeme Cameron Maxwell, KBE, CMG, DSO

Lamb, *Rt. Hon.* Sir Norman Peter, Kt.

Lambert, *Vice-Adm.* Sir Paul, KCB

†Lambert, Sir Peter John Biddulph, Bt. (1711)

Lambert, Sir Richard Peter, Kt.

Lampl, Sir Peter, Kt., OBE

Lamport, Sir Stephen Mark Jeffrey, GCVO

Lancashire, Sir Steve, Kt.

Landau, Sir Dennis Marcus, Kt.

Lander, Sir Stephen James, KCB

Lane, Prof. Sir David Philip, Kt.

Lane, *Hon.* Sir Peter Richard, Kt.

Langham, Sir John Stephen, Bt. (1660)

Langlands, Sir Robert Alan, Kt.

Langley, *Hon.* Sir Gordon Julian Hugh, Kt.

Langrishe, Sir James Hercules, Bt. (I. 1777)

Langstaff, *Hon.* Sir Brian Frederick James, Kt.

Lankester, Sir Timothy Patrick, KCB

Lapli, Sir John Ini, GCMG

Lapthorne, Sir Richard Douglas, Kt., CBE

Large, Sir Andrew McLeod Brooks, Kt.

Latasi, *Rt. Hon.* Sir Kamuta, KCMG, OBE

Latham, *Rt. Hon.* Sir David Nicholas Ramsey, Kt.

Latham, Sir Richard Thomas Paul, Bt. (1919)

Laughton, Sir Anthony Seymour, Kt.

Laurence, *Vice-Adm.* Sir Timothy James Hamilton, KCVO, CB, ADC

Laurie, Sir Andrew Ronald Emilius, Bt. (1834)

Lavender, *Hon.* Sir Nicholas, Kt.

†Lawrence, Sir Aubrey Lyttelton Simon, Bt. (1867)

Lawrence, Sir Clive Wyndham, Bt. (1906)

Lawrence, Sir Edmund Wickham, GCMG, OBE

Lawrence, Sir Henry Peter, Bt. (1858)

Lawrence, Sir Ivan John, Kt., QC

Lawrence-Jones, Sir Christopher, Bt. (1831)

Laws, *Rt. Hon.* Sir John Grant McKenzie, Kt.

Laws, Sir Stephen Charles, KCB

Lawson, Sir Charles John Patrick, Bt. (1900)

Lawson, *Gen.* Sir Richard George, KCB, DSO, OBE

Lawson-Tancred, Sir Andrew Peter, Bt. (1662)

Lawton, *Prof.* Sir John Hartley, Kt., CBE, FRS

Layard, *Adm.* Sir Michael Henry Gordon, KCB, CBE

Lea, Sir Thomas William, Bt. (1892)

Leahy, Sir Daniel Joseph, Kt.

Leahy, Sir Terence Patrick, Kt.

Learmont, *Gen.* Sir John Hartley, KCB, CBE

Leaver, Sir Christopher, GBE

Lechler, *Prof.* Sir Robert Ian, Kt.

Lechmere, Sir Nicholas Anthony Hungerford, Bt. (1818)

†Leeds, Sir John Charles Hildyard, Bt. (1812)

Lees, Sir Christopher James, Bt. (1897), TD

Lees, Sir David Bryan, Kt.

Lees, Sir Thomas Harcourt Ivor, Bt. (1804)

Lees, Sir (William) Antony Clare, Bt. (1937)

Leese, Sir Richard Charles, Kt., CBE

Leeson, *Air Marshal* Sir Kevin James, KCB, CBE

le Fleming, Sir David Kelland, Bt. (1705)

Legard, Sir Charles Thomas, Bt. (1660)

Legg, Sir Thomas Stuart, KCB, QC

Leggatt, *Rt. Hon.* Sir Andrew Peter, Kt.

Leggatt, *Rt. Hon.* Sir George Andrew Midsomer, Kt.

Leggett, *Prof.* Sir Anthony James, KBE

Le Grand, *Prof.* Sir Julian Ernest, Kt.

Leigh, *Rt. Hon.* Sir Edward Julian Egerton, Kt.

Leigh, Sir Geoffrey Norman, Kt.

Leigh, *Dr* Sir Michael, KCMG

Leigh, Sir Richard Henry, Bt. (1918)

Leigh-Pemberton, Sir James Henry, Kt., CVO

Leighton, Sir John Mark Nicholas, Kt.

Leighton, Sir Michael John Bryan, Bt. (1693)

†Leith-Buchanan, Sir Scott Kelly, Bt. (1775)

Le Marchant, Sir Piers Alfred, Bt. (1841)

Lennox-Boyd, *Hon.* Sir Mark Alexander, Kt.

Leon, Sir John Ronald, Bt. (1911)

Lepani, Sir Charles Watson, KBE

†Leslie, Sir Shaun Rudolph Christopher, Bt. (1876)

Lester, Sir James Theodore, Kt.

Lethbridge, Sir Thomas Periam Hector Noel, Bt. (1804)

Letwin, *Rt. Hon.* Sir Oliver, Kt.

Lever, Sir Jeremy Frederick, KCMG, QC

Lever, Sir Paul, KCMG

Lever, Sir (Tresham) Christopher Arthur Lindsay, Bt. (1911)

Leveson, *Rt. Hon.* Sir Brian Henry, Kt.

Levi, Sir Wasangula Noel, Kt., CBE

Levinge, Sir Richard George Robin, Bt. (I. 1704)

Lewinton, Sir Christopher, Kt.

Lewis, *Hon.* Sir Clive Buckland, Kt.

Lewis, Sir David Thomas Rowell, Kt.

Lewis, Sir John Anthony, Kt., OBE

Lewis, Sir John Henry James, Kt., OBE

Lewis, Sir Leigh Warren, KCB

Lewis, Sir Martyn John Dudley, Kt., CBE

Lewis, Sir Terence Murray, Kt., OBE, GM, QPM

Lewison, *Rt. Hon.* Sir Kim Martin Jordan, Kt.

Ley, Sir Christopher Ian, Bt. (1905)

Li, Sir Ka-Shing, KBE

Lickiss, Sir Michael Gillam, Kt.

Lidington, *Rt. Hon.* Sir David Roy, KCB, CBE

Liddington, Sir Bruce, Kt.

Lightman, *Hon.* Sir Gavin Anthony, Kt.

Lighton, Sir Thomas Hamilton, Bt. (I. 1791)

Likierman, *Prof.* Sir John Andrew, Kt.

Lilleyman, *Prof.* Sir John Stuart, Kt.

Lindblom, *Rt. Hon.* Sir Keith John, Kt.

†Lindsay, Sir James Martin Evelyn, Bt. (1962)

Lindsay, *Hon.* Sir John Edmund Frederic, Kt.

†Lindsay-Hogg, Sir Michael Edward, Bt. (1905)

Lipton, Sir Stuart Anthony, Kt.

Lipworth, Sir (Maurice) Sydney, Kt.

Lister, *Vice-Adm.* Sir Simon Robert, KCB, OBE

Lister-Kaye, Sir John Phillip Lister, Bt. (1812), OBE

Lithgow, Sir William James, Bt. (1925)

Llewellyn, Sir Roderic Victor, Bt. (1922)

Llewellyn-Smith, *Prof.* Sir Christopher Hubert, Kt.

Lloyd, *Prof.* Sir Geoffrey Ernest Richard, Kt., FBA

Lloyd, Sir Nicholas Markley, Kt.

Lloyd, *Rt. Hon.* Sir Peter Robert Cable, Kt.

Lloyd, Sir Richard Ernest Butler, Bt. (1960)

Lloyd, *Rt. Hon.* Sir Timothy Andrew Wigram, Kt.

Lloyd-Edwards, *Capt.* Sir Norman, KCVO, RD

Lloyd Jones, *Rt. Hon.* Sir David, Kt. (Lord Lloyd-Jones)

Loader, Air Marshal Sir Clive Robert, KCB, OBE

Lobban, Sir Iain Robert, KCMG, CB

Lockett, Sir Michael Vernon, KCVO

Lockhead, Sir Moir, Kt., OBE

Loder, Sir Edmund Jeune, Bt. (1887)

Logan, Sir David Brian Carleton, KCMG

Long, Sir Richard Julian, Kt., CBE

Longley, *Hon.* Sir Hartman Godfrey, Kt.

Longmore, *Rt. Hon.* Sir Andrew Centlivres, Kt.

Lorimer, *Lt.-Gen.* Sir John Gordon, KCB, MBE, DSO

Lorimer, Sir (Thomas) Desmond, Kt.

Los, *Hon.* Sir Kubulan, Kt., CBE

Loughran, Sir Gerald Finbar, KCB

Lourdenadin, Sir Ninian Mogan, KCMG, KBE

Lovegrove, Sir Stephen Augustus, KCB

Lovestone, *Prof.* Sir Simon, Kt.

Lovill, Sir John Roger, Kt., CBE

Low, *Dr* Sir John Menzies, Kt., CBE

Lowa, *Rt. Revd* Sir Samson, KBE

Lowcock, Sir Mark Andrew, KCB

Lowe, Sir Frank Budge, Kt.

Lowe, Sir Philip Martin, KCMG

Lowe, Sir Thomas William Gordon, Bt. (1918), QC

Lowson, Sir Ian Patrick, Bt. (1951)

†Lowther, Sir Patrick William, Bt. (1824)

Lowy, Sir Frank, Kt.

Loyd, Sir Julian St John, KCVO

Lu, Sir Tseng Chi, Kt.

Lucas, *Prof.* Sir Colin Renshaw, Kt.

†Lucas, Sir Thomas Edward, Bt. (1887)

Lucas-Tooth, Sir (Hugh) John, Bt. (1920)

Luff, Sir Peter James, Kt.

Lumsden, Sir David James, Kt.

Lushington, Sir John Richard Castleman, Bt. (1791)

Lyall Grant, Sir Mark Justin, KCMG

Lyle, Sir Gavin Archibald, Bt. (1929)

Lynch-Blosse, *Capt.* Sir Richard Hely, Bt. (I. 1622)

Lynch-Robinson, Sir Dominick Christopher, Bt. (1920)

Lyne, *Rt. Hon.* Sir Roderic Michael John, KBE, CMG

Lyons, Sir John, Kt.

Lyons, Sir Michael Thomas, Kt.

M–O

McAlinden, *Hon.* Sir Gerald Joseph, Kt.

McAllister, Sir Ian Gerald, Kt., CBE

McAlpine, Sir Andrew William, Bt. (1918)

McCamley, Sir Graham Edward, KBE

McCanny, *Prof.* Sir John Vincent, Kt., CBE

McCarthy, Sir Callum, Kt.

McCartney, *Rt. Hon.* Sir Ian, Kt.

McCartney, Sir (James) Paul, Kt., CH, MBE

†Macartney, Sir John Ralph, Bt. (I. 1799)

McClement, *Vice-Admiral* Sir Timothy Pentreath, KCB, OBE

Macleod, Sir Iain, KCMG

McCloskey, *Hon.* Sir John Bernard, Kt.

McColl, Sir Colin Hugh Verel, KCMG

McColl, *Gen.* Sir John Chalmers, KCB, CBE, DSO

McCollum, *Rt. Hon.* Sir William, Kt.

McCombe, *Rt. Hon.* Sir Richard George Bramwell, Kt.

McConnell, Sir Robert Shean, Bt. (1900)

†McCowan, Sir David James Cargill, Bt. (1934)

McCoy, Sir Anthony Peter, Kt., OBE

McCullin, Sir Donald, Kt., CBE

MacCulloch, *Prof.* Sir Diarmaid Ninian John, Kt.

McCulloch, *Rt. Revd* Nigel Simeon, KCVO

MacDermott, *Rt. Hon.* Sir John Clarke, Kt.

Macdonald, Sir Alasdair Uist, Kt., CBE

MacDonald, *Hon.* Sir Alistair William Orchard, Kt.

Macdonald of Sleat, Sir Ian Godfrey Bosville, Bt. (1625)

McDonald, *Prof.* Sir James, Kt.

Macdonald, Sir Kenneth Carmichael, KCB

McDonald, Sir Simon Gerard, KCMG, KCVO

McDonald, Sir Trevor, Kt., OBE

McDowell, Sir Eric Wallace, Kt., CBE

MacDuff, *Hon.* Sir Alistair Geoffrey, Kt.

Mace, *Lt.-Gen.* Sir John Airth, KBE, CB

McEwen, Sir John Roderick Hugh, Bt. (1953)

MacFadyen, *Air Marshal* Sir Ian David, KCVO, CB, OBE

†McFarland, Sir Anthony Basil Scott, Bt. (1914)

MacFarlane, *Prof.* Sir Alistair George James, Kt., CBE, FRS

McFarlane, *Rt. Hon.* Sir Andrew Ewart, Kt.

Macfarlane, Sir (David) Neil, Kt.

McGeechan, Sir Ian Robert, Kt., OBE

McGrath, Sir Harvey Andrew, Kt.

†Macgregor, Sir Ian Grant, Bt. (1828)

MacGregor of MacGregor, Sir Malcolm Gregor Charles, Bt. (1795)

McGrigor, Sir James Angus Rhoderick Neil, Bt. (1831)

McIntosh, Sir Neil William David, Kt., CBE

McIntyre, Sir Donald Conroy, Kt., CBE

McIntyre, Sir Meredith Alister, Kt.

Mackay, *Hon.* Sir Colin Crichton, Kt.

MacKay, Sir Francis Henry, Kt.

McKay, Sir Neil Stuart, Kt., CB

McKay, Sir William Robert, KCB

Mackay-Dick, *Maj.-Gen.* Sir Iain Charles, KCVO, MBE

Mackechnie, Sir Alistair John, Kt.

McKellen, Sir Ian Murray, Kt., CH, CBE

†Mackenzie, Sir (James William) Guy, Bt. (1890)

Mackenzie, *Gen.* Sir Jeremy John George, GCB, OBE

†Mackenzie, Sir Peter Douglas, Bt. (S. 1673)

†Mackenzie, Sir Roderick McQuhae, Bt. (S. 1703)

Mackeson, Sir Rupert Henry, Bt. (1954)

Mackey, Sir Craig Thomas, Kt., QPM
Mackey, Sir James, Kt.
McKibbin, *Dr* Sir Malcolm, KCB
McKillop, Sir Thomas Fulton Wilson, Kt.
McKinnon, *Rt. Hon.* Sir Donald Charles, GCVO
McKinnon, *Hon.* Sir Stuart Neil, Kt.
Mackintosh, Sir Cameron Anthony, Kt.
Mackworth, Sir Alan Keith, Bt. (1776)
McLaughlin, Sir Richard, Kt.
Maclean of Dunconnel, Sir Charles Edward, Bt. (1957)
Maclean, *Hon.* Sir Lachlan Hector Charles, Bt., (NS 1631), CVO
Maclean, Sir Murdo, Kt.
†McLeod, Sir James Roderick Charles, Bt. (1925)
MacLeod, *Hon.* Sir (John) Maxwell Norman, Bt. (1924)
Macleod, Sir (Nathaniel William) Hamish, KBE
McLintock, Sir Michael William, Bt. (1934)
McLoughlin, Sir Francis, Kt., CBE
McLoughlin, *Rt. Hon.* Sir Patrick Allen, Kt., CH
Maclure, Sir John Robert Spencer, Bt. (1898)
McMahon, Sir Brian Patrick, Bt. (1817)
McMahon, Sir Christopher William, Kt.
McMaster, Sir Brian John, Kt., CBE
McMichael, *Prof.* Sir Andrew James, Kt., FRS
MacMillan, *Very Revd* Gilleasbuig Iain, KCVO
McMillan, Sir Iain Macleod, Kt., CBE
Macmillan, *Dr* Sir James Loy, Kt., CBE
MacMillan, *Lt.-Gen.* Sir John Richard Alexander, KCB, CBE
McMurtry, Sir David, Kt., CBE
Macnaghten, Sir Malcolm Francis, Bt. (1836)
McNair-Wilson, Sir Patrick Michael Ernest David, Kt.
McNulty, Sir (Robert William) Roy, Kt., CBE
MacPhail, Sir Bruce Dugald, Kt.
Macpherson of Cluny, *Hon.* Sir William Alan, Kt., TD
MacRae, Sir (Alastair) Christopher (Donald Summerhayes), KCMG
Macready, Sir Charles Nevil, Bt. (1923)
Mactaggart, Sir John Auld, Bt. (1938)
McVicar, Sir David, Kt.
McWilliam, Sir Michael Douglas, KCMG
McWilliams, Sir Francis, GBE
Madden, Sir Charles Jonathan, Bt. (1919)
Madden, Sir David Christopher Andrew, KCMG
Madejski, Sir John Robert, Kt., OBE
Madel, Sir (William) David, Kt.
Magee, Sir Ian Bernard Vaughan, Kt., CB

Magnus, Sir Laurence Henry Philip, Bt. (1917)
Maguire, *Hon.* Sir Paul Richard, Kt.
Mahon, Sir William Walter, Bt. (1819), LVO
Mahoney, Sir Paul John, KCMG
Maiden, Sir Colin James, Kt., DPHIL
Maini, *Prof.* Sir Ravinder Nath, Kt.
Maino, Sir Charles, KBE
†Maitland, Sir Charles Alexander, Bt. (1818)
Major, *Rt. Hon.* Sir John, KG, CH
Malbon, *Vice-Adm.* Sir Fabian Michael, KBE
Malcolm, Sir Alexander James Elton, Bt. (S. 1665), OBE
Malcolm, *Dr* Noel Robert, Kt., FBA
Males, *Rt. Hon.* Sir Stephen Martin, Kt.
Malet, Sir Harry Douglas St Lo, Bt. (1791)
Mallaby, Sir Christopher Leslie George, GCMG, GCVO
Mallick, *Prof.* Sir Netar Prakash, Kt.
Mallinson, Sir William James, Bt. (1935)
Malpas, Sir Robert, Kt., CBE
Mander, Sir (Charles) Nicholas, Bt. (1911)
Mann, *Hon.* Sir George Anthony, Kt.
Mann, Sir Rupert Edward, Bt. (1905)
Manning, Sir David Geoffrey, GCMG, KCVO
Mano, Sir Koitaga, Kt., MBE
Mans, *Lt.-Gen.* Sir Mark Francis Noel, KCB, CBE
Mansel, Sir Philip, Bt. (1622)
Manuella, Sir Tulaga, GCMG, MBE
Mara, Sir Nambuga, KBE
Margetson, Sir John William Denys, KCMG
Margetts, Sir Robert John, Kt., CBE
Markesinis, *Prof.* Sir Basil Spyridonos, Kt., QC
Markham, *Prof.* Sir Alexander Fred, Kt.
Markham, Sir (Arthur) David, Bt. (1911)
Marling, Sir Charles William Somerset, Bt. (1882)
Marmot, *Prof.* Sir Michael Gideon, Kt.
Marr, Sir Leslie Lynn, Bt. (1919)
Marsden, Sir Jonathan Mark, KCVO
†Marsden, Sir Tadgh Orlando Denton, Bt. (1924)
Marshall, Sir Paul, Kt.
Marshall, Sir Peter Harold Reginald, KCMG
Marshall, *Prof. Emeritus* Sir Woodville Kemble, Kt.
Marsters, *HE* Sir Tom John, KBE
Martin, Sir Clive Haydon, Kt., OBE
Martin, Sir Gregory Michael Gerard, Kt.
Martin, *Prof.* Sir Laurence Woodward, Kt.
Masefield, Sir Charles Beech Gordon, Kt.
Mason, *Hon.* Sir Anthony Frank, KBE
Mason, *Prof.* Sir David Kean, Kt., CBE
Mason, Sir Peter James, KBE

Mason, *Prof.* Sir Ronald, KCB, FRS
Massey, *Vice-Adm.* Sir Alan, KCB, CBE, ADC
Matane, HE Sir Paulias Nguna, GCMG, OBE
Matheson of Matheson, Sir Alexander Fergus, Bt. (1882), LVO
Mathews, *Vice-Adm.* Sir Andrew David Hugh, KCB
Mathewson, Sir George Ross, Kt., CBE, PHD, FRSE
Matthews, Sir Terence Hedley, Kt., OBE
Maughan, Sir Deryck, Kt.
Mawer, Sir Philip John Courtney, Kt.
Maxwell, Sir Michael Eustace George, Bt. (S. 1681)
Maxwell Macdonald (formerly Stirling-Maxwell), Sir John Ronald, Bt. (NS 1682)
Maxwell-Scott, Sir Dominic James, Bt. (1642)
May, *Rt. Hon.* Sir Anthony Tristram Kenneth, Kt.
Mayall, *Lt.-Gen.* Sir Simon Vincent, KBE, CB
Mayfield, Sir Andrew Charles, Kt.
Meadow, *Prof.* Sir (Samuel) Roy, Kt., FRCP, FRCPE
Meale, Sir Joseph Alan, Kt.
Medlycott, Sir Mervyn Tregonwell, Bt. (1808)
Meeran, *His Hon.* Sir Goolam Hoosen Kader, Kt.
Meldrum, Sir Graham, Kt., CBE, QFSM
Melhuish, Sir Michael Ramsay, KBE, CMG
Mellars, *Prof.* Sir Paul Anthony, Kt., FBA
Mellon, Sir James, KCMG
Melmoth, Sir Graham John, Kt.
Melville, *Prof.* Sir David, Kt., CBE
Melville-Ross, Sir Timothy David, Kt., CBE
Merifield, Sir Anthony James, KCVO, CB
Messenger, *Gen.* Sir Gordon Kenneth, KCB, DSO, OBE
Metcalf, *Prof.* Sir David Harry, Kt., CBE
†Meyer, Sir (Anthony) Ashley Frank, Bt. (1910)
Meyer, Sir Christopher John Rome, KCMG
†Meyrick, Sir Timothy Thomas Charlton, Bt. (1880)
Miakwe, *Hon.* Sir Akepa, KBE
Michael, Sir Duncan, Kt.
Michael, *Dr* Sir Jonathan, Kt.
Michael, Sir Peter Colin, Kt., CBE
Michels, Sir David Michael Charles, Kt.
Middleton, Sir John Maxwell, Kt.
Middleton, Sir Peter Edward, GCB
Miers, Sir (Henry) David Alastair Capel, KBE, CMG
Milbank, Sir Edward Mark Somerset, Bt. (1882)

Milborne-Swinnerton-Pilkington, Sir Thomas Henry, Bt. (S. 1635)

Milburn, Sir Anthony Rupert, Bt. (1905)

†Miles, Sir Philip John, Bt. (1859)

Millais, Sir Geoffroy Richard Everett, Bt. (1885)

Millar, *Prof.* Sir Fergus Graham Burtholme, Kt.

Miller, Sir Anthony Thomas, Bt. (1705)

Miller, Sir Donald John, Kt., FRSE, FRENG

Miller, *Air Marshal* Sir Graham Anthony, KBE

Miller, Sir Jonathan Wolfe, Kt., CBE

Miller, Sir Robin Robert William, Kt.

Miller, Sir Ronald Andrew Baird, Kt., CBE

Miller of Glenlee, Sir Stephen William Macdonald, Bt. (1788)

Mills, Sir Ian, Kt.

Mills, Sir Jonathan Edward Harland (John), Kt., FRSE

Mills, Sir Keith Edward, GBE

Mills, Sir Peter Frederick Leighton, Bt. (1921)

Milman, Sir David Patrick, Bt. (1800)

Milne-Watson, Sir Andrew Michael, Bt. (1937)

Milner, Sir Timothy William Lycett, Bt. (1717)

Mitchell, *Rt. Hon.* Sir James FitzAllen, KCMG

Mitchell, *Very Revd* Patrick Reynolds, KCVO

Mitchell, *Hon.* Sir Stephen George, Kt.

Mitting, *Hon.* Sir John Edward, Kt.

Moberly, Sir Patrick Hamilton, KCMG

Moir, Sir Christopher Ernest, Bt. (1916)

Molesworth-St Aubyn, Sir William, Bt. (1689)

Molony, Sir John Benjamin, Bt. (1925)

Moncada, *Prof.* Sir Salvador, Kt.

Montagu, Sir Nicholas Lionel John, KCB

Montagu-Pollock, Sir Guy Maximilian, Bt. (1872)

Montague, Sir Adrian Alastair, Kt., CBE

Montgomery, Sir (Basil Henry) David, Bt. (1801), CVO

Montgomery, *Vice-Adm.* Sir Charles Percival Ross, KBE, ADC

Montgomery, *Prof.* Sir James Robert, Kt.

Montgomery-Cuninghame, Sir John Christopher Foggo, Bt. (NS 1672)

Moody-Stuart, Sir Mark, KCMG

Moollan, Sir Abdool Hamid Adam, Kt.

†Moon, Sir Humphrey, Bt. (1887)

Moor, *Hon.* Sir Philip Drury, Kt.

Moorcroft, Sir William, KBE

Moore, *Most Revd* Desmond Charles, KBE

Moore, Sir Francis Thomas, Kt.

Moore, *Vice Adm.* Sir Michael Antony Claës, KBE, LVO

Moore, Sir Peter Alan Cutlack, Bt. (1919)

Moore, Sir Richard William, Bt. (1932)

Moore-Bick, *Rt. Hon.* Sir Martin James, Kt.

Morauta, Sir Mekere, KCMG, PC

Mordaunt, Sir Richard Nigel Charles, Bt. (1611)

Moree, *Hon.* Sir Brian, Kt.

Morgan, *Vice-Adm.* Sir Charles Christopher, KBE

Morgan, *Rt. Hon.* Sir (Charles) Declan, Kt.

Morgan, Sir Graham, Kt.

Morgan, *Hon.* Sir Paul Hyacinth, Kt.

Morgan, Sir Terence Keith, Kt., CBE

Morison, *Hon.* Sir Thomas Richard Atkin, Kt.

Moritz, Sir Michael Jonathan, KBE

Morland, *Hon.* Sir Michael, Kt.

Morland, Sir Robert Kenelm, Kt.

Morpurgo, Sir Michael Andrew Bridge, Kt., OBE

†Morris, Sir Allan Lindsay, Bt. (1806)

Morris, Sir Andrew Valentine, Kt., OBE

Morris, *Air Marshal* Sir Arnold Alec, KBE, CB

Morris, Sir Derek James, Kt.

Morris, Sir Keith Elliot Hedley, KBE, CMG

Morris, *Prof.* Sir Peter John, Kt.

Morris, *Hon.* Sir Stephen Nathan, Kt.

Morris, Sir Trefor Alfred, Kt., CBE, QPM

Morrison, Sir (Alexander) Fraser, Kt., CBE

Morrison, Sir George Ivan, Kt., OBE

Morrison, Sir Howard Andrew Clive, KCMG, CBE

Morrison-Bell, Sir William Hollin Dayrell, Bt. (1905)

Morrison-Low, Sir Richard Walter, Bt. (1908)

Morritt, *Rt. Hon.* Sir (Robert) Andrew, Kt., CVO

Morse, Sir Amyas Charles Edward, KCB

Moses, *Rt. Hon.* Sir Alan George, Kt.

Moses, *Very Revd* Dr John Henry, KCVO

Moss, Sir David Joseph, KCVO, CMG

Moss, Sir Stephen Alan, Kt.

Moss, Sir Stirling Craufurd, Kt., OBE

Mostyn, *Hon.* Sir Nicholas Anthony Joseph Ghislain, Kt.

Mostyn, Sir William Basil John, Bt. (1670)

Motion, Sir Andrew, Kt.

Mott, Sir David Hugh, Bt. (1930)

Mottley, Sir Elliott Deighton, KCMG, QC

Mottram, Sir Richard Clive, GCB

†Mount, Sir (William Robert) Ferdinand, Bt. (1921)

Mountain, Sir Edward Brian Stanford, Bt. (1922)

Mowbray, Sir John Robert, Bt. (1880)

Moylan, *Rt. Hon.* Sir Andrew John Gregory, Kt.

Moynihan, *Dr* Sir Daniel, Kt.

†Muir, Sir Richard James Kay, Bt. (1892)

Muir-Mackenzie, Sir Alexander Alwyne Henry Charles Brinton, Bt. (1805)

Mulcahy, Sir Geoffrey John, Kt.

Mummery, *Rt. Hon.* Sir John Frank, Kt.

Munby, *Rt. Hon.* Sir James Lawrence, Kt.

Munro, Sir Alan Gordon, KCMG

†Munro, Sir Ian Kenneth, Bt. (S. 1634)

Munro, Sir Keith Gordon, Bt. (1825)

Muria, *Hon.* Sir Gilbert John Baptist, Kt.

Murphy, Sir Jonathan Michael, Kt., QPM

Murray, Sir Andrew, Kt., OBE

Murray, Sir David Edward, Kt.

Murray, *Hon.* Sir Edward Henry, Kt

Murray, Sir Nigel Andrew Digby, Bt. (S. 1628)

Murray, Sir Patrick Ian Keith, Bt. (S. 1673)

Murray, Sir Robert Sydney, Kt., CBE

Murray, Sir Robin MacGregor, Kt.

†Murray, Sir Rowland William, Bt. (S. 1630)

Muscatelli, *Prof.* Sir Vito Antonio, Kt., FRSE

Musgrave, Sir Christopher John Shane, Bt. (I. 1782)

Musgrave, Sir Christopher Patrick Charles, Bt. (1611)

Myers, Sir Derek John, Kt.

Myers, *Prof.* Sir Rupert Horace, KBE

Mynors, Sir Richard Baskerville, Bt. (1964)

Nairn, Sir Michael, Bt. (1904)

Nalau, Sir Jerry Kasip, KBE

Nall, Sir Edward William Joseph, Bt. (1954)

Namaliu, *Rt. Hon.* Sir Rabbie Langanai, KCMG

Napier, Sir Charles Joseph, Bt. (1867)

Napier, Sir John Archibald Lennox, Bt. (S. 1627)

Narey, Sir Martin James, Kt.

Natzler, Sir David Lionel, KCB

Naylor, Sir Robert, Kt.

Naylor-Leyland, Sir Philip Vyvian, Bt. (1895)

Neal, Sir Eric James, Kt., CVO

Neave, Sir Paul Arundell, Bt. (1795)

†Nelson, Sir Jamie Charles Vernon Hope, Bt. (1912)

Nelson, *Hon.* Sir Robert Franklyn, Kt.

New, *Maj.-Gen.* Sir Laurence Anthony Wallis, Kt., CB, CBE

Newbigging, Sir David Kennedy, Kt., OBE

Newby, *Prof.* Sir Howard Joseph, Kt., CBE

Newey, *Rt. Hon.* Sir Guy Richard, Kt.

Newman, Sir Francis Hugh Cecil, Bt. (1912)

Newman, Sir Geoffrey Robert, Bt. (1836)

Newman, *Vice-Adm.* Sir Roy Thomas, KCB

Newman Taylor, *Prof.* Sir Anthony John, Kt., CBE

Newsam, Sir Peter Anthony, Kt.

Newson-Smith, Sir Peter Frank Graham, Bt. (1944)

Newton, *Revd* George Peter Howgill, Bt. (1900)

Newton, Sir John Garnar, Bt. (1924)

Newton, *Lt.-Gen.* Sir Paul Raymond, KBE

Newton, *Hon.* Sir Roderick Brian, Kt.

Nice, Sir Geoffrey, Kt., QC

Nichol, Sir Duncan Kirkbride, Kt., CBE

Nicholas, Sir David, Kt., CBE

Nicholson, Sir Bryan Hubert, GBE, Kt.

Nicholson, Sir Charles Christian, Bt. (1912)

Nicholson, Sir David, KCB, CBE

Nicholson, *Rt. Hon.* Sir Michael, Kt.

Nicholson, Sir Paul Douglas, KCVO, Kt.

Nicholson, Sir Robin Buchanan, Kt., PHD, FRS, FRENG

Nickell, *Prof.* Sir Stephen John, Kt., CBE, FBA

Nicklin, *Hon.* Sir Matthew James, Kt.

Nicol, *Hon.* Sir Andrew George Lindsay, Kt.

Nightingale, Sir Charles Manners Gamaliel, Bt. (1628)

†Nixon, Sir Simon Michael Christopher, Bt. (1906)

Noble, Sir David Brunel, Bt. (1902)

Noble, Sir Timothy Peter, Bt. (1923)

Nombri, Sir Joseph Karl, Kt., ISO, BEM

Norgrove, Sir David Ronald, Kt.

Norman, Sir Nigel James, Bt. (1915)

Norman, Sir Ronald, Kt., OBE

Norman, Sir Torquil Patrick Alexander, Kt., CBE

Normington, Sir David John, GCB

Norrington, Sir Roger Arthur Carver, Kt., CBE

Norris, *Hon.* Sir Alastair Hubert, Kt.

Norriss, *Air Marshal* Sir Peter Coulson, KBE, CB, AFC

North, *Air Marshal* Sir Barry Mark, KCB, OBE

North, Sir Jeremy William Francis, Bt. (1920)

North, Sir Peter Machin, Kt., CBE, QC, DCL, FBA

Norton, Sir Barry, Kt.

Norton, *Maj.-Gen.* Sir George Pemberton Ross, KCVO, CBE

Norton-Griffiths, Sir Michael, Bt. (1922)

Nossal, Sir Gustav Joseph Victor, Kt., CBE

Nott, *Rt. Hon.* Sir John William Frederic, KCB

Novoselov, *Prof.* Sir Konstantin, Kt.

Nugee, *Hon.* Sir Christopher George, Kt.

Nugent, Sir Christopher George Ridley, Bt. (1806)

†Nugent, Sir Nicholas Myles John, Bt. (I. 1795)

Nugent, Sir (Walter) Richard Middleton, Bt. (1831)

Nunn, Sir Trevor Robert, Kt., CBE

Nunneley, Sir Charles Kenneth Roylance, Kt.

Nursaw, Sir James, KCB, QC

Nurse, Sir Paul Maxime, Kt.

Nuttall, Sir Harry, Bt. (1922)

Nutting, Sir John Grenfell, Bt. (1903), QC

Oakeley, Sir Robert John Atholl, Bt. (1790)

Oakes, Sir Christopher, Bt. (1939)

Oakshott, Sir Thomas Hendrie, Bt. (1959)

O'Brien, Sir Robert Stephen, Kt., CBE

O'Brien, *Rt. Hon.* Sir Stephen Rothwell, KBE

†O'Brien, Sir Timothy John, Bt. (1849)

O'Brien, Sir William, Kt.

O'Connell, Sir Bernard, Kt.

O'Connell, Sir Maurice James Donagh MacCarthy, Bt. (1869)

O'Connor, Sir Denis Francis, Kt., CBE, QPM

Odell, Sir Stanley John, Kt.

Odgers, Sir Graeme David William, Kt.

O'Donnell, Sir Christopher John, Kt.

O'Donoghue, *Lt.-Gen.* Sir Kevin, KCB, CBE

O'Dowd, Sir David Joseph, Kt., CBE, QPM

Ogden, *Dr* Sir Peter James, Kt.

Ogden, Sir Robert, Kt., CBE

Ogilvy, Sir Francis Gilbert Arthur, Bt. (S. 1626)

Ogilvy-Wedderburn, Sir Andrew John Alexander, Bt. (1803)

Ognall, *Hon.* Sir Harry Henry, Kt.

O'Hara, *Hon.* Sir John Ailbe

Ohlson, Sir Peter Michael, Bt. (1920)

Oldham, *Dr* Sir John, Kt., OBE

Olisa, Sir Kenneth Aphunezi, Kt., OBE

Oliver, Sir Craig Stewart, Kt.

Oliver, Sir James Michael Yorrick, Kt.

Oliver, Sir Stephen John Lindsay, Kt., QC

†O'Loghlen, Sir Michael, Bt. (1838)

O'Lone, Sir Marcus James, KCVO

Olver, Sir Richard Lake, Kt.

Omand, Sir David Bruce, GCB

Ondaatje, Sir Christopher, Kt., CBE

O'Nions, *Prof.* Sir Robert Keith, Kt., FRS, PHD

Onslow, Sir Richard Paul Atherton, Bt. (1797)

Openshaw, *Hon.* Sir Charles Peter Lawford, Kt.

O'Rahilly, *Prof.* Sir Stephen Patrick, Kt., FRS

Ord, Sir David Charles, Kt.

Orde, Sir Hugh Stephen Roden, Kt., OBE, QPM

O'Regan, *Dr* Sir Stephen Gerard (Tipene), Kt.

O'Reilly, Sir Anthony John Francis, Kt.

O'Reilly, *Prof.* Sir John James, Kt.

Orr-Ewing, *Hon.* Sir (Alistair) Simon, Bt. (1963)

Orr-Ewing, Sir Archibald Donald, Bt. (1886)

Osborn, Sir Richard Henry Danvers, Bt. (1662)

Osborne, Sir Peter George, Bt. (I. 1629)

O'Shea, *Prof.* Sir Timothy Michael Martin, Kt.

Osmotherly, Sir Edward Benjamin Crofton, Kt., CB

Oswald, Sir (William Richard) Michael, KCVO

Ottaway, *Rt. Hon.* Sir Richard Geoffrey James, Kt.

Otton, Sir Geoffrey John, KCB

Otton, *Rt. Hon.* Sir Philip Howard, Kt.

Ouseley, *Hon.* Sir Duncan Brian Walter, Kt.

Outram, Sir Alan James, Bt. (1858)

Owen, Sir Geoffrey, Kt.

Owen, *Prof.* Sir Michael John, Kt.

Owen, *Hon.* Sir Robert Michael, Kt.

Owen-Jones, Sir Lindsay Harwood, KBE

P-S

Packer, Sir Richard John, KCB

Paget, Sir Henry James, Bt. (1871)

Paget, Sir Richard Herbert, Bt. (1886)

Paice, *Rt. Hon.* Sir James Edward Thornton, Kt.

Paine, Sir Christopher Hammon, Kt., FRCP, FRCR

Pakenham, *Hon.* Sir Michael Aiden, KBE, CMG

Palin, Sir Michael Edward, KCMG, CBE

Palin, *Air Chief Marshal* Sir Roger Hewlett, KCB, OBE

Palmer, Sir Albert Rocky, Kt.

Palmer, Sir (Charles) Mark, Bt. (1886)

Palmer, Sir Geoffrey Christopher John, Bt. (1660)

Palmer, *Rt. Hon.* Sir Geoffrey Winston Russell, KCMG

Palmer, *Prof.* Sir Godfrey Henry Oliver, Kt, OBE

†Palmer, Sir Robert John Hudson, Bt. (1791)

Panter, Sir Howard Hugh, Kt.

Pappano, Sir Antonio, Kt.

Parbo, Sir Arvi Hillar, Kt.

Park, *Hon.* Sir Andrew Edward Wilson, Kt.

Parker, Sir Alan, Kt.

Parker, Sir Alan William, Kt., CBE

Parker, Sir Andrew David, KCB

Parker, *Rt. Hon.* Sir Jonathan Frederic, Kt.

Parker, *Hon.* Sir Kenneth Blades, Kt.

Parker, *Maj.* Sir Michael John, KCVO, CBE

Parker, *Gen.* Sir Nicholas Ralph, KCB, CBE

Parker, Sir Richard (William) Hyde, Bt. (1681)

Parker, Sir (Thomas) John, GBE

Parker, Sir William Peter Brian, Bt. (1844)

Parkes, Sir Edward Walter, Kt., FRENG

Parkinson, Sir Michael, Kt., CBE

Parmley, *Dr* Sir Andrew Charles, Kt.

Parry, *Prof.* Sir Eldryd Hugh Owen, KCMG, OBE

Parry, Sir Emyr Jones, GCMG

Parry-Evans, *Air Chief Marshal* Sir David, GCB, CBE

Parsons, Sir John Christopher, KCVO

Partridge, Sir Michael John Anthony, KCB

Partridge, Sir Nicholas Wyndham, Kt., OBE

Pascoe, *Gen.* Sir Robert Alan, KCB, MBE

Pasley, Sir Robert Killigrew Sabine, Bt. (1794)

Paston-Bedingfeld, Sir Henry Edgar, Bt. (1661)

Patey, Sir William Charters, KCMG

Patten, *Rt. Hon.* Sir Nicholas John, Kt.

Pattie, *Rt. Hon.* Sir Geoffrey Edwin, Kt.

Pattison, *Prof.* Sir John Ridley, Kt., DM, FRCPATH

Pattullo, Sir (David) Bruce, Kt., CBE

Pauncefort-Duncombe, Sir David Philip Henry, Bt. (1859)

Payne, *Prof.* Sir David Neil, Kt., CBE, FRS

Peace, Sir John Wilfrid, Kt.

Peach, *Air Chief Marshal* Sir Stuart William, GBE, KCB, ADC

Pearce, Sir (Daniel Norton) Idris, Kt., CBE, TD

Pears, Sir Trevor Stephen, Kt., CMG

Pearse, Sir Brian Gerald, Kt.

Pearson, Sir David Lee, Kt., CBE

Pearson, Sir Francis Nicholas Fraser, Bt. (1964)

Pearson, Sir Keith, Kt.

Pearson, *Gen.* Sir Thomas Cecil Hook, KCB, CBE, DSO

Pease, Sir Joseph Gurney, Bt. (1882)

Pease, Sir Richard Thorn, Bt. (1920)

Peat, Sir Gerrard Charles, KCVO

Peat, Sir Michael Charles Gerrard, GCVO

Peckham, *Prof.* Sir Michael John, Kt.,

Peek, Sir Richard Grenville, Bt. (1874)

Pelgen, Sir Harry Friedrich, Kt., MBE

Pelham, *Dr* Sir Hugh Reginald Brentnall, Kt., FRS

Pelly, Sir Richard John, Bt. (1840)

Pendry, *Prof.* Sir John Brian, Kt., FRS

Penning, *Rt. Hon.* Sir Michael Allan, Kt.

Penny, *Dr* Nicholas Beaver, Kt., FBA

Penrose, *Prof.* Sir Roger, Kt., OM, FRS

Pepper, *Dr* Sir David Edwin, KCMG

Pepper, *Prof.* Sir Michael, Kt.

Pepperall, *Hon.* Sir Edward Brian, Kt

Pepys, *Prof.* Sir Mark Brian, Kt.

Perowne, *Vice-Adm.* Sir James Francis, KBE

†Perring, Sir John Simon Pelham, Bt. (1963)

Perris, Sir David (Arthur), Kt., MBE

Perry, Sir David Howard, KCB

Perry, Sir Michael Sydney, GBE

Pervez, Sir Mohammed Anwar, Kt., OBE

Petchey, Sir Jack, Kt., CBE

Peters, *Prof.* Sir (David) Keith, GBE, FRCP

Pethica, *Prof.* Sir John Bernard, Kt., FRS

Petit, Sir Dinshaw Manockjee, Bt. (1890)

Peto, Sir Francis Michael Morton, Bt. (1855)

Peto, Sir Henry Christopher Morton Bampfylde, Bt. (1927)

Peto, *Prof.* Sir Richard, Kt., FRS

Petrie, Sir Peter Charles, Bt. (1918), CMG

†Philipson-Stow, Sir (Robert) Matthew, Bt. (1907)

Phillips, Sir (Gerald) Hayden, GCB

Phillips, Sir John David, Kt., QPM

Phillips, Sir Jonathan, KCB

Phillips, Sir Peter John, Kt., OBE

Phillips, Sir Robin Francis, Bt. (1912)

Phillips, *Hon.* Sir Stephen Edmund, Kt.

Phillips, Sir Tom Richard Vaughan, KCMG

Pickard, Sir (John) Michael, Kt.

Picken, *Hon.* Sir Simon Derek, Kt.

Pickthorn, Sir James Francis Mann, Bt. (1959)

†Piers, Sir James Desmond, Bt. (I. 1661)

Pigot, Sir George Hugh, Bt. (1764)

Pigott, *Lt.-Gen.* Sir Anthony David, KCB, CBE

†Pigott, Sir David John Berkeley, Bt. (1808)

Pike, *Lt.-Gen.* Sir Hew William Royston, KCB, DSO, MBE

Pike, Sir Michael Edmund, KCVO, CMG

Pilditch, Sir John Richard, Bt. (1929)

Pile, Sir Anthony John Devereux, Bt. (1900), MBE

Pill, *Rt. Hon.* Sir Malcolm Thomas, Kt.

Pilling, Sir Joseph Grant, KCB

Pinsent, Sir Matthew Clive, Kt., CBE

Pinsent, Sir Thomas Benjamin Roy, Bt. (1938)

Pirmohamed, *Prof.* Sir Hussein Munir, Kt.

Pissarides, *Prof.* Sir Christopher Antoniou, Kt., FBA

Pitcher, Sir Desmond Henry, Kt.

Pitchers, *Hon.* Sir Christopher (John), Kt.

Pitoi, Sir Sere, Kt., CBE

Pitt, Sir Michael Edward, Kt.

Platt, Sir Martin Philip, Bt. (1959)

Pledger, *Air Chief Marshal* Sir Malcolm David, KCB, OBE, AFC

Plender, *Hon.* Sir Richard Owen, Kt.

Plumbly, Sir Derek John, KCMG

Pocock, *Dr* Sir Andrew John, KCMG

Poffley, *Lt.-Gen.* Sir Mark William, KCB, OBE

Poh, Sir Sang Chung, Kt., MBE

Pohai, Sir Timothy, Kt., MBE

Pole, Sir John Chandos, Bt. (1791)

Pole, Sir (John) Richard (Walter Reginald) Carew, Bt. (1628), OBE

Poliakoff, *Prof.* Sir Martyn, Kt., CBE

Polkinghorne, *Revd Canon* John Charlton, KBE

Pollard, Sir Charles, Kt.

†Pollen, Sir Richard John Hungerford, Bt. (1795)

Pollock, Sir David Frederick, Bt. (1866)

Pomeroy, Sir Brian Walter, Kt., CBE

Ponder, *Prof.* Sir Bruce Anthony John, Kt.

Ponsonby, Sir Charles Ashley, Bt. (1956)

Poon, Sir Dickson, Kt., CBE

†Poore, Sir Roger Ricardo, Bt. (1795)

Pope, *Lt.-Gen.* Sir Nicholas Arthur William, KCB, CBE

Popplewell, *Hon.* Sir Andrew John, Kt.

Popplewell, *Hon.* Sir Oliver Bury, Kt.

Porritt, *Hon.* Sir Jonathon Espie, Bt. (1963), CBE

Portal, Sir Jonathan Francis, Bt. (1901)

Porter, *Prof.* Sir Keith Macdonald, Kt.

Potter, *Rt. Hon.* Sir Mark Howard, Kt.

Pound, Sir John David, Bt. (1905)

Pountney, Sir David Willoughby, Kt., CBE

Povey, Sir Keith, Kt., QPM

Powell, Sir Ian Clifford, Kt.

†Powell, Sir James Richard Douglas, Bt. (1897)

Powell, Sir John Christopher, Kt.

Power, Sir Alastair John Cecil, Bt. (1924)

Pownall, Sir Michael Graham, KCB

Poya, Sir Nathaniel, Kt.

Prance, *Prof.* Sir Ghillean Tolmie, Kt., FRS

Prendergast, Sir (Walter) Kieran, KCVO, CMG

Prescott, Sir Mark, Bt. (1938)

Preston, *Prof.* Sir Paul, Kt., CBE

Preston, Sir Philip Charles Henry Hulton, Bt. (1815)

Prevost, Sir Christopher Gerald, Bt. (1805)

Price, Sir Francis Caradoc Rose, Bt. (1815)

Price, Sir Frank Leslie, Kt.

†Prichard-Jones, Sir David John Walter, Bt. (1910)

†Primrose, Sir John Ure, Bt. (1903)

Pringle, *Hon.* Sir John Kenneth, Kt.

Pringle, Sir Norman Murray Archibald Macgregor, Bt. (S. 1683)

Proby, Sir William Henry, Bt. (1952), CBE

Proctor-Beauchamp, Sir Christopher Radstock, Bt. (1745)

Prosser, Sir David John, Kt.

Prosser, Sir Ian Maurice Gray, Kt.

Pryke, Sir Christopher Dudley, Bt. (1926)

Puapua, *Rt. Hon.* Sir Tomasi, GCMG, KBE

Pulford, *Air Chief Marshal* Sir Andrew Douglas, GCB, CBE, ADC

Pullman, Sir Philip Nicholas Outram, Kt., CBE

Purves, Sir William, Kt., CBE, DSO

Purvis, *Vice-Adm.* Sir Neville, KCB

Quan, Sir Henry (Francis), KBE

Quilter, Sir Guy Raymond Cuthbert, Bt. (1897)

Radcliffe, Sir Sebastian Everard, Bt. (1813)

Radda, *Prof.* Sir George Karoly, Kt., CBE, FRS

Rae, Sir William, Kt., QPM

Raeburn, Sir Michael Edward Norman, Bt. (1923)

Rake, Sir Michael Derek Vaughan, Kt.

Ralli, Sir David Charles, Bt. (1912)

Ramakrishnan, *Dr* Sir Venkatraman, Kt.

Ramdanee, Sir Mookteswar Baboolall Kailash, Kt.

Ramphal, Sir Shridath Surendranath, GCMG

Ramphul, Sir Baalkhristna, Kt.

Ramphul, Sir Indurduth, Kt.

Ramsay, Sir Alexander William Burnett, Bt. (1806)

Ramsay, Sir Allan John (Hepple), KBE, CMG

†Ramsay-Fairfax-Lucy, Sir Patrick Samuel Thomas Fulke, Bt. (1836)

Ramsden, Sir David Edward John, Kt., CBE

Ramsden, Sir John Charles Josslyn, Bt. (1689)

Ramsey, *Dr* Sir Frank Cuthbert, KCMG

Ramsey, *Hon.* Sir Vivian Arthur, Kt.

Rankin, Sir Ian Niall, Bt. (1898)

Rasch, Sir Simon Anthony Carne, Bt. (1903)

Rashleigh, Sir Richard Harry, Bt. (1831)

Ratcliffe, Sir James Arthur, Kt.

Ratcliffe, *Prof.* Sir Peter John, Kt., FRS

Ratford, Sir David John Edward, KCMG, CVO

Rattee, *Hon.* Sir Donald Keith, Kt.

Rattle, Sir Simon Dennis, Kt., OM, CBE

Rawlins, *Hon.* Sir Hugh Anthony, Kt.

Rawlins, *Prof.* Sir Michael David, GBE, FRCP, FRCPED

Rawlinson, Sir Anthony Henry John, Bt. (1891)

Rea, *Prof.* Sir Desmond, Kt., OBE

Read, *Prof.* Sir David John, Kt.

Reardon-Smith, Sir (William) Antony (John), Bt. (1920)

Reddaway, Sir David Norman, KCMG, MBE

Redgrave, Sir Steven Geoffrey, Kt., CBE

Redmayne, Sir Giles Martin, Bt. (1964)

Redmond, Sir Anthony Gerard, Kt.

Redwood, *Rt. Hon.* Sir John Alan, Kt.

Redwood, Sir Peter Boverton, Bt. (1911)

Reed, *Prof.* Sir Alec Edward, Kt., CBE

Reedie, Sir Craig Collins, GBE

Rees, Sir David Allan, Kt., PHD, DSC, FRS

Rees, Sir Richard Ellis Meuric, Kt., CBE

Reffell, *Adm.* Sir Derek Roy, KCB

Reich, Sir Erich Arieh, Kt.

Reid, Sir Charles Edward James, Bt. (1897)

Reid, Sir David Edward, Kt.

Reid, *Rt. Hon.* Sir George, Kt.

Reid, Sir (Philip) Alan, GCVO

Reid, Sir Robert Paul, Kt.

Reid, Sir William Kennedy, KCB

Reiher, Sir Frederick Bernard Carl, KCMG, KBE

Renals, Sir Stanley Michael, Bt. (1895)

Renouf, Sir Clement William Bailey, Kt.

Renshaw, Sir John David Bine, Bt. (1903)

Renwick, Sir Richard Eustace, Bt. (1921)

Reynolds, Sir James Francis, Bt. (1923)

Reynolds, Sir Peter William John, Kt., CBE

Rhodes, Sir John Christopher Douglas, Bt. (1919)

Ribat, *Most Revd* John, KBE

Rice, *Prof.* Sir Charles Duncan, Kt.

Rice, *Maj.-Gen.* Sir Desmond Hind Garrett, KCVO, CBE

Rice, Sir Timothy Miles Bindon, Kt.

Richard, Sir Cliff, Kt., OBE

Richards, Sir Brian Mansel, Kt., CBE, PHD

Richards, *Rt. Hon.* Sir David Anthony Stewart, Kt.

Richards, Sir David Gerald, Kt.

Richards, Sir Francis Neville, KCMG, CVO

Richards, *Prof.* Sir Michael Adrian, Kt., CBE

Richards, *Rt. Hon.* Sir Stephen Price, Kt.

Richardson, Sir Anthony Lewis, Bt. (1924)

Richardson, Sir Thomas Legh, KCMG

Richardson-Bunbury, Sir Thomas William, Bt. (I. 1787)

Richmond, Sir David Frank, KBE, CMG

Richmond, *Prof.* Sir Mark Henry, Kt., FRS

Ricketts, Sir Stephen Tristram, Bt. (1828)

Ricks, *Prof.* Sir Christopher Bruce, Kt.

Riddell, Sir Walter John Buchanan, Bt. (S. 1628)

Ridgway, *Lt.-Gen.* Sir Andrew Peter, KBE, CB

Ridley, Sir Adam (Nicholas), Kt.

Ridley, Sir Michael Kershaw, KCVO

Rifkind, *Rt. Hon.* Sir Malcolm Leslie, KCMG

Rigby, Sir Anthony John, Bt. (1929)

Rigby, Sir Peter, Kt.

Rimer, *Rt. Hon.* Sir Colin Percy Farquharson, Kt.

Ripley, Sir William Hugh, Bt. (1880)

Ritako, Sir Thomas Baha, Kt., MBE

Ritblat, Sir John Henry, Kt.

Ritchie, *Prof.* Sir Lewis Duthie, Kt., OBE

Rivett-Carnac, Sir Jonathan James, Bt. (1836)

Rix, *Rt. Hon.* Sir Bernard Anthony, Kt.

Robb, Sir John Weddell, Kt.

Robbins, Sir Oliver, KCMG, CB

Roberts, Sir Derek Harry, Kt., CBE, FRS, FRENG

Roberts, *Prof.* Sir Edward Adam, KCMG

Roberts, Sir Gilbert Howland Rookehurst, Bt. (1809)

Roberts, Sir Hugh Ashley, GCVO

Roberts, Sir Ivor Anthony, KCMG

†Roberts, Sir James Elton Denby Buchanan, Bt. (1909)

Roberts, *Dr* Sir Richard John, Kt.

Roberts, Sir Samuel, Bt. (1919)

Roberts, *Maj.-Gen.* Sir Sebastian John Lechmere, KCVO, OBE

Robertson, *Rt. Hon.* Sir Hugh Michael, KCMG

Robertson, Sir Simon Manwaring, Kt.

Robey, Sir Simon Christopher Townsend, Kt.

Robins, Sir Ralph Harry, Kt., FRENG

Robinson, Sir Anthony, Kt.

Robinson, Sir Bruce, KCB

†Robinson, Sir Christopher Philipse, Bt. (1854)

Robinson, Sir Gerrard Jude, Kt.

Robinson, Sir Ian, Kt.

Robinson, Sir John James Michael Laud, Bt. (1660)

Robinson, *Dr* Sir Kenneth, Kt.

Robinson, Sir Peter Frank, Bt. (1908)

Robson, Sir Stephen Arthur, Kt., CB

Roch, *Rt. Hon.* Sir John Ormond, Kt.

Roche, Sir David O'Grady, Bt. (1838)

Roche, Sir Henry John, Kt.

Rodgers, Sir (Andrew) Piers (Wingate Aikin-Sneath), Bt. (1964)

Rogers, *Air Chief Marshal* Sir John Robson, KCB, CBE

Rogers, Sir Mark Ivan, KCMG

Rogers, Sir Peter, Kt.

Rollo, *Lt.-Gen.* Sir William Raoul, KCB, CBE

†Ropner, Sir Henry John William, Bt. (1952)

Ropner, Sir Robert Clinton, Bt. (1904)

Rose, Sir Arthur James, Kt., CBE

Rose, *Rt. Hon.* Sir Christopher Dudley Roger, Kt.

†Rose, Sir David Lancaster, Bt. (1874)

Rose, *Gen.* Sir (Hugh) Michael, KCB, CBE, DSO, QGM

Rose, Sir John Edward Victor, Kt.

Rose, Sir Julian Day, Bt. (1872 and 1909)

Rosenthal, Sir Norman Leon, Kt.

Ross, *Maj.* Sir Andrew Charles Paterson, Bt. (1960)

Ross, *Lt.-Gen.* Sir Robert Jeremy, KCB, OBE

Ross, *Lt.-Col.* Sir Walter Hugh Malcolm, GCVO, OBE

Ross, Sir Walter Robert Alexander, KCVO

Rossi, Sir Hugh Alexis Louis, Kt.

Roth, *Hon.* Sir Peter Marcel, Kt.

Rothschild, Sir Evelyn Robert Adrian de, Kt.

Rowe, *Rear-Adm.* Sir Patrick Barton, KCVO, CBE

Rowe-Ham, Sir David Kenneth, GBE

Rowland, Sir Geoffrey Robert, Kt.

Rowley, Sir Mark Peter, Kt., QPM

Rowley, Sir Richard Charles, Bt. (1786 and 1836)

Rowling, Sir John Reginald, Kt.

Royce, *Hon.* Sir Roger John, Kt.

Royden, Sir John Michael Joseph, Bt. (1905)

Rubin, *Prof.* Sir Peter Charles, Kt.

Rudd, Sir (Anthony) Nigel (Russell), Kt.

Ruddock, Sir Paul, Kt.

Rudge, Sir Alan Walter, Kt., CBE, FRS

†Rugge-Price, Sir James Keith Peter, Bt. (1804)

Ruggles-Brise, Sir Timothy Edward, Bt. (1935)

Rumbold, Sir Henry John Sebastian, Bt. (1779)

Rushdie, Sir (Ahmed) Salman, Kt.

Russell, Sir Charles Dominic, Bt. (1916)

Russell, Sir George, Kt., CBE

Russell, Sir Muir, KCB

Russell, Sir Robert, Kt.

†Russell, Sir Stephen (Steve) Charles, Bt. (1812)

Russell Beale, Sir Simon, Kt., CBE

Rutnam, Sir Philip McDougall, KCB

Rutter, *Prof.* Sir Michael Llewellyn, Kt., CBE, MD, FRS

Ryan, Sir Derek Gerald, Bt. (1919)

Rycroft, Sir Richard John, Bt. (1784)

Ryder, *Rt. Hon.* Sir Ernest Nigel, Kt., TD

Sacranie, Sir Iqbal Abdul Karim Mussa, Kt., OBE

Saini, *Hon.* Sir Pushpinder Singh, Kt.

Sainsbury, *Rt. Hon.* Sir Timothy Alan Davan, Kt.

St Clair-Ford, Sir William Sam, Bt. (1793)

St George, Sir John Avenel Bligh, Bt. (I. 1766)

St John, Sir Walter, KCMG, OBE

St John-Mildmay, Sir Walter John Hugh, Bt. (1772)

St Paul, Sir Lyle Kevin, KCMG

Sainty, Sir John Christopher, KCB

Sakora, *Hon.* Sir Bernard Berekia, KBE

Sales, *Rt. Hon.* Sir Philip James, Kt.

Salika, Sir Gibuna Gibbs, KBE

Salisbury, Sir Robert William, Kt.

Salt, Sir Patrick MacDonnell, Bt. (1869)

Salt, Sir (Thomas) Michael John, Bt. (1899)

Salusbury-Trelawny, Sir John William Richard, Bt. (1628)

Salz, Sir Anthony Michael Vaughan, Kt.

Samani, *Prof.* Sir Nilesh Jayantilal, Kt.

Sampson, Sir Colin, Kt., CBE, QPM

Samuel, Sir John Michael Glen, Bt. (1898)

Samuelson, Sir James Francis, Bt. (1884)

Samuelson, Sir Sydney Wylie, Kt., CBE

Samworth, Sir David Chetwode, Kt., CBE

Sanders, Sir Ronald Michael, KCMG

Sanderson, Sir Frank Linton, Bt. (1920), OBE

Sands, Sir Roger Blakemore, KCB

Sants, Sir Hector William Hepburn, Kt.

Sargent, Sir William Desmond, Kt., CBE

Satchwell, Sir Kevin Joseph, Kt.

Saumarez Smith, *Dr* Sir Charles, Kt., CBE, FBA

Saunders, Sir Bruce Joshua, KBE

Saunders, *Hon.* Sir John Henry Boulton, Kt.

Savill, *Prof.* Sir John Stewart, Kt.

Savory, Sir Michael Berry, Kt.

Sawers, Sir Robert John, GCMG

Saxby, *Prof.* Sir Robin Keith, Kt.

Scarlett, Sir John McLeod, KCMG, OBE

Schama, *Prof.* Sir Simon, Kt., CBE, FBA

Schiemann, *Rt. Hon.* Sir Konrad Hermann Theodor, Kt.

Schiff, Sir András, Kt.

Scholar, Sir Michael Charles, KCB

Scholar, Sir Thomas Whinfield, KCB

Scholey, Sir David Gerald, Kt., CBE

Scipio, Sir Hudson Rupert, Kt.

Scott, Sir Christopher James Anderson, Bt. (1909)

Scott, Sir David Richard Alexander, Kt., CBE

Scott, *Prof.* Sir George Peter, Kt.

Scott, Sir Henry Douglas Edward, Bt. (1913)

Scott, Sir James Jervoise, Bt. (1962)

Scott, Sir John Hamilton, KCVO

Scott, Sir Ridley, Kt.

Scott, Sir Robert David Hillyer, Kt.

Scott, Sir Walter John, Bt. (1907)

Scott-Lee, Sir Paul Joseph, Kt., QPM

Scruton, *Prof.* Sir Roger Vernon, Kt.

Seale, Sir Clarence David, Kt.

Seale, Sir John Robert Charters, Bt. (1838)

Sealy, Sir Austin Llewellyn, Kt.

Seaton, HE Sir Samuel Weymouth Tapley, GCMG, CVO

†Sebright, Sir Rufus Hugo Giles, Bt. (1626)

Sedley, *Rt. Hon.* Sir Stephen John, Kt.

Sedwill, Sir Mark, KCMG

†Seely, Sir William Victor Conway, Bt. (1896)

Seeto, Sir Ling James, Kt., MBE

Seeyave, Sir Rene Sow Choung, Kt., CBE

Seldon, *Dr* Sir Anthony Francis, Kt.

Semple, Sir John Laughlin, KCB

Sergeant, Sir Patrick, Kt.

Serota, *Hon.* Sir Nicholas Andrew, Kt., CH

Setchell, Sir Marcus Edward, KCVO

†Seton, Sir Charles Wallace, Bt. (S. 1683)

Seton, Sir Iain Bruce, Bt. (S. 1663)

Seymour, Sir Julian Roger, Kt., CBE

Shadbolt, *Prof.* Sir Nigel Richard, Kt.

Shakerley, Sir Nicholas Simon Adam, Bt. (1838)

Shakespeare, Sir Thomas William, Bt. (1942)

Sharp, Sir Adrian, Bt. (1922)

Sharp, Sir Fabian Alexander Sebastian, Bt. (1920)

Sharp, Sir Leslie, Kt., QPM

Sharples, Sir James, Kt., QPM

Shaw, Sir Charles De Vere, Bt. (1821)

Shaw, *Prof.* Sir John Calman, Kt., CBE

Shaw, Sir Neil McGowan, Kt.

Shaw-Stewart, Sir Ludovic Houston, Bt. (S. 1667)

Shebbeare, Sir Thomas Andrew, KCVO

Sheffield, Sir Reginald Adrian Berkeley, Bt. (1755)

Sheil, *Rt. Hon.* Sir John, Kt.

Sheinwald, Sir Nigel Elton, GCMG

Sheleg, Sir Ehud, Kt.

Shelley, Sir John Richard, Bt. (1611)

Shepherd, Sir Colin Ryley, Kt.

Shepherd, Sir John Alan, KCVO, CMG

Shepherd, Sir Richard Charles Scrimgeour, Kt.

Sher, Sir Antony, KBE

Sherlock, Sir Nigel, KCVO, OBE

Sherston-Baker, Sir Robert George Humphrey, Bt. (1796)

†Shiffner, Sir Michael Goerge Edward, Bt. (1818)

Shinwell, Sir (Maurice) Adrian, Kt.

Shirreff, *Gen.* Sir Alexander Richard David, KCB, CBE

Shortridge, Sir Jon Deacon, KCB

Shuckburgh, Sir James Rupert Charles, Bt. (1660)

Siedentop, *Dr* Sir Larry Alan, Kt., CBE

Silber, *Rt. Hon.* Sir Stephen Robert, Kt.

Silk, Sir Evan Paul, KCB

Silverman, *Prof.* Sir Bernard Walter, Kt.

†Simeon, Sir Stephen George Barrington, Bt. (1815)

Simmonds, *Rt. Hon. Dr* Sir Kennedy Alphonse, KCMG

Simmons, *Air Marshal* Sir Michael George, KCB, AFC

Simms, Sir Neville Ian, Kt., FRENG

Simon, *Rt. Hon.* Sir Peregrine Charles Hugh, Kt.

Simonet, Sir Louis Marcel Pierre, Kt., CBE

Simpson, Sir Peter Austin, Kt., OBE

Simpson, *Dr* Sir Peter Jeffery, Kt.

Sims, Sir Roger Edward, Kt.

Sinclair, Sir Clive Marles, Kt.

Sinclair, Sir Robert John, Kt.

Sinclair, Sir William Robert Francis, Bt. (S. 1704)

Sinclair-Lockhart, Sir Simon John Edward Francis, Bt. (S. 1636)

Singh, Sir Pritpal, Kt.

Singh, *Rt. Hon.* Sir Rabinder, Kt.

Singleton, Sir Roger, Kt., CBE

Sitwell, Sir George Reresby Sacheverell, Bt. (1808)

Skeggs, Sir Clifford George, Kt.

Skehel, Sir John James, Kt., FRS

Skinner, Sir (Thomas) Keith (Hewitt), Bt. (1912)

Skipwith, Sir Alexander Sebastian Grey d'Estoteville, Bt. (1622)

Slade, *Rt. Hon.* Sir Christopher John, Kt.

Slade, Sir Julian Benjamin Alfred, Bt. (1831)

Slater, *Adm.* Sir John (Jock) Cunningham Kirkwood, GCB, LVO

Sleight, Sir Richard, Bt. (1920)

Sloman, Sir David Morgan, Kt.

Smiley, *Lt.-Col.* Sir John Philip, Bt. (1903)

Smith, *Prof.* Sir Adrian Frederick Melhuish, Kt., FRS

Smith, *Hon.* Sir Andrew Charles, Kt.

Smith, Sir Andrew Thomas, Bt. (1897)

Smith, Sir Cornelius Alvin, GCMG

Smith, Sir David Iser, KCVO

Smith, *Prof.* Sir Eric Brian, Kt., PHD

Smith, *Prof.* Sir James Cuthbert, Kt., FRS

Smith, Sir John Alfred, Kt., QPM

Smith, Sir Joseph William Grenville, Kt.

Smith, Sir Kevin, Kt., CBE

Smith, *Hon.* Sir Marcus Alexander, Kt.

Smith, Sir Martin Gregory, Kt.

Smith, Sir Michael John Llewellyn, KCVO, CMG

Smith, Sir (Norman) Brian, Kt., CBE, PHD

Smith, Sir Paul Brierley, Kt., CBE

Smith, *Hon.* Sir Peter Winston, Kt.

Smith, Sir Robert Courtney, Kt., CBE

Smith, Sir Robert Hill, Bt. (1945)

Smith, *Gen.* Sir Rupert Anthony, KCB, DSO, OBE, QGM

Smith, Sir Steven Murray, Kt.

Smith-Dodsworth, Sir David John, Bt. (1784)

Smith-Gordon, Sir (Lionel) Eldred (Peter), Bt. (1838)

Smith-Marriott, Sir Peter Francis, Bt. (1774)

Smurfit, *Dr* Sir Michael William Joseph, KBE

Smyth, Sir Timothy John, Bt. (1956)

Smyth-Osbourne, *Lt.-Gen.* Sir Edward Alexander, KCVO, CBE

Snowden, *Prof.* Sir Christopher Maxwell, Kt.

Snowden, *Hon.* Sir Richard Andrew, Kt.

Snyder, Sir Michael John, Kt.

Soames, *Rt. Hon.* Sir (Arthur) Nicholas Winston, Kt.

Soar, *Adm.* Sir Trevor Alan, KCB, OBE

Sobers, Sir Garfield St Auburn, Kt.

Solomon, Sir Harry, Kt.

Somare, *Rt. Hon.* Sir Michael Thomas, GCMG, CH

Songo, Sir Bernard Paul, Kt., CMG, OBE

Soole, *Hon.* Sir Michael Alexander, Kt.

Sorabji, *Prof.* Sir Richard Rustom Kharsedji, Kt., CBE

Sorrell, Sir John William, Kt., CBE

Sorrell, Sir Martin Stuart, Kt.

Sosa, Sir Manuel, Kt.

Soulsby, Sir Peter Alfred, Kt.

Souter, Sir Brian, Kt.

Southby, Sir John Richard Bilbe, Bt. (1937)

Southern, *Prof.* Sir Edwin Mellor, Kt.

Southgate, Sir Colin Grieve, Kt.

Southgate, Sir William David, Kt.

Southward, *Dr* Sir Nigel Ralph, KCVO

Sparks, *Prof.* Sir Robert Stephen John, Kt., CBE

Sparrow, Sir John, Kt.

Spearman, Sir Alexander Young Richard Mainwaring, Bt. (1840)

Spencer, Sir Derek Harold, Kt., QC

Spencer, *Hon.* Sir Martin Benedict, Kt.

Spencer, *Vice-Adm.* Sir Peter, KCB

Spencer, *Hon.* Sir Robin Godfrey, Kt.

Spencer-Nairn, Sir Robert Arnold, Bt. (1933)

Spicer, Sir Nicholas Adrian Albert, Bt. (1906)

Spiegelhalter, *Prof.* Sir David John, Kt., OBE, FRS

Spiers, Sir Donald Maurice, Kt., CB, TD

Spring, Sir Dryden Thomas, Kt.

Spurling, Sir John Damian, KCVO, OBE

Stacey, *Air Marshal* Sir Graham Edward, KBE, CB

Stadlen, *Hon.* Sir Nicholas Felix, Kt.

Stagg, Sir Charles Richard Vernon, KCMG

Staite, Sir Richard John, Kt., OBE

Stamer, Sir Peter Tomlinson, Bt. (1809)

Stanhope, *Adm.* Sir Mark, GCB, OBE, ADC

Stanier, Sir Beville Douglas, Bt. (1917)

Stanley, *Rt. Hon.* Sir John Paul, Kt.

Starkey, Sir John Philip, Bt. (1935)

Starkey, Sir Richard, Kt., MBE

Starmer, *Rt. Hon.* Sir Keir, KCB, QC

Stear, *Air Chief Marshal* Sir Michael James Douglas, KCB, CBE

Steel, *Vice-Adm.* Sir David George, KBE

Steel, *Hon.* Sir David William, Kt.

Steer, Sir Alan William, Kt.

Stephens, Sir (Edwin) Barrie, Kt.

Stephens, Sir Jonathan Andrew de Sievrac, KCB

Stephens, *Rt. Hon.* Sir (William) Benjamin Synge, Kt.

†Stephenson, Sir Henry Upton, Bt. (1936)

Stephenson, Sir Paul Robert, Kt., QPM

Stephenson, *Prof.* Sir Terence John, Kt.

Sterling, Sir Michael John Howard, Kt.

Stevens, Sir Michael John, KCVO

Stevenson, Sir Hugh Alexander, Kt.

Stewart, Sir Alan d'Arcy, Bt. (I. 1623)

Stewart, Sir Alastair Robin, Bt. (1960)

Stewart, Sir Brian John, Kt., CBE

Stewart, Sir David James Henderson, Bt. (1957)

Stewart, Sir David John Christopher, Bt. (1803)

Stewart, Sir James Moray, KCB

Stewart, Sir (John) Simon (Watson), Bt. (1920)

Stewart, Sir John Young, Kt., OBE

Stewart, Sir Patrick, Kt., OBE

Stewart, *Lt.-Col.* Sir Robert Christie, KCVO, CBE, TD

Stewart, Sir Roderick David, Kt., CBE

Stewart, *Hon.* Sir Stephen Paul, Kt.

Stewart, *Prof.* Sir William Duncan Paterson, Kt., FRS, FRSE

Stewart-Clark, Sir John, Bt. (1918)

Stewart-Richardson, Sir Simon Alaisdair Ian Neile, Bt. (S. 1630)

Stheeman, Sir Robert Alexander Talma, Kt., CB

Stilgoe, Sir Richard Henry Simpson, Kt., OBE

Stirling, Sir Angus Duncan Aeneas, Kt.

Stirling of Garden, *Col.* Sir James, KCVO, CBE, TD

Stirling-Hamilton, Sir Malcolm William Bruce, Bt. (S. 1673)

Stockdale, Sir Thomas Minshull, Bt. (1960)

Stoddart, *Prof.* Sir James Fraser, Kt.

Stoller, Sir Norman Kelvin, Kt., CBE

Stone, Sir Christopher, Kt.

Stone, Sir Roy Alexander, Kt., CBE

Stonhouse, *Revd* Michael Philip, Bt. (1628 and 1670)

Stonor, *Air Marshal* Sir Thomas Henry, KCB

Stoppard, Sir Thomas, Kt., OM, CBE

Storey, *Hon.* Sir Richard, Bt., CBE (1960)

Storr, Sir Peter, KCB

Stothard, Sir Peter Michael, Kt.

Stott, Sir Adrian George Ellingham, Bt. (1920)

Stoute, Sir Michael Ronald, Kt.

Stoutzker, Sir Ian Isaac, Kt., CBE

Stracey, Sir John Simon, Bt. (1818)
Strachan, Sir Curtis Victor, Kt., CVO
Strachan, Sir Hew Francis Anthony, Kt.
†Strachey, Sir Henry Leofric Benvenuto, Bt. (1801)
Straker, Sir Louis Hilton, KCMG
Strang, *Prof.* Sir John Stanley, Kt.
Strang Steel, Sir (Fiennes) Michael, Bt. (1938), CBE
Stratton, *Prof.* Sir Michael Rudolf, Kt., FRS
Strauss, Sir Andrew John, Kt., OBE
Streeter, Sir Gary Nicholas, Kt.
Strickland-Constable, Sir Frederic, Bt. (1641)
Stringer, Sir Donald Edgar, Kt., CBE
Stringer, Sir Howard, Kt.
Strong, Sir Roy Colin, Kt., CH, PHD, FSA
†Stronge, Sir James Anselan Maxwell, Bt. (1803)
†Stuart, Sir Geoffrey Phillip, Bt. (1660)
Stuart, Sir James Keith, Kt.
†Stuart-Forbes, Sir William Daniel, Bt. (S. 1626)
Stuart-Menteth, Sir Charles Greaves, Bt. (1838)
Stuart-Paul, *Air Marshal* Sir Ronald Ian, KBE
Stuart-Smith, *Hon.* Sir Jeremy Hugh, Kt
Stuart-Smith, *Rt. Hon.* Sir Murray, KCMG
Stubbs, Sir William Hamilton, Kt., PHD
Stucley, *Lt.* Sir Hugh George Coplestone Bampfylde, Bt. (1859)
Studd, Sir Edward Fairfax, Bt. (1929)
Studholme, Sir Henry William, Bt. (1956)
Sturridge, Sir Nicholas Anthony, KCVO
Stuttard, Sir John Boothman, Kt.
†Style, Sir William Frederick, Bt. (1627)
Sullivan, *Rt. Hon.* Sir Jeremy Mirth, Kt.
Sullivan, Sir Richard Arthur, Bt. (1804)
Sunderland, Sir John Michael, Kt.
Supperstone, *Hon.* Sir Michael Alan, Kt.
Sutherland, Sir John Brewer, Bt. (1921)
Sutherland, Sir William George MacKenzie, Kt.
Sutton, Sir Richard Lexington, Bt. (1772)
Swan, Sir John William David, KBE
Swann, Sir Michael Christopher, Bt. (1906), TD
Swayne, *Rt. Hon.* Sir Desmond, Kt., TD
Sweeney, Sir George, Kt.
Sweeney, *Hon.* Sir Nigel Hamilton, Kt.
Sweeting, *Prof.* Sir Martin Nicholas, Kt., OBE, FRS
Swift, *Hon.* Sir Jonathan Mark, Kt

Swire, *Rt. Hon.* Sir Hugo George William, KCMG
Sykes, Sir David Michael, Bt. (1921)
†Sykes, Sir Francis Charles, Bt. (1781)
Sykes, Sir Hugh Ridley, Kt.
Sykes, *Prof.* Sir (Malcolm) Keith, Kt.
Sykes, Sir Richard, Kt.
Sykes, Sir Tatton Christopher Mark, Bt. (1783)
Symons, *Vice-Adm.* Sir Patrick Jeremy, KBE
Syms, *Rt. Hon.* Sir Robert Andrew Raymond, Kt.
†Synge, Sir Allen James Edward, Bt. (1801)

T-Z

Tanner, Sir David Whitlock, Kt., CBE
Tantum, Sir Geoffrey Alan, Kt., CMG, OBE
†Tapps-Gervis-Meyrick, Sir George William Owen, Bt. (1791)
Tate, Sir Edward Nicolas, Bt. (1898)
Taureka, *Dr* Sir Reubeh, KBE
Tauvasa, Sir Joseph James, KBE
Taylor, Sir Hugh Henderson, KCB
Taylor, *Dr* Sir John Michael, Kt., OBE
Taylor, Sir Jonathan McLeod Grigor, KCMG
Taylor, *Prof.* Sir Martin John, Kt., FRS
Taylor, Sir Nicholas Richard Stuart, Bt. (1917)
Taylor, *Prof.* Sir William, Kt., CBE
Taylor, Sir William George, Kt.
Teagle, *Vice-Adm.* Sir Somerford Francis, KBE
Teare, *Hon.* Sir Nigel John Martin, Kt.
Teasdale, *Prof.* Sir Graham Michael, Kt.
Tebbit, Sir Kevin Reginald, KCB, CMG
Temple, *Prof.* Sir John Graham, Kt.
Temple, Sir Richard Carnac Chartier, Bt. (1876)
Temu, *Hon. Dr* Sir Puka, KBE, CMG
Tennyson-D'Eyncourt, Sir Mark Gervais, Bt. (1930)
Terry, *Air Marshal* Sir Colin George, KBE, CB
Thatcher, *Hon.* Sir Mark, Bt. (1990)
Thomas, Sir David John Godfrey, Bt. (1694)
Thomas, Sir Derek Morison David, KCMG
Thomas, *Prof.* Sir Eric Jackson, Kt.
Thomas, Sir Gilbert Stanley, Kt., OBE
Thomas, Sir Jeremy Cashel, KCMG
Thomas, *Prof.* Sir John Meurig, Kt., FRS
Thomas, Sir Keith Vivian, Kt.
Thomas, *Dr* Sir Leton Felix, KCMG, CBE
Thomas, Sir Philip Lloyd, KCVO, CMG
Thomas, Sir Quentin Jeremy, Kt., CB
Thomas, Sir William Michael, Bt. (1919)
Thompson, Sir Christopher Peile, Bt. (1890)

Thompson, Sir Clive Malcolm, Kt.
Thompson, Sir David Albert, KCMG
Thompson, Sir Jonathan Michael, KCB
Thompson, *Prof.* Sir Michael Warwick, Kt., DSc
Thompson, Sir Nicholas Annesley, Bt. (1963)
Thompson, Sir Nigel Cooper, KCMG, CBE
Thompson, Sir Paul Anthony, Bt. (1963)
Thompson, Sir Peter Anthony, Kt.
Thompson, *Dr* Sir Richard Paul Hepworth, KCVO
Thompson, Sir Thomas d'Eyncourt John, Bt. (1806)
Thomson, Sir Adam McClure, KCMG
Thomson, Sir (Frederick Douglas) David, Bt. (1929)
Thomson, Sir Mark Wilfrid Home, Bt. (1925)
Thorne, Sir Neil Gordon, Kt., OBE, TD
Thornicroft, *Prof.* Sir Graham John, Kt.
Thornton, *Air Marshal* Sir Barry Michael, KCB
Thornton, Sir (George) Malcolm, Kt.
Thornton, Sir Peter Ribblesdale, Kt.
†Thorold, Sir (Anthony) Oliver, Bt. (1642)
Thorpe, *Rt. Hon.* Sir Mathew Alexander, Kt.
Thrift, *Prof.* Sir Nigel John, Kt.
Thurecht, Sir Ramon Richard, Kt., OBE
Thwaites, Sir Bryan, Kt., PHD
Tickell, Sir Crispin Charles Cervantes, GCMG, KCVO
Tidmarsh, Sir James Napier, KCVO, MBE
Tilt, Sir Robin Richard, Kt.
Tiltman, Sir John Hessell, KCVO
Timmins, *Col.* Sir John Bradford, KCVO, OBE, TD
Timpson, Sir William John Anthony, Kt., CBE
Tims, Sir Michael David, KCVO
Tindle, Sir Ray Stanley, Kt., CBE
Tirvengadum, Sir Harry Krishnan, Kt.
Tod, *Vice-Adm.* Sir Jonathan James Richard, KCB, CBE
Togolo, Sir Melchior Pesa, Kt.
Toka, Sir Mahuru Dadi, Kt., MBE
†Tollemache, Sir Richard John, Bt. (1793)
Tomkys, Sir (William) Roger, KCMG
Tomlinson, Sir John Rowland, Kt., CBE
Tomlinson, Sir Michael John, Kt., CBE
Tomlinson, *Rt. Hon.* Sir Stephen Miles, Kt.
Tooke, *Prof.* Sir John Edward, Kt.
Tooley, Sir John, Kt.
ToRobert, Sir Henry Thomas, KBE
Torpy, *Air Chief Marshal* Sir Glenn Lester, GCB, CBE, DSO
Torrance, *Very Revd Prof.* Iain Richard, KCVO, TD
Torry, Sir Peter James, GCVO, KCMG

†Touche, Sir Eric MacLellan, Bt. (1962)

Touche, Sir William George, Bt. (1920)

Tovadek, Sir Martin, Kt. CMG

Tovua, Sir Paul Joshua, KCMG

ToVue, Sir Ronald, Kt., OBE

Towneley, Sir Simon Peter Edmund Cosmo William, KCVO

Townsley, Sir John Arthur, Kt.

Traill, Sir Alan Towers, GBE

Trainor, *Prof.* Sir Richard Hughes, KBE

Trawen, Sir Andrew Sean, Kt., CMG, MBE

Treacy, *Rt. Hon.* Sir Colman Maurice, Kt.

Treacy, *Hon.* Sir (James Mary) Seamus, Kt.

Treisman, Sir Richard Henry, Kt., FRS

Trescowthick, Sir Donald Henry, KBE

†Trevelyan, Sir Peter John, Bt. (1662 and 1874)

Trezise, Sir Kenneth Bruce, Kt., OBE

Trippier, Sir David Austin, Kt., RD

Tritton, Sir Jeremy Ernest, Bt. (1905)

Trollope, Sir Anthony Simon, Bt. (1642)

Trotter, Sir Neville Guthrie, Kt.

Troubridge, Sir Thomas Richard, Bt. (1799)

Troup, Sir Edward Astley (John), Kt.

Trousdell, *Lt.-Gen.* Sir Philip Charles Cornwallis, KBE, CB

†Truscott, Sir Ralph Eric Nicholson, Bt. (1909)

Tsang, Sir Donald Yam-keun, KBE

Tuck, Sir Christopher John, Bt. (1910)

Tucker, Sir Paul, Kt.

Tucker, *Hon.* Sir Richard Howard, Kt.

Tuckett, *Prof.* Sir Alan John, Kt., OBE

Tuckey, *Rt. Hon.* Sir Simon Lane, Kt.

Tugendhat, *Hon.* Sir Michael George, Kt.

Tuite, Sir Christopher Hugh, Bt. (I. 1622), PHD

Tully, Sir William Mark, KBE

Tunnock, Sir Archibald Boyd, Kt., CBE

Tunstall, Sir Craig, Kt.

†Tupper, Sir Charles Hibbert, Bt. (1888)

Turing, Sir John Dermot, Bt. (S. 1638)

Turnbull, *Prof.* Sir Douglass Matthew, Kt.

Turner, *Hon.* Sir Mark George, Kt.

Turnquest, Sir Orville Alton, GCMG, QC

Tusa, Sir John, Kt.

Tweedie, *Prof.* Sir David Philip, Kt.

Tyrwhitt, Sir Reginald Thomas Newman, Bt. (1919)

Udny-Lister, Sir Edward Julian, Kt.

Ullmann, Sir Anthony James, Kt.

Underhill, *Rt. Hon.* Sir Nicholas Edward, Kt.

Underwood, *Prof.* Sir James Cressee Elphinstone, Kt.

Unwin, Sir (James) Brian, KCB

Ure, Sir John Burns, KCMG, LVO

Urquhart, Sir Brian Edward, KCMG, MBE

Urquhart, *Rt. Revd* David Andrew, KCMG

Usher, Sir Andrew John, Bt. (1899)

Utting, Sir William Benjamin, Kt., CB

Vallance, *Dr* Sir Patrick John Thompson, Kt.

Vardy, Sir Peter, Kt.

Varney, Sir David Robert, Kt.

Vassar-Smith, Sir John Rathbone, Bt. (1917)

Vavasour, Sir Eric Michael Joseph Marmaduke, Bt. (1828)

Veness, Sir David, Kt., CBE, QPM

Vereker, Sir John Michael Medlicott, KCB

Verey, Sir David John, Kt., CBE

Verity, Sir Gary Keith, Kt.

Verney, Sir Edmund Ralph, Bt. (1818)

†Verney, Sir John Sebastian, Bt. (1946)

Vernon, Sir James William, Bt. (1914)

Vestey, Sir Paul Edmund, Bt. (1921)

Vickers, *Prof.* Sir Brian William, Kt.

Vickers, Sir John Stuart, Kt.

Vickers, *Lt.-Gen.* Sir Richard Maurice Hilton, KCB, CVO, OBE

Vickers, Sir Roger Henry, KCVO

Viggers, *Lt.-Gen.* Sir Frederick Richard, KCB, CMG, MBE

Viggers, Sir Peter John, Kt.

Vincent, Sir William Percy Maxwell, Bt. (1936)

Vineall, Sir Anthony John Patrick, Kt.

Virdee, *Prof.* Sir Tejinder Singh, Kt.

von Friesendorff, Sir Rickard Fredrik Knut, Bt. (1661)

Vos, *Rt. Hon.* Sir Geoffrey Charles, Kt.

Vuatha, Sir Tipo, Kt., LVO, MBE

Vunagi, Rt. Revd David, GCMG

†Vyvyan, Sir Ralph Ferrers Alexander, Bt. (1645)

Waena, Sir Nathaniel Rahumaea, GCMG

Waine, *Rt. Revd* John, KCVO

Wainwright, Sir Robert Mark, KCMG

Waite, *Rt. Hon.* Sir John Douglas, Kt.

Waka, Sir Lucas Joseph, Kt., OBE

Wake, Sir Hereward Charles, Bt. (1621)

Wakefield, Sir (Edward) Humphry (Tyrrell), Bt. (1962)

Wakefield, Sir Norman Edward, Kt.

Wakeford, Sir Geoffrey Michael Montgomery, Kt., OBE

Wakeham, *Prof.* Sir William Arnot, Kt.

†Wakeley, Sir Nicholas Jeremy, Bt. (1952)

Waksman, *Hon.* Sir David Michael, Kt.

Wald, *Prof.* Sir Nicholas John, Kt.

Wales, Sir Robert Andrew, Kt.

Waley-Cohen, Sir Stephen Harry, Bt. (1961)

Walker, *Gen.* Sir Antony Kenneth Frederick, KCB

Walker, Sir Charles Ashley Rupert, KBE

Walker, Sir Christopher Robert Baldwin, Bt. (1856)

Walker, Sir David Alan, Kt.

Walker, *Air Vice-Marshal* Sir David Allan, KCVO, OBE

Walker, Sir Harold Berners, KCMG

Walker, Sir John Ernest, Kt., DPHIL, FRS

Walker, *Air Marshal* Sir John Robert, KCB, CBE, AFC

Walker, Sir Malcolm Conrad, Kt., CBE

Walker, Sir Miles Rawstron, Kt., CBE

Walker, Sir Patrick Jeremy, KCB

Walker, *Hon.* Sir Paul James, Kt.

Walker, Sir Rodney Myerscough, Kt.

Walker, Sir Roy Edward, Bt. (1906)

Walker, *Hon.* Sir Timothy Edward, Kt.

Walker, Sir Victor Stewart Heron, Bt. (1868)

Walker-Okeover, Sir Andrew Peter Monro, Bt. (1886)

Walker-Smith, *Hon.* Sir John Jonah, Bt. (1960)

Wall, Sir (John) Stephen, GCMG, LVO

Wall, *Gen.* Sir Peter Anthony, GCB, CBE, ADC

Wallace, *Prof.* Sir David James, Kt., CBE, FRS

Waller, *Rt. Hon.* Sir (George) Mark, Kt.

Waller, Sir John Michael, Bt. (I. 1780)

Waller, *Revd Dr* Sir Ralph, KBE

Wallis, Sir Peter Gordon, KCVO

Wallis, Sir Timothy William, Kt.

Walmsley, *Vice-Adm.* Sir Robert, KCB

Walport, *Dr* Sir Mark Jeremy, Kt.

†Walsham, Sir Gerald Percy Robert, Bt. (1831)

Walters, Sir Dennis Murray, Kt., MBE

Walters, Sir Frederick Donald, Kt.

Walters, Sir Peter Ingram, Kt.

Wamiri, Sir Akapite, KBE

Warby, *Hon.* Sir Mark David John, Kt.

Ward, *Rt. Hon.* Sir Alan Hylton, Kt.

Ward, Sir Austin, Kt., QC

Ward, *Hon.* Sir (Frederik) Gordon (Roy), Kt., OBE

Ward, *Prof.* Sir John MacQueen, Kt., CBE

Ward, Sir Joseph James Laffey, Bt. (1911)

Ward, Sir Timothy James, Kt.

†Wardlaw, Sir Henry Justin, Bt. (NS. 1631)

Waring, Sir (Alfred) Holburt, Bt. (1935)

Warmington, Sir Rupert Marshall, Bt. (1908)

Warner, Sir Gerald Chierici, KCMG

Warner, Sir Philip Courtenay Thomas, Bt. (1910)

Warren, Sir David Alexander, KCMG

Warren, Sir (Frederick) Miles, KBE

Warren, *Hon.* Sir Nicholas Roger, Kt.

Waterlow, Sir Christopher Rupert, Bt. (1873)

Waterlow, Sir (Thomas) James, Bt. (1930)

Waters, *Gen.* Sir (Charles) John, GCB, CBE

Waters, Sir David Mark Rylance (Mark Rylance), Kt.

Waterstone, Sir Timothy, Kt.

Wates, Sir Christopher Stephen, Kt.

Wates, Sir James Garwood Michael, Kt., CBE

Watson, Sir Graham Robert, Kt.

Watson, Sir (James) Andrew, Bt. (1866)

Watson, *Prof.* Sir Robert Tony, Kt., CMG

Watson, Sir Ronald Matthew, Kt., CBE

Watt, *Gen.* Sir Charles Redmond, KCB, KCVO, CBE, ADC

Watts, Sir Philip Beverley, KCMG

Weatherup, *Hon.* Sir Ronald Eccles, Kt.

Webb, *Prof.* Sir Adrian Leonard, Kt.

Webb, *Rt. Hon.* Sir Steven John, Kt.

Webb-Carter, *Maj.-Gen.* Sir Evelyn John, KCVO, OBE

Webster, *Vice-Adm.* Sir John Morrison, KCB

Wedgwood, Sir Ralph Nicholas, Bt. (1942)

Weekes, Sir Everton DeCourcey, KCMG, OBE

Weinberg, Sir Mark Aubrey, Kt.

Weir, *Hon.* Sir Reginald George, Kt.

Weir, Sir Roderick Bignell, Kt.

Welby, Sir (Richard) Bruno Gregory, Bt. (1801)

Welch, Sir John Reader, Bt. (1957)

Weldon, Sir Anthony William, Bt. (I. 1723)

Wellend, *Prof.* Sir Mark Edward, Kt.

Weller, *Prof.* Sir Ian Vincent Derrick, Kt.

Weller, Sir Nicholas John, Kt.

†Wells, Sir Christopher Charles, Bt. (1944)

Wells, *Prof.* Sir Stanley William, Kt., CBE

Wells, Sir William Henry Weston, Kt., FRICS

Wenge, Rt. Revd Girege, KBE

Wessely, *Prof.* Sir Simon Charles, Kt.

Westmacott, Sir Peter John, GCMG, LVO

Weston, Sir Michael Charles Swift, KCMG, CVO

Weston, Sir (Philip) John, KCMG

Whalen, Sir Geoffrey Henry, Kt., CBE

Wheeler, *Rt. Hon.* Sir John Daniel, Kt.

Wheeler, Sir John Frederick, Bt. (1920)

Wheeler, *Gen.* Sir Roger Neil, GCB, CBE

Wheler, Sir Trevor Woodford, Bt. (1660)

Whitaker, Sir John James Ingham (Jack), Bt. (1936)

Whitbread, Sir Samuel Charles, KCVO

Whitchurch, Sir Graeme Ian, Kt., OBE

White, Sir Adrian Edwin, Kt., CBE

White, *Prof.* Sir Christopher John, Kt., CVO

White, Sir David (David Jason), Kt., OBE

White, Sir David Harry, Kt.

White, Sir George Stanley James, Bt. (1904)

White, Sir John Woolmer, Bt. (1922)

White, *Maj.-Gen.* Sir Martin, KCVO, CB, CBE

White, *Prof.* Sir Nicholas John, KCMG, OBE

White, Sir Nicholas Peter Archibald, Bt. (1802)

White, Sir Willard Wentworth, Kt., CBE

White-Spunner, *Lt.-Gen.* Sir Barnabas William Benjamin, KCB, CBE

Whitehead, Sir Philip Henry Rathbone, Bt. (1889)

Whitmore, Sir Clive Anthony, GCB, CVO

Whitmore, Sir Jason Kevin, Bt. (1954)

Whitson, Sir Keith Roderick, Kt.

Whittam Smith, Sir Andreas, Kt., CBE

Wickerson, Sir John Michael, Kt.

Wicks, Sir Nigel Leonard, GCB, CVO, CBE

Wigan, Sir Michael Iain, Bt. (1898)

Wiggin, Sir Richard Edward John, Bt. (1892)

Wiggins, Sir Bradley Marc, Kt., CBE

Wigram, Sir John Woolmore, Bt. (1805)

Wilbraham, Sir Richard Baker, Bt. (1776)

Wild, Sir John Ralston, Kt., CBE

Wiles, *Prof.* Sir Andrew John, KBE

Wilkie, *Hon.* Sir Alan Fraser, Kt.

Wilkins, Sir Michael, Kt.

Wilkinson, Sir (David) Graham (Brook), Bt. (1941)

Willcocks, *Lt.-Gen.* Sir Michael Alan, KCB, CVO

Williams, Sir Anthony Geraint, Bt. (1953)

Williams, Sir (Arthur) Gareth Ludovic Emrys Rhys, Bt. (1918)

Williams, Sir Charles Othniel, Kt.

Williams, Sir Daniel Charles, GCMG, QC

Williams, *Hon.* Sir David Basil, Kt.

Williams, Sir David Reeve, Kt., CBE

Williams, Sir Donald Mark, Bt. (1866)

Williams, *Prof.* Sir (Edward) Dillwyn, Kt., FRCP

Williams, Sir Francis Owen Garbett, Kt., CBE

Williams, *Hon.* Sir (John) Griffith, Kt.

Williams, Sir Nicholas Stephen, Kt.

Williams, *Prof.* Sir Norman Stanley, Kt.

Williams, Sir Paul Michael, Kt., OBE

Williams, Sir Peter Michael, Kt.

Williams, *Prof.* Sir Robert Hughes, Kt.

Williams, Sir (Robert) Philip Nathaniel, Bt. (1915)

Williams, *HE Dr* Sir Rodney Errey Lawrence, GCMG

Williams, *Prof.* Sir Roger, Kt.

Williams, Sir (William) Maxwell (Harries), Kt.

Williams, *Hon.* Sir Wyn Lewis, Kt.

Williams-Bulkeley, Sir Richard Thomas, Bt. (1661)

Williams-Wynn, Sir David Watkin, Bt. (1688)

Williamson, Sir George Malcolm, Kt.

Williamson, Sir Robert Brian, Kt., CBE

Willink, Sir Edward Daniel, Bt. (1957)

Wills, Sir David James Vernon, Bt. (1923)

Wills, Sir David Seton, Bt. (1904)

Wilmot, Sir Henry Robert, Bt. (1759)

Wilmut, *Prof.* Sir Ian, Kt., OBE

Wilsey, *Gen.* Sir John Finlay Willasey, GCB, CBE

Wilshaw, Sir Michael, Kt.

Wilson, *Prof.* Sir Alan Geoffrey, Kt.

Wilson, Sir David Mackenzie, Kt.

Wilson, Sir Franklyn Roosevelt, KCMG

Wilson, Sir James William Douglas, Bt. (1906)

Wilson, *Brig.* Sir Mathew John Anthony, Bt. (1874), OBE, MC

Wilson, *Rt. Hon.* Sir Nicholas Allan Roy, Kt. (Lord Wilson of Culworth)

Wilson, *Prof.* Sir Robert James Timothy, Kt.

Wilson, Sir Robert Peter, KCMG

Wilson, *Air Chief Marshal* Sir (Ronald) Andrew (Fellowes), KCB, AFC

Wilson, Sir Thomas David, Bt. (1920)

Winkley, Sir David Ross, Kt.

Winnington, Sir Anthony Edward, Bt. (1755)

Winship, Sir Peter James Joseph, Kt., CBE

Winsor, Sir Thomas Philip, Kt.

Winter, *Dr* Sir Gregory Winter, Kt., CBE

Winterton, Sir Nicholas Raymond, Kt.

Wiseman, Sir John William, Bt. (1628)

Witty, Sir Andrew, Kt.

Wolfendale, *Prof.* Sir Arnold Whittaker, Kt., FRS

†Wolseley, Sir James Douglas, Bt. (I. 1745)

Wolseley, Sir Stephen Garnet Hugo Charles, Bt. (1744)

†Wombwell, Sir George Philip Frederick, Bt. (1778)

Womersley, Sir Peter John Walter, Bt. (1945)

Woo, Sir Leo Joseph, Kt., MBE

Woo, Sir Po-Shing, Kt.

Wood, Sir Alan Thorpe Richard, Kt., CBE

Wood, Sir Andrew Marley, GCMG

Wood, Sir Anthony John Page, Bt. (1837)

Wood, Sir Ian Clark, KT, GBE

Wood, Sir James Sebastian Lamin, KCMG

Wood, Sir Martin Francis, Kt., OBE

Wood, Sir Michael Charles, KCMG

Wood, Sir Peter John, Kt., CBE

Wood, *Hon.* Sir Roderic Lionel James, Kt.

Woodard, *Rear Adm.* Sir Robert Nathaniel, KCVO

Woodcock, *Vice-Adm.* Sir (Simon) Jonathan, KCB, OBE

Woodhead, *Vice-Adm.* Sir (Anthony) Peter, KCB

Woods, *Prof.* Sir Kent Linton, Kt.

Woods, Sir Robert Kynnersley, Kt., CBE

Woodward, Sir Clive Ronald, Kt., OBE

Woodward, Sir Thomas Jones (Tom Jones), Kt., OBE

Wootton, Sir David Hugh, Kt.

Wormald, Sir Christopher Stephen, KCB

Worsley, Sir William Ralph, Bt. (1838)

Worsthorne, Sir Peregrine Gerard, Kt.

Worthington, Sir Mark, Kt., OBE

Wratten, *Air Chief Marshal* Sir William John, GBE, CB, AFC

Wraxall, Sir Charles Frederick Lascelles, Bt. (1813)

Wrey, Sir George Richard Bourchier, Bt. (1628)

Wright, Sir Allan Frederick, KBE

Wright, Sir David John, GCMG, LVO

Wright, *Hon.* Sir (John) Michael, Kt.

Wright, *Prof.* Sir Nicholas Alcwyn, Kt.

Wright, Sir Peter Robert, Kt., CBE

Wright, *Air Marshal* Sir Robert Alfred, KBE, AFC

Wright, Sir Stephen John Leadbetter, KCMG

Wright, *Dr* Sir William Thompson, Kt., CBE

Wrightson, Sir Charles Mark Garmondsway, Bt. (1900)

Wrigley, *Prof.* Sir Edward Anthony (Sir Tony), Kt., PHD, PBA

Wrixon-Becher, Sir John William Michael, Bt. (1831)

Wroughton, Sir Philip Lavallin, KCVO

Wu, Sir Gordon Ying Sheung, KCMG

Wynne, Sir Graham Robert, Kt., CBE

Yacoub, *Prof.* Sir Magdi Habib, Kt., OM, FRCS

Yaki, Sir Roy, KBE

Yang, *Hon.* Sir Ti Liang, Kt.

Yarrow, Sir Alan Colin Drake, Kt.

Yarrow, Sir Ross William Grant, Bt. (1916)

Yassaie, *Dr* Sir Hossein, Kt.

Yoo Foo, Sir (François) Henri, Kt.

Young, Sir Colville Norbert, GCMG, MBE

Young, Sir Dennis Charles, KCMG

Young, Sir John Kenyon Roe, Bt. (1821)

Young, Sir John Robertson, GCMG

Young, Sir Nicholas Charles, Kt.

Young, Sir Robin Urquhart, KCB

Young, Sir Stephen Stewart Templeton, Bt. (1945), QC

Young, Sir William Neil, Bt. (1769)

Younger, Sir Alexander, KCMG

Younger, *Capt.* Sir John David Bingham, KCVO

Younger Thieriot, Sir Andrew William, Bt. (1911)

Yuwi, Sir Matiabe, KBE

Zacaroli, *Hon.* Sir Antony James, Kt.

Zacca, *Rt. Hon.* Sir Edward, KCMG

Zahedi, *Prof.* Sir Mir Saeed, Kt., OBE

Zambellas, *Adm.* Sir George Michael, GCB, DSC, ADC

Zissman, Sir Bernard Philip, Kt.

Zumla, *Prof.* Sir Alimuddin, Kt.

Zurenuoc, Sir Manasupe Zure, Kt., OBE

Zurenuoc, Sir Zibang, KBE

THE ORDER OF ST JOHN

THE MOST VENERABLE ORDER OF THE HOSPITAL OF ST JOHN OF JERUSALEM (1888)

GCStJ	Bailiff/Dame Grand Cross
KStJ	Knight of Justice/Grace
DStJ	Dame of Justice/Grace
CStJ	Commander
OStJ	Officer
MStJ	Member

Motto, Pro Fide, Pro Utilitate Hominum
(For the faith and in the service of humanity)

The Order of St John, founded in the early 12th century in Jerusalem, was a religious order with a particular duty to care for the sick. In Britain the order was dissolved by Henry VIII in 1540 but the British branch was revived in the early 19th century. The branch was not accepted by the Grand Magistracy of the Order in Rome but its search for a role in the tradition of the hospitallers led to the founding of the St John Ambulance Association in 1877 and later the St John Ambulance Brigade; in 1882 the St John Ophthalmic Hospital was founded in Jerusalem. A royal charter was granted in 1888 establishing the Order of St John as a British Order of Chivalry with the sovereign as its head.

Since October 1999 the whole order worldwide has been governed by a Grand Council which includes a representative from each of the 11 priories (England, Scotland, Wales, Hong Kong, Kenya, Singapore, South Africa, New Zealand, Canada, Australia and the USA). In addition there are also five commanderies in Northern Ireland, Jersey, Guernsey, the Isle of Man and Western Australia. There are also branches in about 30 other Commonwealth countries. Apart from St John Ambulance, the Order is also responsible for the Eye Hospital in Jerusalem. Admission to the order is usually conferred in recognition of service to either one of these institutions. Membership does not confer any rank, style, title or precedence on a recipient.

SOVEREIGN HEAD OF THE ORDER
HM The Queen

GRAND PRIOR
HRH The Duke of Gloucester, KG, GCVO

Lord Prior, Prof. Mark Compton
Prelate, Rt. Revd Timothy Stevens, CBE
Chancellor, Patrick Burgess, OBE
Sub-Prior, John Mah, QC
Secretary-General, Vice-Adm. Sir Paul Lambert, KCB

International Office, 3 Charterhouse Mews, London EC1M 6BB
T 020-7251 3292 **W** www.stjohninternational.org

DAMES

Style, 'Dame' before forename and surname, followed by
appropriate post-nominal initials. Where such an award is
made to a lady already in possession of a higher title, the
appropriate initials follow her name
Envelope, Dame F_ S_, followed by appropriate post-
nominal letters. *Letter (formal),* Dear Madam; *(social),* Dear
Dame F_. *Spoken,* Dame F_
Husband, Untitled

Dame Grand Cross and Dame Commander are the higher
classes for women of the Order of the Bath, the Order of St
Michael and St George, the Royal Victorian Order, and the
Order of the British Empire. Dames Grand Cross rank after the
wives of Baronets and before the wives of Knights Grand
Cross. Dames Commanders rank after the wives of Knights
Grand Cross and before the wives of Knights Commanders.
   Honorary damehoods may be conferred on women who are
citizens of countries of which the Queen is not head of state.

LIST OF DAMES *as at 31 December 2020*
Women peers in their own right and life peers are not included
in this list. Female members of the royal family are not included
in this list; details of the orders they hold can be found within
the Royal Family section.
   If a dame has a double barrelled or hyphenated surname, she
is listed under the first element of the name.

Abaijah, Dame Josephine, DBE
Abramsky, Dame Jennifer Gita, DBE
Acland Hood Gass, Lady (Elizabeth Periam), DCVO
Airlie, The Countess of, DCVO
Allen, *Hon.* Dame Anita Mildred, DBE
Allen, *Prof.* Dame Ingrid Victoria, DBE
Andrews, *Hon.* Dame Geraldine Mary, DBE
Andrews, Dame Julie, DBE
Angiolini, *Rt. Hon.* Dame Elish, DBE, QC
Anionwu, *Prof.* Dame Elizabeth Nneka, DBE
Anson, Lady (Elizabeth Audrey), DBE
Archer, *Dr* Dame Mary Doreen, DBE
Arden, *Rt. Hon.* Dame Mary Howarth (Mrs Mance), DBE
   (Lady Arden of Heswall)
Ashcroft, *Prof.* Dame Frances Mary, DBE, FRS
Asplin, *Rt. Hon.* Dame Sarah Jane (Mrs Sherwin), DBE
Atkins, Dame Eileen, DBE
Atkins, *Prof.* Dame Madeleine Julia, DBE
August, Dame Kathryn, DBE
Bacon, Dame Patricia Anne, DBE
Bailey, Dame Glenda Adrianne, DBE
Bailey, *Prof.* Dame Susan Mary, DBE
Baird, Dame Vera, DBE
Baker, Dame Janet Abbott (Mrs Shelley), CH, DBE
Barbour, Dame Margaret (Mrs Ash), DBE
Barker, Dame Katharine Mary, DBE
Barker-Welch, *Hon.* Dame Maizie Irene, DBE
Barrow, Dame Jocelyn Anita (Mrs Downer), DBE
Barstow, Dame Josephine Clare (Mrs Anderson), DBE
Bassey, Dame Shirley, DBE
Beale, Dame Inga Kristine, DBE
Beard, *Prof.* Dame (Winifred) Mary, DBE
Beasley, *Prof.* Dame Christine Joan, DBE
Beaurepaire, Dame Beryl Edith, DBE
Beckett, *Rt. Hon.* Dame Margaret Mary, DBE
Beer, *Prof.* Dame Gillian Patricia Kempster, DBE, FBA
Beer, *Prof.* Dame Janet Patricia, DBE
Begg, Dame Anne, DBE
Beral, *Prof.* Dame Valerie, DBE
Bertschinger, *Dr* Dame Claire, DBE
Bevan, Dame Yasmin, DBE

Bibby, Dame Enid, DBE
Black, *Prof.* Dame Carol Mary, DBE
Black, *Rt. Hon.* Dame Jill Margaret, DBE (Lady Black of
   Derwent)
Black, *Prof.* Dame Susan Margaret, DBE, FRSE
Blackadder, Dame Elizabeth Violet, DBE
Blaize, Dame Venetia Ursula, DBE
Blaxland, Dame Helen Frances, DBE
Blume, Dame Hilary Sharon Braverman, DBE
Booth, *Hon.* Dame Margaret Myfanwy Wood, DBE
Bostwick, *Hon.* Dame Janet Gwennett, DBE
Boulding, Dame Hilary, DBE
Bourne, Dame Susan Mary (Mrs Bourne), DBE
Bowe, *Dr* Dame (Mary) Colette, DBE
Bowtell, Dame Ann Elizabeth, DCB
Braddock, *Dr* Dame Christine, DBE
Brain, Dame Margaret Anne (Mrs Wheeler), DBE
Breakwell, *Prof.* Dame Glynis Marie, DBE
Brennan, Dame Maureen, DBE
Brennan, Dame Ursula, DCB
Brewer, *Dr* Dame Nicola Mary, DCMG
Bridges, Dame Mary Patricia, DBE
Brindley, Dame Lynne Janie, DBE
Brittan, Dame Diana (Lady Brittan of Spennithorne), DBE
Brooke, *Rt. Hon.* Dame Annette (Lesley), DBE
Bruce, Dame Susan Margaret, DBE
Bruce, *Prof.* Dame Victoria Geraldine, DBE, FBA, FRSE
Buckland, Dame Yvonne Helen Elaine, DBE
Burnell, *Prof.* Dame Susan Jocelyn Bell, DBE
Burslem, Dame Alexandra Vivien, DBE
Bussell, Dame Darcey Andrea, DBE
Butler, Dame Rosemary Janet Mair, DBE
Byatt, Dame Antonia Susan, DBE, FRSL
Cairncross, Dame Frances Anne, DBE, FRSE
Caldicott, Dame Fiona, DBE, FRCP, FRCPSYCH
Callil, Dame Carmen Thérèse, DBE
Cameron, *Prof.* Dame Averil Millicent, DBE
Campbell-Preston, Dame Frances Olivia, DCVO
Carew Pole, Lady (Mary), DCVO
Carnall, Dame Ruth, DBE
Carnwath, Dame Alison Jane, DBE
Carr, *Rt. Hon.* Dame Sue Lascelles (Mrs Birch), DBE
Cartwright, Dame Silvia Rose, DBE
Chapman, *Prof.* Dame Hilary Anne, DBE
Cheema-Grubb, *Hon.* Dame Bobbie, DBE
Clancy, *Hon.* Dame Claire Elizabeth, DCB
Clark, *Prof.* Dame Jill MacLeod, DBE
Clark, *Prof.* Dame (Margaret) June, DBE, PHD
Cleverdon, Dame Julia Charity, DCVO, CBE
Coates, Dame Sally, DBE
Cockerill, *Hon.* Dame Sara Elizabeth, DBE
Coia, *Dr* Dame Denise Assunta, DBE
Collarbone, Dame Patricia, DBE
Collins, Dame Joan Henrietta, DBE
Connolly, Dame Sarah Patricia, DBE
Contreras, *Prof.* Dame Marcela, DBE
Corley, Dame Elizabeth Pauline Lucy, DBE
Corner, *Prof.* Dame Jessica Lois, DBE
Corsar, *Hon.* Dame Mary Drummond, DBE
Courtice, Dame Veronica Anne (Polly), DBE, LVO
Coward, Dame Pamela Sarah, DBE
Cowley, *Prof.* Dame Sarah Ann, DBE
Cox, *Hon.* Dame Laura Mary, DBE
Cramp, *Prof.* Dame Rosemary Jean, DBE
Cullum, *Prof.* Dame Nicola Anne, DBE
Cunliffe-Lister *Hon.* Dame (Elizabeth) Susan, DCVO
Cutts, *Hon.* Dame Johannah, DBE

Dacon, Dame Monica Jessie, DBE, CMG
Dacre, *Prof.* Dame Jane Elizabeth, DBE
Daniel, Dame Jacqueline Lesley, DBE
Davies, *Prof.* Dame Kay Elizabeth, DBE
Davies, Dame Laura Jane, DBE
Davies, *Rt. Hon.* Dame Nicola Velfor, DBE
Davies, *Prof.* Dame Sally Claire, DBE
Davies, Dame Wendy Patricia, DBE
Davis, Dame Karlene Cecile, DBE
Dawson, *Prof.* Dame Sandra Jane Noble, DBE
de Havilland, Dame Olivia Mary, DBE
De Souza, Dame Rachel Mary, DBE
Dean, *Prof.* Dame Caroline, DBE, FRS
Dell, Dame Miriam Patricia, DBE
Dench, Dame Judith Olivia (Mrs Williams), CH, DBE
Descartes, Dame Marie Selipha Sesenne, DBE, BEM
Dethridge, Dame Kate, DBE
Dick, Dame Cressida Rose, DBE, QPM
Digby, The Lady, DBE
Dobbs, *Hon.* Dame Linda Penelope, DBE
Docherty, Dame Jacqueline, DBE
Dominiczak, *Prof.* Dame Anna Felicja, DBE, FRSE
Donald, *Prof.* Dame Athene Margaret, DBE, FRS
Dowling, *Prof.* Dame Ann Patricia, OM, DBE
Duffield, Dame Vivien Louise, DBE
Duffy, Dame Carol Ann, DBE
Dumont, Dame Ivy Leona, DCMG
Dunnell, Dame Karen, DCB
Dyche, Dame Rachael Mary, DBE
Eady, *Hon.* Dame Jennifer, DBE
Elcoat, Dame Catherine Elizabeth, DBE
Ellison, Dame Jill, DBE
Ellman, Dame Louise Joyce, DBE
Elton, Dame Susan Richenda (Lady Elton), DCVO
Ennis-Hill, Dame Jessica, DBE
Esteve-Coll, Dame Elizabeth Anne Loosemore, DBE
Evans, Dame Anne Elizabeth Jane, DBE
Evans, Dame Madeline Glynne Derval, DBE, CMG
Evans, Dame Oremi, DBE
Fagan, Dame (Florence) Mary, LG, DCVO
Fairbairn, Dame Carolyn Julie, DBE
Falk, *Hon.* Dame Sarah, DBE
Fallowfield, *Prof.* Dame Lesley Jean, DBE
Farbey, *Hon.* Dame Judith Sarah, DBE
Farnham, Dame Marion (Lady Farnham), DCVO
Fawcett, Dame Amelia Chilcott, DBE
Fielding, Dame Pauline, DBE
Finch, *Prof.* Dame Janet Valerie, DBE
Fisher, *Prof.* Dame Amanda Gray, DBE
Fisher, Dame Jacqueline, DBE
Forgan, Dame Elizabeth Anne Lucy, DBE
Foster, *Hon.* Dame Alison Lee Caroline, DBE
Foster, Dame Jacqueline, DBE
Fradd, Dame Elizabeth, DBE
Francis, *Prof.* Dame Jane Elizabeth, DCMG
Fraser, Lady Antonia, CH, DBE
Fraser, Dame Helen Jean Sutherland, DBE
Frost, Dame Barbara May, DBE
Fry, Dame Margaret Louise, DBE
Furse, Dame Clara Hedwig Frances, DBE
Gadhia, Dame Jayne-Anne, DBE
Gai, *Prof.* Dame Pratibha Laxman (Mrs Gai-Boyes), DBE
Gaymer, Dame Janet Marion, DBE, QC
Ghosh, Dame Helen Frances, DCB
Gibb, Dame Moira Margaret, DBE
Gillan, *Rt. Hon.* Dame Cheryl Elise Kendall, DBE
Glenn, *Prof.* Dame Hazel Gillian, DBE
Glennie, *Dr* Dame Evelyn Elizabeth Ann, CH, DBE
Gloag, Dame Ann Heron, DBE
Gloster, *Rt. Hon.* Dame Elizabeth (Lady Popplewell), DBE
Glover, Dame Audrey Frances, DBE, CMG
Glover, *Prof.* Dame Lesley Anne, DBE, FRSE

Goad, Dame Sarah Jane Frances, DCVO
Goodall, *Dr* Dame (Valerie) Jane, DBE
Goodfellow, *Prof.* Dame Julia Mary, DBE
Gordon, Dame Minita Elmira, GCMG, GCVO
Gordon, *Hon.* Dame Pamela Felicity, DBE
Gow, Dame Jane Elizabeth (Mrs Whiteley), DBE
Grafton, Ann, The Duchess of, GCVO
Grainger, *Dr* Dame Katherine Jane, DBE
Grant, Dame Mavis, DBE
Green, Dame Moya Marguerite, DBE
Green, Dame Pauline, DBE
Gretton, Jennifer, Lady, DCVO
Grey, Dame Beryl Elizabeth (Mrs Svenson), CH, DBE
Griffiths, Dame Marianne, DBE
Grimthorpe, Elizabeth, The Lady, DCVO
Guilfoyle, Dame Margaret Georgina Constance, DBE
Guthardt, *Revd Dr* Dame Phyllis Myra, DBE
Hackitt, Dame Judith Elizabeth, DBE
Hakin, *Dr* Dame Barbara Ann, DBE
Hall, *Prof.* Dame Wendy, DBE
Hallett, Dame Nancy Karen, DBE
Hamilton, *Prof.* Dame Carolyn Paula, DBE
Harbison, Dame Joan Irene, DBE
Harper, Dame Elizabeth Margaret Way, DBE
Harris, Dame Pauline (Lady Harris of Peckham), DBE
Harris, Dame Philippa Jill Olivier, DBE
Hassan, Dame Anna Patricia Lucy, DBE
Hay, Dame Barbara Logan, DCMG, MBE
Henderson, Dame Fiona Douglas, DCVO
Hercus, *Hon.* Dame (Margaret) Ann, DCMG
Higgins, *Prof.* Dame Joan Margaret, DBE
Higgins, *Prof.* Dame Julia Stretton, DBE, FRS
Higgins, *Prof.* Dame Rosalyn, GBE, QC
Hill, *Prof.* Dame Judith Eileen, DBE
Hill, *Prof.* Dame Susan Lesley, DBE
Hine, Dame Deirdre Joan, DBE, FRCP
Hodge, *Rt. Hon.* Dame Margaret (Eve), DBE
Hodgson, Dame Patricia Anne, DBE
Hogg, *Hon.* Dame Mary Claire (Mrs Koops), DBE
Hollows, Dame Sharon, DBE
Holmes, Dame Kelly, DBE
Holroyd, Lady (Margaret Drabble), DBE
Holt, Dame Denise Mary, DCMG
Homer, Dame Linda Margaret, DCB
Hoodless, Dame Elisabeth Anne, DBE
Hoyles, *Prof.* Dame Celia Mary, DBE
Hudson, Dame Alice, DBE
Hufton, *Prof.* Dame Olwen, DBE
Humphrey, *Prof.* Dame Caroline (Lady Rees of Ludlow), DBE
Hunt, Dame Vivian, DBE
Husband, *Prof.* Dame Janet Elizabeth Siarey, DBE
Hussey, Dame Susan Katharine (Lady Hussey of North Bradley), GCVO
Hutton, Dame Deirdre Mary, DBE
Hyde, Dame Helen, DBE
Imison, Dame Tamsyn, DBE
Ion, *Dr* Dame Susan Elizabeth, DBE
Isaacs, Dame Albertha Madeline, DBE
James, Dame Naomi Christine (Mrs Haythorne), DBE
Jefford, *Hon.* Dame Nerys Angharad, DBE
Jiang, *Prof.* Dame Xiangqian (Jane), DBE
John, Dame Susan, DBE
Johnson, *Prof.* Dame Anne Mandall, DBE
Johnston, Dame Rotha Geraldine Diane, DBE
Jones, Dame Gwyneth (Mrs Haberfeld-Jones), DBE
Jordan, *Prof.* Dame Carole, DBE
Joseph, Dame Monica Theresa, DBE
Jowett, Dame Susan, DBE
Judd, *Hon.* Dame Frances, DBE
Julius, *Dr* Dame DeAnne Shirley, DCMG, CBE
Karika, Dame Pauline Margaret Rakera George (Mrs Taripo), DBE

Rees, *Prof.* Dame Lesley Howard, DBE
Rees, *Prof.* Dame Teresa Lesley, DBE
Reeves, Dame Helen May, DBE
Refson, Dame Benita, DBE
Rego, Dame Paula Figueiroa, DBE
Reid, Dame Seona Elizabeth, DBE
Reynolds, Dame Fiona Claire, DBE
Rhodes, Dame Zandra Lindsey, DBE
Rice, Lady Susan Ilene, DBE
Richard, Dame Alison (Fettes), DBE
Richardson, Dame Mary, DBE
Rigg, Dame Diana, DBE
Rimington, Dame Stella, DCB
Ritterman, Dame Janet, DBE
Roberts, Dame Jane Elisabeth, DBE
Roberts, *Hon.* Dame Jennifer Mary, DBE
Roberts, *Hon.* Dame Priscilla Jane Stephanie (Lady Roberts),
    DCVO
Robins, Dame Ruth Laura, DBE
Robinson, *Prof.* Dame Ann Louise
Robinson, *Prof.* Dame Carol Vivien, DBE
Robottom, Dame Marlene, DBE
Roe, Dame Marion Audrey, DBE
Roe, Dame Raigh Edith, DBE
Ronson, Dame Gail, DBE
Roscoe, *Dr* Dame Ingrid Mary, DCVO
Rose, *Rt. Hon.* Dame Vivien Judith, DBE
Ross-Wawrzynski, Dame Dana (Mrs Ross-Wawrzynski),
    DBE
Rothwell, *Prof.* Dame Nancy Jane, DBE
Routledge, Dame Katherine Patricia, DBE
Ruddock, *Rt. Hon.* Dame Joan Mary, DBE
Runciman of Doxford, The Viscountess, DBE
Russell, *Hon.* Dame Alison Hunter, DBE
Russell, *Dr* Dame Philippa Margaret, DBE
Ryan, Dame Christine, DBE
Sackler, Dame Theresa, DBE
Salmond, *Prof.* Dame Mary Anne, DBE
Saunders, *Dr* Dame Frances Carolyn, DBE, CB
Savill, Dame Rosalind Joy, DBE
Sawyer, *Rt. Hon.* Dame Joan Augusta, DBE
Scardino, Dame Marjorie, DBE
Scott, Dame Catherine Margaret (Mrs Denton), DBE
Scott Thomas, Dame Kristin, DBE
Seward, Dame Margaret Helen Elizabeth, DBE
Sharp, *Rt. Hon.* Dame Victoria Madeleine, DBE
Shaw, *Prof.* Dame Pamela Jean, DBE
Shirley, Dame Stephanie, CH, DBE
Shovelton, Dame Helena, DBE
Sibley, Dame Antoinette (Mrs Corbett), DBE
Sills, *Prof.* Dame Eileen, DBE
Silver, *Dr* Dame Ruth Muldoon, DBE
Simler, *Rt. Hon.* Dame Ingrid Ann (Mrs Bernstein), DBE
Slade, *Hon.* Dame Elizabeth Ann, DBE
Slingo, *Prof.* Dame Julia Mary, DBE
Smith, Dame Dela, DBE
Smith, *Rt. Hon.* Dame Janet Hilary (Mrs Mathieson), DBE
Smith, *Hon.* Dame Jennifer Meredith, DBE
Smith, Dame Margaret Natalie (Maggie) (Mrs Cross), CH,
    DBE
Snowball, Dame Priscilla (Cilla) Deborah, DBE
Southgate, *Prof.* Dame Lesley Jill, DBE
Spelman, *Rt. Hon.* Dame Caroline Alice, DBE
Spencer, Dame Rosemary Jane, DCMG
Squire, Dame Rosemary Anne, DBE
Stacey, Dame Glenys Jean (Mrs Kyle), DBE
Steel, *Hon.* Dame (Anne) Heather (Mrs Beattie), DBE
Stephens, *Prof.* Dame Elan Cross, DBE
Stocking, Dame Barbara Mary, DBE
Storey, Dame Sarah Joanne, DBE

Strachan, Dame Valerie Patricia Marie, DCB
Strank, *Dr* Dame Angela Rosemary Emily, DBE
Strathern, *Prof.* Dame Anne Marilyn, DBE
Street, Dame Susan Ruth, DCB
Stringer, *Prof.* Dame Joan Kathleen, DBE
Sutherland, Dame Veronica Evelyn, DBE, CMG
Suzman, Dame Janet, DBE
Swift, *Hon.* Dame Caroline Jane (Mrs Openshaw), DBE
Symmonds, Dame Olga Patricia, DBE
Tanner, *Dr* Dame Mary Elizabeth, DBE
Taylor, Dame Meg, DBE
Te Kanawa, Dame Kiri Janette, CH, DBE
Theis, *Hon.* Dame Lucy Morgan, DBE
Thirlwall, *Rt. Hon.* Dame Kathryn Mary, DBE
Thomas, *Prof.* Dame Jean Olwen, DBE
Thomas, Dame Kathrin Elizabeth, DCVO
Thomas, Dame Maureen Elizabeth (Lady Thomas), DBE
Thompson, Dame Emma, DBE
Thompson, Dame Ila Dianne, DBE
Thornton, *Prof.* Dame Janet Maureen, DBE
Thornton, *Hon.* Dame Justine, DBE
Thornton, Dame Sara Joanne, DBE, QPM
Tickell, Dame Clare Oriana, DBE
Tinson, Dame Sue, DBE
Tizard, Dame Catherine Anne, GCMG, GCVO, DBE
Tokiel, Dame Rosa, DBE
Trotter, Dame Janet Olive, DBE
Twelftree, Dame Marcia, DBE
Uchida, Dame Mitsuko, DBE
Uprichard, Dame Mary Elizabeth, DBE
Vitmayer, Dame Janet Mary, DBE
Wagner, Dame Gillian Mary Millicent (Lady Wagner), DBE
Wallace, *Prof.* Dame Helen Sarah, DBE, CMG
Wallis, Dame Sheila Ann, DBE
Walter, Dame Harriet Mary, DBE
Walters, Dame Julie Mary, DBE
Warburton, Dame Anne Arabella, DBE
Warner, *Prof.* Dame Marina Sarah, DBE, FBA
Warwick, Dame Catherine Lilian, DBE
Waterhouse, *Dr* Dame Rachel Elizabeth, DBE
Waterman, *Dr* Dame Fanny, DBE
Watkins, *Prof.* Dame Caroline Leigh, DBE
Watkinson, Dame Angela Eileen, DBE
Webb, *Prof.* Dame Patricia, DBE
Weir, Dame Gillian Constance (Mrs Phelps), DBE
Weller, Dame Rita, DBE
Wells, Dame Rachel Anne, DCVO
Weston, Dame Margaret Kate, DBE
Westwood, Dame Vivienne Isabel, DBE
Whipple, *Hon.* Dame Philippa Jane Edwards, DBE
Whitehead, *Hon.* Dame Annabel Alice Hoyer, DCVO
Whitehead, *Prof.* Dame Margaret McRae, DBE
Whiteread, Dame Rachel, DBE
Wigley, Dame Susan Louise, DCVO
Williams, Dame Josephine, DBE
Willmot, Dame Glenis, DBE
Wilson, Dame Jacqueline, DBE
Wilson-Barnett, *Prof.* Dame Jenifer, DBE
Wilton, Dame Penelope Alice, DBE
Windsor, Dame Barbara, DBE
Winterton, *Rt. Hon.* Dame Rosalie, DBE
Wintour, Dame Anna, DBE
Wolfson de Botton, Dame Janet (Mrs Wolfson de Botton),
    DBE
Wong Yick-ming, Dame Rosanna, DBE
Woodward, Dame Barbara Janet, DCMG, OBE
Woolf, Dame Catherine Fiona, DBE
Wykes, *Prof.* Dame Til Hilary Margaret, DBE
Yip, *Hon.* Dame Amanda Louise, DBE
Zaffar, Dame Naila, DBE

DECORATIONS AND MEDALS

PRINCIPAL DECORATIONS AND MEDALS IN ORDER OF WEAR

VICTORIA CROSS (VC), 1856 (*see* below)
GEORGE CROSS (GC), 1940 (*see* below)

BRITISH ORDERS OF KNIGHTHOOD
(*see also* Orders of Chivalry)

Order of the Garter
Order of the Thistle
Order of St Patrick
Order of the Bath
Order of Merit
Order of the Star of India
Order of St Michael and George
Order of the Indian Empire
Order of the Crown of India
Royal Victorian Order (Classes I, II and III)
Order of the British Empire (Classes I, II and III)
Order of the Companions of Honour
Distinguished Service Order
Royal Victorian Order (Class IV)
Order of the British Empire (Class IV)
Imperial Service Order
Royal Victorian Order (Class V)
Order of the British Empire (Class V)

BARONET'S BADGE

KNIGHT BACHELOR'S BADGE

INDIAN ORDER OF MERIT (MILITARY)

DECORATIONS, MEDALS FOR GALLANTRY AND DISTINGUISHED CONDUCT
Conspicuous Gallantry Cross (CGC), 1995
Distinguished Conduct Medal (DCM), 1854
Conspicuous Gallantry Medal (CGM), 1874
Conspicuous Gallantry Medal (Flying)
George Medal (GM), 1940
Royal West African Field Force Distinguished Conduct Medal (DCM)
Queen's Police Medal for Gallantry
Queen's Fire Service Medal for Gallantry
Royal Red Cross Class I (RRC), 1883
Distinguished Service Cross (DSC), 1914
Military Cross (MC), December 1914
Distinguished Flying Cross (DFC), 1918
Air Force Cross (AFC), 1918
Royal Red Cross Class II (ARRC)
Order of British India (OBI)
Kaisar-i-Hind Medal
Order of St John
Union of South Africa Queen's Medal for Bravery (Gold)
King's African Rifles Distinguished Conduct Medal
Indian Distinguished Service Medal (IDSM)
Union of South Africa Queen's Medal for Bravery (Silver)
Distinguished Service Medal (DSM), 1914
Military Medal (MM)
Distinguished Flying Medal (DFM)
Air Force Medal (AFM)
Constabulary Medal (Ireland)
Medal for Saving Life at Sea (Sea Gallantry Medal)

Indian Order of Merit (Civil)
Indian Police Medal for Gallantry
Ceylon Police Medal for Gallantry
Sierra Leone Police Medal for Gallantry
Sierra Leone Fire Brigades Medal for Gallantry
Colonial Police Medal for Gallantry
Overseas Territories Police Medal for Gallantry
Queen's Gallantry Medal (QGM), 1974
Royal Victorian Medal (RVM) (Gold, Silver and Bronze)
British Empire Medal (BEM)
Canada Medal
Queen's Police Medal for Distinguished Service (QPM)
Queen's Fire Service Medal for Distinguished Service (QFSM)
Queen's Ambulance Service Medal
Queen's Volunteer Reserves Medal
Queen's Medal for Chiefs

BADGE OF HONOUR

CAMPAIGN MEDALS AND STARS
Including any authorised UN, European Community/Union and NATO medals (in order of date of campaign for which awarded).
 World War medals are worn in the following order:
 First World War, 1914 Star; 1914–15 Star; British War Medal; Mercantile Marine War Medal; Victory Medal; Territorial Force War Medal
 Second World War, 1939–45 Star; Atlantic Star; Arctic Star; Air Crew Europe Star; Africa Star; Pacific Star; Burma Star; Italy Star; France & Germany Star; Defence Medal; Canadian/Newfoundland Volunteer Service Medal; War Medal; Africa Service Medal; India Service Medal; New Zealand War Service Medal; Southern Rhodesia Service Medal; Australian Service Medal

POLAR MEDALS *in order of date*

IMPERIAL SERVICE MEDAL

POLICE MEDALS FOR VALUABLE SERVICE
Indian Police Medal for Meritorious Service
Ceylon Police Medal for Merit
Sierra Leone Police Medal for Meritorious Service
Sierra Leone Fire Brigades Medal for Meritorious Service
Colonial Police Medal for Meritorious Service
Overseas Territories Police Medal for Meritorious Service

JUBILEE, CORONATION AND DURBAR MEDALS
Queen Victoria, King Edward VII, King George V, King George VI, Queen Elizabeth II, Visit Commemoration and Long and Faithful Service Medals

EFFICIENCY AND LONG SERVICE DECORATIONS AND MEDALS
Meritorious Service Medal
Accumulated Campaign Service Medal
Accumulated Campaign Service Medal (2011)
Army Long Service and Good Conduct Medal
Naval Long Service and Good Conduct Medal
Medal for Meritorious Service (Royal Navy 1918–28)
Indian Long Service and Good Conduct Medal
Indian Meritorious Service Medal
Royal Marines Meritorious Service Medal (1849–1947)
Royal Air Force Meritorious Service Medal (1918–1928)

Royal Air Force Long Service and Good Conduct Medal
Medal for Long Service and Good Conduct (Ulster Defence Regiment)
Indian Long Service and Good Conduct Medal
Royal West African Frontier Force Long Service and Good Conduct Medal
Royal Sierra Leone Military Forces Long Service and Good Conduct Medal
King's African Rifles Long Service and Good Conduct Medal
Indian Meritorious Service Medal
Police Long Service and Good Conduct Medal
Fire Brigade Long Service and Good Conduct Medal
African Police Medal for Meritorious Service
Royal Canadian Mounted Police Long Service Medal
Ceylon Police Long Service Medal
Ceylon Fire Services Long Service Medal
Sierra Leone Police Long Service Medal
Colonial Police Long Service Medal
Overseas Territories Police Long Service Medal
Sierra Leone Fire Brigades Long Service Medal
Mauritius Police Long Service and Good Conduct Medal
Mauritius Fire Services Long Service and Good Conduct Medal
Mauritius Prisons Service Long Service and Good Conduct Medal
Colonial Fire Brigades Long Service Medal
Overseas Territories Fire Brigades Long Service Medal
Colonial Prison Service Medal
Overseas Territories Prison Service Medal
Hong Kong Disciplined Services Medal
Army Emergency Reserve Decoration (ERD)
Volunteer Officers' Decoration (VD)
Volunteer Long Service Medal
Volunteer Officers' Decoration (for India and the Colonies)
Volunteer Long Service Medal (for India and the Colonies)
Colonial Auxiliary Forces Officers' Decoration
Colonial Auxiliary Forces Long Service Medal
Medal for Good Shooting (Naval)
Militia Long Service Medal
Imperial Yeomanry Long Service Medal
Territorial Decoration (TD), 1908
Ceylon Armed Services Long Service Medal
Efficiency Decoration (ED)
Territorial Efficiency Medal
Efficiency Medal
Special Reserve Long Service and Good Conduct Medal
Decoration for Officers of the Royal Navy Reserve
Decoration for Officers of the Royal Naval Volunteer Reserve
Royal Naval Reserve Long Service Medal
Royal Naval Volunteer Reserve Long Service Medal
Royal Naval Auxiliary Sick Berth Reserve Long Service and Good Conduct Medal
Royal Fleet Reserve Long Service and Good Conduct Medal
Royal Naval Wireless Auxiliary Reserve Long Service and Good Conduct Medal
Royal Naval Auxiliary Service Medal
Air Efficiency Award (AE), 1942
Volunteer Reserves Service Medal
Ulster Defence Regiment Medal
Northern Ireland Home Service Medal
Queen's Medal (for Champion Shots of the RN and RM)
Queen's Medal (for Champion Shots of the New Zealand Naval Forces)
Queen's Medal (for Champion Shots in the Military Forces)
Queen's Medal (for Champion Shots of the Air Forces)
Cadet Forces Medal, 1950
Coastguard Auxiliary Service Long Service Medal
Special Constabulary Long Service Medal
Canadian Forces Decoration
Royal Observer Corps Medal
Civil Defence Long Service Medal

Ambulance Service (Emergency Duties) Long Service and Good Conduct Medal
Royal Fleet Auxiliary Service Medal
Prison Services (Operational Duties) Long Service and Good Conduct Medal
Jersey Honorary Police Long Service and Good Conduct Medal
Merchant Navy Medal for Meritorious Service
Ebola Medal for Service in West Africa
National Crime Agency Long Service and Good Conduct Medal
Rhodesia Medal (1980)
Royal Ulster Constabulary Service Medal
Northern Ireland Prison Service Medal
Union of South Africa Commemoration Medal
Indian Independence Medal
Pakistan Medal
Ceylon Armed Services Inauguration Medal
Ceylon Police Independence Medal (1948)
Sierra Leone Independence Medal
Jamaica Independence Medal
Uganda Independence Medal
Malawi Independence Medal
Fiji Independence Medal
Papua New Guinea Independence Medal
Solomon Islands Independence Medal
Service Medal of the Order of St John
Badge of the Order of the League of Mercy
Voluntary Medical Service Medal
Women's Royal Voluntary Service Medal
South African Medal for War Services
Overseas Territories Special Constabulary Medal
Colonial Special Constabulary Medal

COMMONWEALTH REALM'S ORDERS, DECORATIONS AND MEDALS in order of date

OTHER COMMONWEALTH MEMBER'S ORDERS, DECORATIONS AND MEDALS in order of date

FOREIGN ORDERS, FOREIGN DECORATIONS AND FOREIGN MEDALS in order of date

THE VICTORIA CROSS (1856)

FOR CONSPICUOUS BRAVERY

VC

Ribbon, Crimson, for all Services (until 1918 it was blue for the Royal Navy)

Instituted on 29 January 1856, the Victoria Cross was awarded retrospectively to 1854, the first being held by Lt. C. D. Lucas, RN, for bravery in the Baltic Sea on 21 June 1854 (gazetted 24 February 1857). The first 62 crosses were presented by Queen Victoria in Hyde Park, London, on 26 June 1857.

The Victoria Cross is worn before all other decorations, on the left breast, and consists of a cross-pattée of bronze, 3.8cm in diameter, with the royal crown surmounted by a lion in the centre, and beneath there is the inscription For Valour. In July 2015 the tax-free annuity given to holders of the VC, irrespective of need or other conditions, was increased to £10,000. At the same time, further annual increases to the annuity were linked to the CPI rate of inflation. In 1911, the right to receive the cross was extended to Indian soldiers, and in 1920 to matrons, sisters and nurses, the staff of the nursing services and other services pertaining to hospitals and nursing, and to civilians of either sex regularly or temporarily under the orders, direction or supervision of the naval, military, or air forces of the crown.

SURVIVING RECIPIENTS OF THE VICTORIA CROSS
as at 31 December 2020

Apiata, *Cpl.* B. H., VC (New Zealand Special Air Service)
  2004 *Afghanistan*
Beharry, *LSgt* J. G., VC (Princess of Wales's Royal Regiment)
  2005 *Iraq*
Cruickshank, *Flt Lt.* J. A., VC (RAFVR)
  1944 *World War*
Donaldson, *Cpl.* M. G. S., VC (Australian Special Air Service)
  2008 *Afghanistan*
Keighran, *Cpl.* D. A., VC (Royal Australian Regiment)
  2012 *Afghanistan*
Leakey, *Lance Cpl.* J. M., VC (Parachute Regiment)
  2015 *Afghanistan*
Payne, *WO* K., VC, DSC (USA) (Australian Army Training Team)
  1969 *Vietnam*
Rambahadur Limbu, *Capt.,* VC, MVO (10th Princess Mary's Gurkha Rifles)
  1965 *Sarawak*
Roberts-Smith, *Cpl.* B., VC (Australian Special Air Service)
  2010 *Afghanistan*
Sheean, Ord. Seaman E., (Royal Australian Navy)
  2020 *World War*

THE GEORGE CROSS (1940)
FOR GALLANTRY

GC

Ribbon, Dark blue, threaded through a bar adorned with laurel leaves
Instituted 24 September 1940 (with amendments, 3 November 1942)

The George Cross is worn before all other decorations (except the VC) on the left breast (when worn by a woman it may be worn on the left shoulder from a ribbon of the same width and colour fashioned into a bow). It consists of a plain silver cross with four equal limbs, the cross having in the centre a circular medallion bearing a design showing St George and the Dragon. The inscription *For Gallantry* appears round the medallion and in the angle of each limb of the cross is the royal cypher 'G VI' forming a circle concentric with the medallion. The reverse is plain and bears the name of the recipient and the date of the award. The cross is suspended by a ring from a bar adorned with laurel leaves on dark blue ribbon 3.8cm wide.

The cross is intended primarily for civilians; awards to the fighting services are confined to actions for which purely military honours are not normally granted. It is awarded only for acts of the greatest heroism or of the most conspicuous courage in circumstances of extreme danger. In July 2015 the

tax-free annuity given to holders of the GC, irrespective of need or other conditions, was increased to £10,000. At the same time, further annual increases to the annuity were linked to the CPI rate of inflation. The cross has twice been awarded collectively rather than to an individual: to the island of Malta (1942) and the Royal Ulster Constabulary (1999).

In October 1971 all surviving holders of the Albert Medal and the Edward Medal had their awards translated to the George Cross.

SURVIVING RECIPIENTS OF THE GEORGE CROSS
as at 31 December 2020

If the recipient originally received the Albert Medal (AM) or the Edward Medal (EM), this is indicated by the initials in parentheses.

Bamford, J., GC, 1952
Beaton, J., GC, CVO, 1974
Croucher, *Lance Cpl.* M., GC, 2008
Finney, C., GC, 2003
Gledhill, A. J., GC, 1967
Haberfield, *CSgt.* K. H., GC, 2005
Hughes, *WO2* K. S., GC, 2010
Johnson, *WO1* (*SSM*) B., GC, 1990
Lowe, A. R., GC (AM), 1949
Norton, *Maj.* P. A., GC, 2006
Pratt, M. K., GC, 1978
Purves, Mrs M., GC (AM), 1949
Shephard, S. J., GC, 2014
Troulan, D., GC, QGM, 2017
Walker, C., GC, 1972

THE ELIZABETH CROSS (2009)

EC

Instituted 1 July 2009

The Elizabeth Cross consists of a silver cross with a laurel wreath passing between the arms, which bear the floral symbols of England (rose), Scotland (thistle), Ireland (shamrock) and Wales (daffodil). The centre of the cross bears the royal cypher and the reverse is inscribed with the name of the person for whom it is in honour. The cross is accompanied by a memorial scroll and a miniature.

The cross was created to commemorate UK armed forces personnel who have died on operations or as a result of an act of terrorism. It may be granted to and worn by the next of kin of any eligible personnel who died from 1 January 1948 to date. It offers the wearer no precedence. Those that are eligible include the next of kin of personnel who died while serving on a medal earning operation, as a result of an act of terrorism, or on a non-medal earning operation where death was caused by the inherent high risk of the task.

The Elizabeth Cross is not intended as a posthumous medal for the fallen but as an emblem of national recognition of the loss and sacrifice made by the personnel and their families.

CHIEFS OF CLANS IN SCOTLAND

Only chiefs of whole Names or Clans are included, except certain special instances (marked *) who, though not chiefs of a whole Name, were or are for some reason independent. Under decision (*Campbell-Gray*, 1950) that a bearer of a 'double or triple-barrelled' surname cannot be held chief of a part of such, several others cannot be included in the list at present.

THE ROYAL HOUSE: HM The Queen

AGNEW: Sir Crispin Agnew of Lochnaw, Bt., QC
ANSTRUTHER: Tobias Anstruther of Anstruther and Balcaskie
ARBUTHNOTT: Viscount of Arbuthnott
BANNERMAN: Sir David Bannerman of Elsick, Bt.
BARCLAY: Peter C. Barclay of Towie Barclay and of that Ilk
BORTHWICK: Lord Borthwick
BOYLE: Earl of Glasgow
BRODIE: Alexander Brodie of Brodie
BROUN OF COLSTOUN: Sir Wayne Broun of Colstoun, Bt.
BRUCE: Earl of Elgin and Kincardine, KT
BUCHAN: Charles Buchan of Auchmacoy
BURNETT: James C. A. Burnett of Leys
CAMERON: Donald Cameron of Lochiel, CVO
CAMPBELL: Duke of Argyll
CARMICHAEL: Richard Carmichael of Carmichael
CARNEGIE: Duke of Fife
CATHCART: Earl Cathcart
CHARTERIS: Earl of Wemyss and March
CLAN CHATTAN: K. Mackintosh of Clan Chattan
CHISHOLM: Hamish Chisholm of Chisholm (*The Chisholm*)
COCHRANE: Earl of Dundonald
COLQUHOUN: Sir Malcolm Rory Colquhoun of Luss, Bt.
CRANSTOUN: David Cranstoun of that Ilk
CUMMING: Sir Alastair Cumming of Altyre, Bt.
DARROCH: Duncan Darroch of Gourock
DAVIDSON OF DAVIDSTON: Grant Davidson of Davidston
DEWAR: Michael Dewar of that Ilk and Vogrie
DRUMMOND: Earl of Perth
DUNBAR: Sir James Dunbar of Mochrum, Bt.
DUNDAS: David Dundas of Dundas
DURIE: Andrew Durie of Durie, CBE
ELIOTT: Mrs Margaret Eliott of Redheugh
ERSKINE: Earl of Mar and Kellie
FARQUHARSON: Capt. Alwyne Farquharson of Invercauld, MC
FERGUSSON: Sir Charles Fergusson of Kilkerran, Bt.
FORBES: Lord Forbes
FORSYTH: Alistair Forsyth of that Ilk
FRASER: Lady Saltoun
*FRASER (OF LOVAT): Lord Lovat
GAYRE: Reinold Gayre of Gayre and Nigg
GORDON: Marquess of Huntly
GRAHAM: Duke of Montrose
GRANT: Lord Strathspey
GUNN: Iain Gunn of Gunn
GUTHRIE: Alexander Guthrie of Guthrie
HAIG: Earl Haig
HALDANE: Martin Haldane of Gleneagles
HANNAY: David Hannay of Kirkdale and of that Ilk
HAY: Earl of Erroll

HENDERSON: Alistair Henderson of Fordell
HUNTER: Pauline Hunter of Hunterston
IRVINE OF DRUM: Alexander H. R. Irvine of Drum
JARDINE: Sir William Jardine of Applegirth, Bt.
JOHNSTONE: Earl of Annandale and Hartfell
KEITH: Earl of Kintore
KENNEDY: Marquess of Ailsa
KERR: Marquess of Lothian, PC
KINCAID: Madam Arabella Kincaid of Kincaid
LAMONT: Revd Peter Lamont of that Ilk
LEASK: Jonathan Leask of that Ilk
LENNOX: Edward Lennox of that Ilk
LESLIE: Earl of Rothes
LINDSAY: Earl of Crawford and Balcarres, KT, GCVO, PC
LIVINGSTONE (or MACLEA): Niall Livingstone of the Bachuil
LOCKHART: Ranald Lockhart of the Lee
LUMSDEN: Gillem Lumsden of that Ilk and Blanerne
MACALESTER: William St J. McAlester of Loup and Kennox
MACARTHUR; John MacArthur of that Ilk
MCBAIN: James H. McBain of McBain
MACDONALD: Lord Macdonald (*The Macdonald of Macdonald*)
*MACDONALD OF CLANRANALD: Ranald Macdonald of Clanranald
*MACDONALD OF KEPPOCH: Ranald MacDonald of Keppoch
*MACDONALD OF SLEAT (CLAN HUSTEAIN): Sir Ian Macdonald of Sleat, Bt.
*MACDONELL OF GLENGARRY: Ranald MacDonell of Glengarry
MACDOUGALL: Morag MacDougall of MacDougall
MACDOWALL: Fergus Macdowall of Garthland
MACGREGOR: Sir Malcolm MacGregor of MacGregor, Bt.
MACINTYRE: Donald MacIntyre of Glenoe
MACKAY: Lord Reay
MACKENZIE: Earl of Cromartie
MACKINNON: Anne Mackinnon of Mackinnon
MACKINTOSH: John Mackintosh of Mackintosh (*The Mackintosh of Mackintosh*)
MACLACHLAN: Euan MacLachlan of MacLachlan
MACLAINE: Lorne Maclaine of Lochbuie
MACLAREN: Donald MacLaren of MacLaren and Achleskine
MACLEAN: Hon. Sir Lachlan Maclean of Duart, Bt., CVO
MACLENNAN: Ruaraidh MacLennan of MacLennan
MACLEOD: Hugh MacLeod of MacLeod
MACMILLAN: George MacMillan of MacMillan
MACNAB: James W. A. Macnab of Macnab (*The Macnab*)
MACNAGHTEN: Sir Malcolm Macnaghten of Macnaghten and Dundarave, Bt.
MACNEACAIL: John Macneacail of Macneacail and Scorrybreac
MACNEIL OF BARRA: Rory Macneil of Barra (*The Macneil of Barra*)
MACPHERSON: Hon. Sir William Macpherson of Cluny, TD
MACTAVISH: Steven MacTavish of Dunardry
MACTHOMAS: Andrew MacThomas of Finegand
MAITLAND: Earl of Lauderdale
MAKGILL: Viscount of Oxfuird
MALCOLM (MACCALLUM): Robin N. L. Malcolm of Poltalloch

MAR: Countess of Mar
MARJORIBANKS: Andrew Marjoribanks of that Ilk
MATHESON: Sir Alexander Matheson of Matheson, Bt.
MENZIES: David Menzies of Menzies
MOFFAT: Madam Moffat of that Ilk
MONCREIFFE: Hon. Peregrine Moncreiffe of that Ilk
MONTGOMERIE: Earl of Eglinton and Winton
MORRISON: Dr John Ruairidh Morrison of Ruchdi
MUNRO: Hector Munro of Foulis
MURRAY: Duke of Atholl
NESBITT (or NISBET): Mark Nesbitt of that Ilk
OGILVY: Earl of Airlie, KT, GCVO, PC
OLIPHANT: Richard Oliphant of that Ilk
RAMSAY: Earl of Dalhousie
RIDDELL: Sir Walter Riddell of Riddell, Bt.
ROBERTSON: Alexander Robertson of Struan *(Struan-Robertson)*
ROLLO: Lord Rollo

ROSS: David Ross of that Ilk and Balnagowan
RUTHVEN: Earl of Gowrie, PC
SCOTT: Duke of Buccleuch and Queensberry, KT, KBE
SCRYMGEOUR: Earl of Dundee
SEMPILL: Lord Sempill
SHAW: Iain Shaw of Tordarroch
SINCLAIR: Earl of Caithness, PC
SKENE: Dugald Skene of Skene
STIRLING: Fraser Stirling of Cader
STRANGE: Maj. Timothy Strange of Balcaskie
SUTHERLAND: Earl of Sutherland
SWINTON: John Swinton of that Ilk
TROTTER: Alexander Trotter of Mortonhall, CVO
URQUHART: Wilkins F. Urquhart of Urquhart
WALLACE: Andrew Wallace of that Ilk
WEDDERBURN: The Master of Dundee
WEMYSS: Michael Wemyss of that Ilk

THE PRIVY COUNCIL

The sovereign in council, or Privy Council, was the chief source of executive power until the system of cabinet government developed in the 18th century. Now the Privy Council's main functions are to advise the sovereign and to exercise its own statutory responsibilities independent of the sovereign in council.

Membership of the Privy Council is automatic upon appointment to certain government and judicial positions in the UK, eg cabinet ministers must be Privy Counsellors and are sworn in on first assuming office. Membership is also accorded by the Queen to eminent people in the UK and independent countries of the Commonwealth of which she is Queen, on the recommendation of the prime minister. Membership of the council is retained for life, except for very occasional removals.

The administrative functions of the Privy Council are carried out by the Privy Council Office under the direction of the president of the council, who is always a member of the cabinet. (*see also* Parliament)

President of the Council, Rt. Hon. Jacob Rees-Mogg, MP

Clerk of the Council, Richard Tilbrook

Style The Right (or Rt.) Hon._
Envelope, The Right (or Rt.) Hon. F_ S_. Letter, Dear Mr/Miss/Mrs S_. *Spoken,* Mr/Miss/Mrs S_

It is incorrect to use the letters PC after the name in conjunction with the prefix The Right Hon., unless the Privy Counsellor is a peer below the rank of Marquess and so is styled The Right Hon. because of his/her rank.

MEMBERS *as at 31 December 2020*

HRH The Duke of Edinburgh, 1951
HRH The Prince of Wales, 1977
HRH The Duke of Cambridge, 2016
HRH The Duchess of Cornwall, 2016

Abbott, Diane, 2017
Abernethy, *Hon.* Lord (Alastair Cameron), 2005
Adonis, Lord, 2009
Aikens, Sir Richard, 2008
Ainsworth, Robert, 2005
Airlie, Earl of, 1984
Alebua, Ezekiel, 1988
Alexander, Sir Danny, 2010
Alexander, Douglas, 2005
Amos, Baroness, 2003
Anderson of Swansea, Lord, 2000
Andrews, Dame Geraldine, 2020
Anelay of St Johns, Baroness, 2009
Angiolini, Dame Elish, 2006
Anthony, Douglas, 1971
Arbuthnot of Edrom, Lord, 1998
Arden of Heswall, Lady, 2000
Armstrong of Hill Top, Baroness, 1999
Arnold, Sir Richard, 2019
Arthur, *Hon.* Owen, 1995
Ashcroft, Lord, 2012
Ashton of Hyde, Lord, 2019
Ashton of Upholland, Baroness, 2006
Asplin, Dame Sarah, 2017
Astor of Hever, Lord, 2015
Atkins, Sir Robert, 1995
Auld, Sir Robin, 1995
Baker, Sir Jonathan, 2018
Baker, Norman, 2014
Baker, Sir Thomas, 2002
Baker of Dorking, Lord, 1984
Baldry, Sir Tony, 2013
Balls, Ed, 2007
Barclay, Stephen, 2018
Barker of Battle, Lord, 2012
Barron, Sir Kevin, 2001
Barrow, Dean, 2016
Barwell, Lord, 2017

Bassam of Brighton, Lord, 2009
Bates, Lord, 2015
Battle, John, 2002
Bean, Sir David, 2014
Beatson, Sir Jack, 2013
Beckett, Dame Margaret, 1993
Beith, Lord, 1992
Beldam, Sir Roy, 1989
Benn, Hilary, 2003
Benyon, Richard, 2017
Bercow, John, 2009
Berry, Jake, 2019
Birch, Sir William, 1992
Black of Derwent, Lady, 2010
Blackford, Ian, 2017
Blackstone, Baroness, 2001
Blair, Anthony, 1994
Blanchard, Peter, 1998
Blears, Hazel, 2005
Blencathra, Lord, 1995
Blunkett, Lord, 1997
Boateng, Lord, 1999
Bolger, James, 1991
Bonomy, *Hon.* Lord (Iain Bonomy), 2010
Boothroyd, Baroness, 1992
Bottomley of Nettlestone, Baroness, 1992
Boyd of Duncansby, Lord, 2000
Brabazon of Tara, Lord, 2013
Bracadale, *Hon.* Lord (Alistair Campbell), 2013
Bradley, Karen, 2016
Bradley, Lord, 2001
Bradshaw, Ben, 2009
Brake, Thomas, 2011
Braverman, Suella, 2020
Briggs of Westbourne, Lord, 2013
Brodie, *Hon.* Lord (Philip Brodie), 2013
Brokenshire, James, 2015
Brooke, Dame Annette, 2014
Brooke of Sutton Mandeville, Lord, 1988
Brown, Gordon, 1996

Brown, Nicholas, 1997
Brown, Sir Stephen, 1983
Brown of Eaton-under-Heywood, Lord, 1992
Browne of Ladyton, Lord, 2005
Bruce of Bennachie, Lord, 2006
Buckland, Robert, 2019
Burnett of Maldon, Lord, 2014
Burnham, Andy, 2007
Burns, Conor, 2019
Burns, Sir Simon, 2011
Burnton, Sir Stanley, 2008
Burrows, Lord, 2020
Burstow, Paul, 2012
Burt, Alistair, 2013
Butler of Brockwell, Lord, 2004
Butler-Sloss, Baroness, 1988
Buxton, Sir Richard, 1997
Byers, Stephen, 1998
Byrne, Liam, 2008
Byron, Sir Dennis, 2004
Cable, Sir Vincent, 2010
Caborn, Richard, 1999
Cairns, Alun, 2016
Caithness, Earl of, 1990
Cameron, David, 2005
Cameron of Lochbroom, Lord, 1984
Camoys, Lord, 1997
Campbell, Sir Alan, 2014
Campbell, Sir William, 1999
Campbell of Pittenweem, Lord, 1999
Canterbury, Archbishop of, 2013
Carey of Clifton, Lord, 1991
Carloway, *Hon.* Lord (Colin Sutherland), 2008
Carmichael, Alistair, 2010
Carnwath of Notting Hill, Lord, 2002
Carr, Dame Sue, 2020
Carswell, Lord, 1993
Chadwick, Sir John, 1997
Chakrabarti, Baroness, 2018
Chalfont, Lord, 1964
Chalker of Wallasey, Baroness, 1987
Chan, Sir Julius, 1981
Chartres, Rt. Revd Lord, 1995

Chilcot, Sir John, 2004
Christie, Perry, 2004
Clark, Greg, 2010
Clark, Helen, 1990
Clark of Calton, Baroness, 2013
Clark of Windermere, Lord, 1997
Clarke, Charles, 2001
Clarke, Sir Christopher, 2013
Clarke of Nottingham, Lord, 1984
Clarke, *Hon.* Lord (Matthew Clarke), 2008
Clarke, Thomas, 1997
Clarke of Stone-cum-Ebony, Lord, 1998
Clegg, Sir Nicholas, 2008
Cleverly, James, 2019
Clinton-Davis, Lord, 1998
Clwyd, Ann, 2004
Coffey, Thérèse, 2019
Coghlin, Sir Patrick, 2009
Collins of Mapesbury, Lord, 2007
Cooper, Yvette, 2007
Cope of Berkeley, Lord, 1988
Corbyn, Jeremy, 2015
Corston, Baroness, 2003
Cosgrove, *Hon.* Lady (Hazel Cosgrove), 2003
Coulson, Sir Peter, 2018
Cox, Geoffrey, 2018
Crabb, Stephen, 2014
Crawford and Balcarres, Earl of, 1972
Creech, *Hon.* Wyatt, 1999
Cullen of Whitekirk, Lord, 1997
Cunningham of Felling, Lord, 1993
Curry, David, 1996
Darling of Roulanish, Lord, 1997
Darzi of Denham, Lord, 2009
Davey, Sir Edward, 2012
Davidson, Ruth, 2016
Davies, Dame Nicola, 2018
Davies, Ronald, 1997
Davies of Oldham, Lord, 2006
Davis, David, 1997
Davis, Sir Nigel, 2011
Davis, Terence, 1999
de la Bastide, Michael, 2004
Deben, Lord, 1985
Deeny, Sir Donnell, 2017
Denham, John, 2000
Denham, Lord, 1981
Dholakia, Lord, 2010
Dingemans, Sir James, 2019
Dodds of Duncairn, Lord*, 2010
Donaldson, Sir Jeffrey, 2007
Dorrell, Stephen, 1994
Dorrian, *Hon.* Lady (Leona Dorrian), 2013
Douglas, *Dr* Denzil, 2011
Dowden, Oliver, 2019
Drakeford, Mark, 2019
Drayson, Lord, 2008
Drummond Young, *Hon.* Lord (James Drummond Young), 2013
D'Souza, Baroness, 2009
Duncan, Sir Alan, 2010
Duncan Smith, Iain, 2001
Dunne, Philip, 2019
Dyson, Lord, 2001
Eassie, *Hon.* Lord (Ronald Mackay), 2006
East, Paul, 1998
Edward, Sir David, 2005

Eggar, Timothy, 1995
Elias, Sir Patrick, 2009
Elias, *Hon.* Dame Sian, 1999
Elis-Thomas, Lord, 2004
Ellis, Michael, 2019
Ellwood, Tobias, 2017
Emslie, *Hon.* Lord (George Emslie), 2011
Esquivel, Manuel, 1986
Etherton, Sir Terence, 2008
Eustice, George, 2020
Evans, Sir Anthony, 1992
Evans of Bowes Park, Baroness, 2016
Evennett, Sir David, 2015
Falconer of Thoroton, Lord, 2003
Fallon, Sir Michael, 2012
Featherstone, Baroness, 2014
Feldman of Elstree, Lord, 2015
Fellowes, Lord, 1990
Field of Birkenhead, Lord, 1997
Field, Mark, 2015
Flaux, Sir Julian, 2017
Flint, Caroline, 2008
Floyd, Sir Christopher, 2013
Forsyth of Drumlean, Lord, 1995
Foster, Arlene, 2016
Foster of Bath, Lord, 2010
Foulkes of Cumnock, Lord, 2002
Fowler, Lord, 1979
Fox, Liam, 2010
Francois, Mark, 2010
Freedman, Sir Lawrence, 2009
Freeman, Lord, 1993
Freud, Lord, 2015
Fulford, Sir Adrian, 2013
Gage, Sir William, 2004
Gale, Sir Roger, 2019
Garden of Frognal, Baroness, 2015
Garnier, Lord, 2015
Gauke, David, 2016
Geidt, Lord, 2007
Gibb, Nicolas, 2016
Gibson, Sir Peter, 1993
Gill, *Hon.* Lord (Brian Gill), 2002
Gillan, Dame Cheryl, 2010
Gillen, Sir John, 2014
Girvan, Sir (Frederick) Paul, 2007
Glennie, *Hon.* Lord (Angus Glennie), 2016
Gloster, Dame Elizabeth, 2013
Goldring, Sir John, 2008
Goldsmith, Lord, 2002
Goldsmith of Richmond Park, Lord, 2019
Goodlad, Lord, 1992
Goodwill, Robert, 2018
Gove, Michael, 2010
Gowrie, Earl of, 1984
Graham, Sir Douglas, 1998
Grayling, Chris, 2010
Green, Damian, 2012
Green, Sir Nicholas, 2018
Greening, Justine, 2011
Grieve, Dominic, 2010
Grocott, Lord, 2002
Gross, Sir Peter, 2010
Gummer, Ben, 2016
Haddon-Cave, Sir Charles, 2018
Hague of Richmond, Lord, 1995
Hailsham, Viscount, 1992
Hain, Lord, 2001
Hale of Richmond, Baroness, 1999

Halfon, Robert, 2015
Hamilton, *Hon.* Lord (Arthur Hamilton), 2002
Hamilton of Epsom, Lord, 1991
Hammond of Runnymede, Lord, 2010
Hancock, Matthew, 2014
Hands, Gregory, 2014
Hanley, Sir Jeremy, 1994
Hanson, Sir David, 2007
Hardie, Lord, 1997
Hardie Boys, Sir Michael, 1989
Harman, Harriet, 1997
Harper, Mark, 2015
Hart, Simon, 2019
Haselhurst, Lord, 1999
Hattersley, Lord, 1975
Hayes, Sir John, 2013
Hayman, Baroness, 2000
Heald, Sir Oliver, 2016
Healey, John, 2008
Heath, David, 2015
Heathcoat-Amory, David, 1996
Henderson, Sir Launcelot, 2016
Hendry, Charles, 2010
Henley, Lord, 2013
Henry, John, 1996
Herbertof South Downs Lord, 2010
Heseltine, Lord, 1979
Heseltine, Sir William, 1986
Hesketh, Lord, 1991
Hewitt, Patricia, 2001
Hickinbottom, Sir Gary, 2017
Higgins, Lord, 1979
Higgins, Sir Malachy, 2007
Hill, Keith, 2003
Hill of Oareford, Lord, 2013
Hinds, Damian, 2018
Hodge, Dame Margaret, 2003
Hodge, Lord, 2013
Hoffmann, Lord, 1992
Holroyde, Sir Timothy, 2017
Hoon, Geoffrey, 1999
Hooper, Sir Anthony, 2004
Hope of Craighead, Lord, 1989
Hope of Thornes, Lord, 1991
Hordern, Sir Peter, 1993
Howard of Lympne, Lord, 1990
Howarth, Sir George, 2005
Howarth of Newport, Lord, 2000
Howe, Earl, 2013
Howell of Guildford, Lord, 1979
Howells, Kim, 2009
Hoyle, Sir Lindsay, 2013
Hughes, Sir Simon, 2010
Hughes of Ombersley, Lord, 2006
Hughes of Stretford, Baroness, 2004
Hunt, Jeremy, 2010
Hunt, Jonathon, 1989
Hunt of Kings Heath, Lord, 2009
Hunt of Wirral, Lord, 1990
Hurd, Nicholas, 2017
Hurd of Westwell, Lord, 1982
Hutchison, Sir Michael, 1995
Hutton of Furness, Lord, 2001
Inge, Lord, 2004
Ingraham, Hubert, 1993
Ingram, Adam, 1999
Irvine of Lairg, Lord, 1997
Irwin, Sir Stephen, 2016
Jack, Alister, 2019
Jack, Michael, 1997
Jackson, Sir Peter, 2017

Jackson, Sir Rupert, 2008
Jacob, Sir Robert, 2004
Jacobs, Francis, 2005
Janvrin, Lord, 1998
Javid, Sajid, 2014
Jay of Paddington, Baroness, 1998
Jenrick, Robert, 2019
Johnson, Alan, 2003
Johnson, Boris, 2016
Johnson of Marylebone, 2019
Jones, Carwyn, 2010
Jones, David, 2012
Jones, Kevan, 2018
Jones, Lord, 1999
Jopling, Lord, 1979
Judge, Lord, 1996
Jugnauth, Sir Anerood, 1987
Kakkar, Lord, 2014
Kay, Sir Maurice, 2004
Keen of Elie, Lord, 2017
Keene, Sir David, 2000
Keith, Sir Kenneth, 1998
Kelly, Ruth, 2004
Kennedy, Jane, 2003
Kennedy, Sir Paul, 1992
Kerr of Tonaghmore, Lord, 2004
Khan, Sadiq, 2009
Kilmorey, Earl of, 1994
King, Dame Eleanor, 2014
King of Bridgwater, Lord, 1979
Kingarth, *Hon.* Lord (Derek Emslie), 2006
Kinnock, Lord, 1983
Kitchin, Lord, 2011
Knight, Sir Gregory, 1995
Knight of Weymouth, Lord, 2008
Kramer, Baroness, 2014
Kwarteng, Kwasi, 2019
Laing, Dame Eleanor, 2017
Lamb, Sir Norman, 2014
Laming, Lord, 2014
Lammy, David, 2008
Lamont of Lerwick, Lord, 1986
Lancaster of Kimbolton, Lord, 2017
Lang of Monkton, Lord, 1990
Lansley, Lord, 2010
Latasi, Sir Kamuta, 1996
Latham, Sir David, 2000
Laws, David, 2010
Lawson of Blaby, Lord, 1981
Leadsom, Andrea, 2016
Leggatt, Lord George, 2018
Leigh, Sir Edward, 2019
Letwin, Sir Oliver, 2002
Leveson, Sir Brian, 2006
Lewis, Brandon, 2016
Lewis, Sir Clive, 2020
Lewis, Dr Julian, 2015
Lewison, Sir Kim, 2011
Liddell of Coatdyke, Baroness, 1998
Lidington, Sir David, 2010
Lilley, Lord, 1990
Lindblom, Sir Keith, 2015
Llewellyn of Steep, Lord, 2015
Lloyd, Sir Peter, 1994
Lloyd, Sir Timothy, 2005
Lloyd of Berwick, Lord, 1984
Lloyd-Jones, Lord, 2012
Llwyd, Elfyn, 2011
Longmore, Sir Andrew, 2001
Lothian, Marquess of, 1996
Luce, Lord, 1986

Lyne, Sir Roderic, 2009
McAvoy, Lord, 2003
McCartney, Sir Ian, 1999
McCloskey, Sir Bernard, 2019
McCollum, Sir Liam, 1997
McCombe, Sir Richard, 2012
McConnell of Glenscorrodale, Lord, 2001
MacDermott, Sir John, 1987
Macdonald of Tradeston, Lord, 1999
McDonnell, John, 2016
McFadden, Patrick, 2008
McFall of Alcluith, Lord, 2004
McFarlane, Sir Andrew, 2011
MacGregor of Pulham Market, Lord, 1985
McGuire, Dame Anne, 2008
Macintosh, Kenneth, 2016
Mackay, Andrew, 1998
Mackay of Clashfern, Lord, 1979
McKinnon, Sir Donald, 1992
Maclean, *Hon.* Lord (Ranald MacLean), 2001
McLeish, Henry, 2000
McLoughlin, Lord, 2005
McNally, Lord, 2005
McNulty, Anthony, 2007
Mactaggart, Fiona, 2015
Macur, Dame Julia, 2013
McVey, Esther, 2014
Major, Sir John, 1987
Malcolm, *Hon.* Lord (Colin Campbell), 2015
Males, Sir Stephen, 2019
Malloch-Brown, Lord, 2007
Mance, Lord, 1999
Mandelson, Lord, 1998
Marnoch, *Hon.* Lord (Michael Marnoch), 2001
Marwick, Tricia, 2012
Mates, Michael, 2004
Maude of Horsham, Lord, 1992
May, Sir Anthony, 1998
May, Theresa, 2003
Mellor, David, 1990
Menzies, *Hon.* Lord (Duncan Menzies), 2012
Michael, Alun, 1998
Milburn, Alan, 1998
Miliband, David, 2005
Miliband, Ed, 2007
Miller, Maria, 2012
Millett, Lord, 1994
Milling, Amanda, 2020
Milton, Anne, 2015
Mitchell, Andrew, 2010
Mitchell, Sir James, 1985
Mitchell, Dr Keith, 2004
Moore, Michael, 2010
Moore-Bick, Sir Martin, 2005
Morauta, Sir Mekere, 2001
Mordaunt, Penny, 2017
Morgan, Sir Declan, 2009
Morgan of Cotes, Baroness Nicola, 2014
Morris of Aberavon, Lord, 1970
Morris of Yardley, Baroness, 1999
Morritt, Sir Robert, 1994
Moses, Sir Alan, 2005
Moylan, Sir Andrew, 2017
Mulholland, Frank, 2011
Mullally, Rt. Revd Dame Sarah, 2018

Mummery, Sir John, 1996
Munby, Sir James, 2009
Mundell, David, 2010
Murphy, James, 2008
Murphy of Torfaen, Lord, 1999
Murrison, Dr Andrew, 2019
Musa, Wilbert, 2005
Namaliu, Sir Rabbie, 1989
Naseby, Lord, 1994
Neuberger of Abbotsbury, Lord, 2004
Neville-Jones, Baroness, 2010
Newby, Lord, 2014
Newey, Sir Guy, 2017
Nicholson, Sir Michael, 1995
Nimmo Smith, *Hon.* Lord (William Nimmo Smith), 2005
Nokes, Caroline, 2018
Norman, Jesse, 2019
Northover, Baroness, 2015
Nott, Sir John, 1979
Nugee, Sir Christopher, 2020
O'Brien, Mike, 2009
O'Brien, Sir Stephen, 2013
Oppenheim-Barnes, Baroness, 1979
Osborne, George, 2010
Osborne, *Hon.* Lord (Kenneth Osborne), 2001
Ottaway, Sir Richard, 2013
Otton, Sir Philip, 1995
Owen, Lord, 1976
Paeniu, Bikenibeu, 1991
Paice, Sir James, 2010
Palmer, Sir Geoffrey, 1986
Paraskeva, Dame Janet, 2010
Parker, Sir Jonathan, 2000
Patel, Priti, 2015
Paterson, Owen, 2010
Paton, *Hon.* Lady (Ann Paton), 2007
Patten, Lord, 1990
Patten, Sir Nicholas, 2009
Patten of Barnes, Lord, 1989
Patterson, Percival, 1993
Pattie, Sir Geoffrey, 1987
Paul, Lord, 2009
Peel, Earl, 2006
Pendry, Lord, 2000
Penning, Sir Mike, 2014
Penrose, *Hon.* Lord (George Penrose), 2000
Pentland, *Hon.* Lord (Paul Cullen), 2020
Perry, Claire, 2018
Peters, Winston, 1998
Philip, *Hon.* Lord (Alexander Philip), 2005
Phillips, Sir Stephen, 2020
Phillips of Worth Matravers, Lord, 1995
Pickles, Lord, 2010
Pill, Sir Malcolm, 1995
Pincher, Christopher, 2018
Popplewell, Sir Andrew, 2019
Portillo, Michael, 1992
Potter, Sir Mark, 1996
Prashar, Baroness, 2009
Primarolo, Baroness, 2002
Puapua, Sir Tomasi, 1982
Purnell, James, 2007
Quin, Baroness, 1998
Raab, Dominic, 2018
Radice, Lord, 1999
Rafferty, Dame Anne, 2011

Randall of Uxbridge, Lord, 2010
Raynsford, Nick, 2001
Redwood, Sir John, 1993
Rees-Mogg, Jacob, 2019
Reid, Sir George, 2004
Reid of Cardowan, Lord, 1998
Richards, Sir David, 2016
Richards, Sir Stephen, 2005
Riddell, Peter, 2010
Rifkind, Sir Malcolm, 1986
Rimer, Sir Colin, 2007
Rix, Sir Bernard, 2000
Robathan, Lord, 2010
Robertson, Angus, 2015
Robertson, Sir Hugh, 2012
Robertson of Port Ellen, Lord, 1997
Robinson, Peter, 2007
Roch, Sir John, 1993
Rodgers of Quarry Bank, Lord, 1975
Rooker, Lord, 1999
Rose, Sir Christopher, 1992
Rose, Dame Vivien, 2019
Ross, *Hon.* Lord (Donald MacArthur), 1985
Royall of Blaisdon, Baroness, 2008
Rudd, Amber, 2015
Ruddock, Dame Joan, 2010
Ryan, Joan, 2007
Ryder, Sir Ernest, 2013
Ryder of Wensum, Lord, 1990
Sainsbury, Sir Timothy, 1992
Salisbury, Marquess of, 1994
Salmond, Alex, 2007
Sandiford, Lloyd Erskine, 1989
Saville of Newdigate, Lord, 1994
Saville Roberts, Elizabeth, 2019
Sawyer, Dame Joan, 2004
Schiemann, Sir Konrad, 1995
Scotland of Asthal, Baroness, 2001
Scott of Foscote, Lord, 1991
Sedley, Sir Stephen, 1999
Selkirk of Douglas, Lord, 1996
Sentamu, Rt. revd John, 2005
Shapps, Grant, 2010
Sharma, Alok, 2019
Sharp, Dame Victoria, 2013
Sheil, Sir John, 2005
Shelbrooke, Alec, 2019
Shephard of Northwold, Baroness, 1992
Shipley, Jennifer, 1998
Short, Clare, 1997
Shutt of Greetland, Lord, 2009
Simler, Dame Ingrid, 2019
Simmonds, Sir Kennedy, 1984
Simmonds, Mark, 2014
Simon, Sir Peregrine, 2015
Simpson, Keith, 2015
Sinclair, Ian, 1977

Singh, Sir Rabinder, 2017
Skidmore, Chris, 2019
Slade, Sir Christopher, 1982
Smith, Andrew, 1997
Smith, *Hon.* Lady (Anne Smith), 2013
Smith, Jacqueline, 2003
Smith, Dame Janet, 2002
Smith, Julian, 2017
Smith of Basildon, Baroness, 2009
Smith of Finsbury, Lord, 1997
Soames, Sir Nicholas, 2011
Somare, Sir Michael, 1977
Sopoaga, Enele, 2018
Soubry, Anna, 2015
Spellar, John, 2001
Spelman, Dame Caroline, 2010
Spencer, Mark, 2019
Stanley, Sir John, 1984
Starmer, Sir Keir, 2017
Steel of Aikwood, Lord, 1977
Stephens of Creevyloughgare, Lord, 2017
Stewart, Rory, 2019
Stowell of Beeston, Baroness, 2014
Strang, Gavin, 1997
Strathclyde, Lord, 1995
Straw, Jack, 1997
Stride, Melvyn, 2017
Stuart, Freundel, 2013
Stuart of Edgbaston, Baroness, 2015
Stuart-Smith, Sir Jeremy, 2020
Stuart-Smith, Sir Murray, 1988
Stunell, Lord, 2012
Sturgeon, Nicola, 2014
Sullivan, Sir Jeremy, 2009
Sumption, Lord, 2011
Sunak, Rishi, 2019
Sutherland, *Hon.* Lord (Ranald Sutherland), 2000
Swayne, Sir Desmond, 2011
Swire, Sir Hugo, 2010
Symons of Vernham Dean, Baroness, 2001
Tami, Mark, 2018
Taylor of Bolton, Baroness, 1997
Taylor of Holbeach, Lord, 2014
Tebbit, Lord, 1981
Thirlwall, Dame Kathryn, 2017
Thomas, Edmund, 1996
Thomas of Cwmgiedd, Lord, 2003
Thornberry, Emily, 2017
Thorpe, Sir Matthew, 1995
Thurso, Viscount, 2014
Timms, Stephen, 2006
Tipping, Andrew, 1998
Tomlinson, Sir Stephen, 2010
Touhig, Lord, 2006
Treacy, Sir Colman, 2012
Trefgarne, Lord, 1989

Trevelyan, Anne-Marie, 2020
Trimble, Lord, 1997
Truss, Elizabeth, 2014
Tuckey, Sir Simon, 1998
Turnbull, Lord, 2016
Tyler, Lord, 2014
Tyrie, Lord, 2015
Ullswater, Viscount, 1994
Underhill, Sir Nicholas, 2013
Upton, Simon, 1999
Vadera, Baroness, 2009
Vaizey of Didcot, Lord, 2016
Vaz, Keith, 2006
Vaz, Valerie, 2019
Villiers, Theresa, 2010
Vos, Sir Geoffrey, 2013
Waite, Sir John, 1993
Wakeham, Lord, 1983
Waldegrave of North Hill, Lord, 1990
Walker of Gestingthorpe, Lord, 1997
Wallace, Ben, 2017
Wallace of Saltaire, Lord, 2012
Wallace of Tankerness, Lord, 2000
Waller, Sir Mark, 1996
Ward, Sir Alan, 1995
Warner, Lord, 2006
Warsi, Baroness, 2010
Weatherup, Sir Ronald, 2016
Webb, Sir Steven, 2014
Weir, Sir Reginald, 2016
West of Spithead, Lord, 2010
Wheatley, *Hon.* Lord (John Wheatley), 2007
Wheeler, Sir John, 1993
Whittingdale, John, 2015
Whitty, Lord, 2005
Widdecombe, Ann, 1997
Wigley, Lord, 1997
Willetts, Lord, 2010
Williams of Crosby, Baroness, 1974
Williams of Oystermouth, Lord, 2002
Williamson, Gavin, 2015
Willott, Jennifer, 2014
Wills, Lord, 2008
Wilson, Brian, 2003
Wilson, Sammy, 2017
Wilson of Culworth, Lord, 2005
Wingti, Paias, 1987
Winterton, Dame Rosie, 2006
Wolffe, James, 2016
Woodward, Shaun, 2007
Woolf, Lord, 1986
Woolman, *Hon.* Lord (Stephen Woolman), 2020
Wright, Jeremy, 2014
York, Archbishop of, 2020
Young, Edward, 2017
Young of Cookham, Lord, 1993
Young of Graffham, Lord, 1984

PRIVY COUNCIL OF NORTHERN IRELAND

The Privy Council of Northern Ireland had responsibilities in Northern Ireland similar to those of the Privy Council in Great Britain until the Northern Ireland Act 1974. Membership of the Privy Council of Northern Ireland is retained for life. Since the Northern Ireland Constitution Act 1973 no further appointments have been made. The post-nominal initials PC (NI) are used to differentiate its members from those of the Privy Council.

MEMBERS *as at 10 September 2019*
Bailie, Robin, 1971
Dobson, John, 1969
Kilclooney, Lord, 1970

PARLIAMENT

As at 25 November 2020

The UK constitution is not contained in any single document but has evolved over time, formed by statute, common law and convention. A constitutional monarchy, the UK is governed by ministers of the crown in the name of the sovereign, who is head both of the state and of the government.

The organs of government are the legislature (parliament), the executive and the judiciary. The executive comprises HM government (the cabinet and other ministers), government departments and local authorities (*see* the Government, Public Bodies and Local Government). The judiciary (*see* Law Courts and Offices) pronounces on the law, both written and unwritten, interprets statutes and is responsible for the enforcement of the law; the judiciary is independent of both the legislature and the executive.

THE MONARCHY

The sovereign personifies the state and is, in law, an integral part of the legislature, head of the executive, head of the judiciary, commander-in-chief of all armed forces of the crown and supreme governor of the Church of England. In the Channel Islands and the Isle of Man, which are crown dependencies, the sovereign is represented by a lieutenant-governor. In the member states of the Commonwealth of which the sovereign is head of state, her representative is a governor-general; in UK overseas territories the sovereign is usually represented by a governor, who is responsible to the British government.

Although in practice the powers of the monarchy are now very limited, and restricted mainly to the advisory and ceremonial, there are important acts of government which require the participation of the sovereign. These include summoning, proroguing and dissolving parliament, giving royal assent to bills passed by parliament, appointing important office-holders like government ministers, judges, bishops and governors, conferring peerages, knighthoods and other honours, and granting pardon to a person wrongly convicted of a crime. The sovereign appoints the prime minister; by convention this office is held by the leader of the political party which enjoys, or can secure, a majority of votes in the House of Commons. In international affairs the sovereign, as head of state, has the power to declare war and make peace, to recognise foreign states and governments, to conclude treaties and to annex or cede territory. However, as the sovereign entrusts executive power to ministers of the crown and acts on the advice of her ministers, which she cannot ignore, royal prerogative powers are in practice exercised by ministers, who are responsible to parliament.

Ministerial responsibility does not diminish the sovereign's importance to the smooth working of government. She holds meetings of the Privy Council (*see* below), gives audiences to her ministers and other officials at home and overseas, receives accounts of cabinet decisions, reads dispatches and signs state papers; she must be informed and consulted on every aspect of national life, and she must show complete impartiality.

COUNSELLORS OF STATE

If the sovereign travels abroad for more than a few days or suffers from a temporary illness, it is necessary to appoint members of the royal family, known as counsellors of state, under letters patent to carry out the chief functions of the monarch, including the holding of Privy Councils and giving royal assent to acts passed by parliament. The normal procedure is to appoint two or more members of the royal family remaining in the UK from among the sovereign's spouse and the four adults next in succession, provided they have reached the age of 21. There are currently four members of the royal family from which the counsellors of state are appointed: the Prince of Wales, the Duke of Cambridge, Prince Harry and the Duke of York.

In the event of the sovereign on accession being under the age of 18 years, or by infirmity of mind or body, rendered incapable of performing the royal functions, provision is made for a regency.

THE PRIVY COUNCIL

The sovereign in council, or Privy Council, was the chief source of executive power until the system of cabinet government developed. Its main function today is to advise the sovereign on the approval of various statutory functions and acts of the royal prerogative. These powers are exercised through orders in council and royal proclamations, approved by the Queen at meetings of the Privy Council. The council is also able to exercise a number of statutory duties without approval from the sovereign, including powers of supervision over the registering bodies for the medical and allied professions. These duties are exercised through orders of council.

Although appointment as a privy counsellor is for life, only those who are currently government ministers are involved in the day-to-day business of the council. A full council is summoned only on the death of the sovereign or when the sovereign announces his or her intention to marry. (For a full list of privy counsellors, *see* the Privy Council section.)

There are a number of advisory Privy Council committees whose meetings the sovereign does not attend. Some are prerogative committees, such as those dealing with legislative matters submitted by the legislatures of the Channel Islands and the Isle of Man or with applications for charters of incorporation; and some are provided for by statute, for example those for the universities of Oxford and Cambridge and some Scottish universities.

Administrative work is carried out by the Privy Council Office under the direction of the Lord President of the Council, a cabinet minister.

JUDICIAL COMMITTEE OF THE PRIVY COUNCIL
Supreme Court Building, Parliament Square, London SW1P 3BD
T 020-7960 1500 **W** www.jcpc.uk

The Judicial Committee of the Privy Council is the court of final appeal from courts of the UK dependencies, courts of independent Commonwealth countries which have retained the right of appeal and courts of the Channel Islands and the Isle of Man. It also hears very occasional appeals from a number of ancient and ecclesiastical courts.

The committee is composed of privy counsellors who hold, or have held, high judicial office. Only three or five judges hear each case, and these are usually justices of the supreme court.

Chief Executive, Vicky Fox

PARLIAMENT

Parliament is the supreme law-making authority and can legislate for the UK as a whole or for any parts of it separately (the Channel Islands and the Isle of Man are crown dependencies and not part of the UK). The main functions of parliament are to pass laws, to enable the government to raise taxes and to scrutinise government policy and administration, particularly proposals for expenditure. International treaties and agreements are customarily presented to parliament before ratification.

Parliament can trace its roots to two characteristics of Anglo-Saxon rule: the *witan* (a meeting of the king, nobles and advisors) and the *moot* (county meetings where local matters were discussed). However, it was the parliament that Simon de Montfort called in 1265 that is accepted as the forerunner to modern parliament, as it included non-noble representatives from counties, cities and towns alongside the nobility. The nucleus of early parliaments at the beginning of the 14th century were the officers of the king's household and the king's judges, joined by such ecclesiastical and lay magnates as the king might summon to form a prototype 'House of Lords', and occasionally by the knights of the shires, burgesses and proctors of the lower clergy. By the end of Edward III's reign a 'House of Commons' was beginning to appear; the first known Speaker was elected in 1377.

Parliamentary procedure is based on custom and precedent, partly formulated in the standing orders of both houses of parliament. Each house has the right to control its own internal proceedings and to commit for contempt. The system of debate in the two houses is similar; when a motion has been moved, the Speaker proposes the question as the subject of a debate. Members speak from wherever they have been sitting. Questions are decided by a vote on a simple majority. Draft legislation is introduced, in either house, as a bill. Bills can be introduced by a government minister or a private member, but in practice the majority of bills which become law are introduced by the government. To become law, a bill must be passed by each house (for parliamentary stages, *see* Parliamentary Information) and then sent to the sovereign for the royal assent, after which it becomes an act of parliament.

Proceedings of both houses are public, except on extremely rare occasions. The minutes (called *Votes and Proceedings,* in the Commons and *House of Lords Minutes of Proceedings* in the Lords) and the speeches *(The Official Report of Parliamentary Debates,* Hansard) are published daily. Proceedings are also recorded for transmission on radio and television and stored in the Parliamentary Recording Unit before transfer to the British Library Sound Archive. Television cameras have been allowed into the House of Lords since 1985 and into the House of Commons since 1989; committee meetings may also be televised.

The Fixed Term Parliament Act 2011 fixed the duration of a parliament at five years in normal circumstances, the term being reckoned from the date given on the writs for the new parliament. The term of a parliament has been prolonged by legislation in such rare circumstances as the two World Wars (31 January 1911 to 25 November 1918; 26 November 1935 to 15 June 1945). The life of a parliament is divided into sessions, usually of one year in length, beginning and ending most often in May.

DEVOLUTION

The Scottish parliament and the National Assembly for Wales have legislative power over all devolved matters, for example matters not reserved to Westminster or otherwise outside its powers. The Northern Ireland Assembly has legislative authority in the fields previously administered by the Northern Ireland departments. The assembly was suspended in October 2002 and dissolved in April 2003, before being reinstated on 8 May 2007. The assembly was suspended between January 2017 and January 2020 because of policy disagreements between power-sharing parties. For further information, *see* Devolved Government

THE HOUSE OF LORDS

London SW1A 0PW
T 020-7219 3107
E hlinfo@parliament.uk **W** www.parliament.uk

The House of Lords is the second chamber, or 'Upper House', of the UK's bicameral parliament. Until the beginning of the 20th century, the House of Lords had considerable power, being able to veto any bill submitted to it by the House of Commons. Since the introduction of the Parliament Acts 1911 and 1949, however, it has no powers over money bills and its power of veto over public legislation has been reduced over time to the power to delay bills for up to one session of parliament (usually one year). Today the main functions of the House of Lords are to contribute to the legislative process, to act as a check on the government, and to provide a forum of expertise. Its judicial role as final court of appeal ended in 2009 with the establishment of a new UK Supreme Court (*see* Law Courts and Offices section).

The House of Lords has a number of select committees. Some relate to the internal affairs of the house – such as its House of Lords Commission – while others carry out important investigative work on matters of public interest. The main committees are: the Communications Committee; the Constitution Committee; the Economic Affairs Committee; the European Union Committee; and the Science and Technology Committee. House of Lords' investigative committees look at broad issues and do not mirror government departments as the select committees in the House of Commons do.

The Constitutional Reform Act 2005 significantly altered the judicial function of the House of Lords and the role of the Lord Chancellor as a judge and its presiding officer. The Lord Chancellor is no longer the presiding officer of the House of Lords nor head of the judiciary in England and Wales, but remains a cabinet minister (the Lord Chancellor and Secretary of State for Justice), and is currently a member of the House of Commons. The function of the presiding officer of the House of Lords was devolved to the newly created post of the Speaker of the House of Lords, commonly known as Lord Speaker. The first Lord Speaker elected by the House was the Rt. Hon. Baroness Hayman on 4 July 2006.

Membership of the House of Lords comprises mainly of life peers created under the Life Peerages Act 1958, along with 92 hereditary peers and a small number of Lords of Appeal in Ordinary, for example law lords, who were created under the Appellate Jurisdiction Act 1876*. The Archbishops of Canterbury and York, the Bishops of London, Durham and Winchester, and the 21 senior diocesan bishops of the Church of England are also members.

The House of Lords Act 1999 provides for 92 hereditary peers to remain in the House of Lords until further reform of the House has been carried out. Of these, 75 (42 Conservative, 28 crossbench, three Liberal Democrat and two Labour) were elected by hereditary peers in their political party or crossbench grouping. In addition, 15 office holders were elected by the whole house. Two hereditary peers with royal duties, the Earl Marshal and the Lord Great Chamberlain, have also remained members. Since November 2002, by-elections have been held to replace elected hereditary peers who have died, and since 2014 to replace those who retire permanently from the House. By-elections are held under the Alternative Vote System, and must take place within three months of a vacancy occurring. (*see also* The Peerage).

Peers are disqualified from sitting in the house if they are:
- absent for an entire parliamentary session which is longer than six months (under the House of Lords Reform Act 2014), unless they are on leave of absence (*see* below)

- not a British citizen, a Commonwealth citizen (under the British Nationality Act 1981) or a citizen of the Republic of Ireland
- under the age of 21
- undischarged bankrupts or, in Scotland, those whose estate is sequestered
- holders of a disqualifying judicial office
- members of the European parliament
- convicted of treason

Bishops cease to be members of the house when they retire.

Members who do not wish to attend sittings of the House of Lords may apply for leave of absence for the duration of a parliament. Since the passage of the House of Lords Reform Act 2014, members of the House may also retire permanently by giving notice in writing to the Clerk of the Parliaments.

Members of the House of Lords, who are not paid a salary, may claim a daily allowance of £305 (or may elect to claim a reduced daily allowance of £153) per sitting day – but only if they attend a sitting of the House and/or committee proceedings.

* Although the office of Lord of Appeal in Ordinary no longer exists, law lords created under the Appellate Jurisdiction Act 1876 remain members of the House. Those in office at the time of the establishment of the Supreme Court became justices of the UK Supreme Court and are not permitted to sit or vote in the House of Lords until they retire.

COMPOSITION *as at 19 November 2020*

Archbishops and bishops	26
Life peers under the Appellate Jurisdiction Act 1876 and the Life Peerages Act 1958*	687
Hereditary peers under the House of Lords Act 1999†	86
Total	799

* Excluding 19 peers on leave of absence
† Excluding two peers on leave of absence

STATE OF THE PARTIES* *as at 19 November 2020*

Conservative	259
Crossbench	182
Labour	178
Liberal Democrats	88
Non-affiliated	50
Archbishops and bishops	26
Other parties	15
Lord Speaker	1
Total	799

* Excluding peers on leave of absence

HOUSE OF LORDS PAY FOR SENIOR STAFF 2018–19*

Senior staff are placed in the following pay bands according to their level of responsibility and taking account of other factors such as experience and marketability.

Judicial group 4	£185,197
Senior band 3	£111,500–£158,805
Senior band 2	£90,500–£119,850
Senior band 1A	£75,956–£105,560
Senior band 1	£69,000–£93,380

* Latest available data

OFFICERS AND OFFICIALS

The house is presided over by the Lord Speaker, whose powers differ from those of the Speaker of the House of Commons. The Lord Speaker has no power to rule on matters of order because the House of Lords is self-regulating. The maintenance of the rules of debate is the responsibility of all the members who are present.

A panel of deputy speakers is appointed by Royal Commission. The first deputy speaker is the Chair of Committees, a salaried officer of the house appointed at the beginning of each session. He or she chairs a number of 'domestic' committees relating to the internal affairs of the house. The first deputy speaker is assisted by a panel of deputy chairs, headed by the salaried Principal Deputy Chair of Committees, who is also chair of the European Union Committee of the house.

The Clerk of the Parliaments is the accounting officer and the chief permanent official responsible for the administration of the house. The Lady Usher of the Black Rod is responsible for security and other services and also has royal duties as secretary to the Lord Great Chamberlain.

Lord Speaker, Rt. Hon. Lord Fowler
Senior Deputy Speaker of the House of Lords, Rt. Hon. Lord McFall of Alcluith
Principal Deputy Chair of Committees, Earl of Kinnoull
Clerk of the Parliaments, Edward Ollard
Clerk Assistant, Sarah Davies
Reading Clerk and Clerk of the Overseas Office, Jake Vaughan
Lady Usher of the Black Rod, Sarah Clarke, OBE
Yeoman Usher of the Black Rod, Brig. Neil Baverstock
Commissioner for Lords' Standards, Lucy Scott-Moncrieff, CBE
Counsel to the Chair of Committees, J. Cooper
Registrar of Lords' Interests, Tom Wilson
Clerk of Committees, Tom Goldsmith
Legal Adviser to the Human Rights Committee, Eleanor Hourigan
Director of Library Services, Penny Young
Director of Facilities, Carl Woodall
Finance Director, Fehintola Akinlose
Director of Parliamentary Digital Service, Rob Greig
Director of Human Resources, Nigel Sully
Clerk of Legislation, Liam Smyth
Principal Clerk of Select Committees, Tom Healey
Director of Parliamentary Archives, Adrian Brown

LORD GREAT CHAMBERLAIN'S OFFICE

Lord Great Chamberlain, 7th Marquess of Cholmondeley, KCVO

SELECT COMMITTEES

The main House of Lords select committees, as at November 2020, are as follows:

Committee of Selection – Chair, Rt. Hon. Lord McFall of Alcluith
Common Frameworks Scrutiny – Chair, Baroness Andrews, OBE
Communications and Digital – Chair, Lord Gilbert of Panteg
Conduct – Chair, Rt. Hon. Lord Mance
Constitution – Chair, Rt. Hon. Baroness Taylor of Bolton
COVID-19 – Chair, Baroness Lane-Fox of Soho, CBE
Delegated Powers and Regulatory Reform – Chair, Rt. Hon. Lord Blencathra
Democracy and Digital Technologies – Chair, Lord Puttnam, CBE
Economic Affairs – Chair, Rt. Hon. Lord Forsyth of Drumlean
Electoral Registration Act 2013 – Chair, Rt. Hon. Lord Shutt of Greetland, OBE
European Union – Chair, Earl of Kinnoull
European Union – Sub-committees:
　Environment – Chair, Lord Teverson
　Goods – Chair, Baroness Verma
　International Agreements – Chair, Rt. Hon. Lord Goldsmith, QC

Security and Justice – Chair, Lord Ricketts, GCMG, GCVO
Services – Chair, Baroness Donaghy, CBE, FRSA
Finance – Chair, Baroness Doocey, OBE
Food, Poverty, Health and Environment – Chair, Lord Krebs
Gambling Industry – Chair, Lord Grade of Yarmouth, CBE
High Speed Rail – Chair, Rt. Hon. Lord Hope of Craighead, KT
House – Chair, Rt. Hon. Lord Fowler
Hybrid Instruments – Chair, Rt. Hon. Lord McFall of Alcluith
International Relations and Defence – Chair, Rt. Hon. Baroness Anelay of St Johns, DBE
Liaison – Chair, Rt. Hon. Lord McFall of Alcluith
National Plan for Sport and Recreation – Chair, Lord Willis of Knaresborough
Procedure and Privileges – Chair, Rt. Hon. Lord McFall of Alcluith
Public Services – Chair, Rt. Hon. Baroness Armstrong of Hill Top
Risk Assessment and Risk Planning – Chair, Rt. Hon. Lord Arbuthnot of Erdrom
Science and Technology – Chair, Lord Patel, KT
Secondary Legislation Scrutiny – Chair, Lord Hodgson of Astley Abbotts, CBE
Services – Chair, Rt. Hon. Lord Laming, CBE, DL
Standing Orders (Private Bills) – Chair, Rt. Hon. Lord McFall of Alcluith

THE HOUSE OF COMMONS
London SW1A 0AA
T 020-7219 3000 **W** www.parliament.uk

HOUSE OF COMMONS ENQUIRY SERVICE
14 Tothill Street, London SW1H 9NB
T 020-7219 4272 **E** hcinfo@parliament.uk

The members of the House of Commons are elected by universal adult suffrage. For electoral purposes, the UK is divided into constituencies, each of which returns one member to the House of Commons, the member being the candidate who obtains the largest number of votes cast in the constituency. To ensure equitable representation, the four Boundary Commissions keep constituency boundaries under review and recommend any redistribution of seats which may seem necessary because of population movements etc. At the 2010 general election the number of seats increased from 646 to 650. Of the present 650 seats, there are 533 for England, 40 for Wales, 59 for Scotland and 18 for Northern Ireland.

NUMBER OF SEATS IN THE HOUSE OF COMMONS BY COUNTRY

	2005	2020
England	529	533
Wales	40	40
Scotland	59	59
Northern Ireland	18	18
Total	646	650

ELECTIONS
Elections are by secret ballot, each elector casting one vote; voting is not compulsory. (For entitlement to vote in parliamentary elections, *see* Legal Notes.) When a seat becomes vacant between general elections, a by-election is held.

British subjects and citizens of the Irish Republic can stand for election as MPs provided they are 18 or over and not subject to disqualification. Those disqualified from sitting in the house include:
• undischarged bankrupts
• people sentenced to more than one year's imprisonment
• members of the House of Lords (but hereditary peers not sitting in the Lords are eligible)
• holders of certain offices listed in the House of Commons Disqualification Act 1975, for example members of the judiciary, civil service, regular armed forces, police forces, some local government officers and some members of public corporations and government commissions

A candidate does not require any party backing but his or her nomination for election must be supported by the signatures of ten people registered in the constituency. A candidate must also deposit £500 with the returning officer, which is forfeit if the candidate does not receive more than 5 per cent of the votes cast. All election expenses at a general election, except the candidate's personal expenses, are subject to a statutory limit of £8,700, plus six pence for each elector in a borough constituency or nine pence for each elector in a county constituency.

See also members of parliament for a current alphabetical list.

STATE OF THE PARTIES *as at 20 November 2020*

Party	Seats
Conservative	364
Labour	200
Scottish National Party	47
Liberal Democrats	11
Democratic Unionist Party	8
Sinn Fein (have not taken their seats)	7
Independent*	5
Plaid Cymru	3
Social Democratic and Labour Party	2
Green	1
Alliance	1
The Speaker	1
Total	650

* MPs either suspended or who have had the whip withdrawn: two Labour, one Conservative, one Scottish National Party, one Plaid Cymru.

BUSINESS
The week's business of the house is outlined each Thursday by the leader of the house, after consultation between the chief government whip and the chief opposition whip. A quarter to a third of the time will be taken up by the government's legislative programme and the rest by other business. As a rule, bills likely to raise political controversy are introduced in the Commons before going on to the Lords, and the Commons claims exclusive control in respect of national taxation and expenditure. Bills such as the finance bill, which imposes taxation, and the consolidated fund bills, which authorise expenditure, must begin in the Commons. A bill of which the financial provisions are subsidiary may begin in the Lords, and the Commons may waive its rights in regard to Lords' amendments affecting finance.

The Commons has a public register of MPs' financial and certain other interests; this is published annually as a House of Commons paper. Members must also disclose any relevant financial interest or benefit in a matter before the house when taking part in a debate, in certain other proceedings of the house, or in consultations with other MPs, with ministers or with civil servants.

MEMBERS' PAY AND ALLOWANCES

Since 1911 members of the House of Commons have received salary payments; facilities for free travel were introduced in 1924. Salary rates for the last 30 years are as follows:

1989 Jan – £24,107	2004 Apr – £57,485
1990 Jan – £26,701	2005 Apr – £59,095
1991 Jan – £29,970	2006 Apr – £59,686
1992 Jan – £30,854	2007 Apr – £61,181
1993 Jan – £30,854	2008 Apr – £63,291
1994 Jan – £31,687	2009 Apr – £64,766
1995 Jan – £33,189	2010 Apr – £65,738
1995 Jan – £33,189	2011 Apr – £65,738
1996 Jan – £34,085	2012 Apr – £65,738
1996 Jul – £43,000	2013 Apr – £66,396
1997 Apr – £43,860	2014 Apr – £67,060
1998 Apr – £45,066	2015 May – £74,000
1999 Apr – £47,008	2016 Apr – £74,962
2000 Apr – £48,371	2017 Apr – £76,011
2001 Apr – £49,822	2018 Apr – £77,379
2002 Apr – £55,118	2019 Apr – £79,468
2003 Apr – £56, 358	2020 Apr – £81,932

The Independent Parliamentary Standards Authority (IPSA) was established under the Parliamentary Standards Act 2009 and is responsible for the independent regulation and administration of the MPs' Scheme of Business Costs and Expenses, as well as for paying the salaries of MPs and their staff members. Since May 2011, the IPSA has also been responsible for determining MPs' pay and setting the level of any increase to their salary.

For 2019–20, the office costs expenditure budget is £28,800 for London area MPs and £25,910 for non-London area MPs. The maximum annual staff budget for London area MPs is £188,860 and £177,550 for non-London area MPs.

Since 1972 MPs have been able to claim reimbursement for the additional cost of staying overnight away from their main residence while on parliamentary business. This is not payable to London area MPs and those MPs who reside in 'grace and favour' accommodation. Accommodation expenses for MPs claiming rental payments in the London area is capped at £23,010 a year; outside of the London area each constituency is banded according to rental values in the area and capped at £16,120. For MPs who own their own homes, mortgage interest and associated expenses up to £5,410 are payable.

For ministerial salaries *see* Government Departments.

MEMBERS' PENSIONS

Pension arrangements for MPs were first introduced in 1964. Under the Parliamentary Contributory Pension Fund CARE (career-averaged revalued earnings) scheme, MPs receive a pension on retirement based upon their salary in their final year, and upon accumulating proportions of pensionable earnings over each year of membership. MPs contributions are payable at a rate of 11.09 per cent of pay. Exchequer contributions are paid at a rate recommended by the Government Actuary and meet the balance of the cost of providing MP's retirement benefits. Pensions are normally payable upon retirement at age 65 to those who are no longer MPs. Abated pensions may be payable to members aged 55 or over. Pensions are also payable to spouses and other qualifying partners of deceased scheme members at the rate of three-eighths of the deceased member's pension. In the case of members who die in service, an enhanced spouse's or partner's pension and a lump sum equal to two times pensionable salary is payable. There are also provisions in place for dependants and MPs of any age who retire due to ill health. All pensions are CPI index-linked.

The House of Commons Members' Fund provides for annual or lump sum grants to ex-MPs, their widows or widowers, and children of those who either ceased to serve as an MP prior to the PCPF being established or who are experiencing hardship. Historically, income to the Fund has been derived from individual contributions from MPs (£24 per annum), an Exchequer contribution (a maximum of £215,000 per annum) and the return on investments. Under the provision of the House of Commons Members Fund Act 2016 the trustees can suspend or increase MP contributions up to a maximum of 0.2 per cent of an member's ordinary salary. The 2016 Act also removed the Exchequer contribution.

HOUSE OF COMMONS PAY BANDS FOR SENIOR STAFF

Senior Staff are placed in the following Senior Civil Service pay bands. These pay bands are for 2019–20 and apply to the most senior staff in departments and agencies.

Pay Band 1	£71,000–£117,800
Pay Band 1A*	£71,000–£128,900
Pay Band 2	£93,000–£162,500
Pay Band 3	£120,000–£208,100
Permanent Secretaries	£150,000–£200,000

* Pay Band 1A is now effectively a closed grade, although existing staff will remain on this grade

OFFICERS AND OFFICIALS

The House of Commons is presided over by the Speaker, who has considerable powers to maintain order. A deputy speaker, called the Chairman of Ways and Means, and two deputy chairs may preside over sittings of the House of Commons; they are elected by the house, and, like the Speaker, neither speak nor vote other than in their official capacity.

The staff of the house are employed by a commission chaired by the Speaker. The heads of the six House of Commons departments are permanent officers of the house, not MPs. The Clerk of the House is the principal adviser to the Speaker on the privileges and procedures of the house, the conduct of the business of the house, and committees. The Serjeant-at-Arms is responsible for security and ceremonial functions of the house.

Speaker, Rt. Hon. Sir Lindsay Hoyle, MP
Chairman of Ways and Means, Rt. Hon. Dame Eleanor Laing, DBE, MP
First Deputy Chairman of Ways and Means, Rt. Hon. Dame Rosie Winterton, DBE, MP
Second Deputy Chairman of Ways and Means, Nigel Evans, MP
House of Commons Commission, Rt. Hon. Sir Lindsay Hoyle, MP *(chair);* Ian Ailles *(Director-General of the House of Commons);* Dr John Benger *(Clerk of the House);* Sir Paul Beresford, MP; Jane McCall *(external member);* Dr Rima Makarem *(external member);* Rt. Hon. Jacob Rees-Mogg, MP *(Leader of the House);* Rt. Hon. Valerie Vaz, MP *(Shadow Leader of the House);* Sir Charles Walter, MP; Rt. Hon. Dame Rosie Winterton, DBE, MP; Rt. Hon. Pete Wishart, MP
Secretary of the Commission, Marianne Cwynarski
Assistant Secretary, Robert Cope

OFFICE OF THE SPEAKER

Speaker's Secretary, Helen Wood
Trainbearer, Jim Davey
Speaker's Counsel, Saira Salimi
Chaplain to the Speaker, Revd Canon Patricia Hillas

OFFICE OF THE CLERK OF THE HOUSE

Clerk of the House, Dr John Benger

PARLIAMENTARY COMMISSIONER FOR STANDARDS

Parliamentary Commissioner for Standards, Kathryn Stone, OBE

PARLIAMENTARY SECURITY DIRECTOR
Parliamentary Security Director, Eric Hepburn, CBE

GOVERNANCE OFFICE
Head of Office, Marianne Cwynarski

DEPARTMENT OF CHAMBER AND COMMITTEE
SERVICES
Clerk Assistant and Managing Director, Sarah Davies

COMMITTEE OFFICE
Clerk of Committees, Paul Evans

DEPARTMENTAL SELECT COMMITTEES *as at
September 2019*
Administration – Chair, Sir Charles Walker, KBE, MP
Arms Export Controls – Chair, Mark Garnier, MP
Backbench Business – Chair, Ian Mearns, MP
Business, Energy and Industrial Strategy – Chair, Darren Jones,
    MP
Defence – Chair, Rt. Hon. Tobias Ellwood, MP
Digital, Culture, Media and Sport – Chair, Julian Knight, MP
Education – Chair, Rt. Hon. Robert Halfon, MP
Environment, Food and Rural Affairs – Chair, Neil Parish, MP
Environmental Audit – Chair, Rt. Hon. Philip Dunne, MP
European Scrutiny – Chair, Sir William Cash, MP
European Statutory Instruments – Chair, Andrew Jones, MP
Finance – Chair, Lillian Greenwood, MP
Foreign Affairs – Chair, Tom Tugendhat, MP
Future Relationship with the EU – Chair, Rt. Hon. Hilary Benn,
    MP
Health and Social Care – Chair, Rt. Hon. Jeremy Hunt, MP
Home Affairs – Chair, Rt. Hon. Yvette Cooper, MP
Housing, Communities and Local Government, Chair, Clive Betts,
    MP
International Development – Chair, Sarah Champion, MP
International Trade – Chair, Angus Brendan MacNeil, MP
Justice – Chair, Sir Robert Neill, MP
Liaison – Chair, Sir Bernard Jenkin, MP
Northern Ireland Affairs – Chair, Simon Hoare, MP
Petitions – Chair, Catherine McKinnerll, MP
Privileges – Chair, Chris Bryant, MP
Procedure – Chair, Rt. Hon. Karen Bradley, MP
Public Accounts – Chair, Meg Hillier, MP
Public Administration and Constitutional Affairs – Chair, William
    Wragg, MP
Regulatory Reform – Chair, Stephen McPartland, MP
Science and Technology – Chair, Rt. Hon. Greg Clark, MP
Scottish Affairs – Chair, Pete Wishart, MP
Selection – Chair, Bill Wiggin, MP
Standards – Chair, Chris Bryant, MP
Statutory Instruments – Chair, Jessica Morden, MP
Transport – Chair, Huw Merringham, MP
Treasury – Chair, Rt. Hon. Mel Stride, MP
Welsh Affairs – Chair, Rt. Hon. Stephen Crabb, MP
Women and Equalities – Chair, Rt. Hon. Caroline Nokes, MP
Work and Pensions – Chair, Rt. Hon. Stephen Timms, MP

SCRUTINY UNIT
Head of Unit, David Lloyd
Head of Financial Scrutiny, Larry Honeysett

VOTE OFFICE
Deliverer of the Vote, Tom McVeagh

CHAMBER BUSINESS DIRECTORATE
Clerk of Legislation, Liam Laurence Smyth

OFFICIAL REPORT DIRECTORATE (HANSARD)
Editor, Alex Newton

SERJEANT-AT-ARMS DIRECTORATE
Serjeant-at-Arms, Ugbana Oyet

DEPARTMENT OF FINANCE
Head of Finance, Ebenezer Oduwole

DEPARTMENT OF HUMAN RESOURCES AND
CHANGE
Director-General, Andrew Walker

DEPARTMENT OF INFORMATION SERVICES
Director-General and Librarian, Penny Young
Curator of Works of Art, Melissa Hamnett
Keeper of Historic Collections, Mary-Jane Tsang
Collections Care Manager, Caroline Babington
Collections Information Manager, Natasha Wood

PARLIAMENTARY DIGITAL SERVICE (PDS)
Director of Parliamentary Digital Service, Tracey Jessup

OTHER PRINCIPAL OFFICERS
Clerk of the Crown in Chancery, Ceri King
Parliamentary and Health Service Ombudsman, Robert Behrens,
    CBE

NATIONAL AUDIT OFFICE
157–197 Buckingham Palace Road, London SW1W 9SP
T 020-7798 7000
E enquiries@nao.gsi.gov.uk **W** www.nao.org.uk

The National Audit Office came into existence under the National Audit Act 1983 to replace and continue the work of the former Exchequer and Audit Department. The act reinforced the office's total financial and operational independence from the government and brought its head, the Comptroller and Auditor-General, into a closer relationship with parliament as an officer of the House of Commons.

The National Audit Office (NAO) scrutinises public spending on behalf of parliament, helping it to hold government departments to account and helping public service managers improve performance and service delivery. The NAO audits the financial statements of all government departments and a wide range of other public bodies. It regularly publishes 'value for money' reports on the efficiency and effectiveness of how public resources are used.

Chair, Lord Bichard, KCB
Comptroller and Auditor-General, Gareth Davies
Executive Directors, Abdool Kara; Daniel Lambauer; Elaine
    Lewis; Kate Mathers; Rebecca Sheeran; Max Tse

PARLIAMENTARY INFORMATION

The following is a short glossary of aspects of the work of parliament. Unless otherwise stated, references are to House of Commons procedures.

BILL – Proposed legislation is termed a bill. The stages of a public bill (for private bills, *see* below) in the House of Commons are as follows:

First reading: This stage introduces the legislation to the house and, for government bills, merely constitutes an order to have the bill printed.

Second reading: The debate on the principles of the bill.

Committee stage: The detailed examination of a bill, clause by clause. In most cases this takes place in a public bill committee, or the whole house may act as a committee. Public bill committees may take evidence before embarking on detailed scrutiny of the bill. Very rarely, a bill may be examined by a select committee.

Report stage: Detailed review of a bill as amended in committee, on the floor of the house, and an opportunity to make further changes.

Third reading: Final debate on the full bill in the Commons.

Public bills go through the same stages in the House of Lords, but with important differences: the committee stage is taken in committee of the whole house or in a grand committee, in which any peer may participate. There are no time limits, all amendments are debated, and further amendments can be made at third reading.

A bill may start in either house, and has to pass through both houses to become law. Both houses have to agree the final text of a bill, so that amendments made by the second house are then considered in the originating house, and if not agreed, sent back or themselves amended, until agreement is reached.

CHILTERN HUNDREDS – A nominal office of profit under the crown, the acceptance of which requires an MP to vacate his/her seat. The Manor of Northstead is similar. These are the only means by which an MP may resign.

CONSOLIDATED FUND BILL – A bill to authorise the issue of money to maintain government services. The bill is dealt with without debate.

EARLY DAY MOTION – A motion put on the notice paper by an MP without, in general, the real prospect of its being debated. Such motions are expressions of back-bench opinion.

FATHER OF THE HOUSE – The MP whose continuous service in the House of Commons is the longest. The present Father of the House is the Sir Peter Bottomley, MP.

GRAND COMMITTEES – There are three grand committees in the House of Commons, one each for Northern Ireland, Scotland and Wales; they consider matters relating specifically to that country. In the House of Lords, bills may be sent to a grand committee instead of a committee of the whole house (*see also* Bill).

HOURS OF MEETING – The House of Commons normally meets on Mondays at 2.30pm, Tuesdays and Wednesdays at 11.30am, Thursdays at 9.30am and some Fridays at 9.30am. (*See also* Westminster Hall Sittings, below.) The House of Lords normally meets at 2.30pm Mondays and Tuesdays, 3pm on Wednesdays and at 11am on Thursdays. The House of Lords occasionally sits on Fridays at 10am.

LEADER OF THE OPPOSITION – In 1937 the office of leader of the opposition was recognised and a salary was assigned to the post. In 2020–21 this is £147,103 (including a parliamentary salary of £81,932). The present leader of the opposition is the Rt. Hon. Sir Keir Starmer, KBC, QC, MP.

THE LORD CHANCELLOR – The office of Lord High Chancellor of Great Britain was significantly altered by the Constitutional Reform Act 2005. Previously, the Lord Chancellor was (*ex officio*) the Speaker of the House of Lords, and took part in debates and voted in divisions in the House of Lords. The Department for Constitutional Affairs was created in 2003, and became the Ministry of Justice in 2007, incorporating most of the responsibilities of the Lord Chancellor's department. The role of Speaker has been transferred to the post of Lord Speaker. The Constitutional Reform Act 2005 also brought to an end the Lord Chancellor's role as head of the judiciary. A Judicial Appointments Commission was created in April 2006, and a supreme court (separate from the House of Lords) was established in 2009.

THE LORD GREAT CHAMBERLAIN – The Lord Great Chamberlain is a Great Officer of State, the office being hereditary since the grant of Henry I to the family of De Vere, Earls of Oxford. It is now a joint hereditary office rotating on the death of the sovereign between the Cholmondeley, Carington and Ancaster families.

The Lord Great Chamberlain, currently the 7th Marquess of Cholmondeley, is responsible for the royal apartments in the Palace of Westminster, the Royal Gallery, the administration of the Chapel of St Mary Undercroft and, in conjunction with the Lord Speaker and the Speaker of the House of Commons, Westminster Hall. The Lord Great Chamberlain has the right to perform specific services at a coronation and has particular responsibility for the internal administrative arrangements within the House of Lords for state openings of parliament.

THE LORD SPEAKER – The first Lord Speaker of the House of Lords, the Rt. Hon. Baroness Hayman, took up office on 4 July 2006. The Lord Speaker is independent of the government and elected by members of the House of Lords rather than appointed by the prime minister. Although the Lord Speaker's primary role is to preside over proceedings in the House of Lords, she does not have the same powers as the Speaker of the House of Commons. For example, the Lord Speaker is not responsible for maintaining order during debates, as this is the responsibility of the house as a whole. The Lord Speaker sits in the Lords on one of the woolsacks, which are couches covered in red cloth and stuffed with wool.

MOTHER OF THE HOUSE – Introduced by Theresa May in 2017, the Mother of the House is the female MP whose continuous service is the longest. The inaugural and present Mother of the House is Rt. Hon. Harriet Harman, QC, MP.

OPPOSITION DAY – A day on which the topic for debate is chosen by the opposition. There are 20 such days in a normal session. On 17 days, subjects are chosen by the leader of the opposition; on the remaining three days by the leader of the next largest opposition party.

PARLIAMENT ACTS 1911 AND 1949 – Under these acts, bills may become law without the consent of the Lords, though the House of Lords has the power to delay a public bill for a parliamentary session.

PRIME MINISTER'S QUESTIONS – The prime minister answers questions from 12 to 12.30pm on Wednesdays.

PRIVATE BILL – A bill promoted by a body or an individual to give powers additional to, or in conflict with, the general law, and to which a special procedure applies to enable people affected to object.

PRIVATE MEMBER'S BILL – A public bill promoted by an MP or peer who is not a member of the government.

PRIVATE NOTICE QUESTION – A question adjudged of urgent importance on submission to the Speaker (in the Lords, the Lord Speaker), answered at the end of oral questions.

PRIVILEGE – The House of Commons has rights and immunities to protect it from obstruction in carrying out its duties. These are known as parliamentary privilege and enable Members of Parliament to debate freely. The most important privilege is that of freedom of speech. MPs cannot be prosecuted for sedition or sued for libel or slander over anything said during proceedings in the house. This enables them to raise in the house questions affecting the public good which might be difficult to raise outside owing to the possibility of legal action against them. The House of Lords has similar privileges.

QUESTION TIME – Oral questions are answered by ministers in the Commons from 2.30 to 3.30pm on Mondays, 11.30am to 12.30pm on Tuesdays and Wednesdays, and 9.30 to 10.30am on Thursdays. Questions are also taken for half an hour at the start of the Lords sittings.

ROYAL ASSENT – The royal assent is signified by letters patent to such bills and measures as have passed both Houses of Parliament (or bills which have been passed under the Parliament Acts 1911 and 1949). The sovereign has not given royal assent in person since 1854. On occasion, for instance in the prorogation of parliament, royal assent may be pronounced to the two houses by Lords Commissioners. More usually royal assent is notified to each house sitting separately in accordance with the Royal Assent Act 1967. The old French formulae for royal assent are then endorsed on the acts by the Clerk of the Parliaments.

The power to withhold assent resides with the sovereign but has not been exercised in the UK since 1707.

SELECT COMMITTEES – Consisting usually of 10 to 15 members of all parties, select committees are a means used by both houses in order to investigate certain matters.

Most select committees in the House of Commons are tied to departments: each committee investigates subjects within a government department's remit. There are other select committees dealing with matters such as public accounts (ie the spending by the government of money voted by parliament) and European legislation, and also committees advising on procedures and domestic administration of the house. Major select committees usually take evidence in public; their evidence and reports are published on the parliament website and in hard copy by The Stationery Office (TSO). House of Commons select committees are reconstituted after a general election.

In the House of Lords, select committees do not mirror government departments but cover broader issues. There is a select committee on the European Union (EU), which has six sub-committees dealing with specific areas of EU policy, a select committee on science and technology, a select committee on economic affairs and also one on the constitution. There is also a select committee on delegated powers and regulatory reform and one on privileges and conduct. In addition, *ad hoc* select committees have been set up from time to time to investigate specific subjects. There are also joint committees of the two houses, eg the committees on statutory instruments and on human rights.

THE SPEAKER – The Speaker of the House of Commons is the spokesperson and chair of the Chamber. He or she is elected by the house at the beginning of each parliament or when the previous Speaker retires or dies. The Speaker neither speaks in debates nor votes in divisions except when the voting is equal.

VACANT SEATS – When a vacancy occurs in the House of Commons during a session of parliament, the writ for the by-election is moved by a whip of the party to which the member whose seat has been vacated belonged. If the house is in recess, the Speaker can issue a warrant for a writ, should two members certify to him that a seat is vacant.

WESTMINSTER HALL SITTINGS – Following a report by the Modernisation of the House of Commons Select Committee, the Commons decided in May 1999 to set up a second debating forum. It is known as 'Westminster Hall' and sittings are in the Grand Committee Room on some Mondays from 4.30pm to 7.30pm, Tuesdays and Wednesdays from 9.30am to 11.30am and from 2.30pm to 5.30pm, and Thursdays from 1.30pm to 4.30pm. Sittings are open to the public at the times indicated.

WHIPS – In order to secure the attendance of members of a particular party in parliament, particularly on the occasion of an important vote, whips (originally known as 'whippers-in') are appointed. The written appeal or circular letter issued by them is also known as a 'whip', its urgency being denoted by the number of times it is underlined. Failure to respond to a three-line whip is tantamount in the Commons to secession (at any rate temporarily) from the party. Whips are provided with office accommodation in both houses, and government and some opposition whips receive salaries from public funds.

PARLIAMENTARY ARCHIVES

Houses of Parliament, London SW1A 0PW
T 020-7219 3074 **E** archives@parliament.uk
W www.parliament.uk/archives

Since 1497, the records of parliament have been kept within the Palace of Westminster. They are in the custody of the Clerk of Parliaments. In 1946 the House of Lords Record Office, which became the Parliamentary Archives in 2006, was established to supervise their preservation and their availability to the public. Some 3 million documents are preserved, including acts of parliament from 1497, journals of the House of Lords from 1510, minutes and committee proceedings from 1610, and papers laid before parliament from 1531. Among the records are the Petition of Right, the death warrant of Charles I, the Declaration of Breda, and the Bill of Rights. Records are made available through a public search room.

Director of the Parliamentary Archives, Adrian Brown

GOVERNMENT OFFICE

The government is the body of ministers responsible for the administration of national affairs, determining policy and introducing into parliament any legislation necessary to give effect to government policy. The majority of ministers are members of the House of Commons but members of the House of Lords, or of neither house, may also hold ministerial responsibility. The prime minister is, by current convention, always a member of the House of Commons.

THE PRIME MINISTER

The office of prime minister, which had been in existence for nearly 200 years, was officially recognised in 1905 and its holder was granted a place in the table of precedence. The prime minister, by tradition also First Lord of the Treasury and Minister for the Civil Service, is appointed by the sovereign and is usually the leader of the party which enjoys, or can secure, a majority in the House of Commons. Other ministers are appointed by the sovereign on the recommendation of the prime minister, who also allocates functions among ministers and has the power to dismiss ministers from their posts.

The prime minister informs the sovereign on state and political matters, advises on the dissolution of parliament, and makes recommendations for important crown appointments, ie the award of honours, etc.

As the chair of cabinet meetings and leader of a political party, the prime minister is responsible for translating party policy into government activity. As leader of the government, the prime minister is responsible to parliament and to the electorate for the policies and their implementation.

The prime minister also represents the nation in international affairs, for example summit conferences.

THE CABINET

The cabinet developed during the 18th century as an inner committee of the Privy Council, which was the chief source of executive power until that time. The cabinet is composed of about 20 ministers chosen by the prime minister, usually the heads of government departments (generally known as secretaries of state unless they have a special title, for example Chancellor of the Exchequer), the leaders of the two houses of parliament, and the holders of various traditional offices.

The cabinet's functions are the final determination of policy, control of government and coordination of government departments. The exercise of its functions is dependent upon the incumbent party's (or parties') majority support in the House of Commons. Cabinet meetings are held in private, taking place once or twice a week during parliamentary sittings and less often during a recess. Proceedings are confidential, the members being bound by their oath as privy counsellors not to disclose information about the proceedings.

The convention of collective responsibility means that the cabinet acts unanimously even when cabinet ministers do not all agree on a subject. The policies of departmental ministers must be consistent with the policies of the government as a whole, and once the government's policy has been decided, each minister is expected to support it or resign.

The convention of ministerial responsibility holds a minister, as the political head of his or her department, accountable to parliament for the department's work. Departmental ministers usually decide all matters within their responsibility, although on matters of political importance they normally consult their colleagues collectively. A decision by a departmental minister is binding on the government as a whole.

POLITICAL PARTIES

Before the reign of William and Mary, the principal officers of state were chosen by and were responsible to the sovereign alone, and not to parliament or the nation at large. Such officers acted sometimes in concert with one another but more often independently, and the fall of one did not, of necessity, involve that of others, although all were liable to be dismissed at any moment.

In 1693 the Earl of Sunderland recommended to William III the advisability of selecting a ministry from the political party which enjoyed a majority in the House of Commons, and the first united ministry was drawn in 1696 from the Whigs, to which party the king owed his throne. This group became known as the 'junto' and was regarded with suspicion as a novelty in the political life of the nation, being a small section meeting in secret apart from the main body of ministers. It may be regarded as the forerunner of the cabinet and in the course of time it led to the establishment of the principle of joint responsibility of ministers, so that internal disagreement caused a change of personnel or resignation of the whole body of ministers.

The accession of George I, who was unfamiliar with the English language, led to a disinclination on the part of the sovereign to preside at meetings of his ministers and caused the emergence of a prime minister, a position first acquired by Robert Walpole in 1721 and retained by him without interruption for 20 years and 326 days. The office of prime minister was formally recognised in 1905 when it was established by royal warrant.

DEVELOPMENT OF PARTIES

In 1828 the Whigs became known as Liberals, a name originally given by opponents to imply laxity of principles, but gradually accepted by the party to indicate its claim to be pioneers and champions of political reform and progressive legislation. In 1861 a Liberal Registration Association was founded and Liberal Associations became widespread. In 1877 a National Liberal Federation was formed, with its headquarters in London. The Liberal Party was in power for long periods during the second half of the 19th century and for several years during the first quarter of the 20th century, but after a split in the party in 1931, the numbers elected remained small. In 1988 a majority of the Liberals agreed on a merger with the Social Democratic Party under the title Social and Liberal Democrats; since 1989 they have been known as the Liberal Democrats. A minority continue separately as the Liberal Party.

Soon after the change from Whig to Liberal, the Tory Party became known as Conservative, a name believed to have been invented by John Wilson Croker in 1830 and to have been generally adopted around the time of the passing of the Reform Act of 1832 – to indicate that the preservation of national institutions was the leading principle of the party. After the Home Rule crisis of 1886 the dissentient Liberals entered into a compact with the Conservatives, under which the latter undertook not to contest their seats, but a separate Liberal Unionist organisation was maintained until 1912, when it was united with the Conservatives.

Labour candidates for parliament made their first appearance at the general election of 1892, when there were 27 standing as Labour or Liberal-Labour. In 1900 the Labour Representation Committee (LRC) was set up in order to establish a distinct Labour group in parliament, with its own

whips, its own policy, and a readiness to cooperate with any party which might be engaged in promoting legislation in the direct interests of labour. In 1906 the LRC became known as the Labour Party.

The Scottish National Party (SNP) was founded in 1934 to campaign for independence for Scotland and a referendum on the subject was held in September 2014 which culminated in a 'no' to independence result.

The Democratic Unionist Party (DUP) was founded in 1971 to resist moves by the Ulster Unionist Party which were considered a threat to the Union. Its aim is to maintain Northern Ireland as an integral part of the UK.

Sinn Fein first emerged in the 1900s as a federation of nationalist clubs. It is a left-wing republican party who rejects British Sovereignty following a policy of abstentionism at Westminster and strives for a united Ireland.

Plaid Cymru was founded in 1926 to provide an independent political voice for Wales and to campaign for self-government in Wales.

The Social Democratic and Labour Party is an Irish nationalist party founded in 1970, which during the Troubles (1960s–1998) distinguished itself from Sinn Fein by rejecting violence.

The Alliance Party of Northern Ireland is a non-sectarian centrist party that advocates co-operation between nationalists and unionists; it was founded in 1970.

The Green Party was founded in 1973 and campaigns for social and environmental justice. The party began as 'People', was renamed the Ecology Party, and became the Green Party in 1985.

GOVERNMENT AND OPPOSITION

The government is formed by the party which wins the largest number of seats in the House of Commons at a general election, or which has the support of a majority of members in the House of Commons. By tradition, the leader of the majority party is asked by the sovereign to form a government, while the largest minority party becomes the official opposition with its own leader and a shadow cabinet. Leaders of the government and opposition sit on the front benches of the Commons with their supporters (the back-benchers) sitting behind them.

FINANCIAL SUPPORT

Financial support for opposition parties in the House of Commons was introduced in 1975 and is commonly known as Short Money, after Edward Short, the leader of the house at that time, who introduced the scheme. Short Money is only payable to those parties that secured at least two seats, or one seat and more than 150,000 votes, at the previous general election and is only intended to provide assistance for parliamentary duties. Opposition parties share £201,007 in travel expenses and receive £18,297.43 for every seat won at the most recent general election plus £36.54 for every 200 votes gained by the party (the figures are uprated annually in line with CPI). Short Money allocations for 2019–20 were:

DUP	£195,702.81
Green	£180,826.51
Labour	£6,563,156.52
Liberal Democrats	£898,384.12
Plaid Cymru	£103,693.35
SDPL	£90,980.65
SNP	£1,110,894.19

The sum paid to Sinn Fein and any other party that may choose not to take their seats in the House of Commons is calculated on the same basis as Short Money, but is known as Representative Money. Sinn Fein's allocation in 2019–20 was £165,304.55.

For the financial year which commenced on 1 April 2018, the leader of the opposition's office was allocated £852,491.98 for running costs.

Financial support for opposition parties in the House of Lords was introduced in 1996 and is commonly known as Cranborne Money, after former leader of the house, Viscount Cranborne.

The following list of political parties are those with at least one MP or sitting member of the House of Lords in the present parliament.

CONSERVATIVE PARTY
Conservative Campaign Headquarters, 4 Matthew Parker Street, London SW1H 9HQ
T 020-7222 9000 **W** www.conservatives.com

Parliamentary Party Leader, Rt. Hon. Boris Johnson, MP
Leader in the Lords, Rt. Hon. Baroness Evans of Bowes Park
Leader in the Commons and Lord President of the Council, Rt. Hon. Jacob Rees-Mogg, MP
Co-Chairs, Ben Elliot; Rt. Hon. Amanda Milling, MP
Deputy Chairman, Lord Sharpe of Epsom, OBE
Party Treasurer, Sir Ehud Sheleg

GREEN PARTY
The Biscuit Factory, Unit 201 A Block, 100 Clements Road, London SE16 4DG
T 020-3691 9400 **E** office@greenparty.org.uk
W www.greenparty.org.uk

Party Leaders, Sian Berry, AM; Jonathan Bartley
Deputy Leader, Amelia Womack
Chair, Liz Reason
Finance Coordinator, Jon Nott

LABOUR PARTY
Labour Central, Kings Manor, Newcastle upon Tyne NE1 6PA
T 0845-092 2299 **W** www.labour.org.uk

General Secretary, David Evans
General Secretary, Welsh Labour, Louise Magee
General Secretary, Michael Sharpe

SHADOW CABINET
Leader of the Opposition, Rt. Hon. Sir Keir Starmer, KCB, QC, MP
Deputy Leader, Angela Rayner, MP
Chancellor of the Exchequer, Anneliese Dodds, PHD, MP
Foreign Secretary, Lisa Nandy, MP
Home Secretary, Nick Thomas-Symonds, MP
Cabinet Office, Rachel Reeves, MP
Lord Chancellor and Secretary of State for Justice, Rt. Hon. David Lammy, MP

Secretary of State for Business, Energy and Industrial Strategy, Rt. Hon. Ed Miliband, MP
Secretary of State for Communities and Local Government, Steve Reed, OBE, MP
Secretary of State for Defence, Rt. Hon. John Healey, MP
Secretary of State for Digital, Culture, Media and Sport, Jo Stevens, MP
Secretary of State for Education, Kate Green, OBE, MP
Secretary of State for Employment Rights, Andy McDonald, MP
Secretary of State for Environment, Food and Rural Affairs, Luke Pollard, MP
Secretary of State for Health and Social Care, Jonathan Ashworth, MP
Secretary of State for Housing, Thangam Debbonaire, MP
Secretary of State for International Development, Preet Kaur Gill, MP

Secretary of State for International Trade, Rt. Hon. Emily Thornberry, MP
Secretary of State for Scotland, Ian Murray, MP
Secretary of State for Transport, Jim McMahon, MP
Chief Secretary to the Treasury, Bridget Phillipson, MP
Secretary of State for Wales, Nia Griffith, MP
Secretary of State for Northern Ireland, Louise Haigh, MP
Secretary of State for Work and Pensions, Jonathan Reynolds, MP
Minister for Mental Health, Dr Rosena Allin-Khan, MP
Minister for Voter Engagement and Youth Affairs, Cat Smith, MP
Minister for Women and Equalities, Marsha De Cordova, MP
Leader of the House of Commons, Rt. Hon. Valerie Vaz, MP
Leader of the House of Lords, Rt. Hon. Baroness Smith of Basildon
Attorney General, Lord Falconer of Thoroton, QC

LABOUR WHIPS
Chief Whip (Commons), Rt. Hon. Nick Brown, MP
Chief Whip (Lords), Rt. Hon. Lord McAvoy

LIBERAL DEMOCRATS
8–10 Great George Street, London SW1P 3AE
T 020-7022 0988 **E** info@libdems.org.uk **W** www.libdems.org.uk

Parliamentary Party Leader, Rt. Hon. Sir Ed Davey, MP
Deputy Party Leader, Daisy Cooper, MP
Leader in the Lords, Rt. Hon. Lord Newby, OBE
President, Mark Pack

NORTHERN IRELAND DEMOCRATIC UNIONIST PARTY
91 Dundela Avenue, Belfast BT4 3BU
T 028-9047 1155
E info@mydup.com **W** www.mydup.com

Parliamentary Party Leader, Rt. Hon. Arlene Foster, MLA
Deputy Leader & House of Commons Group Leader, Rt. Hon. Nigel Dodds, OBE, MP
Chair, Lord Morrow, MLA

PLAID CYMRU – THE PARTY OF WALES
Ty Gwynfor, Anson Court, Atlantic Wharf, Caerdydd CF10 4AL
T 029-2047 2272 **E** post@plaidcymru.org **W** www.partyof.wales

Party Leader, Adam Price, AM
Hon. Party President, Rt. Hon. Lord Wigley
Parliamentary Group Leader, Rt. Hon. Liz Saville Roberts, MP
Chair, Alun Ffred Jones
Chief Executive, Gareth Clubb

SCOTTISH NATIONAL PARTY
Gordon Lamb House, 3 Jackson's Entry, Edinburgh EH8 8PJ
T 0800-633 5432 **E** info@snp.org **W** www.snp.org

Westminster Parliamentary Party Leader, Rt. Hon. Ian Blackford, MP
Westminster Parliamentary Party Chief Whip, Patrick Grady, MP
First Minister of Scotland and Leader of the SNP, Rt. Hon. Nicola Sturgeon, MSP
Deputy Leader, Keith Brown, MSP
Party President, Ian Hudghton
National Treasurer, Colin Beattie, MSP
Chief Executive, Peter Murrell

SINN FEIN
53 Falls Road, Belfast BT12 4PD
T 028-9034 7350 **E** admin@sinnfein.ie **W** www.sinnfein.ie

Party President, Mary Lou McDonald, TD
Vice-President, Michelle O'Neill, MLA
Chair, Declan Kearney, MLA

MEMBERS OF PARLIAMENT *as at 20 November 2020*

KEY

* Previously an MP for this seat in the 2017–19 parliament

† Previously an MP for this seat in any parliament prior to the 2017–19 parliament

‡ Previously an MP for a different seat in any previous parliament

§ Currently suspended from the parliamentary Conservative Party

℄ Currently suspended from the parliamentary Labour Party

* **Abbott**, Rt. Hon. Diane (*b.* 1953) *Lab., Hackney North & Stoke Newington,* Maj. 33,188

* **Abrahams**, Debbie (*b.* 1960) *Lab.; Oldham East & Saddleworth,* Maj. 1,499

* **Adams**, Nigel (*b.* 1966) *C., Selby & Ainsty,* Maj. 20,137

* **Afolami**, Bim (*b.* 1986) *C., Hitchin & Harpenden,* Maj. 6,895

* **Afriyie**, Adam (*b.* 1965) *C., Windsor,* Maj. 20,079

Khan, Imran Ahman (*b.* 1973) *C., Wakefield,* Maj. 3, 358

Aiken, Nickie (*b.* 1969) *C. Cities of London and Westminster,* Maj. 3,953

* **Aldous**, Peter (*b.* 1961) *C., Waveney,* Maj. 18,002

* **Ali**, Rushanara (*b.* 1975) *Lab., Bethnal Green & Bow,* Maj. 37,524

Ali, Tahir (*b.)* 1971) *Lab., Birminham Hall Green,* Maj. 28,508

* **Allan**, Lucy (*b.* 1964) *C., Telford,* Maj. 10,941

* **Allen**, Heidi (*b.* 1975) *Ind., Cambridgeshire South,* Maj. 15,952

* **Allin-Khan**, Dr Rosena (*b.* 1977) *Lab., Tooting,* Maj. 14,307

Amesbury, Mike (*b.* 1969) *Lab., Weaver Vale,* Maj. 562

*‡ **Amess**, Sir David (*b.* 1952) *C., Southend West,* Maj. 14,459

Anderson, Fleur (*b.* 1971) *L. Putney,* Maj. 4,774

Anderson, Lee (*b.* 1967) *C. Ashfield,* Maj. 5,733

Anderson, Stuart (*b.* 1976) *C. Wolverhampton South West,* Maj. 1,661

* **Andrew**, Stuart (*b.* 1971) *C., Pudsey,* Maj. 3,517

† **Ansell**, Caroline (*b.* 1971 *) C., Eastbourne* Maj. 4,331

* **Antoniazzi**, Tonia (*b.* 1971) *Lab., Gower,* Maj. 1,837

* **Argar**, Edward (*b.* 1977) *C., Charnwood,* Maj. 22,397

* **Ashworth**, Jonathan (*b.* 1978) *Lab. Co-op, Leicester South,* Maj. 22,675

Atherton, Sarah (*b.* 1967) *C., Wrexham,* Maj. 2,131

* **Atkins**, Victoria (*b.* 1976) *C., Louth & Horncastle,* Maj. 28,868

Bacon, Gareth (*b.* 1972) *C., Orpington* Maj. 22,378

* **Bacon**, Richard (*b.* 1962) *C., Norfolk South,* Maj. 21,275

* **Badenoch**, Kemi (*b.* 1980) *C., Saffron Walden,* Maj. 29,594

Bailey, Shaun (*b.* 1992) *C. West Bromwich West,* Maj. 3,799

Baillie, Siobhan, (*b.* 1981) *C. Stroud,* Maj. 3,840

Baker, Duncan (*b.* 1979) *C., North Norfolk,* Maj. 14,395

* **Baker**, Steve (*b.* 1971) *C., Wycombe,* Maj. 4,214

* **Baldwin**, Harriett (*b.* 1960) *C., Worcestershire West,* Maj. 24,449

* **Barclay**, Rt. Hon. Stephen (*b.* 1972) *C., North East Cambridgeshire,* Maj. 29,993

* **Bardell**, Hannah (*b.* 1984) *SNP, Livingston,* Maj. 13,435

Barker, Paula (*b.* 1972) *Lab., Liverpool Wavertree* Maj. 27,085

* **Baron**, John (*b.* 1959) *C., Basildon & Billericay,* Maj. 20,412

Baynes, Simon (*b.* 1960) *C. Clwyd South,* Maj. 1,239

*‡ **Beckett**, Rt. Hon. Dame Margaret, DBE (*b.* 1943) *Lab., Derby South,* Maj. 6,019

* **Begley**, Órfhlaith (*b.* 1991) *SF, Tyrone West,* Maj. 7,478

Begum, Apsana (*b.* 1990) *L. Poplar and Limehouse* Maj. 28,904

* **Bell**, Aaron (*b.* 1980) *C., Newcastle-under-Lyme,* Maj. 7,446

* **Benn**, Rt. Hon. Hilary (*b.* 1953) *Lab., Leeds Central,* Maj. 19,270

* **Benton**, Scott (*b.* 1960) *C., Blackpool South,* Maj. 3,690

* **Beresford**, Sir Paul (*b.* 1946) *C., Mole Valley,* Maj. 12,041

* **Berry**, Rt. Hon. Jake (*b.* 1978) *C., Rossendale & Darwen,* Maj. 9,522

* **Betts**, Clive (*b.* 1950) *Lab., Sheffield South East,* Maj. 4,289

Bhatti, Saqib, MBE (*b.* 1985) *C. Meriden* Maj. 22,836

* **Black**, Mhairi (*b.* 1994) *SNP, Paisley & Renfrewshire South,* Maj. 10,679

* **Blackman**, Bob (*b.* 1956) *C., Harrow East,* Maj. 8,170

* **Blackman**, Kirsty (*b.* 1986) *SNP, Aberdeen North,* Maj. 12,670

Blake, Olivia (*b.* 1990) *L., Sheffield Hallam,* Maj. 712

* **Blomfield**, Paul (*b.* 1953) *Lab., Sheffield Central,* Maj. 27,273

* **Blunt**, Crispin (*b.* 1960) *C., Reigate,* Maj. 18,310

* **Bone**, Peter (*b.* 1952) *C., Wellingborough,* Maj. 18,540

Bonnar, Steven (*b.* 1982) *SNP, Coatbridge, Chryston and Bellshill,* Maj. 5,624

*‡ **Bottomley**, Sir Peter (*b.* 1944) *C., Worthing West,* Maj. 14,823

* **Bowie**, Andrew (*b.* 1988) *C., Aberdeenshire West & Kincardine,* Maj. 843

* **Brabin**, Tracy (*b.* 1961) *Lab. Co-op, Batley & Spen,* Maj. 3,525

* **Bradley**, Ben (*b.* 1989) *C., Mansfield,* Maj. 16,306

* **Bradley**, Rt. Hon. Karen (*b.* 1970) *C., Staffordshire Moorlands,* Maj. 16,428

* **Bradshaw**, Rt. Hon. Ben (*b.* 1960) *Lab., Exeter,* Maj. 10,403

* **Brady**, Sir Graham (*b.* 1967) *C., Altrincham & Sale West,* Maj. 6,139

* **Brady**, Mickey (*b.* 1950) *SF, Newry & Armagh,* Maj. 9,287

* **Braverman**, Rt. Hon. Suella (*b.* 1980) *C., Fareham,* Maj. 26,086

* **Brennan**, Kevin (*b.* 1959) *Lab., Cardiff West,* Maj. 10,986

* **Brereton**, Jack (*b.* 1991) *C., Stoke-on-Trent South,* Maj. 11,271

* **Bridgen**, Andrew (*b.* 1964) *C., Leicestershire North West,* Maj. 20,400

* **Brine**, Steve (*b.* 1974) *C., Winchester,* Maj. 985

Bristow, Paul (*b.* 1979) *C. Peterborough,* Maj. 2,580

Britcliffe, Sara (*b.* 1995) *C. Hyndburn,* Maj. 2,951

* **Brock**, Deidre (*b.* 1961) *SNP, Edinburgh North & Leith,* Maj. 12,808

*‡ **Brokenshire**, Rt. Hon. James (*b.* 1968) *C., Old Bexley & Sidcup,* Maj. 18,952

* **Brown**, Alan (*b.* 1970) *SNP, Kilmarnock & Loudoun,* Maj. 12,659

* **Brown**, Lyn (*b.* 1960) *Lab., West Ham,* Maj. 32,388

* **Brown**, Rt. Hon. Nick (*b.* 1950) *Lab., Newcastle upon Tyne East,* Maj. 15,463

Browne, Anthony (*b.* 1967) *C., South Cambridgeshire,* Maj. 2,904

* **Bruce**, Fiona (*b.* 1957) *C., Congleton,* Maj. 18,561

* **Bryant**, Chris (*b.* 1962) *Lab., Rhondda,* Maj. 11,115

Buchan, Felicity, *C. Kensington,* Maj. 150

* **Buck**, Karen (*b.* 1958) *Lab., Westminster North,* Maj. 10,759

* **Buckland**, Rt. Hon. Robert (*b.* 1968) *C., Swindon South,* Maj. 6,625

* **Burden**, Richard (*b.* 1954) *Lab., Birmingham Northfield,* Maj. 4,667

* **Burghart**, Alex (*b.* 1977) *C., Brentwood & Ongar,* Maj. 29,065

* **Burgon**, Richard (*b.* 1980) *Lab., Leeds East,* Maj. 5,531

* **Burns**, Rt. Hon. Conor (*b.* 1972) *C., Bournemouth West,* Maj. 10,150

*‡ **Butler**, Dawn (*b.* 1969) *Lab., Brent Central,* Maj. 20,870

Butler, Rob (*b.* 1967) *C., Aylesbury,* Maj. 17,373

Byrne, Ian (*b.* 1972) *Lab., Liverpool West Derby,* Maj. 29,984

* **Eagle**, Maria (*b.* 1961) *Lab., Garston & Halewood,* Maj. 31,624

Eastwood, Colum (*b.* 1983) *SDLP, Foyle,* 17,110

Eastwood, Mark (*b.* 1971) *C., Dewsbury,* 1,561

* **Edwards**, Jonathan (*b.* 1976) *Ind., Carmarthen East & Dinefwr,* Maj. 1,809

Edwards, Ruth, *C., Rushcliffe,* Maj. 7,643

* **Efford**, Clive (*b.* 1958) *Lab., Eltham,* Maj. 3,197

* **Elliott**, Julie (*b.* 1963) *Lab., Sunderland Central,* Maj. 2,964

* **Ellis**, Michael (*b.* 1967) *C., Northampton North,* Maj. 5,507

* **Ellwood**, Rt. Hon. Tobias (*b.* 1966) *C., Bournemouth East,* Maj. 8,806

* **Elmore**, Chris (*b.* 1983) *Lab., Ogmore,* Maj. 7,805

Elphicke, Natalie, OBE (*b.* 1970) *C., Dover,* Maj. 12,278

Eshalmoi, Florence (*b.* 1980) *Lab Co-op, Vauxhall,* Maj. 19,612

* **Esterson**, Bill (*b.* 1966) *Lab., Sefton Central,* Maj. 15,122

* **Eustice**, Rt. Hon. George (*b.* 1971) *C., Camborne & Redruth,* Maj. 8,700

* **Evans**, Chris (*b.* 1976) *Lab. Co-op, Islwyn,* Maj. 15,356

Evans, Dr Luke (*b.* 1983) *C. Bosworth,* Maj. 26,278

* **Evans**, Nigel (*b.* 1957) *C., Ribble Valley,* Maj. 18,439

* **Evennett**, Rt. Hon. Sir David (*b.* 1949) *C., Bexleyheath & Crayford,* Maj. 13,103

* **Fabricant**, Michael (*b.* 1950) *C., Lichfield,* Maj. 23,638

Farris, Laura (*b.* 1978) *C., Newbury,* Maj. 16,047

* **Farron**, Tim (*b.* 1970) *LD, Westmorland & Lonsdale,* Maj. 1,934

Farry, Stephen (*b.* 1971) *Alliance, North Down,* Maj. 2,968

Fell, Simon (*b.* 1980) *C. Barrow and Furness,* Maj. 5,789

* **Fellows**, Marion (*b.* 1949) *SNP, Motherwell & Wishaw,* Maj. 6,268

Ferrier, Margaret (*b.* 1960) *SNP, Rutherglen & Hamilton West,* 5,230

Finucane, John (*b.* 1980) *SF, Belfast North,* 23,078

* **Fletcher**, Colleen (*b.* 1954) *Lab., Coventry North East,* Maj. 7,692

Fletcher, Katherine (*b.* 1976) *C., South Ribble,* Maj. 11,199

Fletcher, Mark (*b.* 1985) *C., Bolsover,* Maj. 5,299

Fletcher, Nick (*b.* 1972) *C., Don Valley,* Maj. 3,630

Flynn, Stephen (*b.* 1988) *SNP, Aberdeen South,* Maj. 3,982

Ford, Vicky (*b.* 1967) *C., Chelmsford,* Maj. 17,621

* **Foster**, Kevin (*b.* 1978) *C., Torbay,* Maj. 17,749

* **Fovargue**, Yvonne (*b.* 1956) *Lab., Makerfield,* Maj. 4,740

* **Fox**, Rt. Hon. Dr Liam (*b.* 1961) *C., Somerset North,* Maj. 17,536

* **Foxcroft**, Vicky (*b.* 1977) *Lab., Lewisham Deptford,* Maj. 32,913

Foy, Mary (*b.* 1968) *Lab., City of Durham,* Maj. 5,025

* **Francois**, Rt. Hon. Mark (*b.* 1965) *C., Rayleigh & Wickford,* Maj. 31,000

* **Frazer**, Lucy (*b.* 1972) *C., Cambridgeshire South East,* Maj. 11,490

* **Freeman**, George (*b.* 1967) *C., Norfolk Mid,* Maj. 22,594

* **Freer**, Mike (*b.* 1960) *C., Finchley & Golders Green,* Maj. 6,562

‡ **Fuller**, Richard (*b.* 1962) *C., North East Bedfordshire,* Maj. 24,283

* **Furniss**, Gill (*b.* 1957) *Lab., Sheffield Brightside & Hillsborough,* Maj. 12,274

* **Fysh**, Marcus (*b.* 1970) *C., Yeovil,* Maj. 16,181

* **Gale**, Rt. Hon. Sir Roger (*b.* 1943) *C., Thanet North,* Maj. 17,189

* **Gardiner**, Barry (*b.* 1957) *Lab., Brent North,* Maj. 8,079

* **Garnier**, Mark (*b.* 1963) *C., Wyre Forest,* Maj. 21,413

* **Ghani**, Nusrat (*b.* 1972) *C., Wealden,* Maj. 25,655

* **Gibb**, Rt. Hon. Nick (*b.* 1960) *C., Bognor Regis & Littlehampton,* Maj. 22,503

* **Gibson**, Patricia (*b.* 1968) *SNP, Ayrshire North & Arran,* Maj. 8,521

Gibson, Peter (*b.* 1975) *C., Darlington,* Maj. 3,294

Gideon, Jo (*b.* 1952) *C., Stoke-on-Trent Central,* Maj. 670

*† **Gildernew**, Michelle (*b.* 1970) *SF, Fermanagh & South Tyrone,* Maj. 57

Gill, Preet (*b.* 1972) *Lab. Co-op, Birmingham Edgbaston,* Maj. 5,614

* **Gillan**, Rt. Hon. Dame Cheryl, DBE (*b.* 1952) *C., Chesham & Amersham,* Maj. 16,223

* **Girvan**, Paul (*b.* 1963) *DUP, Antrim South,* Maj. 2,689

* **Glen**, John (*b.* 1974) *C., Salisbury,* Maj. 19,736

* **Glindon**, Mary (*b.* 1957) *Lab., Tyneside North,* Maj. 9,561

* **Goodwill**, Rt. Hon. Robert (*b.* 1956) *C., Scarborough & Whitby,* Maj. 10,270

* **Gove**, Rt. Hon. Michael (*b.* 1967) *C., Surrey Heath,* Maj. 18,349

* **Grady**, Patrick (*b.* 1980) *SNP, Glasgow North,* Maj. 5,601

* **Graham**, Richard (*b.* 1958) *C., Gloucester,* Maj. 10,277

* **Grant**, Helen (*b.* 1961) *C., Maidstone & The Weald,* Maj. 21,772

* **Grant**, Peter (*b.* 1961) *SNP, Glenrothes,* Maj. 11,757

* **Gray**, James (*b.* 1954) *C., Wiltshire North,* Maj. 17,626

* **Gray**, Neil (*b.* 1986) *SNP, Airdrie & Shotts,* Maj. 5,201

* **Grayling**, Rt. Hon. Chris (*b.* 1962) *C., Epsom & Ewell,* Maj. 17,873

* **Green**, Chris (*b.* 1973) *C., Bolton West,* Maj. 8,855

* **Green**, Rt. Hon. Damian (*b.* 1956) *C., Ashford,* Maj. 24,029

* **Green**, Kate (*b.* 1960) *Lab., Stretford & Urmston,* Maj. 16,417

* **Greenwood**, Lilian (*b.* 1966) *Lab., Nottingham South,* Maj. 12,568

* **Greenwood**, Margaret (*b.* 1959) *Lab., Wirral West,* Maj. 3,003

Griffith, Andrew (*b.* 1971) *C., Arundel & South Downs,* Maj. 22,521

* **Griffith**, Nia (*b.* 1956) *Lab., Llanelli,* Maj. 4,670

Griffiths, Kate (*b.* 1971) *C., Burton,* Maj. 14,496

‡ **Grogan**, John (*b.* 1956) *Lab., Keighley,* Maj. 249

Grundy, James (*b.* 1980) *C., Leigh,* Maj. 1,965

Gullis, Jonathan (*b.* 1990) *C., Stoke-on-Trent North,* Maj. 6,286

* **Gwynne**, Andrew (*b.* 1974) *Lab., Denton & Reddish,* Maj. 6,175

* **Haigh**, Louise (*b.* 1987) *Lab., Sheffield Heeley,* Maj. 8,520

* **Halfon**, Rt. Hon. Robert (*b.* 1969) *C., Harlow,* Maj. 14,063

* **Hall**, Luke (*b.* 1986) *C., Thornbury & Yate,* Maj. 12,369

* **Hamilton**, Fabian (*b.* 1955) *Lab., Leeds North East,* Maj. 17,089

* **Hammond**, Stephen (*b.* 1962) *C., Wimbledon,* Maj. 628

* **Hancock**, Rt. Hon. Matt (*b.* 1978) *C., Suffolk West,* Maj. 23,194

* **Hands**, Rt. Hon. Greg (*b.* 1965) *C., Chelsea & Fulham,* Maj. 11,241

Hanna, Claire (*b.* 1980) *SDLP, Belfast South,* Maj. 15,401

Hanvey, Neale (*b.* 1964) *SNP, Kirkcaldy and Cowdenbeath,* Maj. 1,243

* **Hardy**, Emma (*b.* 1980) *Lab., Hull West & Hessle,* Maj. 2,856

* **Harman**, Rt. Hon. Harriet (*b.* 1950) *Lab., Camberwell & Peckham,* Maj. 33,780

* **Harper**, Rt. Hon. Mark (*b.* 1970) *C., Forest of Dean,* Maj. 15,869

* **Harris**, Carolyn (*b.* 1960) *Lab., Swansea East,* Maj. 7,970

* **Harris**, Rebecca (*b.* 1967) *C., Castle Point,* Maj. 26,634

* **Harrison**, Trudy (*b.* 1976) *C., Copeland,* Maj. 5,842

Hart, Sally-Ann (*b.* 1968) *C., Hastings and Rye,* Maj. 4,043

* **Hart**, Simon (*b.* 1963) *C., Carmarthen West & Pembrokeshire South,* Maj. 7,745

* **Hayes**, Helen (*b.* 1974) *Lab., Dulwich & West Norwood,* Maj. 27,310

* **Hayes**, Rt. Hon. Sir John, CBE (*b.* 1958) *C., South Holland & The Deepings*, Maj. 30,838

* **Hazzard**, Chris (*b.* 1984) *SF, Down South*, Maj. 1,620

* **Heald**, Sir Oliver (*b.* 1954) *C., Hertfordshire North East*, Maj. 18,189

* **Healey**, Rt. Hon. John (*b.* 1960) *Lab., Wentworth & Dearne*, Maj. 2,165

* **Heappey**, James (*b.* 1981) *C., Wells*, Maj. 9,991

* **Heaton-Harris**, Chris (*b.* 1967) *C., Daventry*, Maj. 26,080

* **Henderson**, Gordon (*b.* 1948) *C., Sittingbourne & Sheppey*, Maj. 24,479

* **Hendrick**, Sir Mark (*b.* 1958) *Lab. Co-op, Preston*, Maj. 12,146

* **Hendry**, Drew (*b.* 1964) *SNP, Inverness, Nairn, Badenoch & Strathspey*, Maj. 10,440

Henry, Darren (*b.* 1968) *C., Broxtowe*, Maj. 5,331

Higginbotham, Antony (*b.* 1989) *C., Burnley*, Maj. 1,352

* **Hill**, Mike (*b.* 1963) *Lab., Hartlepool*, Maj. 3, 595

* **Hillier**, Meg (*b.* 1969) *Lab. Co-op, Hackney South & Shoreditch*, Maj. 33,985

* **Hinds**, Rt. Hon. Damian (*b.* 1969) *C., Hampshire East*, Maj. 19,696

* **Hoare**, Simon (*b.* 1969) *C., Dorset North*, Maj. 24,301

* **Hobhouse**, Wera (*b.* 1960) *LD, Bath*, Maj. 12,322

* **Hodge**, Rt. Hon. Dame Margaret, DBE (*b.* 1944) *Lab., Barking*, Maj. 15,427

* **Hodgson**, Sharon (*b.* 1966) *Lab., Washington & Sunderland West*, Maj. 3,723

Holden, Richard (*b.* 1985) *C., North West Durham*, Maj. 1,144

* **Hollern**, Kate (*b.* 1955) *Lab., Blackburn*, Maj. 18,3042

* **Hollinrake**, Kevin (*b.* 1963) *C., Thirsk & Malton*, Maj. 25,154

* **Hollobone**, Philip (*b.* 1964) *C., Kettering*, Maj. 16,765

* **Holloway**, Adam (*b.* 1965) *C., Gravesham*, Maj. 15,581

Holmes, Paul (*b.* 1988) *C., Eastleigh*, Maj. 15,607

Hopkins, Rachel (*b.* 1972) *Lab., Luton South*, Maj. 8,756

* **Hosie**, Stewart (*b.* 1963) *SNP, Dundee East*, Maj. 13,375

* **Howarth**, Rt. Hon. Sir George (*b.* 1949) *Lab., Knowsley*, Maj. 39,942

* **Howell**, John (*b.* 1955) *C., Henley*, Maj. 14,053

* **Hoyle**, Rt. Hon. Sir Lindsay (*b.* 1957) *Speaker, Chorley*, Maj. 17,392

* **Huddleston**, Nigel (*b.* 1970) *C., Worcestershire Mid*, Maj. 28,018

Hudson, Neil, PHD (*b.* 1971) *C., Penrith & The Border*, Maj. 18,519

* **Hughes**, Eddie (*b.* 1968) *C., Walsall North*, Maj. 11,965

Hunt, Jane (*b.* 1966) *C. Loughborough*, Maj. 7,169

* **Hunt**, Rt. Hon. Jeremy (*b.* 1966) *C., Surrey South West*, Maj. 8,817

Hunt, Tom (*b.* 1988) *C., Ipswich*, Maj. 5,479

* **Huq**, Rupa, PHD (*b.* 1972) *Lab., Ealing Central & Acton*, Maj. 13,300

* **Hussain**, Imran (*b.* 1978) *Lab., Bradford East*, Maj. 18,144

* **Jack**, Rt. Hon. Alister (*b.* 1964) *C., Dumfries & Galloway*, Maj. 1,805

* **Jardine**, Christine (*b.* 1960) *LD, Edinburgh West*, Maj. 3,769

* **Jarvis**, Dan (*b.* 1972) *Lab., Barnsley Central*, Maj. 3,571

* **Javid**, Rt. Hon. Sajid (*b.* 1969) *C., Bromsgrove*, Maj. 23,106

* **Jayawardena**, Ranil (*b.* 1986) *C., Hampshire North East*, Maj. 35,280

* **Jenkin**, Sir Bernard (*b.* 1959) *C., Harwich & Essex North*, Maj. 20,182

Jenkinson, Mark (*b.* 1982) *C., Workington*, Maj. 4,176

* **Jenkyns**, Andrea (*b.* 1974) *C., Morley & Outwood*, Maj. 11,267

* **Jenrick**, Rt. Hon. Robert (*b.* 1982) *C., Newark*, Maj. 21,836

*‡ **Johnson**, Rt. Hon. Boris (*b.* 1964) *C., Uxbridge & Ruislip South*, Maj. 7,210

* **Johnson**, Dr Caroline (*b.* 1977) *C., Sleaford & North Hykeham*, Maj. 32,565

* **Johnson**, Dame Diana (*b.* 1966) *Lab., Hull North*, Maj. 7,593

* **Johnson**, Gareth (*b.* 1969) *C., Dartford*, Maj. 19,160

Johnson, Kim (*b.* 1960) *Lab., Liverpool Riverside*, Maj. 41,170

Johnston, David, OBE (*b.* 1981) *C., Wantage*, Maj. 12,653

* **Jones**, Andrew (*b.* 1963) *C., Harrogate & Knaresborough*, Maj. 9,675

* **Jones**, Darren (*b.* 1986) *Lab., Bristol North West*, Maj. 5,692

* **Jones**, Rt. Hon. David (*b.* 1952) *C., Clwyd West*, Maj. 14,402

Jones, Fay (1985) *C., Brecon and Radnorshire*, Maj. 7,131

* **Jones**, Gerald (*b.* 1970) *Lab., Merthyr Tydfil & Rhymney*, Maj. 10,606

* **Jones**, Rt. Hon. Kevan (*b.* 1964) *Lab., Durham North*, Maj. 4,742

* **Jones**, Marcus (*b.* 1974) *C., Nuneaton*, Maj. 13,144

* **Jones**, Ruth, (*b.* 1962) *Lab., Newport West* Maj. 902

* **Jones**, Sarah (*b.* 1972) *Lab., Croydon Central*, Maj. 5,949

* **Jupp**, Simon (*b.* 1985) *C., Devon East*, Maj. 6,708

* **Kane**, Mike (*b.* 1969) *Lab., Wythenshawe & Sale East*, Maj. 10,396

* **Kawczynski**, Daniel (*b.* 1972) *C., Shrewsbury & Atcham*, Maj. 11,217

Kearns, Alicia (*b.* 1988) *C., Rutland and Melton*, Maj. 26,924

* **Keegan**, Gillian (*b.* 1968) *C., Chichester*, Maj. 21,490

* **Keeley**, Barbara (*b.* 1952) *Lab., Worsley & Eccles South*, Maj. 3,219

* **Kendall**, Liz (*b.* 1971) *Lab., Leicester West*, Maj. 4,212

* **Khan**, Afzal, CBE (*b.* 1958) *Lab., Manchester Gorton*, Maj. 30,339

* **Kinnock**, Stephen (*b.* 1970) *Lab., Aberavon*, Maj. 10,490

*‡ **Knight**, Rt. Hon. Sir Greg (*b.* 1949) *C., Yorkshire East*, Maj. 22,787

* **Knight**, Julian (*b.* 1972) *C., Solihull*, Maj. 21,273

Kruger, Danny, MBE (*b.* 1974) *C., Devizes*, Maj. 23,993

* **Kwarteng**, Rt. Hon. Kwasi, PHD (*b.* 1975) *C., Spelthorne*, Maj. 18,393

* **Kyle**, Peter, DPHIL (*b.* 1970) *Lab., Hove*, Maj. 17,044

* **Laing**, Rt. Hon. Dame Eleanor, DBE (*b.* 1958) *C., Epping Forest*, Maj. 22,173

* **Lake**, Ben (*b.* 1993) *PC, Ceredigion*, Maj. 6,329

* **Lammy**, Rt. Hon. David (*b.* 1972) *Lab., Tottenham*, Maj. 30,175

* **Lamont**, John (*b.* 1976) *C., Berwickshire, Roxburgh & Selkirk*, Maj. 5,148

Largan, Robert (*b.* 1987) *C., High Peak*, Maj. 590

* **Latham**, Pauline, OBE (*b.* 1948) *C., Derbyshire Mid*, Maj. 15,385

Lavery, Ian (*b.* 1963) *Lab., Wansbeck*, Maj. 814

* **Law**, Chris (*b.* 1969) *SNP, Dundee West*, Maj. 12,259

* **Leadsom**, Rt. Hon. Andrea, CBE (*b.* 1963) *C., Northamptonshire South*, Maj. 27,761

* **Leigh**, Rt. Hon. Sir Edward (*b.* 1950) *C., Gainsborough*, Maj. 22,967

Levy, Ian (*b.* 1966) *C., Blyth Valley*, Maj. 712

* **Lewell-Buck**, Emma (*b.* 1978) *Lab., South Shields*, Maj. 9,585

* **Lewer**, Andrew (*b.* 1971) *C., Northampton South*, Maj. 4,697

* **Lewis**, Rt. Hon. Brandon, CBE (*b.* 1971) *C., Great Yarmouth*, Maj. 17,663

* **Lewis**, Clive (*b.* 1971) *Lab., Norwich South*, Maj. 12,760

* **Lewis**, Rt. Hon. Julian, DPHIL (*b.* 1951) *Ind., New Forest East*, Maj. 25,251

* **Liddell-Grainger**, Ian (*b.* 1959) *C., Bridgwater & Somerset West*, Maj. 24,439

* **Linden**, David (*b.* 1990) *SNP, Glasgow East*, Maj. 5,566

*‡ **Lloyd**, Tony (*b.* 1950) *Lab., Rochdale*, Maj. 9,668

Lockhart, Carla (*b.* 1985) *DUP, Upper Bann*, Maj. 20,501

Loder, Chris (*b.* 1981) *C., West Dorset*, Maj. 14,106

Logan, Mark, *C., Bolton North East*, Maj., 378

* **Long Bailey**, Rebecca (*b.* 1979) *Lab., Salford & Eccles,* Maj. 16,327

Longhi, Marco (*b.* 1967) *C., Dudley North,* Maj. 11,533

* **Lopez**, Julia (*b.* 1984) *C., Hornchurch & Upminster,* Maj. 23,308

* **Lopresti**, Jack (*b.* 1969) *C., Filton & Bradley Stoke,* Maj. 5,646

* **Lord**, Jonathan (*b.* 1962) *C., Woking,* Maj. 9,767

* **Loughton**, Tim (*b.* 1962) *C., Worthing East & Shoreham,* Maj. 7,441

* **Lucas**, Caroline, PHD (*b.* 1960) *Green, Brighton Pavilion,* Maj. 19,940

* **Lynch**, Holly (*b.* 1986) *Lab., Halifax,* Maj. 2,569

MacAskill, Kenny (*b.* 1958) *SNP, East Lothian,* Maj. 21,156

* **Mackinlay**, Craig (*b.* 1966) *C., Thanet South,* Maj. 10,587

Mackrory, Cherilyn (*b.* 1976) *C., Truro and Falmouth,* Maj. 4,561

* **Maclean**, Rachel (*b.* 1965) *C., Redditch,* Maj. 16,036

* **MacNeil**, Angus (*b.* 1970) *SNP, Na h-Eileanan an Iar,* Maj. 2,438

* **Madders**, Justin (*b.* 1972) *Lab., Ellesmere Port & Neston,* Maj. 8,764

* **Mahmood**, Khalid (*b.* 1961) *Lab., Birmingham Perry Barr,* Maj. 15,317

* **Mahmood**, Shabana (*b.* 1980) *Lab., Birmingham Ladywood,* Maj. 28,582

* **Mak**, Alan (*b.* 1983) *C., Havant,* Maj. 21,792

* **Malhotra**, Seema (*b.* 1972) *Lab. Co-op, Feltham & Heston,* Maj. 7,859

* **Malthouse**, Kit (*b.* 1966) *C., Hampshire North West,* Maj. 26,308

Mangnall, Anthony (*b.* 1989) *C., Totnes,* Maj. 12,724

* **Mann**, Scott (*b.* 1977) *C., Cornwall North,* Maj. 14,752

Marson, Julie (*b.* 1965) *C., Hertford and Stortford,* Maj. 19,620

* **Maskell**, Rachael (*b.* 1972) *Lab. Co-op, York Central,* Maj. 13,545

* **Maskey**, Paul (*b.* 1967) *SF, Belfast West,* Maj. 14,672

* **Matheson**, Chris (*b.* 1968) *Lab., Chester, City of,* Maj. 6,164

* **May**, Rt. Hon. Theresa (*b.* 1956) *C., Maidenhead,* Maj. 18,846

Mayhew, Jerome (*b.* 1970) *C., Broadland,* Maj. 21,861

* **Maynard**, Paul (*b.* 1975) *C., Blackpool North & Cleveleys,* Maj. 8,596

* **McCabe**, Steve (*b.* 1955) *Lab., Birmingham Selly Oak,* Maj. 12,414

* **McCarthy**, Kerry (*b.* 1965) *Lab., Bristol East,* Maj. 10,794

† **McCartney**, Jason (*b.* 1968) *C., Colne Valley,* Maj. 5,103

† **McCartney**, Karl (*b.* 1968) *C., Lincoln,* Maj. 3,514

* **McDonagh**, Siobhain (*b.* 1960) *Lab., Mitcham & Morden,* Maj. 16,482

* **McDonald**, Andy (*b.* 1958) *Lab., Middlesbrough,* Maj. 8,390

* **McDonald**, Stewart (*b.* 1986) *SNP, Glasgow South,* Maj. 9,005

* **McDonald**, Stuart (*b.* 1978) *SNP, Cumbernauld, Kilsyth & Kirkintilloch East,* Maj. 12,976

* **McDonnell**, Rt. Hon. John (*b.* 1951) *Lab., Hayes & Harlington,* Maj. 9,261

* **McFadden**, Rt. Hon. Pat (*b.* 1965) *Lab., Wolverhampton South East,* Maj. 1,235

* **McGinn**, Conor (*b.* 1984) *Lab., St Helens North,* Maj. 12,209

* **McGovern**, Alison (*b.* 1980) *Lab., Wirral South,* Maj. 6,105

* **McKinnell**, Catherine (*b.* 1976) *Lab., Newcastle upon Tyne North,* Maj. 5,765

† **McLaughlin**, Anne (*b.* 1966) *SNP, Glasgow North East,* Maj. 2,548

* **McMahon**, Jim (*b.* 1980) *Lab. Co-op, Oldham West & Royton,* Maj. 11,127

* **McMorrin**, Anna (*b.* 1971) *Lab., Cardiff North,* Maj. 6,982

* **McNally**, John (*b.* 1951) *SNP, Falkirk,* Maj. 14,948

* **McPartland**, Stephen (*b.* 1976) *C., Stevenage,* Maj. 8,592

‡ **McVey**, Rt. Hon. Esther (*b.* 1967) *C., Tatton,* Maj. 17,387

* **Mearns**, Ian (*b.* 1957) *Lab., Gateshead,* Maj. 7,200

* **Menzies**, Mark (*b.* 1971) *C., Fylde,* Maj. 16,611

* **Mercer**, Johnny (*b.* 1981) *C., Plymouth Moor View,* Maj. 12,897

* **Merriman**, Huw (*b.* 1973) *C., Bexhill & Battle,* Maj. 26,059

* **Metcalfe**, Stephen (*b.* 1966) *C., Basildon South & Thurrock East,* Maj. 19,922

* **Miliband**, Rt. Hon. Ed (*b.* 1969) *Lab., Doncaster North,* Maj. 2,370

Millar, Robin (*b.* 1968) *C., Aberconwy,* Maj. 2,034

* **Miller**, Rt. Hon. Maria (*b.* 1964) *C., Basingstoke,* Maj. 14,198

* **Milling**, Rt. Hon. Amanda (*b.* 1975) *C., Cannock Chase,* Maj. 19,879

* **Mills**, Nigel (*b.* 1974) *C., Amber Valley,* Maj. 16,886

Mishra, Navendu (*b.* 1989) *Lab., Stockport,* Maj. 10,039

*‡ **Mitchell**, Rt. Hon. Andrew (*b.* 1956) *C., Sutton Coldfield,* Maj. 19,272

Mohindra, Gagan (*b.* 1978) *C., South West Hertfordshire,* Maj. 14,408

* **Molloy**, Francie (*b.* 1950) *SF, Ulster Mid,* Maj. 9,537

* **Monaghan**, Carol (*b.* 1972) *SNP, Glasgow North West,* Maj. 8,359

* **Moore**, Damien (*b.* 1980) *C., Southport,* Maj. 4,147

Moore, Robbie (*b.* 1984) *C., Keighley,* Maj. 2,218

* **Moran**, Layla (*b.* 1982) *LD, Oxford West & Abingdon,* Maj. 8,943

* **Mordaunt**, Rt. Hon. Penny (*b.* 1973) *C., Portsmouth North,* Maj. 15,780

* **Morden**, Jessica (*b.* 1968) *Lab., Newport East,* Maj. 1,992

* **Morgan**, Stephen (*b.* 1981) *Lab., Portsmouth South,* Maj. 5,363

* **Morris**, Anne Marie (*b.* 1957) *C., Newton Abbot,* Maj. 17,501

* **Morris**, David (*b.* 1966) *C., Morecambe & Lunesdale,* Maj. 6,354

* **Morris**, Grahame (*b.* 1961) *Lab., Easington,* Maj. 6,581

* **Morris**, James (*b.* 1967) *C., Halesowen & Rowley Regis,* Maj. 12,074

Morrissey, Joy (*b.* 1981) *C., Beaconsfield,* Maj. 15,712

* **Morton**, Wendy (*b.* 1967) *C., Aldridge-Brownhills,* Maj. 19,836

Mullan, Dr Kieran (*b.* 1984) *C., Crewe and Nantwich,* Maj. 8,508

Mumby-Croft, Holly (*b.* 1985) *C. Scunthorpe,* Maj. 6,451

* **Mundell**, Rt. Hon. David (*b.* 1962) *C., Dumfriesshire, Clydesdale & Tweeddale,* Maj. 3,781

* **Murray**, Ian (*b.* 1976) *Lab., Edinburgh South,* Maj. 11,095

Murray, James (*b.* 1983) *Lab. Co-op, Ealing North,* Maj. 12,269

* **Murray**, Sheryll (*b.* 1956) *C., Cornwall South East,* Maj. 20,971

* **Murrison**, Rt. Hon. Dr Andrew (*b.* 1961) *C., Wiltshire South West,* Maj. 21,630

* **Nandy**, Lisa (*b.* 1979) *Lab., Wigan,* Maj. 6,728

* **Neill**, Sir Robert (*b.* 1952) *C., Bromley & Chislehurst,* Maj. 10,891

* **Newlands**, Gavin (*b.* 1980) *SNP, Paisley & Renfrewshire North,* Maj. 11,902

Nichols, Charlotte (*b.* 1992) *Lab, Warrington North,* Maj. 1509

Nici, Lia (*b.* 1969) *C., Great Grimsby,* Maj. 7,331

† **Nicolson**, John (*b.* 1961) *SNP, Ochil & South Perthshire,* Maj. 4,498

* **Nokes**, Rt. Hon. Caroline (*b.* 1972) *C., Romsey & Southampton North,* Maj. 10,872

* **Norman**, Rt. Hon. Jesse (*b.* 1962) *C., Hereford & Herefordshire South,* Maj. 19,686

* **Norris**, Alex (*b.* 1984) *Lab. Co-op, Nottingham North,* Maj. 4,490

* **O'Brien**, Neil (*b.* 1978) *C., Harborough,* Maj. 17,278

* **Offord**, Matthew, PHD (*b.* 1969) *C., Hendon,* Maj. 4,230

* **O'Hara**, Brendan (*b.* 1963) *SNP, Argyll & Bute,* Maj. 4,110

† **Olney**, Sarah (*b.* 1977) *LD, Richmond Park,* Maj. 7,766

* **Onwurah**, Chi (*b.* 1965) *Lab., Newcastle upon Tyne Central*, Maj. 12,278
* **Opperman**, Guy (*b.* 1965) *C., Hexham*, Maj. 10,549
Oppong-Asare, Abena (*b.* 1982) *Lab., Erith and Thamesmead*, Maj. 3,758
* **Osamor**, Kate (*b.* 1968) *Lab. Co-op, Edmonton*, Maj. 16,015
Osborne, Kate, *Lab., Jarrow*, Maj. 7,120
† **Oswald**, Kirsten (*b.* 1972) *SNP, East Renfrewshire*, Maj. 5,426
Owatemi, Taiwo (*b.* 1992) *Lab., Coventry North West*, Maj. 208
Owen, Sarah (*b.* 1983) *Lab., Luton North*, Maj. 9,247
* **Paisley**, Hon. Ian (*b.* 1960) *DUP, Antrim North*, Maj. 12,721
* **Parish**, Neil (*b.* 1956) *C., Tiverton & Honiton*, Maj. 24,239
* **Patel**, Rt. Hon. Priti (*b.* 1972) *C., Witham*, Maj. 24,082
* **Paterson**, Rt. Hon. Owen (*b.* 1956) *C., Shropshire North*, Maj. 22,949
* **Pawsey**, Mark (*b.* 1957) *C., Rugby*, Maj. 13,447
* **Peacock**, Stephanie (*b.* 1986) *Lab., Barnsley East*, Maj. 3,217
* **Penning**, Rt. Hon. Sir Mike (*b.* 1957) *C., Hemel Hempstead*, Maj. 14,563
* **Pennycook**, Matthew (*b.* 1982) *Lab., Greenwich & Woolwich*, Maj. 18,464
* **Penrose**, John (*b.* 1964) *C., Weston-Super-Mare*, Maj. 17,121
* **Percy**, Andrew (*b.* 1977) *C., Brigg & Goole*, Maj. 21,941
* **Perkins**, Toby (*b.* 1970) *Lab., Chesterfield*, Maj. 1,451
* **Phillips**, Jess (*b.* 1981) *Lab., Birmingham Yardley*, Maj. 10,659
* **Phillipson**, Bridget (*b.* 1983) *Lab., Houghton & Sunderland South*, Maj. 3,115
* **Philp**, Chris (*b.* 1976) *C., Croydon South*, Maj. 12,339
* **Pincher**, Rt. Hon. Christopher (*b.* 1969) *C., Tamworth*, Maj. 19,634
* **Pollard**, Luke (*b.* 1980) *Lab. Co-op, Plymouth Sutton & Devonport*, Maj. 4,757
* **Poulter**, Dr Dan (*b.* 1978) *C., Suffolk Central & Ipswich North*, Maj. 23,391
* **Pow**, Rebecca (*b.* 1960) *C., Taunton Deane*, Maj. 11,700
* **Powell**, Lucy (*b.* 1974) *Lab. Co-op, Manchester Central*, Maj. 29,089
* **Prentis**, Hon. Victoria (*b.* 1971) *C., Banbury*, Maj. 16,813
* **Pritchard**, Mark (*b.* 1966) *C., Wrekin, The*, Maj. 18,726
* **Pursglove**, Tom (*b.* 1988) *C., Corby*, Maj. 10,268
* **Quin**, Jeremy (*b.* 1968) *C., Horsham*, Maj. 21,127
* **Quince**, Will (*b.* 1982) *C., Colchester*, Maj. 9,423
* **Qureshi**, Yasmin (*b.* 1963) *Lab., Bolton South East*, Maj. 7,598
* **Raab**, Rt. Hon. Dominic (*b.* 1974) *C., Esher & Walton*, Maj. 2,743
Randall Tom, *C., Gedling*, Maj. 679
* **Rayner**, Angela (*b.* 1980) *Lab., Ashton Under Lyne*, Maj. 4,263
* **Redwood**, Rt. Hon. Sir John, DPHIL (*b.* 1951) *C., Wokingham*, Maj. 7,383
* **Reed**, Steve (*b.* 1963) *Lab. Co-op, Croydon North*, Maj. 24,673
* **Rees**, Christina (*b.* 1954) *Lab. Co-op, Neath*, Maj. 5,637
* **Rees-Mogg**, Rt. Hon. Jacob (*b.* 1969) *C., Somerset North East*, Maj. 14,729
* **Reeves**, Ellie (*b.* 1980) *Lab., Lewisham West & Penge*, Maj. 21,543
* **Reeves**, Rachel (*b.* 1979) *Lab., Leeds West*, Maj. 10,564
* **Reynolds**, Jonathan (*b.* 1980) *Lab. Co-op, Stalybridge & Hyde*, Maj. 2,946
Ribeiro-Addy, Bell (*b.* 1985) *Lab, Streatham*, 17,690
Richards, Nicola (*b.* 1994) *C., West Bromwich East*, Maj. 1,593
Richardson, Angela, *C., Guildford*, Maj. 3,337
* **Rimmer**, Marie (*b.* 1947) *Lab., St Helens South & Whiston*, Maj. 19,122
Roberts, Rob, *C., Delyn*, Maj. 865
* **Robertson**, Laurence (*b.* 1958) *C., Tewkesbury*, Maj. 22,410
* **Robinson**, Gavin (*b.* 1984) *DUP, Belfast East*, Maj. 1,819
* **Robinson**, Mary (*b.* 1955) *C., Cheadle*, Maj. 2,336
* **Rodda**, Matt (*b.* 1966) *Lab., Reading East*, Maj. 5,924
* **Rosindell**, Andrew (*b.* 1966) *C., Romford*, Maj. 17,893

* **Ross**, Douglas (*b.* 1983) *C., Moray*, Maj. 513
* **Rowley**, Lee (*b.* 1980) *C., Derbyshire North East*, Maj. 12,876
Russell, Dean (*b.* 1976) *C., Watford*, 4,433
* **Russell-Moyle**, Lloyd (*b.* 1986) *Lab. Co-op, Brighton Kemptown*, Maj. 8,061
* **Rutley**, David (*b.* 1961) *C., Macclesfield*, Maj. 10,711
Sambrook, Gary (*b.* 1989) *C., Birmingham Northfield*, Maj. 1,640
* **Saville Roberts**, Rt. Hon. Liz (*b.* 1964) *PC, Dwyfor Meirionnydd*, Maj. 4,740
Saxby, Selaine (*b.* 1970) *C., North Devon*, Maj. 14,813
* **Scully**, Paul (*b.* 1968) *C., Sutton & Cheam*, Maj. 8,351
* **Seely**, Bob (*b.* 1966) *C., Isle of Wight*, Maj. 23,737
* **Selous**, Andrew (*b.* 1962) *C., Bedfordshire South West*, Maj. 18,583
* **Shah**, Naz (*b.* 1973) *Lab., Bradford West*, Maj. 27,019
* **Shannon**, Jim (*b.* 1955) *DUP, Strangford*, Maj. 7,071
* **Shapps**, Rt. Hon. Grant (*b.* 1968) *C., Welwyn Hatfield*, Maj. 10,955
* **Sharma**, Rt. Hon. Alok (*b.* 1967) *C., Reading West*, Maj. 4,117
* **Sharma**, Virendra (*b.* 1947) *Lab., Ealing Southall*, Maj. 16,084
* **Sheerman**, Barry (*b.* 1940) *Lab. Co-op, Huddersfield*, Maj. 20,509
* **Shelbrooke**, Rt. Hon. Alec (*b.* 1976) *C., Elmet & Rothwell*, Maj. 17,353
* **Sheppard**, Tommy (*b.* 1959) *SNP, Edinburgh East*, Maj. 10,417
* **Siddiq**, Tulip (*b.* 1982) *Lab., Hampstead & Kilburn*, Maj. 14,188
Simmonds, David, CBE (*b.* 1976) *C., Ruislip, Northwood & Pinner*, Maj. 16,394
* **Skidmore**, Rt. Hon. Chris (*b.* 1981) *C., Kingswood*, Maj. 11,220
* **Slaughter**, Andy (*b.* 1960) *Lab., Hammersmith*, Maj. 17,847
Smith, Alyn (*b.* 1973) *SNP, Stirling*, Maj. 9,254
* **Smith**, Cat (*b.* 1985) *Lab., Lancaster & Fleetwood*, Maj. 2,380
* **Smith**, Chloe (*b.* 1982) *C., Norwich North*, Maj. 4,738
Smith, Greg (*b.* 1979) *C., Buckingham*, Maj. 20,411
* **Smith**, Henry (*b.* 1969) *C., Crawley*, Maj. 8,360
* **Smith**, Jeff (*b.* 1963) *Lab., Manchester Withington*, Maj. 27,905
* **Smith**, Rt. Hon. Julian, CBE (*b.* 1971) *C., Skipton & Ripon*, Maj. 23,694
* **Smith**, Nick (*b.* 1960) *Lab., Blaenau Gwent*, Maj. 8,647
* **Smith**, Royston (*b.* 1964) *C., Southampton Itchen*, Maj. 4,498
* **Smyth**, Karin (*b.* 1964) *Lab., Bristol South*, Maj. 9,859
* **Sobel**, Alex (*b.* 1975) *Lab. Co-op, Leeds North West*, Maj. 10,749
† **Solloway**, Amanda (*b.* 1961) *C., Derby North*, Maj. 2,540
*‡ **Spellar**, Rt. Hon. John (*b.* 1947) *Lab., Warley*, Maj. 11,511
* **Spelman**, Rt. Hon. Dame Caroline, DBE (*b.* 1958) *C., Meriden*, Maj. 19,198
Spencer, Dr Ben (*b.* 1981) *C., Runnymede and Weybridge*, Maj. 18,270
* **Spencer**, Rt. Hon. Mark (*b.* 1970) *C., Sherwood*, Maj. 16,186
Stafford, Alexander (*b.* 1987) *C., Rother Valley*, Maj. 14,377
* **Starmer**, Rt. Hon. Sir Keir, KCB (*b.* 1962) *Lab., Holborn & St Pancras*, Maj. 27,763
* **Stephens**, Chris (*b.* 1973) *SNP, Glasgow South West*, Maj. 4,900
* **Stephenson**, Andrew (*b.* 1981) *C., Pendle*, Maj. 6,186
* **Stevens**, Jo (*b.* 1966) *Lab., Cardiff Central*, Maj. 17,196
Stevenson, Jane (*b.* 1971) *C., Wolverhampton North East*, 4,080
* **Stevenson**, John (*b.* 1963) *C., Carlisle*, Maj. 8,319
* **Stewart**, Bob, DSO (*b.* 1949) *C., Beckenham*, Maj. 14,258
* **Stewart**, Iain (*b.* 1972) *C., Milton Keynes South*, Maj. 6,944
* **Stone**, Jamie (*b.* 1954) *LD, Caithness, Sutherland & Easter Ross*, Maj. 204
* **Streeter**, Sir Gary (*b.* 1955) *C., Devon South West*, Maj. 21,430

* **Streeting**, Wes (*b.* 1983) *Lab., Ilford North,* Maj. 5,218

* **Stride**, Rt. Hon. Mel (*b.* 1961) *C., Devon Central,* Maj. 17,721

* **Stringer**, Graham (*b.* 1950) *Lab., Blackley & Broughton,* Maj. 14,402

* **Stuart**, Graham (*b.* 1962) *C., Beverley & Holderness,* Maj. 20,448

* **Sturdy**, Julian (*b.* 1971) *C., York Outer,* Maj. 9,985

Sultana, Zarah (*b.* 1993) *Lab., Coventry South,* Maj. 401

* **Sunak**, Rt. Hon. Rishi (*b.* 1980) *C., Richmond (Yorks),* Maj. 27,210

Sunderland, James (*b.* 1970) *C., Bracknell,* Maj. 31,894

* **Swayne**, Rt. Hon. Sir Desmond, TD (*b.* 1956) *C., New Forest West,* Maj. 24,403

* **Syms**, Sir Robert (*b.* 1956) *C., Poole,* Maj. 19,116

* **Tami**, Rt. Hon. Mark (*b.* 1962) *Lab., Alyn & Deeside,* Maj. 213

Tarry, Sam (*b.* 1982) *Lab., Ilford South,* Maj. 24,101

* **Thewliss**, Alison (*b.* 1982) *SNP, Glasgow Central,* Maj. 6,474

* **Thomas**, Derek (*b.* 1972) *C., St Ives,* Maj. 4,284

* **Thomas**, Gareth (*b.* 1967) *Lab. Co-op, Harrow West,* Maj. 8,692

* **Thomas-Symonds**, Nick (*b.* 1980) *Lab., Torfaen,* Maj. 3,742

Thompson, Owen (*b.* 1978) *SNP, Midlothian,* Maj. 5,705

Thomson, Richard (*b.* 1976) *SNP, Gordon,* 819

* **Thornberry**, Rt. Hon. Emily (*b.* 1960) *Lab., Islington South & Finsbury,* Maj. 17,328

* **Throup**, Maggie (*b.* 1957) *C., Erewash,* Maj. 10,606

* **Timms**, Rt. Hon. Stephen (*b.* 1955) *Lab., East Ham,* Maj. 33,176

‡ **Timpson**, Edward, CBE (*b.* 1973) *C., Eddisbury,* 18,443

* **Tolhurst**, Kelly (*b.* 1978) *C., Rochester & Strood,* Maj. 17,072

* **Tomlinson**, Justin (*b.* 1976) *C., Swindon North,* Maj. 16,171

* **Tomlinson**, Michael (*b.* 1977) *C., Dorset Mid & Poole North,* Maj. 14,898

* **Tracey**, Craig (*b.* 1974) *C., Warwickshire North,* Maj. 17,956

* **Trevelyan**, Rt. Hon. Anne-Marie (*b.* 1969) *C., Berwick-upon-Tweed,* Maj. 14,835

* **Trickett**, Jon (*b.* 1950) *Lab., Hemsworth,* Maj. 1,180

Trott, Laura (*b.* 1984) *C., Sevenoaks,* Maj. 20,818

* **Truss**, Rt. Hon. Elizabeth (*b.* 1975) *C., Norfolk South West,* Maj. 26,195

* **Tugendhat**, Tom (*b.* 1973) *C., Tonbridge & Malling,* Maj. 26,941

* **Turner**, Karl (*b.* 1971) *Lab., Hull East,* Maj. 1,239

* **Twigg**, Derek (*b.* 1959) *Lab., Halton,* Maj. 18,975

* **Twist**, Liz (*b.* 1956) *Lab., Blaydon,* Maj. 5,531

* **Vara**, Shailesh (*b.* 1960) *C., Cambridgeshire North West,* Maj. 25,983

* **Vaz**, Rt. Hon. Valerie (*b.* 1954) *Lab., Walsall South,* Maj. 8,892

* **Vickers**, Martin (*b.* 1950) *C., Cleethorpes,* Maj. 21,418

Vickers, Matt (*b.* 1983) *C., Stockton South,* Maj. 5,260

* **Villiers**, Rt. Hon. Theresa (*b.* 1968) *C., Chipping Barnet,* Maj. 25,745

Wakeford, Christian (*b.* 1984) *C., Bury South,* Maj. 402

* **Walker**, Sir Charles, KBE (*b.* 1967) *C., Broxbourne,* Maj. 19,807

* **Walker**, Robin (*b.* 1978) *C., Worcester,* Maj. 6,758

* **Wallace**, Rt. Hon. Ben (*b.* 1970) *C., Wyre & Preston North,* Maj. 16,781

Wallis, Jamie, PHD (*b.* 1936) *C., Bridgend,* Maj. 1,157

* **Warburton**, David (*b.* 1965) *C., Somerton & Frome,* Maj. 19,213

* **Warman**, Matt (*b.* 1981) *C., Boston & Skegness,* Maj. 25,621

* **Watling**, Giles (*b.* 1953) *C., Clacton,* Maj. 24,702

Webb, Suzanne (*b.* 1966) *C., Stourbridge,* Maj. 27,534

Webbe, Claudia (*b.* 1965) *Ind., Leicester East,* Maj. 6,019

* **West**, Catherine (*b.* 1966) *Lab., Hornsey & Wood Green,* Maj. 19,242

* **Western**, Matt (*b.* 1962) *Lab., Warwick & Leamington,* Maj. 789

* **Whately**, Helen (*b.* 1976) *C., Faversham & Kent Mid,* Maj. 21,976

* **Wheeler**, Heather (*b.* 1959) *C., Derbyshire South,* Maj. 19,335

* **Whitehead**, Alan, PHD (*b.* 1950) *Lab., Southampton Test,* Maj. 6,213

* **Whitford**, Dr Philippa (*b.* 1958) *SNP, Ayrshire Central,* Maj. 5,304

Whitley, Mick (*b.* 1951) *Lab., Birkenhead,* Maj. 17,705

* **Whittaker**, Craig (*b.* 1962) *C., Calder Valley,* Maj. 5,774

* **Whittingdale**, Rt. Hon. John, OBE (*b.* 1959) *C., Maldon,* Maj. 30,041

Whittome, Nadia (*b.* 1996) *Lab., Nottingham East,* 17,393

* **Wiggin**, Bill (*b.* 1966) *C., Herefordshire North,* Maj. 24,856

Wild, James (*b.* 1977) *C., Norfolk North West ,* Maj. 19,922

‡ **Williams**, Craig (*b.* 1985) *C., Montgomeryshire,* Maj. 12,138

* **Williams**, Hywel (*b.* 1953) *PC, Arfon,* Maj. 2,781

* **Williamson**, Rt. Hon. Gavin, CBE (*b.* 1976) *C., Staffordshire South,* Maj. 28,250

Wilson, Munira (*b.* 1978) *LD., Twickenham,* Maj. 14,121

* **Wilson**, Rt. Hon. Sammy (*b.* 1953) *DUP, Antrim East,* Maj. 6,706

Winter, Beth, PHD (*b.* 1974) *Lab., Cynon Valley,* Maj. 8,822

* **Winterton**, Rt. Hon. Dame Rosie, DBE (*b.* 1958) *Lab., Doncaster Central,* Maj. 2,278

* **Wishart**, Pete (*b.* 1962) *SNP, Perth & Perthshire North,* Maj. 7,550

* **Wood**, Mike (*b.* 1976) *C., Dudley South,* Maj. 15,565

* **Wragg**, William (*b.* 1987) *C., Hazel Grove,* Maj. 4,423

* **Wright**, Rt. Hon. Jeremy (*b.* 1972) *C., Kenilworth & Southam,* Maj. 20,353

* **Yasin**, Mohammad (*b.* 1971) *Lab., Bedford,* Maj. 145

Young, Jacob (*b.* 1993) *C., Redcar,* Maj. 3,527

* **Zahawi**, Nadhim (*b.* 1967) *C., Stratford-on-Avon,* Maj. 19,972

* **Zeichner**, Daniel (*b.* 1956) *Lab., Cambridge,* Maj. 9,639

GENERAL ELECTION 2019 RESULTS

UK Turnout

Electorate (E.) 47,587,254 Turnout (T.) 32,026,222 (67.3%)

The results of voting in each of the 650 parliamentary constituencies at the general election on 12 December 2019 are given below.

KEY

swing N/A indicates a constituency for which the swing data cannot be calculated because one of the top two parties in the 2019 General Election did not field a candidate in the seat in 2019.

ABBREVIATIONS OF POLITICAL PARTIES

Active Dem.	Movement for Active Democracy
AD	Apolitical Democrats
Alliance	Alliance Party of Northern Ireland
AP	All People's Party
APNI	APNI Party
AWAP	Abolish the Welsh Assembly Party
AWP	Animal Welfare Party
BA	Brexit Alliance
Blue	Blue Revolution
BNP	British National Party
Bournemouth	Bournemouth Independent Alliance
BPE	Bus-Pass Elvis Party
Bradford	Better for Bradford
Brexit	The Brexit Party
Bristol	Independents for Bristol
C.	Conservative
Change	Alter Change
ChangeUK	The Independent Group for Change
Ch. P.	The Christian Party
CISTA	Cannabis is Safer than Alcohol
Citizens	Citizens Independent Social Thought Alliance
Co. Gd	Common Good
Comm.	Communist Party of Britain
Comm. Lge	Communist League
Community	Communities United Party
Compass	Compass Party
Concordia	Concordia
CPA	Christian Peoples Alliance
Croydon	Putting Croydon First
CSP	Common Sense Party
DDI	Demos Direct Initiative
Digital	Digital Democracy
DUP	Democratic Unionist Party
DVP	Democrats and Veterans Party
Eccentric	The Eccentric Party of Great Britain
Elmo	Give Me Back Elmo
Elvis	Church of the Militant Elvis
Eng. Dem.	English Democrats
Eng. Ind.	English Independence
For Britain	The For Britain Movement
Friends	Friends Party
GM Homeless	Greater Manchester Homeless Voice
Good	The Common Good
Green	Green Party
Green Soc.	Alliance for Green Socialism
Guildford	Guildford Greenbelt Group
Humanity	Humanity
Ind.	Independent
IPP	Immigrants Political Party
JACP	Justice & Anti-Corruption Party
Just	The Just Political Party
Lab.	Labour
Lab. Alt	Labour Alternative
Lab. Co-op	Labour and Co-operative
LD	Liberal Democrat
Lib.	The Liberal Party
Lib. GB	Liberty Great Britain
Libertarian	Libertarian Party
Lincs Ind.	Lincolnshire Independents
Loony	Monster Raving Loony Party
Love	One Love Party
MC	The Magna Carta Party
Money	Money Free Party
ND	No description
NE	The North East Party
NF	National Front
NHAP	National Health Action Party
North	Putting North of England People First
Northern	Northern Party
Open	Open Borders Party
Patria	Patria
PBP	People Before Profit Alliance
PC	Plaid Cymru
Peace	Peace Party
PF	People First
Pilgrim	The Pilgrim Party
Pirate	Pirate Party UK
Poole	The Party for Poole People Ltd
Populist	Populist Party
PUP	Progressive Unionist Party
Radical	The Radical Party
Realist	The Realists' Party
Rebooting	Rebooting Democracy
Referendum	Scotland's Independence Referendum Party
Renew	Renew Party
Respect	The Respect Party
Rochdale	Rochdale First Party
Roman	The Roman Party
S. New	Something New
SCP	Scottish Christian Party
SDLP	Social Democratic and Labour Party
SF	Sinn Fein
SNP	Scottish National Party
Soc.	Socialist Party
Soc. Dem.	Social Democratic Party
Soc. Lab.	Socialist Labour Party
Southampton	Southampton Independents
Southend	Southend Independent Association
Southport	The Southport Party
Sovereign	Independent Sovereign Democratic Britain
Space	Space Navies Party
Speaker	The Speaker
SPGB	The Socialist Party of Great Britain
SSP	Scottish Socialist Party
Thanet	Party for a United Thanet
TUSC	Trade Unionist and Socialist Coalition
TUV	Traditional Unionist Voice
UKEUP	UK European Union Party
UKIP	UK Independence Party
UUP	Ulster Unionist Party
Wessex Reg.	Wessex Regionalists
Wigan	Wigan Independents
Women	Women's Equality Party
Worth	The New Society of Worth
WP	Workers' Party
WRP	Workers' Revolutionary Party
WVPTFP	War Veteran's Pro-Traditional Family Party
Yorks	Yorkshire First
Yorkshire	The Yorkshire Party
Young	Young People's Party UK

ENGLAND

ALDERSHOT
E. 72,617   T. 47,932 (66.01%)   C. hold
Leo Docherty, C.   27,980
Howard Kaye, Lab.   11,282
Alan Hilliar, LD   6,920
Donna Wallace, Green   1,750
C. majority 16,698 (34.84%)
5.70% swing Lab. to C.

ALDRIDGE-BROWNHILLS
E. 60,138   T. 39,342 (65.42%)   C. hold
Wendy Morton, C.   27,850
David Morgan, Lab.   8,014
Ian Garrett, LD   2,371
Bill McComish, Green   771
Mark Beech, Loony   336
C. majority 19,836 (50.42%)
7.43% swing Lab. to C.

ALTRINCHAM & SALE WEST
E. 73,096   T. 54,763 (74.92%)   C. hold
Graham Brady, C.   26,311
Andrew Western, Lab.   20,172
Angela Smith, LD   6,036
Geraldine Coggins, Green   1,566
Neil Taylor, Lib   454
Iram Kiani, Ind.   224
C. majority 6,139 (11.21%)
0.48% swing C. to Lab.

AMBER VALLEY
E. 69,976   T. 45,567 (65.12%)   C. hold
Nigel Mills, C.   29,096
Adam Thompson, Lab.   12,210
Kate Smith, LD   2,873
Lian Pizzey, Green   1,388
C. majority 16,886 (37.06%)
9.47% swing Lab. to C.

ARUNDEL & SOUTH DOWNS
E. 81,726   T. 61,408 (75.14%)   C. hold
Andrew Griffith, C.   35,566
Alison Bennett, LD   13,045
Bella Sankey, Lab.   9,722
Isabel Thurston, Green   2,519
Robert Wheal, Ind.   556
C. majority 22,521 (36.67%)
8.87% swing C. to LD

ASHFIELD
E. 78,204   T. 48,980 (62.63%)   C. gain
Lee Anderson, C.   19,231
Jason Zadrozny, Ashfield   13,498
Natalie Fleet, Lab.   11,971
Martin Daubney, Brexit   2,501
Rebecca Wain, LD   1,105
Rose Woods, Green   674
C. majority 5,733 (11.70%)
7.85% swing Lab. to C.

ASHFORD
E. 89,550   T. 60,059 (67.07%)   C. hold
Damian Green, C.   37,270
Dara Farrell, Lab.   13,241
Adrian Gee-Turner, LD   6,048
Mandy Rossi, Green   2,638
Susannah De Sanvil, Ind.   862
C. majority 24,029 (40.01%)
5.41% swing Lab. to C.

ASHTON-UNDER-LYNE
E. 68,497   T. 38,559 (56.29%)   Lab. hold
Angela Rayner, Lab.   18,544
Dan Costello, C.   14,281
Derek Brocklehurst, Brexit   3,131
George Rice, LD   1,395
Lee Huntbach, Green   1,208
Lab. majority 4,263 (11.06%)
8.67% swing Lab. to C.

AYLESBURY
E. 86,665   T. 60,576 (69.90%)   C. hold
Rob Butler, C.   32,737
Liz Hind, Lab.   15,364
Steven Lambert, LD   10,081
Coral Simpson, Green   2,394
C. majority 17,373 (28.68%)
1.83% swing Lab. to C.

BANBURY
E. 90,113   T. 62,921 (69.82%)   C. hold
Victoria Prentis, C.   34,148
Suzette Watson, Lab.   17,335
Tim Bearder, LD   8,831
Ian Middleton, Green   2,607
C. majority 16,813 (26.72%)
3.29% swing Lab. to C.

BARKING
E. 77,946   T. 44,499 (57.09%)   Lab. hold
Margaret Hodge, Lab.   27,219
Tamkeen Shaikh, C.   11,792
Karen Batley, Brexit   3,186
Ann Haigh, LD   1,482
Shannon Butterfield, Green   820
Lab. majority 15,427 (34.67%)
5.33% swing Lab. to C.

BARNSLEY CENTRAL
E. 65,277   T. 36,903 (56.53%)   Lab. hold
Dan Jarvis, Lab.   14,804
Victoria Felton, Brexit   11,233
Iftikhar Ahmed, C.   7,892
Will Sapwell, LD   1,176
Tom Heyes, Green   900
Ryan Williams, Yorkshire   710
Donald Wood, Ind.   188
Lab. majority 3,571 (9.68%)
swing N/A

BARNSLEY EAST
E. 69,504   T. 38,070 (54.77%)   Lab. hold
Stephanie Peacock, Lab.   14,329
Jim Ferguson, Brexit   11,112
Adam Gregg, C.   10,377
Sophie Thornton, LD   1,330
Richard Trotman, Green   922
Lab. majority 3,217 (8.45%)
swing N/A

BARROW & FURNESS
E. 70,158   T. 46,046 (65.63%)   C. gain
Simon Fell, C.   23,876
Chris Altree, Lab.   18,087
Loraine Birchall, LD   2,025
Ged McGrath, Brexit   1,355
Chris Loynes, Green   703
C. majority 5,789 (12.57%)
6.51% swing Lab. to C.

BASILDON & BILLERICAY
E. 69,906   T. 44,128 (63.12%)   C. hold
John Baron, C.   29,590
Andrew Gordon, Lab.   9,178
Edward Sainsbury, LD   3,741
Stewart Goshawk, Green   1,395
Simon Breedon, Soc Dem   224
C. majority 20,412 (46.26%)
8.21% swing Lab. to C.

BASILDON SOUTH & THURROCK EAST
E. 74,441   T. 45,297 (60.85%)   C. hold
Stephen Metcalfe, C.   29,973
Jack Ferguson, Lab.   10,051
Kerry Smith, Ind.   3,316
Michael Bukola, LD   1,957
C. majority 19,922 (43.98%)
9.80% swing Lab. to C.

BASINGSTOKE
E. 82,926   T. 54,713 (65.98%)   C. hold
Maria Miller, C.   29,593
Kerena Marchant, Lab.   15,395
Sashi Mylvaganam, LD   6,841
Jonathan Jenkin, Green   2,138
Alan Stone, ND   746
C. majority 14,198 (25.95%)
4.52% swing Lab. to C.

BASSETLAW
E. 80,035   T. 50,841 (63.52%)   C. gain
Brendan Clarke-Smith, C.   28,078
Keir Morrison, Lab.   14,065
Debbie Soloman, Brexit   5,366
Helen Tamblyn-Saville, LD   3,332
C. majority 14,013 (27.56%)
18.42% swing Lab. to C.

BATH
E. 67,725   T. 52,138 (76.98%)   LD hold
Wera Hobhouse, LD   28,419
Annabel Tall, C.   16,097
Mike Davies, Lab.   6,639
Jimi Ogunnusi, Brexit   642
Bill Blockhead, Ind.   341
LD majority 12,322 (23.63%)
6.07% swing C. to LD

BATLEY & SPEN
E. 79,558   T. 52,927 (66.53%)
Lab. Co-op hold
Tracy Brabin, Lab. Co-op   22,594
Mark Brooks, C.   19,069
Paul Halloran, Woollen   6,432
John Lawson, LD   2,462
Clive Minihan, Brexit   1,678
Ty Akram, Green   692
Lab. Co-op majority 3,525 (6.66%)
5.00% swing Lab. to C.

BATTERSEA
E. 79,309   T. 59,977 (75.62%)   Lab. hold
Marsha De Cordova, Lab.   27,290
Kim Caddy, C.   21,622
Mark Gitsham, LD   9,150
Lois Davis, Green   1,529
Jake Thomas, Brexit   386
Lab. majority 5,668 (9.45%)
2.53% swing C. to Lab.

BEACONSFIELD
E. 77,720   T. 57,868 (74.46%)   C. gain
Joy Morrissey, C.   32,477
Dominic Grieve, Ind.   16,765
Alexa Collins, Lab.   5,756
Zoe Hatch, Green   2,033
Adam Cleary, Ind.   837
C. majority 15,712 (27.15%)
swing N/A

BECKENHAM
E. 68,671   T. 50,555 (73.62%)   C. hold
Bob Stewart, C.   27,282
Marina Ahmad, Lab.   13,024
Chloe-Jane Ross, LD   8,194
Ruth Fabricant, Green   2,055
C. majority 14,258 (28.20%)
0.51% swing C. to Lab.

BEDFORD
E. 71,579   T. 47,301 (66.08%)   Lab. hold
Mohammad Yasin, Lab.   20,491
Ryan Henson, C.   20,346
Henry Vann, LD   4,608
Adrian Spurrell, Green   960
Charles Bunker, Brexit   896
Lab. majority 145 (0.31%)
0.66% swing Lab. to C.

BEDFORDSHIRE MID
E. 87,795   T. 64,717 (73.71%)   C. hold
Nadine Dorries, C.   38,692
Rhiannon Meades, Lab.   14,028
Rachel McGann, LD   8,171
Gareth Ellis, Green   2,478
Alan Victor, Ind.   812
Ann Kelly, Loony   536
C. majority 24,664 (38.11%)
2.44% swing Lab. to C.

BEDFORDSHIRE NORTH EAST
E. 90,679   T. 65,018 (71.70%)   C. hold
Richard Fuller, C.   38,443
Julian Vaughan, Lab.   14,160
Daniel Norton, LD   7,999
Adam Zerny, Ind.   2,525
Philippa Fleming, Green   1,891
C. majority 24,283 (37.35%)
2.43% swing Lab. to C.

BEDFORDSHIRE SOUTH WEST
E. 79,926   T. 53,307 (66.70%)   C. hold
Andrew Selous, C.   32,212
Callum Anderson, Lab.   13,629
Emma Matanle, LD   5,435
Andrew Waters, Green   2,031
C. majority 18,583 (34.86%)
4.70% swing Lab. to C.

BERMONDSEY & OLD SOUTHWARK
E. 93,313   T. 58,615 (62.82%)   Lab. hold
Neil Coyle, Lab.   31,723
Humaira Ali, LD   15,597
Andrew Baker, C.   9,678
Alex Matthews, Brexit   1,617
Lab. majority 16,126 (27.51%)
2.67% swing LD to Lab.

BERWICK-UPON-TWEED
E. 59,939   T. 42,109 (70.25%)   C. hold
Anne-Marie Trevelyan, C.   23,947
Trish Williams, Lab.   9,112
Tom Hancock, LD   7,656
Thomas Stewart, Green   1,394
C. majority 14,835 (35.23%)
3.66% swing Lab. to C.

BETHNAL GREEN & BOW
E. 88,169   T. 60,562 (68.69%)   Lab. hold
Rushanara Ali, Lab.   44,052
Nicholas Stovold, C.   6,528
Josh Babarinde, LD   5,892
Shahrar Ali, Green   2,570
David Axe, Brexit   1,081
Vanessa Hudson, AWP   439
Lab. majority 37,524 (61.96%)
1.40% swing C. to Lab.

BEVERLEY & HOLDERNESS
E. 79,683   T. 53,542 (67.19%)   C. hold
Graham Stuart, C.   33,250
Chloe Hopkins, Lab.   12,802
Denis Healy, LD   4,671
Andy Shead, Yorkshire   1,441
Isabel Pires, Green   1,378
C. majority 20,448 (38.19%)
6.49% swing Lab. to C.

BEXHILL & BATTLE
E. 81,968   T. 59,093 (72.09%)   C. hold
Huw Merriman, C.   37,590
Christine Bayliss, Lab.   11,531
Martin Saunders, LD   7,280
Jonathan Kent, Green   2,692
C. majority 26,059 (44.10%)
3.41% swing Lab. to C.

BEXLEYHEATH & CRAYFORD
E. 65,466   T. 43,246 (66.06%)   C. hold
David Evennett, C.   25,856
Anna Day, Lab.   12,753
David McBride, LD   2,819
Tony Ball, Green   1,298
Graham Moore, Eng Dem   520
C. majority 13,103 (30.30%)
5.11% swing Lab. to C.

BIRKENHEAD
E. 63,762   T. 42,329 (66.39%)   Lab. gain
Mick Whitley, Lab.   24,990
Frank Field, BSJP   7,285
Claire Rowles, C.   5,540
Stuart Kelly, LD   1,620
Darren Lythgoe, Brexit   1,489
Pat Cleary, Green   1,405
Lab. majority 17,705 (41.83%)
swing N/A

BIRMINGHAM EDGBASTON
E. 68,828   T. 42,328 (61.50%)
                             Lab. Co-op hold
Preet Gill, Lab. Co-op   21,217
Alex Yip, C.   15,603
Colin Green, LD   3,349
Phil Simpson, Green   1,112
David Wilks, Brexit   1,047
Lab. Co-op majority 5,614 (13.26%)
1.30% swing Lab. to C.

BIRMINGHAM ERDINGTON
E. 66,148   T. 35,229 (53.26%)   Lab. hold
Jack Dromey, Lab.   17,720
Robert Alden, C.   14,119
Wendy Garcarz, Brexit   1,441
Ann Holtom, LD   1,301
Rob Grant, Green   648
Lab. majority 3,601 (10.22%)
4.68% swing Lab. to C.

BIRMINGHAM HALL GREEN
E. 80,283   T. 52,911 (65.91%)   Lab. hold
Tahir Ali, Lab.   35,889
Penny-Anne O'Donnell, C.   7,381
Roger Godsiff, Ind.   4,273
Izzy Knowles, LD   3,673
Rosie Cuckston, Brexit   877
Patrick Cox, Green   818
Lab. majority 28,508 (53.88%)
4.31% swing Lab. to C.

BIRMINGHAM HODGE HILL
E. 78,295   T. 45,003 (57.48%)   Lab. hold
Liam Byrne, Lab.   35,397
Akaal Sidhu, C.   6,742
Jill Dagnan, Brexit   1,519
Waheed Rafiq, LD   760
Jane McKears, Green   328
Hilda Johani, CPA   257
Lab. majority 28,655 (63.67%)
1.60% swing Lab. to C.

BIRMINGHAM LADYWOOD
E. 74,912   T. 42,118 (56.22%)   Lab. hold
Shabana Mahmood, Lab.   33,355
Mary Noone, C.   4,773
Lee Dargue, LD   2,228
Alex Nettle, Green   931
Andrew Garcarz, Brexit   831
Lab. majority 28,582 (67.86%)
0.83% swing Lab. to C.

BIRMINGHAM NORTHFIELD
E. 73,694   T. 43,098 (58.48%)   C. gain
Gary Sambrook, C.   19,957
Richard Burden, Lab.   18,317
Jamie Scott, LD   1,961
Keith Rowe, Brexit   1,655
Eleanor Masters, Green   954
Kenneth Lowry, UKIP   254
C. majority 1,640 (3.81%)
7.16% swing Lab. to C.

BIRMINGHAM PERRY BARR
E. 72,006   T. 42,147 (58.53%)   Lab. hold
Khalid Mahmood, Lab.   26,594
Raaj Shamji, C.   11,277
Gerry Jerome, LD   1,901
Annette Willcox, Brexit   1,382
Kefentse Dennis, Green   845
Thomas Braich, Yeshua   148
Lab. majority 15,317 (36.34%)
2.63% swing Lab. to C.

BIRMINGHAM SELLY OAK
E. 82,665   T. 49,467 (59.84%)   Lab. hold
Steve McCabe, Lab.   27,714
Hannah Campbell, C.   15,300
Dave Radcliffe, LD   3,169
Joe Peacock, Green   1,848
Joseph Tawonezvi, Brexit   1,436
Lab. majority 12,414 (25.10%)
2.97% swing Lab. to C.

BIRMINGHAM YARDLEY
E. 74,704   T. 42,678 (57.13%)   Lab. hold
Jess Phillips, Lab.   23,379
Vincent Garrington, C.   12,720
Roger Harmer, LD   3,754
Mary McKenna, Brexit   2,246
Christopher Garghan, Green   579
Lab. majority 10,659 (24.98%)
6.13% swing Lab. to C.

BISHOP AUCKLAND
E. 68,170   T. 44,805 (65.73%)   C. gain
Dehenna Davison, C.   24,067
Helen Goodman, Lab.   16,105
Nicholas Brown, Brexit   2,500
Ray Georgeson, LD   2,133
C. majority 7,962 (17.77%)
9.47% swing Lab. to C.

BLACKBURN
E. 71,229   T. 44,736 (62.81%)   Lab. hold
Kate Hollern, Lab.   29,040
Claire Gill, C.   10,736
Rick Moore, Brexit   2,770
Beth Waller-Slack, LD   1,130
Reza Hossain, Green   741
Rizwan Shah, Ind.   319
Lab. majority 18,304 (40.92%)
0.98% swing Lab. to C.

BLACKLEY & BROUGHTON
E. 73,372   T. 38,618 (52.63%)   Lab. hold
Graham Stringer, Lab.   23,887
Alexander Elias, C.   9,485
James Buckley, Brexit   2,736
Iain Donaldson, LD   1,590
David Jones, Green   920
Lab. majority 14,402 (37.29%)
5.79% swing Lab. to C.

BLACKPOOL NORTH & CLEVELEYS
E. 63,691   T. 38,804 (60.93%)   C. hold
Paul Maynard, C.   22,364
Chris Webb, Lab.   13,768
Sue Close, LD   1,494
Duncan Royle, Green   735
Neil Holden, Ind.   443
C. majority 8,596 (22.15%)
8.61% swing Lab. to C.

BLACKPOOL SOUTH
E. 57,688   T. 32,752 (56.77%)   C. gain
Scott Benton, C.   16,247
Gordon Marsden, Lab.   12,557
David Brown, Brexit   2,009
Bill Greene, LD   1,008
Becky Daniels, Green   563
Gary Coleman, Ind.   368
C. majority 3,690 (11.27%)
9.24% swing Lab. to C.

BLAYDON
E. 67,853   T. 45,681 (67.32%)   Lab. hold
Liz Twist, Lab.   19,794
Adrian Pepper, C.   14,263
Michael Robinson, Brexit   5,833
Vicky Anderson, LD   3,703
Diane Cadman, Green   1,279
Kathy King, Lib   615
Lisabela Marschild, Space   118
Lee Garrett, ND   76
Lab. majority 5,531 (12.11%)
7.96% swing Lab. to C.

BLYTH VALLEY
E. 64,429   T. 40,859 (63.42%)   C. gain
Ian Levy, C.   17,440
Susan Dungworth, Lab. Co-op   16,728
Mark Peart, Brexit   3,394
Thom Chapman, LD   2,151
Dawn Furness, Green   1,146
C. majority 712 (1.74%)
10.19% swing Lab. to C.

BOGNOR REGIS & LITTLEHAMPTON
E. 77,488   T. 51,223 (66.10%)   C. hold
Nick Gibb, C.   32,521
Alan Butcher, Lab.   10,018
Francis Oppler, LD   5,645
Carol Birch, Green   1,826
David Kurten, UKIP   846
Andrew Elston, Ind.   367
C. majority 22,503 (43.93%)
4.93% swing Lab. to C.

BOLSOVER
E. 75,157   T. 45,938 (61.12%)   C. gain
Mark Fletcher, C.   21,791
Dennis Skinner, Lab.   16,492
Kevin Harper, Brexit   4,151
David Hancock, LD   1,759
David Kesteven, Green   758
Ross Walker, Ind.   517
Natalie Hoy, Ind.   470
C. majority 5,299 (11.54%)
11.45% swing Lab. to C.

BOLTON NORTH EAST
E. 67,564   T. 43,556 (64.47%)   C. gain
Mark Logan, C.   19,759
David Crausby, Lab.   19,381
Trevor Jones, Brexit   1,880
Warren Fox, LD   1,847
Liz Spencer, Green   689
C. majority 378 (0.87%)
4.64% swing Lab. to C.

BOLTON SOUTH EAST
E. 69,163   T. 40,604 (58.71%)   Lab. hold
Yasmin Qureshi, Lab.   21,516
Johno Lee, C.   13,918
Mark Cunningham, Brexit   2,968
Kev Walsh, LD   1,411
David Figgins, Green   791
Lab. majority 7,598 (18.71%)
6.15% swing Lab. to C.

BOLTON WEST
E. 73,191   T. 49,298 (67.36%)   C. hold
Chris Green, C.   27,255
Julie Hilling, Lab.   18,400
Rebecca Forrest, LD   2,704
Paris Hayes, Green   939
C. majority 8,855 (17.96%)
8.06% swing Lab. to C.

BOOTLE
E. 74,832   T. 49,174 (65.71%)   Lab. hold
Peter Dowd, Lab.   39,066
Tarsilo Onuluk, C.   4,510
Kim Knight, Brexit   2,610
Rebecca Hanson, LD   1,822
Mike Carter, Green   1,166
Lab. majority 34,556 (70.27%)
0.86% swing Lab. to C.

BOSTON & SKEGNESS
E. 68,895   T. 41,696 (60.52%)   C. hold
Matt Warman, C.   31,963
Ben Cook, Lab.   6,342
Hilary Jones, LD   1,963
Peter Watson, Ind.   1,428
C. majority 25,621 (61.45%)
11.40% swing Lab. to C.

BOSWORTH
E. 81,537   T. 56,432 (69.21%)   C. hold
Luke Evans, C.   36,056
Rick Middleton, Lab.   9,778
Michael Mullaney, LD   9,096
Mick Gregg, Green   1,502
C. majority 26,278 (46.57%)
6.95% swing Lab. to C.

BOURNEMOUTH EAST
E. 74,127   T. 49,274 (66.47%)   C. hold
Tobias Ellwood, C.   24,926
Corrie Drew, Lab.   16,120
Philip Dunn, LD   5,418
Alasdair Keddie, Green   2,049
Ben Aston, ND   447
Emma Johnson, Ind.   314
C. majority 8,806 (17.87%)
0.77% swing Lab. to C.

BOURNEMOUTH WEST
E. 74,211   T. 45,977 (61.95%)   C. hold
Conor Burns, C.   24,550
David Stokes, Lab.   14,400
Jon Nicholas, LD   4,931
Simon Bull, Green   2,096
C. majority 10,150 (22.08%)
2.38% swing Lab. to C.

BRACKNELL
E. 79,206   T. 54,350 (68.62%)   C. gain
James Sunderland, C.   31,894
Paul Bidwell, Lab.   12,065
Kaweh Beheshtizadeh, LD   7,749
Derek Florey, Green   2,089
Olivio Barreto, Ind.   553
C. majority 19,829 (36.48%)
3.91% swing Lab. to C.

BRADFORD EAST
E. 73,206 T. 44,184 (60.36%) Lab. hold
Imran Hussain, Lab.   27,825
Linden Kemkaran, C.   9,681
Jeanette Sunderland, LD   3,316
Jonathan Barras, Brexit   2,700
Andy Stanford, Green   662
Lab. majority 18,144 (41.06%)
1.98% swing Lab. to C.

BRADFORD SOUTH
E. 69,046 T. 39,741 (57.56%) Lab. hold
Judith Cummins, Lab.   18,390
Narinder Sekhon, C.   16,044
Kulvinder Manik, Brexit   2,819
Alun Griffiths, LD   1,505
Matthew Edwards, Green   983
Lab. majority 2,346 (5.90%)
5.21% swing Lab. to C.

BRADFORD WEST
E. 70,694 T. 44,261 (62.61%) Lab. hold
Naz Shah, Lab.   33,736
Mohammed Afzal, C.   6,717
Derrick Hodgson, Brexit   1,556
Mark Christie, LD   1,349
Darren Parkinson, Green   813
Azfar Bukhari, ND   90
Lab. majority 27,019 (61.04%)
6.47% swing C. to Lab.

BRAINTREE
E. 75,208 T. 50,499 (67.15%) C. hold
James Cleverly, C.   34,112
Joshua Garfield, Lab.   9,439
Dominic Graham, LD   4,779
Jo Beavis, Ind.   1,488
David Mansell, Ind.   420
Alan Dorkins, Ind.   261
C. majority 24,673 (48.86%)
6.83% swing Lab. to C.

BRENT CENTRAL
E. 84,204 T. 49,132 (58.35%) Lab. hold
Dawn Butler, Lab.   31,779
David Brescia, C.   10,909
Deborah Unger, LD   4,844
William Relton, Green   1,600
Lab. majority 20,870 (42.48%)
5.53% swing Lab. to C.

BRENT NORTH
E. 83,772 T. 51,879 (61.93%) Lab. hold
Barry Gardiner, Lab.   26,911
Anjana Patel, C.   18,832
Paul Lorber, LD   4,065
Suzie O'Brien, Brexit   951
Simon Rebbitt, Green   850
Noel Coonan, Ind.   169
Elcena Jeffers, Ind.   101
Lab. majority 8,079 (15.57%)
7.33% swing Lab. to C.

BRENTFORD & ISLEWORTH
E. 85,770 T. 58,326 (68.00%) Lab. hold
Ruth Cadbury, Lab.   29,266
Seena Shah, C.   18,752
Helen Cross, LD   7,314
Daniel Goldsmith, Green   1,829
Lucy O'Sullivan, Brexit   1,165
Lab. majority 10,514 (18.03%)
0.87% swing Lab. to C.

BRENTWOOD & ONGAR
E. 75,253 T. 52,941 (70.35%) C. hold
Alex Burghart, C.   36,308
Oliver Durose, Lab.   7,243
David Kendall, LD   7,187
Paul Jeater, Green   1,671
Robin Tilbrook, Eng Dem   532
C. majority 29,065 (54.90%)
4.77% swing Lab. to C.

BRIDGWATER & SOMERSET WEST
E. 85,327 T. 57,652 (67.57%) C. hold
Ian Liddell-Grainger, C.   35,827
Oliver Thornton, Lab.   11,388
Bill Revans, LD   7,805
Mickie Ritchie, Green   1,877
Fares Moussa, Lib   755
C. majority 24,439 (42.39%)
7.94% swing Lab. to C.

BRIGG & GOOLE
E. 65,939 T. 43,402 (65.82%) C. hold
Andrew Percy, C.   30,941
Majid Khan, Lab.   9,000
David Dobbie, LD   2,180
Jo Baker, Green   1,281
C. majority 21,941 (50.55%)
11.56% swing Lab. to C.

BRIGHTON KEMPTOWN
E. 69,833 T. 48,533 (69.50%)
                              Lab. Co-op hold
Lloyd Russell-Moyle, Lab.   25,033
Co-op
Joe Miller, C.   16,972
Ben Thomas, LD   2,964
Alexandra Phillips, Green   2,237
Graham Cushway, Brexit   1,327
Lab. Co-op majority 8,061 (16.61%)
1.72% swing Lab. to C.

BRIGHTON PAVILION
E. 79,057 T. 57,998 (73.36%)
                                  Green hold
Caroline Lucas, Green   33,151
Adam Imanpour, Lab.   13,211
Emma Hogan, C.   10,176
Richard Milton, Brexit   770
Citizen Skwith, Loony   301
Bob Dobbs, Ind.   212
Nigel Furness, UKIP   177
Green majority 19,940 (34.38%)
4.46% swing Lab. to Green

BRISTOL EAST
E. 73,867 T. 52,154 (70.61%) Lab. hold
Kerry McCarthy, Lab.   27,717
Sarah Codling, C.   16,923
Nicholas Coombes, LD   3,527
Conan Connolly, Green   2,106
Tim Page, Brexit   1,881
Lab. majority 10,794 (20.70%)
2.84% swing Lab. to C.

BRISTOL NORTH WEST
E. 76,273 T. 55,885 (73.27%) Lab. hold
Darren Jones, Lab.   27,330
Mark Weston, C.   21,638
Chris Coleman, LD   4,940
Heather Mack, Green   1,977
Lab. majority 5,692 (10.19%)
0.69% swing C. to Lab.

BRISTOL SOUTH
E. 84,079 T. 55,196 (65.65%) Lab. hold
Karin Smyth, Lab.   27,895
Richard Morgan, C.   18,036
Andrew Brown, LD   4,227
Tony Dyer, Green   2,713
Robert de Vito Boutin,   2,325
Brexit
Lab. majority 9,859 (17.86%)
5.77% swing Lab. to C.

BRISTOL WEST
E. 99,253 T. 75,528 (76.10%) Lab. hold
Thangam Debbonaire, Lab.   47,028
Carla Denyer, Green   18,809
Suria Aujla, C.   8,822
Neil Hipkiss, Brexit   869
Lab. majority 28,219 (37.36%)
7.85% swing Lab. to Green

BROADLAND
E. 78,151 T. 56,977 (72.91%) C. hold
Jerome Mayhew, C.   33,934
Jess Barnard, Lab.   12,073
Ben Goodwin, LD   9,195
Andrew Boswell, Green   1,412
Simon Rous, Universal   363
C. majority 21,861 (38.37%)
5.06% swing Lab. to C.

BROMLEY & CHISLEHURST
E. 66,711 T. 45,566 (68.30%) C. hold
Bob Neill, C.   23,958
Angela Wilkins, Lab.   13,067
Julie Ireland, LD   6,621
Mary Ion, Green   1,546
Zion Amodu, CPA   255
Jyoti Dialani, Renew   119
C. majority 10,891 (23.90%)
1.67% swing Lab. to C.

BROMSGROVE
E. 75,079 T. 54,272 (72.29%) C. hold
Sajid Javid, C.   34,408
Rory Shannon, Lab.   11,302
David Nicholl, LD   6,779
Kevin White, Green   1,783
C. majority 23,106 (42.57%)
5.95% swing Lab. to C.

BROXBOURNE
E. 73,182 T. 46,706 (63.82%) C. hold
Charles Walker, C.   30,631
Sean Waters, Lab.   10,824
Julia Bird, LD   3,970
Nicholas Cox, Green   1,281
C. majority 19,807 (42.41%)
4.58% swing Lab. to C.

BROXTOWE
E. 73,895 T. 55,272 (74.80%) C. gain
Darren Henry, C.   26,602
Greg Marshall, Lab.   21,271
Anna Soubry, Change   4,668
Kat Boettge, Green   1,806
Amy Dalla Mura, Eng Dem   432
Teck Khong, Ind.   321
David Bishop, Elvis   172
C. majority 5,331 (9.65%)
4.05% swing Lab. to C.

BUCKINGHAM
E. 83,146   T. 63,458 (76.32%)   C. hold
Greg Smith, C.   37,035
Stephen Dorrell, LD   16,624
David Morgan, Lab.   7,638
Andrew Bell, Brexit   1,286
Ned Thompson, Ind.   681
Antonio Vitiello, Eng Dem   194
C. majority 20,411 (32.16%)
swing N/A

BURNLEY
E. 64,343   T. 38,984 (60.59%)   C. gain
Antony Higginbotham, C.   15,720
Julie Cooper, Lab.   14,368
Gordon Birtwistle, LD   3,501
Stewart Scott, Brexit   3,362
Charlie Briggs, Burnley   1,162
Laura Fisk, Green   739
Karen Helsby Entwistle, Ind.   132
C. majority 1,352 (3.47%)
9.62% swing Lab. to C.

BURTON
E. 75,030   T. 48,738 (64.96%)   C. hold
Kate Griffiths, C.   29,560
Louise Walker, Lab.   15,064
Adam Wain, LD   2,681
Kate Copeland, Green   1,433
C. majority 14,496 (29.74%)
4.81% swing Lab. to C.

BURY NORTH
E. 68,802   T. 46,841 (68.08%)   C. gain
James Daly, C.   21,660
James Frith, Lab.   21,555
Gareth Lloyd-Johnson, LD   1,584
Alan McCarthy, Brexit   1,240
Charlie Allen, Green   802
C. majority 105 (0.22%)
4.68% swing Lab. to C.

BURY SOUTH
E. 75,152   T. 50,274 (66.90%)   C. gain
Christian Wakeford, C.   22,034
Lucy Burke, Lab.   21,632
Richard Kilpatrick, LD   2,315
Andrea Livesey, Brexit   1,672
Ivan Lewis, Ind.   1,366
Glyn Heath, Green   848
Michael Boyle, Ind.   277
Gemma Evans, Women   130
C. majority 402 (0.80%)
6.25% swing Lab. to C.

BURY ST EDMUNDS
E. 89,644   T. 61,957 (69.11%)   C. hold
Jo Churchill, C.   37,770
Cliff Waterman, Lab.   12,782
Helen Geake, Green   9,711
Paul Hopfensperger, Ind.   1,694
C. majority 24,988 (40.33%)
5.33% swing Lab. to C.

CALDER VALLEY
E. 79,287   T. 57,793 (72.89%)   C. hold
Craig Whittaker, C.   29,981
Josh Fenton-Glynn, Lab.   24,207
Javed Bashir, LD   2,884
Richard Phillips, Lib   721
C. majority 5,774 (9.99%)
4.47% swing Lab. to C.

CAMBERWELL & PECKHAM
E. 89,042   T. 56,492 (63.44%)   Lab. hold
Harriet Harman, Lab.   40,258
Peter Quentin, C.   6,478
Julia Ogiehor, LD   5,087
Claire Sheppard, Green   3,501
Cass Cass-Horne, Brexit   1,041
Joshua Ogunleye, WRP   127
Lab. majority 33,780 (59.80%)
2.60% swing Lab. to C.

CAMBORNE & REDRUTH
E. 70,250   T. 50,367 (71.70%)   C. hold
George Eustice, C.   26,764
Paul Farmer, Lab.   18,064
Florence MacDonald, LD   3,504
Karen La Borde, Green   1,359
Paul Holmes, Lib   676
C. majority 8,700 (17.27%)
7.01% swing Lab. to C.

CAMBRIDGE
E. 79,951   T. 53,729 (67.20%)   Lab. hold
Daniel Zeichner, Lab.   25,776
Rod Cantrill, LD   16,137
Russell Perrin, C.   8,342
Jeremy Caddick, Green   2,164
Peter Dawe, Brexit   1,041
Miles Hurley, Ind.   111
Jane Robins, Soc Dem   91
Keith Garrett, Rebooting   67
Lab. majority 9,639 (17.94%)
2.35% swing Lab. to LD

CAMBRIDGESHIRE NORTH EAST
E. 83,699   T. 52,964 (63.28%)   C. hold
Steve Barclay, C.   38,423
Diane Boyd, Lab.   8,430
Rupert Moss-Eccardt, LD   4,298
Ruth Johnson, Green   1,813
C. majority 29,993 (56.63%)
8.36% swing Lab. to C.

CAMBRIDGESHIRE NORTH WEST
E. 94,909   T. 64,533 (67.99%)   C. hold
Shailesh Vara, C.   40,307
Cathy Cordiner-Achenbach,   14,324
Lab.
Bridget Smith, LD   6,881
Nicola Day, Green   3,021
C. majority 25,983 (40.26%)
6.06% swing Lab. to C.

CAMBRIDGESHIRE SOUTH
E. 87,288   T. 66,929 (76.68%)   C. gain
Anthony Browne, C.   31,015
Ian Sollom, LD   28,111
Dan Greef, Lab.   7,803
C. majority 2,904 (4.34%)
14.41% swing C. to LD

CAMBRIDGESHIRE SOUTH EAST
E. 86,769   T. 64,385 (74.20%)   C. hold
Lucy Frazer, C.   32,187
Pippa Heylings, LD   20,697
James Bull, Lab.   10,492
Edmund Fordham, Ind.   1,009
C. majority 11,490 (17.85%)
8.25% swing C. to LD

CANNOCK CHASE
E. 74,813   T. 46,313 (61.91%)   C. hold
Amanda Milling, C.   31,636
Anne Hobbs, Lab.   11,757
Paul Woodhead, Green   2,920
C. majority 19,879 (42.92%)
12.70% swing Lab. to C.

CANTERBURY
E. 80,203   T. 60,113 (74.95%)   Lab. hold
Rosie Duffield, Lab.   29,018
Anna Firth, C.   27,182
Claire Malcomson, LD   3,408
Michael Gould, Ind.   505
Lab. majority 1,836 (3.05%)
1.36% swing C. to Lab.

CARLISLE
E. 65,105   T. 42,873 (65.85%)   C. hold
John Stevenson, C.   23,659
Ruth Alcroft, Lab.   15,340
Julia Aglionby, LD   2,829
Fiona Mills, UKIP   1,045
C. majority 8,319 (19.40%)
6.68% swing Lab. to C.

CARSHALTON & WALLINGTON
E. 72,926   T. 49,098 (67.33%)   C. gain
Elliot Colburn, C.   20,822
Tom Brake, LD   20,193
Ahmad Wattoo, Lab.   6,081
James Woudhuysen, Brexit   1,043
Tracey Hague, Green   759
Ashley Dickenson, CPA   200
C. majority 629 (1.28%)
1.99% swing LD to C.

CASTLE POINT
E. 69,643   T. 44,277 (63.58%)   C. hold
Rebecca Harris, C.   33,971
Katie Curtis, Lab.   7,337
John Howson, LD   2,969
C. majority 26,634 (60.15%)
8.97% swing Lab. to C.

CHARNWOOD
E. 79,556   T. 55,365 (69.59%)   C. hold
Edward Argar, C.   35,121
Gary Godden, Lab.   12,724
Kate Tipton, LD   4,856
Laurie Needham, Green   2,664
C. majority 22,397 (40.45%)
5.42% swing Lab. to C.

CHATHAM & AYLESFORD
E. 71,642   T. 43,340 (60.50%)   C. hold
Tracey Crouch, C.   28,856
Vince Maple, Lab.   10,316
David Naghi, LD   2,866
Geoff Wilkinson, Green   1,090
John Gibson, CPA   212
C. majority 18,540 (42.78%)
9.74% swing Lab. to C.

CHEADLE
E. 74,639   T. 55,903 (74.90%)   C. hold
Mary Robinson, C.   25,694
Tom Morrison, LD   23,358
Zahid Chauhan, Lab.   6,851
C. majority 2,336 (4.18%)
2.04% swing C. to LD

CHELMSFORD

E. 80,481   T. 57,122 (70.98%)   C. hold

Vicky Ford, C.	31,934
Marie Goldman, LD	14,313
Penny Richards, Lab.	10,295
Mark Lawrence, Loony	580

C. majority 17,621 (30.85%)
5.34% swing C. to LD

CHELSEA & FULHAM

E. 67,110   T. 46,821 (69.77%)   C. hold

Greg Hands, C.	23,345
Nicola Horlick, LD	12,104
Matt Uberoi, Lab.	10,872
Samuel Morland, AWP	500

C. majority 11,241 (24.01%)
8.83% swing C. to LD

CHELTENHAM

E. 81,043   T. 59,357 (73.24%)   C. hold

Alex Chalk, C.	28,486
Max Wilkinson, LD	27,505
George Penny, Lab.	2,921
George Ridgeon, Loony	445

C. majority 981 (1.65%)
1.43% swing C. to LD

CHESHAM & AMERSHAM

E. 72,542   T. 55,685 (76.76%)   C. hold

Cheryl Gillan, C.	30,850
Dan Gallagher, LD	14,627
Matt Turmaine, Lab.	7,166
Alan Booth, Green	3,042

C. majority 16,223 (29.13%)
9.26% swing C. to LD

CHESTER, CITY OF

E. 76,057   T. 54,560 (71.74%)   Lab. hold

Chris Matheson, Lab.	27,082
Samantha George, C.	20,918
Bob Thompson, LD	3,734
Nicholas Brown, Green	1,438
Andy Argyle, Brexit	1,388

Lab. majority 6,164 (11.30%)
2.48% swing Lab. to C.

CHESTERFIELD

E. 71,030   T. 45,186 (63.62%)   Lab. hold

Toby Perkins, Lab.	18,171
Leigh Higgins, C.	16,720
John Scotting, Brexit	4,771
Emily Coy, LD	3,985
Neil Jackson, Green	1,148
John Daramy, Ind.	391

Lab. majority 1,451 (3.21%)
8.41% swing Lab. to C.

CHICHESTER

E. 85,499   T. 61,243 (71.63%)   C. hold

Gillian Keegan, C.	35,402
Kate O'Kelly, LD	13,912
Jay Morton, Lab.	9,069
Heather Barrie, Green	2,527
Adam Brown, Libertarian	224
Andrew Emerson, Patria	109

C. majority 21,490 (35.09%)
6.89% swing C. to LD

CHINGFORD & WOODFORD GREEN

E. 65,393   T. 48,444 (74.08%)   C. hold

Iain Duncan Smith, C.	23,481
Faiza Shaheen, Lab.	22,219
Geoff Seeff, LD	2,744

C. majority 1,262 (2.61%)
1.29% swing C. to Lab.

CHIPPENHAM

E. 77,225   T. 57,099 (73.94%)   C. hold

Michelle Donelan, C.	30,994
Helen Belcher, LD	19,706
Martha Anachury, Lab.	6,399

C. majority 11,288 (19.77%)
4.67% swing C. to LD

CHIPPING BARNET

E. 79,960   T. 57,569 (72.00%)   C. hold

Theresa Villiers, C.	25,745
Emma Whysall, Lab.	24,533
Isabelle Parasram, LD	5,932
Gabrielle Bailey, Green	1,288
John Sheffield, Advance	71

C. majority 1,212 (2.11%)
0.73% swing Lab. to C.

CHORLEY

E. 78,177   T. 39,870 (51.00%)   Speaker hold

Lindsay Hoyle, Speaker	26,831
Mark Brexit-Smith, Ind.	9,439
James Melling, Green	3,600

Speaker majority 17,392 (43.62%)
swing N/A

CHRISTCHURCH

E. 71,521   T. 51,951 (72.64%)   C. hold

Christopher Chope, C.	33,894
Mike Cox, LD	9,277
Andrew Dunne, Lab.	6,568
Chris Rigby, Green	2,212

C. majority 24,617 (47.39%)
7.13% swing C. to LD

CITIES OF LONDON & WESTMINSTER

E. 63,700   T. 42,723 (67.07%)   C. hold

Nickie Aiken, C.	17,049
Chuka Umunna, LD	13,096
Gordon Nardell, Lab.	11,624
Zack Polanski, Green	728
Jill McLachlan, CPA	125
Dirk van Heck, Lib	101

C. majority 3,953 (9.25%)
13.14% swing C. to LD

CLACTON

E. 70,930   T. 43,506 (61.34%)   C. hold

Giles Watling, C.	31,438
Kevin Bonavia, Lab.	6,736
Callum Robertson, LD	2,541
Chris Southall, Green	1,225
Andy Morgan, ND	1,099
Colin Bennett, Ind.	243
Just-John Sexton, Loony	224

C. majority 24,702 (56.78%)
10.46% swing Lab. to C.

CLEETHORPES

E. 73,689   T. 46,339 (62.88%)   C. hold

Martin Vickers, C.	31,969
Ros James, Lab.	10,551
Roy Horobin, LD	2,535
Jodi Shanahan, Green	1,284

C. majority 21,418 (46.22%)
12.24% swing Lab. to C.

COLCHESTER

E. 82,625   T. 53,373 (64.60%)   C. hold

Will Quince, C.	26,917
Tina McKay, Lab.	17,494
Martin Goss, LD	7,432
Mark Goacher, Green	1,530

C. majority 9,423 (17.65%)
3.53% swing Lab. to C.

COLNE VALLEY

E. 84,174   T. 60,910 (72.36%)   C. gain

Jason McCartney, C.	29,482
Thelma Walker, Lab.	24,379
Cahal Burke, LD	3,815
Sue Harrison, Brexit	1,286
Darryl Gould, Green	1,068
Owen Aspinall, Yorkshire	548
Melanie Roberts, UKIP	230
Colin Peel, Ind.	102

C. majority 5,103 (8.38%)
4.95% swing Lab. to C.

CONGLETON

E. 80,930   T. 57,233 (70.72%)   C. hold

Fiona Bruce, C.	33,747
Jo Dale, Lab.	15,186
Paul Duffy, LD	6,026
Richard McCarthy, Green	1,616
Jane Smith, AWP	658

C. majority 18,561 (32.43%)
4.99% swing Lab. to C.

COPELAND

E. 61,693   T. 42,523 (68.93%)   C. hold

Trudy Harrison, C.	22,856
Tony Lywood, Lab.	17,014
John Studholme, LD	1,888
Jack Lenox, Green	765

C. majority 5,842 (13.74%)
4.89% swing Lab. to C.

CORBY

E. 86,151   T. 60,484 (70.21%)   C. hold

Tom Pursglove, C.	33,410
Beth Miller, Lab.	23,142
Chris Stanbra, LD	3,932

C. majority 10,268 (16.98%)
6.25% swing Lab. to C.

CORNWALL NORTH

E. 69,935   T. 51,678 (73.89%)   C. hold

Scott Mann, C.	30,671
Danny Chambers, LD	15,919
Joy Bassett, Lab.	4,516
Elmars Liepins, Lib	572

C. majority 14,752 (28.55%)
7.21% swing LD to C.

CORNWALL SOUTH EAST
E. 71,825   T. 53,655 (74.70%)   C. hold
Sheryll Murray, C.	31,807
Gareth Derrick, Lab.	10,836
Colin Martin, LD	8,650
Martha Green, Green	1,493
Jay Latham, Lib	869

C. majority 20,971 (39.08%)
3.15% swing Lab. to C.

COTSWOLDS, THE
E. 81,939   T. 61,176 (74.66%)   C. hold
Geoffrey Clifton-Brown, C.	35,484
Liz Webster, LD	15,270
Alan MacKenzie, Lab.	7,110
Sabrina Poole, Green	3,312

C. majority 20,214 (33.04%)
5.63% swing C. to LD

COVENTRY NORTH EAST
E. 76,002   T. 44,444 (58.48%)   Lab. hold
Colleen Fletcher, Lab.	23,412
Sophie Richards, C.	15,720
Iddrisu Sufyan, Brexit	2,110
Nukey Proctor, LD	2,061
Matthew Handley, Green	1,141

Lab. majority 7,692 (17.31%)
8.10% swing Lab. to C.

COVENTRY NORTH WEST
E. 75,240   T. 47,744 (63.46%)   Lab. hold
Taiwo Owatemi, Lab.	20,918
Clare Golby, C.	20,710
Greg Judge, LD	2,717
Joshua Richardson, Brexit	1,956
Stephen Gray, Green	1,443

Lab. majority 208 (0.44%)
8.39% swing Lab. to C.

COVENTRY SOUTH
E. 70,970   T. 45,044 (63.47%)   Lab. hold
Zarah Sultana, Lab.	19,544
Mattie Heaven, C.	19,143
Stephen Richmond, LD	3,398
James Crocker, Brexit	1,432
Becky Finlayson, Green	1,092
Ed Manning, Ind.	435

Lab. majority 401 (0.89%)
8.01% swing Lab. to C.

CRAWLEY
E. 74,207   T. 49,899 (67.24%)   C. hold
Henry Smith, C.	27,040
Peter Lamb, Lab.	18,680
Khalil Yousuf, LD	2,728
Iain Dickson, Green	1,451

C. majority 8,360 (16.75%)
5.93% swing Lab. to C.

CREWE & NANTWICH
E. 80,321   T. 54,032 (67.27%)   C. gain
Kieran Mullan, C.	28,704
Laura Smith, Lab.	20,196
Matthew Theobald, LD	2,618
Matt Wood, Brexit	1,390
Te Ata Browne, Green	975
Andrew Kinsman, Libertarian	149

C. majority 8,508 (15.75%)
7.92% swing Lab. to C.

CROYDON CENTRAL
E. 81,410   T. 54,045 (66.39%)   Lab. hold
Sarah Jones, Lab.	27,124
Mario Creatura, C.	21,175
Simon Sprague, LD	3,532
Esther Sutton, Green	1,215
Peter Sonnex, Brexit	999

Lab. majority 5,949 (11.01%)
0.55% swing C. to Lab.

CROYDON NORTH
E. 88,466   T. 55,609 (62.86%)
Lab. Co-op hold
Steve Reed, Lab. Co-op	36,495
Donald Ekekhomen, C.	11,822
Claire Bonham, LD	4,476
Rachel Chance, Green	1,629
Chidi Ngwaba, Brexit	839
Candace Mitchell, CPA	348

Lab. Co-op majority 24,673 (44.37%)
4.96% swing Lab. to C.

CROYDON SOUTH
E. 83,977   T. 59,358 (70.68%)   C. hold
Chris Philp, C.	30,985
Olga Fitzroy, Lab.	18,646
Anna Jones, LD	7,503
Peter Underwood, Green	1,782
Kathleen Garner, UKIP	442

C. majority 12,339 (20.79%)
1.08% swing Lab. to C.

DAGENHAM & RAINHAM
E. 71,043   T. 43,735 (61.56%)   Lab. hold
Jon Cruddas, Lab.	19,468
Damian White, C.	19,175
Tom Bewick, Brexit	2,887
Sam Fisk, LD	1,182
Azzees Minott, Green	602
Ron Emin, Ind.	212
Terry London, Ind.	209

Lab. majority 293 (0.67%)
4.74% swing Lab. to C.

DARLINGTON
E. 66,395   T. 43,498 (65.51%)   C. gain
Peter Gibson, C.	20,901
Jenny Chapman, Lab.	17,607
Anne-Marie Curry, LD	2,097
Dave Mawson, Brexit	1,544
Matthew Snedker, Green	1,057
Monty Brack, Ind.	292

C. majority 3,294 (7.57%)
7.45% swing Lab. to C.

DARTFORD
E. 82,209   T. 54,022 (65.71%)   C. hold
Gareth Johnson, C.	34,006
Sacha Gosine, Lab.	14,846
Kyle Marsh, LD	3,735
Mark Lindop, Green	1,435

C. majority 19,160 (35.47%)
5.57% swing Lab. to C.

DAVENTRY
E. 77,493   T. 57,403 (74.08%)   C. hold
Chris Heaton-Harris, C.	37,055
Paul Joyce, Lab.	10,975
Andrew Simpson, LD	7,032
Clare Slater, Green	2,341

C. majority 26,080 (45.43%)
3.19% swing Lab. to C.

DENTON & REDDISH
E. 66,579   T. 38,588 (57.96%)   Lab. hold
Andrew Gwynne, Lab.	19,317
Iain Bott, C.	13,142
Martin Power, Brexit	3,039
Dominic Hardwick, LD	1,642
Gary Lawson, Green	1,124
Farmin Lord F'Tang F'Tang Dave, Loony	324

Lab. majority 6,175 (16.00%)
9.77% swing Lab. to C.

DERBY NORTH
E. 73,212   T. 47,017 (64.22%)   C. gain
Amanda Solloway, C.	21,259
Tony Tinley, Lab.	18,719
Gregory Webb, LD	3,450
Alan Graves, Brexit	1,908
Helen Hitchcock, Green	1,046
Chris Williamson, Ind.	635

C. majority 2,540 (5.40%)
4.77% swing Lab. to C.

DERBY SOUTH
E. 73,079   T. 42,462 (58.10%)   Lab. hold
Margaret Beckett, Lab.	21,690
Ed Barker, C.	15,671
Joe Naitta, LD	2,621
Timothy Prosser, Brexit	2,480

Lab. majority 6,019 (14.18%)
5.33% swing Lab. to C.

DERBYSHIRE DALES
E. 65,060   T. 50,016 (76.88%)   C. hold
Sarah Dines, C.	29,356
Claire Raw, Lab.	11,975
Robert Court, LD	6,627
Matt Buckler, Green	2,058

C. majority 17,381 (34.75%)
2.92% swing Lab. to C.

DERBYSHIRE MID
E. 67,437   T. 49,356 (73.19%)   C. hold
Pauline Latham, C.	29,027
Emma Monkman, Lab.	13,642
Felix Dodds, LD	4,756
Sue MacFarlane, Green	1,931

C. majority 15,385 (31.17%)
4.06% swing Lab. to C.

DERBYSHIRE NORTH EAST
E. 72,360   T. 49,217 (68.02%)   C. hold
Lee Rowley, C.	28,897
Chris Peace, Lab.	16,021
Ross Shipman, LD	3,021
Frank Adlington-Stringer, Green	1,278

C. majority 12,876 (26.16%)
10.24% swing Lab. to C.

DERBYSHIRE SOUTH
E. 79,365   T. 53,381 (67.26%)   C. hold
Heather Wheeler, C.	33,502
Robert Pearson, Lab.	14,167
Lorraine Johnson, LD	3,924
Amanda Baker, Green	1,788

C. majority 19,335 (36.22%)
6.74% swing Lab. to C.

DEVIZES
E. 73,379 T. 50,954 (69.44%) C. hold
Danny Kruger, C. 32,150
Jo Waltham, LD 8,157
Rachael Schneider, Lab. 7,838
Emma Dawnay, Green 2,809
C. majority 23,993 (47.09%)
3.18% swing C. to LD

DEVON CENTRAL
E. 74,926 T. 58,072 (77.51%) C. hold
Mel Stride, C. 32,095
Lisa Robillard Webb, Lab. 14,374
Alison Eden, LD 8,770
Andy Williamson, Green 2,833
C. majority 17,721 (30.52%)
1.70% swing Lab. to C.

DEVON EAST
E. 86,841 T. 64,073 (73.78%) C. hold
Simon Jupp, C. 32,577
Claire Wright, Ind. 25,869
Dan Wilson, Lab. 2,870
Eleanor Rylance, LD 1,771
Henry Gent, Green 711
Peter Faithfull, Ind. 275
C. majority 6,708 (10.47%)
1.42% swing C. to Ind.

DEVON NORTH
E. 75,853 T. 55,581 (73.27%) C. hold
Selaine Saxby, C. 31,479
Alex White, LD 16,666
Finola ONeill, Lab. 5,097
Robbie Mack, Green 1,759
Steve Cotten, Ind. 580
C. majority 14,813 (26.65%)
9.44% swing LD to C.

DEVON SOUTH WEST
E. 72,535 T. 53,367 (73.57%) C. hold
Gary Streeter, C. 33,286
Alex Beverley, Lab. 11,856
Sima Davarian, LD 6,207
Ian Poyser, Green 2,018
C. majority 21,430 (40.16%)
5.12% swing Lab. to C.

DEVON WEST & TORRIDGE
E. 79,831 T. 59,730 (74.82%) C. hold
Geoffrey Cox, C. 35,904
David Chalmers, LD 10,912
Siobhan Strode, Lab. 10,290
Chris Jordan, Green 2,077
Bob Wootton, Ind. 547
C. majority 24,992 (41.84%)
1.51% swing LD to C.

DEWSBURY
E. 81,253 T. 56,389 (69.40%) C. gain
Mark Eastwood, C. 26,179
Paula Sherriff, Lab. 24,618
John Rossington, LD 2,406
Philip James, Brexit 1,874
Simon Cope, Green 1,060
Sir Archibald Earl Eaton
Stanton, Loony 252
C. majority 1,561 (2.77%)
4.32% swing Lab. to C.

DON VALLEY
E. 75,356 T. 45,437 (60.30%) C. gain
Nick Fletcher, C. 19,609
Caroline Flint, Lab. 15,979
Paul Whitehurst, Brexit 6,247
Mark Alcock, LD 1,907
Kate Needham, Green 872
Chris Holmes, Yorkshire 823
C. majority 3,630 (7.99%)
9.61% swing Lab. to C.

DONCASTER CENTRAL
E. 71,389 T. 41,581 (58.25%) Lab. hold
Rosie Winterton, Lab. 16,638
Roberto Weeden-Sanz, C. 14,360
Surjit Duhre, Brexit 6,842
Paul Horton, LD 1,748
Leon French, Yorkshire 1,012
Frank Sheridan, Green 981
Lab. majority 2,278 (5.48%)
9.03% swing Lab. to C.

DONCASTER NORTH
E. 72,362 T. 40,698 (56.24%) Lab. hold
Ed Miliband, Lab. 15,740
Katrina Sale, C. 13,370
Andy Stewart, Brexit 8,294
Joe Otten, LD 1,476
Stevie Manion, Yorkshire 959
Frank Calladine, Eng Dem 309
Eddie Todd, ND 220
Wendy Bailey, Ind. 188
Neil Wood, Ind. 142
Lab. majority 2,370 (5.82%)
13.66% swing Lab. to C.

DORSET MID & POOLE NORTH
E. 65,426 T. 48,930 (74.79%) C. hold
Michael Tomlinson, C. 29,548
Vikki Slade, LD 14,650
Joanne Oldale, Lab. 3,402
Natalie Carswell, Green 1,330
C. majority 14,898 (30.45%)
0.67% swing C. to LD

DORSET NORTH
E. 75,956 T. 56,107 (73.87%) C. hold
Simon Hoare, C. 35,705
David Chadwick, LD 11,404
Pat Osborne, Lab. 6,737
Ken Huggins, Green 2,261
C. majority 24,301 (43.31%)
4.02% swing C. to LD

DORSET SOUTH
E. 72,924 T. 51,058 (70.02%) C. hold
Richard Drax, C. 30,024
Carralyn Parkes, Lab. 12,871
Nick Ireland, LD 5,432
Jon Orrell, Green 2,246
Joseph Green, Ind. 485
C. majority 17,153 (33.60%)
5.53% swing Lab. to C.

DORSET WEST
E. 80,963 T. 60,925 (75.25%) C. gain
Chris Loder, C. 33,589
Edward Morello, LD 19,483
Claudia Sorin, Lab. 5,729
Kelvin Clayton, Green 2,124
C. majority 14,106 (23.15%)
4.44% swing C. to LD

DOVER
E. 76,355 T. 50,701 (66.40%) C. gain
Natalie Elphicke, C. 28,830
Charlotte Cornell, Lab. 16,552
Simon Dodd, LD 2,895
Beccy Sawbridge, Green 1,371
Nathan Sutton, Ind. 916
Eljai Morais, Women 137
C. majority 12,278 (24.22%)
5.91% swing Lab. to C.

DUDLEY NORTH
E. 61,936 T. 36,684 (59.23%) C. gain
Marco Longhi, C. 23,134
Melanie Dudley, Lab. 11,601
Ian Flynn, LD 1,210
Mike Harrison, Green 739
C. majority 11,533 (31.44%)
15.75% swing Lab. to C.

DUDLEY SOUTH
E. 60,731 T. 36,576 (60.23%) C. hold
Mike Wood, C. 24,835
Lucy Caldicott, Lab. 9,270
Jonathan Bramall, LD 1,608
Cate Mohr, Green 863
C. majority 15,565 (42.56%)
11.17% swing Lab. to C.

DULWICH & WEST NORWOOD
E. 84,663 T. 55,778 (65.88%) Lab. hold
Helen Hayes, Lab. 36,521
Jonathan Bartley, Green 9,211
Jane Lyons, C. 9,160
Julia Stephenson, Brexit 571
Anthony Hodgson, CPA 242
John Plume, UKIP 73
Lab. majority 27,310 (48.96%)
9.08% swing Lab. to Green

DURHAM, CITY OF
E. 71,271 T. 48,859 (68.55%) Lab. hold
Mary Foy, Lab. 20,531
William Morgan, C. 15,506
Amanda Hopgood, LD 7,935
Lesley Wright, Brexit 3,252
Jonathan Elmer, Green 1,635
Lab. majority 5,025 (10.28%)
7.65% swing Lab. to C.

DURHAM NORTH
E. 66,796 T. 42,195 (63.17%) Lab. hold
Kevan Jones, Lab. 18,639
Ed Parson, C. 13,897
Peter Telford, Brexit 4,693
Craig Martin, LD 2,879
Derek Morse, Green 1,126
Ken Rollings, Ind. 961
Lab. majority 4,742 (11.24%)
9.33% swing Lab. to C.

DURHAM NORTH WEST
E. 72,166 T. 47,663 (66.05%) C. gain
Richard Holden, C. 19,990
Laura Pidcock, Lab. 18,846
John Wolstenholme, Brexit 3,193
Michael Peacock, LD 2,831
Watts Stelling, Ind. 1,216
David Sewell, Green 1,173
David Lindsay, Ind. 414
C. majority 1,144 (2.40%)
10.38% swing Lab. to C.

EALING CENTRAL & ACTON
E. 75,510   T. 54,807 (72.58%)   Lab. hold
Rupa Huq, Lab.	28,132
Julian Gallant, C.	14,832
Sonul Badiani, LD	9,444
Kate Crossland, Green	1,735
Samir Alsoodani, Brexit	664

Lab. majority 13,300 (24.27%)
0.34% swing Lab. to C.

EALING NORTH
E. 74,473   T. 49,631 (66.64%)
Lab. Co-op hold
James Murray, Lab. Co-op	28,036
Anthony Pickles, C.	15,767
Henrietta Bewley, LD	4,370
Jeremy Parker, Green	1,458

Lab. Co-op majority 12,269 (24.72%)
6.39% swing Lab. to C.

EALING SOUTHALL
E. 64,580   T. 42,217 (65.37%)   Lab. hold
Virendra Sharma, Lab.	25,678
Tom Bennett, C.	9,594
Tariq Mahmood, LD	3,933
Darren Moore, Green	1,688
Rosamund Beattie, Brexit	867
Suzanne Fernandes, CPA	287
Hassan Zulkifal, WRP	170

Lab. majority 16,084 (38.10%)
5.42% swing Lab. to C.

EASINGTON
E. 61,182   T. 34,583 (56.52%)   Lab. hold
Grahame Morris, Lab.	15,723
Clare Ambrosino, C.	9,142
Julie Maughan, Brexit	6,744
Dominic Haney, LD	1,526
Susan McDonnell, NE Party	1,448

Lab. majority 6,581 (19.03%)
10.96% swing Lab. to C.

EAST HAM
E. 97,942   T. 54,628 (55.78%)   Lab. hold
Stephen Timms, Lab.	41,703
Scott Pattenden, C.	8,527
Michael Fox, LD	2,158
Alka Sehgal Cuthbert, Brexit	1,107
Mike Spracklin, Green	883
Kamran Malik, Communities	250

Lab. majority 33,176 (60.73%)
4.85% swing Lab. to C.

EASTBOURNE
E. 79,307   T. 55,134 (69.52%)   C. gain
Caroline Ansell, C.	26,951
Stephen Lloyd, LD	22,620
Jake Lambert, Lab.	3,848
Stephen Gander, Brexit	1,530
Ken Pollock, Ind.	185

C. majority 4,331 (7.86%)
5.33% swing LD to C.

EASTLEIGH
E. 83,880   T. 58,971 (70.30%)   C. hold
Paul Holmes, C.	32,690
Lynda Murphy, LD	17,083
Sam Jordon, Lab.	7,559
Ron Meldrum, Green	1,639

C. majority 15,607 (26.47%)
0.86% swing LD to C.

EDDISBURY
E. 73,700   T. 52,971 (71.87%)   C. gain
Edward Timpson, C.	30,095
Terry Savage, Lab.	11,652
Antoinette Sandbach, LD	9,582
Louise Jewkes, Green	1,191
Andrea Allen, UKIP	451

C. majority 18,443 (34.82%)
5.77% swing Lab. to C.

EDMONTON
E. 65,568   T. 40,341 (61.53%)
Lab. Co-op hold
Kate Osamor, Lab. Co-op	26,217
James Hockney, C.	10,202
David Schmitz, LD	2,145
Benjamin Maydon, Green	862
Sachin Sehgal, Brexit	840
Sabriye Warsame, Ind.	75

Lab. Co-op majority 16,015 (39.70%)
4.32% swing Lab. to C.

ELLESMERE PORT & NESTON
E. 70,327   T. 48,746 (69.31%)   Lab. hold
Justin Madders, Lab.	26,001
Alison Rodwell, C.	17,237
Ed Gough, LD	2,406
Christopher Stevens, Brexit	2,138
Chris Copeman, Green	964

Lab. majority 8,764 (17.98%)
2.19% swing Lab. to C.

ELMET & ROTHWELL
E. 80,957   T. 58,225 (71.92%)   C. hold
Alec Shelbrooke, C.	33,726
David Nagle, Lab.	16,373
Stewart Golton, LD	5,155
Penny Stables, Green	1,775
Matthew Clover, Yorkshire	1,196

C. majority 17,353 (29.80%)
6.67% swing Lab. to C.

ELTHAM
E. 64,084   T. 43,689 (68.17%)   Lab. hold
Clive Efford, Lab.	20,550
Louie French, C.	17,353
Charley Hasted, LD	2,941
Steve Kelleher, Brexit	1,523
Matt Stratford, Green	1,322

Lab. majority 3,197 (7.32%)
3.16% swing Lab. to C.

ENFIELD NORTH
E. 68,066   T. 45,050 (66.19%)   Lab. gain
Feryal Clark, Lab.	23,340
Joanne Lab.an, C.	16,848
Guy Russo, LD	2,950
Isobel Whittaker, Green	1,115
Ike Ijeh, Brexit	797

Lab. majority 6,492 (14.41%)
3.34% swing Lab. to C.

ENFIELD SOUTHGATE
E. 65,055   T. 47,276 (72.67%)   Lab. hold
Bambos Charalambous, Lab.	22,923
David Burrowes, C.	18,473
Rob Wilson, LD	4,344
Luke Balnave, Green	1,042
Parag Shah, Brexit	494

Lab. majority 4,450 (9.41%)
0.20% swing C. to Lab.

EPPING FOREST
E. 74,305   T. 50,268 (67.65%)   C. hold
Eleanor Laing, C.	32,364
Vicky Ashworth Te Velde, Lab.	10,191
Jon Whitehouse, LD	5,387
Steven Neville, Green	1,975
Thomas Hall, Young	181
Jon Newham, Soc Dem	170

C. majority 22,173 (44.11%)
4.09% swing Lab. to C.

EPSOM & EWELL
E. 81,138   T. 59,451 (73.27%)   C. hold
Chris Grayling, C.	31,819
Steve Gee, LD	13,946
Ed Mayne, Lab.	10,226
Janice Baker, Green	2,047
Clive Woodbridge, Ind.	1,413

C. majority 17,873 (30.06%)
8.52% swing C. to LD

EREWASH
E. 72,519   T. 48,814 (67.31%)   C. hold
Maggie Throup, C.	27,560
Catherine Atkinson, Lab.	16,954
James Archer, LD	2,487
Brent Poland, Green	1,115
Des Ball, Ind.	388
Richard Shaw, Ind.	188
Roy Dunn, Ind.	122

C. majority 10,606 (21.73%)
6.31% swing Lab. to C.

ERITH & THAMESMEAD
E. 65,399   T. 41,384 (63.28%)   Lab. hold
Abena Oppong-Asare, Lab.	19,882
Joe Robertson, C.	16,124
Tom Bright, Brexit	2,246
Sam Webber, LD	1,984
Claudine Letsae, Green	876
Richard Mitchell, CPA	272

Lab. majority 3,758 (9.08%)
6.72% swing Lab. to C.

ESHER & WALTON
E. 81,184   T. 63,084 (77.70%)   C. hold
Dominic Raab, C.	31,132
Monica Harding, LD	28,389
Peter Ashurst, Lab.	2,838
Kylie Keens, Ind.	347
Baron Badger, Loony	326
Kyle Taylor, Advance	52

C. majority 2,743 (4.35%)
18.46% swing C. to LD

EXETER
E. 82,043   T. 56,192 (68.49%)   Lab. hold
Ben Bradshaw, Lab.	29,882
John Gray, C.	19,479
Joe Levy, Green	4,838
Leslie Willis, Brexit	1,428
Daniel Page, Ind.	306
Duncan Odgers, UKIP	259

Lab. majority 10,403 (18.51%)
5.28% swing Lab. to C.

FAREHAM

E. 78,337 T. 57,250 (73.08%)   C. hold
Suella Braverman, C.   36,459
Matthew Randall, Lab.   10,373
Matthew Winnington, LD   8,006
Nick Lyle, Green   2,412
C. majority 26,086 (45.57%)
3.88% swing Lab. to C.

FAVERSHAM & KENT MID

E. 73,404 T. 50,394 (68.65%)   C. hold
Helen Whately, C.   31,864
Jenny Reeves, Lab.   9,888
Hannah Perkin, LD   6,170
Hannah Temple, Green   2,103
Gary Butler, Ind.   369
C. majority 21,976 (43.61%)
4.30% swing Lab. to C.

FELTHAM & HESTON

E. 80,932 T. 47,811 (59.08%)
                              Lab. Co-op hold
Seema Malhotra, Lab. Co-op   24,876
Jane Keep, C.   17,017
Hina Malik, LD   3,127
Martyn Nelson, Brexit   1,658
Tony Firkins, Green   1,133
Lab. Co-op majority 7,859 (16.44%)
6.49% swing Lab. to C.

FILTON & BRADLEY STOKE

E. 74,016 T. 53,752 (72.62%)   C. hold
Jack Lopresti, C.   26,293
Mhairi Threlfall, Lab.   20,647
Louise Harris, LD   4,992
Jenny Vernon, Green   1,563
Elaine Hardwick, Citizens   257
C. majority 5,646 (10.50%)
1.13% swing Lab. to C.

FINCHLEY & GOLDERS GREEN

E. 77,573 T. 55,109 (71.04%)   C. hold
Mike Freer, C.   24,162
Luciana Berger, LD   17,600
Ross Houston, Lab.   13,347
C. majority 6,562 (11.91%)
14.22% swing C. to LD

FOLKESTONE & HYTHE

E. 88,273 T. 59,005 (66.84%)   C. hold
Damian Collins, C.   35,483
Laura Davison, Lab.   14,146
Simon Bishop, LD   5,755
Georgina Treloar, Green   2,706
Henry Bolton, Ind.   576
Colin Menniss, Soc Dem   190
Rohen Kapur, Young   80
Andy Thomas, SPGB   69
C. majority 21,337 (36.16%)
4.99% swing Lab. to C.

FOREST OF DEAN

E. 71,438 T. 51,475 (72.06%)   C. hold
Mark Harper, C.   30,680
Di Martin, Lab. Co-op   14,811
Chris McFarling, Green   4,681
Julian Burrett, Ind.   1,303
C. majority 15,869 (30.83%)
6.24% swing Lab. to C.

FYLDE

E. 66,847 T. 46,659 (69.80%)   C. hold
Mark Menzies, C.   28,432
Martin Mitchell, Lab.   11,821
Mark Jewell, LD   3,748
Gina Dowding, Green   1,731
Andy Higgins, Ind.   927
C. majority 16,611 (35.60%)
5.10% swing Lab. to C.

GAINSBOROUGH

E. 76,343 T. 51,046 (66.86%)   C. hold
Edward Leigh, C.   33,893
Perry Smith, Lab.   10,926
Lesley Rollings, LD   5,157
Mary Cavill, Ind.   1,070
C. majority 22,967 (44.99%)
5.95% swing Lab. to C.

GARSTON & HALEWOOD

E. 76,116 T. 53,326 (70.06%)   Lab. hold
Maria Eagle, Lab.   38,578
Neva Novaky, C.   6,954
Kris Brown, LD   3,324
Jake Fraser, Brexit   2,943
Jean-Paul Roberts, Green   1,183
Hazel Williams, Lib   344
Lab. majority 31,624 (59.30%)
0.38% swing Lab. to C.

GATESHEAD

E. 64,449 T. 38,145 (59.19%)   Lab. hold
Ian Mearns, Lab.   20,450
Jane MacBean, C.   13,250
Peter Maughan, LD   2,792
Rachel Cabral, Green   1,653
Lab. majority 7,200 (18.88%)
11.17% swing Lab. to C.

GEDLING

E. 71,438 T. 49,953 (69.92%)   C. gain
Tom Randall, C.   22,718
Vernon Coaker, Lab.   22,039
Anita Prabhakar, LD   2,279
Graham Hunt, Brexit   1,820
Jim Norris, Green   1,097
C. majority 679 (1.36%)
5.22% swing Lab. to C.

GILLINGHAM & RAINHAM

E. 73,549 T. 45,958 (62.49%)   C. hold
Rehman Chishti, C.   28,173
Andy Stamp, Lab.   13,054
Alan Bullion, LD   2,503
George Salomon, Green   1,043
Rob McCulloch Martin,   837
UKIP
Peter Cook, Ind.   229
Roger Peacock, CPA   119
C. majority 15,119 (32.90%)
6.80% swing Lab. to C.

GLOUCESTER

E. 81,332 T. 53,764 (66.10%)   C. hold
Richard Graham, C.   29,159
Fran Boait, Lab. Co-op   18,882
Rebecca Trimnell, LD   4,338
Michael Byfield, Green   1,385
C. majority 10,277 (19.12%)
4.45% swing Lab. to C.

GOSPORT

E. 73,482 T. 48,453 (65.94%)   C. hold
Caroline Dinenage, C.   32,226
Tom Chatwin, Lab.   8,948
Martin Pepper, LD   5,473
Zoe Aspinall, Green   1,806
C. majority 23,278 (48.04%)
6.63% swing Lab. to C.

GRANTHAM & STAMFORD

E. 81,502 T. 56,003 (68.71%)   C. gain
Gareth Davies, C.   36,794
Kathryn Salt, Lab.   10,791
Harrish Bisnauthsing, LD   6,153
Anne Gayfer, Green   2,265
C. majority 26,003 (46.43%)
5.46% swing Lab. to C.

GRAVESHAM

E. 73,234 T. 47,560 (64.94%)   C. hold
Adam Holloway, C.   29,580
Lauren Sullivan, Lab.   13,999
Ukonu Obasi, LD   2,584
Marna Gilligan, Green   1,397
C. majority 15,581 (32.76%)
6.84% swing Lab. to C.

GREAT GRIMSBY

E. 61,409 T. 33,087 (53.88%)   C. gain
Lia Nici, C.   18,150
Melanie Onn, Lab.   10,819
Christopher Barker, Brexit   2,378
Ian Barfield, LD   1,070
Loyd Emmerson, Green   514
Nigel Winn, Ind.   156
C. majority 7,331 (22.16%)
14.69% swing Lab. to C.

GREAT YARMOUTH

E. 71,957 T. 43,462 (60.40%)   C. hold
Brandon Lewis, C.   28,593
Mike Smith-Clare, Lab. Co-   10,930
op
James Joyce, LD   1,661
Anne Killett, Green   1,064
Dave Harding, VPP   631
Adrian Myers, Ind.   429
Margaret McMahon-Morris,   154
Ind.
C. majority 17,663 (40.64%)
11.29% swing Lab. to C.

GREENWICH & WOOLWICH

E. 79,997 T. 53,120 (66.40%)   Lab. hold
Matthew Pennycook, Lab.   30,185
Thomas Turrell, C.   11,721
Rhian O'Connor, LD   7,253
Victoria Rance, Green   2,363
Kailash Trivedi, Brexit   1,228
Eunice Odesanmi, CPA   245
Sushil Gaikwad, Ind.   125
Lab. majority 18,464 (34.76%)
2.12% swing Lab. to C.

GUILDFORD
E. 77,729   T. 58,651 (75.46%)   C. gain
Angela Richardson, C.	26,317
Zoe Franklin, LD	22,980
Anne Rouse, Lab.	4,515
Anne Milton, Ind.	4,356
John Morris, Peace	483

C. majority 3,337 (5.69%)
12.50% swing C. to LD

HACKNEY NORTH & STOKE NEWINGTON
E. 92,451   T. 56,864 (61.51%)   Lab. hold
Diane Abbott, Lab.	39,972
Benjamin Obese-Jecty, C.	6,784
Alex Armitage, Green	4,989
Ben Mathis, LD	4,283
Richard Ings, Brexit	609
Haseeb Ur-Rehman, Renew	151
Lore Lixenberg, ND	76

Lab. majority 33,188 (58.36%)
2.03% swing Lab. to C.

HACKNEY SOUTH & SHOREDITCH
E. 89,380   T. 54,439 (60.91%)
Lab. Co-op hold
Meg Hillier, Lab. Co-op	39,884
Mark Beckett, C.	5,899
Dave Raval, LD	4,853
Tyrone Scott, Green	2,948
Robert Lloyd, Brexit	744
Jonty Leff, WRP	111

Lab. Co-op majority 33,985 (62.43%)
3.05% swing Lab. to C.

HALESOWEN & ROWLEY REGIS
E. 68,300   T. 42,345 (62.00%)   C. hold
James Morris, C.	25,607
Ian Cooper, Lab.	13,533
Ryan Priest, LD	1,738
James Windridge, Green	934
Jon Cross, Ind.	232
Ian Fleming, Ind.	190
Tim Weller, Ind.	111

C. majority 12,074 (28.51%)
8.34% swing Lab. to C.

HALIFAX
E. 71,904   T. 46,458 (64.61%)   Lab. hold
Holly Lynch, Lab.	21,496
Kashif Ali, C.	18,927
Sarah Wood, Brexit	2,813
James Baker, LD	2,276
Bella Jessop, Green	946

Lab. majority 2,569 (5.53%)
2.80% swing Lab. to C.

HALTEMPRICE & HOWDEN
E. 71,062   T. 49,779 (70.05%)   C. hold
David Davis, C.	31,045
George Ayre, Lab.	10,716
Linda Johnson, LD	5,215
Angela Stone, Green	1,764
Richard Honnoraty, Yorkshire	1,039

C. majority 20,329 (40.84%)
5.45% swing Lab. to C.

HALTON
E. 71,930   T. 46,203 (64.23%)   Lab. hold
Derek Twigg, Lab.	29,333
Charles Rowley, C.	10,358
Janet Balfe, Brexit	3,730
Stephen Gribbon, LD	1,800
David O'Keefe, Green	982

Lab. majority 18,975 (41.07%)
5.12% swing Lab. to C.

HAMMERSMITH
E. 74,759   T. 51,966 (69.51%)   Lab. hold
Andy Slaughter, Lab.	30,074
Xingang Wang, C.	12,227
Jessie Venegas, LD	6,947
Alex Horn, Green	1,744
James Keyse, Brexit	974

Lab. majority 17,847 (34.34%)
0.68% swing Lab. to C.

HAMPSHIRE EAST
E. 76,478   T. 56,895 (74.39%)   C. hold
Damian Hinds, C.	33,446
David Buxton, LD	13,750
Gaynor Austin, Lab.	6,287
Zoe Parker, Green	2,600
Jim Makin, UKIP	616
Eddie Trotter, JACP	196

C. majority 19,696 (34.62%)
6.93% swing C. to LD

HAMPSHIRE NORTH EAST
E. 78,954   T. 59,270 (75.07%)   C. hold
Ranil Jayawardena, C.	35,280
Graham Cockarill, LD	15,069
Barry Jones, Lab.	5,760
Culann Walsh, Green	1,754
Tony Durrant, Ind.	831
"Howling Laud" Hope, Loony	576

C. majority 20,211 (34.10%)
9.65% swing C. to LD

HAMPSHIRE NORTH WEST
E. 83,083   T. 58,918 (70.91%)   C. hold
Kit Malthouse, C.	36,591
Luigi Gregori, LD	10,283
Liz Bell, Lab.	9,327
Lance Mitchell, Green	2,717

C. majority 26,308 (44.65%)
3.85% swing C. to LD

HAMPSTEAD & KILBURN
E. 82,432   T. 57,385 (69.61%)   Lab. hold
Tulip Siddiq, Lab.	28,080
Johnny Luk, C.	13,892
Matt Sanders, LD	13,121
David Stansell, Green	1,608
James Pointon, Brexit	684

Lab. majority 14,188 (24.72%)
0.96% swing Lab. to C.

HARBOROUGH
E. 79,366   T. 57,319 (72.22%)   C. hold
Neil O'Brien, C.	31,698
Celia Hibbert, Lab.	14,420
Zuffar Haq, LD	9,103
Darren Woodiwiss, Green	1,709
Robin Lambert, Ind.	389

C. majority 17,278 (30.14%)
4.28% swing Lab. to C.

HARLOW
E. 68,078   T. 43,354 (63.68%)   C. hold
Robert Halfon, C.	27,510
Laura McAlpine, Lab.	13,447
Charlotte Cane, LD	2,397

C. majority 14,063 (32.44%)
8.38% swing Lab. to C.

HARROGATE & KNARESBOROUGH
E. 77,914   T. 56,937 (73.08%)   C. hold
Andrew Jones, C.	29,962
Judith Rogerson, LD	20,287
Mark Sewards, Lab.	5,480
Kieron George, Yorkshire	1,208

C. majority 9,675 (16.99%)
7.51% swing C. to LD

HARROW EAST
E. 72,120   T. 49,491 (68.62%)   C. hold
Bob Blackman, C.	26,935
Pamela Fitzpatrick, Lab.	18,765
Adam Bernard, LD	3,791

C. majority 8,170 (16.51%)
6.53% swing Lab. to C.

HARROW WEST
E. 72,477   T. 47,922 (66.12%)
Lab. Co-op hold
Gareth Thomas, Lab. Co-op	25,132
Anwara Ali, C.	16,440
Lisa-Maria Bornemann, LD	4,310
Rowan Langley, Green	1,109
Richard Jones, Brexit	931

Lab. Co-op majority 8,692 (18.14%)
4.15% swing Lab. to C.

HARTLEPOOL
E. 70,855   T. 41,037 (57.92%)   Lab. hold
Mike Hill, Lab.	15,464
Stefan Houghton, C.	11,869
Richard Tice, Brexit	10,603
Andy Hagon, LD	1,696
Joe Bousfield, Ind.	911
Kevin Cranney, Soc Lab.	494

Lab. majority 3,595 (8.76%)
4.76% swing Lab. to C.

HARWICH & ESSEX NORTH
E. 74,153   T. 51,963 (70.08%)   C. hold
Bernard Jenkin, C.	31,830
Stephen Rice, Lab.	11,648
Mike Beckett, LD	5,866
Peter Banks, Green	1,945
Richard Browning-Smith, Ind.	411
Tony Francis, Ind.	263

C. majority 20,182 (38.84%)
5.38% swing Lab. to C.

HASTINGS & RYE
E. 80,524   T. 54,274 (67.40%)   C. gain
Sally-Ann Hart, C.	26,896
Peter Chowney, Lab.	22,853
Nick Perry, LD	3,960
Paul Crosland, Ind.	565

C. majority 4,043 (7.45%)
3.41% swing Lab. to C.

HAVANT
E. 72,130 T. 45,959 (63.72%) C. hold
Alan Mak, C. 30,051
Rosamund Knight, Lab. 8,259
Paul Gray, LD 5,708
John Colman, Green 1,597
Alan Black, Soc Dem 344
C. majority 21,792 (47.42%)
6.48% swing Lab. to C.

HAYES & HARLINGTON
E. 72,356 T. 43,994 (60.80%) Lab. hold
John McDonnell, Lab. 24,545
Wayne Bridges, C. 15,284
Alexander Cunliffe, LD 1,947
Harry Boparai, Brexit 1,292
Christine West, Green 739
Chika Amadi, CPA 187
Lab. majority 9,261 (21.05%)
8.42% swing Lab. to C.

HAZEL GROVE
E. 65,457 T. 44,269 (67.63%) C. hold
William Wragg, C. 21,592
Lisa Smart, LD 17,169
Tony Wilson, Lab. 5,508
C. majority 4,423 (9.99%)
1.25% swing C. to LD

HEMEL HEMPSTEAD
E. 74,033 T. 51,271 (69.25%) C. hold
Mike Penning, C. 28,968
Nabila Ahmed, Lab. 14,405
Sammy Barry, LD 6,317
Sherief Hassan, Green 1,581
C. majority 14,563 (28.40%)
5.17% swing Lab. to C.

HEMSWORTH
E. 73,726 T. 43,907 (59.55%) Lab. hold
Jon Trickett, Lab. 16,460
Louise Calland, C. 15,280
Waj Ali, Brexit 5,930
Ian Womersley, Ind. 2,458
James Monaghan, LD 1,734
Martin Roberts, Yorkshire 964
Lyn Morton, Green 916
Pete Wilks, Ind. 165
Lab. majority 1,180 (2.69%)
9.73% swing Lab. to C.

HENDON
E. 82,661 T. 55,075 (66.63%) C. hold
Matthew Offord, C. 26,878
David Pinto-Duschinsky, Lab. 22,648
Clareine Enderby, LD 4,628
Portia Vincent-Kirby, Green 921
C. majority 4,230 (7.68%)
2.81% swing Lab. to C.

HENLEY
E. 76,660 T. 58,759 (76.65%) C. hold
John Howell, C. 32,189
Laura Coyle, LD 18,136
Zaid Marham, Lab. 5,698
Jo Robb, Green 2,736
C. majority 14,053 (23.92%)
10.16% swing C. to LD

HEREFORD & HEREFORDSHIRE SOUTH
E. 72,085 T. 49,646 (68.87%) C. hold
Jesse Norman, C. 30,390
Anna-Maria Coda, Lab. 10,704
Lucy Hurds, LD 6,181
Diana Toynbee, Green 2,371
C. majority 19,686 (39.65%)
4.96% swing Lab. to C.

HEREFORDSHIRE NORTH
E. 70,252 T. 51,033 (72.64%) C. hold
Bill Wiggin, C. 32,158
Phillip Howells, LD 7,302
Joe Wood, Lab. 6,804
Ellie Chowns, Green 4,769
C. majority 24,856 (48.71%)
0.78% swing C. to LD

HERTFORD & STORTFORD
E. 82,407 T. 60,094 (72.92%) C. hold
Julie Marson, C. 33,712
Chris Vince, Lab. 14,092
Chris Lucas, LD 8,596
Lucy Downes, Green 2,705
Alistair Lindsay, UKIP 681
Brian Percival, Ind. 308
C. majority 19,620 (32.65%)
0.46% swing Lab. to C.

HERTFORDSHIRE NORTH EAST
E. 76,123 T. 55,327 (72.68%) C. hold
Oliver Heald, C. 31,293
Kelley Green, Lab. 13,104
Amy Finch, LD 8,563
Tim Lee, Green 2,367
C. majority 18,189 (32.88%)
1.29% swing Lab. to C.

HERTFORDSHIRE SOUTH WEST
E. 80,449 T. 61,191 (76.06%) C. gain
Gagan Mohindra, C. 30,327
David Gauke, Ind. 15,919
Ali Aklakul, Lab. 7,228
Sally Symington, LD 6,251
Tom Pashby, Green 1,466
C. majority 14,408 (23.55%)
swing N/A

HERTSMERE
E. 73,971 T. 52,203 (70.57%) C. hold
Oliver Dowden, C. 32,651
Holly Kal-Weiss, Lab. 11,338
Stephen Barrett, LD 6,561
John Humphries, Green 1,653
C. majority 21,313 (40.83%)
4.19% swing Lab. to C.

HEXHAM
E. 61,324 T. 46,150 (75.26%) C. hold
Guy Opperman, C. 25,152
Penny Grennan, Lab. 14,603
Stephen Howse, LD 4,672
Nick Morphet, Green 1,723
C. majority 10,549 (22.86%)
1.44% swing Lab. to C.

HEYWOOD & MIDDLETON
E. 80,162 T. 47,488 (59.24%) C. gain
Chris Clarkson, C. 20,453
Liz McInnes, Lab. 19,790
Colin Lambert, Brexit 3,952
Anthony Smith, LD 2,073
Nigel Ainsworth-Barnes, Green 1,220
C. majority 663 (1.40%)
8.34% swing Lab. to C.

HIGH PEAK
E. 74,343 T. 54,173 (72.87%) C. gain
Robert Largan, C. 24,844
Ruth George, Lab. 24,254
David Lomax, LD 2,750
Alan Graves, Brexit 1,177
Robert Hodgetts-Haley, Green 1,148
C. majority 590 (1.09%)
2.70% swing Lab. to C.

HITCHIN & HARPENDEN
E. 76,321 T. 58,871 (77.14%) C. hold
Bim Afolami, C. 27,719
Sam Collins, LD 20,824
Kay Tart, Lab. 9,959
Sid Cordle, CPA 268
Peter Marshall, Advance 101
C. majority 6,895 (11.71%)
15.37% swing C. to LD

HOLBORN & ST PANCRAS
E. 87,236 T. 56,786 (65.09%) Lab. hold
Keir Starmer, Lab. 36,641
Alexandra Hayward, C. 8,878
Matthew Kirk, LD 7,314
Kirsten De Keyser, Green 2,746
Hector Birchwood, Brexit 1,032
Mohammad Bhatti, UKIP 138
Thomas Scripps, Soc Eq 37
Lab. majority 27,763 (48.89%)
1.41% swing Lab. to C.

HORNCHURCH & UPMINSTER
E. 80,765 T. 53,974 (66.83%) C. hold
Julia Lopez, C. 35,495
Tele Lawal, Lab. 12,187
Thomas Clarke, LD 3,862
Peter Caton, Green 1,920
David Furness, BNP 510
C. majority 23,308 (43.18%)
5.80% swing Lab. to C.

HORNSEY & WOOD GREEN
E. 81,814 T. 61,105 (74.69%) Lab. hold
Catherine West, Lab. 35,126
Dawn Barnes, LD 15,884
Ed McGuinness, C. 6,829
Jarelle Francis, Green 2,192
Daniel Corrigan, Brexit 763
Helen Spiby-Vann, CPA 211
Salah Wakie, Ind. 100
Lab. majority 19,242 (31.49%)
8.93% swing Lab. to LD

HORSHAM
E. 86,730 T. 63,242 (72.92%)   C. hold
Jeremy Quin, C.   35,900
Louise Potter, LD   14,773
Michael Jones, Lab.   9,424
Catherine Ross, Green   2,668
Jim Duggan, Peace   477
C. majority 21,127 (33.41%)
6.90% swing C. to LD

HOUGHTON & SUNDERLAND SOUTH
E. 68,835 T. 39,811 (57.84%) Lab. hold
Bridget Phillipson, Lab.   16,210
Christopher Howarth, C.   13,095
Kevin Yuill, Brexit   6,165
Paul Edgeworth, LD   2,319
Richard Bradley, Green   1,125
Richard Elvin, UKIP   897
Lab. majority 3,115 (7.82%)
10.96% swing Lab. to C.

HOVE
E. 74,313 T. 56,391 (75.88%) Lab. hold
Peter Kyle, Lab.   32,876
Robert Nemeth, C.   15,832
Beatrice Bass, LD   3,731
Ollie Sykes, Green   2,496
Angela Hancock, Brexit   1,111
Dame Dixon, Loony   195
Charlotte Sabel, Ind.   150
Lab. majority 17,044 (30.22%)
1.17% swing Lab. to C.

HUDDERSFIELD
E. 65,525 T. 41,882 (63.92%)
                           Lab. Co-op hold
Barry Sheerman, Lab. Co-op   20,509
Ken Davy, C.   15,572
James Wilkinson, LD   2,367
Andrew Cooper, Green   1,768
Stuart Hale, Brexit   1,666
Lab. Co-op majority 4,937 (11.79%)
7.80% swing Lab. to C.

HULL EAST
E. 65,745 T. 32,442 (49.35%) Lab. hold
Karl Turner, Lab.   12,713
Rachel Storer, C.   11,474
Marten Hall, Brexit   5,764
Bob Morgan, LD   1,707
Julia Brown, Green   784
Lab. majority 1,239 (3.82%)
12.28% swing Lab. to C.

HULL NORTH
E. 65,515 T. 34,203 (52.21%) Lab. hold
Diana Johnson, Lab.   17,033
Holly Whitbread, C.   9,440
Derek Abram, Brexit   4,771
Mike Ross, LD   2,084
Richard Howarth, Green   875
Lab. majority 7,593 (22.20%)
8.12% swing Lab. to C.

HULL WEST & HESSLE
E. 60,409 T. 31,356 (51.91%) Lab. hold
Emma Hardy, Lab.   13,384
Scott Bell, C.   10,528
Michelle Dewberry, Brexit   5,638
David Nolan, LD   1,756
Mike Lammiman, Green   50
Lab. majority 2,856 (9.11%)
7.05% swing Lab. to C.

HUNTINGDON
E. 84,657 T. 59,147 (69.87%)   C. hold
Jonathan Djanogly, C.   32,386
Samuel Sweek, Lab.   13,003
Mark Argent, LD   9,432
Daniel Laycock, Green   2,233
Paul Bullen, Ind.   1,789
Tom Varghese, Ind.   304
C. majority 19,383 (32.77%)
4.27% swing Lab. to C.

HYNDBURN
E. 70,910 T. 42,406 (59.80%)   C. gain
Sara Britcliffe, C.   20,565
Graham Jones, Lab.   17,614
Gregory Butt, Brexit   2,156
Adam Waller-Slack, LD   1,226
Katrina Brockbank, Green   845
C. majority 2,951 (6.96%)
9.91% swing Lab. to C.

ILFORD NORTH
E. 72,963 T. 50,123 (68.70%) Lab. hold
Wes Streeting, Lab.   25,323
Howard Berlin, C.   20,105
Mark Johnson, LD   2,680
Neil Anderson, Brexit   960
David Reynolds, Green   845
Donald Akhigbe, CPA   210
Lab. majority 5,218 (10.41%)
3.90% swing Lab. to C.

ILFORD SOUTH
E. 84,957 T. 53,477 (62.95%) Lab. gain
Sam Tarry, Lab.   35,085
Ali Azeem, C.   10,984
Mike Gapes, Change   3,891
Ashburn Holder, LD   1,795
Munish Sharma, Brexit   1,008
Rosemary Warrington,   714
Green
Lab. majority 24,101 (45.07%)
4.91% swing Lab. to C.

IPSWICH
E. 75,525 T. 49,579 (65.65%)   C. gain
Tom Hunt, C.   24,952
Sandy Martin, Lab.   19,473
Adrian Hyyrylainen-Trett,   2,439
LD
Nicola Thomas, Brexit   1,432
Barry Broom, Green   1,283
C. majority 5,479 (11.05%)
6.34% swing Lab. to C.

ISLE OF WIGHT
E. 113,021 T. 74,442 (65.87%)   C. hold
Bob Seely, C.   41,815
Richard Quigley, Lab.   18,078
Vix Lowthion, Green   11,338
Carl Feeney, Network   1,542
Karl Love, Ind.   874
Daryll Pitcher, Ind.   795
C. majority 23,737 (31.89%)
1.80% swing Lab. to C.

ISLINGTON NORTH
E. 75,162 T. 53,805 (71.59%) Lab. hold
Jeremy Corbyn, Lab.   34,603
Nick Wakeling, LD   8,415
James Clark, C.   5,483
Caroline Russell, Green   4,326
Yosef David, Brexit   742
Nick Brick, Loony   236
Lab. majority 26,188 (48.67%)
7.65% swing Lab. to LD

ISLINGTON SOUTH & FINSBURY
E. 70,489 T. 47,816 (67.83%) Lab. hold
Emily Thornberry, Lab.   26,897
Kate Pothalingam, LD   9,569
Jason Charalambous, C.   8,045
Talia Hussain, Green   1,987
Paddy Hannam, Brexit   1,136
Lord Sandys Of Bunhill,   182
Loony
Lab. majority 17,328 (36.24%)
7.25% swing Lab. to LD

JARROW
E. 65,103 T. 40,736 (62.57%) Lab. gain
Kate Osborne, Lab.   18,363
Nick Oliver, C.   11,243
Richard Monaghan, Brexit   4,122
John Robertson, Ind.   2,991
David Wilkinson, LD   2,360
James Milne, Green   831
Shaun Sadler, Ind.   614
Mark Conway, Soc Dem   212
Lab. majority 7,120 (17.48%)
11.32% swing Lab. to C.

KEIGHLEY
E. 72,778 T. 52,600 (72.27%)
Robbie Moore, C.   25,298
John Grogan, Lab.   23,080
Tom Franks, LD   2,573
Waqas Khan, Brexit   850
Mark Barton, Yorkshire   667
Matthew Rose, Soc Dem   132
C. majority 2,218 (4.22%)
2.35% swing Lab. to C.

KENILWORTH & SOUTHAM
E. 68,156 T. 52,597 (77.17%)   C. hold
Jeremy Wright, C.   30,351
Richard Dickson, LD   9,998
Antony Tucker, Lab.   9,440
Alison Firth, Green   2,351
Nicholas Green, Loony   457
C. majority 20,353 (38.70%)
6.27% swing C. to LD

KENSINGTON

E. 64,609 T. 43,762 (67.73%) C. gain

Felicity Buchan, C.	16,768
Emma Dent Coad, Lab.	16,618
Sam Gyimah, LD	9,312
Vivien Lichtenstein, Green	535
Jay Aston Colquhoun, Brexit	384
Roger Phillips, CPA	70
Harriet Gore, Touch	47
Scott Dore, WRP	28

C. majority 150 (0.34%)
0.20% swing Lab. to C.

KETTERING

E. 73,187 T. 49,361 (67.45%) C. hold

Philip Hollobone, C.	29,787
Clare Pavitt, Lab.	13,022
Chris Nelson, LD	3,367
Jim Hakewill, Ind.	1,642
Jamie Wildman, Green	1,543

C. majority 16,765 (33.96%)
6.29% swing Lab. to C.

KINGSTON & SURBITON

E. 81,975 T. 60,846 (74.23%) LD hold

Ed Davey, LD	31,103
Aphra Brandreth, C.	20,614
Leanne Werner, Lab.	6,528
Sharron Sumner, Green	1,038
Scott Holman, Brexit	788
James Giles, Ind.	458
Chinners Chinnery, Loony	193
Roger Glencross, UKIP	124

LD majority 10,489 (17.24%)
5.30% swing C. to LD

KINGSWOOD

E. 68,972 T. 49,314 (71.50%) C. hold

Chris Skidmore, C.	27,712
Nicola Bowden-Jones, Lab.	16,492
Dine Romero, LD	3,421
Joseph Evans, Green	1,200
Angelika Cowell, AWP	489

C. majority 11,220 (22.75%)
3.68% swing Lab. to C.

KNOWSLEY

E. 84,060 T. 54,938 (65.36%) Lab. hold

George Howarth, Lab.	44,374
Rushi Millns, C.	4,432
Tim McCullough, Brexit	3,348
Paul Woodruff, Green	1,262
Joe Slupsky, LD	1,117
Ray Catesby, Lib	405

Lab. majority 39,942 (72.70%)
1.69% swing Lab. to C.

LANCASHIRE WEST

E. 73,346 T. 52,663 (71.80%) Lab. hold

Rosie Cooper, Lab.	27,458
Jack Gilmore, C.	19,122
Simon Thomson, LD	2,560
Marc Stanton, Brexit	2,275
John Puddifer, Green	1,248

Lab. majority 8,336 (15.83%)
2.83% swing Lab. to C.

LANCASTER & FLEETWOOD

E. 70,059 T. 45,219 (64.54%) Lab. hold

Cat Smith, Lab.	21,184
Louise Thistlethwaite, C.	18,804
Peter Jackson, LD	2,018
Leanne Murray, Brexit	1,817
Caroline Jackson, Green	1,396

Lab. majority 2,380 (5.26%)
4.61% swing Lab. to C.

LEEDS CENTRAL

E. 90,971 T. 49,284 (54.18%) Lab. hold

Hilary Benn, Lab.	30,413
Peter Fortune, C.	11,143
Paul Thomas, Brexit	2,999
Jack Holland, LD	2,343
Ed Carlisle, Green	2,105
William Clouston, Soc Dem	281

Lab. majority 19,270 (39.10%)
5.30% swing Lab. to C.

LEEDS EAST

E. 67,286 T. 39,052 (58.04%) Lab. hold

Richard Burgon, Lab.	19,464
Jill Mortimer, C.	13,933
Sarah Wass, Brexit	2,981
David Dresser, LD	1,796
Shahab Adris, Green	878

Lab. majority 5,531 (14.16%)
8.30% swing Lab. to C.

LEEDS NORTH EAST

E. 70,580 T. 50,500 (71.55%) Lab. hold

Fabian Hamilton, Lab.	29,024
Amjad Bashir, C.	11,935
Jon Hannah, LD	5,665
Rachel Hartshorne, Green	1,931
Inaya Iman, Brexit	1,769
Celia Foote, Green Soc	176

Lab. majority 17,089 (33.84%)
0.89% swing C. to Lab.

LEEDS NORTH WEST

E. 67,741 T. 49,283 (72.75%)
Lab. Co-op hold

Alex Sobel, Lab. Co-op	23,971
Stewart Harper, C.	13,222
Kamran Hussain, LD	9,397
Martin Hemingway, Green	1,389
Graeme Webber, Brexit	1,304

Lab. Co-op majority 10,749 (21.81%)
1.32% swing Lab. to C.

LEEDS WEST

E. 67,727 T. 40,281 (59.48%) Lab. hold

Rachel Reeves, Lab.	22,186
Mark Dormer, C.	11,622
Phillip Mars, Brexit	2,685
Dan Walker, LD	1,787
Victoria Smith, Green	1,274
Ian Cowling, Yorkshire	650
Daniel Whetstone, Soc Dem	46
Mike Davies, Green Soc	31

Lab. majority 10,564 (26.23%)
5.79% swing Lab. to C.

LEICESTER EAST

E. 78,432 T. 49,421 (63.01%) Lab. hold

Claudia Webbe, Lab.	25,090
Bhupen Dave, C.	19,071
Nitesh Dave, LD	2,800
Tara Baldwin, Brexit	1,243
Melanie Wakley, Green	888
Sanjay Gogia, Ind.	329

Lab. majority 6,019 (12.18%)
15.30% swing Lab. to C.

LEICESTER SOUTH

E. 77,665 T. 50,147 (64.57%)
Lab. Co-op hold

Jonathan Ashworth, Lab. Co-op	33,606
Natalie Neale, C.	10,931
Chris Coghlan, LD	2,754
Mags Lewis, Green	1,669
James Potter, Brexit	1,187

Lab. Co-op majority 22,675 (45.22%)
3.38% swing Lab. to C.

LEICESTER WEST

E. 64,918 T. 34,775 (53.57%) Lab. hold

Liz Kendall, Lab.	17,291
Amanda Wright, C.	13,079
Ian Bradwell, LD	1,808
Jack Collier, Brexit	1,620
Ani Goddard, Green	977

Lab. majority 4,212 (12.11%)
8.69% swing Lab. to C.

LEICESTERSHIRE NORTH WEST

E. 78,935 T. 53,821 (68.18%) C. hold

Andrew Bridgen, C.	33,811
Terri Eynon, Lab.	13,411
Grahame Hudson, LD	3,614
Carl Benfield, Green	2,478
Edward Nudd, Ind.	367
Dan Liddicott, Libertarian	140

C. majority 20,400 (37.90%)
6.54% swing Lab. to C.

LEICESTERSHIRE SOUTH

E. 80,520 T. 57,469 (71.37%) C. hold

Alberto Costa, C.	36,791
Tristan Koriya, Lab.	12,787
Phil Knowles, LD	5,452
Nick Cox, Green	2,439

C. majority 24,004 (41.77%)
4.45% swing Lab. to C.

LEIGH

E. 77,417 T. 46,979 (60.68%) C. gain

James Grundy, C.	21,266
Joanne Platt, Lab. Co-op	19,301
James Melly, Brexit	3,161
Mark Clayton, LD	2,252
Ann O'Bern, Ind.	551
Leon Peters, UKIP	448

C. majority 1,965 (4.18%)
12.28% swing Lab. to C.

LEWES
E. 71,503 T. 54,851 (76.71%)   C. hold
Maria Caulfield, C.   26,268
Oli Henman, LD   23,811
Kate Chappell, Lab.   3,206
Johnny Denis, Green   1,453
Paul Cragg, ND   113
C. majority 2,457 (4.48%)
2.84% swing C. to LD

LEWISHAM DEPTFORD
E. 80,617 T. 55,368 (68.68%)   Lab. hold
Vicky Foxcroft, Lab.   39,216
Gavin Haran, C.   6,303
Bobby Dean, LD   5,774
Andrea Carey Fuller, Green   3,085
Moses Etienne, Brexit   789
Tan Bui, Ind.   130
John Lloyd, Green Soc   71
Lab. majority 32,913 (59.44%)
1.94% swing Lab. to C.

LEWISHAM EAST
E. 67,857 T. 44,815 (66.04%)   Lab. hold
Janet Daby, Lab.   26,661
Sam Thurgood, C.   9,653
Ade Fatukasi, LD   5,039
Rosamund Adoo-Kissi-   1,706
Debrah, Green
Wesley Pollard, Brexit   1,234
Maureen Martin, CPA   277
Mark Barber, Ind.   152
Richard Galloway, Young   50
Elder Roger Mighton, Ind.   43
Lab. majority 17,008 (37.95%)
3.50% swing Lab. to C.

LEWISHAM WEST & PENGE
E. 74,615 T. 52,100 (69.83%)   Lab. hold
Ellie Reeves, Lab.   31,860
Aisha Cuthbert, C.   10,317
Alex Feakes, LD   6,260
James Braun, Green   2,390
Teixeira Hambro, Brexit   1,060
Katherine Hortense, CPA   213
Lab. majority 21,543 (41.35%)
1.10% swing Lab. to C.

LEYTON & WANSTEAD
E. 64,852 T. 44,547 (68.69%)   Lab. hold
John Cryer, Lab.   28,836
Noshaba Khiljee, C.   8,028
Ben Sims, LD   4,666
Ashley Gunstock, Green   1,805
Zulf Jannaty, Brexit   785
Henry Scott, Ind.   427
Lab. majority 20,808 (46.71%)
1.13% swing Lab. to C.

LICHFIELD
E. 76,751 T. 53,993 (70.35%)   C. hold
Michael Fabricant, C.   34,844
Dave Robertson, Lab.   11,206
Paul Ray, LD   5,632
Andrea Muckley, Green   1,743
John Madden, Ind.   568
C. majority 23,638 (43.78%)
4.53% swing Lab. to C.

LINCOLN
E. 74,778 T. 50,629 (67.71%)   C. gain
Karl McCartney, C.   24,267
Karen Lee, Lab.   20,753
Caroline Kenyon, LD   2,422
Sally Horscroft, Green   1,195
Reece Wilkes, Brexit   1,079
Rob Bradley, Ind.   609
Charles Shaw, Lib   304
C. majority 3,514 (6.94%)
5.05% swing Lab. to C.

LIVERPOOL RIVERSIDE
E. 80,310 T. 52,789 (65.73%)   Lab. gain
Kim Johnson, Lab.   41,170
Sean Malkeson, C.   4,127
Tom Crone, Green   3,017
Rob McAllister-Bell, LD   2,696
David Leach, Brexit   1,779
Lab. majority 37,043 (70.17%)
2.34% swing Lab. to C.

LIVERPOOL WALTON
E. 62,628 T. 40,786 (65.12%)   Lab. hold
Dan Carden, Lab.   34,538
Alex Phillips, C.   4,018
Ted Grant, Green   814
David Newman, LD   756
Billy Lake, Lib   660
Lab. majority 30,520 (74.83%)
1.16% swing Lab. to C.

LIVERPOOL WAVERTREE
E. 63,458 T. 43,377 (68.36%)   Lab. gain
Paula Barker, Lab.   31,310
Catherine Mulhern, C.   4,225
Richard Kemp, LD   4,055
Adam Heatherington, Brexit   1,921
Kay Inckle, Green   1,365
Mick Coyne, Lib   501
Lab. majority 27,085 (62.44%)
2.54% swing Lab. to C.

LIVERPOOL WEST DERBY
E. 65,640 T. 43,989 (67.02%)   Lab. hold
Ian Byrne, Lab.   34,117
Tom Bradley, C.   4,133
Ray Pearson, Brexit   2,012
Steve Radford, Lib   1,826
Paul Parr, LD   1,296
William Ward, Green   605
Lab. majority 29,984 (68.16%)
2.35% swing Lab. to C.

LOUGHBOROUGH
E. 79,776 T. 54,631 (68.48%)   C. hold
Jane Hunt, C.   27,954
Stuart Brady, Lab.   20,785
Ian Sharpe, LD   4,153
Wes Walton, Green   1,504
Queenie Tea, Ind.   235
C. majority 7,169 (13.12%)
2.62% swing Lab. to C.

LOUTH & HORNCASTLE
E. 79,648 T. 52,332 (65.70%)   C. hold
Victoria Atkins, C.   38,021
Ellie Green, Lab.   9,153
Ross Pepper, LD   4,114
The Iconic Arty-Pole, Loony   1,044
C. majority 28,868 (55.16%)
8.97% swing Lab. to C.

LUDLOW
E. 69,442 T. 50,225 (72.33%)   C. hold
Philip Dunne, C.   32,185
Heather Kidd, LD   8,537
Kuldip Sahota, Lab.   7,591
Hilary Wendt, Green   1,912
C. majority 23,648 (47.08%)
2.57% swing C. to LD

LUTON NORTH
E. 68,185 T. 42,589 (62.46%)   Lab. gain
Sarah Owen, Lab.   23,496
Jeet Bains, C.   14,249
Linda Jack, LD   2,063
Sudhir Sharma, Brexit   1,215
Simon Hall, Green   771
Muhammad Rehman, Ind.   646
Serena Laidley, Women   149
Lab. majority 9,247 (21.71%)
4.55% swing Lab. to C.

LUTON SOUTH
E. 69,338 T. 42,064 (60.67%)   Lab. gain
Rachel Hopkins, Lab.   21,787
Parvez Akhtar, C.   13,031
Gavin Shuker, ND   3,893
Garry Warren, Brexit   1,601
Ben Foley, Green   995
Mohammed Ashraf, Ind.   489
John French, Luton   268
Lab. majority 8,756 (20.82%)
4.68% swing Lab. to C.

MACCLESFIELD
E. 76,216 T. 53,867 (70.68%)   C. hold
David Rutley, C.   28,292
Neil Puttick, Lab.   17,581
Neil Christian, LD   5,684
James Booth, Green   2,310
C. majority 10,711 (19.88%)
2.02% swing Lab. to C.

MAIDENHEAD
E. 76,668 T. 56,492 (73.68%)   C. hold
Theresa May, C.   32,620
Joshua Reynolds, LD   13,774
Patrick McDonald, Lab.   7,882
Emily Tomalin, Green   2,216
C. majority 18,846 (33.36%)
10.09% swing C. to LD

MAIDSTONE & THE WEALD
E. 76,110 T. 51,680 (67.90%)   C. hold
Helen Grant, C.   31,220
Dan Wilkinson, Lab.   9,448
James Willis, LD   8,482
Stuart Jeffery, Green   2,172
Yolande Kenward, Ind.   358
C. majority 21,772 (42.13%)
3.94% swing Lab. to C.

MAKERFIELD
E. 74,190 T. 44,259 (59.66%)   Lab. hold
Yvonne Fovargue, Lab.   19,954
Nick King, C.   15,214
Ross Wright, Brexit   5,817
John Skipworth, LD   2,108
Sheila Shaw, Green   1,166
Lab. majority 4,740 (10.71%)
9.07% swing Lab. to C.

MALDON

E. 72,641   T. 50,408 (69.39%)   C. hold
John Whittingdale, C.   36,304
Stephen Capper, Lab.   6,263
Colin Baldy, LD   5,990
Janet Band, Green   1,851
C. majority 30,041 (59.60%)
6.46% swing Lab. to C.

MANCHESTER CENTRAL

E. 94,247   T. 52,289 (55.48%)
                              Lab. Co-op hold
Lucy Powell, Lab. Co-op   36,823
Shaden Jaradat, C.   7,734
John Bridges, LD   3,420
Sarah Chadwick, Brexit   2,335
Melanie Horrocks, Green   1,870
Dennis Leech, Soc Eq   107
Lab. Co-op majority 29,089 (55.63%)
3.81% swing Lab. to C.

MANCHESTER GORTON

E. 76,419   T. 44,545 (58.29%)   Lab. hold
Afzal Khan, Lab.   34,583
Sebastian Lowe, C.   4,244
Jackie Pearcey, LD   2,448
Eliza Tyrrell, Green   1,697
Lesley Kaya, Brexit   1,573
Lab. majority 30,339 (68.11%)
0.47% swing Lab. to C.

MANCHESTER WITHINGTON

E. 76,530   T. 52,995 (69.25%)   Lab. hold
Jeff Smith, Lab.   35,902
John Leech, LD   7,997
Shengke Zhi, C.   5,820
Lucy Bannister, Green   1,968
Stephen Ward, Brexit   1,308
Lab. majority 27,905 (52.66%)
1.54% swing Lab. to LD

MANSFIELD

E. 77,131   T. 49,273 (63.88%)   C. hold
Ben Bradley, C.   31,484
Sonya Ward, Lab.   15,178
Sarah Brown, LD   1,626
Sid Pepper, Ind.   527
Stephen Harvey, ND   458
C. majority 16,306 (33.09%)
15.49% swing Lab. to C.

MEON VALLEY

E. 75,737   T. 54,829 (72.39%)   C. hold
Flick Drummond, C.   35,271
Lewis North, LD   11,716
Matthew Bunday, Lab.   5,644
Malcolm Wallace, Green   2,198
C. majority 23,555 (42.96%)
5.94% swing C. to LD

MERIDEN

E. 85,368   T. 54,161 (63.44%)   C. hold
Saqib Bhatti, C.   34,358
Teresa Beddis, Lab.   11,522
Laura McCarthy, LD   5,614
Steve Caudwell, Green   2,667
C. majority 22,836 (42.16%)
3.51% swing Lab. to C.

MIDDLESBROUGH

E. 60,759   T. 32,140 (52.90%)   Lab. hold
Andy McDonald, Lab.   17,202
Ruth Betson, C.   8,812
Antony High, Ind.   4,548
Faye Clements, Brexit   2,168
Thomas Crawford, LD   816
Hugh Alberti, Green   546
Lab. majority 8,390 (26.10%)
6.41% swing Lab. to C.

MIDDLESBROUGH SOUTH & CLEVELAND EAST

E. 72,339   T. 47,817 (66.10%)   C. hold
Simon Clarke, C.   28,135
Lauren Dingsdale, Lab.   16,509
Jemma Joy, LD   1,953
Sophie Brown, Green   1,220
C. majority 11,626 (24.31%)
11.09% swing Lab. to C.

MILTON KEYNES NORTH

E. 91,535   T. 62,543 (68.33%)   C. hold
Ben Everitt, C.   30,938
Charlynne Pullen, Lab.   24,683
Aisha Mir, LD   4,991
Catherine Rose, Green   1,931
C. majority 6,255 (10.00%)
3.50% swing Lab. to C.

MILTON KEYNES SOUTH

E. 96,343   T. 64,007 (66.44%)   C. hold
Iain Stewart, C.   32,011
Hannah O'Neill, Lab.   25,067
Saleyha Ahsan, LD   4,688
Alan Francis, Green   1,495
Stephen Fulton, Ind.   539
Amarachi Ogba, CPA   207
C. majority 6,944 (10.85%)
4.09% swing Lab. to C.

MITCHAM & MORDEN

E. 70,014   T. 45,741 (65.33%)   Lab. hold
Siobhain McDonagh, Lab.   27,964
Toby Williams, C.   11,482
Luke Taylor, LD   3,717
Jeremy Maddocks, Brexit   1,202
Pippa Maslin, Green   1,160
Des Coke, CPA   216
Lab. majority 16,482 (36.03%)
4.19% swing Lab. to C.

MOLE VALLEY

E. 74,665   T. 57,110 (76.49%)   C. hold
Paul Beresford, C.   31,656
Paul Kennedy, LD   19,615
Brian Bostock, Lab.   2,965
Lisa Scott-Conte, Green   1,874
Robin Horsley, Ind.   536
Geoffrey Cox, UKIP   464
C. majority 12,041 (21.08%)
10.73% swing C. to LD

MORECAMBE & LUNESDALE

E. 67,397   T. 45,310 (67.23%)   C. hold
David Morris, C.   23,925
Lizzi Collinge, Lab.   17,571
Owen Lambert, LD   2,328
Chloe Buckley, Green   938
Darren Clifford, Ind.   548
C. majority 6,354 (14.02%)
5.48% swing Lab. to C.

MORLEY & OUTWOOD

E. 78,803   T. 51,930 (65.90%)   C. hold
Andrea Jenkyns, C.   29,424
Deanne Ferguson, Lab.   18,157
Craig Dobson, LD   2,285
Chris Bell, Green   1,107
Dan Woodlock, Yorkshire   957
C. majority 11,267 (21.70%)
8.84% swing Lab. to C.

NEW FOREST EAST

E. 73,552   T. 50,786 (69.05%)   C. hold
Julian Lewis, C.   32,769
Julie Hope, Lab.   7,518
Bob Johnston, LD   7,390
Nicola Jolly, Green   2,434
Andrew Knight, AWP   675
C. majority 25,251 (49.72%)
3.45% swing Lab. to C.

NEW FOREST WEST

E. 70,867   T. 50,306 (70.99%)   C. hold
Desmond Swayne, C.   32,113
Jack Davies, LD   7,710
Jo Graham, Lab.   6,595
Nick Bubb, Green   3,888
C. majority 24,403 (48.51%)
4.35% swing C. to LD

NEWARK

E. 75,855   T. 54,722 (72.14%)   C. hold
Robert Jenrick, C.   34,650
James Baggaley, Lab.   12,814
David Watts, LD   5,308
Jay Henderson, Green   1,950
C. majority 21,836 (39.90%)
3.47% swing Lab. to C.

NEWBURY

E. 83,414   T. 59,998 (71.93%)   C. hold
Laura Farris, C.   34,431
Lee Dillon, LD   18,384
James Wilder, Lab.   4,404
Stephen Masters, Green   2,454
Ben Holden-Crowther, Ind.   325
C. majority 16,047 (26.75%)
6.66% swing C. to LD

NEWCASTLE UPON TYNE CENTRAL

E. 57,845   T. 37,474 (64.78%)   Lab. hold
Chi Onwurah, Lab.   21,568
Emily Payne, C.   9,290
Ali Avaei, LD   2,709
Mark Griffin, Brexit   2,542
Tay Pitman, Green   1,365
Lab. majority 12,278 (32.76%)
3.75% swing Lab. to C.

NEWCASTLE UPON TYNE EAST

E. 63,796   T. 43,365 (67.97%)   Lab. hold
Nick Brown, Lab.   26,049
Robin Gwynn, C.   10,586
Wendy Taylor, LD   4,535
Nick Hartley, Green   2,195
Lab. majority 15,463 (35.66%)
5.30% swing Lab. to C.

NEWCASTLE UPON TYNE NORTH
E. 68,486   T. 46,999 (68.63%)   Lab. hold
Catherine McKinnell, Lab.	21,354
Mark Lehain, C.	15,589
Nicholas Cott, LD	4,357
Richard Ogden, Brexit	4,331
Alistair Ford, Green	1,368

Lab. majority 5,765 (12.27%)
4.58% swing Lab. to C.

NEWCASTLE-UNDER-LYME
E. 68,211   T. 44,739 (65.59%)   C. gain
Aaron Bell, C.	23,485
Carl Greatbatch, Lab.	16,039
Nigel Jones, LD	2,361
Jason Cooper, Brexit	1,921
Carl Johnson, Green	933

C. majority 7,446 (16.64%)
8.36% swing Lab. to C.

NEWTON ABBOT
E. 72,533   T. 52,556 (72.46%)   C. hold
Anne Marie Morris, C.	29,190
Martin Wrigley, LD	11,689
James Osben, Lab.	9,329
Megan Debenham, Green	1,508
David Halpin, Ind.	840

C. majority 17,501 (33.30%)
0.81% swing C. to LD

NORFOLK MID
E. 81,975   T. 56,186 (68.54%)   C. hold
George Freeman, C.	35,051
Adrian Heald, Lab.	12,457
Steffan Aquarone, LD	7,739
P J O'Gorman, Ind.	939

C. majority 22,594 (40.21%)
5.66% swing Lab. to C.

NORFOLK NORTH
E. 70,729   T. 50,823 (71.86%)   C. gain
Duncan Baker, C.	29,792
Karen Ward, LD	15,397
Emma Corlett, Lab.	3,895
Harry Gwynne, Brexit	1,739

C. majority 14,395 (28.32%)
17.53% swing LD to C.

NORFOLK NORTH WEST
E. 72,080   T. 46,602 (64.65%)   C. hold
James Wild, C.	30,627
Jo Rust, Lab.	10,705
Rob Colwell, LD	3,625
Andrew De Whalley, Green	1,645

C. majority 19,922 (42.75%)
7.25% swing Lab. to C.

NORFOLK SOUTH
E. 86,214   T. 62,484 (72.48%)   C. hold
Richard Bacon, C.	36,258
Beth Jones, Lab.	14,983
Christopher Brown, LD	8,744
Ben Price, Green	2,499

C. majority 21,275 (34.05%)
3.38% swing Lab. to C.

NORFOLK SOUTH WEST
E. 78,455   T. 51,466 (65.60%)   C. hold
Liz Truss, C.	35,507
Emily Blake, Lab.	9,312
Josie Ratcliffe, LD	4,166
Pallavi Devulapalli, Green	1,645
Earl Elvis Of Outwell, Loony	836

C. majority 26,195 (50.90%)
7.98% swing Lab. to C.

NORMANTON, PONTEFRACT & CASTLEFORD
E. 84,527   T. 48,259 (57.09%)   Lab. hold
Yvette Cooper, Lab.	18,297
Andrew Lee, C.	17,021
Deneice Florence-Jukes, Brexit	8,032
Tom Gordon, LD	3,147
Laura Walker, Yorkshire	1,762

Lab. majority 1,276 (2.64%)
13.42% swing Lab. to C.

NORTHAMPTON NORTH
E. 59,265   T. 39,539 (66.72%)   C. hold
Michael Ellis, C.	21,031
Sally Keeble, Lab.	15,524
Martin Sawyer, LD	2,031
Katherine Pate, Green	953

C. majority 5,507 (13.93%)
5.96% swing Lab. to C.

NORTHAMPTON SOUTH
E. 62,712   T. 40,835 (65.12%)   C. hold
Andrew Lewer, C.	20,914
Gareth Eales, Lab.	16,217
Jill Hope, LD	2,482
Scott Mabbutt, Green	1,222

C. majority 4,697 (11.50%)
4.34% swing Lab. to C.

NORTHAMPTONSHIRE SOUTH
E. 90,840   T. 66,908 (73.65%)   C. hold
Andrea Leadsom, C.	41,755
Gen Kitchen, Lab.	13,994
Chris Lofts, LD	7,891
Denise Donaldson, Green	2,634
Josh Phillips, Ind.	463
Stuart McCutcheon, ND	171

C. majority 27,761 (41.49%)
3.18% swing Lab. to C.

NORWICH NORTH
E. 67,172   T. 46,285 (68.91%)   C. hold
Chloe Smith, C.	23,397
Karen Davis, Lab.	18,659
Dave Thomas, LD	2,663
Adrian Holmes, Green	1,078
David Moreland, UKIP	488

C. majority 4,738 (10.24%)
4.57% swing Lab. to C.

NORWICH SOUTH
E. 77,845   T. 51,673 (66.38%)   Lab. hold
Clive Lewis, Lab.	27,766
Mike Spencer, C.	15,006
James Wright, LD	4,776
Catherine Rowett, Green	2,469
Sandy Gilchrist, Brexit	1,656

Lab. majority 12,760 (24.69%)
2.84% swing Lab. to C.

NOTTINGHAM EAST
E. 66,262   T. 40,004 (60.37%)   Lab. gain
Nadia Whittome, Lab.	25,735
Victoria Stapleton, C.	8,342
Robert Swift, LD	1,954
Chris Leslie, Change	1,447
Damian Smith, Brexit	1,343
Michelle Vacciana, Green	1,183

Lab. majority 17,393 (43.48%)
3.17% swing Lab. to C.

NOTTINGHAM NORTH
E. 66,495   T. 35,320 (53.12%)   Lab. Co-op hold
Alex Norris, Lab. Co-op	17,337
Stuart Bestwick, C.	12,847
Julian Carter, Brexit	2,686
Christina Morgan-Danvers, LD	1,582
Andrew Jones, Green	868

Lab. Co-op majority 4,490 (12.71%)
8.21% swing Lab. to C.

NOTTINGHAM SOUTH
E. 79,485   T. 48,134 (60.56%)   Lab. hold
Lilian Greenwood, Lab.	26,586
Marc Nykolyszyn, C.	14,018
Barry Holliday, LD	3,935
John Lawson, Brexit	2,012
Cath Sutherland, Green	1,583

Lab. majority 12,568 (26.11%)
2.70% swing Lab. to C.

NUNEATON
E. 70,226   T. 45,190 (64.35%)   C. hold
Marcus Jones, C.	27,390
Zoe Mayou, Lab.	14,246
Richard Brighton-Knight, LD	1,862
Keith Kondakor, Green	1,692

C. majority 13,144 (29.09%)
9.40% swing Lab. to C.

OLD BEXLEY & SIDCUP
E. 66,104   T. 46,145 (69.81%)   C. hold
James Brokenshire, C.	29,786
David Tingle, Lab.	10,834
Simone Reynolds, LD	3,822
Matt Browne, Green	1,477
Carol Valinejad, CPA	226

C. majority 18,952 (41.07%)
4.44% swing Lab. to C.

OLDHAM EAST & SADDLEWORTH
E. 72,173   T. 46,164 (63.96%)   Lab. hold
Debbie Abrahams, Lab.	20,088
Tom Lord, C.	18,589
Paul Brierley, Brexit	2,980
Sam Al-Hamdani, LD	2,423
Paul Errock, Oldham	1,073
Wendy Olsen, Green	778
Amoy Lindo, Ind.	233

Lab. majority 1,499 (3.25%)
7.07% swing Lab. to C.

OLDHAM WEST & ROYTON
E. 73,063 T. 44,434 (60.82%)

Lab. Co-op hold

Jim McMahon, Lab. Co-op	24,579
Kirsty Finlayson, C.	13,452
Helen Formby, Brexit	3,316
Garth Harkness, LD	1,484
Dan Jerrome, Green	681
Debbie Cole, Oldham	533
Anthony Prince, UKIP	389

Lab. Co-op majority 11,127 (25.04%)
6.26% swing Lab. to C.

ORPINGTON
E. 68,884 T. 48,721 (70.73%) C. hold

Gareth Bacon, C.	30,882
Simon Jeal, Lab.	8,504
Allan Tweddle, LD	7,552
Karen Wheller, Green	1,783

C. majority 22,378 (45.93%)
3.68% swing Lab. to C.

OXFORD EAST
E. 77,947 T. 49,359 (63.32%)

Lab. Co-op hold

Anneliese Dodds, Lab. Co-op	28,135
Louise Staite, C.	10,303
Alistair Fernie, LD	6,884
David Williams, Green	2,392
Roger Carter, Brexit	1,146
David Henwood, Ind.	238
Chaka Artwell, Ind.	143
Phil Taylor, Ind.	118

Lab. Co-op majority 17,832 (36.13%)
3.54% swing Lab. to C.

OXFORD WEST & ABINGDON
E. 76,953 T. 58,824 (76.44%) LD hold

Layla Moran, LD	31,340
James Fredrickson, C.	22,397
Rosie Sourbut, Lab.	4,258
Allison Wild, Brexit	829

LD majority 8,943 (15.20%)
6.92% swing C. to LD

PENDLE
E. 65,289 T. 44,460 (68.10%) C. hold

Andrew Stephenson, C.	24,076
Azhar Ali, Lab.	17,890
Gordon Lishman, LD	1,548
Clare Hales, Green	678
John Richardson, Ind.	268

C. majority 6,186 (13.91%)
5.53% swing Lab. to C.

PENISTONE & STOCKSBRIDGE
E. 70,925 T. 49,520 (69.82%) C. gain

Miriam Cates, C.	23,688
Francyne Johnson, Lab.	16,478
Hannah Kitching, LD	5,054
John Booker, Brexit	4,300

C. majority 7,210 (14.56%)
8.61% swing Lab. to C.

PENRITH & THE BORDER
E. 67,555 T. 47,824 (70.79%) C. gain

Neil Hudson, C.	28,875
Sarah Williams, Lab. Co-op	10,356
Matt Severn, LD	5,364
Ali Ross, Green	2,159
Jonathan Davies, Cumbria	1,070

C. majority 18,519 (38.72%)
2.24% swing Lab. to C.

PETERBOROUGH
E. 72,560 T. 47,801 (65.88%) C. gain

Paul Bristow, C.	22,334
Lisa Forbes, Lab.	19,754
Beki Sellick, LD	2,334
Mike Greene, Brexit	2,127
Joseph Wells, Green	728
Luke Ferguson, Ind.	260
Tom Rogers, CPA	151
The Very Raving Mr P, Loony	113

C. majority 2,580 (5.40%)
3.33% swing Lab. to C.

PLYMOUTH MOOR VIEW
E. 69,430 T. 44,239 (63.72%) C. hold

Johnny Mercer, C.	26,831
Charlotte Holloway, Lab. Co-op	13,934
Sarah Martin, LD	2,301
Ewan Melling Flavell, Green	1,173

C. majority 12,897 (29.15%)
9.05% swing Lab. to C.

PLYMOUTH SUTTON & DEVONPORT
E. 77,852 T. 53,176 (68.30%)

Lab. Co-op hold

Luke Pollard, Lab. Co-op	25,461
Rebecca Smith, C.	20,704
Ann Widdecombe, Brexit	2,909
Graham Reed, LD	2,545
James Ellwood, Green	1,557

Lab. Co-op majority 4,757 (8.95%)
2.17% swing Lab. to C.

POOLE
E. 73,992 T. 50,451 (68.18%) C. hold

Robert Syms, C.	29,599
Sue Aitkenhead, Lab. Co-op	10,483
Victoria Collins, LD	7,819
Barry Harding-Rathbone, Green	1,702
David Young, Ind.	848

C. majority 19,116 (37.89%)
4.69% swing Lab. to C.

POPLAR & LIMEHOUSE
E. 91,760 T. 61,276 (66.78%) Lab. hold

Apsana Begum, Lab.	38,660
Sheun Oke, C.	9,756
Andrew Cregan, LD	8,832
Neil Jameson, Green	2,159
Catherine Cui, Brexit	1,493
Andy Erlam, Ind.	376

Lab. majority 28,904 (47.17%)
0.03% swing C. to Lab.

PORTSMOUTH NORTH
E. 71,299 T. 45,910 (64.39%) C. hold

Penny Mordaunt, C.	28,172
Amanda Martin, Lab.	12,392
Antonia Harrison, LD	3,419
Lloyd Day, Green	1,304
George Madgwick, ND	623

C. majority 15,780 (34.37%)
6.63% swing Lab. to C.

PORTSMOUTH SOUTH
E. 74,186 T. 47,425 (63.93%) Lab. hold

Stephen Morgan, Lab.	23,068
Donna Jones, C.	17,705
Gerald Vernon-Jackson, LD	5,418
John Kennedy, Brexit	994
Steven George, JACP	240

Lab. majority 5,363 (11.31%)
3.91% swing C. to Lab.

PRESTON
E. 59,672 T. 33,790 (56.63%)

Lab. Co-op hold

Mark Hendrick, Lab. Co-op	20,870
Michele Scott, C.	8,724
Rob Sherratt, Brexit	1,799
Neil Darby, LD	1,737
Michael Welton, Green	660

Lab. Co-op majority 12,146 (35.95%)
4.11% swing Lab. to C.

PUDSEY
E. 73,212 T. 54,215 (74.05%) C. hold

Stuart Andrew, C.	26,453
Jane Aitchison, Lab.	22,936
Ian Dowling, LD	3,088
Quinn Daley, Green	894
Bob Buxton, Yorkshire	844

C. majority 3,517 (6.49%)
2.94% swing Lab. to C.

PUTNEY
E. 65,542 T. 50,467 (77.00%) Lab. gain

Fleur Anderson, Lab.	22,780
Will Sweet, C.	18,006
Sue Wixley, LD	8,548
Fergal McEntee, Green	1,133

Lab. majority 4,774 (9.46%)
6.39% swing C. to Lab.

RAYLEIGH & WICKFORD
E. 78,959 T. 54,901 (69.53%) C. hold

Mark Francois, C.	39,864
David Flack, Lab.	8,864
Ron Tindall, LD	4,171
Paul Thorogood, Green	2,002

C. majority 31,000 (56.47%)
7.04% swing Lab. to C.

READING EAST
E. 77,465 T. 55,918 (72.18%) Lab. hold

Matt Rodda, Lab.	27,102
Craig Morley, C.	21,178
Imogen Shepherd-DuBey, LD	5,035
David McElroy, Green	1,549
Mitchell Feierstein, Brexit	852
Yemi Awolola, CPA	202

Lab. majority 5,924 (10.59%)
1.90% swing C. to Lab.

READING WEST
E. 74,623   T. 50,392 (67.53%)   C. hold
Alok Sharma, C.	24,393
Rachel Eden, Lab. Co-op	20,276
Meri O'Connell, LD	4,460
Jamie Whitham, Green	1,263

C. majority 4,117 (8.17%)
1.31% swing Lab. to C.

REDCAR
E. 65,855   T. 40,842 (62.02%)   C. gain
Jacob Young, C.	18,811
Anna Turley, Lab. Co-op	15,284
Jacqui Cummins, Brexit	2,915
Karen King, LD	2,018
Frankie Wales, Ind.	1,323
Rowan McLaughlin, Green	491

C. majority 3,527 (8.64%)
15.46% swing Lab. to C.

REDDITCH
E. 65,391   T. 44,067 (67.39%)   C. hold
Rachel Maclean, C.	27,907
Rebecca Jenkins, Lab.	11,871
Bruce Horton, LD	2,905
Claire Davies, Green	1,384

C. majority 16,036 (36.39%)
10.05% swing Lab. to C.

REIGATE
E. 74,842   T. 53,156 (71.02%)   C. hold
Crispin Blunt, C.	28,665
Susan Gregory, Lab.	10,355
John Vincent, LD	10,320
Jonathan Essex, Green	3,169
Julia Searle, UKIP	647

C. majority 18,310 (34.45%)
0.86% swing Lab. to C.

RIBBLE VALLEY
E. 79,247   T. 55,284 (69.76%)   C. hold
Nigel Evans, C.	33,346
Giles Bridge, Lab.	14,907
Chantelle Seddon, LD	4,776
Paul Yates, Green	1,704
Tony Johnson, Ind.	551

C. majority 18,439 (33.35%)
4.72% swing Lab. to C.

RICHMOND PARK
E. 82,696   T. 65,067 (78.68%)   LD gain
Sarah Olney, LD	34,559
Zac Goldsmith, C.	26,793
Sandra Keen, Lab.	3,407
Caroline Shah, Ind.	247
John Usher, Ind.	61

LD majority 7,766 (11.94%)
6.00% swing C. to LD

RICHMOND (YORKS)
E. 82,601   T. 57,703 (69.86%)   C. hold
Rishi Sunak, C.	36,693
Thom Kirkwood, Lab.	9,483
Philip Knowles, LD	6,989
John Yorke, Green	2,500
Laurence Waterhouse, Yorkshire	1,077
Nick Jardine, Ind.	961

C. majority 27,210 (47.16%)
3.31% swing Lab. to C.

ROCHDALE
E. 78,909   T. 47,447 (60.13%)   Lab. hold
Tony Lloyd, Lab.	24,475
Atifa Shah, C.	14,807
Chris Green, Brexit	3,867
Andy Kelly, LD	3,312
Sarah Croke, Green	986

Lab. majority 9,668 (20.38%)
4.62% swing Lab. to C.

ROCHESTER & STROOD
E. 82,056   T. 51,926 (63.28%)   C. hold
Kelly Tolhurst, C.	31,151
Teresa Murray, Lab.	14,079
Graham Colley, LD	3,717
Sonia Hyner, Green	1,312
Roy Freshwater, UKIP	1,080
Chris Spalding, Ind.	587

C. majority 17,072 (32.88%)
7.28% swing Lab. to C.

ROCHFORD & SOUTHEND EAST
E. 75,624   T. 46,136 (61.01%)   C. hold
James Duddridge, C.	27,063
Ashley Dalton, Lab.	14,777
Keith Miller, LD	2,822
Navin Kumar, Ind.	1,107
Jason Pilley, PFP	367

C. majority 12,286 (26.63%)
7.44% swing Lab. to C.

ROMFORD
E. 72,350   T. 47,231 (65.28%)   C. hold
Andrew Rosindell, C.	30,494
Angelina Leatherbarrow, Lab.	12,601
Ian Sanderson, LD	2,708
David Hughes, Green	1,428

C. majority 17,893 (37.88%)
5.15% swing Lab. to C.

ROMSEY & SOUTHAMPTON NORTH
E. 68,228   T. 51,390 (75.32%)   C. hold
Caroline Nokes, C.	27,862
Craig Fletcher, LD	16,990
Claire Ransom, Lab.	5,898
Geoff Bentley, UKIP	640

C. majority 10,872 (21.16%)
7.37% swing C. to LD

ROSSENDALE & DARWEN
E. 72,771   T. 48,822 (67.09%)   C. hold
Jake Berry, C.	27,570
Alyson Barnes, Lab.	18,048
Paul Valentine, LD	2,011
Sarah Hall, Green	1,193

C. majority 9,522 (19.50%)
6.55% swing Lab. to C.

ROTHER VALLEY
E. 74,802   T. 48,698 (65.10%)   C. gain
Alexander Stafford, C.	21,970
Sophie Wilson, Lab.	15,652
Allen Cowles, Brexit	6,264
Colin Taylor, LD	2,553
Emily West, Green	1,219
Nigel Short, Ind.	1,040

C. majority 6,318 (12.97%)
10.41% swing Lab. to C.

ROTHERHAM
E. 61,688   T. 35,651 (57.79%)   Lab. hold
Sarah Champion, Lab.	14,736
Gerri Hickton, C.	11,615
Paul Hague, Brexit	6,125
Adam Carter, LD	2,090
Dennis Bannan, Yorkshire	1,085

Lab. majority 3,121 (8.75%)
10.64% swing Lab. to C.

RUGBY
E. 72,340   T. 50,814 (70.24%)   C. hold
Mark Pawsey, C.	29,255
Debbie Bannigan, Lab.	15,808
Rana Das-Gupta, LD	4,207
Becca Stevenson, Green	1,544

C. majority 13,447 (26.46%)
5.23% swing Lab. to C.

RUISLIP, NORTHWOOD & PINNER
E. 73,191   T. 52,904 (72.28%)   C. hold
David Simmonds, C.	29,391
Peymana Assad, Lab.	12,997
Jonathan Banks, LD	7,986
Sarah Green, Green	1,646
Femy Amin, AWP	325
Tracy Blackwell, Ind.	295
Julian Wilson, Ind.	264

C. majority 16,394 (30.99%)
2.40% swing Lab. to C.

RUNNYMEDE & WEYBRIDGE
E. 77,196   T. 53,289 (69.03%)   C. gain
Ben Spencer, C.	29,262
Robert King, Lab.	10,992
Rob O'Carroll, LD	9,236
Benjamin Smith, Green	1,876
Stewart Mackay, Ind.	777
Lorna Rowland, Ind.	670
Nicholas Wood, UKIP	476

C. majority 18,270 (34.28%)
0.34% swing C. to Lab.

RUSHCLIFFE
E. 77,055   T. 60,505 (78.52%)   C. gain
Ruth Edwards, C.	28,765
Cheryl Pidgeon, Lab.	21,122
Jason Billin, LD	9,600
Matthew Faithfull, UKIP	591
John Kirby, Ind.	427

C. majority 7,643 (12.63%)
0.55% swing Lab. to C.

RUTLAND & MELTON
E. 82,711   T. 58,310 (70.50%)   C. hold
Alicia Kearns, C.	36,507
Andy Thomas, Lab.	9,583
Carol Weaver, LD	7,970
Alastair McQuillan, Green	2,875
Marietta King, UKIP	917
Anthony Watchorn, Ind.	458

C. majority 26,924 (46.17%)
3.02% swing Lab. to C.

SAFFRON WALDEN
E. 87,017   T. 63,086 (72.50%)   C. hold
Kemi Badenoch, C.	39,714
Mike Hibbs, LD	12,120
Thomas Van De Bilt, Lab.	8,305
Coby Wing, Green	2,947

C. majority 27,594 (43.74%)
2.02% swing C. to LD

SALFORD & ECCLES
E. 82,202 T. 50,632 (61.59%) Lab. hold
Rebecca Long-Bailey, Lab. 28,755
Attika Choudhary, C. 12,428
Matt Mickler, Brexit 4,290
Jake Overend, LD 3,099
Bryan Blears, Green 2,060
Lab. majority 16,327 (32.25%)
3.97% swing Lab. to C.

SALISBURY
E. 74,560 T. 53,730 (72.06%) C. hold
John Glen, C. 30,280
Victoria Charleston, LD 10,544
Tom Corbin, Lab. 9,675
Rick Page, Green 2,486
King Arthur Pendragon, Ind. 745
C. majority 19,736 (36.73%)
5.05% swing C. to LD

SCARBOROUGH & WHITBY
E. 74,393 T. 49,724 (66.84%) C. hold
Robert Goodwill, C. 27,593
Hugo Fearnley, Lab. 17,323
Robert Lockwood, LD 3,038
Lee Derrick, Yorkshire 1,770
C. majority 10,270 (20.65%)
6.92% swing Lab. to C.

SCUNTHORPE
E. 61,955 T. 37,750 (60.93%) C. gain
Holly Mumby-Croft, C. 20,306
Nic Dakin, Lab. 13,855
Jerry Gorman, Brexit 2,044
Ryk Downes, LD 875
Peter Dennington, Green 670
C. majority 6,451 (17.09%)
12.81% swing Lab. to C.

SEDGEFIELD
E. 64,325 T. 41,566 (64.62%) C. gain
Paul Howell, C. 19,609
Phil Wilson, Lab. 15,096
David Bull, Brexit 3,518
Dawn Welsh, LD 1,955
John Furness, Green 994
Michael Joyce, Ind. 394
C. majority 4,513 (10.86%)
12.71% swing Lab. to C.

SEFTON CENTRAL
E. 69,760 T. 50,880 (72.94%) Lab. hold
Bill Esterson, Lab. 29,254
Wazz Mughal, C. 14,132
Keith Cawdron, LD 3,386
Paul Lomas, Brexit 2,425
Alison Gibbon, Green 1,261
Angela Preston, Lib 285
Carla Burns, Renew 137
Lab. majority 15,122 (29.72%)
0.13% swing Lab. to C.

SELBY & AINSTY
E. 78,715 T. 56,418 (71.67%) C. hold
Nigel Adams, C. 33,995
Malik Rofidi, Lab. 13,858
Katharine Macy, LD 4,842
Mike Jordan, Yorkshire 1,900
Arnold Warneken, Green 1,823
C. majority 20,137 (35.69%)
5.57% swing Lab. to C.

SEVENOAKS
E. 71,777 T. 50,956 (70.99%) C. hold
Laura Trott, C. 30,932
Gareth Willis, LD 10,114
Seamus McCauley, Lab. 6,946
Paul Wharton, Green 1,974
Paulette Furse, Ind. 695
Sean Finch, Libertarian 295
C. majority 20,818 (40.85%)
7.26% swing C. to LD

SHEFFIELD BRIGHTSIDE &
HILLSBOROUGH
E. 69,333 T. 39,600 (57.12%) Lab. hold
Gill Furniss, Lab. 22,369
Hannah Westropp, C. 10,095
Johnny Johnson, Brexit 3,855
Stephen Porter, LD 1,517
Christine Gilligan Kubo, Green 1,179
Shane Harper, UKIP 585
Lab. majority 12,274 (30.99%)
7.36% swing Lab. to C.

SHEFFIELD CENTRAL
E. 89,849 T. 50,913 (56.67%) Lab. hold
Paul Blomfield, Lab. 33,968
Janice Silvester-Hall, C. 6,695
Alison Teal, Green 4,570
Colin Ross, LD 3,237
Paul Ward, Brexit 1,969
Jack Carrington, Yorkshire 416
Barry James, Ind. 30
Chris Marsden, Soc Eq 28
Lab. majority 27,273 (53.57%)
2.19% swing Lab. to C.

SHEFFIELD HALLAM
E. 72,763 T. 56,885 (78.18%) Lab. gain
Olivia Blake, Lab. 19,709
Laura Gordon, LD 18,997
Ian Walker, C. 14,696
Natalie Thomas, Green 1,630
Terence McHale, Brexit 1,562
Michael Virgo, UKIP 168
Elizabeth Aspden, Ind. 123
Lab. majority 712 (1.25%)
1.24% swing Lab. to LD

SHEFFIELD HEELEY
E. 66,940 T. 42,695 (63.78%) Lab. hold
Louise Haigh, Lab. 21,475
Gordon Gregory, C. 12,955
Tracy Knowles, Brexit 3,538
Simon Clement-Jones, LD 2,916
Paul Turpin, Green 1,811
Lab. majority 8,520 (19.96%)
5.66% swing Lab. to C.

SHEFFIELD SOUTH EAST
E. 67,832 T. 41,998 (61.91%) Lab. hold
Clive Betts, Lab. 19,359
Marc Bayliss, C. 15,070
Kirk Kus, Brexit 4,478
Rajin Chowdhury, LD 2,125
Alex Martin, Yorkshire 966
Lab. majority 4,289 (10.21%)
8.42% swing Lab. to C.

SHERWOOD
E. 77,948 T. 52,709 (67.62%) C. hold
Mark Spencer, C. 32,049
Jerry Hague, Lab. 15,863
Timothy Ball, LD 2,883
Esther Cropper, Green 1,214
Simon Rood, Ind. 700
C. majority 16,186 (30.71%)
10.48% swing Lab. to C.

SHIPLEY
E. 74,029 T. 54,004 (72.95%) C. hold
Philip Davies, C. 27,437
Jo Pike, Lab. 21,195
Caroline Jones, LD 3,188
Celia Hickson, Green 1,301
Darren Longhorn, Yorkshire 883
C. majority 6,242 (11.56%)
1.40% swing Lab. to C.

SHREWSBURY & ATCHAM
E. 82,237 T. 59,065 (71.82%) C. hold
Daniel Kawczynski, C. 31,021
Julia Buckley, Lab. 19,804
Nat Green, LD 5,906
Julian Dean, Green 1,762
Hannah Locke, Ind. 572
C. majority 11,217 (18.99%)
3.80% swing Lab. to C.

SHROPSHIRE NORTH
E. 83,257 T. 56,513 (67.88%) C. hold
Owen Paterson, C. 35,444
Graeme Currie, Lab. 12,495
Helen Morgan, LD 5,643
John Adams, Green 1,790
Robert Jones, Salop 1,141
C. majority 22,949 (40.61%)
5.60% swing Lab. to C.

SITTINGBOURNE & SHEPPEY
E. 83,917 T. 51,394 (61.24%) C. hold
Gordon Henderson, C. 34,742
Clive Johnson, Lab. 10,263
Ben Martin, LD 3,213
Monique Bonney, Ind. 1,257
Sam Collins, Green 1,188
Mad Mike Young, Loony 404
Lee McCall, Ind. 327
C. majority 24,479 (47.63%)
9.02% swing Lab. to C.

SKIPTON & RIPON
E. 78,673 T. 58,724 (74.64%) C. hold
Julian Smith, C. 34,919
Brian McDaid, Lab. 11,225
Andrew Murday, LD 8,701
Andy Brown, Green 2,748
Jack Render, Yorkshire 1,131
C. majority 23,694 (40.35%)
2.99% swing Lab. to C.

SLEAFORD & NORTH HYKEHAM
E. 94,761 T. 66,554 (70.23%) C. hold
Caroline Johnson, C. 44,683
Linda Edwards-Shea, Lab. 12,118
Oliver Craven, LD 5,355
Marianne Overton, Lincs 1,999
Simon Tooke, Green 1,742
Caroline Coram, Ind. 657
C. majority 32,565 (48.93%)
5.29% swing Lab. to C.

SLOUGH
E. 87,632   T. 51,038 (58.24%)   Lab. hold
Tan Dhesi, Lab.   29,421
Kanwal Toor Gill, C.   15,781
Aaron Chahal, LD   3,357
Delphine Gray-Fisk, Brexit   1,432
Julian Edmonds, Green   1,047
Lab. majority 13,640 (26.73%)
2.29% swing Lab. to C.

SOLIHULL
E. 78,760   T. 55,344 (70.27%)   C. hold
Julian Knight, C.   32,309
Nick Stephens, Lab. Co-op   11,036
Ade Adeyemo, LD   9,977
Rosemary Sexton, Green   2,022
C. majority 21,273 (38.44%)
1.09% swing Lab. to C.

SOMERSET NORTH
E. 80,194   T. 62,055 (77.38%)   C. hold
Liam Fox, C.   32,801
Hannah Young, Lab.   15,265
Ashley Cartman, LD   11,051
Phil Neve, Green   2,938
C. majority 17,536 (28.26%)
0.34% swing Lab. to C.

SOMERSET NORTH EAST
E. 73,665   T. 56,308 (76.44%)   C. hold
Jacob Rees-Mogg, C.   28,360
Mark Huband, Lab.   13,631
Nick Coates, LD   12,422
Fay Whitfield, Green   1,423
Shaun Hughes, Ind.   472
C. majority 14,729 (26.16%)
3.61% swing Lab. to C.

SOMERTON & FROME
E. 85,866   T. 64,896 (75.58%)   C. hold
David Warburton, C.   36,230
Adam Boyden, LD   17,017
Sean Dromgoole, Lab.   8,354
Andrea Dexter, Green   3,295
C. majority 19,213 (29.61%)
3.21% swing C. to LD

SOUTH HOLLAND & THE DEEPINGS
E. 75,990   T. 49,179 (64.72%)   C. hold
John Hayes, C.   37,338
Mark Popple, Lab.   6,500
Davina Kirby, LD   3,225
Martin Blake, Green   1,613
Rick Stringer, Ind.   503
C. majority 30,838 (62.71%)
6.61% swing Lab. to C.

SOUTH RIBBLE
E. 75,344   T. 53,784 (71.38%)   C. hold
Katherine Fletcher, C.   30,028
Kim Snape, Lab.   18,829
Jo Barton, LD   3,720
Andy Fewings, Green   1,207
C. majority 11,199 (20.82%)
3.64% swing Lab. to C.

SOUTH SHIELDS
E. 62,793   T. 37,882 (60.33%)   Lab. hold
Emma Lewell-Buck, Lab.   17,273
Oni Oviri, C.   7,688
Glenn Thompson, Brexit   6,446
Geoff Thompson, Ind.   3,658
William Shepherd, LD   1,514
Sarah McKeown, Green   1,303
Lab. majority 9,585 (25.30%)
5.14% swing Lab. to C.

SOUTHAMPTON ITCHEN
E. 72,293   T. 47,421 (65.60%)   C. hold
Royston Smith, C.   23,952
Simon Letts, Lab.   19,454
Liz Jarvis, LD   2,503
Osman Sen-Chadun, Green   1,040
Kim Rose, UKIP   472
C. majority 4,498 (9.49%)
4.71% swing Lab. to C.

SOUTHAMPTON TEST
E. 70,113   T. 44,994 (64.17%)   Lab. hold
Alan Whitehead, Lab.   22,256
Steven Galton, C.   16,043
Joe Richards, LD   3,449
Philip Crook, Brexit   1,591
Katherine Barbour, Green   1,433
Kev Barry, ND   222
Lab. majority 6,213 (13.81%)
5.36% swing Lab. to C.

SOUTHEND WEST
E. 69,043   T. 46,537 (67.40%)   C. hold
David Amess, C.   27,555
Aston Line, Lab.   13,096
Nina Stimson, LD   5,312
Seventy-seven Joseph, Ind.   574
C. majority 14,459 (31.07%)
4.94% swing Lab. to C.

SOUTHPORT
E. 70,837   T. 48,180 (68.02%)   C. hold
Damien Moore, C.   22,914
Liz Savage, Lab.   18,767
John Wright, LD   6,499
C. majority 4,147 (8.61%)
1.27% swing Lab. to C.

SPELTHORNE
E. 70,929   T. 49,510 (69.80%)   C. hold
Kwasi Kwarteng, C.   29,141
Pavitar Mann, Lab.   10,748
David Campanale, LD   7,499
Paul Jacobs, Green   2,122
C. majority 18,393 (37.15%)
5.18% swing Lab. to C.

ST ALBANS
E. 73,721   T. 57,599 (78.13%)   LD gain
Daisy Cooper, LD   28,867
Anne Main, C.   22,574
Rebecca Lury, Lab.   5,000
Simon Grover, Green   1,004
Jules Sherrington, ND   154
LD majority 6,293 (10.93%)
10.82% swing C. to LD

ST AUSTELL & NEWQUAY
E. 79,930   T. 55,776 (69.78%)   C. hold
Steve Double, C.   31,273
Felicity Owen, Lab.   14,747
Tim Styles, LD   5,861
Dick Cole, Kernow   1,660
Collin Harker, Green   1,609
Richard Byrne, Lib   626
C. majority 16,526 (29.63%)
4.54% swing Lab. to C.

ST HELENS NORTH
E. 75,593   T. 47,561 (62.92%)   Lab. hold
Conor McGinn, Lab.   24,870
Joel Charles, C.   12,661
Malcolm Webster, Brexit   5,396
Pat Moloney, LD   2,668
David Van Der Burg, Green   1,966
Lab. majority 12,209 (25.67%)
5.49% swing Lab. to C.

ST HELENS SOUTH & WHISTON
E. 79,058   T. 50,313 (63.64%)   Lab. hold
Marie Rimmer, Lab.   29,457
Richard Short, C.   10,335
Daniel Oxley, Brexit   5,353
Brian Spencer, LD   2,886
Kai Taylor, Green   2,282
Lab. majority 19,122 (38.01%)
4.01% swing Lab. to C.

ST IVES
E. 68,795   T. 51,399 (74.71%)   C. hold
Derek Thomas, C.   25,365
Andrew George, LD   21,081
Alana Bates, Lab.   3,553
Ian Flindall, Green   954
Robert Smith, Lib   314
John Harris, People   132
C. majority 4,284 (8.33%)
3.86% swing LD to C.

STAFFORD
E. 72,572   T. 51,149 (70.48%)   C. hold
Theo Clarke, C.   29,992
Joyce Still, Lab.   15,615
Alex Wagner, LD   3,175
Emma Carter, Green   2,367
C. majority 14,377 (28.11%)
6.61% swing Lab. to C.

STAFFORDSHIRE MOORLANDS
E. 65,485   T. 43,656 (66.67%)   C. hold
Karen Bradley, C.   28,192
Darren Price, Lab.   11,764
Andrew Gant, LD   2,469
Douglas Rouxel, Green   1,231
C. majority 16,428 (37.63%)
6.69% swing Lab. to C.

STAFFORDSHIRE SOUTH
E. 73,692   T. 50,005 (67.86%)   C. hold
Gavin Williamson, C.   36,520
Adam Freeman, Lab.   8,270
Chris Fewtrell, LD   3,280
Claire McIlvenna, Green   1,935
C. majority 28,250 (56.49%)
6.01% swing Lab. to C.

STALYBRIDGE & HYDE
E. 73,873   T. 42,368 (57.35%)

Lab. Co-op hold

Jonathan Reynolds, Lab. Co-op	19,025
Tayub Amjad, C.	16,079
Julian Newton, Brexit	3,591
Jamie Dwan, LD	1,827
Julie Wood, Green	1,411
John Edge, Lib	435

Lab. Co-op majority 2,946 (6.95%)
6.04% swing Lab. to C.

STEVENAGE
E. 71,562   T. 47,683 (66.63%)   C. hold

Stephen McPartland, C.	25,328
Jill Borchers, Lab.	16,766
Lisa Nash, LD	4,132
Victoria Snelling, Green	1,457

C. majority 8,562 (17.96%)
5.55% swing Lab. to C.

STOCKPORT
E. 65,457   T. 41,715 (63.73%)   Lab. gain

Navendu Mishra, Lab.	21,695
Isy Imarni, C.	11,656
Wendy Meikle, LD	5,043
Lee Montague-Trenchard, Brexit	1,918
Helena Mellish, Green	1,403

Lab. majority 10,039 (24.07%)
5.39% swing Lab. to C.

STOCKTON NORTH
E. 66,676   T. 41,156 (61.73%)   Lab. hold

Alex Cunningham, Lab.	17,728
Steven Jackson, C.	16,701
Martin Walker, Brexit	3,907
Aidan King, LD	1,631
Mark Burdon, NE Party	1,189

Lab. majority 1,027 (2.50%)
8.95% swing Lab. to C.

STOCKTON SOUTH
E. 76,895   T. 54,802 (71.27%)   C. gain

Matt Vickers, C.	27,764
Paul Williams, Lab.	22,504
Brendan Devlin, LD	2,338
John Prescott, Brexit	2,196

C. majority 5,260 (9.60%)
5.62% swing Lab. to C.

STOKE-ON-TRENT CENTRAL
E. 55,424   T. 32,070 (57.86%)   C. gain

Jo Gideon, C.	14,557
Gareth Snell, Lab. Co-op	13,887
Tariq Mahmood, Brexit	1,691
Steven Pritchard, LD	1,116
Adam Colclough, Green	819

C. majority 670 (2.09%)
6.92% swing Lab. to C.

STOKE-ON-TRENT NORTH
E. 84,357   T. 40,134 (47.58%)   C. gain

Jonathan Gullis, C.	20,974
Ruth Smeeth, Lab.	14,688
Richard Watkin, Brexit	2,374
Peter Andras, LD	1,268
Alan Borgars, Green	508
Matt Dilworth, Ind.	322

C. majority 6,286 (15.66%)
10.65% swing Lab. to C.

STOKE-ON-TRENT SOUTH
E. 64,499   T. 39,604 (61.40%)   C. hold

Jack Brereton, C.	24,632
Mark McDonald, Lab.	13,361
Rosalyn Gordon, LD	1,611

C. majority 11,271 (28.46%)
13.43% swing Lab. to C.

STONE
E. 69,378   T. 49,843 (71.84%)   C. hold

Bill Cash, C.	31,687
Mike Stubbs, Lab.	11,742
Alec Sandiford, LD	4,412
Tom Adamson, Green	2,002

C. majority 19,945 (40.02%)
2.52% swing Lab. to C.

STOURBRIDGE
E. 69,891   T. 45,689 (65.37%)   C. hold

Suzanne Webb, C.	27,534
Pete Lowe, Lab.	13,963
Chris Bramall, LD	2,523
Andi Mohr, Green	1,048
Aaron Hudson, Ind.	621

C. majority 13,571 (29.70%)
6.73% swing Lab. to C.

STRATFORD-ON-AVON
E. 74,038   T. 55,048 (74.35%)   C. hold

Nadhim Zahawi, C.	33,343
Dominic Skinner, LD	13,371
Felix Ling, Lab.	6,222
Dave Passingham, Green	2,112

C. majority 19,972 (36.28%)
6.89% swing C. to LD

STREATHAM
E. 84,788   T. 56,513 (66.65%)   Lab. gain

Bell Ribeiro-Addy, Lab.	30,976
Helen Thompson, LD	13,286
Rory O'Broin, C.	9,060
Scott Ainslie, Green	2,567
Penelope Becker, Brexit	624

Lab. majority 17,690 (31.30%)
15.36% swing Lab. to LD

STRETFORD & URMSTON
E. 72,356   T. 50,067 (69.20%)   Lab. hold

Kate Green, Lab.	30,195
Mussadak Mirza, C.	13,778
Anna Fryer, LD	2,969
Gary Powell, Brexit	1,768
Jane Leicester, Green	1,357

Lab. majority 16,417 (32.79%)
3.23% swing Lab. to C.

STROUD
E. 84,534   T. 65,930 (77.99%)   C. gain

Siobhan Baillie, C.	31,582
David Drew, Lab. Co-op	27,742
Molly Scott Cato, Green	4,954
Desi Latimer, Brexit	1,085
Glenville Gogerly, Libertarian	567

C. majority 3,840 (5.82%)
3.45% swing Lab. to C.

SUFFOLK CENTRAL & IPSWICH NORTH
E. 76,201   T. 56,250 (73.82%)   C. hold

Dan Poulter, C.	35,253
Emma Bonner-Morgan, Lab.	11,862
James Sandbach, LD	6,485
Daniel Pratt, Green	2,650

C. majority 23,391 (41.58%)
5.59% swing Lab. to C.

SUFFOLK COASTAL
E. 81,910   T. 58,308 (71.19%)   C. hold

Therese Coffey, C.	32,958
Cameron Matthews, Lab.	12,425
Jules Ewart, LD	8,719
Rachel Smith-Lyte, Green	2,713
Tony Love, Ind.	1,493

C. majority 20,533 (35.21%)
3.82% swing Lab. to C.

SUFFOLK SOUTH
E. 76,201   T. 53,495 (70.20%)   C. hold

James Cartlidge, C.	33,276
Elizabeth Hughes, Lab.	10,373
David Beavan, LD	6,702
Robert Lindsay, Green	3,144

C. majority 22,903 (42.81%)
5.04% swing Lab. to C.

SUFFOLK WEST
E. 80,192   T. 51,437 (64.14%)   C. hold

Matt Hancock, C.	33,842
Claire Unwin, Lab.	10,648
Elfreda Tealby-Watson, LD	4,685
Donald Allwright, Green	2,262

C. majority 23,194 (45.09%)
6.06% swing Lab. to C.

SUNDERLAND CENTRAL
E. 72,677   T. 43,476 (59.82%)   Lab. hold

Julie Elliott, Lab.	18,336
Tom D'Silva, C.	15,372
Viral Parikh, Brexit	5,047
Niall Hodson, LD	3,025
Rachel Featherstone, Green	1,212
Dale Mckenzie, Ind.	484

Lab. majority 2,964 (6.82%)
7.67% swing Lab. to C.

SURREY EAST
E. 83,148   T. 59,690 (71.79%)   C. gain

Claire Coutinho, C.	35,624
Alex Ehmann, LD	11,584
Frances Rehal, Lab.	8,247
Joseph Booton, Green	2,340
Helena Windsor, Ind.	1,374
Martin Hogbin, Loony	521

C. majority 24,040 (40.27%)
4.45% swing C. to LD

SURREY HEATH
E. 81,349   T. 58,654 (72.10%)   C. hold

Michael Gove, C.	34,358
Alasdair Pinkerton, LD	16,009
Brahma Mohanty, Lab.	5,407
Sharon Galliford, Green	2,252
David Roe, UKIP	628

C. majority 18,349 (31.28%)
11.03% swing C. to LD

SURREY SOUTH WEST
E. 79,129   T. 60,340 (76.26%)   C. hold
Jeremy Hunt, C.   32,191
Paul Follows, LD   23,374
Tim Corry, Lab.   4,775
C. majority 8,817 (14.61%)
15.63% swing C. to LD

SUSSEX MID
E. 85,141   T. 62,762 (73.72%)   C. hold
Mims Davies, C.   33,455
Robert Eggleston, LD   15,258
Gemma Bolton, Lab.   11,218
Deanna Nicholson, Green   2,234
Baron von Thunderclap,   550
Loony
Brett Mortensen, Advance   47
C. majority 18,197 (28.99%)
7.59% swing C. to LD

SUTTON & CHEAM
E. 71,760   T. 50,487 (70.36%)   C. hold
Paul Scully, C.   25,235
Hina Bokhari, LD   16,884
Bonnie Craven, Lab.   7,200
Claire Jackson-Prior, Green   1,168
C. majority 8,351 (16.54%)
3.95% swing C. to LD

SUTTON COLDFIELD
E. 75,638   T. 52,325 (69.18%)   C. hold
Andrew Mitchell, C.   31,604
David Knowles, Lab.   12,332
Jenny Wilkinson, LD   6,358
Ben Auton, Green   2,031
C. majority 19,272 (36.83%)
3.91% swing Lab. to C.

SWINDON NORTH
E. 82,441   T. 55,115 (66.85%)   C. hold
Justin Tomlinson, C.   32,584
Kate Linnegar, Lab.   16,413
Katie Critchlow, LD   4,408
Andy Bentley, Green   1,710
C. majority 16,171 (29.34%)
7.08% swing Lab. to C.

SWINDON SOUTH
E. 73,118   T. 50,746 (69.40%)   C. hold
Robert Buckland, C.   26,536
Sarah Church, Lab. Co-op   19,911
Stan Pajak, LD   4,299
C. majority 6,625 (13.06%)
4.12% swing Lab. to C.

TAMWORTH
E. 71,580   T. 46,056 (64.34%)   C. hold
Christopher Pincher, C.   30,542
Christopher Bain, Lab. Co-op   10,908
op
Rob Wheway, LD   2,426
Andrew Tilley, Green   935
Robert Bilcliff, UKIP   814
John Wright, Ind.   431
C. majority 19,634 (42.63%)
8.21% swing Lab. to C.

TATTON
E. 69,018   T. 48,967 (70.95%)   C. hold
Esther McVey, C.   28,277
James Weinberg, Lab.   10,890
Jonathan Smith, LD   7,712
Nigel Hennerley, Green   2,088
C. majority 17,387 (35.51%)
2.70% swing Lab. to C.

TAUNTON DEANE
E. 88,675   T. 63,733 (71.87%)   C. hold
Rebecca Pow, C.   34,164
Gideon Amos, LD   22,464
Liam Canham, Lab.   4,715
John Hunt, Ind.   2,390
C. majority 11,700 (18.36%)
3.42% swing C. to LD

TELFORD
E. 68,921   T. 42,825 (62.14%)   C. hold
Lucy Allan, C.   25,546
Katrina Gilman, Lab.   14,605
Shana Roberts, LD   2,674
C. majority 10,941 (25.55%)
11.97% swing Lab. to C.

TEWKESBURY
E. 83,958   T. 61,140 (72.82%)   C. hold
Laurence Robertson, C.   35,728
Alex Hegenbarth, LD   13,318
Lara Chaplin, Lab.   9,310
Cate Cody, Green   2,784
C. majority 22,410 (36.65%)
4.92% swing C. to LD

THANET NORTH
E. 72,811   T. 48,178 (66.17%)   C. hold
Roger Gale, C.   30,066
Coral Jones, Lab.   12,877
Angie Curwen, LD   3,439
Rob Edwards, Green   1,796
C. majority 17,189 (35.68%)
6.73% swing Lab. to C.

THANET SOUTH
E. 73,302   T. 48,257 (65.83%)   C. hold
Craig Mackinlay, C.   27,084
Rebecca Gordon-Nesbitt,   16,497
Lab.
Martyn Pennington, LD   2,727
Becky Wing, Green   1,949
C. majority 10,587 (21.94%)
4.55% swing Lab. to C.

THIRSK & MALTON
E. 80,979   T. 56,588 (69.88%)   C. hold
Kevin Hollinrake, C.   35,634
David Yellen, Lab.   10,480
Dinah Keal, LD   6,774
Martin Brampton, Green   2,263
John Hall, Yorkshire   881
Steve Mullins, Ind.   245
Gordon Johnson, ND   184
Michael Taylor, Soc Dem   127
C. majority 25,154 (44.45%)
5.24% swing Lab. to C.

THORNBURY & YATE
E. 69,492   T. 52,243 (75.18%)   C. hold
Luke Hall, C.   30,202
Claire Young, LD   17,833
Rob Logan, Lab.   4,208
C. majority 12,369 (23.68%)
0.07% swing C. to LD

THURROCK
E. 79,655   T. 47,467 (59.59%)   C. hold
Jackie Doyle-Price, C.   27,795
John Kent, Lab.   16,313
Stewart Stone, LD   1,510
James Woollard, Ind.   1,042
Ben Harvey, Green   807
C. majority 11,482 (24.19%)
11.75% swing Lab. to C.

TIVERTON & HONITON
E. 82,953   T. 59,613 (71.86%)   C. hold
Neil Parish, C.   35,893
Liz Pole, Lab.   11,654
John Timperley, LD   8,807
Colin Reed, Green   2,291
Margaret Dennis, UKIP   968
C. majority 24,239 (40.66%)
3.21% swing Lab. to C.

TONBRIDGE & MALLING
E. 77,380   T. 57,003 (73.67%)   C. hold
Tom Tugendhat, C.   35,784
Richard Morris, LD   8,843
Dylan Jones, Lab.   8,286
April Clark, Green   4,090
C. majority 26,941 (47.26%)
4.86% swing C. to LD

TOOTING
E. 76,933   T. 58,473 (76.01%)   Lab. hold
Rosena Allin-Khan, Lab.   30,811
Kerry Briscoe, C.   16,504
Olly Glover, LD   8,305
Glyn Goodwin, Green   2,314
Adam Shakir, Brexit   462
Roz Hubley, Soc Dem   77
Lab. majority 14,307 (24.47%)
1.05% swing Lab. to C.

TORBAY
E. 75,054   T. 50,426 (67.19%)   C. hold
Kevin Foster, C.   29,863
Lee Howgate, LD   12,114
Michele Middleditch, Lab.   6,562
Sam Moss, Green   1,239
James Channer, Ind.   648
C. majority 17,749 (35.20%)
3.64% swing LD to C.

TOTNES
E. 69,863   T. 52,182 (74.69%)   C. gain
Anthony Mangnall, C.   27,751
Sarah Wollaston, LD   15,027
Louise Webberley, Lab.   8,860
John Kitson, ND   544
C. majority 12,724 (24.38%)
8.20% swing C. to LD

TOTTENHAM
E. 75,740   T. 46,856 (61.86%)   Lab. hold
David Lammy, Lab. — 35,621
James Newhall, C. — 5,446
Tammy Palmer, LD — 3,168
Emma Chan, Green — 1,873
Abdul Turay, Brexit — 527
Andrew Bence, Soc Dem — 91
Frank Sweeney, WRP — 88
Jonathan Silberman, Comm Lge — 42
Lab. majority 30,175 (64.40%)
2.85% swing Lab. to C.

TRURO & FALMOUTH
E. 76,719   T. 59,190 (77.15%)   C. hold
Cherilyn Mackrory, C. — 27,237
Jennifer Forbes, Lab. — 22,676
Ruth Gripper, LD — 7,150
Tom Scott, Green — 1,714
Paul Nicholson, Lib — 413
C. majority 4,561 (7.71%)
0.51% swing Lab. to C.

TUNBRIDGE WELLS
E. 74,816   T. 54,650 (73.05%)   C. hold
Greg Clark, C. — 30,119
Ben Chapelard, LD — 15,474
Antonio Weiss, Lab. — 8,098
Christopher Camp, Ind. — 488
Nigel Peacock, Ind. — 471
C. majority 14,645 (26.80%)
10.12% swing C. to LD

TWICKENHAM
E. 84,901   T. 64,503 (75.97%)   LD hold
Munira Wilson, LD — 36,166
Isobel Grant, C. — 22,045
Ranjeev Walia, Lab. — 5,476
Stuart Wells, Brexit — 816
LD majority 14,121 (21.89%)
3.58% swing C. to LD

TYNEMOUTH
E. 77,261   T. 56,034 (72.53%)   Lab. hold
Alan Campbell, Lab. — 26,928
Lewis Bartoli, C. — 22,071
John Appleby, LD — 3,791
Ed Punchard, Brexit — 1,963
Julia Erskine, Green — 1,281
Lab. majority 4,857 (8.67%)
5.92% swing Lab. to C.

TYNESIDE NORTH
E. 78,902   T. 50,429 (63.91%)   Lab. hold
Mary Glindon, Lab. — 25,051
Dean Carroll, C. — 15,490
Andrew Husband, Brexit — 5,254
Chris Boyle, LD — 3,241
John Buttery, Green — 1,393
Lab. majority 9,561 (18.96%)
9.10% swing Lab. to C.

UXBRIDGE & RUISLIP SOUTH
E. 70,369   T. 48,187 (68.48%)   C. hold
Boris Johnson, C. — 25,351
Ali Milani, Lab. — 18,141
Joanne Humphreys, LD — 3,026
Mark Keir, Green — 1,090
Geoffrey Courtenay, UKIP — 283
Lord Buckethead, Loony — 125
Count Binface, Ind. — 69
Alfie Utting, Ind. — 44
Yace Yogenstein, ND — 23
Norma Burke, Ind. — 22
Bobby Smith, ND — 8
William Tobin, ND — 5
C. majority 7,210 (14.96%)
2.09% swing Lab. to C.

VAUXHALL
E. 88,647   T. 56,333 (63.55%)   Lab. Co-op hold
Florence Eshalomi, Lab. Co-op — 31,615
Sarah Lewis, LD — 12,003
Sarah Bool, C. — 9,422
Jacqueline Bond, Green — 2,516
Andrew McGuinness, Brexit — 641
Salah Faissal, Ind. — 136
Lab. Co-op majority 19,612 (34.81%)
0.99% swing Lab. to LD

WAKEFIELD
E. 70,192   T. 45,027 (64.15%)   C. gain
Imran Ahmad-Khan, C. — 21,283
Mary Creagh, Lab. — 17,925
Peter Wiltshire, Brexit — 2,725
Jamie Needle, LD — 1,772
Ryan Kett, Yorkshire — 868
Stephen Whyte, Ind. — 454
C. majority 3,358 (7.46%)
6.08% swing Lab. to C.

WALLASEY
E. 66,310   T. 46,492 (70.11%)   Lab. hold
Angela Eagle, Lab. — 29,901
James Baker, C. — 11,579
Martin York, Brexit — 2,037
Vicky Downie, LD — 1,843
Lily Clough, Green — 1,132
Lab. majority 18,322 (39.41%)
4.41% swing Lab. to C.

WALSALL NORTH
E. 67,177   T. 36,556 (54.42%)   C. hold
Eddie Hughes, C. — 23,334
Gill Ogilvie, Lab. — 11,369
Jennifer Gray, LD — 1,236
Mark Wilson, Green — 617
C. majority 11,965 (32.73%)
12.95% swing Lab. to C.

WALSALL SOUTH
E. 68,024   T. 42,472 (62.44%)   Lab. hold
Valerie Vaz, Lab. — 20,872
Gurjit Bains, C. — 17,416
Gary Hughes, Brexit — 1,660
Paul Harris, LD — 1,602
John Macefield, Green — 634
Akheil Mehboob, Ind. — 288
Lab. majority 3,456 (8.14%)
6.02% swing Lab. to C.

WALTHAMSTOW
E. 70,268   T. 48,335 (68.79%)   Lab. Co-op hold
Stella Creasy, Lab. Co-op — 36,784
Shade Adoh, C. — 5,922
Meera Chadha, LD — 2,874
Andrew Johns, Green — 1,733
Paul Campbell, Brexit — 768
Deborah Longe, CPA — 254
Lab. Co-op majority 30,862 (63.85%)
1.33% swing Lab. to C.

WANSBECK
E. 63,339   T. 40,509 (63.96%)   Lab. hold
Ian Lavery, Lab. — 17,124
Jack Gebhard, C. — 16,310
Eden Webley, Brexit — 3,141
Stephen Psallidas, LD — 2,539
Steve Leyland, Green — 1,217
Michael Flynn, CPA — 178
Lab. majority 814 (2.01%)
11.29% swing Lab. to C.

WANTAGE
E. 90,875   T. 67,173 (73.92%)   C. hold
David Johnston, C. — 34,085
Richard Benwell, LD — 21,432
Jonny Roberts, Lab. — 10,181
Mark Gray, Ind. — 1,475
C. majority 12,653 (18.84%)
10.41% swing C. to LD

WARLEY
E. 62,421   T. 37,239 (59.66%)   Lab. hold
John Spellar, Lab. — 21,901
Chandra Kanneganti, C. — 10,390
Michael Cooper, Brexit — 2,469
Bryan Manley-Green, LD — 1,588
Kathryn Downs, Green — 891
Lab. majority 11,511 (30.91%)
5.04% swing Lab. to C.

WARRINGTON NORTH
E. 72,235   T. 46,667 (64.60%)   Lab. hold
Charlotte Nichols, Lab. — 20,611
Wendy Maisey, C. — 19,102
David Crowther, LD — 3,071
Elizabeth Babade, Brexit — 2,626
Lyndsay McAteer, Green — 1,257
Lab. majority 1,509 (3.23%)
8.26% swing Lab. to C.

WARRINGTON SOUTH
E. 86,015   T. 61,899 (71.96%)   C. gain
Andy Carter, C. — 28,187
Faisal Rashid, Lab. — 26,177
Ryan Bate, LD — 5,732
Clare Aspinall, Brexit — 1,635
Kevin Hickson, Soc Dem — 168
C. majority 2,010 (3.25%)
3.68% swing Lab. to C.

WARWICK & LEAMINGTON
E. 76,373 T. 54,205 (70.97%) Lab. hold
Matt Western, Lab.   23,718
Jack Rankin, C.   22,929
Louis Adam, LD   4,995
Jonathan Chilvers, Green   1,536
Tim Griffiths, Brexit   807
Bob Dhillon, Ind.   153
Xander Bennett, Soc Dem   67
Lab. majority 789 (1.46%)
0.39% swing Lab. to C.

WARWICKSHIRE NORTH
E. 70,271 T. 45,914 (65.34%) C. hold
Craig Tracey, C.   30,249
Claire Breeze, Lab. Co-op   12,293
Richard Whelan, LD   2,069
James Platt, Green   1,303
C. majority 17,956 (39.11%)
10.53% swing Lab. to C.

WASHINGTON & SUNDERLAND WEST
E. 66,278 T. 37,513 (56.60%) Lab. hold
Sharon Hodgson, Lab.   15,941
Valerie Allen, C.   12,218
Howard Brown, Brexit   5,439
Carlton West, LD   2,071
Michal Chantkowski, Green   1,005
Keith Jenkins, UKIP   839
Lab. majority 3,723 (9.92%)
10.98% swing Lab. to C.

WATFORD
E. 83,359 T. 58,065 (69.66%) C. hold
Dean Russell, C.   26,421
Chris Ostrowski, Lab.   21,988
Ian Stotesbury, LD   9,323
Michael McGetrick, Soc   333
Dem
C. majority 4,433 (7.63%)
2.03% swing Lab. to C.

WAVENEY
E. 82,791 T. 51,129 (61.76%) C. hold
Peter Aldous, C.   31,778
Sonia Barker, Lab.   13,776
Elfrede Brambley-Crawshaw,   2,727
Green
Helen Korfanty, LD   2,603
Dave Brennan, CPA   245
C. majority 18,002 (35.21%)
8.86% swing Lab. to C.

WEALDEN
E. 83,038 T. 60,907 (73.35%) C. hold
Nus Ghani, C.   37,043
Chris Bowers, LD   11,388
Angie Smith, Lab.   9,377
Georgia Taylor, Green   3,099
C. majority 25,655 (42.12%)
4.36% swing C. to LD

WEAVER VALE
E. 70,551 T. 50,713 (71.88%) Lab. hold
Mike Amesbury, Lab.   22,772
Adam Wordsworth, C.   22,210
Daniela Parker, LD   3,300
Nicholas Goulding, Brexit   1,380
Paul Bowers, Green   1,051
Lab. majority 562 (1.11%)
3.33% swing Lab. to C.

WELLINGBOROUGH
E. 80,764 T. 51,913 (64.28%) C. hold
Peter Bone, C.   32,277
Andrea Watts, Lab.   13,737
Suzanna Austin, LD   4,078
Marion Turner-Hawes,   1,821
Green
C. majority 18,540 (35.71%)
6.16% swing Lab. to C.

WELLS
E. 84,124 T. 61,295 (72.86%) C. hold
James Heappey, C.   33,336
Tessa Munt, LD   23,345
Kama McKenzie, Lab.   4,034
Dave Dobbs, Ind.   373
Susie Quatermass,   207
Motherworld
C. majority 9,991 (16.30%)
1.92% swing LD to C.

WELWYN HATFIELD
E. 74,892 T. 52,053 (69.50%) C. hold
Grant Shapps, C.   27,394
Rosie Newbigging, Lab.   16,439
Paul Zukowskyj, LD   6,602
Oliver Sayers, Green   1,618
C. majority 10,955 (21.05%)
3.39% swing Lab. to C.

WENTWORTH & DEARNE
E. 74,536 T. 41,557 (55.75%) Lab. hold
John Healey, Lab.   16,742
Emily Barley, C.   14,577
Stephen Cavell, Brexit   7,019
Janice Middleton, LD   1,705
Lucy Brown, Yorkshire   1,201
David Bettney, Soc Dem   313
Lab. majority 2,165 (5.21%)
14.24% swing Lab. to C.

WEST BROMWICH EAST
E. 62,111 T. 35,975 (57.92%) C. gain
Nicola Richards, C.   16,804
Ibrahim Dogus, Lab.   15,211
Christian Lucas, Brexit   1,475
Andy Graham, LD   1,313
Mark Redding, Green   627
George Galloway, Ind.   489
Colin Rankine, Yeshua   56
C. majority 1,593 (4.43%)
12.08% swing Lab. to C.

WEST BROMWICH WEST
E. 64,576 T. 34,459 (53.36%) C. gain
Shaun Bailey, C.   17,419
James Cunningham, Lab.   13,620
Franco D'Aulerio, Brexit   1,841
Flo Clucas, LD   915
Keir Williams, Green   664
C. majority 3,799 (11.02%)
11.69% swing Lab. to C.

WEST HAM
E. 97,942 T. 60,200 (61.46%) Lab. hold
Lyn Brown, Lab.   42,181
Sara Kumar, C.   9,793
Eimear O'Casey, LD   4,161
Danny Keeling, Green   1,780
Emma Stockdale, Brexit   1,679
Paul Jobson, CPA   463
Humera Kamran,   143
Communities
Lab. majority 32,388 (53.80%)
3.37% swing Lab. to C.

WESTMINSTER NORTH
E. 65,519 T. 42,911 (65.49%) Lab. hold
Karen Buck, Lab.   23,240
Jamie Macfarlane, C.   12,481
George Lee, LD   5,593
Holly Robinson, Green   1,064
Cyrus Parvin, Brexit   418
Gabriela Fajardo Palacios,   115
CPA
Lab. majority 10,759 (25.07%)
0.76% swing Lab. to C.

WESTMORLAND & LONSDALE
E. 67,789 T. 52,712 (77.76%) LD hold
Tim Farron, LD   25,795
James Airey, C.   23,861
Phillip Black, Lab.   2,293
Steven Bolton, Brexit   763
LD majority 1,934 (3.67%)
1.08% swing C. to LD

WESTON-SUPER-MARE
E. 82,526 T. 55,614 (67.39%) C. hold
John Penrose, C.   31,983
Tim Taylor, Lab.   14,862
Patrick Keating, LD   6,935
Suneil Basu, Green   1,834
C. majority 17,121 (30.79%)
5.16% swing Lab. to C.

WIGAN
E. 75,680 T. 45,042 (59.52%) Lab. hold
Lisa Nandy, Lab.   21,042
Ashley Williams, C.   14,314
William Malloy, Brexit   5,959
Stuart Thomas, LD   2,428
Peter Jacobs, Green   1,299
Lab. majority 6,728 (14.94%)
9.39% swing Lab. to C.

WILTSHIRE NORTH
E. 73,283 T. 54,758 (74.72%) C. hold
James Gray, C.   32,373
Brian Mathew, LD   14,747
Jon Fisher, Lab.   5,699
Bonnie Jackson, Green   1,939
C. majority 17,626 (32.19%)
5.20% swing C. to LD

WILTSHIRE SOUTH WEST
E. 77,970 T. 54,895 (70.41%) C. hold
Andrew Murrison, C.   33,038
Emily Pomroy-Smith, Lab.   11,408
Ellen Nicholson, LD   8,015
Julie Phillips, Green   2,434
C. majority 21,630 (39.40%)
2.97% swing Lab. to C.

WIMBLEDON
E. 68,232   T. 53,027 (77.72%)   C. hold
Stephen Hammond, C. 20,373
Paul Kohler, LD 19,745
Jackie Schneider, Lab. 12,543
Graham Hadley, Ind. 366
C. majority 628 (1.18%)
15.39% swing C. to LD

WINCHESTER
E. 75,582   T. 58,890 (77.92%)   C. hold
Steve Brine, C. 28,430
Paula Ferguson, LD 27,445
George Baker, Lab. 2,723
Teresa Skelton, JACP 292
C. majority 985 (1.67%)
7.91% swing C. to LD

WINDSOR
E. 75,038   T. 53,750 (71.63%)   C. hold
Adam Afriyie, C. 31,501
Julian Tisi, LD 11,422
Peter Shearman, Lab. 8,147
Fintan McKeown, Green 1,796
David Buckley, Ind. 508
Wisdom Da Costa, Ind. 376
C. majority 20,079 (37.36%)
8.48% swing C. to LD

WIRRAL SOUTH
E. 57,280   T. 43,547 (76.02%)   Lab. hold
Alison McGovern, Lab. 22,284
Stewart Gardiner, C. 16,179
Christopher Carubia, LD 2,917
Martin Waring, Brexit 1,219
Harry Gorman, Green 948
Lab. majority 6,105 (14.02%)
2.20% swing Lab. to C.

WIRRAL WEST
E. 55,550   T. 42,918 (77.26%)   Lab. hold
Margaret Greenwood, Lab. 20,695
Laura Evans, C. 17,692
Andy Corkhill, LD 2,706
John Coyne, Green 965
John Kelly, Brexit 860
Lab. majority 3,003 (7.00%)
2.60% swing Lab. to C.

WITHAM
E. 70,402   T. 49,344 (70.09%)   C. hold
Priti Patel, C. 32,876
Martin Edobor, Lab. 8,794
Sam North, LD 4,584
James Abbott, Green 3,090
C. majority 24,082 (48.80%)
5.47% swing Lab. to C.

WITNEY
E. 83,845   T. 61,305 (73.12%)   C. hold
Robert Courts, C. 33,856
Charlotte Hoagland, LD 18,679
Rosa Bolger, Lab. Co-op 8,770
C. majority 15,177 (24.76%)
5.17% swing C. to LD

WOKING
E. 75,455   T. 53,937 (71.48%)   C. hold
Jonathan Lord, C. 26,396
Will Forster, LD 16,629
Gerry Mitchell, Lab. 8,827
Ella Walding, Green 1,485
Troy De Leon, UKIP 600
C. majority 9,767 (18.11%)
9.22% swing C. to LD

WOKINGHAM
E. 83,957   T. 61,997 (73.84%)   C. hold
John Redwood, C. 30,734
Phillip Lee, LD 23,351
Annette Medhurst, Lab. 6,450
Kizzi Johannessen, Green 1,382
Annabel Mullin, Advance 80
C. majority 7,383 (11.91%)
14.40% swing C. to LD

WOLVERHAMPTON NORTH EAST
E. 61,829   T. 34,281 (55.44%)   C. gain
Jane Stevenson, C. 17,722
Emma Reynolds, Lab. 13,642
Vishal Khatri, Brexit 1,354
Richard Maxwell, LD 960
Andrea Cantrill, Green 603
C. majority 4,080 (11.90%)
12.23% swing Lab. to C.

WOLVERHAMPTON SOUTH EAST
E. 63,006   T. 33,443 (53.08%)   Lab. hold
Pat McFadden, Lab. 15,522
Ahmed Ejaz, C. 14,287
Raj Chaggar, Brexit 2,094
Ruth Coleman-Taylor, LD 1,019
Kathryn Gilbert, Green 521
Lab. majority 1,235 (3.69%)
9.88% swing Lab. to C.

WOLVERHAMPTON SOUTH WEST
E. 60,895   T. 41,136 (67.55%)   C. gain
Stuart Anderson, C. 19,864
Eleanor Smith, Lab. 18,203
Bart Ricketts, LD 2,041
Leo Grandison, Brexit 1,028
C. majority 1,661 (4.04%)
4.60% swing Lab. to C.

WORCESTER
E. 73,475   T. 50,898 (69.27%)   C. hold
Robin Walker, C. 25,856
Lynn Denham, Lab. 19,098
Stephen Kearney, LD 3,666
Louis Stephen, Green 1,694
Martin Potter, Ind. 584
C. majority 6,758 (13.28%)
4.20% swing Lab. to C.

WORCESTERSHIRE MID
E. 78,221   T. 56,123 (71.75%)   C. hold
Nigel Huddleston, C. 37,426
Helen Russell, Lab. 9,408
Margaret Rowley, LD 6,474
Sue Howarth, Green 2,177
Barmy Lord Brockman, 638
Loony
C. majority 28,018 (49.92%)
3.79% swing Lab. to C.

WORCESTERSHIRE WEST
E. 76,267   T. 57,530 (75.43%)   C. hold
Harriett Baldwin, C. 34,909
Beverley Nielsen, LD 10,410
Samantha Charles, Lab. 9,496
Martin Allen, Green 2,715
C. majority 24,499 (42.58%)
4.74% swing C. to LD

WORKINGTON
E. 61,370   T. 41,599 (67.78%)   C. gain
Mark Jenkinson, C. 20,488
Sue Hayman, Lab. 16,312
David Walker, Brexit 1,749
Neil Hughes, LD 1,525
Nicky Cockburn, Ind. 842
Jill Perry, Green 596
Roy Ivinson, ND 87
C. majority 4,176 (10.04%)
9.73% swing Lab. to C.

WORSLEY & ECCLES SOUTH
E. 75,219   T. 44,825 (59.59%)   Lab. hold
Barbara Keeley, Lab. 20,446
Arnie Saunders, C. 17,227
Seamus Martin, Brexit 3,224
Joe Johnson-Tod, LD 2,510
Daniel Towers, Green 1,300
Lab. majority 3,101 (6.92%)
5.72% swing Lab. to C.

WORTHING EAST & SHOREHAM
E. 75,195   T. 53,155 (70.69%)   C. hold
Tim Loughton, C. 27,104
Lavinia O'Connor, Lab. 19,663
Ashley Ridley, LD 4,127
Leslie Groves Williams, 2,006
Green
Sophie Cook, ND 255
C. majority 7,441 (14.00%)
2.19% swing Lab. to C.

WORTHING WEST
E. 78,587   T. 54,648 (69.54%)   C. hold
Peter Bottomley, C. 30,475
Beccy Cooper, Lab. 15,652
Jamie Bennett, LD 6,024
Jo Paul, Green 2,008
David Aherne, Ind. 489
C. majority 14,823 (27.12%)
2.47% swing Lab. to C.

WREKIN, THE
E. 70,693   T. 48,890 (69.16%)   C. hold
Mark Pritchard, C. 31,029
Dylan Harrison, Lab. 12,303
Thomas Janke, LD 4,067
Tim Dawes, Green 1,491
C. majority 18,726 (38.30%)
9.50% swing Lab. to C.

WYCOMBE
E. 78,094   T. 54,756 (70.12%)   C. hold
Steve Baker, C. 24,766
Khalil Ahmed, Lab. 20,552
Toni Brodelle, LD 6,543
Peter Sims, Green 1,454
Julia Wassell, Wycombe 926
Vijay Srao, UKIP 324
Edmund Gemmell, Ind. 191
C. majority 4,214 (7.70%)
2.30% swing C. to Lab.

WYRE & PRESTON NORTH
E. 75,168   T. 52,924 (70.41%)   C. hold
Ben Wallace, C.   31,589
Joanne Ainscough, Lab.   14,808
John Potter, LD   4,463
Ruth Norbury, Green   1,729
David Ragozzino, Ind.   335
C. majority 16,781 (31.71%)
4.22% swing Lab. to C.

WYRE FOREST
E. 78,079   T. 50,561 (64.76%)   C. hold
Mark Garnier, C.   32,960
Robin Lunn, Lab.   11,547
Shazu Miah, LD   4,081
John Davis, Green   1,973
C. majority 21,413 (42.35%)
8.14% swing Lab. to C.

WYTHENSHAWE & SALE EAST
E. 76,313   T. 44,759 (58.65%)   Lab. hold
Mike Kane, Lab.   23,855
Peter Harrop, C.   13,459
Simon Lepori, LD   3,111
Julie Fousert, Brexit   2,717
Rob Nunney, Green   1,559
Caroline Bellamy, Comm   58
Lge
Lab. majority 10,396 (23.23%)
4.68% swing Lab. to C.

YEOVIL
E. 82,468   T. 59,260 (71.86%)   C. hold
Marcus Fysh, C.   34,588
Mick Clark, LD   18,407
Terry Ledlie, Lab.   3,761
Diane Wood, Green   1,629
Tony Capozzoli, Ind.   689
Tom Fox, Constitution   186
C. majority 16,181 (27.31%)
1.26% swing LD to C.

YORK CENTRAL
E. 74,899   T. 49,505 (66.10%)
                              Lab. Co-op hold
Rachael Maskell, Lab. Co-op   27,312
Fabia Tate, C.   13,767
James Blanchard, LD   4,149
Tom Franklin, Green   2,107
Nicholas Szkiler, Brexit   1,479
Andrew Snedden, Yorkshire   557
Andrew Dunn, Soc Dem   134
Lab. Co-op majority 13,545 (27.36%)
3.81% swing Lab. to C.

YORK OUTER
E. 74,673   T. 55,347 (74.12%)   C. hold
Julian Sturdy, C.   27,324
Anna Perrett, Lab.   17,339
Keith Aspden, LD   9,992
Scott Marmion, Ind.   692
C. majority 9,985 (18.04%)
1.80% swing Lab. to C.

YORKSHIRE EAST
E. 80,871   T. 52,769 (65.25%)   C. hold
Greg Knight, C.   33,988
Catherine Minnis, Lab.   11,201
Dale Needham, LD   4,219
Tim Norman, Yorkshire   1,686
Mike Jackson, Green   1,675
C. majority 22,787 (43.18%)
7.69% swing Lab. to C.

WALES

ABERAVON
E. 50,747   T. 31,598 (62.27%)   Lab. hold
Stephen Kinnock, Lab.   17,008
Charlotte Lang, C.   6,518
Glenda Davies, Brexit   3,108
Nigel Hunt, PC   2,711
Sheila Kingston-Jones, LD   1,072
Captain Beany, Ind.   731
Giorgia Finney, Green   450
Lab. majority 10,490 (33.20%)
8.59% swing Lab. to C.

ABERCONWY
E. 44,699   T. 31,865 (71.29%)   C. gain
Robin Millar, C.   14,687
Emily Owen, Lab.   12,653
Lisa Goodier, PC   2,704
Jason Edwards, LD   1,821
C. majority 2,034 (6.38%)
2.20% swing Lab. to C.

ALYN & DEESIDE
E. 62,783   T. 43,008 (68.50%)   Lab. hold
Mark Tami, Lab.   18,271
Sanjoy Sen, C.   18,058
Simon Wall, Brexit   2,678
Donna Lalek, LD   2,548
Susan Hills, PC   1,453
Lab. majority 213 (0.50%)
5.60% swing Lab. to C.

ARFON
E. 42,215   T. 29,074 (68.87%)   PC hold
Hywel Williams, PC   13,134
Steffie Williams Roberts, Lab.   10,353
Gonul Daniels, C.   4,428
Gary Gribben, Brexit   1,159
PC majority 2,781 (9.57%)
4.62% swing Lab. to PC

BLAENAU GWENT
E. 50,736   T. 30,219 (59.56%)   Lab. hold
Nick Smith, Lab.   14,862
Richard Taylor, Brexit   6,215
Laura Jones, C.   5,749
Peredur Owen Griffiths, PC   1,722
Chelsea-Marie Annett, LD   1,285
Stephen Priestnall, Green   386
Lab. majority 8,647 (28.61%)
swing N/A

BRECON & RADNORSHIRE
E. 55,490   T. 41,319 (74.46%)   C. gain
Fay Jones, C.   21,958
Jane Dodds, LD   14,827
Tomos Davies, Lab.   3,944
Lady Lily The Pink, Loony   345
Jeff Green, Christian   245
C. majority 7,131 (17.26%)
1.09% swing C. to LD

BRIDGEND
E. 63,303   T. 42,236 (66.72%)   C. gain
Jamie Wallis, C.   18,193
Madeleine Moon, Lab.   17,036
Jonathan Pratt, LD   2,368
Leanne Lewis, PC   2,013
Robert Morgan, Brexit   1,811
Alex Harris, Green   815
C. majority 1,157 (2.74%)
6.80% swing Lab. to C.

CAERPHILLY
E. 63,166   T. 40,117 (63.51%)   Lab. hold
Wayne David, Lab.   18,018
Jane Pratt, C.   11,185
Lindsay Whittle, PC   6,424
Nathan Gill, Brexit   4,490
Lab. majority 6,833 (17.03%)
6.11% swing Lab. to C.

CARDIFF CENTRAL
E. 64,037   T. 41,822 (65.31%)   Lab. hold
Jo Stevens, Lab.   25,605
Meirion Jenkins, C.   8,426
Bablin Molik, LD   6,298
Gareth Pearce, Brexit   1,006
Sian Caiach, Gwlad   280
Akil Kata, Ind.   119
Brian Johnson, SPGB   88
Lab. majority 17,179 (41.08%)
0.76% swing Lab. to C.

CARDIFF NORTH
E. 68,438   T. 52,666 (76.95%)   Lab. hold
Anna McMorrin, Lab.   26,064
Mo Ali, C.   19,082
Rhys Taylor, LD   3,580
Steffan Webb, PC   1,606
Chris Butler, Brexit   1,311
Michael Cope, Green   820
Richard Jones, Ind.   203
Lab. majority 6,982 (13.26%)
2.62% swing C. to Lab.

CARDIFF SOUTH & PENARTH
E. 78,837   T. 50,579 (64.16%)

	Lab. Co-op hold
Stephen Doughty, Lab. Co-op	27,382
Philippa Broom, C.	14,645
Dan Schmeising, LD	2,985
Nasir Adam, PC	2,386
Tim Price, Brexit	1,999
Ken Barker, Green	1,182

Lab. Co-op majority 12,737 (25.18%)
2.06% swing Lab. to C.

CARDIFF WEST
E. 68,508   T. 46,177 (67.40%)   Lab. hold

Kevin Brennan, Lab.	23,908
Carolyn Webster, C.	12,922
Boyd Clack, PC	3,864
Callum Littlemore, LD	2,731
Nick Mullins, Brexit	1,619
David Griffin, Green	1,133

Lab. majority 10,986 (23.79%)
1.56% swing Lab. to C.

CARMARTHEN EAST & DINEFWR
E. 57,407   T. 41,002 (71.42%)   PC hold

Jonathan Edwards, PC	15,939
Havard Hughes, C.	14,130
Maria Carroll, Lab.	8,622
Peter Prosser, Brexit	2,311

PC majority 1,809 (4.41%)
4.31% swing PC to C.

CARMARTHEN WEST & PEMBROKESHIRE SOUTH
E. 58,629   T. 42,114 (71.83%)   C. hold

Simon Hart, C.	22,183
Marc Tierney, Lab.	14,438
Rhys Thomas, PC	3,633
Alistair Cameron, LD	1,860

C. majority 7,745 (18.39%)
5.51% swing Lab. to C.

CEREDIGION
E. 56,250   T. 40,105 (71.30%)   PC hold

Ben Lake, PC	15,208
Amanda Jenner, C.	8,879
Mark Williams, LD	6,975
Dinah Mulholland, Lab.	6,317
Gethin James, Brexit	2,063
Chris Simpson, Green	663

PC majority 6,329 (15.78%)
2.46% swing C. to PC

CLWYD SOUTH
E. 53,919   T. 36,306 (67.33%)   C. gain

Simon Baynes, C.	16,222
Susan Elan Jones, Lab.	14,983
Chris Allen, PC	2,137
Calum Davies, LD	1,496
Jamie Adams, Brexit	1,468

C. majority 1,239 (3.41%)
7.52% swing Lab. to C.

CLWYD WEST
E. 57,714   T. 40,203 (69.66%)   C. hold

David Jones, C.	20,403
Jo Thomas, Lab.	13,656
Elfed Williams, PC	3,907
David Wilkins, LD	2,237

C. majority 6,747 (16.78%)
4.16% swing Lab. to C.

CYNON VALLEY
E. 51,134   T. 30,236 (59.13%)   Lab. hold

Beth Winter, Lab.	15,533
Pauline Church, C.	6,711
Rebecca Rees-Evans, Brexit	3,045
Geraint Benney, PC	2,562
Andrew Chainey, Cynon	1,322
Steve Bray, LD	949
Ian Mclean, Soc Dem	114

Lab. majority 8,822 (29.18%)
6.22% swing Lab. to C.

DELYN
E. 54,552   T. 38,370 (70.34%)   C. gain

Rob Roberts, C.	16,756
David Hanson, Lab.	15,891
Andrew Parkhurst, LD	2,346
Nigel Williams, Brexit	1,971
Paul Rowlinson, PC	1,406

C. majority 865 (2.25%)
6.51% swing Lab. to C.

DWYFOR MEIRIONNYDD
E. 44,362   T. 29,928 (67.46%)   PC hold

Liz Saville Roberts, PC	14,447
Tomos Davies, C.	9,707
Graham Hogg, Lab.	3,998
Louise Hughes, Brexit	1,776

PC majority 4,740 (15.84%)
0.07% swing PC to C.

GOWER
E. 61,762   T. 44,482 (72.02%)   Lab. hold

Tonia Antoniazzi, Lab.	20,208
Francesca O'Brien, C.	18,371
John Davies, PC	2,288
Sam Bennett, LD	2,236
Rob Ross, Brexit	1,379

Lab. majority 1,837 (4.13%)
1.52% swing Lab. to C.

ISLWYN
E. 55,423   T. 34,350 (61.98%)

	Lab. Co-op hold
Chris Evans, Lab. Co-op	15,356
Gavin Chambers, C.	9,892
James Wells, Brexit	4,834
Zoe Hammond, PC	2,286
Jo Watkins, LD	1,313
Catherine Linstrum, Green	669

Lab. Co-op majority 5,464 (15.91%)
7.86% swing Lab. to C.

LLANELLI
E. 60,513   T. 38,233 (63.18%)   Lab. hold

Nia Griffith, Lab.	16,125
Tamara Reay, C.	11,455
Mari Arthur, PC	7,048
Susan Boucher, Brexit	3,605

Lab. majority 4,670 (12.21%)
8.80% swing Lab. to C.

MERTHYR TYDFIL & RHYMNEY
E. 56,322   T. 32,246 (57.25%)   Lab. hold

Gerald Jones, Lab.	16,913
Sara Jones, C.	6,307
Colin Jones, Brexit	3,604
Mark Evans, PC	2,446
David Hughes, Ind.	1,860
Brendan D'Cruz, LD	1,116

Lab. majority 10,606 (32.89%)
7.90% swing Lab. to C.

MONMOUTH
E. 67,094   T. 50,217 (74.85%)   C. hold

David Davies, C.	26,160
Yvonne Murphy, Lab.	16,178
Alison Willott, LD	4,909
Ian Chandler, Green	1,353
Hugh Kocan, PC	1,182
Martyn Ford, Ind.	435

C. majority 9,982 (19.88%)
1.69% swing Lab. to C.

MONTGOMERYSHIRE
E. 48,997   T. 34,214 (69.83%)   C. hold

Craig Williams, C.	20,020
Kishan Devani, LD	7,882
Kait Duerden, Lab.	5,585
Gwyn Wigley Evans, Gwlad	727

C. majority 12,138 (35.48%)
4.43% swing LD to C.

NEATH
E. 56,416   T. 36,756 (65.15%)

	Lab. Co-op hold
Christina Rees, Lab. Co-op	15,920
Jon Burns, C.	10,283
Daniel Williams, PC	4,495
Simon Briscoe, Brexit	3,184
Adrian Kingston-Jones, LD	1,485
Megan Lloyd, Green	728
Philip Rogers, Ind.	594
Carl Williams, Soc Dem	67

Lab. Co-op majority 5,637 (15.34%)
8.83% swing Lab. to C.

NEWPORT EAST
E. 58,554   T. 36,282 (61.96%)   Lab. hold

Jessica Morden, Lab.	16,125
Mark Brown, C.	14,133
Julie Price, Brexit	2,454
Mike Hamilton, LD	2,121
Cameron Wixcey, PC	872
Peter Varley, Green	577

Lab. majority 1,992 (5.49%)
8.12% swing Lab. to C.

NEWPORT WEST
E. 66,657   T. 43,433 (65.16%)   Lab. hold

Ruth Jones, Lab.	18,977
Matthew Evans, C.	18,075
Ryan Jones, LD	2,565
Cameron Edwards, Brexit	1,727
Jonathan Clark, PC	1,187
Amelia Womack, Green	902

Lab. majority 902 (2.08%)
5.47% swing Lab. to C.

OGMORE
E. 57,581   T. 35,390 (61.46%)   Lab. hold

Chris Elmore, Lab.	17,602
Sadie Vidal, C.	9,797
Christine Roach, Brexit	2,991
Luke Fletcher, PC	2,919
Anita Davies, LD	1,460
Tom Muller, Green	621

Lab. majority 7,805 (22.05%)
7.61% swing Lab. to C.

PONTYPRIDD
E. 60,327 T. 39,060 (64.75%) Lab. hold

Alex Davies-Jones, Lab.	17,381
Sam Trask, C.	11,494
Fflur Elin, PC	4,990
Steve Bayliss, Brexit	2,917
Mike Powell, Ind.	1,792
Sue Prior, Ind.	337
Jonathan Bishop, ND	149

Lab. majority 5,887 (15.07%)
6.81% swing Lab. to C.

PRESELI PEMBROKESHIRE
E. 59,586 T. 42,419 (71.19%) C. hold

Stephen Crabb, C.	21,381
Philippa Thompson, Lab.	16,319
Cris Tomos, PC	2,776
Tom Hughes, LD	1,943

C. majority 5,062 (11.93%)
5.59% swing Lab. to C.

RHONDDA
E. 50,262 T. 29,642 (58.97%) Lab. hold

Chris Bryant, Lab.	16,115
Hannah Jarvis, C.	4,675
Branwen Cennard, PC	4,069
John Watkins, Brexit	3,733
Simon Berman, LD	612
Shaun Thomas, Green	438

Lab. majority 11,440 (38.59%)
7.67% swing Lab. to C.

SWANSEA EAST
E. 58,450 T. 33,579 (57.45%) Lab. hold

Carolyn Harris, Lab.	17,405
Denise Howard, C.	9,435
Tony Willicombe, Brexit	2,842
Geraint Havard, PC	1,905
Chloe Hutchinson, LD	1,409
Chris Evans, Green	583

Lab. majority 7,970 (23.74%)
6.86% swing Lab. to C.

SWANSEA WEST
E. 57,078 T. 35,830 (62.77%)
Lab. Co-op hold

Geraint Davies, Lab. Co-op	18,493
James Price, C.	10,377
Michael O'Carroll, LD	2,993
Gwyn Williams, PC	1,984
Peter Hopkins, Brexit	1,983

Lab. Co-op majority 8,116 (22.65%)
2.89% swing Lab. to C.

TORFAEN
E. 61,743 T. 37,176 (60.21%) Lab. hold

Nick Thomas-Symonds, Lab.	15,546
Graham Smith, C.	11,804
David Thomas, Brexit	5,742
John Miller, LD	1,831
Morgan Bowler-Brown, PC	1,441
Andrew Heygate-Browne, Green	812

Lab. majority 3,742 (10.07%)
8.29% swing Lab. to C.

VALE OF CLWYD
E. 56,649 T. 37,213 (65.69%) C. gain

James Davies, C.	17,270
Chris Ruane, Lab.	15,443
Glenn Swingler, PC	1,552
Peter Dain, Brexit	1,477
Gavin Scott, LD	1,471

C. majority 1,827 (4.91%)
5.53% swing Lab. to C.

VALE OF GLAMORGAN
E. 76,508 T. 54,807 (71.64%) C. hold

Alun Cairns, C.	27,305
Belinda Loveluck-Edwards, Lab.	23,743
Anthony Slaughter, Green	3,251
Laurence Williams, Gwlad	508

C. majority 3,562 (6.50%)
1.21% swing Lab. to C.

WREXHAM
E. 49,734 T. 33,532 (67.42%) C. gain

Sarah Atherton, C.	15,199
Mary Wimbury, Lab. Co-op	13,068
Carrie Harper, PC	2,151
Tim Sly, LD	1,447
Ian Berkeley-Hurst, Brexit	1,222
Duncan Rees, Green	445

C. majority 2,131 (6.36%)
5.79% swing Lab. to C.

YNYS MON
E. 51,925 T. 36,552 (70.39%) C. gain

Virginia Crosbie, C.	12,959
Mary Roberts, Lab.	10,991
Aled Ap Dafydd, PC	10,418
Helen Jenner, Brexit	2,184

C. majority 1,968 (5.38%)
9.73% swing Lab. to C.

SCOTLAND

ABERDEEN NORTH
E. 62,489 T. 37,413 (59.87%)

SNP hold

Kirsty Blackman, SNP	20,205
Ryan Houghton, C.	7,535
Nurul Ali, Lab.	4,939
Isobel Davidson, LD	2,846
Seb Leslie, Brexit	1,008
Guy Ingerson, Green	880

SNP majority 12,670 (33.87%)
7.64% swing C. to SNP

ABERDEEN SOUTH
E. 65,719 T. 45,630 (69.43%) SNP gain

Stephen Flynn, SNP	20,380
Douglas Lumsden, C.	16,398
Ian Yuill, LD	5,018
Shona Simpson, Lab.	3,834

SNP majority 3,982 (8.73%)
9.70% swing C. to SNP

ABERDEENSHIRE WEST & KINCARDINE
E. 72,640 T. 53,345 (73.44%) C. hold

Andrew Bowie, C.	22,752
Fergus Mutch, SNP	21,909
John Waddell, LD	6,253
Paddy Coffield, Lab.	2,431

C. majority 843 (1.58%)
6.91% swing C. to SNP

AIRDRIE & SHOTTS
E. 64,008 T. 39,772 (62.14%)

SNP hold

Neil Gray, SNP	17,929
Helen McFarlane, Lab.	12,728
Lorraine Nolan, C.	7,011
William Crossman, LD	1,419
Rosemary McGowan, Green	685

SNP majority 5,201 (13.08%)
6.28% swing Lab. to SNP

ANGUS
E. 63,952 T. 43,170 (67.50%) SNP gain

Dave Doogan, SNP	21,216
Kirstene Hair, C.	17,421
Ben Lawrie, LD	2,482
Monique Miller, Lab.	2,051

SNP majority 3,795 (8.79%)
7.69% swing C. to SNP

ARGYLL & BUTE
E. 66,525 T. 48,050 (72.23%)

SNP hold

Brendan O'Hara, SNP	21,040
Gary Mulvaney, C.	16,930
Alan Reid, LD	6,832
Rhea Barnes, Lab.	3,248

SNP majority 4,110 (8.55%)
2.90% swing C. to SNP

AYR, CARRICK & CUMNOCK
E. 71,970 T. 46,592 (64.74%) SNP gain

Allan Dorans, SNP	20,272
Martin Dowey, C.	17,943
Duncan Townson, Lab.	6,219
Helena Bongard, LD	2,158

SNP majority 2,329 (5.00%)
5.50% swing C. to SNP

AYRSHIRE CENTRAL
E. 69,742 T. 46,534 (66.72%)

SNP hold

Philippa Whitford, SNP	21,486
Derek Stillie, C.	16,182
Louise McPhater, Lab.	6,583
Emma Farthing, LD	2,283

SNP majority 5,304 (11.40%)
4.29% swing C. to SNP

AYRSHIRE NORTH & ARRAN
E. 73,534   T. 48,154 (65.49%)

	SNP hold
Patricia Gibson, SNP	23,376
David Rocks, C.	14,855
Cameron Gilmore, Lab.	6,702
Louise Young, LD	2,107
David Nairn, Green	1,114

SNP majority 8,521 (17.70%)
5.02% swing C. to SNP

BANFF & BUCHAN
E. 66,655   T. 42,260 (63.40%)

	C. hold
David Duguid, C.	21,182
Paul Robertson, SNP	17,064
Alison Smith, LD	2,280
Brian Balcombe, Lab.	1,734

C. majority 4,118 (9.74%)
0.44% swing SNP to C.

BERWICKSHIRE, ROXBURGH & SELKIRK
E. 74,518   T. 53,146 (71.32%)

	C. hold
John Lamont, C.	25,747
Calum Kerr, SNP	20,599
Jenny Marr, LD	4,287
Ian Davidson, Lab.	2,513

C. majority 5,148 (9.69%)
5.72% swing C. to SNP

CAITHNESS, SUTHERLAND & EASTER ROSS
E. 46,930   T. 31,457 (67.03%)   LD hold

Jamie Stone, LD	11,705
Karl Rosie, SNP	11,501
Andrew Sinclair, C.	5,176
Cheryl McDonald, Lab.	1,936
Sandra Skinner, Brexit	1,139

LD majority 204 (0.65%)
2.98% swing LD to SNP

COATBRIDGE, CHRYSTON & BELLSHILL
E. 72,943   T. 48,221 (66.11%)   SNP gain

Steven Bonnar, SNP	22,680
Hugh Gaffney, Lab.	17,056
Nathan Wilson, C.	6,113
David Stevens, LD	1,564
Patrick McAleer, Green	808

SNP majority 5,624 (11.66%)
7.59% swing Lab. to SNP

CUMBERNAULD, KILSYTH & KIRKINTILLOCH EAST
E. 66,079   T. 45,686 (69.14%)

	SNP hold
Stuart McDonald, SNP	24,158
James McPhilemy, Lab.	11,182
Roz McCall, C.	7,380
Susan Murray, LD	2,966

SNP majority 12,976 (28.40%)
9.34% swing Lab. to SNP

DUMFRIES & GALLOWAY
E. 74,580   T. 51,429 (68.96%)   C. hold

Alister Jack, C.	22,678
Richard Arkless, SNP	20,873
Ted Thompson, Lab.	4,745
McNabb Laurie, LD	3,133

C. majority 1,805 (3.51%)
3.71% swing C. to SNP

DUMFRIESSHIRE, CLYDESDALE & TWEEDDALE
E. 68,330   T. 49,153 (71.93%)   C. hold

David Mundell, C.	22,611
Amanda Burgauer, SNP	18,830
Nick Chisholm, Lab.	4,172
John Ferry, LD	3,540

C. majority 3,781 (7.69%)
5.79% swing C. to SNP

DUNBARTONSHIRE EAST
E. 66,075   T. 53,031 (80.26%)   SNP gain

Amy Callaghan, SNP	19,672
Jo Swinson, LD	19,523
Pam Gosal, C.	7,455
Callum McNally, Lab.	4,839
Carolynn Scrimgeour, Green	916
Rosie Dickson, Ind.	221
Donald MacKay, UKIP	208
Liam McKechnie, Scot Family	197

SNP majority 149 (0.28%)
5.29% swing LD to SNP

DUNBARTONSHIRE WEST
E. 66,517   T. 45,140 (67.86%)

	SNP hold
Martin Docherty, SNP	22,396
Jean Mitchell, Lab.	12,843
Alix Mathieson, C.	6,436
Jennifer Lang, LD	1,890
Peter Connolly, Green	867
Andrew Muir, Ind.	708

SNP majority 9,553 (21.16%)
7.99% swing Lab. to SNP

DUNDEE EAST
E. 66,210   T. 45,277 (68.38%)

	SNP hold
Stewart Hosie, SNP	24,361
Philip Scott, C.	10,986
Rosalind Garton, Lab.	6,045
Michael Crichton, LD	3,573
George Morton, Ind.	312

SNP majority 13,375 (29.54%)
7.03% swing C. to SNP

DUNDEE WEST
E. 64,431   T. 41,579 (64.53%)

	SNP hold
Chris Law, SNP	22,355
Jim Malone, Lab.	10,096
Tess White, C.	5,149
Daniel Coleman, LD	2,468
Stuart Waiton, Brexit	1,271
Quinta Arrey, CPA	240

SNP majority 12,259 (29.48%)
7.94% swing Lab. to SNP

DUNFERMLINE & FIFE WEST
E. 76,652   T. 53,482 (69.77%)

	SNP hold
Douglas Chapman, SNP	23,727
Cara Hilton, Lab. Co-op	13,028
Moira Benny, C.	11,207
Rebecca Bell, LD	4,262
Mags Hall, Green	1,258

SNP majority 10,699 (20.00%)
9.18% swing Lab. to SNP

EAST KILBRIDE, STRATHAVEN & LESMAHAGOW
E. 81,224   T. 56,337 (69.36%)

	SNP hold
Lisa Cameron, SNP	26,113
Monique McAdams, Lab.	12,791
Gail MacGregor, C.	11,961
Ewan McRobert, LD	3,760
Erica Bradley-Young, Green	1,153
David Mackay, UKIP	559

SNP majority 13,322 (23.65%)
8.25% swing Lab. to SNP

EAST LOTHIAN
E. 81,600   T. 58,513 (71.71%)   SNP gain

Kenny MacAskill, SNP	21,156
Martin Whitfield, Lab.	17,270
Craig Hoy, C.	15,523
Robert O'Riordan, LD	4,071
David Sisson, UKIP	493

SNP majority 3,886 (6.64%)
6.08% swing Lab. to SNP

EDINBURGH EAST
E. 69,424   T. 47,815 (68.87%)

	SNP hold
Tommy Sheppard, SNP	23,165
Sheila Gilmore, Lab.	12,748
Eleanor Price, C.	6,549
Jill Reilly, LD	3,289
Claire Miller, Green	2,064

SNP majority 10,417 (21.79%)
6.96% swing Lab. to SNP

EDINBURGH NORTH & LEITH
E. 81,336   T. 59,344 (72.96%)

	SNP hold
Deidre Brock, SNP	25,925
Gordon Munro, Lab. Co-op	13,117
Iain McGill, C.	11,000
Bruce Wilson, LD	6,635
Steve Burgess, Green	1,971
Robert Speirs, Brexit	558
Heather Astbury, Renew	138

SNP majority 12,808 (21.58%)
9.35% swing Lab. to SNP

EDINBURGH SOUTH
E. 66,188   T. 49,732 (75.14%)   Lab. hold

Ian Murray, Lab.	23,745
Catriona MacDonald, SNP	12,650
Nick Cook, C.	8,161
Alan Beal, LD	3,819
Kate Nevens, Green	1,357

Lab. majority 11,095 (22.31%)
5.06% swing Lab. to SNP

EDINBURGH SOUTH WEST
E. 73,501   T. 52,131 (70.93%)

	SNP hold
Joanna Cherry, SNP	24,830
Callum Laidlaw, C.	12,848
Sophie Cooke, Lab.	7,478
Tom Inglis, LD	4,971
Ben Parker, Green	1,265
David Ballantine, Brexit	625
Mev Brown, Soc Dem	114

SNP majority 11,982 (22.98%)
10.38% swing C. to SNP

EDINBURGH WEST
E. 72,507   T. 54,533 (75.21%)   LD hold
Christine Jardine, LD	21,766
Sarah Masson, SNP	17,997
Graham Hutchison, C.	9,283
Craig Bolton, Lab.	4,460
Elaine Gunn, Green	1,027

LD majority 3,769 (6.91%)
0.63% swing SNP to LD

FALKIRK
E. 84,472   T. 55,872 (66.14%)
SNP hold
Johnny McNally, SNP	29,351
Lynn Munro, C.	14,403
Safia Ali, Lab.	6,243
Austin Reid, LD	3,990
Tom McLaughlin, Green	1,885

SNP majority 14,948 (26.75%)
7.00% swing C. to SNP

FIFE NORTH EAST
E. 60,905   T. 45,878 (75.33%)   LD gain
Wendy Chamberlain, LD	19,763
Stephen Gethins, SNP	18,447
Tony Miklinski, C.	5,961
Wendy Haynes, Lab.	1,707

LD majority 1,316 (2.87%)
1.44% swing SNP to LD

GLASGOW CENTRAL
E. 69,230   T. 40,105 (57.93%)
SNP hold
Alison Thewliss, SNP	19,750
Faten Hameed, Lab.	13,276
Flora Scarabello, C.	3,698
Ewan Hoyle, LD	1,952
Elaine Gallagher, Green	1,429

SNP majority 6,474 (16.14%)
4.92% swing Lab. to SNP

GLASGOW EAST
E. 67,381   T. 38,483 (57.11%)
SNP hold
David Linden, SNP	18,357
Kate Watson, Lab.	12,791
Thomas Kerr, C.	5,709
James Harrison, LD	1,626

SNP majority 5,566 (14.46%)
7.13% swing Lab. to SNP

GLASGOW NORTH
E. 57,130   T. 36,191 (63.35%)
SNP hold
Patrick Grady, SNP	16,982
Pam Duncan-Glancy, Lab.	11,381
Tony Curtis, C.	3,806
Andrew Chamberlain, LD	2,394
Cass Macgregor, Green	1,308
Dionne Cocozza, Brexit	320

SNP majority 5,601 (15.48%)
6.15% swing Lab. to SNP

GLASGOW NORTH EAST
E. 61,075   T. 33,925 (55.55%)   SNP gain
Anne McLaughlin, SNP	15,911
Paul Sweeney, Lab. Co-op	13,363
Lauren Bennie, C.	3,558
Nicholas Moohan, LD	1,093

SNP majority 2,548 (7.51%)
4.14% swing Lab. to SNP

GLASGOW NORTH WEST
E. 63,402   T. 39,735 (62.67%)
SNP hold
Carol Monaghan, SNP	19,678
Patricia Ferguson, Lab.	11,319
Ade Aibinu, C.	6,022
James Speirs, LD	2,716

SNP majority 8,359 (21.04%)
7.22% swing Lab. to SNP

GLASGOW SOUTH
E. 70,891   T. 47,443 (66.92%)
SNP hold
Stewart McDonald, SNP	22,829
Johann Lamont, Lab. Co-op	13,824
Kyle Thornton, C.	6,237
Carole Ford, LD	2,786
Dan Hutchison, Green	1,251
Danyaal Raja, Brexit	516

SNP majority 9,005 (18.98%)
7.22% swing Lab. to SNP

GLASGOW SOUTH WEST
E. 64,575   T. 36,847 (57.06%)
SNP hold
Chris Stephens, SNP	17,643
Matt Kerr, Lab. Co-op	12,743
Thomas Haddow, C.	4,224
Ben Denton-Cardew, LD	1,435
Peter Brown, Brexit	802

SNP majority 4,900 (13.30%)
6.56% swing Lab. to SNP

GLENROTHES
E. 65,762   T. 41,546 (63.18%)
SNP hold
Peter Grant, SNP	21,234
Pat Egan, Lab.	9,477
Amy Thomson, C.	6,920
Jane Ann Liston, LD	2,639
Victor Farrell, Brexit	1,276

SNP majority 11,757 (28.30%)
10.11% swing Lab. to SNP

GORDON
E. 79,629   T. 55,916 (70.22%)   SNP gain
Richard Thomson, SNP	23,885
Colin Clark, C.	23,066
James Oates, LD	5,913
Heather Herbert, Lab.	3,052

SNP majority 819 (1.46%)
3.16% swing C. to SNP

INVERCLYDE
E. 60,622   T. 39,903 (65.82%)
SNP hold
Ronnie Cowan, SNP	19,295
Martin McCluskey, Lab.	11,783
Haroun Malik, C.	6,265
Jacci Stoyle, LD	2,560

SNP majority 7,512 (18.83%)
8.92% swing Lab. to SNP

INVERNESS, NAIRN, BADENOCH & STRATHSPEY
E. 78,057   T. 54,810 (70.22%)
SNP hold
Drew Hendry, SNP	26,247
Fiona Fawcett, C.	15,807
Robert Rixson, LD	5,846
Lewis Whyte, Lab.	4,123
Ariane Burgess, Green	1,709
Les Durance, Brexit	1,078

SNP majority 10,440 (19.05%)
4.86% swing C. to SNP

KILMARNOCK & LOUDOUN
E. 74,517   T. 47,631 (63.92%)
SNP hold
Alan Brown, SNP	24,216
Caroline Hollins, C.	11,557
Kevin McGregor, Lab.	9,009
Edward Thornley, LD	2,444
Stef Johnstone, Libertarian	405

SNP majority 12,659 (26.58%)
5.46% swing C. to SNP

KIRKCALDY & COWDENBEATH
E. 72,853   T. 47,005 (64.52%)   SNP gain
Neale Hanvey, SNP	16,568
Lesley Laird, Lab.	15,325
Kathleen Leslie, C.	9,449
Gill Cole-Hamilton, LD	2,903
Scott Rutherford, Green	1,628
Mitch William, Brexit	1,132

SNP majority 1,243 (2.64%)
1.60% swing Lab. to SNP

LANARK & HAMILTON EAST
E. 77,659   T. 53,072 (68.34%)
SNP hold
Angela Crawley, SNP	22,243
Shona Haslam, C.	17,056
Andrew Hilland, Lab.	10,736
Jane Pickard, LD	3,037

SNP majority 5,187 (9.77%)
4.62% swing C. to SNP

LINLITHGOW & FALKIRK EAST
E. 87,044   T. 57,775 (66.37%)
SNP hold
Martyn Day, SNP	25,551
Charles Kennedy, C.	14,285
Wendy Milne, Lab.	10,517
Sally Pattle, LD	4,393
Marc Bozza, Brexit	1,257
Gillian Mackay, Green	1,184
Mark Tunnicliff, VPP	588

SNP majority 11,266 (19.50%)
6.12% swing C. to SNP

LIVINGSTON
E. 82,285   T. 54,592 (66.35%)
SNP hold
Hannah Bardell, SNP	25,617
Damian Timson, C.	12,182
Caitlin Kane, Lab.	11,915
Charles Dundas, LD	3,457
Cameron Glasgow, Green	1,421

SNP majority 13,435 (24.61%)
4.46% swing C. to SNP

MIDLOTHIAN
E. 70,544   T. 48,221 (68.36%)   SNP gain
Owen Thompson, SNP   20,033
Danielle Rowley, Lab.   14,328
Rebecca Fraser, C.   10,467
Steve Arrundale, LD   3,393
SNP majority 5,705 (11.83%)
6.89% swing Lab. to SNP

MORAY
E. 71,035   T. 48,825 (68.73%)   C. hold
Douglas Ross, C.   22,112
Laura Mitchell, SNP   21,599
Jo Kirby, Lab.   2,432
Fiona Campbell Trevor, LD   2,269
Rob Scorer, UKIP   413
C. majority 513 (1.05%)
3.84% swing C. to SNP

MOTHERWELL & WISHAW
E. 68,856   T. 44,420 (64.51%)
                                 SNP hold
Marion Fellows, SNP   20,622
Angela Feeney, Lab.   14,354
Meghan Gallacher, C.   7,150
Christopher Wilson, LD   1,675
Neil Wilson, UKIP   619
SNP majority 6,268 (14.11%)
6.68% swing Lab. to SNP

NA H-EILEANAN AN IAR
E. 21,106   T. 14,477 (68.59%)
                                 SNP hold
Angus MacNeil, SNP   6,531
Alison MacCorquodale, Lab.   4,093
Jennifer Ross, C.   3,216
Neil Mitchison, LD   637
SNP majority 2,438 (16.84%)
5.02% swing Lab. to SNP

OCHIL & PERTHSHIRE SOUTH
E. 78,776   T. 57,813 (73.39%)   SNP gain
John Nicolson, SNP   26,882
Luke Graham, C.   22,384
Lorna Robertson, Lab.   4,961
Iliyan Stefanov, LD   3,204
Stuart Martin, UKIP   382
SNP majority 4,498 (7.78%)
6.99% swing C. to SNP

ORKNEY & SHETLAND
E. 34,211   T. 23,160 (67.70%)   LD hold
Alistair Carmichael, LD   10,381
Robert Leslie, SNP   7,874
Jennifer Fairbairn, C.   2,287
Coilla Drake, Lab.   1,550
Robert Smith, Brexit   900
David Barnard, Ind.   168
LD majority 2,507 (10.82%)
4.39% swing LD to SNP

PAISLEY & RENFREWSHIRE
NORTH
E. 72,007   T. 49,682 (69.00%)
                                 SNP hold
Gavin Newlands, SNP   23,353
Alison Taylor, Lab.   11,451
Julie Pirone, C.   11,217
Ross Stalker, LD   3,661
SNP majority 11,902 (23.96%)
9.18% swing Lab. to SNP

PAISLEY & RENFREWSHIRE
SOUTH
E. 64,385   T. 43,084 (66.92%)
                                 SNP hold
Mhairi Black, SNP   21,637
Moira Ramage, Lab.   10,958
Mark Dougan, C.   7,571
Jack Clark, LD   2,918
SNP majority 10,679 (24.79%)
9.35% swing Lab. to SNP

PERTH & PERTHSHIRE NORTH
E. 72,600   T. 54,076 (74.48%)
                                 SNP hold
Pete Wishart, SNP   27,362
Angus Forbes, C.   19,812
Peter Barrett, LD   3,780
Angela Bretherton, Lab.   2,471
Stuart Powell, Brexit   651
SNP majority 7,550 (13.96%)
6.96% swing C. to SNP

RENFREWSHIRE EAST
E. 72,232   T. 55,357 (76.64%)   SNP gain
Kirsten Oswald, SNP   24,877
Paul Masterton, C.   19,451
Carolann Davidson, Lab.   6,855
Andrew McGlynn, LD   4,174
SNP majority 5,426 (9.80%)
9.29% swing C. to SNP

ROSS, SKYE & LOCHABER
E. 54,229   T. 39,869 (73.52%)
                                 SNP hold
Ian Blackford, SNP   19,263
Craig Harrow, LD   9,820
Gavin Berkenheger, C.   6,900
John Erskine, Lab.   2,448
Kate Brownlie, Brexit   710
Donald Boyd, SCP   460
Richard Lucas, Scot Family   268
SNP majority 9,443 (23.69%)
2.17% swing LD to SNP

RUTHERGLEN & HAMILTON WEST
E. 80,918   T. 53,794 (66.48%)   SNP gain
Margaret Ferrier, SNP   23,775
Ged Killen, Lab. Co-op   18,545
Lynne Nailon, C.   8,054
Mark McGeever, LD   2,791
Janice Mackay, UKIP   629
SNP majority 5,230 (9.72%)
5.12% swing Lab. to SNP

STIRLING
E. 68,473   T. 52,620 (76.85%)   SNP gain
Alyn Smith, SNP   26,895
Stephen Kerr, C.   17,641
Mary Ross, Lab.   4,275
Fayzan Rehman, LD   2,867
Bryan Quinn, Green   942
SNP majority 9,254 (17.59%)
8.94% swing C. to SNP

NORTHERN IRELAND

ANTRIM EAST
E. 64,830   T. 37,261 (57.47%)
                                 DUP hold
Sammy Wilson, DUP   16,871
Danny Donnelly, Alliance   10,165
Steve Aiken, UUP   5,475
Oliver McMullan, SF   2,120
Aaron Rankin, C.   1,043
Angela Mulholland, SDLP   902
Philip Randle, Green   685
DUP majority 6,706 (18.00%)
11.87% swing DUP to Alliance

ANTRIM NORTH
E. 77,134   T. 44,051 (57.11%)
                                 DUP hold
Ian Paisley, DUP   20,860
Robin Swann, UUP   8,139
Patricia O'Lynn, Alliance   6,231
Cara McShane, SF   5,632
Margaret McKillop, SDLP   2,943
Stephen Palmer, Ind.   246
DUP majority 12,721 (28.88%)
11.40% swing DUP to UUP

ANTRIM SOUTH
E. 71,711   T. 42,974 (59.93%)
                                 DUP hold
Paul Girvan, DUP   15,149
Danny Kinahan, UUP   12,460
John Blair, Alliance   8,190
Declan Kearney, SF   4,887
Roisin Lynch, SDLP   2,288
DUP majority 2,689 (6.26%)
0.59% swing DUP to UUP

BELFAST EAST
E. 66,245   T. 42,445 (64.07%)
                                 DUP hold
Gavin Robinson, DUP   20,874
Naomi Long, Alliance   19,055
Carl McClean, UUP   2,516
DUP majority 1,819 (4.29%)
7.74% swing DUP to Alliance

BELFAST NORTH

E. 72,225   T. 49,037 (67.89%)

	SF gain
John Finucane, SF	23,078
Nigel Dodds, DUP	21,135
Nuala McAllister, Alliance	4,824
SF majority 1,943 (3.96%)	
4.25% swing DUP to SF	

BELFAST SOUTH

E. 69,984   T. 47,352 (67.66%)

	SDLP gain
Claire Hanna, SDLP	27,079
Emma Little Pengelly, DUP	11,678
Paula Bradshaw, Alliance	6,786
Michael Henderson, UUP	1,259
Chris McHugh, Aontu	550
SDLP majority 15,401 (32.52%)	
18.55% swing DUP to SDLP	

BELFAST WEST

E. 65,644   T. 38,782 (59.08%)

	SF hold
Paul Maskey, SF	20,866
Gerry Carroll, PBP	6,194
Frank McCoubrey, DUP	5,220
Paul Doherty, SDLP	2,985
Donnamarie Higgins, Alliance	1,882
Monica Digney, Aontu	1,635
SF majority 14,672 (37.83%)	
9.36% swing SF to PBP	

DOWN NORTH

E. 67,099   T. 40,643 (60.57%)

	Alliance gain
Stephen Farry, Alliance	18,358
Alex Easton, DUP	15,390
Alan Chambers, UUP	4,936
Matthew Robinson, C.	1,959
Alliance majority 2,968 (7.30%)	
18.07% swing DUP to Alliance	

DOWN SOUTH

E. 79,175   T. 49,762 (62.85%)

	SF hold
Chris Hazzard, SF	16,137
Michael Savage, SDLP	14,517
Glyn Hanna, DUP	7,619
Patrick Brown, Alliance	6,916
Jill Macauley, UUP	3,307
Paul Brady, Aontu	1,266
SF majority 1,620 (3.26%)	
0.78% swing SF to SDLP	

FERMANAGH & SOUTH TYRONE

E. 72,848   T. 50,762 (69.68%)

	SF hold
Michelle Gildernew, SF	21,986
Tom Elliott, UUP	21,929
Adam Gannon, SDLP	3,446
Matthew Beaumont, Alliance	2,650
Caroline Wheeler, Ind.	751
SF majority 57 (0.11%)	
0.76% swing SF to UUP	

FOYLE

E. 74,346   T. 47,144 (63.41%)

	SDLP gain
Colum Eastwood, SDLP	26,881
Elisha McCallion, SF	9,771
Gary Middleton, DUP	4,773
Anne McCloskey, Aontu	2,032
Shaun Harkin, PBP	1,332
Rachael Ferguson, Alliance	1,267
Darren Guy, UUP	1,088
SDLP majority 17,110 (36.29%)	
18.33% swing SF to SDLP	

LAGAN VALLEY

E. 75,735   T. 45,405 (59.95%)

	DUP hold
Jeffrey Donaldson, DUP	19,586
Sorcha Eastwood, Alliance	13,087
Robbie Butler, UUP	8,606
Ally Haydock, SDLP	1,758
Gary McCleave, SF	1,098
Gary Hynds, C.	955
Alan Love, UKIP	315
DUP majority 6,499 (14.31%)	
17.07% swing DUP to Alliance	

LONDONDERRY EAST

E. 69,246   T. 39,302 (56.76%)

	DUP hold
Gregory Campbell, DUP	15,765
Cara Hunter, SDLP	6,158
Dermot Nicholl, SF	6,128
Chris McCaw, Alliance	5,921
Richard Holmes, UUP	3,599
Sean McNicholl, Aontu	1,731
DUP majority 9,607 (24.44%)	
6.42% swing DUP to SDLP	

NEWRY & ARMAGH

E. 81,226   T. 50,779 (62.52%)

	SF hold
Mickey Brady, SF	20,287
William Irwin, DUP	11,000
Pete Byrne, SDLP	9,449
Jackie Coade, Alliance	4,211
Sam Nicholson, UUP	4,204
Martin Kelly, Aontu	1,628
SF majority 9,287 (18.29%)	
2.51% swing SF to DUP	

STRANGFORD

E. 66,928   T. 37,485 (56.01%)

	DUP hold
Jim Shannon, DUP	17,705
Kellie Armstrong, Alliance	10,634
Philip Smith, UUP	4,023
Joe Boyle, SDLP	1,994
Grant Abraham, C.	1,476
Maurice Macartney, Green	790
Ryan Carlin, SF	555
Robert Stephenson, UKIP	308
DUP majority 7,071 (18.86%)	
14.24% swing DUP to Alliance	

TYRONE WEST

E. 66,259   T. 41,186 (62.16%)

	SF hold
Orfhlaith Begley, SF	16,544
Thomas Buchanan, DUP	9,066
Daniel McCrossan, SDLP	7,330
Stephen Donnelly, Alliance	3,979
Andy McKane, UUP	2,774
James Hope, Aontu	972
Susan Glass, Green	521
SF majority 7,478 (18.16%)	
2.81% swing SF to DUP	

ULSTER MID

E. 70,449   T. 44,620 (63.34%)

	SF hold
Francie Molloy, SF	20,473
Keith Buchanan, DUP	10,936
Denise Johnston, SDLP	6,384
Mel Boyle, Alliance	3,526
Neil Richardson, UUP	2,611
Conor Rafferty, Ind.	690
SF majority 9,537 (21.37%)	
3.12% swing SF to DUP	

UPPER BANN

E. 82,887   T. 50,045 (60.38%)

	DUP hold
Carla Lockhart, DUP	20,501
John O'Dowd, SF	12,291
Eoin Tennyson, Alliance	6,433
Doug Beattie, UUP	6,197
Dolores Kelly, SDLP	4,623
DUP majority 8,210 (16.41%)	
0.41% swing SF to DUP	

THE GOVERNMENT

As at 25 November 2020

THE CABINET

Prime Minister, First Lord of the Treasury, Minister for the Union and Minister for the Civil Service
Rt. Hon. Boris Johnson, MP
Chancellor of the Exchequer
Rt. Hon. Rishi Sunak, MP
Secretary of State for Foreign, Commonwealth and Development Affairs and First Secretary of State
Rt. Hon. Dominic Raab, MP
Secretary of State for the Home Department
Rt. Hon. Priti Patel, MP
Chancellor of the Duchy of Lancaster and Minister for the Cabinet Office
Rt. Hon. Michael Gove, MP
Lord Chancellor and Secretary of State for Justice
Rt. Hon. Robert Buckland, QC, MP
Secretary of State for Defence
Rt. Hon. Ben Wallace, MP
Secretary of State for Health and Social Care
Rt. Hon. Matt Hancock, MP
Secretary of State for Business, Energy and Industrial Strategy
Rt. Hon. Alok Sharma, MP
Secretary of State for International Trade and President of the Board of Trade and Minister for Women and Equalities
Rt. Hon. Elizabeth Truss, MP
Secretary of State for Work and Pensions
Rt. Hon. Thérèse Coffey, MP
Secretary of State for Education
Rt. Hon. Gavin Williamson, CBE, MP
Secretary of State for Environment, Food and Rural Affairs
Rt. Hon. George Eustice, MP
Secretary of State for Housing, Communities and Local Government
Rt. Hon. Robert Jenrick, MP
Secretary of State for Transport
Rt. Hon. Grant Shapps, MP
Secretary of State for Northern Ireland
Rt. Hon. Julian Lewis, MP
Secretary of State for Scotland
Rt. Hon. Alister Jack, MP
Secretary of State for Wales
Rt. Hon. Simon Hart, MP
Leader of the House of Lords and Lord Privy Seal
Rt. Hon. Baroness Evans of Bowes Park
Secretary of State for Digital, Culture, Media and Sport
Rt. Hon. Oliver Dowden, CBE, MP
Minister without Portfolio
Rt. Hon. Amanda Milling, MP

ALSO ATTENDING CABINET MEETINGS
Chief Secretary to the Treasury
Rt. Hon. Steve Barclay, MP
Lord President of the Council and Leader of the House of Commons
Rt. Hon. Jacob Rees-Mogg, MP
Parliamentary Secretary to the Treasury and Chief Whip
Rt. Hon. Mark Spencer, MP
Attorney-General
Rt. Hon. Suella Braverman, QC, MP
Minister for Business, Energy and Clean Growth
Rt. Hon. Kwasi Kwarteng, MP
Minister of State for Housing
Rt. Hon. Christopher Pincher, MP

Minister of State for Media and Data
Rt. Hon. John Whittingdale, OBE, MP
Minister of State for the Middle East and North Africa
Rt. Hon. James Cleverly, MP
Minister of State for Pacific and Environment
Rt. Hon. Lord Zac Goldsmith
Minister of State for School Standards
Rt. Hon. Nick Gibb, MP
Minister of State for Security
Rt. Hon. James Brokenshire, MP
Minister of State for Trade Policy
Rt. Hon. Greg Hands, MP
Deputy Leader of the House of Lords
Rt. Hon. Earl Howe
Finance Secretary to the Treasury
Rt. Hon. Jesse Norman, MP
Paymaster-General
Rt. Hon. Penny Mordaunt, MP
Solicitor General
Rt. Hon. Michael Ellis, QC, MP

LAW OFFICERS

Attorney-General
Rt. Hon. Suella Braverman, QC, MP
Solicitor-General
Rt. Hon. Michael Ellis, QC, MP
Advocate-General for Scotland
Keith Stewart, QC

MINISTERS OF STATE

Business, Energy and Industrial Strategy
Rt. Hon. Kwasi Kwarteng, MP
Cabinet Office
Lord Agnew§
Chloe Smith, MP
Lord True, CBE
Defence
Baroness Goldie, DL
Jeremy Quin
Digital, Culture, Media and Sport
Caroline Dinenage, MP
Rt Hon. John Whittingdale, OBE, MP
Education
Michelle Donelan, MP
Rt. Hon. Nick Gibb, MP
Environment, Food and Rural Affairs
Lord Zac Goldsmith†
Foreign, Commonwealth and Development Office
Lord Ahmad of Wimbledon
Nigel Adams, MP
Rt. Hon. James Cleverly, MP
Health and Social Care
Edward Argar, MP
Nadine Dorries, MP
Helen Whately, MP
Home Office
Rt. Hon. James Brokenshire, MP
Kit Malthouse, MP*

Housing, Communities and Local Government
Lord Stephen Greenhalgh‡
Luke Hall, MP
Rt. Hon. Christopher Pincher, MP
International Trade
Rt. Hon. Greg Hands, MP
Justice
Lucy Frazer, QC, MP
Northern Ireland Office
Robin Walker, MP
Transport
Chris Heaton-Harris, MP
Andrew Stephenson, MP
Work and Pensions
Justin Tomlinson, MP

* Jointly held with the Ministry of Justice
† Jointly held with FCO
‡ Jointly held with the Home Office
§ Jointly held with the Treasury

UNDER-SECRETARIES OF STATE

Business, Energy and Industrial Strategy
Lord Callahan
Paul Scully, MP
Amanda Solloway, MP
Nadhim Zahawi, MP
Cabinet Office
Johnny Mercer, MP*
Defence
James Heappey, MP
Digital, Culture, Media and Sport
Baroness Barran, MBE
Nigel Huddleston, MP††
Matt Warman, MP
Education
Baroness Berridge of The Vale of Catmose†
Vicky Ford, MP
Gillian Keegan, MP
Environment, Food and Rural Affairs
Lord Gardiner of Kimble
Rebecca Pow, MP
Victoria Prentis, MP
Foreign, Commonwealth and Development Office
James Duddridge, MP
Wendy Morton, MO
Health and Social Care
Jo Churchill, MP
Lord Bethell of Romford
Home Office
Victoria Atkins, MP
Kevin Foster, MP
Chris Philp, MP§
Housing, Communities and Local Government
Kelly Tolhurst, MP
International Trade
Kemi Badenoch, MP☪
Baroness Berridge of The Vale of Catmose‡
Ranil Jayawardena, MP
Graham Stuart, MP
Justice
Alex Chalk, MP††
Office of the Secretary of State for Scotland
David Duguid, MP‡‡
Iain Stewart, MP
Transport
Robert Courts, MP
Rachel Maclean, MP
Baroness Vere of Norbiton

Office of the Secretary of State for Wales
David Davies, MP††
Work and Pensions
Mims Davies, MP
Guy Opperman, MP
Will Quince, MP
Baroness Deborah Stedman-Scott, OBE, DL

* Jointly held with the MOD
† Alongside role at DfIT
‡ Alongside role at the DfE
§ Jointly held with the MoJ
☪ Alongside role as Exchequer Secretary to the Treasury
** Jointly held with UK Export Finance
†† Alongside role as Assistant Whip
‡‡ Alongside role as government Whip

OTHER MINISTERS

Business, Energy and Industrial Strategy
Lord Grimstone of Boscobel Kt* *(Minister for Investment)*
Cabinet Office
Julia Lopez, MP *(Parliamentary Secretary)*
Home Office
Baroness Williams of Trafford *(Lords Minister)*
Treasury
Kemi Badenoch, MP *(Exchequer Secretary)*
John Glen, MP *(Economic Secretary)*
* Jointly held with DfIT

GOVERNMENT WHIPS

HOUSE OF LORDS

Lords Chief Whip and Captain of the Honourable Corps of Gentlemen-at-Arms
Rt. Hon. Lord Ashton of Hyde
Deputy Chief Whip and Captain of the Queen's Bodyguard of the Yeomen of the Guard
Earl of Courtown
Lords-in-Waiting
Lord Parkinson of Whitley Bay
Viscount Younger of Leckie
Baronesses-in-Waiting
Baroness Bloomfield of Hinton Waldrist
Baroness Penn
Baroness Scott of Bybrook, OBE

HOUSE OF COMMONS

Chief Whip and Parliamentary Secretary to the Treasury
Rt. Hon. Mark Spencer, MP
Deputy Chief Whip and Treasurer of HM Household
Stuart Andrew, MP
Government Whip and Comptroller of HM Household
Mike Feer, MP
Government Whip and Vice-Chamberlain of HM Household
Marcus Jones, MP
Lords Commissioners of HM Treasury (Whips)
David Duguid, MP*; Rebecca Harris, MP; James Morris, MP; David Rutley, MP; Maggie Throup, MP; Michael Tomlinson, MP
Assistant Whips
Maria Caulfield, MP; Alex Chalk, MP; David Davies, MP†; Leo Docherty, MP; Nigel Huddleston, MP; Eddie Hughes, MP; Tom Pursglove, MP;

*Alongside role as Under-Secretary of State at the Scottish Office
† Alongside role as Under-Secretary of State at the Welsh Office
‡ Alongside role as Under-Secretary of State at the Ministry of Justice
§ Alongside role as Under-Secretary of State at DCMS

GOVERNMENT DEPARTMENTS

THE CIVIL SERVICE

The civil service helps the government develop and deliver its policies as effectively as possible. It works in three types of organisations – departments, executive agencies, and non-departmental government bodies (NDPBs). Under the Next Steps programme, launched in 1988, many semi-autonomous executive agencies were established to carry out much of the work of the civil service. Executive agencies operate within a framework set by the responsible minister which specifies policies, objectives and available resources. All executive agencies are set annual performance targets by their minister. Each agency has a chief executive, who is responsible for the day-to-day operations of the agency and who is accountable to the minister for the use of resources and for meeting the agency's targets. The minister accounts to parliament for the work of the agency.

There are currently 423,770 civil servants on a full-time equivalent (FTE) basis and 456,410 on a headcount basis. FTE is a measure that counts staff according to the proportion of full-time hours that they work. Almost three-quarters of all civil servants work outside London and the south-east. All government departments and executive agencies are responsible for their own pay and grading systems for civil servants outside the senior civil service.

SALARIES 2020–21

MINISTERIAL SALARIES
Ministers who are members of the House of Commons receive a parliamentary salary of £81,932 in addition to the ministerial salary.

Prime minister	£79,936
Cabinet minister (Commons)	£71,673
Cabinet minister (Lords)	£105,216
Minister of state (Commons)	£34,367
Minister of state (Lords)	£82,153
Parliamentary under-secretary (Commons)	£24,678
Parliamentary under-secretary (Lords)	£71,551

SPECIAL ADVISERS' SALARIES
Special advisers to government ministers are paid out of public funds; their salaries are negotiated individually, but are usually in the range of £57,000 to £145,000.

CIVIL SERVICE SALARIES	
Senior Civil Servants	
Permanent secretary	£150,000–£200,000
Band 3	£120,000–£208,100
Band 2	£93,000–£162,500
Band 1	£71,000–£117,800

Staff are placed in pay bands according to their level of responsibility and taking account of other factors such as experience and marketability. Movement within and between bands is based on performance.

GOVERNMENT DEPARTMENTS

For more information on government departments, *see* **W** www.gov.uk/government/organisations

ATTORNEY-GENERAL'S OFFICE
Attorney-General's Office, 120 Petty France, London SW1H 9EA
T 020-7271 2492 **E** correspondence@attorneygeneral.gov.uk
W www.gov.uk/government/organisations/attorney-generals-office

The law officers of the crown for England and Wales are the Attorney-General and the Solicitor-General. The Attorney-General, assisted by the Solicitor-General, is the chief legal adviser to the government and is also ultimately responsible for all crown litigation. They have overall responsibility for the work of the Law Officers' Departments (the Treasury Solicitor's Department, the Crown Prosecution Service – incorporating the Revenue and Customs Prosecutions Office – and the Serious Fraud Office, and HM Crown Prosecution Service Inspectorate). The Attorney-General also oversees the armed forces' prosecuting authority and the government legal service. They have a specific statutory duty to superintend the discharge of their duties by the Director of Public Prosecutions (who heads the Crown Prosecution Service) and the Director of the Serious Fraud Office. The Attorney-General has specific responsibilities for the enforcement of the criminal law and also performs certain public interest functions, for example protecting charities and appealing unduly lenient sentences. They also deal with questions of law arising in bills and with issues of legal policy.

Following the devolution of power to the Northern Ireland Assembly on 12 April 2010, the assembly now appoints the Attorney-General for Northern Ireland. The Attorney-General for England and Wales holds the office of Advocate-General for Northern Ireland, with significantly reduced responsibilities in Northern Ireland. The Attorney-General's Office is supported by four executive agencies and public bodies.

Attorney-General, Rt. Hon. Suella Braverman, QC, MP
Parliamentary Private Secretary, vacant
Principal Private Secretary, Josh Dodd
Deputy Principal Private Secretary, Samuel Chivers
Solicitor-General, Rt. Hon. Michael Ellis, QC, MP

MANAGEMENT BOARD
Director-General (Interim), Shehzad Charania, MBE
Deputy Legal Secretary and Head of Operations, Michelle Crotty

DEPARTMENT FOR BUSINESS, ENERGY AND INDUSTRIAL STRATEGY
1 Victoria Street, London SW1H 0ET
T 020-7215 5000 **E** enquiries@beis.gov.uk **W** www.gov.uk/government/organisations/department-for-business-energy-and-industrial-strategy

The Department for Business, Energy and Industrial Strategy (BEIS) was established in July 2016 following the appointment of Theresa May as prime minister. It merged the Department of Business, Innovation and Skills and the Department of Energy and Climate Change. BEIS brings together responsibilities for business, industrial strategy, science, innovation, energy and climate change, and is supported by 45 executive agencies and public bodies. It is responsible for: developing and delivering a comprehensive industrial strategy and leading the government's relationship with business; ensuring that the UK has secure, reliable, affordable and clean energy supplies; ensuring the UK remains at the forefront of science, research and innovation; and tackling climate change.

Secretary of State for Business, Energy and Industrial Strategy, Rt. Hon. Alok Sharma, MP
Parliamentary Private Secretary, Jo Gideon, MP
Special Advisers, Samantha Magnus; Marc Pooler
Minister of State, Rt. Hon. Kwasi Kwarteng, MP
Parliamentary Private Secretary, Mark Fletcher, MP
Parliamentary Under-Secretary of State, Lord Callanan *(Climate Change and Corporate Responsibility)*
Parliamentary Under-Secretary of State, Paul Scully, MP *(Small Business, Consumers and Labour Markets)*
Parliamentary Under-Secretary of State, Amanda Solloway, MP *(Science, Research and Innovation)*
Parliamentary Under-Secretary of State, Nadim Zahawi, MP *(Business and Industry)*
Minister for Investment, Lord Grimstone of Boscobel Kt*

* Jointly held with DfIT

MANAGEMENT BOARD
Permanent Secretary, Sarah Munby
Members, Julian Critchlow *(Energy Transformation and Clean Growth);* Ashley Ibbett *(Trade, Europe and Analysis);* Prof. Paul Monks *(BEIS Chief Scientific Adviser);* Jee Samant *(Market Frameworks);* Jo Shanmugalingam *(Industrial Strategy, Science and Innovation);* Doug Watkins *(Corporate Services);* Joanna Whittington *(Energy and Security)*
Non-Executive Members, Archie Norman *(Lead);* Nigel Boardman; Stephen Carter; Dame Carolyn McCall, DBE; Leena Nair; Kathryn Parsons; Stuart Quickenden
Special Representatives, Rt. Hon. Anne-Marie Trevelyan, MP *(Adaptation and Resilience for COP26 Presidency)*

BETTER REGULATION EXECUTIVE
1 Victoria Street, London SW1 0ET
T 020-7215 5000 **E** enquiries@beis.gov.uk
W www.gov.uk/government/policy-teams/better-regulation-executive

The Better Regulation Executive (BRE) is a joint BEIS/ Cabinet Office unit which leads on delivering the government's manifesto commitment to reduce the overall burden on business, in order to increase growth and create jobs. Each government department is, however, responsible for delivering its part of the deregulation agenda within the framework put in place by the BRE.

Non-Executive Chair, Lord Curry of Kirkharle, CBE
Chief Executive, Graham Turnock

CABINET OFFICE
70 Whitehall, London SW1A 2AS
T 020-7276 1234
W www.gov.uk/government/organisations/cabinet-office

The Cabinet Office, alongside the Treasury, sits at the centre of the government, with an overarching purpose of making government work better. It supports the prime minister and the cabinet, helping to ensure effective development, coordination and implementation of policy and operations across all government departments. The Cabinet Office also leads work to ensure that the Civil Service provides the most effective and efficient support to the government to meet its objectives. The department is headed by the Minister for the Cabinet Office. The Cabinet Office is responsible for: supporting collective government; supporting the National Security Council and the Joint Intelligence Organisation, coordinating the government's response to crises and managing the UK's cyber security; promoting efficiency and reform across government through innovation, better procurement and project management, and by transforming the delivery of services; promoting the release of government data, and making the way government works more transparent; improving the capability and effectiveness of the Civil Service; and political constitution and reform.

The priorities of the Cabinet Office include: supporting the prime minister and cabinet to deliver the government's programme; driving efficiencies and reforms to improve the government's performance; creating a more united democracy; and strengthening and securing the UK at home and abroad. The Cabinet Office employs around 8,800 staff and is supported by 23 executive agencies and public bodies.

Prime Minister, First Lord of the Treasury, Minister for the Union and Minister for the Civil Service, Rt. Hon. Boris Johnson, MP
Parliamentary Private Secretaries, Alex Burghart, MP; Trudy Harrison, MP
Principal Private Secretary, Martin Reynolds, CMG
Chief of Staff, Baron Ed Udny-Lister
Special Advisers (Senior), Nikki Da Costa *(Legislative Affairs);* David Frost, CMG *(Europe);* Andrew Griffith, MP *(Business);* Oliver Lewis; Munira Mirza *(Policy)*
Chancellor of the Duchy of Lancaster and Minister for the Cabinet Office, Rt. Hon. Michael Gove, MP
Parliamentary Private Secretary, Kevin Hollinrake, MP
Special Advisers, Josh Grimstone; Henry Newman; Charlie Rowley
Lord President of the Council, Rt. Hon. Jacob Rees-Mogg, MP
Parliamentary Private Secretary, Lucy Allan, MP
Special Advisers, Fred de Frossard; Beatrice Timpson
Lord Privy Seal and Leader of the House of Lords, Rt. Hon Baroness Evans of Bowed Park
Parliamentary Private Secretary, Christ Green, MP
Special Advisers, Annabelle Eyre; James Price; Hannah Ellis; Yasmin Kalhori
Minister without Portfolio, Rt. Hon. Amanda Milling, MP
Paymaster-General, Rt. Hon. Penny Mordaunt, MP
Minister of State, Chloe Smith, MP *(Constitution and Devolution)*
Minister of State, Lord Agnew *(Efficiency and Transformation)**
Minister of State, Lord True, CBE
Parliamentary Under-Secretary of State, Johnny Mercer, MP *(Minister for Defence, People and Veterans)†*
Parliamentary Secretary, Julia Lopez, MP

*Jointly held with the Treasury
† Jointly held with the MoD

MANAGEMENT BOARD
Cabinet Secretary and Head of the Civil Service, Simon Case, CVO
Permanent Secretary and Chief Operating Officer for the Civil Service, Alex Chisholm
First Parliamentary Counsel, Elizabeth Gardiner, CB, QC
Chair of the Joint Intelligence Committee, Sir Simon Gass, KCMG, CVO
Chief People Officer, Rupert McNeil
Government Chief Commercial Officer, Gareth Rhys Williams
Executive Director, Government Communications, Alex Aiken
Prime Minister's International Affairs Adviser, Deputy National Security Adviser, David Quarrey, CMG
Director-General, UK Governance, Lucy Smith
Director-General, Government Property, Mike Parsons
Chief Security Officer, Dominic Fortescue
Director-General, Government Digital Service (Interim), Fiona Deans
Chief Executive, Infrastructure and Projects Authority, Nick Smallwood

Director-General, Government Service, Kevin Cunnington
Deputy National Security Adviser, Alex Ellis
Deputy Cabinet Secretary, Helen MacNamara
Lead Non-Executive Board Member, Rt. Hon. Gisela Stuart
Non-Executive Board Members, Anand Aithal; Mike Ashley;
    Karen Blackett, OBE; Henry De Zoete; Baroness Finn;
    Lord Hogan-Howe

SPECIAL REPRESENTATIVE
Kevin Cunnington (Digital Envoy for the UK)*

*Alongside role as Director-General, International Government Service

HONOURS AND APPOINTMENTS BOARD
Room G-39, Horse Guards Road, London SW1A 2HQ
T 020-7276 2777
Chair, Simon Case, CVO

OFFICE OF THE LEADER OF THE HOUSE OF COMMONS
70 Whitehall, London SW1A 2AS
T 020-7276 1005 **E** commonsleader@cabinetoffice.gov.uk
W www.gov.uk/government/organisations/
the-office-of-the-leader-of-the-house-of-commons

The Office of the Leader of the House of Commons is responsible for the arrangement of government business in the House of Commons and for planning and supervising the government's legislative programme. The Leader of the House of Commons upholds the rights and privileges of the house and acts as a spokesperson for the government as a whole.

The leader reports regularly to the cabinet on parliamentary business and the legislative programme. In their capacity as leader of the house, they are a member of the House of Commons Commission. They also chair the cabinet committee on the legislative programme. As Lord President of the Council, they are a member of the cabinet and in charge of the Office of the Privy Council.

The Deputy Leader of the House of Commons supports the leader in handling the government's business in the house. They are responsible for monitoring MPs' and peers' correspondence.

Lord President of the Privy Council and Leader of the House of
    Commons, Rt. Hon. Jacob Rees-Mogg, MP
Parliamentary Private Secretary, Lucy Allan, MP
Special Advisers, Fred de Frossard; Beatrice Timpson

OFFICE OF THE LEADER OF THE HOUSE OF LORDS
Room 20, Principal Floor, West Front, House of Lords, London
SW1A 0PW
T 020-7219 3200 **E** pslseaderofthelords@cabinetoffice.gov.uk
W www.gov.uk/government/organisations/
office-of-the-leader-of-the-house-of-lords

The Office of the Leader of the House of Lords provides support to the leader in their parliamentary and ministerial duties, which include leading the government benches in the House of Lords; the delivery of the government's business in the Lords; taking part in formal ceremonies such as the state opening of parliament; and giving guidance to the House of Lords on matters of procedure and order.

Lord Privy Seal and Leader of the House of Lords, Rt. Hon.
    Baroness Evans of Bowes Park
Parliamentary Private Secretary, Chris Green, MP
Special Advisers, Annabelle Eyre (Senior); Hannah Ellis; Yasmin
    Kalhori; James Price
Deputy Leader of the House of Lords, Rt. Hon. Earl Howe

PRIME MINISTER'S OFFICE
10 Downing Street, London SW1A 2AA
W www.gov.uk/government/organisations/
prime-ministers-office-10-downing-street

Prime Minister, Rt. Hon. Boris Johnson, MP
Parliamentary Private Secretaries, Alex Burghart, MP; Trudy
    Harrison, MP
Principal Private Secretary, Martin Reynolds, CMG
Chief of Staff, Baron Ed Udny-Lister
Special Advisers (Senior), Nikki Da Costa (Legislative Affairs);
    David Frost, CMG (Europe); Andrew Griffith, MP
    (Business); Oliver Lewis; Munira Mirza (Policy)
Special Advisers, Rosie Bate-Williams; Hugh Bennett; Henry
    Cook; Jack Doyle; Lucia Hodgson; Ben Gascoigne; Sophie
    Lis; Damon Poole; Chloe Sarfaty; Sophia True; Cleo
    Watson; Chloe Westley
Director of Communications, vacant
Prime Minister's Official Spokesman, James Slack, CBE
Prime Minister's Official Speech Writer, Alex Marklew
Press Secretary, Allegra Stratton
Head of Operations, Shelley Williams-Walker
Head of Implementation Unit, Jonathan Nancekivell-Smith
Research and Briefing, Declan Lyons; Marcus Natale; Sheridan
    Westlake

PRIVATE OFFICES GROUP
Director-General, Propriety and Ethics and Head of Private Offices
    Group, vacant

UK GOVERNANCE GROUP
Head of UK Governance, Lucy Smith

CABINET OFFICE CORPORATE SERVICES
Executive Director, Government Communications, Alex Aiken
Chief Financial Officer, Richard Hornby
Human Resources Director, Jo Rodrigues

NATIONAL SECURITY
Comprises the National Security Secretariat and the Joint Intelligence Organisation. The National Security Secretariat is responsible for providing policy advice to the National Security Council, where ministers discuss national security issues at a strategic level; coordinating and developing foreign and defence policy across government; coordinating policy, ethical and legal issues across the intelligence community, managing its funding and priorities, and dealing with the Intelligence and Security Committee which calls it to account; developing effective protective security policies and capabilities for government; improving the UK's resilience to respond to and recover from emergencies, and maintaining facilities for the effective coordination of government response to crises; and providing strategic leadership for cyber security in the UK, in line with the National Cyber Security Strategy.

NATIONAL SECURITY SECRETARIAT
Chief Security Officer, Dominic Fortescue
Deputy National Security Advisers, Alex Ellis; David Quarrey,
    CMG

JOINT INTELLIGENCE ORGANISATION
Chair of the Joint Intelligence Committee, Sir Simon Gass, KCMG,
    CVO

INDEPENDENT OFFICES

CIVIL SERVICE COMMISSION
1 Horse Guards Road, London SW1A 2HQ
T 020-7271 0831
W www.civilservicecommission.independent.gov.uk

The Civil Service Commission regulates the requirement that selection for appointment to the Civil Service must be on merit on the basis of fair and open competition; the commission publishes its recruitment principles and audit departments and agencies' performance against these. Commissioners personally chair competitions for the most senior jobs in the civil service. In addition, the commission hears complaints from civil servants under the Civil Service Code.

The commission was established as a statutory body in November 2010 under the provisions of the Constitutional Reform and Governance Act 2010.

Commissioners, Jane Burgess; Jan Cameron; Natalie Campbell; Isabel Doverty; Margaret Edwards; Rosie Glazebrook; Sarah Laessig; June Milligan; Joe Montgomery; Ian Watmore; Kevin Woods

THE COMMISSIONER FOR PUBLIC APPOINTMENTS
G/8, 1 Horse Guards Road, London SW1A 2HQ
T 020-7271 6729 **E** publicappointments@csc.gov.uk
W http://publicappointmentscommissioner.independent.gov.uk

The Commissioner for Public Appointments is responsible for monitoring, regulating and reporting on ministerial appointments (including those made by Welsh government ministers) to public bodies. The commissioner can investigate complaints about the way in which appointments were made.

Commissioner for Public Appointments, Peter Riddell
Chief Executive Commission Secretariat, Peter Lawrence, OBE

OFFICE OF THE PARLIAMENTARY COUNSEL
1 Horse Guards Road, London SW1A 2HQ
T 02-7276 6586 **E** opc@cabinetoffice.gov.uk **W** www.gov.uk/government/organisations/office-of-the-parliamentary-counsel

The Office of the Parliamentary Counsel is a group of government lawyers who specialise in drafting government bills; advising departments on the rules and procedures of Parliament; reviewing orders and regulations which amend Acts of Parliament; and assisting the government on a range of legal and constitutional issues.

Parliamentary Counsel, Elizabeth Gardiner

GOVERNMENT EQUALITIES OFFICE
Sanctuary Buildings, 16–20 Great Smith Street, London SW1P 3BT
T 0808-800 0082 **W** www.gov.uk/government/organisations/government-equalities-office

The Government Equalities Office (GEO) is responsible for the government's overall strategy on equality. Its work includes leading the development of a more integrated approach on equality across government with the aim of improving equality and reducing discrimination and disadvantage for all. The office is also responsible for leading policy on gender equality, sexual orientation and transgender equality matters.

Minister for Women and Equalities, Rt. Hon. Elizabeth Truss, MP*
Parliamentary Under-Secretary of State, Kemi Badenoch *(Equalities)*†
Parliamentary Under-Secretary of State, Baroness Berridge of the Vale of Catmose *(Women)*†
Director (Interim), Elysia McCaffrey

* Alongside role as Secretary of State for International Trade and President of the Board of Trade
† Alongside role as Under-Secretary of State for the School System in the DfE

MINISTRY OF DEFENCE
Main Building, Whitehall, London SW1A 2HB
T 020-7218 9000 **W** www.gov.uk/government/organisations/ministry-of-defence

For further information on the responsibilities and remit of the MoD *see* the Defence Chapter.

Secretary of State for Defence, Rt. Hon. Ben Wallace, MP
Parliamentary Private Secretary, Jack Brereton, MP
Special Adviser, Peter Quentin
Minister of State, Baroness Goldie *(Lords)*
Minister of State, Jeremy Quin, MP *(Defence Procurement)*
Parliamentary Under-Secretary of State and Minister for Armed Forces, James Heappey, MP
Parliamentary Under-Secretary of State and Minister for Defence People and Veterans, Johnny Mercer, MP*

*Jointly held with the Cabinet Office

SENIOR MILITARY OFFICIALS
Chief of the Defence Staff, Gen. Sir Nick Carter, GCB, CBE, DSO, ADC Gen
Vice-Chief of the Defence Staff, Adm. Sir Tim Fraser, KCB, ADC
Chief of Naval Staff and First Sea Lord, Adm. Tony Radakin, CB, ADC
Chief of the General Staff, Gen. Sir Mark Carleton-Smith, KCB, CBE, ADC Gen
Chief of the Air Staff, Air Chief Marshal Mike Wigston, CBE, ADC
Commander of Joint Forces Command, Gen. Sir Patrick Sanders, KCB, CBE, DSO, ADC Gen
Deputy Commander of Strategic Command, Lt.-Gen. Rob Magowan, CB, CBE

MANAGEMENT BOARD
Permanent Secretary, Sir Stephen Lovegrove, KCB
Members, Mike Baker, CBE *(Chief Operating Officer);* Lt.-Gen. Doug Chalmers *(Deputy Chief of Defence Staff (Military Strategy and Operations));* Charlie Forte *(Chief Information Officer);* Prof. Robin Grimes, FRS, FRENG *(Chief Scientific Adviser (Nuclear));* Air Marshal Richard Knighton *(Deputy Chief of the Defence Staff (Financial and Military Capability));* Angus Lapsley *(Strategy and International);* Prof. Dame Angela McLean, DBE *(Chief Scientific Adviser);* Vanessa Nicholls *(Nuclear);* Charlie Pate *(Finance);* Maj.-Gen. James Swift *(Chief of Defence People);* Dominic Wilson *(Security Policy)*
Non-Executive Members, Brian McBride *(Lead);* Danuta Gray; Simon Henry; Robin Marshall

DEPARTMENT FOR DIGITAL, CULTURE, MEDIA AND SPORT
100 Parliament Street, London SW1A 2BQ
E enquiries@culture.gov.uk **W** www.gov.uk/government/organisations/department-for-digital-culture-media-sport

The Department for Digital, Culture, Media and Sport (DCMS) was established in July 1997 (as the Department for Culture, Media and Sport) and aims to improve the quality of life for all those in the UK through cultural and sporting activities while championing the tourism, creative and leisure industries. It is responsible for government policy relating to the arts, sport, the National Lottery, tourism, libraries, museums and galleries, broadcasting, creative industries – including film and the music industry – press freedom and regulation, licensing, gambling, the historic environment, telecommunications and online and media ownership and mergers. In July 2017, the department was rebranded to reflect its growing commitment and responsibility regarding digital infrastructure, communication and cyber security.

The department is also responsible for 45 agencies and public bodies that help deliver the department's strategic aims and objectives, the listing of historic buildings and scheduling of ancient monuments, the export licensing of cultural goods, and the management of the Government Art Collection and the Royal Historic Palaces. It has the responsibility for humanitarian assistance in the event of a disaster, as well as for the organisation of the annual Remembrance Day ceremony at the Cenotaph.

Secretary of State for Digital, Culture, Media and Sport, Rt. Hon. Oliver Dowden, CBE, MP
Special Advisers, Jamie Njoku-Goodwin; Lucy Noakes; Mike Crowhurst
Minister of State, Caroline Dinenage, MP *(Digital and Culture)*
Minister of State, Rt. Hon. John Whittingdale, OBE, MP *(Media and Data)*
Parliamentary Under-Secretary of State, Baroness Barran, MBE *(Civil Society)*
Parliamentary Under-Secretary of State, Nigel Huddleston, MP *(Sport, Tourism and Heritage)**
Parliamentary Under-Secretary of State, Matt Warman, MP *(Digital Infrastructure)*
*Alongside role as Assistant Whip

MANAGEMENT BOARD
Permanent Secretary, Sarah Healey
Members, Clare Dove, CBE *(Voluntary, Community and Social Enterprise Representative);* Jacinda Humphry *(Finance and Commercial Director)* Helen Judge *(Culture, Sport and Civil Society);* Sam Lister *(Strategy and Operations);* Neil Mendoza *(Cultural Recovery and Renewal);* Prof. Tom Rodden *(Chief Scientific Adviser);* Susannah Storey *(Digital and Media);* Non-Executive Members, Charles Alexander *(Lead);* Sherry Coutu, CBE; Hermant Patel; Baroness Laura Wyld

DEPARTMENT FOR EDUCATION
Piccadilly Gate, Store Street, Manchester M1 2WD
T 0370-000 2288 **W** www.gov.uk/government/organisations/department-for-education

The Department for Education (DfE) was established in May 2010 in place of the Department for Children, Schools and Families (DCSF), in order to refocus the department on its core purpose of supporting teaching and learning. The department is responsible for education and children's services, while the Department for Business, Energy and Industrial Strategy is responsible for higher education. The DfE is supported by 18 executive agencies and public bodies.
The department's objectives include keeping pace with academic standards as measured internationally, and improving technical education in line with international systems.

Secretary of State for Education, Rt. Hon. Gavin Williamson, CBE, MP
Parliamentary Private Secretary, Scott Mann, MP
Special Advisers, Iain Mansfield; Innes Taylor; Angus Walker
Minister of State, Rt. Hon. Nick Gibb, MP *(School Standards)*
Minister of State, Michelle Donelan, MP *(Universities)*
Parliamentary Under-Secretary of State, Baroness Berridge of The Vale of Catmose *(School System)*
Parliamentary Under-Secretary of State, Vicky Ford, MP *(Children and Families)*
Parliamentary Under-Secretary of State, Gillian Keegan, MP *(Apprenticeships and Skills)*
* Jointly held with the DfIT

MANAGEMENT BOARD
Permanent Secretary, Susan Acland-Hood
Members, Mike Green *(Chief Operating Officer, Operations Group);* Paul Kett *(Higher and Further Education Group);*

Andrew McCully, CB, CBE *(Early Years and Schools);* Elaine Milner *(ex officio);* Indra Morris *(Social Care, Mobility and Disadvantage);* Lucy Smith *(COVID-19 Response and Schools Recovery)*
Non-Executive Members, Richard Pennycook *(Lead);* Ian Ferguson, CBE; Irene Lucas; Baroness Ruby McGregor-Smith, CBE; Toby Peyton-Jones; Nick Timothy, CBE

DEPARTMENT FOR ENVIRONMENT, FOOD AND RURAL AFFAIRS
Seacole Building, 2 Marsham Street, London SW1P 4DF
T 03459-335577 **E** defra.helpline@defra.gov.uk
W www.gov.uk/government/organisations/department-for-environment-food-rural-affairs

The Department for Environment, Food and Rural Affairs (DEFRA) is responsible for government policy on the environment, rural matters and farming and food production. In association with the agriculture departments of the Scottish government, the National Assembly for Wales and the Northern Ireland Office, the department is responsible for helping negotiating the grounds for Britain's exit from the EU. Its remit includes international agricultural and food trade policy.
The department's strategic priorities are a smooth exit from the EU; climate change adaptation; the protection of natural resources and the countryside; and sustainable rural communities. DEFRA, which is supported by 33 executive agencies and public bodies, is also the lead government department for responding to emergencies in animal and plant diseases, flooding, food and water supply, dealing with the consequences of a chemical, biological, radiological or nuclear incident, and other threats to the environment.

Secretary of State for Environment, Food and Rural Affairs, Rt. Hon. George Eustice, MP
Parliamentary Private Secretary, Caroline Ansell, MP
Special Adviser, Emma Pryor
Minister of State, Rt. Hon. Zac Goldsmith, MP *(Pacific and the Environment)**
Parliamentary Under-Secretary of State, Lord Gardiner of Kimble *(Rural Affairs and Biosecurity)*
Parliamentary Under-Secretary of State, Rebecca Pow, MP
Parliamentary Under-Secretary of State, Victoria Prentis, MP
* Jointly held with the FCDO

MANAGEMENT BOARD
Permanent Secretary, Tamara Finkelstein
Members, Prof. Gideon Henderson *(Chief Scientific Adviser);* David Hill *(Environment, Rural and Marine);* Sarah Homer *(Chief Operating Officer);* Emma Howard Boyd *(ex officio);* Tony Juniper, CBE *(ex officio);* David Kennedy *(Food, Farming and Biosecurity);* James Quinault *(Europe, International and Constitution Group)*
Non-Executive Members, Henry Dimbleby *(Lead);* Elizabeth Buchanan; Colin Day; Ben Goldsmith; Lizzie Noel

FOREIGN, COMMONWEALTH AND DEVELOPMENT OFFICE
King Charles Street, London SW1A 2AH
T 020-7008 5000 **E** fcdo.correspondence@fcdo.gov.uk
W www.gov.uk/government/organisations/foreign-commonwealth-development-office

The Foreign, Commonwealth and Development Office (FCDO) was formed in September 2020 from a merger between the Foreign and Commonwealth Office and the Department for International Development ahead of the UK's presidency of the G7 and COP26 in 2021. It provides the means of communication between the British government and other governments – and international governmental organisations – on all matters falling within the field of international relations and development. The FCDO employs over 17,300 people in 280 places across the world through a network of embassies, consulates, and development programmes that help to protect and promote national interests. FCO diplomats are skilled in understanding and influencing what is happening abroad, supporting British citizens who are travelling and living overseas, helping to manage migration into Britain, promoting British trade and other interests abroad and encouraging foreign investment in the UK.

The FCDO is responsible for promoting sustainable development and reducing poverty, and honouring the UK's international commitments including the United Nations' Sustainable Development Goals. It aims to make British overseas aid more effective by improving transparency and value for money; focusing British international development policy on economic growth and wealth creation; improving the coherence and performance of British development policy in fragile and conflict-affected countries; improving the lives of girls and women through better education, greater choice on family planning and preventing violence; and acting on climate change and encouraging adaptation and low-carbon growth in developing countries. It provides regional and national programmes throughout the world, including in dependent UK Overseas Territories, and gives UK Aid through multi-country global programmes and multilateral institutions like the World Bank and United Nations. The FCDO is supported by 12 executive agencies and public bodies.

Secretary of State for Foreign, Commonwealth and Development Affairs, First Secretary of State, Rt. Hon. Dominic Raab, MP
Parliamentary Private Secretary, Gareth Johnson, MP
Special Advisers, Beth Armstrong; Simon Finkelstien
Minister of State, Nigel Adams, MP *(Asia)*
Minister of State, Lord Ahmad of Wimbledon *(South Asia and the Commonwealth)*
Minister of State, Rt. Hon. James Cleverly, MP *(Middle East and North Africa)*
Minister of State, Rt. Hon. Lord Zac Goldsmith *(Pacific and the Environment)**
Parliamentary Under-Secretary of State, James Duddridge, MP *(Africa)*
Parliamentary Under-Secretary of State, Wendy Morton, MP *(European Neighbourhood and the Americas)*
* Jointly held with DEFRA

SPECIAL REPRESENTATIVES
Lord Ahmad of Wimbledon *(Prime Minister's Special Representative on Preventing Sexual Violence in Conflict);* Gareth Bayley *(Afghanistan and Pakistan);* Nick Bridge *(Climate Change);* Nick Dyer *(Special Envoy for Famine Prevention and Humanitarian Affairs);* Robert Fairweather, OBE *(Sudan and South Sudan);* Philip Parham *(Commonwealth);* Rt. Hon. Lord Pickles *(UK Special Envoy for Post-Holocaust Issues);* Jennifer Townson *(Migration and Modern Slavery Envoy);* Rt. Hon. Marie-Trevelyan, MP *(Adaptation and Resilience for COP26 Presidency)*

MANAGEMENT BOARD
Permanent Under-Secretary, Sir Philip Barton, KCMG, OBE
Political Director, Sir Tim Barrow, GCMG, LVO, MBE
Members, Jenny Bates *(Indo-Pacific);* Juliet Chua *(Finance and Corporate);* Thomas Drew, CMG *(Middle East, North Africa, Afghanistan and Pakistan);* Dr Rachel Glennerster *(Chief*

Economist); Nic Hailey, CMG *(Transformation);* Kumar Iyer *(Delivery);* Sir Iain Macleod, KCMG *(Legal);* Moazzam Malik *(Africa);* Vijay Rangarajan *(Americas and Overseas Territories)*
Non-Executive Members, Baroness Helena Morrissey *(Lead);* John Coffey; Ann Cormack, MBE; Beverley Tew

CDC GROUP
123 Victoria Street, London SW1E 6DE
T 020-7963 4700 E enquiries@cdcgroup.com
W www.cdcgroup.com

Founded in 1948, CDC is the UK's Development Finance Institution wholly owned by the UK government. It invests to create jobs and build businesses in developing countries in Africa and South Asia. In 2019 CDC's new investment commitments totalled £1.66bn to 690 businesses in Africa and 377 businesses in South Asia, helping to create new jobs across these regions. CDC is a public limited company with a portfolio worth £4.7bn.

Chair, Sir Graham Wrigley
Chief Executive, Nick O'Donohoe

DEPARTMENT OF HEALTH AND SOCIAL CARE
39 Victoria Street, London SW1H 0EU
T 020-7210 4850 W www.gov.uk/government/organisations/department-of-health-and-social-care

The Department of Health and Social Care (DHSC) leads, shapes and funds health and social care in England, making sure people have the support, care and treatment they need and that this is delivered in a compassionate, respectful and dignified manner.

The DHSC leads across health and care by creating national policies and legislation to meet current and future challenges. It provides funding, assures the delivery and continuity of services and accounts to parliament in a way that represents the best interests of patients, the public and the taxpayer. The DHSC is supported by 29 executive agencies and public bodies.

Secretary of State for Health and Social Care, Rt. Hon. Matthew Hancock, MP
Parliamentary Private Secretary, Steve Double, MP
Special Advisers, Emma Dean; Allan Nixon; Ed Taylor
Minister of State, Edward Argar, MP *(Health)*
Minister of State, Nadine Dorries, MP *(Patient Safety, Suicide Prevention and Mental Health)*
Minister of State, Helen Whately, MP *(Care)*
Parliamentary Under-Secretary of State, Lord Bethell of Romford *(Innovation)*
Parliamentary Under-Secretary of State, Jo Churchill, MP *(Prevention, Public Health and Primary Care)*

DEPARTMENTAL BOARD
Permanent Secretary, Sir Chris Wormald, KCB
Members, Matthew Gould *(CEO of NHSX);* Jonathan Marron *(Community and Social Care);* Lee McDonough *(Acute Care and Workforce);* Clara Swinson *(Global and Public Health);* Prof. Chris Whitty *(Chief Scientific Adviser, Chief Medical Officer);* David Williams *(Second Permanent Secretary, Finance and Group Operations)*

SPECIAL REPRESENTATIVES
Prof. Dame Sally Davies, DBE *(UK Special Envoy on Antimicrobial Resistance)*

HOME OFFICE

2 Marsham Street, London SW1P 4DF
T 020-7035 4848 **E** public.enquiries@homeoffice.gov.uk
W www.gov.uk/government/organisations/home-office

The Home Office deals with those internal affairs in England and Wales which have not been assigned to other government departments. The Secretary of State for the Home Department is the link between the Queen and the public, and exercises certain powers on her behalf, including that of the royal pardon.

The Home Office aims to build a safe, just and tolerant society and to maintain and enhance public security and protection; to support and mobilise communities so that they are able to shape policy and improvement for their locality, overcome nuisance and anti-social behaviour, maintain and enhance social cohesion and enjoy their homes and public spaces peacefully; to deliver departmental policies and responsibilities fairly, effectively and efficiently; and to make the best use of resources. These objectives reflect the priorities of the government and the home secretary in areas of crime, citizenship and communities, namely to work on the problems caused by illegal drug use; shape the alcohol strategy, policy and licensing conditions; keep the UK safe from the threat of terrorism; reduce and prevent crime, and ensure people feel safe in their homes and communities; secure the UK border and control immigration; consider applications to enter and stay in the UK; issue passports and visas; to support visible, responsible and accountable policing by empowering the public and freeing up the police to fight crime; and oversee the fire and rescue services.

The Home Office delivers these aims through the immigration services, its 30 executive agencies and non-departmental public bodies, and by working with partners in private, public and voluntary sectors, individuals and communities. The home secretary is also the link between the UK government and the governments of the Channel Islands and the Isle of Man.

Secretary of State for the Home Department, Rt. Hon. Priti Patel, MP
Parliamentary Private Secretary, Mike Wood, MP
Special Advisers, Hannah Guerin; Harry Methley; Charlotte Miller; Michael Young
Minister of State, Rt. Hon. James Brokenshire, CBE, MP *(Security)*
Minister of State, Lord Stephen Greenhalgh *(Building Safety and Communities)**
Minister of State, Kit Malthouse, MP *(Crime and Policing)*†
Minister of State, Baroness Williams of Trafford *(Lords)*
Parliamentary Under-Secretary of State, Victoria Atkins, MP *(Safeguarding)*
Parliamentary Under-Secretary of State, Kevin Foster, MP *(Future Borders and Immigration)*
Parliamentary Under-Secretary of State, Chris Philp, MP *(Immigration Compliance and the Courts)*†

* Jointly held with the MHCLG
† Jointly held with the MoJ

MANAGEMENT BOARD
Permanent Secretary, Sir Matthew Rycroft, CBE
Second Permanent Secretary, Shona Dunn
Members, Simon Baugh *(Communications);* Joanna Davinson *(Chief Digital, Data and Technology Officer);* Charu Gorasia *(Capabilities and Resources);* Jill Hatcher *(Chief People Officer);* Tricia Hayes *(Crime, Policing and Fire);* Tyson Hepple *(Immigration Enforcement);* Tom Hurd *(Security and Counter-Terrorism);* Julia Kinniburgh *(Serious and Organised Crime Group);* Paul Lincoln *(Border Force);* Marc Owen, OBE *(Visas and Citizenship);* Abi Tierney *(UK Visas and*

Immigration, Her Majesty's Passport Office); Glyn Williams, CB *(Borders, Immigration and Citizenship)*
Non-Executive Members, Sue Langley, OBE *(Lead);* James Cooper; Michael Fuller, QPM; Suzy Levy; John Paton; Tim Robinson; Phil Swallow

MINISTRY OF HOUSING, COMMUNITIES AND LOCAL GOVERNMENT

2 Marsham Street, London SW1P 4DF
T 0303-444 0000 **W** www.gov.uk/government/organisations/ministry-of-housing-communities-and-local-government

The Ministry of Housing, Communities and Local Government was formed in January 2018 uniting housing, communities and civil renewal functions with responsibility for regeneration, neighbourhood renewal and local government. The ministry is tasked with increasing the national housing supply and home ownership; supporting public services; and devolving power and budgets to boost local growth in England. The ministry is supported by 12 executive agencies and public bodies.

Secretary of State for Housing, Communities and Local Government, Rt. Hon. Robert Jenrick, MP
Parliamentary Private Secretary, Andrea Jenkyns, MP
Special Advisers, Olivia Oates; Tom Kennedy
Minister of State, Luke Hall, MP *(Regional Growth and Local Government)*
Minister of State, Rt. Hon. Christopher Pincher, MP *(Housing)*
Parliamentary Under-Secretary of State, Lord Stephen Greenhalgh *(Building Safety and Communities)**
Parliamentary Under-Secretary of State, Kelly Tolhurst, MP *(Rough Sleeping and Housing)*

* Jointly held with the Home Office

MANAGEMENT BOARD
Permanent Secretary, Jeremy Pocklington
Members, Ruth Bailey *(People Capability and Change);* Lise-Anne Boissiere *(Strategy, Communications and Private Office);* Catherine Frances *(Local Government and Public Services);* Emran Mian *(Decentralisation and Growth);* Prof. Alan Penn *(Chief Scientific Adviser);* Matt Thurstan *(Chief Financial Officer);* Chris Townsend *(Shielding Programme);* Tracey Waltho *(Housing and Planning)*
Non-Executive Members, Michael Jary *(Lead);* Pam Chesters, CBE; Dame Mary Ney, DBE

SPECIAL REPRESENTATIVES
UK Special Envoy for Post-Holocaust Issues, Rt. Hon. Lord Pickles

DEPARTMENT FOR INTERNATIONAL TRADE

King Charles Street, Whitehall, London SW1A 2AH
T 020-7215 5000 **W** www.gov.uk/government/organisations/department-for-international-trade

The Department for International Trade was formed in July 2016 following the UK referendum to leave the European Union. The department is responsible for promoting British trade and investment around the world, striking and extending trade agreements between the UK and non-EU states.

Secretary of State for International Trade and President of the Board of Trade, Rt. Hon. Elizabeth Truss, MP
Parliamentary Private Secretary, Saqib Bhatti, MP
Special Advisers, Sophie Jarvis; Adam Jones
Minister of State, Rt. Hon. Greg Hands, MP *(Trade Policy)*
Minister for Investment, Lord Grimstone of Boscobel Kt*
Parliamentary Under-Secretary of State, Kemi Badenoch, MP *(Equalities)*†

Parliamentary Under-Secretary of State, Baroness Berridge of the
    Vale of Catmose *(Women)*‡
Parliamentary Under-Secretary of State, Ranil Jayawardena, MP
    (International Trade)
Parliamentary Under-Secretary of State, Graham Stuart, MP
    (Exports)§

* Jointly held with the DBEIS
† Alongside role as Exchequer Secretary to the Treasury
‡ Alongside role as Under-Secretary of State for the School System in DfE
§ Jointly held with UK Export Finance

MANAGEMENT BOARD
Permanent Secretary, Antonia Romeo
Second Permanent Secretary and Chief Trade Negotiation Adviser,
    Crawford Falconer
Members, John Alty *(Trade Policy);* John Mahon *(Exports);*
    Mark Slaughter *(Investment);* Louis Taylor *(UK Export
    Finance);* Catherine Vaughan *(Chief Operating Officer)*
Non-Executive Members, Julie Currie, Noel Harwerth, Sir
    Stephen O'Brien

MINISTRY OF JUSTICE
102 Petty France, London SW1H 9AJ
T 020-3334 3555
W www.gov.uk/government/organisations/ministry-of-justice

The Ministry of Justice (MoJ) was established in May 2007.
MoJ is headed by the Lord Chancellor and Secretary of State
for Justice who is responsible for improvements to the justice
system so that it better serves the public. They are also
responsible for some areas of constitutional policy.

The MoJ's key priorities are to reduce reoffending by using
the skills of the public, private and voluntary sectors; build a
prison and probation service that delivers maximum value for
money; to promote the rule of law globally; and to modernise
the courts and justice system. The MoJ has a budget of around
£10bn and is supported by 34 executive agencies and public
bodies to achieve its targets.

The Lord Chancellor and Secretary of State for Justice is the
government minister responsible to parliament for the
judiciary, the court system and prisons and probation. The
Lord Chief Justice has been the head of the judiciary since
2006.

MoJ incorporates HM Prison and Probation Service; HM
Courts and Tribunals Service; the Legal Aid Agency; and the
Youth Justice Board.

Lord Chancellor and Secretary of State for Justice, Rt. Hon. Robert
    Buckland, QC, MP
Parliamentary Private Secretary, Neil O'Brien, MP
Special Advisers, Ben Jafari; Rajiv Shah; Alex Wild
Minister of State, Kit Malthouse, QC, MP *(Crime and Policing)**
Parliamentary Under-Secretary of State, Alex Chalk, MP†
Parliamentary Under-Secretary of State, Chris Philp, MP
    (Immigration Compliance and the Courts)*
HM Advocate-General for Scotland, Keith Stewart, QC

* Jointly held with the Home Office
† Alongside role as Assistant Whip

MANAGEMENT BOARD
Permanent Secretary (Interim), Mike Driver
Members, Susan Acland-Hood *(Chief Executive and Board
    member, HM Courts and Tribunals Service);* Phil Copple
    (Prisons); Jo Farrar *(Chief Executive Officer, HM Prison and
    Probation Service);* Naomi Mallick *(Legal);* James McEwen
    *(Interim Chief Financial Officer, Director General of CFO
    Group);* Amy Rees *(Probation and Wales);* Dr Neil Wooding
    (Chief People Officer)
Non-Executive Members, Mark Rawlinson *(Lead);* Nick
    Campsie; Shirley Cooper; Paul Smith

NORTHERN IRELAND OFFICE
1 Horse Guards Road, London SW1A 2HQ
Stormont House, Stormont Estate, Belfast BT4 3SH
T 028-9052 0700 **E** comms@nio.gov.uk
W www.gov.uk/government/organisations/northern-ireland-office

The Northern Ireland Office was established in 1972, when
the Northern Ireland (Temporary Provisions) Act transferred
the legislative and executive powers of the Northern Ireland
parliament and government to the UK parliament and a
secretary of state. Under the terms of the 1998 Good Friday
Agreement, power was devolved to the Northern Ireland
Assembly in 1999. The assembly took on responsibility for the
relevant areas of work previously undertaken by the
departments of the Northern Ireland Office, covering
agriculture and rural development, the environment, regional
development, social development, education, higher
education, training and employment, enterprise, trade and
investment, culture, arts and leisure, health, social services,
public safety and finance and personnel. In October 2002 the
Northern Ireland Assembly was suspended and Northern
Ireland returned to direct rule, but despite repeated setbacks,
devolution was restored in May 2007. In January 2017 Martin
McGuinness resigned as Deputy First Minister of Northern
Ireland. Under the joint protocols that govern the power-
sharing agreement, which requires the government to be
comprised of both unionists and nationalists, if either the first
minister or the deputy resigns and a replacement is not
nominated by the relevant party within seven days then a snap
election must be called. The assembly was formerly dissolved
on 25 January 2017 and devolved government was not
restored until 10 January 2020, when a new deal was brokered.
For further details, *see* Devolved Government.

The Northern Ireland Office is supported by three executive
agencies and public bodies and is responsible for the smooth
working of the devolution settlement; representing Northern
Ireland interests within the UK government and similarly
representing the UK government in Northern Ireland; working
in partnership with the Northern Ireland Executive for a stable,
prosperous Northern Ireland; and supporting and
implementing political agreements to increase stability.

Secretary of State for Northern Ireland, Rt. Hon. Brandon Lewis,
    CBE, MP
Parliamentary Private Secretary, Sarah Dines, MP
Special Advisers, Isabel Bruce; Oliver Legard; Dr David Sheils
Minister of State, Robin Walker, MP

OFFICE OF THE ADVOCATE-GENERAL
FOR SCOTLAND
Queen Elizabeth House, Edinburgh, EH8 8FT
T 0131-244 0359 **E** enquiries@advocategeneral.gov.uk
Dover House, Whitehall, London SW1A 2AU
T 020-7270 6720
W www.gov.uk/government/organisations/
office-of-the-advocate-general-for-scotland

The Advocate-General for Scotland is one of the three law
officers of the crown, alongside the Attorney-General and the
Solicitor-General for England and Wales. It acts as the legal
adviser to the UK government on Scottish law and supports
the Advocate-General. The office is divided into the Legal
Secretariat, based mainly in London, and the Office of the
Solicitor to the Advocate-General, based in Edinburgh.

The post was created as a consequence of the constitutional
changes set out in the Scotland Act 1998, which created a
devolved Scottish parliament. The Lord Advocate and the
Solicitor-General for Scotland then became part of the Scottish
government and the Advocate-General took over their
previous role as legal adviser to the UK government on Scots
law. *See also* Devolved Government *and* Ministry of Justice.

HM Advocate-General for Scotland and MoJ Spokesperson for the Lords, Keith Stewart, QC
Private Secretary, Nathan Lappin

MANAGEMENT BOARD
Director and Solicitor to the Advocate-General, Neil Taylor
Head of Advisory and Legislation Division, Victoria MacDonald
Members, Shona Bathgate *(Head of HMRC Division);* Fiona Robertson *(Head of Litigation Division);* Chris Stephen *(Legal Secretary to the Advocate General)*

OFFICE OF THE SECRETARY OF STATE FOR SCOTLAND

Dover House, Whitehall, London SW1A 2AU
Queen Elizabeth House, Edinburgh EH8 8FT
T 0131-244 9010 **E** enquiries@scotlandoffice.gsi.gov.uk
W www.gov.uk/government/organisations/office-of-the-secretary-of-state-for-scotland

The Office of the Secretary of State for Scotland represents Scottish interests within the UK government in matters reserved to the UK parliament. The Secretary of State for Scotland maintains the stability of the devolution settlement for Scotland; delivers secondary legislation under the Scotland Act 1998; is responsible for the conduct and funding of the Scottish parliament elections; manages the Scottish vote provision and authorises the monthly payment of funds from the UK consolidated fund to the Scottish consolidated fund; and publishes regular information on the state of the Scottish economy.

Matters reserved to the UK parliament include the constitution, foreign affairs, defence, international development, the civil service, financial and economic matters, national security, immigration and nationality, misuse of drugs, trade and industry, various aspects of energy regulation (for example coal, electricity, oil, gas and nuclear energy), various aspects of transport, social security, employment, abortion, genetics, surrogacy, medicines, broadcasting and equal opportunities. Devolved matters include health and social work, education and training, local government and housing, justice and police, agriculture, forestry, fisheries, the environment, tourism, sports, heritage, economic development and internal transport. It is supported by one public body. *See also* Devolved Government *and* Ministry of Justice.

Secretary of State for Scotland, Rt. Hon. Alister Jack, MP
Parliamentary Private Secretary, Ruth Edwards, MP
Special Advisers, Magnus Gardham
Principal Private Secretary, Victoria Jones
Parliamentary Under-Secretary of State, David Duguid, MP*
Parliamentary Under-Secretary of State, Iain Stewart, MP

* Alongside role as Whip, Lord Commissioner of HM Treasury

MANAGEMENT BOARD
Director, Gillian McGregor, CBE
Members, Alison Evans *(Constitutional Policy);* Rebecca Hackett *(Policy Delivery and Relationship Management);* Rachel Irvine *(Constitutional Policy);* Nick Leake *(Policy Delivery and Relationship Management);* Anna Macmillan *(Communications)*

DEPARTMENT FOR TRANSPORT

Great Minster House, 33 Horseferry Road, London SW1P 4DR
T 0300-330 3000 **W** www.gov.uk/government/organisations/department-for-transport

The Department for Transport (DfT) works with its agencies, partners and local authorities to support the transport network that helps the UK's businesses and gets people and goods travelling around the country. It overseas transport investment and strategic direction in England and Wales, while seeking to promote low-carbon travel and reduce pollution. The DfT sets standards for safety and security in transport and is supported by 24 executive agencies and public bodies.

Secretary of State for Transport, Rt. Hon. Grant Shapps, MP
Parliamentary Private Secretary, Laura Trott, MP
Special Advisers, Rupert Reid; Neil Tweedie
Minister of State, Chris Heaton-Harris, MP
Minister of State, Andrew Stephenson, MP
Parliamentary Under-Secretary of State, Andrew Courts, MP
Parliamentary Under-Secretary of State, Rachel Maclean, MP
Parliamentary Under-Secretary of State, Baroness Vere of Norbiton

MANAGEMENT BOARD
Permanent Secretary, Bernadette Kelly, CB
Members, Prof. Phil Blythe *(Chief Scientific Adviser);* Gareth Davies, *(Aviation, Maritime, International and Security);* Ruth Hannant *(Rail Group);* Nick Joyce *(Resources and Strategy Group);* Clive Maxwell *(High Speed Rail and Major Projects);* Polly Payne *(Rail Group);* Emma Ward *(Roads, laces and Environment Group);* Brett Welch *(Legal Director)*
Non-Executive Members, Ian King *(Lead);* Richard Aitken-Davies; Richard Keys; Tony Poulter; Tracy Westall

HM TREASURY

1 Horse Guards Road, London SW1A 2HQ
T 020-7270 5000 **E** public.enquiries@hmtreasury.gov.uk
W www.gov.uk/government/organisations/hm-treasury

HM Treasury is the country's economics and finance ministry, and is responsible for formulating and implementing the government's financial and economic policy. It aims to raise the rate of sustainable growth, boost prosperity, and provide the conditions necessary for universal economic and employment opportunities. The Lord High Commissioners of HM Treasury are the First Lord of the Treasury (who is also the prime minister), the Chancellor of the Exchequer and six junior lords. This board of commissioners is assisted at present by the chief secretary, the parliamentary secretary (who is also the government chief whip in the House of Commons), the financial secretary, the economic secretary, the exchequer secretary and efficiency and transformation minister. The prime minister as first lord is not primarily concerned with the day-to-day aspects of Treasury business; neither are the parliamentary secretary and the junior lords as government whips. Treasury business is managed by the Chancellor of the Exchequer and the other Treasury ministers, assisted by the permanent secretary.

The chief secretary is responsible for public expenditure, including spending reviews and strategic planning; in-year control; public-sector pay and pensions; Annually Managed Expenditure and welfare reform; efficiency in public services; procurement and capital investment. He also has responsibility for the Treasury's interest in devolution.

The financial secretary has responsibility for financial services policy including banking and financial services reform and regulation; financial stability; city competitiveness; wholesale and retail markets in the UK, Europe and internationally; and the Financial Services Authority. His other responsibilities include banking support; bank lending; UK Financial Investments; Equitable Life; and personal savings and pensions policy. He also provides support to the chancellor on EU and wider international finance issues.

The exchequer secretary is a title only used occasionally, normally when the post of paymaster-general is allocated to a minister outside of the Treasury. The exchequer secretary's responsibilities include strategic oversight of the UK tax system; corporate and small business taxation, with input from the commercial secretary; departmental minister for HM

Revenue and Customs and the Valuation Office Agency; and lead minister on European and international tax issues.

The economic secretary's responsibilities include environmental issues such as taxation of transport, international climate change and energy; North Sea oil taxation; tax credits and child poverty; assisting the chief secretary on welfare reform; charities and the voluntary sector; excise duties and gambling; stamp duty land tax; EU Budget; the Royal Mint; and departmental minister for HM Treasury Group.

The Minister for Efficiency and Transformation is responsible for supporting the Chancellor of the Duchy of Lancaster and the chief secretary to implement cross-government efficiency and public-sector transformation by improved planning and procurement.

HM Treasury is supported by 14 executive agencies and public bodies.

Prime Minister and First Lord of the Treasury, Rt. Hon. Boris Johnson, MP
Parliamentary Private Secretaries, Alex Burghart, MP; James Heappey, MP
Chancellor of the Exchequer, Rt. Hon. Rishi Sunak, MP
Parliamentary Private Secretary, James Cartlidge, MP
Special Advisers, Liam Booth-Smith; Nerissa Chesterfield; Cass Horowitz; Douglas McNeill; Michael Webb; Rupert Yorke
Chief Secretary to the Treasury, Rt. Hon. Steve Barclay, MP
Special Adviser, Aled Maclean-Jones
Financial Secretary to the Treasury, Rt. Hon. Jesse Norman, MP
Economic Secretary to the Treasury, John Glen, MP
Exchequer Secretary to the Treasury, Kemi Badenoch, MP*
Minister of State for Efficiency and Transformation, Lord Agnew†
Parliamentary Secretary to the Treasury (Chief Whip), Rt. Hon. Mark Spencer, MP
Special Advisers, Sophie Bolsover; Simon Burton; David Sforza
Lords Commissioners of HM Treasury (Whips), David Duguid, MP‡; Rebecca Harris, MP§; James Morris; MP; David Rutley, MP; Maggie Throup, MP; Michael Tomlinson, MP℄
Assistant Whips, Maria Caulfield, MP; Alex Chalk, MP**; David Davies, MP††; Leo Docherty, MP; Nigel Huddleston, MP‡‡; Eddie Hughes, MP; Tom Pursglove, MP

* Alongside role at the DfIT
† Jointly held with the Cabinet Office
‡ Alongside role at the Scotland Office
§ Alongside role at the DfT
℄ Alongside role at the DWP
** Alongside role at the MoJ
†† Alongside role at the Wales Office
‡‡ Alongside role at DCMS

MANAGEMENT BOARD
Permanent Secretary, Sir Tom Scholar, KCB
Second Permanent Secretary, Charles Roxburgh
Executive Members, Mark Bowman *(International and EU);* Katharine Braddick *(Financial Services);* Philip Duffy *(Growth and Productivity);* Cat Little *(Public Spending);* Clare Lombardelli *(Chief Economic Adviser);* Beth Russell *(Tax and Welfare)*
Non-Executive Member, Rt. Hon. Lord Hill, CBE *(Lead);* Gay Huey Evans, OBE; Richard Meddings; Tim Score

UK GOVERNMENT INVESTMENTS
1 Victoria Street, London SW1H 0ET
T 020-7215 4720 **E** enquiries@UKGI.org.uk
W www.ukgi.org.uk/

UK Government Investments (UKGI) is the government's centre of expertise in corporate finance and corporate governance. UKGI Limited began operating on 1 April 2016 as a government company, wholly owned by HM Treasury, which brought together the functions of the Shareholder Executive (formerly part of the Department for Business, Energy and Industrial Strategy) and UK Financial Investments. UKGI's principle investments are to: prepare and execute all significant corporate asset sales by the UK government; advise on all major UK government financial interventions into corporate structures; act as shareholder for those arm's length bodies of the UK government that are structured to allow a meaningful shareholder function and for other UK government assets facing complex transformations; and to advise on major UK government negotiations with corporates.

Chief Executive, Mark Russell, CBE

Chair, Charles Donald
Board, Andrew Duff; Lord Jitesh Gadhia; Jane Guyett; Clare Hollingsworth; Robin Lawther; Hon. Sir James Leigh-Pemberton *(Deputy Chair);* Sarah Munby; Charles Roxburgh; Caroline Thompson

OFFICE OF TAX SIMPLIFICATION
HM Treasury, 1 Horse Guards Road, London SW1A 2HQ
E ots@ots.gov.uk
W www.gov.uk/government/organisations/office-of-tax-simplification

The chancellor and exchequer secretary to HM Treasury launched the Office of Tax Simplification (OTS) on 20 July 2010 to provide the government with independent advice on simplifying the UK tax system. The OTS is part of HM Treasury and provides the government with independent advice on simplifying the UK tax system. It carries out projects investigating complex areas of the tax system and makes recommendations to the chancellor in reports which are published on its website.

Chair, Kathryn Cearns, OBE
Tax Director, Bill Dodwell

ROYAL MINT LTD
PO Box 500, Llantrisant, Pontyclun CF72 8YT
W www.royalmint.com

From 1975 the Royal Mint operated as a trading fund and was established as an executive agency in 1990. Since 2010 it has operated as Royal Mint Ltd, a company 100 per cent owned by HM Treasury, with an exclusive contract to supply all coinage for the UK.

The Royal Mint actively competes in world markets for a share of the available circulating coin business and about half of the coins and blanks it produces annually are exported. It is the leading export mint, accounting for around 15 per cent of the world market. The Royal Mint also manufactures special proof and uncirculated quality coins in gold, silver and other metals; military and civil decorations and medals; commemorative and prize medals; and royal and official seals.

Master of the Mint, Chancellor of the Exchequer *(ex officio)*
Chair, Graham Love
Chief Executive, Anne Jessopp

UK EXPORT FINANCE
1 Horse Guards Road, London SW1A 2HQ
T 020-7271 8010 **E** customer.service@ukexportfinance.gov.uk
W www.gov.uk/government/organisations/uk-export-finance

UK Export Finance is the UK's export credit agency. It helps UK exporters by providing insurance to them and guarantees to banks to share the risks of providing export finance. Additionally, it can make loans to overseas buyers of goods and services from the UK. UK Export Finance is the operating name of the Export Credits Guarantee Department.

The priorities of UK Export Finance are to fulfil its statutory remit to support exports; operate within the policy and financial objectives established by the government, which includes international obligations; and to recover the maximum amount of debt in respect of claims paid, taking account of the government's policy on debt forgiveness. It is a ministerial department supported by one public body, the Export Guarantees Advisory Council.

Secretary of State for International Trade and President of the Board of Trade, Rt. Hon. Elizabeth Truss, MP
Special Advisers, Sophie Jarvis; Adam Jones
Parliamentary Under Secretary of State, Graham Stuart, MP *(Minister for Exports)**
* Jointly held with the DfIT

MANAGEMENT BOARD
Chief Executive, Louis Taylor
Chair, Noel Harwerth
Members, Cameron Fox *(Chief Finance and Operating Officer);* Shane Lynch *(Resources);* Davinder Mann *(Legal and Compliance);* Madelaine McTernan *(UK Government Investments);* Samir Parkash *(Chief Risk Officer);* Richard Simon-Lewis *(Business Development, Marketing and Communications);* Gordon Welsh *(Head of the Business Group)*
Non-Executive Members, Alistair Clark; Shalini Khemka; Andrew Mitchell, CMG; Oliver Peterken; Lawrence Weiss; Kimberly Wiehl

OFFICE OF THE SECRETARY OF STATE FOR WALES
Gwydyr House, Whitehall, London SW1A 2NP
T 020-7270 0534 **E** correspondence@walesoffice.gov.uk
1 Caspian Point, Caspian Way, Cardiff CF10 4BQ
W www.gov.uk/government/organisations/office-of-the-secretary-of-state-for-wales

The Office of the Secretary of State for Wales, informally known as the Wales Office, was established in 1999 when most of the powers of the Welsh Office were handed over to the National Assembly for Wales. It is the department of the Secretary of State for Wales, who is the key government figure liaising with the devolved government in Wales and who represents Welsh interests in the cabinet and parliament. The secretary of state has the right to attend and speak at sessions of the National Assembly (and must consult the assembly on the government's legislative programme). *See also* Devolved Government *and* Ministry of Justice.

Secretary of State for Wales, Rt. Hon. Simon Hart, MP
Parliamentary Private Secretary, Sarah Atherton, MP
Special Adviser, Jack Sellers
Principal Private Secretary, Sarah Jennings
Parliamentary Under-Secretary of State, David Davies, MP
* Alongside role as assistant Whip

MANAGEMENT BOARD
Director, Glynne Jones
Members, Ashok Ahir *(Communications);* Louise Parry *(Policy);* Kate Starkey *(Policy);* Geth Williams *(Constitution and Policy)*
Non-Executive Members, Alison White

DEPARTMENT FOR WORK AND PENSIONS
Caxton House, Tothill Street, London SW1H 9NA
W www.gov.uk/government/organisations/department-for-work-pensions

The Department for Work and Pensions was formed in June 2001 from parts of the former Department of Social Security, the Department for Education and Employment and the Employment Service. The department helps unemployed people of working age into work, helps employers to fill their vacancies and provides financial support to people unable to help themselves, through back-to-work programmes. The department also administers the child support system, social security benefits and the social fund. In addition, the department has reciprocal social security arrangements with other countries. It is the largest department in the government, employing 80,790 people in 2020, and is supported by 15 executive agencies and public bodies.

Secretary of State for Work and Pensions, Rt. Hon. Thérèse Coffey, MP
Parliamentary Private Secretary, Bim Afolami, MP
Special Advisers, Alex Hitchcock; Rhiannon Padley
Minister of State, Justin Tomlinson, MP *(Disabled People, Health and Work)*
Parliamentary Under-Secretary of State, Mims Davies, MP *(Employment)*
Parliamentary Under-Secretary of State, Guy Opperman, MP *(Pensions and Financial Inclusion)*
Parliamentary Under-Secretary of State, Will Quince, MP *(Welfare Delivery)*
Parliamentary Under-Secretary of State, Baroness Stedman-Scott, OBE *(Lords)*

MANAGEMENT BOARD
Permanent Secretary, Peter Schofield
Members, Debbie Alder, CB *(People and Capability);* Neil Couling, CBE *(Change and Universal Credit);* Emma Haddad *(Service Excellence);* Nick Joicey *(Finance);* John-Paul Marks *(Work and Health Services);* Jonathan Mills *(Policy Group);* Simon McKinnon *(Digital and Information Officer)*

EXECUTIVE AGENCIES

Executive agencies are well-defined business units that carry out services with a clear focus on delivering specific outputs within a framework of accountability to ministers. They can be set up or disbanded without legislation, and they are organisationally independent from the department they are answerable to. In the following list the agencies are shown in the accounts of their sponsor departments. Legally they act on behalf of the relevant secretary of state. Their chief executives also perform the role of accounting officers, which means they are responsible for the money spent by their organisations. Staff employed by agencies are civil servants.

DEPARTMENT FOR BUSINESS, ENERGY AND INDUSTRIAL STRATEGY

COMPANIES HOUSE
Crown Way, Cardiff CF14 3UZ
T 0303-123 4500 **E** enquiries@companieshouse.gov.uk
W www.gov.uk/government/organisations/companies-house

Companies House incorporates and dissolves limited companies, examines and stores company information delivered under the Companies Act and related legislation; and makes this information available to the public.

Chief Executive, Louise Smyth

THE INSOLVENCY SERVICE
4 Abbey Orchard Street, London SW1P 2HT
T 020-7637 1110
W www.gov.uk/government/organisations/insolvency-service

The role of the service includes administration and investigation of the affairs of bankruptcies, individuals subject to debt relief orders, partnerships and companies in compulsory liquidation; dealing with the disqualification of directors in all corporate failures; authorising and regulating the insolvency profession; providing banking and investment services for bankruptcy and liquidation estate funds; assessing and paying statutory entitlement to redundancy payments when an employer cannot, or will not, pay its employees; and advising ministers and the public on insolvency, redundancy and related issues. The service has around 1,700 staff, operating from 22 locations across Great Britain.

Inspector-General and Chief Executive, Dean Beale

INTELLECTUAL PROPERTY OFFICE
Concept House, Cardiff Road, Newport NP10 8QQ
T 0300-300 2000 **E** information@ipo.gov.uk
W www.gov.uk/government/organisations/
intellectual-property-office

The Intellectual Property Office (an operating name of the Patent Office) was set up in 1852 to act as the UK's sole office for the granting of patents. It was established as an executive agency in 1990 and became a trading fund in 1991. The office is responsible for the granting of intellectual property (IP) rights, which include patents, trade marks, designs and copyright.

Comptroller-General and Chief Executive, Tim Moss

MET OFFICE
FitzRoy Road, Exeter, Devon EX1 3PB
T 0370-900 0100 **E** enquiries@metoffice.gov.uk
W www.metoffice.gov.uk

The Met Office is the UK's National Weather Service, operating as an executive agency of BEIS after having transferred from the MoD in July 2011. Founded in 1854, it is a world leader in providing weather and climate services and processes up to 215 billion weather observations a day from across the world.

Chief Executive, Prof. Penelope Endersby
Chief Scientist, Prof. Stephen Belcher

UK SPACE AGENCY
Polaris House, North Star Avenue, Swindon, Wiltshire SN2 1SZ
T 020-7215 5000 **E** info@ukspaceagency.gov.uk
W www.gov.uk/government/organisations/uk-space-agency

The UK Space Agency was established on 23 March 2010 and became an executive agency on 1 April 2011. It was created to provide a single voice for UK space ambitions, and is responsible for all strategic decisions on the UK civil space programme. Responsibilities of the UK Space Agency include coordinating UK civil space activity; supporting academic research; nurturing the UK space industry; raising the profile of UK space activities at home and abroad; working to increase understanding of space science and its practical benefits; inspiring the next generation of UK scientists and engineers; licencing the launch and operation of UK spacecraft; and promoting co-operation with the European Space programme. It aims to capture 10 per cent of the global market for space by 2030.

Chief Executive, Dr Graham Turnock

CABINET OFFICE

CROWN COMMERCIAL SERVICE
Floor 9, The Capital Building, Old Hall Street, Liverpool L3 9PP
T 0345-410 2222 **E** info@crowncommercial.gov.uk
W www.gov.uk/government/organisations/
crown-commercial-service

The Crown Commercial Service (CCS) is an executive agency of the Cabinet Office, bringing together policy, advice and direct buying; providing commercial services to the public sector; and saving money for the taxpayer. The CCS works with over 17,000 customer organisations in the public sector.

Chief Executive, Simon Tse

GOVERNMENT PROPERTY AGENCY
E enquiries@gpa.gov.uk
W www.gov.uk/government/organisations/
government-property-agency

Formed in April 2018, the Government Property Agency delivers property and workplace solutions across the government, and aims to improve the efficiency and effectiveness of the Government Estate. It owns and operates the central government general purpose estate and aims to improve working environments for civil servants while making efficiency savings.

Chair, Pat Ritchie
Chief Executive, Steven Boyd

MINISTRY OF HOUSING, COMMUNITIES AND LOCAL GOVERNMENT

PLANNING INSPECTORATE
Temple Quay House, 2 The Square, Temple Quay, Bristol BS1 6PN
T 0303-444 5000 **E** enquiries@planninginspectorate.gov.uk
W www.gov.uk/government/organisations/planning-inspectorate

The main work of the inspectorate consists of processing planning and enforcement appeals, national infrastructure planning applications, and holding examinations into local development plans. It also deals with listed building consent appeals; advertisement appeals; rights of way cases; cases arising from the Environmental Protection and Water acts, the Transport and Works Act 1992 and other highways legislation; and reporting on planning applications called in for decision by the Ministry of Housing, Communities and Local Government and the Welsh government. It seeks to foster economic growth through sustainable development, particularly in energy and transport.

Chief Executive, Sarah Richards

THE QUEEN ELIZABETH II CONFERENCE CENTRE
Broad Sanctuary, London SW1P 3EE
T 020-7798 4000 **W** www.qeiicentre.london

The centre provides secure conference facilities for national and international government and private sector use, with a capacity of up to 2,500 delegates.

Chief Executive, Mark Taylor

MINISTRY OF DEFENCE
See also Defence Chapter.

DEFENCE ELECTRONICS AND COMPONENTS AGENCY
Welsh Road, Deeside, Flintshire CH5 2LS **T** 01244-847694
E decainfo@deca.mod.uk
W www.gov.uk/government/organisations/
defence-electronics-and-components-agency

The Defence Electronics and Components Agency (DECA) provides maintenance, repair, overhaul, upgrade and procurement in avionics, electronics and components fields to support the MoD. As a 'trading' executive agency DECA is run along commercial lines, with funding for DECA's activities being generated entirely by payments for delivery of services provided to the MoD and other private sector customers. DECA currently has an annual turnover of around £25m and employs over 400 staff across its head office and main operating centre in North Wales, a site in Stafford and various deployed locations across the UK.

Chief Executive, Geraint Spearing

DEFENCE EQUIPMENT AND SUPPORT

Ministry of Defence, Maple0a,#2043, MoD Abbey Wood, Bristol BS34 8JH **T** 0117-9130893
W www.gov.uk/government/organisations/
defence-electronics-and-components-agency

Defence Equipment and Support is a trading entity that oversees the purchase of equipment and services for the armed forces and MoD, including the procurement of ships, submarines, aircraft, vehicles, weapons, medical supplies, clothing and food. It employs around 12,000 civil servants and military personnel.

Chief Executive, Sir Simon Bollom

DEFENCE SCIENCE AND TECHNOLOGY LABORATORY

Porton Down, Salisbury, Wiltshire SP4 0JQ
T 01980-950000 **E** centralenquiries@dstl.gov.uk
W www.gov.uk/defence-science-and-technology-laboratory

The Defence Science and Technology Laboratory (DSTL) supplies specialist science and technology services to the MoD and wider government.

Chair, Adrian Belton
Chief Executive, Gary Aitkenhead

UK HYDROGRAPHIC OFFICE

Admiralty Way, Taunton, Somerset TA1 2DN
T 01823-484444 **E** customerservices@ukho.gov.uk
W www.gov.uk/uk-hydrographic-office

The UK Hydrographic Office (UKHO) collects and supplies hydrographic and geospatial data for the Royal Navy and merchant shipping to protect lives at sea. Working with other national hydrographic offices, UKHO sets and raises global standards of hydrography, cartography and navigation.

Chief Executive (Acting), Rear-Adm. Peter Sparkes

DEPARTMENT FOR EDUCATION

THE EDUCATION AND SKILLS FUNDING AGENCY

Department for Education, Piccadilly Gate, Shore Street, Manchester M1 2WD
W www.gov.uk/government/organisations/
education-and-skills-funding-agency

Formed in April 2017 after a merger of the Education Funding Agency (EFA) and the Skills Funding Agency (SFA), the Education and Skills Funding Agency (ESFA) is the DfE's delivery agency for funding and compliance. It manages £58bn of funding each year to support all state-provided education and training for children and young people aged 3 to 19, and intervenes where there is evidence of mismanagement of funds or risk of failure. The ESFA also supports the delivery of building and maintenance programmes for schools, academies, free schools and sixth-form colleges. It also administers the National Careers Service, the National Apprenticeship Service and the Learning Records Service.

Chief Executive, Eileen Milner

STANDARDS AND TESTING AGENCY

Ground Floor, South Building, Cheylesmore House, 5 Quinton Road, Coventry CV1 2WT
T 0300-303 3013 **E** assessments@education.gov.uk
W www.gov.uk/government/organisations/
standards-and-testing-agency

The Standards and Testing Agency (STA) opened in October 2011 and is responsible for the development and delivery of all statutory assessments from early years to the end of Key Stage 2.

Chief Executive, Una Bennett

TEACHING REGULATION AGENCY

Ground Floor, South Building, Cheylesmore House, 5 Quinton Road, Coventry CV1 2WT
T 0207-593 5394 **E** qts.enquiries@education.gov.uk
W www.gov.uk/government/organisations/
teaching-regulation-agency

Established in April 2018, the Teaching Regulation Agency is responsible for regulating the teaching profession, maintaining a database of qualified teachers in England and is the awarding body for Qualified Teacher Status (QTS).

Chief Executive, Alan Meyrick

DEPARTMENT FOR ENVIRONMENT, FOOD AND RURAL AFFAIRS

ANIMAL AND PLANT HEALTH AGENCY

Woodham Lane, New Haw, Addlestone, Surrey KT15 3NB
E enquiries@apha.gov.uk
W www.gov.uk/government/organisations/
animal-and-plant-health-agency

The Animal and Plant Health Agency (APHA) was launched in October 2014. It merged the former Animal Health and Veterinary Laboratories Agency with parts of the Food and Environment Research Agency responsible for plant and bee health to create a single agency responsible for animal, plant and bee health.

APHA is responsible for identifying and controlling endemic and exotic diseases and pests in animals, plants and bees, and surveillance of new and emerging pests and diseases; scientific research in areas such as bacterial, viral, prion and parasitic diseases, vaccines and food safety and act as an international reference laboratory for many farm animal diseases; facilitating international trade in animals, products of animal origin, and plants; protecting endangered wildlife through licensing and registration; managing a programme of apiary inspections, diagnostics, research and development, training and advice; and regulating the safe disposal of animal by-products to reduce the risk of potentially dangerous substances entering the food chain.

The agency provides all or some of these services to DEFRA and the Scottish and Welsh governments.

Chief Executive, Chris Hadkiss

CENTRE FOR ENVIRONMENT, FISHERIES AND AQUACULTURE SCIENCE (CEFAS)

Pakefield Road, Lowestoft, Suffolk NR33 0HT
T 01502-562244 **W** www.gov.uk/government/organisations/
centre-for-environment-fisheries-and-aquaculture-science

Established in April 1997, the agency provides research and consultancy services in fisheries science and management, aquaculture, fish health and hygiene, environmental impact assessment, and environmental quality assessment.

Chief Executive (Interim), Tim Green

RURAL PAYMENTS AGENCY

PO Box 69, Reading RG1 3YD
T 0300-0200 301 **E** ruralpayments@defra.gov.uk
W www.gov.uk/government/organisations/rural-payments-agency

The RPA was established in 2001. It pays out over £2bn each year to support the farming and food sector and is responsible for Common Agricultural Policy (CAP) schemes in England. In addition it manages over 40 other rural economy and community schemes. It is also responsible for improving agricultural productivity; boosting rural economies through development schemes; operating cattle tracing services; conducting inspections of farms, processing plants and fresh produce markets in England; providing import and export licences for the agri-food sector; and regulating the dairy and farm produce markets.

Chief Executive, Paul Caldwell

VETERINARY MEDICINES DIRECTORATE
Woodham Lane, New Haw, Addlestone, Surrey KT15 3LS
T 01932-336911 **E** postmaster@vmd.gov.uk
W www.gov.uk/government/organisations/
veterinary-medicines-directorate

The Veterinary Medicines Directorate is responsible for all aspects of the authorisation and control of veterinary medicines, including post-authorisation surveillance of residues in animals and animal products. It is also responsible for the development and enforcement of legislation concerning veterinary medicines and the provision of policy advice to ministers.

Chief Executive, Prof. Peter Borriello

FOREIGN, COMMONWEALTH AND DEVELOPMENT OFFICE

WILTON PARK
Wiston House, Steyning, West Sussex BN44 3DZ
T 01903-815020 **W** www.wiltonpark.org.uk

Wilton Park organises international affairs conferences and is hired out to government departments and commercial users. It organises over 50 events a year, helping to develop international policy and advance practical solutions to global issues.

Chief Executive (Interim), Colin Smith

DEPARTMENT OF HEALTH AND SOCIAL CARE

MEDICINES AND HEALTHCARE PRODUCTS REGULATORY AGENCY (MHRA)
10 South Colonnade, London E14 4PU
T 020-3080 6000 **E** info@mhra.gov.uk **W** www.gov.uk/
government/organisations/
medicines-and-healthcare-products-regulatory-agency

The MHRA, which also includes the National Institute for Biological Standards and Control (NIBSC) and the Clinical Practice Research Datalink (CPRD), is responsible for regulating all medicines, medical devices and blood components for transfusion in the UK by ensuring they work and are acceptably safe.

Chair, Stephen Lightfoot
Chief Executive, Dr June Raine, CBE

PUBLIC HEALTH ENGLAND
Wellington House, 133–155 Waterloo Road, London SE1 8UG
T 020-7654 8000 **E** enquiries@phe.gov.uk
W www.gov.uk/government/organisations/public-health-england

Public Health England (PHE) began operating in April 2013 and is responsible for protecting and improving the health and wellbeing of the nation; reducing health inequalities; protecting the nation from public health hazards; preparing for and responding to public health emergencies; and researching, collecting and analysing data to improve understanding of and solutions to public health problems. PHE employs 5,500 staff who are mostly scientists, researchers and public health professionals. It has eight local centres and four regions in England and works closely with public health professionals in Wales, Scotland, Northern Ireland and internationally.

Chief Executive (Interim), Michael Brodie

MINISTRY OF JUSTICE

CRIMINAL INJURIES COMPENSATION AUTHORITY (CICA)
Alexander Bain House, Atlantic Quay, 15 York Street, Glasgow G2 8JQ **T** 0300-003 3601
W www.gov.uk/government/organisations/
criminal-injuries-compensation-authority

CICA is the executive agency responsible for administering the Criminal Injuries Compensation Scheme in England, Scotland and Wales (separate arrangements apply in Northern Ireland). CICA handles over 30,000 applications for compensation each year, paying more than £130m to victims of violent crime. Appeals against decisions made by CICA can be put to the First-tier Tribunal (Criminal Injuries Compensation) *see* Tribunals.

Chief Executive, Linda Brown

HM COURTS AND TRIBUNALS SERVICE
102 Petty France, London SW1H 9AJ
W www.gov.uk/government/organisations/
hm-courts-and-tribunals-service

HM Courts Service and the Tribunals Service merged in April 2011 to form HM Courts and Tribunals Service, an integrated agency providing support for the administration of justice in courts and tribunals. As an agency within the MoJ it operates as a partnership between the Lord Chancellor, the Lord Chief Justice and the Senior President of Tribunals. It is responsible for the administration of the criminal, civil and family courts and tribunals in England and Wales and non-devolved tribunals in Scotland and Northern Ireland. The agency's work is overseen by a board headed by an independent chair working with non-executive, executive and judicial members.

Chief Executive, Susan Acland-Hood

HM PRISON AND PROBATION SERVICE
102 Petty France, London SW1H 9EX
T 01633-630941 **E** public.enquiries@noms.gsi.gov.uk
W www.gov.uk/government/organisations/
her-majestys-prison-and-probation-service

HM Prison and Probation Service (HMPPS) was established in April 2017, and is responsible for the roll out of government policies concerning the welfare of offenders and communities, and for reducing levels of reoffending by the rehabilitation of offenders through education and training schemes. HM Prison Service operates as an executive agency of HMPPS and is responsible for keeping those sentenced to prison in custody, and helping them lead law-abiding and useful lives both in prison and after they have been released. The agency runs 109 of the 123 prisons in England and Wales, and is also responsible for managing probation services and supporting effective offender management.

Chief Executive, Jo Farrar

LEGAL AID AGENCY
Unit B8, Berkley Way, Viking Business Park, Jarrow NE31 1SF
T 0300-200 2020 **E** contactcivil@justice.gov.uk
W www.gov.uk/government/organisations/legal-aid-agency

The Legal Aid Agency provides civil and criminal legal aid and advice in England and Wales. Formed in April 2013 as part of the Legal Aid, Sentencing and Punishment of Offenders Act 2012, the agency replaced the Legal Services Commission, a non-departmental public body of the MoJ.

Chief Executive (Interim), Jane Harbottle

OFFICE OF THE PUBLIC GUARDIAN
PO Box 16185, Birmingham B2 2WH
T 0300-456 0300 **E** customerservices@publicguardian.gov.uk
W www.gov.uk/government/organisations/
office-of-the-public-guardian

The Office of the Public Guardian (OPG) works within the Mental Capacity Act 2005 and Guardianship (Missing Persons) Act 2017 to support and protect those who lack the mental capacity to make decisions for themselves. It supports the Public Guardian in the registration of Enduring Powers of Attorney (EPA) and Lasting Powers of Attorney (LPA), and the supervision of deputies appointed by the Court of Protection. The OPG also has responsibility for investigating and acting on allegations of abuse by attorneys and deputies. The OPG's responsibility extends across England and Wales.

Chief Executive and Public Guardian, Nick Goodwin

DEPARTMENT FOR TRANSPORT

DRIVER AND VEHICLE LICENSING AGENCY (DVLA)
Longview Road, Swansea SA6 7JL
W www.gov.uk/government/organisations/
driver-and-vehicle-licensing-agency

The DVLA, established as an executive agency in 1990, maintains registers of drivers and vehicles in Great Britain. The information collated by the DVLA helps to improve road safety, reduce vehicle related crime, support environmental initiatives and limit vehicle tax evasion. The DVLA maintains over 49 million driver records and over 40 million vehicle records and collects over £6bn a year in vehicle tax.

Chief Executive, Julie Lennard

DRIVER AND VEHICLE STANDARDS AGENCY
Fourth Floor, The Axis Building, 112 Upper Parliament Street, Nottingham NG1 6LP
W www.gov.uk/government/organisations/
driver-and-vehicle-standards-agency

Formed by the merger of the Driving Standards Agency and the Vehicle and Operator Services Agency in 2014, the Driver and Vehicle Standards Agency (DVSA) is responsible for improving road safety in the UK by setting standards for driving and motorcycling, and ensuring drivers, vehicle operators and MOT garages understand and comply with roadworthiness standards. It additionally provides a range of licensing, testing, education and enforcement services.

Chief Executive, Gareth Llewellyn

MARITIME AND COASTGUARD AGENCY
Spring Place, 105 Commercial Road, Southampton SO15 1EG
T 020-3817 2000 **E** infoline@mcga.gov.uk **W** www.gov.uk/
government/organisations/maritime-and-coastguard-agency

The agency's aims are to prevent loss of life, continuously improve maritime safety and protect the marine environment. It produces legislation and guidance on maritime matters, and oversees certification to seafarers.

Chief Executive, Brian Johnson

VEHICLE CERTIFICATION AGENCY
1 Eastgate Office Centre, Eastgate Road, Bristol BS5 6XX
T 0300-330 5797 **E W** www.vehicle-certification-agency.gov.uk

The agency is the UK authority responsible for ensuring that new road vehicles, agricultural tractors, off-road vehicles and vehicle parts have been designed and constructed to meet internationally agreed standards of safety and environmental protection.

Chief Executive, Pia Wilkes

HM TREASURY

GOVERNMENT INTERNAL AUDIT AGENCY
10 Victoria Street, London SW1H 0NB
E Correspondence@giaa.gov.uk **W** www.gov.uk/government/
organisations/government-internal-audit-agency

Launched in April 2015, the Government Internal Audit Agency (GIAA) helps ensure government and the wider public sector provide services effectively. GIAA offers quality assurance on organisation's systems and processes, based on an objective assessment of the governance, risk management and control arrangements in place.

Chief Executive, Elizabeth Honer

NATIONAL INFRASTRUCTURE COMMISSION
1 Horse Guards Road, London SW1A 2HQ
E Correspondence@giaa.gov.uk **W** www.gov.uk/government/
organisations/government-internal-audit-agency

The National Infrastructure Commission was permanently established in January 2017 to provide the government with expert, impartial advice on significant long-term infrastructure challenges. During each parliament it is tasked with undertaking a national infrastructure assessment and monitoring the government's progress.

Chair, Sir John Armitt, CBE

UK DEBT MANAGEMENT OFFICE
Eastcheap Court, 11 Philpot Lane, London EC3M 8UD
T 020-7862 6500 **W** www.dmo.gov.uk

The UK Debt Management Office (DMO) was launched as an executive agency of HM Treasury in April 1998. The Chancellor of the Exchequer determines the policy and financial framework within which the DMO operates, but delegates operational decisions on debt and cash management and the day-to-day running of the office to the chief executive. The DMO's remit is to carry out the government's debt management policy of minimising financing costs over the long term, and to minimise the cost of offsetting the government's net cash flows over time, while operating at a level of risk approved by ministers in both cases. The DMO is also responsible for providing loans to local authorities through the Public Works Loan Board, and for managing the assets of certain public-sector bodies through the Commissioners for the Reduction of the National Debt.

Chief Executive, Sir Robert Stheeman, CB

NON-MINISTERIAL GOVERNMENT DEPARTMENTS

Non-ministerial government departments are part of central government but are not headed by a minister and are not funded by a sponsor department. They are created to implement specific legislation, but do not have the ability to change it. Departments may have links to a minister, but the minister is not responsible for the department's overall performance. Staff employed by non-ministerial departments are civil servants.

CHARITY COMMISSION
T 0300-066 9197 **W** www.gov.uk/government/organisations/
charity-commission

The Charity Commission is established by law as the independent regulator and registrar of charities in England and Wales. Its aim is to provide the best possible regulation of these charities in order to ensure their legal compliance and increase their efficiency, accountability and effectiveness, as well as to encourage public trust and confidence in them. The commission maintains a register of over 166,000 charities. It is accountable to both parliament and the First-tier Tribunal (Charity), and the chamber of the Upper Tribunal or high court for decisions made in exercising the commission's legal powers. The Charity Commission has offices in London, Liverpool, Taunton and Newport.

Chair, Rt. Hon. Baroness Stowell of Beeston, MBE
Chief Executive, Helen Stephenson, CBE

COMPETITION AND MARKETS AUTHORITY

The Cabot, 25 Cabot Square, London E14 4QZ
T 020-3738 6000 E general.enquiries@cma.gov.uk
W www.gov.uk/government/organisations/
competition-and-markets-authority

The Competition and Markets Authority (CMA) is the UK's primary competition and consumer authority. It is an independent non-ministerial government department with responsibility for carrying out investigations into mergers, markets and the regulated industries and enforcing competition and consumer law. In April 2014 it took over the functions of the Competition Commission and the competition and certain consumer functions of the Office of Fair Trading under the Enterprise Act 2002, as amended by the Enterprise and Regulatory Reform Act 2013.

Chair, Jonathan Scott
Chief Executive, Dr Andrea Coscelli, CBE

CROWN PROSECUTION SERVICE

102 Petty France, London SW1H 9EA
T 020-3357 0899 E enquiries@cps.gov.uk W www.cps.gov.uk

The Crown Prosecution Service (CPS) is the independent body responsible for prosecuting people in England and Wales. The CPS was established as a result of the Prosecution of Offences Act 1985. It works closely with the police to advise on lines of inquiry and to decide on appropriate charges and other disposals in all but minor cases. *See also* Law Courts and Offices.

Director of Public Prosecutions, Max Hill, QC
Chief Executive, Rebecca Lawrence

FOOD STANDARDS AGENCY

Floor 6 & 7, Clive House, 70 Petty France, London SW1H 9EX
T 0330-332 7149 E helpline@food.gov.uk
W www.food.gov.uk

Established in April 2000, the FSA is a non-ministerial government body responsible for food safety and hygiene in England, Wales and Northern Ireland. The agency has the general function of developing policy in these areas and provides information and advice to the government, other public bodies and consumers. The FSA also works with local authorities to enforce food safety regulations and has staff working in UK meat plants to check that the requirements of the regulations are being met.

Chair, Heather Hancock
Chief Executive, Emily Miles

FOOD STANDARDS AGENCY NORTHERN IRELAND, 10C Clarendon Road, Belfast BT1 3BG E infosani@food.gov.uk

FOOD STANDARDS AGENCY WALES, 11th Floor, South Gate House, Wood Street, Cardiff CF10 1EW
E walesadminteam@food.gov.uk

FORESTRY COMMISSION

620 Bristol Business Park, Coldharbour Lane, Bristol BS16 1EJ
T 0300-067 4000 E nationalenquiries@forestrycommission.gov.uk
W www.gov.uk/government/organisations/forestry-commission

The Forestry Commission is the non-ministerial government department responsible for forestry policy in England. It is supported by two executive agencies: Forest Research, which carries out scientific research and technical development relevant to forestry, and Forestry England, responsible for managing around 1,500 woods and forests.

In April 2013 the functions of its Welsh division, Forestry Commission Wales, were subsumed into Natural Resources Wales, a new body established by the Welsh government to regulate and manage natural resources in Wales.

In April 2019 responsibility for forestry in Scotland was devolved to two new Scottish government agencies: Forestry and Land Scotland and Scottish Forestry, who are accountable to the Scottish ministers.

The commission's principal objectives are to protect and expand England's forests and woodlands; enhance the economic value of forest resources; conserve and improve the biodiversity, landscape and cultural heritage of forests and woodlands; develop opportunities for woodland recreation; and increase public understanding of, and community participation in, forestry. It does this by managing public forests in its care to implement these objectives; by supporting other woodland owners with grants, regulation, advice and tree felling licences; and, through its Forest Research agency, by carrying out scientific research and technical development in support of these objectives.

Chair, Sir William Worsley
Chief Executive, Forest Research, Prof. James Pendlebury
Chief Executive, Forestry England, Mike Seddon

GOVERNMENT ACTUARY'S DEPARTMENT

Finlaison House, 15–17 Furnival Street, London EC4A 1AB
T 020-7211 2601 E enquiries@gad.gov.uk
Queen Elizabeth House, 1 Sibbald Walk, Edinburgh EH8 8FT
T 0131-467 0324 E scottish-enquiries@gad.gov.uk
W www.gov.uk/government/organisations/
government-actuarys-department

The Government Actuary's Department (GAD) was established in 1919 and provides actuarial advice to the public sector in the UK and overseas, and also to the private sector, where consistent with government policy. The GAD provides advice on occupational pension schemes, social security and National Insurance, investment and strategic risk management, insurance analysis and advice, financial risk management, and healthcare financing.

Government Actuary, Martin Clarke
Deputy Government Actuary, Colin Wilson

GOVERNMENT LEGAL DEPARTMENT

102 Petty France, Westminster, London SW1H 9GL
T 020-7210 3000 E thetreasurysolicitor@governmentlegal.gov.uk
W www.gov.uk/government/organisations/
government-legal-department

The Treasury Solicitor's Department became the Government Legal Department (GLD) in April 2015. The department provides legal advice to government on the development, design and implementation of government policies and decisions, and represents the government in court. It is superintended by the Attorney-General. The permanent secretary of the GLD, the Treasury Solicitor, is also the Queen's Proctor, and is responsible for collecting ownerless goods *(bona vacantia)* on behalf of the crown.

HM Procurator-General and Treasury Solicitor (Interim), Peter Fish, CB
Directors-General, Stephen Braviner-Roman; Susanna McGibbon
Head of Bona Vacantia, Caroline Harold

HM LAND REGISTRY

Trafalgar House, 1 Bedford Park, Croydon CR0 2AQ
T 0300-006 0411
W www.gov.uk/government/organisations/land-registry

A government department and trading fund of BEIS, HM Land Registry maintains the Land Register – the definitive source of information for more than 25 million property titles in England and Wales. The Land Register has been open to public inspection since 1990.

Chief Land Registrar and Chief Executive, Simon Hayes

HM REVENUE AND CUSTOMS (HMRC)
100 Parliament Street, London SW1A 2BQ
Income Tax Enquiries 0300-200 3300
National Insurance Enquiries 0300-200 3500
VAT Enquiries 0300-200 3700
W www.gov.uk/government/organisations/hm-revenue-customs

HMRC was formed following the integration of the Inland Revenue and HM Customs and Excise, which was made formal by parliament in April 2005. It collects and administers direct taxes (capital gains tax, corporation tax, income tax, inheritance tax and national insurance contributions), indirect taxes (excise duties, insurance premium tax, petroleum revenue tax, stamp duty, stamp duty land tax, stamp duty reserve tax and value-added tax) and environmental taxes (climate change levy, landfill tax, aggregates levy, emissions trading and energy efficiency scheme). HMRC also pays and administers child benefit and tax credits, in addition to being responsible for national minimum wage enforcement and recovery of student loans. HMRC also administers the Government Banking Service.

Chief Executive and First Permanent Secretary, Jim Hara
Deputy Chief Executive and Second Permanent Secretary, Angela
    MacDonald

VALUATION OFFICE AGENCY
Wingate House, 93–107 Shaftesbury Avenue, London W1D 5BU
T 0300-050 1501 (England); 0300-505505 **T** 0300-505505 (Wales)
W www.gov.uk/government/organisations/valuation-office-agency

Established in 1991, the Valuation Office is an executive agency of HM Revenue and Customs. It is responsible for compiling and maintaining the business rating and council tax valuation lists for England and Wales; valuing property throughout Great Britain for the purposes of taxes administered by HMRC; providing statutory and non-statutory property valuation services in England, Wales and Scotland; and giving policy advice to ministers on property valuation matters. In April 2009 the VOA assumed responsibility for the functions of The Rent Service, which provided a rental valuation service to local authorities in England, and fair rent determinations for landlords and tenants.

Chief Executive (Interim), Jonathan Russell, CB

NATIONAL ARCHIVES
Kew, Richmond, Surrey TW9 4DU
T 020-8876 3444 **W** www.nationalarchives.gov.uk

The National Archives is a non-ministerial government department which incorporates the Public Record Office, Historical Manuscripts Commission, Office of Public Sector Information and Her Majesty's Stationery Office. As the official archive of the UK government, it preserves, protects and makes accessible the historical collection of official records.

The National Archives also manages digital information including the UK government web archive which contains over 1.7 billion digital documents, and devises solutions for keeping government records readable now and in the future.

The organisation administers the UK's public records system under the Public Records Acts of 1958 and 1967. The records it holds span 1,000 years – from the Domesday Book to the latest government papers to be released – and fill more than 104 miles of shelving.

Chief Executive and Keeper, Jeff James

NATIONAL CRIME AGENCY
Units 1–6 Citadel Place, Tinworth Street, London SE11 5EF
T 0370-496 7622 **E** communication@nca.gov.uk
W www.nationalcrimeagency.gov.uk

The National Crime Agency (NCA) is an operational crime fighting agency introduced under the Crime and Courts Act 2013, which became fully operational in October 2013. The NCA's remit is to fight serious and organised crime, strengthen UK borders, tackle fraud, modern slavery, human trafficking and cyber crime, and protect children and young people. The agency provides leadership through its organised crime, border policing, economic crime and Child Exploitation and Online Protection Centre commands, the National Cyber Crime Unit and specialist capability teams.

Director-General, Lynne Owens, CBE, QPM

NATIONAL SAVINGS AND INVESTMENTS
Glasgow G58 1SB
T 08085-007007 **W** www.nsandi.com

NS&I (National Savings and Investments) came into being in 1861 when the Palmerston government set up the Post Office Savings Bank, a savings scheme which aimed to encourage working-class wage earners 'to provide for themselves against adversity and ill health'. NS&I was established as a government department in 1969. It is responsible for the design, marketing and administration of savings and investment products for personal savers and investors, including premium bonds. It has over 25 million customers and around £179bn invested. *See also* Banking and Finance, National Savings.

Chief Executive, Ian Ackerley

OFFICE OF GAS AND ELECTRICITY MARKETS (OFGEM)
10 South Colonnade, Canary Wharf, London E14 4PU
T 020-7901 7000 **W** www.ofgem.gov.uk

OFGEM is the regulator for Britain's gas and electricity industries. Its role is to protect and advance the interests of consumers by promoting competition where possible, and through regulation only where necessary. OFGEM operates under the direction and governance of the Gas and Electricity Markets Authority, which makes all major decisions and sets policy priorities for OFGEM. OFGEM's powers are provided for under the Gas Act 1986 and the Electricity Act 1989, as amended by the Utilities Act 2000. It also has enforcement powers under the Competition Act 1998 and the Enterprise Act 2002.

Chair, Martin Cave
Chief Executive, Jonathan Brearley

OFFICE OF RAIL AND ROAD
25 Cabot square, London E14 4QZ
T 020-7282 2000 **E** contact.cct@orr.gov.uk **W** www.orr.gov.uk

The Office of the Rail and Road (ORR) was established in July 2004 under the Railways and Transport Safety Act 2003. It replaced the Office of the Rail Regulator.

In April 2006, ORR assumed new responsibilities as a combined safety and economic regulator under the Railways Act 2005. It also has concurrent jurisdiction with the Competition and Market Authority under the Competition Act 1998 as the competition authority for the railways.

As the railway industry's independent health and safety and economic regulator, its principal functions are to: ensure that Network Rail and HS1 manage the national network efficiently and in a way that meets the needs of its users;

encourage continuous health and safety performance; secure compliance with relevant health and safety law, including taking enforcement action as necessary; develop policy and enhance relevant railway health and safety legislation; and license operators of railway assets, setting the terms for access by operators to the network and other railway facilities, and enforce competition and consumer law in the rail sector.

In April 2015, under the Infrastructure Act 2015, ORR assumed responsibility for monitoring Highways England's management and development of the strategic road network – the motorways and main 'A' roads in England. In this role ORR ensures that the network is managed efficiently, safely and sustainably, for the benefit of road users and the public.

On 16 March 2015, ORR signed an agreement with the French rail regulator ARAF to establish a collaborative regulatory approach for consistent independent regulation across the Channel tunnel network.

ORR is led by a board appointed by the Secretary of State for Transport.

Chair, Declan Collier
Chief Executive (Interim), John Larkinson

OFFICE OF QUALIFICATIONS AND EXAMINATIONS REGULATION (OFQUAL)
Earlsdon Park, 53–55 Butts Road, Coventry CV1 3BH
T 0300-303 3344 **E** public.enquiries@ofqual.gov.uk
W www.gov.uk/government/organisations/ofqual

OFQUAL became the independent regulator of qualifications, examinations and assessments on 1 April 2010. It is responsible for maintaining standards, improving confidence and distributing information about qualifications and examinations, as well as regulating general and vocational qualifications in England.

Chief Regulator, Dame Glenys Stacey
Chair, Roger Taylor

OFFICE FOR STANDARDS IN EDUCATION, CHILDREN'S SERVICES AND SKILLS (OFSTED)
Aviation House, 125 Kingsway, London WC2B 6SE
T 0300-123 1231 **E** enquiries@ofsted.gov.uk
W www.gov.uk/government/organisations/ofsted

Ofsted was established under the Education (Schools Act) 1992 and was relaunched on 1 April 2007 with a wider remit, bringing together four formerly separate inspectorates. It works to raise standards in services through the inspection and regulation of care for children and young people, and inspects education and training for children of all ages. *See also* Education.

HM Chief Inspector, Amanda Spielman
Chair, Dame Christine Ryan

SERIOUS FRAUD OFFICE
2–4 Cockspur Street, London SW1Y 5BS
T 020-7239 7272 **E** public.enquiries@sfo.gov.uk
W www.sfo.gov.uk

The Serious Fraud Office is an independent government department that investigates and, where appropriate, prosecutes serious or complex fraud, bribery and corruption. It is part of the UK criminal justice system with jurisdiction over England, Wales and Northern Ireland but not Scotland, the Isle of Man or the Channel Islands. The office is headed by a director who is superintended by the Attorney-General.

Director, Lisa Osofsky

SUPREME COURT OF THE UNITED KINGDOM
Parliament Square, London SW1P 3BD
T 020-7960 1900 **E** enquiries@supremecourt.uk
W www.supremecourt.uk

The Supreme Court of the United Kingdom is the highest domestic judicial authority; it replaced the appellate committee of the House of Lords (the house functioning in its judicial capacity) in October 2009. It is the final court of appeal for cases heard in Great Britain and Northern Ireland (except for criminal cases from Scotland). Cases concerning the interpretation and application of European Union law, including preliminary rulings requested by British courts and tribunals, are decided by the Court of Justice of the European Union (CJEU), and the supreme court can make a reference to the CJEU in appropriate cases. Additionally, in giving effect to rights contained in the European Convention on Human Rights, the supreme court must take account of any decision of the European Court of Human Rights.

The supreme court also assumed jurisdiction in relation to devolution matters under the Scotland Act 1998 (now partly superseded by the Scotland Act 2012), the Northern Ireland Act 1988 and the Government of Wales Act 2006; these powers were transferred from the Judicial Committee of the Privy Council. Ten of the 12 Lords of Appeal in Ordinary (Law Lords) from the House of Lords transferred to the 12-member supreme court when it came into operation (at the same time one law lord retired and another was appointed Master of the Rolls). All new justices of the supreme court are now appointed by an independent selection commission, and, although styled Rt. Hon. Lord, are not members of the House of Lords. Peers who are members of the judiciary are disqualified from sitting or voting in the House of Lords until they retire from their judicial office.

Chief Executive, Vicky Fox

UK STATISTICS AUTHORITY
1 Drummond Gate, London SW1V 2QQ
E authority.enquiries@statistics.gov.uk
W www.statisticsauthority.gov.uk

The UK Statistics Authority was established in April 2008 by the Statistics and Registration Service Act 2007 as an independent body operating at arm's length from government, reporting to the UK parliament and the devolved legislatures. Its overall objective is to promote and safeguard the production and publication of official statistics and ensure their quality and comprehensiveness. The authority's main functions are the oversight of the Office for National Statistics (ONS); monitoring and reporting on all UK official statistics, which includes around 30 central government departments and the devolved administrations; and the production of a code of practice for statistics and the assessment of official statistics against the code.

BOARD
Chair, Sir David Norgrove
Board Members, Sam Beckett *(Second Permanent Secretary);* Prof. Sir Ian Diamond, FBA, FRSE, FACSS *(National Statistician);* Ed Humpherson *(Director General of Regulation)*
Non-Executive Members, Helen Boaden *(Director General of Regulation)*; Richard Dobbs; Prof. David Hand, OBE; Prof. Jonathan Haskel, OBE; Sian Jones *(Deputy Chair);* Nora Nanayakkara; Prof. David Spiegelhalter; Prof. Anne Trefethen

OFFICE FOR NATIONAL STATISTICS (ONS)
Cardiff Road, Newport NP10 8XG
T 0845-601 3034 **E** info@ons.gov.uk **W** www.ons.gov.uk

The ONS was created in 1996 by the merger of the Central Statistical Office and the Office of Population Censuses and Surveys. In April 2008 it became the executive office of the UK Statistics Authority. As part of these changes, the office's responsibility for the General Register Office transferred to HM Passport Office of the Home Office.

The ONS is responsible for preparing, interpreting and publishing key statistics on the government, economy and society of the UK. Its key responsibilities include designing, managing and running the Census and providing statistics on health and other demographic matters in England and Wales; the production of the UK National Accounts and other economic indicators; the organisation of population censuses in England and Wales and surveys for government departments and public bodies.

National Statistician and Permanent Secretary, John Pullinger

Second Permanent Secretary, Sam Beckett
Director-Generals, Jonathan Athow; Iain Bell; Alison Pritchard

WATER SERVICES REGULATION AUTHORITY (OFWAT)

Centre City Tower, 7 Hill Street, Birmingham B5 4UA
W www.ofwat.gov.uk

OFWAT is the independent economic regulator of the water and sewerage companies in England and Wales. It is responsible for ensuring that the water industry in England and Wales provides household and business customers with a good quality service and value for money. This is done by ensuring that the companies provide customers with a good quality, efficient service at a fair price; limiting the prices companies can charge; monitoring the companies' performance and taking action, including enforcement, to protect customers' interests; setting the companies efficiency targets; making sure the companies deliver the best for consumers and the environment in the long term; and encouraging competition where it benefits consumers.

Chair, Jonson Cox
Chief Executive, Rachel Fletcher

PUBLIC BODIES

The following section is a listing of public bodies and other civil service organisations: it is not a complete list of these organisations, which total over 400.

Whereas executive agencies are either part of a government department or are one in their own right (*see* Government Departments), public bodies carry out their functions to a greater or lesser extent at arm's length from central government. Ministers are ultimately responsible to parliament for the activities of the public bodies sponsored by their department and in almost all cases (except where there is separate statutory provision) ministers make the appointments to their boards. Departments are responsible for funding and ensuring good governance of their public bodies.

The term 'public body' is a general one which includes public corporations, such as the BBC; NHS bodies; and non-departmental public bodies (NDPBs).

ADJUDICATOR'S OFFICE
PO Box 10280, Nottingham NG2 9PF
T 0300-057 1111 **W** www.gov.uk/government/organisations/the-ajudicator-s-office

The Adjudicator's Office investigates complaints from individuals and businesses about the way that HM Revenue and Customs and the Valuation Office Agency have handled a person's affairs. The Adjudicator's Office will only consider a complaint after the respective organisation's internal complaints procedure has been exhausted. It also reviews Home Office decisions on entitlement to compensation under the Windrush Compensation Scheme.

The Adjudicator, Helen Megarry

ADVISORY, CONCILIATION AND ARBITRATION SERVICE (ACAS)
22nd Floor, Euston Tower, 286 Euston Road, London NW1 3JJ
T 0300-123 1100 **W** www.acas.org.uk

The Advisory, Conciliation and Arbitration Service was set up under the Employment Protection Act 1975 (the provisions now being found in the Trade Union and Labour Relations (Consolidation) Act 1992).

ACAS is largely funded by the Department for Business, Energy and Industrial Strategy. A council sets its strategic direction, policies and priorities, and ensures that the agreed strategic objectives and targets are met. It consists of a chair and 11 employer, trade union and independent members, appointed by the Secretary of State for Business, Energy and Industrial Strategy.

ACAS aims to improve organisations and working life through better employment relations, to provide up-to-date information, independent advice and high-quality training, and to work with employers and employees to solve problems and improve performance.

ACAS has regional offices in Birmingham, Bristol, Cardiff, Fleet, Glasgow, Leeds, Manchester, Mildenhall, Newcastle upon Tyne and Nottingham. The head office is in London.

Chair, Sir Brendan Barber
Chief Executive, Susan Clews

ADVISORY COUNCIL ON NATIONAL RECORDS AND ARCHIVES
The National Archives, Kew, Surrey TW9 4DU
T 020-8392 5248
E advisorycouncilsecretary@nationalarchives.gov.uk
W http://www.nationalarchives.gov.uk/about/our-role/advisory-council

The Advisory Council on National Records and Archives advises the Secretary of State for Digital, Culture, Media and Sport on issues relating to public records that are over 20 years old including public access to them. The council meets four times a year, and its main task is to consider requests for the extended closure of public records; it also reaches decisions regarding government departments that want to keep records. It is chaired by the Master of the Rolls.

The Forum on Historical Manuscripts and Academic Research, a sub-committee of the Advisory Council, provides advice to the Chief Executive of The National Archives and Keeper of Public Records on matters relating to historical manuscripts, records and archives, other than public records.

Chair, Rt. Hon. Sir Terence Etherton *(Master of the Rolls)*

AGRICULTURE AND HORTICULTURE DEVELOPMENT BOARD
Stoneleigh Park, Kenilworth, Warwickshire CV8 2TL
T 024-7669 2051 **E** info@ahdb.org.uk **W** www.ahdb.org.uk

The Agriculture and Horticulture Development Board (AHDB) is funded by the agriculture and horticulture industries through statutory levies, with the duty to improve efficiency and competitiveness within six sectors: beef and lamb in England; cereals and oilseeds in the UK; commercial horticulture in Great Britain; milk in Great Britain; pigs in England; and potatoes in Great Britain. The AHDB represents around 70 per cent of total UK agricultural output. Levies raised from the six sectors are ring-fenced to ensure that they can only be used to the benefit of the sectors from which they were raised.

Chair, Nicholas Saphir
Independent members, George Lyon; Sarah Pumfrett; Janet Swadling
Sector members, Hayley Campbell-Gibbons *(Horticulture);* Alison Levett *(Potatoes);* Adam Quinney *(Beef and Lamb);*Mike Sheldon *(Pork);* Richard Soffe *(Dairy);* Paul Temple *(Cereals and Oilseeds)*
Chief Executive, Jane King

ARCHITECTURE AND DESIGN SCOTLAND
9 Bakehouse Close, 146 Canongate, Edinburgh EH8 8DD
T 0131-556 6699 **E** info@ads.org.uk **W** www.ads.org.uk

Architecture and Design Scotland (A&DS) was established in 2005 by the Scottish government as the national champion for good architecture, urban design and planning in the built environment; it works with a wide range of organisations at national, regional and local levels.

Chair, Ann Allen
Chief Executive, Jim MacDonald

ARMED FORCES' PAY REVIEW BODY
8th Floor, Fleetbank House, 2–6 Salisbury Square, London EC4Y 8JX
T 020-7211 8175 **W** www.gov.uk/government/organisations/
armed-forces-pay-review-body

The Armed Forces' Pay Review Body was appointed in 1971. It advises the prime minister and the Secretary of State for Defence on the pay and allowances of members of naval, military and air forces of the Crown.

Chair, Peter Maddison, QPM
Members, Brendan Connor, JP; Jenni Douglas-Todd; Willie Entwisle, OBE, MVO; Kerry Holden; Prof. Ken Mayhew; Julian Miller

ARTS COUNCIL ENGLAND
21 Bloomsbury Street, London WC1B 3HF
E enqiries@artscouncil.org.uk **W** www.artscouncil.org.uk

Arts Council England is the national development agency for the arts in England. Using public money from government and the National Lottery, it supports a range of artistic activities, including theatre, music, literature, dance, photography, digital art, carnival and crafts. Between 2018 and 2022, Arts Council England planned to invest £408m a year in 829 arts organisations, museums and libraries within its national portfolio. However, the economic impact of the coronavirus pandemic in 2020 resulted in significant losses for the entire sector and emergency state funding was announced in July. Administered by Arts Council England, the Cultural Relief Fund allocated £1.57bn of grants, repayable finance and capital investment to institutions and individuals.

The governing body, the national council, comprises 14 members, who are appointed by the Secretary of State for Digital, Culture, Media and Sport usually for a term of four years. There are also five councils, responsible for the agreement of area strategies, plans and priorities for action within the national framework.

Chair, Sir Nicholas Serota, CH
National Council Members, Helen Birchenough; Prof. Roni Brown; Michael Eakin; Ciara Eastell, OBE; Sukhy Johal, MBE; David Joseph; Ruth Mackenzie, CBE; Catherine Mallyon; Andrew Miller; George Mpanga; Elisabeth Murdoch; Paul Roberts, OBE; Tessa Ross; Kate Willard
Chief Executive, Darren Henley, OBE

ARTS COUNCIL OF NORTHERN IRELAND
Linen Hill House, 23 Linenhall Street, Lisburn BT28 1FJ
T 028-9262 3555 **E** info@artscouncil-ni.org
W www.artscouncil-ni.org

The Arts Council of Northern Ireland is the prime distributor of government funds in support of the arts in Northern Ireland. It is funded by the Department for Communities and from National Lottery funds.

Chair, John Edmund
Members, Dr Katy Radford, MBE *(Vice-Chair);* Julie Andrews; Lynne Best; Liam Hannaway; Sean Kelly; Una McRory; Mairtin O Muilleoir; Cian Smyth
Chief Executive, Roisin McDonough

ARTS COUNCIL OF WALES
Bute Place, Cardiff CF10 5AL
T 0330-123 2733 **W** www.arts.wales

The Arts Council of Wales was established in 1994 by royal charter and is the development body for the arts in Wales. It funds arts organisations with funding from the Welsh government and is the distributor of National Lottery funds to the arts in Wales. It is known by its Welsh name, Cyngor Celfyddydau Cymru.

Chair, Phil George
Members, Iwan Bala; Lhosa Daly; Devinda De Silva; Andy Eagle; Kate Eden; Michael Griffiths, OBE; Tadur Hallam; Alison Mears Esswood; Andrew Miller; Victoria Pravis; Dafydd Rhys; Marian Wyn Jones; Sarah Younan
Chief Executive, Nick Capaldi

AUDIT SCOTLAND
102 West Port, Edinburgh EH3 9DN
T 0131-625 1500 **E** info@audit-scotland.gov.uk
W www.audit-scotland.gov.uk

Audit Scotland was set up in 2000 to provide services to the Accounts Commission and the Auditor-General for Scotland. Together they help to ensure that public-sector bodies in Scotland are held accountable for the proper, efficient and effective use of public funds.

Audit Scotland's is responsible for auditing 222 public bodies, including: 72 Scottish government bodies (including the police, fire and Scottish Water) and the Scottish parliament; 23 NHS bodies; 32 councils; 73 joint boards and committees (including 30 health integration boards); 21 further education colleges; and one European Agricultural Fund.

Audit Scotland carries out financial and regularity audits to ensure that public-sector bodies adhere to the highest standards of financial management and governance. It also carries out performance audits to ensure that these bodies achieve the best value for money. All of Audit Scotland's work in connection with local authorities is carried out for the Accounts Commission; its other work is undertaken for the Auditor-General.

Chair, Prof. Alan Alexander, OBE
Auditor-General, Stephen Boyle
Chair of the Accounts Commission (Interim), Elma Murray, OBE

BANK OF ENGLAND
Threadneedle Street, London EC2R 8AH
T 020-3461 4444 **E** enquiries@bankofengland.co.uk
W www.bankofengland.co.uk

The Bank of England was incorporated in 1694 under royal charter. It was nationalised in 1946 under the Bank of England Act of that year which gave HM Treasury statutory powers over the bank. It is the banker of the government and it manages the issue of banknotes. Since 1998 it has been operationally independent and its Monetary Policy Committee has been responsible for setting short-term interest rates to meet the government's inflation target. Its responsibility for banking supervision was transferred to the Financial Services Authority in the same year. As the central reserve bank of the country, the Bank of England keeps the accounts of British banks, and of most overseas central banks; the larger banks and building societies are required to maintain with it a proportion of their cash resources. The bank's core purposes are monetary stability and financial stability. The Banking Act 2009 increased the responsibilities of the bank, including giving it a new financial stability objective and creating a special resolution regime for dealing with failing banks.

In 2012, through the Prudential Regulation Authority (PRA), the bank became responsible for the prudential regulation and supervision of banks, building societies, credit unions, insurers and major investment firms.

COURT OF DIRECTORS
Governor, Andrew Bailey
Deputy Governors, Dr Ben Broadbent *(Monetary Policy);* Sir Jon Cunliffe, CB *(Financial Stability);* Sir Dave Ramsden *(Markets and Banking);* Sam Woods *(Prudential Regulation)*

Non-Executive Members, Bradley Fried *(Chair, Court of Directors);* Anne Glover, CBE; Baroness Harding of Winscombe; Ron Kalifa, OBE; Diana Noble, CBE; Frances O'Grady; Dorothy Thompson

FINANCIAL POLICY COMMITTEE
Members, Andrew Bailey; Dr Colette Bowe, DBE; Alex Brazier; Dr Ben Broadbent; Sir Jon Cunliffe, CB; Jonathan Hall; Anil Kashyap; Donald Kohn; Sir Dave Ramsden; Nikhil Rathi; Charles Roxburgh; Elisabeth Stheeman; Sam Woods

MONETARY POLICY COMMITTEE
Members, Dr Ben Broadbent; Mark Carney; Sir Jon Cunliffe, CB; Andy Haldane; Jonathan Haskel; Sir Dave Ramsden; Michael Saunders; Silvana Tenreyro; Dr Gertian Vlieghe

PRUDENTIAL REGULATION COMMITTEE
Members, Andrew Bailey; David Belsham; Julia Black, CBE, FBA; Dr Ben Broadbent; Norval Bryson; Sir Jon Cunliffe, CB; Jill May; Nikhil Rathi; Sir Dave Ramsden; Sam Woods; Mark Yallop

Chief Operating Officer, Joanna Place
General Counsel, Sonya Branch
Chief Cashier and Director of Notes, Sarah John

BOUNDARY COMMISSIONS

The commissions, established in 1944, are constituted under the Parliamentary Constituencies Act 1986 (as amended). The Speaker of the House of Commons is the *ex officio* chair of all four commissions in the UK.

The last reviews of UK parliament constituencies were undertaken using the electoral register from 1 December 2015; these reviews were submitted by the commissions in September 2018.

ENGLAND
Room 3.26, 1 Horse Guards Road, London SW1A 2HQ
T 020-7276 1102
E information@boundarycommissionengland.gov.uk
W http://boundarycommissionforengland.independent.gov.uk

Deputy Chair, Hon. Mr Justice Nicol

WALES
Hastings House, Fitzalan Court, Cardiff CF24 0BL
T 029-2046 4819 **E** enquiries@boundaries.wales
W www.bcomm-wales.gov.uk

Deputy Chair, Hon. Ms Justice Jefford, DBE, QC

SCOTLAND
Thistle House, 91 Haymarket Terrace, Edinburgh EH12 5HD
T 0131-244 2001 **E** bcs@scottishboundaries.gov.uk
W www.bcomm-scotland.independent.gov.uk

Deputy Chair, Hon. Lord Matthews

NORTHERN IRELAND
The Bungalow, Stormont House, Stormont Estate, Belfast BT4 3SH
T 028-9052 7821 **E** contact@boundarycommission.org.uk
W www.boundarycommission.org.uk

Deputy Chair, Hon. Ms Justice McBride, DBE

BRITISH BROADCASTING CORPORATION (BBC)
BBC Broadcasting House, Portland Place, London W1A 1AA
W www.bbc.co.uk

The BBC was incorporated under royal charter in 1926 as successor to the British Broadcasting Company Ltd. The BBC's current charter, which came into force on 1 January 2017 and extends to 31 December 2027, recognises the BBC's editorial independence and sets out its public purposes. The BBC Board was formed under the new charter and is responsible for ensuring that the Corporation fulfils its mission and public purposes by setting the strategic direction of the BBC, establishing its creative remit, setting the budget and determining the framework for assessing performance. As part of the new charter, The Office of Communications (OFCOM) was awarded sole regulatory responsibility for the BBC. The BBC is financed by television licence revenue to ensure it remains independent from political control.

BBC BOARD
Chair, Sir David Clementi
Director-General, Tim Davie, CBE
National Members, Steve Morrison *(Scotland);* Dr Ashley Steel *(England);* Dame Elan Closs Stephens, DBE *(Wales)*
Members, Tim Davie *(CEO BBC Studios);* Ken MacQuarrie *(Nations and Regions);* Charlotte Moore *(Chief Content Officer);* Nicholas Serota, CH *(Senior Independent Director);* Francesca Unsworth *(News and Current Affairs)*
Non-Executive Members, Shirley Garrood; Baroness Grey-Thompson, DBE; Ian Hargreaves, CBE; Tom Ilube

EXECUTIVE COMMITTEE
Director-General, Tim Davie, CBE
Directors, Kerris Bright *(Chief Customer Officer);* Tom Fussell *(Interim CEO, BBC Studios);* Glyn Isherwood *(Chief Financial Officer);* Ken MacQuarrie *(Nations and Regions);* Charlotte Moore *(Chief Content Officer);* Gautam Rangarajan *(Strategy and Performance);* June Sarpong *(Creative Diversity);* Bob Shennan *(Managing Director);* Francesca Unsworth *(News and Current Affairs)*

CHANNEL AND PLATFORM HEADS
Chief Content Officer, Charlotte Moore
Controller BBC Two, Patrick Holland
Controller BBC Three, Fiona Campbell
Editor BBC Four, Cassian Harrison
Controller of Programming and iPlayer, Dan McGolpin
Director of Sport, Barbara Slater
Head of Content BBC Children's, Cheryl Taylor

GENRE CONTROLLERS
Entertainment, Kate Phillips
Factual, Alison Kirkham
Drama, Piers Wenger
Comedy, Shane Allen

Production, BBC Radio and Music, Bob Shennan

BRITISH COUNCIL
Bridgewater House, 58 Whitworth Street, Manchester M1 6BB
T 0161-957 7755
W www.britishcouncil.org

The British Council was established in 1934, incorporated by royal charter in 1940 and granted a supplemental charter in 1993. It is an independent, non-political organisation which promotes Britain abroad and is the UK's international organisation for educational and cultural relations. The British Council is represented in over 100 countries.

Chair, Stevie Spring, CBE
Chief Executive, Sir Ciarán Devane

BRITISH FILM INSTITUTE
21 Stephen Street, London W1T 1LN
W www.bfi.org.uk

The BFI, established in 1933, offers opportunities for people throughout the UK to experience, learn and discover more about the world of film and moving image culture. It incorporates the BFI National Archive, the BFI Reuben

Library, BFI Southbank, BFI Distribution, the annual BFI London Film Festival as well as the BFI FLARE: London LGBT Film Festival, and the BFI IMAX cinema. It also publishes the monthly *Sight and Sound* magazine and provides advice and support for regional cinemas and film festivals across the UK.

Following the closure of the UK Film Council in April 2011, the BFI became the lead body for film in the UK, in charge of allocating lottery money for the development and production of new British films.

Chair (Interim), Pat Butler
Chief Executive, Ben Roberts

BRITISH LIBRARY
96 Euston Road, London NW1 2DB
Boston Spa, Wetherby, W. Yorks LS23 7BQ
T 0330-333 1144 **E** customer-services@bl.uk **W** www.bl.uk

The British Library was established in 1973. It is the UK's national library and one of the world's greatest research libraries. It aims to serve scholarship, research, industry, commerce and all other major users of information. The Library's collection has developed over 250 years and exceeds 170 million items, including books, journals, manuscripts, maps, stamps, music, patents, newspapers and sound recordings in all written and spoken languages. The library is now based at two sites: London St Pancras and Boston Spa, W. Yorks. The library's sponsoring department is the Department for Digital, Culture, Media and Sport. Up to 3 million digitised items are added to the collection each year.

BRITISH LIBRARY BOARD
Chair, Dame Carol Black, DBE, FRCP
*Members,*Jana Bennett, OBE; Delroy Beverley; Dr Robert Black, CBE, FRSE; Tracy Chevalier, FRSL; Lord Janvrin, GCB, GCVO, QSO, PC; Roly Keating; Patrick Plant; Dr Venki Ramakrishnan; Dr Jeremy Silver; Laela Tabrizi; Dr Simon Thurley, CBE; Dr Wei Yang

EXECUTIVE
Chief Executive, Roly Keating
Chief Librarian, Liz Jolly
Chief Operating Officer, Phil Spence

BRITISH MUSEUM
Great Russell Street, London WC1B 3DG
T 020-7323 8000
W www.britishmuseum.org

The British Museum houses the national collection of antiquities, ethnography, coins and paper money, medals, prints and drawings. The British Museum dates from 7 June 1753, when parliament approved the holding of a public lottery to raise funds for the purchase of the collections of Sir Hans Sloane and the Harleian manuscripts, and for their proper housing and maintenance. The building (Montagu House) was opened in 1759. The existing buildings were erected between 1823 and the present day, and the original collection has increased to its current dimensions by gifts and purchases. Total government grant-in-aid for 2018–19 was £52.5m.

Chair, Sir Richard Lambert
Trustees, Prof. Dame Mary Beard DBE, FSA, FBA; Hon. Nigel Boardman; Cheryl Carolus; Elizabeth Corley, CBE; Patricia Cumper, MBE; Clarissa Farr; Prof. Chris Gosden, FBA; Muriel Gray; Philipp Hildebrand; Dame Vivian Hunt, DBE; Sir Deryck Maughan; Sir Charles Mayfield; Mark Pears, CBE; Grayson Perry, CBE, RA; Sir Paul Ruddock, FSA; Lord Sassoon; Baroness (Minouche) Shafik, DBE *(Deputy Chair)*; George Weston; Prof. Dame Sarah Worthington, DBE, QC (Hon), FBA

OFFICERS
Director, Dr Hartwig Fischer
Deputy Directors, Joanna Mackle; Jonathan Williams; Christopher Yates

KEEPERS
Keeper of Africa, Oceania and the Americas, Lissant Bolton
Keeper of Ancient Egypt and Sudan, Neal Spencer
Keeper of Asia, Jane Portal
Deputy Keeper of Britain, Europe and Prehistory, Jill Cook
Keeper of Coins and Medals, Philip Attwood
Keeper of Greece and Rome, J. Lesley Fitton
Keeper of the Middle East, Jonathan N. Tubb
Keeper of Portable Antiquities and Treasure, Roger Bland
Keeper of Prints and Drawings, Hugo Chapman

BRITISH PHARMACOPOEIA COMMISSION
151 Buckingham Palace Road, London SW1W 9SZ
T 020-3080 6561 **E** bpcom@mhra.gov.uk
W www.pharmacopoeia.com

The British Pharmacopoeia Commission sets standards for medicinal products used in human and veterinary medicines and is responsible for publication of *British Pharmacopoeia* (a publicly available statement of the standard that a medicinal substance or product must meet throughout its shelf-life), *British Pharmacopoeia (Veterinary)* and *British Approved Names.* It has 17 members, including two lay members, who are appointed on behalf of the Secretary of State for Health and Social Care by the Department of Health and Social Care.

Chair, Prof. Kevin Taylor
Vice-Chair, Prof. Alastair Davidson

CARE QUALITY COMMISSION
Citygate, Gallowgate, Newcastle upon Tyne NE1 4PA
T 0300-061 6161 **E** enquiries@cqc.org.uk **W** www.cqc.org.uk

The Care Quality Commission (CQC) is the independent regulator of health and adult social care services in England, ensuring health and social care services provide people with safe, effective, compassionate, high-quality care and encouraging them to improve. CQC monitors, inspects and regulates services to make sure they meet fundamental standards of quality and safety and publishes performance ratings to help people choose care.

Chair, Peter Wyman, CBE
Board Members, Prof. Ted Baker; Rosie Benneyworth; Sir Robert Francis, QC; Jora Gill; Paul Rew; Mark Saxton; Liz Sayce, OBE; Kate Terroni; Kirsty Shaw
Chief Executive, Ian Trenholm

CENTRAL ARBITRATION COMMITTEE
Fleetbank House, 2-6 Salisbury Square, London EC4Y 8JX
T 0330-109 3610 **E** enquiries@cac.gov.uk
W www.gov.uk/government/organisations/central-arbitration-committee

The Central Arbitration Committee (CAC) is a permanent independent body with statutory powers whose main function is to adjudicate on applications relating to the statutory recognition and de-recognition of trade unions for collective bargaining purposes, where such recognition or de-recognition cannot be agreed voluntarily. In addition, the CAC has a statutory role in determining disputes between trade unions and employers over the disclosure of information for collective bargaining purposes, and in resolving applications and complaints under the information and consultation regulations, and performs a similar role in relation to the legislation on the European Works Council, European companies, European cooperative societies and cross-border mergers. The CAC and its predecessors have also provided voluntary arbitration in collective disputes.

Chair, Stephen Redmond

CERTIFICATION OFFICE FOR TRADE UNIONS AND EMPLOYERS' ASSOCIATIONS

Lower Ground Floor, Fleetbank House, 2-6 Salisbury Square, London EC4Y 8JX
T 0330-109 3602 **E** info@certoffice.org
W www.gov.uk/government/organisations/certification-officer

The Certification Office is an independent statutory authority. The Certification Officer is appointed by the Secretary of State for Business, Energy and Industrial Strategy and is responsible for maintaining a list of trade unions and employers' associations; ensuring compliance with statutory requirements and keeping available for public inspection annual returns from trade unions and employers' associations; determining complaints concerning trade union elections, certain ballots and certain breaches of trade union rules; ensuring observance of statutory requirements governing mergers between trade unions and between employers' associations; overseeing the political funds and finances of trade unions and employers' associations; and for certifying the independence of trade unions.

Certification Officer, Sarah Bedwell

CHURCH COMMISSIONERS

Church House, Great Smith Street, London SW1P 3AZ
T 020-7898 1000 **E** commissioners.enquiry@churchofengland.org
W www.churchofengland.org/about/leadership-and-governance/church-commissioners

The Church Commissioners were established in 1948 by the amalgamation of Queen Anne's Bounty (established 1704) and the Ecclesiastical Commissioners (established 1836). They are responsible for the management of some of the Church of England's assets, the income from which is predominantly used to help pay for the stipend and pension of the clergy and to support the church's work throughout the country. The commissioners own UK and global company shares, over 120,000 acres of forestry estate, a residential estate in central London, and commercial property across Great Britain, plus an interest in overseas property via managed funds. They also carry out administrative duties in connection with pastoral reorganisation and closed churches.

The 33 commissioners are: the Archbishops of Canterbury and of York; eleven people elected by the General Synod, comprising four bishops, three clergy and four lay persons; three Church Estates Commissioners; two cathedral deans; nine people appointed by the crown and the archbishops; six holders of state office, comprising the Prime Minister, the Lord Chancellor, the Lord President of the Council, the Secretary of State for Digital, Culture, Media and Sport, the Speaker of the House of Commons and the Lord Speaker.

CHURCH ESTATES COMMISSIONERS
First, Loretta Minghella, OBE
Second, Andrew Selous, MP
Third, Dr Eve Poole

OFFICERS
Chief Executive and Secretary, Gareth Mostyn
Official Solicitor, Revd Alexander McGregor

COAL AUTHORITY

200 Lichfield Lane, Mansfield, Notts NG18 4RG
T 0345-762 6848 **E** thecoalauthority@coal.gov.uk
W www.gov.uk/government/organisations/the-coal-authority

The Coal Authority was established under the Coal Industry Act 1994 to manage certain functions previously undertaken by British Coal, including ownership of unworked coal. It is responsible for licensing coal mining operations and for providing information on coal reserves and past and future coal mining. It settles subsidence damage claims which are not the responsibility of licensed coal mining operators. It deals with the management and disposal of property, and with surface hazards such as abandoned coal mine entries and mine water discharges. The Coal Authority's powers were extended alongside the Energy Act 2011 to enable it to deal with metal mine subsidence issues and deliver a metal mine water treatment programme.

Chair, Stephen Dingle
Chief Executive, Lisa Pinney, MBE

COMMITTEE ON STANDARDS IN PUBLIC LIFE

1 Horse Guards Road, London SW1A 2HQ
T 020-7271 2685 **E** public@public-standards.gov.uk
W www.gov.uk/government/organisations/the-committee-on-standards-in-public-life

The Committee on Standards in Public Life (CSPL) was set up in October 1994. It is formed of 8 people appointed by the prime minister, comprising the chair, three political members nominated by the leaders of the three main political parties and four independent members. The CSPL advises the prime minister on ethical standards across the whole of public life in the UK. It monitors and reports on issues relating to the standards of conduct of all public office holders. It is responsible for promoting the seven principles of public life, being: selflessness; integrity; objectivity; accountability; openness; honesty; and leadership.

Chair, Lord Jonathan Evans of Weardale, KCB, DL
Members, Rt. Hon. Dame Margaret Beckett, DBE, PC, MP; Dr Jane Martin, CBE; Dame Shirley Pearce, DBE; Monisha Shah; Rt. Hon. Lord Andrew Stunell, OBE; Rt. Hon. Jeremy Wright, QC, MP

COMMONWEALTH WAR GRAVES COMMISSION

2 Marlow Road, Maidenhead, Berks SL6 7DX
T 01628-634221 **E** enquiries@cwgc.org **W** www.cwgc.org

The Commonwealth War Graves Commission (CWGC) was founded by royal charter in 1917. It is responsible for the commemoration of around 1.7 million members of the forces of the Commonwealth who lost their lives in the two world wars. More than one million graves are maintained in over 23,000 burial grounds across 154 countries. Over three-quarters of a million men and women who have no known grave or who were cremated are commemorated by name on memorials built by the commission.

The funds of the commission are derived from the six participating governments: the UK, Canada, Australia, New Zealand, South Africa and India.

President, HRH the Duke of Kent, KG, GCMG, GCVO, ADC
Chair, Secretary of State for Defence
Vice-Chair, Lt.-Gen. Sir William Rollo, KCB, CBE
Members, High Commissioners in London for Australia, Canada, India, New Zealand and South Africa; Rt. Hon. Philip Dunne, MP; Sir Tim Hitchens, KCVO, CMG; Vice-Adm. Peter Hudson, CB, CBE; Diana Johnson, MP, DBE;

Dame Judith Mayhew Jonas, DBE; Vasuki Shastry; Air Marshal David Walker, CB, CBE, AFC
Director-General (Acting), Barry Murphy

COMPETITION SERVICE
Victoria House, Bloomsbury Place, London WC1A 2EB
T 020-7979 7979 **W** www.catribunal.org.uk

The Competition Service is the financial corporate body by which the Competition Appeal Tribunal is administered and through which it receives funding for the performance of its judicial functions.

Registrar, Charles Dhanowa, OBE, QC

CONSUMER COUNCIL FOR WATER
Victoria Square House, Victoria Square, Birmingham, B2 4AJ
T 0300-034 2222 **E** enquiries@ccwater.org.uk
W www.ccwater.org.uk

The Consumer Council for Water was established in 2005 under the Water Act 2003 to represent consumers' interests in respect of price, service and value for money from their water and sewerage services, and to investigate complaints from customers about their water company. There are four regional committees in England and one in Wales.

Chair, Robert Light
Chief Executive, Emma Clancy

CORPORATION OF TRINITY HOUSE
Trinity House, Tower Hill, London EC3N 4DH
T 020-7481 6900 **E** enquiries@trinityhouse.co.uk
W www.trinityhouse.co.uk

The Corporation of Trinity House of Deptford Strond is the UK's largest-endowed maritime charity, established formally by royal charter by Henry VIII in 1514, with statutory duties as the General Lighthouse Authority (GLA) for England, Wales, the Channel Islands and Gibraltar. Its remit is to assist the safe passage of a variety of vessels through some of the busiest sea-lanes in the world; it does this by inspecting and auditing almost 11,000 local aids to navigation, ranging from lighthouses to a satellite navigation service. The corporation also has certain statutory jurisdiction over aids to navigation maintained by local harbour authorities and is responsible for marking or dispersing wrecks dangerous to navigation, except those occurring within port limits or wrecks of HM ships.

The statutory duties of Trinity House are funded by the General Lighthouse Fund, which is provided from light dues levied on commercial vessels calling at ports in the British Isles, based on the net registered tonnage of the vessel. Light Dues are paid into the General Lighthouse Fund under the stewardship of the Department for Transport. The fund finances the work of Trinity House and the Northern Lighthouse Board (Scotland and the Isle of Man). The corporation is a deep-sea pilotage authority, authorised by the Secretary of State for Transport to license deep-sea pilots. In addition, Trinity House is a charitable organisation that maintains a number of retirement homes for mariners and their dependants, funds a four-year training scheme for those seeking a career in the merchant navy, and also dispenses grants to a wide range of maritime charities. Trinity House's maritime and corporate charities are entirely self-funded by incomes derived from endowed funds.

The corporation is controlled by a court of 31 elected Elder Brethren, who oversee the corporate and lighthouse boards. The Elder Brethren also act as nautical assessors in marine cases in the Admiralty Division of the High Court.

ELDER BRETHREN
Master, HRH the Princess Royal, KG, KT, GCVO
Deputy Master, Capt. Ian McNaught, CVO
Wardens, Capt. Nigel Palmer, OBE *(Rental);* Rear-Adm. David Snelson, CB *(Nether);* Rear-Adm. David Snelson, CB
Elder Brethren, HRH the Duke of Edinburgh, KG, KT, OM, GBE; HRH the Prince of Wales, KG, KT, GCB; HRH the Duke of York, KG, GCVO, ADC; Capt. Roger Barker; Adm. Lord Boyce, KG, GCB, OBE; Capt. Lord Browne of Madingley, FRS, FRENG; Capt. John Burton-Hall, RD, RNR; Viscount Cobham; Cdre Robert Dorey, RFA; Capt. Sir Malcolm Edge, KCVO; Capt. Ian Gibb, MBE; Malcolm Glaister; Capt. Duncan Glass, OBE; Capt. Stephen Gobbi; Lord Greenway, Bt.; Rear-Adm. Sir Jeremy de Halpert, KCVO, CB; Capt. Nigel Hope, RD, RNR; Lord Mackay of Clashfern, KT, PC; Sir John Major, KG, CH, PC; Capt. Peter Mason, CBE; Cdre Peter Melson, CVO, CBE, RN; Capt. David Orr; Sir John Parker, GBE; Douglas Potter; Capt. Nigel Pryke; Richard Sadler; Lord Robertson of Port Ellen, KT, GCMG, PC; Rear-Adm. Sir Patrick Rowe, KCVO, CBE; Cdre James Scorer, RN; Simon Sherrard; Adm. Sir Jock Slater, GCB, LVO; Cdre David Squire, CBE, RFA; Vice-Adm. Lord Sterling of Plaistow, GCVO, CBE, RNR; Capt. Colin Stewart, LVO; Capt. Thomas Woodfield, OBE; Capt. Richard Woodman, LVO; Cdre William Walworth, CBE; Adm. Sir George Zambellas, CB

OFFICERS
Secretary, Thomas Arculus
Director of Business Services, Ton Damen, RA
Director of Navigational Requirements, Capt. Roger Barker
Director of Operations, Cdre Rob Dorey

CREATIVE SCOTLAND
Waverley Gate, 2–4 Waterloo Place, Edinburgh EH1 3EG
T 0330-333 2000 **E** enquiries@creativescotland.com
W www.creativescotland.com

Creative Scotland is the organisation tasked with leading the development of the arts, creative and screen industries across Scotland. It was created in 2010 as an amalgamation of the Scottish Arts Council and Scottish Screen, and it encourages and sustains the arts through investment in the form of grants, bursaries, loans and equity. It aims to invest in talent; artistic production; audiences, access and participation; and the cultural economy. Total Scottish government grant-in-aid funding for 2019–20 is £62m.

Chair, Robert Wilson
Board, Ewan Angus; David Brew; Duncan Cockburn; Stephanie Fraser; Philip Long; Sarah Munro; Elizabeth Partyka; David Strachan
Chief Executive, Iain Munro

CRIMINAL CASES REVIEW COMMISSION
5 St Philip's Place, Birmingham B3 2PW
T 0121-233 1473 **E** info@ccrc.gov.uk **W** www.ccrc.gov.uk

The Criminal Cases Review Commission is the independent body set up under the Criminal Appeal Act 1995. It is a non-departmental public body reporting to parliament via the Lord Chancellor and Secretary of State for Justice. It is responsible for investigating possible miscarriages of justice in England, Wales and Northern Ireland, and deciding whether or not to refer cases back to an appeal court. Members of the commission are appointed in accordance with the Office of the Commissioner for Public Appointments' code of practice.

Chair, Helen Pitcher, OBE
Members, David Brown, QFSM; Cindy Butts; Ian Comfort; Rachel Ellis; Jill Gramann; Johanna Higgins; Linda Lee; Christine Smith, QC; Robert Ward, CBE, QC (Hon)
Chief Executive, Karen Kneller

CROFTING COMMISSION
Great Glen House, Leachkin Road, Inverness IV3 8NW
T 01463-663439 **E** info@crofting.gov.scot
W www.crofting.scotland.gov.uk

The Crofting Commission was established on 1 April 2012, taking over the regulation of crofting from the Crofters Commission. The aim of the Crofting Commission is to regulate crofting, to promote the occupancy of crofts, active land use, and shared management of the land by crofters, as a means of sustaining and enhancing rural communities in Scotland.

Chief Executive, Bill Barron

CROWN ESTATE
1 St James's Market, London SW1Y 4AH
T 020-7851 5000 **E** enquiries@thecrownestate.co.uk
W www.thecrownestate.co.uk

The Crown Estate is part of the hereditary possessions of the sovereign 'in right of the crown', managed under the provisions of the Crown Estate Act 1961. It had a capital value of £13.4bn in 2020, which included substantial blocks of urban property, primarily in London, sizeable portions of coastal and rural land, and offshore windfarms. The Crown Estate has a duty to maintain and enhance the capital value of estate and the income obtained from it. Under the terms of the act, the estate pays its revenue surplus to the Treasury every year.

Chair and First Commissioner, Robin Budenberg, CBE
Chief Executive and Second Commissioner, Daniel Labbad

DISCLOSURE AND BARRING SERVICE
PO Box 3961, Royal Wootton Bassett SN4 4HF
T 0300-020 0190 **E** customerservices@dbs.gov.uk
W www.gov.uk/government/organisations/disclosure-and-barring-service

The Disclosure and Barring Service (DBS) is an executive non-departmental public body of the Home Office. It helps employers make safer recruitment decisions and prevent unsuitable people from working with vulnerable groups, including children. It was formed in December 2012 and replaced the Criminal Records Bureau (CRB) and Independent Safeguarding Authority (ISA). The DBS is responsible for the children's barred list and adults' barred list for England, Wales and Northern Ireland.

Chair, Dr Gillian Fairfield
Chief Executive, Eric Robinson

ENVIRONMENT AGENCY
PO Box 544, Rotherham S60 1BY
T 0370-850 6506 **E** enquiries@environment-agency.gov.uk
Incident Hotline 0800-807060
W www.gov.uk/government/organisations/environment-agency

Established in 1996 under the Environment Act 1995, the Environment Agency is a non-departmental public body sponsored by the Department for Environment, Food and Rural Affairs. In April 2013, Natural Resources Wales took over the Environment Agency's responsibilities in Wales. Around 68 per cent of the agency's funding is from the government, with the rest raised from various charging schemes. The agency is responsible for pollution prevention and control in England and for the management and use of water resources, including flood defences, fisheries and navigation. Its remit also includes: scrutinising potentially hazardous business operations; helping businesses to use resources more efficiently; taking action against those who do not take environmental responsibilities seriously; looking after wildlife; working with farmers; helping people get the most out of their environment; and improving the quality of inner city areas and parks by restoring rivers and lakes.

The Environment Agency has head offices in Bristol and London, as well as offices across England, divided into 14 regions. Its total grant-in-aid for 2018–19 was £850m.

Chair, Emma Howard Boyd
Board Members, Harvey Bradshaw; John Curtin; John Leyland; Toby Wilson
Chief Executive, Sir James Bevan

EQUALITY AND HUMAN RIGHTS COMMISSION
Arndale House, The Arndale Centre, Manchester M4 3AQ
T 0161-829 8327 **E** correspondence@equalityhumanrights.com
W www.equalityhumanrights.com

The Equality and Human Rights Commission (EHRC) is a statutory body, established under the Equality Act 2006 and launched in October 2007. It inherited the responsibilities of the Commission for Racial Equality, the Disability Rights Commission and the Equal Opportunities Commission. The EHRC's purpose is to reduce inequality, eliminate discrimination, strengthen relations between people, and promote and protect human rights. It enforces equality legislation on age, disability, gender reassignment, marriage and civil partnership, pregnancy and maternity, race, religion or belief, sex and sexual orientation, and encourages compliance with the Human Rights Act 1998 throughout England, Wales and Scotland.

Chair, Baroness Kishwer Falkner of Margravine
Deputy Chair, Caroline Waters, OBE
Commissioners, Suzanne Baxter; Jessica Butcher, MBE; Pavita Cooper; David Goodhart; Alasdair Henderson; Susan Johnston, OBE; Mark McLane; Helen Mahy, CBE; Baron Bernard Ribeiro of Achimota and Ovington, CBE; Dr Lesley Sawers, OBE *(Scotland Commissioner);* Sue-Mei Thompson
Chief Executive, Rebecca Hilsenrath

EQUALITY COMMISSION FOR NORTHERN IRELAND
Equality House, 7–9 Shaftesbury Square, Belfast BT2 7DP
T 028-9050 0600 **E** information@equalityni.org
W www.equalityni.org

The Equality Commission was set up in 1999 under the Northern Ireland Act 1998 and is responsible for promoting equality, keeping the relevant legislation under review, eliminating discrimination on the grounds of age, race, disability, sex and sexual orientation, gender (including marital and civil partner status, gender reassignment, pregnancy and maternity), religion and political opinion, and for overseeing the statutory duties on public authorities to promote equality of opportunity and good relations.

Chief Commissioner, Geraldine McGahey
Deputy Chief Commissioner, Neil Anderson
Chief Executive, Dr Evelyn Collins, CBE

GAMBLING COMMISSION
Victoria Square House, Victoria Square, Birmingham B2 4BP
T 0121-230 6666 **E W** www.gamblingcommission.gov.uk

The Gambling Commission was established under the Gambling Act 2005, and took over the role previously occupied by the Gaming Board for Great Britain in regulating and licensing all commercial gambling – apart from spread betting and the National Lottery – for example casinos, bingo, betting, remote gambling (online and by phone), gaming machines and lotteries. It also advises local and central government on related issues, and is responsible for the protection of children and the vulnerable from being harmed by gambling. In October 2013, the Gambling Commission took over all the responsibilities of the National Lottery Commission in regulating the National Lottery. The commission is sponsored by the Department for Digital, Culture, Media and Sport, with its work funded by licence fees paid by the gambling industry.

Chair, Dr Bill Moyes
Commissioners, Terry Babbs; John Baillie; Brian Bannister; Carol Brady; Stephen Cohen; Jo Hill; Trevor Pearce, CBE, QPM; Catherine Seddon;
Chief Executive, Neil McArthur, MBE

HEALTH AND SAFETY EXECUTIVE
Redgrave Court, Merton Road, Bootle, Merseyside L20 7HS
T 0300-790 6787 **W** www.hse.gov.uk

The Health and Safety Commission (HSC) and the Health and Safety Executive (HSE) merged in April 2008 to form a single national regulatory body – the HSE – responsible for promoting the cause of better health and safety at work. The HSE is sponsored by the Department for Work and Pensions.

HSE regulates all industrial and commercial sectors except operations in the air and at sea. This includes agriculture, construction, manufacturing, services, transport, mines, offshore oil and gas, quarries and major hazard sites in chemicals and petrochemicals.

HSE is responsible for developing and enforcing health and safety law; providing guidance and advice; commissioning research; conducting inspections and accident and ill-health investigations; developing standards; and licensing or approving some work activities such as asbestos removal.

Chair, Sarah Newton, FRSA
Board Members, Janice Crawford; Martin Esom; Susan Johnson, OBE; John McDermid; Prof. Ged Nichols, OBE; Ken Robertson; Kevin Rowan; Claire Sullivan
Chief Executive, Sarah Albon

HER MAJESTY'S OFFICERS OF ARMS

COLLEGE OF ARMS (HERALDS' COLLEGE)
130 Queen Victoria Street, London EC4V 4BT
T 020-7248 2762 **W** www.college-of-arms.gov.uk

The Sovereign's Officers of Arms (King's, Heralds and Pursuivants of Arms) were first incorporated by Richard III in 1484. The powers vested by the crown in the Earl Marshal (the Duke of Norfolk) with regard to state ceremonial are largely exercised through the college. The college is also the official repository of the arms and pedigrees of English, Welsh, Northern Irish and Commonwealth (except Canadian) families and their descendants, and its records include official copies of the records of the Ulster King of Arms, the originals of which remain in Dublin. The 13 officers of the college specialise in genealogical and heraldic work for their respective clients.

Arms have long been, and still are, granted by letters patent from the Kings of Arms. A right to arms can only be established by the registration in the official records of the College of Arms of a pedigree showing direct male line descent from an ancestor already appearing therein as being entitled to arms, or by making application through the College of Arms for a grant of arms. Grants are made to corporations as well as to individuals.

Earl Marshal, the Duke of Norfolk

KINGS OF ARMS
Garter, Thomas Woodcock, CVO, FSA
Clarenceux, Patric Dickinson, LVO
Norroy and Ulster, Timothy Duke, FSA

HERALDS
Lancaster, Robert Noel
Somerset, David White
Richmond, Clive Cheesman, FSA
York, Peter O'Donoghue, FSA
Chester, Hon. Christopher Fletcher-Vane
Windsor, John Allen-Petrie

PURSUIVANTS
Rouge Dragon, Adam Tuck
Bluemantle, Mark Scott
Portcullis, vacant
Rouge Croix, vacant

COURT OF THE LORD LYON
HM New Register House, Edinburgh EH1 3YT
T 0131-556 7255 **E** lyonoffice@gov.scot
W www.courtofthelordlyon.scot

Her Majesty's Officers of Arms in Scotland perform ceremonial duties and, in addition, may be consulted by members of the public on heraldic and genealogical matters in a professional capacity.

KING OF ARMS
Lord Lyon King of Arms, Dr Joseph Morrow, CBE, QC

HERALDS
Rothesay, Sir Crispin Agnew of Lochnaw, Bt., QC
Snawdoun, Elizabeth Roads, LVO, FSA, FSA SCOT
Marchmont, Hon. Adam Bruce, WS

PURSUIVANTS
Dingwall, Yvonne Holton
Unicorn, Liam Devlin
Carrick, George Way of Plean

EXTRAORDINARY OFFICERS
Orkney Herald Extraordinary, vacant
Angus Herald Extraordinary, vacant
Ross Herald Extraordinary, vacant
Islay Herald Extraordinary, vacant
Linlithgow Pursuivant Extraordinary, John Stirling, WS
Falkland Pursuivant Extraordinary, Roderick Macpherson

HIGHLANDS AND ISLANDS ENTERPRISE
An Lòchran, 10 Inverness Campus, Inverness IV2 5NA
T 01463-245245 **E** enquiries@hient.co.uk **W** www.hie.co.uk

Highlands and Islands Enterprise (HIE) was set up under the Enterprise and New Towns (Scotland) Act 1991. Its role is to deliver community and economic development in line with the Scottish government economic strategy. It focuses on four priorities: supporting businesses and social enterprises; strengthening communities and fragile areas; developing growth sectors; and creating the conditions for a competitive and low carbon region. HIE's budget for 2020–21 was £58.2m.

Chair, Alistair Dodds, CBE
Chief Executive, Charlotte Wright

HISTORIC ENGLAND
Cannon Bridge House, 25 Dowgate Hill, London EC4R 2YA
T 0370-333 0607 **E** customers@historicengland.org.uk
W www.historicengland.org.uk

Established under the National Heritage Act 1983, Historic England, officially the Historic Buildings and Monuments Commission for England, has three statutory purposes: to secure the preservation of ancient monuments and historic buildings; to promote the preservation and enhancement of the character and appearance of conservation areas; and to promote the public's enjoyment of, and advance their knowledge of, ancient monuments and historic buildings. In 2018–19 Historic England received £91.6m grant-in-aid from the Department for Digital, Culture, Media and Sport.

Chair, Sir Laurie Magnus
Commissioners, Alex Balfour; Nicholas Boys Smith; Prof. Martin Daunton; Sandie Dawe, CBE; Ben Derbyshire; Sandra Dinneen; Paul Farmer; Prof. Helena Hamerow; Victoria Harley; Rosemarie MacQueen, MBE; Michael Morrison; Patrick Newberry; Charles O'Brien; Susie Thornberry; Richard Upton; Sue Wilkinson
Chief Executive, Duncan Wilson, OBE

HISTORIC ENVIRONMENT SCOTLAND
Longmore House, Salisbury Place, Edinburgh EH9 1SH
T 0131-668 8600 **W** www.historicenvironment.scot

Historic Environment Scotland is the lead public body established to investigate, care for and promote Scotland's historic environment. It is the result of the bringing together of two of Scotland's leading heritage bodies, Historic Scotland and the Royal Commission on Ancient and Historical Monuments Scotland, and has been formed to help deliver the Our Place in Time strategy. It is responsible for more than 300 properties of national importance, including Edinburgh Castle, Skara Brae and Fort George, and for collections that include more than 5 million drawings, photographs, negatives and manuscripts, along with Scotland's National Collection of Aerial Photography, containing more than 26 million aerial images. The Historic Environment Scotland's draft budget from the Scottish government for 2020–21 was £42.8m.

Chair, Jane Ryder, OBE
Trustees, Ian Brennan; Dr Janet Brennan; Trudi Craggs; Andrew Davies; Emma Hard; Terry Levinthal; Dr Coinneach Maclean; Dr Fiona McLean; Ian Robertson; Dr Paul Stollard; Dr Ken Thomson; Jane Williamson
Chief Executive, Alex Paterson

HISTORIC ROYAL PALACES
Apartment 39A, Hampton Court Palace, Surrey KT8 9AU
T 0333-320 6000 **E** info@hrp.org.uk **W** www.hrp.org.uk

Historic Royal Palaces was established in 1998 as a royal charter body with charitable status and is contracted by the Secretary of State for Digital, Culture, Media and Sport to manage unoccupied palaces on his behalf. The palaces – the Tower of London, Hampton Court Palace, the Banqueting House, Kensington Palace and Kew Palace – are owned by the Queen on behalf of the nation. In April 2014, Historic Royal Palaces was also appointed responsible for the management of Hillsborough Castle in Northern Ireland under contract with the Secretary of State for Northern Ireland.

The organisation is governed by a board comprising a chair and 11 non-executive trustees. The chief executive is accountable to the board of trustees and ultimately to parliament. Historic Royal Palaces receives no funding from the government or the Crown.

TRUSTEES
Chair, Rupert Gavin
Appointed by the Queen, Zeinab Badawi; Tim Knox *(ex officio, Director of the Royal Collection Trust);* Sir Michael Stevens, CVO *(ex officio, the Keeper of the Privy Purse)*
Appointed by the Secretary of State, Gen. Lord Houghton of Richmond, GCB, CBE, DL *(ex officio, the Constable of the Tower of London);* Jane Kennedy; Sarah Jenkins; Carole Souter, CBE; Robert Swannell, CBE; Sue Wilkinson, MBE; Dr Jo Twist, OBE; Prof. Michael Wood

OFFICER
Chief Executive, John Barnes

HOMES ENGLAND
50 Victoria Street, Westminster, London SW1H 0TL
T 0300-123 4500 **E** enquiries@homesengland.gov.uk
W www.gov.uk/government/organisations/homes-england

Homes England is an executive non-departmental public body, sponsored by the Ministry of Housing, Communities and Local Government to facilitate delivery of sufficient new homes by bringing together land, money, expertise, planning and compulsory purchase powers. It replaced the Homes and Communities Agency in January 2018, adopting the new trading name Homes England. Along with it, its regulation directorate, which undertakes the functions of the Regulation Committee, refers to itself as the Regulator of Social Housing. Homes England invests mostly in building new homes, but also in creating employment floorspace nationwide, as well as bringing forward public land for development and increasing the speed with which it is made available.

Chief Executive, Nick Walkley
Chief of Staff, Amy Casterton

HUMAN TISSUE AUTHORITY (HTA)
151 Buckingham Palace Road, London SW1W 9SZ
T 020-7269 1900 **E W** www.hta.gov.uk

The Human Tissue Authority (HTA) was established in April 2005 under the Human Tissue Act 2004, and is sponsored and part-funded by the Department of Health and Social Care. It regulates organisations that remove, store and use tissue for research, medical treatment, post-mortem examination, teaching and display in public. The HTA also gives approval for organ and bone marrow donations from living people. Under the EU tissues and cells directives, the HTA is one of the two designated competent authorities for the UK responsible for regulating tissues and cells. The HTA is also the sole competent authority for the UK under the EU organ donation directive.

Chair, Lynne Berry, CBE
Chief Executive, Allan Marriott-Smith

IMPERIAL WAR MUSEUMS (IWM)
Lambeth Road, London SE1 6HZ
T 020-7416 5000 **E W** www.iwm.org.uk

IWM is the world's leading authority on conflict and its impact, focusing on Britain, its former empire and the Commonwealth from the First World War to the present. IWM aims to enrich people's understanding of the causes, course and consequences of war and conflict.

IWM comprises the organisation's flagship, IWM London; IWM North in Trafford, Manchester; IWM Duxford in Cambridgeshire; the Churchill War Rooms in Whitehall; and HMS *Belfast* in the Pool of London.

The total grant-in-aid for 2019–20 is £19.74m.

President, HRH the Duke of Kent, KG, GCMG, GCVO, ADC
Chair, Matthew Westerman
Trustees, Desmond Bowen, CB, CMG; HE Hon. George
Brandis, QC; Hugh Bullock; HE Janice Charette;
Elizabeth Cleaver; HE Bede Cory; Lt.-Gen. Andrew
Figgures, CB, CBE; HE Ruchi Ghanashyam; HE Manisha
Gunasekera; Angus Lapsley; Margaret Macmillan, CH;
Tim Marlow, OBE; HE Mohammad Nafees Zakaria;
Suzanna Raine; HE Nomatemba Tambo; Tamsin Todd;
Mark Urban; Guy Weston
Director-General, Diane Lees, CBE
Directors, John Brown *(Commercial Services and Operations);* Jon
Card *(Collections and Governance);* Graeme Etheridge
(Change); Gill Webber *(Content and Public Programmes)*

INFORMATION COMMISSIONER'S OFFICE
Wycliffe House, Water Lane, Wilmslow, Cheshire SK9 5AF
T 0303-123 1113 **W** www.ico.org.uk

The Information Commissioner's Office (ICO) oversees and
enforces the freedom of information acts of 2000 and 2004,
the Data Protection Act 2018, and the Network and
Information Systems Regulations 2018. Its objective it to
promote public access to official information and protecting
personal information.

The Data Protection Act 2018, which replaced legislation
passed in 1998, sets out rules for the processing of personal
information and applies to records held on computers and some
paper files. The freedom of information acts are designed to
help end the culture of unnecessary secrecy and open up the
inner workings of the public sector to citizens and businesses.

The ICO also enforces and oversees the privacy and electronic
communications regulations 2003 and the environmental
regulations 2004. It also has limited responsibilities under the
INSPIRE regulations 2009 and DRR regulations 2014.

The Information Commissioner reports annually to
parliament on the performance of his/her functions under the
acts and has obligations to assess breaches of the acts. Since
April 2010 the ICO has been able to fine organisations up to
€20m, or 4 per cent of their total annual worldwide turnover,
for serious breaches of the Data Protection Act.

Information Commissioner, Elizabeth Denham, CBE

INDUSTRIAL INJURIES ADVISORY
COUNCIL
First Floor, Caxton House, Tothill Street, London SW1H 9NA
T 020-7449 5618 **E** iiac@dwp.gov.uk
W www.gov.uk/government/organisations/
industrial-injuries-advisory-council

The Industrial Injuries Advisory Council was established under
the National Insurance (Industrial Injuries) Act 1946, which
came into effect on 5 July 1948. Statutory provisions
governing its work are set out in the Social Security
Administration Act 1992 and corresponding Northern Ireland
legislation. The council usually consists of 17 members,
including a chair, appointed by the Secretary of State for Work
and Pensions, and has three roles: to advise on the prescription
of diseases; to consider and advise on draft regulations and
proposals concerning the industrial injuries disablement
benefit scheme referred to the council by the Secretary of State
for Work and Pensions or the Department for Communities in
Northern Ireland; and to advise on any other matter concerning
the scheme or its administration.

Chair, Dr Leslie Rushton, OBE

JOINT NATURE CONSERVATION
COMMITTEE
Monkstone House, City Road, Peterborough PE1 1JY
T 01733-562626 **W** www.jncc.gov.uk

The committee was established under the Environmental
Protection Act 1990, reconstituted by the Natural
Environment and Rural Communities Act 2006, and extended
by the Offshore Marine Conservation (Natural Habitats)
Regulations 2007 and the Marine and Coastal Access Act
2009. It advises the government and devolved administrations
on UK and international nature conservation issues. Its work
contributes to maintaining and enriching biological diversity,
conserving geological features and sustaining natural systems.

Chair, Prof. Chris Gilligan, CBE
Chief Executive, Marcus Yeo

LAW COMMISSION
1st Floor, Tower, 52 Queen Anne's Gate, London SW1H 9AG
T 020-3334 0200 **E** enquiries@lawcommission.gov.uk
W www.lawcom.gov.uk

The Law Commission was set up under the Law Commissions
Act 1965 to make proposals to the government for the
examination of the law in England and Wales and for its
revision to ensure it is fair, modern, simple and cost effective.
It recommends to the lord chancellor programmes for the
examination of different branches of the law and suggests
whether the examination should be carried out by the
commission itself or by some other body. The commission is
also responsible for the preparation of Consolidation and
Statute Law (Repeals) Bills.

Chair, Sir Nicholas Green
Commissioners, Prof. Sarah Green; Prof. Nicholas Hopkins;
Prof. Penney Lewis; Nicholas Paines, QC
Chief Executive, Phil Golding

NATIONAL ARMY MUSEUM
Royal Hospital Road, Chelsea, London SW3 4HT
T 020-7730 0717 **E** info@nam.ac.uk **W** www.nam.ac.uk

The National Army Museum shares the stories of the British
Army and its soldiers. It was established by royal charter in
1960 and moved to its current site in Chelsea in 1971. The
museum re-opened in spring 2017 following a major
redevelopment project. The new museum features five state-of-
the-art galleries, housing a wide array of artefacts, paintings,
photographs, uniforms and equipment; a café; a shop; and
learning and research facilities.

Chair, Gen. Sir Richard Shirreff, KCB, CBE
Council Members, Patrick Aylmer; Dr Jonathan Boff; Judith
Donovan, CBE; John Duncan, OBE; Lt.-Gen. Sir Simon
Mayall, KBE, CB; Guy Perricone; Paul Schreier; Jessica
Spungin; Sabine Vandenbroucke; William Wells
Director, Justin Maciejewski, DSO, MBE

NATIONAL GALLERIES OF SCOTLAND
73 Belford Road, Edinburgh EH4 3DS
T 0131-624 6200 **E** enquiries@nationalgalleries.org
W www.nationalgalleries.org

The National Galleries of Scotland comprise three galleries in
Edinburgh: the National Gallery of Scotland, the Scottish
National Portrait Gallery and the Scottish National Gallery of
Modern Art. There are also partner galleries at Paxton House,
Berwickshire, and Duff House, Banffshire. It also owns the
Granton Centre for Art, a purpose built storage facility.

TRUSTEES
Chair, Benny Higgins
Trustees, Audrey Carlin; Alistair Dodds; Edward Green; Tari Lang; Prof. Nicholas Pearce; Lynn Richmond; Dr Hannah Rudman; Chris Sibbald; Rucelle Soutar; Willie Watt; Andrew Wilson

OFFICERS
Director-General, Sir John Leighton
Directors, Dr Line Clausen Pedersen *(Collection and Research);* Jo Coomber *(Public Engagement);* Jacqueline Ridge *(Conservation and Collection Management);* Bryan Robertson *(Chief Operating Officer)*

NATIONAL GALLERY
Trafalgar Square, London WC2N 5DN
T 020-7747 2885 **E** information@ng-london.org.uk
W www.nationalgallery.org.uk

The National Gallery, which houses a collection of paintings in the western European tradition from the 13th to the 20th century, was founded in 1824, following a parliamentary grant of £57,000 for the purchase of the Angerstein collection of pictures. The present site was first occupied in 1838; an extension to the north of the building with a public entrance in Orange Street was opened in 1975; the Sainsbury Wing was opened in 1991; and the Getty Entrance opened off Trafalgar Square at the east end of the main building in 2004. Total government grant-in-aid for 2019–20 was £24.7m.

BOARD OF TRUSTEES
Chair, Lord Hall of Birkenhead, CBE
Trustees, Dame Moya Greene, DBE; Catherine Goodman, LVO; Doug Gurr; Katrin Henkel; Sir John Kingman; Rosemary Leith; David Marks; Tonya Nelson; Charles Sebag-Montefiore; Stuart Roden; John Singer; Molly Stevens

OFFICERS
Director of the National Gallery, Dr Gabriele Finaldi
Deputy Director, Dr Susan Foister *(Public Programmes and Partnerships)*
Directors, Dr Caroline Campbell *(Collections and Research);* Andy Hibbert *(Finance and Operations);* Dr Chris Michaels *(Digital)*

NATIONAL HERITAGE MEMORIAL FUND
International House, 1 Katherine's Way, London E1W 1UN
T 020-7591 6044 **E** NHMF_Enquiries@nhmf.org.uk
W www.nhmf.org.uk

The National Heritage Memorial Fund was set up under the National Heritage Act 1980 in memory of people who have given their lives for the United Kingdom. The fund provides grants to organisations based in the UK, mainly so that they can buy items of outstanding interest and of importance to the national heritage. These must either be at risk or have a memorial character. The fund is administered by a chair and trustees who are appointed by the prime minister.
   The National Heritage Memorial Fund receives an annual grant from the Department for Digital, Culture, Media and Sport. Under the National Lottery etc. Act 1993, the trustees of the fund became responsible for the distribution of funds for both the National Heritage Memorial Fund and the Heritage Lottery Fund. Total annual government grant-in-aid is £5m.

Chair (Interim), René Olivieri
Trustees, Maria Adebowale-Schwarte; Baroness Andrews, OBE, FSA; Jim Dixon; Dr Claire Feehily; Sarah Flannigan; Perdita Hunt, OBE, DL; Ray Macfarlane; David Stocker
Chief Executive, Ros Kerslake, OBE

NATIONAL LIBRARY OF SCOTLAND
George IV Bridge, Edinburgh EH1 1EW
T 0131-623 3700 **E W** www.nls.uk

The library, which was formally opened as the Advocates' Library in 1689, became the National Library of Scotland in 1925. It contains over 26 million printed items in multiple formats including: books, manuscripts, archives, websites, newspapers, maps, music, moving images and sound, along with the John Murray Archive. One of only six legal deposit libraries, it receives more than 4,000 new items a week. It has an unrivalled Scottish collection as well as online catalogues and digital resources which can be accessed through the Library's website. Material can be consulted in the library branches in Edinburgh and Glasgow, which are open to anyone with a valid library card.
   The National Library of Scotland Act 2012 modernised the composition and responsibilities of the board. Board members are appointed by the Scottish ministers.

Chair (Interim), Simon Learoyd
Board members, Noreen Adams; Elizabeth Carmichal, CBE; Ruth Crawford, QC; Helen Durndell; Dianne Haley; Alan Horn; Iain Marley; Lesley McPherson; Prof. Adrienne Scullion; Amina Shah; Prof. Melissa Terras; Robert Wallen
National Librarian and Chief Executive, Dr John Scally
Heads of Department, John Coll *(Access);* Jackie Cromarty *(External Relations);* Anthony Gillespie *(Business Support);* Stuart Lewis *(Digital);* Joesph Marshall *(Collections Management);* Robin Smith *(Collections and Research)*

NATIONAL LIBRARY OF WALES/ LLYFRGELL GENEDLAETHOL CYMRU
Aberystwyth, Ceredigion, Wales SY23 3BU
T 01970-632800 **E** gofyn@llgc.org.uk **W** www.library.wales

The National Library of Wales was founded by royal charter in 1907, and is funded by the Welsh government. It contains about 6 million books and newspapers, 40,000 manuscripts, four million deeds and documents, 1.5 million maps, prints and drawings, and a sound and moving image collection. It specialises in manuscripts and books relating to Wales and the Celtic peoples. It is the repository for pre-1858 Welsh probate records, manorial records and tithe documents, and certain legal records. Admission to the reading rooms is by reader's ticket, but entry to the exhibition programme is free.
   Funding from the Welsh government totalled £11.8m in 2019–20.

President, Meri Huws

Trustees, Lord Aberdare; Michael Cavanagh; Gwilym Dyfri Jones; Quentin Howard; Dr Anwen Jones; Dr Gwenllian Lansdown Davies; Dr Elin Royles; Dr Elizabeth Siberry; Hugh Thomas; Eleri Twynog Humphries; Carl Williams; Steve Williams; Lee Yale-Helms *(Treasurer)*
Chief Executive and Librarian, Pedr ap Llwyd

NATIONAL MUSEUM OF THE ROYAL NAVY
HM Naval Base (PP66), Portsmouth PO1 3NH
T 023-9289 1370 **W** www.nmrn.org.uk

The National Museum of the Royal Navy comprises ten museums: HMS *Victory,* HMS *Caroline,* HMS *M.33,* HMS *Warrior,* the National Museum of the Royal Navy Portsmouth, the National Museum of the Royal Navy Hartlepool, the Fleet Air Arm Museum, the Royal Navy Submarine Museum, the New Royal Marines Museum, and the Explosion Museum of Naval Firepower. The Fleet Air Museum is located at RNAS Yeovilton, Somerset, and HMS *Caroline* is located at

Alexandra Dock, Belfast, while the other eight are situated in Portsmouth and Gosport.

Chair, Adm. Sir Philip Jones, GCB, DL
Trustees, Mark Anderson; Michael Bedingfield; Katherine Biggs; Philip Dolling; Helen Jackson; Cllr Donna Jones; Mike Gambazzi; Helen Jackson; Vice-Adm. Sir Adrian Johns, KCB, CBE, ADC; Maj.-Gen. Jeffrey Mason, MBE; Rear-Adm. Jonathan Pentreath, CB, OBE; Hon. Mary Montagu-Scott; Tim Schadla-Hall; John Scott; Alison Start; Gavin Whitter
Director-General, Prof. Dominic Tweddle

NATIONAL LOTTERY COMMUNITY FUND
1 Plough Place, London EC4A 1DE
T 0289-568 0143
E general.enquiries@tnlcommunityfund.org.uk
W www.tnlcommunityfund.org.uk

The National Lottery Community Fund, formerly the Big Lottery Fund, awarded over £588m of National Lottery funds in 2019–20; 83.3 per cent in grants under £10,000. The Fund supports health, education, environmental and charitable projects.

Chair (Interim), Tony Burton, CBE
Regional Chairs, Kate Beggs *(Northern Ireland);* Neil Ritch *(Scotland);* Elly de Baker *(England);* John Rose *(Wales)*
Chief Executive, Dawn Austwick, OBE

NATIONAL MUSEUM WALES/ AMGUEDDFA CYMRU
Cathays Park, Cardiff CF10 3NP
T 0300-111 2333 **W** https://museum.wales

National Museum Wales *(Amgueddfa Cymru)* is the body that runs Wales' seven national museums. It comprises National Museum Cardiff; St Fagans: National Waterfront Museum, Swansea; Big Pit: National Coal Museum, Blaenafon; National Roman Legion Museum, Caerleon; National Slate Museum, Llanberis; National Wool Museum, Dre-fach Felindre; and National Collections Centre, Nantgarw.

President, Roger Lewis
Vice-President, Dr Carol Bell
Trustees, Hywel John *(Treasurer);* Baroness Andrews, OBE; Dr Catherine Duigan; Dr Madeleine Havard; Gwyneth Hayward; Carys Howell; Rachel Hughes; Rob Humphries, CBE; Dr Hywel Jones, CMG; Michael Prior
Director-General, David Anderson, OBE

NATIONAL MUSEUMS LIVERPOOL
127 Dale Street, Liverpool L2 2JH
W www.liverpoolmuseums.org.uk

Regulated by the Department of Digital, Culture, Media and Sport, National Museums Liverpool is a group of museums and collections, comprising eight venues: International Slavery Museum, Lady Lever Art Gallery, Merseyside Maritime Museum, Museum of Liverpool, Seized! (UK Border Force National Museum), Sudley House, Walker Art Gallery and World Museum.

Chair, Sir David Henshaw
Trustees, Heather Blyth; James Chapman; Michelle Charters; Sarah Dean; Paul Eccleson; David Fleming; Heather Lauder; Rita McLean; Andrew McCluskey; Philip Price; Ian Rosenblatt, OBE; Max Steinberg, CBE; Virginia Tandy
Director National Museums Liverpool, Laura Pye
Directors, Mark Davies *(People);* Stephanie Donaldson *(Business Resources);* Janet Dugdale *(Museums and Participation);*

Stacey Hammond *(Business Development);* Mairi Johnson *(Estates);* Melanie Lewis *(Commercial and Business Development);* Karen O'Connor *(Commercial Enterprises);* Sandra Penketh *(Galleries and Collections Management);* Fiona Philpott *(Exhibitions);* Carol Rogers *(House of Memories);* David Spilsbury *(Finance);* David Watson *(Audiences and Media)*

NATIONAL MUSEUMS NORTHERN IRELAND
Cultra, Holywood, Northern Ireland BT18 0EU
T 0280-042 8428 **E** info@nmni.com **W** www.nmni.com

Across three unique sites National Museums Northern Ireland cares for and presents inspirational collections reflecting the creativity, innovation, history, culture and people of Northern Ireland and beyond.

Together the Ulster Museum, Ulster Folk and Transport Museum and Ulster American Folk Park contain 1.4 billion objects and offer a unique opportunity to experience the heritage and way of life of Northern Ireland.

Chair, Miceal McCoy
Vice-Chair, Prof. Garth Earls
Trustees, Dr Riann Coulter; Deirdre Devlin; William Duddy; Dr Leon Litvack; Prof. Karen Fleming; Hazel Francey; Daphne Harshaw; Charlotte Jess; Dr Rosemary Kelly, OBE; Alan McFarland; Dr George McIlroy; Catherine Molloy; Dr Robert Whan
Chief Executive, Kathryn Thomson

NATIONAL MUSEUMS SCOTLAND
Chambers Street, Edinburgh EH1 1JF
T 0300-123 6789 **E** info@nms.ac.uk **W** www.nms.ac.uk

National Museums Scotland provides advice, expertise and support to the museums community across Scotland, and undertakes fieldwork that often involves collaboration at local, national and international levels. National Museums Scotland comprises the National Museum of Scotland, the National War Museum, the National Museum of Rural Life, the National Museum of Flight and the National Museums Collection Centre. Its collections represent more than two centuries of collecting and include Scottish and classical archaeology, decorative and applied arts, world cultures and social history and science, technology and the natural world.

Up to 15 trustees can be appointed by the Minister for Culture, Tourism and External Affairs for a term of four years, and may serve a second term.

Chair, Ian Russell, CBE
Trustees, Ann Allen, MBE; Prof. Mary Bownes, OBE, FRSE; Adam Bruce; Gordon Drummond; Chris Fletcher; Dr Brian Lang, CBE, FRSE; Lynda Logan; Dr Catriona Macdonald; Janet Stevenson; Eilidh Wiseman; Dr Laura Young, MBE
Director, Dr Chris Breward

NATIONAL PORTRAIT GALLERY
St Martin's Place, London WC2H 0HE
T 020-7306 0055 **W** www.npg.org.uk

The National Portrait Gallery was established in 1856. Today the Gallery collects portraits of those who have made, or are making, a significant contribution to British history and culture. The Collection is free to visit, and includes works across all media, from painting and sculpture to photography and digital portraits. To complement the Collection, the Gallery stages exhibitions, displays, talks and events throughout the year which explore the nature of portraiture. The Gallery loans exhibitions, displays and individual portraits to organisations across the UK and internationally as part of its ongoing commitment to sharing the Collection as widely as possible.

Chair of the Board of Trustees, David Ross
Director, Dr Nicholas Cullinan

NATURAL ENGLAND

County Hall, Spetchley Road, Worcester WR5 2NP
T 0300-060 3900 **E** enquiries@naturalengland.org.uk
W www.gov.uk/government/organisations/natural-england

Natural England is the government's adviser on the natural environment, providing practical scientific advice on how to look after England's landscapes and wildlife.

The organisation's remit is to ensure sustainable stewardship of the land and sea so that people and nature can thrive.

Natural England works with farmers and land managers; business and industry; planners and developers; national and local government; charities and conservationists; interest groups and local communities to help them improve their local environment.

Chair, Tony Juniper, CBE
Chief Executive, Marian Spain

NATURAL HISTORY MUSEUM

Cromwell Road, London SW7 5BD
T 020-7942 5000 **W** www.nhm.ac.uk

The Natural History Museum, which houses 80 million natural history specimens, originates from the natural history departments of the British Museum, which grew extensively during the 19th century; in 1860 it was agreed that the natural history collections should be separated from the British Museum's collections of books, manuscripts and antiquities. Part of the site of the 1862 International Exhibition in South Kensington was acquired for the new museum, and the museum opened to the public in 1881. In 1963 the Natural History Museum became completely independent, although eight members of the board are still selected by the prime minister, once by the Department for Digital, Culture, Media and Sport, and three by the board itself. The Natural History Museum at Tring, bequeathed by the second Lord Rothschild, has formed part of the museum since 1937. The Geological Museum merged with the Natural History Museum in 1986. In September 2009 the Natural History Museum opened the Darwin Centre, which contains public galleries, a high-tech interactive area known as the Attenborough Studio and scientific research facilities.

Chair, Lord Green of Hurstpierpoint
Trustees, Prof. Sir John Beddington, CMG, FRS; Harris Bokhari, OBE; Dame Frances Cairncross, DBE, FRSE; Prof. Yadvinder Malhi, FRS; Anand Mahindra; Hilary Newiss; Robert Noel; Simon Patterson; Prof. Stephen Sparks, CMG, FRS, CBE; Dr Sarah Thomas; Prof. Dame Janet Thornton, DBE, FRS, FMEDSCI; Dr Kim Winser, OBE
Museum Director, Doug Gurr
Directors, Neil Greenwood *(Finance and Corporate Services);* Dt Tim Littlewood *(Science);* Fiona McWilliams *(Development);* Clare Matterson, CBE *(Engagement)*

NATURAL RESOURCES WALES

Ty Cambria, 29 Newport Road, Cardiff CF24 0TP
T 0300-065 3000 **E** enquiries@naturalresourceswales.gov.uk
W www.naturalresources.wales

Natural Resources Wales *(Cyfoeth Naturiol Cymru)* is the principal adviser to the Welsh government on the environment. It became operational in April 2013 following a

merger of the Countryside Council for Wales, Environment Agency Wales and the Forestry Commission Wales. It is responsible for ensuring that the natural resources of Wales are sustainably maintained, enhanced and used; now and in the future.

Chair, Sir David Henshaw
Board Members, Karen Balmer; Chris Blake; Catherine Brown; Julia Cherrett; Geraint Davies; Howard Davies; Dr Elizabeth Haywood; Zoë Henderson; Prof. Steve Ormerod, FCIEEM; Dr Rosie Plummer; Prof. Peter Rigby, FRS, FMEDSCI
Chief Executive, Clare Pillman

NHS PAY REVIEW BODY

8th Floor, Fleetbank House, 2-6 Salisbury Square, London EC4Y 8JX
T 020-7211 8295 **W** www.gov.uk/government/organisations/nhs-pay-review-body

The NHS Pay Review Body (NHSPRB) advises the prime minister, Secretary of State for Health and ministers in Scotland, Wales and Northern Ireland on the remuneration of all paid staff under agenda for change and employed in the NHS. The review body was established in 1983 for nurses and allied health professionals. Its remit has since expanded to cover just under 1.5 million staff, ie almost all staff in the NHS, with the exception of dentists, doctors and very senior managers.

Chair, Philippa Hird
Members, Richard Cooper; Patricia Gordon; Neville Hounsome; Stephanie Marston; Karen Mumford; Anne Phillimore; Prof. David Ulph, CBE

NORTHERN IRELAND HUMAN RIGHTS COMMISSION

Fourth Floor, Alfred House, 19-21 Alfred Street, Belfast BT2 8ED
T 028-9024 3987 **E** info@nihrc.org **W** www.nihrc.org

The Northern Ireland Human Rights Commission is a non-departmental public body, established by the Northern Ireland Act 1998 and set up in March 1999. Its purpose is to protect and promote human rights in Northern Ireland. Its main functions include reviewing the law and practice relating to human rights, advising government and the Northern Ireland Assembly, and promoting an awareness of human rights. It can also investigate human rights violations and take cases to court. The members of the commission are appointed by the Secretary of State for Northern Ireland.

Chief Commissioner, Les Allamby
Commissioners, Helen Henderson; Jonathan Kearney; David Lavery, CB; Maura Muldoon; Eddie Rooney; Stephen White, OBE
Chief Executive, Dr David Russell

NORTHERN LIGHTHOUSE BOARD

84 George Street, Edinburgh EH2 3DA
T 0131-473 3100 **E** enquiries@nlb.org.uk **W** www.nlb.org.uk

The Northern Lighthouse Board is the general lighthouse authority for Scotland and the Isle of Man and owes its origin to an act of parliament passed in 1786. At present there are 19 commissioners who operate under the Merchant Shipping Act 1995.

The commissioners control 206 lighthouses, 170 lighted and unlighted buoys, 26 beacons, 35 AIS (automatic identification system) stations, 29 radar beacons, four DGPS (differential global positioning system) stations and an ELORAN (long-range navigation) system. *See also* Transport.

Chair, Capt. Michael Brew
Vice-Chair, Capt. Alastair Beveridge

Commissioners, Lord Advocate; Solicitor-General for Scotland; Lord Provosts of Edinburgh, Glasgow, and Aberdeen; Convener of Highland Council; Provost of Argyll and Bute Council; Sheriffs-Principal of South Strathclyde, Dumfries and Galloway, Tayside, Central and Fife, North Strathclyde, Grampian, Highlands and Islands, Lothian and Borders, and Glasgow and Strathkelvin; Brian Archibald; Hugh Shaw, OBE; Elaine Wilkinson; Rob Woodward
Chief Executive, Mike Bullock, MBE

NUCLEAR DECOMMISSIONING AUTHORITY

Herdus House, Westlakes Science and Technology Park, Moor Row, Cumbria CA24 3HU
T 01925-802001 **E** enquiries@nda.gov.uk
W www.gov.uk/government/organisations/nuclear-decommissioning-authority

The Nuclear Decommissioning Authority (NDA) was created under the Energy Act 2004. It is a strategic authority that owns 17 sites plus associated civil nuclear liabilities and assets of the public sector, previously under the control of the UK Energy Authority and British Nuclear Fuels. The NDA's responsibilities include decommissioning and cleaning up civil nuclear facilities; ensuring the safe management of waste products, both radioactive and non-radioactive; implementing government policy on the long-term management of nuclear waste; developing UK-wide low-level waste strategy plans; and scrutinising the decommissioning plans of EDF Energy.
  Total planned expenditure for 2019–20 was £3.112bn, with total grant-in-aid standing at £2.210bn. The remaining £0.902bn will come from commercial operations.

Chair, Dr Ros Rivaz
Chief Executive, David Peattie

OFFICE FOR BUDGET RESPONSIBILITY

14T, 102 Petty France, London SW1H 9AJ
T 020-3334 6117 **E** OBR.Enquiries@obr.uk **W** www.obr.uk

The Office for Budget Responsibility (OBR) was created in 2010 to provide independent and authoritative analysis of the UK's public finances. It has five main roles: producing forecasts for the economy and public finances; judging progress towards the government's fiscal targets; evaluating fiscal risks; assessing the long-term sustainability of the public finances; and scrutinising HM Treasury's costing of tax and welfare spending measures.

Chair, Richard Hughes
Committee Members, Prof. Sir Charles Bean; Andy King

OFFICE OF COMMUNICATIONS (OFCOM)

Riverside House, 2A Southwark Bridge Road, London SE1 9HA
T 0300-123 3000 **W** www.ofcom.org.uk

OFCOM was established in 2003 under the Office of Communications Act 2002 as the independent regulator and competition authority for the UK communications industries with responsibility, for television, video-on-demand, radio, telecommunications and wireless communications services.
  Following the passing of the Postal Services Act 2011, OFCOM also assumed regulatory responsibility for postal services.

Chair, Lord Burns
Deputy Chair, Maggie Carver
Board Members, Kevin Bakhurst; Angela Dean *(Audit and Risk);* Bob Downes *(Scotland);* David Jones *(Wales);* Graham Mather; Tim Suter; Ben Verwaayen
Chief Executive, Melanie Dawes

OFFICE OF MANPOWER ECONOMICS (OME)

8th Floor, Fleetbank House, 2–6 Salisbury Square, London EC4Y 8JX
T 020-7211 8165 **E** omeenquiries@beis.gov.uk **W** www.gov.uk/government/organisations/office-of-manpower-economics

The Office of Manpower Economics (OME) was established in 1971. It is an independent non-statutory organisation responsible for providing an independent secretariat to eight independent review bodies: the Armed Forces' Pay Review Body (AFPRB); the Review Body on Doctors' and Dentists' Remuneration (DDRB); the NHS Pay Review Body (NHSPRB); the Prison Service Pay Review Body (PSPRB); the School Teachers' Review Body (STRB); the Senior Salaries Review Body (SSRB); the Police Remuneration Review Body (PRRB); and the National Crime Agency Remuneration Review Body (NCARRB). In total these pay bodies make recommendations impacting 2.5 million workers – around 45 per cent of public sector staff – and with a total pay bill of £100bn.

Director, David Fry

ORDNANCE SURVEY

Adanac Drive, Southampton SO16 0AS
T 0345-605 0505 **E** customerservices@os.uk
W www.ordnancesurvey.co.uk

Ordnance Survey is the national mapping agency for Great Britain, which can trace its roots back to 1745. It is a public corporation of the Department for Business, Energy and Industrial Strategy.

Chief Executive, Steve Blair

PARADES COMMISSION

2nd Floor, Andras House, 60 Great Victoria Street, Belfast BT2 7BB
T 028-9089 5900 **E** info@paradescommissionni.org
W www.paradescommission.org

The Parades Commission is an independent, quasi-judicial body set up under the Public Processions (Northern Ireland) Act 1998. Its function is to encourage and facilitate local accommodation of contentious parades; where this is not possible, the commission is empowered to make legal determinations about such parades, which may include imposing conditions on aspects of the notified parade (such as restrictions on routes/areas and exclusion of certain groups with a record of bad behaviour).
  The chair and members are appointed by the Secretary of State for Northern Ireland; the membership must, as far as is practicable, be representative of the community in Northern Ireland.

Chair, Anne Henderson
Members, Joelle Black; Sarah Havlin; Paul Hutchinson; Colin Kennedy; Anne Marshall; Geraldine McGahey

PAROLE BOARD FOR ENGLAND AND WALES

3rd Floor, 10 South Colonnade, Canary Wharf, London E14 4PU
T 020-3880 0885 **E** info@paroleboard.gov.uk
W www.gov.uk/government/organisations/parole-board

The Parole Board was established in 1968 under the Criminal Justice Act 1967 and became an independent executive non-departmental public body on 1 July 1996 under the Criminal Justice and Public Order Act 1994. It is the body that protects the public by making risk assessments about prisoners to decide who may safely be released into the community and who must remain in, or be returned to, custody. Board decisions are taken at two main types of panels of up to three members: 'paper panels' for the majority of cases, or oral hearings for decisions concerning prisoners serving life or indeterminate sentences for public protection. The Parole Board held 5,380 oral hearings in 2018–19; 49 per cent were released.

Chair, Caroline Corby
Chief Executive, Martin Jones

PAROLE BOARD FOR SCOTLAND
Saughton House, Broomhouse Drive, Edinburgh EH11 3XD
T 0131-244 8373 **E** enquiries@paroleboard.scot
W www.scottishparoleboard.scot

The board is an independent judicial body directs and advises the Scottish ministers on the release of prisoners on licence, and related matters.

Chair, John Watt

PENSION PROTECTION FUND (PPF)
Renaissance, 12 Dingwall Road, Croydon CR0 2NA
T 0345-600 2541 **E** information@ppf.co.uk
W www.pensionprotectionfund.org.uk

The PPF became operational in 2005. It was established to pay compensation to members of eligible defined-benefit pension schemes, when a qualifying insolvency event in relation to the employer occurs and where there is a lack of sufficient assets in the pension scheme. The PPF also administers the Financial Assistance Scheme, which helps members whose schemes wound-up before 2005. It is also responsible for the Fraud Compensation Fund (which provides compensation to occupational pension schemes that suffer a loss that can be attributed to dishonesty). The chair and board of the PPF are appointed by, and accountable to, the Secretary of State for Work and Pensions, and are responsible for paying compensation, calculating annual levies (which help fund the PPF), and setting and overseeing investment strategy.

Chair, Arnold Wagner, OBE
Chief Executive, Oliver Morley, CBE

PENSIONS REGULATOR
Napier House, Trafalgar Place, Brighton BN1 4DW
T 0345-600 0707 **E** customersupport@tpr.gov.uk
W www.thepensionsregulator.gov.uk

The Pensions Regulator was established in 2005 as the regulator of workplace pension schemes in the UK, replacing the Occupational Pensions Regulatory Authority (OPRA). It aims to make sure employers put their staff into a pension scheme and pay money into it (automatic enrolment) and to protect the benefits of occupational and personal pension scheme members by working with trustees, employers, pension providers and advisers. The regulator's work focuses on encouraging better management and administration of schemes, ensuring that final salary schemes have a sensible funding plan, and encouraging money purchase schemes to provide members with the information that they need to make informed choices about their pension fund. The Pensions Act 2004 and the Pensions Act 2008 gave the regulator a range of powers which can be used to protect scheme members, but a strong emphasis is placed on educating and enabling those responsible for managing pension schemes, and powers are used only where necessary. The regulator offers free online resources to help trustees, employers, professionals and advisers understand their role, duties and obligations.

Chair, Mark Boyle
Chief Executive, Charles Counsell

POLICE ADVISORY BOARD FOR ENGLAND AND WALES
Home Office, 6th Floor Fry, 2 Marsham Street, London SW1P 4DF
E pabewsecretariat@homeoffice.gov.uk
W www.gov.uk/government/organisations/police-advisory-board-for-england-and-wales

The Police Advisory Board for England and Wales was established in 1965 by section 46 of the Police Act 1964 and provides advice to the home secretary on general questions affecting the police in England and Wales. It also considers draft regulations under the Police Act 1996 about matters such as recruitment, diversity and collaboration between forces.

Independent Chair, Elizabeth France

PRISON SERVICE PAY REVIEW BODY
8th Floor, Fleetbank House, 2-6 Salisbury Square, London EC4Y 8JX
T 020-7211 8259 **E** PSPRB@beis.gov.uk
W www.gov.uk/government/organisations/prison-services-pay-review-body

The Prison Service Pay Review Body was set up in 2001. It makes independent recommendations on the pay of prison governors, operational managers, prison officers and related grades for the Prison Service in England and Wales, and for the Northern Ireland Prison Service.

Chair, Tim Flesher, CB
Members, Mary Carter; Luke Corkill; Prof. Andy Dickerson; Judith Gillespie, CBE; Leslie Manasseh, MBE; Paul West, QPM

PRIVY COUNCIL OFFICE
Room G/04, 1 Horse Guards Road, London SW1A 2HQ
E enquiries@pco.gov.uk
W https://privycouncil.independent.gov.uk

The primary function of the office is to act as the secretariat to the Privy Council. It is responsible for the arrangements leading to the making of all royal proclamations and orders in council; for certain formalities connected with ministerial changes; for considering applications for the granting (or amendment) of royal charters; for the scrutiny and approval of by-laws and statutes of chartered institutions and of the governing instruments of universities and colleges; and for the appointment of high sheriffs and Privy Council appointments to governing bodies. Under the relevant acts, the office is responsible for the approval of certain regulations and rules made by the regulatory bodies of the medical and certain allied professions.

The Lord President of the Council is the ministerial head of the office and presides at meetings of the Privy Council. The Clerk of the Council is the administrative head of the Privy Council office.

Lord President of the Council and Leader of the House of Commons, Rt. Hon. Jacob Rees-Mogg
Clerk of the Council, Richard Tilbrook
Head of Secretariat and Deputy Clerk, Ceri King
Deputy Clerk, Christopher Berry

REVIEW BODY ON DOCTORS' AND DENTISTS' REMUNERATION
8th Floor, Fleetbank House, 2-6 Salisbury Square, London EC4Y 8JX
T 020-7211 8184 **W** www.gov.uk/government/organisations/review-body-on-doctors-and-dentists-remuneration

The Review Body on Doctors' and Dentists' Remuneration was set up in 1971. It advises the prime minister, the secretary of state for health and social care, first ministers in Scotland, Wales and Northern Ireland, and the ministers for Health and

Social Care, in England, Scotland, Wales and Northern Ireland on the remuneration of doctors and dentists taking any part in the National Health Service.

Chair, Christopher Pilgrim
Members, David Bingham; Helen Jackson; Prof. Peter Kopelman, MD, FRCP, FFPH; James Malcomson; John Matheson, CBE; Nora Nanayakkara

ROYAL AIR FORCE MUSEUM
Grahame Park Way, London NW9 5LL
T 020-8205 2266 **E** london@rafmuseum.org
W www.rafmuseum.org.uk

The museum has two sites, one at the former airfield at Colindale, in North London, and the second at Cosford, in the West Midlands, both of which illustrate the development of aviation from before the Wright brothers to the present-day RAF. The museum's collection across both sites consists of over 170 aircraft, as well as artefacts, aviation memorabilia, fine art and photographs.

Chair, Air Chief Marshal Sir Andrew Pulford, GCB, CBE, DL
Trustees, Peter Bateson; Laurie Benson; Dr Carol Cole; Dr Rodney Eastwood, MBE; Richard Holman; Catriona Lougher; Julie McGarvey; Andrew Reid; Nick Sanders; Mike Schindler
Chief Executive, Maggie Appleton, MBE

ROYAL BOTANIC GARDEN EDINBURGH
Arboretum Place, Edinburgh EH3 5NZ
T 0172-760254 **W** www.rbge.org.uk

The Royal Botanic Garden Edinburgh (RBGE) originated as the Physic Garden, established in 1670 beside the Palace of Holyroodhouse. The garden moved to its present site at Inverleith, Edinburgh, in 1820. There are also three regional gardens: Benmore Botanic Garden, near Dunoon, Argyll; Logan Botanic Garden, near Stranraer, Wigtownshire; and Dawyck Botanic Garden, near Stobo, Peeblesshire. Since 1986 RBGE has been administered by a board of trustees established under the National Heritage (Scotland) Act 1985. It receives an annual grant from the Scottish government's Environment and Forestry Directorate.

The RBGE is an international centre for scientific research on plant diversity and for horticulture education and conservation. It has an extensive library, a herbarium with almost three million preserved plant specimens, and over 13,500 species in the living collections.

Chair, Dominic Fry
Trustees, Raoul Curtis-Machin; Prof. Beverley Glover; Dr David Hamilton; Dr Ian Jardine; Prof. Thomas Meagher; Diana Murray; Prof. Ian Wall, FRSE
Regius Keeper, Simon Milne, MBE

ROYAL BOTANIC GARDENS, KEW
Kew Gardens, Richmond, London TW9 3AB
T 020-8332 5655 **E** info@kew.org
Wakehurst, Ardingly, W. Sussex RH17 6TN
T 01444-894066 **E** wakehurst@kew.org
W www.kew.org

Kew Gardens was originally laid out as a private garden for the now demolished White House for George III's mother, Princess Augusta, in 1759. The gardens were much enlarged in the 19th century, notably by the inclusion of the grounds of the former Richmond Lodge. In 1965 Kew acquired the gardens at Wakehurst on a long lease from the National Trust. Under the National Heritage Act 1983 a board of trustees was set up to administer the gardens, which in 1984 became an independent body supported by grant-in-aid from the

Department for Environment, Food and Rural Affairs. In 2016, restoration work was completed on Temperate House and the Giant pagoda.

The functions of RBG, Kew are to carry out research into plant sciences, to disseminate knowledge about plants and to provide the public with the opportunity to gain knowledge and enjoyment from the gardens' collections. There are extensive national reference collections of living and preserved plants and a comprehensive library and archive. The main emphasis is on plant conservation and biodiversity; Wakehurst houses the Millennium Seed Bank Partnership, which is the largest *ex situ* conservation project in the world – it is home to 2.4 billion seeds from 97 countries.

Chair, Dame Amelia Fawcett, DBE, CVO
Trustees, Nick Baird, CMG, CVO; Prof. Liam Dolan; Catherine Dugmore; Sarah Flannigan; Valerie Gooding, CBE; Krishnan Guru-Murthy; Prof. Sue Hartley, OBE; Ian Karet; Jantiene Klein Roseboom van der Veer; Michael Lear; Sir Derek Myers
Director, Richard Deverell

ROYAL COMMISSION ON THE ANCIENT AND HISTORICAL MONUMENTS OF WALES
Ffordd Penglais, Aberystwyth SY23 3BU
T 01970-621200 **E** nmr.wales@rcahmw.gov.uk
W www.rcahmw.gov.uk

The Royal Commission on the Ancient and Historical Monuments of Wales, established in 1908, is the investigation body and national archive for the historic environment of Wales. It has the lead role in ensuring that Wales's archaeological, built and maritime heritage is authoritatively recorded, and seeks to promote the understanding and appreciation of this heritage nationally and internationally. The commission is funded by the Welsh government.

Chair, Prof. Nancy Edwards, FSA
Commissioners, Neil Beagrie, FRSA; Chris Brayne; Caroline Crewe-Read, FRSA; Dr Louise Emanuel; Catherine Hardman, FSA; Thomas Lloyd, OBE, FSA; Dr Hayley Roberts; Jonathan Vining
Secretary, Christopher Catling

ROYAL MUSEUMS GREENWICH
National Maritime Museum, Greenwich, London SE10 9NF
T 020-8858 4422 **E** RMGenquiries@rmg.co.uk
W www.rmg.co.uk

Royal Museums Greenwich comprises the National Maritime Museum, the Queen's House and the Royal Observatory Greenwich, and also works in collaboration with the Cutty Sark Trust. The National Maritime Museum provides information on the maritime history of Great Britain and is the largest institution of its kind in the world, with over 2.5 million items related to seafaring, navigation and astronomy. Originally the home of Charles I's Queen, Henrietta Maria, the Queen's House was built between 1616–18, although it was structurally altered between 1629–35. It now contains a fine-art collection. The Royal Observatory, Greenwich is the home of Greenwich Mean Time and the prime meridian of the world. It also contains London's only planetarium, Harrison's timekeepers and the UK's largest refracting telescope.

Chair, Sir Charles Dunstone, CVO
Trustees, Joyce Bridges, CBE; Dr Fiona Butcher; Dr Helen Czerski; Prof. Julian Dowdeswell; Dr Aminul Hoque, MBE; Alastair Marsh; Jeremy Penn; Eric Reynolds; Adm. Sir Mark Stanhope, GCB, OBE
Director, Paddy Rodgers

SCHOOL TEACHERS' REVIEW BODY

8th Floor, Fleetbank House, 2-6 Salisbury Square, London EC4Y 8JX
T 020-7211 8463 **W** www.gov.uk/government/organisations/
school-teachers-review-body

The School Teachers' Review Body was set up under the School Teachers' Pay and Conditions Act 1991. It is required to examine and make recommendations on such matters relating to the statutory conditions of employment of school teachers in England and Wales. It reports to the education secretary and the prime minister.

Chair, Dr Patricia Rice
Members, Sir Robert Burgess; Ken Clark; Harriet Kemp; John Lakin; Lynne Lawrence; Martin Post; Dr Andrew Walker

SCIENCE MUSEUM GROUP

W www.sciencemuseumgroup.org.uk

SCIENCE MUSEUM
Exhibition Road, London SW7 2DD
T 0800-047 8124 **E** info@sciencemuseum.ac.uk
W www.sciencemuseum.org.uk

SCIENCE AND INDUSTRY MUSEUM
Liverpool Road, Castlefield, Manchester M3 4FP
T 0161-832 2244 **E** contact@scienceandindustrymuseum.org.uk
W www.scienceandindustrymuseum.org.uk

NATIONAL RAILWAY MUSEUM AND LOCOMOTION
NRM York, Leeman Road, York YO26 4XJ
T 0333-016 1010 **E** info@railwaymuseum.org.uk
W www.railwaymuseum.org.uk
Locomotion, Shildon, Co. Durham DL4 2RE
T 01904-685780 **E** info@locomotion.org.uk
W www.locomotion.org.uk

NATIONAL SCIENCE AND MEDIA MUSEUM
Pictureville, Bradford BD1 1NQ
T 0844-856 3797 **E** talk.nsmm@scienceandmediamuseum.org.uk
W www.scienceandmediamuseum.org.uk

The Science Museum Group (SMG) consists of the Science Museum; the Science and Industry Museum, Manchester; the National Railway Museum, York; the National Science and Media Museum, Bradford; and Locomotion at Shildon. The Science Museum houses the national collections of science, technology, industry and medicine and attracts around 3.2 million visits annually. The museum began as the science collection of the South Kensington Museum and first opened in 1857. In 1883 it acquired the collections of the Patent Museum and in 1909 the science collections were transferred to the new Science Museum, leaving the art collections with the Victoria and Albert Museum. The Wellcome Wing was opened in July 2000.

The Trustees of the Science Museum Group have statutory duties under the National Heritage Act 1983 for the general management and control of SMG.

Total government grant in aid for 2019–20 was £67.7m.

Chair, Dame Mary Archer, DBE
Trustees, Prof. Brian Cantor; Judith Donovan, CBE; Dr Sarah Dry; Sharon Flood; Prof. Russell Foster, CBE, FRS, FMEDSCI; Dr Hannah Fry; Prof. Ludmilla Jordanova, FRHS, FRSM; Prof. Ajit Lalvani; Iain McIntosh; Lopa Patel; Prof. David Phoenix, OBE; Sarah Staniforth; Steven Underwood; Anton Valk, CBE; Dame Fiona Woolf, CBE
Director of Science Museum, Sir Ian Blatchford
Director of Science & Industry Museum, Sally MacDonald
Director of National Science and Media Museum, Jo Quinton-Tulloch
Director of National Railway Museum, Judith McNicol

SCOTTISH CRIMINAL CASES REVIEW COMMISSION

Portland House, 17 Renfield Street, Glasgow G2 5AH
T 0141-270 7030 **E** info@sccrc.org.uk **W** www.sccrc.org.uk

The commission is a non-departmental public body, funded by the Scottish Government Justice Directorate, and established under the Criminal Procedure (Scotland) Act 1995 in April 1999. It assumed the role previously performed by the Secretary of State for Scotland to consider alleged miscarriages of justice in Scotland and refer cases meeting the relevant criteria to the high court for determination. Members are appointed by the Queen on the recommendation of the first minister; senior executive staff are appointed by the commission.

Chair, Bill Matthews
Members, Prof. Jim Fraser; Raymond McMenamin; Elaine Noad; Dr Alex Quinn; Laura Reilly; Carol Gammie
Chief Executive and Principal Solicitor, Gerard Sinclair

SCOTTISH ENTERPRISE

Atrium Court, 50 Waterloo Street, Glasgow G2 6HQ
T 0300-013 3385
W www.scottish-enterprise.com

Scottish Enterprise was established in 1991 and its purpose is to stimulate the sustainable growth of Scotland's economy. It is mainly funded by the Scottish government and is responsible to the Scottish ministers. Working in partnership with the private and public sectors, Scottish Enterprise invests £300–350m annually to further the development of Scotland's economy by helping ambitious and innovative businesses grow and become more successful. Scottish Enterprise is particularly interested in supporting companies that provide renewable energy, encourage trade overseas, increase innovation, and those that will help Scotland become a low-carbon economy. Total anticipated Scottish government funding for 2019–20 was £295.4m.

Chair, Lord Smith of Kelvin, KT, CH
Chief Executive (Interim), Linda Hannah

SCOTTISH ENVIRONMENT PROTECTION AGENCY (SEPA)

Erskine Court, Castle Business Park, Stirling FK9 4TZ
T 0300-099 6699 **W** www.sepa.org.uk

SEPA was established in 1996 and is the public body responsible for environmental protection in Scotland. It regulates potential pollution to land, air and water; the storage, transport and disposal of controlled waste; and the safekeeping and disposal of radioactive materials. It does this within a complex legislative framework of acts of parliament, EU directives and regulations, granting licences to operations of industrial processes and waste disposal. SEPA also operates Floodline (**T** 0345-988 1188), a public service providing information on the possible risk of flooding 24 hours a day, 365 days a year.

Chair, Bob Downes
Members, Franceska van Dijk; Michelle Francis; Nicola Gordon; Martin Hill; Craig Hume; Julie Hutchinson; Harpreet Kohli; Nick Martin; Philip Matthews
Chief Executive, Terry A'Hearn

SCOTTISH LAW COMMISSION

140 Causewayside, Edinburgh EH9 1PR
T 0131-668 2131 **E** info@scotlawcom.gov.uk
W www.scotlawcom.gov.uk

The Scottish Law Commission, established in 1965, keeps the law in Scotland under review and makes proposals for its development and reform. It is responsible to the Scottish ministers through the Scottish government constitution, law and courts directorate.

Chair, Rt. Hon. Lady Paton
Commissioners, David Bartos; Prof. Gillian Black; Kate Dowdalls, QC; Prof. Frankie McCarthy
Chief Executive, Malcolm McMillan

SCOTTISH LEGAL AID BOARD
Thistle House, 91 Haymarket Terrace, Edinburgh EH12 5HE
T 0131-226 7061 **E** general@slab.org.uk **W** www.slab.org.uk

The Scottish Legal Aid Board was set up under the Legal Aid (Scotland) Act 1986 to manage legal aid in Scotland. It is designed to help individuals on low or modest incomes gain access to the legal system. It reports to the Scottish government. Board members are appointed by Scottish ministers.

Chair, Ray MacFarlane
Members, Brian Baverstock; Rani Dhir, MBE; Marieke Dwarshuis; Stephen Humphreys; Tim McKay; Raymond McMenamin; Sheriff John Morris, QC; Sarah O'Neill; Paul Reid; David Sheldon, QC; Lesley Ward
Chief Executive, Colin Lancaster

SCOTTISH NATURAL HERITAGE (SNH)
Great Glen House, Leachkin Road, Inverness IV3 8NW
T 01463-725000 **E** enquiries@nature.scot **W** www.nature.scot

SNH was established in 1992 under the Natural Heritage (Scotland) Act 1991. It is the government's adviser on all aspects of nature and landscape across Scotland and its role is to help the public understand, value and enjoy Scotland's nature, as well as to support those people and organisations that manage it.

Chair, Dr Mike Cantlay, OBE
Chief Executive and Accountable Officer, Francesca Osowska
Directors, Robbie Kernahan *(Sustainable Growth);* Jane Macdonald *(Business Services and Transformation);* Eileen Stuart *(Nature and Climate Change)*

SEAFISH
18 Logie Mill, Logie Green Road, Edinburgh EH7 4HS
T 0131-558 3331 **E** seafish@seafish.co.uk **W** www.seafish.org

Established under the Fisheries Act 1981, Seafish works with all sectors of the UK seafood industry to satisfy consumers, raise standards, improve efficiency and secure a sustainable and profitable future. Services range from research and development, economic consulting, market research and training and accreditation through to legislative advice for the seafood industry. It is sponsored by the four UK fisheries departments, which appoint the board, and receives 80 per cent of its funding through a levy on seafood.

Chair, Brian Young
Chief Executive, Marcus Coleman

SECURITY AND INTELLIGENCE SERVICES

GOVERNMENT COMMUNICATIONS HEADQUARTERS (GCHQ)
Hubble Road, Cheltenham GL51 0EX
T 01242-221491 **W** www.gchq.gov.uk

GCHQ produces signals intelligence in support of national security and the UK's economic wellbeing, and in the prevention or detection of serious crime. It is the national authority for cyber security and provides advice and assistance to government departments, the armed forces and other national infrastructure bodies on the security of their communications and information systems. GCHQ was placed on a statutory footing by the Intelligence Services Act 1994 and is headed by a director who is directly accountable to the foreign secretary.

Director, Jeremy Fleming

SECRET INTELLIGENCE SERVICE (MI6)
PO Box 1300, London SE1 1BD
Anti-Terrorist Hotline 0800-789 321 **W** www.sis.gov.uk

Established in 1909 as the Foreign Section of the Secret Service Bureau, the Secret Intelligence Service produces secret intelligence in support of the government's security, defence, foreign and economic policies. It was placed on a statutory footing by the Intelligence Services Act 1994 and is headed by a chief, known as 'C', who is directly accountable to the foreign secretary.

Chief, Richard Moore, CMG

SECURITY SERVICE (MI5)
PO Box 3255, London SW1P 1AE
T 0800-111 4645**Anti-Terrorist Hotline** 0800-789 321
W www.mi5.gov.uk

The Security Service is responsible for security intelligence work against covertly organised threats to the UK. It is organised into ten branches, each with dedicated areas of responsibility, which include countering terrorism, espionage and the proliferation of weapons of mass destruction. The Security Service also provides security advice to a wide range of organisations to help reduce vulnerability to threats from individuals, groups or countries hostile to UK interests. The home secretary has parliamentary accountability for the Security Service. There is a network of regional offices around the UK, plus a Northern Ireland headquarters.

Director-General, Ken McCallum

SENIOR SALARIES REVIEW BODY
8th Floor, Fleetbank House, 2-6 Salisbury Square, London EC4Y 8JX
T 020-7211 8315 **E** SSRB@BEIS.gov.uk **W** www.gov.uk/government/organisations/review-body-on-senior-salaries

The Senior Salaries Review Body (formerly the Top Salaries Review Body) was set up in 1971 and advises the prime minister, the Lord Chancellor, the defence secretary, the health secretary and the home secretary on the remuneration of the judiciary, senior civil servants, senior officers of the armed forces, certain senior managers in the NHS, police and crime commissioners and chief police officers. In 1993 its remit was extended to cover the pay, pensions and allowances of MPs, ministers and others whose pay is determined by the Ministerial and Other Salaries Act 1975, and also the allowances of peers. If asked, it advises on the pay of officers and members of the devolved parliament and assemblies.

Chair, Dr Martin Read, CBE
Members, Pippa Greenslade; Sir Adrian Johns, KCB, CBE, DL; Pippa Lambert; Peter Maddison, QPM; David Sissling; Sharon Witherspoon, MBE

STUDENT LOANS COMPANY LTD
100 Bothwell Street, Glasgow G2 7JD
T 0300-100 0607 (England); 0300-200 4050 (Wales); 0300-555 0505 (Scotland); 0300-100 0077 (Northern Ireland)
W www.gove.uk/government/organisations/student-loans-company

The Student Loans Company (SLC) is owned by the Department for Education. It processes and administers financial assistance, in the form of grants and loans, for undergraduates who have secured a place at university or college. The SLC also provides loans for tuition fees, which are paid directly to the university or college. In 2016 the SLC introduced the provision of loans to postgraduates in accordance with government policy. The SLC supports over 1 million students per year and has a loan book worth £156.5bn.

Chair, Peter Lauener
Chief Executive, Paula Sussex

TATE
W www.tate.org.uk

TATE BRITAIN
Millbank, London SW1P 4RG
T 020-7887 8888 **E** information@tate.org.uk

TATE MODERN
Bankside, London SE1 9TG
T 020-7887 8888 **E** information@tate.org.uk

TATE LIVERPOOL
Royal Albert Dock, Liverpool L3 4BB
T 015-1702 7400 **E** visiting.liverpool@tate.org.uk

TATE ST IVES
Porthmeor Beach, St Ives, Cornwall TR26 1TG
T 01736-796226 **E** visiting.stives@tate.org.uk

Tate comprises four art galleries: Tate Britain and Tate Modern in London, Tate Liverpool and Tate St Ives.

Tate Britain, which opened in 1897, displays the national collection of British art from 1500 to the present day – with special attention and dedicated space given to Blake, Turner and Constable.

Opened in May 2000, Tate Modern displays the Tate collection of international modern art dating from 1900 to the present day. It includes works by Dalí, Picasso, and Matisse, as well as many contemporary works. It is housed in the former Bankside Power Station in London, which was redesigned by the Swiss architects Herzog and de Meuron, and in the neighbouring and purpose-built Switch House, which was designed by Herzog and de Meuron and opened in 2016.

Tate Liverpool opened in 1988 and houses mainly 20th-century art, and Tate St Ives, which features work by artists from and working in St Ives and includes the Barbara Hepworth Museum and Sculpture Garden, opened in 1993.

BOARD OF TRUSTEES
Chair, Lionel Barber
Trustees, John Booth; Farooq Chaudhry, OBE; Tim Davie, CBE; Dame Jayne-Anne Gadhia, DBE; Dame Moya Greene, DBE; Katrin Henkel; Anna Loew; Michael Lynton; Dame Seona Reid, DBE; Roland Rudd; James Timpson, OBE; Jane Wilson

OFFICERS
Director, Tate, Maria Balshaw, CBE
Executive Group (Directors), Anne Barlow *(Tate St Ives);* Vicky Cheetham *(COO);* Anna Cutler *(Learning and Research);* Alex Farquharson *(Tate Britain);* Helen Legg *(Tate Liverpool);* Rosemary Lynch *(Collection Care);* Frances Morris *(Tate Modern);* Stephen Wingfield *(Finance and Estates)*

TOURISM BODIES
Visit Britain, Visit Scotland, Visit Wales and the Northern Ireland Tourist Board are responsible for developing and marketing the tourist industry in their respective regions. Visit Wales is not listed here as it is part of the Welsh government, within the Department for Heritage, and not a public body.

VISITBRITAIN
151 Buckingham Palace Road, London SW1W 9SZ
T 020-7578 1000 **W** www.visitbritain.org
Chair, Rt. Hon. Lord McLoughlin, CH
Chief Executive, Sally Balcombe

VISITSCOTLAND
Ocean Point One, 94 Ocean Drive Edinburgh EH6 6JH
T 0131-472 2222 **E** info@visitscotland.com
W www.visitscotland.com
Chair, Lord Thurso
Chief Executive, Malcolm Roughead, OBE

NORTHERN IRELAND TOURIST BOARD
Floors 10–12, Linum Chambers, Bedford Square, Bedford Street, Belfast BT2 7ES **T** 028-9023 1221
E info@tourismni.com **W** www.tourismni.com
Chair, Terence Brannigan
Chief Executive, John McGrillen

TRANSPORT FOR LONDON (TFL)
4th Floor, 14 Pier Walk, London SE10 0ES
T 0343-222 1234 **W** www.tfl.gov.uk

TfL was created in July 2000 and is the integrated body responsible for the capital's transport system. Its role is to implement the Mayor of London's transport strategy and manage the transport services across London, for which the mayor has responsibility. These services include TfL Rail, London's buses, London Underground, London Overground, the Docklands Light Railway (DLR), London Trams, London River Services and Victoria Coach Station. TfL also runs the Emirates Air Line and the London Transport Museum. In a joint venture with the Department for Transport, TfL is responsible for the construction of Crossrail – a new railway linking Reading and Heathrow in the west, to Shenfield and Abbey Wood in the east. The 73-mile section through London, which was due to open in December 2018, is expected to be operational in 2022. In 2017 TfL announced plans for Crossrail 2, a railway running between Surrey and Hertfordshire.

TfL is responsible for managing the Congestion Charging scheme and the Transport for London road network, London's 'red routes', which make up 5 per cent of the city's roads, but carry around 30 per cent of the traffic. It manages, maintains and operates over 6,000 traffic lights and regulates the city's taxis and private hire vehicles. TfL runs the Santander Cycle Hire scheme, allowing customers to hire a bicycle from £2, and the Dial-a-ride scheme, a door-to-door service for disabled people unable to use buses, trams or the London Underground.

Chair, Rt. Hon. Sadiq Khan
Members, Heidi Alexander *(Deputy Chair);* Julian Bell; Kay Carberry, CBE; Prof. Greg Clark, CBE; Bronwen Handyside; Ron Kalifam OBE; Anne McMeel; Dr Alice Maynard, CBE; Dr Mee Ling Ng, OBE; Dr Nelson Ogunshakin, OBE; Mark Phillips; Dr Nina Skorupska, CBE; Dr Lynn Sloman; Ben Story
Commissioner, Mike Brown, MVO

UK ATOMIC ENERGY AUTHORITY
Culham Science Centre, Abingdon, Oxfordshire OX14 3DB
T 01235-528822 **W** www.gov.uk/government/organisations/uk-atomic-energy-authority

The UK Atomic Energy Authority (UKAEA) was established by the Atomic Energy Authority Act 1954 and took over responsibility for the research and development of the sustainable civil nuclear power programme. The UKAEA reports to the Department for Business, Energy and Industrial Strategy and is responsible for managing UK fusion research, including operating the Joint European Torus (JET) on behalf of the UKAEA's European partners at its site in Culham, Oxfordshire. Culham also houses the facilities for Materials Research, Remote Access in Challenging Environments and Oxford Advanced Skills. In October 2009, as part of the government's Operation Efficiency Programme, the authority sold its commercial arm, UKAEA Limited; as a result, the UKAEA no longer provides nuclear decommissioning services.

Chair, Prof. David Gann, CBE
Chief Executive, Prof. Ian Chapman

UK SPORT

21 Bloomsbury Street, London WC1B 3HF
T 020-7211 5100 **E** info@uksport.gov.uk **W** www.uksport.gov.uk

UK Sport was established by royal charter in 1997 and is accountable to parliament through the Department for Digital, Culture, Media and Sport. Its mission is to lead sport in the UK to world-class success. This means working with partner organisations to deliver medals at the Olympic and Paralympic Games and organising, bidding for and staging major sporting events in the UK; increasing the UK's sporting activity and influence overseas; and promoting sporting conduct, ethics and diversity in society. UK Sport is funded by a mix of grant-in-aid and National Lottery income, and invests around £100m a year in high-performance sport.

Chair, Dame Katherine Grainger, DBE
Chief Executive, Sally Munday

VICTORIA AND ALBERT MUSEUM

Cromwell Road, London SW7 2RL
T 020-7942 2000 **E** hello@vam.ac.uk **W** www.vam.ac.uk

The Victoria and Albert Museum (V&A) is the national museum of art, design and performance. It descends directly from the Museum of Manufactures, which opened in Marlborough House in 1852 after the Great Exhibition of 1851. The museum was moved in 1857 to become part of the South Kensington Museum. It was renamed the Victoria and Albert Museum in 1899. It also houses the National Art Library, which holds over 950,000 books dedicated to the study of fine and decorative arts from around the world. V&A Dundee was opened in September 2018 and contains the restored Charles Rennie Macintosh Oak Room; the building was designed by Kengo Kuma and cost £80.1m.

The museum's collections span over 5,000 years of human creativity, including paintings, sculpture, architecture, ceramics, furniture, fashion and textiles, theatre and performance, photography, glass, jewellery, book arts, Asian art and design and metalwork. Materials relating to childhood are displayed at the V&A Museum of Childhood at Bethnal Green, which opened in 1872 and is the most important surviving example of the type of glass and iron construction used by Joseph Paxton for the Great Exhibition.

Chair, Nicholas Coleridge, CBE
Trustees, Jonathan Anderson; Martin Bartle; Allegra Berman; David Bomford; Dr Genevieve Davies; Ben Elliot; Nick Hoffman; Amanda Levete, CBE; Steven Murphy; Prof. Lynda Nead; Kavita Puri; Marc St John; Caroline Silver; Amanda Spielman; Dr Paul Thompson; Nigel Webb
Director, Dr Tristram Hunt

WALLACE COLLECTION

Hertford House, Manchester Square, London W1U 3BN
T 020-7563 9500 **E** collection@wallacecollection.org
W www.wallacecollection.org

The Wallace Collection was bequeathed to the nation by the widow of Sir Richard Wallace, in 1897, and Hertford House was subsequently acquired by the government. The collection contains works by Titian and Rembrandt, and includes porcelain, furniture and an array of arms and armour.

Chair, António Horta-Osório
Trustees, Marilyn Berk; Jennifer Eady, QC; Eric Ellul; Dounia Nadar; Jessica Pulay; Jemima Rellie; Kate de Rothschild-Agius; Dr Ashok Roy; Timothy Schroder
Director, Dr Xavier Bray

DEVOLVED GOVERNMENT

WALES

NATIONAL ASSEMBLY FOR WALES
Cardiff Bay, Cardiff CF99 1NA
T 0300-200 6565 **W** www.assemblywales.org

The National Assembly for Wales has been in existence since 1999, following a 'yes' vote in the 1997 referendum. However, the way the assembly is structured and its powers have changed over time.

The UK Act that created the assembly was the Government of Wales Act 1998. This stated that the Assembly was a 'corporate body' which meant that the Welsh government and the assembly were a single organisation. Also, it could not pass its own acts. It could, however make orders and regulations, known as secondary legislation.

The Government of Wales Act 2006 created a formal legal separation between:

- the legislative branch: the National Assembly for Wales, made up of 60 assembly members, and
- the executive branch: the Welsh government, made up of the First Minister, Welsh cabinet secretaries and the Counsel General

The act allowed the assembly to seek the power to make laws from the UK parliament. The laws were known as 'measures' of the National Assembly for Wales ('assembly measures'). The power to make laws ('legislative competence') was granted through clauses in Westminster bills or through legislative competence orders. These had to be approved by parliament and by the assembly. This is how the third assembly operated between 2007 and 2011.

The Government of Wales Act 2006 also contained provision for the assembly to make its own laws without the permission of the UK parliament. These provisions could only be triggered by:

- two-thirds of all assembly members voting in favour of a referendum
- the approval of the UK government and parliament to hold a referendum
- a 'yes' vote in a referendum of the Welsh public

A referendum held on 3 March 2011 resulted in a 'yes' vote in favour of bringing into force part four of the Government of Wales Act 2006. This has meant that since the 2011 National Assembly of Wales election the assembly has been able to pass laws on all subjects in the devolved areas without first needing the agreement of the UK parliament.

During an assembly election, the people of Wales have two votes. One vote is for their constituency assembly member who represents local areas. Wales is divided into 40 constituencies and each is represented by one assembly member (AM).

The other vote is for a party or independent candidate to represent the voter's region. Wales is divided into five regions – North Wales, Mid and West Wales, South Wales West, South Wales East and South Wales Central.

This system means that the overall number of seats held by each political party more closely reflects the share of the vote that the party receives.

The 60 assembly members who are elected make decisions regarding many things that affect life in Wales – health, education, housing and transport. Their job is to make sure that the Welsh government's decisions are in the best interests of Wales and its people.

The National Assembly for Wales does this by:

- scrutinising the policies the Welsh government sets and the decisions it makes
- scrutinising suggestions for laws, proposing changes and voting on whether they should be passed
- asking questions to Welsh government and making suggestions about policies
- voting on how the Welsh government spends its budget every year

The assembly also makes laws for Wales. A law can be put forward by the Welsh government, an individual assembly member, or an assembly committee or the Assembly Commission. The majority of laws are put forward by the Welsh government.

The assembly operates in both Welsh and English and all its legislation is made bilingually.

In July 2018 the National Assembly of Wales Commission announced plans to lower the minimum voting age for assembly elections to 16 years. They also announced plans to change the name of the assembly to Welsh Parliament/Senedd Cymru. The assembly intends to legislate both changes prior to the next assembly elections in 2021.

ASSEMBLY COMMISSION
The Assembly Commission was created under the Government of Wales Act 2006 to ensure that the assembly is provided with the property, staff and services required for it to carry out its functions. The commission also sets the National Assembly's strategic aims, objectives, standards and values. The Assembly Commission consists of the presiding officer, plus four other assembly members, one nominated by each of the four party groups. The five commissioners are accountable to the National Assembly.

Presiding Officer, Elin Jones, AM
Deputy Presiding Officer, Ann Jones, AM
Commissioners, Suzy Davies, AM; Siân Gwenllian, AM, David Rowlands, AM, Joyce Watson, AM
Chief Executive and Clerk of the Assembly, Manon Antoniazzi

ASSEMBLY COMMITTEES
The Business Committee, chaired by the Presiding Officer and established on 24 May 2016, is responsible for facilitating the effective organisation of assembly proceedings. The rest of the assembly committees *as at* August 2019 are:

Children, Young People and Education
  Chair, Lynne Neagle, AM
Climate Change, Environment and Rural Affairs
  Chair, Mike Hedges, AM
Constitutional and Legislative Affairs
  Chair, Mick Antoniw, AM
Culture, Welsh Language and Communications
  Chair, Bethan Sayed, AM
Economy, Infrastructure and Skills
  Chair, Russell George, AM
Equality, Local Government and Communities
  Chair, John Griffiths, AM
External Affairs and Additional Legislation
  Chair, David Rees, AM
Finance
  Chair, Llyr Gruffydd, AM
Health, Social Care and Sport
  Chair, Dai Lloyd, AM
Petitions
  Chair, Janet Finch-Saunders, AM

Public Accounts
Chair, Nick Ramsay, AM
Scrutiny of the First Minister
Chair, Ann Jones, AM
Standards of Conduct
Chair, Jayne Bryant, AM

SALARIES* 2019–20

First Minister	£147,983
Presiding Officer	£110,987
Cabinet Secretary	£105,701
Minister/Deputy Presiding Officer	£89,846
Assembly Commissioners	£81,390
Assembly Member (AM)	£67,649

* All salaries include the AM salary

MEMBERS OF THE NATIONAL ASSEMBLY FOR WALES *as at 31 August 2019*

KEY
* Elected via a by-election since the 2016 National Assembly election
† Replacement from the party list since the 2016 National Assembly election
‡ Previously AM for PC
§ Previously AM for UKIP
℄ Previously an Ind. AM
** Previously an AM for C.

Antoniw, Mick, *Lab., Pontypridd,* Maj. 5,327
ap Iorwerth, Rhun, *PC, Ynys Môn,* Maj. 9,510
Asghar, Mohammad, *C., South Wales East region*
Bennett, Gareth, *UKIP, South Wales Central region*
Blythyn, Hannah, *Lab., Delyn,* Maj. 3,582
Bowden, Dawn, *Lab., Merthyr Tydfil and Rhymney,* Maj. 5,486
§ **Brown**, Michelle, *Ind., North Wales region*
Bryant, Jayne, *Lab., Newport West,* Maj. 4,115
Burns, Angela, *C., Carmarthen West and South Pembrokeshire,* Maj. 3,373
David, Hefin, *Lab., Caerphilly,* Maj. 1,575
Davies, Alun, *Lab., Blaenau Gwent,* Maj. 650
Davies, Andrew R. T., *C., South Wales Central region*
Davies, Paul, *C., Preseli Pembrokeshire,* Maj. 3,930
Davies, Suzy, *C., South Wales West region*
Drakeford, Rt. Hon. Mark, *Lab., Cardiff West,* Maj. 1,176
‡ **Elis-Thomas**, Rt. Hon. Lord, *Ind., Dwyfor Meirionnydd,* Maj. 6,406
Evans, Rebecca, *Lab., Gower,* Maj. 1,829
Finch-Saunders, Janet, *C., Aberconwy,* Maj. 754
George, Russell, *C., Montgomeryshire,* Maj. 3,339
Gething, Vaughan, *Lab., Cardiff South and Penarth,* Maj. 6,921
Griffiths, John, *Lab., Newport East,* Maj. 4,896
Griffiths, Lesley, *Lab., Wrexham,* Maj. 1,325
Gruffydd, Llyr, *PC, North Wales region*
Gwenllian, Siân, *PC, Arfon,* Maj. 4,162
Hamilton, Neil, *UKIP, Mid and West Wales region*
Hedges, Mike, *Lab., Swansea East,* Maj. 7,452
Howells, Vikki, *Lab., Cynon Valley,* Maj. 5, 994
Hutt, Jane, *Lab., Vale of Glamorgan,* Maj. 777
Irranca-Davies, Huw, *Lab., Ogmore,* Maj. 9,468
Isherwood, Mark, *C., North Wales region*
James, Julie, *Lab., Swansea West,* Maj. 5,080
† **Jewell**, Delyth, *PC, South Wales East region*
Jones, Ann, *Lab., Vale of Clwyd,* Maj. 768
§ **Jones**, Caroline, *Brexit, South Wales West region*
Jones, Rt. Hon. Carwyn, *Lab., Bridgend,* Maj. 5,623
Jones, Elin, *PC, Ceredigion,* Maj. 2,408

Jones, Helen Mary, *PC, Mid and West Wales region*
℄ **Jones**, Mandy, *Brexit, North Wales region*
Lloyd, Dai, *PC, South Wales West region*
‡ **McEvoy**, Neil, *Ind., South Wales Central region*
Melding, David, *C. South Wales Central region*
Miles, Jeremy, *Lab. Neath,* Maj. 2,923
Millar, Darren, *C., Clwyd West,* Maj. 5,063
Morgan, Eluned *Lab., Mid and West Wales region*
Morgan, Julie, *Lab., Cardiff North,* Maj. 3,667
Neagle, Lynne, *Lab., Torfaen,* Maj. 4,498
Passmore, Rhianon, *Lab., Islwyn,* Maj. 5,106
Price, Adam, *PC, Carmarthen East and Dinefwr,* Maj. 8,700
Ramsay, Nick, *C., Monmouth,* Maj. 5,147
Rathbone, Jenny, *Lab., Cardiff Central,* Maj. 817
§ ** **Reckless**, Mark, *Brexit, South Wales East*
Rees, David, *Lab, Aberavon,* Maj. 6,402
§ **Rowlands**, David J., *Brexit, South Wales East region*
* **Sargeant**, Jack, *Lab., Alyn and Deeside* Maj. 6,545
Sayed, Bethan, *PC, South Wales West region*
Skates, Ken, *Lab., Clwyd South,* Maj. 3,016
Waters, Lee, *Lab., Llanelli,* Maj. 382
Watson, Joyce, *Lab., Mid and West Wales region*
Williams, Kirsty, *LD, Brecon and Radnorshire,* Maj. 8,170
Wood, Leanne, *PC, Rhondda,* Maj. 3,359

STATE OF THE PARTIES *as at 31 August 2019*

	Constituency AMs	Regional AMs	AM total
Labour (Lab.)	*27	2	29
Conservative (C.)	6	5	11
Plaid Cymru (PC)	†5	5	10
Brexit Party (Brexit)	0	4	4
UKIP	0	2	2
Independent (Ind.)	1	2	3
Liberal Democrats (LD)	1	0	1
Total	40	20	60

* Includes the Deputy Presiding Officer
† Includes the Presiding Officer

WELSH GOVERNMENT
Cathays Park, Cardiff CF10 3NQ
T 0300-060 4400 W www.gov.wales

The Welsh government is the devolved government of Wales. It is accountable to the National Assembly for Wales, the Welsh legislature which represents the interests of the people of Wales, and makes laws for Wales. The Welsh government and the National Assembly for Wales were established as separate institutions under the Government of Wales Act 2006.

The Welsh government comprises the first minister, who is usually the leader of the largest party in the National Assembly for Wales; up to 14 cabinet secretaries and ministers and deputy ministers; and a counsel-general (the chief legal adviser).

Following the referendum on 3 March 2011 on granting further law-making powers to the National Assembly, the Welsh government's functions now include the ability to propose bills to the National Assembly on subjects within 20 set areas of policy. Subject to limitations prescribed by the Government of Wales Act 2006, acts of the National Assembly may make any provision that could be made by act of parliament. The 20 areas of responsibility devolved to the National Assembly for Wales (and within which Welsh ministers exercise executive functions) are: agriculture, fisheries, forestry and rural development; ancient monuments and historic buildings; culture; economic development; education and training; environment; fire and rescue services and promotion of fire safety; food; health and health services; highways and transport; housing; local government; the National Assembly for Wales; public administration; social welfare; sport and recreation; tourism; town and county planning; water and flood defence; and the Welsh language.

CABINET

Ministers
First Minister of Wales, Rt. Hon. Mark Drakeford, AM
Economy and Transport, Ken Skates, AM
Education, Kirsty Williams, AM
Environment, Energy and Rural Affairs, Lesley Griffiths, AM
Finance and Trefnydd (Leader of the House), Rebecca Evans, AM
Health and Social Services, Vaughan Gething, AM
Housing and Local Government, Julie James, AM
International Relations and the Welsh Language, Eluned Morgan, AM
Counsel-General and Brexit Minister, Jeremy Miles, AM

Deputy Ministers
Culture, Sport and Tourism, Rt. Hon. Lord Elis-Thomas, AM
Economy and Transport, Lee Waters, AM
Health and Social Services, Julie Morgan, AM
Housing and Local Government, Hannah Blythyn, AM
Chief Whip, Jane Hutt, AM

MANAGEMENT BOARD

Permanent Secretary, Dame Shan Morgan, DCMG
Director-Generals, Tracey Burke *(Education and Public Services);* Desmond Clifford *(Office of the First Minister and Brexit);* Dr Andrew Goodall, CBE *(Health and Social Services);* Andrew Slade *(Economy, Skills and Natural Resources)*
Directors, Jeff Godfrey *(Legal Services);* Peter Kennedy *(HR);* David Richards *(Governance and Ethics)*
Head of Organisational Development and Engagement, Natalie Pearson
Board Equality and Diversity Champion, Gillian Baranski
Finance Director, Gawain Evans
Non-Executive Directors, Ellen Donovan; Jeff Farrar; Ann Keane; Gareth Lynn

DEPARTMENTS

Permanent Secretary's Group – Welsh Treasury, Finance, Governance and HR

DIRECTORATES

Office of the First Minister and Brexit
Education and Public Services
Health and Social Services
Economy, Skills and Natural Resources

NATIONAL ASSEMBLY ELECTION RESULTS *as at 5 May 2016*

Electorate (E.) 2,248,050 Turnout (T.) 45.3%
See General Election Results for a list of party abbreviations

ABERAVON (S. WALES WEST)
E. 49,074 T. 20,852 (42.49%)

David Rees, Lab.	10,578
Bethan Jenkins, PC	4,176
Glenda Davies, UKIP	3,119
David Jenkins, C.	1,342
Helen Ceri Clarke, LD	1,248
Jonathan Tier, Green	389

Lab. majority 6,402 (30.70%)
9.31% swing Lab. to PC

ABERCONWY (WALES N.)
E. 44,960 T. 22,038 (49.02%)

Janet Finch-Saunders, C.	7,646
Trystan Lewis, PC	6,892
Mike Priestley, Lab.	6,039
Sarah Lesiter-Burgess, LD	781
Petra Haig, Green	680

C. majority 754 (3.42%)
2.15% swing C. to PC

ALYN AND DEESIDE (WALES N.)
E. 62,697 T. 21,696 (34.60%)

Carl Sargeant, Lab.	9,922
Mike Gibbs, C.	4,558
Michelle Brown, UKIP	3,765
Jacqui Hurst, PC	1,944
Pete Williams, LD	980
Martin Bennewith, Green	527

Lab. majority 5,364 (24.72%)
0.11% swing C. to Lab.

ARFON (WALES N.)
E. 39,269 T. 19,994 (50.92%)

Sian Gwenllian, PC	10,962
Sion Jones, Lab.	6,800
Martin Peet, C.	1,655
Sara Lloyd Williams, LD	577

PC majority 4,162 (20.82%)
4.86% swing PC to Lab.

BLAENAU GWENT (S. WALES EAST)
E. 50,574 T. 21,291 (42.10%)

Alun Davies, Lab.	8,442
Nigel Copner, PC	7,792
Kevin Boucher, UKIP	3,423
Tracey West, C.	1,334
Brendan D'Cruz, LD	300

Lab. majority 650 (3.05%)
27.73% swing Lab. to PC

BRECON AND RADNORSHIRE (WALES MID AND W.)
E. 53,793 T. 30,367 (56.45%)

Kirsty Williams, LD	15,898
Gary Price, C.	7,728
Alex Thomas, Lab.	2,703
Thomas Turton, UKIP	2,161
Freddy Greaves, PC	1,180
Grenville Ham, Green	697

LD majority 8,170 (26.90%)
8.59% swing C. to LD

BRIDGEND (S. WALES WEST)
E. 60,195 T. 26,851 (44.61%)

Carwyn Jones, Lab.	12,166
George Jabbour, C.	6,543
Caroline Jones, UKIP	3,919
James Radcliffe, PC	2,569
Jonathan Pratt, LD	1,087
Charlie Barlow, Green	567

Lab. majority 5,623 (20.94%)
3.62% swing Lab. to C.

CAERPHILLY (S. WALES EAST)
E. 62,449 T. 27,115 (43.42%)

Hefin David, Lab.	9,584
Lindsay Whittle, PC	8,009
Sam Gould, UKIP	5,954
Jane Pratt, C.	2,412
Andrew Creak, Green	770
Aladdin Ayesh, LD	386

Lab. majority 1,575 (5.81%)
6.72% swing Lab. to PC

CARDIFF CENTRAL (S. WALES CENTRAL)
E. 57,177 T. 26,068 (45.59%)

Jenny Rathbone, Lab.	10,016
Eluned Parrott, LD	9,199
Joel Williams, C.	2,317
Glyn Wise, PC	1,951
Mohammed Islam, UKIP	1,223
Amelia Womack, Green	1,150
Jane Croad, Ind.	212

Lab. majority 817 (3.13%)
1.49% swing LD to Lab.

CARDIFF NORTH (S. WALES CENTRAL)
E. 65,927 T. 37,452 (56.81%)

Julie Morgan, Lab.	16,766
Jayne Cowan, C.	13,099
Haydn Rushworth, UKIP	2,509
Elin Walker Jones, PC	2,278
John Dixon, LD	1,130
Fiona Burt, Ind.	846
Chris von Ruhland, Green	824

Lab. majority 3,667 (9.79%)
2.31% swing C. to Lab.

CARDIFF SOUTH AND PENARTH
(S. WALES CENTRAL)
E. 76,110 T. 30,276 (39.78%)

Vaughan Gething, Lab.	13,274
Ben Gray, C.	6,353
Dafydd Davies, PC	4,320
Hugh Moelwyn Hughes, UKIP	3,716
Nigel Howells, LD	1,345
Anthony Slaughter, Green	1,268

Lab. majority 6,921 (22.86%)
0.04% swing C. to Lab.

CARDIFF WEST (S. WALES
CENTRAL)
E. 66,040 T. 31,960 (48.39%)

Mark Drakeford, Lab.	11,381
Neil McEvoy, PC	10,205
Sean Driscoll, C.	5,617
Gareth Bennett, UKIP	2,629
Hannah Pudner, Green	1,032
Cadan ap Tomos, LD	868
Eliot Freedman, Ind.	132
Lee Woolls, FTC	96

Lab. majority 1,176 (3.68%)
11.71% swing Lab. to PC

CARMARTHEN EAST AND
DINEFWR (WALES MID AND W.)
E. 55,395 T. 29,751 (53.71%)

Adam Price, PC	14,427
Stephen Jeacock, Lab.	5,727
Matthew Paul, C.	4,489
Neil Hamilton, UKIP	3,474
William Powell, LD	837
Freya Amsbury, Green	797

PC majority 8,700 (29.24%)
7.17% swing Lab. to PC

CARMARTHEN WEST AND SOUTH
PEMBROKESHIRE (WALES MID
AND W.)
E. 56,886 T. 29,237 (51.40%)

Angela Burns, C.	10,355
Marc Tierney, Lab.	6,982
Simon Thomas, PC	5,459
Allan Brookes, UKIP	3,300
Chris Overton, Ind.	1,638
Val Bradley, Green	804
Alistair Cameron, LD	699

C. majority 3,373 (11.54%)
3.10% swing Lab. to C.

CEREDIGION (WALES MID
AND W.)
E. 51,230 T. 29,485 (57.55%)

Elin T Jones, PC	12,014
Elizabeth Evans, LD	9,606
Gethin James, UKIP	2,665
Felix Aubel, C.	2,075
Iwan Wyn Jones, Lab.	1,902
Brian Williams, Green	1,223

PC majority 2,408 (8.17%)
1.03% swing LD to PC

CLWYD SOUTH (WALES N.)
E. 54,185 T. 22,159 (40.90%)

Ken Skates, Lab.	7,862
Simon Baynes, C.	4,846
Mabon ap Gwynfor, PC	3,861
Mandy Jones, UKIP	2,827
Aled Roberts, LD	2,289
Duncan Rees, Green	474

Lab. majority 3,016 (13.61%)
0.17% swing C. to Lab.

CLWYD WEST (WALES N.)
E. 57,657 T. 26,226 (45.49%)

Darren Millar, C.	10,831
Llyr Gruffydd, PC	5,768
Jo Thomas, Lab.	5,246
David Edwards, UKIP	2,985
Victor Babu, LD	831
Julian Mahy, Green	565

C. majority 5,063 (19.31%)
0.52% swing C. to PC

CYNON VALLEY (S. WALES
CENTRAL)
E. 50,292 T. 19,236 (38.25%)

Vikki Howells, Lab.	9,830
Cerith Griffiths, PC	3,836
Liz Wilks, UKIP	3,460
Lyn Hudson, C.	1,177
John Matthews, Green	598
Michael Wallace, LD	335

Lab. majority 5,994 (31.16%)
1.78% swing Lab. to PC

DELYN (WALES N.)
E. 53,490 T. 23,159 (43.30%)

Hannah Blythyn, Lab.	9,480
Huw Williams, C.	5,898
Nigel Williams, UKIP	3,794
Paul Rowlinson, PC	2,269
Tom Rippeth, LD	1,718

Lab. majority 3,582 (15.47%)
1.52% swing C. to Lab.

DWYFOR MEIRIONNYDD (WALES
MID AND W.)
E. 43,304 T. 20,236 (46.73%)

Dafydd Elis-Thomas, PC	9,566
Neil Fairlamb, C.	3,160
Ian MacIntyre, Lab.	2,443
Frank Wykes, UKIP	2,149
Louise Hughes, Ind.	1,259
Steve Churchman, LD	916
Alice Hooker-Stroud, Green	743

PC majority 6,406 (31.66%)
2.77% swing C. to PC

GOWER (S. WALES WEST)
E. 60,631 T. 30,187 (49.79%)

Rebecca Evans, Lab.	11,982
Lyndon Jones, C.	10,153
Colin Beckett, UKIP	3,300
Harri Roberts, PC	2,982
Sheila Kingston-Jones, LD	1,033
Abi Cherry-Hamer, Green	737

Lab. majority 1,829 (6.06%)
6.05% swing Lab. to C.

ISLWYN (S. WALES EAST)
E. 54,465 T. 22,309 (40.96%)

Rhianon Passmore, Lab.	10,050
Joe Smyth, UKIP	4,944
Lyn Ackerman, PC	4,349
Paul Williams, C.	1,775
Matthew Kidner, LD	597
Katy Beddoe, Green	594

Lab. majority 5,106 (22.89%)

LLANELLI (WALES MID AND W.)
E. 59,651 T. 28,116 (47.13%)

Lee Waters, Lab.	10,267
Helen Mary Jones, PC	9,885
Ken Rees, UKIP	4,132
Stefan Ryszewski, C.	1,937
Sian Caiach, PF	1,113
Guy Smith, Green	427
Gemma Bowker, LD	355

Lab. majority 382 (1.36%)
0.53% swing PC to Lab.

MERTHYR TYDFIL AND RHYMNEY
(S. WALES EAST)
E. 53,754 T. 20,683 (38.48%)

Dawn Bowden, Lab.	9,763
David Rowlands, UKIP	4,277
Brian Thomas, PC	3,721
Elizabeth Simon, C.	1,331
Bob Griffin, LD	1,122
Julie Colbran, Green	469

Lab. majority 5,486 (26.52%)

MONMOUTH (S. WALES EAST)
E. 64,197 T. 31,401 (48.91%)

Nick Ramsay, C.	13,585
Catherine Fookes, Lab.	8,438
Tim Price, UKIP	3,092
Debby Blakebrough, Ind.	1,932
Jonathan Clark, PC	1,824
Veronica German, LD	1,474
Chris Were, Green	910
Stephen Morris, Eng Dem	146

C. majority 5,147 (16.39%)
2.00% swing C. to Lab.

MONTGOMERYSHIRE (WALES MID
AND W.)
E. 48,682 T. 23,600 (48.48%)

Russell George, C.	9,875
Jane Dodds, LD	6,536
Des Parkinson, UKIP	2,458
Aled Morgan Hughes, PC	2,410
Martyn Singleton, Lab.	1,389
Richard Chaloner, Green	932

C. majority 3,339 (14.15%)
2.01% swing LD to C.

NEATH (S. WALES WEST)
E. 55,395 T. 25,363 (45.79%)

Jeremy Miles, Lab.	9,468
Alun Llewelyn, PC	6,545
Richard Pritchard, UKIP	3,780
Peter Crocker-Jaques, C.	2,179
Steve Hunt, Ind.	2,056
Frank Little, LD	746
Lisa Rapado, Green	589

Lab. majority 2,923 (11.52%)
7.63% swing Lab. to PC

NEWPORT EAST (S. WALES EAST)
E. 55,499 T. 20,688 (37.28%)

John Griffiths, Lab.	9,229
James Peterson, UKIP	4,333
Munawar Mughal, C.	3,768
Paul Halliday, LD	1,481
Tony Salkeld, PC	1,386
Peter Varley, Green	491

Lab. majority 4,896 (23.67%)

NEWPORT WEST (S. WALES EAST)
E. 62,169 T. 27,751 (44.64%)

Jayne Bryant, Lab.	12,157
Matthew Evans, C.	8,042
Michael Ford, UKIP	3,842
Simon Coopey, PC	1,645
Liz Newton, LD	880
Pippa Bartolotti, Green	814
Bill Fearnley-Whittingstall, Ind.	333
Gruff Meredith, WSov	38

Lab. majority 4,115 (14.83%)
1.75% swing Lab. to C.

OGMORE (S. WALES WEST)
E. 54,502 T. 23,356 (42.85%)

Huw Irranca-Davies, Lab.	12,895
Tim Thomas, PC	3,427
Elizabeth Kendall, UKIP	3,233
Jamie Wallis, C.	2,587
Anita Davies, LD	698
Laurie Brophy, Green	516

Lab. majority 9,468 (40.54%)
3.36% swing Lab. to PC

PONTYPRIDD (S. WALES CENTRAL)
E. 58,277 T. 25,338 (43.48%)

Mick Antoniw, Lab.	9,986
Chad Rickard, PC	4,659
Joel James, C.	3,884
Edwin Allen, UKIP	3,322
Mike Powell, LD	2,979
Ken Barker, Green	508

Lab. majority 5,327 (21.02%)
8.18% swing Lab. to PC

PRESELI PEMBROKESHIRE (WALES MID AND W.)
E. 56,414 T. 28,397 (50.34%)

Paul Davies, C.	11,123
Dan Lodge, Lab.	7,193
John Osmond, PC	3,957
Howard Lillyman, UKIP	3,286
Bob Kilmister, LD	1,677
Frances Bryant, Green	1,161

C. majority 3,930 (13.84%)
2.92% swing Lab. to C.

RHONDDA (S. WALES CENTRAL)
E. 49,758 T. 23,486 (47.20%)

Leanne Wood, PC	11,891
Leighton Andrews, Lab.	8,432
Stephen Clee, UKIP	2,203
Maria Hill, C.	528
Pat Matthews, Green	259
Rhys Taylor, LD	173

PC majority 3,459 (14.73%)
24.19% swing Lab. to PC

SWANSEA EAST (S. WALES WEST)
E. 57,589 T. 20,576 (35.73%)

Mike Hedges, Lab.	10,726
Clifford Johnson, UKIP	3,274
Dic Jones, PC	2,744
Sadie Vidal, C.	1,729
Charlene Webster, LD	1,574
Tony Young, Green	529

Lab. majority 7,452 (36.22%)

SWANSEA WEST (S. WALES WEST)
E. 54,593 T. 22,202 (40.67%)

Julie James, Lab.	9,014
Craig Lawton, C.	3,934
Dai Lloyd, PC	3,225
Rosie Irwin, UKIP	3,058
Chris Holley, LD	2,012
Gareth Tucker, Green	883
Brian Johnson, SPGB	76

Lab. majority 5,080 (22.88%)
0.77% swing C. to Lab.

TORFAEN (S. WALES EAST)
E. 60,246 T. 22,978 (38.14%)

Lynne Neagle, Lab.	9,688
Susan Boucher, UKIP	5,190
Graham Smith, C.	3,931
Matthew Woolfall-Jones, PC	2,860
Steve Jenkins, Green	681
Alison Willott, LD	628

Lab. majority 4,498 (19.58%)

VALE OF CLWYD (WALES N.)
E. 56,322 T. 24,183 (42.94%)

Ann Jones, Lab.	9,560
Sam Rowlands, C.	8,792
Paul Davies-Cooke, UKIP	2,975
Mair Rowlands, PC	2,098
Gwyn Williams, LD	758

Lab. majority 768 (3.18%)
7.11% swing Lab. to C.

VALE OF GLAMORGAN (S. WALES CENTRAL)
E. 71,177 T. 37,798 (53.10%)

Jane Hutt, Lab.	14,655
Ross England, C.	13,878
Ian Johnson, PC	3,871
Lawrence Andrews, UKIP	3,662
Denis Campbell, LD	938
Alison Haden, Green	794

Lab. majority 777 (2.06%)
4.65% swing Lab. to C.

WREXHAM (WALES N.)
E. 51,567 T. 20,354 (39.47%)

Lesley Griffiths, Lab.	7,552
Andrew Atkinson, C.	6,227
Carrie Harper, PC	2,631
Jeanette Bassford-Barton, UKIP	2,393
Beryl Blackmore, LD	1,140
Alan Butterworth, Green	411

Lab. majority 1,325 (6.51%)
5.67% swing Lab. to C.

YNYS MON (WALES N.)
E. 50,345 T. 25,167 (49.99%)

Rhun ap Iorwerth, PC	13,788
Julia Dobson, Lab.	4,278
Simon Wall, UKIP	3,212
Clay Theakston, C.	2,904
Gerry Wolff, Green	389
Thomas Crofts, LD	334
Daniel ap Eifion Jones, Ind.	262

PC majority 9,510 (37.79%)
11.29% swing Lab. to PC

REGIONS *as at 5 May 2016*
E. 2,248,050 T. 45.3%

MID AND WEST WALES
E. 425,355 T. 215,840 (50.74%)

PC	56,754	(26.29%)
C.	44,461	(20.60%)
Lab.	41,975	(19.45%)
UKIP	25,042	(11.60%)
LD	23,554	(10.91%)
Abolish	10,707	(4.96%)
Green	8,222	(3.81%)
PF	1,496	(0.69%)
Ch. P.	1,103	(0.51%)
Loony	1,071	(0.50%)
Loc. Ind.	1,032	(0.48%)
Welsh Comm	423	(0.20%)

PC majority 12,293 (5.70%)
2.02% swing C. to PC (2011 PC majority 3,479)

ADDITIONAL MEMBERS
Joyce Watson, *Lab.*
Eluned Morgan, *Lab.*
Simon Thomas, *PC*
Neil Hamilton, *UKIP*

NORTH WALES
E. 470,492 T. 204,490 (43.46%)

Lab.	57,528	(28.13%)
PC	47,701	(23.33%)
C	45,468	(22.23%)
UKIP	25,518	(12.48%)
Abolish	9,409	(4.60%)
LD	9,345	(4.57%)
Green	4,789	(2.34%)
Loc Ind.	1,865	(0.91%)
Loony	1,355	(0.66%)
Ind.	926	(0.45%)
Welsh Comm	586	(0.29%)

Lab. majority 9,827 (4.81%)
2.98% swing Lab. to PC (2011 Lab. majority 10,476)

ADDITIONAL MEMBERS
Mark Isherwood, *C.*
Llyr Gruffydd, *PC*
Nathan Gill, *UKIP*
Michelle Brown, *UKIP*

SOUTH WALES CENTRAL
E. 494,758 T. 231,133 (46.72%)

Lab.	78,366	(33.91%)
PC	48,357	(20.92%)
C.	42,185	(18.25%)
UKIP	23,958	(10.37%)
LD	14,875	(6.44%)
Abolish	9,163	(3.96%)
Green	7,949	(3.44%)
Women	2,807	(1.21%)
Loony	1,096	(0.47%)
TUSC	736	(0.32%)
Ind.	651	(0.28%)
Comm	520	(0.22%)
FTC	470	(0.20%)

Lab. majority 30,009 (12.98%)
7.24% swing Lab. to PC (2011 Lab. majority 39,694)

ADDITIONAL MEMBERS
Andrew Davies, *C.*
David Melding, *C.*
Neil McEvoy, *PC*
Gareth Bennett, *UKIP*

SOUTH WALES EAST
E. 463,353 T. 194,091 (41.89%)

Lab.	74,424	(38.34%)
UKIP	34,524	(17.79%)
C.	33,318	(17.17%)
PC	29,686	(15.29%)
Abolish	7,870	(4.05%)
LD	6,784	(3.50%)
Green	4,831	(2.49%)
Loony	1,115	(0.57%)
TUSC	618	(0.32%)
Welsh Comm	492	(0.25%)
NF	429	(0.22%)

Lab. majority 39,900 (20.56%)
9.93% swing Lab. to UKIP (2011 Lab. majority 47,240)

ADDITIONAL MEMBERS
Oscar Asghar, *C.*
Steffan Lewis, *PC*
Mark Reckless, *UKIP*
David Rowlands, *UKIP*

SOUTH WALES WEST
E. 391,979 T. 169,189 (43.16%)

Lab.	66,903	(39.54%)
PC	29,050	(17.17%)
C.	25,414	(15.02%)
UKIP	23,096	(13.65%)
LD	10,946	(6.47%)
Abolish	7,137	(4.22%)
Green	4,420	(2.61%)
Loony	1,106	(0.65%)
TUSC	686	(0.41%)
Welsh Comm	431	(0.25%)

Lab. majority 37,853 (22.37%)
5.17% swing Lab. to PC (2011 Lab. majority 44,309)

ADDITIONAL MEMBERS
Suzy Davies, *C.*
Bethan Jenkins, *PC*
Dai Lloyd, *PC*
Caroline Jones, *UKIP*

SCOTLAND

SCOTTISH PARLIAMENT
Edinburgh EH99 1SP
T 0131-348 5000/ 0800-092 7500
E info@parliament.scot
W www.parliament.scot

In July 1997 the government announced plans to establish a Scottish parliament. In a referendum on 11 September 1997 about 60 per cent of the electorate voted. Of those who voted, 74.3 per cent voted in favour of the parliament and 63.5 per cent voted in support of granting the parliament having tax-raising powers. Elections are normally held every four years, but the current session is scheduled to last for five years. The first elections were held on 6 May 1999, when around 59 per cent of the electorate voted. The first meeting was held on 12 May 1999 and the Scottish parliament was officially opened on 1 July 1999 at the Assembly Hall, Edinburgh. A new building to house the parliament was opened, in the presence of the Queen, at Holyrood on 9 October 2004. On 5 May 2016 the fifth elections to the Scottish parliament took place.

The Scottish parliament has 129 members (including the presiding officer), comprising 73 constituency members and 56 additional regional members, drawn from the party lists. It can introduce primary legislation and has the power to set rates and bands for income tax on non-savings and non-dividend income for Scottish taxpayers.

Members of the Scottish parliament are elected using the additional member system, the same system used to elect London Assembly and Welsh Assembly members. Under the additional member system the electorate has two votes; the first to elect their constituency member via the 'first past the post' method of voting and the second to elect their regional members. The 56 regional seats are filled proportionally from the parties' lists according to their share of the vote on the second ballot paper. By-elections are held for constituency seat vacancies but not for regional seat vacancies which are filled by the next candidate on the list from the same political party in which the vacancy arose.

The areas for which the Scottish parliament is responsible include: civil and criminal justice; education; health; environment; economic development; local government; housing; police; fire services; planning; financial assistance to industry; tourism; heritage and the arts; agriculture; social work; sports; public registers and records; forestry; food standards; some aspects of transport; and some areas of welfare.

SALARIES* *as at 1 April 2019*

First Minister	£155,680
Cabinet Secretary/ Presiding Officer	£111,359
Minister/ Deputy Presiding Officer	£93,510
MSP†	£63,579
Lord Advocate	£126,000
Solicitor-General for Scotland	£108,718
* All salaries include the MSP salary	
† Reduced by two-thirds if the member is also an MP or MEP	

The Presiding Officer, Ken Macintosh, MSP
Deputy Presiding Officers, Linda Fabiani, MSP; Christine Grahame, MSP

MEMBERS OF THE SCOTTISH PARLIAMENT *as at September 2019*

KEY
* Elected via a by-election since the 2016 Scottish parliament election
† Replacement from the party list since the 2016 Scottish parliament election under the additional member system
‡ The Presiding Officer was elected as a regional member for Labour but has no party affiliation while in post

Adam, George, *SNP, Paisley,* Maj. 5,199
Adamson, Clare, *SNP, Motherwell and Wishaw,* Maj. 6,223
Allan, Alasdair, *SNP, Na h-Eileanan an Iar,* Maj. 3,496
Arthur, Tom, *SNP, Renfrewshire South,* Maj. 4,408
Baillie, Jackie, *Lab., Dumbarton,* Maj. 109
Baker, Claire, *Lab., Mid Scotland and Fife region*
Balfour, Jeremy, *C., Lothian region*
† **Ballantyne**, Michelle, *C., South Scotland region*
Beamish, Claudia, *Lab., South Scotland region*
Beattie, Colin, *SNP, Midlothian North and Musselburgh,* Maj. 7,035
Bibby, Neil, *Lab., West Scotland region*
† **Bowman**, Bill, *C., North East Scotland region*
† **Boyack**, Sarah, *Lab., Lothian region*
Briggs, Miles, *C. Lothian region*
Brown, Keith, *SNP, Clackmannanshire and Dunblane,* Maj. 6,721
Burnett, Alexander, *C., Aberdeenshire West,* Maj. 900
Cameron, Donald, *C., Highlands and Islands region*
Campbell, Aileen, *SNP, Clydesdale,* Maj. 5,979
Carlaw, Jackson, CB, *C., Eastwood,* Maj. 1.610
Carson, Finlay, *C., Galloway and West Dumfries,* Maj. 1,514
Chapman, Peter, *C., North East Scotland region*
Coffey, Willie, *SNP, Kilmarnock and Irvine Valley,* Maj. 11,194
Cole-Hamilton, Alex, *LD, Edinburgh Western,* Maj. 2,960
Constance, Angela, *SNP, Almond Valley,* Maj. 8,393
Corry, Maurice, *C., West Scotland region*
Crawford, Bruce, *SNP, Stirling,* Maj. 6,718
Cunningham, Roseanna, *SNP, Perthshire South and Kinross-shire,* Maj. 1,422
Davidson, Ruth, *C., Edinburgh Central,* Maj. 610
Denham, Ash, *SNP, Edinburgh Eastern,* Maj. 5,087
Dey, Graeme, *SNP, Angus South,* Maj. 4,304
Doris, Bob, *SNP, Glasgow Maryhill and Springburn,* Maj. 5,602
Dornan, James, *SNP, Glasgow Cathcart,* Maj. 9,390
Ewing, Annabelle, *SNP, Cowdenbeath,* Maj. 3,041
Ewing, Fergus, *SNP, Inverness and Nairn,* Maj. 10,857
Fabiani, Linda, *SNP, East Kilbride,* Maj. 10,979
Fee, Mary, *Lab., West Scotland region*
Findlay, Neil, *Lab., Lothian region*
Finnie, John, *Green, Highlands and Islands region*
FitzPatrick, Joe, *SNP, Dundee City West,* Maj. 8,828
Forbes, Kate, *SNP, Skye, Lochaber and Badenoch,* Maj. 9,043
Fraser, Murdo, *C., Mid Scotland and Fife region*
Freeman, Jeane, *SNP, Carrick, Cumnock and Doon Valley,* Maj. 6,006
Gibson, Kenneth, *SNP, Cunninghame North,* Maj. 8,724
Gilruth, Jenny, *SNP, Mid Fife and Glenrothes,* Maj. 8,276
Golden, Maurice, *C., West Scotland region*
Gougeon, Mairi, *SNP, Angus North and Mearns,* Maj. 2,472
Grahame, Christine, *SNP, Midlothian South, Tweeddale and Lauderdale,* Maj. 5,868
Grant, Rhoda, *Lab., Highlands and Islands region*
Gray, Iain, *Lab., East Lothian,* Maj. 1,127
Greene, Jamie, *C., West Scotland region*

Greer, Ross, *Green, West Scotland region*
Griffin, Mark, *Lab., Central Scotland region*
† **Halcro Johnston**, Jamie, *C., Highlands and Islands region*
* **Hamilton**, Rachael, *C., Ettrick, Roxburgh and Berwickshire,* Maj. 9,338
Harper, Emma, *SNP, South Scotland region*
Harris, Alison, *C., Central Scotland region*
Harvie, Patrick, *Green, Glasgow region*
Haughey, Clare, *SNP, Rutherglen,* Maj. 3,743
Hepburn, Jamie, *SNP, Cumbernauld and Kilsyth,* Maj. 9,478
Hyslop, Fiona, *SNP, Linlithgow,* Maj. 9,335
Johnson, Daniel, *Lab., Edinburgh Southern,* Maj. 1,123
Johnstone, Alison, *Green, Lothian region*
Kelly, James, *Lab., Glasgow region*
Kerr, Liam, *C., North East Scotland region*
Kidd, Bill, *SNP, Glasgow Anniesland,* Maj. 6,153
Lamont, Johann, *Lab., Glasgow region*
Lennon, Monica, *Lab., Central Scotland region*
Leonard, Richard, *Lab., Central Scotland region*
Lindhurst, Gordon, *C., Lothian region*
Lochhead, Richard, *SNP, Moray,* Maj. 2,875
Lockhart, Dean, *C., Mid Scotland and Fife region*
Lyle, Richard, *SNP, Uddingston and Bellshill,* Maj. 4,809
McAlpine, Joan, *SNP, South Scotland region*
McArthur, Liam, *LD, Orkney Islands,* Maj. 4,534
MacDonald, Angus, *SNP, Falkirk East,* Maj. 8,312
MacDonald, Gordon, *SNP, Edinburgh Pentlands,* Maj. 2,456
Macdonald, Lewis, *Lab., North East Scotland region*
McDonald, Mark, *Ind., Aberdeen Donside,* Maj. 11,630
MacGregor, Fulton, *SNP, Coatbridge and Chryston,* Maj. 3,779
‡ **Macintosh**, Ken, *no party affiliation, West Scotland region*
Mackay, Derek, *SNP, Renfrewshire North and West,* Maj. 7,373
Mackay, Rona, *SNP, Strathkelvin and Bearsden,* Maj. 8,100
McKee, Ivan, *SNP, Glasgow Provan,* Maj. 4,783
McKelvie, Christina, *SNP, Hamilton, Larkhall and Stonehouse,* Maj. 5,437
McMillan, Stuart, *SNP, Greenock and Inverclyde,* Maj. 8,230
McNeill, Pauline, *Lab., Glasgow region*
Macpherson, Ben, *SNP, Edinburgh Northern and Leith,* Maj. 6,746
Maguire, Ruth, *SNP, Cunninghame South,* Maj. 5,693
Marra, Jenny, *Lab., North East Scotland region*
Martin, Gillian, *SNP, Aberdeenshire East,* Maj. 5,837
Mason, John, *SNP, Glasgow Shettleston,* Maj. 7,323
† **Mason**, Tom, *C., North East Scotland region*
Matheson, Michael, *SNP, Falkirk West,* Maj. 11,280
Mitchell, Margaret, *C., Central Scotland region*
Mountain, Edward, *C., Highlands and Islands region*
Mundell, Oliver, *C., Dumfriesshire,* Maj. 1,230
Neil, Alex, *SNP, Airdrie and Shotts,* Maj. 6,192
Paterson, Gil, *SNP, Clydebank and Milngavie,* Maj. 8,432
Rennie, Willie, *LD, North East Fife,* Maj. 3,465
Robison, Shona, *SNP, Dundee City East,* Maj. 10,898
Ross, Gail, *SNP, Caithness, Sutherland and Ross,* Maj. 3,913
Rowley, Alex, *Lab., Mid Scotland and Fife region*
Rumbles, Mike, *LD, North East Scotland region*
Ruskell, Mark, *Green, Mid Scotland and Fife region*
Russell, Michael, *SNP, Argyll and Bute,* Maj. 5,978
Sarwar, Anas, *Lab., Glasgow region*
Scott, John, *C., Ayr,* Maj. 750
Simpson, Graham, *C., Central Scotland region*
Smith, Elaine, *Lab., Central Scotland region*
Smith, Liz, *C., Mid Scotland and Fife region*
Smyth, Colin, *Lab., South Scotland region*
Somerville, Shirley-Anne, *SNP, Dunfermline,* Maj. 4,558
Stevenson, Stewart, *SNP, Banffshire and Buchan Coast,* Maj. 6,583

Stewart, Alexander, *C., Mid Scotland and Fife region*
Stewart, David, *Lab., Highlands and Islands region*
Stewart, Kevin, *SNP, Aberdeen Central,* Maj. 4,349
Sturgeon, Nicola, *SNP, Glasgow Southside,* Maj. 9,593
Swinney, John, *SNP, Perthshire North,* Maj. 3,336
Todd, Maree, *SNP, Highlands and Islands region*
Tomkins, Adam, *C., Glasgow region*
Torrance, David, *SNP, Kirkcaldy,* Maj. 7,395
Watt, Maureen, *SNP, Aberdeen South and North Kincardine,* Maj. 2,755
Wells, Annie, *C., Glasgow region*
Wheelhouse, Paul, *SNP, South Scotland region*
White, Sandra, *SNP, Glasgow Kelvin,* Maj. 4,048
Whittle, Brian, *C., South Scotland region*
Wightman, Andy, *Green, Lothian region*
* **Wishart**, Beatrice, *LD, Shetland Islands* Maj. 1,837
Yousaf, Humza, *SNP, Glasgow Pollok,* Maj. 6,482

STATE OF THE PARTIES *as at August 2019*

	Constituency MSPs	Regional MSPs	Total
Scottish National Party (SNP)	58	4	62
Scottish Conservative and Unionist Party (C.)	7	24	31
Scottish Labour Party (Lab.)	3	20	23
Scottish Green Party (Green)	0	6	6
Scottish Liberal Democrats (LD)	3	1	4
Independent (Ind.)	1	–	1
*Presiding Officer	–	1	1
vacancy	1	0	1
Total	73	56	129

SCOTTISH GOVERNMENT

St Andrew's House, Regent Road, Edinburgh EH1 3DG
T 0300-244 4000
E ceu@gov.scot **W** www.gov.scot

The devolved government for Scotland is responsible for most of the issues of day-to-day concern to the people of Scotland, including health, education, justice, rural affairs and transport.

The Scottish government was known as the Scottish executive when it was established in 1999, following the first elections to the Scottish parliament. There has been a majority Scottish National Party administration since the elections in May 2011.

The government is led by a first minister who is nominated by the parliament and in turn appoints the other Scottish ministers who make up the cabinet.

Civil servants in Scotland are accountable to Scottish ministers, who are themselves accountable to the Scottish parliament.

CABINET
First Minister, Rt. Hon. Nicola Sturgeon, MSP
Deputy First Minister and Cabinet Secretary for Education and Skills, John Swinney, MSP

Cabinet Secretaries
Communities and Local Government, Aileen Campbell, MSP
Culture, Tourism and External Affairs, Fiona Hyslop, MSP
Environment, Climate Change and Land Reform, Roseanna Cunningham, MSP
Finance, Economy and Fair Work, Derek Mackay, MSP
Government Business and Constitutional Relations, Michael Russell, MSP
Health and Sport, Jeane Freeman, MSP
Justice, Humza Yousaf, MSP
Rural Economy, Fergus Ewing, MSP
Social Security and Older People, Shirley-Anne Somerville, MSP
Transport, Infrastructure and Connectivity, Michael Matheson, MSP

Ministers
Business, Fair Work and Skills, Jamie Hepburn, MSP
Childcare and Early Years, Maree Todd, MSP
Community Safety, Ash Denham, MSP
Energy, Connectivity and the Islands, Paul Wheelhouse, MSP
Europe, Migration and International Development, Ben
    Macpherson, MSP
Further Education, Higher Education and Science, Richard
    Lochhead, MSP
Local Government, Housing and Planning, Kevin Stewart, MSP
Mental Health, Clare Haughey, MSP
Older People and Equalities, Christina McKelvie, MSP
Parliamentary Business and Veterans, Graeme Dey, MSP
Public Finance and Digital Economy, Kate Forbes
Public Health, Sport and Wellbeing, Joe FitzPatrick, MSP
Rural Affairs and the Natural Environment, Mairi Gougeon, MSP
Trade, Investment and Innovation, Ivan McKee, MSP

LAW OFFICERS
Lord Advocate, James Wolffe, QC
Solicitor-General for Scotland, Alison di Rollo

STRATEGIC BOARD
Permanent Secretary, Leslie Evans
Director-General Constitution and External Affairs, Ken Thomson
Director-General, Economy, Liz Ditchburn
Director-General, Education, Communities and Justice, Paul
    Johnston
Director-General, Scottish Exchequer, Alyson Stafford
Director-General, Health and Social Care, Malcolm Wright
Director-General, Organisational Development and Operations,
    Lesley Fraser

GOVERNMENT DEPARTMENTS

CONSTITUTION AND EXTERNAL AFFAIRS
St Andrew's House, Regent Road, Edinburgh EH1 3DG
Director-General, Ken Thomson
Directorates: Constitution and Cabinet; EU Directorate; EU
    Exit and Transition; External Affairs; Legal Services
    (Solicitor to the Scottish Government); Parliamentary
    Counsel

ECONOMY
St Andrew's House, Regent Road, Edinburgh EH1 3DG
Director-General, Liz Ditchburn
Directorates: Agriculture and Rural Economy; Chief
    Economist; Culture, Tourism and Major Events; Economic
    Development; Economic Policy and Capability; Energy
    and Climate Change; Environment and Forestry; Fair
    Work, Employability and Skills; International Trade and
    Investment; Marine Scotland; Scottish Development
    International; Scottish National Investment Bank
Executive Agencies: Accountant in Bankruptcy; Drinking Water
    Quality Regulator; Forestry and Land Scotland; James
    Hutton Institute; Moredun Research Institute; National
    Records of Scotland; Scottish Agricultural College;
    Scottish Forestry; Transport Scotland; Waterwatch
    Scotland

EDUCATION, COMMUNITIES AND JUSTICE
St Andrew's House, Regent Road, Edinburgh EH1 3DG
Director-General Paul Johnston
Directorates: Advance Learning and Science; Children and
    Families; Early Learning and Childcare Programme;
    Education Analytical Services; Housing and Social Justice;
    Justice; Learning; Local Government and Communities;
    Safer Communities

Executive Agencies: Disclosure Scotland; Education Scotland;
    HM Chief Inspector of Prosecution in Scotland; HM
    Inspectorate of Constabulary; HM Inspectorate of Prisons;
    Inspectorate of Prosecution in Scotland; Justice of the
    Peace Advisory Committee; Scottish Prison Service;
    Student Awards Agency for Scotland; Visiting Committees
    for Scottish Penal Establishments

SCOTTISH EXCHEQUER
Victoria Quay, Edinburgh, EH6 6QQ
Director-General, Alyson Stafford
Directorates: Budget and Sustainability; Internal Audit and
    Assurance; Performance and Outcomes; Taxation
Executive Agency: Audit Scotland

HEALTH AND SOCIAL CARE
St Andrew's House, Regent Road, Edinburgh EH1 3DG
*Director-General Health and Social Care and Chief Executive NHS
    Scotland,* Malcolm Wright
Directorates: Chief Medical Officer; Chief Nursing Officer;
    Community Health and Social Care; Corporate
    Governance and Value; Health Finance; Health
    Performance and Delivery; Health Workforce, Leadership
    and Service Reform; Healthcare Quality and
    Improvement; Mental Health; Office of the Chief
    Executive NHS Scotland; Performance and Delivery;
    Population Health
Executive Agency: Scottish Children's Reporters
    Administration

ORGANISATIONAL DEVELOPMENT AND OPERATIONS
St Andrew's House, Regent Road, Edinburgh EH1 3DG
Directorates: Communications, Ministerial Support and
    Facilities; Digital; Financial Management; People; Social
    Security; Scottish Procurement and Commercial
Executive Agencies: Scottish Public Pensions Agency; Social
    Security Scotland

NON-MINISTERIAL DEPARTMENTS

FOOD STANDARDS SCOTLAND
Pilgrim House, Old Ford Road, Aberdeen AB11 5RL **T** 01224-285100
W www.foodstandards.gov.scot
Chief Executive, Geoff Ogle
NATIONAL RECORDS OF SCOTLAND
General Register House, 2 Princes Street, Edinburgh EH1 3YY
T 0131-334 0380 **W** www.nrscotland.gov.uk
Registrar General and Keeper of the Records of Scotland, Paul
    Lowe
OFFICE OF THE SCOTTISH CHARITY REGULATOR
2nd Floor, Quadrant House, 9 Riverside Drive, Dundee DD1 4NY
T 01382-220446 **W** www.oscr.org.uk
Chief Executive, Maureen Mallon *(interim)*
REGISTERS OF SCOTLAND
Meadowbank House, 153 London Road, Edinburgh, Midlothian EH8
7AU **T** 0800-169 9391 **W** www.ros.gov.uk
Keeper, Jennifer Henderson
REVENUE SCOTLAND
PO Box 24068, Victoria Quay, Edinburgh EH6 9BR **T** 0300-020 0310
W www.revenue.scot
Chief Executive, Dr Keith Nicholson
SCOTTISH COURTS AND TRIBUNALS SERVICE
Saughton House, Broomhouse Drive, Edinburgh EH11 3XD
T 0131-444 3300 **W** www.scotcourts.gov.uk
Chief Executive, Eric McQueen
SCOTTISH HOUSING REGULATOR
Buchanan House, 58 Port Dundas Road, Glasgow G4 0HF
T 0141-242 5642 **W** www.scottishhousingregulator.gov.uk
Chief Executive, George Walker

SCOTTISH PARLIAMENT ELECTION RESULTS *as at 5 May 2016*

Electorate (E.) 4,099,407 Turnout (T.) 55.6%
See General Election Results for a list of party abbreviations

ABERDEEN CENTRAL
(Scotland North East Region)
E. 57,195 T. 26,704 (46.69%)

Kevin Stewart, SNP	11,648
Lewis Macdonald, Lab.	7,299
Tom Mason, C.	6,022
Ken McLeod, LD	1,735

SNP majority 4,349 (16.29%)
6.92% swing Lab. to SNP

ABERDEEN DONSIDE
(Scotland North East Region)
E. 61,200 T. 30,981 (50.62%)

Mark McDonald, SNP	17,339
Liam Kerr, C.	5,709
Greg Williams, Lab.	5,672
Isobel Davidson, LD	2,261

SNP majority 11,630 (37.54%)
4.82% swing SNP to C.

ABERDEEN SOUTH & KINCARDINE NORTH
(Scotland North East Region)
E. 59,710 T. 32,340 (54.16%)

Maureen Watt, SNP	13,604
Ross Thomson, C.	10,849
Alison Evison, Lab.	5,603
John Waddell, LD	2,284

SNP majority 2,755 (8.52%)
9.49% swing SNP to C.

ABERDEENSHIRE EAST
(Scotland North East Region)
E. 62,844 T. 34,753 (55.30%)

Gillian Martin, SNP	15,912
Colin Clark, C.	10,075
Christine Jardine, LD	6,611
Sarah Flavell, Lab.	2,155

SNP majority 5,837 (16.80%)
16.90% swing SNP to C.

ABERDEENSHIRE WEST
(Scotland North East Region)
E. 59,576 T. 35,198 (59.08%)

Alexander Burnett, C.	13,400
Dennis Robertson, SNP	12,500
Mike Rumbles, LD	7,262
Sarah Christina Duncan, Lab.	2,036

C. majority 900 (2.56%)
12.03% swing SNP to C.

AIRDRIE & SHOTTS
(Scotland Central Region)
E. 53,899 T. 26,573 (49.30%)

Alex Neil, SNP	13,954
Richard Leonard, Lab.	7,762
Eric Holford, C.	4,164
Louise Young, LD	693

SNP majority 6,192 (23.30%)
7.46% swing Lab. to SNP

ALMOND VALLEY
(Lothian Region)
E. 64,901 T. 34,872 (53.73%)

Angela Constance, SNP	18,475
Neil Findlay, Lab.	10,082
Stephanie Smith, C.	5,308
Charles Dundas, LD	1,007

SNP majority 8,393 (24.07%)
3.02% swing Lab. to SNP

ANGUS NORTH & MEARNS
(Scotland North East Region)
E. 54,268 T. 29,379 (54.14%)

Mairi Evans, SNP	13,417
Alex Johnstone, C.	10,945
John Ruddy, Lab.	2,752
Euan Davidson, LD	2,265

SNP majority 2,472 (8.41%)
10.41% swing SNP to C.

ANGUS SOUTH
(Scotland North East Region)
E. 56,278 T. 31,929 (56.73%)

Graeme Dey, SNP	15,622
Kirstene Hair, C.	11,318
Joanne McFadden, Lab.	3,773
Clive Sneddon, LD	1,216

SNP majority 4,304 (13.48%)
12.40% swing SNP to C.

ARGYLL & BUTE
(Highlands and Islands Region)
E. 48,804 T. 29,476 (60.40%)

Michael Russell, SNP	13,561
Alan Reid, LD	7,583
Donald Cameron, C.	5,840
Mick Rice, Lab.	2,492

SNP majority 5,978 (20.28%)
9.07% swing SNP to LD

AYR
(Scotland South Region)
E. 61,558 T. 37,615 (61.10%)

John Scott, C.	16,183
Jennifer Dunn, SNP	15,433
Brian McGinley, Lab.	5,283
Robbie Simpson, LD	716

C. majority 750 (1.99%)
0.67% swing C. to SNP

BANFFSHIRE & BUCHAN COAST
(Scotland North East Region)
E. 59,155 T. 28,683 (48.49%)

Stewart Stevenson, SNP	15,802
Peter Chapman, C.	9,219
Nathan Morrison, Lab.	2,372
David Evans, LD	1,290

SNP majority 6,583 (22.95%)
12.96% swing SNP to C.

CAITHNESS, SUTHERLAND & ROSS
(Highlands and Islands Region)
E. 55,176 T. 32,207 (58.37%)

Gail Ross, SNP	13,937
Jamie Stone, LD	10,024
Struan Mackie, C.	4,912
Leah Franchetti, Lab.	3,334

SNP majority 3,913 (12.15%)
6.96% swing SNP to LD

CARRICK, CUMNOCK & DOON VALLEY
(Scotland South Region)
E. 58,548 T. 31,680 (54.11%)

Jeane Freeman, SNP	14,690
Carol Mochan, Lab.	8,684
Lee Lyons, C.	7,666
Dawud Islam, LD	640

SNP majority 6,006 (18.96%)
4.98% swing Lab. to SNP

CLACKMANNANSHIRE & DUNBLANE
(Mid Scotland and Fife Region)
E. 50,557 T. 29,746 (58.84%)

Keith Brown, SNP	14,147
Craig Miller, Lab.	7,426
Alexander Stewart, C.	6,915
Christopher McKinlay, LD	1,258

SNP majority 6,721 (22.59%)
4.72% swing Lab. to SNP

CLYDEBANK & MILNGAVIE
(Scotland West Region)
E. 54,761 T. 32,838 (59.97%)

Gil Paterson, SNP	16,158
Gail Casey, Lab.	7,726
Maurice Golden, C.	6,029
Frank Bowles, LD	2,925

SNP majority 8,432 (25.68%)
11.58% swing Lab. to SNP

CLYDESDALE
(Scotland South Region)
E. 58,471 T. 33,619 (57.50%)

Aileen Campbell, SNP	14,821
Alex Allison, C.	8,842
Claudia Beamish, Lab.	6,895
Danny Meikle, Ind.	1,332
Bev Gauld, CSSInd.	909
Jennifer Jamieson Ball, LD	820

SNP majority 5,979 (17.78%)
8.88% swing SNP to C.

COATBRIDGE & CHRYSTON
(Scotland Central Region)
E. 54,169 T. 28,334 (52.31%)

Fulton MacGregor, SNP	13,605
Elaine Smith, Lab.	9,826
Robyn Halbert, C.	2,868
John Wilson, Green	1,612
Jenni Lang, LD	423

SNP majority 3,779 (13.34%)
12.56% swing Lab. to SNP

COWDENBEATH
(Mid Scotland and Fife Region)
E. 54,596 T. 29,734 (54.46%)
Annabelle Ewing, SNP	13,715
Alex Rowley, Lab.	10,674
Dave Dempsey, C.	4,251
Bryn Jones, LD	1,094

SNP majority 3,041 (10.23%)
7.54% swing Lab. to SNP

CUMBERNAULD & KILSYTH
(Scotland Central Region)
E. 49,964 T. 28,308 (56.66%)
Jamie Hepburn, SNP	17,015
Mark Griffin, Lab.	7,537
Anthony Newman, C.	3,068
Irene Lang, LD	688

SNP majority 9,478 (33.48%)
9.89% swing Lab. to SNP

CUNNINGHAME NORTH
(Scotland West Region)
E. 55,647 T. 31,965 (57.44%)
Kenneth Gibson, SNP	16,587
Jamie Greene, C.	7,863
Johanna Baxter, Lab.	6,735
Charity Pierce, LD	780

SNP majority 8,724 (27.29%)
5.83% swing SNP to C.

CUNNINGHAME SOUTH
(Scotland South Region)
E. 50,215 T. 25,695 (51.17%)
Ruth Maguire, SNP	13,416
Joe Cullinane, Lab.	7,723
Billy McClure, C.	3,940
Ruby Kirkwood, LD	616

SNP majority 5,693 (22.16%)
5.76% swing Lab. to SNP

DUMBARTON
(Scotland West Region)
E. 55,098 T. 33,598 (60.98%)
Jackie Baillie, Lab.	13,522
Gail Robertson, SNP	13,413
Maurice Corry, C.	4,891
Aileen Morton, LD	1,131
Andrew Muir, Ind.	641

Lab. majority 109 (0.32%)
2.71% swing Lab. to SNP

DUMFRIESSHIRE
(Scotland South Region)
E. 60,698 T. 36,260 (59.74%)
Oliver Mundell, C.	13,536
Joan McAlpine, SNP	12,306
Elaine Murray, Lab.	9,151
Richard Brodie, LD	1,267

C. majority 1,230 (3.39%)
10.99% swing Lab. to C.

DUNDEE EAST
(Scotland North East Region)
E. 55,261 T. 28,437 (51.46%)
Shona Robison, SNP	16,509
Richard McCready, Lab.	5,611
Bill Bowman, C.	4,969
Craig Duncan, LD	911
Leah Ganley, TUSC	437

SNP majority 10,898 (38.32%)
1.57% swing SNP to Lab.

DUNDEE WEST
(Scotland North East Region)
E. 53,830 T. 27,788 (51.62%)
Joe FitzPatrick, SNP	16,070
Jenny Marra, Lab.	7,242
Nicola Ross, C.	2,826
Daniel Coleman, LD	1,008
Jim McFarlane, TUSC	642

SNP majority 8,828 (31.77%)
2.79% swing Lab. to SNP

DUNFERMLINE
(Scotland Mid and Fife Region)
E. 57,740 T. 32,909 (57.00%)
Shirley-Anne Somerville, SNP	14,257
Cara Hilton, Lab.	9,699
James Reekie, C.	5,797
James Calder, LD	3,156

SNP majority 4,558 (13.85%)
5.92% swing Lab. to SNP

EAST KILBRIDE
(Scotland Central Region)
E. 61,134 T. 34,629 (56.64%)
Linda Fabiani, SNP	19,371
LizAnne Handibode, Lab.	8,392
Graham Simpson, C.	5,857
Paul McGarry, LD	1,009

SNP majority 10,979 (31.70%)
12.59% swing Lab. to SNP

EAST LOTHIAN
(Scotland South Region)
E. 60,848 T. 37,913 (62.31%)
Iain Gray, Lab.	14,329
DJ Johnston-Smith, SNP	13,202
Rachael Hamilton, C.	9,045
Ettie Spencer, LD	1,337

Lab. majority 1,127 (2.97%)
1.25% swing SNP to Lab.

EASTWOOD
(Scotland West Region)
E. 53,085 T. 36,255 (68.30%)
Jackson Carlaw, C.	12,932
Stewart Maxwell, SNP	11,321
Ken Macintosh, Lab.	11,081
John Duncan, LD	921

C. majority 1,611 (4.44%)
5.70% swing Lab. to C.

EDINBURGH CENTRAL
(Lothian Region)
E. 59,581 T. 34,169 (57.35%)
Ruth Davidson, C.	10,399
Alison Dickie, SNP	9,789
Sarah Boyack, Lab.	7,546
Alison Johnstone, Green	4,644
Hannah Bettsworth, LD	1,672
Tom Laird, SLP	119

C. majority 610 (1.79%)
9.73% swing SNP to C.

EDINBURGH EASTERN
(Lothian Region)
E. 62,817 T. 35,397 (56.35%)
Ash Denham, SNP	16,760
Kezia Dugdale, Lab.	11,673
Nick Cook, C.	5,700
Cospatric D'Inverno, LD	1,264

SNP majority 5,087 (14.37%)
3.55% swing Lab. to SNP

EDINBURGH NORTHERN & LEITH
(Lothian Region)
E. 67,273 T. 37,102 (55.15%)
Ben Macpherson, SNP	17,322
Lesley Hinds, Lab.	10,576
Iain McGill, C.	6,081
Martin Veart, LD	1,779
Jack Caldwell, Ind.	1,344

SNP majority 6,746 (18.18%)
10.05% swing Lab. to SNP

EDINBURGH PENTLANDS
(Lothian Region)
E. 55,241 T. 33,353 (60.38%)
Gordon MacDonald, SNP	13,181
Gordon Lindhurst, C.	10,725
Blair Heary, Lab.	7,811
Emma Farthing-Sykes, LD	1,636

SNP majority 2,456 (7.36%)
0.76% swing C. to SNP

EDINBURGH SOUTHERN
(Lothian Region)
E. 59,587 T. 38,259 (64.21%)
Daniel Johnson, Lab.	13,597
Jim Eadie, SNP	12,474
Miles Briggs, C.	9,972
Pramod Subbaraman, LD	2,216

Lab. majority 1,123 (2.94%)
2.49% swing Lab. to SNP

EDINBURGH WESTERN
(Lothian Region)
E. 61,666 T. 39,766 (64.49%)
Alex Cole-Hamilton, LD	16,645
Toni Giugliano, SNP	13,685
Sandy Batho, C.	5,686
Cat Headley, Lab.	3,750

LD majority 2,960 (7.44%)
7.74% swing SNP to LD

ETTRICK, ROXBURGH & BERWICKSHIRE
(Scotland South Region)
E. 54,506 T. 33,095 (60.72%)

John Lamont, C.	18,257
Paul Wheelhouse, SNP	10,521
Jim Hume, LD	2,551
Barrie Cunning, Lab.	1,766

C. majority 7,736 (23.38%)
2.43% swing SNP to C.

FALKIRK EAST
(Scotland Central Region)
E. 60,271 T. 32,524 (53.96%)

Angus MacDonald, SNP	16,720
Craig Martin, Lab.	8,408
Callum Laidlaw, C.	6,342
James Munro, LD	1,054

SNP majority 8,312 (25.56%)
6.50% swing Lab. to SNP

FALKIRK WEST
(Scotland Central Region)
E. 59,812 T. 32,083 (53.64%)

Michael Matheson, SNP	18,260
Mandy Telford, Lab.	6,980
Alison Harris, C.	5,877
Gillian Cole-Hamilton, LD	966

SNP majority 11,280 (35.16%)
7.39% swing Lab. to SNP

FIFE MID & GLENROTHES
(Scotland Mid and Fife Region)
E. 53,241 T. 28,547 (53.62%)

Jenny Gilruth, SNP	15,555
Kay Morrison, Lab.	7,279
Alex Stewart-Clark, C.	4,427
Jane-Ann Liston, LD	1,286

SNP majority 8,276 (28.99%)
6.54% swing Lab. to SNP

FIFE NORTH EAST
(Scotland Mid and Fife Region)
E. 54,052 T. 34,063 (63.02%)

Willie Rennie, LD	14,928
Roderick Campbell, SNP	11,463
Huw Bell, C.	5,646
Rosalind Garton, Lab.	2,026

LD majority 3,465 (10.17%)
9.45% swing SNP to LD

GALLOWAY & WEST DUMFRIES
(Scotland South Region)
E. 56,321 T. 33,363 (59.24%)

Finlay Carson, C.	14,527
Aileen McLeod, SNP	13,013
Fiona O'Donnell, Lab.	4,876
Andrew Metcalf, LD	947

C. majority 1,514 (4.54%)
0.83% swing SNP to C.

GLASGOW ANNIESLAND
(Glasgow Region)
E. 57,884 T. 29,016 (50.13%)

Bill Kidd, SNP	15,007
Bill Butler, Lab.	8,854
Adam Tomkins, C.	4,057
James Speirs, LD	1,098

SNP majority 6,153 (21.21%)
10.59% swing Lab. to SNP

GLASGOW CATHCART
(Glasgow Region)
E. 60,871 T. 30,637 (50.33%)

James Dornan, SNP	16,200
Soryia Siddique, Lab.	6,810
Kyle Thornton, C.	4,514
Margot Clark, LD	1,703
Brian Smith, TUSC	909
Chris Creighton, Ind.	501

SNP majority 9,390 (30.65%)
12.29% swing Lab. to SNP

GLASGOW KELVIN
(Glasgow Region)
E. 62,203 T. 28,442 (45.72%)

Sandra White, SNP	10,964
Patrick Harvie, Green	6,916
Michael Shanks, Lab.	5,968
Sheila Mechan, C.	3,346
Carole Ford, LD	1,050
Tom Muirhead, Ind.	198

SNP majority 4,048 (14.23%)

GLASGOW MARYHILL & SPRINGBURN
(Glasgow Region)
E. 53,647 T. 23,612 (44.01%)

Bob Doris, SNP	13,109
Patricia Ferguson, Lab.	7,507
John Anderson, C.	2,305
James Harrison, LD	691

SNP majority 5,602 (23.73%)
15.01% swing Lab. to SNP

GLASGOW POLLOK
(Glasgow Region)
E. 61,350 T. 27,943 (45.55%)

Humza Yousaf, SNP	15,316
Johann Lamont, Lab.	8,834
Thomas Haddow, C.	2,653
Isabel Nelson, LD	585
Ian Leech, TUSC	555

SNP majority 6,482 (23.20%)
12.96% swing Lab. to SNP

GLASGOW PROVAN
(Glasgow Region)
E. 56,169 T. 24,077 (42.87%)

Ivan McKee, SNP	13,140
Paul Martin, Lab.	8,357
Annie Wells, C.	2,062
Tom Coleman, LD	518

SNP majority 4,783 (19.87%)
15.35% swing Lab. to SNP

GLASGOW SHETTLESTON
(Glasgow Region)
E. 58,021 T. 25,375 (43.73%)

John Mason, SNP	14,198
Thomas Rannachan, Lab.	6,875
Thomas Kerr, C.	3,151
Jamie Cocozza, TUSC	583
Giovanni Caccavello, LD	568

SNP majority 7,323 (28.86%)
13.05% swing Lab. to SNP

GLASGOW SOUTHSIDE
(Glasgow Region)
E. 52,141 T. 24,903 (47.76%)

Nicola Sturgeon, SNP	15,287
Fariha Thomas, Lab.	5,694
Graham Hutchison, C.	3,100
Kevin Lewsey, LD	822

SNP majority 9,593 (38.52%)
9.64% swing Lab. to SNP

GREENOCK & INVERCLYDE
(Scotland West Region)
E. 55,171 T. 31,725 (57.50%)

Stuart McMillan, SNP	17,032
Siobhan McCready, Lab.	8,802
Graeme Brooks, C.	4,487
John Watson, LD	1,404

SNP majority 8,230 (25.94%)
13.88% swing Lab. to SNP

HAMILTON, LARKHALL & STONEHOUSE
(Scotland Central Region)
E. 57,656 T. 28,885 (50.10%)

Christina McKelvie, SNP	13,945
Margaret McCulloch, Lab.	8,508
Margaret Mitchell, C.	5,596
Eileen Baxendale, LD	836

SNP majority 5,437 (18.82%)
5.05% swing Lab. to SNP

INVERNESS & NAIRN
(Highlands and Islands Region)
E. 66,619 T. 38,317 (57.52%)

Fergus Ewing, SNP	18,505
Edward Mountain, C.	7,648
David Stewart, Lab.	6,719
Carolyn Caddick, LD	5,445

SNP majority 10,857 (28.33%)
5.80% swing SNP to C.

KILMARNOCK & IRVINE VALLEY
(Scotland South Region)
E. 62,620 T. 34,385 (54.91%)

Willie Coffey, SNP	19,047
Dave Meechan, Lab.	7,853
Brian Whittle, C.	6,597
Rebecca Plenderleith, LD	888

SNP majority 11,194 (32.55%)
6.87% swing Lab. to SNP

KIRKCALDY
(Scotland Mid and Fife Region)
E. 59,533 T. 31,108 (52.25%)

David Torrance, SNP	16,358
Claire Baker, Lab.	8,963
Martin Laidlaw, C.	4,568
Lauren Jones, LD	1,219

SNP majority 7,395 (23.77%)
11.56% swing Lab. to SNP

LINLITHGOW
(Lothian Region)
E. 71,434 T. 38,407 (53.77%)

Fiona Hyslop, SNP	19,362
Angela Moohan, Lab.	10,027
Charles Kennedy, C.	7,699
Dan Farthing-Sykes, LD	1,319

SNP majority 9,335 (24.31%)
6.17% swing Lab. to SNP

MIDLOTHIAN NORTH & MUSSELBURGH
(Lothian Region)
E. 63,360 T. 34,685 (54.74%)

Colin Beattie, SNP	16,948
Bernard Harkins, Lab.	9,913
Jeremy Balfour, C.	6,267
Jacquie Bell, LD	1,557

SNP majority 7,035 (20.28%)
5.12% swing Lab. to SNP

MIDLOTHIAN SOUTH, TWEEDDALE & LAUDERDALE
(Scotland South Region)
E. 60,204 T. 35,581 (59.10%)

Christine Grahame, SNP	16,031
Michelle Ballantyne, C.	10,163
Fiona Dugdale, Lab.	5,701
Kris Chapman, LD	3,686

SNP majority 5,868 (16.49%)
7.63% swing SNP to C.

MORAY
(Highlands and Islands Region)
E. 61,969 T. 33,421 (53.93%)

Richard Lochhead, SNP	15,742
Douglas Ross, C.	12,867
Sean Morton, Lab.	3,547
Jamie Paterson, LD	1,265

SNP majority 2,875 (8.60%)
14.83% swing SNP to C.

MOTHERWELL & WISHAW
(Scotland Central Region)
E. 57,045 T. 29,111 (51.03%)

Clare Adamson, SNP	15,291
John Pentland, Lab.	9,068
Meghan Gallacher, C.	3,991
Yvonne Finlayson, LD	761

SNP majority 6,223 (21.38%)
11.89% swing Lab. to SNP

NA H-EILEANAN AN IAR
(Highlands and Islands Region)
E. 21,695 T. 13,206 (60.87%)

Alasdair Allan, SNP	6,874
Rhoda Grant, Lab.	3,378
Ranald Fraser, C.	1,499
John Cormack, SCP	1,162
Ken MacLeod, LD	293

SNP majority 3,496 (26.47%)
5.10% swing SNP to Lab.

ORKNEY
(Highlands and Islands Region)
E. 16,997 T. 10,534 (61.98%)

Liam McArthur, LD	7,096
Donna Heddle, SNP	2,562
Jamie Halcro Johnston, C.	435
Gerry McGarvey, Lab.	304
Paul Dawson, Ind.	137

LD majority 4,534 (43.04%)
16.20% swing SNP to LD

PAISLEY
(Scotland West Region)
E. 51,673 T. 29,464 (57.02%)

George Adam, SNP	14,682
Neil Bibby, Lab.	9,483
Paul Masterton, C.	3,533
Eileen McCartin, LD	1,766

SNP majority 5,199 (17.65%)
8.34% swing Lab. to SNP

PERTHSHIRE NORTH
(Scotland and Mid Fife Region)
E. 54,255 T. 34,025 (62.71%)

John Swinney, SNP	16,526
Murdo Fraser, C.	13,190
Anna McEwan, Lab.	2,604
Peter Barrett, LD	1,705

SNP majority 3,336 (9.80%)
12.38% swing SNP to C.

PERTHSHIRE SOUTH & KINROSS-SHIRE
(Scotland and Mid Fife Region)
E. 59,397 T. 36,149 (60.86%)

Roseanna Cunningham, SNP	15,315
Liz Smith, C.	13,893
Scott Nicholson, Lab.	3,389
Willie Robertson, LD	3,008
Craig Finlay, Community	544

SNP majority 1,422 (3.93%)
9.51% swing SNP to C.

RENFREWSHIRE NORTH & WEST
(Scotland West Region)
E. 50,555 T. 30,807 (60.94%)

Derek Mackay, SNP	14,718
David Wilson, C.	7,345
Mary Fee, Lab.	7,244
Rod Ackland, LD	888
Jim Halfpenny, TUSC	414
Peter Morton, Ind.	198

SNP majority 7,373 (23.93%)
1.02% swing C. to SNP

RENFREWSHIRE SOUTH
(Scotland West Region)
E. 49,422 T. 29,681 (60.06%)

Thomas Arthur, SNP	14,272
Paul O'Kane, Lab.	9,864
Ann Le Blond, C.	4,752
Tristan Gray, LD	793

SNP majority 4,408 (14.85%)
12.21% swing Lab. to SNP

RUTHERGLEN
(Glasgow Region)
E. 60,702 T. 32,952 (54.28%)

Clare Haughey, SNP	15,222
James Kelly, Lab.	11,479
Taylor Muir, C.	3,718
Robert Brown, LD	2,533

SNP majority 3,743 (11.36%)
8.96% swing Lab. to SNP

SHETLAND ISLANDS
(Highlands and Islands Region)
E. 17,784 T. 11,041 (62.08%)

Tavish Scott, LD	7,440
Danus Skene, SNP	2,545
Robina Barton, Lab.	651
Cameron Smith, C.	405

LD majority 4,895 (44.33%)
4.45% swing SNP to LD

SKYE, LOCHABER & BADENOCH
(Highlands and Islands Region)
E. 59,537 T. 36,505 (61.31%)

Kate Forbes, SNP	17,362
Angela MacLean, LD	8,319
Robbie Munro, C.	5,887
Linda Stewart, Lab.	3,821
Ronnie Campbell, Ind.	1,116

SNP majority 9,043 (24.77%)
4.56% swing LD to SNP

STIRLING
(Scotland and Mid Fife Region)
E. 55,785 T. 34,189 (61.29%)

Bruce Crawford, SNP	16,303
Dean Lockhart, C.	9,585
Rebecca Bell, Lab.	6,885
Elisabeth Wilson, LD	1,416

SNP majority 6,718 (19.65%)
7.03% swing SNP to C.

STRATHKELVIN & BEARSDEN
(Scotland West Region)
E. 62,598 T. 39,188 (62.60%)

Rona Mackay, SNP	17,060
Andrew Polson, C.	8,960
Margaret McCarthy, Lab.	8,288
Katy Gordon, LD	4,880

SNP majority 8,100 (20.67%)
4.21% swing SNP to C.

UDDINGSTON & BELLSHILL
(Central Scotland Region)
E. 57,556 T. 29,543 (51.33%)

Richard Lyle, SNP	14,424
Michael McMahon, Lab.	9,615
Andrew Morrison, C.	4,693
Kaitey Blair, LD	811

SNP majority 4,809 (16.28%)
9.57% swing Lab. to SNP

REGIONS *as at 5 May 2016*
E. 4,099,407 T. 55.6%

GLASGOW
E. 522,988 T. 248,109 (47.44%)

SNP	111,101	(44.78%)
Lab.	59,151	(23.84%)
C.	29,533	(11.90%)
Green	23,398	(9.43%)
LD	5,850	(2.36%)
UKIP	4,889	(1.97%)
Solidarity	3,593	(1.45%)
RISE	2,454	(0.99%)
UP	2,453	(0.99%)
Women	2,091	(0.84%)
Animal	1,819	(0.73%)
SCP	1,506	(0.61%)
Ind.	271	(0.11%)

SNP majority 51,950 (20.94%)
8.05% swing Lab. to SNP (2011 SNP majority 10,078)
ADDITIONAL MEMBERS
Adam Tomkins, *C.* James Kelly, *Lab.*
Annie Wells, *C.* Pauline McNeill, *Lab.*
Anas Sarwar, *Lab.* Patrick Harvie, *Green*
Johann Lamont, *Lab.*

HIGHLANDS AND ISLANDS
E. 348,581 T. 205,313 (58.90%)

SNP	81,600	(39.74%)
C.	44,693	(21.77%)
LD	27,223	(13.26%)
Lab.	22,894	(11.15%)
Green	14,781	(7.20%)
UKIP	5,344	(2.60%)
Ind.	3,689	(1.80%)
SCP	3,407	(1.66%)
RISE	889	(0.43%)
Solidarity	793	(0.39%)

SNP majority 36,907 (17.98%)
8.95% swing SNP to C. (2011 SNP majority 59,198)
ADDITIONAL MEMBERS
Douglas Ross, *C.* David Steward, *Lab.*
Edward Mountain, *C.* Maree Todd, *SNP*
Donald Cameron, *C.* John Finnie, *Green*
Rhoda Grant, *Lab.*

LOTHIAN
E. 565,860 T. 327,178 (57.82%)

SNP	118,546	(36.23%)
C.	74,972	(22.91%)
Lab.	67,991	(20.78%)
Green	34,551	(10.56%)
LD	18,479	(5.65%)
UKIP	5,802	(1.77%)
Women	3,877	(1.18%)
RISE	1,641	(0.50%)
Solidarity	1,319	(0.40%)

SNP majority 43,574 (13.32%)
7.10% swing SNP to C. (2011 SNP majority 40,409)
ADDITIONAL MEMBERS
Miles Briggs, *C.* Neil Findlay, *Lab.*

Gordon Lindhurst, *C.* Alison Johnstone, *Green*
Jeremy Balfour, *C.* Andy Wightman, *Green*
Kezia Dugdale, *Lab.*

SCOTLAND CENTRAL
E. 511,506 T. 270,706 (52.92%)

SNP	129,082	(47.68%)
Lab.	67,103	(24.79%)
C.	43,602	(16.11%)
Green	12,722	(4.70%)
UKIP	6,088	(2.25%)
LD	5,015	(1.85%)
Solidarity	2,684	(0.99%)
SCP	2,314	(0.85%)
RISE	1,636	(0.60%)
Ind.	460	(0.17%)

SNP majority 61,979 (22.90%)
5.92% swing Lab. to SNP (2011 SNP majority 25,802)
ADDITIONAL MEMBERS
Margaret Mitchell, *C.* Monica Lennon, *Lab.*
Graham Simpson, *C.* Mark Griffin, *Lab.*
Alison Harris, *C.* Elaine Smith, *Lab.*
Richard Leonard, *Lab.*

SCOTLAND MID AND FIFE
E. 499,156 T. 291,172 (58.33%)

SNP	120,128	(41.26%)
C.	73,293	(25.17%)
Lab.	51,373	(17.64%)
LD	20,401	(7.01%)
Green	17,860	(6.13%)
UKIP	5,345	(1.84%)
RISE	1,073	(0.37%)
Solidarity	1,049	(0.36%)
SLP	650	(0.22%)

SNP majority 46,835 (16.08%)
7.50% swing SNP to C. (2011 SNP majority 52,068)
ADDITIONAL MEMBERS
Murdo Fraser, *C.* Alex Rowley, *Lab.*
Liz Smith, *C.* Claire Baker, *Lab.*
Dean Lockhart, *C.* Mark Ruskell, *Green*
Alexander Stewart, *C.*

SCOTLAND NORTH EAST
E. 579,317 T. 307,006 (52.99%)

SNP	137,086	(44.65%)
C.	85,848	(27.96%)
Lab.	38,791	(12.64%)
LD	18,444	(6.01%)
Green	15,123	(4.93%)
UKIP	6,376	(2.08%)
SCP	2,068	(0.67%)
Solidarity	992	(0.32%)
Nat Front	617	(0.20%)
RISE	599	(0.20%)
SLP	552	(0.18%)
Comm Brit	510	(0.17%)

SNP majority 51,238 (16.69%)
10.95% swing SNP to C. (2011 SNP majority 96,856)
ADDITIONAL MEMBERS
Alex Johnstone, *C.* Jenny Marra, *Lab.*
Ross Thomson, *C.* Lewis Macdonald, *Lab.*
Peter Chapman, *C.* Mike Rumbles, *LD*
Liam Kerr, *C.*

SCOTLAND SOUTH
E. 533,774 T. 314,192 (58.86%)

SNP	120,217	(38.26%)
C.	100,753	(32.07%)
Lab.	56,072	(17.85%)
Green	14,773	(4.70%)
LD	11,775	(3.75%)
UKIP	6,726	(2.14%)
CSSInd.	1,485	(0.47%)
Solidarity	1,294	(0.41%)
RISE	1,097	(0.35%)

SNP majority 19,464 (6.19%)
7.65% swing SNP to C. (2011 SNP majority 43,675)
ADDITIONAL MEMBERS

Rachel Hamilton, C.	Joan McAlpine, SNP
Brian Whittle, C.	Emma Harper, SNP
Claudia Beamish, Lab.	Paul Wheelhouse, SNP
Colin Smyth, Lab.	

SCOTLAND WEST
E. 538,225 T. 322,076 (59.84%)

SNP	135,827	(42.17%)
Lab.	72,544	(22.52%)
C.	71,528	(22.21%)
Green	17,218	(5.35%)
LD	12,097	(3.76%)
UKIP	5,856	(1.82%)
Solidarity	2,609	(0.81%)
SCP	2,391	(0.74%)
RISE	1,522	(0.47%)
SLP	484	(0.15%)

SNP majority 63,283 (19.65%)
5.44% swing Lab. to SNP (2011 SNP majority 24,776)
ADDITIONAL MEMBERS

Jamie Green, C.	Mary Fee, Lab.
Maurice Golden, C.	Ken Macintosh, Lab.
Maurice Corry, C.	Ross Greer, Green
Neil Bibby, Lab.	

NORTHERN IRELAND

NORTHERN IRELAND ASSEMBLY
Parliament Buildings, Stormont, Belfast BT4 3XX
T 028-9052 1137 **E** info@niassembly.gov.uk
W www.niassembly.gov.uk

The Northern Ireland Assembly was established as a result of the Belfast Agreement (also known as the Good Friday Agreement) in April 1998. The agreement was endorsed through a referendum held in May 1998 and subsequently given legal force through the Northern Ireland Act 1998.

The Northern Ireland Assembly has full legislative and executive authority for all matters that are the responsibility of the government's Northern Ireland departments – known as transferred matters. Excepted and reserved matters are defined in schedules 2 and 3 of the Northern Ireland Act 1998 and remain the responsibility of UK parliament.

The first assembly election occurred on 25 June 1998 and the 108 members elected met for the first time on 1 July 1998.

On 29 November 1999 the assembly appointed ten ministers as well as the chairs and deputy chairs for the ten statutory departmental committees. Devolution of powers to the Northern Ireland Assembly occurred on 2 December 1999, following several delays concerned with Sinn Fein's inclusion in the executive while Irish Republican Army (IRA) weapons were yet to be decommissioned.

Since the devolution of powers, the assembly has been suspended by the Secretary of State for Northern Ireland on four occasions. The first was between 11 February and 30 May 2000, with two 24-hour suspensions on 10 August and 22 September 2001 – all owing to a lack of progress in decommissioning. The final suspension took place on 14 October 2002 after unionists walked out of the executive following a police raid on Sinn Fein's office investigating alleged intelligence gathering.

The assembly was formally dissolved in April 2003 in anticipation of an election, which eventually took place on 26 November 2003. The results of the election changed the balance of power between the political parties, with an increase in the number of seats held by the Democratic Unionist Party (DUP) and Sinn Fein (SF), so that they became the largest parties. The assembly was restored to a state of suspension following the November election while political parties engaged in a review of the Belfast Agreement aimed at fully restoring the devolved institutions.

In July 2005 the leadership of the IRA formally ordered an end to its armed campaign; it authorised a representative to engage with the Independent International Commission on Decommissioning in order to verifiably put the arms beyond use. On 26 September 2005 General John de Chastelain, the chair of the commission, along with two independent church witnesses confirmed that the IRA's entire arsenal of weapons had been decommissioned.

Following the passing of the Northern Ireland Act 2006 the secretary of state created a non-legislative fixed-term assembly, whose membership consisted of the 108 members elected in the 2003 election. It first met on 15 May 2006 with the remit of making preparations for the restoration of devolved government; its discussions informed the next round of talks called by the British and Irish governments held at St Andrews. The St Andrews agreement of 13 October 2006 led to the establishment of the transitional assembly.

The Northern Ireland (St Andrews Agreement) Act 2006 set out a timetable to restore devolution, and also set the date for the third election to the assembly as 7 March 2007. The DUP and SF again had the largest number of Members of the Legislative Assembly (MLAs) elected, and although the initial restoration deadline of 26 March was missed, the leaders of the DUP and SF (Revd Dr Ian Paisley and Gerry Adams respectively) took part in a historic meeting and made a joint commitment to establish an executive committee in the assembly to which devolved powers were restored on 8 May 2007.

RECENT DEVELOPMENTS
Assembly elections took place on 5 May 2016 to elect the 108 members of the legislative assembly for a fifth term. The fifth assembly collapsed on 9 January 2017 when Martin McGuinness resigned as Deputy First Minister. Under the joint protocols that govern the power-sharing agreement, if either the first minister or the deputy resigns and a replacement is not nominated by the relevant party within seven days, then a snap election must be called. The assembly was formerly dissolved at midnight on 25 January 2017 and the most recent assembly elections were held on 2 March 2017 to elect the 90 members of the legislative assembly. Under the Assembly Members (Reduction of Numbers) Act Northern Ireland 2016, the number of assembly members was reduced from 108 to 90 – five members to be elected by each constituency, rather than six.

Following the March 2017 election, negotiations to form an executive missed both the normal three week deadline and an extended deadline of 29 June 2017 set by the Secretary of State for Northern Ireland. The sixth assembly remains suspended until an executive is formed.

THE SINGLE TRANSFERABLE VOTE SYSTEM
Members of the Northern Ireland Assembly are elected by the single transferable vote system from 18 constituencies – five per constituency. Under the single transferable vote system every voter has a single vote that can be transferred from one candidate to another. Voters number their candidates in order of preference. Where candidates reach their quota of votes and are elected, surplus votes are transferred to other candidates according to the next preference on each voter's ballot slip. The candidate in each round with the fewest votes is eliminated and their surplus votes are redistributed according to the voter's next preference. The process is repeated until the required number of members are elected.

SALARIES*

	From 1 January 2019
Speaker	£55,848
Deputy Speaker	£37,388
Commission member	£40,688
MLA	£35,888

* MLA salaries were reduced on 1 November 2018 and further reduced on 1 January 2019 for the present period while there is no executive

NORTHERN IRELAND ASSEMBLY
MEMBERS *as at August 2019*
KEY
* Replacement from the party list since the 2 March 2017 Northern Ireland Assembly election

Agnew, Steven, *Green, Down North*
Aiken, Dr Steve, OBE, *UUP, Antrim South*
Allen, Andy, *UUP, Belfast East*
Allister, Jim, *TUV, Antrim North*
Archibald, Caoimhe, *SF, Londonderry East*
Armstrong, Kellie, *Alliance, Strangford*
Bailey, Clare, *Green, Belfast South*
Barton, Rosemary, *UUP, Fermanagh and South Tyrone*
Beattie, Doug, MC, *UUP, Upper Bann*
Beggs, Roy, *UUP, Antrim East*
* **Blair**, John, *Alliance, Antrim South*

Boylan, Cathal, *SF, Newry and Armagh*
Bradley, Maurice, *DUP, Londonderry East*
Bradley, Paula, *DUP, Belfast North*
Bradley, Sinéad, *SDLP, Down South*
Bradshaw, Paula, *Alliance, Belfast South*
Buchanan, Keith, *DUP, Ulster Mid*
Buchanan, Thomas, *DUP, Tyrone West*
Buckley, Jonathan, *DUP, Upper Bann*
Bunting, Joanne, *DUP, Belfast East*
Butler, Robbie, *UUP, Lagan Valley*
Cameron, Pam, *DUP, Antrim South*
Carroll, Gerry, *PBP, Belfast West*
Catney, Pat, *SDLP, Lagan Valley*
Chambers, Alan, *UUP, Down North*
* Clarke, Trevor, *DUP, Antrim South*
Dallat, John, *SDLP, Londonderry East*
Dickson, Stewart, *Alliance, Antrim East*
Dillon, Linda, *SF, Ulster Mid*
Dolan, Jemma, *SF, Fermanagh and South Tyrone*
Dunne, Gordon, *DUP, Down North*
Durkan, Mark, *SDLP, Foyle*
Easton, Alex, *DUP, Down North*
Eastwood, Colum, *SDLP, Foyle*
Ennis, Sinéad, *SF, Down South*
Farry, Dr Stephen, *Alliance, Down North*
Fearon, Megan, *SF, Newry and Armagh*
Flynn, Órlaithí, *SF, Belfast West*
Foster, Arlene, *DUP, Fermanagh and South Tyrone*
Frew, Paul, *DUP, Antrim North*
* Gildernew, Colm, *SF, Fermanagh and South Tyrone*
Givan, Paul, *DUP, Lagan Valley*
Hamilton, Simon, *DUP, Strangford*
Hanna, Claire, *SDLP, Belfast South*
* Hendron, Máire, *Alliance, Belfast East*
Hilditch, David, *DUP, Antrim East*
Humphrey, William, *DUP, Belfast North*
Irwin, William, *DUP, Newry and Armagh*
Kearney, Declan, *SF, Antrim South*
* Kelly, Catherine, *SF, Tyrone West*
Kelly, Dolores, *SDLP, Upper Bann*
Kelly, Gerry, *SF, Belfast North*
Lockhart, Carla, *DUP, Upper Bann*
Long, Naomi, *Alliance, Belfast East*
Lunn, Trevor, *Alliance, Lagan Valley*
Lynch, Seán, *SF, Fermanagh and South Tyrone*
Lyons, Gordon, *DUP, Antrim East*
Lyttle, Chris, *Alliance, Belfast East*
McAleer, Declan, *SF, Tyrone West*
McCann, Fra, *SF, Belfast West*
McCartney, Raymond, *SF, Foyle*
McCrossan, Daniel, *SDLP, Tyrone West*
McGlone, Patsy, *SDLP, Ulster Mid*
McGrath, Colin, *SDLP, Down South*
McGuigan, Philip, *SF, Antrim North*
* McHugh, Maoliosa, *SF, Tyrone West*
McIlveen, Michelle, *DUP, Strangford*
McNulty, Justin, *SDLP, Newry and Armagh*
Mallon, Nichola, *SDLP, Belfast North*
Maskey, Alex, *SF, Belfast West*
Middleton, Gary, *DUP, Foyle*
* Mullan, Karen, *SF, Foyle*
Murphy, Conor, *SF, Newry and Armagh*
Nesbitt, Mike, *UUP, Strangford*
Newton, Robin, *DUP, Belfast East*
Ní Chuilín, Carál, *SF, Belfast North*
O'Dowd, John, *SF, Upper Bann*
O'Neill, Michelle, *SF, Ulster Mid*
Ó Muilleoir, Máirtín, *SF, Belfast South*
Poots, Edwin, *DUP, Lagan Valley*

Robinson, George, *DUP, Londonderry East*
* Rogan, Emma, *SF, Down South*
Sheehan, Pat, *SF, Belfast West*
* Sheerin, Emma, *SF, Ulster Mid*
Stalford, Christopher, *DUP, Belfast South*
Stewart, John, *UUP, Antrim East*
Storey, Mervyn, *DUP, Antrim North*
Sugden, Claire, *Ind., Londonderry East*
Swann, Robin, *UUP, Antrim North*
Weir, Peter, *DUP, Down North*
Wells, Jim, *DUP, Down South*

STATE OF THE PARTIES *as at 2 March 2017 election*

Party	Seats
Democratic Unionist Party (DUP)	28
Sinn Fein (SF)	27
Social Democratic and Labour Party (SDLP)	12
Ulster Unionist Party (UUP)	10
Alliance Party of Northern Ireland (Alliance)	8
Green Party (Green)	2
People Before Profit Alliance (PBP)	1
Traditional Unionist Voice (TUV)	1
Independents (Ind.)	1
Total	90

NORTHERN IRELAND EXECUTIVE

Stormont Castle, Stormont, Belfast BT4 3TT
T 028-9052 8400
W www.northernireland.gov.uk

The Northern Ireland Executive comprises the first minister, deputy first minister, two junior ministers and eight departmental ministers.

The executive exercises authority on behalf of the Northern Ireland Assembly, and takes decisions on significant issues and matters which cut across the responsibility of two or more ministers.

The executive also agrees proposals put forward by ministers for new legislation in the form of 'executive bills' for consideration by the assembly. It is also responsible for drawing up a programme for government and an agreed budget for approval by the assembly. Ministers of the executive are nominated by the political parties in the Northern Ireland Assembly. The number of ministers which a party can nominate is determined by its share of seats in the assembly. The first minister and deputy first minister are nominated by the largest and second largest parties respectively and act as chairs of the executive. Each executive minister has responsibility for a specific Northern Ireland government department.

EXECUTIVE COMMITTEE OF MINISTERS

There are currently no executive ministers in post since the most recent assembly elections which took place on 2 March 2017. Negotiations to appoint the executive committee of ministers in charge of the nine government departments failed to meet both the three-week deadline following the election and an extended deadline of 29 June 2017 set by the Secretary of State for Northern Ireland. The assembly remains suspended until an executive is formed.

NORTHERN IRELAND EXECUTIVE DEPARTMENTS

THE EXECUTIVE OFFICE, Stormont Castle, Stormont, Belfast
  BT4 3TT **T** 028-9052 8400 **W** www.executiveoffice-ni.gov.uk
**DEPARTMENT OF AGRICULTURE, ENVIRONMENT
  AND RURAL AFFAIRS**, Dundonald House, Upper
  Newtownards Road, Belfast BT4 3SB **T** 0300-200 7850
  W www.daera-ni.gov.uk

DEPARTMENT FOR COMMUNITIES, Causeway Exchange, 1–7 Bedford Street, Belfast BT2 7EG **T** 028-9082 9000
W www.communities-ni.gov.uk

DEPARTMENT FOR THE ECONOMY, Netherleigh, Massey Avenue, Belfast BT4 2JP **T** 028-9052 9900
W www.economy-ni.gov.uk

DEPARTMENT OF EDUCATION, Rathgael House, Balloo Road, Bangor, Co. Down BT19 7PR **T** 028-9127 9279
W www.education-ni.gov.uk

DEPARTMENT OF FINANCE, Clare House, 303 Airport Road, Belfast BT3 9ED **T** 028-9185 8111 **W** www.finance-ni.gov.uk

DEPARTMENT OF HEALTH, Castle Buildings, Stormont, Belfast BT4 3SQ **T** 028-9052 0500 **W** www.health-ni.gov.uk

DEPARTMENT FOR INFRASTRUCTURE, Clarence Court, 10–18 Adelaide Street, Belfast BT2 8GB **T** 028-9054 0540
W www.infrastructure-ni.gov.uk

DEPARTMENT OF JUSTICE, Block B, Castle Buildings, Stormont Estate, Belfast BT4 3SG **T** 028-9076 3000
W www.justice-ni.gov.uk

NORTHERN IRELAND AUDIT OFFICE

106 University Street, Belfast BT7 1EU
T 028-9025 1000 **E** info@niauditoffice.gov.uk
W www.niauditoffice.gov.uk

The Northern Ireland Audit Office supports the Comptroller and Auditor-General in fulfilling his responsibilities. He is responsible for authorising the issue of money from central government funds to Northern Ireland departments and for both financial and value for money audits of central government bodies in Northern Ireland, including, Northern Ireland departments, executive agencies, executive non-departmental public bodies and health and social care bodies.

Comptroller and Auditor-General, Kieran Donnelly, CB

OFFICE OF THE ATTORNEY-GENERAL FOR NORTHERN IRELAND

PO Box 1272, Belfast BT1 9LU
T 028-9072 5333 **E** contact@attorneygeneralni.gov.uk
W www.attorneygeneralni.gov.uk

With the devolution of justice responsibilities on 12 April 2010, the Justice (Northern Ireland) Act 2002 was enacted which established a new post of Attorney-General for Northern Ireland. The Attorney-General acts as the chief legal adviser to the Northern Ireland executive for both civil and criminal matters that fall within the devolved powers of the assembly. He is the executive's most senior representative in the courts and responsible for protecting the public interest in matters of law; overseeing the legal work of the in-house advisers to the executive and its departments; and for the appointment of the director and deputy director of the Public Prosecution Service for Northern Ireland. The Attorney-General participates in the assembly proceedings to the extent permitted by its standing orders, but does not vote in the assembly.

The post of Attorney-General is statutorily independent of the first minister, deputy first minister, the executive and the executive departments.

Attorney-General for Northern Ireland, John Larkin, QC

NORTHERN IRELAND ASSEMBLY ELECTION RESULTS *as at 2 March 2017*

Electorate (E.) 1,254,709 Turnout (T.) 64.8%
First = number of first-preference votes
See General Election Results for a list of party abbreviations

ANTRIM EAST
E. 62,933 T. 37,836 (60.12%)

	First	Round Elected
David Hilditch, DUP	6,000	3
Roy Beggs, UUP	5,121	6
Stewart Dickson, Alliance, DUP	4,179	6
Gordon Lyons, DUP	3,851	8
Oliver McMullan, SF	3,701	
John Stewart, UUP	3,377	9
Stephen Ross, DUP	3,313	
Danny Donnelly, Alliance	1,817	
Noel Jordan, UKIP	1,579	
Ruth Wilson, TUV	1,534	
Margaret McKillop, SDLP	1,524	
Dawn Patterson, Green	777	
Conor Sheridan, Lab. Alt	393	
Alan Dunlop, Lab. C	152	
Ricky Best, Ind.	106	

ANTRIM NORTH
E. 76,739 T. 48,518 (63.22%)

	First	Round Elected
Philip McGuigan, SF	7,600	6
Paul Frew, DUP	6,975	7
Mervyn Storey, DUP	6,857	7
Jim Allister, TUV	6,214	7
Robin Swann, UUP	6,022	6
Phillip Logan, DUP	5,708	
Connor Duncan, SDLP	3,519	
Patricia O'Lynn, Alliance	2,616	
Timothy Gaston, TUV	1,505	
Mark Bailey, Green	530	
Monica Digney, Ind.	435	
Adam McBride, Ind.	113	

ANTRIM SOUTH
E. 68,475 T. 42,726 (62.40%)

	First	Round Elected
Declan Kearney, SF	6,891	4
Steve Aiken, UUP	6,287	5
David Ford, Alliance	5,278	7
Paul Girvan, DUP	5,152	8
Pam Cameron, DUP	4,604	8
Trevor Clarke, DUP	4,522	
Roisin Lynch, SDLP	4,024	
Adrian Cochrane-Watson, UUP	2,505	
Richard Cairns, TUV	1,353	
Ivanka Antova, PBP	530	
David McMaster, Ind.	503	
Eleanor Bailey, Green	501	
Mark Logan, C.	194	

BELFAST EAST
E. 64,788 T. 40,828 (63.02%)

	First	Round Elected
Naomi Long, Alliance	7,610	1
Joanne Bunting, DUP	6,007	9
Andy Allen, UUP	5,275	9
Chris Lyttle, Alliance	5,059	8
Robin Newton, DUP	4,729	11
David Douglas, DUP	4,431	
John Kyle, PUP	2,658	
Georgina Milne, Green	1,447	
Mairead O'Donnell, SF	1,173	
Andrew Girvin, TUV.	917	
Courtney Robinson, CCLA	442	
Sheila Bodel, C.	275	
Séamas de Faoite, SDLP	250	
Jordy McKeag, Ind.	84	

BELFAST NORTH
E. 68,187 T. 42,119 (61.77%)

	First	Round Elected
Gerry Kelly, SF	6,275	7
Caral Ni Chuilin, SF	5,929	7
Nichola Mallon, SDLP	5,431	7
Paula Bradley, DUP	4,835	6
William Humphrey, DUP	4,418	6
Nelson McCausland, DUP	4,056	
Nuala McAllister, Alliance	3,487	
Robert Foster, UUP	2,418	
Julie-Anne Corr-Johnston, PUP	2,053	
Fiona Ferguson, PBP	1,559	
Malachai O'Hara, Green	711	
Gemma Weir, WP	248	
Adam Millar, Ind.	66	

BELFAST SOUTH
E. 61,309 T. 43,465 (70.89%)

	First	Round Elected
Máirtín Ó Muilleoir, SF	7,610	1
Claire Hanna, SDLP	6,559	6
Paula Bradshaw, Alliance	5,595	6
Christopher Stalford, DUP	4,529	9
Emma Little-Pengelly, DUP	4,446	
Clare Bailey, Green	4,247	9
Michael Henderson, UUP	3,863	
Emmet McDonough-Brown, Alliance	2,053	
Naomh Gallagher, SDLP	1,794	
Padraigin Mervyn, PBP	760	
John Hiddleston, TUV	703	
Sean Burns, Lab. Alt	531	
George Jabbour, C.	200	
Lily Kerr, WP	163	

BELFAST WEST
E. 61,309 T. 40,930 (66.76%)

	First	Round Elected
Orlaithi Flynn, SF	6,918	1
Alex Maskey, SF	6,346	3
Fra McCann, SF	6,201	4
Pat Sheehan, SF	5,466	4
Gerry Carroll, PBP	4,903	3
Frank McCoubrey, DUP	4,063	
Alex Attwood, SDLP	3,452	
Michael Collins, PBP	1,096	
Sorcha Eastwood, Alliance	747	
Fred Rodgers, UUP	486	
Connor Campbell, WP	415	
Ellen Murray, Green	251	

DOWN NORTH
E. 64,461 T. 38,174 (59.22%)

	First	Round Elected
Alex Easton, DUP	8,034	1
Alan Chambers, UUP	7,151	1
Stephen Farry, Alliance	7,014	1
Gordon Dunne, DUP	6,118	2
Steven Agnew, Green	5,178	7
Melanie Kennedy, Ind.	1,246	
William Cudworth, UUP	964	
Caoimhe McNeill, SDLP	679	
Frank Shivers, C.	641	
Kieran Maxwell, SF	591	
Chris Carter, Ind.	92	
Gavan Reynolds, Ind.	31	

DOWN SOUTH
E. 75,415 T. 49,934 (66.21%)

	First	Round Elected
Sinéad Ennis, SF	10,256	1
Chris Hazzard, SF	8,827	1
Jim Wells, DUP	7,786	5
Sinéad Bradley, SDLP	7,323	3
Colin McGrath, SDLP	5,110	7
Patrick Brown, Alliance	4,535	
Harold McKee, UUP	4,172	
Lyle Rea, TUV	630	
Hannah George, Green	483	
Patrick Clarke, Ind.	192	
Gary Hynds, C.	85	

FERMANAGH AND SOUTH TYRONE
E. 73,100 T. 53,075 (72.61%)

	First	Round Elected
Arlene Foster, DUP	8,479	2
Michelle Gildernew, SF	7,987	3
Jemma Dolan, SF	7,767	3
Maurice Morrow, DUP	7,102	
Sean Lynch, SF	6,254	4
Rosemary Barton, UUP	6,060	4
Richie McPhillips, SDLP	5,134	
Noreen Campbell, Alliance	1,437	
Alex Elliott, TUV	780	
Donal O'Cofaigh, Lab. Alt	643	
Tanya Jones, Green	550	
Richard Dunn, C.	70	

FOYLE
E. 69,718 T. 45,317 (65.00%)

	First	Round Elected
Elisha McCallion, SF	9,205	1
Colum Eastwood, SDLP	7,240	3
Raymond McCartney, SF	7,145	2
Mark H. Durkan, SDLP	6,948	5
Gary Middleton, DUP	5,975	6
Eamon McCann, PBP	4,760	
Julia Kee, UUP	1,660	
Colm Cavanagh, Alliance	1,124	
Shannon Downey, Green	242	
John Lindsay, CISTA	196	
Stuart Canning, C.	77	
Arthur McGuinness, Ind.	44	

LAGAN VALLEY
E. 72,621 T. 45,440 (62.50%)

	First	Round Elected
Paul Givan, DUP	8,035	1
Robbie Butler, UUP	6,846	7
Trevor Lunn, Alliance	6,105	7
Edwin Poots, DUP	6,013	8
Brenda Hale, DUP	4,566	
Jenny Palmer, UUP	4,492	
Pat Catney, SDLP	3,795	8
Peter Doran, SF	1,801	
Samuel Morrison, TUV	1,389	
Dan Barrios-O'Neill, Green	912	
Jonny Orr, Ind.	856	
Matthew Robinson, C.	183	
Keith John Gray, Ind.	76	

LONDONDERRY EAST
E. 67,392 T. 42,248 (62.69%)

	First	Round Elected
Caoimhe Archibald, SF	5,851	12
Maurice Bradley, DUP	5,444	9
Cathal ohOisin, SF	4,953	
Claire Sugden, Ind.	4,918	8
George Robinson, DUP	4,715	9
Adrian McQuillan, DUP	3,881	
John Dallat, SDLP	3,319	12
William McCandless, UUP	2,814	
Chris McCaw, Alliance	1,841	
Gerry Mullan, Ind.	1,204	
Jordan Armstrong, TUV	1,038	
Russell Watton, PUP	879	
Gavin Campbell, PBP	492	
Anthony Flynn, Green	305	
David Harding, C.	219	

NEWRY AND ARMAGH
E. 80,140 T. 55,625 (69.41%)

	First	Round Elected
William Irwin, DUP	9,760	1
Cathal Boylan, SF	9,197	1
Justin McNulty, SDLP	8,983	2
Megan Fearon, SF	8,881	2
Conor Murphy, SF	8,454	3
Danny Kennedy, UUP	7,256	
Jackie Coade, Alliance	1,418	
Emmet Crossan, CISTA	704	
Rowan Tunnicliffe, Green	265	

STRANGFORD
E. 64,393 T. 39,239 (60.94%)

	First	Round Elected
Simon Hamilton, DUP	6,221	5
Kellie Armstrong, Alliance	5,813	4
Michelle McIlveen, DUP	5,728	9
Mike Nesbitt, UUP	5,323	9
Peter Weir, DUP	3,543	11
Joe Boyle, SDLP	3,045	
Philip Smith, UUP	2,453	
Jimmy Menagh, Ind.	1,627	
Jonathan Bell, Ind.	1,479	
Stephen Cooper, TUV	1,330	
Dermot Kennedy, SF	1,110	
Ricky Bamford, Green	918	
Scott Benton, C.	195	

TYRONE WEST
E. 64,258 T. 44,907 (69.89%)

	First	Round Elected
Thomas Buchanan, DUP	9,064	1
Michaela Boyle, SF	7,714	1
Barry McElduff, SF	7,573	1
Daniel McCrossan, SDLP	6,283	5
Declan McAleer, SF	6,034	5
Alicia Clarke, UUP	3,654	
Stephen Donnelly, Alliance	1,252	
Sorcha McAnespy, Ind.	864	
Charlie Chittick, TUV	851	
Ciaran McClean, Green	412	
Barry Brown, CISTA	373	
Corey French, Ind.	98	
Roisin McMackin, Ind.	85	
Susan-Anne White, Ind.	41	
Roger Lomas, C.	27	

ULSTER MID
E. 69,396 T. 50,228 (72.38%)

	First	Round Elected
Michelle, O'Neill, SF	10,258	1
Keith Buchanan, DUP	9,568	1
Ian Milne, SF	8,143	2
Linda Dillon, SF	7,806	2
Patsy McGlone, SDLP	6,419	5
Sandra Overend, UUP	4,516	
Hannah Loughrin, TUV	1,244	
Fay Watson, Alliance	1,017	
Hugh McCloy, Ind.	247	
Stefan Taylor, Green	243	
Hugh Scullion, WP	217	

UPPER BANN
E. 83,431 T. 52,174 (62.54%)

	First	Round Elected
Carla Lockhart, DUP	9,140	1
John O'Dowd, SF	8,220	5
Jonathan Buckley, DUP	7,745	4
Nuala Toman, SF	6,108	
Doug Beattie, UUP	5,467	5
Jo-Anne Dobson, UUP	5,132	
Dolores Kelly, SDLP	5,127	6
Tara Doyle, Alliance	2,720	
Roy Ferguson, TUV	1,035	
Simon Lee, Green	555	
Colin Craig, WP	218	
Ian Nickels, C.	81	

REGIONAL GOVERNMENT

LONDON

GREATER LONDON AUTHORITY (GLA)

City Hall, The Queen's Walk, London SE1 2AA
T 020-7983 4000 **E** mayor@london.gov.uk **W** www.london.gov.uk

On 7 May 1998 London voted in favour of the formation of
the Greater London Authority (GLA). The first elections to the
GLA took place on 4 May 2000 and the new authority took
over its responsibilities on 3 July 2000. In July 2002 the GLA
moved to one of London's most spectacular buildings, newly
built on a brownfield site on the south bank of the Thames,
adjacent to Tower Bridge. The fifth and most recent election
to the GLA took place on 5 May 2016; the May 2020 mayoral
and assembly elections were delayed until May 2021 due to
the coronavirus pandemic.

The structure and objectives of the GLA stem from its main
areas of responsibility: transport, policing, fire and emergency
planning, economic development, planning, culture and
health. There are five functional bodies which form part of the
wider GLA group and report to the GLA: the Mayor's Office
for Policing and Crime (MOPAC), Transport for London (TfL),
the London Fire Commissioner, the London Legacy
Development Corporation, and the Old Oak and Park Royal
Development Corporation.

The GLA consists of a directly elected mayor, the Mayor of
London, and a separately elected assembly, the London
Assembly. The mayor has the key role in decision making, with
the assembly responsible for regulating and scrutinising these
decisions, and investigating issues of importance to Londoners.
In addition, the GLA has around 950 permanent staff to
support the activities of the mayor and the assembly, which are
overseen by a head of paid service. The mayor may appoint
two political advisers and not more than ten other members of
staff, though he does not necessarily exercise this power, but
he does not appoint the chief executive, the monitoring officer
or the chief finance officer. These must be appointed jointly by
the assembly and the mayor.

Every aspect of the assembly and its activities must be open
to public scrutiny and therefore accountable. The assembly
holds the mayor to account through scrutiny of his strategies,
decisions and actions. Mayor's Question Time, conducted on
ten occasions a year at City Hall, is carried out by direct
questioning at assembly meetings and by conducting detailed
investigations in committee.

People's Question Time, held twice a year, and Talk London
(**W** www.london.gov.uk/talk-london) give Londoners the chance
to question and express their opinions to the mayor and the
assembly about plans, priorities and policies for London.

The role of the mayor can be broken down into a number of
key areas:
- to represent and promote London at home and abroad and
  speak up for Londoners
- to devise strategies and plans to tackle London-wide issues,
  such as crime, transport, housing, planning, economic
  development and regeneration, environment, public
  services, society and culture, sport and health; and to set
  budgets for TfL, MOPAC, London Fire Commissioner and
  the London Legacy Development Corporation
- the mayor is chair of TfL, and is responsible for the
  Metropolitan Police's priorities and performance

The role of the assembly can be broken down into a number
of key areas:
- to hold the mayor to account by examining his decisions and
  actions
- to have the power to amend the mayor's budget by a majority
  of two-thirds
- to have the power to summon the mayor, senior staff of the
  GLA and functional bodies
- to investigate issues of London-wide significance and make
  proposals to appropriate stakeholders
- to examine the work of MOPAC and to review the police
  and crime plan for London through the Police and Crime
  Committee

MAYORAL TEAM
Mayor, Sadiq Khan
Deputy Mayors, Rajesh Agrawal *(Business);* Heidi Alexander
(Transport); Tom Copley *(Housing and Residential
Development);* Sophie Linden *(Policing and Crime);* Joanne
McCartney, AM *(Education and Childcare);* Jules Pipe, CBE
(Planning, Regeneration and Skills); Shirley Rodrigues
(Environment and Energy); Justine Simons, OBE *(Culture and
the Creative Industries);* Dr Fiona Twycross, AM *(Fire and
Resilience);* Debbie Weekes-Bernard *(Social Integration,
Social Mobility and Community Engagement)*
Chief of Staff, David Bellamy
Directors, Dr Nick Bowes *(Policy);* Patrick Hennessy
(Communications); Leah Kreitzman *(External and International
Affairs);* Jack Stenner *(Political and Public Affairs)*
Special Appointments, Theo Blackwell, MBE *(Chief Digital
Officer);* Dr Tom Coffey, OBE *(Health Adviser);* Amy Lamé
(Night Czar); Dr Will Norman *(Walking and Cycling
Commissioner);* Lib Peck *(Director of the Violence Reduction
Unit);* Claire Waxman *(Victims Commissioner)*

ELECTIONS AND VOTING SYSTEMS
The assembly is elected every four years at the same time as the
mayor, and consists of 25 members. There is one member from
each of the 14 GLA constituencies topped up with 11 London-
wide members who are either representatives of political
parties or individuals standing as independent candidates.

Two distinct voting systems are used to appoint the existing
mayor and the assembly. The mayor is elected using the
supplementary vote system (SVS). With SVS, electors have two
votes: one to give a first choice for mayor and one to give a
second choice; they cannot vote twice for the same candidate.
If one candidate gets more than half of all the first-choice votes,
they become mayor. If no candidate gets more than half of the
first-choice votes, the two candidates with the most first-choice
votes remain in the election and all the other candidates drop
out. The second-choice votes on the ballot papers are then
counted. Where these second-choice votes are for the two
remaining candidates, they are added to the first-choice votes
these candidates already have. The candidate with the most
first- and second-choice votes combined becomes the Mayor
of London.

The assembly is appointed using the additional member
system (AMS). Under AMS, electors have two votes. The first
vote is for a constituency candidate. The second vote is for a
party list or individual candidate contesting the London-wide
assembly seats. The 14 constituency members are elected under
the first-past-the-post system, the same system used in general
and local elections. Electors vote for one candidate and the
candidate with the most votes wins. The additional members

are drawn from party lists or are independent candidates; they are chosen using a form of proportional representation.

The Greater London Returning Officer (GLRO) is the independent official responsible for running the election in London. He is supported in this by returning officers in each of the 14 London constituencies.

GLRO for 2016 Election, Jeff Jacobs

TRANSPORT FOR LONDON (TFL)

TfL is the integrated body responsible for London's transport system. Its role is to implement the mayor's transport strategy for London and manage transport services across the capital for which the mayor has responsibility. TfL is directed by a management board whose members are chosen for their understanding of transport matters and are appointed by the mayor, who chairs the board. TfL's role is:

- to manage the London Underground, buses, Croydon Tramlink, London Overground and the Docklands Light Railway (DLR)
- to manage a 580km network of main roads and all 6,000 of London's traffic lights
- to regulate taxis and minicabs
- to run the London River Services, Victoria Coach Station and London Transport Museum
- to help to coordinate the Dial-a-Ride, Capital Call and Taxicard schemes for door-to-door services for transport users with mobility problems

The London Borough Councils maintain the role of highway and traffic authorities for 95 per cent of London's roads. A congestion charge for motorists driving into central London between the hours of 7am and 6.30pm, Monday to Friday (excluding public holidays) was introduced in February 2003. In February 2007, the charge zone roughly doubled in size after a westward expansion and the charging hours were shortened, to finish at 6pm. In January 2011, the westward expansion was removed from the charging zone and an automated payment system was introduced. As at December 2020 the daily congestion charge is £15.00. (**W** www.tfl.gov.uk/modes/driving/congestion-charge).

TfL introduced a low emission zone (LEZ) for London in February 2008; the LEZ covers most of Greater London and is in constant operation for larger vans, minibuses, lorries, buses and other heavy vehicles that do not meet the LEZ emissions standards (cars and motorcycles are exempt). The daily charge is £100 for larger vans, minibuses and other specialist vehicles and £200 for lorries, buses and coaches, although emissions standards are set to become tougher from 1 March 2021. (**W** www.tfl.gov.uk/modes/driving/low-emission-zone).

Since April 2019 a new ultra low emission zone (ULEZ) has operated constantly in central London and covers the same area of central London as the congestion charge. Most vehicles, including cars and vans, need to meet the ULEZ emissions standards or their drivers must pay a daily charge, in addition to the congestion charge and, if applicable, the LEZ, to drive within the zone. As at December 2020 the charge is £12.50 for most vehicle types, including cars, motorcycles and vans (up to and including 3.5 tonnes) and £100 for heavier vehicles, including lorries (over 3.5 tonnes) and buses/coaches (over 5 tonnes). From 25 October 2021 ULEZ is set to expand to create a single larger zone bounded by the north and south circular roads. (**W** www.tfl.gov.uk/modes/driving/ultra-low-emission-zone).

Since January 2009, Londoners over pensionable age (or over 60 if born before 1950) and those with eligible disabilities are entitled to free travel on the capital's transport network at any time. War veterans who are receiving ongoing payments under the war pensions scheme, or those receiving guaranteed income payments under the armed forces compensation scheme can travel free at any time on bus, underground, DLR, tram and London Overground services and at certain times on National Rail services.

In the summer of 2010, the London cycle hire scheme launched with 6,000 new bicycles for hire from 400 docking stations across eight boroughs, the City and the Royal parks. The scheme has been expanded and there are now around 11,500 bicycles available and over 750 docking stations.

Commissioner of TfL, Andy Byford

MAYOR'S OFFICE FOR POLICING AND CRIME (MOPAC)

The Mayor's Office for Policing and Crime (MOPAC) was set up in response to the Police Reform and Social Responsibility Act 2011, replacing the Metropolitan Police Authority. MOPAC is headed by the mayor, or the appointed statutory deputy mayor for policing and crime. Operational responsibility for policing in London belongs to the Metropolitan Police Commissioner. The major areas of focus of MOPAC are:

- operational policing and crime reduction including counter terrorism
- ensuring the Metropolitan Police effectively reduce gang crime and violence in London and coordinating support for communities and local organisations to prevent gang activities
- criminal justice, including preventing reoffending, reducing crime and decreasing demand within the criminal justice system in addition to reducing alcohol and drug abuse.

The Police and Crime Committee consisting of nine elected members of the London Assembly scrutinises the work of MOPAC and meets regularly to hold to account the Deputy Mayor for Policing and Crime.

Deputy Mayor for Policing and Crime, Sophie Linden

LONDON FIRE COMMISSIONER

Under the Policing and Crime Act 2017, the London Fire Commissioner replaced the London Fire and Emergency Planning Authority (LFEPA) and was tasked with overseeing the London Fire Brigade, the fire and rescue authority for London. It consists of three main structural bodies: operational staff and firefighters, control staff and emergency responders, and a non-uniformed support team. Operational staff provide the only full-time fire service in the UK.

The Mayor of London sets its budget, approves its London Safety Plan, and can direct it to act. The London Fire Commissioner is further scrutinised by the Fire, Resilience and Emergency Planning (FREP) Committee of the London Assembly.

Commissioner, Andy Roe

LONDON LEGACY DEVELOPMENT CORPORATION

Following the London 2012 Olympic Games, the London Legacy Development Corporation was made responsible for the long-term planning, development, management and maintenance of the Queen Elizabeth Olympic Park (formerly the Olympic Park) and its facilities. The organisation is tasked with transforming the area into a thriving neighbourhood.

Chair, Sir Peter Hendy, CBE

SALARIES *as at December 2020*

Mayor	£152,734
Chief of Staff	£137,243
Deputy Mayors	
Housing and Residential Development	£132,664
Business	£132,664
Culture and the Creative Industries	£132,664
Transport	£132,664
Environment and Energy	£132,664
Policing and Crime	£127,513
Planning, Regeneration and Skills	£132,664
Social Integration, Social Mobility and Engagement	£132,664
Fire and Resilience	£132,664
Stautory Deputy Mayor (Education and Childcare)	£105,269
Chair of the Assembly	£70,225
Assembly Member	£58,543

STATE OF THE PARTIES *as at December 2020*

Party	Seats
Labour (Lab.)	12
Conservative (C.)	8
Green	2
Brexit Alliance (BA)	2
Liberal Democrats (LD)	1

LONDON ASSEMBLY COMMITTEES
Chair, Audit Panel, Susan Hall, AM
Chair, Budget and Performance Committee, Susan Hall, AM
Chair, Budget Monitoring Sub-Committee, Susan Hall, AM
Chair, Confirmation Hearings Committee, Andrew Boff, AM
Chair, Economy Committee, Leonie Cooper, AM
Chair, Environment Committee, Caroline Russell, AM
Chair, Fire, Resilience and Emergency Planning Committee, Andrew Dismore, AM
Chair, GLA Oversight Committee, Len Duvall, OBE, AM
Chair, Health Committee, Dr Onkar Sahota, AM
Chair, Housing Committee, Murad Queshi, AM
Chair, Planning and Regeneration Committee, Andrew Boff, AM
Chair, Police and Crime Committee, Unmesh Desai, AM
Chair, Transport Committee, Dr Alison Moore

LONDON ASSEMBLY MEMBERS

as at December 2020

Arbour, Tony, *C., South West,* Maj. 21,444
Arnold, Jennette, OBE, *Lab., North East,* Maj. 101,742
Bacon, Gareth, MP, *C., Bexley and Bromley,* Maj. 41,669
Bailey, Shaun, *C., London-wide*
Berry, Sián, *Green, London-wide*
Boff, Andrew, *C., London-wide*
Cooper, Leonie, *Lab., Merton and Wandsworth,* Maj. 4,301
Desai, Unmesh, *Lab., City and East,* Maj. 89,629
Devenish, Tony, *C., West Central,* Maj. 14,564
Dismore, Andrew, *Lab., Barnet and Camden,* Maj. 16,240
Duvall, Len, OBE, *Lab., Greenwich and Lewisham,* Maj. 54,895
Eshalomi, Florence, MP, *Lab., Lambeth and Southwark,* Maj. 62,243
Gavron, Nicky, *Lab., London-wide*
Hall, Susan, *C., London-wide*
Kurten, David, *BA, London-wide*
McCartney, Joanne, *Lab., Enfield and Haringey,* Maj. 51,152
Moore, Dr Alison, *Lab., London-wide*
O'Connell, Steve, *C., Croydon and Sutton,* Maj. 11,614
Pidgeon, Caroline, MBE, *LD, London-wide*
Prince, Keith, *C. Havering and Redbridge,* Maj. 1,438
Murad, Qureshi, *Lab. and Co-op, London-wide*
Russell, Caroline, *Green, London-wide*
Sahota, Dr Onkar, *Lab., Ealing and Hillingdon,* Maj. 15,933
Shah, Navin, *Lab., Brent and Harrow,* Maj. 20,755
Whittle, Peter, *BA, London-wide*

Chair of the London Assembly, Navin Shah

MAYORAL ELECTION RESULTS

as at 5 May 2016

Electorate 5,739,011   Turnout 45.6%

First	Party	Votes	%
Sadiq Khan	Lab.	1,148,716	44.2
Zac Goldsmith	C.	909,755	35.0
Siân Berry	Green	150,673	5.8
Caroline Pidgeon	LD	120,005	4.6
Peter Whittle	UKIP	94,373	3.6
Sophie Walker	Women	53,055	2.0
George Galloway	Respect	37,007	1.4
Paul Golding	Brit. First	31,372	1.2
Lee Harris	CISTA	20,537	0.8
David Furness	BNP	13,325	0.5
Prince Zylinski	Ind.	13,202	0.5
Ankit Love	One Love	4,941	0.2

Second	Party	Votes	%
Sadiq Khan	Lab.	161,427	65.5
Zac Goldsmith	C.	84,859	34.5

LONDON ASSEMBLY ELECTION RESULTS *as at 5 May 2016*

E. Electorate T. Turnout
See General Election Results for a list of party abbreviations

CONSTITUENCIES
E. 5,739,011 T 45.6%

BARNET AND CAMDEN
E. 387,844 T. 47.44%

Andrew Dismore, Lab.	81,482
Daniel Thomas, C.	65,242
Stephen Taylor, Green	16,996
Zack Polanski, LD	11,204
Joseph Langton, UKIP	9,057

Lab. majority 16,240

BEXLEY AND BROMLEY
E. 404,342 T. 46.94%

Gareth Bacon, C.	87,460
Sam Russell, Lab.	45,791
Frank Gould, UKIP	30,485
Roisin Robertson, Green	12,685
Julie Ireland, LD	12,145
Veronica Obadara, APP	1,243

C. majority 41,669

BRENT AND HARROW
E. 381,778 T. 45.76%

Navin Shah, Lab.	79,902
Joel Davidson, C.	59,147
Anton Georgiou, LD	11,534
Jafar Hassan, Green	9,874
Rathy Alagaratnam, UKIP	9,074
Akib Mahmood, Respect GG	5,170

Lab. majority 20,755

CITY AND EAST
E. 503,301 T. 42.01%

Unmesh Desai, Lab.	122,175
Chris Chapman, C.	32,546
Rachel Collinson, Green	18,766
Peter Harris, UKIP	18,071
Elaine Bagshaw, LD	10,714
Rayne Mickail, Respect GG	6,772
Amina Gichinga, TBTC	1,368
Aaron D'Souza, APP	1,009

Lab. majority 89,629

CROYDON AND SUTTON
E. 401,660 T. 45.29%

Steve O'Connell, C.	70,156
Marina Ahmad, Lab.	58,542
Amna Ahmad, LD	18,859
Peter Staveley, UKIP	18,338
Tracey Hague, Green	13,513
Madonna Lewis, APP	1,386
Richard Edmonds, NF	1,106

C. majority 11,614

EALING AND HILLINGDON
E. 444,168 T. 45.25%

Onkar Sahota, Lab.	86,088
Dominic Gilham, C.	70,155
Alex Nieora, UKIP	15,832
Meena Hans, Green	15,758
Francesco Fruzza, LD	13,154

Lab. majority 15,933

ENFIELD AND HARINGEY
E. 377,060 T. 44.73%

Joanne McCartney, Lab.	91,075
Linda Kelly, C.	39,923
Ronald Stewart, Green	15,409
Nicholas da Costa, LD	12,038
Neville Watson, UKIP	9,042
Godson Azu, APP	1,172

Lab. majority 51,152

GREENWICH AND LEWISHAM
E. 362,376 T. 45.08%

Len Duvall, Lab.	85,735
Adam Thomas, C.	30,840
Imogen Solly, Green	20,520
Paul Oakley, UKIP	13,686
Julia Fletcher, LD	11,303
Ajaratu Bangura, APP	1,275

Lab. majority 54,895

HAVERING AND REDBRIDGE
E. 383,234 T. 44.63%

Keith Prince, C.	64,483
Ivana Bartoletti, Lab.	63,045
Lawrence Webb, UKIP	26,788
Lee Burkwood, Green	9,617
Ian Sanderson, LD	7,105

C. majority 1,438

LAMBETH AND SOUTHWARK
E. 426,966 T. 43.98%

Florence Eshalomi, Lab.	96,946
Robert Flint, C.	34,703
Rashid Nix, Green	25,793
Michael Bukola, LD	21,489
Idham Ramadi, UKIP	6,591
Kevin Parkin, SPGB	1,333
Amadu Kanumansa, APP	906

Lab. majority 62,243

MERTON AND WANDSWORTH
E. 374,126 T. 49.56%

Leonie Cooper, Lab.	77,340
David Dean, C.	73,039
Esther Obiri-Darko, Green	14,682
Adrian Hyyrylainen-Trett, LD	10,732
Elizabeth Jones, UKIP	8,478
Thamilini Kulendran, Ind.	1,142

Lab. majority 4,301

NORTH EAST
E. 500,432 T. 45.72%

Jennette Arnold, Lab.	134,307
Sam Malik, C.	32,565
Samir Jeraj, Green	29,401
Terry Stacy, LD	14,312
Freddy Vachha, UKIP	11,315
Tim Allen, Respect GG	5,068
Bill Martin, SPGB	1,293
Jonathan Silberman, Comm L	536

Lab. majority 101,742

SOUTH WEST
E. 435,877 T. 49.04%

Tony Arbour, C.	84,381
Martin Whelton, Lab.	62,937
Rosina Robson, LD	30,654
Andree Frieze, Green	19,745
Alexander Craig, UKIP	14,983
Adam Buick, SPGB	1,065

C. majority 21,444

WEST CENTRAL
E. 348,740 T. 43.96%

Tony Devenish, C.	67,775
Mandy Richards, Lab.	53,211
Jennifer Nadel, Green	14,050
Annabel Mullin, LD	10,577
Clive Egan, UKIP	7,708

C. majority 14,564

LONDON-WIDE MEMBERS

Conservative Party	*Labour Party*
Kemi Badenoch	Fiona Twycross
Andrew Boff	Tom Copley
Shaun Bailey	Nicky Gavron

Green Party	*UKIP*
Sian Berry	Peter Whittle
Caroline Russell	David Kurten

Liberal Democrats
Caroline Pidgeon

LOCAL GOVERNMENT

Major changes in local government were introduced in England and Wales in 1974 and in Scotland in 1975 by the Local Government Act 1972 and the Local Government (Scotland) Act 1973. Additional alterations were made in England by the Local Government Acts of 1985, 1992 and 2000.

The structure in England was based on two tiers of local authorities (county councils and district councils) in the non-metropolitan areas; and a single tier of metropolitan councils in the six metropolitan areas of England and London borough councils in London.

Following reviews of the structure of local government in England by the Local Government Commission (now the Boundary Commission for England), 46 unitary (all-purpose) authorities were created between April 1995 and April 1998 to cover certain areas in the non-metropolitan counties. The remaining county areas continue to have two tiers of local authorities. The county and district councils in the Isle of Wight were replaced by a single unitary authority in April 1995; the former counties of Avon, Cleveland, Humberside and Berkshire were replaced by unitary authorities; and Hereford & Worcester was replaced by a new county council for Worcestershire (with district councils) and a unitary authority for Herefordshire. In April 2009 the county areas of Cornwall, Durham, Northumberland, Shropshire and Wiltshire were given unitary status and two new unitary authorities were created for Bedfordshire (Bedford and Central Bedfordshire) and Cheshire (Cheshire East and Cheshire West & Chester) replacing the two-tier county/district system in these areas.

In April 2019 Dorset's nine councils merged into two unitary authorities. Bournemouth and Poole unitary authorities merged with Christchurch district council to become Bournemouth, Christchurch and Poole (BCP) unitary authority, while Dorset unitary authority was formed from Dorset County Council together with East Dorset, North Dorset, Purbeck, Weymouth & Portland and West Dorset district councils. Also in April 2019, in what is expected to be a continuing trend in order to share resources and make financial savings, a total of six district councils merged into three new district authorities. The three councils, East Suffolk, West Suffolk and Somerset West and Taunton, continue to operate at district level. Similarly, in April 2020 four non-metropolitan districts in Buckinghamshire merged with Buckinghamshire County Council to form a new unitary authority, Buckinghamshire Council.

The Local Government (Wales) Act 1994 and the Local Government etc (Scotland) Act 1994 abolished the two-tier structure in Wales and Scotland with effect from April 1996, replacing it with a single tier of unitary authorities.

In Northern Ireland a reform programme to reduce the number of local authorities from 26 to 11 began in 2012 when legislation finalising the boundaries of the new 11 local government district authorities was approved by the Northern Ireland Assembly. The Local Government Act (Northern Ireland) 2014 received royal assent on 12 May 2014, providing the legislative framework for the 11 new councils. On 1 April 2015 additional functions, previously the responsibility of the Northern Ireland executive, fully transferred to the new district authorities.

ELECTIONS

Local elections are normally held on the first Thursday in May. Generally, all citizens of the UK, the Republic of Ireland, Commonwealth and other European Union citizens who are 18 years or over and resident on the qualifying date in the area for which the election is being held, are entitled to vote at local government elections. A register of electors is prepared and published annually by local electoral registration officers.

A returning officer has the overall responsibility for an election. Voting takes place at polling stations, arranged by the local authority and under the supervision of a presiding officer specially appointed for the purpose. Candidates, who are subject to various statutory qualifications and disqualifications designed to ensure that they are suitable to hold office, must be nominated by electors for the electoral area concerned.

In England, the Local Government Boundary Commission for England is responsible for carrying out periodic reviews of electoral arrangements, to consider whether the boundaries of wards or divisions within a local authority need to be altered to take account of changes in electorate; structural reviews, to consider whether a single, unitary authority should be established in an area instead of an existing two-tier system; and administrative boundary reviews of district or county authorities.

The Local Democracy and Boundary Commission for Wales, the Local Government Boundary Commission for Scotland and the local government boundary commissioner for Northern Ireland (appointed when required by the Boundary Commission for Northern Ireland) are responsible for reviewing the electoral arrangements and boundaries of local authorities within their respective regions.

The Local Government Act 2000 provided for the secretary of state to change the frequency and phasing of elections in England and Wales.

LOCAL GOVERNMENT BOUNDARY COMMISSION FOR ENGLAND, SW1H 0TL1st Floor, Windsor House, 50 Victoria Street, London SW1H 0TL **T** 0330-500 1525 **E** reviews@lgbce.org.uk **W** www.lgbce.org.uk

LOCAL DEMOCRACY AND BOUNDARY COMMISSION FOR WALES, Ground Floor, Hastings House, Fitzalan Court, Cardiff CF24 0BL **T** 029-2046 4819 **E** enquiries@boundaries.wales **W** www.ldbc.gov.wales

LOCAL GOVERNMENT BOUNDARY COMMISSION FOR SCOTLAND, Thistle House, 91 Haymarket Terrace, Edinburgh EH12 5HD **T** 0131-244 2001 **E** lgbcs@scottishboundaries.gov.uk **W** www.lgbc-scotland.gov.uk

BOUNDARY COMMISSION FOR NORTHERN IRELAND, The Bungalow, Stormont House, Stormont Estate, Belfast BT4 3SH **T** 028-9052 7821 **E** contact@boundarycommission.org.uk **W** www.boundarycommission.org.uk

LOCAL GOVERNMENT DEVOLUTION

Local government is a devolved matter in Scotland, Wales and Northern Ireland.

In England, under the Cities and Local Government Devolution Act 2016, multiple local authorities can combine and take on more functions, over and above those they were allowed to take on under previous legislation. In order for a combined or 'regional' authority to be given these extra powers a mayor must be elected for the region by the electorate in the combined-authority area. The first six combined authority mayoral elections took place in May 2017. The exact functions the combined authority and mayor manage varies depending on the devolution agreement reached with central government, but the directly elected 'metro' mayor does have powers and responsibilities to make strategic decisions across whole city regions. This is in contrast to existing city mayors (which are also directly elected) or local council leaders that only make decisions for, and on behalf of, their local authority (*see* Internal Organisation). To date, ten combined authorities have been established, eight of which have a mayor and a devolution agreement with national government (*see* Combined Authorities for a complete list).

INTERNAL ORGANISATION

The council as a whole is the final decision-making body within any authority. Councils are free to a great extent to make their own internal organisational arrangements. The Local Government Act, given royal assent on 28 July 2000, allows councils to adopt one of three broad categories of constitution which include a separate executive:
• A directly elected mayor with a cabinet selected by that mayor
• A cabinet, either elected by the council or appointed by its leader
• A directly elected mayor and council manager

Normally, questions of policy are settled by the full council, while the administration of the various services is the responsibility of committees of councillors. Day-to-day decisions are delegated to the council's officers, who act within the policies laid down by the councillors.

FINANCE

Local government in England, Wales and Scotland is financed from four sources: council tax, non-domestic rates, government grants and income from fees and charges for services.

COUNCIL TAX
Council tax is a local tax levied by each local council. Liability for the council tax bill usually falls on the owner-occupier or tenant of a dwelling which is their sole or main residence. Council tax bills may be reduced because of the personal circumstances of people resident in a property and there are discounts in the case of dwellings occupied by fewer than two adults.

In England, unitary and metropolitan authorities are responsible for collecting their own council tax. In areas where there are two tiers of local authority, each county and district authority sets its own council tax rate; the district authorities collect the combined council tax and the county councils claim their share from the district councils' collection funds. In Wales and Scotland each unitary authority sets its own council tax rate and is responsible for collection.

The tax relates to the value of the dwelling. In England and Scotland each dwelling is placed in one of eight valuation bands, ranging from A to H, based on the property's estimated market value as at 1 April 1991. In Wales there are nine bands, ranging from A to I, based on the estimated market value of property as at 1 April 2003.

The valuation bands and ranges of values in England, Wales and Scotland are:

England

A	Up to £40,000	E	£88,001–£120,000
B	£40,001–£52,000	F	£120,001–£160,000
C	£52,001–£68,000	G	£160,001–£320,000
D	£68,001–£88,000	H	Over £320,001

Wales

A	Up to £44,000	F	£162,001–£223,000
B	£44,001–£65,000	G	£223,001–£324,000
C	£65,001–£91,000	H	£324,001–£424,000
D	£91,001–£123,000	I	Over £424,000
E	£123,001–£162,000		

Scotland

A	Up to £27,000	E	£58,001–£80,000
B	£27,001–£35,000	F	£80,001–£106,000
C	£35,001–£45,000	G	£106,001–£212,000
D	£45,001–£58,000	H	Over £212,000

The council tax within a local area varies between the different bands according to proportions laid down by law. The charge attributable to each band as a proportion of the Band D charge set by the council is:

A	67%	F	144%
B	78%	G	167%
C	89%	H	200%
D	100%	I*	233%
E	122%		

* Wales only

The Band D council tax bill for 2019–20, inclusive of adult social care and parish precepts, for each authority area is given in the complete lists of local authorities for England, London, Wales and Scotland which follow. There may be variations from the given figure within each district council area because of different parish or community precepts being levied, the personal circumstances of the residents in a property or in the case of dwellings occupied by fewer than two adults.

Domestic property in Northern Ireland is subjected to a rateable system based on the capital value of a property as at 1 January 2005 *see* Northern Ireland, Finance for further information.

NON-DOMESTIC RATES
Non-domestic (business) rates are collected by billing authorities; these are the district councils in those areas of England with two tiers of local government and unitary authorities in other parts of England, in Wales and in Scotland. In respect of England and Wales, the Local Government Finance Act 1988 provides for liability for rates to be assessed on the basis of a poundage (multiplier) tax on the rateable value of property (hereditaments). Separate multipliers are set by the Ministry of Housing, Communities and Local Government (MHCLG) in England, the Welsh government and the Scottish government. Rates are collected by the billing authority for the area where a property is located. Rate income collected by billing authorities is paid into a national non-domestic rating (NNDR) pool and redistributed to individual authorities on the basis of the adult population figure as prescribed by MHCLG, the Welsh government or the Scottish government. The rates pools are maintained separately in England, Wales and Scotland. Actual payment of rates in certain cases is subject to transitional arrangements, to phase in the larger increases and reductions in rates resulting from the effects of the latest revaluation.

The most recent rating lists for England, Wales and Scotland came into effect on 1 April 2017. The rateable values on these lists are derived from the rental value of property as at 1 April 2015 and determined on certain statutory assumptions by the Valuation Office Agency in England and Wales, and by local area assessors in Scotland. New property which is added to the list, and significant changes to existing property, necessitate amendments to the rateable value on the same basis. Rating lists (valuation rolls in Scotland) remain in force until the next general revaluation, which usually takes place every five years to reflect changes in the property market.

A revaluation of non-domestic properties in Northern Ireland was completed at the start of 2015, enforced after 1 April 2015, and a revised rate introduced on 1 April 2020 based on the rental value of the property as at 1 April 2018.

Certain types of property are exempt from rates, for example agricultural land and buildings, buildings used for the training or welfare of disabled people and buildings registered for public religious worship. Charities and other non-profit-making organisations may receive full or partial relief and relief schemes for small businesses are available in England, Wales, Scotland and Northern Ireland. Empty commercial property in England and Wales is exempt from business rates for the first three months that the property is vacant, empty industrial property for six months and listed buildings are exempt until re-occupied; after which full business rates are normally payable. In Scotland empty commercial property is entitled to a 50 per cent discount on business rates for the first three months and a 10 per cent discount thereafter, empty industrial buildings are entitled to full relief for six months and a 10 per cent discount thereafter and empty listed buildings and properties with a rateable value of less than £1,700 are entirely exempt. In Northern Ireland all vacant non-domestic property, which has been previously occupied for at least six weeks, is entirely exempt from rates for three months, after this period, rates are billed at 50 per cent of the normal occupied amount.

COMPLAINTS

In England the Local Government and Social Care Ombudsman investigates complaints of injustice arising from maladministration by local authorities about most council services, including planning, some housing issues, social care, some education and schools issues, children's services, housing benefit, council tax, transport and highways, environment and waste, neighbour nuisance and antisocial behaviour and service failure by local authorities, schools and all registered social care providers, including all adult social care complaints. The Local Government Ombudsman will not usually consider a complaint unless the local authority concerned has had an opportunity to investigate and reply to a complainant.

The functions of the Local Government Ombudsman for Wales were subsumed into the office of Public Services Ombudsman for Wales on 1 April 2006 and the Scottish Public Services Ombudsman is responsible for complaints regarding the maladministration of local government in Scotland.

The Office of Northern Ireland Public Services Ombudsman (NIPSO) was established in April 2016, replacing and expanding the functions of the Northern Ireland Assembly Ombudsman and Commissioner for Complaints. NIPSO provides an independent review of complaints of members of the public, where they believe they have sustained an injustice or hardship as a result or inaction of a public service provider. NIPSO additionally ensures that public services improve as a result of the complaints brought to them by the public. The professional, independent and impartial service is provided free of charge to the citizens of Northern Ireland.

LOCAL GOVERNMENT AND SOCIAL CARE OMBUDSMAN, PO Box 4771, Coventry CV4 0EH
T 0300-061 0614 W www.lgo.org.uk
Ombudsman, Michael King
PUBLIC SERVICES OMBUDSMAN FOR WALES, 1 Ffordd yr Hen Gae, Pencoed CF35 5LJ T 0300-790 0203
E ask@ombudsman.wales W www.ombudsman-wales.org.uk
Ombudsman, Nick Bennett

SCOTTISH PUBLIC SERVICES OMBUDSMAN, Bridgeside House, 99 McDonald Road, Edinburgh EH7 4NS
T 0800-377 7330 E ask@spso.org.scot W www.spso.org.uk
Ombudsman, Rosemary Agnew
NORTHERN IRELAND PUBLIC SERVICES OMBUDSMAN, Progressive House, 33 Wellington Place, Belfast BT1 6HN T 028-9023 3821 E nipso@nipso.org.uk
W www.nipso.org.uk
Ombudsman, Margaret Kelly

THE QUEEN'S REPRESENTATIVES

The lord-lieutenant of a county is the permanent local representative of the Crown in that county. The appointment of lord-lieutenants is now regulated by the Lieutenancies Act 1997. They are appointed by the sovereign on the recommendation of the prime minister. The retirement age is 75. The office of lord-lieutenant dates from 1551, and its holder was originally responsible for maintaining order and for local defence in the county. The duties of the post include attending on royalty during official visits to the county, performing certain duties in connection with the armed forces (and in particular the reserve forces), and making presentations of honours and awards on behalf of the Crown. In England, Wales and Northern Ireland, the lord-lieutenant usually also holds the office of *Custos Rotulorum*. As such, he or she acts as head of the county's commission of the peace (which recommends the appointment of magistrates).

The office of sheriff (from the Old English *shire-reeve*) of a county was created in the tenth century. The sheriff was the special nominee of the sovereign, and the office reached the peak of its influence under the Norman kings. The Provisions of Oxford (1258) laid down a yearly tenure of office. Since the mid-16th century the office has been purely civil, with military duties taken over by the lord-lieutenant of the county. The sheriff (commonly known as 'high sheriff') attends on royalty during official visits to the county, acts as the returning officer during parliamentary elections in county constituencies, attends the opening ceremony when a high court judge goes on circuit, executes high court writs, and appoints under-sheriffs to act as deputies. The appointments and duties of the sheriffs in England and Wales are laid down by the Sheriffs Act 1887.

The serving high sheriff submits a list of names of possible future sheriffs to a tribunal, which chooses three names to put to the sovereign. The tribunal nominates the high sheriff annually on 12 November and the sovereign picks the name of the sheriff to succeed in the following year. The term of office runs from 25 March to the following 24 March (the civil and legal year before 1752). No person may be chosen twice in three years if there is any other suitable person in the county.

CIVIC DIGNITIES

District councils in England and local councils in Wales may petition for a royal charter granting borough or 'city' status to the council.

In England and Wales the chair of a borough or county borough council may be called a mayor, and the chair of a city council may be called a lord mayor (if lord mayoralty has been conferred on that city). Parish councils in England and community councils in Wales may call themselves 'town councils', in which case their chair is the town mayor.

In Scotland the chair of a local council may be known as a convenor; a provost is the mayoral equivalent. The chair of the councils for the cities of Aberdeen, Dundee, Edinburgh and Glasgow are lord provosts.

ENGLAND

The country of England lies between 55° 46′ and 49° 57′ 30″ N. latitude (from a few miles north of the mouth of the Tweed to the Lizard), and between 1° 46′ E. and 5° 43′ W. longitude (from Lowestoft to Land's End). England is bounded on the north by the Cheviot Hills; on the south by the English Channel; on the east by the Straits of Dover (Pas de Calais) and the North Sea; and on the west by the Atlantic Ocean, Wales and the Irish Sea. It has a total area of 130,309 sq. km (50,313 sq. miles).

There are currently 339 local authorities, divided into 25 county councils, 188 district councils, 56 unitary authorities (including the Isles of Scilly), and 126 single-tier authorities including 36 metropolitan boroughs and 33 London Boroughs (including the Corporation of London). *See* Local Government, London for information on London Borough councils and the Corporation of London.

POPULATION
The population at the mid-2019 estimate was 56,286,961 (27,827,831 males; 28,459,130 females), a 0.55 per cent increase on mid-2018. The average density of the population at the mid-2019 estimate was 432 persons per sq. km (1,113 per sq. mile).

The populations of most of the unitary authorities are in the range of 100,000 to 500,000. The district councils have populations broadly in the range of 60,000 to 200,000; some, however, have larger populations, because of the need to avoid dividing large towns, or because they were formed from the merger of multiple district councils, and some in mainly rural areas have smaller populations.

The main conurbations outside Greater London – Tyne and Wear, West Midlands, Merseyside, Greater Manchester, West Yorkshire and South Yorkshire – are divided into 36 metropolitan boroughs, most of which have a population of over 200,000.

ELECTIONS
For districts, counties and for around 9,000 towns and parishes, there are elected councils, consisting of directly elected councillors. The councillors elect one of their number as chair annually.

In general, councils can have whole council elections, elections by thirds or elections by halves. However all metropolitan authorities must hold elections by thirds. The electoral cycle of any new unitary authority is specified in the appropriate statutory order under which it is established.

COMBINED AUTHORITIES
Under the Cities and Local Government Devolution Act 2016, multiple local authorities can combine and take on more functions, over and above those they were allowed to take on under previous legislation. In order for a combined or 'regional' authority to be given these extra powers a mayor must be elected for the region by the electorate in the combined-authority area. The first six combined authority mayoral elections took place in May 2017.

The exact functions the combined authority and mayor manage varies depending on the devolution agreement reached with central government, but the directly elected 'metro' mayor does have powers and responsibilities to make strategic decisions across whole city regions. This is in contrast to existing city mayors (which are also directly elected) or local council leaders that only make decisions for, and on behalf of, their local authority.

On 2 November 2018, the North East combined authority was divided into two. The boundaries of the re-constituted North East combined authority now cover the local authorities of Durham, Gateshead, South Tyneside and Sunderland, while the boundaries of the newly created North of Tyne combined authority cover the local authorities of Newcastle, North Tyneside and Northumberland. As at July 2019, ten combined authorities had been established, eight of which have a mayor and a devolution agreement with national government. The combined authorities comprise constituent and non-constituent councils and other local authorities. Constituent councils have full voting rights and cannot be a member of another combined authority. Non-constituent councils usually have restricted voting rights, although this decision rests with the combined authority. In addition, non-constituent councils can be a member of more than one combined authority, as long as this is also on a non-constituent basis. *See* the list of Combined Authorities for details of the devolved regions, their mayors and constituent councils.

COUNCIL FUNCTIONS
In areas with a two-tier system of local governance, functions are divided between the district and county authorities, with those functions affecting the larger area or population generally being the responsibility of the county council. A few functions continue to be exercised over the larger area by joint bodies, made up of councillors from each authority within the area.

Generally the allocation of functions is as follows:

County councils: education; strategic planning; traffic, transport and highways; fire service; consumer protection; refuse disposal; smallholdings; social care; libraries

District councils: local planning; housing; highways (maintenance of certain urban roads and off-street car parks); building regulations; environmental health; refuse collection; cemeteries and crematoria; collection of council tax and non-domestic rates

Unitary and metropolitan councils: their functions are all those listed above, except that the fire service is exercised by a joint body

Concurrently by county and district councils: recreation (parks, playing fields, swimming pools); museums; encouragement of the arts, tourism and industry

PARISH COUNCILS
Parish or town councils are the most local tier of government in England. There are currently 10,219 parishes in England, of which 8,859 have councils. Since February 2008 local councils have been able to create new parish councils without seeking approval from the government. Around 80 per cent of parish councils represent populations of less than 2,500; parishes with no parish council can be grouped with neighbouring parishes under a common parish council. A parish council comprises at least five members, the number being fixed by the district council. Elections are held every four years, at the time of the election of the district councillor for the ward including the parish. Full parish councils must be formed for those parishes with more than 999 electors – below this number, parish meetings comprising the electors of the parish must be held at least twice a year.

Parish council functions include: allotments; encouragement of arts and crafts; community halls, recreational facilities (for example open spaces, swimming pools), cemeteries and crematoria; and many minor functions. They must also be given an opportunity to comment on planning applications. They may, like county and district councils, spend limited sums for the general benefit of the parish. They levy a precept on the district councils for their funds. Parish precepts for 2020–21 total £580m, an increase of 2.9 per cent on 2019–20.

FINANCE

Total revenue expenditure by all local authorities in England for 2020-21 was £102.4bn; of this £33.1bn was estimated to be raised through council tax, £16.5bn from the business rate retention scheme and £51.5bn from government grants. The remainder will be derived from additional COVID-19 government grants, and also drawn from local authority reserves.

Since April 2013 local authorities retain a share of business rates and keep the growth on that share (the 'rate retention scheme'). Revenue support grant is paid to local authorities to enable all authorities in the same class to broadly set the same council tax; in 2020–21 revenue support grant totals £1.6bn. In addition central government pays specific grants in support of revenue expenditure on particular services. Police grant totals £7.9bn in 2020–21. In 2020–21, local authorities' allocated adult social care expenditure increased by £568m on 2019–20, to £17.7bn, and children's social care rose by £529m to £9.8bn.

In response to COVID-19 the government introduced several additional grants in 2020–21, including £3.2bn of emergency funding and £5bn of cashflow support, a £500m hardship fund, and grants to small businesses worth £12.3bn.

In England, the average council tax per dwelling for 2020–21 is £1,385, an increase of 4.4 per cent from 2019–20. The average council tax bill for a Band D dwelling (occupied by two adults, including adult social care and parish precepts) for 2020–21 is £1,818, an increase of 3.9 per cent from 2019–20. The average Band D council tax is £1,895 in shire districts, £1,809 in metropolitan areas, £1,886 in unitary authority areas and £1,534 in London.

The non-domestic rating multiplier for England for 2020–21 is 51.2p (49.9p for small businesses). The City of London is able to set a different multiplier from the rest of England; for 2019–20 this is 52p (50.7p for small businesses).

Under the Local Government and Housing Act 1989, local authorities have four main ways of paying for capital expenditure: borrowing and other forms of extended credit; capital grants from central government towards some types of capital expenditure; 'usable' capital receipts from the sale of land, houses and other assets; and revenue.

The amount of capital expenditure which a local authority can finance by borrowing (or other forms of credit) is effectively limited by the credit approvals issued to it by central government. Most credit approvals can be used for any kind of local authority capital expenditure; these are known as basic credit approvals. Others (supplementary credit approvals) can be used only for the kind of expenditure specified in the approval, and so are often given to fund particular projects or services.

Local authorities can use all capital receipts from the sale of property or assets for capital spending, except in the case of sales of council houses. Generally, the 'usable' part of a local authority's capital receipts consists of 25 per cent of receipts from the sale of council houses and 50 per cent of other housing assets such as shops or vacant land. The balance has to be set aside as provision for repaying debt and meeting other credit liabilities.

EXPENDITURE

Budgeted revenue expenditure for 2020–21 is:

Service	£ million
Education	34,349
Highways and transport	3,915
Children's social care	9,814
Adult social care	17,686
Public health	3,313
Housing (excluding HRA)	1,864
Cultural	2,189
Environmental	5,414
Planning & development	1,378
Police	12,986
Fire and rescue	2,284
Central	3,066
Other	525
Total Service Expenditure	98,782
*Housing benefits	15,899
Parish precepts	580
†Levies & trading account and other adjustments	(522)
Total Net Current Expenditure	114,735
Non-current Expenditure and External Receipts	
Capital expenditure charged to revenue account	1,665
Housing benefits subsidies	(15,857)
Community infrastructure levy	(120)
Capital financing and debt servicing	4,894
REVENUE EXPENDITURE	102,389

HRA = Housing Revenue Account
* Includes all mandatory and non-mandatory housing benefits
† Includes Integrated Transport Authority levy, Waste Disposal Authority levy, London Pensions Fund Authority levy and other levies

RELIEF

There is a marked division between the upland and lowland areas of England. In the extreme north the Cheviot Hills (highest point, the Cheviot, 815m/2,674ft) form a natural boundary with Scotland. Running south from the Cheviots, though divided from them by the Tyne Gap, is the Pennine range (highest point, Cross Fell, 893m/2,930ft), the main orological feature of the country. The Pennines culminate in the Peak District of Derbyshire (Kinder Scout, 636m/2,088ft). West of the Pennines are the Cumbrian mountains, which include Scafell Pike (978m/3,210ft), the highest peak in England, and to the east are the Yorkshire Moors, their highest point being Urra Moor (454m/1,490ft).

In the west, the foothills of the Welsh mountains extend into the bordering English counties of Shropshire (the Wrekin, 407m/1,334ft; Long Mynd, 516m/1,694ft) and Hereford and Worcester (the Malvern Hills – Worcestershire Beacon, 425m/1,394ft). Extensive areas of highland and moorland are also to be found in the south-western peninsula formed by Somerset, Devon and Cornwall, principally Exmoor (Dunkery Beacon, 519m/1,704ft), Dartmoor (High Willhays, 621m/2,038ft) and Bodmin Moor (Brown Willy, 420m/1,377ft). Ranges of low, undulating hills run across the south of the country, including the Cotswolds in the Midlands and southwest, the Chilterns to the north of London, and the North (Kent) and South (Sussex) Downs of the south-east coastal areas.

The lowlands of England lie in the Vale of York, East Anglia and the area around the Wash. The lowest-lying are the Cambridgeshire Fens in the valleys of the Great Ouse and the river Nene, which are below sea-level in places. Since the 17th century extensive drainage has brought much of the Fens under cultivation. The North Sea coast between the Thames and the Humber, low-lying and formed of sand and shingle for the most part, is subject to erosion and defences against further incursion have been built along many stretches.

HYDROGRAPHY

The Severn is the longest river in Great Britain, rising on the north-eastern slopes of Plynlimon (Wales) and entering England in Shropshire, with a total length of 354km (220 miles) from its source to its outflow into the Bristol Channel, where it receives the Bristol Avon on the east and the Wye on the west; its other tributaries are the Vyrnwy, Tern, Stour, Teme and Upper (or Warwickshire) Avon. The Severn is tidal below Gloucester, and a high bore or tidal wave sometimes reverses the flow as high as Tewkesbury (21.75km/13.5 miles above Gloucester). The Severn Tunnel was begun in 1873 and completed in 1886 at a cost of £2m and after many difficulties caused by flooding. It is 7km (4 miles 628 yards) in length (of which 3.67km/2.25 miles are under the river). The Severn road bridge between Haysgate, Gwent, and Almondsbury, Glos, with a centre span of 988m (3,240ft), was opened in 1966.

The longest river wholly in England is the Thames, with a total length of 346km (215 miles) from its source in the Cotswold hills to the Nore. The Thames is tidal to Teddington (111km/69 miles from its mouth) and forms county boundaries almost throughout its course; on its banks are situated London, Windsor Castle, Eton College and Oxford University. Of the remaining English rivers, those flowing into the North Sea are the Tyne, Wear, Tees, Ouse and Trent from the Pennine Range, the Great Ouse (257km/160 miles), which rises in Northamptonshire, and the Orwell and Stour from the hills of East Anglia. Flowing into the English Channel are the Sussex Ouse from the Weald, the Itchen from the Hampshire hills, and the Axe, Teign, Dart, Tamar and Exe from the Devonian hills. Flowing into the Irish Sea are the Mersey, Ribble and Eden from the western slopes of the Pennines and the Derwent from the Cumbrian mountains.

The English Lakes, notable for their picturesque scenery and poetic associations, lie in Cumbria's Lake District, designated a UNESCO World Heritage Site in 2017 for its cultural significance. The largest lakes are Windermere (14.7 sq. km/5.7 sq. miles), Ullswater (8.8 sq. km/3.4 sq. miles) and Derwent Water (5.3 sq. km/2.0 sq. miles).

FLAG

The flag of England is the cross of St George, a red cross on a white field (cross gules in a field argent). The cross of St George, the patron saint of England, has been used since the 13th century.

ISLANDS

The Isle of Wight is separated from Hampshire by the Solent. The capital, Newport, stands at the head of the estuary of the Medina, and Cowes (at the mouth) is the chief port. Other centres are Ryde, Sandown, Shanklin, Ventnor, Freshwater, Yarmouth, Totland Bay, Seaview and Bembridge.

Lundy (the name is derived from the Old Norse for 'puffin island'), 18km (11 miles) north-west of Hartland Point, Devon, is around 5km (3 miles) long and almost 1km (half a mile) wide on average, with a total area of around 452 hectares (1,116 acres), and a population of 28. It became the property of the National Trust in 1969 and is financed, administered and maintained by the Landmark Trust. Lundy is principally a bird sanctuary; the waters around the island were formerly designated as a marine conservation zone in 2013.

The Isles of Scilly comprise around 140 islands and skerries (total area, 10 sq. km/6 sq. miles) situated 45 km (28 miles) south-west of Land's End in Cornwall. Only five are inhabited: St Mary's, St Agnes, Bryher, Tresco and St Martin's. The 2019 mid-year population estimate was 2,242. The entire group has been designated an Area of Outstanding Natural Beauty because of its unique flora and fauna. Tourism and the winter/spring flower trade for the home market form the basis of the economy of the islands.

EARLY HISTORY

Archaeological evidence suggests that England has been inhabited since at least the Palaeolithic period, though the extent of the various Palaeolithic cultures was dependent upon the degree of glaciation. The succeeding Neolithic and Bronze Age cultures have left abundant remains throughout the country; the best-known of these are the henges and stone circles of Stonehenge (ten miles north of Salisbury, Wilts) and Avebury (Wilts). In the latter part of the Bronze Age the Goidels, a people of the Celtic race, invaded the country and brought with them Celtic civilisation and dialects; as a result place names in England bear witness to the spread of the invasion across the whole region.

THE ROMAN CONQUEST

The Roman conquest of Gaul (57–50 BC) brought Britain into close contact with Roman civilisation, but although Julius Caesar raided the south of Britain in 55 and 54 BC, conquest was not undertaken until nearly 100 years later. In AD 43 the Emperor Claudius dispatched Aulus Plautius, with a well-equipped force of 40,000, and himself followed with reinforcements in the same year. Success was delayed by the resistance of Caratacus (Caractacus), the British leader from AD 48–51, who was finally captured and sent to Rome, and by a great revolt in AD 61 led by Boudicca (Boadicea), Queen of the Iceni, but the south of Britain was secured by AD 70, and Wales and the area north to the Tyne by about AD 80.

In AD 122, the Emperor Hadrian visited Britain and built a continuous rampart, since known as Hadrian's Wall, from Wallsend to Bowness (Tyne to Solway). The work was entrusted by the Emperor Hadrian to Aulus Platorius Nepos, legate of Britain from AD 122 to 126, and it was intended to form the northern frontier of the Roman Empire.

The Romans administered Britain as a province under a governor, with a well-defined system of local government, each Roman municipality ruling itself and its surrounding territory, while London was the centre of the road system and the seat of the financial officials of the Province of Britain. Colchester, Lincoln, York, Gloucester and St Albans stand on the sites of five Roman municipalities, and Wroxeter, Caerleon, Chester, Lincoln and York were at various times the sites of legionary fortresses. Well-preserved Roman towns have been uncovered at or near Silchester *(Calleva Atrebatum)*, ten miles south of Reading, Wroxeter *(Viroconium Cornoviorum)*, near Shrewsbury and St Albans *(Verulamium)* in Hertfordshire.

Four main groups of roads radiated from London, and a fifth (the Fosse) ran obliquely from Lincoln through Leicester, Cirencester and Bath to Exeter. Of the four groups radiating from London, one ran south-east to Canterbury and the coast of Kent, a second to Silchester and thence to parts of western Britain and south Wales, a third (later known as Watling Street) ran through St Albans to Chester, with various branches, and the fourth reached Colchester, Lincoln, York and the eastern counties.

In the fourth century Britain was subjected to raids along the east coast by Saxon pirates, which led to the establishment of a system of coastal defences from the Wash to Southampton Water, with forts at Brancaster, Burgh Castle (Yarmouth), Walton (Felixstowe), Bradwell, Reculver, Richborough, Dover, Lympne, Pevensey and Porchester (Portsmouth). The Irish (Scoti) and Picts in the north were also becoming more aggressive and from around AD 350 incursions became more frequent and more formidable. As the Roman Empire came increasingly under attack towards the end of the fourth century, many troops were removed from Britain for service in other parts of the empire. The island was eventually cut off from Rome by the Teutonic conquest of Gaul, and with the withdrawal of the last Roman garrison early in the fifth century, the Romano-British were left to themselves.

SAXON SETTLEMENT
According to legend, the British King Vortigern called in the Saxons to defend his lands against the Picts. The Saxon chieftains Hengist and Horsa landed at Ebbsfleet, Kent, and established themselves in the Isle of Thanet, but the events during the one-and-a-half centuries between the final break with Rome and the re-establishment of Christianity are unclear. However, it would appear that over the course of this period the raids turned into large-scale settlement by invaders traditionally known as Angles (England north of the Wash and East Anglia), Saxons (Essex and southern England) and Jutes (Kent and the Weald), which pushed the Romano-British into the mountainous areas of the north and west. Celtic culture outside Wales and Cornwall survives only in topographical names. Various kingdoms established at this time attempted to claim overlordship of the whole country, hegemony finally being achieved by Wessex (with the capital at Winchester) in the ninth century. This century also saw the beginning of raids by the Vikings (Danes), which were resisted by Alfred the Great (871–899), who fixed a limit on the advance of Danish settlement in the Treaty of Wedmore (878), giving them the area north and east of Watling Street on the condition that they adopt Christianity.

In the tenth century the kings of Wessex recovered the whole of England from the Danes, but subsequent rulers were unable to resist a second wave of invaders. England paid tribute (Danegeld) for many years, and was invaded in 1013 by the Danes and ruled by Danish kings (including Cnut) from 1016 until 1042, when Edward the Confessor was recalled from exile in Normandy. On Edward's death in 1066 Harold Godwinson (brother-in-law of Edward and son of Earl Godwin of Wessex) was chosen to be King of England. After defeating (at Stamford Bridge, Yorkshire, 25 September 1066) an invading army under Harald Hadraada, King of Norway (aided by the outlawed Earl Tostig of Northumbria, Harold's brother), Harold was himself defeated at the Battle of Hastings on 14 October 1066, and the Norman conquest secured the throne of England for Duke William of Normandy, a cousin of Edward the Confessor.

CHRISTIANITY
Christianity reached the Roman province of Britain from Gaul in the third century (or possibly earlier). Alban, traditionally Britain's first martyr, was put to death as a Christian during the persecution of Diocletian (22 June 303) in his native town Verulamium, and the bishops of Londinium, Eboracum (York), and Lindum (Lincoln) attended the Council of Arles in 314. However, the Anglo-Saxon invasions submerged the Christian religion in England until the sixth century: conversion was undertaken in the north from 563 by Celtic missionaries from Ireland led by St Columba, and in the south by a mission sent from Rome in 597 which was led by St Augustine, who became the first archbishop of Canterbury. England appears to have been converted again by the end of the seventh century and followed, after the Council of Whitby in 663, the practices of the Roman Church, which brought the kingdom into the mainstream of European thought and culture.

PRINCIPAL CITIES

There are 51 cities in England and space constraints prevent us from including profiles of them all. Below is a selection of England's principal cities with the date on which city status was conferred in parentheses. Other cities are Bradford (pre-

1900), Chelmsford (2012), Chichester (pre-1900), Coventry (pre-1900), Derby (1977), Ely (pre-1900), Exeter (pre-1900), Gloucester (pre-1900), Hereford (pre-1900), Kingston-upon-Hull (pre-1900), Lancaster (1937), Lichfield (pre-1900), London (pre-1900), Peterborough (pre-1900), Plymouth (1928), Portsmouth (1926), Preston (2002), Ripon (pre-1900), Salford (1926), Stoke-on-Trent (1925), Sunderland (1992), Truro (pre-1900), Wakefield (pre-1900), Wells (pre-1900), Westminster (pre-1900), Wolverhampton (2000) and Worcester (pre-1900).

Certain cities have also been granted a lord mayoralty – this grant confers no additional powers or functions and is purely honorific. Cities with lord mayors are Birmingham, Bradford, Bristol, Canterbury, Chester, Coventry, Exeter, Kingston-upon-Hull, Leeds, Leicester, Liverpool, London, Manchester, Newcastle-upon-Tyne, Norwich, Nottingham, Oxford, Plymouth, Portsmouth, Sheffield, Stoke-on-Trent, Westminster and York.

BATH (PRE-1900)
Bath stands on the river Avon between the Cotswold Hills to the north and the Mendips to the south, and was originally a small roman town (Aquae Sulis) with a baths and temple complex built around naturally occurring hot springs. In the early 18th century Bath became England's premier spa town where the rich and celebrated members of fashionable society gathered to 'take the waters' and enjoy the town's theatres and concert rooms. During this period the architect John Wood laid the foundations of a new Georgian city built using the honey-coloured stone for which Bath is famous today. Since 1987 the city has been listed as a UNESCO World Heritage Site.

Contemporary Bath is a thriving tourist destination and remains a leading cultural, religious and historical centre with many art galleries and historic sites including the Pump Room (1790); the Royal Crescent (1767); the Circus (1754); the 18th-century Assembly Rooms (housing the Museum of Costume); Pulteney Bridge (1771); the Guildhall and the Abbey, now over 500 years old, which is built on the site of a Saxon monastery. In 2006 the Bath Thermae Spa was completed and the hot springs reopened to the public for the first time since 1978.

BIRMINGHAM (PRE-1900)
Birmingham is Britain's second largest city, with a population of over one million. The generally accepted derivation of 'Birmingham' is the ham (dwelling-place) of the ing (family) of Beorma, presumed to have been Saxon. During the Industrial Revolution the town grew into a major manufacturing centre, known as the 'city of a thousand trades', and in 1889 was granted city status. By the 18th century, Birmingham was the main European producer of items such as buckles, medals and coins. Today, around 40 per cent of all the UK's handmade jewellery is produced in Birmingham's Jewellery Quarter. Another product of the Industrial Revolution are the city's 34 miles (56km) of canals.

Recent developments include Millennium Point, which houses Thinktank, the Birmingham science museum, and Brindleyplace, a development of shops, offices and leisure facilities on a former industrial site clustered around canals. In 2003 the Bullring shopping centre was officially opened as part of the city's urban regeneration programme.

The principal buildings are the Town Hall (1834–50), the Council House (1879), Victoria Law Courts (1891), the University of Birmingham (1906–9), the 13th-century church of St Martin in the Bull Ring (rebuilt 1873), the cathedral (formerly St Philip's Church) (1711), the Roman Catholic cathedral of St Chad (1839–41), the Assay Office (1773), the Rotunda (1964) and the National Exhibition Centre (1976).

BRIGHTON AND HOVE (2000)

Brighton and Hove is situated on the south coast of England, around 96km (60 miles) south of London. Originally a fishing village called Brighthelmstone, it was transformed into a fashionable seaside resort in the 18th century when Dr Richard Russell popularised the benefits of his 'sea-water cure'; as one of the closest beaches to London, Brighton began to attract wealthy visitors. One of these was the Prince Regent (the future King George IV), who first visited in 1783 and became so fond of the city that in 1807 he bought the former farmhouse he had been renting, and gradually turned it into Brighton's most recognisable building, the Royal Pavilion. The Pavilion is renowned for its Indo-Saracenic exterior, featuring minarets and an enormous central dome designed by John Nash, combined with the lavish chinoiserie of Frederick Crace's and Robert Jones' interiors. Queen Victoria sold the Pavilion to Brighton's municipal authority in 1850.

Brighton and Hove's Regency heritage can also be seen in the numerous elegant squares and crescents designed by Amon Wilds and Augustin Busby that dominate the seafront.

BRISTOL (PRE-1900)

Bristol was a royal borough before the Norman conquest. The earliest form of the name is *Bricgstow*. Due to the city's position close to the mouth of the River Avon, it was an important location for marine trade for centuries and prospered greatly from the transatlantic slave trade during the 18th century.

The principal buildings include the 12th-century cathedral with Norman chapter house and gateway; the 14th-century church of St Mary Redcliffe; Wesley's Chapel, Broadmead; the Merchant Venturers' Almshouses; the Council House (1956); the Guildhall; the Exchange (erected from the designs of John Wood in 1743); Cabot Tower; the university and Clifton College.

The Clifton Suspension Bridge, with a span of 214m (702ft) over the Avon, was projected by Isambard Kingdom Brunel in 1836 but was not completed until 1864. Brunel's SS *Great Britain,* the first ocean-going propeller-driven ship, now forms a museum at the western dockyard, from where she was originally launched in 1843. The docks themselves have been extensively restored and redeveloped; the 19th-century two-storey former tea warehouse is now the Arnolfini Centre for Contemporary Arts, and an 18th-century sail-loft houses the Architecture Centre. On Princes Wharf, 1950s transit sheds have been renovated and converted into the museum of Bristol, M Shed, which opened in 2011.

CAMBRIDGE (1951)

Cambridge, a settlement far older than its ancient university, lies on the River Cam (or Granta). Its industries include technology research and development, and biotechnology. Among its open spaces are Jesus Green, Sheep's Green, Coe Fen, Parker's Piece, Christ's Pieces, the University Botanic Garden, and the 'Backs' – lawns and gardens through which the Cam winds behind the principal line of college buildings. Historical sites east of the Cam include King's Parade, Great St Mary's Church, Gibbs' Senate House and King's College Chapel.

University and college buildings provide the outstanding features of Cambridge's architecture but several churches (especially St Benet's, the oldest building in the city, and Holy Sepulchre or the Round Church) are also notable. The Guildhall (1937) stands on a site of which at least part has held municipal buildings since 1224. In 2009 the University of Cambridge celebrated its 800th anniversary.

CANTERBURY (PRE-1900)

Canterbury, seat of the Archbishop of Canterbury, the primate of the Church of England, dates back to prehistoric times. It was the Roman *Durovernum Cantiacorum* and the Saxon *Cantwara-byrig* (stronghold of the men of Kent). It was here in 597 that St Augustine began the conversion of the English to Christianity, when Ethelbert, King of Kent, was baptised.

Of the Benedictine St Augustine's Abbey, burial place of the Jutish kings of Kent, only ruins remain. According to Bede, St Martin's Church, on the eastern outskirts of the city, was the place of worship of Queen Bertha, the Christian wife of King Ethelbert, before the advent of St Augustine. In 1170 the rivalry of Church and State culminated in the murder of Archbishop Thomas Becket in Canterbury Cathedral, by Henry II's knights. His shrine became a great centre of pilgrimage, as described in Chaucer's *Canterbury Tales.* After the Reformation pilgrimages ceased, the prosperity of the city was strengthened by an influx of Huguenot refugees, who introduced weaving. The poet and playwright Christopher Marlowe was born and raised in Canterbury and the city is home to the 1,200-seat Marlowe Theatre, which reopened to the public in 2011, following an extensive £25m rebuild.

The cathedral, with its architecture ranging from the 11th to the 15th centuries, is famous worldwide. Visitors are attracted particularly to the Martyrdom, the Black Prince's Tomb and the Warriors' Chapel.

The medieval city walls are built on Roman foundations and the 14th-century West Gate is one of the finest buildings of its kind in the country.

CHESTER (PRE-1900)

Chester is situated on the River Dee. Its recorded history dates from the first century when the Romans founded the fortress of *Deva.* The city's name is derived from the latin *Castra* (a camp or encampment). During the middle ages, Chester was the principal port of north-west England but declined with the silting of the Dee estuary and competition from Liverpool. The city was also an important military centre, notably during Edward I's Welsh campaigns and the Elizabethan Irish campaigns. During the Civil War, Chester supported the king and was besieged from 1643 to 1646. Chester's first charter was granted *c.*1175 and the city was incorporated in 1506. The office of sheriff is the earliest created in the country (1120s), and in 1992 the mayor, who also enjoys the title 'Admiral of the Dee', was made a lord mayor.

The city's architectural features include the city walls (an almost complete two-mile circuit), the unique 13th-century Rows (covered galleries above the street-level shops), the Victorian Gothic town hall (1869), the castle (rebuilt 1788 and 1822) and numerous half-timbered buildings. The cathedral was a Benedictine abbey until the dissolution of the monasteries. Chester racecourse is the oldest racecourse in Britain, believed to have origins in the 13th century. The first recorded horserace was in 1539 during the reign of Henry VIII. Chester also houses the ruins of a Roman amphitheatre, built in the late first century AD.

DURHAM (PRE-1900)

The city of Durham's prominent Norman cathedral and castle are set high on a wooded peninsula overlooking the River Wear. The cathedral was founded as a shrine for the body of St Cuthbert in 995. The present building dates from 1093 and among its many treasures is the tomb of the Venerable Bede (673–735). Durham's prince bishops had unique powers up to 1836, being lay rulers as well as religious leaders. As a palatinate, Durham could have its own army, nobility, coinage and courts. The castle was the main seat of the prince bishops for nearly 800 years; it is now used as a college by the University of Durham. The university, founded in the early 19th century on the initiative of Bishop William Van Mildert, is England's third oldest.

Annual events include Durham's regatta in June (claimed to be the oldest rowing event in Britain) and the annual Durham

Miners' Gala in July. Durham County Cricket Club was established in 1882.

LEEDS (PRE-1900)

Leeds, situated in the lower Aire valley, was first incorporated by Charles I in 1626. The earliest forms of the name are *Loidis* or *Ledes*, the origins of which are obscure.

The principal buildings are the Civic Hall (1933), the Town Hall (1858), the Municipal Buildings and Art Gallery (1884) with the Henry Moore Gallery (1982), the Corn Exchange (1863) and the university. The parish church of St Peter was rebuilt in 1841 and granted minister status in 2012. The 17th-century St John's Church has a fine interior with a famous English Renaissance screen; the last remaining 18th-century church in the city is Holy Trinity in Boar Lane (1727). Kirkstall Abbey (about three miles from the centre of the city), founded by Henry de Lacy in 1152, is one of the most complete examples of a Cistercian house now remaining. The Royal Armouries Museum forms part of a group of museums that house the national collection of antique arms and armour. The Grand Theatre and Opera House is home to Northern Ballet and Opera North.

LEICESTER (1919)

Leicester is situated in central England. The city was an important Roman settlement and also one of the five 'burghs' or boroughs of the Danelaw. In 1485 Richard III was buried in Leicester following his death at the nearby Battle of Bosworth; his remains were subsequently lost during the sixteenth century but rediscovered underneath a car park in 2012, and reburied at Leicester Cathedral in 2015. In 1589 Queen Elizabeth I granted a charter to the city and the ancient title was confirmed by letters patent in 1919.

The textile industry was responsible for Leicester's early expansion and the city still maintains a strong manufacturing base. Cotton mills and factories are now undergoing extensive regeneration and are being converted into offices, apartments, bars and restaurants. The principal buildings include the two universities (the University of Leicester and De Montfort University), as well as the Town Hall, the 13th-century Guildhall, De Montfort Hall, Leicester Cathedral, the Jewry Wall (the UK's highest standing Roman wall), St Nicholas Church and St Mary de Castro church. The motte and Great Hall of Leicester can be seen from the castle gardens, situated next to the River Soar.

LINCOLN (PRE-1900)

Situated 64km (40 miles) inland on the river Witham, Lincoln derives its name from a contraction of *Lindum Colonia,* the settlement founded in AD 48 by the Romans to command the crossing of Ermine Street and Fosse Way. Sections of the third-century Roman city wall can be seen, including an extant gateway (Newport Arch). The Romans also drained the surrounding fenland and created a canal system, laying the foundations of Lincoln's agricultural prosperity and also the city's importance in the medieval wool trade as a port and staple town.

As one of the five 'burghs' or boroughs of the Danelaw, Lincoln was an important trading centre in the ninth and tenth centuries and prosperity from the wool trade lasted until the 14th century. This wealth enabled local merchants to build parish churches, of which three survive, and there are also remains of a 12th-century Jewish community. However, the removal of the staple to Boston in 1369 heralded a decline, from which the city only recovered fully in the 19th century, when improved fen drainage made Lincoln agriculturally important. Improved canal and rail links led to industrial development, mainly in the manufacture of machinery and engineering products.

The castle was built shortly after the Norman Conquest and is unusual in having two mounds; on one motte stands a keep (Lucy's Tower) added in the 12th century. It currently houses one of the four surviving copies of the Magna Carta. The cathedral was begun *c.*1073 but was mostly destroyed by fire and earthquake in the 12th century. Rebuilding was begun by St Hugh and completed over a century later. It is believed the cathedral was the tallest building in the world between 1311 and 1548, when the central tower spire collapsed and was never rebuilt. Other notable architectural features are the 12th-century High Bridge, the oldest in Britain still to carry buildings, and the Guildhall, situated above the 15th-century Stonebow gateway.

LIVERPOOL (PRE-1900)

Liverpool, on the north bank of the river Mersey, 5km (3 miles) from the Irish Sea, is the UK's foremost port for Atlantic trade.

There are 2,100 acres of dockland on both sides of the river and the Gladstone and Royal Seaforth Docks can accommodate tanker-sized vessels. Liverpool Free Port was opened in 1984.

Liverpool was created a free borough in 1207 and was given city status in 1880. From the early 18th century it expanded rapidly with the growth of industrialisation and the transatlantic slave trade. Surviving buildings from this period include the Bluecoat Chambers (1717, formerly the Bluecoat School), and the Town Hall (1754, rebuilt to the original design 1795). Notable from the 19th and 20th centuries are the Anglican cathedral (built from the designs of Sir Giles Gilbert Scott, it took 74 years to construct), and the Catholic Metropolitan Cathedral (designed by Sir Frederick Gibberd, consecrated 1967). Both of these cathedrals are situated on Hope Street, named after the merchant William Hope, which is the only street in the UK with a cathedral at either end. The refurbished Albert Dock (designed by Jesse Hartley) contains the Merseyside Maritime Museum, the International Slavery Museum, the Beatles Story and the Tate Liverpool art gallery. The Museum of Liverpool opened in 2011.

MANCHESTER (PRE-1900)

Manchester (the *Mamucium* of the Romans, who occupied it in AD 79) is a commercial and industrial centre connected with the sea by the Manchester Ship Canal, 57km (35.5 miles) long, opened in 1894 and accommodating ships up to 15,000 tons. During the Industrial Revolution the city had a thriving cotton industry and by 1853 there were over 100 cotton mills, which dominated the city's landscape.

The principal buildings are the Town Hall, erected in 1877 from the designs of Alfred Waterhouse, with a large extension of 1938; the Royal Exchange (1869, enlarged 1921); the Central Library (1934); Heaton Hall; the 17th-century Chetham Library; the Rylands Library (1900), which includes the Althorp collection; the university precinct; the 15th-century cathedral (formerly the parish church); the Manchester Central conference and exhibition centre and the Bridgewater Hall (1996) concert venue. Manchester is the home of the Hallé Orchestra, the Royal Northern College of Music, the Royal Exchange Theatre and numerous public art galleries.

The town received its first charter of incorporation in 1838 and was created a city in 1853.

NEWCASTLE UPON TYNE (PRE-1900)

Newcastle upon Tyne, on the north bank of the River Tyne, is 13km (8 miles) from the North Sea. A cathedral and university city, it is the administrative, commercial and cultural centre for north-east England and the principal port.

The principal buildings include the Castle Keep (12th century), Black Gate (13th century), Blackfriars (13th century), West Walls (13th century), St Nicholas Cathedral (15th century, fine lantern tower), St Andrew's Church (12th–14th century), St John's (14th–15th century), All Saints (1786 by Stephenson), St Mary's Roman Catholic Cathedral (1844), Trinity House (17th century), Sandhill (16th-century houses), Guildhall (Georgian), Grey Street (1834–9), Central Station (1846–50) and the Central Library (1969). Open spaces include the Town Moor (927 acres).

Numerous bridges span the Tyne at Newcastle, including the Tyne Bridge (1928) and the Tilting Millennium Bridge (2001) which links the city with Gateshead to the south.

The city's name is derived from the 'new castle' (1080) erected as a defence against the Scots. In 1265 defensive walls over two miles in length were built around the city as further protection; parts of these walls remain today and can be found to the west of the city centre.

NORWICH (PRE-1900)

Norwich grew from an early Anglo-Saxon settlement near the confluence of the rivers Yare and Wensum, and now serves as the provincial capital for the predominantly agricultural region of East Anglia. The name is thought to relate to the most northerly of a group of Anglo-Saxon villages or *wics*. The city's first known charter was granted in 1158 by Henry II.

Norwich serves its surrounding area as a market town and commercial centre. From the 14th century until the Industrial Revolution, Norwich was the regional centre of the woollen industry. Now the biggest single industry is financial services and principal trades are engineering, printing and shoemaking. The University of East Anglia is on the city's western boundary and admitted its first students in 1963. Norwich is accessible to seagoing vessels by means of the river Yare, entered at Great Yarmouth, 32km (20 miles) to the east.

Among most historic buildings are the cathedral (completed in the 12th century and surmounted by a 15th-century spire 96m (315ft) in height); the keep of the Norman castle (now a museum and art gallery); the 15th-century flint-walled Guildhall; some 30 medieval parish churches; St Andrew's and Blackfriars' Halls; the Tudor houses preserved in Elm Hill and the Georgian Assembly House.

NOTTINGHAM (PRE-1900)

Nottingham stands on the river Trent. *Snotingabam* or *Notingebam,* the 'homestead of the people of Snot', is the Anglo-Saxon name for the Celtic settlement of *Tigguocobauc,* or the house of caves. In 878, Nottingham became one of the five 'burghs' or boroughs of the Danelaw. William the Conqueror ordered the construction of Nottingham Castle, while the town itself developed rapidly under Norman rule. Its laws and rights were formally recognised by Henry II's charter in 1155. The castle became a favoured residence of King John. In 1642 Charles I raised his personal standard at Nottingham Castle at the start of the Civil War.

Architecturally, Nottingham has a wealth of notable buildings, particularly those designed in the Victorian era by T. C. Hine and Watson Fothergill. The city council owns the castle (of Norman origin but restored in 1878), Wollaton Hall (1580–8), Newstead Abbey (once the home of Lord Byron), the Guildhall (1888) and the Council House (1929). St Mary's, St Peter's and St Nicholas' churches are of interest, as is the Roman Catholic cathedral (Pugin, 1842–4). Nottingham was granted city status in 1897.

OXFORD (PRE-1900)

Oxford is a university city, an important industrial centre and a market town.

Oxford is known for its architecture, its oldest specimens being the reputedly Saxon tower of St Michael's Church, the remains of the Norman castle and city walls, and the Norman church at Iffley. It also has many Gothic buildings, such as the Divinity Schools, the Old Library at Merton College, William of Wykeham's New College, Magdalen and Christ Church colleges and many other college buildings. Later centuries are represented by the Laudian Quadrangle at St John's College, the Renaissance Sheldonian Theatre by Sir Christopher Wren, Trinity College Chapel, All Saints Church, Hawksmoor's mock-Gothic at All Souls College, and the 18th-century Queen's College. In addition to individual buildings, High Street and Radcliffe Square both form interesting architectural compositions. Most of the colleges have gardens, those of Magdalen, New College, St John's and Worcester being the largest.

The Oxford University Museum of Natural History, renowned for its spectacular neo-Gothic architecture, houses the university's scientific collections of zoological, entomological and geological specimens and is attached to the neighbouring Pitt Rivers Museum, which houses ethnographic and archaeological objects from around the world. The Ashmolean is the city's museum of art and archaeology and Modern Art Oxford hosts a programme of contemporary art exhibitions.

ST ALBANS (PRE-1900)

The origins of St Albans, situated on the river Ver, stem from the Roman town of *Verulamium.* Named after the first Christian martyr in Britain, who was executed there, St Albans has developed around the Norman abbey and the cathedral church (consecrated 1115), which was built partly of materials from the old Roman city. The museums house Iron Age and Roman artefacts and the Roman theatre, unique in Britain, has a stage as opposed to an amphitheatre. Archaeological excavations in the city centre have revealed evidence of pre-Roman, Saxon and medieval occupation.

The town's significance grew to the extent that it was a signatory and venue for the drafting of the Magna Carta. It was also the scene of riots during the Peasants' Revolt, the French King John was imprisoned there after the Battle of Poitiers, and heavy fighting took place there during the Wars of the Roses.

Previously controlled by the Abbot, the town achieved a charter in 1553 and city status in 1877. The street market, first established in 1553, is still an important feature of the city, as are many hotels and inns, surviving from the days when St Albans was an important coach stop. St Albans is also noted for its clock tower, built between 1403 and 1412, the only remaining medieval town belfry in England.

SALISBURY (PRE-1900)

The history of Salisbury centres around the cathedral and cathedral close. The city evolved from an Iron Age camp a mile to the north of its current position which was strengthened by the Romans and called *Serviodunum.* The Normans built a castle and cathedral on the site and renamed it Sarum. In 1220 Bishop Richard Poore and the architect Elias de Derham decided to build a new Gothic-style cathedral. The cathedral was completed 38 years later and a community known as New Sarum, now called Salisbury, grew around it. Originally the cathedral had a squat tower; the 123m (404ft) spire that makes the cathedral the tallest medieval structure in the world was added *c.*1315. A walled close with houses for the clergy was built around the cathedral; the Medieval Hall still stands today, alongside buildings dating from the 13th to the 20th century, including some designed by Sir Christopher Wren.

A prosperous wool and cloth trade allowed Salisbury to flourish until the 17th century. When the wool trade declined new crafts were established, including cutlery, leather and basket work, saddlery, lacemaking, joinery and malting. By 1750 it had become an important road junction and coaching centre and in the Victorian era the railways enabled a new age of expansion and prosperity.

SHEFFIELD (PRE-1900)

Sheffield is situated at the confluence of the rivers Sheaf, Porter, Rivelin and Loxley with the river Don and was created a city in 1893.

The parish church of St Peter and St Paul, founded in the 12th century, became the cathedral church of the diocese of Sheffield in 1914. The Roman Catholic Cathedral Church of St Marie (founded 1847) was made a cathedral for the new diocese of Hallam in 1980; parts of the present building date from c.1435. The principal buildings are the Town Hall (1897), the Cutlers' Hall (1832), City Hall (1932), Graves Art Gallery (1934), and the Millennium Gallery (2001). The Grade II listed Park Hill housing estate was built between 1957 and 1961, and renovation work is set to be completed in 2022. The City Museum and Mappin Art Gallery (1874) reopened to the public as the Weston Park Museum in 2006 after undergoing a major £19m redevelopment, housing Sheffield's archaeology, natural history, art and social history collections, it underwent further refurbishment in 2016.

The restored Lyceum Theatre, which dates from 1897, reopened in 1990 and The Crucible Theatre (1971), famous for hosting the World Snooker Championship, was refurbished between 2007 and 2009 and officially reopened in 2010. Three major sporting and entertainment venues were opened between 1990 and 1991: Sheffield Arena, now FlyDSA Arena, and Ponds Forge, which houses an Olympic sized swimming pool and the UK's deepest diving pool, home to the GB Diving Squad. The Don Valley Stadium, completed in 1990, was demolished in 2013 and the site redeveloped as the Olympic Legacy Park, which includes a research centre, sport centre and educational facilities for local universities, opened in 2018. The Leadmill, Sheffield's longest-running independent live music venue, opened in 1980.

SOUTHAMPTON (1964)

Southampton is a major seaport on the south coast of England, situated between the mouths of the Test and Itchen rivers. Southampton's natural deep-water harbour has made the area an important settlement since the Romans built the first port (known as Clausentum) in the first century, and Southampton's port has witnessed several important departures, including those of Henry V in 1415 for the Battle of Agincourt, the Mayflower in 1620, and the RMS Titanic in 1912.

The city's strategic importance, not only as a seaport but also as a centre for aircraft production, meant that it was heavily bombed during the Second World War. However, many historically significant structures remain, including the Wool House, dating from 1417 and now used as the Maritime Museum; parts of the Norman city walls, which are among the most complete in the UK; the Bargate, which was originally the main gateway into the city; God's House Tower, now the Museum of Archaeology; St Michael's, the city's oldest church; and the Tudor Merchants Hall.

WINCHESTER (PRE-1900)

Winchester, the ancient capital of England, is situated on the river Itchen. The city is rich in architecture of all types, and especially notable is the cathedral. Built in 1079–93 the cathedral exhibits examples of Norman, early English and Perpendicular styles and is the burial place of author Jane Austen. Winchester College, founded in 1382, is one of the country's most famous public schools, and the original building (1393) remains largely unaltered. St Cross Hospital, another great medieval foundation, lies one mile south of the city. The almshouses were founded in 1136 by Bishop Henry de Blois, and Cardinal Henry Beaufort added a new almshouse of 'Noble Poverty' in 1446. The chapel and dwellings are of great architectural interest, and visitors may still receive the 'Wayfarer's Dole' of bread and ale, a tradition now 900 years old.

Excavations have done much to clarify the origins and development of Winchester. Part of the forum and several of the streets from the Roman town have been discovered. Excavations in the cathedral close have uncovered the entire site of the Anglo-Saxon cathedral (known as the Old Minster) and parts of the New Minster which was built by Alfred the Great's son, Edward the Elder, and is the burial place of the Alfredian dynasty. The original burial place of St Swithun, before his remains were translated to a site in the present cathedral, was also uncovered.

Excavations in other parts of the city have cast much light on Norman Winchester, notably on the site of the Royal Castle (adjacent to which the new Law Courts have been built) and in the grounds of Wolvesey Castle, where the great house built by bishops Giffard and Henry de Blois in the 12th century has been uncovered. The Great Hall, built by Henry III between 1222 and 1236, survives and houses the Arthurian Round Table.

YORK (PRE-1900)

The city of York is an archiepiscopal seat. Its recorded history dates from AD 71, when the Roman Ninth Legion established a base under Petilius Cerealis that would later become the fortress of Eburacum, or Eboracum. In Anglo-Saxon times the city was the royal and ecclesiastical centre of Northumbria, and after capture by a Viking army in AD 866 it became the capital of the Viking kingdom of Jorvik. By the 14th century the city had become a great mercantile centre, mainly because of its control of the wool trade, and was used as the chief base against the Scots. Under the Tudors its fortunes declined, although Henry VIII made it the headquarters of the Council of the North. Excavations on many sites, including Coppergate, have greatly expanded knowledge of Roman, Viking and medieval urban life. The JORVIK Viking Centre (reopened in 2017) takes visitors on a journey through a reconstructed 10th century Viking-age York.

The city is rich in examples of architecture of all periods. The earliest church was built in AD 627 and, from the 12th to 15th centuries, the present Minster was built in a succession of styles.

LORD-LIEUTENANTS AND HIGH SHERIFFS

Area	Lord-Lieutenant	High Sheriff (2020–21)
Bedfordshire	Helen Nellis	Susana Lousada
Berkshire	James Puxley	Mary Riall
Bristol	Peaches Golding, OBE	Dr John Manley
Buckinghamshire	Sir Henry Aubrey-Fletcher, Bt., KCVO	Andrew Farncombe
Cambridgeshire	Julie Spence, OBE, QPM	Brig. Tim Seal, TD
Cheshire	David Briggs, MBE	Nick Hopkinson, MBE
Cornwall	Col. Edward Bolitho, OBE	Kate Holborow
Cumbria	Claire Hensman	Julie Barton
Derbyshire	Elizabeth Fothergill, CBE	Tony Walker, CBE
Devon	David Fursdon	Gerald Hine-Haycock
Dorset	Angus Campbell	George Streatfeild
Durham	Susan Snowden	David Gray
East Riding of Yorkshire	James Dick, OBE	Andrew Horncastle, MBE
East Sussex	Peter Field	Andrew Blackman
Essex	Jennifer Tolhurst	Julie Fosh
Gloucestershire	Edward Gillespie, OBE	Helen Lovatt
Greater London	Sir Kenneth Olisa, OBE	John Garbutt
Greater Manchester	Sir Warren Smith, KVCO	Dr Eamonn O'Neal
Hampshire	Nigel Atkinson	Revd Sue Colman
Herefordshire	Edward Harley, OBE	Patricia Thomas
Hertfordshire	Robert Voss, CBE	The Hon. Henry Holland-Hibbert
Isle of Wight	Susan Sheldon	Caroline Peel
Kent	Lady Annabel Colgrain of Ide Hill	Remony Milwater
Lancashire	Lord Shuttleworth, KG, KCVO	Catherine Penny
Leicestershire	Michael Kapur, OBE	Alison Smith, MBE
Lincolnshire	Toby Dennis	Michael Scott
Merseyside	Mark Blundell	His Hon John Roberts
Norfolk	Lady Dannatt, MBE	Lady Roberts
North Yorkshire	Johanna Ropner	David Kerfoot, MBE
Northamptonshire	James Saunders Watson	Paul Parsons
Northumberland	Duchess of Northumberland	Tom Fairfax
Nottinghamshire	Sir John Peace	Dame Elizabeth Fradd, DBE
Oxfordshire	Tim Stevenson, OBE	Amanda Ponsonby, MBE
Rutland	Dr Sarah Furness	Richard Cole
Shropshire	Anna Turner	Dean Harris
Somerset	Anne Maw	Mary-Clare Rodwell
South Yorkshire	Andrew Coombe	Carole O'Neill
Staffordshire	Ian Dudson, CBE	Commander Charles Bagot-Jewitt
Suffolk	Clare, Countess of Euston	Bridget McIntyre, MBE
Surrey	Michael More-Molyneux	Shahid Azeem
Tyne and Wear	Susan Winfield, OBE	Sarah Stewart, OBE
Warwickshire	Timothy Cox	Joe Greenwall, CBE
West Midlands	John Crabtree, OBE	Wade Lyn, CBE
West Sussex	Susan Pyper	Dr Timothy Fooks
West Yorkshire	Edmund Anderson	Jonathan Thornton
Wiltshire	Sarah Troughton	Maj.-Gen. Ashley Truluck, CB, CBE
Worcestershire	Lt.-Col. Patrick Holcroft, LVO, OBE	Lt.-Col. Mike Jackson, OBE

COMBINED AUTHORITIES

Authority	Constituent Councils*	Pop. †	Mayor, Political Party
Cambridgeshire & Peterborough	Cambridge, Cambridgeshire, E. Cambridgeshire, Fenland, Huntingdonshire, Peterborough, S. Cambridgeshire	855,796	James Palmer, *C.*
Greater Manchester	Bolton, Bury, Manchester, Oldham, Rochdale, Salford, Stockport, Tameside, Trafford, Wigan	2,835,686	Andy Burnham, *Lab.*
Liverpool City Region	Halton, Knowsley, Liverpool, St Helens, Sefton, Wirral	1,559,320	Steve Rotheram, *Lab.*
North East	Durham, Gateshead, S. Tyneside, Sunderland	1,160,830	None
North of Tyne	Newcastle Upon Tyne, N. Tyneside, Northumberland	833,167	Jamie Driscoll, *Lab.*
Sheffield City Region	Barnsley, Doncaster, Rotherham, Sheffield	1,409,020	Dan Jarvis, *Lab.*
Tees Valley	Darlington, Hartlepool, Middlesbrough, Redcar & Cleveland, Stockton-On-Tees	675,944	Ben Houchen, *C.*
West of England	Bath & N. E. Somerset, Bristol, S. Gloucestershire	941,752	Tim Bowles, *C.*
West Midlands	Birmingham, Coventry, Dudley, Sandwell, Solihull, Walsall, Wolverhampton	2,916,458	Andy Street, *C.*
West Yorkshire	Bradford, Calderdale, Kirklees, Leeds, Wakefield	2,332,469	None

COUNTY COUNCILS

Council & Administrative HQ	Telephone	Population†	Council Tax‡	Chief Executive§
Cambridgeshire, Cambridge	0345-045 5200	653,537	£1,359	Gillian Beasley
Cumbria, Carlisle	01228-606060	500,012	£1,441	Katherine Fairclough
Derbyshire, Matlock	01629-580000	802,694	£1,349	E. Alexander; H. Jones; J. Parfrement
Devon, Exeter	0345-155 1015	802,375	£1,439	Dr Phil Norrey
East Sussex, Lewes	0345-608 0190	557,229	£1,492	Becky Shaw
Essex, Chelmsford	0845-7430 430	1,489,189	£1,321	Gavin Jones
Gloucestershire, Gloucester	01452-425000	637,070	£1,345	Peter Bungard
Hampshire, Winchester	0300-555 1375	1,382,542	£1,286	John Coughlan, CBE
Hertfordshire, Hertford	0300-123 4040	1,189,519	£1,414	Owen Mapley
Kent, Maidstone	0300-041 4141	1,581,555	£1,351	David Cockburn
Lancashire, Preston	0300-123 6701	1,219,799	£1,400	Angie Ridgwell
Leicestershire, Leicester	0116-232 3232	706,155	£1,344	John Sinnott
Lincolnshire, Lincoln	01522-552222	761,224	£1,338	Debbie Barnes, OBE
Norfolk, Norwich	0344-800 8020	907,760	£1,417	Tom McCabe
North Yorkshire, Northallerton	01609-780780	618,054	£1,363	Richard Flinton
Northamptonshire, Northampton	0300-126 1000	753,278	£1,285	Theresa Grant
Nottinghamshire, Nottingham	0115-982 3823	828,224	£1,535	Anthony May
Oxfordshire, Oxford	01865-792422	691,667	£1,527	Yvonne Rees
Somerset, Taunton	0300-123 2224	562,225	£1,289	vacant
Staffordshire, Stafford	0300-111 8000	879,560	£1,296	John Henderson, CB
Suffolk, Ipswich	03456-606 6067	761,350	£1,344	Nicola Beach
Surrey, Kingston upon Thames	0345-600 9009	1,196,236	£1,511	Joanna Killian
Warwickshire, Warwick	01926-410410	577,933	£1,489	Monica Fogarty
West Sussex, Chichester	01243-777100	863,980	£1,439	Becky Shaw
Worcestershire, Worcester	01905-763763	595,786	£1,311	Paul Robinson

*See the following pages for information on individual constituent councils
† *Source:* Office for National Statistics – *Mid-2019 Population Estimates* (Crown copyright)
‡ Average 2020–21 Band D council tax in the county area inclusive of the adult social care precept, but exclusive of precepts for fire authorities and Police and Crime Commissioners. County councils claim their share of the combined council tax from the collection funds of the district authorities within their area. Band D council tax bills for the billing authority are given on the following pages
§ Or equivalent postholder

DISTRICT COUNCILS

District Council	Telephone	Pop.*	Council Tax†	Chief Executive‡
Adur	01273-263000	64,301	£1,963	Alex Bailey
Allerdale	01900-702702	97,761	£1,960	Andrew Seekings
Amber Valley	01773-570222	128,147	£1,883	Sylvia Delahay & Julian Townsend
Arun	01903-737500	160,758	£1,903	Nigel Lynn
Ashfield	01623-450000	127,918	£2,045	Carol Cooper-Smith (interim)
Ashford	01233-331111	130,032	£1,848	Tracey Kerly
Babergh	01473-822801	92,036	£1,820	Arthur Charvonia
Barrow-in-Furness	01229-876543	67,049	£1,954	Sam Plum
Basildon	01268-533333	187,199	£1,880	Scott Logan
Basingstoke and Deane	01256-844844	176,582	£1,880	Ian Doll (interim)
Bassetlaw	01909-533533	117,459	£2,059	Neil Taylor
Blaby	0116-275 0555	101,526	£1,920	Jane Toman
Bolsover	01246-242424	80,562	£1,981	Karen Hanson & Lee Hickin
Boston	01205-314200	70,173	£1,842	Rob Barlow
Braintree	01376-552525	152,604	£1,824	Andy Wright
Breckland	01362-656870	139,968	£1,872	Nathan Elvery
Brentwood	01277-312500	77,021	£1,805	Jonathan Stephenson
Broadland	01603-431133	130,783	£1,891	Trevor Holden
Bromsgrove	01527-881288	99,881	£1,876	Kevin Dicks
Broxbourne	01992-785555	97,279	£1,750	Jeff Stack
Broxtowe	0115-917 7777	114,033	£2,039	Ruth Hyde, OBE
Burnley	01282-425011	88,920	£1,996	Mick Cartledge
CAMBRIDGE	01223-457000	124,798	£1,866	Andrew Grant (interim)
Cannock Chase	01543-462621	100,762	£1,845	Tony McGovern
CANTERBURY	01227-862000	165,394	£1,866	Colin Carmichael
CARLISLE	01228-817000	108,678	£1,943	Dr Jason Gooding
Castle Point	01268-882200	90,376	£1,865	David Marchant
Charnwood	01509-263151	185,851	£1,860	Rob Mitchell
CHELMSFORD	01245-606606	178,388	£1,831	Nick Eveleigh
Cheltenham	01242-262626	116,306	£1,823	Gareth Edmundson
Cherwell	01295-227001	150,503	£1,974	Yvonne Rees
Chesterfield	01246-345345	104,900	£1,839	Huw Bowen
Chichester	01243-785166	121,129	£1,868	Diane Shepherd
Chorley	01257-515151	118,216	£1,893	Gary Hall
Colchester	01206-282222	194,706	£1,822	Adrian Pritchard
Copeland	01946-598300	68,183	£1,970	Pat Graham
Corby	01536-464000	72,218	£1,801	Jonathan Waterworth & Paul Goult
Cotswold	01285-623000	89,862	£1,817	Robert Weaver
Craven	01756-700600	57,142	£1,943	Paul Shevlin
Crawley	01293-438000	112,409	£1,848	Natalie Brahma-Pearl
Dacorum	01442-228000	154,763	£1,835	Claire Hamilton
Dartford	01322-343434	112,606	£1,847	Sheri Green & Sarah Martin
Daventry	01327-871100	85,950	£1,858	Ian Vincent
Derbyshire Dales	01629-761100	72,325	£1,926	Paul Wilson
Dover	01304-821199	118,131	£1,894	Nadeem Aziz
East Cambridgeshire	01353-665555	89,840	£1,888	John Hill
East Devon	01395-516551	146,284	£1,967	Mark Williams
East Hampshire	01730-266551	122,308	£1,784	Gill Kneller
East Hertfordshire	01279-655261	149,748	£1,864	Richard Cassidy
East Lindsey	01507-601111	141,727	£1,801	Rob Barlow
East Northamptonshire	01832-742000	94,527	£1,876	David Oliver
East Staffordshire	01283-508000	119,754	£1,875	Andy O'Brien
East Suffolk	03330-162000	249,461	£1,810	Stephen Baker
Eastbourne	01323-410000	103,745	£2,039	Robert Cottrill
Eastleigh	023-8068 8000	133,584	£1,768	Nick Tustian
Eden	01768-817817	53,253	£1,958	vacant
Elmbridge	01372-474474	136,795	£2,009	Robert Moran
Epping Forest	01992-564000	131,689	£1,816	Georgina Blakemore
Epsom and Ewell	01372-732000	80,627	£1,985	Kathryn Beldon
Erewash	0115-907 2244	115,371	£1,857	Jeremy Jaroszek
EXETER	01392-277888	131,405	£1,909	Karime Hassan
Fareham	01329-236100	116,233	£1,732	Peter Grimwood
Fenland	01354-654321	101,850	£1,973	Paul Medd
Folkestone and Hythe	01303-853000	112,996	£1,967	Dr Susan Priest
Forest of Dean	01594-810000	86,791	£1,870	Jan Britton
Fylde	01253-658658	80,780	£1,928	Allan Oldfield

Gedling	0115-901 3901	117,896	£2,033	Mike Hill
GLOUCESTER	01452-396396	129,28	£1,816	Jon McGinty
Gosport	023-9258 4242	84,838	£1,798	David Williams
Gravesham	01474-564422	106,939	£1,853	Stuart Bobby
Great Yarmouth	01493-856100	99,336	£1,863	Sheila Oxtoby
Guildford	01483-505050	148,998	£1,991	James Whiteman
Hambleton	01619-779977	91,594	£1,858	Dr Justin Ives
Harborough	01858-828282	93,807	£1,865	Norman Proudfoot
Harlow	01279-446655	87,067	£1,877	Brian Keane
Harrogate	01423-500600	160,831	£1,966	Wallace Sampson
Hart	01252-622122	97,073	£1,826	Patricia Hughes & Daryl Phillips
Hastings	01424-451066	92,661	£2,058	Jane Hartnell
Havant	023-9244 6019	126,220	£1,776	Gill Kneller
Hertsmere	020-8207 2277	104,919	£1,825	Sajida Bijle
High Peak	0345-129 7777	92,666	£1,869	Andrew Stokes
Hinckley and Bosworth	01455-238141	113,136	£1,836	Bill Cullen
Horsham	01403-215100	143,791	£1,857	Glen Chip
Huntingdonshire	01480-388388	177,963	£1,925	Jo Lancaster
Hyndburn	01254-388111	81,043	£1,934	David Welsby
Ipswich	01473-432000	136,913	£1,936	Russell Williams
Kettering	01536-410333	101,766	£1,824	Graham Soulsby
King's Lynn and West Norfolk	01553-616200	151,383	£1,876	Lorraine Gore
LANCASTER	01524-582000	146,038	£1,931	Kieran Keane
Lewes	01273-471600	103,268	£2,111	Robert Cottrill
Lichfield	01543-308000	104,756	£1,830	Diane Tilley
LINCOLN	01522-881188	99,299	£1,869	Angela Andrews
Maidstone	01622-602000	171,826	£1,933	Alison Broom
Maldon	01621-854477	64,926	£1,858	P. Dodson; R. Holmes; C. Leslie
Malvern Hills	01684-862151	78,698	£1,857	Vic Allison
Mansfield	01623-463463	109,313	£2,039	Hayley Barsby
Melton	01664-502502	51,209	£1,888	Edd de Coverly
Mendip	0300-3038588	115,587	£1,882	Stuart Brown
Mid Devon	01884-255255	82,311	£2,021	Stephen Walford
Mid Suffolk	01449-720711	103,895	£1,812	Arthur Charvonia
Mid Sussex	01444-458166	151,022	£1,883	Kathryn Hall
Mole Valley	01306-885001	87,245	£1,974	Karen Brimacombe
New Forest	023-8028 5000	180,086	£1,836	Bob Jackson
Newark and Sherwood	01636-650000	122,421	£2,100	John Robinson
Newcastle-under-Lyme	01782-717717	129,441	£1,815	Martin Hamilton
North Devon	01271-327711	97,145	£2,006	Ken Miles
North East Derbyshire	01246-231111	101,462	£1,949	Karen Hanson & Lee Hickin
North Hertfordshire	01462-474000	133,570	£1,871	Anthony Roche
North Kesteven	01529-414155	116,915	£1,853	Ian Fytche
North Norfolk	01263-513811	104,837	£1,895	Steve Blatch
North Warwickshire	01827-715341	65,264	£1,990	Steve Maxey
North West Leicestershire	01530-454545	103,611	£1,883	Beverley Smith
Northampton	0300-330 7000	224,610	£1,851	George Candler
NORWICH	0344-980 3333	140,573	£1,949	Stephen Evans
Nuneaton and Bedworth	024-7637 6376	129,883	£1,966	Brent Davis & Simone Hines
Oadby and Wigston	0116-288 8961	57,015	£1,874	Anne Court
OXFORD	01865-249811	152,457	£2,064	Gordon Mitchell
Pendle	01282-661661	92,112	£2,050	Dean Langton & Philip Mousdale
PRESTON	01772-906900	143,135	£2,012	Adrian Phillips
Redditch	01527-64252	85,261	£1,867	Kevin Dicks
Reigate and Banstead	01737-276000	148,748	£2,022	vacant
Ribble Valley	01200-425111	60,888	£1,860	Marshal Scott
Richmondshire	01748-829100	53,730	£1,955	Tony Clark
Rochford	01702-318111	87,368	£1,881	Angela Hutchings *(acting)*
Rossendale	01706-217777	71,482	£1,962	Neil Shaw
Rother	01424-787000	96,080	£2,036	Malcolm Johnston
Rugby	01788-533533	108,935	£1,944	Mannie Ketley
Runnymede	01932-838383	89,424	£1,952	Paul Turrell
Rushcliffe	0115-981 9911	119,184	£2,056	Kath Marriott
Rushmoor	01252-398398	94,599	£1,776	Paul Shackley
Ryedale	01653-600666	55,380	£1,955	Stacey Burlet
ST ALBANS	01727-866100	148,482	£1,840	Amanda Foley
Scarborough	01723-232323	108,757	£1,966	Michael Greene
Sedgemoor	0845-408 2540	123,178	£1,836	Allison Griffin
Selby	01757-705101	90,620	£1,945	Janet Waggott
Sevenoaks	01732-227000	120,750	£1,944	Dr Pav Ramewal

Somerset West and Taunton	0300-304 8000	155,115	£1,814	James Hassett
South Cambridgeshire	0345-045 0500	159,086	£1,907	Liz Watts
South Derbyshire	01283-595795	107,261	£1,844	Frank McArdle
South Hams	01803-861234	87,004	£1,991	Andy Bates
South Holland	01775-761161	95,019	£1,808	Nathan Elvery
South Kesteven	01476-406080	142,424	£1,791	Karen Bradford
South Lakeland	01539-733333	105,088	£1,945	Lawrence Conway
South Norfolk	01508-533633	140,880	£1,917	Trevor Holden
South Northamptonshire	01327-322322	94,490	£1,889	Richard Ellis
South Oxfordshire	01235-520202	142,057	£1,965	Mark Stone
South Ribble	01772-421491	110,788	£1,918	vacant
South Somerset	01935-462462	168,345	£1,874	Alex Parmley
South Staffordshire	01902-696000	112,436	£1,779	Dave Heywood
Spelthorne	01784-451499	99,844	£1,987	Daniel Mouawad
Stafford	01785-619000	137,280	£1,782	Tim Clegg
Staffordshire Moorlands	0345-605 3010	98,435	£1,805	Andrew Stokes
Stevenage	01438-242242	87,845	£1,828	Matt Partridge
Stratford-on-Avon	01789-267575	130,089	£1,933	Dave Buckland
Stroud	01453-766321	119,964	£1,909	Kathy O'Leary
Surrey Heath	01276-707100	89,305	£2,026	Damian Roberts
Swale	01795-417850	150,082	£1,846	Larissa Reed
Tamworth	01827-709709	76,696	£1,780	Anthony Goodwin
Tandridge	01883-722000	88,129	£2,208	Jackie King *(acting)*
Teignbridge	01626-361101	134,163	£2,001	Phil Shears
Tendring	01255-686868	146,561	£1,809	Ian Davidson
Test Valley	01264-368000	126,160	£1,755	Andy Ferrier
Tewkesbury	01684-295010	92,019	£1,788	Mike Dawson
Thanet	01843-577000	141,922	£1,921	Madeline Homer
Three Rivers	01923-776611	93,323	£1,844	Joanne Wagstaffe
Tonbridge and Malling	01732-844522	132,153	£1,909	Julie Beilby
Torridge	01237-428700	68,267	£1,984	Steve Hearse
Tunbridge Wells	01892-526121	118,724	£1,876	William Benson
Uttlesford	01799-510510	91,284	£1,779	Dawn French
Vale of White Horse	01235-520202	136,007	£1,961	Mark Stone
Warwick	01926-410410	143,753	£1,930	Chris Elliott
Watford	01923-226400	96,577	£1,886	Donna Nolan
Waverley	01483-523333	126,328	£2,031	Tom Horwood
Wealden	01323-443322	161,475	£2,091	Trevor Scott
Wellingborough	01933-229777	79,707	£1,786	Liz Elliott
Welwyn & Hatfield	01707-357000	123,043	£1,867	Ka Ng *(interim)*
West Devon	01822-813600	55,796	£2,067	Andy Bates
West Lancashire	01695-577177	114,306	£1,908	Jacqui Sinnott-Lacey
West Lindsey	01427-676676	95,667	£1,878	Ian Knowles
West Oxfordshire	01993-861000	110,643	£1,937	Giles Hughes
West Suffolk	01284-763233	179,045	£1,821	Ian Gallin
WINCHESTER	01962-840222	124,859	£1,798	Laura Taylor
Woking	01483-755855	100,793	£2,027	Ray Morgan, OBE
WORCESTER	01905-722233	101,222	£1,818	David Blake
Worthing	01903-239999	110,570	£1,881	Alex Bailey
Wychavon	01386-565000	129,433	£1,793	Vic Allison
Wyre	01253-891000	112,091	£1,908	Garry Payne
Wyre Forest	01562-732928	101,291	£1,880	Ian Miller

* *Source:* Office for National Statistics – *Mid-2019 Population Estimates* (Crown copyright)
† Band D council tax bill for 2020–21 inclusive of adult social care and parish precepts
‡ Or equivalent postholder
Councils in CAPITAL LETTERS have city status

METROPOLITAN BOROUGH COUNCILS

Metropolitan Borough Council	Telephone	Pop.*	Council Tax†	Chief Executive‡
Barnsley	01226-770770	246,866	£1,820	Sarah Norman
BIRMINGHAM	0121-303 1111	1,141,814	£1,668	Chris Naylor *(interim)*
Bolton	01204-333333	287,550	£1,821	Tony Oakman
BRADFORD	01274-432001	539,776	£1,708	Kersten England
Bury	0161-253 5000	190,990	£1,911	Geoff Little, OBE
Calderdale	01422-288001	211,455	£1,823	Robin Tuddenham
COVENTRY	0500-834 333	371,521	£1,909	Dr Martin Reeves
Doncaster	01302-736000	311,890	£1,707	Damian Allen
Dudley	0300-555 2345	321,596	£1,606	Kevin O'Keefe
Gateshead	0191-433 3000	202,055	£2,045	Sheena Ramsey
Kirklees	01484-221000	439,787	£1,839	Jacqui Gedman
Knowsley	0151-489 6000	150,862	£1,892	Mike Harden
LEEDS	0113-222 4444	793,139	£1,720	Tom Riordan
LIVERPOOL	0151-233 3000	498,042	£2,027	Tony Reeves
MANCHESTER	0161-234 5000	552,858	£1,725	Joanne Roney, OBE
NEWCASTLE UPON TYNE	0191-278 7878	302,820	£1,930	Pat Ritchie
North Tyneside	0191-643 5991	207,913	£1,852	Paul Hanson
Oldham	0161-770 3000	237,110	£1,977	Dr Carolyn Wilkins, OBE
Rochdale	01706-647474	222,412	£1,945	Steve Rumbelow
Rotherham	01709-382121	265,411	£1,885	Sharon Kemp
St Helens	01744-676789	180,585	£1,821	Kath O'Dwyer
SALFORD	0161-794 4711	258,834	£1,940	Tom Stannard
Sandwell	0121-569 2200	328,450	£1,682	David Stevens
Sefton	0345 140 0845	276,410	£1,958	Dwayne Johnson
SHEFFIELD	0114-273 4567	584,853	£1,899	Kate Josephs
Solihull	0121-704 8001	216,374	£1,655	Nick Page
South Tyneside	0191-427 7000	150,976	£1,850	vacant
Stockport	0161-480 4949	293,423	£1,990	Pam Smith
SUNDERLAND	0191-520 5555	277,705	£1,692	Patrick Melia
Tameside	0161-342 8355	226,493	£1,828	Steven Pleasant. MBE
Trafford	0161-912 2000	237,354	£1,644	Sara Todd
WAKEFIELD	0845-850 6506	348,312	£1,735	Merran McRae
Walsall	01922-650000	285,478	£2,007	Dr Helen Paterson
Wigan	01942-244991	328,662	£1,616	Alison McKenzie-Folan
Wirral	0151-606 2000	324,011	£1,896	Paul Satoor
WOLVERHAMPTON	01902-551155	263,357	£1,906	Tim Johnson

* *Source:* Office for National Statistics – *Mid-2019 Population Estimates* (Crown copyright)
† Band D council tax bill for 2020–21 inclusive of adult social care and parish precepts
‡ Or equivalent postholder
Councils in CAPITAL LETTERS have city status

UNITARY COUNCILS

Unitary Council	Telephone	Pop.*	Council Tax†	Chief Executive‡
Bath and North East Somerset	01225-477000	193,282	£1,803	Will Godfrey
Bedford	01234-267422	173,292	£1,908	Philip Simpkins
Blackburn with Darwen	01254-585585	149,696	£1,857	Denise Park
Blackpool	01253-477477	139,446	£1,901	Neil Jack
Bournemouth, Christchurch and Poole (BCP)	01202-451451	395,331	£1,842	Graham Farrant
Bracknell Forest	01344-352000	122,529	£1,716	Timothy Wheadon
BRIGHTON AND HOVE	01273-290000	290,885	£1,955	Geoff Raw
BRISTOL	0117-922 2000	463,377	£2,061	Mike Jackson
Buckinghamshire	0300-131 6000	543,973	£1,903	Rachel Shimmin, OBE
Central Bedfordshire	0300-300 8000	288,648	£1,996	Marcel Coiffait
Cheshire East	0300-123 5500	384,152	£1,851	Lorraine O'Donnell
Cheshire West and Chester	0300-123 8123	343,071	£1,902	Andrew Lewis
Cornwall	0300-123 4100	569,578	£1,943	Kate Kennally
Darlington	01325-380651	106,803	£1,892	Paul Wildsmith
DERBY	01332-293111	257,302	£1,778	Paul Simpson
Dorset	01305-221000	378,508	£2,119	Matt Prosser
DURHAM	0300-026000	530,094	£2,071	John Hewitt (interim)
East Riding of Yorkshire	01482-393939	341,173	£1,875	Caroline Lacey
Halton	0303-333 4300	129,410	£1,789	David Parr, OBE
Hartlepool	01429-266522	93,663	£2,092	Denise McGuckin
Herefordshire	01432-260000	192,801	£1,954	Alistair Neill
Isle of Wight	01983-821000	141,771	£1,965	John Metcalfe
Isles of Scilly§	01720-424000	2,224	£1,550	Paul Masters
KINGSTON-UPON-HULL	01482-609100	259,778	£1,741	Matt Jukes
LEICESTER	0116-254 1000	354,224	£1,915	vacant
Luton	01582-546000	213,052	£1,850	Robin Porter
Medway	01634-333333	278,556	£1,760	Neil Davies
Middlesbrough	01642-245432	140,980	£2,050	Tony Parkinson
Milton Keynes	01908-691691	269,457	£1,747	Michael Bracey
North East Lincolnshire	01472-313131	159,563	£1,923	Rob Walsh
North Lincolnshire	01724-296296	172,292	£1,875	Denise Hyde
North Somerset	01934-888888	215,052	£1,813	Jo Walker
Northumberland	0345-600 6400	322,900	£1,985	Daljit Lally, OBE
NOTTINGHAM	0115-915 5555	332,900	£2,119	Mel Barrett
PETERBOROUGH	01733-747474	201,041	£1,715	Gillian Beasley
PLYMOUTH	01752-668000	262,100	£1,885	Tracey Lee
PORTSMOUTH	023-9282 2251	214,905	£1,733	David Williams
Reading	0118-937 3787	161,780	£1,976	Peter Sloman
Redcar and Cleveland	0164-277 4774	137,150	£1,995	John Sampson
Rutland	01572-722577	39,927	£2,125	Mark Andrews (interim)
Shropshire	0345-678 9000	323,136	£1,850	Andy Begley
Slough	01753-475111	149,539	£1,708	Josie Wragg
South Gloucestershire	01454-868009	285,093	£1,929	Dave Perry
SOUTHAMPTON	023-8083 3000	252,520	£1,847	Sandy Hopkins
Southend-on-Sea	01702-215000	183,125	£1,718	Alison Griffin
Stockton-on-Tees	01642-393939	197,348	£2,006	Julie Danks
STOKE-ON-TRENT	01782-234567	256,375	£1,660	Jon Rouse
Swindon	01793-463000	222,193	£1,828	Susie Kemp
Telford and Wrekin	01952-380000	179,854	£1,733	David Sidaway
Thurrock	01375-652652	174,341	£1,605	Lyn Carpenter
Torbay	01803-201201	136,262	£1,809	Anne-Marie Bond (interim)
Warrington	01925-443322	210,014	£1,881	Prof. Steven Broomhead
West Berkshire	01635-42400	158,450	£1,917	Nick Carter
Wiltshire	0300-456 0100	500,024	£1,935	Terence Herbert
Windsor and Maidenhead	01628-683800	151,422	£1,384	Duncan Sharkey
Wokingham	0118-974 6000	171,119	£1,893	Susan Parsonage
YORK	01904-551550	210,618	£1,734	Ian Floyd

* *Source*: Office for National Statistics – *Mid-2019 Population Estimates* (Crown copyright)
† Band D council tax bill for 2020–21 inclusive of adult social care and parish precepts
‡ Or equivalent postholder
§ Under the Isles of Scilly Clause the council has additional functions to other unitary authorities
Councils in CAPITAL LETTERS have city status

SINGLE-TIER & COUNTY COUNCIL AREAS IN ENGLAND

1 Stockton-on-Tees
2 Middlesbrough
3 Blackpool
4 Blackburn
  with Darwen
5 Bolton
6 Bury
7 Rochdale
8 Salford
9 Oldham
10 Liverpool
11 Knowsley
12 St Helens
13 Halton
14 Warrington
15 Trafford
16 Manchester
17 Tameside
18 Stockport
19 Nottingham
20 Telford and
   Wrekin
21 Wolverhampton

22 Walsall
23 Sandwell
24 Dudley
25 Birmingham
26 Solihull
27 Coventry
28 Peterborough
29 South Glos
30 Bristol
31 Bath and
   NE Somerset
32 Windsor and
   Maidenhead
33 Slough
34 Reading
35 Wokingham
36 Bracknell Forest
37 Thurrock
38 Southend
39 Medway
40 Plymouth
41 Torbay

LONDON

1 Hillingdon
2 Harrow
3 Barnet
4 Enfield
5 Waltham Forest
6 Redbridge
7 Barking and Dagenham
8 Havering
9 Ealing
10 Brent
11 Camden
12 Haringey
13 Islington
14 Hackney
15 Newham
16 Hounslow
17 Hammersmith and Fulham

18 Kensington and Chelsea
19 City of Westminster
20 City of London
21 Tower Hamlets
22 Richmond upon Thames
23 Wandsworth
24 Lambeth
25 Southwark
26 Lewisham
27 Greenwich
28 Bexley
29 Kingston upon Thames
30 Merton
31 Sutton
32 Croydon
33 Bromley

LONDON

The Greater London Council was abolished in 1986 and London was divided into 32 borough councils, which have a status similar to the metropolitan borough councils in the rest of England, and the City of London Corporation.

In March 1998 the government announced proposals for a Greater London Authority (GLA) covering the area of the 32 London boroughs and the City of London, which would comprise a directly elected mayor and a 25-member assembly. A referendum was held in London on 7 May 1998 and 72 per cent of voters balloted in favour of the GLA. A London mayor was elected on 4 May 2000 and the authority assumed its responsibilities on 3 July 2000 (*see also* Regional Government).

LONDON BOROUGH COUNCILS

LONDON BOROUGH COUNCILS
The London boroughs have whole council elections every four years, in the year immediately following the county council election year. The most recent elections took place on 3 May 2018.

The borough councils have responsibility for the following functions: building regulations, cemeteries and crematoria, consumer protection, education, youth employment, environmental health, electoral registration, food, drugs, housing, leisure services, libraries, local planning, local roads, museums, parking, recreation (parks, playing fields, swimming pools), refuse collection and street cleaning, social services, town planning and traffic management.

Council	Telephone	Pop.*	Council Tax†	Chief Executive‡
Barking and Dagenham	020-8592 4500	212,906	£1,617	Claire Symonds
Barnet	020-8359 2000	395,869	£1,606	John Hooton
Bexley	020-8303 7777	248,287	£1,735	Jackie Belton
Brent	020-8937 1234	329,771	£1,645	Carolyn Downs
Bromley	020-8464 3333	332,336	£1,597	Ade Adetosoye, OBE
Camden	020-7974 4444	270,029	£1,624	Jenny Rowlands
CITY OF LONDON CORPORATION	020-7606 3030	9,721	£1,007	John Barradell, OBE
Croydon	020-8726 6000	386,710	£1,784	Katherine Kerswell
Ealing	020-8825 5000	341,806	£1,571	Paul Najsarek
Enfield	020-8379 1000	333,794	£1,696	Ian Davis
Greenwich	020-8854 8888	287,942	£1,548	Debbie Warren
Hackney	020-8356 5000	281,120	£1,512	Tim Shields
Hammersmith and Fulham	020-8748 3020	185,143	£1,124	Kim Smith
Haringey	020-8489 0000	268,647	£1,705	Zina Etheridge
Harrow	020-8863 5611	251,160	£1,855	Sean Harriss
Havering	01708-434343	259,552	£1,796	Andrew Blake-Herbert
Hillingdon	01895-250111	306,870	£1,515	Fran Beasley
Hounslow	020-8583 2000	271,523	£1,607	Niall Bolger
Islington	020-7527 2000	242,467	£1,598	Linzi Roberts-Egan
Kensington and Chelsea	020-7361 3000	156,129	£1,254	Barry Quirk, CBE
Kingston upon Thames	020-8547 5000	177,507	£1,945	Ian Thomas, CBE
Lambeth	020-7926 1000	326,034	£1,502	Andrew Travers
Lewisham	020-8314 6000	305,842	£1,646	Kim Wright
Merton	020-8274 4901	206,548	£1,614	Ged Curran
Newham	020-8430 2000	353,134	£1,383	Althea Loderick
Redbridge	020-8554 5000	305,222	£1,690	Andy Donald
Richmond upon Thames	020-8891 1411	198,019	£1,872	Paul Martin
Southwark	020-7525 5000	318,830	£1,441	Eleanor Kelly
Sutton	020-8770 5000	206,349	£1,761	Helen Bailey
Tower Hamlets	020-7364 5000	324,745	£1,392	Will Tuckley
Waltham Forest	020-8496 3000	276,983	£1,760	Martin Esom
Wandsworth	020-8871 6000	329,677	£800	Paul Martin
WESTMINSTER	020-7641 6000	261,317	£782	Stuart Love

* *Source:* Office for National Statistics – *Mid-2019 Population Estimates* (Crown copyright)
† Band D council tax bill for 2020–21 inclusive of adult social care and parish precepts
‡ Or equivalent postholder
Councils in CAPITAL LETTERS have city status

CITY OF LONDON CORPORATION

The City of London Corporation is the local authority for the City of London. Its legal definition is the 'Mayor and Commonalty and Citizens of the City of London'. It is governed by the Court of Common Council, which consists of the lord mayor, 24 other aldermen and 100 common councillors. The lord mayor and two sheriffs are nominated annually by the City guilds (the livery companies) and elected by the Court of Aldermen. Aldermen and councillors are elected from the 25 wards into which the City is divided; councilmen must stand for re-election every four years. The council is a legislative assembly, and there are no political parties.

The corporation has the same functions as the London borough councils. In addition, it runs the City of London Police; is the health authority for the Port of London; has health control of animal imports throughout Greater London, including at Heathrow airport; owns and manages public open spaces throughout Greater London; runs the central criminal court; and runs Billingsgate, New Spitalfields and Smithfield markets.

The City of London is the historic centre at the heart of London known as 'the square mile', around which the vast metropolis has grown over the centuries. The City's residential population was 9,721 at the mid-2019 estimate and in addition, around 522,000 people work in the City. The City is an international financial and business centre, generating about £30bn a year for the British economy. It includes the head offices of the principal banks, insurance companies and mercantile houses, in addition to buildings ranging from the historic Roman Wall and the 15th-century Guildhall, to the massive splendour of St Paul's Cathedral and the architectural beauty of Christopher Wren's spires.

The City of London was described by Tacitus in AD 62 as 'a busy emporium for trade and traders'. Under the Romans it became an important administration centre and hub of the road system. Little is known of London in Saxon times, when it formed part of the kingdom of the East Saxons. In 886 Alfred recovered London from the Danes and reconstituted it a burgh under his son-in-law. In 1066 the citizens submitted to William the Conqueror who in 1067 granted them a charter, which is still preserved, establishing them in the rights and privileges they had hitherto enjoyed.

THE MAYORALTY

The mayoralty was probably established about 1189, the first mayor being Henry Fitz Ailwyn who filled the office for 23 years and was succeeded by Fitz Alan (1212–14). A new charter was granted by King John in 1215, directing the mayor to be chosen annually, which has been done ever since, though in early times the same individual often held the office more than once. A familiar instance is that of 'Whittington, thrice Lord Mayor of London' (in reality four times: 1397, 1398, 1406 and 1419); and many modern cases have occurred. The earliest instance of the phrase 'lord mayor' in English is in 1414. It was used more generally in the latter part of the 15th century and became invariable from 1535 onwards. At Michaelmas the liverymen in Common Hall choose two aldermen who have served the office of sheriff for presentation to the Court of Aldermen, and one is chosen to be lord mayor for the following mayoral year.

LORD MAYOR'S DAY

The Lord Mayor of the City of London was previously elected on the feast of St Simon and St Jude (28 October), and from the time of Edward I, at least, was presented to the King or to the Barons of the Exchequer on the following day, unless that day was a Sunday. The day of election was altered to 16 October in 1346, and after some further changes was fixed for

Michaelmas Day in 1546, but the ceremonies of admittance and swearing-in of the lord mayor continued to take place on 28 and 29 October respectively until 1751. In 1752, at the reform of the calendar, the lord mayor was continued in office until 8 November, the 'new style' equivalent of 28 October. The lord mayor is now presented to the Lord Chief Justice at the Royal Courts of Justice on the second Saturday in November to make the final declaration of office, having been sworn in at Guildhall on the preceding day. The procession to the Royal Courts of Justice is popularly known as the Lord Mayor's Show.

REPRESENTATIVES

Aldermen are mentioned in the 11th century and their office is of Saxon origin. They were elected annually between 1377 and 1394, when an act of parliament of Richard II directed them to be chosen for life. Aldermen now serve a six-year term of office before submitting themselves for re-election.

The Common Council was, at an early date, substituted for a popular assembly called the *Folkmote*. At first only two representatives were sent from each ward, but now each of the City's 25 wards is represented by an alderman and at least two common councillors (the number depending on the size of the ward). Common councillors are elected every four years at all-out ward elections.

OFFICERS

Sheriffs were Saxon officers; their predecessors were the *wic-reeves* and *portreeves* of London and Middlesex. At first they were officers of the Crown, and were named by the Barons of the Exchequer; but Henry I (in 1132) gave the citizens permission to choose their own sheriffs, and the annual election of sheriffs became fully operative under King John's charter of 1199. The citizens lost this privilege, as far as the election of the sheriff of Middlesex was concerned, by the Local Government Act 1888; but the liverymen continue to choose two sheriffs of the City of London, who are appointed on Midsummer Day and take office at Michaelmas.

The office of chamberlain is an ancient one, the first contemporary record of which is 1237. The Town Clerk (or common clerk) is first mentioned in 1274.

ACTIVITIES

The work of the City of London Corporation is assigned to a number of committees which make decisions on behalf of the Court of Common Council or which make recommendations for decisions by the court. The committees are extensive given the diverse services delivered by the City Corporation and include: Audit and Risk Management; Barbican Centre; Barbican Residential; Board of Governors of the City of London Freeman's School, City of London School, City of London School for Girls and the Guildhall School of Music and Drama; The City Bridge Trust; Community and Children's Services; Culture, Heritage and Libraries; Education; Epping Forest and Commons; Establishment; Finance; Freedom Applications; Gresham (City Side); Hampstead Heath, Highgate Wood and Queen's Park; Health and Wellbeing; Investment; Licensing; Markets; Open Spaces and City Gardens; Pensions Board; Planning and Transportation; Police; Policy and Resources; Port Health and Environmental Services; Standards; and West Ham Park. There are numerous other sub-committees which report to the City of London Corporation's committees.

The City's estate, in the possession of which the City of London Corporation differs from other municipalities, is largely managed by the property investment board.

The Honourable the Irish Society, which manages the City Corporation's estates in Ulster, consists of a governor, two other aldermen and 12 common councilmen.

THE LORD MAYOR 2019–21*

The Rt. Hon. the Lord Mayor, William Russell
Executive Director of Mansion House and the Central Criminal Court, Vic Annells

* Serving a two-year term due to the coronavirus pandemic

THE SHERIFFS 2019–21*

Alderman Michael Mainelli (Broad Street); Christopher Hayward

* Serving a two-year term due to the coronavirus pandemic

OFFICERS, ETC

Town Clerk, John Barradell
Chamberlain, Peter Kane
Chief Commoner (2020), Brian Mooney
Clerk, The Honourable the Irish Society, H. E. J. Montgomery, MBE

THE ALDERMEN

with office held and date of appointment to that office

Name and Ward	Common Councilman	Alderman	Sheriff	Lord Mayor
Ian Luder, *Castle Baynard*	1998	2005	2007	2008
Nicholas Anstee, *Aldersgate*	1987	1996	2003	2009
Sir David Wootton, *Langbourn*	2002	2005	2009	2011
Sir Roger Gifford, *Cordwainer*	–	2004	2008	2012
Sir Alan Yarrow, *Bridge & Bridge Wt.*	–	2007	2011	2014
Dr Sir Andrew Parmley, *Vintry*	1992	2001	2014	2016
Sir Charles Bowman, *Lime Street*	–	2013	2015	2017
Peter Estlin, *Coleman Street*	–	2013	2016	2018
William Russell, *Bread Street*	–	2013	2016	2019

All the above have passed the Civic Chair

	Common Councilman	Alderman	Sheriff
Alison Gowman, *Dowgate*	1991	2002	–
David Graves, *Cripplegate*	–	2008	–
John Garbutt, *Walbrook*	–	2009	–
Timothy Hailes, *Bassishaw*	–	2013	2017
Prof. Michael Mainelli, *Broad Street*	–	2013	2019
Vincent Keaveny, *Farringdon Wn.*	–	2013	2018
Baroness Scotland of Asthal, QC, *Bishopsgate*	–	2015	–
Robert Howard, *Cornhill*	2011	2015	–
Alistair King, *Queenhithe*	–	2016	–
Gregory Jones, QC, *Farringdon Wt.*	2013	2017	–
Prem Goyal, *Portsoken*	2017	2017	–
Nicholas Lyons, *Tower*	2017	2017	–
Emma Edhem, *Candlewick*	2018	2018	–
Robert Hughes-Penney, *Cheap*	2004–12	2018	–
Susan Langley, *Aldgate*	–	2018	–
Bronek Masojada, *Billingsgate*	–	2019	–

THE COMMON COUNCIL

Deputy: each common councillor so described serves as deputy to the alderman of her/his ward.

Abrahams, G. C. (2000) — *Farringdon Wt.*
Absalom, *Deputy* J. D. (1994) — *Farringdon Wt.*
Addy, C. K. (2017) — *Farringdon Wt.*
Ali, M. (2017) — *Portsoken*
Ameer, R. B. (2017) — *Vintry*
Anderson, R. K. (2013) — *Aldersgate*
Barr, A. R. M. (2017) — *Cordwainer*
Barrow, *Deputy* D. G. F. (2007) — *Aldgate*

Bastow, A. M. (2017) — *Aldersgate*
Bell, M. (2017) — *Farringdon Wn.*
Bennett, *Deputy* J. A. (2005) — *Broad Street*
Bennett, P. G. (2016) — *Walbrook*
Bensted-Smith, N. M. (2014) — *Cheap*
Boden, C. P. (2013) — *Castle Baynard*
Bostock, R. M. (2017) — *Cripplegate*
Bottomley, *Deputy* K. D. F. (2015) — *Bridge & Bridge Wt.*
Bradshaw, *Deputy* D. J. (1991) — *Cripplegate Wn.*
Broeke, T. (2017) — *Cheap*
Cassidy, *Deputy* M. J., CBE (1980) — *Coleman Street*
Chadwick, *Deputy* R. A. H., OBE (1994) — *Tower*
Chapman, *Deputy* J. D. (2006) — *Langbourn*
Christian, D. G. (2016) — *Lime Street*
Clementi, T. C. (2017) — *Lime Street*
Colthurst, H. N. A. (2013) — *Lime Street*
Crossan, R. P. (2017) — *Aldersgate*
Dostalova, K. H. (2013) — *Farringdon Wn.*
Duckworth, S. D., OBE (2000) — *Bishopsgate Wn.*
Dunphy, P. G. (2009) — *Cornhill*
Durcan, J. M. (2017) — *Cripplegate*
Edwards, J. E. (2019) — *Farringdon Wn.*
Everett, *Deputy* K. M. (1984) — *Candlewick*
Fairweather, A. H. (2016) — *Tower*
Fernandes, S. A. (2009) — *Coleman Street*
Fletcher, J. W. (2011) — *Portsoken*
Fredericks, M. B. (2008) — *Tower*
Graham, T. (2019) — *Cordwainer*
Haines, C. W. (2017) — *Queenhithe*
Haines, *Deputy* Revd S. D. (2005) — *Cornhill*
Harrower, G. G. (2015) — *Bassishaw*
Hayward, C. M. (2013) — *Broad Street*
Hill, C. (2017) — *Farringdon Wn.*
Hoffman, *Deputy* T. D. D. (2002) — *Vintry*
Holmes, A. (2013) — *Farringdon Wn.*
Hudson, M. (2007) — *Castle Baynard*
Hyde, *Deputy* W. (2011) — *Bishopsgate Wt.*
Ingham Clark, *Deputy* J. (2013) — *Billingsgate*
James, *Deputy* C. (2008) — *Farringdon Wn.*
Jones, *Deputy* H. L. M. (2004) — *Portsoken*
Joshi, S. J. (2018) — *Bishopsgate*
Knowles-Cutler, A. (2017) — *Castle Baynard*
Lawrence, G. A. (2002) — *Farringdon Wt.*
Levene, T. C. (2017) — *Bridge and Bridge Wt.*
Littlechild, V. (2009) — *Cripplegate Wn.*
Lloyd-Owen, N. M. C. (2018) — *Castle Baynard*
Lodge, O. A. W., TD (2009) — *Bread Street*
Lord, *Deputy* C. E., OBE (2001) — *Farringdon Wt.*
Martinelli, P. N. (2013) — *Farringdon Wt.*
Mayer, A. P. (2013) — *Bishopsgate*
Mayhew, J. P. (1996) — *Aldersgate*
McGuinness, *Deputy* C. S. (1997) — *Castle Baynard*
McMurtie, A. S. (2013) — *Coleman Street*
Mead, W., OBE (1997) — *Farringdon Wt.*
Merrett, *Deputy* R. A. (2009) — *Bassishaw*
Meyers, *Deputy* A. G. D. (2017) — *Aldgate*
Mooney, (Chief Commoner) *Deputy* B. D. F. (1998) — *Queenhithe*
Morris, H. F. (2008) — *Aldgate*
Moss, *Deputy* A. M. (2013) — *Cheap*
Moys, S. D. (2001) — *Aldgate*
Murphy, B. D. (2017) — *Bishopsgate*
Nash, *Deputy* J. C., OBE (1983) — *Aldersgate*
Newman, B. P., CBE (1989) — *Aldersgate*
Packham, G. D. (2013) — *Castle Baynard*
Patel, D. (2013) — *Aldgate*
Pearson, S. J. (2017) — *Cripplegate*
Petrie, J. (2018) — *Billingsgate*
Pimlott, W. (2017) — *Cripplegate*

Pleasance, J. L. (2013)	*Langbourn*
Pollard, *Deputy* J. H. G. (2002)	*Dowgate*
Priest, H. J. S. (2009)	*Castle Baynard*
Pritchard, J. P. (2017)	*Portsoken*
Quilter, S. D. (1998)	*Cripplegate Wt.*
Regan, *Deputy* R. D., OBE (1998)	*Farringdon Wn.*
Rogula, *Deputy* E. (2008)	*Lime Street*
de Sausmarez, H. J. (2015)	*Candlewick*
Sayed, R. (2017)	*Farringdon Wt.*
Scott, J. G. S. (1999)	*Broad Street*
Seaton, I. C. N. (2009)	*Cornhill*
Sells, O. M., QC (2017)	*Farringdon Wt.*
Shilson, *Deputy*, G. R. E. (2009)	*Bread Street*
Simons, J. L. (2004)	*Castle Baynard*
Sleigh, *Deputy* T. C. C. (2013)	*Bishopsgate Wt.*
Smith, G. M. (2013)	*Farringdon Wn.*
Snyder, *Deputy* Sir Michael (1986)	*Cordwainer*
Thompson, D. J. (2004)	*Aldgate*
Tomlinson, *Deputy* J. (2004)	*Cripplegate Wt.*
Tumbridge, J. R. (2009)	*Tower*
Upton, J. W. D. (2017)	*Farringdon Wt.*
Wheatley, M. R. P. H. D. (2013)	*Dowgate*
Woodhouse, *Deputy* P. J. (2013)	*Langbourn*
Wright, D. L. (2019)	*Coleman Street*

THE CITY GUILDS (LIVERY COMPANIES)

The livery companies of the City of London grew out of early medieval religious fraternities and began to emerge as trade and craft guilds, retaining their religious aspect, in the 12th century. From the early 14th century, only members of the trade and craft guilds could call themselves citizens of the City of London. The guilds began to be called livery companies, because of the distinctive livery worn by the most prosperous guild members on ceremonial occasions, in the late 15th century.

By the early 19th century the power of the companies within their trades had begun to wane, but those wearing the livery of a company continued to play an important role in the government of the City of London. Liverymen still have the right to nominate the Lord Mayor and sheriffs, and most members of the Court of Common Council are liverymen.

The constitution of the livery companies has been unchanged for centuries. There are three ranks of membership: freemen, liverymen and assistants. A person can become a freeman by patrimony (through a parent having been a freeman); by servitude (through having served an apprenticeship to a freeman); or by redemption (by purchase).

Election to the livery is the prerogative of the company, who can elect any of its freemen as liverymen. Assistants are usually elected from the livery and form a court of assistants which is the governing body of the company. The master (in some companies called the prime warden) is elected annually from the assistants.

The register for 2020 lists 25,949 liverymen of the guilds entitled to vote at elections at common hall.

The order of precedence, omitting extinct companies, is given in parentheses after the name of each company in the list below. In certain companies the election of master or prime warden for the year does not take place until the autumn. In such cases the master or prime warden for 2019–20, rather than 2020–21, is given.

The Twelve Great Companies are given in order of civic precedence and appear first in the list below; the remaining guilds are listed in alphabetical order. Parish clerks and watermen and lightermen have requested to remain with no livery and are marked with a '*'.

MERCERS (1). *Hall*, Mercers' Hall, 6 Frederick's Place, London EC2R 8AB *Livery*, 250.
  Clerk, Rob Abernethy
  Master, Mark Aspinall
GROCERS (2). *Hall*, Grocers' Hall, Princes Street, London EC2R 8AD *Livery*, 360.
  Clerk, Brig. Greville Bibby, CBE
  Master, Rupert Uloth
DRAPERS (3). *Hall*, Drapers' Hall, Throgmorton Avenue, London EC2N 2DQ *Livery*, 290.
  Clerk, Col. Richard Winstanley, OBE
  Master, Timothy Orchard
FISHMONGERS (4). *Hall*, Fishmongers' Hall, London Bridge, London EC4R 9EL *Livery*, 330.
  Clerk, Cdre Toby Williamson, MVO
  Prime Warden, David Jones
GOLDSMITHS (5). *Hall*, Goldsmiths' Hall, Foster Lane, London EC2V 6BN *Livery*, 280.
  Clerk, Sir David Reddaway, KCMG, MBE
  Prime Warden, Richard Fox
MERCHANT TAYLORS (6/7). *Hall*, Merchant Taylors' Hall, 30 Threadneedle Street, London EC2R 8JB *Livery*, 360.
  Clerk, Rear-Adm. John Clink, CBE
  Master, Jane Hall
SKINNERS (6/7). *Hall*, Skinners' Hall, 8 Dowgate Hill, London EC4R 2SP *Livery*, 390.
  Clerk, Maj.-Gen. Andrew Kennett, CB, CBE
  Master, John Emms
HABERDASHERS (8). *Hall*, Haberdashers' Hall, 18 West Smithfield, London EC1A 9HQ *Livery*, 325.
  Clerk, Cdre Philip Thicknesse, RN
  Master, Daniel Hochberg
SALTERS (9). *Hall*, Salters' Hall, 4 London Wall Place, London EC2Y 5DE *Livery*, 180.
  Clerk, vacant
  Master, Dr Elizabeth Nodder
IRONMONGERS (10). *Hall*, Ironmongers' Hall, Shaftesbury Place, London EC2Y 8AA *Livery*, 115.
  Clerk, Col. Charlie Knaggs, OBE
  Master, John Biles
VINTNERS (11). *Hall*, Vintners' Hall, Upper Thames Street, London EC4V 3BG *Livery*, 390.
  Clerk, Brig. Jonathan Bourne-May
  Master, Christopher Davey
CLOTHWORKERS (12). *Hall*, Clothworkers' Hall, Dunster Court, London EC3R 7AH *Livery*, 210.
  Clerk, Joss Stuart-Grumbar
  Master, Alex Nelson
ACTUARIES (91). 2nd Floor, 2 London Wall Place, London EC2Y 5AU *Livery*, 260.
  Clerk, Lyndon Jones
  Master, Julie Griffiths
AIR PILOTS AND AIR NAVIGATORS (81). Air Pilots House, 52A Borough High Street, London SE1 1XN *Livery*, 550.
  Clerk, Paul Tacon
  Master, John Towell
APOTHECARIES (58). *Hall*, Apothecaries' Hall, 14 Black Friars Lane, London EC4V 6EJ *Livery*, 1,200.
  Clerk, Nick Royle
  Master, Prof. Michael Farthing
ARBITRATORS (93). 28 The Meadway, Cuffley EN6 4ES *Livery*, 145.
  Clerk, Biagio Fraulo
  Master, Margaret Bickford-Smith, QC
ARMOURERS AND BRASIERS (22). *Hall*, Armourers' Hall, 81 Coleman Street, London EC2R 5BJ *Livery*, 130.
  Clerk, Peter Bateman
  Master, Mike Goulette
ARTS SCHOLARS (110). 5 Queen Anne's Gate, White House Walk, Farnham GU9 9AN *Livery*, 150.
  Clerk, Lt.-Col. Chris Booth
  Master, John Spanner, TD

BAKERS (19). *Hall*, Bakers' Hall, 9 Harp Lane, London
EC3R 6DP *Livery*, 235.
Clerk, Lance Whitehouse
Master, Christopher Freeman

BARBERS (17). *Hall*, Barber-Surgeons' Hall, Monkwell Square,
London EC2Y 5BL *Livery*, 250.
Clerk, Malachy Doran
Master, Nicolas Goddard

BASKETMAKERS (52). 11 South Way, Seaford
BN25 4JG *Livery*, 200.
Clerk, Sarah Sinclair
Prime Warden, Lewis Block, FCSI

BLACKSMITHS (40). Painters' Hall, 9 Little Trinity Lane, London
EC4V 2AD *Livery*, 260.
Clerk, Jill Moffatt
Prime Warden, Alderman Alastair King

BOWYERS (38). Fosters Lodge, Duck Street, Warminster
BA12 7AL *Livery*, 100.
Clerk, Lt.-Col. Tony Marinos
Master, David Laxton

BREWERS (14). *Hall*, Brewers' Hall, Aldermanbury Square,
London EC2V 7HR *Livery*, 200.
Clerk, Col. Michael O'Dwyer, OBE
Master, Richard Fuller

BRODERERS (48). Orchard House, Vicarage Lane, Steeple
Ashton BA14 6HH *Livery*, 120.
Clerk, Brig. Bill Aldridge, CBE
Master, Toby Gunter

BUILDERS MERCHANTS (88). 4 College Hill, London
EC4R 2RB *Livery*, 210.
Clerk, Virginia Rounding
Master, Stewart Price

BUTCHERS (24). Butchers' Hall, 87 Bartholomew Close, London
EC1A 7EB *Livery*, 650.
Clerk, Maj.-Gen. Jeff Mason, MBE, RM
Master, Andrew Parker

CARMEN (77). Plaisterers' Hall, 1 London Wall, London
EC2Y 5JU *Livery*, 500.
Clerk, Julian Litchfield
Master, Col. Simon Bennett, TD

CARPENTERS (26). *Hall*, Carpenters' Hall, 1 Throgmorton
Avenue, London EC2N 2JJ *Livery*, 150.
Clerk, Brig. Tim Gregson, MBE
Master, Michael Morrison

CHARTERED ACCOUNTANTS (86). 35 Ascot Way, Bicester
OX26 1AG *Livery*, 290.
Clerk, Jonathan Grosvenor
Master, Graeme Gordon

CHARTERED ARCHITECTS (98). 53 Lychgate Drive,
Horndean PO8 9QE *Livery*, 160.
Clerk, Phil Gibbs
Master, John Assael

CHARTERED SECRETARIES AND ADMINISTRATORS
(87). 3rd Floor, Saddlers' Hall, 40 Gutter Lane, London
EC2V 6BR *Livery*, 210.
Clerk, Keith Povey
Master, Edward Nicholl

CHARTERED SURVEYORS (85). 75 Meadway Drive, Horsell,
Woking GU21 4TF *Livery*, 330.
Clerk, Colin Peacock
Master, Ken Morgan

CLOCKMAKERS (61). 1 Throgmorton Avenue, London
EC2N 2BY *Livery*, 285.
Clerk, Camilla Szymanowska
Master, Joanna Migdal

COACHMAKERS AND COACH-HARNESS MAKERS
(72). The Old Barn, Church Lane, Glentham
LN8 2EL *Livery*, 430.
Clerk, Cdr Mark Leaning
Master, Sarah Adams-Diffey

CONSTRUCTORS (99). 5 Delft Close, Southampton
SO31 7TQ *Livery*, 135.
Clerk, Kim Tyrrell
Master, Arthur Seymour

COOKS (35). 18 Solent Drive, Warsash SO31 9HB *Livery*, 70.
Clerk, Vice-Adm. Peter Wilkinson, CB, CVO
Master, Cdre David Smith, CBE

COOPERS (36). *Hall*, Coopers' Hall, 13 Devonshire Square,
London EC2M 4TH *Livery*, 250.
Clerk, Cdr Stephen White
Master, Bill Scott

CORDWAINERS (27). Clothworkers' Hall, Dunster Court,
London EC3R 7AH *Livery*, 170.
Clerk, Penny Graham
Master, Peter Lamble

CURRIERS (29). Oak Lodge, 4 Greenhill Lane, Wimborne
BH21 2RN *Livery*, 110.
Clerk, Adrian Rafferty
Master, Mary McNeill

CUTLERS (18). *Hall*, Cutlers' Hall, Warwick Lane, London
EC4M 7BR *Livery*, 90.
Clerk, Rupert Meacher
Master, Dr Caroline Herbert, MBE

DISTILLERS (69). 1 The Sanctuary, London
SW1P 3JT *Livery*, 320.
Clerk, Edward Macey-Dare
Master, Jonathan Driver

DYERS (13). *Hall*, Dyers' Hall, 10 Dowgate Hill, London
EC4R 2ST *Livery*, 140.
Clerk, Russell Vaizey
Prime Warden, James Rothwell

EDUCATORS (109). 8 Little Trinity Lane, London
EC4V 2AN *Livery*, 200.
Clerk, Christian Jensen
Master, Richard Evans

ENGINEERS (94). Saddlers' House, 44 Gutter Lane, London
EC2V 6BR *Livery*, 310.
Clerk, Col. David Swann, CBE
Master, Prof. Gordon Masterton

ENVIRONMENTAL CLEANERS (97). Woodfield Cottage,
The Street, Mortimer RG7 3DW *Livery*, 160.
Clerk, Philip Morrish
Master, John Shonfeld

FAN MAKERS (76). Skinners' Hall, 8 Dowgate Hill, London
EC4R 2SP *Livery*, 190.
Clerk, Martin Davies
Master, Colin Bramall

FARMERS (80). *Hall*, The Farmers' and Fletchers' Hall, 3 Cloth
Street, London EC1A 7LD *Livery*, 355.
Clerk, Graham Bamford
Master, Richard Whitlock

FARRIERS (55). 19 Queen Street, Chipperfield, Kings Langley
WD4 9BT *Livery*, 330.
Clerk, Charlotte Clifford
Master, John Wilsher

FELTMAKERS (63). Post Cottage, Hook
RG29 1DA *Livery*, 200.
Clerk, Maj. Jollyon Coombs
Master, Lady Gilly Yarrow

FIREFIGHTERS (103). 3rd Floor, Wax Chandlers' Hall, 6
Gresham Street, London EC2V 7AD *Livery*, 140.
Clerk, Steven Tamcken
Master, Frances Blois

FLETCHERS (39). *Hall*, 37 Wallingford Avenue, London
W10 6PZ *Livery*, 150.
Clerk, Kate Pink
Master, Stuart Robbens

FOUNDERS (33). *Hall*, Founders' Hall, 1 Cloth Fair, London
EC1A 7JQ *Livery*, 165.
Clerk, Andrew Bell
Master, Anthony Whiteoak Robinson

FRAMEWORK KNITTERS (64). The Grange, Walton Road,
Lutterworth LE17 5RU *Livery*, 185.
Clerk, Shaun Mackaness
Master, Ian Grundy

FRUITERERS (45). The Old Bakery, Bull Lane, Ketton
PE9 3TB *Livery*, 260.
Clerk, John Grant
Master, David Simmons

FUELLERS (95). Skinners' Hall, 8 Dowgate Hill, London
EC4R 2SP *Livery*, 160.
Clerk, Crde. Bill Walworth, CBE
Master, HRH Prince Edward, Earl of Wessex, KG, GCVO

FURNITURE MAKERS (83). *Hall*, Furniture Makers' Hall, 12
Austin Friars, London EC2N 2HE *Livery*, 220.
Clerk, Jonny Westbrooke
Master, David Woodward .

GARDENERS (66). Ingrams, Ingram's Green, Midhurst
GU29 0LJ *Livery*, 295.
Clerk, Maj. Jeremy Herrtage
Master, Dr Heather Barrett-Modd, OBE

GIRDLERS (23). *Hall*, Girdlers' Hall, Basinghall Avenue, London
EC2V 5DD *Livery*, 80.
Clerk, Brig. Murray Whiteside, OBE
Master, Maj.-Gen. Sir Sebastian Roberts, KCVO, OBE

GLASS SELLERS (71). 238 Nelson Road, Whitton *Livery*, 132.
Clerk, Paul Wenham
Master, Richard Katz

GLAZIERS AND PAINTERS OF GLASS (53). *Hall*, Glaziers'
Hall, 9 Montague Close, London SE1 9DD *Livery*, 180.
Clerk, Liz Wicksteed
Master, Michael Dalton

GLOVERS (62). Seniors Farmhouse, Semley, Shaftesbury
SP7 9AX *Livery*, 250.
Clerk, Lt.-Col. Mark Butler
Master, Richard Morris

GOLD AND SILVER WYRE DRAWERS (74). Lye Green
Forge, Lye Green, Crowborough TN6 1UU *Livery*, 280.
Clerk, Cdr Mark Dickens
Master, Michael Gunston

GUNMAKERS (73). The Proof House, 48–50 Commercial Road,
London E1 1LP *Livery*, 360.
Clerk, Adrian Mundin, MVO
Master, Roderick Richmond-Watson

HACKNEY CARRIAGE DRIVERS (104). 17 Barton Court
Avenue, New Milton BH25 7EP *Livery*, 105.
Clerk, position abolished
Master, Rick Alford

HORNERS (54). 12 Coltsfoot Close, Ixworth
IP31 2NJ *Livery*, 200.
Clerk, Jonathan Mead, FRSA
Master, Martin Muirhead

INFORMATION TECHNOLOGISTS (100). *Hall*, Information
Technologists' Hall, 39A Bartholomew Close, London
EC1A 7JN *Livery*, 380.
Clerk, Susan Hoefling
Master, Mark Holford

INNHOLDERS (32). *Hall*, Innholders' Hall, 30 College Street,
London EC4R 2RH *Livery*, 100.
Clerk, Charles Henty
Master, Keith Harrison

INSURERS (92). PO Box 55873, London N18 9DJ *Livery*, 365.
Clerk, Victoria King
Master, David Sales

INTERNATIONAL BANKERS (106). 12 Austin Friars, London
EC2N 2HE *Livery*, 190.
Clerk, Nicholas Westgarth
Master, Robert Merrett

JOINERS AND CEILERS (41). 3 Dury Road, Barnet
EN5 5PU *Livery*, 130.
Clerk, Alistair MacQueen
Master, James de Sausmarez

LAUNDERERS (89). Glaziers' Hall, 9 Montague Close, London
SE1 9DD *Livery*, 175.
Clerk, Margaret Campbell
Master, Maj. Jack Strachan, MBE

LEATHERSELLERS (15). 7 St Helen's Place, London
EC3A 6AB *Livery*, 150.
Clerk, David Santa-Olalla, DSO, MC
Master, Jonathan Muirhead, OBE, DL

LIGHTMONGERS (96). Tallow Chandlers' Hall, 4 Dowgate Hill,
London EC4R 2SH *Livery*, 150.
Clerk, Victoria McKay
Master, Father Peter Harris

LORINERS (57). 30 Elm Park, Royal Wootton Bassett
SN4 7TA *Livery*, 350.
Clerk, Honor Page
Master, Susan Douthwaite

MAKERS OF PLAYING CARDS (75). 35 Ascot Way, Bicester
E14 3WE *Livery*, 150.
Clerk, Annie Prowse
Master, Giles Stockton

MANAGEMENT CONSULTANTS (105). Skinners' Hall, 8
Dowgate Hill, London EC4R 2SP *Livery*, 130.
Clerk, Julie Fox
Master, Denise Fellows

MARKETORS (90). Plaisterers' Hall, One London Wall, London
EC2Y 5JU *Livery*, 250.
Clerk, John Hammond
Master, Lesley Wilson

MASONS (30). 8 Little Trinity Lane, London
EC4V 2AN *Livery*, 190.
Clerk, Maj. Giles Clapp
Master, Dr Christine Rigden

MASTER MARINERS (78). *Hall*, HQS Wellington, Temple
Stairs, London WC2R 2PN *Livery*, 188.
Clerk, Scott Hanlon
Master, Capt. Derek Chadburn

MUSICIANS (50). 1 Speed Highwalk, Barbican
EC2Y BDX *Livery*, 420.
Clerk, Hugh Lloyd
Master, John Nichols

NEEDLEMAKERS (65). PO Box 73635, London
SW14 9BY *Livery*, 195.
Clerk, Fiona Sedgwick
Master, Andrew Whitton

PAINTER-STAINERS (28). *Hall*, Painters' Hall, 9 Little Trinity
Lane, London EC4V 2AD *Livery*, 270.
Clerk, Christopher Twyman
Master, Peter Huddleston

PATTENMAKERS (70). 3 The High Street, Sutton Valence
ME17 3AG *Livery*, 210.
Clerk, Col. Robert Murfin, TD
Master, Dr David Best

PAVIORS (56). Paviors' House, Charterhouse, London
EC1M 6AN *Livery*, 310.
Clerk, John Freestone
Master, Hugh MacDougald

PEWTERERS (16). *Hall*, Pewterers' Hall, Oat Lane, London
EC2V 7DE *Livery*, 140.
Clerk, Cdre. Mike Walliker, CBE
Master, Chris Hudson, MBE

PLAISTERERS (46). *Hall*, Plaisterers' Hall, 1 London Wall,
London EC2Y 5JU *Livery*, 230.
Clerk, Col. Garth Manger, OBE
Master, Margaret Coates

PLUMBERS (31). Carpenters' Hall, 1 Throgmorton Avenue,
London EC2N 2JJ *Livery*, 340.
Clerk, Adrian Mumford
Master, Dr Peter Rumley

POULTERS (34). 20 Waltham Road, Woodford Green
IG8 8DN *Livery*, 220.
Clerk, Julie Pearce
Master, Reginald Beer

SADDLERS (25). *Hall*, Saddlers' Hall, 40 Gutter Lane, London
EC2V 6BR *Livery*, 90.
Clerk, Brig. Philip Napier, OBE
Prime Warden, Nicholas Mason

SCIENTIFIC INSTRUMENT MAKERS (84). Glaziers' Hall, 9
Montague Close, London SE1 9DD *Livery*, 180.
Clerk, Dr Misha Hebel
Master, Martyn Weatley

SCRIVENERS (44). HQS Wellington, Temple Stairs, Victoria
Embankment, London WC2R 2PN *Livery*, 200.
Clerk, Capt. Arnold Lustman
Master, Barry Theobald-Hicks

SECURITY PROFESSIONALS (108). 4 Holmere Farm Cottages, Goose Green, Ashill IP25 7AS *Livery*, 180.
Clerk, Patricia Boswell
Master, Yasmeen Stratton

SHIPWRIGHTS (59). Ironmonger's Hall, Shaftesbury Place, London EC2Y 8AA *Livery*, 420.
Clerk, Lt.-Col. Richard Cole-Mackintosh
Prime Warden, John Denholm

SOLICITORS (79). 4 College Hill, London EC4R 2RB *Livery*, 410.
Clerk, Linzi James
Master, Robert Bell

SPECTACLE MAKERS (60). Apothecaries' Hall, Black Friars Lane, London EC4V 6EL *Livery*, 380.
Clerk, Helen Perkins
Master, Huntly Taylor

STATIONERS AND NEWSPAPER MAKERS (47). *Hall*, Stationers' Hall, Ave Maria Lane, London EC4M 7DD *Livery*, 530.
Clerk, William Alden, MBE
Master, The Rt. Revd Dr Stephen Platten

TALLOW CHANDLERS (21). *Hall*, Tallow Chandlers' Hall, 4 Dowgate Hill, London EC4R 2SH *Livery*, 180.
Clerk, Brig. David Homer, MBE
Master, Oliver Kirby-Johnson

TAX ADVISERS (107). 10 Deena Close, Queen's Drive W3 0HR *Livery*, 160.
Clerk, Stephen Henderson
Master, Sue Christensen

TIN PLATE WORKERS (ALIAS WIRE WORKERS) (67). PO Box 71002, London W4 9FH *Livery*, 180.
Clerk, Dr Piers Baker
Master, Laurence Mutkin

TOBACCO PIPE MAKERS AND TOBACCO BLENDERS (82). 14 Montpelier Road, Sutton SM1 4QE *Livery*, 135.
Clerk, Sandra Stocker
Master, Adam Bennett

TURNERS (51). Skinner's Hall, 8 Dowgate Hill, London EC4R 2SP *Livery*, 190.
Clerk, Alex Robertson
Master, Melissa Scott

TYLERS AND BRICKLAYERS (37). 15 Heathway, Chaldon Cateram CR3 5DN *Livery*, 160.
Clerk, John Brooks
Master, Dr Michel Saminaden

UPHOLDERS (49). Pembroke Lodge, 162 Tonbridge Road, Hildenborough TN11 9HP *Livery*, 160.
Clerk, Susan Nevard
Master, Wendy Shorter-Blake, MBE

WATER CONSERVATORS (102). The Lark, 2 Bell Lane, Bury St Edmunds IP28 8SE *Livery*, 175.
Clerk, Ralph Riley
Master, Rob Casey

WAX CHANDLERS (20). *Hall*, Wax Chandlers' Hall, 6 Gresham Street, London EC2V 7AD *Livery*, 120.
Clerk, Richard Moule
Master, Susan Green

WEAVERS (42). Saddlers' House, Gutter Lane, London EC2V 6BR *Livery*, 130.
Clerk, James Gaselee
Upper Bailiff, William Makower

WHEELWRIGHTS (68). 90 Fernside Road, London SW12 8LJ *Livery*, 210.
Clerk, Susie Morris
Master, His Excellency Air Chief Marshal Sir Stephen Dalton

WOOLMEN (43). 153 Leathwaite Road, SW11 6RW *Livery*, 160.
Clerk, Duncan Crole
Master, Alderman Sir David Wootton

WORLD TRADERS (101). 13 Hall Gardens, St Albans AL4 0QF *Livery*, 220.
Clerk, Gaye Duffy
Master, Peter Alvey

PARISH CLERKS (90). Acreholt, 33 Medstead Road, Beech, Alton GU34 4AD *Members*, 90.
Clerk, Alana Coombes
Master, Nigel Thompson

WATERMEN AND LIGHTERMEN (No Livery*). *Hall*, Watermen's Hall, 16–18 St Mary at Hill, London EC3R 8EF *Craft Owning Freemen*, 380.
Clerk, Colin Middlemiss
Master, Tony Maynard

WALES

Cymru

The principality of Wales (Cymru) occupies the extreme west of the central southern portion of the island of Great Britain, with a total area of 20,736 sq. km (8,006 sq. miles). It is bordered in the north by the Irish Sea, in the south by the Bristol Channel, in the east by the English counties of Cheshire West and Chester, Shropshire, Herefordshire and Gloucestershire, and in the west by St George's Channel.

Across the Menai Straits is Ynys Mon (Isle of Anglesey) (715 sq. km/276 sq. miles), communication with which is facilitated by the Menai Suspension Bridge (305m/1,000ft long) built by Thomas Telford in 1826, and by the Britannia Bridge (351m/1,151ft), a two-tier road and rail truss arch design, rebuilt in 1972 after a fire destroyed the original tubular railway bridge built by Robert Stephenson in 1850. Holyhead harbour, on Holy Isle (north-west of Anglesey), provides ferry services to Dublin (113km/70 miles).

The Local Government (Wales) Act 1994 abolished the two-tier structure of eight county and 37 district councils which had existed since 1974, and replaced it, from 1 April 1996, with 22 unitary authorities. The new authorities were elected in May 1995. Each unitary authority inherited all the functions of the previous county and district councils, except fire services (which are provided by three combined fire authorities, composed of representatives from the unitary authorities) and national parks (which are the responsibility of three independent national park authorities).

POPULATION

The population at the mid-2019 estimate was 3,138,631 (1,554,678 males; 1,598,201 females). The average density of the population at the mid-2019 estimate was 152 persons per sq. km (392 per sq. mile).

COMMUNITY COUNCILS

In Wales communities are the equivalent of parishes in England. Unlike England, where many areas are not in any parish, communities have been established for the whole of Wales, 870 communities in all. Community meetings may be convened as and when desired.

Community or town councils exist in over 730 of the communities and further councils may be established at the request of a community meeting. Community councils have broadly the same range of powers as English parish councils. Community councillors are elected for a term of four years.

ELECTIONS

Elections usually take place every four years; the last elections took place on 4 May 2017.

FINANCE

Total budgeted revenue expenditure by all local authorities for 2020–21 was £8.7bn, an increase of 4.1 per cent on 2019–20. Total budget requirement, which excludes expenditure financed by specific and special government grants and any use of reserves, was £6.9bn. This comprises revenue support grant of £3.5bn, support from the national non-domestic rate pool of £1.1bn, police grant of £241m and £2.1bn to be raised through council tax. The non-domestic rating multiplier for Wales for 2020–21 is 53.5p. The average Band D council tax levied in Wales for 2020–21 is £1,667, comprising county councils £1,354, police and crime commissioners £275 and community councils £38.

EXPENDITURE

Local authority budgeted revenue expenditure for 2020–21 is:

Service	£ million
Education	2,7893.2
Social services	2,053.8
Housing*	1,022.0
Local environmental services	394.6
Roads and transport	282.3
Libraries, culture, heritage, sport & recreation	193.5
Planning, economic & community development	80.4
Council tax collection	32.1
Debt financing	301.6
Central administrative & other revenue expenditure	398.3
Police	816.6
Fire	166.8
National parks	19.2
Gross revenue expenditure	8,654.7
Less specific & special government grants	(1,897.3)
Net revenue expenditure	6,757.4
Less appropriations from reserves	(118.0)
Council tax reduction scheme	278.2
BUDGET REQUIREMENT	6,917.6

* Includes housing benefit and provision for the homeless, not council owned housing

RELIEF

Wales is a country of extensive tracts of high plateau and shorter stretches of mountain ranges deeply dissected by river valleys. Lower-lying ground is largely confined to the coastal belt and the lower parts of the valleys. The highest mountains are those of Snowdonia in the north-west (Snowdon, 1,085m/3,559ft and Aran Fawddwy, 906m/2,971ft). Snowdonia is also home to Cader Idris (Pen y Gadair, 892m/2,928ft). Other high peaks are to be found in the Cambrian range (Plynlimon, 752m/2,467ft), and the Black Mountains, Brecon Beacons and Black Forest ranges in the south-east (Pen y Fan, 886m/2,906ft; Waun Fâch, 811m/2,660ft; Carmarthen Van, 802m/2,630ft).

HYDROGRAPHY

The principal river in Wales is the Severn, which flows from the slopes of Plynlimon to the English border. The Wye (209km/130 miles) also rises on the slopes of Plynlimon. The Usk (90km/56 miles) flows into the Bristol Channel through Gwent. The Dee (113km/70 miles) rises in Bala Lake and flows through the Vale of Llangollen, where an aqueduct (built by Thomas Telford in 1805) carries the Pontcysyllte branch of the Shropshire Union Canal across the valley. The estuary of the Dee is the navigable portion; it is 23km (14 miles) in length and about 8km (5 miles) in breadth. The Towy (109km/68 miles), Teifi (80km/50 miles), Taff (64km/40 miles), Dovey (48km/30 miles), Taf (40km/25 miles) and Conway (39km/24 miles) are wholly Welsh rivers.

The largest natural lake is Bala (Llyn Tegid) in Gwynedd, nearly 7km (4 miles) long and 1.6km (1 mile) wide. Lake Vyrnwy is an artificial reservoir, about the size of Bala, and forms the water supply of Liverpool; Birmingham's water is supplied from reservoirs in the Elan and Claerwen valleys.

FLAG

The flag of Wales, the Red Dragon *(Y Ddraig Goch)*, is a red dragon on a field divided by white over green *(per fess argent* and vert a dragon passant gules). The flag was augmented in 1953 by a royal badge on a shield encircled with a riband bearing the words *Ddraig Goch Ddyry Cychwyn* and imperially crowned, but this augmented flag is rarely used.

WELSH LANGUAGE

At the 2011 census the percentage of people, aged three years and over, recorded as able to speak Welsh was:

Blaenau Gwent	7.8	Neath Port Talbot	15.3
Bridgend	9.7	Newport	9.3
Caerphilly	11.2	Pembrokeshire	19.2
Cardiff	11.1	Powys	18.6
Carmarthenshire	43.9	Rhondda Cynon Taf	12.3
Ceredigion	47.3	Swansea	11.4
Conwy	27.4	Torfaen	9.8
Denbighshire	24.6	Vale of Glamorgan	10.8
Flintshire	13.2	Wrexham	12.9
Gwynedd	65.4	Ynys Mon	
Merthyr Tydfil	8.9	(Isle of Anglesey)	57.2
Monmouthshire	9.9	*Total in Wales*	19.0

EARLY HISTORY

The earliest inhabitants of whom there is any record appear to have been subdued or exterminated by the Goidels (a people of Celtic race) in the Bronze Age. A further invasion of Celtic Brythons and Belgae followed in the ensuing Iron Age. The Roman conquest of southern Britain and Wales was for some time successfully opposed by Caratacus (Caractacus or Caradog), chieftain of the Catuvellauni and son of Cunobelinus (Cymbeline). South-east Wales was subjugated and the legionary fortress at Caerleon-on-Usk established by around AD 75–7; the conquest of Wales was completed by Agricola around AD 78. Communications were opened up by the construction of military roads from Chester to Caerleon-on-Usk and Caerwent, and from Chester to Conwy (and thence to Carmarthen and Neath). Christianity was introduced in the fourth century, during the Roman occupation.

ANGLO-SAXON ATTACKS

The Anglo-Saxon invaders of southern Britain drove the Celts into the mountain stronghold of Wales, and into Strathclyde (Cumberland and south-west Scotland) and Cornwall, giving them the name of *Waelisc* (Welsh), meaning 'foreign'. The West Saxons' victory of Deorham (AD 577) isolated Wales from Cornwall and the battle of Chester (AD 613) cut off communication with Strathclyde and northern Britain. In the eighth century the boundaries of the Welsh were further restricted by the annexations of Offa, King of Mercia, and counter-attacks were largely prevented by the construction of an artificial boundary from the Dee to the Wye (Offa's Dyke).

In the ninth century Rhodri Mawr (844–878) united the country and successfully resisted further incursions of the Saxons by land and raids of Norse and Danish pirates by sea, but at his death his three provinces of Gwynedd (north), Powys (central) and Deheubarth (south) were divided among his three sons, Anarawd, Mervyn and Cadell. Cadell's son Hywel Dda ruled a large part of Wales and codified its laws but the provinces were not united again until the rule of Llewelyn ap Seisyllt (husband of the heiress of Gwynedd) from 1018 to 1023.

THE NORMAN CONQUEST

After the Norman conquest of England, William I created palatine counties along the Welsh frontier, and the Norman barons began to make encroachments into Welsh territory. The Welsh princes recovered many of their losses during the civil wars of Stephen's reign (1135–54), and in the early 13th century Owen Gruffydd, prince of Gwynedd, was the dominant figure in Wales. Under Llywelyn ap Iorwerth (1194–1240) the Welsh united in powerful resistance to English incursions and Llywelyn's privileges and *de facto* independence were recognised in the Magna Carta. His grandson, Llywelyn ap Gruffydd, was the last native prince; he was killed in 1282 during hostilities between the Welsh and English, allowing Edward I of England to establish his authority over the country. On 7 February 1301, Edward of Caernarvon, son of Edward I, was created Prince of Wales, a title subsequently borne by the eldest son of the sovereign.

Strong Welsh national feeling continued, expressed in the early 15th century in the rising led by Owain Glyndwr, but the situation was altered by the accession to the English throne in 1485 of Henry VII of the Welsh House of Tudor. Wales was politically annexed by England under the Act of Union of 1535, which extended English laws to the principality and gave it parliamentary representation for the first time.

EISTEDDFOD

The Welsh are a distinct nation, with a language and literature of their own; the national bardic festival (Eisteddfod), instituted by Prince Rhys ap Griffith in 1176, is still held annually.

PRINCIPAL CITIES

There are six cities in Wales (with date city status conferred): Bangor (pre-1900), Cardiff (1905), Newport (2002), St Asaph (2012), St David's (1994) and Swansea (1969).

Cardiff and Swansea have also been granted lord mayoralties.

CARDIFF

Cardiff *(Caerdydd)*, at the mouth of the rivers Taff, Rhymney and Ely, is the capital city of Wales. The city has changed dramatically in recent years following the regeneration of Cardiff Bay and construction of a barrage, which has created a permanent freshwater lake and waterfront for the city. As the capital city, Cardiff is home to the National Assembly for Wales and is a major administrative, retail, business and cultural centre.

The city is home to many fine buildings, including the City Hall, Cardiff Castle, Llandaff Cathedral, the National Museum of Wales, university buildings, law courts and the Temple of Peace and Health. The Millennium Stadium opened in 1999 and has hosted high-profile events since 2001.

SWANSEA

Swansea *(Abertawe)* is a seaport with a population of 239,023 at the 2011 census. The Gower peninsula was brought within the city boundary under local government reform in 1974.

The principal buildings are the Norman castle (rebuilt c.1330), the Royal Institution of South Wales, founded in 1835 (including library), the University of Swansea at Singleton and the Guildhall, containing Frank Brangwyn's British Empire panels. The Dylan Thomas Centre, formerly the old Guildhall, was restored in 1995. More recent buildings include the County Hall, the Maritime Quarter Marina, the Wales National Pool and the National Waterfront Museum.

Swansea was chartered by the Earl of Warwick (1158–84), and further charters were granted by King John, Henry III, Edward II, Edward III and James II, Oliver Cromwell and the Marcher Lord William de Breos. It was formally invested with city status in 1969.

LORD-LIEUTENANTS AND HIGH SHERIFFS

Area	Lord-Lieutenant	High Sheriff (2020–21)
Clwyd	Henry Fetherstonhaugh, OBE	David Wynne-Finch
Dyfed	Sara Edwards	Sharron Lusher
Gwent	Brig. Robert Aiken, CBE	Timothy Russen
Gwynedd	Edmund Bailey	David Williams
Mid Glamorgan	Prof. Peter Vaughan, QPM	Jason Edwards
Powys	Tia Jones	Rhian Duggan
S. Glamorgan	Morfudd Meredith	Andrew Howell
W. Glamorgan	Roberta Fleet	Debra Evans-Williams

LOCAL COUNCILS

Council	Administrative HQ	Telephone	Pop.*	Council Tax†	Chief Executive
Blaenau Gwent	Ebbw Vale	01495-311556	69,862	£2,009	Michelle Morris
Bridgend	Bridgend	01656-643643	147,049	£1,862	Mark Shephard
Caerphilly	Hengoed	01443-815588	181,075	£1,471	Christina Harrhy (interim)
CARDIFF	Cardiff	029-2087 2087	366,903	£1,541	Dr Paul Orders
Carmarthenshire	Carmarthen	01267-234567	188,771	£1,667	Wendy Walters
Ceredigion	Aberaeron	01545-570881	72,695	£1,661	Eifion Evans
Conwy	Conwy	01492-574000	117,203	£1,682	Iwan Davies
Denbighshire	Ruthin	01824-706101	95,696	£1,729	Judith Greenhalgh
Flintshire	Mold	01352-752121	156,100	£1,679	Colin Everett
Gwynedd	Caernarfon	01766-771000	124,560	£1,769	Dilwyn Williams
Merthyr Tydfil	Merthyr Tydfil	01685-725000	60,326	£1,944	Ellis Cooper
Monmouthshire	Cwmbran	01633-644644	94,590	£1,717	Paul Matthews
Neath Port Talbot	Port Talbot	01639-686868	143,315	£1,935	Stephen Phillips
NEWPORT	Newport	01633-656656	154,676	£1,478	Bev Owen (interim)
Pembrokeshire	Haverfordwest	01437-764551	125,818	£1,445	Ian Westley
Powys	Llandrindod Wells	01597-827460	132,435	£1,692	Dr Caroline Turner
Rhondda Cynon Taff	Tonypandy	01443-425005	241,264	£1,799	Chris Bradshaw
SWANSEA	Swansea	01792-636000	246,993	£1,696	Phil Roberts
Torfaen	Pontypool	01495-762200	93,961	£1,690	Alison Ward, CBE
Vale of Glamorgan	Barry	01446-700111	133,587	£1,629	Rob Thomas
Wrexham	Wrexham	01978-292000	135,957	£1,575	Ian Barncroft
Ynys Mon (Isle of Anglesey)	Ynys Mon	01248-750057	70,043	£1,642	Annwen Morgan

* Source: Office for National Statistics – Mid-2019 Population Estimates (Crown copyright)
† Band D council tax bill for 2020–21.
Councils in CAPITAL LETTERS have city status

Key	Council	Key	Council
1	Anglesey (Ynys Mon)	12	Merthyr Tydfil
2	Blaenau Gwent	13	Monmouthshire
3	Bridgend	14	Neath Port Talbot
4	Caerphilly	15	NEWPORT
5	CARDIFF	16	Pembrokeshire
6	Carmarthenshire	17	Powys
7	Ceredigion	18	Rhondda Cynon Taff
8	Conwy	19	SWANSEA
9	Denbighshire	20	Torfaen
10	Flintshire	21	Vale of Glamorgan
11	Gwynedd	22	Wrexham

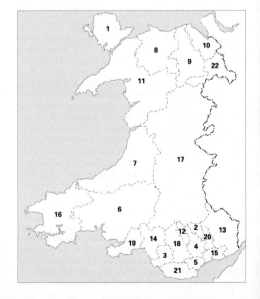

SCOTLAND

Scotland occupies the northern portion of the main island of Great Britain and includes the Inner and Outer Hebrides, Orkney, Shetland and many other islands. It lies between 60° 51′ 30″ and 54° 38′ N. latitude and between 1° 45′ 32″ and 6° 14′ W. longitude, with England to the south-east, the North Channel and the Irish Sea to the south-west, the Atlantic Ocean on the north and west, and the North Sea on the east.

The greatest length of the mainland (Cape Wrath to the Mull of Galloway) is 441km (274 miles), and the greatest breadth (Buchan Ness to Applecross) is 248km (154 miles). The customary measurement of the island of Great Britain is from the site of John o' Groats house, near Duncansby Head, Caithness, to Land's End, Cornwall, a total distance of 970km (603 miles) in a straight line and approximately 1,448km (900 miles) by road.

The Local Government etc (Scotland) Act 1994 abolished the two-tier structure of nine regional and 53 district councils which had existed since 1975 and replaced it, from April 1996, with 29 unitary authorities on the mainland; the three islands councils remained. The new authorities were elected in April 1995.

In July 1999 the Scottish parliament assumed responsibility for legislation on local government.

The total area of Scotland is 77,911 sq. km (30,081 sq. miles).

POPULATION
The population at the mid-2019 estimate was 5,463,300 (2,663,003 males; 2,800,297 females). The average density of the population at the mid-2019 estimate was 70 persons per sq. km (181 per sq. mile).

ELECTIONS
The unitary authorities consist of directly elected councillors. The Scottish Local Government (Elections) Act 2002 moved elections from a three-year to a four-year cycle. The last local authority elections took place in May 2017.

FUNCTIONS
The functions of the councils and islands councils are: education; social work; strategic planning; the provision of infrastructure such as roads; consumer protection; flood prevention; coast protection; valuation and rating; the police and fire services; civil defence; electoral registration; public transport; registration of births, deaths and marriages; housing; leisure and recreation; development and building control; environmental health; licensing; allotments; public conveniences; and the administration of district courts.

COMMUNITY COUNCILS
Scottish community councils differ from those in England and Wales. Their purpose as defined in statute is to ascertain and express the views of the communities they represent, and to take in the interests of their communities such action as appears to be expedient or practicable. Around 1,200 community councils have been established under schemes drawn up by local authorities in Scotland.

FINANCE
The budgeted net revenue expenditure for Scotland's local authorities in 2020–21 was £13.3bn. This was financed by Scottish government grants (£7.8bn), non-domestic rates (£2.8bn), council tax (£2.6bn), and local authority reserves (£95m). Education accounted for over 45 per cent of expenditure, and social care 27 per cent.

The non-domestic tax rate for 2020–21 is 49.8p. Intermediate businesses (rateable value in excess of £51,000) pay 51.1p and higher businesses (rateable value in excess of £95,000) pay 52.4p, which contributes towards the cost of the small business bonus scheme. Non-domestic properties with a rateable value of £15,000 or less do not have to pay business rates. The average Band D council tax for 2020–21 is £1,300.

EXPENDITURE
Local authority budgeted net revenue expenditure for 2020–21 is:

Service	£ million
Education	6,070
Social work	3,572
Environmental services	691
Culture & related service	556
Roads & transport	377
Planning & development	211
All other services	685
Non-service expenditure	1,164
TOTAL	13,327

RELIEF
There are three natural orographic divisions of Scotland. The southern uplands have their highest points in Merrick (843m/2,766ft), Rhinns of Kells (814m/2,669ft) and Cairnsmuir of Carsphairn (797m/2,614ft), in the west; and the Tweedsmuir Hills in the east (Broad Law 840m/2,756ft; Dollar Law 817m/2,682ft; Hartfell 808m/2,651ft).

The central lowlands, formed by the valleys of the Clyde, Forth and Tay, divide the southern uplands from the Highlands, which extend from close to the extreme north of the mainland to the central lowlands, and are divided into a northern and a southern system by the Great Glen.

The Grampian Mountains, the southern Highland system, include in the west Ben Nevis (1,345m/4,412ft), the highest point in the British Isles, and in the east the Cairngorm Mountains (Ben Macdui 1,309m/4,296ft; Braeriach 1,295m/4,248ft; Cairn Gorm 1,245m/4,084ft). The northwest Highlands contain the mountains of Wester and Easter Ross (Carn Eige 1,183m/3,880ft; Sgurr na Lapaich 1,151m/3,775ft).

Created, like the central lowlands, by a major geological fault, the Great Glen (97km/60 miles long) runs between Inverness and Fort William, and contains Loch Ness, Loch Oich and Loch Lochy. These are linked to each other and to the north-east and south-west coasts of Scotland by the Caledonian Canal, providing a navigable passage between the Moray Firth and the Inner Hebrides.

HYDROGRAPHY
The western coast is fragmented by peninsulas and islands, and indented by fjords (sea-lochs), the longest of which is Loch Fyne (68km/42 miles long) in Argyll. Although the east coast tends to be less fractured and lower, there are several great drowned inlets (firths), including the Firth of Forth, Firth of Tay and the Moray Firth, as well as the Firth of Clyde in the west.

The lochs are the principal hydrographic feature. The largest in Scotland and in Britain is Loch Lomond (70 sq. km/27 sq. miles), in the Grampian valleys, and the longest and deepest is Loch Ness (39km/24 miles long and 244m/800ft deep), in the Great Glen.

The longest river is the Tay (188km/117 miles), noted for its salmon. It flows into the North Sea, with Dundee on the estuary, which is spanned by the Tay Bridge (3,136m/10,289ft) opened in 1887 and the Tay Road Bridge (2,245m/7,365ft) opened in 1966. Other noted salmon rivers are the Dee (145km/90 miles) which flows into the North Sea at Aberdeen, and the Spey (177km/110 miles), the swiftest flowing river in the British Isles, which flows into the Moray Firth. The Tweed, which gave its name to the woollen cloth produced along its banks, marks in the lower stretches of its 154km (96 mile) course the border between Scotland and England.

The most important river commercially is the Clyde (171km/106 miles), formed by the junction of the Daer and Portrail water, which flows through the city of Glasgow to the Firth of Clyde. During its course it passes over the picturesque Falls of Clyde, Bonnington Linn (9m/30ft), Corra Linn (26m/84ft), Dundaff Linn (3m/10ft) and Stonebyres Linn (24m/80ft), above and below Lanark. The Forth (106km/66 miles), upon which stands Edinburgh, the capital, is spanned by the Forth Railway Bridge (1890), which is 1,625m (5,330ft) long, and the Forth Road Bridge (1964), which has a total length of 1,876m (6,156ft) (over water) and a single span of 914m (3,000ft).

The highest waterfall in Scotland, and the British Isles, is Eas a'Chùal Aluinn with a total height of 201m (658ft), which falls from Glas Bheinn in Sutherland. The Falls of Glomach, on a head-stream of the Elchaig in Wester Ross, have a drop of 113m (370ft).

GAELIC LANGUAGE
According to the 2011 census, 1.1 per cent (58,000 people) of the population of Scotland aged three and over were able to speak the Scottish form of Gaelic. This was a slight decrease from the 1.2 per cent recorded at the 2001 census.

LOWLAND SCOTTISH LANGUAGE
Several regional lowland Scottish dialects, known variously as Scots, Lallans or Doric, are widely spoken. According to the 2011 census, 43 per cent of the population of Scotland aged three and over stated they could do one or a combination of read, write, speak or understand Scots. A question on Scots was not included in the 2001 census.

FLAG
The flag of Scotland is known as the Saltire. It is a white diagonal cross on a blue field (saltire argent in a field azure) and represents St Andrew, the patron saint of Scotland.

THE SCOTTISH ISLANDS

ORKNEY
The Orkney Islands (total area 972 sq. km/376 sq. miles) lie about 10km (six miles) north of the mainland, separated from it by the Pentland Firth. Of the 90 islands and islets (holms and skerries) in the group, about one-third are inhabited.

The total population at the 2011 census was 21,349; the 2011 populations of the islands shown here include those of smaller islands forming part of the same council district.

Mainland, 17,162	Inner Holm, 1
Auskerry, 4	Norh Ronaldsay, 72
Burray, 409	Papa Westray, 90
Eday, 160	Rousay, 216
Egilsay, 26	Sanday, 494
Flotta, 8	Shapinsay, 307
Gairsay, 3	South Ronaldsay, 909
Graemsay, 28	Stronsay, 349
Holm of Grimbister, 3	Westray, 588
Hoy, 419	Wyre, 29

The islands are rich in prehistoric and Scandinavian remains, the most notable being the Stone Age village of Skara Brae, the burial chamber of Maes Howe, the many brochs (towers) and the 12th-century St Magnus Cathedral. Scapa Flow, between the Mainland and Hoy, was the war station of the British Grand Fleet from 1914 to 1919 and the scene of the scuttling of the surrendered German High Seas Fleet (21 June 1919).

Most of the islands are low-lying and fertile, and farming (principally beef cattle) is the main industry. Flotta, to the south of Scapa Flow, is the site of the oil terminal for the Piper, Claymore and Tartan fields in the North Sea.

The capital is Kirkwall (population 7,045) situated on Mainland.

SHETLAND
The Shetland Islands have a total area of 1,427 sq. km (551 sq. miles) and had a population at the 2011 census of 23,167. They lie about 80km (50 miles) north of the Orkneys, with Fair Isle about half way between the two groups. Out Stack, off Muckle Flugga, 1.6km (one mile) north of Unst, is the most northerly part of the British Isles (60° 51' 30" N. lat.).

There are over 100 islands, of which 16 are inhabited. Populations at the 2011 census were:

Mainland, 18,765	Muckle Roe, 130
Bressay, 368	Papa Stour, 15
Bruray, 24	Trondra, 135
East Burra, 76	Unst, 632
Fair Isle, 68	Vaila, 2
Fetlar, 61	West Burra, 776
Foula, 38	Whalsay, 1,061
Housay, 50	Yell, 966

Shetland's many archaeological sites include Jarlshof, Mousa and Clickhimin, and its long connection with Scandinavia has resulted in a strong Norse influence on its place names and dialect.

Industries include fishing, knitwear and farming. In addition to the fishing fleet there are fish processing factories, and the traditional handknitting of Fair Isle and Unst is now supplemented with machine-knitted garments. Farming is mainly crofting, with sheep being raised on the moorland and hills of the islands. Since 1970s the islands have been at the centre of the North Sea oil industry, with pipelines from the Brent and Ninian fields running to the terminal at Sullom Voe, one of the largest in Europe. Although much quieter than at the height of oil production in the late 1990s, the terminal marked a milestone 40-year anniversary since first oil in November 2018.

The capital is Lerwick (population 6,958) situated on Mainland. Lerwick is the main centre for supply services for offshore oil exploration and development.

THE HEBRIDES
Until the late 13th century the Hebrides included other Scottish islands in the Firth of Clyde, the peninsula of Kintyre (Argyll), the Isle of Man and the (Irish) Isle of Rathlin. The origin of the name is probably the Greek *Eboudai*, latinised as *Hebudes* by Pliny, and corrupted to its present form. The Norwegian name *Sudreyjar* (Southern Islands) was latinised as *Sodorenses*, a name that survives in the Anglican bishopric of Sodor and Man.

There are over 500 islands and islets, of which about 100 are inhabited, though mountainous terrain and extensive peat bogs mean that only a fraction of the total area is under cultivation. Stone, Bronze and Iron Age settlement has left many remains, including those at Callanish on Lewis, and Norse colonisation influenced language, customs and place names. Occupations include farming (mostly crofting and stock-raising), fishing and the manufacture of tweeds and other woollens. Tourism is an important part of the economy.

The Inner Hebrides lie off the west coast of Scotland and are relatively close to the mainland. The largest and best-known is Skye (area 1,665 sq. km/643 sq. miles; pop. 10,008; chief town, Portree), which contains the Cuillin Hills (Sgurr Alasdair, 993m/3,257ft), Bla Bheinn (928m/3,046ft), the Storr (719m/2,358ft) and the Red Hills (Beinn na Caillich, 732m/2,403ft). Other islands in the Highland council area include Raasay (pop. 161), Eigg (pop. 83), Muck (pop. 27) and Rhum (pop. 22).

Further south the Inner Hebridean islands include Arran (pop. 4,629), containing Goat Fell (874m/2,868ft); Coll (pop. 195) and Tiree (pop. 653); Colonsay (pop. 124) and Oronsay (pop. 8); Easdale (pop. 59); Gigha (pop. 163); Islay (area 608 sq. km/235 sq. miles; pop. 3,228); Jura (area 414 sq. km/160 sq. miles; pop. 196), with a range of hills culminating in the Paps of Jura (Beinn-an-Oir, 785m/2,576ft, and Beinn Chaolais, 755m/2,477ft); Lismore (pop. 192); Luing (pop. 195); and Mull (area 950 sq. km/367 sq. miles; pop. 2,800; chief town Tobermory), containing Ben More (1,174m/3,852 ft).

The Outer Hebrides, separated from the mainland by the Minch, now form the Eilean Siar (Western Isles) council (area 2,897 sq. km/1,119 sq. miles; pop. 27,684). The main islands are Lewis with Harris (area 1,994 sq. km/770 sq. miles, pop. 21,031), whose chief town, Stornoway, is the administrative seat; North Uist (pop. 1,254); South Uist (pop. 1,754); Benbecula (pop. 1,303) and Barra (pop. 1,174). Other inhabited islands include Great Bernera (252), Berneray (138), Eriskay (143), Grimsay (169), Scalpay (291) and Vatersay (90).

EARLY HISTORY

There is evidence of human settlement in Scotland dating from the third millennium BC, the earliest settlers being Mesolithic hunters and fishermen. Early in the second millennium BC, Neolithic farmers began to cultivate crops and rear livestock; their settlements were on the west coast and in the north, and included Skara Brae and Maeshowe (Orkney). Settlement by the early Bronze Age 'Beaker Folk', so-called from the shape of their drinking vessels, in eastern Scotland dates from about 1800 BC. Further settlement is believed to have occurred from 700 BC onwards, as tribes were displaced from further south by new incursions from the Continent and the Roman invasions from AD 43.

Julius Agricola, the Roman governor of Britain AD 77–84, extended the Roman conquests in Britain by advancing into Caledonia, culminating with a victory at Mons Graupius, probably in AD 84; he was recalled to Rome shortly after and his forward policy was not pursued. Hadrian's Wall, mostly completed by AD 30, marked the northern frontier of the Roman empire except for the period between about AD 144 and 190 when the frontier moved north to the Forth-Clyde isthmus and a turf wall, the Antonine Wall, was manned.

After the Roman withdrawal from Britain, there were centuries of warfare between the Picts, Scots, Britons, Angles and Vikings. The Picts, generally accepted to be descended from the indigenous Iron Age people of northern Scotland, occupied the area north of the Forth. The Scots, a Gaelic-speaking people of northern Ireland, colonised the area of Argyll and Bute (the kingdom of Dalriada) in the fifth century AD and then expanded eastwards and northwards. The Britons, speaking a Brythonic Celtic language, colonised Scotland from the south from the first century BC; they lost control of south-eastern Scotland (incorporated into the kingdom of Northumbria) to the Angles in the early seventh century but retained Strathclyde (south-western Scotland and Cumbria). Viking raids from the late eighth century were followed by Norse settlement in the western and northern

isles, Argyll, Caithness and Sutherland from the mid-ninth century onwards.

UNIFICATION
The union of the areas which now comprise Scotland began in AD 843 when Kenneth MacAlpin, king of the Scots from c.834, also became king of the Picts, joining the two lands to form the kingdom of Alba (comprising Scotland north of a line between the Forth and Clyde rivers). Lothian, the eastern part of the area between the Forth and the Tweed, seems to have been leased to Kenneth II of Alba (reigned 971–995) by Edgar of England c.973, and Scottish possession was confirmed by Malcolm II's victory over a Northumbrian army at Carham c.1016. At about this time Malcolm II (reigned 1005–34) placed his grandson Duncan on the throne of the British kingdom of Strathclyde, bringing under Scots rule virtually all of what is now Scotland.

The Norse possessions were incorporated into the kingdom of Scotland from the 12th century onwards. An uprising in the mid-12th century drove the Norse from most of mainland Argyll. The Hebrides were ceded to Scotland by the Treaty of Perth in 1266 after a Norwegian expedition in 1263 failed to maintain Norse authority over the islands. Orkney and Shetland fell to Scotland in 1468–9 as a pledge for the unpaid dowry of Margaret of Denmark, wife of James III, although Danish claims of suzerainty were relinquished only with the marriage of Anne of Denmark to James VI in 1590.

From the 11th century, there were frequent wars between Scotland and England, over territory and the extent of England's political influence. The failure of the Scottish royal line with the death of Margaret of Norway in 1290 led to disputes over the throne which were resolved by the adjudication of Edward I of England. He awarded the throne to John Balliol in 1292 but Balliol's refusal to be a puppet king led to war. Balliol surrendered to Edward I in 1296 and Edward attempted to rule Scotland himself. Resistance to Scotland's loss of independence was led by William Wallace, who defeated the English at Stirling Bridge (1297), and Robert Bruce, crowned in 1306, who held most of Scotland by 1311 and routed Edward II's army at Bannockburn (1314). England recognised the independence of Scotland in the Treaty of Northampton in 1328. Subsequent clashes include the disastrous battle of Flodden (1513) in which James IV and many of his nobles fell.

THE UNION
In 1603 James VI of Scotland succeeded Elizabeth I on the throne of England (his mother, Mary Queen of Scots, was the great-granddaughter of Henry VII), his successors reigning as sovereigns of Great Britain. Political union of the two countries did not occur until 1707.

THE JACOBITE REVOLTS
After the abdication (by flight) in 1688 of James VII and II, the crown devolved upon William III (grandson of Charles I) and Mary II (elder daughter of James VII and II). In 1689 Graham of Claverhouse roused the Highlands on behalf of James VII and II, but died after a military success at Killiecrankie. After the death of Anne (younger daughter of James VII and II), the throne devolved upon George I (great-grandson of James VI and I). In 1715, armed risings on behalf of James Stuart (the Old Pretender, son of James VII and II) led to the indecisive battle of Sheriffmuir, and the Jacobite movement died down until 1745, when Charles Stuart (the Young Pretender) defeated the Royalist troops at Prestonpans and advanced to Derby (1746). From Derby, Charles Stuart's forces fell back on the defensive and were finally crushed at Culloden (16 April 1746) by an army led by the Duke of Cumberland, son of George II.

PRINCIPAL CITIES

ABERDEEN

Aberdeen, 209km (130 miles) north-east of Edinburgh, received its charter as a Royal Burgh in 1124. Scotland's third largest city, Aberdeen lies between two rivers, the Dee and the Don, facing the North Sea; the city has a strong maritime history and is today a major centre for offshore oil exploration and production. It is also an ancient university town and distinguished research centre.

Places of interest include King's College, St Machar's Cathedral, Brig o' Balgownie, Duthie Park and Winter Gardens, Hazlehead Park, Kirk of St Nicholas, Mercat Cross, Marischal College and Marischal Museum, Provost Skene's House, Gordon Highlanders Museum, Aberdeen Science Centre (formerly Satrosphere), and Aberdeen Maritime Museum. Closed in 2015 for a major £35m redevelopment, Aberdeen Art Gallery, which first opened in 1885 and comprises the Cowdray Hall concert venue and the city's Remembrance Hall, reopened in November 2019.

DUNDEE

The Royal Burgh of Dundee is situated on the north bank of the Tay estuary. The city's port and dock installations are important to the offshore oil industry and the airport also provides servicing facilities.

The unique City Churches – three churches under one roof, together with the 15th-century St Mary's Tower – are the most prominent architectural feature. Dundee is home to two historic ships: the Dundee-built RRS *Discovery* which took Capt. Scott to the Antarctic lies alongside Discovery Quay, and the frigate *Unicorn,* the only British-built wooden warship still afloat, is moored in Victoria Dock. Places of interest include Mills Observatory, the Tay road and rail bridges, Dundee Contemporary Arts centre, The McManus (Dundee's art gallery and museum), Claypotts Castle, Broughty Castle, Verdant Works (textile heritage centre) and the Dundee Science Centre (formerly Sensation). V&A Dundee was opened in September 2018 at a cost of £80.1m.

EDINBURGH

Edinburgh is the capital city and seat of government in Scotland. The new Scottish parliament building designed by Enric Miralles was completed in 2004 and is open to visitors. The city is built on a group of hills and both the Old and New Towns are inscribed on the UNESCO World Cultural and Natural Heritage List for their cultural significance.

Other places of interest include the castle, which houses the Stone of Scone and also includes St Margaret's Chapel, the oldest building in Edinburgh, and near it, the Scottish National War Memorial; the Palace of Holyroodhouse, the Queen's official residence in Scotland; Parliament House, the present seat of the judicature; Princes Street; three universities (Edinburgh, Heriot-Watt, Napier); St Giles' Cathedral; St Mary's (Scottish Episcopal) Cathedral (Sir George Gilbert Scott); General Register House (Robert Adam); the National Library of Scotland, the Signet Library; the Royal Scottish Academy and National Galleries Scotland – comprising the Scottish National Gallery, the Scottish National Portrait Gallery and the Scottish National Gallery of Modern Art.

GLASGOW

Glasgow, a Royal Burgh, is Scotland's largest city and its principal commercial and industrial centre. The city occupies the north and south banks of the Clyde, formerly one of the chief commercial estuaries in the world.

The chief buildings are the 13th-century Gothic cathedral, the university (Sir George Gilbert Scott), the City Chambers, the Royal Concert Hall, St Mungo Museum of Religious Life and Art, Pollok House, Kelvingrove Art Gallery and Museum, the Gallery of Modern Art, the Riverside Museum: Scotland's Museum of Transport and Travel (Zaha Hadid), Mitchell Library and the Burrell Collection museum, which is currently undergoing a major refurbishment and is due to re-open in Spring 2021. The iconic School of Art designed by Charles Rennie Mackintosh (fully completed in 1909) is being rebuilt after it was devastated by two fires; the first in 2014 and the second in 2018. The city is home to the Royal Scottish National Orchestra, Scottish Opera, Scottish Ballet, BBC Scotland and Scottish Television (STV).

Inverness was granted city status in 2000, Stirling in 2002 and Perth in 2012. Aberdeen, Dundee, Edinburgh and Glasgow have also been granted lord mayoralty/lord provostship.

LORD-LIEUTENANTS

Title	Name
Aberdeen City*	Lord Provost Barney Crockett
Aberdeenshire	Alexander Mason
Angus	Patricia Sawers
Argyll and Bute	Jane MacLeod
Ayrshire & Arran	Iona McDonald
Banffshire	Christopher Simpson
Berwickshire	Jeannna Swan
Caithness	Rt. Hon. Viscount Thurso, PC
Clackmannanshire	Lt.-Col. Johnny Stewart, LVO
Dumfries	Lady Fiona MacGregor of MacGregor (Fiona Armstrong)
Dunbartonshire	Jill Young, MBE
Dundee City*	Lord Provost Ian Borthwick
East Lothian	Maj. Michael Williams, MBE
Edinburgh City*	Rt. Hon. Lord Provost Frank Ross
Eilean Siar (Western Isles)	Donald Martin
Fife	Robert Balfour
Glasgow City*	Rt. Hon. Lord Provost Philip Braat
Inverness	Donald Cameron of Lochiel, CVO
Kincardineshire	Alistair Macphie
Lanarkshire	Lady Susan Haughey, CBE
Midlothian	Lt.-Col. Richard Callander, LVO, OBE, TD
Moray	Maj.-Gen. the Hon. Seymour Monro, CBE, LVO
Nairnshire	George Asher
Orkney	Elaine Grieve
Perth & Kinross	Gordon Leckie
Renfrewshire	Col. Peter McCarthy
Ross & Cromarty	Joanie Whiteford
Roxburgh, Ettrick & Lauderdale	Duke of Buccleuch and Queensberry, KT, KBE
Shetland	Robert Hunter
Stirling & Falkirk	Alan Simpson, OBE
Sutherland	Dr Monica Main, CVO
The Stewartry of Kirkcudbright	Elizabeth Gilroy
Tweeddale	Prof. Sir Hew Strachan
West Lothian	Moira Niven, MBE
Wigtown	Aileen Brewis

* The Lord Provosts of the four cities of Aberdeen, Dundee, Edinburgh and Glasgow are Lord-Lieutenants *ex officio* for those districts

LOCAL COUNCILS

Council	Administrative Headquarters	Telephone	Pop.*	Council Tax†	Chief Executive
ABERDEEN	Aberdeen	0300-020 0291	228,670	£1,377	Angela Scott
Aberdeenshire	Aberdeen	0845-608 1207	261,210	£1,301	Jim Savege
Angus	Forfar	0345-277 7778	116,200	£1,207	Margo Williamson
Argyll and Bute	Lochgilphead	01546-602127	85,870	£1,368	Pippa Milne
Clackmannanshire	Alloa	01259-450000	51,540	£1,305	Nikki Bridle
Dumfries and Galloway	Dumfries	030-3333 3000	148,860	£1,223	Gavin Stevenson
DUNDEE	Dundee	01382-434000	149,320	£1,379	David Martin
East Ayrshire	Kilmarnock	01563-576000	122,010	£1,375	Eddie Fraser
East Dunbartonshire	Kirkintilloch	0300-123 4510	108,640	£1,309	Gerry Cornes
East Lothian	Haddington	01620-827827	107,090	£1,303	Monica Patterson
East Renfrewshire	Giffnock	0141-577 3000	95,530	£1,290	Lorraine McMillan
EDINBURGH	Edinburgh	0131-200 2000	524,930	£1,339	Andrew Kerr
Eilean Siar (Western Isles)	Stornoway	01851-703773	26,720	£1,193	Malcolm Burr
Falkirk	Falkirk	01324-506070	160,890	£1,226	Kenneth Lawrie
Fife	Glenrothes	0345-155 0000	373,550	£1,281	Steve Grimmond
GLASGOW	Glasgow	0141-287 2000	633,120	£1,386	Annemarie O'Donnell
Highland	Inverness	01349-886606	235,830	£1,332	Donna Manson
Inverclyde	Greenock	01475-717171	77,800	£1,332	Aubrey Fawcett
Midlothian	Dalkeith	0131-270 7500	92,460	£1,409	Dr Grace Vickers
Moray	Elgin	01343-543451	95,820	£1,323	Roderick Burns
North Ayrshire	Irvine	01294-310000	134,740	£1,343	Craig Hatton
North Lanarkshire	Motherwell	01698-403200	341,370	£1,221	Des Murray
Orkney	Kirkwall	01856-873535	22,270	£1,208	John Mundell *(interim)*
Perth and Kinross	Perth	01738-475000	151,950	£1,318	Karen Reid
Renfrewshire	Paisley	0300-300 0300	179,100	£1,315	Sandra Black
Scottish Borders	Melrose	01835-824000	115,510	£1,254	Rob Dickson & David Robertson
Shetland	Lerwick	01595-693535	22,920	£1,206	Maggie Sandison
South Ayrshire	Ayr	0300-123 0900	112,610	£1,345	Eileen Howat
South Lanarkshire	Hamilton	0303-123 1015	320,530	£1,203	Cleland Sneddon
STIRLING	Stirling	0845-277 7000	94,210	£1,344	Carol Beattie
West Dunbartonshire	Dumbarton	01389-737000	88,930	£1,294	Joyce White, OBE
West Lothian	Livingston	01506-280000	183,100	£1,276	Graham Hope

* *Source:* Office for National Statistics – *Mid-2019 Population Estimates* (Crown copyright)
† Average Band D council tax bill 2020–21.
Councils in CAPITAL LETTERS have city status

Key	Council	Key	Council
1	Aberdeen City	17	Inverclyde
2	Aberdeenshire	18	Midlothian
3	Angus	19	Moray
4	Argyll and Bute	20	North Ayrshire
5	City of Edinburgh	21	North Lanarkshire
6	Clackmannanshire	22	Orkney
7	Dumfries and Galloway	23	Perth and Kinross
8	Dundee City	24	Renfrewshire
9	East Ayrshire	25	Scottish Borders
10	East Dunbartonshire	26	Shetland
11	East Lothian	27	South Ayrshire
12	East Renfrewshire	28	South Lanarkshire
13	Falkirk	29	Stirling
14	Fife	30	West Dunbartonshire
15	Glasgow City	31	Western Isles (Eilean Siar)
16	Highland	32	West Lothian

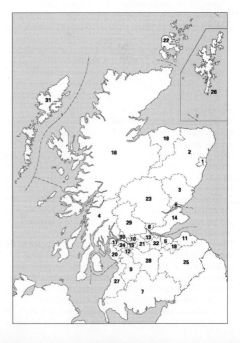

NORTHERN IRELAND

Northern Ireland has a total area of 13,793 sq. km (5,326 sq. miles).

In 2012 a reform programme began to reduce the number of district councils from 26 to 11. The Local Government Act (Northern Ireland) received royal assent on 12 May 2014 providing new governance arrangements for local councils and made transitional provisions for the transfer of staff, assets and liabilities etc to the new 11 councils. On 1 April 2015 additional functions, that were previously the responsibility of the Northern Ireland executive, fully transferred to the new district authorities.

POPULATION

The population of Northern Ireland at the mid-2019 estimate was 1,893,667 (932,717 males; 960,950 females). The estimated average density of population at mid-2019 was 137 persons per sq. km (353 per sq. mile).

ELECTIONS

Elections to the 11 councils took place on 2 May 2019.

FUNCTIONS

The councils are responsible for approving business and financial plans, setting domestic and non-domestic rates. Since April 2016 councils have also been responsible for urban regeneration and community development.

The district councils are responsible for:

Direct Service Provision of a wide range of local services, including: building control-inspection and the regulation of new buildings; byelaw enforcement; cemeteries; community centres; cultural facilities; dog control; environmental health; food safety; health and safety; local economic development; local planning; off-street parking (except park and ride schemes); parks, open spaces and playgrounds; public conveniences; recycling and waste management; registration of births, deaths and marriages; sport, leisure and recreational facilities; and street cleaning. District councils also have a role in community development and safety; sports development; summer schemes; and tourism.

Representation: nominating representatives to sit as members of the various statutory bodies responsible for the administration of regional services such as education, health and social services, libraries and road safety committees

FINANCE

Government in Northern Ireland is part-funded by a system of rates, which supplement the Northern Ireland budget from the UK government. The ratepayer receives a combined tax bill consisting of the regional rate, set by the Northern Ireland executive, and the district rate, which is set by each district council. The regional and district rates are both collected by Land and Property Services (part of the Department of Finance). The product of the district rates is paid over to each council while the product of the regional rate supports expenditure by the departments of the executive and assembly.

Since April 2007 domestic rates bills have been based on the capital value of a property, rather than the rental value. The capital value is defined as the price the property might reasonably be expected to realise had it been sold on the open market on 1 January 2005. Non-domestic rates bills are based on the rental value of the property as at 1 April 2013.

Rate bills are calculated by multiplying the property's net annual rental value (in the case of non-domestic property), or capital value (in the case of domestic property), by the regional and district rate poundages respectively.

For 2020–21 the overall average domestic poundage is 0.8427p compared to 0.8302p in 2012–20. The overall average non-domestic rate poundage in 2020–21 is 53.02p compared to 59.53p in 2019–20.

FLAG

The official national flag of Northern Ireland is the Union Flag.

PRINCIPAL CITIES

In addition to Belfast and Londonderry, three other places in Northern Ireland have been granted city status: Armagh (1994), Lisburn (2002) and Newry (2002).

BELFAST

Belfast, the administrative centre of Northern Ireland, is situated at the mouth of the River Lagan at its entrance to Belfast Lough. The city grew to be a great industrial centre, owing to its easy access by sea to Scottish coal and iron.

The principal buildings are of a relatively young age and include the parliament buildings at Stormont, the City Hall, Waterfront Hall, the Law Courts, the Public Library and the Ulster Museum, situated in the botanic gardens. The Metropolitan Arts Centre (MAC), an award-winning arts venue designed by Belfast-based architectural practice Hall McKnight, was completed in February 2019 and is situated opposite St Anne's Cathedral. In March 2012, Titanic Belfast opened on the banks of the Lagan River on the site of the shipyard where RMS *Titanic* was built and launched. The museum forms the centrepiece of a new mixed-use maritime quarter.

Belfast received its first charter of incorporation in 1613 and was created a city in 1888; the title of lord mayor was conferred in 1892.

LONDONDERRY

Londonderry (originally Derry) is situated on the River Foyle, and has important associations with the City of London. The Irish Society was created by the City of London in 1610, and under its royal charter of 1613 fortified the city and was for a long time closely associated with its administration. Because of this connection the city was incorporated in 1613 under the new name of Londonderry.

The city is famous for the great siege of 1688–9, when for 105 days the town held out against the forces of James II. The city walls are still intact and form a circuit of 1.6 km (one mile) around the old city.

Interesting buildings are the Protestant cathedral of St Columb's (1633) and the Guildhall, reconstructed in 1912 and containing a number of beautiful stained glass windows, many of which were presented by the livery companies of London.

CONSTITUTIONAL HISTORY

Northern Ireland is subject to the same fundamental constitutional provisions which apply to the rest of the UK. It had its own parliament and government from 1921 to 1972, but after increasing civil unrest the Northern Ireland (Temporary Provisions) Act 1972 transferred the legislative and executive powers of the Northern Ireland parliament and government to the UK parliament and a secretary of state. The

Northern Ireland Constitution Act 1973 provided for devolution in Northern Ireland through an assembly and executive, but a power-sharing executive formed by the Northern Ireland political parties in January 1974 collapsed in May 1974 and Northern Ireland returned to direct rule governance under the provisions of the Northern Ireland Act 1974, placing the Northern Ireland department under the direction and control of the Northern Ireland secretary.

In December 1993 the British and Irish governments published the Joint Declaration, complementing their political talks and making clear that any settlement would need to be founded on principles of democracy and consent.

On 12 January 1998 the British and Irish governments issued a joint document, *Propositions on Heads of Agreement*, proposing the establishment of various new cross-border bodies; further proposals were presented on 27 January. A draft peace settlement was issued by the talks' chair, US Senator George Mitchell, on 6 April 1998 but was rejected by the Unionists the following day. On 10 April agreement was reached between the British and Irish governments and the eight Northern Ireland political parties still involved in the talks (the Good Friday Agreement). The agreement provided for an elected Northern Ireland Assembly, a North/South Ministerial Council, and a British-Irish Council comprising representatives of the British, Irish, Channel Islands and Isle of Man governments and members of the new assemblies for Scotland, Wales and Northern Ireland. Further points included the abandonment of the Republic of Ireland's constitutional claim to Northern Ireland, the decommissioning of weapons, the release of paramilitary prisoners and changes in policing.

The agreement was ratified in referendums held in Northern Ireland and the Republic of Ireland on 22 May 1998. In the UK, the Northern Ireland Act received royal assent in November 1998.

On 28 April 2003 the secretary of state again assumed responsibility for the direction of the Northern Ireland departments on the dissolution of the Northern Ireland Assembly, following its initial suspension from midnight on 14 October 2002. In 2006, following the passing of the Northern Ireland Act, the secretary of state created a non-legislative fixed-term assembly which would cease to operate either when the political parties agreed to restore devolution, or on 24 November 2006 (whichever occurred first). In October 2006 a timetable to restore devolution was drawn up (St Andrews Agreement) and a transitional Northern Ireland Assembly was formed on 24 November. The transitional assembly was dissolved in January 2007 in preparation for elections to be held on 7 March; following the elections a power-sharing executive was formed and the new 108-member Northern Ireland Assembly became operational on 8 May 2007.

A breakdown of trust between the parties following the Renewable Heat Incentive scandal resulted in the dissolution of the 5th assembly and executive on 26 January 2017 and a new election took place in March 2017. Following this election negotiations to form an executive missed both the normal three week deadline and an extended deadline of 29 June 2017 and the sixth assembly was suspended until 11 January 2020. For further information *see* Devolved Government.

LORD-LIEUTENANTS AND HIGH SHERIFFS

County	Lord-Lieutenant	High Sheriff (2020)
Antrim	David McCorkell	Rupert Cramsie
Armagh	Earl of Caledon, KCVO	Michael Dickson
Belfast City	Fionnuala Jay-O'Boyle, CBE	Nicola Verner
Down	David Lindsay	Austin Baird
Fermanagh	Viscount Brookeborough, KG	Breda McGrenaghan, BEM
Londonderry	Alison Millar	Ross Wilson, BEM
Londonderry City	Dr Angela Garvey	James Doherty
Tyrone	Robert Scott, OBE	Gordon Aiken, BEM

LOCAL COUNCILS

Council	Telephone	Population*	Chief Executive
Antrim & Newtownabbey	028-9448 1311	143,504	Jacqui Dixon
Ards & North Down	0300-013 3333	161,725	Stephen Reid
Armagh City, Banbridge & Craigavon	0300-030 0900	216,205	Roger Wilson
Belfast City	028-9027 0549	343,542	Suzanne Wylie
Causeway Coast & Glens	028-7034 7034	144,838	David Jackson, MBE
Derry City & Strabane	028-7138 2204	151,284	John Kelpie
Fermanagh & Omagh	0300-303 1777	117,397	Brendan Hegarty
Lisburn & Castlereagh	028-9250 9250	146,002	David Burns
Mid & East Antrim	028-9335 8000	139,274	Anne Donaghy
Mid Ulster	0300-013 2132	148,528	Adrian McCreesh
Newry, Mourne & Down	028-3031 3037	181,368	Marie Ward

* *Source:* Office for National Statistics – *Mid-2019 Population Estimates* (Crown copyright)

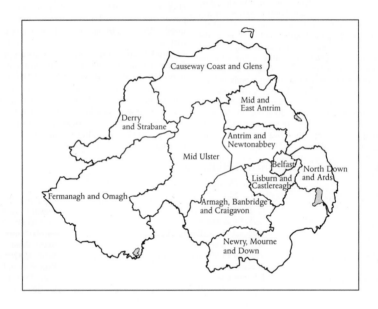

POLITICAL COMPOSITION OF COUNCILS

Most local elections were cancelled in 2020 because of the coronavirus pandemic. Listed are the the composition of councils as at December 2020

Abbreviations

All.	Alliance
C.	Conservative
DUP	Democratic Unionist Party
Green	Green
Ind.	Independent or other party
Lab.	Labour
LD	Liberal Democrat
PC	Plaid Cymru
SDLP	Social Democratic and Labour Party
SF	Sinn Fein
SNP	Scottish National Party
UUP	Ulster Unionist Party
v.	vacant

Total number of seats is given in parentheses after the council name.

ENGLAND

COUNTY COUNCILS

Cambridgeshire (61)	C. 35; LD 16; Lab. 6; Ind. 4
Cumbria (84)	C. 35; Lab. 26; LD 16; Ind. 4; v. 3
Derbyshire (64)	C. 36; Lab. 25; LD 3
Devon (60)	C. 42; Lab. 7; LD 6; Ind. 4; Green 1
East Sussex (50)	C. 29; LD 11; Ind. 5; Lab. 4; v. 1
Essex (75)	C. 52; LD 8; Ind. 7; Lab. 6; Green 1; v. 1
Gloucestershire (53)	C. 29; LD 14; Lab. 5; Green 2; Ind. 2; v. 1
Hampshire (78)	C. 55; LD 19; Lab. 1; Ind. 2; v. 1
Hertfordshire (78)	C. 49; LD 18; Lab. 9; Ind. 2
Kent (81)	C. 64; LD 7; Lab. 5; Green 1; Ind. 3; v. 1
Lancashire (84)	C. 44; Lab. 30; LD 4; Ind. 4; Green 1; v. 1
Leicestershire (55)	C. 36; LD 13; Lab. 6
Lincolnshire (70)	C. 54; Lab. 5; Ind. 9; LD 1; v. 1
Norfolk (84)	C. 54; Lab. 16; LD 9; Ind. 4; v. 1
North Yorkshire (72)	C. 52; Ind. 12; Lab. 4; LD 4
Northamptonshire (57)	C. 40; Lab. 11; Ind. 3; LD 2; v. 1
Nottinghamshire (66)	C. 32; Lab. 22; Ind. 11; LD 1
Oxfordshire (63)	C. 30; Lab. 14; LD 13; Ind. 5
Somerset (55)	C. 33; LD 14; Ind. 3; Lab. 3; Green 2
Staffordshire (62)	C. 51; Lab. 10; Ind. 1
Suffolk (75)	C. 49; Lab. 11; LD 5; Ind. 6; Green 3; v. 1
Surrey (81)	C. 57; Ind. 13; LD 9; Lab. 1; Green 1
Warwickshire (57)	C. 34; Lab. 8; LD 8; Ind. 2; Green 2; v. 3
West Sussex (70)	C. 51; LD 8; Lab. 4; Ind. 6; v. 1
Worcestershire (57)	C. 41; Lab. 8; LD 2; Green 2; Ind. 3; v. 3

DISTRICT COUNCILS

Adur (29)	C. 15; Lab. 7; Ind. 5; v. 2
Allerdale (49)	Ind. 17; C. 15; Lab. 12; v. 5
Amber Valley (45)	Lab. 23; C. 16; Green 1; Ind. 2; v. 3
Arun (54)	C. 21; LD 18; Ind. 11; Green 2; Lab. 1; v. 1
Ashfield (35)	Ind. 29; C. 3; Lab. 2; v. 1
Ashford (47)	C. 25; Ind. 13; Lab. 6; Green 2; v. 1
Babergh (32)	C. 13; Ind. 10; Green 4; LD 3; Lab. 2
Barrow-in-Furness (36)	Lab. 23; C. 11; v. 2
Basildon (42)	C. 19; Lab. 15; Ind. 7; v. 1
Basingstoke and Deane (60)	C. 28; Lab. 13; Ind. 11; LD 7; v. 1
Bassetlaw (48)	Lab. 37; C. 5; Ind. 5; LD 1
Blaby (39)	C. 24; Lab. 6; LD 6; Green 1; Ind. 1; v. 1
Bolsover (37)	Lab. 17; Ind. 15; C. 3; v. 2
Boston (30)	Ind. 15; C. 13; Lab. 2
Braintree (49)	C. 33; Ind. 7; Green 6; Lab. 2; v. 1
Breckland (49)	C. 37; Lab. 6; Ind. 4; Green 2
Brentwood (37)	C. 20; LD 13; Lab. 3; Ind. 1
Broadland (47)	C. 33; LD 12; Lab. 2
Bromsgrove (31)	C. 17; Ind. 8; Lab. 3; LD 3
Broxbourne (30)	C. 27; Lab. 2; Ind. 1
Broxtowe (44)	C. 20; Lab. 14; LD 7; Ind. 3
Burnley (45)	Lab. 22; LD 8; Ind. 7; C. 6; Green 2
Cambridge (42)	Lab. 25; LD 12; Ind. 1; v. 4
Cannock Chase (41)	Lab. 17; C. 14; Ind. 6; LD 2; Green 1; v. 1
Canterbury (39)	C. 22; Lab. 9; LD 6; v. 2
Carlisle (39)	C. 17; Lab. 15; Ind. 5; LD 1; Green 1
Castle Point (41)	C. 24; Ind. 17
Charnwood (52)	C. 37; Lab. 13; Ind. 1; Green 1
Chelmsford (57)	LD 30; C. 21; Ind. 5; v. 1
Cheltenham (40)	LD 31; C. 6; Ind. 3
Cherwell (48)	C. 31; Lab. 9; Ind. 4; LD 2; Green 1; v. 1
Chesterfield (48)	Lab. 28; LD 17; Ind. 3
Chichester (36)	C. 19; LD 10; Ind. 3; Lab. 2; Green 2
Chorley (47)	Lab. 37; C. 7; Ind. 1; v. 2
Colchester (51)	C. 22; LD 13; Lab. 11; Ind. 3; Green 1; v. 1
Copeland (33)	Lab. 16; C. 10; Ind. 6; v. 1
Corby (29)	Lab. 22; C. 4; Ind. 1; v. 2
Cotswolds (34)	LD 18; C. 14; Green 1; Ind. 1
Craven (30)	C. 15; Ind. 8; Lab. 3; Green 2; LD 1; v. 1
Crawley (36)	C. 17; Lab. 17; Ind. 2; v. 1
Dacorum (51)	C. 31; LD 18; Ind. 1; v. 1
Dartford (42)	C. 29; Lab. 9; Ind. 4
Daventry (36)	C. 29; Lab. 4; LD 2; Ind. 1
Derbyshire Dales (39)	C. 20; LD 8; Lab. 6; Ind. 3; Green 2
Dover (32)	C. 19; Lab. 12; Ind. 1
East Cambridgeshire (28)	C. 15; LD 11; Ind. 2
East Devon (60)	Ind. 31; C. 19; LD 8; Green 2
East Hampshire (43)	C. 32; LD 8; Lab. 2; Ind. 1
East Hertfordshire (50)	C. 40; LD 6; Lab. 2; Green 2
East Lindsey (55)	C. 30; Ind. 18; Lab. 6; LD 1
East Northamptonshire (40)	C. 36; Ind. 3; Lab. 1
East Staffordshire (39)	C. 25; Lab. 9; Ind. 2; LD 1; v. 2
East Suffolk (55)	C. 39; Lab. 7; Green 4; LD 3; Ind. 1; v. 1
Eastbourne (27)	LD 17; C. 9; v. 1
Eastleigh (39)	LD 33; Ind. 2; Ind. 3; C. 2; v. 1

Eden (38) — C. 13; LD 11; Ind. 9; Lab. 2; Green 2; v. 1

Elmbridge (48) — Ind. 21; C. 18; LD 7; v. 2

Epping Forest (58) — C. 35; Ind. 15; Green 3; LD 3; v. 2

Epsom and Ewell (38) — Ind. 32; Lab. 3; LD 2; C. 1

Erewash (47) — C. 27; Lab. 18; LD 1; Ind. 1

Exeter (39) — Lab. 28; C. 6; LD 2; Ind. 1; Green 1; v. 1

Fareham (31) — C. 21; Ind. 5; LD 4; v. 1

Fenland (39) — C. 25; Ind. 10; LD 2; Green 1

Folkestone and Hythe (30) — C. 13; Green 6; Lab. 5; LD 2; Ind. 4

Forest of Dean (38) — Ind. 15; C. 9; Green 6; Lab. 5; LD 2; v. 1

Fylde (51) — C. 31; Ind. 19; LD 1

Gedling (41) — Lab. 29; C. 8; Ind. 2; LD 2

Gloucester (39) — C. 19; Lab. 8; LD 9; Ind. 1; v. 2

Gosport (34) — C. 18; LD 14; Lab. 2

Gravesham (44) — Lab. 22; C. 19; Ind. 2; v. 1

Great Yarmouth (39) — C. 20; Lab. 15; Ind. 4

Guildford (48) — Ind. 24; LD 17; C. 4; Lab. 2; v. 1

Hambleton (28) — C. 24; Ind. 2; LD 1; Lab. 1

Harborough (34) — C. 22; LD 11; Lab. 1

Harlow (33) — Lab. 19; C. 12; v. 2

Harrogate (40) — C. 31; LD 7; Ind. 2

Hart (33) — Ind. 11; C. 11; LD 10; v. 1

Hastings (32) — Lab. 23; C. 8; Ind. 1

Havant (38) — C. 33; Lab. 2; Ind. 2; LD 1

Hertsmere (39) — C. 29; Lab. 6; LD 3; v. 1

High Peak (43) — Lab. 22; C. 16; LD 3; Green 2

Hinckley and Bosworth (34) — LD 21; C. 11; Lab. 2

Horsham (48) — C. 32; LD 12; Green 2; Ind. 1; v. 1

Huntingdonshire (52) — C. 30; Ind. 11; LD 7; Lab. 4

Hyndburn (35) — Lab. 25; C. 6; Ind. 2; v. 2

Ipswich (48) — Lab. 36; C. 8; LD 3; v. 1

Kettering (36) — C. 22; Lab. 7; Ind. 4; LD 1; v. 2

King's Lynn and West Norfolk (55) — C. 29; Ind. 15; Lab. 9; LD 1; Green 1

Lancaster (60) — Ind. 21; Lab. 14; C. 12; Green 10; LD 2; v. 1

Lewes (41) — C. 17; LD 9; Green 8; Lab. 3; Ind. 2; v. 2

Lichfield (47) — C. 34; Lab. 10; Ind. 1; LD 1; v. 1

Lincoln City (33) — Lab. 24; C. 9

Maidstone (55) — C. 24; LD 20; Ind. 6; Lab. 4; v. 1

Maldon (31) — Ind. 21; C. 8; v. 2

Malvern Hills (38) — C. 13; Ind. 10; LD 9; Green 5; Lab. 1

Mansfield (36) — Ind. 20; Lab. 14; C. 2

Melton (28) — C. 20; Ind. 7; Green 1

Mendip (47) — LD 24; C. 11; Green 10; Ind. 2

Mid Devon (42) — C. 17; LD 11; Ind. 9; Green 2

Mid Suffolk (34) — C. 16; Green 12; LD 5; Ind. 1

Mid Sussex (54) — C. 34; LD 13; Ind. 3; Green 3; v. 1

Mole Valley (41) — LD 22; C. 11; Ind. 8

New Forest (60) — C. 46; LD 13; Ind. 1

Newark and Sherwood (39) — C. 27; Lab. 7; Ind. 3; LD 2

Newcastle-under-Lyme (44) — Lab. 19; C. 19; Ind. 4; LD 2

North Devon (42) — LD 21; C. 12; Ind. 7; Green 2

North East Derbyshire (53) — C. 30; Lab. 18; LD 3; Ind. 2

North Hertfordshire (49) — C. 21; Lab. 15; LD 11; v. 2

North Kesteven (43) — Ind. 21; C. 21; v. 1

North Norfolk (40) — LD 28; C. 8; Ind. 4

North Warwickshire (35) — C. 20; Lab. 14; Ind. 1

North West Leicestershire (38) — C. 20; Lab. 9; LD 4; Ind. 3; Green 1; v. 1

Northampton (45) — C. 24; Lab. 16; LD 3; Ind. 1; v. 1

Norwich (39) — Lab. 27; Green 8; LD 3; v. 1

Nuneaton and Bedworth (34) — Lab. 17; C. 14; Ind. 2; Green 1

Oadby and Wigston (26) — LD 24; C. 2

Oxford (48) — Lab. 32; LD 8; Green 2; Ind. 3; v. 3

Pendle (49) — C. 20; Lab. 15; LD 10; Ind. 1; v. 3

Preston (48) — Lab. 30; LD 9; C. 8; v. 1

Redditch (29) — C. 18; Lab. 10; v. 1

Reigate and Banstead (45) — C. 29; Ind. 7; Green 5; LD 3; v. 1

Ribble Valley (40) — C. 27; LD 10; Ind. 2; v. 1

Richmondshire (24) — Ind. 11; C. 9; LD 3; Green 1

Rochford (39) — C. 26; Ind. 6; LD 3; Green 2; v. 2

Rossendale (36) — Lab. 19; C. 13; Ind. 4

Rother (38) — C. 14; Ind. 13; LD 7; Lab. 3; Green 1

Rugby (42) — C. 24; LD 9; Lab. 9

Runnymede (41) — C. 25; Ind. 10; LD 3; Lab. 2; Green 1

Rushcliffe (44) — C. 29; Lab. 7; Ind. 3; LD 3; Green 2

Rushmoor (39) — C. 26; Lab. 10; LD 1; v. 2

Ryedale (30) — Ind. 17; C. 11; LD 2

St Albans (58) — LD 24; C. 24; Lab. 5; Ind. 4; Green 1

Scarborough (46) — Ind. 17; C. 14; Lab. 13; Green 2

Sedgemoor (48) — C. 29; Lab. 11; LD 7; Ind. 1

Selby (31) — C. 16; Lab. 8; Ind. 7

Sevenoaks (54) — C. 46; Ind. 4; LD 3; Lab. 1

Somerset West and Taunton (59) — LD 32; Ind. 13; C. 9; Lab. 3; Green 2

South Cambridgeshire (45) — LD 28; C. 11; Ind. 2; Lab. 2; v. 2

South Derbyshire (36) — C. 22; Lab. 14; Ind. 7; v. 3

South Hams (31) — C. 15; LD 10; Green 3; Ind. 2; v. 1

South Holland (37) — C. 24; Ind. 13

South Kesteven (56) — C. 38; Ind. 12; Lab. 3; LD 2; v. 1

South Lakeland (51) — LD 30; C. 13; Lab. 3; Green 1; v. 4

South Norfolk (46) — C. 35; LD 10; Lab. 1

South Northamptonshire (42) — C. 32; LD 6; Ind. 3; v. 1

South Oxfordshire (36) — LD 12; C. 9; Ind. 6; Green 5; Lab. 3; v. 1

South Ribble (50) — C. 23; Lab. 21; LD 5; v. 1

South Somerset (60) — LD 40; C. 14; Green 1; Ind. 5

South Staffordshire (49) — C. 37; Ind. 8; Green 3; Lab. 1

Spelthorne (39) — C. 16; Ind. 12; LD 7; Lab. 2; Green 2

Stafford (40) — C. 22; Lab. 10; Ind. 7; Green 1

Staffordshire Moorlands (56) — C. 25; Ind. 16; Lab. 13; LD 1; v. 1

Stevenage (39) — Lab. 27; C. 7; LD 5

Stratford-on-Avon (36) — C. 19; LD 12; Ind. 4; Green 1

Stroud (51) — C. 21; Lab. 16; Green 9; LD 2; Ind. 2; v. 1

Surrey Heath (35) — C. 16; LD 9; Ind. 6; Green 2; Lab. 1; v. 1

Swale (47) — C. 16; Ind. 13; Lab. 11; LD 5; Green 2

Tamworth (30) — C. 21; Lab. 5; Ind. 4

Tandridge (42) — C. 15; Ind. 15; LD 9; v. 3

Teignbridge (47) — LD 24; C. 12; Ind. 11

Tendring (48) — Ind. 19; C. 19; Lab. 6; LD. 2; v. 2

Test Valley (43) — C. 22; LD 12; Ind. 6; v. 3

Tewkesbury (38) — C. 23; LD 8; Ind. 6; Green 1

Thanet (56) — C. 25; Lab. 19; Ind. 8; Green 3; v. 1

Three Rivers (39) — LD 22; C. 11; Lab. 3; Ind. 3

Tonbridge and Malling (54) — C. 39; LD 9; Ind. 3; Green 2; Lab. 1

Torridge (36) — Ind. 18; C. 11; Lab. 3; LD 2; Green 2
Tunbridge Wells (48) C. 28; LD 10; Ind. 5; Lab. 4; v. 1
Uttlesford (39) Ind. 26; LD 5; C. 4; Ind. 2; v. 2
Vale of White Horse LD 30; C. 6; Green 1; v. 1
(38)
Warwick (44) C. 19; LD 9; Green 8; Lab. 5; Ind. 3
Watford (36) LD 26; Lab. 10
Waverley (57) C. 23; Ind. 16; LD 14; Green 2; Lab. 2
Wealden (45) C. 30; Ind. 6; LD 4; Green 2; v. 3
Wellingborough (36) C. 25; Lab. 9; Ind. 1; v. 1
Welwyn Hatfield (48) C. 23; Lab. 13; LD 12
West Devon (31) C. 15; Ind. 12; LD 2; Green 2
West Lancashire (54) Lab. 29; C. 19; Ind. 6
West Lindsey (36) C. 16; LD 12; Ind. 7; v. 1
West Oxfordshire C. 29; LD 9; Lab. 9; Ind. 2
(49)
West Suffolk (64) C. 37; Ind. 19; Lab. 5; Green 1
Winchester (45) LD 26; C. 15; Ind. 3; v. 1
Woking (30) C. 14; LD 10; Ind. 3; Lab. 3
Worcester (35) C. 16; Lab. 15; Green 3; LD 1
Worthing (37) C. 23; Lab. 10; LD 3; Ind. 1
Wychavon (45) C. 34; LD 6; Green 2; Ind. 2; v. 1
Wyre (50) C. 37; Lab. 8; Ind. 5
Wyre Forest (33) Ind. 15; C. 12; LD 3; Lab. 2; Green 1

LONDON BOROUGH COUNCILS
Barking and Lab. 51
Dagenham (51)
Barnet (63) C. 36; Lab. 24; LD 2; v. 1
Bexley (45) C. 34; Lab. 10; Ind. 1
Brent (63) Lab. 59; C. 3; LD 1
Bromley (60) C. 50; Lab. 8; Ind. 2
Camden (54) Lab. 43; C. 7; LD 3; Green 1
Croydon (70) Lab. 41; C. 29
Ealing (69) Lab. 56; C. 6; LD 4; v. 3
Enfield (63) Lab. 40; C. 16; Ind. 5; v. 2
Greenwich (51) Lab. 40; C. 9; v. 2
Hackney (57) Lab. 49; C. 4; v. 4
Hammersmith and Lab. 35; C. 11
Fulham (46)
Haringey (57) Lab. 41; LD 15; Ind. 1
Harrow (63) Lab. 35; C. 27; Ind. 1
Havering (54) C. 25; Ind. 24; Lab. 5
Hillingdon (65) C. 43; Lab. 21; v. 1
Hounslow (60) Lab. 49; C. 10; v. 1
Islington (48) Lab. 45; C. 1; LD 1; Green 1
Kensington and C. 35; Lab. 13; LD 1; Ind. 1
Chelsea (50)
Kingston upon LD 37; C. 9; Ind. 1; v. 1
Thames (48)
Lambeth (63) Lab. 57; Green 5; C. 1
Lewisham (54) Lab. 51; Ind. 1; v. 2
Merton (60) Lab. 34; C. 17; LD 6; Ind. 3
Newham (60) Lab. 59; v. 1
Redbridge (63) Lab. 49; C. 12; v. 2
Richmond upon LD 39; C. 11; Green 3; v. 1
Thames (54)
Southwark (63) Lab. 48; LD 14; Ind. 1
Sutton (54) LD 33; C. 18; Ind. 3
Tower Hamlets (45) Lab. 41; C. 1; LD 1; Ind. 2
Waltham Forest (60) Lab. 46; C. 13; v. 1
Wandsworth (60) C. 33; Lab. 26; Ind. 1
Westminster (60) C. 41; Lab. 19

METROPOLITAN BOROUGHS
Barnsley (63) Lab. 48; Ind. 7; LD 4; C. 3; v. 1
Birmingham (101) Lab. 64; C. 25; LD 8; Green 1; v. 3
Bolton (60) Con. 18; Lab. 18; Ind. 15; LD 7; v. 2
Bradford (90) Lab. 52; C. 20; LD 7; Ind. 7; Green 2; v. 2
Bury (51) Lab. 28; C. 16; LD 4; Ind. 3

Calderdale (51) Lab. 28; C. 12; LD 7; Ind. 4
Coventry (54) Lab. 39; C. 13; Ind. 1; v. 1
Doncaster (55) Lab. 41; C. 8; Ind. 6
Dudley (72) Lab. 35; C. 34; Ind. 2; v. 1
Gateshead (66) Lab. 51; LD 12; Ind. 2; v. 1
Kirklees (69) Lab. 32; C. 16; LD 10; Ind. 7; Green 3; v. 1
Knowsley (45) Lab. 36; LD 3; Green 3; Ind. 1; v. 2
Leeds (99) Lab. 56; C. 23; LD 7; Ind. 9; Green 3; v. 1
Liverpool (90) Lab. 71; LD 10; Green 4; Ind. 4; v. 1
Manchester (96) Lab. 92; LD 2; v. 2
Newcastle-upon-Tyne Lab. 50; LD 20; Ind. 4; v. 4
(78)
North Tyneside (60) Lab. 49; C. 7; Ind. 1; LD 1; v. 2
Oldham (60) Lab. 46; LD 8; C. 4; Ind. 2
Rochdale (60) Lab. 44; C. 10; LD 3; Ind. 3
Rotherham (63) Lab. 42; Ind. 17; LD 1; v. 3
St Helens (48) Lab. 35; LD 4; C. 3; Green 2; Ind. 2; v. 2
Salford (60) Lab. 50; C. 8; Ind. 1; v. 1
Sandwell (72) Lab. 62; Ind. 5; v. 5
Sefton (66) Lab. 41; LD 12; C. 6; Ind. 5; v. 2
Sheffield (84) Lab. 45; LD 26; Green 8; Ind. 1; v. 4
Solihull (51) C. 26; Green 14; LD 5; Lab. 3; Ind. 2; v. 1
South Tyneside (54) Lab. 44; Ind. 6; Green 1; v. 3
Stockport (63) Lab. 26; LD 26; C. 8; Ind. 3
Sunderland (75) Lab. 50; C. 12; LD 8; Ind. 3; Green 1; v. 1
Tameside (57) Lab. 51; C. 5; Green 1
Trafford (63) Lab. 34; C. 19; LD 3; Green 3; Ind. 1; v. 3
Wakefield (63) Lab. 47; C. 11; Ind. 1; LD 1; v. 3
Walsall (60) C. 31; Lab. 26; LD 2; Ind. 1
Wigan (75) Lab. 57; Ind. 10; C. 7; v. 1
Wirral (66) Lab. 31; C. 19; LD 6; Green 2; Ind. 4; v. 4
Wolverhampton (60) Lab. 47; C. 10; v. 3

UNITARY COUNCILS
Bath and North East LD 37; C. 11; Ind. 6; Lab. 5
Somerset (59)
Bedford (40) LD 15; Lab. 11; C. 11; Green 2; Ind. 1
Blackburn with Lab. 33; C. 12; LD 2; Ind. 2; v. 2
Darwen (51)
Blackpool (42) Lab. 22; C. 14; Ind. 4; v. 2
Bournemouth, C. 36; Ind. 19; LD 14; Lab. 3; Green 2; v. 2
Christchurch & Poole
(BCP) (76)
Bracknell Forest (42) C. 38; Lab. 3; LD 1
Brighton and Hove Green 19; Lab. 17; C. 13; Ind. 5
(54)
Bristol (70) Lab. 34; C. 14; Green 11; LD 9; v. 2
Buckinghamshire C. 151; LD 17; Ind. 16; Lab. 9; Green 1
(194)
Central Bedfordshire C. 42; Ind. 13; LD 3; Lab. 1
(59)
Cheshire East (82) C. 32; Lab. 24; Ind. 21; LD 4; v. 1
Cheshire West and Lab. 34; C. 29; Ind. 3; LD 2; Green 1; v. 1
Chester (70)
Cornwall (123) C. 44; Ind. 40; LD 34; Lab. 4; v. 1
Darlington (50) C. 22; Lab. 19; Ind. 4; LD 3; Green 2
Derby (51) C. 19; Lab. 15; Ind. 9; LD 8
Dorset (82) C. 43; LD 29; Ind. 5; Green 4; Lab. 1
Durham (126) Lab. 70; Ind. 31; LD 15; C. 10
East Riding of C. 47; Ind. 10; LD 9; v. 1
Yorkshire (67)
Halton (56) Lab. 50; LD 3; C. 2; v. 2
Hartlepool (33) Ind. 20; Lab. 6; C. 4; v. 3
Herefordshire (53) Ind. 26; C. 13; Green 7; LD 6; v. 1

Isle of Wight (40) C. 25; Ind. 13; LD 2
*Isles of Scilly (16) Ind. 16
Kingston-upon-Hull Lab. 30; LD 24; C. 2; v. 1
(57)
Leicester (54) Lab. 51; LD 1; Ind. 1; v. 1
Luton (48) Lab. 33; LD 12; C. 3
Medway (55) C. 32; Lab. 20; Ind. 3
Middlesbrough (46) Ind. 25; Lab. 18; C. 3
Milton Keynes (57) Lab. 22; C. 17; LD 15; Ind. 2; v. 1
North East C. 23; Lab. 14; LD 4; Ind. 1
Lincolnshire (42)
North Lincolnshire C. 24; Lab. 14; Ind. 1; v. 1
(43)
North Somerset (50) Ind. 16; C. 13; LD 11; Lab. 6; Green 3; v. 1
Northumberland (67) C. 32; Lab. 23; Ind. 8; LD. 3; v. 1
Nottingham (55) Lab. 50; Ind. 3; C. 2
Peterborough (60) C. 26; Lab. 17; LD 9; Ind. 4; Green 2; v. 2
Plymouth (57) Lab. 30; C. 17; Ind. 10
Portsmouth (42) LD 17; C. 14; Lab. 6; Ind. 5
Reading (46) Lab. 30; C. 10; Green 4; LD 2
Redcar and Ind. 21; Lab. 15; LD 13; C. 8; v. 2
Cleveland (59)
Rutland (27) C. 17; Ind. 6; LD 3; Green 1
Shropshire (74) C. 47; LD 12; Lab. 7; Ind. 7; Green 1
Slough (42) Lab. 35; C. 4; Ind. 2; v. 1
South Gloucestershire C. 32; LD 17; Lab. 11; v. 1
(61)
Southampton (48) Lab. 30; C. 18
Southend-on-Sea (51) C. 20; Lab. 13; Ind. 11; LD 5; v. 2
Stockton-on-Tees Lab. 24; Ind. 15; C. 13; LD 1; v. 3
(56)
Stoke-on-Trent (44) C. 19; Lab. 14; Ind. 10; v. 1
Swindon (57) C. 30; Lab. 22; LD 2; Ind. 2; v. 1
Telford and Wrekin Lab. 35; C. 13; LD 4; Ind. 1; v. 1
(54)
Thurrock (49) C. 28; Lab. 16; Ind. 5
Torbay (36) C. 16; LD 11; Ind. 8; v. 1
Warrington (58) Lab. 42; LD 12; Ind. 2; C. 1; v. 1
West Berkshire (43) C. 24; LD 16; Green 3
Wiltshire (98) C. 63; LD 21; Ind. 10; Lab. 3; v. 1
Windsor and C. 22; LD 10; Ind. 9
Maidenhead (41)
Wokingham (54) C. 31; LD 15; Lab. 4; Ind. 3; v. 1
York (47) LD 21; Lab. 17; Green 3; Ind. 4; C. 2

* Twelve councillors are elected by the residents of the isle of St Mary's and one councillor each are elected by the residents of the four other islands (Bryher, St Agnes, St Martin's and Tresco)

WALES

Blaenau Gwent (41) Ind. 28; Lab. 13; PC 1
Bridgend (54) Lab. 26; Ind. 16; C. 8; PC 2; LD 1; v. 1
Caerphilly (73) Lab. 49; PC 18; Ind. 6
Cardiff (75) Lab. 38; C. 21; LD 11; Ind. 5
Carmarthenshire (74) PC 38; Ind. 19; Lab. 17
Ceredigion (42) PC 20; Ind. 14; LD 8
Conwy (59) Ind. 25; C. 14; PC 9; Lab. 6; LD 4; v. 1
Denbighshire (47) C. 15; Lab. 11; Ind. 11; PC 9; v. 1
Flintshire (70) Lab. 34; Ind. 24; C. 6; LD 5; v. 1
Gwynedd (75) PC 39; Ind. 33; Lab. 1; LD 1; v. 1
Merthyr Tydfil (33) Ind. 18; Lab. 15
Monmouthshire (43) C. 25; Lab. 10; Ind. 5; LD 3

Neath Port Talbot Lab. 38; PC 15; Ind. 9; LD 1' v. 1
(64)
Newport (50) Lab. 30; C. 12; Ind. 5; LD 2
Pembrokeshire (60) Ind. 35; C. 11; Lab. 7; PC 6; LD 1
Powys (73) Ind. 31; C. 17; LD 14; Lab. 8; PC 2; Green 1
Rhondda Cynon Taff Lab. 47; PC 17; Ind. 8; C. 3
(75)
Swansea (72) Lab. 47; C. 9; Ind. 8; LD 7; v. 1
Torfaen (44) Lab. 27; Ind. 12; C. 4; v. 1
Vale of Glamorgan C. 25; Lab. 14; Ind. 14; PC 4
(47)
Wrexham (52) Ind. 25; Lab. 11; C. 9; PC 4; LD 2; v. 1
Ynys Mon (Isle of PC 13; Ind. 12; Lab. 2; LD 1; v. 1
Anglesey) (30)

SCOTLAND

Aberdeen (45) SNP 19; C. 10; Lab. 9; LD 3; Ind. 4
Aberdeenshire (70) SNP 19; C. 18; Ind. 17; LD 14; Green 1; Lab. 1
Angus (28) Ind. 9; SNP 9; C. 8; LD 2
Argyll and Bute (36) SNP 11; Ind. 9; C. 9; LD 5; v. 2
Clackmannanshire SNP 8; Lab. 5; C. 4; Ind. 1
(18)
Dumfries and C. 16; SNP 10; Lab. 9; Ind. 7; LD 1
Galloway (43)
Dundee (29) SNP 14; Lab. 8; C. 3; LD 2; Ind. 2
East Ayrshire (32) SNP 14; Lab. 9; C. 6; Ind. 3
East Dunbartonshire SNP 7; C. 6; LD 6; Lab. 2; Ind. 1
(22)
East Lothian (22) Lab. 9; C. 7; SNP 6
East Renfrewshire C. 5; SNP 5; Lab. 4; LD 1; Ind. 3
(18)
Edinburgh (63) C. 17; SNP 16; Lab. 11; Green 8; LD 6; Ind. 5
Eilean Siar (Western Ind. 22; SNP 7; C. 2
Isles) (31)
Falkirk (30) SNP 12; Lab. 8; C. 6; Ind. 4
Fife (75) SNP 30; Lab. 23; C. 14; LD 7; Ind. 1
Glasgow (85) SNP 36; Lab. 30; C. 7; Green 7; Ind. 4; v. 1
Highland (74) Ind. 32; SNP 18; C. 10; LD 9; Lab. 3; Green 1; v. 1
Inverclyde (22) Lab. 8; SNP 7; Ind. 4; C. 2; LD 1
Midlothian (18) Lab. 6; SNP 7; C. 5
Moray (26) C. 9; SNP 8; Ind. 8; Lab. 1
North Ayrshire (33) Lab. 11; SNP 11; C. 7; Ind. 4
North Lanarkshire Lab. 30; SNP 29; C. 8; Ind. 8; v. 2
(77)
Orkney Islands (21) Ind. 20; Green 1
Perth and Kinross C. 17; SNP 13; LD 5; Ind. 3; Lab. 1; v. 1
(40)
Renfrewshire (43) SNP 19; Lab. 13; C. 8; Ind. 1; LD 1; v. 1
Scottish Borders (34) C. 14; SNP 8; Ind. 9; LD 2; v. 1
Shetland Islands (22) Ind. 21; SNP 1
South Ayrshire (28) C. 12; SNP 9; Lab. 5; Ind. 2
South Lanarkshire SNP 25; Lab. 17; C. 13; LD 3; Ind. 6
(64)
Stirling (23) C. 8; SNP 8; Lab. 4; Green 1; Ind. 1
West Dunbartonshire SNP 10; Lab. 8; Ind. 2; C. 2
(22)
West Lothian (33) SNP 12; Lab. 12; C. 7; Ind. 1; v. 1

NORTHERN IRELAND

Antrim & Newtownabbey (40)	DUP 14; UUP 8; All. 7; SF 5; SDLP 4; Ind. 2
Ards & North Down (40)	DUP 13; All. 10; UUP 8; Ind. 7; SDLP 2
Armagh City, Banbridge & Craigavon (41)	DUP 11; UUP 10; SF 10; SDLP 4; All. 3; Ind. 1; v. 2
Belfast City (60)	SF 18; DUP 14; All. 10; Ind. 10; SDLP 6; UUP 2
Causeway Coast & Glens (40)	DUP 14; SF 9; UUP 6; SDLP 4; All. 2; Ind. 5
Derry City & Strabane (40)	SF 11; SDLP 11; DUP 7; Ind. 6; All. 2; UUP 2; v. 1
Fermanagh & Omagh (40)	SF 14; UUP 10; SDLP 5; DUP 5; Ind. 5; All. 1
Lisburn & Castlereagh (40)	DUP 15; UUP 11; All. 9; SDLP 2; SF 2; Ind. 1
Mid & East Antrim (40)	DUP 16; Ind. 8; All. 7; UUP 6; SF 2; SDLP 1
Mid Ulster (40)	SF 17; DUP 9; UUP 6; SDLP 5; Ind. 3
Newry, Mourne & Down (41)	SF 16; SDLP 11; Ind. 5; UUP 3; DUP 4; All. 2

THE ISLE OF MAN

Ellan Vannin

The Isle of Man is an island situated in the Irish Sea, at latitude 54° 3'–54° 25' N. and longitude 4° 18'–4° 47' W., nearly equidistant from England, Scotland and Ireland. Although the early inhabitants were of Celtic origin, the Isle of Man was part of the Norwegian Kingdom of the Hebrides until 1266, when this was ceded to Scotland. Subsequently granted to the Stanleys (Earls of Derby) in the 15th century and later to the Dukes of Atholl, it was brought under the administration of the Crown in 1765. The island forms the bishopric of Sodor and Man.

The total land area is 572 sq. km (221 sq. miles). The 2016 census showed a resident population of 83,314 (men, 41,269; women, 42,045). The main language in use is English. Around 1,660 people are able to speak the Manx Gaelic language.

CAPITAL – ΨDouglas; population, 26,997 (2016). ΨCastletown (3,216) is the ancient capital; the other towns are ΨPeel (5,374) and ΨRamsey (7,845)

FLAG – A red flag charged with three conjoined armoured legs in white and gold

NATIONAL DAY – 5 July (Tynwald Day)

GOVERNMENT

The Isle of Man is a self-governing Crown dependency, with its own parliamentary, legal and administrative system. The British government is responsible for international relations and defence. Prior to Britain's withdrawal from the European Union, the island's special relationship with the EU was limited to trade alone and did not extend to financial aid; it neither contributed money to nor received funds from the EU budget. The Lieutenant-Governor is the Queen's personal representative on the island.

The legislature, Tynwald, is the oldest parliament in the world in continuous existence. It has two branches: the Legislative Council and the House of Keys. The council consists of the President of Tynwald, the Bishop of Sodor and Man, the Attorney-General (who does not have a vote) and eight members elected by the House of Keys. The House of Keys has 24 members, elected by universal adult suffrage. The branches sit separately to consider legislation and sit together, as Tynwald Court, for most other parliamentary purposes.

The presiding officer of Tynwald Court is the President of Tynwald, elected by the members, who also presides over sittings of the Legislative Council. The presiding officer of the House of Keys is the Speaker, who is elected by members of the house.

The principal members of the Manx government are the chief minister and eight departmental ministers, who comprise the Council of Ministers.

Lieutenant-Governor, HE Sir Richard Gozney, KCMG, CVO
President of Tynwald, Hon. Steve Rodan, OBE
Speaker, House of Keys, Hon. Juan Paul Watterson, SHK
Deputy Speaker, House of Keys, Chris Robertshaw, MHK
The First Deemster and Clerk of the Rolls, His Hon. Andrew Corlett
Clerk of Tynwald, Secretary to the House of Keys and Counsel to the Speaker, Roger Phillips
Clerk of the Legislative Council and Deputy Clerk of Tynwald, Jonathan King
HM Attorney-General, John Quinn, QC
Chief Minister, Hon. Howard Quayle, MHK
Chief Secretary, Will Greenhow

ECONOMY

Much of the income generated in the island is earned in the services sector with financial and professional services accounting for 45.1 per cent of the national income. Two other significant sectors are e-gaming and ICT, contributing 17.6 per cent and 6.9 per cent respectively, to the national income. The island has tariff-free access to EU markets for its engineering, farming and fishing products prior to the end of Britain's withdrawal period from the EU, set to end on 1 January 2021.

In November 2020 the island's unemployment rate was 1.8 per cent and the CPI rate of inflation was 0.2 per cent.

FINANCE

The budget for 2020–21 provides for gross revenue expenditure of £1,066m. The principal sources of government revenue are direct and indirect taxes. Income tax is payable at a rate of 10 per cent on the first £6,500 of taxable income for single resident individuals and 20 per cent on the balance, after personal allowances of £14,250. These bands are doubled for married couples. The rate of income tax for trading companies is zero per cent except for income from banking and major retail operations which is taxed at 10 per cent, and land and property which is taxed at 20 per cent. By agreement with the British government, the island keeps most of its rates of indirect taxation (VAT and duties) the same as those in the UK. However, VAT on tourist accommodation, domestic property, repairs and renovations is charged at 5 per cent. Taxes are also charged on property (rates), but these are comparatively low.

The major government expenditure items are social security payments, health and education. The island makes an annual contribution to the UK for defence and other external services.

Ψ = sea port

THE CHANNEL ISLANDS

The Channel Islands, situated off the north-west coast of France (at a distance of 16km (10 miles) at their closest point), are the only portions of the Dukedom of Normandy still belonging to the Crown, to which they have been attached since the Norman Conquest of 1066. They were the only British territory to come under German occupation during the Second World War, following invasion on 30 June and 1 July 1940. Guernsey and Jersey were relieved by British forces on 9 May 1945, Sark on 10 May 1945 and Alderney on 16 May 1945; 9 May (Liberation Day) is now observed as a bank and public holiday in Guernsey and Jersey.

The islands consist of Jersey (11,630ha/28,717 acres), Guernsey (6,340ha/15,654 acres), and the dependencies of Guernsey: Alderney (795ha/1,962 acres), Brecqhou (30ha/74 acres), Great Sark (419ha/1,035 acres), Little Sark (97ha/239 acres), Herm (130ha/320 acres), Jethou (18ha/44 acres) and Lihou (15ha/38 acres) – a total of 19,474ha/48,083 acres, or 195 sq. km/75 sq. miles.

Official figures estimated the population of Jersey as 106,800 at the end of 2018. Guernsey uses a rolling electronic census system and the most recent figures showed the population of Guernsey to be 63,021 (December 2019) and Alderney 2,019 (March 2018). Sark's population is estimated to be around 600. The official language is English but French is often used for ceremonial purposes. A Norman-French *patois* is also spoken by a few in Jersey, Guernsey and Sark.

GOVERNMENT

The islands are Crown dependencies with their own legislative assemblies (the States of Jersey, the States of Alderney, the States of Deliberation in Guernsey and the Chief Pleas in Sark), systems of local administration and law, and their own courts. *Projets de Loi* (Acts) passed by the States require the sanction of the Queen-in-council. The UK government is responsible for defence and international relations, although the islands are increasingly entering into agreements with other countries in their own right. The Channel Islands are not members of the European Union but had trading rights with the free movement of goods within the EU prior to Britain's withdrawal; as of November 2020 their future arrangement remained unclear. A common customs tariff, levies and agricultural and import measures apply to trade between the islands and non-member countries.

In both Jersey and Guernsey bailiwicks the Lieutenant-Governor and Commander-in-Chief, who is appointed by the Crown, is the personal representative of the Queen and the official channel of communication between the Crown (via the Privy Council) and the islands' governments.

The head of government in both Jersey and Guernsey is the Chief Minister. Jersey has a ministerial system of government; the executive comprises the Council of Ministers and consists of a chief minister and eleven other ministers. The ministers are assisted by up to nine assistant ministers. Members of the States who are not in the executive are able to sit on a number of scrutiny panels and the Public Accounts Committee to examine the policy of the executive and hold ministers to account. Guernsey is administered by a number of committees. The Policy and Resources committee is the senior committee responsible for leadership and coordination of the work of the States and is presided over by the Chief Minister, in addition there are six principal committees with mandated responsibilities. The States of Deliberation is the island's parliamentary assembly. Alderney has a legislature comprising a President and ten members elected by universal suffrage. Sark has a directly elected legislature of 28 members *(conseillers)* who serve on a number of committees.

Justice is administered by the royal courts of Jersey and Guernsey, each consisting of the bailiff and 12 elected jurats. The bailiffs of Jersey and Guernsey, appointed by the Crown, are presidents of the royal courts of their respective islands. Each bailiff is the *ex-officio* presiding officer in their respective parliaments and, by convention, the civic head.

The Church of England in each bailiwick is under the jurisdiction of the Dean of Jersey and the Dean of Guernsey respectively. The Bishop of Dover (Diocese of Canterbury) has episcopal oversight of the Channel Islands.

ECONOMY

A mild climate and good soil have led to the development of intensive systems of agriculture and horticulture. Earnings from tourism are important but the main source of income is banking and finance: the low rates of income and corporation tax and the absence of death duties make the islands an important offshore financial centre. The financial services sector contributes over 50 per cent of GDP in Jersey and 40 per cent of GVA in Guernsey. In addition, there is no VAT or equivalent tax in Guernsey and only small goods and services tax in Jersey (5 per cent since 1 June 2011). The international stock exchange is located in Guernsey, which also has a thriving e-gaming sector.

Principal exports are agricultural produce and flowers; imports are chiefly machinery, manufactured goods, food, fuel and chemicals. Trade with the UK is regarded as internal.

British currency is legal tender in the Channel Islands but each bailiwick issues its own coins and notes (*see* Currency section). They also issue their own postage stamps; UK stamps are not valid.

JERSEY

Lieutenant-Governor and Commander-in-Chief of Jersey, HE Air
    Chief Marshal Sir Stephen Dalton, GCB, *from* 2017
Chief of Staff, Maj. Justin Oldridge
Bailiff of Jersey, Timothy J. Le Cocq, QC
Deputy Bailiff, Robert J. MacRae, QC
Attorney-General, Mark Temple, QC
Receiver-General, David Pett
Solicitor-General, Matthew Jowitt, QC
Greffier of the States, Mark Egan
States Treasurer, Richard Bell
Chief Minister, Senator John Le Fondré

FINANCE

	2018	2019
Revenue income	£799,205,000	£845,370,000
Revenue expenditure	£759,303,000	£782,413,000
Capital expenditure	£18,077,000*	£68,946,000

* Much reduced due to a major new hospital project being postponed.

CHIEF TOWN – Ψ St Helier, on the south coast
FLAG – A white field charged with a red saltire cross, and
    the arms of Jersey in the upper centre

GUERNSEY AND DEPENDENCIES

Lieutenant-Governor and Commander-in-Chief of the Bailiwick of Guernsey and its Dependencies, Vice-Adm. Sir Ian Corder, KBE, CB
Presiding Officer of the Royal Court and of the States of Deliberation, Bailiff Richard McMahon, QC
Deputy Presiding Officer of the Royal Court and States of Deliberation, Deputy Bailiff Jessica Roland
HM Procureur and Receiver-General (Attorney-General), Megan Pullum, QC
HM Comptroller (Solicitor-General), Robert Titterington, QC

GUERNSEY

President of the Policy and Resources Committee, Deputy Peter Ferbrache
Chief Executive, Paul Whitfield

FINANCE

	2018	2019
Revenue income	£455,601,000	£476,876,000
Other income	£38,838,000	£152,778,000
Revenue expenditure	£452,182,000	£479,529,000
Capital expenditure	£37,057,000	£32,487,000
Other expenditure	£21,419,000	£12,082,000

CHIEF TOWNS – ΨSt Peter Port, on the east coast of Guernsey; St Anne on Alderney
FLAG – White, bearing a red cross of St George, with a gold cross of Normandy overall in the centre

ALDERNEY

President of the States, William Tate
Chief Executive, vacant
Greffier, Jonathan Anderson

SARK

Sark was the last European territory to abolish feudal parliamentary representation. Elections for a democratic legislative assembly took place in December 2008, with the *conseillers* taking their seats in the newly constituted Chief Pleas in January 2009.
Seigneur of Sark, Maj. Christopher Beaumont
Seneschal, Jeremy la Trobe-Bateman
Speaker, Lt.-Col. Reginald Guille, MBE
Greffier, Trevor Hamon

OTHER DEPENDENCIES

Herm and Lihou are owned by the States of Guernsey; Herm is leased, Lihou is uninhabited. Jethou is leased by the Crown to the States of Guernsey and is sub-let by the States. Brecqhou is within the legislative and judicial territory of Sark.

Ψ = seaport

LAW COURTS AND OFFICES

SUPREME COURT OF THE UNITED KINGDOM

The Supreme Court of the United Kingdom is the highest domestic judicial authority; it replaced the appellate committee of the House of Lords (the house functioning in its judicial capacity) on 1 October 2009. It is the final court of appeal for cases heard in Great Britain and Northern Ireland (except for criminal cases from Scotland). Cases concerning the interpretation and application of European Union law, including preliminary rulings requested by British courts and tribunals, which are decided by the Court of Justice of the European Union (CJEU) (*see* European Union), and the supreme court can make a reference to the CJEU in appropriate cases. Additionally, in giving effect to rights contained in the European Convention on Human Rights, the supreme court must take account of any decision of the European Court of Human Rights.

The supreme court also assumed jurisdiction in relation to devolution matters under the Scotland Act 1998 (now partly superseded by the Scotland Act 2012), the Northern Ireland Act 1988 and the Government of Wales Act 2006; these powers were transferred from the Judicial Committee of the Privy Council. Ten of the 12 Lords of Appeal in Ordinary (Law Lords) from the House of Lords transferred to the 12-member supreme court when it came into operation (at the same time one law lord retired and another was appointed Master of the Rolls). All new justices of the supreme court are now appointed by an independent selection commission, and, although styled *Rt. Hon. Lord,* are not members of the House of Lords. Peers who are members of the judiciary are disqualified from sitting or voting in the House of Lords until they retire from their judicial office. *See* Life Peers for a list of such peers (§).

President of the Supreme Court (£234,184), Rt. Hon. Lord Reed
　born 1956, *apptd* 2019 (from January 2020)
Deputy President of the Supreme Court (£226,193), vacant

JUSTICES OF THE SUPREME COURT *as at November 2019*
(each £226,193)
Style, The Rt. Hon. Lord/Lady–

Rt. Hon. Lord Kerr of Tonaghmore, *born* 1948, *apptd* 2009
Rt. Hon. Lord Wilson of Culworth, *born* 1945, *apptd* 2011
Rt. Hon. Lord Carnwath of Notting Hill, CVO, *born* 1945,
　apptd 2012
Rt. Hon. Lord Hodge, *born* 1953, *apptd* 2013
Rt. Hon. Lady Black of Derwent, DBE, *born* 1954, *apptd*
　2017
Rt. Hon. Lord Lloyd-Jones, *born* 1952, *apptd* 2017
Rt. Hon. Lord Briggs of Westbourne, *born* 1954, *apptd* 2017
Rt. Hon. Lady Arden of Heswall, DBE, *born* 1947, *apptd*
　2018
Rt. Hon. Lord Kitchin, *born* 1955, *apptd* 2018
Rt. Hon. Lord Sales, *born* 1962, *apptd* 2019

UNITED KINGDOM SUPREME COURT
Parliament Square, London SW1P 3BD **T** 020-7960 1900
Chief Executive, Mark Ormerod, CB

JUDICATURE OF ENGLAND AND WALES

The legal system in England and Wales is divided into criminal law and civil law. Criminal law is concerned with acts harmful to the community and the rules laid down by the state for the benefit of citizens, whereas civil law governs the relationships and transactions between individuals. Administrative law is a kind of civil law usually concerning the interaction of individuals and the state, and most cases are heard in tribunals specific to the subject (*see* Tribunals section). Scotland and Northern Ireland possess legal systems that differ from the system in England and Wales in law, judicial procedure and court structure, but retain the distinction between criminal and civil law.

Under the provisions of the Criminal Appeal Act 1995, a commission was set up to direct and supervise investigations into possible miscarriages of justice and to refer cases to the appeal courts on the grounds of conviction and sentence; these functions were formerly the responsibility of the home secretary.

HIERARCHY OF ENGLISH AND WELSH COURTS

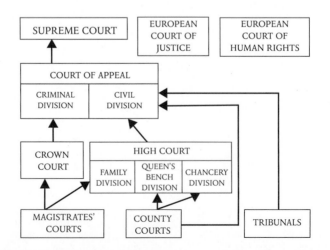

SENIOR COURTS OF ENGLAND AND WALES

The senior courts of England and Wales (until September 2009 known as the supreme court of judicature of England and Wales) comprise the high court, the crown court and the court of appeal. The President of the Courts of England and Wales, a new title given to the Lord Chief Justice under the Constitutional Reform Act 2005, is the head of the judiciary.

The high court was created in 1875 and combined many previously separate courts. Sittings are held at the royal courts of justice in London or at around 120 district registries outside the capital. It is the superior civil court and is split into three divisions – the chancery division, the Queen's bench division and the family division – each of which is further divided. The chancery division is headed by the Chancellor of the High Court and is concerned mainly with equity, trusts, tax and bankruptcy, while also including two specialist courts, the patents court and the companies court. The Queen's bench division (QBD) is the largest of the three divisions, and is headed by its own president. It deals with common law (ie tort, contract, debt and personal injuries), some tax law, eg VAT tribunal appeals, and encompasses the admiralty court and the commercial court. The QBD also administers the technology and construction court. The family division was created in 1970 and is headed by its own president, who is also Head of Family Justice, and hears cases concerning divorce, access to and custody of children, and other family matters. The divisional court of the high court sits in the family and chancery divisions, and hears appeals from the magistrates' courts and county courts.

The crown court was set up in 1972 and sits at 77 centres throughout England and Wales. It deals with more serious (indictable) criminal offences, which are triable before a judge and jury, including treason, murder, rape, kidnapping, armed robbery and Official Secrets Act offences. It also handles cases transferred from the magistrates' courts where the magistrate decides his or her own power of sentence is inadequate, or where someone appeals against a magistrate's decision, or in a case that is triable 'either way' where the accused has chosen a jury trial. The crown court centres are divided into three tiers: high court judges, circuit judges and sometimes recorders (part-time circuit judges), sit in first-tier centres, hearing the most serious criminal offences (eg murder, treason, rape, manslaughter) and some civil high court cases. The second-tier centres are presided over by high court judges, circuit judges or recorders and also deal with the most serious criminal cases. Third-tier courts deal with the remaining criminal offences, with circuit judges or recorders presiding.

The court of appeal hears appeals against both fact and law, and was last restructured in 1966 when it replaced the court of criminal appeal. It is split into the civil division (which hears appeals from the high court, tribunals and in certain cases, the county courts) and the criminal division (which hears appeals from the crown court). Cases are heard by Lords Justices of Appeal and high court judges if deemed suitable for reconsideration.

The Constitutional Reform Act 2005 instigated several key changes to the judiciary in England and Wales. These included the establishment of the independent supreme court, which opened in October 2009; the reform of the post of Lord Chancellor, transferring its judicial functions to the President of the Courts of England and Wales; a duty on government ministers to uphold the independence of the judiciary by barring them from trying to influence judicial decisions through any special access to judges; the formation of a fully transparent and independent Judicial Appointments Commission that is responsible for selecting candidates to recommend for judicial appointment to the Lord Chancellor and Secretary of State for Justice; and the creation of the post of Judicial Appointments and Conduct Ombudsman.

CRIMINAL CASES

In criminal matters the decision to prosecute (in the majority of cases) rests with the Crown Prosecution Service (CPS), which is the independent prosecuting body in England and Wales. The CPS is headed by the director of public prosecutions, who works under the superintendence of the Attorney-General. Certain categories of offence continue to require the Attorney-General's consent for prosecution.

Most minor criminal cases (summary offences) are dealt with in magistrates' courts, usually by a bench of three unpaid lay magistrates (justices of the peace) sitting without a jury and assisted on points of law and procedure by a legally trained clerk. There are approximately 23,000 justices of the peace. In some courts a full-time, salaried and legally qualified district judge (magistrates' court) – formerly known as a stipendiary judge – presides alone. There are 140 district judges and 170 deputy district judges operating in around 330 magistrates' courts in England and Wales. Magistrates' courts deal with 95 per cent of all criminal cases. Magistrates' courts also house some family proceedings courts (which deal with relationship breakdown and childcare cases) and youth courts. Cases of medium seriousness (known as 'offences triable either way') where the defendant pleads not guilty can be heard in the crown court for a trial by jury, if the defendant so chooses. Preliminary proceedings in a serious case to decide whether there is evidence to justify committal for trial in the crown court are dealt with in the magistrates' courts.

The 77 centres that the crown court sits in are divided into seven regions. There are over 600 circuit judges and 1,000 recorders (part-time circuit judges); expected to sit for 30 days a year. A jury is present in all trials that are contested.

Appeals from magistrates' courts against sentence or conviction are made to the crown court, and appeals upon a point of law are made to the high court, which may ultimately be appealed to the supreme court. Appeals from the crown court, either against sentence or conviction, are made to the court of appeal (criminal division). Again, these appeals may be brought to the supreme court if a point of law is contested, and if the house considers it is of sufficient importance.

CIVIL CASES

Most minor civil cases – including contract, tort (especially personal injuries), property, divorce and other family matters, bankruptcy etc – are dealt with by the county courts, of which there are around 200 (see **W** www.justice.gov.uk for further details). Cases are heard by circuit judges, recorders or district judges. For cases involving small claims (with certain exceptions, where the amount claimed is £5,000 or less) there are informal and simplified procedures designed to enable parties to present their cases themselves without recourse to lawyers. Where there are financial limits on county court jurisdiction, claims that exceed those limits may be tried in the county courts with the consent of the parties, subject to the court's agreement, or in certain circumstances on transfer from the high court. Outside London, bankruptcy proceedings can be heard in designated county courts. Magistrates' courts also deal with certain classes of civil case, and committees of magistrates license public houses, clubs and betting shops. For the implementation of the Children Act 1989, a new structure of hearing centres was set up in 1991 for family proceedings cases, involving magistrates' courts (family proceedings courts), divorce county courts, family hearing centres and care centres.

Appeals in certain family matters heard in the family proceedings courts go to the family division of the high court. Appeals from county courts may be heard in the court of appeal (civil division) or the high court, and may go on to the supreme court.

CORONERS' COURTS

Unlike the unified courts system, administered by HM Courts and Tribunals Service, there are 92 separate coroners' jurisdictions in England and Wales. Each jurisdiction is locally funded and resourced by local authorities. Coroners are barristers, solicitors or medical practitioners of not less than five years standing, who continue in their legal or medical practices when not sitting as coroners. Some 32 coroners are 'full-time' coroners and are paid an annual salary regardless of their caseload. The remainder are paid according to the number of cases referred to them. The coroner's jurisdiction is territorial – it is the location of the dead body which dictates which coroner has jurisdiction in any particular case.

The coroners' courts investigate violent and unnatural deaths or sudden deaths where the cause is unknown. Doctors, the police, various public authorities or members of the public may bring cases before a coroner. Where a death is sudden and the cause is unknown, the coroner may order a post-mortem examination to determine the cause of death rather than hold an inquest in court. An inquest must be held, however, if a person died in a violent or unnatural way, or died in prison or other unusual circumstances. If the coroner suspects murder, manslaughter or infanticide, then they must summon a jury.

Coroners are required to appoint a deputy or assistant deputy to act in their stead if they are out of the district or otherwise unable to act. Deputies and assistant deputies have the same professional qualifications as the coroner. In exceptionally high-profile or complex cases, a serving judge may be appointed as a deputy coroner.

SENIOR JUDICIARY OF ENGLAND AND WALES

Lord Chief Justice of England and Wales and Head of Criminal Justice (£262,264), Rt. Hon. Lord Burnett of Maldon, *born* 1958, *apptd* 2017

Master of the Rolls and Head of Civil Justice (£234,184), Rt. Hon. Sir Terence Etherton, *born* 1951, *apptd* 2016

President of the Queen's Bench Division (£226,193), Rt. Hon. Dame Victoria Sharp, DBE, *born* 1956, *apptd* 2019

President of the Family Division and Head of Family Justice (£226,193), Rt. Hon. Sir Andrew McFarlane, *born* 1954, *apptd* 2018

Chancellor of the High Court (£226,193), Rt. Hon. Sir Geoffrey Vos, *born* 1955, *apptd* 2016

SENIOR COURTS OF ENGLAND AND WALES

COURT OF APPEAL

Presiding Judge, Criminal Division, Lord Chief Justice of England and Wales

Presiding Judge, Civil Division, Master of the Rolls

Vice-President, Civil Division (£215,094), Rt. Hon. Sir Nicholas Underhill *born* 1952, *apptd* 2018

Vice-President, Criminal Division (£215,094), Rt. Hon. Lady Heather Hallett, DBE, *born* 1949, *apptd* 2013

LORD JUSTICES OF APPEAL *as at September 2019* (each £215,094)
Style, The Rt. Hon. Lord/Lady Justice [surname]

Rt. Hon. Sir Andrew Longmore, *born* 1944, *apptd* 2001
Rt. Hon. Lady Heather Hallett, DBE, *born* 1949, *apptd* 2005
Rt. Hon. Sir Nicholas Patten, *born* 1950, *apptd* 2009
Rt. Hon. Sir Peter Gross, *born* 1952, *apptd* 2010
Rt. Hon. Dame Anne Rafferty, DBE, *born* 1950, *apptd* 2011
Rt. Hon. Sir Nigel Davis, *born* 1951, *apptd* 2011
Rt. Hon. Sir Kim Lewison, *born* 1952, *apptd* 2011
Rt. Hon. Sir Colman Treacy, *born* 1949, *apptd* 2012
Rt. Hon. Sir Richard McCombe, *born* 1952, *apptd* 2012

Rt. Hon. Sir Ernest Ryder, TD, *born* 1957, *apptd* 2013
Rt. Hon. Sir Nicholas Underhill, *born* 1952, *apptd* 2013
Rt. Hon. Sir Christopher Floyd, *born* 1951, *apptd* 2013
Rt. Hon. Sir Adrian Fulford, *born* 1953, *apptd* 2013
Rt. Hon. Dame Julia Macur, DBE, *born* 1957, *apptd* 2013
Rt. Hon. Sir David Bean, *born* 1954, *apptd* 2014
Rt. Hon. Dame Eleanor King, DBE, *born* 1957, *apptd* 2014
Rt. Hon. Sir Peregrine Simon, *born* 1950, *apptd* 2015
Rt. Hon. Sir Keith Lindblom, *born* 1956, *apptd* 2015
Rt. Hon. Sir David Richards, *born* 1951, *apptd* 2015
Rt. Hon. Sir Nicholas Hamblen, *born* 1957, *apptd* 2016
Rt. Hon. Sir Stephen Irwin, *born* 1953, *apptd* 2016
Rt. Hon. Sir Launcelot Henderson, *born* 1951, *apptd* 2016
Rt. Hon. Sir Julian Flaux, *born* 1955, *apptd* 2016
Rt. Hon. Dame Kathryn Thirlwall, DBE, *born* 1957, *apptd* 2017
Rt. Hon. Sir Gary Hickinbottom, *born* 1955, *apptd* 2017
Rt. Hon. Sir Andrew Moylan, *born* 1953, *apptd* 2017
Rt. Hon. Sir Timothy Holroyde, *born* 1955, *apptd* 2017
Rt. Hon. Sir Peter Jackson, *born* 1955, *apptd* 2017
Rt. Hon Sir Guy Newey, *born* 1959, *apptd* 2017
Rt. Hon Sir Rabinder Singh, *born* 1964, *apptd* 2017
Rt. Hon. Dame Sarah Asplin, DBE, *born* 1959, *apptd* 2017
Rt. Hon. Sir George Leggatt, *born* 1957, *apptd* 2018
Rt. Hon. Sir Peter Coulson, *born* 1958, *apptd* 2018
Rt. Hon. Sir Jonathan Baker, *born* 1955, *apptd* 2018
Rt. Hon. Sir Charles Haddon-Cave, *born* 1956, *apptd* 2018
Rt. Hon. Sir Nicholas Green, *born* 1958, *apptd* 2018
Rt. Hon. Dame Nicola Davies, DBE, *born* 1953, *apptd* 2018
Rt. Hon. Sir Stephen Males, *born* 1955, *apptd* 2019
Rt. Hon. Dame Vivien Rose, DBE, *born* 1960, *apptd* 2019
Rt. Hon. Dame Ingrid Simler, DBE, *born* 1963, *apptd* 2019

Ex Officio Judges, Lord Chief Justice of England and Wales; Master of the Rolls; President of the Queen's Bench Division; President of the Family Division; Chancellor of the High Court

COURTS-MARTIAL APPEAL COURT

Judges, Lord Chief Justice of England and Wales; Master of the Rolls; Lord Justices of Appeal; Judges of the High Court of Justice

HIGH COURT

CHANCERY DIVISION

Chancellor of the High Court (£226,193), Rt. Hon. Sir Geoffrey Vos, *born* 1955, *apptd* 2016
Clerk, Natalie Ford
Legal Secretary, Vannina Ettori

JUDGES *as at September 2019* (each £188,901)
Style, The Hon. Mr/Mrs/Ms Justice [surname]

Hon. Sir George Mann, *born* 1951, *apptd* 2004
Hon. Sir Paul Morgan, *born* 1952, *apptd* 2007
Hon. Sir Alastair Norris, *born* 1950, *apptd* 2007
Hon. Sir Gerald Barling, *born* 1949, *apptd* 2007
Hon. Sir Richard Arnold, *born* 1961, *apptd* 2008
Hon. Sir Peter Roth, *born* 1952, *apptd* 2009
Hon. Sir Robert Hildyard, *born* 1952, *apptd* 2011
Hon. Sir Colin Birss, *born* 1964, *apptd* 2013
Hon. Sir Christopher Nugee, *born* 1959, *apptd* 2013
Hon. Sir Richard Snowden, *born* 1962, *apptd* 2015
Hon. Sir Marcus Smith, *born* 1967, *apptd* 2017
Hon. Sir Antony Zacaroli, *born* 1963, *apptd* 2017
Hon. Sir Timothy Fancourt, *born* 1964, *apptd* 2018
Hon. Dame Sarah Falk, DBE, *born* 1962, *apptd* 2018
The Chancery Division also includes three specialist courts: the Companies Court, the Patents Court and the Bankruptcy Court.

QUEEN'S BENCH DIVISION
President (£226,193), Rt. Hon. Dame Victoria Sharp, DBE,
  born 1956, *apptd* 2019
Vice-President (£215,094), vacant

JUDGES *as at September 2019* (each £188,901)
Style, The Hon. Mr/Mrs/Ms Justice [surname]

Hon. Sir Paul Walker, *born* 1954, *apptd* 2004
Hon. Sir Nigel Teare, *born* 1952, *apptd* 2006
Hon. Sir Nigel Sweeney, *born* 1954, *apptd* 2008
Hon. Sir Andrew Nicol, *born* 1951, *apptd* 2009
Hon. Sir Michael Supperstone, *born* 1950, *apptd* 2010
Hon. Sir Robin Spencer, *born* 1955, *apptd* 2010
Hon. Sir Andrew Popplewell, *born* 1959, *apptd* 2011
Hon. Dame Beverley Lang, DBE, *born* 1955, *apptd* 2011
Hon. Sir Jeremy Stuart-Smith, *born* 1955, *apptd* 2012
Hon. Sir Mark Turner, *born* 1959, *apptd* 2013
Hon. Sir Jeremy Baker, *born* 1958, *apptd* 2013
Hon. Sir Stephen Stewart, *born* 1953, *apptd* 2013
Hon. Sir Robert Jay, *born* 1959, *apptd* 2013
Hon. Sir James Dingemans, *born* 1964, *apptd* 2013
Hon. Sir Clive Lewis, *born* 1960, *apptd* 2013
Hon. Dame Sue Carr, DBE, *born* 1964, *apptd* 2013
Hon. Sir Stephen Phillips, *born* 1961, *apptd* 2013
Hon. Dame Geraldine Andrews, DBE, *born* 1959, *apptd*
  2013
Hon. Dame Elisabeth Laing, DBE, *born* 1956, *apptd* 2014
Hon. Sir William Davis, *born* 1954, *apptd* 2014
Hon. Sir Mark Warby, *born* 1958, *apptd* 2014
Hon. Sir Andrew Edis, *born* 1957, *apptd* 2014
Hon. Sir James Goss, *born* 1953, *apptd* 2014
Hon. Dame Maura McGowan, DBE, *born* 1957, *apptd* 2014
Hon. Sir Robin Knowles, *born* 1960, *apptd* 2014
Hon. Sir Ian Dove, *born* 1963, *apptd* 2014
Hon. Sir David Holgate, *born* 1956, *apptd* 2014
Hon. Sir Timothy Kerr, *born* 1958, *apptd* 2015
Hon. Dame Philippa Whipple, DBE, *born* 1966, *apptd* 2015
Hon. Sir Peter Fraser, *born* 1963, *apptd* 2015
Hon. Sir Neil Garnham, *born* 1959, *apptd* 2015
Hon. Dame Bobbie Cheema-Grubb, DBE *born* 1966, *apptd*
  2015
Hon. Sir Michael Soole, *born* 1954, *apptd* 2015
Hon. Dame Juliet May, DBE, *born* 1961, *apptd* 2015
Hon. Sir Stephen Morris, *born* 1957, *apptd* 2016
Hon. Dame Nerys Jefford, DBE, *born* 1962, *apptd* 2016
Hon. Sir Nicholas Lavender, *born* 1964, *apptd* 2016
Hon. Dame Finola O'Farrell, DBE, *born* 1960, *apptd* 2016
Hon. Sir Andrew Baker, *born* 1965, *apptd* 2016
Hon. Sir Julian Goose, *born* 1961, *apptd* 2017
Hon. Sir Peter Lane, *born* 1953, *apptd* 2017
Hon. Sir Simon Bryan, *born* 1965, *apptd* 2017
Hon. Dame Jane Moulder, DBE, *born* 1960, *apptd* 2017
Hon. Sir Martin Spencer, *born* 1956, *apptd* 2017
Hon. Sir Julian Knowles, *born* 1969, *apptd* 2017
Hon. Dame Amanda Yip, DBE, *born* 1969, *apptd* 2017
Hon. Sir Matthew Nicklin, *born* 1970, *apptd* 2017
Hon. Sir Akhlaq Choudhury, *born* 1967, *apptd* 2017
Hon. Dame Sara Cockerill, DBE, *born* 1968, *apptd* 2017
Hon. Dame Christina Lambert, DBE, *born* 1963, *apptd* 2018
Hon. Sir Christopher Butcher, *born* 1962, *apptd* 2018
Hon. Sir Richard Jacobs, *born* 1956, *apptd* 2018
Hon. Sir David Waksman, *born* 1957, *apptd* 2018
Hon. Dame Johannah Cutts, DBE, *born* 1964, *apptd* 2018
Hon. Sir Jonathan Swift, *born* 1964, *apptd* 2018
Hon. Sir Edward Pepperall, *born* 1966, *apptd* 2018
Hon. Sir Edward Murray, *born* 1958, *apptd* 2018
Hon. Dame Judith Farbey, DBE, *born* 1965, *apptd* 2018
Hon. Clive Freedman, *born* 1955, *apptd* 2018

Hon. Dame Justine Thornton, *born* 1970, *apptd* 2019
Hon. Dame Jennifer Eady, DBE, *born* 1965, *apptd* 2019
Hon. Sir John Cavanagh, *born* 1960, *apptd* 2019
Hon. Dame Alison Foster, *born* 1957, *apptd* 2019
Hon. Sir Pushpinder Saini, *born* 1968, *apptd* 2019
Hon. Sir Jeremy Johnson, *born* 1971, *apptd* 2019
Hon. Sir Martin Chamberlain, *born* 1974, *apptd* 2019

The Queen's Bench Division also includes the Divisional
Court, the Admiralty Court, Commercial Court and
Technology and Construction Court.

FAMILY DIVISION
President (£226,193), Rt. Hon. Sir Andrew McFarlane, *born*
  1954, *apptd* 2018

JUDGES *as at September 2019* (each £188,901)
Style, The Hon. Mr/Mrs/Ms Justice [surname]

Hon. Sir Edward Holman, *born* 1947, *apptd* 1995
Hon. Sir Nicholas Mostyn, *born* 1957, *apptd* 2010
Hon. Dame Lucy Theis, DBE, *born* 1960, *apptd* 2010
Hon. Sir Philip Moor, *born* 1959, *apptd* 2011
Hon. Sir Stephen Cobb, *born* 1962, *apptd* 2013
Hon. Sir Michael Keehan, *born* 1960, *apptd* 2013
Hon. Sir Anthony Hayden, *born* 1961, *apptd* 2013
Hon. Dame Alison Russell, DBE, *born* 1958, *apptd* 2014
Hon. Sir Roderick Newton, *born* 1958, *apptd* 2014
Hon. Dame Jennifer Roberts, DBE, *born* 1953, *apptd* 2014
Hon. Sir Alistair MacDonald, *born* 1970, *apptd* 2015
Hon. Sir Peter Francis, *born* 1958, *apptd* 2016
Hon. Dame Gwynneth Knowles, DBE *born* 1962, *apptd*
  2017
Hon. Sir Jonathan Cohen, *born* 1951, *apptd* 2017
Hon. Sir David Williams, *born* 1961, *apptd* 2017
Hon. Dame Nathalie Lieven, DBE, *born* 1964, *apptd* 2019
Hon. Dame Frances Judd, DBE, *born* 1961, *apptd* 2019

COURTS, DIVISIONS AND OFFICES OF THE HIGH COURT OF ENGLAND AND WALES

ADMINISTRATIVE COURT
Royal Courts of Justice, London WC2A 2LL
T 020-7947 6655
Judge in charge of the Administrative Court (£188,901), Hon. Mr
  Justice Supperstone
*Registrar of Criminal Appeals, Master of the Crown Office and
  Queen's Coroner and Attorney* (£140,289), Master Beldam

ADMIRALTY COURT
Ground Floor, 7 Rolls Building, Fetter Lane, London EC4A 1NL
T 020-7947 6112
Admiralty Judge (£188,901), Hon. Mr Justice Teare
Clerk, Paul Doerr
Registrar (£112,542), vacant

CIRCUIT COMMERCIAL COURT (formerly Mercantile Court)
Ground Floor, 7 Rolls Building, Fetter Lane, London EC4A 1NL
T 020-7947 6112

CHANCERY DIVISION
7 Rolls Building, Fetter Lane, London EC4A 1NL **T** 020-7947 7391
Chief Chancery Master (£140,289), Chief Master Marsh *apptd*
  2014
Masters of Chancery (£112,542), Master Clark *apptd* 2015;
  Master Kaye *apptd* 2019; Master Matthews *apptd* 2015;
  Master Shuman *apptd* 2017; Master Teverson *apptd* 2005

COMMERCIAL COURT
Ground Floor, 7 Rolls Building, Fetter Lane, London EC4A 1NL
T 020-7947 7501
Judge in charge of the Commercial Court (£188,901), Hon. Mr Justice Teare
Clerk, Paul Doerr

COURT OF APPEAL CIVIL DIVISION
Royal Courts of Justice, London WC2A 2LL **T** 020-7947 6916

COURT OF APPEAL CRIMINAL DIVISION
Royal Courts of Justice, London WC2A 2LL **T** 020-7947 6011

COURT OF PROTECTION
First Avenue House, 42–49 High Holborn, London WC1V 6NP
T 0300-456 4600
Senior Judge and Master of the Court of Protection (£140,289), Her Hon. Judge Hilder, *apptd* 2017

FAMILY DIVISION
Royal Courts of Justice, London WC2A 2LL **T** 020-7947 6000

INSOLVENCY AND COMPANIES LIST
7 Rolls Building, Fetter Lane, London EC4A 1NL
T 020-7947 6294
Chief Registrar (140,289), Nicholas Briggs *apptd* 2017
Insolvency and Companies Court Judges (£112,542), Judge Barber *apptd* 2009; Judge Burton *apptd* 2018; Judge Jones *apptd* 2012; Judge Mullen *apptd* 2018; Judge Prentis *apptd* 2018

INTELLECTUAL PROPERTY ENTERPRISE COURT
7 Rolls Building, Fetter Lane, London EC4A 1NL
T 020-7947 7783 **E** ipec@hmcts.gsi.gov.uk
Judge in Charge, His Hon. Judge Hacon
Clerk, Irram Khan

PATENTS COURT
7 Rolls Building, Fetter Lane, London EC4A 1NL
T 020-7073 1789
Judge in Charge, Hon. Mr Justice Arnold
Clerk, Pauline Drewett

PLANNING COURT
Royal Courts of Justice, London WC2A 2LL
T 020-7947 6655

QUEEN'S BENCH DIVISION
Judge in Charge of the Queen's Bench Civil List, Hon. Mr Justice Stewart
Senior Master and Queen's Remembrancer (£140,289), Senior Master Fontaine *apptd* 2014
Masters of the Queen's Bench Division (£112,542), Master Cook *apptd* 2011; Master Davison *apptd* 2016; Master Eastman *apptd* 2009; Master Gidden *apptd* 2012; Master McCloud *apptd* 2010; Master Thornett *apptd* 2016; Master Yoxall *apptd* 2002

SENIOR COURT COSTS OFFICE
Thomas More Building, Royal Courts of Justice, London WC2A 2LL
T 020-7947 6000
Senior Costs Judge (Chief Taxing Master) (£140,289), Chief Master Gordon-Saker *apptd* 2014
Cost Judges (Taxing Masters) (£112,542), Master Brown *apptd* 2016; Master Haworth *apptd* 2006; Master James *apptd* 2015; Master Leonard *apptd* 2010; Master Nagalingam *apptd* 2017; Master Rowley *apptd* 2013; Master Whalan *apptd* 2015

TECHNOLOGY AND CONSTRUCTION COURT (TCC)
Ground Floor, 7 Rolls Building, Fetter Lane, London EC4A 1NL
T 020-7947 7156
Judge in charge of the TCC (£188,901), Hon. Mr Justice Fraser

COURT FUNDS OFFICE
Sunderland SR43 3AB **T** 0300-020 0199 **E** enquiries@cfo.gsi.gov.uk

The Court Funds Office (CFO), established in 1726, provides a banking and administration service for the civil courts throughout England and Wales, including the High Court.

ELECTION PETITIONS OFFICE
Room E113, Royal Courts of Justice, Strand, London WC2A 2LL
T 020-7947 6877

The office accepts petitions and deals with all matters relating to the questioning of parliamentary, European parliament, local government and parish elections, and with applications for relief under the 'representation of the people' legislation.

Prescribed Officer, The Senior Master and Senior Remembrancer (£140,289), B. Fontaine

EXAMINERS OF THE COURT

A panel of 18 advocates and solicitor advocates, of at least three years standing, is empowered to take examination of witnesses in all divisions of the High Court.

Examiners, Tony Baumgartner; Naomi Candlin; Angharad Davies; Judy Dawson; Alison Green; Nicholas Hill; Mathias Kelly; John Leslie; Simon Lewis; Josh Lewison; Susan Lindsey; Andrew McLoughlin; Christopher McNall; Michael Salter; Ashley Serr; Frederico Singarajah; Lara Spencer; John Hamilton

OFFICIAL SOLICITOR AND PUBLIC TRUSTEE
Victory House, 30–34 Kingsway, London WC2B 6EX
E enquiries@ospt.gov.uk

The Official Solicitor and the Public Trustee are independent statutory office holders. Their office (OSPT) is an arms-length body of the Ministry of Justice that exists to support their work. The Official Solicitor provides access to the justice system to those who are vulnerable by virtue of minority or lack of mental capacity. The Public Trustee acts as executor or administrator of estates and as the appointed trustee of settlements, providing an effective executor and trustee service of last resort.

Official Solicitor to the Senior Courts and the Public Trustee, Sarah Castle
Deputy Public Trustee, Janet Peel
Deputy Official Solicitors, Brid Breathnach; Elaine Brown; Janet Ilett

PROBATE REGISTRIES
London Probate Department, 7th Floor, First Avenue House, 42–49 High Holborn, London WC1V 6NP **T** 020-7421 8509

Probate registries issue grants of probate and grants of letters of administration. The principal probate registry is situated in central London and there are 11 district probate registries in Birmingham, Brighton, Bristol, Cardiff, Ipswich, Leeds, Liverpool, Manchester, Newcastle, Oxford and Winchester, and a further 18 probate sub-registries. Probate registries are administered by HM Courts and Tribunals Service.

JUDGE ADVOCATES GENERAL

The Judge Advocate General is the judicial head of the Service justice system, and the leader of the judges who preside over trials in the court martial and other Service courts. The defendants are service personnel from the Royal Navy, the army and the Royal Air Force, and civilians accompanying them overseas.

JUDGE ADVOCATE GENERAL OF THE FORCES
9th Floor, Thomas More Building, Royal Courts of Justice, Strand, London WC2A 2LL **T** 020-7218 8095

Judge Advocate General (£151,497), His Hon. Judge Blackett
Vice-Judge Advocate General (£132,075), Judge Hunter
Assistant Judge Advocates General (£112,542), J. P. Camp; R. D. Hill; A. M. Large; A. J. B. McGrigor
Style, Judge [surname]

CROWN COURT CENTRES

The crown court sits in 77 court centres across England and Wales. It deals with serious criminal cases which include:
* cases sent for trial by magistrates' courts because the offences are 'indictable only' (ie those which can only be heard by the crown court)
* 'either way' offences (which can be heard in a magistrates' court, but can also be sent to the crown court if the defendant chooses a jury trial)
* defendants convicted in magistrates' courts, but sent to the Crown Court for sentencing due to the seriousness of the offence
* appeals against decisions of magistrates' courts

First-tier centres deal with both civil and criminal cases and are served by high court and circuit judges. Second-tier centres deal with criminal cases only and are served by high court and circuit judges. Third-tier centres deal with criminal cases only and are served only by circuit judges.

In London, the high court acts as the first-tier centre, sitting at the Royal Courts of Justice, and the second-tier is the Central Criminal Court.

CIRCUIT JUDGES

Circuit judges are barristers of at least seven years' standing or recorders of at least five years' standing. Circuit judges serve in the county courts and the crown court.

Style, His/Her Hon. Judge [surname]
Senior Presiding Judge, Rt. Hon. Lady Justice Macur, DBE
Deputy Senior Presiding Judge, Rt. Hon Lady Justice Thirlwall, DBE
Senior Circuit Judges, each £151,497
Circuit Judges at the Central Criminal Court, London (Old Bailey Judges), each £151,497
Circuit Judges, each £140,289

MIDLAND CIRCUIT
Presiding Judges, Hon. Mrs Justice Carr; Hon. Mr Justice Jeremy Baker
NORTH-EASTERN CIRCUIT
Presiding Judges, Hon. Mr Justice Goss; Hon. Mr Justice Lavender
NORTHERN CIRCUIT
Presiding Judges, Hon. Mr Justice William Davis; Hon. Mr Justice Dove
SOUTH-EASTERN CIRCUIT
Presiding Judges, Hon. Mrs Justice McGowan; Hon. Mr Justice Edis; Hon. Mrs Justice Whipple; Hon. Mrs Justice Cheema-Grubb
WALES CIRCUIT
Presiding Judges, Hon. Mr Justice Lewis; Hon. Mr Justice Picken

WESTERN CIRCUIT
Presiding Judges, Hon. Mrs Justice May; Hon. Mr Justice Garnham

DISTRICT JUDGES

District judges, formerly known as registrars of the court, are solicitors of at least seven years' standing and serve in county courts.
District Judges, each £112,542

DISTRICT JUDGES (MAGISTRATES' COURTS)

District judges (magistrates' courts), formerly known as stipendiary magistrates, serve in magistrates courts where they hear criminal cases, youth cases and some civil proceedings. Many also hear family cases in the single family court. Some may be authorised to handle extradition proceedings and terrorist cases. District judges (magistrates' courts) are appointed following competition conducted by the Judicial Appointments Commission.
District Judges (Magistrates' Courts), each £112,542

OFFICE OF THE CHIEF MAGISTRATE
181 Marylebone Road, London NW1 5BR
T 020-3126 3100

The Chief Magistrate (senior district judge) is responsible for hearing many of the sensitive or complex cases – extradition and special jurisdiction cases in particular – in the magistrates' courts. The Chief Magistrate also supports and guides district judges (magistrates' courts), and liaises with the senior judiciary and presiding judges on matters pertaining to magistrates' courts.

The Office of the Chief Magistrate provides administration support to both the Chief Magistrate and to all the district judges sitting at magistrates' courts in England and Wales.

Chief Magistrate, Emma Arbuthnot
Deputy Chief Magistrate, Tanweer Ikram

CROWN PROSECUTION SERVICE

102 Petty France, London SW1H 9EA
T 020-3357 0899 **E** enquiries@cps.gov.uk **W** www.cps.gov.uk

The Crown Prosecution Service (CPS) is responsible for prosecuting cases investigated by the police in England and Wales, with the exception of cases conducted by the Serious Fraud Office and certain minor offences.

The CPS is headed by the director of public prosecutions (DPP), who works under the superintendence of the attorney-general. The service is divided into 14 regional teams across England and Wales, with each area led by a chief crown prosecutor.

Director of Public Prosecutions, Max Hill, QC
Chief Executive, Rebecca Lawrence
Directors, Jean Ashton, OBE *(Business Services);* Sue Hemming *(Legal Services);* Gregor McGill *(Legal Services)*

CPS AREAS
EAST MIDLANDS, 2 King Edward Court, King Edward Street, Nottingham NG1 1EL **T** 0115-852 3300
Chief Crown Prosecutor, Janine Smith
EAST OF ENGLAND, County House, 100 New London Road, Chelmsford, Essex CM2 0RG **T** 01245-455800
Chief Crown Prosecutor, Chris Long
LONDON, 1st Floor, Zone A, 102 Petty France, London SW1H 9EA **T** 020-3357 7000
Chief Crown Prosecutor London North, Ed Beltrami, CBE
Chief Crown Prosecutor London South, Claire Lindley

MERSEY–CHESHIRE, 2nd Floor, Walker House, Exchange Flags, Liverpool L2 3YL **T** 0151-239 6400
Chief Crown Prosecutor, Siobhan Blake

NORTH EAST, St Ann's Quay, 112 Quayside, Newcastle Upon Tyne, NE1 3BD **T** 0191-260 4200
Chief Crown Prosecutor, Andrew Penhale

NORTH WEST, 1st Floor, Stocklund House, Castle Street, Carlisle CA3 8SY **T** 01228-882900
Chief Crown Prosecutor, Martin Goldman

SOUTH EAST, Riding Gate House, 37 Old Dover Road, Canterbury, Kent CT1 3JG **T** 01227-866000
Chief Crown Prosecutor, Frank Ferguson

SOUTH WEST, 5th Floor, Kite Wing, Temple Quay House, 2 The Square, Bristol BS1 6PN **T** 0117-930 2800
Chief Crown Prosecutor, Victoria Cook

THAMES AND CHILTERN, Eaton Court, 112 Oxford Road, Reading, Berks RG1 7LL **T** 01727-798700
Chief Crown Prosecutor, Jaswant Kaur Narwal

WALES, 20th Floor, Capital Tower, Greyfriars Road, Cardiff CF10 3PL **T** 029-2080 3800
Chief Crown Prosecutor, Barry Hughes

WESSEX, 3rd Floor, Black Horse House, 8–10 Leigh Road, Eastleigh, Hants SO50 9FH **T** 0238-067 3800
Chief Crown Prosecutor, Joanne Jakymec

WEST MIDLANDS, Colmore Gate, 2 Colmore Row, Birmingham B3 2QA **T** 0121-262 1300
Chief Crown Prosecutor, Grace Ononiwu, OBE

YORKSHIRE AND HUMBERSIDE, 27 Park Place, Leeds LS1 2SZ **T** 0113-290 2700
Chief Crown Prosecutor, Gerry Wareham

HER MAJESTY'S COURTS AND TRIBUNALS SERVICE
1st Floor, 102 Petty France, London SW1H 9AJ
W www.gov.uk/government/organisations/hm-courts-and-tribunals-service

Her Majesty's Courts Service and the Tribunals Service merged on 1 April 2011 to form HM Courts and Tribunals Service. It is an agency of the Ministry of Justice, operating as a partnership between the Lord Chancellor, the Lord Chief Justice and the Senior President of Tribunals. It is responsible for administering the criminal, civil and family courts and tribunals in England and Wales and non-devolved tribunals in Scotland and Northern Ireland.

Chief Executive, Susan Acland-Hood

JUDICIAL APPOINTMENTS COMMISSION
5th Floor, Clive House, 70 Petty France, London SW1H 9EX
T 020-3334 0123 **E** jaas@judicialappointments.gov.uk
W www.judicialappointments.gov.uk

The Judicial Appointments Commission was established as an independent non-departmental public body in April 2006 by the Constitutional Reform Act 2005. Its role is to select judicial office holders independently of government (a responsibility previously held by the Lord Chancellor) for courts and tribunals in England and Wales, and for some tribunals whose jurisdiction extends to Scotland or Northern Ireland. It has a statutory duty to encourage diversity in the range of persons available for selection and is sponsored by the Ministry of Justice and accountable to parliament through the Lord Chancellor. It is made up of a total of 15 commissioners: seven judicial (including one non-legal), two professional, five lay and the chair.

Chair, Rt. Hon. Prof. Lord Kakkar
Vice-Chair, Rt. Hon. Dame Anne Rafferty, DBE
Commissioners, Judge Mathu Asokan; Her Hon. Judge Anuja Dhir; Emir Khan Feisal; Jane Furness, CBE; Sue Hoyle;

Andrew Kennon; Sarah Lee; Judge Fiona Monk; Brie Stevens-Hoare, QC; His Hon. Judge Phillip Sycamore; Sir Simon Wessely; Dame Philippa Whipple, DBE
Chief Executive, Richard Jarvis

JUDICIAL OFFICE
The Judicial Office was established in April 2006 to support the judiciary in discharging its responsibilities under the Constitutional Reform Act 2005. It is led by a chief executive, who reports to the Lord Chief Justice and Senior President of Tribunals rather than to ministers, and its work is directed by the judiciary rather than by the administration of the day. The Judicial Office incorporates the Judicial College, sponsorship of the Family and Civil Justice Councils, the Office for Judicial Complaints and Office of the Chief Coroner.

Chief Executive, Andrew Key

JUDICIAL COMMITTEE OF THE PRIVY COUNCIL
The Judicial Committee of the Privy Council is the final court of appeal for the United Kingdom overseas territories (*see* UK Overseas Territories section), crown dependencies and those independent Commonwealth countries which have retained this avenue of appeal and the sovereign base areas of Akrotiri and Dhekelia in Cyprus. The committee also hears appeals against pastoral schemes under the Pastoral Measure 1983, and deals with appeals from veterinary disciplinary bodies.

Until October 2009, the Judicial Committee of the Privy Council was the final arbiter in disputes as to the legal competence of matters done or proposed by the devolved legislative and executive authorities in Scotland, Wales and Northern Ireland. This is now the responsibility of the UK Supreme Court.

The members of the Judicial Committee are the justices of the supreme court, and Privy Counsellors who hold or have held high judicial office in the United Kingdom or in certain designated courts of Commonwealth countries from which appeals are taken to committee.

JUDICIAL COMMITTEE OF THE PRIVY COUNCIL
Parliament Square, London SW1P 3BD **T** 020-7960 1500
W www.jcpc.uk
Chief Executive, Mark Ormerod
Registrar of the Privy Council, Louise di Mambro

SCOTTISH JUDICATURE
Scotland has a legal system separate from, and differing greatly from, the English legal system in enacted law, judicial procedure and the structure of courts.

In Scotland the system of public prosecution is headed by the Lord Advocate and is independent of the police, who have no say in the decision to prosecute. The Lord Advocate, discharging his functions through the Crown Office in Edinburgh, is responsible for prosecutions in the high court, sheriff courts and justice of the peace courts. Prosecutions in the high court are prepared by the Crown Office and conducted in court by one of the law officers, by an advocate-depute, or by a solicitor advocate. In the inferior courts the decision to prosecute is made and prosecution is preferred by procurators fiscal, who are lawyers and full-time civil servants subject to the directions of the Crown Office. A permanent legally qualified civil servant, known as the crown agent, is responsible for the running of the Crown Office and the organisation of the Procurator Fiscal Service, of which he or she is the head.

Scotland is divided into six sheriffdoms, each with a full-time sheriff principal. The sheriffdoms are further divided into sheriff court districts, each of which has a legally qualified resident sheriff or sheriffs, who are the judges of the court.

In criminal cases sheriffs principal and sheriffs have the same powers; sitting with a jury of 15 members, they may try more serious cases on indictment, or, sitting alone, may try lesser cases under summary procedure. Minor summary offences are dealt with in justice of the peace courts, which replaced district courts formerly operated by local authorities, and presided over by lay justices of the peace (of whom some 500 regularly sit in court) and, in Glasgow only, by stipendiary magistrates. Juvenile offenders (children under 16) may be brought before an informal children's hearing comprising three local lay people. The superior criminal court is the high court of justiciary which is both a trial and an appeal court. Cases on indictment are tried by a high court judge, sitting with a jury of 15, in Edinburgh and on circuit in other towns. Appeals from the lower courts against conviction or sentence are also heard by the high court, which sits as an appeal court only in Edinburgh. There is no further appeal to the UK supreme court in criminal cases.

In civil cases the jurisdiction of the sheriff court extends to most kinds of action. Appeals against decisions of the sheriff may be made to the sheriff principal and thence to the court of session, or direct to the court of session, which sits only in Edinburgh. The court of session is divided into the inner and the outer house. The outer house is a court of first instance in which cases are heard by judges sitting singly, sometimes with a jury of 12. The inner house, itself subdivided into two divisions of equal status, is mainly an appeal court. Appeals may be made to the inner house from the outer house as well as from the sheriff court. An appeal may be made from the inner house to the UK supreme court.

The judges of the court of session are the same as those of the high court of justiciary, with the Lord President of the court of session also holding the office of Lord Justice General in the high court. Senators of the College of Justice are Lords Commissioners of Justiciary as well as judges of the court of session. On appointment, a senator takes a judicial title, which is retained for life. Although styled The Hon./Rt. Hon. Lord, the senator is not a peer, although some judges are peers in their own right.

The office of coroner does not exist in Scotland. The local procurator fiscal inquires privately into sudden or suspicious deaths and may report findings to the crown agent. In some cases a fatal accident inquiry may be held before the sheriff.

COURT OF SESSION AND HIGH COURT OF JUSTICIARY

The Lord President and Lord Justice General (£234,184), Rt. Hon. Lord Carloway, *born* 1954, *apptd* 2015
Private Secretary, Paul Gilmour

INNER HOUSE
Lords of Session (each £215,094)

FIRST DIVISION
The Lord President

Rt. Hon. Lord Menzies (Duncan Menzies), *born* 1953, *apptd* 2012
Rt. Hon. Lady Smith (Anne Smith), *born* 1955, *apptd* 2012
Rt. Hon. Lord Brodie (Philip Brodie), *born* 1950, *apptd* 2012
Rt. Hon. Lady Clark of Calton (Lynda Clark), *born* 1949, *apptd* 2013
Rt. Hon. Lord Glennie (Angus Glennie), *born* 1950, *apptd* 2016

SECOND DIVISION
Lord Justice Clerk (£226,193), Rt. Hon. Lady Dorrian (Leeona Dorrian), *born* 1957, *apptd* 2016

Rt. Hon. Lady Paton (Ann Paton), *born* 1952, *apptd* 2007
Rt. Hon. Lord Drummond Young (James Drummond Young), *born* 1950, *apptd* 2013
Rt. Hon. Lord Malcolm (Colin M. Campbell), *born* 1953, *apptd* 2015
Hon. Lord Turnbull (Alan Turnbull), *born* 1958, *apptd* 2016

OUTER HOUSE
Lords of Session (each £188,901)

Hon. Lord Kinclaven (Alexander F. Wylie, OBE), *born* 1951, *apptd* 2005
Hon. Lord Brailsford (S. Neil Brailsford), *born* 1954, *apptd* 2006
Hon. Lord Uist (Roderick Macdonald), *born* 1951, *apptd* 2006
Hon. Lord Matthews (Hugh Matthews), *born* 1953, *apptd* 2007
Hon. Lord Woolman (Stephen Woolman), *born* 1953, *apptd* 2008
Hon. Lord Pentland (Paul Cullen), *born* 1957, *apptd* 2008
Hon. Lord Bannatyne (Iain Peebles, QC), *born* 1954, *apptd* 2008
Hon. Lady Stacey (Valerie E. Stacey), *born* 1954, *apptd* 2009
Hon. Lord Tyre (Colin Tyre, CBE), *born* 1956, *apptd* 2010
Hon. Lord Doherty (J. Raymond Doherty), *born* 1958, *apptd* 2010
Rt. Hon. Lord Boyd of Duncansby (Colin Boyd), *born* 1953, *apptd* 2012
Hon. Lord Burns (David Burns), *born* 1952, *apptd* 2012
Hon. Lady Scott (Margaret Scott), *born* 1960, *apptd* 2012
Hon. Lady Wise (Morag Wise), *born* 1963, *apptd* 2013
Hon. Lord Armstrong (Iain Armstrong), *born* 1956, *apptd* 2013
Hon. Lady Rae (Rita Rae), *born* 1950, *apptd* 2014
Hon. Lady Wolffe (Sarah Wolffe, QC), *apptd* 2014
Hon. Lord Beckett (John Beckett, QC), *apptd* 2016
Hon. Lord Clark (Alistair Clark, QC), *born* 1955, *apptd* 2016
Hon. Lord Ericht (Andrew Stewart, QC), *born* 1963, *apptd* 2016
Hon. Lady Carmichael (Ailsa Carmichael, QC), *born* 1969, *apptd* 2016
Rt. Hon. Lord Mulholland (Frank Mulholland, QC), *born* 1959, *apptd* 2016
Hon. Lord Summers (Alan Summers, QC), *born* 1964, *apptd* 2017
Hon. Lord Arthurson (Paul Arthurson, QC), *born* 1964, *apptd* 2017

COURT OF SESSION AND HIGH COURT OF JUSTICIARY
Parliament House, Parliament Square, Edinburgh EH1 1RQ
T 0131-225 2595

Director and Principal Clerk of Session and Justiciary, Gillian Prentice
Deputy Principal Clerk of Session, Diane Machin
Deputy Principal Clerk of Justiciary, Joe Moyes
Depute in Charge of the Court of Session Office, Christina Bardsley
Officer in Charge of the Justiciary Office, Ross Martin
Keeper of the Rolls, Trish Fiddes
Assistant Keeper of the Rolls, Grahame Simpson
Appeals Manager, Alex McKay
Clerking Services Manager, Chris Fyffe
Court Manager, Zac Conway

JUDICIAL APPOINTMENTS BOARD FOR SCOTLAND
Thistle House, 91 Haymarket Terrace, Edinburgh EH12 5HE
T 0131-528 5101 W www.judicialappointments.scot

The board's remit is to provide the first minister with the names of candidates recommended for appointment to the court posts of senator of the college of justice, chair of the Scottish Land Court, sheriff principal, sheriff and part-time sheriff. It is also responsible for recommending individuals to the office of vice-president of the Upper Tribunal; chamber and deputy chamber presidents of the First-tier Tribunal; and members of the Upper Tribunal and First-tier Tribunal.

Chair, Nicola Gordon
Chief Executive, John Craig

JUDICIAL OFFICE FOR SCOTLAND
Parliament House, Edinburgh EH1 1RQ
T 0131-240 6677 **W** www.scotland-judiciary.org.uk

The Judicial Office for Scotland came into being on 1 April 2010 as part of the changes introduced by the Judiciary and Courts (Scotland) Act 2008. It provides support for the Lord President in his role as head of the Scottish judiciary with responsibility for the training, welfare, deployment and conduct of judges and the efficient disposal of business in the courts.

Executive Director, Tim Barraclough

SCOTTISH COURTS AND TRIBUNALS SERVICE
Saughton House, Broomhouse Drive, Edinburgh EH11 3XD
T 0131-444 3300 **W** www.scotcourts.gov.uk

The Scottish Courts and Tribunals Service (SCTS) is an independent body which was established on 1 April 2010 under the Judiciary and Courts (Scotland) Act 2008. Its function is to provide administrative support to Scottish courts and tribunals and to the judiciary of courts, including the High Court of Justiciary, Court of Session, sheriff courts and justice of the peace courts, and to the Office of the Public Guardian and Accountant of Court.

Chief Executive, Eric McQueen

SCOTTISH GOVERNMENT JUSTICE DIRECTORATE
St Andrew's House, Edinburgh EH1 3DG
T 0131-244 4000

The Justice Directorate is responsible for the appointment of judges and sheriffs to meet the needs of the business of the supreme and sheriffs court in Scotland. It is also responsible for providing resources for the efficient administration of certain specialist courts and tribunals.

Director (Justice), Neil Rennick

SCOTTISH LAND COURT
126 George Street, Edinburgh EH2 4HH
T 0131-271 4360 **W** www.scottish-land-court.org.uk

The court deals with disputes relating to agricultural and crofting land in Scotland.

Chair (£151,497), Hon. Lord Miningish (Roderick John MacLeod, QC)
Deputy Chair, Iain Maclean
Members, Tom Campbell; John Smith
Principal Clerk, Barbara Brown

SHERIFF COURTS
The majority of cases in Scotland are handled by one of the 39 sheriff courts. Criminal cases are heard by a sheriff and a jury (solemn procedure) but can be heard by a sheriff alone (summary procedure). Civil cases are heard by a single sheriff.
  Scotland is split into six sheriffdoms, each headed by a sheriff principal.

SALARIES
Sheriff Principal, £151,497
Sheriff, £140,289

SHERIFFDOMS
GLASGOW AND STRATHKELVIN
Sheriff Principal, Craig Turnbull
GRAMPIAN, HIGHLAND AND ISLANDS
Sheriff Principal, Derek Pyle
LOTHIAN AND BORDERS
Sheriff Principal, Mhairi Stephen, QC
NORTH STRATHCLYDE
Sheriff Principal, Duncan Murray
SOUTH STRATHCLYDE, DUMFRIES AND GALLOWAY
Sheriff Principal, Ian Abercrombie, QC
TAYSIDE, CENTRAL AND FIFE
Sheriff Principal, Marysia Lewis

JUSTICE OF THE PEACE COURTS
Justice of the peace courts replaced district courts and are a unique feature of Scotland's judicial system. Justices of the peace are lay magistrates who either sit alone, or in a bench of three, and deal with summary crimes such as speeding and careless driving. In court, justices have access to solicitors, who fulfil the role of legal advisers or clerks of court.
  A justice of the peace court can be presided over by a stipendiary magistrate – a legally qualified solicitor or advocate who sits alone. They deal with more serious summary business similar to sheriffs, such as drink driving and assault. All sheriffs principal have powers to appoint stipendiary magistrates, but at present there are no justice of the peace courts in the sheriff court districts of Lerwick, Kirkwall, Wick, Stornoway, Lochmaddy and Portree.

CROWN OFFICE AND PROCURATOR FISCAL SERVICE
25 Chambers Street, Edinburgh EH1 1LA
T 0300-020 3000 **W** www.copfs.gov.uk

The Crown Office and Procurator Fiscal Service (COPFS) is Scotland's prosecution service. COPFS receive reports about crimes from the police and other reporting agencies and then decide what action to take, including whether to prosecute someone. It is also responsible for looking into deaths that need further explanation and investigating allegations of criminal conduct against police officers.

Lord Advocate, Rt. Hon. James Wolffe, QC
Solicitor-General, Alison Di Rollo, QC
Crown Agent, David Harvie

COURT OF THE LORD LYON
HM New Register House, Edinburgh EH1 3YT
T 0131-556 7255 **W** www.courtofthelordlyon.scot

The Court of the Lord Lyon is the Scottish Court of Chivalry (including the genealogical jurisdiction of the *Ri-Sennachie* of Scotland's Celtic kings). The Lord Lyon King of Arms has jurisdiction, subject to appeal to the Court of Session and the House of Lords, in questions of heraldry and the right to bear arms. The court also administers the Public Register of All Arms and Bearings and the Public Register of All Genealogies in Scotland. Pedigrees are established by decrees of Lyon Court and by letters patent. As Royal Commissioner in Armory, the Lord Lyon grants patents of arms to virtuous and well-deserving Scots and to petitioners (personal or corporate) in the Queen's overseas realms of Scottish connection, and also issues birthbrieves. For information on Her Majesty's Officers of Arms in Scotland, *see* the Court of the Lord Lyon in the Public Bodies section.

Lord Lyon King of Arms, Dr Joseph Morrow, CBE, QC
Lyon Clerk and Keeper of the Records, Russell Hunter
Procurator Fiscal, Alexander Green

NORTHERN IRELAND JUDICATURE

In Northern Ireland the legal system and the structure of courts closely resemble those of England and Wales; there are, however, often differences in enacted law.

The court of judicature of Northern Ireland comprises the court of appeal, the high court of justice and the crown court. The practice and procedure of these courts is similar to that in England. The superior civil court is the high court of justice, from which an appeal lies to the Northern Ireland court of appeal; the UK supreme court is the final civil appeal court.

The crown court, served by high court and county court judges, deals with criminal trials on indictment. Cases are heard before a judge and, except those certified by the Director of Public Prosecutions under the Justice and Security Act 2007, a jury. Appeals from the crown court against conviction or sentence are heard by the Northern Ireland court of appeal; the UK supreme court is the final court of appeal.

The decision to prosecute in criminal cases in Northern Ireland rests with the Director of Public Prosecutions.

Minor criminal offences are dealt with in magistrates' courts by a legally qualified district judge (magistrates' courts) and, where an offender is under the age of 18, by youth courts each consisting of a district judge (magistrates' courts) and two lay magistrates (at least one of whom must be a woman). There are approximately 200 lay magistrates in Northern Ireland. Appeals from magistrates' courts are heard by the county court, or by the court of appeal on a point of law or an issue as to jurisdiction.

Magistrates' courts in Northern Ireland can deal with certain classes of civil case but most minor civil cases are dealt with in county courts. Judgments of all civil courts are enforceable through a centralised procedure administered by the Enforcement of Judgments Office.

COURT OF JUDICATURE
The Royal Courts of Justice, Chichester Street, Belfast BT1 3JF
T 0300-200 7812 W www.courtsni.gov.uk

Lord Chief Justice of Northern Ireland (£234,184), Rt. Hon. Sir Declan Morgan, *born* 1952, *apptd* 2009

LORDS JUSTICES OF APPEAL (£215,094)
Style, The Rt. Hon. Lord/Lady Justice [surname]

Rt. Hon. Sir Benjamin Stephens, *born* 1954, *apptd* 2017
Hon. Sir Seamus Treacy, *born* 1956, *apptd* 2017

Hon. Sir Bernard McCloskey, *born* 1956, *apptd* 2019

HIGH COURT JUDGES (£188,901)
Style, The Hon. Mr/Mrs/Ms Justice [surname]

Hon. Sir Paul Maguire, *born* 1952, *apptd* 2012
Hon. Sir Mark Horner, *born* 1956, *apptd* 2012
Hon. Sir John O'Hara, *born* 1956, *apptd* 2013
Hon. Sir Adrian Colton, *born* 1959, *apptd* 2015
Hon. Dame Denise McBride, DBE, *apptd* 2015
Hon. Dame Siobhan Keegan, DBE, *apptd* 2015
Hon. Sir Gerry McAlinden, *apptd* 2018
Hon. Sir Ian Huddleston, *apptd* 2019

MASTERS OF THE HIGH COURT (£112,542)
Presiding Master, Master McCorry, *apptd* 2001
Masters, Master Bell *apptd* 2006; Master Hardstaff, *apptd* 2014; Master Kelly, *apptd* 2005; Master McGivern *apptd* 2015; Master Sweeney, *apptd* 2015; Master Wells, *apptd* 2005

COUNTY COURTS

JUDGES (£151,498†)
Style, His/Her Hon. Judge [surname]

Judge Babington *apptd* 2004; Judge Crawford *apptd* 2015; Judge Devlin *apptd* 2011; Judge Fowler, QC *apptd* 2011; Judge Gilpin *apptd* 2019; Judge Kerr, QC *apptd* 2012; Judge Kinney *apptd* 2012; Judge Lynch, QC *apptd* 2004; Judge McCaffrey *apptd* 2016; Judge McColgan, QC *apptd* 2013; Judge McCormick *apptd* 2018; Judge McFarland *apptd* 1998; Judge McReynolds *apptd* 2004; Judge Miller, QC *apptd* 2009; Judge Rafferty, QC *apptd* 2016; Judge Ramsay, QC *apptd* 2014; Judge Sherrard *apptd* 2012; Judge Smyth *apptd* 2010

† County court judges are paid £151,498 so long as they are required to carry out significantly different work from their counterparts elsewhere in the UK

RECORDERS
Belfast (£163,617), Judge McFarland
Londonderry (£151,497), Judge Babington

DISTRICT JUDGES (£112,542)
Only barristers and solicitors with ten years' standing are eligible to become district judges. There are usually four district judges in Northern Ireland:

Presiding District Judge Brownlie *apptd* 1997; District Judge Collins *apptd* 2000; District Judge Duncan *apptd* 2014

MAGISTRATES' COURTS

DISTRICT JUDGES (MAGISTRATES' COURTS) (£112,542)
There are usually 21 district judges (magistrates' courts) in Northern Ireland:

Presiding District Judge Bagnall *apptd* 2003; District Judge Brady *apptd* 2016; District Judge Broderick *apptd* 2013; District Judge Conner *apptd* 1999; District Judge Copeland *apptd* 1993; District Judge Hamill *apptd* 1999; District Judge Henderson *apptd* 2005; District Judge Kelly *apptd* 1997; District Judge Keown *apptd* 2018; District Judge E. King *apptd* 2005; District Judge P. King *apptd* 2013; District Judge McElholm *apptd* 1998; District Judge McGarrity *apptd* 2019; District Judge McNally *apptd* 2003; District Judge P. Magill *apptd* 2018; District Judge Meehan *apptd* 2002; District Judge Mullan *apptd* 2016; District Judge Prytherch *apptd* 2005; District Judge Ranaghan *apptd* 2017; District Judge Watters *apptd* 1998

NORTHERN IRELAND COURTS AND TRIBUNALS SERVICE
23–27 Oxford Street, Belfast BT1 3LA
T 0300-200 7812 W www.justice-ni.gov.uk/topics/courts-and-tribunals
Chief Executive (acting), Peter Luney

CROWN SOLICITOR'S OFFICE
Royal Courts of Justice, Chichester Street, Belfast BT1 3JE
T 028-9054 2555
Crown Solicitor, Fiona Chamberlain

PUBLIC PROSECUTION SERVICE
Belfast Chambers, 93 Chichester Street, Belfast BT1 3JR
T 028-9089 7100 W www.ppsni.gov.uk
Director of Public Prosecutions, Stephen Herron

TRIBUNALS

Information on all the tribunals listed here, with the exception of the independent tribunals and the tribunals based in Scotland, Wales and Northern Ireland, can be found online (**W** www.gov.uk/government/organisations/hm-courts-and-tribunals-service).

HM COURTS AND TRIBUNALS SERVICE

102 Petty France, London SW1H 9AJ
W www.gov.uk/government/organisations/hm-courts-and-tribunals-service
W www.gov.uk/find-court-tribunal

HM Courts Service and the Tribunals Service merged on 1 April 2011 to form HM Courts and Tribunals Service, an integrated agency providing support for the administration of justice in courts and tribunals. It is an agency within the Ministry of Justice, operating as a partnership between the Lord Chancellor, the Lord Chief Justice and the Senior President of Tribunals. It is responsible for the administration of the criminal, civil and family courts and tribunals in England and Wales and non-devolved tribunals in Scotland

and Northern Ireland. The agency's work is overseen by a board headed by an independent chair working with non-executive, executive and judicial members.

A two-tier tribunal system, comprising the First-tier Tribunal and Upper Tribunal, was established on 3 November 2008 as a result of radical reform under the Tribunals, Courts and Enforcement Act 2007. Both of these tiers are split into a number of separate chambers. These chambers group together individual tribunals (also known as 'jurisdictions') which deal with similar work or require similar skills. Cases start in the First-tier Tribunal and there is a right of appeal to the Upper Tribunal. Some tribunals transferred to the new two-tier system immediately, with more transferring between 2009 and 2011. The exception is employment tribunals, which remain outside this structure. The Act also allowed legally qualified tribunal chairs and adjudicators to swear the judicial oath and become judges.

Senior President, Rt. Hon. Sir Ernest Ryder, TD
Vice-President of the Unified Tribunals, Hon. Sir Keith Lindblom
Chief Executive, Susan Acland-Hood

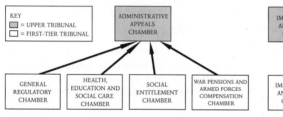

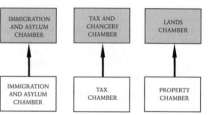

FIRST-TIER TRIBUNAL

The main function of the First-tier Tribunal is to hear appeals by citizens against decisions of the government. In most cases appeals are heard by a panel made up of one judge and two specialists in their relevant field, known as 'members'. Both judges and members are appointed through the Independent Judicial Appointments Commission. Most of the tribunals administered by central government are part of the First-tier Tribunal, which is split into seven separate chambers.

GENERAL REGULATORY CHAMBER

For all jurisdictions: General Regulatory Chamber, HMCTS, PO Box 9300, Leicester LE1 8DJ **T** 0300-123 4504
E grc@justice.gov.uk
Chamber President, Judge McKenna

CHARITY

Under the Charities Act 2011 (only applicable to England and Wales), First-tier Tribunal (Charity) hears appeals against the decisions of the Charity Commission, applications for the review of decisions made by the Charity Commission and considers references from the Attorney-General or the Charity Commission on points of law.

COMMUNITY RIGHT TO BID

The Community Right to Bid jurisdiction of the General Regulatory Chamber was established in January 2013 and hears appeals against review decisions made by local authorities to list your property as a community asset and

give local communities the right to bid for it if you decide to sell. Individuals have the right to appeal against a listing decision under the Localism Act 2011 and the assets of community value (England) regulations 2012.

CONSULTANT LOBBYISTS

Tribunal (Consultant Lobbyists) hears appeals against penalties imposed for an offence under section 12 of the Transparency of Lobbying, Non-Party Campaigning and Trade Union Administration Act 2014 by the Office of the Registrar of Consultant Lobbyists.

CONVEYANCING

The professional regulation jurisdiction hears appeals against decisions made by the Council for Licensed Conveyancers under the Legal Services Act 2007.

COPYRIGHT LICENSING

Under the copyright (regulation of relevant licensing bodies) regulations 2014 a copyright licensing body may appeal to a First-tier Tribunal (Copyright Licensing) against a government decision to fine or impose a code of conduct on their organisation.

DRIVING INSTRUCTORS

First-tier Tribunal (Driving Instructors) hears appeals against decisions made by the Registrar of Approved Driving Instructors under the Road Traffic Act 1988, Transport Act 2000 and the Motor Cars (Driving Instruction) Regulations 2005. Its jurisdiction covers England, Scotland and Wales.

ELECTRONIC COMMUNICATIONS AND POSTAL SERVICES

Hears appeals against decisions made by the Interception of Communications Commissioner under the Regulation of Investigatory Powers (Monetary Penalty Notices and Consents for Interceptions) Regulations 2011.

ENVIRONMENT

First-tier Tribunal (Environment) was created to decide appeals regarding civil sanctions made by environmental regulators. Established in April 2010, the jurisdiction of the tribunal extends to England and Wales.

ESTATE AGENTS

First-tier Tribunal (Estate Agents) hears appeals, under the Estate Agents Act 1979, against decisions made by the Office of Fair Trading pertaining to orders prohibiting a person from being employed as an estate agent when that person has been, for example, convicted of fraud or another offence involving dishonesty. The tribunal also hears appeals relating to decisions refusing to revoke or vary a prohibition order or warning order, as well as appeals regarding the issuing of a warning order when a person has not fulfilled their obligations under the Act.

EXAM BOARDS

Under the Education Act 1997 regulated awarding organisations can appeal to the Exam Board tribunal if they disagree with a decision by OFQUAL or the Welsh government to impose a fine, the amount of the fine, or to recover the costs of taking enforcement action. The board is an independent tribunal and hears appeals across England and Wales.

FOOD

The food jurisdiction of the General Regulatory Chamber was established in January 2013 and hears appeals against some of the decisions taken by the Food Standards Agency, Department for Environment, Food and Rural Affairs and local authority trading standards departments. It also deals with appeals against decisions under the Fish Labelling (England) Regulations.

GAMBLING

First-tier Tribunal (Gambling) hears and decides appeals against decisions made by the Gambling Commission under the Gambling Act 2005.

IMMIGRATION SERVICES

First-tier Tribunal (Welfare of Animals) hears appeals against the removal of licences to sell animals as pets, provide boarding for cats and dogs, hire out horses, breed dogs and keep or train animals for exhibition under the Animal Welfare (Licensing of Activities Involving Animals) Regulations 2018.

INFORMATION RIGHTS

First-tier Tribunal (Information Rights) determines appeals against notices issued by the Information Commissioner under the Freedom of Information Act 2000 and other regulations.

When a minister of the crown issues a certificate on the grounds of national security, the appeal must be transferred to the Administrative Appeals Chamber of the Upper Tribunal on receipt.

LETTING AND MANAGING AGENTS

First-tier Tribunal (Letting and Managing Agents) hears appeals against a decision by a local authority or the Trading Standards Office to impose a fine on an agent for not being a member of an approved complaints scheme or for not clearly publicising fees under The Redress Schemes for Lettings Agency Work and Property Management Work (Requirements to Belong to a Scheme etc) (England) Order 2014 and schedule 9 of the Consumer Rights Act 2015.

MICROCHIPPING DOGS

Established under the Microchipping of Dogs (England) Regulations 2015, appeals can be made to First-Tier Tribunal (Microchipping Dogs) against a decision by the Department for the Environment and Rural Affairs to ban or stop an individual from microchipping dogs or from running a database on microchipped dogs. Dog owners can also appeal against a notice to microchip their dog served by the police or local authority.

PENSIONS REGULATION

First-tier Tribunal (Pensions) hears appeals against decisions made by the Pensions Regulator under section 44 of the Pensions Act 2008. Appeals under section 102 of the Act are heard by the Tax and Chancery Chamber of the Upper Tribunal.

SECONDARY TICKETING

First-tier Tribunal (Secondary Ticketing) hears appeals against penalties issued for failing to comply with the conditions for secondary sale of tickets for cultural sporting and recreation events under section 90 of the Consumer Rights Act of 2015.

WELFARE OF ANIMALS

First-tier Tribunal (Welfare of Animals) hears appeals against the removal of licences to sell animals as pets, provide boarding for cats and dogs, hire out horses, breed dogs and keep or train animals for exhibition under the Animal Welfare (Licensing of Activities Involving Animals) Regulations 2018.

HEALTH, EDUCATION AND SOCIAL CARE CHAMBER

Chamber President, His Hon. Judge Sycamore

CARE STANDARDS

First-tier Tribunal (Care Standards), 1st Floor Darlington Magistrates' Court, Parkgate DL1 1RU
T 01325-289350 **E** cst@justice.gov.uk

First-tier Tribunal (Care Standards) was established under the Protection of Children Act 1999 and considers appeals in relation to decisions made by the Secretary of State for Education, the Secretary of State for Health, the Care Quality Commission, Ofsted or the Care Council for Wales about the inclusion of individuals' names on the list of those considered unsuitable to work with children or vulnerable adults, restrictions from teaching and employment in schools/further education institutions, and the registration of independent schools. It also deals with general registration decisions made about care homes, children's homes, childcare providers, nurses' agencies, social workers, residential family centres, independent hospitals and fostering agencies.

MENTAL HEALTH

PO Box 8793, 5th Floor, Leicester LE1 8BN
T 0300-123 2201 **E** MHRTEnquiries@justice.gov.uk

The First-tier Tribunal (Mental Health) hears applications and references for people detained under the Mental Health Act 1983 (as amended by the Mental Health Act 2007). There are separate mental health tribunals for Wales and Scotland.

PRIMARY HEALTH LISTS
First-tier Tribunal (Primary Health Lists), 1st Floor Darlington Magistrates' Court, Parkgate DL1 1RU **T** 01325-289350

First-tier Tribunal (Primary Health Lists) hears appeals against decisions made by the NHS Commissioning Board to not include, to remove or to change the conditions of inclusion for medical practitioners and providers on the NHS medical, dental, ophthalmic or pharmaceutical lists.

SPECIAL EDUCATIONAL NEEDS AND DISABILITY
First-tier Tribunal (SEND), 1st Floor Darlington Magistrates' Court, Parkgate DL1 1RU
T 01325-289350 **E** send@justice.gov.uk

First-tier Tribunal (Special Educational Needs and Disability) considers parents' appeals against the decisions of local authorities about children's special educational needs if parents cannot reach agreement with the local authority. It also considers claims of disability discrimination in schools.

IMMIGRATION AND ASYLUM CHAMBER
Chamber President, Judge Clements
PO Box 6987, Leicester LE1 6ZX
T 0300-123 1711 **E** customer.service@justice.gov.uk

The Immigration and Asylum Chamber is an independent tribunal dealing with appeals against decisions made by the Home Office concerning immigration, asylum and nationality matters.

PROPERTY CHAMBER
Chamber President, Judge McGrath
10 Alfred Place, London WC1E 7LR
T 020-7291 7250 **E** alr@justice.gov.uk

The First-tier Tribunal (Property Chamber) handles applications, appeals and references relating to disputes over property and land. It serves the private-rented and leasehold property market in England regarding rent increases, leasehold disputes, improvement notices under the Housing Act 2004, land registration matters and agricultural land and drainage matters.

SOCIAL ENTITLEMENT CHAMBER
Chamber President, His Hon. Judge Aitken

ASYLUM SUPPORT
2nd Floor, Anchorage House, 2 Clove Crescent, London E14 2BE
T 0800-681 6509

First-tier Tribunal (Asylum Support) deals with appeals against decisions made by the Home Office. The Home Office decides whether asylum seekers, failed asylum seekers and/or their dependants are entitled to support and accommodation on the grounds of destitution, as provided by the Immigration and Asylum Act 1999. The tribunal can only consider appeals against a refusal or termination of support. It can, if appropriate, require the Secretary of State for the Home Department to reconsider the original decision, substitute the original decision with the tribunal's own decision or dismiss the appeal.

CRIMINAL INJURIES COMPENSATION
20 York Street, Glasgow G2 8GT **T** 0300-790 6234
E cic.enquiries@justice.gov.uk

First-tier Tribunal (Criminal Injuries Compensation) determines appeals against review decisions made by the Criminal Injuries Compensation Authority on applications for compensation made by victims of violent crime.

SOCIAL SECURITY AND CHILD SUPPORT
England and Wales **T** 0300-123 1142
Scotland **T** 0300-790 6234

First-tier Tribunal (Social Security and Child Support) arranges and hears appeals against decisions made by the Department for Work and Pensions and HM Revenue and Customs regarding social security benefits. Appeals considered include those concerned with: attendance, bereavement and carer's allowances; child benefit; child support; the compensation recovery scheme (including NHS recovery claims); diffuse mesothelioma and the industrial injuries disablement benefit payment schemes; income support; jobseeker's allowance; tax credits; universal credit; and vaccine damage payment.

TAX CHAMBER
Chamber President, Judge Sinfield
PO Box 16972, Birmingham B16 6TZ
T 0300-123 1024 **E** taxappeals@justice.gov.uk

First-tier Tribunal Tax Chamber hears most appeals against decisions made by HM Revenue and Customs in relation to income tax, corporation tax, capital gains tax, inheritance tax, stamp duty land tax, statutory sick and maternity pay, national insurance contributions and VAT or duties. The tribunal also hears some appeals relating to goods seized by HM Revenue and Customs or Border Force and against some decisions made by the National Crime Agency. Appeals can be made by individuals or organisations, single taxpayers or large multinational companies. First-tier Tribunal (Tax) also hears appeals against certain decisions made by a compliance officer, an independent office holder appointed by the Independent Parliamentary Standards Authority, the organisation responsible for determining and paying MP expenses. Appeals can be made by current or former MPs under the Parliamentary Standards Act 2009. The jurisdiction is UK-wide.

WAR PENSIONS AND ARMED FORCES COMPENSATION CHAMBER
Acting Chamber President, Judge Sehba Storey
5th Floor, Fox Court, 14 Gray's Inn Road, London WC1X 8HN
T 020-3206 0701 **E** armedforces.chamber@justice.gov.uk

The War Pensions and Armed Forces Compensation Chamber of the First-tier Tribunal hears appeals brought by ex-servicemen and women against decisions by Veterans UK regarding pensions, compensation and other amounts under the war pensions legislation for injuries sustained before 5 April 2005, and under the armed forces compensation scheme for injuries after that date.

UPPER TRIBUNAL

Comprising four separate chambers, the Upper Tribunal deals mostly with appeals from, and enforcement of, decisions taken by the First-tier Tribunal, but it also handles some cases that do not go through the First-tier Tribunal. Additionally, it has assumed some of the supervisory powers of the courts to deal with the actions of tribunals, government departments and some other public authorities. All the decision-makers of the Upper Tribunal are judges or expert members sitting in a panel chaired by a judge, and are specialists in the areas of law they handle. Over time their decisions are expected to build comprehensive case law for each area covered by the tribunals.

ADMINISTRATIVE APPEALS CHAMBER
Chamber President, Hon. Dame Judith Farbey, DBE
England and Wales, 5th Floor, 7 Rolls Building, Fetter Lane,
London EC4A 1NL **T** 020-7071 5662
  E adminappeals@justice.gov.uk
Scotland, George House, 126 George Street, Edinburgh EH2 4HH
  T 0131-271 4310 **E** UTAACmailbox@gov.scot
Northern Ireland, Tribunal Hearing Centre, 2nd Floor, Royal
  Courts of Justice, Chichester Street, Belfast BT1 3JF
  T 028-9072 4883 **E** tribunalsunit@courtsni.gov.uk

The Administrative Appeals Chamber appeals against decisions made by certain lower tribunals and organisations including: social security and child support, war pensions and armed forces compensation, mental health, special education needs or disabilities, disputes heard by the General Regulatory Chamber, decisions made by the Disclosure and Barring Service, decisions made by the Traffic Commissioner (or the Transport Regulation Unit in Northern Ireland), Special Education Needs Tribunal for Wales, Mental Health Review Tribunal for Wales and the Pensions Appeal Tribunal in Northern Ireland (only for assessment appeals under the War Pensions Scheme). It also handles applications for judicial review of decisions made by: First-tier Tribunal (Criminal Injuries Compensation) and other first-tier tribunals where there is no right of appeal.

IMMIGRATION AND ASYLUM CHAMBER
Chamber President, Hon. Sir Peter Lane
1A Field House, 15–25 Bream's Buildings, London EC4A 1DZ
T 0300-123 1711 **E** FieldHouseCorrespondence@justice.gov.uk

The Immigration and Asylum Chamber hears appeals against decisions made by the First-tier Tribunal (Immigration and Asylum) relating to visa and asylum applications and the right to enter or stay in the UK. The chamber also deals with applications for judicial review of certain decisions made by the Home Office relating to immigration, asylum and human rights claims.

LANDS CHAMBER
Chamber President, Hon. Sir David Holgate
5th Floor, 7 Rolls Buildings, London EC4A 1NL
T 020-7612 9710 **E** lands@justice.gov.uk

The Lands Chamber is responsible for handling appeals against decisions made by the First-tier Tribunal (Property Chamber) (except decisions about land registration), the Residential Property Tribunal in Wales and the Leasehold Valuation Tribunal in Wales, It is also responsible for handling applications for cases regarding decisions about rates made by the Valuation Tribunal in England or Wales, compensation for the compulsory purchase of land, discharge or modification of land affected by a 'restrictive covenant', compensation for the effect on land affected by public works, a tree preservation order, compensation for damage to land damaged by subsidence from mining, the valuation of land or buildings for Capital Gains Tax or Inheritance Tax purposes and compensation for blighted land.

TAX AND CHANCERY CHAMBER
Chamber President, Hon. Sir Antony Zacaroli
5th Floor, 7 Rolls Buildings, London EC4A 1NL
T 020-7612 9730 **E** uttc@justice.gov.uk

The Tax and Chancery Chamber hears appeals against decisions made by the First-tier Tribunal (Tax), the land registration division of the First-tier Tribunal (Property Chamber) and the General Regulatory Chamber in cases relating to charities. The chamber also hears appeals against decisions issued by the Financial Conduct Authority, the Prudential Regulation Authority, the Pensions Regulator, the Bank of England, HM Treasury and OFGEM.

SPECIAL IMMIGRATION APPEALS COMMISSION
15–25 Bream's Buildings, London EC4A 1DZ
T 0300-123 1711

The commission was set up under the Special Immigration Appeals Commission Act 1997. It remains separate from the First-tier and Upper Tribunal structure but is part of HM Courts and Tribunals Service. Its main function is to consider appeals against orders for deportation or exclusion, or orders withdrawing or refusing British nationality, in cases which involve considerations of national security.

Chair, Hon. Dame Elisabeth Laing, DBE

EMPLOYMENT TRIBUNALS
Employment Tribunal Central Office England and Wales, PO
  Box 10218, Leicester LE1 8EG **T** 0300-123 1024
Employment Tribunal Central Office Scotland, PO Box 27105,
  Glasgow G2 9JR **T** 0300-790 6234

Employment tribunals hear claims regarding matters of employment law, redundancy, dismissal, contract disputes, sexual, racial and disability discrimination and related areas of dispute which may arise in the workplace.

President (England and Wales), Judge Doyle
President (Scotland), Judge Simon

EMPLOYMENT APPEAL TRIBUNAL
Employment Appeal Tribunal England and Wales, 5th Floor, 7 Rolls
  Buildings, Fetter Lane, London EC4A 1NL **T** 020-7273 1041
  E londoneat@justice.gov.uk
Employment Appeal Tribunal Scotland, George House, 126 George
  Street, Edinburgh, EH2 4HH **T** 0131-225 3963
  E edinburgheat@justice.gov.uk

The Employment Appeal Tribunal hears appeals (on points of law only) arising from decisions made by employment tribunals.

President, Hon. Mr Justice Choudhury

SCOTTISH COURTS AND TRIBUNALS SERVICE
Saughton House, Broomhouse Drive, Edinburgh EH11 3XD
T 0131-444 3300

W www.scotcourts.gov.uk **E** enquiries@scotcourts.gov.uk

The Tribunals (Scotland) Act 2014 created a new, simplified statutory framework for tribunals in Scotland, bringing existing jurisdictions together and providing a structure for new ones. The Act created two new tribunals, the First-tier Tribunal for Scotland and the Upper Tribunal for Scotland.
  The Lord President is the head of the Scottish Courts and Tribunals Service and has delegated various functions to the President of Scottish Tribunals.

President of Scottish Tribunals, Rt. Hon. Lady Smith (Anne
  Smith)

UPPER TRIBUNAL FOR SCOTLAND

The Glasgow Tribunals Centre, 20 York Street, Glasgow G2 8GT
T 0141-302 5880
E uppertribunalforscotland@scotcourtstribunals.gov.uk

The Upper Tribunal hears appeals on decisions of the chambers of the First-tier Tribunal.

FIRST-TIER TRIBUNAL

The First-tier Tribunal is organised into five chambers.

GENERAL REGULATORY CHAMBER
George House, 126 George Street, Edinburgh EH2 4HH
T 0131-271 4340 **E** Charityappeals@scotcourtstribunals.gov.uk

HEALTH AND EDUCATION CHAMBER
20 York Street, Glasgow G2 8GT
T 0141-302 5860

HOUSING AND PROPERTY CHAMBER
20 York Street, Glasgow G2 8GT
T 0141-302 5900

SOCIAL SECURITY CHAMBER
20 York Street, Glasgow G2 8GT
T 0141-302 5858

TAX CHAMBER
George House, 126 George Street, Edinburgh EH2 4HH
T 0131-271 4385 **E** taxchamber@scotcourtstribunals.gov.uk

The Scottish Courts and Tribunals Service currently provides administrative support for the following Scottish tribunals:

COUNCIL TAX REDUCTION REVIEW PANEL, 20 York
  Street, Glasgow G2 8GT **T** 0141-302 5840
  E ctrrpadmin@scotcourtstribunals.gov.uk
  W www.counciltaxreductionreview.scotland.gov.uk
THE LANDS TRIBUNAL FOR SCOTLAND, George House,
  126 George Street, Edinburgh EH2 4HH **T** 0131-271 4350
  E LTS_mailbox@scotcourtstribunals.gov.uk
  W www.lands-tribunal-scotland.org.uk
  President, Hon. Lord Minginish (Roderick MacLeod)
THE MENTAL HEALTH TRIBUNAL FOR SCOTLAND,
  Bothwell House, First Floor, Hamilton Business Park, Caird Park,
  Hamilton ML3 0QA **T** 0800-345 7060
  E mhtsTeam1@scotcourtstribunals.gov.uk
  W www.mhtscotland.gov.uk
  President, Dr Joe Morrow, CBE
THE PENSIONS APPEAL TRIBUNAL SCOTLAND,
  126 George Street, Edinburgh EH2 4HH **T** 0131-271 4340
  E PAT_Info_Mailbox@scotcourtstribunals.gov.uk
  W www.patscotland.org.uk
  President, Marion Caldwell, QC

NORTHERN IRELAND COURTS AND TRIBUNALS SERVICE

Department of Justice, Block B, Castle Buildings, Stormont Estate,
Belfast BT4 3SG
T 028-9076 3000 **W** www.justice-ni.gov.uk/topics/
courts-and-tribunals
Lord Chief Justice of Northern Ireland, Rt. Hon. Sir Declan
Morgan

The Northern Ireland Courts and Tribunals Service currently provides administrative support for the following Northern Ireland tribunals. All the tribunals below, unless otherwise specified, can be contacted at: 2nd Floor, Royal Courts of Justice, Chichester Street, Belfast BT1 3JF **T** 0300-200 7812
E tribunalsunit@courtsni.gov.uk

THE APPEALS SERVICE, 6th Floor, Oyster House, 12
  Wellington Place, Belfast BT1 6GE **T** 028-9054 4000
  E appeals.service.belfast@dsdni.gov.uk
THE CARE TRIBUNAL
  Chairs, Diane Drennan, Stephen Quinn
THE CHARITY TRIBUNAL
CRIMINAL INJURIES COMPENSATION APPEALS
  PANEL NORTHERN IRELAND,
  E cicapnicustomer@courtsni.gov.uk
  Chair, Patricia McKaigue
LANDS TRIBUNAL
MENTAL HEALTH REVIEW TRIBUNAL
NORTHERN IRELAND HEALTH AND SAFETY
  TRIBUNAL
NORTHERN IRELAND TRAFFIC PENALTY TRIBUNAL
NORTHERN IRELAND VALUATION TRIBUNAL
OFFICE OF SOCIAL SECURITY COMMISSIONERS AND
  CHILD SUPPORT COMMISSIONERS
  Chief Commissioner, Kenneth Mullan
PAROLE COMMISSIONERS FOR NORTHERN
  IRELAND, Laganside Court, Mezzanine 1st Floor,
  Oxford Street, Belfast BT1 3LL **T** 028-9041 2969
  E info@parolecomni.org.uk
  Chief Commissioner, Christine Glenn
PENSIONS APPEAL COMMISSIONERS
PENSIONS APPEAL TRIBUNALS
RENT ASSESSMENT PANEL, Cleaver House, 3 Donegall
  Square North, Belfast BT1 5GA **T** 028-9051 8518
  E appeals.service.belfast@dsdni.gov.uk
SPECIAL EDUCATIONAL NEEDS AND DISABILITY
  TRIBUNAL

INDEPENDENT TRIBUNALS

The following represents a selection of tribunals not administered by HM Courts and Tribunals Service.

CIVIL AVIATION AUTHORITY
Aviation House, Beehive Ringroad, Crawley, W. Sussex RH6 0YR
T 0330-022 1500 **W** www.caa.co.uk

The Civil Aviation Authority (CAA) does not have a separate tribunal department as such, but for certain purposes the CAA must conform to tribunal requirements, for example, to deal with appeals against the refusal or revocation of aviation licences and certificates issued by the CAA, and the allocation of routes outside of the EU to airlines.

The chair and non-executive members who may sit on panels for tribunal purposes are appointed by the Secretary of State for Transport.

Chair, Dame Deirdre Hutton, DBE

COMPETITION APPEAL TRIBUNAL
Victoria House, Bloomsbury Place, London WC1A 2EB
T 020-7979 7979 **W** www.catribunal.org.uk

The Competition Appeal Tribunal (CAT) is a specialist tribunal established to hear certain cases in the sphere of UK competition and economic regulatory law. It hears appeals against decisions of the Competition and Markets Authority (CMA) and the sectoral regulators in respect of infringements of competition law and with respect to mergers and markets. The CAT also has jurisdiction to award damages in respect of infringements of EU or UK competition law and to hear appeals against decisions of the Office of Communications (OFCOM) in telecommunications matters.

President, Hon. Sir Peter Roth

COPYRIGHT TRIBUNAL
4 Abbey Orchard Street, London SW1P 2HT
T 020-7034 2836 E copyright.tribunal@ipo.gov.uk
W www.gov.uk/government/organisations/copyright-tribunal

The Copyright Tribunal resolves disputes over the terms and conditions of licences offered by, or licensing schemes operated by, collective management organisations in the copyright and related rights area. Its decisions are appealable to the high court on points of law only.

Chair, His Hon. Judge Hacon

INDUSTRIAL TRIBUNALS AND THE FAIR EMPLOYMENT TRIBUNAL (NORTHERN IRELAND)
Killymeal House, 2 Cromac Quay, Ormeau Road, Belfast BT7 2JD
T 028-9032 7666 E mail@employmenttribunalsni.org
W www.employmenttribunalsni.org

The industrial tribunal system in Northern Ireland was set up in 1965 and has a similar remit to the employment tribunals in the rest of the UK. There is also a Fair Employment Tribunal, which hears and determines individual cases of alleged religious or political discrimination in employment. Employers can appeal to the Fair Employment Tribunal if they consider the directions of the Equality Commission to be unreasonable, inappropriate or unnecessary, and the Equality Commission can make application to the tribunal for the enforcement of undertakings or directions with which an employer has not complied.

President, Eileen McBride, CBE

INVESTIGATORY POWERS TRIBUNAL
PO Box 33220, London SW1H 9ZQ
T 020-7035 3711 E info@ipt-uk.com W www.ipt-uk.com

The Investigatory Powers Tribunal replaced the Interception of Communications Tribunal, the Intelligence Services Tribunal, the Security Services Tribunal and the complaints function of the commissioner appointed under the Police Act 1997.

The Regulation of Investigatory Powers Act 2000 (RIPA) provides for a tribunal made up of senior members of the legal profession, independent of the government and appointed by the Queen, to consider all complaints against the intelligence services and those against public authorities in respect of powers covered by RIPA; and to consider proceedings brought under section 7 of the Human Rights Act 1998 against the intelligence services and law enforcement agencies in respect of these powers.

President, Rt. Hon, Sir Rabinder Singh

SOLICITORS' DISCIPLINARY TRIBUNAL
3rd Floor, Gate House, 1 Farringdon Street, London EC4M 7LG
T 020-7329 4808 E enquiries@solicitorsdt.com
W www.solicitorstribunal.org.uk

The Solicitors' Disciplinary Tribunal is an independent statutory body whose members are appointed by the Master of the Rolls. The tribunal adjudicates upon alleged breaches of the rules and regulations applicable to solicitors and their firms, including the Solicitors' Code of Conduct 2007. It also decides applications by former solicitors for restoration to the Roll.

Chair, Edward Nally

SCOTTISH SOLICITORS' DISCIPLINE TRIBUNAL
Unit 3.5, The Granary Business Centre, Coal Road, Cupar, Fife KY15 5YQ
T 01334-659099 E enquiries@ssdt.org.uk W www.ssdt.org.uk

The Scottish Solicitors' Discipline Tribunal is an independent statutory body with a panel of 24 members, 12 of whom are solicitors appointed by the Lord President of the Court of Session. Its principal function is to consider complaints of misconduct against solicitors in Scotland.

Chair, Nicholas Whyte

TRAFFIC PENALTY TRIBUNAL
Springfield House, Water Lane, Wilmslow, Cheshire SK9 5BG
T 0800-160 1999 E help@trafficpenaltytribunal.gov.uk
W www.trafficpenaltytribunal.gov.uk

The Traffic Penalty Tribunal adjudicators consider appeals in relation to penalty charge notices issued by local authorities in England (outside London) and Wales for parking and bus lane contraventions and, additionally in Wales, moving traffic contraventions. The tribunal also considers appeals in relation to penalties issued by the Secretary of State for Transport for failing to pay a charge at the Dartford river crossing, the Durham peninsular congestion charging zone and the Mersey Gateway bridge crossings.

Chief Adjudicator, Caroline Sheppard, OBE

VALUATION TRIBUNAL FOR ENGLAND
2nd Floor, 120 Leman Street, London E1 8EU
T 020-7246 3900 W www.valuationtribunal.gov.uk

The Valuation Tribunal for England (VTE) came into being on 1 October 2009, replacing 56 valuation tribunals in England. Provision for the VTE was made in the Local Government and Public Involvement in Health Act 2007. The VTE hears appeals concerning council tax and non-domestic (business) rates, as well as a small number of appeals against drainage boards' assessments of drainage rates. A separate panel is constituted for each hearing, and consists of a chair and usually one or two other members.

The Valuation Tribunal Service (VTS) was created as a corporate body by the Local Government Act 2003, and is responsible for providing or arranging the services required for the operation of the Valuation Tribunal for England. The VTS board consists of a chair and members appointed by the secretary of state. The VTS is sponsored by the Ministry of Housing, Communities and Local Government.

President (VTE), Gary Garland
Chair (VTS), Robin Evans

VALUATION TRIBUNAL FOR WALES
W www.valuationtribunal.wales

The Valuation Tribunal for Wales (VTW) was established by the Valuation Tribunal for Wales Regulations 2010, and hears and determines appeals concerning council tax, non-domestic rating and drainage rates in Wales. The governing council, comprising the president, four regional representatives and one member who is appointed by the Welsh government, performs the management functions on behalf of the tribunal. There are a number of VTW offices across Wales and contact details for these can be found on the website listed above.

President, Carol Cobert

OMBUDSMAN SERVICES

The following section is a listing of selected ombudsman services. Ombudsmen are a free, independent and impartial means of resolving certain disputes outside of the courts. These disputes are, in the majority of cases, concerned with whether something has been badly or unfairly handled (for example owing to delay, neglect, inefficiency or failure to follow proper procedures). Most ombudsman schemes are established by statute; they cover various public and private bodies and generally examine matters only after the relevant body has been given a reasonable opportunity to deal with the complaint.

After conducting an investigation an ombudsman will usually issue a written report, which normally suggests a resolution to the dispute and often includes recommendations concerning the improvement of procedures.

OMBUDSMAN ASSOCIATION

PO Box 343, Carshalton, Surrey SM5 9BX
E secretary@ombudsmanassociation.org
W www.ombudsmanassociation.org

The Ombudsman Association was established in 1994 and exists to provide information to the government, public bodies and the public about ombudsmen and other complaint-handling services in the UK and Ireland. An ombudsman scheme must meet four criteria in order to attain full Ombudsman Association membership: independence from the organisations the ombudsman has the power to investigate, fairness, effectiveness and public accountability. Complaint Handler membership is open to complaint-handling bodies that do not meet these criteria in full. Ombudsmen schemes from the UK, Ireland, British crown dependencies and overseas territories may apply to the Ombudsman Association for membership. The Ombudsman Association publishes a quarterly magazine containing news about ombudsmen and complaint-handling services in the UK, Ireland and overseas, along with topical articles of interest to members of the Association.

Chair, Nick Bennett

The following is a selection of organisations that are members of the Ombudsman Association.

FINANCIAL OMBUDSMAN SERVICE

Exchange Tower, London E14 9SR
T 020-7964 1000 E complaint.info@financial-ombudsman.org.uk
W www.financial-ombudsman.org.uk

The Financial Ombudsman Service settles individual disputes between businesses providing financial services and their customers. The service examines complaints about most financial matters, including banking, insurance, mortgages, pensions, savings, loans and credit cards. *See also* Banking and Finance.

Chief Ombudsman and Chief Executive, Caroline Wayman

HOUSING OMBUDSMAN SERVICE

Exchange Tower, London E14 9GE
T 0300-111 3000 E info@housing-ombudsman.org.uk
W www.housing-ombudsman.org.uk

The Housing Ombudsman Service was established in 1997 to deal with complaints and disputes involving tenants and housing associations and social landlords, certain private-sector landlords and managing agents. The ombudsman has a statutory jurisdiction over all registered social landlords in

England. Private and other landlords can join the service on a voluntary basis. On 1 April 2013 a new Housing Ombudsman Service was launched with an extended jurisdiction covering all housing associations and local authorities.

Ombudsman, Andrea Keenoy *(interim)*

INDEPENDENT OFFICE FOR POLICE CONDUCT

90 High Holborn, London WC1V 6BH
T 0300-020 0096 E enquiries@policeconduct.gov.uk
W www.policeconduct.gov.uk

Established under the Policing and Crime Act 2017, the Independent Office for Police Conduct (IOPC) succeeded the Independent Police Complaints Commission (IPCC) in January 2018. The IOPC is responsible for carrying out independent investigations into serious incidents or allegations of misconduct by those serving with the police forces in England and Wales, as well as Police and Crime Commissioners in England and Wales and the London Mayor's Office for Policing and Crime (MOPAC). The IOPC's director-general and its regional directors must not have worked for the police in any capacity prior to their appointment. It has the power to initiate, undertake and oversee investigations and is also responsible for the way in which complaints are handled by local police forces. The IOPC is also responsible for serious complaints and conduct matters relating to staff at the National Crime Agency (NCA), Her Majesty's Revenue and Customs (HMRC), and the Gangmasters and Labour Abuse Authority.

Director-General, Michael Lockwood

LEGAL OMBUDSMAN

PO Box 6806, Wolverhampton WV1 9WJ
T 0300-555 0333 E enquiries@legalombudsman.org.uk
W www.legalombudsman.org.uk

The Legal Ombudsman was set up by the Office for Legal Complaints under the Legal Services Act 2007 and is the single body for all consumer legal complaints in England and Wales. It replaced the Office of the Legal Services Ombudsman in 2010. The Legal Ombudsman aims to resolve disputes between individuals and authorised legal practitioners, including barristers, law cost draftsmen, legal executives, licensed conveyancers, notaries, patent attorneys, probate practitioners, registered European lawyers, solicitors and trade mark attorneys. The Legal Ombudsman is an independent and impartial organisation and deals with various types of complaints against legal services, such as wills, family issues, personal injury and buying or selling a house.

Chief Ombudsman, Rebecca Marsh

LOCAL GOVERNMENT AND SOCIAL CARE OMBUDSMAN

PO Box 4771, Coventry CV4 0EH
T 0300-061 0614 W www.lgo.org.uk

The Local Government and Social Care Ombudsman deals with complaints about most council services, including planning, some housing issues, social care, some education and schools issues, children's services, housing benefit, council tax, transport and highways, environment and waste, neighbour nuisance and antisocial behaviour and service failure by local authorities, schools and all registered social care providers, including all adult social care complaints. The Ombudsman's powers to investigate include complaints about publicly and privately funded social care.

If a complaint is about both health and social care services, a joint investigation with the Health Service Ombudsman can be carried out with the Social Care Ombudsman as the single point of contact.

Local Government and Social Care Ombudsman, Michael King

NORTHERN IRELAND PUBLIC SERVICES OMBUDSMAN

33 Wellington Place, Belfast BT1 6HN
T 028-9023 3821 **E** nipso@nipso.org.uk
W www.nipso.org.uk

The Office of Northern Ireland Public Services Ombudsman (NIPSO) was established in April 2016, replacing and expanding the functions of the Northern Ireland Assembly Ombudsman and Commissioner for Complaints. NIPSO provides an independent review of complaints of members of the public, where they believe they have sustained an injustice or hardship as a result or inaction of a public service provider. NIPSO additionally ensures that public services improve as a result of the complaints brought to them by the public. The professional, independent and impartial service is provided free of charge to the citizens of Northern Ireland.

Ombudsman, Marie Anderson

OFFICE OF THE PENSIONS OMBUDSMAN

10 South Colonnade, Canary Wharf, London E14 4PU
T 0800-917 4487 **E** enquiries@pensions-ombudsman.org.uk
W www.pensions-ombudsman.org.uk

The Pensions Ombudsman can investigate and decide complaints and disputes regarding the way occupational and personal pension schemes are administered and managed. Unless there are special circumstances, this only usually includes issues and disputes that have arisen within the past three years. The Pensions Ombudsman is also the Ombudsman for the Pension Protection Fund (PPF) and the Financial Assistance Scheme (which offers help to those who were a member of an under-funded defined benefit pension scheme that started to wind-up in specific financial circumstances between 1 January 1997 and 5 April 2005).

Pensions Ombudsman, Anthony Arter
Deputy Pensions Ombudsman, Karen Johnston

OMBUDSMAN SERVICES

3300 Daresbury Park, Warrington WA4 4HS
W www.ombudsman-services.org

Ombudsman Services was founded in 2002 and provides independent dispute resolution for the communications, copyright licensing and energy sectors. Ombudsman Services ceased dealing with complaints concerning the property sector in 2018.

Ombudsman Services: Communications investigates complaints from consumers about companies which provide communication services to the public.

Ombudsman Services: Copyright Licensing helps to resolve complaints about bodies that either own or administer, on behalf of third parties, the licensing of copyright materials.

Ombudsman Services: Energy helps to resolve complaints from consumers about energy (gas and electricity companies). This service is also responsible for handling investigations concerning the government's Green Deal policy, which launched in 2013, and offers long-term loans towards energy-saving home improvements.

Chair, Lord Tim Clement-Jones, CBE
Chief Ombudsman, Matthew Vickers

OMBUDSMAN SERVICES: COMMUNICATIONS
PO Box 730, Warrington WA4 6WU
T 0330-440 1614

OMBUDSMAN SERVICES: COPYRIGHT LICENSING
PO Box 1124, Warrington WA4 9GH
T 0330-440 1601

OMBUDSMAN SERVICES: ENERGY
PO Box 966, Warrington WA4 9DF
T 0330-440 1624

PARLIAMENTARY AND HEALTH SERVICE OMBUDSMAN
Millbank Tower, Millbank, London SW1P 4QP
T 0345-015 4033
W www.ombudsman.org.uk

The Parliamentary Commissioner for Administration (commonly known as the Parliamentary Ombudsman) is independent of government and is an officer of parliament. He is responsible for investigating complaints referred to him by MPs from members of the public who claim to have sustained injustice in consequence of maladministration by or on behalf of government departments and certain non-departmental public bodies in the UK. Certain types of action by government departments or bodies are excluded from investigation.

The Health Service Ombudsman is responsible for investigating complaints about services funded by the National Health Service in England that have not been dealt with by the service providers to the satisfaction of the complainant. This includes complaints about doctors, dentists, pharmacists and opticians. Complaints can be referred directly by the member of the public who claims to have sustained injustice or hardship in consequence of the failure in a service provided by a relevant organisation.

The two offices of the Parliamentary and Health Service Ombudsman are traditionally held by the same person.

Parliamentary Ombudsman and Health Service Ombudsman, Robert Behrens, CBE

PRISONS AND PROBATION OMBUDSMAN
Third Floor, 10 South Colonnade, London E14 4PU
T 020-7633 4100 **E** mail@ppo.gov.uk
W www.ppo.gov.uk

The Prisons and Probation Ombudsman investigates complaints from prisoners, people on probation and immigration detainees, deaths of prisoners, residents of probation-service approved premises and those held in immigration removal centres. The ombudsman is appointed by the Secretary of State for Justice and works closely with the Ministry of Justice. All deaths that occur in prison are investigated and an anonymised fatal incident report is written after each investigation.

Ombudsman, Sue McAllister, CB

PROPERTY OMBUDSMAN
Milford House, 43–55 Milford Street, Salisbury SP1 2BP
T 01722-333306
W www.tpos.co.uk

The Property Ombudsman (TPO) scheme was established in 1998 and provides a free, impartial and independent service for dealing with unresolved disputes between property agents and buyers, sellers, tenants and landlords of property in the UK.

The ombudsman's role is to consider complaints against the agents' obligation to act in accordance with the TPO codes of practice and to propose a full and final resolution to the dispute. Consumers are not bound by the Ombudsman's decision, but registered agents are.

TPO is the primary dispute-resolution service for the property industry.

Ombudsman, Katrine Sporle, CBE

PUBLIC SERVICES OMBUDSMAN FOR WALES

1 Ffordd yr Hen Gae, Pencoed CF35 5LJ
T 0300-790 0203 **E** ask@ombudsman-wales.org.uk
W www.ombudsman.wales

The office of Public Services Ombudsman for Wales was established, with effect from 1 April 2006, by the Public Services Ombudsman (Wales) Act 2005. The ombudsman, who is appointed by the Queen, investigates complaints of injustice caused by maladministration or service failure by public services such as the Assembly Commission (and public bodies sponsored by the assembly); Welsh government; National Health Service bodies, including GPs, family health service providers and hospitals; registered social landlords; local authorities, including community councils; fire and rescue authorities; police authorities; the Arts Council of Wales; national park authorities; and countryside and environmental organisations.

Ombudsman, Nick Bennett

REMOVALS INDUSTRY OMBUDSMAN SCHEME

PO Box 1535, High Wycombe HP12 9EE
T 020-8144 3790 **E** ombudsman@removalsombudsman.co.uk
W www.removalsombudsman.co.uk

The Removals Industry Ombudsman Scheme was established to resolve disputes between removal companies that are members of the scheme and their clients, both domestic and commercial. It comprises a board of four members, only one of whom has any connection with the removals industry. The ombudsman investigates complaints such as breaches of contract, unprofessional conduct, delays, excessive charges or breaches in the code of practice. The National Guild of Removers and Storers is currently the principal member.

Ombudsman, Tony Kaye

SCOTTISH PUBLIC SERVICES OMBUDSMAN

Bridgeside House, 99 McDonald Road, Edinburgh EH7 4NS
T 0800-377 7330
W www.spso.org.uk

The Scottish Public Services Ombudsman (SPSO) was established in 2002. The SPSO is the final stage for complaints about public services in Scotland. Its service is free and independent. SPSO investigates complaints about the Scottish government, its agencies and departments; the Scottish Parliamentary Corporate Body; colleges and universities; councils; housing associations; NHS Scotland; prisons; some water and sewerage service providers; and most other Scottish public bodies. The ombudsman looks at complaints regarding poor service or administrative failure and can usually only look at those that have been through the formal complaints process of the organisation concerned. It also has a statutory function in improving complaints handling in public services, which it carries out through its Complaints Standards Authority.

Scottish Public Services Ombudsman, Rosemary Agnew

WATERWAYS OMBUDSMAN

PO Box 854, Altrincham WA15 5JS
T 0161-980 4858 **E** enquiries@waterways-ombudsman.org
W www.waterways-ombudsman.org

Since July 2012, the Waterways Ombudsman has investigated complaints about the Canal and River Trust and its subsidiaries (such as British Waterways Marinas Limited). The ombudsman does not consider complaints about canals in Scotland, which are the responsibility of the Scottish Public Services Ombudsman.

Ombudsman, Sarah Daniel

THE POLICE SERVICE

There are 45 police forces in the United Kingdom: 43 in England and Wales, including the Metropolitan Police and the City of London Police, Police Scotland and the Police Service of Northern Ireland. The Isle of Man, Jersey and Guernsey have their own forces responsible for policing in their respective islands and bailiwicks. The National Crime Agency, which became operational in October 2013, is responsible for preventing organised crime and strengthening UK borders.

Since 1964, police authorities – separate independent bodies for each police force – were responsible for the supervision of local policing in England and Wales. Following the government's white paper *Policing in the 21st Century* it was concluded that, in order to make the police more accountable, police authorities should be replaced with a directly elected commissioner for each force, supported by a police and crime panel made up of representatives from each local authority in a police force area. In November 2012, following the enactment of the Police Reform and Social Responsibility Act 2011, the first elections to install police and crime commissioners (PCCs) were held in November 2012 across England and Wales; the most recent elections took place in May 2016. The PCCs are responsible for appointing the chief constable of their force, establishing local priorities and setting budgets. The PCCs are not in place to run their local force but rather to hold them to account. The Mayor of London, through the Deputy Mayor for Policing and Crime and supported by the Mayor's Office for Policing and Crime (MOPAC), acts as the PCC for the Metropolitan Police. Since 2017 the Mayor of Greater Manchester fulfils the PCC responsibilities for this area's force. The City of London Corporation acts as the police authority for the City of London Police.

Under the Police and Fire Reform (Scotland) Act 2012, Police Scotland was established on 1 April 2013, merging the eight separate territorial police forces, the Scottish Crime and Drug Enforcement Agency and the Association of Chief Police Officers in Scotland. Responsible for policing the whole of Scotland, Police Scotland is the second largest force in the UK after the Metropolitan Police. The service is led by a chief constable who is supported by a team of four deputy constables, assistant chief constables and three directors. The Scottish Police Authority, established in October 2012, is responsible for maintaining policing, promoting policing principles, the continuous improvement of policing and holds the Chief Constable to account. In Northern Ireland, the Northern Ireland Policing Board, an independent public body consisting of 19 political and independent members, fulfils a similar role.

Police forces in England, Scotland and Wales are financed by central and local government grants and a precept on the council tax. The Police Service of Northern Ireland is wholly funded by central government.

The home secretary, the Scottish government and the Northern Ireland Minister of Justice are responsible for the organisation, administration and operation of the police service. They regulate police ranks, discipline, hours of duty and pay and allowances. All police forces are subject to inspection by HM Inspectorate of Constabulary, which reports to the home secretary and the Northern Ireland Minister of Justice. Police forces in Scotland are inspected by HM Inspectorate of Constabulary for Scotland which operates independently of the Scottish government.

COMPLAINTS

Established under the Policing and Crime Act 2017, the Independent Office for Police Conduct (IOPC) succeeded the Independent Police Complaints Commission (IPCC) in January 2018. The IOPC is responsible for carrying out independent investigations into serious incidents or allegations of misconduct by those serving with the police forces in England and Wales, as well as Police and Crime Commissioners in England and Wales and the London Mayor's Office for Policing and Crime (MOPAC). The IOPC's director-general and its regional directors must not have worked for the police in any capacity prior to their appointment. It has the power to initiate, undertake and oversee investigations and is also responsible for the way in which complaints are handled by local police forces. The IOPC is also responsible for serious complaints and conduct matters relating to staff at the National Crime Agency (NCA).

Complaints about the police must first be recorded with the relevant police force and the local force will attempt to resolve the matter internally. Certain serious complaints are automatically referred to the IOPC. The IOPC or police force may refer the case to the Crown Prosecution Service, which will decide whether to bring criminal charges against the officer/s involved.

On 1 April 2013, under the Police and Fire Reform (Scotland) Act 2012 which brought together Scotland's eight police services into the single Police Service of Scotland, the remit of the Police Complaints Commissioner for Scotland (PCCS) was expanded to include investigations into the most serious incidents concerning the police. To reflect this change, the PCCS was renamed the Police Investigations and Review Commissioner (PIRC).

The Police Ombudsman for Northern Ireland provides an independent police complaints system for Northern Ireland, dealing with all stages of the complaints procedure. Complaints that cannot be resolved informally are investigated and the ombudsman recommends a suitable course of action to the Chief Constable of the Police Service of Northern Ireland or the Northern Ireland Policing Board based on the investigation's findings. The ombudsman may recommend that a police officer be prosecuted, but the decision to prosecute a police officer rests with the Director of Public Prosecutions.

INDEPENDENT OFFICE FOR POLICE CONDUCT, PO Box 473, Sale M33 0BW **T** 0300-020 0096
E enquiries@policeconduct.gov.uk
W www.policeconduct.gov.uk
Director-General, Michael Lockwood

POLICE INVESTIGATIONS AND REVIEW COMMISSIONER, Hamilton House, Hamilton Business Park, Caird Park, Hamilton ML3 0QA **T** 01698-542900
E enquiries@pirc.gov.scot **W** www.pirc.scotland.gov.uk
Police Investigations and Review Commissioner, Kate Frame

POLICE OMBUDSMAN FOR NORTHERN IRELAND, New Cathedral Buildings, Writers' Square, 11 Church Street, Belfast BT1 1PG **T** 028-9082 8600 **E** info@policeombudsman.org
W www.policeombudsman.org
Police Ombudsman, Dr Michael Maguire

POLICE SERVICES

COLLEGE OF POLICING

Leamington Road, Ryton-on-Dunsmore, Coventry CV8 3EN
T 0800-496 3322 E contactus@college.pnn.police.uk
W www.college.police.uk

The College of Policing was established in December 2012 as the first professional body set up for policing. It works on behalf of the public to raise professional standards in policing and to assist forces to reduce crime and protect the public. It engages with the public through the Police and Crime Commissioners to ensure that it is responsive to the issues of greatest concern.

The government has designated the college as a centre for reviewing and testing practices and interventions to identify which are effective in reducing crime. It makes this information accessible for all in policing, particularly frontline practitioners. The college also supports continuous professional development and sets national standards for promotion and progression.

Chief Executive, Mike Cunningham, QPM
Chair, Millie Banerjee, CBE

NATIONAL CRIME AGENCY

Units 1–6 Citadel Place, Tinworth Street, London SE11 5EF
T 0370-496 7622
E communication@nca.gov.uk
W www.nationalcrimeagency.gov.uk

Established under the Crime and Courts Act 2013 the National Crime Agency (NCA) became fully operational in October 2013. The NCA is a non-ministerial government department.

The NCA's remit is to fight organised crime, including child sexual exploitation, modern slavery and human trafficking, illegal firearms, cyber crime and money laundering.

The director-general has independent operational direction and control over the NCA's activities and, through the home secretary, is accountable to parliament.

Director-General, Lynne Owens, CBE, QPM

UK MISSING PERSONS UNIT

PO Box 58358, London NW1W 9LA T 0800-234 6034
E ukmpu@nca.gov.uk
W www.missingpersons.police.uk

The UK Missing Persons Unit, part of the National Crime Agency, acts as the centre for the exchange of information connected with the search for missing persons nationally and internationally alongside the police and other related organisations. The unit focuses on cross-matching missing persons with unidentified persons or bodies by maintaining records, including a dental index of ante-mortem chartings of long-term missing persons and post-mortem chartings from unidentified bodies.

Information is supplied and collected for all persons who have been missing in the UK for over 72 hours (or fewer where police deem appropriate), foreign nationals reported missing in the UK, UK nationals reported missing abroad and all unidentified bodies and persons found within the UK.

SPECIALIST FORCES

BRITISH TRANSPORT POLICE

25 Camden Road, London NW1 9LN T 0800-405040
E first_contact@btp.pnn.police.uk
W www.btp.police.uk
Strength (August 2019), 3,069

British Transport Police is the national police force for the railways in England, Wales and Scotland, including the London Underground system, Docklands Light Railway, Glasgow Subway, Midland Metro tram system, Sunderland Metro, London Tramlink and the Emirates Air Line cable car.

The chief constable reports to the British Transport Police Authority. The members of the authority are appointed by the transport secretary and include representatives from the rail industry as well as independent members. Officers are paid the same salary as those in other police forces.

Chief Constable, Paul Crowther, OBE

CIVIL NUCLEAR CONSTABULARY

Building F6, Culham Science Centre, Abingdon,
Oxfordshire OX14 3DB T 0300-313 5400
W www.gov.uk/government/organisations/
civil-nuclear-constabulary
*Strength, c.*1,500

The Civil Nuclear Constabulary (CNC) is overseen by the Civil Nuclear Police Authority, an executive non-departmental public body sponsored by the Department for Business, Energy and Industrial Strategy. The CNC is a specialised armed force that protects civil nuclear sites and nuclear materials. The constabulary is responsible for policing UK civil nuclear industry facilities and for escorting nuclear material between establishments within the UK and worldwide.

Chief Constable, Simon Chesterman, QPM
Deputy Chief Constable, Chris Armitt, QPM

MINISTRY OF DEFENCE POLICE

Ministry of Defence Police HQ, Wethersfield, Braintree, Essex
CM7 4AZ T 01371-854000
W www.mod.police.uk
Strength (July 2018), 2,733

Part of the Ministry of Defence Police and Guarding Agency, the Ministry of Defence Police is a statutory civil police force with particular responsibility for the security and policing of the MoD environment. It contributes to the physical protection of property and personnel within its jurisdiction and provides a comprehensive police service to the MoD as a whole.

Chief Constable, Andy Adams
Deputy Chief Constable, Gareth Wilson

THE SPECIAL CONSTABULARY

Strength (March 2019), 10,640

The Special Constabulary is a force of trained volunteers who support and work with their local police force, usually for a minimum of 16 hours a month. Special constables are thoroughly grounded in the basic aspects of police work, such as self-defence, powers of arrest, common crimes and preparing evidence for court, before they can begin to carry out any police duties. Once they have completed their training, they have the same powers as a regular officer and wear a similar uniform. The Metropolitan Police Service have further information on their website.

POLICE FORCES

The telephone number for each local police force in England, Wales, Scotland and Northern Ireland is **T** 101

Force	Strength†	Chief Constable	Police and Crime Commissioner
ENGLAND			
Avon and Somerset	2,676	Andy Marsh, QPM	Sue Mountstevens
Bedfordshire	1,164	Jon Boutcher, QPM	Kathryn Holloway
Cambridgeshire	1,447	Nick Dean	Jason Ablewhite
Cheshire	2,006	Darren Martland	David Keane
Cleveland	1,198	Richard Lewis	Barry Coppinger
Cumbria	1,160	Michelle Skeer, QPM	Peter McCall
Derbyshire	1,767	Peter Goodman	Hardyal Dhindsa
Devon and Cornwall	3,000	Shaun Sawyer, QPM	Alison Hernandez
Dorset	1,223	James Vaughan, QPM	Martyn Underhill
Durham	1,118	Jo Farrell	Ron Hogg
Essex	3,071	Ben-Julian Harrington	Roger Hirst
Gloucestershire	1,073	Rod Hansen	Martin Surl
Greater Manchester	6,444	Ian Hopkins, QPM	Mayor of Greater Manchester
Hampshire	2,697	Olivia Pinkney	Michael Lane
Hertfordshire	2,009	Charlie Hall, QPM	David Lloyd
Humberside	1,889	Lee Freeman	Keith Hunter
Kent	3,553	Alan Pughsley, QPM	Matthew Scott
Lancashire	2,895	Andy Rhodes	Clive Grunshaw
Leicestershire	1,829	Simon Cole, QPM	Lord Bach
Lincolnshire	1,096	Bill Skelly	Marc Jones
Merseyside	3,396	Andy Cooke, QPM	Jane Kennedy
Norfolk	1,609	Simon Bailey, QPM	Lorne Green
North Yorkshire	1,377	Lisa Winward	Julia Mulligan
Northamptonshire	1,187	Nick Adderley	Stephen Mold
Northumbria	3,081	Winton Keenen	Kim McGuiness
Nottinghamshire	1,936	Craig Guilford	Paddy Tipping
South Yorkshire	2,370	Stephen Watson, QPM	Dr Alan Billings
Staffordshire	1,567	Gareth Morgan	Matthew Ellis
Suffolk	1,172	Steve Jupp	Tim Passmore
Surrey	1,882	Nick Ephgrave	David Munro
Sussex	2,629	Giles York, QPM	Katy Bourne
Thames Valley	4,149	Francis Habgood, QPM	Anthony Stansfeld
Warwickshire	817	Martin Jelley, QPM	Philip Seccombe
West Mercia	1,989	Anthony Bangham	John-Paul Campion
West Midlands	6,495	Dave Thompson, QPM	David Jamieson
West Yorkshire	5,137	John Robins, QPM	Mark Burns-Williamson, OBE
Wiltshire	992	Kier Pritchard	Angus Macpherson
WALES			
Dyfed-Powys	1,145	Mark Collins	Dafydd Llywelyn
Gwent	1,308	Pam Kelly *(acting)*	Jeff Cuthbert
North Wales	1,458	Carl Foulkes	Arfon Jones
South Wales	2,986	Matt Jukes	Rt. Hon. Alun Michael
POLICE SCOTLAND	17,251	Iain Livingstone, QPM	–
POLICE SERVICE OF NORTHERN IRELAND	6,716	Simon Byrne	–

ISLANDS	Strength†	Chief Constable	Telephone
Isle of Man	236	Gary Roberts	01624-631212
States of Jersey	189	Rob Bastable	01534-612612
Guernsey	146	Rauri Hardy	01481-725111

† Size of force (full-time equivalent; excluding long-term absentees) as at 31 March 2019

LONDON FORCES

CITY OF LONDON POLICE

182 Bishopsgate, London EC2M 4NP **T** 020-7601 2222
W www.cityoflondon.police.uk
Strength (June 2019), 756

The City of London has one of the most important financial centres in the world and the force has particular expertise in fraud investigation. The force concentrates on: economic crime, counter terrorism and community policing. It has a wholly elected police authority, the police committee of the City of London Corporation, which appoints the commissioner.

Commissioner, Ian Dyson, QPM
Assistant Commissioner, Alistair Sutherland, QPM
Commander, Karen Baxter *(Economic Crime)*

METROPOLITAN POLICE SERVICE

New Scotland Yard, Broadway, London SW1H 0BG
T 020-7230 1212 **W** www.met.police.uk
*Strength (June 2019),*30,059

Commissioner, Cressida Dick, CBE, QPM
Deputy Commissioner, Sir Stephen House, QPM

The Metropolitan Police Service (MPS) is divided into four main areas for operational purposes:

FRONTLINE POLICING
Most of the day-to-day policing of London is carried out by 32 borough operational command units operating within the same boundaries as the London borough councils.

Assistant Commissioner, Mark Simmons

SPECIALIST OPERATIONS
Counter Terrorism Command is responsible for the prevention and disruption of terrorist activity, domestic extremism and related offences within London and nationally. It provides an explosives disposal and chemical, biological, radiological and nuclear capability in London, assists the security services in fulfilling their roles and provides a point of contact for international partners.
Protection Command is responsible for the protection and security of high-profile persons, such as the royal family, prime minister and visiting heads of state.
Security Command works with authorities at the Houses of Parliament to provide security for peers, MPs, employees and visitors to the Palace of Westminster.

Assistant Commissioner & National Coordinator for Counter Terrorism Policing, Neil Basu

MET OPERATIONS
Met Operations provides two main services: reducing the harm caused by serious crime and criminal networks and providing specialist policing services across London.

Assistant Commissioner, Nick Ephgrave

PROFESSIONALISM
The Directorate of Professionalism's key aims are to uphold and improve professional standards across the MPS. It works with the IOPC to establish good practice, reduce bureaucracy and review decision making. It also works with the CPS to ensure timely investigations of complaints and conduct matters.

Assistant Commissioner, Helen Ball

STAFF ASSOCIATIONS

Police officers are not permitted to join a trade union or to take strike action. All ranks have their own staff associations.
NATIONAL POLICE CHIEFS' COUNCIL (NPCC), 10 Victoria Street, London SW1H 0NN **T** 020-3276 3795
W www.npcc.police.uk
Chair, Barbara Scott

ENGLAND AND WALES
POLICE FEDERATION OF ENGLAND AND WALES, Federation House, Highbury Drive, Leatherhead, Surrey KT22 7UY **T** 01372-352050 **W** www.polfed.org
National Secretary, Alex Duncan
POLICE SUPERINTENDENTS' ASSOCIATION OF ENGLAND AND WALES, 67A Reading Road, Pangbourne, Reading RG8 7JD **T** 0118-984 4005 **W** www.policesupers.com
National Secretary, Chief Supt. Dan Murphy

SCOTLAND
ASSOCIATION OF SCOTTISH POLICE SUPERINTENDENTS, Scottish Police College, Kincardine, Fife FK10 4BE **T** 01259-732122
W www.scottishpolicesupers.org.uk
General Secretary, Craig Suttie
SCOTTISH POLICE FEDERATION, 5 Woodside Place, Glasgow G3 7QF **T** 0300-303 0027 **W** www.spf.org.uk
General Secretary, Calum Steele

NORTHERN IRELAND
POLICE FEDERATION FOR NORTHERN IRELAND, 77–79 Garnerville Road, Belfast BT4 2NX **T** 028-9076 4200
W www.policefed-ni.org.uk
Chair, Mark Lindsay
SUPERINTENDENTS' ASSOCIATION OF NORTHERN IRELAND, **T** 028-9092 2201
E SuptAssociation@psni.pnn.police.uk

RATES OF PAY *as at 1 September 2019*

Chief Constable of Greater Manchester or W. Midlands*	£199,386
Chief Constable	£142,896–£186,099
Deputy Chief Constable	£119,637–£152,871
Assistant Chief Constable/ Commander	£103,023–£116,313
Chief Superintendent	£84,849–£89,511
Superintendent	
in rank on or after 1 April 2014	£68,460–£80,859
in rank before 1 April 2014	£68,460–£79,758
Chief Inspector†	£56,910 (£59,175)–£60,219 (£62,469)
Inspector†	£51,414 (£53,664)–£55,767 (£58,038)
Sergeant	£41,499–£45,099
Constable	
apptd on or after 1 April 2013	£20,880–£40,128
apptd before 1 April 2013	£25,560–£40,128
Metropolitan Police	
Commissioner	£285,792
Deputy Commissioner	£235,944
City of London Police	
Commissioner	£176,802
Assistant Commissioner	£145,830
Police Scotland	
Chief Constable	£214,404
Deputy Chief Constable	£174,741
Assistant Chief Constable	£118,485
Police Service of Northern Ireland	
Chief Constable	£207,489
Deputy Chief Constable	£168,582

* Also applicable to the four Assistant Commissioners of the MPS
† London salary in parentheses. All other officers (not MPS or City of London Commissioners) working in London receive an additional payment of £2,505 per annum

THE PRISON SERVICE

The prison services in the UK are the responsibility of the Secretary of State for Justice, the Scottish Secretary for Justice and the Minister of Justice in Northern Ireland. The chief executive (director-general in Northern Ireland), officers of HM Prison and Probation Service (HMPPS), the Scottish Prison Service (SPS) and the Northern Ireland Prison Service are responsible for the day-to-day running of the system.

There are 122 prison establishments in England and Wales, 15 in Scotland and three in Northern Ireland. Convicted prisoners are classified according to their assessed security risk and are housed in establishments appropriate to that level of security. There are no open prisons in Northern Ireland. Female prisoners are housed in women's establishments or in separate wings of mixed prisons. Remand prisoners are, where possible, housed separately from convicted prisoners. Offenders under the age of 21 are usually detained in a Young Offender Institution, which may be a separate establishment or part of a prison. Appellant and failed asylum seekers are held in Immigration Removal Centres, or in separate units of other prisons.

Fifteen prisons are now run by the private sector in England and Wales, and in England, Wales and Scotland all escort services have been contracted out to private companies. In Scotland, two prisons (Kilmarnock and Addiewell) were built and financed by the private sector and are being operated by private contractors.

There are independent prison inspectorates in England, Wales and Scotland which report annually on conditions and the treatment of prisoners. The Chief Inspector of Criminal Justice in Northern Ireland and HM Inspectorate of Prisons for England and Wales perform an inspectorate role for prisons in Northern Ireland. Every prison establishment also has an independent monitoring board made up of local volunteers.

Any prisoner whose complaint is not satisfied by the internal complaints procedures may complain to the prisons and probation ombudsman for England and Wales, the Scottish public services ombudsman or the prisoner ombudsman for Northern Ireland. The prisons and probation inspectors, the prisons ombudsman and the independent monitoring boards report to the home secretary and to the Minister of Justice in Northern Ireland.

PRISON STATISTICS

The current projections forecast that the prison population in England and Wales will grow to 85,800 by June 2022.

PRISON POPULATION 2019 (UK)

	Remand	Sentenced	Other
ENGLAND AND WALES	8,957	72,860	817
Male	8,437	69,576	739
Female	520	3,284	28
SCOTLAND	1,808	6,416	–
Male	1,697	6,125	–
Female	111	291	–
N. IRELAND*	436	987	–
Male	414	944	–
Female	22	43	–
UK TOTAL	11,201	80,263	1,584

* Figures from September 2018
Sources: MoJ; Scottish Prison Service; NI Prison Service

PRISON CAPACITY (ENGLAND AND WALES)
as at July 2019

Male prisoners	79,211
Female prisoners	3,831
Total	83,042
Useable operational capacity	85,131
Under home detention curfew supervision	2,884

Source: MoJ – *Prisons and Probation Statistics*

SENTENCED PRISON POPULATION BY SEX AND OFFENCE (ENGLAND AND WALES) *as at 31 March 2019*

	Male	Female
Violence against the person	18,342	948
Sexual offences	13,234	125
Robbery	6,840	324
Theft offences	8,494	590
Criminal damage and arson	1,052	95
Drugs offences	10,579	436
Possession of weapons	2,854	113
Public order offences	1,148	41
Miscellaneous crimes against society	2,820	177
Fraud offences	1,079	169
Summary non-motoring	2,502	224
Summary motoring	350	10
Offence not recorded	233	26
Total	69,527	3,278

Source: MoJ – *Prisons and Probation Statistics*

SENTENCED POPULATION BY LENGTH OF SENTENCE (ENGLAND AND WALES) *as at 31 March 2019*

	British	Other Nationalities or Not Recorded
Less than 12 months	4,432	522
12 months to less than 4 years	14,140	1,628
4 years to less than life	31,285	3,441
Indeterminate	8,561	875
Total*	58,418	6,466

* Figures do not include civil (non-criminal) prisoners or fine defaulters
Source: MoJ – *Prisons and Probation Statistics*

AVERAGE DAILY POPULATION BY TYPE OF CUSTODY 2019 (SCOTLAND)

Remand	1,489
Convicted awaiting sentence	319
Sentenced	6,416
Total	8,224

Source: SPS

SUICIDES IN PRISON (ENGLAND AND WALES)
Dec. 2017–Dec. 2018

Total	92

Source: MoJ

THE PRISON SERVICES

HM PRISON AND PROBATION SERVICE

102 Petty France, London SW1H 9AJ
T 0163-363 0941 **E** public.enquiries@noms.gsi.gov.uk
W www.gov.uk/government/organisations/
her-majestys-prison-and-probation-service

HM Prison and Probation Service (HMPPS) was formed on 1 April 2017, incorporating the National Offender Management Service (NOMS) and HM Prisons. HMPPS is responsible for implementing government policy concerning the welfare of prison populations and local communities, working closely with HM Prison Service to oversee the management of public sector prisons in England and Wales.

SALARIES (ENGLAND AND WALES)
from 1 April 2019

All salary ranges given are for the average across England and Wales (includes inner and outer London salaries) and are based on a 37-hour-week inclusive of the required hours allowance (Governors, Deputy Governors and Heads of Function) or the additional 17 per cent unsocial hours payment for all other grades.

Governor	£68,604–£97,859
Deputy Governor	£48,656–£79,520
Head of Function	£43,545–£54,810
Custodial Manager	£31,615–£40,319
Supervising/Specialist Officer	£28,101–£35,988
Prison Officer	£22,293–£29,518
Operational Support Grade	£20,095–£24,829

HM PRISON AND PROBATION SERVICE BOARD
Chief Executive, Jo Farrar
Executive Directors, Ian Blakeman *(Performance);* Phil Copple *(Prisons);* Amy Rees *(HMPPS Wales and Strategy);* Adrian Scott *(Electronic Monitoring Programme and Procurement);* Helga Swindenbank *(Youth Custody Service)*

OPERATING COSTS OF HM PRISON AND PROBATION SERVICE 2018–19

Operating income	(£245,575,000)
Total operating expenditure	£5,072,722,000
Staff costs	£2,146,359,000
Net operating expenditure	£4,827,147,000

Source: HM Prison and Probation Service – *Annual Report and Accounts 2018–19*

SCOTTISH PRISON SERVICE (SPS)

Calton House, 5 Redheughs Rigg, Edinburgh EH12 9HW
T 0131-330 3500 **E** gaolinfo@sps.pnn.gov.uk
W www.sps.gov.uk

SALARIES
from 1 April 2018

Governor in Charge	£64,771–£73,365
Deputy Governor	£52,361–£60,790
Head of Operations	£42,301–£50,547
Unit Manager	£34,440–£42,941
First Line Manager	£28,071–£36,175
Residential Officer	£23,564–£30,356
Operations Officer	£18,871–£23,372

SPS BOARD
Chief Executive, Colin McConnell
Directors, Caroline Johnston *(Strategy and Stakeholder Engagement, interim);* James Kerr *(Operations);* Ruth Sutherland *(Corporate Services, interim)*
Non-Executive Directors, K. Hampton; R. Molan; H. Monro; G. Scott; G. Stillie

OPERATING COSTS OF SPS 2017–18

Staff costs	£170,437,000
Total income	(£7,389,000)
Total operating expenditure	£331,518,000
Net operating expenditure	£324,129,000

Source: SPS – *Annual Report and Accounts 2017–18*

NORTHERN IRELAND PRISON SERVICE

Dundonald House, Upper Newtownards Road, Belfast BT4 3SU
T 028-9052 2922 **E** niprisonservice@nics.gov.uk
W www.justice-ni.gov.uk/topics/prisons

SALARIES
from 1 April 2018

Governor in Charge (Maghaberry)	£75,875–£82,375
Governor in Charge	£68,535–£75,035
Head of Function	£54,350–£58,775
Head of Unit	£48,750–£52,600
Senior Prison Officer	£37,680–£42,276
Main Grade Prison Officer	£34,121–£38,688
Custody Prison Officer	£23,950–£29,470
Operational Support Grade	£23,950
Prisoner Custody Officer (PCO)*	£20,026–£21,798

* 35-hour/week

MANAGEMENT BOARD
Director-General (Chair), Ronnie Armour
Permanent Secretary, Peter May
Directors, Louise Blair *(Finance);* Paul Doran *(Rehabilitation);* Brendan Giffen *(Strategy and Governance);* Austin Treacy, OBE *(Prisons);* Jacqui Wallace *(HR)*
Non-Executive Directors, Dale Ashford; Claire Keatinge

OPERATING COSTS OF NORTHERN IRELAND PRISON SERVICE 2016–17

Staff costs	£61,606,000
Operating income	£2,732,000
Total operating expenditure	£106,602,000
Net operating expenditure	£103,870,000

Source: NI Prison Service – *Annual Report and Accounts 2017–18*

PRISON ESTABLISHMENTS

ENGLAND AND WALES *as at June 2019*

Prison	Address	Capacity	Prisoners	Governor/Director
†‡ ALTCOURSE	Liverpool L9 7LH	1,164	1,147	Steve Williams
ASHFIELD	Bristol BS16 9QJ	400	398	Martin Booth
*‡ ASKHAM GRANGE	York YO23 3FT	128	112	Natalie McKee
‡ AYLESBURY	Bucks HP20 1EH	209	200	Laura Sapwell
BEDFORD	Bedford MK40 1HG	411	347	Patrick Butler
BELMARSH	London SE28 0EB	906	806	Rob Davis, OBE
BERWYN	Wrexham, LL13 9QE	1,400	1,361	Nick Leader
BIRMINGHAM	Birmingham B18 4AS	977	925	Paul Newton
BLANTYRE HOUSE	Kent TN17 2NH	–	–	James Bourke
†‡ BRINSFORD	Wolverhampton WV10 7PY	577	554	Heather Whithead
†‡ BRISTOL	Bristol BS7 8PS	520	463	Steve Cross
BRIXTON	London SW2 5XF	798	737	Dave Bamford
* BRONZEFIELD	Middlesex TW15 3JZ	567	530	Ian Whiteside
BUCKLEY HALL	Lancs OL12 9DP	459	'449	Rob Knight
BULLINGDON	Oxon OX25 1PZ	1,114	1,055	Ian Blakeman
BURE	Norfolk NR10 5GB	656	653	Simon Rhoden
† CARDIFF	Cardiff CF24 0UG	779	722	Helen Ryder
CHANNINGS WOOD	Devon TQ12 6DW	724	690	Richard Luscombe
‡ CHELMSFORD	Essex CM2 6LQ	700	665	Penny Bartlett
COLDINGLEY	Surrey GU24 9EX	426	421	Jo Sims
‡ COOKHAM WOOD	Kent ME1 3LU	188	164	Paul Durham
DARTMOOR	Devon PL20 6RR	640	628	Bridie Oakes-Richards
‡ DEERBOLT	Co. Durham DL12 9BG	387	354	Gavin O'Malley
DONCASTER (private prison)	Doncaster DN5 8UX	1,145	1,081	Jerry Spencer
† DOVEGATE (private prison)	Staffs ST14 8XR	1,160	1,150	John Hewitson
* DOWNVIEW	Surrey SM2 5PD	293	273	Natasha Wilson
* DRAKE HALL	Staffs ST21 6LQ	340	333	Carl Hardwick
† DURHAM	Durham DH1 3HU	996	918	Phil Husband (*acting*)
* EAST SUTTON PARK	Kent ME17 3DF	101	96	Robin Eldridge
* EASTWOOD PARK	Glos GL12 8DB	432	396	Suzy Dymond-White
† ELMLEY	Kent ME12 4DZ	1,212	1,159	Paul Woods
ERLESTOKE	Wilts SN10 5TU	524	507	Tim Knight
†‡ EXETER	Devon EX4 4EX	545	488	Dave Atkinson
FEATHERSTONE	Wolverhampton WV10 7PU	637	611	Babafemi Dada
†‡ FELTHAM	Middx TW13 4ND	568	470	Emily Martin
FORD	W. Sussex BN18 0BX	544	538	Stephen Fradley
‡ FOREST BANK	Salford M27 8FB	1,460	1,430	Matt Spencer
* FOSTON HALL	Derby DE65 5DN	336	286	Andrea Black
FRANKLAND	Durham DH1 5YD	852	838	Gavin O'Malley
FULL SUTTON	York YO41 1PS	574	521	Gareth Sands
GARTH	Preston PR26 8NE	845	817	Steve Pearson
GARTREE	Leics LE16 7RP	'708	678	Ali Barker
GRENDON	Bucks HP18 0TL	568	538	Jamie Bennett
GUYS MARSH	Dorset SP7 0AH	396	387	Jamie Lucas
HATFIELD (AND MOORLAND)	S. Yorks DN7 6EL	1,384	1,328	Julie Spence
HAVERIGG	Cumbria LA18 4NA	269	264	Tony Corcoran
HEWELL	Worcs B97 6QS	1,115	1,094	Clare Pearson
HIGH DOWN	Surrey SM2 5PJ	1,203	1,107	Sally Hill
HIGHPOINT	Suffolk CB8 9YG	1,325	1,279	Nigel Smith
‡ HINDLEY	Lancs WN2 5TH	578	547	Mark Livingston
‡ HOLLESLEY BAY	Suffolk IP12 3JW	485	481	Gary Newnes
HOLME HOUSE	Stockton-on-Tees TS18 2QU	1,210	1,199	Chris Dyer
HULL	Hull HU9 5LS	1,036	989	Anthony Oliver
HUMBER	E. Yorks HU15 2JZ	1,062	937	Marcella Goligher
§ HUNTERCOMBE	Oxon RG9 5SB	480	464	David Redhouse
‡ ISIS	Thamesmead SE28 0NZ	628	622	Emily Thomas
ISLE OF WIGHT	Isle of Wight PO30 5RS	1,053	1,016	Doug Graham
KIRKHAM	Lancs PR4 2RN	657	644	Dan Cooper
KIRKLEVINGTON GRANGE	Cleveland TS15 9PA	283	279	Angie Petit
†‡ LANCASTER FARMS	Lancaster LA1 3QZ	560	551	Peter Francis
LEEDS	Leeds LS12 2TJ	1,212	1,066	Steven Robson
LEICESTER	Leicester LE2 7AJ	411	302	Jim Donaldson
‡ LEWES	E. Sussex BN7 1EA	606	514	Stephen Fradley
LEYHILL	Glos GL12 8BT	515	511	Neil Lavis
† LINCOLN	Lincoln LN2 4BD	629	514	Paul Yates
LINDHOLME	Doncaster DN7 6EE	945	938	Simon Walters
LITTLEHEY	Cambs PE28 0SR	1,220	1,205	Stephen Ruddy
LIVERPOOL	Liverpool L9 3DF	700	670	Pia Sinha
LONG LARTIN	Worcs WR11 8TZ	602	584	Jamie Bennett
* LOW NEWTON	Durham DH1 5YA	352	314	Gabrielle Lee
LOWDHAM GRANGE (private prison)	Notts NG14 7DA	888	878	Mark Hanson

Prison	Address	Average Daily	Max Number	Governor/Director
§ MAIDSTONE	Kent ME14 1UZ	600	585	Dave Atkinson
† MANCHESTER	Manchester M60 9AH	1,072	918	Rob Young
§ MORTON HALL	Lincoln LN6 9PT	392	254	Karen Head
The MOUNT	Herts HP3 0NZ	1,028	990	Kevin Leggett
*‡ NEW HALL	W. Yorks WF4 4XX	425	358	Natalie McKee
NORTH SEA CAMP	Lincs PE22 0QX	420	411	Michelle Quirke
NORTHUMBERLAND	Northumberland NE65 9XG	1,348	1,342	Nick Leader
† NORWICH	Norfolk NR1 4LU	773	719	Declan Moore
NOTTINGHAM	Notts NG5 3AG	800	787	Phil Novis
OAKWOOD	W. Midlands WV10 7QD	2,106	2,080	John McLaughlin
ONLEY	Warks CV23 8AP	734	730	Matthew Tilt
‡ PARC	Bridgend CF35 6AP	1,699	1,631	Janet Wallsgrove
PENTONVILLE	London N7 8TT	1,098	1,065	Darren Hughes
* PETERBOROUGH	Peterborough PE3 7PD	1,240	1,149	Damian Evans
‡ PORTLAND	Dorset DT5 1DL	530	518	Steve Hodson
PRESTON	Lancs PR1 5AB	811	697	Steve Lawrence
RANBY	Notts DN22 8EU	1,038	1,014	Nigel Hirst
RISLEY	Cheshire WA3 6BP	1,014	1,066	Nicki Smith
‡ ROCHESTER	Kent ME1 3QS	695	680	Dean Gardiner
RYE HILL	Warks CV23 8SZ	664	660	Pete Small
* SEND	Surrey GU23 7LJ	282	268	Carlene Dixon
STAFFORD	Stafford ST16 3AW	751	750	Ralph Lubkowski
STANDFORD HILL	Kent ME12 4AA	464	459	Dawn Mauldon
STOCKEN	Rutland LE15 7RD	913	864	Neil Thomas
† STOKE HEATH	Shropshire TF9 2JL	782	755	John Huntington
* STYAL	Cheshire SK9 4HR	486	461	Kate Robinson
‡ SUDBURY	Derbys DE6 5HW	581	579	Adrian Turner
SWALESIDE	Kent ME12 4AX	1,112	1,064	Mark Icke
SWANSEA	Swansea SA1 3SR	497	419	Graham Barrett
‡ SWINFEN HALL	Staffs WS14 9QS	594	574	Ian West
THAMESIDE	London SE28 0FJ	1,232	1,200	Craig Thomson
THORN CROSS	Cheshire WA4 4RL	385	384	Mick Povall
USK/PRESCOED	Monmouthshire NP15 1XP	526	519	Giles Mason
VERNE	Dorset DT5 1EQ	580	480	David Bourne
WAKEFIELD	W. Yorks WF2 9AG	750	723	Tom Wheatley
WANDSWORTH	London SW18 3HU	1,540	1,496	Jeanne Bryant
WARREN HILL	Suffolk IP12 3BF	258	240	Dave Nickolson
WAYLAND	Norfolk IP25 6RL	940	931	Sonia Walsh
WEALSTUN	W. Yorks LS23 7AZ	832	804	Diane Lewis
‡ WERRINGTON	Stoke-on-Trent ST9 0DX	118	116	Ian Darlington
‡ WETHERBY	W. Yorks LS22 5ED	336	223	Andrew Dickinson
WHATTON	Nottingham NG13 9FQ	841	836	Lynn Saunders, OBE
WHITEMOOR	Cambs PE15 0PR	458	451	Will Styles
WINCHESTER	Winchester SO22 5DF	500	474	James Bourke
WOODHILL	Bucks MK4 4DA	622	571	Nicola Marfleet
WORMWOOD SCRUBS	London W12 0AE	1,096	1,039	Sarah Pennington
WYMOTT	Preston PR26 8LW	1,169	1,149	Graham Beck

SCOTLAND *as at June 2019*

Prison	Address	Average Daily	Max. Number	Governor/Director
ADDIEWELL	West Lothian EH55 8QA	696	702	Ian Whitehead
†‡ BARLINNIE	Glasgow G33 2QX	1,127	1,195	Michael Stoney
CASTLE HUNTLY (Open Estate)	Dundee DD2 5HL	189	X	Gerry Michie
*†‡ CORNTON VALE	Stirling FK9 5NU	86	96	Jacqueline Clinton
† DUMFRIES	Dumfries DG2 9AX	172	180	Linda Dorward
*† EDINBURGH	Edinburgh EH11 3LN	872	913	David Abernethy
GLENOCHIL	Tullibody FK10 3AD	641	667	Andrew Hodge
*‡ GRAMPIAN	Peterhead AB42 2YY	449	474	Mike Hebden (*acting*)
*† GREENOCK	Greenock PA16 9AJ	248	257	Karen Smith
† INVERNESS	Inverness IV2 3HH	110	137	Stephen Coyle
† KILMARNOCK (private prison)	Kilmarnock KA1 5AA	499	509	Michael Guy
LOW MOSS	Glasgow G64 2PZ	757	778	James Farish
† PERTH	Perth PH2 8AT	617	654	Fraser Munro
*†‡ POLMONT	Falkirk FK2 0AB	470	522	Brenda Stewart
SHOTTS	Lanarkshire ML7 4LE	531	540	Allister Purdie

NORTHERN IRELAND *as at June 2019*

Prison	Address	Prisoners	Governor/Director
* HYDEBANK WOOD	Belfast BT8 8NA	152	Richard Taylor
†§ MAGHABERRY	Co. Antrim BT28 2NF	857	David Kennedy
MAGILLIGAN	Co. Londonderry BT49 0LR	430	Richard Taylor

* Women's establishment or establishment with units for women
† Remand Centre or establishment with units for remand prisoners
‡ Young Offender Institution or establishment with units for young offenders
§ Immigration Removal Centre or establishment with units for immigration detainees

DEFENCE

The armed forces of the UK comprise the Royal Navy, the Army and the Royal Air Force (RAF). The Queen is Commander-in-Chief of all the armed forces. The Secretary of State for Defence is responsible for the formulation and content of defence policy and for providing the means by which it is conducted. The formal legal basis for the conduct of defence in the UK rests on a range of powers vested by statute and letters patent in the Defence Council, chaired by the Secretary of State for Defence. Beneath the ministers lies the top management of the Ministry of Defence (MoD), headed jointly by the Permanent Secretary and the Chief of the Defence Staff. The Permanent Secretary is the government's principal civilian adviser on defence and has the primary responsibility for policy, finance, management and administration. The Permanent Secretary is also personally accountable to parliament for the expenditure of all public money allocated to defence purposes. The Chief of the Defence Staff is the professional head of the armed forces in the UK and the principal military adviser to the secretary of state and the government.

The Defence Board is the executive of the Defence Council. Chaired by the Permanent Secretary, it acts as the main executive board of the Ministry of Defence, providing senior level leadership and strategic management of defence.

The Central Staff, headed by the Vice-Chief of the Defence Staff and the Second Permanent Under-Secretary of State, is the policy core of the department. Defence Equipment and Support, headed by the Chief of Defence Materiel, is responsible for purchasing defence equipment and providing logistical support to the armed forces.

A permanent Joint Headquarters for the conduct of joint operations was set up at Northwood in 1996. The Joint Headquarters connects the policy and strategic functions of the MoD head office with the conduct of operations and is intended to strengthen the policy/executive division.

The UK pursues its defence and security policies through its membership of NATO (to which most of its armed forces are committed), the Organisation for Security and Cooperation in Europe and the UN (see International Organisations section).

STRENGTH OF THE REGULAR ARMED FORCES

	Royal Navy	Army	RAF	All Services
1975 strength	76,200	167,100	95,000	338,300
2000 strength	42,850	110,050	54,720	207,620
2005 strength	39,940	109,290	51,870	201,100
2010 strength	38,730	108,920	44,050	191,700
2011 strength	37,660	106,240	42,460	186,360
2012 strength	35,540	104,250	40,000	179,800
2013 strength	33,960	99,730	37,030	170,710
2014 strength	33,330	91,070	35,230	159,630
2015 strength	32,740	87,060	33,930	153,720
2016 strength	32,502	85,038	33,456	150,966
2017 strength	32,544	83,561	33,261	149,366
2018 strength	32,483	81,116	32,957	146,556
2019 strength	32,537	79,029	32,862	144,428
2020 strength	33,050	78,876	32,820	144,746

Source: MoD – Defence Statistics (Tri-Service)

UK REGULAR ARMED FORCES BY RANK 2020

Officers	27,752
Other Ranks	117,565

Source: MoD – Defence Statistics (Tri-Service)

UK regular forces include trained and untrained personnel and nursing services, but exclude Gurkhas, full-time reserve service personnel, mobilised reservists and naval activated reservists. As at 1 July 2020 these groups numbered:

All Gurkhas	3,752
Full-time reserve service	5,345
Mobilised reservists	2,854
Army	2,200
RAF	434
Royal Navy	220

Source: MoD – Defence Statistics (Tri-Service)

CIVILIAN PERSONNEL

2000 level	121,300
2005 level	107,680
2006 level	102,970
2007 level	95,790
2008 level	89,499
2009 level	86,621
2010 level	85,850
2011 level	83,063
2012 level	71,008
2013 level	65,400
2014 level	62,501
2015 level	58,161
2016 level	56,243
2017 level	56,675
2018 level	56,865
2019 level	57,760
2020 level	58,256

Source: MoD – Defence Statistics (Tri-Service)

UK REGULAR FORCES: DEATHS

In 2018 there were a total of 61 deaths among the UK regular armed forces, of which 12 were serving in the Royal Navy and Royal Marines, 38 in the Army and 11 in the RAF. The largest single cause of death was cancers, which accounted for 10 deaths (16 per cent of the total) in 2018. Land transport accidents accounted for 10 deaths (16 per cent) and other accidents provisionally accounted for a further 22 deaths (36 per cent). There was one death as a result of hostile action. Suicides and open verdicts accounted for five deaths.

NUMBER OF DEATHS AND MORTALITY RATES

	2015	2016	2017	2018	2019
Total number	60	72	73	61	66
Royal Navy	11	17	12	12	9
Army	39	41	40	38	40
RAF	10	14	11	11	17
Mortality rates per thousand					
Tri-service rate	0.39	0.47	0.42	0.41	0.45
Navy	0.32	0.52	0.36	0.34	0.27
Army	0.45	0.47	0.49	0.46	0.54
RAF	0.28	0.36	0.27	0.29	0.43

Source: MoD National Statistics

NUCLEAR FORCES

The Vanguard Class SSBN (ship submersible ballistic nuclear) provides the UK's strategic nuclear deterrent. Each Vanguard Class submarine is capable of carrying 16 Trident II D5 missiles equipped with nuclear warheads.

There is a ballistic missile early warning system station at RAF Fylingdales in North Yorkshire.

ARMS CONTROL

The 1990 Conventional Armed Forces in Europe (CFE) Treaty, which commits all NATO and former Warsaw Pact members to limiting their holdings of five major classes of conventional weapons, has been adapted to reflect the changed geo-strategic environment and negotiations continue for its implementation. The Open Skies Treaty, which the UK signed in 1992 and entered into force in 2002, allows for the overflight of states parties by other states parties using unarmed observation aircraft.

The UN Convention on Certain Conventional Weapons (as amended 2001), which bans or restricts the use of specific types of weapons that are considered to cause unnecessary or unjustifiable suffering to combatants, or to affect civilians indiscriminately, was ratified by the UK in 1995. In 1968 the UK signed and ratified the Nuclear Non-Proliferation Treaty, which came into force in 1970 and was indefinitely and unconditionally extended in 1995. In 1996 the UK signed the Comprehensive Nuclear Test Ban Treaty and ratified it in 1998. The UK is a party to the 1972 Biological and Toxin Weapons Convention, which provides for a worldwide ban on biological weapons, and the 1993 Chemical Weapons Convention, which came into force in 1997 and provides for a verifiable worldwide ban on chemical weapons.

DEFENCE BUDGET

DEPARTMENTAL EXPENDITURE LIMITS
£ billion

	2020–21
Resource DEL	30.8
Capital DEL	10.6
Total	41.4

Source: HM Treasury – The Budget 2020 (Crown copyright)

MINISTRY OF DEFENCE

Main Building, Whitehall, London SW1A 2HB
T 020-7218 9000
W www.gov.uk/government/organisations/ministry-of-defence

Secretary of State for Defence, Rt. Hon. Ben Wallace, MP
Parliamentary Private Secretary, Jack Brereton, MP
Special Advisers, Peter Quentin
Minister of State, Jeremy Quin, MP (Armed Forces)
Minister of State, Baroness Goldie (Lords)
Parliamentary Under-Secretary of State and Minister for the Armed Forces, James Heappey, MP
Parliamentary Under-Secretary of State and Minister for Defence People and Veterans, Johnny Mercer, MP

CHIEFS OF STAFF

Chief of the Defence Staff, Gen. Sir Nick Carter, GCB, CBE, DSO, ADC
Vice-Chief of the Defence Staff, Adm. Sir Tim Fraser, KCB, ADC
Chief of Naval Staff and First Sea Lord, Adm. Tony Radakin, CB, ADC
Second Sea Lord and Deputy Chief of Naval Staff, Vice-Adm. Nicholas Hine, CB
Chief of the General Staff, Gen. Sir Mark Carleton-Smith, KCB, CBE, ADC
Deputy Chief of the General Staff, Lt.-Gen. Christopher Tickell, CBE

Chief of the Air Staff, Air Chief Marshal Mike Wigston, CBE, ADC
Assistant Chief of the Air Staff, Air Vice-Marshal Ian Gale, MBE
Commander of Strategic Command, Gen. Patrick Sanders, KCB, CBE, DSO, ADC
Deputy Commander of Strategic Command, Lt.-Gen. Rob Magowan, CB, CBE

SENIOR OFFICIALS

Permanent Secretary, Sir Stephen Lovegrove, KCB
Chief Scientific Adviser, Prof. Dame Angela McLean, DBE
Chief Scientific Adviser (Nuclear), Prof. Robin Grimes, FRS, FRENG
Director-General Finance, Charlie Pate

THE DEFENCE COUNCIL

The Defence Council is chaired by the Secretary of State, and comprises the other ministers, the Permanent Under-Secretary, the Chief of Defence Staff and senior service officers and officials who head the armed services and the department's major corporate functions. It provides the formal legal basis for the conduct of UK defence through a range of powers vested in it by statute and letters patent.

THE DEFENCE BOARD

The Defence Board is the main corporate board of the MoD, providing senior level leadership and strategic management of defence. The Defence Board is the highest committee in the MoD, responsible for the full range of defence business, other than the conduct of operations.

MANAGEMENT BOARD

Permanent Secretary, Sir Stephen Lovegrove, KCB
Members, Mike Baker, CBE (Chief Operating Officer); Lt.-Gen. Doug Chalmers (Deputy Chief of Defence Staff (Military Strategy and Operations)); Charlie Forte (Chief Information Officer); Prof. Robin Grimes, FRS, FRENG (Chief Scientific Adviser (Nuclear)); Air Marshal Richard Knighton (Deputy Chief of the Defence Staff (Financial and Military Capability)); Angus Lapsley (Strategy and International); Prof. Dame Angela McLean, DBE (Chief Scientific Adviser); Vanessa Nicholls (Nuclear); Charlie Pate (Finance); Lt.-Gen. James Swift, OBE (Chief of Defence People); Dominic Wilson (Security Policy)
Non-Executive Members, Brian McBride (Lead); Simon Henry; Danuta Gray; Robin Marshall

CENTRAL STAFF

Vice-Chief of the Defence Staff, Adm. Sir Tim Fraser, KCB, ADC

STRATEGIC COMMAND

Commander of Strategic Command, Gen. Patrick Sanders, CBE, DSO, ADC
Deputy Commander of Strategic Command, Lt.-Gen. Rob Magowan, CB, CBE
Commander of Joint Operations, Vice-Adm. Benjamin Key, CBE
Chief of Defence Intelligence, Lt.-Gen. Jim Hockenhull, OBE
Chief Defence Logistics Support, Lt.-Gen. Richard Wardlaw, OBE

FLEET COMMAND

First Sea Lord, Adm. Tony Radakin, CB, ADC
Fleet Commander and Chief Naval Warfare Officer, Vice-Adm. Jeremy Kyd, CBE

NAVAL HOME COMMAND

Second Sea Lord, Vice-Adm. Nicholas Hine, CB

LAND FORCES

Commander Field Army, Lt.-Gen. Ivan Jones, CB
Deputy Commander Field Army, Maj.-Gen. Celia Harvey, OBE, QVRM, TD

AIR COMMAND

Deputy Commander Operations and Air Member for Operations, Air Marshal Gerry Mayhew, CBE

Deputy Commander Capability and Air Member for Personnel and Capability, Air Marshal Andrew Turner, CB, CBE

DEFENCE EQUIPMENT AND SUPPORT

Chief Executive, Sir Simon Bollom

Deputy Chief Executive, Adrian Baguley

Director General (Ships), Vice-Adm. Chris Gardner, CBE

Director General (Land), Chris Bushell

Chief of Materiel (Air), Air Marshal Sir Julian Young, CB, KBE

EXECUTIVE AGENCIES

For a full list, *see* Executive Agencies: Ministry of Defence.

DEFENCE ELECTRONICS AND COMPONENTS AGENCY

Welsh Road, Deeside, Flintshire CH5 2LS **T** 01244-847694

E decainfo@deca.mod.uk

W www.gov.uk/defence-electronics-and-components-agency

The Defence Electronics and Components Agency (DECA) provides maintenance, repair, overhaul, upgrade and procurement in avionics, electronics and components fields to support the MoD. As a 'trading' executive agency DECA is run along commercial lines with funding for DECA's activities being generated entirely by payments for delivery of services provided to the MoD and other private sector customers. DECA currently has an annual turnover of around £25m and employs over 400 staff across its head office and main operating centre in North Wales, a site in Stafford and various deployed locations across the UK.

Chief Executive, Geraint Spearing

DEFENCE SCIENCE AND TECHNOLOGY LABORATORY

Porton Down, Salisbury, Wiltshire SP4 0JQ **T** 01980-950000

E centralenquiries@dstl.gov.uk

W www.gov.uk/defence-science-and-technology-laboratory

The Defence Science and Technology Laboratory (DSTL) supplies specialist science and technology services to the MoD and wider government.

Chief Executive, Adrian Belton

UK HYDROGRAPHIC OFFICE

Admiralty Way, Taunton, Somerset TA1 2DN

T 01823-484444

E customerservices@ukho.gov.uk

W www.gov.uk/uk-hydrographic-office

The UK Hydrographic Office (UKHO) collects and supplies hydrographic and geospatial data for the Royal Navy and merchant shipping, to protect lives at sea. Working with other national hydrographic offices, UKHO sets and raises global standards of hydrography, cartography and navigation.

Chief Executive (Acting), Rear-Adm. Peter Sparkes

ARMED FORCES TRAINING AND RECRUITMENT

From Naval Bases at Portsmouth, Plymouth, the Clyde in Scotland and a small team at Northwood in Middlesex, Flag Officer Sea Training (FOST) provides Fleet Operational Sea Training for all surface ships, submarines, Royal Fleet Auxiliaries and Strike Groups of the Royal Navy. All aspects of naval training are offered by FOST including new entry, officer, Royal Marine, submarine, surface and aviation training. FOST also offers specialist training in a number of areas including hydrography, meteorology, oceanography, marine engineering and diving.

The Army Recruiting and Training Division (ARTD) is responsible for the four key areas of army training: soldier initial training, at the School of Infantry or at one of the army's four other facilities; officer initial training at the Royal Military Academy Sandhurst; trade training at one of the army's specialist facilities; and resettlement training for those about to leave the army. Trade training facilities include: the Armour Centre; the Infantry Battle School; the Infantry Training Centre, Catterick; the Royal School of Military Engineering and the Army Aviation Centre.

The Royal Air Force No. 22 (Training) Group is responsible for the recruitment, selection, initial and professional training of RAF personnel as well as providing trained specialist personnel to the armed forces as a whole, such as providing the army air corps with trained helicopter pilots. The group is split into five areas: RAF College Cranwell; the Air Cadet Organisation (ACO); the Directorate of Flying Training (DFT); the Directorate of Ground Training; and the Defence College of Technical Training.

The Defence College of Technical Training provides technical training to all three services and includes the Defence School of Communications Information Systems (DSCIS); the Defence School of Electronic and Mechanical Engineering (DSEME); and the Defence School of Marine Engineering (DSMarE).

USEFUL WEBSITES

W www.royalnavy.mod.uk

W www.army.mod.uk

W www.raf.mod.uk

THE ROYAL NAVY

In Order of Seniority as at 1 January 2021

LORD HIGH ADMIRAL OF THE UNITED KINGDOM
HRH The Prince Philip, Duke of Edinburgh, KG, KT, OM, GCVO, GBE, GBE, ONZ, QSO, AK, PC, GCL, CMM *apptd* 2011

ADMIRALS OF THE FLEET
HRH The Prince Philip, Duke of Edinburgh, KG, KT, OM, GCVO, GBE, GBE, ONZ, QSO, AK, PC, GCL, CMM, *apptd* 1953
Sir Benjamin Bathurst, GCB, *apptd* 1995
HRH The Prince of Wales, KG, KT, GCB, OM, AK, QSO, CC, ADC, *apptd* 2012
Lord Boyce, KG, GCB, OBE, *apptd* 2014

ADMIRALS
(Former Chiefs or Vice Chiefs of Defence Staff and First Sea Lords who remain on the active list)
Slater, Sir Jock, GCB, LVO, *apptd* 1991
Essenhigh, Sir Nigel, GCB, *apptd* 1998
West of Spithead, Lord, GCB, DSC, PC, *apptd* 2000
Band, Sir Jonathon, GCB, *apptd* 2002
Stanhope, Sir Mark, GCB, OBE, *apptd* 2004
Zambellas, Sir George, GCB, DSC, *apptd* 2012
Jones, Sir Philip, KCB, ADC, *apptd* 2016
Messenger, Sir Gordon, KBC, DSO, *apptd* 2016

ADMIRALS
HRH The Princess Royal, KG, KT, GCVO, QSO *(Adm. Chief Commandant for Women in the Royal Navy; Cdre-in-Chief Portsmouth)*
Radakin, Antony, CB, ADC *(First Sea Lord and Chief of Naval Staff)*
Fraser, Tim, KBC, ADC *(Vice-Chief of the Defence Staff)*

VICE-ADMIRALS
HRH The Duke of York, KG, GCVO, ADC *(Cdre-in-Chief Fleet Air Arm)*
Key, Benjamin, KCB, CBE *(Chief of Joint Operations)*
Bennett, Paul, CB, OBE *(Chief of Staff, Supreme Allied Cdr (Transformation))*
Kyd, Jeremy, CBE *(Fleet Cdr and Chief Naval Warfare Officer)*
Gardner, Chris, CBE *(Director General (Ships))*
Hine, Nicholas, CB *(Second Sea Lord and Deputy Chief of Naval Staff)*
Blount, Keith, CB, OBE *(Cdr Maritime Command)*
Thompson, Richard, CBE *(Director General (Air))*

LIEUTENANT-GENERALS
Magowan, Robert, CB, CBE *(Deputy Cdr UK Strategic Command)*

REAR-ADMIRALS
Beckett, Keith, CBE *(Chief Strategic Systems Executive)*
Hodgson, Timothy, CB, MBE *(Director Submarine Capability)*
Halton, Paul, OBE *(Director Submarine Readiness)*
Robinson, Guy, OBE *(Deputy Cdr Naval Striking and Support Forces NATO)*
Briers, Matthew *(Director Carrier Strike)*
Morley, James *(Director Capability UK Strategic Command)*
Toy, Malcolm *(Director (Technical) Military Aviation Authority)*
Kyte, Andrew, CB *(Assistant Chief of the Defence Staff (Logistics Operations))*

Beard, Hugh *(Assistant Chief of Naval Staff (Capability and Force Design))*
Connell, Martin, CBE *(Director Force Generation)*
Burns, Andrew, OBE *(Director Develop)*
Marshall, Paul, CBE *(Director Naval Acquisition)*
Macleod, James, CB *(Assistant Chief of Defence Staff (Personnel Capability) and Defence Services Secretary)*
Hally, Philip, MBE *(Director People and Training; Naval Secretary)*
Betton, Andrew, OBE *(Deputy Cdr Joint Force Command Norfolk)*
Asquith, Simon, OBE *(Commander Operations)*
Sparkes, Peter *(National Hydrographer; Chief Executive UK Hydrographic Office (acting))*
Utley, Michael, CB, OBE *(Commander UK Strike Force)*
Hatcher, Rhett *(Director Data Acquisition)*
Lower, Iain *(Assistant Chief of the Naval Staff)*

ROYAL MARINES

CAPTAIN-GENERAL
Position in abeyance

GENERAL
Messenger, Sir Gordon, KCB, DSO*, OBE, ADC

MAJOR-GENERALS
Bevis, Timothy, CBE *(Director Operations and Plans, International Military Staff)*
Magowan, Robert, CB, CBE *(Assistant Chief of the Defence Staff (Capability and Force Design))*
Holmes, Matthew, CBE, DSO *(Cdr UK Amphibious Forces and Commandant-General Royal Marines)*
Jenkins, Gwyn, OBE *(Assistant Chief of Naval Staff (Policy))*
Stickland, Charles, CB, OBE *(Assistant Chief of the Defence Staff (Commitments))*
Morris, Jim, DSO *(Director of Joint Warfare)*

The Royal Marines, formed in 1664, are the Royal Navy's elite, amphibious commando force. Capable of operating in the littoral, land and maritime environment their principal operational formation is an all-arms force, 3 Commando Brigade RM, comprising of:
- 40 and 45 Commando RM, based in Taunton and Arbroath, are the force's very high readiness response and forward presence units
- 42 Commando RM, based in Plymouth, is the maritime operations commando unit. They are optimised for boarding operations and maritime interdiction as well as partnering and assistance operations alongside key international allies
- 47 Commando Raiding Group RM, the commando force's surface manoeuvre specialists, provide littoral manoeuvre support to the whole force and enable all its activity. They are based in Devonport Naval Base, Plymouth
- 43 Commando Fleet Protection Group RM provide specialist military support for the protection of the nation's strategic nuclear deterrent. They are based in Faslane Naval Base, Scotland
- 30 Commando Information Exploitation Group RM are the force's information, surveillance and reconnaissance specialists. They are based in Plymouth
- Commando Logistics Regiment RM provide intimate logistical and medical support to every unit in the force. They are located in Chivenor, North Devon

- 24 Commando Royal Engineers and 29 Commando Royal Artillery, based in Chivenor and Plymouth, provide the force with specialist engineering and fires capability

The Royal Marines also provide detachments for warships and land-based naval parties as required.

ROYAL MARINES RESERVES (RMR)

The Royal Marines Reserve is a commando-trained volunteer force with the principal role of supporting the Royal Marines. This can be through mobilisation or other full-time or part-time service. The RMR consists of approximately 670 trained ranks who are distributed between the four RMR Units in the UK. Approximately 10 per cent of the RMR are working with the regular corps on long-term attachments within all of the Royal Marines regular units.

OTHER PARTS OF THE NAVAL SERVICE

FLEET AIR ARM

The Fleet Air Arm (FAA) provides the Royal Navy with a multi-role aviation combat capability able to operate autonomously at short notice worldwide in all environments, over the sea and land. The FAA numbers some 4,500 regulars and 430 reserves. It operates some 200 combat aircraft and more than 50 support/training aircraft.

ROYAL FLEET AUXILIARY (RFA)

The Royal Fleet Auxiliary is a 1,852-strong civilian-manned flotilla of 13 ships owned by the MoD. Its primary role is to supply the Royal Navy and host nations while at sea with fuel, ammunition, food and spares, enabling them to maintain operations away from their home ports. It also provides amphibious support and secure sea transport for military units and their equipment. The ships routinely support and embark Royal Naval Air Squadrons.

ROYAL NAVAL RESERVE (RNR)

The Royal Naval Reserve is an integral part of the Royal Navy. It is an auxiliary and contingent force of around 3,000 trained personnel who provide support to maritime operations and wider defence tasks in peacetime or conflict.

The Royal Naval Reserve has 15 units throughout the UK, one of which, HMS Ferret, provides specialist intelligence capability. Basic training is provided at HMS Raleigh, Torpoint in Cornwall for ratings and at the Britannia Royal Naval College, Dartmouth in Devon for officers.

Reservists usually serve part-time unless mobilised for an operational tour of duty and are expected to fulfil a commitment of 24 days a year, comprising 12 days continuous training and 12 days non-continuous training.

QUEEN ALEXANDRA'S ROYAL NAVAL NURSING SERVICE

The first nursing sisters were appointed to naval hospitals in 1884 and the Queen Alexandra's Royal Naval Nursing Service (QARNNS) gained its current title in 1902. Today QARNNS is a branch of the Royal Naval Medical Service that is committed to supporting the medical component of Royal Naval operational capability. QARNNS trains and employs nurses in a wide variety of specialities including emergency nursing, intensive care, burns and plastics, trauma and orthopaedics, surgical, medical and ophthalmology.

QARNNS is ready to deploy anywhere in the world to support global naval operations; recent deployments have included fighting the Ebola outbreak in Sierra Leone and helping to save lives in the Mediterranean.

Patron, HRH Princess Alexandra, the Hon. Lady Ogilvy, KG, GCVO

Head of the Naval Nursing Service, Capt. Lisa Taylor

HM FLEET

as at December 2020

Submarines	
Vanguard Class	Vanguard, Vengeance, Victorious, Vigilant
Trafalgar Class	Talent, Trenchant, Triumph
Astute Class	Artful, Astute, Ambush, Audacious
Aircraft Carrier	Queen Elizabeth, Prince of Wales
Landing Platform Dock (Albion Class)	Albion, Bulwark
Destroyers	
Daring Class (Type 45)	Daring, Dauntless, Defender, Diamond, Dragon, Duncan
Frigates	
Duke Class (Type 23)	Argyll, Iron Duke, Kent, Lancaster, Monmouth, Montrose, Northumberland, Portland, Richmond, St Albans, Somerset, Sutherland, Westminster
Mine Warfare Vessels	
Hunt Class	Brocklesby, Cattistock, Chiddingfold, Hurworth, Ledbury, Middleton
Sandown Class	Bangor, Blyth, Grimsby, Pembroke, Penzance, Ramsey, Shoreham
Patrol Vessels	
Archer Class P2000 Training Boats	Archer, Biter, Blazer, Charger, Example, Exploit, Explorer, Express, Puncher, Raider, Ranger, Sabre, Scrimatar, Smiter, Tracker, Trumpeter
Pursuer and Dasher Vessels	
Fast Patrol Boats	Sabre, Scimitar
River Class	Forth, Medway, Mersey, Severn, Tamar, Trent, Tyne, Spey
Survey Vessels	
Ice Patrol Ship	Protector
Ocean Survey Vessel	Scott
Coastal Survey Vessel	Magpie
Multi-Role Survey Vessels	Echo, Enterprise

ROYAL FLEET AUXILIARY

Landing Ship Dock (Auxiliary)	RFA Cardigan Bay, RFA Mounts Bay, RFA Lyme Bay
Tide Class	RFS Tideforce, RFA Tiderace, RFA Tidespring, RFA Tidesurge
Wave Class	RFA Wave Knight, RFA Wave Ruler
Fort Class	RFA Fort Austin, RFA Fort Rosalie, RFA Fort Victoria
Casualty Receiving Ship/ Aviation Training Facilities	RFA Argus

THE ARMY

In Order of Seniority as at 1 December 2020

THE QUEEN

FIELD MARSHALS
HRH The Prince Philip, Duke of Edinburgh, KG, KT, OM, GCVO, GBE, GBE, ONZ, QSO, AK, PC, GCL, CMM, *apptd* 1953
Sir John Chapple, GCB, CBE, *apptd* 1992
HRH The Duke of Kent, KG, GCMG, GCVO, ADC, *apptd* 1993
Lord Inge, KG, GCB, PC, *apptd* 1994
HRH The Prince of Wales, KG, KT, GCB, OM, AK, QSO, CC, ADC, *apptd* 2012
Lord Guthrie of Craigiebank, GCB, GCVO, OBE, *apptd* 2012
Lord Walker of Aldringham, GCB, CMG, CBE, *apptd* 2014

FORMER CHIEFS OF STAFF
Gen. Sir Roger Wheeler, GCB, CBE, *apptd* 1997
Gen. Sir Mike Jackson, GCB, CBE, DSO, *apptd* 2003
Gen. Sir Timothy Granville-Chapman, GBE, KCB, *apptd* 2005
Gen. Lord Dannatt, GCB, CBE, MC, *apptd* 2006
Gen. Lord Richards of Herstmonceux, GCB, CBE, DSO, *apptd* 2009
Gen. Lord Houghton of Richmond, GCB, CBE, *apptd* 2009
Gen. Sir Peter Wall, GCB, CBE, *apptd* 2010
Gen. Sir Richard Barrons, KCB, CBE, *apptd* 2013
Gen. Sir Christopher Deverell, KCB, MBE, *apptd* 2016

GENERALS
Carter, Sir Nicholas, KCB, CBE, DSO, ADC *(Chief of the Defence Staff)*
Carleton-Smith, Sir Mark, KCB, CBE, ADC *(Chief of the General Staff)*
Sanders, Sir Patrick, KCB, CBE, DSO, ADC *(Cdr Joint Forces Command)*
Radford, T., CB, DSO, OBE *(Deputy Supreme Allied Cdr Europe)*

LIEUTENANT-GENERALS
Lorimer, Sir John, KCB, DSO, MBE *(Defence Senior Adviser to the Middle East)*
Nugee, R., CB, CVO, CBE *(Climate Change and Sustainability Strategy Lead)*
Cripwell, R., CB, CBE *(Deputy Cdr NATO Land Command Izmir)*
Urch T., CBE *(Cdr Home Command)*
Chalmers, D., DSO, OBE *(Deputy Chief of the Defence Staff (Military Strategy and Operations))*
Hockenhull, J., OBE *(Chief of Defence Intelligence)*
Skeates, S., CBE *(Deputy Cdr Joint Force Command Brunssum)*
Jones, I., CB *(Cdr Field Army)*
Smyth-Osbourne, Sir Edward, KCVO, CBE *(Cdr Allied Rapid Reaction Corps)*
Tickell, C., CBE *(Deputy Chief of the General Staff)*
Wardlaw, R., OBE *(Chief of Defence Logistics and Support)*
Hill, G., CBE *(Deputy Cdr Resolute Support)*
Swift, J., OBE *(Chief of Defence People)*
Bathurst, Sir Ben, KCVO, CBE *(UK Military Representative, HQ NATO)*

MAJOR-GENERALS
Stanford, R., MBE *(Senior British Loan Service Officer – Oman)*
Bramble, W., CBE *(Deputy Cdr NATO Rapid Deployable Corps – Italy)*
Cave, I., CBE *(pending assignment; Cdr Home Command designate (from June 2021))*
Brooks-Ward, S., CVO, OBE, TD, VR *(Assistant Chief of the Defence Staff (Reserves and Cadets))*
Jones, R., CBE *(Standing Joint Force Cdr, Standing Joint Force HQ)*
Hyams, T., OBE *(Military Secretary and General Officer Scotland)*
Borton, N., DSO, MBE *(Chief of Staff (Operations), Permanent Joint HQ; Cdr Allied Rapid Reaction Corps designate (from December 2021))*
Illingworth, J., OBE *(Director Land Warfare)*
Gedney, F., OBE *(pending assignment; Senior Britush Loan Service Officer (Oman) designate (from January 2021))*
Wooddisse, R., CBE, MC *(Assistant Chief of the General Staff; Crd Field Army designate (from April 2021))*
Capps, D., CBE *(Commandant Royal Military Academy Sandhurst)*
Ford, K., CBE *(Director Policy and Capabilities Division, International Military Staff, HQ NATO)*
Copinger-Symes, T., CBE *(Director Military Digitisation)*
Walker, C., DSO *(MoD; Deputy Chief of Defence Staff (Military Strategy and Operations) designate (from June 2021))*
Cole, J., OBE *(Director Information)*
Deakin, G., CBE *(Deputy Chief of Staff Plans, Joint Force Command Naples)*
Cain, P., QHP *(Director Defence Healthcare)*
Ghika, C., CBE *(GOC London District and Maj.-Gen. The Household Division)*
Sexton, N. *(Director Engagement and Communications)*
Weir, C., DSO, MBE *(Chief of Staff Field Army)*
Bennett, J., CBE *(Director Capability)*
Langston, C., CB, QHC, CF *(Chaplain-General)*
Nesmith, S. *(Director Personnel)*
Hamilton, S., CBE *(Director Support)*
Roe, A. *(Chief Executive Defence Academy and Commandant Joint Service Command and Staff College)*
Strickland, G., DSO, MBE *(Deputy Commanding General, HQ III (USA) Corps)*
Harrison, A., DSO, MBE *(Senior British Military Advisor, US Central Command)*
McMahon, S., CBE *(pending assignment)*
Bruce of Crionaich, A., OBE, VR *(Governor of Edinburgh Castle)*
Taylor A. *(Director Army Legal Services)*
Bowder, J., OBE *(GOC 6th Division)*
Mead, J., OBE *(Chief of Staff, Headquarters Allied Rapid Reaction Corps)*
Spencer, R. *(Director Delivery, Intelligence and Expeditionary Services, Defence Digital Service Delivery and Operations)*
Southall, D., CBE *(Director Army Basing and Infrastructure)*
Thomson, R., CBE, DSO, *(Cdr British Forces Cyprus and Administrator of the Sovereign Base Areas)*
Crook, D., *(Director Land Equipment, Defence Equipment and Support)*
Elviss, M., MBE *(GOC 3rd Division)*
Eastman, D., MBE *(GOC Regional Command)*
Hutchings, OBE *(Director Joint Support, UK Strategic Command)*
Harvey, C., OBE, QVRM, TD, VR *(Deputy Cdr Field Army)*
Bell, C., CBE *(GOC ARITC)*
Humphrey, S., CBE *(pending retirement)*

Walton-Knight, R., CBE *(Director Strategy and Planning, Defence Infrastructure Organisation)*
Amison, D., CBE *(Director Development, Concepts and Doctrine Centre)*
Copsey, K., OBE *(Deputy Cdr Combined Joint Task Force, Operation Inherent Resolve)*
Anderton-Brown, R., *(Director Multi-Domain Integration Change Programme, UK Strategic Command)*
Collins, C., DSO, OBE *(GOC 1st Division)*
Graham, S., VR *(Director Reserves)*

CONSTITUTION OF THE ARMY

The army consists of the Regular Army, the Regular Reserve and the Army Reserve. It is commanded by the Chief of the General Staff, who is the professional Head of Service and Chair of the Executive Committee of the Army Board, which provides overall strategic policy and direction to the Commander Land Forces (formerly Commander-in-Chief, Land Forces). There are four subordinate commands that report to the Commander Land Forces: the Field Army; Support Command, headed by the Adjutant General; Force Development and Capability Command and the Joint Helicopter Command. The army is divided into functional arms and services, subdivided into regiments and corps (listed below in order of precedence).

During 2008, as part of the Future Army Structure (FAS) reform programme, the infantry was re-structured into large multi-battalion regiments, which involved amalgamations and changes in title for some regiments. The main changes at divisional, brigade and unit level occurred largely between mid-2014 and mid-2015. As at April 2020 there were 32 Regular Army battalions in the infantry, 16 Army Reserves battalions and 15 Royal Armoured Corps regiments. The 2010 Strategic Defence and Security Review laid out the commitments expected of the UK Armed Forces and, as a result, Army 2020 was created to replace FAS.

All enquiries with regard to records of serving personnel (Regular and Reserve) should be directed to: The Army Personnel Centre Help Desk, Kentigern House, 65 Brown Street, Glasgow G2 8EX T 0345-600 9663. Enquirers should note that the Army is governed in the release of personal information by various acts of parliament.

ORDER OF PRECEDENCE OF CORPS AND REGIMENTS OF THE BRITISH ARMY

ARMS

HOUSEHOLD CAVALRY
  The Life Guards
  The Blues and Royals (Royal Horse Guards and 1st Dragoons)

ROYAL HORSE ARTILLERY
(when on parade, the Royal Horse Artillery take precedence over the Household Cavalry)

ROYAL ARMOURED CORPS
  1st the Queen's Dragoon Guards
  The Royal Scots Dragoon Guards (Carabiniers and Greys)
  The Royal Dragoon Guards
  The Queen's Royal Hussars (The Queen's Own and Royal Irish)
  The Royal Lancers
  The King's Royal Hussars
  The Light Dragoons
  Royal Tank Regiment

ROYAL REGIMENT OF ARTILLERY
(with the exception of the Royal Horse Artillery (*see* above))

CORPS OF ROYAL ENGINEERS

ROYAL CORPS OF SIGNALS

REGIMENTS OF FOOT GUARDS
  Grenadier Guards
  Coldstream Guards
  Scots Guards
  Irish Guards
  Welsh Guards

REGIMENTS OF INFANTRY
  The Royal Regiment of Scotland
  The Princess of Wales's Royal Regiment (Queen and Royal Hampshire's)
  The Duke of Lancaster's Regiment (King's, Lancashire and Border)
  The Royal Regiment of Fusiliers
  The Royal Anglian Regiment
  The Rifles
  The Yorkshire Regiment
  The Mercian Regiment
  The Royal Welsh
  The Royal Irish Regiment
  The Parachute Regiment
  The Royal Gurkha Rifles

SPECIAL AIR SERVICE

ARMY AIR CORPS

SERVICES

ROYAL ARMY CHAPLAINS' DEPARTMENT

THE ROYAL LOGISTIC CORPS

ROYAL ARMY MEDICAL CORPS

CORPS OF ROYAL ELECTRICAL AND MECHANICAL ENGINEERS

ADJUTANT-GENERAL'S CORPS

ROYAL ARMY VETERINARY CORPS

SMALL ARMS SCHOOL CORPS

ROYAL ARMY DENTAL CORPS

INTELLIGENCE CORPS

ROYAL ARMY PHYSICAL TRAINING CORPS

QUEEN ALEXANDRA'S ROYAL ARMY NURSING CORPS

CORPS OF ARMY MUSIC

THE ROYAL MONMOUTHSHIRE ROYAL ENGINEERS (MILITIA) (THE ARMY RESERVE)

THE HONOURABLE ARTILLERY COMPANY (THE ARMY RESERVE)

REST OF THE ARMY RESERVE

EQUIPMENT

VEHICLES

Combat Vehicles	Bulldog, Challenger 2, Stormer, Warrior
Reconnaissance Vehicles	Coyote, FUCHS, Jackal 2, Samaritan, Sampson, Scimitar, Spartan, Sultan
Protected Patrol Vehicles	Foxhound, Husky, Mastiff, Panther, Ridgback, RWMIK Land Rover, Wolfhound
Engineering Equipment	BR90 Bridge, Challenger Armoured Repair & Recovery Vehicle, Explosive Ordnance Disposal, M3 Amphibious Bridging Vehicle, Terrier, Titan Armoured Bridge Launcher, Trojan Armoured Vehicle
Artillery and Air Defence	AS90, Desert Hawk, L118 Light Gun, M270B1 Multiple Launch Rocket System, Rapier, Starstreak High Verlocity Missile
Aircraft	AH-64E Apache Attack Helicopter, Airbus 135 Juno, Bell 212, Gazelle, Watchkeeper, Wildcat Mk1

THE ARMY RESERVE

The Army Reserve (formerly the Territorial Army (TA)) is part of the UK's reserve land forces and provides support to the regular army at home and overseas. The Army Reserve is divided into three types of unit: national, regional, and sponsored. Army Reserve soldiers serving in regional units complete a minimum of 27 days training a year, comprising some evenings, weekends and an annual two-week camp. National units normally specialise in a specific role or trade, such as logistics, IT, communications or medical services. Members of national units have a lower level of training commitment and complete 19 days training a year. Sponsored reserves are individuals who will serve, as members of the workforce of a company contracted to the MoD, in a military capacity and have agreed to accept a reserve liability to be called up for active service in a crisis. In 2012 the Secretary of State for Defence issued a consultation paper *Future Reserves 2020: Delivering the Nation's Security Together,* which outlined plans to invest an additional £1.8bn in the Reserve Forces over a ten-year period, for the Reserve Forces to be more integrated with the regular forces and to have a more significant role within the armed forces as a whole.

QUEEN ALEXANDRA'S ROYAL ARMY NURSING CORPS

The Queen Alexandra's Royal Army Nursing Corps (QARANC) was founded in 1902 as Queen Alexandra's Imperial Military Nursing Service and gained its present title in 1949. The QARANC has trained nurses for the register since 1950 and also trains and employs healthcare assistants. Nursing officers, Nursing soldiers, healthcare assistants and student nurses of the QARANC deliver a high quality, adaptable and dedicated nursing care wherever the Army needs it and can find themselves working in a variety of settings. These can vary from NHS hospitals with military units, to ground based environments such as medical regiments and field hospitals. QARANC personnel deal with a wide range of medical situations, with civilian and military patients in the UK, to military casualties of war and conflict. Work locations vary between clinical roles and instructional positions at training bases. Currently, Army nurses are based and deployed in the UK, Germany, Cyprus, Canada, Poland, Brunei, Nepal, Kenya and Sierra Leone.

Colonel-in-Chief, HRH The Countess of Wessex, GCVO
Colonels Commandant, Col. Jane Davis, OBE, QVRM, TD; Col. Carol Kefford

THE ROYAL AIR FORCE

As at 31 December 2020

THE QUEEN

MARSHALS OF THE ROYAL AIR FORCE
HRH The Prince Philip, Duke of Edinburgh, KG, KT, OM,
GCVO, GBE, GBE, ONZ, QSO, AK, PC, GCL, CMM,
apptd 1953
HRH The Prince of Wales, KG, KT, GCB, OM, AK, QSO,
CC, ADC, *apptd* 2012

FORMER CHIEFS OF THE AIR STAFF

MARSHALS OF THE ROYAL AIR FORCE
Lord Craig of Radley, GCB, OBE, *apptd* 1988
Lord Stirrup, KG, GCB, AFC, *apptd* 2014

AIR CHIEF MARSHALS
Sir Michael Graydon, GCB, CBE, *apptd* 1991
Sir Richard Johns, GCB, KCVO, OBE, *apptd* 1994
Sir Glenn Torpy, GCB, CBE, DSO, *apptd* 2006
Sir Stephen Dalton, GCB, *apptd* 2009
Sir Andrew Pulford, GCB, CBE, *apptd* 2013
Sir Stephen Hillier, KCB, CBE, DFC *apptd* 2016

AIR RANK LIST

AIR CHIEF MARSHALS
Peach, Sir Stuart, GBE, KCB *(Chair of the Military Committee,
NATO)*
Wigston, Sir Michael, KCB, CBE, ADC *(Chief of the Air Staff)*

AIR MARSHALS
Young, J., CB, OBE *(pending retirement)*
Stringer, E., CB, CBE *(Director-General Joint Force
Development)*
Knighton, R., CB *(Deputy Chief of the Defence Staff, Military
Capability)*
Gray, S., CB, OBE *(Director-General Defence Safety Authority)*
Turner, A., CB, CBE *(Deputy Cdr Capability and Air Member for
Personnel and Capability)*
Mayhew, G., CBE *(Deputy Cdr Operations and Air Member for
Operations)*

AIR VICE-MARSHALS
Bethell, K., CBE *(Director Combat Air; pending retirement)*
Byford, M. *(Chief of Staff (Personnel) and Air Secretary)*
Colman, N., OBE *(Commander Joint Helicopter Command)*
Duguid, I., CB, CBE *(Air Officer Commanding No. 11 Group)*
Ellis, J., *(Chaplain-in-Chief and Director-General Chaplaincy
Service (RAF))*
Ellard, S. *(Air Officer Commanding No. 38 Group)*
Gale, I., MBE *(Assistant Chief of the Air Staff (Strategy))*
Gillespie, A., CBE *(Air Officer Commanding No. 2 Group)*
Hart, M., CBE *(Head of Joint Terrorism Analysis Centre)*
Hill, R., CBE *(Director Defence Support Transformation)*
James, W., CBE *(pending retirement)*
Jennings, T., OBE *(Director Legal Services (RAF))*
Maddison, R., OBE *(Air Officer Commanding No. 22 Group)*

Marshall, A., OBE *(Air Officer Commanding No. 1 Group)*
Moore, C., CBE *(Defence Digital Director Service Operations)*
Reid, A., CB, QHP *(Surgeon General)*
Russell, G., CB *(Director Helicopters)*
Sampson, M., CBE, DSO *(Director Ministry of Defence Saudi
Armed Forces Projects)*
Shell, S., CB, CBE *(Director Military Aviation Authority)*
Smeath, M., CBE *(Defence Attaché, British Defence Staff,
Washington D.C.)*
Smith, A., *(Assistant Chief of Defence Staff (Global Engagement
and Military Strategy))*
Smyth, H., OBE *(Director Space)*
Stringer, J., CBE *(Director Strategy, Uk Strategic Command)*
Taylor, L., OBE *(Chief of Staff Capability)*
Tunnicliffe, G., CVO *(Deputy Commandant, Royal College of
Defence Studies)*
Vallely, I., OBE *(Cdr Cyber, Intelligence, Surveillance and
Reconnaissance)*
Walton, C., QHP *(Director Defence Medical Personnel and
Training)*

CONSTITUTION OF THE RAF

The RAF consists of a single command, Air Command, based
at RAF High Wycombe. RAF Air Command was formed on 1
April 2007 from the amalgamation of Strike Command and
Personnel and Training Command.

Air Command consists of four groups, each organised around
specific operational duties. No. 1 Group is the coordinating
organisation for the tactical fast-jet forces responsible for
attack, offensive support and air defence operations. No. 2
Group provides air combat support including air transport and
air-to-air refuelling; intelligence surveillance; targeting and
reconnaissance; and force protection. No. 11 Group, formed in
2018, is a multi-domain operations group tasked with coordinating and integrating data from air, space and cyber
activities into the planning and execution of operations. No.
22 Group recruits personnel and provides trained specialist
personnel to the RAF, as well as to the Royal Navy and the
Army *(see also* Armed Forces Training and Recruitment).

RAF EQUIPMENT

AIRCRAFT

Combat	F35B Lightning II, Typhoon FGR4
Training	Embraer Phenom 100, Hawk T1, Hawk T2, 120TP Prefect, Texan T1, Tutor T1, Viking T1
Surveillance	P-8A Poseidon, MQ-9 Reaper, RC-135W Rivet Joint, Sentinel R1, E-3D Sentry AEW1, Shadow R1
Transport	Atlas, BAe146, C17 Globemaster III, C-130J Hercules, Voyager

HELICOPTERS

Helicopters	Chinook, Griffin HAR2, Puma HC2
Training	Airbus H135 Juno, Airbus H145 Jupiter
Transport	Leonardo GrandNew

ROYAL AUXILIARY AIR FORCE

The Auxiliary Air Force was formed in 1924 to train an elite corps of civilians to serve their country in flying squadrons in their spare time. In 1947 the force was awarded the prefix 'royal' in recognition of its distinguished war service and the Sovereign's Colour for the RAuxAF was presented in 1989. The RAuxAF continues to recruit civilians who undertake military training in their spare time, with a standard minimum commitment of 27 days a year. With the amendments to the reserve service made under the Defence Reform Act 2014, reservists can now be employed to support the RAF across the full spectrum of military tasks. There are currently 27 squadrons with the RAuxAF, with a total establishment of just under 3,200 posts, with reservist posts being available in the majority of trades.

Air Commodore-in-Chief, HM The Queen
Commandant General, Air Vice-Marshal Ranald Munro, CBE, TD, VR, DL
Inspector, Capt. J. White

PRINCESS MARY'S ROYAL AIR FORCE NURSING SERVICE

The Princess Mary's Royal Air Force Nursing Service (PMRAFNS) was formed on 1 June 1918 as the Royal Air Force Nursing Service. In June 1923, His Majesty King George V gave his royal assent for the Royal Air Force Nursing Service to be known as the Princess Mary's Royal Air Force Nursing Service. The Princess Mary's Royal Air Force Nursing Service (PMRAFNS) is committed to providing a skilled, knowledgeable and able nursing workforce to deliver high quality care, whilst being responsive to the dynamic nature of RAF Nursing in peacetime and on operations.

Patron and Air Chief Commandant, HRH Princess Alexandra, The Hon. Lady Ogilvy, KG, GCVO
Matron-in-Chief, Gp Capt. Fionnuala Bradley

SERVICE SALARIES

Pay 16 was introduced on 1 April 2016, replacing the previous Pay 2000 scheme for all regular and reserve personnel on the main pay spines up to and including the rank of Commodore/ Brigadier/ Air Commodore (*see* following page for table of relative rank). Compared with Pay 2000 the total number of increments has been reduced and personnel, with the exception of Lieutenants, remain on the same salary for the first two years in rank.

The following rates of pay apply from 1 April 2020 and are rounded to the nearest pound.

The pay rates shown are for army personnel. The rates also apply to personnel of equivalent rank and pay band in the other services.

Rank	Annual Salary
Second Lieutenant	£27,818
LIEUTENANT	
On appointment	£33,436
After 1 year in rank	£34,610
After 2 years in rank	£35,784
After 3 years in rank	£36,958
CAPTAIN	
On appointment	£42,850
After 2 years in rank	£44,201
After 3 years in rank	£45,552
After 4 years in rank	£46,904
After 5 years in rank	£48,255
After 6 years in rank	£49,606
After 7 years in rank	£50,957
MAJOR	
On appointment	£53,975
After 2 years in rank	£55,753
After 3 years in rank	£57,531
After 4 years in rank	£59,309
After 5 years in rank	£61,087
After 10 years in rank	£68,599
After 12 years in rank	£71,370
LIEUTENANT-COLONEL	
On appointment	£75,754
After 2 years in rank	£77,753
After 3 years in rank	£79,741
After 4 years in rank	£81,735
After 5 years in rank	£83,729
After 6 years in rank	£85,723
After 7 years in rank	£87,716
COLONEL	
On appointment	£91,776
After 2 years in rank	£93,295
After 3 years in rank	£94,814
After 4 years in rank	£96,332
After 5 years in rank	£97,851
After 6 years in rank	£99,369
After 7 years in rank	£100,888
BRIGADIER	
On appointment	£109,368
After 2 years in rank	£110,475
After 3 years in rank	£111,581
After 4 years in rank	£112,688
After 5 years in rank	£113,794

PAY SYSTEM FOR SENIOR MILITARY OFFICERS

Pay rates effective as at 1 April 2020 for all military officers of 2* rank and above (excluding medical and dental officers). All pay rates are rounded to the nearest pound.

Rank	Annual Salary
MAJOR-GENERAL (2*)	
Scale 1	£120,800
Scale 2	£123,160
Scale 3	£125,568
Scale 4	£128,024
Scale 5	£130,529
Scale 6	£133,083
LIEUTENANT-GENERAL (3*)	
Scale 1	£140,549
Scale 2	£147,438
Scale 3	£154,671
Scale 4	£160,746
Scale 5	£165,485
Scale 6	£170,367
GENERAL (4*)	
Scale 1	£184,348
Scale 2	£188,956
Scale 3	£193,681
Scale 4	£198,523
Scale 5	£202,493
Scale 6	£206,543

Field Marshal – appointments to this rank will not usually be made in peacetime. The salary for holders of the rank is equivalent to the salary of a 5-star General, a salary created only in times of war. In peacetime, the equivalent rank to Field Marshal is the Chief of the Defence Staff. As at 1 April 2020, the annual salary range for the Chief of the Defence Staff is £265,588–£281,844.

OFFICERS COMMISSIONED FROM THE SENIOR RANKS

Rank	Annual salary
Level 15	£57,274
Level 14	£56,900
Level 13	£56,506
Level 12	£55,743
Level 11	£54,984
Level 10	£54,216
Level 9	£53,452
Level 8	£52,688
Level 7*	£51,735
Level 6	£51,147
Level 5	£50,550
Level 4†	£49,370
Level 3	£48,782
Level 2	£48,181
Level 1‡	£47,005

* Officers commissioned from the ranks with more than 15 years' service enter on level 7

† Officers commissioned from the ranks with between 12 and 15 years' service enter on level 4

‡ Officers commissioned from the ranks with less than 12 years' service enter on level 1

SOLDIERS' SALARIES

Pay16 was introduced on 1 April 2016, replacing the previous Pay 2000 scheme for all regular and reserve personnel on the main pay spines up to and including the rank of Commodore/ Brigadier/ Air Commodore (*see* below for table of relative rank). Rank remains the key determinant of pay, but the 'high' and 'low' bands under the Pay 2000 scheme were removed and replaced with 4 supplements *(Supp.)* under which trades are allocated. All ranks in a particular trade are treated the same for pay supplement purposes. Compared with Pay 2000 the total number of increments has been reduced and personnel remain on increment Level 1 for the first two years in rank, with the exception of Privates who remain on increment Level 2 for two years.

Rates of pay effective from 1 April 2020 (rounded to the nearest pound) are:

Rank	Supp. 1	Supp. 2	Supp. 3	Supp 4
PRIVATE				
Level 1	20,400	–	–	–
Level 2	21,230	–	–	–
Level 3	22,641	22,908	23,185	23,185
Level 4	23,825	24,902	24,451	24,785
Level 5	24,981	25,340	25,790	26,124
Level 6	26,137	26,656	27,202	27,549
LANCE CORPORAL				
(levels 7 to 9 also applicable to Privates)				
Level 7	27,327	27,961	28,507	29,004
Level 8	28,592	29,342	29,916	30,445
Level 9	29,921	30,748	31,397	32,009

Rank	Supp. 1	Supp. 2	Supp. 3	Supp 4
CORPORAL				
Level 1	31,870	32,797	33,699	34,536
Level 2	32,721	33,668	34,597	35,432
Level 3	33,206	34,338	35,375	36,263
Level 4	33,660	34,807	36,120	37,135
Level 5	34,139	35,285	36,775	37,875
SERGEANT				
Level 1	35,854	37,061	38,628	39,896
Level 2	36,747	38,043	39,615	41,079
Level 3	37,672	39,071	40,588	42,132
Level 4	38,609	40,200	41,601	43,227
Level 5	39,556	41,221	42,666	44,365
STAFF SERGEANT				
Level 1	40,358	42,056	43,581	45,340
Level 2	40,994	42,789	44,361	46,078
Level 3	41,652	43,449	45,142	46,857
Level 4	42,288	44,085	45,943	47,407
Level 5	42,953	44,749	46,866	48,407
WARRANT OFFICER CLASS II				
(also applicable to Staff Sergeants)				
Level 1	43,896	45,930	48,191	49,762
Level 2	44,836	46,870	48,880	50,289
Level 3	45,725	47,520	49,231	50,664
Level 4	46,500	48,166	49,545	50,979
Level 5	47,293	48,798	49,841	51,275
WARRANT OFFICER CLASS I				
Level 1	50,839	–	–	52,314
Level 2	51,133	–	–	52,761
Level 3	51,717	–	–	53,267
Level 4	52,301	–	–	53,779
Level 5	52,837	–	–	54,262

RELATIVE RANK – ARMED FORCES

Royal Navy	*Army*	*Royal Air Force*
1 Admiral of the Fleet	1 Field Marshal	1 Marshal of the RAF
2 Admiral (Adm.)	2 General (Gen.)	2 Air Chief Marshal
3 Vice-Admiral (Vice-Adm.)	3 Lieutenant-General (Lt.-Gen.)	3 Air Marshal
4 Rear-Admiral (Rear-Adm.)	4 Major-General (Maj.-Gen.)	4 Air Vice-Marshal
5 Commodore (Cdre)	5 Brigadier (Brig.)	5 Air Commodore (Air Cdre)
6 Captain (Capt.)	6 Colonel (Col.)	6 Group Captain (Gp Capt.)
7 Commander (Cdr)	7 Lieutenant-Colonel (Lt.-Col.)	7 Wing Commander (Wg Cdr)
8 Lieutenant-Commander (Lt.-Cdr)	8 Major (Maj.)	8 Squadron Leader (Sqn Ldr)
9 Lieutenant (Lt.)	9 Captain (Capt.)	9 Flight Lieutenant (Flt Lt)
10 Sub-Lieutenant (Sub-Lt.)	10 Lieutenant (Lt.)	10 Flying Officer (FO)
11 Midshipman	11 Second Lieutenant (2nd Lt.)	11 Pilot Officer (PO)

EDUCATION

THE UK EDUCATION SYSTEM

The structure of the education system in the UK is a devolved matter with each of the countries of the UK having separate systems under separate governments. There are differences between the school systems in terms of the curriculum, examinations and final qualifications and, at university level, in terms of the nature of some degrees and in the matter of tuition fees. The systems in England, Wales and Northern Ireland are similar and have more in common with one another than the Scottish system, which differs significantly.

Education in England is overseen by the Department for Education (DfE), with university research covered by the Department for Business, Energy and Industrial Strategy (DfBEIS).

Responsibility for education in Wales lies with the Department for Education and Skills (DfES) within the Welsh government. Ministers in the Scottish government are responsible for education in Scotland, led by the directorates of Learning and Lifelong Learning, while in Northern Ireland responsibility lies with the Department of Education and the Department for the Economy within the Northern Ireland government.

DEPARTMENT FOR EDUCATION **T** 0370-000 2288
  W www.gov.uk/government/organisations/
  department-for-education
DEPARTMENT FOR EDUCATION AND SKILLS (DFES)
  T 0300-060 4400 **W** www.gov.wales/topics/educationandskills
SCOTTISH GOVERNMENT – EDUCATION
  T 0300-244 4000 **W** www.gov.scot/education
DEPARTMENT OF EDUCATION (NI) **T** 028-9127 9279
  W www.education-ni.gov.uk
DEPARTMENT FOR THE ECONOMY **T** 028-9052 9900
  W www.economy-ni.gov.uk

RECENT DEVELOPMENTS

All four nations grappled with the fallout from the coronavirus pandemic, with huge financial and learning implications for all. Exams were cancelled in 2020 in all nations, with grades based on teacher assessments. Only Scotland opted to cancel exams in 2021, while England, Wales and Northern Ireland will proceed having made changes to content and assessment. T levels began in earnest in England alongside a focus on further education with changes announced and a white paper planned. Wales continued with moves to reform its education system, with Northern Ireland starting to consider similarly wide ranging reforms.

ENGLAND

- In June 2020 , £1bn was announced to mitigate lost teaching time, including £650m for state schools to lift educational outcomes and a £350m tutoring scheme specifically for the most disadvantaged during 2020–21, while £96m was allocated for small group tutoring to help disadvantaged 16 to 19-year-old students whose studies were disrupted
- GCSE, AS and A-levels were cancelled and grades given based on teachers' judgements in 2020 as a result of Covid-19 disruption to education. In 2021, exams will go ahead with changes to 15 A-level subjects and 25 GCSEs
- From September all new primary school pupils will take the new reception baseline assessment (RBA) that will replace SATs in year 2. The one-to-one exercise done in 20 minutes with a teacher in an informal setting will be taken by all children in their first six weeks of primary school
- 'Early adopter' schools began using the revised Early Years Foundation Stage (EYFS) framework in September, before statutory national roll out in September 2021. The reforms focus on improving outcomes in language, literacy and maths and cut paperwork for teachers so they can spend more time teaching and interacting with pupils
- Pupil funding rose in 2021 to a minimum of £5,150 per secondary pupil and a minimum of £4,000 per primary pupil as part of a £14.4bn three-year settlement
- Up to 3,000 new school places are to be created for children with special educational needs and disabilities (SEND), providing tailored support and specialist equipment. Staffed by specially trained teachers, the 35 new special free schools are expected from September 2022
- Schools in England will get £320m towards sport and physical education in 2020–21
- The government agreed a 3.1 per cent overall pay rise for teachers, including increasing the starting salary for new teachers by 5.5 per cent and the upper and lower boundaries of the pay ranges for all other teachers by 2.75 per cent. There is a commitment to increase teachers' starting salaries to £30,000 by 2022–23. It sought advice on new national professional qualifications to help teachers progress their careers, as part of a teacher recruitment and retention strategy
- The government will help employers and FE providers deliver the high-quality industry placements required of new T Level qualifications by providing new guidance for employers and students, extending the Employer Support Fund pilot and procuring an organisation with the appropriate expertise to support 2020, 2021 and 2022 providers. Over 180 education providers will be able to deliver a range of high-quality T Level courses from 2022, across subject areas such as Law, Engineering and Manufacturing, Digital, Construction, Health, Science and Education. Investment of £95 through the T Level Capital Fund and £15m for the T Level Professional Development (TLPD)
- In August 2019, £400m was announced for school sixth forms and colleges in 2020–21, including: £65m to cover the cost of delivering courses in six expensive subject areas: building and construction, hospitality and catering, engineering, transportation operations and maintenance, manufacturing technologies and science; and £55m for high value courses such as STEM subjects; and £35m for students on level 3 courses (A-level equivalent) who have not yet achieved a GCSE pass in maths and English
- A 10-year schools and colleges rebuilding programme will start in 2020–21 with the first 50 projects, supported by over £1bn in funding. Investment will be targeted at school buildings in the worst condition across England, including substantial investment in the North and the Midlands
- More than 180 colleges will receive a share of £200m to repair and refurbish buildings and campuses, as part of a £1.5bn investment to transform colleges over the next five years
- 20 colleges will divide £5.4m to share good practice, knowledge and experience to drive up the standard of education and training on offer to their local communities, including support to develop high quality digital content to provide improved remote and blended learning

- An overhaul of technical and vocational education in Britain will see lesser known qualifications that sit between A-level and degrees, such as CertHE, DipHE and foundation degrees, rebranded as 'Higher Technical Qualifications' and quality approved to attract more people to study them. Employers will define the skills and requirements needed, then newly approved digital qualifications are due to start in 2022, with health, sciences and construction qualifications to follow in 2023. The Institute for Apprenticeships and Technical Education will work with Ofsted and the Office for Students to make sure the quality of courses is consistently high across HE and FE institutions
- Other measures to transform technical education included £120m to establish up to eight more Institutes of Technology, collaborations between FE colleges, universities and employers offering higher technical education and training mainly at Levels 4 and 5 (above A-levels and T levels but below degree level) in key sectors such as digital, construction, advanced manufacturing and engineering
- Efforts to stabilise university research after Covid-19 were made in May, June and September 2020, including a funding scheme to cover up to 80 per cent of a university's income losses from a decline in international students, £200m to support researchers' salaries across the UK, and £80m redistributed from existing UK Research and Innovation funds. Bureaucracy in universities and research will also be reduced to help focus on high-quality teaching and research
- £100m of public funding was brought forward to 2020–21 to help protect vital university research activities, and around £2.6bn of tuition fee payments to help universities manage financial risks
- A temporary limit was set on the number of full-time undergraduate UK and EU students English higher education providers could recruit for 2020–21, based on their forecasts for the next academic year, plus an additional 5 per cent. The government also allowed for a discretionary 10,000 extra places, with 5,000 ring-fenced for nursing, midwifery or allied health courses to support the country's vital public services
- Students studying to become paramedics, radiographers and physiotherapists will be among those receiving £5,000 maintenance grants from September 2020. Extra payments worth up to £3,000 per academic year will be available for eligible students
- £24m was pledged to 18 universities and partners to deliver 2,500 places on artificial intelligence and data science conversion courses in 28 universities and colleges in England, with 1,000 scholarships offered to students from underrepresented backgrounds
- England's first Space Engineering Technician apprenticeship will be available to students from January 2021. A degree equivalent (level 6) space engineering diploma is expected to be available to students from September 2021
- Students in England could receive university offers only once they have obtained their final grades under proposals to change the current admissions system. The government plans to consult on proposals for post-qualification university admissions that would remove the unfairness of inaccurate predicated grades. This will not affect university applications for 2021 and different options will be assessed after the consultation ends

WALES

- A level, AS, GCSE, Skills Challenge Certificate and Welsh Baccalaureate grades in Wales were awarded on the basis of centre assessment grades. In summer 2021, current AS learners will choose whether to only sit the A2 units, with the A level grade based on their performance in the A2 units, or sit both the AS and A2 units and be awarded the best grade from either route. Those due to sit GCSE will sit only the units they plan to take in summer 2021, with their GCSE grade based on that performance only, or sit the Year 10 units in summer 2021, along with the Year 11 units. They will be awarded the best grade from either route
- A new Early Childhood Education and Care (ECEC) approach launched in 2019 that will reform the provision of early years care to ensure children get the best possible start in life
- Revised guidance on Curriculum for Wales was published and an additional £15m given to support teachers preparing for its implementation
- A new Additional Learning Needs code and regulations are expected to be brought to the assembly in February 2021 to start in September 2021
- The government agreed an overall pay rise of 3.1 per cent – 3.75 per cent for teachers on the main pay scale – while starting salaries for new teachers increased by 8.48 per cent, performance-related pay progression ended and national pay scales were reintroduced. College staff received a pay rise of 2.75 per cent to bring their pay level to that of schoolteachers
- A new all-Wales 'National Masters in Education' programme will be available for teaching from September 2021. The Welsh government will support up to 500 early career education professionals to take the qualification. The aim is to strengthen recruitment and retention, professional learning and the relationship between the HE sector and Wales' education reform programme
- The £10m Skills Development Fund designed for colleges to address gaps in job-specific skills in their areas, as identified by local employers, will continue. £5m will again be available for colleges to invest in staff professional development, including developing digital and Welsh-language skills
- Funding for 2020–21 included £5m to cover the costs of safely bringing back FE learners to take qualifications; £15m for catch up costs of 16–19 learners, £460,000 to support additional costs of allowing Independent Living Skills learners to return to college in September, and nearly £18m to cover the costs of bringing vocational learners safely back for practical face-to-face learning
- A Covid-19 resilience plan stopped performance measures for further education, work-based learning and adult learning outcomes from being produced for 2019–20 and suspended Estyn inspections
- A vision for post compulsory education and training sector (PCET) was unveiled in November 2020 to combat Brexit, Covid-19 and climate change. A new Commission for Tertiary Education and Research (CTER), as proposed in the draft Tertiary Education and Research (Wales) Bill – the introduction of which was delayed to 2021 after Covid-19 – would have extensive funding, planning and regulatory powers, enabling it to improve quality, efficiency and efficacy across the higher education sector. It would bring together further education, including sixth forms, adult community learning, work-based learning and universities

SCOTLAND

- In its work programme for 2020–21, the Scottish government set out measures to help mitigate the impact of Covid-19. These included: a 'Youth Guarantee' to keep 19 to 24-year-olds in training, work or education; £2m to help residential outdoor education; £50m to recruit new teachers and support staff; £1.5m for school staff, and £5m to tackle digital exclusion. An Education Recovery Group was set up to help schools and universities return after lockdown

- In 2020, exams were cancelled and qualifications were awarded based on teacher estimates. Higher and Advanced Higher exams will not go ahead in 2021 either, replaced again with awards based on teacher judgement of pupils' attainment
- Children and young people with additional support needs will be now be directly involved in the decisions that affect them following an independent review. A progress report is due in October 2021
- The government invested a further £182m in the Attainment Scotland Fund and confirmed more than £250m of Pupil Equity Funding will be made available to 97 per cent of schools in 2020–21 and 2021–22
- A new £15m Apprenticeship Employer Grant will help increase the number of employers able to take on an apprentice or help employees obtain new skills. Pathway Apprenticeships will help school leavers up to age 18 train and get qualifications through 1,200 work experience, volunteering and work-based learning opportunities
- A range of measures to support colleges and universities included a one-off £75m to universities to protect world-leading research, £10m for estates development, and early access to £11.4m of Higher Education Hardship Funds. The Scottish Funding Council estimated the country's universities would lose around £72m in academic year 2019–20 as a result of Covid-19 and predicted an operating deficit of between £384m and £651m in 2020–21 as the number of international students decline
- It was confirmed that EU students will have to pay tuition fees from 2021–22 unless Scotland rejoins the EU

NORTHERN IRELAND

- GCSE, AS and A-level exams will go ahead in 2021, with more generous grading across all qualifications, significant reductions in content to be assessed, support materials for GCSE maths and a reserve examination series in early July for A2 candidates who miss exams through illness or self-isolating. Year 14 pupils will not have to take AS examinations and, in the majority of GCSE qualifications a specified module will be omitted from assessment. All assessments in GCSE Maths will be retained but the speaking and listening component of GCSE English Language will be omitted. The timetable for the summer exam series will be delayed by one week with exams starting no earlier than 12 May 2021, but concluding by 30 June. Results will issue at the end of August
- A *New Decade New Approach* set out the priorities of the newly restored Northern Ireland Assembly in January 2020. A wide-ranging review of education will consider the education journey and outcomes of children and young people, support for schools and settings, and system level design. It will begin later in 2021 once an independent panel is appointed. It is expected to last 18 months
- A consultation on how to improve provision of education for children and young people with special educational needs launched, along with £7.5m for a new SEN framework to provide additional resources for schools. Proposed changes include a defined period in which assessments must be carried out and decisions implemented. Children and parents will also have new rights that will ensure services meet their needs. The Education Authority will be required to publish an annual plan of SEN provision arrangements and each child with SEN will be required to have a Personal Learning Plan. Each school will have to have a Learning Support Coordinator
- This followed the Children and Young People's Strategy 2019–29 unveiled in December 2019 that set out a strategic

framework for improving the well-being of children and young people in Northern Ireland. One goal, that children and young people 'learn and achieve', will include a Department of Education led programme to transform the education system

- Almost £64m to help schools manage Education Authority pressures, Covid-19 pressures and for free school meals was announced in October 2020. It included £49.4m to cover additional costs and £12.8m for special educational needs. A further £1.4m went towards providing free school meals over the extended half-term break
- Up to £4m will be invested in new and existing nurture groups across Northern Ireland in 2020–21, including establishing 15 new and funding 31 existing nurture groups in primary schools, and a Nurture Advisory Service in the Education Authority
- A pay rise for teachers was agreed in April 2020, ending all industrial action. All teachers in Northern Ireland were awarded a pay rise of 2.25 per cent payable from September 2017 and an additional 2 per cent payable from September 2018
- Some 12 primary schools, five post-primary schools and one special school will benefit from an estimated capital investment of £45m under the Schools Enhancement Programme
- In FE, the Northern Regional College will get a £40m boost to develop its campus, and £4.6m for 3,000 free online digital skills training places for people whose employment was disrupted by the pandemic
- In HE, £5.6m was set aside to alleviate student hardship in 2020–21

STATE SCHOOL SYSTEM

PRE-SCHOOL

Pre-school education is not compulsory.

In England, a free place is available for every 3- and 4-year-old whose parents want one, although parents may use as little or as much of their entitlement as they choose. All 3- and 4-year-olds, and disadvantaged 2-year-olds, are entitled to 15 hours a week of free early education over 38 weeks of the year until they reach compulsory school age (the term following their fifth birthday). Working parents of 3- and 4-year-old children may be eligible for up to 30 hours free childcare. Free places are funded by local authorities and are delivered by a range of approved providers in the maintained and non-maintained sectors: nursery schools, nursery classes in primary schools, private schools, private day nurseries, voluntary playgroups, pre-schools and registered childminders. In order to receive funding, providers must be working towards the early learning goals and the Early Years Foundation Stage curriculum, must be inspected on a regular basis by Ofsted and must meet any conditions set by the local authority.

In Wales, every child is entitled to receive free Foundation Phase education for a minimum of two hours a day from the term following their third birthday. The Flying Start scheme allows disadvantaged 2- to 3-year-olds 2.5 hours childcare a week for 39 weeks. Up to 30 hours of free childcare is available to working parents of 3- to 4-year-olds from 2020, made up of a minimum of 10 hours early education and a maximum of 20 hours of childcare.

In Scotland, councils have a duty to provide a pre-school education for all 3- and 4-year-olds, and some disadvantaged 2- to 3-year-olds, whose parents request one. From August 2020, education authorities were obliged to offer 1,140 hours of free pre-school education a year, but this was revoked in March 2020 to allow local authorities to focus on the pandemic response (*see also* Recent Developments).

In Northern Ireland, pre-school education is available to all children in the year before they are due to start primary one. Most settings offer 2.5 hours a day, five days a week for at least 38 weeks a year, but some offer full-time places of 4.5 hours a day.

PRIMARY AND SECONDARY SCHOOLS

By law, full-time education starts at the age of five for children in England, Scotland and Wales and at the age of four in Northern Ireland (where the child's age after 1 July determines when they start). In practice, most children in the UK start school before their fifth birthday: in England all children are entitled to a primary school place from the September after their fourth birthday.

Children in England are required to stay in education or training until the end of the academic year in which they turn 18. In all other parts of the UK, compulsory schooling ends at age 16, but children born between certain dates may leave school before their 16th birthday; most young people stay in some form of education until 17 or 18.

Primary education consists mainly of infant schools for children aged 5 to 7, junior schools for those aged 7 to 11, and combined infant and junior schools for both age groups. Scotland has only primary schools with no infant/junior division.

In a few parts of England there are schools catering for ages 5 to 10 as the first stage of a three-tier system of first (lower), middle and secondary (upper) schools.

Children usually leave primary school and move on to secondary school at the age of 11 (or 12 in Scotland). In the few areas of England that have a three-tier system, middle schools cater for children for three to four years between the ages of 8 and 14, depending on the local authority.

Secondary schools cater for children aged 11 to 16 and, if they have a sixth form, for those who choose to stay on to the age of 18. From the age of 16, students may move instead to further education colleges or work-based training.

Most UK secondary schools are co-educational. The largest secondary schools have more than 1,500 pupils and around 60 per cent of secondary pupils in the UK are in schools that take more than 1,000 pupils.

Most state-maintained secondary schools in England, Wales and Scotland are comprehensive schools, which admit pupils without reference to ability. In England there remain some areas with grammar schools, catering for pupils aged 11 to 18, which select pupils on the basis of high academic ability. Nearly two-thirds of state secondary schools in England (2,700) are now academies: academies are funded directly by the state rather than being maintained by local authorities. Northern Ireland still has 66 grammar schools; the 11-plus has been officially discontinued but schools, or consortia of schools, use their own unregulated entry tests.

More than 90 per cent of pupils in the UK attend publicly funded schools and receive free education. The rest (6.5 per cent) attend privately funded 'independent' schools which charge fees, or are educated at home.

The bulk of the UK government's expenditure on school education is through local authorities (Education and Library Boards (ELBs) in Northern Ireland), which pass on state funding to schools and other educational institutions.

SPECIAL EDUCATION

Schools and local authorities in England and Wales, Education and Library Boards (ELBs) in Northern Ireland and education authorities in Scotland are required to identify and secure provision for children with special educational needs and to involve parents in decisions (*see also* Recent Developments.) The majority of children with special educational needs are educated in ordinary mainstream schools, sometimes with supplementary help from outside specialists. Parents of children with special educational needs (referred to as additional support needs in Scotland and additional learning needs in Wales) have a right of appeal to independent tribunals if their wishes are not met.

Special educational needs provision may be made in maintained special schools, special units attached to mainstream schools or in mainstream classes themselves, all funded by local authorities. There are also non-maintained special schools run by voluntary bodies, mainly charities, who may receive grants from central government for capital expenditure and equipment but whose other costs are met primarily from the fees charged to local authorities for pupils placed in the schools. Some independent schools also provide education wholly or mainly for children with special educational needs.

ADDITIONAL SUPPORT NEEDS TRIBUNALS FOR
    SCOTLAND **T** 0141-302 5860
    W www.healthandeducationchamber.scot
FIRST-TIER TRIBUNAL (SPECIAL EDUCATIONAL
    NEEDS AND DISABILITY) **T** 01325-289350
    W www.gov.uk/special-educational-needs-disability-tribunal
INFORMATION ADVICE AND SUPPORT SERVICES
    NETWORK FOR SEND **E** iassn@ncb.org.uk
    W https://councilfordisabledchildren.org.uk/
    information-advice-and-support-services-network
SPECIAL EDUCATIONAL NEEDS TRIBUNAL FOR
    WALES **T** 01597-829800 **W** www.sentw.gov.uk

HOME EDUCATION

In England and Wales parents have the right to educate their children at home and do not have to be qualified teachers to do so. Home-educated children do not have to follow the National Curriculum or take national tests. Nor do they need a fixed timetable, formal lessons or to observe school hours, days or terms. However, by law parents must ensure that the home education provided is full-time and suitable for the child's age, ability and aptitude and, if appropriate, for any special educational needs. Parents have no legal obligation to notify the local authority that a child is being educated at home, but if they take a child out of school, they must notify the school in writing and the school must report this to the local authority. Local authorities can make informal enquiries of parents to establish that a suitable education is being provided. For children in special schools, parents must seek the consent of the local authority before taking steps to educate them at home.

In Northern Ireland, ELBs monitor the quality of home provision and provide general guidance on appropriate materials and exam types through regular home visits.

The home schooling law in Scotland is similar to that of England. One difference, however, is that if parents wish to take a child out of school they must have permission from the local education authority.

HOME EDUCATION ADVISORY SERVICE
    T 01707-371854 **W** www.heas.org.uk
HOME EDUCATION IN NORTHERN IRELAND
    W www.hedni.org
SCHOOLHOUSE HOME EDUCATION ASSOCIATION
    (SCOTLAND) **T** 01307-463120
    E contact@schoolhouse.org.uk **W** www.schoolhouse.org.uk
EDUCATION OTHERWISE **T** 0845-4786345
    W www.educationotherwise.org

FURTHER EDUCATION

In the UK, further education (FE) is generally understood as post-secondary education, ie any education undertaken after an individual leaves school that is below higher education level. FE therefore embraces a wide range of general and vocational study, full-time or part-time, undertaken by people of all ages from 16 upwards who may be self-funded, employer-funded or state-funded.

There are three types of technical and applied qualifications for 16- to 19-year-olds: level 3 tech levels which equip people to specialise in specific technical jobs; level 2 technical certificates to help them get employment or progress to another tech level; and applied general qualifications which prepare them to continue general education at advanced level through applied learning.

FE in the UK is often undertaken at further education colleges, although some takes place on employers' premises. Many of these colleges offer some courses at higher education level; some FE colleges teach certain subjects to 14- to 16-year-olds under collaborative arrangements with schools. Colleges' income comes from public funding, student fees and work for and with employers.

HIGHER EDUCATION

Higher education (HE) in the UK describes courses of study, provided in universities, specialist colleges of higher education and in some FE colleges, where the level of instruction is above that of A-level or equivalent exams.

All UK universities and colleges that provide HE are autonomous bodies with their own internal systems of governance. They are not owned by the state. However, most receive a portion of their income from state funds distributed by the Office for Students in England, the Higher Education Funding Council for Wales, the Scottish Funding Council or the Department for the Economy in Northern Ireland. The rest of their income comes from a number of sources including fees from home and overseas students, government funding for research, endowments and work with or for business.

EXPENDITURE

PUBLIC SECTOR EXPENDITURE ON EDUCATION
(Real terms adjusted to 2019–20 price levels) £bn

2014–15	93.0
2015–16	92.1
2016–17	89.6
2017–18	89.8
2018–19	92.4

Source: HM Treasury – *Public Expenditure Statistical Analyses (PESA)* July 2020

SCHOOLS

UK SCHOOLS BY CATEGORY

	England	Wales
Maintained nursery schools	389	9
*Maintained primary schools	16,784	1,247
Maintained secondary schools	3,456	183
Pupil Referral Units	349	–
Maintained Special schools	993	41
†Non-maintained Special schools	58	–
†Academies	9,041	–
‡Independent schools	2,331	75
Total	24,360	1,555

* Includes 107 middle schools in England and 22 in Wales

† Includes City Technology Colleges, University Technology Colleges, studio schools and free schools; excludes voluntary and private pre-school education centres and academies and free schools alternative provision
‡ Data as at 2019 as not collected in 2020 owing to the coronavirus pandemic
Source: DfE & Welsh government, January 2020

SCOTLAND

Publicly funded schools	5,052
Nursery	2,576
Primary	2,004
Secondary	358
Special	114
Independent schools	92
Total	5,144

Source: Scottish government, December 2020

NORTHERN IRELAND

Maintained nursery schools	95
Maintained primary schools	794
Maintained secondary schools	127
Grammar schools	66
*Special schools	40
Independent schools	14
Total	1,136

* Includes one hospital school
Source: DENI, February 2020

ENGLAND AND WALES

In England and Wales, publicly funded schools are referred to as 'state schools'. Local authorities have a duty to ensure there is a suitable place for every school-age child resident in their area.

The most common types of state funded school are:

- *community schools*, which are sometimes called local authority maintained schools. They are not influenced by business or religious groups and follow the national curriculum
- *foundation schools* and *voluntary schools*, which are funded by the local authority but have more freedom to change the way they do things. Sometimes they are supported by representatives from religious groups
- *academies* and *free schools*, which are run by not-for-profit academy trusts, independent from the local authority. They have more freedom to change how they run things and can follow a different curriculum
- *grammar schools*, which can be run by the local authority, a foundation body or an academy trust; they select pupils based on academic ability

Special schools with pupils aged 11 and older can specialise in one of the four areas of special educational needs: communication and interaction; cognition and learning; social, emotional and mental health; sensory and physical needs.

Faith schools have to follow the national curriculum, but they can choose what they teach in religious studies. They may have different admissions criteria and staffing policies to state schools, although anyone can apply for a place. *Faith academies* do not have to teach the national curriculum and have their own admissions processes.

Free schools are funded by the government but are not run by the local authority so have more control over how they do things and do not have to follow the national curriculum. They are "all-ability" schools so cannot use academic selection processes. They are run on a not-for-profit basis and can be set up by groups like: charities; universities; independent schools; community and faith groups; teachers; parents and businesses.

University technical colleges specialising in subjects like engineering and construction are a type of free school where pupils study academic and practical subjects leading to technical qualifications. *Studio schools* are small free schools teaching mainstream qualifications through project-based learning.

Academies are run by an academy trust with more control over how they do things than community schools. They are inspected by Ofsted and have to follow the same rules on admissions, special educational needs and exclusion as other state schools and students sit the same exams. Academies have greater freedoms over how they use their budgets, set staff pay and conditions and deliver the curriculum. They do not have to follow the national curriculum and can set their own term times.

England now has increasing numbers of Academies. Those set up before the Academies Act 2010 were sponsored by business, faith or voluntary groups who contributed to funding their land and buildings, while the government covered the running costs at a level comparable to other local schools. The Academies Act 2010 streamlined the process of becoming an academy, enabled high-performing schools to convert without a sponsor and allowed primary and special schools to become academies. All academies now receive funding from central government at the level they would have received if still maintained by their local authority, with extra funding only to cover those services the local authority no longer provides. As at October 2020 there were 9,323 open academies, 85.8 per cent of all state-funded schools.

All but three *City technology colleges* – independent schools in urban areas that are free to go to – have now converted into academies.

State boarding schools provide free education but charge fees for boarding. Most are academies, some are free schools and some are run by local authorities.

Private or 'independent' schools charge fees to attend instead of being funded by the government. Pupils do not have to follow the national curriculum. They must be registered with the government and are inspected regularly.

In Wales, Welsh-medium primary and secondary schools were first established in the 1950s and 1960s, originally in response to the wishes of Welsh-speaking parents who wanted their children to be educated through the medium of the Welsh language. Now, many children who are not from Welsh-speaking homes also attend Welsh-medium and bilingual schools throughout Wales. There are 420 Welsh-medium primary schools where instruction is mainly or solely in the Welsh language, six Welsh-medium middle schools and 49 Welsh-medium secondary schools, where more than half of foundation subjects (other than English and Welsh) and religious education are taught wholly or partly in Welsh.

SCOTLAND

Most schools in Scotland, known as 'publicly funded' schools, are state-funded and charge no fees. Funding is met from resources raised by the Scottish local authorities and from an annual grant from the Scottish government. Scotland does not have school governing bodies like the rest of the UK: local authorities retain greater responsibility for the management and performance of publicly funded schools. Headteachers manage at least 80 per cent of a school's budget, covering staffing, furnishings, repairs, supplies, services and energy costs. Spending on new buildings, modernisation projects and equipment is financed by the local authority within the limits set by the Scottish government.

Scotland has 370 state-funded *faith schools*, the majority of which are Catholic. It has no grammar schools.

Integrated community schools form part of the Scottish government's strategy to promote social inclusion and to raise educational standards. They encourage closer and better joint working among education, health and social work agencies and professionals, greater pupil and parental involvement in schools, and improved support and service provision for vulnerable children and young people.

Scotland has eight *grant-aided schools* that are independent of local authorities but supported financially by the Scottish government. These schools are managed by boards and most of them provide education for children and young people with special educational needs.

NORTHERN IRELAND

Most schools in Northern Ireland are maintained by the state and generally charge no fees, though fees may be charged in preparatory departments of some grammar schools. There are different types of state-funded schools, each under the control of management committees, which also employ the teachers.

Controlled schools (nursery, primary, special, secondary and grammar schools) are managed by Northern Ireland's five ELBs through boards of governors consisting of teachers, parents, members of the ELB and transferor representatives (mainly from the Protestant churches).

Catholic maintained schools (nursery, primary, special and secondary) are under the management of boards of governors consisting of teachers, parents and members nominated by the employing authority, the Council for Catholic Maintained Schools (CCMS).

Other maintained schools (primary, special and secondary) are, in the main, Irish-medium schools that provide education in an Irish-speaking environment. The Department of Education has a duty to encourage and facilitate the development of Irish-medium education. Northern Ireland has 29 standalone Irish-medium schools, most of them primary schools, and 11 Irish-medium units attached to English-medium host schools.

Voluntary schools are mainly grammar schools (66 in 2020), which select most pupils according to academic ability. They are managed by boards of governors consisting of teachers, parents and, in most cases, representatives from the Department of Education and the ELB.

Integrated schools (primary and secondary) educate pupils from both the Protestant and Catholic communities as well as those of other faiths and no faith; each school is managed by a board of governors. There are at present 65 integrated schools maintained by the state, 27 of which are controlled schools.

Since 2013 all pupils are guaranteed access to a wide range of courses, with a minimum of 24 courses at Key Stage 4, and 27 at post-16. At least one-third of the courses on offer will be academic and another third will be vocational. Schools work with other schools, FE colleges and other providers to widen the range of courses on offer.

INDEPENDENT SCHOOLS

Around 6.5 per cent of UK schoolchildren are educated by privately funded 'independent' schools that charge fees and set their own admissions policies. Independent schools are required to meet certain minimum standards but need not teach the National Curriculum. *See also* Independent Schools.

INSPECTION

ENGLAND

The Office for Standards in Education, Children's Services and Skills (Ofsted) is the main body responsible for inspecting education in English schools. As well as inspecting all publicly funded and some independent schools, Ofsted inspects a range of other services in England, including childcare, children's homes, pupil referral units, local authority children's services, further education, initial teacher training and publicly funded adult skills training. Inspection reports, recommendations and statistical information are published on Ofsted's website.

Ofsted is an independent, non-ministerial government department that reports directly to parliament, headed by Her Majesty's Chief Inspector (HMCI). Ofsted is required to promote improvement in the public services that it inspects; ensure that these services focus on the interests of their users – children, parents, learners and employers; and see that these services are efficient, effective and promote value for money. A new 'common inspection regime' came into effect in September 2015 to make inspections of different settings with similar age groups more coherent.

Since September 2019, Ofsted adopted a revised inspection framework focused less on exam and test results, more on the quality, breadth and depth of the education provided and on supporting underperforming schools. Inspectors' view of an education provider's overall effectiveness will be based on four other judgements: quality of education; students' behaviour and attitudes; their personal development; and leadership and management. Judgements will still be expressed using continue to be awarded under the current four-point grading scale: outstanding; good; requires improvement; and inadequate.

OFFICE FOR STANDARDS IN EDUCATION,
    CHILDREN'S SERVICES AND SKILLS **T** 0300-123 1231
    W www.gov.uk/government/organisations/ofsted

WALES
Estyn is the education and training inspectorate for Wales. It is independent of, but funded by, the Welsh government and is led by Her Majesty's Chief Inspector of Education and Training in Wales.

Estyn's role is to inspect quality and standards in education and training in Wales, including in primary, secondary, special and independent schools, pupil referral units, publicly funded nursery schools and settings, further education, adult community-based and work-based learning, local authorities and teacher education and training.

Estyn also provides advice on quality and standards in education and training to the Welsh government and others and its remit includes making public good practice based on inspection evidence. Estyn publishes on its website the findings of its inspection reports, its recommendations and statistical information.

The inspection regime will be suspended from September 2020 to August 2021 to enable Estyn to make changes to the system in line with the education reforms in Wales.

HER MAJESTY'S INSPECTORATE FOR EDUCATION
    AND TRAINING IN WALES **T** 029-2044 6446
    W www.estyn.gov.uk

SCOTLAND
Education Scotland is in charge of inspection and review, supporting quality and improvement in Scottish education. The executive agency of the Scottish government operates independently and impartially while being directly accountable to Scottish ministers for the standards of its work. The agency is responsible for delivering measurable year-on-year improvements, with maximum efficiency, by promoting excellence, building on strengths, and identifying and addressing underperformance. Since August 2015, inspections take account of national expectations of progress in implementing Curriculum for Excellence.

Inspection reports and reviews, recommendations, examples of good practice and statistical information are published on Education Scotland's website.

EDUCATION SCOTLAND **T** 0131-244 4330 **W** https:// education.gov.scot

NORTHERN IRELAND
The Education and Training Inspectorate (ETINI) provides inspection services for the Department of Education and the Department for the Economy in Northern Ireland.

ETINI carries out inspections of all schools, pre-school services, special education, further education colleges, initial teacher training, training organisations, and curriculum advisory and support services. ETINI carries out a Sustaining Improvement Inspection (SII) for 'high capacity' special, primary and post-primary schools and Monitoring Inspection (MIn) is more proportionate to risk and aims to focus resources where they will have most impact on learners. Schools are notified 48 hours before either inspection, or two weeks before a full inspection.Since September 2013 regional colleges of further education have received four weeks' notice of inspection, while all other organisations have received two weeks' notice. All inspections were paused on 18 March 2020 until further notice to support schools during the challenge of Covid-19.

The inspectorate's role is to improve services and provide ministers with evidence-based advice to assist in policy formulation. It publishes the findings of its inspection reports, its recommendations and statistical information on its website.

EDUCATION AND TRAINING INSPECTORATE
    T 028-9127 9726 **W** www.etini.gov.uk

THE NATIONAL CURRICULUM

ENGLAND
The National Curriculum, first introduced in 1988, is mandatory in all local authority maintained state schools for children from age five onwards.

Until age five, or the end of Reception Year in primary school, children are in the Early Years Foundation Stage (EYFS), which has its own learning and development requirements for children in nursery and primary schools. Changes to the EYFS came into effect in 2012, 2014 and 2017. These included simplifying the statutory assessment of children's development at age five; reducing the number of early learning goals from 69 to 17; focusing on seven areas of learning and development (communication and language; physical development; personal, social and emotional development; literacy; mathematics; understanding the world; and expressive arts and design) and, for parents, a new progress check on their child's development between the ages of two and three. More reforms in part to help reception age children gain a better grasp of language, literacy and maths are due in September 2021 (*see also* Recent Developments).

After the Foundation Stage the National Curriculum is organised into 'Key Stages', and sets out the core subjects that must be taught and the standards or attainment targets for each subject at each Key Stage.

- Key Stage 1 covers Years 1 and 2 of primary school, for children aged 5–7
- Key Stage 2 covers Years 3 to 6 of primary school, for children aged 7–11
- Key Stage 3 covers Years 7 to 9 of secondary school, for children aged 11–14
- Key Stage 4 covers Years 10 and 11 of secondary school, for children aged 14–16

Within the framework of the National Curriculum, schools may plan and organise teaching and learning in the way that best meets the needs of their pupils, but maintained schools are expected to follow the programmes of study associated with particular subjects. The programmes of study describe the subject knowledge, skills and understanding that pupils are expected to have developed by the end of each Key Stage.

The government brought in a new National Curriculum for England for maintained primary and secondary schools from September 2014. From September 2017 schools have taught the new programmes of study to all pupils in all Key Stages.

COMPULSORY SUBJECTS IN KEY STAGES 1 AND 2	
English	Design and technology
Mathematics	Geography
Science	History
Art and design	Music
Computing	Physical education (incl. swimming)

Foreign languages are compulsory in Key Stage 2, but not Key Stage 1: schools can choose from French, German, Italian, Mandarin, Spanish, Latin and Ancient Greek.

At Key Stage 3, compulsory subjects include those compulsory for Key Stage 2 (though the language taught should be a modern foreign language) plus citizenship.

Pupils in Key Stage 4 study a mix of compulsory and optional subjects in preparation for national examinations such as GCSEs. The compulsory subjects are English, mathematics, science, citizenship, computing and physical education. Key Stage 4 pupils also have to undertake careers education and work-related learning. In addition, schools must offer at least one subject from each of four 'entitlement' areas: arts (art and design, music, dance, drama and media arts); design and technology; humanities (history and geography); and modern foreign languages. To meet the entitlement requirements, schools must ensure that courses in these areas lead to approved qualifications, and must allow pupils to take courses in all four areas if they wish to do so.

Schools must teach religious education (RE) at all key stages, although parents have the right to withdraw children from all or part of the subject. From September 2020, primary schools must teach relationships and health education, while secondary schools must provide sex, relationships and health education.

ASSESSMENT

Statutory assessment must be undertaken for all pupils in publicly funded schools in the relevant years. It first takes place towards the end of reception when teachers assess children's development in 17 early learning goals across seven learning areas to form an early years foundation stage profile (EYFSP).Pupils receive a phonics screening check at the end of the first year in Key Stage 1, repeated the following year if necessary. Teacher assessments in English, mathematics and science take place at the end of Key Stage 1 (Year 2) and Key Stage 2 (Year 6); at the end of Key Stage 3 (Year 9) teachers assess progress in all subjects being studied. National tests in English and mathematics take place in Year 6. At Key Stage 4, national examinations are the main form of assessment.

The assessment process for English at the end of Key Stage 2 now involves three elements: English reading; English grammar, punctuation and spelling.

Key stage 2 results no longer use the previous system of levels. Instead, test results are converted into 'scaled scores', with a score of 100 being the expected standard. Any score below 100 means the pupil is working 'towards the expected standard'; any score above 100 means the pupil is working 'above the expected standard'. Previously the expected standard was a level 4.

From September 2020, children will take a new reception baseline assessment (RBA) within the first six weeks of starting school. This would focus on maths, and literacy, communication and development with the results used to assess how much progress schools are making with their pupils. Results for individual children or schools will not be published (see also Recent Developments). This paves the way for removing national curriculum assessments or SATs at the end of Key Stage 1 from 2022–23. An online multiplication tables check also now takes place in Year 4.

Each year the Department for Education publishes on its website performance tables covering every school, college and local authority. The primary school tables are based mainly on the results of the tests taken by children at the end of Key Stage 2 when they are usually aged 11; since 2010 teacher assessment results are also included.

Headline indicators in the secondary school tables are: pupils' average progress and attainment across eight specified subjects; percentages of pupils achieving passes and strong passes (grades 5 and above) in English and maths; percentages of pupils entering and achieving strong passes in the English Baccalaureate (the EBacc is made up of English, maths, two sciences, a language and history or geography); and the percentage of pupils staying in education or employment for at least two terms after Key Stage 4.

DEPARTMENT FOR EDUCATION T 0370-000 2288
    W www.gov.uk/government/organisations/
    department-for-education

WALES

Guidance on the new curriculum for 3- to 16-year-olds in Wales was published in January 2020 ahead of implementation in 2022 for learners up to and including Year 7. Secondary schools will then be expected to roll out their curricular on a year-by-year basis with Year 8 in September 2023 through to Year 11 in September 2026.

The purposes of the curriculum in Wales are to develop children and young people as:
• Ambitious, capable learners, ready to learn throughout their lives
• Enterprising, creative contributors, ready to play a full part in life and work
• Ethical, informed citizens of Wales and the world
• Healthy, confident individuals, ready to lead fulfilling lives as valued members of society

This will be underpinned by integral skills: creativity and innovation; critical thinking and problem-solving; personal effectiveness; and planning and organising, as well as literacy, numeracy and digital skills. Assessment will be focused on identifying students' progress and preparing them for life after school.

Schools are expected to write their own curriculum, it must include:
• Six areas of learning and experience from age 3 to 16 years
• Three cross-curriculum responsibilities: literacy, numeracy and digital competence
• Progression reference points at ages 5, 8, 11, 14 and 16
• Achievement outcomes which describe expected achievements at each progression reference point

The six Areas of Learning and Experience will be:
• Expressive arts
• Health and well-being
• Humanities (including RE which should remain compulsory to age 16)
• Languages, literacy and communication (including Welsh, which should remain compulsory to age 16, and modern foreign languages)
• Mathematics and numeracy
• Science and technology (including computer science)

Schools must also teach relationships and sexuality education.

Welsh is compulsory for pupils at all key stages, either as a first or as a second language. In 2010, 16.5 per cent of pupils were taught Welsh as a first language. In April 2012, the Minister for Education and Skills approved an action plan to raise standards and attainment in Welsh second language education.

ASSESSMENT

Statutory testing at the end of Key Stage 2 was removed for pupils in Wales from 2004–5, leaving only statutory teacher assessment which takes place at the end of Key Stage 1 (the Foundation Phase) and Key Stage 3, and is being strengthened by moderation and accreditation arrangements.

A National Literacy and Numeracy Framework (LNF), outlining the skills 5- to 15-year-olds are expected to acquire, became statutory from September 2013. For literacy, this means children should become accomplished in reading for information, writing for information and expressing themselves fluently and grammatically in speech. In numeracy, children are expected to develop numerical reasoning and use number skills, measuring skills and data skills.

National reading and numeracy tests – 'personalised assessments' – for pupils in Years 2 to 9 started in Wales in May 2013 and will be entirely online from 2021–22. The tests are designed to give teachers a clearer insight into a learner's development and progress, to allow them to intervene at an earlier stage if learners are falling behind.

The reading test includes a statutory 'core' test, and a set of optional test materials to help teachers to investigate learners' strengths and development needs in more depth.

The numeracy test is split into two papers: numerical procedures and numerical reasoning. The procedural paper consists of a set of questions designed to assess the basic, essential numeracy skills such as addition, multiplication and division. The numerical reasoning test assesses learners' ability to find the most effective ways to solve everyday numeracy problems.

Learners in Welsh-medium schools take a reading test in Welsh only in Years 2 and 3, but in both English and Welsh from Year 4 onwards. Schools have the option to use both tests in Year 3. Learners take the numeracy test in either English or Welsh.

THE WELSH GOVERNMENT – EDUCATION AND
SKILLS **W** https://hwb.gov.wales/curriculum-for-wales

SCOTLAND

The curriculum in Scotland is not prescribed by statute but is the responsibility of education authorities and individual schools. However, schools and authorities are expected to follow the Scottish government's guidance on management and delivery of the curriculum, which is primarily through Education Scotland.

Scotland is now implementing *Curriculum for Excellence,* which aims to provide more autonomy for teachers, greater choice and opportunity for pupils and a single coherent curriculum for all children and young people aged 3 to 18.

The purpose of Curriculum for Excellence is encapsulated in 'the four capacities': to enable each child or young person to be a successful learner, a confident individual, a responsible citizen and an effective contributor. It focuses on providing a broad curriculum that develops skills for learning, skills for life and skills for work, with a sustained focus on literacy and numeracy. The period of education from pre-school through to the end of secondary stage 3, when pupils reach 14, aims to provide every young person in Scotland with this broad general education.

Curriculum for Excellence sets out 'experiences and outcomes', which describe broad areas of learning and what is to be achieved within them. They are:

- Expressive arts (including art and design, dance, drama, music)
- Health and well-being (including physical education, food and health, relationships and sexual health and mental, physical and social well-being)
- Languages
- Mathematics
- Religious and moral education
- Sciences
- Social studies (including history, geography, society and economy)
- Technologies (including business, computing, food and textiles, craft, design, engineering and graphics)

The experiences and outcomes are written at five levels with progression to examinations and qualifications during the senior phase, which covers secondary stages 4 to 6 when students are generally aged 14 to 17. The framework is designed to be flexible so that pupils can progress at their own pace.

Level	Stage
Early	The pre-school years and primary 1 (ages 3–5), or later for some
First	To the end of primary 4 (age 8), but earlier or later for some
Second	To the end of primary 7 (age 11), but earlier or later for some
Third and Fourth	Secondary 1 to secondary 3 (ages 12–14), but earlier for some. The fourth level experiences and outcomes are intended to allow choice, and young people's programmes will not include all of the fourth level outcomes
Senior phase	Secondary 4 to secondary 6 (ages 15–18), and college or other studies

Under the new curriculum, assessment of students' progress and achievements from ages 3 to 15 is carried out by teachers who base their assessment judgments on a range of evidence rather than single assessment instruments such as tests. Teachers have access to an online National Assessment Resource, which provides a range of assessment material and national exemplars across the curriculum areas.

In the senior phase, young people aged 16 to 18, including those studying outside school, build up a portfolio of national qualifications, awarded by the Scottish Qualifications Authority (SQA).

Provision is made for teaching in Gaelic in many parts of Scotland and the number of pupils in Gaelic-medium education, from nursery to secondary, is growing.

EDUCATION SCOTLAND **T** 0113-1244 4330 **W** https://
education.gov.scot

SCOTTISH QUALIFICATIONS AUTHORITY
T 0345-279 1000 **W** www.sqa.org.uk

NORTHERN IRELAND

Children aged four to 16 in all grant-aided schools in Northern Ireland must be taught the curriculum put in place in September 2009. The statutory curriculum for Years 1 to 12 places greater emphasis on developing skills and preparing young people for life and work.

This curriculum includes a Foundation Stage to cover Years 1 and 2 of primary school, to allow a more appropriate learning style for the youngest pupils and to ease the transition from pre-school. Key Stage 1 covers primary Years 3 and 4, until children are 8, and Key Stage 2 covers primary Years 5, 6 and 7, until children are 11. Post-primary, Key Stage 3 covers Years 8, 9 and 10 and Key Stage 4 covers Years 11 and 12.

The primary curriculum is made up of the following areas of learning:
- Language and literacy
- Mathematics and numeracy
- The arts
- The world around us
- Personal development and mutual understanding
- Physical education
- Religious education

The post-primary curriculum includes a new area of learning for life and work, made up of employability, personal development, local and global citizenship and home economics (at Key Stage 3). It is also made up of RE and the following areas of learning:
- Language and literacy
- Mathematics and numeracy
- Modern languages
- The arts
- Environment and society
- Physical education
- Science and technology

At Key Stage 4, there are nine areas of learning, but statutory requirements are reduced to learning for life and work, physical education and RE. The aim is to provide greater choice and flexibility for pupils and allow them access to a wider range of academic and vocational courses provided under the revised curriculum's 'Entitlement Framework' (EF).

Since September 2013, schools have been required to provide pupils with access to at least 18 courses at Key Stage 4 and 21 courses at post-16. This increased to 24 and 27 courses respectively in September 2015. At least one third of the courses must be 'general' with one third 'applied'. The remaining third is at the discretion of each school. Individual pupils decide on the number and mix of courses they wish to follow.

RE is a compulsory part of the Northern Ireland curriculum, although parents have the right to withdraw their children from part or all of RE or collective worship. Schools have to provide RE in accordance with a core syllabus drawn up by the province's four main churches (Church of Ireland, Presbyterian, Methodist and Roman Catholic) and specified by the Department of Education.

Revised assessment and reporting arrangements were introduced when the curriculum was revised. The focus from Foundation to Key Stage 3 is on 'Assessment for Learning'. This programme includes classroom-based teacher assessment, computer-based assessment of literacy and numeracy and pupils deciding on their strengths and weaknesses and how they might progress to achieve their potential. Assessment information is given to parents in an annual report. Pupils at Key Stage 4 and beyond continue to be assessed through public examinations.

The Council for the Curriculum, Examinations and Assessment (CCEA), a non-departmental public body reporting to the Department of Education in Northern Ireland, is unique in the UK in combining the functions of a curriculum advisory body, an awarding body and a qualifications regulatory body. It advises the government on what should be taught in Northern Ireland's schools and colleges, ensures that the qualifications and examinations offered by awarding bodies in Northern Ireland are of an appropriate quality and standard and, as the leading awarding body itself, offers a range of qualifications including GCSEs, A-levels and AS-levels.

The CCEA hosts a dedicated curriculum website covering all aspects of the revised curriculum, assessment and reporting.

COUNCIL FOR THE CURRICULUM, EXAMINATIONS AND ASSESSMENT **T** 028-9026 1200 **W** www.ccea.org.uk

QUALIFICATIONS

ENGLAND, WALES AND NORTHERN IRELAND

There is a very wide range of public examinations and qualifications available, accredited by the Office of Qualifications and Examinations Regulation (OFQUAL) in England, Qualifications Wales in Wales and the Council for the Curriculum, Examinations and Assessment (CCEA) in Northern Ireland. Up-to-date information on all accredited qualifications and awarding bodies is available online at the Register of Regulated Qualifications website.

The qualifications frameworks group all accredited qualifications into levels. All the qualifications within a level place similar demands on individuals as learners. Entry level, for example, covers basic knowledge and skills in English, maths and ICT not geared towards specific occupations, level 3 includes qualifications such as A-levels which are appropriate for those wishing to go on to higher education, level 7 covers Master's degrees and vocational qualifications appropriate for senior professionals and managers and level 8 is equivalent to a doctorate.

Young people aged 14 to 19 in schools or (post-16) colleges or apprenticeships may gain academic qualifications such as GCSEs, AS-levels and A-levels; qualifications linked to particular career fields, like diplomas; vocational qualifications such as BTECs and NVQs; and functional key or basic skills qualifications.

In October 2015, both the National Qualifications Framework (NQF) formerly used in England, Wales and Northern Ireland and its successor the Qualifications and Credit Framework (QCF) for England and Northern Ireland were replaced by the Regulated Qualifications Framework (RQF) for England and the Credit and Qualifications Framework for Wales (CQFW). In Northern Ireland the Council for the Curriculum, Examinations and Assessment (CCEA) regulates qualifications. There is also a Framework for Higher Education Qualifications (FHEQ) for England, Wales and Northern Ireland.

In England, Wales and Northern Ireland there are nine qualification levels:

Entry level – each entry-level qualification is available at three sub-levels: 1, 2 and 3, with level 3 the most difficult. Entry-level qualifications are: entry-level award; entry-level certificate (ELC); entry-level diploma; entry-level English for speakers of other languages (ESOL); entry-level essential skills; entry-level functional skills; Skills for Life.

Level 1 qualifications are: first certificate; GCSE – grade D, E, F or G (3, 2 or 1 in the new grading structure); level 1 award; level 1 certificate; level 1 diploma; level 1 ESOL; level 1 essential skills; level 1 functional skills; level 1 national vocational qualification (NVQ); music grades 1, 2 and 3.

Level 2 qualifications are: CSE – grade 1; GCSE – grade A*, A, B or C (4 or above in the new grading structure); intermediate apprenticeship; level 2 award; level 2 certificate; level 2 diploma; level 2 ESOL; level 2 essential skills; level 2 functional skills; level 2 national certificate; level 2 national diploma; level 2 NVQ; music grades 4 and 5; O level – grade A, B or C.

Level 3 qualifications are: A level – grade A*, A, B, C, D or E; access to higher education; diploma; advanced apprenticeship; applied general; AS level; international Baccalaureate diploma; level 3 award; level 3 certificate; level 3 diploma; level 3 ESOL; level 3 national certificate; level 3 national diploma; level 3 NVQ; music grades 6, 7 and 8; tech level.

Level 4 qualifications are: certificate of higher education (CertHE); higher apprenticeship; higher national certificate (HNC); level 4 award; level 4 certificate; level 4 diploma; level 4 NVQ.

Level 5 qualifications are: diploma of higher education (DipHE); foundation degree; higher national diploma (HND); level 5 award; level 5 certificate; level 5 diploma; level 5 NVQ.

Level 6 qualifications are: degree apprenticeship; degree with honours – for example bachelor of arts (BA) with honours, bachelor of science (BSc) with honours; graduate certificate; graduate diploma; level 6 award; level 6 certificate; level 6 diploma; level 6 NVQ; ordinary degree without honours.

Level 7 qualifications are: integrated master's degree, for example master of engineering (MEng); level 7 award; level 7 certificate; level 7 diploma; level 7 NVQ; master's degree, for example master of arts (MA), master of science (MSc); postgraduate certificate; postgraduate certificate in education (PGCE); postgraduate diploma.

Level 8 qualifications are: doctorate, for example doctor of philosophy (PHD or DPHIL); level 8 award; level 8 certificate; level 8 diploma.

FRAMEWORK FOR HIGHER EDUCATION QUALIFICATIONS (FHEQ)
This framework applies to degrees, diplomas, certificates and other academic awards (other than honorary degrees and higher doctorates) granted by a higher education provider in the exercise of its degree awarding powers. It starts at RQF level 4 and goes up to level 8 and includes the following qualifications: Certificate of Higher Education; Diploma of Higher Education; Bachelor's degrees; Master's degrees; and Doctoral degrees.

COUNCIL FOR THE CURRICULUM, EXAMINATIONS AND ASSESSMENT (NORTHERN IRELAND)
T 028-9026 1200 **W** www.ccea.org.uk

QUALIFICATIONS WALES **T** 01633-373222
   W www.qualificationswales.org

REGISTER OF REGULATED QUALIFICATIONS
   W http://register.ofqual.gov.uk

OFFICE OF QUALIFICATIONS AND EXAMINATIONS REGULATION (OFQUAL) **T** 0300-303 3344
   W www.ofqual.gov.uk

GCSE
The vast majority of pupils in their last year of compulsory schooling in England, Wales and Northern Ireland take at least one General Certificate of Secondary Education (GCSE) exam, though GCSEs may be taken at any age. GCSEs assess the performance of pupils on a subject-specific basis and are mostly taken after a two-year course. They are available in more than 50 subjects, most of them academic subjects, though some, known as vocational or applied GCSEs, involve the study of a particular area of employment and the development of work-related skills. Some subjects are also offered as short-course qualifications, equivalent to half a standard GCSE, or as double awards, equivalent to two GCSEs.

For many years GCSEs were assessed on coursework completed by students during the course as well as exams at the end, and GCSE certificates were awarded on an eight-point scale from A* to G. In most subjects two different papers, higher tier and foundation tier, were provided for different ranges of ability, with grades A*–D available to students taking the higher paper and grades C–G available from the foundation paper.

In England, all traditional GCSEs have been replaced by new GCSEs or, in some subjects, withdrawn. The new GCSEs no longer involve modules and coursework, just exam assessment at the end of the two-year course; a very few subjects (such as music technology) may include an element of non-exam assessment. Only maths, science and foreign language GCSEs will be tiered. New GCSEs are graded 9 to 1, rather than A* to G.

The changeover to new GCSEs was phased in. In September 2015 schools began teaching revised GCSEs in English language, English literature and mathematics, for exams in 2017. Teaching of revised GCSEs in ancient and modern foreign languages, art and design, biology, chemistry, citizenship, computer science, double science, dance, drama, food preparation and nutrition, geography, history, music, physics, physical education and religious studies started in September 2016 for exams in 2018. Teaching in 14 other subjects started in September 2017 for exams in 2019.

In 2017 English language, English literature and maths were the first subjects to be graded from 9 to 1. Another 20 subjects were graded 9 to 1 in 2018, with most others following in 2019. During this transition, students received a mixture of letter and number grades. It will take until summer 2020 for all reformed GCSEs to be graded on the new scale.

In Northern Ireland, new CCEA GCSEs were introduced for first teaching in 2017, with first awards in 2019. They are graded on a 9 grade system from A*-G with a new C* grade.

All GCSE specifications, assessments and grading procedures are monitored by OFQUAL, QW and the CCEA.

Since September 2010 state schools have been allowed to offer pupils International GCSE (iGCSE) qualifications in key subjects including English, mathematics, science and ICT. Though iGCSEs were considered more rigorous than traditional GCSEs, the government regards the new GCSEs in these subjects as superior, and iGCSE results no longer count in school performance tables from 2017, or later, depending on the subject.

GCE A-LEVEL AND AS-LEVEL
GCE (General Certificate of Education) Advanced levels (A-levels) are the qualifications used by most young people in England, Wales and Northern Ireland to gain entry to university.

A-levels are subject-based qualifications. They are mostly taken by UK students aged 16 to 19 over a two-year course in school sixth forms or at college, but can be taken at any age. They are available in more than 45, mostly academic, subjects, though there are some A-levels in vocational areas, often termed 'applied A-levels'.

Traditionally, A-level qualifications consisted of two parts: advanced subsidiary (AS) and A2 units. The AS was a qualification assessed at the standard expected of a learner half way through an A-level course, normally consisting of two units that together contributed 50 per cent towards the full A-level. The A2 was the second half of a full A-level qualification. It was assessed at the standard expected of a learner at the end of a full A-level course, and normally consisted of two units that together made up the remaining 50 per cent of the full A-level qualification. Each unit was graded A–E, with an A* grade available to exceptional candidates since 2010.

An extended project was introduced in September 2008 as a separate qualification. It is a single piece of work on a topic of the student's own choosing that requires a high degree of planning, preparation, research and autonomous working. Awards are graded A–E and the extended project is accredited as half an A-level.

Since September 2013, students in England in their first or second year of A-level studies have not been allowed to sit A-level exams in January. A-levels are still examined unit by unit, but all exams are taken in the summer.

Revised AS and A-levels were introduced in phases from 2015 to 2017. All assessment of the new A-levels now takes place at the end of the two-year course and the AS has become a standalone qualification rather than contributing to a full A-level qualification.

Since September 2015, students have been taught the new-style AS-levels and A-levels in art and design, biology, business, chemistry, computer science, economics, English language, English language and literature, English literature, history, physics, psychology and sociology. New AS and A-levels in ancient languages, dance, drama and theatre, geography, modern foreign languages (French, German and Spanish), music, physical education and religious studies started to be taught in September 2016.

From September 2017, new-style A-levels were introduced in: accounting, ancient history, archaeology, classical civilisation, design and technology, electronics, film studies, geology, government and politics, history of art, law, maths and further maths, media studies, music technology, philosophy and statistics.

As a result of Covid-19 disruption to education, in 2021 exams will go ahead in England, Wales and Northern Ireland with changes to 15 A-level subjects and 25 GCSEs. Changes include: changes to how content is assessed in GCSE geography, history and ancient history; a choice of topics on which students are required to answer questions in their English literature exams; a reduction in geography, geology and environmental science fieldwork at GCSE and A-level; modern foreign languages GCSE students will be given a grade of pass, merit or distinction (or 'not classified') for their spoken language skills by teachers, alongside their 9 to 1 grade; a range of modifications to the non-exam assessment arrangements in a number of subjects to accommodate potential public health requirements, for example, GCSE food preparation and nutrition, GCSE, AS and A level music and GCSE physical education. See also Recent Developments.

INTERNATIONAL BACCALAUREATE

The International Baccalaureate (IB) offers four educational programmes for students aged 3 to 19: IB primary years programme, IB middle years programme, IB diploma programme, IB career-related certificate.

Some 155 'IB World Schools' in the UK offer at least one IB programme.

The IB diploma programme for students aged 16 to 19 is based around detailed academic study of a wide range of subjects, including languages, the arts, science, maths, history and geography, leading to a single qualification recognised by UK universities.

The IB diploma is made up of a compulsory 'core' plus six separate subjects where individuals have some choice over what they study. The compulsory core contains three elements: theory of knowledge; creativity, action and service; and a 4,000-word extended essay.

The IB diploma normally takes two years to complete and most of the assessment is done through externally marked examinations. Candidates are awarded points for each part of the programme, up to a maximum of 45. A candidate must score 24 points or more to achieve a full diploma.

Successfully completing the diploma earns points on the 'UCAS tariff', the UK system for allocating points to qualifications used for entry to higher education. An IB diploma total of 24 points is worth 260 UCAS points – the same as a B and two C grades at A-level. The maximum of 45 points earns 720 UCAS points – equivalent to six A-levels at grade A.

WELSH BACCALAUREATE

The Welsh Baccalaureate Qualification (WBQ), available for 14- to 19-year-olds in Wales, combines a compulsory core, which incorporates personal development skills, with options from existing academic and vocational qualifications, such as A-levels, GCSEs and NVQs, to make one broader award. The WBQ can be studied in English or Welsh, or a combination of the two. Candidates who meet the requirements of the compulsory core and options relevant to each level of the qualification are awarded the Welsh Baccalaureate Foundation, Intermediate or Advanced Diploma as appropriate.

WJEC (Welsh Joint Education Committee), which administers the WBQ, has also developed two new WBQs at level 1 and level 2 suitable for delivery over one year and with a particular focus on employability.

A revised and more rigorous Welsh Baccalaureate has been taught since September 2015. It is based on a graded Skills Challenge Certificate and supporting qualifications. The aim is to enable learners to develop and demonstrate an understanding of, and proficiency in, essential and employability skills: communication, numeracy, digital literacy, planning and organisation, creativity and innovation, critical thinking and problem solving, and personal effectiveness. The emphasis is on applied and purposeful learning and opportunities for assessment in a range of real life contexts through three 'challenge briefs' and an individual project.

APPLIED GENERAL, TECH LEVEL AND T LEVEL QUALIFICATIONS

As part of changes to the 16-19 performance tables, existing vocational qualifications were designated 'Tech levels' if they met specific criteria. Students achieving a Tech level qualification, a level 3 maths qualification and an extended project could be counted as achieving a 'TechBacc' (Technical Baccalaureate) performance measure in the post-16 school and college performance tables from 2016.

From 2017, post-16 performance tables have also recognised Applied General Qualifications, which take the same time to complete as AS-levels and focus on broader study of a technical area. These are advanced (level 3) qualifications that allow 16- to 19-year-old students to develop transferable knowledge and skills. They allow entry to a range of higher education courses, either by meeting the entry requirements in their own right or by adding value to other qualifications such as A-levels.

From September 2020, new 'T Level' qualifications started for students aged 16-19 wanting to specialise in a technical occupation. The two-year courses follow GCSEs and are equivalent to three A-levels and have been developed in collaboration with employers and businesses so that the content meets the needs of industry and prepares students for work, further training or study. T Levels offer students a mixture of classroom learning and 'on-the-job' experience during an industry placement of at least 315 hours (approximately 45 days).

T Levels take as long to complete as A-levels and, like A-levels, are at level 3. They are based on the same standards as apprenticeships, designed by employers, and will offer around 1,800 hours of study over two years, including a 315 hour (45-day) work placement.

T Levels include compulsory elements:
- A technical qualification which includes core skills, theory, and concepts for the industry area
- Specialist occupational skills and knowledge of the career
- An industry placement with an employer
- A minimum standard in maths and English, if students have not already achieved this

Students who complete a T Level will receive an overall grade of pass, merit, distinction or distinction*; a separate grade for the core component using A* to E, and a separate grade for each occupational specialism, shown as pass, merit or distinction. Students will be awarded a nationally recognised certificate showing a breakdown of what they have achieved. It will also confirm that a student has met the minimum requirements for maths and English qualifications.

T-levels in digital production, design and development; design, surveying and planning, and education started in September 2020. From Autumn 2021, T-levels will be available in: building services engineering; digital business services; digital support and services; health; healthcare science; onsite construction; and science. More T-levels are expected from Autumn 2022.

Students who want to go on to higher education must achieve at least an overall pass grade to receive UCAS Tariff points, as Detailed below:

T Level Overall Grade	UCAS Tariffs	A Level
Distinction* (A* on the core and distinction in the occupational specialism)	168	AAA*
Distinction	144	AAA
Merit	120	BBB
Pass (C or above on the core)	96	CCC
Pass (D or E on the core)	72	DDD

BTECS, OCR NATIONALS AND OTHER VOCATIONAL QUALIFICATIONS

Vocational qualifications can range from general qualifications where a person learns skills relevant to a variety of jobs, to specialist qualifications designed for a particular sector. They are available from several awarding bodies, such as City & Guilds, Edexcel and OCR, and can be taken at many different levels. All vocational and work-related qualifications fit into the Regulated Qualifications Framework (RQF).

BTEC qualifications and OCR Nationals are particular types of work-related qualifications, available in a wide range of subjects, including: art and design, business, health and social care, information technology, media, public services, science and sport. The qualifications offer a mix of theory and practice, can include work experience and can be part of an Apprenticeship. They can be studied full-time at college or school, or part-time at college.

Learners complete a range of assignments, case studies and practical activities, as well as a portfolio of evidence that shows what work has been completed.

Since 2016, the quality and assessment of all vocational courses offered by schools and colleges to 14- to 19-year-olds has been strengthened. The standards of reformed BTECs, along with Cambridge OCR National Certificates and Vocational Certificates (V-Certs), equal those of GCSE A*–C grades. All vocational qualifications are graded (previously many were simply pass/fail) and all have a 25 per cent externally examined component. New Substantial Vocational Qualifications at level 2 provide 16- to 19-year-old students seeking entry at a more basic level to a skilled trade or occupation with qualifications that are valued by employers.

NVQs

A National Vocational Qualification (NVQ) is a 'competence-based' qualification that is recognised by employers. Individuals learn practical, work-related tasks designed to help them develop the skills and knowledge to do a particular job effectively. NVQs can be taken in school, at college or by people already in work. There are more than 1,300 different NVQs available from the vast majority of business sectors. NVQs exist at levels 1 to 5 on the RQF. An NVQ qualification at level 2 or 3 can also be taken as part of an Apprenticeship.

Functional Skills

Functional skills qualifications were launched during 2010, for all learners aged 14 and above. They test practical skills that allow people to work confidently, effectively and independently in life, and are available only in England. Wales and Northern Ireland have literacy and numeracy qualifications known as 'Essential Skills'.

In England, the government is reforming functional skills qualifications in English and mathematics, with reformed qualifications first taught from September 2019.

Apprenticeships

Apprenticeships combine on-the-job training with nationally recognised qualifications, allowing individuals to gain skills and qualifications while working and earning a wage. More than 200 different types of apprenticeships are available, offering over 1,500 job roles; they take between one and five years to complete. There are four levels available:

- Intermediate Apprenticeships – at level 2 on the Regulated Qualifications Framework (RQF), they are equivalent to five good GCSE passes (9–4)
- Advanced Apprenticeships – at level 3 on the RQF, they are equivalent to two A-level passes/Level 3 Diploma/International Baccalaureate
- Higher Apprenticeships – levels 4, 5, 6 and 7 equivalent to Foundation degree and above
- Degree Apprenticeships – added in 2015 (RQF level 6 and 7) equivalent to a bachelor's or master's degree

In England, the National Apprenticeship Service (NAS), launched in 2009, is responsible for the delivery of apprenticeships and provides an online vacancy matching system. The way in which the government funds the training and assessment costs of apprenticeships was revised in May 2017, when the apprenticeship levy was introduced and the Institute for Apprenticeships and Technical Education was created. Sponsored by the Department for Education, the institute is focused on supporting employers in developing apprenticeships. In 2018–19, 742,000 people participated in an apprenticeship in England, with 393,400 apprenticeship starts and 185,100 achievements. Degree apprenticeships are growing in number with numerous universities grouping together to offer full bachelor's or master's degree programmes. Currently the scheme is only available in England and Wales, though applications can be made from all parts of the UK. The Welsh government and the Department for the Economy are responsible for the apprenticeship programmes in Wales and Northern Ireland respectively.

INSTITUTE FOR APPRENTICESHIPS AND TECHNICAL EDUCATION **W** www.instituteforapprenticeships.org
NATIONAL APPRENTICESHIP SERVICE (NAS) **T** 0800-015 0400 **W** www.gov.uk/apply-apprenticeship
REGISTER OF APPRENTICESHIP TRAINING PROVIDERS
  W www.gov.uk/guidance/register-of-apprenticeship-training-providers

SCOTLAND

Scotland has its own system of public examinations and qualifications. The Scottish Qualifications Authority (SQA) is Scotland's national body for qualifications, responsible for developing, accrediting, assessing and certificating all Scottish qualifications apart from university degrees and some professional body qualifications.

There are qualifications at all levels of attainment. Almost all school candidates gain SQA qualifications in the fourth year of secondary school and most obtain further qualifications in the fifth or sixth year or in further education colleges. Increasingly, people also take qualifications in the workplace.

SQA, with partners such as Universities Scotland, has introduced the Scottish Credit and Qualifications Framework (SCQF) as a way of comparing and understanding Scottish qualifications. It includes qualifications across academic and vocational sectors and compares them by giving a level and credit points. There are 12 levels in the SCQF, level 1 being the least difficult and level 12 the most difficult. The number of SCQF credit points shows how much learning has to be done to achieve the qualification. For instance, one SCQF credit point equals about 10 hours of learning including assessment.

Since reforms introduced in 2013, qualifications in Scotland are divided into academic National Qualifications and more practical-based Qualifications for Work.

National Qualifications

- National 1 units are assessed as a pass or fail by a teacher or lecturer. They could lead to National 2 courses or awards at SCQF level 1 or 2
- National 2 courses are made up of units assessed as pass or fail by a teacher or lecturer. Learners need to pass all units to achieve the qualification. They could lead to National 3 courses or awards at SCQF level 2 or 3
- National 3 courses comprise three National Units assessed as pass or fail by a teacher or lecturer. They could lead to related courses at National 4, awards at SQCF level 3 or 4, National Certificates or National Progression Awards or employment opportunities
- National 4 courses are made up of units, including an added value unit, which assesses learners' performance across the course. They could lead to National 5 courses, units or awards at SCQF level 4 or 5, National Certificate or National Progression Awards, or Modern Apprenticeships or other employment opportunities
- National 5 courses are assessed through exams, coursework or both, most of which is marked by the Scottish Qualifications Authority. Courses are graded A to D or 'no award'. They could lead to Higher courses, units or awards at SCQF level 5 or 6, National Certificate or National Progression Awards, Foundation Apprenticeships or a Modern Apprenticeship at SCQF level 6
- Higher courses are made up of exams or coursework (units will be removed from 2018–19) or both, marked by the SQA, or teachers or lecturers in some cases. They could lead to Advanced Higher courses, units or awards at SCQF level 6 or 7, National Certificate or National Progression Awards, Higher National Certificate or Higher National Diplomas, or Modern Apprenticeships at SCQF level 7
- Advanced Higher courses are made up of exams or coursework (units will be removed from 2019–20) or both, marked by the SQA, or teachers or lecturers in some cases. They could lead to a Higher National Diploma, undergraduate degree or a Technical Apprenticeship at SCQF level 8
- Skills for Work courses encourage learners to become familiar with the world of work. They are available in a variety of areas such as construction, hairdressing and hospitality (**W** www.sqa.org.uk/skillsforwork)
- Scottish Baccalaureates are qualifications at SCQF level 7, and are available for learners in S5 and S6. They exist in Expressive Arts, Languages, Science, and Social Sciences and are awarded as a pass or distinction. Learners undertake an interdisciplinary project, which allows them to develop and show evidence of initiative, responsibility, and independent working – skills of value in the world of higher education (**W** www.sqa.org.uk/baccalaureates)

Qualifications For Work

- Introduction to Work Place Skills qualification is designed to help 'can do' learners to develop core and employability skills. It comprises an employer-assessed work experience placement of a minimum of 150 hours. Successful completion allows learners to go to Certificate of Work Readiness, further training, education or employment (**W** www.sqa.org.uk/introtowork)
- Certificate of Work Readiness award includes an employer-assessed work experience placement and is available through colleges and training providers working in partnership with employers (**W** www.sqa.org.uk/workready).
- Foundation Apprenticeships are new, work-based learning qualifications for secondary school pupils and allow pupils in S4 to S6 to complete elements of a Modern Apprenticeship while still at school. Depending on their subject, pupils study towards Foundation Apprenticeships alongside their other subjects and spend part of their school week at college or with a local employer. By December 2017, some 18,700 young people had started apprenticeships. (**W** www.apprenticeships.scot/foundation-apprenticeships).
- Modern Apprenticeships offer anyone aged over 16 paid employment combined with the opportunity to train for jobs at craft, technician and management level. They are developed by the industry or sector in which they will be implemented. (**W** www.sqa.org.uk/modernapprenticeships or **W** www.apprenticeships.scot)
- SQA Awards are flexible and nationally recognised. They provide learners with opportunities to acquire skills, recognise achievement and promote confidence
- Wider Achievement qualifications provide young people with the opportunity to have learning and skills formally recognised, whether developed in or outside the classroom. Available at a number of levels in subjects including Employability, Leadership and Enterprise, these qualifications help schools deliver skills for learning, life and work
- Scottish Vocational Qualifications are based on national standards drawn up by people from industry, commerce and education covering a wide range of occupations
- Professional Development Awards develop the skills of those already in professional employment and can be embedded within another qualification such as a Higher National Certificate or Diploma
- National Certificates prepare people for employment, development or progression to advanced study. They are aimed at 16-18 year olds and are at SCQF levels 2 to 6
- National Progression Awards assess a defined set of skills and knowledge in specialist vocational areas, linking to National Occupational Standards, which are the basis of SVQs
- Higher National qualifications are offered by colleges, universities and other training centres. Higher National Certificates, Higher National Diplomas and Professional Development Awards are designed to meet employers' needs and can give candidates access to second or third year entry at university

As part of the Curriculum for Excellence programme SQA developed revised National qualifications that became available in schools from August 2013, replacing Standard Grade, Intermediate and Access qualifications at all levels. New Higher qualifications became available from August 2014 and Advanced Higher qualifications from August 2015:

SCQF level	National qualifications
1 & 2	National 1 & 2
3	National 3
4	National 4
5	National 5
6	Higher
7	Advanced Higher

Revised qualifications were available alongside existing qualifications until 2015–16. Final results for existing Access, Intermediate, Higher and Advanced Higher qualifications were issued in August 2015.

Since 2017–18 mandatory unit assessments have been removed from the National 5 qualification to reduce teacher and pupil workload. Course assessments for National 5 – a combination of exam and coursework – were strengthened to maintain their integrity, breadth and standards.

Mandatory unit assessment was removed for Higher courses from 2018–19 and FOR Advanced Higher courses from 2019–20.

THE SCOTTISH QUALIFICATIONS AUTHORITY (SQA)
    T 0345-279 1000 W www.sqa.org.uk

SCOTTISH CREDIT AND QUALIFICATIONS
    FRAMEWORK (SCQF) T 0845-270 7371
    W www.scqf.org.uk

SKILLS DEVELOPMENT SCOTLAND (SDS)
    T 0800-917 8000 W www.skillsdevelopmentscotland.co.uk

FURTHER EDUCATION AND LIFELONG LEARNING

ENGLAND

The further education (FE) system in England provides a wide range of education and training opportunities for young people and adults. From the age of 16, young people who wish to remain in education, but not in a school setting, can undertake further education (including skills training) in an FE college. There are two main types of college in the FE sector: sixth form colleges and general further education (GFE) colleges. Some FE colleges focus on a particular area, such as art and design or agriculture and horticulture. Each institution decides its own range of subjects and courses. Students at FE colleges can study for a wide and growing range of academic and/or work-related qualifications, from entry level to higher education level.

The Department for Business, Innovation and Skills was responsible for the FE sector and for funding adult FE until July 2016, when these responsibilities passed to the Department for Education, which already funded all education and training for 16- to 18-year-olds.

The proportion of 16- to 18-year-olds in education or training has risen steadily over recent years, driven by increases in state-funded schools and in higher education. The 'September Guarantee', introduced in 2007, offers a place in post-16 education or training to all 16- and 17-year-olds who want one. The latest statistics, for 2019, show 81.6 per cent of young people in full-time education and apprenticeships, with 6.6 per cent not in education, employment or training.

The Education and Skills Funding Agency (ESFA) replaced the Skills Funding Agency and the Education Funding Agency in April 2017. The ESFA is accountable for £59bn of funding for the education and training sector, regulating academies, FE colleges, employers and training providers, intervening where there is risk of failure or where there is evidence of mismanagement of public funds, and delivering major projects in the education and skills sector, such as school capital programmes, the National Careers Service, the digital Apprenticeship Service and National Apprenticeship Service.

In November 2010, the government announced a new strategy for FE, including more adult apprenticeships; fully-funded training for 19- to 24-year-olds undertaking their first full level 2 (GCSE equivalent) or first level 3 qualification; and fully-funded basic skills training for people who left school without basic skills in reading, writing and mathematics. 'Train to Gain', the programme that funded trainees sponsored by employers, was replaced in July 2011 by a programme focused on helping small employers to train low-skilled staff. In April 2012 the National Careers Service was created.

In April 2013, the government announced plans to make the skills system more responsive and to create new traineeships.

There are currently nine centres of training excellence called National Skills Academies, led, funded and designed by employers, in various stages of development. Each academy offers specialist training in a key sector of the economy, working in partnership with colleges, schools and independent training providers.

Among the many voluntary bodies providing adult education, the Workers' Educational Association (WEA) is the UK's largest, operating throughout England and Scotland. It provides part-time courses to adults in response to local need in community centres, village halls, schools, pubs or workplaces. Similar but separate WEA organisations operate in Wales and Northern Ireland.

Since 2016, the Learning and Work Institute promotes lifelong learning opportunities for adults in England and Wales.

LEARNING AND WORK INSTITUTE T 0116-204 4200
    W www.learningandwork.org.uk

THE EDUCATION AND SKILLS FUNDING AGENCY
    W www.gov.uk/government/organisations/
    education-and-skills-funding-agency

WORKERS' EDUCATIONAL ASSOCIATION (WEA)
    T 0300-303346 W www.wea.org.uk

EDUCATION AND TRAINING FOUNDATION
    T 020-3740 8280 W www.et-foundation.co.uk

FEDERATION FOR INDUSTRY SECTOR SKILLS &
    STANDARDS
    W www.fisss.org/sector-skills-council-body/directory-of-sscs/

WALES

In Wales, the aims and makeup of the FE system are similar to those outlined for England. The Welsh government funds a wide range of learning programmes for young people through its 15 FE colleges, local authorities and private organisations. The Welsh government has set out plans to improve learning opportunities for all post-16 learners in the shortest possible time, to increase the engagement of disadvantaged young people in the learning process, and to transform the learning network to increase learner choice, reduce duplication of provision and encourage higher-quality learning and teaching in all post-16 provision.

Responsibility for adult and continuing education lies with the Department for Education and Skills (DfES) within the Welsh government. Wales operates a range of programmes to support skills development, including subsidised work-based training courses for employees and the Workforce Development Programme, where employers can use the free services of experienced skills advisers to develop staff training plans.

COLLEGES WALES **T** 029-2052 2500
  W www.collegeswales.ac.uk
ADULT LEARNING WALES **T** 029-2023 5277
  W www.adultlearning.wales
LEARNING AND WORK INSTITUTE **T** 029-2037 0900
  W www.learningandwork.wales
WEA SOUTH WALES **T** 029-2023 5277
  W www.swales.wea.org.uk

SCOTLAND

Following a series of mergers, Scotland has 26 FE colleges (known simply as colleges), which are at the forefront of lifelong learning, education, training and skills in Scotland. Colleges cater for the needs of learners both in and out of employment and at all stages in their lives. Colleges' courses span much of the range of learning needs, from specialised vocational education and training through to general educational programmes. The level of provision ranges from essential life skills and provision for students with learning difficulties to HNCs and HNDs. Some colleges, notably those in the Highlands and Islands, also deliver degrees and postgraduate qualifications.

A shift in study patterns is taking place within the college sector as colleges concentrate on full-time courses aimed at helping people gain employment and no longer fund short courses lasting less than ten hours. Overall figures are stable, but this change has led to a decline in part-time study and an increase in full-time study.

The Scottish Funding Council (SFC) is the statutory body responsible for funding teaching and learning provision, research and other activities in Scotland's colleges. Overall strategic direction for the sector is provided by the Lifelong Learning Directorate of the Scottish government, which provides annual guidance to the SFC and liaises closely with bodies such as Colleges Scotland, the Scottish Qualifications Authority and the FE colleges themselves to ensure that policies remain relevant and practical.

The Scottish government takes responsibility for community learning and development in Scotland while Skills Development Scotland, a non-departmental public body, is charged with improving Scotland's skills performance by linking skills supply and demand and helping people and organisations to learn, develop and make use of these skills to greater effect.

ILA SCOTLAND **T** 0800-917 8000
  W www.myworldofwork.co.uk/learn-and-train/funding
COLLEGES SCOTLAND **T** 01786-892100
  W www.collegesscotland.ac.uk
SCOTTISH FUNDING COUNCIL **T** 0131-313 6500
  W www.sfc.ac.uk
SKILLS DEVELOPMENT SCOTLAND **T** 0800-917 8000
  W www.skillsdevelopmentscotland.co.uk

NORTHERN IRELAND

FE in Northern Ireland is provided through six regional multi-campus colleges and the College of Agriculture, Food and Rural Affairs. Most secondary schools also have a sixth form which students may attend for two additional years to complete their AS-levels and A-levels.

Colleges Northern Ireland acts as the representative body for the six FE colleges which, like their counterparts in the rest of the UK, are independent corporate bodies each managed by their own governing body. The range of courses that they offer spans essential skills, a wide choice of vocational and academic programmes and higher education programmes. Most full-time students in the six colleges are aged 16 to 19, while most part-time students are over 19.

The Department for the Economy is responsible for the policy, strategic development and financing of the statutory FE sector and for lifelong learning, and also provides support to a small number of non-statutory FE providers. The Educational Guidance Service for Adults, an independent, not-for-profit organisation, has a network of local offices based across Northern Ireland that provide services to adult learners, learning advisers, providers, employers and others interested in improving access to learning for adults.

THE EDUCATIONAL GUIDANCE SERVICE FOR
  ADULTS **E** info@egsa.org.uk **W** www.egsa.org.uk
NI DIRECT FE COLLEGES
  W www.nidirect.gov.uk/contacts/further-education-fe-colleges

FINANCIAL SUPPORT

England has a bursary scheme of up to £1,200 a year for full-time 16- to 19-year-old students facing financial hardship. Two types of bursary exist: vulnerable student bursary and discretionary bursary. Help with transport costs is also possible for some students. This scheme replaced the Education Maintenance Allowance (EMA), which gave 16- to 19-year-olds from low-income families a weekly allowance to continue in education.

There are EMA schemes in Scotland, Wales and Northern Ireland, but with slightly different eligibility conditions. Students must apply to the EMA scheme for the part of the UK where they intend to study. In Northern Ireland 16- to 19-year-old students who meet the relevant criteria and live in a household that has an annual income of £20,500 or less a year (£22,500 if more than one young person in the household qualifies for child benefit) automatically get £30 a week in 2020–21. There is a possibility of two £200 bonus payments too.

Colleges and learning providers award learner support funds directly to new students aged 19 and over.

Care to Learn is available in England to help young parents under the age of 20, who are caring for their own child or children while they are in some form of publicly funded learning (below higher education level), with the costs of childcare and travel. The scheme is not income-assessed and pays up to £160 a week (£175 in London) to cover costs.

Dance and Drama Awards (DaDA) are state-funded scholarships for students aged 16 to 23 enrolled at one of 19 private dance and drama schools in England, who are taking specified courses at National Certificate or National Diploma level. Awards, based on household income, cover some of students' tuition fees and from £1,350 to £5,185 of maintenance in 2020–21.

Young people studying away from home because their chosen course is not available locally may qualify for the *Residential Support Scheme* (up to £3,458 outside London and £4,079 in London for household incomes of less than £21,000).

Information and advice on funding support and applications are available from the Learner Support helpline (**T** 0800-121 8989) or on the GOV.UK website (*see* below).

Discretionary Support Funds (DSF) are available in colleges and school sixth forms to help students who have trouble meeting the costs of participating in further education.

In Wales, students aged 19 or over on FE courses may be eligible for the *Welsh Government Learning Grant FE* (previously the Assembly Learning Grant for Further Education). This is a means-tested payment of up to £1,500 for full-time students and up to £750 for those studying part-time. *Discretionary Assistance Funds* are also available to all students in Wales suffering hardship.

In Scotland, FE students can apply to their college for discretionary support in the form of *Further Education Bursaries,* which can include allowances for maintenance, travel, study, childcare and additional support needs. *Individual Training*

Accounts, which replaced *Individual Learning Accounts* from October 2017, allow eligible students up to £200 towards a single course or training episode per year.

In Northern Ireland, FE students with annual household incomes below £21,330 may be eligible for *Further Education Awards* of up to £2,092, non-refundable assistance, administered on behalf of the five Education and Library Boards by the Western Education and Library Board.

EDUCATION AUTHORITY **W** www.eani.org.uk

GOV.UK **W** www.gov.uk/further-education-courses/financial-help
MY WORLD OF WORK **W** www.myworldofwork.co.uk
STUDENT FINANCE WALES **T** 0300-200 4050
 W www.studentfinancewales.co.uk

HIGHER EDUCATION

Publicly funded higher education (HE) in the UK is provided in universities, higher education colleges and other specialist HE institutions, and in a significant number of FE colleges offering higher education courses.

Since the closure of the Higher Education Funding Council for England (HEFCE) in March 2018, universities and university colleges are funded through UK Research and Innovation (UKRI); *see also* Recent Developments).

The Higher Education Funding Council for Wales (HEFCW) distributes funding for HE in Wales through Wales' eight HEIs, the Open University in Wales and some FE colleges.

The Scottish Funding Council (SFC) – which is also responsible for FE in Scotland – is the national strategic body responsible for funding HE teaching and research in Scotland's 19 HEIs and 26 colleges.

In Northern Ireland, HE is provided by two universities, two university colleges, six regional institutes of further and higher education and the Open University (OU), which operates UK-wide. Northern Ireland has no higher education funding body; the Department for the Economy fulfils that role.

All UK universities and a number of HE colleges award their own degrees and other HE qualifications. HE providers who do not have their own degree-awarding powers offer degrees under 'validation arrangements' with other institutions that do have those powers. The OU, for example, runs a validation service which enables a number of other institutions to award OU degrees, after the OU has assured itself that the academic standards of their courses are as high as the OU's own standards.

Each HE institution is responsible for the standards of the awards it makes and the quality of the education it provides to its students, and each has its own internal quality assurance procedures. External quality assurance for HE institutions throughout the UK is provided by the Quality Assurance Agency for Higher Education (QAA).

The QAA is independent of government, funded by subscriptions from all publicly funded UK universities and colleges of HE. Its main role is to safeguard the standards of HE qualifications. It does this by defining standards for HE through a framework known as the academic infrastructure. QAA carries out reviews of the quality of UK HE institutions via a system known as 'institutional audits', advises on a range of HE quality issues and publishes reports on its website.

DEPARTMENT FOR THE ECONOMY (NI)
 T 028-9052 9900 **W** www.economy-ni.gov.uk

HIGHER EDUCATION FUNDING COUNCIL FOR
 WALES **T** 029-2085 9698 **W** www.hefcw.ac.uk
RESEARCH ENGLAND **T** 0117-905 7600 **W** https://re.ukri.org
SCOTTISH FUNDING COUNCIL **T** 0131-313 6500
 W www.sfc.ac.uk
THE QUALITY ASSURANCE AGENCY FOR HIGHER
 EDUCATION **T** 01452-557000 **W** www.qaa.ac.uk

STUDENTS APPLYING TO UNIVERSITY

	2019	2020	*Difference*
Total applicants by 30 Jan*	638,030	652,790	2%

* Deadline for 2020 cycle
Source: UCAS

STUDENTS IN HIGHER EDUCATION 2018–19*

	Full-time	*Part-time*
HE students	1,883,155	500,810
Postgraduate students	356,650	229,080
Undergraduate students	1,526,505	271,730

* Includes UK, EU and non-EU students
Source: Higher Education Statistics Authority (HESA) 2020

UK HIGHER EDUCATION QUALIFICATIONS AWARDED 2018–19

	Full-time	*Part-time*
First degrees	397,540	27,005
Other undergraduate qualifications	46,620	24,950
Postgraduate Certificate in Education	20,545	930
Other postgraduate research and taught qualifications	203,975	79,570
Total qualifications awarded	668,685	132,450

Source: HESA 2020

COURSES

HE institutions in the UK mainly offer courses leading to the following qualifications. These qualifications go from levels 4 to 8 on England's Regulated Qualifications Framework, levels 7 to 12 on Scotland's Credit and Qualifications Framework. Individual HEIs may not offer all of these.

Certificates of Higher Education (CertHE) are awarded after one year's full-time study (or equivalent). If available to students on longer courses, they certify that students have reached a minimum standard in their first year.

Diplomas of Higher Education (DipHE) and other *Higher Diplomas* are awarded after two to three years' full-time study (or equivalent). They certify that a student has achieved a minimum standard in first- and second-year courses and, in the case of nursing, third-year courses. They can often be used for entry to the third year of a related degree course.

Foundation degrees are awarded after two years of full-time study (or equivalent). These degrees combine academic study with work-based learning, and have been designed jointly by universities, colleges and employers with a particular area of work in mind. They are usually accepted as a basis for entry to the third year of a related degree course. These courses are due to be streamlined and renamed 'Higher Technical Qualifications' under plans to revamp further education in England (see also Recent Developments).

Bachelor's degrees, also referred to as *first degrees,* have different titles, Bachelor of Arts (BA) and Bachelor of Science (BSc) being the most common. In England, Wales and Northern Ireland most Bachelor's degree courses are 'with Honours' and awarded after three years of full-time study, although in some subjects the courses last longer. In Scotland, where young people may leave school and go to university a year younger, HE institutions typically offer Ordinary Bachelor's degrees after three years' study and Bachelor's degrees with Honours after four years. Honours degrees are graded as first, upper second (2:1), lower second (2:2), or third. HEIs in England, Wales and Northern Ireland may allow students who fail the first year of an Honours degree by a small margin to transfer to an Ordinary degree course, if they have one. Ordinary degrees may also be awarded to Honours degree students who do not finish an Honours degree course but complete enough of it to earn a pass.

Postgraduate or *Higher degrees.* Graduates may go on to take *Master's degrees*, which involve one or two years' work and can be taught or research-based. They may also take one-year postgraduate diplomas and certificates, often linked to a specific profession, such as the *Postgraduate Certificate in Education* (PGCE) required to become a state school teacher. A *doctorate*, leading to a qualification such as Doctor of Philosophy – a PHD or DPHIL – usually involves at least three years of full-time research.

The framework for HE qualifications in England, Wales and Northern Ireland (FHEQ) and the framework for qualifications of HE institutions in Scotland can both be found on the QAA website, which describes the achievement represented by HE qualifications.

ADMISSIONS

When preparing to apply to a university or other HE college, individuals can compare facts and figures on institutions and courses using the government's Unistats website. This includes details of students' views from the annual National Student Survey. They can also consult the results of the Teaching Excellence Framework, which is an official survey of teaching quality in universities listed on the Office for Students' website.

For the vast majority of full-time undergraduate courses, individuals need to apply online through UCAS, the organisation responsible for managing applications to HE courses in the UK. More than half a million people wanting to study at a university or college each year use this UCAS service, which has useful online tools to help students find the right course.

UCAS also provides two specialist applications services used by more than 50,000 people each year: the Conservatoires UK Admissions Service (CUKAS), for those applying to UK music conservatoires, and the Graduate Teacher Training Registry (GTTR), for postgraduate applications for initial teacher training courses in England and Wales and some in Scotland. Details of initial teacher training courses in Scotland can also be obtained from Universities Scotland and from Teach in Scotland, the website created by the Scottish government to promote teaching.

Each university or college sets its own entry requirements. These can be in terms of particular exam grades or total points on the 'UCAS tariff' (UCAS's system for allocating points to different qualifications on a common basis), or be non-academic, like having a health check. HE institutions will make 'firm offers' to candidates who have already gained the qualifications they present for entry, and 'conditional offers' to those who have yet to take their exams or obtain their results. Conditional offers often require a minimum level of achievement in a specified subject, for example '300 points to include grade A at A-level Chemistry'. If candidates' achievements are lower than specified in their conditional offers, the university or college may not accept them; then, if they still wish to go into HE, they need to find another institution through the UCAS 'clearing' process.

The government is looking into whether to change to a post-qualification admissions system (*see also* Recent Developments.)

The Open University conducts its own admissions. It is the UK's only university dedicated to distance learning and the UK's largest for part-time HE. Because it is designed to be 'open' to all, no qualifications are needed for entry to the majority of its courses.

Individuals can search thousands of UK postgraduate courses and research opportunities on UK graduate careers website Prospects. The application process for postgraduate

places can vary between institutions. Most universities and colleges accept direct applications and many accept applications through UKPASS, a free, centralised online service run by UCAS that allows individuals to submit up to ten different applications, track their progress and attach supporting material, such as references.

UNISTATS **W** http://unistats.direct.gov.uk
TEACHING EXCELLENCE FRAMEWORK
  W www.officeforstudents.org.uk/advice-and-guidance/teaching
UCAS **T** 0371-468 0468 **W** www.ucas.com
UNIVERSITIES SCOTLAND **T** 0131-226 1111
  W www.universities-scotland.ac.uk
TEACH IN SCOTLAND **T** 0845-345 4745
  W https://teachinscotland.scot
PROSPECTS **T** 0161-277 5200 **W** www.prospects.ac.uk
UKPASS **T** 0371-334 4447 **W** http://ukpass.ac.uk

TUITION FEES AND STUDENT SUPPORT

TUITION FEES

Higher Education institutions (HEIs) in England, Wales and Northern Ireland charge tuition fees for full-time HE courses. Although students from outside the EU can be charged the full cost of their courses, the tuition fees that universities may charge undergraduate degree students from the UK and other EU countries is capped at £9,250 for 2020–21, while for all other international students the fees are variable. In Scotland, tuition fees for 2020–21 are £1,820 for full-time Scottish-domiciled or EU students and capped at £9,250 for full-time students from the rest of the UK (England, Wales and Northern Ireland). In Wales, maximum tuition fees are £, while in Northern Ireland they are £4,275 for resident and EU students, otherwise £9,250.

Full-time students do not have to pay their fees themselves before or during their course, as tuition fee loans are available to cover the full cost; these do not have to be repaid until the student is working and earning more than a specified amount (*see* Student Loans, Grants and Bursaries).

EU students starting courses in 2020–21 will pay home student level fees for the duration of their course. For courses starting in academic year 2021–22, however, EU, other EEA and Swiss nationals will no longer be eligible for home fee status undergraduate, postgraduate, and advanced learner financial support from Student Finance England. This change will also apply to further education funding for those aged 19 or over, and funding for apprenticeships.

STUDENT LOANS, GRANTS AND BURSARIES

England
Students starting their first full-time HE course in 2020–21 can apply through Student Finance England for financial support. Two student loans are available from the government: a tuition fee loan of up to £9,250 for 2020–21, or up to £6,165 for a private university or college, or £11,100 for an accelerated degree course; and a maintenance loan (for students aged under 60) to help with living expenses of up to £9,203 for those living away from home (£12,010 if studying away from home in London), or up to £7,747 for those living with their parents during term time, or up to £10,539 if living and studying abroad for a year.

The tuition fee loan is not affected by household income and is paid directly to the relevant HE institution. A proportion (currently 65 per cent) of the maximum maintenance loan is available irrespective of household income while the rest depends on an income assessment. Student Finance England usually pays the money into the student's own bank account in three instalments, one at the start of each term.

Repayment of both loans does not start until the April after the student has left university or college, or before they are earning £19,390 a year, £1,615 a month or £372 a week in the UK (£21,000 for postgraduate loans).

At this point the individual's employer will deduct 9 per cent of any salary above the starting limit through the Pay As You Earn (PAYE) system (6 per cent for postgraduate loans). The self-employed make repayments through their tax returns. Student loans accrue interest from the date they are paid out, until they are repaid in full. Generally, the interest rate for student loans is set in September each year. The latest rate can be found online (W www.studentloanrepayment.co.uk).

Maintenance loans replaced grants for all new full-time students from 2016. Students can apply in 2020–21 for maintenance loans of up to £9,203 a year (£12,010 in London) – the maximum amount applying only to students with a household income of less than £25,000 a year. Special support grants will also be replaced by maintenance loans.

Students needing extra help may also be entitled to receive disabled students' allowance, adult dependants' grant, childcare grant or parents' learning allowance.

Part-time Higher Education Students are entitled to tuition fee loans (which replaced grants) of up to £5,981 in 2020–21.

Details are available on the Student Finance England website (W www.gov.uk/student-finance/loans-and-grants). There is a student finance calculator on the website to work out what financial support is available.

Universities and other higher education providers offer their own grants and bursaries, with differing criteria. Bursaries do not have to be repaid. Students should always check with the institution they are planning to attend to find out what extra financial support may be available.

If the student's chosen HE institution runs the additional fee support scheme, it could provide extra financial help if the student is on a low income and in certain other circumstances. For students in financial difficulty help may also be available through the institution's access to learning fund.

Wales

Welsh students starting a full-time HE course in 2020–21 can apply through Student Finance Wales for the forms of financial support described below.

The system of tuition fee and maintenance loans and grants in Wales is similar to England's, particularly for new students, but continuing Welsh students can also receive a substantial tuition fee grant. Maximum maintenance loans are: up to £8,100 for students living away from home (£10,124 if studying away from home in London) and up to £6,885 for those living with their parents during term time.

Welsh-domiciled students may apply for a Welsh government learning grant of up to £10,124 to help meet general living costs. This is paid in three instalments, one at the start of each term, like the student maintenance loan. The amount that a student gets depends on household income. The maximum grant is available to those with a household income of £18,370 or under. Those with an income of £59,200 or over will receive £1,000.

There is also a special support grant for single parents, student parents or those with disabilities, which is worth up to £5,161 a year in 2020–21. It is paid directly to students and is not offset against student loan borrowing.

Students can use the student finance calculator on the Student Finance Wales website to work out what financial support they may be entitled to.

Welsh HE institutions also hold financial contingency funds to provide discretionary assistance to students experiencing financial difficulties.

For 2020–21 part-time undergraduate higher education students and continuing students studying at least 25 per cent of an equivalent full-time course are entitled to receive a fee loan of £2,625 (£6,935 for a course at a publicly funded university or college elsewhere in the UK, or £4,625 at a private university or college). The maximum amount of grants and loans available is £5,433.75 depending on household income and course intensity.

Childcare Grants, Parents' Learning Allowance, Adult Dependants' Grant, and Disabled Students' Allowances are also available.

STUDENT FINANCE WALES T 0300-200 4050
W www.studentfinancewales.co.uk

Scotland

Students starting a full-time HE course in 2020–21 can apply through the Student Awards Agency for Scotland for financial support. Full-time Scottish-domiciled or EU students enrolling on a course in 2020 will be eligible to have their tuition fees (£1,285 for a HND/HNC; £1,820 for a degree or equivalent) paid for the duration of their studies through the Student Awards Agency for Scotland (applications for tuition fee payment should be made annually). Tuition fees for full-time students from the rest of the UK (England, Wales and Northern Ireland) are capped at £9,250 for 2020–21, for which loans are available from the relevant body (Student Finance England, Student Finance Wales or Student Finance Northern Ireland). Living cost support is mainly provided through a student loan, the majority of which is income-assessed. The maximum loan for 2020–21 is £7,750.

The young students' bursary (YSB) is available to young students from low-income backgrounds and is non-repayable. Eligible students receive this bursary instead of part of the student loan, thus reducing their level of repayable debt. In 2020–21 the maximum annual support provided through YSB is £2,000 if household income is £20,999 or less a year.

The independent students' bursary (ISB) similarly replaces part of the loan and reduces repayable debt for low-income students independent of parental support. The maximum paid is £1,000 a year to those whose household income is £20,999 or less a year.

In 2020–21, students who have come from a care setting will be eligible to apply for a non-means-tested bursary of £8,100.

Travel expenses are included within the student loan. There are supplementary grants available to certain categories of students such as lone parents (£1,305). Extra help is also available to those who have a disability, learning difficulty or mental health problem.

STUDENT AWARDS AGENCY FOR SCOTLAND
T 0300-555 0505 **W** www.saas.gov.uk

Northern Ireland

Students starting a full-time HE course in 2020–21 can apply through Student Finance Northern Ireland for financial support. The arrangements for both full-time and part-time students are similar to those for England. The main difference is that the income-assessed maintenance grant (or special support grant for students on certain income-assessed benefits) for new full-time students studying at UK universities and colleges is worth up to £3,475 (for household incomes of £19,203 or less).

Universities and colleges in Northern Ireland can charge up to £4,275 for tuition fees in academic year 2020–21, and students can get a loan for up to this amount. There are tuition fee loans of up to £9,250 for students studying in England, Scotland and Wales.

Loans are available for living costs: £3,750 for study in Northern Ireland, £4,840 for study elsewhere in the UK (£6,780 in London).

STUDENT FINANCE NORTHERN IRELAND
T 0300-100 0077 **W** www.studentfinanceni.co.uk

Disabled Students' Allowances
Disabled Students' Allowances (DSAs) are grants available throughout the UK to help meet the extra course costs that full-time, part-time and postgraduate (taught or research) students can face as a direct result of a disability, ongoing health condition, mental health condition or specific learning difficulty. They help disabled people to study in HE on an equal basis with other students. They are paid on top of the standard student finance package and do not have to be repaid. The amount that an individual gets depends on the type of extra help needed, not on household income.

In all parts of the UK, the following three allowances are available: a specialist equipment or large items allowance for the entire course (2020–21 maximum rates vary from £5,849 in Northern Ireland to £5,266 in England); an annual non-medical helper allowance (2020–21 maximum rates for full-time students vary from £23,258 in England to £20,938 in Northern Ireland); and an annual general or basic allowance (2020–21 maximum rates for full-time students vary from £1,954 in England to £1,759 in Northern Ireland). Reasonable spending on extra disability-related travel costs can also be reimbursed. Eligible individuals should apply as early as possible to the relevant UK awarding authority.

POSTGRADUATE AWARDS
In England in 2020–21, postgraduate loans for a masters course of £11,222 and doctoral loans of up to £26,445 are available to cover tuition and living costs for the duration of study, dependent on course, age and nationality or residency as well as other factors. Some courses such as a Postgraduate Certificate in Education (PGCE) allow students to qualify for the finance package usually available only to undergraduates. There are also bursaries available for social work and some medical students.

In Wales, masters loans of up to £17,489 and doctoral loans of up to £26,445 are available, while in Northern Ireland up to £5,500 is available to cover course fees only. In Scotland, eligible full-time and part-time postgraduate students can get tuition fee loans of up to £5,500, while only full-time students can apply for living cost loans of up to £4,500.

There is heavy competition for other postgraduate funding. Individuals can search for postgraduate awards and scholarships on two websites: Hot Courses and Prospects. They can also search for grants available from educational trusts, often reserved for students from poorer backgrounds or for those who have achieved academic excellence, on **W** www.gov.uk/grant-bursary-adult-learners or the Family Action website.

DEPARTMENT FOR THE ECONOMY (DE), NORTHERN IRELAND **T** 028-9052 9900
   W www.nidirect.gov.uk/articles/postgraduate-awards
FAMILY ACTION **T** 020-7254 6251
   W www.family-action.org.uk
HOT COURSES **W** www.hotcourses.com
POSTGRADUATE SEARCH **W** www.postgraduatesearch.com
PROSPECTS **W** www.prospects.ac.uk
STUDENT AWARDS AGENCY FOR SCOTLAND (SAAS)
   T 0300-555 0505 **W** www.saas.gov.uk

TEACHER TRAINING
See Professional Education/Teaching.

EMPLOYEES AND SALARIES

QUALIFIED TEACHERS IN MAINTAINED SCHOOLS
Full-time equivalent, thousands (2019–20)

	England	Wales	Scotland	NI	UK
Nursery and primary schools	*221.2	*14.1	25.8	8.2	269.5
Secondary schools	204.7	10.7	23.5	9.3	248.2
Special schools	24.3	0.8	1.9	0.9	27.9
Total	453.8	25.8	†52.1	18.4	550.1

* Includes middle schools in England and Wales
† Includes all centrally employed teachers
Source: gov.uk; wales.gov; scot.gov and education-ni.gov.uk, 2020

SUPPORT STAFF IN MAINTAINED SCHOOLS, ENGLAND AND WALES (2019–20)
Full-time equivalent, thousands

	England	Wales
Teaching assistants	265.2	15.6
Other support staff	226.8	11.3
Total	492.0	26.8

Source: gov.uk and wales.gov, 2020

ACADEMIC STAFF IN UK HIGHER EDUCATION INSTITUTIONS (2018–19)

	Full-time	Part-time	Total
Professors	16,840	4,680	21,520
Non-professors	126,670	68,875	195,545
Teaching only	19,925	46,430	66,335
Teaching and research	80,880	17,720	98,600
Research only	41,775	9,085	50,860
Neither teaching nor research	930	320	1,250

Source: HESA 2020

SALARIES

State school teachers in England and Wales are employed by local authorities or the governing bodies of their schools. All teachers are eligible for membership of the Teachers' Pension Scheme.

There are teaching and learning responsibility payments for specific posts, special needs work and recruitment and retention factors which may be awarded at the discretion of the school governing body or the local authority. There are separate pay ranges for Headteachers and other school leaders. Academies are free to set their own salaries.

In 2013 every school was required to revise its pay and appraisal policies, setting out how pay progression would, in future, be linked to a teacher's performance. From September 2014, school governing bodies were given more flexibility, within the national pay ranges, to determine the pay of headteachers and other school leaders. In July 2020 the Secretary of State for Education announced a pay award from September 2020 of between 5.5 and 2.75 per cent for teachers on the main scale and of 2.75 per cent for those on upper pay scales. From September 2020 the pay of school leaders ranges from £42,195 to £117,197 a year outside London and from £50,167 to £125,098 a year in Inner London.

After completing initial teacher training and achieving qualified teacher status (QTS), newly qualified teachers (NQTs) in maintained schools can expect to start on a salary of £25,714 a year in England and Wales (or £32,517 in Inner London).

In January 2020, the English government proposed an uplift to £26,000 for starting salaries in England and Wales potentially rising to £30,000 by 2022. In July, the government agreed a 3.1 per cent overall pay rise for teachers (*see also* Recent Developments).

The pay ranges for teachers in England and Wales from September 2020 are:

Main pay range (including NQTs)	
London fringe	£26,948–£38,174
Outer London	£29,915–£41,136
Inner London	£32,157–£42,624
Rest of England and Wales	£25,714–£36,961
Upper pay range	
London fringe	£39,864–£42,780
Outer London	£42,559–£45,766
Inner London	£46,971–£50,935
Rest of England and Wales	£38,690–£41,604

The Scottish Negotiating Committee for Teachers determines teachers' pay in Scotland on a seven-point scale where the entry point is for newly qualified teachers undertaking their probationary year. Experienced, ambitious teachers who reach the top of the main pay scale are eligible to become chartered teachers and earn more on a separate pay spine. However, to do so they must study for further professional qualifications. Headteachers and deputies have a separate pay spine as do 'principals' or heads of department. Additional allowances are payable to teachers in circumstances such as working in distant islands and remote schools. Teaching salaries in Scotland were increased by 1 per cent in April 2017 and by a further 1 per cent in January 2018.

Salary scales for teachers in Scotland from 1 April 2020:

Headteacher/deputy headteacher	£51,207–£98,808
Principal teacher	£45,150–£58,269
Chartered teacher	£42,696–£50,772
Main grade	£27,498–£41,412

Teachers in Northern Ireland have broadly similar pay scales to teachers in England and Wales. Classroom teachers who take on teaching and learning responsibilities outside their normal classroom duties may be awarded one of five teaching allowances. In April 2020, the Department for Education published agreed revised pay scales with a backdated uplift of 2.25 per cent from September 2017 and 2 per cent payable from September 2018 in Northern Ireland. From 1 September 2018, details as follows:

Principal (headteacher)	£45,540–£112,934
School leaders	£40,256–£44,427
Classroom teacher (upper pay scale)	£36,731–£39,498
Classroom teacher (main pay scale)	£23,199–£33,906
Unqualified teacher	£14,760
Teaching allowances	£1,985–£12,800

Since 2007, most academic staff in HE across the UK are paid on a single national pay scale as a result of a national framework agreement negotiated by the HE unions and HE institutions. Staff are paid according to rates on a 51-point national pay spine and academic and academic-related staff are graded according to a national grading structure. As HE institutions are autonomous employers, precise job grades and salaries may vary but the following table outlines salaries that typically tally with certain job roles in HE. As a result of the economic impact of the Covid-19 pandemic, employers opted for a zero per cent uplift in the pay award for 2020–21, so pay remains at previous levels:

Principal lecturer	£50,132–£58,089
Senior lecturer	£39,609–£48,677
Lecturer	£33,199–£38,460
Junior researcher	£26,243–£32,236

UNIVERSITIES

The following is a list of universities, which are those institutions that have been granted degree-awarding powers by either a royal charter or an act of parliament, or have been permitted to use the word 'university' (or 'university college') by the Privy Council. There are other recognised bodies in the UK with degree-awarding powers, as well as institutions offering courses leading to a degree from a recognised body. Further information is available at **W** www.gov.uk/recognised-uk-degrees

Student figures represent the number of undergraduate (UG) and postgraduate (PG) students based on information available at July 2019.

Higher Education institutions in England, Wales and Northern Ireland charge tuition fees for full-time HE courses. Although students from outside the EU can be charged the full cost of their courses, the tuition fees that universities may charge undergraduate degree students from the UK and other EU countries is capped at £9,250 for 2020–21. In Scotland, tuition fees for 2020–21 are £1,820 for full-time Scottish-domiciled or EU students and capped at £9,250 for full-time students from the rest of the UK (England, Wales and Northern Ireland). In Wales, maximum tuition fees are £9,000, while in Northern Ireland they are £4,395 for resident and EU students, otherwise £9,250. For detailed information on tuition fees and student loans, including for the devolved administrations, *see* Education, Higher Education, Tuition Fees and Student Support.

RESEARCH EXCELLENCE FRAMEWORK
The research excellence framework (REF) is the system for assessing the quality of research in UK higher education institutions. The next REF assessment will be published in 2021, further information on this and the existing 2014 REF assessment can be found at **W** www.ref.ac.uk.

TEACHING EXCELLENCE FRAMEWORK
The teaching excellence framework (TEF) rates teaching in universities and colleges and provides information about teaching provision and student outcomes. Participation for institutions is voluntary and open to universities and colleges in England, Wales, Scotland and Northern Ireland. A list of participating institutions and their current ratings (gold, silver, bronze or provisional) can be found on the Office for Students website (**W** www.officeforstudents.org.uk/advice-and-guidance/teaching/tef-outcomes).

UNIVERSITY OF ABERDEEN (1495)
King's College, Aberdeen AB24 3FX **T** 01224-272000
W www.abdn.ac.uk
Students: 10,255 UG; 4,115 PG
Chancellor, HRH the Duchess of Rothesay, GCVO, PC
Vice-Chancellor, Prof. George Boyne
University Secretary, Caroline Inglis

UNIVERSITY OF ABERTAY DUNDEE (1994)
Bell Street, Dundee DD1 1HG **T** 01382-308000
W www.abertay.ac.uk
Students: 3,605 UG; 450 PG
Chancellor, Lord Cullen of Whitekirk, KT, PC, FRSE
Vice-Chancellor, Prof. Nigel Seaton, FRENG
University Secretary, Sheena Stewart

ABERYSTWYTH UNIVERSITY (1872)
Penglais, Aberystwyth SY23 3FL **T** 01970-62311 1
W www.aber.ac.uk
Students: 7,035 UG; 1,150 PG
Chancellor, Lord Thomas of Cwmgiedd, PC, QC
Vice-Chancellor, Prof. Elizabeth Treasure
University Secretary, Geraint Pugh

ANGLIA RUSKIN UNIVERSITY (1992)
Chelmsford Campus, Bishop Hall Lane, Chelmsford CM1 1SQ
T 01245-493131 **E** answers@anglia.ac.uk **W** www.aru.ac.uk
Students: 19,010 UG; 4,490 PG
Chancellor, Lord Ashcroft, KCMG, PC
Vice-Chancellor, Prof. Roderick Watkins
Secretary and Clerk, Paul Bogle

ARTS UNIVERSITY BOURNEMOUTH (2012)
Wallisdown BH12 5HH **T** 01202-533011 **W** www.aub.ac.uk
Students: 3,365 UG; 125 PG
Chancellor, Prof. Sir Christopher Frayling
Vice-Chancellor, Prof. Paul Gough, CBE
University Secretary, Jon Reynard

UNIVERSITY OF THE ARTS LONDON (2003 (Formerly The London Institute (1986), renamed 2004))
272 High Holborn, London WC1V 7EY **T** 020-7514 6000
W www.arts.ac.uk
Students: 15,120 UG; 3,850 PG
Chancellor, Grayson Perry, CBE, RA
Vice-Chancellor, Sir Nigel Carrington
Secretary and Registrar, Stephen Marshall

COLLEGES
CAMBERWELL COLLEGE OF ARTS (1898)
45–65 Peckham Road, London SE5 8UF
T 020-7514 6301
W www.arts.ac.uk/camberwell
Head of College, Prof. David Crow

CENTRAL SAINT MARTINS COLLEGE OF ART AND DESIGN (1854)
Granary Building, 1 Granary Square, London N1C 4AA
T 020-7514 7444
W www.arts.ac.uk/csm
Head of College, Prof. Jeremy Till

CHELSEA COLLEGE OF ARTS (1895)
16 John Islip Street, London SW1P 4JU
T 020-7514 7751
W www.arts.ac.uk/chelsea
Head of College, Prof. David Crow

LONDON COLLEGE OF COMMUNICATION (1894)
Elephant and Castle, London SE1 6SB
T 020-7514 6500
W www.arts.ac.uk/cc
Head of College, Natalie Brett

LONDON COLLEGE OF FASHION (1963)
20 John Prince's Street, London W1G 0BJ
T 020-7514 7400
W www.arts.ac.uk/fashion
Head of College, Prof. Frances Corner, OBE

WIMBLEDON COLLEGE OF ART (1930)
Merton Hall Road, London SW19 3QA
T 020-7514 9641
W www.arts.ac.uk/wimbledon
Head of College, Prof. David Crow

ASTON UNIVERSITY (1966)
Aston Triangle, Birmingham B4 7ET **T** 0121-204 3000
W www2.aston.ac.uk
Students: 11,850 UG; 2,765 PG
Chancellor, Sir John Sunderland
Vice-Chancellor, Prof. Alec Cameron
Chief Operating Officer, Neil Scott

BANGOR UNIVERSITY (1884)
Gwynedd LL57 2DG **T** 01248-3511 51 **W** www.bangor.ac.uk
Students: 8,455 UG; 2,700 PG
Chancellor, George Meyrick
Vice-Chancellor, Prof. Graham Upton (interim)
University Secretary, Dr Kevin Mundy

UNIVERSITY OF BATH (1966)
Bath BA2 7AY **T** 01225-388388 **W** www.bath.ac.uk
Students: 13,275 UG; 4,275 PG
Chancellor, HRH the Earl of Wessex, KG, GCVO
Vice-Chancellor, Prof. Ian White, FRENG
University Secretary, Mark Humphriss

BATH SPA UNIVERSITY (2005)
Newton Park, Bath BA2 9BN **T** 01225-875875
E enquiries@bathspa.ac.uk **W** www.bathspa.ac.uk
Students: 6,320 UG; 1,670 PG
Chancellor, Jeremy Irons
Vice-Chancellor, Prof. Sue Rigby
Registrar, Christopher Ellicott

UNIVERSITY OF BEDFORDSHIRE (1993)
University Square, Luton LU1 3JU **T** 01234-400400
W www.beds.ac.uk
Students: 10,475 UG; 2,325 PG
Chancellor, Rt. Hon. John Bercow, MP
Vice-Chancellor, Bill Rammell
Registrar, Jenny Jenkin

UNIVERSITY OF BIRMINGHAM (1900)
Edgbaston, Birmingham B15 2TT **T** 0121-414 3344
W www.birmingham.ac.uk
Students: 22,710 UG; 12,205 PG
Chancellor, Lord Bilimoria, CBE
Vice-Chancellor and Principal, Prof. Sir David Eastwood
Registrar and Secretary, Lee Sanders

BIRMINGHAM CITY UNIVERSITY (1992)
University House, 15 Bartholemew Row, Birmingham B5 5JU
T 0121-331 5000 **W** www.bcu.ac.uk
Students: 19,790 UG; 4,785 PG
Chancellor, Sir Lenny Henry, CBE
Vice-Chancellor, Prof. Philip Plowden
University Secretary, Karen Stephenson

UNIVERSITY COLLEGE BIRMINGHAM (2012)
Summer Rowe, Birmingham B3 1JB **T** 0121-604 1000
E admissions@ucb.ac.uk **W** www.ucb.ac.uk
Students: 4,425 UG; 520 PG
Vice-Chancellor and Principal, Prof. Ray Linforth, OBE

BISHOP GROSSETESTE UNIVERSITY (2013)
Longdales Road, Lincoln LN1 3DY **T** 01522-527347
E enquiries@bishopg.ac.uk **W** www.bishopg.ac.uk
Students: 1,705 UG; 550 PG
Chancellor, Dame Judith Mayhew-Jonas, DBE
Vice-Chancellor, Revd. Canon Prof. Peter Neil
Registrar and University Secretary, Dr Anne Craven

UNIVERSITY OF BOLTON (2005)
Deane Road, Bolton BL3 5AB **T** 01204-900600
E enquiries@bolton.ac.uk **W** www.bolton.ac.uk
Students: 5,340 UG; 1,205 PG
Chancellor, Earl of St Andrews
Vice-Chancellor, Prof. George E. Holmes
Registrar and Secretary, Sue Duncan, LLD

BOURNEMOUTH UNIVERSITY (1992)
Fern Barrow, Poole BH12 5BB **T** 01202-961916
E enquiries@bournemouth.ac.uk **W** www.bournemouth.ac.uk
Students: 15,420 UG; 3,265 PG
Chancellor, Kate Adie, CBE
Vice-Chancellor, Prof. John Vinney
Chief Operating Officer, Jim Andrews

UNIVERSITY OF BRADFORD (1966)
Richmond Road, Bradford BD7 1DP **T** 01274-232323
W www.bradford.ac.uk
Students: 7,695 UG; 2,420 PG
Chancellor, Kate Swann
Vice-Chancellor and Principal, Prof. Brian Cantor, CBE
University Secretary, Riley Power

UNIVERSITY OF BRIGHTON (1992)
Mithras House, Lewes Road, Brighton BN2 4AT **T** 01273-600900
W www.brighton.ac.uk
Students: 17,700 UG; 3,855 PG
Vice-Chancellor, Prof. Debra Humphris, FRCP
Secretary and Registrar, Stephen Dudderidge

UNIVERSITY OF BRISTOL (1909)
Beacon House, Queens Road, Bristol BS8 1QU **T** 0117-928 9000
W www.bristol.ac.uk
Students: 18,270 UG; 6,585 PG
Chancellor, Sir Paul Nurse, FRS, FMEDSCI
Vice-Chancellor, Prof. Hugh Brady
Registrar, Lucinda Parr

BRUNEL UNIVERSITY LONDON (1966)
Kingston Lane, Uxbridge UB8 3PH **T** 01895-274000
E admissions@brunel.ac.uk **W** www.brunel.ac.uk
Students: 10,545 UG; 3,365 PG
Chancellor, Sir Richard Sykes
Vice-Chancellor, Prof. Julia Buckingham, CBE, PHD, DSc, FRSA
Chief Operating Officer, Paul Thomas, CBE

UNIVERSITY OF BUCKINGHAM (1983)
Buckingham MK18 1EG **T** 01280-814080
E info@buckingham.ac.uk **W** www.buckingham.ac.uk
Students: 1,465 UG; 1,395 PG
Chancellor, The Hon. Lady Keswick
Vice-Chancellor, Sir Anthony Seldon, PHD, FRSA
University Secretary, Emma Potts

BUCKS NEW UNIVERSITY (2007)
High Wycombe Campus, Queen Alexandra Road, High Wycombe
HP11 2JZ **T** 01494-522141 **E** advice@bucks.ac.uk
W www.bucks.ac.uk
Students: 8,030 UG; 1,060 PG
Vice-Chancellor, Prof. Nick Braisby
Academic Registrar and Secretary, Ellie Smith

UNIVERSITY OF CAMBRIDGE (1209)
The Old Schools, Trinity Lane, Cambridge CB2 1TN
T 01223-337733 W www.cam.ac.uk
Students: 12,540 UG; 7,970 PG
Chancellor, Lord Sainsbury of Turville, FRS (King's)
Vice-Chancellor, Prof. Stephen J. Toope (Clare Hall)
High Steward, Lord Watson of Richmond, CBE (Jesus)
Deputy High Steward, Mrs A. Lonsdale, CBE (Murray
    Edwards)
Commissary, Lord Judge, PC (Magdalene)
Pro-Vice-Chancellors, Prof. G. Virgo, QC (Downing); Prof. E.
    Ferran, FBA (St Catharine's); Prof. C. Abell, FRS,
    FMEDSCI (Christ's); Prof. A. Neely (Sidney Sussex); Prof.
    D. Cardwell, FRENG (Fitzwilliam)
Proctors (2019–20), Dr Timothy Dickens (Peterhouse);
    Francis Knights (Fitzwilliam)
Deputy Proctors (2019–20), Dr Gemma Burgess (Newnham);
    Gordon Chesterman (St Edmund's)
Orator, Dr R. Thompson (Selwyn)
Registrary, E. Rampton (Sidney Sussex)
Librarian, Dr J. Gardner (Selwyn)
Director of the Fitzwilliam Museum, L. Syson
Interim Academic Secretary, Dr. R. Coupe
Director of Finance, J. Hughes (Wolfson)
Executive Director of Development, Ms A. Traub
Esquire Bedells, Mrs N. Hardy (Jesus); Ms S. Scarlett (Lucy
    Cavendish)
University Advocate, Dr R. Thornton (Emmanuel)
Deputy University Advocate, Dr J. Seymour (Sidney Sussex)

COLLEGES AND HALLS
(with dates of foundation)
CHRIST'S (1505)
Master, Prof. J. Stapleton, FBA
CHURCHILL (1960)
Master, Prof. Dame Athene Donald, DBE, FRS
CLARE (1326)
Master, Lord Grabiner, QC
CLARE HALL (1966)
President, Prof. D. Ibbetson, FBA
CORPUS CHRISTI (1352)
Master, Prof. C. Kelly
DARWIN (1964)
Master, Prof. C. Fowler, FRAS, FGS
DOWNING (1800)
Master, A. Bookbinder
EMMANUEL (1584)
Master, Dame Fiona Reynolds, DBE
FITZWILLIAM (1966)
Master, Baroness Morgan of Huyton
GIRTON (1869)
Mistress, Prof. S. Smith, FRSE FBA
GONVILLE AND CAIUS (1348)
Master, Dr. P. Rogerson
HOMERTON (1976)
Principal, Prof. G. Ward, FRSA
HUGHES HALL (1885)
President, Dr A. Freeling
JESUS (1496)
Master, Sonita Alleyne, OBE, FRA, FRSA
KING'S (1441)
Provost, Prof. M. Proctor, FRS
LUCY CAVENDISH (1965)
President, Dame Madeleine Atkins, DBE, FACSS
MAGDALENE (1542)
Master, Rt. Revd Lord Williams of Oystermouth, PC, FBA
MURRAY EDWARDS (1954)
President, Dame Barbara Stocking, DBE

NEWNHAM (1871)
Principal, Ms A. Rose
PEMBROKE (1347)
Master, Lord Smith of Finsbury, PC
PETERHOUSE (1284)
Master, Bridget Kendall, MBE
QUEENS' (1448)
President, Prof. Lord Eatwell
ROBINSON (1977)
Warden, Prof. A. D. Yates
ST CATHARINE'S (1473)
Master, Prof. Sir Mark Welland, FRS, FRENG
ST EDMUND'S (1896)
Master, Ms C. Arnold, OBE
ST JOHN'S (1511)
Master, Prof. Sir Christopher Dobson, FRS, FMEDSCI
SELWYN (1882)
Master, R. Mosey
SIDNEY SUSSEX (1596)
Master, Prof. R. Penty, FRENG
TRINITY (1546)
Master, Dame Sally Davies, DBE, FRS
TRINITY HALL (1350)
Master, Revd Canon Dr J. Morris, FRHISTS
WOLFSON (1965)
President, Prof. J. Clarke, FRS, FMEDSCI

CANTERBURY CHRIST CHURCH UNIVERSITY (2005)
North Holmes Road, Canterbury CT1 1QU T 01227-767700
E admissions@canterbury.co.uk W www.canterbury.ac.uk
Students: 11,765 UG; 2,690 PG
Chancellor, Most Revd and Rt. Hon. Archbishop of Canterbury
Vice-Chancellor, Prof. Rama Thirunamachandran
Director of Academic Administration, Cathy Lambert

CARDIFF UNIVERSITY (1883)
Cardiff CF10 3AT T 029-2087 4000 W www.cardiff.ac.uk
Students: 23,480 UG; 8,455 PG
Chancellor, Baroness Randerson
Vice-Chancellor, Prof. Colin Riordan
Chief Operating Officer, Deborah Collins

CARDIFF METROPOLITAN UNIVERSITY (1865)
Western Avenue, Cardiff CF5 2YB T 029-2041 6070
W www.cardiffmet.ac.uk
Students: 8,330 UG; 2,100 PG
President and Vice-Chancellor, Prof. Cara Carmichael Aitchison,
    FACSS, FRGS, FHEA
Chief Operating Officer, John Cappock

UNIVERSITY OF CENTRAL LANCASHIRE (1992)
Preston PR1 2HE T 01772-201201 E cenquiries@uclan.ac.uk
W www.uclan.ac.uk
Students: 18,020 UG; 4,980 PG
Chancellor, Ranvir Singh
Vice-Chancellor, Lynne Livesey (interim)
University Secretary, Ian Fisher

UNIVERSITY OF CHESTER (Founded in 1839 as Chester
Diocesan Training College; gained University status in
2005)
Parkgate Road, Chester CH1 4BJ T 01244-511000
E enquiries@chester.ac.uk W www.chester.ac.uk
Students: 10,945 UG; 4,465 PG
Chancellor, Gyles Brandreth
Vice-Chancellor, Canon Prof. Tim Wheeler
University Secretary, Adrian Lee

UNIVERSITY OF CHICHESTER (2005)
College Lane, Chichester PO19 6PE **T** 01243-816000
E help@chi.ac.uk **W** www.chi.ac.uk
Students: 4,465 UG; 1,055 PG
Vice-Chancellor, Prof. Jane Longmore
University Secretary, Sophie Egleton

COVENTRY UNIVERSITY (1992)
Priory Street, Coventry CV1 5FB **T** 024-7688 7688
W www.coventry.ac.uk
Students: 27,895 UG; 6,230 PG
Chancellor, Margaret Casely-Hayford
Vice-Chancellor, Prof. John Latham
Academic Registrar, Kate Quantrell

CRANFIELD UNIVERSITY (1969)
Cranfield MK43 0AL **T** 01234-750111 **E** info@cranfield.ac.uk
W www.cranfield.ac.uk
Students: 4,355 PG (postgraduate only)
Chancellor, Baroness Young of Old Scone
Vice-Chancellor, Prof. Sir Peter Gregson
University Secretary, Gregor Douglas

UNIVERSITY FOR THE CREATIVE ARTS (2008)
Falkner Road, Farnham GU9 7DS **T** 01252-722441
W www.uca.ac.uk
Students: 6,260 UG; 360 PG
Chancellor, Prof. Magdalene Odundo, OBE
Vice-Chancellor, Prof. Bashir Makhoul
University Secretary, Marion Wilks

UNIVERSITY OF CUMBRIA (2007)
Fusehill Street, Carlisle CA1 2HH **T** 01228-616234
W www.cumbria.ac.uk
Students: 5,860 UG; 1,720 PG
Chancellor, Most Revd and Rt. Hon. Archbishop of York
Vice-Chancellor, Prof. Julie Mennell
Registrar and Secretary, Jean Brown

DE MONTFORT UNIVERSITY (1992)
The Gateway, Leicester LE1 9BH **T** 0116-255 1551
E enquiry@dmu.ac.uk **W** www.dmu.ac.uk
Students: 20,855 UG; 4,845 PG
Chancellor, Baroness Lawrence of Clarendon, OBE
Vice-Chancellor, Prof. Andy Callop (interim)

UNIVERSITY OF DERBY (1992)
Kedleston Road, Derby DE22 1GB **T** 01332-590500
E askadmissions@derby.ac.uk **W** www.derby.ac.uk
Students: 14,595 UG; 3,895 PG
Chancellor, Earl of Burlington
Vice-Chancellor and Principal, Prof. Kathryn Mitchell
Registrar, June Hughes

UNIVERSITY OF DUNDEE (1967)
Nethergate, Dundee DD1 4HN **T** 01382-383000
W www.dundee.ac.uk
Students: 10,715 UG; 4,390 PG
Chancellor, Dame Jocelyn Bell Burnell, DBE, FRS, FRSE, FRAS
Vice-Chancellor and Principal, Prof. Andrew Atherton
University Secretary, Dr James McGeorge

DURHAM UNIVERSITY (1832)
The Palatine Centre, Stockton Road, Durham DH1 3LE
T 0191-334 2000 **W** www.dur.ac.uk
Students: 13,835 UG; 4,495 PG
Chancellor, Sir Thomas Allen, CBE
Vice-Chancellor, Prof. Stuart Corbridge
University Secretary, Jennifer Sewel

COLLEGES
COLLINGWOOD (1972)
Principal, Prof. J. Elliott
GREY (1959)
Master, Prof. T. Allen
HATFIELD (1846)
Master, Prof. A. M. MacLarnon
JOHN SNOW (2001)
Principal, Prof. C. Summerbell
JOSEPHINE BUTLER (2006)
Principal, A. Simpson
ST AIDAN'S (1947)
Principal, S. F. Frenk
ST CHAD'S (1904)
Principal, M. Masson
ST CUTHBERT'S SOCIETY (1888)
Principal, Prof. E. Archibald
ST HILD AND ST BEDE (1839)
Principal, Prof. S. Forrest
ST JOHN'S (1909)
Principal, Revd Dr D. Wilkinson
ST MARY'S (1899)
Principal, Prof. M. Dawn
SOUTH (2020)
Principal, Prof. T. Luckhurst
STEPHENSON (2001)
Principal, Prof. R. Lynes
TREVELYAN (1966)
Principal, Prof. A. Adeyeye
UNIVERSITY (1832)
Master, Dr R. Lawrie (acting)
USTINOV (2003)
Principal, S. Prescott (acting)
VAN MILDERT (1965)
Principal, Prof. D. Harper

UNIVERSITY OF EAST ANGLIA (1963)
Norwich Research Park, Norwich NR4 7TJ **T** 01603-456161
E admissions@uea.ac.uk **W** www.uea.ac.uk
Students: 12,985 UG; 4,970 PG
Chancellor, Karen Jones, CBE
Vice-Chancellor, Prof. David Richardson

UNIVERSITY OF EAST LONDON (1898)
University Way, London E16 2RD **T** 020-8223 3000
E study@uel.ac.uk **W** www.uel.ac.uk
Students: 9,695 UG; 3,390 PG
Chancellor, Shabir Randeree, CBE
Vice-Chancellor, Prof. Amanda Broderick
University Secretary, Tristan Foote (acting)

EDGE HILL UNIVERSITY (2006)
St Helens Road, Ormskirk L39 4QP **T** 01695-575171
W www.edgehill.ac.uk
Students: 11,050 UG; 3,205 PG
Chancellor, Prof. Tanya Byron
Vice-Chancellor, Dr John Cater, CBE
University Secretary, Lynda Brady

UNIVERSITY OF EDINBURGH (1583)
Old College, South Bridge, Edinburgh EH8 9YL **T** 0131-650 1000
E communications.office@ed.ac.uk **W** www.ed.ac.uk
Students: 22,095 UG; 10,795 PG
Chancellor, HRH the Princess Royal, KG, KT, GCVO
Vice-Chancellor and Principal, Prof. Peter Mathieson, FRCP,
  FRCPE
University Secretary, Sarah Smith

EDINBURGH NAPIER UNIVERSITY (1992)
Sighthill Campus, Edinburgh EH11 4BN **T** 0333-900 6040
W www.napier.ac.uk
Students: 10,280 UG; 2,830 PG
Chancellor, David Eustace
Vice-Chancellor, Prof. Andrea Nolan, OBE
Secretary, David Cloy

UNIVERSITY OF ESSEX (1965)
Wivenhoe Park, Colchester CO4 3SQ **T** 01206-873333
E admit@essex.ac.uk **W** www.essex.ac.uk
Students: 11,370 UG; 3,390 PG
Chancellor, Rt. Hon. John Bercow, MP
Vice-Chancellor, Prof. Anthony Forster, DPHIL
Registrar, Bryn Morris

UNIVERSITY OF EXETER (1955)
Stocker Road, Exeter EX4 4PY **T** 01392-661000
W www.exeter.ac.uk
Students: 18,480 UG; 5,565 PG
Chancellor, Lord Myners, CBE
Vice-Chancellor, Prof. Sir Steve Smith, FACSS
Registrar and Secretary, Mike Shore-Nye

FALMOUTH UNIVERSITY (2012)
Falmouth Campus, Woodlane, Falmouth TR11 4RH
T 01326-211077 **W** www.falmouth.ac.uk
Students: 5,605 UG; 400 PG
Chancellor, Dawn French
Vice-Chancellor, Prof. Anne Carlisle, OBE

UNIVERSITY OF GLASGOW (1451)
University Avenue, Glasgow G12 8QQ **T** 0141-330 2000
E student.recruitment@glasgow.ac.uk **W** www.gla.ac.uk
Students: 20,805 UG; 8,920 PG
Chancellor, Prof. Sir Kenneth Calman, KCB, FRCS, FRSE
Vice-Chancellor, Prof. Sir Anton Muscatelli, FRSE, FACSS
Registrar, David Bennion

GLASGOW CALEDONIAN UNIVERSITY (1993)
City Campus, Cowcaddens Road, Glasgow G4 0BA
T 0141-331 3000 **E** ukroenquiries@gcu.ac.uk **W** www.gcu.ac.uk
Students: 13,575 UG; 2,875 PG
Chancellor, Annie Lennox, OBE
Vice-Chancellor, Prof. Pamela Gillies, CBE, FRSE
University Secretary, Jan Hulme

UNIVERSITY OF GLOUCESTERSHIRE (2001)
The Park, Cheltenham GL50 2RH **T** 03330-141414
E admissions@glos.ac.uk **W** www.glos.ac.uk
Students: 7,080 UG; 1,415 PG
Chancellor, Baroness Fritchie, DBE
Vice-Chancellor, Stephen Marston
Secretary and Registrar, Dr Matthew Andrews

UNIVERSITY OF GREENWICH (1992)
Old Royal Naval College, Park Row, London SE10 9LS
T 020-8331 8000 **E** courseinfo@gre.ac.uk **W** www.gre.ac.uk
Students: 14,740 UG; 4,065 PG
Chancellor, Lord Boateng, PC, QC
Vice-Chancellor, Prof. David Maguire
Secretary, Peter Garrod

HARPER ADAMS UNIVERSITY (2012)
Newport TF10 8NB **T** 01952-820280
E admissions@harper-adams.ac.uk **W** www.harper-adams.ac.uk
Students: 4,805 UG; 505 PG
Chancellor, HRH the Princess Royal, KG, KT, GCVO
Vice-Chancellor, David Llewellyn
University Secretary, Dr Catherine Baxter

HARTPURY UNIVERSITY AND COLLEGE (2017)
Hartpury House, Gloucester GL19 3BE
E admissions@hartpury.ac.uk **W** www.hartpury.ac.uk
Students: 1,800
Vice-Chancellor and Chief Executive, Russell Marchant
Vice-Principal and Deputy Chief Executive, Lynn Forrester-Walker

HERIOT-WATT UNIVERSITY (1966)
Edinburgh EH14 4AS **T** 0131-449 5111 **E** enquiries@hw.ac.uk
W www.hw.ac.uk
Students: 7660 UG; 3,250 PG
Chancellor, Dr Robert Buchan
Vice-Chancellor, Prof. Richard A. Williams, OBE, FRSE, FRENG
University Secretary, Ann Marie Dalton-Pillay

UNIVERSITY OF HERTFORDSHIRE (1992)
Hatfield AL10 9AB **T** 01707-284000 **W** www.herts.ac.uk
Students: 18,840 UG; 5,565 PG
Chancellor, Marquess of Salisbury, KG, KCVO, PC
Vice-Chancellor, Prof. Quintin McKellar, CBE
Secretary and Registrar, Sue Grant

UNIVERSITY OF THE HIGHLANDS AND ISLANDS
(2011)
Ness Walk, Inverness IV3 5SQ **T** 01463-279190 **W** www.uhi.ac.uk
Students: 8,470 UG; 850 PG
Chancellor, HRH the Princess Royal, KG, KT, GCVO
Vice-Chancellor, Prof. Crichton Lang (interim)
Chief Operating Officer, Fiona Larg

UNIVERSITY OF HUDDERSFIELD (1992)
Queensgate, Huddersfield HD1 3DH **T** 01484-422288
W www.hud.ac.uk
Students: 14,165 UG; 4,080 PG
Chancellor, HRH the Duke of York, KG, GCVO, ADC(P)
Vice-Chancellor, Prof. Bob Cryan, CBE, DL, FRENG
University Secretary, Michaela Boryslawskyj

UNIVERSITY OF HULL (1927)
Cottingham Road, Hull HU6 7RX **T** 01482-346311
W www.hull.ac.uk
Students: 13,390 UG; 2,200 PG
Chancellor, Baroness Bottomley of Nettlestone, PC
Vice-Chancellor, Prof. Susan Lea, PHD
Registrar, Jeanette Strachan

IMPERIAL COLLEGE LONDON (1907)
South Kensington SW7 2AZ **T** 020-7589 5111
W www.imperial.ac.uk
Students: 9,730 UG; 8,645 PG
President, Prof. Alice Gast
Provost, Prof. Ian Walmsley, FRS
Secretary and Registrar, David Ashton

KEELE UNIVERSITY (1962)
Keele ST5 5BG **T** 01782-732000 **E** admissions@keele.ac.uk
W www.keele.ac.uk
Students: 8,510 UG; 2,360 PG
Chancellor, Sir Jonathon Porritt, CBE
Vice-Chancellor, Prof. Trevor McMillan
Academic Registrar, Dr Helen Galbraith

UNIVERSITY OF KENT (1965)
Canterbury CT2 7NZ **T** 01227-764000 **E** information@kent.ac.uk
W www.kent.ac.uk
Students: 15,905 UG; 3,920 PG
Chancellor, Gavin Esler
Vice-Chancellor & Principal, Prof. Karen Cox
Provost, David Nightingale

KINGSTON UNIVERSITY (1992)
River House, 53–57 High Street, Kingston upon Thames KT1 1LQ
T 020-8417 9000 E admissionsops@kingston.ac.uk
W www.kingston.ac.uk
Students: 13,625 UG; 4,010 PG
Chancellor, Bonnie Greer, OBE
Vice-Chancellor, Prof. Stephen Spier
University Secretary, Keith Brennan

UNIVERSITY OF LANCASTER (1964)
Bailrigg, Lancaster LA1 4YW T 01524-65201
W www.lancaster.ac.uk
Students: 10,220 UG; 3,990 PG
Chancellor, Rt. Hon. Alan Milburn
Vice-Chancellor, Prof. Mark E. Smith, PHD
University Secretary, Nicola Owen

UNIVERSITY OF LEEDS (1904)
Leeds LS2 9JT T 0113-243 1751 W www.leeds.ac.uk
Students: 25,430 UG; 8,990 PG
Chancellor, Prof. Dame Jane Francis, DCMG
Vice-Chancellor, Sir Alan Langlands
University Secretary, Roger Gair

LEEDS ARTS UNIVERSITY (2017)
Blenheim Walk, Leeds LS2 9AQ T 0113-202 8000
W www.leeds-art.ac.uk
Students: 1,570 UG; 35 PG
Vice-Chancellor, Prof. Simone Wonnacott

LEEDS BECKETT UNIVERSITY (1992)
City Campus, Leeds LS1 3HE T 0113-812 0000
W www.leedsbeckett.ac.uk
Students: 18,615 UG; 4,955 PG
Chancellor, Sir Bob Murray, CBE
Vice-Chancellor, Prof. Peter Slee
Secretary and Registrar, Jenny Share

LEEDS TRINITY UNIVERSITY (2012)
Brownberrie Lane, Leeds LS18 5HD T 0113-283 7100
E hello@leedstrinity.ac.uk W www.leedstrinity.ac.uk
Students: 2,725 UG; 640 PG
Chancellor, Deborah McAndrew
Vice-Chancellor, Prof. Margaret House, OBE
Chief Operating Officer, Phill Dixon

UNIVERSITY OF LEICESTER (1957)
University Road, Leicester LE1 7RH T 0116-252 2522
W www.le.ac.uk
Students: 12,555 UG; 4,855 PG
Chancellor, Lord Willets, PC
Vice-Chancellor, Prof. E Burke (acting)
Registrar, David Hall

UNIVERSITY OF LINCOLN (1992)
Brayford Pool, Lincoln LN6 7TS T 01522-882000
E enquiries@lincoln.ac.uk W www.lincoln.ac.uk
Students: 12,645 UG; 2,325 PG
Chancellor, Lord Adebowale, CBE
Vice-Chancellor, Prof. Mary Stuart, CBE
Registrar, Chris Spendlove

UNIVERSITY OF LIVERPOOL (1903)
Brownlow Hill, Liverpool L69 7ZX T 0151-794 2000
W www.liverpool.ac.uk
Students: 22,070 UG; 6,725 PG
Chancellor, Colm Tóibín
Vice-Chancellor, Prof. Dame Janet Beer, DBE

LIVERPOOL HOPE UNIVERSITY (2005)
Hope Park, Liverpool L16 9JD T 0151-291 3000
E enquiry@hope.ac.uk W www.hope.ac.uk
Students: 3,910 UG; 1,290 PG
Chancellor, Lord Guthrie of Craigiebank, GCB, LVO, OBE
Vice-Chancellor and Rector, Prof. Gerald Pillay
University Secretary, Graham Donelan

LIVERPOOL JOHN MOORES UNIVERSITY (1992)
Kingsway House, 2nd Floor, Hatton Garden, Liverpool L3 2QP
T 0151-231 2121 E courses@ljmu.ac.uk W www.ljmu.ac.uk
Students: 18,875 UG; 4,350 PG
Chancellor, Rt. Hon. Sir Brian Leveson
Vice-Chancellor, Mark Power
Registrar, Liz McGough

UNIVERSITY OF LONDON (1836)
Senate House, Malet Street, London WC1E 7HU T 020-7862 8000
W www.london.ac.uk

Chancellor, HRH the Princess Royal, KG, KT, GCVO
Vice-Chancellor, Prof. Wendy Thomson, CBE
University Secretary, Chris Cobb

COLLEGES
BIRKBECK
Malet Street, London WC1E 7HX
Students: 7,155 UG; 4,785 PG
President, Baroness Bakewell, DBE
Master, Prof. David Latchman, CBE
CITY
Northampton Square, London EC1V 0HB
Students: 10,640 UG; 9,140 PG
President, Prof. Sir Paul Curran
COURTAULD INSTITUTE OF ART
Somerset House, Strand, London WC2R 0RN
Students: 205 UG; 300 PG
Director, Prof. Deborah Swallow
GOLDSMITHS
New Cross, London SE14 6NW
Students: 6,545 UG; 3,455 PG
Warden, Patrick Loughrey
INSTITUTE OF CANCER RESEARCH
15 Cotswold Road, Sutton, Surrey SM2 5NG
Students: 290 PG (postgraduate only)
Chief Executive, Prof. Paul Workman
KING'S COLLEGE LONDON
(includes Guy's, King's and St Thomas's Schools of
Medicine, Dentistry and Biomedical Sciences)
Strand, London WC2R 2LS
Students: 18,925 UG; 13,345 PG
Principal, Prof. Edward Byrne
LONDON BUSINESS SCHOOL
Regent's Park, London NW1 4SA
Students: 1,915 PG (postgraduate only)
Dean, François Ortalo-Magné
LONDON SCHOOL OF ECONOMICS AND POLITICAL
SCIENCE
Houghton Street, London WC2A 2AE
Students: 4,835 UG; 6,790 PG
Director, Dame Minouche Shafik, DBE
LONDON SCHOOL OF HYGIENE AND TROPICAL
MEDICINE
Keppel Street, London WC1E 7HT
Students: 1,085 PG (postgraduate only)
Director, Prof. Baron Peter Piot, KCMG, MD, PHD

QUEEN MARY'S
(incorporating St Bartholomew's and the London School of
Medicine and Dentistry)
Mile End Road, London E1 4NS
Students: 13,935 UG; 6,135 PG
Principal, Prof. Colin Bailey
ROYAL ACADEMY OF MUSIC
Marylebone Road, London NW1 5HT
Students: 415 UG; 430 PG
Principal, Prof. Jonathan Freeman-Attwood, CBE
ROYAL CENTRAL SCHOOL OF SPEECH AND DRAMA
Eton Avenue, London NW3 3HY
Students: 685 UG; 405 PG
Principal, Prof. Gavin Henderson, CBE
ROYAL HOLLOWAY
Egham Hill, Egham, Surrey TW20 0EX
Students: 7,725 UG; 2,835 PG
Principal, Prof. Paul Layzell
ROYAL VETERINARY COLLEGE
Royal College Street, London NW1 0TU
Students: 1,995 UG; 545 PG
Principal, Prof. Stuart Reid
SOAS
Thornhaugh Street, Russell Square, London WC1H 0XG
Students: 3,155 UG; 3,115 PG
Director, Baroness Amos, CH, PC
ST GEORGE'S
Cranmer Terrace, London SW17 0RE
Students: 3,935 UG; 1,035 PG
Principal, Prof. Jenny Higham
UCL
(including the Institute of Neurology, Eastman Dental
Institute, School of Pharmacy and Institute of Education)
Gower Street, London WC1E 6BT
Students: 19,705 UG; 20,310 PG
Provost and President, Prof. Michael Arthur, FRCP, FMEDSCI
UNIVERSITY OF LONDON INSTITUTE IN PARIS
9–11 rue de Constantine, 75340 Paris Cedex 07, France
Chief Executive, Dr Tim Gore, OBE

INSTITUTES
SCHOOL OF ADVANCED STUDY
Senate House, Malet Street, London WC1H 0XG
Dean and Chief Executive, Prof. Rick Rylance
The school consists of nine institutes:
INSTITUTE OF ADVANCED LEGAL STUDIES
Charles Clore House, 17 Russell Square, London WC1B 5DR
Director, Prof. Carl Stychin
INSTITUTE OF CLASSICAL STUDIES
Senate House, Malet Street, London WC1E 7HU
Director, Prof. Greg Woolf, FSA
INSTITUTE OF COMMONWEALTH STUDIES
Senate House, Malet Street, London WC1E 7HU
Director, Prof. Philip Murphy
INSTITUTE OF ENGLISH STUDIES
Senate House, Malet Street, London WC1E 7HU
Director, Prof. Clare A. Lees
INSTITUTE OF HISTORICAL RESEARCH
Senate House, Malet Street, London WC1E 7HU
Director, Prof. Jo Fox
INSTITUTE OF LATIN AMERICAN STUDIES
Senate House, Malet Street, London WC1E 7HU
Director, Prof. Linda Newson, OBE
INSTITUTE OF MODERN LANGUAGES RESEARCH
Senate House, Malet Street, London WC1E 7HU
Director, Prof. Catherine Davies
INSTITUTE OF PHILOSOPHY
Senate House, Malet Street, London WC1E 7HU
Director, Prof. Barry Smith

THE WARBURG INSTITUTE
Woburn Square, London WC1H 0AB
Director, Prof. Bill Sherman

LONDON METROPOLITAN UNIVERSITY (2002)
166–220 Holloway Road, London N7 8DB **T** 020-7423 0000
W www.londonmet.ac.uk
Students: 7,920 UG; 2,375 PG
Patron, HRH the Duke of York, KG, GCVO, ADC(P)
Vice-Chancellor, Prof. Lynn Dobbs
University Secretary, Chris Ince

LONDON SOUTH BANK UNIVERSITY (1992)
103 Borough Road, London SE1 0AA **T** 020-7815 7815
E course.enquiry@lsbu.ac.uk **W** www.lsbu.ac.uk
Students: 12,320 UG; 4,810 PG
Chancellor, Sir Simon Hughes, PC
Vice-Chancellor, Prof. David Phoenix
University Secretary, James Stevenson

LOUGHBOROUGH UNIVERSITY (1966)
Epinal Way, Loughborough LE11 3TU **T** 01509-222222
W www.lboro.ac.uk
Students: 13,110 UG; 4,205 PG
Chancellor, Lord Coe, CH, OBE
Vice-Chancellor, Prof. Robert Allison
Chief Operating Officer, Richard Taylor

UNIVERSITY OF MANCHESTER (2004. Formed by the
amalgamation of Victoria University of Manchester (1851;
reorganised 1880 and 1903) and the University of
Manchester Institute of Science and Technology (1824))
Oxford Road, Manchester M13 9PL **T** 0161-306 6000
W www.manchester.ac.uk
Students: 27,505 UG; 12,640 PG
Chancellor, Lemn Sissay, MBE
Vice-Chancellor, Prof. Dame Nancy Rothwell, DBE, FRS
Secretary and Registrar, Patrick Hackett

MANCHESTER METROPOLITAN UNIVERSITY (1992)
All Saints, Manchester M15 6BH **T** 0161-247 2000
W www2.mmu.ac.uk
Students: 26,605 UG; 6,475 PG
Chancellor, Lord Mandelson, PC
Vice-Chancellor, Prof. Malcolm Press
Chief Operating Officer, Prof. Karen Moore

MIDDLESEX UNIVERSITY (1992)
Hendon Campus, London NW4 4BT **T** 020-8411 5555
W www.mdx.ac.uk
Students: 14,920 UG; 4,770 PG
Chancellor, Dame Janet Ritterman, DBE
Vice-Chancellor, Prof. Tim Blackman
Chief Operating Officer, Sophie Bowen, PHD

NEWCASTLE UNIVERSITY (1963)
Newcastle upon Tyne NE1 7RU **T** 0191-208 6000
W www.ncl.ac.uk
Students: 19,860 UG; 6,615 PG
Chancellor, Prof. Sir Liam Donaldson
Vice-Chancellor, Prof. Chris Day, FRS, DPHIL
Registrar, Dr. John Hogan

NEWMAN UNIVERSITY, BIRMINGHAM (2013)
Genners Lane, Birmingham B32 3NT **T** 0121-476 1181
E admissions@newman.ac.uk **W** www.newman.ac.uk
Students: 2,220 UG; 540 PG
Vice-Chancellor, Prof. Scott Davidson
Secretary and Registrar, Andrea Bolshaw

UNIVERSITY OF NORTHAMPTON (2005)
Waterside Campus, University Drive, Northampton NN1 5PH
T 01604-735500 **E** bc.applicationservices@northumbria.ac.uk
W www.northampton.ac.uk
Students: 9,655 UG; 2,310 PG
Chancellor, Revd Richard Coles
Vice-Chancellor, Prof. Nick Petford, PHD, DSc
Chief Operating Officer, Terry Neville, OBE

NORTHUMBRIA UNIVERSITY AT NEWCASTLE (1992)
Ellison Building, Ellison Place, Newcastle upon Tyne NE1 8ST
T 0191-232 6002 **E** course.enquiries@northumbria.ac.uk
W www.northumbria.ac.uk
Students: 21,150 UG; 5,495 PG
Chancellor, Baroness Grey-Thompson, DBE
Vice-Chancellor, Prof. Andrew Wathey, CBE, DPHIL

NORWICH UNIVERSITY OF THE ARTS (2012)
Francis House, 3–7 Redwell Street, Norwich NR2 4SN
T 01603-610561 **E** info@nua.ac.uk **W** www.nua.ac.uk
Students: 2,115 UG; 105 PG
Vice-Chancellor, Prof. John Last, OBE, FRSA
Academic Registrar, Angela Tubb

UNIVERSITY OF NOTTINGHAM (1948)
University Park, Nottingham NG7 2RD **T** 0115-951 5151
W www.nottingham.ac.uk
Students: 24,605 UG; 8,495 PG
Chancellor, Sir Andrew Witty
Vice-Chancellor, Prof. Shearer West
Registrar, Dr Paul Greatrix

NOTTINGHAM TRENT UNIVERSITY (1992)
50 Shakespeare Street, Nottingham NG1 4FQ **T** 0115-941 8418
W www.ntu.ac.uk
Students: 24,520 UG; 6,370 PG
Chancellor, Sir John Peace
Vice-Chancellor, Prof. Edward Peck
Chief Operating Officer, Steve Denton

OPEN UNIVERSITY (1969)
Walton Hall, Milton Keynes MK7 6AA **T** 0300-303 5303
W www.open.ac.uk
Students: 108,990 UG; 8,945 PG
Chancellor, Baroness Lane-Fox of Soho, CBE
Acting Vice-Chancellor, Prof. Mary Kellett
University Secretary, Dr Jonathan Nicholls

UNIVERSITY OF OXFORD (c.12th century)
University Offices, Wellington Square, Oxford OX1 2JD
T 01865-270000 **E** information.office@admin.ox.ac.uk
W www.ox.ac.uk
Students: 14,640 UG; 10,275 PG
Chancellor, Lord Patten of Barnes, CH, PC (Balliol, St Antony's)
Vice-Chancellor, Prof. Louise Richardson, FRSE
Pro-Vice-Chancellors, Dr D. Prout, CB (Queen's); Prof. M.
   Williams (New College); Dr R. Easton (New College);
   Prof. A. Trefethen (St Cross); Prof. Chas Bountra
   (Merton); Prof. P.S. Grant (St Catherine's)
Registrar, G. Aitken
Academic Registrar, Dr S. Shaikh
Public Orator, Dr J. Katz (All Souls)
Director of University Library Services and Bodley's Librarian, R.
   Ovenden (Balliol)
Director of the Ashmolean Museum, Dr A. Sturgis (Worcester)
Director of the Museum of the History of Science, Dr S.
   Ackermann (Linacre)
Director of the Pitt Rivers Museum, Dr L. Van Broekhoven
   (Linacre)
Director of the University Museum of Natural History, Prof. P.
   Smith (Kellogg)
Chief Executive of Oxford University Press, N. Portwood (Exeter)
Keeper of Archives, S. Bailey (Linacre)
Director of Estates, P. Goffin (Jesus)
Director of Finance, L. Pearson (New College)

COLLEGES AND HALLS *(with dates of foundation)*
ALL SOULS (1438)
Warden, Prof. Sir John Vickers, FBA
BALLIOL (1263)
Master, Dame Helen Ghosh, DCB
BLACKFRIARS HALL (1221)
Regent, Very Revd Dr Simon Gaine, OP
BRASENOSE (1509)
Principal, John Bowers, QC
CAMPION HALL (1896)
Master, Revd James Hanvey
CHRIST CHURCH (1546)
Dean, Very Revd Prof. Martyn Percy
CORPUS CHRISTI (1517)
President, Dr Helen Moore
EXETER (1314)
Rector, Prof. Sir Rick Trainor, KBE
GREEN TEMPLETON (2008)
Principal, Prof. Denise Lievesley, CBE
HARRIS MANCHESTER (1889)
Principal, Very Revd Prof. Jane Shaw
HERTFORD (1740)
Principal, Will Hutton
JESUS (1571)
Principal, Prof. Sir Nigel Shadbolt, FRS, FREng
KEBLE (1870)
Warden, Sir Jonathan Phillips, KCB
KELLOGG (1990)
President, Prof. Jonathan M. Michie
LADY MARGARET HALL (1878)
Principal, Alan Rusbridger
LINACRE (1962)
Principal, Dr Nick Brown
LINCOLN (1427)
Rector, Prof. Henry Woudhuysen, FBA
MAGDALEN (1458)
President, Prof. Sir David Clary, FRS
MANSFIELD (1886)
Principal, Helen Mountfield, QC
MERTON (1264)
Warden, Prof. Irene Tracey, FMedSci
NEW COLLEGE (1379)
Warden, Miles Young
NUFFIELD (1958)
Warden, Sir Andrew Dilnot, CBE
ORIEL (1326)
Provost, Neil Mendoza
PEMBROKE (1624)
Master, Dame Lynne Brindley, DBE, FRSA
QUEEN'S (1341)
Provost, Prof. Paul Madden, FRS, FRSE
REGENT'S PARK COLLEGE (1810)
Principal, Revd Dr Robert Ellis
ST ANNE'S (1878)
Principal, Helen King, QPM
ST ANTONY'S (1953)
Warden, Prof. Roger Goodman
ST BENET'S HALL (1897)
Master, Prof. Richard Cooper
ST CATHERINE'S (1963)
Master, Prof. Peter Battle
ST CROSS (1965)
Master, Carole Souter, CBE
ST EDMUND HALL (C. 1278)
Principal, Prof. Katherine Willis, CBE
ST HILDA'S (1893)
Principal, Prof. Sir Gordon Duff, FRCP, FRSE, FMedSci

ST HUGH'S (1886)
Principal, Dame Elish Angiolini, PC, DBE, QC
ST JOHN'S (1555)
President, Prof. Margaret J. Snowling, FBA, CBE
ST PETER'S (1929)
Principal, Mark Damazer, CBE
ST STEPHEN'S HOUSE (1876)
Principal, Revd Canon Dr Robin Ward
SOMERVILLE (1879)
Principal, Baroness Royall of Blaisdon, PC
TRINITY (1554)
President, Dame Hilary Boulding, DBE
UNIVERSITY (1249)
Master, Sir Ivor Crewe
WADHAM (1610)
Warden, Lord Macdonald of River Glaven, QC
WOLFSON (1981)
President, Sir Tim Hitchens, KCVO, CMG
WORCESTER (1714)
Provost, Prof. Sir Jonathan Bate, CBE, FBA, FRSL
WYCLIFFE HALL (1877)
Principal, Revd Michael Lloyd

OXFORD BROOKES UNIVERSITY (1992)
Gipsy Lane, Oxford OX3 0BP T 01865-741111
E query@brookes.ac.uk W www.brookes.ac.uk
Students: 13,120 UG; 4,055 PG
Chancellor, Dame Dr Katherine Grainger, DBE
Vice-Chancellor, Prof. Alistair Fitt
Registrar, Brendan Casey

UNIVERSITY OF PLYMOUTH (1992)
Drake Circus, Plymouth PL4 8AA T 01752-600600
E admissions@plymouth.ac.uk W www.plymouth.ac.uk
Students: 17,740 UG; 3,030 PG
Chancellor, Lord Kestenbaum
Vice-Chancellor, Prof. Judith Petts, CBE
University Secretary, Gordon Stewart

PLYMOUTH MARJON UNIVERSITY (2012)
Derriford Road, Plymouth PL6 8BH T 01752-636700
E admissions@marjon.ac.uk W www.marjon.ac.uk
Students: 2,140 UG; 495 PG
Vice-Chancellor, Prof. Rob Warner
Registrar, Stephen Plant

UNIVERSITY OF PORTSMOUTH (1992)
University House, Winston Churchill Avenue, Portsmouth PO1 2UP
T 023-9284 8484 E info@port.ac.uk W www.port.ac.uk
Students: 20,305 UG; 4,090 PG
Chancellor, Karen Blackett, OBE
Vice-Chancellor, Prof. Graham Galbraith, PHD
Chief Operating Officer, Bernie Topham

QUEEN MARGARET UNIVERSITY (2007)
Edinburgh EH21 6UU T 0131-474 0000 W www.qmu.ac.uk
Students: 3,430 UG; 1,745 PG
Chancellor, Prue Leith, CBE
Vice-Chancellor, Sir Paul Grice, FRSE
Secretary, Prof. Irene Hynd

QUEEN'S UNIVERSITY BELFAST (1908)
University Road, Belfast BT7 1NN T 028-9024 5133
E comms.office@qub.ac.uk W www.qub.ac.uk
Students: 18,630 UG; 5,855 PG
Chancellor, vacant
Vice-Chancellor, Prof. Ian Greer, FRCP,
Registrar, Joanne Clague

RAVENSBOURNE UNIVERSITY LONDON (2018)
Greenwich Peninsula, 6 Penrose Way, London SE10 0EW
T 020-3040 3500 W www.ravensbourne.ac.uk
Students: 2,475 UG; 55 PG
Interim Director and Chief Operating Officer, Andy Cook

UNIVERSITY OF READING (1926)
Whiteknights, PO Box 217, Reading RG6 6AH T 0118-987 5123
W www.reading.ac.uk
Students: 12,380 UG; 4,620 PG
Chancellor, Lord Waldegrave of North Hill, PC
Vice-Chancellor, Prof. Robert Van de Noort
University Secretary, Dr Richard Messer

RICHMOND, AMERICAN INTERNATIONAL
UNIVERSITY (1972 (obtained UK degree awarding powers
2018))
Queens Road, Richmond-upon-Thames TW10 6JP
T 0208 322 8200 W www.richmond.ac.uk
Students: 1,600
Principal and Vice-Chancellor, Prof. Lawrence S. Abeln
Provost, Phil Davies

ROBERT GORDON UNIVERSITY (1992)
Garthdee House, Garthdee Road, Aberdeen AB10 7QB
T 01224-262000 E admissions@rgu.ac.uk W www.rgu.ac.uk
Students: 9,175 UG; 3,355 PG
Chancellor, Sir Ian Wood, KT, GBE
Vice-Chancellor, Prof. John Harper
Academic Registrar, Hilary Douglas

ROEHAMPTON UNIVERSITY (2004)
Erasmus House, Roehampton Lane, London SW15 5PU
T 020-8392 3000 E Info@roehampton.ac.uk
W www.roehampton.ac.uk
Students: 10,155 UG; 1,750 PG
Chancellor, Dame Jacqueline Wilson, DBE, FRSL
Vice-Chancellor, Prof. Jean-Noël Ezingeard
University Secretary, Mark Ellul

ROYAL AGRICULTURAL UNIVERSITY (2013)
Stroud Road, Cirencester GL7 6JS T 01285-652531
E admissions@rau.ac.uk W www.rau.ac.uk
Students: 1,045 UG; 145 PG
Vice-Chancellor, Prof. Joanna Price
Chief Operating Officer, Susan O'Neill

ROYAL COLLEGE OF ART (1967)
Kensington Gore, London SW7 2EU T 020-7590 4444
E info@rca.ac.uk W www.rca.ac.uk
Students: 2,105 PG (postgraduate only)
Chancellor, Sir Jonathan Ive, KBE
Vice-Chancellor, Dr Paul Thompson
Chief Operating Officer (interim), Jocelyn Prudence

UNIVERSITY OF ST ANDREWS (1413)
St Andrews KY16 9AJ T 01334-476161 W www.st-andrews.ac.uk
Students: 8,625 UG; 2,110 PG
Chancellor, Lord Campbell of Pittenweem, CH, CBE, PC, QC
Vice-Chancellor, Prof. Sally Mapstone, FRSE
Academic Registrar, Marie-Noël Earley

ST MARY'S UNIVERSITY (2014)
Waldegrave Road, Strawberry Hill, Twickenham TW1 4SX
T 020-8240 4000 W www.stmarys.ac.uk
Students: 3,860 UG; 1,450 PG
Chancellor, Cardinal Vincent Nichols
Vice-Chancellor, Prof. Francis Campbell
University Secretary, Andrew Bogg

UNIVERSITY OF SALFORD (1967)
The Crescent, Salford M5 4WT **T** 0161-295 5000
W www.salford.ac.uk
Students: 15,985 UG; 4,305 PG
Chancellor, Jackie Kay, MBE
Vice-Chancellor, Prof. Helen Marshall
University Secretary, Alison Blackburn

UNIVERSITY OF SHEFFIELD (1905)
Western Bank, Sheffield S10 2TN **T** 0114-222 2000
E study@sheffield.ac.uk **W** www.sheffield.ac.uk
Students: 19,760 UG; 9,915 PG
Chancellor, Lady Justice Rafferty, DBE, PC
President and Vice-Chancellor, Prof. Koen Lamberts

SHEFFIELD HALLAM UNIVERSITY (1992)
City Campus, Howard Street, Sheffield S1 1WB **T** 011 4-225 5555
E enquiries@shu.ac.uk **W** www.shu.ac.uk
Students: 24,320 UG; 6,410 PG
Chancellor, Baroness Kennedy of The Shaws, FRSA, QC
Vice-Chancellor, Prof. Sir Chris Husbands
Chief Operating Officer, Richard Calvert

UNIVERSITY OF SOUTHAMPTON (1952)
University Road, Southampton SO17 1BJ **T** 023-8059 5000
W www.southampton.ac.uk
Students: 17,000 UG; 7,620 PG
Chancellor, Ruby Wax, OBE
Vice-Chancellor (interim), Prof. Mark Spearing
Chief Operating Officer, Ian Dunn

SOUTHAMPTON SOLENT UNIVERSITY (2005)
East Park Terrace, Southampton SO14 0YN **T** 023-8201 3000
E ask@solent.ac.uk **W** www.solent.ac.uk
Students: 10,015 UG; 560 PG
Chancellor, Theo Paphitis
Vice-Chancellor, Prof. Graham Baldwin
University Secretary, Caroline Carpenter

UNIVERSITY OF SOUTH WALES (1992)
Pontypridd CF37 1DL **T** 0345-576 0101 **W** www.southwales.ac.uk
Students: 18,360 UG; 4,500 PG
Chancellor, Rt. Revd Lord Williams of Oystermouth, PC, DPHIL
Vice-Chancellor, Prof. Julie Lydon, OBE
Academic Registrar, Sara Moggridge

STAFFORDSHIRE UNIVERSITY (1992)
College Road, Stoke-on-Trent ST4 2DE **T** 01782-294000
W www.staffs.ac.uk
Students: 12,305 UG; 2,045 PG
Chancellor, Lord Stafford
Vice-Chancellor, Prof. Liz Barnes
Chief Operating Officer, Ian Blachford

UNIVERSITY OF STIRLING (1967)
Stirling FK9 4LA **T** 01786-473171 **W** www.stir.ac.uk
Students: 8,745 UG; 3,835 PG
Chancellor, Lord McConnell of Glenscorrodale, PC
Vice-Chancellor, Prof. Gerry McCormac, FRSE
University Secretary, Eileen Schofield

UNIVERSITY OF STRATHCLYDE (1964)
16 Richmond Street, Glasgow G1 1XQ **T** 0141-552 4400
E corporatecomms@strath.ac.uk **W** www.strath.ac.uk
Students: 14,860 UG; 7,435 PG
Chancellor, Lord Smith of Kelvin, KT, CH
Vice-Chancellor, Prof. Sir Jim McDonald, FRSE, FRENG
Academic Registrar, Dr Veena O'Halloran

UNIVERSITY OF SUFFOLK (2016)
Waterfront Building, Neptune Quay, Ipswich IP4 1QJ
T 01473-338000 **W** www.uos.ac.uk
Students: 4,910 UG; 465 PG
Chancellor, Dr Helen Pankhurst
Vice-Chancellor, Prof. Helen Langton
Secretary and Registrar, Tim Greenacre

UNIVERSITY OF SUNDERLAND (1992)
Edinburgh Building, Chester Road, Sunderland SR1 3SD
T 0191-515 2000 **E** student.helpline@sunderland.ac.uk
W www.sunderland.ac.uk
Students: 11,320 UG; 2,750 PG
Chancellor, Emeli Sandé, MBE
Vice-Chancellor, Sir David Bell, KCB
Chief Operating Officer, Steve Knight

UNIVERSITY OF SURREY (1966)
Guildford GU2 7XH **T** 01483-300800 **E** admissions@surrey.ac.uk
W www.surrey.ac.uk
Students: 13,225 UG; 3,720 PG
Chancellor, HRH the Duke of Kent, KG, GCMG, GCVO
Vice-Chancellor, Prof. G. Q. Max Lu
Registrar, Sarah Litchfield

UNIVERSITY OF SUSSEX (1961)
Sussex House, Brighton BN1 9RH **T** 01273-606755
E information@sussex.ac.uk **W** www.sussex.ac.uk
Students: 13,000 UG; 4,800 PG
Chancellor, Sanjeev Bhaskar, OBE
Vice-Chancellor, Prof. Adam Tickell
Chief Operating Officer, Dr Tim Westlake

SWANSEA UNIVERSITY (1920)
Singleton Park, Swansea SA2 8PP **T** 01792-205678
W www.swansea.ac.uk
Students: 16,850 UG; 3,565 PG
Chancellor, Prof. Dame Jean Thomas, DBE, FMEDSCI, FLSW, FRS
Vice-Chancellor, Prof. Paul Boyle
Registrar, Andrew Rhodes

TEESIDE UNIVERSITY (1992)
Middlesbrough TS1 3BX **T** 01642-218121 **E** enquiries@tees.ac.uk
W www.tees.ac.uk
Students: 15,830 UG; 2,545 PG
Chancellor, Paul Drechsler, CBE
Vice-Chancellor, Prof. Paul Croney, CBE
Chief Operating Officer, Malcolm Page

UNIVERSITY OF ULSTER (1984)
Cromore Road, Coleraine BT52 1SA **T** 028-7012 3456
W www.ulster.ac.uk
Students: 18,365 UG; 5,350 PG
Chancellor, James Nesbitt, OBE
Vice-Chancellor, Prof. Paddy Nixon
University Secretary, Eamon Mullan

UNIVERSITY OF WALES, TRINITY SAINT DAVID (1828)
Carmarthen Campus, SA31 3EP **T** 01267-676767
W www.uwtsd.ac.uk
Students: 8,495 UG; 1,785 PG
Vice-Chancellor, Prof. Medwin Hughes, FRSA

UNIVERSITY OF WARWICK (1965)
Coventry CV4 7AL **T** 024-7652 3523 **W** www.warwick.ac.uk
Students: 16,520 UG; 9,185 PG
Chancellor, Baroness Ashton of Upholland, GCMG, PC
Vice-Chancellor, Prof. Stuart Croft
Registrar, Rachel Sandby Thomas, CB

UNIVERSITY OF WEST LONDON (1992)
St Mary's Road, London W5 5RF **T** 0800-036 8888
W www.uwl.ac.uk
Students: 8,985 UG; 1,785 PG
Chancellor, Laurence S. Geller, CBE
Vice-Chancellor, Prof. Peter John
University Secretary, Marion Lowe

UNIVERSITY OF WESTMINSTER (1992)
309 Regent Street, London W1B 2HW **T** 020-7911 5000
E course-enquiries@westminster.ac.uk **W** www.westminster.ac.uk
Students: 14,890 UG; 4,350 PG
Chancellor, Lady Sorrell, OBE
Vice-Chancellor and Rector, Dr Peter Bonfield
University Secretary, John Cappock

UNIVERSITY OF THE WEST OF ENGLAND (1992)
Frenchay Campus, Coldharbour Lane, Bristol BS16 1QY
T 0117-965 6261 **E** infopoint@uwe.ac.uk **W** www.uwe.ac.uk
Students: 21,520 UG; 7,270 PG
Chancellor, Sir Ian Carruthers, OBE
Vice-Chancellor, Prof. Steve West, CBE
Registrar, Rachel Cowie

UNIVERSITY OF THE WEST OF SCOTLAND (2007)
Paisley PA1 2BE **T** 0141-848 3000 **E** ask@uws.ac.uk
W www.uws.ac.uk
Students: 13,465 UG; 2,970 PG
Chancellor, Rt. Hon. Dame Elish Angiolini, DBE, QC
Vice-Chancellor and Principal, Prof. Craig Mahoney
Chief Operating Officer, Susan Mitchell

UNIVERSITY OF WINCHESTER (2005)
Winchester SO22 4NR **T** 01962-841515
E enquiries@winchester.ac.uk **W** www.winchester.ac.uk
Students: 6,290 UG; 1,290 PG
Chancellor, Alan Titchmarsh, MBE
Vice-Chancellor, Prof. Joy Carter, CBE
Registrar, Dee Povey

UNIVERSITY OF WOLVERHAMPTON (1992)
Wulfruna Street, Wolverhampton WV1 1LY **T** 01902-321000
E enquiries@wlv.ac.uk **W** www.wlv.ac.uk
Students: 16,055 UG; 3,575 PG
Chancellor, Lord Paul, PC
Vice-Chancellor, Prof. Geoff Layer, OBE
Academic Registrar, Dr Jo Wright

UNIVERSITY OF WORCESTER (1946)
Henwick Grove, Worcester WR2 6AJ **T** 01905-855000
E study@worc.ac.uk **W** www.worcester.ac.uk
Students: 8,945 UG; 1,855 PG
Chancellor, HRH the Duke of Gloucester, KG, GCVO
Vice Chancellor, Prof. David Green, CBE
Registrar, Kevin Pickess

WREXHAM GLYNDWR UNIVERSITY (2008)
Mold Road, Wrexham LL11 2AW **T** 01978-290666
E enquiries@glyndwr.ac.uk **W** www.glyndwr.ac.uk
Students: 5,130 UG; 610 PG
Chancellor, Colin Jackson, CBE
Vice-Chancellor, Maria Hinfelaar

WRITTLE UNIVERSITY COLLEGE (2015)
Lordship Road, Chelmsford CM1 3RR **T** 01245-424200
E info@writtle.ac.uk **W** www.writtle.ac.uk
Students: 720 UG; 90 PG
Chancellor, Baroness Jenkin of Kennington
Vice-Chancellor, Prof. Tim Middleton
University Secretary, Andrew Williamson

UNIVERSITY OF YORK (1963)
York YO10 5DD **T** 01904-320000 **W** www.york.ac.uk
Students: 13,810 UG; 5,010 PG
Chancellor, Prof. Sir Malcolm Grant, CBE
Vice-Chancellor (acting), Prof. Saul Tendler, PHD
Registrar and Secretary, Jo Horsburgh, PHD

YORK ST JOHN UNIVERSITY (2006)
Lord Mayor's Walk, York YO31 7EX **T** 01904-624624
E admissions@yorksj.ac.uk **W** www.yorksj.ac.uk
Students: 5,460 UG; 785 PG
Chancellor, Most Revd and Rt. Hon. Archbishop of York
Vice-Chancellor, Prof. Karen Stanton
University Secretary, Dr Amanda Wilcox

PROFESSIONAL EDUCATION

The organisations selected below provide specialist training, conduct examinations or are responsible for maintaining a register of those with professional qualifications in their sector, thereby controlling entry into a profession.

EU RECOGNITION

It is possible for those with professional qualifications obtained in the UK to have these recognised in other European countries. Further information can be obtained from:

UK NARIC, Suffolk House, 68–70 Suffolk Road, Cheltenham GL50 2ED **T** 0871-330 7033 **W** www.naric.org.uk/naric

ACCOUNTANCY

Salary range for chartered accountants: Certified £25,000 (starting), rising to £26,000–£45,000+ (qualified); £40,000–£100,000+ at senior levels
Management £28,000 (starting); £32,000 (CIMA student); £62,000 (average); £46,000–£129,000+ at senior levels
Public finance £12,000–£35,000 (starting); £35,000–£50,000 (qualified); £50,000–£70,000 (5 years post-qualification experience); £80,000+ at senior levels

Chartered Accountancy trainees can be school-leavers or graduates. They usually undertake a three-year training contract with an approved employer culminating in professional exams provided by ICAEW, ICAS or CAI. Success in the exams and membership of one of the professional bodies, which offers continuous professional development and regulation, allows the use of the designation 'chartered accountant' and the letters ACA, FCA or CA.

The Association of Chartered Certified Accountants (ACCA) is the global body for professional accountants. The ACCA aims to offer business-relevant qualifications to students in a range of business sectors and countries seeking a career in accountancy, finance and management. The ACCA Qualification consists of up to 13 examinations, practical experiences and a professional ethics module. Chartered certified accountants can use the designatory letters ACCA.

Chartered global management accountants focus on accounting for businesses, and most do not work in accountancy practices but in industry, commerce, not-for-profit and public-sector organisations. Graduates who have not studied a business or accounting degree must complete the Chartered Institute of Management Accountants (CIMA) Certificate in Business Accounting before progressing to the CIMA Professional Qualification, which requires three years of practical experience and 12 examinations. In May 2011, CIMA and the American Institute of Certified Public Accountants (AICPA) agreed on the creation of a new professional designation, the Chartered Global Management Accountant (CGMA), which represents a worldwide standard in management accounting.

The Chartered Institute of Public Finance and Accountancy (CIPFA) is the professional body for people working in public finance. Chartered public finance accountants usually work for public bodies, but they can also work in the private sector. To gain chartered public finance accountant status (CPFA), trainees must complete a professional qualification in public sector accountancy. CIPFA also offers a postgraduate diploma for those already working in leadership positions.

ASSOCIATION OF CHARTERED CERTIFIED ACCOUNTANTS (ACCA), The Adelphi, 1–11 John Adam Street, London WC2N 6AU **T** 0141-582 2000 **E** info@accaglobal.com **W** www.accaglobal.com
Chief Executive, Helen Brand, OBE

CHARTERED ACCOUNTANTS IRELAND (CAI), 47–49 Pearse Street, Dublin 2 **T** 0353-1637 7200 **W** www.charteredaccountants.ie
Chief Executive, Barry Dempsey

CHARTERED INSTITUTE OF MANAGEMENT ACCOUNTANTS (CIMA), The Helicon, One South Place, London EC2M 2RB **T** 020-8849 2251 **E** cima.contact@aicpa-cima.com **W** www.cimaglobal.com
Chief Executive, Andrew Harding

CHARTERED INSTITUTE OF PUBLIC FINANCE AND ACCOUNTANCY (CIPFA), 77 Mansell Street, London E1 8AN **T** 020-7543 5600 **E** customerservices@cipfa.org **W** www.cipfa.org
Chief Executive, Rob Whiteman

INSTITUTE OF CHARTERED ACCOUNTANTS IN ENGLAND AND WALES (ICAEW), Chartered Accountants' Hall, Moorgate Place, London EC2R 6EA **T** 020-7920 8100 **E** general.enquiries@icaew.com **W** www.icaew.com
Chief Executive, Michael Izza

INSTITUTE OF CHARTERED ACCOUNTANTS OF SCOTLAND (ICAS), CA House, 21 Haymarket Yards, Edinburgh EH12 5BH **T** 0131-347 0100 **E** enquiries@icas.com **W** www.icas.com
Chief Executive, Bruce Cartwright

ACTUARIAL SCIENCE

Salary range: £25,000–£35,000 for graduate trainees; £40,000–£55,000 after qualification; £60,000+ for senior roles; £200,000+ for senior directors

Actuaries apply financial and statistical theories to solve business problems. These problems usually involve analysing future financial events in order to assess investment risks. To qualify, graduate trainees must complete 15 exams and three years worth of actuarial work-based training; most graduate trainees take between three and six years to qualify. Students can become Associate members of the Institute and Faculty of Actuaries (IFoA) and gain the right to describe themselves as an actuary and to use the letters AIA or AFA. Members of the profession who wish to continue their studies to an advanced level, or who specialise in a particular actuarial field, may take further specialist exams to qualify as a Fellow and bear the designations FIA or FFA.

The IFoA is the UK's chartered professional body dedicated to educating, developing and regulating actuaries based both in the UK and internationally. As at June 2019, the IFoA represent and regulate 32,938 members and oversee their education at all stages of qualification and development throughout their careers.

The Financial Reporting Council (FRC) is the unified independent regulator for corporate reporting, auditing, actuarial practice, corporate governance and the professionalism of accountants and actuaries. In 2012, the FRC assumed responsibility for setting and maintaining technical actuarial standards independently of the profession, as well as overseeing the regulation of the accountancy and actuarial professions by their respective professional bodies.

FINANCIAL REPORTING COUNCIL (FRC), 8th Floor, 125 London Wall, London EC2Y 5AS **T** 020-7492 2300
E enquiries@frc.org.uk **W** www.frc.org.uk
Chief Executive, Stephen Haddrill

INSTITUTE AND FACULTY OF ACTUARIES (IFoA), 7th Floor, Holborn Gate, 326–330 High Holborn, London WC1V 7PP
T 020-7632 2100 **E** careers@actuaries.org.uk
W www.actuaries.org.uk
Chief Executive, Derek Cribb

ARCHITECTURE

Salary range: architectural assistant (part I) £18,000–£22,000; (part II) £22,000–£35,000; fully qualified £32,000–£45,000; senior associate, partner or director £45,000–£70,000

It takes a minimum of seven years to become an architect, involving three stages: a three-year first degree, a two-year second degree or diploma and two years of professional experience followed by the successful completion of a professional practice examination.

The Architects Registration Board (ARB) is the independent regulator for the profession. It was set up by an act of parliament in 1997 and is responsible for maintaining the register of UK architects, prescribing qualifications that lead to registration as an architect, investigating complaints about the conduct and competence of architects and ensuring that only those who are registered offer their services as an architect. Following registration with ARB an architect can apply for chartered membership of the Royal Institute of British Architects (RIBA). RIBA, the UK body for architecture and the architectural profession, received its royal charter in 1837 and validates courses at over 50 schools of architecture in the UK; it also validates overseas courses. RIBA provides support and guidance for its members in the form of training, technical services and events and sets standards for the education of architects.

The Chartered Institute of Architectural Technologists is the international qualifying body for Chartered Architectural Technologists and Architectural Technicians.

ARCHITECTS REGISTRATION BOARD (ARB) 8 Weymouth Street, London W1W 5BU **T** 020-7580 5861
E info@arb.org.uk **W** www.arb.org.uk
Registrar and Chief Executive, Karen Holmes

CHARTERED INSTITUTE OF ARCHITECTURAL TECHNOLOGISTS 397 City Road, London EC1V 1NH
T 020-7278 2206 **E** info@ciat.org.uk **W** www.ciat.org.uk
Chief Executive, Francesca Berriman, MBE

ROYAL INCORPORATION OF ARCHITECTS IN SCOTLAND 15 Rutland Square, Edinburgh EH1 2BE
T 0131-229 7545 **E** info@rias.org.uk **W** www.rias.org.uk
President, Prof. Robin Webster, OBE

ROYAL INSTITUTE OF BRITISH ARCHITECTS (RIBA) 66 Portland Place, London W1B 1AD **T** 020-7580 5533
E info@riba.org **W** www.architecture.com
Chief Executive, Alan Vallance

ENGINEERING

Salary range:
Civil/structural £22,000–£30,000 (graduate); £50,000 (members of the Institution of Civil Engineers (ICE)); £81,447 (fellows of ICE)
Chemical £28,600 average (graduate); £78,500+ (chartered)
Electrical £26,000 (graduate); £35,000–£60,000 with experience; £60,000+ (chartered)

The Engineering Council holds the national registers of Engineering Technicians (EngTech), Incorporated Engineers (IEng), Chartered Engineers (CEng) and Information and Communication Technology Technicians (ICTTech). It also sets and maintains the internationally recognised standards of competence and ethics that govern the award and retention of these titles.

To apply for the EngTech, IEng, CEng or ICTTech titles, an individual must be a member of one of the 36 engineering institutions and societies (listed below) currently licensed by the Engineering Council to assess candidates. Applicants must demonstrate that they possess a range of technical and personal competences and are committed to keeping these up-to-date.

ENGINEERING COUNCIL, 5th Floor, Woolgate Exchange, 25 Basinghall Street, London EC2V 5HA **T** 020-3206 0500
W www.engc.org.uk
Chief Executive, Alasdair Coates

LICENSED MEMBERS

BCS – The Chartered Institute for IT **W** www.bcs.org
British Institute of Non-Destructive Testing **W** www.bindt.org
Chartered Institute of Plumbing and Heating Engineering **W** www.ciphe.org.uk
Chartered Institution of Building Services Engineers **W** www.cibse.org
Chartered Institution of Highways and Transportation **W** www.ciht.org.uk
Chartered Institution of Water and Environmental Management **W** www.ciwem.org
Energy Institute **W** www.energyinst.org
Institute of Acoustics **W** www.ioa.org.uk
Institute of Cast Metals Engineers **W** www.icme.org.uk
Institute of Healthcare Engineering and Estate Management **W** www.iheem.org.uk
Institute of Highway Engineers **W** www.theihe.org
Institute of Marine Engineering, Science and Technology **W** www.imarest.org
Institute of Materials, Minerals and Mining **W** www.iom3.org
Institute of Measurement and Control **W** www.instmc.org
Institute of Physics **W** www.iop.org
Institute of Physics and Engineering in Medicine **W** www.ipem.ac.uk
Institute of Water **W** www.instituteofwater.org.uk
Institution of Agricultural Engineers **W** www.iagre.org
Institution of Chemical Engineers **W** www.icheme.org
Institution of Civil Engineers **W** www.ice.org.uk
Institution of Engineering Designers **W** www.institution-engineering-designers.org.uk
Institution of Engineering and Technology **W** www.theiet.org
Institution of Fire Engineers **W** www.ife.org.uk
Institution of Gas Engineers and Managers **W** www.igem.org.uk
Institution of Lighting Professionals **W** www.theilp.org.uk
Institution of Mechanical Engineers **W** www.imeche.org
Institution of Railway Signal Engineers **W** www.irse.org
Institution of Royal Engineers **W** www.instre.org
Institution of Structural Engineers **W** www.istructe.org
Nuclear Institute **W** www.nuclearinst.com
Permanent Way Institution **W** www.thepwi.org
Royal Aeronautical Society **W** www.aerosociety.com
Royal Institution of Naval Architects **W** www.rina.org.uk
Society of Environmental Engineers **W** www.environmental.org.uk
Society of Operations Engineers **W** www.soe.org.uk
The Welding Institute **W** www.theweldinginstitute.com

HEALTHCARE

CHIROPRACTIC

Salary range: £30,000–£50,000 starting salary; with own practice £50,000–£100,000 (depending on experience and size of practice)

Chiropractors diagnose and treat conditions caused by problems with joints, ligaments, tendons and nerves of the body. The General Chiropractic Council (GCC) is the independent statutory regulatory body for chiropractors and its role and remit is defined in the Chiropractors Act 1994. The GCC sets the criteria for the recognition of chiropractic degrees and for standards of proficiency and conduct. Details of the institutions offering degree programmes are available on the GCC website (*see* below). It is illegal for anyone in the UK to use the title 'chiropractor' unless registered with the GCC.

The British Chiropractic Association, Scottish Chiropractic Association, McTimoney Chiropractic Association and United Chiropractic Association are the representative bodies for the profession and are sources of further information.

BRITISH CHIROPRACTIC ASSOCIATION, 59 Castle Street, Reading RG1 7SN **T** 0150-663 9607
E enquiries@chiropractic-uk.co.uk **W** www.chiropractic-uk.co.uk
Executive Director, Tom Mullarkey, MBE

GENERAL CHIROPRACTIC COUNCIL (GCC), Park House, 186 Kennington Park Road, London SE11 4BT
T 020-7713 5155 **E** enquiries@gcc-uk.org **W** www.gcc-uk.org
Chief Executive and Registrar, Nick Jones

SCOTTISH CHIROPRACTIC ASSOCIATION, The Old Barn, Houston Road, Houston, Renfrewshire PA6 7BH
T 0141-404 0260 **E** admin@sca-chiropractic.org
W www.sca-chiropractic.org
Administrator, Morag Cairns

DENTISTRY

Salary range: see Health: Employees and Salaries

The General Dental Council (GDC) is the organisation that regulates dental professionals in the UK. All dentists, dental hygienists, dental therapists, dental technicians, clinical dental technicians, dental nurses and orthodontic therapists must be registered with the GDC to work in the UK.

There are various different routes to qualify for registration as a dentist, including holding a degree from a UK university, completing the GDC's qualifying examination or holding a relevant European Economic Area or overseas diploma. The GDC's purpose is to protect the public through the regulation of UK dental professionals. It keeps up-to-date registers of dental professionals and works to set standards of dental practice, behaviour and education.

Founded in 1880, the British Dental Association (BDA) is the professional association and trade union for dentists in the UK. It represents dentists working in general practice, in community and hospital settings, in academia, research and the armed forces, and includes dental students.

BRITISH DENTAL ASSOCIATION (BDA), 64 Wimpole Street, London W1G 8YS **T** 020-7935 0875 **E** enquiries@bda.org
W www.bda.org
Chief Executive, Martin Woodrow *(acting)*

GENERAL DENTAL COUNCIL (GDC), 37 Wimpole Street, London W1G 8DQ **T** 020-7167 6000 **E** information@gdc-uk.org
W www.gdc-uk.org
Chief Executive, Ian Brack

MEDICINE

Salary range: see Health: Employees and Salaries

The General Medical Council (GMC) regulates medical education and training in the UK. This covers undergraduate study (usually five years), the two-year foundation programme taken by doctors directly after graduation and all subsequent postgraduate study, including speciality and GP training.

All doctors must be registered with the GMC, which is responsible for protecting the public. It does this by promoting high standards of medical education and training, fostering good medical practice, keeping a register of qualified doctors and taking action where a doctor's fitness to practise is in doubt. Doctors are eligible for full registration upon successful completion of the first year of training after graduation.

Following the foundation programme, many doctors undertake specialist training (provided by the colleges and faculties listed below) to become either a consultant or a GP. Once specialist training has been completed, doctors are awarded the Certificate of Completion of Training (CCT) and are eligible to be placed on either the GMC's specialist register or its GP register.

The British Medical Association (BMA) is a trade union and professional body for doctors in the UK, providing individual and collective representation, as well as information and professional guidance and support.

BRITISH MEDICAL ASSOCIATION (BMA), BMA House, Tavistock Square, London WC1H 9JP **T** 020-7387 4499
E info.public@bma.org.uk **W** www.bma.org.uk
President, Prof. Dinesh Bhugra, CBE

GENERAL MEDICAL COUNCIL (GMC), Regent's Place, 350 Euston Road, London NW1 3JN **T** 0161-923 6602
E gmc@gmc-uk.org **W** www.gmc-uk.org
Chief Executive, Charlie Massey

WORSHIPFUL SOCIETY OF APOTHECARIES OF LONDON, Black Friars Lane, London EC4V 6EJ
T 020-7236 1189 **E** clerksec@apothecaries.org
W www.apothecaries.org
Master, Prof. Martin Rossor

SPECIALIST TRAINING COLLEGES AND FACULTIES

Faculty of Occupational Medicine **W** www.facoccmed.ac.uk
Faculty of Public Health **W** www.fph.org.uk
Joint Committee on Surgical Training **W** www.jcst.org
Joint Royal Colleges of Physicians Training Board
W www.jrcptb.org.uk
Royal College of Anaesthetists **W** www.rcoa.ac.uk
Royal College of Emergency Medicine www.rcem.ac.uk
Royal College of General Practitioners **W** www.rcgp.org.uk
Royal College of Obstetricians and Gynaecologists
W www.rcog.org.uk
Royal College of Ophthalmologists **W** www.rcophth.ac.uk
Royal College of Paediatrics and Child Health
W www.rcpch.ac.uk
Royal College of Pathologists **W** www.rcpath.org
Royal College of Physicians, London **W** www.rcplondon.ac.uk
Royal College of Psychiatrists **W** www.rcpsych.ac.uk
Royal College of Radiologists **W** www.rcr.ac.uk

MEDICINE, SUPPLEMENTARY PROFESSIONS

The standard of professional education for arts therapists, biomedical scientists, chiropodists and podiatrists, clinical scientists, dietitians, hearing aid dispensers, occupational therapists, operating department practitioners, orthoptists, paramedics, physiotherapists, practitioner psychologists, prosthetists and orthotists, radiographers, social workers in England and speech and language therapists are regulated by the Health and Care Professions Council (HCPC), which only registers those practitioners who meet certain standards of training, professional skills, behaviour and health. The HCPC can take action against professionals who do not meet these standards or falsely declare they are registered. Each profession regulated by the HCPC has at least one professional title that is protected by law.

HEALTH AND CARE PROFESSIONS COUNCIL (HCPC), Park House, 184–186 Kennington Park Road, London SE11 4BU **T** 0300-500 6184 **E** registration@hcpc-uk.org **W** www.hcpc-uk.org
Chief Executive and Registrar, Marc Seale

ART, DRAMA AND MUSIC THERAPIES
Salary range: £26,000–£37,000 (starting); £31,000–£43,000 with experience; £40,000–£50,000 (senior and principal therapists)

An art, drama or music therapist encourages people to express their feelings and emotions through art, such as painting and drawing, drama or music. A postgraduate qualification in the relevant therapy is required. Details of accredited training programmes in the UK can be obtained from the following organisations:

BRITISH ASSOCIATION FOR MUSIC THERAPY, 24–27 White Lion Street, London N1 9PD **T** 020-7837 6100 **E** info@bamt.org **W** www.bamt.org
Chair, Ben Saul

BRITISH ASSOCIATION OF ART THERAPISTS, 24–27 White Lion Street, London N1 9PD **T** 020-7686 4216 **E** info@baat.org **W** www.baat.org
Chief Executive, Dr Val Huet

BRITISH ASSOCIATION OF DRAMATHERAPISTS, PO Box 1257, Cheltenham, Gloucestershire GL50 9YX **T** 01242-235515 **E** info@badth.org.uk **W** www.badth.org.uk
Chair, Madeline Anderson-Warren *(acting)*

BIOMEDICAL SCIENCES
Salary range: £22,128–£28,746 (starting); £26,565–£35,577 with experience; £31,696–£48,514 for senior roles

The Institute of Biomedical Science (IBMS) is the professional body for biomedical scientists in the UK. Biomedical scientists carry out investigations on tissue and body fluid samples to diagnose disease and monitor the progress of a patient's treatment. The IBMS sets quality standards for the profession through training, education, assessments, examinations and continuous professional development.

INSTITUTE OF BIOMEDICAL SCIENCE (IBMS), 12 Coldbath Square, London EC1R 5HL **T** 020-7713 0214 **E** mail@ibms.org **W** www.ibms.org
Chief Executive, Jill Rodney

CHIROPODY AND PODIATRY
Salary range: £23,000–£4; £42,000–£85,000 (consultant podiatrist or specialist registrar in practice)

Chiropodists and podiatrists assess, diagnose and treat problems of the lower leg and foot. The College of Podiatry (formerly Society of Chiropodists and Podiatrists) is the professional body and trade union for the profession. Qualifications granted and degrees recognised by the society are approved by the HCPC. HCPC registration is required in order to use the titles chiropodist and podiatrist.

COLLEGE OF PODIATRY, Quartz House, 207 Providence Square, Mill Street, London SE1 2EW **T** 020-7234 8620 **E** reception@scpod.org **W** www.cop.org.uk
Chief Executive, Steve Jamieson

CLINICAL SCIENCE
Salary range: £25,000–£99,000

Clinical scientists conduct tests in laboratories in order to diagnose and manage disease. The Association of Clinical Scientists is responsible for setting the criteria for competence of applicants to the HCPC's register and for presenting a Certificate of Attainment to candidates following a successful assessment. This certificate will allow direct registration with the HCPC.

ASSOCIATION OF CLINICAL SCIENTISTS, 130–132 Tooley Street, London SE1 2TU **T** 020-7940 8960 **E** info@assclinsci.org **W** www.assclinsci.org
Chair, Prof. Richard Lerski

DIETETICS
Salary range: £23,000–£43,000

Dietitians advise patients on how to improve their health and counter specific health problems through diet. The British Dietetic Association, established in 1936, is the professional association for dietitians. Full membership is open to UK-registered dietitians, who must also be registered with the HCPC.

BRITISH DIETETIC ASSOCIATION, 5th Floor, Charles House, 148–149 Great Charles Street Queensway, Birmingham B3 3HT **T** 0121-200 8080 **E** info@bda.uk.com **W** www.bda.uk.com
Chief Executive, Andy Burman

MENTAL HEALTH
Salary range: Clinical psychologist £26,000, rising to £31,000+ after qualification; £48,000–£83,000 at senior levels
Counselling psychologist £26,000–£35,000 (starting), rising to £31,500–£41,500 (qualified) and up to £82,000 at senior levels
Educational psychologist £22,000, rising to £48,211 (fully qualified) and up to £66,000 at senior levels
Psychotherapist £26,250–£35,250 (starting), rising to £55,000 with experience

Psychologists and counsellors are mental health professionals who can work in a range of settings including prisons, schools and hospitals. The British Psychological Society (BPS) is the representative body for psychology and psychologists in the UK. The BPS is responsible for the development, promotion and application of psychology for the public good. The Association of Educational Psychologists (AEP) represents the interests of educational psychologists. The British Association for Counselling and Psychotherapy (BACP) sets educational standards and provides professional support to counsellors, psychotherapists and others working in counselling, psychotherapy or counselling-related roles. The BPS website provides more information on the different specialisations that may be pursued by psychologists.

ASSOCIATION OF EDUCATIONAL PSYCHOLOGISTS (AEP), 4 The Riverside Centre, Frankland Lane, Durham DH1 5TA **T** 0191-384 9512 **E** enquiries@aep.org.uk **W** www.aep.org.uk
President, Lisa O'Connor

BRITISH ASSOCIATION FOR COUNSELLING AND PSYCHOTHERAPY (BACP), BACP House, 15 St John's Business Park, Lutterworth, Leicestershire LE17 4HB **T** 01455-883300 **E** bacp@bacp.co.uk **W** www.bacp.co.uk
President, David Weaver

BRITISH PSYCHOLOGICAL SOCIETY (BPS), St Andrews House, 48 Princess Road East, Leicester LE1 7DR **T** 0116-254 9568 **E** info@bps.org.uk **W** www.bps.org.uk
President, Kate Bullen

OCCUPATIONAL THERAPY
Salary range: £22,000–£41,500; £40,000–£58,000 for consultancy roles

Occupational therapists work with people who have physical, mental and/or social problems, either from birth or as a result of accident, illness or ageing, and aim to make them as independent as possible. The professional qualification and eligibility for registration may be obtained upon successful completion of a validated course in any of the educational institutions approved by the College of Occupational Therapists, which is the professional body for occupational therapy in the UK. The courses are normally degree-level and based in higher education institutions.

COLLEGE OF OCCUPATIONAL THERAPISTS, 106–114 Borough High Street, London SE1 1LB **T** 020-7357 6480 **E** hello@rcot.co.uk **W** www.rcot.co.uk
Chief Executive, Julia Scott

ORTHOPTICS
Salary range: £24,200 (graduate), rising to £30,000–£86,600 in senior posts

Orthoptists undertake the diagnosis and treatment of all types of squint and other anomalies of binocular vision, working in close collaboration with ophthalmologists. The all-graduate workforce comes from three universities: the University of Liverpool, the University of Sheffield and Glasgow Caledonian University.

BRITISH AND IRISH ORTHOPTIC SOCIETY, 5th Floor, Charles House, 148–9 Great Street Queensway, Birmingham B3 3HT **T** 0344-209 0754 **E** bios@orthoptics.org.uk **W** www.orthoptics.org.uk
Chair, Rowena McNamara

PARAMEDICAL SERVICES
Salary range: £23,000–£36,600; £59,000–£71,000 for consultancy roles

Paramedics deal with accidents and emergencies, assessing patients and carrying out any specialist treatment and care needed in the first instance. The body that represents ambulance professionals is the College of Paramedics.

COLLEGE OF PARAMEDICS, The Exchange, Express Park, Bristol Road, Bridgwater TA6 4RR **T** 01278-420014 **E** membership@collegeofparamedics.co.uk **W** www.collegeofparamedics.co.uk
Chief Executive, Gerry Egan

PHYSIOTHERAPY
Salary range: £23,000–£49,000; £60,000 (management roles)

Physiotherapists are concerned with movement and function and deal with problems arising from injury, illness and ageing. Full-time three- or four-year degree courses are available at around 40 higher education institutions in the UK. Information about courses leading to state registration is available from the Chartered Society of Physiotherapy.

CHARTERED SOCIETY OF PHYSIOTHERAPY, 14 Bedford Row, London WC1R 4ED **T** 020-7306 6666 **W** www.csp.org.uk
Chief Executive, Karen Middleton, CBE

PROSTHETICS AND ORTHOTICS
Salary range: £21,000 on qualification, up to £67,000 as a consultant

Prosthetists provide artificial limbs, while orthotists provide devices to support or control a part of the body. It is necessary to obtain an honours degree to become a prosthetist or orthotist. Training is centred at the University of Salford and the University of Strathclyde.

BRITISH ASSOCIATION OF PROSTHETISTS AND ORTHOTISTS, Unit 3010, Mile End Mill, Abbey Mill Business Centre, Paisley PA1 1JS **T** 0141-561 7217 **E** enquiries@bapo.com **W** www.bapo.com
Chair, Lynne Rowley

RADIOGRAPHY
Salary range: £22,000–£43,000, rising to £69,100 in consultancy posts

In order to practise both diagnostic and therapeutic radiography in the UK, it is necessary to have successfully completed a course of education and training recognised by the HCPC. Such courses are offered by around 24 universities throughout the UK and lead to the award of a degree in radiography. Further information is available from the Society of Radiographers, the trade union and professional body which represents the whole of the radiographic workforce in the UK.

SOCIETY OF RADIOGRAPHERS, 207 Providence Square, Mill Street, London SE1 2EW **T** 020-7740 7200 **W** www.sor.org
Chief Executive, Richard Evans, OBE

SPEECH AND LANGUAGE THERAPY
Salary range: £23,000–£43,000

Speech and language therapists (SLTs) work with people with communication, swallowing, eating and drinking problems. The Royal College of Speech and Language Therapists is the professional body for speech and language therapists and support workers. Alongside the HCPC, it accredits education and training courses leading to qualification.

ROYAL COLLEGE OF SPEECH AND LANGUAGE THERAPISTS, 2 White Hart Yard, London SE1 1NX **T** 020-7378 1200 **W** www.rcslt.org
Chief Executive, Kamini Gadhok, MBE

NURSING
Salary range: see Health: Employees and Salaries

In order to practise in the UK, all nurses and midwives must be registered with the Nursing and Midwifery Council (NMC). The NMC is a statutory regulatory body that establishes and maintains standards of education, training, conduct and performance for nursing and midwifery. Courses leading to registration are currently at a minimum of degree level. All take a minimum of three years if undertaken full-time. The NMC approves programmes run jointly by higher education institutions with their healthcare service partners who offer clinical placements. The nursing part of the register has four fields of practice: adult, children's (paediatric), learning disability and mental health nursing. In most cases students must select one specific field to study before applying to an institution. Some universities run courses which offer the simultaneous study of two nursing fields. In addition, those studying to become adult nurses gain experience of nursing in relation to medicine, surgery, maternity care and nursing in the home. The NMC also sets standards for programmes leading to registration as a midwife and a range of post-registration courses including specialist practice programmes, nurse prescribing and those for teachers of nursing and midwifery. The NMC has a part of the register for specialist community public health nurses and approves programmes for health visitors, occupational health nurses and school nurses.

The Royal College of Nursing is the largest professional union for nursing in the UK, representing qualified nurses, midwives, healthcare assistants and nursing students in the NHS and the independent sector.

NURSING AND MIDWIFERY COUNCIL (NMC), 23
Portland Place, London W1B 1PZ **T** 020-7637 7181
E ukenquiries@nmc-uk.org **W** www.nmc.org.uk
Chief Executive and Registrar, Andrea Sutcliffe, CBE

ROYAL COLLEGE OF NURSING, 20 Cavendish Square,
London W1G 0RN **T** 020-7409 3333 **W** www.rcn.org.uk
Chief Executive and General Secretary, Dame Donna Kinnair,
DBE

OPTOMETRY AND DISPENSING OPTICS

Salary range: Optometrist £20,000–£85,000 (NHS); £14,000–
£65,000+ (private)
Dispensing Optician £14,000–£45,000+

There are various routes to qualification as a dispensing
optician. Qualification takes three years in total, and can be
completed by combining a distance learning course or day
release while working as a trainee under the supervision of a
qualified and registered optician. Alternatively, students can do
a two-year full-time course followed by one year of supervised
practice with a qualified and registered optician. Training must
be done at a training establishment approved by the regulatory
body – the General Optical Council (GOC). There are six
training establishments which are approved by the GOC:
ABDO (Association of British Dispensing Opticians) College,
Anglia Ruskin University, Bradford College, City and
Islington College, City University and Glasgow Caledonian
University. After the completion of training to fit contact lenses
and attaining the ABDO Level 6 certificate in contact lens
practice qualification, a Contact Lens Optician may apply to be
included in the GOC Speciality Register. Students are also able
to complete a Foundation or Undergraduate degree in
Ophthalmic Dispensing, offered by ABDO in conjunction
with Canterbury Christ Church University. All routes are
concluded by professional qualifying examinations, successful
completion of which leads to the awarding of the Level 6
Fellowship Diploma of the Association of British Dispensing
Opticians (FBDO) by ABDO. FBDO holders are able to
register with the GOC following the awarding of their
diploma, with registration being compulsory for all practising
dispensing opticians.

Continuing Education and Training (CET) is a statutory
requirement for all registered dispensing opticians and contact
lens opticians to retain GOC registration.

ASSOCIATION OF BRITISH DISPENSING OPTICIANS
(ABDO), Godmersham Park, Godmersham, Canterbury, Kent
CT4 7DT **T** 01227-733905 **E** general@abdo.org.uk
W www.abdo.org.uk
General Secretary, Sir Anthony Garrett, CBE

COLLEGE OF OPTOMETRISTS, 42 Craven Street, London
WC2N 5NG **T** 020-7839 6000 **W** www.college-optometrists.org
Chief Executive, Ian Humphreys

GENERAL OPTICAL COUNCIL (GOC), 10 Old Bailey,
London EC4M 7NG **T** 020-7580 3898 **E** goc@optical.org
W www.optical.org
Chief Executive and Registrar, Lesley Longstone, CB

OSTEOPATHY

Salary Range: £20,000–£100,000+

Osteopathy is a system of diagnosis and treatment for a wide
range of conditions. It works with the structure and function
of the body, and is based on the principle that the well-being
of an individual depends on the skeleton, muscles, ligaments
and connective tissues functioning smoothly together. The
General Osteopathic Council (GOsC) regulates the practice of
osteopathy in the UK and maintains a register of those entitled
to practise. It is a criminal offence for anyone to describe

themselves as an osteopath unless they are registered with the
GOsC.

To gain entry to the register, applicants must hold a
recognised qualification from an osteopathic education
institute accredited by the GOsC; this involves a four- to five-
year honours degree programme combined with clinical
training.

GENERAL OSTEOPATHIC COUNCIL (GOsC), Osteopathy
House, 176 Tower Bridge Road, London SE1 3LU
T 020-7357 6655 **E** info@osteopathy.org.uk
W www.osteopathy.org.uk
Chief Executive and Registrar, Leonie Milliner

PHARMACY

Salary range: £30,000–£70,000 (community); £26,500–
£100,000 (hospital)

Pharmacists are involved in the preparation and use of
medicines, from the discovery of their active ingredients to
their use by patients. Pharmacists also monitor the effects of
medicines, both for patient care and for research purposes.

The General Pharmaceutical Council (GPhC) is the
independent regulatory body for pharmacists in England,
Scotland and Wales, having taken over the regulating function
of the Royal Pharmaceutical Society in 2010. The GPhC
maintains the register of pharmacists, pharmacy technicians
and pharmacy premises; it also sets national standards for
training, ethics, proficiency and continuing professional
development. The Pharmaceutical Society of Northern Ireland
(PSNI) performs the same role in Northern Ireland. In order to
register, students must complete a four-year degree in
pharmacy that is accredited by either the GPhC or the PSNI,
followed by one year of pre-registration training at an
approved pharmacy; they must then pass an entrance
examination.

GENERAL PHARMACEUTICAL COUNCIL (GPhC), 25
Canada Square, London, E14 5LQ **T** 020-3713 8000
E info@pharmacyregulation.org
W www.pharmacyregulation.org
Chief Executive and Registrar, Duncan Rudkin

PHARMACEUTICAL SOCIETY OF NORTHERN
IRELAND (PSNI), 73 University Street, Belfast BT7 1HL
T 028-9032 6927 **E** info@psni.org.uk **W** www.psni.org.uk
Chief Executive, Trevor Patterson

ROYAL PHARMACEUTICAL SOCIETY, 66 East Smithfield,
London, E1W 1AW **T** 020-7572 2737 **E** support@rpharms.com
W www.rpharms.com
Chief Executive, Paul Bennett

INFORMATION MANAGEMENT

Salary range: Archivist £22,443 (newly qualified); £25,000–
£45,000 (with experience); £55,000 in senior posts
Information Officer £18,000–£31,000 (starting); £21,000–
£28,000 (newly qualified); £26,000–£50,000+ in senior and
chartered posts
Librarian £16,000–£20,000 (trainee); £22,500–£29,500
(assistant librarian); £30,000–£40,000 (experienced);
£43,000–£70,000 (chief/head librarian)

The Chartered Institute of Library and Information
Professionals (CILIP) is the leading professional body for
librarians, information specialists and knowledge managers.
The Archives and Records Association is the professional body
for archivists and record managers.

ARCHIVES AND RECORDS ASSOCIATION, Prioryfield
House, 20 Canon Street, Taunton, Somerset TA1 1SW
T 01823-327077 **E** ara@archives.org.uk **W** www.archives.org.uk
Chief Executive, John Chambers

CHARTERED INSTITUTE OF LIBRARY AND
INFORMATION PROFESSIONALS (CILIP), 7 Ridgmount
Street, London WC1E 7AE **T** 020-7255 0500 **E** info@cilip.org.uk
W www.cilip.org.uk
Chief Executive, Nick Poole

JOURNALISM

Salary range: £12,000–£18,000 (trainee); £25,000 for
established journalists, rising to £35,000–£65,000+ for those
with over a decade's experience in print media, as high as
£80,000+ for top/high-profile broadcast journalists.

The National Council for the Training of Journalists (NCTJ)
accredits courses for journalists run by a number of different
education providers throughout the United Kingdom; it also
provides professional support to journalists.
  The Broadcast Journalism Training Council (BJTC) is an
association of the UK's main broadcast journalism employers
and accredits courses in broadcast journalism.

BROADCAST JOURNALISM TRAINING COUNCIL
  (BJTC), Sterling House, 20 Station Road, Gerard's Cross,
  Buckinghamshire, SL9 8EL **T** 0845-600 8789 **E** sec@bjtc.org.uk
  W www.bjtc.org.uk
  Chief Executive, Jon Godel
NATIONAL COUNCIL FOR THE TRAINING OF
  JOURNALISTS (NCTJ), The New Granary, Station Road,
  Newport, Saffron Walden, Essex CB11 3PL **T** 01799-544014
  E info@nctj.com **W** www.nctj.com
  Chief Executive, Joanne Butcher

LAW

There are three types of practising lawyers: barristers, notaries
and solicitors. Solicitors tend to work as a group in firms, and
can be approached directly by individuals. They advise on a
variety of legal issues and must decide the most appropriate
course of action, if any. Notaries have all the powers of a
solicitor other than the conduct of litigation. Most of them
are primarily concerned with the preparation and
authentication of documents for use abroad. Barristers are
usually self-employed. If a solicitor believes that a barrister is
required, he or she will instruct one on behalf of the client;
the client will not have contact with the barrister without the
solicitor being present.
  When specialist expertise is needed, barristers give opinions
on complex matters of law, and when clients require
representation in the higher courts (crown courts, the high
court, the court of appeal and the supreme court), barristers
provide a specialist advocacy service. However, solicitors –
who represent their clients in the lower courts such as
magistrates' courts and county courts – can also apply for
advocacy rights in the higher courts instead of briefing a
barrister.

THE BAR

Salary range: £12,000–£50,000 (pupillage); £50,000–
£200,000 (qualified); £65,000–£1,000,000+ with ten years
experience

The governing body of the Bar of England and Wales is the
General Council of the Bar, also known as the Bar Council.
Since January 2006, the regulatory functions of the Bar
Council (including regulating the education and training
requirements for those wishing to enter the profession) have
been undertaken by the Bar Standards Board.
  In the first (or 'academic') stage of training, aspiring
barristers must obtain a law degree of a good standard (at
least second class). Alternatively, those with a non-law degree
(at least second class) may complete a one-year full-time or

two-year part-time Common Professional Examination (CPE)
or Graduate Diploma in Law (GDL).
  The second (vocational) stage is the completion of the Bar
Professional Training Course (BPTC), which is available at a
number of validated institutions in the UK and must be
applied for one year in advance. All barristers must join one
of the four Inns of Court prior to commencing the BPTC.
  Students are 'called to the Bar' by their Inn after completion
of the vocational stage, but cannot practise as a barrister until
completion of the third stage, which is called 'pupillage'.
Being called to the Bar does not entitle a person to practise as
a barrister – successful completion of pupillage is now a
prerequisite. Pupillage lasts for two six-month periods: the
'first six' and the 'second six'. The former consists of
shadowing an experienced barrister, while the latter involves
appearing in court as a barrister. Chambers can then offer a
long term 'tenancy' to students. Students who are not given
'tenancy' may take a 'third six'.
  In Northern Ireland admission to the Bar is controlled by
the Bar of Northern Ireland; admission as an Advocate to the
Scottish Bar is through the Faculty of Advocates.

BAR STANDARDS BOARD 289-293 High Holborn, London,
  WC1V 7HZ **T** 020-7611 1444
  E contactus@barstandardsboard.org.uk
  W www.barstandardsboard.org.uk
  Chair of the Bar Council, Rt. Hon. Baroness Blackstone
FACULTY OF ADVOCATES, Parliament Square, Edinburgh
  EH1 1RF **T** 0131-226 5071 **E** info@advocates.org.uk
  W www.advocates.org.uk
  Dean, Gordon Jackson, QC
GENERAL COUNCIL OF THE BAR (THE BAR
  COUNCIL), 289–293 High Holborn, London WC1V 7HZ
  T 020-7242 0082 **E** contactus@barcouncil.org.uk
  W www.barcouncil.org.uk
  Chief Executive, Malcolm Cree, CBE
THE BAR OF NORTHERN IRELAND, 91 Chichester Street,
  Belfast BT1 3JQ **T** 028-9024 1523 **W** www.barofni.com
  Chief Executive, David Mulholland

THE INNS OF COURT

HONOURABLE SOCIETY OF GRAY'S INN, 8 South
  Square, London WC1R 5ET **T** 020-7458 7900
  W www.graysinn.org.uk
  Under-Treasurer, Brig. Anthony Harking, OBE
HONOURABLE SOCIETY OF LINCOLN'S INN, Treasury
  Office, Lincoln's Inn, London WC2A 3TL **T** 020-7405 1393
  E mail@lincolnsinn.org.uk **W** www.lincolnsinn.org.uk
  Treasurer, Rt. Hon. Lord Justice McCombe
HONOURABLE SOCIETY OF THE INNER TEMPLE,
  Treasury Office, Inner Temple, 1 Mitre Court, London EC4Y 7BS
  T 020-7797 8250 **E** enquiries@innertemple.org.uk
  W www.innertemple.org.uk
  Treasurer, Rt. Hon. Lord Hughes of Ombersley
HONOURABLE SOCIETY OF THE MIDDLE TEMPLE,
  Treasury Office, Ashley Building, Middle Temple Lane, London
  EC4Y 9BT **T** 020-7427 4800 **E** education@middletemple.org.uk
  W www.middletemple.org.uk
  Chief Executive, Guy Perricone

NOTARIES PUBLIC

Notaries are qualified lawyers with a postgraduate diploma in
notarial practice. Once a potential notary has passed the
postgraduate diploma, they can petition the Court of Faculties
for a 'faculty'. After the faculty is granted, the notary is able
to practise; however, for the first two years this must be under
the supervision of an experienced notary. The admission and

regulation of notaries in England and Wales is a statutory function of the Faculty Office. This jurisdiction was confirmed by the Courts and Legal Services Act 1990. The Notaries Society of England and Wales is the representative body for practising notaries.

THE FACULTY OFFICE, 1 The Sanctuary, Westminster, London SW1P 3JT **T** 020-7222 5381
E faculty.office@1thesanctuary.com
W www.facultyoffice.org.uk
Registrar, Howard Dellar

THE NOTARIES SOCIETY OF ENGLAND AND WALES, PO Box 1023, Ipswich IP1 9XB
E admin@thenotariessociety.org.uk
W www.thenotariessociety.org.uk
Secretary, Christopher Vaughan

SOLICITORS
Salary range: Trainee solicitors paid at least the national minimum wage; £25,000–£65,000 after qualification; £100,000+ (associate or partner)

Graduates from any discipline can train to be a solicitor; however, if the undergraduate degree is not in law, a one-year conversion course – either the Common Professional Examination (CPE) or the Graduate Diploma in Law (GDL) – must be completed. The next stage, and the beginning of the vocational phase, is the Legal Practice Course (LPC), which takes one year and is obligatory for both law and non-law graduates. The LPC provides professional instruction for prospective solicitors and can be completed on a full-time or part-time basis. Trainee solicitors then enter the final stage, which is a paid period of supervised work that lasts two years for full-time contracts. The employer that provides the training contract must be authorised by the Solicitors Regulation Authority (SRA) (the regulatory body of the Law Society of England and Wales), the Law Society of Scotland or the Law Society of Northern Ireland. The SRA also monitors the training contract to ensure that it provides the trainee with the expertise to qualify as a solicitor.

Conveyancers are specialist property lawyers, dealing with the legal processes involved in transferring buildings, land and associated finances from one owner to another. This was the sole responsibility of solicitors until 1987 but under current legislation it is now possible for others to train as conveyancers.

COUNCIL FOR LICENSED CONVEYANCERS (CLC), WeWork, 131 Finsbury Pavement, London EC2A 1NT
T 020-3859 0904 **E** clc@clc-uk.org **W** www.clc-uk.org
Chief Executive, Sheila Kumar

THE LAW SOCIETY OF ENGLAND AND WALES, The Law Society's Hall, 113 Chancery Lane, London WC2A 1PL
T 020-7242 1222 **W** www.lawsociety.org.uk
Chief Executive, Paul Tennant, OBE

LAW SOCIETY OF NORTHERN IRELAND, 96 Victoria Street, Belfast BT1 3GN **T** 028-9023 1614**W** www.lawsoc-ni.org
Chief Executive, Alan Hunter

LAW SOCIETY OF SCOTLAND, Atria One, 144 Morrison Street, Edinburgh EH3 8EX **T** 0131-226 7411
E lawscot@lawscot.org.uk **W** www.lawscot.org.uk
Chief Executive, Lorna Jack

SOLICITORS REGULATION AUTHORITY (SRA), The Cube, 199 Wharfside Street, Birmingham B1 1RN
T 0370-606 2555 **W** www.sra.org.uk
Chief Executive, Paul Philip

SOCIAL WORK
Salary range: £22,000 (newly qualified); £40,000 (with experience); £26,565–£35,577 (NHS)

Social workers tend to specialise in either adult or children's services. Social Work England obtains regulatory responsibility from the Health and Care Professions Council (HCPC) on 2 December 2019, taking on responsibility for setting standards of conduct and practice for social care workers and their employers, regulating the workforce and social work education and training. A degree or postgraduate qualification is needed in order to become a social worker.

SOCIAL WORK ENGLAND, 1 North Bank, Blonk Street, Sheffield S3 8JY **W** www.socialworkengland.org.uk
Chief Executive, Colum Conway

SURVEYING
Salary range: £20,000–£25,000 (starting); £50,000 (senior); up to £100,000+ (partners and directors)

The Royal Institution of Chartered Surveyors (RICS) is the professional body that represents and regulates property professionals including land surveyors, valuers, auctioneers, quantity surveyors and project managers. Entry to the institution, following completion of a RICS-accredited degree, is through completion of the Assessment of Professional Competence (APC), which involves a period of practical training concluded by a final assessment of competence. Entry as a technical surveyor requires completion of the Assessment of Technical Competence (ATC), which mirrors the format of the APC. The different levels of RICS membership are MRICS (member) or FRICS (fellow) for chartered surveyors, and AssocRICS for associate members.

Relevant courses can also be accredited by the Chartered Institute of Building (CIOB), which represents managers working in a range of construction disciplines. The CIOB offers four levels of membership to those who satisfy its requirements: FCIOB (fellow), MCIOB (member), ICIOB (incorporated) and ACIOB (associate).

CHARTERED INSTITUTE OF BUILDING (CIOB), 1 Arlington Square, Downshire Way, Bracknell RG12 1WA **T** 01344-630700 **E** reception@ciob.org.uk **W** www.ciob.org
Chief Executive, Caroline Gumble

ROYAL INSTITUTION OF CHARTERED SURVEYORS (RICS), Parliament Square, London SW1P 3AD **T** 024-7686 8555 **E** contactrics@rics.org **W** www.rics.org
Chief Executive, Sean Tompkins

TEACHING
Salary range: school teachers £24,373–£49,571; school leaders £41,065–£121,749 (for more detailed information *see* Education: Employees and Salaries)

Since 1 April 2018, the Teaching Regulation Agency, an executive agency sponsored by the Department for Education, is responsible for maintaining the register of qualified teachers in England and is the awarding body for Qualified Teacher Status (QTS). The Education Workforce Council in Wales and the General Teaching Council for Scotland fulfil this responsibility in their respective administrations. In Northern Ireland teacher registration is the responsibility of the General Teaching Council for Northern Ireland. Registration is a legal requirement in order to teach in local authority maintained schools. UCAS Teacher Training is the body through which to apply for postgraduate teacher training in the UK. To become a qualified teacher in a state school, all entrants must have a degree and gain QTS, which includes a minimum of 24 weeks in at least two different schools and academic study of teaching. QTS is not required to teach in independent schools, academies or free schools, but it is a definite advantage. Another route is through School-centred Initial Teacher Training (SCITT), where practical, hands-on teacher training is delivered by experienced, practising teachers in their own government-approved school.

Many courses also award an academic qualification known as the Postgraduate Certificate in Education (PGCE) in England and Wales and the Professional Graduate Diploma in Education (PGDE) in Scotland. Once training is completed, applicants spend a year in school as a newly qualified teacher (NQT).

Teachers in Further Education (FE) need not have QTS, though new entrants to FE may be required to work towards a specified FE qualification by employers. A range of courses are offered and usually require one year of study in addition to 100 hours of teaching experience. Similarly, academic staff in Higher Education require no formal teaching qualification, but are expected to obtain a qualification that meets standards set by the Higher Education Academy.

Details of routes to gaining QTS in England are available from the Department for Education, the Teaching Regulation Agency and UCAS. In the devolved administrations information is available from the Welsh government, Teach in Scotland and from the Department of Education in Northern Ireland.

In July 2017, the College of Teaching became the Chartered College of Teaching. Under the terms of its royal charter, it provides professional qualifications and membership to teachers and those involved in education in the UK and overseas.

ADVANCE HE Innovation Way, York Science Park, Heslington, York YO10 5BR **T** 0330–041 6201
E enquiries@advance-he.ac.uk **W** www.advance-he.ac.uk
Chief Executive, Alison Johns

CHARTERED COLLEGE OF TEACHING, 9–11 Endsleigh Gardens, London WC1H 0EH **T** 020-7911 5589
E hello@chartered.college **W** www.chartered.college
Chief Executive, Prof. Dame Alison Peacock, DBE

DEPARTMENT OF EDUCATION NORTHERN IRELAND, Rathgael House, Balloo Road, Rathgill, Bangor BT19 7PR **T** 028-9127 9279 **E** DE.DEWebMail@education-ni.gov.uk
W www.education-ni.gov.uk

EDUCATION WORKFORCE COUNCIL, 9th Floor, Eastgate House, 35–43 Newport Road, Cardiff CF24 0AB
T 029-2046 0099 **E** information@ewc.wales **W** www.ewc.wales
Chief Executive, Hayden Llewellyn

GENERAL TEACHING COUNCIL FOR NORTHERN IRELAND, 3rd Floor, Albany House, 73–75 Great Victoria Street, Belfast BT2 7AF **T** 028-9033 3390 **E** info@gtcni.org.uk
W www.gtcni.org.uk
Chair, David Canning, OBE

GENERAL TEACHING COUNCIL FOR SCOTLAND, Clerwood House, 96 Clermiston Road, Edinburgh EH12 6UT
T 0131-314 6000 **E** gtcs@gtcs.org.uk **W** www.gtcs.org.uk
Chief Executive, Ken Muir

TEACHING REGULATION AGENCY, Ground Floor South, Cheylesmore House, 5 Quinton Road, Coventry CV1 2WT
T 0207 593 5394 **E** qts.enquiries@education.gov.uk
W www.gov.uk/government/organisations/teaching-regulation-agency
Chief Executive, Alan Meyrick

UCAS TEACHER TRAINING, Rosehill, New Barn Lane, Cheltenham GL52 3LZ **T** 0371-468 0469
W www.ucas.com/teaching-in-the-uk
Chief Executive, Clare Marchant

VETERINARY MEDICINE

Salary range: £30,000 (newly qualified); £43,200–£64,870 (with experience); £72,360 (20+ years experience)

The regulatory body for veterinary surgeons in the UK is the Royal College of Veterinary Surgeons (RCVS), which keeps the register of those entitled to practise veterinary medicine, the register of veterinary nurses and veterinary practice premises (on behalf of the Veterinary Medicines Directorate). Holders of recognised degrees from any of the seven UK university veterinary schools that have been approved by the RCVS or from certain EU or overseas universities are entitled to be registered, and holders of certain other degrees may take a statutory membership examination. The UK's RCVS-approved veterinary schools are located at the University of Bristol, the University of Cambridge, the University of Edinburgh, the University of Glasgow, the University of Liverpool, University of Nottingham and the Royal Veterinary College in London; all veterinary degrees last for five years except that offered at Cambridge, which lasts for six.

The British Veterinary Association is the national representative body for the UK veterinary profession. The British Veterinary Nursing Association is the professional body representing veterinary nurses.

BRITISH VETERINARY ASSOCIATION, 7 Mansfield Street, London W1G 9NQ **T** 020-7636 6541 **E** bvahq@bva.co.uk
W www.bva.co.uk
Chief Executive, David Calpin

BRITISH VETERINARY NURSING ASSOCIATION, 79 Greenway Business Centre, Harlow Business Park, Harlow, Essex CM19 5QE **T** 01279-408644 **E** bvna@bvna.co.uk
W www.bvna.org.uk
Honorary Treasurer, Erika Feilberg

ROYAL COLLEGE OF VETERINARY SURGEONS (RCVS), Belgravia House, 62–64 Horseferry Road, London SW1P 2AF **T** 020-7222 2001 **E** info@rcvs.org.uk
W www.rcvs.org.uk
Chief Executive, Lizzie Lockett

INDEPENDENT SCHOOLS

Independent schools (non-maintained mainstream schools) charge fees and are owned privately or managed under special trusts, with profits being used for the benefit of the schools concerned. As at January 2019 there were 2,486 non-maintained mainstream schools in the UK, educating 580,955 pupils; 6.6 per cent of the total school-age population.

The Independent Schools Council (ISC), formed in 1974, acts on behalf of the seven independent schools' associations which constitute it. These associations are:

Association of Governing Bodies of Independent Schools (AGBIS)
Girls' Schools Association (GSA)
Headmasters' & Headmistresses' Conference (HMC)
Independent Association of Prep Schools (IAPS)
Independent Schools Association (ISA)
Independent Schools' Bursars Association (ISBA)
The Society of Heads

In January 2019 there were 536,109 pupils being educated in 1,364 schools in membership of associations within the Independent Schools Council (ISC). Most schools not in membership of an ISC association are likely to be privately owned. The Independent Schools Inspectorate (ISI) was demerged from ISC with effect from 1 January 2008 and is legally and operationally independent of ISC. ISI works as an accredited inspectorate of schools in membership of the ISC associations under a framework agreed with the Department for Education (DfE). A school must pass an ISI accreditation inspection to qualify for membership of an association within ISC.

In 2019 at GCSE 23.1 per cent of all exams taken by candidates in ISC associations' member schools were awarded a grade 9 (compared to the national average of 4.5 per cent), and at A-level 17.2 per cent of entries were awarded an A* grade (national average, 8 per cent). In 2019 a total of 176,633 pupils (34 per cent) at schools in ISC associations were receiving help with their fees, mainly in the form of bursaries and scholarships from the schools. ISC schools provided £864m of assistance with fees.

INDEPENDENT SCHOOLS COUNCIL, First Floor, 27 Queen Anne's Gate, London SW1H 9BU T 020-7766 7070
W www.isc.co.uk

The list of schools below was compiled from the *Independent Schools Yearbook 2018–19* (ed. Judy Mott, published by Bloomsbury Publishing) which includes schools whose heads are members of one of the ISC's five Heads' Associations. Further details are available online (W www.isyb.co.uk).

The fees shown below represent the upper limit payable for the year 2018–19.

School	Web Address	Termly Fees		
		Day	Board	Head
ENGLAND				
Abbey Gate College, Cheshire	www.abbeygatecollege.co.uk	£4,280	–	Mrs T. Pollard
Abbot's Hill School, Herts	www.abbotshill.herts.sch.uk	£6,172	–	Mrs E. Thomas
Abbotsholme School, Derbys, Staffs	www.abbotsholme.co.uk	£7,495	£10,995	R. Barnes
Abingdon School, Oxon	www.abingdon.org.uk	£6,650	£11,070	M. Windsor
Adcote School, Shrops	www.adcoteschool.org.uk	£4,946	£9,032	Mrs D. Browne
AKS Lytham, Lancs	www.akslytham.com	£3,929	–	M. Walton
Aldenham School, Herts	www.aldenham.com	£7,538	£11,078	J. Fowler
Alderley Edge School for Girls, Cheshire	www.aesg.co.uk	£4,150	–	Mrs H. Jeys
Alleyn's School, London, SE22	www.alleyns.org.uk	£6,617	–	Dr G. Savage
Ampleforth College, N. Yorks	www.ampleforth.org.uk/college	£8,212	£11,808	Miss D. Rowe
Ardingly College, W. Sussex	www.ardingly.com	£7,870	£11,470	B. Figgis
Ashford School, Kent	www.ashfordschool.co.uk	£5,600	£12,000	M. Hall
Austin Friars, Cumbria	www.austinfriars.co.uk	£4,880	–	M. Harris
Bablake School, W. Midlands	www.bablake.com	£3,898	–	A. Wright
Badminton School, Bristol	www.badmintonschool.co.uk	£5,475	£12,525	Mrs R. Tear
Bancroft's School, Essex	www.bancrofts.org	£6,041	–	S. Marshall
Barnard Castle School, Durham	www.barnardcastleschool.org.uk	£4,650	£8,400	A. Jackson
Bedales School, Hants	www.bedales.org.uk	£9,505	£12,095	M. Bashaarat
Bede's Senior School, E. Sussex	www.bedes.org	£7,370	£11,720	P. Goodyer
Bedford Girls' School, Beds	www.bedfordgirlsschool.co.uk	£4,468	–	Miss J. MacKenzie
Bedford Modern School, Beds	www.bedmod.co.uk	£4,468	–	A. Tate
Bedford School, Beds	www.bedfordschool.org.uk	£6,344	£10,730	J. Hodgson
Bedstone College, Shrops	www.bedstone.org	£4,885	£8,840	D. Gajadharsingh
Beechwood Sacred Heart School, Kent	www.beechwood.org.uk	£5,375	£9,950	Mrs H. Rowe
Benenden School, Kent	www.benenden.kent.sch.uk	–	£12,650	Mrs S. Price
Berkhamsted, Herts	www.berkhamsted.com	£6,880	£11,530	R. Backhouse
Bethany School, Kent	www.bethanyschool.org.uk	£6,155	£10,500	F. Healy
Birkdale School, S. Yorks	www.birkdaleschool.org.uk	£4,330	–	P. Harris
Birkenhead School, Merseyside	www.birkenheadschool.co.uk	£3,998	–	P. Vicars
Bishop's Stortford College, Herts	www.bishopsstortfordcollege.org	£6,613	£10,237	J. Gladwin
Blackheath High School, London, SE3	www.blackheathhighschool.gdst.net	£5,498	–	Mrs C. Chandler-Thompson
Blundell's School, Devon	www.blundells.org	£7,470	£11,735	B. Wielenga
Bolton School Boys' Division, Lancs	www.boltonschool.org/seniorboys	£3,992	–	P. Britton
Bolton School Girls' Division, Lancs	www.boltonschool.org/seniorgirls	£3,992	–	Miss S. Hincks

School	Website			Head
Bootham School, N. Yorks	www.boothamschool.com	£5,995	£10,155	C. Jeffrey
Bournemouth Collegiate School, Dorset	www.bournemouthcollegiateschool.co.uk	£4,810	£9,890	R. Slatford
Box Hill School, Surrey	www.boxhillschool.com	£6,570	£13,310	C. Lowde
Bradfield College, Berks	www.bradfieldcollege.org.uk	£9,975	£12,468	Dr C. Stevens
Bradford Grammar School, W. Yorks	www.bradfordgrammar.com	£4,223	–	Dr S. Hinchliffe
Bredon School, Glos	www.bredonschool.org	£7,315	£11,715	K. Claeys
Brentwood School, Essex	www.brentwoodschool.co.uk	£6,315	£12,376	D. Davies
Brighton & Hove High School, E. Sussex	www.bhhs.gdst.net	£4,807	–	Ms J. Smith
Brighton College, E. Sussex	www.brightoncollege.org.uk	–	£13,190	R. Cairns
Bristol Grammar School, Bristol	www.bristolgrammarschool.co.uk	£4,870	–	J. Barot
Bromley High School, Kent	www.bromleyhigh.gdst.net	£5,697	–	Mrs A. Drew
Bromsgrove School, Worcs	www.bromsgrove-school.co.uk	£5,555	£12,430	P. Clague
Bruton School for Girls, Somerset	www.brutonschool.co.uk	£5,935	£10,110	Mrs N. Botterill
Bryanston School, Dorset	www.bryanston.co.uk	£10,438	£12,728	Ms S. Thomas
Burgess Hill Girls, W. Sussex	www.burgesshillgirls.com	£6,400	£11,400	Mrs L. Laybourn
Bury Grammar School Boys, Lancs	www.burygrammar.com	£3,585	–	Mrs J. Anderson
Bury Grammar School Girls, Lancs	www.burygrammar.com	£3,585	–	Mrs J. Anderson
Caterham School, Surrey	www.caterhamschool.co.uk	£6,300	£12,190	C. Jones
Channing School, London, N6	www.channing.co.uk	£6,470	–	Mrs B. Elliott
Charterhouse, Surrey	www.charterhouse.org.uk	–	£13,055	Dr A. Peterken
Cheltenham College, Glos	www.cheltenhamcollege.org	£9,195	£12,260	Mrs N. Huggett
Cheltenham Ladies' College, Glos	www.cheltladiescollege.org	£8,270	£12,315	Ms E. Jardine-Young
Chetham's School of Music, Greater Manchester	www.chethams.com	–	–	A. Jones
Chigwell School, Essex	www.chigwell-school.org	£5,995	£10,011	M. Punt
Christ's Hospital, W. Sussex	www.christs-hospital.org.uk	£5,930	£11,480	S. Reid
Churcher's College, Hants	www.churcherscollege.com	£5,140	–	S. Williams
City of London Freemen's School, Surrey	www.freemens.org	£6,081	£10,260	R. Martin
City of London School, London, EC4	www.cityoflondonschool.org.uk	£5,967	–	A. Bird
City of London School for Girls, London, EC2	www.clsg.org.uk	£6,128	–	Mrs E. Harrop
Claremont Fan Court School, Surrey	www.claremontfancourt.co.uk	£5,890	–	W. Brierly
Clayesmore School, Dorset	www.clayesmore.com	£8,740	£11,910	Mrs J. Thomson
Clifton College, Bristol	www.cliftoncollege.com	£8,230	£12,390	Dr T. Greene
Clifton High School, Bristol	www.cliftonhigh.co.uk	£4,985	–	Dr A. Neill
Cobham Hall, Kent	www.cobhamhall.com	£7,401	£11,517	Ms M. Roberts
Cokethorpe School, Oxon	www.cokethorpe.org.uk	£6,400	–	D. Ettinger
Colfe's School, London, SE12	www.colfes.com	£5,643	–	R. Russell
Colston's, Bristol	www.colstons.org	£4,650	–	J. McCullough
Concord College, Shrops	www.concordcollegeuk.com	£4,903	£13,967	N. Hawkins
Cranford House, Oxon	www.cranfordhouse.net	£5,680	–	Dr J. Raymond
Cranleigh School, Surrey	www.cranleigh.org	£10,390	£12,635	M. Reader
Croydon High School, Surrey	www.croydonhigh.gdst.net	£5,552	–	Mrs E. Pattison
Culford School, Suffolk	www.culford.co.uk	£6,500	£10,580	J. Johnson-Munday
Dauntsey's School, Wilts	www.dauntseys.org	£6,330	£10,480	M. Lascelles
Dean Close School, Glos	www.deanclose.org.uk	£8,200	£11,939	Mrs E. Taylor
Denstone College, Staffs	www.denstonecollege.org	£5,293	£8,407	M. Norris
Derby Grammar School, Derbys	www.derbygrammar.org	£4,483	–	Dr R. Norris
Derby High School, Derbys	www.derbyhigh.derby.sch.uk	£4,290	–	Mrs A. Chapman
Dover College, Kent	www.dovercollege.org.uk	£5,350	£10,500	G. Doodes
d'Overbroeck's, Oxon	www.doverbroecks.com	£7,950	£12,900	J. Cuff
Downe House, Berks	www.downehouse.net	£9,165	£12,510	Mrs E. McKendrick
Downside School, Somerset	www.downside.co.uk	£6,417	£11,287	A. Hobbs
Dulwich College, London, SE21	dulwich.org.uk	£6,816	£14,227	Dr J. Spence
Dunottar School, Surrey	www.dunottarschool.com	£5,345	–	M. Tottman
Durham High School for Girls, Durham	www.dhsfg.org.uk	£4,375	–	Mrs S. Niblock
Eastbourne College, E. Sussex	www.eastbourne-college.co.uk	£7,710	£11,750	T. Lawson
Edgbaston High School, W. Midlands	www.edgbastonhigh.co.uk	£4,258	–	Dr R. Weeks
Ellesmere College, Shrops	www.ellesmere.com	£6,123	£10,977	B. Wignall
Eltham College, London, SE9	www.elthamcollege.london	£5,925	–	G. Sanderson
Emanuel School, London, SW11	www.emanuel.org.uk	£6,194	–	R. Milne
Epsom College, Surrey	www.epsomcollege.org.uk	£8,422	£12,421	J. Piggot
Eton College, Berks	www.etoncollege.com	–	£13,556	S. Henderson
Ewell Castle School, Surrey	www.ewellcastle.co.uk	£5,564	–	S. Edmonds
Exeter School, Devon	www.exeterschool.org.uk	£4,410	–	B. Griffin
Farnborough Hill, Hants	www.farnborough-hill.org.uk	£4,932	–	Mrs A. Neil
Farringtons School, Kent	www.farringtons.org.uk	£4,870	£10,560	Mrs D. Nancekievill
Felsted School, Essex	www.felsted.org	£7,850	£11,995	C. Townsend

Forest School, London, E17	www.forest.org.uk	£6,227	– M. Hodges
Framlingham College, Suffolk	www.framcollege.co.uk	£6,642 £10,328	P. Taylor
Francis Holland School, London, NW1	www.fhs-nw1.org.uk	£6,680	– C. Fillingham
Francis Holland School, London, SW1	www.fhs-sw1.org.uk	£6,970	– Mrs L. Elphinstone
Frensham Heights, Surrey	www.frensham.org	£6,410 £9,890	R. Clarke
Fulneck School, W. Yorks	www.fulneckschool.co.uk	£4,375 £8,485	P. Taylor
Gateways School, W. Yorks	www.gatewaysschool.co.uk	£4,538	– Dr T. Johnson
Giggleswick School, N. Yorks	www.giggleswick.org.uk	£6,475 £10,715	M. Turnbull
The Godolphin and Latymer School, London, W6	www.godolphinandlatymer.com	£7,205	– Dr F. Ramsey
Godolphin School, Wilts	www.godolphin.org	£7,030 £10,675	Mrs E. Hattersley
The Grange School, Cheshire	www.grange.org.uk	£3,835	– Mrs D. Leonard
Gresham's School, Norfolk	www.greshams.com	£8,140 £11,660	D. Robb
Guildford High School – Senior School, Surrey	www.guildfordhigh.co.uk	£5,664	– Mrs F. Boulton
The Haberdashers' Aske's Boys' School, Herts	www.habsboys.org.uk	£6,782	– G. Lock
Haberdashers' Aske's School for Girls, Herts	www.habsgirls.org.uk	£6,131	– Miss B. O'Connor
Halliford School, Middx	www.hallifordschool.co.uk	£5,320	– J. Davies
Hampshire Collegiate School, Hants	www.hampshirecs.org.uk	£5,253 £8,925	C. Canning
Hampton School, Middx	hamptonschool.org.uk	£6,685	– K. Knibbs
Harrogate Ladies' College, N. Yorks	www.hlc.org.uk	£5,345 £12,170	Mrs S. Brett
Harrow School, Middx	www.harrowschool.org.uk	– £13,350	A. Land
Headington School, Oxon	www.headington.org	£6,417 £12,762	Mrs C. Jordan
Heathfield School, Berks	www.heathfieldschool.net	£7,600 £12,210	Mrs M. Legge
Hereford Cathedral School, Herefords	www.herefordcs.com	£4,627	– P. Smith
Hethersett Old Hall School, Norfolk	www.hohs.co.uk	£5,210 £8,020	S. Crump
Highclare School, W. Midlands	www.highclareschool.co.uk	£4,215	– Dr R. Luker
Highgate School, London, N6	www.highgateschool.org.uk	£6,990	– A. Pettitt
Hill House School, S. Yorks	www.hillhouse.doncaster.sch.uk	£4,400	– D. Holland
Hurstpierpoint College, W. Sussex	www.hppc.co.uk	£7,950 £9,985	T. Manly
Hymers College, E. Yorks	www.hymerscollege.co.uk	£3,786	– D. Elstone
Ibstock Place School, London, SW15	www.ibstockplaceschool.co.uk	£6,960	– Mrs A. Sylvester-Johnson
Immanuel College, Herts	www.immanuelcollege.co.uk	£5,890	– G. Griffin
Ipswich High School, Suffolk	www.ipswichhighschool.co.uk	£4,708	– Ms O. Carlin
Ipswich School, Suffolk	www.ipswich.school	£5,193 £10,057	N. Weaver
James Allen's Girls' School (JAGS), London, SE22	www.jags.org.uk	£5,997	– Mrs S. Huang
The John Lyon School, Middx	www.johnlyon.org	£6,194	– Miss K. Haynes
Kent College, Kent	www.kentcollege.com	£6,105 £11,497	Dr D. Lamper
Kimbolton School, Cambs	www.kimbolton.cambs.sch.uk	£5,265 £8,760	J. Belbin
King Edward VI High School for Girls, W. Midlands	www.kehs.org.uk	£4,296	– Mrs A. Clark
King Edward VI School, Hants	www.kes.hants.sch.uk	£5,350	– J. Thould
King Edward's School, Somerset	www.kesbath.com	£4,825	– M. Boden
King Edward's School, W. Midlands	www.kes.org.uk	£4,410	– K. Phillips
King Edward's Witley, Surrey	www.kesw.org	£6,820 £10,665	J. Attwater
King Henry VIII School, W. Midlands	www.khviii.com	£3,898	– J. Slack
King William's College, Isle of Man	www.kwc.im	£6,520 £9,882	J. Buchanan
King's College School, London, SW19	www.kcs.org.uk	£7,200	– A. Halls
King's College, Taunton, Somerset	www.kings-taunton.co.uk	£7,460 £11,055	R. Biggs
King's Ely, Cambs	www.kingsely.org	£7,153 £10,355	Mrs S. Freestone
King's High School, Warwicks	www.kingshighwarwick.co.uk	£4,325	– R. Nicholson
The King's School, Kent	www.kings-school.co.uk	£9,165 £12,485	P. Roberts
The King's School, Cheshire	www.kingschester.co.uk	£4,505	– G. Hartley
The King's School, Cheshire	www.kingsmac.co.uk	£4,330	– Dr S. Hyde
King's Rochester, Kent	www.kings-rochester.co.uk	£6,440 £10,530	B. Charles
The King's School, Worcs	www.ksw.org.uk	£4,663	– M. Armstrong
The Kingsley School, Warwicks	www.thekingsleyschool.com	£4,418	– Ms H. Owens
Kingsley School, Devon	www.kingsleyschoolbideford.co.uk	£4,460 £8,945	P. Last
Kingston Grammar School, Surrey	www.kgs.org.uk	£6,410	– S. Lehec
Kingswood School, Somerset	www.kingswood.bath.sch.uk	£5,061 £10,909	S. Morris
Kirkham Grammar School, Lancs	www.kirkhamgrammar.co.uk	£3,875 £7,355	D. Berry
Lady Eleanor Holles, Middx	www.lehs.org.uk	£5,576	– Mrs H. Hanbury
Lancing College, W. Sussex	www.lancingcollege.co.uk	£8,190 £11,995	D. Oliver
Latymer Upper School, London, W6	www.latymer-upper.org	£6,710	– D. Goodhew
The Grammar School at Leeds, W. Yorks	www.gsal.org.uk	£4,596	– Mrs S. Woodroofe
Leicester Grammar School, Leics	www.lgs-senior.org.uk	£4,343	– J. Watson
Leicester High School for Girls, Leics	www.leicesterhigh.co.uk	£4,065	– A. Whelpdale
Leighton Park School, Berks	www.leightonpark.com	£7,326 £11,915	M. Judd

School	Website	Day	Boarding	Head
Leweston School, Dorset	www.leweston.co.uk	£5,140	£10,185	Mrs K. Reynolds
The Leys, Cambs	www.theleys.net	£7,345	£10,975	M. Priestley
Lichfield Cathedral School, Staffs	www.lichfieldcathedralschool.com	£4,605	–	Mrs S. Hannam
Lincoln Minster School, Lincolns	www.lincolnminsterschool.co.uk	£4,608	£9,022	M. Wallace
Lingfield College, Surrey	www.lingfieldcollege.co.uk	£5,104	–	R. Bool
Longridge Towers School, Northumberland	www.lts.org.uk	£4,550	£9,250	J. Lee
Lord Wandsworth College, Hants	www.lordwandsworth.org	£10,600	£11,100	A. Williams
Loughborough Grammar School, Leics	www.lsf.org/grammar	£4,183	£9,584	D. Byrne
Loughborough High School, Leics	www.lsf.org/high	£4,183	–	Dr F. Miles
Luckley House School, Berks	www.luckleyhouseschool.org	£5,540	£9,694	Mrs J. Tudor
LVS Ascot, Berks	www.lvs.ascot.sch.uk	£5,657	£10,077	Mrs C. Cunniffe
Magdalen College School, Oxon	www.mcsoxford.org	£6,159	–	Miss H. Pike
Malvern College, Worcs	www.malverncollege.org.uk	£8,485	£13,153	K. Metcalfe
The Manchester Grammar School, Greater Manchester	www.mgs.org	£4,190	–	Dr M. Boulton
Manchester High School for Girls, Greater Manchester	www.manchesterhigh.co.uk	£3,958	–	Mrs C. Hewitt
Manor House School, Bookham, Surrey	www.manorhouseschool.org	£5,801	–	Ms T. Fantham
The Marist School – Senior Phase, Berks	www.themarist.com	£4,870	–	K. McCloskey
Marlborough College, Wilts	www.marlboroughcollege.org	–	£12,605	Mrs L. Moelwyn-Hughes
Marymount International School, Surrey	www.marymountlondon.com	£7,925	£13,475	Mrs M. Frazier
Mayfield School, E. Sussex	www.mayfieldgirls.org	£7,000	£11,300	Miss A. Beary
The Maynard School, Devon	www.maynard.co.uk	£4,416	–	Miss S. Dunn
Merchant Taylors' Boys' School, Merseyside	www.merchanttaylors.com	£3,798	–	D. Wickes
Merchant Taylors' Girls' School, Merseyside	www.merchanttaylors.com	£3,798	–	Mrs C. Tao
Merchant Taylors' School, Middx	www.mtsn.org.uk	£6,899	–	S. Everson
Mill Hill School, London, NW7	millhill.org.uk	£7,047	£11,239	Mrs J. Sanchez
Millfield, Somerset	millfieldschool.com	£8,535	£12,870	G. Horgan
Milton Abbey School, Dorset	www.miltonabbey.co.uk	£6,750	£12,850	Mrs J. Fremont-Barnes
Monkton Combe School, Somerset	www.monktoncombeschool.com	£6,970	£11,115	C. Wheeler
More House School, London, SW1	www.morehouse.org.uk	£6,650	–	Mrs A. Leach
Moreton Hall, Shrops	www.moretonhall.org	£9,575	£11,625	J. Forster
Mount House School, Herts	www.mounthouse.org.uk	£5,010	–	T. Mullins
Mount Kelly, Devon	www.mountkelly.com	£5,840	£10,190	G. Ayling
Mount St Mary's College, Derbys	www.msmcollege.com	£4,695	£9,995	Dr N. Cuddihy
New Hall School, Essex	www.newhallschool.co.uk	£6,626	£10,002	Mrs K. Jeffrey
Newcastle High School for Girls, Tyne and Wear	www.newcastlehigh.gdst.net	£4,341	–	M. Tippett
Newcastle School for Boys, Tyne and Wear	www.newcastleschool.co.uk	£4,161	–	D. Tickner
Newcastle-under-Lyme School, Staffs	www.nuls.org.uk	£3,993	–	M. Getty
North London Collegiate School, Middx	www.nlcs.org.uk	£6,676	–	Mrs S. Clark
Norwich High School, Norfolk	www.norwichhigh.gdst.net	£4,854	–	Mrs K. Malaisé
Norwich School, Norfolk	www.norwich-school.org.uk	£5,404	–	S. Griffiths
Notre Dame School, Surrey	www.notredame.co.uk	£5,590	–	Mrs A. King
Notting Hill and Ealing High School, London, W13	www.nhehs.gdst.net	£6,187	–	M. Shoults
Nottingham Girls' High School, Notts	www.nottinghamgirlshigh.gdst.net	£4,527	–	Miss J. Keller
Nottingham High School, Notts	www.nottinghamhigh.co.uk	£4,955	–	K. Fear
Oakham School, Rutland	www.oakham.rutland.sch.uk	£6,845	£11,220	N. Lashbrook
Ockbrook School, Derbys	www.ockbrooksch.co.uk	£4,390	–	T. Brooksby
Oldham Hulme Grammar School, Lancs	www.ohgs.co.uk	£3,745	–	C. Mairs
The Oratory School, Oxon	www.oratory.co.uk	£8,322	£11,433	J. Smith
Oundle School, Northants	www.oundleschool.org.uk	£7,935	£12,230	Mrs S. Kerr-Dineen
Our Lady's Abingdon Senior School, Oxon	www.olab.org.uk	£5,350	–	S. Oliver
Oxford High School, Oxon	www.oxfordhigh.gdst.net	£5,182	–	Dr P. Hills
Palmers Green High School, London, N21	www.pghs.co.uk	£5,310	–	Mrs W. Kempster
Pangbourne College, Berks	www.pangbourne.com	£8,295	£11,730	T. Garnier
The Perse Upper School, Cambs	www.perse.co.uk	£5,774	–	E. Elliott
The Peterborough School, Cambs	www.thepeterboroughschool.co.uk	£4,956	–	A. Meadows
Pipers Corner School, Bucks	www.piperscorner.co.uk	£6,130	–	Mrs H. Ness-Gifford
Pitsford School, Northants	www.pitsfordschool.com	£4,902	–	Dr C. Walker
Plymouth College, Devon	www.plymouthcollege.com	£5,225	£9,995	J. Cohen
Pocklington School, E. Yorks	www.pocklingtonschool.com	£4,873	£9,497	T. Seth
Portland Place School, London, W1B	www.portland-place.co.uk	£7,040	–	D. Bradbury
The Portsmouth Grammar School, Hants	www.pgs.org.uk	£5,317	–	Dr A. Cotton
Portsmouth High School, Hants	www.portsmouthhigh.co.uk	£4,662	–	Mrs J. Prescott
Princess Helena College, Herts	www.princesshelenacollege.co.uk	£6,741	£9,800	Mrs S. Davis

School	Website			Head
Princethorpe College, Warwicks	www.princethorpe.co.uk	£4,231	–	E. Hester
Prior Park College, Somerset	www.priorparkschools.com	£5,585	£10,315	J. Murphy-O'Connor
The Purcell School, Herts	www.purcell-school.org	£8,656	£11,025	P. Bambrough
Putney High School, London, SW15	www.putneyhigh.gdst.net	£6,300	–	Mrs S. Longstaff
Queen Anne's School, Berks	www.qas.org.uk	£8,045	£11,860	Mrs J. Harrington
Queen Elizabeth's Hospital (QEH), Bristol	www.qehbristol.co.uk	£4,802	–	S. Holliday
Queen Mary's School, N. Yorks	www.queenmarys.org	£6,325	£8,630	Mrs C. Cameron
Queen's College, London, London, W1G	www.qcl.org.uk	£6,375	–	R. Tillett
Queen's College, Somerset	www.queenscollege.org.uk	£6,150	£10,660	Dr L. Earps
Queen's Gate School, London, SW7	www.queensgate.org.uk	£6,850	–	Mrs R. Kamaryc
Queenswood School, Herts	www.queenswood.org	£8,125	£10,900	Mrs J. Cameron
Radley College, Oxon	www.radley.org.uk	–	£12,775	J. Moule
Ratcliffe College, Leics	www.ratcliffecollege.com	£5,429	£8,653	J. Reddin
The Read School, N. Yorks	www.readschool.co.uk	£4,132	£9,482	Mrs R. Ainley
Reading Blue Coat School, Berks	www.rbcs.org.uk	£5,565	–	J. Elzinga
Reddam House Berkshire, Berks	www.reddamhouse.org.uk	£5,760	£10,935	Mrs T. Howard
Redmaids' High School, Bristol	www.redmaidshigh.co.uk	£5,025	–	Mrs I. Tobias
Reed's School, Surrey	www.reeds.surrey.sch.uk	£8,225	£10,600	M. Hoskins
Reigate Grammar School, Surrey	www.reigategrammar.org	£6,240	–	S. Fenton
Rendcomb College, Glos	www.rendcombcollege.org.uk	£7,775	£10,500	R. Jones
Repton School, Derbys	www.repton.org.uk	£8,831	£11,904	M. Semmence
RGS Worcester, Worcs	www.rgsw.org.uk	£4,360	–	J. Pitt
Rishworth School, W. Yorks	www.rishworth-school.co.uk	£4,220	£9,995	Dr P. Silverwood
Roedean Moira House Girls School, E. Sussex	www.roedeanmoirahouse.co.uk	£6,020	£11,140	A. Wood
Roedean School, E. Sussex	www.roedean.co.uk	£7,165	£12,855	O. Blond
Rossall School, Lancs	www.rossall.org.uk	£4,360	£12,450	J. Quartermain
Royal Grammar School, Surrey	www.rgsg.co.uk	£6,095	–	Dr J. Cox
Royal Grammar School, Tyne and Wear	www.rgs.newcastle.sch.uk	£4,388	–	J. Fern
Royal Hospital School, Suffolk	www.royalhospitalschool.org	£5,830	£10,865	S. Lockyer
The Royal Masonic School for Girls, Herts	www.rmsforgirls.org.uk	£5,825	£9,945	K. Carson
Royal Russell School, Surrey	www.royalrussell.co.uk	£6,160	£12,175	C. Hutchinson
Rugby School, Warwicks	www.rugbyschool.co.uk	£7,479	£11,920	P. Green
Ryde School with Upper Chine, Isle of Wight	www.rydeschool.org.uk	£4,410	–	M. Waldron
Rye St Antony, Oxon	www.ryestantony.co.uk	£5,110	£8,645	Mrs S. Ryan
St Albans High School for Girls, Herts	www.stahs.org.uk	£6,265	–	Mrs J. Brown
St Albans School, Herts	www.st-albans.herts.sch.uk	£6,200	–	J. Gillespie
St Augustine's Priory School, London, W5	www.sapriory.com	£5,231	–	Mrs S. Raffray
St Bede's College, Greater Manchester	www.sbcm.co.uk	£3,775	–	L. d'Arcy
St Benedict's School, London, W5	www.stbenedicts.org.uk	£5,615	–	A. Johnson
St Catherine's School, Surrey	www.stcatherines.info	£6,125	£10,095	Mrs A. Phillips
St Catherine's School, Middx	www.stcatherineschool.co.uk	£4,970	–	Mrs J. McPherson
St Christopher School, Herts	www.stchris.co.uk	£6,025	£10,550	R. Palmer
St Columba's College, Herts	www.stcolumbascollege.org	£5,233	–	D. Buxton
St Dominic's Grammar School, Staffs	www.stdominicsgrammarschool.co.uk	£4,404	–	P. McNabb
St Dunstan's College, London, SE6	www.stdunstans.org.uk	£5,732	–	N. Hewlett
St Edmund's College, Herts	www.stedmundscollege.org	£5,935	£10,305	P. Durán
St Edmund's School Canterbury, Kent	www.stedmunds.org.uk	£6,822	£11,656	E. O'Connor
St Edward's, Oxford, Oxon	www.stedwardsoxford.org	£10,095	£12,615	S. Jones
St Edward's School, Glos	www.stedwards.co.uk	£5,920	–	Mrs P. Clayfield
St Gabriel's, Berks	www.stgabriels.co.uk	£5,806	–	R. Smith
St George's College, Weybridge, Surrey	www.stgeorgesweybridge.com	£6,395	–	Mrs R. Owens
St George's, Ascot, Berks	www.stgeorges-ascot.org.uk	£7,600	£11,820	Mrs E. Hewer
St Helen & St Katharine, Oxon	www.shsk.org.uk	£5,490	–	Mrs R. Dougall
St Helen's School, Middx	www.sthelens.london	£5,816	–	Dr M. Short
St James Senior Boys' School, Surrey	www.stjamesboys.co.uk	£6,310	–	D. Brazier
St James Senior Girls' School, London, W14	www.stjamesgirls.co.uk	£6,700	–	Mrs S. Labram
St John's College, Hants	www.stjohnscollege.co.uk	£4,030	£8,695	Mrs M. Maguire
St Joseph's College, Suffolk	www.stjos.co.uk	£5,050	£11,590	Mrs D. Clarke
St Lawrence College, Kent	www.slcuk.com	£5,333	£11,945	A. Spencer
St Mary's School Ascot, Berks	www.st-marys-ascot.co.uk	£9,210	£12,930	Mrs M. Breen
St Mary's Calne, Wilts	www.stmaryscalne.org	£9,675	£12,975	Dr F. Kirk
St Mary's School, Essex	www.stmaryscolchester.org.uk	£4,995	–	Mrs H. Vipond
St Mary's College, Merseyside	www.stmarys.ac	£3,720	–	M. Kennedy
St Mary's School, Bucks	www.stmarysschool.co.uk	£5,660	–	Mrs P. Adams
St Mary's School, Dorset	www.stmarys.eu	£6,950	£10,490	Mrs M. Young
St Nicholas' School, Hants	www.st-nicholas.hants.sch.uk	£4,786	–	Dr O. Wright
St Paul's Girls' School, London, W6	www.spgs.org	£8,297	–	Mrs S. Fletcher
St Paul's School, London, SW13	www.stpaulsschool.org.uk	£8,344	£12,537	Professor Mark Bailey

School	Website	Fee 1	Fee 2	Contact
St Peter's School, York, N. Yorks	www.stpetersyork.org.uk	£6,025	£10,010	J. Walker
St Swithun's School, Hants	www.stswithuns.com	£6,855	£11,200	Ms J. Gandee
Scarborough College, N. Yorks	www.scarboroughcollege.co.uk	£4,898	£8,267	G. Emmett
Seaford College, W. Sussex	www.seaford.org	£7,130	£11,030	J. Green
Sevenoaks School, Kent	www.sevenoaksschool.org	£7,785	£12,432	Dr K. Ricks
Shebbear College, Devon	www.shebbearcollege.co.uk	£4,325	£8,775	S. Weale
Sheffield High School for Girls, S. Yorks	www.sheffieldhighschool.org.uk	£4,325	–	Mrs N. Gunson
Sherborne Girls, Dorset	www.sherborne.com	£7,095	£11,960	Dr R. Sullivan
Sherborne School, Dorset	www.sherborne.org	£10,125	£12,500	D. Luckett
Shiplake College, Oxon	www.shiplake.org.uk	£7,410	£11,025	A. Davies
Shrewsbury School, Shrops	www.shrewsbury.org.uk	£8,745	£13,040	L. Winkley
Sibford School, Oxon	www.sibfordschool.co.uk	£4,913	£9,548	T. Spence
Solihull School, W. Midlands	www.solsch.org.uk	£4,331	–	D. Lloyd
South Hampstead High School, London, NW3	www.shhs.gdst.net	£6,218	–	Mrs V. Bingham
Stafford Grammar School, Staffs	www.staffordgrammar.co.uk	£4,260	–	M. Darley
Stamford High School, Lincolns	www.ses.lincs.sch.uk	£5,106	£9,482	W. Phelan
Stamford School, Lincolns	www.ses.lincs.sch.uk	£5,106	£9,482	W. Phelan
The Stephen Perse Foundation, Cambs	www.stephenperse.com	£5,850	–	Miss P. Kelleher
Stockport Grammar School, Cheshire	www.stockportgrammar.co.uk	£3,900	–	Dr P. Owen
Stonar, Wilts	www.stonarschool.com	£5,500	£10,135	Dr S. Divall
Stonyhurst College, Lancs	www.stonyhurst.ac.uk	£6,650	£12,100	J. Browne
Stover School, Devon	www.stover.co.uk	£8,730	£4,260	R. Notman
Stowe School, Bucks	www.stowe.co.uk	£6,330	£12,220	Dr A. Wallersteiner
Streatham & Clapham High School, London, SW16	www.schs.gdst.net	£5,874	–	Dr M. Sachania
Sutton Valence School, Kent	www.svs.org.uk	£7,135	£11,115	B. Grindlay
Sydenham High School, London, SE26	www.sydenhamhighschool.gdst.net	£5,579	–	Mrs K. Woodcock
Talbot Heath, Dorset	www.talbotheath.org	£4,801	£8,364	Mrs A. Holloway
Tettenhall College, W. Midlands	www.tettenhallcollege.co.uk	£4,627	£10,533	D. Williams
Thetford Grammar School, Norfolk	www.thetfordgrammar.co.uk	£4,555	–	M. Brewer
Tonbridge School, Kent	www.tonbridge-school.co.uk	£10,114	£13,482	J. Priory
Tormead School, Surrey	www.tormeadschool.org.uk	£5,150	–	Mrs C. Foord
Tring Park School for the Performing Arts, Herts	www.tringpark.com	£7,125	£11,135	S. Anderson
Trinity School, Surrey	www.trinity-school.org	£5,816	–	A. Kennedy
Trinity School, Devon	www.trinityschool.co.uk	£4,100	£9,259	L. Coen
Truro School, Cornwall	www.truroschool.com	£4,690	£9,355	A. Gordon-Brown
Tudor Hall, Oxon	www.tudorhallschool.com	£7,365	£11,870	Miss W. Griffiths
University College School, London, NW3	www.ucs.org.uk	£6,776	–	M. Beard
Uppingham School, Rutland	www.uppingham.co.uk	£8,771	£12,530	Dr R. Maloney
Walthamstow Hall, Kent	www.walthamstow-hall.co.uk	£6,690	–	Miss S. Ferro
Warminster School, Wilts	www.warminsterschool.org.uk	£5,110	£10,880	M. Mortimer
Warwick School, Warwicks	www.warwickschool.org	£4,398	£9,586	Dr D. Smith
Welbeck – The Defence Sixth Form College, Leics	www.dsfc.ac.uk	£6,666	–	J. Middleton
Wellingborough School, Northants	www.wellingboroughschool.org	£5,330	–	A. Holman
Wellington College, Berks	www.wellingtoncollege.org.uk	£9,680	£13,250	J. Thomas
Wellington School, Somerset	www.wellington-school.org.uk	£5,075	£10,270	H. Price
Wells Cathedral School, Somerset	www.wells-cathedral-school.com	£6,124	£10,255	A. Tighe
West Buckland School, Devon	www.westbuckland.com	£5,020	£10,240	P. Stapleton
Westfield School, Tyne and Wear	www.westfield.newcastle.sch.uk	£4,530	–	N. Walker
Westholme School, Lancs	www.westholmeschool.com	£3,760	–	Mrs L. Horner
Westminster School, London, SW1	www.westminster.org.uk	£9,058	£13,084	P. Derham
Westonbirt School, Glos	www.westonbirt.org	£4,995	£9,750	Mrs N. Dangerfield
Wimbledon High School, London, SW19	www.wimbledonhigh.gdst.net	£6,270	–	Mrs J. Lunnon
Winchester College, Hants	www.winchestercollege.org	–	£13,304	Dr T. Hands
Windermere School, Cumbria	www.windermereschool.co.uk	£5,820	£9,950	I. Lavender
Wisbech Grammar School, Cambs	www.wisbechgrammar.com	£4,449	–	C. Staley
Withington Girls' School, Greater Manchester	www.wgs.org	£4,084	–	Mrs S. Haslam
Woldingham School, Surrey	www.woldinghamschool.co.uk	£7,480	£12,180	Mrs A. Hutchinson
Wolverhampton Grammar School, W. Midlands	www.wgs.org.uk	£4,554	–	Mrs K. Crewe-Read
Woodbridge School, Suffolk	www.woodbridgeschool.org.uk	£5,500	£10,295	Dr R. Robson
Woodhouse Grove School, W. Yorks	www.woodhousegrove.co.uk	£4,525	£9,340	J. Lockwood
Worth School, W. Sussex	www.worthschool.org.uk	£7,910	£11,230	S. McPherson
Wrekin College, Shrops	www.wrekincollege.com	£5,975	£8,440	T. Firth
Wychwood School, Oxon	www.wychwoodschool.org	£5,300	£9,300	Mrs A. Johnson
Wycliffe College, Glos	www.wycliffe.co.uk	£6,995	£11,740	N. Gregory
Wycombe Abbey, Bucks	www.wycombeabbey.com	–	£12,980	Mrs R. Wilkinson
The Yehudi Menuhin School, Surrey	www.menuhinschool.co.uk	–	–	Mrs K. Clanchy

WALES

The Cathedral School Llandaff, Cardiff	www.cathedral-school.co.uk	£4,238	– Mrs C. Sherwood
Christ College, Brecon	www.christcollegebrecon.com	£5,892 £9,217	G. Pearson
Howell's School Llandaff, Cardiff	www.howells-cardiff.gdst.net	£4,461	– Mrs S. Davis
Monmouth School for Boys, Monmouth	www.habsmonmouth.org	£5,272 £10,687	Dr A. Daniel
Monmouth School for Girls, Monmouth	www.habsmonmouth.org	£4,926 £10,687	Mrs J. Miles
Myddelton College, Denbigh	www.myddeltoncollege.com	£4,000 £9,366	M. Roberts
Rougemont School, Newport	www.rougemontschool.co.uk	£4,512	– R. Carnevale
Ruthin School, Ruthin	www.ruthinschool.co.uk	£4,666 £11,500	T. Belfield

SCOTLAND

The High School of Dundee, Dundee	www.highschoolofdundee.org.uk	£4,333	– Dr J. Halliday
The Edinburgh Academy, Edinburgh	www.edinburghacademy.org.uk	£3,792	– B. Welsh
Fettes College, Edinburgh	www.fettes.com	£9,400 £11,600	G. Stanford
George Heriot's School, Edinburgh	www.george-heriots.com	£4,174	– Mrs L. Franklin
The Glasgow Academy, Glasgow	www.theglasgowacademy.org.uk	£4,128	– P. Brodie
The High School of Glasgow, Glasgow	www.highschoolofglasgow.co.uk	£4,256	– J. O'Neill
Glenalmond College, Perth	www.glenalmondcollege.co.uk	£8,617 £11,502	H. Ouston
Gordonstoun, Elgin	www.gordonstoun.org.uk	£9,445 £12,765	Mrs L. Kerr
Kelvinside Academy, Glasgow	www.kelvinsideacademy.org.uk	£4,220	– I. Munro
Kilgraston School, Bridge of Earn	www.kilgraston.com	£5,880 £10,045	Mrs D. MacGinty
Lomond School, Helensburgh	www.lomondschool.com	£3,990 £9,250	Mrs J. Urquhart
Loretto School, Musselburgh	www.loretto.com	£7,775 £11,420	G. Hawley
Merchiston Castle School, Edinburgh	www.merchiston.co.uk	£8,070 £10,970	J. Anderson
Morrison's Academy, Crieff	www.morrisonsacademy.org	£4,332	– G. Warren
Robert Gordon's College, Aberdeen	www.rgc.aberdeen.sch.uk	£4,377	– S. Mills
St Aloysius' College, Glasgow	www.staloysius.org	£4,275	– M. Bartlett
St Columba's School, Kilmacolm	www.st-columbas.org	£4,032	– Mrs A. Angus
St Leonards School, St Andrews	www.stleonards-fife.org	£4,736 £11,551	Dr M. Carslaw
St Margaret's School for Girls, Aberdeen	www.st-margaret.aberdeen.sch.uk	£5,292	– Miss A. Tomlinson
Strathallan School, Perth	www.strathallan.co.uk	£7,470 £11,000	M. Lauder

NORTHERN IRELAND

Campbell College, Belfast	www.campbellcollege.co.uk	£930 £4,915	R. Robinson
The Royal School Dungannon, Dungannon	www.royaldungannon.com	£50 £3,550	D. Burnett

CHANNEL ISLANDS

Elizabeth College, Guernsey	www.elizabethcollege.gg	£3,995	– Mrs J. Palmer
Victoria College, Jersey	www.victoriacollege.je	£1,916	– A. Watkins

NATIONAL ACADEMIES OF SCHOLARSHIP

The national academies are self-governing bodies whose members are elected as a result of achievement and distinction in the academy's field. Within their discipline, the academies provide advice, support education and exceptional scholars, stimulate debate, promote UK research worldwide and collaborate with international counterparts.

The UK's four national academies – the Royal Society, the British Academy, the Royal Academy of Engineering and the Academy of Medical Sciences – receive funding from the Department for Business, Energy and Industrial Strategy (BEIS) for key programmes that help deliver government priorities. The total amount of resource funding allocated by BEIS to the four national academies for 2019–20 is £195m. The Royal Society of Edinburgh is aided by funds provided by the Scottish government. In addition to government funding, the national academies generate additional income from donations, membership contributions, trading and investments.

ACADEMY OF MEDICAL SCIENCES (1998)

41 Portland Place, London W1B 1QH
T 020-3141 3200 W www.acmedsci.ac.uk

Founded in 1998, the Academy of Medical Sciences is the independent body in the UK representing the diversity of medical science. The Academy seeks to improve health through research, as well as to promote medical science and its translation into benefits for society.

The academy is self-governing and receives funding from a variety of sources, including the fellowship, charitable donations, government and industry.

Fellows are elected from a broad range of medical sciences: biomedical, clinical and population based. The academy includes in its remit veterinary medicine, dentistry, nursing, medical law, economics, sociology and ethics. Elections are from nominations put forward by existing fellows.

There are around 1,200 fellows and 42 honorary fellows.

President, Prof. Sir Robert Lechler, PMEDSCI
Executive Director, Dr Rachel Quinn *(interim)*

BRITISH ACADEMY (1902)

10–11 Carlton House Terrace, London SW1Y 5AH
T 020-7969 5200 W www.thebritishacademy.ac.uk

The British Academy is an independent, self-governing learned society for the promotion of the humanities and social sciences. It was founded in 1901 and granted a royal charter in 1902. The British Academy supports advanced academic research and is a channel for the government's support of research in those disciplines.

The fellows are scholars who have attained distinction in one of the branches of study that the academy exists to promote. Candidates must be nominated by existing fellows. There are just over 1,000 fellows, around 30 honorary fellows and 300 corresponding fellows overseas.

President, Prof. Sir David Cannadine
Chief Executive, Dr Robin Jackson *(interim)*

ROYAL ACADEMY OF ENGINEERING (1976)

3 Carlton House Terrace, London SW1Y 5DG
T 020-7766 0600 W www.raeng.org.uk

The Royal Academy of Engineering was established as the Fellowship of Engineering in 1976. It was granted a royal charter in 1983 and its present title in 1992. It is an independent, self-governing body whose object is the pursuit, encouragement and maintenance of excellence in the whole field of engineering, in order to promote the advancement of the science, art and practice of engineering for the benefit of the public.

Election to the fellowship is by invitation only, from nominations supported by the body of fellows. There are around 1,500 fellows, 40 honorary fellows and 100 international fellows. The Duke of Edinburgh is the senior fellow and the Princess Royal and the Duke of Kent are both royal fellows.

President, Prof. Dame Ann Dowling, OM, DBE, FRENG, FRS
Chief Executive, Dr Hayaatun Sillem

ROYAL SOCIETY (1660)

6–9 Carlton House Terrace, London SW1Y 5AG
T 020-7451 2500 W www.royalsociety.org

The Royal Society is an independent academy promoting the natural and applied sciences. Founded in 1660 and granted a royal charter in 1662, the society has three roles: as the UK academy of science, as a learned society and as a funding agency. It is an independent, self-governing body under a royal charter, promoting and advancing all fields of physical and biological sciences, of mathematics and engineering, medical and agricultural sciences and their application.

Fellows are elected for their contributions to science, both in fundamental research resulting in greater understanding, and also in leading and directing scientific and technological progress in industry and research establishments. Each year up to 52 new fellows, who must be citizens or residents of the Commonwealth or Ireland, and up to ten foreign members may be elected. In addition one honorary fellow may also be elected annually from those not eligible for election as fellows or foreign members. There are around 1,700 fellows and foreign members and eight honorary members covering all scientific disciplines. The Queen is the patron of the Royal Society, and there are also five royal fellows.

President, Sir Venki Ramakrishnan, PRS
Executive Director, Dr Julie Maxton, CBE

ROYAL SOCIETY OF EDINBURGH (1783)

22–26 George Street, Edinburgh EH2 2PQ
T 0131-240 5000 W www.rse.org.uk

The Royal Society of Edinburgh (RSE) is an educational charity and Scotland's national academy. An independent body with charitable status, its multidisciplinary membership represents a knowledge resource for the people of Scotland. Granted its royal charter in 1783 for the 'advancement of learning and useful knowledge', the society organises conferences, debates and lectures; conducts independent inquiries; facilitates international collaboration and showcases the country's research and development capabilities; provides educational activities for primary and secondary school students; and awards prizes and medals. The society also awards over £2m annually to Scotland's top researchers and entrepreneurs working in Scotland.

There are over 1,750 fellows, including honorary fellows and corresponding fellows overseas.

President, Prof. Dame Anne Glover
Chief Executive, Dr Rebekah Widdowfield

PRIVATELY FUNDED ARTS ACADEMIES

The Royal Academy and the Royal Scottish Academy support the visual arts community in the UK, hold educational events and promote interest in the arts. They are entirely privately funded through contributions by 'friends' (regular donors who receive benefits such as free entry, previews and magazines), bequests, corporate donations and exhibitions.

ROYAL ACADEMY OF ARTS (1768)

Burlington House, Piccadilly, London W1J 0BD
T 020-7300 8000 **W** www.royalacademy.org.uk

Founded by George III in 1768, the Royal Academy of Arts is an independent, self-governing society devoted to the encouragement and promotion of the fine arts.

Membership of the academy is limited to 100 academicians, all of whom are either painters, engravers, printmakers, draughtsmen, sculptors or architects. There must always be at least 14 sculptors, 12 architects and eight printmakers among the academicians. Candidates must be professionally active in the UK and are nominated and elected by the existing academicians. The members are known as royal academicians (RAs) and are responsible for both the governance and direction of the academy. When RAs reach the age of 75, they become senior academicians and can no longer serve as officers or on the committees.

The title of honorary academician is awarded to a small number of distinguished artists who are not resident in the UK; as at July 2019, there were 34 honorary academicians. Unlike the RAs, they do not take part in the governance of the academy and are unable to vote.

President, Christopher Le Brun, PRA
Secretary and Chief Executive, Axel Rüger

ROYAL SCOTTISH ACADEMY (1838)

The Mound, Edinburgh EH2 2EL
T 0131-225 6671 **W** www.royalscottishacademy.org

Founded in 1826 and led by a body of academicians comprising eminent artists and architects, the Royal Scottish Academy (RSA) is an independent voice for cultural advocacy and one of the largest supporters of artists in Scotland. The Academy administers a number of scholarships, awards and residencies and has a historic collection of Scottish artworks, recognised by the Scottish government as being of national significance. The Academy is independent from local or national government funding, relying instead on bequests, legacies, sponsorship and earned income.

Academicians have to be Scots by birth or domicile, and are elected from the disciplines of art and architecture following nominations put forward by the existing membership. There are also a small number of honorary academicians – distinguished artists and architects, writers, historians and musicians – who do not have to be Scottish. As at July 2019 there were 135 academicians and 41 honorary academicians.

President, Joyce W. Cairns, PRSA
Secretary, Robbie Bushe, RSA
Treasurer, Robin Webster, RSA

RESEARCH COUNCILS

The government funds research through nine research councils, supported by the Department for Business, Energy and Industrial Strategy (BEIS) through UK Research and Innovation (for further information *see* W www.ukri.org). The councils support research and training in universities and other higher education and research facilities.

Under the Higher Education and Research Act 2017, the existing seven research councils, Innovate UK and the research and knowledge exchange functions of the former Higher Education Funding Council for England (HEFCE) were subsumed into a new single funding body, UK Research and Innovation (UKRI), which became operational in April 2018. Research England is a new council within UKRI, taking forward the England-only responsibilities of HEFCE in relation to research and knowledge exchange. Innovate UK is a non-departmental public body which works with companies and partner organisations to facilitate scientific and technological development for the UK economy.

Quality-related research funding is administered through UKRI. Additional funds may also be provided by other government departments, devolved administrations and other international bodies. The councils also receive income for research specifically commissioned by government departments and the private sector, and income from charitable sources.

ARTS AND HUMANITIES RESEARCH COUNCIL

Polaris House, North Star Avenue, Swindon SN2 1FL
T 01793-416000 W www.ahrc.ukri.org

The AHRC is the successor organisation to the Arts and Humanities Research Board and was incorporated by royal charter and established in 2005. It provides funding for postgraduate training and research in the arts and humanities; in any one year, the AHRC makes approximately 700 research awards and around 2,000 postgraduate scholarships. Awards are made after a rigorous peer review system, which ensures the quality of applications.

Executive Chair, Prof. Andrew Thompson, DPHIL

BIOTECHNOLOGY AND BIOLOGICAL SCIENCES RESEARCH COUNCIL

Polaris House, North Star Avenue, Swindon SN2 1UH
T 01793-413200 W www.bbsrc.ukri.org

Established by royal charter in 1994, the BBSRC is the UK funding agency for research in the non-clinical life sciences. It funds research into how all living organisms function and behave, benefiting the agriculture, food, health, pharmaceutical and chemical sectors. To deliver its mission, the BBSRC supports research and training in universities and research centres throughout the UK, including providing strategic research grants to the eight institutes listed below. In June 2015, the institutes founded the National Institutes of Bioscience (NIB) partnership in order to increase the impact of bioscience research and to strengthen the UK's reputation in the field.

Chair, Prof. Melanie Welham

INSTITUTES

BABRAHAM INSTITUTE, Babraham Hall, Cambridge CB22 3AT T 01223-496000
Director, Prof. Michael Wakelam

INSTITUTE FOR BIOLOGICAL, ENVIRONMENTAL AND RURAL SCIENCES (ABERYSTWYTH UNIVERSITY), Penglais, Aberystwyth SY23 3DA
T 01970-621986
Director, Prof. Mike Gooding
EARLHAM INSTITUTE, Norwich Research Park, Colney, Norwich NR4 7UZ T 01603-450001
Director, Prof. Neil Hall
JOHN INNES CENTRE, Norwich Research Park, Colney, Norwich NR4 7UH T 01603-450000
Director, Prof. Dale Sanders
PIRBRIGHT INSTITUTE, Ash Road, Woking, Surrey GU24 0NF
T 01483-232441
Director, Dr Bryan Charleston
QUADRAM INSTITUTE, Norwich Research Park, Norwich, Norfolk NR4 7UA T 01603-255000
Director, Prof. Ian Charles
ROSLIN INSTITUTE (UNIVERSITY OF EDINBURGH), Easter Bush, Midlothian EH25 9RG T 0131-651 9100
Director, Prof. Eleanor Riley
ROTHAMSTED RESEARCH, Harpenden, Herts AL5 2JQ
T 01582-763133
Director, Prof. Achim Dobermann

ECONOMIC AND SOCIAL RESEARCH COUNCIL

Polaris House, North Star Avenue, Swindon SN2 1UJ
T 01793-413000 W www.esrc.ukri.org

The ESRC was established by royal charter in 1965 as an organisation for funding and promoting research and postgraduate training in the social sciences. It supports independent research which has an impact on business, the public sector and civil society and also provides advice, disseminates knowledge and promotes public understanding in these areas.

The ESRC has a total budget of around £202m and provides funding to over 4,000 researchers and postgraduate students in academic institutions and independent research institutes.

Executive Chair, Prof. Jennifer Rubin

ENGINEERING AND PHYSICAL SCIENCES RESEARCH COUNCIL

Polaris House, North Star Avenue, Swindon SN2 1ET
T 01793-444000 W www.epsrc.ukri.org

Formed in 1994 by royal charter, the EPSRC is the UK government's main agency for funding research and training in engineering and the physical sciences in universities and other organisations throughout the UK. The EPSRC invests around £800m a year in a broad range of subjects – from mathematics to materials science, and from information technology to structural engineering. It also provides advice, disseminates knowledge and promotes public understanding in these areas.

Executive Chair, Prof. Lynn Gladden, CBE

MEDICAL RESEARCH COUNCIL

Polaris House, North Star Avenue, Swindon SN2 1FL
T 01793-416200 W www.mrc.ukri.org

The MRC is a publicly funded organisation dedicated to improving human health. The MRC supports research across the entire spectrum of medical sciences, in universities, hospitals, centres and institutes.

Chair, Prof. Fiona Watt
Chair, Infections and Immunity Board, Prof. Paul Kaye
Chair, Molecular and Cellular Medicine Board, Prof. Anne Ferguson-Smith
Chair, Neurosciences and Mental Health Board, Prof. Patrick Chinnery
Chair, Population and Systems Medicine Board, Prof. Paul Elliott
Chair, Regenerative Medicine Research Board, Prof. Martin Wilkins

NATURAL ENVIRONMENT RESEARCH COUNCIL

Polaris House, North Star Avenue, Swindon SN2 1EU
T 01793-411500 W www.nerc.ukri.org

NERC is the leading funder of independent research, training and innovation in environmental science in the UK. Its work covers the full range of atmospheric, earth, biological, terrestrial and aquatic sciences. NERC invests around £330m a year in research exploring how we can sustainably benefit from our natural resources, predict and respond to natural hazards and understand environmental change. NERC works closely with policymakers and industry to support sustainable economic growth in the UK and around the world.
Executive Chair, Prof. Duncan Wingham

RESEARCH CENTRES

BRITISH ANTARCTIC SURVEY, High Cross, Madingley Road, Cambridge CB3 OET T 01223-221400
Director, Prof. Dame Jane Francis, DCMG
BRITISH GEOLOGICAL SURVEY, Kingsley Dunham Centre, Keyworth, Nottingham NG12 5GG T 0115-936 3100
Executive Director, Prof. John Ludden
CENTRE FOR ECOLOGY AND HYDROLOGY, Maclean Building, Benson Lane, Crowmarsh Gifford, Wallingford OX10 8BB T 01491-838800
Director, Prof. Mark Bailey
NATIONAL CENTRE FOR ATMOSPHERIC SCIENCE, NCAS Headquarters, School of Earth and Environment, University of Leeds, Leeds LS2 9JT T 0113-343 6408
Director, Prof. Stephen Mobbs

NATIONAL CENTRE FOR EARTH OBSERVATION, Michael Atiyah Building, University of Leicester, University Road, Leicester LE1 7RH T 0116-252 2016
Director, Prof. John Remedios
NATIONAL OCEANOGRAPHY CENTRE, University of Southampton Waterfront Campus, European Way, Southampton SO14 3ZH T 0238-059 6666
Director, Prof. Ed Hill, OBE

SCIENCE AND TECHNOLOGY FACILITIES COUNCIL

Polaris House, North Star Avenue, Swindon SN2 1SZ
T 01793-442000 W www.stfc.ukri.org

Formed by royal charter in 2007, through the merger of the Council for the Central Laboratory of the Research Councils and the Particle Physics and Astronomy Research Council, the STFC is a non-departmental public body reporting to BEIS.
  The STFC invests in large national and international research facilities, while delivering science and technology expertise for the UK. The council is involved in research projects such as the Diamond Light Source Synchrotron and the Large Hadron Collider, and develops new areas of science and technology. The EPSRC has transferred its responsibility for nuclear physics to the STFC.

Executive Chair, Prof. Mark Thompson

RESEARCH CENTRES

BOULBY UNDERGROUND SCIENCE FACILITY, Boulby Mine, Loftus, Saltburn-by-the-Sea, Cleveland TS13 4UZ T 01287-646300
CHILBOLTON OBSERVATORY, Chilbolton, Stockbridge, Hampshire SO20 6BJ T 01264-860391
DARESBURY LABORATORY, SciTech Daresbury, Keckwick Lane, Warrington WA4 4AD T 01925-603000
RUTHERFORD APPLETON LABORATORY, Harwell Campus, Didcot OX11 0QX T 01235-445000
UK ASTRONOMY TECHNOLOGY CENTRE, Royal Observatory Edinburgh, Blackford Hill, Edinburgh EH9 3HJ T 0131-668 8100

HEALTH

NATIONAL HEALTH SERVICE

The National Health Service (NHS) came into being on 5 July 1948 under the National Health Service Act 1946, covering England and Wales and, under separate legislation, Scotland and Northern Ireland. The NHS is now administered by the Secretary of State for Health (in England), the Welsh government, the Scottish government and the Northern Ireland Executive.

The function of the NHS is to provide a comprehensive health service designed to secure improvement in the physical and mental health of the people and to prevent, diagnose and treat illness. It was founded on the principle that treatment should be provided according to clinical need rather than ability to pay, and should be free at the point of delivery.

Hospital, mental, dental, nursing, ophthalmic and ambulance services and facilities for the care of expectant and nursing mothers and young children are provided by the NHS to meet all reasonable requirements. Rehabilitation services such as occupational therapy, physiotherapy, speech therapy and surgical and medical appliances are supplied where appropriate. Specialists and consultants who work in NHS hospitals can also engage in private practice, including the treatment of their private patients in NHS hospitals.

STRUCTURE
The structure of the NHS remained relatively stable for the first 30 years of its existence. In 1974, a three-tier management structure comprising regional health authorities, area health authorities and district management teams was introduced in England, and the NHS became responsible for community health services. In 1979, area health authorities were abolished and district management teams were replaced by district health authorities.

The National Health Service and Community Care Act 1990 provided for more streamlined regional health authorities and district health authorities, and for the establishment of family health services authorities (FHSAs) and NHS trusts. The concept of the 'internal market' was introduced into health care, whereby care was provided through NHS contracts where health authorities or boards and GP fundholders (the purchasers) were responsible for buying health care from hospitals, non-fundholding GPs, community services and ambulance services (the providers). The Act also paved the way for the community care reforms, which were introduced in April 1993, and changed the way care is administered for older people, the mentally ill, the physically disabled and people with learning disabilities.

ENGLAND

Under the Health and Social Care Act 2012, which gained royal assent in March 2012, The NHS in England underwent a complete operational and budgetary restructure at a cost of approximately £1.4bn.

Hospitals were extensively affected by the overhaul, with the cap on income from private hospital patients increased from 1.5 per cent to 49 per cent. All hospitals will become foundation trusts, competing for treatment contracts from clinical commissioning groups (CCGs).

On 1 April 2013 the new commissioning board, NHS England, took on full statutory responsibilities; at the same time, strategic health authorities (SHAs) and primary care trusts (PCTs) which, alongside the Department of Health, had been responsible for NHS planning and delivery, were abolished. NHS England is an executive non-departmental public body of the Department of Health and Social Care (DHSC) with a remit to:
- provide national leadership to improve the quality of care
- oversee the operation of clinical commissioning groups
- allocate resources to clinical commissioning groups
- commission primary care and specialist services

The secretary of state has ultimate responsibility for the provision of a comprehensive health service in England and for ensuring the system works to its optimum capacity to meet the needs of its patients. The DHSC is responsible for strategic leadership of the health and social care systems, but is not the headquarters of the NHS, nor does it directly manage any NHS organisations.

In October 2014, NHS England published *Five Year Forward View* which committed the organisation to further change, including additional decentralisation and a greater emphasis on out-of-hospital care and preventative medicine. In January 2019 the *NHS Long Term Plan* was published outlining NHS England's healthcare plans for the next ten years; subsequently, around 1,250 primary care networks were formed after July 2019 from almost all existing general practices to better work at scale, covering populations of 30,000–50,000 people.

NHS ENGLAND, PO Box 16738, Redditch B97 9PT
T 0300-311 2233 **E** england.contactus@nhs.net
W www.england.nhs.uk
Chief Executive, Simon Stevens

CLINICAL COMMISSIONING GROUPS (CCGS)
On 1 April 2013, PCTs, which controlled 80 per cent of the NHS budget and commissioned most NHS services, were abolished. They were replaced with CCGs which took on many of the functions of the PCTs in addition to some functions previously assumed by the Department of Health. All GP practices now belong to a CCG which also includes other health professionals, such as nurses. CCGs commission most services, including:
- mental health and learning disability services
- planned hospital care
- rehabilitative care
- urgent and emergency care (including out-of-hours)
- most community health services

CCGs can commission any service provider that meets NHS standards and costs. These can be NHS hospitals, social enterprises, charities, or private-sector providers. There are around 135 CCGs in England, which together are responsible for around two-thirds of the NHS budget, around £80bn in 2020–21.

HEALTH AND WELLBEING BOARDS
Every upper-tier local authority has established a health and wellbeing board to act as a forum for local commissioners across the NHS, social care, public health and other services. There are more than 150 health and wellbeing boards in England, which are intended to:
- encourage integrated commissioning of health and social care services
- increase democratic input into strategic decisions about health and wellbeing services
- strengthen working relationships between health and social care

PUBLIC HEALTH ENGLAND (PHE)

Established on 1 April 2013, PHE provides national leadership and expert services to support public health and also works with local government and the NHS to respond to emergencies. PHE's responsibilities are to:

- make the public healthier and reduce differences between the health of different groups by advising the government; supporting action by the NHS, local government and the public; and promoting healthier lifestyles
- protect the public from health hazards
- prepare for and respond to public health emergencies
- share information and expertise, and prepare for future public health challenges
- support the NHS and local authorities to prepare for and provide social care, and develop the public health system and its specialist workforce

REGULATION

Since the restructuring of the NHS in England began in April 2013, some elements of the regulation system have changed. Responsibility for the regulation of particular aspects of care is shared across a number of different bodies, including the Care Quality Commission (CQC), and individual professional regulatory bodies, such as the General Medical Council, Nursing and Midwifery Council, General Dental Council and the Health and Care Professions Council. Regulation of the market is performed by the Department of Health and NHS Improvement.

CARE QUALITY COMMISSION (CQC)

The CQC regulates all health and social care services in England, including those provided by the NHS, local authorities, private companies or voluntary organisations. In addition it protects the interests of people detained under the Mental Health Act. The CQC ensures that all essential standards of quality and safety are met where care is provided, from hospitals to private care homes. By law all NHS providers (such as hospitals and ambulance services) must register with the CQC to show they are protecting people from the risk of infection. The CQC possesses a range of legal powers and duties and will take action if providers do not meet essential standards of quality or safety.

NHS IMPROVEMENT

NHS Improvement is responsible for overseeing NHS foundation trusts, NHS trusts and independent providers, helping them give patients consistently high quality, safe and compassionate care within local health systems that are financially sustainable. In April 2019 NHS Improvement fully integrated into NHS England to act as a single organisation as part of the *NHS Long Term Plan*, but it retains a separate board.

HEALTHWATCH

Healthwatch England was established in October 2012 following the restructuring of the NHS. The organisation functions at a national and local level as an independent consumer body, gathering and representing the views of the public about health and social care services in England.

CARE QUALITY COMMISSION, 151 Buckingham Palace Road, London SW1W 9SZ **T** 03000-616161 **W** www.cqc.org.uk
Chief Executive, Ian Trenholm

NHS IMPROVEMENT, Skipton House, 80 London Road, London SE1 6LH **T** 0113-825 0000
E enquiries@improvement.nhs.uk
Chief Operating Officer, Amanda Pritchard

HEALTHWATCH, 151 Buckingham Palace Road, London SW1W 9SZ **T** 0300-068 3000 **W** www.healthwatch.co.uk
National Director, Imelda Redmond, CBE

AUTHORITIES AND TRUSTS

REGIONS

In April 2019, as outlined in the *NHS Long Term Plan*, all NHS trusts were re-organised into seven integrated regional teams to ensure the commissioning of high quality primary care and specialised services at a local level across England.

ACUTE TRUSTS

Hospitals in England are managed by acute trusts. There were around 135 acute non-specialist trusts, of which 84 have foundation trust status and 17 acute specialist trusts, of which 16 have foundation trust status. Acute trusts ensure hospitals provide high-quality healthcare and spend money efficiently. They employ a large sector of the NHS workforce, including doctors, nurses, pharmacists, midwives and health visitors. Acute trusts also employ those in supplementary medical professions, such as physiotherapists, radiographers and podiatrists, in addition to many other non-medical staff.

AMBULANCE TRUSTS

There are 10 ambulance services (five foundation trusts) in England, providing emergency services to healthcare.

CLINICAL SENATES AND STRATEGIC CLINICAL NETWORKS

Clinical senates are advisory groups of experts from across health and social care. There are 12 senates covering England comprising clinical leaders from across the healthcare system, in addition to members from social care and public health.

There are 12 strategic clinical networks across England, comprising groups of clinical experts covering a particular disease, patient or professional group. They offer advice to CCGs and NHS England.

Neither organisation is a statutory body, and although they comment on CCG plans to NHS England, they are unable to veto them.

FOUNDATION TRUSTS

NHS foundation trusts are independent legal entities with unique governance arrangements. Each NHS foundation trust has a duty to consult and involve a board of governors in the strategic planning of its organisation. They have financial freedoms and can raise capital from both the public and private sectors within borrowing limits determined by projected cash flows and based on affordability.

MENTAL HEALTH TRUSTS

There are 69 mental health trusts in England, 42 of which have foundation trust status.

WALES

The NHS Wales was reorganised according to Welsh Assembly commitments laid out in the *One Wales* strategy which came into effect in October 2009. There are now seven local health boards (LHBs) that are responsible for delivering all health care services within a geographical area, rather than the trust and local health board system that existed previously. Community health councils (CHCs) are statutory lay bodies that represent the public for the health service in their region. There are currently eight CHCs.

NHS TRUSTS

There are three NHS trusts in Wales. The Welsh Ambulance Services NHS Trust is for emergency services; the Velindre NHS Trust offers specialist services in cancer care; while Public Health Wales serves as a unified public health organisation for Wales.

LOCAL HEALTH BOARDS

The websites of the seven LHBs, and contact details for community health councils and NHS trusts, are available in the *NHS Wales Directory* (**W** www.wales.nhs.uk).

ANEURIN BEVAN, Headquarters, Lodge Road, Caerleon, Newport NP18 3XQ **T** 01873-732732
Chief Executive, Judith Paget, CBE

BETSI CADWALADR, Ysbyty Gwynedd, Penrhosgarnedd, Bangor, Gwynedd LL57 2PW **T** 01248-384384
Chief Executive, Gill Harris *(acting)*

CARDIFF AND VALE, Cardigan House, University Hospital of Wales, Heath Park, Cardiff CF14 4XW **T** 029-2074 7747
Chief Executive, Len Richards

CWM TAF MORGANNWG, Ynysmeurig House, Navigation Park, Abercynon CF45 4SN **T** 01443-744800
Chief Executive, Paul Mears

HYWEL DDA, Corporate Offices, Ystwyth Building, Hafan Derwen, Jobswell Road, Carmarthen SA31 3BB **T** 01267-235151
Chief Executive, Steve Moore

POWYS, Glasbury House, Bronllys Hospital, Bronllys, Brecon, Powys LD3 0LS **T** 01874-771661
Chief Executive, Carol Shillabeer

SWANSEA BAY, One Talbot Gateway, Baglan Energy Park, Baglan, Port Talbot SA12 7BR **T** 01656-683344
Chief Executive, Tracy Myhill

SCOTLAND

The Scottish government Health and Social Care directorates are responsible both for NHS Scotland and for the development and implementation of health and community care policy. The chief executive of NHS Scotland leads the central management of the NHS, is accountable to ministers for the efficiency and performance of the service and heads the Health Department which oversees the work of the 14 regional health boards. These boards provide strategic management for the entire local NHS system and are responsible for ensuring that services are delivered effectively and efficiently.

In addition to the 14 regional health boards there are a further seven special boards and one public health body, which provide national services, such as the Scottish ambulance service and NHS Health Scotland. Healthcare Improvement Scotland, was formed on 1 April 2011 by the Public Services Reform Act 2010 to improve the quality of Scottish healthcare.

REGIONAL HEALTH BOARDS

AYRSHIRE AND ARRAN, Eglinton House, Ailsa Hospital, Dalmellington Road, Ayr KA6 6AB **T** 0800-169 1441
W www.nhsaaa.net
Chief Executive, John Burns

BORDERS, Borders General Hospital, Melrose, Roxburghshire TD6 9BS **T** 01896-826000 **W** www.nhsborders.scot.nhs.uk
Chief Executive, Ralph Roberts

DUMFRIES AND GALLOWAY, Mountainhall Treatment Centre, Dumfries DG1 4AP **T** 01387-246246
W www.nhsdg.co.uk
Chief Executive, Jeff Ace

EILEAN SIAR (WESTERN ISLES), 37 South Beach Street, Stornoway, Isle of Lewis HS1 2BB **T** 01851-702997
W www.wihb.scot.nhs.uk
Chief Executive, Gordon Jamieson

FIFE, Hayfield House, Hayfield Road, Kirkcaldy, Fife KY2 5AH **T** 01592-643355 **W** www.nhsfife.org
Chief Executive, Carol Potter

FORTH VALLEY, Carseview House, Castle Business Park, Stirling FK9 4SW **T** 01786-463031 **W** www.nhsforthvalley.com
Chief Executive, Cathie Cowan

GRAMPIAN, Summerfield House, 2 Eday Road, Aberdeen AB15 6RE **T** 0345-456 6000 **W** www.nhsgrampian.org
Chief Executive, Prof. Caroline Hiscox

GREATER GLASGOW AND CLYDE, J. B. Russell House, Gartnavel Royal Hospital Campus, 1055 Great Western Road, Glasgow G12 0XH **T** 0141-201 4444 **W** www.nhsggc.org.uk
Chief Executive, Jane Grant

HIGHLAND, Assynt House, Beechwood Park, Inverness IV2 3BW **T** 01463-704000 **W** www.nhshighland.scot.nhs.uk
Chief Executive, Pam Dudek

LANARKSHIRE, Kirklands, Fallside Road, Bothwell G71 8BB **T** 0300-303 0243 **W** www.nhslanarkshire.org.uk
Chief Executive, Heather Knox *(interim)*

LOTHIAN, Waverley Gate, 2–4 Waterloo Place, Edinburgh EH1 3EG **T** 0131-536 9000 **W** www.nhslothian.scot.nhs.uk
Chief Executive, Calum Campbell

ORKNEY, The Balfour, Foreland Road, Kirkwall, Orkney KW15 1NZ **T** 01856-888100 **W** www.ohb.scot.nhs.uk
Chief Executive, Michael Dickson *(interim)*

SHETLAND, Upper Floor Montfield, Burgh Road, Lerwick ZE1 0LA **T** 01595-743060 **W** www.shb.scot.nhs.uk
Chief Executive, Michael Dickson

TAYSIDE, Ninewells Hospital & Medical School, Dundee DD1 9SY **T** 01382-660111 **W** www.nhstayside.scot.nhs.uk
Chief Executive, Grant Archibald

NORTHERN IRELAND

On 1 April 2009 the four health and social services boards in Northern Ireland were replaced by a single health and social care board for the whole of Northern Ireland. The board, together with its five local commissioning groups are responsible for improving the health and social wellbeing of people in the area for which they are responsible, planning and commissioning services, and coordinating the delivery of services in a cost-effective manner. In March 2016, the health minister announced plans to abolish the health and social care board, with all commissioning powers to be transferred to the Department of Health and a new group being established to hold the five Northern Ireland trusts to account. As at December 2020, no further decision regarding the future of the board had been taken and the board remains operational.

HEALTH AND SOCIAL CARE BOARD, 12–22 Linenhall Street, Belfast BT2 8BS **T** 030-0555 0115
W www.hscboard.hscni.net
Chief Executive, Sharon Gallagher

FINANCE

The NHS is still funded mainly through general taxation, although in recent years more reliance has been placed on the NHS element of national insurance contributions, patient charges and other sources of income.

NHS England's total budget for 2020–21, including the Long Term Plan funding settlement but excluding emergency coronavirus funding, was set at £305bn in March 2020. Expenditure for the NHS in Wales, Scotland and Northern Ireland is set by the devolved governments.

EMPLOYEES AND SALARIES

NHS ENGLAND STAFF 2020
Full-time equivalent

Total	1,161,858
Doctors	121,726
Ambulance staff	17,201
Midwives	21,892
Nurses and health visitors	302,033
Scientific, therapeutic and technical staff	149,144
Clinical support staff	363,448
Infrastructure support staff	184,548
Other staff	1,864

Source: NHS Digital. Excludes dental staff

SALARIES

Many general practitioners (GPs) are self-employed and hold contracts, either on their own or as part of a Clinical Commissioning Group (CCG). The profit of GPs varies according to the services they provide for their patients and the way they choose to provide these services. Salaried GPs who are part of a CCG earn between £60,8455 and £91,228. Most NHS dentists are self-employed contractors. A contract for dentists was introduced on 1 April 2006 which provides dentists with an annual income in return for carrying out an agreed amount, or units, of work. A salaried dentist employed by the NHS, who works mainly with community dental services earns between £41,766 and £89,333.

BASIC SALARIES FOR HOSPITAL MEDICAL AND DENTAL STAFF 2020–21

Consultant (2003 contract)	£82,096–£110,683
Associate specialist	£57,705–£94,988
Speciality doctor	£41,158–£76,751
Core/higher training year 3+	£49,036
Core training year 1 & 2	£38,694
Foundation doctor year 2	£32,691
Foundation doctor year 1	£28,243

NURSES

From 1 December 2004 the *Agenda for Change* pay system was introduced throughout the UK for all NHS staff with the exception of medical and dental staff, doctors in public health medicine and the community health service. Nurses' salaries are incorporated in the *Agenda for Change* nine band pay structure, which provides additional payments for flexible working such as providing out-of-hours services, working weekends and nights and being on-call. There is also additional payments for those staff who work in high-cost areas such as London.

SALARIES FOR NURSES AND MIDWIVES 2020–21

Nurse/Midwife consultant	£53,168–£87,754
Modern matron	£45,753–£51,668
Nurse advanced/team manager	£38,890–£44,503
Midwife higher level	£38,890–£44,503
Nurse specialist/team leader	£31,365–£37,890
Hospital/community midwife	£31,365–£37,890
Registered nurse/entry level midwife*	£24,907–£30,615

*The starting salary in Wales and Northern Ireland is currently the same as in England. The starting salary is £25,100 in Scotland.

HEALTH SERVICES

PRIMARY CARE

Primary care comprises the services provided by general practitioners, community health centres, pharmacies, dental practices and opticians. Primary nursing care includes the work carried out by practice nurses, community nurses, community midwives and health visitors.

PRIMARY MEDICAL SERVICES

In England, primary medical services (PMS) are provided by 35,416 full-time equivalent GPs, working in around 6,800 GP practices, with 60.6 million registered patients.

In Wales, responsibility for primary medical services rests with local health boards (LHBs), in Scotland with the 14 regional health boards and in Northern Ireland with the Health and Social Care Board.

Any vocationally trained doctor may provide general or personal medical services. GPs may also have private fee-paying patients, but not if that patient is already an NHS patient on that doctor's patient list.

A person who is ordinarily resident in the UK is eligible to register with a GP (or PMS provider) for free primary care treatment. Should a patient have difficulty in registering with a doctor, he or she should contact the local CCG for help. When a person is away from home he/she can still access primary care treatment from a GP if they ask to be treated as a temporary resident. In an emergency any doctor in the service will give treatment and advice.

GPs or CCGs are responsible for the care of their patients 24 hours a day, seven days a week, but can fulfil the terms of their contract by delegating or transferring responsibility for out-of-hours care to an accredited provider.

In addition, NHS walk-in centres (WICs) throughout England are usually open seven days a week, from early in the morning until late in the evening. They are nurse-led and provide treatment for minor illnesses and injuries, health information and self-help advice. Some WICs are not able to treat young children.

HEALTH COSTS

Some people are exempt from, or entitled to help with, health costs such as prescription charges, ophthalmic and dental costs, and in some cases help towards travel costs to and from hospital.

The following list is intended as a general guide to those who may be entitled to help, or who are exempt from some of the charges relating to the above:

- children under 16 and young people in full-time education who are under 19
- people aged 60 or over
- pregnant women and women who have had a baby in the last 12 months and have a valid maternity exemption certificate (MatEx)
- people, or their partners, who are in receipt of income support, income-based jobseeker's allowance and/or income-based employment and support allowance
- people in receipt of the pension credit
- diagnosed glaucoma patients, people who have been advised by an ophthalmologist that they are at risk of glaucoma and people aged 40 or over who have an immediate family member who is a diagnosed glaucoma patient
- NHS in-patients
- NHS out-patients for all prescribed contraceptives, medication given at a hospital, NHS walk-in centre, personally administered by a GP or supplied at a hospital or primary care trust clinic for the treatment of tuberculosis or a sexually transmissible infection
- out-patients of the NHS Hospital Dental Service
- people registered blind or partially sighted
- people who need complex lenses
- war pensioners whose treatment/prescription is for their accepted disablement and who have a valid exemption certificate
- people who are entitled to, or named on, a valid NHS tax credit exemption or HC2 certificate
- people who have a medical exemption (MedEx) certificate, including those with cancer or diabetes

People in other circumstances may also be eligible for help; *see* www.nhs.uk/using-the-nhs/help-with-health-costs for further information.

WALES
On 1 April 2007 all prescription charges (including those for medical supports and appliances and wigs) for people living in Wales were abolished. The above guide still applies for NHS dental and optical charges although all people aged under 25 living in Wales are also entitled to free dental examinations.

SCOTLAND
On 1 April 2011 all prescription charges in Scotland were abolished. Those entitled to free prescriptions in Scotland include patients registered with a Scottish GP and receiving a prescription from a Scottish pharmacy, and Scottish patients who have an English GP and an entitlement card.

NORTHERN IRELAND
On 1 April 2010 all prescription charges in Northern Ireland were abolished. All prescriptions dispensed in Northern Ireland are free, even for patients visiting from England, Wales or Scotland.

PHARMACEUTICAL SERVICES
Patients may obtain medicines and appliances under the NHS from any pharmacy whose owner has entered into arrangements with the CCG to provide this service. There are also some suppliers who only provide special appliances. In rural areas, where access to a pharmacy may be difficult, patients may be able to obtain medicines, etc, from a dispensing doctor.

In England, a charge of £9.15 is payable for each item supplied (except for contraceptives for which there is no charge), unless the patient is exempt and the declaration on the back of the prescription form is completed. Prescription prepayment certificates (£29.65 valid for three months, £105.90 valid for a year) may be purchased by those patients not entitled to exemption who require frequent prescriptions.

DENTAL SERVICES
Dentists, like doctors, may take part in the NHS and also have private patients. Dentists are responsible to the local health provider in whose areas they provide services. Patients may go to any dentist who is taking part in the NHS and is willing to accept them. There is a three-tier payment system based on the individual course of treatment required.

NHS DENTAL CHARGES *from 1 April 2020*	
	England/Wales
Band 1* – Examination, diagnosis, preventive care (eg x-rays, scale and polish)	£23.80/£14.70
Band 2 – Band 1 + basic additional treatment (eg fillings and extractions)	£65.20/£47.00
Band 3 – Bands 1 and 2 + all other treatment (eg crowns, dentures and bridges)	£282.80/£203.00
* Urgent and out-of-hours treatment is also charged at this tier	

The cost of individual treatment plans should be known prior to treatment and some dental practices may require payment in advance. There is no charge for writing a prescription or removing stitches and only one charge is payable for each course of treatment even if more than one visit to the dentist is required. If additional treatment is required within two months of visiting the dentist and this is covered by the course of treatment most recently paid for (for example, payment was made for the second tier of treatment but an additional filling is required) then this will be provided free of charge.

SCOTLAND AND NORTHERN IRELAND
Scotland and Northern Ireland have yet to simplify their charging systems. NHS dental patients pay 80 per cent of the cost of the individual items of treatment provided up to a maximum of £384. An NHS dental examination in Scotland is free of charge for everyone.

GENERAL OPHTHALMIC SERVICES
General ophthalmic services are administered by local health providers. Testing of sight may be carried out by any ophthalmic medical practitioner or ophthalmic optician (optometrist). The optician must give the prescription to the patient, who can take this to any supplier of glasses to have them dispensed. Only registered opticians can supply glasses to children and to people registered as blind or partially sighted.

Free eyesight tests and help towards the cost are available to people in certain circumstances. Help is also available for the purchase of glasses or contact lenses. In Scotland eye examinations, which include a sight test, are free to all UK residents. Help is also available for the purchase of glasses or contact lenses to those entitled to help with health costs in the same way it is available to those in England and Wales.

CHILD HEALTH SERVICES
Pre-school services at GP surgeries or child health clinics provide regular monitoring of children's physical, mental and emotional health and development and advise parents on their children's health and welfare.

NHS 111 AND NHS 24
NHS 111 is a website and 24-hour nurse-led advice telephone service for England, Wales and Northern Ireland, dealing with non-urgent health issues. It provides medical advice as well as directing people to the appropriate part of the NHS for treatment if necessary. (T 111 W www.111.nhs.uk & www.111.wales.nhs.uk).

NHS 24 provides an equivalent service for Scotland (T 111 W www.nhs24.scot).

SECONDARY CARE AND OTHER SERVICES

HOSPITALS
NHS hospitals provide acute and specialist care services, treating conditions which normally cannot be dealt with by primary care specialists, and provide for medical emergencies. The figures below are representative of the period 1 April 2019–31 March 2020. As such, they exclude the significant increase in bed capacity that was introduced by the government in early April 2020 in response to the coronavirus pandemic.

HOSPITAL CHARGES
Acute or foundation trusts can provide hospital accommodation in single rooms or small wards, if not required for patients who need privacy for medical reasons. The patient is still an NHS patient, but there may be a charge for these additional facilities. Acute or foundation trusts can charge for certain patient services that are considered to be additional treatments over and above the normal hospital service provision. There is no blanket policy to cover this and each case is considered in the light of the patient's clinical need. However, if an item or service is considered to be an integral part of a patient's treatment by their clinician, then a charge should not be made.

In some NHS hospitals, accommodation and services are available to the treatment of private patients where it does not interfere with care for NHS patients. Income generated by treating private patients is then put back into local NHS services. Private patients undertake to pay the full costs of medical treatment, accommodation, medication and other related services. Charges for private patients are set locally.

NUMBER OF BEDS 2019–20

	Average daily	
	available beds	occupation of beds
England	142,745	126,758
Wales*	10,564	9,170
Scotland	13,156	11,406
Northern Ireland	5,780	4,831

* Figures are for 2018–19
Sources: NHS England, Welsh government, ISD Scotland, Northern Ireland Executive

WAITING LISTS
During 2020, the COVID-19 pandemic adversely affected the NHS, and consequently the figures listed below are significantly lower than in previous years.

England
During June 2020, 94,354 referral to treatment (RTT) patients started admitted treatment and 662,634 started non-admitted treatment. Of the admitted patients, 92 per cent were waiting up to 37.4 weeks, and for patients waiting to start treatment 52 per cent were treated within 18 weeks of referral. The median waiting time was 17.6 weeks.
Wales
During September 2020, 72.2 per cent of 232,127 patients were treated within 26 weeks and 84.8 per cent were treated within 36 weeks of the date the referral letter was received by the hospital.
Scotland
In the quarter ending September 2020, 66.9 per cent of patients with fully measurable journeys were seen within the 18 week referral to treatment (RTT) standard. In the same quarter, 72.1 per cent of patients waiting for a new outpatient appointment were seen within 12 weeks.
Northern Ireland
By September 2020 the aim was for at least 50 per cent of patients to wait no longer than 9 weeks for a first out-patient appointment, with no patient waiting longer than 52 weeks. The total number of people waiting for a first outpatient appointment at the end of September 2020 was 160,663, of these 65.4 per cent had been waiting over 9 weeks and 44.8 per cent had been waiting over 26 weeks.

AMBULANCE SERVICE
The NHS provides emergency ambulance services free of charge via the 999 emergency telephone service. Air ambulances, provided through local charities and partially funded by the NHS, are used throughout the UK. They assist with cases where access may be difficult or heavy traffic could hinder road progress. Non-emergency ambulance services are provided free to patients who are deemed to require them on medical grounds.
 Since 1 April 2001 all services have had a system of call prioritisation. Since 2017, ambulances have been expected to reach Red 1 – calls requiring a defibrillator – and Red 2 emergency calls within seven minutes, at least 75 per cent of the time. Non-emergency calls are categorised as Green 1, 2, 3 or 4, with category Green 4 calls being the least serious. Green calls are generally responded to between 20 minutes and one hour.
 In 2016 it was agreed that all ambulance staff were to be re-banded from a band 5 to a band 6 under the *Agenda for Change* pay scale. In 2020, the NHS employed 18,299 qualified ambulance staff in England earning between £19,737 (emergency care assistant) and £37,890 (senior paramedic).

BLOOD AND TRANSPLANT SERVICES
There are four national bodies which coordinate the blood donor programme and transplant and related services in the UK. Donors give blood at local centres on a voluntary basis.

NHS BLOOD AND TRANSPLANT, 500, North Bristol Park, Filton, Bristol, BR34 7QH **T** 0300-123 2323
 W www.nhsbt.nhs.uk

WELSH BLOOD SERVICE, Ely Valley Road, Talbot Green, Pontyclun CF72 9WB **T** 0800-252 2266
 W www.welsh-blood.org.uk
SCOTTISH NATIONAL BLOOD TRANSFUSION SERVICE, The Jack Copland Centre, 52 Research Avenue North, Herriot-Watt Research Park, Edinburgh EH14 4BE
 T 0131-314 5510 **W** www.scotblood.co.uk
NORTHERN IRELAND BLOOD TRANSFUSION SERVICE, Lisburn Road, Belfast BT9 7TS **T** 028-9032 1414
 W www.nibts.hscni.net

HOSPICES
Hospice or palliative care may be available for patients with life-threatening illnesses. It may be provided at the patient's home, in a voluntary or NHS hospice or at hospital, and is intended to ensure the best possible quality of life for the patient, and to provide help and support to both the patient and the patient's family. Hospice UK coordinates NHS and voluntary services in England, Wales and Northern Ireland; the Scottish Partnership for Palliative Care performs the same function in Scotland.

HOSPICE UK, Hospice House, 34–44 Britannia Street, London WC1X 9JG **T** 020-7520 8200 **W** www.hospiceuk.org
SCOTTISH PARTNERSHIP FOR PALLIATIVE CARE, CBC House, 24 Canning Street, Edinburgh EH3 8EG
 T 0131-272 2735 **W** www.palliativecarescotland.org.uk

COMPLAINTS

Patient advice and liaison services (PALS) have been established for every NHS and PCT in England. PALS can give advice on local complaints procedure, or resolve concerns informally. If the case is not resolved locally or the complainant is not satisfied with the way a local NHS body or practice has dealt with their complaint, they may approach the Parliamentary and Health Service Ombudsman in England, the Scottish Public Services Ombudsman, Public Services Ombudsman for Wales or the Northern Ireland Public Services Ombudsman. *See* Ombudsman Services.

HEALTH ADVICE AND MEDICAL TREATMENT ABROAD

IMMUNISATION
Country-by-country guidance is set out on the website **W** www.fitfortravel.nhs.uk

RECIPROCAL ARRANGEMENTS
Prior to 1 Jan 2021, the European Health Insurance Card (EHIC) had allowed UK residents access to state-provided healthcare while temporarily travelling in all European Economic Area (EEA) countries and Switzerland, either free or at a reduced cost. From 1 January 2021, the EHIC was no longer valid for most travellers except pensioners living in the EU, EU nationals living in the UK before the end of 2020, students studying in the EEA, 'frontier workers' living and working in different states, and dependents of these groups. A card is free, valid for up to five years and should be obtained before travelling. Full eligibility criteria can be found online (**W** www.ehic.org.uk), where applications can also be made.
 Visitors from countries with which the UK has bilateral health care agreements are currently able to receive emergency health care on the NHS on the same terms as is available to UK residents. After 1 January 2021, when the Brexit transition period ends, European Economic Area nationals may lose this entitlement or it will be dependent on arrangements made with individual countries. The UK also has bilateral agreements with several other countries, including Australia and New Zealand, for the free provision of urgent medical treatment.

SOCIAL WELFARE

SOCIAL SERVICES

The Secretary of State for Health (in England), the Welsh government, the Scottish government and the Secretary of State for Northern Ireland are responsible, under the Local Authority Social Services Act 1970, for the provision of social services for older people, disabled people, families and children, and those with mental disorders. Personal social services are administered by local authorities according to policies, with standards set by central and devolved government. Each authority has a director and a committee responsible for the social services functions placed upon them. Local authorities provide, enable and commission care after assessing the needs of their population. The private and voluntary sectors also play an important role in the delivery of social services, and an estimated 7 million people in the UK provide substantial regular care for a member of their family.

The Care Quality Commission (CQC) was established in April 2009, bringing together the independent regulation of health, mental health and adult social care. Prior to 1 April 2009 this work was carried out by three separate organisations: the Healthcare Commission, the Mental Health Act Commission and the Commission for Social Care Inspection. The CQC is responsible for the registration of health and social care providers, the monitoring and inspection of all health and adult social care, issuing fines, public warnings or closures if standards are not met and for undertaking regular performance reviews. Since April 2007 the Office for Standards in Education, Children's Services and Skills (Ofsted) has been responsible for inspecting and regulating all care services for children and young people in England. Both Ofsted and CQC collate information on local care services and make this information available to the public.

The Care Inspectorate Wales, an operationally independent part of the Welsh government, is responsible for the regulation and inspection of all social care services in Wales.

In Scotland, the Care Inspectorate, is the independent care services regulator for Scotland.

The Department of Health is responsible for social care in Northern Ireland.

CARE QUALITY COMMISSION (CQC), Citygate, Gallowgate, Newcastle upon Tyne NE1 4PA **T** 0300-061 6161 **W** www.cqc.org.uk

OFFICE FOR STANDARDS IN EDUCATION, CHILDREN'S SERVICES AND SKILLS (Ofsted), Piccadilly Gate, Store Street, Manchester M1 2WD **T** 0300-123 1231 **E** enquiries@ofsted.gov.uk **W** www.gov.uk/government/organisations/ofsted

CARE INSPECTORATE WALES (CIW), Welsh Government Office, Sarn Mynach, Llandudno Junction LL31 9RZ **T** 0300-790 0126 **E** ciw@gov.wales **W** www.careinspectorate.wales

CARE INSPECTORATE, Compass House, 11 Riverside Drive, Dundee DD1 4NY **T** 0345 600 9527 **E** enquiries@careinspectorate.com **W** www.careinspectorate.com

DEPARTMENT OF HEALTH, Castle Buildings, Stormont, Belfast BT4 3SQ **T** 028-9052 0500 **E** webmaster@health-ni.gov.uk **W** www.health-ni.gov.uk

ADULT SOCIAL CARE WORKFORCE ESTIMATES (ENGLAND)

Total: all job roles	1,600,000
Managerial	119,000
Regulated professional	83,000
Direct care	1,220,000
Other	180,000

Source: Skills for Care, 2018

OLDER PEOPLE

Services for older people are designed to enable them to remain living in their own homes for as long as possible. Local authority services include advice, domestic help, meals in the home, alterations to the home to aid mobility, emergency alarm systems, day and/or night attendants, laundry services and the provision of day centres and recreational facilities. Charges may be made for these services. Respite care may also be provided in order to allow carers temporary relief from their responsibilities.

Local authorities and the private sector also provide 'sheltered housing' for older people, sometimes with resident wardens.

If an older person is admitted to a residential home, charges are made according to a means test; if the person cannot afford to pay, the costs are met by the local authority.

DISABLED PEOPLE

Services for disabled people are designed to enable them to remain living in their own homes wherever possible. Local authority services include advice, adaptations to the home, meals in the home, help with personal care, occupational therapy, educational facilities and recreational facilities. Respite care may also be provided in order to allow carers temporary relief from their responsibilities.

Special housing may be available for disabled people who can live independently, and residential accommodation for those who cannot.

FAMILIES AND CHILDREN

Local authorities are required to provide services aimed at safeguarding the welfare of children in need and, wherever possible, allowing them to be brought up by their families. Services include advice, counselling, help in the home and the provision of family centres. Many authorities also provide short-term refuge accommodation for women and children.

DAY CARE

In allocating day care places to children, local authorities give priority to children with special needs, whether in terms of their health, learning abilities or social needs. Since September 2001, Ofsted has been responsible for the regulation and registration of all early years childcare and education provision in England (previously the responsibility of the local authorities). All day care and childminding services that care for children under eight years of age for more than two hours a day must register with Ofsted and are inspected at least every two years. In 2018 there were an estimated 81,500 childcare providers in England.

CHILD PROTECTION

Children considered to be at risk of physical injury, neglect or sexual abuse are placed on the local authority's child protection register. Local authority social services staff, schools, health visitors and other agencies work together to prevent and detect cases of abuse. As at 31 March 2018, there was a total of 61,500 children on child protection registers or subject to a child protection plan in the UK. In England, there were 53,790 children on child protection registers, of these, 25,820 were at risk of neglect, 4,120 of physical abuse, 2,180 of sexual abuse and 18,860 of emotional abuse. At 31 March (July in Scotland) 2018 there were 2,960 children on child protection registers in Wales, 2,668 in Scotland and 2,082 in Northern Ireland.

LOCAL AUTHORITY CARE

Local authorities are required to provide accommodation for children who have no parents or guardians or whose parents or guardians are unable or unwilling to care for them. A family proceedings court may also issue a care order where a child is being neglected or abused, or is not attending school; the court must be satisfied that this would positively contribute to the well-being of the child.

The welfare of children in local authority care must be properly safeguarded. Children may be placed with foster families, who receive payments to cover the expenses of caring for the child or children, or in residential care.

Children's homes may be run by the local authority or by the private or voluntary sectors; all homes are subject to inspection procedures. As at 31 March 2018, 75,420 children in England were in the care of local authorities, of these, 55,200 were in foster placements and 8,530 were in children's homes, hostels or secure units.

ADOPTION

Local authorities are required to provide an adoption service, either directly or via approved voluntary societies. In the year to 31 March 2018, 2,230 children in local authority care in England were placed for adoption.

PEOPLE WITH LEARNING DISABILITIES

Services for people with learning disabilities are designed to enable them to remain living in the community wherever possible. Local authority services include short-term care, support in the home, the provision of day care centres, and help with other activities outside the home. Residential care is provided for the severely or profoundly disabled.

MENTALLY ILL PEOPLE

Under the care programme approach, mentally ill people should be assessed by specialist services and receive a care plan. A key worker should be appointed for each patient and regular reviews of the person's progress should be conducted. Local authorities provide help and advice to mentally ill people and their families, and places in day centres and social centres. Social workers can apply for a mentally disturbed person to be compulsorily detained in hospital. Where appropriate, mentally ill people are provided with accommodation in special hospitals, local authority accommodation, or at homes run by private or voluntary organisations. Patients who have been discharged from hospitals may be placed on a supervision register.

NATIONAL INSURANCE

The National Insurance (NI) scheme operates under the Social Security Contributions and Benefits Act 1992 and the Social Security Administration Act 1992, and orders and regulations made thereunder. The scheme is financed by contributions payable by earners, employers and others (see below). Money collected under the scheme is used to finance the National Insurance Fund (from which contributory benefits are paid) and to contribute to the cost of the National Health Service.

NATIONAL INSURANCE FUND

Estimated receipts, payments and statement of balances of the National Insurance Fund for 2019–20:

Receipts	£ million
Net national insurance contributions	108,706
Compensation from the Consolidated Fund for statutory payments recoveries	2,760
Income from investments	305
State scheme premiums	0
Other receipts	0
TOTAL RECEIPTS	111,771

Payments	£ million
Benefits	
At present rates	102,008
Increase due to proposed rate changes	2,515
Administration costs	743
Redundancy fund payments	295
Transfer to Northern Ireland	737
Other payments	188
TOTAL PAYMENTS	106,486

Balances	£ million
Balance at the beginning of the year	27,337
Excess of receipts over payments	5,285
BALANCE AT END OF YEAR	32,622

CONTRIBUTIONS

There are six classes of National Insurance contributions (NICs):

Class 1	paid by employees and their employers
Class 1A	paid by employers who provide employees with certain benefits in kind for private use, such as company cars
Class 1B	paid by employers who enter into a pay as you earn (PAYE) settlement agreement (PSA) with HM Revenue and Customs
Class 2	paid by self-employed people
Class 3	voluntary contributions paid to protect entitlement to the state pension for those who do not pay enough NI contributions in another class
Class 4	paid by the self-employed on their taxable profits over a set limit. These are normally paid by self-employed people in addition to class 2 contributions. Class 4 contributions do not count towards benefits.

The lower and upper earnings limits and the percentage rates referred to below apply from April 2019 to April 2020.

CLASS 1

Class 1 primary (employee) contributions are paid where a person:
- is an employed earner (employee), office holder (eg company director) or employed under a contract of service in Great Britain or Northern Ireland
- is 16 or over and under state pension age
- earns at or above the earnings threshold of £166.00 per week (including overtime pay, bonus, commission, etc, without deduction of superannuation contributions)

Class 1 contributions are made up of primary and secondary contributions. Primary contributions are those paid by the employee and these are deducted from earnings by the employer. Since 6 April 2001 the employee's and employer's earnings thresholds have been the same. Primary contributions are not paid on earnings below the earnings threshold of £166.00 per week. However, between the lower earnings limit of £118.00 per week and the earnings threshold of £166.00 per week, NI contributions are treated as having been paid to protect the benefit entitlement position of lower earners. Contributions are payable at the rate of 12 per cent on earnings between the earnings threshold and the upper earnings limit of £962.00 per week. Above the upper earnings limit 2 per cent is payable.

Some married women or widows pay a reduced rate of 5.85 per cent on earnings between the earnings threshold and upper earnings limits and 2 per cent above this. It is no longer possible to elect to pay the reduced rate but those who had reduced liability before 12 May 1977 may retain it for as long as certain conditions are met.

Secondary contributions are paid by employers of employed earners at the rate of 13.8 per cent on all earnings above the earnings threshold of £166.00 per week. There is a zero rate between the earnings threshold and the upper threshold of £962 per week for employers of relevant apprentices and employed earners under the age of 21.

CLASS 2

Class 2 contributions are paid where a person is self-employed and is 16 or over and under state pension age. Contributions are paid at a flat rate of £3.00 per week regardless of the amount earned. However, those with profits of less than £6,365 a year can apply for small profits exception. Those granted exemption from class 2 contributions may pay class 2 or class 3 contributions voluntarily. Self-employed earners (whether or not they pay class 2 contributions) may also be liable to pay class 4 contributions based on profits. There are special rules for those who are concurrently employed and self-employed.

Married women and widows can no longer choose not to pay class 2 contributions but those who elected not to pay class 2 contributions before 12 May 1977 may retain the right for as long as certain conditions are met.

Class 2 contributions are assessed and collected annually by HM Revenue and Customs (HMRC) as part of the self-assessment tax bill. For self-employed people that do not pay tax through self-assessment, a bill is issued by HMRC by the end of October.

CLASS 3

Class 3 contributions are voluntary flat-rate contributions of £15.00 per week payable by persons over the age of 16 who would otherwise be unable to qualify for retirement pension and certain other benefits because they have an insufficient record of class 1 or class 2 contributions. This may include those who are not working, those not liable for class 1 or class 2 contributions, or those excepted from class 2 contributions. Married women and widows who on or before 11 May 1977 elected not to pay class 1 (full rate) or class 2 contributions cannot pay class 3 contributions while they retain this right. Class 3 contributions are collected by HMRC by quarterly bills or monthly direct debit. One-off payments can also be made.

CLASS 4

Self-employed people whose profits and gains are over £8,632 a year pay class 4 contributions in addition to class 2 contributions. This applies to self-employed earners over 16 and under the state pension age. Class 4 contributions are calculated at 9 per cent of annual profits or gains between £8,632 and £50,000 and 2 per cent above. Class 4 contributions are assessed and collected annually by HMRC as part of the self-assessment tax bill. It is possible, in some circumstances, to apply for exceptions from liability to pay class 4 contributions or to have the amount of contribution reduced.

PENSIONS

Many people will qualify for a state pension; however, there are further pension choices available, such as workplace, personal and stakeholder pensions. There are also other non-pension savings and investment options.

STATE PENSION

From 6 April 2016, the system of basic and additional state pension was replaced with a new scheme for people reaching state pension age after that date (ie men born on or after 6 April 1951, and women born on or after 6 April 1953).

Those that reached state pension age before this date continue to receive their state pension in line with the old rules.

The earliest state pension can be claimed is at state pension age, people can delay claiming it to earn weekly state pension or a lump sum payment.

NEW STATE PENSION

The full rate of the new state pension, for people reaching state pension age on or after 6 April 2016, is £168.60 per week for a single person in 2019–20. The amount received is based on the individual's national insurance record.

An individual's 'starting amount', part of the new state pension, is based on NI contributions and credits made before 6 April 2016 and will be the higher of either:
- the amount received under the old state pension rules (including basic state pension and additional state pension)
- the amount received if the new state pension had been in place from the start of their working life

A deduction may be made to these amounts for periods an individual was contracted out of the additional state pension because they were in a certain type of workplace, personal or stakeholder pension.

If the individual's starting amount is less than the full new state pension (£168.60 per week) more qualifying years can be added to their national insurance record after 5 April 2016 until the individual reaches the full rate of new state pension or reaches state pension age – whichever is first. If the individual's starting amount is more than the full new state pension of £168.60 per week, then the amount above the full new state pension (the 'protected payment') is paid on top of the full new state pension.

If an individual did not make NI contributions or get NI credits prior to 6 April 2016 than their state pension will be calculated entirely under the new state pension rules.

Further information about the new state pension can be found online (www.gov.uk/new-state-pension).

CATEGORY A OR B STATE PENSION

The category A or B state pension scheme is paid to individuals who reached state pension age before 6 April 2016 and is based on their own contributions or those made by a deceased spouse or civil partner. The full weekly rate in 2019–20 is £129.20.

For further information see Benefits, State Pension: Categories A and B.

WORKING LIFE

The working life is from the start of the tax year (6 April) in which a person reaches 16 to the end of the tax year (5 April) before the one in which they reach state pension age (see State Pension Age).

QUALIFYING YEARS

A 'qualifying year' is a tax year in which a person has sufficient earnings upon which they have paid, are treated as having paid, or have been credited with national insurance (NI) contributions (see National Insurance Credits).

For people reaching state pension age on or after 6 April 2016 a full new state pension (£168.60 per week in 2019–20) is payable to those individuals who have 35 qualifying years on their national insurance record. Individuals usually need at least ten qualifying years and will receive a proportion of the new state pension if they have between ten and 35 qualifying years.

For people who reached state pension age between 6 April 2010 and 5 April 2016 a full category A or B pension (£129.20 per week in 2019–20) is payable to those individuals who have 30 qualifying years on their national insurance record. Someone with less than 30 qualifying years will be entitled to a proportion of the full category A or B pension based on the number of qualifying years they have. Just one qualifying year, achieved through paid or credited contributions, will give entitlement to the basic state pension worth one-thirtieth of the full basic state pension.

For people who reached state pension age before 6 April 2010, women normally needed 39 qualifying years for a full basic state pension (£129.20 per week in 2019–20) and men normally needed 44 qualifying years. A reduced-rate basic state pension was payable if the number of qualifying years was less than 90 per cent of the individual's working life, but to receive any state pension at all, a person must have had enough qualifying years, normally ten or 11, to receive a basic state pension of at least 25 per cent of the full rate.

The state pension of transgender people may be affected for those that changed their gender or started claiming state pension before 4 April 2005; claims for those who legally changed their gender and started claiming state pension on or after 4 April 2005 are based on the individual's legal gender.

NATIONAL INSURANCE CREDITS

Those in receipt of carer's allowance, working tax credit (with a disability premium), jobseeker's allowance, employment and support allowance, unemployability supplement, statutory sick pay, maternity allowance, statutory maternity, paternity or statutory adoption pay may have class 1 NI contributions credited to them each week. People may also get credits if they are unemployed and looking for work or too sick to work, even if they are not in receipt of any benefit, although the credits must be applied for in these circumstances. Since April 2010, spouses and civil partners of members of HM forces may get credits if they are on an accompanied assignment outside the UK. Those who reach state pension age on or after 6 April 2016 can apply for NI credits for periods before April 2010 during which they were married to, or in a civil partnership with, a member of HM forces and accompanied them on a posting outside the UK. Persons undertaking certain training courses or jury service or who have been wrongly imprisoned for a conviction which is quashed on appeal may also get class 1 NI credits for each week they fulfil certain conditions. Class 1 credits may also be available to men approaching state pension age, born before 6 October 1953 who live in the UK for at least 183 days a year and who don't work, earn enough to make a qualifying year or are self-employed with profits of less than £6,365. Class 1 NI credits count toward all future contributory benefits.

A class 3 NI credit for basic state pension and bereavement benefit purposes is awarded, where required, for each week universal credit, working tax credit (without a disability premium) or child benefit, for a child under 12, has been received. Class 3 credits may also be awarded, on application, to approved foster carers and people caring for others for at least 20 hours a week. Since 6 April 2011, class 3 credits have been available to adults under state pension age who care for a family member under 12. Further information regarding eligibility for NI credits is available online (www.gov.uk/national-insurance-credits/eligibility)

STATE PENSION AGE

From 6 November 2018 state pension age is 65 for both men and women and this will increase to age 66 for both men and women by October 2020. The Pensions Act 2014 makes provision for a regular review of state pension age. Reviews will take place at least once every six years and will take into account up-to-date life expectancy data and the findings of an independently led review, which will consider wider factors such as variation in life expectancy and employment opportunities for older workers. Further information can be obtained from the online state pension calculator (W www.gov.uk/state-pension-age).

USING THE NI CONTRIBUTION RECORD OF ANOTHER TO CLAIM A STATE PENSION

Married people or civil partners who reached state pension age before 6 April 2016 whose own NI record is incomplete may get a lower-rate basic state pension calculated using their partner's NI contribution record. This can be up to £77.45 a week in 2019–20.

People who reached state pension age before 6 April 2016 will continue to be able to use these provisions, even if their spouse or civil partner reaches state pension age on or after that date. However, contributions their spouse or civil partner pays, or is credited with, following implementation of the new system will only count towards their own state pension. This means that only the NI record of the spouse or civil partner up to and including 2015–16 will be used to calculate any derived entitlement.

People who reached state pension age on or after 6 April 2016 will not be able to claim state pension on their spouse's or civil partner's NI record. There will be special arrangements for women who had opted to pay the married women's and widows reduced rate contributions before May 1977.

NON-CONTRIBUTORY STATE PENSIONS

A non-contributory state pension may be payable to those aged 80 or over who live in England, Scotland or Wales, and have done so for a total of ten years or more for any continuous period in the 20 years after their 60th birthday, if they are not entitled to another category of state pension, or are entitled to one below the rate of £77.45 a week in 2019–20 (see also Benefits, State Pension for people aged 80 and over).

GRADUATED RETIREMENT BENEFIT

Graduated Retirement Benefit (GRB) is based on the amount of graduated NI contributions paid into the GRB scheme between April 1961 and April 1975 (see also Benefits, Graduated Retirement Benefit). It is normally paid as an increase to a main state pension. For those reaching state pension age under the new state pension rules, it will be included in the calculation of their basic amount.

HOME RESPONSIBILITIES PROTECTION

From 6 April 1978 until 5 April 2010, it was possible for people who had low income or were unable to work because they cared for children or a sick or disabled person at home to reduce the number of qualifying years required for basic state pension. This was called home responsibilities protection (HRP); the number of years for which HRP was given was deducted from the number of qualifying years needed. HRP could, in some cases, also qualify the recipient for additional state pension. From April 2003 to April 2010 HRP was also available to approved foster carers.

From 6 April 2010, HRP was replaced by weekly credits for parents and carers. A class 3 national insurance credit is also given, where eligible, towards state pension and bereavement benefits for spouses and civil partners. An earnings factor credit towards additional state pension was also awarded. Any years of HRP accrued before 6 April 2010 were converted into qualifying years of credits for people reaching state pension age after that date, up to a maximum of 22 years for state pension purposes.

ADDITIONAL STATE PENSION

The additional state pension is an extra sum paid on top of a basic state pension to men born before 6 April 1951 or women born before 1953. Individuals born after these dates will get the new state pension instead and won't qualify for the additional state pension, although they might still be able to inherit additional state pension from their partner. Additional state pension is paid automatically if an individual is eligible for it, unless they contracted out of it. There is no fixed amount for the additional state pension, the amount paid depends on the amount of earnings a person has, or is treated as having, between the lower and upper earnings limits for each complete tax year between 6 April 1978 and the tax year before they reach state pension age. The additional state pension is paid with the basic state pension.

From 1978 to 2002, additional state pension was called the State Earnings-Related Pension Scheme (SERPS). SERPS covered all earnings by employees from 6 April 1978 to 5 April 1997 on which standard rate class 1 NI contributions had been paid, and earnings between 6 April 1997 and 5 April 2002 if the standard rate class 1 NI contributions had been contracted-in.

In 2002, SERPS was reformed through the state second pension, by improving the pension available to low and moderate earners and extending access to certain carers and people with long-term illness or disability. If earnings on which class 1 NI contributions have been paid or can be treated as paid are above the annual NI lower earnings limit (£6,136 for 2019–2020) but below the primary threshold (£8,632 for 2019–2020), the state second pension regards this as earnings of £8,632 and it is treated as equivalent. Certain carers and people with long-term illness and disability will be considered as having earned at the primary threshold for each complete tax year since 2002–3 even if they do not work at all, or earn less than the annual NI lower earnings limit.

The amount of additional state pension paid also depends on when a person reaches state pension age; changes phased in from 6 April 1999 mean that pensions are calculated differently after that date.

ADDITIONAL STATE PENSION INHERITANCE

Men or women widowed before 6 October 2002 may inherit all of their late spouse's SERPS pension. Since 6 October 2002, the maximum percentage of SERPS pension that a person can inherit from a late spouse or civil partner depends on their late spouse's or civil partner's date of birth:

Maximum SERPS entitlement	d.o.b. (men)	d.o.b. (women)
100%	5/10/37 or earlier	5/10/42 or earlier
90%	6/10/37 to 5/10/39	6/10/42 to 5/10/44
80%	6/10/39 to 5/10/41	6/10/44 to 5/10/46
70%	6/10/41 to 5/10/43	6/10/46 to 5/10/48
60%	6/10/43 to 5/10/45	6/10/48 to 5/7/50
50%	6/10/45 or later	6/7/50 or later

The maximum state second pension a person can inherit from a spouse or civil partner is 50 per cent. If a person is bereaved before they have reached their state pension age, inherited SERPS or state second pension can be paid as part of widowed parent's allowance (in the case of a person who has dependent children) or otherwise only from state pension age. If they remarry or form a new civil partnership before state pension age they lose the right to inherit any state pension.

NEW STATE PENSION INHERITANCE

A person who reached state pension age before 6 April 2016 will still be able to inherit additional state pension under the existing rules. However, if their late spouse or civil partner reaches state pension age on or after that date, the amount they can inherit will be based on the deceased's contributions up to 5 April 2016 only.

A person reaching state pension age on or after 6 April 2016 whose deceased spouse or civil partner reached state pension age or died before that date will be able to inherit additional state pension under the current rules. If the deceased spouse or civil partner is also in the new state pension the survivor may inherit half of any 'protected payment'. A person will have a protected payment if their state pension calculated under current rules is more than the full rate of new state pension at April 2016. The protected payment is the amount of the excess.

In order for a person reaching state pension age on or after 6 April 2016 to qualify for an inherited amount the marriage or civil partnership must have begun before that date; and, in the case of a person widowed under state pension age, they must not remarry or form a new civil partnership before state pension age.

STATE PENSION STATEMENTS

The Department for Work and Pensions provide state pension statements. These statements give an estimate of the state pension an individual may get based on their current NI contribution record.

There is also an online state pension calculator (**W** www.gov.uk/check-state-pension).

PRIVATE PENSIONS

CONTRACTED-OUT PENSIONS

From 6 April 2012, employees have not been able to contract-out of the state second pension through a money purchase (defined contribution) occupational pension scheme or a personal or stakeholder pension. Anyone contracted-out via these schemes, from that date, was automatically contracted back into the additional state pension. Although those rights built up before the abolition date can be used to provide pension benefits. These changes did not affect contracting-out via a salary-related occupational pension scheme (also known as contracted-out defined benefit (DB) or final salary schemes), which provide a pension related to earnings and the length of pensionable service. However, the introduction of the single-tier pension scheme in April 2016 closed the additional state pension for those reaching state pension age after this date, and contracting out on a DB basis ended.

STAKEHOLDER PENSION SCHEMES

Introduced in 2001, stakeholder pensions are available to everyone but are principally for moderate earners who do not have access to a good value company pension scheme. Stakeholder pensions must meet minimum standards to make sure they are flexible, portable and annual management charges are capped. The minimum contribution is £20.

AUTOMATIC ENROLMENT INTO WORKPLACE PENSIONS

Under the Pensions Act 2008 automatic enrolment into workplace pensions was phased in between October 2012 and February 2018, from when all employers must automatically enrol their workers who meet the age and earnings criteria into a workplace pension. This applies to people who are not already in a qualifying workplace pension scheme and who:
- earn at least £10,000 per annum
- are aged 22 or over
- are under state pension age
- ordinarily work in the UK

Employees who meet the above requirements are entitled to opt out of the scheme at any time if they wish to do so; if they opt out within one calendar month of enrolment they will get back any money already paid in, otherwise payments will usually stay in the pension until retirement. Employees can opt back in at any time by writing to their employer, although they do not have to accept the employer back into their workplace scheme if they they have opted in and opted out within the past 12 months. Employers will automatically re-enrol those that have opted out every three years (from the date they were first enrolled) and will write to the employee when they do this. Employees can leave the scheme again, but only once they have been re-enrolled.

Additionally certain employees can also choose to opt in to the scheme. Currently, employees can opt in if they are:
• aged 16 to 21, or state pension age to 74
• earning above £6,032 up to and including £10,000 per annum

If they remain in the scheme, they, together with their employer, will pay into it every month. The government will also contribute through tax relief. Further information is available at **W** www.gov.uk/workplace-pensions

COMPLAINTS

The Pensions Advisory Service provides information and guidance to members of the public, on state, company, personal and stakeholder schemes. They also help any member of the public who has a problem, complaint or dispute with their occupational or personal pensions.

There are two bodies for pension complaints. The Financial Ombudsman Service deals with complaints which predominantly concern the sale and/or marketing of occupational, stakeholder and personal pensions. The Pensions Ombudsman deals with complaints regarding the management (after sale or marketing) of occupational, stakeholder and personal pensions.

The Pensions Regulator is the UK regulator for work-based pension schemes; it concentrates its resources on schemes where there is the greatest risk to the security of members' benefits, promotes good administration practice for all work-based schemes and works with trustees, employers and professional advisers to put things right when necessary.

WAR PENSIONS AND THE ARMED FORCES COMPENSATION SCHEME

Veterans UK is part of the Ministry of Defence. It was formed on 1 April 2007 to provide services to both serving personnel and veterans.

Veterans UK is responsible for the administration of the war pensions scheme and the armed forces compensation scheme (AFCS) to members of the armed forces in respect of disablement or death due to service. They are also responsible for the administration of the armed forces pension scheme (AFPS), which provides occupational pensions for ex-service personnel.

THE WAR PENSIONS SCHEME

War disablement pension is awarded for the disabling effects of any injury, wound or disease which was the result of, or was aggravated by, service in the armed forces prior to 6 April 2005. Claims are only considered once the person has left the armed forces. The amount of pension paid depends on the severity of disablement, which is assessed by comparing the health of the claimant with that of a healthy person of the same age and sex. The person's earning capacity or occupation are not taken into account in this assessment. A pension is awarded if the person has a disablement of 20 per cent or more and a lump sum is usually payable to those with a disablement of less than 20 per cent. No award is made for noise-induced sensorineural hearing loss where the assessment

of disablement is less than 20 per cent. Where an assessment of disablement is at 40 per cent or more, an age addition is automatically given when the pensioner reaches 65.

A pension is payable to war widows, widowers and surviving civil partners where the spouse's or civil partner's death was due to, or hastened by, service in the armed forces prior to 6 April 2005 or where the spouse or civil partner was in receipt of a war disablement pension constant attendance allowance (or would have been if not in hospital) at the time of death. A pension is also payable to widows, widowers or surviving civil partners if the spouse or civil partner was receiving the war disablement pension at the 80 per cent rate or higher in conjunction with unemployability supplement at the time of death. War widows, widowers and surviving civil partners receive a standard rank-related rate, but a lower weekly rate is payable to war widows, widowers and surviving civil partners of personnel of the rank of Major or below who are under the age of 40, without children and capable of maintaining themselves. This is increased to the standard rate at age 40. Allowances are paid for children and adult dependants. An age allowance is automatically given when the widow, widower or surviving civil partner reaches 65 and increased at ages 70 and 80.

Pensioners living overseas receive the same pension rates as those living in the UK. All war disablement pensions and allowances and pensions for war widows, widowers and surviving civil partners are tax-free in the UK; this does not always apply in overseas countries due to different tax laws.

SUPPLEMENTARY ALLOWANCES

A number of supplementary allowances may be awarded to a war pensioner and are intended to meet various needs. The principal supplementary allowances are unemployability supplement, allowance for lowered standard of occupation, constant attendance allowance and war pensions mobility supplement. Others include exceptionally severe disablement allowance, severe disablement occupational allowance, treatment allowance, comforts allowance, clothing allowance, age allowance and widow/widower/surviving civil partner's age allowance. Rent and children's allowances are also available with pensions for war widows, widowers and surviving civil partners.

ARMED FORCES COMPENSATION SCHEME

The armed forces compensation scheme (AFCS) became effective on 6 April 2005 and covers all regular (including Gurkhas) and reserve personnel whose injury, ill health or death is caused predominantly by service on or after 6 April 2005. There are time limits under this scheme and generally claims must be made within seven years of the injury occurring or from first seeking medical advice about an illness. There are some exceptions to this time limit, the main one being for a late-onset illness. Claims for a late-onset illness can be made, after discharge, at any time after the event to which it relates, providing the claim is made within three years of medical advice being sought.

The AFCS provides compensation where service in the armed forces is the only or predominant cause of injury, illness or death. Any other personal accident cover held by the individual is not taken into account when determining an AFCS award. Under the terms of the scheme a tax-free lump sum is payable to service or ex-service personnel based on a 15-level tariff, graduated according to the seriousness of the injury. If multiple injuries are sustained in the same incident compensation for each injury, up to the scheme maximum, is awarded. For those with the most serious injuries and illness a tax-free, index-linked monthly payment – a guaranteed income payment or GIP – is paid for life from the point of discharge. A taxable survivor's GIP (SGIP) will also be paid to surviving spouses, civil partners and unmarried partners who meet certain criteria. GIP and SGIP are calculated by multiplying the pensionable pay of the service person by a factor that depends on the age at the person's last birthday. The younger the person, the higher the factor, because there are more years to normal retirement age.

ARMED FORCES INDEPENDENCE PAYMENT

Armed forces independence payment (AFIP) is designed to provide financial support for service personnel and veterans who have been seriously injured to cover the extra costs they may incur as a result of their injury. It is administered by Veterans UK as part of AFCS although payments are made by the Department for Work and Pensions (DWP). It is non-taxable and non-means-tested.

Service personnel and veterans awarded a GIP of 50 per cent or higher under the AFCS are eligible. Those eligible for AFIP are not required to undergo an assessment and will keep the payment for as long as they are entitled to receive a GIP of 50 per cent or higher.

DEPARTMENT FOR WORK AND PENSIONS BENEFITS

Payments under the AFCS and the war pensions scheme may affect income related benefits from the DWP. In particular any supplementary allowances in payment with war pensions. Any state pension for which a war widow, widower or surviving civil partner qualifies for on their own NI contribution record can be paid in addition to monies received under the war pensions scheme.

CLAIMS AND QUESTIONS

Further information on the war pensions scheme, the AFCS and contact details for Veterans Welfare Service centres can be obtained from Veterans UK (**T** 0808-191 4218, if calling from the UK or, if living overseas, **T** (+44) (1253) 866-043).

VETERANS UK, Norcross Lane, Thornton-Cleveleys FY5 3WP **E** veterans-uk@mod.gov.uk **W** www.gov.uk/government/organisations/veterans-uk

TAX CREDITS

Tax credits are administered by HM Revenue and Customs (HMRC). They are based on an individual's or couple's household income and current circumstances. Adjustments can be made during the year to reflect changes in income and/or circumstances. Tax credits are being replaced by universal credit. Further information regarding the qualifying conditions for tax credits, how to claim and the rates payable is available online at (**W** www.gov.uk/browse/benefits/tax-credits).

WORKING TAX CREDIT

Working tax credit is a payment from the government to support people on low incomes. New claims may only be made by those who are in receipt of a severe disability premium. Those who do not meet this criteria may be eligible for universal credit if they are of working age, or pension credits if they are of qualifying age.

For those in receipt of working tax credit (where this has not been replaced by universal credit) the amount received depends on individual circumstances and income. The basic amount is up to £1,960 per annum and extra 'elements' are paid on top of this:

Element	Amount per annum
Couple applying together	up to £2,010
Single parent	up to £2,010
An individual working at least 30 hours a week	up to £810
An individual with a disability	up to £3,165
An individual with a severe disability	up to £1,365*

* Usually in addition to the disability payment

Childcare Element
Those already in receipt of tax credits, may still be able to claim for the childcare element. In families with children where a lone parent works at least 16 hours a week, or couples who work at least 24 hours a week between them with one partner working at least 16 hours a week, or where one partner works at least 16 hours a week and the other is disabled, an in-patient in hospital, or in prison, the family is entitled to the childcare element of working tax credit. Depending on circumstances this payment can contribute up to £122.50 a week towards childcare costs for one child and up to £210.00 a week for two or more children. Families can only claim if they use an approved childcare provider.

CHILD TAX CREDIT

Child tax credit has been replaced by universal credit for most people. The credit is made up of a main 'family' element of up to £545 a year with an additional 'child' payment of up to £2,780 a year for each child in a household born before 6 April 2017. For children born after this date, only the 'child' element of child tax credit will apply for the first two children in a household with no 'family element', however there are exceptions to this two-child rule. An additional payment is paid for children with a disability, plus a further payment for children who are severely disabled. New child tax credit claims are still possible for individuals who are eligible for a severe disability premium and have legal responsibility and care for any child who is 16 years and younger.

BENEFITS

The following is intended as a general guide to the benefits system. Conditions of entitlement and benefit rates change annually and all prospective claimants should check exact entitlements and rates of benefit directly with their local Jobcentre Plus office, pension centre or online (**W** www.gov.uk/browse/benefits). Leaflets relating to the various benefits and contribution conditions for different benefits are available from local Jobcentre Plus offices.

UNIVERSAL CREDIT

Universal credit (UC) is a single benefit which combines benefits for in and out of work support, housing and childcare costs, with additional payments for people who have disabilities or caring responsibilities. UC is gradually being rolled out to all new and existing claimants in all local authority areas in the country, replacing six means-tested benefits with a single monthly payment. The six benefits being replaced by UC are:
- Income-based jobseeker's allowance (JSA)
- Income-related employment and support allowance (ESA)
- Income support
- Child tax credit
- Working tax credit
- Housing benefit

The UC full service completed its roll-out for all new claimants in December 2018 and is available in all parts of the UK. It is expected that existing claimants of the above six benefits will be moved to UC between November 2020 and December 2023. This will follow a pilot involving up to 10,000 people moved between July 2019 and July 2020.

The amount of UC awarded is determined by the circumstances of the claimant, this includes income and number of dependants in the household. It consists of a basic 'standard allowance' and additional payments as applicable to the claimant's circumstances. UC can be claimed while working, but the monthly payment will reduce gradually as the claimant earns more.

Standard monthly allowance from April 2019

Single, under 25	£251.77
Single, over 25	£317.82
Couple, both under 25	£395.20
Couple, one or both over 25	£498.89

Additional monthly payments from April 2019

Disability or health condition	£336.20
Carer allowance	£160.20
First child born before 6 April 2017	£277.08
First child born after 6 April 2017	£231.67
Second child	£231.67
Childcare for one child (max.)	£646.35
Childcare for two or more children (max.)	£1,108.04
Child with a disability	
Lower rate addition	£126.11
Higher rate addition	£392.08

For more information and to check eligibility visit **W** www.gov.uk/universal-credit

CONTRIBUTORY BENEFITS

Entitlement to contributory benefits depends on national insurance contribution conditions being satisfied either by the claimant or by someone on the claimant's behalf (depending on the kind of benefit). The class or classes of national insurance contribution relevant to each benefit are:

Jobseeker's allowance (contribution-based)	Class 1
Employment and Support Allowance (contributory)	Class 1 or 2
Widow's benefit and bereavement benefit	Class 1, 2 or 3
State pensions, categories A and B	Class 1, 2 or 3

The system of contribution conditions relates to yearly levels of earnings on which national insurance (NI) contributions have been paid.

JOBSEEKER'S ALLOWANCE

Jobseeker's allowance (JSA) replaced unemployment benefit and income support for unemployed people under state pension age from 7 October 1996. There are three different types of JSA: 'new style' JSA, contribution-based JSA and income-based JSA. Following the roll out of universal credit (UC) new claimants can only claim contribution-based JSA if they are entitled to the severe disability premium, existing claimants will transfer to 'new style' JSA in line with UC roll-out in their area. JSA is paid at a personal rate (ie additional benefit for dependants is not paid) to those who have made sufficient Class 1 NI contributions in the previous two or three tax years. Savings and partner's earnings are not taken into account and payment can be made for up to six months. Rates of JSA correspond to income support rates.

Claims are made through Jobcentre Plus. A person wishing to claim JSA must generally be unemployed or working on average less than 16 hours a week, capable of work and available for any work which he or she can reasonably be expected to do, usually for at least 40 hours a week. The claimant must agree and sign a 'jobseeker's agreement', which will set out his or her plans to find work, and must actively seek work. If the claimant refuses work or training the benefit may be sanctioned for between one and 26 weeks. On successfully claiming the 'new style' JSA, UC payments will be reduced.

A person will be sanctioned from JSA for up to 26 weeks if he or she has left a job voluntarily without just cause or through misconduct. In these circumstances, it may be possible to receive hardship payments, particularly where the claimant or the claimant's family is vulnerable, eg if sick or pregnant, or with children or caring responsibilities.

Weekly Rates from April 2019

Person aged under 25	£57.90
Person aged 25 or over	£73.10

EMPLOYMENT AND SUPPORT ALLOWANCE

From 27 October 2008, employment and support allowance (ESA) replaced incapacity benefit and income support paid on the grounds of incapacity or disability. There are three different types of ESA: 'new style' ESA, contribution-based ESA and income-related ESA. Those eligible for UC may be able to get UC at the same time or instead of 'new style' ESA. Contributory ESA is available to those who have limited capability for work but cannot get statutory sick pay from their employer; new claimants must be in receipt of the severe disability premium otherwise they can only apply for 'new style' ESA. Those over pensionable age are not entitled to ESA. Apart from those who qualify under the special provisions for people incapacitated in youth, entitlement to contributory ESA is based on a person's NI contribution record. The amount of contributory ESA payable may be reduced where the person receives more than a specified amount of occupational or personal pension. Contributory ESA is paid only in respect of the person claiming the benefit – there are no additional amounts for dependants.

Those with the most severe health conditions or disabilities will receive the support component, which is more than the work-related activity component. Claimants in receipt of the support component are not required to engage in work-related activities, although they can volunteer to do so or undertake permitted work if their condition allows.

Weekly Rates from April 2019

ESA plus work-related activity component	up to £102.15
ESA plus support component	up to £111.65

BEREAVEMENT SUPPORT PAYMENT

Bereavement support payment replaced bereavement payment, widowed parent's allowance and bereavement allowance for those whose spouse or civil partner died on or after 6 April 2017. It may be paid to those under state pension age at the time of their spouse or civil partner's death and whose spouse or civil partner had paid National Insurance contributions for at least 25 weeks or died because of an accident at work or a disease caused by work.

It consists of an initial one-off payment followed by up to 18 monthly payments. There are two rates: those in receipt of, or entitled to, child benefit or those who were pregnant when their spouse or civil partner died receive the higher rate. In order to receive the full amount claims must be made within three months of the death of the spouse or civil partner. After three months, claims can still be made up to 21 months after the spouse or civil partner's death but the payments will be less.

Rates from April 2019

Standard rate	
lump sum	£2,500.00
monthly payment	£100.00
Higher rate	
lump sum	£3,500.00
monthly payment	£350.00

NEW STATE PENSION

The new state pension is payable to men and women who reach state pension age on or after 6 April 2016 (ie men born on or after 6 April 1951 or women born on or after 6 April

1953). Those that reached state pension age before this date continue to receive state pension under the old rules.

The full new state pension of £168.60 a week in 2019–20 is payable to those individuals who have 35 qualifying years on their national insurance record. Individuals usually need at least ten qualifying years and will receive a proportion of the new state pension if they have between ten and 35 qualifying years. The starting amount is the higher of the amount receivable under the old state pension rules (category A and B) and the amount the individual would receive had the new state pension been in place at the start of their working life. The amount received includes a deduction for those who were contracted out of the additional state pension.

Each qualifying year on an individual's national insurance record after 5 April 2016 adds £4.82 a week to the new state pension. The exact amount can be calculated by dividing £168.60 by 35 and then multiplying by the number of qualifying years after 5 April 2016. Additional qualifying years can be added to a person's national insurance record until the person reaches the full new state pension amount or the state pension age – whichever is first.

Those individuals who have accrued an amount, before 5 April 2016, which is above the new full state pension – a 'protected payment' – have this paid on top of the full new state pension.

The new state pension increases each year by whichever is the highest:

- earnings – the average percentage growth in wages (in Great Britain)
- prices – the percentage growth in prices in the UK as measured by the Consumer Prices Index (CPI)
- 3 per cent

Any protected payment increases each year in line with the CPI.

The new state pension can be deferred beyond state pension age and will increase by 1 per cent for every nine weeks it is deferred, as long as it is deferred for at least nine weeks. This equates to just under 5.8 per cent for every full year a new state pension is deferred. The new state pension can only be deferred once and for a period of at least nine weeks (there is no upper limit).

Weekly Rate from April 2019	
Full new state pension	£168.60

STATE PENSION: CATEGORIES A AND B

Category A pension is payable for life to men and women who reach state pension age, who satisfy the contributions conditions and who claim for it. Category B pension may be payable to married women, married men and civil partners who are not entitled to a basic state pension on their own NI contributions or whose own basic state pension entitlement is less than £77.45 a week in 2019–20. It is based on their spouse or civil partner's NI contributions and is payable when both members of the couple have reached state pension age. Married men and civil partners may only be able to qualify for a category B pension if their wife or civil partner was born on or after 6 April 1950. Category B pension is also payable to widows, widowers and surviving civil partners who are bereaved before state pension age if they were previously entitled to widowed parent's allowance or bereavement allowance based on their late spouse's or civil partner's NI contributions. If they were receiving widowed parent's allowance on reaching state pension age, they could qualify for a category B pension payable at the same rate as their widowed parent's allowance comprising a basic pension, plus, if applicable, the appropriate share of their late spouse's or late civil partner's additional state pension. If their widowed

parent's allowance had stopped before they reached state pension age, or they had been getting bereavement allowance at any time before state pension age, their category B pension will consist of inheritable additional state pension only. No basic state pension is included, although they may qualify for a basic state pension or have their own basic state pension improved by substituting their late spouse's or late civil partner's NI records for their own.

Widows who are bereaved when over state pension age can qualify for a category B pension regardless of the age of their husband when he died. This is payable at the same rate as the basic state pension the widow's late husband was entitled to (or would have been entitled to) at the time of his death. It can also be paid to widowers and civil partners who are bereaved when over state pension age if their wife or civil partner had reached state pension age when they died. Widowers and surviving civil partners who reached state pension age on or after 6 April 2010 and bereaved when over state pension age can qualify for a category B pension regardless of the age of their wife or civil partner when they died.

Where a person is entitled to both a category A and category B pension then they can be combined to give a composite pension, but this cannot be more than the full rate pension. Where a person is entitled to more than one category A or category B pension then only one can be paid. In such cases the person can choose which to get; if no choice is made, the most favourable one is paid.

A person may defer claiming their pension beyond state pension age. In doing so they may earn increments which will increase the weekly amount paid by 1 per cent per five weeks of deferral (equivalent to 10.4 per cent/year) when they claim their state pension. If a person delays claiming for at least 12 months they are given the option of a one-off taxable lump sum, instead of a pension increase, based on the weekly pension deferred, plus interest of at least 2 per cent above the Bank of England base rate. Since 6 April 2010, a category B pension has been treated independently of the spouse's or partner's pension. It is possible to take a category B pension even if the spouse or partner has deferred theirs.

It is no longer possible to claim an increase on a state pension for another adult (known as adult dependency increase). Those who received the increase before April 2010 can keep receiving it until the conditions are no longer met or until 5 April 2020, whichever is first.

Provision for children is made through universal credit. An age addition of 25p a week is payable with a state pension if a pensioner is aged 80 or over.

Since 1989 pensioners have been allowed to have unlimited earnings without affecting their state pension. *See also* Pensions.

Weekly Rates from April 2019	
Category A or B pension for a single person	£129.20
Category B pension based on spouse or civil partner's NI contributions	£77.45

GRADUATED RETIREMENT BENEFIT

Graduated retirement benefit (GRB) is based on the amount of graduated NI contributions paid into the GRB scheme between April 1961 and April 1975; however, it is still paid in addition to any state pension to those who made the relevant contributions. A person will receive graduated retirement benefit based on their own contributions, even if not entitled to a basic state pension. Widows, widowers and surviving civil partners may inherit half of their deceased spouse's or civil partner's entitlement, but none that the deceased spouse or civil partner may have been eligible for from a former spouse or civil partner. If a person defers making a claim beyond state pension age, they may earn an increase or a one-off lump sum payment in respect of their deferred graduated retirement benefit; calculated in the same way as for a category A or B state pension.

NON-CONTRIBUTORY BENEFITS
These benefits are paid from general taxation and are not dependent on NI contributions.

JOBSEEKER'S ALLOWANCE (INCOME-BASED)
Those who do not qualify for contribution-based jobseeker's allowance (JSA) and those who have exhausted their entitlement to contribution-based JSA may qualify for income-based JSA. Universal credit and 'new style' Jobseeker's Allowance (JSA) has replaced income-based JSA for most people, only those in receipt of, or eligible for, a benefit with a severe disability premium and those who recently stopped getting a benefit with a severe disability premium and still meet the eligibility requirements can make a new claim for income-based JSA.

The amount paid depends on age, whether they are single or a couple and amount of income and savings. To get income-based JSA the claimant must usually be aged 18 or over but below state pension age, although there are some exceptions for 16- or 17-year-olds. The rules of entitlement are the same as for contribution-based JSA.

Weekly Rates from April 2019	
Person aged under 25	£57.90
Person aged 25 or over	£73.10
Couple, both aged 18 or over	£114.85

MATERNITY ALLOWANCE
Maternity allowance (MA) is a benefit available for pregnant women who cannot get statutory maternity pay (SMP) from their employer or have been employed/self-employed during or close to their pregnancy. In order to qualify for payment, a woman must have been employed and/or self-employed for at least 26 weeks in the 66-week period up to and including the week before the baby is due (test period). These weeks do not have to be in a row and any part weeks worked will count towards the 26 weeks. She must also have an average weekly earning of at least £30 (maternity allowance threshold) over any 13 weeks of the woman's choice within the test period.

Self-employed women who pay class 2 NI contributions or who hold a small earnings exception certificate are deemed to have enough earnings to qualify for MA.

A woman can choose to start receiving MA from the 11th week before the week in which the baby is due (if she stops work before then) up to the day following the day of birth. The exact date MA starts will depend on when the woman stops work to have her baby or if the baby is born before she stops work. However, where the woman is absent from work wholly or partly due to her pregnancy in the four weeks before the week the baby is due to be born, MA will start the day following the first day of absence from work. MA is paid for a maximum of 39 weeks.

Women who are not eligible for statutory maternity pay or the higher amount of MA may be eligible for a reduced rate of MA for either a 39-week or a 14-week period. For example, women who have not made enough Class 2 NI contributions or who take part in the business of their self-employed spouse or civil partner, for at least 26 weeks in the 66 weeks before their baby is due, and the work they do is unpaid.

Weekly Rates from April 2019	
Standard rate	£148.68 or 90 per cent of the woman's average weekly earnings if less than £148.68
39-week reduced rate	£27.00
14-week reduced rate	£27.00

CHILD BENEFIT
A person responsible for one or more children under 16 (or under 20 if they stay in approved education or training) is entitled to claim child benefit. There's no limit to the number of children that can be claimed for, but only one person can receive child benefit for a child. Child benefit is taxable if the claimant or their partner's individual income is over £50,000. An individual can choose not to receive child benefit payments, but they should still fill in the claim form in order to get National Insurance credits and to ensure the child is registered to get a National Insurance number when they become 16-years-old

Weekly Rates from April 2019	
Eldest/only child	£20.70
Each subsequent child	£13.70

GUARDIAN'S ALLOWANCE
Guardian's allowance is payable to a person who is bringing up a child or young person because the child's parents have died, or in some circumstances, where only one parent has died. To receive the allowance the person must be in receipt of child benefit for the child or young person, although they do not have to be the child's legal guardian.

Weekly Rate (in addition to child benefit) from April 2019	
Each child	£17.60

CARER'S ALLOWANCE
Carer's allowance (CA) is a benefit payable to people who spend at least 35 hours a week caring for a severely disabled person. To qualify for CA a person must be caring for someone in receipt of one of the following benefits:
- attendance allowance
- disability living allowance (middle or highest care rate)
- personal independence payment (daily living component)
- constant attendance allowance, paid at not less than the normal maximum rate with an industrial injuries disablement benefit or at the basic (full-day) rate with a war disablement pension
- armed forces independence payment

Weekly Rate from April 2019	
Carer's allowance	£66.15

ATTENDANCE ALLOWANCE
This may be payable to people aged 65 or over who need help with personal care because they are physically or mentally disabled, and who have needed help for a period of at least six months. Attendance allowance has two rates: the lower rate is for day or night care, and the higher rate is for day and night care. People not expected to live for more than six months because of a progressive disease can receive the highest rate of attendance allowance straight away.

Weekly Rates from April 2019	
Higher rate	£87.65
Lower rate	£58.70

PERSONAL INDEPENDENCE PAYMENT (PIP)

Personal independence payment (PIP) replaced disability living allowance (DLA) for people aged 16 to 64 on 8 April 2013. PIP has two components: the daily living component and the mobility component, with each offering two different benefit rates: standard and enhanced. Whether one or both components are claimed depends on the requirements of the individual. Claimants are assessed on their ability to carry out everyday activities, with the majority of claims evaluated via an interview. Claimants with a terminal illness automatically receive the enhanced daily living component.

Weekly Rates from April 2019	
Daily living component	
Standard	£58.70
Enhanced	£87.65
Mobility component	
Standard	£23.20
Enhanced	£61.20

STATE PENSION FOR PEOPLE AGED 80 AND OVER

A state pension, referred to as category D pension, is provided for people aged 80 and over if they are not entitled to another category of state pension or are entitled to a state pension that is less than £77.45 a week. The person must live in Great Britain and have done so for a period of ten years or more in any continuous 20-year period since their 60th birthday.

Weekly Rate from April 2019	
Single person	£77.45
Age addition	£0.25

INCOME SUPPORT

Broadly speaking income support is a benefit for those aged between 16 and pension credit qualifying age, whose income is below a certain level, work on average less than 16 hours a week and are:

- bringing up children alone
- registered sick or disabled
- a student who is also a lone parent or disabled
- caring for someone who is sick or elderly

Income support is being replaced by universal credit, new claims for income support can only be made by those entitled to the severe disability premium or those in receipt of it in the last month and who are still eligible.

Income support is not payable if the claimant, or claimant and partner, have capital or savings in excess of £16,000 – and deductions are made for capital and savings in excess of £6,000. For people permanently in residential care and nursing homes, deductions apply for capital over £10,000. A permanent address is not needed to claim income support.

Sums payable depend on fixed allowances laid down by law for people in different circumstances. If both partners are eligible for income support, either may claim it for the couple. People receiving income support may be able to receive housing benefit and help with healthcare. They may also be eligible for help with exceptional expenses from the Social Fund. Special rates may apply to some people living in residential care or nursing homes.

INCOME SUPPORT PREMIUMS

Income support premiums are extra weekly payments for those with additional needs. People qualifying for more than one premium will normally only receive the highest single premium for which they qualify. However, family premium, disabled child premium, severe disability premium and carer premium are payable in addition to other premiums.

Child tax credit replaced premiums for people with children for all new income support claims from 6 April 2004. People with children who were already in receipt of income support in April 2004 and have not claimed child tax credit may qualify for:

- the family premium if they have at least one child
- the disabled child premium if they have a child who receives disability living allowance or is registered blind
- the enhanced disability child premium if they have a child in receipt of the higher rate disability living allowance care component

Carers may qualify for the carer premium if they or their partner are in receipt of carer's allowance and Long-term sick or disabled people may qualify for the disability premium, the severe disability premium or the enhanced disability premium. People with a partner at state pension age may qualify for the pensioner premium.

WEEKLY RATES OF INCOME SUPPORT
from April 2019

Single person	
Aged under 18	£57.90
aged 25+	£73.10
Aged under 18 and a single parent	£57.90
Aged 18+ and a single parent	£73.10

Couples	
Both under 18	£57.90
Both under 18, in certain circumstances	£87.50
One under 18, one under 25	£57.90
One under 18, one aged 25+	£73.10
Both aged 18+	£114.85

Premiums	
Carer premium	£36.85
Severe disability premium	£65.85
Enhanced disability premium	
Single person	£16.80
Couples	£24.10
Pensioner premium (couple)	£140.40

PENSION CREDIT

To qualify for pension credit you must have reached state pension age. Since 15 May 2019 only couples where both parties have both reached state pension age, or one party is in receipt of housing benefit for people aged over state pension age, are eligible for pension credit. Couples not in receipt of pension credit could backdate their claim until 13 August 2019. Those already in receipt of pension credit under the old rules on 15 May 2019 will continue to receive it while they remain eligible. If their entitlement stops for any reason they can not start getting it again until they are eligible under the new rules. Those not entitled to pension credit can apply for universal credit instead.

Income from state pension, private pensions, earnings and most benefits are taken into account when calculating the pension credit. For savings and capital in excess of £10,000, £1 for every £500 or part of £500 held is taken into account as income when working out entitlement to pension credit.

There are two elements to pension credit:

THE GUARANTEE CREDIT

The guarantee credit guarantees a minimum income of £167.25 for single people and £255.25 for couples, with additional elements for people who have severe disabilities and caring responsibilities.

Weekly Rates from April 2019	
Additional amount for severe disability	
Single person	£65.85
Couple (one qualifies)	£65.85
Couple (both qualify)	£131.70
Additional amount for carers	£36.85

THE SAVINGS CREDIT

Savings Credit is only available to individuals and couples that reached state pension age before 6 April 2016. Those that have been in receipt of savings credit since before 6 April 2016, will continue to receive it as long as there are no breaks in their entitlement. If eligibility ceases the individual or couple will not be able to claim it again.

The savings credit is calculated by taking into account any qualifying income above the savings credit threshold. For 2019–20 the threshold is £144.38 for single people and £229.67 for couples. The maximum savings credit is £13.73 a week (£15.35 a week for couples).

HOUSING BENEFIT

Housing benefit is designed to help people with rent (including rent for accommodation in guesthouses, lodgings or hostels), but does not cover mortgage payments. This benefit is being replaced by universal credit (UC). Since May 2019, only new claimants in receipt of a severe disability premium, who have reached state pension age or who live in temporary accommodation or sheltered housing are eligible to make a claim for housing benefit. Couples are only eligible if both have reached state pension age or one party has reached state pension age and started claiming housing benefit or pension credit (as a couple) before 15 May 2019.

The amount of benefit paid depends on:
- the income of the claimant, and partner if there is one, including earned income, unearned income (any other income including some other benefits) and savings
- number of dependants
- certain extra needs of the claimant, partner or any dependants
- number and gross income of people sharing the home who are not dependent on the claimant
- how much rent is paid

Housing benefit is not payable if the claimant, or claimant and partner, have savings in excess of £16,000. The amount of benefit is affected if savings held exceed £6,000 (£10,000 for people living in residential care and nursing homes). Housing benefit is not paid for meals, fuel or certain service charges that may be included in the rent. Deductions are also made for most non-dependants who live in the same accommodation as the claimant (and their partner). If the claimant is living with a partner or civil partner there can only be one claim.

The maximum amount of benefit (which is not necessarily the same as the amount of rent paid) may be paid where the claimant is in receipt of income support, income-based jobseeker's allowance, the guarantee element of pension credit or where the claimant's income is less than the amount allowed for their needs. Any income over that allowed for their needs will mean that their benefit is reduced.

LOCAL HOUSING ALLOWANCE

Local Housing Allowance (LHA) is the name given to housing benefit for private renters. LHA rates are calculated for every local area based on local rents. The maximum amount of support a household can claim will depend on where they live, the minimum number of bedrooms they need and their income.

COUNCIL TAX REDUCTION

From April 2013, council tax benefit was replaced by council tax reduction. Nearly all the rules that apply to housing benefit apply to council tax reduction, which helps people on low incomes to pay council tax bills. The amount payable depends on how much council tax is paid and who lives with the claimant. The benefit may be available to those receiving income support, income-based jobseeker's allowance, the guarantee element of pension credit or to those whose income is less than that allowed for their needs. Any income over that allowed for their needs will mean that they will receive less help with their council tax reduction. Deductions are made for non-dependants.

A full council tax bill is based on at least two adults living in a home. Residents may receive a 25 per cent reduction on their bill if they count as an adult for council tax and live on their own. If the property is the resident's main home and there is no-one who counts as an adult, the reduction is 50 per cent.

THE SOCIAL FUND

REGULATED PAYMENTS

Sure Start Maternity Grant

Sure start maternity grant (SSMG) is a one-off payment of £500 (or £1,000 for multiple births of three or more) to help people in England, Wales and Northern Ireland on low incomes pay for essential items for new babies that are expected, born, adopted, the subject of a parental order (following a surrogate birth) or, in certain circumstances, the subject of a residency order. SSMG can be claimed any time within 11 weeks of the expected birth and up to six months after the birth, adoption or date of parental or residency order. Those eligible are people in receipt of universal credit, income support, income-based jobseeker's allowance, pension credit, child tax credit at a rate higher than the family element or working tax credit where a disability or severe disability element is in payment. SSMG is only available if there are no other children under 16 in the family, unless the claimant is expecting a multiple birth. There are also exceptions for those who have taken on responsibility for another's child (eg through adoption, legal guardianship or a parental order). Expectant parents in Scotland may be eligible for a pregnancy and baby payment as part of the 'best start' grant. *See* www.mygov.scot/best-start-grant for further information.

Funeral Expenses Payment

Payable to help cover the necessary cost of burial or cremation, a new burial plot, moving the body, the purchase of official documents and certificates and certain other expenses plus an additional payment of £700 for any other funeral expenses, such as the funeral director's fees, the coffin or flowers. Those eligible are people receiving universal credit, income support, income-based jobseeker's allowance, pension credit, child tax credit at a higher rate than the family element, working tax credit where a disability or severe disability element is in payment, council tax benefit or housing benefit who have good reason for taking responsibility for the funeral expenses, such as partner, child or parent of the deceased. These payments are recoverable from any estate of the deceased.

Cold Weather Payments

A payment of £25 per seven-day period between 1 November and 31 March when the average temperature is recorded at or forecast to be 0°C or below over seven consecutive days in the qualifying person's area. Payments are made to people on universal credit, pension credit or child tax credit with a disability element, those on income support whose benefit includes a pensioner or disability premium, and those on income-based jobseeker's allowance or employment and support allowance who have a child who is disabled or under the age of five. Payments are made automatically and do not have to be repaid.

Winter Fuel Payments

For 2019–20 the winter fuel payment is £200 for households with someone born on or before 5 April 1954 and £300 for households with someone aged 80 or over. The rate paid is based on the person's age and circumstances in the 'qualifying week' between 16 and 22 September 2019. The majority of eligible people are paid automatically between November and December, although a few need to claim. Payments do not have to be repaid.

Christmas Bonus

The Christmas bonus is a one-off tax-free £10 payment made before Christmas to those people in receipt of a qualifying benefit in the qualifying week (usually the first full week of December).

DISCRETIONARY PAYMENTS

Finance Support – Northern Ireland

The Northern Ireland (Welfare Reform) Act 2016 introduced Finance Support to replace Crisis Loans and Community Care Grants on 31 October 2016. Since 31 October 2016, people suffering a financial crisis are able to apply for a discretionary support loan or short term benefit advance from the Finance Support Service (**W** www.nidirect.gov.uk/contacts/contacts-az/finance-support-service-times-crisis-and-need). To receive discretionary support, the applicant must have a crisis which places themselves or their family's health, safety or wellbeing at significant risk. Applicants must be a resident of Northern Ireland and be over 18-years-old (16-years-old if they do not have any parental support) and be earning less than the national living wage. If eligible, the applicant may be offered a discretionary support loan or grant; usually no more than three loans and one grant can be awarded within a 12-month period.

Short-term benefit advances are available to those that have an urgent financial need that may impact the applicant or their family's health, safety or wellbeing. The applicant must be able to afford to repay the advance within 12 weeks.

If an applicant's combined discretionary support and short-term benefit advance debt is £1,000 or more they will not be able to get further support until their debt falls below this limit.

Budgeting Loans

These are interest-free loans to people who have been receiving universal credit, income support, income-based jobseeker's allowance or income-related employment and support allowance or pension credit for the past six months, for intermittent expenses that may be difficult to budget for. Those claiming universal credit can apply for a budgeting advance instead. The smallest borrowable amount is £100.

SAVINGS

Savings of £1,000 (£2,000 if the applicant or their partner is aged 63 or over) are taken into account for budgeting loans. Savings are not taken into account for sure start maternity grant, funeral payments, cold weather payments, winter fuel payments or the Christmas bonus.

INDUSTRIAL INJURIES AND DISABLEMENT BENEFITS

The Industrial Injuries Scheme, administered under the Social Security Contributions and Benefits Act 1992, provides a range of benefits designed to compensate for disablement resulting from an industrial accident (ie an accident arising out of and in the course of an earner's employment) or from a prescribed disease due to the nature of a person's employment. Those who are self-employed are not covered by this scheme.

INDUSTRIAL INJURIES DISABLEMENT BENEFIT

A person may be able to claim industrial injuries disablement benefit if they are ill or disabled due to an accident or incident that happened at work or in connection with work in England, Scotland or Wales. The amount of benefit awarded depends on the person's age and the degree of disability as assessed by a doctor.

The benefit is payable whether the person works or not and those who are incapable of work are entitled to draw other benefits, such as statutory sick pay or incapacity benefit, in addition to industrial injuries disablement benefit. It may also be possible to claim the following allowances:

- reduced earnings allowance for those who are unable to return to their regular work or work of the same standard and who had their accident (or whose disease started) before 1 October 1990. At state pension age this is converted to retirement allowance
- constant attendance allowance for those with a disablement of 100 per cent who need constant care. There are four rates of allowance depending on how much care the person needs
- exceptionally severe disablement allowance can be claimed in addition to constant care attendance allowance at one of the higher rates for those who need constant care permanently

Weekly Rates from April 2019

Degree of disablement	Aged 18+ or with dependants
100 per cent	£179.00
90	£161.10
80	£143.20
70	£125.30
60	£107.40
50	£89.50
40	£71.60
30	£53.70
20	£35.80
Unemployability supplement	£110.65
Reduced earnings allowance (max)	£71.60
Retirement allowance (max)	£17.90
Constant attendance allowance (normal max rate)	£71.60
Exceptionally severe disablement allowance	£71.60

OTHER BENEFITS

People who are disabled because of an accident or disease that was the result of work that they did before 5 July 1948 are not entitled to industrial injuries disablement benefit. They may, however, be entitled under the Workmen's Compensation Scheme or the Pneumoconiosis, Byssinosis and Miscellaneous Diseases Benefit Scheme. People who suffer from certain industrial diseases caused by dust can make a claim for an additional payment under the Pneumoconiosis Act 1979 if they are unable to get damages from the employer responsible.

Diffuse Mesothelioma Payments (2008 Scheme)

Since 1 October 2008 any person suffering from the asbestos-related disease, diffuse mesothelioma, who is unable to make a claim under the Pneumoconiosis Act 1979, have not received payment in respect of the disease from an employer, via a civil claim or elsewhere, and are not entitled to compensation from a MoD scheme, can claim a one-off lump sum payment. The scheme covers people whose exposure to asbestos occurred in the UK and was not as a result of their work (ie they lived near a factory using asbestos). The amount paid depends on the age of the person when the disease was diagnosed, or the date of the claim if the diagnosis date is not known. The current rate is £92,259 for those who were diagnosed aged 37 and under to £14,334 for persons aged 77 and over at the time of diagnosis. Since 1 October 2009 claims must be received within 12 months of the date of diagnosis. If the sufferer has died, their dependants may be able to claim, but must do so within 12 months of the date of death.

CLAIMS AND QUESTIONS

Entitlement to benefit and regulated Social Fund payments is determined by a decision maker on behalf of the Secretary of State for the Department for Work and Pensions. A claimant who is dissatisfied with that decision can ask for an explanation. He or she can dispute the decision by applying to have it revised or, in particular circumstances, superseded. The claimant can appeal to the First-tier Tribunal (Social Security and Child Support). There is a further right of appeal to the Administrative Appeals Chamber of the Upper Tribunal (*see* Tribunals).

Decisions on claims and applications for housing benefit and council tax benefit are made by local authorities. The explanation, dispute and appeals process is the same as for other benefits.

All decisions on applications to the discretionary Social Fund are made by Jobcentre Plus Social Fund decision makers. Applicants can ask for a review of the decision within 28 days of the date on the decision letter. As above, the claimant has a right of appeal to the First-tier Tribunal (Social Security and Child Support).

EMPLOYER PAYMENTS

STATUTORY MATERNITY PAY

Employers pay statutory maternity pay (SMP) to pregnant women who have been employed by them, full or part-time, continuously for at least 26 weeks into the 15th week before the week the baby is due, and whose earnings on average at least equal the lower earnings limit applied to NI contributions (£118 a week if the end of the qualifying week is in the 2019–20 tax year). SMP can be paid for a period of up to 39 weeks. If the qualifying conditions are met women will receive a payment of 90 per cent of their average earnings for the first six weeks, followed by 33 weeks at £148.68 or 90 per cent of the woman's average weekly earnings if this is less than £148.68. SMP can be paid, at the earliest, 11 weeks before the week in which the baby is due, up to the day following the birth. Women can decide when they wish their maternity leave and pay to start and can work until the baby is born. However, where the woman is absent from work wholly or partly due to her pregnancy in the four weeks before the week the baby is due to be born, SMP will start the day following the first day of absence from work.

Employers are reimbursed for 92 per cent of the SMP they pay. Small employers with annual gross NI payments of £45,000 or less recover 103 per cent of the SMP paid out.

STATUTORY PATERNITY PAY

Employers pay statutory paternity pay (SPP) to employees who are taking leave when a child is born or placed for adoption. To qualify the employee must:

• be the father or the intended parent (ie in a surrogacy arrangement)
• be the husband or partner of the mother (or adopter) – this includes same-sex partners
• be the child's adopter
• have been employed continuously by the same employer for at least 26 weeks ending with the 15th week before the baby is due (or the week in which the adopter is notified of having been matched with a child)

• continue working for the employer up to the child's birth (or placement for adoption) and give the correct notice
• be earning an average of at least £118 a week (before tax)

Employees who meet these conditions receive payment of £148.68 or 90 per cent of the employee's average weekly earnings if this is less than £148.68. The employee can choose to be paid for one or two consecutive weeks. The SPP period can not start before the birth of the child or date of placement for adoption and must be completed within eight weeks of that date. SPP is not payable for any week in which the employee works. Employers are reimbursed in the same way as for statutory maternity pay.

STATUTORY ADOPTION PAY

Employers pay statutory adoption pay (SAP) to employees taking adoption leave from their employers. To qualify for SAP the employee must:

• have been continuously employed by the same employer for at least 26 weeks ending up to any day in the week in which they were matched with a child
• be earning an average of at least £118 a week (before tax) during the 'relevant' eight week period
• have given the correct notice and provided proof of the adoption or surrogacy
• have permission from a UK authority, in cases where the child is being adopted from abroad

Employees who meet these conditions receive payment of £148.68 or 90 per cent of their average weekly earnings if this is less than £148.68 for up to 39 weeks. The earliest SAP can be paid from is two weeks before the expected date of placement (UK adoptions), on the date the employee is matched with a child (UK adoptions), on arrival of the child in the UK or within 28 days of this date (overseas adoptions) or the day or day after the child's birth in surrogacy arrangements. Where a couple adopt a child, only one of them may receive SAP, the other may be able to receive statutory paternity pay if they meet the eligibility criteria. Employers are reimbursed in the same way as for statutory maternity pay.

STATUTORY SHARED PARENTAL PAY

The Children and Families Act 2014 provided parents greater flexibility to maternity and paternity provisions. Shared parental leave (SPL) provides up to 50 weeks of leave and 37 weeks of pay for couples having a baby or adopting a child. The leave and pay is shared between the couple in the first year after the birth or, in the case of adoption, placement of the child. SPL is flexible and can be used in blocks separated by periods of work, or taken all in one go. Couples can also choose to be off work together or to stagger the leave and pay. There are different eligibility criteria for birth and adoptive parents. For further information *see* **W** www.gov.uk/shared-parental-leave-and-pay

The current rate of statutory shared parental pay is £148.68 a week or 90 per cent of the employee's average weekly earnings if this is less than £148.68. The earnings threshold is the same as for SMP and SPP (£118 a week (before tax)).

STATUTORY SICK PAY

Employers pay statutory sick pay (SSP) for up to 28 weeks, to any employee incapable of work for four or more consecutive days (including non-working days). Employees must have done some work under their contract of service, have average weekly earnings of at least £118 a week (before tax) and inform their employer they are sick before their employer's deadline, or within seven days if their employer does not have a deadline. SSP is a daily payment and is usually paid for the days that an employee would normally work. SSP is paid at £94.25 a week and is subject to PAYE and NI contributions.

THE WATER INDUSTRY

In the UK, the water industry provides clean and safe drinking water to over 60 million homes and has an estimated annual economic impact of over £15bn. It supplies around 17 billion litres of water a day to domestic and commercial customers and collects and treats more than 16 billion litres of wastewater a day. It also manages assets that include around 1,400 water treatment and 9,350 wastewater treatment works, 550 impounding reservoirs, over 6,500 service reservoirs/water towers and 800,000km of water mains and sewers.

Water services in England and Wales are provided by private companies. In Scotland and Northern Ireland there are single authorities, Scottish Water and Northern Ireland Water, that are publicly owned companies answerable to their respective governments. In drinking water quality tests carried out in 2018 by the Drinking Water Inspectorate, the water industry in England and Wales achieved 99.95 per cent compliance with the standards required by the EU Drinking Water Directive; Scotland achieved 99.91 per cent and Northern Ireland 99.88 per cent.

In 2016, the Drinking Water Inspectorate (DWI) introduced the Compliance Risk Index (CRI) to illustrate the risk arising from failing to meet water safety standards and the proportion of consumers potentially at risk. In 2019, the CRI for England and Wales was 2.80, an improvement on 3.87 in 2018.

Water UK is the industry association that represents all UK water and wastewater service suppliers at national and European level and is funded directly by its members, the service suppliers for England, Scotland, Wales and Northern Ireland, of which each has a seat on the Water UK Council.

WATER UK, 3rd Floor, 36 Broadway, London SW1H 0BH
  T 020-7344 1844 W www.water.org.uk
  Chief Executive, Christine McGourty

ENGLAND AND WALES

In England and Wales, the Secretary of State for Environment, Food and Rural Affairs and the Welsh government have overall responsibility for water policy and oversee environmental standards for the water industry.

The statutory consumer representative body for water services is the Consumer Council for Water.

CONSUMER COUNCIL FOR WATER, 1st Floor, Victoria Square House, Victoria Square, Birmingham B2 4AJ
  T 0300-034 2222 (England) & 0300-034 3333 (Wales)
  W www.ccwater.org.uk

REGULATORY BODIES
The Water Services Regulation Authority (OFWAT) was established in 1989 when the water and sewerage industry in England and Wales was privatised. Its statutory role and duties are laid out under the Water Industry Act 1991 and it is the independent economic regulator of the water and sewerage companies in England and Wales. OFWAT's main duties are to ensure that the companies can finance and carry out their statutory functions and to protect the interests of water customers. OFWAT is a non-ministerial government department headed by a board following a change in legislation introduced by the Water Act 2003.

Under the Competition Act 1998, from 1 March 2000 the Competition Appeal Tribunal has heard appeals against the regulator's decisions regarding anti-competitive agreements and abuse of a dominant position in the marketplace. The Water Act 2003 placed a new duty on OFWAT to contribute to the achievement of sustainable development.

The Environment Agency has statutory duties and powers in relation to water resources, pollution control, flood defence, fisheries, recreation, conservation and navigation in England and Wales. It is also responsible for issuing permits, licences, consents and registrations such as industrial licences to extract water and fishing licences.

The Drinking Water Inspectorate (DWI) is the drinking water quality regulator for England and Wales, responsible for assessing the quality of drinking water supplied by the water companies and investigating any incidents affecting drinking water quality, initiating prosecution where necessary. The DWI science and policy group provides scientific advice on drinking water policy to DEFRA and the Welsh government.

OFWAT, Centre City Tower, 7 Hill Street, Birmingham B5 4UA
  W www.ofwat.gov.uk
  Chair, Jonson Cox
  Chief Executive, Rachel Fletcher

METHODS OF CHARGING
In England and Wales, most domestic customers still pay for domestic water supply and sewerage services through charges based on the rateable value of their property. Currently around half of household customers in England and Wales have a metered supply. Nearly all non-household customers are charged according to consumption.

Under the Water Industry Act 1999, water companies can continue basing their charges on the old rateable value of the property. Domestic customers can continue paying on an unmeasured basis unless they choose to pay according to consumption. After having a meter installed (which is free of charge), a customer can revert to unmeasured charging within 12 months. However, water companies may charge by meter for new homes, or homes where there is a high discretionary use of water. Domestic, school and hospital customers cannot be disconnected for non-payment.

In December 2019, OFWAT finalised its 2019 price review decisions for household water bills for the five-year period to 2025. This means that average bills for water and wastewater customers in England and Wales will decreased by around 12 per cent, before adjustments for inflation, between 2020 and 2025; an average household bill decrease of around £50 compared with the previous period.

AVERAGE HOUSEHOLD BILLS 2018–21 *(£)*
WATER AND SEWERAGE COMPANIES

| | 2018–19 | 2019–20 | 2020–21 |
	(£)	(£)	(£)
Anglian	429	438	412
Dwr Cymru	445	445	451
Hafren Dyfrdwy	289	296	300
Northumbrian	403	411	326
Severn Trent	347	356	358
South West	499	487	470
Southern	396	440	391
Thames	385	396	394
United Utilities	435	443	420
Wessex	489	487	447
Yorkshire	387	392	406
Average	404	413	397

WATER ONLY COMPANIES

	2018–19	2019–20	2020–21
	(£)	(£)	(£)
Affinity*	191	188	175
Bournmouth	147	150	136
Bristol	184	187	177
Cambridge	141	139	139
Essex and Suffolk	258	257	223
Portsmouth	105	106	102
South East	210	211	210
South Staffs	147	146	149
SES	195	199	187
Average	191	192	186

* Average figures from central, east and south-east regions
Source: Water UK

SCOTLAND

In 2002 the three existing water authorities in Scotland (East of Scotland Water, North of Scotland Water and West of Scotland Water) merged to form Scottish Water. Scottish Water, which serves more than 2.5 million households and provides 1.4 billion litres of water per day while removing almost one billion litres of waste water, is a public sector company, structured and managed like a private company, but remains answerable to the Scottish parliament. Scottish Water is regulated by the Water Industry Commission for Scotland (established under the Water Services (Scotland) Act 2005), the Scottish Environment Protection Agency (SEPA) and the Drinking Water Quality Regulator for Scotland. The Water Industry Commissioner is responsible for regulating all aspects of economic and customer service performance, including water and sewerage charges. SEPA, created under the Environment Act 1995, is responsible for environmental issues, including controlling pollution and promoting the cleanliness of Scotland's rivers, lochs and coastal waters. The Public Services Reform (Scotland) Act 2010 transferred the complaints handling function of Waterwatch Scotland regarding Scottish Water, to the Scottish Public Services Ombudsman. Consumer Futures represented the views and interests of Scottish Water customers but became part of Citizens Advice Scotland in 2014.

METHODS OF CHARGING
Scottish Water sets charges for domestic and non-domestic water and sewerage provision through charges schemes which are regulated by the Water Industry Commission for Scotland. In February 2004 the harmonisation of all household charges across the country was completed following the merger of the separate authorities under Scottish Water. In October 2010 the Water Industry Commission for Scotland published *The Strategic Review of Charges 2021–2027*, stating that annual price rises would not increase at more than £2 a month above inflation for any Scottish household. For the year 2020–21, the combined service charge, covering the water supply and waste water collection, increased by 0.9 per cent on the previous year; resulting in an annual average household bill of £372.

CITIZENS ADVICE SCOTLAND, W www.cas.org.uk

DRINKING WATER QUALITY REGULATOR FOR
SCOTLAND, Area 3-J South, Victoria Quay, Edinburgh EH6 6QQ T 0131-244 0190 W www.dwqr.scot

SCOTTISH ENVIRONMENT PROTECTION AGENCY,
Third Floor, Silvan House, 231 Corstorphine Road, Edinburgh EH12 7AT T 0131-449 7296 W www.sepa.org.uk

SCOTTISH PUBLIC SERVICES OMBUDSMAN,
Bridgewater House, 99 McDonald Rd, Edinburgh EH7 4NS T 0800-377 7330 W www.spso.org.uk

SCOTTISH WATER, Castle House, 6 Castle Drive, Dunfermline KY11 8GG T 0800-077 8778 W www.scottishwater.co.uk
Chief Executive, Douglas Millican

WATER INDUSTRY COMMISSION FOR SCOTLAND,
First Floor, Moray House, Forthside Way, Stirling FK8 1QZ
T 01786-430200 W www.watercommission.co.uk

NORTHERN IRELAND

Formerly an executive agency of the Department for Regional Development, Northern Ireland Water is a government-owned company but with substantial independence from government. Northern Ireland Water was set up as a result of government reform of water and sewerage services in April 2007. It is responsible for policy and coordination with regard to the supply, distribution and cleanliness of water, and the provision and maintenance of sewerage services. It supplies 560 million litres of clean water a day to around 840,000 households and treats 330 million litres of waste water each day. The Northern Ireland Authority for Utility Regulation (known as the Utility Regulator) is responsible for regulating the water services provided by Northern Ireland Water. The Drinking Water Inspectorate, a unit in the Northern Ireland Environment Agency (NIEA), regulates drinking water quality. Another NIEA unit, the Water Management Unit, has responsibility for the protection of the aquatic environment. The Consumer Council for Northern Ireland is the consumer representative body for water services.

METHODS OF CHARGING
The water and sewerage used by metered domestic customers in Northern Ireland is currently paid for by the Department for Infrastructure (un-metered domestic customers pay 50 per cent of the full charge), however the future of the subsidy system is uncertain. Non-domestic customers in Northern Ireland became subject to water and sewerage charges and trade effluent charges where applicable in April 2008.

CONSUMER COUNCIL FOR NORTHERN IRELAND,
Seatem House, 28–32 Alfred Street, Belfast BT2 8EN
T 028-9025 1600 W www.consumercouncil.org.uk

NORTHERN IRELAND AUTHORITY FOR UTILITY
REGULATION, Queens House, 14 Queen Street, Belfast BT1 6ED T 028-9031 1575 W www.uregni.gov.uk

NORTHERN IRELAND WATER, Westland House, 40 Old
Westland Road, Belfast BT14 6TE T 0345-744 0088
W www.niwater.com
Chief Executive, Sara Venning

WATER SERVICE COMPANIES

WATER UK MEMBERS
AFFINITY WATER, Tamblin Way, Hatfield, Herts AL10 9EZ
T 0345-357 2407 W www.affinitywater.co.uk

ALBION WATER, Harpenden Hall, Southdown Road,
Harpenden, Herts AL5 1TE T 03300-342020
W www.albionwater.co.uk

ANGLIAN WATER SERVICES LTD, Lancaster House,
Lancaster Way, Huntington PE29 6YJ T 01480-32300
W www.anglianwater.co.uk

BRISTOL WATER PLC, Bridgwater Road, Bristol BS13 7AX
T 0345-702 3797 W www.bristolwater.co.uk

CAMBRIDGE WATER COMPANY, 90 Fulborn Road,
Cambridge CB1 9JN T 01223-706050
W www.cambridge-water.co.uk

DWR CYMRU (WELSH WATER), Pentwyn Road, Nelson,
Treharris, Mid Glamorgan CF46 6LY T 0800-052 0145
W www.dwrcymru.co.uk

ESSEX & SUFFOLK WATER PLC (subsidiary of Northumbrian Water Ltd), Sandon Valley House, Cannon Barnes Road, Chelmsford CM3 8BD **T** 0345-782 0111 **W** www.eswater.co.uk

HAFREN DYFRDWY WATER Packsaddle/ Wrexham Road, Rhostyllen, Wrexham, Clwyd LL14 4EH **T** 0330-678 0679 **W** www.hdcymru.co.uk

ICOSA WATER LTD, Sophia House, 28 Cathedral Road, Cardiff CF11 9LI **T** 0330-111 0780 **W** www.icosawater.co.uk

INDEPENDENT WATER NETWORKS, Driscoll 2, Ellen Street, Cardiff CF10 4BP **T** 029-2002 8711 **W** www.iwnl.co.uk

LEEP UTILITIES, The Greenhouse, MediaCityUK, Salford M50 2EQ **T** 0345-122 6786 **W** www.leeputilities.co.uk

NORTHERN IRELAND WATER, Westland House, Old Westland Road, Belfast BT14 6TE **T** 0345-733 0088 **W** www.niwater.com

NORTHUMBRIAN WATER LTD, Northumbria House, Abbey Road, Pity Me, Durham DH1 5FJ **T** 0345-717 1100 **W** www.nwl.co.uk

PORTSMOUTH WATER PLC, PO Box 99, West Street, Havant, Hants PO9 1LG **T** 023-9249 9888 **W** www.portsmouthwater.co.uk

SCOTTISH WATER, Castle House, 6 Castle Drive, Carnegie Campus, Dunfermline KY11 8GG **T** 0800-077 8778 **W** www.scottishwater.co.uk

SEVERN TRENT WATER PLC, PO Box 407, Darlington DL1 9WD **T** 0345-570 0500 **W** www.stwater.co.uk

SOUTH EAST WATER LTD, Rocfort Road, Snodland, Kent ME6 5AH **T** 0333-000 0001 **W** www.southeastwater.co.uk

SOUTH STAFFS WATER PLC, Green Lane, Walsall WS2 7PD **T** 0845-607 0456 **W** www.south-staffs-water.co.uk

SOUTH WEST WATER LTD, Peninsula House, Rydon Lane, Exeter EX2 7HR **T** 0344-346 1010 **W** www.southwestwater.co.uk

SOUTHERN WATER SERVICES LTD, Southern House, Yeoman Road, Worthing BN13 3NX **T** 0330-303 0277 **W** www.southernwater.co.uk

SES WATER PLC, London Road, Redhill, Surrey RH1 1LJ **T** 01737-772000 **W** www.seswater.co.uk

THAMES WATER UTILITIES LTD, Clearwater Court, Vastern Road, Reading RG1 8DB **T** 0800-980 8800 **W** www.thameswater.co.uk

UNITED UTILITIES WATER PLC, Haweswater House, Lingley Mere Business Park, Great Sankey, Warrington WA5 3LP **T** 0345-672 2888 **W** www.unitedutilities.com

VEOLIA WATER PROJECTS, 210 Pentonville Road, London N1 9JY**T** 020-7812 5000 **W** www.veolia.co.uk

WESSEX WATER SERVICES LTD, Claverton Down, Bath BA2 7WW **T** 0345-6004 600 **W** www.wessexwater.co.uk

YORKSHIRE WATER SERVICES LTD, Western House, Western Way, Bradford BD6 2LZ **T** 0345-124 2424 **W** www.yorkshirewater.com

ASSOCIATE MEMBERS
(not members of Water UK)

GUERNSEY WATER, PO Box 30, Brickfield House, St Andrew, Guernsey GY1 3AS **T** 01481-239500 **W** www.water.gg

IRISH WATER (UISCE EIREANN), Colvill House, 24–26 Talbot Street, Dublin 1 **T** (+353) (1) 707 2828 **W** www.water.ie

JERSEY WATER, Mulcaster House, Westmount Road, St Helier, Jersey JE1 1DG **T** 01534-707300 **W** www.jerseywater.je

TIDEWAY (BAZALGETTE TUNNEL LTD), Cottons Centre, Cottons Land, London SE1 2QG **T** 0800-308 080 **W** www.tideway.london

ENERGY

The main primary sources of energy in Britain are coal, oil, natural gas, renewables and nuclear power. The main secondary sources are electricity, coke and smokeless fuels and petroleum products. The UK was a net importer of fuels in the 1970s, however as a result of growth in oil and gas production from the North Sea, the UK became a net exporter of energy for most of the 1980s. Output decreased in the late 1980s following the Piper Alpha disaster until the mid-1990s, after which the UK again became a net exporter. Since 2004, the UK has reverted back to become a net importer of energy. However, in 2019 the UK net import gap decreased for the sixth consecutive year – from the 2013 peak of 104 million tonnes of oil equivalent – to 70 million tonnes of oil equivalent, accounting for 35.2 per cent of the total energy used in the UK.

The Department for Business, Energy and Industrial Strategy (DBEIS) is responsible for promoting energy efficiency.

INDIGENOUS PRODUCTION OF PRIMARY FUELS
Million tonnes of oil equivalent

	2018	2019
Primary oils	55.7	56.8
Natural gas	38.9	37.8
Primary electricity	20.5	20.4
Coal	1.8	1.5
Bioenergy and waste	13.5	13.8
Total	130.4	130.2

Source: DBEIS

INLAND ENERGY CONSUMPTION BY PRIMARY FUEL
Million tonnes of oil equivalent

	2018	2019
Natural gas	75.3	74.3
Petroleum	68.8	68.0
Coal	8.6	6.1
Nuclear electricity	14.1	13.3
Bioenergy and waste	17.5	18.9
Wind and hydro electricity	6.5	7.2
Net Imports	1.6	1.8
Total	192.4	189.5

Source: DBEIS

TRADE IN FUELS AND RELATED MATERIALS (2019)

	Quantity, million tonnes of oil equivalent	Value £m
Imports		
Crude oil	57.1	19,480
Petroleum products	36.3	16,375
Natural gas	44.5	6,965
Coal and other solid fuel	10.5	1,600
Electricity	2.1	1,015
Total	150.6	45,435
Exports		
Crude oil	49.1	18,290
Petroleum products	22.7	11,245
Natural gas	7.5	1,125
Coal and other solid fuel	0.9	90
Electricity	0.3	140
Total	80.5	30,890

Source: DBEIS, ONS

OIL

Until the 1960s Britain imported almost all its oil supplies. In 1969 oil was discovered in the Arbroath field in the North Sea. The first oilfield to be brought into production was Argyll in 1975, and since the mid-1970s Britain has been a major producer of crude oil.

To date, the UK has produced around 3.9 billion tonnes of oil. It is estimated that there are around 481 million tonnes remaining to be produced. Licences for exploration and production are granted to companies by the Oil and Gas Authority. As at July 2019, there were 285 offshore oil and gas fields in production. Total UK oil production peaked in 1999 but is now on a long-term trajectory of gradual decline. Production stood at 52.2 million tonnes in 2019, just over a third of the 1999 level. Profits from oil production are subject to a special tax regime with different taxes applying depending on the date of approval of each field.

INDIGENOUS PRODUCTION AND REFINERY RECEIPTS
Thousand tonnes

	2018	2019
Indigenous production	51,234	52,186
Crude oil	47,550	48,743
*NGLs	3,320	3,074
Refinery receipts	58,397	59,158

* Natural Gas Liquids: condensates and petroleum gases derived at onshore treatment plants
Source: DBEIS

DELIVERIES OF PETROLEUM PRODUCTS FOR INLAND CONSUMPTION BY ENERGY USE
Thousand tonnes

	2018	2019
Transport	49,999	49,470
Industry	2,397	2,153
Domestic	2,290	2,267
Other	3,351	3,381
Total	58,388	57,271

Source: DBEIS

COAL

Mines were in private ownership until 1947 when they were nationalised and came under the management of the National Coal Board, later the British Coal Corporation. The corporation held a near monopoly on coal production until 1994 when the industry was restructured. Under the Coal Industry Act 1994, the Coal Authority was established to take over ownership of coal reserves and to issue licences to private mining companies. The Coal Authority is also responsible for the physical legacy of mining, eg subsidence damage claims that are not the responsibility of licensees, and for holding and making available all existing records. It also publishes current data on the coal industry on its website (**W** www.gov.uk/government/organisations/the-coal-authority).

The mines owned by the British Coal Corporation were sold as five separate businesses in 1994 and coal production is now undertaken entirely in the private sector. Coal output was around 50 million tonnes a year in 1994 but has since declined. In 2019, coal output stood at a record low of 2.2 million tonnes, a decrease of 16 per cent on 2018 and about 7 per cent of the value recorded at the start of the century. The decrease was mainly due to a decrease in demand for coal fired electricity. Deep mine production of coal virtually ceased and accounted for only 5 per cent of production, while surface mined production decreased by 19 per cent. As at 31 December 2019, there were eight deep mines and nine surface mines in production in the UK, additionally one deep mine and one surface mine are in 'care and maintenance'.

The main consumer of coal in the UK is the electricity supply industry. Coal supplies 3 per cent of the UK's electricity needs, but as indigenous production has declined imports have continued to make up the shortfall and now represent 82 per cent of UK coal supply, 37 per cent of which is currently supplied from Russia.

UK government policy is to meet the long-term challenges posed by climate change while continuing to ensure secure, clean and affordable energy. Coal's carbon emissions are high compared to other fuels so the UK government is committed to ending unabated coal generation by 2024. In the future generating mix carbon emissions will need to be managed through the introduction of abatement technologies including carbon capture and storage (CCS).

CCS attempts to mitigate the effects of global warming by capturing the carbon dioxide emissions from power stations that burn fossil fuels, preventing the gas from being released into the atmosphere, and storing it in underground geological formations. CCS is still in its infancy and only through its successful demonstration and development will it be possible for coal to remain a part of a low-carbon UK energy mix. As part of a wider package of reforms to the electricity market, the government will also be introducing an Emissions Performance Standard, which will limit the emissions from new fossil fuel power stations.

INLAND COAL USE
Thousand tonnes

	2018	2019
Fuel producers		
Electricity generators	6,655	2,906
Coke manufacture	1,766	1,809
Blast furnaces	1,156	1,135
Heat generation	6	6
Patent fuel manufacture	194	144
Final consumption		
Industry	1,581	1,426
Transport	15	15
Domestic	518	492
Public administration	26	19
Commercial	5	5
Agriculture	0	0
Miscellaneous	7	7

Source: DBEIS

COAL PRODUCTION AND FOREIGN TRADE
Thousand tonnes

	2018	2019
Surface mining	2,556	2,067
Deep-mined	24	99
Imports	10,144	6,529
Exports	(634)	(740)
*Total supply	11,922	7,971
Total demand	11,929	7,963

* Includes stock change
Source: DBEIS

GAS

From the late 18th century gas in Britain was produced from coal. In the 1960s town gas began to be produced from oil-based feedstocks using imported oil. In 1965 gas was discovered in the North Sea in the West Sole field, which became the first gasfield in production in 1967, and from the late 1960s natural gas began to replace town gas. From October 1998 Britain was connected to the continental European gas system via a pipeline from Bacton, Norfolk to Zeebrugge, Belgium. Gas is transported through 278,000km of mains pipeline including 7,600km of high-pressure gas pipelines owned and operated in the UK by National Grid Gas plc.

The gas industry in Britain was nationalised in 1949 and operated as the Gas Council. The Gas Council was replaced by the British Gas Corporation in 1972 and the industry became more centralised. The British Gas Corporation was privatised in 1986 as British Gas plc. In 1993 the Monopolies and Mergers Commission found that British Gas's integrated business in Great Britain as a gas trader and the owner of the gas transportation system could operate against the public interest. In February 1997, British Gas demerged its trading arm to become two separate companies, BG plc and Centrica plc. In February 2016, Royal Dutch Shell announced that it had acquired BG Group, whose principal business was finding and developing gas reserves and building gas markets. Its core operations are located in the UK, South America, Egypt, Trinidad and Tobago, Kazakhstan and India. Centrica runs the trading and services operations under the British Gas brand name in Great Britain. In October 2000 BG demerged its pipeline business, Transco, which became part of Lattice Group, finally merging with the National Grid Group in 2002 to become National Grid Transco plc.

In July 2005 National Grid Transco plc changed its name to National Grid plc and Transco plc became National Grid Gas plc. In the same year National Grid Gas also completed the sale of four of its eight gas distribution networks. The distribution networks transport gas at lower pressures, which eventually supply the consumers such as domestic customers. The Scotland and south-east of England networks were sold to Scotia Gas Networks. The Wales and south-west network was sold to Wales & West Utilities and the network in the north-east to Northern Gas Networks. This was the biggest change in the corporate structure of gas infrastructure since privatisation in 1986.

Competition was gradually introduced into the industrial gas market from 1986. Supply of gas to the domestic market was opened to companies other than British Gas, starting in April 1996 with a pilot project in the West Country and Wales, with the rest of the UK following soon after.

Declines in UK indigenous gas production and increasing demand led to the UK becoming a net importer of gas once more in 2004. With the depletion of the UK Continental Shelf reserves, UK annual gas production has experienced decline since the turn of the century, where annual production is 65 per cent below the peak recorded in 2000. As part of the Energy Act 2008, the government planned to strengthen regulation of the offshore gas supply infrastructure, to allow private sector investment to help maintain UK energy supplies.

In 2012, it was estimated that there could be over 200 trillion cubic feet of untapped gas underneath Lincolnshire. Trapped inside rock formations, the gas is known as shale gas and the process to release the gas is called hydraulic fracturing or fracking, whereby water, chemicals and sand are pumped into a drilled well at high pressure. A further investigation by the British Geological Survey in 2012 claimed that there could in fact be up to 1,300 trillion cubic feet of gas but opponents to the process raised concerns that fracking results in more greenhouse gas emissions than conventional gas, damages the environment significantly and that it may cause seismic tremors.

CENTRICA PLC, Millstream, Maidenhead Road, Windsor, Berkshire SL4 5GD T 01753-494000 W www.centrica.com
Chair, Scott Wheway
Chief Executive, Chris O'Shea

NATIONAL GRID PLC, 1–3 Strand, London WC2N 5EH
T 0207-0043 000 W www.nationalgrid.com
Chair, Sir Peter Gershon, CBE
Chief Executive, John Pettigrew

UK GAS CONSUMPTION BY INDUSTRY
GWh

	2018	2019
Domestic	312,770	309,934
Industry	102,966	101,766
Public administration	37,697	36,961
Commercial	47,541	47,871
Agriculture	995	1,078
Non-energy use	4,807	4,663
Miscellaneous	10,105	9,837
Total gas consumption	516,880	512,110

Source: DBEIS

ELECTRICITY

The first power station in Britain generating electricity for public supply began operating in 1882. In the 1930s a national transmission grid was developed, and it was reconstructed and extended in the 1950s and 1960s. Power stations were operated by the Central Electricity Generating Board.

Under the Electricity Act 1989, 12 regional electricity companies, responsible for the distribution of electricity from the national grid to consumers, were formed from the former area electricity boards in England and Wales. Four companies were formed from the Central Electricity Generating Board: three generating companies (National Power plc, Nuclear Electric plc and Powergen plc) and the National Grid Company plc, which owned and operated the transmission system in England and Wales. National Power and Powergen were floated on the stock market in 1991.

National Power was demerged in October 2000 to form two separate companies: International Power plc and Innogy plc, which manages the bulk of National Power's UK assets. Nuclear Electric was split into two parts in 1996.

The National Grid Company was floated on the stock market in 1995 and formed a new holding company, National Grid Group. National Grid Group completed a merger with Lattice in 2002 to form National Grid Transco, a public limited company (*see* Gas).

Following privatisation, generators and suppliers in England and Wales traded via the Electricity Pool. A competitive wholesale trading market known as NETA (New Electricity Trading Arrangements) replaced the Electricity Pool in March 2001, and was extended to include Scotland via the British Electricity Transmissions and Trading Arrangements (BETTA) in 2005. As part of BETTA, National Grid became the system operator for all transmission. The introduction of competition into the domestic electricity market was completed in May 1999.

In Scotland, three new companies were formed under the Electricity Act 1989: Scottish Power plc and Scottish Hydro-Electric plc, which were responsible for generation, transmission, distribution and supply; and Scottish Nuclear Ltd. Scottish Power and Scottish Hydro-Electric were floated on the stock market in 1991. Scottish Hydro-Electric merged with Southern Electric in 1998 to become Scottish and Southern Energy plc. Scottish Nuclear was incorporated into British Energy in 1996. In 2009, British Energy was acquired by French multinational EDF and rebranded EDF Energy.

In Northern Ireland, Northern Ireland Electricity plc (NIE) was set up in 1993 under a 1991 Order in Council. In 1993 it was floated on the stock market and in 1998 it became part of the Viridian Group (now Energia Group) and was responsible for distribution and supply until NIE was sold to the Electricity Supply Board of Ireland in December 2010. In June 2010, Airtricity became the first new electricity supplier since the Northern Ireland electricity market was opened to competition in 2007.

On 14 December 2020 the government published 'Powering our Net Zero Future', a White Paper with net zero and efforts to fight climate change at its core. This built on a 2011 White Paper 'Planning Our Electric Future: a White Paper for Secure, Affordable and Low-carbon Electricity' which recognised that extensive investment was needed to update the grid and build new power stations. Currently, 17.3 per cent of the UK electricity generation comes from nuclear reactors, a process by which uranium atoms are split to produce heat through a chemical process known as fission. While nuclear power stations will close gradually over the next decade, with only one expected to produce power beyond 2030, there are plans in place for a new generation of reactors to be built, the first of which is expected to be running by 2025. A significant proportion of the UK's electricity still comes from burning fossil fuels and, in 2019, natural gas provided 40.6 per cent of electricity generation, coal provided 2.1 per cent – a record low – and 0.3 per cent was provided from oil. However, the picture is changing; renewables generated a record of 37.1 per cent of the UK's electricity in 2019, up from 33.1 per cent in 2018.

Interconnecting cables import and export electricity to Europe. These link the UK to the grids of France, the Netherlands and Ireland. A new 'interconnector' was launched in January 2019, connecting the UK to the Belgian grid. In 2019, the UK was a net importer of electricity via these cables, totalling 21.1TWh (terawatt hours), or 6.1 per cent of electricity supplied to the UK grid. The UK's only net exporting system was the Ireland-Wales interconnector.

On 30 September 2003 the Electricity Association, the industry's main trade association, was replaced with three separate trade bodies: the Association of Electricity Producers; the Energy Networks Association; and the Energy Retail Association. In April 2012, following a merger between the Association of Electricity Producers, the Energy Retail Association and the UK Business Council for Sustainable Energy, Energy UK – the new trade association for the gas and electricity sector – was established.

ENERGY NETWORKS ASSOCIATION, 4 More London Riverside, London SE1 2AU T 020-7706 5100
W www.energynetworks.org
Chief Executive, David Smith

ENERGY UK, 1st Floor, 26 Finsbury Square, London EC2A 1DS
T 020-7930 9390 W www.energy-uk.org.uk
Chief Executive, Emma Pinchbeck

ELECTRICITY PRODUCTION, SUPPLY AND CONSUMPTION
GWh

	2018	2019
Electricity produced		
Nuclear	65,064	56,184
Hydro	5,444	5,935
Wind, wave and solar photovoltaics	69,651	77,267
Coal	16,831	6,891
Oil	1,063	1,119
Gas	131,490	131,931
Other renewables	34,954	37,314
Other	5,780	6,363
Total	330,277	323,005
Electricity supplied		
Production	330,277	323,005
*Other sources	2,498	1,756
Imports	21,332	24,556
Exports	(2,225)	(3,385)
Total	351,883	345,931
Electricity consumed		
Industry	93,871	91,617
Transport	4,984	5,456
Other	201,589	198,187
Domestic	105,065	103,825
Public administration	18,248	17,744
Commercial	73,961	72,413
Agriculture	4,316	4,205
Total	300,444	295,259

* Pumped storage production
Source: DBEIS

GAS AND ELECTRICITY SUPPLIERS

With the gas and electricity markets open, most suppliers offer their customers both services. The majority of gas/electricity companies have become part of larger multi-utility companies, often operating internationally.

As part of measures to reduce the UK's carbon output, the government has outlined plans to introduce 'smart meters' to all UK homes. Smart meters perform the traditional meter function of measuring energy consumption, in addition to more advanced functions such as allowing energy suppliers to communicate directly with their customers and removing the need for meter readings and bill estimates. The meters also allow domestic customers to have direct access to energy consumption information.

The following list comprises a selection of major suppliers offering gas and electricity. After E.ON absorbed Npower, one of its major competitors, in April 2019, the 'Big Six' energy suppliers in the UK became the 'Big Five'. In 2020, SSE Energy Services was sold to OVO Energy, a new challenger and now a major supplier. Nonetheless, in recent years the dominance of these companies has been declining. The 'Big Five', including OVO Energy, claimed a combined market share 72.8 per cent in 2020, down from 90.2 per cent in 2015. Organisations in italics are subsidiaries of the companies listed in capital letters directly above.

ENGLAND, SCOTLAND AND WALES

CENTRICA PLC, Millstream, Maidenhead Road, Windsor, Berkshire SL4 5GD T 01753-494000 W www.centrica.com
British Gas, PO Box 227, Rotherham S98 1PD T 0800-072 8625 W www.britishgas.co.uk
EDF ENERGY, 90 Whitfield Street, London W1T 4EZ T 0333-200 5100 W www.edfenergy.com
E.ON UK, Westward Way Business Park, Coventry, CV4 8LG T 0345-052 0000 W www.eonenergy.com
Npower, Windmill Business Park, Whitehall Way, Swindon SN5 6PB T 0800-073 3000 W www.npower.com

OVO ENERGY, 1 Rivergate Temple Quay, Bristol, BS1 6ED T 0330-303 5063 W www.ovoenergy.com
SCOTTISH POWER, 320 St Vincent Street, Glasgow G2 5AD T 0800-027 0072 W www.scottishpower.co.uk

NORTHERN IRELAND

AIRTRICITY (a member of SSE plc), Millennium House, 25 Great Victoria Street, Belfast BT2 7AQ T 0345-600 9093 W www.sseairtricity.com/uk
ELECTRIC IRELAND, 1 Cromac Quay, The Gasworks, Belfast BT7 2JD T 0345-600 5335 W www.electricireland.com
POWERNI (a member of Energia Group), 120 Malone Road, Belfast BT9 5HT T 0345-745 5455 W www.powerni.co.uk

REGULATION OF THE GAS AND ELECTRICITY INDUSTRIES

The Office of Gas and Electricity Markets (OFGEM) regulates the gas and electricity industries in Great Britain. It was formed in 1999 by the merger of the Office of Gas Supply and the Office of Electricity Regulation. OFGEM's overriding aim is to protect and promote the interests of all gas and electricity customers by promoting competition and regulating monopolies. It is governed by an authority and its powers are provided for under the Gas Act 1986, the Electricity Act 1989, the Competition Act 1998, the Utilities Act 2000, the Enterprise Act 2002 and the Consumer Rights Ace 2015.

THE OFFICE OF GAS AND ELECTRICITY MARKETS (OFGEM), 10 South Colonnade, Canary Wharf, London E14 4PU T 020-7901 7000 W www.ofgem.gov.uk

NUCLEAR POWER

Nuclear reactors began to supply electricity to the national grid in 1956. There are presently 15 reactors at eight sites which generated 17.3 per cent of the UK's electricity in 2019. Approximately half of this capacity is due to be retired by 2025. In December 2015, the final Magnox reactor, and last remaining nuclear plant in Wales (Wylfa 1) began decommissioning after 44 years of operation. This left 14 active advanced gas-cooled reactors (AGR) and one pressurised water reactor (PWR), Sizewell B in Suffolk. The AGRs and PWR are owned by a private company, EDF Energy. Apart from Sizewell B, which first produced power in 1995, the seven other sites are expected to close by 2035. The UK's ageing nuclear power stations have seen the decline of nuclear generation over the past decade, as a result of prolonged outages which have reduced operational nuclear capacity, with the 2019 share of generation the lowest since 2010.

In June 2011, eight new sites across the UK were selected for locations of new nuclear power stations, and EDF Energy was contracted to construct four new European Pressurised Reactors (EPRs), two of which were scheduled to be established at Hinkley Point, with the other two at Sizewell. However, the future many of these projects looks uncertain due to delays, lower energy demand, cheaper renewable energy and developers pulling out. The fate of the two EPRs at Sizewell C has yet to be determined.

Hinkley Point C, which was the first new nuclear power plant to begin construction in the UK in 20 years, is due to commission in the mid-2020s. The French firm EDF Energy, which is set to finance two-thirds of the site, had approved the funding but critics warned of environmental damage, increasing costs and concern over the implications of nuclear sites being built in the UK by foreign investors. However, in September 2016, the prime minister gave the go ahead for the nuclear power station after the government imposed significant new safeguards for future projects. The initial estimated cost of £18bn has since increased to £21.5–22.5bn. The combined 3.2GW capacity of its two EPRs is expected to deliver around 7 per cent of the country's current electricity needs, which is enough to power the equivalent of six million homes. Nuclear power continues to be a reliable source of low carbon electricity, with analysis suggesting that additional nuclear beyond Hinkley Point C will be required as the UK seeks to achieve net-zero carbon emissions by 2050.

The UK Energy White Paper, published in December 2020, outlines plans for advanced nuclear innovation, including a £385 million fund for the development of Small Modular Reactors (SMRs) and Advanced Modular Reactors (AMRs). The estimated worth of the global market for SMRs and AMRs is expected to be between £250bn and £400bn by 2035. With the controversially high costs associated with large-scale nuclear power plants, SMRs have the potential to provide cost-competitive nuclear power by the early-2030s and may be suitable for a wide range of sites across the country.

In April 2005 the responsibility for the decommissioning of civil nuclear reactors and other nuclear facilities used in research and development was handed to the Nuclear Decommissioning Authority (NDA). The NDA is a non-departmental public body, funded mainly by the DBEIS. The total planned expenditure for the NDA in 2020–21 was £3.5bn. Until April 2007, UK Nirex was responsible for the disposal of intermediate and some low-level nuclear waste. After this date Nirex was integrated into the NDA and renamed the Radioactive Waste Management directorate.

There are currently 17 nuclear sites owned by the NDA that are in various stages of decommissioning, including the world's first commercial power station at Calder Hall on the Sellafield site in Cumbria and Windscale, which produced plutonium in the 1950s to be used for military purposes. The responsibilities of the NDA include: decommissioning and cleaning up nuclear facilities; ensuring that all waste, including radioactive and non-radioactive products, are safely managed; developing nationwide strategies and plans for Low Level Waste; implementing a long-term plan for the management of nuclear waste; and scrutinising EDF Energy's decommissioning plans, which includes the fleet of AGR nuclear stations.

In 2019, electricity supplied from nuclear sources accounted for 56TWh, equating to 17.3 per cent of total electricity generation or 7.3 per cent of total energy supplied.

Nuclear power has its advantages: reactors emit virtually no carbon dioxide and uranium prices remain relatively steady. However, the advantages of low emissions are countered by the high costs of construction and difficulties in disposing of nuclear waste. Currently, the only method is to store it securely until it has slowly decayed to safe levels. Public distrust persists despite the advances in safety technology. Following the tsunami which struck Japan in March 2011 and the level 7 meltdowns of three reactors in the Fukushima Daiichi Nuclear Plant, the safety of nuclear reactors was brought further into public interest and became a government priority.

SAFETY AND REGULATION

The Office for Nuclear Regulation (ONR) is responsible for regulation of nuclear safety and security across the UK. The Civil Nuclear Constabulary, a specialised armed force created in April 2005, is responsible for policing the industry.

RENEWABLE SOURCES

Progress was made towards the UK's target of consuming 15 per cent of energy from renewable sources by 2020, introduced in the 2009 EU Renewable Directive, as 12.3 per cent of energy consumption came from renewable sources in 2019, up from 11.2 per cent in 2018. Renewable sources provided 37.1 per cent of the electricity generated in the UK in 2019, up from 33.1 per cent in 2018, with record annual generations for wind, solar and bioenergy. This rise is attributed to a 6.5 per cent increase in capacity and a decrease in total electricity generation. Yearly weather conditions were unfavourable (for wind) but sunlight hours (solar) and average rainfall (hydro) were up slightly on 2018.

In 2019 onshore wind was the leading technology in terms of capacity for a second year in a row, at 29.9 per cent, closely followed by solar photovoltaics (28.3 per cent), which had been the leading technology from 2015 and 2017. Onshore wind capacity increased by 4.2 per cent from 2018, and average wind speeds were up so that onshore wind generation increased by 6.5 per cent. The largest increase in capacity was for offshore wind which increased by 21 per cent from 2018, generation from offshore wind also increased by 20 per cent in 2019. Despite no new capacity in 2019, hydro generation increased by 9.0 per cent as a result of more rainfall. Solar photovoltaic generation grew by just 1.4 per cent as average sunlight hours were down and capacity increased by just 2.1 per cent. Meanwhile, heat generation from renewable sources increased by 2.4 per cent, primarily due to increases in generation from wood fuel.

The government's principal mechanism for developing renewable energy sources is the Contracts for Difference (CfD) scheme. The CfD scheme recently replaced the Renewables Obligation (RO) which had been in place since 2002. It aims to increase the contribution of electricity from renewables in the UK by offering long-term contracts to new low carbon electricity generators. These guarantee a certain price for their generated electricity, which helps to tackle the risks and uncertainties associated with investing in renewables. The RO closed to new capacity in March 2017, but will continue to provide support to existing generators for 20 years.

The Feed-in Tariff (FIT) scheme has run alongside CfDs and the RO, providing incentives to encourage the uptake of small-scale low carbon electricity generation technologies, principally renewables such as solar photovoltaics, wind and hydro-electricity. The scheme was hugely successful in attracting investment; however, the scheme closed to new registrations in April 2019. Following this, the government laid legislation in June 2019 to introduce a new supplier-led smart export guarantee (SEG) in Great Britain from 1 January 2020. Under the SEG, licensed electricity suppliers (with 150,000 domestic customers or more) are required to offer small-scale low-carbon generators a price per kWh for electricity exported to the grid.

In addition to these schemes, the Renewable Heat Incentive (RHI) aims to promote the use of renewable heating systems. The RHI was originally introduced in November 2011 to provide a long-term financial incentive to support the uptake of renewable heat in the non-domestic sector. In April 2014, the RHI was extended to cover the domestic sector replacing the renewable heat premium payment scheme which closed in March 2013. Participants of the scheme receive tariff payments for the heat generated from an eligible renewable heating system which is heating a single dwelling.

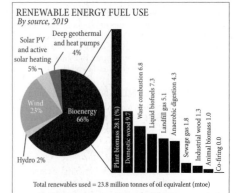

RENEWABLE ENERGY FUEL USE
By source, 2019

Total renewables used = 23.8 million tonnes of oil equivalent (mtoe)

Source: Department for Business, Energy and Industrial Strategy, 2019

TRANSPORT

CIVIL AVIATION

Since the privatisation of British Airways in 1987, UK airlines have been operated entirely by the private sector. In 2019, total capacity of British airlines amounted to 58 billion tonne-km. UK airlines carried around 153 million passengers; 142 million on scheduled services and 11 million on charter flights. Passenger traffic through UK airports increased by 2 per cent in 2019. Traffic at the six main London area airports (Gatwick, Heathrow, London City, Luton, Southend and Stansted) increased by 2 per cent over 2018 and other UK regional airports saw an increase of 1 per cent.

Leading British airlines include British Airways, EasyJet, Tui Airways and Virgin Atlantic. Irish airline Ryanair also operates frequent flights from the UK.

There are around 126 licensed civil aerodromes in Britain, with Heathrow and Gatwick handling the highest volume of passengers.

The Civil Aviation Authority (CAA), an independent statutory body, is responsible for the regulation of UK airlines. This includes economic and airspace regulation, air safety, consumer protection and environmental research and consultancy. All commercial airline companies must be granted an air operator's certificate, which is issued by the CAA to operators meeting the required safety standards. The CAA issues airport safety licences, which must be obtained by any airport used for public transport and training flights. All British-registered aircraft must be granted an airworthiness certificate, and the CAA issues professional licences to pilots, flight crew, ground engineers and air traffic controllers. The CAA also manages the Air Travel Organiser's Licence (ATOL), the UK's principal travel protection scheme. The CAA's costs are met entirely from charges on those whom it regulates; there is no direct government funding of the CAA's work.

The Transport Act 2000 separated the CAA from its subsidiary, National Air Traffic Services (NATS), which provides air traffic control services to aircraft flying in UK airspace and over the eastern part of the North Atlantic. NATS is a public private partnership (PPP) between the Airline Group (a consortium of UK airlines), which holds 42 per cent of the shares; NATS staff, who hold 5 per cent; UK airport operator LHR Airports Limited, which holds 4 per cent, and the government, which holds 49 per cent and a golden share. NATS handled 2.6m flights in 2019, from its centres at Swanwick, Hampshire and Prestwick, Ayrshire. NATS also provides air traffic services at 14 UK airports; at Gibraltar Airport, and, in a joint venture with Ferrovial, at several airport towers in Spain.

AIR PASSENGERS 2019

All UK Airports: Total	296,924,188
Aberdeen	2,912,883
Barra	14,599
Belfast City	2,455,259
Belfast International	6,278,563
Benbecula	34,691
Birmingham	12,650,607
Blackpool	15,213
Bournemouth	803,307
Bristol	8,964,242
Cambridge	–
Campbeltown	8,086
Cardiff	1,656,085
City of Derry (Eglinton)	203,777
Doncaster Sheffield	1,407,862
Dundee	20,917
Durham Tees Valley	142,080
East Midlands	4,675,411
Edinburgh	14,737,497
Exeter	1,021,784
Gatwick	46,086,089
Glasgow	8,847,100
Gloucestershire	–
Heathrow	80,890,031
Humberside	204,463
Inverness	938,232
Islay	34,992
Isle of Man	854,676
Isles of Scilly (St Mary's)	93,927
Kirkwall	172,625
Lands End (St Just)	64,056
Leeds Bradford	3,992,862
Lerwick (Tingwall)	3,309
Liverpool	5,045,991
London City	5,122,271
Luton	18,216,207
Lydd	39
Manchester	29,397,357
Newcastle	5,203,624
Newquay	461,478
Norwich	530,238
Oxford (Kidlington)	–
Prestwick	640,055
Scatsta	109,480
Shoreham	–
Southampton	1,781,457
Southend	2,035,535
Stansted	28,124,292
Stornoway	131,441
Sumburgh	267,456
Teeside	150,735
Tiree	12,178
Wick	13,149
Channel Islands Airports	2,698,478
Alderney	53,155
Guernsey	882,374
Jersey	1,762,949

Source: Civil Aviation Authority

CAA, Aviation House, Beehive Ringroad, Crawley, West Sussex RH6 0YR T 0330-022 1500 W www.caa.co.uk

Heathrow Airport	**T** 0844-335 1801
Gatwick Airport	**T** 0344-892 0322
Manchester Airport	**T** 0808-169 7030
Stansted Airport	**T** 0844-335 1803

BRITISH AIRLINES

BRITISH AIRWAYS, PO Box 365, Waterside, Harmondsworth UB7 0GB T 0844-493 0787 W www.britishairways.com

EASYJET, Hangar 89, London Luton Airport LU2 9PF T 0330-365 5000 W www.easyjet.com

TUI AIRWAYS, Wigmore House, Wigmore Place, Wigmore Lane, Luton, Beds LU2 9TN T 0203-451 2688 W www.tui.co.uk

VIRGIN ATLANTIC, Fleming Way, Crawley, W. Sussex RH10 9DF T 0344-874 7747 W www.virginatlantic.com

RAILWAYS

The railway network in Britain was developed by private companies in the 19th century. In 1948 the main railway companies were nationalised and were run by a public authority, the British Transport Commission. The commission was replaced by the British Railways Board in 1963, operating as British Rail. On 1 April 1994, responsibility for managing the track and railway infrastructure passed to a newly formed company, Railtrack plc. In October 2001 Railtrack was put into administration under the Railways Act 1993. In October 2002 Railtrack was taken out of administration and replaced by the not-for-profit company Network Rail. The British Railways Board continued as operator of all train services until 1996–7, when they were sold or franchised to the private sector.

The Strategic Rail Authority (SRA) was created to provide strategic leadership to the rail industry and formally came into being on 1 February 2001 following the passing of the Transport Act 2000. In January 2002 it published its first strategic plan, setting out the strategic priorities for Britain's railways over the next ten years. In addition to its coordinating role, the SRA was responsible for allocating government funding to the railways and awarding and monitoring the franchises for operating rail services.

On 15 July 2004 the transport secretary announced a new structure for the rail industry in the white paper *The Future of Rail*. These proposals were implemented under the Railways Act 2005, which abolished the SRA, passing most of its functions to the Department for Transport; established the Rail Passengers Council as a single national body, dissolving the regional committees; and gave devolved governments in Scotland and Wales more say in decisions at a local level. In addition, responsibility for railway safety regulation was transferred to the Office of Rail Regulation from the Health and Safety Executive.

OFFICE OF RAIL AND ROAD

The Office of Rail and Road (ORR), previously known as the Office of Rail Regulation, was established on 5 July 2004 by the Railways and Transport Safety Act 2003, replacing the Office of the Rail Regulator. In April 2015 it acquired responsibility for monitoring Highways England in addition to its existing role as the railway industry's economic and safety regulator and changed its name to better reflect its functions. The ORR regulates Network Rail's stewardship of the national network, licenses operators, approves network access agreements, and enforces domestic competition law. The ORR is a non-ministerial government department led by a board appointed by the Secretary of State for Transport and chaired by Declan Collier.

SERVICES

For privatisation, under the Railways Act 1993, domestic passenger services were divided into 25 train operating units, which were franchised to private sector operators via a competitive tendering process. The train operators formed the Association of Train Operating Companies (ATOC) to act as the official voice of the passenger rail industry and provide its members with a range of services enabling them to comply with conditions imposed on them through their franchise agreements and operating licences.

As at December 2020 there were 31 passenger train operating companies: Avanti West Coast, c2c, Caledonian Sleeper, Chiltern Railways, CrossCountry, East Midlands Railway, Eurostar, Gatwick Express, Grand Central, Great Northern, Great Western Railway, Greater Anglia, Heathrow Express, Hull Trains, Island Line, London North Eastern Railway, London Northwestern Railway, London Overground, London Underground, Merseyrail, Northern, ScotRail, South Western Railway, Southeastern, Southern, Stansted Express, TfL Rail, Thameslink, TransPennine Express, Transport for Wales, West Midlands Railway.

Network Rail publishes a national timetable which contains details of rail services operated over the UK network and sea ferry services which provide connections with Ireland, the Isle of Man, the Isle of Wight, the Channel Islands and some European destinations.

The national rail enquiries service offers information about train times and fares for any part of the country, Transport for London (TfL) provides London-specific travel information for all modes of travel and Eurostar provides information for international channel tunnel rail services:

NATIONAL RAIL ENQUIRIES
T 0345-748 4950 W www.nationalrail.co.uk

TRANSPORT FOR LONDON
T 0343-222 1234 W www.tfl.gov.uk

EUROSTAR
T 0343-186186 W www.eurostar.com

CONSUMER WATCHDOGS

Previously known as Passenger Focus, Transport Focus is the national consumer watchdog for bus, tram, coach and rail passengers in England. Under The Infrastructure Act 2015 Transport Focus's role was expanded to also represent users of the strategic road network. The entity is funded by the Department for Transport and is an executive non-departmental public body.

Established in July 2000, London TravelWatch is the operating name of the official watchdog organisation representing the interests of transport users in and around the capital. Officially known as the London Transport Users' Committee, it is sponsored and funded by the London Assembly and is independent of the transport operators. London TravelWatch represents users of buses, the Underground, river and rail services in and around London, including Eurostar and Heathrow Express, Croydon Tramlink and the Docklands Light Railway. The interests of pedestrians, cyclists and motorists are also represented, as are those of taxi users.

FREIGHT

On privatisation in 1996, British Rail's bulk freight operations were sold to North and South Railways – subsequently called English, Welsh and Scottish Railways (EWS). In 2007, EWS was bought by Deutsche Bahn and is now DB Cargo UK. The other major companies in the rail freight sector are: Colas Rail, Direct Rail Services, Freightliner and GB Railfreight (GBRf). In 2019–20 total volume of freight moved by rail amounted to 16.6 billion net tonne-kilometres, the lowest total since 1996–7 due to the coronavirus pandemic and a sharp fall in coal transportation.

NETWORK RAIL

Network Rail is responsible for the tracks, bridges, tunnels, level crossings, viaducts and main stations that form Britain's rail network. In addition to providing the timetables for the passenger and freight operators, Network Rail is also responsible for all the signalling and electrical control equipment needed to operate the rail network and for monitoring and reporting performance across the industry.

In September 2014, Network Rail was reclassified as a public body after being privately run since 2002 as a commercial business which was directly accountable to its members. The members had similar rights to those of shareholders in a public company except they did not receive dividends or share capital and thereby had no financial interest in Network Rail. On 1 July 2015, the 46 public members were dismissed and the company is now accountable directly to parliament through the Secretary of State for Transport. Network Rail is regulated by the ORR and all of its profits are reinvested into maintaining and upgrading the rail infrastructure. In 2019–20 a total of 1.7 billion passenger journeys were made on the rail network, a reduction of 0.8 per cent on 2018–19.

LONDON TRAVELWATCH, Europoint 5–11, Lavington Street, London SE1 0NZ **T** 020-3176 2999 **W** www.londontravelwatch.org.uk

NETWORK RAIL, 1 Eversholt Street, London NW1 2DN **T** 0345-711 4141 **W** www.networkrail.co.uk

OFFICE OF RAIL AND ROAD, 25 Cabot Square, London E14 4QZ **T** 020-7282 2000 **W** www.orr.gov.uk

TRANSPORT FOCUS, Fleetbank House, 2–6 Salisbury Square, London EC4Y 8AE **T** 0300-123 2350 **W** www.transportfocus.org.uk

RAIL SAFETY
On 1 April 2006 responsibility for health and safety policy and enforcement on the railways transferred from the Health and Safety Executive to the Office of Rail Regulation (ORR).

ACCIDENTS ON RAILWAYS

	2018–19	2019–20
Rail incident fatalities		
Passengers	17	12
Railway employees	2	4

SUICIDES AND ATTEMPTED SUICIDES 2019–20
Fatalities	283

Source: RSSB – *Annual Safety Performance Report 2019–20*

OTHER RAIL SYSTEMS
Responsibility for the London Underground passed from the government to the Mayor and Transport for London on 15 July 2003, with a public-private partnership already in place. Plans for a public-private partnership for London Underground were pushed through by the government in February 2002 despite opposition from the Mayor of London and a range of transport organisations. Under the PPP, long-term contracts with private companies were estimated to enable around £16bn to be invested in renewing and upgrading the London Underground's infrastructure over 15 years. In July 2007, Metronet, which was responsible for two of three PPP contracts, went into administration; TfL took over both contracts. Responsibility for stations, trains, operations, signalling and safety remains in the public sector. In 2019–20, there were 2.1 billion passenger journeys.

In addition to Glasgow Subway (12.7 million passenger journeys in 2019–20) and Edinburgh Trams (7.45 million passenger journeys in 2019), Britain has eight other light rail and tram systems: Blackpool Tramway, Docklands Light Railway (DLR), London Tramlink, Manchester Metrolink, Midland Metro, Nottingham Express Transit (NET), Sheffield Supertram and Tyne and Wear Metro. These eight accounted for 263.4 million passenger journeys in 2019–20; a decrease of 4.2 per cent on 2018–19 figures.

THE CHANNEL TUNNEL
The earliest recorded scheme for a submarine transport connection between Britain and France was in 1802. Tunnelling began simultaneously on both sides of the Channel three times: in 1881, in the early 1970s, and on 1 December 1987, when construction workers bored the first of the three tunnels which form the Channel Tunnel. Engineers 'holed through' the first tunnel (the service tunnel) on 1 December 1990 and tunnelling was completed in June 1991. The tunnel was officially inaugurated by the Queen and President Mitterrand of France on 6 May 1994.

The submarine link comprises two rail tunnels, each carrying trains in one direction, which measure 7.6m (24.93ft) in diameter. Between them lies a smaller service tunnel, measuring 4.8m (15.75ft) in diameter. The service tunnel is linked to the rail tunnels by 130 cross-passages for maintenance and safety purposes. The tunnels are 50km (31 miles) long, 38km (24 miles) of which is under the seabed at an average depth of 40m (132ft). The rail terminals are situated at Folkestone and Calais, and the tunnels go underground at Shakespeare Cliff, Dover and Sangatte, west of Calais.

HIGH SPEED 1
The Channel Tunnel rail link, High Speed 1, runs from Folkestone to St Pancras station, London, with intermediate stations at Ashford and Ebbsfleet in Kent.

Construction of the rail link was financed by the private sector with a substantial government contribution. A private sector consortium, London and Continental Railways Ltd (LCR), comprising Union Railways and the UK operator of Eurostar, owns the rail link and was responsible for its design and construction. The rail link was constructed in two phases: phase one, from the Channel Tunnel to Fawkham Junction, Kent, began in October 1998 and opened to fare-paying passengers on 28 September 2003; phase two, from Southfleet Junction to St Pancras, was completed in November 2007.

Eurostar provides direct services from the UK (London) to Avignon (5 hours 49 minutes), Calais (55 minutes), Disneyland Paris (2 hours 49 minutes), Lille (1 hour 22 minutes), Lyon (4 hours 41 minutes), Marseille (6 hours 26 minutes) and Paris (2 hours 16 minutes) in France; Brussels (1 hour 53 minutes) in Belgium; and Amsterdam (3 hours 52 minutes) and Rotterdam (3 hours 13 minutes) in the Netherlands.

HIGH SPEED 2
A second high speed rail link connecting London and Birmingham, with branches to Manchester and Leeds, was first proposed in 2009 and the legislative process started in 2012. Following significant opposition, particularly from environmental groups, an independent review was conducted in 2019 and Prime Minister Boris Johnson confirmed the project would proceed in February 2020. Construction started in September on phase one, between London and Birmingham, and is set to be completed in 2031. The second phase is expected to open in 2040, at a total cost of £106bn. It is Europe's largest infrastructure project.

ROADS

HIGHWAY AUTHORITIES
The powers and responsibilities of highway authorities in England and Wales are set out in the Highways Act 1980; for Scotland there is separate legislation.

Responsibility for motorways and other trunk roads in Great Britain rests in England with the Secretary of State for Transport, in Scotland with the Scottish government, and in Wales with the Welsh government. The highway authority for non-trunk roads in England, Wales and Scotland is, in general, the local authority in whose area the roads lie. With the establishment of the Greater London Authority in July 2000, Transport for London became the highway authority for roads in London.

In Northern Ireland the Department for Infrastructure is responsible for public roads and their maintenance and construction.

FINANCE

In England all aspects of trunk road and motorway funding are provided directly by the government to Highways England, which operates, maintains and improves a network of motorways and trunk roads around 6,920km (4,300 miles) long, on behalf of the secretary of state. Since 2001 the length of the network that the Highways England is responsible for has been decreasing owing to a policy of de-trunking, which transfers responsibility for non-core roads to local authorities. The government's second road investment strategy, published in 2020, outlines Highways England's five-year objectives which include 12 major new road projects and 52 other schemes. The budget for 2020–25 is £27.4bn, and this includes maintenance, major schemes, traffic management, technology improvements, other programmes and administration costs.

Government support for local authority capital expenditure on roads and other transport infrastructure is provided through grant and credit approvals as part of the Local Transport Plan (LTP). Local authorities bid for resources on the basis of a five-year programme built around delivering integrated transport strategies. As well as covering the structural maintenance of local roads and the construction of major new road schemes, LTP funding also includes smaller-scale safety and traffic management measures with associated improvements for public transport, cyclists and pedestrians.

In Northern Ireland all roads, some 26,000km (16,160 miles) are managed by the Department for Infrastructure (DfI) for Northern Ireland as the sole road authority. The road network is made up of some 300km (185 miles) of motorway, 1,300km (810 miles) of trunk roads and 25,000km (15,534miles) of other roads. The department is also responsible for maintaining some 10,000km (6,210 miles) of footpaths and 5,800 bridges.

For the financial year 2020–21 the DfI open resourcing budget was £418m, and planned expenditure on all infrastructure was £544m. This included maintenance, capital schemes, traffic management and technology improvements.

The Transport Act 2000 gave English and Welsh local authorities (outside London) powers to introduce road-user charging or workplace parking levy schemes. The act requires that the net revenue raised is used to improve local transport services and facilities for at least ten years. The aim is to reduce congestion and encourage greater use of alternative modes of transport. Schemes developed by local authorities require government approval. The UK's first toll road, the M6 Toll, opened in December 2003 and runs for 43.5km (27 miles) around Birmingham from junction 3a to junction 11a on the M6.

Charging schemes in London are allowed under the 1999 Greater London Authority Act. The Central London Congestion Charge Scheme began on 17 February 2003 (*see also* Regional Government London).

ROAD LENGTHS 2019
Miles

	England	Wales	Scotland	Great Britain
Major Roads	22,355	2,720	6,734	31,809
Motorways	1,941	88	296	2,325
Minor Roads	166,793	18,306	30,146	215,246
Total	189,148	21,026	36,880	247,055

Source: Department for Transport

BUSES

The majority of bus services outside London are provided on a commercial basis by private operators. Local authorities have powers to subsidise services where needs are not being met by a commercial service.

Since April 2008 men and women who have attained the state pension age and disabled people who qualify under the categories listed in the Transport Act 2000 have been able to travel for free on any local bus across England between 9.30am and 11pm Monday to Friday and all day on weekends and bank holidays. Local authorities recompense operators for the reduced fare revenue. The age of eligibility for concessionary travel is the female state pension age, regardless of your gender. A similar scheme from age 60 operates in Wales and within London, although there is no time restriction. In Scotland, people aged 60 and over and disabled people have been able to travel for free on any local or long-distance bus since April 2006.

In London, Transport for London (TfL) has overall responsibility for setting routes, service standards and fares for the bus network. Almost all routes are competitively tendered to commercial operators.

In Northern Ireland, passenger transport services are provided by Ulsterbus, Metro (formerly Citybus) and Glider, a new service added in 2018, three wholly owned subsidiaries of the Northern Ireland Transport Holding Company. Along with Northern Ireland Railways, Ulsterbus, Metro and Glider operate under the brand name of Translink and are publicly owned. Ulsterbus is responsible for virtually all bus services in Northern Ireland except Belfast city services, which are operated by Metro and Glider, which connects East Belfast, West Belfast and the Titanic Quarter through the city centre. People living in Northern Ireland aged 60 and over can travel on buses and trains for free once they have obtained a SmartPass from Translink.

LOCAL BUS PASSENGER JOURNEYS 2019–20
No. of journeys (millions)

England	4,069
London	2,091
Scotland	366
Wales	89
Total	4,524

Source: Department for Transport

TAXIS AND PRIVATE HIRE VEHICLES

A taxi is a public transport vehicle with fewer than nine passenger seats, which is licensed to 'ply for hire'. This distinguishes taxis from private hire vehicles (PHVs) which must be booked in advance through an operator. In London, taxis and private hire vehicles are licensed by the Public Carriage Office (PCO), part of TfL. At the end of March 2020 there were 19,000 taxis and 96,000 PHVs licensed in London. Outside London, local authorities are responsible for the licensing of taxis and private hire vehicles operational in their respective administrative areas. At the end of March 2020 there were 67,900 licensed taxis and 230,900 licensed PHVs in England.

ROAD TRAFFIC BY VEHICLE TYPE (UK) 2019

	Billion vehicle miles
All motor vehicles	356.5
Cars & taxis	278.2
Light goods vehicles	55.5
Heavy goods vehicles	17.4
Motorcycles	3
Buses & coaches	2.4

Source: Department for Transport

ROAD SAFETY

The key findings from the Department for Transport's 2019 annual road casualty report found that the total number of reported casualties of all severities in Great Britain in 2019 was 153,158; a 5 per cent decrease from 2018. Of these a total of 1,752 people were killed in 2019; a decrease of almost 2 per cent from 2018. Serious injuries accounted for 25,945 of the casualties and slight injuries for 125,461. Total reported child casualties (0–15 years) decreased by 5 per cent to 13,574 in 2019.

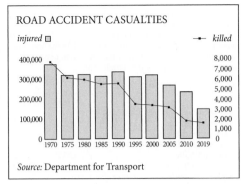

ROAD ACCIDENT CASUALTIES

injured □   ● killed

(Chart: y-axis left "injured" 0 to 400,000 in increments of 100,000; y-axis right "killed" 0 to 8,000 in increments of 1,000; x-axis years 1970 1975 1980 1985 1990 1995 2000 2005 2010 2019)

Source: Department for Transport

DRIVING LICENCES

It is necessary to hold a valid full licence in order to drive unaccompanied on public roads in the UK. Learner drivers must obtain a provisional driving licence before starting to learn to drive and must then pass theory and practical tests to obtain a full driving licence.

There are separate tests for driving motorcycles, cars, passenger-carrying vehicles (PCVs) and large goods vehicles (LGVs). Drivers must hold full car entitlement before they can apply for PCV or LGV entitlements.

The Driver and Vehicle Licensing Agency (DVLA) ceased the issue of paper licences in March 2000, but those currently in circulation will remain valid until they expire or the details on them change. The photocard driving licence was introduced to comply with the second EC directive on driving licences. This requires a photograph of the driver to be included on all UK licences issued from July 2001. The photocard licence must be renewed every ten years, with fines of up to £1,000 for failure to do so.

To apply for a first photocard driving licence, individuals are required to either apply online or complete the form *Application for a Driving Licence* (D1) and submit by post.

The minimum age for driving motor cars, light goods vehicles up to 3.5 tonnes and motorcycles is 17 (moped, 16). Drivers who collect 12 or more penalty points within three years of qualifying lose their licence and are required to take another test. Forms and leaflets are available from post offices and online (**W** www.gov.uk/dvlaforms or **W** www.gov.uk/government/organisations/driver-and-vehicle-licensing-agency).

The DVLA is responsible for issuing driving licences, registering and licensing vehicles, and collecting excise duty in Great Britain. The Driver and Vehicle Agency (DVA), has similar responsibilities in Northern Ireland.

DRIVING LICENCE FEES *as at December 2020*

	online*/postal
Provisional licence	
Car, motorcycle or moped	£34/£43
Bus or lorry	Free
Changing a provisional licence to a full licence	Free
Renewal	
Renewing an expired licence (must be renewed every 10 years)	£14/£17
At age 70 and over	Free
For medical reasons	Free
Bus or lorry driver entitlement	Free
After disqualification	£65
After disqualification for some drink driving offences†	£90
After revocation (under the New Drivers Act)	£50
Replacing a lost, stolen, defaced or destroyed licence	£20/£20
Adding an entitlement to a full licence	Free
Exchanging	
a paper licence for a photocard licence‡	£20/£20
a full Northern Ireland licence for a full GB licence	Free
a full GB licence for a full EU/EEA or other designated foreign licence	Free
a full EU/EEA or other designated foreign licence for a full GB licence	£43
Changing	
name or address	Free
photo	£14/£17

* Not all services are available online; in these instances just the postal fee is shown. Licence fees differ in Northern Ireland (**W** www.nidirect.gov.uk/the-cost-of-a-driving-licence).

† For an alcohol-related offence where the DVLA need to arrange medical enquiries

‡ If a paper licence is exchanged for a photocard at the same time as name or address details are changed there is no charge

DRIVING TESTS

The Driver and Vehicle Standards Agency (DVSA) is responsible for improving road safety in Great Britain by setting standards for driving and motorcycling and making sure drivers, vehicle operators and MOT garages understand and follow roadworthiness standards. The agency also provides a range of licensing, testing, education and enforcement services.

DRIVING TESTS TAKEN AND PASSED
2019–2020

	Number Taken	Percentage Passed
Practical Test		
Car	1,599,504	45.9
Motorcycle Module 1	51,921	72.1
Motorcycle Module 2	50,993	71.0
PCV	7,345	60.0
LGV	70,288	58.9
Theory Test		
Car	1,865,740	47.1
Motorcycle	64,924	70.7
PCV		
Multiple choice	8,210	62.9
Hazard perception	6,874	79.8
Driver CPC*	5,334	52.7
LGV		
Multiple choice	55,110	60.7
Hazard perception	43,882	81.2
Driver CPC*	33,510	68.8

LGV = Large goods vehicle; PCV = Passenger-carrying vehicle
* Driver Certificate of Professional Competence – legal requirement for all professional bus, coach and lorry drivers
Source: DVSA

The theory and practical driving tests can be booked online (**W** www.gov.uk/book-driving-test) or by phone (**T** 0300-2001122).

DRIVING TEST FEES *as at December 2020*

	Weekday/evening, weekend & bank holidays
Theory tests	
Car and motorcycle	£23.00/£23.00
Bus and lorry	
Multiple choice	£26.00/£26.00
Hazard perception	£11.00/£11.00
Driver CPC†	£23.00/£23.00
Practical tests	
Car	£62.00/£75.00
Tractor and other specialist vehicles	£62.00/£75.00
Motorcycle	
Module 1 (off-road)	£15.50/£15.50
Module 2 (on-road)	£75.00/£88.50
Lorry and bus	£115.00/£141.00
Driver CPC†	£55.00/£63.00
Car and trailer	£115.00/£141.00
Extended tests for disqualified drivers	
Car	£124.00/£150.00
Motorcycle Module 1 (on-road)	£150.00/£177.00

* After 4.30pm
† Driver Certificate of Professional Competence – legal requirement for all professional bus, coach and lorry drivers

VEHICLE LICENCES

Registration and first licensing of vehicles is through local offices of the DVLA in Swansea. Local facilities for relicensing are available at any post office which deals with vehicle licensing. Applicants will need to take their vehicle registration document (V55/5) or, if this is not available, the applicant must complete form V62. Forms are available at post offices and online (**W** www.gov.uk/dvlaforms)

MOTOR VEHICLES LICENSED (UK)

As at 30 September 2020

	Thousands
All cars	32,869.9
Light goods vehicles	4,342.5
Motorcycles	1,384.3
Heavy goods vehicles	507.9
Buses and coaches	144.4
Other vehicles*	806.3
Total	40,055.4

* Includes rear diggers, lift trucks, rollers, ambulances, Hackney Carriages, three-wheelers and agricultural vehicles
Source: Department for Transport

VEHICLE EXCISE DUTY

Details of the present duties chargeable on motor vehicles are available at post offices and online (**W** www.gov.uk/government/publications/rates-of-vehicle-tax-v149). The Vehicle Excise and Registration Act 1994 provides *inter alia* that any vehicle kept on a public road but not used on roads is chargeable to excise duty as if it were in use. All non-commercial vehicles constructed before 1 January 1973 are exempt from vehicle excise duty. Any vehicle licensed on or after 31 January 1998, not in use and not kept on public roads must be registered as SORN (Statutory Off Road Notification) to be exempted from vehicle excise duty. From 1 January 2004 the registered keeper of a vehicle remains responsible for taxing a vehicle or making a SORN declaration until that liability is formally transferred to a new keeper.

All rates of duty can also be paid by direct debit – the 6-month direct debit rate is slightly cheaper than the non-direct debit rate listed below. There is also the option to pay vehicle duty by direct debit monthly instalments.

RATES OF DUTY *from 1 April 2020*

	6 months	12 months
Cars registered on or after 1 April 2017*†		
petrol/diesel car	£82.50	£150.00
alternative fuel car	£77.00	£140.00
Cars registered on or after 1 March 2001		
Under 1,549cc	£90.75	£165.00
Over 1,549cc	£148.50	£270.00
Light goods vehicles registered on or after 1 March 2001		
	£77.00	£140.00
Euro 4 light goods vehicles registered between 1 March 2003 and 31 December 2006		
	£77.00	£140.00
Euro 5 light goods vehicles registered between 1 January 2009 and 31 December 2010		
	£77.00	£140.00
Motorcycles (with or without sidecar)		
Not over 150cc	–	£20.00
151–400cc	–	£44.00
401–600cc	£36.85	£67.00
600cc+	£51.15	£93.00
Tricycles		
Not over 150cc	–	£20.00
All others	£51.15	£93.00

* Different first year licence rates based on CO_2 emissions are payable at first registration
† Cars with a list price of over £40,000 at first registration pay an additional £325 on the standard 12-month rate above for five years from the start of the second tax payment

RATES OF DUTY FOR CARS REGISTERED BETWEEN 1 MARCH 2001 AND 1 APRIL 2017

from 1 April 2020

	CO_2 Emissions	Petrol and Diesel Car		Alternative Fuel Car	
	(g/km)	6 months	12 months	6 months	12 months
A	Up to 100	–	£0.00	–	£0.00
B	101–110	–	£20.00	–	£10.00
C	111–120	–	£30.00	–	£20.00
D	121–130	£68,75	£125.00	£63.25	£115.00
E	131–140	£82.50	£150.00	£77.00	£140.00
F	141–150	£90.75	£165.00	£85.25	£155.00
G	151–165	£112.75	£205.00	£107.25	£195.00
H	166–175	£132.00	£240.00	£126.50	£230.00
I	176–185	£145.75	£265.00	£140.25	£255.00
J	186–200	£167.75	£305.00	£162.25	£295.00
K*	201–255	£181.50	£330.00	£176.00	£320.00
L	226–255	£310.75	£565.00	£305.25	£555.00
M	255+	£319.00	£580.00	£313.50	£570.00

* Includes cars that have a CO_2 emission figure over 225g/km but were registered before 23 March 2006

MOT TESTING

Cars, motorcycles, motor caravans, light goods and dual-purpose vehicles more than three years old must be covered by a current MOT test certificate. However, some vehicles (ie minibuses, ambulances and taxis) may require a certificate at one year old. All certificates must be renewed annually. Only MOT testing stations showing a blue sign with three triangles and an official 'MOT: Test: Fees and Appeals' poster may carry out an approved MOT. The MOT testing scheme is administered by the Driver and Vehicle Standards Agency (DVSA) on behalf of the Secretary of State for Transport.

A fee is payable to MOT testing stations. The current maximum fees are:

For cars, private hire and public service vehicles, motor caravans, dual purpose vehicles, ambulances and taxis (all up to eight passenger seats)	£54.85
For motorcycles	£29.65
For motorcycles with sidecar	£37.80
For three-wheeled vehicles (up to 450kg unladen weight)	£37.80

*Private passenger vehicles and ambulances with:

9–12 passenger seats	£57.30 (£64.00)
13–16 passenger seats	£59.55 (£80.50)
16+ passenger seats	£80.65 (£124.50)
Goods vehicles (3,000–3,500kg)	£58.60

* Figures in parentheses include seatbelt installation check

SHIPPING AND PORTS

Sea trade has always played a central role in Britain's economy. By the 17th century Britain had built up a substantial merchant fleet and by the early 20th century it dominated the world shipping industry. In 2019 the UK registered trading fleet decreased by 34 per cent in gross tonnage (GT) compared to 2018, to 10.5 million GT, the 24th largest trading fleet in the world. At the end of 2019, the number of UK registered trading vessels was 1,177, an annual decrease of 10 per cent. This sharp decline, after several years of stability, was likely due to uncertainty over the UK's exit from the EU. The UK registered share of the world fleet fell to 0.5 per cent on a deadweight tonnage basis and 0.7 per cent when measured using GT, compared with 0.8 per cent and 1.1 per cent respectively in 2018.

Freight is carried by liner and bulk services, almost all scheduled liner services being containerised. About 95 per cent by weight of Britain's overseas trade is carried by sea. Passengers and vehicles are carried by roll-on, roll-off ferries, hovercraft, cruise ships and high-speed catamarans. In 2019 the number of international short-sea route passengers to and from the UK decreased by 6 per cent to 18.4 million.

Lloyd's of London provides the most comprehensive shipping intelligence service in the world. *Lloyd's List* (www.lloydslistintelligence.com) lists over 126,000 ocean-going vessels and gives the latest known report of each.

PORTS

There are 51 major ports in the UK. Total freight tonnage handled by UK ports in 2019 was 486.1 million tonnes, broadly level with 2018 (483.3 million tonnes). The largest ports in terms of freight tonnage in 2018 were Grimsby and Immingham (54.1 million tonnes), London (54 million tonnes), Milford Haven (35 million tonnes), Liverpool (34.3 million tonnes) and Southampton (33.2 million tonnes). Belfast (18.5 million tonnes) is the principal freight port in Northern Ireland.

Broadly speaking, ports are owned and operated by private companies, local authorities or self-owning bodies, known as trust ports. The largest operator is Associated British Ports which owns 21 ports.

MARINE SAFETY

The Maritime and Coastguard Agency (MCA) is an executive agency of the Department for Transport responsible for implementing the government's maritime safety policy in the UK and works to prevent the loss of life on the coast and at sea.

HM Coastguard maintains a 24-hour search and rescue response and coordination capability for the whole of the UK coast and the internationally agreed search and rescue region. HM Coastguard is responsible for mobilising and organising resources in response to people in distress at sea, or at risk of injury or death on the UK's cliffs or shoreline.

The MCA also inspects and surveys ships to ensure that they are meeting UK and international safety rules, provides certification to seafarers, registers vessels and responds to pollution from shipping and offshore installations.

Locations hazardous to shipping in coastal waters are marked by lighthouses and other lights and buoys. The lighthouse authorities are the Corporation of Trinity House (for England, Wales and the Channel Islands), the Northern Lighthouse Board (for Scotland and the Isle of Man), and the Commissioners of Irish Lights (for Northern Ireland and the Republic of Ireland). Trinity House maintains 66 lighthouses, nine light vessels/floats, 508 buoys, 18 beacons, 52 radar beacons, seven DGPS (differential global positioning system) stations* and three AIS (automatic identification system) stations. The Northern Lighthouse Board maintains 206 lighthouses, 204 buoys, 25 beacons, 29 radar beacons, 46 AIS stations and four DGPS stations; and Irish Lights looks after 67 lighthouses, 183 buoys, 20 beacons, and three DGPS stations, with AIS in operation on 48 lighthouses.

Harbour authorities are responsible for pilotage within their harbour areas; and the Ports Act 1991 provides for the transfer of lights and buoys to harbour authorities where these are used mainly for local navigation.

* DGPS is a satellite-based navigation system

UK-OWNED TRADING VESSELS
500 gross tons and over, as at end 2019

Type of vessel	No.	Gross tonnage
Tankers	98	2,945,000
Fully cellular container	73	3,172,000
Dry bulk carriers	68	2,660,000
Ro-Ro (passenger & cargo)	77	901,000
Passenger (incl cruise)	33	2,044,000
Other general cargo	110	355,000
Specialised carriers	12	413,000
All vessels	471	12,485,000

Source: Department for Transport

UK SEA PASSENGER* MOVEMENTS 2019

Type of journey	No. of passenger movements
Short-sea routes	18,404,000
Cruises beginning or ending at a UK port*	2,171,000
Long sea journeys	75,000
Total	20,651,000

* Passengers are included at both departure and arrival if their journeys begin and end at a UK seaport
Source: Department for Transport

UK SHIPPING FORECAST AREAS

Weather bulletins for shipping are broadcast daily on BBC Radio 4 at 00h 48m, 05h 20m, 12h 01m and 17h 54m. All transmissions are broadcast on long wave at 198kHz and the 00h 48m and 05h 20m transmissions are also broadcast on FM 92–95. The bulletins consist of a gale warning summary, general synopsis, sea-area forecasts and coastal station reports. In addition, gale warnings are broadcast at the first available programme break after receipt. If this does not coincide with a news bulletin, the warning is repeated after the next news bulletin. Shipping forecasts and gale warnings are also available on the Met Office and BBC Weather websites.

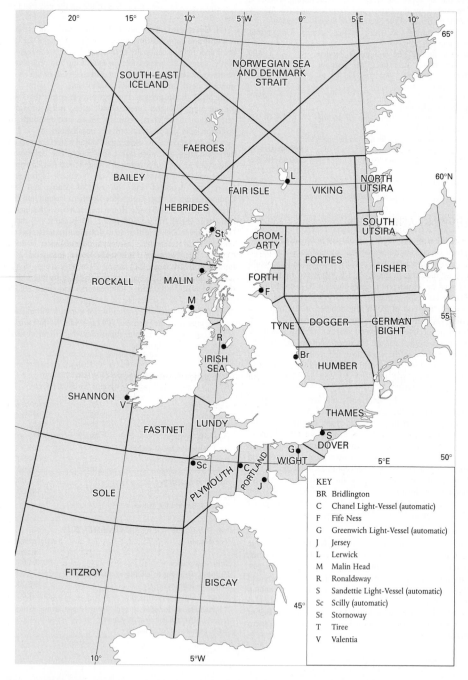

KEY

BR Bridlington
C   Chanel Light-Vessel (automatic)
F   Fife Ness
G   Greenwich Light-Vessel (automatic)
J   Jersey
L   Lerwick
M   Malin Head
R   Ronaldsway
S   Sandettie Light-Vessel (automatic)
Sc Scilly (automatic)
St Stornoway
T   Tiree
V   Valentia

RELIGION IN THE UK

The 2011 census in England and Wales included a voluntary question on religion; 92.8 per cent of the population chose to answer the question. Christianity remained the largest religion, despite a decrease of 4 million people from the 2001 census, to 33.2 million adherents, or 59.3 per cent of the population. The second largest religious group were Muslims with 2.7 million people identifying themselves as such, an increase of 1.2 million since 2001. The number of people reporting that they had 'no religion' was 14.1 million, around a quarter of the population. Of those reporting that they had no religion, the majority identified themselves as white (93 per cent) and born in the UK (also 93 per cent); in terms of age, the largest demographic were those aged 20 to 24 (1.4 million or 10 per cent). More than 240,000 people listed 'other religion' on the census, which included, among many others, 176,632 Jedi Knights, 56,620 Pagans and 39,061 Spiritualists. Norwich remained the city with the highest proportion reporting no religion (42.5 per cent), while London was the most diverse region with the largest proportion of people classifying themselves as Buddhist, Hindu, Jewish and Muslim. Knowsley, in Merseyside, was the local authority with the highest proportion of Christians at 80.9 per cent, while Tower Hamlets in London had the highest population of Muslims at 34.5 per cent.

In Northern Ireland, the religion question was phrased differently; 738,033 (41 per cent) identified themselves as Roman Catholic, 752,555 (42 per cent) as 'Protestant and other Christian', 14,859 (0.8 per cent) belonged to an 'other religion' and 183,164 (10 per cent) stated they had no religion.

CENSUS 2011 RESULTS – RELIGION IN ENGLAND, WALES AND SCOTLAND*

	thousands	per cent
Christian	36,093	58.8
Buddhist	261	0.4
Hindu	833	1.4
Jewish	269	0.4
Muslim	2,783	4.5
Sikh	432	0.7
Other religion	256	0.4
All religions	40,927	66.6
No religion	16,038	26.1
Not stated	4,406	7.2
All no religion/not stated	20,444	33.3
TOTAL	61,371	100

* Figures from the 2011 census for Northern Ireland did not contain a full breakdown of each major religion
Source: Census 2011

INTER-CHURCH AND INTER-FAITH COOPERATION

The main umbrella body for the Christian churches in the UK is Churches Together in Britain and Ireland. There are also ecumenical bodies in each of the constituent countries of the UK: Churches Together in England, Action of Churches Together in Scotland, CYTUN (Churches Together in Wales), and the Irish Council of Churches. The Free Churches Group (formerly the Free Churches Council), which is closely associated with Churches Together in England, represents most of the free churches in England and Wales, and the Evangelical Alliance represents evangelical Christians.

The Inter Faith Network for the United Kingdom promotes cooperation between faiths, and the Council of Christians and

Jews works to improve relations between the two religions. Churches Together in Britain and Ireland also has a commission on inter-faith relations.

ACTION OF CHURCHES TOGETHER IN SCOTLAND, Jubilee House, Forthside Way, Stirling FK8 1QZ **T** 01259-216980 **W** www.acts-scotland.org
General Secretary (interim), Revd Ian Boa

CHURCHES TOGETHER IN BRITAIN AND IRELAND, Interchurch House, 35 Lower Marsh, London SE1 7RL **T** 020-3794 2288 **E** info@ctbi.org.uk **W** www.ctbi.org.uk
General Secretary, Bob Fyffe

CHURCHES TOGETHER IN ENGLAND, 27 Tavistock Square, London WC1H 9HH **T** 020-7529 8131 **E** office@cte.org.uk **W** www.cte.org.uk
General Secretary, Revd Dr Paul Goodliff

COUNCIL OF CHRISTIANS AND JEWS, Mary Sumner House, 24 Tufton Street, London SW1P 3RB **T** 020-3515 3003 **E** cjrelations@ccj.org.uk **W** www.ccj.org.uk
Director, Elizabeth Harris-Sawczenko

CYTUN (CHURCHES TOGETHER IN WALES), 58 Richmond Road, Cardiff CF24 3AT **T** 029-2046 4204 **E** post@cytun.cymru **W** www.cytun.co.uk
Chief Executive, Revd Aled Edwards, OBE

EVANGELICAL ALLIANCE, 176 Copenhagen Street, London N1 0ST **T** 020-7520 3830 **E** info@eauk.org **W** www.eauk.org
General Director, Steve Clifford

FREE CHURCHES GROUP, 27 Tavistock Square, London WC1H 9HH **T** 020-3651 8334 **E** info@freechurches.org.uk **W** www.freechurches.org.uk
General Secretary, Revd Paul Rochester

INTERFAITH NETWORK FOR THE UK, 2 Grosvenor Gardens, London SW1W 0DH **T** 020-7730 0410 **W** www.interfaith.org.uk
Director, Dr Harriet Crabtree, OBE

IRISH COUNCIL OF CHURCHES, 48 Elmwood Avenue, Belfast BT9 6AZ **T** 028-9066 3145 **E** info@irishchurches.org **W** www.irishchurches.org
General Secretary, Dr Nicola Brady

RELIGIONS AND BELIEFS

BAHA'I FAITH

Baha'u'llah ('Glory of God'), the founder of the Baha'i faith, was born in Iran in 1817. He was imprisoned in 1852 for advocating the teachings of the Bab ('Gate'), a prophet who was martyred in 1850. Baha'u'llah was banished and sent into successive stages of exile, first to Baghdad – where in 1863 he announced that he was the 'promised one' foretold by the Bab – and then to Constantinople, Adrianople and eventually Acre, in present day Israel. He died in 1892 and was succeeded by his son, Abdu'l-Baha, as head of the Baha'i faith, under whose guidance the faith spread to Europe and North America. He was in turn succeeded by Shoghi Effendi, his grandson, who oversaw the establishment of the administrative order and the spread of the faith around the world until his death in 1957. The Universal House of Justice, an elected international governing council, was formed in 1963 in accordance with Baha'u'llah's teachings.

The Baha'i faith espouses the oneness of humanity and of religion and teaches that there is only one God, whose will has been revealed to mankind by a series of messengers, such as Zoroaster, Abraham, Moses, Buddha, Krishna, Christ, Muhammad, the Bab and Baha'u'llah, who were seen as the founders of separate religions, but whose common purpose was to bring God's message to mankind. The Baha'i faith attributes the differences in teachings between religions to humanity's changing needs. Baha'i teachings include that all races and both sexes are equal and deserving of equal opportunities and treatment, that education is a fundamental right and that extremes of wealth and poverty should be eliminated. In addition, the faith exhorts mankind to establish a world federal system to promote peace and unity.

In an effort to translate these principles into action, Baha'is have initiated an educational process across the world that seeks to raise the capacity of people of all ages and from all backgrounds to contribute towards the betterment of society. There is no clergy; each local community elects a local spiritual assembly to tend to its administrative needs. A national spiritual assembly is elected annually by locally elected delegates, and every five years the national spiritual assemblies meet together to elect the Universal House of Justice, the supreme international governing body of the Baha'i Faith. Worldwide there are over 13,000 local spiritual assemblies and nearly 7 million followers, with around 7,000 in the UK.

BAHA'I COMMUNITY OF THE UK, 27 Rutland Gate, London SW7 1PD **T** 020-7584 2566 **E** opa@bahai.org.uk
W www.bahai.org.uk
Director, Office of Public Affairs, Padideh Sabeti

BUDDHISM

Buddhism originated in what is now the Bihar area of northern India in the teachings of Siddhartha Gautama, who became the *Buddha* ('Enlightened One'). In the Thai or Suriyakati calendar the beginning of the Buddhist era is dated from the death of Buddha; the year 2020 is therefore 2563 by the Thai Buddhist reckoning.

Fundamental to Buddhism is the concept of rebirth, whereby each life carries with it the consequences of the conduct of earlier lives (known as the law of *karma*) and this cycle of death and rebirth is broken only when the state of *nirvana* has been reached. Buddhism steers a middle path between belief in personal continuity and the belief that death results in total extinction.

While doctrine does not have a pivotal position in Buddhism, a statement of four 'Noble Truths' is common to all its schools and varieties. These are: suffering is inescapable in even the most fortunate of existences; craving is the root cause of suffering; abandonment of the selfish mindset is the way to end suffering; and bodily and mental discipline, accompanied by the cultivation of wisdom and compassion, provides the spiritual path ('Noble Eightfold Path') to accomplish this. Buddhists deny the idea of a creator and prefer to emphasise the practical aspects of moral and spiritual development.

The schools of Buddhism can be broadly divided into three: *Theravada,* the generally monastic-led tradition practised in Sri Lanka and South East Asia; *Mahayana,* the philosophical and popular traditions of the Far East; and *Esoteric,* the Tantric-derived traditions found in Tibet and Mongolia and, to a lesser extent, China and Japan. The extensive Theravada scriptures are contained in the *Pali Canon,* which dates in its written form from the first century BC. Mahayana and Esoteric schools have Sanskrit-derived translations of these plus many more additional scriptures as well as exegetical material.

In the East the new and full moons and the lunar quarter days were (and to a certain extent, still are) significant in determining the religious calendar. Most private homes contain a shrine where offerings, worship and other spiritual practices (such as meditation, chanting or mantra recitation)

take place on a daily basis. Buddhist festivals vary according to local traditions within the different schools and there is little uniformity – even in commemorating the birth, enlightenment and death of the Buddha.

There is no governing authority for Buddhism in the UK. Communities representing all schools of Buddhism operate independently. The Buddhist Society was established in 1924; it runs courses, lectures and meditation groups, and publishes books about Buddhism. The Network of Buddhist Organisations was founded in 1993 to promote fellowship and dialogue between Buddhist organisations and to facilitate cooperation in matters of common interest.

There are estimated to be at least 490 million Buddhists worldwide. Of the 248,000 Buddhists in England and Wales (according to the 2011 census), 72,000 are white British (the majority are converts), 49,000 Chinese, 93,000 'other Asian' and 36,000 are 'other ethnic'.

THE BUDDHIST SOCIETY, 58 Eccleston Square, London SW1V 1PH **T** 020-7834 5858 **E** info@thebuddhistsociety.org
W www.thebuddhistsociety.org
President, Dr Desmond Biddulph, CBE

LONDON BUDDHIST CENTRE, 51 Roman Road, London E2 0HU **T** 020-8981 1225 **E** contact@lbc.org.uk
W www.lbc.org.uk
Chair, Dharmachari Subhuti

THE NETWORK OF BUDDHIST ORGANISATIONS, PO Box 4147, Maidenhead SL60 1DN **T** 0845-345 8978
E nboadmin@nbo.org.uk **W** www.nbo.org.uk
Chair, Juliet Hackney

SOKA GAKKAI UK, Taplow Court Grand Cultural Centre, Cliveden Road, Taplow, Berkshire SL6 0ER **T** 01628-773163
W www.sgi-uk.org
General Director, Robert Harrap

TIBET HOUSE TRUST, Tibet House, 1 Culworth Street, London NW8 7AF **T** 020-7722 5378
E secretary@tibet-house-trust.co.uk
W www.tibet-house-trust.co.uk
Chair, Sonam Tsering Frasi

CHRISTIANITY

Christianity is a monotheistic faith based on the person and teachings of Jesus Christ, and all Christian denominations claim his authority. Central to its teaching is the concept of God and his son Jesus Christ, who was crucified and resurrected in order to enable mankind to attain salvation.

The Jewish scriptures predicted the coming of a *Messiah,* an 'anointed one', who would bring salvation. To Christians, Jesus of Nazareth, a Jewish rabbi (teacher) who was born in Palestine, was the promised Messiah. Jesus' birth, teachings, crucifixion and subsequent resurrection are recorded in the *Gospels,* which, together with other scriptures that summarise Christian belief, form the *New Testament.* This, together with the Hebrew scriptures – entitled the *Old Testament* by Christians – makes up the Bible, the sacred texts of Christianity.

Christians believe that sin distanced mankind from God, and that Jesus was the son of God, sent to redeem mankind from sin by his death. In addition, many believe that Jesus will return again at some future date, triumph over evil and establish a kingdom on earth, thus inaugurating a new age. The Gospel assures Christians that those who believe in Jesus and obey his teachings will be forgiven their sins and will be resurrected from the dead.

The Apostles were Jesus' first converts and are recognised by Christians as the founders of the Christian community. Early Christianity spread rapidly throughout the eastern provinces of the Roman Empire but was subjected to great persecution until AD 313, when Emperor Constantine's Edict of Toleration confirmed its right to exist. Christianity was established as the religion of the Roman Empire in AD 381.

Between AD 325 and 787 there were seven Oecumenical Councils at which bishops from the entire Christian world assembled to resolve various doctrinal disputes. The estrangement between East and West began after Constantine moved the centre of the Roman Empire from Rome to Constantinople, and it grew after the division of the Roman Empire into eastern and western halves. Linguistic and cultural differences between Greek East and Latin West served to encourage separate ecclesiastical developments which became pronounced in the tenth and early 11th centuries. Administration of the church was divided between five ancient patriarchates: Rome and all the West, Constantinople (the imperial see – the 'New Rome'), Jerusalem and all of Palestine, Antioch and all the East, and Alexandria and all of Africa. Of these, only Rome was in the Latin West and after the schism in 1054, Rome developed a structure of authority centralised on the Papacy, while the Orthodox East maintained the style of localised administration. Papal authority over the doctrine and jurisdiction of the church in Western Europe was unrivalled after the split with the Eastern Orthodox Church until the Protestant Reformation in the 16th century.

Christian practices vary widely between different Christian churches, but prayer, charity and giving (for the maintenance of the church buildings, for the work of the church, and to those in need) are common to all. In addition, certain days of observance, ie the Sabbath, Easter and Christmas, are celebrated by most Christians. The Orthodox, Roman Catholic and Anglican churches celebrate many more days of observance, based on saints and significant events in the life of Jesus. The belief in sacraments, physical signs believed to have been ordained by Jesus Christ to symbolise and convey spiritual gifts, varies greatly between Christian denominations; baptism and the Eucharist are practised by most Christians. Baptism, symbolising repentance and faith in Jesus, is an act marking entry into the Christian community; the Eucharist, the ritual re-enactment of the Last Supper, Jesus' final meal with his disciples, is also practised by most denominations. Other sacraments, such as anointing the sick, the laying on of hands to symbolise the passing on of the office of priesthood or to heal the sick, and speaking in tongues, where it is believed that the person is possessed by the Holy Spirit, are less common. In denominations where infant baptism is practised, confirmation (where the person confirms the commitments made on their behalf in infancy) is common. Matrimony and the ordination of priests are also widely believed to be sacraments. Many Protestants regard only baptism and the Eucharist to be sacraments; the Quakers and the Salvation Army reject the use of sacraments.

See Churches for contact details of the Church of England, the Roman Catholic Church and other Christian churches in the UK.

HINDUISM

Hinduism has no historical founder but had become highly developed in India by c.2500 BC. Its adherents originally called themselves Aryans; Muslim invaders first called the Aryans 'Hindus' (derived from 'Sindhu', the name of the river Indus) in the eighth century.

Most Hindus hold that satya (truthfulness), honesty, sincerity and devotion to God are essential for good living. They believe in one supreme spirit (Brahman), and in the transmigration of atman (the soul). Most Hindus accept the doctrine of karma (consequences of actions), the concept of samsara (successive lives) and the possibility of all atmans achieving moksha (liberation from samsara) through jnana (knowledge), yoga (meditation), karma (work or action) and bhakti (devotion).

Most Hindus offer worship to murtis (images of deities) representing different incarnations or aspects of Brahman, and follow their dharma (religious and social duty) according to the traditions of their varna (social class), ashrama (stage in life), jaiti (caste) and kula (family).

Hinduism's sacred texts are divided into shruti ('that which is heard'), including the Vedas, and smriti ('that which is remembered'), including the Ramayana, the Mahabharata, the Puranas (ancient myths), and the sacred law books. Most Hindus recognise the authority of the Vedas, the oldest holy books, and accept the philosophical teachings of the Upanishads, the Vedanta Sutras and the Bhagavad-Gita.

Hindus believe Brahman to be omniscient, omnipotent, limitless and all-pervading. Brahman is usually worshipped in its deity form. Brahma, Vishnu and Shiva are the most important deities or aspects of Brahman worshipped by Hindus; their respective consorts are Saraswati, Lakshmi and Durga or Parvati, also known as Shakti. There are believed to have been ten avatars (incarnations) of Vishnu, of whom the most important are Rama and Krishna. Other popular gods are Ganesha, Hanuman and Subrahmanyam. All Hindu gods are seen as aspects of the supreme spirit (Brahman), not as competing deities.

Orthodox Hindus revere all gods and goddesses equally, but there are many denominations, including the Hare-Krishna movement (ISKCon), the Arya Samaj and the Swaminarayan Hindu mission, in which worship is concentrated on one deity. The guru (spiritual teacher) is seen as the source of spiritual guidance.

Hinduism does not have a centrally trained and ordained priesthood. The pronouncements of the shankaracharyas (heads of monasteries) of Shringeri, Puri, Dwarka and Badrinath are heeded by the orthodox but may be ignored by the various sects.

The commonest form of worship is puja, in which water, flowers, food, fruit, incense and light are offered to the deity. Puja may be done either in a home shrine or a mandir (temple). Many British Hindus celebrate samskars (purification rites), to name a baby, for the sacred thread (an initiation ceremony), marriage and cremation.

The largest communities of Hindus in Britain are in Leicester, London, Birmingham and Bradford, and developed as a result of immigration from India, eastern Africa and Sri Lanka.

There are an estimated 800 million Hindus worldwide; there are around 817,000 adherents, according to the 2011 census in England and Wales, and around 135 temples in the UK.

ARYA SAMAJ LONDON, 69 Argyle Road, London W13 0LY
T 020-8991 1732 **E** aryasamajlondon@yahoo.co.uk
W www.aryasamajlondon.org.uk
General Secretary, Amrit Lal Bhardwaj

BHARATIYA VIDYA BHAVAN, 4A Castletown Road, London W14 9HE **T** 020-7381 3086 **E** info@bhavan.net
W www.bhavan.net
Executive Director, Dr N. M Nandakumara

BHAKTIVEDANTA MANOR: INTERNATIONAL SOCIETY FOR KRISHNA CONSCIOUSNESS (ISKCON), Bhaktivedanta Manor, Dharam Marg, Hilfield Lane, Aldenham, Watford, Herts WD25 8EZ **T** 01923-851000
E info@krishnatemple.com **W** www.bhaktivedantamanor.co.uk
Temple President, Gauri Das

NATIONAL COUNCIL OF HINDU TEMPLES (UK), c/o
Shree Sanatan Mandir, 84 Weymouth Street, Leicester LE4 6FQ
T 0771-781 4357 **E** info@nchtuk.org **W** www.nchtuk.org
General Secretary, Satish K. Sharma

SWAMINARAYAN HINDU MISSION (SHRI
  SWAMINARAYAN MANDIR), 105–119 Brentfield Road,
  London NW10 8
  LD **T** 020-8965 2651 **E** info@londonmandir.baps.org
  W www.londonmandir.baps.org

HUMANISM

Humanism traces its roots back to ancient times, with Chinese,
Greek, Indian and Roman philosophers expressing Humanist
ideas some 2,500 years ago. Confucius, the Chinese
philosopher who lived *c.*500 BC, believed that religious
observances should be replaced with moral values as the basis
of social and political order and that 'the true way' is based
on reason and humanity. He also stressed the importance of
benevolence and respect for others, and believed that the
individual situation should be considered rather than the
global application of traditional rules.

Humanists believe that there is no God or other supernatural
being, that humans have only one life (Humanists do not
believe in an afterlife or reincarnation) and that humans can
live ethical and fulfilling lives without religious beliefs
through a moral code derived from a shared history, personal
experience and thought. There are no sacred Humanist texts.
Particular emphasis is placed on science as the only reliable
source of knowledge of the universe. Many Humanists
recognise a need for ceremonies to mark important occasions
in life and the British Humanist Association has a network of
celebrants who are trained and accredited to conduct baby
namings, weddings and funerals. The British Humanist
Association's campaigns for a secular state (a state based on
freedom of religious or non-religious belief with no privileges
for any particular set of beliefs) are based on equality and
human rights. The association also campaigns for inclusive
schools that meet the needs of all parents and pupils,
regardless of their religious or non-religious beliefs. According
to figures from the 2011 census, there are just over 15,000
Humanists in England and Wales.

BRITISH HUMANIST ASSOCIATION, 39 Moreland Street,
  London EC1V 8BB **T** 020-7324 3060 **E** info@humanism.org.uk
  W www.humanism.org.uk
  Chief Executive, Andrew Copson

ISLAM

Islam (which means 'peace arising from submission to the will
of Allah' in Arabic) is a monotheistic religion which was
taught in Arabia by the Prophet Muhammad, who was born
in Mecca (Al-Makkah) in 570 AD. Islam spread to Egypt,
north Africa, Spain and the borders of China in the century
following the Prophet's death, and is now the predominant
religion in Indonesia, the near and Middle East, northern and
parts of western Africa, Pakistan, Bangladesh, Malaysia and
some of the former Soviet republics. There are also large
Muslim communities in other countries.

For Muslims (adherents of Islam), there is one God *(Allah)*,
who holds absolute power. Muslims believe that Allah's
commands were revealed to mankind through the prophets,
who include Abraham, Moses and Jesus, but that Allah's
message was gradually corrupted until revealed finally and in
perfect form to Muhammad through the angel *Jibril* (Gabriel)
over a period of 23 years. This last, incorruptible message is
said to have been recorded in the *Qur'an* (Koran), which
contains 114 divisions called *surahs,* each made up of *ayahs* of
various lengths, and is held to be the essence of all previous
scriptures. The *Ahadith* are the records of the Prophet
Muhammad's deeds and sayings (the *Sunnah*) as practised and
recounted by his immediate followers. A culture and a system
of law and theology gradually developed to form a distinctive
Islamic civilisation. Islam makes no distinction between sacred
and worldly affairs and provides rules for every aspect of

human life. The *Shariah* is the sacred law of Islam based
primarily upon prescriptions derived from the *Qur'an* and the
Sunnah of the Prophet.

The 'five pillars of Islam' are *shahadah* (a declaration of faith
in the oneness and supremacy of Allah and the messengership
of Muhammad); *salat* (formal prayer, to be performed five
times a day facing the *Ka'bah* (the most sacred shrine in the
holy city of Mecca)); *zakat* (welfare due, paid annually on all
savings at the rate of 2.5 per cent); *sawm* (fasting during the
month of Ramadan from dawn until sunset); and *hajj*
(pilgrimage to Mecca made once in a lifetime if the believer is
financially and physically able). Some Muslims would add
jihad as the sixth pillar (striving for the cause of good and
resistance to evil).

Two main groups developed among Muslims. *Sunni* Muslims
accept the legitimacy of Muhammad's first four *caliphs*
(successors as head of the Muslim community) and of the
authority of the Muslim community as a whole. About 90 per
cent of Muslims are Sunni Muslims.

Shi'ites recognise only Muhammad's son-in-law Ali as his
rightful successor and the *Imams* (descendants of Ali, not to be
confused with *imams,* who are prayer leaders or religious
teachers) as the principal legitimate religious authority. The
largest group within Shi'ism is *Twelver Shi'ism,* which has
been the official school of law and theology in Iran since the
16th century; other subsects include the *Ismailis,* the *Druze*
and the *Alawis,* the latter two differing considerably from the
main body of Muslims. The *Ibadis* of Oman are neither Sunni
nor Shia, deriving from the strictly observant *Khariji*
(Seceders). There is no organised priesthood, but learned men
such as imams, *ulama,* and *ayatollahs* are accorded great respect.
The *Sufis* are the mystics of Islam. Mosques are centres for
worship and teaching and also for social and welfare activities.
Islam was first recorded in western Europe in the eighth
century AD when 800 years of Muslim rule began in Spain.
Later, Islam spread to eastern Europe. More recently, Muslims
came to Europe from Africa, the Middle East and Asia in the
late 19th century. Both the Sunni and Shia traditions are
represented in Britain, but the majority of Muslims in Britain
adhere to Sunni Islam. Efforts to establish a representative
national body for Muslims in Britain resulted in the founding,
in 1997, of the Muslim Council of Britain. In addition, there
are many other Muslim organisations in the UK. There are
around 1.6 billion Muslims worldwide, with around 2.8
million adherents in England, Wales and Scotland and about
1,500 mosques in the UK.

ISLAMIC CULTURAL CENTRE – THE LONDON
  CENTRAL MOSQUE, 146 Park Road, London NW8 7RG
  T 020-7724 3363 **E** info@iccuk.org **W** www.iccuk.org
  Director-General, Dr Ahmad Al-Dubayan

MUSLIM COUNCIL OF BRITAIN, PO Box 57330, London
  E1 2WJ **T** 0845-262 6786 **E** admin@mcb.org.uk
  W www.mcb.org.uk
  Secretary-General, Harun Rashid Khan

MUSLIM LAW (SHARIAH) COUNCIL UK, 20–22 Creffield
  Road, London W5 3RP **T** 0208-992 6636
  E info@shariahcouncil.org **W** www.shariahcouncil.org
  Chair, Dr Mohamed Benotman

MUSLIM WORLD LEAGUE LONDON, 46 Goodge Street,
  London W1T 4LU **T** 020-7636 7568 **E** info@mwllo.org.uk
  W www.mwllo.org.uk
  Director, Dr Ahmed Makhdoom

JAINISM

Jainism traces its history to Vardhamana Jnatriputra, known
as *Tirthankara Mahavira* ('the Great Hero') whose traditional
dates were 599–527 BC. Jains believe he was the last of the
current era in a series of 24 *Jinas* (those who overcome all
passions and desires) or *Tirthankaras* (those who show a way
across the ocean of life) stretching back to remote antiquity.

Born to a noble family in north-eastern India (presently the state of Bihar), he renounced the world for the life of a wandering ascetic and after 12 years of austerity and meditation he attained enlightenment. He then preached his message until, at the age of 72, he left the mortal world and achieved total liberation *(moksha)* from the cycle of death and rebirth.

Jains declare that the Hindu rituals of transferring merit are not acceptable as each living being is responsible for its own actions. They recognise some of the minor deities of the Hindu pantheon, but the supreme objects of worship are the Tirthankaras. The pious Jain does not ask favours from the Tirthankaras, but seeks to emulate their example in his or her own life.

Jains believe that the universe is eternal and self-subsisting, that there is no omnipotent creator God ruling it and the destiny of the individual is in his or her own hands. *Karma,* the fruit of past actions, is believed to determine the place of every living being and rebirth may be in the heavens, on earth as a human, an animal or other lower being, or in the hells. The ultimate goal of existence for Jains is *moksha,* a state of perfect knowledge and tranquillity for each individual soul, which can be achieved only by gaining enlightenment.

The Jainist path to liberation is defined by the three jewels: *Samyak Darshan* (right perception), *Samyak Jnana* (right knowledge) and *Samyak Charitra* (right conduct). Of the five fundamental precepts of the Jains, *Ahimsa* (non-injury to any form of being, in any mode: thought, speech or action) is the first and foremost, and was popularised by Gandhi as *Ahimsa paramo dharma* (non-violence is the supreme religion).

The largest population of Jains can be found in India but there are approximately 30,000 Jains in Britain, with sizeable communities in North America, East Africa, Australia and smaller groups in many other countries.

INSTITUTE OF JAINOLOGY, Unit 18, Silicon Business Centre, 28 Wadsworth Road, Perivale, Greenford, Middx UB6 7JZ
T 020-8997 2300 **E** info@jainology.org **W** www.jainology.org
Chair, Nemu Chandaria, OBE

JUDAISM

Judaism is the oldest monotheistic faith. The primary text of Judaism is the Hebrew bible or *Tanakh,* which records how the descendants of Abraham were led by Moses out of their slavery in Egypt to Mount Sinai where God's law *(Torah)* was revealed to them as the chosen people. The *Talmud,* which consists of commentaries on the *Mishnah* (the first text of rabbinical Judaism), is also held to be authoritative, and may be divided into two main categories: the *halakeh* dealing with legal and ritual matters) and the *aggadah* (dealing with theological and ethical matters not directly concerned with the regulation of conduct). The *midrash* comprises rabbinic writings containing biblical interpretations in the spirit of the aggadah. The halakah has become a source of division: orthodox Jews regard Jewish law as derived from God and therefore unalterable; progressive Jews seek to interpret it in the light of contemporary considerations; and conservative Jews aim to maintain most of the traditional rituals but to allow changes in accordance with tradition. Reconstructionist Judaism, a 20th-century movement, regards Judaism as a culture rather than a theological system and accepts all forms of Jewish practice.

The family is the basic unit of Jewish ritual, with the synagogue playing an important role as the centre for public worship and religious study. A synagogue is led by a group of laymen who are elected to office. The Rabbi is primarily a teacher and spiritual guide. The *Sabbath* is the central religious observance. Most British Jews are descendants of either the *Ashkenazim* of central and eastern Europe or the *Sephardim* of Spain, Portugal and the Middle East.

The Chief Rabbi of the United Hebrew Congregations of the Commonwealth is appointed by a Chief Rabbinate Conference, and is the rabbinical authority of the mainstream Orthodox sector of the Ashkenazi Jewish community, the largest body of which is the United Synagogue. His formal ecclesiastical authority is not recognised by the Reform Synagogues of Great Britain (the largest progressive group), the Union of Liberal and Progressive Synagogues, the Spanish and Portuguese Jews' Congregation or the Assembly of Masorti Synagogues. He is, however, generally recognised both outside the Jewish community and within it as the public religious representative of the totality of British Jewry. The Chief Rabbi is President of the London *Beth Din* (Court of Judgment), a rabbinic court. The *Dayanim* (Judges) adjudicate in disputes or on matters of Jewish law and tradition; they also oversee dietary law administration, marriage, divorce and issues of personal status.

The Board of Deputies of British Jews, established in 1760, is the representative body of British Jewry. The basis of representation is through the election of deputies by synagogues and communal organisations. It protects and promotes the interests of British Jewry, acts as the central voice of the community and seeks to counter anti-Jewish discrimination and anti-Semitic activities.

There are approximately 13.9 million Jews worldwide; in the UK there are an estimated 290,000 adherents and over 400 synagogues.

OFFICE OF THE CHIEF RABBI, 305 Ballards Lane, London N12 8GB **T** 020-8343 6301 **E** info@chiefrabbi.org
W www.chiefrabbi.org
Chief Rabbi, Ephraim Mirvis

BETH DIN (THE UNITED SYNAGOGUE), 305 Ballards Lane, London N12 8GB **T** 020-8343 6270 **E** info@bethdin.org.uk
W www.theus.org.uk
President, Michael Goldstein
Dayanim, Menachem Gelley *(Rosh Beth Din);* Ivan Binstock; Shmuel Simons

MASORTI JUDAISM, Alexander House, 3 Shakespeare Road, London N3 1XE **T** 020-8349 6650 **E** enquiries@masorti.org.uk
W www.masorti.org.uk
Executive Director, Matt Plen

BOARD OF DEPUTIES OF BRITISH JEWS, 1 Torriano Mews, London NW5 2RZ **T** 020-7543 5400 **E** info@bod.org.uk
W www.bod.org.uk
Chief Executive, Gillian Merron

FEDERATION OF SYNAGOGUES, 65 Watford Way, London NW4 3AQ **T** 020-8202 2263
E info@federationofsynagogues.com
W www.federationofsynagogues.com
Chief Executive, Rabbi Ari Lazarus

LIBERAL JUDAISM, The Montagu Centre, 21 Maple Street, London W1T 4BE **T** 020-7580 1663
E montagu@liberaljudaism.org **W** www.liberaljudaism.org
Chief Executive, Rabbi Danny Rich

THE MOVEMENT FOR REFORM JUDAISM, The Sternberg Centre for Judaism, 80 East End Road, London N3 2SY
T 020-8349 5640 **E** admin@reformjudaism.org.uk
W www.reformjudaism.org.uk
Senior Rabbi, Laura Janner-Klausner

THE SEPHARDI COMMUNITY, 119–121 Brent Street, London NW4 2DX **T** 020-7289 2573 **E** admin@spsyn.org.uk
W www.sephardi.org.uk
Executive Director, David Arden

UNITED SYNAGOGUE HEAD OFFICE, Adler House, 735 High Road, London N12 0US **T** 020-8343 8989
W www.theus.org.uk
Chief Executive, Dr Stephen Wilson

PAGANISM

Paganism draws on the ideas of the Celtic people of pre-Roman Europe and is closely linked to Druidism. The first historical record of Druidry comes from classical Greek and Roman writers of the third century BC, who noted the existence of Druids among a people called the Keltoi who inhabited central and southern Europe. The word druid may derive from the Indo-European 'dreo-vid', meaning 'one who knows the truth'. In practice it was probably understood to mean something like 'wise-one' or 'philosopher-priest'.

Paganism is a pantheistic nature-worshipping religion which incorporates beliefs and ritual practices from ancient times. Pagans place much emphasis on the natural world and the ongoing cycle of life and death is central to their beliefs. Most Pagans believe that they are part of nature and not separate from, or superior to it, and seek to live in a way that minimises harm to the natural environment (the word Pagan derives from the Latin *Paganus,* meaning 'rural'). Paganism strongly emphasises the equality of the sexes, with women playing a prominent role in the modern Pagan movement and goddess worship featuring in most ceremonies. Paganism cannot be defined by any principal beliefs because it is shaped by each individual's experiences.

The Pagan Federation was founded in 1971 to provide information on Paganism, campaigns on issues which affect Paganism and provides support to members of the Pagan community. Within the UK the Pagan Federation is divided into 12 districts each with a district manager and a regional coordinator. Local meetings are called 'moots' and take place in private homes, pubs or coffee bars. The Pagan Federation publishes a quarterly journal, *Pagan Dawn,* formerly *The Wiccan* (founded in 1968). The federation also publishes other material, arranges members-only and public events and maintains personal contact by letter with individual members and the wider Pagan community. Regional gatherings and conferences are held throughout the year.

THE PAGAN FEDERATION, Suite 1, The Werks, 45 Church Road, Hove BN3 2BE **E** info@paganfederation.co.uk **W** www.paganfed.org
President, Robin Taylor

SIKHISM

The Sikh religion dates from the birth of Guru Nanak in the Punjab in 1469. 'Guru' means teacher but in Sikh tradition has come to represent the divine presence of God giving inner spiritual guidance. Nanak's role as the human vessel of the divine guru was passed on to nine successors, the last of whom (Guru Gobind Singh) died in 1708. The immortal guru is now held to reside in the sacred scripture, *Guru Granth Sahib,* and so to be present in all Sikh gatherings.

Guru Nanak taught that there is one God and that different religions are like different roads leading to the same destination. He condemned religious conflict, ritualism and caste prejudices. The fifth Guru, Guru Arjan Dev, largely compiled the Sikh Holy scripture, a collection of hymns *(gurbani)* known as the *Adi Granth.* It includes the writings of the first five gurus and the ninth guru, and selected writings of Hindu and Muslim saints whose views are in accord with the gurus' teachings. Guru Arjan Dev also built the Golden Temple at Amritsar, the centre of Sikhism. The tenth guru, Guru Gobind Singh, passed on the guruship to the sacred scripture, Guru Granth Sahib, and founded the *Khalsa,* an order intended to fight against tyranny and injustice. Male initiates to the order added 'Singh' to their given names and women added 'Kaur'. Guru Gobind Singh also made the wearing of five symbols obligatory: *kaccha* (a special undergarment), *kara* (a steel bangle), *kirpan* (a small sword),

kesh (long unshorn hair, and consequently the wearing of a turban) and *kangha* (a comb). These practices are still compulsory for those Sikhs who are initiated into the Khalsa (the *Amritdharis*). Those who do not seek initiation are known as *Sehajdharis.*

There are no professional priests in Sikhism; anyone with a reasonable proficiency in the Punjabi language can conduct a service. Worship can be offered individually or communally, and in a private house or a *gurdwara* (temple). Sikhs are forbidden to eat meat prepared by ritual slaughter; they are also asked to abstain from smoking, alcohol and other intoxicants. Such abstention is compulsory for the Amritdharis.

There are about 24 million Sikhs worldwide and, according to the 2011 census, there are 432,000 adherents in England, Wales and Scotland. Every gurdwara manages its own affairs; there is no central body in the UK. The Sikh Missionary Society provides an information service.

SIKH MISSIONARY SOCIETY UK, 10 Featherstone Road, Southall, Middx UB2 5AA **T** 020-8574 1902 **E** info@sikhmissionarysociety.org **W** www.sikhmissionarysociety.org

ZOROASTRIANISM

Zoroastrians are followers of the Iranian prophet Spitaman Zarathushtra (or Zoroaster in its hellenised form) who lived *c.*1200–1500 BC. Zoroastrians were persecuted in Iran following the Arab invasion of Persia in the seventh century AD and a group (who are known as Parsis) migrated to India in the ninth century AD to avoid harassment and persecution. Zarathushtra's words are recorded in 17 hymns called the *Gathas,* which, together with other scriptures, form the *Avesta.*

Zoroastrianism teaches that there is one God, *Ahura Mazda* ('Wise Lord'), and that all creation stems ultimately from God; the Gathas teach that human beings have free will, are responsible for their own actions and can choose between good and evil. It is believed that choosing *Asha* (truth or righteousness), with the aid of *Vohu Manah* (good mind), leads to happiness for the individual and society, whereas choosing evil leads to unhappiness and conflict. The *Gathas* also encourage hard work, good deeds and charitable acts. Zoroastrians believe that after death the immortal soul is judged by God, and is then sent to paradise or hell, where it will stay until the end of time to be resurrected for the final judgment.

In Zoroastrian places of worship, an urn containing fire is the central feature; the fire symbolises purity, light and truth and is a visible symbol of the *Fravashi* or *Farohar* (spirit), the presence of Ahura Mazda in every human being. Zoroastrians respect nature and much importance is attached to cultivating land and protecting air, earth and water.

The Zoroastrian Trust Funds of Europe is the main body for Zoroastrians in the UK. Founded in 1861 as the Religious Funds of the Zoroastrians of Europe, it disseminates information on the Zoroastrian faith, provides a place of worship and maintains separate burial grounds for Zoroastrians. It also holds religious and social functions and provides assistance to Zoroastrians as considered necessary, including the provision of loans and grants to students of Zoroastrianism, and participates in inter-faith educational activities.

There are approximately 150,000 Zoroastrians worldwide, of which around 4,000 reside in England and Wales, mainly in London and the South East.

ZOROASTRIAN TRUST FUNDS OF EUROPE, Zoroastrian Centre, 440 Alexandra Avenue, Harrow, Middx HA2 9TL **T** 020-8866 0765 **E** secretary@ztfe.com **W** www.ztfe.com
President, Malcolm Deboo

CHURCHES

There are two established (ie state) churches in the UK: the Church of England and the Church of Scotland. There are no established churches in Wales or Northern Ireland, though the Church in Wales, the Scottish Episcopal Church and the Church of Ireland are members of the Anglican Communion.

THE CHURCH OF ENGLAND

The Church of England is divided into the two provinces of Canterbury and York, each under an archbishop. The two provinces are subdivided into 42 dioceses, the newest of which came into existence on 20 April 2014. The new Diocese of Leeds was formed from the amalgamation of the former dioceses of Bradford, Ripon and Leeds and Wakefield.

Legislative provision for the Church of England is made by the General Synod, established in 1970. It also discusses and expresses opinion on any other matter of religious or public interest. The General Synod has 483 members in total, divided between three houses: the House of Bishops, the House of Clergy and the House of Laity. It is presided over jointly by the Archbishops of Canterbury and York and normally meets twice a year. The synod has the power, delegated by parliament, to frame statute law (known as a 'measure') on any matter concerning the Church of England. A measure must be laid before both houses of parliament, who may accept or reject it but cannot amend it. Once accepted the measure is submitted for royal assent and then has the full force of law. In addition to the General Synod, there are synods at diocesan level. The entire General Synod is re-elected once every five years. The tenth General Synod was inaugurated by the Queen on 23 November 2015.

THE ARCHBISHOPS' COUNCIL

The Archbishops' Council was established in January 1999. Its creation was the result of changes to the Church of England's national structure proposed in 1995 and subsequently approved by the synod and parliament. The council's purpose, set out in the National Institutions Measure 1998, is 'to coordinate, promote and further the work and mission of the Church of England'. It reports to the General Synod. The Archbishops' Council comprises the Archbishops of Canterbury and York, *ex officio*, the prolocutors elected by the convocations of Canterbury and York, the chair and vice-chair of the House of Laity, two bishops, two clergy and two lay persons elected by their respective houses of the General Synod, the Church Estates Commissioner, and up to six persons appointed jointly by the two archbishops.

There are also a number of national boards, councils and other bodies working on matters such as social responsibility, mission, Christian unity and education, which report to the General Synod through the Archbishops' Council.

GENERAL SYNOD OF THE CHURCH OF ENGLAND/
ARCHBISHOPS' COUNCIL, Church House, Great Smith Street, London SW1P 3AZ **T** 020-7898 1000
Secretary-General, William Nye, LVO

THE ORDINATION AND CONSECRATION OF WOMEN

The canon making it possible for women to be ordained to the priesthood was promulgated in the General Synod in February 1994 and the first 32 women priests were ordained on 12 March 1994.

On 14 July 2014 the General Synod approved the Bishops and Priests (Consecration and Ordination of Women) Measure which made provision for the consecration of women as bishops and for the continuation of provision for the ordination of women. The Revd Elizabeth Lane was consecrated as the first female bishop on 26 January 2015 when she became Bishop Suffragan of Stockport in the diocese of Chester. The first female diocesan bishop, Rachel Treweek, was consecrated as the 41st Bishop of Gloucester on 22 July 2015.

PORVOO DECLARATION

The Porvoo Declaration was approved by the General Synod of the Church of England in July 1995. Churches that approve the declaration regard baptised members of each other's churches as members of their own, and allow free interchange of episcopally ordained ministers within the rules of each church.

MEMBERSHIP AND MINISTRY

	Full-time Diocesan Clergy 2017		Electoral Roll Membership 2017
	Male	Female	
Bath and Wells	132	52	29,800
Birmingham	108	42	15,800
Blackburn	132	24	28,200
Bristol	70	29	14,700
Canterbury	97	27	20,700
Carlisle	72	16	17,600
Chelmsford	222	85	40,800
Chester	138	53	38,900
Chichester	217	31	47,000
Coventry	79	29	15,300
Derby	94	38	15,000
Durham	95	43	18,900
Ely	75	41	17,500
Europe	63	5	11,600
Exeter	154	33	26,000
Gloucester	77	40	21,400
Guildford	119	48	26,300
Hereford	58	25	14,700
Leeds	218	89	38,900
Leicester	79	37	15,900
Lichfield	179	56	38,200
Lincoln	102	53	21,300
Liverpool	119	60	23,800
London	427	86	76,100
Manchester	135	63	28,000
Newcastle	86	32	13,800
Norwich	125	45	17,800
Oxford	264	96	51,800
Peterborough	94	47	17,900
Portsmouth	64	27	14,300
Rochester	145	40	25,900
St Albans	163	70	31,800
St Edmundsbury and Ipswich	79	36	19,000
Salisbury	132	60	35,200
Sheffield	94	32	15,500
Sodor and Man	15	3	2,000
Southwark	231	87	43,600
Southwell and Nottingham	76	31	17,500
Truro	48	34	13,200
Winchester	119	33	28,200
Worcester	74	34	14,500
York	139	54	28,600
Channel Islands	26	4	–
Total	5,235	1,870	1,053,000

In 2017, 102,250 people were baptised, 38,420 people were married in parish churches, the Church of England had an electoral roll membership of 1.05 million, and each week an average 895,300 people (all ages) attended services. There were 15,583 churches; 377 senior clergy (including bishops, archdeacons and cathedral clergy); 7,270 parochial stipendiary clergy; 100 non-parochial stipendiary clergy; 3,060 self-supporting ministers; 1,070 ordained chaplains; 5,180 readers or licensed lay ministers in active ministry; and 3,310 readers or licensed lay ministers with permission to officiate (active emeriti).

STIPENDS

The stipends below are for those appointed on or after 1 April 2004; transitional arrangements are in place for those appointed prior to this date. The national minimum stipend from 1 April 2019 is £24,770; under common tenure all full-time office-holders must receive stipend, or stipend together with other income related to their office, of at least this amount.

	2019–20
Archbishop of Canterbury	£83,400
Archbishop of York	£71,470
Bishop of London	£65,510
Diocesan bishops	£45,270
Suffragan bishops	£36,930
Deans	£36,930
Archdeacons	£35,400
Residentiary canons	*£28,580
Incumbents and clergy of similar status	*£26,470

* National stipend benchmark: adjusted regionally to reflect variations in the cost of living

CANTERBURY

105TH ARCHBISHOP AND PRIMATE OF ALL ENGLAND

Most Revd and Rt. Hon. Justin Welby, *cons.* 2011, *apptd* 2013; Lambeth Palace, London SE1 7JU
Signs Justin Cantuar:

BISHOPS SUFFRAGAN

Dover, vacant

Ebbsfleet, Rt. Revd Jonathan Goodall, *cons.* 2013, *apptd* 2013; Hill House, Treetops, The Mount, Caversham, Reading RG4 7RE
Richborough, Rt. Revd Norman Banks, *cons.* 2011, *apptd* 2011; Parkside House, Abbey Mill Lane, St Albans AL3 4HE
Maidstone, Rt. Revd Roderick Thomas, *cons.* 2015, *apptd* 2015; The Bishop's Lodge, Church Road, Worth, Crawley RH10 7RT

DEAN

Very Revd Robert Willis, *apptd* 2001

Dean of Jersey (A Peculiar), Very Revd Mike Keirle, *apptd* 2017
Dean of Guernsey (A Peculiar), Very Revd Tim Barker, *apptd* 2015

Organist (Canterbury Cathedral), David Flood, FRCO, *apptd* 1988

ARCHDEACONS

Ashford, Ven. Darren Miller, *apptd* 2018
Canterbury, Ven. Jo Kelly Moore *apptd* 2017
Maidstone, Ven. Stephen Taylor, *apptd* 2011

Vicar-General of Province and Diocese, Chancellor Sheila Cameron, QC
Commissary-General, Morag Ellis, QC
Joint Registrars of the Province, Canon John Rees; Stephen Slack
Diocesan Registrar and Legal Adviser, Owen Carew Jones

Diocesan Secretary, Julian Hills, Diocesan House, Lady Wootton's Green, Canterbury CT1 1NQ **T** 01227-459401

YORK

97TH ARCHBISHOP AND PRIMATE OF ENGLAND

Most Revd and Rt. Hon. Dr John Sentamu, *cons.* 1996, *trans.* 2005; Bishopthorpe, York YO23 2GE
Signs Sentamu Ebor:

BISHOPS SUFFRAGAN

Hull, Rt. Revd Alison White, *cons.* 2015, *apptd* 2015; Hullen House, Woodfield Lane, Hessle, Hull HU13 0ES
Selby, Rt. Revd John Thomson, *cons.* 2014, *apptd* 2014; 6 Pinfold Garth, Malton YO17 7XQ
Whitby, Rt. Revd Paul Ferguson, *cons.* 2014, *apptd* 2014; 21 Thornton Road, Stainton TS8 9DS

PRINCIPAL EPISCOPAL VISITOR

Beverley, Rt. Revd Glyn Webster, *cons.* 2013, *apptd* 2013; Holy Trinity Rectory, Micklegate, York YO1 6LE

DEAN

Very Revd Jonathan Frost, *apptd* 2019

Director of Music, Robert Sharpe, *apptd* 2008

ARCHDEACONS

Cleveland, Ven. Samantha Rushton, *apptd* 2015
East Riding, Ven. Andy Broom, *apptd* 2014
York, vacant

Chancellor of the Diocese, His Hon. Judge Collier, QC, *apptd* 2006
Acting Registrar and Legal Secretary, Louise Connacher
Diocesan Secretary, Canon Peter Warry, Diocesan House, Amy Johnson Way, York YO30 4XT **T** 01904-699500

LONDON (CANTERBURY)

133RD BISHOP

Rt. Revd Dame Sarah Mullally, DBE, *cons.* 2015, *apptd* 2017; Bishop of London's Office, St Michael Paternoster Royal, College Hill, London EC4R 2RL
Signs Sarah Londin:

AREA BISHOPS

Edmonton, Rt. Revd Robert Wickham, *cons.* 2015, *apptd* 2015; 27 Thurlow Road, London NW3 5PP
Kensington, Rt. Revd Graham Tomlin, *cons.* 2015, *apptd* 2015; Dial House, Riverside, Twickenham TW1 3DT
Stepney, Rt. Revd Joanne Grenfell, *cons.* 2019, *apptd* 2019; 63 Coburn Road, London E3 2DB
Willesden, Rt. Revd Peter Broadbent, *cons.* 2001, *apptd* 2001; 173 Willesden Lane, London NW6 7YN

BISHOP SUFFRAGAN

Islington, Rt. Revd Ric Thorpe, *cons.* 2015, *apptd* 2015; St Edmund the King, Lombard Street, London, EC3V 9EA
Fulham, Rt. Revd Jonathan Baker, *cons.* 2011, *apptd* 2013; The Vicarage, 5 St Andrew Street, London EC4A 3AF

DEAN OF ST PAUL'S

Very Revd Dr David Ison, PHD, *apptd* 2012

Director of Music, Andrew Carwood, *apptd* 2007

ARCHDEACONS

Hackney, Ven. Liz Adekunle, *apptd* 2016
Hampstead, Ven. John Hawkins, *apptd* 2015
London, Ven. Luke Miller, *apptd* 2016
Middlesex, Ven. Stephan Welch, *apptd* 2006
Northolt, Ven. Duncan Green, *apptd* 2013
Two Cities, vacant

Chancellor, Nigel Seed, QC, *apptd* 2002
Registrar and Legal Secretary, Paul Morris
Diocesan Secretary, Richard Gough, London Diocesan House, 36 Causton Street, London SW1P 4AU **T** 020-7932 1100

DURHAM (YORK)

74TH BISHOP

Rt. Revd Paul Butler, *cons.* 2004, *trans.* 2013; Auckland Castle, Bishop Auckland DL14 7NR
Signs Paul Dunelm:

BISHOP SUFFRAGAN

Jarrow, Rt. Revd Sarah Clark, *cons.* 2019, *apptd* 2019; Bishop's House, 25 Ivy Lane, Low Fell, Gateshead NE9 6QD

DEAN

Very Revd Andrew Tremlett, *apptd* 2015

Organist, Daniel Cook, *apptd* 2017

ARCHDEACONS

Auckland, Ven. Rick Simpson, *apptd* 2017
Durham, Ven. Ian Jagger, *apptd* 2006
Sunderland, Ven. Bob Cooper, *apptd* 2018

Chancellor, Adrian Iles, *apptd* 2017
Registrar and Legal Secretary, Philip Wills, *apptd* 2018
Diocesan Secretary, Andrew Thurston, Diocesan Office, Cuthbert House, Stonebridge, Durham DH1 3RY **T** 01388-660010

WINCHESTER (CANTERBURY)

97TH BISHOP

Rt. Revd Tim Dakin, cons. 2012, *apptd* 2011; Bishop's Office, Wolvesey, Winchester SO23 9ND
Signs Tim Winton:

BISHOPS SUFFRAGAN

Basingstoke, Rt. Revd David Williams, *cons.* 2014, *apptd* 2014; Diocesan Office, Old Alresford Place, Alresford, Hants SO24 9DH
Southampton, Rt. Revd Deborah Sellin, *cons.* 2019, *apptd* 2019; Diocesan Office, Old Alresford Place, Alresford, Hants SO24 9DH

DEAN

Very Revd Catherine Ogle, *apptd* 2017

Director of Music, Andrew Lumsden, *apptd* 2002

ARCHDEACONS

Bournemouth, Ven. Dr Peter Rouch, *apptd* 2011
Winchester, Ven. Richard Brand, *apptd* 2016
For Mission Development, Ven. Paul Moore, *apptd* 2014

Chancellor, Cain Ormondroyd, *apptd* 2017
Registrar and Legal Secretary, Sue de Candole
Chief Executive, Andrew Robinson, Old Alresford Place, Alresford, Hants SO24 9DH **T** 01962-737300

BATH AND WELLS (CANTERBURY)

79TH BISHOP

Rt. Revd Peter Hancock, *cons.* 2010, *apptd* 2014; The Bishop's Palace, Wells, Somerset BA5 2PD
Signs Peter Bath & Wells:

BISHOP SUFFRAGAN

Taunton, Rt. Revd Ruth Worsley, *cons.* 2015, *apptd* 2015; The Bishop's Palace, Market Place, Wells BA5 2PD

DEAN

Very Revd John Davies, *apptd* 2016

Organist, Matthew Owens, *apptd* 2005

ARCHDEACONS

Bath, Ven. Dr Adrian Youings, *apptd* 2017
Taunton, Ven. Simon Hill, *apptd* 2016
Wells, Ven. Anne Gell, *apptd* 2017

Chancellor, Timothy Briden, *apptd* 1993
Registrar and Legal Secretary, Roland Callaby
Diocesan Secretary, Nick May, The Old Deanery, St Andrew's Street, Wells, Somerset BA5 2UG **T** 01749-670777

BIRMINGHAM (CANTERBURY)

9TH BISHOP

Rt. Revd David Urquhart, KCMG *cons.* 2000, *apptd* 2006; Bishop's Croft, Old Church Road, Harborne, Birmingham B17 0BG
Signs David Birmingham:

BISHOP SUFFRAGAN

Aston, Anne Hollinghurst, *cons.* 2015, *apptd* 2015, Bishop's Lodge, 16 Coleshill Street, Sutton Coldfield B72 1SH

DEAN

Very Revd Matt Thompson, *apptd* 2017

Director of Music, David Hardie, *apptd* 2018

ARCHDEACONS

Aston, Ven. Simon Heathfield, *apptd* 2014
Birmingham, Ven. Jenny Tomlinson, *apptd* 2019

Chancellor, Mark Powell, QC, *apptd* 2012
Registrar and Legal Secretary, Vicki Simpson
Diocesan Secretary, Andrew Halstead, 1 Colmore Row, Birmingham B3 2BJ **T** 0121-426 0400

BLACKBURN (YORK)

9TH BISHOP

Rt. Revd Julian Henderson, *cons.* 2013, *apptd* 2013; Bishop's House, Ribchester Road, Blackburn BB1 9EF
Signs Julian Blackburn

BISHOPS SUFFRAGAN

Burnley, Rt. Revd Philip North, *cons.* 2015, *apptd* 2015; Dean House, 449 Padiham Road, Burnley BB12 6TE
Lancaster, Rt. Revd Dr Jill Duff, *cons.* 2018, *apptd* 2018; Shireshead Vicarage, Whinney Brow, Forton, Preston PR3 0AE

DEAN

Very Revd Peter Howell-Jones, *apptd* 2016

Organist and Director of Music, John Robinson, *apptd* 2019

ARCHDEACON

Blackburn, Ven. Mark Ireland, *apptd* 2015
Lancaster, vacant

Chancellor, His Hon. Judge Bullimore, *apptd* 1990
Registrar and Legal Secretary, Revd Paul Benfield
Diocesan Secretary, Graeme Pollard, Diocesan Office, Clayton House, Walker Office Park, Blackburn BB1 2QE **T** 01254-503070

BRISTOL (CANTERBURY)

56TH BISHOP

Rt. Revd Vivienne Faull, *cons.* 2018, *apptd* 2018; 58A High Street, Winterbourne, Bristol BS36 1JQ
Signs Vivienne Bristol

BISHOP SUFFRAGAN

Swindon, Rt. Revd Dr Lee Rayfield, *cons.* 2005, *apptd* 2005; Mark House, Field Rise, Swindon, Wiltshire SN1 4HP

DEAN
Very Revd David Hoyle, *apptd* 2010

Organist and Director of Music, Mark Lee, *apptd* 1998

ARCHDEACONS
Bristol, Ven. Neil Warwick, *apptd* 2019
Malmesbury, Ven. Christopher Bryan, *apptd* 2019

Chancellor, Revd Justin Gau
Registrar and Legal Secretary, Roland Callaby

Diocesan Secretary, Oliver Home, First Floor, Hillside House, 1500 Parkway North, Stoke Gifford, Bristol BS34 8YU **T** 0117-9060100

CARLISLE (YORK)

67TH BISHOP

Rt. Revd James Newcome, *cons.* 2002, *apptd* 2009; Bishop's House, Ambleside Road, Keswick CA12 4DD
Signs James Carliol

BISHOP SUFFRAGAN
Penrith, Revd Dr Emma Ineson, *cons.* 2019, *apptd* 2018; Holm Croft, 13 Castle Road, Kendal, Cumbria LA9 7AU

DEAN
Very Revd Mark Boyling, *apptd* 2004

Director of Music, Mark Duthie, *apptd* 2017

ARCHDEACONS
Carlisle, Ven. Lee Townend, *apptd* 2017
West Cumberland, Ven. Dr Richard Pratt, *apptd* 2009
Westmorland and Furness, Ven. Vernon Ross, *apptd* 2017

Chancellor, Geoffrey Tattersall, QC, *apptd* 2003
Registrar and Legal Secretary, Jane Lowdon
Diocesan Secretary, Derek Hurton, Church House, 19–24 Friargate, Penrith, Cumbria CA11 7XR **T** 01768-807777

CHELMSFORD (CANTERBURY)

10TH BISHOP

Rt. Revd Stephen Cottrell, *cons.* 2004, *apptd* 2010; Bishopscourt, Main Road, Margaretting, Ingatestone, Essex CM4 0HD
Signs Stephen Chelmsford

BISHOPS SUFFRAGAN
Barking, Rt. Revd Peter Hill, *cons.* 2014, *apptd* 2014; Barking Lodge, Verulam Avenue, London E17 8ES
Bradwell, Rt. Revd Dr John Perumbalath, *cons.* 2018, *apptd* 2018; Bishop's House. Orsett Road, Horndon-on-the-Hill, Essex SS17 8NS
Colchester, Rt. Revd Roger Morris, *cons.* 2014, *apptd* 2014; 1 Fitzwater Road, Colchester, Essex CO3 3SS

DEAN
Very Revd Nicholas Henshall, *apptd* 2013

Director of Music, James Davy, *apptd* 2012

ARCHDEACONS
Barking, Ven. Christopher Burke, *apptd* 2019
Chelmsford, Ven. Elizabeth Snowden, *apptd* 2016
Colchester, Ven. Ruth Patten, *apptd* 2019
Harlow, Ven. Vanessa Herrick, *apptd* 2017
Southend, Ven. Mike Lodge, *apptd* 2017
Stansted, Ven. Robin King, *apptd* 2013
West Ham, Ven. Elwin Cockett, *apptd* 2007

Chancellor, George Pulman, QC, *apptd* 2001
Registrar and Legal Secretary, Aiden Hargreaves-Smith
Chief Executive, Joel Gowen, 53 New Street, Chelmsford, Essex CM1 1AT **T** 01245-294400

CHESTER (YORK)

41ST BISHOP
vacant

BISHOPS SUFFRAGAN
Birkenhead, Rt. Revd Keith Sinclair, *cons.* 2007, *apptd* 2007; Bishop's Lodge, 67 Bidston Road, Prenton CH43 6TR
Stockport, vacant; Bishop's Lodge, Back Lane, Dunham, Altrincham WA14 4SG

DEAN
Very Revd Dr Timothy Stratford, *apptd* 2018

Organist and Director of Music, Philip Rushforth, FRCO, *apptd* 2008

ARCHDEACONS
Chester, Ven. Dr Michael Gilbertson, *apptd* 2010
Macclesfield, Ven. Ian Bishop, *apptd* 2011

Chancellor, His Hon. Judge Turner, QC, *apptd* 1998
Registrar and Legal Secretary, Lisa Moncur
Diocesan Secretary, George Colville, Church House, 5500 Daresbury Park, Daresbury, Warrington WA4 4GE **T** 01928-718834

CHICHESTER (CANTERBURY)

103RD BISHOP

Rt. Revd Dr Martin Warner, *cons.* 2010, *apptd* 2012; The Palace, Chichester PO19 1PY
Signs Martin Cicestr:

BISHOPS SUFFRAGAN
Horsham, vacant

Lewes, Rt. Revd Richard Jackson, *cons.* 2014, *apptd* 2014; Ebenezer House, Kingston Ridge, Kingston, Lewes BN7 3JU

DEAN
Very Revd Stephen Waine, *apptd* 2015

Organist, Charles Harrison, *apptd* 2014

ARCHDEACONS
Brighton and Lewes, Ven. Martin Lloyd Williams, *apptd* 2015
Chichester, Ven. Luke Irvine-Capel, *apptd* 2019
Horsham, Ven. Fiona Windsor, *apptd* 2014
Hastings, Ven. Edward Dowler, *apptd* 2016

Chancellor, Prof. Mark Hill, QC
Deputy Registrar and Legal Secretary, Darren Oliver
Diocesan Secretary, Gabrielle Higgins, Diocesan Church House, 211 New Church Road, Hove, E. Sussex BN3 4ED **T** 01273-421021

COVENTRY (CANTERBURY)

9TH BISHOP

Rt. Revd Dr Christopher Cocksworth, *cons.* 2008, *apptd* 2008; The Bishop's House, 23 Davenport Road, Coventry CV5 6PW
Signs Christopher Coventry

BISHOP SUFFRAGAN
Warwick, Rt. Revd John Stroyan, *cons.* 2005, *apptd* 2005; Warwick House, School Hill, Offchurch, Leamington Spa CV33 9AL

DEAN
Very Revd John Witcombe, *apptd* 2013

Director of Music, Mr Kerry Beaumont, *apptd* 2006

ARCHDEACONS
Archdeacon Missioner, Ven. Barry Dugmore, *apptd* 2019
Archdeacon Pastor, Ven. Sue Field *apptd* 2017

Chancellor, His Hon. Judge Eyre, *apptd* 2009
Registrar and Legal Secretary, Mary Allanson

Diocesan Secretary, Ruth Marlow, Cathedral & Diocesan Offices, 1 Hilltop, Coventry CV1 5AB **T** 024-7652 1200

DERBY (CANTERBURY)

8TH BISHOP

Rt. Revd. Elizabeth Lane, *cons.* 2015, *apptd* 2019; The Bishop's Office, 6 King Street, Duffield DE56 4EU
Signs Elizabeth Derby

BISHOP SUFFRAGAN

Repton, Rt. Revd Jan McFarlane, *cons.* 2016, *apptd* 2016; Repton House, 39 Hickton Road, Swanwick, Alfreton DE55 1AF

DEAN
Very Revd Dr Stephen Hance, *apptd* 2017

Director of Music, Alexander Binns, *apptd* 2019

ARCHDEACONS
Chesterfield, Ven. Carol Coslett, *apptd* 2018
Derby, Ven. Dr Christopher Cunliffe, *apptd* 2006

Chancellor, His Hon. Judge Bullimore, *apptd* 1981
Registrar and Legal Secretary, Nadine Waldron

Diocesan Secretary, Rachel Morris, Derby Church House, Full Street, Derby DE1 3DR **T** 01332-388650

ELY (CANTERBURY)

69TH BISHOP

Rt. Revd Stephen Conway, *cons.* 2006, *apptd* 2011; The Bishop's House, Ely CB7 4DW
Signs Stephen Ely

BISHOP SUFFRAGAN

Huntingdon, Rt. Revd Dr Dagmar Winter, *cons.* 2019, *apptd* 2019; 14 Lynn Road, Ely, Cambs CB6 1DA

DEAN
Very Revd Mark Bonney, *apptd* 2012

Director of Music, Edmund Aldhouse, *apptd* 2018

ARCHDEACONS
Cambridge, Ven. Dr Alex Hughes, *apptd* 2014
Huntingdon and Wisbech, Ven. Hugh McCurdy, *apptd* 2005

Chancellor, His Hon. Judge Leonard, QC
Registrar, Howard Dellar

Diocesan Secretary, Paul Evans, Bishop Woodford House, Barton Road, Ely, Cambs CB7 4DX **T** 01353-652701

EXETER (CANTERBURY)

71ST BISHOP

Rt. Revd Robert Atwell, *cons.* 2008, *apptd* 2014; The Palace, Exeter EX1 1HY
Signs Robert Exon:

BISHOPS SUFFRAGAN

Crediton, Rt. Revd Jackie Searle, *cons.* 2018, *apptd* 2018; 32 The Avenue, Tiverton EX16 4HW
Plymouth, Rt. Revd Nick McKinnel, *cons.* 2012, *trans.* 2015; 108 Molesworth Road, Stoke, Plymouth PL3 4AQ

DEAN
Very Revd Jonathan Greener, *apptd* 2017

Director of Music, Timothy Noon, *apptd* 2016

ARCHDEACONS
Barnstaple, Ven. Mark Butchers, *apptd* 2015
Exeter, Ven. Andrew Beane, *apptd* 2019
Plymouth, Ven. Nick Shutt, *apptd* 2019
Totnes, Ven. Douglas Dettmer, *apptd* 2015

Chancellor, Hon. Sir Andrew McFarlane
Registrar and Legal Secretary, Alison Stock

Diocesan Secretary, Stephen Hancock, The Old Deanery, The Cloisters, Exeter EX1 1HS **T** 01392-272686

GIBRALTAR IN EUROPE (CANTERBURY)

4TH BISHOP

Rt. Revd Robert Innes, PHD, *cons.* 2014, *apptd* 2014; Office of the Bishop in Europe, 47, rue Capitaine Crespel – boite 49, 1050 Brussels, Belgium

BISHOP SUFFRAGAN

In Europe, Rt. Revd David Hamid, *cons.* 2002, *apptd* 2002; 14 Tufton Street, London SW1P 3QZ

Dean, Cathedral Church of the Holy Trinity, Gibraltar, vacant

Chancellor, Pro-Cathedral of St Paul, Valletta, Malta, Canon Simon Godfrey
Chancellor, Pro-Cathedral of the Holy Trinity, Brussels, Belgium, Ven. Dr Paul Vrolijk

ARCHDEACONS
Eastern, Canon Adèle Kelham *(acting)*
France, Ven. Meurig Williams
Germany and Northern Europe, Canon John Newsome *(acting)*
Gibraltar, Ven. Geoffrey Johnston *(interim)*
Italy and Malta, Ven. Geoffrey Johnston *(acting)*
North-West Europe, Ven. Dr Paul Vrolijk
Switzerland, Canon Adèle Kelham

Chancellor, Prof. Mark Hill, QC
Registrar and Legal Secretary, Aiden Hargreaves-Smith

Diocesan Secretary, Andrew Caspari 14 Tufton Street, London SW1P 3QZ **T** 020-7898 1155

GLOUCESTER (CANTERBURY)

41ST BISHOP

Rt. Revd Rachel Treweek, *cons.* 2015, *apptd* 2015; 2 College Green, Gloucester GL1 2LR
Signs Rachel Gloucestr

BISHOP SUFFRAGAN

Tewkesbury, Rt. Revd Robert Springett, *cons.* 2016, *apptd* 2016; 2 College Green, Gloucester GL1 2LR

DEAN
Very Revd Stephen Lake, *apptd* 2011

Director of Music, Adrian Partington, *apptd* 2007

ARCHDEACONS
Cheltenham, Ven. Phil Andrew, *apptd* 2017
Gloucester, Ven. Hilary Dawson, *apptd* 2019

Chancellor and Vicar-General, June Rodgers, *apptd* 1990
Registrar and Legal Secretary, Jos Moule

Diocesan Secretary, Ben Preece Smith, Church House, College Green, Gloucester GL1 2LY **T** 01452-410022

GUILDFORD (CANTERBURY)

10TH BISHOP
Rt. Revd Andrew Watson, *cons.* 2008, *apptd* 2014; Willow Grange, Woking Road, Guildford, Surrey GU4 7QS
Signs Andrew Guildford

BISHOP SUFFRAGAN
Dorking, Rt Revd Jo Wells, *cons.* 2016, *apptd* 2016; Dayspring, 13 Pilgrim's Way, Guildford, Surrey GU4 8AD

DEAN
Very Revd Dianna Gwilliams, *apptd* 2013

Organist, Katherine Dienes-Williams, *apptd* 2007

ARCHDEACONS
Dorking, vacant
Surrey, Ven. Paul Davies, *apptd* 2017

Chancellor, Andrew Jordan
Registrar and Legal Secretary, Howard Dellar
Diocesan Secretary, Peter Coles, Church House, 20 Alan Turing Road, Guildford GU2 7YF **T** 01483-790300

HEREFORD (CANTERBURY)

105TH BISHOP
Rt. Revd Richard Frith, cons. 1998, apptd 2014; Bishop's House, The Palace, Hereford HR4 9BN
Signs Richard Hereford

BISHOP SUFFRAGAN
Ludlow, Rt. Revd Alistair Magowan, *cons.* 2009, *apptd* 2009; Bishop's House, Corvedale Road, Craven Arms, Shropshire SY7 9BT

DEAN
Very Revd Michael Tavinor, *apptd* 2002

Organist and Director of Music, Geraint Bowen, FRCO, *apptd* 2001

ARCHDEACONS
Hereford, Ven. Derek Chedzey, *apptd* 2018
Ludlow, Rt. Revd Alistair Magowan, *apptd* 2009

Chancellor, His Hon. Judge Kaye, QC
Registrar and Legal Secretary, Howard Dellar
Diocesan Secretary, Sam Pratley, The Palace, Hereford HR4 9BL **T** 01432-373300

LEEDS (YORK)

1ST BISHOP OF LEEDS
Rt. Revd Nicholas Baines, *cons.* 2003, *apptd* 2014; Hollin House, Weetwood Avenue, Leeds LS16 5NG
Signs Nicholas Leeds

AREA BISHOPS
Bradford, Rt. Revd Dr Toby Howarth, *cons.* 2014, *apptd* 2014; 47 Kirkgate, Shipley BD18 3EH
Huddersfield, Rt. Revd Jonathan Gibbs, *cons.* 2014, *apptd* 2014; University of Huddersfield, Ground Floor, Sir John Ramsden Court, Huddersfield HD1 3AQ
Ripon, Rt. Revd Dr Helen-Ann Hartley, *cons.* 2014, *apptd* 2018; The Bishop's Office, Redwood, New Road, Sharow, Ripon HG4 5BS
Wakefield, Rt. Revd Anthony Robinson, *cons.* 2002, *apptd* 2014; Pontefract House 181A Manygates Lane, Sandal, Wakefield WF2 7DR

SUFFRAGAN BISHOP
Richmond, Rt. Revd Paul Slater, *cons.* 2015, apptd 2015; Church House, 17–19 York Place, Leeds LS1 2EX

DEANS
Bradford, Very Revd Jerry Lepine, *apptd* 2013
Ripon, Very Revd John Dobson, *apptd* 2014
Wakefield, Very Revd Simon Cowling, *apptd* 2018

Directors of Music, Alexander Berry (Bradford), *apptd* 2017; Andrew Bryden (Ripon), *apptd* 2003; Thomas Moore (Wakefield), *apptd* 2010

ARCHDEACONS
Bradford, Ven. Andrew Jolley, *apptd* 2016
Halifax, Ven. Dr Anne Dawtry, *apptd* 2011
Leeds, Ven. Paul Ayers, *apptd* 2017
Richmond and Craven, Ven. Jonathan Gough, *apptd* 2019
Pontefract, Ven. Peter Townley, *apptd* 2008

Chancellor, Prof. Mark Hill, QC
Registrar and Legal Secretary, Peter Foskett
Diocesan Secretary, Debbie Child; Church House, 17–19 York Place, Leeds LS1 2EX **T** 0113-200 0540

LEICESTER (CANTERBURY)

7TH BISHOP
Rt Revd Martyn Snow, *cons.* 2013, *apptd* 2016; Bishop's Lodge, 10 Springfield Road, Leicester LE2 3BD
Signs Martyn Leicester

SUFFRAGAN BISHOP
Loughborough, Rt. Revd Guli Francis-Dehqani, *cons.* 2017, *apptd* 2017; c/o Bishop's Lodge, 10 Springfield Road, Leicester LE2 3BD

DEAN
Very Revd David Monteith, *apptd* 2013

Director of Music, Dr Christopher Ouvry-Johns

ARCHDEACONS
Leicester, Ven. Richard Worsfold, *apptd* 2018
Loughborough, Ven. Claire Wood, *apptd* 2017

Chancellor, Mark Blackett-Ord
Registrar and Legal Secretary, Lee Coley
Diocesan Secretary, Jonathan Kerry, St Martin's House, 7 Peacock Lane, Leicester LE1 5PZ **T** 0116-261 5200

LICHFIELD (CANTERBURY)

99TH BISHOP
Rt. Revd Dr Michael Ipgrave, OBE, *cons.* 2012, *apptd* 2016; 22 The Close, Lichfield, WS13 7LG
Signs Michael Lich:

AREA BISHOPS
Shrewsbury, Rt. Revd Sarah Bullock, *cons.* 2019, *apptd* 2019; Athlone House, 68 London Road, Shrewsbury SY2 6PG
Stafford, Rt. Revd Geoffrey Annas, *cons.* 2010, *apptd* 2010; Ash Garth, Broughton Crescent, Barlaston, Stoke-on-Trent ST12 9DD
Wolverhampton, Rt. Revd Clive Gregory, *cons.* 2007, *apptd* 2007; 61 Richmond Road, Wolverhampton WV3 9JH

DEAN
Very Revd Adrian Dorber, *apptd* 2005

Director of Music, Ben Lamb, *apptd* 2010
Organist, Martyn Rawles, *apptd* 2010

ARCHDEACONS
Lichfield, vacant
Salop, Ven. Paul Thomas, *apptd* 2011
Stoke-on-Trent, Ven. Matthew Parker, *apptd* 2013
Walsall, Ven. Julian Francis, *apptd* 2019

Chancellor, His Hon. Judge Eyre, *apptd* 2012
Joint Registrars and Legal Secretaries, Niall Blackie; Andrew Wynne

Diocesan Secretary, Julie Jones, St Mary's House, The Close, Lichfield, Staffs WS13 7LD **T** 01543-306030

LINCOLN (CANTERBURY)

72ND BISHOP
Rt. Revd Christopher Lowson, *cons.* 2011, *apptd* 2011; Bishop's Office, The Old Palace, Minster Yard, Lincoln LN2 1PU
Signs Christopher Lincoln

BISHOPS SUFFRAGAN
Grantham, Rt. Revd Dr Nicholas Chamberlain, *cons.* 2015, *apptd* 2015; The Old Palace, Minster Yard, Lincoln LN2 1PU
Grimsby, Rt. Revd Dr David Court (acting diocesan bishop), *cons.* 2014, *apptd* 2014; The Old Palace, Minster Yard, Lincoln LN2 1PU

DEAN
Very Revd Christine Wilson, *apptd* 2016 (currently on leave of absence)

Director of Music, Aric Prentice, *apptd* 2003

ARCHDEACONS
Boston, Ven. Dr Justine Allain Chapman, *apptd* 2013
Lincoln, Ven. Gavin Kirk, *apptd* 2016
Stow and Lindsey, Ven. Mark Steadman, *apptd* 2015

Chancellor, His Hon. Judge Bishop
Registrar and Legal Secretary, Ian Blaney
Diocesan Secretary, Revd David Dadswell, Edward King House, Minster Yard, Lincoln LN2 1PU **T** 01522-504050

LIVERPOOL (YORK)

8TH BISHOP
Rt. Revd Paul Bayes, *cons.* 2010, *apptd* 2014; Bishop's Lodge, Woolton Park, Liverpool L25 6DT
Signs Paul Liverpool

BISHOP SUFFRAGAN
Warrington, Rt. Revd Bev Mason, *cons.* 2018, *apptd* 2018; 34 Central Avenue, Eccleston Park, Prescot L34 2QP

DEAN
Very Revd Susan Jones, PHD, *apptd* 2018

Director of Music, Lee Ward, *apptd* 2017

ARCHDEACONS
Liverpool, Ven. Mike McGurk, *apptd* 2017
Knowsley & Sefton, Ven. Pete Spiers *apptd* 2015
St Helens & Warrington, Ven. Peter Preece, *apptd* 2015
Wigan & West Lancashire, Ven. Jennifer McKenzie, *apptd* 2015

Chancellor, His Hon. Judge Wood, QC
Registrar and Legal Secretary, Howard Dellar
Diocesan Secretary, Mike Eastwood, St James House, 20 St James Street, Liverpool L1 7BY **T** 0151-709 9722

MANCHESTER (YORK)

12TH BISHOP
Rt. Revd Dr David Walker, *cons.* 2000, *apptd* 2013; Bishopscourt, Bury New Road, Salford M7 4LE
Signs David Manchester

BISHOPS SUFFRAGAN
Bolton, Rt. Revd Mark Ashcroft, *cons.* 2016, *apptd* 2016; Bishop's Lodge, Walkenden Road, Walkenden M28 2WH
Middleton, Rt. Revd Mark Davies, *cons.* 2008, *apptd* 2008; The Hollies, Manchester Road, Rochdale OL11 3QY

DEAN
Very Revd Rogers Govender, *apptd* 2006

Organist, Christopher Stokes, *apptd* 1992

ARCHDEACONS
Bolton, Ven. Jean Burgess, *apptd* 2018
Manchester, Ven. Karen Lund, *apptd* 2017
Rochdale, Ven. Cherry Vann, *apptd* 2008
Salford, Ven. David Sharples, *apptd* 2009

Chancellor, Canon Geoffrey Tattersall, QC
Registrar and Legal Secretary, Jane Monks
Diocesan Secretary, Helen Platts, Diocesan Church House, 90 Deansgate, Manchester M3 2GH **T** 0161-828 1400

NEWCASTLE (YORK)

12TH BISHOP
Rt. Revd Christine Elizabeth Hardman, *cons.* 2015, apptd 2015; Bishop's House, 29 Moor Road South, Gosforth, Newcastle upon Tyne NE3 1PA
Signs Christine Newcastle

SUFFRAGAN BISHOP
Berwick Rt. Revd Mark Tanner, *cons.* 2016, *apptd* 2016; Berwick House, Longhirst Road, Pegswood, Morpeth NE61 6XF

DEAN
Very Revd Geoff Miller, *apptd* 2018

Director of Music, Ian Roberts, *apptd* 2016

ARCHDEACONS
Lindisfarne, Ven. Dr Peter Robinson, *apptd* 2008
Northumberland, Ven. Mark Wroe, *apptd* 2019

Chancellor, Euan Duff, *apptd* 2013
Registrar and Legal Secretary, Jane Lowdon
Diocesan Secretary, Canon Shane Waddle, Church House, St John's Terrace, North Shields NE29 6HS **T** 0191-270 4100

NORWICH (CANTERBURY)

72ND BISHOP
Rt. Revd Graham Usher, *cons.* 2014, *apptd* 2019; Bishop's House, Norwich NR3 1SB
Signs Graham Norvic:

BISHOPS SUFFRAGAN
Lynn, Rt. Revd Jonathan Meyrick, *cons.* 2011, *apptd* 2011; The Old Vicarage, Castle Acre, King's Lynn PE32 2AA
Thetford, Rt. Revd Alan Winton, PHD, *cons.* 2009, *apptd* 2009; The Red House, 53 Norwich Road, Stoke Holy Cross, Norwich NR14 8AB

DEAN
Very Revd Jane Hedges, *apptd* 2014

Master of Music, Ashley Grote, *apptd* 2012

ARCHDEACONS
Lynn, Ven. Ian Bentley, *apptd* 2018
Norfolk, Ven. Steven Betts, *apptd* 2012
Norwich, Ven. Karen Hutchinson, *apptd* 2016

Chancellor, Ruth Arlow, *apptd* 2012
Registrar and Legal Secretary, Stuart Jones

Diocesan Secretary, Richard Butler, Diocesan House, 109
    Dereham Road, Easton, Norwich, Norfolk NR9 5ES **T** 01603-
    880853

OXFORD (CANTERBURY)

44TH BISHOP

Rt. Revd Steven Croft, *cons.* 2009, *apptd* 2016; Church House
    Oxford, Langford Locks, Kidlington, Oxford OX5 1GF
    Signs Steven Oxon:

AREA BISHOPS

Buckingham, Rt. Revd Dr Alan Wilson, *cons.* 2003, *apptd*
    2003; Sheridan, Grimms Hill, Great Missenden, Bucks HP16 9BD
Dorchester, Rt. Revd Colin Fletcher, *cons.* 2000, *apptd* 2000;
    Arran House, Sandy Lane, Yarnton, Oxon OX5 1PB
Reading, vacant; Bishop's House, Tidmarsh Lane, Tidmarsh,
    Reading RG8 8HA

DEAN OF CHRIST CHURCH
Very Revd Martyn Percy, PHD, *apptd* 2014

Organist, Steven Grahl, *apptd* 2018

ARCHDEACONS
Berkshire, Ven. Olivia Graham, *apptd* 2013
Buckingham, Ven. Guy Elsmore, *apptd* 2016
Dorchester, Ven. Judy French, *apptd* 2014
Oxford, Ven. Martin Gorick, *apptd* 2013

Chancellor, His Hon. Judge Hodge, QC, *apptd* 2019
Joint Registrars and Legal Secretaries, Darren Oliver; Revd
    Canon John Rees

Diocesan Secretary, Mark Humphriss, Church House Oxford,
    Langford Locks, Kidlington, Oxford OX5 1GF **T** 01865-208200

PETERBOROUGH (CANTERBURY)

38TH BISHOP

Rt. Revd Donald Allister, *cons.* 2010, *apptd* 2009; Bishop's
    Lodging, The Palace, Peterborough PE1 1YA
    Signs Donald Petriburg:

BISHOP SUFFRAGAN

Brixworth, Rt. Revd John Holbrook, *cons.* 2011, *apptd* 2011;
    Orchard Acre, 11 North Street, Mears Ashby, Northants NN6
    0DW

DEAN
Very Revd Christopher Dalliston, *apptd* 2018

Director of Music, Tansy Castledine, *apptd* 2018

ARCHDEACONS
Northampton, Ven. Richard Ormston, *apptd* 2014
Oakham, Ven. Gordon Steele, *apptd* 2012

Chancellor, David Pittaway, QC, *apptd* 2005
Registrar and Legal Secretary, Anna Spriggs

Diocesan Secretary, Andrew Roberts, Diocesan Office, The Palace,
    Peterborough PE1 1YB **T** 01733-887000

PORTSMOUTH (CANTERBURY)

9TH BISHOP

Rt. Revd Christopher Foster, *cons.* 2010, *apptd* 2010;
    Bishopsgrove, 26 Osborn Road, Fareham, Hants PO16 7DQ
    Signs Christopher Portsmouth

DEAN
Very Revd Anthony Cane, *apptd* 2019

Organist, David Price, *apptd* 1996

ARCHDEACONS
Isle of Wight, Ven. Peter Leonard, *apptd* 2019
Portsdown, vacant
The Meon, Ven. Gavin Collins, *apptd* 2011

Chancellor, His Hon. Judge Waller, CBE
Registrar and Legal Secretary, Hilary Tyler

Diocesan Secretary, Victoria James, Diocesan Offices, 1st Floor,
    Peninsular House, Wharf Road, Portsmouth PO2 8HB
    T 023-9289 9664

ROCHESTER (CANTERBURY)

107TH BISHOP

Rt. Revd James Langstaff, *cons.* 2004, *apptd* 2010;
    Bishopscourt, 24 St Margaret's Street, Rochester ME1 1TS
    Signs, James Roffen:

BISHOP SUFFRAGAN

Tonbridge, Rt. Revd Simon Burton-Jones, *cons.* 2018, *apptd*
    2018; 25 Shoesmith Lane, Kings Hill, Kent ME19 4FF

DEAN
Very Revd Dr Philip Hesketh, *apptd* 2016

Interim Director of Music, Adrian Bawtree, *apptd* 2018

ARCHDEACONS
Bromley & Bexley, Ven. Dr Paul Wright, *apptd* 2003
Rochester, Ven. Andrew Wooding Jones, *apptd* 2018
Tonbridge, Ven. Julie Conalty *apptd* 2017

Chancellor, The Worshipful John Gallagher
Registrar and Legal Secretary, Owen Carew-Jones

Diocesan Secretary, vacant, St Nicholas Church, Boley Hill,
    Rochester ME1 1SL **T** 01634-560000

ST ALBANS (CANTERBURY)

10TH BISHOP

Rt. Revd Dr Alan Smith, *cons.* 2001, *apptd* 2009, *trans.* 2009;
    Abbey Gate House, St Albans AL3 4HD
    Signs Alan St Albans

BISHOPS SUFFRAGAN

Bedford, Rt. Revd Richard Atkinson, OBE, *cons.* 2012, *apptd*
    2012; Bishop's Lodge, Bedford Road, Cardington, Bedford
    MK44 3SS
Hertford, Rt. Revd Dr Michael Beasley, *cons.* 2015, *apptd*
    2015; Bishopswood, 3 Stobarts Close, Knebworth SG3 6ND

DEAN
Very Revd Dr Jeffrey John, *apptd* 2004

Organist, Andrew Lucas, *apptd* 1998

ARCHDEACONS
Bedford, Ven. Dave Middlebrook, *apptd* 2019
Hertford, Ven. Janet Mackenzie, *apptd* 2016
St Albans, Ven. Jonathan Smith, *apptd* 2008

Chancellor, Lyndsey de Mestre, QC
Deputy Registrars, Jonathan Baldwin; Owen Carew-Jones

Diocesan Secretary, Susan Pope, Holywell Lodge, 41 Holywell Hill,
    St Albans AL1 1HE **T** 01727-854532

ST EDMUNDSBURY AND IPSWICH (CANTERBURY)

11TH BISHOP

Rt. Revd Martin Seeley, *cons.* 2015, *apptd* 2015; The Bishop's House, 4 Park Road, Ipswich IP1 3ST
Signs Martin St Edmundsbury and Ipswich

BISHOP SUFFRAGAN

Dunwich, Rt. Revd Michael Harrison, PHD, *cons.* 2016, *apptd* 2015; Robin Hall, Chapel Lane, Mendlesham, Stowmarket IP14 5SQ

DEAN

Very Revd Joe Hawes, *apptd* 2018

Director of Music, James Thomas, *apptd* 1997

ARCHDEACONS

Ipswich, Ven. Rhiannon King, *apptd* 2019
Sudbury, Ven. Dr David Jenkins, *apptd* 2010
Suffolk, Ven. Ian Morgan, *apptd* 2012
Rural Mission, Ven. Sally Gaze, *apptd* 2019

Chancellor, David Etherington, QC
Registrar and Legal Secretary, James Hall

Diocesan Secretary, Anna Hughes, Diocesan Office, St Nicholas Centre, 4 Cutler Street, Ipswich IP1 1UQ **T** 01473-298500

SALISBURY (CANTERBURY)

78TH BISHOP

Rt. Revd Nicholas Holtam, *cons.* 2011, *apptd* 2011; South Canonry, 71 The Close, Salisbury SP1 2ER
Signs Nicholas Sarum

BISHOPS SUFFRAGAN

Ramsbury, Rt. Revd Dr Andrew Rumsey, *cons.* 2019, *apptd* 2018; Church House, Crane Street, Salisbury SP1 2QB
Sherborne, Rt. Revd Karen Gorham, *cons.* 2016, *apptd* 2015; The Sherborne Office, St Nicholas' Church Centre, 30 Wareham Road, Corfe Mullen BH21 3LE

DEAN

Very Revd Nicholas Papadopulos *apptd* 2018

Director of Music, David Halls, *apptd* 2005

ARCHDEACONS

Dorset, Ven. Antony MacRow-Wood, *apptd* 2015
Sarum, Ven. Alan Jeans, *apptd* 2003
Sherborne, Ven. Penny Sayer, *apptd* 2018
Wilts, Ven. Sue Groom, *apptd* 2016

Chancellor, Canon Ruth Arlow, *apptd* 2016
Registrar and Legal Secretary, Sue de Candole

Diocesan Secretary, David Pain, Church House, Crane Street, Salisbury SP1 2QB **T** 01722-411922

SHEFFIELD (YORK)

8TH BISHOP

Rt. Revd Dr Peter Wilcox, *cons.* 2017, *apptd* 2017; Bishopscroft, Snaithing Lane, Sheffield S10 3LG
Signs Peter Sheffield

BISHOP SUFFRAGAN

Doncaster, vacant

DEAN

Very Revd Peter Bradley, *apptd* 2003

Director of Music, Thomas Corns, *apptd* 2017

ARCHDEACONS

Doncaster, Ven. Steve Wilcockson, *apptd* 2012
Sheffield and Rotherham, Ven. Malcolm Chamberlain, *apptd* 2013

Chancellor, Her Hon. Judge Sarah Singleton, QC, *apptd* 2014
Registrar and Legal Secretary, Andrew Vidler

Diocesan Secretary, Heidi Adcock, Church House, 95–99 Effingham Street, Rotherham S65 1BL **T** 01709-309100

SODOR AND MAN (YORK)

82ND BISHOP

Rt. Revd Peter Eagles, *cons.* 2017, *apptd* 2017; Thie yn Aspick, 4 The Falls, Douglas, Isle of Man IM4 4PZ
Signs Peter Sodor as Mannin

ARCHDEACON OF MAN

Ven. Andrew Brown, *apptd* 2011

Vicar-General and Chancellor, Howard Connell
Registrar, Louise Connacher

Diocesan Secretary, Andrew Swithinbank, c/o Thie yn Aspick, 4 The Falls, Douglas, Isle of Man IM4 4PZ **T** 07624-314590

SOUTHWARK (CANTERBURY)

10TH BISHOP

Rt. Revd Christopher Chessun, *cons.* 2005, *apptd* 2011; Trinity House, 4 Chapel Court, Borough High Street, London SE1 1HW
Signs Christopher Southwark

AREA BISHOPS

Croydon, Rt. Revd Jonathan Clark, *cons.* 2012, *apptd* 2012; St Matthew's House, 100 George Street, London CR0 1PE
Kingston upon Thames, Rt. Revd Dr Richard Cheetham, *cons.* 2002, *apptd* 2002; 620 Kingston Road, Raynes Park, London SW20 8DN
Woolwich, Rt. Revd Dr Karowei Dorgu, *cons.* 2017, *apptd* 2017; Trinity House, 4 Chapel Court, Borough High Street, London SE1 1HW

DEAN

Very Revd Andrew Nunn, *apptd* 2011

Director of Music, Ian Keatley, *apptd* 2019

ARCHDEACONS

Croydon, Ven. Christopher Skilton, *apptd* 2013
Lambeth, Ven. Simon Gates, *apptd* 2013
Lewisham & Greenwich, Ven. Alastair Cutting, *apptd* 2013
Reigate, Ven. Moira Astin, *apptd* 2016
Southwark, Ven. Dr Jane Steen, *apptd* 2013
Wandsworth, Ven. John Kiddle, *apptd* 2015

Chancellor, Philip Petchey
Registrar and Legal Secretary, Paul Morris

Diocesan Secretary, Ruth Martin, Trinity House, 4 Chapel Court, Borough High Street, London SE1 1HW **T** 020-7939 9400

SOUTHWELL AND NOTTINGHAM (YORK)

12TH BISHOP

Rt. Revd Paul Williams, *cons.* 2009, *trans.* 2015; Jubilee House, Westgate, Southwell NG25 0JH
Signs Paul Southwell and Nottingham

BISHOP SUFFRAGAN

Sherwood, Rt. Revd Anthony Porter, *cons.* 2006, *apptd* 2006; Jubilee House, Westgate, Southwell NG25 0JH

DEAN
Very Revd Nicola Sullivan, *apptd* 2016

Rector Chori, Paul Provost, *apptd* 2017

ARCHDEACONS
Newark, Ven. David Picken, *apptd* 2012
Nottingham, Ven. Phil Williams, *apptd* 2019

Chancellor, His Hon. Judge Ockelton
Registrar and Legal Secretary, Amanda Redgate
Chief Executive, Nigel Spraggins, Jubilee House, Westgate,
Southwell, Notts NG25 0JH **T** 01636-814331

TRURO (CANTERBURY)

16TH BISHOP
Rt. Revd Philip Mounstephen, *cons.* 2018, *apptd* 2018; Lis
Escop, Feock, Truro TR3 6QQ
Signs Philip Truro

BISHOP SUFFRAGAN
St Germans, Rt. Revd Christopher Goldsmith, DPHIL, *cons.*
2013, *apptd* 2013; Lis Escop, Feock, Truro TR3 6QQ

DEAN
Very Revd Roger Bush, *apptd* 2012

Organist and Director of Music, Chris Gray, *apptd* 2008

ARCHDEACONS
Bodmin, Ven. Audrey Elkington, *apptd* 2011
Cornwall, Ven. Paul Bryer, *apptd* 2019

Chancellor, Timothy Briden, *apptd* 1998
Registrar and Legal Secretary, Jos Moule
Diocesan Secretary, Esther Pollard, Church House, Woodlands
Court, Truro Business Park, Threemilestone, Truro TR4 9NH
T 01872-274351

WORCESTER (CANTERBURY)

113TH BISHOP
Rt. Revd Dr John Inge, *cons.* 2003, *apptd* 2007; The Bishop's
Office, The Old Palace, Deansway, Worcester WR1 2JE
Signs John Wigorn

SUFFRAGAN BISHOP
Dudley, vacant; Bishop's House, 60 Bishop's Walk, Cradley Heath,
West Midlands B64 7RH

DEAN
Very Revd Dr Peter Atkinson, *apptd* 2006

Director of Music, Samuel Hudson, *apptd* 2018

ARCHDEACONS
Dudley, Ven. Nikki Groarke, *apptd* 2014
Worcester, Ven. Robert Jones, *apptd* 2014

Chancellor, Charles Mynors, *apptd* 1999
Registrar and Legal Secretary, Stuart Ness
Diocesan Secretary, John Preston, The Old Palace, Deansway,
Worcester WR1 2JE **T** 01905-20537

ROYAL PECULIARS

WESTMINSTER
The Collegiate Church of St Peter

Dean, vacant
Canon Steward, Revd Anthony Ball

Chapter Clerk, Receiver-General and Registrar, Paul Baumann,
CBE; Chapter Office, 20 Dean's Yard, London SW1P 3PA
Organist, James O'Donnell, *apptd* 2000
Legal Secretary, Christopher Vyse, *apptd* 2000

WINDSOR
The Queen's Free Chapel of St George within Her Castle of Windsor

Dean, Rt. Revd David Conner, KCVO, *apptd* 1998
Chapter Clerk, Charlotte Manley, CVO, OBE, *apptd* 2003;
Chapter Office, The Cloisters, Windsor Castle, Windsor, Berks
SL4 1NJ
Director of Music, James Vivian, *apptd* 2013

OTHER ANGLICAN CHURCHES

THE CHURCH IN WALES

The Anglican Church was the established church in Wales
from the 16th century until 1920, when the estrangement of
the majority of Welsh people from Anglicanism resulted in
disestablishment. Since then the Church in Wales has been an
autonomous province consisting of six sees. The bishops are
elected by an electoral college comprising elected lay and
clerical members, who also elect one of the diocesan bishops
as Archbishop of Wales.

The legislative body of the Church in Wales is the Governing
Body, which has 138 members divided between the three
orders of bishops, clergy and laity. Its president is the
Archbishop of Wales and it meets twice annually. Its decisions
are binding upon all members of the church. The church's
property and finances are the responsibility of the
Representative Body. There are 44,875 members of the
Church in Wales, with 410 stipendiary clergy and 563
parishes.

THE REPRESENTATIVE BODY OF THE CHURCH IN
WALES, 2 Callaghan Square, Cardiff CF10 5BT
T 029-2034 8200 *Secretary,* Simon Lloyd
13TH ARCHBISHOP OF WALES, Most Revd John Davies
(Bishop of Swansea and Brecon), *elected* 2017
Signs John Cambrensis

BISHOPS
Bangor (81st), Rt. Revd Andrew John, *b.* 1964, *cons.* 2008,
elected 2008; Ty'r Esgob, Bangor, Gwynedd LL57 2SS
Signs Andrew Bangor. *Stipendiary clergy,* 45
Llandaff (103rd), Rt. Revd June Osborne, *b.* 1953, *cons.*
2017, *elected* 2017; Llys Esgob, The Cathedral Green, Llandaff,
Cardiff CF5 2YE
Signs June Landav. *Stipendiary clergy,* 107
Monmouth (11th), vacant; Bishopstow, Stow Hill, Newport NP20
4EA
Stipendiary clergy, 45
St Asaph (76th), Rt. Revd Gregory Cameron, *b.* 1959, *cons.*
2009, *elected* 2009; Esgobty, Upper Denbigh Road, St Asaph,
Denbighshire LL17 0TW
Signs Gregory Llanelwy. *Stipendiary clergy,* 76
St David's (129th), Rt. Revd Joanna Penberthy, *b.* 1960, *cons.*
2017, *elected* 2016; Llys Esgob, Abergwili, Carmarthen SA31
2JG
Signs Joanna Tyddewi. *Stipendiary clergy,* 82
Swansea and Brecon (9th), Most Revd John Davies (also
Archbishop of Wales), *b.* 1953, *cons.* 2008, *trans.* 2017; Ely
Tower, Castle Square, Brecon, Powys LD3 9DJ
Signs John Cambrensis. *Stipendiary clergy,* 55

The stipend for a diocesan bishop of the Church in Wales is
£45,956 a year for 2019–20.

SCOTTISH EPISCOPAL CHURCH
The Scottish Episcopal Church was founded after the Act of
Settlement (1690) established the presbyterian nature of the
Church of Scotland. The Scottish Episcopal Church is a
member of the worldwide Anglican Communion. The
governing authority is the General Synod, which consists of

the Church's seven bishops, the conveners of the provincial Standing Committee, the conveners of the boards, the Church's representatives on the Anglican Consultative Council and 124 elected members (62 from the clergy and 62 from the laity). The General Synod meets once a year. The bishop who convenes and presides at meetings of the General Synod is called the 'primus' and is elected by his fellow bishops.

As at December 2018 there were 28,647 members of the Scottish Episcopal Church, seven bishops, around 500 serving clergy and 300 churches and places of worship.

THE GENERAL SYNOD OF THE SCOTTISH EPISCOPAL CHURCH, 21 Grosvenor Crescent, Edinburgh EH12 5EE **T** 0131-225 6357 **W** www.scotland.anglican.org
Secretary-General, John Stuart

PRIMUS OF THE SCOTTISH EPISCOPAL CHURCH, Most Revd Mark Strange (Bishop of Moray, Ross and Caithness), *elected* 2017

BISHOPS
Aberdeen and Orkney, Rt. Revd Anne Dyer, *b.* 1957, *cons.* 2018, *elected* 2017. *Clergy,* 50
Argyll and the Isles, Rt. Revd Kevin Pearson, *b.* 1954, *cons.* 2011, *elected* 2010. *Clergy,* 25
Brechin, Rt. Revd Andrew Swift, *b.* 1968, *cons.* 2018, *elected* 2018. *Clergy,* 30
Edinburgh, Rt. Revd Dr John Armes, *b.* 1955, *cons.* 2012, *elected* 2012. *Clergy,* 160
Glasgow and Galloway, vacant. *Clergy,* 110
Moray, Ross and Caithness, Most Revd Mark Strange, *b.* 1961, *cons.* 2007, *elected* 2007. *Clergy,* 60
St Andrews, Dunkeld and Dunblane, Rt. Revd Ian Paton, *elected* 2018. *Clergy,* 75
The minimum stipend of a diocesan bishop of the Scottish Episcopal Church for 2019 is £39,705 (ie 1.5 times the standard clergy stipend of £26,470).

CHURCH OF IRELAND

The Anglican Church was the established church in Ireland from the 16th century but never secured the allegiance of the majority and was disestablished in 1871. The Church of Ireland is divided into the provinces of Armagh and Dublin, each under an archbishop. The provinces are subdivided into 12 dioceses.

The legislative body is the General Synod, which has 660 members in total, divided between the House of Bishops (12 members) and the House of Representatives (216 clergy and 432 laity). The Archbishop of Armagh is elected by the House of Bishops; other episcopal elections are made by an electoral college.

There are around 375,000 members of the Church of Ireland, 249,000 in Northern Ireland and 126,000 in the Republic of Ireland. There are two archbishops, ten bishops and 441 stipendiary clergy.

CENTRAL OFFICE, Church of Ireland House, Church Avenue, Rathmines, Dublin D06 CF67 **T** (+353) (1) 497 8422
Chief Officer and Secretary-General of the Representative Church Body, David Ritchie

PROVINCE OF ARMAGH
Archbishop of Armagh, Primate of all Ireland and Metropolitan, Most Revd Richard Clarke, PHD, *b.* 1949, *cons.* 1996, *trans.* 2012. *Clergy,* 42

BISHOPS
Clogher, Rt. Revd John McDowell, *b.* 1956, *cons.* 2011, *elected* 2011. *Clergy,* 23
Connor, Rt. Revd Alan Abernethy, *b.* 1957, *cons.* 2007, *elected* 2007. *Clergy,* 70

Derry and Raphoe, vacant. *Clergy,* 46
Down and Dromore, Rt. Revd Harold Miller, *b.* 1950, *cons.* 1997, *elected* 1997. *Clergy,* 79
Kilmore, Elphin and Ardagh, Rt. Revd Ferran Glenfield, PHD *b.* 1954, *cons.* 2013, *elected* 2013. *Clergy,* 22
Tuam, Killala and Achonry, Rt. Revd Patrick Rooke, *b.* 1955, *cons.* 2011, *elected* 2011. *Clergy,* 10

PROVINCE OF DUBLIN
Archbishop of Dublin, Bishop of Glendalough, Primate of Ireland and Metropolitan, Most Revd Michael Jackson, PHD, DPHIL, *b.* 1956, *cons.* 2002, *trans.* 2011. *Clergy,* 61

BISHOPS
Cashel, Ferns and Ossory, Rt. Revd Michael Burrows, *b.* 1961, *cons.* 2006, *elected* 2006. *Clergy,* 32
Cork, Cloyne and Ross, Rt. Revd Paul Colton, PHD, *b.* 1960, *cons.* 1999, *elected* 1999. *Clergy,* 25
Limerick, Killaloe and Ardfert, Rt. Revd Kenneth Kearon, *b.* 1953, *cons.* 2015, *elected* 2014. *Clergy,* 16
Meath and Kildare, Most Revd Patricia Storey, *b.* 1960, *cons.* 2013, *elected* 2013. *Clergy,* 15

OVERSEAS

PRIMATES
Primates and Archbishops of Aotearoa, New Zealand and Polynesia, Most Revd Philip Richardson; Most Revd Don Tamihere
Primate of Australia, Most Revd Phillip Freier
Primate of Brazil, Most Revd Naudal Alves Gomes
Archbishop of the Province of Burundi, Most Revd Martin Nyaboho
Primate of Canada, Most Revd Linda Nicholls
Archbishop of the Province of Central Africa, Most Revd Albert Chama
Primate of the Central Region of America, Rt. Revd Julio Thompson
Primate of Chile, Most Revd Héctor Zavala Muñoz
Archbishop of the Province of Congo, Most Revd Zacharie Masimango Katanda
Archbishop of Hong Kong Sheng Kung Hui, Most Revd Paul Kwong
Archbishop of the Province of the Indian Ocean, Most Revd James Wong Yin Song
Primate of Japan (Nippon Sei Ko Kai), Most Revd Nathaniel Makoto Uematsu
Archbishop of Jerusalem and the Middle East, Most Revd Suheil Dawani
Primate and Archbishop of All Kenya, Most Revd Jackson Ole Sapit
Primate of Korea, Most Revd Moses Nagjun Yoo
Archbishop of Melanesia, Most Revd George Takeli
Presiding Bishop of Mexico, Most Revd Francisco Moreno
Archbishop of the Province of Myanmar (Burma), Most Revd Stephen Oo
Metropolitan and Primate of All Nigeria, Most Revd Nicholas Okoh
Archbishop of Papua New Guinea, Rt. Revd Allan Migi
Prime Bishop of the Philippines, Most Revd Joel Atiwag Pachao
Archbishop of the Province of Rwanda, Most Revd Laurent Mbanda
Archbishop of the Province of South East Asia, Most Revd Ng Moon Hing
Primate of Southern Africa, Most Revd Dr Thabo Makgoba
Presiding Bishop of South America, Most Revd Gregory Venables
Primate of the Province of South Sudan, Most Revd Justin Badi Arama
Archbishop of the Province of Sudan, Most Revd Ezekiel Kumir Kondo

Archbishop of Tanzania, Most Revd Maimbo Mndolwa
Archbishop of the Province of Uganda, Most Revd Stanley
   Ntagali
Presiding Bishop of the USA, Most Revd Michael Curry
Primate and Metropolitan of the Province of West Africa, Most
   Revd Dr Daniel Sarfo
Archbishop of the Province of the West Indies, Most Revd
   Howard Gregory

OTHER CHURCHES AND EXTRA-PROVINCIAL
DIOCESES
Anglican Church of Bermuda, extra-provincial to Canterbury
   Bishop, Rt. Revd Nicholas Dill
Church of Ceylon, extra-provincial to Canterbury
   Bishop of Colombo, Rt. Revd Dhiloraj Canagasabey
   Bishop of Kurunegala, Rt. Revd Keerthisiri Fernando
Episcopal Church of Cuba, Rt. Revd Griselda Del Carpio
Falkland Islands, extra-provincial to Canterbury
   Bishop, Rt. Revd Timothy Thornton (Bishop to the Forces)
Lusitanian Church (Portuguese Episcopal Church), extra-provincial
   to Canterbury
   Bishop, Rt. Revd Jose Cabral
Reformed Episcopal Church of Spain, extra-provincial to Canterbury
   Bishop, Rt. Revd Carlos López-Lozano

MODERATION OF CHURCHES IN FULL
COMMUNION WITH THE ANGLICAN
COMMUNION
Church of Bangladesh, Most Revd Samuel Mankhin
Church of North India, Most Revd Dr Prem Chand Singh
Church of South India, Most Revd Thomas Oommen
Church of Pakistan, Most Revd Humphrey Peters

CHURCH OF SCOTLAND

The Church of Scotland is the national church of Scotland. The
church is reformed in doctrine, and presbyterian in
constitution; ie based on a hierarchy of courts of ministers and
elders and, since 1990, of members of a diaconate. At local
level the Kirk Session consists of the parish minister and ruling
elders. At district level the presbyteries, of which there are 44
in Britain, consist of all the ministers in the district, one ruling
elder from each congregation, and those members of the
diaconate who qualify for membership. The General Assembly
is the supreme authority, and is presided over by a Moderator
chosen annually by the Assembly. The sovereign, if not present
in person, is represented by a Lord High Commissioner who
is appointed each year by the Crown. In May 2019 the General
Assembly voted in favour of replacing the Council of Assembly
with a new 12-person body, the Assembly Trustees, from June
2019. The Assembly Trustees appoint a chief officer, who has
oversight of budgets and staff, and other office bearers.
   The Church of Scotland has around 360,000 members, 780
parish ministers and 30,000 elders. The majority of parishes
are in Scotland, but there are also churches in England, Europe
and overseas.

Lord High Commissioner (2019–20), Duke of Buccleuch and
   Queensberry, KT, KBE
Moderator of the General Assembly (2019–20), Rt. Revd Colin
   Sinclair
Principal Clerk, Revd Dr George Whyte
Procurator, James McNeill, QC
Law Agent and Solicitor of the Church, Mary Macleod
Parliamentary Officer, Chloe Clemmons
General Treasurer, Anne Macintosh
Convener to the Assembly Trustees, Very Revd D John Chalmers
CHURCH OFFICE, 121 George Street, Edinburgh EH2 4YN
   T 0131-225 5722

PRESBYTERIES AND CLERKS
Aberdeen, Revd Dr John Ferguson
Abernethy, Revd James MacEwan
Angus, Revd Dr Ian McLean
Annandale and Eskdale, Revd Adam Dillon
Ardrossan, Jean Hunter
Argyll, Dr Christopher Brett
Ayr, Revd Kenneth Elliott
Buchan, Revd Sheila Kirk
Caithness, Revd Ronald Johnstone
Dumbarton, David Sinclair
Dumfries and Kirkcudbright, Revd Donald Campbell
Dundee, Revd James Wilson
Dunfermline, Revd Iain Greenshields
Dunkeld and Meigle, Revd John Russell
Duns, David Philp
Edinburgh, Revd Marjory McPherson
England, Revd Alistair Cumming
Falkirk, Revd Andrew Sarle
Glasgow, Revd George Cowie
Gordon, Revd Euan Glen
Greenock and Paisley, Revd Dr Peter McEnhill
Hamilton, Revd Dr Gordon McCracken
International, Revd Jim Sharp
Inverness, Revd Trevor Hunt
Irvine and Kilmarnock, Steuart Dey
Jedburgh, Revd Lisa-Jane Rankin
Jerusalem, Revd Joanna Oakley-Levstein
Kincardine and Deeside, Revd Hugh Conkey
Kirkcaldy, Revd Alan Kimmitt
Lanark, Revd Bryan Kerr
Lewis, John Cunningham
Lochaber, Revd Donald McCorkindale
Lochcarron-Skye, Revd John Murray
Lothian, John McCulloch
Melrose and Peebles, Revd Victoria Linford
Moray, Revd Alastair Gray
Orkney, Dr Mike Partridge
Perth, Revd Colin Caskie
Ross, Cath Chambers
St Andrews, Revd Nigel Robb
Shetland, Revd Deborah Dobby
Stirling, Revd Alan Miller
Sutherland, Revd Ian McCree
Uist, Revd Gavin Elliott
West Lothian, Revd Duncan Shaw
Wigtown and Stranraer, Sam Scobie
The stipends for ministers in the Church of Scotland in 2019
range from £27,585–£33,899, depending on length of
service.

ROMAN CATHOLIC CHURCH

The Roman Catholic Church is a worldwide Christian church
acknowledging as its head the Bishop of Rome, known as the
Pope (father). Despite its widespread usage, 'Pope' is actually
an unofficial term. The Annuario Pontificio, (Pontifical
Yearbook) lists eight official titles: Bishop of Rome, Vicar of
Jesus Christ, Successor of the Prince of the Apostles, Supreme
Pontiff of the Universal Church, Primate of Italy, Archbishop
and Metropolitan of the Roman Province, Sovereign of the
State of the Vatican City and Servant of the Servants of God.
   The Pope leads a communion of followers of Christ, who
believe they continue His presence in the world as servants of
faith, hope and love to all society. The Pope is held to be the
successor of St Peter and thus invested with the power which
was entrusted to St Peter by Jesus Christ. A direct line of
succession is therefore claimed from the earliest Christian
communities. With the fall of the Roman Empire the Pope also

became an important political leader. His territory is now limited to the 0.44 sq. km (0.17 sq. miles) of the Vatican City State, created to provide some independence to the Pope from Italy and other nations. The episcopal jurisdiction of the Roman Catholic Church is called the Holy See.

The Pope exercises spiritual authority over the church with the advice and assistance of the Sacred College of Cardinals, the supreme council of the church. The number of cardinals was fixed at 70 by Pope Sixtus V in 1586 but has increased steadily since the pontificate of John XXIII. On 28 February 2013, the date of Pope Benedict XVI's resignation, there were 207 cardinals.

Following the death or resignation of the Pope, the members of the College of Cardinals under the age of 80 are called to the Vatican to elect a successor. They are known as cardinal electors and form an assembly called the conclave. The conclave, which comprised 115 cardinal electors when it convened in March 2013, conducts a secret ballot in complete seclusion to elect the next Pope. A two-thirds majority is necessary before the vote can be accepted as final. When a cardinal receives the necessary number of votes, the Dean of the Sacred College formally asks him if he will accept election and the name by which he wishes to be known. On his acceptance of the office of Supreme Pontiff, the conclave is dissolved and the first Cardinal Deacon announces the election to the assembled crowd in St Peter's Square.

The Pope has full legislative, judicial and administrative power over the whole Roman Catholic Church. He is aided in his administration by the curia, which is made up of a number of departments. The Secretariat of State is the central office for carrying out the Pope's instructions and is presided over by the Cardinal Secretary of State. It maintains relations with the departments of the curia, with the episcopate, with the representatives of the Holy See in various countries, governments and private persons. The congregations and pontifical councils are the Pope's ministries and include departments such as the Congregation for the Doctrine of Faith, whose field of competence concerns faith and morals; the Congregation for the Clergy and the Congregation for the Evangelisation of Peoples, the Pontifical Council for the Family and the Pontifical Council for the Promotion of Christian Unity.

The Holy See, composed of the Pope and those who help him in his mission for the church, is recognised by the Conventions of Vienna as an international moral body. Apostolic nuncios are the Pope's diplomatic representatives; in countries where no formal diplomatic relations exist between the Holy See and that country, the papal representative is known as an apostolic delegate.

According to the 2019 Pontifical Yearbook the number of baptised Roman Catholics worldwide was 1,313 million in 2017 and there were 414,582 priests.

SUPREME PONTIFF
His Holiness Pope Francis (Jorge Mario Bergoglio), *born* Buenos Aires, Argentina, 17 December 1936; *ordained priest* 13 December 1969; *appointed Archbishop* (of Buenos Aires), 28 February 1998; *created Cardinal* 21 February 2001; *assumed pontificate* 13 March 2013

PONTIFF EMERITUS
His Holiness Pope Benedict XVI (Joseph Ratzinger), *born* Bavaria, Germany, 16 April 1927; *ordained priest* 29 June 1951; *appointed Archbishop* (of Munich), 24 March 1977; *created Cardinal* 27 June 1977; *assumed pontificate* 19 April 2005; *resigned pontificate* 28 February 2013

SECRETARIAT OF STATE
Secretary of State, His Eminence Cardinal Pietro Parolin
First Section (General Affairs), Most Revd Edgar Peña Parra (Titular Archbishop of Thélepte)
Second Section (Relations with Other States), Most Revd Paul Gallagher (Titular Archbishop of Hodelm)

BISHOPS' CONFERENCE
The Catholic Bishops' Conference of England and Wales is the permanent assembly of Catholic Bishops and Ordinaries in the two member countries. The membership of the Conference comprises the Archbishops, Bishops and Auxiliary Bishops of the 22 Dioceses within England and Wales, the Bishop of the Forces (Military Ordinariate), the Apostolic Eparchs of the Ukrainian Church and Syro-Malabar Catholics in Great Britain, the Ordinary of the Personal Ordinariate of Our Lady of Walsingham, and the Apostolic Prefect of the Falkland Islands. The Conference is headed by a president and vice-president. There are six departments, each with an episcopal chair: Christian Life and Worship, Dialogue and Unity, Education and Formation, Evangelisation and Catechesis, International Affairs, and Social Justice.

The Bishops' Conference Standing Committee is made up of two directly elected bishops in addition to the Metropolitan Archbishops and chairs from each of the above departments. The committee has general responsibility for continuity of policy between the plenary sessions of the conference, preparing the conference agenda and implementing its decisions.

The administration of the Bishops' Conference is funded by a levy on each diocese, according to income. A general secretariat in London coordinates and supervises the Bishops' Conference administration activities. There are also other agencies and consultative bodies affiliated to the conference.

The Bishops' Conference of Scotland is the permanently constituted assembly of the eight bishops of Scotland. The conference is headed by the president (Rt. Revd. Hugh Gilbert, Bishop of Aberdeen). The conference establishes various agencies which perform advisory functions in relation to the conference. The more important of these agencies are called commissions; each one is headed by a bishop president who, with the other members of the commissions, are appointed by the conference.

The Irish Catholic Bishops' Conference (also known as the Irish Episcopal Conference) has as its president the Most Revd Eamon Martin (Archbishop of Armagh and Primate of All Ireland). Its membership comprises all the archbishops and bishops of Ireland. It appoints various commissions and agencies to assist with the work of the Catholic Church in Ireland.

The Catholic Church in the UK has over 900,000 mass attendees, 5,500 priests and 4,550 churches.
Bishops' Conferences secretariats:
ENGLAND AND WALES, 39 Eccleston Square, London SW1V 1BX **T** 020-7630 8220 **W** www.cbcew.org.uk
General Secretary, Revd Christopher Thomas
SCOTLAND, 64 Aitken Street, Airdrie ML6 6LT **T** 01236-764061 **W** www.bcos.org.uk
General Secretary, Fr James Grant
IRELAND, Columba Centre, Maynooth, County Kildare W23 P6D3 **T** (+353) (1) 505 3000 **E** info@catholicbishops.ie **W** www.catholicbishops.ie
Episcopal Secretary, Most Revd Kieran O'Reilly (Archbishop of Cashel and Emly)
Executive Secretary, Mgr Gearóid Dullea

GREAT BRITAIN

APOSTOLIC NUNCIO TO GREAT BRITAIN

HE Most Revd Edward Joseph Adams (Titular Archbishop of Scala), *apptd* 2017. *Apostolic Nunciature*, 54 Parkside, London SW19 5NE **T** 020-8944 7189

ENGLAND AND WALES

THE MOST REVD ARCHBISHOPS

Westminster, HE Cardinal Vincent Nichols, *cons.* 1992, *apptd* 2009 *Auxiliaries,* John Sherrington, *cons.* 2011; Nicholas Hudson, *cons.* 2014; Paul McAleenan, *cons.* 2016; John Sherrington, *cons.* 2011. *Clergy,* 318. *Archbishop's House,* Ambrosden Avenue, London SW1P 1QJ **T** 020-7798 9033

Birmingham, Bernard Longley, *cons.* 2003, *apptd* 2009 *Auxiliaries,* William Kenney, *cons.* 1987; David McGough, *cons.* 2005; Robert Byrne, *cons.* 2014. *Clergy,* 430. *Archbishop's House,* 8 Shadwell Street, Birmingham B4 6EY **T** 0121-236 9090

Cardiff, George Stack, *cons.* 2001, *apptd* 2011. *Clergy,* 47. *Archbishop's House,* 41–43 Cathedral Road, Cardiff CF11 9HD **T** 029-2022 0411

Liverpool, Malcolm McMahon, *cons.* 2000, *apptd* 2014 *Auxiliary,* Tom Williams, *cons.* 2003. *Clergy,* 402. *Archbishop's House,* 19 Salisbury Road, Cressington Park, Liverpool L19 0PH **T** 0151-494 0686

Southwark, John Wilson, *cons.* 2016, *apptd* 2019 *Auxiliaries,* Patrick Lynch, *cons.* 2006; Paul Hendricks, *cons.* 2006. *Clergy,* 366. *Archbishop's House,* 150 St George's Road, London SE1 6HX **T** 020-7928 2495

THE RT. REVD BISHOPS

Arundel and Brighton, Richard Moth, *cons.* 2009, *apptd* 2015. *Clergy,* 95. *Bishop's House,* High Oaks, Old Brighton Road North, Pease Pottage RH11 9AJ **T** 01293-526428

Brentwood, Alan Williams, *cons.* 2014, *apptd* 2014. *Clergy,* 170. *Bishop's Office,* Cathedral House, Ingrave Road, Brentwood, Essex CM15 8AT **T** 01277-232266

Clifton, Declan Lang, *cons.* 2001, *apptd* 2001. *Clergy,* 153. *Bishop's House,* St Ambrose, North Road, Leigh Woods, Bristol BS8 3PW **T** 0117-973 3072

East Anglia, Alan Hopes, *cons.* 2003, *apptd* 2013. *Clergy,* 129. *Diocesan Curia,* The White House, 21 Upgate, Poringland, Norwich NR14 7SH **T** 01508-492202

Hallam, Ralph Heskett, *cons.* 2010, *apptd* 2014. *Clergy,* 71. *Bishop's House,* 75 Norfolk Road, Sheffield S2 2SZ **T** 0114-278 7988

Hexham and Newcastle, Robert Byrne, *cons.* 2014, *apptd* 2019. *Clergy,* 164. *Bishop's House,* 800 West Road, Newcastle upon Tyne NE5 2BJ **T** 0191-228 0003

Lancaster, Paul Swarbrick, *cons.* 2018, *apptd* 2018. *Clergy,* 97. *Bishop's Office,* The Pastoral Centre, Balmoral Road, Lancaster LA1 3BT **T** 01524-596050

Leeds, Marcus Stock, *cons.* 2014, *apptd* 2014. *Clergy,* 193. *Diocesan Curia,* Hinsley Hall, 62 Headingley Lane, Leeds LS6 2BX **T** 0113-230 4533

Menevia (Wales), vacant. *Clergy,* 60. *Diocesan Office,* 27 Convent Street, Swansea SA1 2BX **T** 01792-644017

Middlesbrough, Terence Drainey, *cons.* 2008, *apptd* 2007. *Clergy,* 50. *Diocesan Curia,* 16 Cambridge Road, Middlesbrough TS5 5NN **T** 01642-850505

Northampton, Peter Doyle, *cons.* 2005, *apptd* 2005. *Clergy,* 116. *Bishop's House,* Marriott Street, Northampton NN2 6AW **T** 01604-715635

Nottingham, Patrick McKinney, *cons.* 2015, *apptd* 2015. *Clergy,* 166. *Bishop's House,* 27 Cavendish Road East, The Park, Nottingham NG7 1BB **T** 0115-947 4786

Plymouth, Mark O'Toole, *cons.* 2014, *apptd* 2013. *Clergy,* 50. *Bishop's House,* 45 Cecil Street, Plymouth PL1 5HW **T** 01752-224414

Portsmouth, Philip Egan, *cons.* 2012, *apptd* 2012. *Clergy,* 214. *Bishop's House,* Bishop Crispian Way, Portsmouth, Hants PO1 3HG **T** 023-9282 0894

Salford, John Arnold, *cons.* 2006, *apptd* 2014. *Clergy,* 218. *Diocesan Curia,* Wardley Hall, Worsley, Manchester M28 2ND **T** 0161-794 2825

Shrewsbury, Mark Davies, *cons.* 2010, *apptd* 2010. *Clergy* 112. *Diocesan Curia,* 2 Park Road South, Prenton, Wirral CH43 4UX **T** 0151-652 9855

Wrexham (Wales), Peter Brignall, *cons.* 2012, *apptd* 2012. *Clergy,* 16. *Bishop's House,* Sontley Road, Wrexham LL13 7EW **T** 01978-262726

SCOTLAND

THE MOST REVD ARCHBISHOPS

St Andrews and Edinburgh, Leo Cushley, *cons.* 2013, *apptd* 2013. *Clergy,* 50. *Archdiocesan Offices,* 100 Strathearn Road, Edinburgh EH9 1BB **T** 0131-623 8900

Glasgow, Philip Tartaglia, *cons.* 2005, *apptd* 2012. *Clergy,* 198. *Diocesan Curia,* 196 Clyde Street, Glasgow G1 4JY **T** 0141-226 5898

THE RT. REVD BISHOPS

Aberdeen, Hugh Gilbert, *cons.* 2011, *apptd* 2011. *Clergy,* 47. *Bishop's House,* 3 Queen's Cross, Aberdeen AB15 4XU **T** 01224-319154

Argyll and the Isles, Brian McGee, *cons.* 2016, *apptd* 2015. *Clergy,* 32. *Diocesan Office* Bishop's House, Esplanade, Oban, Argyll PA34 5AB **T** 01631-567436

Dunkeld, Stephen Robson, *cons.* 2012, *apptd* 2013. *Clergy,* 43. *Diocesan Curia,* 24–28 Lawside Road, Dundee DD3 6XY **T** 01382-225453

Galloway, William Nolan, *cons.* 2015, *apptd* 2014. *Clergy,* 19. *Diocesan Office,* 8 Corsehill Road, Ayr KA7 2ST **T** 01292-266750

Motherwell, Joseph Toal, *cons.* 2008, *trans.* 2014. *Clergy,* 123. *Diocesan Curia,* Coursington Road, Motherwell ML1 1PP **T** 01698-269114

Paisley, John Keenan, *cons.* 2014, *apptd* 2014. *Clergy,* 75. *Diocesan Curia,* Cathedral Precincts, Incle Street, Paisley PA1 1HR **T** 0141-847 6131

BISHOPRIC OF THE FORCES

Rt. Revd Paul Mason, *cons.* 2016, *apptd* 2018. *Administration,* RC Bishopric of the Forces, Wellington House, St Omer Barracks, Thornhill Road, Aldershot, Hants GU11 2BG **T** 01252-348234

IRELAND

There is one hierarchy for the whole of Ireland. Several of the dioceses have territory partly in the Republic of Ireland and partly in Northern Ireland.

APOSTOLIC NUNCIO TO IRELAND

Most Revd Jude Thaddeus Okolo (Titular Archbishop of Novica), *apptd* 2017. *Apostolic Nunciature,* 183 Navan Road, Dublin 7 **T** (+353) (1) 838 0577

THE MOST REVD ARCHBISHOPS

Armagh, Eamon Martin (*also* Primate of All Ireland), *cons.* 2013, *apptd* 2014. *Archbishop Emeritus,* HE Cardinal Seán Brady *cons.* 1995, *elevated* 2007. *Auxiliary,* Michael Router, *cons.* 2019. *Clergy,* 135. *Bishop's Residence,* Ara Coeli, Cathedral Road, Armagh BT61 7QY **T** 028-3752 2045

Cashel and Emly, Kieran O'Reilly, *cons.* 2010, *apptd* 2015. *Clergy,* 83. *Archbishop's House,* Thurles, Co. Tipperary **T** (+353) (504) 21512

Dublin, Diarmuid Martin (*also* Primate of Ireland), *cons.* 1999, *apptd* Coadjutor Archbishop 2003, *succeeded as Archbishop* 2004. *Auxiliary,* Éamonn Walsh, *cons.* 1990. *Clergy,* 389. *Archbishop's House,* Drumcondra, Dublin 9 **T** (+353) (1) 837 3732

Tuam, Dr Michael Neary, *cons.* 1992, *apptd* 1995. *Clergy*, 110. *Archbishop's House*, Tuam, Co. Galway T (+353) (93) 24166

THE MOST REVD BISHOPS

Achonry, vacant. *Clergy*, 50. *Bishop's House*, Edmondstown, Ballaghaderreen, Co. Roscommon T (+353) (94) 986 0034
Ardagh and Clonmacnois, Francis Duffy, *cons.* 2013, *apptd* 2013. *Clergy*, 60. *Diocesan Office*, St Mel's, Longford T (+353) (43) 334 6432
Clogher, Lawrence Duffy, *cons.* 2019, *apptd* 2019. *Clergy*, 74. *Bishop's House*, Monaghan T (+353) (47) 81019
Clonfert, John Kirby, *cons.* 1988, *apptd* 1988. *Clergy*, 37. *Bishop's House*, Coorheen, Loughrea, Co. Galway T (+353) (91) 841560
Cloyne, William Crean, *cons.* 2013, *apptd* 2013. *Clergy*, 126. *Diocesan Office*, Cobh, Co. Cork T (+353) (21) 481 1430
Cork and Ross, Fintan Gavin, *cons.* 2019, *apptd* 2019. *Clergy*, 133. *Diocesan Office*, Cork and Ross Offices, Redemption Road, Cork T (+353) (21) 430 1717
Derry, Dónal McKeown, *cons.* 2001, *apptd* 2014. *Clergy*, 108. *Bishop's House*, PO Box 227, Derry BT48 9YG T 028-7126 2302
Down and Connor, Noël Treanor, *cons.* 2008, *apptd* 2008. *Clergy*, 199. *Bishop's Residence*, Lisbreen, 73 Somerton Road, Belfast, Co. Antrim BT15 4DE T 028-9077 6185
Dromore, vacant. *Clergy*, 83. *Bishop's House*, 44 Armagh Road, Newry, Co. Down BT35 6PN T 028-3026 2444
Elphin, Kevin Doran, *cons.* 2014, *apptd* 2014. *Clergy*, 66. *Bishop's House*, Temple St, St Mary's, Sligo T (+353) (71) 915 0106
Ferns, Denis Brennan, *cons.* 2006, *apptd* 2006. *Clergy*, 88. *Bishop's House*, Summerhill, Wexford T (+353) (53) 912 2177
Galway, Kilmacduagh and Kilfenora, Brendan Kelly, *cons.* 2008, *apptd* 2018. *Clergy*, 57. *Diocesan Office*, The Cathedral, Galway T (+353) (91) 563566
Kerry, Ray Browne, *cons.* 2013, *apptd* 2013. *Clergy*, 88. *Bishop's House*, Killarney, Co. Kerry T (+353) (64) 663 1168
Kildare and Leighlin, Denis Nulty, *cons.* 2013, *apptd* 2013. *Clergy*, 72. *Bishop's House*, Old Dublin Road, Carlow Town T (+353) (59) 917 6725
Killala, John Fleming, *cons.* 2002, *apptd* 2002. *Clergy*, 40. *Bishop's House*, Ballina, Co. Mayo T (+353) (96) 21518
Killaloe, Fintan Monahan, *cons.* 2016, *apptd* 2016. *Clergy*, 95. *Diocesan Office*, Westbourne, Ennis, Co. Clare T (+353) (65) 682 8638
Kilmore, vacant. *Clergy*, 67. *Bishop's House*, Cullies, Cavan, Co. Cavan T (+353) (49) 433 1496
Limerick, Brendan Leahy, *cons.* 2013, *apptd* 2013. *Clergy*, 109. *Diocesan Office*, Social Service Centre, Henry Street, Limerick T (+353) (61) 315856
Meath, Thomas Deenihan, *cons.* 2018, *apptd* 2018. *Clergy*, 120. *Bishop's House*, Dublin Road, Mullingar, Co. Westmeath T (+353) (44) 934 8841
Ossory, Dermot Farrell, *cons.* 2018, *apptd* 2018. *Clergy*, 81. *Diocesan Office*, James's Street, Kilkenny T (+353) (56) 776 2448
Raphoe, Alan McGuckian, *cons.* 2017, *apptd* 2017. *Clergy*, 80. *Bishop's House*, Ard Adhamhnáin, Letterkenny, Co. Donegal T (+353) (74) 912 1208
Waterford and Lismore, Alphonsus Cullinan, *cons.* 2015, *apptd* 2015. *Clergy*, 114. *Bishop's House*, John's Hill, Waterford T (+353) (51) 874463

OTHER CHURCHES IN THE UK

ASSOCIATED PRESBYTERIAN CHURCHES OF SCOTLAND

The Associated Presbyterian Churches came into being in 1989 as a result of a division within the Free Presbyterian Church of Scotland. The Associated Presbyterian Churches is reformed and evangelistic in nature and emphasises the importance of doctrine based primarily on the Bible and secondly on the Westminster Confession of Faith. There are an estimated 500 members, 8 ministers and 18 congregations in Scotland. There are also congregations in Canada.

ASSOCIATED PRESBYTERIAN CHURCHES OF SCOTLAND, Bruach Taibh, 2 Borve, Arnisort, Isle of Skye IV51 9PS T 01470-582264 W www.apchurches.org
Presbytery Clerk, Revd J.R. Ross Macaskill

BAPTIST CHURCH

Baptists trace their origins to John Smyth, who in 1609 in Amsterdam reinstituted the baptism of conscious believers as the basis of the fellowship of a gathered church. Members of Smyth's church established the first Baptist church in England in 1612. They came to be known as 'General' Baptists and their theology was Arminian, whereas a later group of Calvinists who adopted the baptism of believers came to be known as 'Particular' Baptists. The two sections of the Baptists were united into one body in 1891: the Baptist Union of Great Britain and Ireland (renamed the Baptist Union of Great Britain in 1988).

Baptists emphasise the complete autonomy of the local church, although individual churches are linked in various kinds of associations. There are international bodies (such as the Baptist World Alliance) and national bodies, but some Baptist churches belong to neither. However, in Great Britain the majority of churches and associations belong to the Baptist Union of Great Britain. There are also Baptist unions in Wales, Scotland and Ireland and there is some overlap of membership.

There are currently around 135,000 members, 2,500 ministers and 2,080 churches associated with the Baptist Union of Great Britain. The Baptist Union of Great Britain is one of the founder members of the European Baptist Federation (1948) and the Baptist World Alliance (1905); the latter represents 42 million members worldwide.

In the Baptist Union of Wales (Undeb Bedyddwyr Cymru) there are 11,355 members, 88 pastors and 386 churches, including those in England.

In the Baptist Union of Scotland there are 11,500 members and 161 churches.

BAPTIST UNION OF GREAT BRITAIN, Baptist House, PO Box 44, 129 Broadway, Didcot, Oxon OX11 8RT T 01235-517700 W www.baptist.org.uk
President (2019–20), Revd Ken Benjamin
General Secretary, Lynn Green

BAPTIST UNION OF WALES, Y Llwyfan, College Road, Carmarthen SA31 3EQ T 01267-245660 E mennajones@ubc.cymru W www.buw.org.uk
President of the Welsh Assembly (2019–20), David Peregrine
President of the English Assembly (2019–20), Janet Matthews
General Secretary of the Baptist Union of Wales, Revd Judith Morris

BAPTIST UNION OF SCOTLAND, 48 Speirs Wharf, Glasgow G4 9TH T 0141-423 6169 E admin@scottishbaptist.org.uk W www.scottishbaptist.com
General Director, Revd Martin Hodson

THE BRETHREN

The Brethren was founded in Dublin in 1827–8, basing itself on the structures and practices of the early church and rejecting denominationalism and clericalism. Many groups sprang up; the group at Plymouth became the best known, resulting in its designation by others as the 'Plymouth Brethren'. Early worship had a prescribed form but quickly assumed an unstructured, non-liturgical format.

There are services devoted to worship, usually involving the breaking of bread, and separate preaching meetings. There is no salaried ministry.

A theological dispute led in 1848 to schism between the Open Brethren and the Closed or Exclusive Brethren, each branch later suffering further divisions.

Open Brethren churches are run by appointed elders and are completely independent, but freely cooperate with each other. Exclusive Brethren churches believe in a universal fellowship between congregations. They do not have appointed elders, but use respected members of their congregation to perform certain administrative functions.

There are a number of publishing houses that publish Brethren-related literature. Chapter Two is the main supplier of such literature in the UK; it also has a Brethren history archive which is available for use by appointment.

CHAPTER TWO, 3 Conduit Mews, London SE18 7AP
T 020-8316 5389 E info@chaptertwobooks.org.uk
W www.chaptertwobooks.org.uk

CONGREGATIONAL FEDERATION

The Congregational Federation was founded by members of Congregational churches in England and Wales who did not join the United Reformed Church in 1972. There are also churches in Scotland and France affiliated to the federation. The federation exists to encourage congregations of believers to worship in free assembly, but it has no authority over them and emphasises their right to independence and self-governance.

The federation has around 7,000 members, 187 accredited ministers and 265 churches in England, Wales and Scotland.

CONGREGATIONAL FEDERATION, 8 Castle Gate,
Nottingham NG1 7AS T 0115-911 1460
E admin@congregational.org.uk W www.congregational.org.uk
President of the Federation (2019–20), Revd Dr Janet Wootton
General Secretary, Yvonne Campbell

FELLOWSHIP OF INDEPENDENT EVANGELICAL CHURCHES

The Fellowship of Independent Evangelical Churches (FIEC) was founded by Revd E. J. Poole-Connor (1872–1962) in 1922. In 1923 the fellowship published its first register of non-denominational pastors, evangelists and congregations who had accepted the doctrinal basis for the fellowship.

Members of the fellowship have two primary convictions: firstly to defend the evangelical faith, and secondly that evangelicalism is the bond that unites the fellowship, rather than forms of worship or church government.

The FIEC exists to promote the welfare of non-denominational Bible churches and to give expression to the fundamental doctrines of evangelical Christianity. It supports individual churches by providing resources and advising churches on current theological, moral, social and practical issues.

There are currently around 600 churches affiliated to the fellowship.

FELLOWSHIP OF INDEPENDENT EVANGELICAL
CHURCHES, 39 The Point, Market Harborough, Leics LE16
7QU T 01858-434540 E admin@fiec.org.uk W www.fiec.org.uk
National Director, John Stevens

FREE CHURCH OF ENGLAND

The Free Church of England, otherwise called the Reformed Episcopal Church, is an independent episcopal church, constituted according to the historic faith, tradition and practice of the Church of England. Its roots lie in the 18th century, but it started to grow significantly from the 1840s onwards, as clergy and congregations joined it from the established church in protest against the Oxford Movement. The historic episcopate was conferred on the English church in 1876 through bishops of the Reformed Episcopal Church (which had broken away from the Protestant Episcopal Church in the USA in 1873). A branch of the Reformed Episcopal Church was founded in the UK and this merged with the Free Church of England in 1927 to create the present church. The Orders of the Free Church of England are recognised by the Church of England.

Worship is according to the *Book of Common Prayer* and some modern liturgy is permissible. Only men are ordained to the orders of deacon, presbyter and bishop.

The Free Church of England has two dioceses, 19 congregations and around 900 members in England. There is one congregation in St Petersburg, Russia and three congregations and six missions in Brazil.

THE FREE CHURCH OF ENGLAND, 329 Wolverhampton
Road West, Willenhall, W. Midlands WV13 2RL T 01902-607335
W www.fcofe.org.uk
Bishop Primus, Rt. Revd Dr John Fenwick (Bishop of the Northern Diocese)
General Secretary, Rt. Revd Paul Hunt (Bishop of the Southern Diocese)

FREE CHURCH OF SCOTLAND

The Free Church of Scotland was formed in 1843 when over 400 ministers withdrew from the Church of Scotland as a result of interference in the internal affairs of the church by the civil authorities. In 1900, all but 26 ministers joined with others to form the United Free Church (most of which rejoined the Church of Scotland in 1929). In 1904 the remaining 26 ministers were recognised by the House of Lords as continuing the Free Church of Scotland.

The church maintains strict adherence to the Westminster Confession of Faith (1648) and accepts the Bible as the sole rule of faith and conduct. Its general assembly meets annually. It also has links with reformed churches overseas. The Free Church of Scotland has about 13,000 members, 90 ministers and 100 congregations.

FREE CHURCH OF SCOTLAND, 15 North Bank Street,
The Mound, Edinburgh EH1 2LS T 0131-226 5286
E offices@freechurchofscotland.org.uk W www.freechurch.org
Chief Executive, Scott Matheson

FREE PRESBYTERIAN CHURCH OF SCOTLAND

The Free Presbyterian Church of Scotland was formed in 1893 by two ministers of the Free Church of Scotland who refused to accept a Declaratory Act passed by the Free Church General Assembly in 1892. The Free Presbyterian Church of Scotland is Calvinistic in doctrine and emphasises observance of the Sabbath. It adheres strictly to the Westminster Confession of Faith (1648).

The church has about 700 members in Scotland. It has 17 ministers and 40 churches in the UK.

FREE PRESBYTERIAN CHURCH OF SCOTLAND,
133 Woodlands Road, Glasgow G3 6LE
E outreach@fpchurch.org.uk W www.fpchurch.org.uk
Moderator (2019–20), Revd Roderick McLeod
Clerk of the Synod, Revd Keith Watkins

HOLY APOSTOLIC CATHOLIC ASSYRIAN CHURCH OF THE EAST

The Holy Apostolic Catholic Assyrian Church of the East traces its beginnings to the middle of the first century. It spread from Upper Mesopotamia throughout the territories of the Persian Empire. The Assyrian Church of the East became theologically separated from the rest of the Christian community following the Council of Ephesus in 431. The church is headed by the Catholicos Patriarch and is episcopal in government. The liturgical language is Syriac (Aramaic). The Assyrian Church of the East and the Roman Catholic Church agreed a common Christological declaration in 1994, and a process of dialogue between the Assyrian Church of the East and the Chaldean Catholic Church, which is in communion with Rome but shares the Syriac liturgy, was instituted in 1996.

The church has around 325,000 members in the Middle East, India, Russia, Europe, North America and Australasia. In Great Britain there is one parish, which is situated in London. The church in Great Britain forms part of the Diocese of Europe under HG Mar Odisho Oraham.

HOLY APOSTOLIC CATHOLIC ASSYRIAN CHURCH OF THE EAST, St Mary's Church Hall, 62 Greenford Avenue, Hanwell, London W7 3QP **T** 0786-873 7112

INDEPENDENT METHODIST CHURCHES

The Independent Methodist Churches were formed in 1805 and remained independent when the Methodist Church in Great Britain was formed in 1932. They are mainly concentrated in the industrial areas of the north of England.

The churches are Methodist in doctrine but their organisation is congregational. All the churches are members of the Independent Methodist Connexion of Churches. The controlling body of the Connexion is the Annual Meeting, to which churches send delegates. The Connexional President is elected every two years. Between annual meetings the affairs of the Connexion are handled by the Connexional Committee and departmental committees. Ministers are appointed by the churches and trained through the Connexion. The ministry is open to both men and women.

There are 1,600 members, 70 ministers and 74 churches in Great Britain.

INDEPENDENT METHODIST RESOURCE CENTRE, The Resource Centre, Fleet Street, Wigan WN5 0DS **T** 01942-223526 **E** resourcecentre@imchurches.org.uk **W** www.imchurches.org.uk *General Secretary,* Brian Rowney

LUTHERAN CHURCH

Lutheranism is based on the teachings of Martin Luther, the German leader of the Protestant Reformation. The authority of the scriptures is held to be supreme over church tradition. The teachings of Lutheranism are explained in detail in 16th-century confessional writings, particularly the Augsburg Confession. Lutheranism is one of the largest Protestant denominations and it is particularly strong in northern Europe and the USA. Some Lutheran churches are episcopal, while others have a synodal form of organisation; unity is based on doctrine rather than structure. Most Lutheran churches are members of the Lutheran World Federation, based in Geneva.

Lutheran services in Great Britain are held in 15 languages to serve members of different nationalities. Services usually follow ancient liturgies. English-language congregations are members either of the Lutheran Church in Great Britain or of the Evangelical Lutheran Church of England. The Lutheran Church in Great Britain and other Lutheran churches in Britain are members of the Lutheran Council of Great Britain, which represents them and coordinates their common work.

There are around 70 million Lutherans worldwide, with around 180,000 members in Great Britain.

THE LUTHERAN COUNCIL OF GREAT BRITAIN, 30 Thanet Street, London WC1H 9QH **T** 020-7554 9753 **E** enquiries@lutheran.org.uk **W** www.lutheran.org.uk *Chair,* Revd Torbjorn Holt *General Secretary,* Malcolm Bruce

METHODIST CHURCH

The Methodist movement started in England in 1729 when the Revd John Wesley, an Anglican priest, and his brother Charles met with others in Oxford and resolved to conduct their lives by 'rule and method'. In 1739 the Wesleys began evangelistic preaching and the first Methodist chapel was founded in Bristol in the same year. In 1744 the first annual conference was held, at which the Articles of Religion were drawn up. Doctrinal emphases included repentance, faith, the assurance of salvation, social concern and the priesthood of all believers. After John Wesley's death in 1791 the Methodists withdrew from the established church to form the Methodist Church. Methodists gradually drifted into many groups, but in 1932 the Wesleyan Methodist Church, the United Methodist Church and the Primitive Methodist Church united to form the Methodist Church in Britain.

The governing body is the Conference. The Conference meets annually and consists of two parts: the ministerial and representative sessions. The Methodist Church is structured as a 'Connexion' of churches, circuits and districts. The local churches in a defined area form a circuit, and a number of these 368 circuits make up each of the 31 districts. The latest 2019 *Statistics for Mission* show that as at October 2018 the Methodist Church in Britain had 173,000 members, 1,600 active ministers and 4,271 local churches.

THE METHODIST CHURCH IN BRITAIN, Methodist Church House, 25 Marylebone Road, London NW1 5JR **T** 020-7486 5502 **E** enquiries@methodistchurch.org.uk **W** www.methodist.org.uk *Conference President (2019–20),* Revd Barbara Glasson *Conference Vice-President (2019–20),* Clive Marsh *Conference Secretary,* Doug Swanney

THE METHODIST CHURCH IN IRELAND

The Methodist Church in Ireland is autonomous but has close links with British Methodism. As at December 2014 it had 45,828 members, 121 active ministers and 270 lay preachers.

METHODIST CHURCH IN IRELAND, 1 Fountainville Avenue, Belfast BT9 6AN **T** 028-9032 4554 **E** secretary@irishmethodist.org **W** www.irishmethodist.org *President of the Conference (2019–20),* Revd Sam McGuffin *Lay Leader of the Conference (2019–20),* Lynda Neilands *Secretary,* Revd Tom McKnight

ORTHODOX CHURCHES

EASTERN ORTHODOX CHURCH

The Eastern (or Byzantine) Orthodox Church is a communion of self-governing Christian churches that recognises the honorary primacy of the Ecumenical Patriarch of Constantinople.

The position of Orthodox Christians is that the faith was fully defined during the period of the Oecumenical Councils. In doctrine it is strongly trinitarian, and stresses the mystery and importance of the sacraments. It is episcopal in government. The structure of the Orthodox Christian year differs from that of western churches.

Orthodox Christians throughout the world are estimated to number about 300 million; there are around 300,000 in the UK.

GREEK ORTHODOX CHURCH (PATRIARCHATE OF ANTIOCH)

The church is led by John X, Patriarch of Antioch, who was enthroned in February 2013. The Archdiocese of the British Isles and Ireland has 18 parishes, including St George's Cathedral in London, and 27 clergy.

ANTIOCHIAN ORTHODOX ARCHDIOCESE OF THE BRITISH ISLES AND IRELAND, St George's Cathedral, 1A Redhill Street, London NW1 4BG **T** 020-7383 0403
E fr.s.gholam@antiochianorth.co.uk
W www.antiochian-orthodox.co.uk
Archbishop, Metropolitan Silouan Oner

GREEK ORTHODOX CHURCH (PATRIARCHATE OF CONSTANTINOPLE)

The presence of Greek Orthodox Christians in Britain dates back at least to 1677 when Archbishop Joseph Geogirenes of Samos fled from Turkish persecution and came to London. The present Greek cathedral in Moscow Road, Bayswater, was opened for public worship in 1879, and the Diocese of Thyateira and Great Britain was established in 1922. There are now around 100 parishes and one monastery in the UK, served by one archbishop, three bishops and around 120 clergy.

THE PATRIARCHATE OF CONSTANTINOPLE IN GREAT BRITAIN, Archdiocese of Thyateira and Great Britain, Thyateira House, 5 Craven Hill, London W2 3EN
T 020-7723 4787 **E** mail@thyateira.org.uk
W www.thyateira.org.uk
Archbishop, Nikitas of Thyateira and Great Britain

THE RUSSIAN ORTHODOX CHURCH (PATRIARCHATE OF MOSCOW)

The records of Russian Orthodox Church activities in Britain date from the visit to England of Tsar Peter I in the early 18th century. Clergy were sent from Russia to serve the chapel established to minister to the staff of the Imperial Russian Embassy in London.

In 2007, after an 80-year division, the Russian Orthodox Church Outside Russia agreed to become an autonomous part of the Russian Orthodox Church, Patriarchate of Moscow. The reunification agreement was signed by Patriarch Alexy II, 15th Patriarch of Moscow and All Russia and Metropolitan Laurus, leader of the Russian Orthodox Church Outside Russia on 17 May at a ceremony at Christ the Saviour Cathedral in Moscow. Patriarch Alexy II died on 5 December 2008. Metropolitan Kirill of Smolensk and Kaliningrad was enthroned as the 16th Patriarch of Moscow and All Russia on 1 February 2009, having been elected by a secret ballot of clergy on 27 January 2009.

The diocese of Sourozh is the diocese of the Russian Orthodox Church in Great Britain and Ireland and is led by Bishop Matthew of Sourozh.

DIOCESE OF SOUROZH, Diocesan Office, Cathedral of the Dormition of the Mother of God and All Saints, 67 Ennismore Gardens, London SW7 1NH **T** 020-7584 0096
W www.sourozh.org
Diocesan Hierarch, Bishop Matthew of Sourozh

SERBIAN ORTHODOX CHURCH (PATRIARCHATE OF SERBIA)

There are seven parishes in Great Britain and around 4,000 members. Great Britain is part of the Diocese of Great Britain and Scandinavia, which is led by Bishop Dositey. The church can be contacted via the church of St Sava in London.

SERBIAN ORTHODOX CHURCH IN GREAT BRITAIN, Church of Saint Sava, 89 Lancaster Road, London W11 1QQ
T 020-7727 8367 **E** crkva@spclondon.org.uk
W www.spclondon.org.uk
Archpriest, Very Revd Goran Spaic

OTHER NATIONALITIES

The Patriarchates of Romania and Bulgaria (Diocese of Western Europe) have memberships estimated at 20,000 and 2,000 respectively, while the Georgian Orthodox Church has around 500 members. The Belarusian (membership estimated at 2,400) and Latvian (membership of around 100).

ORIENTAL ORTHODOX CHURCHES

The term 'Oriental Orthodox Churches' is now generally used to describe a group of six ancient eastern churches (Armenian, Coptic, Eritrean, Ethiopian, Indian (Malankara) and Syrian) which rejected the Christological definition of the Council of Chalcedon (AD 451). There are around 50 million members worldwide of the Oriental Orthodox Churches and over 20,000 in the UK.

ARMENIAN ORTHODOX CHURCH (CATHOLICOSATE OF ETCHMIADZIN)

The Armenian Orthodox Church is led by HH Karekin II, Catholicos of All Armenians. HG Bishop Hovakim Manukyan was appointed Primate of the Armenian Church in the UK and Ireland in 2015.

ARMENIAN CHURCH IN THE UK AND IRELAND, The Armenian Vicarage, 27 Haven Green, London W5 2NZ
T 020-8998 9210 **W** www.armeniandiocese.org.uk
Primate, HG Bishop Hovakim Manukyan

COPTIC ORTHODOX CHURCH

The Coptic Orthodox Church is headed by Pope Tawadros II, who was appointed in November 2012. There are three dioceses in the UK: the Midlands, led by HG Bishop Missael; Ireland, Scotland and north-east England, led by HG Bishop Antony; and the Papal Diocese which is led by HG Bishop Angaelos and covers all the remaining parishes in the UK.

CATHEDRAL OF ST GEORGE AT THE COPTIC ORTHODOX CHURCH CENTRE, Shephalbury Manor, Broadhall Way, Stevenage, Herts SG2 8NP **T** 020-7993 9001
W www.copticcentre.com
Bishop, HG Bishop Angaelos

BRITISH ORTHODOX CHURCH

The British Orthodox Church is a small autonomous Orthodox jurisdiction, originally deriving from the Syrian Orthodox Church. It was canonically part of the Coptic Orthodox Patriarchate of Alexandria from 1994–2015. As it ministers to British people, all of its services are in English.

THE BRITISH ORTHODOX CHURCH, 10 Heathwood Gardens, Charlton, London SE7 8EP **T** 020-8854 3090
E info@britishorthodox.org **W** www.britishorthodox.org
Metropolitan, Abba Seraphim

ERITREAN ORTHODOX TEWAHEDO CHURCH

The Eritrean Orthodox Church was granted independence in 1994 by Pope Shenouda III, following the declaration of Eritrea's independence from Ethiopia in 1993. In 2006, the Eritrean government removed the third patriarch, Abune Antonios, from office and imprisoned him; the government replaced him with Abune Dioskoros in 2007, although the Oriental Orthodox Churches continue to recognise Antonios as the rightful patriarch. The diocesan bishop for North America, Europe and the Middle East is HG Abune Makarios.

ETHIOPIAN ORTHODOX TAWAHEDO CHURCH

The Ethiopian Orthodox Church was administratively part of the Coptic Orthodox Church of Alexandria until 1959, when it was granted its own patriarch by the Coptic Orthodox Pope of Alexandria and Patriarch of All Africa, Cyril VI. The current patriarch is HH Abune Mathias. The church in London was established in 1976.

ETHIOPIAN ORTHODOX TAWAHEDO CHURCH, St
Mary of Zion, PO Box 56856, London N13 5US **T** 020-8807 5885
E pc@tserhasion.org.uk **W** www.stmaryofzion.co.uk
Priest-in-Charge, Melake Sion Habte Mariam

INDIAN ORTHODOX CHURCH
The Indian Orthodox Church, also known as the Malankara
Orthodox Church, traces its origins to the first century. The
head of the Malankara Orthodox Church is HH Baselios
Marthoma Paulose II. The mother church of all the parishes
in the UK and the Republic of Ireland is St Gregorios Church
in London. The London parish has around 280 families as
practising members.

INDIAN ORTHODOX CHURCH, St Gregorios Indian
Orthodox Church, Cranfield Road, Brockley, London SE4 1UF
T 020-8691 9456 **E** ioclondon@gmail.com
W www.ioclondon.co.uk
Diocesan Metropolitan, HG Dr Mathews Mar Thimothios
Vicar, Revd Fr Aby P Varghese

SYRIAN ORTHODOX CHURCH
The Syrian (Syriac) Orthodox Church of Antioch is an
Oriental Orthodox Church based in the Eastern Mediterranean
headed by HH Moran Mor Ignatius Aphrem II. The
Patriarchate Vicariate in the UK is represented by HE
Archbishop Mor Athanasius Toma Dawod.

SYRIAN ORTHODOX CHURCH IN THE UK, St Thomas
Cathedral, 7–11 Armstrong Road, London W3 7JL
T 020-8749 5834 **E** enquiry-uk@syrianorthodoxchurch.net
W www.syrianorthodoxchurch.net
Archbishop, HE Mor Athanasius Toma Dawod

PENTECOSTAL CHURCHES
Pentecostalism is inspired by the descent of the Holy Spirit
upon the apostles at Pentecost. The movement began in Los
Angeles, USA, in 1906 and is characterised by baptism with
the Holy Spirit, divine healing, speaking in tongues
(glossolalia) and a literal interpretation of the scriptures.
The Pentecostal movement in Britain dates from 1907.
Initially, groups of Pentecostalists were led by laymen and
did not organise formally. However, in 1915 the Elim
Foursquare Gospel Alliance (more commonly called the Elim
Pentecostal Church) was founded in Ireland by George
Jeffreys and currently has about 550 churches, 68,500
adherents and 650 accredited ministers. In 1924 about 70
independent assemblies formed a fellowship called Assemblies
of God in Great Britain and Ireland, which now incorporates
around 600 churches, around 75,000 adherents and 1,000
ministers.
The Apostolic Church grew out of the 1904–5 Christian
revivals in South Wales and was established in 1916. The
Apostolic Church has around 90 churches, 7,000 adherents
and 100 ministers in the UK. The New Testament Church of
God was established in England in 1953 and has over 130
congregations, 11,000 members and over 300 ministers
across England and Wales.
There are about 105 million Pentecostalists worldwide, with
over 350,000 adherents in the UK.

THE APOSTOLIC CHURCH, Suite 105, Crystal House, New
Bedford Road, Luton LU1 1HS **T** 020-7587 1802
E admin@apostolic-church.org **W** www.apostolic-church.org
National Leader, Tim Jack

ASSEMBLIES OF GOD, National Ministry Centre, Mattersey,
Doncaster DN10 5HD **T** 017-7781 7663 **E** info@aog.org.uk
W www.aog.org.uk

THE ELIM PENTECOSTAL CHURCH, Elim International
Centre, De Walden Road, Malvern WR14 4DF **T** 0345-302 6750
W www.elim.org.uk
General Superintendent, Chris Cartwright

THE NEW TESTAMENT CHURCH OF GOD, 3 Cheyne
Walk, Northampton NN1 5PT **T** 01604-824222
E mmcc@ntcg.org.uk **W** www.ntcg.org.uk
Administrative Bishop, Donald Bolt

PRESBYTERIAN CHURCH IN IRELAND
Irish Presbyterianism traces its origins back to the Plantation
of Ulster in 1606, when English and Scottish Protestants
began to settle on the land confiscated from the Irish
chieftains. The first presbytery was established in Ulster in
1642 by chaplains of a Scottish army that had been sent to
crush a Catholic rebellion in 1641.
The Presbyterian Church in Ireland is reformed in doctrine
and belongs to the World Alliance of Reformed Churches.
Structurally, the 536 congregations are grouped in 19
presbyteries under the General Assembly. This body meets
annually and is presided over by a moderator who is elected
for one year. The ongoing work of the church is undertaken
by boards under which there are specialist committees.
There are over 225,000 members and 326 active ministers
of Irish presbyterian churches in Ireland and Northern
Ireland.

THE PRESBYTERIAN CHURCH IN IRELAND, Assembly
Buildings, 2–10 Fisherwick Place, Belfast BT1 6DW
T 028-9032 2284 **E** info@presbyterianireland.org
W www.presbyterianireland.org
Moderator (2019–20), Rt. Revd Dr William Henry
Clerk of Assembly and General Secretary, Revd Trevor Gribben

PRESBYTERIAN CHURCH OF WALES
The Presbyterian Church of Wales or Calvinistic Methodist
Church of Wales is Calvinistic in doctrine and presbyterian in
constitution. It was formed in 1811 when Welsh Calvinists
severed the relationship with the established church by
ordaining their own ministers. It secured its own confession
of faith in 1823 and a Constitutional Deed in 1826, and
since 1864 the General Assembly has met annually, presided
over by a moderator elected for a year. The doctrine and
constitutional structure of the Presbyterian Church of Wales
was confirmed by act of parliament in 1931–2.
The Church has 20,000 members, 55 ministers and 600
congregations.

THE PRESBYTERIAN CHURCH OF WALES, Tabernacle
Chapel, 81 Merthyr Road, Whitchurch, Cardiff CF14 1DD
T 029-2062 7465 **E** swyddfa.office@ebcpcw.org.uk
W www.ebcpcw.cymru
Moderator (2019–20), Revd Brian Matthews
General Secretary, Revd Meirion Morris

RELIGIOUS SOCIETY OF FRIENDS (QUAKERS)
Quakerism is a religious denomination which was founded in
the 17th century by George Fox and others in an attempt to
revive what they saw as the original 'primitive Christianity'.
The movement, at first called Friends of the Truth, started in
the Midlands, Yorkshire and north-west England, but there
are now Quakers all over the UK and in 36 countries around
the world. The colony of Pennsylvania, founded by William
Penn, was originally a Quaker settlement.
Quakers place an emphasis on the experience of God in
daily life rather than on sacraments or religious occasions.
There is no church calendar. Worship is largely silent and
there are no appointed ministers; the responsibility for
conducting a meeting is shared equally among those present.
Religious tolerance and social reform have always been
important to Quakers, together with a commitment to peace
and non-violence in resolving disputes.
There are more than 23,000 'friends' or Quakers in Great
Britain. There are around 475 places where Quaker meetings
are held, many of them Quaker-owned Friends Meeting

Houses. The Britain Yearly Meeting is the name given to the central organisation of Quakers in Britain.

THE RELIGIOUS SOCIETY OF FRIENDS (QUAKERS) IN BRITAIN, Friends House, 173–177 Euston Road, London NW1 2BJ **T** 020-7663 1000 **E** enquiries@quaker.org.uk
W www.quaker.org.uk
General Secretary, Oliver Robertson

SALVATION ARMY

The Salvation Army is an international Christian organisation working in 126 countries worldwide. As a church and registered charity, The Salvation Army is funded through donations from its members, the general public and, where appropriate, government grants.

The Salvation Army was founded by Methodists William and Catherine Booth in the East End of London in 1865 and marked its 150th anniversary on 2 July 2015. It now has around 40,000 members and 1,067 Salvation Army Officers (full-time ministers) in the UK. There are over 700 local church and community centres, 62 residential support centres for homeless people, 16 care homes for older people and six substance-misuse centres. It also runs a clothing recycling programme, charity shops, foodbanks, a prison-visiting service and a family-tracing service. In 1878 it adopted a quasi-military command structure intended to inspire and regulate its endeavours and to reflect its view that the church was engaged in spiritual warfare.

UK TERRITORIAL HEADQUARTERS, 101 Newington Causeway, London SE1 6BN **T** 020-7367 4500
E info@salvationarmy.org.uk **W** www.salvationarmy.org.uk
UK Territorial Leaders, Commissioners Anthony and Gillian Cotterill

SEVENTH-DAY ADVENTIST CHURCH

The Seventh-day Adventist Church is a worldwide Christian church marked by its observance of Saturday as the Sabbath and by its emphasis on the imminent second coming of Jesus Christ. Adventists summarise their faith in '28 fundamental beliefs'.

The church grew out of the Millerite movement in the USA during the mid-19th century and was formally established in 1863. The church has a worldwide membership of over 17 million. In the UK and Ireland there are 37,917 members worshipping in around 300 churches and companies.

SEVENTH-DAY ADVENTIST CHURCH HQ, Stanborough Park, Watford WD25 9JZ **T** 01923-672251
E info@adventist.org.uk **W** www.adventist.org.uk
President, Pastor Ian Sweeney
Executive Secretary, John Sturridge

THE (SWEDENBORGIAN) NEW CHURCH

The New Church is based on the teachings of the 18th-century Swedish scientist and theologian Emanuel Swedenborg (1688–1772), who believed that Jesus Christ appeared to him and instructed him to reveal the spiritual meaning of the Bible. He claimed to have visions of the spiritual world, including heaven and hell, and conversations with angels and spirits. He published several theological works, including descriptions of the spiritual world and a Bible commentary.

Swedenborgians believe that the second coming of Jesus Christ is taking place, being not an actual physical reappearance of Christ, but rather his return in spirit. It is also believed that concurrent with our life on earth is life in a parallel spiritual world, of which we are usually unconscious until death. There are around 30,000 Swedenborgians worldwide, with around 600 members, 18 churches and five ministers in the UK.

THE GENERAL CONFERENCE OF THE NEW CHURCH, Purley Chase Centre, Purley Chase Lane, Mancetter, Atherstone CV9 2RQ **T** 01827-712370
W www.generalconference.org.uk

UNDEB YR ANNIBYNWYR CYMRAEG

Undeb Yr Annibynwyr Cymraeg (the Union of Welsh Independents) was formed in 1872 and is a voluntary association of Welsh Congregational churches and personal members. It is mainly Welsh-speaking. Congregationalism in Wales dates back to 1639 when the first Welsh Congregational church was opened in Gwent.

Member churches are traditionally congregationalist in organisation and Calvinistic in doctrine, although a wide range of interpretations are permitted. Each church has complete independence in the governance and administration of its affairs.

The Union has around 24,000 members, 80 ministers and 400 member churches.

UNDEB YR ANNIBYNWYR CYMRAEG, 5 Axis Court, Riverside Business Park, Swansea Vale, Swansea SA7 0AJ
T 01792-795888 **E** undeb@annibynwyr.org
W www.annibynwyr.org
President, Revd Jill-Hailey Harries
President Elect, Revd Beti-Wyn James
General Secretary, Revd Dyfrig Rees

UNITED REFORMED CHURCH

The United Reformed Church (URC) was first formed by the union of most of the Congregational churches in England and Wales with the Presbyterian Church of England in 1972. It is Calvinistic in doctrine, and its followers form independent self-governing congregations bound under God by covenant, a principle laid down in the writings of Robert Browne (1550–1633). From the late 16th century the movement was driven underground by persecution, but the cause was defended at the Westminster Assembly in 1643 and the Savoy Declaration of 1658 laid down its principles. Congregational churches formed county associations and in 1832 these associations merged to form the Congregational Union of England and Wales.

In the 1960s there was close cooperation locally and nationally between congregational and presbyterian churches. This led to union negotiations and a Scheme of Union, supported by an act of parliament in 1972. In 1981 a further unification took place, with the Reformed Association of Churches of Christ becoming part of the URC. In 2000 a third union took place, with the Congregational Union of Scotland. At its basis the URC reflects local church initiative and responsibility with a conciliar pattern of oversight.

The URC is divided into 13 synods, each with a synod moderator. There are 1,406 churches which serve 49,517 members. There are 401 stipendiary ministers.

The General Assembly is the central body, and comprises around 400 representatives, mainly appointed by the synods, of which half are lay persons and half are ministers. Since 2010 the General Assembly has met biennially to elect two moderators (one lay and one ordained), who then become the public representatives of the URC.

UNITED REFORMED CHURCH, 86 Tavistock Place, London WC1H 9RT **T** 020-7916 2020 **E** urc@urc.org.uk
W www.urc.org.uk
Moderators of the General Assembly 2018–20, Revd Nigel Uden; Derek Estill
General Secretary, Revd John Proctor

WESLEYAN REFORM UNION

The Wesleyan Reform Union was founded by Methodists who left or were expelled from Wesleyan Methodism in 1849 following a period of internal conflict. Its doctrine is conservative evangelical and its organisation is congregational, each church having complete independence in the government and administration of its affairs. The union has around 1,250 members, 20 ministers and 96 churches.

THE WESLEYAN REFORM UNION, Church Street, Jump,
   Barnsley S74 0HZ **T** 01226-891608 **E** admin@thewru.co.uk
   W www.thewru.com
   President, Revd Colin Braithwaite

NON-TRINITARIAN CHURCHES

CHRISTADELPHIAN

Christadelphians believe that the Bible is the word of God and that it reveals both God's dealings with mankind in the past and his plans for the future. These plans centre on the work of Jesus Christ, who it is believed will return to Earth to establish God's kingdom. The Christadelphian group was founded in the USA in the 1850s by Englishman Dr John Thomas.

THE CHRISTADELPHIAN MAGAZINE AND
   PUBLISHING ASSOCIATION, 404 Shaftmoor Lane, Hall
   Green, Birmingham B28 8SZ **T** 0121-777 6328
   W www.thechristadelphian.com

CHURCH OF CHRIST, SCIENTIST

The Church of Christ, Scientist was founded by Mary Baker Eddy in the USA in 1879 to 'reinstate primitive Christianity and its lost element of healing'. Christian Science teaches the need for spiritual regeneration and salvation from sin, but it is best known for its reliance on prayer alone in the healing of sickness. Adherents believe that such healing is the result of divine laws, or divine science, and is in direct line with that practised by Jesus Christ (revered, not as God, but as the son of God) and by the early Christian church.

The denomination consists of The First Church of Christ, Scientist, in Boston, Massachusetts, USA ('The Mother Church') and its branch churches in almost 80 countries worldwide. The Bible and Mary Baker Eddy's book, *Science and Health with Key to the Scriptures,* are used for daily spiritual guidance and healing by all members and are read at services. There are no clergy; those engaged in full-time healing are called Christian Science practitioners, of whom there are around 1,500 worldwide.

No membership figures are available, since Mary Baker Eddy felt that numbers are no measure of spiritual vitality and ruled that such statistics should not be published. There are almost 2,000 branch churches worldwide, including 100 in the UK.

CHRISTIAN SCIENCE COMMITTEE ON PUBLICATION
   UK AND IRELAND, Golden Cross House, 8 Duncannon
   Street, London WC2N 4JF **T** 020-8150 0245
   E londoncs@csps.com **W** http://ukchristianscience.com
   District Manager for the UK and Ireland, Robin Harragin
   Hussey

CHURCH OF JESUS CHRIST OF LATTER-DAY SAINTS

The Church of Jesus Christ of Latter-day Saints ('Mormons') was founded in New York State, USA, in 1830, and came to Britain in 1837.

Mormons are Christians who claim to belong to the 'restored church' of Jesus Christ. They believe that true Christianity died when the last original apostle died, but that it was given back to the world by God and Jesus Christ through Joseph Smith, the church's founder and first president. They accept and use the Bible as scripture, but believe in continuing revelation from God; Mormons also use additional scriptures, including *The Book of Mormon: Another Testament of Jesus Christ.* The importance of the family is central to the church's beliefs and practices. Polygamy was formally discontinued in 1890.

The church has no paid ministry: local congregations are headed by a leader chosen from among their number. The world governing body, based in Utah, USA, is led by a president, believed to be the chosen prophet, and his two counsellors. There are over 15 million members worldwide, with 185,848 members and 333 congregations in the UK.

THE CHURCH OF JESUS CHRIST OF LATTER-DAY
   SAINTS, London Temple Visitors' Centre, West Park Road,
   Newchapel, Surrey RH7 6HW **T** 01342-831400
   W www.lds.org.uk

JEHOVAH'S WITNESSES

The movement now known as Jehovah's Witnesses grew from a Bible study group formed by Charles Taze Russell in 1872 in Pennsylvania, USA. In 1896 it adopted the name of the Watch Tower Bible and Tract Society, and in 1931 its members became known as Jehovah's Witnesses.

Jehovah's Witnesses believe in the Bible as the word of God, and consider it to be inspired and historically accurate. They take the scriptures literally, except where there are obvious indications that they are figurative or symbolic, and reject the doctrine of the Trinity. Witnesses also believe that all those approved of by Jehovah will have eternal life on a cleansed and beautified earth; only 144,000 will go to heaven to rule with Jesus Christ. They believe that the second coming of Christ began in 1914, that his thousand-year reign over the earth is imminent, and that armageddon (a final battle in which evil will be defeated) will precede Christ's rule of peace. Jehovah's Witnesses refuse to take part in military service and do not accept blood transfusions.

The world governing body is based in New York, USA. There is no paid ministry, but each congregation has elders assigned to look after various duties and every Witness takes part in the public ministry in their neighbourhood. There are 8.3 million Jehovah's Witnesses worldwide, with around 136,000 Witnesses in Great Britain organised into around 1,500 congregations.

BRITISH HEADQUARTERS, The Ridgeway, London NW7 1RN
   T 020-8906 2211 **W** www.jw.org/en

UNITARIAN AND FREE CHRISTIAN CHURCHES

Unitarianism has its historical roots in the Judaeo-Christian tradition but rejects the deity of Christ and the doctrine of the Trinity. There is no fixed creed and it allows the individual to take insights from all of the world's faiths and philosophies. It is accepted that beliefs may evolve in the light of personal experience.

Unitarian communities first became established in Poland and Transylvania in the 16th century. The first avowedly Unitarian place of worship in Britain opened in London in 1774. The General Assembly of Unitarian and Free Christian Churches came into existence in 1928 as the result of the amalgamation of two earlier organisations.

There are around 3,400 Unitarians in Great Britain in 170 self-governing congregations and fellowship groups.

GENERAL ASSEMBLY OF UNITARIAN AND FREE
   CHRISTIAN CHURCHES, Essex Hall, 1–6 Essex Street,
   London WC2R 3HY **T** 020-7240 2384 **E** info@unitarian.org.uk
   W www.unitarian.org.uk
   President (2019–20), Revd Celia Cartwright
   Chief Officer, Liz Slade

COMMUNICATIONS

POSTAL SERVICES

On 15 October 2013, under the Postal Services Act 2011, Royal Mail was privatised when it was listed on the London Stock Exchange. The government initially retained a 30 per cent stake in Royal Mail, however it sold its remaining shares in 2015. Royal Mail Group ltd operates Royal Mail, Parcelforce Worldwide and General Logistics Systems (GLS). Under the same 2011 Act, the Post Office became independent of Royal Mail Group on 1 April 2012. The government, through the Department for Business, Energy and Industrial Strategy (BEIS), holds a special share in Post Office ltd. The Post Office has a strategic agreement in place to continue to supply Royal Mail products and services through its network and also has the same group holding company (Royal Mail Holdings plc), which holds shares in both Post Office ltd and Royal Mail Group ltd. Neither Royal Mail Holdings plc, nor BEIS, have any involvement in the day-to-day operations of the Post Office.

Royal Mail is the sole provider of the 'universal service': postal products and associated minimum service standards that must be available to all addresses in the UK.

Following the passing of the Postal Services Act 2011, the Office of Communications (OFCOM) assumed regulatory responsibility for postal services. OFCOM's primary responsibility is to secure the provision of a universal postal service with regard to its financial sustainability.

ROYAL MAIL GROUP LTD, 100 Victoria Embankment, London EC4Y 0HQ **T** 0345-774 0740
W www.royalmailgroup.com
OFCOM, Riverside House, 2A Southwark Bridge Road, London SE1 9HA **T** 0207-981 3000
W www.ofcom.org.uk

PRICING IN PROPORTION

Since 2006 Royal Mail has priced mail according to its size as well as its weight. The system is intended to reflect the fact that larger, bulkier items cost more to handle than smaller, lighter ones. There are five basic categories of correspondence:

LETTER: *Length* up to 240mm, *width* up to 165mm, *thickness* up to 5mm, *weight* up to 100g; eg most cards and postcards
LARGE LETTER: *Length* up to 353mm, *width* up to 250mm, *thickness* up to 25mm, *weight* up to 750g; eg most A4 documents and magazines
SMALL PARCEL: *Length* up to 450mm, *width* up to 350mm, *depth* up to 160mm, *weight* up to 2kg; eg books, clothes and gifts
MEDIUM PARCEL: *Length* up to 610mm, *width* up to 460mm, *depth* up to 460mm, *weight* up to 20kg; eg gifts, shoes, heavy or bulky items
ROLLED OR CYLINDER SHAPED PARCEL: The length of the item plus twice the diameter must not exceed 104cm, with the greatest dimension being no more than 90cm; eg posters and prints

Items larger than those listed above can only be sent via Parcelforce:

STANDARD PARCELFORCE: *Length* up to 150cm, with a combined length and girth of less than 300cm, *weight* up to 30kg
LARGE PARCELFORCE*: *Length* up to 250cm, with a combined length and girth of less than 500cm, *weight* up to 30kg

* Only available at selected Post Office branches

INLAND POSTAL SERVICES

Following are the details of a number of popular postal services along with prices correct as at December 2020. For a full list of prices *see* **W** www.royalmail.com

FIRST AND SECOND CLASS

Format	Maximum weight	First class	Second class
Letter/postcard	100g	£0.85	£0.66
Large letter	100g	£1.29	£0.96
	250g	£1.83	£1.53
	500g	£2.39	£1.99
	750g	£3.30	£2.70
Small parcel	1,000g	£3.85	£3.20
	2,000g	£5.57	£3.20
Medium parcel	1,000g	£6.00	£5.30
	2,000g	£9.02	£5.30
	5,000g	£15.85	£8.99
	10,000g	£21.90	£20.25
	20,000g	£33.40	£28.55

First class post is normally delivered on the following working day and second class within three working days. Prices are exempt from VAT.

STANDARD PARCELFORCE

Maximum weight	Lowest tariff*
2kg	£12.12
5kg	£13.14
10kg	£16.62
15kg	£23.40
20kg	£28.80
25kg	£40.08
30kg	£44.22

* The rate listed includes VAT, compensation up to £100 and is for delivery within 48 hours

OVERSEAS POSTAL SERVICES

For charging purposes Royal Mail divides the world into four zones: UK, Europe, World Zone 1 (including the Americas, Africa, the Middle East, the Far East and S. E. Asia) and World Zone 2 (including Australia, British Indian Ocean Territory, Fiji, New Zealand, Papua New Guinea, Singapore and Samoa). There is a complete listing on the Royal Mail website (**W** www.royalmail.com/international-zones)

INTERNATIONAL ECONOMY MAIL RATES*

Maximum weight		Standard tariff
Letters up to 100g†		
10g		£1.45
20g		£1.45
100g		£1.45

	Large letters	Small parcels/ printed papers
100g	£3.00	£4.85
250g	£4.00	£5.20
500g	£4.90	£7.45
750g	£5.90	£8.70
1,000g	–	£9.50
2,000g	–	£12.95

* Formerly Surface Mail
† Can only be sent by International Economy to destinations outside of Europe

Printed papers only add £1.35 for each additional 250g, or part thereof, up to 5,000g

INTERNATIONAL STANDARD MAIL RATES*

Weight up to and including	Europe	World Zone 1	World Zone 2
Letters			
10g	£1.70	£1.70	£1.70
20g	£1.70	£1.70	£1.70
100g	£1.70	£2.55	£2.55
Large letters			
100g	£3.25	£4.20	£4.20
250g	£4.25	£5.70	£6.80
500g	£5.25	£8.00	£9.85
750g	£6.25	£10.65	£13.55
Small parcels and printed papers			
100g	£5.80	£7.15	£8.35
250g	£5.95	£8.30	£9.90
500g	£7.80	£12.10	£14.50
750g	£9.05	£14.85	£17.60
1,000g	£10.20	£17.65	£20.85
2,000g	£13.00	£23.30	£28.55

Printed papers only add £1.40 for Europe, £1.90 for World Zone 1 or £2.35 for World Zone 2 for each additional 250g, or part thereof, up to 5,000g

* Formerly Airmail

SPECIAL DELIVERY SERVICES

INTERNATIONAL TRACKED AND SIGNED FOR SERVICES

There are various services available: *International Tracked & Signed* provides full end-to-end tracking, signature on delivery and online delivery confirmation to over 60 destinations; *International Tracked* provides the same, but without a signature on delivery, to over 50 destinations; and *International Signed* is tracked within the UK, a signature is taken on delivery and is available to over 155 destinations. All Tracked and Signed For services deliver to Europe within 3–5 working days, and worldwide within 5–7 working days. Proof of posting and compensation up to £50 is provided as standard. Additional compensation up to £250 can be provided for an extra fee.

SAME DAY

A courier service which provides same day delivery of urgent items in most places in the UK. With collection within the hour of booking, satellite tracking, delivery confirmation and automatic compensation up to £2,500, and for an additional fee, up to £10,000, the service is charged on a loaded mile basis **T** 0330-088 5522

SIGNED FOR

A service which offers proof of delivery including a signature from the receiver and compensation cover up to £50. The first class service is delivered the next working day and prices vary from £2.25 to £34.40 depending on the size and weight of the item. The second class service allows two to three working days for delivery with charges of £2.06 to £29.55.

SPECIAL DELIVERY GUARANTEED

A guaranteed next working day delivery service by 9am or 1pm with a refund option guaranteed for late delivery. With many options available, Royal Mail offers a full list of prices online **W** www.royalmail.com/personal/uk-delivery/special-delivery

OTHER SERVICES

KEEPSAFE

Mail is held for up to 100 days while the addressee is away, and is delivered when the addressee returns. Prices start at £16.00 for 10 days up to £82.00 for 100 days.

PASSPORT CHECK & SEND

For a fee, paper and child passport applications are checked to ensure they meet the requirements set by HM Passport Office and are dispatched to HM Passport Office by secure post.

In November 2018 a digital check and send passport service, available at over 700 branches, was launched for the renewal of adult passports. For a fee of £16.00, and on submission of the old passport, counter staff will take photographs, submit an electronic application and dispatch the old passport to HM Passport Office by special delivery. The new passport will be received from HM Passport Office within three weeks. **W** www.postoffice.co.uk/passport-check-send.

POST OFFICE BOX

A Post Office (PO) Box provides a short and memorable alternative address. Mail is held at a local delivery office until the addressee is ready to collect it, or delivered to a street address for an extra fee. Prices start at £35.10 for one month or £168.00 for six months or £283.50 for a year.

POSTCODE FINDER

Customers can search an online database to find UK postcodes and addresses. For more information *see* Royal Mail's postcode finder **W** www.royalmail.com/postcode-finder

REDELIVERY

Customers can request a redelivery of an item for up to 18 days if it was unable to be delivered and the person is unable to collect from the address on the delivery notification card. A 48-hour notice period is required for redelivery. Redelivery can be arranged to the customer's house, an alternative local address or, for a fee of £0.70 payable on collection, to a local post office branch.

REDIRECTION

Customers may arrange the redirection of their mail via post, at the Post Office or online, subject to verification of their identity. The service is available for three months, six months or 12 months. Prices start at £33.99 for redirection to a UK destination for a single applicant; a full price list is available at **W** www.royalmail.com/personal/receiving-mail/redirection

TRACK AND TRACE

An online service for customers to track the progress of items sent using any special delivery tracked and signed for service. It is accessible from **W** www.royalmail.com/track-your-item

CONTACTS

PARCELFORCE **T** 0344-800 4466 **W** www.parcelforce.com
POST OFFICE **T** 0345-722 3355 **W** www.postoffice.co.uk

TELECOMMUNICATIONS

4G AND 5G

Mobile network technology has improved dramatically since the launch in 1985 of the first-generation global system for mobile communications (GSM), which offered little or no data capability. In 1992 Vodafone launched a new GSM network, usually referred to as 2G or second generation, which used digital encoding and allowed voice and low-speed data communications. This technology was extended, via the enhanced data transfer rate of 2.5G, to 3G – a family of mobile standards that provide high bandwidth support to applications such as voice- and video-calling, data transfer, television streaming and full internet access.

EE was the first operator to launch 4G in late 2012 and by April 2013 the service was available in ten cities where the broadband speed was doubled to more than 20 megabits per second (Mbps). O2 and Vodafone subsequently launched their 4G networks in late August 2013 while 3 began their service in December 2013.

By the end of 2017, there were 58.4 million 4G subscribers, an increase of 6 million (11.5 per cent) from the previous year. The number of 4G subscribers at the end of 2017 comprised 63.5 per cent of the total number of all active mobile subscribers in the UK. 4G coverage improved in 2017, with 58 per cent of all indoor premises covered by all four networks, up from 40 per cent in 2016. Geographic areas covered by all four networks increased from 21 per cent in 2016 to 43 per cent in 2017 and geographic areas with no coverage from any network decreased from 37 per cent in 2016 to 22 per cent in 2017. The ability to connect to a good 4G service continues to vary according to location; in urban areas, good 4G data services of a least 2Mbps is available at 83 per cent of premises, in contrast, only 41 per cent of premises can access good quality data services in rural areas.

In February 2015, OFCOM stated that 5G data connections could be available in the UK by 2020 and in December 2017, the organisation that governs cellular standards, The 3rd Generation Partnership Project (3GPP), signed off on a universal standard, called 5G NR. EE officially switched on its 5G services in Belfast, Birmingham, Cardiff, Edinburgh, London and Manchester on 30 May 2019, becoming the first company to launch 5G in the UK. EE planned to extend 5G to a further ten cities in the UK by the end of 2019 and launched a 5G home broadband service in June 2019. O2 launched 5G in the UK's four capital cities in 2019 and Vodafone launched in 19 cities in 2019, starting with seven cities in July. 3 launched its 5G services in the second half of 2019. All four mobile network providers have 5G-capable devices on the market.

The headline benefit of 5G is speed. 5G is expected to reach speeds in excess of 1,000Mbps or 1Gbps (1 gigabit per second). In comparison maximum download speeds are 384Kbps (kilobits per second) for 3G, 100Mbps for 4G and 300Mbps for 4G+. However, actual download speeds depend on a variety of factors, such as distance from a base station and how many other people are using the network at the same time. As at April 2019 EE provided the fastest 4G connection with an average download speed of 29.6 Mbps; Vodafone, 3 and O2 offered average download speeds of 21.0Mbps, 18.0Mbps and 14.1Mbps respectively. So, although 5G is targeting a download speed of over 1Gbps, average mobile download speeds are expected to be in the region of 80 to 100 Mbps.

FIXED-LINE SERVICES

The total number of fixed-line services in the UK declined for the first time in 2017; from a total of 33.6 million connections in 2016 to 33.1 million in 2017. The decrease in landlines was as a result of businesses switching to mobile and voice over internet protocol (VoIP) services, such as Skype. Fixed voice call minutes continued to decline, from 54 billion in 2017, to 9.5 billion in 2019; part of a steady decline from the 103 billion minutes recorded in 2012.

The decrease in business lines was partly offset by a 1 per cent increase in the number of residential landlines, attributed to growing fixed broadband take-up – most households in the UK need a landline to be able to access fixed broadband services. Fixed broadband connections totalled 26.8 million in 2019, compared to 26.0 million in 2017.

MOBILE PHONE USAGE

At the end of 2019 the total number of mobile subscriptions in the UK had increased by 0.9 million to 84.9 million since the previous year. The volume of SMS and MMS messages sent continued to decline, decreasing to 2.7 billion; a further decline from 90 billion in 2016. The decline in text messaging is likely to be a result of the increasing number of smartphones being used for communication, with social media platforms and instant messaging services such as Whatsapp and iMessenger providing alternatives to SMS. Total outgoing mobile calls decreased to 39.6 billion minutes in 2019, compared with an increase from 143 to 151 billion minutes from 2015 to 2016. Average monthly data use per mobile connection further increased from 1.3 gigabytes in 2016 to 1.9 gigabytes in 2017 and from just 0.9 gigabytes in 2015.

UK adults spent most of their time online on the smartphone in March 2018. Of the total minutes spent online by the entire UK digital population in March 2018, 62 per cent was via the smartphone, followed by the desktop/ laptop (25 per cent) and tablet (13 per cent). In 2018, nearly half (48 per cent) of UK internet users stated that smartphones were their most important device for accessing the internet. This was higher for younger adults, with 72 per cent regarding their smartphones as their most important device for accessing the internet. In contrast, only 17 per cent of those aged over 54 perceived the smartphone as the most important device.

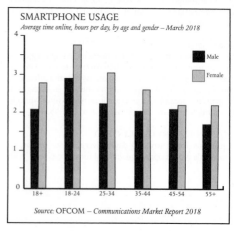

SMARTPHONE USAGE
Average time online, hours per day, by age and gender – March 2018

Source: OFCOM – Communications Market Report 2018

HEALTH

In 1999 the Independent Expert Group on Mobile Phones (IEGMP) was established to examine the possible effects on health of mobile phones, base stations and transmitters. The main findings of the IEGMP's report *Mobile Phones and Health,* published in May 2000, were:

- exposure to radio frequency radiation below guideline levels did not cause adverse health effects to the general population
- the use of mobile phones by drivers of any vehicle can increase the chance of accidents
- the widespread use of mobile phones by children for non-essential calls should be discouraged as if there are unrecognised adverse health effects children may be more vulnerable
- there is no general risk to the health of people living near to base stations on the basis that exposures are expected to be much lower than guidelines set by the International Commission on Non-Ionising Radiation Protection

The government set up the Mobile Telecommunications Health and Research (MTHR) programme in 2001 to undertake independent research into the possible health risks from mobile telephone technology. The MTHR programme published its report in September 2007 concluding that, in the short term, neither mobile phones nor base stations have been found to be associated with any biological or adverse health effects. An international cohort study into the possible long-term health effects of mobile phone use was launched by the MTHR in April 2010. The study is known as COSMOS and aims to follow the health of 250,000 mobile phone users from five countries over 20 to 30 years. Details of the study can be found on the COSMOS website (**W** www.thecosmosproject.org).

A national measurement programme to ensure that emissions from mobile phone base stations do not exceed the ICNIRP guideline levels is overseen by OFCOM and annual audits of these levels can be found on the sitefinder part of its website. Public Health England is responsible for providing information and advice on the health effects of electromagnetic fields, including those emitted from mobile phones and base stations. In April 2012, the HPA's independent Advisory Group on Non-ionising Radiation published a report concluding that there was no convincing evidence that mobile phone technologies cause adverse effects on human health.

In 2014, the Department of Health and Social Care commissioned the world's biggest study into the effects of mobile phone usage on children and adolescents, known as the Study of Cognition, Adolescents and Mobile Phones (SCAMP). The first round of follow-up data collection ended in July 2018. Details of this study can be found on the SCAMP website (**W** www.scampstudy.org).

SAFETY WHILE DRIVING

Under legislation that came into effect in December 2003 it is illegal for drivers to use a hand-held mobile phone while driving. Since March 2017 the fixed penalty for using a hand-held mobile device while driving is £200 and six penalty points. If the driver passed their driving test in the last two years, they will lose their licence. Three penalty points can also be issued to a driver for not having proper control of a vehicle while using a hands-free device or if the device blocks the driver's view of the road and traffic ahead. If the police or driver chooses to take the case to court rather than issue or accept a fixed penalty notice, the driver may be disqualified from driving in addition to a maximum fine of £1,000 for car drivers and £2,500 for drivers of buses, coaches or heavy goods vehicles. The only exceptions for using a mobile phone while driving are to call the emergency services, when it is unsafe or impractical to stop, or when the driver is safely parked.

REGULATION

Under the Communications Act 2003, OFCOM is the independent regulator and competition authority for the UK communications industries, with responsibilities across television, radio, telecommunications and wireless communications services. Competition in the communications market is also regulated by the Competition and Markets Authority, although OFCOM takes the lead in competition investigations in the UK market. The Competition Appeal Tribunal hears appeals against OFCOM's decisions.

CONTACTS

OFCOM, Riverside House, 2A Southwark Bridge Road, London SE1 9HA **T** 020-7981 3000
W www.ofcom.org.uk

INTERNET

The UK ranks 31st in the world for broadband speed with an average speed of 16.51Mbps. At May 2017, OFCOM reported 100 per cent coverage in the UK at a download speed of 44Mbps, up from 37Mbps in 2016. Superfast broadband is now available in 91 per cent of the UK at a speed of 77Mbps and OFCOM are continually working to boost superfast and ultrafast connections. There were 26 million fixed broadband connections in the UK at the end of 2017, 49 per cent of which were superfast connections.

In 2018 87 per cent of UK adults (aged 16+) had broadband internet access at home. The most frequently cited reason for not having internet access was that they did not need it (45 per cent). Of adults without home internet access, 14 per cent said they were likely to get it in the next year. Home internet access varies significantly according to age group. At the beginning of 2019, 95 per cent of those aged 16 to 24 reported they had home internet access, as opposed to only 75 per cent of those aged over 55+.

In 2018 the most popular internet activity was general browsing, with 69 per cent of adults having browsed the internet in the past week. Sending emails was the second most common activity, with 66 per cent of adults reporting to have done this in the last week. Just under half of adults (44 per cent) reported they had shopped online in the last week, a reduction from 76 per cent in 2017, and around half of UK adults had used online banking and social media in the last week. In 2016, 42 per cent of internet users claimed to use the same password for most, if not all websites and in 2018, a quarter of internet users said they did not carry out appropriate checks before entering their personal or financial information online.

In the UK 77 per cent of internet users had a profile or account on a social media or messaging site or app in 2018, unchanged since 2016. Facebook remained the most-visited social platform, reaching 41 million internet users aged 13+ in 2018 (90 per cent of the total UK internet audience). However Facebook began to see a downward trend in the number of people aged under 35 accessing the platform; with the number of people aged 18 to 24 decreasing by 4 per cent in the year to March 2018, in contrast, visitors among those aged over 54 increased to 24 per cent (2.2 million people) in the same period. Snapchat and Facebook-owned Instagram saw an increase in online audiences, with 22.7 million adults visiting Snapchat in March 2018, fractionally less than Instagram with 23.1 million. However, Snapchat had much larger year-on-year growth than Instagram (122 per cent, compared with 22 per cent). Much of the growth was driven by an increased number of adults aged 25+ visiting the platform.

In March 2018 the organisation with the largest online audience in the UK was Google (41.9 million unique visitors aged 18+), closely followed by Facebook and BBC (40.2 million and 39.5 million respectively) and Amazon (37.7 million), pushing Microsoft down to fifth place with 37 million unique visitors. Within the Google portfolio, YouTube was the most popular platform (40 million), followed by Google Search (37 million), Google Maps (25 million) and Gmail (23 million).

GLOSSARY OF TERMS

The following is a list of selected internet terms. It is by no means exhaustive but is intended to cover those that the average computer user might encounter.

BANNER AD: An advertisement on a web page that links to a corresponding website when clicked.

BLOG: Short for 'web log' – an online personal journal that is frequently updated and intended to be read by the public. Blogs are kept by 'bloggers' and are commonly available as RSS feeds.

BOOKMARKS: A method of storing links or automatic pathways within web browsers which allow a user to quickly return to a webpage. Referred to as 'Favourites' in Internet Explorer.

BROWSER: Typically refers to a 'web browser' program that allows a computer user to view web page content on their computer, eg Firefox, Internet Explorer or Safari.

CLICK-THROUGH: The number of times a web user 'clicks through' a paid advertisement link to the corresponding website.

CLOUD COMPUTING: The use of IT resources as an on-demand service across a network; through cloud computing, software, advanced computation and archived information can be accessed remotely, without the user needing local dedicated hardware.

COOKIE: A piece of information placed on a user's hard disk by a web server. Cookies contain data about the user's activity on a website, and are returned to the server whenever a browser makes further requests. They are important for remembering information such as login and registration details, 'shopping cart' data, user preferences etc, and are often set to expire after a fixed period.

DOMAIN: A set of words or letters, separated by dots, used to identify an internet server, eg www.whitakersalmanack.com, where 'www' denotes a web (http) server, 'whitakersalmanack' denotes the organisation name and 'com' denotes that the organisation is a company.

ENCRYPTION: The conversion of information or data into a code in order to prevent unauthorised access.

FIREWALL: A protection system designed to prevent unauthorised access to or from a private network.

FTP: File Transfer Protocol – a set of network rules enabling a user to exchange files with a remote server.

HACKER: A person who attempts to break or 'hack' into websites. Motives typically involve the desire to procure personal information such as addresses, passwords or credit card details. Hackers may also delete code or incorporate traces of malicious code to damage the functionality of a website.

HIT: A single request from a web browser for a single item from a web server. In order for a web browser to display a page that contains three graphics, four 'hits' would occur at the server: one for the HTML page and one for each of the three graphics. Therefore the number of hits on a website is not synonymous with the number of visitors.

HTML: HyperText Mark-up Language – a programming language used to denote or mark up how an internet page should be presented to a user from an HTTP server via a web browser.

HTTP: HyperText Transfer Protocol – an internet protocol whereby a web server sends web pages, images and files to a web browser.

HYPERLINK: A piece of specially coded text that users can click on to navigate to the web page, or element of a web page, associated with that link's code. Links are typically distinguished through the use of bold, underlined or differently coloured text.

JAVA: A programming language used widely on the internet.

MALWARE: A combination of the words 'malicious' and 'software'. Malware is software designed with the intention of infiltrating a computer and damaging its system.

OPEN-SOURCE: Describes a computer program that has its source code (the instructions that make up a program) freely available for viewing and modification.

PAGERANK: A link analysis algorithm used by search engines that assigns a numerical value based on a website's relevance and reputation. In general, a site with a higher pagerank has more traffic than a site with a lower one.

PHISHING: The fraudulent practice of sending emails to acquire personal information by masquerading as a legitimate company.

PODCAST: A form of audio and video broadcasting using the internet. Although the word is a portmanteau of 'iPod' and broadcasting, podcasting does not require the use of an iPod. A podcaster creates a list of files and makes it available in the RSS 2.0 format. The list can then be obtained using podcast 'retriever' software which makes the files available to digital devices (including iPods); users may then listen or watch at their convenience.

RSS FEED: Rich Site Summary or RDF Site Summary or Real Simple Syndication – a commonly used protocol for syndication and sharing of content, originally developed to facilitate the syndication of news articles, now widely used to share the content of blogs.

SEO: Search Engine Optimisation – the process of optimising the content of a web page to ensure that it is indexed by search engines.

SERVER: A node on a network that provides service to the terminals on the network. These computers have higher hardware specifications, ie more resources and greater speed, in order to handle large amounts of data.

SOCIAL NETWORKING: The practice of using a web-hosted service such as Facebook or Twitter to upload and share content and build friendship networks.

SPAM: A term used for unsolicited, generally junk, email.

TRAFFIC: The number of visitors to a website.

TWITTER: An online microblogging service that allows users to stay connected through the exchange of 140-character posts, known as 'tweets'.

URL: Uniform Resource Locator – address of a file accessible on the internet, eg http://www.whitakersalmanack.com

USER-GENERATED CONTENT (UGC): Refers to various media content produced or primarily influenced by end-users, as opposed to traditional media producers such as licensed broadcasters and production companies. These forms of media include digital video, blogging, podcasting, mobile phone photography and wikis.

WIKI: A website or database developed collaboratively by a community of users, allowing any user to add or edit content.

CONSERVATION AND HERITAGE

NATIONAL PARKS

ENGLAND AND WALES

There are ten national parks in England, and three in Wales. In addition, the Norfolk and Suffolk Broads are considered to have equivalent status to a national park. Under the National Parks and Access to the Countryside Act 1949, as clarified by the Natural Environment and Rural Communities Act 2006, the two purposes of the national parks are to conserve and enhance the parks' natural beauty, wildlife and cultural heritage, and to promote opportunities for the understanding and enjoyment of the special qualities of national parks by the public. If there is a conflict between the two purposes, then conservation takes precedence.

Natural England is the statutory body that has the power to designate national parks in England, and Natural Resources Wales (formerly Countryside Council for Wales) is responsible for national parks in Wales. Designations in England are confirmed by the Secretary of State for Environment, Food and Rural Affairs and those in Wales by the Welsh government. The designation of a national park does not affect the ownership of the land or remove the rights of the local community. The majority of the land in the national parks is owned by private landowners (around 75 per cent) or by bodies such as the National Trust and the Forestry Commission. The national park authorities own only a small percentage of the land themselves.

The Environment Act 1995 replaced the existing national park boards and committees with free-standing national park authorities (NPAs). NPAs are the sole local planning authorities for their areas and as such influence land use and development, and deal with planning applications. NPAs are responsible for carrying out the statutory purposes of national parks stated above.

In pursuing these purposes they have a statutory duty to seek to foster the economic and social well-being of the communities within national parks. The NPAs publish management plans setting out overarching policies for their area and appoint their own officers and staff.

The Broads Authority was established under the Norfolk and Suffolk Broads Act 1988 and meets the requirement for the authority to have a navigation function in addition to a regard for the needs of agriculture, forestry and the economic and social interests of those who live or work in the Broads.

MEMBERSHIP
Membership of English NPAs comprises local authority appointees, members directly appointed by the Secretary of State for Environment, Food and Rural Affairs and members appointed by the secretary after consultation with local parishes. Under the Natural Environment and Rural Communities Act 2006 every district, county or unitary authority with land in a national park is entitled to appoint at least one member unless it chooses to opt out. The total number of local authority and parish members must exceed the number of national members.

Brecon Beacons, Northumberland, Pembrokeshire Coast and Snowdonia NPAs have 18 members; Dartmoor has 19; the Lake District and North York Moors have 20; the Broads has 21; Exmoor, the New Forest 22; Yorkshire Dales 25; South Downs 27; and the Peak District 30.

In Wales, two-thirds of NPA members are appointed by the constituent local authorities and one-third by the Welsh government, advised by Natural Resources Wales.

FUNDING
Core funding for the English NPAs and the Broads Authority is provided by central government through the Department for Environment, Food and Rural Affairs (DEFRA) National Park Grant.

In Wales, the three national parks are funded by the Welsh government; for 2020–21 budgeted gross revenue expenditure totals £19.2m and capital expenditure £5.4m.

All NPAs and the Broads Authority can take advantage of grants from other bodies including lottery and European grants.

The national parks (with date that designation was confirmed) are:

BRECON BEACONS (1957), Powys (66 per cent)/ Carmarthenshire/Rhondda, Cynon and Taff/Merthyr Tydfil/Blaenau Gwent/Monmouthshire, 1,344 sq. km/ 519 sq. miles – The park is centred on the Brecon Beacons mountain range, which includes the three highest mountains in southern Britain (Pen y Fan, Corn Du and Cribyn), but also includes the valleys of the rivers Usk and Wye, the Black Mountains to the east and the Black Mountain to the west. There is a visitor centre at Libanus, a tourist information centre at Abergavenny and community run information centres in Llandovery and Brecon.
National Park Authority, Plas y Ffynnon, Cambrian Way, Brecon, Powys LD3 7HP **T** 01874-624437 **W** www.beacons-npa.gov.uk
Chief Executive, Vacant

BROADS (1989), Norfolk/Suffolk, 303 sq. km/117 sq. miles – The Broads is located between Norwich and Great Yarmouth on the flood plains of the six rivers flowing through the area to the sea. The area is one of fens, winding waterways, woodland and marsh. The 60 or so broads are man-made, and many are connected to the rivers by dykes, providing over 200km (125 miles) of navigable waterways. There are information centres at Hoveton, Whitlingham Country Park and How Hill National Nature Reserve. There are yacht stations at Norwich, Reedham and Great Yarmouth.
Broads Authority, Yare House, 62–64 Thorpe Road, Norwich NR1 1RY **T** 01603-610734 **W** www.broads-authority.gov.uk
Chief Executive, Dr John Packman

DARTMOOR (1951), Devon, 953 sq. km/368 sq. miles – The park consists of moorland and rocky granite tors, and is rich in prehistoric remains. There are visitor centres at Haytor, Princetown (main visitor centre) and Postbridge.
National Park Authority, Parke, Bovey Tracey, Devon TQ13 9JQ **T** 01626-832093 **E** hq@dartmoor.gov.uk
W www.dartmoor.gov.uk
Chief Executive, Kevin Bishop

EXMOOR (1954), Somerset (71 per cent)/Devon (29 per cent), 694 sq. km/268 sq. miles – Exmoor is a moorland plateau, with steep wooded slopes that extend along the coastline and is inhabited by wild Exmoor ponies and red deer. There are many ancient remains and burial mounds. There are national park centres at Dunster, Dulverton and Lynmouth.
National Park Authority, Exmoor House, Dulverton, Somerset TA22 9HL **T** 01398-323665 **E** info@exmoor-nationalpark.gov.uk
W www.exmoor-nationalpark.gov.uk
Chief Executive, Sarah Bryan

LAKE DISTRICT (1951), Cumbria, 2,362 sq. km/912 sq. miles – The Lake District includes England's highest mountains (Scafell Pike, Helvellyn and Skiddaw) but it is most famous for its glaciated lakes. In 2017 the Lake District was inscribed as a UNESCO World Heritage Site for its cultural significance *see also* World Heritage Sites. There are national park information centres at Bowness-on-Windermere, Keswick, Ullswater and a visitor centre at Brockhole, Windermere.
National Park Authority, Murley Moss, Oxenholme Road, Kendal, Cumbria LA9 7RL **T** 01539-724555
E hq@lakedistrict.gov.uk **W** www.lakedistrict.gov.uk
Chief Executive, Richard Leafe

NEW FOREST (2005), Hampshire, 570 sq. km/220 sq. miles – The forest has been protected since 1079 when it was declared a royal hunting forest. The area consists of forest, ancient woodland, heathland, farmland, coastal saltmarsh and mudflats. Managed by the ancient system of commoning, the landscape is shaped by grazing animals and contains a range of rare plants and animals.
National Park Authority, Town Hall, Avenue Road, Lymington, Hants SO41 9ZG **T** 01590-646600
E enquiries@newforestnpa.gov.uk **W** www.newforestnpa.gov.uk
Chief Executive, Alison Barnes

NORTH YORK MOORS (1952), North Yorkshire (96 per cent)/Redcar and Cleveland, 1,434 sq. km/554 sq. miles – The park consists of dales woodland, moorland and coast, and includes the Hambleton Hills and the Cleveland Way national trail. There are national park centres at Danby and Sutton Bank.
National Park Authority, The Old Vicarage, Bondgate, Helmsley, York YO62 5BP **T** 01439-772700
E general@northyorkmoors.org.uk
W www.northyorkmoors.org.uk
Chief Executive, Tom Hind

NORTHUMBERLAND (1956), Northumberland, 1,049 sq. km/405 sq. miles – The park is an area of hill country, comprising open moorland, blanket bogs and very small patches of ancient woodland, stretching from Hadrian's Wall to the Scottish border. Visitor information is available from the Sill National Landscape Discovery Centre on Hadrian's Wall.
National Park Authority, Eastburn, South Park, Hexham, Northumberland NE46 1BS **T** 01434-605555
E enquiries@nnpa.org.uk
W www.northumberlandnationalpark.org.uk
Chief Executive, Tony Gates

PEAK DISTRICT (1951), Derbyshire (64 per cent)/Staffordshire/South Yorkshire/Cheshire/West Yorkshire/Greater Manchester, 1,437 sq. km/555 sq. miles – The Peak District includes the gritstone moors of the Dark Peak, the limestone dales of the White Peak and the crags and rolling farmland of the South West Peak. There are information centres at Bakewell, Castleton, Edale and Upper Derwent.
National Park Authority, Aldern House, Baslow Road, Bakewell, Derbyshire DE45 1AE **T** 01629-816200
E customer.service@peakdistrict.gov.uk
W www.peakdistrict.gov.uk
Chief Executive, Sarah Fowler

PEMBROKESHIRE COAST (1952 and 1995), Pembrokeshire, 615 sq. km/240 sq. miles – The park includes cliffs, moorland and a number of islands, including Skomer and Ramsey, and the 186-mile Pembrokeshire Coast Path National Trail. There is a gallery and visitor centre at Oriel y Parc, St Davids. The park also manages Castell Henllys Iron Age Village and Carew Castle and Tidal Mill.
National Park Authority, Llanion Park, Pembroke Dock, Pembrokeshire SA72 6DY **T** 01646-624800
E info@pembrokeshirecoast.org.uk
W www.pembrokeshirecoast.wales
Chief Executive, Tegryn Jones

SNOWDONIA/ERYRI (1951), Gwynedd/Conwy, 2,132 sq. km/823 sq. miles – Snowdonia, which takes its name from Snowdon, is an area of deep valleys and rugged mountains. There are information centres at Aberdyfi, Beddgelert and Betws y Coed.
National Park Authority, Penrhyndeudraeth, Gwynedd LL48 6LF **T** 01766-770274 **E** park@snowdonia.gov.wales
W www.snowdonia.gov.wales
Chief Executive, Emyr Williams

THE SOUTH DOWNS (2010), West Sussex/Hampshire, 1,624 sq. km/627 sq. miles – The South Downs contains a diversity of natural habitats, including flower-studded chalk grassland, ancient woodland, flood meadow, lowland heath and rare chalk heathland. There are visitor centres at Beachy Head, Queen Elizabeth Country Park in Hampshire and Seven Sisters Country Park in East Sussex.
National Park Authority, North Street, Midhurst, W. Sussex GU29 9DH **T** 01730-814810 **W** www.southdowns.gov.uk
Chief Executive, Trevor Beattie

YORKSHIRE DALES (1954), North Yorkshire (71 per cent)/Cumbria (28 per cent)/Lancashire (1 per cent), 2,179 sq. km/841 sq. miles – The Yorkshire Dales is composed primarily of limestone overlaid in places by millstone grit. The three peaks of Ingleborough, Whernside and Pen-y-ghent are within the park. There are information centres at Grassington, Hawes, Aysgarth Falls, Malham and Reeth.
National Park Authority, Yoredale, Bainbridge, Leyburn, N. Yorks DL8 3EL **T** 0300-456 0030 **E** info@yorkshiredales.org.uk
W www.yorkshiredales.org.uk
Chief Executive, David Butterworth

SCOTLAND

On 9 August 2000 the national parks (Scotland) bill received royal assent, giving parliament the ability to create national parks in Scotland. The Act gives Scottish parks wider powers than in England and Wales, including statutory responsibilities for the local economy and rural communities. The board of the Cairngorms NPA comprises 19 members; seven appointed by the Scottish ministers, a further seven nominated to the board by the five local authorities in the park area and five locally elected members. The board of Loch Lomond and the Trossachs NPA comprises 17 members; five elected by the community and 12 appointed by Scottish Ministers, six of whom are nominated by local authorities. In Scotland, the national parks are central government bodies and are wholly funded by the Scottish government. Due to the financial hardships caused by COVID-19, the budget for 2020–21 will run a deficit of £398,000.

CAIRNGORMS (2003), North-East Scotland, 4,528 sq. km/1,748 sq. miles – The Cairngorms national park is the largest in the UK, covering around 6 per cent of Scotland. It displays a vast collection of landforms, including five of the six highest mountains in the UK and contains 25 per cent of Britain's threatened species. The near natural woodlands contain remnants of the original ancient Caledonian pine forest. There are 13 visitor centres within the park.
National Park Authority, 14 The Square, Grantown-on-Spey, Morayshire PH26 3HG **T** 01479-873535
E enquiries@cairngorms.co.uk **W** www.cairngorms.co.uk
Chief Executive, Grant Moir

LOCH LOMOND AND THE TROSSACHS (2002), Argyll and Bute/Perth and Kinross/Stirling/West Dunbartonshire, 1,865 sq. km/720 sq. miles – The park boundaries encompass lochs, rivers, forests, 21 mountains above 914m (3,000ft) including Ben More, the highest at 1,174m (3,852ft) and a further 20 mountains between 762m (2,500ft) and 914m (3,000ft). There is a national park centre in Balmaha and several other visitor centres across the park which are administered by VisitScotland.
National Park Authority, Carrochan, Carrochan Road, Balloch G83 8EG **T** 01389-722600 **E** info@lochlomond-trossachs.org
W www.lochlomond-trossachs.org
Chief Executive, Gordon Watson

NORTHERN IRELAND

There is a power to designate national parks in Northern Ireland under the Nature Conservation and Amenity Lands Order (Northern Ireland) 1985, but there are currently no national parks in Northern Ireland.

AREAS OF OUTSTANDING NATURAL BEAUTY

ENGLAND AND WALES

Under the National Parks and Access to the Countryside Act 1949, provision was made for the designation of areas of outstanding natural beauty (AONBs). Natural England is responsible for designating AONBs in England and Natural Resources Wales for the Welsh AONBs. Designations in England are confirmed by the Secretary of State for Environment, Food and Rural Affairs and those in Wales by the Welsh government. The Countryside and Rights of Way (CROW) Act 2000 placed greater responsibility on local authorities to protect AONBs and made it a statutory duty for relevant authorities to produce a management plan for their AONB area. The CROW Act also provided for the creation of conservation boards for larger and more complex AONBs.

The primary objective of the AONB designation is to conserve and enhance the natural beauty of the area. Where an AONB has a conservation board, it has the additional purpose of increasing public understanding and enjoyment of the special qualities of the area; the board has greater weight should there be a conflict of interests between the two. In addition, the board is also required to foster the economic and social well-being of the local communities but without incurring significant expenditure in doing so. Overall responsibility for AONBs lies with the relevant local authorities or conservation board. To coordinate planning and management responsibilities between local authorities in whose area they fall, AONBs are overseen by a joint advisory committee (or similar body) which includes representatives from the local authorities, landowners, farmers, residents and conservation and recreation groups. Core funding for AONBs is provided by central government through DEFRA, local authorities and Natural Resources Wales.

The 46 AONBs (with date designation confirmed) are:

ARNSIDE AND SILVERDALE (1972), Cumbria/Lancashire, 75 sq. km/29 sq. miles
BLACKDOWN HILLS (1991), Devon/Somerset, 370 sq. km/143 sq. miles
CANNOCK CHASE (1958), Staffordshire, 68 sq. km/26 sq. miles
CHICHESTER HARBOUR (1964), Hampshire/West Sussex, 74 sq. km/29 sq. miles
CHILTERNS (1965; extended 1990), Bedfordshire/Buckinghamshire/Hertfordshire/Oxfordshire, 839 sq. km/324 sq. miles
CLWYDIAN RANGE AND DEE VALLEY (1985; extended 2011), Denbighshire/Flintshire, 389 sq. km/150 sq. miles
CORNWALL (1959; Camel Estuary 1983), 958 sq. km/370 sq. miles
COTSWOLDS (1966; extended 1990), Gloucestershire/Oxfordshire/Warwickshire/Wiltshire/Worcestershire, 2,046 sq. km/790 sq. miles
CRANBORNE CHASE AND WEST WILTSHIRE DOWNS (1983), Dorset/Hampshire/Somerset/Wiltshire, 983 sq. km/380 sq. miles
DEDHAM VALE (1970; extended 1978, 1991), Essex/Suffolk, 90 sq. km/35 sq. miles
DORSET (1959), Dorset/Somerset, 1,129 sq. km/436 sq. miles
EAST DEVON (1963), 268 sq. km/103 sq. miles
FOREST OF BOWLAND (1964), Lancashire/North Yorkshire, 803 sq. km/310 sq. miles
GOWER (1956), Swansea, 188 sq. km/73 sq. miles
HIGH WEALD (1983), East Sussex/Kent/Surrey/West Sussex, 1,461 sq. km/564 sq. miles
HOWARDIAN HILLS (1987), North Yorkshire, 204 sq. km/79 sq. miles
ISLE OF WIGHT (1963), 189 sq. km/73 sq. miles
ISLES OF SCILLY (1976), 16 sq. km/6 sq. miles
KENT DOWNS (1968), 878 sq. km/339 sq. miles
LINCOLNSHIRE WOLDS (1973), 558 sq. km/215 sq. miles
LLYN (1957), Gwynedd, 155 sq. km/60 sq. miles
MALVERN HILLS (1959), Gloucestershire/Worcestershire, 105 sq. km/41 sq. miles
MENDIP HILLS (1972; extended 1989), Somerset, 198 sq. km/76 sq. miles
NIDDERDALE (1994), North Yorkshire, 603 sq. km/233 sq. miles
NORFOLK COAST (1968), 451 sq. km/174 sq. miles
NORTH DEVON (1960), 171 sq. km/66 sq. miles
NORTH PENNINES (1988), Cumbria/Durham/North Yorkshire/Northumberland, 1,983 sq. km/766 sq. miles

NORTH WESSEX DOWNS (1972), Hampshire/
Oxfordshire/Wiltshire, 1,730 sq. km/668 sq. miles
NORTHUMBERLAND COAST (1958), 138 sq. km/64 sq.
miles
QUANTOCK HILLS (1957), Somerset, 99 sq. km/38 sq.
miles
SHROPSHIRE HILLS (1959), 804 sq. km/310 sq. miles
SOLWAY COAST (1964), Cumbria, 115 sq. km/44 sq.
miles
SOUTH DEVON (1960), 337 sq. km/130 sq. miles
SUFFOLK COAST AND HEATHS (1970), 403 sq. km/156
sq. miles
SURREY HILLS (1958), 419 sq. km/162 sq. miles
TAMAR VALLEY (1995), Cornwall/Devon, 190 sq. km/73
sq. miles
WYE VALLEY (1971), Gloucestershire/Herefordshire/
Monmouthshire, 326 sq. km/126 sq. miles
YNYS MON (ISLE OF ANGLESEY) (1967), 221 sq. km/85
sq. miles

NORTHERN IRELAND

The Department of Agriculture, Environment and Rural Affairs
(Northern Ireland), with advice from the Council for Nature
Conservation and the Countryside, designates AONBs in
Northern Ireland. Dates given are those of designation.

ANTRIM COAST AND GLENS (1988), Co. Antrim, 725
sq. km/280 sq. miles
BINEVENAGH (2006), Co. Londonderry, 166 sq. km/64
sq. miles
CAUSEWAY COAST (1989), Co. Antrim, 42 sq. km/ 16
sq. miles
LAGAN VALLEY (1965), Co. Down, 39 sq. km/15 sq.
miles
MOURNE (1986), Co. Down, 580 sq. km/224 sq. miles
RING OF GULLION (1991), Co. Armagh, 153 sq. km/59
sq. miles
SPERRIN (1968; extended 2008), Co. Tyrone/Co.
Londonderry, 1,182 sq. km/456 sq. miles
STRANGFORD LOUGH (2010), Co. Down, 528 sq. km/
204 sq. miles

NATIONAL SCENIC AREAS

In Scotland, national scenic areas have a broadly equivalent
status to AONBs. Scottish Natural Heritage recognises areas of
national scenic significance. As at October 2020, there were
40, covering a land area of 1,020,495 hectares (2,521,694
acres) and a marine area of 357,864 hectares (884,299 acres).
  Development within national scenic areas is dealt with by
local authorities, who are required to consult Scottish Natural
Heritage concerning certain categories of development.
Disagreements between Scottish Natural Heritage and local
authorities are referred to the Scottish government. Land
management uses can also be modified in the interest of scenic
conservation.

ASSYNT-COIGACH, Highland, 129,824ha/222,884 acres
BEN NEVIS AND GLEN COE, Highland, 92,278ha/
228,024 acres
CAIRNGORM MOUNTAINS, Highland/Aberdeenshire/
Moray, 65,541ha/161,955 acres
CUILLIN HILLS, Highland, 27,320ha/67,509 acres
DEESIDE AND LOCHNAGAR, Aberdeenshire, 39,787ha/
98,316 acres
DORNOCH FIRTH, Highland, 15,782ha/38,998 acres
EAST STEWARTRY COAST, Dumfries and Galloway,
9,620ha/23,772 acres
EILDON AND LEADERFOOT, Borders, 3,877ha/9,580
acres

FLEET VALLEY, Dumfries and Galloway, 5,854ha/14,466
acres
GLEN AFFRIC, Highland, 18,837ha/46,547 acres
GLEN STRATHFARRAR, Highland, 4,027ha/9,951 acres
HOY AND WEST MAINLAND, Orkney Islands,
24,407ha/60,311 acres
JURA, Argyll and Bute, 30,317ha/74,915 acres
KINTAIL, Highland, 17,149/42,376 acres
KNAPDALE, Argyll and Bute, 32,832ha/81,130 acres
KNOYDART, Highland, 50,696ha/125,272 acres
KYLE OF TONGUE, Highland, 24,488ha/60,511 acres
KYLES OF BUTE, Argyll and Bute, 5,739ha/14,181 acres
LOCH LOMOND, Argyll and Bute, 28,077ha/69,380 acres
LOCH NA KEAL, Mull, Argyll and Bute, 44,250ha/
109,344 acres
LOCH RANNOCH AND GLEN LYON, Perthshire and
Kinross, 48,625ha/120,155 acres
LOCH SHIEL, Highland, 13,045ha/32,235 acres
LOCH TUMMEL, Perthshire and Kinross, 9,013ha/22,272
acres
LYNN OF LORN, Argyll and Bute, 15,726ha/38,860 acres
MORAR, MOIDART AND ARDNAMURCHAN, Highland,
36,956ha/91,320 acres
NITH ESTUARY, Dumfries and Galloway, 14,337ha/
35,427 acres
NORTH ARRAN, North Ayrshire, 27,304ha/67,470 acres
NORTH-WEST SUTHERLAND, Highland, 26,565ha/
65,643 acres
RIVER EARN, Perthshire and Kinross, 3,108ha/7,680 acres
RIVER TAY, Perthshire and Kinross, 5,708ha/14,105 acres
ST KILDA, Eilean Siar (Western Isles), 6,966ha/17,213
acres
SCARBA, LUNGA AND THE GARVELLACHS, Argyll and
Bute, 6,542ha/16,166 acres
SHETLAND, Shetland Isles, 41,833ha/130,371 acres
SMALL ISLANDS, Highland, 47,235ha/116,720 acres
SOUTH LEWIS, HARRIS AND NORTH UIST, Eilean Siar
(Western Isles), 202,388ha/500,111 acres
SOUTH UIST MACHAIR, Eilean Siar (Western Isles),
13,314ha/32,900 acres
THE TROSSACHS, Stirling, 4,850ha/11,985 acres
TROTTERNISH, Highland, 7,916ha/19,561 acres
UPPER TWEEDDALE, Borders, 12,770ha/31,555 acres
WESTER ROSS, Highland, 163,456ha/403,908 acres

THE NATIONAL FOREST

The National Forest is one of the UK's biggest environmental
projects, creating a forest across 518.5 sq. km (200.2 sq. miles)
of Derbyshire, Leicestershire and Staffordshire. Since the early
1990s, more than 8.9 million trees have been planted to create
over 7,000ha of new woodland landscapes. Forest cover has
increased from 6 per cent to 20 per cent, with the aim of
eventually covering approximately one-third of the designated
area.
  Since its establishment in 1995, the National Forest
Company leads the project and is responsible for delivery of
the government-approved National Forest Strategy, sponsored
by DEFRA. Priorities include continued forest creation and
management, economic development of the area for recreation
and tourism, and engaging local communities in the forest to
improve quality of life.

NATIONAL FOREST COMPANY, Enterprise Glade, Bath
  Yard, Moira, Swadlincote, Derbyshire DE12 6BA
  T 01283-551211 **W** www.nationalforest.org
  Chief Executive, John Everitt

SITES OF SPECIAL SCIENTIFIC INTEREST

A site of special scientific interest (SSSI) is a legal notification applied to land in England, Scotland or Wales which Natural England (NE), Scottish Natural Heritage (SNH) or Natural Resources Wales (NRW) identifies as being of special interest because of its flora, fauna, geological or physiographical features. In some cases, SSSIs are managed as nature reserves.

NE, SNH and NRW must notify the designation of an SSSI to the local planning authority, every owner/occupier of the land, and the environment secretary, the Scottish ministers or the Welsh government. The Environment Agency (in England), water companies and internal drainage authorities and a number of other interested parties are also formally notified.

Objections to the notification of an SSSI can be made and ultimately considered at a full meeting of the board of NE or, in Wales, a subgroup committee of the NRW board. In Scotland an objection will be dealt with by the main board of SNH or an appropriate subgroup.

The protection of these sites depends on the cooperation of individual landowners and occupiers. Owner/occupiers must consult NE, SNH or NRW and gain written consent before they can undertake certain listed activities on the site. Funds are available through management agreements and grants to assist owners and occupiers in conserving sites' interests. Sites can also be protected by management schemes, management notices and other enforcement mechanisms. As a last resort a site can be purchased.

SSSIs in Britain as at June 2019:

	Number	Hectares	Acres
England	4,125	1,096,608	2,709,777
Scotland	1,423	1,022,883	2,527,599
Wales	1,077	262,233	647,993

Sources: Natural England; © Natural Resources Wales and database right (all rights reserved); Scottish Natural Heritage

NORTHERN IRELAND

In Northern Ireland areas of special scientific interest (ASSIs) are designated by the Department of Agriculture, Environment and Rural Affairs (Northern Ireland).

NATIONAL NATURE RESERVES

National Nature Reserves are defined in the National Parks and Access to the Countryside Act 1949 as modified by the Natural Environment and Rural Communities Act 2006. National Nature Reserves may be managed solely for the purpose of conservation, or for both the purposes of conservation and recreation, providing this does not compromise the conservation purpose.

NE, SNH or NRW can declare as a national nature reserve land which is held and managed as a nature reserve under an agreement; land held and managed by NE, SNH or NRW; or land held and managed as a nature reserve by an approved body. NE, SNH or NRW can make by-laws to protect reserves from undesirable activities; these are subject to confirmation by the Secretary of State for Environment, Food and Rural Affairs, the Welsh government or the Scottish ministers.

National nature reserves in Britain as at June 2019:

	Number	Hectares	Acres
England	224	93,912	232,062
Scotland	43	154,262	381,190
Wales	76	26,362	65,143

Sources: Natural England; © Natural Resources Wales and database right (all rights reserved); Scottish Natural Heritage

NORTHERN IRELAND

Nature reserves are established and managed by the Department of Agriculture, Environment and Rural Affairs (Northern Ireland), with advice from the Council for Nature Conservation and the Countryside. Nature reserves are declared under the Nature Conservation and Amenity Lands (Northern Ireland) Order 1985.

LOCAL NATURE RESERVES

Local Nature Reserves are defined in the National Parks and Access to the Countryside Act 1949 (as amended by the Natural Environment and Rural Communities Act 2006) as land designated for the study and preservation of flora and fauna, or of geological or physiographical features. Local Nature Reserves also have a statutory obligation to provide opportunities for the enjoyment of nature or open air recreation, providing this does not compromise the conservation purpose of the reserve. Local authorities in England, Scotland and Wales have the power to acquire, declare and manage reserves in consultation with NE, SNH and NRW. There is similar legislation in Northern Ireland, where the consulting organisation is the Environment Agency.

Any organisation, such as water companies, educational trusts, local amenity groups and charitable nature conservation bodies, such as wildlife trusts, may manage local nature reserves, provided that a local authority has a legal interest in the land. This means that the local authority must either own it, lease it or have a management agreement with the landowner.

Designated local nature reserves in Britain as at June 2019:

	Number	Hectares	Acres
England	1,622	41,954	103,671
Scotland	75	10,780	26,638
Wales	95	6,187	15,289

Sources: Natural England; © Natural Resources Wales and database right (all rights reserved); Scottish Natural Heritage

There are also local nature reserves in Northern Ireland.

FOREST RESERVES

The Forestry Commission is the government department responsible for forestry policy throughout Great Britain. Forestry is a devolved matter, with the separate Forestry Commissions for England, Scotland and Wales reporting directly to their appropriate minister. The equivalent body in Northern Ireland is the Forest Service, an agency of the Department of Agriculture and Rural Development for Northern Ireland. The Forestry Commission in each country is led by a director who is also a member of the GB Board of Commissioners. As at October 2020, UK woodland certified by the Forestry Commission (including Forestry Commission-managed woodland) amounted to around 1,394,000ha (3,444,644 acres): 323,000ha (798,149 acres) in England, 145,000ha (360,773 acres) in Wales, 859,000ha (2,122,632 acres) in Scotland and 66,000ha (163,089 acres) in Northern Ireland.

There are forest nature reserves in Northern Ireland, designated and administered by the Forest Service.

MARINE NATURE RESERVES

Marine protected areas provide protection for marine flora and fauna, and geological and physiographical features on land covered by tidal waters or parts of the sea in or adjacent to the UK. These areas also provide opportunities for study and research.

ENGLAND AND WALES

The Marine and Coastal Access Act 2009 created a new kind of statutory protection for marine protected areas in England and Wales, marine conservation zones (MCZs), which are designed to increase the protection of species and habitats deemed to be of national importance. The Secretary of State for Environment, Food and Rural Affairs and the Welsh ministers have the power to designate MCZs. Individual MCZs can have varying levels of protection: some include specific activities that are appropriately managed, while others prohibit all damaging and disturbing activities. The act converted the waters around Lundy Island, a former marine protected area, to MCZ status in 2010 and this was formerly designated as such in 2013. Similarly, the marine nature reserve in the waters around Skomer was reclassified and designated an MCZ in 2014; forming the only MCZ solely in Welsh waters.

In 2009, Natural England and the Joint Nature Conservation Committee (JNCC) gave sea-users and stakeholders the ability to recommend potential MCZs to the UK government by establishing four regional projects. On 21 November 2013, the government announced the creation of 27 MCZs, covering an area of around 9,700 sq. km, to protect wildlife including seahorses, coral reefs and oyster beds from dredging and bottom-trawling. In January 2016, 23 additional MCZs were designated and in May 2019, a further 41 sites were added to the list, bringing the total to 91. The new MCZ designations means that around 30 per cent of English waters are considered protected. Information on all 91 MCZs (with date designation confirmed) can be found online **W**   www.gov.uk/government/collections/marine-conservation-zone-designations-in-england

SCOTLAND

In July 2014, under the Marine (Scotland) Act 2010, the Scottish government designated 17 marine protected areas (MPAs) in Scottish inshore territorial waters (Clyde Sea Sill; East Caithness Cliffs; Fetlar to Haroldswick; Loch Creran; Loch Sunart; Loch Sunart to the Sound of Jura; Loch Sween; Lochs Duich, Long and Alsh; Monarch Isles; Mousa to Boddam; Noss Head; Papa Westray; Small Isles; South Arran; Upper Loch Fyne and Loch Goil; Wester Ross; and Wyre and Rousay Sounds). In 2017 Loch Carron was designated an inshore MPA.

A further 13, also in July 2014, were designated in offshore waters under the UK Marine and Coastal Access Act 2009. These are: Central Fladen; East of Gannet and Montrose Fields; Faroe–Shetland Sponge Belt; Firth of Forth Banks Complex; Geikie Slide and Hebridean Slope; Hatton–Rockall Basin; North-east Faroe Shetland Channel; North-west Orkney; Norwegian Boundary Sediment Plain; Rosemary Bank Seamount; The Barra Fan and Hebrides Terrace Seamount; Turbot Bank; and West Shetland Shelf.

NORTHERN IRELAND

The Marine Act (Northern Ireland) 2013 includes provisions for establishing Marine Conservation Zones (MCZs), as well as a system of marine planning, fisheries management and marine licensing. MCZs may be designated for various purposes including the conservation of marine species and habitats, taking fully into account any economic, cultural or social consequences of doing so. The Act also allows the NI Department of Agriculture, Environment and Rural Affairs to make byelaws to protect MCZs from damage caused by unregulated activities such as anchoring, kite surfing or jet skiing. It is an offence to intentionally or recklessly destroy or damage a protected feature of an MCZ.

As at October 2020 there were five MCZs in Northern Ireland. Strangford Lough was Northern Ireland's only marine nature reserve, established in 1995 under the Nature Conservation and Amenity Lands Order (Northern Ireland) 1985, but it was redesignated as Northern Ireland's first MCZ on the introduction of the Marine Act (Northern Ireland) 2013. After a consultation period, the NI Department of Agriculture, Environment and Rural Affairs announced four new MCZ's in December 2016; Carlingford Lough, Outer Belfast Lough, Rathlin and Waterfoot.

INTERNATIONAL CONVENTIONS

The UK is party to a number of international conventions.

BERN CONVENTION

The 1979 Bern Convention on the Conservation of European Wildlife and Natural Habitats came into force in the UK in June 1982. There are 51 contracting parties and a number of other states attend meetings as observers.

The aims are to conserve wild flora and fauna and their habitats, especially where this requires the cooperation of several countries, and to promote such cooperation. The convention imposes legal obligations on contracting parties, protecting over 500 wild plant species and more than 1,000 wild animal species.

All parties to the convention must promote national conservation policies and take account of the conservation of wild flora and fauna when setting planning and development policies. The contracting parties are invited to submit reports to the standing committee every four years.

SECRETARIAT OF THE BERN CONVENTION STANDING COMMITTEE, Council of Europe, Avenue de l'Europe, F-67075 Strasbourg Cedex, France **W** www.coe.int/bernconvention

BIOLOGICAL DIVERSITY

The UK ratified the Convention on Biological Diversity (CBD) in June 1994. As at October 2020 there were 196 parties to the convention.

There are seven programmes addressing agricultural biodiversity, marine and coastal biodiversity and the biodiversity of inland waters, dry and sub-humid lands, islands, mountains and forests. On 29 January 2000 the Conference of the Parties adopted a supplementary agreement to the convention known as the Cartagena Protocol on Biosafety. The protocol seeks to protect biological diversity from potential risks that may be posed by introducing modified living organisms, resulting from biotechnology, into the environment. As at October 2020, 173 countries were party to the protocol; the UK joined on 17 February 2004. The Nagoya Protocol on Access and Benefit-sharing was adopted in October 2010 and entered into force on 12 October 2014. It provides international rules and procedure on liability and redress for damage to biodiversity resulting from living modified organisms. As at October 2020, 128 countries were party to the protocol; the UK became party on 22 May 2016. The Nagoya-Kuala Lumpur Supplementary Protocol on Liability and Redress was adopted as a supplementary agreement to the Cartagena Protocol on Biosafety. It aims to contribute to the conservation and sustainable use of biodiversity by providing international rules and procedures in the field of liability and redress relating to living modified organisms; requiring that response measures are taken in the event of damage resulting from living modified organisms, or where there is sufficient likelihood that damage will result if timely response measures are not taken. The Nagoya-Kuala Lumpur Supplementary Protocol entered into force on 5 March 2018; as at October 2020 44 countries, including the UK, were party to the protocol.

The UK Biodiversity Action Plan (UKBAP), published in 1994, was the UK government's response to the CBD at the 1992 Rio Earth Summit. The UK Post-2010 Biodiversity Framework replaced UKBAP when it was published in 2012 by DEFRA and the devolved administrations. The framework covers the period 2011–20 and forms the UK government's response to the strategic plan of the CBD. It includes five internationally agreed strategic goals to be achieved by 2020: to address the underlying causes of biodiversity loss by making biodiversity a mainstream issue across government and society; to reduce the direct pressures on biodiversity and promote sustainable use; to safeguard ecosystems, species and genetic diversity; to enhance the benefits to all from biodiversity and ecosystem services; and to enhance implementation through participatory planning, knowledge management and capacity building. The list of priority species and habitats under the biodiversity framework covers 1,150 species and 65 habitats and is administered by the Joint Nature Conservation Committee (JNCC).

SECRETARIAT OF THE CONVENTION ON
BIOLOGICAL DIVERSITY, 413, Saint Jacques Street, suite 800, Montreal, QC H2Y 1N9 Canada
T +1514-288 2220 E secretariat@cbd.int W www.cbd.int
JNCC, Monkstone House, City Road, Peterborough PE1 1JY
T 01733-562626 W www.jncc.defra.gov.uk

BONN CONVENTION

The 1979 Convention on Conservation of Migratory Species of Wild Animals (also known as the CMS or Bonn Convention) came into force in the UK in October 1985. As at October 2020, 131 countries were party to the convention.

It requires the protection of listed endangered migratory species and encourages international agreements covering these and other threatened species.

Seven agreements have been concluded to date under the convention. They aim to conserve African-Eurasian migratory waterbirds; albatrosses and petrels; European bats; cetaceans of the Black Sea, Mediterranean and contiguous Atlantic area; small cetaceans in the Baltic, north-east Atlantic, Irish and North Seas; gorillas and their habitats; and seals in the Wadden Sea. A further 19 memorandums of understanding have been agreed for West-African populations of the African elephant, aquatic warbler, bukhara deer, cetaceans of the Pacific Islands, dugongs (large marine mammals), middle-European population of the great bustard, high Andean flamingos, huemuls (Andean deer). manatee and small cetaceans of Western Africa and Macaronesia, marine turtles of the Atlantic coast of Africa, Indian Ocean and South East Asia, migratory birds of prey in Africa and Eurasia, migratory grassland birds of southern South America, migratory sharks, eastern-Atlantic populations of the Mediterranean monk seal, ruddy-headed goose, saiga antelope, Siberian crane and the slender-billed curlew. In addition, there are four special species initiatives for: African carnivores, central Asian mammals, Sahelo–Saharan megafauna and the central Asian flyway.

UNEP/CMS SECRETARIAT, Platz der Vereinten Nationen 1, 53113 Bonn, Germany T (+49) (228) 815 2401
E cms.secretariat@cms.int W www.cms.int

CITES

The 1973 Convention on International Trade in Endangered Species of Wild Fauna and Flora (CITES), which entered into force in 1975, is an agreement between governments to ensure that international trade in specimens of wild animals and plants does not threaten their survival. The convention came into force in the UK in October 1976 and there are currently 183 member countries. Countries party to the convention ban commercial international trade in an agreed list of endangered species and regulate and monitor trade in other species that might become endangered. The convention accords varying degrees of protection to approximately 30,000 species of plants and 5,800 species of animals, whether they are traded as live specimens or as products derived from them.

The Conference of the Parties to CITES meets every two to three years to review the convention's implementation. The Animal and Plant Health Agency at the Department for Environment, Food and Rural Affairs carries out the government's responsibilities under CITES.

CITES is implemented in the EU through a series of EC regulations known as the Wildlife Trade Regulations.

CITES SECRETARIAT, Palais des Nations, Avenue de la Paix 8-14, 1211 Genève 10, Switzerland T (+41) (22) 917 8139/40
E info@cites.org W www.cites.org

INTERNATIONAL CONVENTION FOR THE REGULATION OF WHALING

The International Convention for the Regulation of Whaling was signed in Washington DC in 1946 and currently has 89 member countries.

The measures in the convention provide for the complete protection of certain species; designate specified areas as whale sanctuaries; set limits on the numbers and size of whales which may be taken; prescribe open and closed seasons and areas for whaling; and prohibit the capture of suckling calves and female whales accompanied by calves. The International Whaling Commission meets biennially to review and revise these measures.

INTERNATIONAL WHALING COMMISSION, The Red House, 135 Station Road, Impington, Cambridge CB24 9NP
T 01223-233971 E secretariat@iwc.int W www.iwc.int

OSPAR

The Convention for the Protection of the Marine Environment of the North-East Atlantic (the OSPAR Convention) was adopted in Paris, France in September 1992 and entered into force in March 1998. The OSPAR Convention replaced both the Oslo Convention (1972) and the Paris Convention (1974), with the intention of providing a comprehensive approach to addressing all sources of pollution which may affect the maritime area, and matters relating to the protection of the maritime environment. An annex on biodiversity and ecosystems was adopted in 1998 to cover non-polluting human activities that can adversely affect the sea.

Fifteen countries plus the European Union are party to the convention; the UK ratified OSPAR in 1998. The OSPAR Commission makes decisions and recommendations and sets out actions to be taken by the contracting parties. The OSPAR Secretariat administers the work under the convention, coordinates the work of the contracting parties and runs the formal meeting schedule of OSPAR.

OSPAR COMMISSION, The Aspect, 12 Finsbury Square, London EC2A 1AS T 020-7430 5200 E secretariat@ospar.org
W www.ospar.org

RAMSAR CONVENTION

The 1971 Convention on Wetlands of National Importance, called the Ramsar Convention, is an inter-governmental treaty that provides for the conservation and sustainable use of wetlands and their resources. The Convention entered into force in the UK in 1976.

Governments that are contracting parties to the convention must designate wetlands for inclusion in the List of Wetlands of International Importance (the 'Ramsar List') and include wetland conservation considerations in their land-use planning. As at October 2020, the Convention's 171 contracting parties had designated 2,414 wetland sites, covering 252,537,889 hectares. The UK currently has 175 designated sites covering 1,283,040 hectares.

The contracting parties meet every three years to assess progress. The 13th Meeting of the Conference of the Contracting Parties to the Ramsar Convention on Wetlands took place in Dubai, UAE in October 2018.

RAMSAR CONVENTION SECRETARIAT, Rue Mauverney 28, CH-1196 Gland, Switzerland T (+41) (22) 999 0170 E ramsar@ramsar.org W https://www.ramsar.org

UK LEGISLATION

The Wildlife and Countryside Act 1981 gives legal protection to a wide range of wild animals and plants. Every five years the statutory nature conservation agencies (Natural England, Natural Resources Wales and Scottish Natural Heritage), working jointly through the Joint Nature Conservation Committee, are required to review schedules 5 (animals, other than birds) and 8 (plants) of the Wildlife and Countryside Act 1981. They make recommendations to the Secretary of State for Environment, Food and Rural Affairs, the Welsh ministers and the Scottish government for changes to these schedules. The most recent variations of schedules 5 and 8 for England came into effect on 1 October 2011, following the fifth quinquennial review. The sixth review was submitted to DEFRA, the Welsh government and the Scottish government in April 2014; once these governments have considered the review, they will respond formally and publish amendments to the Wildlife and Countryside Act (1981).

Under section 9 of the act it is an offence to kill, injure, take, possess or sell (whether alive or dead) any wild animal included in schedule 5 of the act and to disturb its place of shelter and protection or to destroy that place. However certain species listed on schedule 5 are protected against some, but not all, of these activities.

Under section 13 of the act it is illegal without a licence to pick, uproot, sell or destroy plants listed in schedule 8. Since January 2001, under the Countryside and Rights of Way Act 2000, persons found guilty of an offence under part 1 of the Wildlife and Countryside Act 1981 face a maximum penalty of up to £5,000 and/or up to a six-month custodial sentence per specimen.

BIRDS

The act lays down a close season for birds (listed on Schedule 2, part 1) from 1 February to 31 August inclusive, each year. Variations to these dates are made for:

Black grouse – 10 December to 20 August (10 December – 1 September for Somerset, Devon and New Forest)
Capercaillie – 1 February to 30 September (England and Wales only)
Grey partridge – 1 February to 1 September
Pheasant – 1 February to 1 October
Ptarmigan and Red grouse – 10 December to 12 August
Red-legged partridge – 1 February to 1 September
Snipe – 1 February to 11 August

Woodcock – 1 February to 30 September (England and Wales); 1 February to 31 August (Scotland)
Birds listed on schedule 2, part 1 (below high water mark) (see below) – 21 February to 31 August
Wild duck and wild geese, in or over any area below the high-water mark of ordinary spring tides – 21 February to 31 August
Sundays and Christmas Day in Scotland, and Sundays for any area of England or Wales prescribed by the Secretary of State.

Birds listed on schedule 2, part 1, which may be killed or taken outside the close season are: capercaillie (England and Wales only); coot; certain wild duck (gadwall, goldeneye, mallard, Northern pintail, common pochard, Northern shoveler, teal, tufted duck, Eurasian wigeon); certain wild geese (Canada, greylag, pink-footed, white-fronted (in England and Wales only); golden plover; moorhen; snipe; and woodcock.

Section 16 of the 1981 act allows licences to be issued on either an individual or general basis, to allow the killing, taking and sale of certain birds for specified reasons such as public health and safety. All other wild birds are fully protected by law throughout the year.

ANIMALS PROTECTED BY SCHEDULE 5

Adder *(Vipera berus)*
Anemone, Ivell's Sea *(Edwardsia ivelli)*
Anemone, Starlet Sea *(Nematosella vectensis)*
Apus *(Triops cancriformis)*
Bat, Horseshoe, all species *(Rhinolophidae)*
Bat, Typical, all species *(Vespertilionidae)*
Beetle *(Hypebaeus flavipes)*
Beetle, Bembridge Water *(Paracymus aeneus)*
Beetle, Lesser Silver Water *(Hydrochara caraboides)*
Beetle, Mire Pill *(Curimopsis nigrita)*
Beetle, Moccas *(Hypebaeus flavipes)*
Beetle, Rainbow Leaf *(Chrysolina cerealis)*
Beetle, Spangled Water *(Graphoderus zonatus)*
Beetle, Stag *(Lucanus cervus)*
Beetle, Violet Click *(Limoniscus violaceus)*
Beetle, Water *(Paracymus aeneus)*
Burbot *(Lota lota)*
Butterfly, Adonis Blue *(Lysandra bellargus)*
Butterfly, Black Hairstreak *(Strymonidia pruni)*
Butterfly, Brown Hairstreak *(Thecla betulae)*
Butterfly, Chalkhill Blue *(Lysandra coridon)*
Butterfly, Chequered Skipper *(Carterocephalus palaemon)*
Butterfly, Duke of Burgundy Fritillary *(Hamearis lucina)*
Butterfly, Glanville Fritillary *(Melitaea cinxia)*
Butterfly, Heath Fritillary *(Mellicta athalia* or *Melitaea athalia)*
Butterfly, High Brown Fritillary *(Argynnis adippe)*
Butterfly, Large Blue *(Maculinea arion)*
Butterfly, Large Copper *(Lycaena dispar)*
Butterfly, Large Heath *(Coenonympha tullia)*
Butterfly, Large Tortoiseshell *(Nymphalis polychloros)*
Butterfly, Lulworth Skipper *(Thymelicus acteon)*
Butterfly, Marsh Fritillary *(Eurodryas aurinia)*
Butterfly, Mountain Ringlet *(Erebia epiphron)*
Butterfly, Northern Brown Argus *(Aricia artaxerxes)*
Butterfly, Pearl-bordered Fritillary *(Boloria euphrosyne)*
Butterfly, Purple Emperor *(Apatura iris)*
Butterfly, Silver Spotted Skipper *(Hesperia comma)*
Butterfly, Silver-studded Blue *(Plebejus argus)*
Butterfly, Small Blue *(Cupido minimus)*
Butterfly, Swallowtail *(Papilio machaon)*
Butterfly, White Letter Hairstreak *(Stymonida w-album)*
Butterfly, Wood White *(Leptidea sinapis)*
Cat, Wild *(Felis silvestris)*
Cicada, New Forest *(Cicadetta montana)*
Crayfish, Atlantic Stream *(Austropotamobius pallipes)*

Cricket, Field *(Gryllus campestris)*
Cricket, Mole *(Gryllotalpa gryllotalpa)*
Damselfly, Southern *(Coenagrion mercuriale)*
Dolphin, all species *(Cetacea)*
Dormouse *(Muscardinus avellanarius)*
Dragonfly, Norfolk Aeshna *(Aeshna isosceles)*
Frog, Common *(Rana temporaria)*
Frog, Pool, Northern Clade *(Pelophylax lessonae)*
Goby, Couch's *(Gobius couchii)*
Goby, Giant *(Gobius cobitis)*
Grasshopper, Wart-biter *Decticus verrucivorus*
Hatchet Shell, Northern *(Thyasira gouldi)*
Hydroid, Marine *(Clavopsella navis)*
Lagoon Snail, De Folin's *(Caecum armoricum)*
Lagoon Worm, Tentacled *(Alkmaria romijni)*
Leech, Medicinal *(Hirudo medicinalis)*
Lizard, Sand *(Lacerta agilis)*
Lizard, Viviparous *(Lacerta vivipara)*
Marten, Pine *(Martes martes)*
Moth, Barberry Carpet *(Pareulype berberata)*
Moth, Black-veined *(Siona lineata or Idaea lineata)*
Moth, Fiery Clearwing *(Bembecia chrysidiformis)*
Moth, Fisher's Estuarine *(Gortyna borelii)*
Moth, New Forest Burnet *(Zygaena viciae)*
Moth, Reddish Buff *(Acosmetia caliginosa)*
Moth, Slender Scotch Burnet *(Zygaena loti)*
Moth, Sussex Emerald *(Thalera fimbrialis)*
Moth, Talisker Burnet *(Zygaena lonicerae)*
Mussel, Fan *(Atrina fragilis)*
Mussel, Freshwater Pearl *(Margaritifera margaritifera)*
Newt, Great Crested (or Warty) *(Triturus cristatus)*
Newt, Palmate *(Triturus helveticus)*
Newt, Smooth *(Triturus vulgaris)*
Otter, Common *(Lutra lutra)*
Porpoise, all species *(Cetacea)*
Sandworm, Lagoon *(Armandia cirrhosa)*
Sea Fan, Pink *(Eunicella verrucosa)*
Sea Slug, Lagoon *(Tenellia adspersa)*
Sea-mat, Trembling *(Victorella pavida)*
Seahorse, Short Snouted (England only) *(Hippocampus hippocampus)*
Seahorse, Spiny (England only) *(Hippocampus guttulatus)*
Shad, Allis *(Alosa alosa)*
Shad, Twaite *(Alosa fallax)*
Shark, Angel (England only) *(Squatina squatina)*
Shark, Basking *(Cetorhinus maximus)*
Shrimp, Fairy *(Chirocephalus diaphanus)*
Shrimp, Lagoon Sand *(Gammarus insensibilis)*
Shrimp, Tadpole (Apus) *(Triops cancriformis)*
Skate, White *(Rostroraja alba)*
Slow-worm *(Anguis fragilis)*
Snail, Glutinous *(Myxas glutinosa)*
Snail, Roman (England only) *(Helix pomatia)*
Snail, Sandbowl *(Catinella arenaria)*
Snake, Grass *(Natrix natrix or Natrix helvetica)*
Snake, Smooth *(Coronella austriaca)*
Spider, Fen Raft *(Dolomedes plantarius)*
Spider, Ladybird *(Eresus niger)*
Squirrel, Red *(Sciurus vulgaris)*
Sturgeon *(Acipenser sturio)*
Toad, Common *(Bufo bufo)*
Toad, Natterjack *(Bufo calamita)*
Turtle, Flatback *(Cheloniidae/Natator Depressus)*
Turtle, Green Sea *(Chelonia mydas)*
Turtle, Hawksbill *(Eretmochelys imbricate)*
Turtle, Kemp's Ridley Sea *(Lepidochelys kempii)*
Turtle, Leatherback Sea *(Dermo chelys coriacea)*
Turtle, Loggerhead Sea *(Caretta caretta)*
Turtle, Olive Ridley *(Lepidochelys olivacea)*

Vendace *(Coregonus albula)*
Vole, Water *(Arvicola terrestris)*
Walrus *(Odobenus rosmarus)*
Whale, all species *(Cetacea)*
Whitefish *(Coregonus lavaretus)*

PLANTS PROTECTED BY SCHEDULE 8
Adder's Tongue, Least *(Ophioglossum lusitanicum)*
Alison, Small *(Alyssum alyssoides)*
Anomodon, Long-leaved *(Anomodon longifolius)*
Beech-lichen, New Forest *(Enterographa elaborata)*
Blackwort *(Southbya nigrella)*
Bluebell *(Hyacinthoides non-scripta)*
Bolete, Royal *(Boletus regius)*
Broomrape, Bedstraw *(Orobanche caryophyllacea)*
Broomrape, Oxtongue *(Orobanche loricata)*
Broomrape, Thistle *(Orobanche reticulata)*
Cabbage, Lundy *(Rhynchosinapis wrightii)*
Calamint, Wood *(Calamintha sylvatica)*
Caloplaca, Snow *(Caloplaca nivalis)*
Catapyrenium, Tree *(Catapyrenium psoromoides)*
Catchfly, Alpine *(Lychnis alpina)*
Catillaria, Laurer's *(Catellaria laureri)*
Centaury, Slender *(Centaurium tenuiflorum)*
Cinquefoil, Rock *(Potentilla rupestris)*
Cladonia, Convoluted *(Cladonia convoluta)*
Cladonia, Upright Mountain *(Cladonia stricta)*
Clary, Meadow *(Salvia pratensis)*
Club-rush, Triangular *(Scirpus triquetrus)*
Colt's-foot, Purple *(Homogyne alpina)*
Cotoneaster, Wild *(Cotoneaster integerrimus)*
Cottongrass, Slender *(Eriophorum gracile)*
Cow-wheat, Field *(Melampyrum arvense)*
Crocus, Sand *(Romulea columnae)*
Crystalwort, Lizard *(Riccia bifurca)*
Cudweed, Broad-leaved *(Filago pyramidata)*
Cudweed, Jersey *(Gnaphalium luteoalbum)*
Cudweed, Red-tipped *(Filago lutescens)*
Cut-grass *(Leersia oryzoides)*
Diapensia *(Diapensia lapponica)*
Dock, shore *(Rumex rupestris)*
Earwort, Marsh *(Jamesoniella undulifolia)*
Eryngo, Field *(Eryngium campestre)*
Fern, Dickie's Bladder *(Cystopteris dickieana)*
Fern, Killarney *(Trichomanes speciosum)*
Flapwort, Norfolk *(Leiocolea rutheana)*
Fleabane, Alpine *(Erigeron borealis)*
Fleabane, Small *(Pulicaria vulgaris)*
Fleawort, South Stack *(Tephroseris integrifolia ssp maritima)*
Frostwort, Pointed *(Gymnomitrion apiculatum)*
Fungus, Hedgehog *(Hericium erinaceum)*
Galingale, Brown *(Cyperus fuscus)*
Gentian, Alpine *(Gentiana nivalis)*
Gentian, Dune *(Gentianella uliginosa)*
Gentian, Early *(Gentianella anglica)*
Gentian, Fringed *(Gentianella ciliata)*
Gentian, Spring *(Gentiana verna)*
Germander, Cut-leaved *(Teucrium botrys)*
Germander, Water *(Teucrium scordium)*
Gladiolus, Wild *(Gladiolus illyricus)*
Goblin Lights *(Catolechia wahlenbergii)*
Goosefoot, Stinking *(Chenopodium vulvaria)*
Grass-poly *(Lythrum hyssopifolia)*
Grimmia, Blunt-leaved *(Grimmia unicolor)*
Gyalecta, Elm *(Gyalecta ulmi)*
Hare's-ear, Sickle-leaved *(Bupleurum falcatum)*
Hare's-ear, Small *(Bupleurum baldense)*
Hawk's-beard, Stinking *(Crepis foetida)*
Hawkweed, Northroe *(Hieracium northroense)*

Hawkweed, Shetland *(Hieracium zetlandicum)*
Hawkweed, Weak-leaved *(Hieracium attenuatifolium)*
Heath, Blue *(Phyllodoce caerulea)*
Helleborine, Red *(Cephalanthera rubra)*
Helleborine, Young *(Epipactis youngiana)*
Horsetail, Branched *(Equisetum ramosissimum)*
Hound's-tongue, Green *(Cynoglossum germanicum)*
Knawel, Perennial *(Scleranthus perennis)*
Knotgrass, Sea *(Polygonum maritimum)*
Lady's-Slipper *(Cypripedium calceolus)*
Lecanactis, Churchyard *Lecanactis hemisphaerica)*
Lecanora, Tarn *(Lecanora archariana)*
Lecidea, Copper *(Lecidea inops)*
Leek, Round-headed *(Allium sphaerocephalon)*
Lettuce, Least *(Lactuca saligna)*
Lichen, Arctic Kidney *(Nephroma arcticum)*
Lichen, Ciliate Strap *(Heterodermia leucomelos)*
Lichen, Coralloid Rosette *(Heterodermia propagulifera)*
Lichen, Ear-lobed Dog *(Peltigera lepidophora)*
Lichen, Forked Hair *(Bryoria furcellata)*
Lichen, Golden Hair *(Teloschistes flavicans)*
Lichen, Orange-fruited Elm *(Caloplaca luteoalba)*
Lichen, River Jelly *(Collema dichotomum)*
Lichen, Scaly Breck *(Squamarina lentigera)*
Lichen, Starry Breck *(Buellia asterella)*
Lily, Snowdon *(Lloydia serotina)*
Liverwort *(Petallophyllum ralfsi)*
Liverwort, Lindenberg's Leafy *(Adelanthus lindenbergianus)*
Lungwort, Tree *(Lobaria pulmonaria)*
Marsh-mallow, Rough *(Althaea hirsuta)*
Marshwort, Creeping *(Apium repens)*
Milk-parsley, Cambridge *(Selinum carvifolia)*
Moss *(Drepanocladius vernicosus)*
Moss, Alpine Copper *(Mielichoferia mielichoferi)*
Moss, Baltic Bog *(Sphagnum balticum)*
Moss, Blue Dew *(Saelania glaucescens)*
Moss, Blunt-leaved Bristle *(Orthotrichum obtusifolium)*
Moss, Bright Green Cave *(Cyclodictyon laetevirens)*
Moss, Cordate Beard *(Barbula cordata)*
Moss, Cornish Path *(Ditrichum cornubicum)*
Moss, Derbyshire Feather *(Thamnobryum angustifolium)*
Moss, Dune Thread *(Bryum mamillatum)*
Moss, Flamingo *(Desmatodon cernuus)*
Moss, Glaucous Beard *(Barbula glauca)*
Moss, Green Shield *(Buxbaumia viridis)*
Moss, Hair Silk *(Plagiothecium piliferum)*
Moss, Knothole *(Zygodon forsteri)*
Moss, Large Yellow Feather *(Scorpidium turgescens)*
Moss, Millimetre *(Micromitrium tenerum)*
Moss, Multi-fruited River *(Cryphaea lamyana)*
Moss, Nowell's Limestone *(Zygodon gracilis)*
Moss, Polar Feather *(Hygrohypnum polare)*
Moss, Rigid Apple *(Bartramia stricta)*
Moss, Round-leaved Feather *(Rhyncostegium rotundifolium)*
Moss, Schleicher's Thread *(Bryum schleicheri)*
Moss, Triangular Pygmy *(Acaulon triquetrum)*
Moss, Vaucher's Feather *(Hypnum vaucheri)*
Mudwort, Welsh *(Limosella australis)*
Naiad, Holly-leaved *(Najas marina)*
Naiad, Slender *(Najas flexilis)*
Nail, Rock *(Calicium corynellum)*
Orache, Stalked *(Halimione pedunculata)*
Orchid, Early Spider *(Ophrys sphegodes)*

Orchid, Fen *(Liparis loeselii)*
Orchid, Ghost *(Epipogium aphyllum)*
Orchid, Lapland Marsh *(Dactylorhiza lapponica)*
Orchid, Late Spider *(Ophrys fuciflora)*
Orchid, Lizard *(Himantoglossum hircinum)*
Orchid, Military *(Orchis militaris)*
Orchid, Monkey *(Orchis simia)*
Pannaria, Caledonia *(Panneria ignobilis)*
Parmelia, New Forest *(Parmelia minarum)*
Parmentaria, Oil Stain *(Parmentaria chilensis)*
Pear, Plymouth *(Pyrus cordata)*
Penny-cress, Perfoliate *(Thlaspi perfoliatum)*
Pennyroyal *(Mentha pulegium)*
Pertusaria, Alpine Moss *(Pertusaria bryontha)*
Physcia, Southern Grey *(Physcia tribacioides)*
Pigmyweed *(Crassula aquatica)*
Pine, Ground *(Ajuga chamaepitys)*
Pink, Cheddar *(Dianthus gratianopolitanus)*
Pink, Childing *(Petroraghia nanteuilii)*
Pink, Deptford (England and Wales only) *(Dianthus armeria)*
Plantain, Floating Water *(Luronium natans)*
Polypore, Oak *(Buglossoporus pulvinus)*
Pseudocyphellaria, Ragged *(Pseudocyphellaria lacerata)*
Psora, Rusty Alpine *(Psora rubiformis)*
Puffball, Sandy Stilt *(Battarraea phalloides)*
Ragwort, Fen *(Senecio paludosus)*
Ramping-fumitory, Martin's *(Fumaria martinii)*
Rampion, Spiked *(Phyteuma spicatum)*
Restharrow, Small *(Ononis reclinata)*
Rock-cress, Alpine *(Arabis alpina)*
Rock-cress, Bristol *(Arabis stricta)*
Rustwort, Western *(Marsupella profunda)*
Sandwort, Norwegian *(Arenaria norvegica)*
Sandwort, Teesdale *(Minuartia stricta)*
Saxifrage, Drooping *(Saxifraga cernua)*
Saxifrage, Marsh *(Saxifraga hirilus)*
Saxifrage, Tufted *(Saxifraga cespitosa)*
Solenopsora, Serpentine *(Solenopsora liparina)*
Solomon's-seal, Whorled *(Polygonatum verticillatum)*
Sow-thistle, Alpine *(Cicerbita alpina)*
Spearwort, Adder's-tongue *(Ranunculus ophioglossifolius)*
Speedwell, Fingered *(Veronica triphyllos)*
Speedwell, Spiked *(Veronica spicata)*
Spike-rush, Dwarf *(Eleocharis parvula)*
Star-of-Bethlehem, Early *(Gagea bohemica)*
Starfruit *(Damasonium alisma)*
Stonewort, Bearded *(Chara canescens)*
Stonewort, Foxtail *(Lamprothamnium papulosum)*
Strapwort *(Corrigiola litoralis)*
Sulphur-tresses, Alpine *(Alectoria ochroleuca)*
Threadmoss, Long-leaved *(Bryum neodamense)*
Turpswort *(Geocalyx graveolens)*
Violet, Fen *(Viola persicifolia)*
Viper's-grass *(Scorzonera humilis)*
Water-plantain, Ribbon-leaved *(Alisma gramineum)*
Wood-sedge, Starved *(Carex depauperata)*
Woodsia, Alpine *(Woodsia alpina)*
Woodsia, Oblong *(Woodsia ilvenis)*
Wormwood, Field *(Artemisia campestris)*
Woundwort, Downy *(Stachys germanica)*
Woundwort, Limestone *(Stachys alpina)*
Yellow-rattle, Greater *(Rhinanthus serotinus)*

WORLD HERITAGE SITES

The Convention Concerning the Protection of the World Cultural and Natural Heritage was adopted by the United Nations Educational, Scientific and Cultural Organization (UNESCO) in 1972 and ratified by the UK in 1984. As at October 2020, 194 states were party to the convention. The convention provides for the identification, protection and conservation of cultural and natural sites of outstanding universal value.

Cultural sites may be:
- an extraordinary exponent of human creative genius
- sites representing architectural and technological innovation or cultural interchange
- sites of artistic, historic, aesthetic, archaeological, scientific, ethnologic or anthropologic value
- 'cultural landscapes', ie sites whose characteristics are marked by significant interactions between human populations and their natural environment
- exceptional examples of a traditional settlement or land- or sea-use, especially those threatened by irreversible changes.
- unique or exceptional examples of a cultural tradition or a civilisation either still present or extinct

Natural sites may be:
- those displaying critical periods of earth's history
- superlative examples of on-going ecological and biological processes in the evolution of ecosystems
- those exhibiting remarkable natural beauty and aesthetic significance or those where extraordinary natural phenomena are witnessed
- the habitat of threatened species and plants

Governments which are party to the convention nominate sites in their country for inclusion in the World Heritage List. Nominations are considered by the World Heritage Committee, an inter-governmental committee composed of 21 representatives of the parties to the convention. The committee is advised by the International Council on Monuments and Sites (ICOMOS), the International Centre for the Study of the Preservation and Restoration of Cultural Property (ICCROM) and the International Union for the Conservation of Nature (IUCN). ICOMOS evaluates and reports on proposed cultural and mixed sites, ICCROM provides expert advice and training on how to conserve and restore cultural property and IUCN provides technical evaluations of natural heritage sites and reports on the state of conservation of listed sites.

A prerequisite for inclusion in the World Heritage List is the existence of an effective legal protection system in the country in which the site is situated and a detailed management plan to ensure the conservation of the site. Inclusion in the list does not confer any greater degree of protection on the site than that offered by the national protection framework.

If a site is considered to be in serious danger of decay or damage, the committee may add it to the World Heritage in Danger List. Sites on this list may benefit from particular attention or emergency measures to allay threats and allow them to retain their world heritage status, or in extreme cases of damage or neglect they may lose their world heritage status completely. A total of 53 sites are currently inscribed on the World Heritage in Danger List.

Financial support for the conservation of sites on the World Heritage List is provided by the World Heritage Fund, administered by the World Heritage Committee. The fund's income is derived from compulsory and voluntary contributions from the states party to the convention and from private donations.

WORLD HERITAGE CENTRE, UNESCO, 7 Place de Fontenoy, 75352 Paris 07 SP, France **W** https://whc.unesco.org

DESIGNATED SITES

As at 10 July 2019, following the 43rd session of the World Heritage Committee, 1,121 sites across 167 countries were on the World Heritage List. The 44th session of the World Heritage Committee was delayed until 2021, due to COVID-19; no new UNESCO sites were designated in 2020. Of these, 28 are in the UK and four in UK overseas territories; 27 are listed for their cultural significance (†), four for their natural significance (*) and one for both cultural and natural significance. Liverpool's Maritime Mercantile City is the only UK site on the List of World Heritage in Danger. The year in which sites were designated appears in the first set of parentheses. The number in the second set of parentheses denotes the position of each site on the map below.

WORLD HERITAGE SITES IN THE UK

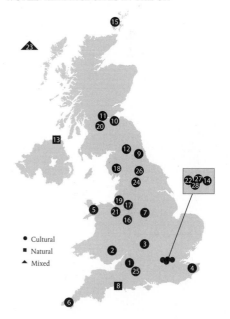

● Cultural
■ Natural
▲ Mixed

UNITED KINGDOM
†Bath – the city (1987). (1)
†Blaenarvon industrial landscape, Wales (2000). (2)
†Blenheim Palace and Park, Oxfordshire (1987). (3)
†Canterbury Cathedral, St Augustine's Abbey, St Martin's Church, Kent (1988). (4)
†Castle and town walls of King Edward I, north Wales – Beaumaris, Caernarfon Castle, Conwy Castle, Harlech Castle (1986). (5)
†Cornwall and west Devon mining landscape (2006). (6)
†Derwent Valley Mills, Derbyshire (2001). (7)
*Dorset and east Devon coast (2001). (8)
†Durham Cathedral and Castle (1986). (9)
†Edinburgh old and new towns (1995). (10)
†Forth Bridge, Firth of Forth, Scotland (2015). (11)

†Frontiers of the Roman Empire – Hadrian's Wall, northern England; Antonine Wall, central Scotland (1987, 2005, 2008). (12)

*Giant's Causeway and Causeway coast, Co. Antrim (1986). (13)

†Greenwich, London – maritime Greenwich, including the Royal Naval College, Old Royal Observatory, Queen's House, town centre (1997). (14)

†Heart of Neolithic Orkney (1999). (15)

†Ironbridge Gorge, Shropshire – the world's first iron bridge and other early industrial sites (1986). (16)

†Jodrell Bank Observatory, Cheshire (2019). (17)

†Lake District, Cumbria (2017). (18)

†Liverpool – six areas of the maritime mercantile city (2004). (19)

†New Lanark, South Lanarkshire, Scotland (2001). (20)

†Pontcysyllte Aqueduct and Canal, Wrexham, Wales (2009). (21)

†Royal Botanic Gardens, Kew (2003). (22)

†*St Kilda, Eilean Siar (Western Isles) (1986). (23)

†Saltaire, West Yorkshire (2001). (24)

†Stonehenge, Avebury and related megalithic sites, Wiltshire (1986). (25)

†Studley Royal Park, Fountains Abbey, St Mary's Church, N. Yorkshire (1986). (26)

†Tower of London (1988). (27)

†Westminster Abbey, Palace of Westminster, St Margaret's Church, London (1987). (28)

UK OVERSEAS TERRITORIES

*Henderson Island, Pitcairn Islands, South Pacific Ocean (1988)

*Gough Island and Inaccessible Island (part of Tristan da Cunha), South Atlantic Ocean (1995)

†Historic town of St George and related fortifications, Bermuda (2000)

†Gorham's Cave Complex, Gibraltar (2016)

HISTORIC BUILDINGS AND MONUMENTS

ENGLAND

Under the Planning (Listed Buildings and Conservation Areas) Act 1990, the Secretary of State for Digital, Culture, Media and Sport has a statutory duty to approve buildings or groups of buildings in England that are of special architectural or historic interest. Since April 2015 the list of such buildings is maintained by Historic England who are also responsible for making recommendations to the secretary of state for additions, removals and amendments to the list. Under the Ancient Monuments and Archaeological Areas Act 1979 as amended by the National Heritage Act 1983, the secretary of state is also responsible for compiling a schedule of ancient monuments. Decisions are taken on the advice of Historic England. A searchable database of all nationally designated heritage assets, The National Heritage List for England (NHLE), is available online: **W** www.historicengland.org.uk/listing/the-list.

LISTED BUILDINGS

Listed buildings are classified into Grade I, Grade II* and Grade II. As at October 2020, there were approximately 400,000 listed buildings in England, of which approximately 90 per cent are Grade II listed. Almost all pre-1700 buildings are listed, as are most buildings of 1700 to 1850. Historic England surveys particular types of buildings with a view to making recommendations for listing. The main purpose of listing is to ensure that care is taken in deciding the future of a building. No changes which affect the architectural or historic character of a listed building can be made without listed building consent (in addition to planning permission where relevant). Applications for consent are normally dealt with by the local planning authority, although Historic England is always consulted about proposals affecting Grade I and Grade II* properties. It is a criminal offence to demolish a listed building, or alter it in such a way as to affect its character, without consent.

SCHEDULED MONUMENTS

As at October 2020, there were approximately 20,000 scheduled monuments in England. All monuments proposed for scheduling are considered to be of national importance. Where buildings are both scheduled and listed, ancient monuments legislation takes precedence. The main purpose of scheduling a monument is to preserve it for the future and to protect it from damage, destruction or any unnecessary interference. Once a monument has been scheduled, scheduled monument consent is required before any works can be carried out. The scope of the control is more extensive and more detailed than that applied to listed buildings, but certain minor works, as detailed in the Ancient Monuments (Class Consents) Order 1994, may be carried out without consent. It is a criminal offence to carry out unauthorised work to scheduled monuments.

WALES

Under the Planning (Listed Buildings and Conservation Areas) Act 1990 and the Ancient Monuments and Archaeological Areas Act 1979, the National Assembly for Wales is responsible for listing buildings and scheduling monuments in Wales on the advice of Cadw (the Welsh government's historic environment division) and the Royal Commission on the Ancient and Historical Monuments of Wales (RCAHMW). The criteria for evaluating buildings are similar to those in England

and the same listing system is used. As at Octobe 2020, there were approximately 30,000 listed buildings and 4,200 scheduled monuments in Wales. A list of National Historic Assets of Wales is available online: **W** https://cadw.gov.wales/historicenvironment/recordsv1.

SCOTLAND

Under the Planning (Listed Buildings and Conservation Areas) (Scotland) Act 1997 and the Ancient Monuments and Archaeological Areas Act 1979, Scottish ministers are responsible for listing buildings and scheduling monuments in Scotland on the advice of Historic Environment Scotland. The Historic Environment Scotland Act 2014 sets out Historic Environment Scotland's role and legal status. The criteria for evaluating buildings are similar to those in England but an A, B, C categorisation is used. As at October 2020, there were approximately 47,500 listed buildings and 8,300 scheduled monuments in Scotland. A list of historic buildings and monuments in Scotland is available online: **W** https://portal.historicenvironment.scot/search.

NORTHERN IRELAND

Under the Planning (Northern Ireland) Act 2011 and the Historic Monuments and Archaeological Objects (Northern Ireland) Order 1995, the Historic Environment Division (part of the Department for Communities, Northern Ireland) is responsible for listing buildings and scheduling monuments. The Historic Buildings Council for Northern Ireland and the relevant district council must be consulted on listing proposals, and the Historic Monuments Council for Northern Ireland must be consulted on scheduling proposals. The criteria for evaluating buildings are similar to those in England but an A, B+, B1 and B2 categorisation is used. As at As at May 2019 the most up to date figure was recorded as 8,916 listed buildings and 1,994 scheduled monuments in Norther Ireland.

ENGLAND

English Heritage cares for over 400 historic monuments, buildings and places. For more information on English Heritage properties, including those listed below, the official website is **W** www.english-heritage.org.uk

For more information on National Trust properties in England, including those listed below, the official website is **W** www.nationaltrust.org.uk

KEY
(EH) English Heritage property
(NT) National Trust property
* UNESCO World Heritage Site (*see also* World Heritage Sites)

A LA RONDE (NT), Exmouth, Devon EX8 5BD **T** 01395-265514
Unique 16-sided house completed *c.*1796

ALNWICK CASTLE, Alnwick, Northumberland NE66 1NG
T 01665-511100 **W** www.alnwickcastle.com
Seat of the Dukes of Northumberland since 1309; Italian Renaissance-style interior; gardens with spectacular water features

ALTHORP, Northants NN7 4HQ **T** 01604-770006
W www.spencerofalthorp.com
Spencer family seat built in 1508; home to the annual Althorp Literary Festival and Althorp Food and Drink Festival

ANGLESEY ABBEY (NT), Quy Road, Lode, Cambridge CB25 9EJ **T** 01223-810080
Jacobean house (*c.*1600) with gardens and a working watermill (Lode Mill) on the site of a 12th-century priory; fine furnishings and a unique clock collection

APSLEY HOUSE (EH), London W1J 7NT **T** 020-7499 5676
Built by Robert Adam 1771–8; home of the Dukes of Wellington since 1817 and known as 'No. 1 London'; collection of fine and decorative arts

ARUNDEL CASTLE, Arundel, W. Sussex BN18 9AB
T 01903-882173 **W** www.arundelcastle.org
Castle dating from the Norman Conquest; seat of the Dukes of Norfolk

AUDLEY END HOUSE AND GARDENS (EH), Saffron Walden, Essex, CB11 4JF **T** 01799-522842 **T** 01799-522842
Jacobean house converted from a Benedictine monastery; given to Sir Thomas Audley by King Henry VIII.

AVEBURY (EH/NT), Wilts SN8 1RF **T** 01672-539250
Remains of stone circles constructed 4,000 years ago enclosing part of the later village of Avebury

BANQUETING HOUSE, Whitehall, London SW1A 2ER
T 020-3166 6000 **W** www.hrp.org.uk/banquetinghouse
Designed by Inigo Jones in 1619; ceiling paintings by Rubens; site of the execution of Charles I

BASILDON PARK (NT), Reading, Berks RG8 9NR
T 01491-672382
Palladian mansion built in 1776–83 by John Carr

BATTLE ABBEY (EH), Battle, E. Sussex TN33 0AD **T** 870 333 1181
Remains of the abbey founded by William the Conqueror on the site of the Battle of Hastings

BEESTON CASTLE (EH), Cheshire CW6 9TX **T** 01829-260464
Built in the 13th century by Ranulf, sixth Earl of Chester, on the site of an Iron Age hillfort

BELVOIR CASTLE, Grantham, Lincs NG32 1PE
T 01476-871001 **W** www.belvoircastle.com
Seat of the Dukes of Rutland; 19th-century Gothic-style castle; notable art collection

BERKELEY CASTLE, Glos GL13 9BQ **T** 01453-810303
W www.berkeley-castle.com
Completed late 12th century; site of the murder of Edward II (1327)

BIRDOSWALD ROMAN FORT (EH), Brampton, Cumbria CA8 7DD **T** 01697-747602
Stretch of Hadrian's Wall with Roman wall fort, turret and milecastle

*BLENHEIM PALACE, Woodstock, Oxon OX20 1UL
T 01993-810530 **W** www.blenheimpalace.com
Seat of the Dukes of Marlborough and Winston Churchill's birthplace; house designed by Vanbrugh; landscaped parkland by Capability Brown

BLICKLING ESTATE (NT), Blickling, Norfolk NR11 6NF
T 01263-738030
Jacobean house with state rooms; extensive gardens, temple and 18th-century orangery

BODIAM CASTLE (NT), Bodiam, E. Sussex TN32 5UA
T 01580-830196
Well-preserved medieval moated castle built in 1385

BOLSOVER CASTLE (EH), Bolsover, Derbys S44 6PR
T 01246-822844
17th-century castle on site of medieval fortress

BOSCOBEL HOUSE (EH), Bishops Wood, Shrops ST19 9AR
T 01902-850244
Timber-framed 17th-century hunting lodge; refuge of fugitive Charles II from parliamentary troops

BOUGHTON HOUSE, Kettering, Northants NN14 1BJ
T 01536-515731 **W** www.boughtonhouse.org.uk
17th-century house with French-style additions; home of the Dukes of Buccleuch and Queensbury

BOWOOD HOUSE, Calne, Wilts SN11 0LZ **T** 01249-812102
W www.bowood.org/bowood-house-gardens/house/
18th-century house in Capability Brown park, featuring Robert Adam orangery and renowned pinetum and arboretum

BUCKFAST ABBEY, Buckfastleigh, Devon TQ11 0EE
T 01364-645500 **W** www.buckfast.org.uk
Benedictine monastery on medieval foundations

BUCKINGHAM PALACE, London SW1A 1AA
T 030-3123 7300 **W** www.royalcollection.org.uk
Purchased by George III in 1761, and the Sovereign's official London residence since 1837; 19 state rooms, including the Throne Room, and Queen's Gallery

BUCKLAND ABBEY (NT), Yelverton, Devon PL20 6EY
T 01822-853607
13th-century Cistercian monastery; home of Sir Francis Drake

BURGHLEY HOUSE, Stamford, Lincs PE9 3JY **T** 01780-752451
W www.burghley.co.uk
Late Elizabethan house built by William Cecil, first Lord Burghley

CARISBROOKE CASTLE (EH), Newport, Isle of Wight PO30 1XY **T** 01983-522107
Norman castle; museum; prison of Charles I 1647–8

CARLISLE CASTLE (EH), Carlisle, Cumbria CA3 8UR
T 01228-591922
Medieval castle; prison of Mary, Queen of Scots

CASTLE ACRE PRIORY (EH), King's Lynn, Norfolk PE32 2XD
T 01760-755394
Remains include 12th-century church and prior's lodgings

CASTLE DROGO (NT), Drewsteignton, Devon EX6 6PB
T 01647-433306
Granite castle designed by Lutyens in 1911

CASTLE HOWARD, N. Yorks YO60 7DA **T** 01653-648333
W www.castlehoward.co.uk
Designed by Vanbrugh 1699–1726; mausoleum designed by Hawksmoor

CASTLE RISING CASTLE (EH), King's Lynn, Norfolk PE31 6AH **T** 01553-631330 **W** www.castlerising.co.uk
12th-century keep with gatehouse and bridge, surrounded by 20 acres of defensive earthworks

CHARLES DARWIN'S HOME (DOWN HOUSE) (EH), Downe, Kent BR6 7JT **T** 01689-859119
The family home where Darwin wrote *On the Origin of Species*

CHARTWELL (NT), Westerham, Kent TN16 1PS
T 01732-868381
Home and studio of Sir Winston Churchill

CHATSWORTH, Bakewell, Derbys DE45 1PP **T** 01246-565300
W www.chatsworth.org
Tudor mansion set in magnificent parkland; seat of the Dukes of Devonshire

CHESTERS ROMAN FORT (EH), Chollerford, Northumberland NE46 4EU **T** 870 333 1181
Roman cavalry fort built to guard Hadrian's Wall

CHYSAUSTER ANCIENT VILLAGE (EH), Penzance, Cornwall TR20 8XA **T** 870 333 1181
Remains of nearly 2,000-year-old Celtic settlement; eight stone-walled homesteads

CLANDON PARK (NT), Guildford, Surrey GU4 7RQ
T 01483-222482
18th-century Palladian mansion and gardens, with an original Maori meeting house, brought back from New Zealand in 1892

CLIFFORD'S TOWER (EH), York YO1 9SA **T** 01904-646940
13th-century keep built on a mound; remains of a castle built by William the Conqueror

CORBRIDGE ROMAN TOWN (EH), Corbridge, Northumberland NE45 5NT T 870 333 1181
Excavated central area of a Roman garrison town

CORFE CASTLE (NT), Wareham, Dorset BH20 5EZ T 01929-481294
Former royal castle, dating from the 11th century and partially ruined during the English Civil War

CROFT CASTLE AND PARKLAND (NT), Yarpole, Herefordshire HR6 9PW T 01568-780246
17th-century quadrangular manor house with Georgian-Gothic interior; built close to the ruin of pre-Conquest border castle

DEAL CASTLE (EH), Deal, Kent CT14 7BA T 870 333 1181
Largest of the coastal defence forts built by Henry VIII; shaped like a rose with six inner and outer bastions

*DERWENT VALLEY MILLS, Belper, Derbyshire DE56 1YD T 01629-536831 W www.derwentvalleymills.org
Series of 18th- and 19th-century cotton mills; birthplace of the modern factory

DOVER CASTLE (EH), Dover, Kent CT16 1HU T 01304-211067
Castle with Roman, Saxon and Norman features; tunnels used as secret wartime operations rooms

DR JOHNSON'S HOUSE, London EC4A 3DE T 020-7353 3745 W www.drjohnsonshouse.org
300-year-old townhouseme of Samuel Johnson 1748–59

DUNSTANBURGH CASTLE (EH/NT), Alnwick, Northumberland NE66 3TT T 01665-576231
14th-century castle ruins on a headland, with a substantial twin-towered gatehouse-keep

ELTHAM PALACE (EH), Greenwich, London SE9 5QE T 020-8294 2548
Art Deco mansion next to remains of medieval palace once occupied by Henry VIII; moated gardens

FARLEIGH HUNGERFORD CASTLE (EH), Bath, Somerset BA2 7RS T 01225-754026
Late 14th-century castle with inner and outer courts; chapel with rare medieval wall paintings

FARNHAM CASTLE KEEP (EH), Farnham, Surrey GU9 0AG T 01252-721194 W www.farnhamcastle.com
Large 14th-century castle keep with motte and bailey wall

FISHBOURNE ROMAN PALACE,Chichester, W. Sussex PO19 3QR T 01243-785859 W http://sussexpast.co.uk
Excavated Roman palace with largest collection of in situ mosaics in the UK

*FOUNTAINS ABBEY (NT), Ripon, N. Yorks HG4 3DY T 01765-608888
Ruined Cistercian monastery and corn mill; site includes Studley Royal, a Georgian water garden and deer park

FRAMLINGHAM CASTLE (EH), Framlingham, Suffolk IP13 9BP T 870 333 1181
Castle (c.1200) with high curtain walls enclosing an almshouse (1639); once the refuge of Mary I

FURNESS ABBEY (EH), Barrow-in-Furness, Cumbria LA13 0PJ T 01229-823420
Remains of an abbey founded in 1124 by Stephen, later king of England

GLASTONBURY ABBEY, Glastonbury, Somerset BA6 9EL T 01458-832267 W www.glastonburyabbey.com
12th-century abbey, destroyed by fire in 1184 and later rebuilt; site of early Christian settlement; ruined in 1539 during dissolution of monasteries

GOODRICH CASTLE (EH), Ross-on-Wye, Herefordshire HR9 6HY T 01600-890538
Remains of 12th- and 13th-century castle; contains a famous mortar that ruined the castle in 1646

GREENWAY (NT), Brixham, Devon TQ5 0ES T 01803-842382
Large woodland; walled garden; location of Agatha Christie's holiday home and inspiration for several settings in her books, including the murder in *Dead Man's Folly*

*GREENWICH, London SE10 9NF T 020-8305 5235 W www.visitgreenwich.org.uk
Former Royal Observatory (founded 1675) home to the Meridian Line, *Cutty Sark* and National Maritime Museum; the Queen's House, designed for Queen Anne, wife of James I, by Inigo Jones; Painted Hall and neoclassical Chapel (Old Royal Naval College)

GRIME'S GRAVES (EH), Thetford, Norfolk IP26 5DE T 01842-810656
Neolithic flint mines, dug over 5,000 years ago; one shaft has been excavated

GUILDHALL, London EC2V 7HH T 020-7332 1313 W www.guildhall.cityoflondon.gov.uk
Centre of civic government of the City of London built c.1441; facade built 1788–9

HADDON HALL, Bakewell, Derbys DE45 1LA T 01629-812855 W www.haddonhall.co.uk
Well-preserved 12th-century manor house

HAILES ABBEY (EH), Cheltenham, Glos GL54 5PB T 01242-602398
Ruins of a 13th-century Cistercian monastery

HAM HOUSE AND GARDEN (NT), Richmond, Surrey TW10 7RS T 020-8940 1950
Grand Stuart house with lavish interiors and formal gardens

HAMPTON COURT PALACE, East Molesey, Surrey KT8 9AU T 020-3166 6000 W www.hrp.org.uk/hampton-court-palace
Palace originally built for Cardinal Wolsey in the early 16th-century, famous as the home of Henry VIII, his wives and children, with a 17th-century Baroque palace by Wren commissioned by William III and Mary II in 1689; Royal Tennis Court and world-renowned maze

HARDWICK HALL (NT), Chesterfield, Derbys S44 5QJ T 01246-850430
Elizabethan house built for Bess of Hardwick

HARDY'S COTTAGE (NT), Higher Bockhampton, Dorset DT2 8QJ T 01305-262366
Birthplace and home of Thomas Hardy

HAREWOOD HOUSE, Leeds, W. Yorks LS17 9LG T 0113-218 1010 W https://harewood.org
18th-century house designed by John Carr and Robert Adam; park by Capability Brown

HATFIELD HOUSE, Hatfield, Herts AL9 5NB T 01707-287010 W www.hatfield-house.co.uk
Jacobean house built by Robert Cecil; features surviving wing of Royal Palace of Hatfield (c.1485), the childhood home of Elizabeth I

HELMSLEY CASTLE (EH), Helmsley, N. Yorks YO62 5AB T 01439-770442
12th-century keep and curtain wall with 16th-century buildings; spectacular earthwork defences

HEVER CASTLE, Edenbridge, Kent TN8 7NG T 01732-865224 W www.hevercastle.co.uk
13th-century double-moated castle; childhood home of Anne Boleyn

HOLKHAM HALL, Wells-next-the-Sea, Norfolk NR23 1AB T 01328-710227 W www.holkham.co.uk
Palladian mansion; notable fine art collection

HOUSESTEADS ROMAN FORT (EH), Hexham, Northumberland NE47 6NN T 870 333 1181
Excavated Roman infantry fort on Hadrian's Wall with museum

*IRONBRIDGE GORGE, Ironbridge, Shropshire T 01952-433424W www.ironbridge.org.uk
Important Industrial Revolution site, featuring the world's first iron bridge

KEDLESTON HALL (NT), Derbys DE22 5JH **T** 01332-842191
Palladian mansion built 1759–65; complete Robert Adam
interiors; museum of Asian artefacts

KELMSCOTT MANOR, Lechlade, Glos GL7 3HJ
T 01367-252486 **W** www.sal.org.uk/kelmscott-manor/
Built c.1600; summer home of William Morris, with
products of Morris and Co.

KENILWORTH CASTLE (EH), Kenilworth, Warks CV8 1NG
T 01926-852078
Largest castle ruin in England; Norman keep with 13th-
century outer walls; once home to Robert Dudley

KENSINGTON PALACE, Kensington Gardens, London W8 4PX
T 020-3166 6000 **W** www.hrp.org.uk/kensington-palace
Built in 1605 and enlarged by Wren; birthplace of Queen
Victoria

KENWOOD HOUSE (EH), Hampstead , London NW3 7JR
T 020-8348 1286
Neoclassical villa on the edge of Hampstead Heath,
housing the Iveagh bequest of paintings and furniture

KEW PALACE, Richmond, Surrey TW9 3AE **T** 020-3166 6000
W www.hrp.org.uk/kew-palace
Red-brick mansion (c.1631); includes Queen Charlotte's
Cottage, used by King George III and family as a
summerhouse

KINGSTON LACY (NT), Wimborne Minster, Dorset BH21 4EA
T 01202-883402
17th-century mansion with 19th-century alterations;
important art collection

KNEBWORTH HOUSE, Knebworth, Herts SG3 6PY
T 01438-812661 **W** www.knebworthhouse.com
Tudor manor house concealed by 19th-century Gothic
decoration; Lutyens gardens

KNOLE (NT), Sevenoaks, Kent TN15 0RP **T** 01732-462100
House built in 1456, set in 1,000-acre deer park; fine art
and furniture collection; birthplace of Vita Sackville-West

LAMBETH PALACE, London SE1 7JU **T** 020-7898 1200
W www.archbishopofcanterbury.org/about-lambeth-palace
Official residence of the Archbishop of Canterbury since
the 13th century

LANERCOST PRIORY (EH), nr Brampton, Cumbria CA8 2HQ
T 01697-73030 **W** www.lanercostpriory.org.uk
The nave of the Augustinian priory's church, c.1166, is
still used; remains of other claustral buildings and
beautifully preserved cloisters

LANHYDROCK (NT), Bodmin, Cornwall PL30 5AD
T 01208-265950
House dating from the 17th century; 50 rooms, including
kitchen and nursery

LEEDS CASTLE, Maidstone, Kent ME17 1PL **T** 01622-765400
W www.leeds-castle.com
Castle dating from the 12th century, situated in 500 acres
of parkland and gardens; used as a royal palace by Henry
VIII

LEVENS HALL, nr Kendal, Cumbria LA8 0PD **T** 01539-560321
W www.levenshall.co.uk
Elizabethan house with unique topiary garden (1694);
steam engine collection

LINCOLN CASTLE, Lincoln, Lincs LN1 3AA **T** 01522-554559
W www.lincolncastle.com
Built by William the Conqueror in 1068 on a Roman site;
one of only two double-motted castles in Britain

LINDISFARNE PRIORY (EH), Holy Island, Northumberland
TD15 2RX **T** 01289-389200
Founded in AD 635; re-established in the 12th century as
a Benedictine priory, now ruined

LITTLE MORETON HALL (NT), Congleton, Cheshire CW12
4SD **T** 01260-272018
Iconic timber-framed moated Tudor manor house with
knot garden

LONGLEAT HOUSE, Warminster, Wilts BA12 7NW
T 01985-844400 **W** www.longleat.co.uk
Elizabethan house in Italian Renaissance style; Capability
Brown parkland with lakes; safari park

LULLINGSTONE ROMAN VILLA (EH), Eynsford, Kent DA4
0JA **T** 870 333 1181
Large villa occupied for much of the Roman period;
collection of Roman artefacts and unique Christian
paintings

MIDDLEHAM CASTLE (EH), Middleham, N. Yorks DL8 4QG
T 01969-623899
12th-century keep within later fortifications; childhood
home of Richard III

MONTACUTE HOUSE (NT), Montacute, Somerset TA15 6XP
T 01935-823289
Elizabethan Renaissance mansion, with collection of
portraits from the period

MOUNT GRACE PRIORY (EH), Northallerton, N. Yorks DL6
3JG **T** 01609-883494
Well-preserved Carthusian priory with remains of
monastic buildings

OLD SARUM (EH), Salisbury, Wilts SP1 3SD **T** 01722-335398
Iron Age hill fort enclosing remains of Norman castle and
cathedral

ORFORD CASTLE (EH), Orford, Suffolk IP12 2ND **T** 870 333
1181
Polygonal tower keep c.1170 and remains of coastal
defence castle built by Henry II

OSBORNE HOUSE (EH), East Cowes, Isle of Wight PO32 6JT
T 01983-200022
Queen Victoria's seaside residence; built by Thomas
Cubitt in Italian Renaissance style; summer house, Swiss
Cottage and museum

OSTERLEY PARK AND HOUSE (NT), Isleworth, Middx TW7
4RB **T** 020-8232 5050
18th-century neoclassical mansion with Tudor stable
block

PENDENNIS CASTLE (EH), Falmouth, Cornwall TR11 4LP
T 01326-316594
Well-preserved 16th-century coastal defence castle

PENSHURST PLACE, Penshurst, Kent TN11 8DG
T 01892-870307 **W** www.penshurstplace.com
Medieval house featuring Baron's Hall (1341) and
gardens (1346); toy museum

PETWORTH HOUSE (NT), Petworth, W. Sussex GU28 9LR **T**
01798-342207
Late 17th-century house set in Capability Brown
landscaped deer park; fine art collection

PEVENSEY CASTLE (EH), Pevensey, E. Sussex BN24 5LE
T 870 333 1181
Walls of a fourth-century Roman fort; remains of an 11th-
century castle

POLESDEN LACEY (NT), nr Dorking, Surrey RH5 6BD
T 01372-452048
Regency villa remodelled in the Edwardian era; fine
paintings and furnishings; walled rose garden

PORTCHESTER CASTLE (EH), Portchester, Hants PO16 9QW
T 02392-378291
Walls of a late Roman fort enclosing a Norman keep and
an Augustinian priory church

POWDERHAM CASTLE, Kenton, Devon EX6 8JQ
T 01626-890243 **W** www.powderham.co.uk
Medieval castle with 18th- and 19th-century alterations,
including James Wyatt music room

RABY CASTLE, Staindrop, Co. Durham DL2 3AH
T 01833-660202 **W** www.raby.co.uk
14th-century castle with walled gardens

RAGLEY HALL, Alcester, Warks B49 5NJ **T** 01789-762090
W www.ragley.co.uk
17th-century Palladian house with gardens and lake

RICHBOROUGH ROMAN FORT (EH), Sandwich, Kent
CT13 9JW **T** 01304-612013
Remains of a Roman Saxon Shore fortress; landing-site of
the Claudian invasion in AD 43

RICHMOND CASTLE (EH), Richmond, N. Yorks DL10 4QW
T 870 333 1181
12th-century keep with 11th-century curtain wall

RIEVAULX ABBEY (EH), nr Helmsley, N. Yorks YO62 5LB
T 01439-798228
Remains of a Cistercian abbey founded c.1132

ROCHESTER CASTLE (EH), Rochester, Kent ME1 1SW
T 01634-335882
11th-century castle partly on the Roman city wall, with a
well-preserved square keep of c.1127

ROCKINGHAM CASTLE, Market Harborough, Leics LE16 8TH
T 01536-770240 **W** www.rockinghamcastle.com
Built by William the Conqueror; formal gardens and 400-
year-old 'elephant' hedge

ROMAN BATHS, Abbey Church Yard, Bath BA1 1LZ
T 01225-477785 **W** www.romanbaths.co.uk
Extensive remains of a Roman temple and bathing
complex which still flows with natural thermal water;
museum

ROYAL PAVILION, Brighton BN1 1EE **T** 03000-290900
W https://brightonmuseums.org.uk/royalpavilion
Unique palace of George IV, in Indo-gothic style with
chinoiserie interiors and Regency gardens

ST AUGUSTINE'S ABBEY (EH), Canterbury, Kent CT1 1PF
T 01227-767345
Remains of Benedictine monastery founded in 598

ST MAWES CASTLE (EH), St Mawes, Cornwall TR2 5DE
T 01326-270526
Coastal defence castle built by Henry VIII

ST MICHAEL'S MOUNT (NT), Marazion, Cornwall TR17 0HS
T 01736-710265 **W** www.stmichaelsmount.co.uk
12th-century church and castle with later additions,
situated on an iconic rocky island

*SALTAIRE VILLAGE, nr Shipley, W. Yorks **T** 01274-433678
W www.saltairevillage.info
Victorian industrial village founded by mill owner Titus
Salt for his workers; see also World Heritage Sites

SANDRINGHAM, Norfolk PE35 6EN **T** 01485-545400
W www.sandringhamestate.co.uk
The Queen's private residence; neo-Jacobean house built
in 1870 with gardens and country park

SCARBOROUGH CASTLE (EH), Scarborough, N. Yorks YO11
1HY **T** 01723-372451
Remains of 12th-century keep and curtain walls

SHERBORNE CASTLE, Sherborne, Dorset DT9 5NR
T 01935-813182 **W** www.sherbornecastle.com
16th-century castle built by Sir Walter Raleigh set in
Capability Brown landscaped gardens

SHUGBOROUGH ESTATE (NT), Milford, Staffs ST17 0XB
T 01889-880166
Late 17th century house in 18th-century park with
monuments, temples and pavilions in the Greek Revival
style; seat of the Earls of Lichfield

SISSINGHURST CASTLE GARDEN (NT), Nr Cranbrook,
Kent TN17 2AB **T** 01580-710700
Early 16th century site, purchased by Vita Sackville-West
in the 1930s where the writer, poet and Bloomsbury
Group member created the famous gardens

SKIPTON CASTLE, Skipton, N. Yorks BD23 1AW
T 01756-792442 **W** www.skiptoncastle.co.uk
Well-preserved D-shaped medieval castle with six round
towers and inner courtyard

SMALLHYTHE PLACE (NT), Tenterden, Kent TN30 7NG
T 01580-762334
Half-timbered 16th-century house

*STONEHENGE (EH), nr Amesbury, Wilts SP4 7DE
T 0370-333 1181
World-famous prehistoric monument comprising
concentric stone circles surrounded by a ditch and bank

STONOR PARK, Henley-on-Thames, Oxon RG9 6HF
T 01491-638587 **W** www.stonor.com
Medieval house with Georgian facade; refuge for Catholic
recusants after the Reformation

STOURHEAD (NT), Nr Mere, Wilts BA12 6QD **T** 01747-841152
18th-century Palladian mansion with world-renowned
landscape gardens; King Alfred's Tower

STRATFIELD SAYE HOUSE, Hants RG7 2BT **T** 01256-882694
W www.wellingtonestates.co.uk/stratfield-saye-house
House built 1630–40; home of the Dukes of Wellington
since 1817

STRATFORD-UPON-AVON, Warks **T** 01789-868191
W www.stratford-upon-avon.co.uk
Shakespeare's Birthplace Trust with Shakespeare Centre;
Anne Hathaway's Cottage; Holy Trinity Church, where
Shakespeare is buried

STRAWBERRY HILL HOUSE, Twickenham TW1 4ST
T 020-8744 1241 **W** www.strawberryhillhouse.org.uk
Early Gothic Revival villa built between 1749 and 1776
for Horace Walpole (1717–97)

SUDELEY CASTLE, Winchcombe, Glos GL54 5JD
T 01242-604244 **W** www.sudeleycastle.co.uk
Castle built in 1442; once owned by Richard III and
former home of Catherine Parr, sixth wife of Henry VIII;
restored in the 19th century

SULGRAVE MANOR, nr Banbury, Oxon OX17 2SD
T 01295-760205 **W** www.sulgravemanor.org.uk
Tudor and Georgian house; home of George
Washington's family

SUTTON HOUSE (NT), Hackney, London E9 6JQ
T 020-8986 2264
Tudor house, built in 1535 by Sir Ralph Sadleir

SYON HOUSE, Brentford, Middx TW8 8JF **T** 020-8560 0882
W www.syonpark.co.uk
Built on the site of a former monastery; Robert Adam
interior; Capability Brown park

TINTAGEL CASTLE (EH), Tintagel, Cornwall PL34 0HE
T 01840-770328
13th-century cliff-top castle and 5th–6th-century Celtic
settlement; linked with Arthurian legend

TOWER OF LONDON, London EC3N 4AB **T** 020-3166 6000
W www.hrp.org.uk/tower-of-london
Royal palace and fortress begun by William the
Conqueror in 1078; houses the Crown Jewels

TYNEMOUTH PRIORY AND CASTLE (EH), Tyne and Wear
NE30 4BZ **T** 01912-571090
Remains of a Benedictine priory, founded c.1090, moated
castle-towers, a gatehouse and keep on Saxon monastic
site

UPPARK (NT), Petersfield, W. Sussex GU31 5QR
T 01730-825415
17th-century house, restored after fire; Fetherstonhaugh
art collection; 18th-century dolls' house

WALMER CASTLE (EH), Deal, Kent CT14 7LJ **T** 01304-364288
One of Henry VIII's coastal defence castles, now the
residence of the Lord Warden of the Cinque Ports

WARKWORTH CASTLE (EH), Warkworth, Northumberland
NE65 0UJ **T** 01665-711423
14th-century keep amid earlier ruins, with hermitage
upstream

WHITBY ABBEY (EH), Whitby, N. Yorks YO22 4JT
T 01947-603568
Remains of Norman church on the site of a monastery
founded in AD 657
WILTON HOUSE, nr Salisbury, Wilts SP2 0BJ **T** 01722-746700
W www.wiltonhouse.com
17th-century house on the site of a Tudor house and
ninth-century nunnery; Palladian bridge
WINDSOR CASTLE, Windsor, Berks SL4 1NJ **T** 030-3123 7304
W www.rct.org.uk/visit/windsor-castle
Official residence of the Queen; oldest royal residence still
in regular use; largest inhabited castle in the world. Also
St George's Chapel; Queen Mary's Dolls' House
WOBURN ABBEY, Woburn, Beds MK17 9WA **T** 01525-290333
W www.woburn.co.uk
Built on the site of a Cistercian abbey; seat of the Dukes
of Bedford; art collection
WROXETER ROMAN CITY (EH), nr Shrewsbury, Shropshire
SY5 6PH **T** 01743-761330
Second-century public baths and part of the forum of the
Roman town of *Viroconium*

WALES

For more information on Cadw properties, including those
listed below, the official website is **W** www.cadw.wales.gov.uk
For more information on National Trust properties in Wales,
including those listed below, the official website is
W www.nationaltrust.org.uk

KEY
(C) Property of Cadw: Welsh Historic Monuments
(NT) National Trust property
* UNESCO World Heritage Site (*see also* World Heritage Sites)

*BEAUMARIS CASTLE (C), Anglesey LL58 8AP
T 01248-810361
Concentrically planned 13th-century castle, still virtually
intact
*BLAENAVON, Blaenavon NP4 9AS **T** 01495-742333
W www.visitblaenavon.co.uk
18th- and 19th-century industrial landscape associated
with coal and iron production
CAERLEON ROMAN BATHS AND AMPHITHEATRE
(C), Newport NP18 1AE **T** 01633-422518
Rare example of a legionary bath-house and late first-
century arena surrounded by bank for spectators
*CAERNARFON CASTLE (C), Gwynedd LL55 2AY
T 01286-677617 **W** www.caernarfon-castle.co.uk
Huge fortress with polygonal towers built between 1283
and 1330, initially for King Edward I of England; setting
for the investiture of Prince Charles in 1969
CAERPHILLY CASTLE (C), Caerphilly CF83 1JD
T 029-2088 3143
Concentrically planned castle (*c.*1270) notable for its scale
and use of water defences
CARDIFF CASTLE, Cardiff CF10 3RB **T** 029-2087 8100
W www.cardiffcastle.com
Norman keep built on site of Roman fort; 'fairytale'
gothic-revival mansion added in the 19th century
CASTELL COCH (C), Tongwynlais, Cardiff CF15 7JS
T 029-2081 0101
'Fairytale'-style castle, rebuilt 1872–91 on medieval
foundations
CHEPSTOW CASTLE (C), Monmouthshire NP16 5EY
T 01291-624065
Rectangular keep amid extensive fortifications; developed
throughout the Middle Ages
*CONWY CASTLE (C), Gwynedd LL32 8AY **T** 01492-592358
Built for Edward I in 1283–9 on narrow rocky outcrop;
features eight towers and two barbicans

CRICCIETH CASTLE (C), Gwynedd LL52 0DP
T 01766-522227
Native Welsh 13th-century castle, taken and altered by
Edward I and Edward II
DENBIGH CASTLE (C), Denbighshire LL16 3NB
T 01745-813385
Remains of the castle (begun 1282), including triple-
towered gatehouses
DYFFRYN GARDENS (NT), St Nicholas, Cardiff CF5 6SU
T 029-2059 3328
Edwardian gardens designed by Thomas Mawson,
overlooked by a grand Edwardian mansion
*HARLECH CASTLE (C), Gwynedd LL46 2YH **T** 01766-780552
Well-preserved castle, constructed 1283–95, on an
outcrop above the former shoreline; withstood seven-year
siege 1461–8
PEMBROKE CASTLE, Pembrokeshire SA71 4LA
T 01646-681510 **W** https://pembrokecastle.co.uk
Castle founded in 1093; Great Tower built in late 12th
century; birthplace of King Henry VII
PENRHYN CASTLE (NT), Bangor, Gwynedd LL57 4HT
T 01248-353084
Neo-Norman castle built in the 19th century; railway and
dolls' museums; private art collection
*PONTCYSYLLTE AQUEDUCT AND CANAL, Trevor,
Wrexham LL20 7TY **T** 01978-822912
W www.pontcysyllte-aqueduct.co.uk
Longest and highest aqueduct in Great Britain; designed
by Thomas Telford and finished in 1805
POWIS CASTLE (NT), Welshpool, Powys SY21 8RF
T 01938-551944
Medieval castle with interior in variety of styles; 17th-
century gardens; Clive of India museum
RAGLAN CASTLE (C), Monmouthshire NP15 2BT
T 01291-690228
Remains of 15th-century castle with moated hexagonal
keep
ST DAVIDS BISHOP'S PALACE (C), Pembrokeshire SA62 6PE
T 01437-720517
Remains of residence of Bishops of St Davids built 1328–
47
TINTERN ABBEY (C), Tintern, Monmouthshire NP16 6SE
T 01291-689251
Remains of 13th-century church and conventual buildings
of a 12th-century Cistercian monastery
TRETOWER COURT AND CASTLE (C), Nr Crickhowell,
Powys NP8 1RD **T** 01874-730279
Medieval manor house rebuilt in the 15th century, with
remains of 12th-century castle nearby

SCOTLAND

For more information on Historic Environment Scotland
properties, including those listed below, the official website is
W www.historicenvironment.scot
For more information on National Trust for Scotland
properties, including those listed below, the official website is
W www.nts.org.uk

KEY
(HES) Historic Environment Scotland property
(NTS) National Trust for Scotland property
* Part of the Heart of Neolithic Orkney UNESCO World
Heritage Site

ABBOTSFORD HOUSE, Melrose, Roxburghshire TD6 9BQ
T 01896-752043 **W** www.scottsabbotsford.co.uk
Home of Sir Walter Scott; features historic Scottish relics
and formal gardens

BALMORAL CASTLE, Ballater, Aberdeenshire AB35 5TB
T 01339-742534 W www.balmoralcastle.com
Baronial-style castle built for Victoria and Albert; the
Queen's private residence

BLACKHOUSE, ARNOL (HES), Lewis, Western Isles HS2 9DB
T 01851-710395
Traditional Lewis thatched house

BLAIR CASTLE, Blair Atholl, Perthshire PH18 5TL
T 01796-481207 W www.blair-castle.co.uk
Mid-18th-century mansion with 13th-century tower; seat
of the Dukes and Earls of Atholl

BOWHILL, Selkirk, Scottish Borders TD7 5ET T 01750-22204
W www.bowhillhouse.co.uk
Present house dates mainly from 1812; Seat of the Dukes
of Buccleuch and Queensberry; fine collection of paintings

BROUGH OF BIRSAY (HES), Orkney KW17 2LX
T 01856-841815
Remains of Norse and Pictish village on the tidal island of
Birsay

CAERLAVEROCK CASTLE (HES), Glencaple, Dumfries and
Galloway DG1 4RU T 01387-770244
Unique triangular 13th-century moated castle with
classical Renaissance additions

CAIRNPAPPLE HILL (HES), Torphichen, West Lothian
T 01506-634622
Neolithic ceremonial site and Bronze Age burial chambers

CALANAIS STANDING STONES (HES), Lewis, Western Isles
HS2 9DY T 01851-621422
Standing stones in a cross-shaped setting, dating from
between 2900 and 2600 BC

CATERTHUNS (BROWN AND WHITE) (HES), Menmuir,
nr Brechin, Angus
Two large Iron Age hill forts

CAWDOR CASTLE, Nairn, Moray IV12 5RD T 01667-404401
W www.cawdorcastle.com
14th-century keep with 15th- and 17th-century additions

CLAVA CAIRNS (HES), nr Inverness, Inverness-shire IV2 5EU
T 0131-668 8600
Bronze Age cemetery complex of cairns and standing
stones

CRATHES CASTLE (NTS), nr Banchory, Aberdeenshire AB31
5QJ T 01330-844525
16th-century baronial castle in woodland, fields and
gardens

CULZEAN CASTLE (NTS), Maybole, Ayrshire KA19 8LE
T 01655-884455
18th-century Robert Adam castle with oval staircase and
circular saloon

DRYBURGH ABBEY (HES), nr Melrose, Roxburghshire TD6
0RQ T 01835-822381
12th-century abbey containing the tomb of Sir Walter
Scott

DUNVEGAN CASTLE, Skye IV55 8WF T 01470-521206
W www.dunvegancastle.com
13th-century castle with later additions; home of the
chiefs of the Clan MacLeod

EDINBURGH CASTLE (HES), Edinburgh EH1 2NG
T 0131-225 9846 W www.edinburghcastle.scot
Fortress perched on extinct volcano; houses the Scottish
Crown Jewels, Scottish National War Memorial, Scottish
United Services Museum

EDZELL CASTLE (HES), nr Brechin, Angus DD9 7UE
T 01356-648631
Ruined 16th-century tower house on medieval
foundations; early 17th-century walled garden

EILEAN DONAN CASTLE, Dornie, Ross and Cromarty IV40
8DX T 01599-555202 W www.eileandonancastle.com
13th-century castle situated at the meeting point of three
sea lochs; Jacobite relics

ELGIN CATHEDRAL (HES), Moray IV30 1HU T 01343-547171
13th-century cathedral and octagonal chapterhouse

FLOORS CASTLE, Kelso, Roxburghshire TD5 7SF
T 01573-223333 W www.floorscastle.com
Largest inhabited castle in Scotland; seat of the Dukes of
Roxburghe; built in the 1720s by William Adam

FORT GEORGE (HES), Ardersier, Inverness-shire IV2 7TD
T 01667-460232
18th-century fort; still a working army barracks

GLAMIS CASTLE, Forfar, Angus DD8 1RJ T 01307-840393
W www.glamis-castle.co.uk
Seat of the Lyon family (later Earls of Strathmore and
Kinghorne) since 1372; the setting for Shakespeare's
Macbeth

GLASGOW CATHEDRAL (HES), Lanarkshire G4 0QZ
T 0141-552 8198 W www.glasgowcathedral.org.uk
Late 12th-century cathedral with vaulted crypt

GLENELG BROCHS (HES), Glenelg, Ross and Cromarty
T 0131-668 8600
Two 2,000-year-old broch towers (Dun Telve and Dun
Troddan) with well-preserved structural features

HOPETOUN HOUSE, South Queensferry, West Lothian EH30
9RW T 0131-331 2451 W www.hopetoun.co.uk
Designed by Sir William Bruce in 1699 and enlarged by
William Adam 1721–48

HUNTLY CASTLE (HES), Aberdeenshire AB54 4SH
T 01466-793191
Ruin of a 16th- and 17th-century baronial residence

INVERARAY CASTLE, Argyll PA32 8XE T 01499-302203
W www.inveraray-castle.com
Gothic-style 18th-century castle designed by William
Adam and Roger Morris; seat of the Dukes of Argyll

IONA ABBEY (HES), Iona, Argyll PA76 6SQ T 01681-700512
Monastery founded by St Columba in AD 563; remains a
popular Christian pilgrimage site

JARLSHOF (HES), Sumburgh Head, Shetland ZE3 9JN
T 01950-460112
Prehistoric settlement with later ninth-century Norse
additions

JEDBURGH ABBEY (HES), Roxburghshire TD8 6JQ
T 01835-863925
Ruined Augustinian abbey founded c.1138; display of
early Christian artefacts

KISIMUL CASTLE (HES), Castlebay, Barra, Western Isles HS9
5UZ T 01871-810313
Medieval island home of the Clan MacNeil

LINLITHGOW PALACE (HES), Kirkgate, Linlithgow, West
Lothian EH49 7AL T 01506-842896
Ruined royal palace, founded in 1424, set in park;
birthplace of James V and Mary, Queen of Scots

*MAESHOWE (HES), Stenness, Orkney KW16 3LB
Neolithic chambered tomb with Viking runes

MEIGLE SCULPTURED STONES (HES), Meigle, Perthshire
PH12 8SB T 01828-640612
Twenty-six carved Pictish stones dating from the late
eighth to the late tenth centuries

MELROSE ABBEY (HES), Roxburghshire TD6 9LG
T 01896-822562
Ruin of Cistercian abbey founded c.1136 by David I;
museum of medieval objects

MOUSA BROCH (HES), Island of Mousa, Shetland ZE2 9HP
Finest surviving Iron Age broch tower c.100 BC

NEW ABBEY CORN MILL (HES), Dumfriesshire DG2 8BX
T 01387-850260
Working water-powered mill built in the late 18th
century
*NEW LANARK, South Lanarkshire ML11 9DB T 01555-661345
W www.newlanark.org
18th-century village built around a cotton mill
PALACE OF HOLYROODHOUSE, Edinburgh EH8 8DX
T 0303-123 7306 W www.royalcollection.org.uk
The Queen's official Scottish residence; home to Mary,
Queen of Scots; main part of the palace built 1671–9
close to ruined 12th-century Augustinian abbey
*RING OF BRODGAR (HES), Stenness, Orkney
T 01856-841815
Neolithic circle of upright stones surrounded by circular
ditch
ROSSLYN CHAPEL, Roslin, Midlothian EH25 9PU
T 0131-440 2159 W www.rosslynchapel.com
Historic church built between 1446 and 1484 with
unique stone carvings
ST ANDREWS CASTLE AND CATHEDRAL (HES), Fife
KY16 9AR (castle); 9QL (cathedral) T 01334-477196 (castle);
01334-472563 (cathedral)
Ruins of 13th-century castle, the former residence of
bishops of St Andrews, and remains of the largest
cathedral in Scotland; museum
SCONE PALACE, Perth, Perthshire PH2 6BD T 01738-552300
W www.scone-palace.co.uk
Georgian-Gothic house built 1802–12; originally the site
of a 12th-century church
*SKARA BRAE (HES), Sandwick, Orkney KW16 3LR
T 01856-841815
Neolithic village with adjacent replica house
SMAILHOLM TOWER (HES), nr Kelso, Roxburghshire TD5
7PG T 01573-460365
Well-preserved 15th-century tower-house
STIRLING CASTLE (HES), Stirlingshire FK8 1EJ
T 01786-450000 W www.stirlingcastle.scot
Great Hall and gatehouse built for James IV c.1500;
palace built for James V in 1538; site of coronations
including Mary, Queen of Scots
*STONES OF STENNESS (HES), Stenness, Orkney KW16 3JZ
T 0131-668 8600
Four surviving Neolithic standing stones and the uprights
of a three-stone dolmen
TANTALLON CASTLE (HES), North Berwick, East Lothian
EH39 5PN T 01620-892727
Ruined 14th-century curtain wall with towers
THREAVE CASTLE (HES), Dumfries, Kirkcudbrightshire DG7
1TJ T 07711-223101
Ruined late 14th-century tower on an island; accessible
only by boat
URQUHART CASTLE (HES), Drumnadrochit, Inverness-shire
IV63 6XJ T 01456-450551
13th-century castle remains on the banks of Loch Ness

NORTHERN IRELAND

For the Northern Ireland Department for Communities, the
official website is W www.discovernorthernireland.com
For more information on National Trust properties in Northern
Ireland, including those listed below, the official website is
W www.nationaltrust.org.uk

KEY
(NIDC) Property in the care of the Northern Ireland
Department for Communities
(NT) National Trust property

CARRICKFERGUS CASTLE (NIDC), Carrickfergus, Co.
Antrim BT38 7BG T 028-9335 1273
Castle built in 1177 and taken by King John in 1210;
garrisoned until 1928. From March 2019 the Inner Ward
and Great Tower are closed to the public for renovation
CASTLE COOLE (NT), Enniskillen, Co. Fermanagh BT74 6JY
T 028-6632 2690
18th-century neoclassical mansion in parkland; designed
by James Wyatt
CASTLE WARD (NT), Strangford, Co. Down BT30 7BA
T 028-4488 1204
18th-century house with Classical and Gothic facades
DEVENISH MONASTIC SITE (NIDC), nr Enniskillen, Co.
Fermanagh T 028-9082 3207
Island monastery founded in the sixth century by St
Molaise; church dating from 13th century
DOWNHILL DEMESNE AND HEZLETT HOUSE (NT),
Castlerock, Co. Londonderry BT51 4RP T 028-7084 8728
Ruins of 18th-century mansion and a 17th-century
cottage in landscaped estate including Mussenden Temple
DUNLUCE CASTLE (NIDC), Bushmills, Co. Antrim BT57 8UY
T 028-2073 1938
Ruins of 16th-century stronghold of the McDonnells
FLORENCE COURT (NT), Enniskillen, Co. Fermanagh BT92
1DB T 028-6634 8249
Mid-18th-century house with Rococo decoration
GREY ABBEY (NIDC), Greyabbey, Co. Down BT22 2NQ
T 028-9082 3207
Substantial remains of a Cistercian abbey founded in
1193 set in landscaped parkland
MOUNT STEWART (NT), Newtownards, Co. Down BT22 2AD
T 028-4278 8387
19th-century neoclassical house; octagonal Temple of the
Winds
NENDRUM MONASTIC SITE (NIDC), Mahee Island, Co.
Down T 028-9082 3207
Pre-Norman island monastery founded in the fifth century
by St Machaoi; has links to St. Patrick
PATTERSON'S SPADE MILL (NT), Templepatrick, Co. Antrim
BT39 0AP T 028-9443 3619
Last working water-driven spade mill in the UK
TULLY CASTLE (NIDC), Derrygonnelly, Co. Fermanagh
T 028-9082 3207
Remains of a fortified house and bawn built c.1619

MUSEUMS AND GALLERIES

There are approximately 2,500 museums and galleries in the UK. As at October 2020, 1,572 of these were fully accredited by Arts Council England and a further 170 museums held provisional accreditation. Accreditation indicates that the museum or gallery has an appropriate constitution, is soundly financed, has adequate collection management standards and public services and has access to professional curatorial advice. These applications are assessed by either Arts Council England; the Museums, Archives and Libraries division of the Welsh government; Museums Galleries Scotland or the Northern Ireland Museums Council.

The following is a selection of museums and art galleries in the UK. Opening hours and admission charges vary. Further information about museums and galleries in the UK is available from the Museums Association (**T** 020-7566 7800 **W** www.museumsassociation.org).

W www.weareculture24.org.uk includes a database of all the museums and galleries in the UK.

ENGLAND
* England's national museums and galleries, which receive funding from a government department, such as the DCMS or MoD. These institutions are deemed to have collections of national importance, and the government is able to call upon their staff for expert advice.

ALTON
Jane Austen's House Museum, Chawton, Hants GU34 1SD
 T 01420-83262 **W** www.janeaustens.house
 17th-century house which tells the author's story
BARNARD CASTLE
The Bowes Museum, Co. Durham DL12 8NP **T** 01833-690606
 W www.thebowesmuseum.org.uk
 Public gallery in a French châteaux style featuring archaeology, fashion and ceramics. Houses one of the largest collections of Spanish art in the country
BATH
American Museum, Claverton Manor BA2 7BD **T** 01225-460503
 W www.americanmuseum.org
 American decorative arts from the 17th to 20th centuries
Fashion Museum, Bennett Street BA1 2QH **T** 01225-477789
 W www.fashionmuseum.co.uk
 Fashion from the 17th century to the present day
Victoria Art Gallery, Bridge Street BA2 4AT **T** 01225-477233
 W www.victoriagal.org.uk
 European Old Masters and British art since the 15th century
BEAMISH
Beamish Museum, Co. Durham DH9 0RG **T** 0191-370 4000
 W www.beamish.org.uk
 Living working museum of a northern industrial town during Georgian, Victorian and Edwardian times
BEAULIEU
National Motor Museum, Hants SO42 7ZN **T** 01590-612345
 W www.beaulieu.co.uk
 Former royal estate within the New Forest national park home to Beaulieu Abbey, Palace House and the National Motor Museum
BIRMINGHAM
Aston Hall, Trinity Road B6 6JD **T** 0121-348 8100
 W www.birminghammuseums.org.uk/aston
 Jacobean House containing paintings, furniture and tapestries from the 17th to 19th centuries

Barber Institute of Fine Arts, University of Birmingham, Edgbaston B15 2TS **T** 0121-414 7333 **W** www.barber.org.uk
 Extensive coin collection; fine arts, including Old Masters
Birmingham Museum and Art Gallery, Chamberlain Square B3 3DH
 T 0121-348 8000 **W** www.birminghammuseums.org.uk/bmag
 Includes notable collection of Pre-Raphaelite art
Museum of the Jewellery Quarter, Vyse Street, B18 6HA
 T 0121-348 8140
 W www.birminghammuseums.org.uk/jewellery
 Preserved jewellery workshop
Sarehole Mill, Cole Bank Road, B13 0BD **T** 0121-348 8160
 W www.birminghammuseums.org.uk/sarehole
 A 250-year-old watermill renowned for its association with author J. R. R. Tolkien
Thinktank, Curzon Street B4 7XG **T** 0121-348 8000
 W www.birminghammuseums.org.uk/thinktank
 Science museum featuring over 200 hands-on displays and a Planetarium
BOURNEMOUTH
Russell-Cotes Art Gallery and Museum, East Cliff Promenade BH1 3AA **T** 01202-451858 **W** www.russellcotes.com
 Seaside villa housing 19th- and 20th-century art and sculptures from around the world
BOVINGTON
Tank Museum, Dorset BH20 6JG **T** 01929-405096
 W www.tankmuseum.org
 Collection of 300 tanks from their invention in 1915 to the modern conflict in Afghanistan
BRADFORD
Bradford Industrial Museum, Moorside Mills, Moorside Road, Eccleshill BD2 3HP **T** 01274-435900
 W www.bradfordmuseums.org
 Steam power, machinery and motor vehicle exhibits
Cartwright Hall Art Gallery, Lister Park BD9 4NS **T** 01274-431212
 W www.bradfordmuseums.org
 British 19th- and 20th-century fine art, contemporary prints and south Asian art
National Science and Media Museum,* BD1 1NQ **T 0800-047 8124
 W www.scienceandmediamuseum.org.uk
 The science and culture of image and sound technologies, film and television with interactive exhibits and experiments; features an IMAX cinema and the only permanent Cinerama screen in Europe
BRIGHTON
Booth Museum of Natural History, Dyke Road BN1 5AA
 T 03000-290900 **W** www.brightonmuseums.org.uk/booth
 Zoology, botany and geology collections; British birds in recreated habitats
Brighton Museum and Art Gallery, Royal Pavilion Gardens BN1 1EE
 T 03000-290900 **W** www.brightonmuseums.org.uk/brighton
 Includes fine art and design, fashion, world art; Sussex history
Royal Pavilion, 4/5 Pavilion Buildings BN1 1EE **T** 0300-0290900
 W https://brightonmuseums.org.uk/royalpavilion
 Regency seaside pleasure palace for George IV built in the visual style of India and China; includes the Prince Regent and Indian Military Hospital galleries
BRISTOL
Arnolfini, Narrow Quay BS1 4QA **T** 0117-917 2300
 W www.arnolfini.org.uk
 Experimental contemporary visual arts, dance, performance, music; talks and workshops

Blaise Castle House Museum, Henbury Road BS10 7QS
   T 0117-903 9818
   W www.bristolmuseums.org.uk/blaise-castle-house-museum
   18th-century mansion; social history collections
Bristol Museum and Art Gallery, Queen's Road BS8 1RL
   T 0117-922 3571
   W www.bristolmuseums.org.uk/bristol-museum-and-art-gallery
   Includes Victorian, Edwardian and French fine art;
   archaeology, local history and natural sciences
M Shed, Prince's Wharf BS1 4RN **T** 0117-352 6600
   W www.bristolmuseums.org.uk/m-shed
   The story of Bristol's heritage of engineering, transport,
   music and industry
Red Lodge Museum, Park Row BS1 5LJ **T** 0117-921 1360
   W www.bristolmuseums.org.uk/red-lodge-museum
   House museum showcasing original historical interiors
   from the Tudor to Victorian periods
CAMBRIDGE
Fitzwilliam Museum, Trumpington Street CB2 1RB
   T 01223-332900 **W** www.fitzmuseum.cam.ac.uk
   Antiquities, fine and applied arts, clocks, ceramics,
   manuscripts, furniture, sculpture, coins and medals
*Imperial War Museum Duxford, Duxford CB22 4QR
   T 01223-835000 **W** www.iwm.org.uk/visits/iwm-duxford
   Displays of military and civil aircraft, tanks and naval
   exhibits
Museum of Archaeology and Anthropology, Downing Street CB2
   3DZ **T** 01223-333516 **W** www.maa.cam.ac.uk
   Global archaeological and anthropological collections;
   photography and modern art collections
Museum of Zoology, Downing Street CB2 3EJ **T** 01223-336650
   W www.museum.zoo.cam.ac.uk
   Extensive assortment of zoological specimens; includes the
   collections of Charles Darwin and Alfred Russel Wallace
Sedgwick Museum of Earth Sciences, Downing Street CB2 3EQ
   T 01223-333456 **W** www.sedgwickmuseum.org
   Extensive geological collection
Whipple Museum of the History of Science, Free School Lane CB2
   3RH **T** 01223-330906 **W** www.hps.cam.ac.uk/whipple
   Scientific instruments from the 14th century to the present
CARLISLE
Tullie House Museum and Art Gallery, Castle Street CA3 8TP
   T 01228-618718 **W** www.tulliehouse.co.uk
   Jacobean house with fine art, local social history,
   prehistoric archaeology and natural sciences including
   Hadrian's Wall exhibit
CHATHAM
The Historic Dockyard, ME4 4TE **T** 01634-823800
   W www.thedockyard.co.uk
   Maritime attractions including HMS *Cavalier,* the UK's last
   Second World War destroyer
Royal Engineers Museum, Prince Arthur Road, Gillingham ME7 1UR
   T 01634-822312 **W** www.re-museum.co.uk
   Regimental history, ethnography, decorative art and
   photography
CHELTENHAM
The Wilson Art Gallery and Museum, Clarence Street GL50 3JT
   T 01242-387488 **W** www.cheltenhammuseum.org.uk
   Arts and crafts, local heroes, fine art and natural history
CHESTER
Grosvenor Museum, Grosvenor Street CH1 2DD **T** 01244-972197
   W www.grosvenormuseum.westcheshiremuseums.co.uk
   Roman collections, natural history, art, Chester silver,
   local history and costume
CHICHESTER
Weald and Downland Open Air Museum, Singleton PO18 0EU
   T 01243-811363 **W** www.wealddown.co.uk
   Rebuilt vernacular buildings from south-east England;
   includes medieval houses and a working watermill; craft
   demonstrations, Tudor kitchen and cooking

COLCHESTER
Colchester Castle Museum, Castle Park CO1 1TJ **T** 01206-282939
   W www.colchestercastlepark.co.uk/colchester-castle
   Largest Norman keep in Europe standing on foundations
   of the Roman Temple of Claudius
COVENTRY
Coventry Transport Museum, Hales Street CV1 1JD
   T 024-7623 4270 **W** www.transport-museum.com
   Extensive collection of motor vehicles and bicycles; land
   speed record-holding car
Herbert Art Gallery and Museum, Jordan Well CV1 5QP
   T 024-7623 7521 **W** www.theherbert.org
   Local history, archaeology, industry and visual arts
DERBY
Derby Museum and Art Gallery, The Strand DE1 1BS
   T 01332-641901 **W** www.derbymuseums.org/museumartgallery
   Includes paintings by Joseph Wright of Derby, origins of
   Derby and military history
Pickford's House Museum, Friar Gate DE1 1DA **T** 01332-715181
   W www.derbymuseums.org/pickfords-house
   Georgian town house designed by architect Joseph
   Pickford; museum of Georgian life and costume
DEVIZES
Wiltshire Museum, Library and Gallery, Long Street SN10 1NS
   T 01380-727369 **W** www.wiltshiremuseum.org.uk
   Natural and local history; art gallery; archaeological finds
   from prehistoric, Roman and Saxon sites
DOVER
Dover Museum, Market Square CT16 1PH **T** 01304-201066
   W www.dovermuseum.co.uk
   Contains the Dover Bronze Age Boat Gallery and
   archaeological finds from Bronze Age, Roman and Saxon
   sites
EXETER
Royal Albert Memorial Museum and Art Gallery, Queen Street EX4
   3RX **T** 01392-265858 **W** www.rammuseum.org.uk
   Natural history; archaeology; worldwide fine and
   decorative art including Exeter silver
GATESHEAD
BALTIC Centre for Contemporary Art, NE8 3BA **T** 0191-478 1810
   W www.baltic.art
   Contemporary art exhibitions and events
Shipley Art Gallery, Prince Consort Road NE8 4JB **T** 0191-477 1495
   W www.shipleyartgallery.org.uk
   Contemporary crafts
GAYDON
British Motor Museum, Banbury Road, Warks CV35 0BJ
   T 01926-641188 **W** www.britishmotormuseum.co.uk
   The world's largest collection of British cars with nearly
   300 vehicles spanning the classic, vintage and veteran eras
GLOUCESTER
Gloucester Waterways Museum, Gloucester Docks GL1 2EH
   T 01452-318200 **W** www.gloucesterwaterwaysmuseum.org.uk
   200-year history of Britain's canals and inland waterways
GOSPORT
Royal Navy Submarine Museum, Haslar Jetty Road, Hants PO12 2AS
   T 023-9251 0354 **W** www.nmrn.org.uk/submarine-museum
   Underwater warfare exhibition, including submarines
   HMS *Alliance* and HMS *Holland 1* – the Royal Navy's first
   submarine
GRASMERE
Dove Cottage and the *Wordsworth Museum,* Cumbria LA22 9SH
   T 015394-35544 **W** www.wordsworth.org.uk
   William Wordsworth's manuscripts, home and garden
HOVE
Hove Museum and Art Gallery, New Church Road BN3 4AB
   T 03000-290900 **W** www.brightonmuseums.org.uk/hove
   Toys, cinema, local history and fine art collections

HULL

Ferens Art Gallery, Queen Victoria Square HU1 3RA
   T 01482-300300 **W** www.hcandl.co.uk/ferens-art-gallery
   European Old Masters, Victorian, Edwardian and
   contemporary British art

Hull and East Riding Museum of Archaeology, High Street, HU1
   1NQ **T** 01482-300300
   W www.hcandl.co.uk/hull-and-east-riding-museum
   Local history from the pre-historic to the present day

Hull Maritime Museum, Queen Victoria Square HU1 3DX
   T 01482-300300 **W** www.hcandl.co.uk/maritime-museum
   Hull's maritime heritage including whaling, fishing,
   navigation and merchant trade

Wilberforce House, 23–25 High Street HU1 1NQ **T** 01482-300300
   W www.hcandl.co.uk/wilberforce-house
   Birthplace of abolitionist William Wilberforce; history of
   the transatlantic slave trade

HUNTINGDON

The Cromwell Museum, Grammar School Walk PE29 3LF
   T 01480-708008 **W** www.cromwellmuseum.org
   Portraits and memorabilia relating to Oliver Cromwell

IPSWICH

Christchurch Mansion and *Wolsey Art Gallery,* Christchurch Park
   IP4 2BE **T** 01473-433554 **W** www.cimuseums.org.uk
   Tudor house with paintings by Gainsborough, Constable
   and other Suffolk artists; furniture and 18th-century
   ceramics; temporary exhibitions

KEIGHLEY

The Brontë Parsonage Museum, Haworth, W. Yorks BD22 8DR
   T 01535-642323 **W** www.bronte.org.uk
   The former home of the literary Brontë family

KESWICK

Derwent Pencil Museum, Southey Works CA12 5NG
   T 01900-609590 **W** www.derwentart.com
   500-year history of the pencil; demonstration events and
   workshops throughout the year

LEEDS

Armley Mills, Leeds Industrial Museum, Canal Road, Armley
   LS12 2QF **T** 0113-378 3173
   W museumsandgalleries.leeds.gov.uk/armleymills
   Once the world's largest woollen mill, now a museum for
   textiles and Leeds' industrial heritage

Leeds Art Gallery, The Headrow LS1 3AA **T** 0113-378 5350
   W museumsandgalleries.leeds.gov.uk/artgallery
   Includes English watercolours, sculpture, contemporary
   art and prints from the region's artists

*Royal Armouries Museum, Armouries Drive LS10 1LT
   T 0113-220 1961 **W** www.royalarmouries.org
   National collection of over 8,500 items of arms and
   armour from BC to present over five galleries: War,
   Tournament, Oriental, Self Defence and Hunting

LEICESTER

New Walk Museum and Art Gallery, 53 New Walk LE1 7EA
   T 0116-255 4900
   W www.leicester.gov.uk/leisure-and-culture/
   museums-and-galleries
   Natural and cultural history; ancient Egypt gallery;
   European art including works by the German
   expressionists and ceramics by Picasso

LINCOLN

The Collection, Danes Terrace LN2 1LP **T** 01522-782040
   W www.thecollectionmuseum.com
   Artefacts from the Stone Age to the Roman, Viking and
   Medieval eras; adjacent art gallery; collections of
   contemporary art and craft, sculpture, porcelain, clocks
   and watches

Museum of Lincolnshire Life, Burton Road LN1 3LY
   T 01522-782040
   W www.lincolnshire.gov.uk/museumoflincolnshirelife
   Social history; agricultural, industrial, military and
   commercial exhibits

LIVERPOOL

*International Slavery Museum, Royal Albert Dock L3 4AQ
   T 0151-478 4499 **W** www.liverpoolmuseums.org.uk/ism
   Explores historical and contemporary aspects of slavery

*Lady Lever Art Gallery, Wirral CH62 5EQ **T** 0151-478 4136
   W www.liverpoolmuseums.org.uk/ladylever
   Paintings, furniture and porcelain

*Merseyside Maritime Museum, Royal Albert Dock L3 4AQ
   T 0151-478 4499 **W** www.liverpoolmuseums.org.uk/maritime
   Floating exhibits, working displays and craft
   demonstrations; incorporates the *UK Border Agency
   National Museum*

*Museum of Liverpool, Pier Head L3 1DG **T** 0151-478 4545
   W www.liverpoolmuseums.org.uk/mol
   Explores the significance of the city's geography, history
   and culture

* *Sudley House,* Mossley Hill Road L18 8BX **T** 0151-478 4016
   W www.liverpoolmuseums.org.uk/sudley
   Late 18th- and 19th-century paintings in former
   shipowner's home

*Tate Liverpool, Albert Dock L3 4BB **T** 0151-1702 7400
   W www.tate.org.uk/liverpool
   20th-century paintings and sculpture

*Walker Art Gallery, William Brown Street L3 8EL
   T 0151-478 4199 **W** www.liverpoolmuseums.org.uk/walker
   Paintings and decorative arts from the 13th century to the
   present day

*World Museum Liverpool, William Brown Street L3 8EN
   T 0151-478 4393 **W** www.liverpoolmuseums.org.uk/wml
   Includes Egyptian mummies, weapons and classical
   sculpture; planetarium, aquarium, vivarium and natural
   history centre

LONDON: GALLERIES

Barbican Art Gallery, Barbican Centre, Silk Street EC2Y 8DS
   T 020-7638 4141 **W** www.barbican.org.uk
   Art, music, theatre, dance and film exhibitions

Courtauld Institute of Art Gallery, Somerset House, Strand
   WC2R 0RN **T** 020-3947 7777 **W** www.courtauld.ac.uk
   Fine art from the early renaissance to the 20th century,
   including impressionist and post-impressionist paintings

Dennis Severs' House, 18 Folgate Street E1 6BX **T** 020-7247 4013
   W www.dennissevershouse.co.uk
   Candlelit recreation of a Huguenot silk weaver's home

Dulwich Picture Gallery, Gallery Road SE21 7AD **T** 020-8693 5254
   W www.dulwichpicturegallery.org.uk
   England's first public art gallery; designed by Sir John
   Soane to house 17th- and 18th-century paintings

Estorick Collection of Modern Italian Art, Canonbury Square
   N1 2AN **T** 020-7704 9522 **W** www.estorickcollection.com
   Early 20th-century Italian drawings, paintings, sculptures
   and etchings, with an emphasis on Futurism

Hayward Gallery, Belvedere Road SE1 8XX **T** 020-7960 4200
   W www.southbankcentre.co.uk
   Temporary exhibitions

*National Gallery, Trafalgar Square WC2N 5DN **T** 020-7747 2885
   W www.nationalgallery.org.uk
   Western painting from the 13th to 19th centuries; early
   Renaissance collection in the Sainsbury Wing

*National Portrait Gallery, St Martin's Place WC2H 0HE
   T 020-7306 0055 **W** www.npg.org.uk
   Portraits of eminent people in British history

Photographers' Gallery, Ramillies Street W1F 7LW **T** 020-7087 9300
   W www.thephotographersgallery.org.uk
   Temporary exhibitions; permanent camera obscura

The Queen's Gallery, Buckingham Palace SW1A 1AA
  T 020-7766 7300 **W** www.rct.uk
  Art from the Royal Collection
Royal Academy of Arts, Burlington House, Piccadilly W1J 0BD
  T 020-7300 8090 **W** www.royalacademy.org.uk
  British art since 1768 and temporary exhibitions; annual
  Summer Exhibition
Saatchi Gallery, Duke of York's HQ, King's Road SW3 4RY
  T 020-7811 3070 **W** www.saatchigallery.com
  Contemporary art including paintings, photographs,
  sculpture and installations
Serpentine Gallery, Kensington Gardens W2 3XA **T** 020-7402 6075
  W www.serpentinegallery.org
  Temporary exhibitions of British and international
  contemporary art
*Tate Britain, Millbank SW1P 4RG **T** 020-7887 8888
  W www.tate.org.uk/britain
  British art from the 16th century to the present;
  international modern art
*Tate Modern, Bankside SE1 9TG **T** 020-7887 8888
  W www.tate.org.uk/modern
  International modern art from 1900 to the present
*Wallace Collection, Manchester Square W1U 3BN
  T 020-7563 9500 **W** www.wallacecollection.org
  Old Masters; French 18th-century paintings, furniture,
  armour, porcelain, clocks and sculpture
Whitechapel Art Gallery, Whitechapel High Street E1 7QX
  T 020-7522 7888 **W** www.whitechapelgallery.org
  Temporary exhibitions of modern art
LONDON: MUSEUMS
Bank of England Museum, Bartholomew Lane EC2R 8AH
  T 020-3461 4444 **W** www.bankofengland.co.uk/museum
  History of the Bank of England since 1694
*British Museum, Great Russell Street WC1B 3DG **T** 020-7323 8000
  W www.britishmuseum.org
  Collection of art and antiquities spanning 2 million years
  of human history; temporary exhibitions; houses the Elgin
  Marbles from the Parthenon
Brunel Museum, Rotherhithe SE16 4LF **T** 020-7231 3840
  W www.brunel-museum.org.uk
  Explores the engineering achievements of Isambard
  Kingdom Brunel and his father, Marc Brunel
Charles Dickens Museum, Doughty Street WC1N 2LX
  T 020-7405 2127 **W** www.dickensmuseum.com
  Dickens's home from 1837–9; manuscripts, personal
  items and paintings
*Churchill War Rooms, King Charles Street SW1A 2AQ
  T 020-7416 5000 **W** www.iwm.org.uk/visits/churchill-war-rooms
  Underground rooms used by Churchill and the
  government during the Second World War
Cutty Sark, King William Walk SE10 9HT **T** 020-8858 4422
  W www.rmg.co.uk/cuttysark
  The world's last remaining tea clipper; re-opened in April
  2012 following extensive restoration
Design Museum, Kensington High Street W8 6AG **T** 020-3862 5900
  W www.designmuseum.org
  The development of design and the mass-production of
  consumer objects
Garden Museum, Lambeth Palace Road SE1 7LB **T** 020-7401 8865
  W www.gardenmuseum.org.uk
  History and development of gardens and gardening;
  temporary exhibitions, symposia and events
*HMS Belfast, The Queen's Walk SE1 2JH **T** 020-7940 6300
  W www.iwm.org.uk/hms-belfast
  Life and work on board a Second World War cruiser
*Horniman Museum and Gardens, London Road SE23 3PQ
  T 020-8699 1872 **W** www.horniman.ac.uk
  Museum of anthropology, musical instruments and natural
  history; aquarium; reference library; gardens

*Imperial War Museum, Lambeth Road SE1 6HZ **T** 020-7416 5000
  W www.iwm.org.uk
  All aspects of the two World Wars and other military
  operations involving Britain and the Commonwealth since
  1914
Jewish Museum, Albert Street NW1 7NB **T** 020-7284 7384
  W www.jewishmuseum.org.uk
  Jewish life, history, art and religion
London Metropolitan Archives, Northampton Road EC1R 0HB
  T 020-7332 3820 **W** www.cityoflondon.gov.uk/lma
  Material on the history of London and its people dating
  from 1067 to the present day
London Museum of Water and Steam, Green Dragon Lane TW8 0EN
  T 020-8568 4757 **W** www.waterandsteam.org.uk
  Large collection of steam engines; reopened in 2014 after
  refurbishment
London Transport Museum, Covent Garden Piazza WC2E 7BB
  T 034-3222 5000 **W** www.ltmuseum.co.uk
  Vehicles, photographs and graphic art relating to the
  history of transport in London
MCC Museum, Lord's Cricket Ground, St John's Wood NW8 8QN
  T 020-7616 8500 **W** www.lords.org/tours-and-museum
  Cricket exhibits including the Ashes Urn, kits, paintings
  and W. G. Grace exhibit
Migration Museum, Lambeth High Street SE1 7AG
  E info@migrationmuseum.org **W** www.migrationmuseum.org
  Opened in 2017, tells the story of migration through the
  ages and how it has affected and transformed Britain
*Museum of Childhood (V&A), Cambridge Heath Road E2 9PA
  T 020-7942 2000 **W** www.vam.ac.uk/moc
  Toys, games and exhibits relating to the social history of
  childhood from the 17th century to the present
*Museum of London, London Wall EC2Y 5HN **T** 020-7001 9844
  W www.museumoflondon.org.uk
  History of London from prehistoric times to the present
  day; Galleries of Modern London
Museum of London Docklands, West India Quay, Canary Wharf
  E14 4AL **T** 020-7001 9844
  W www.museumoflondon.org.uk/docklands
  Explores the story of London's river, port and people over
  2,000 years; includes the London Sugar Slavery Gallery
National Archives Museum, Kew TW9 4DU **T** 020-8876 3444
  W www.nationalarchives.gov.uk/museum
  Displays treasures from the archives, including the
  Domesday Book and Magna Carta
*National Army Museum, Royal Hospital Road SW3 4HT
  T 020-7730 0717 **W** www.nam.ac.uk
  Five-hundred-year history of the British soldier; exhibits
  include model of the Battle of Waterloo and recreated
  First World War trench
*National Maritime Museum, Romney Road SE10 9NF
  T 020-8858 4422
  W www.rmg.co.uk/national-maritime-museum
  Maritime history of Britain; collections include globes,
  clocks, telescopes and paintings; comprises the main
  building, the Royal Observatory and the Queen's House
*Natural History Museum, Cromwell Road SW7 5BD
  T 020-7942 5000 **W** www.nhm.ac.uk
  Natural history collections and interactive Darwin Centre
Petrie Museum of Egyptian Archaeology, University College London,
  Malet Place WC1E 6BT **T** 020-3108 9000
  W www.ucl.ac.uk/museums/petrie
  Egyptian and Sudanese archaeology featuring around
  80,000 objects
Postal Museum, 15–20 Phoenix Place, WC1X 0DL **T** 0300-030 0700
  W www.postalmuseum.org
  British postal service and communications from Tudor
  times to the present; interactive galleries, archives and
  subterranean mail train ride

Royal Air Force Museum, Grahame Park Way NW9 5LL
   T 020-8205 2266 **W** www.rafmuseum.org.uk
   Aviation from before the Wright brothers to the present
Royal Mews, Buckingham Palace SW1W 0QH **T** 020-7766 7302
   W www.rct.uk/visit/royalmews
   State vehicles, including the Queen's gold state coach;
   home to the Queen's horses; guided tours
Science Museum, Exhibition Road SW7 2DD **T** 0800-047 8124
   W www.sciencemuseum.org.uk
   Science, technology, industry and medicine exhibitions;
   children's interactive gallery; IMAX cinema
Shakespeare's Globe Exhibition, New Globe Walk, Bankside SE1 9DT
   T 020-7902 1400 **W** www.shakespearesglobe.com
   Recreation of Elizabethan theatre using 16th-century
   techniques; includes a tour of the theatre
Sir John Soane's Museum, Lincoln's Inn Fields WC2A 3BP
   T 020-7405 2107 **W** www.soane.org
   Art and antiquities collected by Soane throughout his
   lifetime; authentic Georgian and Victorian interior
Tower Bridge Exhibition, SE1 2UP **T** 020-7403 3761
   W www.towerbridge.org.uk
   History of the bridge and display of Victorian steam
   machinery; panoramic views from walkways
Victoria and Albert Museum, Cromwell Road SW7 2RL
   T 020-7942 2000 **W** www.vam.ac.uk
   Includes the National Art Library and the Gilbert
   Collection; fine and applied art and design; furniture,
   glass, textiles, theatre and dress collections; temporary
   exhibitions
Wellcome Collection, Euston Road NW1 2BE **T** 020-7611 2222
   W www.wellcomecollection.org
   Contemporary and historic exhibitions and collections
   including the Wellcome Library
Wimbledon Lawn Tennis Museum, Church Road SW19 5AE
   T 020-8944 1066 **W** www.wimbledon.com/museum
   Tennis trophies, fashion and memorabilia; view of Centre
   Court
MALTON
Eden Camp, N. Yorks YO17 6RT **T** 01653-697777
   W www.edencamp.co.uk
   Restored POW camp and Second World War
   memorabilia
MANCHESTER
Gallery of Costume, Platt Hall, Rusholme M14 5LL **T** 0161-245 7245
   W www.manchesterartgallery.org
   Exhibits from the 17th century to the present day
Imperial War Museum North, Trafford Wharf Road M17 1TZ
   T 0207-416 5000 **W** www.iwm.org.uk/north
   History of war from the 20th century to the present
Manchester Art Gallery, Mosley Street M2 3JL **T** 0161-235 8888
   W www.manchesterartgallery.org
   European fine and decorative art from the 17th to 20th
   centuries
Manchester Museum, Oxford Road M13 9PL **T** 0161-275 2648
   W www.museum.manchester.ac.uk
   Collections include decorative arts, natural history and
   zoology; three Ancient Worlds galleries
Museum of Science and Industry, Liverpool Road M3 4FP
   T 0800-047 8124 **W** www.scienceandindustrymuseum.org.uk
   On site of world's oldest passenger railway station;
   galleries relating to space, energy, power, transport,
   aviation, textiles and social history
National Football Museum, Cathedral Gardens M4 3BG
   T 0161-605 8200 **W** www.nationalfootballmuseum.com
   Home to the FIFA, FA and Football League collections
   including the 1966 World Cup final ball
People's History Museum, Left Bank, Spinningfields M3 3ER
   T 0161-838 9190 **W** www.phm.org.uk
   History of British political and working life

The Whitworth, Oxford Road M15 6ER **T** 0161-275 7450
   W www.whitworth.manchester.ac.uk
   Fine and modern art, wallpapers, prints, textiles and
   sculptures
MILTON KEYNES
Bletchley Park National Codes Centre, Bucks MK3 6EB
   T 01908-640404 **W** www.bletchleypark.org.uk
   Home of British codebreaking during the Second World
   War; Enigma machine; computer museum and Alan
   Turing gallery
The National Museum of Computing Block H, Bletchley Park, MK3
   6EB **T** 01908-374708 **W** www.tnmoc.org
   Charts the development of computing from the 1940s
   onwards and houses the world's largest collection of
   functional historical computers, including the Colossus
   and the WITCH
NEWCASTLE UPON TYNE
Discovery Museum, Blandford Square NE1 4JA **T** 0191-232 6789
   W www.discoverymuseum.org.uk
   Science and industry, local history, fashion; Tyneside's
   maritime history; digital jukebox of 2,000 film and TV
   titles from the BFI National Archive
Great North Museum: Hancock, Barras Bridge NE2 4PT
   T 0191-222 6765 **W** www.greatnorthmuseum.org.uk
   Natural and ancient history; planetarium; Living Planet
   display incorporates live animal tanks and aquaria
Laing Art Gallery, New Bridge Street NE1 8AG **T** 0191-278 1611
   W www.laingartgallery.org.uk
   19th and 20th century art including local painters;
   ceramics, glass, Japanese decorative arts and prints
NEWMARKET
*Palace House: National Heritage Centre for Horseracing and
   Sporting Art,* Palace Street CB8 8EP **T** 01638-667314
   W www.palacehousenewmarket.co.uk
   Collection of horseracing memorabilia, British Sporting
   Art from around the UK and home of the retraining of
   racehorses
NORTH SHIELDS
Stephenson Railway Museum, Middle Engine Lane NE29 8DX
   T 0191-277 7135 **W** www.stephensonrailwaymuseum.org.uk
   Locomotive engines and rolling stock; open April through
   November and school holidays outside this period
NOTTINGHAM
Natural History Museum, Wollaton Hall, Wollaton NG8 2AE
   T 0115-876 3100 **W** www.wallatonhall.org.uk
   Geology, botany and zoology specimens housed in an
   Elizabethan mansion
OXFORD
Ashmolean Museum, Beaumont Street OX1 2PH **T** 01865-278000
   W www.ashmolean.org
   Art and archaeology including Egyptian, Minoan, Anglo-
   Saxon and Chinese exhibits; largest collection of Raphael
   drawings in the world
Modern Art Oxford, Pembroke Street OX1 1BP **T** 01865-722733
   W www.modernartoxford.org.uk
   Temporary exhibitions
Museum of the History of Science, Broad Street OX1 3AZ
   T 01865-277293 **W** www.hsm.ox.ac.uk
   Displays include early scientific instruments, chemical
   apparatus, clocks and watches
Oxford University Museum of Natural History, Parks Road
   OX1 3PW **T** 01865-272950 **W** www.oumnh.ox.ac.uk
   Entomology, geology, mineralogy and petrology, and
   zoology
Pitt Rivers Museum, South Parks Road OX1 3PP **T** 01865-613000
   W www.prm.ox.ac.uk
   Anthropological and archaeological artefacts

PLYMOUTH
The Box Plymouth, Tavistock Place PL4 8AX
W www.theboxplymouth.com
Local archives and study; fine and decorative arts; world cultures; temporary exhibitions
PORTSMOUTH
Charles Dickens Birthplace, Old Commercial Road PO1 4QL
T 023-9282 1879 **W** www.charlesdickensbirthplace.co.uk
Reproduction Regency house; Dickens memorabilia
The D-Day Story, Clarence Esplanade, Southsea PO5 3NT
T 023-9288 2555 **W** www.theddaystory.com
The evacuation of Dunkirk, the D-Day landings and the Battle of Normandy exhibitions with over 10,000 objects and artefacts including the Overlord embroidery
Portsmouth Historic Dockyard, HM Naval Base PO1 3LJ
T 023-9283 9766 **W** www.historicdockyard.co.uk
Incorporates the *National Museum of the Royal Navy** (PO1 3NH **T** 023-9289 1370 **W** www.nmrn.org.uk), HMS *Victory* (PO1 3NH **T** 023-9283 9766 **W** www.hms-victory.com), HMS *Warrior* (PO1 3QX **T** 023-9283 9766 **W** www.hmswarrior.org), *Mary Rose* (PO1 3LX **T** 077-166 3973 **W** www.maryrose.org) and *Action Stations* (PO1 3LJ **T** 023-9283 9766 **W** www.actionstations.org)
History of the Royal Navy and of the dockyard; warships and technology spanning 500 years
PRESTON
Harris Museum and Art Gallery, Market Square PR1 2PP
T 01772-258248 **W** www.theharris.org.uk
British art since the 18th century; ceramics, glass, costume and local history; contemporary exhibitions
ST ALBANS
Verulamium Museum, St Michael's Street AL3 4SW
T 01727-751810 **W** www.stalbansmuseums.org.uk
Remains of Iron Age settlement and the third-largest city in Roman Britain
ST IVES
*Tate St Ives, Porthmeor Beach, Cornwall TR26 1TG
T 01736-796226 **W** www.tate.org.uk/stives
Modern art, much by artists associated with St Ives; includes the Barbara Hepworth Museum and Sculpture Garden; open after 2014 part closure
SALISBURY
Salisbury & South Wiltshire Museum, The Close SP1 2EN
T 01722-332151 **W** www.salisburymuseum.org.uk
Local history and archaeology; Stonehenge exhibits
SHEFFIELD
Graves Gallery, Surrey Street S1 1XZ **T** 0114-278 2600
W www.museums-sheffield.org.uk
Twentieth-century British art; European art spanning four centuries
Millennium Galleries, Arundel Gate S1 2PP **T** 0114-278 2600
W www.museums-sheffield.org.uk
Incorporates four different galleries: the Special Exhibition Gallery, the Craft and Design Gallery, the Metalwork Gallery and the Ruskin Gallery, which houses John Ruskin's collection of paintings, drawings, books and medieval manuscripts
Weston Park Museum, Western Bank S10 2TP **T** 0114-278 2600
W www.museums-sheffield.org.uk
World and local history; art and temporary exhibitions
SOUTHAMPTON
City Art Gallery, Commercial Road SO14 7LP **T** 023-8083 3007
W www.southamptoncityartgallery.com
Western art from the Renaissance to the present
SeaCity Museum, Havelock Road SO14 7FY **T** 023-8083 3007
W www.seacitymuseum.co.uk
Opened in 2012, the museum tells the story of the city's maritime past and present

SOUTH SHIELDS
Arbeia Roman Fort, Baring Street NE33 2BB **T** 0191-277 2170
W www.arbeiaromanfort.org.uk
Excavated ruins; reconstructions of original buildings
South Shields Museum and Art Gallery, Ocean Road NE33 2JA
T 0191-211 5599 **W** www.southshieldsmuseum.org.uk
South Tyneside history; interactive art gallery
STOKE-ON-TRENT
Etruria Industrial Museum, Lower Bedford Street ST4 7AF
T 07900-267711 **W** www.etruriamuseum.org.uk
Britain's sole surviving steam-powered potter's mill
Gladstone Pottery Museum, Uttoxeter Road, Longton ST3 1PQ
T 01782-237777 **W** www.stokemuseums.org.uk
The last complete Victorian pottery factory in Britain
Potteries Museum and Art Gallery, Bethesda Street ST1 3DW
T 01782-232323 **W** www.stokemuseums.org.uk/pmag
Pottery, china and porcelain collections and a Mark XVI Spitfire
The Wedgwood Museum, Barlaston ST12 9ER **T** 01782-371900
W www.wedgwoodmuseum.org.uk
The story of Josiah Wedgwood and the company he founded
SUNDERLAND
Sunderland Museum and Winter Gardens, Burdon Road SR1 1PP
T 0191-553 2323 **W** www.sunderlandculture.org.uk
Fine and decorative art, local history and gardens
TELFORD
Ironbridge Gorge Museums, TF8 7DQ **T** 01952-433424
W www.ironbridge.org.uk
Ten museums including The Museum of the Gorge; The Iron Bridge and Tollhouse; Blists Hill (late Victorian working town); Brosely Pipeworks; Coalbrookdale Museum of Iron; Coalport China Museum; Jackfield Tile Museum; Tar Tunnel; Darby Houses
WAKEFIELD
Hepworth Wakefield, Gallery Walk WF1 5AW **T** 01924-247360
W www.hepworthwakefield.org
Historic and modern art; temporary exhibitions of contemporary art
National Coal Mining Museum for England, New Road, Overton WF4 4RH **T** 01924-848806 **W** www.ncm.org.uk
Includes underground tours of one of Britain's oldest working mines
Yorkshire Sculpture Park, West Bretton WF4 4LG **T** 01924-832631
W www.ysp.co.uk
Open-air sculpture gallery including works by Henry Moore, Barbara Hepworth and others in 500 acres of parkland
WEYBRIDGE
Brooklands Museum, Brooklands Road KT13 0QN **T** 01932-857381
W www.brooklandsmuseum.com
Birthplace of British motorsport; world's first purpose-built motor racing circuit
WILMSLOW
Quarry Bank Mill and Styal Estate, Wilmslow SK9 4LA
T 01625-527468 **W** www.nationaltrust.org.uk/quarry-bank
Europe's most powerful working waterwheel owned by the National Trust illustrating history of cotton industry; costumed guides at restored Apprentice House
WINCHESTER
Winchester Science Centre and Planetarium, Telegraph Way, Hants SO21 1HZ **T** 01962-863791
W www.winchestersciencecentre.org
Interactive science centre and planetarium
WORCESTER
City Art Gallery and Museum, Foregate Street WR1 1DT
T 01905-25371
W www.museumsworcestershire.org.uk/museums/worcester-city-art-gallery-museum

Includes the Regimental museum, 19th-century chemist shop and changing art exhibitions

Museum of Royal Worcester, Severn Street WR1 2ND
   T 01905-21247 **W** www.museumofroyalworcester.org
   Worcester porcelain from 1751 to the present day

YEOVIL

Fleet Air Arm Museum, RNAS Yeovilton, Somerset BA22 8HT
   T 01935-840565 **W** www.fleetairarm.com
   History of naval aviation; historic aircraft, including Concorde 002

YORK

Beningbrough Hall, Beningbrough YO30 1DD **T** 01904-472027
   W www.nationaltrust.org.uk/beningbrough-hall
   18th-century house with portraits from the National Portrait Gallery; parklands and gardens

JORVIK Viking Centre, Coppergate YO1 9WT **T** 01904-615505
   W www.jorvikvikingcentre.co.uk
   Reconstruction of Viking York based on archaeological evidence

*National Railway Museum, Leeman Road YO26 4XJ
   T 0800-047 8124 **W** www.railwaymuseum.org.uk
   Includes locomotives, rolling stock and carriages

York Art Gallery, Exhibition Square, YO1 7EW **T** 01904 687687
   W www.yorkartgallery.org.uk
   600 years of British and European painting; ceramics and sculpture

York Castle Museum, Eye of York YO1 9RY **T** 01904-687687
   W www.yorkcastlemuseum.org.uk
   Includes Kirkgate, a reconstructed Victorian street; costume and military collections

Yorkshire Museum, Museum Gardens YO1 7FR **T** 01904-687687
   W www.yorkshiremuseum.org.uk
   Yorkshire life from Roman to medieval times; geology and biology; York observatory

WALES
* Members of National Museum Wales, a public body that receives its core funding from the Welsh government

ABERYSTWYTH

Ceredigion Museum, Terrace Road SY23 2AQ **T** 01970-633088
   W www.ceredigionmuseum.wales
   Local history, housed in a restored Edwardian theatre

Silver Mountain Experience, Ponterwyd SY23 3AB **T** 01970-890620
   W www.silvermountainexperience.co.uk
   Tours of an 18th-century silver mine, with interactive challenges and games for children

BLAENAFON

*Big Pit National Coal Museum, Torfaen NP4 9XP
   T 030-0111 2333 **W** www.museum.wales/bigpit
   Colliery with an underground tour and exhibitions of modern mining equipment

BODELWYDDAN

Bodelwyddan Castle, Denbighshire LL18 5YA **T** 01745-584060
   W www.bodelwyddan-castle.co.uk
   Art gallery within an historic house; features temporary art exhibits

CAERLEON

*National Roman Legion Museum, NP18 1AE **T** 030-0111 2333
   W www.museum.wales/roman
   Features the oldest recorded piece of writing in Wales; pottery, Roman era gemstones

CARDIFF

*National Museum Cardiff, Cathays Park CF10 3NP
   T 030-0111 2333 **W** www.museum.wales/cardiff
   Houses Wales's national art, archaeology and natural history collections

*St Fagans: National History Museum, St Fagans CF5 6XB
   T 030-0111 2333 **W** www.museum.wales/stfagans
   Open-air museum with re-erected buildings, agricultural equipment and costume

TECHNIQUEST, Stuart Street CF10 5BW **T** 029-2047 5475
   W www.techniquest.org
   Interactive science exhibits, planetarium and science theatre

CRICCIETH

Lloyd George Museum, Llanystumdwy LL52 0SH **T** 01766-522071
   W www.gwynedd.llyw.cymru
   Childhood home of David Lloyd George

DRE-FACH FELINDRE

*National Wool Museum, Llandysul SA44 5UP **T** 030-0111 2333
   W www.museum.wales/wool
   Exhibitions, a working woollen mill and craft workshops

LLANBERIS

*National Slate Museum, Gwynedd LL55 4TY **T** 030-0111 2333
   W www.museum.wales/slate
   Former slate quarry with original machinery and plant; slate crafts demonstrations; working waterwheel

LLANDRINDOD WELLS

National Cycle Collection, Automobile Palace, Temple Street
   LD1 5DL **T** 01597-825531 **W** www.cyclemuseum.org.uk
   Approximately 250 bicycles on display, from 1819 to the present

PRESTEIGNE

Judge's Lodging Museum, Broad Street LD8 2AD **T** 01544-260650
   W www.judgeslodging.org.uk
   Restored apartments, courtroom, cells and servants' quarters

SWANSEA

Glynn Vivian Art Gallery, Alexandra Road SA1 5DZ
   T 01792-516900 **W** www.swansea.gov.uk/glynnvivian
   Fine art and ceramics from 1700 to the present

*National Waterfront Museum, Oystermouth Road SA1 3RD
   T 030-0111 2333 **W** www.museum.wales/swansea
   Wales during the Industrial Revolution

Swansea Museum, Victoria Road SA1 1SN **T** 01792-653763
   W www.swanseamuseum.co.uk
   Paintings, Egyptian artifacts, transport and nautical collections; war time Swansea

TENBY

Tenby Museum and Art Gallery, Castle Hill SA70 7BP **T** 01834-842809 **W** www.tenbymuseum.org.uk
   Local archaeology, history, geology and art

SCOTLAND
* Members of National Museums Scotland or National Galleries of Scotland, which are non-departmental public bodies funded by, and accountable to, the Scottish government

ABERDEEN

Aberdeen Art Gallery, Schoolhill AB10 1FQ **T** 0300-020 0293
   W www.aagm.co.uk
   Paintings, sculptures and graphics; temporary exhibitions

Aberdeen Maritime Museum, Shiprow AB11 5BY **T** 0300-020 0293
   W www.aagm.co.uk
   Maritime history, including shipbuilding and North Sea oil

AYR

Robert Burns Birthplace Museum, Murdoch's Lone, Alloway
   KA7 4PQ **T** 0129-244 3700 **W** www.burnsmuseum.org.uk
   Comprises Burns Cottage, birthplace of the poet, gardens and a museum

EDINBURGH

Britannia, Leith EH6 6JJ **T** 0131-555 5566
   W www.royalyachtbritannia.co.uk
   Former royal yacht with royal barge and royal family picture gallery

City Art Centre, Market Street EH1 1DE **T** 0131-529 3993
   W www.edinburghmuseums.org.uk
   Rolling programme of exhibitions including historic and
   modern photography; contemporary art, design and
   architecture
Museum of Childhood, High Street EH1 1TG **T** 0131-529 4142
   W www.edinburghmuseums.org.uk
   Toys, games, clothes and exhibits relating to the social
   history of childhood
Museum of Edinburgh, Canongate, Royal Mile EH8 8DD
   T 0131-529 4143 **W** www.edinburghmuseums.org.uk
   Local history, silver, glass and Scottish pottery
*National Museum of Flight, East Fortune Airfield, East Lothian
   EH39 5LF **T** 0300-123 6789 **W** www.nms.ac.uk/flight
   Aviation from the early 20th century to the present
*National Museum of Scotland, Chambers Street EH1 1JF
   T 0300-123 6789 **W** www.nms.ac.uk/scotland
   Scottish history; world cultures; natural world; art and
   design; science and technology
*National War Museum of Scotland, Edinburgh Castle EH1 2NG
   T 0300-123 6789 **W** www.nms.ac.uk/war
   Scotland's military history housed within Edinburgh
   Castle
*Scottish National Gallery, The Mound EH2 2EL **T** 0131-624 6200
   W www.nationalgalleries.org
   Fine art from the early Renaissance to the end of the 19th
   century
*Scottish National Gallery of Modern Art, Belford Road EH4 3DR
   T 0131-624 6200 **W** www.nationalgalleries.org
   Contemporary art featuring British, French and Russian
   collections; outdoor sculpture park
*Scottish National Portrait Gallery, Queen Street EH2 1JD
   T 0131-624 6200 **W** www.nationalgalleries.org/portraitgallery
   Portraits of eminent people in Scottish history;
   Photography Gallery; Victorian Library
The Writers' Museum, Lady Stair's Close EH1 2PA
   T 0131-529 4901 **W** www.edinburghmuseums.org.uk
   Exhibitions relating to Robert Burns, Sir Walter Scott and
   Robert Louis Stevenson
FORT WILLIAM
West Highland Museum, Cameron Square PH33 6AJ
   T 01397-702169 **W** www.westhighlandmuseum.org.uk
   Highland life; Military, Victorian and Jacobite collections
GLASGOW
Burrell Collection, Pollokshaws Road G43 1AT **T** 0141-287 2550
   W www.glasgowlife.org.uk/museums
   Paintings by major artists; medieval art, Chinese and
   Islamic art
Gallery of Modern Art, Royal Exchange Square G1 3AH
   T 0141-287 3050 **W** www.glasgowlife.org.uk/museums
   Collection of contemporary Scottish and world art
Hunterian, University of Glasgow G12 8QQ **T** 0141-330 4221
   W www.gla.ac.uk/hunterian
   Rennie Mackintosh and Whistler collections; coins;
   Scottish paintings; Pacific ethnographic collection;
   archaeology; medicine
Kelvingrove Art Gallery & Museum, Argyle Street G3 8AG
   T 0141-357 3929 **W** www.glasgowlife.org.uk/museums
   Includes Old Masters; natural history; arms and armour
Museum of Piping, McPhater Street G4 0HW **T** 0141-353 0220
   W www.thepipingcentre.co.uk
   The history and origins of bagpiping

*Museum of Rural Life, Philipshill Road, East Kilbride G76 9HR
   T 0300-123 6789 **W** www.nms.ac.uk/rural
   History of rural life and work
People's Palace and Winter Gardens, Glasgow Green G40 1AT
   T 0141-276 0788 **W** www.glasgowlife.org.uk/museums
   Social history of Glasgow since 1750
Riverside Museum, 100 Pointhouse Place G3 8RS **T** 0141-287 2720
   W www.glasgowlife.org.uk/museums
   Scotland's museum of transport and travel; the Tall Ship
   Glenlee, a Clyde-built sailing ship, is berthed alongside
St Mungo Museum of Religious Art and Life, Castle Street G4 0RH
   T 0141-276 1625 **W** www.glasgowlife.org.uk/museums
   Exhibits detailing the world's major religions; oldest Zen
   garden in Britain

NORTHERN IRELAND
* Members of National Museums Northern Ireland, a public
body sponsored by the Department for Communities,
Northern Ireland executive.

ARMAGH
*Armagh County Museum, The Mall East BT61 9BE
   T 028-3752 3070 **W** www.nimc.co.uk
   Local history; fine art; archaeology; crafts
BANGOR
North Down Museum, Town Hall BT20 4BT **T** 028-9127 1200
   W www.andculture.org.uk
   Local history from the Bronze age to the present
BELFAST
Titanic Belfast, Queen's Road, Titanic Quarter BT3 9EP
   T 028-9076 6386 **W** www.titanicbelfast.com
   The story of RMS *Titanic* from her conception to demise;
   Shipyard ride and ocean exploration centre
*Ulster Museum, Botanic Gardens BT9 5AB **T** 0289-044 0000
   W www.nmni.com/um
   Irish antiquities; natural and local history; fine and applied
   arts
*W5, Queen's Quay BT3 9QQ **T** 028-9046 7700
   W www.w5online.co.uk
   Interactive science and technology centre
HOLYWOOD
*Ulster Folk and Transport Museum, Cultra BT18 0EU
   T 028-9042 8428 **W** www.nmni.com/uftm
   Open-air museum with original buildings from Ulster
   town and rural life *c.*1900; indoor galleries including Irish
   rail and road transport
LONDONDERRY
The Tower Museum, Union Hall Place BT48 6LU **T** 028-7137 2411
   W www.derrystrabane.com/towermuseum
   Tells the story of Ireland through the history of
   Londonderry
NEWTOWNARDS
The Somme Heritage Centre, Bangor Road BT23 7PH
   T 028-9182 3202 **W** www.sommeassociation.com
   Commemorates the part played by Irish forces in the First
   World War
OMAGH
*Ulster American Folk Park, Castletown, Co. Tyrone BT78 5QU
   T 028-8224 3292 **W** www.nmni.com/uafp
   Open-air museum telling the story of Ulster's emigrants to
   America; restored or recreated dwellings and workshops;
   ship and dockside gallery

SIGHTS OF LONDON

For historic buildings, museums and galleries in London, *see* the Historic Buildings and Monuments, and Museums and Galleries sections.

BRIDGES

The bridges over the Thames in London, from east to west, are:

Tower Bridge (268m/880ft by 18m/60ft), architect: Horace Jones, engineer: John Wolfe Barry, opened 1894

London Bridge (262m/860ft by 32m/105ft), original 13th-century stone bridge rebuilt and opened 1831 (engineer: John Rennie), reconstructed in Arizona when current London Bridge opened 1973 (architect: Lord Holford, engineer: Mott, Hay and Anderson)

Cannon Street Railway Bridge (261m/855ft), engineers: John Hawkshaw and John Wolfe Barry, originally named Alexandra Bridge, opened 1866; renovated 1979–82

Southwark Bridge (244m/800ft by 17m/56ft), engineer: John Rennie, originally named Queen Street Bridge, opened 1819; rebuilt 1912–21 (architect: Ernest George, engineer: Mott, Hay and Anderson)

Millennium Bridge (325m/1,066ft by 4m/13ft), architect: Foster and Partners, engineer: Ove Arup and Partners, opened 2000; reopened after modification 2002

Blackfriars Railway Bridge (284m/933ft), engineers: John Wolfe Barry and Henri Marc Brunel, originally named St Paul's Railway Bridge, opened 1886

Blackfriars Bridge (294m/963ft by 32m/105ft), engineer: Robert Mylne, opened 1769; rebuilt 1869 (engineer: Joseph Cubitt); widened 1909

Waterloo Bridge (366m/1,200ft by 24m/80ft), engineer: John Rennie, opened 1817; rebuilt 1945 (architect: Sir Giles Gilbert Scott, engineer: Rendel, Palmer and Triton)

Golden Jubilee Bridges (325m/1,066ft by 4.7m/15ft), architect: Lifschutz Davidson, engineer: WSP Group, opened 2002; commonly known as the Hungerford Footbridges

Hungerford Railway Bridge (366m/1,200ft), engineer: Isambard Kingdom Brunel, suspension bridge opened 1845; present railway bridge opened 1864 (engineer: John Hawkshaw); widened in 1886

Westminster Bridge (228m/748ft by 26m/85ft), engineer: Charles Labelye, opened 1750; rebuilt 1862 (architect: Charles Barry, engineer: Thomas Page)

Lambeth Bridge (237m/776ft by 18m/60ft), engineer: Peter W. Barlow, original suspension bridge opened 1862; current structure opened 1932 (architect: Reginald Blomfield, engineer: George W. Humphreys)

Vauxhall Bridge (231m/759ft by 24m/80ft), engineer: James Walker, opened 1816; redesigned and opened 1906 (architect: William Edward Riley, engineers: Alexander Binnie and Maurice Fitzmaurice)

Grosvenor Railway Bridge (213m/699ft), engineer: John Fowler, opened 1860; rebuilt 1965; also known as the Victoria Railway Bridge

Chelsea Bridge (213m/699ft by 25m/83ft), original suspension bridge opened 1858 (engineer: Thomas Page); rebuilt 1937 (architects: George Topham Forrest and E. P. Wheeler, engineer: Rendel, Palmer and Triton)

Albert Bridge (216m/710ft by 12m/40ft), engineer: Rowland M. Ordish, opened 1873; restructured 1884 (engineer: Joseph Bazalgette); strengthened 1971–3

Battersea Bridge (204m/670ft by 17m/56ft), engineer: Henry Holland, opened 1771; rebuilt 1890 (engineer: Joseph Bazalgette)

Battersea Railway Bridge (204m/670ft), engineer: William Baker, opened 1863; also known as Cremorne Bridge

Wandsworth Bridge (189m/619ft by 18m/60ft), engineer: Julian Tolmé, opened 1873; rebuilt 1940 (architect: E. P. Wheeler, engineer: T. Pierson Frank)

Putney Railway Bridge (229m/750ft), engineers: W. H. Thomas and William Jacomb, opened 1889; also known as the Fulham Railway Bridge or the Iron Bridge – it has no official name

Putney Bridge (213m/699ft by 23m/74ft), architect: Jacob Ackworth, original wooden bridge opened 1729; current granite structure completed in 1886 (engineer: Joseph Bazalgette). The starting point of the Boat Race

Hammersmith Bridge (210m/688ft by 10m/33ft), engineer: William Tierney Clarke; the first suspension bridge in London, originally built 1827; rebuilt 1887 (engineer: Joseph Bazalgette)

Barnes Railway Bridge (also footbridge, 110m/360ft), engineer: Joseph Locke, opened 1849; rebuilt 1895 (engineers: London and South Western Railway); the original structure stands unused

Chiswick Bridge (137m/450ft by 21m/70ft), architect: Herbert Baker, engineer: Alfred Dryland, opened 1933. The bridge marks the end point of the Boat Race

Kew Railway Bridge (175m/575ft), engineer: W. R. Galbraith, opened 1869

Kew Bridge (110m/360ft by 17m/56ft), engineer: Robert Tunstall, original timber bridge built 1759; replaced by a Portland stone structure in 1789 (engineer: James Paine); current granite bridge renamed King Edward VII Bridge in 1903, but still known as Kew Bridge (engineers: John Wolfe Barry and Cuthbert Brereton)

Richmond Lock (91m/300ft by 11m/36ft), engineer: F. G. M. Stoney, lock and footbridge opened 1894

Twickenham Bridge (85m/280ft by 21m/70ft), architect: Maxwell Ayrton, engineer: Alfred Dryland, opened 1933

Richmond Railway Bridge (91m/300ft), engineer: Joseph Locke, opened 1848; rebuilt 1906–8 (engineer: J. W. Jacomb-Hood)

Richmond Bridge (85m/280ft by 10m/33ft), architect: James Paine, engineer: Kenton Couse, built 1777; widened 1939

Teddington Lock (198m/650ft), engineer: G. Pooley, two footbridges opened 1889; marks the end of the tidal reach of the Thames

Kingston Railway Bridge architects: J. E. Errington and W. R. Galbraith, engineer: Thomas Brassey, opened 1863

Kingston Bridge (116m/382ft), engineer: Edward Lapidge, built 1825–8; widened 1911–14 (engineers: Basil Mott and David Hay) and 1999–2001

Hampton Court Bridge, engineers: Samuel Stevens and Benjamin Ludgator, built 1753; replaced by iron bridge 1865; present bridge opened 1933 (architect: Edwin Lutyens, engineer: W. P. Robinson)

CEMETERIES

In 1832, in response to the overcrowding of burial grounds in London, the government authorised the establishment of seven non-denominational cemeteries that would encircle the city. These large cemeteries, known as the 'magnificent seven', were seen by many Victorian families as places in which to demonstrate their wealth and stature, and as a result there are some highly ornate graves and tombs.

THE MAGNIFICENT SEVEN

Abney Park, Stoke Newington, N16 (13ha/32 acres), established 1840; tomb of William and Catherine Booth, founders of the Salvation Army, and memorials to many nonconformists and dissenters

Brompton, Old Brompton Road, SW10 (16.5ha/40 acres), established 1840; graves of Sir Henry Cole, Emmeline Pankhurst, John Wisden

Highgate, Swains Lane, N6 (15ha/38 acres), established 1839; graves of Douglas Adams, George Eliot, Eric Hobsbawm, Michael Faraday, Karl Marx, Ralph Miliband and Christina Rossetti

Kensal Green, Harrow Road, W10 (29ha/72 acres), established 1833; tombs of Charles Babbage, Isambard Kingdom Brunel, Wilkie Collins, George Cruikshank, Tom Hood, Leigh Hunt, Harold Pinter, William Makepeace Thackeray, Anthony Trollope

Nunhead, Linden Grove, SE15 (21ha/52 acres), established 1840; closed in 1969, restored and opened for burials

Tower Hamlets, Southern Grove, E3 (11ha/27 acres), established 1841, 350,000 interments; bombed heavily during the Second World War and closed to burials in 1966; now a nature reserve

West Norwood Cemetery and Crematorium, Norwood High Street, SE27 (17ha/42 acres), established 1837; tombs of C. W. Alcock, Mrs Beeton, Sir Henry Tate and Joseph Whitaker *(Whitaker's Almanack)*

OTHER CEMETERIES

Bunhill Fields, City Road, EC1 (1.6ha/4 acres), 17th-century nonconformist burial ground containing the graves of William Blake, John Bunyan and Daniel Defoe

City of London Cemetery and Crematorium, Aldersbrook Road, E12 (81ha/200 acres), established 1856; grave of Bobby Moore

Golders Green Crematorium, Hoop Lane, NW11 (5ha/12 acres), established 1902; retains the ashes of Kingsley Amis, Lionel Bart, Enid Blyton, Marc Bolan, Sigmund Freud, Keith Moon, Ivor Novello, Bram Stoker and H. G. Wells

Hampstead, Fortune Green Road, NW6 (10.5ha/26 acres), established 1876; graves of Alan Coren, Kate Greenaway, Joseph Lister and Marie Lloyd

MARKETS

Billingsgate, Trafalgar Way, E14 (fish), a market site for over 1,000 years, with the Lower Thames Street site dating from 1876; moved to the Isle of Dogs in 1982; owned and run by the City of London Corporation

Borough, Southwark Street, SE1 (vegetables, fruit, meat, dairy, bread), established on present site in 1756; privately owned and run

Brick Lane, E1 (jewellery, vintage clothes, bric-a-brac, food), open Saturday and Sunday

Brixton, SW9 (African-Caribbean food, music, clothing), open Monday to Saturday

Broadway, E8 (food, fashion, crafts), re-established in 2004, open Saturday

Camden Lock, NW1 (second-hand clothing, jewellery, alternative fashion, crafts), established in 1973

Columbia Road, E2 (flowers), dates from 19th century; became dedicated flower market in the 20th century

Covent Garden, WC2 (antiques, handicrafts, jewellery, clothing, food), originally a fruit and vegetable market (*see* New Covent Garden market); it has been trading in its current form since 1980

Grays, Davies Street, W1K (antiques), indoor market in listed building, established 1977

Greenwich, SE10 (crafts, fashion, food), market revived in the 1980s

Leadenhall, Gracechurch Street, EC3V (meat, poultry, cheese, clothing), site of market since 14th century; present hall built 1881; owned and run by the City of London Corporation

New Covent Garden, SW8 (wholesale vegetables, fruit, flowers), established in 1670 under a charter of Charles II; relocated from central London in 1974

New Spitalfields, E10 (vegetables, fruit), established 1682, modernised 1928, moved out of the City to Leyton in 1991, open Monday to Saturday

Old Spitalfields, E1 (arts, crafts, books, clothes, organic food, antiques), continues to trade on the original Spitalfields site on Commercial Street

Petticoat Lane, Middlesex Street, E1, a market has existed on the site for over 500 years, now a Sunday morning market selling almost anything

Portobello Road, W11, originally for herbs and horse-trading from 1870; became famous for antiques after the closure of the Caledonian Market in 1948

Smithfield, EC1 (meat, poultry), built 1866–8, refurbished 1993–4; the site of St Bartholomew's Fair from 12th to 19th century; owned and run by the City of London Corporation, open Monday to Friday

MONUMENTS

CENOTAPH

Whitehall, SW1. The Cenotaph (from the Greek meaning 'empty tomb') was built to commemorate 'The Glorious Dead' and is a memorial to all ranks of the sea, land and air forces who gave their lives in the service of the Empire during the First World War. Designed by Sir Edwin Lutyens and constructed in plaster as a temporary memorial in 1919, it was replaced by a permanent structure of Portland stone and unveiled by George V on 11 November 1920, Armistice Day. An additional inscription was made in 1946 to commemorate those who gave their lives in the Second World War

FOURTH PLINTH

Trafalgar Square, WC2. The fourth plinth (1841) was designed for an equestrian statue that was never built due to lack of funds. From 1999 temporary works have been displayed on the plinth including *Ecce Homo* (Mark Wallinger), *Monument* (Rachel Whiteread), *Alison Lapper Pregnant* (Marc Quinn) and *One & Other* (Antony Gormley). Since March 2018 *The Invisible Enemy Should Not Exist* (Michael Rakowitz) a recreation of the Lamassu, a winged bull and protective deity that stood at the entrance to the Nergal Gate of Nineveh from *c.*700 BC until it was destroyed by Islamic State in 2015, has occupied the plinth. The Lamassu is made from 10,500 empty Iraqi date syrup cans, representing a once-renowned industry now decimated by war. In 2020 it will be replaced by *The End* (Heather Phillipson); a sculpture portraying a giant dollop of cream upon which sits a fly, a cherry and a drone that will film Trafalgar Square from above

LONDON MONUMENT

(Commonly called the Monument), Monument Street, EC3. Built to designs by Sir Christopher Wren and Robert Hooke between 1671 and 1677, the Monument commemorates the Great Fire of London, which broke out in Pudding Lane on 2 September 1666. The fluted Doric column is 36.6m

(120ft) high, the moulded cylinder above the balcony supporting a flaming vase of gilt bronze is an additional 12.8m (42ft), and the column is based on a square plinth 12.2m (40ft) high (with fine carvings on the west face), making a total height of 61.6m (202ft) – the tallest isolated stone column in the world, with views of London from a gallery at the top (311 steps)

OTHER MONUMENTS

(sculptor's name in parentheses):

7 July Memorial (Carmody Groarke), Hyde Park
Afghanistan and Iraq War Memorial (Day), Victoria Embankment
African and Caribbean War Memorial, Windrush Square, Brixton
Viscount Alanbrooke (Roberts-Jones), Whitehall
Albert Memorial (Scott), Kensington Gore
Battle of Britain (Day), Victoria Embankment
Beatty (Wheeler), Trafalgar Square
Belgian Gratitude (setting by Blomfield, statue by Rousseau), Victoria Embankment
Boadicea (or *Boudicca*), *Queen of the Iceni* (Thornycroft), Westminster Bridge
Brunel (Marochetti), Victoria Embankment
Burghers of Calais (Rodin), Victoria Tower Gardens, Westminster
Burns (Steell), Embankment Gardens
Canada Memorial (Granche), Green Park
Carlyle (Boehm), Chelsea Embankment
Cavalry (Jones), Hyde Park
Edith Cavell (Frampton), St Martin's Place
Charles I (Le Sueur), Trafalgar Square
Charles II (Gibbons), Royal Hospital, Chelsea
Churchill (Roberts-Jones), Parliament Square
Cleopatra's Needle (20.9m/68.5ft high, *c.*1500 BC, erected in London in 1878; the sphinxes are Victorian), Thames Embankment
Clive (Tweed), King Charles Street
Captain Cook (Brock), The Mall
Oliver Cromwell (Thornycroft), outside Westminster Hall
Cunningham (Belsky), Trafalgar Square
Gen. Charles de Gaulle (Conner), Carlton Gardens
Diana, Princess of Wales Memorial Fountain (Gustafson Porter), Hyde Park
Disraeli, Earl of Beaconsfield (Raggi), Parliament Square
Duke of Cambridge (Jones), Whitehall
Duke of York (37.8m/124ft column, with statue by Westmacott), Carlton House Terrace
Edward VII (Mackennal), Waterloo Place
Elizabeth I (Kerwin, 1586, oldest outdoor statue in London; from Ludgate), Fleet Street
Eros (Shaftesbury Memorial) (Gilbert), Piccadilly Circus
Lord Dowding (Winter), Strand
Millicent Fawcett (Wearing), Parliament Square
Marechal/Marshall Foch (Mallisard, copy of one in Cassel, France), Grosvenor Gardens
Charles James Fox (Westmacott), Bloomsbury Square
Yuri Gagarin (Novikov, copy of Russian statue), The Mall
Mahatma Gandhi (Jackson), Parliament Square
George III (Cotes Wyatt), Cockspur Street
George IV (Chantrey), Trafalgar Square
George V (Reid Dick and Scott), Old Palace Yard
George VI (McMillan), Carlton Gardens
Gladstone (Thornycroft), Strand
Guards' (Crimea; Bell), Waterloo Place
Guards Division (Ledward, figures, Bradshaw, cenotaph), Horse Guards' Parade
Haig (Hardiman), Whitehall
Sir Arthur (Bomber) Harris (Winter), Strand
Gen. Henry Havelock (Behnes), Trafalgar Square
International Brigades Memorial (Spanish Civil War) (Ian Walters), Jubilee Gardens, South Bank

Irving (Brock), north side of National Portrait Gallery
Isis (Gudgeon), Hyde Park
James II (Gibbons), Trafalgar Square
Jellicoe (McMillan), Trafalgar Square
Samuel Johnson (Fitzgerald), opposite St Clement Danes
Kitchener (Tweed), Horse Guards' Parade
Abraham Lincoln (Saint-Gaudens, copy of one in Chicago), Parliament Square
Mandela (Walters), Parliament Square
Milton (Montford), St Giles, Cripplegate
Mountbatten (Belsky), Foreign Office Green
Gen. Charles James Napier (Adams), Trafalgar Square
Nelson (Railton), Trafalgar Square, with Landseer's lions (cast from guns recovered from the wreck of the *Royal George)*
Florence Nightingale (Walker), Waterloo Place
Palmerston (Woolner), Parliament Square
Sir Keith Park (Johnson), Waterloo Place
Peel (Noble), Parliament Square
Pitt (Chantrey), Hanover Square
Portal (Nemon), Embankment Gardens
Prince Albert (Bacon), Holborn Circus
Queen Elizabeth Gate (Lund and Wynne), Hyde Park Corner
Queen Mother (Jackson), Carlton Gardens
Raleigh (McMillan), Greenwich
Richard I (Coeur de Lion) (Marochetti), Old Palace Yard
Roberts (Bates), Horse Guards' Parade
Franklin D. Roosevelt (Reid Dick), Grosvenor Square
Royal Air Force (Blomfield), Victoria Embankment
Royal Air Force Bomber Command Memorial (O'Connor), Green Park
Royal Artillery (Great War) (Jagger and Pearson), Hyde Park Corner
Royal Artillery (South Africa) (Colton), The Mall
Captain Scott (Lady Scott), Waterloo Place
Shackleton (Jagger), Kensington Gore
Shakespeare (Fontana, copy of one by Scheemakers in Westminster Abbey), Leicester Square
Smuts (Epstein), Parliament Square
Sullivan (Goscombe John), Victoria Embankment
Trenchard (McMillan), Victoria Embankment
Victoria Memorial (Webb and Brock), in front of Buckingham Palace
Raoul Wallenberg (Jackson), Great Cumberland Place
George Washington (Houdon copy), Trafalgar Square
Wellington (Boehm), Hyde Park Corner
Wellington (Chantrey), outside Royal Exchange
John Wesley (Adams Acton), City Road
Westminster School (Crimea) (Scott), Broad Sanctuary
William III (Bacon), St James's Square
Wolseley (Goscombe John), Horse Guards' Parade

PARKS, GARDENS AND OPEN SPACES

CITY OF LONDON CORPORATION OPEN SPACES

W www.cityoflondon.gov.uk

Ashtead Common (202ha/500 acres), Surrey
Burnham Beeches and *Fleet Wood* (220ha/540 acres), Bucks. Acquired by the City of London for the benefit of the public in 1880, Fleet Wood (26ha/65 acres) being presented in 1921
Coulsdon Common (51ha/127 acres), Surrey
Epping Forest (2,476ha/6,118 acres), Essex. Acquired by the City of London in 1878 and opened to the public in 1882. The Queen Elizabeth Hunting Lodge, built for Henry VIII in 1543, lies at the edge of the forest. The present forest is 19.3km (12 miles) long by around 3km (2 miles) wide, approximately one-tenth of its original area
Epping Forest Buffer Land (735ha/1,816 acres), Waltham Abbey/Epping

Farthing Downs and New Hill (95ha/235 acres), Surrey
Hampstead Heath (275ha/680 acres), NW3. Including Golders Hill (15ha/36 acres) and Parliament Hill (110ha/271 acres)
Highgate Wood (28ha/70 acres), N6/N10
Kenley Common (56ha/139 acres), Surrey
Queen's Park (12ha/30 acres), NW6
Riddlesdown (43ha/104 acres), Surrey
Spring Park (20ha/50 acres), Kent
Stoke Common (80ha/198 acres), Bucks. Ownership was transferred to the City of London in 2007
West Ham Park (31ha/77 acres), E15
West Wickham Common (10ha/26 acres), Kent
  Also over 150 smaller open spaces within the City of London, including *Finsbury Circus* and *St Dunstan-in-the-East*
* Includes Copped Hall Park, Woodredon Estate and Warlies Park

OTHER PARKS AND GARDENS

CHELSEA PHYSIC GARDEN, 66 Royal Hospital Road SW3 4HS **T** 020-7352 5646 **W** www.chelseaphysicgarden.co.uk
  A garden of general botanical research and education, maintaining a wide range of rare and unusual plants; established in 1673 by the Society of Apothecaries
HAMPTON COURT PARK AND GARDENS (328ha/810 acres), Surrey KT8 9AU **T** 0844-482 7777 **W** www.hrp.org.uk
  Also known as Home Park, the park lies beyond the palace's formal gardens. It contains a herd of deer and a 750-year-old oak tree from the original park
HOLLAND PARK (22.5ha/54 acres), Ilchester Place W8 **T** 020-7361 3000 **W** www.rbkc.gov.uk
  The largest park in the Royal Borough of Kensington and Chelsea, includes the Kyoto Garden
KEW, ROYAL BOTANIC GARDENS (120ha/300 acres), Richmond, Surrey TW9 3AB **T** 020-8332 5655 **W** www.kew.org
  Founded in 1759 and declared a UNESCO World Heritage Site in 2003
THAMES BARRIER PARK (9ha/22acres), North Woolwich Road E16 2HP **T** 020-7476 3741 Opened in 2000, landscaped gardens with spectacular views of the Thames Barrier

ROYAL PARKS

W www.royalparks.org.uk
Bushy Park (450ha/1,099 acres), Middx. Adjoins Hampton Court; contains an avenue of horse-chestnuts enclosed in a fourfold avenue of limes planted by William III
Green Park (19ha/47 acres), W1. Between Piccadilly and St James's Park, with Constitution Hill leading to Hyde Park Corner
Greenwich Park (74ha/183 acres), SE10. Enclosed by Humphrey, Duke of Gloucester, and laid out by Charles II from the designs of Le Nôtre. On a hill in Greenwich Park is the Royal Observatory (founded 1675). Its buildings are now managed by the National Maritime Museum (**T** 020-8858 4422 **W** www.rmg.co.uk) and the earliest building is named Flamsteed House, after John Flamsteed (1646–1719), the first astronomer royal
Hyde Park (142ha/350 acres), W1/W2. From Park Lane to Kensington Gardens and incorporating the Serpentine lake, Apsley House, the Achilles Statue, Rotten Row and the Ladies' Mile; fine gateway at Hyde Park Corner. To the north-east is Marble Arch, originally erected by George IV at the entrance to Buckingham Palace and re-erected in the present position in 1851. At Hyde Park Corner stands Wellington Arch, built in 1825–7, it opened to the public in 2012 following major renovation
Kensington Gardens (107ha/265 acres), W2/W8. From the western boundary of Hyde Park to Kensington Palace; contains the Albert Memorial, Serpentine Gallery, Diana, Princess of Wales' Memorial Playground and the Peter Pan statue

The Regent's Park and *Primrose Hill* (197ha/487 acres), NW1. From Marylebone Road to Primrose Hill surrounded by the Outer Circle; divided by the Broad Walk leading to the Zoological Gardens
Richmond Park (1,000ha/2,500 acres), Surrey. Designated a National Nature Reserve, a Site of Special Scientific Interest and a Special Area of Conservation
St James's Park (23ha/57 acres), SW1. From Whitehall to Buckingham Palace; ornamental lake of 4.9ha (12 acres); the Mall leads from Admiralty Arch to Buckingham Palace

PLACES OF HISTORICAL AND CULTURAL INTEREST

1 Canada Square
  Canary Wharf E14 5AB **T** 020-7418 2000
  W www.canarywharf.com
  Also known as 'Canary Wharf', the steel and glass skyscraper is designed to sway 35cm in the strongest winds
20 Fenchurch Street
  W https://skygarden.london
  Designed by architect Rafael Viñoly the skyscraper was completed in March 2014. The top three storeys are home to the Sky Garden, London's highest public garden with viewing platforms, bars, restaurants and an open air terrace. Access to the Sky Garden is free, but tickets must be booked in advance
30 St Mary Axe
  EC3A 8BF **W** www.30stmaryaxe.com
  Completed in 2004 and commonly known as the 'Gherkin', each of the floors rotates five degrees from the one below
122 Leadenhall Street
  EC3V 4AB **T** 020-7220 8950 **W** www.theleadenhallbuilding.com
  The distinctive 225m (737ft) asymmetrical Leadenhall Building, designed by architects Rogers Stirk Harbour & Partners, was completed in 2014
Alexandra Palace
  Alexandra Palace Way N22 7AY **T** 020-8365 2121
  W www.alexandrapalace.com
  The Victorian palace was severely damaged by fire in 1980 but was restored, and reopened in 1988. Alexandra Palace now provides modern facilities for exhibitions, conferences, banquets and leisure activities. There is a winter ice rink, a boating lake and a conservation area. Restoration of the east wing and Victorian theatre was completed in 2018
Barbican Centre
  Silk Street EC2Y 8DS **T** 020-7638 4141 **W** www.barbican.org.uk
  Owned, funded and managed by the City of London Corporation, the Barbican Centre opened in 1982 and houses the Barbican Theatre, a studio theatre called The Pit and the Barbican Hall; it is also home to the London Symphony Orchestra. There are three cinemas, six conference rooms, two art galleries, a sculpture court, a lending library, trade and banqueting facilities and a conservatory
British Library
  St Pancras, 96 Euston Road NW1 2DB **T** 0330-333 1144
  W www.bl.uk
  The largest building constructed in the UK in the 20th century with basements extending 24.5m underground. Holdings include the *Magna Carta*, the Gutenburg Bible, Shakespeare's First Folio, Beatles manuscripts and the first edition of *The Times* from 1788. Holds temporary exhibitions on a range of topics

Central Criminal Court
Old Bailey EC4M 7EH **T** 020-7192 2739
W www.cityoflondon.gov.uk
The highest criminal court in the UK, the 'Old Bailey' is located on the site of the old Newgate Prison. Trials held here have included those of Oscar Wilde, Dr Crippen and the Yorkshire Ripper. The courthouse has been rebuilt several times since 1674; Edward VII officially opened the current neo-baroque building in 1907

Charterhouse
Charterhouse Square EC1M 6AN **T** 020-7253 9503
W www.thecharterhouse.org
A Carthusian monastery from 1371 to 1538, purchased in 1611 by Thomas Sutton, who endowed it as a residence for aged men 'of gentle birth' and a school for poor scholars (removed to Godalming in 1872)

Downing Street
SW1A 2AA **W** www.number10.gov.uk
Number 10 Downing Street is the official town residence of the prime minister and number 11 of the Chancellor of the Exchequer. The street was named after Sir George Downing, Bt., soldier and diplomat, who was MP for Morpeth 1660–84

George Inn
The George Inn Yard SE1 1NH **T** 020-7407 2056
W www.nationaltrust.org.uk/george-inn
The last galleried inn in London, built in 1677. Now owned by the National Trust and run as an ordinary public house

Horse Guards
Whitehall SW1
Archway and offices built about 1753. The changing of the guard takes place daily at 11am (10am on Sundays) and the inspection at 4pm. Only those with the Queen's permission may drive through the gates and archway into *Horse Guards Parade*, where the colour is 'trooped' on the Queen's official birthday

HOUSES OF PARLIAMENT
T 020-7219 3000 **W** www.parliament.uk
House of Commons, Westminster SW1A 0AA
House of Lords, Westminster SW1A 0PW
The royal palace of Westminster, originally built by Edward the Confessor, was the normal meeting place of Parliament from about 1340. St Stephen's Chapel was used from about 1550 for the meetings of the House of Commons, which had previously been held in the Chapter House or Refectory of Westminster Abbey. The House of Lords met in an apartment of the royal palace. The fire of 1834 destroyed much of the palace, and the present Houses of Parliament were erected on the site from the designs of Sir Charles Barry and Augustus Welby Pugin between 1840 and 1867. The chamber of the House of Commons was destroyed by bombing in 1941, and a new chamber designed by Sir Giles Gilbert Scott was used for the first time in 1950. *Westminster Hall and the Crypt Chapel* was the only part of the old palace of Westminster to survive the fire of 1834. It was built by William II from 1097 to 1099 and altered by Richard II between 1394 and 1399. The hammerbeam roof of carved oak dates from 1396–8. The Hall was the scene of the trial of Charles I. *The Victoria Tower* of the House of Lords is 98.5m (323ft) high and *The Elizabeth Tower* of the House of Commons is 96.3m (316ft) high and contains 'Big Ben', the hour bell said to be named after Sir Benjamin Hall, First Commissioner of Works when the original bell was cast in 1856. This bell, which weighed 16 tons 11 cwt, was found to be cracked in 1857. The present bell (13.5 tons) is a recasting of the original and was first brought into use in 1859. The dials of the clock are 7m (23ft) in diameter, the hands being 2.7m (9ft) and 4.3m (14ft) long (including balance piece).

During session, tours of the Houses of Parliament are only available to UK residents who have made advance arrangements through an MP or peer. Overseas visitors are no longer provided with permits to tour the Houses of Parliament during session, although they can tour on Saturdays and during the summer opening and attend debates for both houses in the Strangers' Galleries. During the summer recess, tickets for tours of the Houses of Parliament can be booked online, by telephone (**T** 020-7219 4114) or bought on site at the ticket office located at the front of Portcullis House SW1A 2LW. The Strangers' Gallery of the House of Commons is open to the public when the house is sitting. To acquire tickets in advance, UK residents should write to their local MP and overseas visitors should apply to their embassy or high commission in the UK for a permit. If none of these arrangements has been made, visitors should join the public queue outside St Stephen's Entrance, where there is also a queue for entry to the House of Lords Gallery

INNS OF COURT
The Inns of Court are ancient unincorporated bodies of lawyers which for more than five centuries have had the power to call to the Bar those of their members who have qualified for the rank or degree of Barrister-at-Law. There are four Inns of Court as well as many lesser inns:

Lincoln's Inn, WC2A 3TL **T** 020-7405 1393
W www.lincolnsinn.org.uk
The most ancient of the inns with records dating back to 1422. The hall and library buildings are from 1845, although the library is first mentioned in 1474; the old hall (late 15th century) and the chapel were rebuilt *c.*1619–23

Inner Temple, King's Bench Walk EC4Y 7HL **T** 020-7797 8250
W www.innertemple.org.uk
Middle Temple, Middle Temple Lane EC4Y 9BT
T 020-7427 4800 **W** www.middletemple.org.uk
Records for the Inner and Middle Temple date back to the beginning of the 16th century. The site was originally occupied by the Order of Knights Templar *c.*1160–1312. The two inns have separate halls thought to have been formed *c.*1350. The division between the two societies was formalised in 1732 with Temple Church and the Masters House remaining in common. The Inner Temple Garden is normally open to the public on weekdays between 12.30pm and 3pm

Temple Church, EC4Y 7BB **T** 020-7353 8559
W www.templechurch.com
The nave forms one of five remaining round churches in England

Gray's Inn, South Square WC1R 5ET **T** 020-7458 7800
W www.graysinn.info
Founded early 14th century; hall 1556–8
No other 'Inns' are active, but there are remains of *Staple Inn*, a gabled front on Holborn (opposite Gray's Inn Road). *Clement's Inn* (near St Clement Danes Church), *Clifford's Inn*, Fleet Street, and *Thavies Inn*, Holborn Circus, are all rebuilt. *Serjeants' Inn*, Fleet Street, and another (demolished 1910) of the same name in Chancery Lane, were composed of Serjeants-at-Law, the last of whom died in 1922

Institute of Contemporary Arts
The Mall SW1Y 5AH **T** 020-7930 3647 **W** www.ica.art
Exhibitions of modern art in the fields of film, theatre, new media and the visual arts

Lloyd's
Lime Street EC3M 7HA **T** 020-7327 1000 **W** www.lloyds.com
International insurance market which evolved during the 17th century from Lloyd's Coffee House. The present

building was opened for business in May 1986, and houses the Lutine Bell. Underwriting is on three floors with a total area of 10,591 sq. m (114,000 sq. ft). The Lloyd's building is not open to the general public

London Central Mosque and the Islamic Cultural Centre
Park Road NW8 7RG **T** 020-7725 2152 **W** www.iccuk.org
The focus for London's Muslims; established in 1944 but not completed until 1977, the mosque can accommodate about 5,000 worshippers; guided tours are available

London Eye
South Bank SE1 7PB **W** www.londoneye.com
Opened in March 2000 as London's millennium landmark, this 137m (450ft) observation wheel is the tallest cantilevered observation wheel in the world. The wheel provides a 30-minute ride offering panoramic views of the capital

London Zoo
Regent's Park NW1 4RY **T** 0344-225 1826 **W** www.zsl.org
Opened in 1828 by the Zoological Society of London (ZSL) to house an array of exotic and endangered animals with an emphasis on scientific research and conservation

Madame Tussauds
Marylebone Road NW1 5LR **T** 0871-894 3000
W www.madametussauds.com
Waxwork exhibition

Mansion House
Cannon Street EC4N 8BH **T** 020-7626 2500
W www.cityoflondon.gov.uk
The official residence of the Lord Mayor. Built in the 18th century in the Palladian style. Open to groups by appointment only

Marlborough House
Pall Mall SW1Y 5HX **T** 020-7747 6500
W www.thecommonwealth.org
Built by Wren for the first Duke of Marlborough and completed in 1711, the house reverted to the Crown in 1835. In 1863 it became the London house of the Prince of Wales and was the London home of Queen Mary until her death in 1953. In 1959 Marlborough House was given by the Queen as the headquarters for the Commonwealth Secretariat and it was opened as such in 1965. The Queen's Chapel, Marlborough Gate, was begun in 1623 from the designs of Inigo Jones for the Infanta Maria of Spain, and completed for Queen Henrietta Maria. Marlborough House is not open to the public

Neasden Temple
BAPS Shri Swaminarayan Mandir, Brentfield Road, Neasden NW10 8LD **T** 020-8965 2651 **W** http://londonmandir.baps.org
When built, it was the first and largest traditional Hindu Mandir outside of India; opened in 1995

Port of London
Port of London Authority, Royal Pier Road, Kent DA12 2BG
T 01474-562200 **W** www.pla.co.uk
The Port of London covers the tidal section of the river Thames from Teddington to the seaward limit (the outer Tongue buoy and the Sunk light vessel), a distance of 153km (95 miles). The governing body is the Port of London Authority (PLA). Cargo is handled at privately operated riverside terminals between Fulham and Canvey Island, including the enclosed dock at Tilbury, 40km (25 miles) below London Bridge. Passenger vessels and cruise liners can be handled at moorings at Greenwich, Tower Bridge and Tilbury

Queen Elizabeth Olympic Park
Stratford E20 **T** 0800-072 2110
W www.queenelizabetholympicpark.co.uk
Built for the London 2012 Olympic and Paralympic Games, the park, which included the Olympic Stadium,

Velodrome and Aquatics Centre has been redeveloped to provide 227ha (560 acres) of parkland with play areas, outside arts and theatre spaces, waterways and wetlands. The north of the park, which includes the Copper Box Arena sport venue, re-opened to the public in 2013. The south of the park, which re-opened in April 2014, incorporates three venues for arts and sports events and the *ArcelorMittal Orbit,* designed by Sir Anish Kapoor and Cecil Balmond; it is the UK's tallest sculpture (114.5m/376ft) and has two accessible observation floors

Roman Remains
The city wall of Roman *Londinium* was largely rebuilt during the medieval period but sections may be seen near the White Tower in the Tower of London; at Tower Hill; at Coopers' Row; at All Hallows, London Wall, its vestry being built on the remains of a semi-circular Roman bastion; at St Alphage, London Wall, showing a succession of building repairs from the Roman until the late medieval period; and at St Giles, Cripplegate. Sections of the great forum and basilica, more than 165 sq. m (1,776 sq. ft), have been encountered during excavations in the area of Leadenhall, Gracechurch Street and Lombard Street. Traces of Roman activity along the river include a massive riverside wall built in the late Roman period, and a succession of Roman timber quays along Lower and Upper Thames Street. Finds from these sites can be seen at the Museum of London.
Other major buildings are the amphitheatre at Guildhall, remains of bath-buildings in Upper and Lower Thames Street, and the temple of Mithras in Walbrook

Royal Albert Hall
Kensington Gore SW7 2AP **T** 020-7589 3203
W www.royalalberthall.com
The elliptical hall, one of the largest in the world, was completed in 1871; since 1941 it has been the venue each summer for the Promenade Concerts founded in 1895 by Sir Henry Wood. Other events include pop and classical music concerts, dance, opera, sporting events, conferences and banquets

Royal Courts of Justice
Strand WC2A 2LL **T** 020-7947 6000 **W** www.justice.gov.uk
Victorian Gothic building that is home to the high court. Visitors are free to watch proceedings

Royal Hospital, Chelsea
Royal Hospital Road SW3 4SR **T** 020-7881 5200
W www.chelsea-pensioners.co.uk
Founded by Charles II in 1682, and built by Wren; opened in 1692 for old and disabled soldiers. The extensive grounds include the former Ranelagh Gardens and are the venue for the Chelsea Flower Show each May

Royal Naval College
Greenwich SE10 9NN **T** 020-8269 4747 **W** www.ornc.org
The building was the Greenwich Hospital until 1869. It was built by Charles II, largely from designs by John Webb, and by Queen Mary II and William III, from designs by Wren. It stands on the site of an ancient abbey, a royal house and Greenwich Palace, which was constructed by Henry VII. Henry VIII, Mary I and Elizabeth I were born in the royal palace and Edward VI died there. The Painted Hall, designed by Wren, reopened in March 2019 after a major two-year conservation project to restore its vividly painted interior by Sir James Thornhill

Royal Opera House
Covent Garden WC2E 9DD **T** 020-7240 1200 **W** www.roh.org.uk
Home of The Royal Ballet (1931) and The Royal Opera (1946). The Royal Opera House is the third theatre to be built on the site, opening 1858; the first was opened in 1732

St James's Palace
Pall Mall SW1A 1BQ **W** www.royal.uk
Built by Henry VIII, only the Gatehouse and Presence
Chamber remain; later alterations were made by Wren and
Kent. Representatives of foreign powers are still
accredited 'to the Court of St James's'. *Clarence House*
(1825), the official London residence of the Prince of
Wales, stands within the St James's Palace estate

St Paul's Cathedral
St Paul's Churchyard EC4M 8AD **T** 020-7246 8350
W www.stpauls.co.uk
Built 1675–1710. The cross on the dome is 111m (365ft)
above ground level, the inner cupola 66.4m (218ft) above
the floor. 'Great Paul' in the south-west tower weighs
nearly 17 tons. The organ by Father Smith (enlarged by
Willis and rebuilt by Mander) is in a case carved by
Grinling Gibbons, who also carved the choir stalls

Shakespeare's Globe
New Globe Walk SE1 9DT **T** 020-7902 1500
W www.shakespearesglobe.com
Reconstructed in 1997, the open-air playhouse is a unique
resource for the works of William Shakespeare through
performance and education; a new indoor replica Jacobean
theatre staged its first public performance in January 2014

Shard
London Bridge SE1 **T** 0344 449-7222 **W** www.the-shard.com
Completed in May 2012, the skyscraper stands at 310m
(1,016ft) and possesses a unique facade of 11,000 glass
panels and a 360-degree viewing gallery

Somerset House
Strand WC2R 1LA **T** 020-7845 4600
W www.somersethouse.org.uk
The river facade (183m/600ft long) was built in 1776–
1801 from the designs of Sir William Chambers; the
eastern extension, which houses part of King's College,
was built by Smirke in 1829–35. Somerset House was the
property of Lord Protector Somerset, at whose attainder in
1552 the palace passed to the Crown, and it was a royal
residence until 1692. Somerset House has recently
undergone extensive renovation and is home to the
Embankment Galleries and the Courtauld Gallery. Open-
air concerts and ice-skating (Nov–Jan) are held in the
courtyard

SOUTH BANK, SE1
Arts complex on the south bank of the river Thames
which consists of:
BFI Southbank **T** 020-7928 3232 **W** www.bfi.org.uk
Opened in 1952 and administered by the British Film
Institute, which has four auditoria of varying capacities. Venue
for the annual London Film Festival
The *Royal Festival Hall* **T** 020-7960 4200
W www.southbankcentre.co.uk
Opened in 1951 for the Festival of Britain, adjacent are
the *Queen Elizabeth Hall*, the *Purcell Room* and the *Hayward
Gallery*
The *Royal National Theatre*, **T** 020-7452 3000
W www.nationaltheatre.org.uk
Opened in 1976; comprises the Olivier, the Lyttelton and
Dorfman theatres. The Cottesloe Theatre closed in
February 2013 and, following refurbishment reopened in
2014 as the Dorfman Theatre

Southwark Cathedral
London Bridge SE1 9DA **T** 020-7367 6700
W www.cathedral.southwark.anglican.org
Mainly 13th century, but the nave is largely rebuilt. The
tomb of John Gower (1330–1408) is between the Bunyan
and Chaucer memorial windows in the north aisle;
Shakespeare's effigy, backed by a view of Southwark and
the Globe Theatre, is in the south aisle; the tomb of
Bishop Andrewes (*d.* 1626) is near the screen. The Lady
Chapel was the scene of the consistory courts of the reign
of Mary (Gardiner and Bonner) and is still used as a
consistory court. John Harvard, after whom Harvard
University is named, was baptised here in 1607, and the
chapel by the north choir aisle is his memorial chapel

Thames Embankments
Sir Joseph Bazalgette (1819–91) constructed the *Victoria
Embankment*, on the north side from Westminster to
Blackfriars for the Metropolitan Board of Works, 1864–
70 (the seats, of which the supports of some are a
kneeling camel, laden with spicery, and of others a
winged sphinx, were presented by the Grocers' Company
and by W. H. Smith, MP, in 1874); the *Albert Embankment*,
on the south side from Westminster Bridge to Vauxhall,
1866–9, and the Chelsea Embankment, 1871–4. The
total cost exceeded £2m. Bazalgette also inaugurated the
London main drainage system, 1858–65. A medallion
(Flumini vincula posuit) has been placed on a pier of the
Victoria Embankment to commemorate the engineer

Thames Flood Barrier
W www.environment-agency.gov.uk
Officially opened in May 1984, though first used in
February 1983, the barrier consists of ten rising sector
gates which span approximately 520m from bank to bank
of the Thames at Woolwich Reach. When not in use the
gates lie horizontally, allowing shipping to navigate the
river normally; when the barrier is closed, the gates turn
through 90 degrees to stand vertically more than 50 feet
above the river bed. The barrier took eight years to
complete and can be raised within about 90 minutes

Trafalgar Tavern
Park Row, Greenwich SE10 9NW **T** 020-3887 9886
W www.trafalgartavern.co.uk
Regency-period riverside public house built in 1837.
Charles Dickens and William Gladstone were patrons

Wembley Stadium
Wembley HA9 0WS **W** www.wembleystadium.com
The second largest stadium in Europe; hosts major
sporting events and music concerts

Westminster Abbey
SW1P 3PA **T** 020-7222 5152 **W** www.westminster-abbey.org
Founded as a Benedictine monastery over 1,000 years
ago, the church was rebuilt by Edward the Confessor in
1065 and again by Henry III in the 13th century. The
abbey is the resting place for monarchs including Edward
I, Henry III, Henry V, Henry VII, Elizabeth I, Mary I and
Mary, Queen of Scots, and has been the setting of
coronations since that of William the Conqueror in 1066.
In Poets' Corner there are memorials to many literary
figures, and many scientists and musicians are also
remembered here. The grave of the Unknown Warrior is
to be found in the nave

Westminster Cathedral
Francis Street SW1P 1QW **T** 020-7798 9055
W www.westminstercathedral.org.uk
Roman Catholic cathedral built 1895–1903 from the
designs of John Francis Bentley. The campanile is 83m
(273ft) high

Wimbledon All England Lawn Tennis Club
Church Road SW19 5AE **T** 020-8944 1066
W www.wimbledon.com
Venue for the Wimbledon Championships. Includes the
Wimbledon Lawn Tennis Museum

HALLMARKS

Hallmarks are the symbols stamped on gold, silver, palladium or platinum articles to indicate that they have been tested at an official Assay Office and that they conform to one of the legal standards. The marking of gold and silver articles to identify the maker was instituted in England in 1363 under a statute of Edward III. In 1478 the Assay Office in Goldsmiths' Hall was established and all gold and silversmiths were required to bring their wares to be date-marked by the Hall, hence the term 'hallmarked'.

With certain exceptions, all gold, silver, palladium or platinum articles are required by law to be hallmarked before they are offered for sale. Current hallmarking requirements come under the UK Hallmarking Act 1973 and subsequent amendments. The act is built around the principle of description, where it is an offence for any person to apply to an unhallmarked article a description indicating that it is wholly or partly made of gold, silver, palladium or platinum. There is an exemption by weight: compulsory hallmarks are not needed on gold and palladium under 1g, silver under 7.78g and platinum under 0.5g. Also, some descriptions, such as rolled gold and gold plate, are permissible. The British Hallmarking Council is a statutory body created as a result of the Hallmarking Act. It ensures adequate provision for assaying and hallmarking, supervises the assay offices and ensures the enforcement of hallmarking legislation. The four assay offices at London, Birmingham, Sheffield and Edinburgh operate under the act.

BRITISH HALLMARKING COUNCIL Secretariat, c/o Shakespeare Martineau, 60 Gracechurch Street, London EC3V 0HR **W** www.gov.uk/government/organisations/british-hallmarking-council

COMPULSORY MARKS

Since January 1999 UK hallmarks have consisted of three compulsory symbols – the sponsor's mark, the millesimal fineness (purity) mark and the assay office mark. The distinction between UK and foreign articles has been removed, and more finenesses are now legal, reflecting the more common finenesses elsewhere in Europe.

SPONSOR'S MARK

Formerly known as the maker's mark, the sponsor's mark was instituted in England in 1363. Originally a device such as a bird or fleur-de-lis, now it consists of a combination of at least two initials (usually a shortened form of the manufacturer's name) and a shield design. The London Assay Office offers 45 standard shield designs but other designs are possible by arrangement.

MILLESIMAL FINENESS MARK

The millesimal fineness (purity) mark indicates the number of parts per thousand of pure metal in the alloy. The current finenesses allowed in the UK are:

Gold	999; 990; 916 (22 carat); 750 (18 carat); 585 (14 carat); 375 (9 carat)
Silver	999; 958 (Britannia); 925 (sterling); 800
Palladium	999; 950; 500
Platinum	999; 950; 900; 850

ASSAY OFFICE MARK

This mark identifies the particular assay office at which the article was tested and marked. The British assay offices are:

 LONDON, Goldsmiths' Hall, Gutter Lane, London EC2V 8AQ **T** 020-7606 8971 **W** www.assayofficelondon.co.uk

 BIRMINGHAM, 1 Moreton Street, Birmingham B1 3AX **T** 0121-236 6951 **W** www.theassayoffice.co.uk

 SHEFFIELD, Guardians' Hall, Beulah Road, Hillsborough, Sheffield S6 2AN **T** 0114-231 2121 **W** www.assayoffice.co.uk

 EDINBURGH, Goldsmiths' Hall, 24 Broughton Street, Edinburgh EH1 3RH **T** 0131-556 1144 **W** www.edinburghassayoffice.co.uk

Assay offices formerly existed in other towns, eg Chester, Exeter, Glasgow, Newcastle, Norwich and York, each having its own distinguishing mark.

OPTIONAL MARKS

Since 1999 traditional pictorial marks such as a crown for gold, the Britannia for 958 silver, the lion passant for 925 Sterling silver (lion rampant in Scotland) and the orb for 950 platinum may be added voluntarily to the millesimal mark. In 2010 a pictorial mark of the Greek goddess Pallas Athene was introduced for 950 palladium.

 Gold – a crown

 Sterling silver (Scotland)

 Britannia silver

 Platinum – an orb

 Sterling silver (England)

 Palladium – the Greek goddess Pallas Athene

DATE LETTER

The date letter shows the year in which an article was assayed and hallmarked. Each alphabetical cycle has a distinctive style of lettering or shape of shield. The date letters were different at the various assay offices and the particular office must be established from the assay office mark before reference is made to tables of date letters. Date letter marks became voluntary from 1 January 1999.

The table which follows shows one specimen shield and letter used by the London Assay Office on silver articles for each alphabetical cycle from 1498. The same letters are found on gold articles but the surrounding shield may differ. Until 1 January 1975, each hallmark covered two calendar years as the letter changed annually in May on St Dunstan's Day (the patron saint of silversmiths). Since 1 January 1975, each date letter has indicated a calendar year from January to December and each office has used the same style of date letter and shield for all articles.

LONDON (GOLDSMITHS' HALL) DATE LETTERS

	from	*to*		*from*	*to*
	1498–9	1517–18		1756–7	1775–6
	1518–19	1537–8		1776–7	1795–6
	1538–9	1557–8		1796–7	1815–16
	1558–9	1577–8		1816–17	1835–6
	1578–9	1597–8		1836–7	1855–6
	1598–9	1617–18		1856–7	1875–6
	1618–19	1637–8		1876–7 (A to M square shield, N to Z as shown)	1895–6
	1638–9	1657–8		1896–7	1915–16
	1658–9	1677–8		1916–17	1935–6
	1678–9	1696–7		1936–7	1955–6
	1697 (from March, 1697 only)	1715–16		1956–7	1974
	1716–17	1735–6		1975	1999
	1736–7	1738–9		2000	
	1739–40	1755–6			

OTHER MARKS

FOREIGN GOODS

Foreign goods imported into the UK are required to be hallmarked before sale, unless they already bear a convention mark or a hallmark struck by an independent assay office in the European Economic Area which is deemed to be equivalent to a UK hallmark.

The following are the assay office marks used for gold imported articles until the end of 1998. For silver and platinum the symbols remain the same but the shields differ in shape.

 London   *Sheffield*

 Birmingham   *Edinburgh*

CONVENTION HALLMARKS

The UK has been a signatory to the International Convention on Hallmarks since 1972. A convention hallmark struck by the UK assay offices is recognised by all member countries in the convention and, similarly, convention marks from member countries are legally recognised in the UK. There are currently 20 members of the hallmarking convention: Austria, Croatia, Cyprus, Czech Republic, Denmark, Finland, Hungary, Ireland, Israel, Latvia, Lithuania, the Netherlands, Norway, Poland, Portugal, Slovakia, Slovenia, Sweden, Switzerland, and the UK.

A convention hallmark comprises four marks: a sponsor's mark, a common control mark, a fineness mark, and an assay office mark.

Examples of common control marks (figures differ according to fineness, but the style of each mark remains the same for each article):

GOLD	SILVER	PALLADIUM	PLATINUM

COMMEMORATIVE MARKS

There are other marks to commemorate special events: the silver jubilee of King George V and Queen Mary in 1935, the coronation of Queen Elizabeth II in 1953, her silver jubilee in 1977, and her golden jubilee in 2002. During 1999 and 2000 there was a voluntary additional Millennium Mark. A mark to commemorate the Queen's diamond jubilee in 2012 was available from July 2011 to October 2012:

BANKING AND FINANCE

BRITISH CURRENCY

The unit of currency is the pound sterling (£) of 100 pence. The decimal system was introduced on 15 February 1971.

COIN

Gold Coins	*Nickel-Brass Coins*
One hundred pounds £100*	Two pounds £2 (pre-1997)ℂ
Fifty pounds £50*	One pound £1
Twenty-five pounds £25*	
Ten pounds £10*	*Cupro-Nickel Coins*
Five pounds £5	Crown £5 (since 1990)ℂ
Two pounds £2	50 pence 50p
Sovereign £1	Crown 25p (pre-1990)ℂ
Half-sovereign 50p	20 pence 20p
Silver Coins	*Nickel-plated Steel Coins***
(Britannia coins)*	10 pence 10p
Two pounds £2	5 pence 5p
One pound £1	
50 pence 50p	*Bronze Coins*
Twenty pence 20p	2 pence 2p
	1 penny 1p
Maundy Money†	
Fourpence 4p	*Copper-plated Steel Coins††*
Threepence 3p	2 pence 2p
Twopence 2p	1 penny 1p
Penny 1p	
Bi-colour Coins‡	
Two pounds £2	
One pound £1§	

* Britannia coins: gold bullion introduced 1987; silver, 1997
† Ceremonial money given annually by the sovereign on Maundy Thursday to as many elderly men and women as there are years in the sovereign's age
‡ Cupro-nickel centre and nickel-brass outer ring
§ The 12-sided £1 entered circulation on 28 March 2017
ℂ Commemorative coins; not intended for general circulation
** Since September 1992; in 1998 the 2p was additionally struck in bronze
†† Pre-2012 the 10p and 5p coins were struck in cupro-nickel

GOLD COIN

Gold ceased to circulate during the First World War. Since then controls on buying, selling and holding gold coin have been imposed at various times but have subsequently been revoked. Under the Exchange Control (Gold Coins Exemption) Order 1979, gold coins may now be imported and exported without restriction, except gold coins which are more than 50 years old and valued at a sum in excess of £8,000.

Value Added Taxation on the sale of gold coins was revoked in 2000.

SILVER COIN

Prior to 1920 silver coins were struck from sterling silver, an alloy of which 925 parts in 1,000 were silver. In 1920 the proportion of silver was reduced to 500 parts. Since 1947 all 'silver' coins, except Maundy money, have been struck from cupro-nickel, an alloy of 75 parts copper and 25 parts nickel, except for the 20p, composed of 84 parts copper, 16 parts nickel. Maundy coins continue to be struck from sterling silver.

BRONZE COIN

Bronze, introduced in 1860 to replace copper, is an alloy consisting mainly of copper with small amounts of zinc and tin. Bronze was replaced by copper-plated steel in September 1992 with the exception of 1998 when the 2p was made in both copper-plated steel and bronze.

LEGAL TENDER *as at May 2019*

	Legal up to
Gold*	any amount
£2	any amount
£1	any amount
50p	£10
20p	£10
10p	£5
5p	£5
2p	20p
1p	20p

* Dated 1838 onwards, if not below least current weight

£5 (Crown since 1990) and 25p (Crown pre-1990) up to £10 are also legal tender under the Coinage Act 1971 but, as for all commemorative coins, are not designed for general circulation and are unlikely to be accepted by banks and shops.

The following coins have ceased to be legal tender:

Farthing	31 Dec 1960
Halfpenny (½d)	31 Jul 1969
Half-crown	31 Dec 1969
Threepence	31 Aug 1971
Penny (1d)	31 Aug 1971
Sixpence	30 Jun 1980
Halfpenny (½p)	31 Dec 1984
Old 5 pence	31 Dec 1990
Old 10 pence	30 Jun 1993
Old 50 pence	28 Feb 1998
Old £1 (nickel-brass/round)	15 Oct 2017

The Channel Islands and the Isle of Man issue their own coinage, which is legal tender only in the island of issue.

COIN STANDARDS

	Metal	Standard weight (g)	Standard diameter (mm)
1p	bronze	3.56	20.30
1p	copper-plated steel	3.56	20.30
2p	bronze	7.12	25.90
2p	copper-plated steel	7.12	25.90
5p	cupro-nickel	3.25	18.00
5p	nickel-plated steel	3.25	18.00
10p	nickel-plated steel	6.50	24.50
20p	cupro-nickel	5.00	21.40
25p Crown	cupro-nickel	28.28	38.61
50p	cupro-nickel	8.00	27.30
£1	nickel-brass, nickel-plated brass alloy	8.75	23.43
£2	nickel-brass	15.98	28.40
£2	nickel-brass, cupro-nickel	12.00	28.40
£5 Crown	cupro-nickel	28.28	38.61

The 'remedy' is the amount of variation from standard permitted in weight and fineness of coins when first issued from the Royal Mint.

THE TRIAL OF THE PYX

The Trial of the Pyx is the examination by a jury to ascertain that coins made by the Royal Mint, which have been set aside in the pyx (or box), are of the proper weight, diameter and composition required by law. The trial is held annually, presided over by the Queen's Remembrancer, with a jury of freemen of the Company of Goldsmiths.

BANKNOTES

Bank of England notes are issued in denominations of £5, £10, £20 and £50 for the amount of the fiduciary note issue, and are legal tender in England and Wales.

LEGAL TENDER

A new-style £20 note, the first in series F, was introduced in March 2007. A £50 note, the second in the F series, and the first banknote issued by the Bank of England to feature two portraits on the reverse, was issued in November 2011. The first polymer G series banknote, a £5 note featuring Sir Winston Churchill, was issued in September 2016, a £10 polymer note featuring Jane Austen followed in September 2017 and a £20 polymer note featuring the artist J. M. W. Turner will be issued in 2020.

The historical figures portrayed in the F and G series are:

£5	Sep 2016–date	Sir Winston Churchill
£10	Sep 2017–date	Jane Austen
£20	Mar 2007–date	Adam Smith
£50	Nov 2011–date	Matthew Boulton and James Watt

NOTE CIRCULATION

Note circulation is highest at the two peak spending periods of the year: around Christmas and during the summer holiday period.

The Bank of England measures the value of notes in circulation on the last day of February each year. The value of notes in circulation (£ million) at the end of February 2018 and 2019 was:

	2018	2019
£5	1,910	1,979
£10	7,789	10,524
£20	42,692	40,129
£50	16,508	17,210
Other notes*	4,351	4,330
Total	73,250	74,171

* Includes higher value notes used as backing for the note issues of authorised banks in Scotland and Northern Ireland

WITHDRAWN BANKNOTES

Banknotes which are no longer legal tender are payable when presented at the head office of the Bank of England in London.

The white notes for £10, £20, £50, £100, £500 and £1,000, which were issued until April 1943, ceased to be legal tender in May 1945, and the white £5 note in March 1946.

The white £5 note issued between October 1945 and September 1956, the £5 notes issued between 1957 and 1963 (bearing a portrait of Britannia) and the first series to bear a portrait of the Queen, issued between 1963 and 1971, ceased to be legal tender in March 1961, June 1967 and September 1973 respectively.

The series of £1 notes issued during the years 1928 to 1960 and the 10 shilling notes issued from 1928 to 1961 (those without the royal portrait) ceased to be legal tender in May and October 1962 respectively. The £1 note first issued in March 1960 (bearing on the back a representation of Britannia) and the £10 note first issued in February 1964 (bearing a lion on the back), both bearing a portrait of the Queen on the front, ceased to be legal tender in June 1979. The £1 note first issued in 1978 ceased to be legal tender on 11 March 1988. The 10 shilling note was replaced by the 50p coin in October 1969, and ceased to be legal tender on 21 November 1970.

The D series of banknotes was introduced from 1970 and ceased to be legal tender from the dates shown below. The predominant identifying feature of each note was the portrayal on the back of a prominent figure from British history:

£1	Feb 1978–Mar 1988	Sir Isaac Newton
£5	Nov 1971–Nov 1991	Duke of Wellington
£10	Feb 1975–May 1994	Florence Nightingale
£20	Jul 1970–Mar 1993	William Shakespeare
£50	Mar 1981–Sep 1996	Sir Christopher Wren

The £1 coin was introduced on 21 April 1983 to replace the £1 note. No £1 notes have been issued since 1984 and in March 1998 the outstanding notes were written off in accordance with the provision of the Currency Act 1983.

The E series of notes was introduced from June 1990, replacing the D series. E series notes were withdrawn from circulation on the dates shown below:

£5	Jun 1990–Nov 2003	George Stephenson
£5	May 2002–May 2017	Elizabeth Fry
£10	Apr 1992–Jul 2003	Charles Dickens
£10	Nov 2000–Mar 2018	Charles Darwin
£20	Jun 1991–Feb 2001	Michael Faraday
£20	Jun 1999–Jun 2010	Sir Edward Elgar
£50	Apr 1994–Apr 2014	Sir John Houblon

Scotland – Banknotes are issued by three Scottish banks. The Royal Bank of Scotland issues notes for £1, £5, £10, £20, £50 and £100. Bank of Scotland and the Clydesdale Bank issue notes for £5, £10, £20, £50 and £100. All three banks have replaced paper £5 and £10 with polymer notes. Scottish notes are not legal tender in the UK but they are an authorised currency.

Northern Ireland – Banknotes are issued by four banks in Northern Ireland. The Bank of Ireland and the Ulster Bank issue notes for £5 (polymer), £10 (polymer), £20, £50 and £100. The First Trust Bank retains the right to issue notes for £10, £20, £50 and £100 until midnight on 30 June 2020, when it will cease to do so. Danske Bank (formerly Northern Bank) issue notes for £10 (polymer) and £20. Northern Ireland notes are not legal tender in the UK but they are an authorised currency.

Channel Islands – The States of Guernsey issues its own currency notes and coinage. The notes are for £1, £5, £10, £20 and £50, and the coins are for 1p, 2p, 5p, 10p, 20p, 50p and £2. The Guernsey round £1 coin was withdrawn from circulation in October 2017 with the introduction of the UK 12-sided coin, which is used alongside the £1 note.

The States of Jersey issues its own currency notes and coinage. The notes are for £1, £5, £10, £20, £50 and £100, and the coins are for 1p, 2p, 5p, 10p, 20p, 50p and £2. The Jersey round £1 coin was withdrawn from circulation in October 2017 with the introduction of the UK 12-sided coin, which is used alongside the £1 note.

The Isle of Man – The Isle of Man government issues notes for £1, £5, £10, £20 and £50. Although these notes are only legal tender in the Isle of Man, they may be exchanged at face value at certain UK banks at their discretion. The Isle of Man issues coins for 1p, 2p, 5p, 10p, 20p, 50p, £1, £2 and £5.

BANKING AND PERSONAL FINANCE

There are two main types of deposit-taking institutions: banks and building societies, although National Savings and Investments also provides savings products. Banks and building societies are regulated by the Prudential Regulation Authority, part of the Bank of England (*see* Financial Services Regulation), and National Savings and Investments is accountable to HM Treasury.

The main institutions within the British banking system are the Bank of England (the central bank), retail banks, investment banks and overseas banks. In its role as the central bank, the Bank of England acts as banker to the government and as a note-issuing authority; it also oversees the efficient functioning of payment and settlement systems.

Since May 1997, the Bank of England has had operational responsibility for monetary policy. At monthly meetings of its monetary policy committee the Bank sets the interest rate at which it will lend to the money markets.

OFFICIAL INTEREST RATES 2006–19	
3 August 2006	4.75%
9 November 2006	5.00%
11 January 2007	5.25%
10 May 2007	5.50%
5 July 2007	5.75%
6 December 2007	5.50%
7 February 2008	5.25%
10 April 2008	5.00%
8 October 2008	4.50%
6 November 2008	3.00%
4 December 2008	2.00%
8 January 2009	1.50%
5 February 2009	1.00%
5 March 2009	0.50%
4 August 2016	0.25%
2 November 2017	0.50%
2 August 2018	0.75%

RETAIL BANKING

Retail banks offer a wide variety of financial services to individuals and companies, including current and deposit accounts, loan and overdraft facilities, credit and debit cards, investment services, pensions, insurance and mortgages. All banks offer internet and telephone banking facilities and the majority also offer traditional branch services.

The Financial Ombudsman Service provides independent and impartial arbitration in disputes between banks and their customers (*see* Financial Services Regulation).

PAYMENT CLEARINGS

The Payment Systems Regulator (PSR), a subsidiary of the Financial Conduct Authority (*see* Financial Services Regulation), is the economic regulator for the £81 trillion payment systems industry in the UK. Funded by an annual levy on the firms it regulates, it was established on 1 April 2015. The PSR's statutory objectives are:

- to ensure that payment systems are operated and developed in a way that considers and promotes the interests of all the businesses and consumers that use them
- to promote effective competition in the markets for payment systems and services – between operators, payment service providers and infrastructure providers
- to promote development and innovation in payment systems, in particular the infrastructure used to operate these systems

DESIGNATED PAYMENT SYSTEMS

The PSR can only use its regulatory powers in relation to payment systems designated by HM Treasury, which regularly reviews this list. The current designated payment systems are: BACS, C&C (Cheque & Credit), CHAPS, Faster Payments Scheme (FPS), LINK, Northern Ireland Cheque Clearing (NICC), MasterCard, Visa Europe (Visa).

PSR, 12 Endeavour Square, Stratford, London E20 1JN
T 020-7066 1000 **E** contactus@psr.org.uk **W** www.psr.org.uk
Chair, Charles Randell, CBE

MAJOR RETAIL BANKS' FINANCIAL RESULTS 2018

Bank group	Profit/(loss) before taxation £ million	Profit/(loss) after taxation £ million	Total assets £ million
Barclays Bank	3,494	2,372	1,133,283
Cooperative Bank	(141)	(69)	23,103
HSBC UK Bank	1,064	763	238,939
Lloyds Banking Group	5,960	4,400	797,598
RBS Group	3,359	2,084	694,235
Santander UK	1,545	1,104	283,372
TSB Banking Group	(105)	(63)	41,124
Virgin Money Group	119	81	45,116

GLOSSARY OF FINANCIAL TERMS

The following provides a glossary of a selection of financial terms currently in general use and does not constitute any sort of financial advice which should always be sort from a regulated provider *see also* Financial Services Regulation.

ACCIDENT, SICKNESS AND UNEMPLOYMENT (ASU) INSURANCE – Is a short-term income protection policy that replaces an individual's income for a pre-defined amount of time, should they become unable to work due to accident, sickness or involuntary redundancy. Unemployment protection insurance can also be brought as a standalone product, as can accident and sickness protection. *See also* PPI.

AER (ANNUAL EQUIVALENT RATE) – A notional rate quoted on savings and investment products which demonstrates the return on interest, when compounded and paid annually.

APR (ANNUAL PERCENTAGE RATE) – Calculates the total amount of interest payable over the whole term of a product (such as an investment or loan), allowing consumers to compare rival products on a like-for-like basis. Companies offering loans, credit cards, mortgages or overdrafts are required by law to provide the APR rate. Where typical APR is shown, it refers to the company's typical borrower and so is given as a best example; rate and costs may vary depending on individual circumstances.

ANNUITY – A type of insurance policy that provides regular income in exchange for a lump sum. The annuity can be bought from a company other than the existing pension provider.

ATM (AUTOMATED TELLER MACHINES) – Commonly referred to as cash machines. Users can access their bank accounts using a card for simple transactions such as withdrawing money and viewing an account balance. Some banks and independent ATM deployers charge for transactions.

BANKER'S DRAFT – A cheque drawn on a bank against a cash deposit. Considered to be a secure way of receiving money in instances where a cheque could 'bounce' or where it is not desirable to receive cash.

BASE RATE – The interest rate set by the Bank of England at which it will lend to financial institutions. This acts as a benchmark for all other interest rates.

BASIS POINT – Unit of measure (usually one-hundredth of a percentage point) used to express movements in interest rates, foreign rates or bond yields.

BUY-TO-LET – The purchase of a residential property for the sole purpose of letting to a tenant. Not all lenders provide mortgage finance for this purpose. Buy-to-let lenders assess projected rental income (typical expectations are between 125 and 130 per cent of the monthly interest payment) in addition to, or instead of, the borrower's income. Buy-to-let mortgages are available as either interest only or repayment.

CAPITAL GAIN/LOSS – Increase/decrease in the value of a capital asset when it is sold or transferred compared to its initial worth.

CAPPED RATE MORTGAGE – The interest rate applied to a loan is guaranteed not to rise above a certain rate for a set period of time; the rate can therefore fall but will not rise above the capped rate. The level at which the cap is fixed is usually higher than for a fixed rate mortgage for a comparable period of time. The lender normally imposes early redemption penalties within the first few years.

CASH CARD – Issued by banks and building societies for withdrawing cash from ATMs.

CHARGE CARD – Charge cards, eg American Express and Diners Club, can be used in a similar way to credit cards but the debt must be settled in full each month.

CHIP AND PIN CARD – A credit/debit card which incorporates an embedded chip containing unique owner details. When used with a PIN, such cards offer greater security as they are less prone to fraud.

CONTACTLESS PAYMENT – A system that uses radio-frequency identification (RFID) or near-field communication (NFC) for making secure payments via a credit, debit or smart card or another device, such as a smartphone, with an embedded chip and antenna which need to be in close proximity to a reader at the point of sale. Occasional PIN verification is required to authenticate the user and purchases are typically limited to small value sales.

CREDIT CARD – Normally issued with a credit limit, credit cards can be used for purchases until the limit is reached. There is normally an interest-free period on the outstanding balance of up to 56 days. Charges can be avoided if the balance is paid off in full within the interest-free period. Alternatively part of the balance can be paid and in most cases there is a minimum amount set by the issuer (normally a percentage of the outstanding balance) which must be paid on a monthly basis. Some card issuers charge an annual fee and most issuers belong to at least one major credit card network, eg Mastercard or Visa.

CREDIT RATING – Overall credit worthiness of a borrower based on information from a credit reference agency, such as Experian or Equifax, which holds details of credit agreements, payment records, county court judgments etc for all adults in the UK. This information is supplied to lenders who use it in their credit scoring or underwriting systems to calculate the risk of granting a loan to an individual and the probability that it will be repaid. Each lender sets their own criteria for credit worthiness and may accept or reject a credit application based on an individual's credit rating.

CRITICAL ILLNESS COVER – Insurance that covers borrowers against critical illnesses such as stroke, heart attack or cancer and is designed to protect mortgage or other loan payments.

DEBIT CARD – Debit cards were introduced on a large scale in the UK in the mid-1980s, replacing cash and cheques to purchase goods and services. Funds are automatically withdrawn from an individual's bank account after making a purchase and no interest is charged. They can also be used to withdraw cash from ATMs in the UK and abroad.

DIRECT DEBIT – An instruction from a customer to their bank, which authorises the payee to charge costs to the customer's bank account.

DISCOUNTED MORTGAGE – Discounted mortgages guarantee an interest rate set at a margin below the standard variable rate for a period of time. The discounted rate will move up or down with the standard variable rate, but the payment rate will retain the agreed differential below the standard variable rate. The lender normally imposes early redemption penalties within the first few years.

EARLY REDEMPTION PENALTY – *see* Redemption Penalty

ENDOWMENT MORTGAGE – Refers to a mortgage loan arranged on an interest-only basis where the capital is intended to be repaid by one or more endowment policies. The borrower has two distinct arrangements: one with the lender for the mortgage and one with the insurer for the endowment policy. The borrower can change either arrangement if they wish.

EQUITY – When applied to real estate, equity is the difference between the value of a property and the amount outstanding on any loan secured against it. Negative equity occurs when the loan is greater than the market value of the property.

FIXED RATE MORTGAGE – A repayment mortgage where the interest rate on the loan is fixed for a set amount of time, normally a period of between one and ten years. The interest rate does not vary with changes to the base rate resulting in the monthly mortgage payment remaining the same for the duration of the fixed period. The lender normally imposes early redemption penalties within the first few years.

ISA (INDIVIDUAL SAVINGS ACCOUNT) – A means by which investors can save (in a cash ISA) and invest (in a stocks and shares ISA) without paying any tax on the proceeds. There are limits on the amount that can be invested during any given tax year (*see* Taxation).

INTEREST ONLY MORTGAGE – Only interest is paid by the borrower and capital remains constant for the term of the loan. The onus is on the borrower to make provision to repay the capital at the end of the term. This is usually achieved through an investment vehicle such as an endowment policy or pension.

LOAN TO VALUE (LTV) – This is the ratio between the size of a mortgage loan sought and the mortgage lender's valuation. On a loan of £55,000, for example, on a property valued at £100,000, the loan to value is 55 per cent. This means that there is sufficient equity in the property for the lender to be reassured that if interest or capital repayments were stopped, it could sell the property and recoup the money owed. Fewer options are available to borrowers requiring high LTV.

LONDON INTERBANK OFFERED RATE (LIBOR) – Is the interest rate that London banks charge when lending to one another on the wholesale money market. LIBOR is set by supply and demand of money as banks lend to each other in order to balance their books on a daily basis.

MIG (MORTGAGE INDEMNITY GUARANTEE) – An insurance for the lender paid by the borrower on high LTV mortgages (typically more than 90 per cent). It is a policy designed to protect the lender against loss in the event of the borrower defaulting or ceasing to repay a mortgage and is usually paid as a one-off premium or can be added to the value of the loan. It offers no protection to the borrower. Not all lenders charge MIG premiums.

OVERDRAFT – An 'authorised' overdraft is an arrangement made between customer and bank allowing the balance of the customer's account to go below zero; interest is normally charged at an agreed rate and sometimes an arrangement fee is charged. If the negative balance exceeds the agreed terms or a prior arrangement for an overdraft facility has not been made (an 'unauthorised' overdraft) then additional penalty fees may be charged and higher interest rates may apply. Interest-free overdrafts are available for customers in certain circumstances, such as full-time higher education students and recent graduates.

PERSONAL PENSION SCHEME (PPS) – A tax-privileged individual investment vehicle, with the primary purpose of building a capital sum to provide retirement benefits,

although it will usually also provide death benefits. Contributions can be made to a PPS by both the individual and, if they are not self-employed, their employer. Contributions are exempt from tax and the retirement age may be selected at any time, usually from age 55. Up to 25 per cent of the pension fund may be taken as a tax-free cash sum on retirement. *See also* Social Welfare, Pensions.

PHISHING – A fraudulent attempt to obtain bank account details and security codes through an email. The email purports to come from a *bona fide* organisation, such as a bank or building society, and attempts to steer the recipient, usually under the pretext that the institution is updating its security arrangements, to a website which requests personal details.

PIN (PERSONAL IDENTIFICATION NUMBER) – A PIN is issued alongside a cash card to allow the user to access a bank account via an ATM. PINs are also issued with smart, credit and debit cards and, since 14 February 2006, have been compulsory as a security measure in the majority of purchases.

PORTABLE MORTGAGE – A mortgage product that can be transferred to a different property in the event of a house move. Preferable where early redemption penalties are charged.

PPI (PAYMENT PROTECTION INSURANCE) – A credit protection, or loan repayment, insurance taken out by a borrower to cover repayment of credit in the event of illness, disablement, redundancy, death or another circumstance that could prevent the borrower from earning income to service the debt.

REDEMPTION PENALTY – A charge levied for paying off a loan, debt balance or mortgage before a date agreed with the lender.

REPAYMENT MORTGAGE – In contrast to the interest only mortgage, the monthly repayment includes an element of the capital sum borrowed in addition to the interest charged.

SHARE – A share is a divided-up unit of the value of a company. If a company is worth £100m, and there are 50 million shares in issue, then each share is worth £2 (usually listed as pence). As the overall value of the company fluctuates so does the share price.

STANDING ORDER – An instruction made by the customer to their bank, which allows the transfer of a set amount to a payee at regular intervals.

UNIT TRUST – A 'pooled' fund of assets, usually shares, owned by a number of individuals. Managed by professional, authorised fund-management groups, unit trusts have traditionally delivered better returns than average cash deposits, but do rise and fall in value as their underlying investment varies in value.

VARIABLE RATE MORTGAGE – Repayment mortgages where the interest rate set by the lender increases or decreases in relation to the base interest rate which can result in fluctuating monthly repayments.

WITH-PROFITS – Usually applies to pensions, endowments, savings schemes or bonds. The intention is to smooth out the rises and falls in the stock market for the benefit of the investor. Actuaries working for the insurance company, or fund managers, hold back some profits in good years in order to make up the difference in years when shares perform badly.

BANK FAMILY TREE

Includes the major retail banks operating in the UK as at April 2019. For financial results for these banks *see* Banking and Personal Finance. Building societies are only included in instances where they demutualised to become a bank.

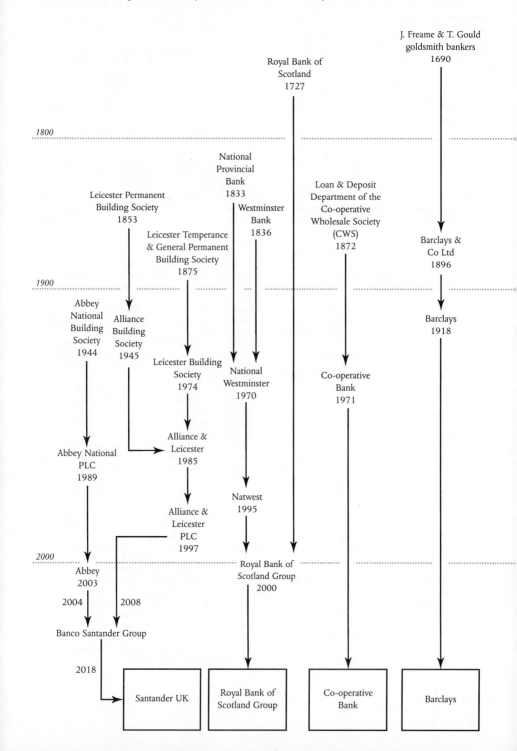

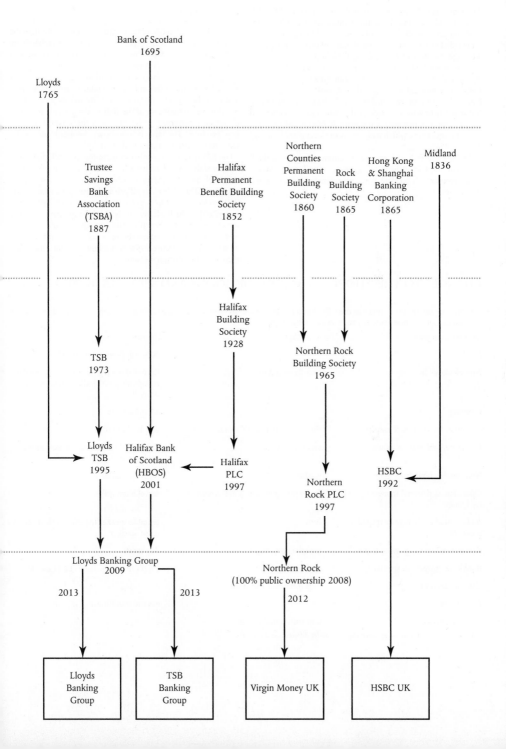

COST OF LIVING AND INFLATION RATES

The first cost of living index to be calculated took July 1914 as 100 and was based on the pattern of expenditure of working-class families in 1914. The cost of living index was superseded in 1947 by the general index of retail prices (RPI), although the older term is still popularly applied.

The Harmonised Index of Consumer Prices (HICP) was introduced in 1997 to enable comparisons within the European Union using an agreed methodology. In 2003 the National Statistician renamed the HICP the Consumer Prices Index (CPI) to reflect its role as the main target measure of inflation for macroeconomic purposes. In March 2013 CPIH, an additional index which includes owner-occupiers' housing costs, was introduced.

The RPI and indices based on it continue to be published alongside the CPI. Private-sector pensions and index-linked gilts continue to be calculated with reference to RPI or its derivatives.

CPI AND RPI

The CPI and RPI measure the changes month by month in the average level of prices of goods and services purchased by households in the UK. The indices are compiled using a selection of around 700 goods and services, and the prices charged for these items are collected at regular intervals at about 140 locations throughout the country, from the internet and over the phone. The Office for National Statistics (ONS) reviews the components of the indices once a year to reflect changes in consumer preferences and the establishment of new products. The table below shows changes made by the ONS to the CPI 'shopping basket' in 2019.

The CPI excludes a number of items that are included in the RPI, mainly related to housing, such as council tax, and a range of owner-occupier housing costs, such as mortgage payments. The CPI covers all private households, whereas the RPI excludes the top 4 per cent by income and pensioner households which derive at least three-quarters of their income from state benefits. The two indices use different methodologies to combine the prices of goods and services, which means that since 1996 the CPI inflation measure is less than the RPI inflation measure.

CHANGES TO THE 'SHOPPING BASKET' OF GOODS AND SERVICES IN 2019

The table below shows changes to the CPI* basket of goods and services made by the ONS in 2019 in order to reflect changes in consumer preferences and the establishment of new products.

Goods and services group	Removed items	New items
Food	–	popcorn; peanut butter
Non-alcoholic beverages	cola flavoured drink	flavoured tea (eg herbal/ fruit); regular cola drink (bottle); diet/ sugar-free cola drink (bottle)
Clothing	–	adult hat/ cap
Furniture, furnishings & carpets	three-piece non-leather suite	non-leather settee
Glassware, tableware & household utensils	crockery set	bakeware (baking tray or roasting tin); dinner plate
Non-durable household goods	washing powder	washing liquid/ gel
Operation of personal transport equipment	brake fitting in fast-fit auto centre	wheel alignment
Audio-visual equipment & related products	hi-fi	portable speaker (eg Bluetooth speaker); smart speaker
Recreational items, gardens & pets	complete dry dog food	dog treats
Books, newspapers & stationery	envelopes	child's fiction book, 6–12-years-old
Catering services	staff restaurant soft drink	–
Personal care	–	electric toothbrush
Financial services	unit trust initial charge	–

* RPI goods and services are grouped together under different classifications

INFLATION RATE

The 12-monthly percentage change in the 'all items' index of the RPI or CPI is referred to as the rate of inflation. As the most familiar measure of inflation, the RPI is often referred to as the 'headline rate of inflation'. The CPI is the main measure of inflation for macroeconomic purposes and forms the basis of the government's inflation target, which is currently 2 per cent. The percentage change in prices between any two months/years can be obtained using this formula:

$$\frac{\text{Later date RPI/CPI} - \text{Earlier date RPI/CPI}}{\text{Earlier date RPI/CPI}} \times 100$$

For example, to find the CPI rate of inflation for 2006, using the annual averages for 2005 and 2006:

$$\frac{79.9 - 78.1}{78.1} \times 100 = 2.3$$

On 16 February 2016 the reference year for all CPI indices was re-based to 2015=100, replacing the 2005=100 series. The change of reference period does not apply to the RPI, which remains unchanged. The CPI rate of inflation figure given in the Annual Indices table may differ by plus or minus 0.1 percentage points from the figure calculated by the above equation.

The RPI and CPI figures are published around the the middle of each month in an indices bulletin on the ONS website (**W** www.ons.gov.uk/economy/inflationandpriceindices).

PURCHASING POWER OF THE POUND

Changes in the internal purchasing power of the pound may be defined as the 'inverse' of changes in the level of prices: when prices go up, the amount which can be purchased with a given sum of money goes down. To find the purchasing power of the pound in one month or year, given that it was 100p in a previous month or year, the calculation would be:

$$100p \times \frac{\text{Earlier month/year RPI}}{\text{Later month/year RPI}}$$

Thus, if the purchasing power of the pound is taken to be 100p in 1975, the comparable purchasing power in 2000 would be:

$$100p \times \frac{34.2}{170.3} = 20.1p$$

For longer term comparisons, it has been the practice to use an index which has been constructed by linking together the RPI for the period 1962 to date; an index derived from the consumers' expenditure deflator for the period from 1938 to 1962; and the pre-war 'cost of living' index for the period 1914 to 1938. This long-term index enables the internal purchasing power of the pound to be calculated for any year from 1914 onwards. It should be noted that these figures can only be approximate.

ANNUAL INDICES

	Annual average RPI (1987 = 100)	Purchasing power of £ (1998 = 1.00)	Annual average CPI (2015 = 100)*	Annual average CPIH† (2015=100)*	Rate of inflation (RPI/ CPI/ CPIH)†
1914	2.8	58.18			
1915	3.5	46.54			
1920	7.0	23.27			
1925	5.0	32.58			
1930	4.5	36.20			
1935	4.0	40.72			
1938	4.4	37.02			
There are no official figures for 1939–45					
1946	7.4	22.01			
1950	9.0	18.10			
1955	11.2	14.54			
1960	12.6	12.93			
1965	14.8	11.00			
1970	18.5	8.80			
1975	34.2	4.76			
1980	66.8	2.44			
1985	94.6	1.72			
1990	126.1	1.29			9.5/ 7.0
1995	149.1	1.09			3.5/ 2.6
1998	162.9	1.00	71.2		3.4/ 1.6
2000	170.3	0.96	72.7		3.0/ 0.8
2005	192.0	0.85	78.1	79.4	2.8/ 2.1
2006	198.1	0.82	79.9	81.4	3.2/ 2.3/ 2.5
2007	206.6	0.79	81.8	83.3	4.3/ 2.3/ 2.4
2008	214.8	0.76	84.7	86.2	4.0/ 3.6/ 3.5
2009	213.7	0.76	86.6	87.9	−0.5/ 2.2/ 2.0
2010	223.6	0.73	89.4	90.1	4.6/ 3.3/ 2.5
2011	235.2	0.69	93.4	93.6	5.2/ 4.5/ 3.8
2012	242.7	0.67	96.1	96.0	3.2/ 2.8/ 2.6
2013	250.1	0.65	98.5	98.2	3.0/ 2.6/ 2.3
2014	256.0	0.64	100.0	99.6	2.4/ 1.5/ 1.5
2015	258.5	0.63	100.0	100.0	1.0/ 0.0/ 0.4
2016	263.1	0.62	100.7	101.0	1.8/ 0.7/ 1.0
2017	272.5	0.60	103.4	103.6	3.6/ 2.7/ 2.6
2018	281.6	0.58	105.9	106.0	3.3/ 2.5/ 2.3

ECONOMIC STATISTICS

TRADE

TRADE IN GOODS
£ million

	Exports	Imports	Balance
2014	293,116	415,187	(122,071)
2015	286,752	404,562	(117,810)
2016	299,073	431,725	(132,652)
2017	338,739	475,774	(137,035)
2018	350,651	488,744	(138,093)

Source: ONS (Crown copyright)

BALANCE OF PAYMENTS, 2018

Current Account	£ million
Trade in goods and services	
Trade in goods	(138,093)
Trade in services	107,124
Total trade in goods and services	(30,969)
Income	
Compensation of employees	(171)
Investment income	(25,376)
Other	(1,103)
Total income	(26,650)
Total secondary income	(24,025)
TOTAL (CURRENT BALANCE)	(81,644)

Source: ONS (Crown copyright)

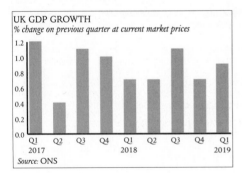

UK GDP GROWTH
% change on previous quarter at current market prices

Source: ONS

UK EMPLOYMENT

DISTRIBUTION OF THE WORKFORCE

	Mar 2018	Mar 2019
Workforce jobs	34,949,000	35,537,000
HM forces	154,000	152,000
Self-employment jobs	4,496,000	4,657,000
Employees jobs	30,271,000	30,701,000
Government-supported trainees	28,000	27,000

Source: ONS – Labour Market Statistics 2019 (Crown copyright)

EMPLOYED AND UNEMPLOYED
thousands, all aged 16+

	Apr–Jun 2018		Apr–Jun 2019	
	Number	Rate (%)	Number	Rate (%)
Employed	32,386	61.1	32,811	61.6
Unemployed	1,362	4.0	1,329	3.9

Source: ONS – Labour Market Statistics 2019 (Crown copyright)

DURATION OF UNEMPLOYMENT, APR–JUN 2019

All unemployed	1,329,000
Less than 6 months	793,000
6 months–1 year	194,000
1 year +	342,000
2 years +	169,000

Source: ONS – Labour Market Statistics 2019 (Crown copyright)

MEDIAN EARNINGS, 2018
full-time, £

	All	Male	Female
Gross annual	24,006.00	29,425.00	18,735.00
Gross weekly	460.00	555.00	369.90
Hourly	12.78	14.10	11.50

Source: ONS (Crown copyright)

LABOUR STOPPAGES BY DURATION, 2018

1 day	12
2–3 days	22
4 days	6
5–10 days	23
11+ days	18
All stoppages	81

Source: ONS (Crown copyright)

LABOUR DISPUTES BY INDUSTRY, 2018

Industry Group	Working Days Lost
Mining, quarrying, electricity, gas, air con.	100
Manufacturing	3,000
Sewage, waste management, water supply	4,600
Construction	5,800
Wholesale & retail, motor vehicles, accommodation, food	900
Transport & storage	42,600
Information & Communication	10,600
Financial, professional, scientific, administration	4,000
Public administration & defence	15,900
Education	179,400
Human health and social work	4,900
Other	800
All industries & services	272,600

Source: ONS (Crown copyright)

TRADE UNIONS

Year	No. of unions	Total membership
2013–14	166	7,086,116
2014–15	160	7,010,527
2015–16	160	6,948,725
2016–17	151	6,865,056
2017–18	146	6,875,231

Source: Annual Report of the Certification Officer 2017–18

FINANCIAL SERVICES REGULATION

Under the Financial Services and Markets Act 2000, as amended by the Financial Services Act (2012), the Financial Conduct Authority and the Prudential Regulation Authority are responsible for financial regulation in the UK.

FINANCIAL CONDUCT AUTHORITY

The Financial Conduct Authority (FCA) is responsible for supervising the conduct of over 58,000 financial services firms and financial markets in the UK and for regulating the prudential standards of those firms – over 18,000 – not regulated by the Prudential Regulation authority. The FCA has three statutory objectives:
• to secure an appropriate degree of protection for consumers
• to protect and enhance the integrity of the UK financial system
• to promote effective market competition in the interests of consumers
The FCA is accountable to HM Treasury and therefore to parliament, but is operationally independent of the government and is funded entirely by the firms which it regulates. The FCA is governed by a board appointed by HM Treasury, but day-to-day decisions and staff management are the responsibility of the executive committee.

The FCA's annual budget for ongoing regulatory activity (ORA) in 2019–20 is £537.7m, a 2 per cent increase from 2018–19. The 2019–20 annual funding requirement totals £558.5m, an increase of 2.7 per cent due to the increase in the ORA budget and an additional £5m allocated for the costs associated with withdrawing from the European Union.

THE FINANCIAL SERVICES REGISTER
The Financial Services Register lists financial services firms and individuals in the UK who are authorised by the FCA and PRA (see Prudential Regulation Authority) to do business and specifies which activity each firm or individual is regulated to undertake and what products or services each is approved to provide.

FINANCIAL CONDUCT AUTHORITY, 12 Endeavour Square, London E20 1JN **T** 020-7066 1000 **W** www.fca.org.uk
Chair, Charles Randell, CBE
Chief Executive, Andrew Bailey

PRUDENTIAL REGULATION AUTHORITY

The Prudential Regulation Authority (PRA), part of the Bank of England, works alongside the FCA and is responsible for the prudential regulation and supervision of around 1,500 banks, building societies, credit unions, insurers and major investment firms. The PRA has three statutory objectives:
• to promote the safety and soundness of the firms it regulates
• to contribute to securing an appropriate degree of protection for those who are, or may become, insurance policyholders
• to facilitate effective competition
The members of the PRA's committee are: the Governor of the Bank of England (chair); the three Deputy Governors for Financial Stability, Markets and Banking, and Prudential Regulation; the chief executive of the FCA; a member appointed by the Governor with the approval of the chancellor; and six other external members appointed by the chancellor.
The PRA's budget for 2019–20 is £273m.

PRUDENTIAL REGULATION AUTHORITY, 20 Moorgate, London EC2R 6DA **T** 020-3461 4444
E enquiries@bankofengland.co.uk
W www.bankofengland.co.uk/prudential-regulation
Chief Executive, Sam Woods

COMPENSATION

Created under the Financial Services and Markets Act (2000), the Financial Services Compensation Scheme (FSCS) is the UK's statutory fund of last resort for customers of authorised financial services firms. It provides compensation if a firm authorised by the FCA or PRA is unable, or likely to be unable, to pay claims against it. In general this is when a firm has stopped trading and has insufficient assets to meet claims, or is in insolvency. This includes, banks, building societies and credit unions; firms providing debt management, mortgage and endowment advice; insurance firms; insurance brokers; investment firms; payment protection insurance firms and pension companies. The FSCS is independent of the UK regulators (FCA and PRA), with separate staff and premises. However, the FCA and PRA appoint the directors. The chair's appointment (and removal) is subject to HM Treasury approval. The FSCS is funded by an annual levy on every firm authorised by the UK regulators.

The Pension Protection Fund (PPF) is a statutory fund established under the Pensions Act 2004 and became operational on 6 April 2005. The fund was set up to pay compensation to members of eligible defined benefit pension schemes, where there is a qualifying insolvency event in relation to the employer and where there are insufficient assets in the pension scheme to cover PPF levels of compensation. Compulsory annual levies are charged on all eligible schemes to help fund the PPF, in addition to investment of PPF assets. The PPF is also responsible for the Fraud Compensation Fund – a fund that will provide compensation to occupational pension schemes that suffer a loss attributable to dishonesty.

FINANCIAL SERVICES COMPENSATION SCHEME, Beaufort House, 15 St Botolph Street, 10th Floor, London EC3A 7QU **T** 0800-678 1100 **W** www.fscs.org.uk
Chair, Marshall Bailey
Chief Executive, Caroline Rainbird

PENSION PROTECTION FUND, Renaissance, 12 Dingwall Road, Croydon CR0 2NA **T** 0345-600 2541
E information@ppf.co.uk **W** www.ppf.co.uk
Chair, Arnold Wagner, OBE
Chief Executive, Oliver Morley, CBE

DESIGNATED PROFESSIONAL BODIES

Professional firms are exempt from requiring direct regulation by the FCA if they carry out only certain restricted activities that arise out of, or are complementary to, the provision of professional services, such as arranging the sale of shares on the instructions of executors or trustees, or providing services to small, private companies. These firms are, however, supervised by designated professional bodies (DPBs). There are a number of safeguards to protect consumers dealing with firms that do not require direct regulation. These arrangements include:
• the FCA's power to ban a specific firm from taking advantage of the exemption and to restrict the regulated activities permitted to the firms

- rules which require professional firms to ensure that their clients are aware that they are not authorised persons
- a requirement for the DPBs to supervise and regulate the firms and inform the FCA on how the professional firms carry on their regulated activities

See Professional Education section for contact details of the following DPBs:

Association of Chartered Certified Accountants
Council for Licensed Conveyancers
Institute of Actuaries
Institute of Chartered Accountants in England and Wales
Institute of Chartered Accountants in Ireland
Institute of Chartered Accountants of Scotland
Law Society of England and Wales
Law Society of Northern Ireland
Law Society of Scotland
Royal Institution of Chartered Surveyors

RECOGNISED INVESTMENT EXCHANGES

The FCA currently supervises seven recognised investment exchanges (RIEs) in the UK; recognition confers an exemption from the need to be authorised to carry out regulated activities in the UK. The RIEs are organised markets on which member firms can trade investments such as equities and derivatives. The RIEs are listed with their year of recognition in parentheses:

CBOE EUROPE (2013), 5th Floor, The Monument Building, 11 Monument Street, London EC3R 8AF **T** 020-7012 8900 **W** https://markets.cboe.com

EURONEXT LONDON (2014), 10th Floor, 110 Cannon Street, London EC4N 6EU **T** 020-7076 0900 **W** www.euronext.com/en

ICE FUTURES EUROPE (2001), 5th Floor Milton Gate, 60 Chiswell Street, London EC1Y 4SA **T** 020-7065 7700 **W** www.theice.com

INTERNATIONAL PROPERTY SECURITIES EXCHANGE (IPSX) UK (2019), 8–10 Hill Street, London W1J 5NG **T** 020-3931 8800 **W** www.ipsx.com

LONDON METAL EXCHANGE (2001), 10 Finsbury Square, London EC2A 1AJ **T** 020-7113 8888 **W** www.lme.com

LONDON STOCK EXCHANGE (2001), 10 Paternoster Square, London EC4M 7LS **T** 020-7797 1000 **W** www.londonstockexchange.com

NEX EXCHANGE (2007), London Fruit and Wool Exchange, 1 Duval Square, London E1 6PW **T** 020-7818 9774 **W** www.nexexchange.com

RECOGNISED CLEARING HOUSES AND CENTRAL COUNTERPARTIES

The Bank of England is responsible for recognising and supervising central counterparties (CCPs) and clearing houses (RCHs). CCPs and RCHs provide clearing and settlement services for transactions in foreign exchange, securities, options and derivatives on recognised investment exchanges. There are currently three UK CCPs authorised under the European Market Infrastructure regulation (EMIR) and one recognised RCH (dates of authorisation and recognition are given in parentheses):

EUROCLEAR UK AND IRELAND (RCH, 2001), 33 Cannon Street, London EC4M 5SB **T** 020-7849 0000 **W** www.euroclear.com

ICE CLEAR EUROPE (CCP, 2016), 5th Floor, Milton Gate, 60 Chiswell Street, London EC1Y 4SA **T** 020-7065 7600 **W** www.theice.com/clear-europe

LCH (LONDON CLEARING HOUSE) (CCP, 2014), Aldgate House, 33 Aldgate High Street, London EC3N 1EA **T** 020-7426 7000 **W** www.lch.com

LME (LONDON METAL EXCHANGE) CLEAR (CCP, 2014), 10 Finsbury Square, London EC2A 1AJ **T** 020-7113 8888 **W** www.lme.com/LME-Clear

OMBUDSMAN SCHEMES

The Financial Ombudsman Service was set up by the Financial Services and Markets Act 2000 to provide consumers with a free, independent service for resolving disputes with authorised financial firms. It can consider complaints about most financial matters including: banking; credit cards and store cards; financial advice; hire purchase and pawnbroking; insurance; loans and credit; money transfer; mortgages; payday lending and debt collecting; payment protection insurance; pensions; savings and investments; stocks, shares, unit trusts and bonds.

Complainants must first complain to the firm involved. They do not have to accept the ombudsman's decision and are free to go to court if they wish, but if a decision is accepted, it is binding for both the complainant and the firm.

The Pensions Ombudsman can investigate and decide complaints and disputes regarding the way occupational and personal pension schemes are administered and managed. Unless there are special circumstances, this only usually includes issues and disputes that have arisen within the past three years. The Pensions Ombudsman is also the Ombudsman for the Pension Protection Fund (PPF) and the Financial Assistance Scheme (which offers help to those who were a member of an under-funded defined benefit pension scheme that started to wind-up in specific financial circumstances between 1 January 1997 and 5 April 2005).

FINANCIAL OMBUDSMAN SERVICE, Exchange Tower, Harbour Exchange, London E14 9SR **Helpline** 0800-023 4567 **T** 020-7964 1000 **W** www.financial-ombudsman.org.uk
Chief Ombudsman, Caroline Wayman

PENSIONS OMBUDSMAN, 10 South Colonnade, Canary Wharf, London E14 4PU **T** 0800-917 4487 **E** enquiries@pensions-ombudsman.org.uk **W** www.pensions-ombudsman.org.uk
Pensions Ombudsman, Anthony Arter
Deputy Pensions Ombudsman, Karen Johnston

THE TAKEOVER PANEL

The Panel on Takeovers and Mergers is an independent body, established in 1968, whose main functions are to issue and administer the City code and to ensure equality of treatment and opportunity for all shareholders in takeover bids and mergers. The panel's statutory functions are set out in the Companies Act 2006.

The panel comprises up to 36 members representing a spread of expertise in takeovers, securities markets, industry and commerce. The chair, at least one deputy chair and up to 20 other members are nominated by the panel's own nomination committee. The remaining 12 members are nominated by professional bodies representing the accountancy, financial advice, insurance, investment and pension industries; the Association for Financial Markets in Europe; the Confederation of British Industry; the Quoted Companies Alliance; and UK Finance.

THE TAKEOVER PANEL, One Angel Court, London EC2R 7HJ **T** 020-7382 9026 **E** supportgroup@thetakeoverpanel.org.uk **W** www.thetakeoverpanel.org.uk
Chair, Michael Crane, QC

INSURANCE

AUTHORISATION AND REGULATION OF INSURANCE COMPANIES

Since 1 April 2013, under the Financial Services Act 2012, the prudential supervision of over 60,000 banks, insurers and other financial services firms is the responsibility of the Prudential Regulation Authority (PRA), an operationally independent subsidiary of the Bank of England. The Financial Conduct Authority (FCA) is responsible for consumer protection, promoting competition and markets oversight. All life insurers, general insurers, reinsurers, insurance and reinsurance brokers, financial advisers and composite firms are statutorily regulated. *See also* Financial Services Regulation.

Firms wishing to effect or carry out contracts of insurance must be granted authorisation to do so. The PRA assesses applicant insurers from a prudential perspective, using the same framework that is employed for supervision of existing insurers. The FCA then assesses applicants from a conduct perspective. Although the PRA manages the authorisation process, an insurer will be granted authorisation only where both the FCA and the PRA are satisfied that they meet their relevant requirements.

There are around over 1,200 insurance organisations and friendly societies with authorisation to transact one or more class of insurance business in the UK. Although the UK left the EU on 31 January 2020, it continued to be treated for most purposes as if it was still an EU member state during the transition period and most EU law continued to apply. *See also* Brexit.

COMPLAINTS

Disputes between consumers and financial businesses can be referred to the Financial Ombudsman Service (FOS). Consumers with a complaint about any form of money matter, including bank accounts, insurance, mortgages, savings, credit and claims management companies must first take the matter to the highest level within the provider. The provider has to provide a 'final response' within eight weeks. If the complaint remains unresolved consumers can refer the complaint, free of charge, to the FOS. Since 1 April 2020 the FOS compensation limits are £355,000 for acts or omissions by firms on or after 1 April 2019 and £160,000 for acts or omissions by firms before 1 April 2019, even if the complaint is referred to the FOS after this date. Award limits are automatically adjusted each year in line with inflation as measured by the Consumer Prices Index (CPI).

Businesses falling under the EU definition of a micro enterprise (businesses with a turnover of up to €2m and fewer than ten employees) may also refer a matter to the FOS. In 2018–19, 39 per cent of new complaints about financial services companies related to payment protection insurance (down 45 per cent). Other types of insurance, such as motor, buildings and life insurance, accounted for 10 per cent (down from 11 per cent) of the total number of 1.6 million complaints received. *See also* Financial Services Regulation.

ASSOCIATION OF BRITISH INSURERS

Over 90 per cent of the domestic business of UK insurance companies is transacted by the 200 members of the Association of British Insurers (ABI). The ABI is a trade association which protects and promotes the interests of all its insurance company members. Only insurers authorised in the EU are eligible for membership. Brokers, intermediaries, financial advisers and claims handlers may not join the ABI, but may have their own trade associations. Legal firms, consultants, price comparison websites and other firms which help insurers deliver their services may join the ABI as associate members.

ASSOCIATION OF BRITISH INSURERS (ABI), One America Square, 17 Crosswall, London EC3N 2LB
T 020-7600 3333 **W** www.abi.org.uk
Chair, Amanda Blanc (Group Chief Executive Officer, AVIVA plc)
Director-General, Huw Evans

BALANCE OF PAYMENTS

In 2018, financial and insurance services contributed £132bn to the UK economy, 6.9 per cent of the total. The UK trade surplus for insurance and pensions was around £63bn.

WORLDWIDE MARKET

In 2019 the UK insurance industry was the largest in Europe and the fourth largest in the world behind the USA, China and Japan. China continued to be the biggest growth area, increasing its premium income by 7.4 per cent in 12 months.

Market	Premium income ($bn)
USA	2,460
China	617
Japan	459
UK	366

TAKEOVERS AND MERGERS

In an industry as competitive as insurance, where products can be very similar, price can often be the most important factor for consumers when choosing a product. This makes increasing a company's market share through increased sales extremely difficult. An alternative strategy can be through takeovers and mergers.

Allianz continued to be among the most active in 2019–20 with the announcement in May 2019 of their purchase of LV General Insurance from Liverpool Victoria Friendly Society for £1.08bn and the general insurance division of Legal and General for £242m. Both deals were completed in January 2020 and moved Allianz to the UK's second largest general insurer.

In January 2019, Markerstudy Group announced the purchase of Co-op Insurance Services for £185m. Progress on this acquisition was slow due to the COVID-19 pandemic, opposition from the trade union UNITE and the complicated structure of the deal. The sale was finally completed in December 2020.

Over the last few years RSA has been linked with a number of companies as a takeover or merger target. These have included Aviva, Zurich and Allianz but nothing had been agreed until November 2020 when it was confirmed that Canadian insurer Intact Financial Corp. and Danish insurer Tryg A/S had agreed to purchase RSA Insurance Group Plc for a total of £7.2bn, the biggest acquisition of a UK-listed company in 2020. Under the deal, RSA will be broken up with Tryg taking the Swedish and Norwegian operations for £4.2bn and Intact taking the Canadian, UK and international business for £3bn. Both companies will jointly own RSA's Danish company.

In August 2020 motor Insurer Hastings Direct was purchased by Finnish Insurer SAMPO and South African consortium RMI for £1.66bn, and in October 2020 Ageas insurance sold their 50 per cent stake in Tesco underwriting to Tesco Bank, giving the latter full ownership of the company.

BREXIT

Although COVID-19 has grabbed much of the world's attention, the issue of Brexit and its impact on the UK Insurance Industry has not gone away.

The Insurance and financial services sector are very important to the UK and its economy. The UK is the fourth largest insurance and long-term savings industry in the world and the largest in the EU. Certainly, the insurance industry made no secret of being firmly in the 'remain' camp in the Brexit debate, with the ABI, British Insurance Brokers' Association (BIBA) and Lloyd's all stressing the volatility and uncertainty they believed a 'leave' vote would create. But the result in June 2016 proved that their lobbying had not persuaded enough voters.

While leaving the EU may present opportunities to expand global markets and the demand for insurance products will certainly not reduce, the referendum result left the industry with a number of concerns, not least the need for the UK government to negotiate a very complicated trade agreement, or at least interim measures, in a short space of time.

The UK formally left the EU on 31 January 2020, entering into an 11-month transition period. At the time of writing it is still not clear whether or not a trade deal can be agreed and whether insurance and financial services will be included in any deal and on what terms.

In the absence of a specific agreement, the main effect on insurance consumers will be that from 1 January 2021 anyone travelling to Europe will need to have health insurance cover to replace the provisions of the European Health Insurance Card (EHIC). This card had guaranteed to provide a UK traveller with the same state-provided healthcare that was available to a resident of the EU country they are visiting. This provision will cease on 1 January.

In the same way, if there is no agreement on the UK's participation in the Green Card Free Circulation Zone, which is separate from the main negotiations, anyone taking their vehicle to the EU will be required to carry with them a Green Card. This is a document that has to be issued by insurers to confirm correct insurance cover is in place to satisfy the law in the countries to be visited. Having a Green Card every time a vehicle crosses into or out of an EU country could add additional delay and inconvenience to every private and commercial driver, particularly those who regularly drive between Northern Ireland and the Republic.

For insurance companies, after 1 January 2020, if there is no specific agreement, UK insurers and brokers will not have 'passporting rights' to EU countries. This currently allows firms registered in the EEA to do business in all other EEA states without additional authorisation from each country. Many insurers have already opened EU-based subsidiaries to avoid the complication the loss of passporting rights will present.

As has been the case since the referendum, the insurance industry will wait for definite news on the outcome of trade negotiations.

COVID-19 AND THE INSURANCE INDUSTRY

Like all others, the insurance industry has been hit by restrictions and lockdowns imposed to reduce the spread of COVID-19. As a result, insurance staff joined the 49 per cent of UK workers who were working from home. Where this was not possible, the industry adapted its working practices and IT systems, as appropriate.

There were, however, specific areas of cover that were impacted directly or were altered as a result of the pandemic.

LIFE INSURANCE

With a very small number of exceptions, life insurance policies all pay out on death by any cause. As a result, between 1 March and 31 May 2020 the life insurance industry paid out over £90m in COVID-19 related death claims.

Some insurers were also prepared to offer payment holidays for some types of life insurance.

BUSINESS INSURANCE

Early in the pandemic there was criticism by some business leaders and politicians because business interruption insurers refused claims for lost profits caused by business closures, due to lockdown. In May 2020, in an open letter to the Association of British Insurers, almost 700 business owners accused the industry of an 'abrogation of responsibility.' A week later a beer and pub industry coalition sent a similar open letter. The industry responded by pointing out that it was not possible to buy a policy covering business interruption caused by a COVID-19 pandemic anywhere in the world. A very small number of firms had covered themselves for closure caused by notifiable diseases but these diseases were usually specifically listed in the policy and did not include COVID-19, as it was a very new virus.

TRAVEL INSURANCE

Initially, the main focus of travel insurers was dealing with claims for curtailment of trips and repatriation of people caught in areas closed or locked-down following COVID-19 outbreaks. The majority of travel insurance policies also covered medical expenses for people needing treatment for COVID-19 related conditions contracted while abroad and cancellation of trips where the Foreign, Commonwealth and Development Office (FCDO) had advised against travel. These claims had cost around £275m by December 2020.

Going forward, travel insurance will not cover anyone travelling against FCDO advice but will be automatically extended for travellers unable to return home due to quarantine or lockdowns.

HOME INSURANCE

In March 2020, as the COVID-19 restrictions and the first lockdown were announced, household insurers confirmed that any office-based worker who needed to work from home during the pandemic could do so without affecting their home contents insurance cover or needing to tell their insurers.

MOTOR INSURANCE

A number of additional support measures were announced for private car policyholders:

- If a person could not work from home and needed to drive to their workplace, insurers agreed to include this 'commuting cover' without notification and free of charge
- Anyone using their vehicle to help with community activity like delivering medicines or groceries or voluntary responders carrying patients or equipment were also covered automatically

- Key workers who needed to drive to a different place of work because of re-deployment or who had to work on multiple sites were automatically given cover for these activities

CHARITABLE

Possibly as a result of the bad publicity over business interruption insurance, in May 2020 the insurance and long-term savings industry launched a COVID-19 Support Fund to provide immediate relief to charities affected by COVID-19, as well as a longer-term programme of support for people, communities, and issues where there is the greatest need. It was supported by members of the ABI (Association of British Insurers), The British Insurance Brokers' Association (BIBA), Lloyd's, and The London Market Group (LMG). Its aim was to raise £100m which was achieved by September 2020.

UK insurance companies (ie excluding Lloyd's and London Market insurers) estimated that the cost of claims arising from the COVID-19 pandemic will be over £1.2bn.

GENERAL INSURANCE

In October 2018, the Financial Conduct Authority announced a market study into how insurers charge their customers for the most common types of general insurance, home and motor cover. The study was prompted by suggestions in the media and from consumer organisations that customers who remained with the same insurer over a period of years were paying more for exactly the same product than new customers. An interim report was published in October 2019 and the final report was released in September 2020. The FCA concluded that the pricing of these products was unclear and that some loyal customers could find themselves worse off than new ones. The FCA produced a number of proposals including:

- An automatic remedy for customers who find they are not being given the same deal as new customers
- Requirements on insurers to submit pricing data to FCA so they can check the new rules are being followed
- Moves towards the prohibition of automatic renewal of policies

The FCA believes the proposed remedies will improve competition, lower costs for supplying insurance, and, on average, reduce the prices paid by consumers. The FCA estimates that its proposals will save consumers £3.7bn over 10 years.

Flood and storm damage claims continued to be a headache for property insurers. Storms and flooding in the North of England and the Midlands in October and November 2019 costing £110m were swiftly followed by Storms Ciara and Dennis in February 2020, which produced 82,000 further claims costing around £363m. Following these flooding events the government asked Amanda Blanc, CEO of AVIVA Insurance, to conduct a review of the extent of insurance coverage in Doncaster, one of the worst hit areas. The report found that although a substantial number of homes and businesses had insurance cover some policies excluded flood cover despite it being available with other insurers. Private landlords were also criticised for not being transparent with tenants about the cover they had.

Finally, motor insurance policyholders had some good news in 2020 as the cost of an average comprehensive motor policy remained at a four-year low. The average price in 2020 was £460, £8 lower than in 2019.

TOP FIVE GENERAL INSURANCE COMPANIES IN THE UK 2018

Insurance Company	Gross written premium (£bn)
1. AVIVA	11.2
2. AIG	5.3
3. AXA	4.5
4. RSA	4.1
5. Zurich	3.6

LONDON INSURANCE MARKET

In recent years it has become increasingly difficult to define the London Insurance Market business. Many businesses operate in London as branch offices of parent companies located elsewhere in the world and may no longer separately identify as London Market premiums. What is acknowledged is that, despite the growth of other international centres, London remains the world's leading market for internationally traded insurance and reinsurance, its business comprising mainly overseas non-life large and high-exposure risks. The market is centred on the square mile of the City of London, which provides the required financial, banking, legal and other support services. Around 56 per cent of London market business is transacted at Lloyd's of London, the remainder through insurance companies and protection and indemnity clubs. In 2018 the market had a written gross premium income of £63.96bn. Around 200 Lloyd's brokers service the market.

The trade association for the international insurers and reinsurers writing primarily non-marine insurance and all classes of reinsurance business in the London market is the International Underwriting Association (IUA).

INTERNATIONAL UNDERWRITING ASSOCIATION, 1 Minster Court, Mincing Lane, London EC3R 7AA
T 020-7617 4444 **W** www.iua.co.uk
Chair, Malcolm Newman
Chief Executive, Dave Matcham

LLOYD'S OF LONDON

Lloyd's of London is an international market for almost all types of general insurance. Lloyd's currently has the capacity to accept insurance premiums of around £33bn. Much of this business comes from outside the UK and makes a valuable contribution to the balance of payments.

A policy is underwritten at Lloyd's by a mixture of private and corporate members. Specialist underwriters accept insurance risks at Lloyd's on behalf of members (referred to as 'names') grouped in syndicates. There are currently 93 syndicates of varying sizes, each managed by one of the 53 underwriting agents approved by the Council of Lloyd's.

Members divide into three categories: corporate organisations, individuals who have no limit to their liability for losses, and those who have an agreed limit (known as NameCos). Currently there are around 2,000 members of which around 200 are individuals.

Lloyd's is incorporated by an act of parliament (Lloyd's Acts 1871 onwards) and was governed by an 18-person council, and an 11-person Lloyd's Franchise Board. In November 2019 it was announced that as from 1 June 2020 these two boards would be merged into a single 15-member body – the Lloyd's Council.

Lloyd's corporation is a non-profit making body chiefly financed by its members' subscriptions. It provides the premises, administrative staff and services for Lloyd's underwriting syndicates. It does not, however, assume corporate liability for the risks accepted by its members. Individual members are responsible to the full extent of their personal means for their underwriting affairs unless they have converted to limited liability companies.

Lloyd's syndicates have no direct contact with the public. All business is transacted through insurance brokers accredited by the Corporation of Lloyd's. In addition, non-Lloyd's brokers in the UK, when guaranteed by Lloyd's brokers, are able to deal directly with Lloyd's motor syndicates, a facility that has made the Lloyd's market more accessible to the insuring public.

Under the Financial Services and Markets Act 2000, Lloyd's is regulated by the FCA and the PRA. However, in situations where Lloyd's internal regulatory and compensation arrangements are more far-reaching – as for example with the Lloyd's Central Fund which safeguards claim payments to policyholders – the regulatory role is delegated to the Council of Lloyd's.

DEVELOPMENTS IN 2019–20

Like all businesses, the Lloyd's market found the spring of 2020 extremely difficult as COVID-19 spread rapidly around the world causing devastation for individuals, communities and the world economy.

The market was able to continue to function through a programme of remote working (even Lloyd's famous underwriting room was forced to close), the use of a digital platform for arranging cover known as PPL and the use of the previously designed Lloyd's emergency trading protocol. The significant volatility of global financial markets had its effect on the value of the market's assets but these have been closely monitored and a plan put in place to mitigate the risks as far as possible. The extent of the market's liability for claims arising from COVID-19 is not yet clear but, as with any potential large loss event, market reports are already being collected and assessed.

2019 saw Lloyd's net resources increase by 9 per cent to £30.6bn.

It also proved to be a better year for the market with an overall profit of £2.5bn compared to losses of £2.0bn in 2017 and £1.0bn in 2018. Most underwriting results were better as a result of improved pricing. Pre-covid investment returns also showed signs of improvement at £3,537m (2018: £504m), a return of 4.8 per cent (2018: 0.7 per cent).

The greatest turnaround in underwriting results saw property underwriting move to a small £12m profit from a loss of £700m in 2018. The motor insurance underwriting result remained stable with a small profit of £12m (£11m in 2018).

Major claims (catastrophes) for the market cost £1.81bn, down from £2.91bn in 2018 net of reinsurance. After a quiet first half of 2019, Japan was hit, firstly by Typhoon Faxai then Typhoon Hagibis causing extensive flood and wind damage. Hurricane Dorian caused substantial damage in the Bahamas. There were also wildfires in the US and Australia and rioting in Chile.

2019 was also the first full year of trading for Lloyd's Europe (previously called Lloyd's Brussels) which will enable the market to continue to underwrite European business irrespective of the outcome of Brexit trade talks.

LLOYD'S OF LONDON, One Lime Street, London EC3M 7HA
T 020-7327 1000 **W** www.lloyds.com
Chair, Bruce Carnegie-Brown
Chief Executive, John Neal

LLOYD'S SEGMENTAL RESULTS 2019 *(£m)*

	Gross written premiums	Net earned premiums	Underwriting result
Reinsurance	11,418	7,841	(434)
Casualty	9,459	6,793	(390)
Property	9,856	6,815	(12)
Marine Aviation and Transit	2,802	2,343	(199)
Motor	1,053	955	11
Energy	1,500	1,008	27
Life	87	66	1
Total from syndicate operations	35,905	25,821	(972)

HEALTH AND PRIVATE MEDICAL INSURANCE

Over the four-year period between 2015 and 2019, the number of people covered by personal health insurance dropped to 1.2 million – a fall of nearly 10 per cent. Over the same period corporate health insurance saw a 5 per cent drop to 3.5 million. The industry laid the blame for these falls firmly at the door of the government, pointing out that over the same period Insurance Premium Tax had doubled from 6 per cent to 12 per cent, one of the highest rates in Europe. Other contributing factors included price rises of 15 per cent for personal cover and 8 per cent for corporate insurance. These were blamed on increases in medical costs driven by the use of more sophisticated technologies and treatments.

BRITISH INSURANCE COMPANIES

The following insurance company figures refer to members and certain non-members of the ABI.

DOMESTIC PROPERTY CLAIMS STATISTICS 2018

Type	Payment (£m)
Theft	422
Fire	520
Weather	585
Escape of water	877
Domestic subsidence	195
Accidental damage	325
other domestic claims	325
Total	3,249

WORLDWIDE GENERAL BUSINESS TRADING RESULTS *(£m)*

	2017	2018
Net written premiums	45,959	48,214
Underwriting results	1,679	1,935
Investment income	2,136	1,969
Overall trading profit	3,815	3,904
Profit as percentage of premium income	8%	8%

LIFE AND LONG-TERM INSURANCE AND PENSIONS

Although regulatory and product development activity was severely restricted by the pandemic, there were developments in a number of on-going issues, particularly in the pensions area.

In 2015 the government introduced a series of reforms that removed the requirement that pension pots had to be invested in a guaranteed income for life. Instead, savers who had reached 55 were able to access their pension savings and have total freedom over whether its left alone, invested for their retirement or spent.

To mark five years since those reforms, the ABI published a report in February 2020 calling for further measures to address a number of issues:

- The risk that savers may face a retirement in poverty because they have used their pension savings for holidays or consumer goods (this has become more pertinent as there is now evidence that the financial hardships caused by the COVID-19 pandemic may force more people to withdraw funds)
- The lack of suitable financial advice to enable savers to make informed decisions
- That the true impact of the reforms may not be apparent for decades

The Government and regulators have yet to respond.

Work continued throughout 2019 and 2020 on the establishment of a pensions dashboard. This is the online system that will allow individuals to see, in one place, all the private and company pensions they have contributed to in their working life. A system of this kind requires complex setting up and data standards as well as stringent security and privacy measures. The next steps, in 2021, will be the building integration and testing of the digital architecture.

Since 2013 the payment of commission by life insurance and pension companies to financial advisers who sell their investment products has been banned. It was replaced by a fee-based system involving an initial charge for becoming a client and an ongoing annual percentage charge. The intention was to create a fairer system that avoids mis-selling but a survey by the Association of British Insurers (ABI) found that 72 per cent of people were not prepared to pay for financial advice. The most popular alternative options were Government websites (29 per cent), family members (23 per cent) and online information (22 per cent). The FCA will now consider the report and decide if reform is needed.

PROTECTION INSURANCE CLAIMS 2019

Type of product	No. of claims paid*	% of new claims paid	Total value paid (£ thousand)	Average claim paid (£)
Critical illness	17,995	91.60	1,215,957	67,573.28
Term Life	39,638	97.40	3,073,382	77,535.28
Total permanent disability	474	71.70	32,345	68,174.00
Whole of life	229,197	99.99	794,106	3,464.73
Income protection	16,591	87.20	669,397	17,728.80
All protection products	303,896	98.30	5,785,187	19,037.00

* Figures are for new claims, as well as all income protection claims in payment

UK LONG-TERM INSURANCE NET PREMIUM INCOME

Year	Life & annuities	Individual pensions	Occupational pensions	Income protection & other business	Total
2008	36,300	30,523	62,820	1,541	131,183
2009	20,336	27,725	68,988	1,473	118,521
2010	19,241	28,218	64,033	1,482	112,975
2011	16,008	27,401	71,680	1,456	116,545
2012	14,893	33,219	71,148	1,862	121,122
2013	9,944	25,119	80,192	1,457	116,712
2014	9,985	23,721	70,826	1,290	105,822
2015	10,461	35,194	76,188	1,290	123,133
2016	12,679	29,684	75,634	1,553	119,551
2017	11,685	59,817	91,039	2,511	165,052
2018	10,275	49,462	110,582	2,489	172,807

THE NATIONAL DEBT

HISTORY

The early 1700s saw the meteoric rise of the banking and financial markets in Great Britain, with the emerging stock market revolving around government funds. The ability to raise money by means of creating debt through the issue of bills and bonds heralded the beginning of the national debt.

The war years of 1914–18 saw an increase in the national debt from £650m at the start of the war to £7,500m by 1919. The Treasury developed new expertise in foreign exchange, currency, credit and price control in order to manage the post-war economy. The slump of the 1930s necessitated the restructuring of the UK economy following the Second World War (the national debt stood at £21bn by its end) and the emphasis was placed on economic planning and financial relations.

The relatively high period of inflation in the 1970s and 1980s led to the rise of the national debt in nominal terms from £36bn in 1972 to £197bn in 1987 and then to £419bn in March 1998. Although in nominal terms the national debt has risen sharply in recent years, as a percentage of GDP it has decreased dramatically since the end of the Second World War, when it stood at 250 per cent of GDP (for current figures, *see* table below).

THE UK DEBT MANAGEMENT OFFICE

The decision in 1997 to transfer monetary policy to the Bank of England, while the Treasury retained control of fiscal policy, led to the creation of the UK Debt Management Office (DMO) as an executive agency of HM Treasury in April 1998. Initially the DMO was responsible only for the management of government marketable debt and for issuing gilts. In April 2000 responsibility for exchequer cash management and for issuing Treasury bills (short-dated securities with maturities of less than one year) was transferred from the Bank of England to the DMO. The national debt also includes the (non-marketable) liabilities of National Savings and Investments and other public sector and foreign currency debt.

In 2002 the operations of the long-standing statutory functions of the Public Works Loan Board, which lends capital to local authorities, and the Commissioners for the Reduction of the National Debt, which manages the investment portfolios of certain public funds, were integrated within the DMO.

UK PUBLIC SECTOR NET DEBT

	£ billion	per cent of GDP
2017–18 (outturn)	1,779	85.0
2018–19 (forecast)	1,810	83.7
2019–20 (forecast)	1,851	82.8

Source: HM Treasury – *The Budget 2018* (Crown copyright)

NATIONAL SAVINGS AND INVESTMENTS

NS&I (National Savings and Investments) is both a non-ministerial government department and an executive agency of the Chancellor of the Exchequer. It is one of the UK's largest savings organisations, with 25 million customers and around £157bn invested. When people invest in NS&I they are lending money to the government which pays them interest or prizes in return. All deposits are 100 per cent financially secure because they are guaranteed by HM Treasury.

TAX-FREE PRODUCTS

PREMIUM BONDS
Introduced in 1956, premium bonds enable savers to enter a regular draw for tax-free prizes, while retaining the right to get their money back. A sum equivalent to interest on each bond is put into a prize fund and distributed by monthly prize draws. The prizes are drawn by ERNIE (electronic random number indicator equipment) and are free of all UK income tax and capital gains tax. Two £1m jackpots are drawn each month in addition to other tax-free prizes ranging in value from £25 to £100,000.

Bonds are in units of £1, with a minimum purchase of £25, up to a maximum holding limit of £50,000 per person. Bonds become eligible for prizes once they have been held for one clear calendar month following the month of purchase. Each £1 unit can win only one prize per draw, but it will be awarded the highest for which it is drawn. Bonds remain eligible for prizes until they are repaid.

The scheme offers a facility to reinvest prize wins automatically. Upon completion of an automatic prize reinvestment mandate, holders receive new bonds which are immediately eligible for future prize draws. Bonds can only be held in the name of an individual and not by organisations.

INDIVIDUAL SAVINGS ACCOUNTS
Since April 1999 NS&I has offered cash individual savings accounts (ISAs). Its Direct ISA, launched in April 2006, can be opened and managed online and by telephone with a minimum investment of £1 and a maximum investment of £20,000 in the 2019–20 tax year. Interest for the Direct ISA is calculated daily, added to the account annually on 6 April and is free of tax.

Its Junior ISA, launched in August 2017 as a successor to children's bonds, can be opened for children under 18 by those with parental responsibility or, by a young person aged 16 or 17 for themselves. There is a minimum investment of £1 and a maximum investment of £4,368 in the 2019–20 tax year. It can only be opened and managed online and there are no withdrawals allowed until the young person reaches 18. Interest is accrued daily, added to the account annually on 6 April and is free of tax.

OTHER PRODUCTS

INCOME BONDS
NS&I income bonds were introduced in 1982. They are suitable for those who want to receive regular monthly payments of interest while preserving the full cash value of their capital. The minimum holding for each investment is £500 and the maximum £1m per person. A variable rate of interest is calculated on a day-to-day basis and paid monthly. Interest is taxable but is paid gross without deduction of tax at source.

GUARANTEED GROWTH AND GUARANTEED INCOME BONDS
Guaranteed growth and guaranteed income bonds, re-launched in December 2017, offer a lump sum investment that earns a fixed rate of interest over either a one-year term or a three-year term. The minimum holding is £500 to a maximum of £10,000 per person or trust per issue. For the guaranteed growth bond interest is calculated daily and added to the bond on each anniversary of the investment. The guaranteed income bond has interest paid monthly. Interest on both bonds is taxable but is paid gross without deduction of tax at source.

SAVINGS AND INVESTMENT ACCOUNTS
The direct saver account was launched in March 2010. Accounts can be opened by an individual aged at least 16, or jointly. Customers are able to invest between £1 and £2m per person. The account can be managed online or by telephone and funds can be withdrawn at any time. Interest is paid gross without deduction of tax at source.

The investment account can be opened with a minimum balance of £20 and has a maximum limit of £1m. The interest is paid gross without deduction of tax at source.

FURTHER INFORMATION
Further information regarding products and their current availability can be obtained online (**W** www.nsandi.com), by telephone (**T** 0808-500 7007) or by writing to: NS&I, Glasgow G58 1SB.

THE LONDON STOCK EXCHANGE

The London Stock Exchange Group (LSEG) serves the needs of companies by providing facilities for raising capital. It also operates marketplaces for members to trade financial instruments. including equities, bonds and derivatives, on behalf of investors and institutions such as pension funds and insurers.

LSEG's key subsidiary companies are the London Stock Exchange, Borsa Italiana, MTS (a trading platform for European government and corporate bonds), Turquoise (a trading platform for European equities) and FTSE (a global index provider).

Headquartered in London, with significant operations in Italy, France, North America and Sri Lanka, the group employs around 4,500 people.

HISTORY

The London Stock Exchange is one of the world's oldest stock exchanges, dating back more than 300 years to its origins in the coffee houses of 17th-century London. It was formally established as a membership organisation in 1801.

MAJOR DEVELOPMENTS

'BIG BANG'
In 1986 a package of reforms which are now known as 'Big Bang' transformed the London Stock Exchange and the City of London, liberalising the way in which banks and stockbroking firms operated and facilitating greater foreign investment. The London Stock Exchange ceased granting voting rights to individual members and became a private company. The 'Big Bang' also saw the start of a move towards fully electronic trading and the closure of the trading floor.

INTRODUCTION OF SETS
In October 1997, the Exchange introduced SETS, its electronic order book. The system enhanced the efficiency and transparency of trading on the Exchange, allowing trades to be executed automatically and anonymously rather than negotiated by telephone.

DEMUTUALISATION AND LISTING
The London Stock Exchange demutualised in 2000 and listed on its own main market in 2001.

MERGER WITH BORSA ITALIANA
In October 2007 the London Stock Exchange merged with the Italian stock exchange, Borsa Italiana, creating London Stock Exchange Group (LSEG).

DIVERSIFICATION
Since 2009 LSEG has diversified its business beyond the listing and trading of UK and Italian equities:
• In 2009 LSEG purchased Sri Lankan technology company MillenniumIT which provides technology to stock

exchanges, brokerages and regulators around the world. It also supplies the trading technology to LSEG's own markets
• In 2010 LSEG acquired a majority stake in Turquoise, a platform facilitating the trading of stocks listed in 19 European countries and the USA
• In 2011 LSEG became the owner of FTSE, the international business which creates and manages financial indices
• In 2013 LSEG purchased a majority stake in LCH (London Clearing House) (*see also* Financial Services Regulation, Recognised Clearing Houses and Central Counterparties)

UK EQUITY MARKETS

LSEG offers a range of listing options for companies, according to their size, history and requirements:
• The Main Market has the highest standards of regulation and disclosure obligations and is overseen by the UK Listing Authority (UKLA), a division of the Financial Conduct Authority (FCA). A Main Market listing enables established companies to raise capital, widen their investor base and have their shares traded alongside global peers. They are also eligible for inclusion in key indices, such as the FTSE 100 and the FTSE 250
• The Alternative Investment Market (AIM), established in June 1995, is specially designed to meet the needs of small and growing companies. It enables them to raise capital and broaden their investor base in a more flexible regulatory environment, while still being traded on an internationally recognised market. AIM companies retain an experienced Nominated Adviser (or 'Nomad') firm, which is responsible for ensuring the company's suitability for the market
• The Professional Securities Market (PSM), established in July 2005, allows companies to target professional investors only, on a market that offers greater flexibility in accounting standards
• The Specialist Fund Segment (SFS), established as the Specialist Fund Market (SFM) in November 2007, is a part of the London Stock Exchange's regulated Main Market designed for highly specialised investment entities, such as hedge funds or private equity funds, that wish to target institutional, professional, professionally advised and knowledgeable investors

As at 30 April 2019 there were 5,739 companies listed on LSEG's primary markets, with a combined market value of £2,052,073m: 1,770 on the Main Market (1,431 on the UK main market and 398 on the international main market), 3,852 on the AIM, 16 on the PSM and 35 entities on the SFS.

LONDON STOCK EXCHANGE, 10 Paternoster Square, London EC4M 7LS **T** 020-7797 1000
W www.londonstockexchange.com
Chair, Don Robert
Chief Executive, David Schwimmer

TAXATION

The government raises money to pay for public services such as education, health and the social welfare system through tax. Each year the Chancellor of the Exchequer's Budget sets out how much it will cost to provide these services and how much tax is therefore needed to pay for them. The tax is collected by HM Revenue and Customs (HMRC). There are several different types of tax:

- income tax payable on earnings, pensions, state benefits, savings and investments
- capital gains tax (CGT) payable on the disposal of certain assets
- inheritance tax (IHT) payable on estates upon death and certain lifetime gifts
- stamp duty payable when purchasing property and shares
- value added tax (VAT) payable on goods and services
- certain other duties such as fuel duty on petrol and excise duty on alcohol and tobacco

Corporation tax raises funds from companies and small businesses.

New taxation measures and changes to the administration of the taxation system are normally announced by the incumbent Chancellor of the Exchequer in the government's annual Budget in the autumn, with a spring statement on government spending forecasts.

The government has a stated policy of investing resources into reducing tax evasion and avoidance by both individuals and companies. Information and updates on the latest measures can be found on the government's website: www.gov.uk/government/policies/tax-evasion-and-avoidance).

The government also has an ongoing drive to simplify the UK tax system via the Office of Tax Simplification (OTS). Details of the OTS and its work can also be found on the government's website (**W** www.gov.uk/government/organisations/office-of-tax-simplification). The OTS welcomes views from individuals and can be contacted via email (**E** ots@ots.gov.uk).

HELP AND INFORMATION ON TAXATION

For information and help on any aspect of personal taxation, call the HMRC helpline (**T** 0300-200 3300). The lines are open 8am to 8pm from Monday to Friday, 8am to 4pm on Saturday, and 9am to 5pm on Sunday. For general queries (not specific cases) you can also use Twitter, starting your query with @HMRCcustomers.

HMRC no longer has a network of enquiry centres, because visitor numbers had dropped dramatically.

The HMRC website (**W** www.gov.uk/government/organisations/hm-revenue-customs) provides wide-ranging information.

INCOME TAX

Income tax is assessed on different sorts of income. Not all types of income are taxable and individuals are entitled to certain reliefs and allowances which reduce or, in some cases, cancel out their income tax bill.

An individual's taxable income is assessed each tax year, starting on 6 April and ending on 5 April the following year. The information below relates specifically to the year of assessment 2019–20, ending on 5 April 2020, and has only limited application to earlier years. Changes due to come into operation at a later date are briefly mentioned where information is available. Types of income that are taxable include:

- earnings from employment or profits from self-employment
- most pensions income, including state, company and personal pensions

- interest over the savings allowance
- income (dividends) from shares
- income from property
- income received from a trust
- certain state benefits
- an individual's share of any joint income

There are certain sorts of income on which individuals never pay tax. These are ignored altogether when working out how much income tax an individual may need to pay. Types of income that are not taxable include:

- certain state benefits and tax credits, such as child benefit, working tax credit, child tax credit, pension credit, attendance allowance, personal independence payment, housing benefit and maternity allowance
- winter fuel payments
- income from National Savings and Investments savings certificates
- interest, dividends and other income from various tax-free investments, notably individual savings accounts (ISAs)
- premium bond and national lottery prizes

PERSONAL ALLOWANCE

Every individual resident in the UK has a 'personal allowance' for tax purposes. This is the amount of taxable income that an individual can earn or receive each year tax-free. This tax year (2019–20) the basic personal allowance or tax-free amount is £12,500, an increase of £650 from the 2018–19 figure of £11,850. The personal allowance is for all taxpayers regardless of age.

Income tax is only due on an individual's taxable income that is above his or her tax-free allowance. Spouses and civil partners are taxed separately, with each entitled to his or her personal allowance. Each spouse or civil partner may obtain other allowances and reliefs where the required conditions are satisfied.

The personal allowance is available for all individuals with income up to £100,000. Those individuals with an 'adjusted net income' above the £100,000 limit have their personal allowance reduced by half the excess (£1 for every £2) they have over that limit until their personal allowance is reduced to nil.

An individual's 'adjusted net income' is calculated in a series of steps. The starting point is 'net income', which is the total of the individual's income subject to income tax less specified deductions such as payments made gross to pension schemes or trading losses. This net income is then reduced by the grossed-up amount of the individual's Gift Aid contributions to charities and the grossed-up amount of the individual's pension contributions that have received tax relief at source. The final step is to add back any relief for payments to trade unions or police organisations deducted in arriving at the individual's net income. The result is the individual's adjusted net income.

MARRIAGE ALLOWANCE

Some married couples and civil partners, made up of one non-taxpayer and one basic rate taxpayer, are eligible for a marriage allowance, which lets them share some of the non-taxpayer's unused annual income tax allowance. In the 2019–20 tax year, the allowance allows a spouse or civil partner with an income less than £12,500 to transfer up to £1,250 of their unused personal allowance to their higher-income partner. So long as the person receiving the transfer is a basic rate taxpayer, which, in most cases, means having an income of between £12,500 and £50,000 (£43,430 in Scotland), this transferable tax allowance is worth up to £250 in 2019–20.

BLIND PERSON'S ALLOWANCE

If an individual is registered blind or is unable to perform any work for which eyesight is essential, he or she can claim blind person's allowance, an extra amount of tax-free income added to the personal allowance. In 2019–20 the blind person's allowance is £2,450, irrespective of age or income. If an individual is married or in a civil partnership and cannot use all of the allowance because of insufficient income, the unused part of the allowance can be passed to the spouse or civil partner.

PROPERTY AND TRADING ALLOWANCES

These allowances benefit 'micro-entrepreneurs' who use one or more of a wide range of money-making activities to supplement their income. Individuals with property or trading income do not need to declare or pay tax on the first £1,000 they earn from each source per year. If they earn more than that amount they will have to declare it to HMRC, but they can still take advantage of the allowance.

Property income qualifying for relief under the property allowance could be any income that an individual makes from renting out a residence, home, building, property or land – even from renting out a driveway as a parking space, for example, or renting out a room via websites like Airbnb.

Trading income qualifying for the allowance can be income from any sale of goods or services. An individual could do tasks such as cleaning or odd jobs, hiring out their own equipment such as power tools, or selling goods through websites like eBay or Etsy.

INCOME TAX ALLOWANCES

	2018–19	2019–20
Personal allowance	£11,850	£12,500
Income limit for personal allowance	£100,000	£100,000
Marriage allowance	£1,190	£1,250
Blind person's allowance	£2,390	£2,450
Property allowance	£1,000	£1,000
Trading allowance	£1,000	£1,000

CALCULATING INCOME TAX DUE

Individuals' liability to pay income tax is determined by establishing their level of taxable income for the year. For married couples and civil partners, income must be allocated between the couple by reference to the individual who is beneficially entitled to that income. Where income arises from jointly held assets, it is normally apportioned equally between the partners. If, however, the beneficial interests in jointly held assets are not equal, in most cases couples can make a special declaration to have income apportioned by reference to the actual interests in that income.

To work out an individual's liability for tax, his or her taxable income must be allocated between three different types:
- earned income (excluding income from savings and dividends)
- income from savings
- company dividends from shares and other equity-based investments

After the tax-free personal allowance plus any deductible allowances and reliefs have been taken into account, the amount of tax an individual pays is calculated using different tax rates and a series of tax bands. Each tax band applies to a slice of an individual's income after tax allowances and any reliefs have been taken into account.

SCOTLAND

Since the start of the tax year 2017–18, the Scottish government has been able to set the rates and bands for tax on income from earnings, pensions and most other taxable income in Scotland. The tax raised is paid to the Scottish government.

Income from savings and dividends continues to be taxed at the same rate as in the rest of the UK.

UK INCOME TAX BANDS AND RATES 2018–19

England, Wales & NI	Band*	Rate
Basic rate	£0–37,500	20%
Higher rate	£37,501–150,000	40%
Additional rate	£150,000+	45%
Scotland		
Starter rate	£0–2,049	19%
Basic rate	£2,050–12,444	20%
Intermediate rate	£12,445–30,930	21%
Higher rate	£30,931–£150,000	40%
Top rate	£150,000+	46%

The first calculation is applied to earned income, which includes income from employment or self-employment, most pension income and rental income, plus the value of a wide range of employee 'benefits in kind' such as company cars, living accommodation and private medical insurance (for more information on benefits in kind, *see* later section on Payment of Income Tax). In working out the amount of an individual's net taxable earnings, all expenses incurred 'wholly, exclusively and necessarily' in the performance of his or her employment duties, together with the cost of business travel, may be deducted. Fees and subscriptions to certain professional bodies may also be deducted. Redundancy payments and other sums paid on the termination of an employment are assessable income, but the first £30,000 is normally tax-free provided the payment is not linked with the recipient's retirement or performance.

For UK taxpayers other than Scottish residents, the first £37,500 of taxable income remaining after the tax-free allowance and any deductible allowances and reliefs have been taken into account is taxed at the basic rate of 20 per cent. Taxable income between £37,501 and £150,000 is taxed at the higher rate of 40 per cent. Taxable income above £150,001 is taxed at the additional rate of 45 per cent.

Savings and dividend income is added to an individual's other taxable income and taxed last. This means that tax on such sorts of income is based on an individual's highest income tax band.

SAVINGS INCOME

The second calculation is applied to any income from savings received by an individual. Savings income includes interest paid on bank and building society accounts, interest paid on accounts from providers like credit unions or National Savings and Investments, interest distributions (but not dividend distributions) from authorised unit trusts, open-ended investment companies and investment trusts, interest from peer-to-peer lending, government or company bonds and life annuity payments.

The appropriate rate at which savings income must be taxed is determined by adding income from savings to an individual's other taxable income (excluding dividends). Savings interest may be set against the personal allowance (if that is not used up on income from employment or pension), the starting rate for savings income and the personal savings allowance.

The starting rate of tax for savings income allows an individual to earn up to £5,000 of interest tax-free in 2019–20, but this amount is reduced by £1 for every £1 of their non-savings income above the personal allowance threshold. For example, a person earning £16,000 from their employment:

- their personal allowance of £12,500 is set against their income, leaving £3,500 taxable
- this taxable amount reduces their starting rate for savings, but they can still receive up to £1,500 (£5,000 less £3,500) of tax-free interest on their savings

In addition, the personal savings allowance (PSA) allows a basic rate taxpayer to earn their first £1,000 of savings income tax-free. A higher rate taxpayer may earn their first £500 of savings income tax-free. Additional rate taxpayers do not get a PSA. Interest from ISAs (see Tax-Free Savings) do not count towards this limit.

It is an individual's responsibility to inform HMRC if they earn savings income above the PSA on which tax is payable; any tax owed will normally be collected via the individual's tax code.

Tax on interest over the allowance is paid at the individual's usual rate of income tax, that is for a taxpayer not resident in Scotland 20 per cent for basic rate taxpayers, 40 per cent for higher rate taxpayers and 45 per cent for additional rate taxpayers. If savings income falls on both sides of a tax band, the relevant amounts are taxed at the rates for each tax band.

DIVIDEND INCOME

The third and final income tax calculation is on UK dividends, which means income from shares in UK companies and other share-based investments.

All taxpayers now have a £2,000 tax-free dividend allowance. This means that individuals do not have to pay tax on the first £2,000 of their dividend income, no matter what non-dividend income they have. The allowance is available to anyone who has dividend income.

Dividends received that exceed the £2,000 allowance are treated as the top band of income. This means that if an individual's divided income takes them from one income tax band into the next, they will then pay the higher dividend rate on that portion of income.

TAX RATES ON DIVIDENDS OVER £2,000

Band	2019–20
Basic rate	7.5%
Higher rate	32.5%
Additional rate	38.1%

If there is significant change to an individual's savings or other income, whatever his or her current tax bracket, it is the individual's responsibility to contact HMRC immediately, even if he or she does not normally complete a tax return. This enables HMRC to work out whether more tax should be paid, or if a refund is due.

TAX-FREE SAVINGS

There is a small selection of savings and investment products that are tax-free. This means that there is no tax to pay on any income generated in the form of interest or dividends, nor on any increase in the value of the capital invested. Their tax-efficient status has been granted by the government in order to give people an incentive to save more. For this reason there are usually limits and restrictions on the amount of money an individual may invest in such savings and investments.

Individual savings accounts (ISAs) are the best known among tax-efficient savings and investments. There are four types: cash ISAs, stocks and shares ISAs, innovative finance ISAs (earning interest and capital gains free of tax on loans made via peer-to-peer lending platforms) and lifetime ISAs. Money may be invested in one of each type of ISA each tax year, up to an overall annual subscription limit, which is

£20,000 in 2019–20. This may be paid into one ISA or split between some or all of the other types, although no more than £4,000 may be paid into a lifetime ISA in one tax year.

To be eligible to invest in ISAs and receive all profits free of tax, individuals must be:

- aged 16 or over to hold a cash ISA
- aged 18 or over for a stocks and shares or innovative finance ISA
- aged 18 or over but under 40 for a lifetime ISA
- resident in the UK or, if not resident in the UK, a Crown servant or their spouse or civil partner

An ISA must be in an individual's name and cannot be held jointly with another person, but spouses and civil partners may inherit their partner's ISA allowance after death.

The lifetime ISA introduced in April 2017 may be opened by UK residents between the ages of 18 and 40, and allows individuals to save up to £4,000 a year between the ages of 18 and 50. Savings put into the account before their 50th birthday will qualify for a government bonus of 25 per cent, up to £1,000 a year. An individual may use their savings and bonus towards the purchase of a first-time home worth up to £450,000. Alternatively, they may choose to keep the account as retirement savings until their 60th birthday, after which date they can withdraw all the money tax-free.

There are also long-term, tax-free savings accounts for children called Junior ISAs. The investment limit for these in 2019–20 is £4,368 per child. Parents or guardians with parental responsibility can open Junior ISAs for children aged under 18 who live in the UK. However, while parents can open and manage Junior ISAs for their children, the invested money belongs to the child, who can take control of their account when they are 16 and withdraw the money when they are 18. Children aged 16 and 17 can open their own Junior ISA as well as an adult cash ISA. Junior ISAs automatically turn into an adult ISA when the child turns 18.

The Help to Buy ISA is one of a number of government measures to help individuals save towards buying their first home. Aspiring first-time buyers aged 16 or over who open a Help to Buy ISA before 30 November 2019 may continue to save up to £200 a month and the government boosts their savings by 25 per cent, up to a maximum of £3,000 per person. If, therefore, an individual saves £12,000, the government bonus boosts their total savings to £15,000. The minimum government bonus is £400, meaning that the individual must save at least £1,600 to qualify for the scheme. There is no monthly minimum investment.

Savings held in a Help to Buy ISA can be accessed at any time, but the government payment is only added if and when the savings are used as a deposit on a first and only home in the UK. The bonus is available on home purchases of up to £450,000 in London and up to £250,000 outside London. Qualifying properties must be purchased with a mortgage and must be lived in by the purchaser and not rented out.

Those who hold an account may continue saving into their account, but must claim their bonus by 1 December 2030.

Further details about ISAs are available via the HMRC's savings helpline (T 0300-200 3300).

DEDUCTIBLE ALLOWANCES AND RELIEF

Income taxpayers may be entitled to certain tax-deductible allowances and reliefs as well as their personal allowances. Examples include the married couple's allowance and maintenance payments relief, see below. Unlike the tax-free allowances, these are not amounts of income that an individual can receive tax-free but amounts by which their tax bill can be reduced.

MARRIED COUPLE'S ALLOWANCE

A married couple's allowance (MCA) is available to taxpayers who are married or are in a civil partnership where at least one partner was born before 6 April 1935 and they usually live together. Eligible couples can start to claim the MCA from the year of marriage or civil partnership registration.

The MCA is restricted to give relief at a fixed rate of 10 per cent, which means that – unlike the personal allowance – it is not income that can be received without paying tax. Instead, it reduces an individual's tax bill by up to a fixed amount of 10 per cent of the amount of the allowance to which they are entitled.

In 2019–20, the maximum MCA is £8,915 and is therefore worth £891.50 off a couple's tax bill. In 2019–20 this maximum is reduced by £1 for every £2 the highest earner's income exceeds £29,600, to a minimum MCA of £3,450. The minimum always applies, regardless of the level of the highest earner's income.

For marriages before 5 December 2005, the allowance is based on the husband's income; for marriages and civil partnerships after that date, the allowance is based on the income of the highest earner. A couple can decide to have the minimum amount of the allowance split equally between them, or transfer the whole of the minimum MCA from one to the other. If an individual does not have enough income to use all of his or her share of the MCA, the unused part of it can be transferred to his or her spouse or civil partner. A couple must inform HMRC of their decision before the start of the new tax year in which they want the decision to take effect.

MAINTENANCE PAYMENTS RELIEF

An allowance is available to reduce an individual's tax bill for maintenance payments he or she makes to his or her ex-spouse or former civil partner in certain circumstances. To be eligible:
- one or other partner must have been born before 6 April 1935
- the couple must be legally separated or divorced
- the maintenance payments being made must be under a court order
- the payments must be for the maintenance of an ex-spouse or former civil partner (provided he or she is not now remarried or in a new civil partnership) or for children who are under 21.

For the tax year 2019–20, this allowance can reduce an individual's tax bill by:
- 10 per cent of £3,260 (maximum £326) – this applies where an individual makes maintenance payments of £3,260 or more a year
- 10 per cent of the amount the individual has actually paid – this applies where an individual makes maintenance payments of less than £3,260 a year

An individual cannot claim a tax reduction for any voluntary payments he or she makes for a child, ex-spouse or former civil partner. To claim maintenance payments relief, individuals should call the HMRC helpline (**T** 0300-200 3300).

TAX RELIEF FOR LANDLORDS

Up to April 2017 individual landlords were able to deduct all their costs, including mortgage interest, from their profits before they paid tax. Wealthier landlords received tax relief at 40 per cent and 45 per cent.

This calculation has been changing for properties other than furnished holiday lettings. From April 2020, tax relief on financing costs will only be at the basic rate. Property profits (excluding interest costs) and other income will be assessed, and then amount of tax due will be reduced by the amount of the interest multiplied by the basic rate of income tax. This change only applies to landlords who are individuals, including where they operate through a partnership. It does not apply to companies who rent out property. *See* **W** www.gov.uk/government/news/changes-to-tax-relief-for-residential-landlords.

CHARITABLE DONATIONS

A number of charitable donations qualify for tax relief. Individuals can increase the value of regular or one-off charitable gifts of money, however small, by using the Gift Aid scheme that allows charities or community amateur sports clubs (CASCs) to reclaim 20 per cent basic rate tax relief on donations they receive. If a taxpayer gives £10 using Gift Aid, for example, the donation is worth £12.50 to the charity or CASC.

Individuals who pay 40 per cent higher rate income tax can claim back the difference between the 40 per cent and the 20 per cent basic rate of income tax on the total (gross) value of their donations. For example, a 40 per cent tax payer donates £100; the total value of this donation to the charity or CASC is £125, of which the individual can claim back 20 per cent (£25) for themselves. Similarly, those who pay 45 per cent additional rate income tax can claim back the difference between the 45 per cent and the 20 per cent basic rate on the total (gross) value of their donations. On a £100 donation, this means they can claim back £31.25. Scottish taxpayers who pay tax at rates higher than the basic 20 per cent rate can claim extra tax relief.

In order to make a Gift Aid donation, individuals need to make a Gift Aid declaration. The charity or CASC will normally ask an individual to complete a simple form. One form can cover every gift made to the same charity or CASC for whatever period chosen, including both gifts made in the past and in the future. Charities are able to claim a Gift Aid-type tax refund on small donations in various circumstances, *see* **W** www.gov.uk/claim-gift-aid/small-donations-scheme.

Individuals can use Gift Aid provided the amount of income tax and/or capital gains tax they have paid in the tax year in which their donations are made is at least equal to the amount of basic rate tax the charity or CASC is reclaiming on their gifts. It is the responsibility of the individual to make sure this is the case. If an individual makes Gift Aid donations and has not paid sufficient tax, they may have to pay the shortfall to HMRC. The Gift Aid scheme is not available for non-taxpayers.

Individuals who complete a tax return and are due a tax refund can ask HMRC to treat all or part of it as a Gift Aid donation.

For employees or those in receipt of an occupational pension, a tax-efficient way of making regular donations to charities is to use the payroll giving scheme. It allows the donations to be paid from a salary or pension before income tax is deducted. This effectively reduces the cost of giving for donors, which may allow them to give more.

For example, it costs a basic rate taxpayer only £8 in take-home pay to give £10 to charity from their pre-tax pay. Where a donor pays 40 per cent higher rate tax, that same £10 donation costs the taxpayer £6, and for donors who pay the additional 45 per cent rate tax, it costs £5.50.

Anyone who pays tax through the pay as you earn (PAYE) system (*see* Payment of Income Tax) can give to any charity of their choosing in this way, providing their employer or pension provider offers the payroll giving scheme. There is no limit to the amount individuals can donate.

Details of tax-efficient charitable giving methods can be found at **W** www.gov.uk/donating-to-charity.

TAX RELIEF ON PENSION CONTRIBUTIONS

Pensions are long-term investments designed to help ensure that people have enough income in retirement. The government encourages individuals to save towards a pension by offering tax relief on their contributions. Tax relief reduces an individual's tax bill or increases their pension fund.

The way tax relief is given on pension contributions depends on whether an individual pays into a company, public service or personal pension scheme.

For employees who pay into a company or public service pension scheme, most employers take the pension contributions from the employee's pay before deducting tax, which means that the individual – whether they pay income tax at the basic or higher rate – gets full tax relief straight away. Some employers, however, use the same method of paying pension contributions as that used by personal pension scheme payers described below.

Individuals who pay into a personal pension scheme normally make contributions from their net salary; that is, after tax has been deducted. For each pound that individuals contribute to their pension from net salary, the pension provider claims tax back from the government at the basic rate of 20 per cent and reinvests it on behalf of the individual into the scheme. In practice this means that for every £80 an individual pays into their pension, they receive £100 in their pension fund.

Subject to certain income related limits (*see* below) higher rate taxpayers currently get 40 per cent tax relief on money they put into a pension. On contributions made from net salary, the first 20 per cent is claimed back from HMRC by the pension scheme in the same way as for a lower rate taxpayer. It is then up to individuals to claim back the other 20 per cent from HMRC, either when they fill in their annual tax return. In a similar fashion, individuals subject to the 45 per cent additional rate of income tax can get 45 per cent tax relief on their pension contributions.

Non-taxpayers can still pay into a personal pension scheme and benefit from 20 per cent basic rate relief on the first £2,880 a year they contribute. In practice this means that the government tops up their £2,880 contribution to make it £3,600, which is the current universal pension allowance. Such pension contributions may be made on behalf of a non-taxpayer by another individual. An individual may, for example, contribute to a pension on behalf of a husband, wife, civil partner, child or grandchild. Tax relief will be added to their contribution at the basic rate, again on up to £2,880 a year benefiting the recipient, but their own tax bill will not be affected.

In any one tax year, individuals can get tax relief on pension contributions made into any number and type of registered pension schemes of up to 100 per cent of their annual earnings, irrespective of age, up to a maximum 'annual allowance'. For the tax year 2019–20 the annual allowance for most individuals is £40,000. This £40,000 annual allowance is reduced by £1 for every £2 of income between £150,000 and £210,000, so that those earning £210,000 and over have a £10,000 annual allowance.

Everyone also has a 'lifetime allowance' which defines the total amount a taxpayer can save in their pension fund and still get tax relief at their highest rate of income tax on all their contributions. The lifetime allowance is £1.055m in 2019–20, increased from £1.03m in 2018–19.

For information on pensions and tax relief visit **W** www.gov.uk/browse/working/workplace-personal-pensions. Another useful source of information and advice is the Pensions Advisory Service (TPAS), an independent voluntary organisation grant-aided by the government, at **W** www.pensionsadvisoryservice.org.uk; or the pensions helpline is on **T** 0300-123 1047.

PAYMENT OF INCOME TAX

Employees have their income tax deducted from their wages throughout the year by their employer, who sends it on to HMRC. Those in receipt of a company pension have their tax deducted in the same way by their pension provider. This system of collecting income tax is known as 'pay as you earn' (PAYE).

BENEFITS IN KIND

The PAYE system is also used to collect tax on certain employee benefits or 'benefits in kind' that employees or directors receive from their employer as part of their remuneration package. These include company cars, living accommodation, private medical insurance paid for by the employer or cheap or free loans from the employer. Some of these benefits are tax-free, including employer-paid contributions into an employee's pension fund, cheap or free canteen meals, works buses, in-house sports facilities, reasonable relocation expenses, provision of a mobile phone and workplace nursery places provided for the children of employees. Tax is paid on the 'taxable value' of any taxable benefit.

Employers submit returns for individual employees to HMRC on form P11D, with details of any benefits they have been given. Employees should get a copy of this form by 6 July following the end of the tax year and must enter the value of the benefits they have received on their tax return for the relevant year, even if tax has already been paid on them under PAYE. Benefits in kind may be taxed under PAYE by being offset against personal tax allowances in an individual's PAYE code. Otherwise tax will be collected after the end of the tax year by the issue of an assessment on the value of the benefits.

SELF ASSESSMENT

Individuals who are not on PAYE, notably the self-employed, need to complete a self assessment tax return each year online (**W** www.gov.uk/log-in-file-self-assessment-tax-return), and pay any income tax owed in twice-yearly instalments. Some individuals with more complex tax affairs, such as those who earn money from rents or investments above a certain level, may also need to make a self assessment return even if they are on PAYE. HMRC uses the figures supplied on the tax return to work out the individual's tax bill, or they can choose to work it out themselves. It is called self assessment because individuals are responsible for making sure the details they provide are correct.

Some people still prefer to file a paper tax return. The forms can be downloaded from **W** www.gov.uk/government/publications/self-assessment-tax-return-sa100, but it should be noted that the deadline for returning a paper form is earlier than the online version.

Central to the self assessment system is the requirement for individuals to register online if they should complete a self assessment return. Individuals have six months from when the tax year ends to report any new income. The registration process is online (**W** www.gov.uk/log-in-file-self-assessment-tax-return), but it is important to allow enough time for the process – HMRC recommend allowing up to 20 working days extra for a first online return.

TAX RETURN FILING AND PAYMENT DEADLINES

There are also key deadlines for filing (sending in) completed tax returns and paying the tax due. Failure to do so can incur penalties, interest charges and surcharges.

KEY FILING DATES FOR SELF ASSESSMENT RETURNS

Date	Why the date is important
31 Oct*	Deadline for filing paper returns* for tax year ending the previous 5 April
30 Dec	Deadline for online filing where the amount owed for tax year ending the previous 5 April is less than £3,000 and the taxpayer wants HMRC to collect any tax due through their PAYE tax code
31 Jan†	Deadline for online filing of returns for tax year ending the previous 5 April

* Or three months from the date the return was requested if this was after 31 July

† Or three months from the date the return was requested if this was after 31 October

KEY SELF ASSESSMENT PAYMENT DATES

Date	What payment is due?
31 Jan	Deadline for paying the balance of any tax owed – the 'balancing payment' – for the tax year ending the previous 5 April. It is also the date by which a taxpayer must make any first 'payment on account' (advance payment) for the current tax year. For example, on 31 January 2020 a taxpayer may have to pay both the balancing payment for the year 2018–19 and the first payment on account for 2019–20.
31 Jul	Deadline for making a second payment on account for the current tax year

LATE FILING AND PAYMENT PENALTIES

Late filing of tax returns incurs an automatic £100 penalty, although individuals may appeal against the penalty if they have a reasonable excuse.

- Over three months late – £10 each day, up to a maximum of £900, in addition to the penalty above
- Over six months late – an additional £300 or 5 per cent of the tax due, whichever is the higher, in addition to the penalty above
- Over 12 months late – a further £300 or 5 per cent of the tax due, whichever is the higher. In serious cases HMRC reserve the right to ask for 100 per cent of the tax due instead. In both instances this is in addition to the penalty above

Late payment of tax owing incurs interest at 3.25 per cent.

Interest is due on all outstanding amounts, including any unpaid penalties, until payment is received in full. Individuals may calculate the penalties they owe for late self assessment tax returns and payments online (**W** www.gov.uk/estimate-self-assessment-penalties).

TAX CREDITS

Child tax credit, working tax credit and the new universal credit are paid to qualifying individuals. Although the titles of these credits incorporate the word 'tax', they do not affect the amount of income tax payable or repayable. They are forms of social security benefits. *See* Social Welfare.

CAPITAL GAINS TAX

Capital gains tax (CGT) is a tax on the gain or profit that an individual makes when they sell, give away or otherwise dispose of certain assets, for example shares, land or buildings. An individual potentially has to pay CGT on gains they make from any disposal of taxable assets during a tax year. There is a tax-free allowance and some additional reliefs that may reduce an individual's CGT bill. The following information relates to the tax year 2019–20 ending on 5 April 2020.

CGT is paid by individuals who are either resident or ordinarily resident in the UK for the tax year, executors or administrators – 'personal representatives' – responsible for a deceased person's financial affairs and trustees of a settlement. Non-residents are not usually liable to CGT unless they carry on a business in the UK through a branch or agency. However, from April 2015, the government introduced a CGT charge on gains made by non-residents disposing of UK residential property. Special CGT rules apply to individuals who used to live and work in the UK but have since left the country.

CAPITAL GAINS CHARGEABLE TO CGT

Typically, individuals have made a gain if they sell an asset for more than they paid for it. It is the gain that is taxed, not the amount the individual receives for the asset. For example, a man buys shares for £1,000 and later sells them for £3,000.

He has made a gain of £2,000 (£3,000 less £1,000). If someone gives an asset away, the gain will be based on the difference between what the asset was worth when originally acquired and its worth at the time of disposal. The same is true when an asset is sold for less than its full worth in order to give away part of the value. For example, a woman buys a property for £120,000 and three years later, when the property's market value has risen to £180,000, she gives it to her son. The son may pay nothing for the property, or pay less than its true worth, for example £100,000. Either way, she has made a gain of £60,000 (£180,000 less £120,000).

If an individual disposes of an asset he or she received as a gift, the gain is worked out according to the market value of the asset when it was received. For example, a man gives his sister a painting worth £8,000. She pays nothing for it. Later she sells the painting for £10,000. For CGT purposes, she is treated as making a gain of £2,000 (£10,000 less £8,000). If an individual inherits an asset, the estate of the person who died does not pay CGT at the time. If the inheritor later disposes of the asset, the gain is worked out by looking at the market value at the time of the death (the probate value). For example, a woman acquires some shares for £5,000 and leaves them to her niece when she dies. No CGT is payable at the time of death when the shares are worth £8,000. Later the niece sells the shares for £10,000. She has made a gain of £2,000 (£10,000 less £8,000).

Individuals may also have to pay CGT if they dispose of part of an asset or exchange one asset for another. Similarly, CGT may be payable if an individual receives a capital sum of money from an asset without disposing of it, for example where he or she receives compensation when an asset is damaged.

Assets that may lead to a CGT charge when they are disposed of include:

- shares in a company that are not held in an ISA or PEP
- units in a unit trust
- land and buildings (though not normally an individual's main home – *see* 'Disposal of a home' section for details)
- personal possessions, including jewellery, paintings, antiques and other personal effects, individually worth £6,000 or more
- business assets

EXEMPT GAINS

Certain kinds of assets do not give rise to a chargeable gain when they are disposed of. Assets exempt from CGT include:

- a car
- an individual's main home, if certain conditions are met
- tax-free investments such as assets held in an ISA or PEP
- UK government gilts or 'bonds' (including premium bonds)
- personal belongings, including jewellery, paintings and antiques, individually worth £6,000 or less
- betting, lottery or pools winnings

DISPOSAL OF A HOME: PRIVATE RESIDENCE RELIEF

When an individual sells their own home they automatically qualify for private residence relief, which means they do not have to pay any CGT provided that:

- the property has been their only home or main residence since they bought it, and
- they have used it as their home and for no other purpose

Even if an individual has not lived in the property for all of the time that they owned it, they may still be entitled to full relief.

Under the relief rules, the final 18 months of ownership are always treated as if the individual lived in the property even if they did not. This means that if an individual moves out of one home and into a new one, they have up to 18 months in which to sell their former home without incurring any CGT on the sale proceeds.

Full relief is granted to individuals when they sell their home if they could not live in it for periods because they were working abroad. Full relief is also granted if an individual is prevented from living in the home for periods totalling a maximum of four years because their job required them to work elsewhere in the UK. In both cases, however, for the property to qualify for full relief, the general rule is that it must have been the individual's only or main home both before and after they worked away.

Individuals can also get full relief when they sell their home if they have lived away from it for reasons other than working away, provided all of the following apply:
- they were not living away from the home for more than three years in total during the time they owned the property
- they were not entitled to private residence relief on any other property during that time
- the property was their only or main home both before and after they lived elsewhere

There are instances when individuals may not get the full amount of private residence relief when they sell their home. These include if:
- the grounds, including all buildings, are larger than 5,000 square metres
- any part of the home has been used exclusively for business purposes
- all or part of the home has been let out (or more than one lodger has been taken in at a time). The owner may, however, be entitled to another form of CGT relief – letting relief – instead
- the main reason the property was bought was to make a profit from a quick sale

If an individual lives in – not just owns – more than one property, they can 'nominate' which should be treated as their main home for private residence relief purposes. Married couples or those in a civil partnership must make such a nomination jointly as they are only entitled to private residence relief on one house between them.

There is a calculator to help individuals work out how much private residence relief they may be entitled to when selling their main residence at **W** www.gov.uk/tax-relief-selling-home.

OTHER TRANSACTIONS NOT CHARGEABLE TO CGT

Certain other kinds of disposal similarly do not give rise to a chargeable gain. For example, individuals who are married or in a civil partnership and live together may sell or give assets to their spouse or civil partner without having to pay CGT. Individuals may not, however, give or sell assets cheaply to their children without having to consider CGT. There is no CGT to pay on assets given to a registered charity.

CALCULATING CGT

CGT is worked out for each tax year and is charged on the total of an individual's taxable gains after taking into account certain costs and reliefs that can reduce or defer chargeable gains, allowable losses made on assets to which CGT normally applies and an annual exempt (tax-free) amount that applies to every individual. If the total of an individual's net gains in a tax year is less than the annual exempt amount (AEA), the individual will not have to pay CGT. For the tax year 2019–20 the AEA is £12,000. If an individual's net gains are more than the AEA, they pay CGT on the excess. Should any part of the exemption remain unused, this cannot be carried forward to a future year.

There are certain reliefs available that may eliminate, reduce or defer CGT. Some reliefs are available to many people while others are available only in special circumstances. Some reliefs are given automatically while others are given only if they are claimed. Some of the costs of buying, selling and improving assets may be deducted from total gains when working out an individual's chargeable gain.

RATES OF TAX

The net gains remaining, if any, calculated after subtracting the AEA, deducting costs and taking into account all CGT reliefs, incur liability to capital gains tax. Individuals pay CGT at a rate of 10 per cent on gains up to the unused amount of the basic rate income tax band (if any) and at 20 per cent on gains above that amount. Rates for individuals for gains on residential property not eligible for private residence relief (*see* above) are charged at a rate of 18 per cent up to any unused amount of the basic rate income tax band and at 28 per cent on gains above that amount. The CGT rate charged to trustees and personal representatives is 28 per cent on residential property and 20 per cent on other chargeable assets.

An individual can report any CGT they need to pay (*see* below):
- straight away using the 'real time' Capital Gains Tax service
  W   www.gov.uk/capital-gains-tax/report-and-pay-capital-gains-tax*
- annually in a self assessment tax return

* It should be noted that if the 'real time' service is used but the individual needs to submit a tax return for another reason, then their gains have to be reported again through self assessment

VALUATION OF ASSETS

The disposal proceeds (the amount received as consideration for the disposal of an asset) are the sum used to establish the gain or loss once certain allowable costs have been deducted. In most cases this is straightforward because the disposal proceeds are the amount actually received for disposing of the asset. This may include cash payable now or in the future and the value of any asset received in exchange for the asset disposed of. However, in certain circumstances, the disposal proceeds may not accurately reflect the value of the asset and the individual may be treated as disposing of an asset for an amount other than the actual amount (if any) that they received. This applies, in particular, where an asset is transferred as a gift or sold for a price known to be below market value. Disposal proceeds in such transactions are deemed to be equal to the market value of the asset at the time it was disposed of rather than the actual amount (if any) received for it.

Market value represents the price that an asset might reasonably be expected to fetch upon sale in the open market. In the case of unquoted shares or securities, it is assumed that the hypothetical purchaser in the open market would have available all the information that a prudent prospective purchaser of shares or securities might reasonably require if that person were proposing to purchase them from a willing vendor by private treaty and at arm's length. The market value of unquoted shares or securities will often be established following negotiations with the specialist HMRC Shares and Assets Valuation department. The valuation of land and interests in land in the UK is dealt with by the Valuation Office Agency. Special rules apply to determine the market value of shares quoted on the London Stock Exchange.

ALLOWABLE COSTS

When working out a chargeable gain, once the actual or notional disposal proceeds have been determined, certain allowable costs may be deducted. There is a general rule that no costs that could be taken into account when working out income or losses for income tax purposes may be deducted. Subject to this, allowable costs are:
- acquisition costs – the actual amount spent on acquiring the asset or, in certain circumstances, the equivalent market value

- incidental costs of acquiring the asset, such as fees paid for professional advice, valuation costs, stamp duty and advertising costs to find a seller
- enhancement costs – incurred for the purpose of enhancing the value of the asset (not including normal maintenance and repair costs)
- expenditure on defending or establishing a person's rights over the asset
- incidental costs of disposing of the asset, such as fees paid for professional advice, valuation costs, stamp duty and advertising costs to find a buyer

If an individual disposes of part of his or her interest in an asset, or part of a holding of shares of the same class in the same company, or part of a holding of units in the same unit trust, he or she can deduct the relevant part of the allowable costs of the asset or holding when working out the chargeable gain.

ENTREPRENEURS' RELIEF

Entrepreneurs' relief allows individuals in business and some trustees to claim relief on the first £10m of gains made on the disposal of any of the following:

- all or part of a business
- the assets of a business after it has ceased
- certain shares in a company.

The relief is available to taxpayers as individuals if they are in business, for example as a sole trader or as a partner in a trading business, or if they hold shares in their own personal trading company. This relief is not available for companies.

Depending on the type of disposal, certain qualifying conditions need to be met throughout a qualifying one-year period. For example, if an individual is selling all or part of their business, they must have owned the business during a one-year period that ends on the date of the disposal.

Where all gains qualify for entrepreneurs' relief, CGT is charged at 10 per cent. An individual can make claims for this relief on more than one occasion as long as the lifetime total of all their claims does not exceed £10m of gains qualifying for relief.

BUSINESS ASSET ROLLOVER RELIEF

When certain types of business asset are sold or disposed of and the proceeds are reinvested in new qualifying trading assets, business asset rollover relief makes it possible to 'rollover' or postpone the payment of any CGT that would normally be due. The gain is deducted from the base cost of the new asset and only becomes chargeable to CGT on the eventual disposal of that replacement asset, unless a further rollover situation then develops. Full relief is available if all the proceeds from the original asset are reinvested in the qualifying replacement asset.

For example, a trader sells a freehold office for £75,000 and makes a gain of £30,000. All of the proceeds are reinvested in a new freehold business premises costing £90,000. The trader can postpone the whole of the £30,000 gain made on the sale of the old office, as all of the proceeds have been reinvested. When the trader eventually sells the new business premises and the CGT bill becomes payable, the cost of the new premises will be treated as £60,000 (£90,000 less the £30,000 gain).

If only part of the proceeds from the disposal of an old asset is reinvested in a new one, different rules may apply, but it may still be possible to postpone paying tax on part of the gain until the eventual disposal of the new asset.

Relief is only available if the acquisition of the new asset takes place within a period between 12 months before and 36 months after the disposal of the old asset. However, HMRC may extend this time limit at their discretion where there is a clear intention to acquire a replacement asset. The most common types of business asset that qualify for rollover relief are land, buildings occupied and used for the purposes of trade, and fixed plant and machinery. Assets used for the commercial letting of furnished holiday accommodation qualify if certain conditions are satisfied.

GIFT HOLD-OVER RELIEF

The gift of an asset is treated as a disposal made for a consideration equal to market value, with a corresponding acquisition by the transferee at an identical value. In the case of gifts of business assets made by individuals and a limited range of trustees, a form of hold-over relief may be available. This relief, which must be claimed, in effect enables liability for CGT to be deferred and passed to the person to whom the gift is made. Relief is limited to the transfer of certain assets, including the following:

- gifts of assets used for the purposes of a business carried on by the donor or his or her personal company
- gifts of shares in trading companies that are not listed on a stock exchange
- gifts of shares or securities in the donor's personal trading company
- gifts of agricultural land and buildings that would qualify for inheritance tax agricultural property relief
- gifts that are chargeable transfers for inheritance tax purposes
- certain types of gifts that are specifically exempt from inheritance tax

Hold-over relief is automatically due on certain sorts of gifts, including gifts to charities and community amateur sports clubs, and gifts of works of art where certain undertakings have been given. There are certain rules to prevent gifts hold-over relief being used for tax avoidance purposes. For example, restrictions may apply where an individual gifts assets to trustees administering a trust in which the individual retains an interest, or the assets transferred comprise a dwelling-house. Subject to these exceptions, the effect of a valid claim for hold-over relief is similar to a claim for rollover relief on the disposal of business assets.

OTHER CGT RELIEFS

There are certain other CGT reliefs available on the disposal of property, shares and business assets. For detailed information on all CGT reliefs and for more general guidance on CGT, visit **W** www.gov.uk/personal-tax/capital-gains-tax.

REPORTING AND PAYING CGT

Individuals are responsible for telling HMRC about capital gains on which they have to pay tax, either:

- on their self assessment tax return by filling in the capital gains supplementary pages (the return explains how to obtain these pages if needed), or
- by visiting **W** www.gov.uk/capital-gains-tax/report-and-pay-capital-gains-tax, which explains what information to gather before following the link on that page to the 'real time' capital gains tax service

There is a time limit for claiming capital losses. The deadline is four years from 31 January after the end of the tax year in which the loss was made.

INHERITANCE TAX

Inheritance tax (IHT) is a tax on the value of a person's estate on death and on certain gifts made by an individual during his or her lifetime, usually payable within six months of death. Broadly speaking, a person's estate is everything he or she owned at the time of death, including property, possessions, money and investments, less his or her debts. Not everyone pays IHT. It only applies if the taxable value of an estate is above the current IHT threshold. If an estate, including any assets held in trust and gifts made within seven years of death, is less than the threshold (in the nil-rate band), no IHT will be due.

A claim can be made to transfer any unused IHT nil-rate band on a person's death to the estate of their surviving spouse or civil partner. This applies where the IHT nil-rate band of the first deceased spouse or civil partner was not fully used in calculating the IHT liability of their estate. When the surviving spouse or civil partner dies, the unused amount may be added to their own nil-rate band (*see* below for details).

IHT used to be something only very wealthy individuals needed to consider. This is no longer the case. The fact that the IHT threshold has not kept pace with house price inflation in recent years means that the estates of some 'ordinary' taxpayers are now liable for IHT purely because of the value of their home. However, there are a number of ways that individuals – while still alive – can legally reduce the IHT bill that will apply to their estates on death. Several valuable IHT exemptions are available (explained further below) which allow individuals to pass on assets during their lifetime or in their will without any IHT being due. Detailed information on IHT is available at **W** www.gov.uk/inheritance-tax. Further help is also available from the probate and inheritance tax helpline (**T** 0300-123 1072).

DOMICILE

Liability to IHT depends on an individual's domicile at the time of any gift or on death. Domicile is a complex legal concept and what follows explains some of the main issues. An individual is domiciled in the country where he or she has a permanent home. Domicile is different from nationality or residence, and an individual can only have one domicile at any given time.

A 'domicile of origin' is normally acquired from the individual's father on birth, so this may not be the country in which the individual is born. For example, a child born in Germany to a father who is working there, but whose permanent home is in the UK, will have the UK as his or her domicile of origin. Until a person legally changes his or her domicile, it will be the same as that of the person on whom they are legally dependent.

Individuals can legally acquire a new domicile – a 'domicile of choice' – from the age of 16 by leaving the current country of domicile, settling in another country and providing strong evidence of intention to live there permanently or indefinitely. Women who were married before 1974 acquired their husband's domicile and still retain it until they legally acquire a new domicile.

For IHT purposes, there is a concept of 'deemed domicile'. This means that even if a person is not domiciled in the UK under general law, he or she is treated as domiciled in the UK at the time of a transfer (ie at the time of a lifetime gift or on death) if he or she was:
- domiciled in the UK at any time in the three years immediately before the transfer, or
- 'resident' in the UK in at least 17 of the 20 income tax years of assessment ending with the year in which a transfer is made

Where a person is domiciled, or treated as domiciled, in the UK at the time of a gift or on death, the location of assets is immaterial and full liability to IHT arises. A non-UK domiciled individual is also liable to IHT, but only on chargeable property in the UK.

The assets of spouses and registered civil partners are not merged for IHT purposes, except that the IHT value of assets owned by one spouse or civil partner may be affected if the other also owns similar assets (eg shares in the same company or a share in their jointly owned house). Each spouse or partner is treated as a separate individual entitled to receive the benefit of his or her exemptions, reliefs and rates of tax.

IHT EXEMPTIONS

There are some important exemptions that allow individuals to legally pass assets on to others, both before and after their death – without being subject to IHT.

Exempt Beneficiaries
Assets can be given away to certain people and organisations without any IHT having to be paid. These gifts, which are exempt whether individuals make them during their lifetime or in their will, include gifts to:
- a spouse or civil partner, even if the couple is legally separated (but not if they are divorced or the civil partnership has been dissolved). Note that gifts to an unmarried partner or a partner with whom the donor has not formed a civil partnership are not exempt
- a 'qualifying' charity established in the EU or another specified country
- some national institutions, including national museums, universities and the National Trust
- UK political parties

Annual Exemption
The first £3,000 of gifts made each tax year by each individual is exempt from IHT. If this exemption is not used, or not wholly used in any year, the balance may be carried forward to the following year only. A couple, therefore, may give away a total of £6,000 per tax year between them or £12,000 if they have not used their previous year's annual exemptions.

Wedding Gifts/Civil Partnership Ceremony Gifts
Some gifts are exempt from IHT because of the type of gift or reason for making it. Wedding or civil partnership ceremony gifts made to either of the couple are exempt from IHT up to certain amounts:
- gifts by a parent or step-parent, £5,000
- gifts by a grandparent or great-grandparent, £2,500
- gifts by anyone else, £1,000
The gift must be made on or shortly before the date of the wedding or civil partnership ceremony. If the ceremony is called off but the gift is made, this exemption will not apply.

Small Gifts
An individual can make small gifts, up to the value of £250, to any number of people in any one tax year without them being liable for IHT. However, a larger sum such as £500 cannot be given and exemption claimed for the first £250. Note that this exemption cannot be used with any other exemption when giving to the same person. For example, a parent cannot combine a 'small gifts exemption' with a 'wedding/civil partnership ceremony gift exemption' to give a child £5,250 when he or she gets married or forms a civil partnership. Neither may an individual combine a 'small gifts exemption' with the 'annual exemption' to give someone £3,250. Note that it is possible to use the 'annual exemption' with any other exemption, such as the 'wedding/civil partnership ceremony gift exemption'. For example, if a child marries or forms a civil partnership, the parent who has not made any other taxable transfers in the year can give him or her a total IHT-free gift of £8,000 by combining £5,000 under the wedding/civil partnership gift exemption and £3,000 under the annual exemption.

Normal Expenditure
Any gifts made out of an individual's after-tax income (not capital) are exempt from IHT if they are part of their normal expenditure and do not result in a fall in their standard of living. These can include regular payments to someone, such as an

allowance or gifts for Christmas or a birthday, and regular premiums paid on a life insurance policy for someone else.

Maintenance Gifts

An individual can make IHT-free maintenance payments to his or her spouse or registered civil partner, ex-spouse or former civil partner, relatives dependent because of old age or infirmity, and children (including adopted children and step-children) who are under 18 or in full-time education.

POTENTIALLY EXEMPT TRANSFERS

If an individual makes a gift to either another individual or a certain type of trust and it is not covered by one of the above exemptions, it is known as a 'potentially exempt transfer' (PET). A PET is only free of IHT on two strict conditions:

- the gift must be made at least seven years before the donor's death; if the donor does not survive seven years after making the gift, it will be liable for IHT
- the gift must be made as a true gift with no strings attached (technically known as a 'gift with reservation of benefit'). This means that the donor must give up all rights to the gift and stop benefiting from it in any way

If a gift is made and the donor does retain some benefit from it, then it will still count as part of the donor's estate no matter how long he or she lives after making it. For example, a father could make a lifetime gift of his home to his child, on condition that he continue to live in it. HMRC would not accept this as a true gift unless he paid his child a full commercial rent to do so, because he would be considered to still have a material interest in the gifted home. Its value, therefore, would still be liable for IHT.

In some circumstances a gift with strings attached might give rise to an income tax charge on the donor based on the value of the benefit he or she retains. In this case the donor can choose whether to pay the income tax or have the gift treated as a gift with reservation.

CHARGEABLE TRANSFERS

Any remaining lifetime gifts that are not (potentially or otherwise) exempt transfers are chargeable transfers or 'chargeable gifts', meaning that they incur liability to IHT. Chargeable transfers comprise mainly gifts to or from companies and gifts to particular types of trust. There is an immediate charge to IHT on chargeable gifts, and additional tax may be payable if the donor dies within seven years of making a chargeable gift.

DEATH

Immediately before the time of death an individual is deemed to make a transfer of value. This transfer will comprise the value of assets forming part of the deceased's estate after subtracting most liabilities. Any exempt transfers may be excluded, such as transfers for the benefit of a surviving spouse or civil partner and charities. Death may also trigger three additional liabilities:

- on a PET made within the seven years before death, which loses its potential status and becomes chargeable to IHT
- on the value of gifts made with reservation may incur liability if any benefit was enjoyed within the seven years before the death
- additional tax may become payable for chargeable lifetime transfers made within the seven years before the death

The 'personal representative' (the person nominated to handle the affairs of the deceased person) arranges to value the estate and pay any IHT that is due. One or more personal representatives can be nominated in a person's will, in which case they are known as the 'executors'. If a person dies without leaving a will a court can nominate the personal representative, who is then known as the 'administrator'. Valuing the deceased person's estate is one of the first things a personal representative

needs to do. The representative will not normally be able to take over management of the estate (called 'applying for probate') until all or some of any IHT that is due has been paid.

VALUATIONS

When valuing a deceased person's estate, all assets (property, possessions and money) owned at the time of death and certain assets given away during the seven years before death must be included. The valuation must accurately reflect what those assets would reasonably fetch in the open market at the date of death. The value of all of the assets that the deceased owned should include:

- his or her share of any assets owned jointly with someone else, for example a house owned with a partner
- any assets that are held in a trust, from which the deceased had the right to benefit
- any assets given away, but in which he or she kept an interest (gifts with reservation)
- PETs given away within the last seven years

Most estate assets can be valued quite easily, for example money in bank accounts or stocks and shares. In other instances the help of a professional valuer may be needed. Advice on how to value different assets, including joint or trust assets, is available at **W** www.gov.uk/valuing-estate-of-someone-who-died.

When valuing an estate, special relief is made available for certain assets. The two main reliefs are agricultural property relief and business relief, outlined below. Once all assets have been valued, the next step is to deduct from the total assets everything that the deceased person owed, such as unpaid bills, outstanding mortgages, other loans and their funeral expenses.

The value of all of the assets, less the deductible debts, is their estate. IHT is only payable on any value above the threshold for the tax year. It is payable at the current rate of 40 per cent. This rate is reduced to 36 per cent where 10 per cent or more of a net estate (after deducting IHT exemptions, reliefs and the nil-rate band) is left to charity.

RELIEF FOR SELECTED ASSETS

Agricultural Property

If an individual owns agricultural property and it is part of a working farm, it is possible to pass on some of this property free of IHT, either during that individual's lifetime or on their death. Agricultural property generally includes land or pasture used in the growing of crops or intensive rearing of animals for food consumption. It can also include farmhouses and farm cottages. The agricultural property can be owner-occupied or let. Relief is only due if the transferor has owned the property and it has been occupied for agricultural purposes for a minimum period.

The chargeable value transferred, either in a lifetime gift or on death, must be determined. This value may then be reduced by a percentage. Depending on the type of property, it will normally qualify for relief of 100 per cent.

Business Relief

Business relief is available on transfers of certain types of business and of business assets if they qualify as relevant business property and the transferor has owned them for a minimum period. The relief can be claimed for transfers made during the person's lifetime or on their death. Where the chargeable value transferred is attributable to relevant business property, the business relief reduces that value by either 50 or 100 per cent, depending on the type of asset. Business relief may be claimed on relevant business property, including property and buildings or assets such as unlisted shares or machinery.

It is a general requirement that the property must have been retained for a period of two years before the transfer or death, and restrictions may be necessary if the property has not been used wholly for business purposes. The same property cannot obtain both business property relief and the relief available for agricultural property.

CALCULATION OF TAX PAYABLE

The calculation of IHT payable adopts the use of a cumulative or 'running' total. Each chargeable lifetime transfer is added to the total if it was made within seven years of the donor's death. To the running total this produces is added the total value of the estate at death. If the total exceeds the inheritance tax threshold (the 'nil-rate band') IHT becomes payable. The rate of tax that is paid is determined by the element that causes the estate to exceed the threshold; gifts use up all or part of the nil-rate band first.

Lifetime Chargeable Transfers

The value transferred by total chargeable transfers during the deceased's lifetime must be added to the seven-year running total to calculate whether any IHT is due. If the nil-rate band is exceeded, tax will be imposed on the excess at the rate of 20 per cent. However, if the donor dies within a period of seven years from the date of the chargeable lifetime transfer, additional tax may be due. This is calculated by applying tax at the full rate of 40 per cent (rather than 20 per cent). The amount of tax is then reduced by applying taper relief, which is a percentage of the full rate of 40 per cent. This percentage is governed by the number of years from the date of the lifetime gift to the date of death, as follows:

TAPER RELIEF

Years between transfer and death	Taper relief %
More than 3 but not more than 4	20%
More than 4 but not more than 5	40%
More than 5 but not more than 6	60%
More than 6 but not more than 7	80%

Should this exercise produce liability greater than that previously paid at the 20 per cent rate on the lifetime transfer, the difference must be paid in additional tax. Where the calculation shows an amount falling below tax paid on the lifetime transfer, no additional liability can arise nor will the shortfall become repayable.

Taper relief is only available if the calculation discloses a liability to IHT. There is no liability if the lifetime transfer falls within the nil-rate band.

Potentially Exempt Transfers

Where a PET loses immunity from liability to IHT because the donor dies within seven years of making the transfer, the value transferred enters into the running total. Any liability to IHT will be calculated by applying the full rate of 40 per cent, reduced by taper relief if applicable. Again, liability to IHT can only arise if the nil-rate band is exceeded.

Death

On death, IHT is due on the value of the deceased's estate plus the running total of gifts made in the seven years before death if that comes to more than the nil-rate band. IHT is then charged at the full rate of 40 per cent on the amount in excess of the nil-rate band.

Settled Property and Trusts

Trusts are special legal arrangements that can be used by individuals to control how their assets are distributed to their beneficiaries and minimise their IHT liability. Complex rules apply to establish IHT liability on 'settled property' which includes property held in trust, and individuals are advised to take expert legal advice when setting up trusts.

RATES OF TAX

There are four rates:

- nil-rate
- lifetime rate of 20 per cent
- full rate of 40 per cent
- reduced rate of 36 per cent applicable to taxable estates where 10 per cent of the net estate has been left to charity (*see* above)

The basic nil-rate band threshold is £325,000 for 2019–20. In 2015 the government announced that the nil-rate band would remain at this figure until April 2021. Any excess over this level is taxable at the relevant rate.

ADDITIONAL THRESHOLD (RNRB)

The additional threshold (or residence nil-rate band) was introduced from April 2017, applying where a residence the deceased owns and has lived in passes on their death to direct descendants. The additional threshold is £150,000 in 2019–20 and £175,000 in 2020–21. It will increase in line with the consumer prices index (CPI) from 2021–22 onwards. Any unused nil-rate band may be transferred to the surviving spouse or civil partner.

The RNRB will also be available when an individual downsizes or ceases to own a home and other assets of an equivalent value are passed on death to direct descendants. These changes apply for deaths on or after 6 April 2017 where the deceased downsized or disposed of a property after 7 July 2015.

There is a tapered withdrawal of the RNRB for estates with a net value of more than £2m. This will be at a rate of £1 for every £2 over the additional threshold. Guidance on the additional threshold can be found at **W** www.gov.uk/guidance/inheritance-tax-residence-nil-rate-band.

TRANSFER OF NIL-RATE BAND

Transfers of property between spouses or civil partners are generally exempt from IHT. This means that someone who dies leaving some or all of their property to their spouse or civil partner may not have fully used up their nil-rate band. Any nil-rate band unused on the first death can be used when the surviving spouse or civil partner dies. A transfer of unused nil-rate band from a deceased spouse or civil partner may be made to the estate of their surviving spouse or civil partner.

Where a valid claim to transfer unused nil-rate band is made, the nil-rate band that is available when the surviving spouse or civil partner dies is increased by the proportion of the nil-rate band unused on the first death. For example, if on the first death the chargeable estate is £150,000 and the nil-rate band is £300,000, 50 per cent of the nil-rate band would be unused. If the nil-rate band when the survivor dies is £329,000, then that would be increased by 50 per cent to £493,500. The amount of the nil-rate band that can be transferred does not depend on the value of the first spouse or civil partner's estate. Whatever proportion of the nil-rate band is unused on the first death is available for transfer to the survivor.

The amount of additional nil-rate band that can be accumulated by any one surviving spouse or civil partner is limited to the value of the nil-rate band in force at the time of their death. This may be relevant where a person dies having survived more than one spouse or civil partner.

Where these rules have effect, personal representatives do not have to claim for the unused nil-rate band to be transferred at the time of the first death. Any claims for transfer of unused nil-rate band amounts are made by the personal representatives of the estate of the second spouse or civil partner to die when they make an IHT return.

Guidance on how to transfer the nil-rate band can be found at **W** www.gov.uk/government/publications/claim-the-residence-nil-rate-band-rnrb-iht435.

PAYMENT OF TAX

IHT is normally due six months after the end of the month in which the death occurs or the chargeable transaction takes place. This is referred to as the 'due date'. Tax on some assets, such as business property, certain shares and securities and land and buildings (including the deceased person's home), can be deferred and paid in equal instalments over ten years, though interest will be charged in most cases. If IHT is due on lifetime gifts and transfers, the person who received the gift or assets (the transferee) is normally liable to pay the IHT, though any IHT already paid at the time of a transfer into a trust or company will be taken into account. If tax owed is not paid by the due date, interest is charged on any unpaid IHT, no matter what caused the delay in payment.

HMRC has developed an online service to support the administration of IHT. This does away with the need to complete paper forms and enables individuals to proceed with their application for probate and submit IHT accounts online:

* if you are dealing with the estate of someone who has died, there is some guidance about the basic processes at **W** www.gov.uk/valuing-estate-of-someone-who-died and this page also gives links to make the relevant return
* to get a payment reference number, go to **W** www.gov.uk/paying-inheritance-tax/get-a-reference-number at least three weeks before the payment is due
* forms and worksheets for calculating IHT liabilities are available at **W** www.gov.uk/government/publications/inheritance-tax-inheritance-tax-account-iht100

CORPORATION TAX

Corporation tax is a tax on a company's profits, including all its income and gains. This tax is payable by UK resident companies and by non-resident companies carrying on a trade in the UK through a permanent establishment. The following comments are confined to companies resident in the UK. The word 'company' is also used to include:

* members' clubs, societies and associations
* trade associations
* housing associations
* groups of individuals carrying on a business but not as a partnership (for example, cooperatives)

A company's taxable income is charged by reference to income or gains arising in its 'accounting period', which is normally 12 months long. In some circumstances accounting periods can be shorter than 12 months, but never longer. The accounting period is normally the period for which a company's accounts are drawn up, but the two periods do not have to coincide.

If a company is liable to pay corporation tax on its profits, several things must be done. HMRC must be informed that the company exists and is liable for tax. A self assessment company tax return plus full accounts and calculation of tax liability must be filed by the statutory filing date, normally 12 months after the end of the accounting period. Companies have to work out their own tax liability and have to pay their tax without prior assessment by HMRC. Records of all company expenditure and income must be kept in order to work out the tax liability correctly. Companies are liable to penalties if they fail to carry out these obligations.

There is a radically simpler way for small self-employed businesses, such as sole traders and partnerships, to calculate their tax. Such businesses with receipts of £150,000 or less are able to work out their income on a cash basis and use simplified expenses rules, rather than having to follow the rules for larger businesses. Limited companies and limited liability partnerships can not use the cash basis. If a small business uses cash basis accounting and the business grows during the tax year, it can stay in the scheme up to a total business turnover of £300,000 a year.

Corporation tax information is available at **W** www.gov.uk/browse/business/business-tax and companies may file their company tax returns online (**W** www.gov.uk/file-your-company-accounts-and-tax-return).

RATE OF TAX

The rate of corporation tax is fixed for a financial year starting on 1 April and ending on the following 31 March. If a company's accounting period does not coincide with the financial year, its profits must be apportioned between the financial years and the tax rates for each financial year applied to those profits. The corporation tax liability is the total tax for both financial years.

The rate of corporation tax has been 19 per cent since 1 April 2017, but will decrease to 17 per cent for the financial year commencing 1 April 2020.

ALLOWANCES AND RELIEFS

Businesses can claim capital allowances, on certain purchases or investments. This means that a proportion of these costs can be deducted from a business' taxable profits and reduce its tax bill. Capital allowances are currently available on plant and machinery such as equipment and business vehicles. Reliefs are also available for research and development, profits from patented inventions and certain creative industries. The amount of the allowance or relief depends on what is being claimed for.

Detailed information on allowances and reliefs is available at **W** www.gov.uk/corporation-tax-rates/allowances-and-reliefs.

PAYMENT OF TAX

Corporation tax liabilities are normally due and payable in a single lump sum not later than nine months and one day after the end of the accounting period. For 'large' companies – those with profits over £1.5m – there is a requirement to pay corporation tax in four quarterly instalments. Where a company is a member of a group, the profits of the entire group must be merged to establish whether the company is 'large'.

HMRC runs a Business Payment Support Service (BPSS) which allows businesses facing temporary financial difficulties more time to pay their tax bills. Traders concerned about their ability to meet corporation tax, VAT or other payments owed to HMRC can call the BPSS Line (**T** 0300-200 3835) seven days a week. This helpline is for new enquiries only, not for traders who have already been contacted by HMRC about an overdue payment. For details of the service, visit **W** www.gov.uk/government/organisations/hm-revenue-customs/contact/business-payment-support-service.

CAPITAL GAINS

Chargeable gains arising to a company are calculated in a manner similar to that used for individuals. However, companies are not entitled to the CGT annual exemption. Companies incur liability to corporation tax rather than CGT on chargeable gains. Tax is due on the full chargeable gain of an accounting period after subtracting relief for any losses.

GROUPS OF COMPANIES

Each company within a group is separately charged corporation tax on profits, gains and income. However, where one group member realises a trading loss for which special rules apply, a claim may be made to offset the taxable loss against profits of some other member of the same group. These rules do not apply to capital losses. The transfer of capital assets from one member of a group to a fellow member will usually incur no liability to tax on chargeable gains.

SPORTS CLUBS

Though corporation tax is payable by unincorporated associations (including most sports clubs) on their profits, a substantial exemption from liability to corporation tax is available to qualifying registered community amateur sports clubs (CASCs). Sports clubs that are registered as CASCs are exempt from liability to corporation tax on:

- profits from trading where the turnover of the trade is less than £50,000 in a 12-month period
- income from letting property where the gross rental income is less than £30,000 in a 12-month period
- bank and building society interest received
- chargeable gains
- any Gift Aid donations

All of the exemptions depend upon the club having been a registered CASC for the whole of the relevant accounting period and the income or gains being used only for qualifying purposes. If the club has only been a registered CASC for part of an accounting period the exemption amounts of £50,000 (for trading) and £30,000 (for income from property) are reduced proportionally. Only interest and gains received after the club is registered are exempted. Full details can be found at **W** www.gov.uk/government/publications/community-amateur-sports-clubs-detailed-guidance-notes.

CHARITIES

Charities do not pay corporation tax on profits from their charitable activities. To minimise their liability, they often operate their trading activities through a subsidiary company.

VALUE ADDED TAX

Value added tax (VAT) is a tax on consumption which is collected at each stage in the supply chain. It is included in the sale price of taxable goods and services and paid at the point of purchase. Each EU country has its own rates of VAT. VAT is charged on most business transactions involving the supply of goods and services by VAT registered traders in the UK and Isle of Man. It is also charged on goods and some services imported from places outside the EU and on goods and some services coming into the UK from the other EU countries. VAT is administered by HMRC. A wide range of information on VAT, including VAT forms, is available online (**W** www.gov.uk/topic/business-tax/vat) and HMRC also runs a VAT enquiries helpline (**T** 0300-200 3700).

HMRC have confirmed that the UK will continue to have a VAT system after it leaves the EU. The revenue that VAT provides is vital for funding public services. The VAT rules relating to UK domestic transactions will continue to apply to businesses as they do now.

RATES OF TAX

There are three rates of VAT in the UK:
- the standard rate, payable on most goods and services in the UK, is 20 per cent
- the reduced rate – currently 5 per cent – is payable on certain goods and services, including domestic fuel and power, children's car seats, women's sanitary products, smoking cessation products and the installation of energy-saving materials such as wall insulation and solar panels
- the zero rate applies to certain items, including, children's clothes, books, newspapers, most food and drink, and drugs and aids for disabled people. There are numerous exceptions to the zero-rated categories, including: confectionery, potato crisps, alcoholic drinks, soft drinks and items sold for consumption in a restaurant or café. Takeaway cold items such as sandwiches are zero-rated, but hot foods like fish and chips are not.

REGISTRATION

All traders, including professional persons and companies, must register for VAT if they are making 'taxable supplies' of a value exceeding the registration threshold. All goods and services that are VAT rated are defined as 'taxable supplies'. This includes zero-rated items, which must be included when calculating the total value of a trader's taxable supplies – his or her 'taxable turnover'. The limits that govern mandatory registration are amended periodically.

An unregistered trader must register for VAT if:
- at the end of any month the total value of his or her taxable turnover (not just profit) for the past 12 months or less is more than the current VAT threshold of £85,000

or
- at any time he or she has reasonable grounds to expect that his or her taxable turnover will be more than the current registration threshold of £85,000 in the next 30 days alone

VAT registration must be completed within 30 days. Most businesses register online, but some need to download a form (**W** www.gov.uk/vat-registration/how-to-register). Traders who do not register at the correct time can be fined. Traders must charge VAT on their taxable supplies from the effective date of registration.

Traders who only supply zero-rated goods may not have to register for VAT even if their taxable turnover goes above the registration threshold. However, a trader in this position must inform HMRC first and apply to be 'exempt from registration'.

A trader whose taxable turnover does not reach the mandatory registration limit may choose to register for VAT voluntarily. This step may be thought advisable to recover input tax (*see* below) or to compete with other registered traders.

Registered traders may submit an application for deregistration if their taxable turnover subsequently falls. An application for deregistration can be made if the taxable turnover for the 12 months beginning on the application date is not expected to exceed £83,000.

INPUT TAX

Traders suffer input tax when buying in goods or services for the purposes of their business. It is the VAT that traders pay out to their suppliers on goods and services coming *in* to their business. Relief can usually be obtained for input tax suffered by registered traders, either by setting that tax against output tax due on sales or by repayment. Most items of input tax can be relieved in this manner. Where a registered trader makes both exempt supplies and taxable supplies to his customers or clients, there may be some restriction in the amount of input tax that can be recovered.

OUTPUT TAX

When making a taxable supply of goods or services, registered traders must account for output tax on the value of that supply. Output tax is the term used to describe the VAT on the goods and services that they supply or sell, so the goods or services are going *out* of the business. It is collected from customers on each sale by increasing the price by the VAT. Failure to make the required addition will not remove liability to pay the output tax to HMRC.

The liability to account for output tax, and also relief for input tax, may be affected where a trader is using a special secondhand goods scheme.

EXEMPT SUPPLIES

VAT is not chargeable on certain goods and services because the law deems them 'exempt' from VAT. These include:
- the provision of burial and cremation facilities
- insurance
- loans of money
- certain types of education and training
- most property transactions, unless the owner has opted to tax the property

Exempt supplies do not enter into the calculation of taxable turnover that governs liability to mandatory registration (*see* above). Such supplies made by a registered trader may limit the amount of input tax that can be relieved.

COLLECTION OF TAX

Registered traders submit VAT returns for accounting periods usually of three months in duration, but arrangements can be made to submit returns on a monthly basis. Very large traders – those whose annual VAT liability exceeds £2.3m – must make payments on account on a monthly basis, with the quarterly return used to determine the balancing payment. The return will show the output tax due for supplies made by the trader in the accounting period and the input tax for which relief is claimed. If the output tax exceeds input tax the balance must be remitted at the time of the VAT return. Where input tax suffered exceeds the output tax due, the registered trader may claim the excess from HMRC.

In this way, each trader in the supply chain collects the tax relating to the value added by their business. Where the supply is made to a person who is not a registered trader there can be no recovery of input tax and it is on this person that the final burden of VAT eventually falls.

As part of the Making Tax Digital initiative, most registered traders are required to use the Making Tax Digital service to keep records digitally and use software to submit their VAT returns from 1 April 2019. From 1 October 2019 the following organisations will also need to use the digital service:

• trusts
• not-for-profit organisations that are not set up as a company
• VAT divisions and groups
• public sector entities required to provide additional information on their VAT return (eg government departments and NHS trusts)
• local authorities
• public corporations
• traders based overseas
• those required to make payments on account
• annual accounting scheme users

For further information see **W** www.gov.uk/guidance/making-tax-digital-for-vat.

Exemptions from Making Tax Digital are available to those:
• that can not use computers, software or the internet due to age, disability or where they live
• or whose business are subject to an insolvency procedure
• that object to using computers on religious grounds

Applications for exemptions should be made to: HMRC – VAT Written Enquiries Team, Portcullis House, 21 India Street, Glasgow G2 4PZ or **T** 0300-200 3700. Applicants must state their VAT registration number, business name and address, details of how they currently file their VAT Return, and the reason they think they're exempt from Making Tax Digital.

Where goods are acquired by a UK trader from a supplier within the EU, the trader must also account for the tax due on acquisition. At the time of writing, the future of these arrangements is uncertain.

There are a number of simplified arrangements to make VAT accounting easier for businesses, particularly small businesses, and there is advice on the HMRC website about how to choose the most appropriate scheme for a business:

Cash Accounting Scheme
This scheme allows businesses to only pay VAT on the basis of payments received from their customers rather than on invoice dates or time of supply. This is useful for businesses with cash flow problems. Businesses may use the cash accounting scheme if estimated taxable turnover is £1.35m or less for the next 12 months. There is no need to apply for the scheme – eligible businesses may start using it at the beginning of a new tax period. If a trader opts to use this scheme, he or she can do so until the taxable turnover reaches £1.6m. For further information see **W** www.gov.uk/vat-cash-accounting-scheme.

Annual Accounting Scheme
If estimated taxable turnover is £1.35m or less in the next 12 months, the trader may join the annual accounting scheme which allows them to make nine monthly or three quarterly instalments during the year based on an estimate of their total annual VAT bill. At the end of the year they submit a single return and any balance due. The advantages of this scheme for businesses are easier budgeting and cash flow planning, because fixed payments are spread regularly throughout the year. Once a trader has joined the annual accounting scheme, membership may continue until the annual taxable turnover reaches £1.6m. This scheme is not helpful where businesses receive a refund of VAT, because it delays receipt of the refund. For more information see **W** www.gov.uk/vat-annual-accounting-scheme.

Flat Rate Scheme
This scheme allows small businesses with an annual taxable turnover of £150,000 or less to save on administration by paying VAT as a set flat percentage of their annual turnover instead of accounting internally for VAT on each individual 'in and out'. The percentage rate used is governed by the trade sector into which the business falls. The scheme can no longer be used once annual income exceeds £230,000.

Under this scheme, it is not possible to reclaim the VAT on purchases, except for certain assets over £2,000. For further information see **W** www.gov.uk/vat-flat-rate-scheme.

A business can not use the Flat Rate Scheme and the Cash Accounting Scheme at the same time.

Retail Schemes
There are special schemes that offer retailers an alternative if it is impractical for them to issue invoices for a large number of supplies direct to the public. These schemes include a provision to claim relief from VAT on bad debts where goods or services are supplied to a customer who does not pay for them. For further information see **W** www.gov.uk/vat-retail-schemes.

VAT FACT SUMMARY *from 1 April 2019*

Standard rate	20%
Reduced rate	5%
Registration (last 12 months or next 30 days)	over £85,000
Deregistration (next 12 months)	under £83,000
Cash accounting scheme	up to £1,350,000
Exit limit	£1,600,000
Annual accounting scheme	up to £1,350,000
Exit limit	£1,600,000
Flat rate scheme	up to £150,000
Exit limit	£230,000

STAMP DUTY

Stamp duty is payable by the buyer based on the purchase price of a property, stocks and shares. For the majority of people, contact with stamp duty arises when they buy a property. This section aims to provide a broad overview of stamp duty as it may affect the average person.

STAMP DUTY LAND TAX

Stamp duty land tax (SDLT) covers the purchase of houses, flats and other land, buildings and certain leases in the UK.

Buyers of property are responsible for completing a land transaction return form, SDLT1, which contains all information regarding the purchase that is relevant to HMRC and paying SDLT, though the solicitor or licensed conveyancer acting for them in a land transaction will normally complete the relevant paperwork. Once HMRC has received the completed land transaction return and the payment of any SDLT due, a certificate, SDLT5, will be issued that enables a solicitor or licensed conveyancer to register the property in the new owner's name at the land registry.

The threshold for notification of residential property is currently £40,000. This means that taxpayers entering into a transaction involving residential or non-residential property where the chargeable consideration is less than £40,000 do not need to notify HMRC about the transaction. Further information can be found online: **W** www.gov.uk/government/organisations/hm-revenue-customs/contact/stamp-duty-land-tax.

Since 1 April 2015 stamp duty has no longer applied to land transactions in Scotland. These are now subject to land and buildings transaction tax, details of which can be found online (**W** www.gov.uk/sdlt-scottish-transactions).

RATES OF SDLT
SDLT is charged at different rates and has thresholds for different types of property and different values of transaction. The tax rate and payment threshold can vary according to whether the property is in residential or non-residential use and whether it is freehold or leasehold.

SDLT on purchases of residential property is charged at increasing rates for each portion of the price.

SDLT ON RESIDENTIAL PROPERTY 2018–19

Portion of the transaction value	SDLT is charged at
Up to £125,000	zero
Between £125,001 and £250,000	2 per cent
Between £250,001 and £925,000	5 per cent
Between £925,001 and £1,500,000	10 per cent
Over £1,500,000	12 per cent

For example, on a property bought for £275,000, a total of £3,750 is payable in SDLT. This is made up of: nothing on the first £125,000, £2,500 (2 per cent) on the next £125,000, and £1,250 (5 per cent) on the remaining £25,000.

Higher rates of SDLT apply to purchases of additional residential properties such as second homes and buy-to-let properties. The higher rates are 3 per cent above the standard rates of SDLT. They do not apply to purchases of caravans, mobile homes, houseboats or property under £40,000.

HIGHER RATE SDLT ON ADDITIONAL RESIDENTIAL PROPERTY 2018–19

Portion of the transaction value	SDLT is charged at
Up to £125,000	3 per cent
Between £125,001 and £250,000	5 per cent
Between £250,001 and £925,000	8 per cent
Between £925,001 and £1,500,000	13 per cent
Over £1,500,000	15 per cent

Each of these higher rates again applies to the portion of the consideration that falls within each rate band. For example, on a buy-to-let property bought for £300,000, a total of £14,000 is payable in higher rate SDLT. This is made up of: £3,750 (3 per cent) on the first £125,000, £6,250 (5 per cent) on the next £125,000, and £4,000 (8 per cent) on the remaining £50,000.

The SDLT on purchases of non-residential and mixed-use property is charged at increasing rates for each portion of the price (in the same way that it is charged on purchases of residential property).

SDLT ON NON-RESIDENTIAL AND MIXED USE PROPERTY PURCHASES 2018–19

Portion of the transaction value	SDLT is charged at
Up to £150,000	zero
Between £150,001 and £250,000	2 per cent
Over £250,001	5 per cent

FIRST TIME BUYERS
From November 2017, first time buyers of homes worth between £300,000 and £500,000 will not pay SDLT on the first £300,000. They will pay the normal rates of SDLT on the price above that. This will save £1,660 on the average first-time property. This zero rate does not apply to first time buy-to-let or holiday home purchases, although those that are investing in buy-to-let property as first time buyers, will still get some relief as they will pay the standard residential rates rather than the higher buy-to-let rates. It is estimated that 80 per cent of people buying their first home will pay no SDLT.

This relief does not apply for those buying properties over £500,000.

CALCULATING SDLT
To work out the amount of SDLT payable on residential or non-residential property, a SDLT calculator is available online (**W** www.tax.service.gov.uk/calculate-stamp-duty-land-tax/#/intro).

STAMP DUTY RESERVE TAX
Stamp duty or stamp duty reserve tax (SDRT) is payable at the rate of 0.5 per cent when shares are purchased. Stamp duty is payable when the shares are transferred using a stock transfer form, whereas SDRT is payable on 'paperless' share transactions where the shares are transferred electronically without using a stock transfer form. Most share transactions nowadays are paperless and settled by stockbrokers through CREST (the electronic settlement and registration system). SDRT therefore now accounts for the majority of taxation collected on share transactions effected through the London Stock Exchange.

The flat rate of 0.5 per cent is based on the amount paid for the shares, not what they are worth. If, for example, shares are bought for £2,000, £10 SDRT is payable, whatever the value of the shares themselves. If shares are transferred for free, no SDRT is payable.

A higher rate of 1.5 per cent is payable where shares are transferred into a 'depositary receipt scheme' or a 'clearance service'. These are special arrangements where the shares are held by a third party.

CREST automatically deducts the SDRT and sends it to HMRC. A stockbroker will settle up with CREST for the cost of the shares and the SDRT and then bill the purchaser for these and the broker's fees. If shares are not purchased through CREST, the stamp duty must be paid by the purchaser to HMRC.

UK stamp duty or SDRT is not payable on the purchase of foreign shares, though there may be foreign taxes to pay. SDRT is already accounted for in the price paid for units in unit trusts or shares in open-ended investment companies.

Further information on SDRT is available via the stamp taxes helpline on **T** 0300-200 3510 or the government information website (**W** www.gov.uk/topic/business-tax/stamp-duty-on-shares).

LEGAL NOTES

These notes outline certain aspects of the law as they might affect the average person. They are intended only as a broad guideline and are by no means definitive. The law is constantly changing so expert advice should always be taken. In some cases, sources of further information are given in these notes.

It is always advisable to consult a solicitor without delay. Anyone who does not have a solicitor can contact the following for assistance in finding one: Citizens Advice (**W** www.citizensadvice.org.uk), the Community Legal Service (**W** www.gov.uk) or the Law Society of England and Wales. For assistance in Scotland, contact Citizens Advice Scotland (**W** www.cas.org.uk) or the Law Society of Scotland.

Legal aid schemes exist to make the help of a lawyer available to those who would not otherwise be able to afford one. Entitlement for most types of legal aid depends on an individual's means but a solicitor or Citizens Advice will be able to advise on this.

LAW SOCIETY OF ENGLAND AND WALES, 113 Chancery Lane, London WC2A 1PL **T** 020-7242 1222
  W www.lawsociety.org.uk

LAW SOCIETY OF SCOTLAND, Atria One, 144 Morrison Street, Edinburgh EH8 8EX **T** 0131-226 7411
  W www.lawscot.org.uk

ABORTION

Abortion is governed by the Abortion Act 1967. Under its provisions, a legally induced abortion must be:
- performed by a registered medical practitioner
- carried out in an NHS hospital or other approved premises
- certified by two registered medical practitioners, acting in good faith, on the basis of one or more of the following grounds:
1. that the pregnancy has not exceeded its 24th week and that the continuance of the pregnancy would involve risk, greater than if the pregnancy were terminated, of injury to the physical or mental health of the pregnant woman or any existing children of her family
2. that the termination is necessary to prevent grave permanent injury to the physical or mental health of the pregnant woman
3. that the continuance of the pregnancy would involve risk to the life of the pregnant woman, greater than if the pregnancy were terminated
4. that there is a substantial risk that if the child were born it would suffer from such physical or mental abnormalities as to be seriously handicapped.

In determining whether the continuance of a pregnancy would involve such risk of injury to health as is mentioned in the first and second grounds, account may be taken of the pregnant woman's actual or reasonably foreseeable environment.

The requirements relating to the opinion of two registered medical practitioners and to the performance of the abortion at an NHS hospital or other approved place cease to apply in circumstances where a registered medical practitioner is of the opinion, formed in good faith, that a termination is immediately necessary to save the life, or to prevent grave permanent injury to the physical or mental health, of the pregnant woman.

The Abortion Act 1967 does not apply to Northern Ireland. Despite a 2015 high court ruling that Northern Ireland's law on abortion is inconsistent with the European Convention on Human Rights, abortion is only permitted where there is a serious long-term risk to the health of the mother.

FAMILY PLANNING ASSOCIATION (UK), 23–28 Penn Street, London N1 5DL **T** 020-7608 5240 **W** www.fpa.org.uk

BRITISH PREGNANCY ADVISORY SERVICE (BPAS), 20 Timothys Bridge Road, Stratford-upon-Avon CV37 9BF **T** 0345-730 4030 **W** www.bpas.org

ADOPTION OF CHILDREN

The Adoption and Children Act 2002 reformed the framework for domestic and intercountry adoption in England and Wales and some parts of it extend to Scotland and Northern Ireland. The Children and Adoption Act 2006, recently amended by the Children and Families Act 2014, introduced further provisions for adoptions involving a foreign element.

WHO MAY APPLY FOR AN ADOPTION ORDER

A couple (whether married or two people living as partners in an enduring family relationship) may apply for an adoption order where both of them are over 21 or where one is only 18 but the natural parent and the other is 21. An adoption order may be made for one applicant where that person is 21 and: a) the court is satisfied that person is the partner of a parent of the person to be adopted; or b) they are not married and are not civil partners; or c) married or in a civil partnership but they are separated from their spouse or civil partner and living apart with the separation likely to be permanent; or d) their spouse/civil partner is either unable to be found, or their spouse/civil partner is incapable by reason of ill-health of making an application. There are certain qualifying conditions an applicant must meet, eg residency in the British Isles.

ARRANGING AN ADOPTION

Adoptions may generally only be arranged by an adoption agency or by way of an order from the high court; breach of the restrictions on who may arrange an adoption would constitute a criminal offence. When deciding whether a child should be placed for adoption, the court or adoption agency must consider all the factors set out in the 'welfare checklist' – the paramount consideration being the child's welfare, throughout his or her life. These factors include the child's wishes, needs, age, sex, background and any harm which the child has suffered or is likely to suffer. At all times, the court or adoption agency must bear in mind that delay is likely to prejudice a child's welfare.

ADOPTION ORDER

Once an adoption has been arranged, a court order is necessary to make it legal; this may be obtained from the high court, county court or magistrates' court (including the family proceedings court). An adoption order may not be given unless the court is satisfied that the consent of the child's natural parents (or guardians) has been given correctly. Consent can be dispensed with on two grounds: where the parent or guardian cannot be found or is incapable of giving consent, or where the welfare of the child so demands.

An adoption order extinguishes the parental responsibility that a person other than the adopters (or adopter) has for the child. Where an order is made on the application of the partner of the parent, that parent keeps parental responsibility. Once adopted, the child has the same status as a child born to the adoptive parents, but may lose rights to the estates of those losing their parental responsibility.

REGISTRATION AND CERTIFICATES

All adoption orders made in England and Wales are required to be registered in the Adopted Children Register which also contains particulars of children adopted under registrable foreign adoptions. The General Register Office keeps this register from which certificates may be obtained in a similar way to birth certificates. The General Register Office also has equivalents in Scotland and Northern Ireland.

TRACING NATURAL PARENTS OR CHILDREN WHO HAVE BEEN ADOPTED

An adult adopted person may apply to the Registrar-General to obtain a certified copy of his/her birth certificate. Adoption agencies and adoption support agencies should provide services to adopted persons to assist them in obtaining information about their adoption and facilitate contact with their relatives. There is an Adoption Contact Register which provides a safe and confidential way for birth parents and other relatives to assure an adopted person that contact would be welcome. CoramBAAF (*see* below) can provide addresses of organisations which offer advice, information and counselling to adopted people, adoptive parents and people who have had their children adopted.

CORAMBAAF ADOPTION AND FOSTERING
ACADEMY, 41 Brunswick Square, London WC1N 1AZ
T 020-7520 0300 W https://corambaaf.org.uk

SCOTLAND

The relevant legislation is the Adoption and Children (Scotland) Act 2007 which came into force on 28 September 2009. In addition, adoptions with a foreign element are governed by the Adoptions with a Foreign Element (Scotland) Regulations 2009. Pre-2009 adoptions are governed by Part IV of the Adoption (Scotland) Act 1978. The provisions of the 2007 act are similar to those described above. In Scotland, petitions for adoption are made to the sheriff court or the court of session.

ADOPTION AND FOSTERING ALLIANCE SCOTLAND,
Foxglove Offices/GF2, 14 Links Place, Edinburgh EH6 7EZ
T 0131-322 8490 W www.afascotland.com

BIRTHS (REGISTRATION)

It is the duty of the parents of a child born in England or Wales to register the birth within 42 days of the date of birth at the register office in the district in which the baby was born. If it is inconvenient to go to the district where the birth took place, the information for the registration may be given to a registrar in another district, who will send your details to the appropriate register office. Failure to register the birth within 42 days without reasonable cause may leave the parents liable to a penalty. If a birth has not been registered within 12 months of its occurrence it is possible for the late registration of the birth to be authorised by the Registrar-General, provided documentary evidence of the precise date and place of birth are satisfactory.

Births that take place in England may only be registered in English, but births that take place in Wales may be registered bilingually in Welsh and English. In order to do this, the details must be given in Welsh and the registrar must be able to understand and write in Welsh.

If the parents of the child were married to each other at the time of the birth (or conception), either the mother or the father may register the birth alone. If the parents were not married to each other at the time of the child's birth (or conception), the father's particulars may be entered in the register only where he attends the register office with the mother and they sign the birth register together or the mother can choose to register the child's birth without the father's details. Where an unmarried parent is unable to attend the register office, either parent may submit to the registrar a statutory declaration of acknowledgement of parentage (this form may be obtained from any registrar in England or Wales or online at W www.gro.gov.uk); alternatively a parental responsibility agreement or appropriate court order may be produced to the registrar.

If the father's details are not included in the birth register, it may be possible to re-register the birth at a later date. If the parents can not register the birth of their child the following people may do so:

- an administrative member of staff of the hospital where the child was born
- a person who was present at the birth
- a person who is responsible for the child

Upon registration of the birth a short (containing only the child's details) or full (containing the child's and parents' details) certificate can be issued at a cost of £11.00 each. It may be possible to register the birth while still at hospital. Hospitals will advise individually whether this is possible.

SAME-SEX COUPLES

Male couples must get a parental order from the court before they can be registered as parents. Female couples can include both of their names on the child's birth certificate when registering the birth; however the rules differ depending on whether or not they are in a civil partnership.

In the case of female civil partners, either woman can register the birth on her own if all of the following are true:

- the mother had the child by donor insemination or fertility treatment
- she was married or in a civil partnership at the time of the treatment

When a mother is not in a civil partnership, her partner can be seen as the child's second parent if both women:

- were treated together in the UK by a licensed clinic
- have made a 'parenthood agreement'

However, for both parents' details to be recorded on the birth certificate, the parents must do one of the following:

- register the birth jointly
- complete a 'statutory declaration of acknowledgement of parentage' form and one parent takes the signed form when she registers the birth
- get a document from the court (eg a court order) giving the second female parent parental responsibility and one parent shows the document when she registers the birth

BIRTHS ABROAD

A child's birth abroad must be registered according to the regulations in the country where the child was born. The local authorities will issue a local birth certificate. The local birth certificate should be accepted in the UK, for example when registering a child with a school or doctor, but the certificate may be required to be translated and certified in English.

Once the child's birth has been registered locally, the birth may be registered with the UK authorities (only if the child was born on or after 1 January 1983). There is no obligation to register a child's birth with the UK authority; however, by registering the birth with the UK authority the birth will be recorded with the General Register Offices and a consular birth registration certificate can be ordered.

SCOTLAND

In Scotland the birth of a child must be registered within 21 days at the registration office of any registration district in Scotland.

If the child is born, either in or out of Scotland, on a ship, aircraft or land vehicle that ends its journey at any place in Scotland, the child, in most cases, will be registered as if born in that place.

CERTIFICATES OF BIRTHS, DEATHS OR MARRIAGES

Certificates of births, marriages and deaths that have taken place in England and Wales since 1837 can be obtained from the General Register Office (GRO).

Marriage or death certificates may also be obtained from the minister of the church in which the marriage or funeral took place. Any register office can advise about the best way to obtain certificates.

The fees for certificates are:

Online application:
- full certificate of birth, marriage, death or adoption, £14.00
- full certificate of birth, marriage, death or adoption with GRO reference supplied, £11.00

By postal/phone/fax application:
- full certificate of birth, marriage, death or adoption, £14.00
- full certificate of birth, marriage, death or adoption with GRO reference supplied, £11.00
- extra copies of the same birth, marriage or death certificate issued at the same time, £11.00

A priority service is available for a fee of £35.00 with GRO reference supplied and £38.00 without.

A complete set of the GRO indexes including births, deaths and marriages, civil partnerships, adoptions and provisional indexes for births and deaths are available at the British Library, City of Westminster Archives Centre, Manchester Central Library, Newcastle City Library, Library of Birmingham, Bridgend Reference and Information Library and Plymouth Central Library. Copies of GRO indexes may also be held at some libraries, family history societies, local records offices and The Church of Jesus Christ of Latter Day Saints family history centres. Some organisations may not hold a complete record of indexes and a small fee may be charged by some of them. GRO indexes are also available online.

The Society of Genealogists has many records of baptisms, marriages and deaths prior to 1837.

SCOTLAND

Certificates of births, deaths or marriages that have taken place in Scotland since 1855 can be obtained from the National Records of Scotland (formerly the General Register Office for Scotland) or from the appropriate local registrar.

Applicable fees – local registrar:
- each extract or abbreviated certificate of birth, death, marriage, civil partnership or adoption within a month of registration, £10.00
- each extract or abbreviated certificate of birth, death, marriage, civil partnership or adoption outwith a month of registration, £15.00

A priority service is available for an additional fee.

The National Records of Scotland also keeps the Register of Divorces (including decrees of declaration of nullity of marriage), and holds parish registers dating from before 1855.

Applicable fees – National Records of Scotland:
- personal application, or postal, telephone or fax order: £15.00

A priority service for a response within 24 hours is available for an additional fee of £15.00. Online fees (excluding postage) are £12.00 or £27.00 for a priority service.

A search of birth, death and marriage records including records of Church of Scotland parishes and other statutory records can be done at the Scotland's People Centre. There are also indexes to some of the old parish registers death and burial records in the library at the centre and indexes and images of census records from 1841–1911 are available. The charges for a full or part-day search pass is £15.00.

Online searching is also available. For more information, visit **W** www.scotlandspeople.gov.uk

THE GENERAL REGISTER OFFICE, General Register Office, Certificate Services Section, PO Box 2, Southport PR8 2JD **T** 0300-123 1837 **W** www.gro.gov.uk/gro/content/certificates

THE NATIONAL RECORDS OF SCOTLAND, HM General Register House, 2 Princes Street, Edinburgh EH1 3YT **T** 0131-334 0380 **W** www.nrscotland.gov.uk

SCOTLAND'S PEOPLE CENTRE, General Register House, 2 Princes Street, Edinburgh EH1 3YY **W** www.scotlandspeople.gov.uk

THE SOCIETY OF GENEALOGISTS, 14 Charterhouse Buildings, Goswell Road, London EC1M 7BA **T** 020-7251 8799 **W** www.sog.org.uk

BRITISH NATIONALITY

There are different types of British nationality status: British citizenship; British overseas citizenship; British national (overseas); British overseas territories citizenship; British protected persons; and British subjects. The most widely held of these is British citizenship. Everyone born in the UK before 1 January 1983 became a British citizen when the British Nationality Act 1981 came into force, with the exception of children born to certain diplomatic staff working in the UK at the time. Individuals born outside the UK before 1 January 1983 but who at that date were citizens of the UK and colonies and had a right of abode in the UK also became British citizens. British citizens have the right to live permanently in the UK and are free to leave and re-enter the UK at any time.

A person born on or after 1 January 1983 in the UK (including, for this purpose, the Channel Islands and the Isle of Man) is entitled to British citizenship if he/she falls into one of the following categories:
- he/she has a parent who is a British citizen
- he/she has a parent who is settled in the UK
- he/she is a newborn infant found abandoned in the UK
- his/her parents subsequently settle in the UK or become British citizens and an application is made before he/she is 18
- he/she lives in the UK for the first ten years of his/her life and is not absent for more than 90 days in each of those years
- he/she is adopted in the UK and one of the adopters is a British citizen
- the home secretary consents to his/her registration while he/she is a minor
- if he/she has always been stateless and lives in the UK for a period of five years before his/her 22nd birthday
- if he/she has been born on or after 13 January 2010 to a parent who is a member of the UK armed forces
- if he/she has been born on or after 13 January 2010 and a parent becomes a member of the UK armed forces, and an application is made before he/she is 18

A person born outside the UK may acquire British citizenship if he/she falls into one of the following categories:
- he/she has a parent who is a British citizen otherwise than by descent, eg a parent who was born in the UK

- he/she has a parent who is a British citizen serving the crown or a European community institution overseas and was recruited to that service in the UK (including qualifying territories for those born on or after 21 May 2002) or in the European Community (for services within an EU institution); or if the applicant himself/herself has at any time been in crown, or similar, service under the government of a British overseas territory
- if he/she has been born on or after 13 January 2010 to a parent who is a member of the UK armed forces serving outside the UK and qualifying territories, is of good character and (if he/she is a minor at the time of application) all parents then alive consent in signed writing
- the home secretary consents to his/her registration while he/she is a minor
- he/she is a British overseas territories citizen, a British overseas citizen, a British subject or a British protected person and has been lawfully resident in the UK for five years
- he/she is a British overseas territories citizen who acquired that citizenship from a connection with Gibraltar
- he/she is adopted or naturalised

Where parents are married, the status of either may confer citizenship on their child. Since July 2006, both parents are able to pass on nationality even if they are not married, provided that there is satisfactory evidence of paternity. For children born before July 2006, it must be shown that there is parental consent and that the child would have an automatic claim to citizenship or entitlement to registration had the parents been married. Where parents are not married, the status of the mother determines the child's citizenship.

Under the 1981 act, Commonwealth citizens and citizens of the Republic of Ireland were entitled to registration as British citizens before 1 January 1983. In 1983, citizens of the Falkland Islands were granted British citizenship.

Renunciation of British citizenship must be registered with the home secretary and will be revoked if no new citizenship or nationality is acquired within six months. If the renunciation was required in order to retain or acquire another citizenship or nationality, the citizenship may be reacquired only once. If the renunciation was for another reason, the home secretary may allow reacquisition more than once, depending on the circumstances. The secretary of state may deprive a person of a citizenship status if he or she is satisfied that the person has done anything seriously prejudicial to the vital interests of the UK, or a British overseas territory, unless making the order would have the effect of rendering such a person stateless. A person may also be deprived of a citizenship status which results from his registration or naturalisation if the secretary of state is satisfied that the registration or naturalisation was obtained by fraud, false representation or concealment of a material fact.

BRITISH DEPENDENT TERRITORIES CITIZENSHIP
Since 26 February 2002, this category of nationality no longer exists and has been replaced by British overseas territory citizenship.

If a person had this class of nationality only by reason of a connection to the territory of Hong Kong, they lost it automatically when Hong Kong was returned to the People's Republic of China. However, if after 30 June 1997, they had no other nationality and would have become stateless, or were born after 30 June 1997 and would have been born stateless (but had a parent who was a British national (overseas) or a British overseas citizen), they became a British overseas citizen.

BRITISH OVERSEAS CITIZENSHIP
Under the 1981 act, as amended by the British Overseas Territories Act 2002, this type of citizenship was conferred on any UK and colonies citizens who did not become either a British citizen or a British overseas territories citizen on 1 January 1983 and as such is now, for most purposes, only acquired by persons who would otherwise be stateless.

BRITISH OVERSEAS TERRITORIES CITIZENSHIP
This category of nationality replaced British dependent territories citizenship. Most commonly, this form of nationality is acquired where, after 31 December 1982, a person was a citizen of the UK and colonies and did not become a British citizen, and that person, and their parents or grandparents, were born, registered or naturalised in the specified British overseas territory. However, on 21 May 2002, people became British citizens if they had British overseas territories citizenship by connection with any British overseas territory, except for the sovereign base areas of Akrotiri and Dhekelia in Cyprus.

RESIDUAL CATEGORIES
British subjects, British protected persons and British nationals (overseas) may be entitled to registration as British citizens on completion of five years' legal residence in the UK.

Citizens of the Republic of Ireland who were also British subjects before 1 January 1949 can retain that status if they fulfil certain conditions.

EUROPEAN UNION CITIZENSHIP
At the time of writing, British citizens (including Gibraltarians who are registered for this purpose) are also EU citizens and are entitled to travel freely to other EU countries to work, study, reside and set up a business. EU citizens have the same rights with respect to the UK. However, on the day the UK leaves the EU, European freedom of movement will end for all EU citizens (including citizens of Switzerland, Norway, Iceland and Liechtenstein) and their family members in the UK, and for all British citizens living in the EU.

The EU and the UK have negotiated the terms of the UK's withdrawal from the EU. Under the withdrawal agreement, EU law, in the main, would continue to apply in the UK from when the UK leaves the EU until 31 December 2020. This means that the freedom of movement would also continue until this date. In the case of no agreement between the UK and the EU, the freedom of movement would end after the withdrawal date.

NATURALISATION
Naturalisation is granted at the discretion of the home secretary. The basic requirements are lawful residence in the UK in the five years immediately preceding application (three years if the applicant is married to, or is the civil partner of a British citizen), good character, adequate knowledge of the English, Welsh or Scottish Gaelic language, passing the UK citizenship test and an intention to reside permanently in the UK.

The good character requirement applies to adults and children over the age of 10 and in assessing this the Home Office will take into account a range of factors, including any convictions, cautions, civil judgements, bankruptcies, financial soundness and any instances of failure to comply with immigration laws. If a person is deemed not to be of good character their naturalisation application will be refused. In January 2019 the Home Office updated its guidance as to how caseworkers should assess whether or not someone meets the good character requirement. The changes to the guidance apply to all applications made after 16 January 2019 and mainly relate to children, certain immigration offences and genuine mistakes made by the applicant.

STATUS OF ALIENS
Aliens, being persons without any of the above forms of British nationality, may not hold public office or vote in

Britain and they may not own a British ship or aircraft. Citizens of the Republic of Ireland and Commonwealth citizens are not deemed to be aliens. Certain provisions of the Immigration and Asylum Act 1999 make provision about immigration and asylum and about procedures in connection with marriage by superintendent registrar's certificate.

CONSUMER LAW

SALE OF GOODS

The law in this area is enacted to protect buyers who deal as 'consumers' (where the seller is selling in the course of a business, the goods are of a type ordinarily bought for private use and the goods are purchased by a buyer who is not a business buyer).

A sale of goods contract is the most common type of contract. These are governed by the Consumer Rights Act 2015 (CRA), which was designed to modernise and simplify the law in this area by codifying consumer legislation, most notably incorporating the Sale of Goods Act 1979.

The CRA provides protection for buyers by implying terms into every business-to-consumer sale of goods contract. These terms include:

- that the goods must be of a standard such that a reasonable person would deem them to be of satisfactory quality, considering, among other relevant factors, any description of the goods given by the seller and their price. The goods should be of satisfactory quality for the purpose for which they are usually intended, as well as in appearance, and they should not pose safety concerns. Should, prior to purchase, any issue affecting the quality of the goods be made clear to the consumer, then the term will not be applied. The same is true if, prior to purchase, the consumer has the opportunity to make a reasonable examination of the goods or a sample of them which would reveal any issue affecting their quality

- that goods must be suitable for the purpose for which the consumer has, expressly or implicitly, stated that they are intended. This term is applicable regardless of whether or not goods of such a nature are usually intended for this purpose, unless the consumer is advised otherwise by the trader and ignores such advice

- that any description of the goods provided by the seller must be accurate. If the seller provides both a description and a sample, the goods must ultimately correspond with the description, irrespective of whether they mostly correspond with the sample. This term is included even when the goods have been exposed for supply prior to purchase and selected by the consumer

- that goods will match any sample or model provided by the seller before purchase. In the case of the provision of a sample or a model, the goods must match the sample or model with the exception of any difference made clear to the consumer prior to purchase. Where a sample is provided, there must be no defect to the goods that a reasonable examination of the sample would not reveal

- that, in the event that the contract includes the installation of the goods, it is the duty of the seller to install or ensure that the goods are installed correctly

- that, in the event that goods include digital content, such digital content must comply with the contract for the provision of such content, or the goods will be considered as breaching the contract; and

- that the seller has the right to sell the goods, and that the goods have and will continue to have no charge or encumbrance that has not been made clear to the consumer prior to purchase. In the case of the hire of goods, the trader must have the right to transfer the goods for such a purpose

Under the CRA, which draws together and slightly amends the pre-existing rules under the Unfair Contract Terms Act 1977 and the Unfair Terms in Consumer Contracts Regulations 1999, these terms can not be excluded from contracts by the seller.

In a sale of secondhand goods by auction (at which individuals have the opportunity of attending the sale in person), a buyer does not deal as a consumer.

HIRE-PURCHASE AGREEMENTS

Terms similar to those implied in contracts of sales of goods are implied into contracts of hire-purchase, under the CRA. The Act limits the exclusion of these implied terms as before.

SUPPLY OF GOODS AND SERVICES

Before the CRA, the Supply of Goods and Services Act 1982 regulated other types of contracts (including for services, contracts under which ownership of goods pass and contracts for hire of goods). This Act has now also been amalgamated into the CRA. Similar terms to those above are implied into such contracts, however there are additional terms including:

- that the supplier will use reasonable care and skill in carrying out the service
- that the supplier will carry out the service in a reasonable time (unless the time has been agreed)
- that the supplier will make a reasonable charge (unless the charge or mechanism for its calculation has already been agreed)

The CRA Act limits the exclusion of these implied terms in a similar manner as before.

DIGITAL CONTENT

The CRA is the first statute to address the sale and supply of digital products, defined as 'data which are produced and supplied in digital form.' The Act applies to any digital content which is purchased or that which comes free alongside purchased services or goods. As above, implied terms for quality, fitness for purpose and adherence to description will be imposed on all consumer contracts. However, there is an extra term for contracts for digital content: that the seller has the right to provide such content.

These terms also apply to any future update or modification of the content. Should such future alterations fail to meet these standards, then the breach will be treated as having occurred at the time of supply rather than the point at which it was adapted.

Where digital content causes damage to other digital content or devices, and this could have been prevented where the seller had exercised reasonable skill and care, then that seller will be required to remedy the breach.

UNFAIR TERMS

The CRA has also consolidated the provisions of the Unfair Terms in Consumer Contracts Regulations 1999 that protected consumers against the imposition of unfair consumer contract terms. Where the terms have not been individually negotiated (ie where the terms were drafted in advance so that the consumer was unable to influence those terms), a term will be deemed unfair if it operates to the detriment of the consumer (ie causes a significant imbalance in the parties' rights and obligations arising under the contract). An unfair term does not bind the consumer but the contract may continue to bind the parties if it is capable of existing without the unfair term. The CRA contains a non-exhaustive list of terms that are regarded as potentially unfair. When a term does not fall into such a category, whether it will be regarded as fair or not will depend on many factors, including the nature of the goods or services, the surrounding circumstances (such as the bargaining strength of both parties) and the other terms in the contract.

CONSUMER PROTECTION

The Consumer Protection from Unfair Trading Regulations 2008 (CPRs) replaced much previous consumer protection regulation, including the majority of the Trade Descriptions Act 1968. The CPRs prohibit 31 specific practices, including pyramid schemes. In addition the CPRs prohibit business sellers from making misleading actions and misleading omissions, which cause, or are likely to cause, the average consumer to take a different transactional decision. There is also a general duty not to trade unfairly. The CPRs were amended by the Consumer Protection (Amendment) Regulations 2014, which entered into force on 1 October 2014 and introduced a new direct civil right of redress for consumers against businesses for misleading and aggressive practices, as well as extending the CPRs to cover misleading and aggressive demands for payment.

Under the Consumer Protection Act 1987, producers of goods are liable for any injury, death or damage to any property exceeding £275 caused by a defect in their product (subject to certain defences).

Consumers are also afforded protection under the Consumer Contracts (Information, Cancellation and Additional Charges) Regulations 2013 (CCRs), which came into force on 13 June 2014 and require certain information to be provided to the consumer.

The Financial Guidance and Claims Act 2018 makes provision to ensure members of the public are able to access free and impartial money guidance, pensions guidance and debt advice, and to ensure that they are able to access high-quality claims handling services by strengthening the regulation of claims management companies.

The CPA, CPRs and CCRs implement EU legislation and will be amended accordingly on the day that the UK exits the EU.

CONSUMER CREDIT

In matters relating to the provision of credit (or the supply of goods on hire or hire-purchase), consumers are also protected by the Consumer Credit Act 1974 (as amended by the Consumer Credit Act 2006). The Act was most recently amended by a number of statutory instruments made under the Financial Services and Markets Act 2000. These came into force on 1 April 2014 and represent a major overhaul of the consumer credit regime which was carried out in order to implement the recent EU Consumer Credit Directive. Under the new regime, responsibility for consumer credit regulation has been transferred from the Office of Fair Trading (OFT), which has ceased to exist, to the Financial Conduct Authority (FCA). Previously, a licence issued by the OFT was required in order to conduct a consumer credit, consumer hire or an ancillary credit business, subject to certain exemptions. The requirement to obtain a licence from the OFT has been replaced by the need to obtain authorisation from the FCA to carry out a consumer credit 'regulated' activity, which is likewise subject to certain exemptions. Provisions of the 1974 Act as amended include:

- in order for a creditor to enforce a regulated agreement, the agreement must comply with certain formalities and must be properly executed. An improperly executed regulated agreement is enforceable only on an order of the court. The debtor must also be given specified information by the creditor or his/her broker or agent during the negotiations which take place before the signing of the agreement. The agreement must also state certain information to ensure that the debtor or hirer is aware of the rights and duties conferred or imposed on him/her and the protection and remedies available to him/her under the Act
- the right to withdraw from or cancel some contracts depending on the circumstances. For example, subject to certain exceptions, a borrower may withdraw from a regulated credit agreement within 14 days without giving any reason. The exceptions include agreements for credit exceeding £60,260 and agreements secured on land. The right to withdraw applies only to the credit agreement itself and not to goods or services purchased with it. The borrower must also repay the credit and any interest
- if the debtor is in breach of the agreement, the creditor must serve a default notice before taking any action such as repossessing the goods
- if the agreement is a hire purchase or conditional sale agreement, the creditor cannot repossess the goods without a court order if the debtor has paid one third of the total price of the goods
- in agreements where the relationship between the creditor and the debtor is unfair to the debtor, the court may alter or set aside some of the terms of the agreement

It is intended that the statutory basis of consumer credit regulation, under the 1974 Act, will be replaced by a rules-based approach under the new regime. The FCA will be reviewing the statutory framework over the next few years and will develop rule-based alternatives where possible.

Consumer credit legislation will be amended on the day the UK exits the EU.

SCOTLAND

The legislation governing the sale and supply of goods applies to Scotland as follows:

- the Consumer Rights Act 2015 (with the exception of chapter three)
- the Sale of Goods Act 1979 applies with some modifications and it has been amended by the Sale and Supply of Goods Act 1994
- the Supply of Goods (Implied Terms) Act 1973 applies
- the Supply of Goods and Services Act 1982 does not extend to Scotland but some of its provisions were introduced by the Sale and Supply of Goods Act 1994
- only Parts II and III of the Unfair Contract Terms Act 1977 apply
- the Trade Descriptions Act 1968 applies with minor modifications
- the Consumer Credit Act 1974 applies
- the Consumer Credit Act 2006 applies
- the Consumer Protection Act 1987 applies
- the General Product Safety Regulations 2005 apply
- the Unfair Terms in Consumer Contracts (Amendment) Regulations 2001 apply
- the Consumer Protection (Distance Selling) Regulations 2000 apply
- the Consumer Protection from Unfair Trading Regulations 2008 apply

PROCEEDINGS AGAINST THE CROWN

Until 1947, proceedings against the Crown were generally possible only by a procedure known as a petition of right, which put the private litigant at a considerable disadvantage. The Crown Proceedings Act 1947 placed the Crown (not the sovereign in his/her private capacity, but as the embodiment of the state) largely in the same position as a private individual and made proceedings in the high court involving the Crown subject to the same rules as any other case. The act did not, however, extinguish or limit the Crown's prerogative or statutory powers, and it continued the immunity of HM ships and aircraft. It also left certain Crown privileges unaffected. The act largely abolished the special procedures which previously applied to civil proceedings by and against the Crown. Civil proceedings may be initiated against the appropriate government department or, if there is doubt regarding which is the appropriate department, against the attorney-general.

In Scotland proceedings against the Crown founded on breach of contract could be taken before the 1947 act and no special procedures applied. The Crown could, however, claim certain special pleas. The 1947 act applies in part to Scotland and brings the practice of the two countries as closely together as the different legal systems permit. As a result of the Scotland Act 1998, actions against government departments should be raised against the Lord Advocate or the advocate-general. Actions should be raised against the Lord Advocate where the department involved administers a devolved matter. Devolved matters include agriculture, education, housing, local government, health and justice. Actions should be raised against the advocate-general where the department is dealing with a reserved matter. Reserved matters include defence, foreign affairs and social security.

DEATHS

WHEN A DEATH OCCURS

If the death (including stillbirth) was expected, the doctor who attended the deceased during their final illness should be contacted. If the death was sudden or unexpected, the family doctor (if known) and police should be contacted. If the cause of death is quite clear, the doctor will provide:

- a medical certificate that shows the cause of death
- a formal notice that states that the doctor has signed the medical certificate and that explains how to get the death registered
- if the death was known to be caused by a natural illness but the doctor wishes to know more about the cause of death, he/she may ask the relatives for permission to carry out a post-mortem examination

In England and Wales a coroner is responsible for investigating deaths occurring:

- when there is no doctor who can issue a medical certificate of cause of death
- no doctor has treated the deceased during his or her last illness or when the doctor attending the patient did not see him or her within 14 days before death, or after death
- the death occurred during an operation or before recovery from the effect of an anaesthetic
- the death was sudden and unexplained or attended by suspicious circumstances
- the death might be due to an industrial injury, disease or poisoning
- the death might be due to accident, violence, neglect or abortion
- the death occurred in prison or in police custody
- the cause of death is unknown

The doctor will write on the formal notice that the death has been referred to the coroner; if the post-mortem shows that death was due to natural causes, the coroner may issue a notification which gives the cause of death so that the death can be registered. If the cause of death was violent or unnatural, is still undetermined after a post-mortem, or took place in prison or police custody, the coroner must hold an inquest. The coroner must hold an inquest in these circumstances even if the death occurred abroad (and the body has been returned to England or Wales).

In Scotland the office of coroner does not exist. The local procurator fiscal inquires into sudden or suspicious deaths. A fatal accident inquiry will be held before the sheriff where the death has resulted from an accident during the course of the employment of the person who has died, or where the person who has died was in legal custody or a child required to be kept or detained in secure accommodation, or where

the Lord Advocate deems it in the public interest that an inquiry be held.

REGISTERING A DEATH

In England and Wales the death can be registered at any register office, although if it is registered by the registrar of births and deaths for the district in which it occurred, the necessary documents can be obtained on the same day. A death which occurs in Scotland can be registered in any registration district in Scotland. Information concerning a death can be given before any registrar of births and deaths in England and Wales. The registrar will pass the relevant details to the registrar for the district where the death occurred, who will then register the death.

In England and Wales the death must normally be registered within five days (unless the registrar says this period can be extended); in Scotland within eight days. If the death has been referred to the coroner/local procurator fiscal it cannot be registered until the registrar has received authority from the coroner/local procurator fiscal to do so. Failure to register a death involves a penalty in England and Wales and may lead to a court decree being granted by a sheriff in Scotland. A stillbirth normally needs to be registered within 42 days, and at the latest within three months. In many cases this can be done at the hospital or at the local register office. In Scotland this must be done within 21 days.

If the death occurred at a house or hospital, the death may be registered by:

- any relative of the deceased
- any person present at the death
- any person making the funeral arrangements
- an administrator from the hospital
- in Scotland, the deceased's executor or legal representative

For deaths that took place elsewhere, the death may be registered by:

- any relative of the deceased
- someone present at the death
- someone who found the body
- a person in charge of the body
- any person making the funeral arrangements

The majority of deaths are registered by a relative of the deceased. The registrar would normally allow one of the other listed persons to register the death only if there were no relatives available.

The person registering the death should take the medical certificate of the cause of death (signed by a doctor) with them; it is also useful, though not essential, to take the deceased's birth and marriage/civil partnership certificates, council tax bill, driving licence, passport or NHS medical card. The details given to the registrar must be absolutely correct, otherwise it may be difficult to change them later. The person registering the death should check the entry carefully before it is signed. The registrar will issue a certificate for burial or cremation, and a certificate of registration of death (form BD8, commonly known as a 'death certificate' which is issued for social security purposes if the deceased received a state pension or benefits) – both free of charge. A death certificate is a certified copy of the entry in the death register; copies can be provided on payment of a fee and may be required for the following purposes, in particular by the executor or administrator when sorting out the deceased's affairs:

- the will
- bank and building society accounts
- savings bank certificates and premium bonds
- insurance policies
- pension claims

If the death occurred abroad or on a foreign ship or aircraft, the death should be registered according to the local regulations of the relevant country and a death certificate should be obtained. In many countries the death can also be registered with the British consulate in that country and a record will be kept at the General Register Office. This avoids the expense of bringing the body back.

After 12 months (three months in Scotland) of death or the finding of a dead body, no death can be registered without the written authority of the registrar-general.

BURIAL AND CREMATION

In most circumstances in England and Wales a certificate for burial or cremation must be obtained from the registrar before the burial or cremation can take place. If the death has been referred to the coroner, an order for burial or a certificate for cremation must be obtained. In Scotland a death or still birth must be registered in order that the appropriate certificate can be obtained to allow burial or cremation of the body.

Funeral costs can normally be repaid out of the deceased's estate and should be given priority over any other claims. If the deceased has left a will it may contain directions concerning the funeral; however, these directions need not be followed by the executor.

The deceased's papers should also indicate whether a grave space had already been arranged. This information will be contained in a document known as a 'Deed of Grant'. Most town churchyards and many suburban churchyards are no longer open for burial because they are full. Most cemeteries are non-denominational and may be owned by local authorities or private companies; fees vary.

If the body is to be cremated, an application form, two cremation certificates, one signed by the doctor who issued the medical certificate and the other signed by a different doctor confirming the first certificate (for which there is a charge) or a certificate for cremation if the death was referred to the coroner must be completed in addition to the certificate for burial or cremation (the form is not required if the coroner has issued a certificate for cremation). All the forms are available from the funeral director or crematorium. Most crematoria are run by local authorities; the fees can include the medical referee's fee and the use of the chapel. Ashes may be scattered, buried in a churchyard or cemetery, or kept.

The registrar must be notified of the date, place and means of disposal of the body within 96 hours (England and Wales) or three days (Scotland).

If the death occurred abroad or on a foreign ship or aircraft, a local burial or cremation may be arranged. If the body is to be brought back to England or Wales, a death certificate from the relevant country or an authorisation for the removal of the body from the country of death from the coroner or relevant authority, together with a certificate of embalming, will be required. The British consulate can help to arrange this documentation. To arrange a funeral in England or Wales, a certified translation of a foreign death certificate or a death certificate issued in Scotland or Northern Ireland which must show the cause of death, is needed, together with a certificate of no liability to register from the registrar in England and Wales in whose sub-district it is intended to bury or cremate the body. If burial is intended they will issue a certificate for burial. If it is intended to cremate the body, a cremation order will be required from the Home Office or a certificate for cremation. If the body is to be cremated in Scotland, a certificate permitting this must be obtained from the Death Certification Review Service run by Healthcare Improvement Scotland.

THE GENERAL REGISTER OFFICE, General Register Office, PO Box 2, Southport PR8 2JD **T** 0300-123 1837 **W** www.gro.gov.uk/gro/content/certificates

THE NATIONAL RECORDS OF SCOTLAND, New Register House, 3 West Register Street, Edinburgh EH1 3YT **T** 0131-334 0380 **W** www.nrscotland.gov.uk

DIVORCE, DISSOLUTION AND RELATED MATTERS

Divorce is the legal process which ends a marriage. The process is the same whether the parties are of the opposite or same sex pursuant to the Marriage (Same Sex Couples) Act 2013. Dissolution is a similar process which ends a civil partnership. Divorce and dissolution should be distinguished from judicial separation which does not legally dissolve the marriage/civil partnership but removes the legal requirement for a married couple to live together.

DIVORCE

There are two bars to divorce and dissolution: the 'one-year rule' and jurisdiction.

An application for a matrimonial order for divorce may only be presented to the court after one year of marriage. The spouse who lodges this document is known as the 'applicant petitioner' throughout the divorce proceedings and the other spouse is the 'respondent'.

Whether the English court may or may not have jurisdiction to deal with any divorce will depend on where the parties spent their married life and whether or not one party has retained their residence or domicile in England (and Wales). If there is a dispute as to which of two jurisdictions should host the divorce, where the two jurisdictions likely to be relevant are EU countries then the usual rule is that the divorce takes place in the country where the petition is filed first. The exception to this rule is Denmark, which opted out of the EU regulation which determines forums in this way.

If the two countries are not within the EU, or one of them is Denmark, then the forum of divorce may be determined by which is the more appropriate or convenient *(forum conveniens)*. In these circumstances, an election of a jurisdiction in a pre-nuptial agreement can be very important in resolving that dispute, although it cannot override the 'first in time' rule between EU countries (except Denmark) referred to above (save in the case of maintenance claims).

Some EU countries have signed up to the Convention on the Recognition of Divorces and Legal Separations which would allow a couple to elect a choice of law even in EU countries whereby one country would be required to apply the law of another. For the time being, England has not signed up to that convention and would apply English law only.

The UK's withdrawal from the EU will undoubtedly have an impact on the law in this area, since various European instruments apply (as outlined above) in determining in which country and jurisdiction a couple get divorced. In the case of a no-deal Brexit, the 'first-in-time' rules will no longer apply between the UK and the remaining EU member states and the UK would revert to the pre-EU *forum conveniens* rules.

There is only one ground for divorce, namely that the marriage has broken down irretrievably. This ground must be 'proved' by one of the five following facts:
- the respondent has committed adultery and the petitioner finds it intolerable to live with the respondent (an applicant can not file for divorce based on their own adultery)
- the respondent has behaved in such a way that the petitioner cannot reasonably be expected to live with the respondent
- the respondent has deserted the petitioner for a continuous period of at least two years immediately prior to the petition
- the applicant and respondent have lived apart for a continuous period of two years immediately prior to the petition and the respondent agrees to a divorce
- the applicant and respondent have lived apart for a continuous period of five years immediately prior to the petition

If the court is satisfied that the petitioner has proved one of those facts then it must grant a decree nisi (*see* below) unless it is satisfied that the marriage has not broken down.

Periods of up to six months' cohabitation are permitted for attempts at reconciliation without prejudicing the matrimonial proceedings. If the parties continue to live together for more than six months following discovery of adultery, the applicant will not be able to rely on the fact of adultery to prove the marriage has irretrievably broken down and may also adversely affect the applicant's chances of establishing arguments of unreasonable behaviour.

NO-FAULT DIVORCE

The majority of people are not prepared to wait two or five years to divorce and so are forced by the current legislation to apportion blame (adultery or unreasonable behaviour). Following the supreme court case of *Owens v Owens* in 2018, the government announced plans to introduce no-fault divorce and, in April 2019, it was confirmed the government will introduce new legislation to implement the planned changes. Removing blame from the divorce process has come as a welcome development to family lawyers. Following reform, a couple (or one party) would need to notify the court that their marriage has irretrievably broken down. The 'five facts' will be removed, a minimum six-month period will be required to enable couples to 'reflect' on their decision and the ability to contest a divorce will be abolished. Parallel changes will be made to the law governing the dissolution of civil partnerships. The proposed legislation will not cover other areas of matrimonial law such as financial provision.

DECREE NISI

If the judge is satisfied that the petitioner has proved the marriage has irretrievably broken down, a date will be set for the pronouncement of the decree nisi in open court. The decree nisi confirms the grounds for divorce have been met; the marriage will not be legally dissolved until the decree absolute. Neither party needs to attend and all the proceedings up to this point are usually carried out on paper.

DECREE ABSOLUTE

The final step in the divorce procedure is to obtain a decree absolute which formally ends the marriage. The petitioner can apply for this six weeks and one day after the date of the decree nisi. If the petitioner does not apply the respondent can apply, but only after three months from the earliest date on which the petitioner could have applied.

A decree absolute will not usually be granted until the parties have agreed, or the court has dealt with, the parties' financial situation (*see* below for details of financial provision).

DISSOLUTION OF CIVIL PARTNERSHIPS

The legal process for dissolution of a civil partnership follows a model closely based on divorce. Irretrievable breakdown of the partnership is the sole ground for dissolution. The facts to be proved to establish this are the same as for divorce, with the exception of adultery which, due to its legal definition, can only apply to opposite sex couples. Sexual activity with a third party can, however, be used as an example of unreasonable behaviour.

FINANCIAL RELIEF ANCILLARY TO DIVORCE, NULLITY AND JUDICIAL SEPARATION

Following a petition for divorce, nullity or judicial separation, it is open to either spouse or former spouse to make a claim for financial provision provided they have not remarried. It is common practice for such an application to be made at the same time, or shortly after, a divorce petition has been issued. Although most are agreed or settled by the parties themselves, where the parties are unable to agree, the courts have wide powers to make financial provision where a marriage breaks down. Orders can be made for:
- spousal maintenance (periodical payments) which can be capitalised into a lump sum

- lump sum payments
- adjustment or transfer of interests in property
- adjustment of interests in trusts and settlements
- orders relating to pensions

EXERCISE OF THE COURT'S POWERS TO ORDER FINANCIAL PROVISION

The court must exercise its powers so as to achieve an outcome which is fair between the parties, although it has a wide discretion in determining what is a fair financial outcome. It will consider the worldwide assets of both parties, whether liquid or illiquid. In exercising its discretion, the court has to consider a range of statutory factors including:
- the income, earning capacity, property and other financial resources which either party has or is likely to have in the foreseeable future, including, in the case of earning capacity, any increase in that capacity which it would in the opinion of the court be reasonable to expect a party to the marriage to take steps to acquire
- the financial needs, obligations and responsibilities which each of the parties to the marriage has or is likely to have in the foreseeable future
- the standard of living enjoyed by the family before the breakdown of the marriage
- the age of each party to the marriage and the duration of the marriage
- any physical or mental disability of either of the parties to the marriage
- the contribution which each of the parties has made or is likely to make in the foreseeable future to the welfare of the family, including any contribution by looking after the home or caring for the family
- the conduct of each of the parties, if that conduct is such that it would in the opinion of the court be inequitable to disregard it
- the value to each of the parties to the marriage of any benefit which, by reason of the dissolution of that marriage, that party will lose the chance of acquiring

When considering the above factors, the court must give first consideration to the welfare of any child of the family.

The court has a duty when exercising its powers to consider whether a 'clean break' would be appropriate. A clean break severs the financial ties between the parties and would provide no continuing capital payments or spousal periodical payments.

The court has a wide discretion in considering these factors in order to achieve an outcome it considers to be fair. The court's approach changed dramatically following the House of Lords decision of *White v White* in October 2000 where it was said that, after providing for the parties' reasonable needs, the remaining assets should be shared. In that case, it was established that the contributions made by both breadwinner and homemaker are to be regarded as equal and the court's main objective must be to achieve a fair outcome. More recent case law has gone further in establishing that the starting point should be an equal division of matrimonial assets. In lower net worth cases, any departure from an equal division is usually justified on the basis of need.

In high net worth cases, however, a departure from equality is frequently justified not just on the basis of need but also of compensation and non-matrimonial property. In the House of Lords cases of Miller and McFarlane the court refined the thinking in the White case to say that the court should strive to achieve a fair result by considering three strands:
- the needs of the parties going forward
- compensation for any economic disparity between the parties (such as where one party has sacrificed their career to become a full-time parent)
- sharing

NUPTIAL AGREEMENTS

Nuptial agreements are legal agreements drawn up prior to (pre-nuptial) or during (post-nuptial) marriage or civil partnership to regulate financial arrangements and division of assets in the event of divorce or dissolution. Such agreements are not currently binding in England and Wales. In October 2010, the supreme court gave judgment in *Radmacher v Granatino* which made it clear that a nuptial agreement can carry considerable weight (and will most likely be binding) provided the spouses freely and fully agree to its terms, are aware of its implications and it is fair to hold the parties to it, given the circumstances at the time of the court hearing. However, the court will still be able to decide as to whether the agreement is fair and whether the terms setting out the financial provision on divorce should be enforced in whole or in part. The supreme court gave some guidelines on when a pre-nuptial agreement would be considered 'fair', but ultimately it depends on the facts of the individual case.

FINANCIAL PROVISION ON DISSOLUTION OF A CIVIL PARTNERSHIP

The Civil Partnership Act 2004 makes provisions for financial relief for civil partners generally and extends the same rights and responsibilities invoked by marriage. Again the court must consider a number of factors when exercising its discretion and must take into account all of the circumstances of the case while giving first consideration to the welfare of any child of the family who is under 18. The list of statutory factors the court must consider resemble those for marriage and it is likely that the interpretation of these factors will be based on the court's interpretation of the factors relating to marriage.

COHABITING COUPLES

There is no such thing as a common law spouse. Unmarried couples do not benefit from the same statutory protection afforded to married couples. Instead, the rights of cohabitees are based on property law and trust interests. Therefore, it is advisable to consider entering into a contract, or 'cohabitation agreement', which establishes how money, property and the care of any children should be divided in the event of a relationship breakdown.

The Cohabitation Rights bill 2017–19 seeks to introduce certain protections for cohabitees during their lifetime and on death, it received its first reading in the House of Lords on 5 July 2017 and second reading on 15 March 2019, but has made no further progress. Thus, cohabitation agreements continue to be governed by the same general principles of property, trust, and contract law.

FINANCIAL PROVISION FOR CHILDREN

Under the Child Support Act 1991, all parents are under a legal obligation to support their children financially. A parent who does not have day-to-day care of a child is under a duty to pay child maintenance to the parent who does.

Parents can arrange child maintenance themselves (a so-called 'family based arrangement') or, where the parties are not able to reach an agreement, one party may apply to the Child Maintenance Service (CMS), (formerly the Child Support Agency (CSA)) to carry out an assessment.

Since 31 December 2017, CMS handles all child maintenance arrangements. The CSA no longer takes on new cases but still handles cases opened before 25 November 2013.

There is a £20 application fee for applying to CMS (unless the applicant is under the age of 18, a victim of domestic abuse, or lives in Northern Ireland), which covers the costs for calculating the amount of child maintenance, the provision to both parties of a yearly updated calculation using HMRC data and provision of information about payment services.

There are three different methods of calculating child support under the statutory child maintenance schemes:

- the 'old' scheme (for all applications up until 3 March 2003)
- the net income scheme (for applications from 3 March 2003)
- the gross income scheme (for all new applications since 25 November 2013)

All CMS child maintenance calculations will be dealt with under the gross income scheme. CMS uses the paying parent's gross weekly income (using information obtained from HMRC) as a starting point to work out the rate of child maintenance a non-resident parent should be liable for. Once the gross income information is received, the CMS applies a specific formula to work out the level of child maintenance payable. The child maintenance calculation may only be reassessed annually, unless the income variation is 25 per cent or more or in cases involving long-term illness or redundancy. It is a criminal offence to make a false statement or representation to or withhold information from the CMS and also to fail to notify CMS of a change of address or other change of circumstances.

Under the gross income scheme, it is mandatory for parents to have a conversation with the Child Maintenance Options (CMO) team to discuss their choices and consider alternatives before they proceed with their application. The CMO will discuss the various options available to parents if they cannot agree a 'family-based arrangement' between themselves:

- 'Direct Pay' (previously known as 'Maintenance Direct' under CSA arrangements) which enables parents to keep control of making and receiving payments. The statutory service works out the payment amounts for parents but will not be involved in collection
- 'Collect and Pay' (previously known as the 'full collection service' under CSA arrangements) whereby CMS calculates how much maintenance the paying parent owes. If the Collect and Pay Service is used, parties will be required to pay a fee for use of the service. Paying parents are required to pay a 20 per cent fee on top of their regular child maintenance payment and receiving parents will have 4 per cent of their child maintenance payment deducted from the total they receive

If payments are not made on time there is a spectrum of collection actions and enforcement powers (the range of which was increased in December 2018) available to the CMS to collect arrears, although they can only be used if a case is on the 'Collect and Pay' scheme. CMS will contact the paying parent to seek continuing payments. Where there is persistent non-payment, the CMS is able to take money directly from the paying parent, either from their earnings or bank account, or to take court action. There are CMS fees for pursuing enforcement action, which may affect the eventual amount of child maintenance received by the receiving party. Since December 2018, the government has had the power to write-off arrears that accumulated when a case was administered by the CSA, if no payment towards those arrears has been made for three months, and subject to certain other conditions. Further changes were introduced in December 2018 including how CMS calculates child maintenance for complex earnings giving CMS the right to make deductions from joint accounts and unlimited partnership accounts and the power to disqualify a payment parents from holding or obtaining a passport if they have consistently avoided paying their child maintenance debt.

Provision is also made under Schedule 1 of the Children Act 1989 for unmarried parents, step-parents and guardians to apply to the court for periodical payments, lump sum and property adjustment orders.

SCOTLAND

Although some provisions are similar to those for England and Wales, there is separate legislation for Scotland covering nullity of marriage, judicial separation, divorce and ancillary matters. The principal legislation in relation to family law in Scotland is the Family Law (Scotland) Act 1985. The Family Law (Scotland) Act 2006 came in to force on 4 May 2006, and introduced reforms to various aspects of Scottish family law. The following is confined to major points on which the law in Scotland differs from that of England and Wales.

An action for judicial separation or divorce may be raised in the court of session; it may also be raised in the sheriff court if either party was resident in the sheriffdom for 40 days immediately before the date of the action or for 40 days ending not more than 40 days before the date of the action and has no known residence in Scotland at that date. The fee for starting a divorce petition in the sheriff court is £156.

The grounds for raising an action of divorce in Scotland are set down in The Divorce (Scotland) Act 1976 and have been subject to reform in terms of the 2006 act. The current grounds for divorce are:

• the defender has committed adultery. When adultery is cited as proof that the marriage has broken down irretrievably, it is not necessary in Scotland to prove that it is also intolerable for the pursuer to live with the defender

• the defender's behaviour is such that the pursuer cannot reasonably be expected to cohabit with the defender

• there has been no cohabitation between the parties for one year prior to the raising of the action for divorce, and the defender consents to the granting of decree of divorce

• there has been no cohabitation between the parties for two years prior to the raising of the action for divorce

• the marriage has broken down irretrievably

• an interim gender recognition certificate under the Gender Recognition Act 2004 has, after the date of marriage, been issued to either party to the marriage. However, as a result of changes under the Marriage and Civil Partnership (Scotland) Act 2014, this ground of divorce will sometimes not be available where a full gender recognition certificate has been issued under the 2004 Act

The previously available ground of desertion was abolished by the 2006 Act.

A simplified procedure for 'do-it-yourself divorce' was introduced in 1983 for certain divorces. If the action is based on one or two years' separation and will not be opposed or because a gender recognition certificate has been issued; there are no children under 16; no financial claims; there is no sign that the applicant's spouse is unable to manage his or her affairs through mental illness or handicap; and there are no other court proceedings underway which might result in the end of the marriage, the applicant can access the appropriate forms to enable him or her to proceed on the Scottish Courts and Tribunals' website. From 25 April 2019 the fee is £125, however the applicant may be exempt from paying the fee if they are in receipt of certain benefits; or if legal advice and assistance is being provided by a solicitor in terms of the Legal Aid (Scotland) Act 1986.

Where a divorce action has been raised, it may be put on hold for a variety of reasons. In all actions for divorce an extract decree, which brings the marriage to an end, will be made available 14 days after the divorce has been granted. Unlike in England, there is no decree nisi, only a final decree of divorce. Parties must ensure that all financial issues have been resolved prior to divorce, as it is not possible to seek further financial provision after divorce has been granted.

FINANCIAL PROVISION

In relation to financial provision on divorce, the first, and most important, principle is fair sharing of the matrimonial property. There is a presumption that fair share means an equal share of the matrimonial property, which can be departed from if justified by special circumstances. In terms of Scots law matrimonial property is defined as all property acquired by either spouse from the date of marriage up to the date of separation. Property acquired before the marriage is not deemed to be matrimonial unless it was acquired for use by the

parties as a family home or as furniture for that home. Property acquired after the date of separation is not matrimonial property. Any property acquired by either of the parties by way of gift or inheritance during the marriage is excluded and does not form part of the matrimonial property.

When considering whether to make an award of financial provision a court shall also take account of any economic advantage derived by either party to the marriage as a result of contributions, financial or otherwise, by the other, and of any economic disadvantage suffered by either party for the benefit of the other party. The court must also ensure that the economic burden of caring for a child under the age of 16 is shared fairly between the parties.

A court can also consider making an order requiring one party to pay the other party a periodical allowance for a certain period of time following divorce. Such an order may be appropriate in cases where there is insufficient capital to effect a fair sharing of the matrimonial property. Orders for periodical allowance are uncommon, as courts will favour a 'clean break' where possible.

CHILDREN

The court has the power to award a residence order in respect of any children of the marriage or to make an order regulating the child's contact with the non-resident parent. The court will only make such orders if it is deemed better for the child to do so than to make no order at all, and the welfare of the children is of paramount importance. The fact that a spouse has caused the breakdown of the marriage does not in itself preclude him/her from being awarded residence.

NULLITY

An action for 'declaration of nullity' can be brought if someone with a legitimate interest is able to show that the marriage is void or voidable. Although the grounds on which a marriage may be void or voidable are similar to those on which a marriage can be declared invalid in England, there are some differences. Where a spouse is capable of sexual intercourse but refuses to consummate the marriage, this is not a ground for nullity in Scots law, though it could be a ground for divorce. Where a spouse was suffering from venereal disease at the time of marriage and the other spouse did not know, this is not a ground for nullity in Scots law, neither is the fact that a wife was pregnant by another man at the time of marriage without the knowledge of her husband.

COHABITING COUPLES

The law in Scotland now provides certain financial and property rights for cohabiting couples in terms of the Family Law (Scotland) Act 2006, or 'the 2006 Act'. The relevant 2006 Act provisions do not place cohabitants in Scotland on an equal footing with married couples or civil partners, but provide some rights for cohabitants in the event that the relationship is terminated by separation or death. The provisions relate to couples who cease to cohabit after 4 May 2006.

The legislation provides for a presumption that most contents of the home shared by the cohabitants are owned in equal shares. A former cohabitant can also seek financial provision on termination of the relationship in the form of a capital payment if they can successfully demonstrate that they have been financially disadvantaged, and that conversely the other cohabitant has been financially advantaged, as a consequence of contributions made (financial or otherwise). An order can also be made in respect of the economic burden of caring for a child of whom the cohabitants are the parents. Such a claim must be made no later than one year after the day on which the cohabitants cease to cohabit.

The 2006 Act also provides that a cohabitant may make a claim on their partner's estate in the event of that partner's death, providing that there is no will. A claim of this nature must be made no later than six months after the date of the partner's death.

THE CENTRAL FAMILY COURT, First Avenue House, 42–49 High Holborn, London WC1V 6NP **T** 020-7421 8594

THE COURT OF SESSION, Parliament House, Parliament Square, Edinburgh EH1 1RQ **T** 0131-225 2595
W www.scotcourts.gov.uk

THE CHILD MAINTENANCE SERVICE, **T** 0800-171 2033
W www.gov.uk/child-maintenance

EMPLOYMENT LAW

EMPLOYEES

A fundamental distinction in UK employment law is that drawn between an employee and someone who is self-employed. Further, there is an important, intermediate category introduced by legislation: 'workers' covers all employees but also catches others who do not have full employment status. An 'employee' is someone who has entered into or works under a contract of employment, while a 'worker' has entered into or works under a contract whereby he undertakes to do or perform personally any work or services for another party whose status is not that of a client or customer. Whether or not someone is an employee or a worker as opposed to being genuinely self-employed is an important and complex question, for it determines that person's statutory rights and protections. For certain purposes, such as protection against discrimination, protection extends to some genuinely self-employed people as well as workers and employees.

The greater the level of control that the employer has over the work carried out, the greater the depth of integration of the employee in the employer's business, and the closer the obligations to provide and perform work between the parties, the more likely it is that the parties will be employer and employee.

PAY AND CONDITIONS

The Employment Rights Act 1996 consolidated the statutory provisions relating to employees' rights. Employers must give each employee employed for one month or more a written statement containing the following information:
- names of employer and employee
- date when employment began and the date on which the employee's period of *continuous* employment began (taking into account any employment with a previous employer which counts towards that period)
- the scale, rate or other method of calculating remuneration and intervals at which it will be paid
- job title or description of job
- hours and the permitted place(s) of work and, where there are several such places, the address of the employer
- holiday entitlement and holiday pay
- provisions concerning incapacity for work due to sickness and injury, including provisions for sick pay
- details of pension scheme(s)
- length of notice the employee is obliged to give and entitled to receive in order to terminate the contract of employment
- if the employment is not intended to be permanent, the period for which it is expected to continue or, if it is for a fixed term, the end date of the contract
- details of any collective agreement (including the parties to the agreement) which directly affects the terms of employment
- details of disciplinary and grievance procedures (including the individual to whom a complaint should be made and the process of making that complaint) except those which relate to health and safety at work
- if the employee is to work outside the UK for more than one month, the period of such work and the currency in which

payment is made and any additional remuneration or benefits payable to them
- a note stating whether a contracting-out certificate is in force

This must be given to the employee within two months of the start of their employment.

If the employer does not provide the written statement within two months (or a statement of any changes to these particulars within one month of the changes being made) then the employee can complain to an employment tribunal, which can specify the information that the employer should have given. When, in the context of an employee's successful tribunal claim, the employer is also found to have been in breach of the duty to provide the written statement at the time proceedings were commenced, the tribunal must award the employee two weeks' pay, and may award four weeks' pay, subject to the statutory cap, unless it would be unjust or inequitable to do so.

The Working Time Regulations 1998, the National Minimum Wage Act 1998, Employment Relations Act 1999, the Employment Act 2002 and the Employment Act 2008 now supplement the 1996 Act.

The Employment Rights (Employment Particulars and Paid Annual Leave) (Amendment) Regulations 2018 will come into force on 6 April 2020 and provides that a written statement of terms must be given on or before the first day of employment, rather than within two months of employment starting. In addition, they increase the amount of information that must be included in the statement.

The Employment Rights (Miscellaneous Amendments) Regulations 2019 will also extend the right to a written statement of terms to all workers, rather than just employees, for all new joiners on or after 6 April 2020.

FLEXIBLE WORKING

The Flexible Working Regulations 2014 gives all employees, from 30 June 2014, the right to apply for flexible working after continuously working for the same employer for at least 26 weeks. An employer must consider and decide upon a request within three months and must have a sound business reason for rejecting any request. If an application under the act is not dealt with in accordance with a prescribed procedure, or is rejected on other than specific grounds, the employee may complain to an employment tribunal. In Northern Ireland an employer must hold a meeting with an employee within 28 days of a request for flexible working, and give reasons in writing within a further 14 days.

SICK PAY

Employees absent from work through illness or injury are entitled to receive Statutory Sick Pay (SSP) from the employer from the fourth day of absence for a maximum period of 28 weeks. The right to SSP will cease where an employee has had linked periods of sickness that have spanned a period of three years.

MATERNITY AND PARENTAL RIGHTS

Under the Employment Relations Act 1999, the Employment Act 2002, the Maternity and Parental Leave Regulations 1999 (as amended in 2001, 2002, 2006, 2013 and 2014), the Paternity and Adoption Leave Regulations 2002 and 2003, the Additional Paternity Leave Regulations 2010 and the Shared Parental Leave Regulations 2014, both men and women are entitled to take leave when they become a parent (including by adoption). Women are protected from discrimination, detriment or dismissal by reason of their pregnancy or maternity, including discrimination by association and by perception. Men and adoptive parents are protected from suffering a detriment or dismissal for taking paternity, adoption or parental leave.

Any woman who needs to attend an antenatal appointment on the advice of a registered medical professional is entitled to paid leave from work to attend. All pregnant women are entitled to a maximum period of maternity leave of 52 weeks. This comprises 26 weeks' ordinary maternity leave, followed immediately by 26 weeks' additional maternity leave. A woman who takes ordinary maternity leave normally has the right to return to the job in which she was employed before her absence. If she takes additional maternity leave, she is entitled to return to the same job or, if that is not reasonably practicable, to another job that is suitable and appropriate for her to do. There is a two-week period of compulsory maternity leave, immediately following the birth of the child, wherein the employer is not permitted to allow the mother to work.

A woman will qualify for Statutory Maternity Pay (SMP), which is payable for up to 39 weeks, if she has been continuously employed for not less than 26 weeks by the end of the 15th week before the expected week of childbirth. For further information *see* Social Welfare, Employer Payments.

Employees are entitled to adoption leave and adoption pay (at the same rates as SMP) subject to fulfilment of similar criteria to those in relation to maternity leave and pay. Where a couple is adopting a child, either one (but not both) of the parents may take adoption leave, and the other may take paternity leave.

Certain employees are entitled to paternity leave on the birth or adoption of a child. To be eligible, the employee must be the child's father, or the partner of the mother or adopter, and meet other conditions. These conditions are, firstly, that they must have been continuously employed for not less than 26 weeks prior to the 15th week before the expected week of childbirth (or, in the case of adoptions, 26 weeks ending with the week in which notification of the adoption match is given) and, secondly, that the employee must have or expect to have responsibility for the upbringing of the child. The employee may take either one week's leave, or two consecutive weeks' leave. This leave may be taken at any time between the date of the child's birth (or placement for adoption) and 56 days later. A statutory payment is available during this period.

For births on or after 5 April 2015, eligible parents are entitled to shared parental leave (SPL) whereby they will be able to share a pot of leave of up to 50 weeks and 37 weeks of pay, after the initial two weeks of maternity leave that is compulsory for the mother (or the equivalent two-week period for the adopter in adoption cases). During that 50 week period, parents can decide to be off work at the same time and/or take it in turns to have periods of leave to look after their child. To be eligible, the employee must be the child's mother, father, adopter, or partner of the mother or adopter, and must have worked for the same employer for not less than 26 weeks prior to the end of the 15th week before the expected week of childbirth (or, in case of adoptions, 26 weeks ending with the week in which notification of the adoption match is given). The amount of leave available is calculated using the mother's entitlement to maternity leave. If a mother reduces maternity leave she and/or her partner may opt to take SPL for the remaining weeks. On taking SPL, a woman will be entitled to statutory shared parental pay, which will generally be at the same rate as SMP, except in the first six weeks of maternity leave, during which a cap applies to shared parental pay but not to SMP.

For more information *see* Social Welfare, Employer Payments.

Any employee with one at least year's continuous service who has, or expects to have, responsibility for a child may take parental leave to care for the child. Each parent is entitled to a total of 18 weeks unpaid parental leave for each child or adopted child. This leave must be taken (at the rate of no more than four weeks a year, and in blocks of whole weeks only) before the child's 18th birthday.

The Parental Bereavement (Leave and Pay) Act 2018 is expected to come into force in April 2020 and will provide the right for all employed parents to take two weeks' leave if they lose a child under the age of 18, or suffer a stillbirth from 24 weeks of pregnancy, together with the right to statutory parental bereavement pay if certain eligibility criteria are met. It is likely that any such leave will need to be taken within 56 days of the child's death.

SUNDAY TRADING

The Sunday Trading Act 1994 allows shops to open on Sunday. The Employment Rights Act 1996 gives shop workers and betting workers the right not to be dismissed, selected for redundancy or to suffer any detriment (such as the denial of overtime, promotion or training) if they refuse to work only on Sundays. This does not apply to those who, under their contracts, are employed to work on Sundays.

TERMINATION OF EMPLOYMENT

An employee may be dismissed without notice if guilty of gross misconduct but in other cases a period of notice must be given by the employer. The minimum periods of notice specified in the Employment Rights Act 1996 are:

- one week if the employee has been continuously employed for one month or more but for less than two years
- one week for each complete year of continuous employment, if the employee has been employed for two years or more, up to a maximum of 12 weeks' notice
- longer periods apply if these are specified in the contract of employment

If an employee is dismissed with less notice than he/she is entitled to by statute, or under their contract if longer, he/she will have a wrongful dismissal claim (unless the employer paid the employee in lieu of notice in accordance with a contractual provision entitling it to do so). This claim for wrongful dismissal can be brought by the employee either in the civil courts or the employment tribunal, but if brought in the tribunal the maximum amount that can be awarded is £25,000.

REDUNDANCY

An employee dismissed because of redundancy may be entitled to redundancy pay. This applies if:

- the employment commenced before 6 April 2012 and the employee has at least one year's continuous service or the employment commenced on or after 6 April 2012 and the employee has at least two years' continuous service
- the employee is dismissed by the employer by reason of redundancy (this can include cases of voluntary redundancy)

Redundancy can mean closure of the entire business, closure of a particular site of the business, or a reduction in the need for employees to carry out work of a particular kind.

An employee may not be entitled to a redundancy payment if offered a suitable alternative job by the same (or an associated) employer. The amount of statutory redundancy pay depends on the employee's length of service, age, and their earnings, subject to a weekly maximum of (currently) £525 (£547 in Northern Ireland). The maximum payment that can be awarded is £15,750. The redundancy payment is guaranteed by the government in cases where the employer becomes insolvent.

UNFAIR DISMISSAL

Complaints of unfair dismissal are dealt with by an employment tribunal. Any employee whose employment commenced before 6 April 2012 with at least one year's continuous service or any employee whose employment commenced on or after 6 April 2012 with at least two year's continuous service (subject to exceptions, including in relation to whistleblowers – *see* below) can make a complaint to the tribunal. At the tribunal, it is for the employee to show that the employer dismissed them either expressly or constructively and it is for the employer to prove that the dismissal was due to one or more potentially fair reasons: a statutory restriction preventing the continuation of the employee's contract; the employee's capability or qualifications for the job he/she was employed to do; the employee's conduct; redundancy; or some other substantial reason.

If the employer succeeds in showing this, the tribunal must then decide whether the employer acted reasonably in dismissing the employee for that reason. If the employee is found to have been unfairly dismissed, the tribunal can order that he/she be reinstated, re-engaged or compensated. Any person believing that they may have been unfairly dismissed should contact their local Citizens Advice bureau or seek legal advice. A claim must be brought within three months of the date of effective termination of employment.

The normal maximum compensatory award for unfair dismissal is £86,444 as at April 2019 (£86,614 in Northern Ireland). If the dismissal occurred after 6 April 2009 and the employer unreasonably failed to follow the ACAS Code of Practice on Disciplinary and Grievance Procedures in carrying out the dismissal, the tribunal may increase the employee's compensation by up to 25 per cent.

Employees in Northern Ireland can make a complaint to the tribunal if they have at least one year's continuous service.

WHISTLEBLOWING

Under the whistleblowing legislation (Public Interest Disclosure Act 1998, which inserted provisions into the Employment Rights Act 1996) dismissal of an employee is automatically unfair if the reason or principal reason for the dismissal is that the employee has made a protected disclosure. The legislation also makes it unlawful to subject workers (a broad category that includes employees and certain other individuals, such as agency workers) who have made a protected disclosure to any detriment on the ground that they have done so.

For a disclosure to qualify for protection, the claimant must show that he or she has disclosed information, which in his or her reasonable belief tends to show one or more of the following six categories of wrongdoing: criminal offences; breach of any legal obligation; miscarriages of justice; danger to the health and safety of any individual; damage to the environment; or the deliberate concealing of information about any of the other categories. The malpractices can be past, present, prospective or merely alleged.

A qualifying disclosure will only be protected if the manner of the disclosure fulfils certain conditions, which varies according to the type of disclosure. With effect from 25 June 2013, there is no requirement for the disclosure to have been made in 'good faith', although where it appears to the tribunal that the protected disclosure was not made in good faith, the tribunal may reduce any compensatory award it makes by up to 25 per cent if it considers that it is just and equitable to do so in all the circumstances.

Any whistleblower claim in the employment tribunal must normally be brought within three months of the date of dismissal or other act leading to a detriment.

An individual does not need to have been working with the employer for any particular period of time to be able to bring such a claim and compensation is uncapped (and can include an amount for injury to feelings).

DISCRIMINATION

Discrimination in employment on the grounds of sex (including gender reassignment), sexual orientation, being pregnant or on maternity leave, race, colour, nationality, ethnic or national origins, religion or belief, marital or civil partnership status, age or disability is unlawful. Discrimination legislation generally covers direct discrimination, indirect discrimination, harassment and victimisation. Only in limited circumstances can such discrimination be justified (rendering it lawful).

An individual does not need to be employed for any particular period of time to be able to claim discrimination (discrimination can be alleged at the recruitment phase), and discrimination compensation is uncapped (and can include an amount for injury to feelings). These features distinguish the discrimination laws from, for example, the unfair dismissal laws.

The Equality Act 2010 was passed on 8 April 2010 and its main provisions came into force on 1 October 2010. It unifies several pieces of discrimination legislation, providing one definition of direct discrimination, indirect discrimination, harassment and victimisation. The Act applies to those employed in Great Britain but not to employees in Northern Ireland; it is only likely to apply to those predominantly working abroad if there is a strong connection between their work and Great Britain.

The Act provides that:

* it is unlawful to discriminate on the grounds of sex, gender reassignment, being pregnant or on maternity leave, or marital/civil partner status (all but the last of these categories include discrimination by association and by perception). This covers all aspects of employment (including advertising for jobs), but there are some limited exceptions, such as where the essential nature of the job requires it to be given to someone of a particular sex, or where decency and privacy requires it. The act entitles men and women to equality of remuneration for equivalent work or work of the same value
* individuals have the right not to be discriminated against on the grounds of race, colour, nationality, or ethnic or national origins and this applies to all aspects of employment. Employers may also take lawful positive action, including in relation to recruitment and promotion
* discrimination against a disabled person in all aspects of employment is unlawful. This includes protecting carers from discrimination by association with the disabled persons that they look after. The act also imposes a duty on employers to make 'reasonable adjustments' to the arrangements and physical features of the workplace if these place disabled people at a substantial disadvantage compared with those who are not disabled. The definition of a 'disabled person' is wide and includes people diagnosed with HIV, cancer and multiple sclerosis
* discrimination against a person on the grounds of religion or belief (or lack of belief) including discrimination by association and by perception, in all aspects of employment, is unlawful
* discrimination against an individual on the grounds of sexual orientation, including discrimination by association and by perception, in all aspects of employment, is unlawful
* age discrimination in the workplace is unlawful. However, it is lawful to discriminate because of age in relation to benefits based on length of service, redundancy pay (provided that any enhanced redundancy payment scheme operated by the employer is sufficiently similar to the statutory redundancy payment scheme), national minimum wage and insurance benefits.

The responsibility for monitoring equality in society rests with the Equality and Human Rights Commission.

In Northern Ireland similar provisions exist to those that were in force in Great Britain prior to the coming into force of the Equality Act but are contained in separate legislation (although the Disability Discrimination Act 1995 does extend to Northern Ireland).

In Northern Ireland there is one combined body working towards equality and eliminating discrimination, the Equality Commission for Northern Ireland.

WORKING TIME

The Working Time Regulations 1998 impose rules that limit working hours and provide for rest breaks and holidays. The regulations apply to workers and so cover not only employees but also other individuals who undertake to perform personally any work or services (eg freelancers). The regulations are complex and subject to various exceptions and qualifications but the basic provisions relating to adult day workers are as follows:

- No worker is permitted to work more than an average of 48 hours per week (unless they have made a genuine voluntary opt-out of this limit – it is not generally thought to be sufficient to make it a term of the contract that the worker opts out), and a worker is entitled to, but is not required to take, the following breaks:
- 11 consecutive hours' uninterrupted rest in every 24-hour period
- an uninterrupted rest period of 24 hours in each 7-day period or 48 hours in each fortnight (in addition to the daily rest period)
- 20 minutes' rest break provided that the working day is longer than 6 hours
- 5.6 weeks' paid annual leave (28 days full-time). This equates to 4 weeks plus public holidays

There are specific provisions relating to night work, young workers (ie those over school leaving age but under 18) and a variety of workers in specialised sectors (such as off-shore oil rig workers).

HUMAN RIGHTS

On 2 October 2000 the Human Rights Act 1998 came into force in the UK. This act incorporates the European Convention on Human Rights into the law of the UK. The main principles of the act are as follows:

- all legislation must be interpreted and given effect by the courts as compatible with the Convention so far as it is possible to do so. Before the second reading of a new bill the minister responsible for the bill must provide a statement regarding its compatibility with the Human Rights Act
- subordinate legislation (eg statutory instruments) which is incompatible with the Convention can be struck down by the courts
- primary legislation (eg an act of parliament) which is incompatible with the Convention cannot be struck down by a court, but the higher courts can make a declaration of incompatibility which is a signal to parliament to change the law
- all public authorities (including courts and tribunals) must not act in a way which is incompatible with the Convention
- individuals whose Convention rights have been infringed by a public authority may bring proceedings against that authority, but the act is not intended to create new rights as between individuals

The main human rights protected by the Convention are the right to life (article 2); protection from torture and inhuman or degrading treatment (article 3); protection from slavery or forced labour (article 4); the right to liberty and security of the person (article 5); the right to a fair trial (article 6); the right not to be subject to retrospective criminal offences (article 7); the right to respect for private and family life (article 8); freedom of thought, conscience and religion (article 9); freedom of expression (article 10); freedom of association and peaceful assembly (article 11); the right to marry and found a family (article 12); protection from discrimination (article 14); the right to protection of property (article 1 of protocol No.1); the right to education (article 2 of protocol No.1); and the right to free elections (article 3 protocol No.1). Most of the Convention rights are subject to limitations which deem the

breach of the right acceptable on the basis it is 'necessary in a democratic society'.

Human rights are also enshrined in the common law (of tort). Although this is of historical significance, the common law (for example the duty of confidentiality) remains especially important regarding violations of human rights that occur between private parties, where the Human Rights Act 1998 does not apply.

PARENTAL RESPONSIBILITY

The Children Act 1989 (as amended by the Children and Families Act 2014) gives both the mother and father parental responsibility for the child if the parents are married to each other at the time of the child's birth. If the parents are not married, only the mother has parental responsibility. The father may acquire it in accordance with the provisions of section 4 of the Children Act 1989. He can do this in one of several ways, including: by being registered as the father on the child's birth certificate with the consent of the mother (only for fathers of children born after 1 December 2003, following changes to the Adoption and Children Act 2002); by applying to the court for a parental responsibility order; by entering into a parental responsibility agreement with the mother which must be in the prescribed form; or by marrying the mother of the child.

Following changes to the Children Act 1989 (introduced by the Children and Families Act 2014), if a court makes a child arrangements order in favour of a father, providing that the child lives with that father, the court must make a parental responsibility order in his favour. If the child arrangements order provides that the child spend time or otherwise have contact with the father, the court must consider whether to make a parental responsibility order (residence orders were replaced by child arrangement orders under the Children and Families Act 2014, but if obtained prior to 22 April 2014 are still valid).

Where a child's parent, who has parental responsibility, marries or enters into a civil partnership with a person who is not the child's parent, the child's parent(s) with parental responsibility can agree for the step-parent to have parental responsibility by entering into a parental responsibility agreement, or the step-parent may acquire parental responsibility by order of the court (section 4A(1) Children Act 1989).

If a child is conceived after 6 April 2009 by female civil partners or female same-sex spouses, under the Human Fertilisation and Embryology Act (HFEA) 2008, both individuals will have parental responsibility for that child. A female, who is not in a civil partnership or same-sex marriage with the mother at the date of the child's birth, but is the child's other parent (by virtue of HFEA 2008), can acquire parental responsibility in the same way as set out above in relation to a father. Parental responsibility will also be acquired if the mother and the child's other parent enter into a civil partnership or (from 13 March 2014) a same-sex marriage after the child's date of birth.

Where the court makes a child arrangements order and a person (who is not the parent or guardian of the child) is named in the order as a person with whom the child is to live, that person will have parental responsibility while the order remains in force. Where the person (who is not the parent or guardian of the child) is named in the order as a person with whom the child is to spend time or otherwise have contact (but not with whom the child is to live), the court may provide in the order for that person to have parental responsibility for the child, while the provisions in the order continue.

An adoption order gives parental responsibility for the child to the adopters. It extinguishes parental responsibility that any person had for the child immediately before the making of the order.

In Scotland, the relevant legislation is the Children (Scotland) Act 1995, which gives the mother parental rights and responsibilities for her child whether or not she is married to the child's father. A father who is married to the mother, either at the time of the child's conception or subsequently, will also have automatic parental rights and responsibilities. Section 3 of the 2006 act provides that an unmarried father will obtain automatic parental responsibilities and rights if he is registered as the father on the child's birth certificate. For unmarried fathers who are not named on the birth certificate, or whose children were born before the 2006 act came into force, it is possible to acquire parental responsibilities and rights by applying to the court or by entering into a parental responsibilities and rights agreement with the mother. The father of any child, regardless of parental rights, has a duty to aliment that child until he/she is 18 (or under 25 if the child is still at an educational establishment or training for employment or for a trade, profession or vocation).

LEGITIMATION

Under the Legitimacy Act 1976, an illegitimate person automatically becomes legitimate when his/her parents marry. This applies even where one of the parents was married to a third person at the time of the birth. In such cases it is necessary to re-register the birth of the child. In Scotland, the status of illegitimacy has been abolished by section 21 of the 2006 act. The Family Law Reform Act 1987 reformed the law so as to remove so far as possible the legal disadvantages of illegitimacy.

JURY SERVICE

In England and Wales, the law concerning juries is largely consolidated in the Juries Act 1974 (as amended by the Criminal Justice and Courts Act 2015). In England and Wales, a person charged with a serious criminal offence is entitled to have their trial heard by a jury in a crown court, except in cases where there is a danger of jury tampering or where jury tampering has taken place.

In civil cases, there is a right to a jury in the Queen's Bench Division of the high court in cases where the person applying for a jury has been accused of fraud, as well as in cases of malicious prosecution or false imprisonment. The same applies to the county court. In all other cases in the Queen's Bench Division only the judge has discretion to order trial with a jury, though such an order is seldom made. In the chancery division of the high court a jury is never used. The same is true in the family division of the high court.

No right to a jury trial exists in Scotland, although more serious offences are heard before a jury. In England and Wales criminal cases and civil cases in the high court are generally heard by a jury of 12 members, but in the county court the jury is smaller, normally consisting of eight members. In the event that a juror is excused the trial can proceed so long as there are at least seven remaining jurors in the county court and nine in the case of the high court or crown court. At an inquest, there must be at least seven and no more than 11 members. In Scotland there are 12 members of a jury in a civil case in the court of session and certain sheriff court cases, and 15 in a criminal trial in the high court of justiciary. Jurors are normally asked to serve for ten working days, during which time they could sit on more than one case. Jurors selected for longer cases are expected to sit for the duration of the trial.

In England and Wales, every 'registered' parliamentary or local government elector between the ages of 18 and 75 who has lived in the UK (including, for this purpose, the Channel Islands and the Isle of Man) for any period of at least five years since reaching the age of 13 is qualified to serve on a jury unless he/she is disqualified.

Those disqualified from jury service include:

- those who have at any time been sentenced by a court in the UK (including, for this purpose, the Channel Islands and the Isle of Man) to a term of imprisonment or youth custody of five years or more
- those who have within the previous ten years served any part of a sentence of imprisonment, youth custody or detention, been detained in a young offenders' institution, received a suspended sentence of imprisonment or order for detention, or received a community order
- those who are on bail in criminal proceedings
- those who have been convicted of a jury misconduct offence
- those who are liable to be detained, who are under guardianship or who are under a community treatment order under the Mental Health Act 1983 or who are in resident in a hospital on account of mental disorder
- Those who lack capacity, as defined under the Mental Capacity Act 2005, to serve as a juror

The court has the discretion to excuse a juror from service, or defer the date of service, if the juror can show there is good reason why he/she should be excused from attending or good reason why his/her attendance should be deferred. It is an offence (punishable by a fine) to fail to attend when summoned, to serve knowing that you are disqualified from service, or to make false representations in an attempt to evade service. If a juror fails to turn up for service, or attends but cannot serve due to being under the influence of drink or drugs, this is punishable as contempt of court. Any party can object to any juror if he/she can show cause to the trial judge.

It may be appropriate for a judge to excuse a juror from a particular case if he is personally concerned in the facts of the particular case, or closely connected with a party to the proceedings or with a prospective witness. The judge may also discharge any juror who, from a mental or physical incapacity, temporary or permanent, or alternatively due to linguistic difficulties, cannot pay proper attention to the evidence.

An individual juror (or the entire jury) can be discharged if it is shown that they or any of their number have, among other things, separated from the rest of the jury without the leave of the court; talked to any person out of court who is not a member of the jury; determined the verdict of the trial by drawing lots; come to a compromise on the verdict; been drunk, or otherwise incapacitated, while carrying out their duties as a juror; exerted improper pressure on the other members of the jury (eg harassment or bullying); declined to take part in the jury's functions; displayed actual or apparent bias (eg racism, sexism or other discriminatory or deliberate hostility); or inadvertently possessed knowledge of the bad character of a party to the proceedings which has not been adduced as evidence in the proceedings. The factual situations that arise are many, and include falling asleep during the trial, asking friends on Facebook for help in making a decision, consulting an ouija board in the course of deliberations, making telephone calls after retirement, and lunching with a barrister not connected with the proceedings.

The Criminal Justice and Courts Act 2015 has introduced four new offences of juror misconduct with a penalty of up to two years in prison. A juror commits an offence if he: (a) intentionally seeks information during a trial where he knows, or ought to reasonably know, that the information sought is or may be relevant to the case; (b) passes on to another juror information obtained through such research; (c) engages in conduct from which it may reasonably be concluded that he intends to try the issue otherwise than on the basis of the evidence presented in the proceedings on the issue; and (d) discloses information about the jury's deliberations, subject to specified exceptions. A person who has been convicted of one of the above offences within the last ten years will be disqualified from jury duty. A judge now has a discretionary power to order members of a jury to surrender their electronic communication devices for a period of time, and a court security officer is authorised to search a juror for a device that a judge has ordered be surrendered.

In England and Wales, the jury's verdict need not be unanimous. In criminal proceedings, and civil proceedings in the high court, the agreement of ten jurors will suffice when there are not fewer than 11 people on the jury (or nine in a jury of ten). In civil proceedings in the county court the agreement of seven or eight jurors will suffice. Where a majority verdict is given, the court must be satisfied that the jury had reasonable time to consider its verdict based on the nature and complexity of the case. In criminal proceedings this must be no less than two hours and ten minutes (allowing time for the jury to settle after retiring).

A juror is immune from prosecution or civil claim in respect of anything said or done by him or her in the discharge of their office. It is an offence for a juror to disclose what happened in the jury room even after the trial is over. A juror may claim travelling expenses, a subsistence allowance and an allowance for other financial loss (eg loss of earnings or benefits, fees paid to carers or child-minders) up to a stated limit. For more information on jury service, visit **W** www.gov.uk/jury-service/overview

SCOTLAND

Qualification criteria for jury service in Scotland are similar to those in England and Wales, except that members of the judiciary are ineligible for ten years after ceasing to hold their post, and others concerned with the administration of justice are only eligible for service five years after ceasing to hold office. Certain persons have the right to apply to be excused – full-time members of the medical, dental, nursing, veterinary and pharmaceutical professions, full-time members of the armed forces, ministers of religion, persons who have served on a jury within the previous five years, persons who have attended court to serve on a jury but were not selected by ballot within the previous two years, members of the Scottish parliament, members of the Scottish government, junior Scottish ministers and those aged 71 years or over. Those who are incapable by reason of a mental disorder may also be excused. Such an application will be accepted if the application is made within 7 days of the person being notified that they may have to serve. For civil trials there is an age limit of 65 years. Those convicted of a crime and sentenced to a period of imprisonment of 5 years or more are automatically disqualified. The maximum fine for a person serving on a jury while knowing himself/herself to be ineligible is £1,000. The maximum fine for failing to attend without good cause in criminal trials is also £1,000, however in civil proceedings the maximum fine is £200.

HER MAJESTY'S COURTS AND TRIBUNALS SERVICE, 102 Petty France, London SW1H 9AJ **T** 0845-456 8770

JURY CENTRAL SUMMONING BUREAU, Freepost LON 19669, Pocock Street, London SE1 0YG **T** 0300-456 1024
E jurysummoning@justice.gov.uk

SCOTTISH COURTS AND TRIBUNALS SERVICE, Saughton House, Broomhouse Drive, Edinburgh EH11 3XD
T 0131-444 3300
W www.scotcourts.gov.uk

LANDLORD AND TENANT

RESIDENTIAL LETTINGS

The provisions outlined here apply only where the tenant lives in a separate dwelling from the landlord and where the dwelling is the tenant's only or main home. It does not apply to licensees such as lodgers, guests or service occupiers.

The 1996 Housing Act radically changed certain aspects of the legislation referred to below; in particular, the grant of assured and assured shorthold tenancies under the Housing Act 1988.

ASSURED SHORTHOLD TENANCIES

If a tenancy was granted on or after 15 January 1989 and before 28 February 1997, the tenant would have an assured tenancy unless the landlord served notice under section 20 in the prescribed form prior to the commencement of the tenancy, stating that the tenancy is to be an assured shorthold tenancy and the tenancy is for a minimum fixed term period of six months (*see* below). An assured tenancy gives that tenant greater security. The tenant could, for example, stay in possession of the dwelling for as long as the tenant observed the terms of the tenancy. The landlord cannot obtain possession from such a tenant unless the landlord can establish a specific ground for possession (set out in the Housing Act 1988) and obtains a court order. The rent payable is that agreed with the landlord at the start of the tenancy. The landlord has the right to increase the rent annually by serving a notice. If that happens the tenant can apply to the Residential Property Tribunal in England (or a rent assessment committee in Wales) to assess the open market rent for the property. The tenant or the landlord may request that the committee sets the rent in line with open market rents for that type of property.

Under the Housing Act 1996, all new lettings (below an annual rent threshold of £100,000 since October 2010 in England or December 2011 in Wales) entered into on or after 28 February 1997 (for whatever term) will be assured shorthold tenancies unless the landlord serves a notice stating that the tenancy is not to be an assured shorthold tenancy. This means that the landlord is entitled to possession at the end of the tenancy provided he serves a notice under section 21 Housing Act 1988 and commences the proceedings in accordance with the correct procedure. The landlord must obtain a court order, however, to obtain possession if the tenant refuses to vacate at the end of the tenancy. If the tenancy is an assured shorthold tenancy, the court must grant the order.

REGULATED TENANCIES

Before the Housing Act 1988 came into force on 15 January 1989 there were regulated tenancies; some are still in existence and are protected by the Rent Act 1977. Under this act it is possible for the landlord or the tenant to apply to the local rent officer to have a 'fair' rent registered. The fair rent is then the maximum rent payable.

SECURE TENANCIES

Secure tenancies are generally given to tenants of local authorities, housing associations (before 15 January 1989) and certain other bodies. This gives the tenant security of tenure unless the terms of the agreement are broken by the tenant and it is reasonable to make an order for possession. Those with secure tenancies may have the right to buy their property. In practice this right is generally only available to council tenants. However, the Housing and Planning Act 2016 enables housing associations voluntarily to extend the right to buy. A roll out of the extended right to buy regime has now taken place as the Department for Communities and Local Government published its guidance in April 2018.

The Prevention of Social Housing Fraud Act came into force in October 2013. It creates criminal offences for unlawful sub-letting by secure and assured tenants of social housing.

AGRICULTURAL PROPERTY

Tenancies in agricultural properties are governed by the Agricultural Holdings Act 1986, the Agricultural Tenancies

Act 1995 (both amended by the Regulatory Reform (Agricultural Tenancies) (England and Wales) Order 2006), the Tribunals, Courts and Enforcement Act 2007, the Legal Services Act 2007 and the Rent (Agriculture) Act 1976, which give similar protections to those described above, eg security of tenure, right to compensation for disturbance, etc. Similar provisions are applied to Scotland by the Agricultural Holdings (Scotland) Act 2003 for those leases entered into on or after 27 November 2003. The Agricultural Holdings (Scotland) Act 1991 continues to apply to those leases in Scotland entered into prior to this date and in certain other circumstances outlined by the 2003 act. However, one distinction to note between the 1991 act and the 2003 act is that those leases governed by the former have full security of tenure, subject to certain exceptions, whereas leases under the 2003 act are fixed term arrangements of various durations.

EVICTION

The Protection from Eviction Act 1977 (as amended by the Housing Act 1988 and Nationality, Immigration and Asylum Act 2002) sets out the procedure a landlord must follow in order to obtain possession of property. It is unlawful for a landlord to evict a tenant otherwise than in accordance with the law. For common law tenancies and for Rent Act tenants a notice to quit in the prescribed form giving 28 days notice is required. For secure and assured tenancies a notice seeking possession must be served. It is unlawful for the landlord to evict a person by putting their belongings on to the street, by changing the locks and so on. It is also unlawful for a landlord to harass a tenant in any way in order to persuade him/her to give up the tenancy. The tenant may be able to obtain an injunction to restrain the actions of the landlord and get back into the property and be awarded damages.

LANDLORD RESPONSIBILITIES

Under the Landlord and Tenant Act 1985, where the term of the lease is less than seven years, the landlord is responsible for maintaining the structure and exterior of the property, for sanitation, for heating and hot water, and all installations for the supply of water, gas and electricity.

While the responsibility of maintaining the premises remains intact, since July 2012 landlords are no longer permitted to enter the rental premises for the purpose of viewing their state and condition. This power of entry was revoked by the Protection of Freedoms Act 2012.

LEASEHOLDERS

Strictly speaking, leaseholders have bought a long lease rather than a property and in certain limited circumstances the landlord can end the tenancy. Under the Leasehold Reform Act 1967 (as amended by the Housing Acts 1969, 1974, 1980 and 1985), leaseholders of houses, as opposed to flats, may have the right to buy the freehold or to take an extended lease for a term of 50 years. This applies to leases where the term of the lease is more than 21 years and where the leaseholder has occupied the house as his/her only or main residence for the last two years, or for a total of two years over the last ten. It was the case that a low rent and rateable value test applied to the right to buy the freehold, this is generally no longer the case, although they do remain applicable to the right for a lease extension. The tenant must give the landlord written notice of his desire to acquire the freehold or extend the leasehold.

The Leasehold Reform, Housing and Urban Development Act came into force in 1993 and allows the leaseholders of flats in certain circumstances to buy the freehold of the building in which they live. Owners of certain long leases of flats may also have the right to take an extended act of 90 years plus the unexpired residue of their current lease: although technically a grant of a new lease, these are commonly called 'lease extensions'.

Responsibility for maintenance of the structure, exterior and interior of the building should be set out in the lease. Usually the upkeep of the interior of his/her part of the property is the responsibility of the leaseholder, and responsibility for the structure, exterior and common interior areas is shared between the freeholder and the leaseholder(s).

If leaseholders are dissatisfied with charges made in respect of lease extensions, they are entitled to have their situation evaluated by the First-tier Tribunal (Property Chamber).

The Commonhold and Leasehold Reform Act 2002 makes provision for the freehold estate in land to be registered as commonhold land and for the legal interest in the land to be vested in a 'commonhold association', ie a private limited company.

BUSINESS LETTINGS

The Landlord and Tenant Acts 1927 and 1954 (as amended) give security of tenure to the tenants of most business premises. The landlord can only evict the tenant on one of the grounds laid down in the 1954 act, and in some cases where the landlord repossesses the property the tenant may be entitled to compensation. However, it is commonplace for landlords and tenants to agree that these provisions will not apply to their lease, meaning that no security of tenure is granted.

SCOTLAND

In Scotland assured and short assured tenancies exist for residential lettings entered into after 2 January 1989 and before December 2017 are similar to assured shorthold tenancies in England and Wales. The relevant legislation for these is the Housing (Scotland) Act 1988. However, under the provisions of the Private Housing (Tenancies) (Scotland) Act 2016 all new tenancies for private residential lettings from 1 December 2017 take the form of a private rental tenancy. They provide more security for tenants as the 'no fault ground of repossession' (the equivalent of recovering possession under section 21 of the Housing Act 1988 in England) has been abolished. The act also introduced a model tenancy agreement, rent controls and move the adjudication of disputes from the sheriff court to the Housing and Property Chamber of the First-tier Tribunal.

Most tenancies created before 2 January 1989 were regulated tenancies and the Rent (Scotland) Act 1984 still applies where these exist. The act defines, among other things, the circumstances in which a landlord can increase the rent when improvements are made to the property. It does not apply to tenancies where the landlord is the Crown, a local authority or a housing corporation.

The Antisocial Behaviour etc (Scotland) Act 2004 provides that all private landlords letting property in Scotland must register with the local authority in which the let property is situated, unless the landlord is a local authority, or a registered social landlord. Exceptions also apply to holiday lets, owner-occupied accommodation and agricultural holdings. The act applies to partnerships, trusts and companies as well as to individuals.

Tenancy Deposit Schemes (Scotland) Regulations 2011 require that a landlord must pay deposits taken from tenants into an approved scheme and ensure that the money is held by an approved scheme for the duration of the tenancy. Evidence of registration with the relevant local authority in terms of the 2004 Act must be provided when the deposit is paid over.

Landlords who provide a private residential tenancy must provide new tenants with a Tenant Information Pack. The Tenant Information Pack includes information on the Repairing Standard, and its provision satisfies the separate obligation of a landlord to provide a tenant with written information about the landlord's duty to repair and maintain in terms of the Housing (Scotland) Act 2006.

The Housing (Scotland) Acts of 1987 and 2001 relate to local authority and registered social landlord responsibilities for housing, the right to buy, and local authority secured tenancies. The Housing (Scotland) Act 2010 reformed right-to-buy provisions, modernised social housing regulation, introduced the Scottish social housing charter and replaced the regulatory framework established by the 2001 act. Right-to-buy provisions were then abolished by the Housing (Scotland) Act 2014.

In Scotland, business premises are not controlled by statute to the same extent as in England and Wales, although the Tenancy of Shops (Scotland) Act 1949 gives some security to tenants of shops. Tenants of shops can apply to the sheriff, within 21 days of being served a notice to quit, for a renewal of tenancy if threatened with eviction. This application may be dismissed on various grounds, including where the landlord has offered to sell the property to the tenant at an agreed price or, in the absence of agreement as to price, at a price fixed by a single arbiter appointed by the parties or the sheriff. The act extends to properties where the Crown or government departments are the landlords or the tenants.

Under the Leases Act 1449 the landlord's successors (either purchasers or creditors) are bound by the agreement made with any tenants so long as the following conditions are met:
• the lease, if for more than one year, must be in writing
• there must be a rent
• there must be a term of expiry
• the tenant must have entered into possession
• the subjects of the lease must be land
• the landlord, if owner, must be the proprietor with a recorded title, ie the title deeds recorded in the Register of Sasines or registered in the Land Register

On 28 November 2013 certain leases which were granted for more than 175 years and under which the rent does not exceed £100 a year, converted to heritable titles. Therefore the tenants under these leases will become the owners of the property. Conversion of the lease will be automatic, provided certain conditions are met, unless the tenant opts out. It is possible for the landlord to claim compensation for their loss of income.

LEGAL AID

The Access to Justice Act 1999 transformed what used to be known as the Legal Aid system. The Legal Aid Board was replaced by the Legal Services Commission, which was responsible for the development and administration of two legal funding schemes in England and Wales, namely the Criminal Defence Service and the Community Legal Service. The Criminal Defence Service assisted people who were under police investigation or facing criminal charges. The Community Legal Service was designed to increase access to legal information and advice by involving a much wider network of funders and providers in giving publicly funded legal services. In Scotland, provision of legal aid is governed by the Legal Aid (Scotland) Act 1986, the Legal Profession and Legal Aid (Scotland) Act 2007 and the Scottish Civil Justice Council and Criminal Legal Assistance Act 2013, and administered by the Scottish Legal Aid Board.

Under the Legal Aid, Sentencing and Punishment of Offenders Act 2012 (LASPO), which came into force on 1 April 2013, the Legal Services Commission was abolished and replaced by the newly created Legal Aid Agency. The act has also limited the areas of law that fall within the scope of legal aid funding, especially those related to civil legal services. However, the act does include provisions for funding in exceptional cases, such as where failure to provide legal aid

would result in a violation of an individual's human rights or where providing legal aid would serve a wider public interest. Further, the act allows for areas of law to be added or omitted from the scope of legal aid independently, without subsequent legislation.

LASPO took whole areas of law out of scope for legal aid; some areas only qualify if they meet certain criteria. Broadly, the following categories of cases are now out of such scope: (a) family cases where there is no proof of domestic violence, forced marriage or child abduction; (b) immigration cases that do not involve asylum or detention; (c) housing and debt matters unless they constitute an immediate risk to the home; (d) welfare benefit cases except appeals to the upper tribunal or high court; (e) almost all clinical negligence cases; and (f) employment cases that do not involve human trafficking or a contravention of the Equality Act 2010. Funding for cases that fall outside of the scope of legal aid may be available under the Exceptional Case Funding scheme.

The Ministry of Justice published a review of LASPO in February 2019 and a Legal Support Action Plan which outlines changes the government intends to make and the future direction for legal aid support.

LEGAL AID AGENCY, **W** www.gov.uk/government/organisations/legal-aid-agency

CIVIL LEGAL AID

From 1 January 2000, only organisations (such as solicitors or Citizens Advice) with a contract with the Legal Services Commission (now Legal Aid Agency) have been able to give initial help in any civil matter. Moreover, from that date decisions about funding were devolved from the Legal Services Commission to contracted organisations in relation to any level of publicly funded service in family and immigration cases. For other types of case, applications for public funding are made through a solicitor (or other contracted legal services providers) in much the same way as the former Legal Aid.

Under the civil funding scheme there are broadly six levels of service available:
• legal help
• help at court
• family help – either family help (lower) or family help (higher)
• legal representation – either investigative help or full representation
• family mediation
• such other services as authorised by specific orders

ELIGIBILITY

Eligibility for funding from the Legal Aid Agency depends broadly on five factors:
• the level of service sought (*see* above)
• whether the applicant qualifies financially
• the merits of the applicant's case
• a costs-benefits analysis (if the costs are likely to outweigh any benefit that might be gained from the proceedings, funding may be refused)
• whether there is any public interest in the case being litigated (ie whether the case has a wider public interest beyond that of the parties involved, eg a human rights case)

The limits on capital and income above which a person is not entitled to public funding vary with the type of service sought. As of Spring 2017, there is a consultation on government proposals seeking to amend the legal financial eligibility system to accommodate the expansion of Universal Credit. Nothing in the consultation will affect the scope of or eligibility threshold for legal aid, but instead when claimants are passported and so would not have to undergo a full assessment of their means. The consultation closed on 11 May 2017 and the outcome is pending.

The 2012 act also amended the merits criteria so that legal aid may be refused where the case is suitable for alternative funding, such as Conditional Fee Agreements. Children, and individuals on certain welfare benefits, may be relieved from means testing and from the liability to make contributions. Financial eligibility requirements may be waived for individuals applying for an order for protection from domestic violence or forced marriage (though a contribution may be required). The government intend to extend the relief of means testing to parents opposing applications for placement orders or adoption orders by summer 2019.

CONTRIBUTIONS
Some of those who qualify for Legal Aid Agency funding will have to contribute towards their legal costs. Contributions must be paid by anyone who has a disposable income or disposable capital exceeding a prescribed amount. The rules relating to applicable contributions are complex and detailed information can be obtained from the Legal Aid Agency. Individuals on certain welfare benefits may not have to contribute.

STATUTORY CHARGE
A statutory charge is made if a person keeps or gains money or property in a case for which they have received legal aid. This means that the amount paid by the Legal Aid Agency fund on their behalf is deducted from the amount that the person receives. This does not apply if the court has ordered that the costs be paid by the other party (unless the amount paid by the other party does not cover all of the costs). In certain circumstances, the Legal Aid Agency may waive or postpone payment.

CONTINGENCY OR CONDITIONAL FEES
This system was introduced by the Courts and Legal Services Act 1990. It can offer legal representation on a 'no win, no fee' basis. It provides an alternative form of assistance, especially for those cases which are ineligible for funding by the Legal Aid Agency. The main area for such work is in the field of personal injuries.

Not all solicitors offer such a scheme and different solicitors may well have different terms. The effect of the agreement is that solicitors may not make any charges, or may waive some of their charges, until the case is concluded successfully. If a case is won then the losing party will usually have to pay towards costs, with the winning party contributing around one third.

SCOTLAND
Civil legal aid is available for cases in the following:
- the sheriff courts
- the Court of Session
- the Supreme Court
- the Lands Valuation Appeal Court
- the Scottish Land Court
- the Sheriff Appeal Court
- the Lands Tribunal for Scotland
- the Employment Appeal Tribunal
- the Proscribed Organisations Appeal Commission
- the Upper Tribunal for Scotland
- certain appeals before the Social Security Commissioners

Civil legal aid is not available for election petitions, some simple procedure actions, simplified divorce procedures or petitions by a debtor for his own sequestration. In defamation actions additional criteria must be met in order for legal aid to be available.

Eligibility for civil legal aid is assessed in a similar way to that in England and Wales, though the financial limits differ in some respects. A person shall be eligible for civil legal aid if their disposable income does not exceed £26,239 a year. A person may be refused civil aid if their disposable capital exceeds £13,017 and it appears to the Legal Aid board that they can afford to pay without legal aid. Additionally:
- if disposable capital is between £7,853 and £13,017, the applicant will be required to pay a contribution which will be equal to the difference between £7,853 and their disposable capital
- if disposable income is between £3,522 and £11,540, a contribution of one third of the difference between £3,522 and the disposable income may be payable
- if disposable income is between £11,541 and £15,743, one third of the difference between £3,522 and £11,540 plus half the difference between £11,541 and the disposable income may be payable
- if disposable income is between £15,744 and £26,239, a contribution of the following: one third of the difference between £3,522 and £11,540, plus half the difference between £11,541 and £15,743, plus all the remaining disposable income between £15,744 and £26,239 – will be payable

CRIMINAL LEGAL AID
The Legal Aid Agency provides defendants facing criminal charges with free legal representation if they pass a merits test and a means test although children and individuals on certain welfare benefits may be relieved from means testing.

Criminal legal aid covers the cost of preparing a case and legal representation in criminal proceedings. It is also available for appeals against verdicts or sentences in magistrates' courts, the crown court or the court of appeal. It is not available for bringing a private prosecution in a criminal court.

If granted criminal legal aid, either the person may choose their own solicitor or the court will assign one. Contributions to the legal costs may be required. The rules relating to applicable contributions are complex and detailed information can be obtained from the Legal Aid Agency.

DUTY SOLICITORS
LASPO also provides for free initial advice and initial assistance to anyone questioned by the police (whether under arrest or helping the police with their enquiries). No means test or contributions are required for this.

SCOTLAND
Legal advice and assistance operates in a similar way in Scotland. A person is eligible:
- if disposable income does not exceed £245 a week. If disposable income is between £105 and £245 a week, contributions are payable
- if disposable capital does not exceed £1,716 (if the person has dependent relatives, the savings allowance is higher)
- if receiving income support or income-related job seeker's allowance they qualify automatically provided their disposable capital is not over the limit

The procedure for application for criminal legal aid depends on the circumstances of each case. In solemn cases (more serious cases, such as murder) heard before a jury, a person is automatically entitled to criminal legal aid until they are given bail or placed in custody. Thereafter, it is for the court to decide whether to grant legal aid. The court will do this if the person accused cannot meet the expenses of the case without undue hardship on him or his dependants. In less serious cases the procedure depends on whether the person is in custody:
- anyone taken into custody has the right to free legal aid from the duty solicitor up to and including the first court appearance

- if the person is not in custody and wishes to plead guilty, they are not entitled to criminal legal aid but may be entitled to legal advice and assistance, including assistance by way of representation

However, regardless of whether the person is in custody if they wish to plead not guilty, they can apply for criminal legal aid. This must be done within 14 days of the first court appearance at which they made the plea.

The criteria used to assess whether or not criminal legal aid should be granted is similar to the criteria for England and Wales. When meeting with your solicitor, take evidence of your financial position such as details of savings, bank statements, pay slips, pension book or benefits book.

Under the relevant provisions of the Scottish Civil Justice Council and Criminal Legal Assistance Act 2013, a person in receipt of criminal legal aid or criminal assistance by way of representation will be required, in most circumstances, to make contributions where their weekly disposable income is £82 or above or if their disposable capital is £750 or more. The Scottish government has delayed the implementation of these provisions and no timetable has yet been proposed.

THE SCOTTISH LEGAL AID BOARD, Thistle House, 91 Haymarket Terrace, Edinburgh EH12 5HE **T** 0131-226 7061 **W** www.slab.org.uk

MARRIAGE

Any two persons may marry provided that:
- they are at least 16 years old on the day of the marriage (in England and Wales persons under the age of 18 must generally obtain the consent of their parents or guardian; if consent is refused an appeal may be made to the high court or the family court)
- they are not related to one another in a way which would prevent their marrying
- they are unmarried (a person who has already been married must produce documentary evidence that the previous marriage has been ended by death, divorce or annulment)
- they are capable of understanding the nature, duties and responsibilities of a marriage
- they consent to the marriage

It is now lawful for same sex couples to marry by way of civil or religious ceremony following the passing of the Marriage (Same Sex Couples) Act 2013, which came into force in March 2014. In addition, an existing marriage will now be able to continue where one or both parties change their legal gender and both parties wish to remain married. Civil partnerships are also still available for same sex couples, although The Marriage (Same Sex Couples) Act 2013 provides that couples in civil partnerships may convert their relationship to a marriage if they wish.

The parties should check the marriage will be recognised as valid in their home country if either is not a British citizen.

DEGREES OF RELATIONSHIP

A marriage between persons within the prohibited degrees of consanguinity, affinity or adoption is void.

Neither party may marry his or her parent, child, grandparent, grandchild, sibling, parent's sibling, sibling's child, adoptive parent, former adoptive parent, adoptive child or former adoptive child. All references to siblings include half-brothers/sisters.

Under the Marriage (Prohibited Degrees of Relationship) Act 1986, some exceptions to the law permit a person to marry certain step-relatives or in-laws.

In addition to the above, a person may not marry a child of their former civil partner, a child of a former spouse, the former civil partner of a grandparent, the former civil partner of a parent, the former spouse of a grandparent, the former spouse of a parent, the grandchild of a former civil partner or the grandchild of a former spouse, unless that relationship is the only reason they cannot marry and both persons are over 21 and the younger party has not at any time before attaining the age of 18 been a child of the family in relation to the other party.

ENGLAND AND WALES

TYPES OF MARRIAGE CEREMONY

It is possible to marry by either religious or civil ceremony. A religious ceremony can take place at a church or chapel of the Church of England or the Church in Wales, or at any other place of worship which has been formally registered by the Registrar-General. Same-sex marriages can also take place in a religious building, provided that the premises have been registered for the marriage of same-sex couples. Applications to register are made to the superintendent register of the registration district where the building is located and then forwarded to the General Register Office to be recorded. It is not possible, however, for same-sex marriages to take place in an Anglican church (although the Church of England is currently considering proposals to give same-sex marriage blessings).

A civil ceremony can take place at a register office, a venue approved by the local authority or any religious premises where permission has been given by the relevant religious organisation and is approved by the local authority.

An application for an approved premises licence must be made by the owners or trustees of the building concerned; it cannot be made by the prospective marriage couple. Approved premises must be regularly open to the public for marriages and civil partnerships; be a seemly and dignified venue; and the venue must be deemed to be a permanent and immovable structure. Open-air ceremonies are prohibited.

Non-Anglican marriages may also be solemnised following the issue of a Registrar-General's licence in other premises where one of the parties is seriously ill, is not expected to recover, and cannot be moved to premises where the marriage could normally be solemnised. The marriage must be solemnised in the place stated on the relevant notice of marriage, which may be one of the parties' place of residence. Detained and house-bound persons may also be married at their usual place of residence on the authority of a superintendent registrar's certificates with proper notice and consents.

MARRIAGE IN THE CHURCH OF ENGLAND OR THE CHURCH IN WALES

Marriage by banns

The marriage can take place in a parish in which one of the parties lives, or in a church in another parish if it is the usual place of worship of either or both of the parties. Further to measures introduced in October 2008, marriages can also take place in a parish where one of the parties has a 'qualifying connection', ie in: a parish where one of the parties was baptised (but not if it was part of a combined rite) or confirmed (where the confirmation was entered into the register book of confirmation for a church or chapel in that parish); a parish where one of the parties lived or habitually attended worship for six months or more; a parish where one of the parents of either of the parties lived for six months or more in the child's lifetime; a parish where one of the parents of either of the parties has habitually attended public worship for six months or more in the child's lifetime; or a parish where a parent or grandparent of either of the parties was married. The banns (ie the announcement of the marriage ceremony) must be called in the parish in which the marriage is to take place on three Sundays before the day of the ceremony; if either or both of the parties lives in a different parish the banns must also be called there. After three months the banns are no longer valid. The minister will not perform the marriage unless satisfied that the banns have been properly called.

Marriage by common licence
The couple and the member of the church who is to conduct the marriage will arrange for a common licence to be issued by the local diocese; this dispenses with the necessity for banns. One of the parties must reside in the parish, must usually worship at the parish church or authorised chapel of that parish, or otherwise have a 'qualifying connection' to the parish. The party must swear that they believe there is no lawful impediment to hinder the solemnisation of the marriage in accordance with the licence. If either party is under 18 years old, evidence of consent by their parent or guardian will be required. Any further eligibility requirements vary from diocese to diocese. The licence is valid for three months.

Marriage by special licence
A special licence is granted at the discretion of the Archbishop of Canterbury where a party has a genuine connection to a particular church or chapel but does not satisfy the legal requirements to marry there. They are also used where the building is not authorised for marriages, such as a private chapel. The parties are usually required to demonstrate that they have a genuine worshipping connection to the church or chapel. The special licence will usually be issued to the officiating priest approximately three weeks prior to the date of the wedding and expire three months after the date of issue. An application for the special licence must be made in hard copy to the registrar of the Faculty Office: 1 The Sanctuary, London SW1P 3JT **T** 020-7222 5381.

Marriage by certificate
The marriage can be conducted on the authority of a superintendent registrar's certificate, provided that the consent of the minister of the church or chapel where the celebration of the marriage is to take place is obtained. Since 2 March 2015, the marriage of non-EU nationals in the Church of England must take place by superintendent registrar's certificate (unless a special marriage licence is required or certain transitional arrangements apply to them), and will be allowed in any situation where the couple would otherwise have qualified for marriage by banns. In the case of British/EU nationals, the certificate procedure will be only be available if one of the parties lives in the parish for at least seven days or usually worships at the church/chapel.

Registration of the Marriage
Immediately following the solemnisation of a marriage according to the rites of the Church of England, the marriage must be registered in duplicate in two marriage register books provided by the Registrar-General for England and Wales. The entry must contain the particulars of the marriage in the prescribed form and must be signed by the clergyman, the parties to the marriage and two witnesses.

MARRIAGE BY OTHER RELIGIOUS CEREMONY
The parties will need to give notice to the register office at least 28 days before the ceremony. One of the parties must normally live in the registration district where the marriage is to take place or usually worship in the building where they wish to be married. If the building where the parties wish to be married has not been registered, the couple can still have a religious ceremony there, but this will have to follow a separate civil marriage ceremony for it to be valid. If the building is registered, in addition to giving notice to the superintendent registrar it may also be necessary to book a registrar, or authorised person to be present at the ceremony.

CIVIL MARRIAGE
A marriage may be solemnised at any register office, registered building or approved premises in England and Wales, without either of the parties being resident in the same district. The superintendent registrar of the district should be contacted and given notice, and, if the marriage is to take place at approved premises, the necessary arrangements at the venue must also be made.

NOTICE OF MARRIAGE
Where a marriage is intended to take place on the authority of a superintendent registrar's certificates, a notice of the marriage must be given in person to the superintendent registrar of the relevant district.

Both parties must have lived in a registration district in England or Wales for at least seven days immediately before giving notice personally at the local register office. If they live in different registration districts, notice must be given in both districts by the respective party in person. The marriage can take place in any register office or other approved premises in England and Wales no sooner than 28 days after notice has been given, when the superintendent registrar issues a certificate. The parties must get married or register the civil partnership within one year of giving notice.

When giving notice of the marriage it is necessary to provide evidence of name and surname, date of birth, place of residence and nationality, for example, with a passport or birth certificate and a recent bank statement. It will also be necessary to produce official proof, if relevant, that any previous marriage has ended in divorce or death by producing the original decree absolute or death certificate (or a certified copy). If the divorce or annulment documents were granted outside the UK, Channel Islands or Isle of Man the registrar may need to get in touch with the General Register Office to confirm their validity, which will incur further costs of between £50 and £75.

If either party is under 18 years old, evidence of consent by their parent or guardian is required. There are special procedures for those wishing to get married in the UK that are subject to immigration control; the register office will be able to advise on these.

SOLEMNISATION OF THE MARRIAGE
On the day of the wedding there must be at least two other people present who are prepared to act as witnesses and sign the marriage register. A registrar of marriages must be present at a marriage in a register office or at approved premises, but an authorised person may act in the capacity of registrar in a registered building.

If the marriage takes place at approved premises, the room must be separate from any other activity on the premises at the time of the ceremony, and no food or drink can be sold or consumed in the room during the ceremony or for one hour beforehand. In addition, proceedings conducted on approved premises cannot be religious in nature (although predominantly non-religious music and/or readings with incidental references to deities may be included).

The marriage must be solemnised with open doors. At some time during the ceremony the parties must make a declaration that they know of no legal impediment to the marriage and they must also say the contracting words; the declaratory and contracting words may vary according to the form of service. It may also be possible to embellish the marriage vows taken by the couple.

CIVIL FEES
Notice and registration of Marriage at a Register Office
By superintendent registrar's certificate, £35 per person for the notice of the marriage (which is not refundable if the

marriage does not in fact take place) and £46 for the registration of the marriage.

Marriage at a Register Office/Approved Premises
Fees for marriage at a register office are set by the local authority responsible. An additional fee will also be payable for the registrar's attendance at the marriage on an approved premises. This is also set locally by the local authority responsible. A further charge is likely to be made by the owners of the building for the use of the premises.

For marriages taking place in a registered religious building, an additional fee (determined by the local authority) is payable for the registrar's attendance at the marriage unless an 'authorised person' has agreed to register the marriage. Additional fees may be charged by the trustees and/or proprietors of the building for the wedding and by the person who performs the ceremony.

ECCLESIASTICAL FEES
(Church of England and Church in Wales)

Marriage by banns
For publication of banns, £30*
For certificate of banns issued at time of publication, £14*
For marriage service, £455*
For marriage certificate at time of registration £11 and £11 thereafter
* These fees are revised from 1 January each calendar year. Some may not apply to the Church in Wales

Marriage by common licence
The fee will be specified by each individual diocese
Marriage by special licence £250*
* This fee is revised on 1 April each calendar year

SCOTLAND

REGULAR MARRIAGES
A regular marriage is one which is celebrated by a minister of religion or authorised registrar or other celebrant. Each of the parties must complete a marriage notice form and return it to the district registrar for the area in which they are to be married, irrespective of where they live, within the three month period prior to the date of the marriage and not later than 29 days prior to that date. The district registrar must then enter the date of receipt and certain details in a marriage book kept for this purpose, and must also enter the names of the parties and the proposed date of marriage in a list which is displayed in a conspicuous place at the registration office until the date of the marriage has passed. All persons wishing to enter into a regular marriage in Scotland must follow the same preliminary procedure regardless of whether they intend to have a religious or civil ceremony. Before the marriage ceremony takes place any person may submit an objection in writing to the district registrar.

A marriage schedule, which is prepared by the registrar, will be issued to one or both of the parties in person up to seven days before a religious marriage; for a civil marriage the schedule will be available at the ceremony. The schedule must be handed to the celebrant before the ceremony starts and it must be signed immediately after the wedding. For religious marriages the schedule must be sent within three days by the parties to the district registrar who must register the marriage as soon as possible thereafter. In civil marriages, the district registrar must register the marriage as soon as possible.

The authority to conduct a religious marriage is deemed to be vested in the authorised celebrant rather than the building in which it takes place; open-air religious ceremonies are therefore permissible in Scotland.

From 10 June 2002 it has been possible, under the Marriage (Scotland) Act 2002, for venues or couples to apply to the local council for a licence to allow a civil ceremony to take place at a venue other than a registration office. To obtain further information, a venue or couple should contact the district registrar in the area they wish to marry.

MARRIAGE BY COHABITATION WITH HABIT AND REPUTE
Prior to the enactment of the Family Law (Scotland) Act 2006, if two people had lived together constantly as husband and wife and were generally held to be such by the neighbourhood and among their friends and relations, a presumption could arise from which marriage could be inferred. Before such a marriage could be registered, however, a decree of declarator of marriage had to be obtained from the court of session. Section 3 of the 2006 act provides that it will no longer be possible for a marriage to be constituted by cohabitation with habit and repute, but it will still be possible for couples whose period of cohabitation began before commencement of the 2006 act to seek a declarator under the old rule of law.

SAME-SEX MARRIAGES
On 12 March 2014 the Scottish government passed the Marriage and Civil Partnership (Scotland) Act 2014. This permits same-sex couples to get married, either in a civil ceremony or a 'religious or belief' ceremony where the religious or belief body has opted-in to solemnising same-sex marriage. Also, certain same-sex couples who have entered into a civil partnership have the option under the act to change their civil partnership to a marriage.

It is still possible for same-sex couples to enter into a civil partnership and this may be a 'religious or belief' civil partnership if the religious or belief body has agreed to perform these.

CIVIL FEES
The fee for submitting a notice of marriage to the district registrar is £30.00 per person. Solemnisation of a civil marriage costs £55.00, while the extract of the entry in the register of marriages attracts a fee of £10.00. The costs of religious marriage ceremonies can vary.

THE GENERAL REGISTER OFFICE, PO Box 2, Southport PR8 2JD T 0300-123 1837 W www.gro.gov.uk/gro/content/certificates

THE NATIONAL RECORDS OF SCOTLAND, New Register House, 3 West Register Street, Edinburgh EH1 3YT T 0131-314 0380 W www.nrscotland.gov.uk

TOWN AND COUNTRY PLANNING

There are a number of acts governing the development of land and buildings in England and Wales and advice should always be sought from Citizens Advice or the local planning authority before undertaking building works on any land or property. If development takes place which requires planning permission without permission being given, enforcement action may take place and the situation may need to be rectified. Planning law in Scotland is similar but certain Scotland-specific legislation applies so advice should always be sought.

PLANNING PERMISSION
Planning permission may be needed if the work involves:
• making a material change in use, such as dividing off part of a house for commercial use, eg for a workshop
• subdivision of a residential house into two or more separate homes
• going against the terms of the original planning permission, eg there may be a pre-existing restriction on fences in front gardens within an 'open-plan' estate

- building, engineering or mining works, except for the permitted developments below
- new or wider access to a main road
- additions or extensions to flats or maisonettes
- work which might obstruct the view of road users

Planning permission is not needed to carry out internal alterations or work which does not affect the external appearance of the building, and are not works for making good war damage or works begun after 5 December 1968 for the alteration of a building by providing additional space in it underground.

Under regulations which came into effect on 15 April 2015, there are certain types of development for which the Secretary of State for the Environment, Food and Rural Affairs has granted general permissions (permitted development rights). These include house extensions and additions, outbuildings and garages, other ancillary garden buildings such as swimming pools or ponds, and laying patios, paths or driveways for domestic use. However, all such developments will still be subject to a number of conditions.

Before carrying out any of the above permitted developments you should contact your local planning authority to find out whether the general permission has been modified in your area. For more information, visit **W** www.gov.uk/planning-permission-england-wales/when-you-dont-need-it

OTHER RESTRICTIONS

It may be necessary to obtain other types of permissions before carrying out any development. These permissions are separate from planning permission and apply regardless of whether or not planning permission is needed, eg:

- building regulations will probably apply if a new building is to be erected, if an existing one is to be altered or extended, or if the work involves building over a drain or sewer. The building control department of the local authority will advise on this
- listed building consent must be obtained from the local authority in order to make any alterations to a listed building. This applies to the main building, as well as possibly other structures within the curtilage of the building and/ or its grounds
- local authority approval is necessary if a building (or, in some circumstances, gates, walls, fences or railings) in a conservation area is to be demolished; each local authority keeps a register of all local buildings that are in conservation areas
- many trees are protected by tree preservation orders and must not be pruned or taken down without local authority consent
- bats and many other species are protected, and so Natural England or Natural Resources Wales must be notified before any work is carried out that will affect the habitat of protected species, eg timber treatment, renovation or extensions of lofts
- developments in areas with special designations, such as National Parks, Areas of Outstanding Natural Beauty, National Scenic Areas or in the Norfolk or Suffolk Broads, are subject to greater restrictions. The local planning authority will advise or refer enquirers to the relevant authority

There may also be restrictions contained in the title to the property which require you to get someone else's agreement before carrying out certain developments, and which should be considered when works are planned.

VOTERS' QUALIFICATIONS

Those entitled to vote at parliamentary and local government elections are those who, at the date of taking the poll, are:
- on the electoral roll
- aged 18 years or older (although for Scottish parliament and local government elections in Scotland those aged 16 and older can vote)
- British citizens, qualifying Commonwealth citizens or citizens of the Irish Republic who are resident in the UK
- those who suffer from no other legal bar to voting (eg prisoners). It should be noted that there is some uncertainty regarding the future of the legal bar on prisoners' voting following a decision taken by the European Court of Human Rights
- citizens of any EU member state may vote in local elections if they meet the criteria listed above (save for the nationality requirements). There is some uncertainty regarding future voting rights of EU citizens in light of Brexit. However, it should be noted that there will be no change to the voting rights of EU citizens living in the UK while the UK remains in the EU
- registered to vote as a Crown Servant
- registered to vote as a service voter

British citizens resident abroad are entitled to vote, provided they have been registered to vote in the UK within the last 15 years, as overseas electors in domestic parliamentary elections in the constituency in which they were last resident if they are on the electoral roll of the relevant constituency. The government released a policy statement in October 2016 proposing to abolish the current 15 year time limit for British citizens registering as overseas electors although it is unclear when this proposal will be legislated for. Members of the armed forces and their spouses or civil partners, Crown servants and employees of the British Council who are overseas, along with their spouses and civil partners, are entitled to vote regardless of how long they have been abroad. British citizens who had never been registered as an elector in the UK are not eligible to register as an overseas voter unless they left the UK before they were 18, providing they left the country no more than 15 years ago. Overseas electors may opt to vote by proxy or by postal vote. Overseas voters may not vote in local government elections.

The main categories of people who are not entitled to vote at general elections are:
- sitting peers in the House of Lords
- convicted persons detained in pursuance of their sentences (though remand prisoners, unconvicted prisoners and civil prisoners can vote if on the electoral register). This is currently subject to review, as detailed above
- those convicted within the previous five years of corrupt or illegal election practices
- EU citizens (who may only vote in EU and local government elections)

Under the Representation of the People Act 2000, several new groups of people are permitted to vote for the first time. These include: people who live on barges; people in mental health hospitals (other than those with criminal convictions) and homeless people who have made a 'declaration of local connection'.

REGISTERING TO VOTE

Voters must be entered on an electoral register. The Electoral Registration Officer (ERO) for each council area is responsible for preparing and publishing the register for his area by 1 December each year. Names may be added to the register to reflect changes in people's circumstances as they occur and each month during December to August, the ERO publishes a list of alterations to the published register.

On 10 May 2012, the government introduced the electoral registration and administration bill, which received royal assent on 31 January 2013. The act replaced household registration with individual elector registration, meaning each elector must apply individually to be registered to vote. Individuals will also be asked for identifying information such as date of birth and national insurance number. The act also introduced a number of changes relating to electoral administration and the conduct of elections. Anyone failing to supply information to the ERO when requested, or supplying false information, may be fined by up to £1,000. Further, the ERO may impose a civil penalty on those who fail to make an application for registration when required to do so by the ERO. Application forms and more information are available from the Electoral Commission (**W** www.aboutmyvote.co.uk).

VOTING

Voting is not compulsory in the UK. Those who wish to vote do so in person at the allotted polling station. Postal votes are now available to anyone on request and you do not need to give a reason for using a postal vote.

A proxy (whereby the voter nominates someone to vote in person on their behalf) can be appointed to act in a specific election, for a specified period of time or indefinitely. For the appointment of an indefinite or long-term proxy, the voter needs to specify physical employment, study reasons or a disability to explain why they are making an application. With proxy votes where a particular election is specified, the voter needs to provide details of the circumstances by which they cannot reasonably be expected to go to the polling station. Applications for a proxy are normally available up to six working days before an election, but should the voter fall ill on election day, it is possible to appoint a proxy up until polling day.

On 4 April 2019, a new campaign 'Let Us Vote' was launched with the aim of giving everyone living in the UK the right to vote in elections and referendums. The campaign is seeking new legislation which would allow all UK residents, plus British citizens living abroad, to vote in general elections regardless of their citizenship.

WILLS

A will is used to appoint executors (who will administer the estate), give directions as to the disposal of the body, appoint guardians for children and determine how and to whom property is to be passed. A well-drafted will can operate to reduce the level of inheritance tax which the estate pays. It is best to have a will drawn up by a solicitor, but if a solicitor is not employed the following points must be taken into account:
- if possible the will must not be prepared on behalf of another person by someone who is to benefit from it or who is a close relative of a major beneficiary
- the language used must be clear and unambiguous and it is better to avoid the use of legal terms where the same thing can be expressed in plain language
- it is better to rewrite the whole document if a mistake is made. If necessary, alterations can be made by striking through the words with a pen, and the signature or initials of the testator and the witnesses must be put in the margin opposite the alteration. No alteration of any kind should be made after the will has been executed
- if the person later wishes to change the will or part of it, it is better to write a new will revoking the old. The use of codicils (documents written as supplements or containing modifications to the will) should be left to a solicitor

- the will should be typed or printed, or if handwritten be legible and preferably in ink

The form of a will varies to suit different cases, a solicitor will be able to advise as to wording, however, 'DIY' will-writing kits can be purchased from good stationery shops and many banks offer a will-writing service.

LAPSED LEGATEES

If a person who has been left property in a will dies before the person who made the will, the gift fails and will pass to the person entitled to everything not otherwise disposed of (the residuary estate). If the beneficiary of the residuary estate dies before the person who made the will, the gift of the residuary estate also fails and passes to the closest relative(s) of the testator in accordance with the intestacy rules.

It is always better to draw up a new will if a beneficiary predeceases the person who made the will.

EXECUTORS

It is usual to appoint two executors, although one is sufficient. No more than four persons can deal with the estate of the person who has died. The name and address of each executor should be given in full (the addresses are not essential but including them adds clarity to the document). Executors should be 18 years of age or over. An executor may be a beneficiary of the will.

WITNESSES

A person who is a beneficiary of a will, or the spouse or civil partner of a beneficiary at the time the will is signed, must not act as a witness or else he/she will be unable to take his/her gift. There is nothing preventing the spouse or civil partner of the person making the will from acting as a witness, but as it is rare for a spouse or civil partner not to benefit from the will of his/her spouse or civil partner, an independent witness is usually better.

It is also better that a person does not act as an executor and as a witness, as he/she can take no benefit (including remuneration) under a will to which he/she is witness. In relation to deaths on or after 1 February 2001, however, a professional executor who is also a witness can receive payments due to him or her under a term in the will for services provided as executor.

The identity of the witnesses should be made as explicit as possible, such as by stating their names, addresses, and occupations.

EXECUTION OF A WILL

The person making the will should sign his/her name in the presence of the two witnesses. It is advisable to sign at the foot of the document, so as to avoid uncertainty about the testator's intention. The witnesses must then sign their names while the person making the will looks on. If this procedure is not adhered to, the will may be considered invalid. There are certain exceptional circumstances where these rules are relaxed, eg where the person may be too ill to sign.

CAPACITY TO MAKE A WILL

Anyone aged 18 or over can make a will. However, if there is any suspicion that the person making the will is not, through reasons of infirmity or age, fully in command of his/her faculties, it is advisable to arrange for a medical practitioner to examine the person making the will as near to the time that the testator gives instructions for the will and to when the will is executed (to verify his/her mental capacity and to record that medical opinion in writing), and to ask the examining practitioner to act as a witness. If a person is not mentally able to make a will, the court of protection may do this for him/her by virtue of the Mental Capacity Act 2005.

REVOCATION

A will may be revoked or cancelled in a number of ways:
- a later will revokes an earlier one if it says so; otherwise the

earlier will is by implication revoked by the later one to the extent that it contradicts or repeats the earlier one

- a will is revoked if the original physical document on which it is written is destroyed by the person whose will it is. There must be an intention to revoke the will and an act of destruction. It may not be sufficient to obliterate the will with a pen
- a will is revoked by the testator making a written declaration to this effect executed in the same way as a will
- a will is also revoked when the person marries or forms a civil partnership, unless it is clear from the will that the person intended the will to stand after that particular marriage or civil partnership. A will is not revoked, however, by the conversion of a civil partnership to a marriage, or when the testator is treated as having formed a civil partnership on 5 December 2005 because he/she registered a recognised overseas relationship before that date.
- where a marriage or civil partnership ends in divorce or dissolution or is annulled or declared void, gifts to the spouse or civil partner and the appointment of the spouse or civil partner as executor fail unless the will says that this is not to happen. A former spouse or civil partner is treated as having predeceased the testator. A separation does not change the effect of a married person or civil partner's will.

PROBATE AND LETTERS OF ADMINISTRATION
The grant of probate is granted to the executors named in a will and once granted, the executors are obliged to carry out the instructions of the will. Letters of administration are granted where the deceased died intestate or did not leave a valid will. Letters of administration with will annexed are granted when the deceased did not appoint an executor in the will or the appointed executor(s) are not able or willing to act. The letters of administration give a person, often the next of kin, similar powers and duties to those of an executor.

Applications for the grant of probate or for letters of administration can be made to the Principal Registry of the Family Division, to a district probate registry or to a probate sub-registry. Applicants not using a solicitor will need to send the following documents to the main probate registry of choice: the Probate Application Form (PA1A if the deceased did not leave a will or PA1P if the deceased had a will); the original will and codicils (if any) and three copies of the same; an official copy of the death certificate; and the appropriate tax form (an 'IHT 205' if no inheritance tax is owed; otherwise an 'IHT 421' stamped by HMRC confirming payment of inheritance tax), in addition to a cheque for the relevant probate fee. The applicant will then be invited to an interview at the probate registry of choice where they will swear an oath. Where an applicant is using a solicitor, the PA1 is not necessary and the appropriate oath (for executors or administrators) will be included in the documents to be sent to the probate registry; there is no interview. In both cases, where the estate of the deceased is below £5,000, there is no probate fee to pay. Certain property, up to the value of £5,000, may be disposed of without a grant of probate or letters of administration, as can assets that do not pass under the will such as jointly owned assets which pass automatically on the death of one of the joint holders to the survivor, life policies written in trust, or discretionary pension death benefits.

A new probate regime was scheduled to be in force by April 2019, but due to the immediacy of Brexit, the approval process had been delayed, and at the time of writing there had been no indication from the Ministry of Justice as to when it may come into force. Notwithstanding, the new regime will come into force 21 days after the order is made, unless the approval motion is rejected by parliament and the issue has to be debated and voted on. The new regime stipulates that probate fees will maintained at the current level for estates worth below £50,000 and increased to £6,000 for estates worth over £2m, with a sliding scale for estates worth between £50,000 and £2m.

WHERE TO FIND A PROVED WILL
Since 1858 wills which have been proved, that is wills on which probate or letters of administration have been granted, must have been proved at the Principal Registry of the Family Division or at a district probate registry. The Lord Chancellor has power to direct where the original documents are kept but most are filed where they were proved and may be inspected there and a copy obtained. You can search for a probate record online or by post. The Principal Registry also holds copies of all wills proved at district probate registries and these may be inspected at First Avenue House, High Holborn, London. An index of all grants, both of probate and of letters of administration, is compiled by the Principal Registry and may be seen either at the Principal Registry or at a district probate registry.

It is also possible to discover when a grant of probate or letters of administration is issued by requesting a standing search. In response to a request and for a small fee, a district probate registry will supply the names and addresses of executors or administrators and the registry in which the grant was made, of any grant in the estate of a specified person made in the previous six months or following six months.

PRINCIPAL REGISTRY (FAMILY DIVISION), 7th Floor, 42–49 High Holborn, First Avenue House, London WC1V 6NP
T 020-7421 8509

INTESTACY
Intestacy occurs when someone dies without leaving a will or leaves a will which is invalid or which does not take effect for some reason. Intestacy can be partial, for instance, if there is a valid will which disposes of some but not all of the testator's property. In such cases the person's estate (property, possessions, other assets following the payment of debts) passes to certain members of the family. If a will has been written that disposes of only part of a person's property, these rules apply to the part which is undisposed of.

Some types of property do not follow the intestacy rules, for example, property held as joint tenants, insurance policies taken out for specified individuals or assigned into trust during the testator's lifetime and death benefits under a pension scheme.

Following a lengthy review by the Law Commission, the intestacy rules changed on 1 October 2014.

If the person (intestate) leaves a spouse or a civil partner who survives for 28 days and children (legitimate, illegitimate and adopted children and other descendants), the estate is divided as follows:

- if the estate is worth more than £250,000, the spouse or civil partner takes the 'personal chattels' (household articles, including cars, but nothing used for business purposes or held solely as an investment), £250,000 and half of the rest of the estate absolutely
- the rest of the estate goes to the children*

If the intestate leaves a spouse or civil partner who survives for 28 days but no children, the spouse or civil partner will take the estate in its entirety, regardless of its value.

If there is no surviving spouse or civil partner, the estate is distributed among those who survive the intestate as follows (these provisions remained unchanged at 1 October 2014):

- to surviving children*, but if none to
- parents (equally, if both alive), but if none to
- brothers and sisters of the whole blood* (including issue of deceased ones), but if none to
- brothers and sisters of the half blood* (including issue of deceased ones), but if none to
- grandparents (equally, if more than one), but if none to
- aunts and uncles of the whole blood*, but if none to
- aunts and uncles of the half blood*, but if none to

- the Crown, Duchy of Lancaster or the Duke of Cornwall *(bona vacantia)*

* To inherit, a member of these groups must survive the intestate and attain the age of 18, or marry under that age. If they die under the age of 18 (unless married under that age), their share goes to others, if any, in the same group. If any member of these groups predeceases the intestate leaving children, their share is divided equally among their children.

In England and Wales the provisions of the Inheritance (Provision for Family and Dependants) Act 1975 may allow other people to claim provision from the deceased's assets. This act also applies to cases where a will has been made and allows a person to apply to the court if they feel that the will or rules of intestacy (or both) do not make adequate provision for them. The court can order payment from the deceased's assets or the transfer of property from them if the applicant's claim is accepted. The application must be made within six months of the grant of probate or letters of administration and the following people can make an application:

- the spouse or civil partner
- a former spouse or civil partner who has not remarried or formed a subsequent civil partnership
- a child of the deceased
- someone treated as a child of the deceased's family where the deceased stood in the role of a parent to the applicant
- someone maintained wholly or partly by the deceased
- where the deceased died on or after 1 January 1996, someone who has cohabited for two years before the death in the same household as the deceased and was living as the husband or wife or civil partner of the deceased

SCOTLAND

In Scotland any person over 12 and of sound mind can make a will. The person making the will can only freely dispose of the heritage and what is known as the 'dead's part' of the estate because:

- the spouse or civil partner has the right to inherit one-third of the moveable estate if there are children or other descendants, and one-half of it if there are not
- children are entitled to one-third of the moveable estate if there is a surviving spouse or civil partner, and one-half of it if there is not

The remaining portion of the moveable estate is the dead's part, and legacies and bequests are payable from this. Debts are payable out of the whole estate before any division.

From August 1995, wills no longer needed to be 'holographed' and it is now only necessary to have one witness. The person making the will still needs to sign each page. It is better that the will is not witnessed by a beneficiary although the attestation would still be sound and the beneficiary would not have to relinquish the gift.

As a result of the changes brought in by the Succession (Scotland) Act 2016, from 1 November 2016 a divorce, dissolution or annulment (granted by a UK court) will revoke any provision in a will which confers a benefit or power of appointment on the former spouse or civil partner unless the will expressly provides that the benefit or appointment should still apply in the event of a divorce, dissolution or annulment. Subsequent marriage or civil partnership does not revoke a will but the birth of a child who is not provided for may do so. A will may be revoked by a subsequent will, either expressly or by implication, but in so far as the two can be read together both have effect. If a subsequent will is revoked, the earlier will may be revived provided it was not physically destroyed.

Wills may be registered in the sheriff court Books of the Sheriffdom in which the deceased lived or in the Books of Council and Session at the Registers of Scotland.

CONFIRMATION

Confirmation (the Scottish equivalent of probate) is obtained in the sheriff court of the sheriffdom in which the deceased was domiciled at the time of death. Executors are either 'nominate' (named by the deceased in the will) or 'dative' (appointed by the court in cases where no executor is named in a will or in cases of intestacy). Applicants for confirmation must first provide an inventory of the deceased's estate and a schedule of debts, with an affidavit. In estates under £36,000 gross, confirmation can be obtained under a simplified procedure at reduced fees, with no need for a solicitor. The local sheriff clerk's office can provide assistance.

PRINCIPAL REGISTRY (FAMILY DIVISION), First Avenue House, 42–49 High Holborn, London WC1V 6NP
T 020-7947 6000

REGISTERS OF SCOTLAND, Meadowbank House, 153 London Road, Edinburgh EH8 7AU **T** 0800-169 9391
W www.ros.gov.uk

INTESTACY

The rules of distribution are contained in the Succession (Scotland) Act 1964 and are extended to include civil partners by the Civil Partnership Act 2004.

A surviving spouse or civil partner is entitled to 'prior rights'. Prior rights mean that if certain conditions are met the spouse or civil partner has the right to inherit:

- the matrimonial or family home up to a value of £473,000, or one matrimonial or family home if there is more than one, or, in certain circumstances, the value of the home
- the furnishings and contents of that home, up to the value of £29,000
- a cash sum of £50,000 if the deceased left children or other descendants, or £89,000 if not

These figures are increased from time to time by regulations.

Once prior rights have been satisfied legal rights are settled. Legal rights are:

- *Jus relicti(ae) and rights under the section 131 of the Civil Partnership Act 2004* – the right of a surviving spouse or civil partner to one-half of the net moveable estate, after satisfaction of prior rights, if there are no surviving children; if there are surviving children, the spouse or civil partner is entitled to one-third of the net moveable estate
- *Legitim and rights under the section 131 of the Civil Partnership Act 2004* – the right of surviving children to one-half of the net moveable estate if there is no surviving spouse or civil partner; if there is a surviving spouse or civil partner, the children are entitled to one-third of the net moveable estate after the satisfaction of prior rights

Once prior and legal rights have been satisfied, the remaining estate will be distributed in the following order:

- to descendants
- if no descendants, then to collaterals (ie brothers and sisters) and parents with each being entitled to half of the estate, or if only either parents or collaterals survive, the whole of the estate
- surviving spouse or civil partner
- if no collaterals, parents, spouse or civil partner, then to ascendants collaterals (ie aunts and uncles), and so on in an ascending scale
- if all lines of succession fail, the estate passes to the Crown

Relatives of the whole blood are preferred to relatives of the half blood. Also the right of representation, ie the right of the issue of a person who would have succeeded if he/she had survived the intestate, applies.

The Family Law (Scotland) Act 2006 makes provision to allow an unmarried cohabitant to make a financial claim against the estate of a cohabitant who dies intestate. In general a claim must be made within six months of the deceased's death. The court must take into account certain factors when considering such a claim. If the claim is successful the court has the power to order payment of a capital sum and transfer of property.

In February 2019 the Scottish government launched a consultation on changes to the law of intestate succession.

INTELLECTUAL PROPERTY

Intellectual property is a broad term covering a number of legal rights provided by the government to help people protect their creative works and encourage further innovation. By using these legal rights people can own the things they create and control the way in which others use their innovations. Intellectual property owners can take legal action to stop others using their intellectual property, they can license their intellectual property to others or they can sell it on. Different types of intellectual property utilise different forms of protection including copyright, designs, patents and trade marks, which are all covered below in more detail.

CHANGES TO INTELLECTUAL PROPERTY LAW
Reforms to the Copyright, Designs and Patents Act 1988 came into force on 1 June 2014, giving a number of sectors a legal framework suitable for the digital age, removing unnecessary regulations and enabling these sectors to better preserve and use copyright material. Under the reforms, researchers benefit from a text and data mining exception for non-commercial research and schools, colleges and universities can obtain a licence to use copyright material on interactive whiteboards and in presentations without accidentally infringing copyright. An existing preservation exception was expanded to cover all types of copyright work, and now applies to museums and galleries as well as libraries and archives. The reforms also provided exceptions to copyright for the benefit of disabled people, allowing those with any type of disability which affected access to copyright works to make accessible copies of these works (eg music, film, books) when no commercial alternative existed. Under the Marrakesh Treaty, which entered into force on 11 October 2018, the commercial availability restrictions were removed to allow disabled persons to make accessible copies even when the material is commercially available.

The Intellectual Property Act 2014 came into effect on 1 October 2014. The act modernised intellectual property law to help UK businesses better protect their rights. It also implemented reforms to design legislation and introduced a number of changes to patent law, making it cheaper and easier to use and defend patents. Additional patent rule changes came into effect on 1 October 2016 and 6 April 2017. These streamlined the application process, made procedures more flexible and increased the legal certainty of patents that are granted.

The Intellectual Property (Unjustified Threats) Act 2017 came into effect on 1 October 2017. The act serves to protect businesses against unfair threats of legal action, when no infringement of intellectual property has actually taken place, and to help businesses negotiate fairly over intellectual property disputes and avoid costly litigation.

COPYRIGHT

Copyright protects all original literary, dramatic, musical and artistic works, as well as sound and film recordings and broadcasts. Among the works covered by copyright are novels, computer programs, newspaper articles, sculptures, technical drawings, websites, maps and photographs. Under copyright the creators of these works can control the various ways in which their material may be exploited, the rights broadly covering copying, adapting, issuing (including renting and lending) copies to the public, performing in public, and broadcasting the material (including online). The transfer of copyright works to formats accessible to visually impaired persons without infringement of copyright was enacted in 2002.

Copyright protection in the UK is automatic and there is no official registration system. The creator of a work can help to protect it by including the copyright symbol ©, the name of the copyright owner, and the year in which the work was created. In addition, steps can be taken by the work's creator to provide evidence that they had the work at a particular time (eg by depositing a copy with a bank or solicitor). The main legislation is the Copyright, Designs and Patents Act 1988 (as amended). The term of copyright protection for literary, dramatic, musical (including song lyrics and musical compositions) and artistic works lasts for 70 years after the death of the creator. For film, copyright lasts for 70 years after the director, authors of the screenplay and dialogue, or the composer of any music specially created for the film have all died. Sound recordings are protected for 50 years after their publication (or their first performance if they are not published), and broadcasts for 50 years from the end of the year in which the broadcast/transmission was made. The typographical arrangement of published editions remains under copyright protection for 25 years from the end of the year in which the particular edition was published.

The main international treaties protecting copyright are the Berne Convention for the Protection of Literary and Artistic Works (administered by the World Intellectual Property Organization (WIPO)), the Rome Convention for the Protection of Performers, Producers of Phonograms and Broadcasting Organisations (administered by the the International Labour Organisation, UNESCO and WIPO), the Geneva Phonograms Convention (administered by WIPO), and the Universal Copyright Convention (developed by UNESCO); the UK is a signatory to these conventions. Copyright material created by UK nationals or residents is protected in the countries that have signed one of the above-named conventions by the national law of that country. A list of participating countries may be obtained from the UK Intellectual Property Office. The World Trade Organization's Trade-Related Aspects of Intellectual Property Rights (TRIPS) agreement may also provide copyright protection abroad.

In May 2001 the EU passed a new directive (which became law in the UK in 2003) aimed at harmonising copyright law throughout the EU to take account of the internet and other technologies. More information can be found online (**W** www.ipo.gov.uk).

LICENSING
Use of copyright material without seeking permission in each instance may be permitted under 'blanket' licences available from national copyright licensing agencies. The International Federation of Reproduction Rights Organisations facilitates agreements between its member licensing agencies and on behalf of its members with organisations such as WIPO, UNESCO, the EU and the Council of Europe. More information can be found online (**W** www.ifrro.org).

DESIGN PROTECTION

Design protection covers the outward appearance of an article, and in the UK it takes two forms: registered design and design right, which are not mutually exclusive. Registered design protects the aesthetic appearance of an article, including shape, configuration, pattern or ornament; artistic works such as sculptures are excluded, being generally protected by copyright. To achieve design protection the owner of the design must apply to the Intellectual Property Office. In order to qualify for protection, a design must be new and materially different from earlier UK published designs. Initial registration lasts for five years and can be extended in five-year increments to a maximum of 25 years. The current legislation is the Registered Designs Act 1949 (as amended).

UK applicants wishing to protect their designs in the EU can do so by applying for a Registered Community Design with the EU Intellectual Property Office. Outside the EU separate applications must be made in each country in which protection is sought.

Design right is an automatic right which applies to the shape or configuration of articles and does not require registration. Unlike registered design, two-dimensional designs do not qualify for protection but designs of electronic circuits are protected by design right. Designs must be original and non-commonplace. The term of design right is ten years from first marketing of the design, or 15 years after the creation of the design, whichever is earlier. This right is effective only in the UK. After five years anyone is entitled to apply for a licence of right, which allows others to make and sell products copying the design. The current legislation is Part 3 of the Copyright, Designs and Patents Act 1988.

PATENTS

A patent is a document issued by the UK Intellectual Property Office relating to an invention. It gives the proprietor the right for a limited period to stop others from making, using, importing or selling the invention without the inventor's permission. The patentee pays a fee to cover the costs of processing the patent and must publicly disclose details of the invention.

To qualify for a patent, an invention must be new, must be functional or technical, must exhibit an inventive step, and must be capable of industrial application. The patent is valid for a maximum of 20 years, subject to renewal on the fourth anniversary of when the application was first filed and annually thereafter. The UK Intellectual Property Office, established in 1852, is responsible for ensuring that all stages of an application comply with the Patents Act 1977, and that the invention meets the criteria for a patent. An online patent renewal service is available at: www.gov.uk/renew-patent.

WIPO is responsible for administering many of the international conventions on intellectual property. The Patent Cooperation Treaty allows inventors to file a single application for patent rights in some or all of the contracting states. This application is searched by an International Searching Authority to confirm the invention is novel and that the same concept has not already been made publicly available. The application and search report are then published by the International Bureau of WIPO. It may also be the subject of an (optional) international preliminary examination. Applicants must then deal directly with the patent offices in the countries where they are seeking patent rights. The European Patent Convention allows inventors to obtain patent rights in all the contracting states by filing a single application with the European Patent Office. More information can be found at: **W** www.ipo.gov.uk.

RESEARCH DISCLOSURES

Research disclosures are publicly disclosed details of inventions. Once published, an invention is considered no longer novel and becomes 'prior art'. Publishing a disclosure is significantly cheaper than applying for a patent; however, unlike a patent, it does not entitle the author to exclusive rights to use or license the invention. Instead, research disclosures are primarily published to ensure the inventor the freedom to use the invention. This works because publishing legally prevents other parties from patenting the disclosed innovation and, in the UK, patent law dictates that by disclosing details of an invention, even the inventor relinquishes their right to a patent.

In theory, publishing details of an invention anywhere should be enough to constitute a research disclosure. However, to be effective, a research disclosure needs to be published in a location which patent examiners will include in their prior art searches. To ensure global legal precedent it must be included in a publication with a recognised date stamp and made publicly available throughout the world.

Research Disclosure, established in 1960 and operated by Questel Ireland Ltd, is the primary publisher of research disclosures. It is the only disclosure service recognised by the Patent Cooperation Treaty as a mandatory search resource which must be consulted by the international search authorities. (**W** www.researchdisclosure.com).

TRADE MARKS

Trade marks are a means of identification, enabling traders to make their goods and services readily distinguishable from those supplied by others. Trade marks can take the form of words, a logo or a combination of both. Registration prevents other traders using the same or similar trade marks for similar products or services.

In the UK trade marks are registered at the UK Intellectual Property Office. In order to qualify for registration, a trade mark must be capable of distinguishing its proprietor's goods or services from those of other undertakings; it should be non-deceptive, should not describe the goods and services or any characteristics of them, should not be contrary to law or morality and should not be similar or identical to any earlier trade marks for the same or similar goods or services. The owner of a registered trade mark may include an ® symbol next to it, and must renew their registration every ten years to keep it in force. The relevant current legislation is the Trade Marks Act 1994 (as amended).

It is possible to obtain an international trade mark registration, effective in up to 120 countries, under the Madrid system for the international registration of marks, to which the UK is party. British companies can obtain international trade mark registration in those countries party to the system through a single application to WIPO.

EU trade mark regulation is administered by the EU Intellectual Property Office, which registers Community trade marks, valid throughout the EU. The registration of trade marks in individual member states continues in parallel with EU trade marks.

DOMAIN NAMES

An internet domain name (eg www.whitakersalmanack.com) has to be registered separately from a trade mark, and this can be done through a number of registrars which charge varying rates and compete for business. For each top-level domain name (eg uk.com), there is a central registry to store the unique internet names and addresses using that suffix. A list of accredited registrars can be found online (**W** www.icann.org).

CONTACTS

COPYRIGHT LICENSING AGENCY LTD, 5th Floor, Shackleton House, 4 Battle Bridge Lane, London SE1 2HX **T** 020-7400 3100 **W** www.cla.co.uk

EUROPEAN PATENT OFFICE, 80298 Munich, Germany **T** (+49) 89 2399-0 **W** www.epo.org

INTELLECTUAL PROPERTY OFFICE, Concept House, Cardiff Road, Newport NP10 8QQ **T** 0300-300 2000 **W** www.ipo.gov.uk

WORLD INTELLECTUAL PROPERTY ORGANIZATION, 34 chemin des Colombettes, CH-1211 Geneva 20, Switzerland **T** (+41) 22 338 9111 **W** www.wipo.int

THE MEDIA

CROSS-MEDIA OWNERSHIP

The rules surrounding cross-media ownership were overhauled as part of the 2003 Communications Act. The act simplified and relaxed existing rules to encourage dispersion of ownership and new market entry while preventing the most influential media in any community being controlled by too narrow a range of interests. However, transfers and mergers are not solely subject to examination on competition grounds by the competition authorities. The Secretary of State for Digital, Culture, Media and Sport has a broad remit to decide if a transaction is permissible and can intervene on public interest grounds (relating both to newspapers and cross-media criteria, if broadcasting interests are also involved). The Office of Communications (OFCOM) has an advisory role in this context. Government and parliamentary assurances were given that any intervention into local newspaper transfers would be rare and exceptional. Following a request from the Secretary of State for Digital, Culture, Media and Sport in June 2010 for a removal of all restrictions from the ownership of local media, OFCOM recommended the liberalisation of local cross-media regulations to enable a single owner to control newspapers, a TV licence and radio stations in one area.

REGULATION

OFCOM is the regulator for the communication industries in the UK and has responsibility for television, radio, telecommunications and wireless communications services. OFCOM is required to report annually to parliament and exists to further the interests of consumers by balancing choice and competition with the duty to foster plurality; protect viewers and listeners and promote cultural diversity in the media; and to ensure full and fair competition between communications providers.

OFFICE OF COMMUNICATIONS (OFCOM), Riverside House, 2A Southwark Bridge Road, London SE1 9HA
T 020-7981 3000 **W** www.ofcom.org.uk
Chair, Lord Burns, GCB

COMPLAINTS

Under the Communications Act 2003 OFCOM's licensees are obliged to adhere to the provisions of its codes (including advertising, programme standards, fairness, privacy and sponsorship). Complainants should contact the broadcaster in the first instance (details can be found on OFCOM's website); however, if the complainant wishes the complaint to be considered by OFCOM, it will do so. Complaints must be submitted within 20 working days of broadcast, as broadcasters are only required to keep recordings for the following periods: radio, 42 days; television, 90 days; cable and satellite, 60 days. OFCOM can fine a broadcaster, revoke a licence or take programmes off the air. Since November 2004 complaints relating to individual advertisements on TV or radio have been dealt with by the Advertising Standards Authority.

ADVERTISING STANDARDS AUTHORITY Mid City Place, 71 High Holborn, London WC1V 6QT **T** 020-7492 2222
W www.asa.org.uk
Chief Executive, Guy Parker

TELEVISION

There are six major television channel owners who are responsible for the biggest audience share. They are the British Broadcasting Corporation (BBC), Independent Television (ITV), Channel 4, Channel 5, Sky and UKTV. Overall there are around 480 channels available to viewers, through free-to-air, free-to-view and subscription-based services. Following the completion of the switchover to a digital format in October 2012, analogue transmissions ended and digital-only content was broadcast through a range of services, including terrestrial, satellite, cable and IP.

Beginning as a radio station in 1922, the BBC is the oldest broadcaster in the world. The corporation began a London-only television service from Alexandra Palace in 1936 and achieved nationwide coverage 15 years later. A second station, BBC Two, was launched in 1964. The BBC's other free-to-air channels available in the UK comprise BBC Four, BBC News, BBC Parliament, the children's channels, CBeebies and CBBC, and regional channels including BBC Alba, a gaelic-language channel in Scotland. Many of the BBC's channels have a corresponding HD (high definition) service and there are additionally several local channels. BBC's iPlayer service was launched on Christmas Day 2007 and allows users to view and listen to content instantly, stream live television and download programmes on to a computer, tablet or mobile device for up to 30 days. An integrated service for radio was launched in June 2008. In 2009, iPlayer was extended to more than 20 devices, including mobile phones and games consoles, and an HD service was launched. The BBC services are funded by the licence fee. The corporation also has a commercial arm, BBC Worldwide, which was formed in 1994 and exists to maximise the value of the BBC's programme and publishing assets for the benefit of the licence payer. Its businesses include international programming distribution, magazines, other licensed products, live events and media monitoring.

The ITV (Independent Television) network began broadcasting in 1955 on Channel 3 in the London area, under the Television Act 1954 which made provision for commercial television in the UK. The ITV network originally comprised a number of independent licensees, the majority of which have now merged to form ITV plc. The network generates funds through broadcasting television advertisements. The ITV network channels now include ITV2, ITV3, ITV4, ITVBe, ITV Encore and CiTV, while the network also owns UTV Ireland. The majority of ITV channels have corresponding HD services. ITV Player, similar to iPlayer, was launched December 2008 and rebranded as ITV Hub in November 2015. ITV Network Centre is wholly owned by the ITV companies and undertakes commissioning and scheduling of programmes shown across the ITV network and, as with the other terrestrial channels, 25 per cent of programmes must come from independent producers.

Channel 4 and S4C (Sianel Pedwar Cymru – Channel Four Wales) were launched in 1982 to provide programmes with a distinctive character that appeal to interests not catered for by ITV. Channel 4 has a remit to be innovative, experimental and distinctive. Although publicly owned, Channel 4 receives no public funding and is financed predominantly through advertising, but unlike ITV, Channel 4 is not shareholder-owned. It has expanded to create the stations E4, More4, Film4, 4Music and, in July 2012, catchup channel 4seven. All 4 is Channel 4's online service which enables viewers to download and revisit programmes from the last 30 days as well as access an older archive of footage. All 4 replaced Channel 4's first online platform 4oD (launched in 2006) in March 2015 and in March 2019 a subscription service was added, All 4+, which removes ads from the platform. S4C, the Welsh language public service broadcaster, receives annual funding, £15m in 2018–19, from the Department for Digital, Culture, Media and Sport (DCMS). In March 2018, the government decided that S4C would be entirely funded through the TV licence from 2022, which currently fulfils 90 per cent of its budget. S4C will remain independent and be entitled to receive UK government funding and generate its own revenue. The on-demand service is called S4C Clic and some S4C programmes are also available through BBC iPlayer.

Channel 5 began broadcasting in 1997. It was rebranded Five in 2002 but reverted to its original name, Channel 5, after the station was acquired by Northern & Shell in July 2010. Digital stations 5USA and 5Star (formerly Five Life, then Fiver) were launched in October 2006. My5 (formerly Demand 5) is an online service, launched in June 2008, where viewers can watch and download content from the last 30 days on various platforms.

BSkyB was formed after the merger in 1990 of Sky Television and British Sky Broadcasting. Now known as Sky plc, the company operates across five countries: Italy, Germany, Austria, the UK and Ireland and serves 22 million customers. Sky is one of the UK's largest pay-TV broadcasters and Its television service includes Sky Sports, Sky Cinema, Sky Arts and Sky Atlantic. In 2007, Freeview overtook Sky as the UK's most popular digital service.

In February 2011, a new version of OFCOM's Broadcasting Code came into force, permitting product placement for the first time in UK-produced television programmes. A large 'P' logo designed by OFCOM and broadcasters is displayed at the beginning and end of each programme containing product placement. The first instance of product placement occurred on 28 February 2011.

THE TELEVISION LICENCE

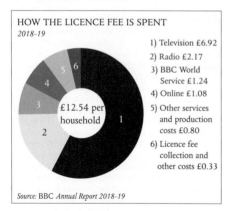

HOW THE LICENCE FEE IS SPENT
2018-19

£12.54 per household

1) Television £6.92
2) Radio £2.17
3) BBC World Service £1.24
4) Online £1.08
5) Other services and production costs £0.80
6) Licence fee collection and other costs £0.33

Source: BBC *Annual Report 2018-19*

In the UK and its dependencies, a television licence is required to receive any publicly broadcast television service, regardless of its source, including commercial, satellite and cable programming. A TV licence registered to a home address allows the viewer to watch television on laptops, tablets and mobile phones outside the place of residence. Since 1 September 2016 a TV licence is required for services such as BBC iPlayer, even if the programme is not being watched live.

The TV licence is classified as a tax, therefore non-payment is a criminal offence. A fine of up to £1,000 can be imposed on those successfully prosecuted. The TV licence is issued on behalf of the BBC as the licensing authority under the

Communications Act 2003. In 2018–19 25,927,000 TV licences were purchased, a 37,000 decrease on the number purchased in 2017–18, resulting in a 3.8 per cent decrease in revenue to £3,690m. As at 1 April 2019, an annual colour television licence costs £154.50 and a black and white licence £52.00. Concessions are available for the elderly and people with disabilities. In June 2019, the BBC announced its intention to end free TV licences for those aged 75 and over from June 2020; only households with someone aged 75 and over who is in receipt of pension credit will remain eligible to apply for a free licence. Further details can be found at **W** www.tvlicensing.co.uk/information

DIGITAL TELEVISION

The Broadcasting Act 1996 provided for the licensing of 20 or more digital terrestrial television (DTT) channels (on six frequency channels or 'multiplexes'). The first digital services went on air in autumn 1998.

In June 2002, following the collapse of ITV Digital, the digital terrestrial television licence was awarded to a consortium made up of the BBC, BSkyB and transmitter company Crown Castle by the Independent Television Commission. Freeview was launched on 30 October 2002 with 25 free-to-air channels: it now offers over 70 digital channels, up to 15 HD channels and 30 radio stations and requires the one-off purchase of a set-top box, but is subsequently free of charge with no subscription. In Autumn 2005 ITV and Channel 4 officially became shareholders, each taking a 20 per cent stake. As at 2018, around 20 million homes use Freeview on at least one set, amounting to around 30 per cent of UK households. There is an additional Freeview+ service which works in a similar fashion to Sky+, allowing viewers to record programmes. Over 97 per cent of UK homes have access to digital television.

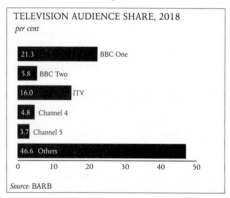

TELEVISION AUDIENCE SHARE, 2018
per cent

	per cent
BBC One	21.3
BBC Two	5.8
ITV	16.0
Channel 4	4.8
Channel 5	3.7
Others	46.6

Source: BARB

RECENT DEVELOPMENTS

The internet has now firmly established itself as an alternative to live and programmed TV, particularly for those aged 16 to 34. Since the launch of 4oD in 2006 and BBC iPlayer in 2007, there has been a noticeable shift in the way viewers can watch their favourite programmes. Technological advancements have also contributed to this phenomenon; more than half of the UK population uses a tablet, over 90 per cent of UK homes and businesses have access to superfast broadband and there are millions of public Wi-Fi hotspots across the UK. There is now a much bigger emphasis on catch-up, and subscription video on demand (SVOD) services then ever before, with BBC iPlayer recording 356 million requests in January 2019, an average of 11.5 million requests a day. SVOD services such as Netflix, Now TV and Amazon Prime Video have experienced a surge in popularity, with subscribers able to stream programmes through computers, mobiles, tablets and games consoles on up to four devices at a time. Both Netflix and Amazon Prime Video commission and distribute their own programmes, available exclusively to their subscribers, contributing to their popularity. UK subscriptions to Netflix surpassed those to Sky for the first time in December 2018. and 47 per cent of all UK households currently have an active subscription to at least one SVOD service. The BBC has provided exclusive content and programmes on iPlayer since 2014 and in 2016 moved BBC Three to an online-only service. ITV and Channel 4 both launched their own SVOD services (ITV Hub+, All 4+) in 2018 and 2019 respectively.

Despite the rise in the popularity of tablets, traditional TV sets are still the most popular way to watch television. HD TV provides more vibrant colours, greater detail and increased picture clarity, along with improved sound quality. An HD television screen uses 1,280 by 720 pixels and up to 1,920 by 1,080 pixels. HD Ready TVs operate at 720p while full HD TVs tend to operate on 1080p or 1080i; the differences between these three settings are down to the number of lines in the resolution and the type of scanning technology. 'HD Ready' simply means the TV will only operate a higher definition once plugged into a decoder, whereas full HD has this built in. In 2017, the average screen size in the UK was 43.7 inches wide and this is expected to increase to 48.9 inches by 2020, indicating a rapidly increasing trend towards bigger screens. Sales of Smart TVs, which can access apps, browse the internet and stream video, are increasing; around 48 per cent of UK households now own a Smart TV.

In April 2010, Samsung released the first consumer 3D TV; in the same month Sky launched the UK's first dedicated 3D channel. Several sporting events were broadcast in 3D, including the Wimbledon Championships. The BBC began a two-year 3D trial in 2011 but announced in July 2013 it would suspend 3D programming for an indefinite period of time due to a lack of public appetite for the technology and the sale of new 3D TV sets and services has now essentially ceased in the UK. In June 2018, the Facebook owned virtual reality (VR) headset company Oculus launched Oculus TV, intended to create a fully immersive experience.

In September 2012, OFCOM awarded its first local TV licences after announcing plans to broadcast 21 channels in total. In November 2013, Estuary TV, based in Grimsby, was the first to be launched. In March 2013, OFCOM stated plans for a further 30 areas to invite bids for local television services. However in April 2018, OFCOM announced its intention to halt the roll out of new local TV stations due several service providers facing financial difficulties and poor audience figures.

CONTACTS

THE BRITISH BROADCASTING CORPORATION (BBC)

BBC Broadcasting House, Portland Place, London W1A 1AA
W www.bbc.co.uk
BBC North, Media City UK, Bridge House, Salford Quays, Manchester M50 2BH
Chair, BBC Board, Sir David Clementi
Director-General, Lord Hall of Birkenhead, CBE

BBC Worldwide, 1 Television Centre, Wood Lane, London W12 7FA W www.bbcworldwide.com

INDEPENDENT TELEVISION (ITV)

London Television Centre, 2 Waterhouse Square, 138-142 Holborn, London EC1N 2AE W www.itv.com
Chair, Sir Peter Bazalgette
Chief Executive, Dame Carolyn McCall, DBE

INDEPENDENT TELEVISION (ITV) REGIONS

Anglia (eastern England), W www.itv.com/anglia
Border (Borders and the Isle of Man), W www.itv.com/border
Calendar (Yorkshire), W www.itv.com/calendar
Central (east, west and south Midlands), W www.itv.com/central
Channel (Channel Islands), W www.itv.com/channel
Granada (north-west England), W www.itv.com/granada
London, W www.itv.com/london
Meridian (south and south-east England), W www.itv.com/meridian
STV (Scotland), W www.stv.tv
Tyne Tees (north-east England), W www.itv.com/tynetees
Ulster (Northern Ireland), W www.itv.com/utv
Wales, W www.itv.com/wales
West, W www.itv.com/west

OTHER TELEVISION COMPANIES

Channel 4 Television, 124 Horseferry Road, London SW1P 2TX
T 020-7396 4444 W www.channel4.com
Channel 5 Broadcasting Ltd, 10 Lower Thames Street, London EC3R 6EN T 020-8612 7700 W www.channel5.com
Independent Television Network (ITN), 200 Gray's Inn Road, London WC1X 8XZ T 020-7833 3000 W www.itn.co.uk
Provides news programming and services for ITV, Channel 4 and Channel 5, as well as content for international news providers.
Sianel Pedwar Cymru (S4/C), Canolfan S4/C, Yr Egin, Carmarthen SA31 3EQ T 0870-600 4141 W www.s4c.cymru
Freeview, DTV Services Ltd, 27 Mortimer Street, London W1T 3JF W www.freeview.co.uk

DIRECT BROADCASTING BY SATELLITE TELEVISION

Sky plc, Grant Way, Isleworth, Middlesex TW7 5QD
T 033-3100 0333 W www.sky.com
Chief Executive, Stephen van Rooyen

RADIO

UK domestic radio services are broadcast across three wavebands: FM, medium wave and long wave (used by BBC Radio 4). In the UK the FM waveband extends in frequency from 87.5MHz to 108MHz and the medium waveband from 531kHz to 1602kHz. A number of radio stations are broadcast in both analogue and digital as well as a growing number in digital alone. As at June 2019, the BBC Radio network controlled around 51.4 per cent of the listening market (*see* BBC Radio section), and the independent sector (*see* Independent Radio section) 45.7 per cent. As at June 2019, a listener tunes into an average of 20.9 hours of radio per week.

ESTIMATED AUDIENCE SHARE

	Percentage		
	Apr–Jun 2017	Apr–Jun 2018	Apr–Jun 2019
BBC Radio 1	6.2	5.9	5.7
BBC Radio 2	16.8	17.9	17.4
BBC Radio 3	1.2	1.2	1.2
BBC Radio 4	12.3	11.7	11.9
BBC Radio Five Live	3.4	3.1	3.4
Five Live Sports Extra	0.3	0.3	0.1
BBC 6 Music	1.9	2.4	2.4
BBC Asian Network UK	0.3	0.3	0.2
1Xtra	0.5	0.4	0.4
BBC Local/Regional	7.3	6.7	6.6
BBC World Service	0.9	0.7	0.7
All BBC	52.3	45.0	51.4
All independent	45.0	45.7	45.7
All national independent	16.7	18.1	19.9
All local independent	28.4	27.6	25.9
Other	2.8	2.5	2.8
Source: RAJAR			

DIGITAL RADIO

The UK has the world's largest digital radio network, with 103 transmitters, two national Digital Audio Broadcasting (DAB) ensembles and a total of 48 local and regional DAB ensembles, which broadcast around 250 independent and 34 BBC radio stations. The BBC began test transmissions of the DAB Eureka 147 digital radio service in 1990 from the Crystal Palace transmitting station and the service was publicly launched in 1995. As well as DAB, digital televisions, car radios, games consoles, mobile devices and the internet are commonly employed as platforms to listen to radio in the UK. One of the major benefits of DAB is better sound quality than analogue radio, and the availability of a wider choice of stations, in addition to the lack of interference experienced by other broadcast media.

The UK government intends to migrate the majority of AM and FM analogue radio services to digital, based on certain conditions being met such as coverage, listening figures and agreements in relation to funding. In the second quarter of 2018, 50.2 per cent of all radio listening hours in the UK were through digital platforms. From this 50.2 per cent, DAB made up the majority of listenership with 72 per cent. In 2018, over 63 per cent of all UK households were believed to have access to DAB radio.

The BBC's national DAB ensemble has coverage across the UK of around 97 per cent and broadcasts on the frequency 225.648 MHz. Owned and operated by the BBC, the multiplex of broadcasts is transmitted across the UK from a number of sites. Local and regional ensembles, which cover 71.7 per cent of the UK, are transmitted through a number of DAB multiplex operators across the UK, including Digital One and Sound Digital – the two national operators – in addition to local multiplex operators.

There are two criteria that must be met for digital migration to occur:

- at least 50 per cent of radio listening is digital
- national DAB coverage is comparable to FM coverage, and local DAB reaches 90 per cent of the population and all major roads

LICENSING

The Broadcasting Act 1996 provided for the licensing of digital radio services (on multiplexes, where a number of stations share one frequency to transmit their services). To allocate the multiplexes, OFCOM advertises licences for which interested parties can bid. Once the licence has been awarded, the new owner seeks out services to broadcast on the multiplex. The BBC has a separate national multiplex for its services. There are local multiplexes around the country, each broadcasting an average of seven services, plus the local BBC station.

INNOVATIONS

The internet offers a number of advantages compared to other digital platforms such as DAB, including higher sound quality, a greater range of channel availability and flexibility in listening opportunity. Listeners can tune in to the majority of radio stations live on the internet or listen again online generally up to seven days after broadcast. DAB radio does not allow the same interactivity: the data is only able to travel one-way from broadcaster to listener whereas the internet allows a two-way flow of information.

Increases in Wi-Fi hotspots also means listening to radio, podcasts and catch-up programmes is easy to do through tablets and mobile phones; in 2018, over 50 per cent of all reported radio listening was via a digital service. The increase in music streaming services and radio-related apps has had a major effect on music discovery and sharing. In the UK in 2018 the number of streams per week averaged around 550 million. Since 6 July 2014 the UK Official Charts Company has included streaming services in its compilation, with 100 streams the equivalent to one purchase.

Since 2005 most radio stations offer all or part of their programmes as downloadable files, known as podcasts, to listen to on computers, mobiles or tablets. Podcasting technology allows listeners to subscribe in order to automatically receive the latest episodes of regularly transmitted programmes as soon as they become available.

The relationship between radio stations and their audiences is also undergoing change. The quantity and availability of music on the internet has led to the creation of shows dedicated entirely to music sent in by listeners. Another new development in internet-based radio has been personalised radio stations, such as SoundCloud and Spotify. SoundCloud allows users to upload, record, promote and share their music and sounds. Artists who upload their music are given a URL, allowing their music to be embedded anywhere, making it easier to share through social media platforms such as Twitter and Facebook. Users can also create their own playlists and link them to social media platforms. Spotify, available as an app on most smart phones and tablets as well as online, allows listeners access to the track, artist or genre of their choice, or to share and create playlists. It has seen steady growth in popularity since its launch in 2008, with 83 million paying subscribers and 180 million active users globally, as at June 2018. Spotify 'learns as you listen' and makes product recommendations based on user choices. Radioplayer (W www.radioplayer.co.uk), a not-for-profit company backed by the BBC and commercial radio, allows audiences to listen to live and catch-up radio from one place. Over 6 million people per month use the Radioplayer service. There are over 400 stations available and a 'recommended' service which offers station suggestions depending on location, what is trending and the type of music the user likes. Radioplayer launched as a mobile app in 2012 and a tablet app in 2013. Through the tablet app, users sample an average of 4.6 stations a week in comparison with just 2.1 for analogue users. In November 2018, the BBC launched BBC Sounds (W www.bbc.co.uk/sounds), a digital platform for all BBC radio and podcast output with the intention of streamlining their audio content on to a single platform, personalised to the individual listener's preferences.

BBC RADIO

BBC Radio broadcasts network services to the UK, Isle of Man and the Channel Islands, with around 34.7 million listeners each week. There is also a tier of national services in Wales, Scotland and Northern Ireland and around 40 local radio stations in England and the Channel Islands. In Wales and Scotland there are also dedicated language services in Welsh and Gaelic respectively. The frequency allocated for digital BBC broadcasts is 225.648MHz.

BBC Radio, Broadcasting House, Portland Place, London W1A 1AA
W www.bbc.co.uk/radio

BBC NETWORK RADIO STATIONS

Radio 1 (contemporary pop music and entertainment news) – 24 hours a day, Frequencies: 97–99 FM and digital

Radio 1Xtra (contemporary urban and hip-hop music, culture and entertainment) – 24 hours a day, digital only

Radio 2 (popular music, entertainment, comedy and the arts) – 24 hours a day, Frequencies: 88–91 FM and digital

Radio 3 (classical music, classic drama, documentaries and features) – 24 hours a day, Frequencies: 90–93 FM and digital

Radio 4 (news, documentaries, drama, entertainment and cricket on long wave in season) – 5.20am–1am daily, with BBC World Service overnight, Frequencies: 92–95 FM/ 103–105 FM and 198 LW and digital

Radio Five Live (news and sport) – 24 hours a day, *Frequencies:* 909/693 MW and digital*Five Live Sports Extra* (live sport) – schedule varies, digital only

6 Music (contemporary and classic pop and rock music) – 24 hours a day, digital only

Asian Network (news, music and sport) – 5am–1am, with Radio 1Xtra overnight, *Frequencies:* various MW frequencies in Midlands and digital

BBC NATIONAL RADIO STATIONS

Radio Cymru (Welsh-language), *Frequencies:* 92–105 FM and digital

Radio Foyle, Frequencies: 93.1 FM and 792 MW and digital

Radio nan Gaidheal (Gaelic service), *Frequencies:* 103–105 FM and digital

Radio Scotland, Frequencies: 92–95 FM and 810 MW and digital. Local programmes for Orkney, Shetland and Highlands and Islands

Radio Ulster, Frequencies: 1341 MW and 92–95 FM and digital. Local programmes on Radio Foyle

Radio Wales, Frequencies: 657/882 MW and 93–104 FM and digital

BBC WORLD SERVICE

The BBC World Service broadcasts to an estimated weekly audience of 1.5 million people in the UK and 280 million worldwide, in 40 languages including English, and is now available in around 150 capital cities. It no longer broadcasts in Dutch, French for Europe, German, Hebrew, Italian, Japanese or Malay because it was found that most speakers of these languages preferred to listen to the English broadcasts. In 2006 services in ten languages (Bulgarian, Croatian, Czech, Greek, Hungarian, Kazakh, Polish, Slovak, Slovene and Thai) were terminated to provide funding for a new Arabic television channel, which was launched in March 2008. In August 2008 the BBC's Romanian World Service broadcasts were discontinued after 68 years. In January 2011 the BBC announced five more language services would be terminated: Albanian, Caribbean English, Macedonian, Portuguese for Africa and Serbian. The BBC World Service website offers interactive news services in 28 languages including English, Arabic, Chinese, Hindi, Persian, Portuguese for Brazil, Russian, Spanish and Urdu with audiostreaming available.

LANGUAGES

Afaan Oromoo, Amharic, Arabic, Azeri, Bengali, Burmese, Cantonese, English, French, Gujarati, Hausa, Hindi, Igbo, Indonesian, Kinyarwanda, Kirundi, Korean, Kyrgyz, Marathi, Nepali, Nigerian, Nigerian Pidgin, Pashto, Persian, Portuguese, Punjabi, Russian, Sinhala, Somali, Spanish, Swahili, Tamil, Telugu, Tigrinya, Turkish, Ukrainian, Urdu, Uzbek, Yoruba and Vietnamese.

UK frequencies: digital; overnight on BBC Radio 4.

BBC Learning English teaches English worldwide through radio, television and a wide range of published and online courses.

BBC Media Action is a registered charity established in 1999 by BBC World Service, known as the BBC World Service Trust until December 2011. It promotes development through the innovative use of the media in the developing world.

BBC Monitoring tracks the global media for the latest news reports emerging around the world.

BBC WORLD SERVICE, Broadcasting House, Portland Place, London W1A 1AA **W** www.bbc.co.uk/worldservice

INDEPENDENT RADIO

Until 1973, the BBC had a legal monopoly on radio broadcasting in the UK. During this time, the corporation's only competition came from pirate stations located abroad, such as Radio Luxembourg. Christopher Chataway, Minister for Post and Telecommunications, changed this by creating the first licences for commercial radio stations. The Independent Broadcasting Authority (IBA) awarded the first of these licences to the London Broadcasting Company (LBC) to provide London's news and information service. LBC was followed by Capital Radio, to offer the city's entertainment service, Radio Clyde in Glasgow and BRMB in Birmingham.

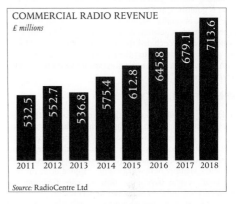

COMMERCIAL RADIO REVENUE
£ millions

2011	2012	2013	2014	2015	2016	2017	2018
532.5	552.7	536.8	575.4	612.8	645.8	679.1	713.6

Source: RadioCentre Ltd

The IBA was dissolved when the Broadcasting Act of 1990 de-regulated broadcasting, to be succeeded by the less rigid Radio Authority (RA). The RA began advertising new licences for the development of independent radio in January 1991. It awarded national and local radio, satellite and cable services licences, and long-term restricted service licences for stations serving non-commercial establishments such as hospitals and universities. The first national commercial digital multiplex licence was awarded in October 1998 and a number of local digital multiplex licences followed. At the end of 2003 the RA was replaced by OFCOM, which now carries out the licensing administration.

RadioCentre was formed in July 2006 as a result of the merger between the Radio Advertising Bureau (RAB) and the Commercial Radio Companies Association (CRCA), the former non-profit trade body for commercial radio companies in the UK, to operate essentially as a union for commercial radio stations.

RadioCentre, 6th Floor, 55 New Oxford Street, London WC1A 1BS
T 020-7010 0600 **W** www.radiocentre.org
Chief Executive, Siobhan Kenny

THE PRESS

The newspaper and periodical press in the UK is large and diverse, catering for a wide variety of views and interests. There is no state control or censorship of the press; however, it is subject to the laws on publication.

The press is not state-subsidised and receives few tax concessions. The income of most newspapers and periodicals is derived largely from sales and from advertising. The Advertising Association reported in July 2018 that national newspaper brands experienced their first increase in advertising spend in seven years in 2017. The UK advertising market in general grew to an estimated £23.5bn in 2018, an increase of 6 per cent.

LEVESON REPORT

The Leveson Inquiry, established under the Inquiries Act 2005, was announced by the prime minister on 13 July 2011 to investigate the role of press and police in the *News of the World* phone-hacking scandal. Lord Justice Leveson was appointed as chair of the inquiry. The hearings began on 14 November 2011 and ended on 24 July 2012 following the testimonies of 650 witnesses.

The Leveson Report was published in late November 2012 and featured several broad and complex recommendations as to how the press should be regulated. The report generally recommended that the press should continue to be self-regulated, with the government allowed no direct power over what is published, and that a new press standards body, with a new code of conduct, should be established by legislation in order to ensure regulation is independent and effective. Lord Justice Leveson concluded that this arrangement should give the public confidence that their complaints would be dealt with seriously and ensure the press would be protected from interference.

SELF-REGULATION

Following the publication of the Leveson Report the Press Complaints Commission (PCC), which had been established in January 1991 as a non-statutory body to operate the press's self-regulation, was closed and replaced by the Independent Press Standards Organisation (IPSO) on 8 September 2014. While the majority of newspapers have signed up to the new regulator, several have not, including *The Guardian*, the *Financial Times* and the *London Evening Standard*.

In 2013 a royal charter on press regulation was granted by the Privy Council to create a watchdog to oversee a new regulator. On 3 November 2014, a fully independent body, the Press Recognition Panel (PRP) was established to consider whether press regulators meet the criteria recommended in the Leveson Report and, if so, to afford these regulators official recognition.

IPSO has not sought recognition from the PRP, but another regulator, IMPRESS, was awarded recognition by the PRP in October 2016.

INDEPENDENT PRESS STANDARDS ORGANISATION, Gate House, 1 Farringdon Street, London EC4M 7LH
T 0300-123 2220 **E** inquiries@ipso.co.uk **W** www.ipso.co.uk
Chair, Rt. Hon. Sir Alan Moses

PRESS RECOGNITION PANEL, Mappin House, 4 Winsley Street, London W1W 8HF
E contact@pressrecognitionpanel.org.uk
W www.pressrecognitionpanel.org.uk
Chair, Dr David Wolfe, QC

NEWSPAPERS

Newspapers are mostly financially independent of any political party, though most adopt a political stance in their editorial comments, usually reflecting proprietorial influence. Ownership of the national and regional daily newspapers is concentrated in the hands of large corporations whose interests cover publishing and communications, although *The Guardian* and *The Observer* are owned by the Scott Trust, formed in 1936 to protect the financial and editorial independence of *The Guardian* in perpetuity. The rules on cross-media ownership, as amended by the Broadcasting Act 1996, which limited the extent to which newspaper organisations may become involved in broadcasting, have been relaxed by the Communications Act 2003: newspapers with over a 20 per cent share of national circulation may own national and/or local radio licences.

In October 2010, *The Independent* launched a concise newspaper, *i*, the first new daily newspaper since 1986 but the final editions of *The Independent* and *The Independent on Sunday* were published in March 2016 as the paper moved to digital only. In July 2011, *News of the World* was closed by its parent company, News International, following accusations of phone-hacking. In February 2012 News International printed the first edition of *The Sun on Sunday*, a Sunday format of the daily tabloid paper *The Sun*. In November 2014, The Herald and Times Group launched the Scottish daily *The National,* the first newspaper to actively support Scottish independence. In September 2018, *The Sunday National* was launched to replace *The Sunday Herald* which ceased publication on 2 September 2018. In February 2016, Trinity Mirror launched a compact daily newspaper, *The New Day* – the first new standalone paper since *The Independent* in 1986 – but it ceased publication in May 2016 after a sharp drop in circulation. There are 11 daily and Sunday national papers and several hundred local papers that are published daily, weekly or twice-weekly. Scotland, Wales and Northern Ireland all have at least one daily and one Sunday national paper.

National Daily Newspapers	June 2018	June 2019	% +/-
The Sun	1,451,584	1,277,947	−12.72
Daily Mail	1,264,810	1,175,653	−7.31
Daily Mirror	562,523	488,829	−14.02
Daily Star	364,448	310,246	−16.07
The Daily Telegraph	370,613	327,345	−12.40
The Times	428,034	399,672	−6.85
Daily Express	338,527	307,662	−9.57
i	248,234	288,801	−8.14
Financial Times	183,319	175,512	−4.35
The Guardian	138,082	132,821	−3.88
Daily Record	145,724	111,543	−26.57
National Sunday Newspapers			
The Sun on Sunday	1,224,119	1,066,147	−13.80
The Mail on Sunday	1,056,916	986,385	−6.90
The Sunday Times	721,808	686,819	−4.97
Sunday Mirror	475,976	403,350	−16.52
The Sunday Telegraph	288,484	258,394	−11.0
Sunday Express	295,294	268,096	−10.12
Daily Star Sunday	220,684	184,914	−17.63
Sunday People	183,784	151,523	−19.24
The Observer	166,317	159,568	−4.14
Sunday Mail	131,716	113,712	−14.67
Sunday Post	115,973	96,422	−18.41

Source: Audit Bureau of Circulations Ltd

Newspapers are usually published in either broadsheet or smaller, tabloid format. The 'quality' daily papers – ie those providing detailed coverage of a wide range of public matters – have traditionally been broadsheets, the more populist newspapers tabloid. In 2004 this correlation between format and content was redefined when two traditionally broadsheet newspapers, *The Times* and *The Independent*, switched to tabloid-sized editions, while *The Guardian* launched a 'Berliner' format in September 2005. In October 2005 *The Independent on Sunday* became the first Sunday broadsheet to be published in the tabloid (or 'compact') size. *The Observer,* like its daily counterpart *The Guardian,* began publishing in the Berliner format in January 2006 and began publishing in tabloid format in January 2018.

NEWSPAPERS ONLINE

The demand to read news instantly and while on the move has increased the popularity of newspaper websites. Most newspapers now operate their own websites in line with their print editions, often including the same material as seen in daily printed editions but can also include video and audio features. Many articles and columns additionally have the option of reader contributions and debate. Certain newspapers charge a subscription fee to access their websites but the majority are free to browse.

NATIONAL PRESS WEBSITE DAILY AVERAGE BROWSERS

National Press Website	June 2017	June 2018	% +/−
MailOnline	15,406,452	12,622,077	−18.07
metro.co.uk	2,676,403	1,689,148	−36.89
Reach PLC*	10,121,154	8,976,593	−11.31
thesun.co.uk	5,281,981	5,410,691	2.44

* Formerly known as Trinity Mirror Group PLC
Source: Audit Bureau of Circulations Ltd

NATIONAL DAILY NEWSPAPERS

DAILY EXPRESS
Northern & Shell Building, 10 Lower Thames Street, London
EC3R 6EN **T** 020-8612 7000 **W** www.express.co.uk
Editor, Gary Jones

DAILY MAIL
Northcliffe House, 2 Derry Street, London W8 5TT **T** 020-7938 6000
W www.dailymail.co.uk
Editor, Geordie Greig

DAILY MIRROR
1 Canada Square, Canary Wharf, London E14 5AP
T 020-7293 3000 **W** www.mirror.co.uk
Editor, Allison Phillips

DAILY RECORD
1 Central Quay, Glasgow G3 8DA **T** 0141-309 3000
W www.dailyrecord.co.uk
Editor, David Dick

DAILY STAR
Northern & Shell Building, 10 Lower Thames Street, London
EC3R 6EN **T** 020-8612 7000 **W** www.dailystar.co.uk
Editor, Jon Clark

THE DAILY TELEGRAPH
111 Buckingham Palace Road, London SW1W 0DT
T 020-7931 2000 **W** www.telegraph.co.uk
Editor, Chris Evans

FINANCIAL TIMES
Bracken House, 1 Friday Street, London EC4M 9BT
T 020-7873 3000 **W** www.ft.com
Editor, Lionel Barber

THE GUARDIAN
Kings Place, 90 York Way, London N1 9GU **T** 020-3353 2000
W www.theguardian.com
Editor-in-Chief, Katharine Viner

THE HERALD
200 Renfield Street, Glasgow G2 3QB **T** 0141-302 7000
W www.heraldscotland.com
Editor, Graeme Smith

i
2 Derry Street, London W8 5HF **T** 020-7005 2000
W www.inews.co.uk
Editor, Oliver Duff

MORNING STAR
William Rust House, 52 Beachy Road, London E3 2NS
T 020 8510-0815 **W** www.morningstaronline.co.uk
Editor, Ben Chacko

THE NATIONAL
200 Renfield Street, Glasgow, G2 3QB **T** 0141-302 7000
W www.thenational.scot
Editor, Callum Baird

THE SCOTSMAN
Orchard Brae House, 30 Queensferry Road, Edinburgh EH4 2HS
T 0131-311 7311 **W** www.scotsman.com
Editorial Director, Frank O'Donnell

THE SUN
1 London Bridge Street, London SE1 9GF **T** 020-7782 4000
W www.thesun.co.uk
Editor, Tony Gallagher

THE TIMES
1 London Bridge Street, London SE1 9GF **T** 0800-018 5177
W www.thetimes.co.uk
Editor, John Witherow

WEEKLY NEWSPAPERS

DAILY STAR SUNDAY
Northern & Shell Building, 10 Lower Thames Street, London
EC3R 6EN **T** 020-8612 7000 **W** www.dailystar.co.uk/sunday
Editor, Denis Mann

MAIL ON SUNDAY
Northcliffe House, 2 Derry Street, London W8 HFT **T** 020-7938 6000
W www.mailonsunday.co.uk
Editor, Ted Verity

THE OBSERVER
Kings Place, 90 York Way, London N1 9GU **T** 020-3353 2000
W www.theguardian.com/observer
Editor, Paul Webster

THE SUNDAY PEOPLE
1 Canada Square, Canary Wharf, London E14 5AP
T 020-7293 3000 **W** www.people.co.uk
Editor, Peter Willis

SCOTLAND ON SUNDAY
Orchard Brae House, 30 Queensferry Road, Edinburgh EH4 2HS
T 0131-311 7311 **W** www.scotlandonsunday.com
Editorial Director, Frank O'Donnell

THE SUN ON SUNDAY
1 London Bridge Street, London SE1 9GF **T** 020-7782 4000
W www.thesun.co.uk
Editor, Victoria Newton

SUNDAY EXPRESS
Northern & Shell Building, 10 Lower Thames Street, London
EC4R 6EN **T** 020-8612 7000 **W** www.sundayexpress.co.uk
Editor, Gary Jones

SUNDAY MAIL
1 Central Quay, Glasgow G3 8DA **T** 0141-309 3000
W www.sundaymail.com
Editor, Brendan McGinty

SUNDAY MIRROR
1 Canada Square, Canary Wharf, London E14 5AP
T 020-7293 3000 **W** www.sundaymirror.co.uk
Editor, Lloyd Embley

SUNDAY NATIONAL
200 Renfield Street, Glasgow, G2 3QB **T** 0141 302-7000
W www.thenational.scot
Editor, Richard Walker

SUNDAY POST
Skypark, 8 Elliot Place, Glasgow G3 8EP **T** 01382-223131
W www.sundaypost.com
Editor, Richard Prest

SUNDAY TELEGRAPH
111 Buckingham Palace Road, London SW1W 0DT
T 020-7931 2000 **W** www.telegraph.co.uk
Editor, Allister Heath

THE SUNDAY TIMES
1 London Bridge Street, London SE1 9GF **T** 020-7782 5000
W www.thesundaytimes.co.uk
Editor, Martin Ivens

REGIONAL NEWSPAPERS
EAST ANGLIA

CAMBRIDGE NEWS
Cambridge Research Park, Waterbeach CB25 9PD **T** 01223-632200
W www.cambridge-news.co.uk
Editor, David Bartlett

EAST ANGLIAN DAILY TIMES
Portman House, 120 Princes Street, Ipswich IP1 1RS
T 01473-230023 **W** www.eadt.co.uk
Editor, Brad Jones

EASTERN DAILY PRESS
Prospect House, Rouen Road, Norwich NR1 1RE **T** 01603-628311
W www.edp24.co.uk
Editor, David Powles

IPSWICH STAR
Portman House, 120 Princes Street, Ipswich IP1 1RS
T 01473-230023 **W** www.ipswichstar.co.uk
Editor, Brad Jones

NORWICH EVENING NEWS
Prospect House, Rouen Road, Norwich NR1 1RE **T** 01603-628311
W www.eveningnews24.co.uk
Editor, David Powles

EAST MIDLANDS

DERBY TELEGRAPH
2 Siddals Road, Derby DE1 2PB **T** 01332-411888
W www.derbytelegraph.co.uk
Editor, Julie Bayley

THE LEICESTER MERCURY
16 New Walk, Leicester LE1 6TF **T** 0116-251 2512
W www.leicestermercury.co.uk
Editor, George Oliver

LINCOLNSHIRE ECHO
Witham Wharf, Brayford Wharf East, Lincoln LN5 7AY
T 01522-804300 **W** www.lincolnshirelive.co.uk
Editor, Adam Moss

NORTHAMPTON CHRONICLE & ECHO
400 Pavilion Drive, Northants NN4 7PA **T** 01604-467032
W www.northamptonchron.co.uk
Editor, David Summers

NOTTINGHAM POST
City Gate, Tollhouse Hill, Notts NG1 5FS **T** 0115-948 2000
W www.nottinghampost.com
Editor, Mike Sassi

LONDON

EVENING STANDARD
Northcliffe House, 2 Derry Street, London W8 5TT **T** 020-3367 7000
W www.standard.co.uk
Editor, George Osborne

METRO
Northcliffe House, 2 Derry Street, London W8 5TT **T** 020-3615 3480
W www.metro.co.uk
Editor, Ted Young

NORTH EAST

EVENING CHRONICLE
2nd Floor, Eldon Court, Percy Street, Newcastle upon Tyne NE1 7JB
T 0191-201 6446 **W** www.chroniclelive.co.uk
Editor-in-Chief, Neil Hodgkinson

HARTLEPOOL MAIL
North East Business & Innovation Centre, Westfield Enterprise Park
East, Sunderland SR5 2TA **T** 0191-516 6127
W www.hartlepoolmail.co.uk
Editor, Joy Yates

THE JOURNAL
2nd Floor, Eldon Court, Percy Street, Newcastle upon Tyne NE1 7JB
T 0191-201 6446 **W** www.thejournal.co.uk
Editor, Neil Hodgkinson

THE NORTHERN ECHO
PO Box 14, Priestgate, Darlington, Co. Durham DL1 1NF
T 01325-381313 **W** www.thenorthernecho.co.uk
Editor, Hannah Chapman

THE SHIELDS GAZETTE
North East Business & Innovation Centre, Westfield Enterprise Park
East, Sunderland SR5 2TA **T** 0191-516 6127
W www.shieldsgazette.com
Editor, Joy Yates

THE SUNDAY SUN
2nd Floor, Eldon Court, Percy Street, Newcastle upon Tyne NE1 7JB
T 0191-201 6446 **W** www.sundaysun.co.uk
Editor, Neil Hodgkinson

SUNDERLAND ECHO
North East Business & Innovation Centre, Westfield Enterprise Park
East, Sunderland SR5 2TA **T** 0191-501 5800
W www.sunderlandecho.com
Editor, Joy Yates

TEESIDE GAZETTE
1st Floor, Hudson Quay, The Halyard, Middlehaven, Middlesbrough
TS3 6RT **T** 01642-234262 **W** www.gazettelive.co.uk
Editor, Neil Hodgkinson

NORTH WEST

THE BLACKPOOL GAZETTE
Avroe House, Avroe Crescent, Blackpool FY4 2DP **T** 01253-400888
W www.blackpoolgazette.co.uk
Editor, Simon Drury

THE BOLTON NEWS
The Wellsprings, Civic Centre, Bolton BL1 1AR **T** 01204-522345
W www.theboltonnews.co.uk
Editor, Karl Holbrook

CARLISLE NEWS AND STAR
Newspaper House, Dalston Road, Carlisle CA2 5UA
T 01228-612600 **W** www.newsandstar.co.uk
Editor, Chris Story

LANCASHIRE EVENING POST
Stuart House, 89 Caxton Road, Fulwood, Preston PR2 9ZB
T 01772-254841 **W** www.lep.co.uk
Editor, Gillian Parkinson

LANCASHIRE TELEGRAPH
50–54 Church Street, Blackburn, Lancs. BB1 5AL **T** 01254 678678
W www.lancashiretelegraph.co.uk
Editor, Steven Thompson

LIVERPOOL ECHO
5 St Paul's Square, Liverpool L3 9SL **T** 0151-472 2507
W www.liverpoolecho.co.uk
Editor, Alastair Machray

MANCHESTER EVENING NEWS
Mitchell Henry House, Hollinwood Avenue, Chadderton OL9 8EF
T 0161-832 7200 **W** www.manchestereveningnews.co.uk
Editor, Darren Thwaites

NORTH-WEST EVENING MAIL
Abbey Road, Barrow-in-Furness, Cumbria LA14 5QS
T 01229-840100 **W** www.nwemail.co.uk
Editor, Vanessa Sims

SOUTH EAST

THE ARGUS
Dolphin House, 2–5 Manchester Street, Brighton BN2 1TF
T 01273-021400 **W** www.theargus.co.uk
Editor, vacant

ECHO
Newspaper House, Chester Hall Lane, Basildon, Essex SS14 3BL
T 01268-522792 **W** www.echo-news.co.uk
Editor, Chris Hatton

MEDWAY MESSENGER
Medway House, Ginsbury Close, Sir Thomas Longley Road,
Rochester, Kent ME2 4DU **T** 01634-227800
W www.kentonline.co.uk/medway
Editor, Matt Ramsden

THE NEWS, PORTSMOUTH
1000 Lakeside, North Harbour, Portsmouth PO6 3EN
T 023-9266 4488 **W** www.portsmouth.co.uk
Editor, Mark Waldron

OXFORD MAIL
Newsquest Oxfordshire & Wiltshire, Osney Mead, Oxford OX2 0EJ
T 01865-425262 **W** www.oxfordmail.co.uk
Managing Editor, Samantha Harmon

READING CHRONICLE
2–10 Bridge Street, Reading, Berks. RG1 2LU **T** 0118-955 3333
W www.readingchronicle.co.uk
Group Editor, Andrew Colley

THE SOUTHERN DAILY ECHO
Newspaper House, Test Lane, Redbridge, Southampton SO16 9JX
T 023-8042 4777 **W** www.dailyecho.co.uk
Editor, Gordon Sutter

SOUTH WEST

BRISTOL POST
Temple Way, Bristol BS2 0BY **T** 0117-934 3331
W www.bristolpost.co.uk
Editor, Mike Norton

BOURNEMOUTH ECHO
Richmond Hill, Bournemouth BH2 6HH **T** 01202-554601
W www.bournemouthecho.co.uk
Editor, Andy Martin

CORNISH TIMES
The Tindle Suite, Webbs House, Liskeard PL14 6AH
T 01579-342174 **W** www.cornish-times.co.uk
Editor, Andrew Townsend

DORSET ECHO
Fleet House, Hampshire Road, Weymouth, Dorset DT4 9XD
T 01305-830930 **W** www.dorsetecho.co.uk
Editor, Diarmuid MacDonagh

EXETER EXPRESS & ECHO
Queens House, Little Queen Street, Exeter EX4 3LJ **T** 01392-346763
W www.exeterexpressandecho.co.uk
Editor, Rich Booth

GLOUCESTER CITIZEN
Gloucester Quays, St Ann Way, Gloucester GL1 5SH
T 01452-689320 **W** www.gloucestershirelive.co.uk
Editor, Rachael Sugden

GLOUCESTERSHIRE ECHO
Gloucester Quays, St Ann Way, Gloucester GL1
5SH**T** 01452 689320 **W** www.gloucestershirelive.co.uk
Editor, Rachael Sugden

THE HERALD
3rd Floor, Millbay Road, Plymouth PL1 3LF **T** 01752-293000
W www.plymouthherald.co.uk
Editor, Edd Moore

SUNDAY INDEPENDENT
Indy House, Lighterage Hill, Truro TR1 2XR **T** 01579-556970
W www.indyonline.co.uk
Editor, John Collings

SWINDON ADVERTISER
Richmond House, Edison Park, Swindon SN3 3RB **T** 01793-528144
W www.swindonadvertiser.co.uk
Editor, Pete Gavan

TORQUAY HERALD EXPRESS
Queens House, Little Queen Street, Exeter EX4 3LJ **T** 01392-346763
W www.devonlive.com
Editor, Rich Booth

WESTERN DAILY PRESS
Temple Way, Bristol BS99 7HD **T** 0117-934 3000
W www.somersetlive.co.uk
Editor, vacant

THE WESTERN MORNING NEWS
3rd Floor, Millbay Road, Plymouth PL1 3LF **T** 01752-293000
W www.thisiswesternmorningnews.co.uk
Editor, Bill Martin

WEST MIDLANDS

BIRMINGHAM MAIL
Embassy House, 60 Church Street, Birmingham B3 2DJ
T 0121-234 5000 **W** www.birminghammail.co.uk
Editor, Anna Jeys

COVENTRY TELEGRAPH
Corporation Street, Coventry CV1 1FP **T** 024-7663 3633
W www.coventrytelegraph.net
Editor, Keith Perry

EXPRESS & STAR
51–53 Queen Street, Wolverhampton WV1 1ES **T** 01902-313131
W www.expressandstar.com
Editor, Martin Wright

THE SENTINEL
Sentinel House, Bethesda Street, Stoke-on-Trent ST1 3GN
T 01782-864100 **W** www.stokesentinel.co.uk
Editor, Martin Tideswell

SHROPSHIRE STAR
Waterloo Road, Ketley, Telford TF1 5HU **T** 01952-242424
W www.shropshirestar.com
Editor, Martin Wright

WORCESTER NEWS
Berrows House, Hylton Road, Worcester WR2 5JX **T** 01905-748200
W www.worcesternews.co.uk
Editor, Michael Purton

YORKSHIRE AND HUMBERSIDE

GRIMSBY TELEGRAPH
Heritage House, Fisherman's Wharf, Grimsby DN31 1SY
T 01472-808000 **W** www.grimsbytelegraph.co.uk
Editor, Jamie Macaskill

HALIFAX COURIER
The Fire Station, Dean Clough Mills, Halifax HX3 5AX
T 01422-260252 **W** www.halifaxcourier.co.uk
Editor, John Kenealy

THE HUDDERSFIELD DAILY EXAMINER
Pennine Business Park, Longbow Close, Bradley Road, Huddersfield
HD2 1GQ **T** 01484-430000 **W** www.examiner.co.uk
Editor, Wayne Ankers

HULL DAILY MAIL
Blundell's Corner, Beverley Road, Hull HU3 1XS **T** 01482-327111
W www.hulldailymail.co.uk
Editor, Neil Hodgkinson

THE PRESS
PO Box 29, 76–86 Walmgate, York YO1 9YN **T** 01904-567131
W www.yorkpress.co.uk
Editor, Nigel Burton

SCARBOROUGH NEWS
17–23 Aberdeen Walk, Scarborough, N. Yorks YO11 1BB
T 01723-60100 **W** www.thescarboroughnews.co.uk
Editor, Jean MacQuarrie

SHEFFIELD STAR
The Balance, 2 Pinfold Street, Sheffield S1 2GU **T** 0114-276 7676
W www.thestar.co.uk
Editor, Nancy Fielder

TELEGRAPH & ARGUS
Hall Ings, Bradford BD1 1JR **T** 01274-729511
W www.thetelegraphandargus.co.uk
Editor, Nigel Burton

YORKSHIRE EVENING POST
26 Whitehall Road, Leeds LS12 1BE **T** 0113-238 8917
W www.yorkshireeveningpost.co.uk
Editor, Hannah Thaxter

YORKSHIRE POST
26 Whitehall Road, Leeds LS12 1BE **T** 0113-238 8427
W www.yorkshirepost.co.uk
Editor, James Mitchinson

SCOTLAND

THE COURIER
2 Albert Square, Dundee DD1 1DD **T** 01382-575291
W www.thecourier.co.uk
Editor, Richard Neville

DUNDEE EVENING TELEGRAPH
2 Albert Square, Dundee DD1 1DD **T** 01382-575950
W www.eveningtelegraph.co.uk
Editor, Dave Lord

EDINBURGH EVENING NEWS
Orchard Brae House, 30 Queensferry Road, Edinburgh EH4 2HS
T 0131-311 7311 **W** www.edinburghnews.scotsman.com
Editor, Euan McGrory

EVENING EXPRESS
1 Marischal Square, Broad Street, Aberdeen AB10 1BL
T 01224-691212 **W** www.eveningexpress.co.uk
Editor, Craig Walker

GLASGOW EVENING TIMES
200 Renfield Street, Glasgow G2 3QB **T** 0141-302 6600
W www.eveningtimes.co.uk
Editor, Donald Martin

INVERNESS COURIER
New Century House, Stadium Road, Inverness IV1 1FF
T 01463-246575 **W** www.inverness-courier.co.uk
Editor, Andrew Dixon

PAISLEY DAILY EXPRESS
1 Central Quay, Glasgow G3 8DA **T** 0141-887 7911
W www.paisleydailyexpress.co.uk
Editor, Cheryl McEvoy

THE PRESS AND JOURNAL
1 Marischal Square, Broad Street, Aberdeen AB10 1BL
T 01224-690222 **W** www.pressandjournal.co.uk
Editor, Alan McCabe

WALES

THE LEADER
Mold Business Park, Mold, Flintshire CH7 1XY **T** 01352-707707
W www.leaderlive.co.uk
Group Editor, Susan Perry

SOUTH WALES ARGUS
Cardiff Road, Maesglas, Newport NP20 3QN **T** 01633-810000
W www.southwalesargus.co.uk
Editor, Nicole Garnon

SOUTH WALES ECHO
6 Park Street, Cardiff CF10 1XR **T** 029-2024 3602
W www.walesonline.co.uk
Editor, Tryst Williams

SOUTH WALES EVENING POST
Urban Village, High Street, Swansea SA1 1NW **T** 01792-545515
W www.southwales-eveningpost.co.uk
Editor, Jonathan Roberts

WESTERN MAIL
6 Park Street, Cardiff CF10 1XR **T** 029-2024 3635
W www.walesonline.co.uk
Editor, Catrin Pascoe

NORTHERN IRELAND

BELFAST TELEGRAPH
124–144 Royal Avenue, Belfast BT1 1DN **T** 028-9026 4000
W www.belfasttelegraph.co.uk
Editor, Gail Walker

IRISH NEWS
113–117 Donegall Street, Belfast BT1 2GE **T** 028-9032 2226
W www.irishnews.com
Editor, Noel Doran

NEWS LETTER
Arthur House, 41 Arthur Street, Belfast BT1 4GB **T** 028-3839 5577
W www.newsletter.co.uk
Editor, Alistair Bushe

SUNDAY LIFE
124–144 Royal Avenue, Belfast BT1 1EB **T** 028-9026 4000
W www.belfasttelegraph.co.uk/sunday-life
Editor, Martin Breen

CHANNEL ISLANDS

GUERNSEY PRESS
PO Box 57, Braye Road, Vale, Guernsey GY1 3BW **T** 01481-240240
W www.guernseypress.com
Editor, Shaun Green

JERSEY EVENING POST
Guiton House, Five Oaks, St Saviour, Jersey JE4 8XQ
T 01534-611611 **W** www.jerseyeveningpost.com
Editor, Andy Sibcy

PERIODICALS

ART

AESTHETICA
PO Box 371, York YO23 1WL **T** 01904-629137
W www.aestheticamagazine.com
Editor, Cherie Federico

APOLLO
22 Old Queen Street, London SW1H 9HP **T** 020-7961 0150
W www.apollo-magazine.com
Editor, Thomas Marks

ART MONTHLY
12 Carlton House Terrace, London SW1Y 5AH **T** 020-7240 0389
W www.artmonthly.co.uk
Editor, Patricia Bickers

ARTREVIEW
1 Honduras Street, London EC1Y 0TH **T** 020-7490 8138
W www.artreview.com
Editor, Mark Rappolt

TATE ETC.
Tate, Millbank, London SW1P 4RG **T** 020-7887 8724
W www.tate.org.uk/tate-ect
Editor, Simon Grant

BUSINESS AND FINANCE

THE ECONOMIST
20 Cabot Square, London E14 4QW **T** 020-7576 8000
W www.economist.com
Editor, Zanny Minton Beddoes

MANAGEMENT TODAY
Bridge House, 69 London Road, Twickenham TW1 3SP
T 020-8267 5000 **W** www.managementtoday.co.uk
Editor, Adam Gale

MARKETING WEEK
79 Wells Street, London W1T 3QN **T** 020-7292 3711
W www.marketingweek.co.uk
Editor, Russell Parsons

MONEYWEEK
31–32 Alfred Place, London WC1E 7DP**T** 0330-333 9688
W www.moneyweek.com
Editor-in-Chief, Merryn Somerset Webb

PUBLIC FINANCE
78 Chamber Street, London E1 8BL **T** 020-7880 6200
W www.publicfinance.co.uk
Managing Editor, John Watkins

CELEBRITY

CLOSER
Endeavour House, 189 Shaftesbury Avenue, London WC2H 8JG
T 020-7295 5000 **W** www.closeronline.co.uk
Editor, Lisa Burrow

HEAT
Endeavour House, 189 Shaftesbury Avenue, London WC2H 8JG
T 020-7437 9011 **W** www.heatworld.com
Editor, Suzy Cox

HELLO!
Wellington House, 69–71 Upper Ground, London SE1 9PQ
T 020-7667 8901 **W** www.hellomagazine.com
Editor, Rosie Nixon

OK!
10 Lower Thames Street, London EC3R 6EN **T** 020-8612 7000
W www.ok.co.uk
Editor, Kirsty Tyler

CHILDREN'S AND FAMILY

THE BEANO
185 Fleet Street, London EC4A 2HS **W** www.beano.com
Editor, John Anderson

MOTHER & BABY
Bauer Media Group, Media House, Lynchwood, Peterborough
Business Park, Peterborough PE2 6EA **T** 01733- 468000
W www.motherandbaby.co.uk
Editor, Sally Saunders

YOUR CAT
Warners Group Publications, The Maltings, West Street, Bourne,
Lincs PE10 9PH**T** 0177-839 5070 **W** www.yourcat.co.uk
Editor, Emily Wardle

YOUR DOG
Warners Group Publications, The Maltings, West Street, Bourne,
Lincs PE10 9PH **T** 0177-839 5070 **W** www.yourdog.co.uk
Editor, Sarah Wright

CLASSICAL MUSIC AND OPERA

BBC MUSIC
Immediate Media Company Bristol Ltd, Tower House, Colston Avenue, Bristol BS1 4ST **T** 0117-927 9009
W www.classical-music.com
Editor, Oliver Condy

CLASSICAL MUSIC
Rhinegold House, 20 Rugby Street, London WC1N 3QZ
T 020-7333 1729 **W** www.classicalmusicmagazine.org
Editor, Lucy Thraves

GRAMOPHONE
c/o Mark Allen Group, St Jude's Church, Dulwich Road, London SE24 0PB **T** 020-7738 5454 **W** www.gramophone.co.uk
Editor, Martin Cullingford

OPERA
36 Black Lion Lane, London W6 9BE **T** 020-8563 8893
W www.opera.co.uk
Editor, John Allison

COMPUTERS AND TECHNOLOGY

PC PRO
31–32 Alfred Place, London WC1E 7DP **T** 020-3890 3890
W www.alphr.com
Editorial Director, Victoria Woollaston

STUFF
Blackfriars Foundry, 154–156 Blackfriars Road, London SE1 8EN
T 020-8267 5036 **W** www.stuff.tv
Editor, James Day

T3
T3 magazine, 5 Pinesway Industrial Estate, Bath BA2 3QS
W www.t3.com
Editor, Matt Bolton

WEB USER
Dennis Publishing, 30 Cleveland Street, London W1T 4JD
T 020-7907 6000 **W** www.webuser.co.uk
Group Editor, Daniel Booth

WIRED
Condé Nast, Vogue House, Hanover Square, London W1S 1JU
T 0844-848 5202 **W** www.wired.co.uk
Editor-in-Chief, Nicholas Thompson

CRAFT

CARDMAKING & PAPERCRAFT
Immediate Media, Vineyard House, 44 Brook Green, London W6 7BT **T** 0117-933 8081 **W** www.cardmakingandpapercraft.com
Editor, Hayley Hawes

SIMPLY KNITTING
Immediate Media, Vineyard House, 44 Brook Green, London W6 7BT **T** 0117-3008 253 **W** www.immediate.co.uk/brands/simply-knitting
Commissioning Editor, Kirstie McLeod

THE WORLD OF CROSS STITCHING
Immediate Media, Vineyard House, 44 Brook Green, London W6 7BT **T** 0117-314 8351 **W** www.cross-stitching.com
Editor, Hannah Kelly

ENTERTAINMENT

EMPIRE
Endeavour House, 189 Shaftesbury Avenue, London WC2H 8JG
T 020-7437 9011 **W** www.empireonline.com
Editor-in-Chief, Terri White

RADIO TIMES
Vineyard House, 44 Brook Green, London W6 7BT
T 020-7150 5800 **W** www.radiotimes.com
Editorial Director, Mark Frith

SIGHT & SOUND
BFI, 21 Stephen Street, London W1T 1LN **T** 020-7255 1444
W www.bfi.org.uk/sightandsound
Editor, vacant

TIME OUT LONDON
77 Wicklow Street, London WC1X 9JY **T** 020-7813 3000
W www.timeout.com
Editor, Caroline McGinn

TOTAL FILM
Future Publishing Ltd, 1–10 Praed Mews, London W2 1QY
T 020-7042 4831 **W** www.gamesradar.com/totalfilm
Editor, Jane Crowther

FASHION AND BEAUTY

COSMOPOLITAN
House of Hearst, 30 Panton Street, London SW1Y 4AJ
T 020-7439 5000 **W** www.cosmopolitan.co.uk
Editor, Claire Hodgson

ELLE
House of Hearst, 30 Panton Street, London SW1Y 4AJ
T 020-7150 7000 **W** www.elleuk.com
Editor, Farrah Storr

GLAMOUR
Condé Nast, Vogue House, Hanover Square, London W1S 1JU
T 020-7499 9080 **W** www.glamourmagazine.co.uk
Editor-in-Chief, Deborah Joseph

GRAZIA
Endeavour House, 189 Shaftesbury Avenue, London WC2H 8JG
T 0845-601 1356 **W** www.graziadaily.co.uk
Editor, Hattie Brett

HARPER'S BAZAAR
House of Hearst, 30 Panton Street, London SW1Y 4AJ
T 0844-848 5203 **W** www.harpersbazaar.co.uk
Editor-in-Chief, Justine Picardie

MARIE CLAIRE
161 Marsh Wall, London E14 9AP **T** 020-3148 5000
W www.marieclaire.co.uk
Editor-in-Chief, Trish Halpin

VOGUE
Condé Nast, Vogue House, Hanover Square, London W1S 1JU
T 0844-848 5202 **W** www.vogue.co.uk
Editor, Edward Enninful

FOOD AND DRINK

FOOD AND TRAVEL
Suite 51, The Business Centre, Ingate Place, London SW8 3NS
T 020-7501 0511 **W** www.foodandtravel.com
Editor, Michelle Hather

GOOD FOOD
44 Vineyard House, Brook Green, London W6 7BT
T 020-7150 5022 **W** www.bbcgoodfood.com
Editor, Christine Hayes

OLIVE
Vineyard House, 44 Brook Green, London W6 7BT
T 020-7150 5024 **W** www.olivemagazine.com
Editor, Laura Rowe

WHISKY
6 Woolgate Court, St Benedicts Street, Norwich NR2 4AP
T 01603-633 808 **W** www.whiskymag.com
Editor, Rob Allanson

GENERAL INTEREST

BBC HISTORY
Tower House, Fairfax Street, Bristol BS1 3BN **T** 0117-927 9009
W www.historyextra.com
Editor, Rob Attar

BOOKSELLER
Floor 10, Westminster Tower, 3 Albert Embankment, London SE1 7SP **T** 020-3358 0365 **W** www.thebookseller.com
Editor, Philip Jones

HISTORY TODAY
2nd Floor, 9 Staple Inn, London WC1V 7QH **T** 020-3219 7810
W www.historytoday.com
Editor, Paul Lay

LITERARY REVIEW
44 Lexington Street, London W1F OLW **T** 020-7437 9392
W www.literaryreview.co.uk
Editor, Nancy Sladek

NEW STATESMAN
Standard House, 12–13 Essex Street, London WC2R
3AA**T** 020-7936 6400 **W** www.newstatesman.com
Editor, Jason Cowley

PRIVATE EYE
6 Carlisle Street, London W1D 3BN **T** 020-7437 4017
W www.private-eye.co.uk
Editor, Ian Hislop

PROSPECT
5th Floor, 23 Savile Row, London W1S 2ET **T** 020-7255 1281
W www.prospectmagazine.co.uk
Editor, Tom Clark

READER'S DIGEST
The Maltings, West Street, Bourne BH24 9PH **T** 0330-333 2220
W www.readersdigest.co.uk
Editor, Fiona Hicks

SAGA
Saga Publishing Ltd, Enbrook Park, Folkestone, Kent CT20 3SE
T 01303-771111 **W** www.saga.co.uk
Editor, Louise Robinson

THE SPECTATOR
22 Old Queen Street, London SW1H 9HP **T** 020-7961 0200
W www.spectator.co.uk
Editor, Fraser Nelson

TLS (THE TIMES LITERARY SUPPLEMENT)
1 London Bridge Street, London SE1 9GF **T** 020-7782 5000
W www.the-tls.co.uk
Editor, Stig Abell

THE WEEK
31–32 Alfred Place, London WC1E 7DP **T** 020-3890 3890
W www.theweek.co.uk
Editor-in-Chief, Jeremy O'Grady

WHO DO YOU THINK YOU ARE?
Tower House, Fairfax Street, Bristol BS1 3BN **T** 0117-314 7400
W www.whodoyouthinkyouaremagazine.com
Editor, Sarah Williams

HEALTH AND FITNESS

MEN'S FITNESS
31–32 Alfred Place, London WC1E 7DP **T** 020-3890 3890
W www.coachmag.co.uk
Editor, Isaac Williams

RUNNER'S WORLD
33 Broadwick Street, London W1F 9EP **T** 020-7339 4409
W www.runnersworld.co.uk
Editor, Andy Dixon

WW MAGAZINE
The River Group, 1 Neal Street, London WC2H 9QL
T 020-7306 0304 **W** www.weightwatchers.co.uk
Editor, vacant

WOMEN'S HEALTH
House of Hearst, 30 Panton Street, London SW1Y 4AJ
T 0844-322 1773 **W** www.womenshealthmag.com/uk
Editor, Claire Sanderson

HOBBIES AND GAMES

AIRFIX MODEL WORLD
Key Publishing Ltd, PO Box 100, Stamford PE9 1XQ
T 01780-755131 **W** www.airfixmodelworld.com
Editor, Stuart Fone

ANGLING TIMES
Bauer Media Group, Media House, Lynchwood, Peterborough PE2
6EA **T** 01733-395097 **W** www.anglingtimes.co.uk
Editor-in-Chief, Steve Fitzpatrick

BRITISH RAILWAY MODELLING
Warners Group Publications, The Maltings, West Street, Bourne,
Lincs PE10 9PH **T** 01778-391000 **W** www.world-of-railways.co.uk/
brm
Editor, Steve Cole

BRITISH CHESS MAGAZINE
Albany House, 14 Shute End, Wokingham RG40 1BJ
T 01252-514372 **W** www.britishchessmagazine.co.uk
Editors, Milan Dinic; Shaun Taulbut

COIN NEWS
Token Publishing Ltd, 40 Southernhay East, Exeter, Devon EX1 1PE
T 01404-46972 **W** www.tokenpublishing.com
Editor, John Russell

HORNBY
Key Publishing Ltd, PO Box 100, Stamford PE9 1XQ
T 01780-755131 **W** www.hornbymagazine.com
Editor, Mike Wild

HOME AND GARDEN

BBC GARDENERS' WORLD
Immediate Media, 5th Floor, Vineyard House, 44 Brook Green,
London W6 7BT **T** 020-7150 5700 **W** www.gardenersworld.com
Editor, Lucy Hall

GOOD HOUSEKEEPING
House of Hearst, 30 Panton Street, London SW1Y 4AJ
T 020-7439 5000 **W** www.goodhousekeeping.co.uk
Editor-in-chief, Gaby Huddart

HOUSE & GARDEN
Condé Nast Publications, Vogue House, Hanover Square, London
W1S 1JU **T** 020-7499 9080 **W** www.houseandgarden.co.uk
Editor, Hatta Byng

LIVING ETC
TI Media, 161 Marsh Wall, London E14 9SJ **T** 020-3148 5000
W www.housetohome.co.uk/livingetc
Editor, Sarah Spiteri

MEN'S LIFESTYLE

ESQUIRE
House of Hearst, 30 Panton Street, London SW1Y 4AJ
T 020-7439 5000 **W** www.esquire.co.uk
Editor, Alex Bilmes

GAY TIMES
Millivres Prowler Group, Spectrum House, 32-34 Gordon House
Road, London NW5 1LP **T** 020-7424 7400 **W** www.gaytimes.co.uk
Editor, Tag Warner

GQ
Vogue House, 1 Hanover Square, London W1S 1JU
T 020-7499 9080 **W** www.gq-magazine.co.uk
Editor, Dylan Jones

MOTORING

BIKE
Bauer Media, Media House, Lynchwood, Peterborough PE2 6EA
T 01733-468000 **W** www.bikemagazine.co.uk
Editor, Hugo Wilson

CARAVAN
Warners Group Publications, The Maltings, West Street, Bourne,
Lincs PE10 9PH **T** 01778-392450 **W** www.outandaboutlive.co.uk
Editor, Daniel Attwood

F1 RACING
Autosport Media, 1 Eton Street, Richmond TW9 1AG
T 020-3405 8100 **W** www.f1racing.co.uk
Editor, Ben Anderson

PRACTICAL CARAVAN
Haymarket Ltd, Bridge House, 69 London Road, Twickenham TW1
3SP **T** 020-8267 5712 **W** www.practicalcaravan.com
Editor, Sarah Wakely

TOP GEAR
Energy Centre, Media Centre, 201 Wood Lane, London W12 7TQ
T 020-7150 5558 **W** www.topgear.com
Editor, Charlie Turner

PHOTOGRAPHY

AMATEUR PHOTOGRAPHER
Pinehurst 2, Pinehurst Road, Farnborough, Hants. GU14 7BF
T 01252-555213 **W** www.amateurphotographer.co.uk
Group Editor, Nigel Atherton

DIGITAL CAMERA
Future Publishing Ltd Quay House, The Ambury, Bath BA1 1UA
W www.digitalcameraworld.com
Editor, James Artaius

DIGITAL PHOTOGRAPHER
Future Publishing Ltd, Quay House, The Ambury, Bath BA1 1UA
T 01202-586200 **W** www.dphotographer.co.uk
Editor-in-Chief, Amy Squibb

POPULAR MUSIC

CLASH
Studio 86, Hackney Downs Studios, 17 Amhurst Terrace, London E8
2BT **T** 020-7628 2312 **W** www.clashmusic.com
Editor-in-Chief, Simon Harper

CLASSIC ROCK
Future Publishing Ltd, Quay House, The Ambury, Bath BA1 1UA
W www.loudersound.com/classic-rock
Editor, Siân Llewellyn

DIY
2nd Floor, Unit 23, Tileyard Studios, Tileyard Road, London N7 9AH
W www.diymag.com
Editor, Sarah Jamieson

GUITARIST
Future Publishing Ltd, Beauford Court, 30 Monmouth Street, Bath
BA1 2BW **T** 01225-442244 **W** www.musicradar.com/guitarist
Editor, Jamie Dickson

MOJO
Endeavour House, 189 Shaftesbury Avenue, London WC2H 8JG
T 020-7208 3443 **W** www.mojo4music.com
Editor, John Mulvey

Q
Endeavour House, 189 Shaftesbury Avenue, London WC2H 8JG
T 020-7295 5000 **W** www.qthemusic.com
Editor-in-Chief, John Mulvey

UNCUT
TI Media, 161 Marsh Wall, London E14 9SJ **T** 020-3148 5000
W www.uncut.co.uk
Editor, Michael Bonnier

SCIENCE AND NATURE

BBC WILDLIFE
Immediate Media, Eagle House, Colston Avenue, Bristol BS1 4ST
T 0117-927 9009 **W** www.discoverwildlife.com
Editor, Paul McGuinness

BIRD WATCHING
Bauer Media, Media House, Lynch Wood, Peterborough PE2 6EA
T 01733-468000 **W** www.birdwatching.co.uk
Editor, Matthew Merritt

COUNTRYFILE
9th Floor, Tower House, Fairfax Street, Bristol BS1 3BN
T 0117-927 9009 **W** www.countryfile.com
Editor, Fergus Collins

BBC SCIENCE FOCUS
Immediate Media, Eagle House, Colston Avenue, Bristol BS1 4ST
T 0117-927 9009 **W** www.sciencefocus.com
Editor, Daniel Bennett

HOW IT WORKS
Future Publishing Limited Quay House, The Ambury, Bath BA1 1UA
W www.howitworksdaily.com
Editor-in-Chief, Dave Harfield

NEW SCIENTIST
110 High Holborn, London WC1V 6EU **T** 020-7611 1206
W www.newscientist.com
Editor-in-Chief, Emily Wilson

BBC SKY AT NIGHT
Immediate Media, Eagle House, Colston Avenue, Bristol BS1
4ST**T** 0117-927 9009 **W** www.skyatnightmagazine.com
Editor, Chris Bramley

SPORT

BOXING MONTHLY
Kelsey Media, Cudham Tithe Barn, Berry's Hill, Cudham, Kent TN16
3AG **T** 020-8986 4141 **W** www.boxingmonthly.com
Editor, Graham Houston

THE CRICKETER
Court House, Cleaver Street, London SE11 4DZ **T** 020-3198 1359
W www.thecricketer.com
Editor, Simon Hughes

FOURFOURTWO
Future Publishing Ltd, Quay House, The Ambury, Bath BA1 1UA
T 0844-848 2852 **W** www.fourfourtwo.com
Editor, James Brown

GOLF MONTHLY
TI Media Ltd, Pinehurst 2, Pinehurst Road, Farnborough Business
Park, Farnborough, Hants GU14 7BF **T** 01252-555197
W www.golf-monthly.co.uk
Editor, Michael Harris

HORSE & HOUND
TI Media Ltd, 161 Marsh Wall, London E14 9SJ **T** 01252-555029
W www.horseandhound.co.uk
Editor, Pippa Roome

MATCH
Kelsey Media, Cudham Tithe Barn, Berrys Hill, Cudham, Kent, TN16
3AG **T** 01959-541444 **W** www.matchfootball.co.uk
Editor, Stephen Fishlock

RUGBY WORLD
TI Media Ltd, 2nd Floor, Pinehurst 2, Pinehurst Road, Farnborough
Business Park, Farnborough, Hants GU14 7BF **T** 01252-555271
W www.rugbyworld.com
Editor, Sarah Mockford

TENNISHEAD
Advantage Publishing (UK) Ltd, Trinity House, Sculpins Lane,
Braintree, Essex CM7 4AY **T** 020-8408 7148
W www.tennishead.net
Consultant Editor, Paul Newman

WISDEN CRICKET MONTHLY
PO Box 33, 4th Floor, Kia Oval, Kennington, London, England, SE11
5SS **T** 01293 312094 **W** www.wisden.com
Editor, Phil Walker

WORLD SOCCER
TI Media Ltd, 2nd Floor, Pinehurst 2, Pinehurst Road, Farnborough
Business Park, Farnborough, Hants GU14 7BF **T** 020-3148 4817
W www.worldsoccer.com
Editor, Gavin Hamilton

TRAVEL

CONDÉ NAST TRAVELLER
Vogue House, Hanover Square, London W1S 1JU **T** 0844-848 2851
W www.cntraveller.com
Editor, Melinda Stevens

FRANCE
Archant House, 3 Oriel Road, Cheltenham GL50 1BB
T 01242-216050 **W** www.completefrance.com
Editor, Karen Tait

LONELY PLANET
Immediate Media, Eagle House, Colston Avenue, Bristol BS1 4ST
T 0207-150 5000 **W** www.lonelyplanet.com
Editor, Peter Grunert

NATIONAL GEOGRAPHIC TRAVELLER
Unit 310 Highgate Studios, 53–79 Highgate Road, London NW5 1TL
T 020-7253 9906 **W** www.natgeotraveller.co.uk
Editor, Pat Riddell

TRADE AND PROFESSIONAL BODIES

The following is a list of employers' and trade associations and other professional bodies in the UK. It does not represent a comprehensive list. For further professional bodies *see* Professional Education.

ASSOCIATIONS

ABTA – THE TRAVEL ASSOCIATION 30 Park Street, London SE1 9EQ **W** www.abta.com
Chief Executive, Mark Tanzer

ADVERTISING ASSOCIATION Lynton House 7-12, Tavistock Square, London WC1H 9LT **T** 020-7340 1100
E aa@adassoc.org.uk **W** www.adassoc.org.uk
Chief Executive, Stephen Woodford

AEROSPACE DEFENCE SECURITY Salamanca Square, 9 Albert Embankment, London SE1 7SP **T** 020-7091 4500
W www.adsgroup.org.uk
Chief Executive, Paul Everitt

AGRICULTURAL ENGINEERS ASSOCIATION Samuelson House, 62 Forder Way, Peterborough PE7 8JB **T** 0845-644 8748
E info@aea.uk.com **W** www.aea.uk.com
Chief Executive, Ruth Bailey

ASBESTOS REMOVAL CONTRACTORS ASSOCIATION Unit 1, Stretton Business Park 2, Brunel Drive, Stretton DE13 0BY
T 01283-566467 **E** info@arca.org.uk **W** www.arca.org.uk
Chief Executive, Steve Sadley

ASSOCIATION FOR CONSULTANCY AND ENGINEERING Alliance House, 12 Caxton Street, London SW1H 0QL **T** 020-7222 6557 **E** consult@acenet.co.uk
W www.acenet.co.uk
Chief Executive, Hannah Vickers

ASSOCIATION OF ACCOUNTING TECHNICIANS 140 Aldersgate Street, London EC1A 4HY **T** 020-3735 2468
E customersupport@aat.org.uk **W** www.aat.org.uk
Chief Executive, Mark Farrar

ASSOCIATION OF ANAESTHETISTS OF GREAT BRITAIN AND IRELAND 21 Portland Place, London W1B 1PY **T** 020-7631 1650 **E** info@aagbi.org **W** www.aagbi.org
Executive Director, Karin Pappenheim

ASSOCIATION OF BRITISH INSURERS One America Square, London EC3N 2LB **T** 020-7600 3333 **E** info@abi.org.uk
W www.abi.org.uk
Director-General, Huw Evans

ASSOCIATION OF BUSINESS RECOVERY PROFESSIONALS 8th Floor, 120 Aldersgate Street, London EC1A 4JQ **T** 020-7566 4200 **E** association@r3.org.uk
W www.r3.org.uk
Chief Executive, Liz Bingham

ASSOCIATION OF CONVENIENCE STORES LTD Federation House, 17 Farnborough Street, Farnborough GU14 8AG **T** 01252-515001 **E** acs@acs.org.uk
W www.acs.org.uk
Chief Executive, James Lowman

ASSOCIATION OF CORPORATE TREASURERS 69 Leadenhall Street, London EC3A 2BG **T** 020-7847 2540
W www.treasurers.org
Chief Executive, Caroline Stockmann

ASSOCIATION OF DRAINAGE AUTHORITIES Rural Innovation Centre, Avenue H, Stoneleigh Park CV8 2LG
T 024-7699 2889 **E** admin@ada.org.uk **W** www.ada.org.uk
Chief Executive, Innes Thomson, CENG

BOOKSELLERS ASSOCIATION 6 Bell Yard, London WC2A 2JR **T** 020-7421 4640 **E** mail@booksellers.org.uk
W www.booksellers.org.uk
Chief Executive, Meryl Halls

BRITISH ANTIQUE DEALERS' ASSOCIATION 21 John Street, London WC1N 2BF **T** 020-7589 4128 **E** info@bada.org
W www.bada.org
President, Vacant

BRITISH ASSOCIATION OF SOCIAL WORKERS 37 Waterloo Street, Birmingham B2 5PP **T** 0121-622 3911
W www.basw.co.uk
Chief Executive, Dr Roth Allen

BRITISH BEER & PUB ASSOCIATION Ground Floor, 61 Queen Street, London EC4R 1EB **T** 020-7627 9191
E contact@beerandpub.com **W** www.beerandpub.com
Chief Executive, Emma McClarkin

BRITISH CHAMBERS OF COMMERCE 65 Petty France, London SW1H 9EU **T** 020-7654 5800
W www.britishchambers.org.uk
Director-General, Adam Marshall

BRITISH ELECTROTECHNICAL AND ALLIED MANUFACTURERS ASSOCIATION (BEAMA) Rotherwick House, 3 Thomas More Street, London E1W 1YZ
T 020-7793 3000 **E** info@beama.org.uk **W** www.beama.org.uk
Chief Executive, Dr Howard Porter

BRITISH HOROLOGICAL INSTITUTE Upton Hall, Upton, Newark NG23 5TE **T** 01636-813795 **E** info@bhi.co.uk
W www.bhi.co.uk
President, Rt. Hon. Viscount Middleton, FBHI

BRITISH INSTITUTE OF PROFESSIONAL PHOTOGRAPHY The Artistry House, 16 Winckley Square, Preston PR1 3JJ **T** 01772-367968 **E** admin@bipp.com
W www.bipp.com
Chief Executive, Martin Baynes

BRITISH INSURANCE BROKERS' ASSOCIATION 8th Floor, John Stow House, 18 Bevis Marks, London EC3A 7JB
T 0344-770 0266 **E** enquiries@biba.org.uk **W** www.biba.org.uk
Chief Executive, Steve White

BRITISH MARINE FEDERATION Marine House, Thorpe Lea Road, Egham TW20 8BF **T** 01784-473377
E info@britishmarine.co.uk **W** www.britishmarine.co.uk
Chief Executive, Lesley Robinson

BRITISH MEDICAL ASSOCIATION BMA House, Tavistock Square, London WC1H 9JP **T** 020-7387 4499
W www.bma.org.uk
Chief Executive, Tom Grinyer

BRITISH OFFICE SUPPLIES AND SERVICES (BOSS) FEDERATION c/o British Printing Industries Federation, 2 Villiers Court, Copse Drive CV5 9RN **T** 01676-526030
W www.bossfederation.co.uk
Chief Executive, Amy Hutchinson

BPI (BRITISH PHONOGRAPHIC INDUSTRY) Riverside Building, County Hall, Westminster Bridge Road, London SE1 7JA
T 020-7803 1300 **E** general@bpi.co.uk **W** www.bpi.co.uk
Chief Executive, Geoff Taylor

BRITISH PLASTICS FEDERATION 6 Bath Place, London EC2A 3JE **T** 020-7457 5000 **E** reception@bpf.co.uk
W www.bpf.co.uk
Director-General, Philip Law

BRITISH PORTS ASSOCIATION 1st Floor, 30 Park Street, London SE1 9EQ T 020-7260 1780 E info@britishports.org.uk W www.britishports.org.uk
Chief Executive, Richard Ballantyne

BRITISH PRINTING INDUSTRIES FEDERATION Unit 2, Villiers Court, Meriden Business Park CV5 9RN T 01676-526030 W www.britishprint.com
Chief Executive, Charles Jarrold

BRITISH PROPERTY FEDERATION 5th Floor, St Albans House, 57–59 Haymarket, London SW1Y 4QX T 020-7802 0110 E info@bpf.org.uk W www.bpf.org.uk
Chief Executive, Melanie Leech

BRITISH RETAIL CONSORTIUM 100 Avebury Blvd., Milton Keynes MK9 1FH T 020-7854 8900 E info@brc.org.uk W www.brc.org.uk
Director-General, Helen Dickinson, OBE

BRITISH TYRE MANUFACTURERS' ASSOCIATION 5 Berewyk Hall Court, White Colne, Colchester CO6 2QB T 01787-226995 W www.btmauk.com
Chief Executive, Graham Willson

BUILDING SOCIETIES ASSOCIATION 6th Floor, York House, London WC2B 6UJ T 020-7520 5900 W www.bsa.org.uk
Chief Executive, Robin Fieth

CHARTERED ASSOCIATION OF BUILDING ENGINEERS Lutyens House, Billing Brook Road, Northampton NN3 8NW T 01604-404121 W www.cbuilde.com
Chief Executive, Dr Gavin Dunn

CHARTERED INSTITUTE FOR ARCHAEOLOGISTS Power Steele Building, Wessex Hall, Whiteknights Road, Reading RG6 6DE T 0118-966 2841 E admin@archaeologists.net W www.archaeologists.net
Chief Executive, Peter Hinton

CHARTERED INSTITUTE OF ENVIRONMENTAL HEALTH Chadwick Court, 15 Hatfields, London SE1 8DJ T 020-7827 5800 E info@cieh.org W www.cieh.org
Chief Executive, Dawn Welham

CHARTERED INSTITUTE OF JOURNALISTS 2 Dock Offices, Surrey Quays Road, London SE16 2XU T 020-7252 1187 E memberservices@cioj.co.uk W www.cioj.co.uk
General Secretary, Dominic Cooper

CHARTERED INSTITUTE OF PURCHASING AND SUPPLY Easton House, Church Street, Stamford PE9 3NZ T 08458-801188 W www.cips.org
Chief Executive, Malcolm Harrison

CHARTERED INSTITUTE OF TAXATION 30 Monck Street, London SW1P 2AP T 020-7340 0550 W www.tax.org.uk
Chief Executive, Helen Whiteman

CHARTERED INSURANCE INSTITUTE 42–48 High Road, London E18 2JP T 020-8989 8464 E customer.serv@cii.co.uk W www.cii.co.uk
Chief Executive, Sian Fisher

CHARTERED MANAGEMENT INSTITUTE Management House, Cottingham Road, Corby NN17 1TT T 01536-207360 E cmi@managers.org.uk W www.managers.org.uk
Chief Executive, Anne Francke

CHARTERED QUALITY INSTITUTE 2nd Floor North, Chancery Exchange, London EC4A 1AB T 020-7245 6722 E membership@quality.org W www.quality.org
Chief Executive, Vincent Desmond

CHARTERED TRADING STANDARDS INSTITUTE 1 Sylvan Court, Sylvan Way, Basildon SS15 6TH T 01268-582200 E institute@tsi.org.uk W www.tradingstandards.uk
Chief Executive, Leon Livermore

CHEMICAL INDUSTRIES ASSOCIATION Kings Buildings, Smith Square, London SW1P 3JJ T 020-7834 3399 E enquiries@cia.org.uk W www.cia.org.uk
Chief Executive, Steve Elliott

CONFEDERATION OF PAPER INDUSTRIES 1 Rivenhall Road, Swindon SN5 7BD T 01793-889600 E cpi@paper.org.uk W www.paper.org.uk
Director-General, Andrew Large

CONFEDERATION OF PASSENGER TRANSPORT UK Fifth Floor Offices (South), Chancery House, London WC2A 1QS T 020-7240 3131 E admin@cpt-uk.org W www.cpt-uk.org
Chief Executive, Graham Vidler

CONSTRUCTION PRODUCTS ASSOCIATION The Building Centre, 26 Store Street, London WC1E 7BT T 020-7323 3770 W www.constructionproducts.org.uk
Chief Executive, Peter Caplehorn

DAIRY UK 6th Floor, London WC1V 7EP T 020-7405 1484 E info@dairyuk.org W www.dairyuk.org
Chief Executive, Dr Judith Bryans

ENERGY UK 26 Finsbury Square, London EC2A 1DS T 020-7930 9390 W www.energy-uk.org.uk
Chief Executive, Emma Pinchbeck

FEDERATION OF BAKERS 6th Floor, 10 Bloomsbury Way, London WC1A 2SL T 020-7420 7190 E info@fob.uk.com W www.fob.uk.com
Director, Gordon Polson

FEDERATION OF MASTER BUILDERS David Croft House, 25 Ely Place, London EC1N 6TD T 0330-333 7777 W www.fmb.org.uk
Chief Executive, Brian Berry

FSPA (FEDERATION OF SPORTS AND PLAY ASSOCIATIONS) Office 8, Rural Innovation Centre, Unit 169– Avenue H, Kenilworth CV8 2LG T 024-7641 4999 E info@sportsandplay.com W www.sportsandplay.com
Chair, Jack Osborne

FINANCE AND LEASING ASSOCIATION 2nd Floor, Imperial House, 8 Kean Street, London WC2B 4AS T 020-7836 6511 E info@fla.org.uk W www.fla.org.uk
Director-General, Stephen Haddrill

FOOD AND DRINK FEDERATION 6th Floor, London WC1A 2SL T 020-7836 2460 W www.fdf.org.uk
Chief Executive, Ian Wright

FREIGHT TRANSPORT ASSOCIATION LTD Hermes House, St John's Road, Tunbridge Wells TN4 9UZ T 01892-52617 E enquiry@logistics.org.uk W www.logistics.org.uk
President, David Wells

GLASGOW CHAMBER OF COMMERCE 30 George Square, Glasgow G2 1EQ T 0141-204 2121 E chamber@glasgowchamberofcommerce.com W www.glasgowchamberofcommerce.com
Chief Executive, Stuart Patrick

INSTITUTE OF BREWING AND DISTILLING 44A Curlew Street, London SE1 2ND T 020-7499 8144 E customer.support@ibd.org.uk W www.ibd.org.uk
Chief Executive, Dr Jerry Avis

INSTITUTE OF BRITISH ORGAN BUILDING 13 Ryefields, Bury St Edmunds IP31 3TD T 01359-233433 W www.ibo.co.uk
President, Andrew Moyes

INSTITUTE OF CHARTERED FORESTERS 59 George Street, Edinburgh EH2 2JG E icf@charteredforesters.org W www.charteredforesters.org
Executive Director, Shireen Chambers

INSTITUTE OF CHARTERED SECRETARIES AND ADMINISTRATORS Saffron House, 6–10 Kirby Street, London EC1N 8TS **T** 020-7580 4741 **E** enquiries@icsa.org.uk **W** www.icsa.org.uk
Chief Executive, Sara Drake

INSTITUTE OF CHARTERED SHIPBROKERS
30 Park Street, London SE1 9EQ **T** 020-7357 9722 **E** enquiries@ics.org.uk **W** www.ics.org.uk
Interim Director, Robert Hill, FICS

INSTITUTE OF DIRECTORS 116 Pall Mall, London SW1Y 5ED **T** 020-3855 4738 **E** businessinfo@iod.com **W** www.iod.com
Director-General, Johnathan Geldart

INSTITUTE OF EXPORT AND INTERNATIONAL TRADE Export House, Minerva Business Park, Peterborough PE2 6FT **T** 01733-404400 **W** www.export.org.uk
Chair, Terry Scuoler, CBE

INSTITUTE OF FINANCIAL ACCOUNTANTS
CS111, Clerkenwell Workshops, 27–31 Clerkenwell Close, London EC1R 0AT **T** 020-3567 5999 **E** mail@ifa.org.uk **W** www.ifa.org.uk
Chief Executive, John Edwards

INSTITUTE OF HEALTHCARE MANAGEMENT
33 Cavendish Square, London W1G 0PW **T** 020-7182 4066 **E** contact@ihm.org.uk **W** www.ihm.org.uk
Chief Executive, Jon Wilks

INSTITUTE OF HOSPITALITY 14 Palmerston Road, Surrey SM1 4QL **T** 020-8661 4900 **E** info@instituteofhospitality.org **W** www.instituteofhospitality.org
Chief Executive, Peter Ducker

INSTITUTE OF INTERNAL COMMUNICATION Scorpio House, Rockingham Drive, MK14 6LY **T** 01908-232168 **E** enquiries@ioic.org.uk **W** www.ioic.org.uk
Chief Executive, Jennifer Sproul

INSTITUTE OF MANAGEMENT SERVICES Lichfield Business Village, Friary Way, Lichfield WS13 6AA **T** 01543-308605 **E** admin@ims-productivity.com **W** www.ims-productivity.com
Chairman, Dr Andrew Muir

INSTITUTE OF QUARRYING McPherson House, 8A Regan Way, Chilwell NG9 6RZ **T** 0115-972 9995 **E** mail@quarrying.org **W** www.quarrying.org
Chief Executive, James Thorne

INSTITUTE OF THE MOTOR INDUSTRY Fanshaws, Hertford SG13 8PQ **T** 01992-519025 **E** comms@theimi.org.uk **W** www.theimi.org.uk
Chief Executive, Steve Nash

INSTITUTION OF OCCUPATIONAL SAFETY AND HEALTH The Grange, Highfield Drive, Wigston LE18 1NN **T** 0116-257 3100 **E** reception@iosh.co.uk **W** www.iosh.co.uk
Chief Executive, James Quinn

IP FEDERATION 60 Gray's Inn Road, London WC1X 8AQ **T** 020-7242 3923 **E** admin@ipfederation.com **W** www.ipfederation.com
President, Scott Roberts

LEATHER UK Leather Trade House, Kings Park Road, Northampton NN3 6JD **T** 01604-679999 **E** info@leatheruk.org **W** www.leatheruk.org
Director, Dr Kerry Senior

MAGISTRATES' ASSOCIATION 10A Flagstaff House, St George Wharf, London SW8 2LE **T** 020-7387 2353 **E** information@magistrates-association.org.uk **W** www.magistrates-association.org.uk
Chief Executive, Jon Collins

MAKE UK, THE MANUFACTURERS' ORGANISATION Broadway House, Tothill Street, London SW1H 9NQ **T** 0808-168 5874 **E** enquiries@makeuk.org **W** www.makeuk.org
Chief Executive, Stephen Phipson, CBE

MANAGEMENT CONSULTANCIES ASSOCIATION
5th Floor, 36–38 Cornhill, London EC3V 3NG **T** 020-7645 7950 **E** info@mca.org.uk **W** www.mca.org.uk
Chief Executive, Tamzen Isacsson

MASTER LOCKSMITHS ASSOCIATION 1 Prospect Park, Rugby CV21 1TF **T** 01327-262255 **E** enquiries@locksmiths.co.uk **W** www.locksmiths.co.uk
Director, Maria Ging

NATIONAL ASSOCIATION OF BRITISH MARKET AUTHORITIES The Guildhall, Shropshire SY11 1PZ **T** 01691-680713 **E** nabma@nabma.com **W** www.nabma.com
Chief Executive, David Preston

NATIONAL ASSOCIATION OF ESTATE AGENTS Arbon House, 6 Tournament Court, Warwick CV34 6LG **T** 01926-496800 **W** www.naea.co.uk
President, Kirsty Finney

NATIONAL FARMERS' UNION (NFU) Agriculture House, Stoneleigh Park, Stoneleigh CV8 2LZ **T** 024-7685 8500 **W** www.nfuonline.com
Director-General, Terry Jones

NATIONAL FEDERATION OF RETAIL NEWSAGENTS Bede House, Belmont Business Park, Durham DH1 1TW **T** 020-7017 8880 **E** connect@nrfn.org.uk **W** www.nfrn.org.uk
Chief Executive, Paul Baxter

NATIONAL LANDLORDS ASSOCIATION 212 Washway Road, Manchester M33 6RN **T** 0300-121 6400 **W** www.nrla.org.uk
Chief Executive, Ben Beadle

NATIONAL MARKET TRADERS FEDERATION Hampton House, Hawshaw Lane, Barnsley S74 0HA **T** 01226-749021 **E** genoffice@nmtf.co.uk **W** www.nmtf.co.uk
Chief Executive, John Dyson

NATIONAL PHARMACY ASSOCIATION Mallinson House, 38–42 St Peter's Street, Herts AL1 3NP **T** 01727-858687 **E** npa@npa.co.uk **W** www.npa.co.uk
Chief Executive, Mark Lyonette

NEWS MEDIA ASSOCIATION 16-18 New Bridge Road, London ECV4 6AG **T** 020-3848 9620 **E** nma@newsmediauk.org **W** www.newsmediauk.org
Chief Executive, David Newell

OIL AND GAS UK *1st Floor,* Paternoster House, 65 St. Paul Churchyard, London EC4M 8AB **T** 020-7802 2400 **E** info@oilandgasuk.co.uk **W** www.oilandgasuk.co.uk
Chief Executive, Deirdre Michie

PROPERTY CARE ASSOCIATION 11 Ramsay Court, Kingfisher Way, Huntingdon PE29 6FY **T** 0148-400 000 **E** pca@property-care.org **W** www.property-care.org
Chief Executive, Stephen Hodgson

PUBLISHERS ASSOCIATION 50 Southwark Street, London SE1 1UN **T** 020-7378 0504 **E** mail@publishers.org.uk **W** www.publishers.org.uk
Chief Executive, Stephen Lotinga

RADIOCENTRE 6th Floor, 55 New Oxford Street, London WC1A 1BS **T** 020-7010 0600 **E** info@radiocentre.org **W** www.radiocentre.org
Chief Executive, Siobhan Kenny

ROAD HAULAGE ASSOCIATION LTD Roadway House, Bretton Way, Peterborough PE3 8DD **T** 01733-261131 **W** www.rha.uk.net
Chief Executive, Richard Burnett

ROYAL ASSOCIATION OF BRITISH DAIRY FARMERS
Dairy House, Unit 31, Abbey Park, Kenilworth CV8 2LY
T 024-7663 9317 E office@rabdf.co.uk W www.rabdf.co.uk
Managing Director, Matthew Knight

ROYAL FACULTY OF PROCURATORS IN GLASGOW
12 Nelson Mandela Place, Glasgow G2 1BT T 0141-332 3593
E library@rfpg.org W www.rfpg.org
Chief Executive, John McKenzie

SHELLFISH ASSOCIATION OF GREAT BRITAIN
Fishmongers' Hall, London Bridge, London EC4R 9EL
T 020-7283 8305 E projects@shellfish.org.uk
W www.shellfish.org.uk
Director, David Jarrad

SOCIETY OF LOCAL AUTHORITY CHIEF EXECUTIVES AND SENIOR MANAGERS (SOLACE) Off Southgate,
Pontefract, West Yorkshire WF8 1NT T 0207-233 0081
E contact@solace.org.uk W www.solace.org.uk
Directors, Graeme McDonald; Terry McDougall

SOCIETY OF MOTOR MANUFACTURERS AND TRADERS LTD 71 Great Peter Street, London SW1P 2BN
T 020-7235 7000 W www.smmt.co.uk
Chief Executive, Mike Hawes

TIMBER TRADE FEDERATION The Building Centre, 26
Store Street, London WC1E 7BT T 020-3205 0067 E ttf@ttf.co.uk
W www.ttf.co.uk
Managing Director, David Hopkins

UK CHAMBER OF SHIPPING 30 Park Street, London
SE1 9EQ T 020-7417 2800 E query@ukchamberofshipping.com
W www.ukchamberofshipping.com
Chief Executive, Bob Sanguinetti

UK FASHION AND TEXTILE ASSOCIATION 3 Queen
Square, London WC1N 3AR T 020-7843 9460 E info@ukft.org
W www.ukft.org
Chief Executive, Adam Mansell

UK FINANCE 5th Floor, 1 Angel Court, London EC2R 7HJ
T 020-7706 3333 W www.ukfinance.org.uk
COO, Alastair Gilmartin Smith

UKHOSPITALITY 10 Bloomsbury Way, London WC1A 2SL
T 020-7404 7744 W www.ukhospitality.org.uk
Chairman, Steve Richards

UK PETROLEUM INDUSTRY ASSOCIATION LTD 37–
39 High Holborn, London WC1V 6AA T 020-7269 7600
E info@ukpia.com W www.ukpia.com
Director-General, Stephen Marcos Jones

ULSTER FARMERS' UNION 475 Antrim Road, Belfast
BT15 3DA T 028-9037 0222 E info@ufuhq.com
W www.ufuni.org
Chief Executive, Wesley Aston

THE WINE AND SPIRIT TRADE ASSOCIATION
International Wine and Spirit Centre, 39–45 Bermondsey Street,
London SE1 3XF T 020-7089 3877 E info@wsta.co.uk
W www.wsta.co.uk
Chief Executive, Miles Beale

CBI
Cannon Place, 78 Cannon Street, London EC4N 6HN
T 020-7379 7400 E enquiries@cbi.org.uk W www.cbi.org.uk

The CBI was founded in 1965 and is an independent non-party political body financed by industry and commerce. It works with the UK government, international legislators and policymakers to help UK businesses compete effectively. It is the recognised spokesman for the business viewpoint and is consulted as such by the government.

The CBI speaks for some 190,000 businesses that together employ approximately one-third of the private sector workforce. Member companies, which decide all policy positions, include FTSE 100 index listed companies, small- and medium-size firms, micro businesses, private and family owned businesses, start-ups and trade associations.

The CBI board is chaired by the president and meets four times a year. It is assisted by 14 expert standing committees which advise on the main aspects of policy. There are nine regional councils for England and three national councils for, Wales, Scotland and Northern Ireland. There are also offices in Beijing, Brussels, New Delhi and Washington DC.

President, Lord Karan Bilimoria, CBEDL
Director-General, Tony Danker

WALES, 2 Caspian Point, Caspian Way, Cardiff Bay, Cardiff
CF10 4DQ T 029-2097 7600 E wales.mail@cbi.org.uk
Regional Director, Ian Price

SCOTLAND, 160 West George Street, Glasgow G2 2HQ
T 0141-222 2184 E scotland@cbi.org.uk
Regional Director, Tracy Black

NORTHERN IRELAND, Hamilton House, 3 Joy Street, Belfast
BT2 8LE T 028-9010 1100 E ni.mail@cbi.org.uk
Regional Director, Angela McGowan

TRADE UNIONS

A trade union is an organisation of workers formed for the purpose of collective bargaining over pay and working conditions. Trade unions may also provide legal and financial advice, sickness benefits and education facilities to their members. Legally any employee has the right to join a trade union, but not all employers recognise all or any trade unions. Conversely an employee also has the right not to join a trade union, in particular since the practice of a 'closed shop' system, where all employees have to join the employer's preferred union, is no longer permitted.

THE CENTRAL ARBITRATION COMMITTEE

Fleetbank House, 2–6 Salisbury Square, London EC4Y 8JX
T 0330-109 3610 **E** enquiries@cac.gov.uk
W www.gov.uk/government/organisations/central-arbitration-committee

The Central Arbitration Committee's main role is concerned with requests for trade union recognition and de-recognition under the statutory procedures of Schedule A1 of the Employment Rights Act 1999. It also determines disclosure of information complaints under the Trade Union and Labour Relations (Consolidation) Act 1992, considers applications and complaints under the Information and Consultation Regulations 2004, and performs a similar role in relation to European works councils, companies, cooperative societies and cross-border mergers.

Chair, Sir Stephen Redmond
Acting Chief Executive, Maverlie Tavares

TRADES UNION CONGRESS (TUC)

Congress House, 23–28 Great Russell Street, London WC1B 3LS
T 020-7636 4030 **E** info@tuc.org.uk
W www.tuc.org.uk

The Trades Union Congress (TUC), founded in 1868, is an independent association of trade unions. The TUC promotes the rights and welfare of those in work and helps the unemployed. The TUC brings Britain's unions together to draw up common polices; lobbies the government to implement policies that will benefit people at work; campaigns on economic and social issues; represents working people on public bodies and at the UN employment body – the International Labour Organisation; carries out research on employment-related issues; runs training and education programmes for union representatives; helps unions to develop new services for their members and negotiate with each other; and builds links with other trade union bodies worldwide.

The governing body of the TUC is the annual congress which sets policy. Between congresses, business is conducted by a 56-member general council, which meets every two months to oversee the TUC's work programme and sanction new policy initiatives. Each year, at its first post-congress meeting, the general council appoints an executive committee and the TUC president for that congress year. The executive committee meets monthly to implement and develop policy, manage TUC financial affairs and deal with any urgent business. The president chairs general council and executive meetings and is consulted by the General Secretary on all major issues.

President (2020–21), Gail Cartmail
General Secretary, Frances O'Grady

SCOTTISH TRADES UNION CONGRESS (STUC)

Red Tree Business Unit, 24 Stonelaw Road, Glasgow G73 3TW
T 0141-337 8100
E info@stuc.org.uk **W** www.stuc.org.uk

The congress was formed in 1897 and acts as a national centre for the trade union movement in Scotland. The STUC promotes the rights to welfare of those in work and helps the unemployed. It helps its member unions to promote membership in new areas and industries, and campaigns for rights at work for all employees, including part-time and temporary workers, whether union members or not. It also makes representations to government and employers. In 2016 the STUC had over 540,000 members from 37 affiliated unions and 20 trade union councils.

The annual congress in April elects a 36-member general council on the basis of six sections.

General Secretary, Roz Foyer

WALES TUC

Wales TUC was established in 1974 to ensure that the role of the TUC was effectively undertaken in Wales. Its structure reflects the four economic regions of Wales and matches the regional committee areas of the National Assembly of Wales. The regional committees oversee the implementation of Wales TUC policy and campaigns in the relevant regions, and liaise with local government, training organisations and regional economic development bodies. The Wales TUC seeks to reduce unemployment, increase the levels of skill and pay, and eliminate discrimination.

The governing body of Wales TUC is the conference, which meets annually in May and elects a general council (usually of around 50 people) that oversees the work of the TUC throughout the year.

There are 49 affiliated unions representing around 400,000 workers.

Acting General Secretary, Shavanah Taj

TUC-AFFILIATED UNIONS
As at December 2020

ACCORD Simmons House, 46 Old Bath Road, Reading RG10 9QR **T** 0118-934 1808 **E** info@accordhq.org
W www.accord-myunion.org
General Secretary, Ged Nichols
Membership: 24,431

ADVANCE 2nd Floor, 16–17 High Street, Tring HP23 5AH
T 01442-891122 **E** info@advance-union.org
W www.advance-union.org
General Secretary, Linda Rolph
Membership: 6,848

AEGIS THE UNION 1–3 Lochside Crescent, Edinburgh EH12 9SE **T** 0131-549 5665 **E** members@aegistheunion.co.uk
W www.aegistheunion.co.uk
General Secretary, Brian Linn
Membership: 4,570

AEP (ASSOCIATION OF EDUCATIONAL PSYCHOLOGISTS) 4 The Riverside Centre, Durham DH1 5TA
T 0191-384 9512 **E** enquiries@aep.org.uk **W** www.aep.org.uk
General Secretary, Kate Fallon
Membership: 3,396

AFA (ASSOCIATION OF FLIGHT ATTENDANTS) 32 Wingford Road, London SW2 4DS **T** 0208-276 6723 **E** afalhr@unitedafa.org **W** www.afacwa.org
General Secretary, Michael Schwaabe
Membership: 500

ARTISTS' UNION ENGLAND Old Bakery, Carlow Street, London NW1 7LH **E** info@artistsunionengland.org.uk **W** www.artistsunionengland.org.uk
General Secretary, Vacant
Membership: 295

ASLEF (ASSOCIATED SOCIETY OF LOCOMOTIVE ENGINEERS AND FIREMEN) 77 St John Street, London EC1M 4NN **T** 020-7324 2400 **E** info@aslef.org.uk **W** www.aslef.org.uk
General Secretary, Michael Whelan
Membership: 22,078

BALPA (BRITISH AIRLINE PILOTS ASSOCIATION) BALPA House, 5 Heathrow Boulevard, 278 Bath Road, West Drayton UB7 0DQ **T** 020-8476 4000 **E** balpa@balpa.org **W** www.balpa.org
General Secretary, Brian Strutton
Membership: 8,012

BDA (BRITISH DIETETIC ASSOCIATION) 3rd Floor, Interchange Place, 151-165 Edmund Street, Birmingham B3 2TA **T** 0121-200 8021 **W** www.bda.uk.com
General Secretary, Annette Mansell-Green
Membership: 9,073

BFAWU (BAKERS, FOOD AND ALLIED WORKERS' UNION) Stanborough House, Great North Road, Welwyn Garden City AL8 7TA **T** 01707-260150 **E** info@bfawu.org **W** www.bfawu.org
General Secretary, Sarah Woolley
Membership: 17,595

BOS TU (BRITISH ORTHOPTIC SOCIETY TRADE UNION) 5th Floor, Charles House, 148/9 Great Charles Street Queensway, Birmingham B3 3HT **T** 0121-728 5633 **E** bios@orthoptics.org.uk **W** www.orthoptics.org.uk
Chair, Samantha Aitkenhead
Membership: 1,782

COMMUNITY 465C Caledonian Road, London N7 9GX **T** 0800 389 6332 **E** info@community-tu.org **W** www.community-tu.org
General Secretary, Roy Rickhuss
Membership: 31,866

COP (COLLEGE OF PODIATRY) Quartz House, London SE1 2EW **T** 020-7234 8639 **E** reception@scpod.org **W** www.cop.org.uk
General Secretary, Steve Jamieson
Membership: 9,512

CSP (CHARTERED SOCIETY OF PHYSIOTHERAPY) 14 Bedford Row, London WC1R 4ED **T** 020-7306 6666 **E** enquiries@csp.org.uk **W** www.csp.org.uk
Chief Executive, Claire Sullivan
Membership: 40,050

CWU (COMMUNICATION WORKERS UNION) 150 The Broadway, London SW19 1RX **T** 020-8971 7200 **E** info@cwu.org **W** www.cwu.org
General Secretary, Dave Ward
Membership: 191,437

EIS (EDUCATIONAL INSTITUTE OF SCOTLAND) 46 Moray Place, Edinburgh EH3 6BH **T** 0131-225 6244 **E** enquiries@eis.org.uk **W** www.eis.org.uk
General Secretary, Larry Flanagan
Membership: 54,702

EQUITY Guild House, Upper St Martin's Lane, London WC2H 9EG **T** 020-7379 6000 **E** info@equity.org.uk **W** www.equity.org.uk
General Secretary, Paul Flemming
Membership: 43,555

FBU (FIRE BRIGADES UNION) Bradley House, 68 Coombe Road, Kingston upon Thames KT2 7AE **T** 020-8541 1765 **E** office@fbu.org.uk **W** www.fbu.org.uk
General Secretary, Matthew Wrack
Membership: 33,042

FDA Centenary House, 93-95 Borough High Street, London SE1 1NL **T** 020-7401 5555 **E** info@fda.org.uk **W** www.fda.org.uk
General Secretary, Dave Penman
Membership: 16,744

GMB 22 Stephenson Way, London NW1 2HD **T** 020-7391 6700 **E** info@gmb.org.uk **W** www.gmb.org.uk
General Secretary, John Phillips
Membership: 614,494

HCSA (HOSPITAL CONSULTANTS' AND SPECIALISTS' ASSOCIATION) 1 Kingsclere Road, Basingstoke RG25 3JA **T** 01256-771777 **E** conspec@hcsa.com **W** www.hcsa.com
Chief Executive, Dr Paul Donaldson
Membership: 3,229

MU (MUSICIANS' UNION) 60–62 Clapham Road, London SW9 0JJ **T** 020-7582 5566 **E** info@theMU.org **W** www.musiciansunion.org.uk
General Secretary, Horace Trubridge
Membership: 30,421

NAHT (NATIONAL ASSOCIATION OF HEAD TEACHERS) 1 Heath Square, Haywards Heath RH16 1BL **T** 0300-303 0333 **E** info@naht.org.uk **W** www.naht.org.uk
General Secretary, Paul Whiteman
Membership: 28,600

NAPO (TRADE UNION AND PROFESSIONAL ASSOCIATION FOR FAMILY COURT AND PROBATION STAFF) 160 Falcon Road, London SW11 2NY **T** 020-7223 4887 **E** info@napo.org.uk **W** www.napo.org.uk
General Secretary, Ian Lawrence
Membership: 4,996

NARS (NATIONAL ASSOCIATION OF RACING STAFF) The Racing Centre, Fred Archer Way, Newmarket CB8 8NT **T** 01638-663411 **E** admin@naors.co.uk **W** www.naors.co.uk
Chief Executive, George McGrath
Membership: 2,137

NASUWT (NATIONAL ASSOCIATION OF SCHOOLMASTERS/ UNION OF WOMEN TEACHERS) Orion Centre, 5 Upper St Martins Lane, London WC2H 9EA **T** 020-7420 9670 **E** nasuwt@mail.nasuwt.org.uk **W** www.nasuwt.org.uk
General Secretary, Patrick Roach
Membership: 295,565

NATIONAL HOUSE BUILDING COUNCIL STAFF ASSOCIATION NHBC House, Davey Avenue, Milton Keynes MK5 8FP **E** lheritage@nhbc.co.uk **W** www.nhbc.co.uk
Acting Chair, Julia Georgiou
Membership: 686

NAUTILUS INTERNATIONAL 1–2 The Shrubberies, George Lane, London E18 1BD **T** 020-8989 6677 **E** enquiries@nautilusint.org **W** www.nautilusint.org
General Secretary, Mark Dickinson
Membership: 14,590

NEU (NATIONAL EDUCATION UNION) Hamilton House, Mabledon Place, London WC1H 9BD **T** 0345-811 8111 **W** www.neu.org.uk
General Secretaries, Dr Mary Bousted; Kevin Courtney
Membership: 450,150

NGSU (NATIONWIDE GROUP STAFF UNION) Middleton Farmhouse, 37 Main Road, Middleton Cheney OX17 2QT **T** 07793 596244 **E** ngsu@ngsu.org.uk **W** www.ngsu.co.uk
General Secretary, Tim Rose
Membership: 12,666

NSEAD (NATIONAL SOCIETY FOR EDUCATION IN ART AND DESIGN) 3 Mason's Wharf, Potley Lane, Corsham SN13 9FY T 01225-810134 E info@nsead.org W www.nsead.org
General Secretary, Michele Gregson
Membership: 1,240

NUJ (NATIONAL UNION OF JOURNALISTS) 72 Acton Street, London WC1X 9NB T 020-7843 3700 E info@nuj.org.uk W www.nuj.org.uk
General Secretary, Michelle Stanistreet
Membership: 30,261

NUM (NATIONAL UNION OF MINEWORKERS) Miners' Offices, 2 Huddersfield Road, Barnsley S70 2LS T 01226-215555 E chris.kitchen@num.org.uk W www.num.org.uk
National Secretary, Chris Kitchen
Membership: 319

PCS (PUBLIC AND COMMERCIAL SERVICES UNION) 160 Falcon Road, London SW11 2LN T 020-7924 2727 W www.pcs.org.uk
General Secretary, Mark Serwotka
Membership: 177,750

PFA (PROFESSIONAL FOOTBALLERS' ASSOCIATION) 20 Oxford Court, Manchester M2 3WQ T 0161-236 0575 E info@thepfa.co.uk W www.thepfa.com
Chief Executive, Gordon Taylor , OBE *Membership:* 2,168

POA (PROFESSIONAL TRADE UNION FOR PRISON, CORRECTIONAL AND SECURE PSYCHIATRIC WORKERS) Cronin House, 245 Church Street, London N9 9HW T 020-8803 0255 E general@poauk.org.uk W www.poauk.org.uk
General Secretary, Steve Gillan
Membership: 30,011

PROSPECT New Prospect House, 8 Leake Street, London SE1 7NN T 020-7902 6600 E enquiries@prospect.org.uk W www.prospect.org.uk
General Secretary, Mike Clancy
Membership: 143,770

RCM (ROYAL COLLEGE OF MIDWIVES) 15 Mansfield Street, London W1G 9NH T 030-0303 0444 W www.rcm.org.uk
General Secretary, Gill Walton
Membership: 35,428

RMT (NATIONAL UNION OF RAIL, MARITIME AND TRANSPORT WORKERS) Unity House, 39 Chalton Street, London NW1 1JD T 020-7387 4771 E info@rmt.org.uk W www.rmt.org.uk
General Secretary, Mick Cash
Membership: 85,474

SOR (SOCIETY OF RADIOGRAPHERS) 207 Providence Square, Mill Street, London SE1 2EW T 020-7740 7200 W www.sor.org
Chief Executive, Richard Evans
Membership: 23,320

TSSA (TRANSPORT SALARIED STAFFS' ASSOCIATION) 2nd Floor, 17 Devonshire Square, London EC2M 4SQ T 020-7387 2101 E enquiries@tssa.org.uk W www.tssa.org.uk
General Secretary, Manuel Cortes
Membership: 18,494

UCAC (UNDEB CENEDLAETHOL ATHRAWON CYMRU/ NATIONAL UNION OF THE TEACHERS OF WALES) Prif Swyddfa UCAC, Ffordd Penglais, Aberystwyth SY23 3EU T 01970-639950 E ucac@ucac.cymru W www.ucac.cymru
General Secretary, Dilwyn Roberts-Young
Membership: 4,028

UCU (UNIVERSITY AND COLLEGE UNION) Carlow Street, London NW1 7LH T 020-7756 2500 W www.ucu.org.uk
General Secretary, Jo Grady
Membership: 108,515

UNISON 130 Euston Road, London NW1 2AY T 0800-085 7857 W www.unison.org.uk
General Secretary, Dave Prentis
Membership: 1,193,991

UNITE 128 Theobald's Road, London WC1X 8TN T 020-7611 2500 W www.unitetheunion.org
General Secretary, Len McCluskey
Membership: 1,233,646

URTU (UNITED ROAD TRANSPORT UNION) Almond House, Oak Green, Cheadle, Hulme SK8 6QL T 0800-526 639 E info@urtu.com W www.urtu.com
General Secretary, Robert Monks
Membership: 9,400

USDAW (UNION OF SHOP, DISTRIBUTIVE AND ALLIED WORKERS) 188 Wilmslow Road, Manchester M14 6LJ T 0161-224 2804 E enquiries@usdaw.org.uk W www.usdaw.org.uk
General Secretary, Paddy Lillis
Membership: 433,260

WGGB (WRITERS' GUILD OF GREAT BRITAIN) 134 Tooley Street, London SE1 2TU T 020-7833 0777 E admin@writersguild.org.uk W www.writersguild.org.uk
General Secretary, Ellie Peers
Membership: 2,242

NON-AFFILIATED UNIONS
As at December 2020

ASCL (ASSOCIATION OF SCHOOL AND COLLEGE LEADERS) 130 Regent Road, Leicester LE1 7PG T 0116-299 1122 E info@ascl.org.uk W www.ascl.org.uk
General Secretary, Geoff Barton
Membership: 20,500

BDA (BRITISH DENTAL ASSOCIATION) 64 Wimpole Street, London W1G 8YS T 020-7935 0875 E enquiries@bda.org W www.bda.org
General Secretary, Eddie Crouch
Membership: 15,000

CIOJ (CHARTERED INSTITUTE OF JOURNALISTS) T 020-7252 1187 E memberservices@cioj.co.uk W www.cioj.co.uk
General Secretary, Dominic Cooper
Membership: 1,000 (est.)

SOCIETY OF AUTHORS 24 Bedford Row, London WC1R 4EH T 020-7373 6642 E info@societyofauthors.org W www.societyofauthors.org
Chief Executive, Nicola Solomon
Membership: 10,000 (est.)

SSTA (SCOTTISH SECONDARY TEACHERS' ASSOCIATION) West End House, 14 West End Place, Edinburgh EH11 2ED T 0131-313 7300 E info@ssta.org.uk W www.ssta.org.uk
General Secretary, Seamus Searson
Membership: 6,500 (est.)

SPORTS BODIES

SPORTS COUNCILS

SPORT AND RECREATION ALLIANCE Holborn Tower,
137–145 High Holborn, London WC1V 6PL **T** 020-7976 3900
E info@sportandrecreation.org.uk
W www.sportandrecreation.org.uk
Chief Executive, Lisa Wainwright
SPORT ENGLAND 21 Bloomsbury Street, London WC1B 3HF
T 0345-850 8508 **E** info@sportengland.org
W www.sportengland.org
Chief Executive, Tim Hollingsworth
SPORT NORTHERN IRELAND House of Sport, 2A Upper
Malone Road, Belfast BT9 5LA **T** 028-9038 1222
E info@sportni.net **W** www.sportni.net
Chief Executive, Antoinette McKeown
SPORTSCOTLAND Doges, Templeton on the Green, 62
Templeton Street, Glasgow G40 1DA **T** 0141-534 6500
E sportscotland.enquiries@sportscotland.org.uk
W www.sportscotland.org.uk
Chief Executive, Stewart Harris
SPORT WALES Sophia Gardens, Cardiff CF11 9SW
T 0300-300 3111 **E** info@sportwales.org.uk **W** www.sport.wales
Chief Executive, Sarah Powell
UK SPORT 21 Bloomsbury Street, London WC1B 3HF
T 020-7211 5100 **E** info@uksport.gov.uk
W www.uksport.gov.uk
Chief Executive, Liz Nicholl, CBE

AMERICAN FOOTBALL

BRITISH AMERICAN FOOTBALL ASSOCIATION
1 Franchise Street, Kidderminster DY11 6RE
E human.resources@britishamericanfootball.org
W www.britishamericanfootball.org
Chair, Nichole McCulloch

ANGLING

ANGLING TRUST Eastwood House, 6 Rainbow Street,
Herefordshire HR6 8DQ **T** 0343-507 7006
E admin@anglingtrust.net **W** www.anglingtrust.net
Chief Executive, Mark Lloyd

ARCHERY

ARCHERY GB Lilleshall National Sports Centre, Newport
TF10 9AT **T** 0195-267 7888 **E** enquiries@archerygb.org
W www.archerygb.org
Chief Executive, Neil Armitage

ASSOCIATION FOOTBALL

ENGLISH FOOTBALL LEAGUE EFL House, 10-12 West Cliff,
Preston PR1 8HU **T** 01772-325800 **E** enquiries@efl.com
W www.efl.com
Chief Executive, Shaun Harvey
FOOTBALL ASSOCIATION Wembley Stadium, PO Box 1966,
London SW1P 9EQ **T** 0800-169 1863 **E** info@thefa.com
W www.thefa.com
Chief Executive, Martin Glenn
FOOTBALL ASSOCIATION OF WALES 11–12 Neptune
Court, Vanguard Way, Cardiff CF24 5PJ **T** 029-2043 5830
E info@faw.co.uk **W** www.faw.cymru
Chief Executive, Jonathan Ford
IRISH FOOTBALL ASSOCIATION Donegal Avenue, Belfast
BT12 6LU **T** 028-9066 9458 **E** info@irishfa.com
W www.irishfa.com
Chief Executive, Patrick Nelson

PREMIER LEAGUE 30 Gloucester Place, London W1U 8PL
T 020-7864 9000 **E** info@premierleague.com
W www.premierleague.com
Chief Executive, vacant
SCOTTISH FOOTBALL ASSOCIATION Hampden Park,
Glasgow G42 9AY **T** 0141-616 6000 **E** info@scottishfa.co.uk
W www.scottishfa.co.uk
Chief Executive, Ian Maxwell
SCOTTISH PROFESSIONAL FOOTBALL LEAGUE
Hampden Park, Glasgow G42 9DE **T** 0141-620 4140
E info@spfl.co.uk **W** www.spfl.co.uk
Chief Executive, Neil Doncaster

ATHLETICS

BRITISH ATHLETICS Athletics House, Alexander Stadium,
Birmingham B42 2BE **T** 0121-713 8400
E majorevents@britishathletics.org.uk
W www.britishathletics.org.uk
Chief Executive, Nigel Holl (interim)
ATHLETICS NORTHERN IRELAND Athletics House, Old
Coach Road, Belfast BT9 5PR **T** 028-9060 2707
E info@athleticsni.org **W** www.athleticsni.org
General Secretary, John Allen
SCOTTISH ATHLETICS Caledonia House, Edinburgh
EH12 9DQ **T** 0131-539 7320 **E** admin@scottishathletics.org.uk
W www.scottishathletics.org.uk
Chief Executive, Mark Munro
WELSH ATHLETICS Cardiff International Sports Stadium,
Leckwith Road, Cardiff CF11 8AZ **T** 029-2064 4870
E office@welshathletics.org **W** www.welshathletics.org
Chief Executive, Matt Newman

BADMINTON

BADMINTON ENGLAND National Badminton Centre,
Bradwell Road, Milton Keynes MK8 9LA **T** 01908-268400
E enquiries@badmintonengland.co.uk
W www.badmintonengland.co.uk
Chief Executive, Adrian Christy
BADMINTON SCOTLAND Sir Craig Reedie Badminton
Centre, 40 Bogmoor Place, Glasgow G51 4TQ **T** 0141-445 1218
E enquiries@badmintonscotland.org.uk
W www.badmintonscotland.org.uk
Chief Executive, Keith Russell
BADMINTON WALES Sport Wales National Centre, Sophia
Gardens, Cardiff CF11 9SW **T** 029-2033 4938
E enquiries@badminton.wales **W** www.badminton.wales
General Manager, Gareth Hall

BASEBALL

BASEBALLSOFTBALL UK Marathon House, 190 Great Dover
Street, London SE1 4YB **T** 020-7453 7055
W www.baseballsoftballuk.com
Chief Executive, John Boyd
BRITISH BASEBALL FEDERATION Marathon House, 190
Great Dane Street, London SE1 4YB **T** 0207-7453 7055
W www.britishbaseballfederation.org
President, Gerry Perez

BASKETBALL

BASKETBALL ENGLAND Etihad Stadium, Rowsley Street,
Manchester M11 3FF **T** 0300-600 1170
E info@basketballengland.co.uk
W www.basketballengland.co.uk
Chief Executive, Stewart Kellett

BASKETBALL SCOTLAND Caledonia House, Edinburgh
EH12 9DQ **T** 0131-317 7260
E enquiries@basketball-scotland.com
W www.basketballscotland.co.uk
Chief Executive, Kevin Pringle

BILLIARDS AND SNOOKER

WORLD SNOOKER 75 Whiteladies Road, Bristol BS8 2NT
T 0117-317 8200 **E** info@worldsnooker.com
W www.worldsnooker.com
Chief Executive, Steve Dawson

BOBSLEIGH

BRITISH BOBSLEIGH & SKELETON ASSOCIATION
University of Bath, Claverton Down, Bath BA2 7AY
T 01225-384343 **E** office@thebbsa.co.uk **W** www.thebbsa.co.uk
Chair, Christopher Rodrigues

BOWLS

BOWLS ENGLAND Riverside House, Milverton Hill, Royal
Leamington Spa CV32 5HZ **T** 01926-334609
E enquiries@bowlsengland.com **W** www.bowlsengland.com
Chief Executive, Tony Allcock, MBE
BRITISH ISLES BOWLS COUNCIL
E bibcsecretary@aol.co.uk **W** www.britishislesbowls.com
President, David Graham, OBE
ENGLISH INDOOR BOWLING ASSOCIATION David
Cornwell House, Bowling Green, Melton Mowbray LE13 0FA
T 01664-481900 **E** enquiries@eiba.co.uk **W** www.eiba.co.uk
Chief Executive, Peter Thompson

BOXING

BRITISH BOXING BOARD OF CONTROL 14 North Road,
Cardiff CF10 3DY **T** 029-2036 7000 **E** admin@bbbofc.com
W www.bbbofc.com
General Secretary, Robert Smith
ENGLAND BOXING English Institute of Sport, Coleridge Road,
Sheffield S9 5DA **T** 0114-223 5654
E enquiries@englandboxing.org **W** www.abae.co.uk
Chief Executive, Gethin Jenkins

CANOEING

BRITISH CANOEING National Water Sport Centre, Adbolton
Lane, Nottingham NG12 2LU **T** 0300-011 9500
E info@britishcanoeing.org.uk **W** www.britishcanoeing.org.uk
Chief Executive, David Joy

CHESS

ENGLISH CHESS FEDERATION The Watch Oak, Chain Lane,
Battle TN33 0YD **T** 01424-775222 **E** office@englishchess.org.uk
W www.englishchess.org.uk
Chief Executive, Mike Truran

CRICKET

ENGLAND AND WALES CRICKET BOARD Lord's Cricket
Ground, St John's Wood Road, London NW8 8QZ
T 020-7432 1200 **W** www.ecb.co.uk
Chief Executive, Tom Harrison
MCC Lord's Cricket Ground, London NW8 8QN **T** 020-7616 8500
E reception@mcc.org.uk **W** www.lords.org
Chief Executive and Secretary, Guy Lavender

CROQUET

CROQUET ASSOCIATION Old Bath Road, Cheltenham
GL53 7DF **T** 01242-242318 **E** caoffice@croquet.org.uk
W www.croquet.org.uk
Manager, Mark Suter

CURLING

BRITISH CURLING c/o The Royal Caledonian Curling Club,
Ochil House, Stirling FK7 7XE **E** info@britishcurling.com
W www.britishcurling.org.uk
Chief Executive, Bruce Crawford
SCOTTISH CURLING Ochil House, Stirling FK7 7XE
T 0131-333 3003 **E** office@scottishcurling.org
W www.scottishcurling.org
Chief Executive, Bruce Crawford

CYCLING

BRITISH CYCLING FEDERATION Stuart Street, Manchester
M11 4DQ **T** 0161-274 2000 **E** info@britishcycling.org.uk
W www.britishcycling.org.uk
Chief Executive, Julie Harrington

DARTS

BRITISH DARTS ORGANISATION Unit 4, Glan-y-Llyn
Industrial Estate, Cardiff CF15 7JD **T** 029-2081 1815
E contact@bdodarts.com **W** www.bdodarts.com
Chairman, Derek Jacklin

EQUESTRIANISM

BRITISH EQUESTRIAN FEDERATION Abbey Park,
Kenilworth CV8 2RH **T** 024-7669 8871 **E** info@bef.co.uk
W www.bef.co.uk
Chief Executive, Nick Fellows
BRITISH EVENTING Abbey Park, Kenilworth CV8 2RN
T 024-7669 8856 **E** info@britisheventing.com
W www.britisheventing.com
Chief Executive, David Holmes

ETON FIVES

ETON FIVES ASSOCIATION 45 Sandhills Crescent, Solihull
B91 3UE **T** 07833-600230 **W** www.etonfives.com
Chair, Chris Davies

FENCING

BRITISH FENCING 1 Baron's Gate, 33 Rothschild Road,
London W4 5HT **T** 020-8742 3032
E headoffice@britishfencing.com **W** www.britishfencing.com
Chief Executive, Georgina Usher

GLIDING

BRITISH GLIDING ASSOCIATION 8 Merus Court, Meridian
Business Park, Leicester LE19 1RJ **T** 0116-289 2956
E office@gliding.co.uk **W** www.gliding.co.uk
Chief Executive, Pete Stratten

GOLF

ENGLAND GOLF The National Golf Centre, Woodhall Spa
LN10 6PU **T** 01526-354500 **E** info@englandgolf.org
W www.englandgolf.org
Chief Executive, Nick Pink
THE ROYAL AND ANCIENT GOLF CLUB Golf Place, St
Andrews KY16 9JD **T** 01334-460000
E thesecretary@randagc.org **W** www.randa.org
Chief Executive and Secretary, Martin Slumbers

GYMNASTICS

BRITISH GYMNASTICS Ford Hall, Lilleshall National Sports
Centre, Newport TF10 9NB **T** 0345-129 7129
E information@british-gymnastics.org
W www.british-gymnastics.org
Chief Executive, Jane Allen

HANDBALL

ENGLAND HANDBALL The Halliwell Jones Stadium, Winwick Road, Warrington WA2 7NE **T** 01925-246482
E office@englandhandball.com **W** www.englandhandball.com
Chief Executive, David Meli

HOCKEY

ENGLAND HOCKEY Bisham Abbey National Sports Centre, Marlow SL7 1RR **T** 01628-897500
E enquiries@englandhockey.co.uk **W** www.englandhockey.co.uk
Chief Executive, Sally Munday
HOCKEY WALES Sport Wales National Centre, Sophia Close, Cardiff CF11 9SW **T** 0300-300 3126 **E** info@hockeywales.org.uk
W www.hockeywales.org.uk
Chief Executive, Ria Male (interim)
SCOTTISH HOCKEY UNION Glasgow National Hockey Centre, 8 King's Drive, Glasgow G40 1HB **T** 0141-550 5999
W www.scottish-hockey.org.uk
Chief Executive, David Sweetman

HORSERACING

BRITISH HORSERACING AUTHORITY 75 High Holborn, London WC1V 6LS **T** 020-7152 0000
E info@britishhorseracing.com **W** www.britishhorseracing.com
Chief Executive, Nick Rust
THE JOCKEY CLUB 75 High Holborn, London WC1V 6LS
T 020-7611 1800 **E** info@thejockeyclub.co.uk
W www.thejockeyclub.co.uk
Chief Executive, Simon Bazalgette

ICE SKATING

NATIONAL ICE SKATING ASSOCIATION English Institute of Sport, Coleridge Road, Sheffield S9 5DA **T** 0115-988 8060
E info@iceskating.org.uk **W** www.iceskating.org.uk
Chair, Rob Jones

LACROSSE

ENGLISH LACROSSE ASSOCIATION National Squash Centre and Regional Arena, Gate 13, Manchester M11 3FF
T 0161-974 7757 **E** info@englandlacrosse.co.uk
W www.englandlacrosse.co.uk
Chief Executive, Mark Coups

LAWN TENNIS

LAWN TENNIS ASSOCIATION National Tennis Centre, 100 Priory Lane, London SW15 5JQ **T** 020-8487 7000
E info@lta.org.uk **W** www.lta.org.uk
Chief Executive, Scott Lloyd

MARTIAL ARTS

BRITISH JUDO ASSOCIATION Floor 1, Kudhail House, 238 Birmingham Road, Great Barr B43 7AH **T** 0121-728 6920
E bja@britishjudo.org.uk **W** www.britishjudo.org.uk
Chief Executive, Andrew Scoular
BRITISH JU JITSU ASSOCIATION 5 Avenue Parade, Accrington BB5 6PN **T** 03333-202039 **E** bjjagb@icloud.com
W www.bjjagb.com
Chairman, Prof. Martin Dixon
BRITISH TAEKWONDO Manchester Regional Arena, Rowsley Street, Manchester M11 3FF **T** 01623-382020
E admin@britishtaekwondo.org
W www.britishtaekwondo.org.uk
Chair, Jonny Cowan (interim)

MODERN PENTATHLON

PENTATHLON GB Sports Training Village, University of Bath, Bath BA2 7AY **T** 01225-386808 **E** admin@pentathlongb.org
W www.pentathlongb.org
Chief Executive, Sara Heath

MOTOR SPORTS

AUTO-CYCLE UNION ACU House, Rugby CV21 2YX
T 01788-566400 **E** admin@acu.org.uk **W** www.acu.org.uk
General Secretary, Gary Thompson, MBE
MOTORSPORT UK Motorsport UK House, Riverside Park, Colnbrook SL3 0HG **T** 01753-765000 **W** www.motorsportuk.org
Chief Executive, Hugh Chambers
SCOTTISH AUTO CYCLE UNION 28 West Main Street, Uphall EH52 5DW **T** 01506-858354 **E** office@sacu.co.uk
W www.sacu.co.uk
Chair, Sandy Mack

MOUNTAINEERING

BRITISH MOUNTAINEERING COUNCIL The Old Church, 177–179 Burton Road, Manchester M20 2BB **T** 0161-445 6111
E office@thebmc.co.uk **W** www.thebmc.co.uk
Chief Executive, Dave Turnbull

MULTI-SPORTS BODIES

ACTIVITY ALLIANCE Loughborough University, 3 Oakwood Drive, LE11 3QF **T** 01509-227750 **W** www.activityalliance.org.uk
Chief Executive, Barry Horne
BRITISH OLYMPIC ASSOCIATION 60 Charlotte Street, London W1T 2NU **T** 020-7842 5700 **E** boa@boa.org.uk
W www.teamgb.com
Chief Executive, Bill Sweeney
BRITISH PARALYMPIC ASSOCIATION 60 Charlotte Street, London W1T 2NU **T** 020-7842 5789 **E** info@paralympics.org.uk
W www.paralympics.org.uk
Chief Executive, Mike Sharrock
BRITISH UNIVERSITIES AND COLLEGES SPORT 20–24 Kings Bench Street, London SE1 0QX **T** 020-7633 5080
E info@bucs.org.uk **W** www.bucs.org.uk
Chief Executive, Vince Mayne
COMMONWEALTH GAMES ENGLAND 5th floor, Holborn Tower, 137–144 High Holborn, London WC1V 6PL
T 020-7831 3444 **E** info@teamengland.org
W www.teamengland.org
Chief Executive, Paul Blanchard
COMMONWEALTH GAMES FEDERATION Commonwealth House, 55–58 Pall Mall, London SW1Y 5JH
T 020-7747 6427 **E** info@thecgf.com **W** www.thecgf.com
Chief Executive, David Grevemberg, CBE

NETBALL

ENGLAND NETBALL SportPark, 3 Oakwood Drive, Loughborough LE11 3QF **T** 01509-277850
E info@englandnetball.co.uk **W** www.englandnetball.co.uk
Chief Executive, Joanna Adams
NETBALL NI Unit F, Curlew Pavilion, Portside Business Park, Belfast BT3 9ED **T** 028-9073 6320
E bookingsandadmin@netballni.org **W** www.netballni.org
Chair, Geoff Wilson
NETBALL SCOTLAND Emirates Arena, 1000 London Road, Glasgow G40 3HY **T** 0141-428 3460
E membership@netballscotland.com
W www.netballscotland.com
Chief Executive, Claire Nelson
WELSH NETBALL ASSOCIATION Sport Wales National Centre, Sophia Gardens, Cardiff CF11 9SW **T** 029-2033 4950
E welshnetball@welshnetball.com **W** www.welshnetball.com
Chief Executive, Sarah Jones

ORIENTEERING

BRITISH ORIENTEERING Scholes Mill, Old Coach Road, Matlock DE4 5FY **T** 01629-583037
E info@britishorienteering.org.uk
W www.britishorienteering.org.uk
Chief Executive, Peter Hart

POLO

THE HURLINGHAM POLO ASSOCIATION Manor Farm, Little Coxwell, Faringdon SN7 7LW **T** 01367-242828 **E** enquiries@hpa-polo.co.uk **W** www.hpa-polo.co.uk
Chief Executive, David Woodd

RACKETS AND REAL TENNIS

TENNIS AND RACKETS ASSOCIATION c/o The Queen's Club, Palliser Road, London W14 9EQ **T** 020-7835 6937 **E** office@tennisandrackets.com **W** www.tennisandrackets.com
Chief Executive, C. S. Davies

ROWING

BRITISH ROWING 6 Lower Mall, London W6 9DJ
T 020-8237 6700 **E** info@britishrowing.org
W www.britishrowing.org
Chief Executive, Andy Parkinson
HENLEY ROYAL REGATTA Regatta Headquarters, Henley-on-Thames RG9 2LY **T** 01491-572153 **W** www.hrr.co.uk
Secretary, Daniel Grist

RUGBY LEAGUE

BRITISH AMATEUR RUGBY LEAGUE ASSOCIATION West Yorkshire House, 4 New North Parade, Huddersfield HD1 5JP **T** 01484-510682 **E** secretary@barla.org.uk
W www.barla.org.uk
Chair, Sue Taylor
RUGBY FOOTBALL LEAGUE Red Hall, Red Hall Lane, Leeds LS17 8NB **T** 0330-111 1113 **E** enquiries@rfl.uk.co.uk
W www.rugby-league.com
Chief Executive, Ralph Rimmer

RUGBY UNION

IRISH RUGBY FOOTBALL UNION 10–12 Lansdowne Road, Dublin 4 **T** (+353) 1647 3800 **E** info@irishrugby.ie
W www.irishrugby.ie
Chief Executive, Philip Browne
RUGBY FOOTBALL UNION Rugby House, Twickenham Stadium, 200 Whitton Road, Twickenham TW2 7BA
T 0871-222 2120 **E** enquiries@therfu.com
W www.englandrugby.com
Chief Executive, Bill Sweeney
RUGBY FOOTBALL UNION FOR WOMEN Rugby House, Twickenham Stadium, 200 Whitton Road, Twickenham TW2 7BA **T** 0871-222 2120 **E** enquiries@therfu.com
W www.englandrugby.com
Managing Director, Rosie Williams
SCOTTISH RUGBY UNION BT Murrayfield, Edinburgh EH12 5PJ **T** 0131-346 5000 **E** feedback@sru.org.uk
W www.scottishrugby.org
Chief Executive, Mark Dodson
SCOTTISH WOMEN'S RUGBY UNION BT Murrayfield, Edinburgh EH12 5PJ **T** 0131-346 5000 **E** feedback@sru.org.uk
W www.scottishrugby.org
Chief Executive, Mark Dodson
WELSH RUGBY UNION Principality Stadium, Westgate Street, Cardiff CF10 1NS **T** 0844-249 1999 **E** info@wru.co.uk
W www.wru.wales
Chief Executive, Martyn Phillips

SHOOTING

BRITISH SHOOTING Bisham Abbey National Sports Centre, Marlow Road, Marlow SL7 1RR **T** 01628-488800
E admin@britishshooting.org.uk **W** www.britishshooting.org.uk
Chief Executive, Hamish McInnes
CLAY PIGEON SHOOTING ASSOCIATION Edmonton House, National Shooting Centre, Brookwood, Woking GU24 0NP **T** 01483-485400 **E** info@cpsa.co.uk
W www.cpsa.co.uk
Chief Executive, Iain Parker

NATIONAL RIFLE ASSOCIATION Bisley Camp, Brookwood GU24 0PB **T** 01483-797777 **E** info@nra.org.uk
W www.nra.org.uk
Chief Executive, John Webster
NATIONAL SMALL-BORE RIFLE ASSOCIATION Lord Roberts Centre, Bisley Camp, Woking GU24 0NP
T 01483-485502 **W** www.nsra.co.uk
Chair, Robert Newman

SKIING AND SNOWBOARDING

GB SNOWSPORT 60 Charlotte Street, London W1T 2NU
T 020-7842 5764 **E** info@gbsnowsport.com
W www.gbsnowsport.com
Chief Executive, Victoria Gosling, OBE

SPEEDWAY

BRITISH SPEEDWAY ACU Headquarters, Wood Street, Rugby CV21 2YX **T** 01788-560648 **E** office@speedwaygb.co.uk
W www.speedwaygb.co.uk
Chair, Keith Chapman

SQUASH

ENGLAND SQUASH National Squash Centre, Manchester M11 3FF **T** 0161-231 4499 **W** www.englandsquash.com
Chief Executive, Keir Worth
SCOTTISH SQUASH Oriam, Edinburgh EH14 4AS
T 0131-451 8525 **E** info@scottishsquash.org
W www.scottishsquash.org
Chief Executive, Maggie Still
WALES SQUASH AND RACKETBALL Sport Wales National Centre, Sophia Close, Cardiff CF11 9SW **T** 0300-300 3121
W www.walessquashandracketball.co.uk
General Manager, Gareth Hall

SUB-AQUA

BRITISH SUB-AQUA CLUB Telford's Quay, South Pier Road, Ellesmere Port CH65 4FL **T** 0151-350 6200 **E** info@bsac.com
W www.bsac.com
Chief Executive, Mary Tetley

SWIMMING

SWIM ENGLAND Pavilion 3, Sport Park, Loughborough LE11 3QF **T** 01509-618700 **E** customerservices@swimming.org
W www.swimming.org
Chief Executive, Jane Nickerson
SCOTTISH SWIMMING National Swimming Academy, University of Stirling, FK9 4LA **T** 01786-466520
E info@scottishswimming.com **W** www.scottishswimming.com
Chief Executive, Forbes Dunlop
SWIM WALES WNPS, Sketty Lane, Swansea SA2 8QG
T 01792-513636 **W** www.swimwales.org
Chief Executive, Fergus Feeney

TABLE TENNIS

TABLE TENNIS ENGLAND Bradwell Road, Milton Keynes MK8 9LA **T** 01908-208860 **E** help@tabletennisengland.co.uk
W www.tabletennisengland.co.uk
Chief Executive, Sara Sutcliffe
TABLE TENNIS SCOTLAND Caledonia House, South Gyle, Edinburgh EH12 9DQ **T** 0131-317 8077
E info@tabletennisscotland.co.uk
W www.tabletennisscotland.co.uk
Chair, Terry McLernon, MBE
TABLE TENNIS WALES Glanrhyd, Ebbw View, Ebbw Vale NP23 5NU **T** 01244-571335 **W** www.tabletennis.wales
Company Secretary, Neil O'Connell

TRIATHLON

BRITISH TRIATHLON PO Box 25, Loughborough LE11 3WX
T 01509-226161 **E** info@britishtriathlon.org
W www.britishtriathlon.org
Chief Executive, Andy Salmon

VOLLEYBALL

NORTHERN IRELAND VOLLEYBALL ASSOCIATION 7
Greengage Cottages, Ballymoney BT53 6GZ
W www.nivolleyball.com
General Secretary, Paddy Elder
SCOTTISH VOLLEYBALL ASSOCIATION 48 The
Pleasance, Edinburgh EH8 9TJ **T** 0131-556 4633
E info@scottishvolleyball.org **W** www.scottishvolleyball.org
Chief Executive, Margaret Ann Fleming
VOLLEYBALL ENGLAND SportPark, Loughborough University,
3 Oakwood Drive, Loughborough LE11 3QF **T** 01509-227722
E info@volleyballengland.org **W** www.volleyballengland.org
Chief Executive, Janet Inman
VOLLEYBALL WALES 13 Beckgrove Close, Cardiff CF24 2SE
T 029-2041 6537 **E** yperkins@cardiffmet.ac.uk
W www.volleyballwales.org
Chair, Yvonne Perkins

WALKING

RACE WALKING ASSOCIATION Hufflers, Heard's Lane,
Brentwood CM15 0SF **T** 01277-220687
E racewalkingassociation@btinternet.com
W www.racewalkingassociation.com
Hon. General Secretary, Colin Vesty

WATER SKIING

BRITISH WATER SKI AND WAKEBOARD The Forum,
Hanworth Lane, Chertsey KT16 9JX **T** 01932-560007
E info@bwsf.co.uk **W** www.bwsw.org.uk
Chief Executive, Patrick Donovan

WEIGHTLIFTING

BRITISH WEIGHT LIFTING St Ann's Mill, Kirkstall Road,
Leeds LS5 3AE **T** 0113-224 9402
E enquiries@britishweightlifting.org
W www.britishweightlifting.org
Chief Executive, Ashley Metcalfe

WRESTLING

BRITISH WRESTLING ASSOCIATION 41 Great Clowes St,
Salford M7 1RQ **T** 0161-835 2112 **E** admin@britishwrestling.org
W www.britishwrestling.org
Chief Executive, Colin Nicholson

YACHTING

ROYAL YACHTING ASSOCIATION RYA House, Ensign
Way, Southampton SO31 4YA **T** 023-8060 4100
E enquiries@rya.org.uk **W** www.rya.org.uk
Chief Executive, Sarah Treseder

CHARITIES AND SOCIETIES

The following is a selection of charities, societies and non-profit organisations in the UK and does not represent a comprehensive list. For professional and employment-related organisations, *see* Professional Education and Trade and Professional Bodies.

ABBEYFIELD SOCIETY (1956), St Peter's House, 2 Bricket Road, St Albans AL1 3JW T 01727-857536
E post@abbeyfield.com W www.abbeyfield.com
Chief Executive, David McCullough

ACTIONAID (1972), 33–39 Bowling Green Lane, London EC1R 0BJ T 01460 238000 E supportercontact@actionaid.org
W www.actionaid.org
Chief Executive, Girish Menon

ACTION FOR CHILDREN (1869), 3 The Boulevard, Watford WD18 8AG T 0300 123-2112 E ask.us@actionforchildren.org.uk
W www.actionforchildren.org.uk
Chief Executive, Julie Bentley

ACTION MEDICAL RESEARCH (1952), Vincent House, Horsham RH12 2DP T 01403-210406 E info@action.org.uk
W www.action.org.uk
Chief Executive, Julie Buckler

ACTION ON HEARING LOSS (1911), 1–3 Highbury Station Road, London N1 1SE
T 0808-808 0123, **Textphone** 0808-808 9000
E informationline@hearingloss.org.uk
W www.actiononhearingloss.org.uk
Chief Executive, Mark Atkinson

ACTORS' BENEVOLENT FUND (1882), 6 Adam Street, London WC2N 6AD T 020-7836 6378 E office@abf.org.uk
W www.actorsbenevolentfund.co.uk
General Secretary, Jonathan Ellicott

ACTORS' CHILDREN'S TRUST (1896), 58 Bloomsbury Street, London WC1B 3QT T 020-7636 7868
E robert@actorschildren.org W www.actorschildren.org
Executive Director, Robert Ashby

ADAM SMITH INSTITUTE (1977), 23 Great Smith Street, London SW1P 3DJ T 020-7222 4995 E info@adamsmith.org
W www.adamsmith.org
Director, Dr Eamonn Butler

ADDACTION (1967), Gate House, 1–3 St John's Square, London EC1M 4DH T 020-7251 5860 E info@addaction.org.uk
W www.addaction.org.uk
Chief Executive, Mike Dixon

ADVERTISING STANDARDS AUTHORITY (1962), Mid City Place, 71 High Holborn, London WC1V 6QT
T 020-7492 2222 W www.asa.org.uk
Chief Executive, Guy Parker

AFASIC (1968), 209–211 City Road, London EC1V 1JN
T 020-7490 9410 W www.afasic.org.uk
Chief Executive, Linda Lascelles

AGE CYMRU (2010), Ground Floor, Mariners House, East Moors Road CF24 5TD T 029-2043 1555
E advice@agecymru.org.uk W www.ageuk.org.uk/cymru
Chief Executive, Victoria Lloyd (interim)

AGE SCOTLAND (1943), Causewayside House, 160 Causewayside, Edinburgh EH9 1PR T 0333-323 2400
E info@agescotland.org.uk W www.ageuk.org.uk/scotland
Chief Executive, Brian Sloan

AGE UK (2010), Tavis House, 1–6 Tavistock Square, London WC1H 9NA T 0800-169 8787 E contact@ageuk.org.uk
W www.ageuk.org.uk
Chief Executive, Steph Harland

ALEXANDRA ROSE CHARITY (1912), 5 Mead Lane, Farnham GU9 7DY T 01252-726171 E info@alexandrarose.org
W www.alexandrarose.org.uk
Chief Executive, Jonathan Pauling

ALZHEIMER'S SOCIETY (1979), 43–44 Crutched Friars, London EC3N 2AE T 0330-333 0804
E enquiries@alzheimers.org.uk W www.alzheimers.org.uk
Chief Executive, Jeremy Hughes

AMNESTY INTERNATIONAL UK (1961), The Human Rights Action Centre, 17–25 New Inn Yard, London EC2A 3EA
T 020-7033 1500 E sct@amnesty.org.uk
W www.amnesty.org.uk
UK Director, Kate Allen

AMREF UK (1957), 15–18 White Lion Street, London N1 9PD
T 020-7269 5520 E info@amrefuk.org W www.amrefuk.org
Chief Executive, Frances Longley

ANGLO-BELGIAN SOCIETY (1982), 15 Westmoreland Terrace, London SW1V 4AG
E secretary@anglobelgiansociety.com
W www.anglobelgiansociety.com
Chair, Caroline Colvin, OBE

ANGLO-DANISH SOCIETY (1924), 43 Maresfield Gardens, London NW3 5TF T 07934-236686
E info@anglo-danishsociety.org.uk
W www.anglo-danishsociety.org.uk
Chair, Wayne Harber, OBE

ANGLO-NORSE SOCIETY (1918), 25 Belgrave Square, London SW1X 8QD T 01825 840-043 E info@anglo-norse.org.uk
W www.anglo-norse.org.uk
Chair, Sir Richard Dales, KCVO, CMG

ANIMAL HEALTH TRUST (1942), Lanwades Park, Newmarket CB8 7UU T 01638-751000 E info@aht.org.uk
W www.aht.org.uk
Chief Executive, Dr Mark Vaudin

ANTHONY NOLAN (1974), 2 Heathgate Place, 75–87 Agincourt Road, London NW3 2NU T 0303-303 0303
W www.anthonynolan.org
Chief Executive, Henny Braund

ANTI-SLAVERY INTERNATIONAL (1839), Thomas Clarkson House, The Stableyard, London SW9 9TL
T 020-7501 8920 E info@antislavery.org W www.antislavery.org
CEO, Jasmine O'Connor

ARCHITECTS BENEVOLENT SOCIETY (1850), 43 Portland Place, London W1B 1QH T 020-7580 2823
E help@absnet.org.uk W www.absnet.org.uk
Chief Executive, Robert Ball

ARCHITECTURAL HERITAGE FUND (1976), 3 Spital Yard, London E1 6AQ T 020-7925 0199 E ahf@ahfund.org.uk
W www.ahfund.org.uk
Chief Executive, Matthew McKeague

ARLIS/UK AND IRELAND (1969), National Art Library, Victoria & Albert Museum, London SW7 2RL E info@arlis.net
W www.arlis.net
Chair, Carla Marchesan

ART FUND (1903), 2 Granary Square, King's Cross, London N1C 4BH T 020-7225 4800 E info@artfund.org
W www.artfund.org
Director, Dr Stephen Deuchar

ASSOCIATION FOR LANGUAGE LEARNING (1990), 1A Duffield Road, Derby DE21 5DR T 01332-227779
E info@all-languages.org.uk W www.all-languages.org.uk
Director, Rachel Middleton

ASSOCIATION FOR SCIENCE EDUCATION (1901), College Lane, Hatfield AL10 9AA **T** 01707-283000 **E** info@ase.org.uk **W** www.ase.org.uk
Chief Executive, Shaun Reason

ASSOCIATION FOR THE PROTECTION OF RURAL SCOTLAND (1926), Dolphin House, 4 Hunter Square, Edinburgh EH1 1QW **T** 0131-225 7012 **E** info@aprs.scot **W** www.aprs.scot
Director, John Mayhew

ASSOCIATION OF FINANCIAL MUTUALS (1995), 7 Castle Hill, Caistor LN7 6QL **T** 0844-879 7863 **E** martin@financialmutuals.org **W** www.financialmutuals.org
Chief Executive, Martin Shaw

ASSOCIATION OF GENEALOGISTS AND RESEARCHERS IN ARCHIVES (1968), Box A, 14 Charterhouse Buildings, Goswell Road, London EC1M 7BA **E** info@agra.org.uk **W** www.agra.org.uk
Chair, Sharon Grant

ASSOCIATION OF ROYAL NAVY OFFICERS (1920), 70 Porchester Terrace, London W2 3TP **T** 020-7402 5231 **E** enquiries@arno.org.uk **W** www.arno.org.uk
Director, Cdr Mike Goldthorpe

ASTHMA UK (1927), 18 Mansell Street, London E1 8AA **T** 0300-222 5800 **E** info@asthma.org.uk **W** www.asthma.org.uk
Chief Executive, Kay Boycott

AUDIT BUREAU OF CIRCULATIONS LTD (1931), Saxon House, 211 High Street, Berkhamsted HP4 1AD **T** 01442-870800 **E** enquiries@abc.org.uk **W** www.abc.org.uk
Chair, Derek Morris

AUTISM INITIATIVES (1971), Sefton House, Bridle Road, Merseyside L30 4XR **T** 0151-330 9500 **E** info@autisminitiatives.org **W** www.autisminitiatives.org
Chair, Brian Williams

AUTOMOBILE ASSOCIATION (1905), Fanum House, Basing View, Basingstoke RG21 4EA **T** 0345-607 6727 **E** customersupport@theaa.com **W** www.theaa.com
CEO, Simon Breakwell

BALTIC EXCHANGE (1744), St Mary Axe, London EC3A 8BH **T** 020-7283 9300 **W** www.balticexchange.com
Chief Executive, Mark Jackson

BARNARDO'S (1866), Tanners Lane, Ilford IG6 1QG **T** 020-8550 8822 **W** www.barnardos.org.uk
Chief Executive, Javed Khan

BBC MEDIA ACTION (1999), Ibex House, 42–47 Minories, London EC2N 1DY **T** 020-7481 9797 **E** media.action@bbc.co.uk **W** www.bbc.co.uk/mediaaction
Executive Director, Caroline Nursey, OBE

BCS, THE CHARTERED INSTITUTE FOR IT (1957), 1st Floor, Block D, North Star House, North Star Avenue, Swindon SN2 1FA **T** 01793-417417 **W** www.bcs.org
Chief Executive, Paul Fletcher

BEAT (1989), Unit 1 Chalk Hill House, 19 Rosary Road, Norwich NR1 1SZ
T 0300-123 3355 **Helpline** 0808-801 0677 **Youthline** 0808-801 0711 **E** info@b-eat.co.uk **W** www.beateatingdisorders.org.uk
Chief Executive, Andrew Radford

BIBLE SOCIETY (1804), Stonehill Green, Swindon SN5 7DG **T** 01793-418222 **W** www.biblesociety.org.uk
Chief Executive, Paul Williams

BIBLIOGRAPHICAL SOCIETY (1892), c/o University of London, Institute of English Studies, Senate House, London WC1E 7HU **E** admin@bibsoc.org.uk **W** www.bibsoc.org.uk
Hon. Secretary, Karen Limper-Herz

BIPOLAR UK (1983), 11 Belgrave Road, London SW1V 1RB **T** 0333-323 3880 **E** info@bipolaruk.org.uk **W** www.bipolaruk.org
Chief Executive, Simon Kitchen

BLIND VETERANS UK (1915), 12–14 Harcourt Street, London W1H 4HD **T** 0300 111-2233 **E** info@blindveterans.org.uk **W** www.blindveterans.org.uk
Chief Executive, Maj.-Gen. Nick Caplin, CB

BLISS (1979), Fourth Floor, Maya House, London SE1 1LB **T** 020-7378 1122 **E** ask@bliss.org.uk **W** www.bliss.org.uk
Chief Executive, Caroline Lee-Davey

BLOODWISE (1960), 39–40 Eagle Street, London WC1R 4TH **T** 020-7504 2200 **W** bloodwise.org.uk
Chief Executive, Gemma Peters

BLUE CROSS (1897), Shilton Road, Burford OX18 4PF **T** 0300-777 1897 **W** www.bluecross.org.uk
Chief Executive, Sally de la Bedoyere

BOOK AID INTERNATIONAL (1954), 39–41 Coldharbour Lane, London SE5 9NR **T** 020-7733 3577 **E** info@bookaid.org **W** www.bookaid.org
Chief Executive, Alison Tweed

BOOK TRADE CHARITY (BTBS) (1837), The Foyle Centre, The Retreat, Kings Langley WD4 8LT **T** 01923-263128 **E** info@booktradecharity.org **W** www.btbs.org
Chief Executive, David Hicks

BOOKTRUST (1926), G8 Battersea Studios, 80 Silverthorne Road, London SW8 3HE **T** 020-7801 8800 **E** query@booktrust.org.uk **W** www.booktrust.org.uk
Chief Executive, Diana Gerald

BOTANICAL SOCIETY OF BRITAIN AND IRELAND (1836), 29 West Farm Court, Durham DH7 7RN **T** 07725-862957 **E** enquiries@bsbi.org.uk **W** www.bsbi.org
Chair, Christopher Miles

BOTANICAL SOCIETY OF SCOTLAND (1836), c/o Royal Botanic Garden Edinburgh, 20A Inverleith Row, Edinburgh EH3 5LR **T** 0131-552 7171 **W** www.botanical-society-scotland.org.uk
General Secretaries, Julia Wilson; Liz Lavery

BRISTOL AND GLOUCESTERSHIRE ARCHAEOLOGICAL SOCIETY (1876), 10 Paddock Gardens, Gloucester GL2 0ED **T** 01452-414279 **E** secretary@bgas.org.uk **W** www.bgas.org.uk
Hon. General Secretary, Dr Graham Barton

BRITISH ASSOCIATION FOR EARLY CHILDHOOD EDUCATION (1923), 54 Clarendon Road, Watford WD17 1DU **T** 01923-438995 **E** office@early-education.org.uk **W** www.early-education.org.uk
Chief Executive, Beatrice Merrick

BRITISH ASSOCIATION FOR LOCAL HISTORY (1982), Chester House, 68 Chestergate, Macclesfield SK11 6DY **T** 01625-664524 **E** admin@balh.org.uk **W** www.balh.org.uk
President, Professor Caroline Barron

BRITISH ASTRONOMICAL ASSOCIATION (1890), Burlington House, London W1J 0DU **T** 020-7734 4145 **W** www.britastro.org
President, Callum Potter

BRITISH BOARD OF FILM CLASSIFICATION (1912), 3 Soho Square, London W1D 3HD **T** 020-7440 1570 **E** feedback@bbfc.co.uk **W** www.bbfc.co.uk
President, Patrick Swaffer

BRITISH CATTLE BREEDERS CLUB (1946), Underhill Farm, Glutton Bridge, Buxton SK17 0RN **T** 07966-032079 **E** heidi.bradbury@cattlebreeders.org.uk **W** www.cattlebreeders.org.uk
Chair, Mike Coffey

BRITISH COPYRIGHT COUNCIL (1965), 2 Pancras Square, London N1C 4AG **T** 020-3290 1444 **E** info@britishcopyright.org **W** www.britishcopyright.org
Chairman, Trevor Cook

BRITISH DEAF ASSOCIATION (1890), 3rd Floor, 356 Holloway Road, London N7 6PA **T** 020-7697 4140 **E** bda@bda.org.uk **W** www.bda.org.uk
Executive Director, Damian Barry

BRITISH ECOLOGICAL SOCIETY (1913), Charles Darwin House, 12 Roger Street, London WC1N 2JU **T** 020-7685 2500 **E** hello@britishecologicalsociety.org **W** www.britishecologicalsociety.org
Chief Executive, Dr Hazel Norman

BRITISH FEDERATION OF WOMEN GRADUATES (1907), 4 Mandeville Courtyard, 142 Battersea Park Road, London SW11 4NB **T** 020-7498 8037 **E** office@bfwg.org.uk **W** www.bfwg.org.uk
President, Patrice Wellesley-Cole

BRITISH HEART FOUNDATION (1961), Greater London House, 180 Hampstead Road, London NW1 7AW **T** 020-7554 0000 **W** www.bhf.org.uk
Chief Executive, Simon Gillespie, OBE

BRITISH HEDGEHOG PRESERVATION SOCIETY (1982), Hedgehog House, Dhustone, Ludlow SY8 3PL **T** 01584-890801 **E** info@britishhedgehogs.org.uk **W** www.britishhedgehogs.org.uk
Chief Executive, Fay Vass

BRITISH HERPETOLOGICAL SOCIETY (1947), 11 Strathmore Place, Montrose DD10 8LQ **E** info@thebhs.org **W** www.thebhs.org
Secretary, Trevor Rose

BRITISH HORSE SOCIETY (1947), Abbey Park, Stareton, Kenilworth CV8 2XZ **T** 024-7684 0500 **E** enquiry@bhs.org.uk **W** www.bhs.org.uk
Chief Executive, Sarah Phillips

BRITISH LUNG FOUNDATION (1985), 73–75 Goswell Road, London EC1V 7ER **T** 020-7688 5555, **Helpline** 03000-030 555 **W** www.blf.org.uk
Chief Executive, Dr Penny Woods

BRITISH MENSA LTD (1946), St John's House, St John's Square, Wolverhampton WV2 4AH **T** 01902-772771 **W** www.mensa.org.uk
Chief Executive, John Stevenage

BRITISH NATURALISTS' ASSOCIATION (1905), BM 8129, London WC1N 3XX **T** 0844-892-1817 **E** info@bna-naturalists.org **W** www.bna-naturalists.org
Hon. Chair, Steven Rutherford

BRITISH NUTRITION FOUNDATION (1967), New Derwent House, 69–73 Theobalds Road, London WC1X 8TA **T** 020-7557 7930 **E** postbox@nutrition.org.uk **W** www.nutrition.org.uk
Director-General, Prof. Judith Buttriss, PHD

BRITISH ORNITHOLOGISTS' UNION (1858), PO Box 417, Peterborough PE7 3FX **T** 01733-844820 **E** bou@bou.org.uk **W** www.bou.org.uk
Chief Operations Officer, Steve Dudley

BRITISH PHARMACOLOGICAL SOCIETY (1931), The Schild Plot, 16 Angel Gate, London EC1V 2PT **T** 020-7239 0171 **W** www.bps.ac.uk
Chief Executive, Jonathan Brüin

BRITISH POLIO FELLOWSHIP (1939), CP House, Otterspool Way, Watford WD25 8HR **T** 0800-043 1935 **E** info@britishpolio.org.uk **W** www.britishpolio.org.uk
National Chairman, David Mitchell

BRITISH RED CROSS (1870), 44 Moorfields, London EC2Y 9AL **T** 0344-871 11 11 , **Textphone** 020-7562 2050 **E** contactus@redcross.org.uk **W** www.redcross.org.uk
Chief Executive, Mike Adamson

BRITISH SAFETY COUNCIL (1957), 70 Chancellors Road, London W6 9RS **T** 020-3510 8355 **E** customer.service@britsafe.org **W** www.britsafe.org
Chief Executive, Michael Robinson

BRITISH SCIENCE ASSOCIATION (1831), Wellcome Wolfson Building, London SW7 5HD **E** info@britishscienceassociation.org **W** www.britishscienceassociation.org
Chief Executive, Katherine Mathieson

BRITISH SUNDIAL SOCIETY (1989), c/o The Royal Astronomical Society, London W1J 0BQ **E** secretary@sundialsoc.org.uk **W** www.sundialsoc.org.uk
Chair, Dr Frank King

BRITISH TRUST FOR ORNITHOLOGY (1933), The Nunnery, Thetford IP24 2PU **T** 01842-750050 **E** info@bto.org **W** www.bto.org
Director, Dr Andy Clements

BUCKINGHAMSHIRE ARCHAEOLOGICAL SOCIETY (1847), County Museum, Church Street, Aylesbury HP20 2QP **T** 01296-397200 **E** help@bucksas.org.uk **W** www.bucksas.org.uk
Chair, Peter Marsden

BUILD AFRICA (1978), 14th Floor, Tower Building, London SE1 7NX **T** 01892-519619 **E** hello@build-africa.org.uk **W** www.build-africa.org
Chief Executive, Martin Realey

CAFOD (CATHOLIC AGENCY FOR OVERSEAS DEVELOPMENT) (1962), Romero House, 55 Westminster Bridge Road, London SE1 7JB **T** 020-7733 7900 **E** cafod@cafod.org.uk **W** www.cafod.org.uk
Director, Christine Allen

CALOUSTE GULBENKIAN FOUNDATION (1956), 50 Hoxton Square, London N1 6PB **T** 020-7012 1400 **E** info@gulbenkian.org.uk **W** gulbenkian.pt/uk-branch/
Director, Andrew Barnett

CAMBRIAN ARCHAEOLOGICAL ASSOCIATION (1847), Braemar, SA31 2PB **T** 01248-364865 **E** info@cambrians.org.uk **W** www.cambrians.org
General Secretary, Heather James

CAMERON FUND (1970), BMA House, Tavistock Square, London WC1H 9JP **T** 020-7388 0796 **E** info@cameronfund.org.uk **W** www.cameronfund.org.uk
Chief Executive, Jill Rowlinson

CAMPAIGN FOR FREEDOM OF INFORMATION (1984), Free Word Centre, 60 Farringdon Road, London EC1R 3GA **T** 020-7324 2519 **E** admin@cfoi.org.uk **W** www.cfoi.org.uk
Director, Maurice Frankel

CAMPAIGN FOR NUCLEAR DISARMAMENT (1958), Mordechai Vanunu House, 162 Holloway Road, London N7 8DQ **T** 020-7700 2393 **E** enquiries@cnduk.org **W** www.cnduk.org
General Secretary, Kate Hudson

CAMPAIGN FOR THE PROTECTION OF RURAL WALES (1928), Tŷ Gwyn, 31 High Street, Welshpool SY21 7YD **T** 01938-552525 **E** info@cprwmail.org.uk **W** www.cprw.org.uk
Chair, Peter Alexander-Fitzgerald

CANCER RESEARCH UK (2002), Angel Building, 407 St John Street, London EC1V 4AD **T** 0300-123 1022 **W** www.cancerresearchuk.org
Chief Executive, Michelle Mitchell, OBE

CAREERS RESEARCH AND ADVISORY CENTRE (1964), 22 Signet Court, Swanns Road, Cambridge CB5 8LA **T** 01223-460277 **E** enquiries@crac.org.uk **W** www.crac.org.uk
Chief Executive, Clare Viney

CARERS TRUST (2012), Unit 101, 164-180 Union Street, London SE1 0LH **T** 0300-772 9600 **E** info@carers.org **W** www.carers.org
Chief Executive, Giles Meyer

CARERS UK (1965), 20 Great Dover Street, London SE1 4LX **T** 020-7378 4999 **E** info@carersuk.org **W** www.carersuk.org
Chief Executive, Helen Walker

CARNEGIE UNITED KINGDOM TRUST (1913), Andrew Carnegie House, Pittencrieff Street, Dunfermline KY12 8AW **T** 01383-721445 **E** info@carnegieuk.org **W** www.carnegieuktrust.org.uk
President, William Thomson, CBE

CATHEDRALS FABRIC COMMISSION FOR ENGLAND (1991), Church House, 27 Great Smith Street, London SW1P 3AZ T 020-7898 1000 E enquiries.ccb@c-of-e.org.uk W www.churchcare.co.uk/cathedrals
Secretary, Thomas Ashley

CATHOLIC TRUTH SOCIETY (1868), 42–46 Harleyford Road, London SE11 5AY T 020-7640 0042 E info@ctsbooks.org W www.ctsbooks.org
General Secretary, Fergal Martin

CATHOLIC UNION OF GREAT BRITAIN (1870), St Maximillian Kolbe House, 63 Jeddo Road, London W12 9EE T 020-8749 1321 W www.catholicunion.org.uk
President, Rt. Hon. Sir Edward Leigh, MP

CAVELL NURSES' TRUST (1917), Grosvenor House, Prospect Hill, Redditch B97 4DL T 01527-595999 E admin@cavellnursestrust.org W www.cavellnursestrust.org
Chief Executive, John Orchard

CENTRAL AND CECIL HOUSING TRUST (1927), Cecil House, 266 Waterloo Road, London SE1 8RQ T 020-7922 5300 E contact-us@ccht.org.uk W www.ccht.org.uk
Chief Executive, Julia Ashley

CENTREPOINT (1969), Central House, 25 Camperdown Street, London E1 8DZ T 0800-587 5158 W www.centrepoint.org.uk
Chief Executive, Seyi Obakin, OBE

CEREDIGION HISTORICAL SOCIETY (1909), 78 Maesceinion, Aberystwyth SY23 3QJ E ymholiadau@cymdeithashanesceredigion.org W www.ceredigionhistoricalsociety.org
Hon. Secretary, Siän Bowyer

CHANGING FACES (1992), The Squire Centre, 33–37 University Street, London WC1E 6JN T 0345-450 0275 E info@changingfaces.org.uk W www.changingfaces.org.uk
Chief Executive, Becky Hewitt

CHARITIES AID FOUNDATION (1924), 25 Kings Hill Avenue, West Malling ME19 4TA T 0300-012 3000 W www.cafonline.org
Chief Executive, Sir John Low, CBE

CHARTERED INSTITUTE OF ARBITRATORS (1915), 12 Bloomsbury Square, London WC1A 2LP T 020-7421 7444 E info@ciarb.org W www.ciarb.org
Director-General, Anthony Abrahams

CHARTERED INSTITUTE OF LINGUISTS (1910), 7th floor, 167 Fleet Street, London EC4A 2EA T 020-7940 3100 E info@ciol.org.uk W www.ciol.org.uk
Chief Executive, Ann Carlisle

CHARTERED SOCIETY OF FORENSIC SCIENCES (1959), Office 40, Flexspace, Harrogate HG3 2XA T 01423-534646 E info@csofs.org W www.csofs.org
Chief Executive, Dr Anya Hunt

CHATHAM HOUSE (1920), The Royal Institute of International Affairs, Chatham House, 10 St James's Square, London SW1Y 4LE T 020-7957 5700 E contact@chathamhouse.org W www.chathamhouse.org
Director, Dr Robin Niblett, CMG

CHILD POVERTY ACTION GROUP (1965), 30 Micawber Street, London N1 7TB T 020-7837 7979 E info@cpag.org.uk W www.cpag.org.uk
Chief Executive, Alison Garnham

CHILDREN 1ST (1884), 83 Whitehouse Loan, Edinburgh EH9 1AT T 0131-446 2300 E cfs@children1st.org.uk W www.children1st.org.uk
Chief Executive, Mary Glasgow

CHILDREN'S SOCIETY (1881), Edward Rudolf House, Margery Street, London WC1X 0JL T 0300-303 7000 E supportercare@childrenssociety.org.uk W www.childrenssociety.org.uk
Chief Executive, Matthew Reed

CHOICE SUPPORT (1987), 1 Hermitage Court, Maidstone Me16 9NT T 01622-722400 E enquiries@choicesupport.org.uk W www.choicesupport.org.uk
Chief Executive, Sarah Maguire

CHRISTIAN AID (1945), 35–41 Lower Marsh, London SE1 7RL T 020-7620 4444 E info@christian-aid.org W www.christianaid.org.uk
Chief Executive, Amanda Mukwashi

CHRISTIAN AID SCOTLAND (1945), Augustine United Church, 41 George IV Bridge, Edinburgh EH1 1EL T 0131-220 1254 E edinburgh@christian-aid.org W www.christianaid.org.uk/scotland
Head of Christian Aid Scotland, Sally Foster-Fulton

CHRISTIAN EDUCATION (2001), 5/6 Imperial Court, 12 Sovereign Road, Birmingham B30 3FH T 0121-458 3313 E sales@christianeducation.org.uk W www.christianeducation.org.uk
Secretary, Zöe Keens

CHURCH BUILDINGS COUNCIL (1921), Church House, 27 Great Smith Street, London SW1P 3NZ T 020-7898 1874 E churchcare@churchofengland.org W www.churchcare.co.uk
Senior Church Buildings Officer, Dr David Knight

CHURCH LADS' AND CHURCH GIRLS' BRIGADE (1891), St Martin's House, 2 Barnsley Road, Barnsley S63 6PY T 01709-876535 E contactus@clcgb.org.uk W www.clcgb.org.uk
Chief Executive, Audrey Simm

CHURCH MISSION SOCIETY (1799), Watlington Road, Oxford OX4 6BZ T 01865-787400 E info@churchmissionsociety.org W www.churchmissionsociety.org
Chief Executive, Alastair Bateman

CHURCH MONUMENTS SOCIETY (1979), c/o The Society of Antiquaries, Burlington House, London W1J 0BD T 0147-658 5012 E secretarychurchmonuments@gmail.com W www.churchmonumentssociety.org
President, Mark Downing

CHURCH UNION (1859), c/o Additional Curates Society, 16 Commercial Street, Birmingham B1 1RS T 0121-382 5533 E membership@churchunion.co.uk W www.churchunion.co.uk
Chair, Father Darren Smith

CITIZENS ADVICE (1939), 3rd Floor North, 200 Aldersgate, London EC1A 4HD T 03000-231231 W www.citizensadvice.org.uk
Chief Executive, Gillian Guy, CBE

CITY BUSINESS LIBRARY (1970), Aldermanbury, London EC2V 7HH T 020-7332 1812 E cbl@cityoflondon.gov.uk W www.cityoflondon.gov.uk/cbl
Manager, Alexandra Leader

CLASSICAL ASSOCIATION (1903), Cardinal Point, Park Road, Rickmansworth WD3 1RE T 07926-632598 E office@classicalassociation.org W www.classicalassociation.org
Hon. Secretary, Dr J. Robson

CLIMATE GROUP (2004), 2nd Floor, Riverside Building, County Hall, London SE1 7PB T 020-7960 2970 E info@theclimategroup.org W www.theclimategroup.org
Chief Executive, Helen Clarkson

COMBAT STRESS (1919), Tyrwhitt House, Oaklawn Road, Leatherhead KT22 0BX T 01372-587000 E contactus@combatstress.org.uk W www.combatstress.org.uk
Chief Executive, Sue Freeth

COMMUNITY INTEGRATED CARE (1988), Old Market Court, Miners Way, Widnes WA8 7SP T 0151 420 3637 E information@c-i-c.co.uk W www.c-i-c.co.uk
Chief Executive, Mark Adams

CONCERN WORLDWIDE (1968), 13–14 Calico House, Clove Hitch Quay, London SW11 3TN T 020-7801 1850 W www.concern.org.uk
Executive Director, Rose Caldwell

THE CONSERVATION VOLUNTEERS (1959), Sedum House, Mallard Way, Doncaster DN4 8DB **T** 01302-388883 **E** information@tcv.org.uk **W** www.tcv.org.uk
Chief Executive, Darren York

CONTEMPORARY APPLIED ARTS (1948), 6 Paddington Street, London W1U 5QG **T** 020-7620 0086 **E** shop@caa.org.uk **W** www.caa.org.uk
Executive Director, Christine Lalumia

CO-OPERATIVES UK (1869), Holyoake House, Hanover Street, Manchester M60 0AS **T** 0161-214 1750 **E** info@uk.coop **W** www.uk.coop
Secretary-General, Ed Mayo

CORAM FAMILY (1739), Coram Campus, 41 Brunswick Square, London WC1N 1AZ **T** 020-7520 0300 **W** www.coram.org.uk
Chief Executive, Dr Carol Homden, CBE

CORONERS' SOCIETY OF ENGLAND AND WALES (1846), HM Coroner's Court, Gerard Majella Courthouse, Liverpool L5 2QD **W** www.coronersociety.org.uk
Chief Coroner, Hon. Judge Mark Lucraft, QC

CORPORATION OF THE CHURCH HOUSE (1888), Church House, Great Smith Street, London SW1P 3AZ **T** 020-7898 1311 **W** www.churchhouse.org.uk
Secretary, Christopher Palmer, CBE

COUNCIL FOR BRITISH ARCHAEOLOGY (1944), Beatrice de Cardi House, 66 Bootham, York YO30 7BZ **T** 01904-671417 **E** info@archaeologyuk.org **W** www.archaeologyuk.org
Director, Dr Mike Heyworth, MBE

COUNCIL FOR WORLD MISSION (1977), 6th Floor, Regus, 50 Broadway, London SW1H 0RG **T** 020-7222 4214 **E** council.uk@cwmission.org **W** www.cwmission.org
General Secretary, Revd Dr Collin Cowan

COUNCIL OF UNIVERSITY CLASSICAL DEPARTMENTS (1972), Institute of Classical Studies, Senate House, Malet Street, London WC1E 7HU **E** director.ics@sas.ac.uk **W** cucd.blogs.sas.ac.uk
Chair, Prof. Helen Lovatt

COUNTRY LAND & BUSINESS ASSOCIATION (1907), 16 Belgrave Square, London SW1X 8PQ **T** 020-7235 0511 **E** mail@cla.org.uk **W** www.cla.org.uk
President, Tim Breitmeyer

COUNTRYSIDE ALLIANCE (1997), 1 Spring Mews, Tinworth Street, London SE11 5AN **T** 020-7840 9220 **W** www.countryside-alliance.org.uk
Chief Executive, Tim Bonner

CPRE (CAMPAIGN TO PROTECT RURAL ENGLAND) (1926), 5–11 Lavington Street, London SE1 0NZ **T** 020-7981 2800 **E** info@cpre.org.uk **W** www.cpre.org.uk
Chief Executive, Crispin Truman

CRAFTS COUNCIL (1971), 44A Pentonville Road, London N1 9BY **T** 020-7806 2500 **E** reception@craftscouncil.org.uk **W** www.craftscouncil.org.uk
Executive Director, Rosy Greenlees, OBE

CRANSTOUN (1969), Thames Mews, Esher KT10 9AD **T** 020-8335 1830 **E** info@cranstoun.org.uk **W** www.cranstoun.org
Chair, Richard Pertwee

CROHN'S AND COLITIS UK (1979), 1 Bishop Square, Hatfield Business Park AL10 9NE **T** 01727-830038 **E** info@crohnsandcolitis.org.uk **W** www.crohnsandcolitis.org.uk
Chief Executive, Sarah Sleet

CRUELTY FREE INTERNATIONAL (1898), 16A Crane Grove, London N7 8NN **T** 020-7700 4888 **E** info@crueltyfreeinternational.org **W** www.crueltyfreeinternational.org
Chief Executive, Michelle Thew

CRUSE BEREAVEMENT CARE (1959), Unit 01, One Victoria Villas, Richmond TW9 2GW **T** 020-8939 9530, **Helpline** 0808-808 1677 **E** info@cruse.org.uk **W** www.cruse.org.uk
Chief Executive, Steven Wibberley

CUMBRIA PAST (1866), Westlands, Westbourne Drive, Lancaster LA1 5EE **T** 01524-67523 **W** www.cumbriapast.com
General Secretary, Marion E. M. McClintock, MBE

CYCLING UK (1878), Parklands, Railton Road, Guildford GU2 9JX **T** 01483-238301 **E** cycling@cyclinguk.org **W** www.cyclinguk.org
Chief Executive, Paul Tuohy

CYSTIC FIBROSIS TRUST (1964), One Aldgate, 2nd Floor, London EC3N 1RE **T** 020-3795 1555 **E** enquiries@cysticfibrosis.org.uk **W** www.cysticfibrosis.org.uk
Chief Executive, David Ramsden

DEMOS (1994), 76 Vincent Square, London SW1P 2PD **T** 020-3878 3955 **E** hello@demos.co.uk **W** www.demos.co.uk
Chief Executive, Polly Mackenzie

DESIGN AND TECHNOLOGY ASSOCIATION (1989), 11 Manor Park, Banbury OX16 3TB **T** 01789-470007 **E** info@data.org.uk **W** www.data.org.uk
Chief Executive, Tony Ryan

DEVON ARCHAEOLOGICAL SOCIETY (1929), Royal Albert Memorial Museum, Queen Street, Exeter EX4 3RX **E** dashonsec@devonarchaeologicalsociety.org.uk **W** www.devonarchaeologicalsociety.org.uk
Hon. Secretary, Debbie Griffiths

DIABETES UK (1934), Wells Lawrence House, 126 Back Church Lane, London E1 1FH **T** 0345-123 2399 **E** helpline@diabetes.org.uk **W** www.diabetes.org.uk
Chief Executive, Chris Askew

DISABILITY RIGHTS UK (1977), Plexal, 14 East Bay Lane, Queen Elizabeth Olympic Park E20 3BS **T** 0330-995 0400 **E** enquiries@disabilityrightsuk.org **W** www.disabilityrightsuk.org
Chief Executive, Kamran Mallick

DITCHLEY FOUNDATION (1958), Ditchley Park, Chipping Norton OX7 4ER **T** 01608-677346 **E** info@ditchley.co.uk **W** www.ditchley.co.uk
Director, James Arroyo, OBE

DOWN'S SYNDROME ASSOCIATION (1970), Langdon Down Centre, 2A Langdon Park, Teddington TW11 9PS **T** 0333-1212300 **E** info@downs-syndrome.org.uk **W** www.downs-syndrome.org.uk
Chief Executive, Carol Boys

EARLY YEARS ALLIANCE (1961), 50 Featherstone Street, London EC1Y 8RT **T** 020-7697 2500 **E** info@eyalliance.org.uk **W** www.eyalliance.org.uk
Chief Executive, Neil Leitch

ECCLESIOLOGICAL SOCIETY (1879), 68 Scholars Road, Balham SW12 0PG **E** admin@ecclsoc.org **W** www.ecclsoc.org
Chairman, Mark Kirby

EDINBURGH CHAMBER OF COMMERCE (1785), Chamber Business Centre, 40 George Street, Edinburgh EH2 2LE **T** 0131-221 2999 **E** info@edinburghchamber.co.uk **W** www.edinburghchamber.co.uk
Chief Executive, Liz McAreavey

EDUCATION SUPPORT PARTNERSHIP (1877), 40A Drayton Park, London N5 1EW **T** 020-7697 2750, **Helpline** 0800-056 2561 **E** enquiries@edsupport.org.uk **W** www.educationsupportpartnership.org.uk
Chief Executive, Sinéad McBrearty

EGYPT EXPLORATION SOCIETY (1882), 3 Doughty Mews, London WC1N 2PG **T** 020-7242 1880 **E** contact@ees.ac.uk **W** www.ees.ac.uk
Director, Dr Carl Graves

ELECTORAL REFORM SOCIETY (1884), 3rd Floor, News
Building, 3 London Bridge Street, London SE1 9SG
T 020-3743 6066 **E** ers@electoral-reform.org.uk
W www.electoral-reform.org.uk
Chief Executive, Darren Hughes

ELGAR SOCIETY (1951), 6 Carriage Close, Worcester
WR2 6AE **T** 01905-339371 **E** vice.chair@elgar.org
W elgar.org/elgarsoc/
Chairman (acting), Stuart Freed

EMERGENCY PLANNING SOCIETY (1993), The Hawkhills,
Easingwold, York YO61 3EG **T** 01347-821972
E info@the-eps.org **W** www.the-eps.org
Chair, Jacqui Semple

ENABLE SCOTLAND (1954), Inspire House, 3 Renshaw Place,
Glasgow ML1 4UF **T** 01698-737000
E enabledirect@enable.org.uk **W** www.enable.org.uk
Chief Executive, Theresa Shearer

ENERGY INSTITUTE (2003), 61 New Cavendish Street,
London W1G 7AR **T** 020-7467 7100 **E** info@energyinst.org
W www.energyinst.org
Chief Executive, Louise Kingham, OBE

ENGLISH ASSOCIATION (1906), University of Leicester,
University Road, Leicester LE1 7RH **T** 0116-229 7622
E engassoc@le.ac.uk **W** www.le.ac.uk/engassoc
Chief Executive, Dr Rebecca Fisher

ENGLISH CHESS FEDERATION (1904), The Watch Oak,
Chain Lane, Battle TN33 0YD **T** 01424-775222
E office@englishchess.org.uk **W** www.englishchess.org.uk
Chief Executive, Mike Truran

ENGLISH FOLK DANCE AND SONG SOCIETY (1932),
Cecil Sharp House, 2 Regent's Park Road, London NW1 7AY
T 020-7485 2206 **E** info@efdss.org **W** www.efdss.org
Chief Executive, Katy Spicer

ENGLISH-SPEAKING UNION OF THE
COMMONWEALTH (1918), Dartmouth House, 37 Charles
Street, London W1J 5ED **T** 020-7529 1550 **E** esu@esu.org
W www.esu.org
Director-General, Jane Easton

EPILEPSY SOCIETY (1892), Chesham Lane, Chalfont St Peter
SL9 0RJ **T** 01494-601300, **Helpline** 01494-601400
W www.epilepsysociety.org.uk
Chief Executive, Clare Pelham

EQUINOX CARE (1986), 1 Waterloo Gardens, London N1 1TY
T 020-3668 9270 **E** enquiries@equinoxcare.org.uk
W www.equinoxcare.org.uk
Chief Executive, Gill Arukpe

ESPERANTO ASSOCIATION OF BRITAIN (1976),
Esperanto House, Station Road, Stoke-on-Trent ST12 9DE
T 01782-372 141 **E** eab@esperanto.org.uk
W www.esperanto.org.uk
President, Ian Carter

FABIAN SOCIETY (1884), 61 Petty France, London SW1H 9EU
T 020-7227 4900 **E** info@fabians.org.uk **W** www.fabians.org.uk
General Secretary, Andrew Harrop

FAITH AND THOUGHT (VICTORIA INSTITUTE)
(1865), 15 The Drive, Harlow CM20 3QD
E admin@faithandthought.org **W** www.faithandthought.org
President, Prof. Sir Colin J. Humphreys, CBE

FAMILY ACTION (1869), 24 Angel Gate, City Road, London
EC1V 2PT **T** 020-7254 6251 **E** info@family-action.org.uk
W www.family-action.org.uk
Chief Executive, David Holmes, CBE

FAUNA & FLORA INTERNATIONAL (1903), The David
Attenborough Building, Pembroke Street, Cambridge CB2 3QZ
T 01223-571000 **E** info@fauna-flora.org
W www.fauna-flora.org
Chief Executive, Mark Rose

FEDERATION OF FAMILY HISTORY SOCIETIES
(1974), 2 Primrose Avenue, Manchester M41 0TY
T 01263-824 951 **E** info@ffhs.org.uk
W www.familyhistoryfederation.com
President, Dr Nick Barratt

FEDERATION OF SMALL BUSINESSES (1974), Sir Frank
Whittle Way, Blackpool FY4 2FE **T** 0808-2020 888
E customerservices@fsb.org.uk **W** www.fsb.org.uk
National Chairman, Mike Cherry, OBE

FIELDS IN TRUST (1925), Unit 2D, Woodstock Studios, 36
Woodstock Grove, London W12 8LE **T** 020-7427 2110
E info@fieldsintrust.org **W** www.fieldsintrust.org
Chief Executive, Helen Griffiths

FIELD STUDIES COUNCIL (1943), Preston Montford,
Shrewsbury SY4 1HW **T** 01743-852100
E enquiries@field-studies-council.org
W www.field-studies-council.org
Chief Executive, Mark Castle, OBE

FIGHT FOR SIGHT (1965), 18 Mansell Street, London E1 8AA
T 020-7264 3900 **E** info@fightforsight.org.uk
W www.fightforsight.org.uk
Chief Executive, Sherine Krause

FIRE FIGHTERS CHARITY (1943), Level 6, Belvedere, Basing
View, Basingstoke RG21 4HG **T** 01256-366566
W www.firefighterscharity.org.uk
Chief Executive, Jill Tolfrey

FIRE PROTECTION ASSOCIATION (1946), London Road,
Moreton-in-Marsh, Glos GL56 0RH **T** 01608-812500
E fpa@thefpa.co.uk **W** www.thefpa.co.uk
Managing Director, Jonathan O'Neill, OBE

FLAG INSTITUTE (1971), HQS Wellington, Victoria
Embankment, London WC2R 2PN **E** info@flaginstitute.org
W www.flaginstitute.org
President, Capt. Malcolm Farrow, OBE, FFI, RN

FOREIGN PRESS ASSOCIATION IN LONDON (1888),
8 St James's Square, London SW1Y 4JU **T** 020-3727 4319
W www.fpalondon.net
Director, Deborah Bonetti

FOUNDATION FOR CREDIT COUNSELLING (STEP
CHANGE) (1993), Wade House, Merrion Centre, Leeds
LS2 8NG **T** 0800-138 1111 **W** www.stepchange.org
Chief Executive, Phil Andrew

FRANCO-BRITISH SOCIETY (1924), 3 Dovedale Studios,
465 Battersea Park Road, London SW11 4LR
E francobritsoc@gmail.com **W** www.franco-british-society.org
Executive Secretary, Isabelle Gault

FRIENDS OF CATHEDRAL MUSIC (1956), 27 Old
Gloucester Street, London WC1N 3XX **T** 020-3637 2172
E info@fcm.org.uk **W** www.fcm.org.uk
Chair, Peter Allwood

FRIENDS OF FRIENDLESS CHURCHES (1957), St Ann's
Vestry Hall, 2 Church Entry, London EC4V 5HB **T** 020-7236 3934
E office@friendsoffriendlesschurches.org.uk
W www.friendsoffriendlesschurches.org.uk
Director, Rachel Morley

FRIENDS OF THE BODLEIAN (1925), Bodleian Library,
Broad Street, Oxford OX1 3BG **T** 01865-277162
E reader.services@bodleian.ox.ac.uk
W www.bodleian.ox.ac.uk/bodley/friends
Librarian, Richard Ovenden

FRIENDS OF THE EARTH SCOTLAND (1978), Thorn
House, 5 Rose Street, Edinburgh EH2 2PR **T** 0131-243 2700
W www.foe.scot
Director, Dr Richard Dixon

FRIENDS OF THE ELDERLY (1905), 40–42 Ebury Street,
London SW1W 0LZ **T** 020-7730 8263 **E** enquiries@fote.org.uk
W www.fote.org.uk
Chief Executive, Steve Allen

FRIENDS OF THE NATIONAL LIBRARIES (1931),
PO Box 4291, Reading RG8 9JA
W www.friendsofnationallibraries.org.uk
Chair, Geordie Greig

FUTURES FOR WOMEN (SPTW) (1859), 11 Church Street,
Rugby CV23 9RL E futuresforwomen@btinternet.com
W futuresforwomen.org.uk
Secretary, Ms Jane Hampson

GALLIPOLI ASSOCIATION (1969), 5 Mews House, Roffey
Park, Colegate RH12 4TD T 028-2177 2996
E secretary@gallipoli-association.org
W www.gallipoli-association.org
Hon. Secretary, Sarah Kellam

GAME AND WILDLIFE CONSERVATION TRUST
(1969), Burgate Manor, Fordingbridge SP6 1EF
T 01425-652381 E info@gwct.org.uk W www.gwct.org.uk
Chief Executive, Teresa Dent

GARDENS TRUST (1965), 70 Cowcross Street, London
EC1M 6EJ T 020-7608 2409 E enquiries@thegardenstrust.org
W thegardenstrust.org
Chairman, Dr James Bartos

GEMMOLOGICAL ASSOCIATION OF GREAT BRITAIN
(GEM-A) (1931), 21 Ely Place, London EC1N 6TD
T 020-7404 3334 E information@gem-a.com
W www.gem-a.com
Chief Executive, Alan Hart

GENERAL MEDICAL COUNCIL (1858), 3 Hardman Street,
Manchester M3 3AW T 0161-923 6602 E gmc@gmc-uk.org
W www.gmc-uk.org
Chief Executive, Charlie Massey

GENERAL OPTICAL COUNCIL (1958), 10 Old Bailey,
London EC4M 7NG T 020-7580 3898 E goc@optical.org
W www.optical.org
Chief Executive/Registrar, Vicky McDermott

GEOGRAPHICAL ASSOCIATION (1893), 160 Solly Street,
Sheffield S1 4BF T 0114-296 0088 E info@geography.org.uk
W www.geography.org.uk
Chief Executive, Alan Kinder

GEOLOGICAL SOCIETY OF LONDON (1807),
Burlington House, Piccadilly, London W1J 0BG T 020-7434 9944
E enquiries@geolsoc.org.uk W www.geolsoc.org.uk
President, Prof. Nick Rogers

GEORGIAN GROUP (1937), 6 Fitzroy Square, W1T 5DX
T 020-7529 8920 E office@georgiangroup.org.uk
W www.georgiangroup.org.uk
Secretary, David Adshead

GIRLGUIDING (1910), 17–19 Buckingham Palace Road,
SW1W 0PT T 020-7834 6242 E info@girlguiding.org.uk
W www.girlguiding.org.uk
Chief Guide, Amanda Medler

GIRLS' FRIENDLY SOCIETY IN ENGLAND AND
WALES (1875), Unit 30 Angel Gate, 326 City Road, London
EC1V 2PT T 020-7837 9669 E enquiries@girlsfriendlysociety.org.uk
W girlsfriendlysociety.org.uk
Executive Director, Paul Rompani

GLADSTONE'S LIBRARY (1894), Church Lane, Hawarden
CH5 3DF T 01244-532350 E enquiries@gladlib.org
W www.gladstoneslibrary.org
Warden, Revd Peter Francis

GREENPEACE UK (1979), Canonbury Villas, N1 2PN
T 020-7865 8100 W www.greenpeace.org.uk
Executive Director, John Sauven

GUIDE DOGS (1934), Hillfields, Burghfield Common, Reading
RG7 3YG T 0118-983 5555 E guidedogs@guidedogs.org.uk
W www.guidedogs.org.uk
Chief Executive, Thomas Wright, CBE

GUILD OF FREEMEN OF THE CITY OF LONDON
(1908), Rooms 78/79, 65 London Wall, London EC2M 5TU
T 020-7239 9016 E clerk@guild-freemen-london.co.uk
W www.guild-freemen-london.co.uk
Clerk to the Guild, Christine Cook

GUILD OF GLASS ENGRAVERS (1975), c/o Red House Glass
Cone, High Street, Stourbridge DY8 4AZ T 07834-549925
E enquiries@gge.org.uk W www.gge.org.uk
President, Tracey Sheppard

GUILD OF PASTORAL PSYCHOLOGY (1937), GPP
Administration, Unit 1 Chapleton Lodge, Blackborough End
PE32 1SF T 01553-849849
E administration@guildofpastoralpsychology.org.uk
W www.guildofpastoralpsychology.org.uk
Chair, Jim Keeling

GURKHA WELFARE TRUST (1969), PO Box 2170, 22 Queen
Street, Salisbury SP2 2EX T 01722-323955 E info@gwt.org.uk
W www.gwt.org.uk
Director, Al Howard

GUY'S AND ST THOMAS' CHARITY (1553), Francis House,
9 King's Head Yard, SE1 1NA T 020-7089 4550
E info@gsttcharity.org.uk W www.gsttcharity.org.uk
Chief Executive, Kieron Boyle

HAEMOPHILIA SOCIETY (1950), Willcox House, 140–148
Borough High Street, London SE1 1LB T 020-7939 0780
E info@haemophilia.org.uk W www.haemophilia.org.uk
Chief Executive, Liz Carroll

HAIG HOUSING TRUST (2009), Alban Dobson House, Green
Lane, Morden SM4 5NS T 020-8685 5777
E enquiries@haighousing.org.uk W www.haighousing.org.uk
Chief Executive, James Richardson

HAKLUYT SOCIETY (1846), c/o Map Library, The British
Library, London NW1 2DB T 07568-468066
E office@hakluyt.com W www.hakluyt.com
President, Prof. Jim. Bennett

HANSARD SOCIETY (1944), 5th Floor, 9 King Street,
EC2V 8EA T 020-7710 6070 E contact@hansardsociety.org.uk
W www.hansardsociety.org.uk
Director, Dr Ruth Fox

HARVEIAN SOCIETY OF LONDON (1831), Lettsom
House, 11 Chandos Street, W1G 9EB T 020-7580 1043
E harveiansoclondon@btconnect.com
W www.harveiansocietyoflondon.btck.co.uk
Executive Secretary, Cdr Mike Flynn, FCMI MCPID

HEARING LINK (1947), The Grange, Wycombe Road, Princes
Risborough HP27 9NS T 07526-123255
E enquiries@hearinglink.org W www.hearinglink.org
Chief Operating Officer, Dr Lorraine Gailey

HELP FOR HEROES (2007), Unit 14, Parkers Close, Salisbury
SP5 3RB T 0300-303 9888 W www.helpforheroes.org.uk
Chief Executive, Melanie Waters, OBE

HELP MUSICIANS (MUSICIANS BENEVOLENT FUND)
(1921), 7–11 Britannia Street, London WC1X 9JS
T 020-7239 9100 E info@helpmusicians.org.uk
W www.helpmusicians.org.uk
Chief Executive, James Ainscough

HERALDRY SOCIETY (1947), 53 Hitchin Street, Baldock
SG7 6AQ E info@theheraldrysociety.com
W www.theheraldrysociety.com
Hon. Secretary, John Tunesi of Liongam

HIGH SHERIFFS' ASSOCIATION OF ENGLAND &
WALES (1971), Heritage House, PO Box 21, Baldock SG7 5SH
T 01462-896688 E secretary@highsheriffs.com
W www.highsheriffs.com
Chair, Hon. Hugh Tollemache

HISPANIC AND LUSO BRAZILIAN COUNCIL
(CANNING HOUSE) (1943), Canning House, 126 Wigmore
Street, W1U 3RZ T 020-7811 5600 E events@canninghouse.org
W www.canninghouse.org
Chief Executive, Cristina Cortes

HISTORICAL ASSOCIATION (1906), 59A Kennington Park
Road, London SE11 4JH **T** 0300-100 0223
E enquiries@history.org.uk **W** www.history.org.uk
Chief Executive, Rebecca Sullivan

HISTORIC HOUSES ASSOCIATION (1973), 2 Chester
Street, London SW1X 7BB **T** 020-7259 5688 **E** info@hha.org.uk
W www.historichouses.org
Director-General, Ben Cowell

HONG KONG ASSOCIATION (1961), Swire House, 59
Buckingham Gate, London SW1E 6AJ **T** 020-7963 9447
E communications@hkas.org.uk **W** www.hkas.org.uk
Executive Director, Lindsay Jones

HONOURABLE SOCIETY OF CYMMRODORION
(1751), 157–163, Grays Inn Road, London WC1X 8UE
E secretary@cymmrodorion.org **W** www.cymmrodorion.org
Honorary Secretary, Dr Lynn Williams, FLSW

HOSPITAL SATURDAY FUND (1873), 24 Upper Ground,
London SE1 9PD **T** 020-7202 1365 **E** charity@hsf.eu.com
W www.hospitalsaturdayfund.org
Chief Executive, Paul Jackson

HOUSING JUSTICE (2003), 256 Bermondsey Street, London
SE1 3UJ **T** 020-3544 8094 **E** info@housingjustice.org.uk
W www.housingjustice.org.uk
Chief Executive, Kathy Mohan

THE HUMANE RESEARCH TRUST (1962), Brook House,
29 Bramhall Lane South, Stockport SK7 2DN **T** 0161-439 8041
E info@humaneresearch.org.uk **W** www.humaneresearch.org.uk
Chair, L. M. Rhoades

I CAN (1888), 31 Angel Gate (Gate 5), Goswell Road, London
EC1V 2PT **T** 020-7843 2510 **E** info@ican.org.uk
W www.ican.org.uk
Chief Executive, Bob Reitemeier, CBE

INCORPORATED COUNCIL OF LAW REPORTING
FOR ENGLAND AND WALES (1865), Megarry House, 119
Chancery Lane, WC2A 1PP **T** 020-7242 6471
E enquiries@iclr.co.uk **W** www.iclr.co.uk
Chief Executive, Kevin Laws

INCORPORATED SOCIETY OF MUSICIANS (1882), 4–
5 Inverness Mews, London W2 3JQ **T** 020-7221 3499
E membership@ism.org **W** www.ism.org
Chief Executive, Deborah Annetts

INDEPENDENT SCHOOLS' BURSARS ASSOCIATION
(1932), Bluett House, Unit 11–12, Cliddesden RG25 2JB
T 01256-330369 **E** office@theisba.org.uk
W www.theisba.org.uk
Chief Executive, David Woodgate

INDEPENDENT AGE (1863), 18 Avonmore Road, W14 8RR
T 020-7605 4200 **E** charity@independentage.org
W www.independentage.org
Chief Executive, Shan Nicholas

INDUSTRY AND PARLIAMENT TRUST (1977),
Suite 101, 3 Whitehall Court, SW1A 2EL **T** 020-7839 9400
E enquiries@ipt.org.uk **W** www.ipt.org.uk
Chief Executive, Nick Maher

INSTITUTE FOR PUBLIC POLICY RESEARCH (1988),
Ground Floor, 14 Buckingham Street, London WC2N 6DF
T 020-7470 6100 **E** info@ippr.org **W** www.ippr.org
Director, Tom Kibasi

INSTITUTE OF CANCER RESEARCH (1909), 123 Old
Brompton Road, London SW7 3RP **T** 020-7352 8133
W www.icr.ac.uk
Chief Executive, Prof. Paul Workman

INSTITUTE OF ECONOMIC AFFAIRS (1955), 2 Lord North
Street, London SW1P 3LB **T** 020-7799 8900 **E** iea@iea.org.uk
W www.iea.org.uk
Director-General, Mark Littlewood

INSTITUTE OF FOOD SCIENCE AND TECHNOLOGY
(1964), 5 Cambridge Court, 210 Shepherd's Bush Road, London
W6 7NJ **T** 020-7603 6316 **E** info@ifst.org **W** www.ifst.org
Chief Executive, Jon Poole

INSTITUTE OF HEALTH PROMOTION AND
EDUCATION (1962), PO BOX 7409, Lichfield WS14 4LS
E admin@ihpe.org.uk **W** www.ihpe.org.uk
President, Sylvia Cheater

INSTITUTE OF HERALDIC AND GENEALOGICAL
STUDIES (1961), 79–82 Northgate, Canterbury CT1 1BA
T 01227-768664 **E** enquiries@ihgs.ac.uk **W** www.ihgs.ac.uk
Principal, Dr Richard Baker

INSTITUTE OF MASTERS OF WINE (1955), 6 Riverlight
Quay, London SW11 8EA **T** 020-7383 9130
E info@mastersofwine.org **W** www.mastersofwine.org
Executive Director, Rufus Olins

INSTITUTE OF MATHEMATICS AND ITS
APPLICATIONS (1964), Catherine Richards House, 16
Nelson Street, Southend-on-Sea SS1 1EF **T** 01702-354020
E post@ima.org.uk **W** www.ima.org.uk
Executive Director, David Youdan

INSTITUTE OF PHYSICS AND ENGINEERING IN
MEDICINE (1997), Fairmount House, 230 Tadcaster Road,
York YO24 1ES **T** 01904-610821 **E** office@ipem.ac.uk
W www.ipem.ac.uk
Chief Executive, Rosemary Cook, CBE

INSTITUTION OF ENGINEERING AND TECHNOLOGY
(1871), Michael Faraday House, Six Hills Way, Stevenage
SG1 2AY **T** 01438-313311 **E** postmaster@theiet.org
W www.theiet.org
Chief Executive & Secretary, Nigel Fine

INTERCONTINENTAL CHURCH SOCIETY (1823), Unit
11, Ensign Business Centre, Westwood Way, Coventry CV4 8JA
T 024-7646 3940 **W** www.ics-uk.org
Mission Director, Revd Richard Bromley

INTERNATIONAL AFRICAN INSTITUTE (1926), School
of Oriental and African Studies, Thornhaugh Street, London
WC1H 0XG **T** 020-7898 4420 **E** iai@soas.ac.uk
W www.internationalafricaninstitute.org
Honorary Director, Prof. Philip Burnham

INTERNATIONAL CHURCHILL SOCIETY UK (1968),
Churchill College, Storey's Way, Cambridge CB3 0DS
T 01223-331646 **E** asmith@winstonchurchill.org
W www.winstonchurchill.org
Executive Director, Andrew Smith

INTERNATIONAL INSTITUTE FOR CONSERVATION
OF HISTORIC AND ARTISTIC WORKS (1950),
3 Birdcage Walk, London SW1H 9JJ **T** 020-7799 5500
E iic@iiconservation.org **W** www.iiconservation.org
Secretary-General, Jane Henderson

INTERNATIONAL RESCUE COMMITTEE UK (1997),
100 Wood Street, London EC2V 7AN **T** 020-3983 2727
E contactus@rescue-uk.org **W** www.rescue-uk.org
Executive Director, Sanj Srikanthan

INTERNATIONAL STUDENTS HOUSE (1962),
229 Great Portland Street, London W1W 5PN **T** 020-7631 8300
E accom@ish.org.uk **W** www.ish.org.uk
Chief Executive, Martin Chalker

INTERNATIONAL TREE FOUNDATION (1924), 1 Kings
Meadow, Oxford OX2 0DP **T** 01865-922430
E info@internationaltreefoundation.org
W www.internationaltreefoundation.org
Chief Executive, Andy Egan

IRAN SOCIETY (1911), 1a St Martin's House, London
NW1 1QB **T** 020-7235 5122 **E** info@iransociety.org
W www.iransociety.org
President, Sir Richard Dalton, KCMG

JAPAN SOCIETY (1891), 13–14 Cornwall Terrace, London
NW1 4QP **T** 020-7935 0475 **E** info@japansociety.org.uk
W www.japansociety.org.uk
Chief Executive, Heidi Potter

THE JERUSALEM AND THE MIDDLE EAST CHURCH ASSOCIATION (1929), 1 Hart House, The Hart, Farnham GU9 7HJ T 01252-726994 E information@jmeca.org.uk W www.jmeca.org.uk
Chair, John Clark

JEWISH CARE (1990), Amélie House, Maurice and Vivienne Wohl Campus, London NW11 9DQ T 020-8922 2000 E info@jcare.org W www.jewishcare.org
Chair, Steven Lewis

JOURNALISTS' CHARITY (1864), Dickens House, 35 Wathen Road, Dorking RH4 1JY T 01306-887511 E enquiries@journalistscharity.org.uk W www.journalistscharity.org.uk
Chief Executive, James Brindle

KENT ARCHAEOLOGICAL SOCIETY (1857), Maidstone Museum, St Faith's Street, Maidstone ME14 1LH E secretary@kentarchaeology.org.uk W www.kentarchaeology.org.uk
Hon. General Secretary, Dr Clive Drew

KING'S FUND (1897), 11–13 Cavendish Square, London W1G 0AN T 020-7307 2400 E enquiry@kingsfund.org.uk W www.kingsfund.org.uk
Chief Executive, Richard Murray

LCIA (LONDON COURT OF INTERNATIONAL ARBITRATION) (1892), 70 Fleet Street, London EC4Y 1EU T 020-7936 6200 E enquiries@lcia.org W www.lcia.org
Director-General, Dr Jacomijn van Haersolte-van Hof

LEAGUE OF THE HELPING HAND (1908), PO Box 342, Burgess Hill RH15 5AQ T 01444-236099 E secretary@lhh.org.uk W www.lhh.org.uk
Chair and Director, Moira Parrott

THE LEPROSY MISSION, ENGLAND, WALES, THE CHANNEL ISLANDS AND THE ISLE OF MAN (1874), Goldhay Way, Peterborough PE2 5GZ T 01733-370505 E post@tlmew.org.uk W www.leprosymission.org.uk
National Director, Peter Waddup

LIBERTY (NATIONAL COUNCIL FOR CIVIL LIBERTIES) (1934), Liberty House, 26–30 Strutton Ground, London SW19 2HR T 020-7403 3888 W www.libertyhumanrights.org.uk
Director (acting), Corey Stoughton

LINNEAN SOCIETY OF LONDON (1788), Burlington House, London W1J 0BF T 020-7434 4479 E info@linnean.org W www.linnean.org
Executive Secretary, Dr Elizabeth Rollinson

LISTENING BOOKS (1959), 12 Lant Street, London SE1 1QH T 020-7407 9417 E info@listening-books.org.uk W www.listening-books.org.uk
Chief Executive, Bill Dee

LIVABILITY (c.1840), 6 Mitre Passage, London SE10 0ER T 020-7452 2000 E info@livability.org.uk W www.livability.org.uk
Chief Executive, Helen England

LOCAL GOVERNMENT ASSOCIATION (1997), 18 Smith Square, London SW1P 3HZ T 020-7664 3000 E info@local.gov.uk W www.local.gov.uk
Chief Executive, Mark Lloyd

LOCAL SOLUTIONS (1974), Mount Vernon Green, Hall Lane, Liverpool L7 8TF T 0151-709 0990 E info@localsolutions.org.uk W www.localsolutions.org.uk
Chief Executive, Steve Hawkins

LONDON AND MIDDLESEX ARCHAEOLOGICAL SOCIETY (1855), c/o Museum of London, London EC2Y 5HN T 020-7410 2228 W www.lamas.org.uk
Hon. Secretary, Karen Thomas

LONDON CITY MISSION (1835), Nasmith House, 175 Tower Bridge Road, London SE1 2AH T 020-7407 7585 E enquiries@lcm.org.uk W www.lcm.org.uk
Chief Executive, Graham Miller

LONDON COLLEGE OF OSTEOPATHIC MEDICINE (1946), 8–10 Boston Place, London NW1 6QH T 020-7262 1128 W www.lcom.org.uk
Director, Brian McKenna

LONDON CATALYST (1873), 45 Westminster Bridge Road, London SE1 7JB T 020-3828 4204 E london.catalyst@peabody.org.uk W www.londoncatalyst.org.uk
Director, Victor Willmott

LONDON COUNCILS (2000), 59½ Southwark Street, London SE1 0AL T 020-7934 9999 E info@londoncouncils.gov.uk W www.londoncouncils.gov.uk
Chief Executive, John O'Brien

LONDON INSTITUTE OF FINANCE AND BANKING (1879), 8th Floor, Peninsular House, London EC3R 8LJ T 01227-818609 E customerservices@libf.ac.uk W www.libf.ac.uk
Chief Executive, Alex Fraser

LONDON LIBRARY (1841), 14 St James's Square, London SW1Y 4LG T 020-7766 4700 E reception@londonlibrary.co.uk W www.londonlibrary.co.uk
Director, Philip Marshall

LONDON PLAYING FIELDS FOUNDATION (1890), 58 Bloomsbury Street, London WC1B 3QT T 020-7323 0331 E enquiries@lpff.org.uk W www.lpff.org.uk
Chief Executive, Alex Welsh

LONDON SOCIETY (1912), Mortimer Wheeler House, 46 Eagle Wharf Road, London N1 7ED E info@londonsociety.org.uk W www.londonsociety.org.uk
Chair, Peter Murray

LOTTERIES COUNCIL (1979), 66 Lincoln's Inn Fields, London WC2A 3LH T 07954-723224 E tina@lotteriescouncil.org.uk W www.lotteriescouncil.org.uk
Chair, Tony Vick

LULLABY TRUST (1971), 11 Belgrave Road, London SW1V 1RB T 020-7802 3200 E office@lullabytrust.org.uk W www.lullabytrust.co.uk
Chief Executive, Jenny Ward (acting)

MACMILLAN CANCER SUPPORT (1911), 89 Albert Embankment, London SE1 7UQ T 020-7840 7840 W www.macmillan.org.uk
Chief Executive, Lynda Thomas

MAKING MUSIC, THE NATIONAL FEDERATION OF MUSIC SOCIETIES (1935), 8 Holyrood Street, London SE1 2EL T 020-7939 6030 W www.makingmusic.org.uk
Chief Executive, Barbara Eifler

MARIE CURIE CANCER CARE (1948), 89 Albert Embankment, SE1 7TP T 0800-716146 E supporter.relations@mariecurie.org.uk W www.mariecurie.org.uk
Chief Executive, Matthew Reed

MARINE BIOLOGICAL ASSOCIATION OF THE UK (1884), The Laboratory, Citadel Hill, Plymouth PL1 2BP T 01752-426493 E info@mba.ac.uk W www.mba.ac.uk
President, Prof. Sir John Beddington, CMG FRS

MARINE SOCIETY AND SEA CADETS (1756), 202 Lambeth Road, London SE1 7JW T 020-7654 7000 E info@ms-sc.org W www.ms-sc.org
Chief Executive, Martin Coles

MASONIC CHARITABLE FOUNDATION (1982), 60 Great Queen Street, London WC2B 5AZ T 020-3146 3333 E info@mcf.org.uk W www.mcf.org.uk
Chief Executive, David Innes

MATERNITY ACTION (2008), 52–54 Featherstone Street, London EC1Y 8RT T 020-7253 2288 W www.maternityaction.org.uk
Director, Rosalind Bragg

MATHEMATICAL ASSOCIATION (1871), 259 London Road, Leicester LE2 3BE **T** 0116-221 0013 **E** office@m-a.org.uk **W** www.m-a.org.uk
President, Prof. Mike Askew

ME ASSOCIATION (1976), 7 Apollo Office Court, Radclive Road, Gawcott MK18 4DF **T** 01280-818964 **W** www.meassociation.org.uk
Chair, Neil Riley

MEDIAWATCH-UK (1965), 3 Willow House, Kennington Road, Ashford TN24 0NR **T** 01233-633936 **E** info@mediawatchuk.org **W** www.mediawatchuk.org
Director, Helen Lewington

MEDICAL SOCIETY OF LONDON (1773), Lettsom House, 11 Chandos Street, London W1G 9EB **T** 020-7580 1043 **E** info@medsoclondon.org **W** www.medsoclondon.org
Registrar, Cdr Mike Flynn, FCMI MCPID

MEDICAL WOMEN'S FEDERATION (1917), Tavistock House North, Tavistock Square, London WC1H 9HX **T** 020-7387 7765 **E** admin@medicalwomensfederation.org.uk **W** www.medicalwomensfederation.org.uk
President, Dr Henrietta Bowden-Jones

MENCAP (ROYAL MENCAP SOCIETY) (1946), 123 Golden Lane, EC1Y 0RT **T** 020-7454 0454 **E** helpline@mencap.org.uk **W** www.mencap.org.uk
Chief Executive, Jan Tregelles

MENTAL HEALTH FOUNDATION (1972), Colechurch House, 1 London Bridge Walk, London SE1 2SX **T** 020-7803 1100 **W** www.mentalhealth.org.uk
Chief Executive, Mark Rowland

MERCHANT NAVY WELFARE BOARD (1948), 8 Cumberland Place, Southampton SO15 2BH **T** 023-8033 7799 **E** enquiries@mnwb.org.uk **W** www.mnwb.org
Chief Executive, Peter Tomlin, MBE

MHA (1943), Epworth House, 3 Stuart Street, Derby DE1 2EQ **T** 01332-296200 **E** enquiries@mha.org.uk **W** www.mha.org.uk
Chief Executive, Sam Monaghan

MILITARY HISTORICAL SOCIETY (1948), Lower Brook Farm, Smithy Lane, Rainow SK10 5VP **T** 0121-711 4712 **E** flers99@yahoo.com **W** www.themilitaryhistoricalsociety.co.uk
Chair, Clive Elderton, CBE

MIND (NATIONAL ASSOCIATION FOR MENTAL HEALTH) (1946), 15–19 Broadway, London E15 4BQ **T** 020-8519 2122, **Infoline** 0300-123 3393 **E** supporterrelations@mind.org.uk **W** www.mind.org.uk
Chief Executive, Paul Farmer, CBE

MINERALOGICAL SOCIETY (1876), 12 Baylis Mews, Twickenham TW1 3HQ **T** 020-8891 6600 **E** info@minersoc.org **W** www.minersoc.org
Executive Director, Kevin Murphy

MISSING PEOPLE (1993), 284 Upper Richmond Road West, London SW14 7JE **T** 020-8392 4590 **W** www.missingpeople.org.uk
Chief Executive, Jo Youle

MISSION TO SEAFARERS (1856), St Michael Paternoster Royal, College Hill, London EC4R 2RL **T** 020-7248 5202 **E** info@missiontoseafarers.org **W** www.missiontoseafarers.org
Secretary General, Revd Andrew Wright

MULTIPLE SCLEROSIS SOCIETY (1953), MS National Centre, 372 Edgware Road, London NW2 6ND **T** 020-8438 0700 **E** supportercare@mssociety.org.uk **W** www.mssociety.org.uk
Chief Executive, Nick Moberly

MUSEUMS ASSOCIATION (1889), 42 Clerkenwell Close, London EC1R 0AZ **T** 020-7566 7800 **E** info@museumsassociation.org **W** www.museumsassociation.org
Director, Sharon Heal

NABS (1916), 10 Hills Place, London W1F 7SD **T** 020-7290 7070 **W** www.nabs.org.uk
Chief Executive, Diana Tickell

NACRO, THE SOCIAL JUSTICE CHARITY (1966), 1st Floor, 46 Loman Street, London SE1 0EH **T** 0300-123 1889 **E** helpline@nacro.org.uk **W** www.nacro.org.uk
Chief Executive, Campbell Robb

NAT (NATIONAL AIDS TRUST) (1987), Aztec House, 397–405 Archway Road, London N6 4EY **T** 020-7814 6767 **E** info@nat.org.uk **W** www.nat.org.uk
Chief Executive, Deborah Gold

NATIONAL BENEVOLENT CHARITY (1812), Peter Hervé House, Eccles Court, Tetbury GL8 8EH **T** 01666-505500 **E** office@natben.org.uk **W** www.natben.org.uk
Chief Executive, Paul Rossi

NATIONAL CAMPAIGN FOR THE ARTS LTD (1985), c/o Cog Design, 11 Greenwich Centre Business Park, London SE10 9QF **T** 020-8269 1800 **E** hello@forthearts.org.uk **W** forthearts.org.uk
Executive Chair, Michael Smith

NATIONAL CAMPAIGN FOR COURTESY (1986), Walmere, Wrigglebrook Lane, Kingsthorne HR2 8AW **T** 020-3633 4650 **E** courtesy@campaignforcourtesy.org.uk **W** www.campaignforcourtesy.org.uk
Chair, John Stokes

NATIONAL CHILDBIRTH TRUST (1956), 30 Euston Square, London NW1 2FB **T** 0300-330 0770 **E** enquiries@nct.org.uk **W** www.nct.org.uk
Chief Executive, Nick Wilkie

NATIONAL COUNCIL OF WOMEN GREAT BRITAIN (1895), 81 Bondgate, Darlington DL3 7JT **T** 01325-367375 **E** info@ncwgb.org **W** www.ncwgb.org
President, Dr Andrena Telford

NATIONAL EXTENSION COLLEGE (1963), Michael Young Centre, School House, Cambridge CB2 8EB **T** 0800-389 2839 **E** info@nec.ac.uk **W** www.nec.ac.uk
Chief Executive, Dr Ros Morpeth

NATIONAL FAMILY MEDIATION (1981), Civic Centre, Paris Street, Exeter EX1 1JN **T** 0300-400 0636 **E** general@nfm.org.uk **W** www.nfm.org.uk
Chief Executive, Jane Robey

NATIONAL FEDERATION OF WOMEN'S INSTITUTES (1915), 104 New Kings Road, London SW6 4LY **T** 020-7371 9300 **W** www.thewi.org.uk
General Secretary, Melissa Green

NATIONAL FOUNDATION FOR EDUCATIONAL RESEARCH IN ENGLAND AND WALES (1946), The Mere, Upton Park, Slough SL1 2DQ **T** 01753-574123 **E** enquiries@nfer.ac.uk **W** www.nfer.ac.uk
Chief Executive, Carole Willis

NATIONAL GARDENS SCHEME CHARITABLE TRUST (1927), East Wing, Hatchlands Park, Guildford GU4 7RT **T** 01483-211535 **E** hello@ngs.org.uk **W** www.ngs.org.uk
Chair, Martin McMillan, OBE

NATIONAL OPERATIC AND DRAMATIC ASSOCIATION (NODA) (1899), 15 The Metro Centre, Peterborough PE2 7UH **T** 01733-374790 **E** info@noda.org.uk **W** www.noda.org.uk
Chief Operating Officer, Dale Freeman

NATIONAL SECULAR SOCIETY (1866), 25 Red Lion Square, London WC1R 4RL **T** 020-7404 3126 **E** enquiries@secularism.org.uk **W** www.secularism.org.uk
President, K. P. Wood

NATIONAL TRUST (1895), Heelis, Kemble Drive, Swindon SN2 2NA **T** 0344-800 1895 **E** enquiries@thenationaltrust.org.uk **W** www.nationaltrust.org.uk
Director-General, Hilary McGrady

NATIONAL TRUST FOR SCOTLAND (1931), Hermiston Quay, Edinburgh EH11 4DF **T** 0131-458 0200 **E** information@nts.org.uk **W** www.nts.org.uk
Chief Executive, Simon Skinner

NATIONAL UNION OF STUDENTS (NUS) (1922), Ian King House, Snape Road, Macclesfield SK10 2NZ T 0300-303 8602 W www.nus.org.uk
President, Zamzam Ibrahim

NATIONAL WOMEN'S REGISTER (1966), Unit 23, Vulcan House, Norwich NR6 6AQ T 01603-406767 E office@nwr.org.uk W www.nwr.org.uk
Chair of Trustees, Josephine Burt

NEWCOMEN SOCIETY (1920), The Science Museum, London SW7 2DD T 020-7371 4445 E office@newcomen.com W www.newcomen.com
President, Robert Taylor

NHS CONFEDERATION (1997), Floor 15, Portland House, London SW1E 5BH T 020-7799 6666 E enquiries@nhsconfed.org W www.nhsconfed.org
Chief Executive, Niall Dickson, CBE

NOISE ABATEMENT SOCIETY (1959), 44 Grand Parade, Brighton BN2 9QA T 01273-823850
E info@noise-abatement.org
W www.noiseabatementsociety.com
Chief Executive, Gloria Elliott

NORFOLK AND NORWICH ARCHAEOLOGICAL SOCIETY (1846), 64 The Close, Norwich NR1 4DH
E secretary@nnas.info W www.nnas.info
Hon. Secretary, Edmund Perry

NORTH OF ENGLAND ZOOLOGICAL SOCIETY (1934), Chester Zoo, Chester CH2 1LH T 01244-380280
E reception@chesterzoo.co.uk W www.chesterzoo.org
Chief Executive Officer, Dr Mark Pilgrim

NSPCC (1884), Weston House, 42 Curtain Road, London EC2A 3NH T 0808-800 5000 E help@nspcc.org.uk W www.nspcc.org.uk
Chief Executive, Peter Wanless

NUCLEAR INSTITUTE (1962), Phoenix House, 18 King William Street, London EC4N 7BP T 020-7816 2600
E admin@nuclearinst.com W www.nuclearinst.com
President, John Clarke

NUFFIELD FOUNDATION (1943), 28 Bedford Square, London WC1B 3JS T 020-7631 0566
E info@nuffieldfoundation.org W www.nuffieldfoundation.org
Director, Timothy Gardam

NUFFIELD TRUST (1940), 59 New Cavendish Street, London W1G 7LP T 020-7631 8450 E info@nuffieldtrust.org.uk W www.nuffieldtrust.org.uk
Chief Executive, Nigel Edwards

NUTRITION SOCIETY (1941), 10 Cambridge Court, 210 Shepherds Bush Road, London W6 7NJ T 020-7602 0228
E office@nutritionsociety.org W www.nutritionsociety.org
Chief Executive, Mark Hollingsworth

OFFICERS' ASSOCIATION (1919), First Floor, Mountbarrow House, London SW1W 9RB T 020-7808 4160
E info@officersassociation.org.uk
W www.officersassociation.org.uk
Chief Executive, Lee Holloway

OPEN-AIR MISSION (1853), 4 Harrier Court, Woodside Road, Luton LU1 4DQ T 01582-841141 E email@oamission.com W www.oamission.com
General Secretary, Andy Banton

OPEN SPACES SOCIETY (1865), 25A Bell Street, Henley-on-Thames RG9 2BA T 01491-573535 E hq@oss.org.uk W www.oss.org.uk
General Secretary, Kate Ashbrook

OVERSEAS DEVELOPMENT INSTITUTE (1960), 203 Blackfriars Road, London SE1 8NJ T 020-7922 0300
E odi@odi.org W www.odi.org
Executive Director, Simon Gill (acting)

OXFAM GREAT BRITAIN (1942), Oxfam House, John Smith Drive, Oxford OX4 2JY T 0300-200 1300
E enquiries@oxfam.org.uk W www.oxfam.org.uk
Chief Executive, Dr Dhananjayan Sriskandarajah

OXFORD PRESERVATION TRUST (1927), 10 Turn Again Lane, Oxford OX1 1QL T 01865-242918
E info@oxfordpreservation.org.uk
W www.oxfordpreservation.org.uk
Director, Debbie Dance OBE

OXFORDSHIRE ARCHITECTURAL AND HISTORICAL SOCIETY (1839), 99 Wellington Street, Thame OX9 3BW
E secretary@oahs.org.uk W www.oahs.org.uk
President, Geoffrey Tyack

OXFORD UNIVERSITY SOCIETY (1932), University Alumni Office, Wellington Square, Oxford OX1 2JD T 01865-611610
E enquiries@alumni.ox.ac.uk W www.alumni.ox.ac.uk
Chair, Nicholas Segal

THE PALAEONTOLOGICAL ASSOCIATION (1957), Alport House, 35 Old Elvet, Durham DH1 3HN T 0191-386 1482 W www.palass.org
Executive Officer, Dr Jo Hellawell

PARLIAMENTARY AND SCIENTIFIC COMMITTEE (1939), 3 Birdcage Walk, London SW1H 9JJ T 020-7222 7085
E office@scienceinparliament.org.uk
W www.scienceinparliament.org.uk
Chair, Stephen Metcalfe, MP

PATIENTS ASSOCIATION (1963), PO Box 935, Harrow HA1 3YJ T 020-8423 9111, **Helpline** 020-8423 8999
E helpline@patients-association.com
W www.patients-association.com
Chair, Lucy Watson

PEABODY (1862), 45 Westminster Bridge Road, London SE1 7JB T 020-7021 4444 E customercareline@peabody.org.uk W www.peabody.org.uk
Chief Executive, Brendan Sarsfield

PEN INTERNATIONAL (1921), Unit A Koops Mill Mews, 162–164 Abbey Street, London SE1 2AN T 020-7405 0338
E info@pen-international.org W www.pen-international.org
President, Jennifer Clement

PENSIONS ADVISORY SERVICE (1983), 11 Belgrave Road, London SW1V 1RB T 0800-011 3797
W www.pensionsadvisoryservice.org.uk
Chief Executive, Caroline Siarkiewicz (acting)

PERENNIAL (1839), 115–117 Kingston Road, Leatherhead KT22 7SU T 0800-093 8510 E info@perennial.org.uk W www.perennial.org.uk
Chief Executive, Peter Newman

PHYSIOLOGICAL SOCIETY (1876), Hodgkin Huxley House, 30 Farringdon Lane, London EC1R 3AW T 020-7269 5710
E contactus@physoc.org W www.physoc.org
Chief Executive, Dariel Burdass

PILGRIM TRUST (1930), 23 Lower Belgrave Street, London SW1W 0NR T 020-7834 6510 E info@thepilgrimtrust.org.uk W www.thepilgrimtrust.org.uk
Director, Georgina Nayler

PLAIN ENGLISH CAMPAIGN (1979), 20 Union Road, High Peak Sk22 3ES T 01663-744409 E info@plainenglish.co.uk W www.plainenglish.co.uk
Director, Ms C. Maher, OBE

POETRY SOCIETY (1909), 22 Betterton Street, London WC2H 9BX T 020-7420 9880 E info@poetrysociety.org.uk W www.poetrysociety.org.uk
Director, Judith Palmer

POTENTIAL PLUS UK (1967), The Mansion, Bletchley Park, Sherwood Drive, Milton Keynes MK3 6EB T 01908-646433 W www.potentialplusuk.org
Chief Executive, Julie Taplin

PRAYER BOOK SOCIETY (1975), The Studio, Copyhold Farm, Reading RG8 7RT T 01189-842582
E pbs.admin@pbs.org.uk W www.pbs.org.uk
Chairman, Prudence Dailey

PRINCE'S TRUST (1976), 9 Eldon Street, London EC2M 7LS
T 0800-842 842 E webinfops@princes-trust.org.uk
W www.princes-trust.org.uk
Chief Executive, Dame Martina Milburn, DCVO, CBE

PRISONERS ABROAD (1978), 89–93 Fonthill Road, London
N4 3JH T 020-7561 6820 E info@prisonersabroad.org.uk
W www.prisonersabroad.org.uk
Chief Executive, Pauline Crowe, OBE

PRIVATE LIBRARIES ASSOCIATION (1956), Ravelston,
South View Road, Pinner HA5 3YD E info@plabooks.org
W www.plabooks.org
Hon. Secretary, Jim Maslen

PROFESSIONAL ASSOCIATION FOR CHILDCARE
AND EARLY YEARS (1971), Northside House, Third Floor,
69 Tweedy Road, Bromley BR1 3WA T 0300-003 0005
E info@pacey.org.uk W www.pacey.org.uk
Chief Executive, Liz Bayram

PROFESSIONAL PUBLISHERS ASSOCIATION (1970),
White Collar Factory, 1 Old Street Yard, London EC1Y 8AF
T 020-7404 4166 E info@ppa.org.uk W www.ppa.co.uk
Chief Executive, Barry McIlheney

PROSTATE CANCER UK (1996), Fourth Floor, The Counting
House, 53 Tooley Street, London SE1 2QN T 020-3310 7000
E info@prostatecanceruk.org W www.prostatecanceruk.org
Chief Executive, Angela Culhane

QUAKER PEACE AND SOCIAL WITNESS (2000),
Friends House, 173–177 Euston Road, London NW1 2BJ
T 020-7663 1000 E enquiries@quaker.org.uk
W www.quaker.org.uk
General Secretary, Oliver Robertson

QUEEN ELIZABETH'S FOUNDATION FOR DISABLED
PEOPLE (1934), Leatherhead Court, Woodlands Road,
Leatherhead KT22 0BN T 01372-841100 E info@qef.org.uk
W www.qef.org.uk
Chief Executive, Karen Deacon

QUEEN'S NURSING INSTITUTE (1887), 1A Henrietta Place,
London W1G 0LZ T 020-7549 1400 E mail@qni.org.uk
W www.qni.org.uk
Chief Executive, Dr Crystal Oldman, CBE

RAILWAY BENEFIT FUND (1858), 1st Floor, Millennium
House, Crewe CW2 6AD T 0345-241 2885
E info@railwaybenefitfund.org.uk
W www.railwaybenefitfund.org.uk
Chief Executive, Jason Tetley

RAMBLERS' ASSOCIATION (1935), 2nd Floor, Camelford
House, 87–90 Albert Embankment, London SE1 7TW
T 020-3961 3300 E ramblers@ramblers.org.uk
W www.ramblers.org.uk
Chief Executive, Vanessa Griffiths

RARE BREEDS SURVIVAL TRUST (1973), Stoneleigh Park,
Nr. Kenilworth CV8 2LG T 024-7669 6551
E enquiries@rbst.org.uk W www.rbst.org.uk
CEO, Christopher Price

REFUGEE COUNCIL (1951), PO Box 68614, London E15 9DQ
T 020-7346 6700 E info@refugeecouncil.org.uk
W www.refugeecouncil.org.uk
Chief Executive, Maurice Wren

REGIONAL STUDIES ASSOCIATION (1965), Sussex
Innovation Centre, Falmer Brighton BN1 9SB T 01273-698017
E office@regionalstudies.org W www.regionalstudies.org
Chief Executive, Sally Hardy

RELATE (1938), Premier House, Carolina Court, Doncaster
DN4 5RA T 0300-100 1234 E relate.enquiries@relate.org.uk
W www.relate.org.uk
Chief Executive, Aidan Jones, OBE

RETHINK (1972), 89 Albert Embankment, London SE1 7TP
T 0121-522 7007 E info@rethink.org W www.rethink.org
Chief Executive, Mark Winstanley

RFEA (REGULAR FORCES EMPLOYMENT
ASSOCIATION LTD) (1885), 1st Floor, Mountbarrow
House, 12 Elizabeth Street, London SW1W 9RB
T 0121-262 3058 E info@rfea.org.uk W www.rfea.org.uk
Chief Executive, Alistair Halliday

RICHARD III SOCIETY (1924), 18 Berberis Close, Milton
Keynes MK7 7DZ E secretary@richardiii.net W www.richardiii.net
Chair, Dr Phil Stone

ROYAL AERONAUTICAL SOCIETY (1866),
4 Hamilton Place, London W1J 7BQ T 020-7670 4300
E raes@aerosociety.com W www.aerosociety.com
President, Prof. Jonathan Cooper, MBE

ROYAL AGRICULTURAL BENEVOLENT INSTITUTION
(1860), Shaw House, 27 West Way, Oxford OX2 0QH
T 01865-724931 E info@rabi.org.uk W www.rabi.org.uk
Chief Executive, Alicia Chivers

ROYAL AGRICULTURAL SOCIETY OF THE
COMMONWEALTH (1957), c/o Royal Norfolk Agricultural
Association, Norfolk Showground, Norwich NR5 0TT
T 01603-731977 E info@therasc.com W www.therasc.com
Hon. Secretary, Michael Lambert

ROYAL AIR FORCE BENEVOLENT FUND (1919), 67
Portland Place, London W1B 1AR T 020-7580 8343
E mail@rafbf.org.uk W www.rafbf.org
Controller, Air Vice-Marshal Hon. David Murray, CVO, OBE

ROYAL AIR FORCES ASSOCIATION (1943), Atlas House,
41 Wembley Road, Leicester LE3 1UT T 0800-018 2361
W www.rafa.org.uk
Secretary General, Nick Bunting

ROYAL ARTILLERY ASSOCIATION (1920), Artillery
House, Royal Artillery Barracks, Salisbury SP4 8QT
T 01980-845233 E sarah.davies119@mod.gov.uk
W www.thegunners.org.uk
General Secretary, Lt.-Col. I. A. Vere Nicoll, MBE

ROYAL ASIATIC SOCIETY (1823), 14 Stephenson Way,
London NW1 2HD T 020-7388 4539
E info@royalasiaticsociety.org W www.royalasiaticsociety.org
President, Dr. A. Stockwell

ROYAL ASSOCIATION FOR DEAF PEOPLE (1841),
Block F, Parkside Office Village, Nesfield Road, Colchester
CO4 3ZL T 0300-688 2525 E info@royaldeaf.org.uk
W www.royaldeaf.org.uk
Chief Executives, A. Casson-Webb; L. Frearson; S. Mountford

ROYAL ASTRONOMICAL SOCIETY (1820), Burlington
House, London W1J 0BQ T 020-7734 4582 W www.ras.ac.uk
Executive Director, Philip Diamond

ROYAL BRITISH LEGION (1921), 199 Borough High Street,
London SE1 1AA T 0808-802 8080 E info@britishlegion.org.uk
W www.britishlegion.org.uk
Director-General, Charles Byrne

ROYAL BRITISH LEGION SCOTLAND (1921), New Haig
House, Logie Green Road, Edinburgh EH7 4HQ T 0131-550 1586
E info@legionscotland.org.uk W www.legionscotland.org.uk
Chief Executive Officer, Claire Armstrong

ROYAL CAMBRIAN ACADEMY (1882), Crown Lane,
Conwy LL32 8AN T 01492-593413 E rca@rcaconwy.org
W www.rcaconwy.org
President, Jeremy Yates

ROYAL CELTIC SOCIETY (1820), 25 Rutland Street,
Edinburgh EH1 2RN T 0131-228 6449
E info@royalcelticsociety.scot W www.royalcelticsociety.scot
Secretary, J. Gordon Cameron, WS

ROYAL COMMISSION FOR THE EXHIBITION OF 1851
(1850), 453 Sherfield Building, Imperial College SW7 2AZ
T 020-7594 8790 E royalcom1851@imperial.ac.uk
W www.royalcommission1851.org.uk
Secretary, Nigel Williams, CENG

ROYAL GEOGRAPHICAL SOCIETY (WITH THE
INSTITUTE OF BRITISH GEOGRAPHERS) (1830),
1 Kensington Gore, SW7 2AR T 020-7591 3000 W www.rgs.org
Director, Prof. Joe Smith

ROYAL HIGHLAND AND AGRICULTURAL SOCIETY
OF SCOTLAND (1784), Ingliston House, Royal Highland
Centre, Edinburgh EH28 8NB T 0131-335 6200
E info@rhass.org.uk W www.rhass.org.uk
Chief Executive, Alan Laidlaw

ROYAL HISTORICAL SOCIETY (1868), University College
London, Gower Street, WC1E 6BT T 020-7387 7532
E enquiries@royalhistsoc.org W www.royalhistsoc.org
Executive Secretary, Dr S. E. Carr

ROYAL HORTICULTURAL SOCIETY (1804), 80 Vincent
Square, London SW1P 2PE T 020-3176 5800 W www.rhs.org.uk
Director-General, Sue Biggs

ROYAL HOSPITAL FOR NEURO-DISABILITY (1854),
West Hill, London SW15 3SW T 020-8780 4500
E info@rhn.org.uk W www.rhn.org.uk
Chief Executive, Paul Allen

ROYAL HUMANE SOCIETY (1774), 50–51 Temple
Chambers, 3–7 Temple Avenue, London EC4Y 0HP
T 020-7936 2942 E info@royalhumanesociety.org.uk
W www.royalhumanesociety.org.uk
Secretary, Lt-Col. Andrew Chapman

ROYAL INSTITUTE OF NAVIGATION (1947),
1 Kensington Gore, SW7 2AT T 020-7591 3134
E admin@rin.org.uk W www.rin.org.uk
Director, J R Pottle, BSC, MBA, FIET

ROYAL INSTITUTE OF OIL PAINTERS (1882), 17 Carlton
House Terrace, London SW1Y 5BD T 020-7930 6844
E enquiries@theroi.org.uk W www.theroi.co.uk
President, Tim Benson

ROYAL INSTITUTE OF PAINTERS IN WATER
COLOURS (1831), 17 Carlton House Terrace, London
SW1Y 5BD T 020-7930 6844
W www.royalinstituteofpaintersinwatercolours.org
President, Rosa Sepple

ROYAL INSTITUTE OF PHILOSOPHY (1925), 14 Gordon
Square, London WC1H 0AR T 020-7387 4130
W www.royalinstitutephilosophy.org
Managing Director, Dr James Garvey

ROYAL INSTITUTION OF GREAT BRITAIN (1799),
21 Albemarle Street, London W1S 4BS T 020-7670 2955
E ri@ri.ac.uk W www.rigb.org
Director, Dr Shaun Fitzgerald

ROYAL LIFE SAVING SOCIETY UK (1891), Red Hill House,
227 London Road, Worcester WR5 2JG T 0300-323 0096
E info@rlss.org.uk W www.rlss.org.uk
Chief Executive Officer, Robert Gofton

ROYAL LITERARY FUND (1790), 3 Johnson's Court, off
Fleet Street, London EC4A 3EA T 020-7353 7150
W www.rlf.org.uk
Chief Executive, Eileen Gunn

ROYAL MEDICAL BENEVOLENT FUND (1836), 24 Kings
Road, London SW19 8QN T 020-8540 9194 E info@rmbf.org
W www.rmbf.org
Chief Executive, Steve Crone

ROYAL MICROSCOPICAL SOCIETY (1839), 37–38 St
Clements, Oxford OX4 1AJ T 01865-254760 E info@rms.org.uk
W www.rms.org.uk
Chief Executive, Allison Winton

ROYAL MUSICAL ASSOCIATION (1874), 4 Chandos Road,
Chorlton-cum-Hardy M21 0ST T 0161-861 7542
E exec@rma.ac.uk W www.rma.ac.uk
President, Prof. Simon McVeigh

ROYAL NATIONAL COLLEGE FOR THE BLIND (1872),
Venns Lane, Hereford HR1 1DT T 01432-265725
E info@rnc.ac.uk W www.rnc.ac.uk
Principal, Mark Fisher

ROYAL NATIONAL INSTITUTE OF BLIND PEOPLE
(1868), 105 Judd Street, London WC1H 9NE T 030-3123 9999
E helpline@rnib.org.uk W www.rnib.org.uk
Chief Executive, Matt Stringer

ROYAL NATIONAL LIFEBOAT INSTITUTION (1824),
West Quay Road, Poole BH15 1HZ T 0300-300 9990
W www.rnli.org
Chief Executive, Mark Dowie

ROYAL NAVAL ASSOCIATION (1949), Room 209, Royal
Semaphore Tower, PP70, HM Naval Base, Portsmouth PO1 3LT
T 023-9272 3747 E admin@royalnavalassoc.com
W www.royal-naval-association.co.uk
General Secretary, Capt. Bill Oliphant, RN

ROYAL NAVAL BENEVOLENT TRUST (1922), Castaway
House, 311 Twyford Avenue, Portsmouth PO2 8RN
T 023-9269 0112 E rnbt@rnbt.org.uk W www.rnbt.org.uk
Chief Executive, Cdr Rob Bosshardt, RN

ROYAL OSTEOPOROSIS SOCIETY (1986), Bath BA2 0PJ
T 01761-471771, Helpline 0808-800 0035
E info@theros.org.uk W www.theros.org.uk
Chief Executive, Claire Severgnini

ROYAL PHILATELIC SOCIETY LONDON (1869),
41 Devonshire Place, London W1G 6JY T 020-7486 1044
E secretary@rpsl.org.uk W www.rpsl.org.uk
President, Richard Stock

ROYAL PHILHARMONIC SOCIETY (1813), 48 Great
Marlborough Street, London W1F 7BB T 020-7289 0019
E web@royalphilharmonicsociety.org.uk
W www.royalphilharmonicsociety.org.uk
Chief Executive, James Murphy

ROYAL PHOTOGRAPHIC SOCIETY (1853), RPS House,
337 Paintworks, Bristol BS4 3AR T 0117-316 4450
E FrontofHouse@rps.org W www.rps.org
President, Robert Albright, HONFRPS

ROYAL SCHOOL OF CHURCH MUSIC (1927), 19 The
Close, Salisbury SP1 2EB T 01722-424848 E enquiries@rscm.com
W www.rscm.org.uk
Director, Hugh Morris

ROYAL SCHOOL OF NEEDLEWORK (1872), Apartment
12A, Hampton Court Palace KT8 9AU T 020-3166 6932
E enquiries@royal-needlework.org.uk
W www.royal-needlework.org.uk
Chief Executive, Dr Susan Kay-Williams

ROYAL SOCIETY FOR ASIAN AFFAIRS (1901),
1a St Martin's House, Polygon Road, London NW1 1QB
T 020-7235 5122 E info@rsaa.org.uk W www.rsaa.org.uk
Chief Executive, Michael Ryder, CMG

ROYAL SOCIETY FOR BLIND CHILDREN (1838), 52–58
Arcola Street, London E8 2DJ T 020-3198 0225
E enquiries@rsbc.org.uk W www.rsbc.org.uk
Chief Executive, Dr Tom Pey

ROYAL SOCIETY FOR THE ENCOURAGEMENT OF
ARTS, MANUFACTURES AND COMMERCE (RSA)
(1754), 8 John Adam Street, London WC2N 6EZ
T 020-7930 5115 E general@rsa.org.uk W www.thersa.org
Chief Executive, Matthew Taylor

THE ROYAL SOCIETY FOR THE PREVENTION OF
ACCIDENTS (1916/17), 28 Calthorpe Road, Birmingham
B15 1RP T 0121-248 2000 E help@rospa.com
W www.rospa.com
Chief Executive, Errol Taylor

ROYAL SOCIETY FOR THE PREVENTION OF
CRUELTY TO ANIMALS (1824), Wilberforce Way,
Horsham RH13 9RS T 0300-123 0346 W www.rspca.org.uk
Chief Executive, Chris Sherwood

ROYAL SOCIETY FOR THE PROTECTION OF BIRDS
(1889), The Lodge, Potton Road, Sandy SG19 2DL
T 01767-680551 W www.rspb.org.uk
Chief Executive, Beccy Speight

ROYAL SOCIETY OF BIOLOGY (2009), 1 Naoroji Street, London WC1X 0GB T 020-3925 3440 E info@rsb.org.uk W www.rsb.org.uk
Chief Executive, Dr Mark Downs

ROYAL SOCIETY OF CHEMISTRY (1841), Burlington House, London W1J 0BA T 020-7437 8656 W www.rsc.org
Chief Executive, Dr Robert Parker

ROYAL SOCIETY OF LITERATURE (1820), Somerset House, London WC2R 1LA T 020-7845 4679 E info@rsliterature.org W www.rsliterature.org
President, Dame Marina Warner, DBE, FRSL

ROYAL SOCIETY OF MARINE ARTISTS (1939), 17 Carlton House Terrace, London SW1Y 5BD T 020-7930 6844 E rsma.contact@gmail.com W www.rsma-web.co.uk
President, Benjamin Mowll

ROYAL SOCIETY OF MEDICINE (1805), 1 Wimpole Street, London W1G 0AE T 020-7290 2900 E info@rsm.ac.uk W www.rsm.ac.uk
Chief Executive, Michele Acton

ROYAL SOCIETY OF MINIATURE PAINTERS, SCULPTORS AND GRAVERS (1895), 89 Roseberry Road, Dursley GL11 4PU T 01454-269268 E info@royal-miniature-society.org.uk W www.royal-miniature-society.org.uk
President, Elizabeth Meek, MBE

THE ROYAL SOCIETY OF MUSICIANS OF GREAT BRITAIN (1738), 26 Fitzroy Square, London W1T 6BT T 020-7629 6137 E enquiries@royalsocietyofmusicians.org W www.royalsocietyofmusicians.org
President, Judith Weir, CBE

ROYAL SOCIETY OF PAINTER-PRINTMAKERS (1880), Bankside Gallery, 48 Hopton Street, SE1 9JH T 020-7928 7521 E info@banksidegallery.com W www.re-printmakers.com
President, David Ferry

ROYAL SOCIETY OF PORTRAIT PAINTERS (1891), 17 Carlton House Terrace, London SW1Y 5BD T 020-7930 6844 E enquiries@therp.co.uk W www.therp.co.uk
President, Richard Foster

ROYAL SOCIETY OF ST GEORGE (1894), PO Box 397, Loughton IG10 9GN T 020-3225 5011 E info@rssg.org.uk W http://rssg.org.uk
Chairman, Joanna M. Cadman

ROYAL SOCIETY OF TROPICAL MEDICINE AND HYGIENE (1907), Northumberland House, 303–306 High Holborn, London WC1V 7JZ T 020-7405 2628 E amelia.fincham@rstmh.org W www.rstmh.org
Chief Executive, Tamar Ghosh

ROYAL STAR AND GARTER HOMES (1916), 15 Castle Mews, Hampton TW12 2NP T 020-8481 7676 E general.enquiries@starandgarter.org W www.starandgarter.org
Chief Executive, Andy Cole, OBE

ROYAL THEATRICAL FUND (1839), 11 Garrick Street, London WC2E 9AR T 020-7836 3322 E admin@trtf.com W www.trtf.com
President, Robert Lindsay

ROYAL UNITED SERVICES INSTITUTE FOR DEFENCE AND SECURITY STUDIES (1831), Whitehall, London SW1A 2ET T 020-7747 2600 W www.rusi.org
Director-General, Dr Karin von Hippel

ROYAL VOLUNTARY SERVICE (1938), Beck Court, Cardiff Gate Business Park, Cardiff CF23 8RP T 0330-555 0310 W www.royalvoluntaryservice.org.uk
Chief Executive, Catherine Johnstone, CBE

ROYAL WATERCOLOUR SOCIETY (1804), Bankside Gallery, 48 Hopton Street, London SE1 9JH T 020-7928 7521 E info@royalwatercoloursociety.com W www.royalwatercoloursociety.co.uk
President, Jill Leman

ROYAL ZOOLOGICAL SOCIETY OF SCOTLAND (1909), Edinburgh Zoo, 134 Corstorphine Road, Edinburgh EH12 6TS T 0131-334 9171 E info@rzss.org.uk W www.rzss.org.uk
Chief Executive, Barbara Smith

ST JOHN AMBULANCE (1877), St John's Gate, 27 St John's Lane, London EC1M 4BU T 0870-010 4950 W www.sja.org.uk
Chief Executive, Martin Houghton-Brown

SALTIRE SOCIETY (1936), 9 Fountain Close, 22 High Street, Edinburgh EH1 1TF T 0131-556 1836 E saltire@saltiresociety.org.uk W www.saltiresociety.org.uk
Convener, Prof Alan Riach

SAMARITANS (1953), The Upper Mill, Ewell KT17 2AF T 020-8394 8300, Helpline 116 123 E admin@samaritans.org W www.samaritans.org
Chief Executive, Ruth Sutherland

SANE (1986), St Mark's Studios, 14 Chillingworth Street, London N7 8QJ T 020-3805 1790, Helpline 0300-304 7000 E info@sane.org.uk W www.sane.org.uk
Chief Executive, Marjorie Wallace, CBE

SAVE THE CHILDREN (1919), 1 St John's Lane, London EC1M 4AR T 020-7012 6400 E supportercare@savethechildren.org.uk W www.savethechildren.org.uk
Chief Executive, Kevin Watkins

SCHOOL LIBRARY ASSOCIATION (1937), 1 Pine Court, Swindon SN2 8AD T 01793-530166 E info@sla.org.uk W www.sla.org.uk
Director, Alison Tarrant

SCOPE (1952), Here East Press Centre, 14 East Bay Lane, London E15 2GW T 020-7619 7100, Helpline 0808-800 3333 E supportercare@scope.org.uk W www.scope.org.uk
Chief Executive, Mark Atkinson

SCOTTISH ASSOCIATION FOR MARINE SCIENCE (1884), Scottish Marine Institute, Argyll PA37 1QA T 01631-559000 E info@sams.ac.uk W www.sams.ac.uk
Director, Prof. Nicholas Owens

SCOTTISH ASSOCIATION FOR MENTAL HEALTH (1923), Brunswick House, 51 Wilson Street, Glasgow G1 1UZ T 0141-530 1000 E enquire@samh.org.uk W www.samh.org.uk
Chief Executive, Billy Watson

SCOTTISH CHAMBERS OF COMMERCE (1948), Strathclyde Business School, 199 Cathedral Street, Glasgow G4 0QU T 0141-444 7500 E admin@scottishchambers.org.uk W www.scottishchambers.org.uk
Chief Executive, Liz Cameron, OBE

SCOTTISH COUNCIL FOR VOLUNTARY ORGANISATIONS (1943), Mansfield Traquair Centre, 15 Mansfield Place, Edinburgh EH3 6BB T 0131-474 8000 E enquiries@scvo.org.uk W www.scvo.org.uk
Chief Executive, Anna Fowlie

SCOTTISH LAND AND ESTATES (1906), Stuart House, Eskmills Business Park, Musselburgh EH21 7PB T 0131-653 5401 E info@scottishlandandestates.co.uk W www.scottishlandandestates.co.uk
Chief Executive, Sarah-Jane Laing

SCOTTISH SOCIETY FOR THE PREVENTION OF CRUELTY TO ANIMALS (1839), Kingseat Road, Dunfermline KY11 8RY T 03000-999 999 E info@scottishspca.org W www.scottishspca.org
Chief Executive, Kirsteen Campbell

SCOTTISH WILDLIFE TRUST (1964), Harbourside House, 110 Commercial Street, Edinburgh EH6 6NF T 0131-312 7765 E enquiries@scottishwildlifetrust.org.uk W www.scottishwildlifetrust.org.uk
Chief Executive, Jo Pike

SCOUT ASSOCIATION (1907), Gilwell Park, Chingford, London E4 7QW T 0345-300 1818 E info.centre@scouts.org.uk W www.scouts.org.uk
Chief Executive, Matt Hyde

SEEABILITY (1799), Newplan House, 41 East Street, Epsom KT17 1BL T 01372-755000 E enquiries@seeability.org W www.seeability.org
Chief Executive, Lisa Hopkins

SELDEN SOCIETY (1887), School of Law, Queen Mary, London E1 4NS T 020-7882 3968 E selden-society@qmul.ac.uk W www.selden-society.ac.uk
Secretary, Prof. Michael Lobban

SENSE (1955), 101 Pentonville Road, N1 9LG T 0300-330 9256 E info@sense.org.uk W www.sense.org.uk
Chief Executive, Richard Kramer

SHELTER (NATIONAL CAMPAIGN FOR HOMELESS PEOPLE) (1966), 88 Old Street, London EC1V 9HU T 0300-330 1234, Helpline 0808-800 4444 E info@shelter.org.uk W www.shelter.org.uk
Chief Executive, Polly Neate

SIGHTSAVERS (ROYAL COMMONWEALTH SOCIETY FOR THE BLIND) (1950), Bumpers Way, Bumpers Farm, Chippenham SN14 6NG T 01444-446600 E info@sightsavers.org W www.sightsavers.org
Chief Executive, Dr Caroline Harper, CBE

SOCIÉTÉ JERSIAISE (1873), 7 Pier Road, St Helier JE2 4XW T 01534-758314 E info@societe-jersiaise.org W www.societe-jersiaise.org
Administrative Secretary, Ms C. Cornick

SOCIETY FOR PROMOTING CHRISTIAN KNOWLEDGE (SPCK) (1698), 36 Causton Street, London SW1P 4ST T 020-7592 3900 E spck@spck.org.uk W www.spckpublishing.co.uk
CEO, Sam Richardson

SOCIETY FOR THE PROMOTION OF HELLENIC STUDIES (1879), Senate House, Malet Street, London WC1E 7HU T 020-7862 8730 E secretary@hellenicsociety.org.uk W www.hellenicsociety.org.uk
President, Prof. Judith Mossman

SOCIETY FOR THE PROMOTION OF ROMAN STUDIES (1910), Senate House, Malet Street, London WC1E 7HU T 020-7862 8727 E office@romansociety.org W www.romansociety.org
President, Prof. Tim Cornell

SOCIETY OF ANTIQUARIES OF LONDON (1707), Burlington House, London W1J 0BE T 020-7479 7080 E admin@sal.org.uk W www.sal.org.uk
General-Secretary, John S. C. Lewis, FSA

SOCIETY OF ANTIQUARIES OF NEWCASTLE UPON TYNE (1813), Great North Museum: Hancock, Barras Bridge, Newcastle upon Tyne NE2 4PT T 0191-231 2700 E admin@newcastle-antiquaries.org.uk W www.newcastle-antiquaries.org.uk
President, Nick Hodgson

SOCIETY OF ANTIQUARIES OF SCOTLAND (1780), National Museums Scotland, Chambers Street, Edinburgh EH1 1JF T 0131-247 4133 E info@socantscot.org W www.socantscot.org
Director, Dr Simon Gilmour, FSA, FSA SCOT, MIFA

SOCIETY OF BOTANICAL ARTISTS (1985), 1 Knapp Cottages, Gillingham SP8 4NQ T 01747-825718 E info@soc-botanical-artists.org W www.soc-botanical-artists.org
Executive Secretary, Pam Henderson

SOCIETY OF EDITORS (1999), University Centre, Granta Place, Cambridge CB2 1RU T 01223-304080 E office@societyofeditors.org www.societyofeditors.org
Executive Director, Ian Murray

SOCIETY OF GENEALOGISTS (1911), 14 Charterhouse Buildings, Goswell Road, London EC1M 7BA T 020-7251 8799 E genealogy@sog.org.uk W www.sog.org.uk
Chief Executive, June Perrin

SOCIETY OF GLASS TECHNOLOGY (1917), 9 Churchill Way, Sheffield S35 2PY T 0114-263 4455 E info@sgt.org W www.sgt.org
Managing Editor, David Moore

SOCIETY OF INDEXERS (1957), Woodbourn Business Centre, 10 Jessell Street, Sheffield S9 3HY T 0114-244 9561 E admin@indexers.org.uk W www.indexers.org.uk
Chair, Nicola King

SOCIETY OF LEGAL SCHOLARS (1908), School of Law, Southampton University, Southampton SO17 1BJ T 023-8059 4039 E admin@legalscholars.ac.uk W www.legalscholars.ac.uk
Hon. Secretary, Prof. Paula Giliker

SOCIETY OF SCRIBES AND ILLUMINATORS (1921), Art Workers Guild, 6 Queen Square, London WC1N 3AT E honsec@calligraphyonline.org W www.calligraphyonline.org
Chair, Julie Chaney

SOCIETY OF SOLICITORS IN THE SUPREME COURT OF SCOTLAND (1784), SSC Library, Parliament House, Edinburgh EH1 1RF T 0131-225 6268 E enquiries@ssclibrary.co.uk W www.ssclibrary.co.uk
Secretary, Robert Shiels

SOCIETY OF WOMEN ARTISTS (1855), The Mall Galleries, The Mall, London T 07528-477002 E info@society-women-artists.org.uk W www.society-women-artists.org.uk
Executive Secretary, Rebecca Cotton

SOCIETY OF WRITERS TO HM SIGNET (1594), The Signet Library, Parliament Square, Edinburgh EH1 1RF T 0131-220 3249 E reception@wssociety.co.uk W www.wssociety.co.uk
Chief Executive, Robert Pirrie

SOIL ASSOCIATION (1946), Spear House, 51 Victoria Street, Bristol BS1 6AD T 0300-330 0100 W www.soilassociation.org
Chief Executive, Helen Browning, OBE

SOMERSET ARCHAEOLOGICAL AND NATURAL HISTORY SOCIETY (1849), Somerset Heritage Centre, Brunel Way, Taunton TA2 6SF T 01823-272429 E office@sanhs.org W www.sanhs.org
Chair, Christine Jessop

SOUND AND MUSIC (1967), 3rd Floor, South Wing, Somerset House, London WC2R 1LA T 020-7759 1800 E info@soundandmusic.org W www.soundandmusic.org
Chief Executive, Susanna Eastburn, MBE

SOUND SEEKERS (1959), The Green House, 244-254 Cambridge Heath Road, London T 020-35596673 E help@sound-seekers.org.uk W www.sound-seekers.org.uk
Chief Executive, Kavita Prasad

SPURGEONS (1867), 74 Wellingborough Road, Rushden NN10 9TY T 01933-412412 E info@spurgeons.org W www.spurgeons.org
Chief Executive, Ross Hendry

STANDING COUNCIL OF THE BARONETAGE (1903), 1 Tarrel Farm Cottages, Tain IV20 1SL T 01862-870177 E secretary@baronetage.org W www.baronetage.org
Chair, Sir Henry Bedingfeld, BT.

STOLL (SIR OSWALD STOLL FOUNDATION) (1916), 446 Fulham Road, London SW6 1DT T 020-7385 2110 E info@stoll.org.uk W www.stoll.org.uk
Chief Executive, Ed Tytherleigh

SUFFOLK INSTITUTE OF ARCHAEOLOGY AND HISTORY (1848), 116 Hardwick Lane, IP33 2LE T 01284-753228 E generalsecretary@suffolkinstitute.org.uk W www.suffolkinstitute.org.uk
Hon. Secretary, Jane Carr

SURREY ARCHAEOLOGICAL SOCIETY (1854), Castle Arch, Guildford GU1 3SX T 01483-532454 E info@surreyarchaeology.org.uk W www.surreyarchaeology.org.uk
Hon. Secretary, David Calow

SUSSEX ARCHAEOLOGICAL SOCIETY (1846),
Bull House, 92 High Street, Lewes BN7 1XH **T** 01273-486260
E adminlewes@sussexpast.co.uk **W** www.sussexpast.co.uk
Chief Executive, Tristan Bareham

SUSTRANS (1977), Head Office, 2 Cathedral Square, Bristol
BS1 5DD **T** 0117 926 8893 **E** reception@sustrans.org.uk
W www.sustrans.org.uk
Chief Executive, Xavier Brice

SUZY LAMPLUGH TRUST (1986), 17 Oval Way, London
SE11 5RR **T** 020-7091 0014 **E** info@suzylamplugh.org
W www.suzylamplugh.org
Chief Executive, Rachel Griffin

SWEDENBORG SOCIETY (1810), 20–21 Bloomsbury Way,
London WC1A 2TH **T** 020-7405 7986
E admin@swedenborg.org.uk **W** www.swedenborg.org.uk
Executive Director, Stephen McNeilly

TAVISTOCK INSTITUTE (1947), 30 Tabernacle Street,
London EC2A 4UE **T** 020-7417 0407 **E** hello@tavinstitute.org
W www.tavinstitute.org
Chief Executive, Dr Eliat Aram

TERRENCE HIGGINS TRUST (1982), 314–320 Gray's Inn
Road, London WC1X 8DP **T** 020-7812 1600 **E** info@tht.org.uk
W www.tht.org.uk
Chief Executive, Ian Green

THEATRES TRUST (1976), 22 Charing Cross Road, London
WC2H 0QL **T** 020-7836 8591 **E** info@theatrestrust.org.uk
W www.theatrestrust.org.uk
Director, Jon Morgan

THORESBY SOCIETY (1889), The Leeds Library, 18
Commercial Street, Leeds LS1 6AL **E** secretary@thoresby.org.uk
W www.thoresby.org.uk
President, Mrs E. Bradford

TOGETHER FOR MENTAL WELLBEING (1879),
52 Walnut Tree Walk, London SE11 6DN **T** 020-7780 7300
E contact-us@together-uk.org **W** www.together-uk.org
Chief Executive, Linda Bryant

TOWN AND COUNTRY PLANNING ASSOCIATION
(1899), 17 Carlton House Terrace, London SW1Y 5AS
T 020-7930 8903 **E** tcpa@tcpa.org.uk **W** www.tcpa.org.uk
Chief Executive, Fiona Howie

TREE COUNCIL (1974), 4 Docks Offices, Surrey Quays Road,
London SE16 2XU **T** 020-7407 9992 **E** info@treecouncil.org.uk
W www.treecouncil.org.uk
Chief Executive, Sarah Lom

TURN2US (1897), Hythe House, 200 Shepherds Bush Road,
London W6 7NL **T** 020-8834 9200 **W** www.turn2us.org.uk
Chair, Sally O'Sullivan

UK YOUTH (1911), 8th Floor, Kings Buildings, 16 Smith Square,
London SW1P 3HQ **T** 0203-137 3810 **E** info@ukyouth.org
W www.ukyouth.org
Chief Executive, Anna Smee

UNDERSTANDING ANIMAL RESEARCH (2008), Abbey
House, 74–76 St John Street, London EC1M 4DZ
E office@uar.org.uk **W** www.uar.org.uk
Chief Executive, Wendy Jarrett

UNITED GRAND LODGE OF ENGLAND (1717),
Freemasons' Hall, 60 Great Queen Street, London WC2B 5AZ
T 020-7831 9811 **E** enquiries@ugle.org.uk **W** www.ugle.org.uk
Grand Master, HRH the Duke of Kent, KG, GCMG, GCVO

UNITED REFORMED CHURCH HISTORY SOCIETY
(1972), Westminster College, Madingley Road, Cambridge
CB3 0AA **T** 01223-330620 **E** mt212@cam.ac.uk
W www.westminster.cam.ac.uk/rcl/about/urc-history-society
Hon. Secretary, Mrs M. Thompson

UNIVERSITIES FEDERATION FOR ANIMAL WELFARE
(1926), The Old School, Brewhouse Hill, Wheathampstead
AL4 8AN **T** 01582-831818 **E** ufaw@ufaw.org.uk
W www.ufaw.org.uk
Chief Executive & Scientific Director, Dr R. C. Hubrecht

UNIVERSITIES UK (2000), Woburn House, 20 Tavistock
Square, London WC1H 9HQ **T** 020-7419 4111
E info@universitiesuk.ac.uk **W** www.universitiesuk.ac.uk
Chief Executive, Alistair Jarvis

VEGAN SOCIETY (1944), Donald Watson House, 34–35
Ludgate Hill, Birmingham B3 1EH **T** 0121-523 1730
E info@vegansociety.com **W** www.vegansociety.com
Chief Executive, George Gill

VEGETARIAN SOCIETY OF THE UNITED KINGDOM
LTD (1847), Parkdale, Dunham Road, Cheshire WA14 4QG
T 0161-925 2000 **E** hello@vegsoc.org **W** www.vegsoc.org
Chair, Dale Hoyland

VERNACULAR ARCHITECTURE GROUP (1952),
Kangaroo House, Colby, Appleby-in-Westmorland CA16 6BD
E secretary@vag.org.uk **W** www.vag.org.uk
President, Dr Adam Menuge

VERSUS ARTHRITIS (1947), Copeman House, St Mary's
Court, St Mary's Gate, Chesterfield S41 7TD **T** 0300-790 0400
E enquiries@versusarthritus.org **W** www.versusarthritis.org
Chief Executive, Liam O'Toole

VICTIM SUPPORT (1979), Octavia House, 50 Banner Street,
London EC1Y 8ST **T** 020-7268 0200, **Helpline** 0808-1689 111
W www.victimsupport.org.uk
Chief Officer, Diana Fawcett

VICTIM SUPPORT SCOTLAND (1985), 15–23 Hardwell
Close, Edinburgh EH8 9RX **T** 0131-668 4486
E info@victimsupportsco.org.uk
W www.victimsupportsco.org.uk
Chief Executive, Kate Wallace

VICTORIA CROSS AND GEORGE CROSS
ASSOCIATION (1956), Horse Guards, Whitehall, London
SW1A 2AX **T** 020-7930 3506 **E** secretary@vcandgc.org
W vcgca.org
Secretary, Rebecca Maciejewska

VICTORIAN SOCIETY (1958), 75 Cowcross Street,
EC1M 6EJ **T** 020-8994 1019 **E** admin@victoriansociety.org.uk
W www.victoriansociety.org.uk
Director, Christopher Costelloe

VOLUNTEERING MATTERS (1962), The Levy Centre, 18–24
Lower Clapton Road, London E5 0PD **T** 020-3780 5870
W www.volunteeringmatters.org.uk
Chief Executive, Oonagh Aitken

VSO (VOLUNTARY SERVICE OVERSEAS) (1958), 100
London Road, Kingston-Upon-Thames KT2 6QJ **T** 020-8780 7500
E enquiry@vso.org **W** www.vsointernational.org
Chief Executive, Dr Philip Goodwin

WAR WIDOWS ASSOCIATION OF GREAT BRITAIN
(1971), 199 Borough High Street, SE1 1AA **T** 0845-241 2189
E info@warwidows.org.uk **W** www.warwidows.org.uk
Chairman, Mary Moreland

WELLBEING OF WOMEN (1965), First Floor, Fairgate House,
78 New Oxford Street, WC1A 1HB **T** 020-3697 7000
E hello@wellbeingofwomen.org.uk
W www.wellbeingofwomen.org.uk
Chief Executive, Janet Lindsay

WESTMINSTER FOUNDATION FOR DEMOCRACY
(1992), Artillery House, 11 –19 Artillery Row, London SW1P 1RT
T 020-7799 1311 **W** www.wfd.org
Chief Executive, Anthony Smith, CMG

WHICH? (1957), 2 Marylebone Road, London NW1 4DF
T 020-7770 7000 **W** www.which.co.uk
Chair, Tim Gardam

WILDFOWL AND WETLANDS TRUST (1946), Slimbridge
GL2 7BT **T** 01453-891900 **E** enquiries@wwt.org.uk
W www.wwt.org.uk
Chief Executive, Martin Spray, CBE

WILLIAM MORRIS SOCIETY AND KELMSCOTT
FELLOWSHIP (1955), Kelmscott House, 26 Upper Mall,
London W6 9TA **T** 020-8741 3735
E info@williammorrissociety.org.uk
W www.williammorrissociety.org.uk
Hon. Secretary, Natalia Martynenko-Hunt

WILTSHIRE ARCHAEOLOGICAL AND NATURAL
HISTORY SOCIETY (1853), Wiltshire Heritage Museum, 41
Long Street, Devizes SN10 1NS **T** 01380-727369
E hello@wiltshiremuseum.org.uk
W www.wiltshiremuseum.org.uk/society
Director, David Dawson

WOMEN'S ENGINEERING SOCIETY (1919), c/o The IET,
Michael Faraday House, Stevenage SG1 2AY **T** 01438-765506
E info@wes.org.uk **W** www.wes.org.uk
President, Dawn Childs

WOMEN'S ROYAL NAVAL SERVICE BENEVOLENT
TRUST (1941), Castaway House, 311 Twyford Avenue,
Portsmouth PO2 8RN **T** 023-9265 5301
E generalsecretary@wrnsbt.org.uk **W** www.wrnsbt.org.uk
General Secretary, Sarah Ayton

WOODLAND TRUST (1972), Kempton Way, Grantham
NG31 6LL **T** 0330-333 3300 **E** england@woodlandtrust.org.uk
W www.woodlandtrust.org.uk
Chief Executive, Beccy Speight

WORKING FAMILIES (2003), Spaces, City Point, London
EC2Y 9AW **T** 020-7153 1230 **E** office@workingfamilies.org.uk
W www.workingfamilies.org.uk
Chief Executive, Jane van Zyl

YMCA (1844), 10–11 Charterhouse Square, London EC1M 6EH
T 020-7186 9500 **E** enquiries@ymca.org.uk
W www.ymca.org.uk
Chief Executive, Denise Hatton

YORKSHIRE ARCHAEOLOGICAL AND HISTORICAL
SOCIETY (1863), Stringer House, 34 Lupton Street, Leeds
LS10 2QW **T** 0113-245 7910 **E** yahs.office@gmail.com
W www.yas.org.uk
President, David Asquith

YOUNG WOMEN'S TRUST (1855), Unit D, 15–18 White Lion
Street, London N1 9PD **T** 020-7837 2019
E contact@youngwomenstrust.org
W www.youngwomenstrust.org
Chief Executive, Sophie Walker

YOUTH HOSTELS ASSOCIATION (ENGLAND &
WALES) (1930), Trevelyan House, Dimple Road, Matlock
DE4 3YH **T** 01629-592700 **E** customerservices@yha.org.uk
W www.yha.org.uk
Chief Executive, James Blake

ZOOLOGICAL SOCIETY OF LONDON (1826), Outer
Circle, Regent's Park, London NW1 4RY **T** 0344-225 1826
E generalenquiries@zsl.org **W** www.zsl.org
Director-General, Dominic Jermey, CVO, OBE

THE WORLD

THE WORLD IN FIGURES

THE EARTH

The shape of the Earth is that of an oblate spheroid or solid of revolution whose meridian sections are ellipses, while the sections at right angles are circles.

DIMENSIONS

Equatorial diameter = 12,742.01km (7,917.51 miles)
Polar diameter = 12,713.50km (7,899.80 miles)
Equatorial circumference = 40,030.20km (24,873.6 miles)
Polar circumference = 40,007.86km (24,859.73 miles)
Mass = 5,972,190,000,000,000,000,000,000kg
$\quad$ (5.972×10^{24}kg)

The equatorial circumference is divided into 360 degrees of longitude, which is measured in degrees, minutes and seconds east or west of the Greenwich (or 'prime') meridian (0°) to 180°; the meridian 180° E coinciding with 180° W. This was internationally ratified in 1884.

$\quad$ Distance north and south of the equator is measured in degrees, minutes and seconds of latitude. The equator is 0°, the North Pole is 90°N. and the South Pole is 90°S. The tropics lie at 23° 27′ N. (tropic of cancer) and 23° 27′ S. (tropic of capricorn). The Arctic Circle lies at 66° 33′ N. and the Antarctic Circle at 66° 33′ S. (Note the tropics and the Arctic and Antarctic circles are affected by the slow decrease in obliquity of the ecliptic, of about 0.47 arcseconds a year. The effect of this is that the Arctic and Antarctic circles are currently moving towards their respective poles by about 14m per annum, while the tropics move towards the equator by the same amount.)

AREA ETC

The surface area of the Earth is 510,064,472km² (196,936,994 miles²), of which the water area is 70.92 per cent and the land area is 29.08 per cent.

$\quad$ The radial velocity on the Earth's surface at the equator is 1,669.79km per hour (1,037.56mph). The Earth's mean velocity in its orbit around the Sun is 107,218km per hour (66,622mph). The Earth's mean distance from the Sun is 149,598,262km (92,956,050 miles).

OCEANS

LARGEST BY AREA

	km²	miles²
Pacific	165,250,000	63,800,000
Atlantic	82,440,000	31,830,000
Indian	73,440,000	28,360,000
Southern	20,327,000	7,848,300
Arctic	14,090,000	5,440,000

The equator divides the Pacific into the North and South Pacific and the Atlantic into the North and South Atlantic. In 2000 the International Hydrographic Organisation approved the description of the 20,327,000km² (7,848,300 miles²) of circum-Antarctic waters up to 60°S. as the Southern Ocean.

GREATEST KNOWN OCEAN DEPTHS

Greatest depth	Location	metres	feet
Mariana Trench	Pacific	10,994	36,070
Puerto Rico Trench	Atlantic	8,380	27,493
Java Trench	Indian	8,290	23,917
South Sandwich Trench	Southern	7,235	23,737
Molloy Deep	Arctic	5,607	18,397

On 23 January 1960, Jacques Piccard (Switzerland) and Don Walsh (USA) descended in the bathyscaphe *Trieste* to the floor of the Mariana Trench, a depth later calculated as 10,916m (35,814ft). The current depth was calculated by the Japanese remote-controlled probe *Kaiko* on 24 March 1995. On 1 June 2009, sonar mapping of the Challenger Deep in the Mariana Trench by the US oceanographic research vessel *Kilo Moana* indicated a possible depth of 10,971m (35,994ft).

$\quad$ Previously, the Diamantia Trench was listed as the deepest depth in the India Ocean. However, research published in 2019 claimed that the Diamantia Trench is not a trench but a fracture zone. Therefore, it is actually the Java Trench that is the deepest spot in the Indian Ocean.

SEAS

LARGEST BY AREA

	km²	miles²
South China	3,685,000	1,423,000
Caribbean	2,753,000	1,063,000
Mediterranean	2,509,900	969,100
Bering	2,304,000	890,000
Okhotsk	1,582,000	611,000
Gulf of Mexico	1,550,000	600,000
Japan	978,000	377,600
Hudson Bay	819,000	316,000
Andaman	798,000	308,000
East China	750,000	290,000
North Sea	570,000	220,000
Red Sea	453,000	174,900
Black Sea	422,000	163,000

GREATEST KNOWN SEA DEPTHS

Greatest depth	metres	feet
Caribbean (Cayman Trench)	7,686	25,216
Philippine Sea (Ryukyu Trench)	7,507	24,629
Mediterranean (Calypso Deep)	5,267	17,280
Gulf of Mexico (Sigsbee Deep)	5,203	17,070
South China	5,016	16,457
Andaman	4,400	14,500
Bering (Bowers Basin)	4,097	13,442
Japan	3,742	12,276
Okhotsk	3,372	11,063
Red Sea	3,040	9,974
Black Sea	2,212	7,257
North Sea	700	2,300

THE CONTINENTS

There are generally considered to be seven continents: Africa, North America, South America, Antarctica, Asia, Australia and Europe. Europe and Asia are sometimes considered a single continent: Eurasia, and North and South America are sometimes referred to together as the Americas.

$\quad$ AFRICA is surrounded by sea except for the narrow isthmus of Suez in the north-east, through which was cut the Suez Canal (opened 17 November 1869). Its extreme longitudes are 17° 20′ W. at Cabo Verde, Senegal, and 51° 24′ E. at Raas Xaafuun, Somalia. The extreme latitudes are 37° 20′ N. at Cape Blanc, Tunisia, and 34° 50′ S. at Cape Agulhas, South Africa, about 7,081km (4,400 miles) apart. The equator passes across Gabon, Republic of the Congo, Uganda, Kenya and Somalia in the middle of the continent.

NORTH AMERICA, including Mexico, is surrounded by ocean except in the south, where the isthmian states of Central America link North America with South America. Its extreme longitudes are 168° 5′ W. at Cape Prince of Wales, Alaska, and 55° 40′ W. at Cape Charles, Newfoundland. The extreme continental latitudes are the tip of the Boothia peninsula, NW Territories, Canada (71° 51′ N.) and 14° 22′ N. in southern Mexico near La Victoria, Guatemala.

SOUTH AMERICA lies mostly in the southern hemisphere, the equator passing across Ecuador, Colombia and Brazil in the north of the continent. It is surrounded by ocean except where it is joined to Central America in the north by the narrow isthmus through which was cut the Panama Canal (opened 15 August 1914). Its extreme longitudes are 34° 47′ W. at Cape Branco in Brazil and 81° 20′ W. at Punta Pariña, Peru. The extreme continental latitudes are 12° 25′ N. at Punta Gallinas, Colombia, and 53° 54′ S. at the southernmost tip of Peninsula de Brunswick, Chile. Cape Horn, on Cape Island, Chile, lies in 55° 59′ S.

ANTARCTICA lies almost entirely within the Antarctic Circle (66° 33′ S.) and is the largest of the world's glaciated areas. Ninety-eight per cent of the continent is permanently covered in ice. The ice amounts to some 29 million km³ (7 million miles³) and represents more than 70 per cent of the world's fresh water. The ice sheet is on average 2.45km (1.5 miles) thick; if it were to melt, the world's seas would rise by more than 60m (197ft). The environment is too hostile for unsupported human habitation.

ASIA is the largest continent and occupies 29.6 per cent of the world's land surface. The extreme longitudes are 26° 05′ E. at Baba Buran, Turkey, and 169° 40′ W. at Mys Dezhneva, Russia, a distance of about 9,656km (6,000 miles). Its extreme northern latitude is 77° 45′ N. at Mys Chelyuskin, Russia, and it extends over 8,046km (5,000 miles) south to Tanjong Piai, Malaysia.

AUSTRALIA is the smallest of the continents and lies in the southern hemisphere. It is entirely surrounded by ocean. Its extreme longitudes are 113° 11′ E. at Steep Point, Western Australia, and 153° 11′ E. at Cape Byron, New South Wales. The extreme latitudes are 10° 42′ S. at Cape York, Queensland, and 39°S. at South East Point, Tasmania. Australia, together with New Zealand (Australasia), Papua New Guinea and the Pacific Islands, comprises Oceania.

EUROPE, including European Russia, is the smallest continent in the northern hemisphere. Its extreme latitudes are 71° 11′ N. at Nord Kapp in Norway, and 36° 23′ N. at Akra Tainaron (Matapas) in southern Greece, a distance of about 3,862km (2,400 miles). Its breadth from Cabo Carvoeiro in Portugal (9° 34′ W.) in the west to the Kara River, north of the Urals (66° 30′ E.) in the east is about 5,310km (3,300 miles). The division between Europe and Asia is generally regarded as the watershed of the Ural Mountains; down the Ural river to Atyrau, Kazakhstan; across the Caspian Sea to Apsheronskiy Poluostrov, near Baku; along the watershed of the Caucasus Mountains to Anapa and then across the Black Sea to the Bosporus in Turkey; across the Sea of Marmara to Canakkale Bogazi (Dardanelles).

	Area km²	Area miles²
Asia	44,614,000	17,226,000
Africa	30,365,000	11,724,000
North America	24,230,000	9,355,000
South America	17,814,000	6,878,000
Antarctica	14,200,000	5,500,000
Europe*	9,699,000	3,745,000
Australia	7,702,501	2,973,952

* Includes 5,571,000km² (2,151,000miles²) of former USSR territory, including the Baltic states, Belarus, Moldova, Ukraine and the part of Russia west of the Ural Mountains and Kazakhstan west of the Ural river. European Turkey (24,378km²/9,412 miles²) comprises territory to the west and north of the Bosporus and the Dardanelles

GLACIATED AREAS

It is estimated that around 14,800,000km² (5,712,800 miles²) or 10 per cent of the world's land surface is permanently covered with ice. Glacial retreat and thinning occurs where glaciers melt faster than they are created. The phenomenon has been observed since the mid-19th century but has accelerated since about 1980 as a result of global warming and is most notable in the Antarctic. The largest glacier is the 400km (250 miles) long and 100km (60 miles) wide Lambert-Fisher Ice Passage, Mac Robertson Land, Eastern Antarctica.

Location	km²	miles²
South Polar regions	13,829,000	5,340,000
North Polar regions (incl. Greenland)	1,965,000	758,500

LARGEST ISLANDS

	km²	miles²
Greenland (Kalaallit Nunaat), Arctic	2,166,086	836,330
New Guinea, Pacific	785,753	303,381
Borneo, Pacific	743,330	287,000
Madagascar, Indian	587,041	226,657
Baffin Island, Arctic	507,451	195,928
Sumatra, Indian	473,606	182,860
Honshu, Pacific	227,898	87,992
Great Britain, Atlantic	218,077	84,200
Victoria Island, Arctic	217,291	83,896
Ellesmere Island, Arctic	196,236	75,767

LARGEST DESERTS

	km²	miles²
Antarctica	14,000,000	5,400,000
Sahara, N. Africa	8,600,000	3,320,000
Arabian, Middle East	2,330,000	900,000
Gobi, Mongolia/China	1,300,000	500,000
Kalahari, Botswana/Namibia/ S. Africa	930,000	360,000
Patagonian, Argentina/Chile	670,000	260,000
Syrian, Middle East	518,000	200,000
Great Basin, USA	492,000	190,000
Great Victoria, Australia	424,400	163,900
Chihuahuan, USA/Mexico	362,600	140,000

DEEPEST DEPRESSIONS

The depth given is the maximum depth below sea level.

	metres	feet
Dead Sea, Jordan/Israel	413	1,354
Lake Assal, Djibouti	157	515
Turfan Depression, Sinkiang, China	155	508
Qattara Depression, Egypt	133	435
Batyr Depression, Kazakhstan	130	425
Kobar Sink, Ethiopia	116	381
Death Valley, California, USA	86	282
Salton Sea, California, USA	69	227
Caspian Depression, Russia/Kazakhstan	27	90

The world's largest exposed depression is the Caspian Depression covering the hinterland of the northern third of the Caspian Sea, which is itself 27m (90ft) below sea level.

Western Antarctica and central Greenland largely comprise crypto-depressions under ice burdens. The Antarctic Bentley subglacial trench has a bedrock 2,538m (8,326ft) below sea level. In Greenland (lat. 73° N., long. 39° W.) the bedrock is 365m (1,197ft) below sea level.

Around 26 per cent of the area of the Netherlands lies marginally below sea level, an area of more than 10,000km² (3,860 miles²).

CAVES

DEEPEST CAVES

The world's deepest cave was discovered in January 2001 by a team of Ukrainian cave explorers in the Arabikskaya system in the western Caucasus mountains of Georgia. It is a branch of the Voronya or 'Crow's Cave'.

	metres	feet
Krubera (Voronya), Georgia	2,191	7,188
Illyuzia-Mezhonnogo-Snezhnaya, Georgia	1,753	5,751
Lamprechtsofen Vogelschacht, Austria	1,632	5,354
Gouffre Mirolda, France	1,626	5,335
Réseau Jean Bernard, France	1,602	5,256
Torca del Cerro del Cuevon/Torca de las Saxifragas, Spain	1,589	5,213
Sarma, Georgia	1,543	5,062
Shakta Vyacheslav, Georgia	1,508	4,947
Sima de la Cornisa (Torca Magali), Spain	1,507	4,944
Cehi 2, Slovenia	1,502	4,928
Sistema Cheve (Cuicateco), Mexico	1,484	4,868
Sistema Huautla, Mexico	1,475	4,839

LONGEST CAVE SYSTEMS

	km	miles
Mammoth Cave System, Kentucky, USA	643.7	400
Jewel Cave, South Dakota, USA	241.6	150
Optymistychna, Ukraine	232.0	144
Wind Cave, South Dakota, USA	218.4	136
Sistema Sac Actun, Mexico (submerged, but dry)	217.4	135
Lechuguilla Cave, New Mexico, USA	209.6	130
Hölloch, Switzerland	195.9	122
Fisher Ridge System, Kentucky, USA	183.6	114
Sistema Ox Bel Ha, Mexico (submerged)	182.2	113
Gua Air Jernih, Malaysia	175.7	109
Siebenhengste-hohgant, Switzerland	156.0	97
Schoenbergsystem, Austria	130.2	81

LONGEST MOUNTAIN RANGES

	km	miles
Cordillera de Los Andes, South America	8,900	5,500
Rocky Mountains, North America	4,800	3,000
Great Dividing Range, Australia	3,700	2,300
Transantarctic Mountains, Antarctica	3,200	2,000
West Sumatran-Javan Range, Indonesia	2,900	1,800
Serra do Mar, Brazil	2,600	1,600
Himalaya, Central Asia	2,500	1,550
Tien Shan, Central Asia	2,400	1,500
New Guinea Highlands, New Guinea	2,010	1,250

HIGHEST MOUNTAINS

Mountain (first ascent)	metres	feet
Mt Everest* [Qomolangma] (29 May 1953)	8,850	29,035
K2 [Qogir]† (31 July 1954)	8,611	28,251
Kangchenjunga (25 May 1955)	8,586	28,169
Lhotse (18 May 1956)	8,516	27,940
Makalu (15 May 1955)	8,463	27,766
Cho Oyu (19 October 1954)	8,201	26,906
Dhaulagiri I (13 May 1960)	8,167	26,795
Manaslu I [Kutang I] (9 May 1956)	8,163	26,781
Nanga Parbat [Diamir] (3 July 1953)	8,126	26,660
Annapurna I (3 June 1950)	8,091	26,545

* Named after Sir George Everest (1790–1866), Surveyor-General of India 1830–43, in 1863. He pronounced his name 'Eve-rest'.

† Formerly named after Col. Henry Haversham Godwin-Austen (1834–1923), who worked on the Trigonometrical Survey of India, which established the heights of the Himalayan peaks, including Everest

The culminating summits in the other major mountain ranges are:

	metres	feet
Victory Peak [Pik Pobedy], Tien Shan	7,439	24,406
Mt Aconcagua, Cordillera de Los Andes	6,959	22,831
Denali (S. Peak), Alaska Range	6,190	20,310
Kilimanjaro (Kibo), Tanzania	5,895	19,340
Hkakabo Razi, Myanmar	5,881	19,296
Mt Elbrus, (W. Peak), Caucasus	5,642	18,510
Citlaltépetl [Orizaba], Mexico	5,610	18,406
Jaya Peak, Central New Guinea Range	5,030	16,500
Vinson Massif, Antarctica	4,892	16,050
Mt Blanc, Alps	4,807	15,771

HIGHEST ACTIVE VOLCANOES

Although it displays fumarolic activity, emitting steam and gas, no major eruption has ever been observed of the world's highest volcano and second highest peak in the western hemisphere, the 6,893m (22,615ft) Ojos del Salado, in the Andes on the Argentina/Chile border. For comparison, Eyjafjallajokull, the Icelandic volcano which erupted in 2010 causing air transport chaos, has an elevation of 1,666m (5,466ft).

The volcanoes listed below include only those that have had activity recorded since 1960.

Volcano, location (most recent activity)	metres	feet
San Pedro, Andes, Chile (1960)	6,145	20,161
Aracar, Andes, Argentina (1993)	6,082	19,954
Volcan Guallatiri, Andes, Chile (1960)	6,071	19,918
Tupungatito, Andes, Chile (1987)	6,000	19,685
Sabancaya, Andes, Peru (ongoing)	5,967	19,577
San José, Andes, Argentina/Chile (1960)	5,856	19,213
Lascar, Andes, Chile (2015)	5,592	18,346
Popocatepetl, Mexico (ongoing)	5,426	17,802
Nevado del Ruiz, Colombia (2016)	5,321	17,457
Sangay, Andes, Ecuador (2016)	5,230	17,159
Irruputuncu, Chile (1995)	5,163	16,939
Tungurahua, Ecuador (2016)	5,023	16,479

LAKES

LARGEST LAKES

The areas of some of the lakes listed are subject to seasonal variation. The most voluminous lakes are the Caspian Sea (saline) with 78,200km³ (18,800 miles³) and Baikal (fresh water) with 23,000km³ (5,518 miles³). Baikal is also the world's deepest lake (*see* below). It is estimated that it contains as much water as the entire Great Lakes system in North America – more than 20 per cent of the world's fresh water and some 90 per cent of all the fresh water in Russia.

The Aral was once the fifth largest in the world, with an area of 68,000km² (26,255 miles²), but since the 1960s many of its feeder rivers have been diverted for irrigation, as a result of which its area shrank to 17,160km² (6,626 miles²). Its salinity was almost three times that of seawater, and pollution led to the extinction of many aquatic species. Since the construction of the Kok-Aral dam (2005), water levels are rising again, especially in the north.

Lake and location	Area		Length	
	km²	miles²	km	miles
Caspian Sea, Iran/ Azerbaijan/Russia/ Turkmenistan/Kazakhstan	386,400	149,200	1,200	750
Michigan–Huron, USA/ Canada*	117,610	45,300	1,010	627
Superior, Canada/USA	82,100	31,700	563	350
Victoria, Uganda/ Tanzania/Kenya	69,484	26,828	337	210
Tanganyika, Dem. Rep. of Congo/Tanzania/Zambia/ Burundi	32,900	12,700	660	410
Baikal, Russia	31,500	12,200	636	395
Great Bear, Canada	31,328	12,096	320	200
Malawi [Nyasa], Tanzania/ Malawi/Mozambique	29,604	11,430	584	363
Great Slave, Canada	28,568	11,030	480	298
Erie, Canada/USA	25,670	9,910	388	241

* Lakes Michigan and Huron may be regarded as lobes of the same lake. The Michigan lobe has an area of 57,750km² (22,300 miles²) and the Huron lobe an area of 59,570km² (23,000 miles²)

UNITED KINGDOM (BY COUNTRY)

Lake and location	km²	miles²	km	miles
Lough Neagh, Northern Ireland	396.00	153.00	28.90	18.00
Loch Lomond, Scotland	71.12	27.46	36.44	22.64
Windermere, England	14.74	5.69	16.90	10.50
Lake Vyrnwy, Wales (artificial)	4.53	1.75	7.56	4.70
Llyn Tegid [Bala], Wales	4.38	1.69	5.80	3.65

LARGEST MANMADE LAKES

by volume

Dam/lake* (year of completion)	km³	miles³
Nalubaale dam [Owen Falls], Uganda/ Kenya/Tanzania (1954)	204.80	49.13
Kariba, Zimbabwe/Zambia (1959)	180.60	43.33
Bratsk, Russia (1967)	169.27	40.61
Nasser, Egypt (1970)	168.90	40.52
Volta, Ghana (1965)	153.00	36.71
Manicouagan [Daniel Johnson dam], Canada (1968)	141.85	34.03
Guri [Raul Leoni], Venezuela (1986)	138.00	33.11
Krasnoyarskoye, Russia (1967)	73.30	17.58
Wadi-Tatar, Iraq (1967)	72.80	17.46
Williston (W. A. C. Bennett dam), Canada (1967)	70.31	16.87

* Formed as a result of dam construction

The UK's largest reservoir is Kielder Water, Northumberland (1982) with a volume of 0.2km³ (0.048 miles³)

DEEPEST LAKES

Lake, location	metres	feet
Baikal, Russia	1,637	5,371
Tanganyika, Burundi/Tanzania/Dem. Rep. of Congo/Zambia	1,470	4,823
Caspian Sea, Azerbaijan/Iran/Kazakhstan/ Russia/Turkmenistan	1,025	3,363
O'Higgins [San Martin], Chile/Argentina	836	2,743
Malawi [Nyasa], Malawi/Mozambique/ Tanzania	706	2,316
Ysyk, Kyrgyzstan	668	2,192
Great Slave, Canada	614	2,015
Quesnel, Canada	610	2,001
Crater, Oregon, USA	594	1,949
Matano, South Sulawesi, Indonesia	590	1,936
Buenos Aires [General Carrera], Argentina/ Chile	586	1,923
Hornindalsvatnet, Norway	514	1,686
Sarez, Tajikistan	505	1,657
Toba, Sumatra, Indonesia	505	1,657
Argentino, Argentina	500	1,640
Tahoe, California/Nevada, USA	500	1,640

Loch Morar, Highland, Scotland is the UK's deepest lake at 310m (1,017ft).

LONGEST RIVERS

River, source–outflow	km	miles
Nile [Bahr-el-Nil], R. Luvironza, Burundi–E. Mediterranean Sea	6,650	4,132
Amazon [Amazonas], Lago Villafro, Peru–S. Atlantic Ocean	6,448	4,007
Yangtze [Chang Jiang], Kunlun Mts, W. China–Yellow Sea	6,300	3,915
Mississippi-Missouri-Red Rock, Montana– Gulf of Mexico	5,971	3,710
Yenisey-Selenga, W. Mongolia–Kara Sea	5,539	3,442
Huang He [Yellow River], Bayan Har Shan range, Central China–Yellow Sea	5,464	3,395
Ob-Irtysh, W. Mongolia–Kara Sea	5,410	3,362
Congo [Zambia], R. Lualaba, Dem. Rep. of Congo-Zambia–S. Atlantic Ocean	4,665	2,900
Amur-Argun, R. Argun, Khingan Mts, N. China–Sea of Okhotsk	4,416	2,744
Lena, R. Kirenga, W. of Lake Baikal–Laptev Sea, Arctic Ocean	4,400	2,734

BRITISH ISLES

River, source–outflow	km	miles
Shannon, Co. Cavan, Rep. of Ireland–Atlantic Ocean	372	231
Severn, Powys, Wales–Bristol Channel	354	220
Thames, Gloucestershire, England–North Sea	346	215
Tay, Perthshire, Scotland–North Sea	193	120
Clyde, Lanarkshire, Scotland–Firth of Clyde	170	106
Tweed, Scottish Borders–North Sea	155	97
Bann (Upper and Lower), Co. Down, N. Ireland–Atlantic Ocean	129	80

WATERFALLS

GREATEST BY HEIGHT

	Total drop		Greatest single leap	
	metres	feet	metres	feet
Angel, Carrao Auyan Tepui, Venezuela	979	3,212	807	2,648
Tugela, Tugela, S. Africa (5 leaps)	947	3,110	411	1,350
Ramnefjellsfossen, Jostedal Glacier, Norway	800	2,625	600	1,970
Mongefossen, Monge, Norway	773	2,535	–	–
Gocta, Cocahuayco, Peru	771	2,531	–	–
Mutarazi, Mutarazi, Zimbabwe	762	2,499	479	1,572
Yosemite, Yosemite Creek, USA	740	2,425	436	1,430
Ostre Mardola Foss, Mardals, Norway*	655	2,149	296	974
Tyssestrengene, Tysso, Norway*	646	2,120	289	948
Kukenaam, Arabopo, Venezuela	610	2,000	–	–

* Volume much affected by hydroelectric harnessing

POPULATIONS

MOST POPULOUS COUNTRIES IN THE WORLD

Country	Population*	Area (sq. km)	Area: world comparison†
China	1,394,015,977	9,596,961	4
India	1,326,093,247	3,287,263	7
USA	332,639,102	9,826,675	3
Indonesia	267,026,366	1,904,569	15
Pakistan	233,500,636	8,514,877	36
Nigeria	214,028,302	796,095	32
Brazil	211,715,973	923,768	5
Bangladesh	162,650,853	143,998	94
Russia	141,722,205	17,098,242	1
Mexico	128,649,565	377,915	14

* 2020 estimate
† Country's position in terms of area when compared against all the countries of the world, with '1' (Russia) having the largest land area

POPULATION GROWTH RATE

Top 10		Bottom 10	
Country	Growth Rate (%)*	Country	Growth Rate (%)*
Syria	4.25	Lebanon	−6.68
Niger	3.66	Cook Islands	−2.59
Angola	3.43	Puerto Rico	−1.59
Benin	3.40	American Samoa	−1.40
Uganda	3.34	St Pierre and Miquelon	−1.15
Malawi	3.30	Lithuania	−1.13
Chad	3.18	Latvia	−1.12
Dem. Rep. Congo	3.18	Moldova	−1.08
Mali	2.95	Estonia	−0.65
Zambia	2.89	Bulgaria	−0.65

* 2020 estimate

DAMS

TALLEST DAMS

Dam, location (year of completion)	metres	feet
Jinping-I, China (2014)	305	1,001
Nurek, Tajikistan (1980)	300	984
Xiaowan, China (2010)	292	958
Grande Dixence, Switzerland (1961)	285	935
Xiluodu, China (2014)	278	912
Enguri, Georgia (1980)	272	892
Vajont, Italy (1961)	262	859
Nuozhadu, China (2013)	262	858
Manuel Moreno Torres, Mexico (1981)	261	856

TALLEST

All heights are in accordance with the Council on Tall Buildings and Urban Habitat's regulations, which measure from the ground level of the main entrance to the architectural tip of the building and include spires but not antennae, signage or flag poles.

INHABITED BUILDINGS

Building and location (year of completion)	metres	feet
Burj Khalifa, Dubai, UAE (2010)	828	2,717
Shanghai Tower, Shanghai, China (2015)	632	2,073
Makkah Royal Clock Tower, Mecca, Saudi Arabia (2012)	601	1,972
Ping An Finance Center, Shenzhen, China (2016)	599	1,965
Goldin Finance 117, Tianjin, China (2022)*	597	1,957
Lotte World Tower, Seoul, South Korea (2016)	555	1,819
One World Trade Centre, New York, USA (2014)	541	1,776
Guangzhou CTF Finance Centre, Guangzhou, China (2016)	530	1,739
Tianjin CTF Finance Center, Tianjin, China (2019)	530	1,739
CITIC (China Zun) Tower, Beijing, China (2018)	528	1,731
TAIPEI 101, Taipei, Taiwan (2004)	508	1,667
Shanghai World Financial Center, Shanghai, China (2008)	492	1,614
International Commerce Centre, Hong Kong, China (2010)	484	1,588
Wuhan Greenland Center, Wuhan, China (2022)*	476	1,560
Lakhta Center, St. Petersburg, Russia (2019)	462	1,516
Vincom Landmark 81, Ho Chi Minh City, Vietnam (2018)	461	1,513
Changsha IFS Tower T1, Changsha, China (2018)	452	1,483
Petronas Towers I and II, Kuala Lumpur, Malaysia (1998)	452	1,483
Suzhou IFS, Suzhou, China (2019)	450	1,476
Zifeng Tower, Nanjing, China (2010)	450	1,476

* Scheduled completion date

TWIN TOWERS

Structure, location (year of completion)	Floors	metres	feet
Petronas Towers, Kuala Lumpur, Malaysia (1998)	88	452	1,483
JW Marriott Marquis Dubai, Dubai, UAE (2012)	82	355	1,166
Huaguoyuan Towers, Guiyang, China (2018)	74	335	1,099
SPG Global Twin Towers, Suzhou, China (2010)	54	282	925
The Cullinan, Hong Kong, China (2008)	68	270	886
Al Kazim Towers, Dubai, UAE (2008)	53	265	869
Grand Gateway, Shanghai, China (2005)	54	262	859
Dual Towers, Manama, Bahrain (2007)	53	260	853
The Imperial, Mumbai, India (2009)	60	256	840
The Palm Towers, Doha, Qatar (2011)	58	250	820

Destroyed 2001

	Floors	metres	feet
World Trade Center One New York City (1972)	110	417	1,368
World Trade Center Two New York City (1973)	110	415	1,362

STRUCTURES

Structure, location (year of completion)	metres	feet
Tokyo Skytree, Tokyo, Japan (2012)	634	2,080
KVLY (formerly KTHI)-TV Mast, North Dakota (guyed), USA (1963)*	629	2,063
Canton, Guangzhou, China (2010)	600	1,968
CN Tower, Toronto, Canada (1976)	553	1,815
Ostankino Tower, Moscow, Russia (1967)	540	1,772

* The USA has numerous other guyed TV towers above 600m (1,969ft)

CHURCHES

Structure, location (year of completion)	metres	feet
Sagrada Família, Barcelona, Spain (2026*)	170	560
Ulm Minster, Ulm, Germany (1890)	162	530
Our Lady of Peace Basilica, Yamoussoukro, Côte d'Ivoire (1990)	158	518
Cologne Cathedral, Cologne, Germany (1880)	157	515
Notre-Dame Cathedral, Rouen, France (1876)	151	495
St Nicholas Church, Hamburg, Germany (1874)	148	485
Notre-Dame Cathedral, Strasbourg, France (1439)	144	472
Queen of Peace Shrine and Basilica, Lichen, Poland (2004)	140	459
Basilica of St Peter, Rome, Italy (1626)	138	452
St Stephen's Cathedral, Vienna, Austria (1433)	137	448

* Scheduled completion date, the 100th anniversary of the death of its architect, Antoni Gaudí; open for worship following its consecration by Pope Benedict XVI in 2010

The Chicago Methodist Temple, Chicago, USA (completed 1924) is 173m (568ft) high, but is sited atop a 25-storey, 100m (328ft) building. Salisbury Cathedral (1521), at 123m (404ft), is the UK's tallest religious building. St Paul's Cathedral, London, and Liverpool Anglican Cathedral are the only others in the UK over 100m (328ft) tall. At 94m (309ft) the Church of St Walburge, Preston, Lancashire is the tallest church in Britain that is not a cathedral.

TALLEST STRUCTURES – A CHRONOLOGY

Structure and location	Year	metres	feet
Djoser's Step Pyramid, Saqqara, Egypt	c.2650 BC	62	204
Pyramid of Meidum, Egypt	c.2600 BC	92	302
Snefru's Bent Pyramid, Dahshur, Egypt	c.2600 BC	102	336
Red Pyramid, Dahshur, Egypt	c.2590 BC	104	341
Great Pyramid, Giza, Egypt*	c.2580 BC	147	481
Liuhe (Six Harmonies) Pagoda, Hangzhou, China†	AD 970	150	492
Lincoln Cathedral, Lincoln, England‡	1311–1400	160	525
St Paul's Cathedral, London, England§	1315	149	489
St Mary's Church, Stralsund, Germany	1384–1478	151	495
St Olaf's Church, Tallinn, Estonia⟪	1438–1519	159	522
Notre-Dame Cathedral, Strasbourg, France	1439	142	466
St Nicholas Church, Hamburg, Germany	1874	147	482
Notre-Dame Cathedral, Rouen, France	1876	151	495
Cologne Cathedral, Cologne, Germany	1880	157	515
Washington Monument, Washington DC, USA	1884	169	555
Eiffel Tower, Paris, France	1889	300	984
Chrysler Building, New York, USA	1930	319	1,046
Empire State Building, New York, USA	1931	381	1,250
KWTV Mast, Oklahoma City, USA	1954	481	1,577
KOBR-TV Tower, Caprock, USA	1960	490	1,608
KFVS TV Mast, Egypt Mills, USA	1960	511	1,677
KVLY (formerly KTHI)-TV Mast, Blanchard, USA	1963	629	2,063
Warszawa Radio Mast, Konstantynow, Poland**	1974	646	2,120
Burj Khalifa, Dubai, UAE	2010	828	2,717

* Later reduced through loss of topstone to 137m (449ft)
† Destroyed in 1121
‡ Destroyed in 1549
§ Destroyed in 1561
⟪ Spire burned down in 1625; renovated in 1931 to present height of 123m (403ft)
** Collapsed in 1991 during renovation

BRIDGES

The longest stretch of bridging of any kind is the Danyang–Kunshan Grand Bridge (2010) in China at 164km (102 miles).

LONGEST SUSPENSION SPANS

Bridge, location (year of completion)	metres	feet
Akashi-Kaikyo, Japan (1998)	1,991	6,532
Yangsigang Yangtze River Bridge, China (2019)	1,770	5,577
Humen Second Bridge, Dongguan, China (2019)	1,688	5,538
Xihoumen, China (2009)	1,650	5,413
Great Belt Bridge, Denmark (1998)	1,624	5,328
Osman Gazi, Turkey (2016)	1,550	5,085
Yi Sun-sin, South Korea (2012)	1,545	5,069
Runyang, China (2005)	1,490	4,888
Dongtinghu Second Bridge, Yueyang, China (2018)	1,480	4,856
Nanjing Fourth Yangtze, China (2012)	1,418	4,652

LONGEST CANTILEVER SPANS

Bridge, location (year of completion)	metres	feet
Pont de Québec, St Lawrence, Canada (1917)	549	1,800
Forth, Scotland (two spans of 1,710ft each) (1890)	521	1,710
Minato, Japan (1974)	510	1,673
Commodore Barry, New Jersey/Pennsylvania, USA (1974)	501	1,644
Crescent City Connection, Louisiana, USA (I 1958, II 1988)	480	1,575
Howrah, India (1943)	457	1,500
Veterans Memorial, Louisiana, USA (1995)	445	1,460
Tokyo Gate, Japan (2012)	440	1,443
San Francisco Oakland Bay, California, USA (1936)	426	1,400
J. C. Van Home, New Brunswick, Canada (1961)	380	1,247

LONGEST ARCH SPANS

Bridge, location (year of completion)	metres	feet
Ping'nan Third Bridge, China (2020)	575	1,886
Chaotianmen, China (2009)	552	1,811
Lupu, China (2003)	550	1,804
Bosideng, China (2012)	530	1,740
New River Gorge, West Virginia, USA (1977)	518	1,700
Bayonne, New Jersey/New York, USA (1931)	510	1,675
Sydney Harbour, Australia (1932)	503	1,650
Chenab, India (2020*)	467	1,532
Wushan, China (2005)	460	1,509
Mingzhou, China (2011)	450	1,476

* Scheduled completion date

LONGEST SHIP CANALS

Canal	Length km	miles	Min. depth metres	feet
White Sea–Baltic [formerly Stalin] (1933), of which canalised river 51.5km (32 miles)	227	141.00	5.0	16.5
Rhine–Main–Danube, Germany (1992)	171	106.25	4.0	13.1
*Suez (1869), links Red and Mediterranean Seas	162	100.60	12.9	42.3
V. I. Lenin Volga–Don, Russia (1952), links Black and Caspian Seas	100	62.20	3.6	11.8
Kiel (or North Sea), Germany (1895), links North and Baltic Seas	98	60.90	11.0	37.0
Alphonse XIII, Spain (1926), gives Seville access to Atlantic Ocean	85	53.00	7.6	25.0
Panama (1914), links Pacific Ocean and Caribbean Sea; lake chain, 78.9km (49 miles) dug	82	50.71	13.0	43.0
*Houston, USA (1940), links inland city with Gulf of Mexico	81	50.50	11.0	36.0
Danube–Black Sea, Romania (1984)	64.4	40.02	7.0	23.0
Manchester Ship, UK (1894), links city with Irish Channel	58	36.00	8.5	28.0

* Has no locks

The first section of China's Grand Canal, running 1,782km (1,107 miles) from Beijing to Hangzhou, was opened in AD 610 and completed in 1283. Today it is limited to 2,000-tonne vessels.

The St Lawrence Seaway comprises the Beauharnois, Welland and Welland Bypass and Seaway 54–59 canals, and allows access to Duluth, Minnesota, USA via the Great Lakes from the Atlantic end of Canada's Gulf of St Lawrence, a distance of 3,769km (2,342 miles). The St Lawrence Canal, completed in 1959, is 293km (182 miles) long.

TRAVEL OVERSEAS

PASSPORT REGULATIONS

Application forms for UK passports can be obtained from Her Majesty's Passport Office's telephone advice line or website, regional passport offices or from main post offices.

HM PASSPORT OFFICE, T 0300-222 0000
  W www.gov.uk/government/organisations/hm-passport-office
Regional Passport Offices
BELFAST, Law Society House, Ground Floor, 90–106 Victoria Street, Belfast BT1 3GN
DURHAM, Freeman's Reach, Durham DH1 1SL
GLASGOW, 3 Northgate, 96 Milton Street, Cowcaddens, Glasgow G4 0BT
LIVERPOOL, 101 Old Hall Street, Liverpool L3 9BD
LONDON, Globe House, 89 Eccleston Square, London SW1V 1PN
NEWPORT, Nexus House, Mission Court, Newport NP20 2DW
PETERBOROUGH, Aragon Court, Northminster Road, Peterborough PE1 1QG

Passport offices are open Monday to Saturday on an appointment-only basis (appointments should be arranged by calling the central telephone number listed above). For an additional fee, passport offices provide either a premium one-day service (not available for a first adult or child passport, extending a limited passport, replacing a lost, stolen or damaged passport or for complex amendments) or a one-week fast track service (except for first adult passports).

Standard postal applications take at least three weeks to be processed. Application forms are provided by post offices. The completed application form should be posted, with the appropriate supporting documents and fee, to the regional passport office indicated on the addressed envelope which is provided with each application form. Accompanying cheques should be made payable to 'Her Majesty's Passport Office', or to 'Post Office Ltd' when using the Check & Send service.

Applications can also be submitted through Check & Send outlets at selected post offices, who, for a handling fee, will forward the application form to the relevant regional passport office after having checked that it has been completed correctly with the appropriate documents attached. These applications take a minimum of two weeks (first adult passport applications may take six weeks including a passport interview).

Online applications can be made (W www.gov.uk/apply-renew-passport). The applicant must be over 16, reside in the UK, already possess a passport and have only British nationality. No changes to the applicant's name can be made through this service.

A passport cannot be issued or extended on behalf of a person already abroad; such persons should apply online (W https://passportapplication.service.gov.uk) or to the nearest local embassy, British High Commission or Consulate.

UK passports are granted to British citizens, British nationals (overseas), British overseas territories citizens, British overseas citizens, British subjects and British protected persons, and are generally available for travel to all countries. The possession of a passport does not exempt the holder from compliance with any immigration regulations in force in British or foreign countries, or from the necessity of obtaining a visa where required (*see* below for a list of countries for which UK citizens do not require a visa).

Biometric passports were introduced in 2006. The design and security features, including a chip containing the biometrics (the facial image and biographical data of the holder), render the passport more secure against forgery and aid border controls.

ADULTS

A passport granted to a person over 16 will normally be valid for ten years. Thereafter, or if at any time the passport contains no further space for visas, a new passport must be obtained.

British nationals born on or before 2 September 1929 are eligible for a free standard passport.

CHILDREN

Since 5 October 1998 all children under the age of 16 travelling abroad are required to have their own passport. This is primarily to help prevent child abductions. The passports are initially valid for five years, but can be renewed for a further five years at the end of this period.

COUNTERSIGNATURES

A countersignature is needed if the application is for a first passport, to replace a lost, stolen or damaged passport, or to renew a passport for a child aged 11 or under. A countersignature is also needed for renewals if the applicant's appearance has significantly changed and the photograph in their previous passport is unrecognisable. The signatory must be willing to enter their own passport number on to the form. A countersignatory must be a friend, neighbour, or colleague (not just a professional acquaintance); be a person of good standing in their community who has known the applicant for at least two years; and who lives in the UK and who holds a British or Irish passport. A relative or partner, someone living at the same address as the applicant, or an employee of HM Passport Office must not countersign the application.

PHOTOGRAPHS

Two identical, unmounted, recent colour photographs of the applicant must be sent. These photographs should measure 45mm by 35mm, be printed on plain white photographic paper and should be taken full face against a plain cream or light grey background. The photo must show the applicant's full face, looking straight at the camera, with a neutral expression and with their mouth closed. If a countersignature is required for the application, the person who countersigned the form should also certify one photograph as a true likeness of the applicant.

DOCUMENTATION

In addition to two photographs, the applicant's current or previous British passport, and other documents in support of the statements made in the application, must be produced at the time of applying. Details of which documents are required are set out in the notes accompanying the application form.

If the passport applicant is a British national by naturalisation or registration, the certificate proving this must be produced with the application, unless the applicant holds a previous British passport issued after registration or naturalisation.

INTERVIEWS

Interviews for adults applying for their first passport (not including those who held their own passport as a child) were introduced on 1 June 2007 to combat passport fraud and forgery. After applying for a passport, applicants will be sent a letter asking them to book an interview at one of the offices in the UK. Interviews last for approximately 30 minutes. HM Passport Office recommends that new applicants allow six weeks to receive their passport. There is no one-week fast-track service for first adult passports.

50-PAGE PASSPORTS

The 50-page 'jumbo' passport is intended to meet the needs of frequent travellers who fill standard passports well before the validity has expired. It is valid for ten years but is not available for children.

PASSPORT FEES*

Adult passport†	£85.00 (£75.50)
Child passport†	£58.50 (£49.00)
50-page passport	£95.00 (£85.50)
People born on or before 2 Sep 1929	Free

* Standard postal (online) application fees. Applications made at UK regional offices have a higher fee

† New passports, renewals or amendments are priced at the same rate

HEALTH ADVICE

The NHS Choices website provides health advice for those travelling abroad, including information on immunisations and reciprocal health agreements with other countries. *See* **W** www.nhs.uk/livewell/travelhealth.*See also* National Health Service, Health Advice and Medical Treatment Abroad.

VISA REQUIREMENTS

It is advisable to check specific visa requirements with the appropriate embassy before making final travel arrangements (*see* Countries of the World section for foreign embassy contact details). The lists below are intended as a guide.

If the UK withdraws from the EU without a deal in place, travel requirements could change *see* **W** www.gov.uk/check-a-passport-for-travel-to-europe. At the time of printing, the countries listed below do not require British citizens to hold a valid visa or tourist card before arrival on short visits:

All EU member states and their overseas territories (*see* The European Union) except Ascension Island and Tristan da Cunha; Albania, Andorra, Antigua and Barbuda, Argentina, Armenia, Bahamas, Barbados, Belarus, Belize, Bolivia, Bosnia and Hercegovina, Botswana, Brazil, Brunei, Canada, Chile, Colombia, Costa Rica, Dominica, Ecuador, El Salvador, eSwatini, Fiji, Gambia, Georgia, Grenada, Guatemala, Guyana, Haiti, Honduras*, Hong Kong, Iceland, Indonesia, Israel, Jamaica, Japan, Kazakhstan, Kiribati, Kosovo, Kuwait‡, Republic of Korea (South Korea), Kyrgyzstan, Lebanon*, Lesotho*, Liechtenstein, Macau, Malaysia, Maldives*, Mauritius, Mexico*, Micronesia (Federated States of)*, Moldova, Monaco, Montenegro, Morocco, Namibia, New Zealand, Nicaragua, North Macedonia, Norway, Palau, Panama‡, Paraguay, Peru, the Philippines, Samoa, San Marino, Senegal, Serbia, Seychelles, Singapore, Solomon Islands, South Africa, St Kitts and Nevis, St Lucia, St Vincent and the Grenadines, Switzerland, Taiwan, Thailand, Tonga, Trinidad and Tobago, Tunisia, Tuvalu, Ukraine, United Arab Emirates*, Uruguay, USA†, Vanuatu, Venezuela‡, Vietnam, Western Sahara.

* Upon entry to these countries a visa or tourist card will be issued at no extra charge

† Those travelling to the USA under the Visa Waiver Programme must provide details online (the Electronic System for Travel Authorisation) at least 72 hours in advance of travel

‡ Only applicable when arriving by air, those arriving at overland crossings or by sea should arrange documentation in advance

Brunei, Iraq, Solomon Islands, Sudan and Yemen bar entry to travellers with HIV/AIDS. Jordan, Papua New Guinea, Qatar, Russia and UAE have some entry restrictions for visitors with HIV/AIDS.

Residents of the following countries must hold a valid visa for every entry to the UK:
Afghanistan, Albania, Algeria, Angola, Armenia, Azerbaijan, Bahrain, Bangladesh, Belarus, Benin, Bhutan, Bolivia, Bosnia and Hercegovina, Burkina Faso, Burundi, Cabo Verde, Cambodia, Cameroon, Central African Republic, Chad, China, Colombia, Comoros, Dem. Rep. of Congo, Rep. of Congo, Côte d'Ivoire, Cuba, Cyprus, Djibouti, Dominican Republic, Ecuador, Egypt, Equatorial Guinea, Eritrea, Eswatini, Ethiopia, Fiji, Gabon, Gambia, Georgia, Ghana, Guinea, Guinea-Bissau, Guyana, Haiti, India, Indonesia, Iran, Iraq, Jamaica, Jordan, Kazakhstan, Kenya, Dem. People's Republic of Korea (North Korea), Kosovo, Kuwait, Kyrgyzstan, Laos, Lebanon, Lesotho, Liberia, Libya, Macedonia, Madagascar, Malawi, Mali, Mauritania, Moldova, Mongolia, Montenegro, Morocco, Mozambique, Myanmar, Nepal, Niger, Nigeria, Oman*, Pakistan, Palestinian Authority, Peru, Philippines, Qatar*, Russian Federation, Rwanda, Sao Tome and Príncipe, Saudi Arabia, Senegal, Serbia, Sierra Leone, Somalia, South Africa, South Sudan, Sri Lanka, Sudan, Suriname, Syria, Taiwan†, Tajikistan, Tanzania, Thailand, Togo, Tunisia, Turkey, Turkmenistan, Uganda, Ukraine, United Arab Emirates*, Uzbekistan, Vietnam, Venezuela, Yemen, Zambia, Zimbabwe.

* An electronic visa waiver should be obtained online prior to travel

† Passports containing personal ID numbers do not require visas

BAGGAGE RESTRICTIONS

Individual airlines may set their own limits for hand luggage sizes, and travellers should check these before arriving at the airport: oversized baggage may have to be checked in as hold luggage, which often incurs a fee. Since January 2008, some airports have allowed passengers to take more than one item into the aircraft cabin. Other airports in the UK still have a one-bag restriction in place, and individual airlines may operate their own policies.

Passengers are allowed to carry small amounts of liquids as cabin luggage. These must be in containers not greater than 100ml, and placed in a single, clear resealable bag which must not exceed 1 litre in capacity. Liquids are classified as drinks, make-up such as mascara or lipstick, sprays, pastes and gels. Medicines that are larger than 100ml must be accompanied by relevant documentation, such as a doctor's letter, and prior approval should be sought from the airline and departure airport. When travelling with a baby, enough liquid baby food, milk and sterilised water for the journey can be taken on board but containers may be screened by security. One lighter is permitted as cabin luggage carried separately in a clear bag for the duration of the flight and not placed in the main hand luggage bag.

Sharp items must not be carried in hand luggage. Prohibited sharp items include knives, large scissors, razor blades, tools, hiking poles and corkscrews. Other prohibited items include ammunition, chemical and toxic substances, work tools, sporting equipment, fireworks, party poppers, cork screws and non-safety matches.

Electrical equipment such as charged laptops, mobile phones and cameras are allowed in hand luggage but they must be removed and screened separately prior to boarding. Some electronic equipment is prohibited from use at certain times during a flight. Electrictronics taken on flights to the UK from Egypt, Jordan, Lebanon, Saudi Arabia and Turkey must be put in the hold if larger than 16cm by 9.3cm by 1.5cm.

The amount passengers can check-in to the hold is determined by each airline. The airline will usually set a 'free baggage allowance' according to the number of items and the weight of each item; if this is exceeded charges may apply.
W www.gov.uk/hand-luggage-restrictions

THE EUROPEAN UNION

MEMBER STATE	ACCESSION DATE	POPULATION*	Population Percentage	EP Seats
Austria	1 Jan 1995	8,859,449	1.98 per cent	19
Belgium	1 Jan 1958	11,720,716	2.58 per cent	21
Bulgaria	1 Jan 2007	6,966,899	1.55 per cent	17
Croatia	1 July 2013	4,227,746	0.91 per cent	12
Cyprus	1 May 2004	1,266,676	0.20 per cent	6
Czechia	1 May 2004	10,702,498	2.35 per cent	21
Denmark	1 Jan 1973	5,869,410	1.30 per cent	14
Estonia	1 May 2004	1,228,624	0.30 per cent	7
Finland	1 Jan 1995	5,571,665	1.23 per cent	14
France	1 Jan 1958	67,848,156	14.97 per cent	79
Germany	1 Jan 1958	80,159,662	18.54 per cent	96
Greece	1 Jan 1981	10,607,051	2.39 per cent	21
Hungary	1 May 2004	9,771,827	2.18 per cent	20
Ireland	1 Jan 1973	5,176,569	1.11 per cent	13
Italy	1 Jan 1958	62,402,659	13.58 per cent	76
Latvia	1 May 2004	1,881,232	0.43 per cent	8
Lithuania	1 May 2004	2,731,464	0.62 per cent	11
Luxembourg	1 Jan 1958	628,381	0.14 per cent	6
Malta	1 May 2004	457,267	0.11 per cent	6
The Netherlands	1 Jan 1958	17,280,397	3.91 per cent	29
Poland	1 May 2004	38,282,325	8.47 per cent	52
Portugal	1 Jan 1986	10,302,674	2.30 per cent	21
Romania	1 Jan 2007	21,302,893	4.31 per cent	33
Slovakia	1 May 2004	5,440,602	1.22 per cent	14
Slovenia	1 May 2004	2,102,678	0.47 per cent	8
Spain	1 Jan 1986	50,015,792	10.56 per cent	59
Sweden	1 Jan 1995	10,202,491	2.30 per cent	21

* July 2020 estimate
† Under the Lisbon Treaty the total number of MEPs was set at 751 from the 2014 election. Following the UK's withdrawal from the EU, the total number of seats will be reduced to 705, with 27 of the current 73 UK seats redistributed among the remaining member states.
Sources: CIA World Factbook; www.europa.eu

LEGISLATION

The core of the European Union (EU) policy-making process is a dialogue between the European Commission (EC), which initiates and implements policy, and the Council of the European Union and the European Parliament, which take policy decisions.

The original legislative process is known as the consultation procedure. The commission drafts a proposal which it submits to the council and to the parliament. The council then consults the Economic and Social Committee, the parliament and the Committee of the Regions; the parliament may request that amendments are made. With or without these amendments, the proposal is then adopted by the council and becomes law. The consultation procedure now only applies to cases not specifically subject to one of the other procedures.

The Single European Act introduced the assent procedure (now the consent procedure), whereby an absolute majority of the parliament must vote to approve laws in certain fields before they are passed. Issues covered by the procedure include uniform procedure for elections, some international agreements, violation of human rights and the accession of new member states.

The Maastricht Treaty introduced the co-decision procedure as an extension of the cooperation procedure; if, after the parliament's second reading of a proposal, the council and parliament fail to agree, a conciliation committee of the two will aim to reach a compromise. If a compromise is not reached, the parliament can reject the legislation by the vote of an absolute majority of its members. The Amsterdam Treaty extended the co-decision procedure to all areas covered by qualified majority voting, with the exception of measures related to the European Monetary Union.

The Lisbon Treaty extended the use of the co-decision procedure to several new fields, and renamed it the ordinary legislative procedure. The treaty strengthens the role of the European parliament so that it is involved in almost all new legislation. The changes give the European parliament equal powers in areas such as legal immigration, crime prevention and police cooperation. As a result of the Lisbon Treaty, the Council of the European Union must now vote in public on any new legislation, and if one-third of national parliaments disagree with a proposal then it can be sent back to be reviewed.

The council, commission and parliament can issue the following legislation:

- regulations, which are binding in their entirety and directly applicable to all member states; they do not need to be incorporated into national law to come into effect
- directives, which are less specific, binding as to the result to be achieved but leaving the method of implementation open to member states; a directive thus has no force until it is incorporated into national law
- decisions, which are also binding but are addressed solely to one or more member states or individuals in a member state
- recommendations or opinions, which are merely persuasive.

The council and parliament also have certain budgetary powers and determine all expenditure together. The final decision on whether the budget should be adopted or rejected lies with the parliament.

The European Central Bank (ECB) has legislative powers within its field of competence. The commission also has limited legislative powers, where it has been delegated the power to implement or revise legislation by the council.

SCHENGEN AGREEMENT

The Schengen agreement was signed by France, Germany, Belgium, Luxembourg and the Netherlands in 1985. The agreement committed the five states to abolishing internal border controls, erecting external frontiers against illegal immigrants, drug traffickers, terrorists and organised crime, and it implemented the Schengen Information System which enables national border control, customs and police authorities from Schengen member states to share and access data on specific individuals, such as a person who may have been involved in a serious crime, or vehicles, documents or objects which may have been stolen, lost or misappropriated. The second-generation Schengen Information System (SIS II) entered into operation in April 2013. SIS II has improved functionalities such as new types of alerts and the potential to enter biometrics. It also contains copies of European arrest warrants, facilitating the detention of persons wanted for arrest, surrender or extradition.

Subsequently signed by Portugal and Spain, the agreement was ratified by the seven signatory states and entered into force in March 1995 with the removal of internal frontier, passport, customs and immigration controls. Austria and Italy became full members of the agreement in 1997; Greece in 2000; and Denmark, Finland and Sweden in 2001. The Czech Republic, Estonia, Hungary, Latvia, Lithuania, Malta, Poland, Slovakia and Slovenia joined in 2007. Although not members of the EU, Iceland and Norway joined the agreement in 2001 and Switzerland in 2008. The European Council granted Liechtenstein membership in 2011. There is no date set for Bulgaria, Croatia, Cyprus or Romania to join. The UK and the Republic of Ireland have not signed the agreement and are only partial participants, since their border controls have been maintained.

The Schengen agreement originated as an intergovernmental agreement and was adopted by the EU following the signing of the Amsterdam Treaty.

MAASTRICHT TREATY

Agreed in Maastricht, the Netherlands, in 1991, the treaty came into effect in November 1993 following ratification by the member states. Three pillars formed its basis:

- the European Community (removing Economic from its name) with its established institutions and decision-making processes
- a common foreign and security policy charged with providing a forum for member states and EU institutions to consult on foreign affairs
- cooperation in justice and home affairs, with the Council of the European Union coordinating policies on asylum, immigration, conditions of entry, cross-border crime, drug trafficking and terrorism

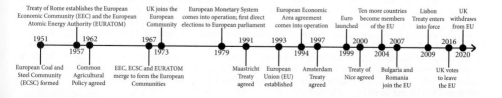

The treaty established a common European citizenship for nationals of all member states and introduced the principle of subsidiarity, whereby decisions are taken at the most appropriate level (national, regional or local). It extended European Community competency into the areas of environmental and industrial policies, consumer affairs, health, and education and training, and extended qualified majority voting in the Council of the European Union to some areas which had previously required a unanimous vote. The powers of the European parliament over the budget and over the EC were also enhanced, and a co-decision procedure enabled the parliament to override decisions made by the council in certain policy areas. A separate protocol to the Maastricht Treaty on social policy was agreed by 11 states and was incorporated into the Amsterdam Treaty in 1997 following adoption by the UK.

AMSTERDAM TREATY

The treaties of Rome and Maastricht were amended through the Amsterdam Treaty, which was signed in 1997 and came into effect on 1 May 1999. It extended the scope of qualified majority voting and the powers of the European parliament. It also included a formal commitment to fundamental human rights, gave additional powers to the European Court of Justice and provided for the reform of common foreign and security policy.

LISBON TREATY

The Lisbon Treaty was drawn up to replace the original European constitution, which was rejected in referendums in France and the Netherlands in 2005. It amends, rather than replaces, existing EU and European Community treaties. Ireland, the only country to hold a referendum on the Lisbon Treaty, voted against ratification on 12 June 2008. It held a second referendum on 2 October 2009 in which 67 per cent voted in favour, and – as a result of all EU countries approving the treaty – it came into force on 1 December 2009.

The Lisbon Treaty granted 'legal personality' (the right under international law to adopt laws and treaties) to the EU. The three pillars created by the Maastricht Treaty (*see* above) merged to make the EU a single legal entity, replacing the European Community. The Lisbon Treaty introduced a number of changes to the EU: a new president was appointed to the European Council for a two-and-a-half year term to replace the previous system of a six-month rotating presidency (this still exists in a reduced capacity for the Council of the European Union). The position of High Representative of the Union for Foreign Affairs and Security Policy was created, to enhance the EU's relations with other countries. The European parliament was strengthened and given more legislative and budgetary powers, and the number of MEPs was set at 751 from the 2014 election. The system of qualified majority voting was extended to new policy areas and since 2014 has been based on a double majority of member states and people; a decision must be agreed by 55 per cent of member states representing at least 65 per cent of the EU population. The treaty establishes the principle of 'mutual recognition', whereby each member state acknowledges that legal decisions by other member states are valid; the UK has an opt-out clause with regard to some policies, such as external borders, asylum and immigration.

Following the UK's withdrawal from the EU, the total number of seats in the European parliament will be reduced to 705, with 27 of the current 73 UK seats redistributed among the remaining member states. France and Spain will gain the most seats at five each, increasing from 74 to 79 and 54 to 59 respectively. Italy and the Netherlands will each gain three seats, from 73 to 76 and 26 to 29, and Ireland will gain two seats. Austria, Croatia, Denmark, Estonia, Finland, Poland, Romania, Slovakia, and Sweden will all be allocated one additional seat. The remaining 13 countries will keep their current allocation.

MEMBERSHIP AND EXTERNAL RELATIONS

ACCESSION

The procedure for accession to the EU is laid down in the Treaty of Rome; states must be stable European democracies governed by the rule of law with free-market economies. A membership application is studied by the EC, which produces an 'opinion'. If the opinion is positive, negotiations may be opened leading to an accession treaty that must be approved by all member state governments and parliaments, the European parliament, and the applicant state's government and parliament.

Cyprus, the Czech Republic, Estonia, Hungary, Latvia, Lithuania, Malta, Poland, Slovakia and Slovenia became full members of the EU on 1 May 2004. Bulgaria and Romania joined the EU on 1 January 2007, and Croatia on 1 July 2013. The Council of the EU recalled the offer of an accession partnership to Turkey in 2002, following the commission's conclusion that Turkey did not yet fully meet the required political criteria. However, at its December 2004 meeting in Brussels, the council decided that Turkey sufficiently met the Copenhagen political criteria, and accession negotiations began in October 2005. However, in November 2016, negotiations again stalled after a non-binding vote in the EU parliament resulted overwhelmingly in favour of a motion to suspend negotiations with Turkey due to concerns over human rights and rule of law abuses in the country. Montenegro was granted candidate status in December 2005 and accession negotiations began on 29 June 2012. Macedonia was granted candidate status in December 2005, but accession negotiations have not yet begun. Iceland applied for membership in July 2009 and accession negotiations started in June 2010, but were put on hold by the Icelandic government in May 2013 and in March 2015 Iceland formally retracted its membership application. Serbia applied for membership in December 2009 and accession negotiations commenced in January 2014 while Albania was granted candidate status in June 2014. There are currently two potential candidates for membership of the EU: Bosnia and Hercegovina, and Kosovo.

UK WITHDRAWAL FROM THE EU

A referendum was held in the UK on 23 June 2016 in which the UK electorate (turnout 72 per cent) voted to leave the EU (52 per cent).

The UK government invoked Article 50 of the Lisbon Treaty on 29 March 2017 therefore setting the country on course to leave the EU by 29 March 2019. Official negotiations between the EU and the UK to decide the terms of the UK's withdrawal from the EU began on 19 June 2017. A draft withdrawal agreement was published on 19 March 2018 and the EU and UK negotiators aimed to finalise the agreement in October 2018 so that it could be ratified before 29 March 2019. However, the agreement was rejected by the UK parliament leading to the postponement of the date of the UK's withdrawal until 31 October 2019. On 19 October 2019 Britain submitted a further extension request to postpone the withdrawal date which was granted by the EU Ambassadors. On 31 January 2020 the UK left the EU and entered a transition period which ended at 11pm on 31 December 2020.

EU AGREEMENTS WITH OTHER STATES

The EU has several types of agreements with other European and non-European states. Association agreements (AAs), which must be ratified by all EU member states, can include commitments to reforming the country's trade, human rights, economy or political system in exchange for financial assistance or trade agreements. Partnership and cooperation agreements (PCAs) are legal frameworks, based on respect for democratic principles and human rights, setting out the political, economic and trade relationship between the EU and its partner countries. Each PCA is a ten-year bilateral treaty signed and ratified by the EU and the individual state. After the ten-year period expires the agreements are automatically renewed annually unless one of the parties objects. Agreements have been implemented (date when PCA entered into force in parentheses) with Russia (1997), Moldova and Ukraine (1998), Armenia, Azerbaijan, Georgia, Kazakhstan, Kyrgyzstan and Uzbekistan (1999), Tajikistan (2010), Indonesia (2014) and the Philippines and Vietnam (2015). In 2003 the PCA council summit strengthened EU cooperation with the Russian Federation by establishing a permanent partnership council (PPC). Negotiations for a new agreement to replace and update the existing PCA between the EU and Russia began in 2008 but have since been suspended. There are PCAs under ratification with Iraq (2012), Belarus (1995), Kazakhstan (Enhanced) (2015), and Turkmenistan (1998), and in negotiations with Malaysia, Singapore, and Thailand.

Trade and cooperation agreements are intended to foster trade and economic relations, and include a commitment to respect the human rights and democratic principles of both parties. The EC has negotiated around 120 agreements worldwide.

While the EU has agreements with over 60 trade partners, it does not have current agreements with some of the largest economies such as China, India, Japan, and the USA. There are ongoing trade negotiations with Australia, Chile, Japan, Mexico and New Zealand. Trade negotiations with the USA through the Transatlantic Trade and Investment Partnership (TTIP) are uncertain due to US President Trump's reversion of trade terms in 2017. The Comprehensive Economic and Trade Agreement between the EU and Canada was signed in 2016. On 28 June 2019 a comprehensive trade agreement was reached between the EU and MERCOSUR (Argentina, Brazil, Paraguay and Uruguay).

The European neighbourhood policy was developed in 2004 and applies to the enlarged EU's immediate neighbours. It aims to strengthen stability and security through economic integration and deeper political relationships based on a mutual commitment to European common values (democracy, human rights, rule of law, good governance and market economy).

A stabilisation and association agreement (SAA) – which is tailored to the western Balkan states – provides the contractual framework for relations to enable accession to the EU. Candidate or potential candidate countries with SAAs in force are Macedonia (2004), Albania (2009), Montenegro (2010), Serbia (2013), Bosnia and Hercegovina (2015) and most recently Kosovo (1 April 2016).

TREATY OF NICE

The Treaty of Nice was signed in 2001 and came into effect in 2003. It enabled the EU to accommodate up to 13 new member states, and extended qualified majority voting to 30 further articles of the treaties that previously required unanimity. The weighting of votes in the European Council was altered from 1 January 2005 for the new member states.

To obtain a qualified majority, a decision requires a specified number of votes (to be reviewed following each accession); the decision has to be approved by a majority of member states and represent at least 62 per cent of the total population of the EU. The treaty also set the number of MEPs that both existing and new member states would have following enlargement.

The Maastricht Treaty established the right of groups of member states to work together without requiring the participation of all members (enhanced cooperation); the Treaty of Nice removed the right of individual member states to veto the launch of enhanced cooperation.

ECONOMY

BUDGET OF THE EUROPEAN UNION

The principles of funding the European Union budget were established by the Treaty of Rome and remain, with modifications, to this day. There is a legally binding limit on the overall level of resources (known as 'own resources') that the EU can raise from its member states; this limit is defined as a percentage of gross national income (GNI). Budget revenue and expenditure must balance, and there is therefore no deficit financing. The 'own resources' decision, which came into effect in 1975 and has been regularly updated, states that there are four sources of funding under which each member state makes contributions:

- duties charged on agricultural imports into the EU from non-member states
- customs duties on imports from non-member states
- contributions based on member states' shares of a notional EU-harmonised VAT base
- contributions based on member states' shares of total GNI

The latter source above is the budget-balancing item and covers the difference between total expenditure and the revenue from the other three sources. On 3 July 2013 the European parliament voted in favour of a budget for 2014–20; the budget was officially adopted following a vote on the legislation in November 2013. The overall budget for the seven-year period is €963bn in commitments and €908bn in payments (at 2011 prices).

The EU's multi-annual financial framework (MFF) for 2014–20 is 3.5 per cent less than the commitment appropriations under the MFF 2007–13 and 3.7 per cent less than the payment appropriations for the same period. In line with the political priorities of the EU, a strong emphasis was put on expenditure aimed at boosting growth and creating jobs, with an increase of 37 per cent over the 2007–13 model dedicated to 'competitiveness for growth and jobs'.

In 2017, an extra €6bn in commitments was pledged to help member states tackle the refugee crisis. Measures included, the creation of reception centres, resettlement and integration programmes for those refugees with the right to remain, counter terrorism activities and border control enhancement.

In February 2018 the EU adopted legislation enabling the European Investment Bank (EIB) to lend an additional €5.3bn to projects outside the EU, with €3.7bn of this allocated for projects addressing migration issues. The EU provides a maximum budgetary guarantee to the EIB of €30bn (€27bn plus €3bn in reserve) for the 2014–20 period. The new rules release the €3bn kept in reserve, of which €1.4bn is for public sector projects addressing the root causes of migration, plus an additional €2.3bn for private sector lending for migration-related projects; increasing the EU's guarantee to the EIB to €32.3bn.

EU BUDGET 2020

€m	CA	PA
Smart and inclusive growth*	83,931	72,354
Sustainable growth	59,907	57,905
Security and citizenship	3,729	3,685
Global Europe	10,262	8,929
Administration	9,10,272	10,275
Special Instruments	588	419
Total	€168,688m	€153,566m

(1 euro = £0.90 as at 1 December 2020)
* Includes 'competitiveness for growth and jobs' and 'economic, social and territorial cohesion'
CA = commitment appropriations (maximum value of commitments to pay future bills)
PA = payment appropriations (actual amounts to pay for previous commitments)
Source: www.consilium.europa.eu

SINGLE MARKET

Even after the removal of tariffs and quotas between member states in the 1970s and 1980s, the European Community was still separated into a number of national markets by a series of non-tariff barriers. It was to overcome these internal barriers to trade that the concept of the single market was developed. The measures to be undertaken were codified in the commission's 1985 white paper on completing the internal market.

The white paper included articles removing obstacles distorting the internal market: the elimination of frontier controls; the mutual recognition of professional qualifications; the harmonisation of product specifications, largely by the mutual recognition of national standards; open tendering for public procurement contracts; the free movement of capital; the harmonisation of VAT and excise duties; and the reduction of state aid to particular industries. The Single European Act (SEA) aided the completion of the single market by changing the legislative process within the European Community, particularly with the introduction of qualified majority voting in the Council of the European Union for some policy areas, and the introduction of the assent procedure in the European parliament. The Single European Act also extended European Community competence into the fields of technology, the environment, regional policy, monetary policy and external policy. The single market came into effect on 1 January 1993, though full implementation of the elimination of frontier controls and the harmonisation of taxes have been repeatedly delayed. A fundamental review of the single market was completed in 2007, which resulted in an operational set of initiatives intended to modernise single market policy. Following the abolition of the European Community in 2009 as a result of the Lisbon Treaty, the single market policy now applies to the EU.

EUROPEAN ECONOMIC AREA

The single market programme spurred European non-member states to open negotiations with the European Community on preferential access for their goods, services, labour and capital to the single market. Principal among these states were European Free Trade Association (EFTA) members who opened negotiations on extending the single market to EFTA by the formation of the European Economic Area (EEA), encompassing all 19 European Community and EFTA states. Agreement was reached in 1992, but the operation of the EEA was delayed by its rejection in a Swiss referendum, necessitating an additional protocol agreed by the remaining 18 states. The EEA came into effect in 1994 after ratification by 17 member states (Liechtenstein joined in 1995 after adapting its customs union with Switzerland).

Austria, Finland and Sweden joined the EU on 1 January 1995, leaving only Iceland, Liechtenstein and Norway as the non-EU EEA members. Under the EEA agreement, the three states adopted the EU's *acquis communautaire,* apart from in the fields of agriculture, fisheries, and coal and steel.

The EEA is controlled by regular ministerial meetings and by a joint EU-EFTA committee which extends relevant EU legislation to EEA states. Apart from single market measures, there is cooperation in several areas, including education, civil protection, research and development, consumer policy and tourism. An EFTA court has been established in Luxembourg and an EFTA surveillance authority in Brussels to supervise the implementation of the EEA Agreement.

The EEA Enlargement Agreement came into force on 1 May 2004, which allowed the simultaneous expansion of both the EU and the EEA without disruption of the internal market. A similar process took place to ensure that Bulgaria and Romania could become contracting parties to the EEA upon joining the EU in 2007 and Croatia in 2013.

EUROPEAN MONETARY SYSTEM AND THE SINGLE CURRENCY

The European Monetary System (EMS) began operation in March 1979 with three main purposes. The first was to establish monetary stability in Europe, initially in exchange rates between European Community member state currencies through the Exchange Rate Mechanism (ERM), and in the longer term as part of a wider stabilisation process, overcoming inflation and budget and trade deficits. The second purpose was to overcome the constraints resulting from the interdependence of European Community economies, and the third was to aid the long-term process of European monetary integration.

The Maastricht Treaty set in motion timetables for achieving economic and monetary union (EMU) and a single currency (the euro). In May 1998, 11 member states were judged to fulfil or be close to fulfilling the necessary convergence criteria for participation in the first stage of EMU: Austria, Belgium, Finland, France, Germany, Ireland, Italy, Luxembourg, the Netherlands, Portugal and Spain. The criteria were that:

- the budget deficit should be 3 per cent or less of gross domestic product (GDP)
- total national debt must not exceed 60 per cent of GDP
- inflation should be no more than 1.5 per cent above the average rate of the three best performing economies in the EU
- long-term interest rates should be no more than 2 per cent above the average of the three best-performing economies in the EU in the previous 12 months
- applicants must have been members of the ERM for two years without having realigned or devalued their currency

Under the terms of a stability and growth pact agreed in December 1996 and revised in 2005, penalties may be imposed on EMU members with high budget deficits. Governments with deficits exceeding 3 per cent of GDP will receive a warning and will be obliged to pay up to 0.5 per cent of their GDP into a fund after ten months. This will become a fine if the budget deficit is not rectified within two years. A member state with negative growth will be allowed to apply for an exemption from the fine by referring to a number of relevant factors outlined in the pact.

As a result of the global economic downturn, by May 2010, 24 out of 27 countries in the EU had a deficit exceeding 3 per cent of GDP. The EC revised its existing recommendations in November 2009 and proposed extended deadlines for each country to correct its budget deficit.

On 1 January 1999 the 11 qualifying member states adopted the euro at irrevocably fixed exchange rates, the European Central Bank (ECB) took charge of the single monetary policy, and the euro replaced the ECU (an artificial currency adopted by European Community member states in 1979 as an internal accounting unit for the EMS).

Subsequent member states who have fulfilled the criteria for participation and adopted the euro includes Greece on 1 January 2001, Slovenia on 1 January 2007, Cyprus and Malta on 1 January 2008, Slovakia on 1 January 2009, Estonia on 1 January 2011, Latvia on 1 January 2014 and Lithuania on 1 January 2015. Referendums on the adoption of the euro have been held in Denmark and Sweden, but participation was rejected. In June 2003 the UK announced that it would not be adopting the euro.

The euro is now the legal currency in 19 participating states, which together constitute the eurozone. Euro notes and coins were introduced on 1 January 2002 and circulated alongside national currencies for a period of up to two months, after which time national notes and coins ceased to be legal tender.

The ECB meets twice a month in Frankfurt to set the following month's monetary policy applicable to the countries participating in the euro. Its governing council has 25 members: the six members of the ECB's executive board and the 19 governors of the national central banks of the participating states.

THE EURO CRISIS

Greece

Early in 2010, Greece's soaring budget deficit and the escalating cost of servicing the country's debt brought it to the verge of economic meltdown. In May 2010 the EC, ECB and IMF agreed a rescue package totalling €110bn (£95bn) and in February 2012 provided a further bailout package worth €130bn (£110bn). In November 2012, faced with the possibility of defaulting on its repayments, the Greek parliament passed a number of austerity measures. In June–July 2015 Greece defaulted on an IMF repayment, the ECB withdrew emergency funding and the government had to impose capital controls and close banks. International creditors offered a further bailout plan on the basis of the introduction of additional austerity measures; the rescue package was rejected by 60 per cent of the population in a referendum held on 5 July. Subsequently, a third bailout package totalling €86bn (£62bn), with different, but equally stringent, austerity measures was secured in August 2015, essentially to avoid Greece's departure from the eurozone.

Other Countries

In November 2010 the near collapse of the banking system in Ireland led to the approval of an €85bn (£72bn) rescue package by the EU and the IMF. In April 2011 Portugal requested financial assistance from the EU after rising borrowing costs left the government unable to pay its debts, and in May 2011 European finance ministers finalised the terms of a three-year bailout agreement worth €78bn (£69bn). The Spanish government requested a eurozone rescue loan of around €100bn (£77bn) on 10 June 2012; eurozone finance ministers approved the loan on the same day. On 25 June, Cyprus became the fifth eurozone member to ask for financial assistance, citing significant exposure to the crippled Greek economy. A €10bn support package was agreed on 25 March 2013.

COMMON AGRICULTURAL POLICY

The Common Agricultural Policy (CAP) was established to increase agricultural production, provide a fair standard of living for farmers and ensure the availability of food at reasonable prices. This aim was achieved by a number of mechanisms, including import levies, intervention purchase and export subsidies.

These measures stimulated production but also placed increasing demands on the budget, which was exacerbated by the increase in EC members and yields enlarged by technological innovation; the CAP now accounts for over 40 per cent of EU expenditure. To surmount these problems reforms were agreed in 1984, 1988, 1992, 1997, 1999, 2003, 2008 and 2013.

REFORMS

The 1984 reforms created the system of co-responsibility levies: farm payments to the EC by volume of product sold. This system was supplemented by national quotas for particular products, such as milk. The 1988 reforms emphasised 'set-aside', whereby farmers are given direct grants to take land out of production as a means of reducing surpluses. The set-aside reforms were extended in 1993 for another five years and to every farm in the EC. The 1999 reforms further reduced surpluses of cereals, beef and milk by cutting the intervention prices by up to 20 per cent and compensating producers by making area payments. Under the reforms, CAP rules were also simplified, eliminating inconsistencies between policies.

In 2003, EU farm ministers adopted a fundamental reform of the CAP, which included the following provisions:
- a single farm payment for EU farmers, independent of production (begun in 2005)
- payment to be linked to meeting environmental, food safety, animal and plant health and animal welfare standards, and the requirement to keep all farmland in good condition
- a strengthened rural development policy with more EU money to help farmers meet EU production standards (begun in 2005)
- a reduction in direct payments for bigger farms
- a mechanism for financial discipline to ensure that the farm budget fixed until 2013 is not exceeded

The ten EU members that joined in 2004 were also given access to a special €5.8bn (£3.9bn) three-year funding package.

A CAP 'health check' was carried out in 2008 and resulted in proposals intended to further modernise and streamline EU agricultural policy, and to allow farmers to follow market signals by breaking the link between direct payments and production. These include abolishing the requirement for farmers to leave 10 per cent of their arable land fallow, a gradual increase in milk quotas before their abolition in 2015 and a general reduction in market intervention.

On 13 March 2013, MEPs voted to adopt a controversial package of legislation, including approving both the extension of quotas and the rural development programme that involves shared financing with national governments. The stated aim of the CAP reform was to strengthen the competitiveness and sustainability of agriculture and maintain its presence in all regions, to guarantee European citizens healthy and quality food production, and to preserve the environment and develop rural areas. On 26 June 2013, a political agreement on the CAP 2014–20 reforms was reached between the European Commission, parliament and council and on 16 December 2013, the council of EU agriculture ministers formally adopted the four basic regulations for the reformed CAP in addition to the transition rules for 2014. The CAP 2014–20 reforms saw an investment of almost €28bn in the UK farming sector and rural areas. On 1 June 2018, the European Commission presented new legislative proposals on the future of the CAP after 2020.

INSTITUTIONS

EUROPEAN PARLIAMENT
E eplondon@europarl.europa.eu W www.europarl.europa.eu; www.europarl.org.uk

The European parliament (EP) originated as the common assembly of the ECSC, acquiring its present name in 1962. The parliament now comprises 751 seats representing citizens of the 28 countries in the EU, although this number will decrease to 705 when the UK leaves the EU. Members (MEPs), initially appointed from the membership of national parliaments, have been directly elected at five-year intervals since 1979. Elections to the parliament are held on differing bases throughout the EU; British MEPs have been elected by a regional list system of proportional representation since June 1999. The most recent elections were held in May 2019.

MEPs serve on committees which scrutinise draft EU legislation and the activities of the EC. A minimum of 12 plenary sessions a year are held in Strasbourg and six additional shorter plenary sessions a year are held in Brussels; committees meet in Brussels, and the secretariat's headquarters is in Luxembourg.

The influence of the EP has gradually expanded within the EU since the Single European Act 1985, which introduced the cooperation procedure; the Maastricht Treaty, which extended the cooperation procedure and introduced the co-decision (now ordinary legislative) procedure (see Legislation); the Amsterdam Treaty, which effectively extended the ordinary legislative procedure to all areas except economic and monetary union, and taxation; and the Lisbon Treaty, which gave parliament legislative powers comparable with the Council of the European Union. The EP has general powers of supervision over the EC, and powers of consultation and co-decision with the Council of the European Union; it votes to approve a newly appointed commission and can dismiss it at any time by a two-thirds majority. Under the Maastricht Treaty it has the right to be consulted on the appointment of the new commission, and can also veto its appointment. Under the Lisbon Treaty, the parliament elects the president of the commission on the proposal of the European Council. The EP has an equal right to decide on budgetary matters as the Council of the European Union, and they work together to approve and adopt the entire annual budget. In accordance with the Maastricht Treaty, the EP appoints the European Ombudsman to provide citizens with redress against maladministration by EU institutions.

The EP's organisation is deliberately biased in favour of multinational political groupings; recognition of a political grouping in the parliament entitles it to offices, funding, representation on committees and influence in debates and legislation. A political group must be composed of a minimum of 25 MEPs representing one quarter of the member states. For a list of UK MEPs, see European Parliament.

President, David Sassoli (Italy)

PARLIAMENT, allée du Printemps, F-67070 Strasbourg Cedex, France/ Wiertzstraat 60, B-1047 Brussels, Belgium
SECRETARIAT, Centre Européen, Plateau du Kirchberg, BP 1601, L-2929 Luxembourg T (+352) 43001
OMBUDSMAN, 1 avenue du Président Robert Schuman, CS 30403, F-67001 Strasbourg Cedex, France
　W www.ombudsman.europa.eu
　Ombudsman, Emily O'Reilly (Ireland)
EUROPEAN PARLIAMENT LIAISON OFFICE IN THE UK, Europe House, 32 Smith Square, London SW1P 3EU
　T 020-7227 4300 E eplondon@europarl.europa.eu

EUROPEAN PARLIAMENT LIAISON OFFICE IN EDINBURGH, The Tun, 4 Jackson's Entry, Holyrood Road, Edinburgh EH8 8PJ T 0131-557 7866
　E epedinburgh@europarl.europa.eu

COUNCIL OF THE EUROPEAN UNION
Wetstraat 175, Rue de la Loi, B-1048 Brussels, Belgium
W www.consilium.europa.eu

The Council of the European Union (Council of Ministers) is the main decision-making body of the EU, and formally comprises the ministers of the member states. Depending on the issue on the agenda, each country will be represented by the minister responsible for that subject. It passes laws, usually legislating jointly with the European parliament; coordinates the broad economic policies of the member states; approves the EU's budget jointly with the European parliament; defines and implements the EU's common foreign and security policy; concludes agreements between the EU and other states or international organisations; and coordinates the actions of member states and adopts measures in the area of police and judicial cooperation.

Council decisions are taken using one of three methods: by qualified majority vote, by a simple majority, or by unanimity. The treaties define which one of the three methods should be used in each subject area. Unanimity votes are taken on sensitive issues such as taxation and defence, but the qualified majority vote (QMV) is now used for the majority of council decisions. Under the provisions of the Lisbon Treaty, a new system of QMV began on 1 November 2014, under which a qualified majority is achieved if:

- at least 55 per cent of member states approve (72 per cent where the council does not act on a proposal from the commission) *and*
- these member states represent at least 65 per cent of the EU's population

This system therefore assigns a vote to each member state while taking account of their demographic weight.

The presidency of the Council of the European Union is held in rotation for six-month periods, setting the agenda for and chairing council meetings in all policy areas except foreign affairs. The holders of the presidency for the years 2020–21 are:

2021 Jan–Jun, Portugal　　　2021 Jul–Dec, Slovenia
2022 Jan–Jun, France　　　　2022 Jul–Dec, Czechia

In the area of foreign affairs, council meetings are chaired by the High Representative of the Union for Foreign Affairs and Security Policy.

High Representative of the Union for Foreign Affairs and Security Policy, Josep Borrell (Spain)

GENERAL SECRETARIAT OF THE COUNCIL OF THE EUROPEAN UNION, Wetstraat 175, rue de la Loi, B-1048 Brussels, Belgium W www.consilium.europa.eu
Secretary-General of the Council of the European Union (2020–25), Jeppe Tranholm-Mikkelsen (Denmark)

EUROPEAN COUNCIL
The European Council, formed in 1974, was given formal recognition by the Single European Act in 1987; on 1 December 2009, under the Lisbon Treaty it has become a fully fledged institution of the EU with a permanent president. It normally meets four times a year, unless a special meeting is convened by the president, and comprises the heads of state or government of each EU member state and the president of the EC. Meetings are chaired by the president of the council.

The primary function of the European Council is to give political guidance in all areas of EU activity at both European and national levels. The European Council can issue declarations and resolutions expressing the opinions of the heads of state and governments, but its decisions are not legally binding.

President of the European Council, Charles Michel (Belgium)

EUROPEAN COMMISSION

Wetstraat 200, rue de la Loi, B-1049 Brussels, Belgium

The European Commission (EC) consists of a college of 27 commissioners, one per member state. The members of the commission are appointed for five-year renewable terms by the agreement of the member states; the terms run concurrently with the terms of the European parliament. The president and the other commissioners are nominated by the governments of the member states, and, under the terms of the Lisbon Treaty, the appointments are approved by the European parliament. The commissioners pledge sole allegiance to the EU. The commission initiates and implements EU legislation and is the guardian of the EU treaties. It is the exponent of community-wide interests rather than the national preoccupations of the council. Each commissioner is supported by advisers and oversees the departments assigned to them, known as directorates-general.

Ursula von der Leyen (Germany) was elected president of the EC by the members of the European parliament on 16 July 2019, receiving 383 votes – more than the 374 majority required. Mrs von der Leyen took office on 1 November 2019.

At the time of going to press, a list of candidate commissioners, one for each member state, had been submitted to the president elect for consideration for the 2019–24 commission. The incoming commissioners were due to be confirmed following a vote by MEPs in October 2019. On 22 August 2019, the UK's Permanent Representative to the EU Sir Tim Barrow confirmed that the UK would not be nominating a candidate for the 2019–24 commission.

The commission has a total staff of around 33,000 permanent civil servants and temporary agents.

President, Ursula von der Leyen (Germany)

EC REPRESENTATION OFFICES

UK, Europe House, 32 Smith Square, London SW1P 3EU
 T 020-7973 1992

COURT OF JUSTICE OF THE EUROPEAN UNION

Palais de la Cour de Justice, boulevard Konrad Adenauer, Kirchberg, L-2925 Luxembourg
 W www.curia.europa.eu

The Lisbon Treaty gave a new framework to the EU court system. The court of justice of the European Union is now composed of two courts: the court of justice and the general court.

COURT OF JUSTICE

The court of justice exists to safeguard the law in the interpretation and application of EU treaties, to decide on the legality of EU legislation, and to determine infringements of the treaties. Cases may be brought to it directly by the member states and EU institutions. Questions on EU law may be referred to the court of justice by national courts. The decisions of the court are directly binding in the member states. The court's powers were extended by the Maastricht Treaty, allowing it to impose fines on member states who breach EU law. The court comprises 28 judges – one from each member state – and 11 advocates-general. These positions are appointed for renewable six-year terms by the member governments.

President, Koen Lenaerts (Belgium)

GENERAL COURT

Established under powers conferred by the Single European Act, the general court has jurisdiction to hear and determine direct actions brought by individuals, companies and, in some cases, EU governments against any of the institutions, bodies, agencies or offices of the EU, except those cases reserved for the court of justice. Additionally, the general court hears actions seeking compensation for damage caused by the institutions of the EU or their staff. It also has jurisdiction to hear actions brought by member states against the EC and actions relating to community trade marks. The court is composed of at least one judge from each member state (47 judges in 2017), increasing to 56 judges, or two from each member state, in 2019. Judges are appointed for renewable six-year terms by the individual national governments.

President, Marc van der Woude (The Netherlands)

EUROPEAN COURT OF AUDITORS

12 rue Alcide de Gasperi, L-1615 Luxembourg
 W www.eca.europa.eu

The European Court of Auditors, established in 1977, examines the accounts of all revenue and expenditure of the EU. It evaluates whether all revenue has been received and all expenditure incurred in a lawful and regular manner and in accordance with the principles of sound financial management. The court issues an annual report and a statement of assurance as to the reliability of the accounts and the legality and regularity of the underlying transactions. It also publishes special reports on specific topics and delivers opinions on financial matters. The court has one member from each member state, appointed for a renewable six-year term by the Council of the European Union following consultation with the European parliament. The President is elected for a renewable term of three years.

President, Klaus-Heiner Lehne (Germany)

FINANCIAL BODIES

EUROPEAN CENTRAL BANK

Kaiserstrasse 29, D-60311 Frankfurt am Main, Germany
 E info@ecb.europa.eu **W** www.ecb.europa.eu

The ECB, which superseded the European Monetary Institute, became fully operational on 1 January 1999 and defines and implements the single monetary policy for the euro area. The ECB's main task is to maintain the euro's purchasing power and price stability in the 19 EU countries that have introduced the currency since 1999. Its decision-making bodies are the executive board, the governing council and the general council. The executive board consists of the president, the vice-president and four other members. All members are appointed by the governments of the states participating in the single currency, at the level of heads of state and government. The governing council, the main decision-making body of the ECB, comprises the six members of the executive board and the governors of the national central banks of the 19 euro area states. The general council comprises the president and vice-president and the 28 governors of the national central banks of all the member states of the EU, the other members of the executive board being entitled to participate but not to vote. The ECB is independent of national governments and of all other EU institutions.

President, Christine Lagarde (France)
Vice-President, Luis de Guindos (Spain)

EUROPEAN INVESTMENT BANK
100 boulevard Konrad Adenauer, L-2950 Luxembourg
E info@eib.org **W** www.eib.org

The European Investment Bank (EIB) was set up in 1958 under the terms of the Treaty of Rome and is the financing arm of the EU. The EIB's main activity is to provide long-term loans in support of investments undertaken by private or public promoters, for projects furthering European integration.

The EIB also operates outside the EU, in support of EU development and cooperation policies in partner countries including the enlargement area of Europe (both candidate and potential candidate countries), the Mediterranean, Russia and the southern Caucasus, Africa, the Caribbean, the Pacific, Asia and Latin America.

The bank is not dependent on the EU budget, and raises its own resources on the capital markets. It is one of the biggest supranational bond issuers and lenders in the world with an AAA credit rating. In 2018 the EIB lent a total of €64.2bn and invested €1.55bn in the UK.

The UK-EU withdrawal draft agreed that the EIB will reimburse the UK's paid-in capital in 12 annual instalments, starting in 2019, in return the UK will guarantee its paid-in and callable capital and retain EIB board privileges and immunities until EIB lending undertaken while a member is recovered. The EIB will not reimburse the UK a share of the EIBs accumulated profits and, after withdrawal, UK projects will not be eligible for EIB operations reserved for member states.

The shareholders of the EIB are the 28 member states, whose ministers of economy and finance constitute its board of governors. This body lays down general directives on the credit policy of the bank and appoints members to the board of directors. The board of directors consists of 28 members nominated by the member states, and one by the European Commission. It takes decisions on the granting and raising of loans and the fixing of interest rates. The management committee, composed of the bank's president and eight vice-presidents and also appointed by the board of governors, is responsible for the day-to-day operations of the bank.

President, Werner Hoyer (Germany)

ADVISORY BODIES

COMMITTEE OF THE REGIONS
Bâtiment Jacques Delors, rue Belliard 99–101, B-1040 Brussels, Belgium
W www.cor.europa.eu

The Committee of the Regions (CoR) was established in 1994 and is the political assembly which provides local and regional authorities with a voice within the EU. The Lisbon Treaty obliges the EC, the Council of the European Union and the European parliament to consult the CoR whenever new legislative proposals are made in areas which have repercussions at regional or local level. The CoR then issues opinions on these proposals for EU laws, and also has the right to comment on any amendments to proposed legislation by MEPs. The CoR has the right to challenge new EU laws in the European court of justice if it believes it has not been correctly consulted by the commission, parliament or council or for any infringement of the subsidiarity principle.

The committee has 350 full members; the proportion of members from each of the 28 member states of the EU approximately reflects the size of the individual country's population. Committee members are proposed by the member states to the Council of the European Union, which appoints them for a five-year renewable term of office. Members must hold a regional or local authority electoral mandate or be politically accountable to an elected assembly. They participate in the work of seven specialist commissions which are responsible for drafting the CoR's opinions and resolutions on a wide range of topics.

President, Apostolos Tzitzikostas (Greece)
Secretary-General, Petr Blizkovsky (Belgium)

EUROPEAN ECONOMIC AND SOCIAL COMMITTEE
rue Belliard 99, B-1040 Brussels, Belgium **W** www.eesc.europa.eu

The European Economic and Social Committee (EESC) is a consultative body of the EU. It comprises 350 members drawn from economic and social interest groups in Europe; these members are appointed by the governments of the 28 member states for a five-year renewable term. The last renewal occurred in October 2015 for the 2015–20 mandate. The EESC is divided into three groups: employers, workers, and other interest groups such as consumers, farmers and the self-employed. Every two-and-a-half years the EESC elects a bureau made up of 40 members, including a president and two vice-presidents chosen from each of the three groups in rotation. The EESC issues opinions on draft EU legislation, which are forwarded to the commission, council and parliament. The EESC's competencies have increased as a result of revisions to the Treaty of Rome, and the Lisbon Treaty strengthens the committee's role.

President, Christa Schweng (Austria)
Secretary-General, Gianluca Brunetti (Italy)

AGENCIES

EUROPEAN ENVIRONMENT AGENCY
Kongens Nytorv 6, DK-1050 Copenhagen K, Denmark
T (+45) 3336 7100 **W** www.eea.europa.eu

The European Environment Agency (EEA) aims to support sustainable development and to help achieve significant and measurable improvement in Europe's environment, through the provision of information to policy-making agents and the public. The EEA has been operational since 1994, and now has 33 member countries. It is an EU body but is open to non-EU countries that share its objectives. The management board consists of representatives of the member countries, two representatives of the EC and two representatives designated by the European parliament.

Executive Director, Hans Bruyninckx (Belgium)

EUROPEAN JUDICIAL COOPERATION UNIT (EUROJUST)
Johan de Wittlaan 9, 2517 JR The Hague, The Netherlands
E info@eurojust.europa.eu **W** www.eurojust.europa.eu

The European Union's Judicial Cooperation Unit (Eurojust) was established in 2002 with the aim of developing Europe-wide cooperation in cases involving serious crime committed across more than one member state's jurisdiction. Eurojust also facilitates the provision of international mutual legal assistance and helps to implement extradition requests. It is a key interlocutor with the European parliament, the Council of the European Union and the EC.

The college of Eurojust is composed of 28 national members, one nominated by each member state. These members are experienced prosecutors, judges or police officers.

President, Ladislav Hamran (Slovakia)
Director, Nick Panagiotopoulos (Greece)

EUROPEAN POLICE OFFICE (EUROPOL)

Eisenhowelaan 73, 2517 KK The Hague, The Netherlands
W www.europol.europa.eu

The European Police Office (Europol) came into being on 1 October 1998 and assumed its full powers on 1 July 1999. It superseded the Europol Drugs Unit and exists to improve police cooperation between member states and to combat terrorism, illicit traffic in drugs and other serious forms of organised international crime. It is ultimately responsible to the Council of the European Union. Each member state has a national unit to liaise with Europol, and the units send at least one liaison officer to represent its interests at Europol headquarters. Europol employs over 1,000 staff at its headquarters, with around 100 criminal analysts, handling around 40,000 international investigations each year. It works closely with law enforcement agencies in the 28 EU member states and non-EU partner states, including Australia, the USA and Canada.

Executive Director, Catherine De Bolle (Belgium)

EUROPEAN PARLIAMENT POLITICAL GROUPINGS *as at 1 December 2020*

	EPP	S&D	Renew	Greens/EFA	ID	ECR	GUE/NGL	Others	Total
Austria	7	5	1	3	3	–	–	–	19
Belgium	4	3	4	3	3	3	–	–	*21
Bulgaria	7	5	3	–	–	2	–	–	17
Croatia	4	4	1	–	–	1	–	2	12
Cyprus	2	2	–	–	–	–	–	–	*6
Czechia	5	–	6	3	2	4	–	–	*21
Denmark	1	3	6	2	1	–	–	–	*14
Estonia	1	2	3	–	1	–	–	–	7
Finland	3	2	3	2	3	–	–	–	*14
France	8	6	23	13	23	–	–	–	*79
Germany	29	16	7	25	11	1	–	2	*96
Greece	8	2	–	–	–	1	–	4	*21
Hungary	12	5	2	–	–	–	–	1	20
Ireland	5	–	2	2	–	–	–	–	*13
Italy	8	18	1	4	28	6	–	11	76
Latvia	2	2	1	1	–	2	–	–	8
Lithuania	4	2	2	2	–	1	–	–	11
Luxembourg	2	1	2	1	–	–	–	–	6
Malta	2	4	–	–	–	–	–	–	6
The Netherlands	6	6	7	3	1	4	–	1	*29
Poland	17	7	–	1	–	27	–	–	52
Portugal	7	9	–	1	–	–	–	–	*21
Romania	14	10	7	–	–	1	–	1	33
Slovakia	5	3	2	–	–	2	–	2	14
Slovenia	4	2	2	–	–	–	–	–	8
Spain	13	21	9	3	–	4	–	–	*59
Sweden	6	5	3	3	–	3	–	–	*20
Total	186	145	97	75	73	62	0	27	*704

* Due to Brexit a number of member states have vacant seats.

EPP – European People's Party (Christian Democrats)
W www.eppgroup.eu
S&D – Progressive Alliance of Socialists and Democrats in the European Parliament
W www.socialistsanddemocrats.eu
Renew – Renew Europe
W www.reneweuropegroup.eu

Greens/EFA – Greens/European Free Alliance
W www.greens-efa.eu
ID – Identity and Democracy Group
ECR – European Conservatives and Reformists
W www.ecrgroup.eu
GUE/NGL – European United Left/Nordic Green Left
W www.guengl.eu

INTERNATIONAL ORGANISATIONS

International organisations are intergovernmental bodies, whose membership can only include either sovereign states or other international organisations. They are subject to international law and are capable of entering into agreements among themselves or with states. They do not include private non-governmental organisations with an international scope. International organisations are usually established by a treaty providing them with legal recognition, which distinguishes them from collections of states such as the G7.

AFRICAN UNION

PO Box 3243, Roosvelt Street W21K19, Addis Ababa, Ethiopia
T (+251) (1) 1551 7700 **E** DIC@africa-union.org **W** www.au.int

The African Union (AU) was launched in 2002 as a successor to the amalgamated Organisation of African Unity (OAU) and the African Economic Community. It currently has 55 members, representing every African country. The AU aims to further African unity, solidarity and democracy, to coordinate political, economic, social and defence policies, and to intervene in regional conflicts on a humanitarian basis.

Chief AU governing organs include the assembly of heads of state or government, the ultimate decision-making body; the executive council, composed of foreign ministers from member states and which advises the assembly; the African Commission, which is the AU secretariat and consists of one chair, one deputy chair and eight commissioners, each with a separate portfolio, who elect a chair to a four-year term; the peace and security council, modelled on that of the UN and capable of military intervention; and the pan-African parliament, established in 2004 to advise heads of state.

In 2013 the AU launched the Agenda 2063 pan-African plan outlining 20 goals and 14 flagship projects that each aim to accelerate economic growth and development by improving or expanding infrastructure, education, science and technology, arts and culture, as well as other initiatives. Agenda 2063 is divided into five ten-year implementation plans that set short-term targets in order to drive long-term goals. The first ten-year plan is due for assessment in 2023 and will be the first evaluation of the agenda.

Chair 2020, Cyril Ramaphosa (South Africa)
Chair of the Commission, Moussa Faki Mahamat

ANDEAN COMMUNITY

General Secretariat, Av. Paseo de la República 3895, San Isidro, Lima 27, Peru
T (+51) (1) 710 6400 **E** correspondencia@comunidadandina.org
W www.comunidadandina.org

The Andean Community (CAN), known as the Andean Pact until 1996, began operating formally on 21 November 1969 when its commission was established. It comprises four member states – Bolivia, Colombia, Ecuador and Peru – and the organisations and institutions of the Andean Integration System (AIS). Argentina, Brazil, Chile, Paraguay and Uruguay are associated states, Spain is an observer state.

The community's objectives are to facilitate economic growth, create jobs and facilitate regional integration towards the goal of a Latin American common market. It also aims to reduce the inequalities in development between member states. It pursues its objectives through a programme of trade liberalisation, a common external tariff, the relaxation of border controls, coordination between national legislatures and the promotion of industrial, agricultural and technological

development. The community also promotes democratic practices, respect for human rights and environmental sustainability. Additionally, CAN supports cultural integration by providing media platforms for sharing documentaries, news and other cultural programming.

The general secretariat of the Andean Community is its executive body, responsible for administration and dispute resolution. The general secretariat operates under the direction of the secretary-general, who is elected by the Andean Council of Foreign Ministers (ACFM). It can propose decisions or suggestions to the ACFM; it also manages the integration process, ensures that community commitments are fulfilled and maintains relations with the member countries and the executive bodies of other international organisations.

The Andean presidential council is the highest-level body of the AIS and comprises the presidents of the member states. Its responsibilities include setting new policies, evaluating the integration process and communicating with other bodies. The chairmanship is rotated among the members of the council each calendar year.

Since 2005, a policy of free flow of persons has enabled citizens to travel, work and study throughout the area without a visa.

Secretary-General, Dr Jorge Hernando Pedraza (Colombia)

ARAB MAGHREB UNION

73 Boulevard Tensift, Agdal, Rabat, Morocco
T (+212) (5) 376 81371 **E** sg.uma@maghrebarabe.org
W www.maghrebarabe.org

The Treaty establishing the Arab Maghreb Union (AMU) was signed on 17 February 1989 by the heads of state of the five member states: Algeria, Libya, Mauritania, Morocco and Tunisia. The AMU aims to strengthen ties between the member countries by developing agriculture and commerce, working towards a customs union and economic common market.

Decisions must be unanimous and are made by a council of heads of state, which is briefed by a council of foreign affairs ministers. The council of heads of state has not assembled since 1994 because of a dispute over the status of Western Sahara. A consultative assembly – consisting of 30 representatives from each member state – is based in Algiers; the secretariat is in Rabat; and the court of justice, with two judges from each country, operates in Nouakchott, Mauritania.

Secretary-General, Dr Al-Tayeb El-Bakoush (Tunisia)

ARCTIC COUNCIL

Fram Centre, Postboks 6606 Langnes, 9296 Tromsø, Norway
T (+47) 9112 0370S **E** acs@arctic-council.org
W www.arctic-council.org

The Arctic Council was founded in 1996 in Ottawa, Canada, and is a regional forum for socio-economic development and scientific research within the Arctic region, with particular emphasis on environmental conservation and sustainable developments. It comprises eight states: Canada, Denmark (including Greenland and the Faroe Islands), Finland, Iceland, Norway, Russia, Sweden and the USA. A further six organisations representing indigenous peoples are granted permanent participatory status and include the Saami Council, Inuit Circumpolar Conference and the Arctic Athabaskan Council. Thirteen states (China, France, Germany, India, Italy, Japan, the Netherlands, Poland, Singapore, South Korea, Spain, Switzerland and the UK) have observer status.

Decisions within the Arctic Council are made at biennial ministerial meetings attended by foreign ministers or designates of the member states. The chairmanship of the council and secretariat also rotate on a biennial basis. Between these meetings, the operation of the council is administered by the Committee of Senior Arctic Officials, which meets biannually.

Arctic Council initiatives are carried out by six working groups, each focusing on specific issues such as the monitoring and prevention of pollution, climate change, biodiversity, and public health.

Chair 2019–21, Gudlaugur Thor Thordarson (Iceland)
Director of the Secretariat, Nina Buvang Vaaja (Norway)

ASIA COOPERATION DIALOGUE

Al Salam, Block 7, Street 27, House 14, Kuwait City, Kuwait
E acd.secretariat@gmail.com **W** www.acd-dialogue.org

The Asia Cooperation Dialogue (ACD) was initiated by the former prime minister of Thailand, Thaksin Shinawatra, and inaugurated in June 2002. It currently has 34 members, with Morocco granted development partner status.

Its purpose is to provide a continent-wide forum to assist development in countries in Asia, with the ultimate goal of creating a consolidated Asian trade community to enhance competitiveness in the global market and to reduce poverty. It aims to achieve these objectives through promoting interdependence among Asian countries, improving quality of life and expanding the continent's trade and financial markets.

Representatives from each of the member states (typically foreign ministers) meet annually to discuss ACD developments, issues of regional cooperation and methods of enhancing Asian unity. In addition, ministers also meet during the annual UN general assembly to discuss the implementation of policy and a common approach to international issues.

Secretary-General, Dr Pornchai Danvivathana

ASIAN-AFRICAN LEGAL CONSULTATIVE ORGANIZATION

29 C, Rizal Marg, Diplomatic Enclave, Chanakyapuri, New Delhi 110021, India
T (+91) (11) 2419 7000 **E** mail@aalco.int **W** www.aalco.int

The Asian-African Legal Consultative Organization (AALCO), founded as a result of the Bandung Conference of 1955, was previously known as both the Asian Legal Consultative Committee and the Asian-African Legal Consultative Committee before its name was changed again in 2001. It was initially established as a non-permanent committee for a five-year term which was repeatedly extended until 1981, when it was granted permanent status. It has 48 member states and two permanent observer states.

The functions of the AALCO include serving as an advisory body to its member states in the field of international law, operating as a forum for common concerns among its members and making recommendations to governments and other international organisations.

Representatives from member states meet for the annual session which is hosted on a rotational basis and is attended by members of government, observers from other organisations and members of the International Court of Justice and International Law Commission.

The secretariat is located in New Delhi and is responsible for the day-to-day functioning of the organisation. It is headed by a secretary-general, who is elected to a four-year term that can be renewed once. Other infrastructure includes four regional arbitration centres, located in Egypt, Iran, Malaysia and Nigeria.

Secretary-General, Prof. Kennedy Gastorn (Tanzania)

ASIAN DEVELOPMENT BANK

6 ADB Avenue, Mandaluyong City 1550, Metro Manila, The Philippines
T (+63) (2)8632 4444 **W** www.adb.org

The Asian Development Bank (ADB), founded in 1966, is a multilateral financial institution dedicated to reducing poverty in Asia and the Pacific. It has 68 member countries from across the world; 49 within Asia and 19 non-regional. The ADB extends loans, equity investments and technical assistance to governments and public and private enterprises in its member countries, and promotes the investment of public and private capital for development. The bank's programmes prioritise economic growth, human development, good governance, environmental protection, private sector growth and regional cooperation.

The ADB is controlled by its board of governors, which meets annually and consists of a representative from each of the member states. It elects and delegates its powers to a board of directors which is responsible for administration and policy review.

The ADB raises funds through members' contributions and issuing bonds on the world's capital markets.

President, Masatsugu Asakawa (Japan)

ASIA-PACIFIC ECONOMIC COOPERATION

35 Heng Mui Keng Terrace, Singapore 119616
T (+65) 6891 9690 **E** info@apec.org **W** www.apec.org

The Asia-Pacific Economic Cooperation (APEC) is an economic forum for Pacific Rim countries to discuss regional economy, cooperation, trade and investment. APEC was founded in 1989 in response to the growing interdependence among Asia-Pacific economies. The 1994 Declaration of Common Resolve envisaged free and open trade between member states with industrialised economies by 2010, extending to members with developing economies by 2020. At the 2016 summit in Lima, Peru, APEC leaders issued the twenty-fourth APEC economic leaders' declaration in which they committed to increased regional economic integration and quality growth, enhancing the regional food market, working towards modernising small- and medium-sized businesses in the region, and developing human capital. Its 21 members define and fund work programmes for APEC's four committees, 16 working groups and other special task groups.

APEC's chairmanship rotates annually among member states and the chair is responsible for hosting the annual leaders' meeting, as well as meetings of foreign affairs and trade ministers. The permanent secretariat, based in Singapore, is responsible for implementing policy, and is headed by an executive director selected by member states to serve a three-year term.

Executive Director, Dr Rebecca Fatima Sta Maria (Malaysia)

ASSOCIATION OF SOUTH-EAST ASIAN NATIONS

Jalan Sisingamangaraja 70a, Jakarta 12110, Indonesia
T (+62) (21) 726 2991/724 3372 **E** public@aseansec.org
W www.asean.org

The Association of South-East Asian Nations (ASEAN) is a geo-political and economic organisation formed in 1967 with the aim of accelerating economic growth, social progress and cultural development, and ensuring regional stability. It currently has ten member states.

The ASEAN summit, a biannual meeting of the heads of government, is the organisation's highest authority. The biannual ASEAN foreign ministers' meeting (ASEAN Coordinating Council) is responsible for preparing summit meetings, implementing their policies, and coordinating ASEAN's activities. The ASEAN economic ministers meet annually to coordinate economic policy.

An ASEAN free trade area was implemented in 2003, while a common preferential tariff was introduced in 1993. At the ASEAN summit in 1995, a South East Asia nuclear-weapon-free zone was declared. In December 2008 a new charter came into force which gave ASEAN legal status and a new institutional framework, committed it to the promotion of democracy, and provided for the establishment of the intergovernmental commission on human rights. The ASEAN Economic Community was formed at the end of 2015 with the aim of establishing a common market and therefore regional economic integration.

The secretary-general of ASEAN is appointed by rotation and can initiate, advise on, coordinate and implement ASEAN activities. In addition to the ASEAN secretariat based in Jakarta, each member state has a national secretariat in its foreign ministry which organises and implements activities at a national level.

Secretary-General 2018–22, Dato Lim Jock Hoi (Brunei)

BALTIC ASSEMBLY

Citadeles Street 2–616, Riga, LV-1010, Latvia
T (+371) 6722 5178 **W** www.baltasam.org

Established in November 1991, the Baltic Assembly (BA) is an international organisation for cooperation between the parliaments of Estonia, Latvia and Lithuania. Each member state appoints between 12 and 16 parliamentarians to the assembly, including a chair and vice-chair of the national delegation. The political allegiances of the appointees reflect party proportions in each of the domestic parliaments. The BA holds an annual session in each of the member states in rotation. Several permanent and *ad hoc* committees also meet up to three times a year. The Baltic council of ministers, which comprises the heads of government and ministers of the member states, meets with the BA once a year and promotes intergovernmental and regional cooperation between the Baltic states; the joint sessions are known as the Baltic council.

President 2020, Aadu Must (Estonia)

CAB INTERNATIONAL

Nosworthy Way, Wallingford, Oxon OX10 8DE
T 01491-832111 **W** www.cabi.org

Founded in 1910, CAB International (CABI) (formerly the Commonwealth Agricultural Bureau) is a non-profit organisation that provides scientific expertise to assist sustainable development and environmental protection. The organisation consists of 43 countries, five British overseas territories and one associate member (the Netherlands); each is represented on both the executive council, which meets biannually, and the review conference, held every five years to appraise policy and set future goals. A governing board provides guidance on policy issues.

CABI has three divisions: publishing, development projects and research, and microbial services. Each division undertakes research and provides consultancy aimed at raising agricultural productivity, conserving biological resources, protecting the environment and controlling disease. Any country is eligible to apply for membership.

Chief Executive, Daniel Elger (UK)

CARIBBEAN COMMUNITY

Turkeyen, Greater Georgetown, Guyana
T (+592) 222 0001 **E** communications@caricom.org
W www.caricom.org

The Caribbean Community (CARICOM) was established as the Caribbean Community and Common Market in 1973 with the signing of the Treaty of Chaguaramas, which was updated in 2002. The objectives of CARICOM is to improve member states' working and living standards, boost employment levels, promote economic development and competitiveness, coordinate foreign and economic policies and enhance cooperation in the delivery of services such as health and education.

The supreme organ is the Conference of Heads of Government, which determines policy and resolves conflict. The Community Council of Ministers consists of ministers of government assigned to CARICOM affairs and is responsible for economic and strategic planning. The principal administrative arm is the secretariat, based in Guyana. The Bureau of the Conference of Heads of Government is the executive body; it comprises the chair of the conference, the outgoing chair and the secretary-general, who are all authorised to initiate proposals and to secure the implementation of decisions. In addition, there are five ministerial councils dealing with trade and economic development, foreign and community relations, human and social development, finance and planning, and national security and law enforcement.

There are 15 member states of CARICOM plus five associate members, 13 of which are party to the Revised Treaty of Chaguaramas, which established the Caribbean Community including the CARICOM single market and economy (CSME) in 2006.

Secretary-General, Irwin LaRocque (Dominica)

THE COMMONWEALTH

The Commonwealth is a voluntary association of 54 sovereign and independent states together with their associated states and dependencies. All of the states were formerly parts of the British Empire or League of Nations (later the UN) mandated territories, except for Mozambique and Rwanda which were admitted because of their history of cooperation with neighbouring Commonwealth nations.

The status and relationship of member nations were first defined by the inter-imperial relations committee of the 1926 Imperial Conference, when the six existing dominions (Australia, Canada, the Irish Free State, Newfoundland, New Zealand and South Africa) were described as 'autonomous communities within the British Empire, equal in status, in no way subordinate one to another in any aspect of their domestic or external affairs, though united by a common allegiance to the Crown and freely associated as members of the British Commonwealth of Nations'. This formula was given legal substance by the statute of Westminster in 1931.

This concept of a group of countries owing allegiance to a single crown changed in 1949 when India became a republic. India's continued membership of the Commonwealth was agreed by the other members on the basis of its 'acceptance of the monarch as the symbol of the free association of its independent member nations and as such the head of the Commonwealth'. This enabled subsequent new republics to join the association. Member nations agreed at the time of the accession of Queen Elizabeth II to recognise Her Majesty as the new head of the Commonwealth. However, the position is not vested in the British Crown.

THE MODERN COMMONWEALTH

As the UK's former colonies joined, after India and Pakistan in 1947, the Commonwealth was transformed into a multiracial association of equal nations, increasingly focused on promoting development and racial equality. South Africa withdrew in 1961 when it became clear that its reapplication for membership on becoming a republic would be rejected over its policy of apartheid.

The new goals of advocating democracy, the rule of law, good government and social justice were enshrined in the Harare Commonwealth Declaration (1991), which formed the basis of new membership guidelines agreed in Cyprus in 1993. Following the adoption of measures at the New Zealand summit in 1995 against serious or persistent violations of these principles, Nigeria was suspended in 1995 and Sierra Leone was suspended in 1997 for anti-democratic behaviour. Sierra Leone's suspension was revoked the following year when a legitimate government was returned to power. Similarly, Nigeria's suspension was lifted in 1999, the day a newly elected civilian president took office. The Edinburgh Commonwealth Economic Declaration (1997) established a set of economic principles for the Commonwealth, promoting economic growth while protecting smaller member states from the negative effects of globalisation. Zimbabwe was suspended from the councils of the Commonwealth in March 2002, and in 2003 the Zimbabwean government officially confirmed its departure from the association. Following the bloodless coup led by General Pervez Musharraf in 1999, Pakistan faced its first suspension from the Commonwealth. It was readmitted in 2004 only to be suspended again in 2007 after the imposition of emergency rule. The suspension was lifted after successful democratic elections in February 2008. Fiji's Commonwealth membership was suspended in September 2009 after its military government refused to commit to elections in 2010, but was reinstated in September 2014 following democratically held elections that took place earlier in the same month. In February 2018 The Gambia rejoined the Commonwealth after a near five-year absence in an attempt by the government to end international isolation; Yahya Jammeh, president 1996 to 2017, had pulled the country out of the Commonwealth in 2013. The Maldives rejoined in 2020.

INTERGOVERNMENTAL AND OTHER LINKS

The main forum for consultation is the Commonwealth Heads of Government Meetings, held biennially to discuss international developments and to consider cooperation among members. Decisions are reached by consensus and the views of the meeting are set out in a communiqué. There are also annual meetings of finance ministers and frequent meetings of ministers and officials in other fields, such as education, health, gender and youth affairs. Intergovernmental links are complemented by the activities of some 80 Commonwealth non-governmental organisations linking professionals, sportsmen and sportswomen, and interest groups. The Commonwealth Games take place every four years.

COMMONWEALTH SECRETARIAT

The Commonwealth has a secretariat, established in 1965 in London, which is funded by member governments. This is the main agency for multilateral communication between member governments on issues relating to the Commonwealth as a whole. It promotes consultation and cooperation, disseminates information on matters of common concern, organises meetings including the biennial summits, coordinates Commonwealth activities and provides technical assistance for economic and social development through the Commonwealth fund for technical cooperation.

The Commonwealth Foundation was established by Commonwealth governments in 1965 as an autonomous body with a board of governors representing Commonwealth governments that fund the foundation. It promotes and funds exchanges and other activities aimed at strengthening the skills and effectiveness of professionals and non-governmental organisations. It also promotes culture, rural development, social welfare, human rights and gender equality.

MEMBERSHIP

Membership of the Commonwealth involves acceptance of the association's basic principles and is subject to the approval of existing members. There are 54 members at present, of which 16 have Queen Elizabeth II as head of state, 32 are republics and five have national monarchies. (The date of joining the Commonwealth is shown in parentheses.)

*Antigua and Barbuda (1981)	Mozambique (1995)
*Australia (1931)	Namibia (1990)
*The Bahamas (1973)	Nauru (1968)
Bangladesh (1972)	*New Zealand (1931)
*Barbados (1966)	Nigeria (1960)
Belize (1981)	Pakistan (1947)
Botswana (1966)	*Papua New Guinea (1975)
Brunei (1984)	Rwanda (2009)
Cameroon (1995)	*St Kitts and Nevis (1983)
*Canada (1931)	*St Lucia (1979)
Cyprus (1961)	*St Vincent and the
Dominica (1978)	Grenadines (1979)
†eSwatini (1968)	Samoa (1970)
Fiji (1970)	Seychelles (1976)
The Gambia (1965)	Sierra Leone (1961)
Ghana (1957)	Singapore (1965)
*Grenada (1974)	*Solomon Islands (1978)
Guyana (1966)	South Africa (1931)
India (1947)	Sri Lanka (1948)
*Jamaica (1962)	Tanzania (1961)
Kenya (1963)	Tonga (1970)
Kiribati (1979)	Trinidad and Tobago (1962)
Lesotho (1966)	*Tuvalu (1978)
Malawi (1964)	Uganda (1962)
Malaysia (1957)	*United Kingdom (1931)
The Maldives (1982)	Vanuatu (1980)
Malta (1964)	Zambia (1964)
Mauritius (1968)	

* Realms of Queen Elizabeth II
† Formerly Swaziland

COUNTRIES THAT HAVE LEFT THE COMMONWEALTH

Republic of Ireland (1949)
South Africa (1961, rejoined 1994)
Pakistan (1972, rejoined 1989; suspended 1999, suspension lifted 2004; suspended 2007, suspension lifted 2008)
Zimbabwe (2003)
The Gambia (2013, rejoined 2018)
The Maldives (2016, rejoined 2020)

In each of the realms where Queen Elizabeth II is head of state (except for the UK), she is personally represented by a governor-general, who holds in all essential respects the same position in relation to the administration of public affairs in the realm as is held by Her Majesty in the UK. The governor-general is appointed by the Queen on the advice of the government of the state concerned.

COMMONWEALTH SECRETARIAT, Marlborough House, Pall Mall, London SW1Y 5HX **T** 020-7747 6500
E info@commonwealth.int **W** www.thecommonwealth.org
Secretary-General, Rt. Hon. Baroness Scotland of Asthal, QC (Dominica)

COMMONWEALTH FOUNDATION, Marlborough House, Pall Mall, London SW1Y 5HY **T** 020-7930 3783
E foundation@commonwealth.int
W www.commonwealthfoundation.com
Chair, Shree Baboo Chekitan Servansing (Mauritius)
COMMONWEALTH EDUCATION TRUST, 7-14 Great Dover Street, London SE1 4YR **T** 020-3096 7721
E hello@commonwealtheducationtrust.org
W www.commonwealtheducationtrust.org
Chair, Jeff Twentyman (UK)

COMMONWEALTH OF INDEPENDENT STATES

St. Kirov 17, Minsk 220030, Belarus
T (+375) (17) 215 50 01 **E** cr@cis.minsk.by **W** www.cis.minsk.by

The Commonwealth of Independent States (CIS) is a multilateral grouping of 11 former Soviet republics, including nine full members; Ukraine, a participating member; and Turkmenistan, an associate member. It was formed in 1991 and its charter was signed by ten states in 1993–4. The CIS acts as a coordinating mechanism for foreign, defence and economic policies and as a forum for addressing problems common to former members of the USSR. These matters are addressed in more than 80 inter-state, intergovernmental coordinating and consultative statutory bodies.

The two supreme CIS organs are the council of heads of state, which meets twice a year, and the council of heads of government. The executive committee, based in Minsk and Moscow, provides administrative support. There are also numerous ministerial, parliamentary, economic and security councils.

On becoming members of the CIS, the member states agreed to recognise their existing borders, respect one another's territorial integrity and reject the use of military force or coercion to settle disputes. A treaty on collective security was signed in 1992 by six states, and a joint peacemaking force, to intervene in CIS conflicts, was agreed upon by nine states. Russia concluded bilateral and multilateral agreements with other CIS states under the supervision of the council of heads of collective security (established 1993). These agreements became the Collective Security Treaty, enabling Russia to station troops in eight of the CIS states, and giving Russian forces *de facto* control of virtually all of the former USSR's external borders. Only Ukraine and Moldova remained outside the defence cooperation framework and did not sign the treaty. In 1999, Azerbaijan, Georgia and Uzbekistan withdrew from the treaty and formed a new defensive union (GUAM) with Moldova and Ukraine. Georgia withdrew from the organisation entirely in August 2009, following the country's war with Russia in 2008. In May 2014, Ukraine announced that it would begin the process of withdrawing from the CIS. However, in September 2015 Ukraine confirmed that it would not withdraw completely from the CIS but would instead participate on a selective basis.

In 1991, 11 republics signed a treaty forming an economic community. Members agreed to refrain from economic actions that would damage each other and to coordinate economic and monetary policies. A coordinating consultative committee, an economic arbitration court and an inter-state bank were established. Members also affirmed the principles of private ownership, free enterprise and competition as the basis for economic recovery.

The 11 CIS members who signed the Establishment of an Economic Union Treaty in September 1993 committed themselves to a common economic space with free movement of goods, services, capital and labour. In 2000 the presidents of the five countries approved a treaty establishing the Eurasian Economic Community, and in 2010 Russia, Belarus

and Kazakhstan formed a customs union, which Kyrgyzstan and Armenia joined in 2015. In April 2011 the economic council approved a draft agreement for the development of a free trade zone that would include all of the CIS member states: the agreement was signed by the CIS states with the exception of Azerbaijan, Uzbekistan and Turkmenistan in October 2011. On 1 January 2012 the customs union of Russia, Belarus and Kazakhstan transformed into an single economic space (SES), a higher form of economic integration, ensuring freedom of movement of goods, services, capital, labour, and equal treatment of economic entities within the three countries. Russia assumed the presidency of the Commonwealth on 1 January 2017.

Executive Secretary, Sergei Lebedev (Russia)

COUNCIL OF EUROPE

Avenue de l'Europe, F-67075 Strasbourg-Cedex, France
T (+33) (3) 8841 2000 **W** www.coe.int

The Council of Europe was founded in 1949. Its aim is to achieve greater unity between its members, to safeguard their European heritage and to facilitate their progress in economic, social, cultural, educational, scientific, legal and administrative matters, and to further pluralist democracy, human rights and fundamental freedoms. It has 47 member states, including the 28 members of the European Union, plus six observer states.

The organs are the committee of ministers, consisting of the foreign ministers of member countries, and the parliamentary assembly of 324 members (and 324 substitutes), elected or chosen by the national parliaments of member countries in proportion to the relative strength of political parties.

The committee of ministers is the executive organ. The majority of its conclusions take the form of international agreements (known as European conventions) or recommendations to governments. Decisions of the ministers may also be embodied in partial agreements to which a limited number of member governments are party.

One of the principal achievements of the Council of Europe is the European Convention on Human Rights (1950), which entered into force on 3 September 1953, and under which the European Court of Human Rights was established in 1959. The court oversees the implementation of the convention in the member states. It sits in chambers of seven judges or, exceptionally, as a grand chamber of 17 judges. Litigants must exhaust legal processes in their own country prior to bringing cases before the court.

Among other conventions and agreements are the European Convention for the Prevention of Torture, the European Social Charter, the Framework Convention for the protection of national minorities, the Istanbul Convention which combats violence against women, the Lanzarote Convention to protect children against sexual abuse and the Convention on Cyber Crime.

In 1990 the Venice Commission, an independent legal advisory body, was set up to assist in developing legislative, administrative and constitutional reforms in both European and non-European countries; it currently has 62 member states (47 Council of Europe members and 15 other countries), four observers and one associate member.

Non-member states take part in certain Council of Europe activities, such as educational, cultural and sports activities on a regular or *ad hoc* basis.

The council's ordinary budget for 2020 totals €255m (£230.3m).

President, Anders Knape (Sweden)
Secretary-General, Marija Pejcinovic Buric (Croatia)

COUNCIL OF THE BALTIC SEA STATES

Momma Reenstiernas Palats, Wollmar Yxkullsgatan 23, 118 50 Stockholm, Sweden
T (+46) 8440 1920 **E** cbss@cbss.org **W** www.cbss.org

The Council of the Baltic Sea States was established in 1992 with the aim of creating a regional forum to increase cooperation and coordination among the countries that border the Baltic Sea. The organisation focuses mainly on the environment, economic development, energy, education and culture, civil security and humanitarian issues. It currently has 12 members (the 11 countries of the Baltic Sea region and the European Union) while a further ten countries (including the UK and the USA) hold observer status.

The council consists of the foreign ministers of each member state and a member of the European Commission. The presidency of the council rotates among the member states on an annual basis, and the annual session is held in the presiding country. The foreign minister of the presiding country is responsible for coordinating the council's activities and is assisted by the committee of senior officials; a permanent international secretariat established in Stockholm, Sweden in 1998 and financed jointly by the member states. The council does not have a general budget or project fund; member countries are responsible for funding common activities and/ or for seeking and coordinating financing from other sources.

In 2020 the council completed the implementation of a reforms project aimed at increasing the relevancy and efficiency of the Council of the Baltic Sea States.

Presidency 2020–21, Lithuania

ECONOMIC COMMUNITY OF WEST AFRICAN STATES

101 Yakubu Gowon Crescent, Asokoro District, PMB 401, Abuja, Nigeria **T** (+234) (9) 314 76479 **E** info@ecowas.int
W www.ecowas.int

The Economic Community of West African States (ECOWAS) was founded in 1975 and came into operation in 1977. It aims to promote the economic, social and cultural development of West Africa through mutual cooperation, and to prevent and control regional conflicts.

The supreme authority of ECOWAS is vested in the annual summit of heads of government of all 15 member states. A council of ministers meets biannually to monitor the organisation and make recommendations to the summit. Since restructuring in 2007, ECOWAS has been managed by a commission, headed by the president. The ECOWAS parliament was inaugurated in November 2000 and judges for the court of justice were appointed in January 2001. Chad currently holds observer status.

An ECOWAS travel certificate is issued allowing free movement within the community, and nine of the 15 member states have a common passport.

An ECOWAS peacekeeping force has been involved in attempts to restore peace in Liberia (1990–6), Sierra Leone (1997–9) and in Guinea-Bissau (1998–9). In December 2010 the Côte d'Ivoire was suspended from ECOWAS following the failure of its *de facto* president, Laurent Gbagbo, to step down after a presidential election; the country was reinstated the following year following Mr Gbagbo's arrest. In March 2011 both Guinea and Niger were reinstated to the organisation; their memberships had been suspended, for failure to hold satisfactory democratic elections in 2009. ECOWAS suspended Mali in March 2012 and, a few weeks later, in April, Guinea-Bissau, demanding the immediate restoration of constitutional order in both states following military coups in both countries. Both countries were subsequently reinstated.

President 2018–22, Jean-Claude Brou (Côte d'Ivoire)

EUROPEAN BANK FOR RECONSTRUCTION AND DEVELOPMENT

One Exchange Square, London EC2A 2JN
T 020-7338 6000 **W** www.ebrd.com

Since its establishment in 1991, the European Bank for Reconstruction and Development (EBRD) has become the largest financial investor in a region that stretches from central Europe and the Western Balkans to central Asia. The Bank, currently owned by 69 countries, the EU and the European Investment Bank, has been working since 2011 to expand their operations into new countries with a focus on the Mediterranean region, bringing in countries such as Cyprus (2014), Greece (2015) and Lebanon (2017).

The main forms of EBRD financing are loans, equity investments and guarantees. EBRD's charter stipulates that at least 60 per cent of lending must go to the private sector, reflecting its particular interest in strengthening the financial sector and to promoting small and medium-sized businesses. It works in cooperation with national governments, private companies and international organisations such as the OECD, the IMF, the World Bank and the UN specialised agencies. The EBRD is also able to borrow on world capital markets.

The EBRD's highest authority is the board of governors; each member appoints one governor and one alternate. The governors delegate most powers to a 23-member board of directors; the directors are responsible for the EBRD's operations and budget, and are elected by the governors for three-year terms. The governors also elect the president of the board of directors, who acts as the bank's president for a four-year term.

In 2019 it delivered an investment of €10.1bn (£9.1bn) across 452 projects.

President, Odile Renaurd-Basso (France)

EUROPEAN FREE TRADE ASSOCIATION

9–11 rue de Varembé, CH-1211 Geneva 20, Switzerland
T (+41) (22) 332 2600 **E** mail.gva@efta.int **W** www.efta.int

The European Free Trade Association (EFTA) was founded in 1960 on the premise of free trade as a means of achieving growth and prosperity among its member states as well as promoting closer economic cooperation between the Western European countries. The immediate aim of the Association was to provide a framework for the liberalisation of trade in goods among its member states.

EFTA was founded by seven countries: Austria, Denmark, Norway, Portugal, Sweden, Switzerland and the UK. Finland joined in 1961, Iceland in 1970 and Liechtenstein in 1991. In 1973, the UK and Denmark left EFTA to join the European Community. They were followed by Portugal in 1986 and by Austria, Finland and Sweden in 1995. Today the four EFTA member states are Iceland, Liechtenstein, Norway and Switzerland.

The Agreement on the European Economic Area (EEA) was signed in 1992 and entered into force in January 1994. The agreement brings together the 27 European Union member states and the three EEA EFTA states – Iceland, Liechtenstein and Norway – in a single market, referred to as the 'internal market'. Switzerland is not a member of the EEA, but has a series of bilateral agreements with the EU. The secretariat in Brussels provides support for the management of the EEA agreement, including the preparation of new legislation.

Currently, the EFTA states have free trade agreements with the following partners: Albania; Bosnia and Hercegovina; Canada; Central American States (Costa Rica, Guatemala and Panama); Chile; Colombia; Ecuador; Egypt; Georgia; Hong Kong, China; Gulf Cooperation Council (GCC); Indonesia; Israel; Jordan; the Rep. of Korea; Lebanon; Macedonia;

Mexico; Montenegro; Morocco; the Palestinian Authority; Peru; the Philippines; Saudi Arabia; Serbia; Singapore; Southern African Customs Union; Tunisia; Turkey; and Ukraine. Negotiations on free trade agreements are ongoing with India; Malaysia; MERCOSUR and Vietnam.

The EFTA Council is the governing body. Member states usually meet eight times a year at ambassadorial level in Geneva.

Secretary-General, Henri Getaz (Sweden)

EUROPEAN ORGANISATION FOR NUCLEAR RESEARCH (CERN)
Esplanade des Particules 1, CH-1211 Geneva 23, Switzerland
T (+41) (22) 767 8484 **E** cern.reception@cern.ch **W** www.cern.ch

The convention establishing the European Organisation for Nuclear Research (CERN) came into force in 1954. CERN promotes European collaboration in high-energy physics with scientific goals and no military implication. It has 23 member states, two associate member states in the pre-stage to membership, six associate member states, and six members with observer status, including the European Commission and UNESCO.

The council, which is the highest policy-making body, comprises two delegates from each member state and is chaired by the president, who is elected by the council in session. The council also appoints a director-general, who is responsible for the internal organisation of CERN. The director-general heads a workforce of approximately 2,500 civil servants from the 23 member states. At present more than 12,200 scientists from all over the world use CERN's facilities.

Tim Berners-Lee developed the World Wide Web while working at CERN in 1989, and in 2008 CERN completed construction work on the Large Hadron Collider, the world's largest and most powerful particle accelerator. In 2012 the Higgs-Boson particle was discovered through experiments using the Large Hadron Collider.

Director-General, Dr Fabiola Gianotti (Italy)

EUROPEAN SPACE AGENCY
24 rue du General Bertrand, CS 30798 75345 Paris Cedex 7, France
T (+33) (1) 5369 7654 **E** contactesa@esa.int **W** www.esa.int

The European Space Agency (ESA) was created in 1975 by the merger of the European Space Research Organisation and the European Launcher Development Organisation. Its aims include the advancement of space research and technology and the implementation of European space policy. ESA has 22 member states, one associate member and seven cooperating states. ESA's mandatory activities are funded by contributions from all member states and calculated in accordance with each country's gross national income. In 2020, ESA's budget amounted to €4.87bn (£4.43bn).

The agency is directed by a council composed of the representatives of its member states; its chief officer is the director-general who is appointed by the council. ESA has liaison offices in Belgium (for the EU), the USA and Russia, while a launch base is stationed in French Guiana.

Director-General, Johann-Dietrich Wörner (Germany)

EUROPEAN UNION

See European Union section

FOOD AND AGRICULTURE ORGANIZATION OF THE UNITED NATIONS
Viale delle Terme di Caracalla, 00153 Rome, Italy
T (+39) (06) 57051 **E** fao-hq@fao.org **W** www.fao.org

The Food and Agriculture Organization (FAO) is a specialised UN agency, established in 1945. It assists rural populations by raising levels of nutrition and living standards, and by encouraging greater efficiency in food production and distribution. It analyses and publishes information on agriculture and natural resources. The FAO also advises governments on national agricultural policy and planning through its investment centre and collaboration with the World Bank and other financial institutions. The FAO's field programme covers a range of activities, including strengthening crop yields, rural development and livestock heath and productivity.

The FAO's priorities are sustainable agriculture, rural development and food security. The organisation monitors potential famine areas, channels emergency aid from governments and other agencies, assists in rehabilitation and responds to urgent or unforeseen requests for technical assistance.

The FAO has 195 members (194 states plus the European Union) and two associate members (the Faroe Islands and Tokelau). It is governed by a biennial conference of its members which sets a programme and budget. The budget for 2018–19 was US$2.6bn (£2bn) funded by member countries in proportion to their gross national income. The FAO is also funded by donor governments and other institutions.

The conference elects a director-general and a 49-member council which governs between conferences. The regular and field programmes are administered by a secretariat, headed by the director-general. Five regional, ten sub-regional and numerous national offices help administer the field programme.

Director-General, Qu Dongyu (China)

GULF COOPERATION COUNCIL
PO Box 7153, Riyadh 11-462, Saudi Arabia
T (+966) (11) 482 7777 **W** www.gcc-sg.org

The Gulf Cooperation Council (GCC), or the Cooperation Council for the Arab States of the Gulf, was established on 25 May 1981. Its main objectives are increasing coordination and integration, harmonising economic, commercial, educational and social policies and promoting scientific and technical innovation among its member states. It established a common market in 2008, and set up a customs union in 2003 which became fully operational in 2015. The GCC has six members: Bahrain, Kuwait, Oman, Qatar, Saudi Arabia and the United Arab Emirates.

The highest authority of the GCC is the supreme council, whose presidency rotates among members' heads of states. It holds one regular session every year, but extraordinary sessions may be convened if necessary.

The ministerial council, which ordinarily meets every three months, consists of the foreign ministers of the member states or other delegated ministers. It is authorised to propose policies and recommendations.

Secretary-General, H.E. Dr Nayef Falah M. Al-Hajraf (Bahrain)

INTERNATIONAL ATOMIC ENERGY AGENCY
Vienna International Centre, PO Box 100,1400 Vienna, Austria
T (+43) (1) 26000 **W** www.iaea.org

The International Atomic Energy Agency (IAEA) was established in 1957. It is an intergovernmental organisation that reports to, but is not a specialised agency of, the UN.

The IAEA aims to enhance the contribution of atomic energy to peace, health and prosperity. It does not advocate the use of atomic energy for military purposes. It establishes atomic energy safety standards and offers services to its member states to upgrade safety and security measures for their nuclear installations and material, and for radioactive sources, material and waste. It is the focal point for international conventions on the early notification of a nuclear accident, accident assistance, civil liability for nuclear damage, physical protection of nuclear material and the safety of spent fuel and radioactive waste management. The IAEA also encourages research and training in nuclear power. It is additionally charged with drawing up safeguards and verifying their enforcement in accordance with several international nuclear weapons treaties.

The IAEA has 172 members that meet annually in a general conference. The conference decides policy, a programme and a budget as well as electing a director-general and a 35-member board of governors. The board meets five times a year to review and formulate policy, address budgetary concerns and consider applications for membership. Project and policy changes are implemented by the secretariat.

Director-General, Rafael Mariano Grossi (Argentina)

INTERNATIONAL CIVIL AVIATION ORGANISATION

999 Robert-Bourassa Boulevard, Montréal, Québec H3C 5H7, Canada
T (+1) (514) 954 8219 **E** icaohq@icao.int **W** www.icao.int

The International Civil Aviation Organisation (ICAO) was founded with the signing of the Chicago Convention on International Civil Aviation in 1944 and became a specialised agency of the UN in 1947. It sets international technical standards and regulations for aviation safety, security and efficiency, as well as environmental protection.

ICAO has 193 members and is governed by an assembly, which convenes triennially. A council of 36 members is elected, which represents leading air transport nations as well as less developed countries. The council elects the president, appoints the secretary-general and supervises the organisation through subsidiary committees, serviced by a secretariat.

President of the Council, Salvatore Sciacchitano (Italy)
Secretary-General, Dr Fang Liu

INTERNATIONAL CRIMINAL POLICE ORGANISATION (INTERPOL)

200 quai Charles de Gaulle, F-69006 Lyon, France
W www.interpol.int

Interpol was set up in 1923 to establish an international criminal records office and to harmonise extradition procedures. The organisation has a global membership of 194 countries. Interpol's aims are to promote cooperation between criminal police authorities and to support government agencies concerned with combating crime, while respecting national sovereignty. It is financed largely by annual contributions from the governments of the member countries and supplementary funding from private and commercial sources.

Interpol policy is formulated by the general assembly which meets annually and is composed of delegates appointed by the member countries. The 13-member executive committee is elected by the general assembly from the member countries' delegates and is chaired by the president, who serves a four-year term of office. The permanent administrative organ is the general secretariat, headed by the secretary-general, who is appointed by the general assembly.

The UK Interpol National Central Bureau is operated by the National Crime Agency (NCA).

Secretary-General, Jürgen Stock (Germany)

INTERNATIONAL ENERGY AGENCY

31–35 rue de la Fédération, 75739 Paris Cedex 15, France
T (+33) (1) 4057 6500 **E** info@iea.org **W** www.iea.org

The International Energy Agency (IEA), founded in 1974, is an autonomous agency within the framework of the Organisation for Economic Cooperation and Development (OECD). The IEA's objectives include the improvement of energy cooperation worldwide, development of alternative energy sources and the promotion of relations between oil-producing and oil-consuming countries. The IEA also maintains an emergency system to alleviate the effects of severe oil supply disruptions.

The main decision-making body is the governing board, composed of senior energy officials from member countries. The IEA secretariat, with a staff of energy experts, carries out the work of the governing board and its subordinate bodies. The executive director is appointed by the board. The IEA has 30 member states; eight associate states; and the European Union also participates in its work.

Executive Director, Fatih Birol (Turkey)

INTERNATIONAL FRANCOPHONE ORGANISATION

Cabinet du Secrétaire général, 19–21 avenue Bosquet, 75007 Paris, France
T (+33) (1) 4437 3325 **W** www.francophonie.org

The International Francophone Organisation *(International Organisation of La Francophonie* – IOF) is an intergovernmental organisation founded in 1970 by 21 French-speaking countries. Its 88 member states and governments, 54 members, 7 associate members, and 27 observers, together represent over 900 million people; 300 million of which speak French regularly, with varying degrees of fluency. The IOF organises political activities and actions multilateral cooperation that benefits French-speaking populations. It represents its member states internationally, promotes French language and francophone cultural industries with the aim of preventing conflict and promoting development.

The conference of heads of state and government of countries with French as a common language – also known as La Francophonie summit – takes place biennially. Other institutions include the permanent ministerial conference and the permanent council.

Secretary-General, Louise Mushikiwabo (Rwanda)

INTERNATIONAL FUND FOR AGRICULTURAL DEVELOPMENT

44 Via Paolo di Dono, 00142 Rome, Italy
T (+39) (06) 54591 **E** ifad@ifad.org **W** www.ifad.org

The International Fund for Agricultural Development (IFAD) began operations as a UN specialised agency in 1977. It develops and finances agricultural and rural projects in developing countries and aims to promote employment and additional income for poor farmers, reduce malnutrition and improve food security systems.

IFAD has 177 member states divided into three lists: List A (primarily OECD countries), List B (primarily OPEC countries), and List C (developing countries) which is subdivided into C1 (Africa), C2 (Europe, Asia and the Pacific) and C3 (Latin America and the Caribbean). All powers are vested in a governing council of all member states, which meets annually. It elects an executive board which is composed of 18 members and 18 alternate members and is chaired by the president of the IFAD. The president serves a four-year term that can be renewed once.

President, Gilbert F. Houngbo (Togo)

INTERNATIONAL HYDROGRAPHIC ORGANIZATION
4b quai Antoine 1er, B.P. 445, MC 98011, Monaco
T (+377) 9310 8100 E info@iho.int W www.iho.int

The International Hydrographic Organization (IHO) began operating in 1921 with 19 member states and headquarters in the Principality of Monaco. In 1970 its name was changed from the International Hydrographic Bureau. The IHO is an intergovernmental organisation that has a purely consultative role and aims to support safety in international navigation, set policy for marine conservation and improve coordination between national hydrographic institutions. The IHO has a membership of 93 states that meet at triennial assemblies to set policy, approve budget, review progress and adopt programmes of work. Each member is represented at these conferences by their most senior hydrographer. All member states have an opportunity to initiate new proposals for IHO consideration. Outside of its membership, the IHO acts to promote hydrography and facilitate the exchange of technology with developing countries. It is also the source that defines the boundaries between seas and oceans.

Secretary-General, Dr Mathias Jonas (Germany)

INTERNATIONAL LABOUR ORGANIZATION
4 route des Morillons, CH-1211, Geneva 22, Switzerland
T (+41) (22) 799 6111 E ilo@ilo.org W www.ilo.org

The International Labour Organization (ILO) was established in 1919 as an autonomous body of the League of Nations and became the UN's first specialised agency in 1946. The ILO aims to promote employment, improve working conditions, extend social protection and promote dialogue between government, workers' and employers' organisations.

It sets minimum international labour standards through the drafting of international conventions. Member countries are obliged to submit these to their domestic authorities for ratification, and thus undertake to bring their domestic legislation in line with the conventions. Members must report to the ILO periodically on how these regulations are being implemented. The ILO is also a principal resource centre for information, analysis and guidance on labour and employment.

The ILO has 187 member states and is composed of the International Labour Conference, the governing body and the International Labour Office. The conference of members meets annually and is attended by national delegations. It adopts international labour conventions and recommendations, provides a forum for discussion of economic and social issues and approves the ILO's programme and budget.

The 56-member governing body is composed of 28 government, 14 worker and 14 employer members and acts as the ILO's executive council. It convenes three times a year. Ten governments, including the UK, hold permanent seats on the governing body because of their industrial importance. There are also various regional conferences and advisory committees. The ILO acts as a secretariat and as a centre for operations, publishing and research.

Director-General, Guy Ryder (UK)

INTERNATIONAL MARITIME ORGANIZATION
4 Albert Embankment, London SE1 7SR
T 020-7735 7611 E info@imo.org W www.imo.org

Originally named the Inter-Governmental Maritime Consultative Organisation, the International Maritime Organisation (IMO) was established as a UN specialised agency in 1948. Owing to delays in treaty ratification it did not commence operations until 1958.

The IMO fosters intergovernmental cooperation in technical matters relating to international shipping, particularly regarding safety and security at sea, efficiency in navigation and protecting the marine environment from pollution caused by shipping. The IMO is responsible for convening maritime conferences and drafting marine conventions. It also provides technical aid to countries wishing to develop their activities at sea.

The IMO has 174 members and three associate members. It is governed by an assembly comprising delegates of all its members. It meets biennially to formulate policy, set a budget, to vote on specific recommendations on pollution, maritime safety and security, and to elect the council. The council, which meets twice a year, fulfils the functions of the assembly between sessions and appoints a secretary-general. It consists of 40 members: ten from the world's largest shipping nations, ten from the nations most dependent on seaborne trade and 20 other members to ensure a fair geographical representation. The IMO acts as the secretariat for the London Convention (1972) and its 1996 protocol which regulates the disposal of land-generated waste at sea.

Secretary-General, Kitack Lim (Republic of Korea)

INTERNATIONAL MONETARY FUND
700 19th Street NW, Washington DC 20431, USA
T (+1) (202) 623 7000 E publicaffairs@imf.org W www.imf.org

The International Monetary Fund (IMF) was established at the UN Monetary and Financial Conference at Bretton Woods, New Hampshire, in 1944. Its articles of agreement entered into force in 1945 and it began operations in 1947.

The IMF exists to promote international monetary cooperation and the expansion of world trade to ensure international economic stability. It advises members on their economic and financial policies; promotes policy coordination among the major industrial countries; gives technical assistance in central banking, balance of payments accounting, taxation and other financial matters; and provides loans to states with weak economies. The IMF serves as a forum for members to discuss monetary policy issues and seeks the balanced growth of international trade. It has 190 members; Tuvalu joined in June 2010, South Sudan in April 2012, Nauru in April 2016 and Andorra in January 2020.

Upon joining the IMF, a member is assigned a quota based on that member's relative standing in the world economy and its balance of payments. The quota determines the maximum size of the member's capital subscription to the fund, access to IMF resources, voting power and share in the allocation of special drawing rights (SDRs). Quotas are reviewed at regular intervals (usually every five years) and adjusted accordingly. After the 13th general review in 2008 the IMF board of governors adopted a reform package which would grant *ad hoc* quota increases to 54 countries found to be under-represented, and triple the number of basic votes to all members, thereby enhancing the representation of emerging and low-income countries. These reforms became effective in March 2011. In December 2010 the board of governors approved recommendations of the 14th general review – namely the doubling of all available quotas, a shift in 6 per cent of quotas from over- to under-represented countries, and an overall realignment in quota shares to reflect emerging markets and developing countries (EDMCs). Under these reforms, China will become the third largest member country and three further EDMCs (Brazil, India and Russia) will be among the top ten shareholders. These reforms will become effective upon their acceptance by three-fifths of members having 85 per cent of total voting power. Work on the 15th general review was delayed, pending implementation of the 2010 reforms. In February 2015, the board of governors adopted a resolution calling for the completion of the 15th review by 15 December 2015. The deadline was extended until the commencement of the October 2019 annual meeting where it was determined there would be no increases in IMF quotas. A deadline for the 16th review has been set for 15 December 2023.

The SDR (special drawing rights), the reserve currency created by the IMF in 1969, is calculated daily on a basket of usable currencies and is the IMF's unit of account; as at 15 October 2020, 1 SDR equalled US$1.41 (£1.09). SDRs are allocated at intervals to supplement members' reserves and thereby improve international financial liquidity. Total quotas currently stand at SDR477bn, a doubling of quotas from 2015, following the implementation of the reforms of the 14th general review on 26 January 2016.

The IMF is not a bank and does not lend money; it provides temporary financial assistance by selling a member's SDRs or other members' currencies in exchange for the member's own currency. The member can then use the purchased currency to alleviate its balance of payments difficulties. IMF financial resources derive primarily from members' capital subscriptions, which are proportionally related to their quotas. In addition, the IMF is authorised to borrow from official lenders. It may also draw on a line of credit from 40 member countries and institutions under the new arrangements to borrow (NAB). Once activated, NAB can provide supplementary resources of up to SDR182bn to the IMF. In limited cases the IMF can also access a potential amount totalling SDR17bn from 11 countries under the so-called general arrangements to borrow (GAB), with an additional SDR1.5bn available under an associated arrangement with Saudi Arabia.

Benign market conditions between 2004 and 2008 prompted many countries to start repaying their outstanding loans and demand for the fund's resources dropped dramatically; however, in 2008 the IMF increased its lending in response to the global financial crisis. In March 2009 the IMF announced a number of reforms to its lending framework, intended to provide greater speed and flexibility in lending arrangements, doubled access limits on loans and more closely tailor the conditionality of loans to fit the recipient state's requirements. In February 2010 a defined poverty line was introduced under which countries would qualify to access low-cost concessional loans under the poverty reduction and growth trust. In 2011 the IMF further refined its lending options to better meet the needs of its member countries as global growth continued to weaken in response to the ongoing crisis in the euro area. The 2011 measures included the introduction of a precautionary credit line to enable the IMF to provide upfront liquidity, including for countries with sound policies that had been affected by economic shocks beyond their control, and a rapid financing instrument for emergency assistance to support member countries experiencing a range of urgent balance of payments needs, without the need for a fully fledged programme. As at 31 October 2020 total outstanding IMF credits amounted to SDR99.15bn.

The IMF supports long-term efforts at economic reform and transformation as well as medium-term programmes under the extended fund facility, which runs for three to four years and is aimed at overcoming balance of payments difficulties stemming from macroeconomic and structural problems. Typically, measures are introduced to reform taxation and the financial sector, to privatise state-owned enterprises and to make labour markets more flexible.

The IMF is headed by a board of governors, comprising one representative and one alternate representative of each member state, which meets annually. The governors delegate powers to 24 executive directors, who are appointed or elected by member countries. The executive directors are responsible for the daily operation of the fund and the election of the managing director.

Managing Director, Kristalina Georgieva

INTERNATIONAL ORGANIZATION FOR MIGRATION

17 Route des Morillons, PO Box 17, CH-1211 Geneva 19, Switzerland
T (+41) (22) 717 9111 E hq@iom.int W www.iom.int

The International Organization for Migration (IOM) was founded in 1951 to resettle European displaced persons and refugees. During the 1960s and 1970s the IOM developed links with the United Nations High Commissioner for Refugees and began a programme of assistance and reintegration outside of Europe.

The role of the IOM is to help ensure the orderly and humane management of migration; its remit includes migration health services, international migration law, counter-trafficking measures, emergency and post-crisis management and assisted voluntary returns. More than 9,000 staff are employed in over 480 field locations. There are 173 member states and eight states with observer status.

The IOM is led by a director-general who is elected for a five-year term. The director-general's office has the constitutional authority to manage the organisation, carry out the activities within its mandate and develop current policies, procedures and strategies.

Director-General, Antonio Vitorino (Portugal)

INTERNATIONAL RED CROSS AND RED CRESCENT MOVEMENT

International Committee of the Red Cross, 19 Avenue de la paix, 1202 Geneva, Switzerland
T (+41) (22) 734 6001 W www.icrc.org

The International Red Cross and Red Crescent Movement is composed of three elements – the International Committee of the Red Cross, the International Federation of Red Cross and Red Crescent Societies, and the National Red Cross and Red Crescent Societies.

The International Committee of the Red Cross (ICRC), the organisation's founding body, was formed in 1863. It aims to protect and assist victims of armed conflict. It also seeks to ensure the application of the Geneva Conventions regarding prisoners of war and detainees.

The International Federation of Red Cross and Red Crescent Societies (IFRC) was founded in 1919 to assist the humanitarian activities of national societies, coordinate their relief operations for victims of natural disasters and care for refugees outside areas of conflict. There are Red Cross and Red Crescent societies in 190 countries and it has more than 60 field delegations internationally.

The international conference of the Red Cross and Red Crescent meets every four years, bringing together delegates of the ICRC, the International Federation and the national societies, as well as representatives of all states party to the Geneva Conventions.

Director-General of the ICRC, Robert Mardini (Lebanon)
President of the IFRC, Peter Maurer (Switzerland)

INTERNATIONAL TELECOMMUNICATION UNION

Place des Nations, 1211 Geneva 20, Switzerland
T (+41) (22) 730 5111 E itumail@itu.int W www.itu.int

The International Telecommunication Union (ITU) was founded in Paris in 1865 as the International Telegraph Union and became a UN specialised agency in 1947.

ITU is an intergovernmental organisation for information and communication technologies. It comprises 193 member states, almost 900 sector members and associates who represent public and private organisations involved in telecommunications. Its mission is to promote the development of information and communication technologies and to offer assistance to developing countries.

For more than 150 years, ITU has coordinated the shared global use of the radio spectrum, promoted international cooperation in assigning satellite orbits, worked to improve communication infrastructure in the developing world and established the worldwide standards for the interconnection of a vast range of communications systems: from broadband networks to new-generation wireless technologies, aeronautical and maritime navigation, radio astronomy, satellite-based meteorology and converging fixed-line and mobile telephone, internet and broadcasting technologies.

Secretary-General, Houlin Zhao (China)

INTERNATIONAL TRADE UNION CONFEDERATION

Boulevard du Roi Albert II, 5 B 1, B-1210 Brussels, Belgium
T (+32) (2) 224 0211 **E** info@ituc-csi.org **W** www.ituc-csi.org

The International Trade Union Confederation (ITUC) was created in 2006 by the merger between the International Confederation of Free Trade Unions (ICFTU), the World Confederation of Labour (WCL) and other independent unions. Through public and industrial advocacy work it seeks to assert and defend the rights and interests of workers, and to foster international cooperation between trade unions. The ITUC represents 200 million workers in 163 countries and territories and had 332 national affiliates.

The congress, the supreme authority of the ITUC, meets once every four years to review and propose policy and to elect the 78-member general council. Council members are elected according to population-weighted geographical regions, with six seats reserved for nomination by the women's committee, and two by the youth committee. The council, and the general secretary elected at each congress, govern the organisation. It also elects a 25-member executive bureau from among its members which deals with urgent issues and those delegated to it by the council; it also makes decisions on finances and formulates the annual budget for council approval.

The ITUC has regional organisations for Africa (ITUC-AF), the Americas (TUCA), Asia-Pacific (ITUC-AP), and Europe (the pan-European regional council, or PERC), along with the Arab Trade Union Confederation (ATUC). It also cooperates closely with the Global Union Federations, the Trade Union Advisory Committee to the Organisation for Economic Cooperation and Development (OECD), the European Trade Union Confederation, the International Labour Organisation, a number of other UN specialised agencies and national and regional unions and organisations.

General Secretary, Sharan Burrow (Australia)

INTERNATIONAL WHALING COMMISSION

The Red House, 135 Station Road, Impington, Cambridge CB24 9NP
T 01223-233971 **W** www.iwc.int

The International Whaling Commission (IWC) was set up under the International Convention for the Regulation of Whaling, signed in Washington DC in 1946. It has 100 member states. The purpose of the IWC is to provide for the conservation of whale stocks, enabling the development of the whaling industry. The measures in the convention provide for the complete protection of certain species; designate specified areas as whale sanctuaries; set limits on the numbers and size of whales which may be taken; prescribe open and closed seasons and areas for whaling; and prohibit the capture of suckling calves and female whales accompanied by calves. The IWC meets biennially to review and revise these measures.

The IWC has three main committees, responsible for scientific, finance and administration, and conservation matters. There are further sub-committees and working groups concerned with subjects including aboriginal subsistence whaling, infractions, small cetaceans, whale-watching, whale-killing methods and animal welfare.

Executive Secretary, Dr Rebecca Lent (USA)

LEAGUE OF ARAB STATES

Al-Tahrir Square, PO Box 11642, Cairo, Egypt
T (+20) (2) 2575 0511 **W** www.lasportal.org

The League of Arab States was founded in 1945 to protect the independence and sovereignty of its member states, supervise the affairs and interests of Arab countries and promote coordination among them. The organisation has 22 members, including Palestine. The League itself has observer status at the United Nations.

The heads of member states meet annually at the Arab League summit, while foreign ministers convene every six months as part of the Arab League council. Member states participate in various specialised agencies which develop specific areas of cooperation between Arab states. These include the Arab Monetary Fund; the Arab Satellite Communications Organisation; the Arab Academy for Science, Technology and Maritime Transport; the Arab Bank for Economic Development in Africa; the Arab League Educational, Cultural and Scientific Organisation; and the Council of Arab Economic Unity.

Secretary-General, Ahmed Ali Aboul Gheit (Egypt)

MERCOSUR

Dr. Luis Piera 1992, Piso 1, 11200-Montevideo, Uruguay
T (+598) (2) 412 9024 **W** www.mercosur.int

MERCOSUR (the Southern Common Market) was created by the Treaty of Asunción, signed by Argentina, Brazil, Paraguay and Uruguay on 26 March 1991. Venezuela signed an adhesion protocol in 2006 and became a full member in 2012, but was suspended indefinitely as a member in August 2017. Bolivia, which had been an associate member since 1997, became a full member on 17 July 2015. Six other countries (Chile, Colombia, Ecuador, Guyana, Peru and Suriname) have associate member status. Bolivia is in the process of ascension. New Zealand and Mexico are observer states.

The Common Market Council (CMC) is the highest-level agency of MERCOSUR, with authority to formulate policy and enforce member states' compliance with the Treaty of Asunción. The CMC comprises ministers of foreign affairs and economic ministers of the member states; it meets at least once a year.

The Common Market Group is the executive body of MERCOSUR and is coordinated by the foreign ministries of the member states. Its function is to implement decisions made by the CMC and resolve disputes, and if necessary, establish subgroups to work on particular issues. Other bodies include a joint parliamentary committee, a trade commission and a socio-economic advisory forum. The presidency of MERCOSUR rotates alphabetically between member states every six months.

In 2005, Argentina, Brazil, Paraguay and Uruguay became associate members of the Andean Community, reciprocating MERCOSUR's action to grant associate membership to all Andean Community nations. In December 2005, the Colombian president ratified a free trade agreement (FTA) with MERCOSUR giving Colombian products preferential access to MERCOSUR countries. MERCOSUR signed an FTA with Israel in December 2007, the bloc's first such agreement outside Latin America. On 28 June 2019, 20 years since negotiations first began, MERCOSUR and the EU reached a landmark trade agreement.

Presidency Jan–Jun 2020, Mario Abdo Benítez (Paragay)
Presidency Jul–Dec 2020, Luis Lacalle Pou (Uruguay)

NORDIC COUNCIL

Ved Stranden 18, 1061 Copenhagen K, Denmark
T (+45) 3396 0200 **E** receptionen@norden.org **W** www.norden.org

The Nordic Council was established in March 1952 as an advisory body on economic and social cooperation, comprising parliamentary delegates from Denmark, Iceland, Norway and Sweden. It was subsequently joined by Finland (1955), and representatives from the Faroes (1970), the Aland Islands (1970) and Greenland (1984).

Cooperation is regulated by the Helsinki Treaty, signed in 1962. This was amended in 1971 to create a Nordic council of ministers, which discusses all matters except defence and foreign affairs. Decisions of the council of ministers, which are taken by consensus, are binding, although if ratification by member parliaments is required, decisions only become effective following parliamentary approval. The council of ministers is advised by the Nordic Council, to which it reports annually. There are ministers for Nordic cooperation in every member government.

The Nordic Council comprises 87 elected members. Denmark, Finland, Norway, and Sweden each have 20 members and Iceland has seven members. Of these, two of the Danish representatives are from the Faroe Islands and two are from Greenland, while Finland has two representatives from Aland. The council comprises members of the national parliaments nominated by their party groups. The council meets biannually – the ordinary session in the autumn and the theme session in the spring, at which decisions are made on issues that are then implemented by the national governments. The president, vice-president, and the 11 members of the presidium for the forthcoming year are elected at the ordinary session. The presidency of the Nordic Council rotates between the five countries, and the presiding country hosts the council sessions.

The on-going political work of the council is conducted through committees and party groups. The council is served by a secretariat that shares its premises with the secretariat to the council of ministers in Copenhagen. There is also a national secretariat in each of the Nordic parliaments.

President 2020, Silja Dögg Gunnarsdóttir (Iceland)

NORTH AMERICAN FREE TRADE AGREEMENT

The leaders of Canada, Mexico and the USA signed the North American Free Trade Agreement (NAFTA) on 17 December 1992 in their respective capitals; it came into force in January 1994 after being ratified by the legislatures of the three member states. This treaty was replaced by the United States-Mexico-Canada Agreement (USMCA) which took effect on 1 July 2020.

NORTH ATLANTIC TREATY ORGANISATION

Blvd Leopold III, Brussels B-1110, Belgium
W www.nato.int

The North Atlantic Treaty Organisation (NATO) is a political and military alliance designed to provide common security for its members through cooperation and consultation in political, military and economic as well as scientific and other non-military fields.

The North Atlantic Treaty (Treaty of Washington) was signed in 1949 by Belgium, Canada, Denmark, France, Iceland, Italy, Luxembourg, the Netherlands, Norway, Portugal, the UK and the USA. Greece and Turkey acceded to the treaty in 1952, the Federal Republic of Germany in 1955 (the reunited Germany acceded in October 1990), Spain in 1982, and the Czech Republic, Hungary and Poland in 1999. Bulgaria, Estonia, Latvia, Lithuania, Romania, Slovakia and Slovenia signed membership protocols in March 2003 and officially joined NATO in March 2004. Albania and Croatia became official members in April 2009, having signed membership accords in September 2008, while Montenegro joined in 2017, and North Macedonia joined in 2020.

STRUCTURE

The North Atlantic council (NAC), chaired by the secretary-general, is the highest authority of the alliance and is composed of permanent representatives of the 30 member countries. It meets weekly, but also holds meetings at higher levels involving foreign and defence ministers and heads of government. The permanent representatives (ambassadors) head national delegations of advisers and experts. The nuclear planning group (NPG) is composed of all member countries, with the exception of France, and meets at ministerial level at least once a year. The NATO secretary-general chairs the council and the NPG. Much of the NAC policy is prepared and drafted by the senior political committee, a group of deputy permanent representatives and policy advisers.

The senior military authority in NATO, which advises the council, is the military committee, composed of the chief of defence staffs of each member country except Iceland, which has no military forces and is represented by a civilian. The military committee, which is assisted by an integrated international military staff, also meets in permanent session with permanent military representatives and is responsible for making recommendations to the council on measures considered necessary for the common defence of the NATO area and for supplying guidance on military matters to the NATO strategic commanders. The chair of the military committee, elected for a period of two to three years, represents the committee on the council.

The alliance's military command structure is divided between two functional strategic commands: Allied Command Operations (ACO) is responsible for all NATO military operations, whereas Allied Command Transformation (ACT) is charged with training and restructuring NATO military forces and capabilities. The headquarters of ACO is at the Supreme Headquarters of the Allied Powers Europe (SHAPE) at Mons, Belgium, and comes under the command of the Supreme Allied Commander Europe (SACEUR). The headquarters of ACT is at Norfolk, Virginia, USA, and is under the command of the Supreme Allied Commander Transformation (SACT). There is also a regional planning group for Canada and the USA.

POST COLD WAR DEVELOPMENTS

The Euro-Atlantic Partnership Council (EAPC) was established in 1997 to develop closer security links with Eastern European and former Soviet states. Replacing the North Atlantic Cooperation Council (NACC) as the first institutional framework for cooperation between NATO member countries and former adversaries from Central and Eastern Europe, the EAPC focuses on defence planning, defence industry conversion, defence management and force structuring. Its membership comprises the 29 NATO members and Armenia, Austria, Azerbaijan, Belarus, Bosnia and Hercegovina, Finland, Georgia, Ireland, Kazakhstan, Kyrgyzstan, Macedonia, Malta, Moldova, Russia, Serbia, Sweden, Switzerland, Tajikistan, Turkmenistan, Ukraine and

Uzbekistan. The EAPC provides the multilateral, political framework for the Partnership for Peace programme (PFP). The PFP is the basis for practical, bilateral security cooperation between NATO and all partner countries in the fields of defence planning and budgeting, military exercises and civil emergency operations. It also works to improve the interoperability between the forces of partner and member countries to enable them to undertake joint operations and has provided the context for cooperation by many of the partner countries in NATO-led peacekeeping and peace-support operations in Bosnia and Hercegovina, Kosovo and Afghanistan.

NATO and Russia committed themselves to helping build a stable and secure partnership based on mutual interest when they signed the 1997 Founding Act on mutual relations, cooperation and security, which provided for the creation of a NATO-Russia Permanent Joint Council (PJC). In 2002 it was replaced by the NATO-Russia Council (NRC). In April 2014, following Russia's military intervention in Ukraine, NATO suspended all practical cooperation with Russia, including the NRC, save for high level communications at ambassadorial level and above, but meetings of the council resumed in 2016. Three meetings of the NRC took place in 2016 and three in 2017. The first meeting in 2018 took place on 31 May. NATO remains open to a periodic, focused and meaningful political dialogue with Russia on the basis of reciprocity, as agreed at the NATO Summit in Warsaw in July 2016.

The establishment of the NATO-Ukraine Commission (NUC) in 1997 committed both parties to developing their relationship under a programme of consultation and cooperation on political and security issues, and cooperation has been intensified since Russia's intervention in 2014. The NATO-Georgia Commission (NGC), created in 2008, is pursuing political dialogue between NATO and Georgia, and helping to supervise Georgia's progress towards membership of NATO. The NGC is also co-ordinating support to help the country recover from the summer 2008 conflict.

NATO's Mediterranean dialogue, launched in 1994, aims to improve trust and understanding of NATO's goals and objectives among the countries of the southern Mediterranean area: Algeria, Egypt, Israel, Jordan, Mauritania, Morocco and Tunisia.

At its summit meeting in 2004, the alliance launched the Istanbul Cooperation Initiative (ICI), promoting practical cooperation with the Gulf Cooperation Council (GCC) and other interested countries in the Middle East. To date Bahrain, Qatar, Kuwait and the United Arab Emirates have joined the ICI.

The development of a European security and defence identity, which would strengthen NATO's European pillar, was agreed at the 1999 NATO summit meeting in Washington. Subsequent developments have served to strengthen cooperation between NATO and the European Union and to establish a strategic partnership.

At the 2002 Prague summit, further measures to improve defence capabilities were taken on the basis of a new capabilities commitment, in which member countries agreed to specific targets and time frames for improvements. A military concept for defence against terrorism was also agreed, and additional initiatives taken in the areas of nuclear, biological and chemical weapons defence and protection against cyber attacks. The NATO response force (NRF), a rapid-reaction unit comprising land, sea and air special forces, was officially launched at the Prague summit and became fully operational in 2006. The Lisbon summit in 2010 saw the publication of NATO's strategic concept, a statement of core principles that emphasised the importance of international cooperation in defence, security and crisis management, with particular reference to strengthening NATO's relationships with the EU

and UN. At the 2014 Wales summit, it was decided to enhance the NATO response force by establishing a very high readiness joint task force (VJTF) to deploy within just a few days to challenges that arise. The VJTF was deployed for exercises for the first time in June 2015 and has been on active standby since that time.

Ahead of the Brussels summit in July 2018, NATO and the EU signed a new joint declaration enhancing cooperation in areas such as military mobility, cyber security, and counter-terrorism. The 2018 Brussels summit also assessed NATO progress achieved following the 2016 Warsaw and 2017 Brussels summits.

AFGHANISTAN

From January 2001, following the establishment of the Afghan Transitional Authority, an international security assistance force (ISAF) was created on the basis of a UN mandate to provide the security required to allow infrastructure reconstruction and create a stable democratic government. In 2002, NATO began providing support for ISAF at the request of the lead nations and, in August 2003, assumed full responsibility for the leadership of ISAF. In accordance with an October 2003 UN security council mandate, ISAF gradually extended its authority from the capital, Kabul, to assume responsibility for the security, reconstruction and development of the entire country in October 2006. The gradual transition of security responsibility from ISAF to the Afghan national security forces commenced in 2010 and was completed at the end of 2014. In January 2015, a new non-combat resolute support mission was launched to train, assist and advise Afghan security forces. It was agreed in May 2016 that this mission would extend beyond the end of the year and that a civilian-led presence would remain in Afghanistan following the end of the mission in order to help Afghan security forces become self-sufficient. NATO and its partners have committed to providing financial support to sustain the Afghan forces until the end of 2024.

KOSOVO

NATO has been leading a peace-support operation in Kosovo since June 1999 in support of wider international efforts to build peace and stability in the area. Approximately 3,400 troops from the NATO-led Kosovo Force (KFOR), provided by 26 countries, are currently deployed in the region.

TURKEY

In December 2012, the Turkish government requested support for its air defence system in the wake of the escalating conflict in Syria. The request was prompted by several incidents of cross-border fire and resulting civilian casualties. Germany, The Netherlands and the USA agreed to provide patriot air defence systems for purely defensive deployment in Adana, Gaziantep and Kahramanmaras. All defence systems have been operational under NATO command and control since February 2013. In January 2015, Spanish troops replaced the Dutch unit stationed in Adana.

AFRICA

NATO counter-piracy operations were active between October and December 2008, and again between March and July 2009, in response to the growing threat presented by piracy in the Horn of Africa region. Operation Ocean Shield – approved by the North Atlantic Council in August 2009 and ended in November 2016 – focused on at-sea operations, but also offered assistance to regional states in developing their capacity to combat piracy.

Since June 2007, NATO has assisted the African Union Mission in Somalia (AMISOM) by providing airlift support. Following renewed African Union requests, the alliance agreed to extend its support by periods of six to twelve months and has done this on several occasions. NATO also continues to work with the African Union in identifying further areas where NATO could support the African Standby Force, a continental on-call security force. At the 2016 Warsaw Summit heads of state and government agreed to further strengthen and expand NATO's political and practical partnership with the African Union.

Secretary-General and Chair of the North Atlantic Council, of the DPC and of the NPG, Jens Stoltenberg (Norway)

ORGANISATION FOR ECONOMIC COOPERATION AND DEVELOPMENT
2 rue André Pascal, 75016 Paris Cedex 16, France
T (+33) 1 4524 8200 **W** www.oecd.org

The Organisation for Economic Cooperation and Development (OECD) was formed in 1961 to replace the Organisation for European Economic Cooperation. It is the instrument for international cooperation among industrialised member countries on economic and social policies. Its objectives are to assist its member governments in creating policies designed to achieve high, sustained economic growth and maintain financial stability, to contribute to world trade on a multilateral basis and to stimulate members' aid to developing countries. The OECD has 38 member countries, most of which have developed, high-income economies. Colombia joined in 2020 as the 38th member state. The European Commission is involved in the work of the OECD but is not a member of the organisation.

The council is the supreme body of the organisation. It is composed of one representative for each member country plus one representative of the European Commission (the European Commission does not have the right to vote) and meets at permanent representative level under the chairmanship of the secretary-general, and at ministerial level (usually once a year) under the chair of a minister. Decisions and recommendations are adopted by consensus. Most of the OECD's work is undertaken by around 250 specialised committees and working parties. These are serviced by an international secretariat headed by a secretary-general.

In 2007 the OECD council opened accession discussions with Chile, Estonia, Israel, Russia and Slovenia: Chile, Estonia, Israel and Slovenia became members in 2010. In 2013 the council launched accession discussions with Colombia and Latvia and, in April 2015, also invited Costa Rica and Lithuania to open formal talks. Latvia became a member in 2016. Following its meeting in March 2014, the council postponed accession negotiations with Russia.

The funding of the OECD is divided according to a member state's economy and population size; the USA, the largest contributor, supplies almost 21 per cent of the organisation's budget (€386m (£325m) in 2019).

Secretary-General, Angel Gurría (Mexico)

ORGANIZATION FOR SECURITY AND COOPERATION IN EUROPE
6 Wallnerstrasse, 1010 Vienna, Austria
T (+43) 1 514360 **E** pm@osce.org **W** www.osce.org

The Organization for Security and Cooperation in Europe (OSCE) was launched in 1975 as the Conference on Security and Cooperation in Europe (CSCE) under the Helsinki Final Act. This established agreements between NATO members, Warsaw Pact members, and neutral and non-aligned European countries covering security, cooperation and human rights. It was renamed in 1994.

The Charter of Paris for a New Europe, signed in November 1990, committed members to support multiparty democracy,

free-market economics, the rule of law and human rights. The signatories also agreed to regular meetings of heads of government, ministers and officials. The first CSCE summit was held in Helsinki in July 1992, at which the Helsinki Document was adopted. This declared the CSCE to be a regional organisation under the UN charter and defined the structures of the organisation.

Three structures have been established: the ministerial council, which comprises the foreign ministers of participating states and meets at least once a year; the permanent council, which is the main regular body for political consultation, meeting weekly in Vienna; and the forum for security cooperation, also meeting weekly. The chair of the OSCE rotates annually and the post of chair-in-office is held by the foreign minister of a participating state.

The OSCE has 16 field operations in Europe, the Caucasus and Central Asia. The OSCE observes elections throughout its 57 participating states. It also provides technical assistance to improve the legislative and administrative framework for elections in specific countries. In 1999, the charter on European security committed the OSCE to cooperating with other organisations and institutions concerned with the promotion of security within the OSCE area. In 2020 its budget was €138m (£125m).

Chair, Edi Rama (Albania)

ORGANIZATION OF AMERICAN STATES
17th Street and Constitution Avenue, NW, Washington DC 20006–4499, USA
T (+1) (202) 370 5000 **W** www.oas.org

Originally founded in 1890 for largely commercial purposes, the Organization of American States (OAS) adopted its present name and charter in 1948. The charter entered into force in 1951 and was amended in 1970, 1988, 1996 and 1997. OAS has 35 member states, though the membership of Honduras was suspended in July 2009 following a coup against President Jose Zelaya; its suspension was lifted in June 2011. The European Union and 72 non-American states have permanent observer status.

The OAS aims to strengthen the peace and security of the Americas; to promote and consolidate representative democracy; to prevent or resolve any political, judicial or economic issues which may arise among member states; to promote their economic, social and cultural development; and to achieve an effective limitation of conventional weapons.

Policy is determined by the annual general assembly, the organisation's supreme authority, which elects the secretary-general for a five-year term. The meeting of consultation of ministers of foreign affairs considers urgent problems on an *ad hoc* basis. The permanent council, comprising one ambassador from each member state, implements the policies approved by the general assembly, acts as an intermediary in cases of disputes arising between states and oversees the general secretariat, the main administrative body. The inter-American council for integral development was created in 1996 by the ratification of the protocol of Managua to promote sustainable development and eliminate poverty.

Secretary-General, Luis Almagro (Uruguay)

ORGANIZATION OF ARAB PETROLEUM EXPORTING COUNTRIES
PO Box 20501, Safat 13066, Kuwait
T (+965) 2495 9000 **E** oapec@oapecorg.org **W** www.oapecorg.org

The Organization of Arab Petroleum Exporting Countries (OAPEC) was founded in 1968. Its objectives are to promote cooperation in economic activities, unite efforts to ensure the flow of oil to consumer markets and create a favourable climate for capital investment and the development of the petroleum industry. OAPEC has 11 member states, although Tunisia's membership has been inactive since 1986.

The ministerial council is composed of oil ministers from the member countries and meets twice a year to determine policy and approve the budgets and accounts of the general secretariat and the judicial tribunal. The judicial tribunal is composed of between seven and 11 judges who rule on disputes between member countries and between countries and oil companies. The executive organ of OAPEC is the general secretariat.

The active members are Algeria, Bahrain, Egypt, Iraq, Kuwait, Libya, Qatar, Saudi Arabia, Syria and the United Arab Emirates.

Secretary-General, Ali Sabt Bensabt (Kuwait)

ORGANIZATION OF THE BLACK SEA ECONOMIC COOPERATION

Darüşşafaka Cad. Seba Center iş Merkezi, No:45 Kat 3, Istinye, 34460 Sar7#x0131₃r-Istanbul, Turkey
T (+90) (212) 229 6330/6335 **E** info@bsec-organization.org
W www.bsec-organization.org

The Black Sea Economic Cooperation (BSEC) resulted from the Istanbul Summit Declaration and the adoption of the Bosphorus statement on 25 June 1992; it acquired a permanent secretariat in 1994. A charter was inaugurated to found the Organization of the Black Sea Economic Cooperation in May 1999 following the Yalta Summit of the heads of state or government in June 1998. It has 12 member states.

The organisation aims to promote closer political and economic cooperation between the countries in the Black Sea region and to foster greater security, foreign investment and good governance.

The council of the ministers of foreign affairs is the highest decision-making authority; it elects the organisation's secretary-general and meets twice-yearly. The meetings rotate among the member states and the chair is the foreign minister of the state in which the meeting is held. There is also a committee of senior officials, and a number of working groups which deal with specific areas of cooperation. BSEC has a permanent secretariat based in Istanbul.

Secretary-General, Michael B. Christides (Greece)

ORGANISATION OF ISLAMIC COOPERATION

PO Box 178, Jeddah 21411, Saudi Arabia
T (+966) (12) 651 5222 **W** www.oic-oci.org

The Organisation of Islamic Cooperation (OIC) was established in 1969 with the purpose of promoting solidarity and cooperation between its member states. It also has the specific aims of supporting the formation of a Palestinian state, coordinating the views of member states in international forums such as the UN, and improving cooperation in the fields of economics, culture and science.

The OIC has three main bodies: the Islamic summit, the organisation's supreme authority composed of the heads of member states, which meets triennially; the annual conference of foreign ministers; and the general secretariat, which implements policy and is headed by a secretary-general elected by the conference of foreign ministers for a once-renewable five-year term.

In addition to this structure, the OIC has several subsidiary bodies, institutions and standing committees. These include the Islamic Solidarity Fund, to aid Islamic institutions in member countries; the Islamic Development Bank, to finance development projects in member states and the Islamic Educational, Scientific and Cultural Organisation.

Since 1991, the OIC has spoken out in protest of violence against Muslims in India, the Occupied Territories and Bosnia-Hercegovina. From 1993 to 1995 the OIC coordinated the offering of troops to the UN by Muslim states to protect Muslim areas of Bosnia-Hercegovina.

The organisation has 57 members (27 states in Africa; 24 in the Middle East, central and South East Asia plus the Palestinian Authority; three in Europe, and two in South America) and five observer states.

Secretary-General, Dr. Yousef bin Ahmad Al-Othaimeen (Saudi Arabia)

ORGANIZATION OF THE PETROLEUM EXPORTING COUNTRIES

Helferstorferstrasse 17, A-1010 Vienna, Austria
W www.opec.org

The Organization of the Petroleum Exporting Countries (OPEC) was created in 1960 as a permanent intergovernmental organisation with the principal aims of unifying and coordinating the petroleum policies of its 14 member countries (Qatar terminated its membership in January 2019), and stabilising prices and supply in international oil markets.

The supreme authority is the conference of ministers, which generally comprises the oil and energy ministers of the member countries. The conference meets in formal session twice a year to discuss oil policy, energy and administrative matters. The board of governors implements conference resolutions and oversees the running of the OPEC secretariat located in Vienna, Austria.

According to the *OPEC Annual Statistical Bulletin 2020* OPEC's 13 member countries held 83.1 per cent of the world's proven oil reserves at the end of 2019.

Secretary-General, Mohammad Sanusi Barkindo (Nigeria)

PACIFIC COMMUNITY

95 Promenade Roger Laroque, BP D5, 98848 Noumea, New Caledonia **T** (+687) 262 000 **E** spc@spc.int **W** www.spc.int

The Secretariat of the Pacific Community (SPC) (formerly the South Pacific Commission) was established in 1947 by Australia, France, the Netherlands, New Zealand, the UK and the USA with the aim of promoting the economic and social stability of the islands in the region. The community now numbers 26 member states and territories: the four remaining founder states (the Netherlands and the UK have withdrawn) and the other 22 states and territories of Melanesia, Micronesia and Polynesia.

The SPC is a technical assistance agency with programmes in marine and land development and health and social policy. The governing body is the conference of the Pacific community, which meets every two years.

Director-General, Stuart Minchin (Australia)

PACIFIC ISLANDS FORUM

Secretariat, Private Mail Bag, Suva, Fiji
T (+679) 331 2600 **E** info@forumsec.org **W** www.forumsec.org

The Pacific Islands Forum (PIF), formerly the South Pacific Forum, was established in 1971 and represents heads of governments of 18 independent and self-governing Pacific island countries. It aims to foster cooperation between its governments and to represent the interests of the region in international organisations. The PIF meets annually, after which a dialogue is conducted at ministerial level with 17 forum dialogue partner states and the European Union.

The PIF secretariat is governed by the forum officials committee (FOC), composed of senior figures from each member country. It comprises divisions dealing with development and economic policy, trade and investment, political and international affairs and services, and is responsible for implementing the forum's decisions.

Tokelau became an associate member in 2014. The African, Caribbean and Pacific Group of States, American Samoa, the Asian Development Bank, the Commonwealth, Commonwealth of the Northern Marianas, Guam, the International Organization for Migration, Timor-Leste, the United Nations, Wallis and Futuna, Western and Central Pacific Fisheries Commission and the World Bank currently hold observer status.

Secretary-General, Dame Meg Taylor, DBE (Papua New Guinea)

PARTNERS IN POPULATION AND DEVELOPMENT

Block-F, Plot 17/B&C, Sher-E-Bangla Nagar, Administrative Zone, Agargaon, Dhaka-1207, Bangladesh
T (+88) (2) 4811 7941 **E** partners@ppdsec.org
W www.partners-popdev.org

Partners in Population and Development (PPD) is an intergovernmental organisation launched at the UN International Conference on Population and Development in Cairo in 1994. It has 27 member states. PPD was created specifically for the purpose of expanding and improving South-to-South collaboration in the fields of reproductive health, population, and development and is dedicated to forming partnerships between and among individuals, organisations and the governments of developing countries.

PPD is controlled by a board of directors consisting of ministers or other high-ranking officials in the field of population and development from member countries. The responsibilities of the board include setting policy, promoting cooperation among members and providing advice to the secretariat. The secretariat is based in Dhaka, Bangladesh, and is mandated to serve as the administrative centre of the organisation. It ensures policies are implemented and identifies new areas for collaboration. PPD also has an international programme advisory committee consisting of specialists who advise the board and secretariat on current trends in population, development and reproductive health.

PPD is a permanent observer at the United Nations.

Chair, Dr Li Bin (China)

SHANGHAI COOPERATION ORGANISATION

7 Ritan Road, Chaoyang District, 100600 Beijing, China
T (+86) (10) 6532 9807 **E** sco@sectsco.org **W** http://eng.sectsco.org

The Shanghai Cooperation Organisation (SCO) is a permanent intergovernmental organisation. It was established in 1996 as the Shanghai Five, when China, Kazakhstan, Kyrgyzstan, Russia and Tajikistan signed an agreement on cooperating to resolve disputes along the former Sino-Soviet border. It was renamed in 2001 when Uzbekistan became an official member. India and Pakistan joined the organisation in June 2017, while Afghanistan, Belarus, Iran and Mongolia have observer status. The SCO also works with six dialogue partners including Azerbaijan, Armenia, Cambodia, Nepal, Turkey, and Sri Lanka.

The main principle of the SCO is strengthening cooperation among member states across a range of fields, including politics, economics, science, culture, energy, transport, environmental protection and tourism.

The heads of state council is the organisation's supreme body and meets annually to formulate SCO policy. The heads of government council also holds annual meetings to discuss cooperation strategies and approve budgets. The SCO has two permanent bodies: a secretariat based in Beijing and a regional anti-terrorist structure in Tashkent. The secretary-general and the director of the executive committee are appointed by the council of heads of state for a period of three years.

Secretary-General, Vladimir Norov (Uzbekistan)

SOUTH ASIAN ASSOCIATION FOR REGIONAL COOPERATION

PO Box 4222, Tridevi Marg, Kathmandu, Nepal
T (+977) (1) 422 1785/ 6350 **E** saarc@saarc-sec.org
W www.saarc-sec.org

The South Asian Association for Regional Cooperation (SAARC) was established in 1985 by Bangladesh, Bhutan, India, the Maldives, Nepal, Pakistan and Sri Lanka; Afghanistan was admitted as its eighth member in 2007. Its primary objective is the acceleration of economic and social development in member states through collective action in agreed areas of cooperation. These include agricultural development, climate change, science and technology, health, education, transport, energy and communications.

A SAARC preferential trading arrangement, designed to reduce tariffs on trade between SAARC member states, was signed in 1993 and entered into force in 1995. The South Asian free trade area (SAFTA) was agreed in 2004 and came into effect in 2006.

The highest authority rests with the heads of state or government of each member state. The council of ministers, which meets twice a year, is made up of the foreign ministers of the member states and is responsible for formulating policy. The standing committee is composed of the foreign secretaries of the member states and monitors and coordinates SAARC programmes; it meets as often as is necessary. Technical committees are assigned to individual areas of SAARC's activities. Its secretariat monitors, facilitates and promotes SAARC's activities and serves as a channel of communication between the association and other regional and intergovernmental institutions.

In 2005, as the only country in South Asia not to be a member of SAARC, Iran declared its wish to join and has since become an observer member, along with seven other states and the European Union.

Secretary-General, H.E. Esala Ruwan Weerakoon (Sri Lanka)

SOUTHERN AFRICAN DEVELOPMENT COMMUNITY

Plot No. 54385, Central Business District, Private Bag 0095, Gaborone, Botswana
T (+267) 395 1863 **E** registry@sadc.int **W** www.sadc.int

The Southern African Development Community (SADC) was formed in 1992 by the members of its predecessor, the Southern African Development Coordination Conference. The latter was founded in 1980 to harmonise economic development among southern Africa's 'majority ruled' countries and reduce their dependence on then apartheid South Africa. The SADC now comprises 16 countries, including South Africa. Madagascar's membership was reactivated in January 2014 after years of suspension following a coup in March 2009. The Comoros became a full member in August 2018 at the 38th Summit of Heads of State and Government.

The SADC aims to evolve common political values, promote economic growth, regional security, sustainable development and the interdependence of member states. An annual summit attended by members' heads of state is the SADC's supreme authority, and its policies are implemented by a secretariat.

Executive Secretary, Dr Stergomena Lawrence Tax (Tanzania)

UNITED NATIONS

Headquarters, 405 East 42nd Street, New York, NY 10017, USA
T (+1) (212) 963 1234 **W** www.un.org
Regional Information Centre, rue de la Loi 155, Block C2, 7th Floor,
　Brussels 1040, Belgium **T** (+32) (2) 788 8484 **E** info@unric.org
　W www.unric.org

The United Nations (UN) is an intergovernmental organisation dedicated, through signature of the UN charter, to the maintenance of international peace and security and the solution of economic, social and political problems through international cooperation.

The UN was founded as a successor to the League of Nations and inherited many of its procedures and institutions. The name United Nations was first used in the Washington Declaration of 1942 to describe the 26 states that had allied to fight the Axis powers. The UN charter developed from discussions at the Moscow conference of the foreign ministers of China, the Soviet Union, the UK and the USA in 1943. Further progress was made at Dumbarton Oaks, Washington, in 1944 during talks involving the same states. The role of the security council was formulated at the Yalta conference in 1945. The charter was formally drawn up by 50 allied nations at the San Francisco conference between April and June 1945, when it was signed. Following ratification, the UN came into effect on 24 October 1945, which is celebrated annually as United Nations Day. The UN flag is light blue with the UN emblem centred in white.

The principal organs of the UN are the general assembly, the security council, trusteeship council, the economic and social council, the secretariat and the international court of justice. The economic and social council is an auxiliary, charged with assisting and advising the general assembly, security council and member states, and coordinating the economic and social aspects of the work of UN agencies and commissions. The official languages used are Arabic, Chinese, English, French, Russian and Spanish; the working languages of the secretariat and the international court of justice are English and French.

THE GENERAL ASSEMBLY
UN Plaza, New York, NY 10017, USA

The general assembly is the main deliberative organ of the UN. It consists of all members, each entitled to five representatives but having only one vote. The annual session begins on the third Tuesday of September, when the president is elected, and usually continues until mid-December. Special sessions are held on specific issues and emergency special sessions can be called within 24 hours.

The assembly is empowered to discuss any matter within the scope of the charter – except when it is under consideration by the security council – and to make recommendations. Under the peace resolution, adopted in 1950, the assembly may also take action to maintain international peace and security when the security council fails to do so because of a lack of unanimity of its permanent members. Important decisions (such as those on peace and security, the election of officers, the budget, etc) need a two-thirds majority. Others need a simple majority. The assembly has effective power only over the internal operations of the UN itself; external recommendations are not legally binding.

The work of the general assembly is divided among a number of committees, on each of which every member has the right to be represented. Subjects include human rights, the use of torture, peacekeeping, assistance to developing countries and discrimination. In addition, the general assembly appoints *ad hoc* committees to consider more specific issues. All committees consider items referred to them by the assembly and recommend draft resolutions to its plenary meeting.

The assembly is assisted by a number of functional committees. The general committee coordinates its

proceedings and operations, while the credentials committee verifies the representatives.

President of the General Assembly, Volkan Bozkir (Turkey)

SPECIALISED BODIES

The assembly has created a large number of specialised bodies, some of which are supervised jointly with the economic and social council. They are supported by UN and voluntary contributions from governments, non-governmental organisations and individuals. These organisations include:

CONFERENCE ON DISARMAMENT
Palais des Nations, CH-1211 Geneva 10, Switzerland

The Conference on Disarmament (CD) was established in 1979 as the international community's multilateral disarmament negotiating forum. Originally comprising 40 member states, the CD has expanded to 65 members. The Non-Proliferation of Nuclear Weapons Treaty entered into force on 5 March 1970 and has so far been ratified by 191 states. The Biological Weapons Convention, the first multilateral disarmament treaty banning the development, production and stockpiling of an entire category of weapons of mass destruction, was opened for signature on 10 April 1972 and entered into force on 26 March 1975. A chemical weapons convention was agreed in Paris in 1993 and came into force in April 1997 after being ratified by 87 countries. Currently 193 states participate in the convention, which bans the use, production, stockpiling and transfer of all chemical weapons. A convention prohibiting the use of cluster munitions, agreed in Dublin in 2008 and currently ratified by 106 states, entered into force on 1 August 2010.

The CD and its predecessors have negotiated such major multilateral arms limitation and disarmament agreements as the Treaty on the Non-Proliferation of Nuclear Weapons, the Convention on the Prohibition of Military or Any Other Hostile Use of Environmental Modification Techniques, the Treaty on the Prohibition of the Emplacement of Nuclear Weapons and Other Weapons of Mass Destruction on the Sea-Bed and the Ocean Floor and in the Subsoil thereof, the Convention on the Prohibition of the Development, Production and Stockpiling of Bacteriological (Biological) and Toxin Weapons and on their Destruction, the Convention on the Prohibition of the Development, Production, Stockpiling and Use of Chemical Weapons and on Their Destruction and Comprehensive Nuclear-Test-Ban Treaty.

UNITED NATIONS CHILDREN'S FUND (UNICEF)
3 UN Plaza, New York, NY 10017, USA **T** (+1) 212 326 7000
W www.unicef.org
UNICEF House, 30A Great Sutton St, London EC1V 0DU
T 020-7490 2388

Established in 1946 to assist children and mothers in the immediate post-war period, UNICEF now concentrates on developing countries. It provides primary healthcare and health education, and conducts programmes in oral hydration, immunisation against common diseases, HIV/AIDS treatment and prevention and child growth monitoring. It also works to provide children with equal access to quality education.

UNITED NATIONS DEVELOPMENT PROGRAMME (UNDP)
1 UN Plaza, New York, NY 10017, USA **T** (+1) 212 906 5000
W www.undp.org

Established in 1965 from the merger of the UN expanded programme of technical assistance and the UN special fund, UNDP is the central funding agency for economic and social development projects around the world. Much of its annual expenditure is channelled through UN specialised agencies, governments and non-governmental organisations.

UNITED NATIONS HIGH COMMISSIONER FOR REFUGEES (UNHCR)
Case Postale 2500, CH-1211 Geneva 2 Depot, Switzerland
T (+41) 22 739 8111 **W** www.unhcr.org

Established in 1950 to protect the rights and interests of refugees, UNHCR organises emergency relief and longer-term solutions, such as voluntary repatriation, local integration or resettlement. UNHCR is also mandated to assist stateless people.

UNITED NATIONS RELIEF AND WORKS AGENCY FOR PALESTINE REFUGEES IN THE NEAR EAST (UNRWA)
HQ Gaza, PO Box 338, Gaza City
T (+972) 8 288 7701 **W** www.unrwa.org

The UNRWA was established in 1949 to bring relief to the Palestinians displaced by the Arab-Israeli conflict. The UN general assembly has repeatedly voted every three years to extend its mandate, most recently until 2023.

UNITED NATIONS HUMAN RIGHTS COUNCIL (UNHRC)
Palais des Nations, CH-1211 Geneva 10, Switzerland
T (+41) (22) 917 9220 **E** infodesk@ohchr.org **W** www.ohchr.org

The UNHRC is a 47-member council, established in 2006, replacing the United Nations Commission on Human Rights (UNCHR). The UNHRC has a mandate to promote (and prevent violations of) human rights by engaging in dialogue with governments and international organisations. It is also responsible for the coordination of all UN human rights activities and reports to, and is directly elected by, the general assembly.

THE SECURITY COUNCIL
UN Plaza, New York, NY 10017, USA
W www.un.org/en/sc

The security council is the senior arm of the UN and has the primary responsibility for maintaining world peace and security. It consists of 15 members, each with one representative and one vote. There are five permanent members – China, France, Russia, the UK and the USA – and ten non-permanent members. Each of the non-permanent members is elected for a two-year term by a two-thirds majority of the general assembly and is ineligible for immediate re-election. Five of the elective seats are allocated to Africa and Asia, one to eastern Europe, two to Latin America and two to western Europe and remaining countries. Decisions on procedural matters require affirmative votes from at least nine of the 15 members. Other matters require the same, but must include the affirmative votes of the permanent members; they thus have a right of veto. The abstention of a permanent member does not constitute a veto. The presidency rotates each month by state in (English) alphabetical order. Parties in a dispute, other non-members and individuals can be invited to participate in security council debates but are not permitted to vote.

The security council is empowered to settle or adjudicate in disputes or situations which threaten international peace and security. It can adopt political, economic and military measures to achieve this end. Any matter considered to be a threat to or breach of the peace or an act of aggression can be brought to the security council's attention by any member state or by the secretary-general. The charter envisaged members placing at the disposal of the security council armed forces and other facilities which would be coordinated by the military staff committee, composed of military representatives of the five permanent members. The security council is also supported by a committee of experts, to advise on procedural and technical matters, and a committee on admission of new members.

Owing to superpower disunity, the security council has rarely played the decisive role set out in the charter; the military staff committee was effectively suspended from 1948 until 1990, when a meeting was convened during the Gulf crisis on the formation and control of UN-supervised armed forces. In 1992, heads of government laid plans to transform the UN in light of the changed post-Cold War world. The secretary-general produced *An Agenda for Peace,* a report which centred on the establishment of a UN army composed of national contingents on permanent standby, as envisaged at the time of the UN's formation. However, enthusiasm for UN intervention waned during the rest of the decade after a problematic mission in Somalia during which 42 UN personnel were killed. The security council has since been criticised for its failure to intervene in subsequent conflicts, including the genocide in Rwanda and the ongoing situation in Darfur. More recently it has applied sanctions to Iran, North Korea, the Pakistani militant group Lashkar-e-Taiba, and figures within Libya, the Côte d'Ivoire and South Sudan.

The security council also has the power to elect judges to the international court of justice and to recommend to the general assembly the election of a secretary-general.

PEACEKEEPING FORCES
The security council has established a number of peacekeeping forces since its foundation, comprising contingents provided mainly by neutral and non-aligned UN members. As at December 2020, current operations were:

Continent	UN Code	Year implemented	Uniformed personnel deployed
Africa			
Western Sahara	MINURSO	1991	462
Dem. Rep. of the Congo	MONUSCO	2010	17,467
South Sudan	UNMISS	2011	19,195
Sudan	UNISFA	2011	3,679
Mali	MINUSMA	2013	15,916
Central African Rep.	MINUSCA	2014	14,943
The Americas			
No Active Operations			
Asia			
India and Pakistan	UNMOGIP	1949	117
Europe			
Cyprus	UNFICYP	1964	1,028
Kosovo	UNMIK	1999	350
Middle East	UNTSO	1948	365
Syria	UNDOF	1974	1,224
Lebanon	UNIFIL	1978	10,830

TOP FIVE CONTRIBUTORS TO UN PEACEKEEPING MISSIONS *as at* 31 December 2020	
Country	Number of Troops
Bangladesh	6,798
Rwanda	6,383
Ethiopia	6,307
Nepal	5,715
India	5,425
Source: www.un.org/en/peacekeeping	

MECHANISM FOR INTERNATIONAL CRIMINAL TRIBUNALS (MICT)
AICC Complex, PO Box 6016, Arusha, Tanzania
T (+31) (07) 0512 5691 **E** mict-press@un.org **W** www.unmict.org

On 22 December 2010, the MICT was established to oversee the outstanding work of the International Criminal Tribunal of the Former Yugoslavia (ICTY) and the International Tribunal for Rwanda (ICTR). There was an overlap as these organisations completed their respective mandates before the MICT took over the ICTR in July 2012 and the ICTY in July 2013. The MICT carries out the same essential functions as the ICTR and ICTY and will continue the tribunals' work of tracking and prosecuting fugitives; protecting victims and witnesses; and supervising the enforcement of sentences. The progress of the MICT was reviewed in 2018 and will continue to be reviewed every two years.

President, Judge Carmel Agius (Malta)

THE ECONOMIC AND SOCIAL COUNCIL
UN Plaza, New York, NY 10017, USA
W www.un.org/ecosoc

The economic and social council is responsible under the general assembly for the economic and social work of the UN and for the coordination of the activities of the specialised agencies and other UN bodies. It makes reports and recommendations on economic, social, cultural, educational, health and related matters, often in consultation with non-governmental organisations, passing the reports to the general assembly and other UN bodies. It also drafts conventions for submission to the assembly and calls conferences on matters within its remit.

The council consists of 54 members, who are elected by the general assembly for overlapping three-year terms. Each member has one vote and can be immediately re-elected. The council elects a president and four vice-presidents each year: this five-member bureau proposes the council's agenda, draws up a programme of work and organises the substantive session. This session is held each July, and decisions are reached by a simple majority vote of those present.

The council has established a number of functional commissions and standing committees on particular issues. These include commissions on social development, sustainable development, population and development, the status of women, crime prevention and criminal justice, narcotic drugs, and science and technology for development, as well as five regional economic commissions.

President, Munir Akram (Pakistan)

THE SECRETARIAT
UN Plaza, New York, NY 10017, USA

The secretariat services the other principal UN organs and administers their programmes and policies. It is headed by a secretary-general elected by a majority vote of the general assembly on the recommendation of the security council. He is assisted by some 44,000 staff worldwide. The secretary-general is charged with bringing to the attention of the security council any matter which he considers poses a threat to international peace and security. He may also bring other matters to the attention of the general assembly and other UN bodies and may be entrusted by them with additional duties. As chief administrator to the UN, the secretary-general is present in person or via representatives at all meetings of the other five main organs of the UN. He may also act as a mediator in disputes between member states.

The power and influence of the secretary-general has been determined largely by the character of the office-holder and by the state of relations between the superpowers. The improvement of these relations since the mid-1980s has increased the effectiveness of the UN, particularly in its attempts to intervene in international disputes.

Secretary-General, António Guterres (Portugal)
Deputy Secretary-General, Amina J. Mohammed (Nigeria)

FORMER SECRETARIES-GENERAL	
1946–52	Trygve Lie (Norway)
1953–61	Dag Hammarskjold (Sweden)
1961–71	U Thant (Myanmar)
1972–81	Kurt Waldheim (Austria)
1982–91	Javier Pérez de Cuéllar (Peru)
1992–96	Boutros Boutros-Ghali (Egypt)
1997–2006	Kofi Annan (Ghana)
2007–16	Ban Ki-moon (South Korea)

UK MISSION TO THE UN, 1 Dag Hammarskjold Plaza, 885 Second Avenue, New York, NY 10017, USA **T** (+1) (212) 745 9200 **W** www.ukun.fco.gov.uk
Permanent Representative to the UN and Representative on the Security Council, Dame Barbara Woodward, DCMG OBE, *apptd* 2020

UK MISSION TO THE UN AND OTHER INTERNATIONAL ORGANISATIONS IN GENEVA, 58 Avenue Louis Casaï, Case Postale 6, 1216 Cointrin, Geneva, Switzerland **T** (+41) (22) 918 2300
Permanent UK Representative, HE Julian Braithwaite, *apptd* 2015

UK MISSION TO THE UN IN VIENNA, Jaurèsgasse 12, A-1030 Vienna, Austria **T** (+43) (1) 716 130
W www.ukinaustria.fco.gov.uk
Permanent UK Representative, HE Leigh Turner, CMG, *apptd* 2015

REGIONAL UN INFORMATION CENTRE, Residence Palace, 155 rue de la Loi, Brussels 1040, Belgium **T** (+32) 2788 8484 **E** info@unric.org **W** www.unric.org

THE INTERNATIONAL COURT OF JUSTICE
Peace Palace, Carnegieplein 2, 2517 KJ, The Hague, The Netherlands **T** (+31) (70) 302 2323 **W** www.icj-cij.org

The international court of justice is the principal judicial organ in the UN, and its statute is an integral part of the UN charter; all members of the UN are *ipso facto* parties to it. The court is composed of 15 judges, elected by both the general assembly and the security council for nine-year terms, which are renewable. Judges may deliberate over cases in which their country is involved. If no judge on the bench is from a country that is party to a dispute under consideration, that party may designate a judge to participate *ad hoc* in that particular deliberation. If any party to a case fails to adhere to the judgment of the court, the other party may have recourse to the security council.

President, Abdulqawi Ahmed Yusuf (Somalia)
Vice-President, Xue Hanqin (China)

Judges, James Crawford (Australia); Antonio A. Cancado Trindade (Brazil); Xue Hanqin (China); Ronny Abraham (France); Georg Nolta (Germany); Dalveer Bhandari (India); Patrick Robinson (Jamaica); Yuji Iwasawa (Japan); Nawaf Salam (Lebanon); Mohamed Bennouna (Morocco); Kirill Gevorgian (Russia); Peter Tomka (Slovakia); Abdulqawi Ahmed Yusuf (Somalia); Julia Sebutinde (Uganda); Joan Donoghue (USA)

MEMBERSHIP

Membership is open to all countries that accept the charter and its principle of peaceful co-existence. New members are admitted by the general assembly on the recommendation of the security council. The original membership of 51 states has grown to 193.

Members of the UN

Afghanistan
Albania
Algeria
Andorra
Angola
Antigua and Barbuda
Argentina*
Armenia
Australia
Austria
Azerbaijan
Bahamas
Bahrain
Bangladesh
Barbados
Belarus
Belgium*
Belize
Benin
Bhutan
Bolivia
Bosnia and Hercegovina
Botswana
Brazil*
Brunei
Bulgaria
Burkina Faso
Burundi
Cabo Verde
Cambodia
Cameroon
Canada*
Central African Republic
Chad
Chile*
China*
Colombia*
Comoros
Congo, Dem. Rep. of
Congo, Republic of the
Costa Rica*
Côte d'Ivoire
Croatia
Cuba*
Cyprus
Czech Republic
Denmark*
Djibouti
Dominica

Dominican Republic
Ecuador*
Egypt*
El Salvador*
Equatorial Guinea
Eritrea
Estonia
eSwatini†
Ethiopia*
Fiji
Finland
France
Gabon
The Gambia
Georgia
Germany
Ghana
Greece
Grenada
Guatemala*
Guinea
Guinea-Bissau
Guyana
Haiti*
Honduras*
Hungary
Iceland
India*
Indonesia
Iran*
Iraq*
Ireland
Israel
Italy
Jamaica
Japan
Jordan
Kazakhstan
Kenya
Kiribati
Korea, D. P. R.
Korea, Rep. of
Kuwait
Kyrgyzstan
Laos
Latvia
Lebanon*
Lesotho
Liberia

Libya
Liechtenstein
Lithuania
Luxembourg*
Macedonia
Madagascar
Malawi
Malaysia
Maldives
Mali
Malta
Marshall Islands
Mauritania
Mauritius
Mexico*
Micronesia, Fed. States of
Moldova
Monaco
Mongolia
Montenegro
Morocco
Mozambique
Myanmar
Namibia
Nauru
Nepal
The Netherlands*
New Zealand*
Nicaragua*
Niger
Nigeria
Norway*
Oman
Pakistan
Palau
Panama*
Papua New Guinea
Paraguay*
Peru*
The Philippines*
Poland*
Portugal
Qatar
Romania
Russian Federation*
Rwanda
St Kitts and Nevis
St Lucia

St Vincent and the Grenadines
Samoa
San Marino
São Tomé and Principe
Saudi Arabia*
Senegal
Serbia
Seychelles
Sierra Leone
Singapore
Slovakia
Slovenia
Solomon Islands
Somalia
South Africa
South Sudan
Spain
Sri Lanka
Sudan
Suriname
Sweden
Switzerland
Syria*
Tajikistan
Tanzania
Thailand
Timor-Leste
Togo
Tonga
Trinidad and Tobago
Tunisia
Turkey*
Turkmenistan
Tuvalu
Uganda
Ukraine*
United Arab Emirates
United Kingdom*
United States of America
Uruguay*
Uzbekistan
Vanuatu
Venezuela*
Vietnam
Yemen
Zambia
Zimbabwe

* Original member (ie from 1945). Czechoslovakia, Yugoslavia and the USSR were all original members until their dissolution.
† Formerly Swaziland

OBSERVERS

Permanent observer status is held by the Holy See and the State of Palestine.

UNITED NATIONS EDUCATIONAL, SCIENTIFIC AND CULTURAL ORGANIZATION

7 place de Fontenoy, F-75007 Paris, France
T (+33) (01) 4568 1004 **W** www.unesco.org

The United Nations Educational, Scientific and Cultural Organization (UNESCO) was established in 1945. It promotes collaboration among its member states in education, science, culture and communication. It aims to promote a universal respect for human rights, justice and the rule of law, without distinction of race, sex, language or religion, in accordance with the UN charter.

UNESCO runs a number of programmes to improve education and extend access to it. It provides assistance to ensure the free flow of information and its wider dissemination without any barriers to freedom of expression, to safeguard cultural heritages and encourage sustainable development. It fosters research and study in the social and environmental sciences. The UNESCO world heritage list, decided upon by an intergovernmental committee of 21 representatives from states party to the convention, includes 1,121 cultural and natural sites of 'outstanding universal value'.

UNESCO has 193 member states, 11 associate members, and two permanent observers. The general conference, consisting of representatives of all the members, meets biennially to decide the programme and the budget. It elects the 58-member executive board, which supervises operations, and appoints a director-general who heads a secretariat responsible for carrying out the organisation's programmes. In most member states national commissions liaise with UNESCO to execute its policies.

Director-General, Audrey Azoulay (France)

UNITED NATIONS INDUSTRIAL DEVELOPMENT ORGANIZATION

Vienna International Centre, Wagramerstrasse 5, PO Box 300, A-1400 Vienna, Austria
T (+43) (1) 260 260 **E** unido@unido.org **W** www.unido.org

The United Nations Industrial Development Organization (UNIDO) was established in 1966 by the UN general assembly to act as the central coordinating body for industrial activities within the UN. It became a UN specialised agency in 1979. UNIDO aims to help countries with developing and transitional economies by increasing the productivity and competitiveness of their agricultural, technological and energy industries.

As at October 2020, 170 states were members of UNIDO. It is funded by regular and operational budgets, together with contributions for technical cooperation activities. The regular budget is derived from member states' contributions. Technical cooperation is funded mainly through voluntary contributions from donor countries and institutions and by intergovernmental and non-governmental organisations. A general conference of all the members meets biennially to discuss strategy and policy, elect the director-general and approve the budget. The 2020–21 budget is €179.9m (£162m). The industrial development board is composed of representatives from 53 member states and reviews the work programme and the budget, which is prepared by the programme and budget committee of 27 member states.

Director-General, Li Yong (China)

UNIVERSAL POSTAL UNION

PO Box 312, CH-3000 Berne 15, Switzerland
W www.upu.int

The Universal Postal Union (UPU) was established by the Treaty of Bern 1874, taking effect from 1875, and became a UN specialised agency in 1948. The UPU exists to form and regulate a single postal territory of all member countries for the reciprocal exchange of correspondence without discrimination. With a total of 192 members, it also assists and advises on the improvement of postal services.

The universal postal congress is the UPU's supreme authority and meets every four years. The council of administration meets annually to supervise the union's work between congresses, to investigate regulatory developments and policy issues, to approve the budget and to examine proposed treaty changes. The postal operations council, first convened in 2013, is responsible for assessing operational, commercial, technical, and economic issues affecting members. The four UPU bodies are served by the international bureau, a secretariat headed by a director-general.

Funding is provided by members according to a scale of contributions drawn up by the congress. The council of administration sets the annual budget.

Director-General, Bishar Abdirahman Hussein (Kenya)

UNREPRESENTED NATIONS AND PEOPLES ORGANIZATION

Rue du Pépin 54, Brussels, B-1000, Belgium
T (+32) (0) 251 31459 **E** unpo@unpo.org **W** www.unpo.org

The Unrepresented Nations and Peoples Organization (UNPO) was founded in 1991 to offer an international forum for occupied nations, indigenous peoples and national minorities who are not represented in other international organisations.

The UNPO does not aim to represent these nations and peoples, but rather to assist and empower them to represent themselves more effectively, and provides professional services and facilities as well as education and training in the fields of diplomacy, international and human rights law, democratic processes, institution building, conflict management and resolution, and environmental protection.

Participation is open to all nations and peoples who are inadequately represented at the UN and who declare allegiance to five principles relating to the right of self-determination of all peoples: human rights, democracy, tolerance, non-violence and respect for the rights of minorities. Applicants must show that they constitute a nation or people and that the organisation applying for membership is representative of that nation or people.

As at October 2020 UNPO had 42 members.

General Secretary, Ralph Bunche (USA)

WORLD BANK GROUP

1818 H Street NW, Washington, DC 20433, USA
T (+1) (202) 473 1000 **W** www.worldbank.org

The World Bank Group was founded in 1944 from the consolidation of five major development organisations and is one of the world's largest sources of development assistance. It has 189 member states. Originally directed towards post-war reconstruction in Europe, the bank subsequently turned towards assisting less-developed countries worldwide, and in 2019 provided US$62.3bn (£48.2bn) for projects across the developing world. It works with government agencies, non-governmental organisations and the private sector to formulate assistance strategies. Its local offices implement the bank's programme in each country.

The World Bank is owned by the governments of member countries and its capital is subscribed by its members. It finances its lending primarily from borrowing in world capital markets, and derives a substantial contribution to its resources from its retained earnings and the repayment of loans.

The World Bank Group consists of two institutions and three affiliates. The International Bank for Reconstruction and Development (IBRD) provides loans and development assistance to middle-income countries and credit-worthy poorer countries (total loans for 2019 US$23.2bn (£18bn)). The International Development Association (IDA) performs the same function as the IBRD but primarily to less-developed countries and on terms that bear less heavily on their balance of payments than IBRD loans (total loans for 2019 US$22bn (£17bn)).

The three affiliates are the International Finance Corporation (IFC), which has 185 members and promotes private sector investment in developing countries by mobilising domestic and foreign capital; the Multilateral Investment Guarantee Agency (MIGA), which has 182 members and promotes foreign direct investment in developing states by insuring investors against political risk and helping member countries to improve their investment climates; and the International Centre for Settlement of Investment Disputes (ICSID), which has 154 full members (known as contracting states) and provides facilities for resolving disputes between foreign investors and their host countries.

The IBRD, IDA and the affiliates are financially and legally distinct but share headquarters. The IBRD is headed by a board of governors, which meets annually and consists of one governor and one alternate governor appointed by each member country; most IBRD governors also serve on the separate boards of the IDA, IFC and MIGA. Twenty-five executive directors exercise all powers of the World Bank (except those reserved to the board of governors). The president, elected by the board of executive directors, conducts the business of the bank, assisted by an international staff. Membership in both the IFC and the IDA is open to all IBRD countries. The IDA is administered by the same staff as the bank; the IFC has its own personnel but can draw on the IBRD for administrative and other support. All share the same president.

President, David Malpass (USA)

WORLD CUSTOMS ORGANIZATION
30 rue de Marché, B-1210, Brussels, Belgium
T (+32) 2209 9211 W www.wcoomd.org

Established in 1952 as the Customs Cooperation Council, the World Customs Organization (WCO) is an independent intergovernmental organisation whose primary mission is to enhance the effectiveness and efficiency of customs administrations worldwide. It is the only international body specialising in customs matters, and is recognised as the voice of the global customs community and a centre of customs expertise.

Comprising 183 member customs administrations that process approximately 98 per cent of international trade, the WCO is governed by a council which meets annually and in which each member has one vote. The council is supported by a policy commission, a finance committee, an audit committee, various technical committees, and a permanent secretariat charged with implementing council decisions.

Secretary-General, Kunio Mikuriya (Japan)

WORLD HEALTH ORGANIZATION
Avenue Appia 20, 1211 Geneva 27, Switzerland
T (+41) (22) 791 2111 W www.who.int

The UN International Health Conference, held in 1946, established the World Health Organization (WHO) as a UN specialised agency, with effect from 1948. It is dedicated to attaining the highest possible level of health for all. It collaborates with member governments, UN agencies and other bodies to improve health standards, control communicable diseases and promote all aspects of family and environmental health. It seeks to raise the standards of health teaching and training, and promotes research through collaboration with research centres worldwide.

WHO has 194 members and is governed by an annual assembly of members. This sets policy, approves the budget, appoints a director-general, and adopts health conventions and regulations. It also elects 34 member states to designate one expert each to serve on the executive board. The board sets the assembly's agenda and implements its policies, suggests initiatives, and is empowered to deal with emergencies. A secretariat, headed by the director-general, supervises the activities of six regional offices.

In 2020 the USA gave notice that it would withdraw from the WHO, the USA withdraw will become effective on 6 July 2021.

Director-General, Dr Tedros Adhanom Ghebreyesus (Ethiopia)

WORLD INTELLECTUAL PROPERTY ORGANIZATION
34 chemin des Colombettes, CH-1211, Geneva 20, Switzerland
T (+41) (22) 338 9111 W www.wipo.int

The World Intellectual Property Organization (WIPO) was established in Stockholm in 1967 by the signing of the WIPO Convention, which entered into force in 1970. WIPO administers 26 treaties that deal with different legal and administrative aspects of intellectual property, notably the Paris Convention for the protection of industrial property and the Bern Convention for the protection of literary and artistic works. WIPO became a UN specialised agency in 1974.

Intellectual property falls into two main branches: industrial property (inventions, trademarks, industrial designs and geographical indications) and copyright (literary, musical, photographic, audiovisual and artistic works, etc). WIPO helps ensure that creative intellectual activity is rewarded, and facilitates technology transfer, particularly to developing countries.

WIPO's mission is to promote the protection of intellectual property rights worldwide. The organisation's activities fall into three broad categories: the progressive development of international intellectual property law, assistance to developing countries, and the provision of services which facilitate the process of obtaining intellectual property rights in multiple countries.

WIPO had 193 members as at October 2020. The biennial session of the general assembly, the conference and the coordination committee set policy, a programme and a budget. A separate agency, the International Union for the Protection of New Varieties of Plants (UPOV), established by convention in 1961, is linked to WIPO and has 76 members.

Director-General, Daren Tang (Singapore)

WORLD METEOROLOGICAL ORGANIZATION
7 bis, avenue de la Paix, PO Box 2300, CH-1211 Geneva 2, Switzerland
T (+41) (22) 730 8111 W http://public.wmo.int/en

The World Meteorological Organization (WMO) was established in 1950 and became a UN specialised agency in

1951, succeeding the International Meteorological Organization founded in 1873. It facilitates cooperation in the establishment of networks for making, processing and exchanging meteorological, climatological, hydrological and geophysical observations. It also fosters collaboration between meteorological and hydrological services, and furthers the application of meteorology to aviation, shipping, environment, water problems, agriculture and the mitigation of natural disasters.

In October 2020, the WMO had 187 member states and six member territories. Six regional associations are responsible for the coordination of activities within their own regions. There are also eight technical commissions, which study meteorological and hydrological problems, establish methodology and procedures, and make recommendations to the executive council and the congress. The supreme authority is the world meteorological congress, which meets every four years to determine general policy and set the budget (SFr271.5m (£219.6m) for the period 2020–22). It also elects 31 members of the 37-member executive council which supervises the implementation of congress decisions, initiates studies and makes recommendations on matters requiring international action. The secretariat is headed by a secretary-general, appointed by the congress.

Secretary-General (2020–26), Petteri Taalas (Finland)

WORLD TOURISM ORGANISATION
Poeta Joan Maragall 42, 28020 Madrid, Spain
T (+34) 9156 78100 **E** info@unwto.org **W** www.unwto.org

The World Tourism Organisation (UNWTO) was officially launched in 1975 to act as an executing agency of the United Nations Development Programme. Primarily concerned with developing public and private sector partnerships, the UNWTO also promotes the global code of ethics for tourism, a framework of policy aimed at tour operators, governments, labour organisations and travellers. There are 159 member states, six associate member states, and two observer states.

The general assembly is the principal gathering of the UNWTO and meets every two years in order to approve policy and budget. Every four years, the assembly elects a secretary-general. The executive council is UNWTO's governing board and meets at least twice a year to ensure the organisation adheres to policy and budget. It is composed of 32 members of the general assembly. As host country of UNWTO's headquarters, Spain has a permanent seat on the executive council.

Secretary-General (2018–21), Zurab Pololikashvili (Georgia)

WORLD TRADE ORGANIZATION
Centre William Rappard, 154 rue de Lausanne, CH-1211 Geneva 21, Switzerland
T (+41) (22) 739 5111 **E** enquiries@wto.org **W** www.wto.org

The World Trade Organization was established on 1 January 1995 as the successor to the General Agreement on Tariffs and Trade (GATT).

The GATT was dedicated to the expansion of non-discriminatory international trade and progressively extended free trade via 'rounds' of multilateral negotiations. The final act of the comprehensive Uruguay round of negotiations was signed by trade ministers from the 123 GATT negotiating states and the EU in Marrakesh, Morocco, in 1994. New talks on agriculture and services began in 2000 and were incorporated into a broader agenda launched at the 2001 ministerial conference in Doha, Qatar.

The WTO is the legal and institutional foundation of the multilateral trading system. It provides the contractual obligations determining how governments frame and implement trade policy, and provides the forum for the debate, negotiation and adjudication of trade issues. The WTO's principal aims are to liberalise world trade and place it on a secure basis; it seeks to achieve this through the combination of an agreed set of trade rules and market-access agreements and further trade liberalisation negotiations. The WTO also administers and implements multilateral agreements in fields such as agriculture, industrial goods, services, government procurement, rules of origin and intellectual property.

The highest authority of the WTO is the ministerial conference composed of all members, which usually meets once every two years. The general council meets as required and acts on behalf of the ministerial conference in regard to the regular working of the WTO. The general council also convenes in two particular forms: as the dispute-settlement body, dealing with disagreements between members arising from WTO agreements or commitments; and as the trade policy review body, conducting regular reviews of the trade policies of members. A secretariat of 625 staff, headed by a director-general, services WTO bodies and provides trade performance and trade policy analysis.

As at October 2020, the WTO has 164 members and 25 observer governments. The most recent member – Afghanistan – joined the WTO in 2016. The WTO budget for 2020 was SFr197.2m (£166.1m), with members' contributions calculated on the basis of their share of international trade. The official languages of the WTO are English, French and Spanish.

On 31 August 2020 Roberto Azevedo stepped down from office one year before his term ended. Four Deputy Director-Generals are acting in place of the Director-General until the seat is filled.

Director-General, Vacant

COUNTRIES OF THE WORLD A–Z

DEFINITIONS, ABBREVIATIONS AND SOURCES

est = estimate

IDD = International direct dialling

AIRPORTS – figures reference airports with paved runways only, unless otherwise specified

BIRTH RATE – figures are per 1,000 population

CORRUPTION PERCEPTIONS INDEX (CPI) SCORE – the perception of the degree of public sector corruption as seen by business people and country analysts; ranging from 0 (highly corrupt) to 100 (very clean). Overall position given in parentheses. *Corruption Perceptions Index 2019* © 2020 by Transparency International. (**W** www.transparency.org).

DEATH PENALTY:

Retained (not used) – countries that retain the death penalty for ordinary crimes such as murder but can be considered to have abolished it in practice

Retained for certain crimes – countries whose laws provide for the death penalty only for exceptional crimes ('Last used' = date of last execution)

Retained – countries that retain the death penalty for ordinary crimes

Abolitionist and Retentionist Countries 2019 © 2020 Amnesty International (**W** www.amnesty.org).

GROSS ENROLMENT RATIO – the ratio of total enrolment, regardless of age, to the total population of the relevant age group expressed as a percentage; this figure can be above 100 per cent where, for example, a greater number of children are attending classes designed for six-year-olds than there are six-year-olds in the country, owing to some children starting school late or skipping a year

GROSS NATIONAL INCOME (GNI) – using the Atlas Method, this is the total income earned by a country's residents; the second figure is GNI divided by the population to give a per capita figure

HIV/AIDS ADULT PREVALENCE – estimate of the percentage of the total adult population (aged 15–49) infected with HIV/AIDS

INFANT MORTALITY RATE – averages for male and female infants under one year old and per 1,000 live birth

LIFE EXPECTANCY – averages, at birth, for males and females

LITERACY (ADULT) – the World Bank defines literacy as the percentage of the population aged 15 and above that can read and write a short statement on their everyday life. Where the World Bank figure is not available the statistic provided is that given by the government of that country. This figure is not always comparable due to differing definitions of what constitutes adult literacy. *World Development Indicators 2019* published by The World Bank.

MILITARY EXPENDITURE – figures are the most recent available at current 2019 prices and exchange rates. When data is highly uncertain a figure for an earlier year is given and these are at constant 2018 prices and exchange rates © Stockholm International Peace Research Institute (SIPRI) (**W** www.sipri.org).

MORTALITY RATE – figures are per 1,000 population. This indicator is significantly affected by age distribution, and most countries will eventually show a rise in the overall death rate, in spite of continued decline in mortality at all ages, as declining fertility results in an ageing population

POPULATION BELOW POVERTY LINE – although strict definitions of poverty vary considerably between nations, this figure most commonly represents the percentage of the adult population whose income is less than US$1 per day

TOTAL EXTERNAL DEBT – the total public and private debt owed to non-residents repayable in foreign currency, goods or services

WORLD PRESS FREEDOM INDEX (WPFI) SCORE – the perception of press freedom based on assessments carried out by journalists and human rights activists, ranging from 0 (low censorship) to 100 (high censorship). The score is calculated by combining two scores: the first is based on six criteria – pluralism, media independence, environment and self-censorship, legislative framework, transparency and infrastructure; the second combines the first six indicators with a seventh, measuring abuses and acts of violence against journalists. The country's final score is the greater of the two scores; those above 55.01 are considered very serious. The overall international position is given in parentheses. *Press Freedom Score 2020* © Reporters Without Borders (**W** https://rsf.org/en/world-press-freedom-index).

Sources (in addition to those already indicated): *Human Development Indicators 2019* published by the UN Development Programme and *UN Statistics* published by UN Data; *World Economic Outlook Database 2019* © International Monetary Fund; UNESCO Institute for Statistics (UIS) (**W** www.uis.unesco.org/datacentre).

Government cabinet lists are sourced from *People in Power* © Cambridge International Reference on Current Affairs Ltd (**W** www.circaworld.com). People in Power provides a constantly updated service at www.peopleinpower.com

AFGHANISTAN

Jamhuri-ye Eslami-ye Afghanestan – Islamic Republic of Afghanistan

Area – 652,230 sq. km

Capital – Kabul; population, 4,012,000 (2018 est)

Major cities – Herat, Jalalabad, Kandahar, Mazar-e-Sharif

Currency – Afghani (Af) of 100 puls

Population – 36,643,815 rising at 2.38 per cent a year (2020 est); Pashtun, Tajik, Hazara, Uzbek

Religion – Muslim 99.7 per cent (Sunni 85 per cent, Shia 15 per cent est) (est); Islam is the state religion

Language – Dari, Pashto (both official); Balochi, Nuristani, Pamiri, Pashai, Turkmen and Uzbek are official in some areas

Population density – 57 per sq. km (2019)

Urban population – 25.8 per cent (2019 est)

Median age (years) – 19.5 (2020 est)

National anthem – 'Milli Surud' 'National Anthem'

National day – 19 August (Independence Day)

Death penalty – Retained
CPI score – 16 (173)
Military expenditure – US$198m (2018)

CLIMATE AND TERRAIN

Mountains, chief among which are the Hindu Kush, cover three-quarters of the country, with plains in the north and south-west. Elevation extremes range from 7,485m (Noshak, a peak in the Hindu Kush) to 258m (Amu Darya). There are three great river basins: the Amu Dar'ya (Oxus), Helmand and Kabul. Natural hazards are flooding, drought and earthquakes. Average annual rainfall is around 247mm per year. Temperatures in Afghanistan average 0.7°C in January and 25.7°C in July.

POLITICS

Under the 2004 constitution, the executive president, who is directly elected for a five-year term, appoints the government, subject to the approval of the lower house of the legislature. The bicameral National Assembly, the *Jirga,* comprises the House of the People *(Wolesi Jirga),* the lower house and the House of Elders *(Meshrano Jirga).* The House of the People has 250 members directly elected for a five-year term. The House of Elders has 102 members: 34 elected by provincial councils for a three-year term, 34 elected by district councils for a four-year term and 34 appointed by the president for a five-year term; 17 must be women, two must represent the Kuchi nomads and two must represent the disabled.

Hamid Karzai was elected president in 2004, and was re-elected in 2009; he stepped down when his second term concluded in 2014, after NATO handed control to the Afghan state. Following the disputed June 2014 presidential elections, it was declared on 21 September that Ashraf Ghani would become president, ending months of political deadlock. He was re-elected in 2020. The Taliban, ousted in the US-led 2001 invasion, have increasingly grown in strength in recent years, as has IS militants, and have contributed to rising political instability and violence. Over 10,000 civilians were killed or injured in armed conflict in 2019, a slight decrease on 2018.

HEAD OF STATE
President, Ashraf Ghani Ahmadzai, *sworn in* 29 September 2014, re-elected 18 February 2020
First Vice-President, Amrullah Saleh
Second Vice-President, Sarwar Danish

SELECTED GOVERNMENT MEMBERS *AS AT NOVEMBER* 2020
Chair of National Reconciliation, Abdullah Abdullah
Defence (acting), Asadullah Khalid
Finance (acting), Abdul Hadi Arghandiwal
Foreign Affairs (acting), Mohammad Hanif Atmar

EMBASSY OF THE ISLAMIC REPUBLIC OF AFGHANISTAN
31 Princes Gate, London SW7 1QQ
T 020-7225 4743 **E** consulate@afganistanembassy.org.uk
W www.afghanistanembassy.org.uk/english

Ambassador Extraordinary and Plenipotentiary, HE Said Tayeb Jawad, *apptd* 2017

BRITISH EMBASSY
PO Box 334, 15th Street, Roundabout Wazir Akbar Khan, Kabul
T (+93) (0) 700 102 000 **E** britishembassy.kabul@fco.gov.uk
W www.gov.uk/government/world/afghanistan
Ambassador Extraordinary and Plenipotentiary, HE Alison Blake, CMG, *apptd* 2019

ECONOMY AND TRADE

The economy, devastated by almost 40 years of conflict, has improved significantly since 2001. Economic growth has been sustained over the decade, although security problems, weak governance, poor infrastructure and corruption continue to hamper reconstruction. Several years of drought led to warnings in 2018 that half the rural population, around 10.6 million people, were at risk of famine and an estimated 250,000 people had been internally displaced. Poverty is being reduced through substantial civilian aid donations, including an additional US$16bn (£10.5bn) pledged in July 2012, and US$3.8bn (£2.9bn) annual development aid pledge between 2017 and 2020. Eradication of the opium trade (which constituted as much as 60 per cent of the economy but has been reduced to about 15 per cent), and exploration for oil and gas in the north are two major long-term policy objectives. Since 2011, the Afghan and US governments have pursued a policy of turning Afghanistan into a regional trade hub for central Asian commodities, such as gas and cotton, although there has been a rise in both IS and Taliban activity since mid-2016.

Around 44 per cent of the workforce is engaged in agriculture, both subsistence and commercial, which accounts for some 23 per cent of GDP. The main agricultural products are opium, wheat, fruit, nuts, wool, meat, sheepskins and lambskins. Natural gas, coal, copper and semi-gemstones are extracted. The withdrawal of nearly 100,000 troops since 2014 has negatively impacted growth, especially in the services sector. The main trading partners are Pakistan and India. Principal exports are agricultural products, handwoven carpets and gemstones. Imports are chiefly machinery and other capital goods, food, textiles and petroleum products.
GNI – US$20.7bn; US$540 per capita (2019)
Annual average growth of GDP – 2.7 per cent (2017 est)
Inflation rate – 5.0 per cent (2017 est)
Population below poverty line – 54.5 per cent (2017 est)
Imports – US$8,675m (2017 est)
Exports – US$1,228m (2017 est)

BALANCE OF PAYMENTS
Trade – US$7,446m deficit (2017)
Current Account – US$3,792m deficit (2019)

Trade with UK	2018	2019
Imports from UK	£29,858,114	£75,005,217
Exports to UK	£2,127,932	£3,074,861

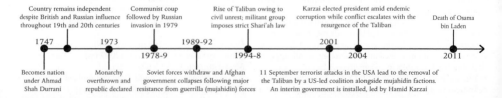

| Country remains independent despite British and Russian influence throughout 19th and 20th centuries | Communist coup followed by Russian invasion in 1979 | Rise of Taliban owing to civil unrest; militant group imposes strict Shari'ah law | Karzai elected president amid endemic corruption while conflict escalates with the resurgence of the Taliban | Death of Osama bin Laden |

1747   1973   1989-92   2001   2011
1978-9   1994-8   2004

Becomes nation under Ahmad Shah Durrani | Monarchy overthrown and republic declared | Soviet forces withdraw and Afghan government collapses following major resistance from guerrilla (mujahidin) forces | 11 September terrorist attacks in the USA lead to the removal of the Taliban by a US-led coalition alongside mujahidin factions. An interim government is installed, led by Hamid Karzai

COMMUNICATIONS

Airports – 43; two international: Kabul and Kandahar
Waterways – The Amu Dar'ya river makes up most of the 1,200km of inland waterways; the main river ports are Kheyrabad and Shir Khan
Roadways – 34,903km (2017)
Telecommunications – 118,769 fixed lines and 23.9 million mobile subscriptions (2017); there were 4.7 million internet users in 2018
Internet code and IDD – af; 93 (from UK), 44 (to UK)
Major broadcasters – The principal and state-owned broadcaster is National Radio Television Afghanistan (RTA), alongside 150 private radio stations and 50 television stations (2018)
Press – There are nine daily newspapers, including the privately owned *Hasht-e Sobh* and *Mandegar,* and the government sponsored *Hewad*
WPFI score – 37.70 (122)

EDUCATION AND HEALTH

Education is free and nominally compulsory; elementary schools have been established in most centres.
Literacy rate – 43 per cent (2018 est)
Gross enrolment ratio (percentage of relevant age group – primary 104 per cent, secondary 55.4 per cent, tertiary 9.7 per cent (2018 est)
Health expenditure (per capita) – US$67 (2017)
Hospital beds (per 1,000 people) – 0.5 (2014)
Life expectancy (years) – 52.8 (2020 est)
Mortality rate – 12.7 (2020 est)
Birth rate – 36.7 (2020 est)
Infant mortality rate – 104.3 (2020 est)
HIV/AIDS adult prevalence – 0.1 per cent (2019 est)

ALBANIA

Republika e Shqiperise – Republic of Albania

Area – 28,748 sq. km
Capital – Tirana; population, 494,000 (2020 est)
Major towns – Durres, Elbasan, Shkoder, Vlore
Currency – Lek (Lk) of 100 qindarka
Population – 3,074,579 rising at 0.28 per cent a year (2020 est); Albanian (82.6 per cent), Greek (0.9 per cent) (2011 est)
Religion – Muslim 56.7 per cent (Sunni), Christian (Roman Catholic 10 per cent, Orthodox 6.8 per cent), Bektashi 2.1 per cent (est). Religious observance was banned in 1967; private religious practice has been permitted since 1990
Language – Albanian (official), Greek, Macedonian, Vlach, Romani, Turkish, Italian, Serbo-Croatian
Population density – 105 per sq. km (2019)
Urban population – 61.2 per cent (2019 est)

Median age (years) – 34.3 (2020 est)
National anthem – 'Himni i Flamurit' 'Hymn to the Flag'
National day – 28 November (Independence Day)
Death penalty – Abolished for all crimes (since 2007)
CPI score – 35 (106)
Military expenditure – US$180m (2018)

CLIMATE AND TERRAIN

About two-thirds of the country is mountainous, and 36 per cent is covered by forest. Elevation extremes range from 2,764m (Maja e Korabit, a peak on the Macedonian border) to 0m (Adriatic Sea). The climate is Mediterranean on the coast and continental in the interior. The average daily temperature ranges between 2.1°C in January and 21.8°C in July and August.

POLITICS

Under the 1998 constitution, the president is elected by the legislature for a five-year term, renewable once. The unicameral legislature, the People's Assembly, has 140 members directly elected for four-year terms. The president appoints the prime minister, who must be approved by the People's Assembly. The assembly elects the council of ministers.

Ilir Meta, of the Socialist Movement for Integration (LSI), was elected president in 2017 in the fourth round of voting. Legislative elections were held in June 2017 and won by the incumbent prime minister Edi Rama and his Socialist Party of Albania (PS), which increased its share of seats to 74.

Albania applied to join the EU in 2009 and obtained candidate status in 2014.

HEAD OF STATE
President, Ilir Meta, *elected* 28 April 2017

SELECTED GOVERNMENT MEMBERS *AS AT NOVEMBER* 2020
Prime Minister, Foreign Affairs, Edi Rama
Deputy Prime Minister, Erion Brace
Defence, Olta Xhacka
Finance, Anila Denaj

EMBASSY OF THE REPUBLIC OF ALBANIA
33 St George's Drive, London SW1V 4DG
T 020-7828 8897 **E** embassy.london@mfa.gov.al
W www.ambasadat.gov.al/united-kingdom/en
Ambassador Extraordinary and Plenipotentiary, HE Qirjako Qirko, *apptd* 2016

BRITISH EMBASSY
Rruga Skenderbeg 12, Tirana
T (+355) (4) 223 4973 **W** www.gov.uk/government/world/albania
Ambassador Extraordinary and Plenipotentiary, HE Duncan Norman, MBE, *apptd* 2016

ECONOMY AND TRADE

Albania is one of the poorest countries in Europe, although liberalisation measures have resulted in gradual growth since 1993. Trade and banking sector ties with the fragile economies of Greece and Italy, high levels of public debt, corruption and organised crime remain significant economic challenges. The economy is increasingly able to cope with a decline in remittances from expatriate workers, which has fallen from between 12 and 15 per cent of GDP before 2008 to less than 6 per cent in 2015, and has grown steadily since 2014. The inefficient energy and transport sectors have been improved by investment, although they remain underdeveloped by European standards.

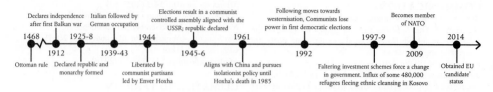

Declares independence after first Balkan war — 1468

Italian followed by German occupation — 1925-8

Elections result in a communist controlled assembly aligned with the USSR; republic declared — 1944

Following moves towards westernisation, Communists lose power in first democratic elections — 1961

Becomes member of NATO — 1997-9

2014

1912 — Ottoman rule

1939-43 — Declared republic and monarchy formed

1945-6 — Liberated by communist partisans led by Enver Hoxha

1992 — Aligns with China and pursues isolationist policy until Hoxha's death in 1985

2009 — Faltering investment schemes force a change in government. Influx of some 480,000 refugees fleeing ethnic cleansing in Kosovo

Obtained EU 'candidate' status

Agriculture accounts for 41.4 per cent of employment but only 21.7 per cent of GDP. The main crops are wheat, corn, potatoes, vegetables, fruit, olives and livestock products. The principal industries are food processing, footwear and clothing, timber, oil, cement, chemicals, mining (base metals) and hydroelectric power.

Trade is mainly with Italy, Turkey, Spain, Greece and Kosovo. Exports include textiles and footwear, asphalt, metals and metal ores, crude oil, tobacco, fruit and vegetables. Imports include machinery and equipment, foodstuffs, textiles and chemicals.

GNI – US$14.9bn; US$5,240 per capita (2019)
Annual average growth of GDP – 2.24 per cent (2019 est)
Inflation rate – 2 per cent (2017 est)
Population below poverty line – 14.3 per cent (2012 est)
Unemployment – 5.83 per cent (2019 est)
Total external debt – US$9.505bn (2017 est)
Imports – US$6,118m (2017)
Exports – US$4,139m (2017)

BALANCE OF PAYMENTS
Trade – US$1,978m deficit (2017)
Current Account – US$1,218m deficit (2019)

Trade with UK	2018	2019
Imports from UK	£17,812,934	£18,738,133
Exports to UK	£7,215,776	£6,401,245

COMMUNICATIONS
Airports – 4; three international: Kukes, Tirana, Vlore
Roadways and railways – 3,945km; 677km
Telecommunications – 248,631 fixed lines and 2.7 million mobile subscriptions (2018); there were 2.2 million internet users in 2018
Internet code and IDD – al; 355 (from UK), 44 (to UK)
Major broadcasters – Albanian Radio and TV (RTSh), Top Channel and TV Klan
Press – There are 25 daily newspapers, including *Shekulli, Gazeta Shqiptare* and the *Tirana Times*
WPFI score – 30.25 (84)

EDUCATION AND HEALTH
Literacy rate – 98.1 per cent (2018 est)
Gross enrolment ratio (percentage of relevant age group) – primary 104.8 per cent, secondary 95.1 per cent, tertiary 59.8 per cent (2019 est)
Health expenditure (per capita) – US$272 (2014)
Hospital beds (per 1,000 people) – 2.9 (2013)
Life expectancy (years) – 79 (2020 est)
Mortality rate – 7.1 (2020 est)
Birth rate – 13 (2020 est)
Infant mortality rate – 10.8 (2020 est)
HIV/AIDS adult prevalence – 0.1 per cent (2019 est)

ALGERIA
Al-Jumhuriyah al-Jaza'iriyah ad Dimuqratiyah ash Sha'biyah – People's Democratic Republic of Algeria

Area – 2,381,740 sq. km
Capital – Algiers (El Djazair, Al Jaza'ir); population, 2,760,000 (2020 est)
Major cities – Annaba, Blida, Constantine (Qacentina), Oran (Wahran)
Currency – Algerian dinar (DA) of 100 centimes
Population – 42,972,878 rising at 1.52 per cent a year (2020 est); Arab-Berber (99 per cent) (est)
Religion – Muslim 99 per cent (predominantly Sunni) (est); Islam is the state religion
Language – Arabic (official), French, Berber (also official), Berber dialects
Population density – 18 per sq. km (2019)
Urban population – 273.2 per cent (2019 est)
Median age (years) – 28.9 (2020 est)
National anthem – 'Kassaman' 'We Pledge'
National day – 1 November (Revolution Day)
Death penalty – Retained (last used 1993)
CPI score – 35 (106)
Military expenditure – US$10,637m (2016)
Conscription – 19–30 years of age; 12 months

CLIMATE AND TERRAIN
Algeria, the largest country in Africa, is dominated by the Sahara desert, which covers more than 80 per cent of its territory. Elevation extremes range from 3,003m (Mt Tahat) to −40m (Chott Melrhir, a salt lake). The mountains are subject to earthquakes, and to flooding during the rainy season (November–March). The temperate northern coastal areas receive the greatest and most frequent rainfall, whereas the interior plateaux are drier and experience cold winters and hot summers.

POLITICS
Algeria's 1976 constitution was amended in 1989 to reintroduce political pluralism. It was revised in 2008, most notably to remove the limit on presidential terms, but a two-term limit was reinstated in February 2016. The president is directly elected for a five-year term. The bicameral *Barlaman* comprises the National People's Assembly, the lower house and Council of the Nation. The assembly has 462 members,

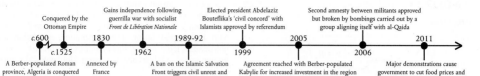

Conquered by the Ottoman Empire	Gains independence following guerrilla war with socialist *Front de Libération Nationale*	Elected president Abdelaziz Bouteflika's 'civil concord' with Islamists approved by referendum	Second amnesty between militants approved but broken by bombings carried out by a group aligning itself with al-Qaida	
*c.*600	1830	1989-92	2005	2011
*c.*1525	1962	1999	2006	
A Berber-populated Roman province, Algeria is conquered by Arabs and converted to Islam	Annexed by France	A ban on the Islamic Salvation Front triggers civil unrest and a state of emergency	Agreement reached with Berber-populated Kabylie for increased investment in the region and greater recognition of the Berber language	Major demonstrations cause government to cut food prices and lift the 19-year state of emergency

including eight seats for Algerians living abroad, directly elected for a five-year term. The National Council has 144 members; 48 are appointed by the president, and 96 are indirectly elected for a six-year term by electoral colleges formed by local councils; half of these elected members are re-elected every three years. Although Algeria is no longer a one-party state, parties based on religion or on race, language, gender or region are banned under the constitution.

In the 2017 legislative election, the ruling National Liberation Front-led coalition won the most seats and retained control in the assembly. In April 2014, President Abdelaziz Bouteflika was re-elected for a fourth term despite not campaigning due to ill health. In February 2019, large nonviolent protests were held over Bouteflika's decision to run for a fifth term despite a ban on demonstrations. In March, Bouteflika's promise to implement constitutional change failed to quell the protests and he resigned soon after, ending two decades of rule. Former prime minister Abelmajid Tebboune won the subsequent 2019 election.

HEAD OF STATE
President, Defence, Abelmajid Tebboune, *appointed* 12 December 2019

SELECTED GOVERNMENT MEMBERS *AS AT NOVEMBER 2020*
Prime Minister, Abdelazis Djerad
Finance, Aymen Benabderahmane
Foreign Affairs, Sabri Boukadoum

ALGERIAN EMBASSY
6 Hyde Park G, London SW7 5EW
T 020-7589 6885 **E** info@algerianembassy.org.uk
W www.algerianembassy.org.uk
Ambassador Extraordinary and Plenipotentiary, HE Abderrahmane Benguerrah, *apptd* 2019

BRITISH EMBASSY
3 Chemin Capitaine Hocine Slimane, Hydra, Algiers
T (+213) (770) 085 000 **E** britishembassy.algiers@fco.gov.uk
W www.gov.uk/government/world/algeria
Ambassador Extraordinary and Plenipotentiary, HE Barry Lowen, *apptd* 2017

ECONOMY AND TRADE
After independence, Algeria's economy was dominated by the state until a privatisation programme was introduced in 1997. Reform, combined with high oil prices, resulted in trade surpluses, record foreign exchange reserves and the reduction of foreign debt, despite recent blocks on the privatisation process. Low oil prices since 2014 have dented the economy and significantly cut its previously high foreign currency reserves, while diversification away from the energy sector and development of the financial system has been hampered by a lack of foreign investment. This has led to increasingly protectionist policies to encourage domestic production, including the indefinite suspension of the importation of around 850 products in January 2018.

Algeria has substantial oil and gas reserves, and the hydrocarbon industry accounts for 30 per cent of GDP, nearly 60 per cent of government revenue and over 95 per cent of export earnings. Services provide 47.4 per cent of GDP, industry 39.3 per cent and agriculture 13.3 per cent. Industries other than oil and gas production include mining, electrical goods, food processing and light industries.

Algeria's main trading partners are China, France, Italy, other EU countries and the USA. The chief imports are capital goods, foodstuffs and consumer goods.

GNI – US$170.7bn; US$3,970 per capita (2019)
Annual average growth of GDP – 1.7 per cent (2017 est)
Inflation rate – 1.9 per cent (2019 est)
Population below poverty line – 23 per cent (2006 est)
Unemployment – 11.7 per cent (2017 est)
Total external debt – US$8.163bn (2017 est)
Imports – US$60,384m (2017)
Exports – US$37,830m (2017)

BALANCE OF PAYMENTS
Trade – US$22,554m deficit (2017)
Current Account – US$17,147m deficit (2019)

Trade with UK	2018	2019
Imports from UK	£337,802,282	£360,270,124
Exports to UK	£2,200,712,713	£1,988,616,030

COMMUNICATIONS
Airports and waterways – 64, including Algiers and Constantine; major ports are at Algiers and Bejaia
Roadways and railways – 104,000km; 3,973km
Telecommunications – 3.3 million fixed lines and 50 million mobile subscriptions (2017); there were 17.3 million internet users in 2016
Internet code and IDD – dz; 213 (from UK), 44 (to UK)
Major broadcaster – Enterprise Nationale de Télévision (ENTV) is the state broadcaster
Press – There are more than 80 newspapers available in Algiers, including *El Khabar, Ech Chourouk* and *Le Quotidien d'Oran*
WPFI score – 45.52 (146)

EDUCATION AND HEALTH
Literacy rate – 81.4 per cent (2018 est)
Gross enrolment ratio (percentage of relevant age group) – primary 107.3 per cent (2019 est); secondary 95 per cent (2016 est); tertiary 51.4 per cent (2018 est)
Health expenditure (per capita) – US$258 (2017)
Hospital beds (per 1,000 people) – 1.9 (2015)
Life expectancy (years) – 77.5 (2020 est)
Mortality rate – 4.4 (2020 est)
Birth rate – 20 (2020 est)
Infant mortality rate – 17.6 (2020 est)
HIV/AIDS adult prevalence – 0.1 per cent (2019 est)

ANDORRA

Principat d'Andorra – Principality of Andorra

Area – 468 sq. km
Capital – Andorra la Vella; population, 23,000 (2018 est)
Major cities – Encamp, Les Escaldes-Engordany, Sant Julià de
    Lòria
Currency – Euro (€) of 100 cents
Population – 77,000 falling at 0.06 per cent a year (2020 est);
    Andorran (48.8 per cent), Spanish (25.1 per cent),
    Portuguese (12 per cent), French (4.4 per cent) (est)
Religion – Christian (predominantly Roman Catholic)
Language – Catalan (official), French, Spanish (Castilian),
    Portuguese
Population density – 164 per sq. km (2019)
Urban population – 88.0 per cent (2019 est)
Median age (years) – 46.2 (2020 est)
National anthem – 'El Gran Carlemany' 'The Great
    Charlemagne'
National day – 8 September (Our Lady of Meritxell Day)
Death penalty – Abolished for all crimes (since 1990)
Health expenditure (per capita) – US$4,041 (2019)
Life expectancy (years) – 83 (2020 est)
Mortality rate – 7.7 (2020 est)
Birth rate – 7 (2020 est)
Infant mortality rate – 3.5 (2020 est)

CLIMATE AND TERRAIN

Andorra is a country of dramatic mountains interspersed by
narrow valleys; over a third of the country is forested.
Elevation extremes range from 2,946m (Pic de Coma
Pedrosa) to 840m (Riu Runer). The climate is alpine, with
heavy snowfall in winter and warm summers. Average
temperature ranges from 1.6°C in January to 18.3°C in
August.

HISTORY AND POLITICS

Conquered by Charlemagne from Moorish rule in 803,
Andorra is a neutral principality that was formed by a *paréage*
(a type of feudal treaty) in 1278 and since then has owed dual
allegiance to two co-princes, the Spanish Bishop of Urgell and
the head of state of France. Andorra became an independent
democratic parliamentary co-principality in 1993. The
country subsequently formalised its links with the EU, and
joined the UN and the Council of Europe.
  Andorra has a unicameral legislature, the General Council of
the Valleys *(Consell General de las Valls)*, whose minimum of 28
members are directly elected for a four-year term by
proportional representation. The council appoints the
president of the executive council, who nominates
government members.
  Under the 1993 constitution, the heads of state are two co-
princes, the President of France and the Bishop of Urgell,
Spain. They are represented in Andorra by the permanent

delegates (the Spanish vicar-general of the diocese of Urgell
and the French prefect of the Pyrenees Orientales
department), but their powers now relate solely to relations
with France and Spain. The constitution established an
independent judiciary and allows Andorra to conduct its own
foreign policy, while its people may now join political parties
and trade unions.
  In the April 2019 legislative election, the Democrats for
Andorra remained the largest party despite losing four seats,
winning 11 of the 30 seats in the general council.

HEADS OF STATE

The President of France, Emmanuel Macron
The Bishop of Urgell, Joan Enric Vives i Sicilia
Permanent French Delegate, Patrick Strzoda
Permanent Episcopal Delegate, Josep Maria Mauri i Prior

SELECTED GOVERNMENT MEMBERS *AS AT*
NOVEMBER 2020
President of the Executive Council, Xavier Espot
Finance, Eric Jover
Foreign Affairs, Maria Ubach
Interior and Justice, Josep Maria Rossell

BRITISH CONSULATE-GENERAL

Ambassador, HE Hugh Elliott, CMG, *apptd* 2019, resident at
    Madrid, Spain

ECONOMY AND TRADE

The economy is largely based on tourism, banking and retail
sales, which together account for over 75 per cent of GDP.
Following pressure from the EU, controversial bank secrecy
laws were reformed in 2009 and the country's low tax
economy modified by the introduction of corporation tax in
2012 and the nation's first income tax in 2015, a flat rate of
10 per cent. The country has actively sought foreign
investment and businesses to diversity its economy since
2008. Other activities include tourism, perfume and cosmetics
production, forestry, furniture-making and sheep-farming.
Andorra is a member of the EU Customs Union and is treated
as an EU member for trade in manufactured goods and as a
non-EU member for agricultural products.
GNI – US$3,284bn (2015 est); US$43,270 per capita
    (2013)
Annual average growth of GDP – 1.1 per cent (2015 est)
Inflation rate – –0.9 per cent (2015 est)
Population below poverty line – 3.7 (2016 est)
Imports – US$1,355m (2016)
Exports – US$100m (2016)

BALANCE OF PAYMENTS
Trade – US$1,255m deficit (2016)

Trade with UK	2018	2019
Imports from UK	£7,926,770	£15,462,323
Exports to UK	£1,827,123	£379,775

COMMUNICATIONS

Roadways – 320km
Telecommunications – 39,375 fixed lines and 82,614 mobile
subscriptions (2018); there were 78,483 internet users in
2018
Internet code and IDD – ad; 376 (from UK), 44 (to UK)
Major broadcaster – Radio i Televisio d'Andorra
Press – Major newspapers include *Diari d'Andorra* and
El Periodic d'Andorra
WPFI score – 23.23 (37)

ANGOLA

Republica de Angola – Republic of Angola

Area – 1,246,700 sq. km; includes the exclave of Cabinda
Capital – Luanda; population, 8,330,000 (2020 est)
Major cities – Benguela, Huambo, Lubango
Currency – Kwanza (Kzrl) of 100 centimos
Population – 32,522,339 rising at 3.43 per cent a year (2020 est); Ovimbundu (37 per cent), Kimbundu (25 per cent), Bakongo (13 per cent), Mestico (2 per cent), other African, including Lunda-Chokwe and Ngangela (22 per cent) (est)
Religion – Christian (Roman Catholic 41.1 per cent, Protestant 38.1 per cent), other 8.2 per cent (including indigenous beliefs) (est)
Language – Portuguese (official), Umbundu, Kikongo, Kimbundu, Chokwe, Nhaneca, Nganguela, Fiote, Kwanhama, Muhumbi
Population density – 25 per sq. km (2019)
Urban population – 66.2 per cent (2019 est)
Median age (years) – 15.9 (2020 est)
National anthem – 'Angola Avante' 'Forward Angola'
National day – 11 November (Independence Day)
Death penalty – Abolished for all crimes (since 1992)
CPI score – 26 (146)
Military expenditure – US$7,798m (2014)
Conscription – 20–45 years of age for compulsory male service, mandatory registration at 18; 20–45 years of age for voluntary female service, 2 year obligation
Literacy rate – 71.1 per cent (2018 est)
Gross enrolment ratio (percentage of relevant age group) – primary 113.5 per cent (2015 est); secondary 50.7 per cent, tertiary 9.3 per cent (2016 est)
Health expenditure (per capita) – US$114 (2017)
Hospital beds (per 1,000 people) – 0.8 (2005)
Life expectancy (years) – 61.3 (2020 est)
Mortality rate – 835 (2020 est)
Birth rate – 42.7 (2020 est)
Infant mortality rate – 62.3 (2020 est)
HIV / AIDS adult prevalence – 1.6 per cent (2019 est)

CLIMATE AND TERRAIN

The land rises from a narrow coastal plain to a vast interior plateau, with desert to the south. The highest point of elevation is 2,620m (Morro do Moco) and the lowest is 0m (Atlantic Ocean). The climate is tropical in the north – with a cool, dry season from April to September and a hot, rainy season from October to March – and subtropical in the south and along the coast to Luanda.

POLITICS

Under the 2010 constitution, the president is the head of the party with the largest number of seats in the legislature. The unicameral National Assembly has 220 members, elected by proportional representation for a five-year term.

Political pluralism was introduced under the 1991 peace agreement and multiparty elections were held in 1992, though the National Union for Total Independence of Angola (UNITA) refused to accept the results. The first legislative elections since 1992, held in 2008, were won by the People's Movement for the Liberation of Angola (MPLA); it retained its majority in the 2012 and 2017 legislative elections, the latter with 150 seats to UNITA's 51. The new constitution, introduced in 2010, ended direct election of the president, created the office of vice-president and abolished the post of prime minister. After legislative elections in August 2017, Jose Eduardo dos Santos stood down as president after 38 years in power and was replaced by Joao Lourenco.

HEAD OF STATE
President, Joao Lourenco, *took office* 26 September 2017
Vice-President, Bornito De Sousa

SELECTED GOVERNMENT MEMBERS *AS AT NOVEMBER 2020*
Defence, Joao Dos Santos
Finance, Vera Daves
Foreign Affairs, Tete Antonio
Interior, Eugenio Cesar Laborinho

EMBASSY OF THE REPUBLIC OF ANGOLA
22 Dorset Street, London W1U 6QY
T 020-7299 9850 **E** embassy@angola.org.uk **W** www.angola.org.uk
Ambassador Extraordinary and Plenipotentiary, HE Geraldo Nunda, *apptd* 2020

BRITISH EMBASSY
Rua 17 de Setembro 4, Caixa, Luanda 1244
T (+244) (22) 233 4583 **E** postmaster.luand@fco.gov.uk
W www.gov.uk/government/world/angola
Ambassador Extraordinary and Plenipotentiary, HE Jessica Hand, *apptd* 2018

SECESSION
In the oil-rich northern exclave of Cabinda, separatists have conducted a low-level guerrilla war since the mid-1970s. The government has been unable to end the fighting either through negotiation or by military means. A ceasefire and peace agreement reached in 2006 has not been observed by all parties.

ECONOMY AND TRADE

The economy is still recovering from decades of corruption, mismanagement and civil war, but liberalisation and stabilisation are being achieved. Post-war increases in oil, diamond and agricultural production have driven strong economic growth, although the economy contracted in 2009 as the global downturn reduced demand for exports. The extractive industries and infrastructure projects have attracted foreign investment despite the corruption and stifling bureaucracy that have deterred investors in other sectors.

Angola, especially Cabinda, is rich in natural resources. The main industries involve extracting and processing oil (Angola is Africa's largest producer of oil, above Nigeria, with production and related activities accounting for around 50 per cent of GDP and 90 per cent of exports), diamonds, metals

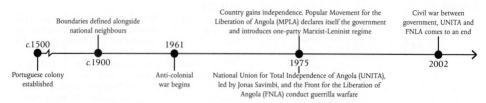

Boundaries defined alongside national neighbours

Country gains independence. Popular Movement for the Liberation of Angola (MPLA) declares itself the government and introduces one-party Marxist-Leninist regime

Civil war between government, UNITA and FNLA comes to an end

*c.*1500   1961

*c.*1900   1975   2002

Portuguese colony established

Anti-colonial war begins

National Union for Total Independence of Angola (UNITA), led by Jonas Savimbi, and the Front for the Liberation of Angola (FNLA) conduct guerrilla warfare

and other minerals, forestry, fishing, food processing and the manufacture of cement, metal products, tobacco products and textiles, and ship repair. Angola has large areas of good farmland, but the prevalence of unexploded landmines has reduced the area under cultivation and forced many areas back to subsistence agriculture, although coffee, sisal and cotton are produced for export. Agriculture contributes just 10 per cent of GDP but employs 85 per cent of the labour force. A dependence on imported consumable goods (Angola imports around 50 per cent of its food), poor infrastructure and high property prices have caused Luanda to become one of the world's most expensive cities.

The main trading partners are China, the USA, India and Portugal. The principal exports are crude oil, diamonds, refined petroleum products, coffee, sisal, fish, timber and cotton. The main imports are machinery and electrical equipment, vehicles and spare parts, medicines, food, textiles and military goods.

GNI – US$97bn; US$3,050 per capita (2019)
Annual average growth of GDP – 2.5 per cent (2017 est)
Inflation rate – 30.9 per cent (2017 est)
Population below poverty line – 36.6 per cent (2008 est)
Unemployment – 6.6 per cent (2016 est)
Total external debt – US$27.34bn (2017 est)
Imports – US$28,753m (2017)
Exports – US$35,287m (2017)

BALANCE OF PAYMENTS
Trade – US$6,534m surplus (2016)
Current Account – US$5,137m surplus (2019)

Trade with UK	2018	2019
Imports from UK	£196,718,530	£228,374,790
Exports to UK	£88,098,984	£49,528,742

COMMUNICATIONS
Airports and waterways – 32; main ports include Cabinda, Lobito, Luanda and Namibe
Roadways and railways –26,000km; 2,852km
Telecommunications – 171,858 fixed lines and 13.3 million mobile subscriptions (2018); there were 4.3 million internet users in 2018
Internet code and IDD – ao; 244 (from UK), 44 (to UK)
Major broadcasters – Only the government-owned Televisao Publica de Angola (TPA) and Radio National de Angola (RNA) have national coverage
Press – The government owned *Jornal de Angola* is the only daily newspaper
WPFI score – 33.92 (106)

ANTIGUA AND BARBUDA

Antigua and Barbuda

Area – 442.6 sq. km: Antigua 280 sq. km; Barbuda 161 sq. km; Redonda 1.6 sq. km
Capital – St John's; population, 21,000 (2018 est)
Currency – East Caribbean dollar (EC$) of 100 cents
Population – 98,179 rising at 1.18 per cent a year (2020 est)
Religion – Christian (Protestant 68.3 per cent, Roman Catholic 8.2 per cent, other 12.2 per cent est)
Language – English (official), Antiguan creole
Population density – 219 per sq. km (2019)
Urban population – 24.5 per cent (2019 est)
Median age (years) – 32.7 (2020 est)
National anthem – 'Fair Antigua, We Salute Thee'
National day – 1 November (Independence Day)
Death penalty – Retained
Literacy rate – 99 per cent (2015 est)
Gross enrolment ratio (percentage of relevant age group) – primary 105 per cent, secondary 111.2 per cent (2018 est); tertiary 24.8 per cent (2012 est)
Health expenditure (per capita) – US$674 (2017)
Life expectancy (years) – 77.3 (2020 est)
Mortality rate – 5.8 (2020 est)
Birth rate – 15.4 (2020 est)
Infant mortality rate – 11.1 (2020 est)

CLIMATE AND TERRAIN
Unlike most other Leeward Islands, Antigua has few high hills and little forest cover. Its elevation extremes range from 402m (Boggy Peak) to 0m (Caribbean Sea). Barbuda, 48km north of Antigua, is a flat coral island with a large lagoon. Both islands are tropical, but drier than most of the West Indies. They lie within the hurricane belt and are subject to tropical storms and hurricanes between August and October.

HISTORY AND POLITICS
Prehistoric settlers were succeeded by the Arawaks, then the Caribs. Although the islands were discovered by Columbus in 1493, the European (English) settlement of Antigua began only in 1632. Barbuda was colonised from Antigua in 1661. Administered as part of the Leeward Islands Federation from 1871 to 1956, it became internally self-governing in 1967 and fully independent on 1 November 1981.

The head of state is Queen Elizabeth II, represented by the governor-general. The bicameral parliament comprises a senate of 17 members, appointed by the governor-general on the advice of the prime minister and opposition leader, and a House of Representatives of 18 directly elected members; both chambers serve a five-year term.

The Antigua Labour Party won the 2018 legislative elections, claiming 15 seats.

Governor-General, HE Dr Sir Rodney Williams, GCMG, *apptd* 2014

SELECTED GOVERNMENT MEMBERS *AS AT NOVEMBER 2020*
Prime Minister, Finance, Gaston Browne
Foreign Affairs, Paul Greene
Tourism, Charles Fernandez

HIGH COMMISSION FOR ANTIGUA AND BARBUDA
2nd Floor, 45 Crawford Place, London W1H 4LP
T 020-7258 0070 **E** enquiries@antigua-barbuda.com
W www.antigua-barbuda.com
High Commissioner, HE Karen-Mae Hill, *apptd* 2016

BRITISH HIGH COMMISSION
High Commissioner, HE Janet Douglas, CMG, *apptd* 2017, resident at Bridgetown, Barbados

ECONOMY AND TRADE

The economy is largely based on tourism and related services (contributing nearly 60 per cent of GDP), with petroleum products and light manufacturing (bedding, handicrafts, electronic components) for export, and agriculture (livestock, sea island cotton, market gardening, fishing) for local consumption. Economic growth and fiscal reform between 2004 and 2007 enabled the government to reduce public debt. However, from 2009, a severe decline in tourism caused by the global economic downturn and the collapse of Allen Stanford's Antigua-based financial group (which included Antigua's major financial institution) hit the economy badly. The bleak economic outlook was exacerbated in September 2017 by hurricanes Irma and Maria, which left Barbuda barely habitable and the government struggling to pay a reconstruction bill estimated at US$200m.

GNI – US$1.6bn; US$16,660 per capita (2019)
Annual average growth of GDP – 2.8 per cent (2017 est)
Inflation rate – 2.5 per cent (2017 est)
Unemployment – 11 per cent (2014 est)
Total external debt – US$441.2m (2012 est)
Imports – US$866m (2016)
Exports – US$1,040m (2016)

BALANCE OF PAYMENTS
Trade – US$173m surplus (2016)
Current Account – US$113m deficit (2018)

Trade with UK	2018	2019
Imports from UK	£17,633,270	£14,440,918
Exports to UK	£5,084,330	£3,062,759

COMMUNICATIONS

Airports and waterways – Three; the main port is at St John's
Roadways – 1,170km
Telecommunications – 22,504 fixed lines and 180,000 mobile subscriptions (2017); there were 72,870 internet users in 2018
Internet code and IDD – ag; 1 268 (from UK), 011 44 (to UK)

Major broadcasters – The Antigua and Barbuda Broadcasting Service (ABS) is the state broadcaster; private and public TV and radio stations are affiliated with political parties
Press – *Antigua Sun* is the only daily newspaper
WPFI score – 23.78 (44)

ARGENTINA

República Argentina – Argentine Republic

Area – 2,780,400 sq. km
Capital – Buenos Aires; population, 15,154,000 (2020 est)
Major cities – Córdoba, La Plata, Mendoza, Rosario, San Miguel de Tucumán
Currency – Argentine Peso of 100 centavos
Population – 45,479,118 rising at 0.86 per cent a year (2020 est)
Religion – Christian (Roman Catholic 92 per cent, Protestant 2 per cent), Jewish (2 per cent) (est)
Language – Spanish (official), Italian, English, German, French; Mapudungun and Quechua (both indigenous)
Population density – 16 per sq. km (2019)
Urban population – 92 per cent (2019 est)
Median age (years) – 32.4 (2020 est)
National anthem – 'Himno Nacional Argentina' 'Argentine National Anthem'
National day – 25 May (Revolution Day)
Death penalty – Abolished for all crimes (since 2008)
CPI score – 45 (66)
Military expenditure – US$3,980m (2006)

CLIMATE AND TERRAIN

The Andes mountain range runs the full length of the country, along its western border with Chile, and the area is prone to earthquakes. East of the Andes, the north is mostly subtropical rainforest, the centre contains the vast grasslands of the pampas, and the southern Patagonian plateau is arid and desolate, with glaciers in the far south. The highest point of elevation is 6,960m (Cerro Aconcagua) and the lowest is −105m (Laguna del Carbon). Temperatures range from subtropical in the north to subantarctic in the south. Average temperatures range from 20.5°C in January to 7.3°C in July.

POLITICS

Following constitutional amendments agreed in 1994, the executive president is directly elected for a four-year term, renewable once. The bicameral National Congress consists of a 72-member senate (three members for each province and three for Buenos Aires) and a 257-member Chamber of Deputies. Deputies are directly elected for a four-year term, with half of the seats renewable every two years. Senators are directly elected for a six-year term, with one-third of seats renewable every two years.

The Argentine Republic is a federation of 23 provinces, each with an elected governor and legislature, plus the federal

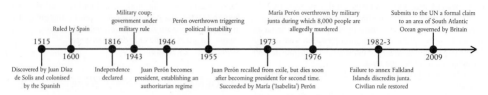

Ruled by Spain — 1515
Discovered by Juan Díaz de Solís and colonised by the Spanish — 1600

Military coup; government under military rule — 1816
Independence declared — 1943

Perón overthrown triggering political instability — 1946
Juan Perón becomes president, establishing an authoritarian regime — 1955

— 1973
Juan Perón recalled from exile, but dies soon after becoming president for second time. Succeeded by María ('Isabelita') Perón

María Perón overthrown by military junta during which 8,000 people are allegedly murdered — 1976

Submits to the UN a formal claim to an area of South Atlantic Ocean governed by Britain — 1982-3
Failure to annex Falkland Islands discredits junta. Civilian rule restored — 2009

district of Buenos Aires, which has an elected mayor and autonomous government.

The October 2019 presidential election was won by Alberto Fernández of the Frente de Todos ('Everyone's Front') coalition, defeating incumbent Mauricio Macri, leader of the centre-right Cambiemos coalition. Simultaneous legislative elections saw Todos claim a majority in the senate and 64 of the 130 seats competed for in the Chamber of Deputies.

HEAD OF STATE
President, Alberto Fernández, *elected* 27 October 2019, *sworn in* 10 December 2019
Vice-President, Cristina Fernandez de Kirchner

SELECTED GOVERNMENT MEMBERS *AS AT NOVEMBER 2020*
Defence, Agustin Rossi
Economy, Martin Guzman
Foreign Relations, Felipe Sola
Interior, Eduardo de Pedro

EMBASSY OF THE ARGENTINE REPUBLIC
65 Brook Street, London W1K 4AH
T 020-7318 1300 E info@argentine-embassy-uk.org
W www.argentine-embassy-uk.org
Ambassador Extraordinary and Plenipotentiary, HE Javier Esteban Figueroa, *apptd* 2020

BRITISH EMBASSY
Dr Luis Agote 2412, 1425 Buenos Aires
T (+54) (11) 4808 2200 W www.gov.uk/government/world/argentina
Ambassador Extraordinary and Plenipotentiary, HE Mark Kent, *apptd* 2016

ECONOMY AND TRADE
The economy recovered rapidly from the economic collapse of 2001–2, experiencing strong growth from 2003, but has experienced a sharp recession in recent years. Argentina restructured its defaulted debt in 2005 and repaid its IMF loan in 2006, but experienced a contraction in 2008–9 caused by the global downturn. Following a US court ruling in July 2014 in favour of bond holders who had not accepted previous debt restructuring – mainly US hedge funds – the government chose to default on its debt for the eighth time in Argentinian history. Despite high levels of inflation and the devaluing of the peso, which in January 2014 saw its sharpest one-day fall against the dollar since the 2002 crisis, the economy slightly rebounded after 2010, initially by increased state intervention and latterly through liberalisation policies. Nonetheless, inflation nearly reached 30 per cent in 2017, and a sharp fall in the value of the peso meant President Macri asked for the early release of a US$57.1bn loan from the IMF – the largest funding arrangement ever issued by the organisation – to tackle the crisis in 2018. The situation failed to improve in 2019, as very high inflation was sustained and unemployment jumped to over ten per cent by July, and the impact of the coronavirus pandemic in 2020 only exacerbated the nation's debt crisis.

The country is rich in natural resources, particularly lead, zinc, tin, copper, iron ore, manganese, uranium, oil and coal.

The fertile pampas supports a strong and export-orientated agricultural sector; the main crops are cereals, oil-bearing seeds, fruit, tea, tobacco and livestock products, especially beef, mutton and wool.

The main industrial activities are food processing (meat-packing, flour-milling, sugar-refining, wine production) and the production of motor vehicles, consumer durables, textiles, chemicals, petrochemicals, printing, metallurgy and steel.

The main trading partners are Brazil, China and the USA. The principal exports include soya beans and derivatives, petroleum and gas, motor vehicles and cereals. The major imports are machinery, motor vehicles, petroleum and natural gas, organic chemicals and plastics.
GNI – US$503.1bn; US$11,200 per capita (2019)
Annual average growth of GDP – -2.03 per cent (2019 est)
Inflation rate – 25.7 per cent (2017 est)
Population below poverty line – 32.2 per cent (2016 est)
Unemployment – 9.84 per cent (2019 est)
Total external debt – US$214.9bn (2017 est)
Imports – US$88,061m (2017)
Exports – US$72,822m (2017)

BALANCE OF PAYMENTS
Trade – US$15,239m deficit (2017)
Current Account – US$3,997m deficit (2019)

Trade with UK	2018	2019
Imports from UK	£366,508,954	£392,289,310
Exports to UK	£634,632,954	£684,299,467

COMMUNICATIONS
Airports and waterways – 161, major airports include Buenos Aires, Córdoba, Rio Gallegos and Salta; 11,000km of waterways
Roadways and railways – 281,290km; 36,917km
Telecommunications – 9.8 million fixed lines and 58.6 million mobile subscriptions (2018); there were 33.2 million internet subscribers in 2018
Internet code and IDD – ar; 54 (from UK), 44 (to UK)
Major broadcasters – The privately owned Telefe and Canal 13 are the leading television broadcasters; Radio Nacional is the state-run radio broadcaster
Press – There are over 150 daily newspapers, including *Clarin, La Nación* and *Cronica*
WPFI score – 28.78 (64)

EDUCATION AND HEALTH
Education is compulsory until the age of 14.
Literacy rate – 99 per cent (2018 est)
Gross enrolment ratio (percentage of relevant age group) – primary 109.7 per cent, secondary 108.7 per cent, tertiary 90 per cent (2017 est)
Health expenditure (per capita) – US$1,324
Hospital beds (per 1,000 people) – 5 (2014)
Life expectancy (years) – 77.8 (2020 est)
Mortality rate – 7.4 (2020 est)
Birth rate – 16 (2020 est)
Infant mortality rate – 9 (2020 est)
HIV/AIDS adult prevalence – 0.4 per cent (2019 est)

ARGENTINE ANTARCTIC TERRITORY

The Argentine Antarctic Territory consists of the Antarctic Peninsula and a triangular section extending to the South Pole, defined as the area between 25°W. and 74°W. and 60°S. This overlaps with both Britain's and Chile's claimed areas (*see also* The North and South Poles). Administratively, the territory is a department of the province of Tierra del Fuego, Antarctica and South Atlantic Islands. The population varies seasonally between approximately 150 and 660 people, all of whom are scientific researchers and their dependants.

ARMENIA

Hayastani Hanrapetut'yun – Republic of Armenia

Area – 29,743 sq. km
Capital – Yerevan; population, 1,086,000 (2020 est)
Major cities – Gyumri, Vanadzor
Currency – Dram of 100 luma
Population – 3,021,324 falling at 0.3 per cent a year (2020 est); Armenian (98.1 per cent), Yezidi (1.2 per cent) (est)
Religion – Christian (Armenian Apostolic 92.6 per cent, other Christian 3.4 per cent) (est). The kingdom of Armenia was the first state to adopt Christianity as its official religion, in AD 301
Language – Armenian (official), Kurdish
Population density – 104 per sq. km (2019)
Urban population – 63.2 per cent (2019 est)
Median age (years) – 36.6 (2020 est)
National anthem – 'Mer Hayrenik' 'Our Fatherland'
National day – 21 September (Independence Day)
Death penalty – Abolished for all crimes (since 2003)
CPI score – 42 (77)
Military expenditure – US$609m (2018)
Conscription – 18–27 years of age; 2 years

CLIMATE AND TERRAIN

Landlocked Armenia is situated in the southwestern part of the Caucasus region. It lies at a high altitude and consists of vast plateaux surrounded by mountain ranges. The elevation extremes range from 4,090m (Mt Aragats) to 400m (Debed river). The climate is continental, with hot summers, cold winters and low rainfall. Armenia experiences occasional droughts and severe earthquakes.

POLITICS

The 1995 constitution has been amended by referendums multiple times, most recently in 2015. The unicameral National Assembly *(Azgayin Joghov)* has a minimum of 101 members who are directly elected for a five-year term. Changes to the constitution adopted in December 2015 aimed to transform the government to a parliamentary system: the prime minister is nominated by the ruling party for approval by assembly, and the president is elected by the National Assembly for a non-renewable, seven-year term.

Former president Serzh Sargsyan's Republican Party of Armenia (RPA) remained the largest party in the legislature following the 2017 election. The March 2018 election was the first in which the National Assembly elected its president; Armen Sarkisyan was chosen and the outgoing Sargsyan was appointed prime minister, but popular protests forced Sargsyan to resign six days after taking office. Opposition leader Nikol Pashinyan replaced him, but his Armenian National Congress party held no parliamentary majority. A snap parliamentary election was held in December 2018 in which Pashinyan's coalition, the My Step Alliance, won a landslide victory.

HEAD OF STATE
President, Armen Sarkisyan, *elected* 9 April 2018

SELECTED GOVERNMENT MEMBERS *AS AT NOVEMBER 2020*
Prime Minister, Nikol Pashinyan
Deputy Prime Ministers, Tigran Avinyan, Mher Grigoryan
Defence, Davit Tonoyan
Finance, Atom Janjughazyan

EMBASSY OF THE REPUBLIC OF ARMENIA
25A Cheniston Gardens, London W8 6TG
T 020-7938 5435 **E** armembassyuk@mfa.am
W http://uk.mfa.am/en
Ambassador Extraordinary and Plenipotentiary, vacant

BRITISH EMBASSY
34 Baghramyan Avenue, Yerevan 0019
T (+374) (10) 264 301 **E** enquiries.yerevan@fco.gov.uk
W www.gov.uk/government/world/armenia
Ambassador Extraordinary and Plenipotentiary, HE Judith Farnworth, *apptd* 2015

FOREIGN RELATIONS
There is a longstanding dispute with Azerbaijan over the predominantly Armenian-populated Azeri region of Nagorny-Karabakh; Armenia claims this territory as historically native land arbitrarily granted to Soviet Azerbaijan by Stalin in 1921–2. The territory's government voted to transfer to Armenia in 1988 but this was rejected by the USSR. When the USSR collapsed in 1991, the territory declared independence. Azeri attempts to reassert control were met with resistance, which escalated into a war that lasted from 1992 until a ceasefire was agreed between Armenia, Azerbaijan and Nagorny-Karabakh in 1994. By this time, Nagorno-Karabakh forces, supported by Armenia, had captured all of Nagorny-Karabakh, all Azeri territory that

Becomes part of the Roman Empire	East forcibly incorporated into Russian Empire, which concludes wars with Persia in 1813 and 1828		Declares independence		Accedes to the USSR	
*c.*190	1600	1915-8		1920		1991
64		1813	1918		1922	
First Armenian state founded	Incorporated into the Ottoman Empire; eastern areas fall under Persian control	Areas under Ottoman rule experience pogroms and over 1.5 million are deported or killed	Invaded by Soviet forces. Soviet Socialist Republic declared		Some 99 per cent of the electorate vote for independence, which is declared on 21 September	

separated Nagorny-Karabakh from Armenia and all mountainous Azeri territory around the enclave. Talks mediated by the Organisation for Security and Cooperation in Europe failed to make any progress towards a peaceful resolution until 2008, when Armenia and Azerbaijan agreed to intensify efforts, although recent years have seen stalled negotiations and regular ceasefire breaches. In September 2020 renewed fighting broke out, further complicated by Turkish support for Azerbaijan, that by November 2020 had resulted in several thousand casualties. The region, renamed the Republic of Artsakh in 2017, has limited international recognition and has remained closely reliant on Armenia.

ECONOMY AND TRADE

The economy experienced a severe decline following the break-up of the USSR in 1991, adding to existing problems arising from the 1988 earthquake and subsequently exacerbated by the Nagorny-Karabakh conflict and the consequent trade embargos imposed by Azerbaijan and Turkey, both of which are still in place. Economic liberalisation from 1994 brought sustained high growth and falls in inflation and poverty levels until the global economic crisis. Although a recovery began in 2010, corruption, the poor performance of the eurozone and Russian economies, and diplomatic isolation remain long-term threats to growth. High public debt, which led to a tightening of fiscal policies in recent years, has been exacerbated by the coronavirus pandemic and conflict with Azerbaijan in 2020. Armenia was a founding member of the Russia-led Eurasian Economic Union in January 2015, but has since forged closer ties with the EU.

The agricultural sector produces fruit, vegetables and livestock as cash crops, and grain; it contributes 16.7 per cent of GDP and employs 36.3 per cent of the workforce. There are large mineral deposits, including iron and copper ore, and non-ferrous metals. Industry, which contributes 28.2 per cent of GDP, is diversified and most small- and medium-sized enterprises are now privatised. The main activities are diamond-processing, the production of industrial machinery, vehicles and parts, textiles and clothing, chemicals, instruments, microelectronics, jewellery, software development and food processing. Remittances from expatriates working in Russia contribute 12 to 14 per cent of GDP.

The main trading partners are Russia, EU countries, Iran, other former Soviet bloc states, China and Iraq. Principal exports are pig iron, copper, non-ferrous metals, diamonds, mineral products, food and energy. The main imports are natural gas, petrol, tobacco products, foodstuffs and diamonds.

GNI – US$13.8bn; US$4,680 per capita (2019)
Annual average growth of GDP – 7.5 per cent (2017 est)
Inflation rate – 0.9 per cent (2017 est)
Population below poverty line – 32 per cent (2013 est)
Unemployment – 18.9 per cent (2017 est)
Total external debt – US$10.41bn (2017 est)
Imports – US$5,651m (2017)
Exports – US$4,132m (2017)

BALANCE OF PAYMENTS

Trade – US$1,518m deficit (2017)
Current Account – US$987.5m deficit (2019)

Trade with UK	2018	2019
Imports from UK	£13,893,420	£14,467,880
Exports to UK	£2,065,932	£1,679,607

COMMUNICATIONS

Airports – Ten
Roadways and railways – 7,700km; 780km
Telecommunications – 477,932 fixed lines and 3.6 million mobile subscriptions (2018); there were 2 million internet users in 2018
Internet code and IDD – am; 374 (from UK), 44 (to UK)
Major broadcasters – Public TV of Armenia (state-run) and Armenia TV (commercial), alongside 24 private television stations
Press – Daily newspapers include *Aravot, Aykakan Zhanamak* and the state-operated *Ayastani Anrapetutyun*
WPFI score – 28.60 (61)

EDUCATION AND HEALTH

State education is free and compulsory for all children aged seven to 14. Senior secondary school may be attended from the ages of 14 to 16.
Literacy rate – 99.7 per cent (2017 est)
Gross enrolment ratio (percentage of relevant age group) – primary 91.8 per cent, secondary 86.5 per cent, tertiary 51.5 per cent (2019 est)
Health expenditure (per capita) – US$408 (2017)
Hospital beds (per 1,000 people) – 4.2 (2015)
Life expectancy (years) – 75.6 (2020 est)
Mortality rate – 9.5 (2020 est)
Birth rate – 11.9 (2020 est)
Infant mortality rate – 11.5 (2020 est)
HIV/AIDS adult prevalence – 0.2 per cent (2019 est)

AUSTRALIA

Commonwealth of Australia

Area – 7,741,220 sq. km (excluding overseas territories)
Capital – Canberra; population, 457,000 (2020 est)
Major cities – Adelaide, Brisbane, Melbourne, Perth, Sydney
Currency – Australian dollar ($A) of 100 cents
Population – 25,466,459 rising at 1.4 per cent a year (2020 est)
Religion – Christian (Protestant 23.1 per cent, Roman Catholic 22.6 per cent, Orthodox 2.3 per cent), Muslim 2.6 per cent, Buddhist 2.4 per cent, Hindu 1.9 per cent (est)
Language – English, Mandarin, Italian, Arabic, Greek, Cantonese, Vietnamese, Aboriginal languages
Population density – 3 per sq. km (2019)
Urban population – 86.1 per cent (2019 est)
Median age (years) – 37.5 (2020 est)
National anthem – 'Advance Australia Fair'
National day – 26 January (Australia Day)
Death penalty – Abolished for all crimes (since 1985)
CPI score – 77 (12)
Military expenditure – US$26,712m (2018)

CLIMATE AND TERRAIN

The majority of Australia is a plateau, with hills, low mountain ranges and sparsely populated deserts in the interior, and tropical wetlands and rainforest in the north-east. Mountain ranges running down the east coast are the source of the Murray and Darling river systems, which flow across the densely populated fertile plain in the south-east. Off the north-east coast is the Great Barrier Reef, the world's largest coral reef. Elevation ranges from 2,229m (Mt Kosciuszko) to −15m (Lake Eyre). The climate is arid or semi-arid in the interior, tropical in the north and temperate in the south and east.

POLITICS

Under the 1901 constitution, the Commonwealth of Australia is a federation of six states. The constitution defines the powers of the federal government, and residuary legislative power remains with the states.

The head of state is Queen Elizabeth II, represented by the governor-general, who is appointed on the advice of the Australian prime minister. The bicameral parliament consists of the senate and the House of Representatives. The constitution provides that the number of members of the House of Representatives shall be proportionate to the population of each state, with a minimum of five members for each state, and that the number of senators shall be, as nearly as is practicable, half the number of representatives. There are currently 151 members, including two members for the Northern Territory and two for the Australian Capital Territory; they are directly elected for a three-year term. There are 76 senators; each state returns 12 senators, who are directly elected for a six-year term, with half retiring every third year. The Australian Capital Territory and the Northern Territory each return two senators, who are directly elected for a three-year term.

Each of the six states has its own constitution, executive, legislature and judicature. Executive authority is vested in a governor (appointed by the Crown), assisted by a council of ministers or executive council headed by a state premier. There are ten territories, and two – the Northern Territory and Australian Capital Territory – have limited self-government. Northern Territory has an executive authority headed by an administrator (appointed by the governor-general), and legislative assembly led by a chief minister; authority over Australian Capital Territory rests with the governor-general acting on the advice of the federal government. The other territories are directly administered by the federal government.

The Liberal–National coalition, led by Tony Abbott of the Liberal Party of Australia, defeated the incumbent Australian Labor Party (ALP) in the September 2013 federal elections, winning a significant overall majority in the House of Representatives, but not in the Senate. His victory ended seven years of government by the ALP and followed a divisive leadership battle within the party that saw deputy prime minister Julia Gillard challenge Kevin Rudd and become Australia's first woman prime minister in June 2010 and then relinquish the premiership back to him exactly three years later. In September 2015, Malcolm Turnbull replaced Tony Abbott as prime minister after the Liberal Party carried out a leadership ballot following plummeting opinion polls. Turnbull claimed victory in the closely fought July 2016 federal elections, but was replaced by the socially conservative Scott Morrison in August 2018 following a leadership contest. The Liberal–National coalition pulled off a surprise victory in the May 2019 legislative elections, winning a slim majority in the lower house.

Governor-General, HE David Hurley, *apptd* 2019

SELECTED GOVERNMENT MEMBERS *AS AT NOVEMBER 2020*
Prime Minister, Scott Morrison *sworn in* 24 August 2018
Deputy Prime Minister, Infrastructure and Transport, Michael McCormack
Defence, Linda Reynolds
Finance, Simon Birmingham
Foreign Affairs, Marise Payne

AUSTRALIAN HIGH COMMISSION
Australia House, Strand, London WC2B 4LA
T 020-7379 4334 **W** www.uk.embassy.gov.au
High Commissioner, HE George Brandis, CMG, MVO *apptd* 2019

BRITISH HIGH COMMISSION
Commonwealth Avenue, Yarralumla, Canberra, ACT 2600
T (+61) (2) 6270 6666 **E** canberra.enquiries@fconet.fco.gov.uk
W www.gov.uk/government/world/australia
High Commissioner, HE Victoria Treadell, *apptd* 2019

ECONOMY AND TRADE

Australia has a highly diversified and internationally competitive market economy that saw sustained strong growth from 1992 to 2016. It weathered the global downturn better than most developed countries, avoiding recession through a government fiscal stimulus package and low interest rates. Recent problems have been climate-related, with floods, droughts and extensive bush fires all affecting agriculture, mining and infrastructure, while the economy faces falls in key export commodity prices coupled with reduced demand from Asia and China. In September 2020 it entered its first recession since 1991 and experienced a record fall in economic activity due to the coronavirus pandemic. The service sector contributes 71.2 per cent of GDP and employs 75.3 per cent of the workforce, industry accounts for 25.3 per cent of GDP and 21.1 per cent of labour, and agriculture contributes 3.6 per cent of GDP and employs 3.6 per cent of the workforce.

The diversity of Australia's climate and soil conditions means that a wide range of crops can be grown, although most are confined to specific regions. Scant or erratic rainfall, limited scope for irrigation and unsuitable soils or topography have restricted intensive agriculture, although wheat is a major export, and sugar cane and fruit are important crops. Cattle and sheep ranching is widespread, providing meat, meat derivatives, wool and dairy products.

Significant natural resources include bauxite, coal, copper, diamonds, gold, iron ore, lead, mineral salts, nickel, silver, tin, tungsten, uranium, zinc, oil and natural gas. The main industrial activities are mining, the production of industrial

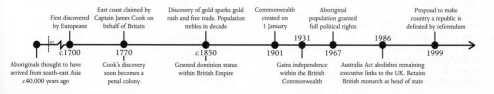

	East coast claimed by	Discovery of gold sparks gold	Commonwealth	Aboriginal		Proposal to make
First discovered by Europeans	Captain James Cook on behalf of Britain	rush and free trade. Population trebles in decade	created on 1 January	population granted full political rights		country a republic is defeated by referendum
				1931	1986	
c.1700	1770	*c*.1850	1901	1967		1999
Aboriginals thought to have arrived from south-east Asia *c*.40,000 years ago	Cook's discovery soon becomes a penal colony	Granted dominion status within British Empire	Gains independence within the British Commonwealth	Australia Act abolishes remaining executive links to the UK. Retains British monarch as head of state		

STATES AND TERRITORIES

	Capital	Premier	Area (sq. km)	Pop. (2020 est)
Australian Capital Territory (ACT)	Canberra	Andrew Barr*	2,358	429,800
New South Wales (NSW)	Sydney	Gladys Berejiklian	800,642	8,157,700
Northern Territory (NT)	Darwin†	Michael Gunner*	1,349,129	245,400
Queensland (Qld)	Brisbane	Annastacia Palaszczuk	1,730,648	5,160,000
South Australia (SA)	Adelaide	Steven Marshall	983,482	1,767,200
Tasmania (Tas.)	Hobart	Peter Gutwein	68,401	539,600
Victoria (Vic.)	Melbourne	Daniel Andrews	227,416	6,689,400
Western Australia (WA)	Perth	Mark McGowan	2,529,875	2,656,200

* Chief Minister
† Seat of Administration

and transport equipment, chemicals and steel, and food processing. Production and processing of hydrocarbon in the Timor Sea has controversially contributed billions to government revenue due to an unratified maritime border with Timor-Leste.

Over the past 20 years, the focus of Australia's trade, like its foreign policy, has shifted from Europe to Asia and the Pacific region. It is a leading member of the Asia-Pacific Economic Cooperation forum, and a free-trade agreement (FTA) between Australia and the Association of Southeast Asian Nations (ASEAN) countries entered into force in 2010; it also has FTAs with China (since 2015), Japan, Chile, South Korea and Malaysia. Major trading partners include China, Japan, South Korea, India, the USA and Thailand. The chief exports are coal, iron ore, gold, meat, wool, alumina, wheat, natural gas and alcohol. The main imports are machinery and transport equipment, computers, office and telecoms equipment, crude oil and petroleum products.
GNI – US$1,392.8bn; US$54,910 per capita (2019)
Annual average growth of GDP – 1.84 per cent (2019 est)
Inflation rate – 2.0 per cent (2017 est)
Unemployment – 5.16 per cent (2019 est)
Total external debt – US$1.71 trillion (2017 est)
Imports – US$288,611m (2017)
Exports – US$296,337m (2017)

BALANCE OF PAYMENTS
Trade – US$7,726m surplus (2017)
Current Account – US$8,400m surplus (2019)

Trade with UK	2018	2019
Imports from UK	£4,413,766,677	£4,327,584,778
Exports to UK	£2,960,505,676	£8,649,523,010

COMMUNICATIONS
Airports – 349; there are international airports in each of the eight territories
Waterways – 2,000km; major ports in all of the state capitals except Hobart
Roadways and railways – 873,573km; 36,064km
Telecommunications – 8.1 million fixed lines and 28.3 million mobile subscriptions (2018); there were 21.4 million internet subscribers in 2018
Internet country code and IDD – au; 61 (from UK), 11 41 (to UK)
Major broadcasters – The Australian Broadcasting Corporation (ABC) and Special Broadcasting Service (SBS), both public, provide radio and TV coverage; other major television networks include Australia Network and Foxtel (owned by News Corporation)
Press – Two major media groups – News Corp Australia and Fairfax Media – account for 85 per cent of newspaper sales; major titles include *The Sydney Morning Herald, The Australian* and *The Daily Telegraph*

WPFI score – 20.21 (26)

EDUCATION AND HEALTH
Education is administered by each state and territory, and is compulsory between the ages of five and 17.
Gross enrolment ratio (percentage of relevant age group) – primary 100.2 per cent, secondary 132.8 per cent, tertiary 107.8 per cent (2018 est)
Health expenditure (per capita) – US$408 (2017)
Hospital beds (per 1,000 people) – 3.8 (2014)
Life expectancy (years) – 82.4 (2020 est)
Mortality rate – 6.9 (2020 est)
Birth rate – 12.4 (2020 est)
Infant mortality rate – 3.1 (2020 est)
HIV/AIDS adult prevalence – 0.2 per cent (2019 est)

EXTERNAL TERRITORIES
Most of the territories are administered by the federal government through the Department of Regional Australia, Regional Development and Local Government; the Australian Antarctic Territory and the Territory of Heard Island and McDonald Islands are administered through the Australian Antarctic Division of the Department of Sustainability, Environment, Water, Population and Communities.

ASHMORE AND CARTIER ISLANDS
The Ashmore Islands (comprising Middle, East and West Islands) and Cartier Island are situated in the Indian Ocean 320km off Australia's north-west coast. The islands became an Australian territory in 1933. A nature reserve was established on Ashmore Reef in 1983 and a marine reserve around Cartier Island in 2000.

AUSTRALIAN ANTARCTIC TERRITORY
The Australian Antarctic Territory was established in 1933 and is 5,896,500 sq. km. It comprises all the islands and territories, other than Adélie Land, that are situated south of latitude 60°S. and lying between 160°E. longitude and 45°E. longitude. (*See also* The North and South Poles.)

CHRISTMAS ISLAND
Area – 135 sq. km
Population – 2,205 (2016 est) rising at 1.11 per cent a year (2014 est); Chinese (70 per cent), European (20 per cent), Malay (10 per cent) (est)
Religion – Muslim 19.4 per cent, Buddhist 18.3 per cent, Christian (Roman Catholic 8.8 per cent, Protestant 6.5 per cent, other Christian 3.3 per cent) (est)
Christmas Island is situated in the Indian Ocean about 1,565km north-west of Northwest Cape in Western Australia. The island was annexed by Britain in 1888. Sovereignty was transferred to Australia in 1958. The Shire of Christmas Island (SOCI) is responsible for local government services on the island; its council has nine members directly elected for a four-

year term. The main activities are phosphate mining, tourism and the government sector.

Administrator, Natasha Griggs, *apptd* 2018

COCOS (KEELING) ISLANDS
Area – 14 sq. km
Population – 596 (2014 est)
Religion – Muslim (predominantly Sunni) 75 per cent, Christian (Anglican 3.5 per cent, Roman Catholic 2.2 per cent) (2016 est)

The Cocos (Keeling) Islands are two separate atolls (North Keeling Island and, 24km to the south, the main atoll) comprising 27 small coral islands, situated in the Indian Ocean, about 2,950km north-west of Perth. The two inhabited islands of the southern atoll are West Island and Home Island, where around 80 per cent of the population lives, including most of the Cocos Malay community.

The islands were declared a British possession in 1857. In 1886 Queen Victoria granted all land in the islands to George Clunies-Ross and his heirs, who established coconut plantations worked by imported Malay labour. Sovereignty was transferred to Australia in 1955, and the government purchased the Clunies-Ross land and property in 1978, 1984 and 1993. The land is held in trust for the residents, with the local government body, the Shire of the Cocos (Keeling) Islands, as trustee. In 1984 the Cocos community, in a UN-supervised Act of Self-Determination, voted to integrate with Australia. The seven-member Shire Council of Cocos (Keeling) Islands is responsible for local government services. The public sector is the main employer and there is a little tourism; coconuts are the only cash crop.

Administrator, Natasha Griggs, *apptd* 2018

CORAL SEA ISLANDS TERRITORY
The Coral Sea Islands Territory lies east of Queensland between the Great Barrier Reef and longitude 156° 06′ E., and between latitudes 12°S. and 24°S. It comprises scattered islands, spread over a sea area of 780,000 sq. km. There is a manned meteorological station on Willis Island but otherwise the islands are uninhabited. Established in 1969, the territory is now a nature reserve, administered jointly by the Department of Sustainability, Environment, Water, Population and Communities, and the Department of Agriculture, Fisheries and Forestry.

HEARD ISLAND AND MCDONALD ISLANDS
The Territory of Heard Island and the McDonald Islands, about 4,100km south-west of Perth, comprises all the islands and rocks lying between 52° 30′ and 53° 30′ S. latitude and 72° and 74° 30′ E. longitude. The subantarctic islands, which have active volcanoes, were discovered in the 1850s and sovereignty was transferred from Britain to Australia in 1947. The islands are now part of a marine reserve established in 2002.

JERVIS BAY TERRITORY
Area – 76 sq. km
Population – 391 (2016 census)

The territory consists of 66 sq. km of land on the southern shore of Jervis Bay, 9 sq. km of marine waters and Bowen Island (0.5 sq. km), and lies about 200km south of Sydney. Originally part of New South Wales, the territory was acquired by the federal government in 1915 to provide Canberra with access to the sea. Much of the land and water now comprises Booderee National Park, leased from the Wreck Bay Aboriginal Community, who since the 1980s have been granted 90 per cent of the land. The main economic activity is tourism.

NORFOLK ISLAND
Area – 36 sq. km
Population – 1,748 (2016 census); Australian (22.8 per cent), English (22.4 per cent), Pitcairn (20 per cent) (est)
Religion – Christian (Protestant 46.8 per cent, Roman Catholic 12.6 per cent, other Christian 2.9 per cent) (est)
Seat of government – Kingston
National day – 8 June (Bounty Day)

Discovered by Captain Cook in 1774, Norfolk Island is situated in the South Pacific Ocean, about 1,600km north-east of Sydney. In 1856, 194 descendants of the *Bounty* mutineers accepted an invitation to leave Pitcairn and settle on Norfolk Island, which had served as a penal colony.

The island became a territory in 1914 and internally self-governing in 1979, but after financial difficulties it was absorbed into the state of New South Wales in 2016. A five-seat regional council is responsible for planning and managing public services. The economy is dependent on tourism; other economic activities include the sale of postage stamps and pine and palm seeds, livestock-rearing and agriculture.

Administrator, Eric Hutchinson, *apptd* 2017

AUSTRIA
Republik Österreich – Republic of Austria

Area – 83,871 sq. km
Capital – Vienna (Wien); population, 1,930,000 (2020 est)
Major cities – Graz, Innsbruck, Klagenfurt, Linz, Salzburg
Currency – Euro (€) of 100 cents
Population – 8,859,449 rising at 0.35 per cent a year (2020 est)
Religion – Christian (Catholic 57 per cent, Orthodox 8.7 per cent), Muslim 7.9 per cent (est)
Language – German (official), Croatian and Hungarian (official in Burgenland), Slovene (official in Carinthia), Turkish, Serbian
Population density – 107 per sq. km (2019)
Urban population – 58.5 per cent (2019 est)
Median age (years) – 44.5 (2020 est)
National anthem – 'Land der Berge, Land am Strome' 'Land of the Mountains, Land by the River'
National day – 26 October (date law of neutrality passed, 1955)
Death penalty – Abolished for all crimes (since 1968)
CPI score – 77 (12)
Military expenditure – US$3,367m (2018)
Conscription – 18–50 years of age, male only; 6 months

CLIMATE AND TERRAIN
The north and east of the country feature rolling hills in the river Danube basin, while the west and south contain the eastern Alps, which cover nearly two-thirds of the country. The highest point of elevation is 3,798m (Grossglockner) and the lowest is 115m (Neusiedler See). The climate is continental in the lowlands and alpine in the mountains, with average

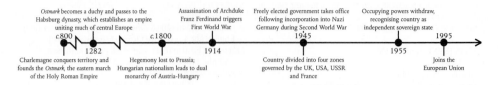

Ostmark becomes a duchy and passes to the Habsburg dynasty, which establishes an empire uniting much of central Europe
c.800

Assassination of Archduke Franz Ferdinand triggers First World War

Freely elected government takes office following incorporation into Nazi Germany during Second World War
1945

Occupying powers withdraw, recognising country as independent sovereign state
1995

1282
1914
1955

Charlemagne conquers territory and founds the Ostmark, the eastern march of the Holy Roman Empire

Hegemony lost to Prussia; Hungarian nationalism leads to dual monarchy of Austria-Hungary
c.1800

Country divided into four zones governed by the UK, USA, USSR and France

Joins the European Union

temperatures in Vienna ranging from −2.1°C in January to 16.4°C in July and August.

POLITICS

Under the 1955 constitution, the federal president is directly elected for a six-year term, renewable once. There is a bicameral legislature, the *Parlament,* consisting of the National Council *(Nationalrat),* which has 183 members directly elected for a four-year term, and the Federal Council *(Bundesrat),* which has 61 members elected for terms of five to six years by the provincial assemblies. Some powers may only be exercised by both houses acting together as the Federal Assembly *(Bundesversammlung).* The executive is headed by the federal chancellor, who is appointed by the president.

In the 2013 legislative elections, the Social Democrats (SPÖ) and the Austrian People's Party (ÖVP) remained the largest parties but both lost ground to the right-wing Freedom Party of Austria (FPÖ). In the October 2017 legislative elections the ÖVP, led by 31-year-old Sebastian Kurz, emerged as the largest party and formed a coalition with the far-right Freedom Party (FPO). The government collapsed in May 2019 after footage emerged of FPO leader Heinz-Christian Strache offering public contracts in return for Russian investment. Kurz was ousted by a vote of no confidence and Brigitte Bierlein was appointed chancellor of a nonpartisan interim government, and became the first woman to hold the post. Early elections were called for September 2019, in which the FPO and SPÖ lost substantial support in favour of the ÖVP and Green Party, the latter two forming a coalition government in January 2020. Kurz was re-appointed as chancellor.

The independent Alexander Van der Bellen won the December 2016 presidential election, defeating far-right candidate Norbert Hofer.

HEAD OF STATE

Federal President, Alexander Van der Bellen, *elected* 4 December 2016, *sworn in* 26 January 2017

SELECTED GOVERNMENT MEMBERS *AS AT NOVEMBER 2020*

Chancellor, Sebastian Kurz
Vice-Chancellor, Werner Kogler
Defence, Thomas Starlinger
Finance, Gernot Blümel

EMBASSY OF AUSTRIA

18 Belgrave Mews West, London SW1X 8HU
T 020-7344 3250 **E** london-ob@bmeia.gv.at
W www.bmeia.gv.at/london
Ambassador Extraordinary and Plenipotentiary, HE Michael Zimmerman, *apptd* 2018

BRITISH EMBASSY

Jaurèsgasse 12, 1030 Vienna
T (+43) (1) 716 130 **E** viennaconsularenquiries@fco.gov.uk
W www.gov.uk/government/world/austria
Ambassador Extraordinary and Plenipotentiary, HE Leigh Turner, CMG, *apptd* 2016

FEDERAL STRUCTURE

There are nine provinces *(Bundesländer):* Burgenland, Carinthia, Lower Austria, Salzburg, Styria, Tyrol, Upper Austria, Vienna and Vorarlberg. Each has its own assembly and government.

ECONOMY AND TRADE

Austria has a well-developed market economy, which is closely linked to other EU states. Its strong commercial links with central, eastern and southeastern Europe, an attraction for foreign investors in the past, increased its vulnerability in the global economic downturn, and its financial sector required state support. A combination of austerity policies since 2012 and the pro-business government elected in 2017 strengthened economic growth and reduced national debt, but the 2020 coronavirus pandemic pushed the economy into its deepest recession since the Second World War.

The services sector contributes most to GDP (70.3 per cent in 2017), followed by industry (28.4 per cent) and the small but highly developed agricultural sector (1.3 per cent). The main industries include tourism, construction, manufacturing of machinery, vehicles and parts, food processing, timber, production of metals and metal goods, chemicals, paper and cardboard, and electronics.

Austria's main trading partners are Germany, the USA, Italy and Switzerland. Exports, which account for around 60 per cent of GDP, principally include the goods produced by the main industries, iron and steel, and textiles. The main imports are machinery and equipment, vehicles, chemical products, metal goods, oil and oil products, and foodstuffs.

GNI – US$455.4bn; US$51,300 per capita (2019)
Annual average growth of GDP – 1.42 per cent (2019 est)
Inflation rate – 2.2 per cent (2019 est)
Population below poverty line – 3 per cent (2017 est)
Unemployment – 7.35 per cent (2019 est)
Total external debt – US$630.8bn (2017 est)
Imports – US$210,770m (2017)
Exports – US$223,437m (2017)

BALANCE OF PAYMENTS

Trade – US$12,667m surplus (2017)
Current Account – US$12,666m surplus (2019)

Trade with UK	2018	2019
Imports from UK	£2,001,564,938	£1,870,867,440
Exports to UK	£3,833,249,221	£3,932,180,987

COMMUNICATIONS

Airports – 50; principal airports include Vienna, Salzburg and Innsbruck
Waterways – 358km of navigable waterways; considerable trade through Danube ports (Vienna, Krems, Enns, Linz)
Roadways and railways – 137,039km; 5,800km
Telecommunications – 3.8 million fixed lines and 10.9 million mobile subscriptions (2018); there were 7.7 million internet subscribers in 2018
Internet code and IDD – at; 43 (from UK), 44 (to UK)
Major broadcasters – Österreichischer Rundfunk (ÖRF) (public) and ATV (commercial)

Press – Regional newspapers compete effectively against national publications. Leading titles include *Die Presse, Kleine Zeitung* (Graz), *Wiener Zeitung* (Vienna), *Der Standard* and *Der Kurier*
WPFI score – 15.78 (18)

EDUCATION AND HEALTH

Education is free and compulsory from six to 15.
Gross enrolment ratio (percentage of relevant age group) – primary 103.3 per cent, secondary 100 per cent, tertiary 86.7 per cent (2018 est)
Health expenditure (per capita) – US$4,940 (2017)
Hospital beds (per 1,000 people) – 7.6 (2013)
Life expectancy (years) – 81.9 (2020 est)
Mortality rate – 9.8 (2020 est)
Birth rate – 9.5 (2020 est)
Infant mortality rate – 3.3 (2020 est)

AZERBAIJAN

Azarbaycan Respublikasi – Republic of Azerbaijan

Area – 86,600 sq. km
Capital – Baku (Baki); population, 2,341,000 (2020 est)
Major cities – Ganca, Sumqayit
Currency – New Manat of 100 gopik
Population –10,205,810 rising at 0.77 per cent a year (2020 est); Azeri (91.6 per cent), Lezghin (2 per cent), Armenian (1.3 per cent), Russian (1.3 per cent), Talysh (1.3 per cent) (2009). There are more Azeris in Iran than in Azerbaijan. Almost all of the Armenian population lives in the Nagorny-Karabakh enclave
Religion – Muslim 96.9 per cent (predominantly Shia), Christian 3 per cent (est)
Language – Azeri (official), Russian, Armenian
Population density – 120 per sq. km (2019)
Urban population – 56 per cent (2019 est)
Median age (years) – 32.6 (2020 est)
National anthem – 'Azerbaijan Marsi' 'March of Azerbaijan'
National day – 28 May (founding of the republic, 1918)
Death penalty – Abolished for all crimes (since 1998)
CPI score – 30 (126)
Military expenditure – US$1,709m (2018)
Conscription – 18–35 years of age, male only; 18 months, or 12 months for university graduates

CLIMATE AND TERRAIN

Azerbaijan lies on the western shore of the Caspian Sea, in the eastern part of the Caucasus region. It includes the exclave of Nakhichevana, separated from it by Armenia. The north-east of Azerbaijan rises to the southeastern end of the main Great Caucasus mountain range; to the country's south-west lie the lower Caucasus hills, and in its southeastern corner the spurs of the Talysh Ridge. Central Azerbaijan lies in a low plain irrigated by the river Kura and the lower reaches of its tributary the Araks. Elevation ranges from 4,485m (Bazarduzu Dagi) to −28m (Caspian Sea). Climate and landscape vary greatly, but rainfall is generally low.

POLITICS

The 1995 constitution was amended in 2002 when the limit on presidential terms was restricted to two terms, but this was subsequently abolished in 2009 and presidential terms extended from five to seven years in 2016. The executive president is directly elected, as is the unicameral National Assembly *(Milli Majlis),* which has 125 members serving five-year terms. The president appoints the prime minister and the cabinet.

Ilham Aliyev was re-elected for a fourth term in 2018. The New Azerbaijan Party, which is aligned with President Aliyev, retained its majority in the February 2020 legislative elections; observers noted that the restrictive political environment and limits on freedom restricted genuine competition. For dispute with Armenia over the Nagorny-Karabakh region *see* Armenia, Foreign Relations.

HEAD OF STATE
President, Ilham Aliyev, *sworn in* 31 October 2003, *re-elected* 2008, 2013, 2018

SELECTED GOVERNMENT MEMBERS *AS AT NOVEMBER 2020*
Prime Minister, Ali Asadov
First Deputy Prime Minister, Yagub Abdulla Eyyubov
Deputy Prime Ministers, Ali Ahmadov; Shahin Mustafayev
Defence, Col.-Gen. Zakir Hasanov

EMBASSY OF THE REPUBLIC OF AZERBAIJAN
4 Kensington Court, London W8 5DL
T 020-7938 3412 **E** london@mission.mfa.gov.az
W www.azembassy.org.uk
Ambassador Extraordinary and Plenipotentiary, HE Tahir Taghizade, *apptd* 2014

BRITISH EMBASSY
45 Khagani Street, Baku AZ 1010
T (+994) (12) 437 7878 **E** generalenquiries.baku@fco.gov.uk
W www.gov.uk/government/world/azerbaijan
Ambassador Extraordinary and Plenipotentiary, HE James Sharp, *apptd* 2019

ECONOMY AND TRADE

Despite high economic growth in recent years, Azerbaijan's transition from a command to a market economy is slow. This has been exacerbated by its failure to attract foreign investment in sectors other than energy, widespread corruption and systemic inefficiencies. The economy is dominated by oil and natural gas extraction and related industries, centred in Baku and Sumqayit, and exploited through co-production deals with foreign companies. Oil pipelines (1,424km) link the Azeri oilfields to Black Sea ports in Russia, Georgia and Turkey. The completion of the Southern Gas Corridor between Azerbaijan and Europe, expected around 2021, will also boost revenues. Diversifying the economy is a long-term goal, but efforts have been hindered by a struggling state-owned financial sector. Although the country's sovereign oil fund remains one of the wealthiest in the world, the sharp fall in oil prices and tourism due to the coronavirus pandemic in 2020 resulted in economic contraction.

Although agriculture contributes only 6.1 per cent of GDP, it employs 37 per cent of the workforce. The main crops are cotton, cereals, rice, fruit, vegetables, tea, tobacco and

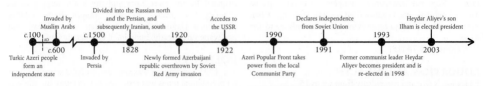

livestock. Industry, which contributes 53.5 per cent of GDP, produces oil, natural gas, petroleum products, oilfield equipment, steel, iron ore, cement, chemicals, petrochemicals and textiles.

Russia and other former Soviet republics are increasingly being replaced as trade partners by Turkey, China, the USA and various European countries. Oil and gas constitute around 90 per cent of exports, which also include machinery, cotton and foodstuffs. Principal imports are machinery and equipment, foodstuffs, metals and chemicals.

GNI – US$44.9bn; US$4,480 per capita (2019)
Annual average growth of GDP – 0.1 per cent (2017 est)
Inflation rate – 13.0 per cent (2017 est)
Population below poverty line – 4.9 per cent (2015 est)
Unemployment – 5 per cent (2017 est)
Total external debt – US$16.62bn (2017 est)
Imports – US$17,105m (2017)
Exports – US$19,840m (2017)

BALANCE OF PAYMENTS
Trade – US$2,735m surplus (2017)
Current Account – US$4,365m surplus (2019)

Trade with UK	2018	2019
Imports from UK	£969,530,352	£1,941,163,011
Exports to UK	£288,324,390	£205,766,948

COMMUNICATIONS
Airports – 23; international airports at Baku, Ganca, Lankaran and Nakhichevan
Waterways – The Baku International Sea Trade port provides links to Turkmenistan and other trade and passenger routes
Roadways and railways – 24,981km; 2,944km
Telecommunications – 1.7 million fixed lines and 10.4 million mobile telephone subscriptions (2014); there were 8 million internet users in 2016
Internet – az; 994 (from UK), 44 (to UK)
Major broadcasters – AzTV, Azerbaijan Radio (state-run), iTV and ANS TV
Press – Printing presses are generally reserved for pro-government titles such as *Azarbaycan;* opposition newspapers include *Azadliq* and *Yeni Musavat*
WPFI score – 58.48 (168)

EDUCATION AND HEALTH
Education up to university level is free.
Literacy rate – 99.8 per cent (2017 est)
Gross enrolment ratio (percentage of relevant age group) – primary 98 per cent, secondary 94.8 per cent, tertiary 31.5 per cent (2019 est)
Health expenditure (per capita) – US$1,720 (2017)
Hospital beds (per 1,000 people) – 4.7 (2013)
Life expectancy – 73.6 (2020 est)
Mortality rate – 7 (2020 est)
Birth rate – 14.5 (2020 est)
Infant mortality rate – 21.3 (2020 est)
HIV/AIDS adult prevalence – 0.2 per cent (2019 est)

THE BAHAMAS
Commonwealth of the Bahamas

Area – 13,880 sq. km
Capital – Nassau, on New Providence; population, 280,000 (2018 est)
Major city – Freeport, on Grand Bahama
Currency – Bahamian dollar (B$) of 100 cents
Population – 337,721 rising at 0.75 per cent a year (2020 est)
Religion – Christian (Protestant 69.9 per cent, Roman Catholic 12 per cent, other Christian 13 per cent) (est)
Language – English (official), Creole
Population density – 39 per sq. km (2019)
Urban population – 83.1 per cent (2019 est)
Median age (years) – 32.8 (2020 est)
National anthem – 'March on, Bahamaland'
National day – 10 July (Independence Day)
Death penalty – Retained
CPI score – 64 (29)
Health expenditure (per capita) – US$1,772 (2017)
Life expectancy (years) – 73.3 (2020 est)
Mortality rate – 7.4 (2020 est)
Birth rate – 14.8 (2020 est)
Infant mortality rate – 10.6 (2020 est)
HIV/AIDS adult prevalence – 3.2 per cent (2019 est)

CLIMATE AND TERRAIN
The Bahamas consist of more than 700 islands and 2,400 cays, all low-lying. The highest point is 63m (Mt Alvernia, on Cat Island) and the lowest 0m (Atlantic Ocean). The principal islands include: Abaco Islands, Acklins, Andros, Berry Islands, Bimini, Cat Island, Crooked Island, Eleuthera, Exuma, Grand Bahama, Great Inagua, Harbour Island, Long Island, Mayaguana, New Providence, Ragged Island, Rum Cay, San Salvador and Spanish Wells. The 14 major islands are inhabited, as are a few of the smaller islands. The climate is semitropical. The hurricane season is June to November.

HISTORY AND POLITICS
The islands were discovered by Columbus in 1492, settled by the British from the 17th century and became a crown colony in 1717. The Bahamas became internally self-governing in 1964 and gained independence on 10 July 1973.

The Progressive Liberal Party (PLP) held power for 25 years until the Free National Movement (FNM) won an absolute majority in the 1992 general election. Power has subsequently alternated between the two parties. The FNM, led by Hubert Minnis, overturned the PLP's majority in legislative elections in May 2017.

The head of state is Queen Elizabeth II, who is represented by a governor-general. The bicameral parliament has a senate of 16 appointed members and a House of Assembly of 39 members; both chambers serve a five-year term.

Governor-General, HE Sir Cornelius Smith, GCMG, *apptd* 2019

SELECTED GOVERNMENT MEMBERS *AS AT NOVEMBER 2020*
Prime Minister, Hubert Minnis
Deputy Prime Minister, Finance, Peter Turnquest
Foreign Affairs, Darren Henfield

HIGH COMMISSION OF THE COMMONWEALTH OF THE BAHAMAS
10 Chesterfield Street, London W1J 5JL
T 020-7408 4488 **E** information@bahamashclondon.net
W www.bahamashclondon.net
High Commissioner, HE Ellison Greenslade, *apptd* 2017

BRITISH HIGH COMMISSION
High Commissioner, HE Sarah Dickson, *apptd* 2019

ECONOMY AND TRADE
The economy, one of the wealthiest in the Caribbean, is dominated by tourism and offshore financial services, which together contribute around 65 per cent of GDP. The economy entered recession in 2007–11 when the service industry was disrupted by the global financial crisis and the number of tourists from the USA (about 80 per cent of all visitors) declined. The economy contracted slightly, returned to growth in 2017, but was significantly impacted by loss of tourism in 2020 due to the coronavirus pandemic. The island chain is vulnerable to environmental change, especially hurricanes that have increased the nation's high level of public debt in recent years; Hurricane Dorian caused an estimated US$3.4bn of damage in September 2019. The country remains a low-tax state, charging neither corporation nor income tax, though a sales tax was introduced for the first time in January 2015.

Manufacturing and agriculture account for 10 per cent of GDP and 12 per cent of employment. Agriculture centres mainly on fresh vegetables, citruses, meat and eggs. Mineral reserves produce aragonite and salt for export. Other industries include rum, pharmaceuticals and the provision of oil trans-shipment services.

The main trading partners are the USA (83 per cent of imports and 63.9 per cent of exports) and Namibia. The chief exports are mineral products, lobsters and polystyrene products. Imports are chiefly machinery and transport equipment, manufactured articles, chemicals, fuel, foodstuffs and livestock.
GNI – US$12.4bn; US$31,780 per capita (2019)
Annual average growth of GDP – 1.4 per cent (2017 est)
Inflation rate – 1.4 per cent (2017 est)
Population below poverty line – 9.3 per cent (2010 est)
Unemployment – 10.1 per cent (2017 est)
Total external debt – US$17.56bn (2013 est)
Imports – US$5,177m (2017)
Exports – US$3,434m (2017)

BALANCE OF PAYMENTS
Trade – US$1,713m deficit (2017)
Current Account – US$84m surplus (2019)

Trade with UK	2018	2019
Imports from UK	£51,436,077	£35,524,999
Exports to UK	£6,315,385	£5,565,843

COMMUNICATIONS
Airports – 54; international airports are operated from Andros, Chubb Cay, Eleuthera, Exuma, Grand Bahama and New Providence
Waterways – The main ports are Nassau (New Providence), Freeport and South Riding Point (Grand Bahama); the Bahamas is a major ship registry
Roadways – 2,700km
Telecommunications – 113,455 fixed lines and 381,591 mobile phone subscriptions (2018); there were 282,739 internet users in 2016
Internet code and IDD – bs; 1 242 (from UK), 011 44 (to UK)
Major broadcasters – The public Broadcasting Corporation of the Bahamas (BCB) operates ZNS TV and ZNS Bahamas (radio)
Press – Daily newspapers include *The Nassau Guardian, The Tribune* and *The Freeport News*

BAHRAIN
Mamlakat al-Bahrayn – Kingdom of Bahrain

Area – 760 sq. km
Capital – Manama; population, 635,000 (2020 est)
Major towns – Al Muharraq, Ar Rifa, Madinat Hamad
Currency – Bahraini dinar (BD) of 1,000 fils
Population – 1,505,003 rising at 2.08 per cent a year (2020 est); Bahraini (46 per cent), Asian (45.5 per cent) (est)
Religion – Muslim 73.7 per cent, Christian 9.3 per cent, other 16.9 (est); Islam is the state religion
Language – Arabic (official), English, Farsi, Urdu
Population density – 2,017 per sq. km (2019)
Urban population – 89.4 per cent (2019 est)
Median age (years) – 32.9 (2020 est)
National anthem – 'Bahrainona' 'Our Bahrain'
National day – 16 December (date of independence from British protection, 1971)
Death penalty – Retained
CPI score – 47 (77)
Military expenditure – US$1,397m (2018)
Literacy rate – 97.5 per cent (2018 est)
Gross enrolment ratio (percentage of relevant age group) – primary 98 per cent, secondary 97.1 per cent, tertiary 55.6 per cent (2019 est)
Health expenditure (per capita) – US$1,127 (2017)
Life expectancy (years) – 79.4 (2020 est)
Mortality rate – 2.8 (2020 est)
Birth rate – 12.7 (2020 est)
Infant mortality rate – 8.3 (2020 est)

CLIMATE AND TERRAIN

Bahrain consists of an archipelago of 36 low-lying islands situated approximately halfway down the Persian Gulf, some 32km off the east coast of Saudi Arabia. The largest of these, Bahrain Island, is about 48km long and 16km wide at its broadest. Elevation extremes range from 122m (Jabal ad Dukhan) to 0m at sea level. The climate is arid, hot and humid, with average maximum temperatures ranging from 16°C in January to 37.1°C in July.

HISTORY AND POLITICS

Bahrain was ruled by Persia (Iran) from 1602 until it was ousted in 1783 by the al-Khalifa family, which remains in power. The emirate was a British protectorate from 1820 until 1971, when it became independent. In 1975 the legislature was suspended and the emir assumed virtually absolute power after clashes between Sunni and Shia factions. Moves to return to democratic rule were made in response to civil agitation in the 1990s, until Sheikh Hamad succeeded to the throne and initiated the transition to a constitutional monarchy. The 2002 constitution established Bahrain as a kingdom and a constitutional monarchy, and legalised elections. There has been ongoing agitation for further democratisation, particularly by the Shia majority against the predominantly Sunni authorities.

In February 2011 this flared up into mass demonstrations that the government repressed brutally from March, when martial law was declared and the Pearl monument, the focal point of the demonstrations in Manama, was demolished. A report into the unrest, commissioned by Sheikh Hamad, was released in November 2011 and confirmed the practice of torture and infringements of human rights; in response, the ruler vowed to 'learn lessons' from the unrest and promised to reform the country's laws to make them compatible with international standards. In October 2014, one month before legislative elections, al-Wefaq, the main Shia political organisation, was banned from operating for three months, although it had previously announced it would boycott the vote, maintaining that the current electoral system fails to represent the country's Shia majority.

A resolution to the unrest has failed to materialise. The 2014 legislative elections saw low voter turnout as al-Wefaq lost all of its 18 seats. The November 2018 elections were labelled a 'sham' by UN officials amid a clampdown on dissent and press freedom; al-Wefaq claimed voter turnout was below 30 per cent.

Under the 2002 constitution, the country is a hereditary constitutional monarchy with the king as head of state. The king appoints the cabinet. The bicameral National Assembly consists of a lower house, the Council of Representatives, and an upper house, the Consultative Council. The lower house has 40 members directly elected for a four-year term, and the upper house has 40 members appointed by the king for a four-year term. The 2002 constitution granted women the right to vote and to stand for election.

HEAD OF STATE

HH The King of Bahrain, Sheikh Hamad bin Isa al-Khalifa, KCMG, *C-in-C of the Armed Forces, succeeded as emir* 6 March 1999, *proclaimed king* 14 February 2002
Crown Prince, First Deputy Prime Minister, HRH Sheikh Salman bin Hamad al-Khalifa

SELECTED GOVERNMENT MEMBERS *AS AT NOVEMBER 2020*
Prime Minister, HH Sheikh Khalifa bin Salman al-Khalifa
Deputy Prime Ministers, Sheikh Khalid bin Abdulla al-Khalifa; Sheikh Ali bin Khalifa al-Khalifa; Sheikh Mohammad bin Mubarak al-Khalifa; Sheikh Jawad bin Salim al-Arrayed

Defence, Maj.-Gen. Abdulla bin Hassan al-Nuaimi
Finance, Sheikh Salman bin Khalifa al-Khalifa
Foreign Affairs, SAbdullatif bin Rashid al-Zayani

EMBASSY OF THE KINGDOM OF BAHRAIN
30 Belgrave Square, London SW1X 8QB
T 020-7201 9170 **E** information@bahrainembassy.co.uk
W www.bahrainembassy.co.uk
Ambassador Extraordinary and Plenipotentiary, HE Sheikh Fawaz bin Mohammad al-Khalifa, *apptd* 2015

BRITISH EMBASSY
PO Box 114, 21 Government Avenue, Manama 306
T (+973) 1757 4100 **W** www.gov.uk/government/world/bahrain
Ambassador Extraordinary and Plenipotentiary, HE Roderick Drummond, CMG, *apptd* 2019

ECONOMY AND TRADE

Bahrain was one of the first Gulf states to discover oil, in the 1930s, but reserves and production are lower than in neighbouring countries. Despite attempting to diversify its economy, particularly as a regional financial and business centre, low oil prices resulted in a budget deficit of nearly 10 per cent of GDP in 2017, which was further exacerbated by sharp fall in prices during the 2020 coronavirus pandemic. Petroleum production and refining still accounts for 85 per cent of government revenue and around 70 per cent of total export receipts. Other industries include petrochemicals, aluminium smelting, tourism, ship repair and fertilisers. Bahrain's main trading partners are the UAE, Saudi Arabia, China and the USA, with whom a Free Trade Agreement was agreed in 2006.

GNI – US$36.3bn; US$22,110 per capita (2019)
Annual average growth of GDP – 2.5 per cent (2019 est)
Inflation rate – 1.4 per cent (2017 est)
Unemployment – 3.6 per cent (2017 est)
Total external debt – US$52.2bn (2017 est)
Imports – US$23,718m (2017)
Exports – US$26,505m (2017)

BALANCE OF PAYMENTS
Trade – US$2,787m surplus (2017)
Current Account – US$2,434m deficit (2018)

Trade with UK	2018	2019
Imports from UK	£491,798,378	£504,031,606
Exports to UK	£284,362,945	£287,110,122

COMMUNICATIONS

Airports – Four; Bahrain International Airport is a major air traffic centre in the Gulf
Waterways – The main ports are Khalifa bin Salman and Mina Salman
Roadways – There are 4,122km of paved roadways; the four main islands are connected by causeways, and a 25km causeway links Bahrain to Saudi Arabia
Telecommunications – 274,733 fixed lines and 2.1 million mobile phone subscriptions (2018); there were 1.4 million internet users in 2016
Internet code and IDD – bh; 973 (from UK), 44 (to UK)
Major broadcasters – State-run Bahrain Radio and Television Corporation (BRTC) operates radio networks and five terrestrial TV networks. Bahrain suspended the Saudi-financed al-Arab satellite news TV channel from operating in February 2015
Press – Six daily newspapers are published, including *Akhbar al-Khaleej, Al-Ayam* and *Al-Wasat*
WPFI score – 60.13 (169)

BANGLADESH

Gana Prajatantri Bangladesh – People's Republic of Bangladesh

Area – 148,460 sq. km
Capital – Dhaka; population, 21,006,000 (2020 est)
Major cities – Chittagong, Gazipur, Khulna, Narayanganj
Currency – Taka (Tk) of 100 paisa
Population – 162,650,853 rising at 0.98 per cent a year
   (2020 est); Bengali (98 per cent) (est)
Religion – Muslim 89.1 per cent (predominantly Sunni),
   Hindu 10 per cent (est)
Language – Bangla (official), English
Population density – 1,240 per sq. km (2019)
Urban population – 37.4 per cent (2019 est)
Median age (years) – 27.9 (2020 est)
National anthem – 'Amar Shonar Bangla' 'My Golden Bengal'
National day – 26 March (Independence Day)
Death penalty – Retained
CPI score – 26 (146)
Military expenditure – US$3,895m (2018)

CLIMATE AND TERRAIN

Although hilly in the south-east and north-east, over 75 per cent of the country is less than 3m above sea level, situated on the alluvial plain and delta of the Ganges (Padma)–Brahmaputra (Jamuna)–Meghna river system, which empties into the Bay of Bengal, the largest estuarine delta in the world. The highest elevation is 1,230m (Keokradong) and the lowest 0m at the Indian Ocean. The climate is tropical, with a monsoon season (June–September) during which heavy rainfall causes flooding in around one-third of the country each year; annual average rainfall is up to 2,339mm.

HISTORY AND POLITICS

Bangladesh consists of what was the eastern part of Bengal province and the Sylhet district of Assam province in British India. On independence in 1947, these territories acceded to Pakistan, forming the province of East Bengal (renamed East Pakistan in 1955). Tensions between East and West Pakistan (separated by over 1,600km) caused the East to secede in 1971. After months of civil war, and following the intervention of India, Bangladesh achieved independence from Pakistan on 16 December 1971.

Since independence, Bangladesh has experienced periods of political instability, with a number of coups and attempted coups, the assassinations of President Mujibar Rahman (1975) and President Zia (1981), and periods of government under martial law (1975–8, 1982–6) or a state of emergency (1987–8, 2007–8). Since 2014 the country has faced a campaign of high-profile violence by Islamists against atheists and secular intellectuals.

Parliamentary government has remained in place since 1991, despite occasional boycotts of parliament. Governments have been formed, or coalition governments led, by one of the two main parties: the Bangladesh Nationalist Party (BNP), led by Khaleda Zia (widow of President Zia), in 1991–6 and 2001–6; and the Awami League, led by Sheikh Hasina Wajed (daughter of President Rahman), in 1996–2001 and since January 2009.

A boycott of the 2014 legislative election by the BNP resulted in a default win and overwhelming majority for the Awami League (AL), with the party gaining 234 seats to the BNP's 34. Mohammad Abdul Hamid (AL) was elected president unopposed in 2013, and was re-elected unopposed in February 2018. Political unrest in early 2015, which aimed to bring about early elections, resulted in at least 50 deaths, with the BNP leader herself charged with instigating an arson attack that killed seven people. The first contested election in a decade took place in December 2018, with a landslide win for the AL-led Grand Alliance, which claimed 96 per cent of seats. Opposition parties rejected the results.

The head of state is the president, elected by the legislature for a five-year term, renewable once. The unicameral parliament, *Jatiya Sangsad,* has 300 directly elected members and 50 women members indirectly elected, all serving five-year terms. The president appoints as prime minister the majority party leader in parliament, and president selects the cabinet on the advice of the prime minister.

HEAD OF STATE
President, Mohammad Abdul Hamid, *elected* 22 April 2013,
   re-elected 7 February 2018

SELECTED GOVERNMENT MEMBERS *AS AT NOVEMBER 2020*
Prime Minister, Defence, Sheikh Hasina Wajed
Finance, Abu Hena Mohammed Mustafa Kamal
Foreign Affairs, Abul Kalam Abdul Momen

HIGH COMMISSION FOR THE PEOPLE'S REPUBLIC OF BANGLADESH
28 Queen's Gate, London SW7 5JA
T 020-7584 0081 E info@bhclondon.org.uk
W www.bhclondon.org.uk
High Commissioner, HE Saida Muna Tasneem, *apptd* 2018

BRITISH HIGH COMMISSION
PO Box 6079, United Nations Road, Baridhara, Dhaka 1212
T (+880) (2) 882 2705 E press.dhaka@fco.gov.uk
W www.gov.uk/government/world/bangladesh
High Commissioner, HE Robert Chatterton Dickson, *apptd* 2019

ECONOMY AND TRADE

Bangladesh has a fast-growing but poor economy, highly dependent on foreign aid. Nearly a quarter of the population lives below the poverty line. Many migrate to the Gulf states and south-east Asia to find work, and their remittances, which totalled US$13bn in 2016–17, and garment manufacturing (80 per cent of exports) are the mainstay of the economy. These fuelled steady growth of 6 per cent a year from the mid-1990s, which continued throughout the global downturn and rose to 7.9 per cent in 2019, before the coronavirus pandemic resulted in a small contraction in 2020. Political instability, poor infrastructure, slow implementation of economic reforms, corruption, inflation and unreliable power supplies are obstacles to greater growth.

The service and industrial sectors account for 56.5 per cent and 29.3 per cent of GDP respectively. Although the smallest contributor to GDP (14.2 per cent), agriculture is the primary occupation of 42.7 per cent of the workforce. The chief industries are based on processing agricultural and fisheries products such as cotton, jute, tea, sugar, fish and seafood, the manufacture of textiles, garments, newsprint, cement and fertiliser, and light engineering. Most exports are to the USA and EU countries; imports come mainly from China, India and Singapore.

GNI – US$316bn; US$1,940 per capita (2019)
Annual average growth of GDP – 7.4 per cent (2017 est)
Inflation rate – 5.6 per cent (2017 est)
Population below poverty line – 24.3 per cent (2016 est)
Unemployment – 4.4 per cent (2017 est)
Total external debt – US$50.26bn (2017 est)
Imports – US$56,820m (2017)
Exports – US$39,158m (2017)

BALANCE OF PAYMENTS
Trade – US$17,661m deficit (2017)
Current Account – US$3,434m deficit (2019)

Trade with UK	2018	2019
Imports from UK	£298,065,115	£407,699,438
Exports to UK	£2,737,173,139	£3,027,521,304

COMMUNICATIONS
Airports – 16, including international airports at Dhaka, Chittagong and Sylhet
Waterways – Principal seaports are Chittagong and Mongla, and there are smaller ports in Chalna and Khulna; the 8,370km of waterways are a key element of the transport infrastructure, although reduced to 5,200km in dry season
Roadways and railways – There are 110,311 paved roads and 258,794 unpaved roads; 2,460km
Telecommunications – 1.5 million fixed lines and 161.7 million mobile phone subscriptions (2018); there were 23.9 million internet users in 2018
Internet country code and IDD – bd; 880 (from UK), 44 (to UK)
Major broadcasters – The government-run Bangladesh Television (BTV) and Radio Bangladesh are the principal channels; private broadcasters include ATN Bangla, Channel i and NTV
Press – Leading titles include English-language dailies *New Age, The New Nation* and *The Independent,* and the Bangla *Daily Prothom Alo, Dainik Ittefaq* and *Dainik Jugantor*
WPFI score – 49.37 (151)

EDUCATION AND HEALTH
Education is compulsory and free for children aged six to ten, but drop-out rates are high.
Literacy rate – 74.7 per cent (2019 est)
Gross enrolment ratio (percentage of relevant age group) – primary 116.5 per cent (2018 est); secondary 72.6 per cent, tertiary 24 per cent (2019 est)
Health expenditure (per capita) – US$36 (2017)
Hospital beds (per 1,000 people) – 0.8 (2015)
Life expectancy (years) – 74.2 (2020 est)
Mortality rate – 5.5 (2020 est)
Birth rate – 18.1 (2020 est)
Infant mortality rate – 28.3 (2020 est)
HIV/AIDS adult prevalence – 0.1 per cent (2019 est)

BARBADOS

Area – 430 sq. km
Capital – Bridgetown, in the parish of St Michael; population, 89,000 (2018 est)
Currency – Barbados dollar (BD$) of 100 cents
Population – 294,560 rising at 0.23 per cent a year (2020 est)
Religion – Christian (Protestant 66.4 per cent, including 23.9 per cent Anglican, Roman Catholic 3.8 per cent), Rastafarian 1 per cent (est)
Language – English (official), Bajan
Population density – 667 per sq. km (2019)
Urban population – 31.2 per cent (2019 est)
Median age (years) – 39.5 (2019 est)
National anthem – 'In Plenty and in Time of Need'
National day – 30 November (Independence Day)
Death penalty – Retained
CPI score – 62 (30)

CLIMATE AND TERRAIN
Barbados is the most easterly of the Caribbean islands. The land rises gently to central highlands, and elevation extremes range from 336m (Mt Hillaby) to 0m (Atlantic Ocean). The climate is tropical with a wet season from July to November, when the island is subject to occasional hurricanes.

HISTORY AND POLITICS
Early settlers were succeeded by the Arawaks and then the Caribs. The island was uninhabited when settled by the English in 1627 and was a crown colony from 1652, achieving self-government in 1961. It became an independent state on 30 November 1966.

Since independence, power has alternated between the two main political parties, the Barbados Labour Party (BLP) and the Democratic Labour Party (DLP). In the 2008 general election the DLP defeated the BLP and took office under David Thompson. He died in October 2010 and was succeeded as prime minister by his deputy, Freundel Stuart. The DLP narrowly retained power in 2013, before the BLP won every parliamentary seat in the May 2018 elections. Mia Mottley was named prime minister, the first woman to hold the position.

The head of state is Queen Elizabeth II, represented by the governor-general. The bicameral parliament consists of a senate of 21 appointed members and a House of Assembly of 30 directly elected members; both chambers serve a five-year term.

Local government is divided into 11 administrative districts (parishes) and the city of Bridgetown: Christ Church, St Andrew, St George, St James, St John, St Joseph, St Lucy, St Michael, St Peter, St Philip and St Thomas.

Governor-General, HE Dame Sandra Mason, DCMG *apptd* 2018

SELECTED GOVERNMENT MEMBERS *AS AT NOVEMBER 2020*
Prime Minister, Finance, Mia Mottley
Foreign Affairs, Jerome Walcott
Home Affairs, Wilfred Abrahams

BARBADOS HIGH COMMISSION
1 Great Russell Street, London WC1B 3ND
T 020-7631 4975 **E** london@foreign.gov.bb
High Commissioner, HE Milton Inniss, *apptd* 2019

BRITISH HIGH COMMISSION
PO Box 676, Lower Collymore Rock, Bridgetown
T (+1) (246) 430 7800 **E** ukinbarbados@fco.gov.uk
W www.gov.uk/government/world/barbados
High Commissioner, HE Janet Douglas, CMG, *apptd* 2017

ECONOMY AND TRADE

The wealthiest country in the Eastern Caribbean, historically Barbados' chief products were sugar, rum and molasses. Since independence, tourism, offshore finance and information services, and light industry have become more significant. The global economic downturn affected tourism in particular, causing the economy to enter recession in 2009 and producing high levels of public debt. GDP growth rose above 1 per cent for the first time in nine years in 2016, but the economy has contracted steadily since, even before the coronavirus pandemic negatively impacted its tourism and finance industries in 2020.

The main trading partners are Trinidad and Tobago, the USA and Guyana. Chief exports are manufactured goods, sugar and molasses, rum, other food and beverages, chemicals and electronic components.

GNI – US$5.0bn; US$17,380 per capita (2019)
Annual average growth of GDP – -0.2 per cent (2017 est)
Inflation rate – 4.4 per cent (2017 est)
Unemployment – 10.1 per cent (2017 est)
Imports – US$2,362m (2017)
Exports – US$2,024m (2017)

BALANCE OF PAYMENTS

Trade – US$337m deficit (2017)
Current Account – US$453m deficit (2016)

Trade with UK	2018	2019
Imports from UK	£38,252,124	£44,323,650
Exports to UK	£10,056,383	£8,728,117

COMMUNICATIONS

Airports – The Grantley Adams International near Bridgetown is the only international airport on the island
Waterways – Bridgetown, the only port of entry, has a deep-water harbour
Roadways – 1,700km
Telecommunications – 128,043 fixed lines and 329,326 mobile phone subscriptions (2018); there were 239,664 internet users in 2018
Internet country code and IDD – bb; 1 246 (from UK), 011 44 (to UK)
Major broadcasters – Caribbean Broadcasting Corporation (CBC) is the sole TV station and operates a number of public and commercial channels
Press – Major newspapers include *The Barbados Advocate* and *The Nation*

EDUCATION AND HEALTH

Education is free in government schools at primary (ages four to 11), secondary (ages 11 to 18) and tertiary levels, and is compulsory until the age of 16.

Literacy rate – 99.6 per cent (2014 est)
Gross enrolment ratio (percentage of relevant age group) – primary 100.3 per cent, secondary 102.7 per cent (2019 est); tertiary 65.4 per cent (2011 est)
Health expenditure (per capita) – US$1,183 (2017)
Hospital beds (per 1,000 people) – 5.8 (2014)
Life expectancy (years) – 76 (2020 est)
Mortality rate – 8.8 (2020 est)
Birth rate – 11.3 (2020 est)
Infant mortality rate – 9.6 (2020 est)
HIV/AIDS adult prevalence – 1.8 per cent (2019 est)

BELARUS

Respublika Byelarus' – Republic of Belarus

Area – 207,600 sq. km
Capital – Minsk (the administrative centre of the CIS); population, 2,028,000 (2020 est)
Major cities – Brest, Homyel, Hrodna, Mahilyow, Vitsyebsk
Currency – Belarusian rouble (Br) of 100 kopeks
Population – 9,477,918 falling at 0.27 per cent a year (2020 est); Belarusian (83.7 per cent), Russian (8.3 per cent), Polish (3.1 per cent), Ukrainian (1.7 per cent) (est)
Religion – Christian (Orthodox 48.3 per cent, Catholic 7.1 per cent) (est)
Language – Belarusian, Russian (both official), Polish, Ukrainian
Population density – 47 per sq. km (2019)
Urban population – 79 per cent (2019 est)
Median age (years) – 40.9 (2020 est)
National anthem – 'My Belarusy' 'We, the Belarusians'
National day – 3 July (Independence Day)
Death penalty – Retained
CPI score – 45 (66)
Military expenditure – US$715m (2018)
Conscription – 18–27 years of age; 12–18 months dependent on level of education

CLIMATE AND TERRAIN

Much of Belarus is a plain, with many lakes, swamps and marshes, and forest cover is around 43 per cent. Its main rivers are the upper reaches of the Dnieper, the Nyoman and the Western Dvina. Elevation extremes range from 346m (Dzyarzhynskaya Hara) to 90m (Nyoman river). The climate is continental, with cold winters and warm, humid summers.

HISTORY AND POLITICS

In the 13th century the area was absorbed into the grand duchy of Lithuania, which entered into the Polish Commonwealth from the 16th until the 18th centuries. Following the partitions of Poland in the late 18th century it became part of the expanding Russian Empire. It was the site of fierce fighting during the First World War, but its brief period of independence in 1918 ended, after a war over the territory, in partition between Poland and the USSR. The Polish territory was largely regained by the USSR after the Second World War, which devastated Belarus; over a quarter of the population was killed.

Belarus declared its independence from the USSR after a failed coup in Moscow in 1991. Stanislav Shuskevich became Belarusian leader at the head of a coalition of communists and democrats, but he was forced to resign in 1994. He was replaced by Gen. Mecheslav Grib, who pursued closer political, economic and trade relations with Russia.

Alexander Lukashenko was elected to the newly created post of president in 1994. Since coming to power, President Lukashenko has opposed privatisation and economic liberalisation, subverted political processes and repressed opposition and the media, creating what Condoleezza Rice, the former US Secretary of State, referred to in 2005 as the 'last dictatorship in Europe'. The EU and USA have imposed sanctions several times because of the regime's poor human rights record and obstructiveness towards international election monitors.

Following the 2020 presidential election, in which President Lukashenko was returned for a sixth time with 80.1 per cent of the vote, the largest protests in the nation's history erupted against the allegedly falsified results, which were also rejected by the EU. Despite further international sanctions, nationwide strikes and sustained protests, as of November 2020 Lukashenko was unmoved. The UN Human Rights Office reported hundreds of incidents of torture and ill-treatment of civilians during the violent suppression of the protests. No opposition candidate won a seat in the 2019 parliamentary election, which international observers determined was neither free nor fair.

Under the 1994 constitution, the president is directly elected for a five-year term; this was renewable only once until a 2004 constitutional amendment removed the two-term limit. The legislature is the bicameral National Assembly, comprising a 110-member House of Representatives (lower chamber), directly elected for a four-year term, and a Council of the Republic, with 56 members elected by regional *soviets* (councils) and eight members appointed by the president, for a four-year term.

The president may appoint half the members of the constitutional court and the electoral commission.

HEAD OF STATE

President, Alexander Lukashenko, *elected* 10 July 1994, *re-elected* 2001, 2006, 2010, 2015, 2020

SELECTED GOVERNMENT MEMBERS *AS AT NOVEMBER 2020*

Prime Minister, Roman Golovchenko
First Deputy Prime Minister, Nikolai Snopkov
Deputy Prime Ministers, Anatoly Sivak; Yuri Nazarov; Igor Petrishenko; Aleksander Subbotin
Foreign Affairs, Vladimir Makey

EMBASSY OF THE REPUBLIC OF BELARUS

6 Kensington Court, London W8 5DL
T 020-7937 3288 **E** uk.london@mfa.gov.by
W http://uk.mfa.gov.by/en

Ambassador Extraordinary and Plenipotentiary, HE Maksim Yermalovich, *apptd* 2020

BRITISH EMBASSY

37 Karl Marx Street, 220030 Minsk
T (+375) (172) 298 200 **E** ukin.belarus@fconet.fco.gov.uk
W www.gov.uk/government/world/belarus
Ambassador Extraordinary and Plenipotentiary, HE Jacqueline Perkins, *apptd* 2019

FOREIGN RELATIONS

Belarus was a founder member of the Commonwealth of Independent States (CIS) in 1991. President Lukashenko, who opposed the break-up of the Soviet Union, has sought closer relations with Russia. In 1997 a treaty was signed with Russia providing for closer political and economic integration, and in 1999 the two countries signed a treaty that committed them to becoming a confederal state. In 2011, Belarus formed an economic union with Kazakhstan and Russia, removing tariffs and customs control along their shared borders. In January 2015, Belarus and Russia became founding members of the Eurasian Economic Union (EEU), establishing a common market, commission, bank and supranational court between the two countries, and Armenia and Kazakhstan.

ECONOMY AND TRADE

Although prosperous under the Soviet regime, the country experienced a dramatic decline after independence. Since 1994 President Lukashenko has resisted structural reform of the economy and reimposed state control of prices and currency exchange rates. Some privatised businesses have been renationalised, and the small private sector is subject to pressure and intervention by the state, circumstances that continue to discourage foreign investment. The country is highly dependent on Russia for its energy needs, and economic growth in recent years was largely based on the re-export at market prices of heavily discounted oil and natural gas from Russia. Russian economic dominance over Belarus further increased in November 2011 in a deal that agreed the sale of oil to Belarus at a discount of 60 per cent below other European states in exchange for Russian ownership of Belarusian oil pipeline firm Beltransgaz. After years of stagnation, the poor Russian economy pushed the nation into recession in 2015–16, but it returned to modest growth in 2017 thanks to improved external conditions. Due to widespread strikes and the impact of the coronavirus pandemic, the economy is expected to shrink by 6 per cent in 2020.

The main economic activities are oil-refining and the manufacture of heavy machinery and equipment, vehicles, domestic appliances, chemicals and textiles. These commodities, along with oil, mineral products, metals and foodstuffs, constitute the main exports and the main imports. The main trading partner is Russia.

GNI – US$59.5bn; US$6,280 per capita (2019)
Average annual growth of GDP – 1.22 per cent (2019 est)
Inflation rate – 6 per cent (2017 est)
Population below poverty line – 5.7 per cent (2016 est)
Unemployment – 0.8 per cent (2017 est)
Total external debt – US$39.92bn (2017 est)
Imports – US$36,405m (2017)
Exports – US$36,499m (2017)

BALANCE OF PAYMENTS

Trade – US$94m surplus (2017)
Current Account – US$1,258m deficit (2019)

Trade with UK	2018	2019
Imports from UK	£159,450,928	£138,461,743
Exports to UK	£58,565,000	£85,496,904

COMMUNICATIONS

Airports – 33, including an international airport in Minsk plus six other major domestic airports

Waterways – Belarus has an extensive 2,500km canal and river system, but its use is limited by shallowness or remoteness

Roadways and railways – 86,600km; 5,528km

Telecommunications – 4.5 million fixed lines and 11.6 million mobile phone subscriptions (2018); there were 7.5 million internet users in 2018

Internet code and IDD – by; 375 (from UK), 810 44 (to UK)

Major broadcasters – The four national TV channels, including Belarusian TV, are state-run; the government-owned Belarusian Radio is the principal radio broadcaster. Exile groups operate radio stations and TV channels from Poland, such as Belsat (TV) and Radio Racja

Press – Major government newspapers include *Sovetskaya Belorussiya* (Russian-language daily) and *Zvyazda* (Belarusian-language daily); independent titles, such as *Narodnaya Volya*, operate but face harassment

WPFI score – 49.75 (153)

EDUCATION AND HEALTH

Education is compulsory between the ages of six and 15.

Literacy rate – 99.8 per cent (2019 est)

Gross enrolment ratio (percentage of relevant age group) – primary 100.5 per cent, secondary 102.4 per cent, tertiary 87.4 per cent (2018 est)

Health expenditure (per capita) – US$342 (2017)

Hospital beds (per 1,000 people) – 11 (2013)

Life expectancy (years) – 73.8 (2020 est)

Mortality rate – 13.1 (2020 est)

Birth rate – 9.5 (2020 est)

Infant mortality rate – 3.5 (2020 est)

HIV/AIDS adult prevalence – 1.5 per cent (2019 est)

BELGIUM

*Koninkrijk Belgie/Royaume de Belgique/Königreich Belgien –
Kingdom of Belgium*

Area – 30,528 sq. km

Capital – Brussels; population, 2,081,000 (2020 est)

Major cities – Antwerp, Bruges, Charleroi, Ghent, Liège

Currency – Euro (€) of 100 cents

Population – 11,720,716 rising at 0.63 per cent a year (2020 est)

Religion – Christian (Roman Catholic 50 per cent, Protestant and other Christian 2.5 per cent), Muslim 5 per cent (est)

Language – Dutch (Flemish), French, German (all official)

Population density – 377 per sq. km (2019)

Urban population – 98 per cent (2019 est)

Median age (years) – 41.6 (2020 est)

National anthem – 'La Brabançonne' 'The Song of Brabant'

National day – 21 July (Accession of King Leopold I, 1831)

Death penalty – Abolished for all crimes (since 1996)

CPI score – 75 (17)

Military expenditure – US$4,960m (2018)

CLIMATE AND TERRAIN

There are two distinct regions: the west is generally low-lying and fertile, while in the east the forested hills of the Ardennes are more rugged with poorer soil. Elevation extremes range from 694m (Signal de Botrange) to 0m on the North Sea coast. The polders near the coast, which are protected against floods by dykes, cover an area of around 500 sq. km. Average temperatures range from 3.2°C in January to 18.3°C in July and August.

POLITICS

Belgium is a constitutional monarchy with a hereditary monarch as head of state. Amendments to the constitution since 1968 have devolved power to the regions. The national government retains competence only in foreign and defence policies, the national budget and monetary policy, social security, and the judicial, legal and penal systems. The bicameral legislature, the Federal Chambers, consists of a senate and a Chamber of Representatives. The latter has 150 members, directly elected by proportional representation for a five-year term. The senate has 60 members, with 50 members indirectly elected by community and regional parliaments and ten elected by other senators; members serve five-year terms.

There are three language communities: Flemish, Francophone and Germanophone. Each community has its own assembly, which elects the community government. At this level, Flanders is covered by the Flemish community assembly; most of Wallonia is covered by the Francophone community assembly, and areas of Wallonia lying in the German-speaking communities of Eupen and Malmédy are covered by the Germanophone community assembly; Brussels is covered by a joint community commission of the Flemish and Francophone community assemblies.

At regional level, Belgium is divided into three: the Brussels capital region, the Flemish region and Walloon region. Each region has its own directly elected assembly and government.

The ten provinces of Belgium are: Antwerp, East Flanders, Flemish Brabant, Hainaut, Liège, Limburg, Luxembourg, Namur, Walloon Brabant and West Flanders. In addition, 589 communes form the lowest level of local government.

Prince Philippe ascended the throne in July 2013 following the abdication of his father, King Albert, due to ill health. In the May 2014 legislative elections, the Flemish nationalist New Flemish Alliance (N-VA) emerged as the largest party, as it had done in the 2010 elections, and was nominated to form a ruling coalition. In October, following months of negotiations, Charles Michel of the centre-right Francophone Reform Movement party formed a coalition government with the N-VA, but the coalition collapsed in December 2018 over divisions on immigration. Michel continued as head of a minority government until the May 2019 elections, which were marked by strong gains for the far-left and far-right at the expense of centrist parties, and initiated another lengthy round of coalition talks. A seven-party coalition was finally agreed in October 2020, after almost 500 days of negotiations.

Minister-President of the Brussels Capital Government, Rudi Vervoort

Minister-President of the Flemish Community and Flemish Region, Jan Jambon

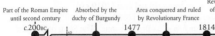

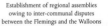

Part of the Roman Empire until second century c.200BC — Invaded by Germanic tribes and becomes part of the Frankish Empire

Absorbed by the duchy of Burgundy 1385 — 1477 — Under the rule of the Spanish, then Austrian, Habsburgs

Area conquered and ruled by Revolutionary France 1794 — 1814 — Unites with the Netherlands following the collapse of the Napoleonic regime

Revolution leads to the declaration of independence and, in 1831, a constitutional monarchy 1830 — 1914-44 — Invasion and occupation by Germany during both world wars

Establishment of regional assemblies owing to inter-communal disputes between the Flemings and the Walloons 1980 — 1989 — Adopts a federal constitution

Joins the eurozone 2002

Minister-President of the French Community and Walloon Region, Elio Di Rupio
Minister-President of the German-speaking Community, Oliver Paasch

HEAD OF STATE
HM The King of the Belgians, King Philippe, *born* 15 April 1960, *acceded* 21 July 2013
Heir, HRH Princess Elisabeth, *born* 25 October 2001

SELECTED GOVERNMENT MEMBERS *AS AT NOVEMBER 2020*
Prime Minister, Alexander De Croo
Deputy Prime Ministers, Pierre-Yves Dermagne *(Economy);* Sophie Wilmes *(Foreign Affairs);* Georges Gilkinet; Frank Vandenbroucke; Petra De Sutter; Vincent van Quickenborne *(Justice)*
Interior, Annelies Verlinden

EMBASSY OF BELGIUM
17 Grosvenor Crescent, London SW1X 7EE
T 020-7470 3700 **E** london@diplobel.fed.be
W www.unitedkingdom.diplomatie.belgium.be
Ambassador Extraordinary and Plenipotentiary, HE Bruno van der Pluijm, *apptd* 2020

BRITISH EMBASSY
Avenue d'Auderghem 10, 1040 Brussels
T (+32) (2) 287 6211 **E** public.brussels@fco.gov.uk
W www.gov.uk/government/world/belgium
Ambassador Extraordinary and Plenipotentiary, HE Martin Shearman, *apptd* 2019

ECONOMY AND TRADE
Belgium has a free-market economy with highly diversified industrial and commercial sectors. With few natural resources, industry is based largely on processing imported raw materials for export, which makes the economy dependent on the state of world markets. Belgium's high level of integration into the struggling eurozone, spiralling labour costs and high public debt are restraints to growth. The country's regional and political divide is reflected in the Belgian economy. Flanders, including the major ports of Antwerp, Brussels and Ghent, has higher levels of employment and productivity. Wallonia, the richer portion of the country in the 19th century, has become poorer due to the declining importance of its heavy industry, although Liège and Charleroi remain important industrial centres. Efforts to reduce public debt have resulted in low growth in recent years, and joblessness, particularly in Wallonia, has remained high. These issues have been exacerbated by the coronavirus pandemic; the economy is expected to contract by 6.9 per cent in 2020.

Principal industries are engineering and metal products, vehicle assembly, transport equipment, scientific instruments, food processing and beverages, chemicals, base metals, textiles, glass, petroleum and diamonds. Industry accounts for 22.1 per cent of GDP and 18.6 per cent of employment. There is a large service sector, partly owing to the location in Brussels of EU institutions, NATO headquarters and a number of other international organisations. The service sector accounts for 77.2 per cent of GDP and 80.1 per cent of employment. There is a small agricultural sector amounting to 0.7 per cent of GDP.

Around three-quarters of trade is with other EU states, especially the UK, Germany, France and the Netherlands. External trade statistics relate to Luxembourg as well as Belgium, as the two countries formed an economic union in 1921.
GNI – US$544bn; US$47,350 per capita (2019)
Annual average growth of GDP – 1.41 per cent (2019 est)
Inflation rate – 2.2 per cent (2017 est)
Population below poverty line – 15.1 per cent (2013 est)
Unemployment – 5.36 per cent (2019 est)
Total external debt – US$1.281 trillion (2016 est)
Imports – US$420,228m (2017)
Exports – US$422,844m (2017)

BALANCE OF PAYMENTS
Trade – US$2,616m surplus (2017)
Current Account – US$1,842m surplus (2019)

Trade with UK	2018	2019
Imports from UK	£14,212,009,751	£12,928,385,326
Exports to UK	£25,966,780,959	£25,331,528,736

COMMUNICATIONS
Airports – 26; the main airports are at Antwerp, Brussels, Liège and Ostend-Bruges
Waterways – There are 2,043km of inland waterways, of which 1,528km are in regular commercial use; ship canals and the Meuse (Maas), Sambre and Schelde rivers form an integral part of the network. The major inland ports are located in Brussels, Ghent and Antwerp
Roadways – 118,414km, including 1,756km of motorways
Railways – The rail system is run by Belgian National Railways (NMBS/SNCB) and, at 3,233km, the network is one of the densest in the world
Telecommunications – 4.3 million main lines and 12 million mobile phone subscriptions (2017); there were 9.9 million internet users in 2016
Internet code and IDD – be; 32 (from UK), 44 (to UK)
Major broadcasters – Television and radio broadcasters include French-language RTBF and Dutch-language VRT
Press – Major newspapers include Dutch-language daily *Het Nieuwsblad* and French-language daily *Le Soir*
WPFI score – 12.57 (12)

EDUCATION AND HEALTH
Nursery schools provide free education for children from two-and-a-half to six years of age. The official school-leaving age is 18.
Gross enrolment ratio (percentage of relevant age group) – primary 103.4 per cent, secondary 156 per cent, tertiary 79 per cent (2018 est)
Health expenditure (per capita) – US$4,507 (2017)
Hospital beds (per 1,000 people) – 6.2 (2014)
Life expectancy (years) – 81.4 (2020 est)
Mortality rate – 9.8 (2020 est)
Birth rate – 11.1 (2020 est)
Infant mortality rate – 3.3 (2020 est)

BELIZE

Area – 22,966 sq. km
Capital – Belmopan; population, 23,000 (2018 est)
Major towns – Belize City (the former capital), Orange Walk, San Ignacio
Currency – Belize dollar (BZ$) of 100 cents; the Belize dollar is tied to the US dollar
Population – 399,598 rising at 1.72 per cent a year (2020 est); mestizo (52.9 per cent), Creole (25.9 per cent), Maya (11.3 per cent), Garifuna (6.1 per cent) (est)
Religion – Christian (Roman Catholic 40.1 per cent, Protestant 31.5), other 10.5 per cent (includes Buddhist, Hindu, Muslim, Rastafarian) (est)
Language – English (official), Spanish, Creole, Mayan dialects, Garifuna, German
Population density – 17 per sq. km (2019)
Urban population – 45.9 per cent (2019 est)
Median age (years) – 23.9 (2020 est)
National anthem – 'Land of the Free'
National day – 21 September (Independence Day)
Death penalty – Retained
Military expenditure – US$23.1m (2018)

CLIMATE AND TERRAIN

Belize comprises a large coastal plain, swamps in the north, fertile land in the south and the Maya mountains in the southwest. The highest point of elevation is 1,160m (Doyle's Delight), the lowest is 0m (Caribbean Sea). Part of the Mesoamerican barrier reef system, the western hemisphere's longest, runs nearly the entire length of the coastline. The climate is subtropical but is cooled by trade winds. The hurricane season is from May to November.

HISTORY AND POLITICS

Numerous ruins in the area indicate that Belize was heavily populated by the Maya. The first British settlement was established in 1638 but was subject to repeated attacks by the Spanish, who claimed sovereignty until their defeat by the British navy and settlers in 1798. In 1862 the settlement was given colonial status as British Honduras. The colony became self-governing in 1964. In 1973 it was renamed Belize and it was granted independence on 21 September 1981.

Since independence, power has alternated between the two main political parties, the People's United Party (PUP) and the United Democratic Party (UDP). The UDP gained seats from the PUP in the November 2015 legislative elections, and retained its overall majority for a record third term under Prime Minister Dean Barrow.

Under the 1981 constitution, the head of state is Queen Elizabeth II, represented by a governor-general. There is a bicameral National Assembly, comprising a House of Representatives with 31 members directly elected for a five-year term, and a senate of 13 members appointed by the governor-general, including six on the advice of the prime minister, three on the advice of the opposition leader, three representing various sectors of society and a senate president elected by the representatives. A referendum in 2008 approved the reform of the senate into an elected chamber, effective from the next elections. The prime minister is appointed by the governor-general and is responsible to the legislature.
Governor-General, HE Sir Colville Young, GCMG, *apptd* 17 November 1993

SELECTED GOVERNMENT MEMBERS *AS AT NOVEMBER 2020*
Prime Minister, Finance, Dean Barrow
Economy, Erwin Contreras
Foreign Affairs, Wilfred Elrington

BELIZE HIGH COMMISSION
3rd Floor, 45 Crawford Place, London W1H 4LP
T 020-7723 3603 **E** info@belizehighcommission.co.uk
W www.belizehighcommission.co.uk
High Commissioner, HE Perla Maria Perdomo, *apptd* 2012

BRITISH HIGH COMMISSION
North Ring Road, Melhado Parade PO Box 91, Belmopan
T (+501) 822 2981 **E** brithicom@btl.net
W www.gov.uk/government/world/belize
High Commissioner, HE Claire Evans, *apptd* 2018

FOREIGN RELATIONS
There is a longstanding territorial dispute with Guatemala, which claims the southern part of Belize. In February 2015, 37 Belizeans were arrested by Guatemalan authorities after they took part in an excursion into the disputed territory. After years of discussions, a referendum in Guatemala in April 2018 resulted in public support for mediation through the International Court of Justice, and a referendum in Belize in May 2019 also backed this measure to settle the dispute.

ECONOMY AND TRADE

The economy grew steadily from 1999 to 2007, bolstered from 2006 by commercial exploitation of oil reserves. It contracted sharply in 2009 owing to the global downturn, natural disasters and the drop in international oil prices, and grew sluggishly between 2010 and 2019. In January 2013 the government announced the restructure of its US$544m commercial external debt, or 'superbond', on which it defaulted in 2012, and by 2019 public debt had slightly decreased. Partly due to low oil prices and a sharp fall in tourism resulting from the coronavirus pandemic, growth is expected to contract by 12 per cent in 2020. Crime and corruption, inequality, high unemployment and a growing trade deficit remain concerns.

The services sector has grown as tourism has developed, and accounts for 68 per cent of GDP; industry contributes around 21.6 per cent, and agriculture and fisheries around 10.3 per cent. The main industries apart from tourism are garment manufacturing, food processing, construction and oil production. The chief trading partners are the USA, the UK, Mexico and China. The major exports are sugar, bananas, citrus fruits and juice, garments, fish products, molasses and crude oil. Imports are primarily machinery and transport equipment, manufactured goods, fuel, chemicals, pharmaceuticals, food, beverages and tobacco.
GNI – US$1.7bn; US$4,450 per capita (2019)
Annual average growth of GDP – 0.8 per cent (2017 est)
Inflation rate – 1.1 per cent (2017 est)
Population below poverty line – 41 per cent (2013 est)
Unemployment – 9 per cent (2017 est)

Total external debt – US$1.315bn (2017 est)
Imports – US$1,086m (2017)
Exports – US$1,038m (2017)

BALANCE OF PAYMENTS
Trade – US$47m deficit (2017)
Current Account – US$177m deficit (2019)

Trade with UK	2018	2019
Imports from UK	£7,057,707	£7,707,832
Exports to UK	£71,273,719	£77,096,752

COMMUNICATIONS
Airports – 6, including the international airport at Belize City
Waterways – Although there are 825km of waterways, these are only accessible by small craft
Roadways – 3,281km
Telecommunications – 20,869 fixed lines and 327,629 mobile phone subscriptions (2018); there were 157,735 internet users in 2016
Internet code and IDD – bz; 501 (from UK), 44 (to UK)
Major broadcasters – Commercial broadcasters include Channels 5 and 7 (TV), Love FM and Krem FM (radio); in 2014, a court approved the nationalisation of Belize Telemedia, the country's largest telecoms provider
Press – The country has no daily newspapers
WPFI score – 27.50 (53)

EDUCATION AND HEALTH
Education is free and compulsory for eight years.
Gross enrolment ratio (percentage of relevant age group) – primary 110.5 per cent, secondary 86.4 per cent, tertiary 25 per cent (2019 est)
Health expenditure (per capita) – US$280 (2017)
Hospital beds (per 1,000 people) – 1.3 (2014)
Life expectancy (years) – 75.3 (2020 est)
Mortality rate – 4.1 (2020 est)
Birth rate – 22 (2020 est)
Infant mortality rate – 11.2 (2020 est)
HIV / AIDS adult prevalence rate – 1.8 per cent (2019 est)

BENIN

République du Bénin – Republic of Benin

Area – 112,622 sq. km
Capital – Porto-Novo; population, 285,000 (2018 est); Cotonou, the seat of government, population, 682,000 (2020 est)
Major cities – Abomey-Calavi, Bohicon, Djougou, Parakou
Currency – Franc CFA of 100 centimes
Population – 12,864,634 rising at 3.4 per cent a year (2020 est); Fon (38.4 per cent), Adja (15.1 per cent),

Yoruba (12 per cent), Bariba (9.6 per cent), Fulani (8.6 per cent), Ottamari (6.1 per cent) (est)
Religion – Muslim 27.7 per cent, Christian (Roman Catholic 25.5 per cent, Protestant 13.5 per cent, other Christian 9.5 per cent), Vodoun (voodoo) 11.6 per cent (est); many Christians and Muslims also practise voodoo, which originated in this region of Africa, or other indigenous religions
Language – French (official), Fon, Yoruba and other African languages
Population density – 102 per sq. km (2019)
Urban population – 47.9 per cent (2019 est)
Median age (years) – 17 (2020 est)
National anthem – 'L'Aube Nouvelle' 'The Dawn of a New Day'
National day – 1 August (Independence Day)
Death penalty – Abolished for all crimes (since 2016)
CPI score – 41 (80)
Military expenditure – US$90.2m (2018)
Conscription – 18–35 years of age; 18 months (selective)
Literacy rate – 42.4 per cent (2018 est)
Gross enrolment ratio (percentage of relevant age group) – primary 116.7 per cent (2019 est); secondary 59 per cent (2016 est); tertiary 12.5 per cent (2018 est)
Health expenditure (per capita) – US$31 (2017)
Hospital beds (per 1,000 people) – 0.5 (2010)
Life expectancy (years) – 61.4 (2020 est)
Mortality rate – 8.4 (2020 est)
Birth rate – 42.1 (2020 est)
Infant mortality rate – 58.7 (2020 est)
HIV / AIDS adult prevalence – 1.0 per cent (2019 est)

CLIMATE AND TERRAIN
Benin has a short coastline of 121km on the Gulf of Guinea, but extends northwards inland for over 700km. The coast is a sandbar backed by lagoons that are fed by rivers. The land rises to a central plateau with the Atacora massif in the north-west, and falls to plains in the Niger basin in the north-east. Elevation extremes range from 658m (Mt Sokbaro) to 0m (Atlantic Ocean) at the lowest. The climate is tropical in the south and semi-arid in the north.

POLITICS
Under the 1990 constitution, the executive president is directly elected for a five-year term, renewable only once. The unicameral National Assembly has 83 members, directly elected for a four-year term. The president appoints and chairs the council of ministers.

The March 2016 presidential election was won in the second round by businessman Patrice Talon, an independent candidate, after Thomas Yayi Boni served his maximum two five-year terms. In the 2019 legislative elections, both participating blocs declared support for Talon and were subsequently boycotted by opposition groups; the election was characterised by violent demonstrations and only 23 per cent voter turnout.

HEAD OF STATE
President, Defence, Patrice Talon, *elected* 20 March 2016

SELECTED GOVERNMENT MEMBERS *AS AT NOVEMBER 2020*
Economy, Finance, Romuald Wadagni
Foreign Affairs, Aurélien Agbénonci
Interior, Security, Sacca Lafia

EMBASSY OF THE REPUBLIC OF BENIN
87 Avenue Victor Hugo, 75116 Paris, France
T (+33) 1 4500 9882 **E** ambassade.benin@gofornet.com
Ambassador Extraordinary and Plenipotentiary, vacant

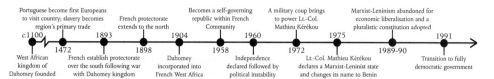

West African kingdom of Dahomey founded — c.1100

1472 — West African kingdom of Dahomey founded

1893 — Portuguese become first Europeans to visit country; slavery becomes region's primary trade

1898 — French establish protectorate over the south following war with Dahomey kingdom

French protectorate extends to the north — 1893

1904 — Dahomey incorporated into French West Africa

1958 — Dahomey incorporated into French West Africa

Becomes a self-governing republic within French Community — 1904

1960 — Independence declared followed by political instability

1972 — Lt.-Col. Mathieu Kérékou declares a Marxist-Leninist state and changes its name to Benin

A military coup brings to power Lt.-Col. Mathieu Kérékou — 1960

1975 — A military coup brings to power Lt.-Col. Mathieu Kérékou

Marxist-Leninism abandoned for economic liberalisation and a pluralistic constitution adopted — 1975

1989–90 — Transition to fully democratic government

1991 — Marxist-Leninism abandoned for economic liberalisation and a pluralistic constitution adopted

Transition to fully democratic government

BRITISH HIGH COMMISSION

High Commissioner, HE Tom Hartley, *apptd* 2018, resident in Accra, Ghana

ECONOMY AND TRADE

Although the economy is underdeveloped and still burdened by foreign debt, Benin has benefited from increased competitiveness and debt reduction or relief since its economic restructuring commenced. Privatisation of industries, including utilities, began in 2001 and public debt has fallen in recent years. However, rapid population growth has meant a third of the population lives below the poverty line. The economy is based on agriculture, particularly cotton production, and re-export trade with neighbouring countries; customs receipts provide over 40 per cent of government revenue, but much of the re-export trade operates outside the official economy and is unrecorded. The economy is vulnerable to commodity price fluctuations, thus contracting in 2017 but sharply rising in 2018 and 2019. Efforts to attract foreign investment and tourism by improving the nation's infrastructure have been given IMF support in 2017, and the electricity network has significantly improved in recent years.

Agriculture is mostly at subsistence level and contributes 26.1 per cent to GDP, while industry contributes 22.8 per cent and services 51.1 per cent. The main cash crops are cotton, cashew nuts, shea butter, palm products and seafood, and the principal industrial activities are textiles and food processing. The main trading partners are Bangladesh, India, and Thailand.

GNI – US$14.8bn; US$1,250 per capita (2019)
Annual average growth of GDP – 5.6 per cent (2017 est)
Inflation rate – 0.1 per cent (2017 est)
Population below poverty line – 36.2 per cent (2011 est)
Total external debt – US$2.804bn (2017 est)
Imports – US$3,108m (2016)
Exports – US$2,110m (2016)

BALANCE OF PAYMENTS

Trade – US$998m deficit (2016)
Current Account – US$648m deficit (2018)

Trade with UK	2018	2019
Imports from UK	£18,744,242	£27,860,303
Exports to UK	£2,773,157	£2,040,344

COMMUNICATIONS

Airports and waterways – One, serving Cotonou, which is also the major seaport
Roadways and railways – There are 1,400 paved roads; 438km
Telecommunications – 48,508 fixed lines and 9.5 million mobile telephones in use (2018); there were 2.4 million internet users in 2018
Internet code and IDD – bj; 229 (from UK), 44 (to UK)
Major broadcasters – Television Nationale and Radio Nationale are the official state broadcasters

Press – Dozens of newspapers and periodicals are published, including *Le Matinal, Fraternité* and *La Nation;* the International Press Institute rates Benin as having one of West Africa's most plural media landscapes, but has experienced less freedom under President Talon's rule
WPFI score – 35.11 (113)

BHUTAN

Druk Gyalkhap – Kingdom of Bhutan

Area – 38,394 sq. km
Capital – Thimphu; population, 203,000 (2018 est)
Major towns – Geylegphug, Paro, Phodrang, Phuentsholing, Tashigang, Wangdue
Currency – Ngultrum (Nu) of 100 chetrum (Indian currency is also legal tender)
Population – 782,318 rising at 1.02 per cent a year (2020 est); Ngalop (Bhote) (50 per cent), ethnic Nepali (35 per cent), indigenous or migrant tribes (15 per cent) (est)
Religion – Lamaistic Buddhist 75.3 per cent, Hindu 22.1 per cent (est)
Language – Dzongkha (official), Sharchhopka, Lhotshamkha
Population density – 20 per sq. km (2019)
Urban population – 41.6 per cent (2019 est)
Median age (years) – 29.1 (2020 est)
National anthem – 'Druk Tsendhen' 'The Thunder Dragon Kingdom'
National day – 17 December (inauguration of first hereditary monarch, 1907)
Death penalty – Abolished for all crimes (since 2004)
CPI score – 68 (25)
Literacy rate – 66.6 per cent (2018 est)
Gross enrolment ratio (percentage of relevant age group) – primary 100.1 per cent, secondary 90.1 per cent, tertiary 15.6 per cent (2018 est)
Health expenditure (per capita) – US$97 (2017)
Life expectancy (years) – 72.1 (2020 est)
Mortality rate – 6.3 (2020 est)
Birth rate – 16.3 (2020 est)
Infant mortality rate – 27 (2020 est)
HIV/AIDS adult prevalence – 0.13 per cent (2013 est)

CLIMATE AND TERRAIN

Bhutan is crossed by numerous rivers, and most of the population and cultivated land is found in the deep, fertile valleys of the highlands. There is a mountainous northern region that is infertile and sparsely populated, central highlands and densely forested foothills in the south, which are mainly inhabited by Nepalese settlers and indigenous tribespeople. Extremes of elevation range from 7,570m (Gangkar Puensum) to 97m (Drangeme Chhu). The climate is determined by altitude, varying from subtropical in the south to alpine in the north. There is heavy annual rainfall of up to 1,000mm in the central valleys and 5,000mm in the south, which experiences monsoons from June to September.

HISTORY AND POLITICS

Bhutan's external relations were under the guidance of Britain from the 19th century until 1947, and of India from 1947 until 2007; a 2007 revision of the friendship treaty between the two countries left Bhutan free to manage its external relations without India's advice.

Although the country has opened up since the 1970s, the monarchy has taken measures to preserve its indigenous culture and the environment, including the compulsory wearing of national dress and restrictions on tourism. The emphasis on the majority culture has caused tension with the sizeable Nepali minority. Many were denied citizenship in the 1990s and obliged to leave, which resulted in over 100,000 becoming refugees in Nepal, where most remain, living in refugee camps.

Bhutan's transition from an absolute monarchy to a democracy began in the 1950s, with the establishment of an elected legislature in 1953, and the transfer of powers from the king to the legislature in 1969 and 1989. The 2008 constitution formally established Bhutan as a parliamentary democracy with a constitutional monarchy, and provided for universal suffrage. King Jigme Singye Wangchuk abdicated in 2006 in favour of the Crown Prince.

In July 2013, elections to the National Assembly resulted in an unexpected win for the People's Democratic Party (PDP) which overtook the ruling Bhutan Peace and Prosperity Party (DPT). The PDP lost all of its 32 seats in the October 2018 election and the DPT claimed 17 seats. The Social Democrat Party won 30 seats and formed the new government.

Under the 2008 constitution, the head of state is a hereditary constitutional monarch, who must retire at the age of 65 and who may be required to abdicate by a two-thirds majority of the legislature. The bicameral parliament comprises a National Assembly with 47 directly elected members and a non-partisan National Council with 25 members: 20 directly elected and five appointed by the king. Both chambers serve a fixed five-year term. The cabinet is appointed by the king on the recommendation of the prime minister, who may serve two parliamentary terms. In April 2018 a new National Council was elected.

HEAD OF STATE

HM The King of Bhutan, Jigme Khesar Namgyal Wangchuk, born 21 February 1980, acceded 14 December 2006, crowned 6 November 2008

SELECTED GOVERNMENT MEMBERS AS AT NOVEMBER 2020
Prime Minister, Lotay Tshering
Finance, Namgay Tshering
Foreign Affairs, Tandi Dorji
Home and Cultural Affairs, Sherub Gyeltshen

BRITISH DEPUTY HIGH COMMISSION
British Deputy High Commissioner, Nick Low, apptd 2019, resident at Kolkata, India

ECONOMY AND TRADE

The growing economy is being cautiously modernised but is still based on agriculture (16.2 per cent of GDP) in what is largely a self-sufficient rural society. Industry (41.8 per cent of GDP) is on a small scale, and the growing services sector (42 per cent of GDP) is mostly the result of increased tourism. Agriculture and animal husbandry, much at subsistence level, engage over 58 per cent of the workforce, although the mountainous terrain and heavy forest cover limit the area under cultivation. The further construction of hydropower dams designed to export electricity to India, which already accounts for 40 per cent of total exports and 25 per cent of government revenue, should ensure future sustainable growth if chronic construction delays are overcome. The principal food crops are rice, cereals, vegetables and fruit, especially oranges. Industries include forestry, mining (limestone, gypsum, dolomite, graphite, coal), cement and calcium carbide production, food processing, distilling and tourism.

The main trading partner is India, which accounts for 89.5 per cent of imports and 95.3 per cent of exports. The principal exports are electricity, ferrosilicon, cement, calcium carbide, metal products and vegetable oil. The main imports are fuel and lubricants, passenger vehicles, machinery and rice.

GNI – US$2.2bn; US$2,970 per capita (2018)
Annual average growth of GDP – 7.4 per cent (2017 est)
Inflation rate – 5.8 per cent (2017 est)
Population below poverty line – 12 per cent (2012 est)
Unemployment – 3.2 per cent (2017 est)
Total external debt – US$2.671bn (2017 est)
Imports – US$1,234m (2017)
Exports – US$8,801m (2017)

BALANCE OF PAYMENTS
Trade – US$520m deficit (2017)
Current Account – US$511m deficit (2019)

Trade with UK	2018	2019
Imports from UK	£1,218,552	£1,145,214
Exports to UK	£6,223,032	£65,993

COMMUNICATIONS

Airports – Two, including an international airport in Paro
Roadways – 12,205km
Telecommunications – 22,015 fixed lines and 703,554 mobile subscriptions (2018); there were 368,714 internet users in 2018
Internet code and IDD – bt; 975 (from UK), 44 (to UK)
Major broadcasters – Fear that outside influences would undermine Bhutanese culture meant that radio broadcasting began only in 1973, and television broadcasting and internet access in 1999; radio and television services are provided by the state-owned Bhutan Broadcasting Services (BBS)
Press – The country's two daily newspapers are Kuensel and Bhutan Today, which was launched in English in 2008
WPFI score – 28.90 (67)

BOLIVIA

Estado Plurinacional de Bolivia – Plurinational State of Bolivia

Area – 1,098,581 sq. km
Capital – La Paz, the seat of government; population, 1,858,000 (2020 est); Sucre, the legal capital and seat of the judiciary; population, 278,000 (2018 est)
Major cities – Cochabamba, El Alto, Oruro, Santa Cruz
Currency – Boliviano ($b) of 100 centavos
Population – 11,639,909 rising at 1.44 per cent a year (2020 est); mestizo (68 per cent), indigenous (20 per cent) (est)
Religion – Christian (Roman Catholic 76.8 per cent, Evangelical and Pentecostal 8.1 per cent, Protestant 7.9 per cent) (est)
Language – Spanish, 36 indigenous languages (all official); Quechua and Aymara are the main indigenous languages
Population density – 10 per sq. km (2019)
Urban population – 69.8 per cent (2019 est)
Median age (years) – 25.3 (2020 est)
National anthem – 'Cancion Patriotica' 'Patriotic Song'
National day – 6 August (Independence Day)
Death penalty – Abolished for all crimes (since 2009)
CPI score – 31 (123)
Military expenditure – US$619m (2018)
Conscription – 14–49 years of age; 12 months (only if volunteers fall short)

CLIMATE AND TERRAIN
Landlocked Bolivia's main topographical feature is its great central plateau, the Altiplano. Over 800km in length and at an average altitude of 3,750m above sea level, this plateau lies between two great chains of the Andes that traverse the country from north to south. Lake Titicaca, shared with Peru, lies on the Altiplano. Elevation extremes range from 6,542m (Nevado Sajama) to 90m (Rio Paraguay). The low-lying north and eastern plains are drained by the principal rivers, the Beni, Itenez, Madre de Dios and Mamoré. The climate varies dramatically between regions: on the lowlands of the Amazon basin, temperatures average around 25°C; above 500m on the Altiplano, conditions are subpolar. The south is prone to droughts. The wet season is October to April.

POLITICS
The 1967 constitution was revised in 1994, 2009 and 2017. It provides for an executive president who is directly elected, with no term limits since they were abolished in 2017. The bicameral Plurinational Legislative Assembly, or National Congress, consists of a 36-member Chamber of Senators and a 130-member Chamber of Deputies; members of both chambers are directly elected for a five-year term.

President Evo Morales, leader of the Movement Towards Socialism (MAS), won the 2005 presidential election, and was re-elected in 2009. After the Constitutional Court ruled that

Morales could stand for a third term, the president subsequently won the October 2014 presidential election. In February 2016 President Morales lost a referendum to alter the constitution to allow the president and vice-president to run for re-election in 2019, however the constitutional court subsequently inscribed the changes in November 2017. Following two weeks of civil unrest in November 2019, caused by the disputed re-election of Morales, the president was forced from office by the military. Fresh elections took place in October 2020, which were delayed due to the coronavirus pandemic, in which MAS's Luis Acre comfortably won and the party secured majorities in both chambers.

HEAD OF STATE
Interim President, Jenine Chávez, *sworn in* 12 November 2019
President-elect Luis Arce *elected* 18 October 2020
Vice-President-elect, David Choquehuanca

SELECTED GOVERNMENT MEMBERS *AS AT NOVEMBER 2020*
Defence, Luis Lopez
Economy, vacant
Foreign Affairs, Karen Longeric

BOLIVIAN EMBASSY
106 Eaton Square, London SW1W 9AD
T 020-7235 4248 **E** embol@bolivianembassy.co.uk
W www.bolivianembassy.co.uk
Ambassador Extraordinary and Plenipotentiary, vacant

BRITISH EMBASSY
Avenida Arce 2732, La Paz
T (+591) (2) 243 3424 **E** BELaPaz@fco.gov.uk
W www.gov.uk/government/world/bolivia
Ambassador Extraordinary and Plenipotentiary, HE Jeffrey Glekin, *apptd* 2019

ECONOMY AND TRADE
The country is rich in resources but one of the most underdeveloped and least affluent in South America, although steady growth since the 1990s has lowered the proportion of the population living below the poverty line to less than 40 per cent. The government of Evo Morales implemented a wide-reaching socialist agenda when in power, including nationalising the oil and gas sectors. The state energy company YPFB has a $30bn (£21bn) investment programme for 2015–25 with an emphasis on maintaining and expanding the gas supplies on which the country is largely reliant. While the economy grew annually by around 5 per cent for a decade from 2006, particularly between 2010 and 2014, it remains vulnerable to falling commodity prices and integration with the struggling Argentinian and Brazilian economies. Public debt, inflation and unemployment have remained low, but due to the coronavirus pandemic the economy is expected to shrink by 2.9 per cent in 2020.

Mining (principally for zinc, tin and gold) and smelting, natural gas and oil production, agriculture and textiles are the principal industries. Industry contributes 37.8 per cent of GDP, agriculture 13.8 per cent and services 48.2 per cent.

The main trading partners are Brazil, the USA, Argentina and China. Principal exports are natural gas, soya beans and soya products, crude oil, zinc ore and silver. The main imports are petroleum products, machinery, vehicles, iron and steel, and plastics.

GNI – US$40.6bn; US$3,530 per capita (2019)
Annual average growth of GDP – 2.22 per cent (2019 est)
Inflation rate – 2.8 per cent (2017 est)
Population below poverty line – 38.6 per cent (2015 est)
Unemployment – 4 per cent (2017 est)

Conquered by the Spanish
*c.*1450

Ruled by military juntas
1825

Austerity measures introduced to curb rising inflation and attract foreign investment, widen social divisions and create civil unrest
1964–82

Morales seeks to give greater political power to the indigenous population through constitutional changes; he wins a recall referendum and presses ahead with a draft constitution
2006

1525
Assimilated into the Inca Empire

Gained independence after a war of liberation led by Simón Bolívar

1936-52
Ruled by military juntas

1983
Former coca growers' leader, Evo Morales, elected first indigenous president. He renationalises the energy industry and reduces restrictions on coca cultivation

2008

Total external debt – US$12.81bn (2017 est)
Imports – US$11,647m (2017)
Exports – US$8,081m (2017)

BALANCE OF PAYMENTS
Trade – US$3,566m deficit (2017)
Current Account – US$1,324m deficit (2019)

Trade with UK	2018	2019
Imports from UK	£31,771,665	£19,870,081
Exports to UK	£19,385,571	£22,732,798

COMMUNICATIONS
Airports – 21, including four international airports serving the major cities
Waterways – There are 10,000km of commercially navigable waterways, with an inland port on the river Paraguay at the border with Brazil; Bolivia has free port privileges at seaports in Argentina, Brazil, Chile and Paraguay, and a lease on a free-trade zone at the Peruvian port of Ilo
Roadways and railways – 9,792km of paved roads and 80,776 of unpaved roads; the 3,960km of railways form an eastern network and an Andean network
Telecommunications – 711,961 fixed lines and 11.5 million mobile subscriptions (2018); there were 5 million internet users in 2018
Internet code and IDD – bo; 591 (from UK), 10/11/12/13 44 (to UK; depends on area and/or carrier)
Major broadcasters – Evo Morales acquired several media outlets and allowed little journalistic freedom; the leading state-run broadcasters are Bolivia TV and Radio Patria Nueva. In 2013, a law was passed requiring that private media companies publish government messages, damaging the finances of many by limiting commercial advertising space
Press – Daily newspapers are published on a regional basis; leading titles include *La Razon* (La Paz), *Los Tiempos* (Cochabamba) and *El Deber* (Santa Cruz)
WPFI score – 35.37 (114)

EDUCATION AND HEALTH
Elementary education is free and officially, though often not in practice, compulsory from the ages of six to 13.
Literacy rate – 92.5 per cent (2015 est)
Gross enrolment ratio (percentage of relevant age group) – primary 98.2 per cent, secondary 89.7 per cent (2018 est)
Health expenditure (per capita) – US$220 (2017)
Hospital beds (per 1,000 people) – 1.1 (2014)
Life expectancy (years) – 70.4 (2020 est)
Mortality rate – 6.3 (2020 est)
Birth rate – 20.8 (2020 est)
Infant mortality rate – 32.2 (2020 est)
HIV/AIDS adult prevalence – 0.2 per cent (2019 est)

BOSNIA AND HERCEGOVINA

Bosna i Hercegovina – *Bosnia and Hercegovina*

Area – 51,197 sq. km
Capital – Sarajevo; population, 343,000 (2020 est)
Major towns – Banja Luka, Bijeljina, Mostar, Tuzla, Zenica
Currency – Convertible mark (KM) of 100 fenings
Population – 3,835,586 falling at 0.19 per cent a year (2020 est); Bosniak (50.1 per cent), Serb (30.8 per cent), Croat (15.4 per cent) (est)
Religion – Muslim 50.7 per cent (predominantly Sunni), Christian (Orthodox 30.7 per cent, Roman Catholic 15.2 per cent) (est)
Language – Bosnian, Croatian, Serbian (all official)
Population density – 65 per sq. km (2019)
Urban population – 48.6 per cent (2019 est)
Median age (years) – 43.3 (2020 est)
National anthem – 'Drzavna Himna Bosne i Hercegovine' 'National Anthem of Bosnia and Hercegovina'
National day – 25 November (formation of the anti-fascist resistance council, 1943)
Death penalty – Abolished for all crimes (since 2001)
CPI score – 36 (101)
Military expenditure – US$221m (2018)
Literacy rate – 98.5 per cent (2015 est)
Gross enrolment ratio (percentage of relevant age group) – primary 88 per cent, secondary 90 per cent (2010 est); tertiary 40.2 per cent (2019 est)
Health expenditure (per capita) – US$460 (2017)
Hospital beds (per 1,000 people) – 3.5 (2013)
Life expectancy (years) – 77.5 (2020 est)
Mortality rate – 10.2 (2020 est)
Birth rate – 8.6 (2020 est)
Infant mortality rate – 5.2 (2019 est)

CLIMATE AND TERRAIN
The mountainous centre of the country is split by deep valleys, while the north is lower-lying, falling to the basin of the river Sava, which forms the northern border with Croatia. The Dinaric Alps lie along the western border. The highest point of elevation is 2,386m (Maglic), the lowest point is 0m (Adriatic Sea). Average temperatures range from 0°C in January to 20.3°C in July and August.

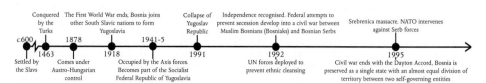

Timeline: c.600 — 1463 — 1878 — 1918 — 1941–5 — 1991 — 1992 — 1995

Settled by the Slavs | Comes under Austro-Hungarian control | Occupied by the Axis forces. Becomes part of the Socialist Federal Republic of Yugoslavia | UN forces deployed to prevent ethnic cleansing | Civil war ends with the Dayton Accord, Bosnia is preserved as a single state with an almost equal division of territory between two self-governing entities

POLITICS

Under the Dayton Peace Accord, the Bosnian republican (national) government is responsible for foreign affairs, currency, citizenship and immigration. The head of state is a collective presidency comprising a representative from each of the three main ethnic groups, all directly elected for a four-year term; the chair of the presidency rotates among its members every eight months. Legislative authority is vested in the bicameral Parliamentary Assembly, comprising a House of Peoples and a House of Representatives. Both houses have four-year terms. The House of Peoples has 15 members – five Bosniak, five Croat and five Serb – who are appointed from the House of Representatives. The House of Representatives has 42 members who are directly elected to the two constituent chambers: the Chamber of Deputies of the Federation, which has 28 members, and the Chamber of Deputies of the Republika Srpska, which has 14 members.

In the Bosniak-Croat Federation, the president and vice-president are elected by the Bosniak and Croat members of the House of Peoples for a four-year term; a second vice-president is elected to represent the Serb population. There is a bicameral Assembly comprising a 58-member House of Peoples elected on an ethnic basis and a House of Representatives with 98 directly elected members.

In the Republika Srpska, the president is directly elected for a four-year term. There is a unicameral National Assembly with 83 members directly elected for a four-year term.

There is a national council of ministers and each of the entities also has its own executive. All appointments to the executives are in consultation with the UN High Representative, who has the power of veto.

Legislative elections in October 2018 mirrored the results of October 2014. The Bosniak-dominated Party of Democratic Action (SDA) won the largest number of seats in the House of Representatives of the Federation of Bosnia and Hercegovina, at the expense of the mixed Social Democratic Party (SDP). In the Republika Srpska, the Alliance of Independent Social Democrats under its president Milorad Dodik won the largest number of seats.

In the simultaneous presidential elections, Milorad Dodik (Serb) and Zeljko Komsic (Croat) were elected to the collective federal presidency, and Sefik Dzaferovic elected as the Bosniak member. Zelijka Cvijanovic was elected president of Republika Srpska. The presidential election in the Bosniak-Croat Federation in February 2015 was won by Marinko Cavara.

REPUBLIC OF BOSNIA AND HERCEGOVINA

HEADS OF STATE
Presidency Members, Zeljko Komsic *(Croat),* Milorad Dodik *(Serb),* Sefik Dzaferovic *(Bosniak)*

SELECTED GOVERNMENT MEMBERS *AS AT NOVEMBER 2020*
Chair of the Council of Ministers, Zoran Tegeltija
Defence, Sifet Podzic
Finance, Vjekoslav Bevanda
Foreign Affairs, Bisera Turkovic

FEDERATION OF BOSNIA AND HERCEGOVINA
President, Marinko Cavara
Vice-Presidents, Milan Dunovic; Melika Mahmutbegovic

SELECTED GOVERNMENT MEMBERS *AS AT NOVEMBER 2021*
Prime Minister, Fadil Novalic
Deputy Prime Ministers, Finance, Jelka Milicevic
Interior, Aljosa Campara

REPUBLIKA SRPSKA
President, Zelijka Cvijanovic
Vice-Presidents, Josip Jerkovic; Ramiz Salkic

SELECTED GOVERNMENT MEMBERS *AS AT NOVEMBER 2020*
Prime Minister, Randovan Viskovic
Finance, Zora Vidovic
Internal Affairs, Dragan Lukac

OFFICE OF THE UN HIGH REPRESENTATIVE/EU SPECIAL REPRESENTATIVE
UN High Representative, Dr Valentin Inzko, *apptd* 2009
EU Special Representative, Johann Sattler, *apptd* 2019

EMBASSY OF BOSNIA AND HERCEGOVINA
5–7 Lexham Gardens, London W8 5JJ
T 020-7373 0867 **E** embassy@bhembassy.co.uk
W www.bhembassy.co.uk
Ambassador Extraordinary and Plenipotentiary, HE Vanja Filipovic *apptd* 2019

BRITISH EMBASSY
39a Hamdije Cemerlica Street, 71000 Sarajevo
T (+387) (0) 33 282 200 **E** britemb@bih.net.ba
W www.gov.uk/government/world/bosnia-and-herzegovina
Ambassador Extraordinary and Plenipotentiary, HE Matthew Field, *apptd* 2018

ECONOMY AND TRADE

When the civil war broke out, the structure of the economy – dominated by state-owned industries, mainly of a military nature – still reflected the central planning of the communist era. Economic restructuring, such as privatisation, has been slow and uneven, although the financial sector is now largely privatised and the government continues to promote greater competition. There has been political deadlock, however, on the reforms needed to pave the way for EU accession. The difficulties inherent in tackling problems such as the large public sector, large deficits and high unemployment are exacerbated by the duplication of administrative functions and reluctant cooperation between its decentralised government. There is a large unofficial economy, but undeclared activity has declined since the introduction of VAT in 2006. In 2016, a three-year IMF loan programme was agreed with Bosnia but it has struggled to meet the economic benchmarks needed to ensure all funding instalments. Corruption and high levels of joblessness, long-term problems for the nation, are have been exacerbated by the coronavirus pandemic which contracted growth in the economy in 2020.

Most agricultural products are for domestic consumption and foodstuffs also have to be imported. The main industrial activities include mining (metals, minerals and coal), production of steel, textiles, tobacco products, wooden furniture, ammunition and domestic appliances, assembly of vehicles, and oil refining. The country produces enough hydroelectric power for its needs and exports electricity. The main trading partners are Germany, Croatia, Serbia, Slovenia and Italy. Principal exports are metals, clothing and wood products, and the main imports are machinery and equipment, chemicals, fuels and foodstuffs.

GNI – US$20.3bn; US$6,150 per capita (2019)
Annual average growth of GDP – 3 per cent (2017 est)
Inflation rate – 1.2 per cent (2017 est)
Population below poverty line – 16.9 per cent (2015 est)
Unemployment – 33.3 per cent (2019 est)
Total external debt – US$10.87bn (2017 est)
Imports – US$10,238m (2017)
Exports – US$7,255m (2017)

BALANCE OF PAYMENTS
Trade – US$2,983m deficit (2017)
Current Account – US$623m deficit (2019)

Trade with UK	2018	2019
Imports from UK	£25,328,218	£26,137,727
Exports to UK	£19,411,470	£16,841,284

COMMUNICATIONS
Airports – Seven, including international airports in Sarajevo, Banja Luka, Mostar and Tuzla
Waterways – Although the country has 20km of coastline on the Adriatic Sea, there are no seaports
Roadways and railways – 22,926km; 965km
Telecommunications – 792,535 fixed lines and 3.5 million mobile subscriptions (2018); there were 2.7 million internet users in 2018
Internet code and IDD – ba; 387 (from UK), 44 (to UK)
Major broadcasters – More than 200 commercial TV and radio stations are on the air in Bosnia; national broadcaster BHTV1 operates alongside two separate-entity broadcasters. Major radio broadcasters include the Bosniak-Croat Radio FBiH and the Bosnian Serb station RTRS
Press – There are five major daily newspapers, including *Oslobodjenje*, *Nezavisne Novine* and *Dnevni List*
WPFI score – 28.50 (58)

BOTSWANA

Republic of Botswana

Area – 581,730 sq. km
Capital – Gaborone; population, 269,000 (2018 est)
Major cities – Francistown, Maun, Molepolole, Selebi-Phikwe
Currency – Pula (P) of 100 thebe

Population – 2,317,233 rising at 1.48 per cent a year (2020 est); Tswana (79 per cent), Kalanga (11 per cent), Basarwa (3 per cent) (est)
Religion – Christian 79.1 per cent (predominantly Protestant), Badimo 4.1 per cent, other 1.4 per cent (including Baha'i, Hindu, Muslim and Rastafarian) (est)
Language – English (official), Setswana, Kalanga, Sekgalagadi
Population density – 4 per sq. km (2019)
Urban population – 70.2 per cent (2019 est)
Median age (years) – 25.7 (2020 est)
National anthem – 'Fatshe Leno La Rona' 'Blessed Be This Noble Land'
National day – 30 September (Botswana Day)
Death penalty – Retained
CPI score – 61 (34)
Military expenditure – US$529m (2018)

CLIMATE AND TERRAIN
Botswana lies on an undulating plateau and is covered by the Kalahari desert in the south and west. To the east, streams run into the Marico, Notwani and Limpopo rivers. In the north lies a flat region comprising the Makgadikgadi salt pans and the swampland of the Okavango delta. Elevation extremes range from 1,489m (Tsodilo Hills) to 513m (junction of the Limpopo and Shashe rivers). The climate is subtropical in the north, arid in the south and west, and more temperate in the east, which has regular rain. Average temperatures range from 15°C in July to 26.7°C in January.

HISTORY AND POLITICS
The Tswana people were predominant in the area from the 17th century. In 1885, at the request of indigenous chiefs fearing invasion by the Boers, Britain formally took control of Bechuanaland, and the northern part of the territory was declared the Bechuanaland Protectorate, while land to the south of the Molopo river became British Bechuanaland, which was later incorporated into the Cape Colony and eventually South Africa. In 1964, the Bechuanaland Protectorate became self-governing, and on 30 September 1966 it became an independent republic under the name Botswana. Since independence, Botswana has been stable and relatively prosperous, owing to the diamond mining industry. There is a high level of HIV/AIDS among the population, and although an advanced treatment programme, in place since 2001, is reducing the level of infection, the country faces serious demographic and social problems.

President Festus Mogae stood down in 2008, having completed two terms of office, and was succeeded by the vice-president, Lt.-Gen. Ian Khama, son of the country's first president. Khama stepped down in April 2018 having completed the constitutionally mandated ten-year term limit, and was replaced by vice-president Mokgweetsi Masisi. The Botswana Democratic Party (BDP) was re-elected to power in the October 2019 legislative elections, winning 38 of 65 seats.

Under the 1966 constitution, the executive president is elected by the legislature for a five-year term, renewable once. He appoints the vice-president and the cabinet. The unicameral National Assembly has 57 members directly elected for a five-year term, plus a variable number of members (currently six) nominated by the president and elected by the assembly, and two *ex officio* members. A 35-member House of Chiefs advises on tribal matters and constitutional changes.

HEAD OF STATE
President, Mokgweetsi Masisi, *sworn in* 1 April 2018
Vice-President, Slumber Tsogwane

SELECTED GOVERNMENT MEMBERS *AS AT NOVEMBER 2020*

Defence, Kagiso Mmusi
Finance and Economy, Thapelo Matsheka
International Affairs, Lemogang Kwape

BOTSWANA HIGH COMMISSION
6 Stratford Place, London W1C 1AY
T 020-7499 0031 **E** bohico@govbw.com
High Commissioner, HE Dr John Seakgosing, *apptd* 2019

BRITISH HIGH COMMISSION
Plot 1079–1084, Main Mall, off Queens Road, Gaborone
T (+267) 395 2841 **E** bhc@botsnet.bw
W www.gov.uk/government/world/botswana
High Commissioner, HE Sian Price, *apptd* 2020

ECONOMY AND TRADE

One of the poorest nations in the world when it achieved its independence, Botswana has since been relatively prosperous because of its mining industry, political stability, low levels of corruption and sound economic management. Despite this, around 20 per cent of the population lives below the poverty line and a similar number are unemployed. Longer-term problems are the impact of the high levels of HIV/AIDS among the workforce and the levelling off of diamond production, which accounts for 85 per cent of export earnings and a third of government revenues; diamond exports declined owing to the global downturn, causing the economy to contract sharply in 2009. The government has sought to reduce the economy's dependence on the diamond industry by diversifying. A major drought and power shortages restricted economic growth in 2012 and 2013, but the economy grew by 4.5 per cent in 2018 thanks to increased diamond exports. However, the coronavirus pandemic is expected to shrink GDP by around 5.2 per cent in 2020. Safari tourism and financial services have grown in recent years, and the services sector contributes 70.6 per cent of GDP. The industrial sector contributes 27.5 per cent of GDP, mainly from mining diamonds, copper, nickel, salt, soda ash, potash, coal, iron ore and silver. Agriculture is mostly pastoral and accounts for 1.8 per cent of GDP.

The main trading partners are the EU, southern African countries and India. Principal exports are diamonds, copper, nickel, soda ash, meat and textiles. The main imports are foodstuffs, machinery, electrical goods, transport equipment, textiles, fuel and petroleum products.

GNI – US$17.6bn; US$7,660 per capita (2019)
Annual average growth of GDP – 2.4 per cent (2017 est)
Inflation rate – 3.3 per cent (2017 est)
Population below poverty line – 19.3 per cent (2009 est)
Unemployment – 20 per cent (2013 est)
Total external debt – US$2.187bn (2017 est)
Imports – US$5,736m (2017)
Exports – US$7,291m (2017)

BALANCE OF PAYMENTS

Trade – US$1,555m surplus (2017)
Current Account – US$1,396m deficit (2019)

Trade with UK	2018	2019
Imports from UK	£33,690,932	£31,472,719
Exports to UK	£13,743,187	£423,446

COMMUNICATIONS

Airports – Ten, including the international airport in Gaborone
Roadways – 31,747km, of which 9,810km are paved
Railways – The only railway is the 888km line from Zimbabwe to South Africa, which passes through eastern Botswana
Telecommunications – 142,481 fixed lines and 3.4 million mobile subscriptions (2018); there were 1 million internet users in 2018
Internet code and IDD – bw; 267 (from UK), 44 (to UK)
Major broadcasters – State-run television broadcaster Botswana TV was established in 2000 and a private station is hosted by eBotswana; state-run Radio Botswana operates a commercial FM station from Gaborone, while other stations such as Yarona FM operate a private service
Press – Major daily newspapers include the state-run *Daily News* and the privately owned *Mmegi*
WPFI score – 23.56 (39)

EDUCATION AND HEALTH

Botswana does not have a compulsory education policy, although many children receive 12 years of education (seven years of primary education, three years of junior secondary and two years of senior secondary). In 2006 fees were reintroduced for state secondary schools, which had been free of charge for over 20 years.

Literacy rate – 88.5 per cent (2018 est)
Gross enrolment ratio (percentage of relevant age group) – primary 103.2 per cent (2015 est); secondary 80 per cent (2011 est); tertiary 25.1 per cent (2019 est)
Health expenditure (per capita) – US$466 (2017)
Hospital beds (per 1,000 people) – 1.8 (2010)
Life expectancy (years) – 64.8 (2020 est)
Mortality rate – 9.2 (2020 est)
Birth rate – 20.9 (2020 est)
Infant mortality rate – 26.8 (2020 est)
HIV/AIDS adult prevalence – 20.7 per cent (2019 est)

BRAZIL

Republica Federativa do Brasil – Federative Republic of Brazil

Area – 8,515,770 sq. km
Capital – Brasilia; population, 4,646,000 (2020 est)
Major cities – Belo Horizonte, Fortaleza, Porto Alegre, Recife, Rio de Janeiro (the former capital), Salvador, Sao Paulo
Currency – Real (R$) of 100 centavos
Population – 211,715,973 rising at 0.67 per cent a year (2020 est)
Religion – Christian (Roman Catholic 64.6 per cent, Protestant 22.2 per cent), Spiritist 2.2 per cent (est)
Language – Portuguese (official), Spanish, German, Italian, Japanese, English, Amerindian languages
Population density – 25 per sq. km (2019)

Urban population – 86.8 per cent (2019 est)
Median age (years) – 33.2 (2020 est)
National anthem – 'Hino Nacional Brasileiro' 'Brazilian National Anthem'
National day – 7 September (Independence Day)
Death penalty – Retained for certain crimes (last used 1855)
CPI score – 35 (106)
Military expenditure – US$27,766m (2018)
Conscription – 18–45 years of age; 10–12 months

CLIMATE AND TERRAIN

Brazil has six distinct topographical areas: the Amazon basin (north and west of the country), the Parana-Paraguay river basin (south; the Parana drains the Pantanal, the world's largest freshwater wetland), the Guiana Highlands (north of the Amazon), the Mato Grosso plateau (centre), the Brazilian Highlands (south of the Amazon) and the coastal strip. Elevation extremes range from 2,994m (Pico da Neblina) to 0m (Atlantic Ocean). Brazil has the world's largest rainforest, as well as large expanses of savannah *(cerrado)*. The climate is mostly tropical, with the equator passing through the north and the Tropic of Capricorn through the south-east. The Amazon basin sees annual rainfall of up to 2,300mm a year and there is no dry season. The north-east is the driest area of the country and can experience long periods of drought. The southern states have a seasonal temperate climate.

POLITICS

The Federative Republic of Brazil is composed of the Federal District of Brasilia, in which the capital lies, and 26 states: Acre, Alagoas, Amapa, Amazonas, Bahia, Ceara, Espirito Santo, Goias, Maranhao, Mato Grosso, Mato Grosso do Sul, Minas Gerais, Para, Paraiba, Parana, Pernambuco, Piaui, Rio de Janeiro, Rio Grande do Norte, Rio Grande do Sul, Rondonia, Roraima, Santa Catarina, Sao Paulo, Sergipe and Tocantins. Each state has its own governor and legislative assembly.

Under the 1988 constitution (amended in 1997), the executive president is directly elected for a four-year term, which is renewable once. The National Congress consists of an 81-member federal senate (three senators per state plus three from the federal distict, directly elected for an eight-year term) and a 513-member Chamber of Deputies, which is directly elected every four years; the number of deputies per state depends upon the state's population.

The October 2018 presidential election was won by Jair Bolsonaro of the Social Liberal Party (PSL), the far-right candidate who replaced Dilma Rousseff who won the previous two elections representing the Workers' Party (PT). Rousseff's government was dogged by allegations of corruption, and in August 2016 Rousseff was impeached for illegally manipulating government accounts and Michel Temer was sworn in as president. In the simultaneous legislative election, centrist and left-wing parties experienced heavy losses as the PSL made large gains, but the PT remained the largest party.

HEAD OF STATE
President, Jair Bolsonaro, *sworn in* 1 January 2019
Vice-President, Hamilton Mourao

SELECTED GOVERNMENT MEMBERS *AS AT NOVEMBER 2020*
Defence, Fernando Azevedo
Economy, Paulo Guedes
Foreign Affairs, Ernesto Araujo

EMBASSY OF BRAZIL
14/16 Cockspur Street, London SW1Y 5BL
T 020-7747 4500 **E** info.london@itamaraty.gov.br
W www.brazil.org.uk
Ambassador Extraordinary and Plenipotentiary, HE Fred Arruda, *apptd* 2018

BRITISH EMBASSY
Setor de Embaixadas Sul, Quadra 801, Lote 8, CEP 70408-900, Brasilia DF
T (+55) (61) 3329 2300 **W** www.gov.uk/government/world/brazil
Ambassador Extraordinary and Plenipotentiary, HE Peter Wilson, CMG, *apptd* 2020

ECONOMY AND TRADE

Historically subject to boom and bust cycles, the economy was stabilised by reforms in the 1990s. Tight fiscal management, IMF programmes, a growth in output and an expanding export base produced steady growth from 2003. Brazil's economy, the eighth largest in the world, is based on well-developed agriculture, mining, manufacturing and service sectors. Unemployment and income inequality have decreased steadily in the past 15 years, although poverty is still widespread. In 2015–16 the nation experienced the worst recession in its history due to rising inflation and decreasing demand from China. Multiple corruption scandals involving politicians and private companies resulted in government sanctions and limited business opportunities, but increased infrastructure spending and the reduction of barriers to foreign investment helped the economy recover prior to the coronavirus pandemic. The virus was widespread in Brazil, with over 5 million cases by November 2020, and pushed the economy back into recession.

The country is rich in mineral deposits, including iron ore (haematite), bauxite, gold, manganese, nickel, platinum and uranium. It produces oil, gas and hydroelectricity, and is close to self-sufficiency in oil. Brazil is the world's largest producer of coffee; the other main agricultural products are soya beans, wheat, rice, maize, sugar cane, cocoa, citrus fruit and beef. The expansion of agriculture and forestry threaten the rainforest, although recent governments' attempts to prevent further depredations by loggers and farmers have slowed the rate of deforestation considerably. Tourism is a growing industry. In 2017, services generated 72.7 per cent of GDP, industry 20.7 per cent and agriculture 6.6 per cent.

Brazil's main trading partners are the USA, China, and Argentina. Principal exports are transport equipment, iron ore, soya beans, footwear, coffee and vehicles. The main imports are machinery, electrical and transport equipment, chemical products, vehicle parts and electronics.
GNI – US$1,926.3bn; US$9,130 per capita (2019)
Annual average growth of GDP – 1.13 per cent (2019 est)
Inflation rate – 3.4 per cent (2017 est)

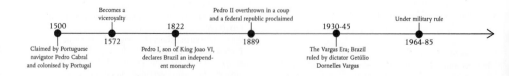

| 1500 | 1572 | 1822 | 1889 | 1930-45 | 1964-85 |

Becomes a viceroyalty — 1572

Pedro II overthrown in a coup and a federal republic proclaimed

Under military rule

Claimed by Portuguese navigator Pedro Cabral and colonised by Portugal

Pedro I, son of King Joao VI, declares Brazil an independent monarchy

The Vargas Era; Brazil ruled by dictator Getúlio Dornelles Vargas

Population below poverty line – 4.2 per cent (2016 est)
Unemployment – 11.9 per cent (2019 est)
Total external debt – US$547.4bn (2017 est)
Imports – US$221,543m (2017)
Exports – US$251,721m (2017)

BALANCE OF PAYMENTS
Trade – US$30,177m surplus (2017)
Current Account – US$50,927m deficit (2019)

Trade with UK	2018	2019
Imports from UK	£1,911,388,725	£1,929,384,330
Exports to UK	£2,391,985,489	£2,638,009,201

COMMUNICATIONS
Airports – 698; international flights operate to the major cities
Waterways – In remote regions, transport is primarily by air or water, utilising the 50,000km of navigable waterways
Roadways and railways – There are 2 million km of roadways, of which 246,000km are paved; the Trans-Amazonian Highway connects the Amazon region with the rest of the country, although it is mostly unpaved and often becomes impassable in the rainy season; 29,850km
Telecommunications – 38.3 million fixed lines and 207 million mobile subscriptions (2018); there were 140.9 million internet users in 2018
Internet code and IDD – br; 55 (from UK), 14/15/21/23/31 44 (to UK, varies depending on area and/or carrier)
Major broadcasters – Domestic conglomerates – most notably Globo – dominate the market and run television and radio networks, newspapers and subscription television stations
Press – There are six major daily newspapers, including *O Dia*, *O Correio Brazilinese* and *Jornal do Brasil*
WPFI score – 34.05 (107)

EDUCATION AND HEALTH
Public education is free at all levels, and is compulsory between the ages of seven and 14.
Literacy rate – 93.2 per cent (2018 est)
Gross enrolment ratio (percentage of relevant age group) – primary 115.3 per cent, secondary 99.7 per cent, tertiary 50.6 per cent (2015 est)
Health expenditure (per capita) – US$929 (2017)
Hospital beds (per 1,000 people) – 2.2 (2014)
Life expectancy (years) – 74.7 (2020 est)
Mortality rate – 6.9 (2019 est)
Birth rate – 13.6 (2020 est)
Infant mortality rate – 15.9 (2020 est)
HIV/AIDS adult prevalence – 0.5 per cent (2019 est)

BRUNEI
Negara Brunei Darussalam – Brunei Darussalam

Area – 5,765 sq. km
Capital – Bandar Seri Begawan; population, 241,000 (2011 est)

Major towns – Kampong Ayer, Kuala Belait, Seria, Tutong
Currency – Brunei dollar (B$) of 100 sen (fully interchangeable with Singapore currency)
Population – 464,478 rising at 1.51 per cent a year (2020 est); Malay (65.7 per cent), Chinese (10.3 per cent) (est)
Religion – Muslim 78.8 per cent (predominantly Sunni), Christian 8.7 per cent, Buddhist 7.8 per cent, other 4.7 per cent (including indigenous beliefs); Islam is the state religion
Language – Malay (official), English, Chinese languages
Population density – 81 per sq. km (2019)
Urban population – 77.9 per cent (2019 est)
Median age (years) – 31.1 (2020 est)
National anthem – 'Allah Peliharakan Sultan' 'God Bless the Sultan'
National day – 23 February (date of independence from British protection, 1984)
Death penalty – Retained (no known use since 1957)
CPI score – 60 (35)
Military expenditure – US$347m (2018)

CLIMATE AND TERRAIN
The country lies on the north-west coast of the island of Borneo. It is surrounded and divided in two by the Malaysian state of Sarawak. The terrain is estimated to be around 70 per cent rainforest, with extensive mangrove swamps along the coastal plain. There are mountains on the border with Sarawak. Elevation extremes range from 1,850m (Bukit Pagon) to 0m (South China Sea). The climate is tropical, with high humidity, and an annual average daily temperature of 26.3°C.

HISTORY AND POLITICS
Formerly a powerful Muslim sultanate that controlled Borneo and parts of the Philippines, Brunei was reduced to its present size by the mid-19th century and came under British protection in 1889. It chose to remain a British dependency in 1963 rather than joining the Federation of Malaysia. Internally self-governing from 1959, Brunei gained full independence on 1 January 1984.

In 1962 the legislative election was annulled after it was won by a party that sought to remove the sultan; a state of emergency was declared and the sultan has ruled by decree ever since. A ministerial system of government was introduced in 1984. Some political liberalisation and modernisation has taken place since 2004, when the legislature was reconvened after 20 years. In April 2014, Brunei became the first East Asian country to adopt Shari'ah law, causing widespread international condemnation, and further alienated western allies after announcing stricter punishments in April 2019, which included death by stoning for gay sex.

Parts of the 1959 constitution have been suspended since the state of emergency began in 1962. Supreme executive authority is vested in the sultan, a hereditary monarch who presides over and is advised by a privy council, a religious council and the council of cabinet ministers. The legislative council was reconvened in 2004 with 21 members appointed by the sultan; it has passed constitutional amendments to increase its size to 36 members.
HM The Sultan of Brunei, Prime Minister, Defence, Finance, Foreign Affairs, HM Hassanal Bolkiah, GCB, *acceded* 5 October 1967, *crowned* 1 August 1968
Heir, Senior Minister in the Prime Minister's Office, HM Crown Prince Al-Muhtadee Billah

SELECTED GOVERNMENT MEMBERS *AS AT NOVEMBER 2020*
Energy, Mat Suny bin Haji Mohammad Yusof
Home Affairs, Abu Bakar bin Haji Apong

BRUNEI DARUSSALAM HIGH COMMISSION
19–20 Belgrave Square, London SW1X 8PG
T 020-7581 0521 **E** info@bdhcl.co.uk
High Commissioner, HE Pengiran Dato Norazmi Penigran Haji Muhammad, *apptd* 2020

BRITISH HIGH COMMISSION
2.01, 2nd Floor, Block D, Kompleks Yayasan Sultan Haji Hassanal Bolkiah, Jalan Pretty, PO Box 2197, Brunei
T (+673) (2) 222 231 **E** ukinbrunei@fco.gov.uk
W www.gov.uk/government/world/brunei
High Commissioner, HE John Virgoe, *apptd* 2020

ECONOMY AND TRADE
The economy is based on the production of oil and natural gas and the income from overseas investments. Royalties and taxes from these operations form the bulk of government revenue and have enabled the construction of free health, education and welfare services; Brunei's GDP per capita is one of the highest in the world, however, oil and gas reserves, which make up 65 per cent of GDP and 95 per cent of exports, are declining and Brunei is now trying to diversify its economy, developing Islamic financial services, tourism and communications technology. Trade has increased in the past few years following regional economic integration with the ASEAN economic community, but the economy remains vulnerable to fluctuations in the price of hydrocarbons.

Agriculture accounts for 1.2 per cent of GDP, industry 56.6 per cent and services 42.3 per cent. The main trading partners are Japan, Singapore, South Korea, China and Malaysia. The main imports are machinery and transport equipment, manufactured goods, food (over 80 per cent of domestic requirements are imported) and chemicals.
GNI – US$14bn; US$32,230 per capita (2019)
Annual average growth of GDP – 1.3 per cent (2017 est)
Inflation rate – –0.2 per cent (2017 est)
Unemployment – 6.9 per cent (2017 est)
Imports – US$4,462m (2017)
Exports – US$6,005m (2017)

BALANCE OF PAYMENTS
Trade – US$1,524m surplus (2017)
Current Account – US$893m surplus (2019)

Trade with UK	2018	2019
Imports from UK	£47,960,831	£57,019,610
Exports to UK	£110,811,190	£6,582,830

COMMUNICATIONS
Airports and waterways – There is one international airport; the largest port is at Muara and the 209km of internal waterways are navigable only by shallow craft
Roadways – 2,976km
Telecommunications – 82,588 fixed lines (2018) and 565,949 mobile subscriptions (2018); there were 426,000 internet users in 2018
Internet code and IDD – bn; 673 (from UK), 44 (to UK)
Major broadcasters – The only broadcast media organisation, Radio Television Brunei (RTB), is state-owned and heavily censored; it broadcasts in Malay and English
Press – Daily newspapers include the English-language *Borneo Bulletin* and *Brunei Times,* and Malay *Media Permata*
WPFI score – 49.65 (152)

EDUCATION AND HEALTH
All levels of education are free but not compulsory; most children receive a minimum of 12 years of schooling.
Literacy rate – 97.2 per cent (2018 est)
Gross enrolment ratio (percentage of relevant age group) – primary 100.1 per cent, secondary 92.1 per cent, tertiary 31.4 per cent (2019 est)
Health expenditure (per capita) – US$671 (2017)
Hospital beds (per 1,000 people) – 2.7 (2015)
Life expectancy (years) – 77.9 (2020 est)
Mortality rate – 3.8 (2020 est)
Birth rate – 16.5 (2020 est)
Infant mortality rate – 8.8 (2020 est)

BULGARIA

Republika Balgariya – Republic of Bulgaria

Area – 110,879 sq. km
Capital – Sofia; population, 1,281,000 (2020 est)
Major cities – Burgas, Plovdiv, Varna
Currency – Lev of 100 stotinki
Population – 6,966,899 falling at 0.65 per cent a year (2020 est); Bulgarian (76.9 per cent), Turkish (8 per cent), Roma (4.4 per cent) (est); Romani populations are usually underestimated and may represent 9–11 per cent of the population
Religion – Eastern Orthodox 59.4 per cent, Muslim 7.8 per cent (predominantly Sunni) (est)
Language – Bulgarian (official), Turkish, Romani
Population density – 65 per sq. km (2019)
Urban population – 75.3 per cent (2019 est)
Median age (years) – 43.7 (2020 est)
National anthem – 'Mila Rodino' 'Dear Homeland'
National day – 3 March (Liberation Day)
Death penalty – Abolished for all crimes (since 1998)
CPI score – 43 (74)
Military expenditure – US$1,096m (2018)

CLIMATE AND TERRAIN
The Balkan mountains cross the country from west to east, averaging 2,000m in height, and the Rhodope mountains in the south-west climb to almost 3,000m. Elevation extremes range from 2,925m (Musala) to 0m (Black Sea). The lowland plains of the north and south-east are in the basins of the main rivers: the Danube in the north, which forms much of the border with Romania, and the Maritsa, which divides the Balkan and Rhodope ranges. The climate is temperate, with cold, damp winters and hot, dry summers. Average temperatures in Sofia range from 0°C in January to 22.3°C in July.

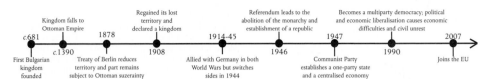

Kingdom falls to Ottoman Empire — 1878 — Regained its lost territory and declared a kingdom — 1914-45 — Referendum leads to the abolition of the monarchy and establishment of a republic — 1947 — Becomes a multiparty democracy; political and economic liberalisation causes economic difficulties and civil unrest — 2007

c.681 — c.1390 — 1908 — 1946 — 1990

First Bulgarian kingdom founded — Treaty of Berlin reduces territory and part remains subject to Ottoman suzerainty — Allied with Germany in both World Wars but switches sides in 1944 — Communist Party establishes a one-party state and a centralised economy — Joins the EU

POLITICS

Under the 1991 constitution, the president is directly elected for a five-year term, renewable once. The head of government is the prime minister, who is elected by the National Assembly, and is usually the leader of the largest party in the legislature. There is a unicameral National Assembly of 240 members who are directly elected for a four-year term.

Early legislative elections arranged for October 2014 saw eight parties win seats in an election with a turnout as low as 50 per cent. In November, former prime minister Boyko Borissov of the centre-right Citizens for European Development of Bulgaria (GERB) party formed a minority government in coalition with three other parties. However, Borissov resigned in December 2016 after voters rejected his party in presidential elections, when socialist candidate Rumen Radev was declared the victor. Nevertheless, the GERB emerged once again as the largest party in new legislative elections in March 2017.

HEAD OF STATE
President, Rumen Radev, *elected* 13 November 2016, *sworn in* 19 January 2017
Vice-President, Iliana Yotova

SELECTED GOVERNMENT MEMBERS *AS AT NOVEMBER 2020*
Prime Minister, Boyko Borissov
Deputy Prime Ministers, Tomislav Donchev; Ekaterina Gecheva-Zaharieva *(Foreign Affairs)*; Krasimir Karakachanov *(Defence)*; Mariana Nikolova *(Economy)*
Finance, Kiril Ananiev

EMBASSY OF THE REPUBLIC OF BULGARIA
186–188 Queen's Gate, London SW7 5HL
T 020-7584 9400 **E** info@bulgarianembassy.org.uk
W www.bulgarianembassy-london.org
Ambassador Extraordinary and Plenipotentiary, HE Marin Raykov, *apptd* 2019

BRITISH EMBASSY
9 Moskovska Street, Sofia 1000
T (+359) (2) 933 9222 **E** britishembassysofia@fco.gov.uk
W www.gov.uk/government/world/bulgaria
Ambassador Extraordinary and Plenipotentiary, HE Dr Rob Dixon, *apptd* 2020

ECONOMY AND TRADE

The government adopted radical economic reforms in 1996 and the economy achieved stability and attracted significant foreign investment, although continues to suffer from administrative corruption, a weak judiciary and organised crime. Despite EU entry in 2007, steady economic growth in 2004–8 and responsible fiscal management, the economy contracted in the global economic downturn as industrial production and exports declined. Strong domestic demand, low energy imports and rising tourism have boosted growth in recent years and contributed to budget surpluses, but the coronavirus pandemic is expected to push the economy back into recession in 2020.

Natural resources include copper, lead, zinc, other minerals, coal and timber. Fertile arable land produces vegetables, fruit, tobacco, wine, wheat, barley, sunflowers and livestock. Agriculture employs 6.8 per cent of the workforce and accounts for 4.3 per cent of GDP. Industries include energy generation, food processing, beverages, tobacco, machinery and equipment, base metals, chemicals, mining and oil refining.

The main trading partners are EU countries, Russia and Turkey. Principal exports are clothing and footwear, iron and steel, machinery and equipment, and fuels. The main imports are predominantly machinery and raw materials for the industrial sector.
GNI – US$65.6bn; US$9,410 per capita (2019)
Annual average growth of GDP – 3.39 per cent (2019 est)
Inflation rate – 1.2 per cent (2017 est)
Population below poverty line – 23.4 per cent (2016 est)
Unemployment – 5.66 per cent (2019 est)
Total external debt – US$42.06bn (2017 est)
Imports – US$36,441m (2017)
Exports – US$39,100m (2017)

BALANCE OF PAYMENTS
Trade – US$2,658m surplus (2017)
Current Account – US$2,025m surplus (2019)

Trade with UK	2018	2019
Imports from UK	£441,061,184	£377,011,369
Exports to UK	£506,423,139	£601,025,664

COMMUNICATIONS

Airports and waterways – 57, the main airports are at Sofia, Plovdiv, Burgas and Varna; the main ports are Burgas and Varna on the Black Sea, and there are 470km of waterways
Roadways and railways – 19,512km; 5,114km
Telecommunications – 1.1 million fixed lines and 8.4 million mobile telephone subscriptions (2018); there were 4.6 million internet users in 2018
Internet code and IDD – bg; 359 (from UK), 44 (to UK)
Major broadcasters – Public service broadcasters Bulgarian National Radio and Bulgarian National Television share the radio and TV markets with a vigorous commercial sector that provides national and regional broadcasting
Press – Major daily newspapers include *Dnevnik*, *Trud* and *24 Chasa*
WPFI score – 35.06 (111)

EDUCATION AND HEALTH

Education is free and compulsory from seven to 16 years.
Literacy rate – 98.4 per cent (2015 est)
Gross enrolment ratio (percentage of relevant age group) – primary 87.4 per cent, secondary 96.8 per cent, tertiary 71.5 per cent (2018 est)
Health expenditure (per capita) – US$664 (2017)
Hospital beds (per 1,000 people) – 6.8 (2013)
Life expectancy (years) – 75 (2020 est)
Mortality rate – 14.6 (2020 est)
Birth rate – 8.3 (2020 est)
Infant mortality rate – 8.1 (2020 est)

BURKINA FASO

MALI

NIGER

BURKINA FASO

Ouagadougou

Bobo-Dioulasso

GHANA

BENIN

CÔTE
D'IVOIRE

TOGO

Area – 274,200 sq. km
Capital – Ouagadougou; population, 2,780,000 (2020 est)
Major city – Bobo-Dioulasso
Currency – Franc CFA of 100 centimes
Population – 20,835,401 rising at 2.66 per cent a year (2020 est); there are 63 ethnic groups, of which Mossi (52 per cent) is the largest (est)
Religion – Muslim 61.5 per cent (predominantly Sunni), Christian (Roman Catholic 23.2 per cent, animist 7.8 per cent, Protestant 6.5 per cent) (est)
Language – French (official), various African languages (spoken by 90 per cent of the population)
Population density – 72 per sq. km (2019)
Urban population – 30 per cent (2019 est)
Median age (years) – 17.9 (2020 est)
National anthem – 'Le Ditanye' 'Anthem of Victory'
National day – 11 December (Republic Day)
Death penalty – Retained for certain crimes (last used 1988)
CPI score – 40 (85)
Military expenditure – US$312m (2018)

CLIMATE AND TERRAIN
The landlocked state occupies a plateau dissected by the White, Black and Red Volta rivers. There are tropical savannahs in the south and the north is semi-desert. Elevation extremes range from 749m (Tena Kourou) to 200m (Mouhoun, or Black Volta, river). The climate is tropical, with a wet season from May to September; there are recurring droughts. Average temperatures range from 25.2°C in January to 32.7°C in April.

HISTORY AND POLITICS
Burkina Faso (Upper Volta until 1983) was part of the Mossi Empire in the 18th and 19th centuries. It was administered as part of other French colonies between 1932 and 1947, and in 1958 it became autonomous within the French Community; independence was achieved on 5 August 1960.

In the three decades after independence there was a succession of military regimes; the last military coup, in 1987, brought to power Captain Blaise Compaoré. Military rule ended in 1991 when a new constitution was adopted and multiparty elections were held in 1992. Despite the constitutional restriction on the number of terms that a president may serve, President Compaoré was re-elected for a fourth term in 2010. In January 2014, protests took place across the country after President Compaoré announced that he would look to alter the constitution in order to stand in the 2015 elections. In October, demonstrators stormed the presidential palace, causing the president to resign and flee to the Côte d'Ivoire after 27 years in power. In simultaneous presidential and legislative elections in November 2015, Roch Marc Kaboré was elected president and his People's Movement for Progress (MPP) won 55 seats. In October 2016 it was reported that a coup by forces loyal to Compaoré

had been thwarted. In recent years, Islamist extremists in the Sahel region have gained a significant presence.

The 1991 constitution was amended in 2000 to reduce the presidential term from seven years. The president is directly elected for a five-year term, renewable once. The unicameral National Assembly has 127 members who are directly elected for a five-year term. Executive power is vested jointly in the president and the council of ministers, both responsible to the legislature.

HEAD OF STATE
President, Roch Marc Christian Kaboré, *elected* 29 November 2015, *sworn in* 29 December 2015

SELECTED GOVERNMENT MEMBERS *AS AT NOVEMBER 2020*
Prime Minister, Christophe Dabiré
Economy and Finance, Lassané Kaboré
Foreign Affairs, Alpha Barry

EMBASSY OF THE REPUBLIC OF BURKINA FASO
16 Place Guy d'Arezzo, 1180 Brussels, Belgium
T (00) (+32) (2) 345 9912 **E** ambassade.burkina@skynet.be
W www.ambassadeduburkina.be
Ambassador Extraordinary and Plenipotentiary, HE Zaba Nikiema, *appt* 2018

BRITISH AMBASSADOR
Ambassador Extraordinary and Plenipotentiary, HE Iain Walker, *apptd* 2017, resident in Accra, Ghana

ECONOMY AND TRADE
The country is one of the poorest in the world, with around 80 per cent of the population engaged in subsistence agriculture and animal husbandry, which are vulnerable to periodic droughts. With few natural resources, the economy is heavily dependent on cotton and gold exports and therefore also exposed to the vagaries of global price fluctuations. Civil war in neighbouring Côte d'Ivoire harmed trade by cutting off transport routes, and caused many expatriate Burkinabes to return home, adding to the unemployment problem and depriving the economy of their remittances. During 2013, unrest in Mali caused similar problems and a number of public protests were held about socio-economic issues; the government reduced income taxes and price controls to alleviate discontent. Despite these difficulties, the economy grew rapidly between 2013 and 2019 thanks to gold and cotton production, although major terrorist attacks like that on Ouagadougou's Splendid Hotel in January 2016 has limited investment. Major infrastructure projects begun in 2014 include road building and the construction of a new airport in Ouagadougou, while a three-year IMF programme agreed in 2018 has facilitated increased public investment.

Agriculture contributes 31 per cent of GDP; the main product apart from cotton is livestock. Gold extraction is increasing and exploration for other minerals has begun. The processing of cotton and other agricultural products, gold mining and the manufacturing of beverages, soap, cigarettes and textiles are the main industries, contributing 23.9 per cent to GDP. Services account for 44.9 per cent of GDP.

The main export markets are Switzerland and India. Principal exports are cotton, livestock and gold. The chief import providers are China, Côte d'Ivoire and the USA, supplying capital goods, foodstuffs and fuel.
GNI – US$16.1bn; US$790 per capita (2019)
Annual average growth of GDP – 6.4 per cent (2017 est)
Inflation rate – 0.4 per cent (2017 est)
Population below poverty line – 40.1 per cent (2009 est)
Total external debt – US$3.056bn (2017 est)
Imports – US$4,065m (2016)
Exports – US$3,269m (2016)

BALANCE OF PAYMENTS

Trade – US$795m deficit (2016)
Current Account – US$664m deficit (2018)

Trade with UK	2018	2019
Imports from UK	£16,996,116	£40,228,193
Exports to UK	£5,015,830	£2,629,227

COMMUNICATIONS

Airports – Two; the main international airport is at Ouagadougou
Roadways and railways – 15,304km; 622km
Telecommunications – 76,760 fixed lines and 19.3 million mobile subscriptions (2018); there were 3.2 million internet users in 2018
Internet code and IDD – bf; 226 (to UK), 44 (from UK)
Major broadcasters – Radio is the most popular medium with the state-run Radio Burkina the largest broadcaster; state-run Television Nationale du Burkina is one of the largest television broadcasters
Press – There are five daily national newspapers, including the government-run *Sidwaya, L'Observateur Paalga* and *Le Pays*
WPFI score – 23.47 (38)

EDUCATION AND HEALTH

Education is nominally compulsory from age six to 16 but the prohibitive cost of school supplies and a lack of resources prevent many children from attending.
Literacy rate – 41.2 per cent (2018)
Gross enrolment ratio (percentage of relevant age group) – primary 94.5 per cent, secondary 41.3 per cent, tertiary 7.1 per cent (2019 est)
Health expenditure (per capita) – US$44 (2017)
Hospital beds (per 1,000 people) – 0.4 (2010)
Life expectancy (years) – 62.7 (2020 est)
Mortality rate – 8.2 (2020 est)
Birth rate – 35.1 (2020 est)
Infant mortality rate – 52 (2020 est)
HIV/AIDS adult prevalence – 0.7 per cent (2019 est)

BURUNDI

Republika y'u Burundi / République du Burundi – Republic of Burundi

Area – 27,830 sq. km
Capital – Gitega; population, 135,000 (2020 est)
Major towns – Bujumbura, Bubanza, Muyinga, Ngozi, Ruyigi
Currency – Burundi franc (FBu) of 100 centimes
Population – 11,865,821 rising at 2.85 per cent a year (2020 est); Hutu (85 per cent), Tutsi (14 per cent) (est)
Religion – Christian (Roman Catholic 62.1 per cent, Protestant 23.9 per cent), Muslim 2.5 per cent (est)
Language – Kirundi, French (both official), Swahili, English

Population density – 435 per sq. km (2019)
Urban population – 13.4 per cent (2019 est)
Median age (years) – 17.7 (2020 est)
National anthem – 'Burundi Bwacu' 'Our Burundi'
National day – 1 July (Independence Day)
Death penalty – Abolished for all crimes (since 2009)
CPI score – 19 (165)
Military expenditure – US$63.9m (2017)
Literacy rate – 68.4 per cent (2017 est)
Gross enrolment ratio (percentage of relevant age group) – primary 119 per cent, secondary 45.1 per cent (2019 est); tertiary 4.1 per cent (2018 est)
Health expenditure (per capita) – US$24 (2017)
Hospital beds (per 1,000 people) – 0.8 (2014)
Life expectancy (years) – 66.7 (2020 est)
Mortality rate – 6.2 (2020 est)
Birth rate – 36.5 (2020 est)
Infant mortality rate – 40.1 (2020 est)
HIV/AIDS adult prevalence – 1 per cent (2019 est)

CLIMATE AND TERRAIN

Burundi lies across the Nile–Congo watershed in central Africa. A hilly interior rises from an average altitude of 1,700m to the country's highest point at 2,670m (Heha) and falls to a plateau in the east. The river Ruzizi forms part of the north-western border with the Democratic Republic of the Congo, along with Lake Tanganyika (the lowest elevation in the country at 772m) in the south-west. The climate is equatorial, moderated by altitude; the average temperature in the lower regions is 29°C, and in the higher regions is 20°C. There are two rainy seasons: February to April and October to December.

POLITICS

Under the 2005 constitution, amended following a referendum in 2018, the executive president is directly elected for a seven-year term, renewable once. The bicameral *Parlement* comprises the National Assembly and the senate; members of both serve a five-year term. The National Assembly has 100 directly elected members, three co-opted members from the Twa ethnic group, and 21 members co-opted to ensure a 60 per cent Hutu and 40 per cent Tutsi split and that 30 per cent of the total are women. The senate has 43 members: 36 indirectly elected by an electoral college of provincial councils; three co-opted Twa members; four former presidents; and enough women to make the number of women senators up to 30 per cent of the total. The constitution also specifies the proportion of Hutu, Tutsi and female members of the council of ministers.

Pierre Nkurunziza of the National Council for the Defence of Democracy-Forces for the Defence of Democracy (CNDD-FDD), a Hutu party, was elected president by the newly elected legislature in 2005 and by direct presidential elections in June 2010 and July 2015. In May 2015, Burundi's constitutional court ruled that President Nkurunziza could stand for a third term of office, notwithstanding the constitution limiting incumbents to two terms. The decision sparked protests across Burundi, which killed dozens of people and caused over 150,000 to flee to neighbouring states. The 2018 referendum extended presidential terms from five to seven years, but Nkurunziza died in June 2020.

The CNDD-FDD retained large majorities in the 2015 and 2020 legislative elections, and Nkurunziza's appointed successor, Evariste Ndayishimiye, won the simultaneous presidential election in May 2020 with 71 per cent of the vote. Opposition groups claimed the elections were fraudulent.

HEAD OF STATE
President, Evariste Ndayishimiye, *sworn in* 18 June 2020
First Vice-President, Bazombanza Prosper

		Breaks union with Rwanda and becomes independent	Monarchy overthrown	First multiparty elections end Tutsi dominance with the election of a Hutu president, Melchior Ndadaye	Legislative elections take place

Area annexed and included in German East Africa

c.1600 — 1890 — 1918 — 1962 — 1966 — 1993-4 — 2000 — 2005

Ruled by Tutsi kings despite a majority Hutu population

Administered by Belgium as part of the League of Nations-mandated territory of Ruanda-Urundi

Becomes a one-party state republic under a series of brutal regimes dominated by the Tutsi minority

Assassinations of President Ndadaye and successor Cyprien Ntaryamira spark civil war

Arusha (Tanzania) peace accords signed

SELECTED GOVERNMENT MEMBERS *AS AT NOVEMBER 2020*
Prime Minister, Allaine Guillaume Bunyoni
Defence, Alaine Tribert Mutabazi
Finance, Domitien Ndihokubwayo
Interior, Gervais Ndirakobuca

EMBASSY OF THE REPUBLIC OF BURUNDI
Uganda House, 2nd Floor, 58–59 Trafalgar Square, London WC2N 5DX
T 020-7930 4958 **E** info@burundiembassy.org.uk
W www.burundiembassy.org.uk
Ambassador Extraordinary and Plenipotentiary, HE Ernest Ndabashinze, *apptd* 2017

BRITISH AMBASSADOR
HE Joanne Lomas, *apptd* 2018, resident at Kigali, Rwanda

ECONOMY AND TRADE

Economic activity has increased since the civil war ended, but reform and reconstruction are hampered by a lack of administrative capacity, a poorly educated workforce, limited access to healthcare, a malaria epidemic, malnutrition, high levels of inflation, corruption and poor law enforcement. Agriculture is the mainstay of the economy, contributing 39.5 per cent of GDP and employing around 90 per cent of the workforce. Around 65 per cent of the population live below the poverty line. Exports of coffee and tea account for over half of foreign exchange earnings, leaving the economy vulnerable to the effects of global price fluctuations and weather conditions. Industry is relatively small-scale and employs around 2.3 per cent of the workforce but contributes 16.4 per cent of GDP. The main activities are light manufacturing, food processing, the assembly of imported components and public sector construction. Since 2013 there has been major investment in infrastructure projects, but economic growth was dented by the political turmoil of 2015–16. Burundi is heavily reliant upon foreign aid, which constituted over one-third of national income in 2016.

Most trade is with the DRC, India, China, Switzerland and the UAE, but it is constrained by the poor transport infrastructure and landlocked location. The main exports are coffee, tea, sugar, cotton and hides. The principal imports are capital goods, petroleum products and food.
GNI – US$3.2bn; US$280 per capita (2019)
Annual average growth of GDP – 0.0 per cent (2017 est)
Inflation rate – 16.6 per cent (2017 est)
Population below poverty line – 64.6 per cent (2014 est)
Total external debt – US$610.9m (2017 est)
Imports – US$741m (2017)
Exports – US$197m (2017)

BALANCE OF PAYMENTS
Trade – US$544m deficit (2016)
Current Account – US$362m deficit (2019)

Trade with UK	2018	2019
Imports from UK	£4,147,088	£5,471,090
Exports to UK	£336,594	£386,566

COMMUNICATIONS

Airports and waterways – Bujumbura has the only airport with a surfaced runway and the only port, while movement around Lake Tanganyika is by water
Roadways – A limited road network, of which only 1,500km is paved, is concentrated around Bujumbura
Railways – There are no railways at present but the East African railways master plan, a project designed to expand the rail network in this region of Africa, is in its planning stage
Telecommunications – 24,810 fixed lines and 6.3 million mobile subscriptions (2018); there were 300,00 internet users in 2018
Internet code and IDD – bi; 257 (from UK), 44 (to UK)
Major broadcasters – The government-controlled Radio Télévision Nationale du Burundi (RTNB) runs the main national television and radio stations
Press – The only regularly published newspaper is the government-owned *Le Renouveau*
WPFI score – 55.33 (160)

CABO VERDE

Republica de Cabo Verde – Republic of Cabo Verde

Area – 4,033 sq. km; comprises the Windward Islands (Boa Vista, Sal, Santa Antao, Santa Luzia, Sao Nicolau, Sao Vicente) and Leeward Islands (Brava, Fogo, Maio and Sao Tiago)
Capital – Praia, on Sao Tiago; population, 168,000 (2018 est)
Major town – Mindelo
Currency – Escudo Caboverdiano ($) of 100 centavos
Population – 583,255 rising at 1.28 per cent a year (2020 est)
Religion – Christian (Roman Catholic 77.3 per cent, Protestant 4.6 per cent, other Christian 3.4 per cent), Muslim 1.8 per cent (est)
Language – Portuguese (official), Crioulo (a blend of Portuguese and West African words)
Population density – 135 per sq. km (2019)
Urban population – 66.2 per cent (2019 est)
Median age (years) – 26.8 (2020 est)
National anthem – 'Cantico da Liberdade' 'Song of Freedom'
National day – 5 July (Independence Day)
Death penalty – Abolished for all crimes (since 1981)

CPI score – 58 (41)
Military expenditure – US$10.7m (2018)
Conscription – 18–35 years of age; 24 months (selective)
Literacy rate – 86.8 per cent (2016 est)
Gross enrolment ratio (percentage of relevant age group) – primary 104 per cent, secondary 88.2 per cent, tertiary 23.6 per cent (2018 est)
Health expenditure (per capita) – US$168 (2017)
Life expectancy (years) – 73.2 (2020 est)
Mortality rate – 5.9 (2020 est)
Birth rate – 19.1 (2020 est)
Infant mortality rate – 19.7 (2020 est)
HIV/AIDS adult prevalence – 0.6 per cent (2019 est)

CLIMATE AND TERRAIN

The archipelago of ten islands of volcanic origin lies 600km off the west African coast. Elevation extremes range from 2,829m (Mt Fogo, an active volcano on Fogo island) to 0m (Atlantic Ocean). The climate is hot and dry, with periodic droughts.

HISTORY AND POLITICS

The islands were first discovered and colonised *c*.1460 by Portugal. Administered with Portuguese Guinea until 1879, they became an overseas province in 1951. The country achieved independence on 5 July 1975 after a campaign by the African Party for the Independence of Guinea Bissau and Cape Verde (PAIGC).

The republic was a one-party state under the African Party for the Independence of Cape Verde (PAICV) until 1990. Multiparty elections in 1991 were won by the opposition Movement for Democracy (MPD), but 2001 legislative elections returned the PAICV to power and the party retained its overall majority in the 2006 and 2011 elections. MPD leader Jorge Fonseca was re-elected in the 2016 presidential election, and the MPD won 54.5 per cent of the vote in the March 2016 legislative elections.

Under the 1992 constitution, the president is directly elected for a five-year term, renewable once. There is a unicameral National Assembly with 72 members directly elected for a five-year term. The prime minister appoints the council of ministers.

HEAD OF STATE
President, Jorge Fonseca, *elected* 21 August 2011, *re-elected* 2 October 2016

SELECTED GOVERNMENT MEMBERS *AS AT NOVEMBER 2020*
Prime Minister, Ulisses Correia e Silva
Deputy Prime Minister, Finance, Olavo Correia
Defence, Foreign Affairs, Luis Filipe Tavares
Internal Affairs, Paulo Costa Rocha

EMBASSY OF THE REPUBLIC OF CABO VERDE
Avenue Jeanne 29, 1050 Brussels, Belgium
T (+32) (2) 643 6270
Ambassador Extraordinary and Plenipotentiary, vacant

BRITISH AMBASSADOR
HE George Hodgson, *apptd* 2018, resident at Lisbon, Portugal

ECONOMY AND TRADE

The islands have few natural resources, little fresh water and are subject to periods of prolonged drought. It has produced steady growth nevertheless, despite high public debt and unemployment, and further reforms are intended to attract foreign investment to aid diversification and development of the private sector. The government is dependent on foreign aid and remittances; owing to large-scale emigration the expatriate population is larger than the resident one, and remittances are one of the highest in Sub-Saharan Africa. The service sector dominates, with commerce, tourism, transport and public services accounting for 73.7 per cent of GDP. Industry contributes 17.5 per cent and agriculture 8.9 per cent; fishing resources are not fully exploited. The main industries are the production of food, beverages, garments and footwear, fishing and fish processing, salt mining and ship repair.

The main trading partners are Portugal, Spain and the Netherlands. Exports are fuel, footwear, garments, fish and hides. Imports include foodstuffs (over 80 per cent of food is imported), industrial products, transport equipment and fuel.
GNI – US$2bn; US$3,630 per capita (2019)
Annual average growth of GDP – 4.0 per cent (2017 est)
Inflation rate – 0.8 per cent (2017 est)
Population below poverty line – 30 per cent (2000 est)
Total external debt – US$1.713bn (2017 est)
Unemployment – 9 per cent (2017 est)
Imports – US$1,210m (2017)
Exports – US$845m (2017)

BALANCE OF PAYMENTS
Trade – US$364m deficit (2017)
Current Account – US$6m deficit (2019)

Trade with UK	2018	2019
Imports from UK	£1,604,689	£3,597,598
Exports to UK	£56,904	£1,934,413

COMMUNICATIONS

Airports and waterways – Nine, including airports at Praia and on Sal; the main ports are Praia and Mindelo
Roadways – 1,350km
Telecommunications – 62,680 fixed lines and 610,328 mobile subscriptions (2018); there were 320,623 internet users in 2018
Internet code and IDD – cv; 238 (from UK), 44 (to UK)
Major broadcasters – Radio and television services are operated by the state-run Radiotelevisao Caboverdiana
WPFI score – 20.15 (25)

CAMBODIA

Preahreacheanachakr Kampuchea – *Kingdom of Cambodia*

Area – 181,035 sq. km
Capital – Phnom Penh; population, 2,078,000 (2020 est)
Major towns – Battambang, Poipet, Siem Reap, Sihanoukville

Currency – Riel of 100 sen; the US dollar is widely used

Population – 16,926,984 rising at 1.4 per cent a year (2020 est); Khmer (97.6 per cent) (est)

Religion – Buddhist 97.9 per cent, Muslim 1.1 per cent (est); Buddhism is the state religion

Language – Khmer (official)

Population density – 92 per sq. km (2019)

Urban population – 23.8 per cent (2019 est)

Median age (years) – 26.4 (2020 est)

National anthem – 'Nokoreach' 'Royal Kingdom'

National day – 9 November (Independence Day)

Death penalty – Abolished for all crimes (since 1989)

CPI score – 20 (162)

Military expenditure – US$346m (2015)

Literacy rate – 80.5 per cent (2018 est)

Gross enrolment ratio (percentage of relevant age group) – primary 106.5 per cent (2019 est); secondary 34 per cent (2011 est); tertiary 14.7 per cent (2019 est)

Health expenditure (per capita) – US$82 (2017)

Hospital beds (per 1,000 people) – 0.8 (2015)

Life expectancy (years) – 65.9 (2020 est)

Mortality rate – 7.3 (2020 est)

Birth rate – 21.3 (2020 est)

Infant mortality rate – 43.7 (2020 est)

HIV/AIDS adult prevalence – 0.5 per cent (2019 est)

CLIMATE AND TERRAIN

Cambodia is a mostly flat country, apart from the Cardamom mountains in the south-west and the uplands of the north-east. The fertile central plains are drained by rivers that run into Tonle Sap, the largest lake in south-east Asia, and into the Mekong river, which flows through the country from north to south. The highest point of elevation is 1,810m (Phnum Aoral) while the lowest is 0m (Gulf of Thailand). The climate is tropical, with a monsoon season from May to November.

POLITICS

Under the 1993 constitution, Cambodia is a pluralist liberal democracy with a constitutional monarchy. The monarch is chosen from eligible royal males by a Council of the Throne elected by parliament. Executive power rests with the government, which is responsible to parliament. The bicameral parliament comprises the National Assembly, which has 125 members directly elected for a five-year term, and the senate, which has 62 members, 58 of whom are elected for a six-year term by the National Assembly and commune councils, with two members appointed by the king and two appointed by the National Assembly.

King Sihanouk abdicated in 2004 and was succeeded by his son, Prince Norodom Sihamoni. In the 2013 election the Cambodian People's Party (CPP) won 68 seats in the National Assembly – losing the large majority that, in the 2008 elections, had allowed it to form a government without a coalition for the first time. In the 2018 elections, the CPP overwhelmingly extended its mandate, claiming 114 seats amid a crackdown on the press and suppression of the leading opposition party. Long-serving Prime Minister Hun Sen (CPP) was sworn in for a further five-year term, having ruled since 1985.

HEAD OF STATE

HM The King of Cambodia, Norodom Sihamoni, *crowned* 29 October 2004

President of the National Assembly, Heng Samrin

SELECTED GOVERNMENT MEMBERS *AS AT NOVEMBER 2020*

Prime Minister, Hun Sen

Deputy Prime Ministers, Gen. Tea Banh *(Defence);* Aun Porn Moniroth *(Economy and Finance);* Prak Sokhonn *(Foreign Affairs);;* Sar Kheng *(Interior);* Yim Chhai Ly; Bin Chhin; Ke Kim Yan; Hor Namhong; Men Sam An; Chea Sophara

ROYAL EMBASSY OF CAMBODIA

64 Brondesbury Park, London NW6 7AT

T 020-8451 7997 **E** cambodianembassy@btconnect.com

W www.cambodianembassy.org.uk

Ambassador Extraordinary and Plenipotentiary, HE Soeung Rathchavy, *apptd* 2017

BRITISH EMBASSY

27–29 Street 75, Sangat Srah Chak, Khan Daun Penh, Phnom Penh 12201

T (+855) (0) 23 427 124

W www.gov.uk/government/world/cambodia

Ambassador Extraordinary and Plenipotentiary, HE Tina Redshaw, *apptd* 2018

SECURITY PROBLEMS

The Khmer Rouge continued to fight a guerrilla war until 1996, when it was weakened by internal divisions. Pol Pot was tried by the Khmer Rouge in 1997 and died in captivity in 1998. The remaining Khmer Rouge soldiers surrendered in 1999. A UN-backed tribunal was established in 2007 to try former leaders of the Khmer Rouge regime for atrocities committed during its rule.

Relations with Thailand deteriorated after 2008 because of a long-running dispute over the border in the area of the Preah Vihear temple, with sporadic exchanges of fire and occasional fighting between the two countries' forces. In November 2013 the International Court of Justice ruled that Thailand must withdraw its troops from the temple and granted most of the territory to Cambodia.

ECONOMY AND TRADE

Since 1999 the government has made progress with economic reform and development but the country remains very poor. The demographic imbalance (over half the population is around 25), lack of education and skills, deeply ingrained corruption and an absence of basic infrastructure also pose serious problems. Nevertheless, the economy grew at an average rate of 8 per cent between 2000 and 2010, and around 7 per cent between 2011 and 2019. Economic growth has been driven by the expansion of garment manufacturing (68 per cent of exports), construction, agriculture, tourism (visitors more than tripled between 2007 and 2018) and mining, which is attracting foreign investment, but the benefits are largely limited to urban areas. The discovery of oil and gas deposits in territorial waters promises additional revenue once exploitation begins. While poverty is

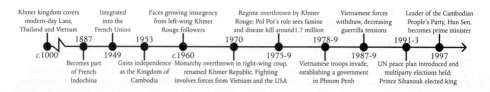

| c.1000 | 1887 | 1949 | 1953 | c.1960 | 1970 | 1975-9 | 1978-9 | 1987-9 | 1991-3 | 1997 |

Khmer kingdom covers modern-day Laos, Thailand and Vietnam — 1887

Integrated into the French Union — 1953

Faces growing insurgency from left-wing Khmer Rouge followers — 1970

Regime overthrown by Khmer Rouge; Pol Pot's rule sees famine and disease kill around 1.7 million — 1978-9

Vietnamese forces withdraw, decreasing guerrilla tensions — 1991-3

Leader of the Cambodian People's Party, Hun Sen, becomes prime minister — 1997

*c.*1000

Becomes part of French Indochina — 1949

Gains independence as the Kingdom of Cambodia — c.1960

Monarchy overthrown in right-wing coup, renamed Khmer Republic. Fighting involves forces from Vietnam and the USA — 1975-9

Vietnamese troops invade, establishing a government in Phnom Penh — 1987-9

UN peace plan introduced and multiparty elections held; Prince Sihanouk elected king — 1997

declining, around a fifth of government expenditure comes from foreign donations and public debt has steadily grown thanks to a sustained current account deficit.

The service sector contributes 41.9 per cent of GDP, agriculture 25.3 per cent and industry 32.8 per cent. Agriculture engages 48.7 per cent of the workforce; the main crops are rice, rubber, maize, vegetables, cashew nuts and cassava. The main industrial activities are tourism, garment and textiles manufacturing, processing of agricultural and forestry products, fishing and mining gemstones. The main trading partners are the USA (21.5 per cent of exports), China (34.1 per cent of imports), the UK, Singapore and Thailand.

GNI – US$22.4bn; US$1,480 per capita (2019)
Annual average growth of GDP – 6.9 per cent (2017 est)
Inflation rate – 2.9 per cent (2017 est)
Population below poverty line – 16.5 per cent (2016 est)
Unemployment – 0.3 per cent (2017 est)
Total external debt – US$11.87bn (2017 est)
Imports – US$17,588m (2017)
Exports – US$15,917m (2017)

BALANCE OF PAYMENTS
Trade – US$1,671m deficit (2017)
Current Account – US$4,064m deficit (2019)

Trade with UK	2018	2019
Imports from UK	£55,419,289	£45,981,731
Exports to UK	£872,891,393	£862,233,730

COMMUNICATIONS
Airports – Six; the main airports are at Phnom Penh, Siem Reap and Sihanoukville
Waterways – There are 3,700km of navigable waterways, mostly on the Mekong river, and ships of up to 2,500 tonnes can sail as far as Phnom Penh all year round
Roadways and railways – 12,239km of paved roadways; 690km
Telecommunications – 88,157 fixed lines and 19.4 million mobile phone subscriptions (2018); there were 6.6 million internet users in 2018
Internet code and IDD – kh; 855 (from UK), 1 44 (to UK)
Major broadcasters – There are 11 TV broadcasters, including the government-run National Television of Cambodia (TVK); there are roughly 160 radio broadcasters
Press – Daily newspapers include the pro-government *Reaksmei Kampuchea* (Khmer), and the English-language *Cambodia Daily* and *Phnom Penh Post*
WPFI score – 45.46 (144)

CAMEROON
République du Cameroun – Republic of Cameroon

Area – 475,440 sq. km
Capital – Yaoundé; population, 3,922,000 (2020 est)
Major cities – Bafoussam, Bamenda, Douala, Garoua
Currency – Franc CFA of 100 centimes

Population – 27,744,989 rising at 2.78 per cent a year (2020 est); Bamileke-Bamu (24.3 per cent), Beti/Bassa/Mbam (21.6 per cent), Biu-Mandara (14.6 per cent), Arab-Choa/Hausa/Kanuri (11 per cent), Adamawa-Ubangi (9.8 per cent), Grassfields (7.7 per cent), other African (6.7 per cent) (est)
Religion – Christian (Roman Catholic 38.3 per cent, Protestant 25.5 per cent, other Christian 6.9 per cent), Muslim 24.4 per cent, animist 2.2 per cent (est)
Language – English, French (both official), about 24 African languages
Population density – 53 per sq. km (2019)
Urban population – 57 per cent (2019 est)
Median age (years) – 18.5 (2020 est)
National anthem – 'O Cameroun, Berceau de nos Ancetres' 'O Cameroon, Cradle of Our Forefathers'
National day – 20 May (Republic Day)
Death penalty – Retained (last used 1997)
CPI score – 25 (153)
Military expenditure – US$430m (2018)
Literacy rate – 77.1 per cent (2018 est)
Gross enrolment ratio (percentage of relevant age group) – primary 105.7 per cent (2019 est); secondary 60.1 per cent (2016 est); tertiary 14.3 per cent (2018 est)
Health expenditure (per capita) – US$68 (2017)
Hospital beds (per 1,000 people) – 1.3 (2010)
Life expectancy (years) – 62.3 (2020 est)
Mortality rate – 8.1 (2020 est)
Birth rate – 36.3 (2020 est)
Infant mortality rate – 51.5 (2020 est)
HIV/AIDS adult prevalence – 3.1 per cent (2019 est)

CLIMATE AND TERRAIN
There are three main geographic zones: desert plains and savannah in the north (the Lake Chad basin), mountains and plateaux in the central region and tropical rainforests in the south and east. Elevation extremes range from 4,095m (Fako on Mt Cameroon, an active volcano) to 0m (Atlantic Ocean). The climate varies from tropical in the south to arid in the north. There is a wet season from April to September in the north, while there is low rain from March to June and heavy rain from September to November in the south.

POLITICS
The 1972 constitution was amended in 1990 to enable a return to multiparty rule, in 1996 to extend the presidential term and to provide for the establishment of a second legislative chamber (not implemented until 2013), and in 2008 to remove the limit on the number of presidential terms.

The president is directly elected for a seven-year term and appoints the prime minister and cabinet. The bicameral Parliament consists of the National Assembly (lower house) with 180 directly elected members, and the Senate with 100 members, 70 indirectly elected by regional councils and 30 appointed by the president. All members serve five-year terms.

In the 2020 election, the Cameroon People's Democratic Movement (RDPC) retained its overwhelming majority in the National Assembly, winning 139 seats. The RDPC also won 63 of the 70 seats available in the Senate in the 2018 elections. In October 2018, Paul Biya won a seventh continuous term as president after claiming 71.3 per cent of the vote, in an election marred by voter intimidation.

Cameroon has experienced an increasing number of cross-border raids by the Nigeria-based Islamist group Boko Haram since 2014. In response, a multinational task force consisting of troops from Cameroon and Chad has carried out attacks on Boko Haram bases in northern Nigeria. Separatist conflict in the anglophone south-west region, beginning in 2016 and

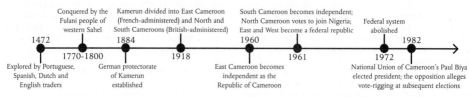

Conquered by the Fulani people of western Sahel — 1472

1770-1800 — Explored by Portuguese, Spanish, Dutch and English traders

1884 — Kamerun divided into East Cameroon (French-administered) and North and South Cameroons (British-administered)

German protectorate of Kamerun established

1918

1960 — South Cameroon becomes independent; North Cameroon votes to join Nigeria; East and West become a federal republic

1961 — East Cameroon becomes independent as the Republic of Cameroon

Federal system abolished — 1982

1972 — National Union of Cameroon's Paul Biya elected president; the opposition alleges vote-rigging at subsequent elections

escalating in 2017, were violently repressed and by September 2019 it was estimated more than 3,000 people had died in the ongoing conflict.

HEAD OF STATE
President, Paul Biya, *took power* 6 November 1982, *elected* 14 January 1984, *re-elected* 1988, 1992, 1997, 2004, 2011, 2018

SELECTED GOVERNMENT MEMBERS *AS AT NOVEMBER 2020*
Prime Minister, Joseph Dion Nguté
Defence, Joesph Beti Assomo
Economy, Alamine Ousmane Mey
External Relations, Lejeune Mbella Mbella

HIGH COMMISSION FOR THE REPUBLIC OF CAMEROON
84 Holland Park, London W11 3SB
T 020-7727 0771 **E** info@cameroonhighcommission.co.uk
W www.cameroonhighcommission.co.uk
High Commissioner, HE Albert Njoteh Fotabong, *apptd* 2018

BRITISH HIGH COMMISSION
PO Box 547, Avenue Winston Churchill, Yaoundé, Centre Region 547
T (+237) 2222 0796 **E** bhc.yaounde@fco.gov.uk
W www.gov.uk/government/world/cameroon
High Commissioner, HE Rowan Laxton, *apptd* 2017

ECONOMY AND TRADE
Natural resources such as oil and timber have enabled diverse agricultural, industrial and infrastructural development. Coupled with the growth of domestic demand and implementation of large-scale projects, the economy was able to counteract the effects of the global downturn. Nonetheless, around 40 per cent of the population live in poverty. Cameroon has a large and top-heavy public sector that suffers from endemic corruption, and recent IMF funding and debt relief have been conditional on progress towards privatisation and greater financial transparency. The emergence of Boko Haram in Nigeria presents a long-term threat to tourist revenue and international investment. Significant resources are directed towards infrastructure projects including the Lom Pangar Hydroelectric Dam and a deep seaport at Kribi, but the country struggles to attract foreign investment.

Industry contributes 26.5 per cent to GDP, agriculture 16.7 per cent and services 56.8 per cent. Around 70 per cent of the workforce is engaged in agriculture. The main industrial activity is oil production and refining. Revenue is also earned from the oil pipeline passing through the country from Chad.

The main trading partners are EU countries, China and Thailand. Principal exports are crude oil and petroleum products, timber, cocoa, aluminium, coffee and cotton. Imports are chiefly machinery, electrical and transport equipment, fuel and food.

GNI – US$38.9bn; US$1,500 per capita (2019)
Annual average growth of GDP – 3.5 per cent (2017 est)
Inflation rate – 0.6 per cent (2017 est)
Population below poverty line – 30 per cent (2001 est)

Unemployment – 4.3 per cent (2014 est)
Total external debt – US$9.375bn (2017 est)
Imports – US$7,026m (2017)
Exports – US$6,221m (2017)

BALANCE OF PAYMENTS
Trade – US$804m deficit (2016)
Current Account – US$1,695m deficit (2019)

Trade with UK	2018	2019
Imports from UK	£44,824,815	£43,842,482
Exports to UK	£46,999,105	£56,347,277

COMMUNICATIONS
Airports – 11; the main airports are at Douala, Garoua and Yaoundé
Waterways – The main seaports are at Douala and the Limboh terminal; the river Benue is navigable up to Garoua in the rainy season
Roadways and railways – 5,133km paved roadways; 1,245km
Telecommunications – There are 902,253 fixed lines and 18.5 million mobile subscriptions (2018); there were 6.1 million internet users in 2018
Internet code and IDD – cm; 237 (from UK), 44 (to UK)
Major broadcasters – The state-run Cameroon Radio-Television Corporation (CRTV) held a monopoly on broadcast media until liberalisation in 2001 allowed commercial television and radio stations to be established; other major broadcasters include Canal 2 and Radio Siantou
Press – The government-owned *Cameroon Tribune* is the main daily national newspaper
WPFI score – 43.28 (134)

CANADA

Area – 9,984,670 sq. km
Capital – Ottawa; population, 1,393,000 (2020 est)
Major cities – Calgary, Edmonton, Hamilton, Montréal, Québec, Toronto, Vancouver, Winnipeg
Currency – Canadian dollar (C$) of 100 cents
Population – 37,694,085 rising at 0.81 per cent a year (2020 est)
Religion – Christian (Catholic 32.3 per cent, Protestant 20.3 per cent, other Christian 7.9 per cent), Muslim 3.2 per cent, Hindu 1.5 per cent, Sikh 1.4 per cent, Buddhist 1.1 per cent, Jewish 1 per cent (est)

Language – English, French (both official), Punjabi, Italian, Spanish, German, Cantonese, Tagalog, Arabic
Population density – 4 per sq. km (2019)
Urban population – 81.5 per cent (2019 est)
Median age (years) – 41.8 (2020 est)
National anthem – 'O Canada'
National day – 1 July (Canada Day)
Death penalty – Abolished for all crimes (since 1998)
CPI score – 77 (12)
Military expenditure – US$21,621m (2018)

CLIMATE AND TERRAIN

The six main geographic divisions of Canada are: the Appalachian–Acadian region; the Canadian Shield, which comprises more than half the country; the St Lawrence–Great Lakes lowland; the interior plains; the Cordilleran region; and the Arctic archipelago, which lies under continuous permafrost. The most southerly point is Middle Island in Lake Erie. Elevation extremes range from 5,959m (Mt Logan) to 0m (Atlantic Ocean). The climate varies from temperate in the south to subarctic and arctic in the north. The east and centre experience greater extremes than in corresponding latitudes in Europe, but the climate is milder in the southwestern part of the prairie region and the southern parts of the Pacific slope. The tornado season is April to September, peaking in June and early July in southern Ontario, Alberta, Québec, Saskatchewan and Manitoba through to Thunder Bay. The interior of British Columbia and western New Brunswick are also tornado zones.

POLITICS

Under the 1982 constitution, the head of state is Queen Elizabeth II, represented by a governor-general appointed on the advice of the Canadian prime minister.

The bicameral parliament consists of a senate and a House of Commons. The senate comprises 105 members, who serve until the age of 75, appointed by the governor-general on the recommendation of the prime minister; seats are assigned on a regional basis. The House of Commons has 338 members, directly elected for a four-year term. Representation is proportional to the population of each province. Each province is largely self-governing, with its own lieutenant-governor and unicameral legislative assembly. The territories are administered by the federal government.

In snap general elections in 2006 and 2008, the Conservative Party won the most seats, but not a majority, and formed minority governments under Stephen Harper. His government won a snap general election in 2011, increasing its seats to achieve an overall majority, however in October 2015 the Liberal Party won 184 seats in federal elections, allowing it to form a majority government led by Justin Trudeau. The Liberals lost the popular vote in the October 2019 federal election but formed a minority government with 157 seats.

GOVERNOR-GENERAL

Governor-General, HE Julie Payette, OC *apptd* 2017

SELECTED GOVERNMENT MEMBERS *AS AT NOVEMBER* 2020

Prime Minister, Justin Trudeau, *elected* 19 October 2015, *sworn in* 4 November 2015
Defence, Harjit Sajjan
Finance, Chrystia Freeland
Foreign Affairs, Francois-Phillippe Champagne

CANADIAN HIGH COMMISSION

Canada House, Trafalgar Square, London SW1Y 5BJ
T 020-7004 6000 **W** www.unitedkingdom.gc.ca
High Commissioner, HE Janice Charette, *apptd* 2016

BRITISH HIGH COMMISSION

80 Elgin Street, Ottawa, Ontario K1P 5K7
T (+1) (613) 237 1530 **E** ukincanada@fco.gov.uk
W www.gov.uk/government/world/canada
High Commissioner, HE Susan le Jeune d'Allegeersheceque, CMG, *apptd* 2017

ECONOMY AND TRADE

Canada has a highly developed, industrialised and diversified market economy, which was transformed from a predominantly rural to an industrial economy in the second half of the 20th century by the growth of mining, manufacturing and services. Tight management of government finances resulted in balanced budgets from the late 1990s until 2007, and free-trade agreements with the USA in 1989 and 1994 (NAFTA) stimulated trade. The economy went into recession in 2008 owing to the global downturn; recovery began in 2010 and marginal growth was achieved in 2012–16 despite the global decline in crude oil prices, and a stronger rate of 3 per cent was achieved in 2017. Lower levels of growth in 2018 and 2019 are likely to be followed by a fall of roughly 6.2 per cent in 2020 owing to the coronavirus pandemic.

Canada's wealth of natural resources make it the world's largest exporter of timber, pulp and newsprint (over half the land is tree-covered), and it is one of the world's largest exporters of minerals, particularly uranium (of which it is the world's second-largest single producer) and diamonds. In 2012 around 7.2 per cent of the land area was farmed, of which 4.6 per cent was under cultivation, mostly in the prairie region of western Canada. The country is one of the world's leading food producers, particularly of wheat, barley, oilseed, fruit, vegetables and dairy products. The fishing industry is also significant but has declined in recent years because of restrictions introduced to protect stocks after decades of overfishing. Oil, natural gas and hydroelectricity production is high enough for Canada to be a net exporter of energy; oil production, in particular, has become a significant economic driver, and Canada's oil reserves are ranked third in the world behind Saudi Arabia and Venezuela. The government has plans to develop the oil and gas-rich Arctic area but the assertion of its sovereignty has attracted criticism from other Arctic countries and is complicated by the lack of international agreement on countries' territorial claims.

In 2017, the services sector contributed 70.2 per cent of GDP, industry 28.2 per cent and agriculture 1.6 per cent.

England claims St John's, Newfoundland	Hudson's Bay Company founded; it opens up the interior of the country	Treaty of Paris awards almost all of France's North American territory to Britain		Constitution patriated (severed from the British government)	
1497	1608	1713	1867		2006
1583	1670	1763	1982		

First recorded landing by John Cabot — Québec founded by French — Britain gains large areas of the country under the Treaty of Utrecht — The British North America Act forms a dominion under the name of Canada, comprising four provinces: Ontario, Québec, New Brunswick and Nova Scotia — Parliament recognises Québecois as nation within a united Canada

FEDERAL STRUCTURE

Provinces or Territories (with official contractions)	Capital	Premier	Area (sq. km)	Pop. (2019)
Alberta (AB)	Edmonton	Jason Kenney	661,848	4,354,737
British Columbia (BC)	Victoria	John Horgan	944,735	5,020,302
Manitoba (MB)	Winnipeg	Brian Pallister	647,797	1,360,396
New Brunswick (NB)	Fredericton	Blaine Higgs	72,908	772,094
Newfoundland and Labrador (NL)	St John's	Andrew Furey	405,212	523,790
Northwest Territories (NT)	Yellowknife	Caroline Cochrane	1,346,106	44,598
Nova Scotia (NS)	Halifax	Stephen McNeil	55,284	965,382
Nunavut (NU)	Iqaluit	Joe Savikataaq	2,093,190	38,787
Ontario (ON)	Toronto	Doug Ford	1,076,395	14,446,515
Prince Edward Island (PE)	Charlottetown	Dennis King	5,660	154,748
Québec (QC)	Québec City	Francois Legault	1,542,056	8,433,301
Saskatchewan (SK)	Regina	Scott Moe	651,036	1,168,423
Yukon Territory (YT)	Whitehorse	Sandy Silver	482,443	40,369

The USA and Canada enjoy the world's most comprehensive trade and economic partnership, with 51.5 per cent of Canada's imports arriving from the US and 76.4 per cent of exports destined for its southern neighbour. The main exports are motor vehicles and parts, industrial machinery, aircraft, telecommunications equipment, chemicals, plastics, fertilisers, forestry products, energy products (including crude oil, natural gas and electricity) and aluminium.

GNI – US$1,742.8bn; US$46,370 per capita (2019)
Annual average growth of GDP – 1.66 per cent (2019 est)
Inflation rate – 1.6 per cent (2017 est)
Population below poverty line – 9.4 per cent (2008 est)
Unemployment – 5.67 per cent (2019 est)
Total external debt – US$1.608 trillion (2016 est)
Imports – US$548,449m (2017)
Exports – US$510,168m (2017)

BALANCE OF PAYMENTS
Trade – US$38,280m deficit (2017)
Current Account – US$35,408m deficit (2019)

Trade with UK	2018	2019
Imports from UK	£5,412,985,928	£5,215,266,940
Exports to UK	£11,310,106,151	£12,891,907,084

COMMUNICATIONS
Airports – There are 523 paved airports and airstrips, of which 26 serve major cities
Waterways – There are 636km of waterways and over 300 ports, the most significant of which are Vancouver and Prince Rupert on the Pacific coast and Montréal, Halifax, Port Cartier, Sept-Iles/Pointe Noire, Saint John and Québec in the east. Most deep-water ports are open all year, and Churchill, on Hudson's Bay, is ice-free for longer periods as a result of climate change. In addition, the Great Lakes/St Lawrence Seaway system, the world's longest inland waterway for ocean-going shipping, provides access to the North American interior
Roadways and railways – 415,600km paved roadways, including 17,000km of motorways; 77,932km
Telecommunications – There are 13.8 million fixed lines and 33.2 million mobile telephones subscriptions (2018); there were 33.7 million internet users in 2018
Internet code and IDD – ca; 1 (from UK), 011 44 (to UK)
Major broadcasters – The public broadcaster, the Canadian Broadcasting Corporation (CBC), transmits programmes in English and French, and provides services for indigenous peoples in the north of the country. Société Radio-Canada is the French-language public broadcasting service

Press – Major newspapers include *The Toronto Sun, National Post* and *Le Journal de Montréal* (French-language)
WPFI score – 15.29 (16)

EDUCATION AND HEALTH
Education is compulsory from age six to 16 (18 in Ontario and New Brunswick).
Gross enrolment ratio (percentage of relevant age group) – primary 101.5 per cent, secondary 114.1 per cent, tertiary 70.1 per cent (2018 est)
Health expenditure (per capita) – US$4,755 (2017)
Hospital beds (per 1,000 people) – 2.7 (2012)
Life expectancy (years) – 83.4 (2020 est)
Mortality rate – 7.9 (2020 est)
Birth rate – 10.2 (2020 est)
Infant mortality rate – 4.3 (2020 est)

CENTRAL AFRICAN REPUBLIC

République Centrafricaine – Central African Republic

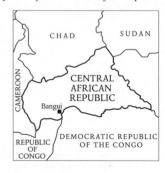

Area – 622,984 sq. km
Capital – Bangui; population, 889,000 (2020 est)
Major cities – Berbérati, Bimbo, Carnot
Currency – Franc CFA of 100 centimes
Population – 5,990,855 rising at 2.09 per cent a year (2020 est); Baya (28.8 per cent), Banda (22.9 per cent), Mandjia (9.9 per cent), Sara (7.9 per cent), M'Baka-Bantu (7.9 per cent), Mbum (6 per cent), Ngbanki (5.5 per cent), Zande-Nzakara (3 per cent), other Central African Republic ethnic groups (11 per cent) (est)
Religion – Indigenous beliefs 35 per cent, Christian (Protestant 25 per cent, Roman Catholic 25 per cent, animism strongly influences Christian practice), Muslim 15 per cent (est)
Language – French (official), Sangho, other African languages

Population density – 7 per sq. km (2019)
Urban population – 41.8 per cent (2019 est)
Median age (years) – 20 (2020 est)
National anthem – 'La Renaissance' 'The Renaissance'
National day – 1 December (Republic Day)
Death penalty – Retained (last used 1981)
CPI score – 26 (153)
Military expenditure – US$30.95m (2018)
Literacy rate – 37.4 per cent (2017 est)
Gross enrolment ratio (percentage of relevant age group) – primary
    102 per cent (2016 est); secondary 17.1 per cent (2017
    est); tertiary 3 per cent (2012 est)
Health expenditure (per capita) – US$24 (2017)
Hospital beds (per 1,000 people) – 1 (2011)
Life expectancy (years) – 54.2 (2020 est)
Mortality rate – 12.3 (2020 est)
Birth rate – 33.2 (2020 est)
Infant mortality rate – 80.6 (2020 est)
HIV/AIDS adult prevalence – 3.5 per cent (2019 est)

CLIMATE AND TERRAIN
This landlocked state lies on a plateau between the Chad and
Congo river basins, with mostly savannah in the north and
rainforest in the south. The main river is the Oubangui, which
is the lowest point of elevation (335m). The highest point is
Mt Ngaoui (1,420m). The climate is tropical, with a wet season
in the north from May to September and in the south from May
to October. The north can experience average temperatures of
up to 34°C between January and April, and the humidity can
be extreme. Seasonal temperatures vary slightly, ranging from
24.3°C in August to 27.7°C in March.

POLITICS
Under the 2004 constitution, the president is elected for a five-
year term, renewable once. The unicameral National Assembly
has 140 members, directly elected for a five-year term. The
prime minister is appointed by the president and appoints the
ministers.

François Bozizé seized power in 2003 and won presidential
elections in 2005 and 2011. Legislative elections in January
and March 2011 were won by the Kwa Na Kwa (KNK)
coalition, a group loyal to the president. In March 2013 the
New Seleka rebel coalition took the capital by force, forcing
President Bozizé to flee; the rebel leader Michel Djotodia
suspended the constitution and dissolved parliament. Djotodia
was forced to resign in January 2014 after he failed to stop
sectarian violence between Seleka and Christian militias. On
20 January Catherine Samba Panza was elected interim
president and she remained in post as continued violence in
2015 delayed fresh elections. One-time prime minister
Faustin-Archange Touadéra, a former maths professor, won a
presidential run-off in February 2016, while the National
Union for Democracy and Progress (UNDP) and the Union for
Central African Renewal (URCA) emerged as the two largest
parties in legislative elections in the same month.

HEAD OF STATE
President, Faustin-Archange Touadéra, *elected* February 2016

SELECTED GOVERNMENT MEMBERS *AS AT*
NOVEMBER 2020
Prime Minister, Firmin Ngrebada
Defence, Marie-Noelle Koyara
Finance, Henri-Marie Dondra
Foreign Affairs, Sylvie Baipo-Temon

EMBASSY OF THE CENTRAL AFRICAN REPUBLIC
30 Rue des Perchamps, 75016 Paris, France
T (+33) (1) 4525 3974
Ambassador Extraordinary and Plenipotentiary, vacant

BRITISH AMBASSADOR
HE Rowan Laxton, *apptd* 2017, resident at Yaoundé,
    Cameroon

ECONOMY AND TRADE
The economy is largely undeveloped owing to decades of
conflict and misrule, but is becoming more stable.
Development is still hindered by political factionalism, a
landlocked position and poor transport infrastructure, an
unskilled workforce, massively unequal income distribution,
and corruption. The country is dependent on international aid
and the amount received only partially meets humanitarian
needs. Despite working closely with the IMF since 2009,
including receiving infrastructure funding in 2012 and
extended credit in 2016, the economy has struggled to match
pre-2013 levels when sectarian fighting caused a 34.2 per cent
drop in GDP growth. Over 70 per cent of the population live
below the poverty line.

Natural resources include diamonds, gold, uranium and
timber; diamond and gold mining, and forestry are among the
main industrial activities but the economy still depends mostly
on agriculture, which accounts for 42.3 per cent of GDP. Most
production is at subsistence level but cotton, coffee and timber
form the main exports along with diamonds. The main imports
are food, textiles, fuels and machinery. Trade is mainly with
France, the USA and China.
GNI – US$2.4bn; US$520 per capita (2019)
Annual average growth of GDP – 4.3 per cent (2017 est)
Inflation rate – 4.1 per cent (2017 est)
Unemployment – 6.9 per cent (2017 est)
Total external debt – US$779.9m (2017 est)
Imports – US$507m (2016)
Exports – US$227m (2016)

BALANCE OF PAYMENTS
Trade – US$279m deficit (2016)
Current Account – US$45,287m deficit (2018)

Trade with UK	2018	2019
Imports from UK	£4,751,526	£2,363,826
Exports to UK	£33,660	£47,965

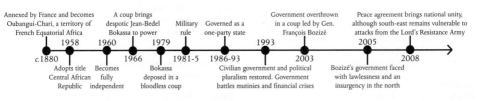

						Government overthrown	Peace agreement brings national unity,
Annexed by France and becomes	A coup brings					in a coup led by Gen.	although south-east remains vulnerable to
Oubangui-Chari, a territory of	despotic Jean-Bedel	Military	Governed as a			François Bozizé	attacks from the Lord's Resistance Army
French Equatorial Africa	Bokassa to power	rule	one-party state				
1958	1960	1979		1993			2005

c.1880   1966   1981-5   1986-93   2003   2008

Adopts title — Becomes — Bokassa deposed in a bloodless coup — Civilian government and political pluralism restored. Government battles mutinies and financial crises — Bozizé's government faced with lawlessness and an insurgency in the north
Central African — fully
Republic — independent

COMMUNICATIONS

Airports – One; the principal airport is at Bangui
Waterways – There are 2,800km of waterways, mostly on the Oubangui and Sangha rivers, that are navigable all year and are important passenger and freight transport routes
Roadways – 24,000km, of which only 700km are paved
Telecommunications – There are 2,193 fixed lines and 1.3 million mobile telephone subscriptions (2018); there were 249,000 internet users in 2018
Internet code and IDD – cf; 236 (from UK), 44 (to UK)
Major broadcasters – Major broadcasters include the state-run Télévision Centrafricaine and Radio Centrafique; Radio Ndeke Luka operates nationally and is funded by the UN and foreign NGOs
Press – There are five privately owned daily newspapers, including *Le Citoyen*, *Le Confident* and *L'Hirondelle*
WPFI score – 42.87 (132)

CHAD

République du Tchad/Jumhuriyat Tshad – Republic of Chad

Area – 1,284,000 sq. km
Capital – N'Djamena; population, 1,423,000 (2020 est)
Major cities – Abéché, Moundou, Sarh
Currency – Franc CFA of 100 centimes
Population – 16,877,357 rising at 3.18 per cent a year (2020 est); the population is made up of around 200 ethnic groups, of which Sara is the largest (30.5 per cent) (est)
Religion – Muslim 52.1 per cent, Christian (Protestant 23.9 per cent, Roman Catholic 20 per cent) (est)
Language – French, Arabic (both official), Sara (in the south)
Population density – 12 per sq. km (2019)
Urban population – 23.3 per cent (2019 est)
Median age (years) – 16.1 (2020 est)
National anthem – 'La Tchadienne' 'People of Chad'
National day – 11 August (Independence Day)
Death penalty – Retained
CPI score – 20 (162)
Military expenditure – US$233m (2018)
Conscription – 20 years of age, male only; 36 months (women are subject to 12 months of military or civic service at age 21)
Literacy rate – 22.3 per cent (2018 est)
Gross enrolment ratio (percentage of relevant age group) – primary 89.2 per cent, secondary 20.6 per cent (2019 est); tertiary 3.3 per cent (2015 est)
Health expenditure (per capita) – US$30 (2017)
Life expectancy (years) – 58.3 (2020 est)
Mortality rate – 10 (2020 est)
Birth rate – 41.7 (2020 est)
Infant mortality rate – 68.6 (2020 est)
HIV/AIDS adult prevalence – 1.2 per cent (2019 est)

CLIMATE AND TERRAIN

The population is concentrated in the fertile lowlands of the south, away from the arid central and northern desert areas. The highest point of elevation is 3,415m (Emi Koussi) and the lowest is 160m (the Djourab depression). The climate is desert in the north and tropical in the south, with a wet season from July to September.

HISTORY AND POLITICS

Chad was colonised by France from the 1890s, becoming part of French Equatorial Africa. It became self-governing after the Second World War and independent on 11 August 1960. A one-party state was declared in 1963 by the president, a southerner, which in 1965 prompted a rebellion in the north against a perceived pro-southern bias in the government. Regional and ethnic tensions, most notably between the Muslim Arab north and the Christian and animist African south have made the country politically unstable since independence. Chad's instability was exacerbated from the 1970s to the 1990s by Libya's support for some rebels and its annexation of territory in northern Chad, and since 2004 by the overspill of the Darfur conflict in Sudan.

Idriss Déby seized power in 1990 after leading a rebellion in eastern Chad, and initiated a transition to democracy. A new constitution was introduced in 1996, and the first multiparty elections were held.

Déby won the first multiparty presidential election in 1996 and was re-elected in 2001, 2006, 2011 and 2016, amid opposition boycotts and doubts over the integrity of the polls. The 2011 legislative election was won by Déby's Patriotic Salvation Movement (MPS) and its allies. That parliamentary term was due to end in June 2015 but has been habitually extended, first by constitutional law until November 2018, then until May 2019, and is now due to take place in October 2021. In May 2018, Albert Pahimi Padacké resigned as prime minister along with his government, in protest over constitutional changes which further extended Déby's powers. The amendments were subsequently passed, allowing Déby to rule without a prime minister.

The 1996 constitution was amended in 2005 to remove the limit on the number of terms a president may serve. The president is directly elected for a five-year term. The unicameral National Assembly of 188 members is directly elected for a four-year term.

HEAD OF STATE
President, Idriss Déby, *took power* December 1990, *elected* 3 July 1996, *re-elected* 2001, 2006, 2011, 2016

SELECTED GOVERNMENT MEMBERS *AS AT NOVEMBER 2020*
Economy, Issa Doubregné
Finance, Hamid Tahir Guilim
Foreign Affairs, Amine Abba Sidik

EMBASSY OF THE REPUBLIC OF CHAD
Boulevard Lambermont 52, 1030 Brussels, Belgium
T (+32) (2) 215 1975 **E** ambassade.tchad@chello.be
W www.ambassadedutchad.be
Ambassador Extraordinary and Plenipotentiary, HE Ousmane Matar Breme, *apptd* 2015

BRITISH AMBASSADOR
HE Rowan Laxton, *apptd* 2017, resident at Yaoundé, Cameroon

INSURGENCIES
The series of insurgencies over the decades since independence means that no government has ever controlled

the whole of the country. Rebel offensives reached the capital in 2006 and 2008 before being repulsed. In 2009, eight rebel groups united to form the Union of Resistance Forces alliance.

From 2004, the east and south-east were further destabilised by the overspill of fighting from Sudan's Darfur region. The EU/UN mission deployed in 2008 to protect Sudanese refugees in Chad was withdrawn in 2010, and relations with Sudan have now been normalised and the border reopened. In 2012, the leader of rebel group the Popular Front for Recovery (FPR), Abdel Kader Baba Ladde, surrendered to military forces in the Central African Republic and returned to Chad. In 2013, following a coup in the Central African Republic, a regional summit in Chad agreed that neighbouring countries should send troops to restore security to the region.

In July 2014, France announced it would set up a new military operation in the Sahel region in an effort to stop the emergence of militant Islamist groups. As of 2020 the operation, based in the Chadian capital N'Djamena, involved around 5,000 French troops, along with troops from Burkina Faso, Chad, Mali and Mauritania.

ECONOMY AND TRADE
Economic development has been limited by political instability, corruption, the landlocked location and poor transport infrastructure. About 80 per cent of the workforce is occupied in subsistence agriculture, herding and fishing, which contributes 52.3 per cent of GDP, and the remaining 20 per cent are practically all employed in services, which contribute 33.1 per cent of GDP. Nearly 40 per cent of the population live below the poverty line. The main focus of development, funded by foreign investment and international aid, is to further exploit oil deposits in the Doba basin in the south, which came into production in 2003; the oil is exported via a pipeline through Cameroon. Efforts to reduce public finances resulted in the restructuring of a US$1.45bn oil-backed loan in February 2018, but the ensuing cuts to public spending prompted strikes and protests; the government has continued to work multinational partners to relieve its high public debt. Other industries include processing cotton (the main industry before oil) and other agricultural products, and light manufacturing. Industry generates 14.7 per cent of GDP.

An oil refinery was constructed in N'Djamena in 2011 and production from new oil wells allowed growth to reach double digits in 2014. In October 2014, the government also received compensation from the China National Petroleum Corporation (CNPC) after the company was found to have dumped crude oil in the Koudalwa region in 2013. Oil provides about 60 per cent of export earnings, making the country vulnerable to price fluctuations, and since 2016 it has sought to diversify its economy through joint public-private development but with little success.

Chad's main trading partners are the USA, France, China and Cameroon. Principal exports are oil, cattle, cotton and gum arabic. The main imports are machinery and transport equipment, industrial goods, food and textiles.
GNI – US$11.2bn; US$700 per capita (2019)
Annual average growth of GDP – 3.1 per cent (2017 est)
Inflation rate – -0.9 per cent (2017 est)
Population below poverty line – 46.7 per cent (2011 est)
Total external debt – US$1.724bn (2017 est)
Imports – US$2,200m (2015)
Exports – US$2,900m (2015)

BALANCE OF PAYMENTS
Trade – US$700m surplus (2015)
Current Account – US$187m deficit (2018)

Trade with UK	2018	2019
Imports from UK	£20,838,061	£28,808,345
Exports to UK	£226,380	£762,232

COMMUNICATIONS
Airports and waterways – Nine, the principal airport is at N'Djamena; the Chari and Legone rivers are navigable only in the wet season
Roadways – 40,000km, of which only 206km of urban roads are paved
Telecommunications – There are 9,000 fixed lines and 7 million mobile subscriptions (2018); there were 1 million internet users in 2016
Internet code and IDD – td; 235 (from UK), 15 44 (to UK)
Major broadcasters – Al-Nassour and the state-owned Télé-Tchad are the only two TV stations; Radiodiffusion Nationale Tchadienne is the state-controlled radio station
Press – Le Progres is the country's only daily newspaper; other privately owned periodicals include *N'Djamena Bi-Hebdo*
WPFI score – 39.70 (123)

CHILE

República de Chile – Republic of Chile

Area – 756,102 sq. km
Capital – Santiago; population, 6,767,000 (2020 est)
Major cities – Antofagasta, Concepción, Puente Alto, San Bernardo, Temuco, Valparaíso, Viña del Mar
Currency – Chilean peso ($) of 100 centavos
Population – 18,186,770 rising at 0.71 per cent a year (2020 est)
Religion – Christian (Roman Catholic 66.7 per cent, Evangelical and Protestant 16.4 per cent) (est)
Language – Spanish (official), English, Mapudungun and other indigenous languages
Population density – 25 per sq. km (2019)
Urban population – 87.6 per cent (2019 est)
Median age (years) – 35.5 (2020 est)
National anthem – 'Himno Nacional de Chile' 'National Anthem of Chile'
National day – 18 September (Independence Day)
Death penalty – Retained for certain crimes (last used 1985)
CPI score – 67 (26)
Military expenditure – US$5,571m (2018)

CLIMATE AND TERRAIN
Chile extends over 4,600km from the arid north around Arica to Cape Horn, with an average breadth of 180km. The Atacama desert lies in the north. In the central zone there is a fertile valley between the Andes and the low coastal range of mountains, with a Mediterranean climate; two-thirds of the population live here. Chilean Patagonia, in the south, extends

into subantarctic terrain, with glaciers and icefields; the climate is cool with high precipitation. Elevation extremes range from 6,880m (Nevado Ojos del Salado) to 0m (Pacific Ocean). Its Pacific island possessions include the Juan Fernández group and Easter Island, and the Chilean Antarctic Territory covers the Antarctic peninsula and an area of the landmass that extends from 53°W. to 90°W. along a latitude of 60°S.

HISTORY AND POLITICS

Chile was conquered in the 16th century by the Spanish, who subjugated the indigenous population. It remained under Spanish rule until 1810, when the first autonomous government was established. Independence was achieved in 1818 after a revolutionary war.

A military coup in 1973 overthrew the Marxist president Salvador Allende. General Augusto Pinochet, the coup leader, assumed the presidency and retained the office until elections were held in 1989, beginning the transition to full democracy. Between 1998 and his death in 2006, a number of unsuccessful attempts were made to bring Gen. Pinochet to trial for human rights atrocities committed during his time in office.

In the 2017 legislative elections, the centre-left New Majority Coalition extended its mandate by winning 68 seats in the lower chamber, and 19 of the 38 seats in the senate. Conservative business tycoon Sebastián Piñera, the former president who led the country from 2010–14, returned to power in 2018.

The 1981 constitution, drafted to promote private sectors to control public services, has been amended many times. The executive president is directly elected for a four-year term that is not renewable. The bicameral National Congress comprises a senate of 43 members elected for an eight-year term (half renewed every four years) and a Chamber of Deputies of 155 members directly elected for a four-year term. However, in October 2020 the country overwhelmingly voted to rewrite the neoliberal constitution, which will be drafted by a popularly elected body.

HEAD OF STATE
President, Sebastián Piñera, *elected* 17 December 2017, *sworn in* 11 March 2018

SELECTED GOVERNMENT MEMBERS *AS AT NOVEMBER 2020*
Defence, Mario Desbordes
Finance, Ignacio Briones
Foreign Affairs, Andres Allamand
Interior, Victor Perez

EMBASSY OF CHILE
37–41 Old Queen Street, London SW1H 9JA
T 020-7222 2361 **E** embachile@embachile.co.uk
W www.chileabroad.gov.cl/reino-unido
Ambassador Extraordinary and Plenipotentiary, HE David Gallagher Patrickson, *apptd* 2018

BRITISH EMBASSY
Avda. El Bosque Norte 0125, Las Condes, Santiago
T (+56) (2) 370 4100 **E** embsan@britemb.cl
W www.gov.uk/government/world/chile
Ambassador Extraordinary and Plenipotentiary, HE James Bowden, *apptd* 2018

ECONOMY AND TRADE

Economic reforms in the late 1970s and the 1980s, and sound financial management, have made Chile one of the most successful economies in Latin America; in 2010 it became the first South American country to join the OECD, and by 2019 had 26 trade agreements covering 60 countries. Growth is based on high copper prices (20 per cent of government revenue), a strong export base and growing domestic demand, but the falling price of copper has slowed growth and in 2015 the government used US$5.5bn (£3.68bn) of its healthy sovereign wealth fund to stimulate the economy. Growth has slowed in recent years and the economy is expected to shrink in 2020, partly owing to the coronavirus pandemic.

Chile is the world's largest producer of copper, and the world's only commercial producer of nitrate of soda (Chile saltpetre) from natural resources. The chief industries are mining, forestry, fishing, food and fish processing, and winemaking.

Agriculture provides 4.2 per cent of GDP, industry 32.8 per cent and services 63 per cent. The main trading partners are China, the USA, Brazil and Japan. Principal exports are copper, fruit, fish products, paper and pulp, chemicals and wine. The main imports are petrol and petroleum products, chemicals, electrical and telecommunications equipment, industrial machinery, vehicles and natural gas.

GNI – US$284.5bn; US$15,010 per capita (2019)
Annual average growth of GDP – 1.03 per cent (2019 est)
Inflation rate – 2.2 per cent (2017 est)
Population living below poverty line – 14.4 per cent (2013 est)
Unemployment – 7.22 per cent (2019 est)
Total external debt – US$183.4bn (2017 est)
Imports – US$74,370m (2017)
Exports – US$79,439m (2017)

BALANCE OF PAYMENTS
Trade – US$5,069m surplus (2017)
Current Account – US$10,932m deficit (2019)

Trade with UK	2018	2019
Imports from UK	£582,886,342	£696,388,648
Exports to UK	£943,225,275	£848,835,205

COMMUNICATIONS

Airports and waterways – 90, the principal airport is at Santiago; the main ports are Arica, Antofagasta, Coquimbo, San Antonio, Talcahuano and Valparaíso
Roadways and railways – 77,801km; 7,282km of railways
Telecommunications – 3 million fixed lines and 25.2 million mobile subscriptions (2018); there were around 14.7 million internet users in 2018
Internet code and IDD – cl; 56 (from UK), 44 (to UK)
Major broadcasters – The National Television of Chile is state-owned but not under direct government control; Radio Cooperativa is a news-based private network that broadcasts alongside numerous other private radio stations
Press – Major newspaper publications include *El Mercurio* and *La Tercera;* the government-owned *La Nación* was privatised in January 2014
WPFI score – 27.31 (51)

EDUCATION AND HEALTH

Education is free and compulsory from age six to 17, although the education system has suffered from underinvestment and mismanagement, resulting in ongoing student protests.
Literacy rate – 96.4 per cent (2018 est)
Gross enrolment ratio (percentage of relevant age group) – primary 102.2 per cent, secondary 102.4 per cent, tertiary 90.9 per cent (2018 est)

Health expenditure (per capita) – US$1,382 (2017)
Hospital beds (per 1,000 people) – 2.2 (2013)
Life expectancy (years) – 79.4 (2020 est)
Mortality rate – 6.5 (2020 est)
Birth rate – 13.1 (2020 est)
Infant mortality rate – 6.2 (2020 est)
HIV/AIDS adult prevalence – 0.5 per cent (2019 est)

CHINA

Zhonghua Renmin Gongheguo – *People's Republic of China*

Area – 9,596,960 sq. km
Capital – Beijing; population, 20,463,000 (2020 est)
Major cities – Chengdu, Chongqing, Dongguan, Foshan,
   Guangzhou, Nanjing, Shanghai, Shenyang, Shenzhen,
   Tianjin, Wuhan, Xi'an
Currency – Renminbi (RMB) or yuan (Y) of ten jiao or
   100 fen
Population – 1,394,015,977 rising at 0.32 per cent a year
   (2020 est); the Chinese Government officially recognises
   56 ethnic groups, of which Han Chinese (91.6 per cent) is
   the largest (est)
Religion – officially atheist, but permits four state-registered
   religions: Buddhism (18.2 per cent est), Christianity (5.1
   per cent est), Islam (1.8 per cent est) and Taoism. It is
   difficult to estimate numbers, as many congregations
   worship in private
Language – Mandarin (official), Cantonese, Shanghainese,
   Fuzhou, Xiang, Gan, Taiwanese; common speech, or
   putonghua (often referred to as Mandarin), is based on the
   northern dialect and is promoted throughout the country
Population density – 148 per sq. km (2019)
Urban population – 60.3 per cent (2019 est)
Median age (years) – 38.4 (2020 est)
National anthem – 'Yiyongjun Jinxingqu' 'The March of the
   Volunteers'
National day – 1 October (Founding of People's Republic)
Death penalty – Retained
CPI score – 41 (80)
Military expenditure – US$249,997m (2018 est)
Conscription – 18–22 years of age; 24 months (selective)

CLIMATE AND TERRAIN
China is twice the size of western Europe and contains a vast range of landscapes and climates. The highest mountains are on the Tibetan plateau, in the west of the country, where the highest elevation is 8,850m (Mt Everest). To the north of the Tibetan plateau, the land drops to the arid, semi-desert steppes bisected by the Tian Shan mountains; the country's lowest elevation is −154m at Turpan Pendi. The southern plains and east coast have the most fertile land, irrigated by the Huang He (Yellow), Chang Jiang (Yangtze) and Xi Jiang (West) rivers, and are the most heavily populated areas.

There are seven climate zones. The north-east has cold winters, fierce winds, warm and humid summers, and erratic rainfall. The mountainous south-west has mild winters and warm summers. Inner Mongolia has cold winters and hot summers. Central China has warm and humid summers with occasional tropical cyclones. South China is partly tropical with heavy rainfall. The high Tibet plateau is subject to harsh winters. Xinjiang and the west have a desert climate, with cold winters and little rain.

POLITICS
The Communist Party of China is the dominant political party, and all elements of the political system are subordinate to it. A party congress is held every five years and elects the Politburo and its standing committee. This standing committee is the policy- and decision-making body and the *de facto* government.

Under the 1982 constitution, the National People's Congress (NPC) is the highest organ of state power. It has 2,980 members, indirectly elected for a five-year term, and holds only one full session a year; between sessions, its work is delegated to its standing committee. The congress elects the premier and, on his nomination, the State Council. The head of state is the president, also elected by the congress. In 2018, a constitutional amendment abolished presidential limits, allowing Xi Jinping to rule indefinitely and marking a possible return to lifelong rule.

Deputies to people's congresses at the primary level are directly elected by the voters from a list of approved candidates. These congresses elect the deputies to the congress at the next highest level. Deputies to the NPC are elected by the provincial and municipal people's congresses, and by the armed forces.

Local government is conducted through people's governments at provincial/municipal, prefecture/city, county/district, township and village levels. There are 22 provinces (Taiwan is claimed as a 23rd province), four municipalities directly under the central government, five autonomous regions, and two special administrative areas; provinces may contain autonomous counties or towns for ethnic minorities.

In 2012 Xi Jinping took over as General Secretary of the Communist Party of China, becoming president in 2013. He stated that he aimed to make corruption-free governance and economic growth key elements of his administration, the former of which has resulted in several high-profile purges of senior officials. Xi Jingping was unanimously re-elected in March 2018. Li Keqiang was elected premier by the 12th National People's Congress in 2013.

HEAD OF STATE
President, Xi Jinping, *elected* 14 March 2013, *re-elected* 17
   March 2018
Vice-President, Wang Qishan

STATE COUNCIL *AS AT NOVEMBER 2020*
Premier, Li Keqiang
Vice-Premiers, Han Zheng; Hu Chunhua; Liu He; Sun
   Chunlan
State Councillors, Wang Yong; Wei Fenghe; Xiao Jie; Zhao
   Kazhi

SELECTED GOVERNMENT MEMBERS
Civil Affairs, Huang Shuxian
Finance, Liu Kun
Foreign Affairs, Wang Yi

EMBASSY OF THE PEOPLE'S REPUBLIC OF CHINA
49–51 Portland Place, London W1B 1JL
T 020-7299 4049 **W** www.chinese-embassy.org.uk

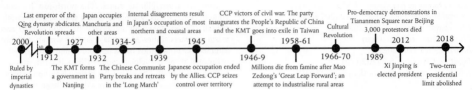

<table>
<tr><td>Last emperor of the
Qing dynasty abdicates.
Revolution spreads</td><td>Japan occupies
Manchuria and
other areas</td><td>Internal disagreements result
in Japan's occupation of most
northern and coastal areas</td><td>CCP victors of civil war. The party
inaugurates the People's Republic of China
and the KMT goes into exile in Taiwan</td><td>Cultural
Revolution</td><td>Pro-democracy demonstrations in
Tiananmen Square near Beijing
3,000 protestors died</td></tr>
</table>

| 2000 | 1927 | 1934-5 | 1945 | 1958-61 | 2012 | 2018 |

| 1912 | 1932 | 1939 | 1946-9 | 1966-70 | 1989 |

| Ruled by imperial dynasties | The KMT forms a government in Nanjing | The Chinese Communist Party breaks and retreats in the 'Long March' | Japanese occupation ended by the Allies. CCP seizes control over territory | Millions die from famine after Mao Zedong's 'Great Leap Forward'; an attempt to industrialise rural areas | Xi Jinping is elected president | Two-term presidential limit abolished |

Ambassador Extraordinary and Plenipotentiary, HE Liu
Xiaoming, *apptd* 2010

BRITISH EMBASSY
11 Guang Hua Lu, Jian Guo Men Wai, 100600, Beijing, China
T (+86) 0(10) 5192 4000 **W** www.gov.uk/government/world/china
Ambassador Extraordinary and Plenipotentiary, HE Caroline
Wilson, CMG *apptd* 2020

HUMAN RIGHTS
China's political system has become more liberal since 1978, when economic reforms allowing for greater amounts of personal freedom were introduced, with further liberalisation taking place during the regime of Deng Xiaoping from 1981 to 1987. The constitution was amended to officially recognise human rights in 2004, and National Human Rights Action Plans, issued by the State Council, were released in 2009 and 2012. While the practice of sending prisoners to labour camps for 're-education' was officially abolished in 2007, and the majority of camps were independently confirmed to have been closed in 2014, Chinese authorities claimed over 13,000 Muslim 'terrorists' had been detained between 2014 and 2019 in its western region of Xinjiang. In March 2019, human rights groups estimated the number of Muslims held in internment camps was over a million.

Despite reform, the state continues to tightly control freedom of expression, religion, association and reproduction rights. Ethnic minorities in Tibet, Inner Mongolia and Xinjiang, home to the Uygur Muslim separatist movement, experience widespread discrimination. The country is thought to have executed approximately 4,000 people in 2014, more than every other country in the world combined, and applies the death sentence to a variety of non-violent crimes, including corruption. Prominent critics of the regime are frequently subjected to house arrest and torture. Notable dissidents include: Chen Guangcheng, a blind human rights lawyer who fled to the USA in 2012; Liu Xiaobo, winner of the Nobel Peace prize in 2010, who died of cancer in custody in July 2017; and the artist Ai Weiwei. In April 2014, President Xi Jinping stated that China would never develop into a pluralist, Western-style democracy.

ECONOMY AND TRADE
Liberalisation since the 1980s has transformed the economy, developing a more autonomous state sector, a rapidly growing private sector and a leading presence in global trade and investment. A massive industrial base and transport infrastructure have been constructed, especially in the coastal regions, and the economy has become a free market in all but name, with several stock markets and Shanghai's emergence as a financial centre. China attracts considerable foreign investment and has become a major investor overseas. GDP has grown more than ten-fold since 1978, and China is now the largest exporter and trading nation in the world, and the largest economy when measured on a purchasing power parity basis.

Although some 500 million people who migrated to urban areas in the past 35 years have been lifted out of poverty, the effects of the rapid transformation have been unevenly distributed. In 2012, it was reported that China's city dwellers outnumber China's rural population for the first time; there are wide income differences between urban and rural areas, poor healthcare provision, lack of access to public services for migrant workers, rampant official corruption and environmental degradation of land, water and air. The government is also keen to increase domestic consumption (a priority of the 2011–16 and 2016–21 five-year plans), and so reduce the economy's reliance on exports for growth. The economy grew in real terms by an average of 7 per cent between 2013 and 2017. Growth is expected to remain relatively modest as China gradually transitions from a heavy manufacturing focus to a service economy, but an ongoing trade dispute with the US, starting in early 2018, has affected this and in July 2019 China declared its slowest quarterly growth rate in 27 years. As a result of the coronavirus pandemic, growth is expected to sharply reduce in 2020, to around 1.2 per cent.

China's expansion boosted its need for oil and coal, met initially by imports but increasingly by domestic production. However, to achieve its aim of reducing environmental degradation, China is looking to nuclear power and alternative energy generation, such as hydroelectric power from the Three Gorges Dam. In 2015, a 10-year 'Made in China' plan was initiated, which aimed to develop the country's robotics, information technology and aerospace industries; in January 2019, China landed the first spacecraft on the far side of the moon.

Although rural areas have seen few benefits from the economic transformation and are suffering the effects of rural depopulation and pollution, agriculture remains important; it contributes 7.9 per cent of GDP but employs 27.7 per cent of the workforce. The main crops are rice, cereals, potatoes, vegetables, peanuts, tea, fruit, cotton and oilseed crops. Livestock is raised in large numbers. Silk farming is one of the oldest industries. Cotton, woollen and silk textiles are manufactured in large quantities.

The highly diversified industrial sector, encompassing heavy industry, manufacturing and construction, contributes 40.5 per cent of GDP and employs 28.8 per cent of the workforce. The services sector accounts for 51.6 per cent of GDP and 43.5 per cent of employment. Tourism is now a major industry.

The world's largest importer and exporter of goods, China's exports include machinery, electrical equipment, data processing equipment, garments, textiles, iron and steel, and optical and medical equipment. The principal imports are electrical and other machinery, oil and mineral fuels, optical and medical equipment, metal ores, plastics and organic chemicals. The main trading partners are the USA, Hong Kong, Japan, Germany and South Korea, although trade with Latin America and Africa is growing.

GNI – US$14,554.3bn; US$10,410 per capita (2019)
Annual average growth of GDP – 6.14 per cent (2019 est)
Inflation rate – 1.6 per cent (2017 est)
Population below poverty line – 3.3 per cent (2016 est)
Unemployment – 3.64 per cent (2019 est)
Total external debt – US$1.598 trillion (2017 est)
Imports – US$2,207,901m (2017)
Exports – US$2,444,548m (2017)

BALANCE OF PAYMENTS
Trade – US$236,646m surplus (2017)
Current Account – US$141,335m surplus (2019)

Trade with UK	2018	2019
Imports from UK	£20,751,852,255	£23,610,392,457
Exports to UK	£42,560,391,933	£46,374,612,777

COMMUNICATIONS
Airports – There are 510 airports and airfields and several national air carriers
Waterways – The main seaports are Shanghai and Dalian in the north, and Guangzhou in the south; there are 110,000km of navigable waterways, Nanjing is the largest river port, and the Huang He (Yellow), Chang Jiang (Yangtze) and Xi Jiang (West) are the most significant river routes
Roadways and railways – 4,388,600km of paved roadways, including 136,500km of motorways; 131,000km
Telecommunications – 192 million fixed lines and 1.6 billion mobile subscriptions (2018); there were 751 million internet users in 2018
Internet code and IDD – cn; 86 (from UK), 44 (to UK)
Major broadcasters – The Communist Party maintains a firm grip on media and the internet. Television, provided by Chinese Central TV (CCTV), is the most popular medium; there are around 3,300 channels and 418 million households have access to television. All of China's 2,600 radio stations are state-owned
Press – Every city has its own newspaper – approximately 1,900 newspapers are published every week; national dailies include *Renmin Ribao* (Communist Party newspaper), *Zhongguo Qingnian Bao* and *China Daily* (English-language)
WPFI score – 78.48 (177)

EDUCATION AND HEALTH
Primary education lasts six years and secondary education six years (three years in junior middle school and three optional years in senior middle school).
Literacy rate – 96.8 per cent (2018 est)
Gross enrolment ratio (percentage of relevant age group) – primary 102 per cent (2019 est); secondary 94.3 per cent (2014 est); tertiary 53.8 per cent (2019 est)
Health expenditure (per capita) – US$441 (2017)
Hospital beds (per 1,000 people) – 4.2 (2012)
Life expectancy (years) – 76.1 (2020 est)
Mortality rate – 8.2 (2020 est)
Birth rate – 11.6 (2020 est)
Infant mortality rate – 11.4 (2020 est)
HIV/AIDS adult prevalence – 0.1 per cent (2012 est)

TIBET
Area – 1,199,164 sq. km
Population – 3,180,000 (2014 est)
Capital – Lhasa
Tibet is a plateau, seldom lower than 3,000m, in south-west China. It forms the frontier with India (boundary imperfectly demarcated), from which it is separated by the Himalayas from Kashmir to Myanmar; Nepal and Bhutan also border it to the south. The Indus, Brahmaputra, Mekong and Yangtze rivers all rise on the Tibet plateau.
  Tibet was under Mongol rule almost continuously from the 13th to the 17th centuries. Chinese control grew from the 18th century and direct rule began in 1910, but with the collapse of the Chinese Empire in 1911, Tibet declared its independence and the Dalai Lama ruled undisturbed until communist rule was established in China. In 1950, Chinese communist forces invaded Tibet, and in 1951 the Tibetan

authorities signed a treaty agreeing joint Chinese–Tibetan rule. A series of revolts against Chinese rule culminated in a 1959 uprising in the capital, which was crushed following several days of fighting, after which military rule was imposed. The Dalai Lama fled to India, where he and his followers were granted political asylum, and established a government in exile. Tibet became an Autonomous Region of China in 1965. Martial law was declared in Tibet in 1989.
  The Panchen Lama, the second-highest Lama, remained in Lhasa after 1959; when he died in 1989, China rejected the Dalai Lama's choice of successor and enthroned its own candidate. Subsequent appointments have been handled in a similar manner. Despite occasional talks between the Chinese government and representatives of the Dalai Lama, relations remain poor. In March 2011, the Dalai Lama announced his intention to withdraw from political life, transferring leadership to Lobsang Sangay, prime minister of the Tibetan parliament. In September 2012 his title was amended to political leader *(Sikyong)*.
  Another source of tension is the large number of Chinese migrants who have settled in Tibet since the 1970s, a development that the Tibetan government-in-exile regards as an attempt to eradicate the culture of the Tibetan people. Chinese now considerably outnumber Tibetans and have benefited disproportionately from the economic development of recent years.
  Peaceful anti-Chinese demonstrations in Tibet increased in early 2008 as the imminence of the Beijing Olympics put China's human rights record under greater international scrutiny. The violence of the Chinese crackdown was condemned worldwide, and pro-Tibet activists abroad disrupted the Olympic torch relay in several countries. Resistance and unrest continue: in 2009, in a show of passive resistance, farmers in Tibet and neighbouring provinces refused to till the fields or plant crops; in 2011, demonstrations sparked by the self-immolation of a Tibetan monk in the Sechuan province led to hundreds of arrests. More than 130 other self-immolations have taken place since.

SPECIAL ADMINISTRATIVE REGIONS

HONG KONG
Xianggang Tebie Xingzhengqu – Hong Kong Special Administrative Region
Area – 1,108 sq. km
Currency – Hong Kong dollar (HK$) of 100 cents
Population – 7,249,907 rising at 0.24 per cent a year (2020 est)
Population density – 7,096 per sq. km (2019)
Median age – 45.6 (2020 est)
Flag – Red, with a white bauhinia flower of five petals each containing a red star
National day – 1 July (Establishment Day)
Death penalty – Abolished for all crimes (since 2003)
CPI score – 76 (16)

CLIMATE AND TERRAIN
Hong Kong consists of Hong Kong Island, Kowloon and the New Territories (on a peninsula of the mainland in Guangdong province) and over 260 islands, including Lantau Island. Hong Kong Island is about 18km long and 3–8km wide. It is separated from the mainland by a narrow strait. The highest point is Tai Mo Shan (958m). The climate is subtropical, with hot, wet summers and cool, dry winters. Mean monthly temperatures range from 16°C to 29°C. Tropical cyclones occur between May and November, and over 75 per cent of the average annual rainfall of 2,180mm falls between May and September.

HISTORY AND POLITICS

Hong Kong developed as a major regional trading port because of its location on the main Far Eastern trade routes. Hong Kong Island was first occupied by Britain in 1841 and formally ceded to Britain in 1842. Kowloon was acquired in 1860, and the New Territories by a 99-year lease signed in 1898.

In 1984, the UK and China agreed that China would resume sovereignty over Hong Kong in 1997, and on 1 July 1997, Hong Kong became a Special Administrative Region (SAR) of the People's Republic of China. The 1984 joint declaration and the Basic Law (1990) guarantee that the SAR's social and economic systems will remain unchanged for 50 years and grant it a high degree of autonomy, known as the 'one country, two systems' principle.

Although the Basic Law provides for the development of democratic processes, political reform has been slow, prompting frequent demonstrations to demand full democracy or to oppose measures perceived to be repressive. In 2007 the Chinese government said that the chief executive could be directly elected from 2017 and the legislature members from 2020, although neither reform has yet been introduced. In 2017, China's foreign ministry simultaneously announced that China viewed the Sino-British joint declaration of 1984 as a 'historical document' to which it no longer felt bound.

Proposed electoral reforms in 2014, that were perceived as restrictive, sparked widespread sit-in protests known as the Umbrella Movement. A subsequent bill that would have allowed the transfer of political fugitives to mainland China provoked months of popular, sustained, and violent demonstrations starting in June 2019. Although the bill was retracted in September, pro-democracy protests calling for universal suffrage and direct elections continued; by late August it was estimated a quarter of the population (1.7 million people) attended a pro-democracy march through the city. Nonetheless, in June 2020 China passed a wide-ranging security law that critics claimed restricted freedoms, protest and Hong Kong's autonomy; in November a further bill disqualifying 'unpatriotic' opposition resulted in the resignation of all opposition lawmakers.

The Basic Law, approved in 1990, has served as Hong Kong's constitution since 1997. Its government is headed by the chief executive, who is elected by a 1,200-member electoral committee and serves a five-year term. The chief executive is aided by an executive council consisting of 15 principal officials, who are the heads of administrative departments, and 14 non-official members. The legislative council consists of 70 members, 35 directly elected by geographic constituencies, five directly elected by all voters in 'super seats', and 30 elected by functional, occupation-based constituencies; they serve a four-year term.

Carrie Lam was elected chief executive in March 2017, replacing Leung Chun-ying. In the 2016 legislative elections, pro-China parties won 40 seats and pro-democracy parties won 29.

Chief Executive, Carrie Lam, *elected* 26 March 2017, *sworn in* 1 July 2017

SELECTED GOVERNMENT MEMBERS *AS AT NOVEMBER 2020*

Chief Secretary for Administration, Matthew Cheung
Financial Secretary, Paul Chan Mo-po
Secretary for Justice, Teresa Cheng Yeuk-wah

BRITISH CONSULATE-GENERAL

PO Box 528, 1 Supreme Court Road, Central Hong Kong
T (+852) 2901 3000 **E** hongkong.consular@fco.gov.uk
W www.gov.uk/government/world/hong-kong
Consul-General, Andrew Heyn, OBE, *apptd* 2016

ECONOMY AND TRADE

The economy has moved away from manufacturing (which has mostly relocated to mainland China) and is service-based, with a high reliance on international trade and re-exports. It has developed into a regional corporate and banking centre, and has benefited in recent years from closer integration with China through increased trade, tourism and financial links. Although badly affected by the global economic downturn in 2008–9, and vulnerable to future volatility, the strength of the Chinese economy helped it to recover quickly. In 2014, Hong Kong signed the Closer Economic Partnership Arrangement with China, which aims to eliminate trade barriers and liberalise trade between the two economies.

The economy is dominated by the service sector, which accounted for 92.3 per cent of GDP in 2017. The main contributors to this are tourism, financial services and shipping. Industry contributes 7.6 per cent of GDP. Principal products are textiles, clothing, electronics, plastics, toys, clocks and watches.

The principal export markets are China (54.1 per cent), and the USA. China is also Hong Kong's principal supplier of imported goods (44.6 per cent).

GNI – US$381.74bn; US$50,840 per capita (2020)
Annual average growth of GDP – -1.25 per cent (2019 est)
Inflation rate – 1.5 per cent (2017 est)
Population below poverty line – 19.9 per cent (2016 est)
Unemployment – 2.93 per cent (2019 est)
Total external debt – US$633.6bn (2017 est)
Imports – US$516,411m (2016)
Exports – US$462,284m (2016)

BALANCE OF PAYMENTS

Trade – US$54,127m deficit (2016)
Current Account – US$22,467m surplus (2019)

Trade with UK	2018	2019
Imports from UK	£7,718,456,621	£8,769,731,856
Exports to UK	£6,932,302,229	£8,333,222,319

COMMUNICATIONS

Airports – There are two airports, one accommodating international flights
Waterways – Hong Kong has one of the world's finest natural harbours, and is the third-busiest container port in the world
Roadways – 2,107km (2017)
Telecommunications – 4.2 million fixed lines and 19.9 million mobile subscriptions (2018); there were 6.5 million internet users in 2018
Internet code and IDD – hk; 852 (from UK), 1 44 (to UK)
WPFI score – 29,65 (80)

EDUCATION AND HEALTH

Education is free and compulsory for children up to age 15.
Literacy rate – 99.2 per cent (2012 est)
Gross enrolment ratio (percentage of age group) – primary 109.3 per cent, secondary 107.7 per cent, tertiary 81 per cent (2019 est)
Life expectancy (years) – 83.2 (2020 est)
Mortality rate – 7.9 (2020 est)
Birth rate – 8.4 (2020 est)
Infant mortality rate – 2.7 (2020 est)

MACAU (AOMEN)

Aomen Tebie Xingzhengqu – Macau Special Administrative Region
Area – 28.2 sq. km
Currency – Pataca (MOP$) of 100 avos
Population – 614,458 rising at 0.64 per cent a year (2020 est)
Religion – Folk religions 58.9 per cent, Buddhist 17.3 per cent, Christian 7.2 per cent, other 1.2 per cent (est)

Population density – 20,778 per sq. km (2019)
Median age (years) – 40.8 (2020 est)
Flag – Green, with a white lotus flower above a white stylised bridge and water, under a large gold five-point star and four gold stars in crescent
National day – 20 December (Establishment Day)
Internet code and IDD – mo; 853 (from UK), 44 (to UK)

CLIMATE AND TERRAIN
Macau consists of the Macau peninsula and the islands of Coloane and Taipa. It is situated at the western side of the mouth of the Pearl river, bordering Guangdong province in south-east China. It is 64km from Hong Kong. Its area has nearly doubled since the 19th century due to land reclamation. The highest point is Coloane Alto (172m). The climate is subtropical.

HISTORY AND POLITICS
The first Portuguese ship arrived at Macau in 1513 and trade with China commenced in 1553. Macau became a Portuguese colony in 1557; China recognised Portugal's sovereignty over Macau by treaty in 1887. An agreement to transfer the administration of Macau to China was signed in 1987, and Macau became the Macau Special Administrative Region (MSAR) of China on 20 December 1999. Fernando Chui was elected unopposed as chief executive in 2009 and was re-elected in 2014 and 2018. The most recent legislative election was held in September 2017, returning a solid pro-government majority.

The Basic Law (1993) has served as Macao's constitution since 1999. The chief executive is elected by a 400-member election committee and serves a five-year term of office, which may be renewed once. The chief executive is assisted by the ten-member executive council. The legislative assembly has 33 members, who serve for four years; 14 are directly elected in proportional representation, 12 are indirectly elected by an electoral college of commercial and professional interest groups, and seven are appointed by the chief executive.
Chief Executive, Ho Iat Seng, elected August 2019, sworn in 20 December 2019

SELECTED GOVERNMENT MEMBERS *AS AT NOVEMBER 2020*
Economy and Finance, Leong Vai Tac
Secretary for Administration and Justice, Andre Cheong Weng Chon

CONSUL-GENERAL
Andrew Heyn, *apptd* 2016, resident at Hong Kong

ECONOMY AND TRADE
The economy is based on tourism and gambling, which have grown rapidly since 2001, and garment and textile manufacturing, which is in decline. Visitors totalled 30.95 million in 2016, the majority coming from mainland China, where gambling is illegal. The service sector contributes about 88.7 per cent of GDP and industry 11.4 per cent. The principal products and exports are clothing, textiles, footwear, toys, electronics, machinery and parts. The main trading partners are Hong Kong, China – with whom a Comprehensive Economic Partnership Agreement was signed in 2013 – and EU nations.
GNI – US$49.7bn; US$78,640 per capita (2018)
Annual average growth of GDP – 9.1 per cent (2017 est)
Inflation rate – 1.2 per cent (2017 est)
Unemployment – 2 per cent (2017 est)
Imports – US$8,925m (2016)
Exports – US$1,257m (2016)

BALANCE OF PAYMENTS
Trade – US$7,668m deficit (2016)
Current Account – US$17,695m surplus (2019)

Trade with UK	2018	2019
Imports from UK	£61,931,666	£53,483,392
Exports to UK	£11,557,390	£11,904,947

COLOMBIA

República de Colombia – Republic of Colombia

Area – 1,138,910 sq. km
Capital – Bogotá; population, 10,978,000 (2020 est)
Major cities – Barranquilla, Cali, Cartagena, Medellín
Currency – Colombian peso ($) of 100 centavos
Population – 49,084,841 rising at 0.93 per cent a year (2020 est)
Religion – Christian (Roman Catholic 79 per cent, Protestant 14 per cent) (est)
Language – Spanish (official)
Population density – 45 per sq. km (2019)
Urban population – 81.1 per cent (2019 est)
Median age (years) – 31.2 (2020 est)
National anthem – 'Himno Nacional de la República de Colombia' 'National Anthem of the Republic of Colombia'
National day – 20 July (Independence Day)
Death penalty – Abolished for all crimes (since 1910)
CPI score – 37 (96)
Military expenditure – US$10,603m (2018)
Conscription – 18–24 years of age; 18 months

CLIMATE AND TERRAIN
The western, central and eastern ranges of the Andes run from the south-west to north-east of Colombia, separating the arid northeastern peninsula and the tropical coastal regions in the north and west from the densely forested southeastern lowlands and the vast tablelands in the east. This last region, having a temperate climate, is the most densely populated part of the country. Elevation extremes range from 5,775m (Pico Simon Bolívar and Picó Cristóbal Colón) to 0m (Pacific Ocean). The principal rivers are the Magdalena, which flows into the Caribbean; the Guaviare and Meta, tributaries of the Orinoco; and the Caquetá and Putumayo, which drain into the Amazon basin. The predominantly tropical climate is moderated by altitude in the interior.

HISTORY AND POLITICS
Spanish settlement of the region began in 1525, and Colombia was ruled as part of a viceroyalty until 1810, when independence was declared. In 1819, Simón Bolivar established the Republic of Gran Colombia, consisting of the territories now known as Colombia, Panama, Venezuela and Ecuador, after finally defeating the Spanish. In 1829–30

Venezuela and Ecuador withdrew, and in 1831 the remaining territories formed a separate state, which adopted the name of Colombia in 1866; Panama seceded in 1903.

Power alternated between the Conservative and Liberal parties from the mid-19th century. In 1949, a civil war broke out that lasted until 1957, when the Conservative and Liberal parties formed a coalition government known as the National Front. This arrangement continued until 1974 and was revived in 1978 in an attempt to maintain the rule of law in the face of violence by drug cartels, a left-wing insurgency and counter-attacks by right-wing paramilitaries. In 2016, the government agreed a fragile and controversial peace deal with the left-wing guerilla group the Revolutionary Armed Forces of Colombia (FARC). Despite foreign assistance and increased military spending, drug trafficking continues to be widespread, although it has become less of a threat to civil order.

The 2018 presidential election, the first peacetime election in 52 years, was won by conservative candidate Iván Duque, who replaced Juan Manuel Santos Calderón after he reached his two-term limit. In the 2018 legislative elections, right-wing parties opposed to the 2016 peace deal won the most votes in both chambers but fell short of an overall majority.

The 1991 constitution, amended in 2005, allowed for the directly elected president to govern for two four-year terms, but an amendment in 2015 reduced this to a single term. The bicameral congress comprises the 171-member Chamber of Representatives and the 108-member senate. All members are elected for a four-year term. Two senate seats are reserved for representatives of indigenous people, and five for FARC members as per the 2016 peace deal.

HEAD OF STATE
President, Iván Duque, *elected* 17 June 2018, *sworn in* 7 August 2018
Vice-President, Martha Lucia Ramirez

SELECTED GOVERNMENT MEMBERS *AS AT NOVEMBER* 2020
Defence, Carlos Trujillo
Finance, Carlos Carrasquilla
Foreign Affairs, Claudia Blum
Justice, Javier Sarmiento

EMBASSY OF COLOMBIA
3 Hans Crescent, London SW1X 0LN
T 020-7589 9177 **E** egranbretana@cancilleria.gov.co
W www.colombianembassy.co.uk
Ambassador Extraordinary and Plenipotentiary, Antonio Ardila *apptd* 2019

BRITISH EMBASSY
Carrera 9, No 76–49, Piso 8, Edificio ING Barings, Bogotá
T (+57) (1) 326 8300 **E** embajadabritanica.bogota@fco.gov.uk
W www.gov.uk/government/world/colombia
Ambassador Extraordinary and Plenipotentiary, HE Colin Martin-Reynolds, CMG, *apptd* 2019

INSURGENCIES
Colombia has been dogged by violence since the 1960s, initially from insurgency by left-wing guerrilla groups, mainly the FARC and the National Liberation Army (ELN), countered by right-wing paramilitaries affiliated with the United Self-Defence Forces of Colombia (AUC), which was suspected of having links with the security forces. In the 1980s, lawlessness increased with the rise of drug-producing and drug-trafficking cartels. An estimated 220,000 people, mainly civilians, were killed during the conflict.

Action against the insurgents and drug cartels since 2002 has extended state control to the extent that the government now has a presence in every municipality. Talks with the AUC from 2004 led to the demobilisation of most units in 2006, and in November 2012 FARC rebels declared a two-month ceasefire and began talks in Havana, Cuba. Negotiations wers suspended in November 2014 after FARC kidnapped a Colombian general. Talks resumed in January 2015 after FARC declared an indefinite ceasefire and a final peace settlement was reached on 23 June 2016. After the deal was rejected by voters in a referendum in October 2016, a revised version was ratified by Congress on 1 December 2016. Peacetime negotiations with the ELN and FARC dissidents were suspended by President Duque following the bombing of a police academy in Bogotá in January 2019, which killed 22 people.

ECONOMY AND TRADE
The economy is heavily dependent on its energy, mining and agricultural exports, and hindered by its vulnerability to commodity price fluctuations, an inadequate transport infrastructure, poverty and drug trafficking. An improving security situation, economic liberalisation and international investment aided economic growth from 2002 to 2008 until the economy contracted in 2009 owing to the global downturn. GDP growth soon returned to an average rate of over 4 per cent while high global coffee prices allowed the government to abolish expensive farming subsidies in 2014. Growth slowed after 2016 due to low oil prices, which accounts for almost 50 per cent of exports, and the economy is likely to slightly contract in 2020 owing to the coronavirus pandemic.

Services account for around 62.1 per cent of GDP, industry 30.8 per cent and agriculture 7.2 per cent. Coal, oil, natural gas and hydroelectricity resources are exploited, and coal accounts for the majority of mining output; iron ore, nickel, gold, emeralds, copper and other minerals account for the remainder. Major cash crops are coffee, bananas and cut flowers. Cattle are raised in large numbers, and forestry is also important.

The principal trading partners are the USA, China, Mexico and Panama. Main exports are oil, coffee, coal, nickel, emeralds, garments, bananas and cut flowers. Imports include industrial and transport equipment, consumer goods, chemicals, paper products and fuels.

GNI – US$327.7bn; US$2,750 per capita (2019)
Annual average growth of GDP – 3.26 per cent (2019 est)
Inflation rate – 4.3 per cent (2017 est)
Population below poverty line – 28 per cent (2017 est)
Unemployment – 10.5 per cent (2019 est)
Total external debt – US$124.6bn (2017 est)
Imports – US$56,196m (2017)
Exports – US$48,138m (2017)

BALANCE OF PAYMENTS
Trade – US$8,058m deficit (2017)
Current Account – US$13,747m deficit (2019)

Trade with UK	2018	2019
Imports from UK	£396,442,211	£540,162,167
Exports to UK	£434,258,819	£470,468,843

COMMUNICATIONS
Airports – 121; the principal airports are at Bogotá, Barranquilla and Cali
Waterways – 18,300km of navigable waterways; the main seaports are Barranquilla and Cartagena on the Caribbean Sea and Buenaventura on the Pacific coast
Roadways and railways – 206,500km; 2,141km

Telecommunications – 7 million fixed lines and 62.2 million mobile subscriptions (2017); there were 27.5 million internet users in 2016

Internet code and IDD – co; 57 (from UK), 5/7/9 44 (to UK)

Major broadcasters – The state-run Senal Colombia is one of the largest television broadcasters in the country; Caracol runs several radio networks across the country alongside the state-run Radio Nacional de Colombia

Press – Daily newspapers include *El Tiempo, El Nuevo Siglo* and *El Espacio*

WPFI score – 42.66 (130)

EDUCATION AND HEALTH
Elementary education is free and compulsory from age six to 15. Healthcare is provided through a mixture of contributory and subsidised health schemes by both the private and the public sector.

Literacy rate – 95.1 per cent (2018 est)

Gross enrolment ratio (percentage of relevant age group) – primary 114.5 per cent, secondary 97.5 per cent, tertiary 55.3 per cent (2018 est)

Health expenditure (per capita) – US$459 (2017)

Hospital beds (per 1,000 people) – 1.5 (2014)

Life expectancy (years) – 76.6 (2020 est)

Mortality rate – 5.6 (2020 est)

Birth rate – 15.4 (2020 est)

Infant mortality rate – 12.3 (2020 est)

HIV/AIDS adult prevalence – 0.5 per cent (2019 est)

THE COMOROS

Udzima wa Komori/Jumhuriyat al-Qamar al-Muttahidah/Union des Comores – Union of the Comoros

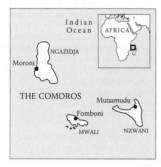

Area – 2,235 sq. km (excluding Mayotte). The Comoros includes the islands of Ngazidja (formerly Grande Comore), Nzwani (Anjouan), Mwali (Moheli) and certain islets in the Indian Ocean. Mayotte, the easternmost island of the archipelago, is a French dependency

Capital – Moroni, on Ngazidja; population, 62,000 (2018 est)

Major towns – Domoni, Fomboni, Mutsamudu

Currency – Comoran franc (KMF) of 100 centimes. The Franc CFA of 100 centimes is also used

Population – 846,281 rising at 1.47 per cent a year (2020 est)

Religion – Sunni Muslim 98 per cent, other 2 per cent (including Shia Muslim and Christian) (est); Sunni Islam is the state religion

Language – Arabic, French, Shikomoro (a blend of Swahili and Arabic) (all official)

Population density – 447 per sq. km (2018)

Urban population – 29 per cent (2018 est)

Median age (years) – 20.9 (2020 est)

National anthem – 'Udzima wa ya Masiwa' 'The Union of the Great Islands'

National day – 6 July (Independence Day)

Death penalty – Retained

CPI score – 25 (153)

Literacy rate – 58.8 per cent (2018 est)

Gross enrolment ratio (percentage of relevant age group) – primary 99.5 per cent, secondary 59.5 per cent (2018 est); tertiary 8.9 per cent (2014 est)

Health expenditure (per capita) – US$59 (2017)

Life expectancy (years) – 65.7 (2020 est)

Mortality rate – 6.9 (2020 est)

Birth rate – 23.6 (2020 est)

Infant mortality rate – 55 (2020 est)

HIV/AIDS adult prevalence – 0.1 per cent (2019 est)

CLIMATE AND TERRAIN
Located in the Mozambique Channel between Africa and Madagascar, Ngazidja, Nzwani and Mwali are mountainous volcanic islands in the Comoros archipelago. The highest point is Karthala (2,360m) on Ngazidja, an active volcano that last erupted in 2007, and the lowest is 0m (Indian Ocean). The climate is tropical, with a hot, rainy season from October to April; the islands are prone to cyclones during the rainy season.

HISTORY AND POLITICS
The islands were settled by a variety of peoples before becoming part of the trading empire of the Shirazis of Persia, who established sultanates in the 15th to 16th centuries. In 1886, France established protectorates over the islands, making them a colony in 1912. They achieved internal self-government in 1961. In a 1974 referendum, the residents of three of the main islands voted in favour of independence, which was declared on 6 July 1975; Mayotte voted to remain part of France.

The republic experienced over 20 coups or attempted coups between 1975 and 1999. Nzwani and Mwali seceded in 1997 but after a coup in 1999, the military took control of all the islands' governments and reunited the state. Talks on the secessionist crisis produced a new constitution, introducing a federal structure with greater autonomy for the individual islands. Another constitutional crisis arose in June 2007 when the incumbent president of Nzwani, Mohamed Bacar, refused to stand down and then held elections that he claimed to have won. The federal government declared the elections null and void, and in March 2008 federal troops, supported by African Union forces, ousted Bacar.

The April 2016 presidential election was rerun in May following violence and irregularities, and was won by Azali Assoumani, a one-time coup leader. Assoumani was re-elected in the first round of voting in March 2019 with over 60 per cent of the vote. Post-election violence resulted in several deaths and the arrest of an opposition leader. The January 2020 legislative election was boycotted by major opposition parties owing to allegations of political repression and fraud, which was won by President Assoumani's Convention for the Renewal of the Comoros.

The 2002 constitution created a federal structure. Constitutional amendments approved in 2009 downgraded the islands' presidents to governors and harmonised presidential and legislative terms by extending those of the president and governors. In 2018, the nation overwhelmingly voted to extend presidential term limits to two consecutive five-year terms, and ended the policy of rotating the office of the president among the three islands.

The executive president appoints the union ministers. The unicameral Assembly of the Union has 33 members; three are appointed by each of the three island assemblies and 24 are directly elected for a five-year term.

Each island has its own governor and legislative assembly, and each governor may appoint eight ministers to form a government. Governors serve a five-year term. The islands' governments deal with local issues; foreign affairs, finance, defence, judicial and religious matters remain the responsibility of the union government. There are still areas of dispute, principally over security, budget control and customs revenue.

HEAD OF STATE
President of the Union, Azali Assoumani, *elected* 15 May 2016, *sworn in* 26 May 2016, *re-elected* 24 March 2019

SELECTED GOVERNMENT MEMBERS *AS AT NOVEMBER 2020*
Finance, Said Ali Said Chayhane
Foreign Affairs, Dhoihir Dhoulkamal
Interior, Mohamed Daoudou

BRITISH AMBASSADOR
Ambassador Extraordinary and Plenipotentiary, HE Dr Philip Boyle, *apptd* 2018, resident at Antananarivo, Madagascar

ECONOMY AND TRADE
The Comoros is very poor and heavily dependent on foreign aid and technical assistance. It has few natural resources, an uneducated workforce and poor transport infrastructure. It is susceptible to extreme weather and imports roughly 70 per cent of its food. Unemployment is high and remittances from 300,000 Comorans living abroad contribute around 25 per cent to the nation's GDP. In December 2012 the IMF and World Bank supported US$176m in debt relief for the Comoros, allowing a 59 per cent decrease in future external debt over a period of 40 years. Since 2016 the government has sought to improve infrastructure, particularly electricity access, and reduce expenditure. Agriculture, fishing and forestry account for 47.7 per cent of GDP and employ around 80 per cent of the population; service industries account for about 40.5 per cent and the manufacturing industry 11.8 per cent. The main industries are fishing, tourism and perfume distillation. The main trading partners are India, France, China, Pakistan and the UAE. Principal exports are vanilla, perfume essence and cloves; coconuts, bananas and cassava are also cultivated.

GNI – US$1.205bn; US$1,420 per capita (2019)
Annual average growth of GDP – 2.7 per cent (2017 est)
Inflation rate – 1.0 per cent (2017 est)
Population below poverty line – 44.8 per cent (2004 est)
Unemployment – 6.5 per cent (2014 est)
Total external debt – US$199.8m (2017 est)
Imports – US$263m (2014)
Exports – US$24m (2014)

BALANCE OF PAYMENTS
Trade – US$260m deficit (2013)
Current Account – US$37m deficit (2019)

Trade with UK	2018	2019
Imports from UK	£1,270,457	£1,772,275
Exports to UK	£349,107	£85,913

COMMUNICATIONS
Airports and waterways – Four; the main international airport is based on Moroni; the principal ports are based at Moroni and Mutsamudu
Roadways – 880km
Telecommunications –10,320 fixed lines and 498,903 mobile subscriptions (2018); there were 69,635 internet users in 2018

Internet code and IDD – km; 269 (from UK), 44 (to UK)
Major broadcasters – National radio and television broadcasting is provided by state-run networks, and some island governments run radio and television stations
Press – No daily newspapers are published; the state-owned *Al-Watwan* is published weekly
WPFI score – 29.77 (75)

DEMOCRATIC REPUBLIC OF THE CONGO

République Démocratique du Congo – Democratic Republic of the Congo

Area – 2,344,858 sq. km
Capital – Kinshasa; population, 14,342,000 (2020 est)
Major cities – Bukavu, Kananga, Kisangani, Kolwezi, Likasi, Lubumbashi, Mbuji-Mayi
Currency – Congolese franc (FC) of 100 centimes
Population – 101,780,263 rising at 3.18 per cent a year (2020 est); there are over 200 African ethnic groups, of which Bantu is the largest
Religion – Christian (Roman Catholic 29.9 per cent, Protestant 26.7 per cent), Kimbanguist 2.8 per cent, Muslim 1.3 per cent, other 1.2 per cent (including indigenous beliefs) (est)
Language – French (official), Lingala, Kingwana (a Swahili dialect), Kikongo, Tshiluba
Population density – 37 per sq. km (2019)
Urban population – 45 per cent (2019 est)
Median age (years) – 16.7 (2020 est)
National anthem – 'Debout Congolais' 'Arise, Congolese'
National day – 30 June (Independence Day)
Death penalty – Retained
CPI score – 18 (168)
Military expenditure – US$295m (2018)
Conscription – 18–45 years of age
Literacy rate – 77 per cent (2016 est)
Gross enrolment ratio (percentage of relevant age group) – primary 118.5 per cent (2018 est); secondary 46.2 per cent (2015 est); tertiary 6.6 per cent (2016 est)
Health expenditure (per capita) – US$19 (2017)
Life expectancy (years) – 61 (2020 est)
Mortality rate – 8.4 (2020 est)
Birth rate – 41 (2020 est)
Infant mortality rate – 64.5 (2020 est)
HIV/AIDS adult prevalence – 0.8 per cent (2019 est)

CLIMATE AND TERRAIN
Africa's second-largest country lies on the equator, most of it in the basin of the river Congo and its principal tributaries, the Lualaba and the Kasai. A chain of mountains and lakes (Albert, Edward, Kivu and Tanganyika) runs along the eastern border. Elevation extremes range from 5,110m (Mt Ngaliema, also known as Mt Stanley) to 0m (Atlantic Ocean). The climate is

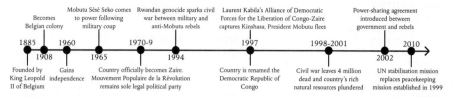

Timeline:

- **1885** Founded by King Leopold II of Belgium
- **1908** Becomes Belgian colony
- **1960** Gains independence
- **1965** Mobutu Sésé Seko comes to power following military coup. Country officially becomes Zaire. Mouvement Populaire de la Révolution remains sole legal political party
- **1970-9**
- **1994** Rwandan genocide sparks civil war between military and anti-Mobutu rebels
- **1997** Laurent Kabila's Alliance of Democratic Forces for the Liberation of Congo-Zaire captures Kinshasa; President Mobutu flees. Country is renamed the Democratic Republic of Congo
- **1998-2001** Civil war leaves 4 million dead and country's rich natural resources plundered
- **2002** UN stabilisation mission replaces peacekeeping mission established in 1999
- **2010** Power-sharing agreement introduced between government and rebels

tropical, though cooler in the eastern and southern highlands. There are different climatic cycles either side of the equator, which passes through the north of the country, with a wet season in the north from April to November and in the south from October to May.

POLITICS

Under the 2006 constitution, the executive president is directly elected for a five-year term, renewable once. The bicameral *Parlement* consists of the National Assembly, which has 500 members directly elected for a five-year term, and the senate, which has 108 members elected by the provincial assemblies to serve a five-year term, plus former elected presidents, who are senators for life.

Joseph Kabila succeeded his father Laurent (assassinated in 2001) as president. After a period of transitional government, a new constitution came into effect in 2006 and presidential and legislative elections were held. The presidential election was won in the second round by President Kabila, who went on to win re-election in November 2011. Violent protests broke out in Kinshasa in January 2015 after President Kabila suggested he would consider changing the constitution to allow him to seek a third term of office. Political instability and violence continued into 2018, with thousands killed and an estimated 4 million people displaced in the country. Legislative elections, due in 2016 but postponed until December 2018, were overwhelmingly won by the pro-Kabila Joint Front for Congo. The simultaneous presidential election results were delayed almost two weeks before Félix Tshisekedi was unexpectedly announced the winner, beating both Kabila's preferred successor, Emmanuel Shadary, and popular opposition leader Martin Fayulu. Catholic church election monitors estimated Fayulu won 60 per cent of the vote.

HEAD OF STATE
President, Félix Tshisekedi, *sworn in* 24 January 2019

SELECTED GOVERNMENT MEMBERS *AS AT NOVEMBER 2020*
Prime Minister, Sylvestre Ilunga Ilukamba
Deputy Prime Ministers (acting), Gilbert Kankonde Malambe *(Interior)*; Wily Ngoopos Sunzhel; Elysee Munembwe Tamukumwe; Jean Mayo Manbeke
Defence, Aime Ngoy Mukena
Economy, Acacia Bandubola Mbongo

EMBASSY OF THE DEMOCRATIC REPUBLIC OF THE CONGO
45–49 Great Portland Street, London W1W 7LD
T 020-7580 3931 **E** missionrdclondres@gmail.com
W http://ambardc-londres.gouv.cd
Ambassador Extraordinary and Plenipotentiary, HE Marie Ndjeka Opombo, *apptd* 2017

BRITISH EMBASSY
83 Avenue du Roi Baudouin, Gombe, Kinshasa
T (+243) 81 556 6200 **E** ambassade.britannique@fco.gov.uk
W www.gov.uk/government/world/democratic-republic-of-congo

Ambassador Extraordinary and Plenipotentiary, HE Emily Maltman, *apptd* 2020

ECONOMY AND TRADE

A decade of civil war left the country with huge external debt, little infrastructure, widespread corruption, a significant informal economy and an environment that discourages foreign investment. Improved stability since 2003 has allowed some economic growth, although the global downturn caused the economy to contract in 2008–9. Growth returned in 2010–11, and government reforms, international aid and debt relief continue to help the economy recover. The economy averaged strong growth of 8 per cent between 2012 and 2015, but low commodity prices reduced this and the economy is expected to shrink in 2020, partly owing to the coronavirus pandemic. The fall in copper prices since 2015 has coincided with considerable inflation, which peaked at nearly 50 per cent in mid-2017. Ebola outbreaks have been exacerbated by ongoing political instability, with an increased number of cases and deaths reported in 2018 and 2019; in July 2019, the World Health Organization declared this outbreak an international health emergency. The east of the country was disproportionately affected by the civil war and remains particularly underdeveloped.

The country has great potential wealth in the form of immense natural resources, including copper, cobalt, diamonds, gold, silver, uranium, other minerals, coal, oil, timber and hydroelectric power; mining is the largest source of export income. Agriculture contributes 19.7 per cent of GDP, the services sector 36.7 per cent and industry 43.6 per cent. Apart from mining and mineral processing, the main industrial activities are the production of textiles, plastics, footwear, cigarettes, metal products, processed food, beverages, timber and cement, and ship repair. Oil deposits are exploited off the Congo estuary, and hydroelectric schemes on the river Congo supply power to the major cities.

The main trading partners are China, South Africa, Belgium, South Korea and Zimbabwe. Principal exports are diamonds, gold, copper, cobalt, wood products, crude oil and coffee. The main imports are foodstuffs, industrial machinery, transport equipment and fuels.

GNI – US$45.3bn; US$520 per capita (2019)
Annual average growth of GDP – 3.4 per cent (2017 est)
Inflation rate – 41.5 per cent (2017 est)
Population below poverty line – 63 per cent (2014 est)
Total external debt – US$4.963bn (2017 est)
Imports – US$12,021m (2016)
Exports – US$8,785m (2016)

BALANCE OF PAYMENTS
Trade – US$3,236m deficit (2016)
Current Account – US$1,693m deficit (2019)

Trade with UK	2018	2019
Imports from UK	£28,165,612	£25,895,474
Exports to UK	£1,563,897	£3,514,004

COMMUNICATIONS

Airport – 26, the principal airports being at Kinshasa, Kananga, Goma, Gemena and Mbandaka

Waterways – The river Congo and its main tributaries provide 15,000km of waterways, with the principal ports in Banana, Boma and Matadi

Roadways and railways – There are 3,047km of paved roads; the 4,007km rail system links the interior to the rivers and to the great lakes in the east

Telecommunications – 36.5 million mobile subscriptions (2018); there were 8.2 million internet users in 2018

Internet code and IDD – cd; 243 (from UK), 44 (to UK)

Major broadcasters – The state-controlled Radio-Télévision Nationale Congolaise (RTNC) and the popular radio station La Voix du Congo approach national coverage; the UN and foreign NGOs sponsor Radio Okapi

Press – Major dailies include *Le Potentiel, La Reference Plus* and *L'Avenir*

WPFI score – 49.09 (150)

REPUBLIC OF THE CONGO

République du Congo – Republic of the Congo

Area – 342,000 sq. km

Capital – Brazzaville; population, 2,388,000 (2020 est)

Major cities – Loubomo, Pointe-Noire

Currency – Franc CFA of 100 centimes

Population – 5,293,070 rising at 2.26 per cent a year (2020 est); Kongo (40.5 per cent), Teke (16.9 per cent), Mbochi (13.1 per cent), Sangha (5.6 per cent) (est)

Religion – Christian (Roman Catholic 33.1 per cent, Awakening Churches 22.3 per cent, Protestant 19.9 per cent), Muslim 1.6 per cent, Kimbanguist 1.5 per cent (est)

Language – French (official), Lingala, Monokutuba, Kikongo

Population density – 15 per sq. km (2020)

Urban population – 67.4 per cent (2020 est)

Median age (years) – 19.5 (2020 est)

National anthem – 'La Congolaise' 'The Congolese'

National day – 15 August (Independence Day)

Death penalty – Abolished for all crimes (since 2015)

CPI score – 19 (165)

Military expenditure – US$292m (2018)

CLIMATE AND TERRAIN

The republic, which lies on the equator, is covered by grassland, mangrove and dense rainforest. The land rises from the narrow Atlantic coastal plain to a central plateau; in the north and east it falls to the northern part of the basin of the river Congo, which forms part of the border with the Democratic Republic of the Congo, and to the valleys of the Sangha and Alima rivers in the north. Elevation extremes range from 903m (Mt Berongou) to 0m (Atlantic Ocean). The climate is tropical. Average temperatures range from 23.5°C in July to 26°C in March. Outside the main dry season between June and September, the country is prone to flooding.

HISTORY AND POLITICS

The first European visitors to the area were the Portuguese, who established slave trading in the 16th century. The French established a colonial presence in the area in the 1880s and, as Middle Congo, it was part of French Equatorial Africa from 1910. It became independent as the Republic of the Congo on 17 August 1960.

One-party socialism was introduced in 1964; the Congolese Labour Party (PCT) was set up shortly after a military coup in 1968 and continued to rule until 1990, when Marxism was renounced and the PCT abandoned its monopoly of power. Elections in 1993 left the PCT a minority party, and the power shift destabilised the country, with factional fighting after the 1993 election, a civil war between 1997 and 1999 following Denis Sassou-Nguesso's deposition of the elected president, and a renewed insurgency by opponents of the PCT over the manipulation of the 2002 elections. A peace accord ended the insurgency in 2003 but the peace remains fragile, and remnants of the rebel militias are still active in the south of the country.

Sassou-Nguesso was elected president in 2002 and was re-elected in 2009 and 2016; the legitimacy of all three victories was suspect after the barring or withdrawal of opponents, fraud and other irregularities. In 2015, President Sassou-Nguesso pushed through reforms to the country's constitution that allowed him to be elected for a third term. In the 2017 legislative elections the PCT maintained its large majority, taking 89 of the 151 seats available.

Under the 2002 constitution, parties organised on regional, ethnic or religious lines are banned. The executive president is directly elected for a five-year term, renewable twice, and appoints the cabinet. The bicameral *Parlement* comprises the National Assembly, with 151 members directly elected for a five-year term, and the senate, which has 72 members indirectly elected for a six-year term, half of the members retiring every three years.

HEAD OF STATE

President, Denis Sassou-Nguesso, *took power* October 1997, *elected* 10 March 2002, *re-elected* 2009, 2016

SELECTED GOVERNMENT MEMBERS *AS AT NOVEMBER 2020*

Prime Minister, Clément Mouamba

Defence, Charles Richard Mondjo

Economy, Gilbert Mokoki

Foreign Affairs, Jean-Claude Gakosso

EMBASSY OF THE REPUBLIC OF THE CONGO

37 bis Rue Paul Valéry, 75116 Paris, France

T (+33) (1) 4500 6057

Ambassador Extraordinary and Plenipotentiary, vacant

BRITISH AMBASSADOR

HE Emily Maltman, *apptd* 2020, resident at Kinshasa, Democratic Republic of the Congo

ECONOMY AND TRADE

A decade of civil conflict left the country with a high external debt, a devastated infrastructure and widespread poverty. Since 2003 the government has made efforts to address these problems and has benefited from debt relief in 2006, 2007 and 2010. Years of recession meant the government sought further macroeconomic adjustments from the IMF in 2018, but was told public spending reductions were first needed, and later signed a debt restructuring agreement with China in 2019.

However, the economy recorded negative growth in 2019, and the impact of the coronavirus pandemic will likely exacerbate this recession. Fluctuating oil prices, high unemployment, a contracting economy and public sector strikes continue to be a problem.

Oil production is the backbone of the economy and declining production and falling global commodity prices represent a major threat to the economy. Mining (particularly of diamonds), forestry, brewing, agricultural processing and cement production are the other main industries; new projects, notably the mining of iron ore, are expected to add around US$1bn to annual revenue. Industry accounts for 51 per cent of GDP, services for 39.7 per cent and agriculture, which is mostly at subsistence level, for 9.3 per cent.

The main trading partners are China, France and Belgium. Principal exports are oil, timber, plywood, sugar, cocoa, coffee and diamonds. Imports are mainly capital equipment, construction materials and foodstuffs.

GNI – US$9.4bn; US$1,750 per capita (2019)
Annual average growth of GDP – –3.1 per cent (2017 est)
Inflation rate – 0.5 per cent (2017 est)
Population below poverty line – 46.5 per cent (2011 est)
Total external debt – US$4.605bn (2017 est)
Imports – US$9,132m (2016)
Exports – US$4,757m (2016)

BALANCE OF PAYMENTS
Trade – US$4,374m deficit (2016)
Current Account – US$208m deficit (2018)

Trade with UK	2018	2019
Imports from UK	£30,513,634	£28,863,659
Exports to UK	£24,049,598	£16,045,763

COMMUNICATIONS
Airports – Eight, including an international airport at Brazzaville
Waterways – Pointe-Noire is the main seaport and also the centre of the offshore oil industry. Brazzaville is the main river port, lying on the river Congo which, with the river Oubangui, provides 1,120km of commercially navigable waterways
Roadways and railways – The road network is comprised of 23,324km classified roadways, 3,111km of which are paved; there are 510km of railways
Telecommunications – 17,000 fixed lines (2016) and 5 million mobile subscriptions (2018); there were 4378,000 internet users in 2018
Internet code and IDD – cg; 242 (from UK), 44 (to UK)
Major broadcasters – TV Congo is the only television station and is controlled by the state. Two government radio stations, Radio Congo and Radio Brazzaville, exist alongside commercial and community stations
Press – The government-run *La Nouvelle République* is the country's only daily newspaper
WPFI score – 36.56 (118)

EDUCATION AND HEALTH
Schooling is free and compulsory between the ages of six and 16.
Literacy rate – 80.3 per cent (2018 est)
Gross enrolment ratio (percentage of relevant age group) – primary 105.7 per cent (2016 est); secondary 52.6 per cent (2012 est); tertiary 12.6 per cent (2017 est)
Health expenditure (per capita) – US$50 (2017)
Life expectancy (years) – 61.3 (2020 est)
Mortality rate – 8.7 (2020 est)

Birth rate – 32.6 (2020 est)
Infant mortality rate – 50.7 (2020 est)
HIV/AIDS adult prevalence – 3.1 per cent (2014 est)

COSTA RICA
República de Costa Rica – Republic of Costa Rica

Area – 51,100 sq. km
Capital – San José; population, 1,400,000 (2020 est)
Major towns – Alajuela, Liberia, Limón, Paraíso, San Francisco
Currency – Costa Rican colón of 100 céntimos
Population – 5,097,988 rising at 1.08 per cent a year (2020 est)
Religion – Christian (Roman Catholic 71.8 per cent, Evangelical and Pentecostal 12.3 per cent) (est)
Language – Spanish (official), English
Population density – 98 per sq. km (2019)
Urban population – 80.1 per cent (2019 est)
Median age (years) – 31.7 (2018 est)
National anthem – 'Himno Nacional de Costa Rica' 'National Anthem of Costa Rica'
National day – 15 September (Independence Day)
Death penalty – Abolished for all crimes (since 1877)
CPI score – 56 (44)
Literacy rate – 97.9 per cent (2018 est)
Gross enrolment ratio (percentage of relevant age group) – primary 116.2 per cent, secondary 141.4 per cent, tertiary 57.7 per cent (2019 est)
Health expenditure (per capita) – US$869 (2017)
Hospital beds (per 1,000 people) – 1.1 (2014)
Life expectancy (years) – 79.2 (2020 est)
Mortality rate – 4.9 (2020 est)
Birth rate – 14.8 (2020 est)
Infant mortality rate – 7.5 (2020 est)
HIV/AIDS adult prevalence – 0.4 per cent (2019 est)

CLIMATE AND TERRAIN
The Cordillera de Guanacaste (north-west), Cordillera de Talamanca and Cordillera Central (south-east) form a chain of volcanic mountain ranges that traverse the country from north to south. A central valley lies between the ranges, and the land slopes to plains on the Pacific and Caribbean coasts. Elevation extremes range from 3,810m (Cerro Chirripó Grande) to 0m (Pacific Ocean). The climate is tropical, with average temperatures ranging from 24.3°C in November to 26.8°C in April, and a wet season from May to November. The area is subject to occasional earthquakes, hurricanes, flooding and landslides.

HISTORY AND POLITICS
Visited by Columbus in 1502, Costa Rica was colonised by the Spanish from the 1560s and remained under Spanish rule until Central America gained its independence in 1821. Costa Rica was part of a Central American federation of former Spanish provinces from 1823 until its secession in 1838. Political unrest in the mid-20th century led to a brief civil war

in 1948, after which the army was abolished and replaced with a national guard. Subsequently power alternated between the two main political parties, the National Liberation Party (PLN) and the Social Christian Unity Party (PUSC), but in recent years the scandal-ridden PUSC has lost ground to emerging new parties.

In the 2018 legislative elections the PLN remained the largest party, despite losing votes for a third consecutive election. The simultaneous presidential election was won by the centre-left Citizens' Action party candidate Carlos Alvarado Quesada.

Under the 1949 constitution, the executive president is directly elected for a four-year term and is eligible for non-consecutive terms. The unicameral legislative assembly has 57 members directly elected for a four-year term.

HEAD OF STATE
President, Carlos Alvarado Quesada, *elected* 2 April 2018, *sworn in* 8 May 2018
First Vice-President, Epsy Campbell Barr
Second Vice-President, Marvin Rodriquez Cordero

SELECTED GOVERNMENT MEMBERS *AS AT NOVEMBER 2020*
Economy, Victoria Hernandez Mora
Foreign Affairs, Rodolfo Solano Quiros

EMBASSY OF COSTA RICA
23 Woodstock Street, London W1C 2AS
T 020-7706 8844 **E** info@costaricanembassy.co.uk
W www.costaricanembassy.co.uk
Ambassador Extraordinary and Plenipotentiary, HE Rafael Ortiz Fábrega, *apptd* 2018

BRITISH EMBASSY
Edificio Centro Colón, Paseo Colón and Streets 38 and 40, San Jose, Apartado 815–1007
T (+506) 2258 2025 **E** ukin.costarica@fco.gov.uk
W www.gov.uk/government/world/costa-rica
Ambassador Extraordinary and Plenipotentiary, HE Ross Denny, *apptd* 2015

ECONOMY AND TRADE
Sixty years of political stability have allowed steady economic growth, the creation of a social welfare system, one of the highest levels of foreign direct investment in Latin America and a reduction in poverty to less than 25 per cent of the population, though the social benefit system is becoming increasingly strained due to restrictions on government spending and increased immigration. Costa Rica introduced a floating exchange rate regime for the Costa Rican colón on 2 February 2015 in order to create more flexible exchange rates and to manage inflation. Despite strong growth in recent years, rising public debt has meant the country's credit rating was downgraded in 2015 and then again in 2017.

Tourism is the largest single industry, and with one-third of the country now national parkland or nature reserve, eco-tourism is on the increase. Services account for about 73.9 per cent of GDP while the increasingly diverse manufacturing industry accounts for 20.6 per cent, the principal products being microprocessors, foodstuffs, medical equipment, textiles, clothing, construction materials, fertiliser and plastic goods. The agricultural sector contributes 5.5 per cent of GDP; the principal products are tropical fruit, coffee, ornamental plants, sugar, rice, vegetables, meat and timber.

The main trading partners are the USA, China and Mexico. The chief exports are tropical fruit, coffee, plants, sugar, beef, seafood, electrical components and medical equipment. The

chief imports are raw materials, consumer goods, capital equipment, petrol and construction materials.
GNI – US$59.1bn; US$11,700 per capita (2019)
Annual average growth of GDP – 3.3 per cent (2017 est)
Inflation rate – 1.6 per cent (2017 est)
Population below poverty line – 21.7 per cent (2014 est)
Unemployment – 8.1 per cent (2017 est)
Total external debt – US$26.83bn (2017 est)
Imports – US$18,914m (2017)
Exports – US$19,828m (2017)

BALANCE OF PAYMENTS
Trade – US$913m surplus (2017)
Current Account – US$1,415m deficit (2019)

Trade with UK	2018	2019
Imports from UK	£64,843,493	£57,077,532
Exports to UK	£238,175,190	£267,068,106

COMMUNICATIONS
Airports and waterways – 47; the principal airports are at San José and Limón; the chief seaports are Limón on the Atlantic coast, and Puntarenas and de Caldera on the Pacific coast
Roadways and railways – 5,035km; 278km
Telecommunications – 774,303 fixed lines and 8.5 million mobile subscriptions (2018); there were 3.7 million internet users in 2018
Major broadcasters – Public broadcasting is provided by Canal 13 (TV) and Radio Nacional; cable television is widely available
Press – Media are generally free from state interference; daily newspapers include *Al Día, Diario Extra* and *La Nación*
Internet code and IDD – cr; 506 (from UK), 44 (to UK)
WPFI score – 10.53 (7)

CÔTE D'IVOIRE

République de Côte d'Ivoire – Republic of Côte d'Ivoire

Area – 322,463 sq. km
Capital – Yamoussoukro (since 1983); population, 231,000 (2018 est); slow progress in transferring functions means that the former capital, Abidjan (population, 4,921,000; 2018 est), remains the seat of government at present
Major cities – Abidjan, Bouaké, Daloa, Korhogo
Currency – Franc CFA of 100 centimes
Population – 27,481,086 rising at 2.26 per cent a year (2020 est); Akan (28.8 per cent), Voltaique or Gur (16.1 per cent), Northern Mande (14.5 per cent), Kru (8.5 per cent), Southern Mande (6.9 per cent) (est)
Religion – Muslim 42.9 per cent, Christian (Catholic 17.2 per cent, Evangelical 11.8 per cent, Methodist 1.7 per cent), animist 3.6 per cent (est)

Language – French (official), around 60 native dialects of which Dioula is the most widely spoken
Population density – 79 per sq. km (2019)
Urban population – 51.2 per cent (2019 est)
Median age (years) – 20.3 (2018 est)
National anthem – 'L'Abidjanaise' 'Song of Abidjan'
National day – 7 August (Independence Day)
Death penalty – Abolished for all crimes (since 2000)
CPI score – 35 (106)
Military expenditure – US$608m (2018)
Literacy rate – 47.2 per cent (2018 est)
Gross enrolment ratio (percentage of relevant age group) – primary 100.3 per cent, secondary 54.6 per cent (2019 est); tertiary 9.3 per cent (2017 est)
Health expenditure (per capita) – US$70 (2017)
Life expectancy (years) – 61.3 (2020 est)
Mortality rate – 7.9 (2020 est)
Birth rate – 29.1 (2020 est)
Infant mortality rate – 59.1 (2020 est)
HIV/AIDS adult prevalence – 2.4 per cent (2019 est)

CLIMATE AND TERRAIN

The land rises from a coastal plain to a large interior plateau with mountains in the north and west. Coastal lagoons give way to tropical rainforest in the centre and savannah in the north; deforestation means that the area of savannah is increasing. The country is dissected by the Sassandra, Bandama and Komoé rivers, the first two forming large central lakes. Elevation extremes range from 1,752m (Mt Nimba) to 0m (Gulf of Guinea). The climate is tropical in the south and semi-arid in the north. The south has two rainy seasons (May to July, October to November) and the north has one (June to September). The average annual temperature is 26.8°C.

POLITICS

Since the turn of the century Côte d'Ivoire has seen increased civil unrest and ethnic tensions. Following an election in 2010 the incumbent president Laurent Gbagbo refused to concede to the internationally acknowledged victor, Alassane Ouattara; after a four-month stalemate Ouattara took office by force. In the 2011 parliamentary elections, President Ouattara and his allies obtained a majority and the president was re-elected in October 2015 with 83.66 per cent of the vote. Opposition groups claimed Ouattara's candidacy in the October 2020 election was illegal and boycotted the election, which the incumbent won with 94 per cent of the vote.

Under the new constitution adopted in 2016, the executive president is directly elected for a five-year term and limited to two terms beginning with the 2020 election. The president appoints the prime minister and the other ministers, who are nominated by the prime minister. The bicameral Parliament consists of the National Assembly, which has 255 directly elected members, and a 99-seat Senate with 66 members indirectly elected by the National Assembly and 33 appointed by the president; both houses serve five-year terms. The Senate was introduced in the 2016 constitution and elections first held in March 2018. Ouattara's Rally of the Republicans party won 167 seats in the December 2016 parliamentary

elections. In recent years the country has been the target of attacks by Islamist militants on hotels and beach resorts.

HEAD OF STATE
President, C-in-C of the Armed Forces, Defence, Alassane Ouattara, *elected* 28 November 2010, *sworn in* 6 May 2011, *re-elected* 28 October 2015, 31 October 2020

SELECTED GOVERNMENT MEMBERS *AS AT NOVEMBER 2020*
Prime Minister, Defence, Hamed Bakayoko
Economy and Finance, Adama Coulibaly
Foreign Affairs, Ally Coulibaly

EMBASSY OF THE REPUBLIC OF CÔTE D'IVOIRE
2 Upper Belgrave Street, London SW1X 8BJ
T 020-7235 6991
Ambassador Extraordinary and Plenipotentiary, vacant

BRITISH EMBASSY
Cocody, Quartier Ambassades, Rue l'Impasse du Belier, Rue A 58, 01 BP 2581, Abidjan 01
T (+225) 2244 2669 **E** uk_abidjan@yahoo.fr
W www.gov.uk/government/world/cote-d-ivoire
Ambassador Extraordinary and Plenipotentiary, HE Josephine Gauld, *apptd* 2016

ECONOMY AND TRADE

The country was one of the most prosperous in the region, attracting large numbers of migrant workers from neighbouring countries, until the political turbulence of the late 1990s caused many to return home. The civil war particularly damaged the economy in the cotton-growing north, and although it is vulnerable to price fluctuations in its key exports the nation's economic recovery is progressing well. Since 2006, revenue from oil, gas and refined products has outstripped earnings from cocoa, and offshore exploration for other deposits continues. The economy grew steadily in 2013–19, enjoying one of the highest growth rates in the world thanks to foreign investment and high cocoa revenues, but is expected to slow in 2020 due to the coronavirus pandemic.

In 2014 the UN overturned a ban on the export of the country's diamonds, which had been put in place in 2005 in order to stop the trade funding armed rebel groups. Improved political stability allowed the African Development Bank to return to Abidjan in 2014, having relocated to Tunisia for 11 years during the civil war. Poor infrastructure and business practices are a barrier to future growth, with Côte d'Ivoire having one of the most complex tax codes in Africa. Over 45 per cent live below the poverty line.

Services account for 53.8 per cent of GDP, agriculture for 20.1 per cent and industry for 26.6 per cent. Agriculture employs around 68 per cent of the workforce, producing cocoa (of which Côte d'Ivoire is the world's largest producer and exporter), coffee, cotton, bananas, pineapples and palm oil for export. The principal industries are food processing, forestry, oil refining, vehicle assembly, gold mining, textiles, building materials, fertiliser and hydroelectric power; the

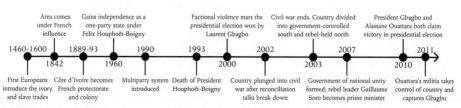

Area comes under French influence **1460-1600**
First Europeans introduce the ivory and slave trades **1842**

Gains independence as a one-party state under Felix Houphoët-Boigny **1889-93**
Côte d'Ivoire becomes French protectorate and colony **1960**

1990
Multiparty system introduced

Factional violence mars the presidential election won by Laurent Gbagbo **1993**
Death of President Houphoët-Boigny **2000**

Civil war ends. Country divided into government-controlled south and rebel-held north **2002**
Country plunged into civil war after reconciliation talks break down **2003**

2007
Government of national unity formed; rebel leader Guillaume Soro becomes prime minister

President Gbagbo and Alassane Ouattara both claim victory in presidential election **2011**
Ouattara's militia takes control of country and captures Gbagbo **2010**

country is a net exporter of electricity. The main trading partners are Nigeria, France, other EU and west African states, and China.
GNI – US$58.9bn; US$2,290 per capita (2019)
Annual average growth of GDP – 7.8 per cent (2017 est)
Inflation rate – 0.8 per cent (2017 est)
Population below poverty line – 46.3 per cent (2015 est)
Total external debt – US$13.07bn (2017 est)
Imports – US$10,712m (2016)
Exports – US$10,975m (2016)

BALANCE OF PAYMENTS
Trade – US$262m surplus (2016)
Current Account – US$2,077m deficit (2018)

Trade	2018	2019
Imports from UK	£89,969,671	£69,694,008
Exports to UK	£194,504,573	£227,874,802

COMMUNICATIONS
Airports – Seven, the principal international airport being at Abidjan
Waterways – There are 980km of navigable rivers, canals and lagoons; the main seaports are Abidjan and San Pedro
Roadways and railways – 6,502km of paved roads; 660km
Telecommunications – 302,398 fixed lines and 33.8 million mobile telephone subscriptions (2018); there were 12.3 million internet users in 2018
Internet code and IDD – ci; 225 (from UK), 44 (to UK)
Major broadcasters – The state broadcaster, Radiodiffusion Télévision Ivoirienne (RTI), operates two national radio stations and two television channels; in 2012 the government allowed private companies to enter the radio and TV markets for the first time
Press – Nine newspapers are published daily, including the state-owned *Fraternité Matin* and the privately owned *Le Nouveau Reveil*
WPFI score – 28.94 (68)

CROATIA
Republika Hrvatska – Republic of Croatia

Area – 56,594 sq. km
Capital – Zagreb; population, 685,000 (2020 est)
Major cities – Osijek, Rijeka (Fiume), Split, Zadar
Currency – Kuna of 100 lipa
Population – 4,277,746 falling at 0.50 per cent a year (2020 est)
Religion – Christian (Roman Catholic 86.3 per cent, Orthodox 4.4 per cent, Muslim 1.5 per cent (est)
Language – Croatian (official), Serbian
Population density – 73 per sq. km (2019)

Urban population – 57.2 per cent (2019 est)
Median age (years) – 43.9 (2020 est)
National anthem – 'Lijepa Nasa Domovino' 'Our Beautiful Homeland'
National day – 8 October (Independence Day)
Death penalty – Abolished for all crimes (since 1990)
CPI score – 47 (63)
Military expenditure – US$890m (2018)

CLIMATE AND TERRAIN
There are three major geographic areas: the plains of the Pannonian region in the north, the central mountain belt, and the Adriatic coast region of Istria and Dalmatia, which has 1,185 islands and islets and 1,777km of coastline. Elevation extremes range from 1,831m (Dinara) to 0m (Adriatic Sea). The climate varies significantly between the Dalmatian coast, where the winters are mild and the summers hot, and inland areas, which have colder temperatures and rain in the summer. Average temperatures range from 1.8°C in January to 28°C in July.

POLITICS
The 1990 constitution was amended in 2000 to increase the powers of the legislature, making the presidency a largely ceremonial role, and in 2001 to abolish the upper house of the legislature. The head of state is a president, who is directly elected for a five-year term, renewable once. The legislature, the Croatian Assembly, has one chamber, the *Hrvatski Sabor,* which has 151 members directly elected for a four-year term, with 11 representatives elected to serve ethnic minorities. The prime minister is appointed by the legislature and appoints the cabinet.

Following a vote of no confidence in Prime Minister Tihomir Oreskovic and his governing coalition in June 2016, the cente-right Croatian Democratic Union's (HDZ) Andrei Plenkovic was elected prime minister in legislative elections in September 2016. The HDZ slightly extended its mandate in the July 2020 elections, claiming 66 seats. The 2020 presidential election was won by former prime minister Zoran Milanovic of the Social Democratic Party in the second round of voting. Croatia became a member of the EU in July 2013.

HEAD OF STATE
President, Zoran Milanovic, *elected* 5 December 2020, *sworn in* 19 February 2020

SELECTED GOVERNMENT MEMBERS *AS AT NOVEMBER 2020*
Prime Minister, Andrej Plenkovic
Deputy Prime Ministers, Brig.-Gen. Tomo Medved; Davor Bozinovic *(Interior)*; Zdravko Maric *(Finance)*; Boris Milosevic

EMBASSY OF THE REPUBLIC OF CROATIA
21 Conway Street, London W1T 6BN
T 020-7387 2022 **E** vrhlon@mvep.hr **W** http://uk.mvp.hr
Ambassador Extraordinary and Plenipotentiary, HE Igor Pokaz, *apptd* 2017

BRITISH EMBASSY
Ivana Lucica 4, 10000 Zagreb
T (+385) 600 9100 **E** british.embassyzagreb@fco.gov.uk
W www.gov.uk/government/world/croatia
Ambassador Extraordinary and Plenipotentiary, HE Andrew Dalgleish, *apptd* 2016

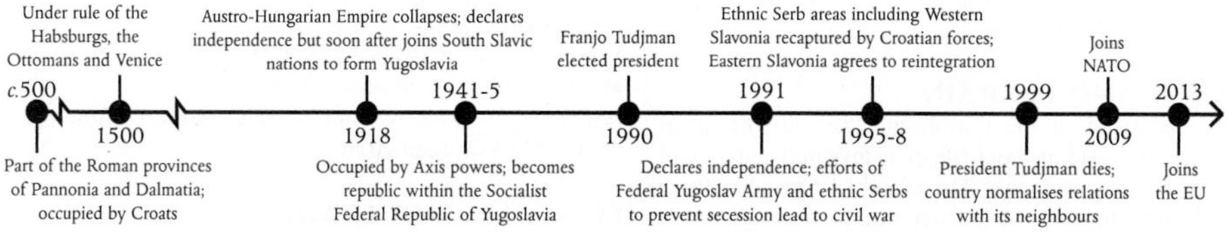

Under rule of the Habsburgs, the Ottomans and Venice	Austro-Hungarian Empire collapses; declares independence but soon after joins South Slavic nations to form Yugoslavia	Franjo Tudjman elected president	Ethnic Serb areas including Western Slavonia recaptured by Croatian forces; Eastern Slavonia agrees to reintegration	Joins NATO	
c.500	1941-5	1991	1999	2013

(Timeline markers)
- **1500** — Part of the Roman provinces of Pannonia and Dalmatia; occupied by Croats
- **1918** — Occupied by Axis powers; becomes republic within the Socialist Federal Republic of Yugoslavia
- **1990**
- **1995-8** — Declares independence; efforts of Federal Yugoslav Army and ethnic Serbs to prevent secession lead to civil war
- **2009** — President Tudjman dies; country normalises relations with its neighbours
- Joins the EU

ECONOMY AND TRADE

As part of Yugoslavia, Croatia was a prosperous and industrialised area, but the conflict in 1991–5 damaged its infrastructure, large areas of farmland, industrial productivity and the tourist industry. From 2000 to 2007 there was steady economic growth, led by a recovery in tourism, banking and public investment. However, a growing trade deficit, high unemployment, the size of the public sector and the economy's over-reliance on tourism are longer-term problems that left the economy vulnerable in the global economic downturn in 2008. The country joined the EU in 2013 but does not yet qualify to join the Economic and Monetary Union, but plans to adopt the Euro by 2024. Following six years of recession, Croatia entered the EU's excessive-deficit procedure in 2014 but recovered enough to exit it in 2017. Reductions in tax and economic reforms since 2017 were designed to stimulate domestic consumption and foreign investment following a sharp fall in public debt, but the economy is expected to shrink by 9 per cent in 2020 due to the coronavirus pandemic.

The service sector accounts for 70.1 per cent of GDP, industry for 26.2 per cent and agriculture for 3.7 per cent. Tourism is a major economic contributor, at 19.6 per cent of GDP. Industry produces chemicals and plastics, machine tools, metals and metal products, electronics, wood products, construction materials and textiles, and includes food processing, shipbuilding and oil refining. Agricultural production includes cereals, pulses, fruit and vegetables, livestock and dairy products. Most trade is with EU and neighbouring countries.

GNI – US$60.6bn; US$14,910 per capita (2019)
Annual average growth of GDP – 2.94 per cent (2019 est)
Inflation rate – 1.1 per cent (2017 est)
Population below poverty line – 19.5 per cent (2015 est)
Unemployment – 8.07 per cent (2019 est)
Total external debt – US$48.1bn (2017 est)
Imports – US$28,106m (2017)
Exports – US$29,826m (2017)

BALANCE OF PAYMENTS
Trade – US$1,720m surplus (2017)
Current Account – US$1,455m surplus (2019)

Trade with UK	2018	2019
Imports from UK	£244,960,801	£210,876,662
Exports to UK	£141,762,695	£168,289,291

COMMUNICATIONS

Airports and waterways – 24; there are 785km of inland waterways and frequent ferry services to the many Adriatic islands
Roadways and railways – 26,958km, including 1,416km of motorways; 2,722km
Telecommunications – 1.4 million fixed lines and 4.4 million mobile subscriptions (2018); there were 3.1 million internet users in 2018
Internet code and IDD – hr; 385 (from UK), 44 (to UK)

Major broadcasters – Croatian Radio-Television (HRT) is the national state-owned public service broadcaster
Press – Leading daily newspapers include *Vecernji List, Jutarnji List* and *Slobodna Dalmacija*
WPFI score – 28.51 (59)

EDUCATION AND HEALTH

Education is free and compulsory for all children from age six to 15.
Literacy rate – 99.3 per cent (2015 est)
Gross enrolment ratio (percentage of relevant age group) – primary 94.6 per cent, secondary 100.1 per cent, tertiary 67.7 per cent (2018 est)
Health expenditure (per capita) – US$902 (2017)
Hospital beds (per 1,000 people) – 5.6 (2015)
Life expectancy (years) – 76.7 (2020 est)
Mortality rate – 12.8 (2020 est)
Birth rate – 8.7 (2020 est)
Infant mortality rate – 8.6 (2020 est)
HIV/AIDS adult prevalence – 0.1 per cent (2019 est)

CUBA

República de Cuba – Republic of Cuba

Area – 110,860 sq. km
Capital – Havana; population, 2,140,000 (2020 est)
Major cities – Camagüey, Guantánamo, Holguín, Santa Clara, Santiago de Cuba
Currency – Cuban peso ($) of 100 centavos
Population – 11,059,062 falling at 0.25 per cent a year (2020 est)
Religion – Christian 59.2 per cent (est); many practise Santería (African religions syncrinised with Christianity). Religious activity is tightly controlled; house churches must be state-registered
Language – Spanish (official)
Population density – 109 per sq. km (2019)
Urban population – 77.1 per cent (2019 est)
Median age (years) – 42.1 (2020 est)
National anthem – 'La Bayamese' 'The Bayamo Song'
National day – 1 January (Triumph of the Revolution)
Death penalty – Retained
CPI score – 48 (60)
Military expenditure – US$123m (2017)

Conscription – 17–28 years of age; 24 months for men, optional for women

CLIMATE AND TERRAIN
The largest island in the Caribbean, Cuba is part of an archipelago that also includes Isla de la Juventud and around 1,600 other islets and cays. The island of Cuba has three mountainous ranges running from east to west. Elevation extremes range from 2,005m (Pico Turquino) to 0m (Caribbean Sea). The climate is subtropical, with an average annual temperature of 25.5°C.

POLITICS
The Communist Party of Cuba (PCC) is the only authorised political party. The 1976 constitution was amended in 1991 to allow direct election of the National Assembly by secret ballot, in 2002 to enshrine socialism in the constitution, and in 2019 to introduce modest market liberalisation. The president is elected by the legislature for a five-year term, renewable once. The unicameral National Assembly of the People's Power has 605 members directly elected for a five-year term; all candidates are approved by the PCC and stand unopposed. Between its sessions, the assembly is represented by the Council of State, whose members are elected by the assembly.

A referendum on a new constitution, approved by the National Assembly in July 2018, was overwhelmingly supported in February 2019. While it ensured the continuation of a one-party socialist system, mild reforms included the recognition of private property, foreign investment, and small businesses.

Fidel Castro (1926–2016), who had been president since 1959, announced in February 2008 that he would not accept another term in office due to ill health. His brother, Raúl Castro, who had been acting president since July 2006, was elected head of state and head of government later that month by the National Assembly; he stepped down in April 2018 and was replaced by Miguel Díaz-Canel, ending almost 60 years of Castro rule.

HEAD OF STATE
President of Council of State and Council of Ministers, Miguel Díaz-Canel, *elected* 18 April 2018
First Vice-President of Council of State, Salvador Valdés Mesa

SELECTED GOVERNMENT MEMBERS *AS AT NOVEMBER 2020*
Prime Minister, Manuel Marrero
Deputy Prime Ministers, Roberto Morales; Ines Chapman; Jose Tapia; Alejandro Gil *(Economy)*; Ricardo Cabrisas
Foreign Relations, Bruno Rodriguez

EMBASSY OF THE REPUBLIC OF CUBA
167 High Holborn, London WC1V 6PA
T 020-7240 2488 **E** secembajador@uk.embacuba.cu
W misiones.minrex.gob.cu/en/united-kingdom/ embassy-cuba-united-kingdom
Ambassador Extraordinary and Plenipotentiary, HE Barbara Montalvo Alvarez, *apptd* 2020

BRITISH EMBASSY
Calle 34, No 702, Miramar, Playa, Havana
T (+53) (0) 7214 2200 **E** embrit@enet.cu
W www.gov.uk/government/world/cuba
Ambassador Extraordinary and Plenipotentiary, HE Dr Antony Stokes, LVO, *apptd* 2016

ECONOMY AND TRADE
After the revolution, virtually all land and industrial and commercial enterprises were nationalised. With the collapse of communism in Europe in 1989–91, the economy deteriorated sharply, necessitating rationing of energy, food and consumer goods, and obliging the government to introduce reforms. Since 1993, liberalisation has gradually opened up the economy to limited private enterprise and foreign ownership of property and business enterprises, and introduced price rises for some goods and services and income tax. The reforms resulted in steady growth, in particular stimulating tourism and the oil and mining industries. The global economic downturn resulted in a fall in tourism and nickel prices, which led to a further easing of restrictions on private enterprise and consumption since 2011, as well as a reduction in public sector jobs.

In 2014, the Obama administration announced that it would re-establish communications with Cuba, paving the way for greater foreign travel and business interaction with the USA. In January 2015, the two governments began talks to remove the embargo entirely and President Obama made a historic visit to Cuba in March 2016, but the Trump administration reversed many aspects of the rapprochement, including tightening trade and travel rules. Since 2016, Venezuela's spiralling economy has impacted upon Cuba and resulted in slow economic growth.

Agriculture contributes 4 per cent of GDP and employs around 18 per cent of the workforce. Industrial activities include sugar refining, oil production, tobacco processing, construction, nickel mining and the production of steel, cement, agricultural machinery and pharmaceuticals. Industry contributes 22.7 per cent of GDP, and the service sector 73.4 per cent. As of December 2015, roughly 500,000 Cubans were self-employed.

The main trading partners are China, Spain, Venezuela and Russia; Venezuela has provided Cuba with 100,000 subsidised barrels of oil a day since 2000, although in recent years this number may have halved. Principal exports are petroleum, sugar, nickel, tobacco, fish, medical products, citrus fruits and coffee. The main imports are oil, food, machinery and equipment, and chemicals.

GNI – US$66,397m; US$5,890 per capita (2011)
Annual average growth of GDP – 1.6 per cent (2017 est)
Inflation rate – 5.5 per cent (2017 est)
Unemployment – 2.6 per cent (2017 est)
Total external debt – US$30.06bn (2017 est)
Imports – US$13,442m (2017)
Export – US$14,975m (2017)

BALANCE OF PAYMENTS
Trade – US$1,532m surplus (2017)
Current Account – US$145.7m (2015 est)

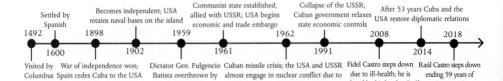

Settled by Spanish	Becomes independent; USA retains naval bases on the island	Communist state established, allied with USSR; USA begins economic and trade embargo	Collapse of the USSR; Cuban government relaxes state economic controls	After 53 years Cuba and the USA restore diplomatic relations
1492	1898	1959	1962	2008	2018
1600	1902	1961	1991	2014
Visited by Columbus	War of independence won; Spain cedes Cuba to the USA	Dictator Gen. Fulgencio Batista overthrown by Fidel Castro	Cuban missile crisis; the USA and USSR almost engage in nuclear conflict due to missile site construction on Cuba	Fidel Castro steps down due to ill-health; he is replaced by his brother Raúl	Raúl Castro steps down ending 59 years of dynastic rule

Trade with UK	2018	2019
Imports from UK	£11,189,224	£13,350,727
Exports to UK	£7,391,011	£7,030,804

COMMUNICATIONS

Airports – 64; the main international airport is at Havana
Waterways – There are 240km of navigable waterways; the main ports are Havana, Cienfuegos and Matanzas
Roadways and railways – 60,000km, of which 20,000km are paved; 8,367km, 4,533km of which are used exclusively by sugar plantations
Telecommunications – 1.4 million fixed line users and 5.4 million mobile subscriptions (2018); there were 6.4 million internet users in 2018
Internet code and IDD – cu; 53 (from UK), 44 (to UK)
Major broadcasters – The government operates four television channels and six radio stations including Cubavision (TV) and Radio Rebelde; Radio-TV Marti, a US government-backed station, transmits from Florida
Press – Cuba is Latin America's worst media freedom violator; the official Communist Party newspaper is *Granma*
WPFI score – 63.81 (171)

EDUCATION AND HEALTH

Education is free of charge and compulsory between the ages of six and 15. Healthcare is free.
Literacy rate – 100 per cent (2015 est)
Gross enrolment ratio (percentage of relevant age group) – primary 102.9 per cent, secondary 100.3 per cent; tertiary 41.4 per cent (2018 est)
Health expenditure (per capita) – US$988 (2017)
Hospital beds (per 1,000 people) – 5.2 (2014)
Life expectancy (years) – 79.2 (2020 est)
Mortality rate – 9.1 (2020 est)
Birth rate – 10.4 (2020 est)
Infant mortality rate – 4.3 (2020 est)
HIV/AIDS adult prevalence – 0.4 per cent (2019 est)

CYPRUS

Kypriaki Dimokratia/Kibris Cumhuriyeti – Republic of Cyprus

Area – 9,251 sq. km, of which 3,355 sq. km are in the Turkish Cypriot-administered area
Capital – Nicosia; population, 269,000 (2018 est)
Major cities – Larnaca, Limassol, Strovolos (south of the partition); Famagusta, Kyrenia (north)
Currency – Euro (€) of 100 cents (south), Turkish lira (north)
Population – 1,266,676 rising at 1.15 per cent a year (2020 est)
Religion – Christian (Orthodox 89.1 per cent, Roman Catholic 2.9 per cent); data only representative of the government-controlled region of Cyprus (est)

Language – Greek, Turkish (both official), English, Romanian, Russian, Bulgarian, Arabic, Filipino
Population density – 129 per sq. km (2019)
Urban population – 66.8 per cent (2019 est)
Median age (years) – 37.9 (2020 est)
National anthem – 'Ymnos eis tin Eleutherian' 'Hymn to Liberty'
National day – 1 October (Independence Day); Turkish Cypriots celebrate Republic Day on 15 November
Death penalty – Abolished for all crimes (since 2002)
CPI score – 58 (41)
Military expenditure – US$382m (2018)
Conscription – 18–50 years of age, Greek Cypriot males only; 14 months
Literacy rate – 99.9 per cent (2015 est)
Gross enrolment ratio (percentage of relevant age group) – primary 99.8 per cent, secondary 100.3 per cent, tertiary 81.3 per cent (2018 est)
Health expenditure (per capita) – US$1,732 (2017)
Life expectancy (years) – 79.3 (2020 est)
Mortality rate – 7 (2020 est)
Birth rate – 10.9 (2020 est)
Infant mortality rate – 7.4 (2020 est)
HIV/AIDS adult prevalence – 0.06 per cent (2013 est)

CLIMATE AND TERRAIN

Cyprus is the third-largest island in the Mediterranean. It has two mountain ranges, the Pentadaktylos along the north coast, and the Troodos in the centre and west. Plains lie between the two ranges and on parts of the south coast. Elevation extremes range from 1,951m (Mt Olympus, Troodos range) to 0m (Mediterranean Sea). The climate is Mediterranean, with very warm summers.

POLITICS

The 1960 constitution provides for power-sharing between the Greek and Turkish Cypriots but some of these provisions have been in abeyance since 1963, when the Turkish Cypriots withdrew from the power-sharing arrangements. The executive president is directly elected for a five-year term. The unicameral legislature, the House of Representatives, has 80 members, directly elected for a five-year term; elections to the 24 seats reserved for Turkish Cypriots have not taken place since 1963. The area administered by Turkish Cypriots has its own 50-seat unicameral Assembly of the Republic, where members are directly elected for a five-year term.

In legislative elections held in May 2016, the right-wing Democratic Rally (DISY) party consolidated its position in the government-controlled House of Representatives, following a drop in support for all the major parties including the second-placed Progressive Party of the Working People (AKEL) and the Democratic Party (DIKO). DISY's Nikos Anastasiades was re-elected president in February 2018. Peace talks with Northern Cyprus resumed in May 2015 after they had been suspended in October 2014, when Cyprus claimed it had been prevented by Turkey from exploring for potential gas fields off the south coast of the island. However, UN-backed talks in 2017 closed without reaching an agreement, and Turkey has continued to claim the right to drill in the region despite opposition from the EU.

HEAD OF STATE
President, Nikos Anastasiades, *elected* 24 February 2013, *sworn in* 28 February 2013, *re-elected* 4 February 2018

SELECTED GOVERNMENT MEMBERS *AS AT NOVEMBER 2020*
Defence, Charalambos Petrides
Finance, Constantinos Petrides

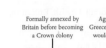

Formally annexed by Britain before becoming a Crown colony	Agreement signed between Britain, Greece and Turkey stipulating that Cyprus would become an independent republic	Tensions between Greek and Turkish Cypriots cause power-sharing to break down, leading to intercommunal conflict	A Greece-backed coup leads Turkey to invade and occupy the northern third of the island, displacing over 160,000 Greek Cypriots
1878	1950-4	1960	1964	2004
1914-25	1959	1961-71	1974	
Administration taken over by Britain from Turkey	Demands for union with Greece (*enosis*) leads to guerrilla warfare against the British administration	Island becomes independent with Britian retaining sovereignty over two military bases	UN peacekeeping force deployed to region	Greek Cypriots reject UN-sponsored reunification plan

Foreign Affairs, Nikos Christodoulides

HIGH COMMISSION FOR THE REPUBLIC OF CYPRUS
13 St James's Square, London SW1Y 4LB
T 020-7321 4100 **E** cyphclondon@btconnect.com
W www.mfa.gov.cy/highcomlondon/london.nsf
High Commissioner, HE Euripides L. Evriviades, *apptd* 2013

BRITISH HIGH COMMISSION
PO Box 21978, Alexander Pallis Street, 1587 Nicosia
T (+357) 2286 1100 **E** brithc.2@cytanet.com.cy
W www.gov.uk/government/world/cyprus
High Commissioner, HE Stephen Lillie, CMG, *apptd* 2018

BRITISH SOVEREIGN BASE AREAS
The Sovereign Base Areas (SBAs) of Akrotiri and Dhekelia are those parts of Cyprus that remained under British sovereignty and jurisdiction after independence, and have the status of a UK overseas territory. They are around 231 sq. km in size. There are approximately 15,700 residents: 7,700 Cypriots, and 8,000 military and UK-based civilian personnel and their dependants.
Administrator of the British Sovereign Base Areas, Major-General Robert Thomson, *apptd* 2019

TURKISH REPUBLIC OF NORTHERN CYPRUS
In 1974, a Greece-backed coup against the Cypriot government led Turkey, fearing the coup was a precursor to the union of Cyprus with Greece, to invade northern Cyprus and occupy over a third of the island. The following year, a Turkish Federated State of Cyprus was declared, and in 1983 a declaration of statehood was issued, which purported to establish the Turkish Republic of Northern Cyprus. This was condemned by the UN Security Council and only Turkey has recognised the republic. A constitution was adopted in 1985, and elections have been held at regular intervals since.

Reunification talks were unsuccessful in the 1980s and 1990s, and although Turkish Cypriots approved a UN-sponsored reunification plan put to simultaneous referendums in 2004, it was rejected by Greek Cypriots. Since 2004, the EU has given aid to the area to promote and ease reunification, and UN-facilitated talks began in 2008.

Following the 2018 legislative election, a left-wing coalition was formed between four parties but it collapsed in May 2019 and was replaced by a centre-right National Unity Party minority government. Far-right candidate and former prime minister Ersin Tatar won the 2020 presidential election, whose advocation of closer ties with Turkey may further endanger reunification talks.

DE FACTO HEAD OF STATE
President, Mustafa Akinci, *elected* 11 October 2020, *sworn in* 23 October 2020
Prime Minister, vacant

ECONOMY AND TRADE
The Greek Cypriot economy is dominated by the service sector, which accounted for 85.5 per cent of GDP; this was derived mainly from tourism and financial services. Tourism represents a major part of the total GDP, making the economy vulnerable to fluctuations. Shipping services are also important; about 20 per cent of the world's shipping is Cypriot-registered. Industry contributes 12.5 per cent of GDP and agriculture 2 per cent. The main products for export are citrus fruits, potatoes, pharmaceuticals, cement and garments. Imports are primarily consumer goods, fuel and lubricants, machinery and transport equipment. The main trading partners are EU nations, Libya and China.

Between 2009 and 2013, the economy contracted by a total of 8.2 per cent following a banking crisis triggered by excessive exposure to the damaged Greek economy. In 2013, Cyprus received a US$13bn (£7.6bn) economic bailout from the European Commission, the European Central Bank and the IMF (the 'Troika'). Conditions included the privatisation of state-owned enterprises and the downsizing and restructuring of the banking sector. In March 2016, Cyprus exited the EU/IMF bailout programme. The economy returned to real GDP growth in 2015 and grew steadily until 2020, when the impact of the coronavirus pandemic, especially to tourism, is expected to result in negative growth of 6.5 per cent. Exploitation of hydrocarbon deposits in Cypriot waters remains a long-term goal, but disagreements with Turkey over ownership have caused the project to stall.

The Turkish Cypriot economy suffers from a small domestic market, international isolation and a bloated public sector. It is heavily dependent on financial support from the Turkish government. It is about one-fifth the size of its southern neighbour. Services accounted for about 58.7 per cent of GDP in 2012 (the latest year for which data is available), industry for 35.1 per cent and agriculture for 6.2 per cent. The main products for export are citrus fruits, dairy products, potatoes and textiles. The main imports are vehicles, fuel, cigarettes, food, minerals, chemicals and machinery.

GNI – US$24.4bn; US$27,710 per capita (2019)
Annual average growth of GDP – 3.08 per cent (2019 est)
Inflation rate – 0.7 per cent (2017 est)
Unemployment – 7.07 per cent (2019 est)
Total external debt – US$95.28m (2013 est)
Imports – US$14,880m (2017)
Exports – US$13,496m (2017)

BALANCE OF PAYMENTS
Trade – US$1,384m deficit (2017)
Current Account – US$1,577m deficit (2019)

Trade with UK	2018	2019
Imports from UK	£395,529,285	£432,691,587
Exports to UK	£164,287,729	£239,470,757

COMMUNICATIONS

Airports and waterways – 13, including Larnaca and Paphos (Greek area); flight connections to Turkish area are via Turkey; principal ports are Limassol, Larnaca and Vasilikos (Greek area), and Famagusta and Kyrenia (Turkish area)
Roadways – 19,901km
Telecommunications – 311,559 fixed lines and 1.2 million mobile subscriptions (2018); there were 1 million internet users in 2018
Internet code and IDD – cy; 357 (from UK), 44 (to UK)
Major broadcasters – The state-run Cyprus Broadcasting Corporation competes with a number of privately owned television and radio stations; the Turkish north has its own public broadcaster, Bayrak Radio-TV
Press – Major daily newspapers include *Cyprus Mail* (English-language), *Politis* (Greek-language) and *Kibris Gazete* (Turkish-language)
WPFI score – 20.45 (27) (Greek area); 29.79 (77) (Turkish area)

CZECHIA

Ceska Republika – Czech Republic

Area – 78,867 sq. km
Capital – Prague (Praha); population, 1,306,000 (2020 est)
Major cities – Brno (Brünn), Ostrava, Plzen (Pilsen)
Currency – Koruna (Kc) of 100 haleru
Population – 10,702,498 rising at 0.06 per cent a year (2020 est)
Religion – Christian (Roman Catholic 10.4 per cent, Protestant 1.1 per cent) (est)
Language – Czech (official), Slovak
Population density – 138 per sq. km (2019)
Urban population – 73.9 per cent (2019 est)
Median age (years) – 43.3 (2020 est)
National anthem – 'Kde Domov Muj?' 'Where is My Homeland?'
National day – 28 October (Founding Day)
Death penalty – Abolished for all crimes (since 1990)
CPI score – 56 (44)
Military expenditure – US$2,710m (2018)

CLIMATE AND TERRAIN

The landlocked republic is composed of Bohemia (the west and centre) and Moravia (the east). Bohemia contains the fertile plains of the river Elbe and the surrounding low mountains, while the hilly region of Moravia extends towards the basin of the river Danube. Roughly a third of the country is covered by forest. Elevation extremes range from 1,602m (Snezka) to 115m (river Elbe). The climate is continental, with warm, humid summers and cold, dry winters. The average temperature in Prague ranges from −1.4°C in January to 18.2°C in July and August.

POLITICS

The 1992 constitution provided for the separation of the Czech Republic and Slovakia; federal laws remain in place unless superseded by Czech ones. The president is elected by popular vote for a five-year term, renewable once; prior to 2012 the president was elected by a joint session of both chambers of the legislature. The bicameral *Parlament* comprises a 200-member Chamber of Deputies, directly elected for a four-year term, and an 81-member senate directly elected for a six-year term, one-third being elected every two years. The council of ministers is appointed by the president on the recommendation of the prime minister. In April 2016 the country changed its official short geographic name to Czechia.

Early legislative elections in October 2013 gave a combined majority to three centre-left parties – the Czech Social Democratic Party (CSSD), the Christian Democratic Union/Czech People's Party (KDU–CSL) and the Movement of Dissatisfied Citizens (ANO) – which formed a coalition government under CSSD chairman Bohuslav Sobotka. The CSSD retained its position as the largest party in the senate in October 2016 elections. The ANO, led by billionaire Andrej Babis, won legislative elections in October 2017, but the minority government resigned in January 2018 over corruption allegations regarding Babis, initiating over eight months of coalition talks. Prime Minister Babis maintained his position with the help of the CSSD, but in June 2019 his leadership was subject to the largest political demonstrations since 1989. Milos Zeman (CCSD) was elected president in January 2013 and was narrowly re-elected in January 2018.

HEAD OF STATE

President, Milos Zeman, *elected* 25 January 2013, *sworn in* 8 March 2013, *re-elected* 25 January 2018

SELECTED GOVERNMENT MEMBERS *AS AT NOVEMBER 2020*

Prime Minister, Andrej Babis
First Deputy Prime Minister, Interior, Jan Hamacek
Deputy Prime Ministers, Alena Schillerova *(Finance);* Karel Havlicek
Foreign Affairs, Tomas Petricek

EMBASSY OF THE CZECH REPUBLIC

26–30 Kensington Palace Gardens, London W8 4QY
T 020-7243 1115 E london@embassy.mzv.cz
W www.mzv.cz/london
Ambassador Extraordinary and Plenipotentiary, HE Libor Secka, *apptd* 2016

BRITISH EMBASSY

Thunovska 14, 11800 Prague 1
T (+420) (2) 5740 2111 E ukinczechrepublic@fco.gov.uk
W www.gov.uk/government/world/czech-republic
Ambassador Extraordinary and Plenipotentiary, HE Nicholas Archer, MVO, *apptd* 2018

ECONOMY AND TRADE

Economic reforms and accession to the EU have produced a stable and successful market economy, as well as contributing to steady growth by expanding export markets and encouraging foreign investment. The global economic downturn caused the economy to contract in 2009, largely because of a reduced demand for the country's exports, particularly automobiles, which constitute around 80 per cent of GDP. The economy came out of two years of recession in 2014 thanks to the manufacturing sector, internal consumption, tourism and international investment. Between

| Collapse of Austro-Hungarian Empire; creation of Czechoslovakia, an amalgamation of Bohemia, Moravia, Slovakia and Ruthenia | Liberated by Soviet and US forces | The Communist Party embarks on a reform programme (the Prague Spring) which is abandoned after Gustav Husak becomes leader | The Communist Party is defeated in first free elections | Joins NATO | Joins the EU | Adopts Czechia as its official short name |

1526   1939   1948   1989   1992   —→
1918   1945   1968-9   1990   1999 2004   2016

Medieval kingdom of Bohemia comes under rule of the Habsburg dynasty — German forces invade Czech lands; Slovakia becomes a puppet state — Soviets take power in a coup — The Communist Party forced to concede its monopoly on power following mass protests — Leaders of the Czech and Slovak republics agree to dissolve the federation and form two sovereign states

2017 and 2019 it had one of the highest growth rates and lowest levels of unemployment in the EU, but the economy is expected to shrink by 6.5 per cent in 2020.

Services account for 60.8 per cent of GDP, industry for 36.9 per cent and agriculture for 2.3 per cent. The principal agricultural products are cereal crops, sugar beet, potatoes and meat. The country has been industrialised since the 19th century, and motor vehicles, metals, machinery, glass and armaments are major products. Electricity is also exported. The principal trading partners are EU countries – especially Germany – and China.

GNI – US$234.7bn; US$22,000 per capita (2020)
Annual average growth of GDP – 2.27 per cent (2019 est)
Inflation rate – 2.4 per cent (2017 est)
Population below poverty line – 9.7 per cent (2015 est)
Unemployment – 2.8 per cent (2017 est)
Total external debt – US$205.2bn (2017 est)
Imports – US$156,140m (2017)
Exports – US$171,323m (2017)

BALANCE OF PAYMENTS
Trade – US$15,182m surplus (2017)
Current Account – US$676m deficit (2019)

Trade with UK	2018	2019
Imports from UK	£2,210,836,018	£2,212,847,069
Exports to UK	£5,864,310,173	£6,063,845,083

COMMUNICATIONS
Airports and waterways – There are 41 airports, with the principal airport at Prague; the 664km of waterways include the Elbe, Vltava and Oder rivers
Roadways and railways – 55,744km; 9,408km
Telecommunications – 1.5 million fixed lines and 12.7 million mobile subscriptions (2018); there were 8.6 million internet users in 2018
Internet code and IDD – cz; 420 (from UK), 44 (to UK)
Major broadcasters – The public broadcaster Ceska Televize (CT) runs two networks and a 24-hour news channel alongside two major private television stations; Czech public radio, Cesky Rozhlas (CRo), operates three national networks and local services
Press – Major daily newspapers include *Lidove Noviny, Mlada Fronta Dnes* and *Pravo*
WPFI score – 23.57 (40)

EDUCATION AND HEALTH
Education is free and compulsory for all children from the age of six to 15.
Literacy rate – 99.8 per cent (2016 est)
Gross enrolment ratio (percentage of relevant age group) – primary 100.5 per cent, secondary 102.3 per cent, tertiary 63.8 per cent (2018 est)
Health expenditure (per capita) – US$1,476 (2017)
Hospital beds (per 1,000 people) – 6.5 (2015)
Life expectancy (years) – 79.3 (2020 est)
Mortality rate – 10.7 (2020 est)
Birth rate – 8.9 (2020 est)
Infant mortality rate – 2.6 (2020 est)

DENMARK
Kongeriget Danmark – Kingdom of Denmark

Area – 43,094 sq. km (excluding the Faroe Islands and Greenland)
Capital – Copenhagen; population, 1,346,000 (2020)
Major cities – Aalborg, Aarhus, Esbjerg, Odense
Currency – Danish krone (DKr) of 100 ore
Population – 5,869,410 rising at 0.48 per cent a year (2020 est)
Religion – Christian (officially Evangelical Lutheran 74.7 per cent), Muslim 5.5 per cent, other (including other Christian, Jewish and Buddhist) 19.8 per cent (est)
Language – Danish (official), Faroese, Greenlandic, German; English is widely spoken as a second language
Population density – 138 per sq. km (2020)
Urban population – 88 per cent (2020 est)
Median age (years) – 42 (2020 est)
National anthem – 'Det er et Yndigt Land' 'There is a Lovely Country'
National day – 5 June (Constitution Day)
Death penalty – Abolished for all crimes (since 1978)
CPI score – 87 (1)
Military expenditure – US$4,228m (2017)
Conscription – 18 years of age; 4–12 months

CLIMATE AND TERRAIN
Denmark consists of most of the Jutland peninsula and 406 islands, mainly in the Baltic Sea or among the northern Frisian Islands in the North Sea. The largest islands are Sjaelland (Zealand), Fyn, Lolland, Faister and Bornholm. It is a low-lying country, indented by fjords on its east coast and with lagoons and sand dunes along the west coast; Lim Fjord nearly bisects the north of Jutland. Elevation extremes range from 171m (Mollehoj) to −7m (Lammefjord). The climate is temperate, with cold winters and warm summers. Average temperatures range from 1.1°C in January to 17.4°C in July.

HISTORY AND POLITICS
The Danes were at the forefront of Viking expansionism from the eighth century. Denmark was unified in the tenth century and was the centre of a short-lived empire, also including Norway and England, created by Cnut (Canute) in the 11th century. The Union of Kalmar (1397) brought Norway and Sweden (including Finland) under Danish rule. Danish power waned during the 16th century, enabling Sweden to re-

establish its independence in 1523, and Norway was ceded to Sweden under the Treaty of Kiel in 1814. Denmark was neutral during the First World War, but in the Second World War it was invaded and occupied by Germany until May 1945.

Denmark joined the European Community in 1973. In a 2000 referendum, it rejected adopting the euro.

In the 2011 legislative election, the Liberal Party remained the largest party in parliament, but a surge of support for the Red Bloc (a political alliance consisting of centre-left parties) gave them an overall majority with 97 seats and they formed a coalition, taking office in October 2011. In January 2015, the coalition continued as a minority government after the withdrawal of the Socialist People's party. After the June 2015 legislative election, negotiations within the centre-right Blue Bloc coalition proved unsuccessful despite a one-seat majority, and the Liberal Party formed a minority government. In November 2016 two Blue Bloc parties entered into coalition with the Liberal Party but still failed to form a majority. In June 2019, the Red Bloc returned to power, again forming a minority government, led by Mette Frederiksen, who became the country's youngest ever prime minister.

The country is a constitutional monarchy, with a hereditary monarch as head of state. The head of government is the prime minister, who appoints the cabinet. The unicameral legislature, the *Folketing*, has 179 members, including two for the Faroes and two for Greenland; members are elected for a four-year term by proportional representation.

HEAD OF STATE
HM *The Queen of Denmark,* Queen Margrethe II, KG, *born* 16 April 1940, *acceded* 14 January 1972
Heir, HRH Crown Prince Frederik, *born* 26 May 1968

SELECTED GOVERNMENT MEMBERS *AS AT NOVEMBER 2020*
Prime Minister, Mette Frederiksen
Defence, Trine Bramsen
Finance, Nicolai Wammen
Foreign Affairs, Jeppe Kofod

ROYAL DANISH EMBASSY
55 Sloane Street, London SW1X 9SR
T 020-7333 0200 **E** lonamb@um.dk **W** www.storbrittanien.um.dk
Ambassador Extraordinary and Plenipotentiary, HE Lars Thuesen, *apptd* 2017

BRITISH EMBASSY
Kastelsvej 36–40, DK-2100 Copenhagen
T (+45) 3544 5200 **E** enquiry.copenhagen@fco.gov.uk
W www.gov.uk/government/world/denmark
Ambassador Extraordinary and Plenipotentiary, HE Dominic Schroeder, *apptd* 2016

ECONOMY AND TRADE
Denmark has a diversified and industrialised market economy with a high dependence on exports. It is a net exporter of food and energy (oil and natural gas). Slowing growth from 2007 and then the global downturn pushed the economy into recession in 2009; a modest recovery began in 2010 but the economy re-entered a technical recession at the beginning of 2011. The economy achieved modest growth between 2014 and 2019 before the coronavirus pandemic, which is expected to result in negative growth of 6.5 per cent in 2020. The service sector contributes 75.8 per cent of GDP, industry 22.9 per cent and the highly efficient agricultural sector 1.3 per cent. Metals, pharmaceuticals, shipping and renewable energy are key industries. An equitable income distribution,

comprehensive government welfare and low public dept is offset by an aging population and vulnerability to market fluctuations.

The main trading partners are other EU countries, especially Germany and Sweden. Principal exports are machinery and instruments, meat and meat products, dairy products, fish, pharmaceuticals, furniture and windmills. The main imports are machinery and equipment, industrial raw materials and semi-manufactures, chemicals, grain and foodstuffs, and consumer goods.

GNI – US$367.9bn; US$63,420 per capita (2019)
Annual average growth of GDP – 2.85 per cent (2019 est)
Inflation rate – 1.1 per cent (2017 est)
Population below poverty line – 13.4 per cent (2011)
Unemployment – 3.05 per cent (2019 est)
Total external debt – US$484.8bn (2016 est)
Imports – US$156,396m (2017)
Exports – US$178,073m (2017)

BALANCE OF PAYMENTS
Trade – US$21,676m surplus (2017)
Current Account – US$30,937m surplus (2019)

Trade with UK	2018	2019
Imports from UK	£2,742,633,258	£2,682,017,982
Exports to UK	£6,657,872,123	£6,631,809,777

COMMUNICATIONS
Airports and waterways – 28, the principal airports are at Copenhagen, Aarhus, Aalborg and near Vejle; the main ports are Aarhus, Odense, Copenhagen, Aalborg and Esbjerg
Roadways and railways – 74,558km; 3,476km
Telecommunications – 1.1 million fixed lines and 7.2 million mobile subscriptions (2018); there were 5.7 million internet users in 2018
Internet code and IDD – dk; 45 (from UK), 44 (to UK)
Major broadcasters – The public broadcaster is Danmarks Radio, which operates two television networks, and national and regional radio stations
Press – There are six major daily newspapers, including *Morgenavisen Jyllands-Posten* (English-language pages), *Berlingske Tidende* and *Ekstra Bladet*
WPFI score – 8.13 (3)

EDUCATION AND HEALTH
Education is free and compulsory for nine years.
Gross enrolment ratio (percentage of relevant age group) – primary 100.5 per cent, secondary 129.7 per cent, tertiary 81.2 per cent (2018 est)
Health expenditure (per capita) – US$5,800 (2017)
Hospital beds (per 1,000 people) – 2.5 (2015)
Life expectancy (years) – 81.2 (2020 est)
Mortality rate – 9.5 (2020 est)
Birth rate – 11.1 (2020 est)
Infant mortality rate – 3.2 (2020 est)
HIV/AIDS adult prevalence – 0.16 per cent (2014 est)

THE FAROE ISLANDS
Area – 1,393 sq. km
Capital – Torshavn; population, 21,000 (2018 est)
Population – 51,628 rising at 0.6 per cent a year (2020 est)
Religion – Christian 89.3 per cent (predominantly Evangelical Lutheran) (est)
Population density – 35 per sq. km (2019)
Urban population – 42.2 per cent (2019 est)
Median age (years) – 37.2 (2020 est)
National day – 29 July (Olaifest)

Internet code and IDD – fo; 298 (from UK), 44 (to UK)
The Faroe (Sheep) Islands are a group of 18 rugged islands (17 inhabited) and a few islets in the North Atlantic Ocean, between the Shetland Islands and Iceland. First settled in the ninth century, the islands were a Norwegian province and, with Norway, came under Danish rule in the 14th century. Since 1948 the Faroes have been self-governing and are not part of the EU.

The sovereign is represented in the islands by a high commissioner, and the islands elect two representatives to the Danish legislature. The Faroese government *(Landsstyri)* is responsible for internal affairs. The parliament *(Loegting)* has 33 members, elected for a four-year term. Following the 2019 election, a centre-right coalition of three parties formed a government under Prime Minister Barour a Steig Nielsen.
Prime Minister, Barour a Steig Nielsen, *sworn in* 16 September 2019

ECONOMY AND TRADE
The economy grew significantly before the the global downturn. It remains highly dependent on fishing and fish processing; fish and fish products account for 97 per cent of exports. Offshore oil discoveries raise the possibility of future diversification and less dependence on Danish government subsidies. High public debt has been addressed by budget surpluses in recent years.
Imports – US$980m (2016)
Exports – US$1,192m (2016)

BALANCE OF PAYMENTS
Trade – US$212m surplus (2016)
Current Account – US$194m deficit (2011)

Trade with UK	2018	2019
Imports from UK	£30,231,856	£24,982,873
Exports to UK	£207,107,224	£251,769,794

BRITISH CONSULATE
P/F Damfar, PO Box 1154, Niels Finsengota 5, FR-110 Torshavn
T (+298) 35 00 77
Honorary Consul, Joannes Hansen

GREENLAND KALAALLIT NUNAAT
Area – 2,166,086 sq. km
Capital – Nuuk (Godthab); population, 18,000 (2018)
Population – 57,616 falling at 0.08 per cent a year (2020 est)
Urban population – 87.1 per cent (2020 est)
Median age (years) – 34.3 (2020 est)
National day – 21 June (longest day)
Internet code and IDD – gl; 299 (from UK), 44 (to UK)
Greenland, the world's largest island, lies between the Atlantic and Arctic oceans, to the east of Canada and to the west of Iceland. Most of Greenland is within the Arctic Circle, with permafrost covering about 80 per cent of the island, although this ice cap is beginning to melt (*see also* The North and South Poles). Elevation extremes range from 3,700m (Gunnbjorn) to 0m (Atlantic Ocean).

Greenland was first discovered by small groups of hunters and nomadic groups who migrated from Canada *c.*500 BC. In the late tenth century Icelanders established settlements along the southeastern coast, but these colonies had died out by the 16th century. Danish colonisation began in the 18th century. Greenland was integrated into Denmark in 1953 and was granted internal autonomy in 1979; greater autonomy was granted in 2009. Greenland negotiated its withdrawal from the EU, without discontinuing relations with Denmark, and left in 1985. The USA maintains air bases on the island.

The sovereign is represented by a high commissioner, and Greenland elects two representatives to the Danish legislature. The Greenlandic government *(Landsstyri)* is elected by the parliament *(Landsting),* which has 31 members, elected for a four-year term. Aleqa Hammond became the country's first female prime minister in 2013. Snap elections in December 2014, called after Hammond resigned following a corruption scandal and fears over the economy, were won by the governing centre-left Siumut (Forward) party. In the 2018 election to the *Landsting,* Siumut lost two seats but remained the largest party.
Prime Minister, Kim Kielsen, *sworn in* 10 December 2014

ECONOMY AND TRADE
The economy is dependent on Danish subsidies (over 50 per cent of government revenue) and fishing; fish and fish products comprise over 90 per cent of exports. Natural resources include zinc, iron ore, lead, coal, molybdenum, gold, platinum and uranium, some of which are mined. Mineral exploration and mining operations are being extended as the ice cap shrinks. This is also benefiting offshore oil exploration, and global warming is extending the growing season. Tourism is being encouraged.
Imports – US$631m (2016)
Exports – US$551m (2016)

Trade with UK	2018	2019
Imports from UK	£2,261,997	£2,445,451
Exports to UK	£692,114	£2,475,953

DJIBOUTI
Jumhuriyat Jibuti/République de Djibouti – Republic of Djibouti

Area – 23,200 sq. km
Capital – Djibouti; population, 576,000 (2020 est)
Currency – Djibouti franc (DJF) of 100 centimes
Major cities – Ali Sabin, Danan, Tadjoura
Population – 921,804 rising at 2.07 per cent a year (2020 est); Somali 60 per cent, Afar 35 per cent (est)
Religion – Muslim 94 per cent, Christian 6 per cent (est)
Language – French, Arabic (both official), Somali, Afar
Population density – 41 per sq. km (2019)
Urban population – 77.9 per cent (2019 est)
Median age (years) – 24.9 (2020 est)
National anthem – 'Jabuuti' 'Djibouti'
National day – 27 June (Independence Day)
Death penalty – Abolished for all crimes (since 1995)
CPI score – 30 (126)
Military expenditure – US$44.5m (2008)
Gross enrolment ratio (percentage of relevant age group) – primary 75.3 per cent, secondary 52 per cent (2019 est); tertiary 5.3 (2011 est)
Health expenditure (per capita) – US$70 (2017)
Life expectancy (years) – 64.7 (2020 est)

Mortality rate – 7.3 (2020 est)
Birth rate – 22.7 (2020 est)
Infant mortality rate – 41.6 (2020 est)
HIV/AIDS adult prevalence – 00.8 per cent (2019 est)

CLIMATE AND TERRAIN

Djibouti is situated on the strait linking the Gulf of Aden with the Red Sea, close to busy shipping lanes. The coastal plain is separated from an inland plateau by the central mountains. Elevation extremes range from 2,028m (Moussa Ali) to −155m (Lake Assal). Although the climate is semi-arid with a hot season between April and October, occasional heavy rains can cause flash floods. The country is also prone to cyclones, drought and earthquakes. Djibouti experienced a ninth consecutive year of drought in 2016.

POLITICS

Under the 1992 constitution, amended several times, the president is directly elected for a five-year term, with no term limits. The president appoints the council of ministers. The unicameral National Assembly has 65 members, directly elected for a five-year term.

In the 2008 legislative elections, which were boycotted by the opposition, the Union for a Presidential Majority (UMP) retained all 65 seats in the legislature. Though opposition parties took part in the February 2013 parliamentary elections, the ruling party took 49 seats; the Union of National Salvation issued a statement claiming the vote was rigged. The major opposition parties again boycotted the 2018 elections, with the UMP winning 58 seats. The 2011 presidential election was also boycotted, and in 2016 President Guelleh won a fourth term in office.

HEAD OF STATE
President, Ismail Omar Guelleh, *elected* 9 April 1999, *re-elected* 2005, 2011, 2016

SELECTED GOVERNMENT MEMBERS *AS AT NOVEMBER 2020*
Prime Minister, Abdoulkader Kamil
Defence, Hassan Omar Mohamed Bourhan
Economy and Finance, Ilyas Moussa Dawaleh
Foreign Affairs, Mahamoud Ali Youssouf

EMBASSY OF THE REPUBLIC OF DJIBOUTI
26 Rue Emile Ménier, 75116 Paris, France
T (+33) (1) 4727 4922 **E** webmaster@amb-djibouti.org
Ambassador Extraordinary and Plenipotentiary, HE Ayeid Mousseid Yahya, *apptd* 2015

BRITISH AMBASSADOR
HE Alastair McPhail, CMG, OBE, *apptd* 2019, resident at Addis Ababa, Ethiopia

ECONOMY AND TRADE

A barren country with few natural resources and little industry, Djibouti's chief asset is its location on major shipping lanes. It is a transit port for neighbouring landlocked countries, especially Ethiopia, an international trans-shipment and refuelling centre, and a military base for US and EU forces because of its strategic position. The country is heavily dependent on foreign aid, has high levels of unemployment and has to import nearly all its food. The service sector accounts for 80.2 per cent of GDP, industry for 17.3 per cent and agriculture for 2.4 per cent. In recent years it has started to modernise with large infrastructure projects, largely financed by China, which includes a significant port extension (Port of Doraleh) and the Djibouti-Addis Ababa Railway. It

aims to become a logistics and commercial hub for East Africa by 2035.

The main trading partners are Ethiopia, Somalia, France and the UAE. Principal exports are re-exports (mainly coffee), hides and skins, and scrap metal. The main imports are food, beverages, clothing, transport equipment, chemicals and petroleum products.
GNI – US$2.1m; US$2,180 per capita (2018)
Annual average growth of GDP – 7.0 per cent (2017 est)
Inflation rate – 3.0 per cent (2017 est)
Population below poverty line – 23 per cent (2015 est)
Unemployment – 40 per cent (2017 est)
Total external debt – US$1.554bn (2017 est)
Imports – US$914m (2016)
Exports – US$544m (2016)

BALANCE OF PAYMENTS
Trade – US$359m deficit (2016)
Current Account – US$21,172m surplus (2017)

Trade with UK	2018	2019
Imports from UK	£10,803,058	£18,552,644
Exports to UK	£10,296,407	£13,515,079

COMMUNICATIONS

Airports and waterways – The main port and principal airport are located in Djibouti
Roadways and railways – 2,893km; the Addis Ababa-Djibouti Railway, opened in 2018, connects Ethiopia and the Port of Doraleh
Telecommunications – 36,855 fixed lines and 395,037 mobile telephones in use (2018); there were 492,221 internet users in 2018
Internet code and IDD – dj; 253 (from UK), 44 (to UK)
Press – The government owns the two major newspapers: *La Nation* (French-language) and *Al-Qarn* (Arabic-language)
Major broadcasters – Radiodiffusion-Télévision de Djibouti (RTD) is the national broadcaster and operates a radio station (Radio Djibouti) and television channel (Télé Djibouti 1). Opposition parties operate media outlets from overseas, including La Voix de Djibouti radio
WPFI score – 76.73 (176)

DOMINICA

Commonwealth of Dominica

Area – 751 sq. km
Capital – Roseau; population, 15,000 (2018 est)
Currency – East Caribbean dollar (EC$) of 100 cents
Population – 74,243 rising at 0.13 per cent a year (2020 est)
Religion – Christian (Roman Catholic 61.4 per cent, Protestant 28.6 per cent) (est)

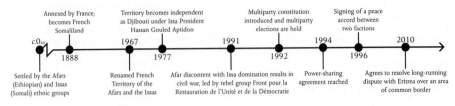

Annexed by France; becomes French Somaliland

Territory becomes independent as Djibouti under Issa President Hassan Gouled Aptidon

Multiparty constitution introduced and multiparty elections are held

Signing of a peace accord between two factions

*c.0*ᴬᴰ   1888   1967   1977   1991   1992   1994   1996   2010

Settled by the Afars (Ethiopian) and Issas (Somali) ethnic groups

Renamed French Territory of the Afars and the Issas

Afar discontent with Issa domination results in civil war, led by rebel group Front pour la Restauration de l'Unité et de la Démocratie

Power-sharing agreement reached

Agrees to resolve long-running dispute with Eritrea over an area of common border

Language – English (official), French patois
Population density – 96 per sq. km (2019)
Urban population – 70.8 per cent (2019 est)
Median age (years) – 34.9 (2020 est)
National anthem – 'Isle of Beauty'
National day – 3 November (Independence Day)
Death penalty – Retained
CPI score – 55 (48)
Gross enrolment ratio (percentage of relevant age group) – primary 100.4 per cent, secondary 101.1 per cent (2019 est)
Health expenditure (per capita) – US$440 (2017)
Life expectancy (years) – 77.7 (2020 est)
Mortality rate – 8 (2020 est)
Birth rate – 14.5 (2020 est)
Infant mortality rate – 9.7 (2020 est)

CLIMATE AND TERRAIN
Dominica, the most northerly of the Windward Islands, is 46km long and 25km wide, with a mountainous and forested centre. Its peaks include volcanic craters, one of which contains Boiling Lake, the world's second-largest thermally active lake. Elevation extremes range from 1,447m (Morne Diablotins) to 0m (Caribbean Sea). The climate is tropical, with an average temperature of 23.3°C. The island is located within the hurricane zone.

HISTORY AND POLITICS
Dominica was discovered by Columbus in 1493, when it was a stronghold of the Caribs, the sole inhabitants of the island until the French founded settlements in the 18th century. It was ceded to the British in 1763 but passed back and forth between France and Britain until 1805, after which British possession was unchallenged. From 1871 until the 1960s Dominica was administered by Britain as part of various federations of West Indian islands. Internal self-government from 1967 was followed on 3 November 1978 by independence as a republic.

The Dominica Labour Party (DLP) won the legislative election in 2019, the party's fifth general election victory in a row. Charles Savarin was elected president in 2013; the main opposition United Workers Party boycotted the election, claiming the process was unconstitutional. He was re-elected in 2018.

Under the 1978 constitution, the president is elected by the legislature for a five-year term, renewable once. The unicameral House of Assembly has 32 members, 21 directly elected, two *ex-officio* and nine appointed senators; all members serve a five-year term.

HEAD OF STATE
President, Charles Savarin, *elected* October 2013, *re-elected* October 2018

SELECTED GOVERNMENT MEMBERS *AS AT* *NOVEMBER* 2020
Prime Minister, Finance, Roosevelt Skerrit
Senior Minister, Reginald Austrie
Foreign Affairs, Kenneth Darroux

OFFICE OF THE HIGH COMMISSIONER FOR THE COMMONWEALTH OF DOMINICA
1 Collingham Gardens, London SW5 0HW
T 020-7370 5194 **E** info@dominicahighcommission.co.uk
W www.dominicahighcommission.co.uk
High Commissioner, vacant

BRITISH HIGH COMMISSIONER
HE Janet Douglas, CMG, *apptd* 2017, resident at Bridgetown, Barbados

ECONOMY AND TRADE
The economy, traditionally dependent on banana exports, struggled in the early 2000s as EU preferential access for the fruit was phased out; the industry also suffered serious hurricane damage in 2007 and 2017. Economic restructuring from 2003 led to steady growth, with an emphasis on eco-agriculture and eco-tourism, until the global downturn caused the economy to contract in 2009, and again in 2013. Diversification into offshore financial services, medical education and light industry is also being encouraged, alongside exploitation of geothermal energy, fishing and forestry resources. However, following the destruction caused by Hurricane Maria in September 2017, the government's short-term priorities have been reconstruction and managing mounting public debt.

Agriculture is the principal occupation, employing 40 per cent of the workforce and producing 22.3 per cent of GDP. Services contribute 65.1 per cent of GDP and industry 12.6 per cent. The main trading partners are the USA, other Caribbean countries and Saudi Arabia. Principal exports are bananas, soap, bay oil, vegetables and citrus fruits. The main imports are manufactured goods, machinery and equipment, food and chemicals.
GNI – US$0.58bn; US$8,090 per capita (2019)
Annual average growth of GDP – -4.7 per cent (2017 est)
Inflation rate – 0.6 per cent (2016 est)
Population below poverty line – 29 per cent (2009 est)
Total external debt – US$280.4m (2017 est)
Imports – US$313m (2016)
Exports – US$280m (2016)

BALANCE OF PAYMENTS
Trade – US$33m deficit (2016)
Current Account – US$225m deficit (2018)

Trade with UK	2018	2019
Imports from UK	£10,115,672	£10,578,704
Exports to UK	£516,842	£776,713

COMMUNICATIONS
Airports and waterways – The principal airports are Melville Hall on the north-east tip of the island and Canefield, just outside Roseau; the main seaports are located at Portsmouth and Roseau
Roadways – 762km of paved roadways
Telecommunications – 2,660 fixed lines and 75,771 mobile subscriptions (2018); there were 51,538 internet users in 2018

Internet code and IDD – dm; 1 767 (from UK), 011 44 (to UK)
Press – There are no daily newspapers
Major broadcasters – There is no national television on the island, but cable television provider Marpim Telecom and Broadcasting covers parts of the island; DBS Radio is operated by the state broadcaster
WPFI score – 23,78 (44)

DOMINICAN REPUBLIC

República Dominicana – Dominican Republic

Area – 48,670 sq. km
Capital – Santo Domingo; population, 3,318,000 (2020)
Major cities – La Romana, Los Alcarrizos, San Pedro de Macorís, Santiago de los Caballeros
Currency – Dominican Republic peso (RD$) of 100 centavos
Population – 10,499,707 rising at 0.95 per cent a year (2020 est)
Religion – Christian (Roman Catholic 47.8 per cent, Protestant 21.3 per cent), other 5 per cent (est)
Language – Spanish (official)
Population density – 220 per sq. km (2019)
Urban population – 81.8 per cent (2019)
Median age (years) – 27.9 (2020 est)
National anthem – 'Himno Nacional' 'National Anthem'
National day – 27 February (Independence Day)
Death penalty – Abolished for all crimes (since 1966)
CPI score – 28 (137)
Military expenditure – US$603m (2018)
Literacy rate – 93.8 per cent (2016)
Gross enrolment ratio (percentage of relevant age group) – primary 112.2 per cent, secondary 81.6 per cent (2019 est); tertiary 60 per cent (2017 est)
Health expenditure (per capita) – US$433 (2017)
Hospital beds (per 1,000 people) – 1.62 (2014)
Life expectancy (years) – 72 (2020 est)
Mortality rate – 6.3 (2020 est)
Birth rate – 18.5 (2020 est)
Infant mortality rate – 20.9 (2020 est)
HIV/AIDS adult prevalence – 0.9 per cent (2019 est)

CLIMATE AND TERRAIN

The republic forms the eastern two-thirds of the island of Hispaniola and is crossed from the north-west to the south-east by the Cordillera Central mountain range, which has a number of peaks over 3,000m. Elevation extremes range from 3,175m (Pico Duarte) to −46m (Lake Enriquillo). The climate is maritime tropical, with an average temperature of 24.8°C.

HISTORY AND POLITICS

The island was discovered by Columbus in 1492, and a Spanish colony was established in 1496. The eastern province of Santo Domingo remained under Spanish rule after the partition of Hispaniola in 1697, but was ceded to France in 1795. It was restored to Spain in 1809, but rebelled in 1821 and achieved independence briefly before being annexed by

Haiti in 1822. Haitian rule ended in 1844 when independence was declared as the Dominican Republic, although the country was voluntarily under Spanish rule again from 1861 to 1865. A long dictatorship at the end of the 19th century was followed by revolution and bankruptcy, which led to occupation by US forces from 1916 until 1924. A military coup in 1930 established the dictatorship of Gen. Rafael Trujillo, whose corrupt rule continued until his assassination in 1961. After a period of political instability, a new constitution was adopted in 1966 and democracy was restored.

The Modern Revolutionary Party won both houses in the July 2020 general election and Luis Abinader was appointed president, replacing two-time winner Danilo Medina of the Dominican Liberation Party (PLD); the PLD had ruled for the previous 16 years.

In 2015, the 2010 constitution was changed to allow the president to run for a second term. The bicameral National Congress comprises the House of Representatives, which has 190 members, and the senate, with 32 members; both chambers are directly elected for a four-year term.

HEAD OF STATE
President, Luis Abinader, *elected* 5 July 2020, *sworn in* 16 August 2020
Vice-President, Raquel Peña

SELECTED GOVERNMENT MEMBERS *AS AT NOVEMBER* 2020
Defence, Carlos Diaz
Finance, Jose Vicente
Foreign Affairs, Roberto Alvarez
Interior, Jesus Vasquez

EMBASSY OF THE DOMINICAN REPUBLIC
81 Cromwell Road, London SW7 5BW
T 020-7727 7091 E info@dominicanembassy.org.uk
W www.dominicanembassy.org.uk
Ambassador Extraordinary and Plenipotentiary, HE Hugo Maximiliano Guiliani Cury, *apptd* 2019

BRITISH EMBASSY
Edificio Corominas Pepín, 7th–8th Floor, Ave 27 de Febrero No 233, Santo Domingo
T (+1) (829) 472 7111
W www.gov.uk/government/world/dominican-republic
Ambassador Extraordinary and Plenipotentiary, HE Mockbul Ali, OBE, *apptd* 2020

ECONOMY AND TRADE

In recent years, tourism and the free trade zones have overtaken agriculture as the mainstay of the economy, and services now account for over 61.4 per cent of GDP. Industry accounts for 33 per cent and agriculture 5.6 per cent. The main crops are sugar, coffee, cotton, cocoa, tobacco, rice, vegetables and bananas, and the main industrial activities are sugar processing, mining and the production of textiles, cement and tobacco products. Remittances from expatriate workers are equivalent to roughly two-thirds of tourism receipts. The economy returned to growth from 2010 after the global recession and the country's budget deficit was halved from 2012 to 2014. Government revenues have been boosted by the opening of the Pueblo Viejo mine, one of the largest gold mines in the world. Despite being one of the fastest growing economies in Latin America, poverty, inequality and unemployment rates remain high.

The main trading partner is the USA, which claims over half of all exports and provides 41.4 per cent of imports. Principal exports are sugar, gold, silver, coffee, cocoa, tobacco, meats

and consumer goods. The chief imports are foodstuffs, fuel, cotton and fabrics, chemicals and pharmaceuticals.
GNI – US$86.9bn; US$8,090 per capita (2019)
Annual average growth of GDP – 4.6 per cent (2017 est)
Inflation rate – 3.3 per cent (2017 est)
Population below poverty line – 30.5 per cent (2016 est)
Unemployment – 5.1 per cent (2017 est)
Total external debt – US$29.16bn (2017 est)
Imports – US$21,019m (2017)
Exports – US$17,455m (2017)

BALANCE OF PAYMENTS
Trade – US$3,754m deficit (2017)
Current Account – US$1,204m deficit (2019)

Trade with UK	2018	2019
Imports from UK	£103,497,832	£99,676,137
Exports to UK	£106,655,632	£111,624,309

COMMUNICATIONS
Airports and waterways – 16, the principal airport is at Santo Domingo; Santo Domingo, Rio Haina and Caucedo are the main seaports
Roadways and railways – There are 9,872km of surfaced roads, and 496km of railways
Telecommunications – 1.3 million fixed lines and 8.9 million mobile subscriptions (2018); there were 7.7 million internet users in 2018
Internet code and IDD – do; 1 809/829 (from UK), 011 44 (to UK)
Major broadcasters – Combination of state-owned and privately owned broadcast media, including over 300 radio stations. The state-owned broadcaster is Corporacion Estatal de Radio y Television (CERTV)
Press – Five main daily newspapers are published in Spanish
WPFI score – 27.90 (55)

ECUADOR

República del Ecuador – Republic of Ecuador

Area – 283,561 sq. km
Capital – Quito; population, 2,994,000 (2020 est)
Major cities – Cuenca, Guayaquil, Machala, Manta, Santo Domingo de los Colorados
Currency – US dollar (US$) of 100 cents
Population – 16,904,867 rising at 1.2 per cent a year (2020 est)
Religion – Christian (Roman Catholic 74 per cent, Protestant 10.4 per cent), other 6.4 per cent (including Buddhist, Jewish, Muslim, Hindu, indigenous religions (est)
Language – Spanish (official), Quechua, other Amerindian languages

Population density – 69 per sq. km (2020)
Urban population – 64 per cent (2020 est)
Median age (years) – 28.8 (2020 est)
National anthem – 'Salve, Oh Patria' 'We Salute You, Our Homeland'
National day – 10 August (Independence Day)
Death penalty – Abolished for all crimes (since 1906)
CPI score – 38 (93)
Military expenditure – US$2,549m (2018)
Conscription – 18 years of age; 12 months (selective), currently suspended

CLIMATE AND TERRAIN
The Andes run north to south through the centre of Ecuador, dividing the coastal plain in the west from the low-lying rainforest in the east, and between two local Andean chains lie the central highlands. Elevation extremes range from 6,267m (Chimborazo) to 0m (Pacific Ocean). Other Andean peaks include Cotopaxi (5,896m) and Cayambe (5,790m) in the Eastern Cordillera. Ecuador is located in an earthquake zone and five of its volcanoes have erupted since 2000 – most recently Tungurahua in April 2014. The country has four different climatic zones and is one of the most biodiverse countries on earth; its territory includes the Galápagos Islands in the Pacific Ocean. The average temperature is 21.9°C.

HISTORY AND POLITICS
The kingdom of the Caras, around Quito, was conquered by the Incas in the 15th century. After the Spanish defeated the Incas in Peru, Ecuador was conquered in 1534 and added to the Spanish viceroyalty of Peru. Independence from Spain was achieved in a revolutionary war that culminated in the battle of Mt Pichincha (1822). Ecuador then formed part of Gran Colombia with Colombia, Panama and Venezuela, but left this union to become a fully independent state in 1830. After independence, the country experienced periods of political instability interspersed with dictatorships and military rule. Democratic rule under civilian government was restored in 1979.

The exploitation of oil reserves funded economic and social transformation from the 1970s onwards but also caused rapid inflation and increased foreign debt. In recent years, these problems have worsened because of economic recession, leading to strikes and demonstrations. Civil unrest forced three presidents from office between 1997 and 2003.

Presidential and legislative elections were held in 2009 after a new constitution was approved by a national referendum in 2008, and in 2013 President Correa was elected for a third term – and his second four-year term. He did not contest presidential elections in February 2017, which resulted in a narrow victory for his vice-president Lenín Moreno over right-wing candidate Guillermo Lasso. In the simultaneous legislative elections, the left-wing PAIS Alliance won 39 per cent of the vote. Moreno's running partner and vice-president, Jorge Glas, was jailed for six years in December 2017 for bribery.

The 2008 constitution provides for an executive president who is directly elected for a four-year term, renewable once. The unicameral National Assembly has 137 members elected on a party-list proportional representation basis for a four-year term. The republic is divided into 24 provinces.

HEAD OF STATE
President, Lenín Moreno, *elected* 2 April 2017, *sworn in* 24 May 2017
Vice-President, Maria Muñoz

SELECTED GOVERNMENT MEMBERS *AS AT NOVEMBER 2020*
Defence, Oswaldo Jarrin
Economy and Finance, Maurico Pozo
Foreign Affairs, Luis Gallegos

EMBASSY OF ECUADOR
Flat 3B, 3 Hans Crescent, London SW1X 0LS
T 020-7584 1367 **E** eecugranbretania@mmrree.gob.ec
W www.consuladoecuador.org.uk
Ambassador Extraordinary and Plenipotentiary, HE Jaime Marchán-Romero, *apptd* 2019

BRITISH EMBASSY
PO Box 17-17-830, Citiplaza Building, Av. Naciones Unidas y Republica de El Salvador, Piso 14, Quito
T (+593) (2) 2970 800 **E** quito.consular@fco.gov.uk
W www.gov.uk/government/world/ecuador
Ambassador Extraordinary and Plenipotentiary, HE Christopher Campbell, *apptd* 2020

ECONOMY AND TRADE

Structural reforms in 2000, including the adoption of the US dollar in response to the severe economic crisis of 1999, paved the way for strong growth from 2002 to 2006. Growth then slowed owing to the uncertainty created by windfall taxes imposed on foreign oil companies, a fall in oil production since 2007, the government defaulting on 30 per cent of public external debt in 2008, and the cancellation of a number of bilateral investment treaties in 2009. The economy, already in recession in 2015, struggled after April 2016's 7.8-magnitude earthquake, which killed more than 650 people and caused up to US$3bn (£2bn) of damage. In 2019, the country agreed an IMF package worth US$4.2bn as it sought to reduce its public debt, but austerity has stifled domestic demand; there was nil growth in 2019 and the economy is expected to shrink by 6.3 per cent in 2020 largely due to the coronavirus pandemic.

Oil is Ecuador's principal export, accounting for around a third of export earnings. After oil, agriculture, fishing and forestry are the most important activities, providing products both for export and for the food- and wood-processing industries. The main exports are oil, bananas, cut flowers, fish, cacao, coffee, hemp and timber. The main imports are industrial materials, fuels and lubricants, and consumer goods. Principal trading partners are the USA and China.

GNI – US$105.6bn; US$6,080 per capita (2019)
Annual average growth of GDP – 0.06 per cent (2019 est)
Inflation rate – 0.4 per cent (2017 est)
Population below poverty line – 21.5 per cent (2017 est)
Unemployment – 5.71 per cent (2019 est)
Total external debt – US$39.29bn (2017 est)
Imports – US$22,602m (2017)
Exports – US$21,918m (2017)

BALANCE OF PAYMENTS
Trade – US$684m deficit (2017)
Current Account – US$53m deficit (2019)

Trade with UK	2018	2019
Imports from UK	£94,464,041	£96,410,050
Exports to UK	£153,412,555	£139,341,678

COMMUNICATIONS

Airports and waterways – 104, with international flights operating to Quito and Guayaquil; the main ports are Guayaquil and Esmeraldas

Roadways and railways – There are 43,216km of roadways, 8,161km of which are surfaced, and 965km of railways
Telecommunications – 2.4 million fixed lines and 15.8 million mobile subscriptions (2018); there were 9.5 million internet users in 2018
Internet code and IDD – ec; 593 (from UK), 44 (to UK)
Major broadcasters – Combination of privately owned and nationally owned outlets; 60 media outlets are recognised as national, with the Ecuadorian government controlling 12 national outlets and multiple radio stations. There are multiple television stations and over 300 radio channels (2018)
Press – Six newspapers are published daily, including *El Comercio, El Tiempo* and the Guayaquil-based daily *El Universo*
WPFI score – 32.62 (98)

EDUCATION AND HEALTH

Elementary education is free and compulsory until age 14.
Literacy rate – 92.8 per cent (2017 est)
Gross enrolment ratio (percentage of relevant age group) – primary 103.3 per cent, secondary 101.4 per cent (2018 est); tertiary 44.9 per cent (2015 est)
Health expenditure (per capita) – US$518 (2017)
Hospital beds (per 1,000 people) – 1.5 (2012)
Life expectancy (years) – 77.5 (2020 est)
Mortality rate – 5.2 (2020 est)
Birth rate – 17 (2020 est)
Infant mortality rate – 15 (2020 est)
HIV/AIDS adult prevalence – 0.4 per cent (2019 est)

GALÁPAGOS ISLANDS

The Galápagos (Giant Tortoise) Islands, about 960km from the mainland, were annexed by Ecuador in 1832. The 12 large and several hundred smaller islands lie on the equator, and most form part of a national park where unique marine birds, iguanas and giant tortoises are conserved. This wildlife provided naturalist Charles Darwin (1809–82) with inspiration and research material for his theory of evolution by natural selection, expounded in *On the Origin of Species* (1859). The islands were declared a UNESCO World Heritage site in 1978.

EGYPT

Jumhuriyat Misr al-Arabiyah – Arab Republic of Egypt

Area – 1,001,450 sq. km
Capital – Cairo; population, 20,901,000 (2020 est); stands on the Nile about 22km from the head of the delta
Major cities – Alexandria (founded 332 BC by Alexander the Great; the capital for over 1,000 years), Giza, Port Said, Shubra al-Khema, Suez
Currency – Egyptian pound (£E) of 100 piastres

Population – 104,124,440 rising at 2.28 per cent a year (2020 est)
Religion – Muslim 90 per cent (predominantly Sunni), Christian 10 per cent (predominantly Coptic Orthodox) (est)
Language – Arabic (official), English, French
Population density – 99 per sq. km (2019)
Urban population – 42.7 per cent (2019 est)
Median age (years) – 24.1 (2020 est)
National anthem – 'Biladi, Biladi, Biladi' 'My Homeland, My Homeland, My Homeland'
National day – 23 July (Revolution Day)
Death penalty – Retained
CPI score – 35 (106)
Military expenditure – US$3,110m (2018)
Conscription – 18–30 years of age, male only; 18–36 months, followed by a nine-year reserve obligation

CLIMATE AND TERRAIN

There are four broad regions: the Western Desert, which covers nearly two-thirds of the country to the west of the Nile valley; the Eastern Desert, which lies between the Nile and the mountains along the Red Sea coast; the fertile Nile valley and delta, where most of the population lives; and the Sinai peninsula, where a coastal plain on the Mediterranean rises to mountains in the south. The deserts are arid plateaux, with depressions in the Western Desert whose springs irrigate oases, while the Eastern Desert is dissected by wadis (dry watercourses). Elevation extremes range from 2,629m (Mt Catherine, Sinai) to −133m (Qattara depression). The country has a desert climate, with hot, dry summers and mild winters. Temperatures increase further south, and rainfall increases nearer the coast. Average daily temperatures range from 13°C in January to 30.4°C in August.

POLITICS

The 1971 constitution was suspended after President Mubarak's resignation in 2011 and substantial changes to it were approved by referendum in March 2011. A new constitution was approved in January 2014, which provides the army with greater political powers, established Shari'ah as the basis of the country's laws and provides for an executive president who is directly elected.

Under the 2014 constitution the legislature is unicameral, with 448 of the 596 members of the House of Representatives directly elected by an individual candidacy system, 120 members elected in constituencies by majority vote, and 28 appointed by the president. All members serve five-year terms.

The first legislative election since President Mubarak's departure from office was held in November 2011 and saw the Freedom and Justice Party (FJP, founded by the Muslim Brotherhood) win the most seats but fail to win a majority. The People's Assembly was suspended in July 2013 and legislative elections under the new 2014 constitution were held in July 2014.

The first presidential election in the country's history was won by FJP candidate Mohammed Mursi and was inaugurated in June 2012. Following mass demonstrations, Mursi was deposed by the army in July 2013; in April 2015, Mursi and 12 others were sentenced to 20 years in jail for the arrest and torture of protestors and incitement to violence, and in June 2015 a court confirmed a death sentence handed to Mursi and 105 others for their role in the 2011 Wadi al-Natrun prison break. In 2014, amid boycotts from opposition parties and claims that rivals had been intimidated, independent candidate and Commander-in-Chief of the Egyptian armed forces Abdel al-Sisi won the presidential election with 90 per cent of the vote. His re-election was confirmed in April 2018 with 97 per cent of the vote following an election in March 2018 with no public debates or legitimate opposition. The constitution was subsequently amended following a popular referendum in April 2019 to extend presidential terms from four to six years, expand military power in politics and give President Sisi greater control over the judiciary. The amendment passed amid a crackdown on dissent and could allow Sisi to stay in power until 2030.

HEAD OF STATE

President, C-in-C of the Armed Forces, Abdel Fattah al-Sisi, *elected* 29 May 2014, *sworn in* 8 June 2014, *re-elected* 2 April 2018
Vice-President, Ahmed Khaled Hassan

SELECTED GOVERNMENT MEMBERS *AS AT NOVEMBER 2020*

Prime Minister, Moustafa Kamal Madbouli
Head of the Supreme Council of the Armed Forces, Defence, Lt.-Gen. Mohamed Ahmed Zaki
Finance, Mohamed Maeet
Foreign Affairs, Sameh Hassan Shoukry
Interior, Mahmoud Tawfik

EMBASSY OF THE ARAB REPUBLIC OF EGYPT

26 South Street, London W1K 1DW
T 020-7499 3304 **E** eg.emb_london@mfa.gov.eg
Ambassador Extraordinary and Plenipotentiary, HE Tarek Adel, *apptd* 2018

BRITISH EMBASSY

7 Ahmed Ragheb Street, Garden City, Cairo
T (+20) (2) 2791 6000 **E** consular.cairo@fco.gov.uk
W www.gov.uk/government/world/egypt
Ambassador Extraordinary and Plenipotentiary, HE Sir Geoffrey Adams, KCMG, *apptd* 2018

ECONOMY AND TRADE

Economic liberalisation in recent decades has attracted foreign investment and promoted exports, producing strong growth in GDP, but political uncertainty significantly reduced government revenues in 2012. In 2011 and 2012, the government drew down foreign exchange reserves by 50 per cent. Although the dams on the Nile have expanded the area of land under cultivation, other factors, such as population growth, put a greater strain on resources, while terrorist attacks have affected tourism. In November 2016, Egypt devalued its currency by 48 per cent and announced that its value would be allowed to float, in order to meet a key IMF demand ahead of securing a US$12bn loan. This resulted in

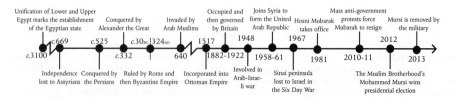

Unification of Lower and Upper Egypt marks the establishment of the Egyptian state — c.3100

Conquered by Alexander the Great — c.525

Conquered by Arab Muslims — c.30ᴮᶜ–324ᴬᴰ

Invaded by Britain — 1517

Occupied and then governed by Britain — 1948

Joins Syria to form the United Arab Republic — 1967

Hosni Mubarak takes office

Mass anti-government protests force Mubarak to resign — 2012

Mursi is removed by the military

Independence lost to Assyrians — c.332

Conquered by the Persians

Ruled by Rome and then Byzantine Empire — 640

Incorporated into Ottoman Empire — 1882–1922

Involved in Arab-Israeli war — 1958–61

Sinai peninsula lost to Israel in the Six Day War — 1981

The Muslim Brotherhood's Mohammed Mursi wins presidential election — 2010–11 / 2013

high levels of inflation, but also significant levels of foreign investment and a return to growth. Political uncertainty, security issues and internal repression continue to hamper growth and investment.

The services sector contributes 54 per cent to GDP and employs 49.1 per cent of the workforce. Tourism is the largest component of this sector (estimated to have contributed 7.5 per cent of GDP in 2014), along with Suez Canal revenues and expatriate remittances. Industry accounts for 34.3 per cent of GDP and 25.1 per cent of employment, but despite increasing industrialisation, agriculture still employs 25.8 per cent of the workforce, contributing 11.7 per cent of GDP. Egypt is a net importer of foodstuffs, especially grain, and a food security programme has been set up with the aim of achieving self-sufficiency.

The main cash crop is cotton, of which Egypt is one of the world's main producers. Other important crops are rice, maize, wheat, vegetables, fruit and livestock. Industry is centred on oil and gas extraction, processing hydrocarbons, cotton and other agricultural products, producing textiles, metal products and chemicals. Oil is the backbone of the economy and helps, alongside considerable reserves of natural gas and the hydroelectric power produced by the Aswan High Dam, to make Egypt self-sufficient in energy.

The main trading partners are China, the UAE, the USA, and EU nations. Principal exports are crude oil and petroleum products, cotton, textiles, metal products, chemicals and processed food. The main imports are machinery and equipment, foodstuffs, chemicals, wood products and fuels.

GNI – US$270.2bn; US$2,690 per capita (2019)
Annual average growth of GDP – 4.2 per cent (2017 est)
Inflation rate – 23.5 per cent (2017 est)
Population below poverty line – 27.8 per cent (2016 est)
Unemployment – 7.86 per cent (2019 est)
Total external debt – US$77.47bn (2017 est)
Imports – US$69,802m (2017)
Exports – US$43,372m (2017)

BALANCE OF PAYMENTS
Trade – US$26,430m deficit (2017)
Current Account – US$10,221m deficit (2019)

Trade with UK	2018	2019
Imports from UK	£1,147,271,302	£1,276,403,342
Exports to UK	£817,866,928	£868,221,224

COMMUNICATIONS
Airports – 72; the principal airports are at Cairo, Sharm el-Sheikh, Luxor, Alexandria and Hurghada (2013)
Waterways – Egypt has 3,500km of waterways, including the Nile river and Lake Nasser, the Alexandria–Cairo waterway, numerous small canals in the Nile delta and the Suez Canal (opened 1869; closed 1967–75); the main seaports are Alexandria, Damietta and Port Said on the Mediterranean Sea and Suez on the Red Sea
Roadways and railways – 65,050km; 5,085km
Telecommunications – 7.9 million fixed lines and 93 million mobile subscriptions (2018); there were 46.6 million internet users in 2016
Internet code and IDD – eg; 20 (from UK), 44 (to UK)
Major broadcasters – Combination of state-run and privately owned media broadcasting outlets. State-run national television channels and regional channels compete with the country's thriving satellite television industry, which is watched throughout the Arab-speaking world. State-run media operates two national and six regional television

networks and approximately 30 radio outlets across eight networks (2019)
Press – A number of daily newspapers are published, including *Al-Ahram,* the oldest newspaper in the Arab world. Mixture of publications in different languages, including Arabic, Armenian, English, and French; includes state-run newspapers. One of the biggest jailers of journalists in the world.
WPFI score – 56.82 (166)

EDUCATION AND HEALTH
Education is free between the ages of six and 15.
Literacy rate – 71.2 per cent (2017 est)
Gross enrolment ratio (percentage of relevant age group) – primary 106.4 per cent, secondary 89.5 per cent (2019 est); tertiary 35.2 per cent (2017 est)
Health expenditure (per capita) – US$106 (2017)
Hospital beds (per 1,000 people) – 1.6 (2015)
Life expectancy (years) – 73.7 (2020 est)
Mortality rate – 4.4 (2020 est)
Birth rate – 27.2 (2020 est)
Infant mortality rate – 17.1 (2020 est)
HIV/AIDS adult prevalence – 0.1 per cent (2019 est)

EL SALVADOR
República de El Salvador – Republic of El Salvador

Area – 21,041 sq. km
Capital – San Salvador; population, 1,106,000 (2020 est)
Major cities – San Miguel, Santa Ana, Soyapango
Currency – US dollar (US$) of 100 cents
Population – 6,481,102 rising at 0.83 per cent a year (2020 est)
Religion – Christian (Roman Catholic 50 per cent, Protestant 36 per cent) (est)
Language – Spanish (official), Nawat
Population density – 310 per sq. km (2019)
Urban population – 72.7 per cent (2019 est)
Median age (years) – 27.7 (2020 est)
National anthem – 'Himno Nacional de El Salvador' 'National Anthem of El Salvador'
National day – 15 September (Independence Day)
Death penalty – Retained for certain crimes (no known use since 1973)
CPI score – 34 (113)
Military expenditure – US$266m (2018 est)
Conscription – 18 years of age; 12 months (selective)

CLIMATE AND TERRAIN
El Salvador is mountainous, with narrow coastal plains and a central plateau. Many of its peaks are volcanoes; most are extinct, but Ilamatepec (or Santa Ana) erupted in 2005. There are also numerous volcanic lakes. Elevation extremes range from 2,730m (Cerro El Pital) to 0m (Pacific Ocean). The climate is tropical on the coast but more temperate at higher

altitudes. The average annual temperature in San Salvador is 25.4°C. Earthquakes and volcanic activity are common, and the country is also susceptible to hurricanes and tropical storms.

HISTORY AND POLITICS

El Salvador was part of the Aztec kingdom conquered in 1524 by Pedro de Alvarado, and formed part of the Spanish viceroyalty of Guatemala until 1821. It was part of a Central American federation of former Spanish provinces from 1823 until the federation's dissolution in 1838, becoming fully independent in 1840.

There was political unrest in the 1970s, and guerrilla activity by the left-wing Farabundo Martí National Liberation Front (FMLN), which intensified from 1977 amid reports of human rights abuses by government troops and right-wing death squads. Decades of military rule ended in 1979, but elections in 1982 were boycotted by left-wing parties and the right-wing Nationalist Republican Alliance (ARENA) took office. The civil war between the FMLN and the US-backed government lasted throughout the 1980s, until a UN-sponsored peace agreement was signed in 1992. The FMLN was recognised as a political party, and it won seats in the 1994 election.

In 2014 the FMLN candidate and former guerrilla fighter Salvador Sanchez Ceren was elected president. However in February 2019, the 25-year two-party system was ended with the election of Nayib Bukele on an anti-corruption platform. The conservative Nationalist Republican Alliance (ARENA) was the largest single party after the March 2018 elections, though the FMLN continued to govern as part of a coalition.

Under the 1983 constitution, the executive president is directly elected for a five-year term, which is not renewable. The unicameral legislative assembly has 84 members, who are directly elected for a three-year term. The president appoints the Council of State. The country is divided into 14 departments.

HEAD OF STATE

President, Nayib Bukele, *elected* 3 February 2019, *took office* 1 June 2019
Vice-President, Felix Ulloa

SELECTED GOVERNMENT MEMBERS *AS AT NOVEMBER 2020*

Defence, Rene Francis Merino
Economy, Maria Luisa Hayem
Foreign Affairs, Juana Alexandra Hill

EMBASSY OF EL SALVADOR

8 Dorset Square, 1st & 2nd Floors, London NW1 6PU
T 020-7224 9800 **E** embajadalondres@rree.gob.sv
Ambassador Extraordinary and Plenipotentiary, HE Gilda Guadalupe Verásquez-Paz, *apptd* 2019

BRITISH EMBASSY

Edificio Torre Futura, 14th Floor, Colonia Escalon, San Salvador
T (+503) 2511 5757 **E** britishembassy.elsalvador@fco.gov.uk
W www.gov.uk/government/world/el-salvador
Ambassador Extraordinary and Plenipotentiary, HE David Lelliott, *apptd* 2019

ECONOMY AND TRADE

The country is one of the most industrialised in Central America and has the region's fourth-largest economy despite being its smallest country and having few natural resources. Recovery after the civil war was set back by a series of natural disasters, but the economy has been transformed from a mainly agricultural to a service-based economy with a growing manufacturing sector. Government diversification efforts have promoted textile production, international port services and tourism. In September 2014, El Salvador was awarded US$277m by US government agency the Millennium Challenge Corporation with the aim of stimulating economic growth and reducing poverty, but US aid was suspended between March and October 2019 over allegations the country failed to stop migrants fleeing to the US. El Salvador has struggled to attract foreign investment, not least because drug trafficking has made it the world's most violent country that is not at war. Expatriate remittances are received by about a third of households. Historically low public debt has been rising for several years.

Services, through tourism, commerce and financial services, contribute 60.3 per cent of GDP. Industry contributes 27.7 per cent of GDP, mostly through assembly for re-export, food processing, beverages, oil, chemicals, fertiliser, textiles, furniture and light metals. Agriculture contributes 12 per cent to GDP and employs 21 per cent of the workforce. The principal agricultural products are coffee, sugar, maize, rice, beans, oilseed, cotton, sorghum, beef and dairy products.

The main trading partners are the USA and other Central American states. Principal exports are offshore assembly products, coffee, sugar, textiles, garments, gold, ethanol, chemicals and electricity. The chief imports are raw materials, consumer goods, capital goods, fuels, foodstuffs, oil and electricity.

GNI – US$25.8bn; US$4,000 per capita (2019)
Annual average growth of GDP – 2.3 per cent (2017 est)
Inflation rate – 1.0 per cent (2017 est)
Population below poverty line – 32.7 per cent (2016 est)
Unemployment – 7 per cent (2017 est)
Total external debt – US$15.51bn (2017 est)
Imports – US$11,365m (2017)
Exports – US$7,220m (2017)

BALANCE OF PAYMENTS

Trade – US$4,145m deficit (2017)
Current Account – US$557m deficit (2019)

Trade with UK	2018	2019
Imports from UK	£28,142,176	£43,065,393
Exports to UK	£13,663,366	£13,672,903

COMMUNICATIONS

Airports and waterways – Five; the principal ports are Cutuco and Acajutla, and ports in Honduras and Guatemala are also used
Roadways and railways – There are 5,341km of paved roads; 13km
Telecommunications – 923,029 fixed lines and 9.5 million mobile subscriptions (2018); there were 2.2 million internet users in 2018
Internet code and IDD – sv; 503 (from UK), 44 (to UK)
Major broadcasters – Digital transition to begin in 2018, adding to hundreds of private television and radio outlets, including Teledos and Canal Cuatro; there are hundreds of radio broadcasters, including the state-run Radio Nacional de El Salvador (2017)
Press – There are five main daily newspapers: *Diario Co Latino, La Prensa Grafica, El Mundo, El Diario de Hoy* and *El Diario Co Latino*
WPFI score – 29.70 (74)

EDUCATION AND HEALTH

Primary education is state-run, compulsory and free.

Literacy rate – 89 per cent (2018 est)
Gross enrolment ratio (percentage of relevant age group) – primary 94.8 per cent, secondary 71.7 per cent, tertiary 29.4 per cent (2018 est)
Health expenditure (per capita) – US$282 (2017)
Hospital beds (per 1,000 people) – 1.3 (2014)
Life expectancy (years) – 74.8 (2020 est)
Mortality rate – 5.9 (2020 est)
Birth rate – 18.6 (2020 est)
Infant mortality rate – 11.8 (2020 est)
HIV/AIDS adult prevalence – 0.5 per cent (2019 est)

EQUATORIAL GUINEA

República de Guinea Ecuatorial/République de Guinée Equatoriale – Republic of Equatorial Guinea

Area – 28,051 sq. km
Capital – Malabo, on Bioko; population, 297,000 (2018 est)
Major towns – Bata, the principal town and port of Río Muni; Ebebiyín
Currency – Central African CFA franc of 100 centimes
Population – 836,178 rising at 2.35 per cent a year (2020 est); Fang (85.7 per cent), Bubi (6.5 per cent) (est)
Religion – Nominally Christian (predominantly Roman Catholic)
Language – Spanish, French, Portuguese (all official), Fang, Bubi
Population density – 47 per sq. km (2019)
Urban population – 72.6 per cent (2019 est)
Median age (years) – 20.3 (2020 est)
National anthem – 'Caminemos pisando las sendas de nuestra inmensa felicidad' 'Let Us Tread the Path of our Immense Happiness'
National day – 12 October (Independence Day)
Death penalty – Retained
CPI score – 16 (173)
Military expenditure – US$18.6m (2016 est)
Conscription – 18 years of age; 24 months (selective)
Literacy rate – 95.3 per cent (2015 est)
Gross enrolment ratio (percentage of relevant age group) – primary 79.1 per cent (2015 est)
Health expenditure (per capita) – US$301 (2017)
Life expectancy (years) – 65.7 (2020 est)
Mortality rate – 7.3 (2020 est)
Birth rate – 30.7 (2020 est)
Infant mortality rate – 59.7 (2020 est)
HIV/AIDS adult prevalence – 7.2 per cent (2019 est)

CLIMATE AND TERRAIN

The country consists of several islands off the Cameroon coast and a small area on the mainland, Río Muni, where 80 per cent of the population lives. The islands, of which Bioko is the largest, are of volcanic origin. The mainland rises from a narrow coastal plain to a mountainous interior plateau, and is covered in dense vegetation. Elevation extremes range from 3,008m (Pico Basile) to 0m (Atlantic Ocean). The climate is tropical, with a rainy season from July to January on Bioko, and from April to May and October to December on the mainland.

HISTORY AND POLITICS

The island of Fernando Po (Bioko) was claimed by the Portuguese in 1494 and held until 1777, when it was ceded to Spain. The mainland territory of Río Muni came under Spanish rule in 1844, and the two territories became one colony, subsequently known as Spanish Guinea, in 1904. The colony became autonomous in 1963, and independent in 1968 under its present name.

The first president, Francisco Macías Nguema, established a one-party state in 1970. His brutal regime was overthrown in 1979 in a military coup led by his nephew, Col. Obiang Nguema. A military regime was established after the coup, and only presidential nominees were allowed to stand in the 1983 and 1988 elections. Constitutional amendments were introduced in 1991 to allow multiparty elections, but President Nguema and the Democratic Party of Equatorial Guinea (PDGE) have retained power since 1992; most elections have been boycotted by the opposition parties because of election irregularities and intimidation. The regime has been accused of human rights abuses and the suppression of political opposition, and in 2003 opposition leaders set up a 'government-in-exile' in Spain. There is also a separatist movement on Bioko.

In the 2017 legislative election, the PDGE retained total control over the senate and claimed 99 of the 100 seats in the Chamber of Deputies. President Nguema was re-elected in April 2016 with 94 per cent of the vote in his first term since 2011's constitutional referendum.

The 1991 constitution introduced a multiparty system. The president is directly elected for a seven-year term; constitutional amendments approved by referendum in November 2011 introduced a two-term limit. Constitutional amendments in 2012 created a bicameral system with a lower chamber, the Chamber of Deputies, with 100 members, and an upper chamber, the senate, containing 55 elected officials and 15 presidential appointments.

HEAD OF STATE

President, Brig.-Gen. Teodoro Obiang Nguema, *took power* August 1979, *re-elected* 1989, 1996, 2002, 2009, 2016
Vice-President, Defence, Teodoro Nguema Obiang

SELECTED GOVERNMENT MEMBERS *AS AT NOVEMBER 2020*
Prime Minister, Francisco Pascual Obama Asue
Deputy Prime Ministers, Clemente Engonga Nguema; Angel Mesie Mibuy; Alfonso Nsue Mokuy
Economy, César Augusto Mba Abogo
Foreign Affairs, Simeon Oyono Esono

EMBASSY OF THE REPUBLIC OF EQUATORIAL GUINEA
13 Park Place, St James's, London SW1A 1LP
T 020-7499 6867 **E** embarege-londres@embarege-londres.org
W www.embarege-londres.org
Ambassador Extraordinary and Plenipotentiary, vacant

BRITISH HIGH COMMISSION
High Commissioner, HE Rowan Laxton, *apptd* 2017, resident at Yaounde, Cameroon

ECONOMY AND TRADE

Large oil and natural gas deposits discovered off Bioko in the 1990s have transformed the economy, which has grown dramatically since production began in 1996. The country has the reputation of being one of the most corrupt in the world; oil exploitation has not benefited much of the population as most businesses are owned by government officials or their families. The economy entered recession in 2013 and has continued to decline sharply with the fall in oil prices. The nation is attempting to diversify its economy, and in December 2019 entered a three-year credit arrangement with the IMF worth US$282.2m. Cocoa production, which was the nation's primary export before the 1990s, has given way to subsistence farming. Major economic concerns include a dependency on declining oil revenues, falling public investment, corruption and a lack of foreign investment.

Industry contributes 54.6 per cent of GDP, services 42.9 per cent and agriculture 2.5 per cent. The oil-driven growth in the GDP masks stagnation in other sectors; agriculture has declined owing to neglect and lack of investment. The main crops are coffee, cocoa, rice, fruit, nuts, livestock and timber. Industrial activities other than oil and natural gas production include fishing and timber processing.

The main trading partners are Spain, China and the USA. Principal exports are petroleum and timber. The main imports are oil-industry and other industrial equipment.

GNI – US$8.8bn; US$6,460 per capita (2019)
Annual average growth of GDP – –3.2 per cent (2017 est)
Inflation rate – 0.7 per cent (2017 est)
Population below poverty line – 44 per cent (2011)
Total external debt – US$1.211bn (2017 est)
Imports – US$3,458m (2016)
Exports – US$4,426m (2016)

BALANCE OF PAYMENTS
Trade – US$968m surplus (2016)
Current account – US$1,242m deficit (2018)

Trade with UK	2018	2019
Imports from UK	£26,705,160	£42,307,319
Exports to UK	£23,826,161	£34,910,257

COMMUNICATIONS
Airports – Six paved airports, the principal airport is based in Malabo
Roadways – 2,880km
Telecommunications – 10,848 fixed lines and 591,223 mobile subscriptions (2018); there were 209,253 internet users in 2018
Internet code and IDD – gq; 240 (from UK), 44 (to UK)
Broadcasters – Television and radio broadcasts are state-controlled
Press – *Ebano* is the government-run newspaper; privately owned newspapers are unable to publish regularly due to financial and political pressure
WPFI score – 56.38 (165)

ERITREA

Hagere Ertra – State of Eritrea

Area – 117,600 sq. km
Capital – Asmara; population, 963,000 (2020 est)
Major towns – Assab, Keren, Massawa
Currency – Nakfa (Nfk) of 100 cents

Population – 6,081,196 rising at 0.93 per cent a year (2020 est); Tigrinya (55 per cent), Tigre (30 per cent) (est)
Religion – Muslim (Sunni), Christian (Coptic Christian, Roman Catholic, Protestant); only Christians and Muslims may meet freely
Language – Arabic, English, Tigrinya (all official), Tigre, Afar, Kunama
Population density – 32 per sq. km (2011)
Urban population – 40.7 per cent (2019 est)
Median age (years) – 20.3 (2020 est)
National anthem – 'Ertra, Ertra, Ertra' 'Eritrea, Eritrea, Eritrea'
National day – 24 May (Independence Day)
Death penalty – Retained (last used 1989)
CPI score – 23 (160)
Military expenditure – US$182m (2003 est)
Conscription – 18–40 years of age; 18 months
Literacy rate – 76.6 per cent (2018 est)
Gross enrolment ratio (percentage of relevant age group) – primary 68.4 per cent, secondary 47.7 per cent (2018 est); tertiary 3.4 per cent (2016 est)
Health expenditure (per capita) – US$33 (2017)
Hospital beds (per 1,000 people) – 0.7 (2011)
Life expectancy (years) – 66.2 (2020 est)
Mortality rate – 6.9 (2020 est)
Birth rate – 27.9 (2020 est)
Infant mortality rate – 43.3 (2020 est)
HIV/AIDS adult prevalence – 0.6 per cent (2019 est)

CLIMATE AND TERRAIN
The northern end of the Ethiopian Highlands extends into central Eritrea, where the average altitude is over 2,000m. The mountains fall in the west to a plateau, which then rises to the hills on the Sudanese border. To the east of the mountains, the land falls to the narrow coastal plain. The coastal strip extending to the Djibouti border is low-lying, while the border with Ethiopia runs along the edge of the Danakil desert. Elevation extremes range from 3,018m (Soira) to –75m (Danakil depression). Average temperatures range from 23°C in January to 30.6°C in June.

HISTORY AND POLITICS
Part of the Axum empire from the first century AD, the area came under the control of the Ottoman Empire in the mid-16th century. It was occupied by Italy in the late 19th century and was the base for Italy's 1936 invasion of Abyssinia (now Ethiopia). After the Italian defeat in North Africa in 1941, Eritrea became a British protectorate until 15 September 1952, when a federation with Ethiopia was established by the UN. In 1962, Ethiopia annexed Eritrea outright.

The Eritrean Liberation Front (ELF) fought a guerrilla war for independence from 1961, and the Eritrean People's Liberation Front (EPLF) – a breakaway faction of the ELF – emerged in the 1970s, becoming the dominant rebel group in the 1980s. The EPLF joined with Ethiopian resistance groups to fight the Mengistu regime, which was overthrown in 1991. The EPLF secured the whole of Eritrea and formed an autonomous provisional government. The new Ethiopian government agreed to an Eritrean referendum on independence, held in April 1993, which recorded a 99.89 per cent vote in favour. Independence was declared on 24 May 1993.

Following independence, a transitional government for a four-year period was formed under Isaias Afewerki, and the EPLF became the ruling political party, renaming itself the People's Front for Democracy and Justice (PFDJ) in 1994. The post-independence regime has become increasingly authoritarian, and since 2001 has dealt harshly with anyone openly critical of the government. In 2015, the UN reported that Eritreans are routinely subjected to a number of abuses by the government, including torture, sexual abuse and indefinite service in the country's military.

Few of the provisions outlined in the 1997 constitution have been enacted and no presidential or legislative elections have been held, so the transitional president, state council (cabinet) and legislature remain in place. Under the constitution, the president is elected for a five-year term by the legislature, renewable once, and the 150-member unicameral National Assembly is elected for a four-year term. PFDJ is the only legal political party.

HEAD OF STATE
President, Chairman of the State Council and of the National Assembly, C-in-C of the Armed Forces, Isaias Afewerki, *elected by the National Assembly* 22 May 1993

SELECTED GOVERNMENT MEMBERS *AS AT NOVEMBER 2020*
Defence, vacant
Finance, vacant
Foreign Affairs, Osman Mohammed Saleh

EMBASSY OF THE STATE OF ERITREA
96 White Lion Street, London N1 9PF
T 020-7713 0096 **E** eriemba@eriembauk.com
Ambassador Extraordinary and Plenipotentiary, HE Estifanos Habtemariam Ghebreyesus, *apptd* 2014

BRITISH EMBASSY
PO Box 5584, 66–68 Mariam Ghimbi Street, Asmara
T (+291) (1) 120 145 **E** asmara.enquiries@fco.gov.uk
W www.gov.uk/government/world/eritrea
Ambassador Extraordinary and Plenipotentiary, HE Alisdair Walker, *apptd* 2019

FOREIGN RELATIONS
Since independence, Eritrea has been involved in disputes with Yemen, Ethiopia and Djibouti over territory, while Sudan has accused Eritrea of supporting rebels in eastern Sudan. The dispute with Yemen was over the Hanish and Mohabaka islands in the Red Sea; possession was divided between Yemen and Eritrea by international arbitration.

There has been fighting with Ethiopia in disputes over border territory, especially in the Tigray region, since 1998. Fighting escalated in 1999–2000 into a war that left thousands of people dead. An independent boundary commission defined the international border between the two countries in 2002, but both countries failed to abide by successive rulings.

Fighting broke out on the part of the border disputed with Djibouti in 2008. Following border disputes in early 2011, Ethiopia announced that it would support Eritrean rebels fighting President Afewerki.

In July 2011, a UN report accused Eritrea of planning to attack an African Union Summit in Ethiopia and further tightened sanctions soon after, owing to Eritrea's alleged support for Islamist insurgents in Somalia. In March 2012 Ethiopia attacked three military camps in Eritrea, claiming the country was supporting Ethiopian rebels who mounted attacks on western tourists. Following a change of government in Ethiopia, a peace deal was agreed between the two countries in July 2018 that ended nearly 20 years of military stalemate. Ethiopia's prime minister, Abiy Ahmed, was awarded the 2019 Nobel peace prize for resolving the conflict.

Political repression and human rights abuses have increasingly led to Eritreans seeking political asylum abroad. Nearly a quarter of refugees attempting to enter Europe via boat in 2015 were Eritrean, and in 2017 the UN estimated Eritreans comprised the ninth-largest refugee group in the would, with over 486,000 forcibly displaced.

ECONOMY AND TRADE
Over 30 years of conflict left the country's economy devastated, and the restrictive policies of the post-independent regime have hampered recovery. The command economy has concentrated business ownership in military and party hands. Agricultural output is restricted by lack of labour owing to the failure to demobilise the large army, the conflict with Ethiopia, which officially ended 2018, and the frequent droughts and ensuing famines. Nevertheless, agriculture and herding are the means of subsistence for around 80 per cent of the population and contributes 11.7 per cent of GDP. The industrial sector has contracted since trade with Ethiopia halted in 1998, and the principal ports have suffered from the loss of this transit trade. The Zara mining project, a new gold mine in the centre of the country, began production in early 2016.

Mineral reserves include zinc, potash, gold, copper and possibly oil; these are not fully exploited at present, although mining production began in 2010. Industries include food processing, beverages, clothing and textiles, salt, cement and light manufacturing. A free trade zone opened at Massawa in 2008 with the aim of boosting revenues, which are heavily dependent on remittances from expatriates.

Principal exports (62 per cent destined for China) are gold and other minerals, livestock, sorghum, textiles, food and light manufactures. The main imports are machinery, petroleum products, food and manufactured goods.
GNI – US$3,063m; US$490 per capita (2013)
Annual average growth of GDP – 5 per cent (2017 est)
Inflation rate – 9.0 per cent (2017 est)
Population below poverty line – 50 per cent (2004 est)
Unemployment – 792.7 per cent (2017 est)
Total external debt – US$869.9m (2017 est)
Imports – US$2,359m (2014)
Exports – US$15m (2014)

BALANCE OF PAYMENTS
Trade – US$418m deficit (2010)
Current Account – US$494m deficit (2018)

Trade with UK	2018	2019
Imports from UK	£4,399,699	£1,881,895
Exports to UK	£18,000	£64,991

COMMUNICATIONS
Airports and waterways – Four, with the main international airport at Asmara; the principal seaports are at Assab and Massawa
Roadways and railways – There are 16,000km of roadways of which 1,600km are paved; 306km of railways, which link Massawa to Sudan via Asmara
Telecommunications – There are 66,086 fixed lines and 506,000 mobile subscriptions (2016); there were 78,215 internet users in 2018
Internet code and IDD – er; 291 (from UK), 44 (to UK)
Broadcasters – Eritrea is the only country in Africa without any privately owned broadcasting media; Eri TV, Voice of the Broad Masses of Eritrea and Radio Zara are state-run. There are three radio stations, including educational radio available in nine languages
Press – Hadas Eritrea (Tigrinya language) and Al-Hadisa (Arabic) are the government-owned newspaper publications, along with two additional weekly papers
WPFI score – 83.50 (178)

ESTONIA

Eesti Vabariik – Republic of Estonia

Area – 45,228 sq. km
Capital – Tallinn; population, 445,000 (2020 est)
Major towns – Kohtla-Jarve, Narva, Parnu, Tartu
Currency – Euro (€) of 100 cents
Population – 1,228,624 falling at 0.65 per cent a year (2020
   est); Estonian (68.7 per cent), Russian (24.8 per cent) (est)
Religion – Christian (Orthodox 16.2 per cent, Lutheran
   9.9 per cent) (est)
Language – Estonian (official), Russian, Ukrainian
Population density – 30 per sq. km (2019)
Urban population – 69.1 per cent (2019 est)
Median age (years) – 43.7 (2020 est)
National anthem – 'Mu Isamaa, Mu Onn Ja Room' 'My
   Fatherland, My Pride and Joy'
National day – 24 February (Independence Day)
Death penalty – Abolished for all crimes (since 1998)
CPI score – 74 (18)
Military expenditure – US$618m (2018)
Conscription – 18–27 years of age; 8–11 months, depending
   on education

CLIMATE AND TERRAIN

The country is mostly a plain of lakes, marshes and forests,
with a range of low hills in the south-east. Elevation extremes
range from 318m (Suur Munamagi) to 0m (Baltic Sea). Part of
the border with Russia runs through the large Lake Peipsi.
The climate is maritime, with average temperatures ranging
from −3.9°C in February to 17.7°C in July.

HISTORY AND POLITICS

The area came under Swedish control between 1561 and
1629, and was ceded to the Russian Empire in 1721. An
Estonian nationalist movement developed in the late 19th
century and fought against occupying German forces during
the First World War. Estonia declared its independence in
February 1918 and defended it against Soviet forces until
1920, when independence was recognised by the USSR.
However, the USSR annexed Estonia in 1940, and the
country was subsequently occupied by German forces when
they invaded the USSR in 1941. In 1944 the USSR expelled
the Germans and reannexed the country, beginning a process
of 'Sovietisation'.

There was a resurgence of nationalist sentiment in the
1980s, and in 1989 the Estonian Supreme Soviet declared the
republic to be sovereign and its 1940 annexation by the
USSR to be illegal. In 1990, the Communist Party's
monopoly on power was abolished and, following multiparty
elections in which pro-independence candidates won the
majority of seats, a period of transition to independence was
inaugurated, culminating in its declaration on 20 August
1991. The last Russian troops withdrew in 1994. Since

independence, Estonia has pursued pro-Western policies. It
joined NATO and the EU in 2004.

In the 2015 legislative election, the Reform Party, the main
partner in the coalition government since 2005, remained the
largest party and formed a coalition with the Social
Democratic Party and centre-right Res Publica. In November
2016, Prime Minister Taavi Roivas lost a confidence vote in
parliament and centre-left Center Party chairman Juri Ratas
was sworn in as his replacement. Ratas and the Centre Party
retained power following elections in March 2019, forming a
coalition with the far-right Conservative People's Party and
centre-right Pro Patria. In October 2016, parliament selected
the country's first female president, Kersti Kaljulaid.

Under the 1992 constitution, the president is elected for a
five-year term by the legislature by a two-thirds majority or,
if no candidate receives this majority after three rounds of
voting, by an electoral assembly composed of the legislature
members and local government representatives. The
unicameral legislature, the *Riigikogu,* has 101 members,
directly elected for a four-year term. The prime minister is
appointed by the president and nominates the government.

HEAD OF STATE

President, Kersti Kaljulaid, *elected by electoral assembly*
   3 October 2016, *sworn in* 10 October 2016

SELECTED GOVERNMENT MEMBERS *AS AT*
NOVEMBER 2020

Prime Minister, Juri Ratas
Defence, Juri Luik
Finance, Martin Helme
Foreign Affairs, Urmas Reinsalu
Interior, Mart Helme

EMBASSY OF THE REPUBLIC OF ESTONIA

44 Queen's Gate Terrace, London SW7 5PJ
T 020-7589 3428 **E** london@mfa.ee **W** www.estonia.gov.uk
Ambassador Extraordinary and Plenipotentiary, HE Tiina
   Intelmann, *apptd* 2017

BRITISH EMBASSY

Wismari 6, Tallinn 10136
T (+372) 667 4700 **E** infotallinn@fco.gov.uk
W www.gov.uk/government/world/estonia
Ambassador Extraordinary and Plenipotentiary, HE Theresa
   Bubbear, *apptd* 2016

ECONOMY AND TRADE

Economic reforms and restructuring since 1992 have resulted
in a export-orientated market economy, the growth of which
was boosted by the country's accession to the EU in 2004.
Estonia entered recession in 2008 after an investment and
consumption slump, and a drop in demand for exports.
Prudent financial management has enabled the economy to
recover slowly, and it met the accession criteria for the
eurozone, which Estonia joined in January 2011; between
2012 and 2017 it had one of the highest GDP growth rates
and lowest debt-to-GDP ratios in Europe. However, its
exposure to the Russian economy meant growth slowed in
2018 and 2019, and is expected to shrink by around 7.5 per
cent in 2020 due to the coronavirus pandemic.

Agriculture engages 2.7 per cent of the workforce and
accounts for 2.8 per cent of GDP, the main products being
cereals, vegetables, livestock, dairy products and fish. Industry
accounts for 20.5 per cent of employment and 29.2 per cent
of GDP, concentrating on engineering, electronics, wood and
wood products, textiles, information technology and
telecommunications; electronics and telecommunications are

particularly strong. The services sector accounts for 68.1 per cent of employment and 76.8 per cent of GDP.

The main trading partners are other EU countries, particularly Finland, Sweden and Germany. Principal exports are machinery and electrical equipment, mineral fuels, food products, wood and wood products, metals, furniture, vehicles and parts and textiles. The main imports are machinery and electrical equipment, fuels, foodstuffs, vehicles and chemicals. Estonia remains dependent on Russian natural gas supplies.

GNI – US$30.8bn; US$23,220 per capita (2019)
Annual average growth of GDP – 5.0 per cent (2019 est)
Inflation rate – 3.7 per cent (2017 est)
Population below poverty line – 21.1 per cent (2016)
Unemployment – 4.94 per cent (2019 est)
Total external debt – US$19.05bn (2016 est)
Imports – US$17,639m (2017)
Exports – US$20,379m (2017)

BALANCE OF PAYMENTS
Trade – US$1,242m surplus (2017)
Current Account – US$616m surplus (2019)

Trade with UK	2018	2019
Imports from UK	£265,358,305	£254,773,211
Exports to UK	£215,000,789	£249,347,246

COMMUNICATIONS
Airports and waterways – 13 with paved runways, with the principal international airport in Tallinn; there are 335km of year-round navigable waterways, and the main seaports are at Talinn, Parnu Reid and Haapsalu Jahtklubi
Roadways and railways – There are 58,412km of roadways, of which 10,427km are paved; 2,146km
Telecommunications – 345,690 fixed lines and 1.9 million mobile subscriptions (2018); there were 1.1 million internet users in 2018
Internet code and IDD – ee; 372 (from UK), 44 (to UK)
Major broadcasters – Publicly owned broadcaster Eesti Rahvusringhaaling (EER) operates three television and five radio channels; there is a growing number of privately owned broadcasting outlets regionally and nationally
Press – Major newspapers include *Postimees* (Estonian and Russian editions) and *Eesti Paevaleht*
WPFI score – 12.61 (14)

EDUCATION AND HEALTH
Primary and secondary level education is compulsory between the ages of seven and 15.
Literacy rate – 100 per cent (2015 est)
Gross enrolment ratio (percentage of relevant age group) – primary 97.7 per cent, secondary 116.7 per cent, tertiary 70.4 per cent (2018 est)
Health expenditure (per capita) – US$1,300 (2017)
Hospital beds (per 1,000 people) – 5 (2015)
Life expectancy (years) – 77.4 (2020 est)
Mortality rate – 12.9 (2020 est)
Birth rate – 9.3 (2020 est)
Infant mortality rate – 3.7 (2020 est)
HIV/AIDS adult prevalence – 1.3 per cent (2013 est)

ESWATINI

Umbuso weSwatini – Kingdom of eSwatini

Area – 17,364 sq. km
Capital – Mbabane; population, 68,000 (2018). Lobamba is the legislative and royal capital
Major town – Manzini
Currency – Lilangeni (E; plural *Emalangeni*) of 100 cents; the Lilangeni has a par value with the South African rand, which is also in circulation
Population – 1,104,479 rising at 0.77 per cent a year (2020 est)
Religion – Christian 90 per cent (Zionist 40 per cent, Roman Catholic 20 per cent), Muslim 2 per cent, other 8 per cent (including Baha'i, Buddhist, Hindu and Jewish) (est)
Language – English, siSwati (both official)
Population density – 66 per sq. km (2019)
Urban population – 24 per cent (2019 est)
Median age (years) – 23.7 (2020 est)
National anthem – 'Nkulunkulu Mnikati wetibusiso temaSwati' 'Oh God, Bestower of Blessings on the Swazi'
National day – 6 September (Independence Day)
Death penalty – Retained (last used 1983)
CPI score – 34 (113)
Military expenditure – US$81.1m (2015 est)
Literacy rate – 88.4 per cent (2018 est)
Gross enrolment ratio (percentage of relevant age group) – primary 114.7 per cent (2018 est); secondary 82.4 (2016 est); tertiary 6.7 per cent (2013 est)
Health expenditure (per capita) – US$225 (2017)
Hospital beds (per 1,000 people) – 2.1 (2011)
Life expectancy (years) – 58.6 (2020 est)
Mortality rate – 10.1 (2020 est)
Birth rate – 24.5 (2020 est)
Infant mortality rate – 42.8 (2020 est)
HIV/AIDS adult prevalence – 27 per cent (2019 est)

CLIMATE AND TERRAIN
The main regions of the landlocked country are: the densely forested and mountainous Highveld along the western border, with an average altitude of 1,219m; the Middleveld, a mixed farming area, which averages about 609m in altitude, and the Lowveld, which was mainly scrubland until the introduction of sugar cane plantations, in the centre; and the Lubombo ridge, along the eastern edge of the Lowveld. Elevation extremes range from 1,862m (Emlembe) to 21m (Great Usutu river). Four rivers, the Komati, Usutu, Mbuluzi and Ngwavuma, flow from west to east.

The climate varies; the Highveld is humid and temperate, the Middleveld and Lubombo are subtropical, and the Lowveld is tropical and semi-arid. Average temperatures in Mbabane, in the Highveld, range from 15.8°C in July to 24°C in February.

HISTORY AND POLITICS

The Swazi people are believed to have arrived in the area in the 16th century, and by the mid-17th century had developed a strong kingdom three times the size of the present country. This became a protectorate of the Boer republic of the Transvaal in 1884, and subsequently of Britain. The Kingdom of Swaziland became independent in 1968, and was renamed the Kingdom of eSwatini in 2018 – its 'ancient name' – to mark 50 years of independence.

In 1973 King Sobhuza II suspended the constitution, banned political parties and assumed absolute power. The parliamentary system was replaced by traditional tribal communities *(tinkhundla)*. Sobhuza II died in 1982, and was succeeded by a son who was a minor. The regency between 1982 and 1986 led to power struggles within the royal family, but the real power passed to the Dlamini clan, which continues to dominate the government.

The 2005 constitution retains the executive powers of the king; it appears to permit political parties while maintaining the ban on their members standing for election. The head of state is a hereditary king who is effectively an absolute monarch who rules by decree. There is a bicameral parliament comprising a 30-member senate and a 65-member House of Assembly; members of both serve a five-year term. Each of the country's 55 administrative districts *(tinkhundla)* directly elects one member to the House of Assembly and the king appoints ten members; there is also a provision for four female members to be regionally elected if the total percentage of women is less than 30 per cent. The members of the House of Assembly elect ten of their own number to the senate and a further 20 senators are appointed by the king.

HEAD OF STATE

HM The King of eSwatini, King Mswati III, *crowned* 25 April 1986

SELECTED GOVERNMENT MEMBERS *AS AT NOVEMBER 2020*

Prime Minister, Ambrose Mandvulo Dlamini
Deputy Prime Minister, Themba Masuku
Finance, Neil Reikenburg
Foreign Affairs, Thulisile Dladla

KINGDOM OF ESWATINI HIGH COMMISSION

20 Buckingham Gate, London SW1E 6LB
T 020-7630 6611 **E** enquiries@swaziland.org.uk
High Commissioner, HE Christian Muzie Nkambule, *apptd* 2017

BRITISH HIGH COMMISSIONER

HE John Lindfield, MBE, *apptd* 2019

ECONOMY AND TRADE

The country is very poor, with 38.6 per cent of the population living below the international poverty line and a 22.1 per cent unemployment rate. Customs dues from the South African Customs Union and remittances from expatriates working in South Africa are a vital supplement to the domestic economy; customs revenue dropped sharply in the global downturn and the government applied for international financial assistance. Overgrazing, soil depletion, drought and floods are potential future problems.

eSwatini has the highest levels of HIV/AIDS infection in the world, more than a quarter of the adult population, and consequently faces serious demographic, economic and social problems.

Subsistence agriculture occupies 10.7 per cent of the population and contributes 6.5 per cent of GDP. Sugar cane, cotton, citrus fruits and pineapples are the main cash crops and the basis of industries producing sugar, canned fruit and soft drink concentrates. Coal mining has become less important since the 1980s with diversification into small-scale gold and diamond mining, alongside manufacturing products such as textiles, clothing, wood pulp and refrigerators. Industry contributes 45 per cent of GDP and services 48.6 per cent.

South Africa accounts for 94 per cent of exports and over 80 per cent of imports. Principal exports are the products of agriculture and manufacturing. The main imports are vehicles, machinery, transport equipment, foodstuffs, petroleum products and chemicals.

GNI – US$4.1bn; US$3,590 per capita (2019)
Annual average growth of GDP – 1.6 per cent (2017 est)
Inflation rate – 6.2 per cent (2017 est)
Population below poverty line – 63 per cent (2010)
Total external debt – US$526.3m (2017 est)
Imports – US$1,960m (2017)
Exports – US$1,919m (2017)

BALANCE OF PAYMENTS

Trade – US$41m deficit (2017)
Current Account – US$195m surplus (2019)

Trade with UK	2018	2019
Imports from UK	£2,747,105	£3,411,921
Exports to UK	£9,769,729	£3,135,505

COMMUNICATIONS

Airports – Two paved airports; the international airports are in Manzini: Matsapha and Mswati III International Airport
Roadways and railways – 3,769km; 301km of railway connect with the Mozambique port of Maputo and the South African railway to Richards Bay and Durban
Telecommunications – 42,000 fixed lines and 995,000 mobile subscriptions (2016); there were 510,984 internet users in 2018
Internet code and IDD – sz; 268 (from UK), 44 (to UK)
Media – One state-owned television channel, three radio channels; one private radio channel (2017). Swaziland Broadcasting and Information Service (radio) and Swazi TV are the state broadcasters; the only daily newspapers are *The Times of Swaziland* and *The Swazi Observer*
WPFI score – 45.15 (141)

ETHIOPIA

Ityop'iya Federalawi Demokrasiyawi Ripeblik – Federal Democratic Republic of Ethiopia

Area – 1,104,300 sq. km
Capital – Addis Ababa; population, 4,794,000 (2020 est)
Major cities – Bahir Dar, Dese, Dire Dawa, Gonder, Mek'ele, Nazret

Currency – Birr (EB) of 100 cents
Population – 108,113,150 rising at 2.56 per cent a year
(2020 est); Oromo (34.9 per cent), Amhara (27.9 per
cent), Tigray (7.3 per cent), Somali (2.7 per cent) (est)
Religion – Christian (Ethiopian Orthodox 43.8 per cent,
Protestant 22.8 per cent), Muslim 31.3 per cent (mostly
Sunni) (2007 est)
Language – Amharic, English, Arabic (all official), Oromo
Tigrinya, Somali, Guaragigna, Sidamo
Population density – 109 per sq. km (2019)
Urban population – 21.2 per cent (2019 est)
Median age (years) – 19.8 (2020 est)
National anthem – 'Wodefit Gesgeshi Widd Innat Ityopp'ya'
'March Forward, Dear Mother Ethiopia'
National day – 28 May (defeat of Mengistu government,
1991)
Death penalty – Retained
CPI score – 37 (96)
Military expenditure – US$448m (2015)

CLIMATE AND TERRAIN

Ethiopia is dominated by a central plateau, rising to the
mountains of the Ethiopian Highlands, which are divided by
the Great Rift valley. The western mountains are the source of
the Blue Nile. The land drops to desert plains in the east
(Ogaden) and north-east (Danakil desert). Elevation extremes
range from 4,533m (Ras Dejen) to −125m (Danakil
depression). There is a tropical monsoon climate, with
variations according to altitude. The wet season is from April
to September.

POLITICS

The 1994 constitution provides for a federal government
responsible for foreign affairs, defence and economic policy,
and nine ethnically based states. The president is elected by
both houses of the legislature for a six-year term, renewable
once. The prime minister is appointed by the lower chamber
of the legislature and appoints the government. The Federal
Parliamentary Assembly is bicameral. The lower chamber, the
House of People's Representatives, has 547 members, directly
elected for a five-year term. The House of the Federation has
153 members, elected for a five-year term by the government
councils of the nine states in the federation. These regional
administrations have considerable autonomy and the right to
secede.

Border disputes, ethnic violence, food crises and political
insurgencies have plagued the nation in recent decades.
Military conflicts with Eritrea over border territories flared in
1998, resulting in a war between 1999 and 2000 and
subsequent clashes before a peace deal was agreed in July 2018
(*see* Eritrea). Ethiopia intervened in Somalia in 2006 in support
of the Somali transitional government and formally withdrew
its forces in January 2009, in accordance with a 2008 peace
agreement between the Somali government and rebels. In
January 2014, 4,000 Ethiopian troops reinforced African
Union soldiers fighting the al-Qaida-aligned al-Shabab group
in northern Somalia.

Ethnic violence between the Oromo and Gedeo people in
southern Ethiopia flared up in 2017 and resulted in a

humanitarian crisis in which hundreds died and an estimated
2.6 million people were displaced, which was more than any
other country in 2018.

In the 2015 legislative elections, the ruling Ethiopian
People's Revolutionary Democratic Front and its allies won all
seats in the House of People's Representatives; observers and
opposition groups claimed the polls were not fair due to
government restrictions on free speech. In 2018, Prime
Minister Hailemariam Desalegn resigned after months of
protests for democratic change, following an initially violent
response from the government. He was replaced by Abiy
Ahmed, who pursued a radical, democratic reform agenda
including appointing half of cabinet positions to women in
October 2018. Mulatu Teshome was replaced as president by
Sahle-Work Zewde in October 2018. Zewde became
Ethiopia's first woman president and the only female head of
state in Africa.

HEAD OF STATE
President, Sahle-Work Zewde, *sworn in* 25 October 2018

SELECTED GOVERNMENT MEMBERS *AS AT*
NOVEMBER 2020
Prime Minister, Abiy Ahmed Ali
Deputy Prime Minister, Demeke Mekonnen
Finance, Ahmed Shide
Foreign Affairs, Gedu Andargachew

EMBASSY OF THE FEDERAL DEMOCRATIC REPUBLIC
OF ETHIOPIA
17 Princes Gate, London SW7 1PZ
T 020-7589 7212 **E** info@ethioembassy.org.uk
W www.ethioembassy.org.uk
Ambassador Extraordinary and Plenipotentiary, HE Fesseha
Shawel Gebre, *apptd* 2019

BRITISH EMBASSY
Comoros Street, Addis Ababa 858
T (+251) (11) 61 70100 **E** britishembassy.addisababa@fco.gov.uk
W www.gov.uk/government/world/ethiopia
Ambassador Extraordinary and Plenipotentiary, HE Alastair
McPhail, *apptd* 2019

ECONOMY AND TRADE

The economy is highly dependent on agriculture, and therefore
reliant on the rains; recurring droughts led to famine conditions
in 1984–5, 1992, 1997, 2000, 2002, 2009, 2011 and 2015–
16. Although most foreign debt was cancelled in 2005,
emergency IMF funding was needed to cushion the country
from the effects of the global downturn. Economic reform has
subsequently been supported by the IMF, which agreed to
provide US$2.9bn of extended credit in December 2019.
Ethiopia has experienced more than a decade of strong growth,
with GDP growing by 8–11 per cent annually between 2006
and 2019, but nonetheless is one of the poorest countries in
the world. In recent years government has invested revenue in
improving the country's infrastructure and manufacturing base,
and in 2017 devalued the birr by 15 per cent in order to boost
exports.

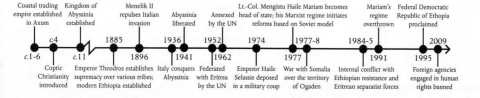

Agriculture and herding account for 34.8 per cent of GDP, and 72.7 per cent of the population is dependent upon the land for a living. The main crops are cereals, pulses, coffee, oilseed, cotton, sugar, potatoes, qat (or khat, a flowering plant chewed for its stimulant properties), cut flowers, livestock products and fish. Natural resources, including gold, platinum, copper, potash, oil and natural gas, are largely unexploited; most industrial activity involves the processing of agricultural products, gold mining and metalworking, and textiles. Work continues on three major dams, which is intended to generate electricity for domestic consumption and export, despite protests from the Egyptian government that the Grand Ethiopian Renaissance Dam could threaten Egypt's water supply. Completion of this dam is ongoing.

The main trade partners are China, Saudi Arabia, Sudan, Switzerland and India. Principal exports are coffee, vegetables, gold, leather products, livestock and oilseeds. The main imports are petroleum products, electronics, chemicals, machinery, vehicles, metal and metal products.

GNI – US$95.1bn; US$850 per capita (2019)
Annual average growth of GDP – 10.9 per cent (2017 est)
Inflation rate – 9.9 per cent (2017 est)
Population below poverty line – 29.6 per cent (2014 est)
Unemployment – 17.5 per cent (2012 est)
Total external debt – US$26.05bn (2017 est)
Imports – US$19,908m (2016)
Exports – US$5,903m (2016)

BALANCE OF PAYMENTS

Trade – US$14,005m deficit (2016)
Current Account – US$4,611m deficit (2018)

Trade with UK	2018	2019
Imports from UK	£272,927,046	£485,588,258
Exports to UK	£178,254,365	£328,243,681

COMMUNICATIONS

Airports and waterways – 17; this landlocked country uses ports in Djibouti city and Berbera in Somalia
Roadways and railways – 120,171km; the only railway line links Addis Ababa and the Port of Doraleh in Djibouti, which was completed in 2018
Telecommunications – 1.2 million fixed lines and 62.6 million mobile subscriptions (2017); there were 19.1 million internet users in 2018
Internet country code and IDD – et; 251 (from UK), 44 (to UK)
Major broadcasters – The state-owned Ethiopian Television and Radio Ethiopia operate national and regional stations
Press – There are six public television outlets and ten public radio channels alongside seven private and 19 commercial radio stations. *Addis Zemen* and *Ethiopian Herald* are the state-owned dailies, *The Daily Monitor* and *Addis Admass* are privately owned publications (2017). Significant progress has been made since 2018, with the restoration of 200 news websites and blogs that had previously been blocked.
WPFI score – 32.82 (99)

EDUCATION AND HEALTH

Non-compulsory elementary and secondary education is provided by government schools in the major population centres; there are also mission schools.

Literacy rate – 51.8 per cent (2017 est)
Gross enrolment ratio (percentage of relevant age group) – primary 101.0 per cent, secondary 35.0 per cent (2015 est); tertiary 8.1 per cent (2014 est)
Health expenditure (per capita) – US$25 (2017)
Hospital beds (per 1,000 people) – 0.3 (2015)

Life expectancy (years) – 67.5 (2020 est)
Mortality rate – 5.9 (2020 est)
Birth rate – 31.6 (2020 est)
Infant mortality rate – 35.8 (2020 est)
HIV/AIDS adult prevalence – 0.9 per cent (2019 est)

FIJI

Matanitu ko Viti – Republic of Fiji

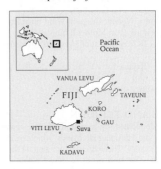

Area – 18,274 sq. km
Capital – Suva, on Viti Levu; population, 178,000 (2018)
Major towns – Lautoka, Nasinu, Nausori
Currency – Fijian dollar (F$) of 100 cents
Population – 935,974 rising at 0.5 per cent a year (2020 est); iTaukei (56.8 per cent), Indo-Fijian (37.5 per cent) (est)
Religion – Christian (Protestant 45 per cent, Roman Catholic 9.1 per cent, other Christian 10.4 per cent), Hindu 27.9 per cent, Muslim 6.3 per cent (est)
Language – English, Fijian (both official), Hindustani
Population density – 48 per sq. km (2019)
Urban population – 56.8 per cent (2019 est)
Median age (years) – 29.9 (2020 est)
National anthem – 'Meda Dau Doka' 'God Bless Fiji'
National day – 10 October (Independence Day)
Death penalty – Abolished for all crimes since 2015
Military expenditure – US$48.4m (2018)
Literacy rate – 99.1 per cent (2017 est)
Gross enrolment ratio (percentage of relevant age group) – primary 116.5 per cent (2019 est); secondary 89.8 per cent (2012 est)
Health expenditure (per capita) – US$188 (2017)
Life expectancy (years) – 73.7 (2020 est)
Mortality rate – 6.3 (2020 est)
Birth rate – 17.4 (2020 est)
Infant mortality rate – 8.8 (2020 est)
HIV/AIDS adult prevalence – 0.2 per cent (2019 est)

CLIMATE AND TERRAIN

Fiji comprises a group of about 330 islands (around 110 are permanently inhabited) and over 500 islets in the South Pacific, about 1,770km north of New Zealand. The group extends 480km from east to west and 480km north to south. The international date line has been diverted to the east of the island group. The largest islands are Viti Levu and Vanua Levu. The terrain is mountainous and volcanic, with tropical rainforest and grassland, and most islands are surrounded by coral reefs. Elevation extremes range from 1,324m (Tomanivi, on Viti Levu) to 0m (Pacific Ocean). Fiji has a tropical maritime climate with high humidity and an average annual temperature of 24.3°C.

HISTORY AND POLITICS

The islands were settled by Melanesian peoples. European contact began with the visit of the Dutch explorer Abel Tasman in 1643; later visitors included Captain Cook in 1774. The islands became a British colony in 1874, and sugar plantations, employing more than 60,000 indentured Indian labourers, were established. Fiji became independent as a constitutional monarchy on 10 October 1970, and became a republic after the 1987 coups.

The growing size and political strength of the ethnic Indian population caused political instability in the late 1980s. There were two coups in 1987 and one in 2000 as indigenous Fijians attempted to reassert their political dominance and entrench this in the constitution. A fourth coup occurred in 2006 over the government's proposed amnesty for those involved in the 2000 coup.

In 2007 President Ratu Josefa Iloilo was reinstated and 2006 coup leader Commodore 'Frank' Bainimarama became prime minister. In response to a court of appeal ruling in April 2009 stating that the military government was illegal, President Iloilo suspended the constitution, dismissed the judiciary, reappointed Bainimarama as interim prime minister and declared a state of emergency. President Iloilo retired in July 2009.

Political instability and failure to hold elections caused Fiji to be suspended from the Commonwealth of Nations between 1987 and 1997, from 2000 to 2001 and from 2009 to 2014. The first legislative elections in eight years were held in September 2014; the Fiji First Party (FFP) emerged as the largest single party, winning 32 of the 50 seats in the legislature, in elections deemed credible by many international observers. The FFP narrowly retained its majority in the November 2018 elections and Frank Bainimarama remained prime minister; international observers considered the elections credible despite opposition complaints. Jioji Konusi Konrote was elected president in October 2015 and re-elected unopposed in August 2018.

In September 2013, Fiji's fourth constitution was signed into law, the first to abolish race-based electoral rolls and seat quotas. It vests sole legislative authority in the single-chamber, 51-seat parliament. The president is elected by parliament for a three-year term, renewable once, and members serve four-year terms.

HEAD OF STATE

President, Jioji Konusi Konrote, *elected* 12 October 2015, *sworn in* 12 November 2015, *re-elected* 31 August 2018

SELECTED GOVERNMENT MEMBERS *AS AT NOVEMBER 2020*

Prime Minister, Foreign Affairs, Josaia ('Frank') Bainimarama
Attorney-General, Economy, Aiyaz Sayed-Khaiyum
Defence, Inia Batikoto Seruirata

HIGH COMMISSION OF THE REPUBLIC OF FIJI

34 Hyde Park Gate, London SW7 5DN
T 020-7584 3661 **E** mail@fijihighcommission.org.uk
W www.fijihighcommission.org.uk
High Commissioner, HE Jitoko Tikovelu, *apptd* 2016

BRITISH HIGH COMMISSION

47 Gladstone Road, Suva
T (+679) 322 9100 **E** publicdiplomacy@fco.gov.uk
W www.gov.uk/government/world/fiji
High Commissioner, HE Melanie Hopkins, *apptd* 2016

ECONOMY AND TRADE

Fiji has abundant natural resources and one of the more developed economies in the region. However, the economy suffered after the 1987 coups because of the mass emigration of Indian Fijians, and was contracting until recently owing to structural problems, inefficiency and political instability. Tourism, the mainstay of the economy, declined after the 2006 coup but recovered following the country's return to democracy, notwithstanding the damage wrought by Cyclone Winston in February 2016. Over 870,000 people visited the island in 2018 and private investment had risen sharply since 2014, but the impact of the coronavirus pandemic was significant, especially to tourism, and the economy is expected to shrink by 21 per cent in 2020.

Agriculture, much of it at subsistence level, accounts for 13.5 per cent of GDP and employs 44.2 per cent of the workforce. The principal cash crop is sugar cane, but revenue has been affected by cuts in EU subsidies. The other main agricultural products are coconuts, cassava, rice, sweet potatoes, livestock and fish. The main industries are tourism, sugar processing, garment manufacturing, copra production, gold and silver mining, forestry and small cottage industries. Expatriate remittances are also an important economic contributor. The main trade partners are Australia, New Zealand, China, the USA and Singapore. Principal exports are bottled water, fuel, sugar, garments, gold, timber, fish, molasses and coconut oil. The chief imports are manufactured goods, machinery and transport equipment, petroleum products, food and chemicals.

GNI – US$5.2bn; US$5,860 per capita (2019)
Annual average growth of GDP – 3.0 per cent (2017 est)
Inflation rate – 3.4 per cent (2017 est)
Unemployment – 4.5 per cent (2017 est)
Total external debt – US$100,022m (2017 est)
Imports – US$2,678m (2017)
Exports – US$2,414m (2017)

BALANCE OF PAYMENTS

Trade – US$263m deficit (2017)
Current Account – US$696m deficit (2019)

Trade with UK	2018	2019
Imports from UK	£16,248,694	£12,720,059
Exports to UK	£11,317,131	£20,637,602

COMMUNICATIONS

Airports and waterways – Four, including international airports at Suva and Nadi; the main seaports are Suva and Lautoka
Roadways and railways – 3,440km; 597km of railway track, principally used by the sugar industry
Telecommunications – 76,522 fixed lines and 1 million mobile subscriptions (2018); there were 462,860 internet users in 2018
Internet code and IDD – fj; 679 (from UK), 44 (to UK)
Major broadcasters – There are two main television networks: national Fiji TV Ltd and the commercial Mai TV; Fiji Broadcasting Corporation is the state-owned radio broadcaster; six radio stations, two public broadcasters and four commercial broadcasters are operated by Fiji Broadcasting (2017)
Press – Newspapers include the daily *Fiji Times* (English language), and Hindi weeklies *Sartaj* and *Shanti Dut*
WPFI score – 27.41 (52)

FINLAND

Suomen tasavalta/Republiken Finland – Republic of Finland

Area – 338,145 sq. km
Capital – Helsinki (Helsingfors); population, 1,305,000
   (2020 est)
Major cities – Espoo (Esbo), Oulu (Uleaborg), Tampere
   (Tammerfors), Turku (Aabo), Vantaa (Vanda)
Currency – Euro (€) of 100 cents
Population – 5,571,665 rising at 0.3 per cent a year (2020
   est)
Religion – Christian (Lutheran 69.8 per cent, Orthodox 1.1
   per cent) (est)
Language – Finnish, Swedish (both official), Russian
Population density – 18 per sq. km (2019)
Urban population – 85.4 per cent (2019 est)
Median age (years) – 42.8 (2020 est)
National anthem – 'Maamme' 'Our Land'
National day – 6 December (Independence Day)
Death penalty – Abolished for all crimes (since 1972)
CPI score – 86 (3)
Military expenditure – US$3,849m (2018)
Conscription – 18 years of age, male only; 6–12 months

CLIMATE AND TERRAIN

Much of the centre of the country is a glaciated plateau of
forests and lakes, with low hills along the eastern border with
Russia and in the far north. Forests cover around 70 per cent
of the country, including those of the coastal peatlands in the
south-west. There are over 60,000 lakes, with an average
depth of 7m. Elevation extremes range from 1,328m
(Haltiatunturi, or Halti) to 0m (Baltic Sea). A quarter of the
country lies north of the Arctic Circle; temperatures there can
range from −9.4°C in February to 15.6°C in July. Average
temperatures in Helsinki range from −6°C in February to
16°C in July.

Owing to isostatic uplift (the rise of landmass no longer
depressed by the weight of glaciers), the surface area of
Finland is growing by around 7 sq. km a year.

HISTORY AND POLITICS

Finland was part of the Swedish Empire from the 12th
century until it was ceded to Russia in 1809, when it became
an autonomous grand duchy of the Russian Empire. After the
Russian Revolution in 1917, Finland declared its
independence. An attempted coup by Finnish Bolsheviks led
to a short civil war that ended in their defeat in 1918, and in
1919 a republic was established. It resisted the 1939 invasion
by the USSR but was defeated in 1940 and forced to cede
territory; in the hope of recovering this territory it joined
Germany's attack on the USSR in 1941. After agreeing an
armistice with the USSR in 1944, Finland concluded a peace
treaty in 1947 that conceded further territory to the USSR
and obliged it to pay reparations. A Soviet-Finnish

cooperation treaty in 1948 forced Finland to demilitarise its
Soviet border and to adopt a stance of neutrality; these terms
lasted until the demise of the USSR in 1991.

Finland joined the EU in 1995 and the European Monetary
Union in 1998.

In the 2015 legislative election, the Centre Party emerged as
the largest party, winning 49 of 200 parliamentary seats, and
formed a centre-right coalition that included the far-right
Eurosceptic Finns party. The government was replaced by a
coalition of five centre-left parties following the April 2019
legislative election, led by Antti Rinne of the Social
Democratic Party (SDP). Rinne resigned in the wake of a
major postal strike and was replaced by 33-year-old Sanna
Marin (SDP) in December 2019. Sauli Niinisto of the centre-
right National Coalition Party was re-elected president in
January 2018.

Under the 2000 constitution, the president is directly elected
for a six-year term, renewable once. There is a unicameral
legislature, the *Eduskunta*, with 200 members directly elected
for a four-year term. The prime minister is elected by the
Eduskunta and appointed by the president.

HEAD OF STATE

President, Sauli Niinisto, *elected* 5 February 2012, *inaugurated*
   1 March 2012, *re-elected* 28 January 2018

SELECTED GOVERNMENT MEMBERS *AS AT*
NOVEMBER 2020
Prime Minister, Sanna Marin
Finance, Matti Vanhanen
Defence, Antti Kaikkonen
Foreign Affairs, Pekka Haavisto
Interior, Maria Ohisalo

EMBASSY OF FINLAND
38 Chesham Place, London SW1X 8HW
T 020-7838 6200 **E** sanomat.lon@formin.fi **W** www.finemb.org.uk
Ambassador Extraordinary and Plenipotentiary, HE Markku
   Tapio Keinanen, *apptd* 2019

BRITISH EMBASSY
Itainen Puistotie 17, 00140 Helsinki
T (+358) (9) 2286 5100 **E** info.helsinki@fco.gov.uk
W www.gov.uk/government/world/finland
Ambassador Extraordinary and Plenipotentiary, HE Thomas
   Dodd, *apptd* 2018

ECONOMY AND TRADE

The country has a highly industrialised market economy that
has thrived as a result of its telecommunications and
electronics industries, particularly the manufacture of mobile
phones, as well as its traditional timber and metals industries.
The economy entered recession in 2012, due to a lack of
economic competitiveness, high wages and an aging
population. The economy is vulnerable to fluctuations in trade
with Russia, particularly due to the economic sanctions
imposed on the country in 2014. Growth returned in 2016
and was maintained until 2019 thanks to rising investment,
but the economy entered recession in May 2020 as exports
fell due to the coronavirus pandemic.

The main trade partners are Germany, Sweden and Russia.
Principal exports are electrical and optical equipment,
machinery, transport equipment, paper and pulp, chemicals,
base metals and timber. The main imports are foodstuffs
(especially grain), petroleum and petroleum products,
chemicals, transport equipment, iron and steel, machinery,
textile yarn and fabrics, and components for manufactured
goods. Finland is a net importer of energy.
GNI – US$263.9bn; US$47,820 per capita (2018)

Annual average growth of GDP – 1.15 per cent (2019 est)
Inflation rate – 0.8 per cent (2017 est)
Unemployment – 6.63 per cent (2019 est)
Total external debt – US$150.6bn (2016 est)
Imports – US$96,302m (2017)
Exports – US$96,446m (2017)

BALANCE OF PAYMENTS
Trade – US$143m surplus (2017)
Current Account – US$604m deficit (2019)

Trade with UK	2018	2019
Imports from UK	£1,427,358,585	£1,313,592,638
Exports to UK	£2,462,373,725	£2,430,021,666

COMMUNICATIONS
Airports and waterways – 74 airports with paved runways; the principal airports are at Helsinki, Turku and Tampere; the main seaports are Helsinki, Kotka, Rauma and Turku
Roadways and railways – There are 454,000km of roadways, of which 350,000km are private and forest roads; 5,926km of railways
Telecommunications – 323,000 fixed lines and 7.2 million mobile telephone subscriptions (2018); there were 4.9 million internet users in 2018
Internet code and IDD – fi; 358 (from UK), 44 (to UK)
Major broadcasters – There are both commercial and state-owned broadcasters; the state broadcaster, Yleisradio Oy (YLE), is funded by licence fees and provides radio and television services in Swedish and Finnish, with radio in Sami (Lappish)
Press – Major publications include *Helsingin Sanomat* (Finnish), *Hufvudstadsbladet* (Swedish) and the English-language *Helsinki Times*
WPFI score – 7.93 (2)

EDUCATION AND HEALTH
Basic education is free and compulsory for children from seven to 16 years.
Gross enrolment ratio (percentage of relevant age group) – primary 100.2 per cent, secondary 154.8 per cent, tertiary 90.3 per cent (2018 est)
Health expenditure (per capita) – US$4,206 (2017)
Hospital beds (per 1,000 people) – 4.4 (2015)
Life expectancy (years) – 81.3 (2020 est)
Mortality rate – 10.3 (2020 est)
Birth rate – 10.6 (2020 est)
Infant mortality rate – 2.5 (2020 est)

FRANCE

République française – French Republic

Area – 551,500 sq. km (excluding overseas territories)
Capital – Paris; population, 11,017,000 (2020 est)
Major cities – Bordeaux, Lille, Lyon, Marseille, Montpellier, Nantes, Nice, Reims, Rennes, Strasbourg, Toulouse. The chief towns of Corsica are Ajaccio and Bastia

Currency – Euro (€) of 100 cents
Population – 67,848,156 (excluding overseas territories), rising at 0.35 per cent a year (2020 est)
Religion – Christian 63–6 per cent (mainly Roman Catholic), Muslim 7–9 per cent (est)
Language – French (official)
Population density – 122 per sq. km (2019)
Urban population – 80.7 per cent (2019 est)
Median age (years) – 41.7 (2018 est)
National anthem – 'La Marseillaise' 'The Song of Marseille'
National day – 14 July (Fête de la Fédération/Fête Nationale)
Death penalty – Abolished for all crimes (since 1981)
CPI score – 69 (23)
Military expenditure – US$63,800m (2018)

CLIMATE AND TERRAIN
The north and west consist of flat plains, particularly in the basins of the Somme, Seine, Loire and Garonne rivers, with some low hills. The centre of the south is occupied by the Massif Central plateau, which is divided by the valley of the Rhone and Soane rivers from the mountains – the French Alps, the Jura and the Vosges – on the eastern border. The Pyrenees range lies along the southern border with Spain. Elevation extremes range from 4,807m (Mt Blanc, Alps) to −2m (Rhône delta). The climate is generally temperate, though the south has a Mediterranean climate and the east a continental climate.

POLITICS
Under the 1958 constitution, the head of state is a president directly elected for a five-year term, which is renewable once. The legislature, the *Parlement,* consists of the National Assembly and the senate. The National Assembly has 577 deputies, 556 for metropolitan France and 21 for the overseas departments and territories; members are directly elected for a five-year term. The senate has been enlarged gradually over the past decade; since the September 2011 elections there are 348 senators (328 for metropolitan France and the overseas departments, eight for overseas collectivities and territories, and 12 for French nationals abroad) elected by an electoral college to serve a six-year term, with half elected every three years.

The prime minister is nominated by the National Assembly and appointed by the president, as is the council of ministers. They are responsible to the legislature, but as the executive is constitutionally separate from the legislature, ministers may not sit in the legislature and must hand over their seats to a substitute.

The constitution was amended in 2003 to pave the way for the devolution to the 13 metropolitan regions and 96 metropolitan departments of powers over economic development, transport, tourism, culture and further education.

In the 2012 legislative elections, the Socialist Party (PS) won an overall majority, defeating Nicolas Sarkozy's Union for a Popular Movement party by 86 seats. Emmanuel Macron, leader of the centrist La République En Marche party, won the May 2017 presidential elections, beating the Front National's Marine Le Pen in the second round by more than 32 per cent of the vote. En Marche and their allies took 350 seats in the National Assembly in legislative elections in June 2017, with the PS experiencing heavy losses. Jean Castex was appointed prime minister in July 2020.

Marcon's presidency has been marked by widespread protests and strikes organised by groups on both the right and left, angered by high taxes, rising inequality and Macron's unpopular political reforms. On 17 November 2018, anti-government protests by the far-right *gilets jaunes* movement

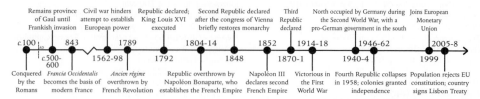

Remains province of Gaul until Frankish invasion | Civil war hinders attempt to establish European power | Republic declared; King Louis XVI executed | Second Republic declared after the congress of Vienna briefly restores monarchy | Third Republic declared | North occupied by Germany during the Second World War, with a pro-German government in the south | Joins European Monetary Union

c.100 AD   843   1789   1804-14   1852   1914-18   1946-62   2005-8
c.500-600   1562-98   1792   1848   1870-1   1940-4   1999

Conquered by the Romans | Francia Occidentalis becomes the basis of modern France | Ancien régime overthrown by French Revolution | Republic overthrown by Napoléon Bonaparte, who establishes the French Empire | Napoléon III declares second French Empire | Victorious in the First World War | Fourth Republic collapses in 1958; colonies granted independence | Population rejects EU constitution; country signs Lisbon Treaty

began, initially to oppose rising fuel taxes, and violent weekend protests lasted for months, particularly in Paris.

HEAD OF STATE
President of the French Republic, Emmanuel Macron, *elected* 7 May 2017, *took office* 14 May 2017

SELECTED GOVERNMENT MEMBERS *AS AT NOVEMBER 2020*
Prime Minister, Jean Castex
Economy, Bruno Le Maire
Europe, Foreign Affairs, Jean-Yves Le Drian
Interior, Gérald Darmanin

EMBASSY OF FRANCE
58 Knightsbridge, London SW1X 7JT
T 020-7073 1000 **W** www.ambafrance-uk.org
Ambassador Extraordinary and Plenipotentiary, HE Catherine Colonna, *apptd* 2019

BRITISH EMBASSY
35 rue du Faubourg St Honoré, 75383 Paris Cédex 08
T (+33) (1) 4451 3100 **W** www.gov.uk/government/world/france
Ambassador Extraordinary and Plenipotentiary, HE the Rt Hon. Baron Llewellyn of Steep, OBE, *apptd* 2016

INSURGENCIES
Except for a ceasefire in 2003–5, Corsican separatists pursued a campaign of bombings and shootings from the 1970s until 2016, when the main separatist faction announced it was ceasing military operations. The National Liberation Front of Corsica (FNLC) said it did not want to interfere with the work of the island's assembly, which has been led by nationalists since regional elections in 2015. The French government's proposals to combine the island's two departments and to give the Corsican regional parliament greater autonomy were narrowly rejected in a 2003 referendum.

ECONOMY AND TRADE
The economy, the world's seventh largest, is in transition from extensive government ownership and intervention to a more liberal and market-oriented form with many large, state-run companies becoming privatised; reform was initiated in response to poor economic growth and high unemployment. Implementation has been slow because of strong resistance to the government's plans for privatisation and reform of labour, pensions and welfare. Since 2017, President Macron has pursued policies designed to weaken labour laws, decrease public spending and reduce corporation tax in order to improve competitiveness, but these reforms have caused widespread protests and strikes. Economic recovery between 2014 and 2019 was sluggish and public debt grew, but the coronavirus pandemic hit the nation particularly hard and the economy is expected to contract by 9.8 per cent in 2020.

Over one-third of the land area of metropolitan France is utilised for agricultural production and a further quarter is covered by forests. Viniculture is extensive, although France has lost market share to other countries in recent years. Cognac, liqueurs and cider are also produced. Other important agricultural products include cereals, sugar beet, potatoes, beef, dairy products and fish. Agriculture employs 2.8 per cent of the workforce and contributes 1.7 per cent of GDP.

Oil is produced from fields in the Landes area, but France is a net importer of crude oil, for processing by its oil-refining industry. Natural gas is produced in the foothills of the Pyrenees.

Industry accounts for 19.5 per cent of GDP and employs 20 per cent of the workforce. The sector is highly diversified and includes the production of machinery, iron, steel, aluminium, chemicals, vehicles, aircraft, electronic goods, textiles and processed food. The service sector contributes 78.8 per cent of GDP and employs 77.2 per cent of the workforce. Tourism is an important contributor to GDP: France is the most-visited country in the world.

The main trading partners are other EU countries, especially Germany. Principal exports are machinery, vehicles, aircraft, plastics, chemicals, pharmaceutical products, iron and steel, and beverages. The main imports are raw materials for industry (eg crude oil, chemicals, plastics), machinery, vehicles and aircraft.

GNI – US$2,834bn; US$42,400 per capita (2019)
Annual average growth of GDP – 1.49 per cent (2019 est)
Inflation rate – 1.2 per cent (2017 est)
Population below poverty line – 14.2 per cent (2015 est)
Unemployment – 8.12 per cent (2017 est)
Total external debt – US$5.36 trillion (2019 est)
Imports – US$847,895m (2017)
Exports – US$802,610m (2017)

BALANCE OF PAYMENTS
Trade – US$45,285m deficit (2017)
Current Account – US$18,418m deficit (2019)

Trade with UK	2018	2019
Imports from UK	£23,989,362,568	£24,630,003,455
Exports to UK	£27,559,029,654	£29,870,310,800

COMMUNICATIONS
Airports – 294 with paved runways; there are two international airports serving Paris, and many regional airports capable of accepting international flights
Waterways – The principal seaports are Marseille on the Mediterranean Sea, Bordeaux and Nantes on the Atlantic coast, and Le Havre, Calais and Dunkirk on the Channel coast; there are 8,501km of navigable inland waterways, 1,621km navigable by large vessels, and Paris, Rouen and Strasbourg are significant river ports. The French mercantile marine consisted in 2011 of 162 ships of 1,000 gross tonnage or over, 151 of which are registered overseas
Roadways and railways – 1,053,215km; 29,640km
Telecommunications – 38.6 million fixed lines and 70.4 million mobile subscriptions (2018); there were 55.3 million internet users in 2018
Internet code and IDD – fr; 33 (from UK), 44 (to UK)
Major broadcasters – TV5 is an international French-language television channel co-financed by Belgium, Canada, France

and Switzerland. The main domestic channel, TF1, was privatised in 1987. A global news channel, France 24, was launched in 2006 and broadcasts in French, English and Arabic

Press – France has more than 100 daily newspapers, including *Le Monde, Le Figaro* and *Libération*

WPFI score – 22.92 (34)

EDUCATION AND HEALTH

Education is compulsory and free between the ages of six and 16. There are three types of *lycée* – *général, technique* and *professionnel* – and each leads to its own *baccalauréat* qualification. Specialist schools are numerous.

Gross enrolment ratio (percentage of relevant age group) – primary 102.9 per cent, secondary 104.1 per cent, tertiary 67.6 per cent (2018 est)

Health expenditure (per capita) – US$4,380 (2017)

Hospital beds (per 1,000 people) – 6.5 (2013)

Life expectancy (years) – 82.2 (2020 est)

Mortality rate – 9.6 (2020 est)

Birth rate – 11.9 (2020 est)

Infant mortality rate – 3.2 (2020 est)

HIV/AIDS adult prevalence – 0.3 (2019 est)

OVERSEAS DEPARTMENTS/REGIONS

French Guiana, Guadeloupe, Martinique and Réunion have had departmental status since 1946. They were given regional status with greater powers of self-government and elected assemblies in 1982, and were redesignated as Overseas Regions in 2003. Their regional and departmental status is identical to that of regions and departments of metropolitan France, and they can choose to replace these with a single structure by merging their regional and departmental assemblies. The French government is represented by a *prefect* in each. In referendums in 2010, French Guiana and Martinique rejected proposals for granting greater autonomy to their local governments.

FRENCH GUIANA

Area – 83,534 sq. km

Capital – Cayenne; population, 61,268 (2017 est)

Population – 290,691 (2020 est)

Situated on the northeastern coast of South America, French Guiana is flanked by Suriname to the west and by Brazil to the south and east. Under the administration of French Guiana are the Îles du Salut group of islands (St Joseph, Île Royal and Île du Diable). The European Space Agency rocket launch site is situated at Kourou and accounts for 25 per cent of GDP. Fishing, forestry and mining are the main activities, and the economy is dependent on government subsidies. The main exports are timber, shrimp and gold. Tourism is restricted by the lack of infrastructure, as much of the interior is only accessible by river.

Prefect, Mark Del Grande, *apptd* 2019

GUADELOUPE

Area – 1,705 sq. km

Capital – Basse-Terre; population, 11,730 (2011 est), on Guadeloupe

Population – 400,149 (2020 est)

The Guadeloupe archipelago consists of a number of islands in the Leeward Islands group in the West Indies, including Guadeloupe (or Basse-Terre), Grande-Terre, Marie-Galante, La Désirade and the Îles des Saintes. The main towns are Les Abymes, Pointe-à-Pitre (Grande-Terre) and Grand Bourg (Marie-Galante). The main industries are tourism, agriculture, sugar refining and rum distilling. Bananas, sugar, rum and vanilla are the main exports.

Prefect, Phillipe Gustin, *apptd* 2018

MARTINIQUE

Area – 1,100 sq. km

Capital – Fort-de-France; population, 82,502 (2015 est)

Population – 376,480 (2016)

An island in the Windward Islands group in the West Indies, Martinique lies between Dominica in the north and St Lucia in the south. It is dominated by Mt Pelée (1,397m), an active volcano that last erupted in 1902. Tourism is a major industry. The main exports are bananas, rum and petroleum products.

Prefect, Ange Mancini, *apptd* 2007

MAYOTTE

Area – 374 sq. km

Capital – Mamoudzou; population, 71,437 (2017 est)

Population – 270,372 (2019 est)

Part of the Comoros archipelago, Mayotte remained a French dependency when the other three islands became independent as the Comoros Republic in 1975. It became a *collectivité territoriale* in 1976, and an Overseas Department/Region in 2011. The main products are vanilla, ylang-ylang (perfume essence), coffee, copra, lobster and shrimp. The economy is dependent on French subsidies.

Prefect, Jean-François Colombet, *apptd* 2019

RÉUNION

Area – 2,507 sq. km

Capital – St-Denis; population, 149,311 (2017 est)

Population – 859,959 (2020 est)

A French possession since 1638, Réunion lies in the Indian Ocean, about 650km east of Madagascar and 180km southwest of Mauritius. The main industries are tourism and sugar, and rum production.

Prefect, Jacques Billant, *apptd* 2019

TERRITORIAL COLLECTIVITIES

Overseas *collectivités* are administrative divisions with a degree of autonomy but without the status of a similar administrative division in metropolitan France; each has its own laws and an elected assembly and president. The French government is represented by a *prefect* or high commissioner in each. Constitutional changes in 2003 redesignated most of the former overseas territories as *collectivités*.

FRENCH POLYNESIA

Area – 4,167 sq. km

Capital – Papeete, on Tahiti; population, 136,000 (2018 est)

Population – 295,121 rising at 0.79 per cent a year (2020 est); Polynesian (78 per cent), Chinese (12 per cent), French (10 per cent) (est)

Religion – Christian (Protestant 54 per cent, Roman Catholic 30 per cent), other 10 per cent (est)

Population density – 76 per sq. km (2019)

Urban population – 61.9 per cent (2019 est)

Median age (years) – 33.3 (2020 est)

French Polynesia consists of over 118 volcanic or coral islands and atolls in the South Pacific. There are five archipelagos: the Society Islands (Windward Islands group includes Makatea, Mehetia, Moorea, Tahiti, Tetiaroa, Tubuai Manu; Leeward Islands group includes Bora-Bora, Huahine, Maupiti, Raiatea, Tahaa); the Tuamotu Islands (Hao, Rangiroa, Turéia, etc); the Gambier Islands (Mangareva etc); the Tubuai Islands (Raivavae, Rapa, Rimatara, Rurutu, Tubuai, etc); and the Marquesas Islands (Fatu-Hiva, Hiva-Oa, Nuku-Hiva, Tahuata, Ua Huka, etc). Some of the atolls were used by France for testing nuclear weapons between 1966 and 1996. The main industries are tourism, pearl-farming, deep-sea fishing, coconut products and vanilla production.

High Commissioner, Dominique Sorain, *apptd* 2019

NEW CALEDONIA

Area – 18,575 sq. km
Capital – Nouméa; population, 189,000 (2018 est)
Population – 290,009 rising at 1.25 per cent a year (2020 est); Kanak (39.1 per cent), European (27.1 per cent) (est)
Religion – Christian (Roman Catholic 60 per cent, Protestant 30 per cent), other 10 per cent (est)
Population density – 16 per sq. km (2019)
Urban population – 71.1 per cent (2019 est)
Median age (years) – 32.9 (2020 est)

New Caledonia, a 'special' collectivity, is a large island in the western Pacific, 1,120km off the eastern coast of Australia. Its dependencies are the Isle of Pines, the Loyalty Islands (Mahé, Lifou, Urea, etc), the Bélep Archipelago, the Chesterfield Islands, the Huon Islands and Walpole. New Caledonia was discovered in 1774 and annexed by France in 1853. Agitation for independence from the 1980s ended with the Nouméa accord in 1998, under which an increasing degree of autonomy was transferred to the territory up to 2018. In November 2018, the island rejected independence in a long-awaited referendum. The territory is divided into three provinces, each with a provincial assembly; these combine to form the territorial assembly.

Over one-tenth of the world's nickel deposits are found in the territory, and nickel mining and smelting are the main industries, along with tourism and fishing. Ferronickel, nickel ore and fish are the main exports. About 20 per cent of food has to be imported.

High Commissioner, Laurent Prévost, *apptd* 2019

ST BARTHÉLEMY

Area – 21 sq. km
Capital – Gustavia
Population – 7,122 (2020 est)
Median age (years) – 45.6 (2020 est)

The island lies in the Caribbean Sea about 240km north-west of Guadeloupe. It was settled by the French from 1648. France sold the island to Sweden in 1784 but bought it back again in 1878 and it was under the administration of Guadeloupe until 2007, when it became a *collectivité territoriale*. The economy is based on luxury tourism and duty-free commerce in luxury goods. Freshwater sources are limited, so all food and energy and most manufactured goods are imported.

Prefect, Sylvie Feucher, *apptd* 2018

ST MARTIN

Area – 54.4 sq. km
Capital – Marigot
Population – 32.556 (2020 est)
Population density – 672 per sq. km (2019)
Median age (years) – 33.3 (2020 est)

The territory occupies the northern part of the island of St Martin, 250km to the north-west of Guadeloupe; the southern part (Sint Maarten) is a territory of the Netherlands. The island was claimed for Spain by Columbus in 1493 but the Spanish relinquished it in 1648 to the Dutch and French, who divided the island between them. The French part was administered from Guadeloupe until it was made a *collectivité territoriale* in 2007. The economy is dependent on tourism, which employs 85 per cent of the workforce. Nearly all food, energy and manufactured goods are imported.

Prefect, Sylvie Feucher, *apptd* 2018

ST PIERRE AND MIQUELON

Area – 242 sq. km
Capital – St-Pierre; population, 6,000 (2018 est)
Population – 5,347 falling at 1.15 per cent a year (2020 est)
Religion – Roman Catholic 99 per cent (est)
Urban population – 89.9 per cent (2019 est)

Median age (years) – 48.5 (2020 est)

These two small groups of eight islands off the south coast of Newfoundland became a *collectivité territoriale* in 1985. The main industry of fishing and servicing fishing fleets has declined in step with the decline in cod stocks, and fish farming, crab fishing and agriculture are being developed. Tourism is of growing importance, but the economy is dependent on government subsidies.

Prefect, Thierry Devimeux, *apptd* 2018

WALLIS AND FUTUNA ISLANDS

Area – 142 sq. km
Capital – Mata-Utu, on Uvea, the main island of the Wallis group; population, 1,000 (2018 est)
Population – 15,854 rising at 0.28 per cent a year (2020 est)
Religion – Roman Catholic 99 per cent (est)
Median age (years) – 34 (2020 est)

The two groups of islands (the Wallis Archipelago and the Îles de Horne) lie in the South Pacific, north-east of Fiji. They became a French protectorate from the 1840s and were administered from New Caledonia until 1961. The main products are copra, vegetables, bananas, livestock products, fish and timber.

Administrator Superior, Thierry Queffelec, *apptd* 2018

OVERSEAS TERRITORIES

TERRITORY OF THE FRENCH SOUTHERN AND ANTARCTIC LANDS

Created in 1955 from former Réunion dependencies, the territory comprises the islands of Amsterdam (55 sq. km) and St Paul (7 sq. km), the Kerguelen Islands (7,215 sq. km) and Crozet Islands (352 sq. km) archipelagos, Adélie Land (about 500,000 sq. km) in the Antarctic continent and, since 2007, the islands of Bassas da India (80 sq. km), Europa (28 sq. km), les Glorieuses (5 sq. km), Juan de Nova (4.4 sq. km) and Tromelin (1 sq. km). The population consists only of staff of the meteorological and scientific research stations.

Administrator, Cécile Pozzo Di Borgo, *apptd* 2014

THE FRENCH COMMUNITY OF STATES

The 1958 constitution envisaged the establishment of a French Community of States. A number of former French colonies in Africa have seceded from the community but for all practical purposes continue to enjoy the same close links with France as do those that remain formal members. Most former French African colonies are closely linked to France by financial, technical and economic agreements.

GABON

République Gabonaise – Gabonese Republic

Area – 267,667 sq. km
Capital – Libreville; population, 834,000 (2018 est)
Major towns – Franceville (Masuku), Moanda, Oyem, Port-Gentil

Currency – Central African CFA franc of 100 centimes
Population – 2,230,908 rising at 2.5 per cent a year (2020 est); over 40 predominantly Bantu tribes, of which Fang, Shira-Punu, Nzabi-Duma, Mbede-Teke, Myene and Kota-Kele are the largest tribal groupings
Religion – Christian (Catholic 42.3 per cent, other Christian 27.4 per cent, Protestant 12.3 per cent), Muslim 9.8 per cent (est); many people combine elements of Christian and indigenous beliefs
Language – French (official), Fang, Myene, Nzebi, Bapounou, Bandjabi
Population density – 8 per sq. km (2019)
Urban population – 89.7 per cent (2019 est)
Median age (years) – 21 (2020 est)
National anthem – 'La Concorde' 'The Concord'
National day – 17 August (Independence Day)
Death penalty – Abolished for all crimes (since 2010)
CPI score – 31 (123)
Military expenditure – US$261m (2018 est)
Literacy rate – 84.7 per cent (2018 est)
Health expenditure (per capita) – US$204 (2017)
Hospital beds (per 1,000 people) – 6.3 (2010)
Life expectancy (years) – 69 (2020 est)
Mortality rate – 5.9 (2020 est)
Birth rate – 26.3 (2020 est)
Infant mortality rate – 30.3 (2020 est)
HIV/AIDS adult prevalence – 3.5 per cent (2019 est)

CLIMATE AND TERRAIN
The country lies on the equator. It rises from a narrow coastal plain to a hilly interior; approximately 85 per cent of the land is rainforest, with savannah in the east and south, although by 2006 as much as half of the country's forest was being leased for timber. In 2002, 10 per cent of the country was designated as national park. Elevation extremes range from 1,575m (Mt Iboundji) to 0m (Atlantic Ocean). The climate is tropical, with an average temperature of 25.2°C. There are two wet seasons each year, from January to June and September to December.

HISTORY AND POLITICS
The first Europeans to visit the region were the Portuguese in the 15th century; Dutch, French and English traders arrived soon after. Sovereignty was signed over to the French in 1839 by a local Mpongwe ruler. In 1849, slaves freed by the French formed a settlement, which they called Libreville, now the capital. The country was occupied by the French in 1885 and became part of French Equatorial Africa in 1910. Gabon became autonomous within the French Community in 1958 and gained independence on 17 August 1960.

Omar Bongo succeeded to the presidency in 1967 after the death of the first president, and in 1968 he established a one-party state with the *Parti Démocratique Gabonais* (PDG) as the only party. By the late 1980s, the deteriorating economy was provoking unrest and demands for greater democracy, and in 1991 a multiparty system was reintroduced.

Under the multiparty system, the PDG has remained in power (amid allegations of electoral fraud) although it has included opposition party members in coalition governments since 1994. The PDG and its coalition partners maintained power in the 2011 legislative election, which was boycotted by the main opposition party, and retained its two-thirds majority in the October 2018 elections despite some losses. President Bongo was re-elected for a sixth term of office in 2005; he died in June 2009, and was succeeded by his son, Ali Bongo Ondimba, who was elected president in August 2009 amid allegations of vote-rigging. He was narrowly re-elected in August 2016. Following an attempted military coup in January 2019, the cabinet has been shuffled numerous times. Rose

Christiane Raponda was appointed prime minister in July 2020, the first woman to hold the position.

The 1991 constitution, amended in 1995, 1997, 2003, and 2011, provides for a president who is directly elected for a seven-year term; since 2003, there has been no limit on the number of terms a president may serve. The president appoints the prime minister, who then appoints the council of ministers. There is a bicameral *Parlement,* comprising the 143-member National Assembly, directly elected for five-year terms, and the senate, which does not fix the number of members elected (currently 102) for a six-year term by municipal and regional councillors.

HEAD OF STATE
President, Ali Bongo Ondimba, *elected* 30 August 2009, *sworn in* 16 October 2009, *re-elected* August 2016
Vice-President, vacant

SELECTED GOVERNMENT MEMBERS *AS AT NOVEMBER 2020*
Prime Minister, Rose Christiane Raponda
Defence, Michael Adamo
Economy, Jean-Marie Ogandaga
Foreign Affairs, Pacôme Moubelet Boubeya

EMBASSY OF THE GABONESE REPUBLIC
27 Elvaston Place, London SW7 5NL
T 020-7823 9986
Ambassador Extraordinary and Plenipotentiary, HE Aichatou Sanni Aoudou, *apptd* 2015

BRITISH HIGH COMMISSION
HE Rowan Laxton, *apptd* 2017, resident at Yaoundé, Cameroon

ECONOMY AND TRADE
Gabon is one of the most prosperous countries in Africa, largely owing to its small population and abundance of oil and mineral resources. The economy is heavily dependent on oil (which contributes 45 per cent of GDP) and other mineral resources, including manganese and uranium, and timber, but the government is investing in diversification to reduce vulnerability to fluctuating commodity prices and the gradual decline in oil production as reserves become exhausted. Despite the country's wealth, over a third of the population live below the poverty line and weak fiscal management has resulted in a high foreign debt, which has had to be restructured several times. Economic challenges also include frequent power cuts and water shortages, corruption and high levels of unemployment. Following poor growth due to low oil prices, in June 2017 Gabon signed a three-year agreement with the IMF. Plans to develop eco-tourism have been set back by the coronavirus pandemic; the economy is expected to contract by 2.7 per cent in 2020.

Industry contributes 44.7 per cent of GDP and employs 12 per cent of the workforce, mainly in oil and mineral extraction, oil refining, chemicals, ship repair, textiles, and processing agricultural and forestry products. Agriculture is largely at subsistence level, employing 64 per cent of the workforce but contributing only 5 per cent of GDP. It is restricted by the forest cover and lack of suitable land. The main products include cocoa, coffee, sugar, palm oil, rubber, cattle, timber and fish.

The main trading partners are France, Belgium and China. Principal exports are crude oil (about 80 per cent), timber, manganese and uranium. The main imports are machinery and equipment, food, chemicals and construction materials.
GNI – US$15.7bn; US$7,210 per capita (2019)
Annual average growth of GDP – 0.5 per cent (2017 est)

Inflation rate – 2.7 per cent (2017 est)
Total external debt – US$6.49bn (2017 est)
Imports – US$3,033m (2015)
Exports – US$5,074m (2015)

BALANCE OF PAYMENTS
Trade – US$2,040m surplus (2015)
Current Account – US$19,584m deficit (2018)

Trade with UK	2018	2019
Imports from UK	£28,321,077	£40,594,014
Exports to UK	£4,602,550	£4,843,525

COMMUNICATIONS

Airports and waterways – 14, including international airports in Libreville and Port-Gentil; there are 1,600km of navigable waterways and the principal seaport is in Port-Gentil
Roadways and railways – 14,300km, of which only 900km are paved; 649km
Telecommunications – 21,235 fixed lines and 2.9 million mobile subscriptions (2018); there were 1.3 million internet users in 2018
Internet code and IDD – ga; 241 (from UK), 44 (to UK)
Broadcasters – State-controlled broadcaster Radiodiffusion-Télévision Gabonaise operates two television channels and two radio networks; pan-African radio broadcaster Africa No. 1 is based in Gabon
Press – The only two daily newspapers, *L'Union* and *Gabon Matin,* are operated by the government
WPFI score – 37.20 (121)

THE GAMBIA

Republic of The Gambia

Area – 11,300 sq. km
Capital – Banjul; population, 451,000 (2020 est)
Major towns – Bakau, Brikama, Farafenni, Serekunda
Currency – Dalasi (D) of 100 butut
Population – 2,173,999 rising at 1.87 per cent a year (2020 est); Mandinka (34 per cent), Fulani (22.4 per cent), Wolof (12.6 per cent), Jola (10.7 per cent), Serahuleh (6.6 per cent) (est)
Religion – Muslim 95.7 per cent (majority Malikite Sufi), Christian 4.2 per cent (predominantly Roman Catholic) (est)
Language – English (official), Mandinka, Wolof, Fula
Population density – 225 per sq. km (2019)
Urban population – 61.9 per cent (2019 est)
Median age (years) – 21.8 (2020 est)
National anthem – 'For The Gambia, Our Homeland'
National day – 18 February (Independence Day)
Death penalty – Retained

CPI score – 37 (96)
Military expenditure – US$11.49m (2018)

CLIMATE AND TERRAIN

The Gambia consists of a narrow strip of land along the river Gambia, mostly comprising the basin and flood plain of the river, flanked by savannah and low hills. Elevation extremes range from 53m to 0m (Atlantic Ocean). The climate is tropical, with a wet season from June to November.

HISTORY AND POLITICS

The Gambia river basin was part of an area dominated from the 10th to 16th centuries by the Mali and Songhai kingdoms. The Portuguese reached the river Gambia in 1447 and established trading posts along the river. In 1816 a British garrison was stationed on an island at the river mouth; this became the capital of a small British colony, and a crown colony in 1843. The boundaries of the country were agreed by France and Britain in 1889; British territory would extend 10km from the upper river on either bank. The Gambia became independent on 18 February 1965 and a republic in 1970. The country withdrew from the Commonwealth in 2013, but rejoined in February 2018 in an attempt by the government to end international isolation.

The post-independence prime minister, Sir Dawda Jawara (1924–2019) was president from 1970 until 1994, when he was overthrown in a military coup. The coup leader, Lt. (later Col.) Yahya Jammeh, assumed the presidency and a civilian-military government was formed to govern in conjunction with the ruling military council. Civilian government was restored after elections in 1996 and 1997, following the approval of a new constitution. Jammeh was elected president and his Alliance for Patriotic Reorientation and Construction (APRC) won an overall majority of the legislative seats.

Property developer and independent candidate Adama Barrow won the December 2016 presidential election, but incumbent president Jammeh refused to step down after 22 years in power. In January 2017, troops from neighbouring Senegal entered the country and Jammeh fled, allowing Barrow to be installed as president. Barrow pledged to resign after three years in office, but later refused and cracked down on subsequent protests in January 2020. The previously dominant APRC was heavily defeated in the April 2017 legislative elections, losing 38 seats to the centre-left United Democratic Party.

Under the 1997 constitution, the executive president is directly elected for a five-year term; there is no limit on re-election. The unicameral National Assembly has 58 members, of whom 53 are directly elected and five are appointed by the president, for a five-year term.

HEAD OF STATE
President, Defence, C-in-C of the Armed Forces, Adama Barrow, *elected* 2 December 2016, *sworn in* 19 January 2017
Vice-President, Isatou Jarra Touray

SELECTED GOVERNMENT MEMBERS *AS AT NOVEMBER 2020*
Finance and Economic Affairs, Mambury Njie
Foreign Affairs, Mamadou Tangara
Interior, Yankuba Sonko

THE GAMBIA HIGH COMMISSION
57 Kensington Court, London W8 5DG
T 020-7229 9225 **E** gambiahighcomuk@btconnect.com
W www.gambiaembassy.org.uk
High Commissioner, HE Francis Blain, *apptd* 2017

BRITISH HIGH COMMISSION
PO Box 507, 48 Atlantic Road, Fajara, Banjul
T (+220) 449 5133 **E** ukinthegambia@fco.gov.uk
W www.gov.uk/government/world/gambia
High Commissioner, HE Sharon Wardle, *apptd* 2017

ECONOMY AND TRADE

The country has limited natural resources and underutilised agricultural potential. Historically, the mainstay of the economy was re-export trade with neighbouring countries, but this has declined since the late 1990s, owing to the vagaries of government policies and trade and transport disputes with Senegal. There are high levels of public and foreign debt and the country is dependent on financial and technical aid from foreign donors. Over 60 per cent of the population live in poverty. Remittances from Gambians working abroad account for around 20 per cent of GDP. The economy slowed following the Ebola outbreak of 2014, affecting the previously flourishing tourism sector, but following President Jammeh's departure in 2017 the new regime successfully steered the economy back to high levels of growth. However, a large reduction in tourists due to the coronavirus pandemic is likely to see the economy slightly contract in 2020. With less than half of arable land under cultivation, the government has also prioritised agricultural investment.

The services sector employs only 6 per cent of the workforce but contributes 65.4 per cent of GDP. About 75 per cent of the population is dependent on subsistence agriculture, which contributes 20.4 per cent of GDP. The chief product, peanuts, is also the main export and the basis of the main industrial activity, leaving the economy vulnerable to market fluctuations and the weather. Industry contributes 14.2 per cent to GDP, chiefly through processing peanuts, fish and hides, assembling agricultural machinery, metalworking, woodworking and the production of beverages and clothing.

The main trade partners are Guinea-Bissau, Vietnam, Brazil, Côte d'Ivoire and Senegal. Principal exports (nearly 80 per cent are re-exports) are peanut products, fish, cotton lint and palm kernels. The main imports are foodstuffs, manufactures, fuel, machinery and transport equipment.

GNI – US$1.7bn; US$740 per capita (2019)
Annual average growth of GDP – 4.6 per cent (2017 est)
Inflation rate – 8.0 per cent (2017 est)
Population below poverty line – 48.4 per cent (2010 est)
Total external debt – US$586.8m (2017 est)
Imports – US$537m (2017)
Exports – US$236m (2017)

BALANCE OF PAYMENTS
Trade – US$300m deficit (2017)
Current Account – US$332m deficit (2019)

Trade with UK	2018	2019
Imports from UK	£27,873,908	£32,821,041
Exports to UK	£2,796,979	£3,894,425

COMMUNICATIONS

Airports and waterways – There is an international airport at Banjul; there are 390km of navigable waterways on the Gambia river
Roadways – 518km of paved roadways
Telecommunications – 44,000 fixed lines and 3.2 million mobile subscriptions (2018); there were 406,918 internet users in 2017
Internet code and IDD – gm; 220 (from UK), 44 (to UK)

Major broadcasters – Gambia Television (GRTS TV) and Radio Gambia are the state broadcasters; private television stations are banned while independent radio stations self-censor content; one state-run TV-channel; one privately-owned TV-station; one state-owned radio station and 15 privately owned radio stations; six community radio stations; transmissions of multiple international broadcasters are available (2018)
Press – Major publications include the *Daily Observer, The Standard* and *The Daily News*
WPFI score – 30.62 (87)

EDUCATION AND HEALTH

Education is compulsory between the ages of seven and 12.
Literacy rate – 50.8 per cent (2015 est)
Gross enrolment ratio (percentage of relevant age group) – primary 101.7 per cent (2019 est); secondary 50.1 per cent (2010 est); tertiary 2.7 per cent (2012 est)
Health expenditure (per capita) – US$23 (2017)
Hospital beds (per 1,000 people) – 1.1 (2011)
Life expectancy (years) – 65.8 (2020 est)
Mortality rate – 6.7 (2020 est)
Birth rate – 27 (2020 est)
Infant mortality rate – 54.9 (2020 est)
HIV/AIDS adult prevalence – 1.9 per cent (2019 est)

GEORGIA

Sak'art'velo – Georgia

Area – 69,700 sq. km
Capital – Tbilisi; population, 1,078,000 (2020 est)
Major cities – Batumi, Kutaisi, Poti, Rustavi, Zugdidi
Currency – Lari of 100 tetri
Population – 4,997,000 rising at 0.05 per cent a year (2020 est); Georgian (86.8 per cent), Azeri (6.3 per cent), Armenian (4.5 per cent est)
Religion – Christian (officially Orthodox 83.4 per cent, Armenian Apostolic 2.9 per cent), Muslim 10.7 per cent (est)
Language – Georgian (official), Russian, Armenian, Azeri, Abkhaz (official in Abkhazia)
Population density – 65 per sq. km (2020)
Urban population – 59 per cent (2020 est)
Median age (years) – 38.6 (2020 est)
National anthem – 'Tavisupleba' 'Freedom'
National day – 26 May (Independence Day, 1918)
Death penalty – Abolished for all crimes (since 1997)
CPI score – 56 (44)
Military expenditure – US$317m (2018 est)
Conscription – 18–27 years of age; 12 months
Literacy rate – 99.4 per cent (2017 est)
Gross enrolment ratio (percentage of relevant age group) – primary 99.3 per cent, secondary 106.2 per cent, tertiary 63.9 per cent (2019 est)
Health expenditure (per capita) – US$293 (2017)
Hospital beds (per 1,000 people) – 2.6 (2013)

Life expectancy (years) – 77 (2020 est)
Mortality rate – 11 (2020 est)
Birth rate – 11.6 (2020 est)
Infant mortality rate – 13.8 (2020 est)
HIV/AIDS adult prevalence – 0.4 per cent (2019 est)

CLIMATE AND TERRAIN
Georgia lies in the western part of the Caucasus region, on the eastern shore of the Black Sea. It is mountainous, with the Great Caucasus mountain range along the northern border with Russia, and the Lesser Caucasus in the south. These are divided by the Kolkhida lowland in the west and the Mtkvari (Kura) river basin in the east, between which runs the valley of the Mtkvari river. Elevation extremes range from 5,201m (Mt Shkhara) to 0m (Black Sea). The climate is almost tropical in summer, while cold winters affect both the mountains and valleys. Average temperatures range from −6.4°C in January to 18.6°C in August.

POLITICS
The 1995 constitution provides for a federal republic with a unicameral legislature, to become bicameral 'following the creation of appropriate conditions'. It was amended in 2010 to transfer some of the president's powers to the legislature and prime minister. The president is directly elected for a five-year term, renewable once. The unicameral parliament has 150 members, 73 elected in single-member constituencies and 77 by proportional representation, who serve for a four-year term. Constitutional amendments passed in 2017 and due to be implemented in 2024 will transform the country into a parliamentary system where the president will be elected by lawmakers.

In November 2013, Irakli Garibashvili, aged 31, of the centrist Georgian Dream party became the country's prime minister and the world's youngest elected leader at the time, but he resigned in December 2015 amid increasing public dissatisfaction with the government. Anti-government protests also resulted in resignations from his successors, Giorgi Kvirikashvili in June 2018 and Mamuka Bakhtadze in September 2019. Georgian Dream won the October 2016 legislative elections with an increased majority. The November 2018 presidential election was won by pro-European Salome Zurabishvili, making her the last popularly elected president.

HEAD OF STATE
President, Salome Zurabishvili, *sworn in* 16 December 2018

SELECTED GOVERNMENT MEMBERS *AS AT NOVEMBER 2020*
Prime Minister, Giorgi Gakharia
Deputy Prime Ministers, Maia Tskitishvili; Tea Tsulukiani
Foreign Affairs, Davit Zalkaliani
Defence, Irakli Gharibashvili

EMBASSY OF GEORGIA
20 St George's Square, London SW1V 2HP
T 020-7348 1941 **E** embassy@geoemb.plus.com
W www.uk.mfa.gov.ge

Ambassador Extraordinary and Plenipotentiary, HE Sophie Katsarava, *apptd* 2020

BRITISH EMBASSY
51 Krtsanisi Street, 0144 Tbilisi
T (+995) (32) 227 47 47 **E** british.embassy.tbilisi@fco.gov.uk
W www.gov.uk/government/world/georgia
Ambassador Extraordinary and Plenipotentiary, HE Justin McKenzie Smith, *apptd* 2016

SECESSION
Fears that Georgian independence would deprive them of their own autonomy led to unilateral declarations of independence by the central region of South Ossetia (1991) and the northwestern region of Abkhazia (1992) followed by a year of conflict in both separatist areas. In August 2008, clashes between Georgian troops and South Ossetian separatists escalated into a brief war between Georgia and Russia, in which Georgian forces were expelled from South Ossetia and Abkhazia. Russia has not fully complied with an EU-brokered ceasefire, maintaining a military presence in the areas and a 'buffer zone' around them; only Russia and a handful of its allies recognise their unilateral declarations of independence. Russia signed integration treaties with Abkhazia in 2014 and South Ossetia in 2015, paving the way for greater Russian involvement in the breakaway regions. In June 2019, a pro-independence speech by a Russian MP in the Georgian parliament caused violent riots in the capital.

Relations between Georgia and Ajaria, a semi-autonomous region in the south-west and a key trade hub, deteriorated briefly in 2004 when Aslan Abashidze, Ajaria's leader since 1991, refused to recognise the authority of the newly elected President Saakashvili, and accused Georgia of planning to invade Ajaria. Public demonstrations against Abashidze forced him to resign. The Georgian parliament granted the Ajarian assembly powers over local affairs but the Georgian president retains the power to nominate the region's head of government and to dissolve its government and assembly.

ECONOMY AND TRADE
The economy grew rapidly from 2003, making good progress towards recovery following near-collapse in the 1990s. Reform of the tax system nearly quadrupled government revenue, while added impetus in privatisation and anti-corruption programmes attracted foreign investment. However, the economy slowed in 2008 following the war with Russia and contracted in 2009 as the global economic downturn affected the regional economy and led to a decline in foreign investment and expatriates' remittances. The fuel crises in 2005–6 prompted the renovation of hydroelectric power plants and the repair of a pipeline from Azerbaijan; the country now meets the majority of its energy needs, but imports nearly all its supplies of gas and oil. In 2014, Georgia signed an association agreement with the EU that provided Georgian firms with greater access to European markets, and in 2017 signed a free trade agreement with China. Economic growth prior to the 2020 coronavirus pandemic was built higher domestic demand and closer integration with global economies.

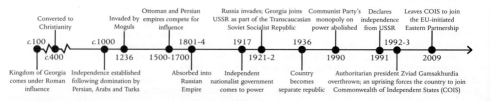

Converted to Christianity	Invaded by Moguls	Ottoman and Persian empires compete for influence	Russia invades; Georgia joins USSR as part of the Transcaucasian Soviet Socialist Republic	Communist Party's monopoly on power abolished	Declares independence from USSR	Leaves COIS to join the EU-initiated Eastern Partnership
*c.*100	*c.*1000	1801-4	1917	1936	1992-3	
*c.*400	1236	1500-1700	1921-2	1990	1991	2009
Kingdom of Georgia comes under Roman influence	Independence established following domination by Persian, Arabs and Turks	Absorbed into Russian Empire	Independent nationalist government comes to power	Country becomes separate republic	Authoritarian president Zviad Gamsakhurdia overthrown; an uprising forces the country to join Commonwealth of Independent States (COIS)	

Agriculture employs 55.6 per cent of the workforce and generates 8.2 per cent of GDP, with a concentration on grapes for winemaking, tea, citrus fruits and hazelnuts. Industry, which contributes 23.7 per cent of GDP, produces steel, machine tools, electrical appliances, manganese, copper, gold, chemicals, wood products and wine.

The main trading partners are Turkey, Azerbaijan and Russia. Principal exports are vehicles, ferro-alloys, fertilisers, scrap metal, gold, fruit and nuts. The main imports are fuels, vehicles, machinery and parts, food (especially grain) and pharmaceuticals.

GNI – US$17.6bn; US$4,740 per capita (2019)
Annual average growth of GDP – 5.0 per cent (2017 est)
Inflation rate – 6.0 per cent (2017 est)
Population below poverty line – 9.2 per cent (2012)
Unemployment – 11.5 per cent (2017 est)
Total external debt – US$16.99bn (2017 est)
Imports – US$9,335m (2017)
Exports – US$7,542m (2017)

BALANCE OF PAYMENTS

Trade – US$1,792m deficit (2017)
Current Account – US$960m deficit (2019)

Trade with UK	2018	2019
Imports from UK	£60,420,302	£80,071,738
Exports to UK	£11,674,811	£19,939,146

COMMUNICATIONS

Airports – 18 with paved runways, including an international terminal in Tbilisi
Roadways and railways – 20,295km; 1,612km
Telecommunications – 604,438 fixed lines and 5.5 million mobile subscriptions (2018); there were 3.2 million internet users in 2018
Internet code and IDD – ge; 995 (from UK), 810 44 with no extra zeros (to UK)
Major broadcasters – Government-funded Georgian Public Broadcasting provides two television and two radio networks, alongside a host of private cable operators and major commercial stations
Press – Daily titles include *Rezonansi* and *The Messenger* (English language)
WPFI score – 28.59 (60)

GERMANY

Bundesrepublik Deutschland – Federal Republic of Germany

Area – 357,022 sq. km
Capital – Berlin; population, 3,562,000 (2020 est)
Major cities – Bremen, Cologne, Dortmund, Dresden, Düsseldorf, Essen, Frankfurt, Hamburg, Hannover, Leipzig, Munich, Nuremberg, Stuttgart

Currency – Euro (€) of 100 cents
Population – 80,159,662 falling at 0.19 per cent a year (2020 est)
Religion – Christian (Roman Catholic 27.7 per cent, Protestant 25.5 per cent, Orthodox 1.9 per cent), Muslim 5.1 per cent (est)
Language – German (official)
Population density – 237 per sq. km (2019)
Urban population – 77.4 per cent (2019 est)
Median age (years) – 47.8 (2020 est)
National anthem – 'Das Lied der Deutschen' 'Song of the Germans'
National day – 3 October (Unity Day)
Death penalty – Abolished for all crimes (since 1949 in FRG and 1987 in GDR)
CPI score – 80 (9)
Military expenditure – US$49,471m (2018)

CLIMATE AND TERRAIN

The north of the country is low-lying, rising in the centre to uplands and Alpine foothills, then to the Bavarian Alps in the south. Elevation extremes range from 2,963m (Zugspitze, Bavaria) to −3.54m (Neuendorf bei Wilster). The Rhine, Weser and Elbe rivers flow from the south to the North Sea, the Oder and Neisse rivers flow north to the Baltic Sea, and the Danube flows east from its source in the south of the country to the Austrian border. Nearly a third of the land is covered by forest or woodland. The climate is temperate, with average temperatures ranging from 0.9°C in January to 18.2°C in July.

POLITICS

The Basic Law was adopted in 1949 as the constitution of West Germany; at unification in 1990, Berlin and the five reformed *Länder* (states) of East Germany acceded to the Federal Republic. The president is elected for a five-year term by the *Bundesversammlung*, an electoral college comprising the members of the *Bundestag* (*see* below) and an equal number of representatives elected by the state legislatures. The bicameral legislature comprises a lower house, the Federal Assembly *(Bundestag)*, with 709 members elected by a mixed constituency and proportional representation system for a four-year term. The Federal Council *(Bundesrat)* has 69 members appointed by the governments of the *Länder* in proportion to their populations; their term of office is determined by their *Land's* constitution. The head of government is the chancellor, who is proposed by the president and elected by the *Bundestag*.

Angela Merkel, leader of the Christian Democratic Union of Germany and the Christian Social Union of Bavaria (CDU/CSU), became Germany's first female chancellor in 2005 at the head of a CDU/CSU and Social Democratic Party (SPD) coalition, governing without the latter following re-election in 2009. In 2013 the CDU again formed a 'grand coalition' with the SPD after the CDU fell five seats short of claiming a historic majority in the *Bundestag* with 41.5 per cent of the vote. In the 2017 legislative election, the arrival of the far-right party Alternative for Germany (AFD) significantly cut the support of both the CDU and the SPD, resulting in political stalemate for almost six months before another 'grand coalition' was negotiated between the CDU/CSU and the SPD, with Merkel remaining as chancellor. It was the longest the country had been without a government in its postwar history.

Former foreign minister Frank-Walter Steinmeier of the SPD won the 2017 presidential election, winning 931 of 1,239 valid votes.

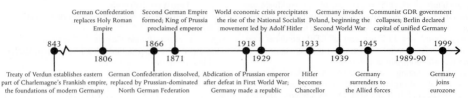

German Confederation replaces Holy Roman Empire — 843 / 1806 — Treaty of Verdun establishes eastern part of Charlemagne's Frankish empire, the foundations of modern Germany

Second German Empire formed; King of Prussia proclaimed emperor — 1866 / 1871 — German Confederation dissolved, replaced by Prussian-dominated North German Federation

World economic crisis precipitates the rise of the National Socialist movement led by Adolf Hitler — 1918 / 1929 — Abdication of Prussian emperor after defeat in First World War; Germany made a republic

Germany invades Poland, beginning the Second World War — 1933 / 1939 — Hitler becomes Chancellor

Communist GDR government collapses; Berlin declared capital of unified Germany — 1945 / 1989-90 — Germany surrenders to the Allied forces

1999 — Germany joins eurozone

HEAD OF STATE

Federal President, Frank-Walter Steinmeier, *elected* 12 February 2017, *sworn in* 22 March 2017

SELECTED GOVERNMENT MEMBERS *AS AT NOVEMBER 2020*

Federal Chancellor, Angela Merkel
Defence, Annegret Kramp-Karrenbauer
Finance, Olaf Scholz
Foreign Affairs, Heiko Maas

EMBASSY OF THE FEDERAL REPUBLIC OF GERMANY

23 Belgrave Square, London SW1X 8PZ
T 020-7824 1300 **W** www.london.diplo.de
Ambassador Extraordinary and Plenipotentiary, HE Andreas Michaelis, *apptd* 2020

BRITISH EMBASSY

Wilhelmstrasse 70/71, 10117 Berlin
T (+49) (30) 204 570 **E** ukingermany@fco.gov.uk
W www.gov.uk/government/world/germany
Ambassador Extraordinary and Plenipotentiary, HE Sir Sebastian Wood, KCMG, *apptd* 2015

FEDERAL STRUCTURE

Germany is a federal republic composed of 16 states *(Länder)* (ten from the former Federal Republic of Germany (FRG), five from the former German Democratic Republic (GDR), and Berlin). Each *Land* has its own directly elected legislature and government led by a minister-president (prime minister) or equivalent. The 1949 Basic Law vests executive power in the *Länder* governments except in those areas reserved for the federal government.

State *(Capital, where name differs)*	Population (millions) (2019 est)
Baden-Württemberg (Stuttgart)	11.10
Bavaria (Munich)	13.14
Berlin	3.67
Brandenburg (Potsdam)	2.52
Bremen	0.68
Hamburg	1.85
Hesse (Wiesbaden)	6.29
Lower Saxony (Hannover)	7.99
Mecklenburg-West Pomerania (Schwerin)	1.61
North Rhine-Westphalia (Düsseldorf)	17.95
Rhineland-Palitanate (Mainz)	4.09
Saarland (Saarbrücken)	0.99
Saxony (Dresden)	4.07
Saxony-Anhalt (Magdeburg)	2.19
Schleswig-Holstein (Kiel)	2.90
Thuringia (Erfurt)	2.13

ECONOMY AND TRADE

Germany has the world's fourth-largest economy and the largest in Europe, but decades of strong economic performance gave way in the 1990s to a severe recession, largely an aftermath of reunification and of macroeconomic stagnation. Although the economy as a whole began to grow again in 2006, in the east it remains far weaker despite costly modernisation and integration measures. However, the revival was largely export-led and a decline in demand due to the global economic downturn caused a recession in 2008–9. The government's economic stimulus measures pushed the budget deficit slightly beyond the eurozone's 3 per cent threshold in 2010, but since 2012 surpluses have been recorded and by 2019 its debt-to-GDP ratio had fallen below 60 per cent. The country suffers from a lack of internal investment, and consequently €15bn was spent improving its infrastructure between 2016 and 2018. The country is the world's third-largest exporter and Germany's reliance on exports means the economy has been hampered by slowdowns in the eurozone, and Russian and Chinese economies, and latterly by the coronavirus pandemic. Although Germany's handling of the virus was better than most of its large European neighbours, the economy is expected to contract by 6 per cent in 2020.

The country has a modern, diverse, highly industrialised and technologically advanced market economy. The services sector contributes 68.6 per cent of GDP, industry 30.7 per cent and agriculture 0.7 per cent. The industrial sector is among the world's largest producers of iron, steel, coal, cement, chemicals, machinery, vehicles, machine tools, electronics, food and beverages, ships and textiles. Germany depends on imports to meet its oil and natural gas needs, but it remains a net exporter of electricity; in the wake of Japan's Fukushima crisis in 2011, the German government committed itself to closing all 17 nuclear reactors by 2022, and replacing them with renewable energy. Between 2000 and 2017 renewable energy consumption rose from just 9 per cent to 52 per cent.

The main trading partners are EU nations, the USA and China. Machinery, vehicles, chemicals, metals and manufactures, foodstuffs and textiles are the principal imports and exports.

GNI – US$4,033.5bn; US$48,520 per capita (2019)
Annual average growth of GDP – 0.59 per cent (2019 est)
Inflation rate – 1.7 per cent (2017 est)
Population below poverty line – 16.7 per cent (2015 est)
Unemployment – 4.98 per cent (2019 est)
Total external debt – US$5.326 trillion (2016 est)
Imports – US$1,455,834m (2017)
Exports – US$1,735,279m (2017)

BALANCE OF PAYMENTS

Trade – US$279,444m surplus (2017)
Current Account – US$273,136m surplus (2019)

Trade with UK	2018	2019
Imports from UK	£35,518,174,752	£36,307,232,875
Exports to UK	£68,295,185,477	£66,909,850,317

COMMUNICATIONS

Airports – 318 with paved runways; the busiest airport is at Frankfurt, other major airports include Berlin, Munich and Bonn

Waterways – Around 20 per cent of domestic freight is carried on 7,467km of inland waterways. The Rhine and the Danube are linked by the Rhine–Maine–Danube (RMD) canal,

creating a through route from the North Sea to the Black Sea. The Kiel canal links the North Sea and the Baltic Sea. The main river ports are Duisburg, Frankfurt, Karlsruhe and Mainz; the main seaports are Hamburg, Bremen, Bremerhaven, Lübeck, Rostock and Wilhelmshaven
Roadways and railways – 625,000km; 33,590km
Telecommunications – 42.5 million fixed lines and 107.5 million mobile subscriptions (2018); there were 72.2 million internet users in 2018
Internet code and IDD – de; 49 (from UK), 44 (to UK)
Major broadcasters – National and regional public television competes with a large private sector, with about 90 per cent of households having access to cable or satellite stations; broadcasters include ARD (which operates Das Erste, the main national public TV channel) and ZDF
Press – Major newspapers include *Frankfurter Allgemeine Zeitung, Süddeutsche Zeitung* and *Die Welt*
WPFI score – 12.16 (11)

EDUCATION AND HEALTH
Education is free and compulsory between the ages of six and 18.
The largest universities are in Munich, Berlin, Hamburg, Bonn, Frankfurt and Cologne. Germany's oldest university is Heidelberg, founded in 1386.
Gross enrolment ratio (percentage of relevant age group) – primary 103.9 per cent, secondary 97.6 per cent, tertiary 70.3 per cent (2018 est)
Health expenditure (per capita) – US$5,033 (2017)
Hospital beds (per 1,000 people) – 8.3 (2013)
Life expectancy (years) – 81.1 (2020 est)
Mortality rate – 12.1 (2020 est)
Birth rate – 8.6 (2020 est)
Infant mortality rate – 3.3 (2020 est)
HIV/AIDS adult prevalence – 0.15 per cent (2013 est)

GHANA

Republic of Ghana

Area – 238,533 sq. km
Capital – Accra; population, 2,514,000 (2020 est)
Major cities – Kumasi, Sekondi-Takoradi, Tamale
Currency – Cedi of 100 pesewas
Population – 29,340,248 rising at 2.15 per cent a year (2020 est); Akan (47.5 per cent), Mole-Dagbon (16.6 per cent), Ewe (13.9 per cent) (est)
Religion – Christian 71.2 per cent, Muslim 17.6 per cent (predominantly Sunni), indigenous and other religions 6 per cent (est)
Language – English (official), Asante, Ewe, Fante, Boron, Dagomba, Dangme, Dagarte, Akyem, Ga, Akuapem
Population density – 131 per sq. km (2019)
Urban population – 56.7 per cent (2019 est)

Median age (years) – 21.4 (2020 est)
National anthem – 'God Bless Our Homeland Ghana'
National day – 6 March (Independence Day)
Death penalty – Retained (last used 1993)
CPI score – 41 (80)
Military expenditure – US$218m (2018)

CLIMATE AND TERRAIN
Ghana consists mostly of plains dissected by the Volta river basin and the great central Lake Volta, rising to the Ashanti plateau in the west. There is dense rainforest in the south and west and forested hills in the north, with savannah in the east and far north. Elevation extremes range from 885m (Mt Afadjato) to 0m (Atlantic Ocean). The climate is tropical but with cooler temperatures on the south-east coast, and less rainfall in the south-east and north. Average temperatures range between 25.6°C in August and 29.94°C in March.

HISTORY AND POLITICS
First reached by Europeans in the 15th century, after which it became a centre for gold and slave trading, the constituent parts of Ghana came under British administration at various times. The original Gold Coast colony was constituted in 1874 and Ashanti and the Northern Territories Protectorate in 1901. Trans-Volta-Togoland, part of the former German colony of Togo, was mandated to Britain by the League of Nations after the First World War and was integrated with the Gold Coast colony in 1956 following a plebiscite. The colony became independent as Ghana on 6 March 1957. It was proclaimed a republic in 1960.
Ghana became a one-party state in 1964 and from 1966 experienced long periods of military rule (1966–9, 1972–9, 1981–91) interspersed with short-lived civilian governments (1969–72, 1979–81). Flt.-Lt. Jerry Rawlings, who had ousted the military regime in 1979 and deposed the civilian government in 1981, was elected president in 1992 when the country returned to multiparty politics after a referendum approved a new constitution.
Since the mid-1990s there have been intermittent clashes over land ownership between ethnic groups in the north; a state of emergency was in place there for two years after the last major outbreak of ethnic violence in 2002.
In the 2008 elections, John Atta Mills, the candidate of the National Democratic Congress (NDC), was elected president, and the NDC became the largest party in the legislature, winning half the seats. Vice-President John Dramani Mahama took over the presidency following the death of Mills in July 2012 and was elected president in December. Parliamentary elections in December 2016 were won by the liberal-conservative New Patriotic Party and the party's candidate, Nana Akufo-Addo, was elected president.
Under the 1993 constitution, the executive president is directly elected for a four-year term, renewable once. The president appoints members of the council of ministers subject to approval by the legislature. The unicameral parliament has 275 members who are directly elected for a four-year term.

HEAD OF STATE
President, Nana Akufo-Addo, *apptd* 7 January 2017
Vice-President, Mahamadu Bawumia

SELECTED GOVERNMENT MEMBERS *AS AT NOVEMBER 2020*
Defence, Dominic Nittiwul
Finance, Ken Offori-Atta
Foreign Affairs, Shirley Ayorkor Botchway
Interior, Ambrose Dery

OFFICE OF THE HIGH COMMISSIONER FOR GHANA
13 Belgrave Square, London SW1X 8PN
T 020-7201 5900 **W** www.ghanahighcommissionuk.com
High Commissioner, HE Papa Owusu-Ankomah, *apptd* 2017

BRITISH HIGH COMMISSION
PO Box 296, Osu Link, off Gamel Abdul Nasser Avenue, Accra
T (+233) (302) 213 250 **E** high.commission.accra@fco.gov.uk
W www.gov.uk/government/world/ghana
High Commissioner, HE Iain Walker, *apptd* 2017

ECONOMY AND TRADE

Ghana has abundant natural resources, but high foreign debt and budget and trade deficits make it dependent on international financial and technical aid to fund its economic and social development programmes. It has benefited from tighter government management of the economy since 2001, and from debt relief in 2002 and 2006; in 2015, Ghana received a US$920m loan from the IMF to improve financial stability and help job creation. Ghana was re-categorised as a lower middle-income country in 2010. Between 2008 and 2019 the economy grew strongly, by an average of around 6 per cent, which was largely driven by the service sector and industry. The opening of several oil and gas fields in 2016 and 2017 further strengthened the economy, but poverty and unemployment remain widespread and growth is expected to slow significantly in 2020 due to the coronavirus pandemic.

Agriculture, mostly at subsistence level, forms the basis of the economy, along with forestry and fishing. The sector employs 44.7 per cent of the workforce and generates 18.3 per cent of GDP. The main cash crops are cocoa, timber and tuna. Industry employs 14.4 per cent of the workforce and contributes 24.5 per cent of GDP, mainly from mining (gold, manganese, bauxite, diamonds), forestry, light manufacturing, aluminium smelting, food processing and shipbuilding. Services employ 40.9 per cent of the workforce and account for 57.2 per cent of GDP. Hydroelectric power is generated at dams on Lake Volta and is transmitted to most of Ghana, and to Togo and Benin. Oil was discovered offshore in 2007 and production began in 2010.

The main export markets are India, the UAE and China. Principal exports are gold, oil, cocoa, timber, tuna, metals, minerals and diamonds. Imports are provided mainly by China, the USA and the UK. The main imports are capital equipment, fuel and foodstuffs.
GNI – US$67.5bn; US$2,220 per capita (2019)
Annual average growth of GDP – 5.9 per cent (2017 est)
Inflation rate – 12.4 per cent (2017 est)
Population below poverty line – 24.2 per cent (2013 est)
Unemployment – 11.9 per cent (2015 est)
Total external debt – US$22.14bn (2017 est)
Imports – US$22,097m (2017)
Exports – US$20,694m (2017)

BALANCE OF PAYMENTS
Trade – US$1,403m deficit (2017)
Current Account – US$1,863m deficit (2019)

Trade with UK	2018	2019
Imports from UK	£353,803,348	£368,988,674
Exports to UK	£424,947,552	£288,218,429

COMMUNICATIONS

Airports and waterways – 10, including an international terminal in Accra; there are 1,293km of navigable waterways
Roadways and railways – 13,787km of paved roads; 947km
Telecommunications – 278,379 fixed lines and 40.1 million mobile subscriptions (2018); there were 11 million internet users in 2018

Broadcasters – Ghana has a diverse media environment with state-run and private media outlets, though journalists face occasional harassment from the government. Ghana Broadcasting Corporation (GBC) operates the TV and two radio stations, and competes with a number of private companies
Press – Major daily titles include *The Ghanaian Chronicle, Daily Guide* and *The Ghanaian Times*
Internet code and IDD – gh; 233 (from UK), 44 (to UK)
WPFI score – 22.26 (30)

EDUCATION AND HEALTH

The government provides ten years of compulsory basic education for all children free of charge. Ghana has one of Africa's oldest universities, at Legon in Accra (established in 1948).
Literacy rate – 79.0 per cent (2018 est)
Gross enrolment ratio (percentage of relevant age group) – primary 104.8 per cent, secondary 74.7 per cent, tertiary 17.2 per cent (2019 est)
Health expenditure (per capita) – US$67 (2017)
Hospital beds (per 1,000 people) – 0.9 (2011)
Life expectancy (years) – 68.2 (2020 est)
Mortality rate – 6.6 (2020 est)
Birth rate – 29.6 (2020 est)
Infant mortality rate – 32.1 (2020 est)
HIV/AIDS adult prevalence – 1.6 per cent (2016 est)

GREECE

Elliniki Dhimokratia – Hellenic Republic

Area – 131,957 sq. km
Capital – Athens; population, 3,153,000 (2020 est)
Major cities – Iraklion (Heraklion) on Crete, Larisa, Patrai (Patras), Piraeus, Rhodes on Rhodes, Thessaloniki (Salonika)
Currency – Euro (€) of 100 cents
Population – 10,607,051 falling at 0.31 per cent a year (2020 est)
Religion – Christian (officially Greek Orthodox 81–90 per cent), Muslim 2 per cent (est)
Language – Greek (official)
Population density – 83 per sq. km (2019)
Urban population – 79.4 per cent (2019 est)
Median age (years) – 45.3 (2020 est)
National anthem – 'Ymnos eis tin Eleutherian' 'Hymn to Liberty'
National day – 25 March (Independence Day)
Death penalty – Abolished for all crimes (since 2004)
CPI score – 48 (60)
Military expenditure – US$5,227m (2018)
Conscription – 19–45 years of age, male only; 9–12 months

CLIMATE AND TERRAIN

The main areas of Greece are: Macedonia, Thrace, Epirus, Thessaly, Continental Greece, the Peloponnese and Attica on the mainland and the island of Crete. The main island groups are the Sporades, the Dodecanese (or Southern Sporades) and the Cyclades in the Aegean Sea, and the Ionian islands, including Corfu, to the west of the mainland. Low-lying coastal areas rise to a hilly or mountainous interior on the mainland and the islands. The Pindos mountains form a spine down the centre of the mainland, continuing down the Peloponnese, which is divided from the mainland by the Gulf of Corinth, the largest of the gulfs and bays indenting the coast. Elevation extremes range from 2,917m (Mt Olympus) to 0m (Mediterranean Sea). The climate is temperate; the coastline and islands have a Mediterranean climate but the weather is cooler at higher altitudes. The average temperature ranges from 6.4°C in January to 25°C in July.

POLITICS

Under the 1975 constitution, the head of state is the president, elected by the legislature for a five-year term, renewable once. The unicameral legislature, the *Vouli*, has 300 members directly elected for a four-year term.

The centre-right New Democracy party (ND) won the most seats in the 2012 legislative elections but was unable to form a coalition government; the party increased its number of seats in the subsequent election and ND leader Antonis Samaras was sworn into office in June 2012. Katerina Sakellaropoulos replaced Prokopis Pavlopoulos as president in January 2020. In the early 2015 legislative elections, called after parliament failed to initially elect a president in 2014, left-wing Syriza became the largest party in the *Vouli*, and formed a coalition with the far-right, anti-austerity Independent Greeks (ANEL). In July 2015, voters rejected the terms of a proposed EU bailout by 61.3 per cent to 38.7 per cent in a national referendum. On 20 September, the ruling coalition was re-elected following snap legislative elections in which Syriza won 145 seats, but continued economic pressures meant the ND returned to power after another snap election in July 2019.

HEAD OF STATE
President of the Hellenic Republic, Katerina Sakellaropoulos
    elected 22 January 2020, *sworn in* 13 March 2020

SELECTED GOVERNMENT MEMBERS *AS AT NOVEMBER 2020*
Prime Minister, Kyriakos Mitsotakis
Deputy Prime Minister, Panagiotis Pikrammenos
Defence, Nikos Panagiotopoulos
Finance, Christos Staikouras
Foreign Affairs, Nikos Dendias

EMBASSY OF GREECE
1A Holland Park, London W11 3TP
T 020-7229 3850 **E** gremb.lon@mfa.gr **W** www.mfa.gr/uk
Ambassador Extraordinary and Plenipotentiary, HE Dimitris
    Caramitzos-Tziras, *apptd* 2016

BRITISH EMBASSY
1 Ploutarchou Street, 106 75 Athens
T (+30) (210) 727 2600 **E** consular.athens@fco.gov.uk
W www.gov.uk/government/world/greece
Ambassador Extraordinary and Plenipotentiary, HE Kate Smith,
    CMG *apptd* 2017

ECONOMY AND TRADE

Greece experienced rapid economic growth in the final quarter of the 20th century, owing largely to increased tourism and its accession to the European Community, but has been tackling a major debt crisis, high unemployment and a thriving black market for the past decade.

In the 2000s, high government spending, low fiscal revenue and recession contributed to a growing budget deficit, which soared to over 15 per cent of GDP in 2009 and left the country particularly vulnerable in the global economic downturn. The New Democracy government failed to address the public finance crisis but the following Panhellenic Socialist Movement (Pasok) government's austerity measures, and financial assistance from the IMF and other EU countries, saw the budget deficit reduced to 9 per cent of GDP in 2011. Against a backdrop of protests, in 2012 and 2013 further austerity measures were agreed in order to pave the way for more bailout funds. In 2014, the government balanced the 2013 budget and the economy recorded the first quarter of growth since 2008, and a third bailout was agreed with EU partners in August 2015. In the same month, the Syriza government approved its first privatisation. In July 2017, the EU Commission recommended that the excessive debt procedure for Greece be closed. The economy grew slightly in 2016 and performed better between 2017 and 2019 as unemployment and the deficit fell, but the 2020 coronavirus pandemic is expected to contract the economy by around 10 per cent. Greece's black market is estimated to account for 20–25 per cent of GDP.

The service sector employs 72.4 per cent of the workforce and generates 79.1 per cent of GDP; much of this is derived from tourism, which accounts for about 18 per cent of GDP, and shipping. Greece is a net importer of energy, including oil for refining and re-export. Industrial activities, which contribute 16.9 per cent of GDP, include food and tobacco processing, textiles, chemicals, metal products, mining and petroleum production. Despite substantial industrialisation in the 20th century, agriculture still employs 12.6 per cent of the workforce, contributing 4.1 per cent of GDP. The most important agricultural products are cereals, vegetables, fruit, tobacco, olives, beef and dairy products.

The main trading partners are Germany, Russia, Italy and Turkey. Principal exports are food and drink, manufactured goods, petroleum products, chemicals and textiles. The main imports are machinery, transport equipment, fuels and chemicals.

GNI – US$217.8bn; US$20,320 per capita (2019)
Annual average growth of GDP – 1.87 per cent (2019 est)
Inflation rate – 1.1 per cent (2017 est)
Population below poverty line – 36.0 per cent (2014 est)
Unemployment – 17.3 per cent (2019 est)
Total external debt – US$506.6bn (2016 est)

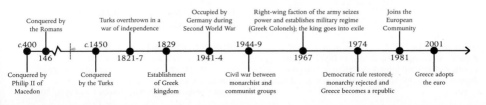

Conquered by the Romans	Turks overthrown in a war of independence	Occupied by Germany during Second World War	Right-wing faction of the army seizes power and establishes military regime (Greek Colonels); the king goes into exile	Joins the European Community
c.400	c.1450	1829	1944-9	1974	2001
146	1821-7	1941-4	1967	1981	
Conquered by Philip II of Macedon	Conquered by the Turks	Establishment of Greek kingdom	Civil war between monarchist and communist groups	Democratic rule restored; monarchy rejected and Greece becomes a republic	Greece adopts the euro

Imports – US$64,464m (2017)
Exports – US$63,696m (2017)

BALANCE OF PAYMENTS
Trade – US$768m deficit (2017)
Current Account – US$3,112m deficit (2019)

Trade with UK	2018	2019
Imports from UK	£1,169,661,159	£1,025,525,334
Exports to UK	£906,340,743	£953,791,762

COMMUNICATIONS
Airports – 68 with paved runways, the largest of which are at Athens, Thessaloniki, Iraklion (Crete) and Corfu town (Corfu)
Waterways – The main seaports are Piraeus, Thessaloniki and Patrai on the mainland, and Iraklion on Crete. An extensive ferry system connects the islands to one another and to the mainland. The 6km Corinth canal across the Corinth isthmus shortens the sea journey by 325km
Roadways and railways – There are 41,357km of paved roads, including 1,091km of motorways; 2,548km
Telecommunications – 5.1 million fixed lines and 12.2 million mobile subscriptions (2018); there were 7.8 million internet users in 2018
Internet code and IDD – gr; 30 (from UK), 44 (to UK)
Major broadcasters – In 2013 state broadcaster ERT was closed as part of the country's ongoing austerity measures. A new public broadcaster, New Hellenic Radio, Internet and TV (NERIT), was established in 2014; private broadcasters include Mega TV and Athena 984 (radio)
Press – There are three major daily news publications: *Eleftherotypia*, *Ta Nea* and *Kathimerini*
WPFI score – 28.80 (65)

EDUCATION AND HEALTH
Education is free and compulsory between the ages of six and 14, and is maintained by state grants.
Literacy rate – 97.9 per cent (2018 est)
Gross enrolment ratio (percentage of relevant age group) – primary 99.4 per cent, secondary 104.9 per cent, tertiary 142.9 per cent (2018 est)
Health expenditure (per capita) – US$1,517 (2017)
Hospital beds (per 1,000 people) – 4.3 (2015)
Life expectancy (years) – 81.1 (2020 est)
Mortality rate – 12 (2020 est)
Birth rate – 7.8 (2020 est)
Infant mortality rate – 3.7 (2020 est)
HIV/AIDS adult prevalence – 0.3 per cent (2015 est)

GRENADA

Area – 344 sq. km
Capital – St. George's; population, 39,000 (2018 est)
Currency – East Caribbean dollar (EC$) of 100 cents
Population – 113,094 rising at 0.38 per cent a year (2020 est)

Religion – Christian (Protestant 49.2 per cent, Roman Catholic 36 per cent) (est)
Language – English (official), French patois
Population density – 328 per sq. km (2019)
Urban population – 36.4 per cent (2019 est)
Median age (years) – 33.3 (2020 est)
National anthem – 'Hail Grenada'
National day – 7 February (Independence Day)
Death penalty – Retained (last used 1978)
CPI score – 53 (51)
Literacy rate – 98.6 per cent (2014 est)
Gross enrolment ratio (percentage of relevant age group) – primary 106.9 per cent, secondary 120.1 per cent, tertiary 104.6 per cent (2018 est)
Health expenditure (per capita) – US$497 (2017)
Life expectancy (years) – 75.2 (2020 est)
Mortality rate – 8.3 (2020 est)
Birth rate – 14.6 (2020 est)
Infant mortality rate – 8.9 (2020 est)

CLIMATE AND TERRAIN
The most southerly of the Windward Islands, Grenada comprises three islands: Grenada (the largest at 18km in length and 34km in width), Carriacou and Petite Martinique. Elevation extremes range from 840m (Mt St Catherine) to 0m (Caribbean Sea). The climate is subtropical, with the wettest weather from July to November. Grenada lies in a hurricane zone.

HISTORY AND POLITICS
Discovered by Columbus in 1498 and named Concepción, Grenada was colonised from the mid-17th century by the French, who subdued the native Caribs; the island was ceded to Britain in 1763. It became a crown colony in 1877, a self-governing associated state in 1967 and an independent nation on 7 February 1974.

The government was overthrown in 1979 by the New Jewel Movement led by Maurice Bishop, and the People's Revolutionary Government (PRG) was set up, with Bishop as prime minister. In 1983, disagreements within the PRG led to the deposition and execution of Bishop, whose government was replaced by a revolutionary military council. These events prompted the intervention of Caribbean and US forces. After a period of interim government, democracy was restored and a general election held in 1984. Since the restoration of democracy, power has alternated between the New National Party (NNP) and the National Democratic Congress (NDC). In 2018 the NNP won all 15 seats in parliamentary elections; Keith Mitchell returned as prime minister.

Under the 1974 constitution, reinstated in 1984, the head of state is Queen Elizabeth II, represented locally by a governor-general. The bicameral parliament consists of the House of Representatives, with 15 directly elected members, and a senate with 13 appointed members, ten of whom are appointed by the government and three by the opposition; both chambers serve a five-year term.
Governor-General, HE Dame Cécile La Grenade, GCMG, OBE apptd 2013

SELECTED GOVERNMENT MEMBERS *AS AT NOVEMBER 2020*
Prime Minister, Home Affairs, Keith Mitchell
Foreign Affairs, Oliver Joseph

HIGH COMMISSION FOR GRENADA
The Chapel, Archel Road, London W14 9QH
T 020-7385 4415 **E** office@grenada-highcommission.co.uk
W www.grenada-highcommission.co.uk
High COmmissioner, HE Lakisha Abba Grant apptd 2019

BRITISH HIGH COMMISSIONER
HE Janet Douglas, CMG, *apptd* 2017, resident at
Bridgetown, Barbados

ECONOMY AND TRADE
The economy has grown considerably in recent decades owing to diversification into tourism, offshore financial services and other service industries. St George's University provides the main source of foreign exchange earnings. Tourism and agriculture recovered from severe hurricane damage in 2004 and 2005, but the global downturn's effect on tourism and remittances caused the economy to contract in 2009 and stagnate in 2010–14. Between 2015 and 2019 public debt was reduced, GDP steadily grew and the government passed measures to ensure fiscal discipline, but the loss of tourism due to the coronavirus pandemic is expected to contract the economy by 11.8 per cent in 2020.

Agriculture now employs only 11 per cent of the workforce and produces 6.8 per cent of GDP. Industry consists of processing agricultural products, textile manufacturing, light assembly operations and construction, and contributes 15.5 per cent of GDP. The service sector, including tourism and offshore financial services, accounts for 69 per cent of employment and 77.7 per cent of GDP.

The main trading partners are the USA, Trinidad and Tobago, and other Caribbean countries. Principal exports are bananas, cocoa, nutmeg, fruit, vegetables, clothing and mace. Imports include food, manufactured goods, machinery, chemicals and fuels.

GNI – US$1.1bn; US$9,980 per capita (2019)
Annual average growth of GDP – 5.1 per cent (2017 est)
Inflation rate – 0.9 per cent (2017 est)
Unemployment – 24.0 per cent (2013)
Total external debt – US$793.5m (2017 est)
Imports – US$546m (2016)
Exports – US$594m (2016)

BALANCE OF PAYMENTS
Trade – US$47m deficit (2016)
Current Account – US$7,348m deficit (2018)

Trade with UK	2018	2019
Imports from UK	£13,626,316	£9,489,442
Exports to UK	£360,931	£372,564

COMMUNICATIONS
Airports and waterways – The main airport and port are based at St George's
Roadways – 1,127km
Telecommunications – 32,491 fixed lines and 113,177 mobile subscriptions (2017); there were 66,281 internet users in 2018
Internet code and IDD – gd; 1 473 (from UK), 011 44 (to UK)
Major broadcasters and press – The Grenada Broadcasting Network is jointly owned by the government and the Caribbean Communications Network; there are no daily newspapers but several weeklies, including *Grenada Today* and *The Grenada Informer*

GUATEMALA
República de Guatemala – Republic of Guatemala

Area – 108,889 sq. km
Capital – Guatemala City; population, 2,935,000 (2020 est)
Major cities – Mixco, Quezaltenango, Santo Tomás de Castilla, Villa Nueva
Currency – Quetzal (Q) of 100 centavos
Population – 17,153,288 rising at 1.68 per cent a year (2020 est); mestizo and European (60.1 per cent), Maya (41.7 per cent) (est)
Religion – Christian (Roman Catholic and Protestant), indigenous Maya
Language – Spanish, 23 Amerindian languages (all official)
Population density – 153 per sq. km (2019)
Urban population – 51.4 per cent (2019 est)
Median age (years) – 23.2 (2020 est)
National anthem – 'Himno Nacional de Guatemala' 'National Anthem of Guatemala'
National day – 15 September (Independence Day)
Death penalty – Retained for certain crimes (last used 2000)
CPI score – 26 (146)
Military expenditure – US$278m (2018)
Conscription – 18–50 years of age, male only; 12–24 months (selective)

CLIMATE AND TERRAIN
Narrow tropical plains on both the north (Caribbean) and south (Pacific) coasts rise to a mountainous interior in the centre and south. The mountains fall in the north to lowlands covered in tropical jungle. Elevation extremes range from 4,211m (Tajumulco volcano) to 0m (Pacific Ocean). There are 37 volcanoes, three active, in the central plateau. The climate is tropical but is cooler in the highlands. The wet season runs from May to September, when mudslides and hurricanes can occur. There are also frequent minor earth tremors and some earthquakes.

HISTORY AND POLITICS
Mayan and Aztec civilisations flourished in the area until the Spanish conquest in 1523–4, after which the area became a Spanish colony. It gained independence in 1821, and formed part of a Central American federation of former Spanish provinces from 1823 to 1839. After independence, the country was ruled by a series of dictatorships and military regimes, interspersed with periods of democratic government. In 1960 a civil war between military governments, right-wing vigilantes and left-wing guerrillas began, lasting 36 years and during which over 200,000 people died or disappeared.

In 1996 the democratically elected civilian government concluded a peace agreement with the left-wing Guatemalan Revolutionary National Unity guerrillas that ended the civil war. In 1999, an independent commission found that 93 per cent of human rights abuses during the war had been instigated by the security forces, and in 2000 and 2004 the state formally admitted guilt in several human rights cases, paying damages to the victims. At present, only a small number of the military personnel found to be responsible for the atrocities have been prosecuted.

In the 2019 legislative election, the centre-left National Unity of Hope party became the largest party in Congress, with 54 seats. After President Otto Perez Molina resigned in September 2015 following a bribery scandal, former TV comic 'Jimmy' Ernesto Morales won the October presidential election in the second round. The 2019 presidential elections were won by conservative Alejandro Giammattei. Following the results of a referendum in April 2018, the nation filed a claim with the International Court of Justice demanding sovereignty over 53 per cent of neighbouring Belize.

Under the 1986 constitution, the executive president is directly elected for a four-year term, which is not renewable. He or she is responsible to the congress and appoints the cabinet. The unicameral Congress of the Republic has 158 members, who are directly elected for a four-year term.

For foreign relations see Belize.

HEAD OF STATE
President, Alejandro Giammattei, elected 16 June 2019, sworn in 14 January 2020
Vice-President, Guillermo Castillo

SELECTED GOVERNMENT MEMBERS AS AT NOVEMBER 2020
Defence, Gen. Juan Aleman
Economy, Roberto Malouf
Foreign Affairs, Pedro Brolo

EMBASSY OF GUATEMALA
105a Westbourne Grove, London W2 4UW
T 020-7221 1525 E inglaterra@minex.gob.gt
Ambassador Extraordinary and Plenipotentiary, HE Acisclo Valladares Molina, apptd 2010

BRITISH EMBASSY
Edificio Torre Internacional, Nivel 11, 16 Calle 0–55, Zona 10, Guatemala City
T (+502) 2380 7300 E embassy@intelnett.com
W www.gov.uk/government/world/guatemala
Ambassador Extraordinary and Plenipotentiary, HE Nick Whittingham, apptd 2019

ECONOMY AND TRADE
Since the civil war, IMF funding and foreign aid have underpinned the government's economic reforms and stabilisation programmes, but the trade deficit, poor infrastructure, volcanic eruptions, security problems and high levels of corruption still deter foreign investment despite potential for tourism and increased trade. The country suffers from a huge imbalance in wealth, and over half the population lives below the poverty line and 23 per cent live in extreme poverty. Remittances, largely from Guatemala's large expatriate community in the USA, contributes about 10 per cent of GDP.

Nearly one-third of the population is dependent on agriculture, which contributes 13.3 per cent of GDP and accounts for a high proportion of exports. In recent years the climate crisis has, however, has caused drought and famine that has dented production and contributed to a growing exodus of Guatemalans migrating to the USA. Industry accounts for 23.4 per cent of GDP, and the services sector, which includes tourism, for 63.2 per cent of GDP.

The main trading partners are the USA, El Salvador, Honduras and China. The principal exports are coffee, sugar, petroleum, garments, bananas, other fruit, vegetables and cardamom. The chief imports are fuels, machinery and transport equipment, construction materials, grain, fertilisers and electricity.

GNI – US$79.5bn; US$4,610 per capita (2020)
Annual average growth of GDP – 2.8 per cent (2017 est)
Inflation rate – 4.4 per cent (2017 est)
Population below poverty line – 59.3 per cent (2014 est)
Unemployment – 2.3 per cent (2017 est)
Total external debt – US$22.92bn (2017 est)
Imports – US$20,382m (2017)
Exports – US$13,936m (2017)

BALANCE OF PAYMENTS
Trade – US$6,446m deficit (2017)
Current Account – US$1,853m surplus (2019)

Trade with UK	2018	2019
Imports from UK	£33,532,631	£59,366,179
Exports to UK	£80,099,801	£92,243,069

COMMUNICATIONS
Airports – 16; the principal international airport is based in Guatemala City
Waterways – There are 990km of navigable waterways, of which only 260km are navigable all year round; the main seaports are at Quetzal on the Pacific Ocean and Santo Tomás de Castilla on the Gulf of Honduras
Roadways and railways – 7,489km of paved roads; 800km
Telecommunications – 2.4 million fixed lines and 20.5 million mobile subscriptions (2018); there were 10.8 million internet users in 2018
Internet code and IDD – gt; 502 (from UK), 44 (to UK)
Major broadcasters – Private broadcasters dominate the media; four national television stations, including Canal 3, share the same owner
Press – There are four main daily newspapers, including Prensa Libre and El Periodico
WPFI score – 35.73 (116)

EDUCATION AND HEALTH
There are nine years of compulsory education.
Literacy rate – 95.4 per cent (2015 est)
Gross enrolment ratio (percentage of relevant age group) – primary 101.9 per cent, secondary 51.1 per cent (2019 est); tertiary 21.8 per cent (2015)
Health expenditure (per capita) – US$260 (2017)
Hospital beds (per 1,000 people) – 0.6 (2014)
Life expectancy (years) – 72.4 (2020 est)
Mortality rate – 4.9 (2020 est)
Birth rate – 23.3 (2020 est)
Infant mortality rate – 21.8 (2020 est)
HIV/AIDS adult prevalence – 0.3 per cent (2019 est)

GUINEA

République de Guinée – Republic of Guinea

Area – 245,857 sq. km
Capital – Conakry; population, 1,938,000 (2020 est)

Major cities – Guéckédou, Kankan, Nzérékoré
Currency – Guinea franc (GNF) of 100 centimes
Population – 12,527,440 rising at 2.76 per cent a year (2020 est); Fulani (33.4 per cent), Malinke (29.4 per cent), Susu (21.2 per cent) (est)
Religion – Muslim 89.1 per cent (predominantly Sunni), Christian 6.8 per cent, indigenous beliefs (animist 1.6 per cent) (est)
Language – French (official), Eastern Maninkakan, Guinea Kpelle, Northern Kissi, Pular, Susu, Toma
Population density – 51 per sq. km (2019)
Urban population – 36.5 per cent (2019 est)
Median age (years) – 19.1 (2020 est)
National anthem – 'Liberté' 'Freedom'
National day – 2 October (Independence Day)
Death penalty – Abolished for all crimes (since 2017)
CPI score – 29 (130)
Military expenditure – US$209m (2018)
Literacy rate – 30.4 per cent (2015 est)
Gross enrolment ratio (percentage of relevant age group) – primary 92.7 per cent, secondary 39.3 per cent, tertiary 11.6 per cent (2014 est)
Health expenditure (per capita) – US$34 (2017)
Hospital beds (per 1,000 people) – 0.3 (2011)
Life expectancy (years) – 63.2 (2020 est)
Mortality rate – 8.4 (2020 est)
Birth rate – 36.1 (2020 est)
Infant mortality rate – 36.1 (2020 est)
HIV / AIDS adult prevalence – 1.4 per cent (2019)

CLIMATE AND TERRAIN

Guinea has a flat coastal plain that rises to the hilly Fouta Djallon plateau in the north-west, where the Gambia and Senegal rivers rise. East of the plateau is the central savannah, the source of the Niger river, with rainforest in the south-east. Elevation extremes range from 1,752m (Mt Nimba) to 0m (Atlantic Ocean). The climate is tropical, with a wet season from April to November; the average daily temperature is 26.1°C.

POLITICS

Under the 2010 constitution, the executive president is directly elected for a five-year term, renewable once. The unicameral National Assembly has 114 members, who are directly elected for a five-year term. The president appoints the council of ministers.

The presidential election in 2010, the first democratic election since independence, was won by Alpha Condé; the second round of voting was delayed by allegations of fraud in the first round, and his victory sparked off several weeks of intercommunal violence. Delayed 2013 legislative elections resulted in Alpha Condé's ruling Rally of the Guinean People party (RPG) winning 53 seats and forming a coalition with smaller parties. Opposition parties declared the result invalid and violent demonstrations occurred in the capital. Condé was re-elected president by 58 per cent of the vote in October 2015, although the opposition alleged fraud and vote-rigging. A constitutional referendum, once again characterised by violent opposition, passed in March 2020 that reset presidential term limits; in the simultaneous parliamentary elections RPG won 79 seats. Condé subsequently won the October 2020 presidential election, which opposition groups alleged was fraudulent, and secured a third consecutive term in office.

HEAD OF STATE

President, Alpha Condé, *elected* 7 November 2010, *sworn in* 21 December, *re-elected* 17 October 2015, 18 October 2020

SELECTED GOVERNMENT MEMBERS *AS AT NOVEMBER 2020*
Prime Minister, Ibrahima Kassory Fofana
Economy and Finance, Mamady Camara
Foreign Affairs, Mamadi Touré
Defence, Mohamed Diane

EMBASSY OF THE REPUBLIC OF GUINEA

239 Old Marylebone Road, London NW1 5QT
T 020-7258 9640 **E** embassyofguinea@gmail.com
Ambassador Extraordinary and Plenipotentiary, HE Paul Goa Zoumanigui, *apptd* 2013

BRITISH EMBASSY

Villa 1, Residence 2000, Corniche Sud Conakry
T (+224) 6335 5329 **E** britembconakry@hotmail.com
W www.gov.uk/government/world/guinea
Ambassador Extraordinary and Plenipotentiary, HE David McIlroy, *apptd* 2019

ECONOMY AND TRADE

Although Guinea is the second-largest producer of bauxite in the world and despite an abundance of natural resources, including fertile soil, mineral deposits, high-grade iron ore and hydroelectric potential, decades of mismanagement and corruption have left the economy undeveloped. Foreign aid was suspended following the 2008 coup and resumed in 2012 following democratic elections in 2010. The 2014–15 Ebola outbreak is thought to have cost the economy US$540m (£348m), due to the disruption caused to trade and a reduction in investor confidence; nevertheless, GDP grew by 6–7 per cent between 2017 and 2019 because of increased mining, agricultural output and public investment.

Mining attracts foreign investment and a new mining code introduced in 2011 and amended in 2013 includes provisions to combat corruption. Agriculture, much of it at subsistence level, employs 76 per cent of the population and contributes 19.8 per cent of GDP. Industry accounts for 32.1 per cent of GDP, mostly through mining and the processing of minerals and agricultural produce.

The main trading partners are China, Ghana and EU countries, especially the Netherlands. Principal exports are bauxite, gold, diamonds, coffee, fish and other agricultural products. The main imports are petroleum products, metals, machinery, transport equipment, textiles, grain and other foodstuffs.

GNI – US$12.1bn; US$950 per capita (2019)
Annual average growth of GDP – 8.2 per cent (2017 est)
Inflation rate – 8.9 per cent (2017 est)

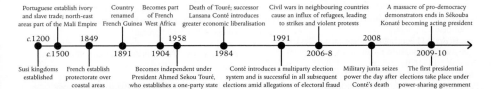

Portuguese establish ivory and slave trade; north-east areas part of the Mali Empire	Country renamed French Guinea	Becomes part of French West Africa	Death of Touré; successor Lansana Conté introduces greater economic liberalisation	Civil wars in neighbouring countries cause an influx of refugees, leading to strikes and violent protests		A massacre of pro-democracy demonstrators ends in Sékouba Konaté becoming acting president
*c.*1200	1849		1958		1991	2008
*c.*1500	1891	1904	1984		2006-8	2009-10
Susi kingdoms established	French establish protectorate over coastal areas	Becomes independent under President Ahmed Sekou Touré, who establishes a one-party state	Conté introduces a multiparty election system and is successful in all subsequent elections amid allegations of electoral fraud	Military junta seizes power the day after Conté's death		The first presidential elections take place under power-sharing government

Population below poverty line – 55.2 per cent (2012 est)
Unemployment rate – 2.7 per cent (2017 est)
Total external debt – US$1.458bn (2017 est)
Imports – US$5,138m (2016)
Exports – US$2,467m (2016)

BALANCE OF PAYMENTS
Trade – US$2,670m deficit (2016)
Current Account – US$314m deficit (2019)

Trade with UK	2018	2019
Imports from UK	£21,710,029	£24,510,143
Exports to UK	£148,156	£599,503

COMMUNICATIONS

Airports – Four with paved runways; the principal airport is at Conakry
Waterways – The major seaports are Conakry and Kamsar; there are 1,300km of waterways
Roadways and railways – 3,346km of paved roadways;1,086km
Telecommunications – 18,000 fixed lines (2012) and 12 million mobile telephone lines in use (2018); there were 2.1 million internet users in 2018
Internet code and IDD – gn; 224 (from UK), 44 (to UK)
Major broadcasters – Radiodiffusion-Télévision Guinéenne is the principal, state-run broadcaster
Press – Horoya is the main government-owned daily
WPFI score – 34.34 (110)

GUINEA-BISSAU

Republica da Guine-Bissau – Republic of Guinea-Bissau

Area – 36,125 sq. km
Capital – Bissau; population, 600,000 (2020 est)
Major cities – Bolama, Gabú
Currency – West African CFA franc of 100 centimes
Population – 1,927,104 rising at 2.51 per cent a year (2020 est); Fulani (28.5 per cent), Balanta (22.5 per cent), Mandinga (14.7 per cent), Papel (9.1 per cent), Manjaco (8.3 per cent) (est)
Religion – Muslim 45.1 per cent, Christian 22.1 per cent, indigenous beliefs (animist 14.9 per cent) (est)
Language – Portuguese (official), Creole, Pular, Mandingo
Population density – 67 per sq. km (2020)
Urban population – 43.8 per cent (2020 est)
Median age (years) – 18 (2020 est)
National anthem – 'Esta e a Nossa Patria Bem Amada' 'This is Our Beloved Country'
National day – 24 September (Independence Day)
Death penalty – Abolished for all crimes (since 1993)
CPI score – 18 (168)
Military expenditure – US$17.7m (2015)
Conscription – 18–25 years of age (selective)

Literacy rate – 77.3 per cent (2015 est)
Gross enrolment ratio (percentage of relevant age group) – primary 118.7 per cent (2010 est)
Health expenditure (per capita) – US$52 (2017)
Hospital beds (per 1,000 people) – 1 (2009)
Life expectancy (years) – 62.8 (2020 est)
Mortality rate – 7.9 (2020 est)
Birth rate – 36.9 (2020 est)
Infant mortality rate – 36.9 (2020 est)
HIV / AIDS adult prevalence – 3.4 per cent (2019 est)

CLIMATE AND TERRAIN

Guinea-Bissau has a low coastal plain that rises to savannah in the east. The coast is heavily indented and covered with mangrove swamps. Elevation extremes range from 300m (in the north-east) to 0m (Atlantic Ocean). The climate is tropical, with a wet season from July to September.

HISTORY AND POLITICS

A part of the ancient African empire of Mali, Guinea-Bissau was once the kingdom of Gabu, which became independent of the empire in 1546 and survived until 1867. In 1446, Portuguese traders discovered the coast and established slave trading there, subsequently administering Guinea-Bissau with the Cape Verde islands; it became a separate colony in 1879. After a guerrilla war led by the left-wing African Party for the Independence of Guinea and Cape Verde (PAIGC), Guinea-Bissau declared independence unilaterally in 1973 and Portugal recognised this in 1974.

After independence Guinea-Bissau became a one-party socialist state under the PAIGC, led by Luis Cabral. He was deposed in 1980, in a military coup led by General Joao Vieira, and the country was under military rule until 1994. A multiparty system was introduced in 1991 after popular agitation, but the following 15 years saw a short civil war (1998–9) and two more military coups (1999, 2003); democratic government was restored in 2004–5.

Following a military coup in April 2012, Guinea-Bissau was ruled by the Transitional National Council. The 2014 legislative election was won by the formerly-Marxist Independence party (PAIGC), whose candidate, Jose Mario Vaz, was elected president. However, internal political instability led to a series of new governments and prime ministers. In the November 2018 legislative elections, which were delayed until March 2019, the PAIGC lost its majority but remained the largest party, forming a coalition government with three other parties. The PAIGC, having ruled the country since independence, lost the contested December 2019 presidential election to Madem G15 candidate and former prime minister Umaro Sissoco Embalò; the party was formed in 2018 by former members of the PAIGC.

Under the 1999 constitution, the executive president is directly elected for a five-year term, with no term limits. The president appoints the council of ministers. The unicameral National People's Assembly has 102 members, who are directly elected for a four-year term.

HEAD OF STATE
President, Umaro Sissoco Embalò, elected 29 December 2019, sworn in 27 February 2020

SELECTED GOVERNMENT MEMBERS AS AT NOVEMBER 2020
Prime Minister, Nuno Gomes Nabian
Economy and Finance, Geraldo Joao Martins
Foreign Affairs, Suzi Barbosa

EMBASSY OF THE REPUBLIC OF GUINEA-BISSAU
94 rue St Lazare, 75009 Paris, France
T (+33) (1) 4874 3639
Ambassador Extraordinary and Plenipotentiary, vacant

BRITISH CONSULATE
Ambassador Extraordinary and Plenipotentiary, HE George
  Hodgson, *appdt* 2015, resident at Dakar, Senegal

ECONOMY AND TRADE
The economy is in a poor state owing to decades of
mismanagement and corruption, the devastating effects of the
1998–9 civil war and ongoing political instability. Successful
elections in 2014 allowed the country to resume receiving
international aid, but subsequent political turmoil has resulted
in weak governance and limited international assistance. A
planned three-year IMF extended credit programme was
resumed in 2017 but its major donors (the EU, World Bank
and African Development Bank) later withdrew their support.
Over one-third of the country live below the absolute poverty
line.

   Although Guinea-Bissau has mineral resources, including oil,
the high cost of exploiting these inhibits development and the
economy is based almost exclusively on agriculture (mainly
cashew nuts, which provides over 80 per cent of export
receipts) and fishing; drug trafficking is the most lucrative
industry in the country, and illegal logging is also common.
The agricultural sector employs 82 per cent of the population
and contributes half of GDP. The industrial sector generates
13.1 per cent of GDP, mainly through processing agricultural
products, and beer and soft drink production.

   The main trading partners are India (67.1 per cent of exports),
Portugal and Vietnam. Principal exports include fish, cashew
nuts, peanuts, palm kernels and timber. The main imports are
foodstuffs, machinery and transport equipment, and fuels.
GNI – US$1.6bn; US$820 per capita (2019)
Annual average growth of GDP – 5.9 per cent (2017 est)
Inflation rate – 1.1 per cent (2017 est)
Population below poverty line – 67 per cent (2015 est)
Imports – US$218m (2016)
Exports – US$185m (2016)

BALANCE OF PAYMENTS
Trade – US$33m deficit (2016)
Current Account – US$1,894m deficit (2018)

Trade with UK	2018	2019
Imports from UK	£732,523	£483,271
Exports to UK	£134,714	£297,514

COMMUNICATIONS
Airports – Two; the principal airport is at Bissau
Waterways – The main rivers are navigable for part of their
lengths, and shallow-draught craft can access much of the
interior via creeks and inlets; Bissau is the main seaport
Roadways – There are 453km of paved roads
Telecommunications – 5,000 fixed lines (2014) and 1.5 million
mobile subscriptions (2018); there were 66,169 internet users
in 2018
Internet code and IDD – gw; 245 (from UK), 44 (to UK)
Major broadcasters – The state-run Radio Televisao de Guine-
Bissau is the main broadcaster
Press – Major newspapers include state-run weekly *No Pintcha*
and the privately run *Gazeta de Noticias*
WPFI score – 32.06 (94)

GUYANA
Cooperative Republic of Guyana

Area – 214,969 sq. km
Capital – Georgetown; population, 110,000 (2018 est)
Major towns – Linden, New Amsterdam
Currency – Guyana dollar (G$) of 100 cents
Population – 750,204 rising at 0.72 per cent a year (2020
  est)
Religion – Christian (Protestant 34.8 per cent, Roman
  Catholic 7.1 per cent per cent), Hindu 24.8 per cent,
  Muslim 6.8 per cent (est)
Language – English (official), Amerindian dialects, Creole,
  Indian dialects, Chinese
Population density – 4 per sq. km (2019)
Urban population – 26.7 per cent (2019 est)
Median age (years) – 27.5 (2020 est)
National anthem – 'Dear Land of Guyana, of Rivers and Plains'
National day – 23 February (Republic Day)
Death penalty – Retained
CPI score – 40 (85)
Military expenditure – US$59.8m (2018)
Literacy rate – 94.4 per cent (2015 est)
Gross enrolment ratio (percentage of relevant age group) – primary
  97.8 per cent, secondary 97.7 per cent, tertiary 11.6 per
  cent (2012 est)
Health expenditure (per capita) – US$231 (2017)
Life expectancy (years) – 69.5 (2020 est)
Mortality rate – 7.5 (2020 est)
Birth rate – 15.5 (2020 est)
Infant mortality rate – 27.6 (2020 est)
HIV/AIDS adult prevalence – 1.4 per cent (2019 est)

CLIMATE AND TERRAIN
The land rises from a narrow coastal plain to forested
highlands in the west and savannah on the southern border;
about 90 per cent of the population lives on the coastal plain,
which constitutes 5 per cent of the land area. Around 79 per
cent of the country is covered by rainforest. Elevation
extremes range from 2,835m (Mt Roraima) to 0m (Atlantic
Ocean). The climate is tropical, with an average daily
temperature of 26°C, and two wet seasons, from April to July
and from November to January.

HISTORY AND POLITICS
Carib and Arawak peoples inhabited the coastal region of
Guyana when Dutch merchants founded the first European
settlement in the late 16th century. Guyana became an
important producer of sugar, grown on plantations worked
first by African slaves and then, after the abolition of slavery
in 1834, by indentured labourers, mostly from India. Several

areas were ceded to Britain in 1815, and consolidated as British Guiana in 1831. The country became independent, as Guyana, on 26 May 1966, and became a republic in 1970.

Guyana's first political party, the People's Progressive Party (PPP), split along ethnic lines in the 1950s; the PPP continued as a predominantly Indian party under Cheddi Jagan, while those of African descent formed the People's National Congress (PNC), led by Forbes Burnham. Burnham dominated political life after independence, first as prime minister (1966–80) and then as executive president until his death in 1985. Under his autocratic rule, politics became characterised by suspect elections and a disregard for civil liberties and human rights. The PPP's electoral victory in 1992 ended the PNC's monopoly of power but persistent ethnic tensions continue to destabilise politics.

The 2011 legislative election was won by the PPP, securing its fifth consecutive term of office but without an overall majority. In the May 2015 legislative elections, the Partnership for National Unity and Alliance for Change coalition (APNU-AFC) emerged as the single largest party, and APNU's leader, David Granger, was sworn in as president. The government narrowly lost a vote of no confidence in December 2018 and was constitutionally obliged to hold fresh elections by mid-March 2019, but the coalition challenged the validity of the vote, which was subsequently rejected by the Caribbean Court of Justice. Allegations of fraud in the delayed March 2020, in which Granger claimed victory, resulted in a five-month legal battle that eventually declared the PPP the winners, with 33 seats, and Irfaan Ali was sworn in as president in August. The election stakes had been raised following the discovery of vast offshore oil reserves.

Under the 1980 constitution, the executive president is nominated by the majority party in the legislature after each legislative election, and serves a five-year term with no term limits. The unicameral National Assembly has 65 members serving five-year terms.

HEAD OF STATE
President, Irfaan Ali, *sworn in* 2 August 2020
Vice-President, Finance, Bharrat Jagdeo

SELECTED GOVERNMENT MEMBERS *AS AT NOVEMBER 2020*
Prime Minister, Mark Phillips
Foreign Affairs, Hugh Todd

HIGH COMMISSION FOR GUYANA
3 Palace Court, Bayswater Road, London W2 4LP
T 020-7229 7684 **E** info@guyanahclondon.co.uk
W www.guyanahclondon.co.uk
High Commissioner, HE Frederick Hamley Case, *apptd* 2016

BRITISH HIGH COMMISSION
PO Box 10849, 44 Main Street, Georgetown
T (+1592) 226 5881 **W** www.gov.uk/government/world/guyana
High Commissioner, HE Gregory Quinn, *apptd* 2015

ECONOMY AND TRADE
The economy grew from 2001 to 2008 owing to expansion in agriculture and mining, the cancellation of over one-third of Guyana's external debt, and increases in foreign direct investment and remittances from expatriate workers. Attempts to develop tourism, hindered by poor infrastructure and skills shortages, are also likely to be offset by new investment in gold mining and offshore oil extraction. The discovery of offshore oil reserves, which has made Guyana the country with the most amount of oil per person in the world, and its exploitation will likely result in significant growth. Prior to

the coronavirus pandemic, the IMF expected the economy to grow by 52.8 per cent in 2020. Prior to 2020, nearly 60 per cent of GDP was derived from gold, sugar, bauxite, prawns, timber and rice, many of which were weather-dependent and vulnerable to fluctuations in prices. Sugar production is undergoing a planned and sizeable reduction.

Agriculture accounted for 15.4 per cent of GDP and provided the raw materials for the major industries of sugar processing and rice milling. Non-agricultural activities are growing in importance, and include bauxite and gold mining, forestry, fishing and textile manufacturing; industry accounted for 15.3 per cent of GDP.

The main trading partners are the USA, Trinidad and Tobago, Canada and China. Principal exports include sugar, gold, bauxite, alumina, rice, shrimp, molasses, rum and timber. The main imports are manufactured goods, machinery, fuel and food.

GNI – US$4.1bn; US$5,180 per capita (2019)
Annual average growth of GDP – 2.1 per cent (2017 est)
Inflation rate – 2.0 per cent (2017 est)
Unemployment – 11.1 per cent (2013 est)
Total external debt – US$1.69bn (2017 est)
Imports – US$2,085m (2017)
Exports – US$1,569m (2017)

BALANCE OF PAYMENTS
Trade – US$515m deficit (2017)
Current Account – US$1,696m deficit (2019)

Trade with UK	2018	2019
Imports from UK	£28,621,720	£46,628,497
Exports to UK	£29,078,418	£33,446,004

COMMUNICATIONS
Airports and waterways – 11; 330km of navigable waterways (principally the Berbice, Demerara and Essequibo rivers) form the main arteries of communication
Roadways – There are 799km of paved roads
Telecommunications – 135,795 fixed lines and 643,210 mobile subscriptions (2017); there were 276,498 internet users in 2018
Internet code and IDD – gy; 592 (from UK), 1 44 (to UK)
Major broadcasters – The state-owned National Communications Network operates national television and radio networks
Press – There are three major daily newspapers: the government-owned *Guyana Chronicle, Stabroek News* and *Kaieteur News*
WPFI score – 26.63 (49)

HAITI
République d'Haïti / Repiblik d'Ayiti – Republic of Haiti

Area – 27,750 sq. km
Capital – Port-au-Prince; population, 2,774,000 (2020 est)

Major cities – Cap-Haïtien, Gonaïves, Pétionville
Currency – Gourde (G) of 100 centimes
Population – 11,067,777 rising at 1.26 per cent a year (2020 est)
Religion – Christian (Roman Catholic 54.7 per cent, Protestant 28.5 per cent) (est); many Christians also practise Voodoo
Language – French, Creole (both official)
Population density – 404 per sq. km (2019)
Urban population – 56.2 per cent (2019 est)
Median age (years) – 24.1 (2020 est)
National anthem – 'La Dessalinienne' 'The Song of Dessalines'
National day – 1 January (Independence Day)
Death penalty – Abolished for all crimes (since 1987)
CPI score – 18 (168)
Literacy rate – 61.7 per cent (2016 est)
Health expenditure (per capita) – US$62 (2017)
Hospital beds (per 1,000 people) – 0.3 (2011)
Life expectancy (years) – 65.3 (2020 est)
Mortality rate – 7.4 (2020 est)
Birth rate – 21.7 (2020 est)
Infant mortality rate – 42.6 (2020 est)
HIV/AIDS adult prevalence – 1.9 per cent (2019 est)

CLIMATE AND TERRAIN

The country occupies the western third of the island of Hispaniola. The terrain is mountainous, with coastal plains and a large central plateau. Elevation extremes range from 2,680m (Châine de la Selle) to 0m (Caribbean Sea). The climate is tropical, and semi-arid where the eastern mountains block the trade winds, with two wet seasons (April–June, August–November) and a hurricane season from June to November.

POLITICS

Under the 1987 constitution, the president is directly elected for a five-year term that may be renewed once but not consecutively. The bicameral National Assembly comprises a lower house, the Chamber of Deputies, with 119 members directly elected for a four-year term, and the senate, with 30 members directly elected for a six-year term; one-third of the senators are elected every two years. The president appoints the prime minister, who must be approved by the legislature.

After a delay of more than three years legislative elections were held in late 2015, with the Haitian Tet Kale Party (PHTK) winning the largest number of seats in the Chamber of Deputies (13). In January 2017, the country's electoral commission confirmed that Jovenel Moïse of the PHTK had won November 2016's presidential election with 55.6 per cent of the vote. Violent protests against Prime Minister Jack Guy Lafontant's plans to raise fuel prices forced him from power in July 2018, and he was replaced by Jean-Henry Céant. More violent unrest followed in February 2019 over corruption allegations concerning a missing £3.1bn development fund, and in March the government was ousted after comprehensively losing a vote of no confidence. Elections that were planned for 2019 have been delayed until 2021, as President Moïse sought constitutional changes to concentrate more power in his office; in January 2020 he started ruling by decree.

HEAD OF STATE
President, Jovenel Moïse, *elected* 20 November 2016, *sworn in* 7 February 2017

SELECTED GOVERNMENT MEMBERS *AS AT NOVEMBER 2020*
Prime Minister, Joseph Jouthe
Economy and Finance, Michel Patrick Boisvert
Foreign Affairs, Claude Joseph
Interior, Audin Fils Bernadel

EMBASSY OF THE REPUBLIC OF HAITI
21 Bloomsbury Way, London WC1A 2TH
T 020-3771 1427
    Ambassador Extraordinary and Plenipotentiary, vacant

BRITISH AMBASSADOR
HE Sharon Campbell, *apptd* 2015, resident at Santo Domingo, Dominican Republic

ECONOMY AND TRADE

The country is the poorest in the Americas with most of the population living below the poverty line and more than half in abject poverty. Its economy, damaged by years of political instability, violence and corruption as well as the natural disasters to which it is vulnerable, experienced moderate growth from 2005. However the 2010 earthquake and Hurricane Matthew in October 2016 reversed these gains, devastating infrastructure and continuing the government's dependence on foreign aid; foreign debt was written off in 2009 and 2010. The economy contracted slightly in 2019, and this is set to continue into 2020 partly due to the coronavirus pandemic. Remittances from the estimated one in six Haitians who live abroad, principally in the USA, are the main source of foreign revenue, worth around a quarter of GDP. Two-fifths of the population depend on agriculture – predominantly small-scale subsistence farming – which contributes 22.1 per cent of GDP. Industrial activities include production of textiles and garments, sugar refining, flour milling and assembly of goods, especially vehicle parts, for re-export.

The main trading partners are the USA (which takes 80.6 per cent of exports) and China. Garments account for over 90 per cent of exports, but Haiti also exports manufactured goods, essential oils, cocoa, mangoes and coffee. The main imports are food, manufactured goods, machinery and transport equipment, fuels and raw materials.

GNI – US$8.9bn; US$790 per capita (2019)
Annual average growth of GDP – 1.2 per cent (2017 est)
Inflation rate – 14.7 per cent (2017 est)
Population below poverty line – 58.5 per cent (2012 est)
Total external debt – US$2.762bn (2017 est)
Imports – US$4,723m (2017)
Exports – US$1,623m (2017)

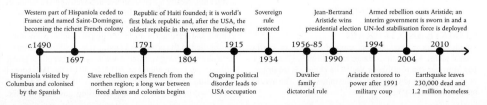

Western part of Hispaniola ceded to France and named Saint-Domingue, becoming the richest French colony	Republic of Haiti founded; it is world's first black republic and, after the USA, the oldest republic in the western hemisphere	Sovereign rule restored	Jean-Bertrand Aristide wins presidential election	Armed rebellion ousts Aristide; an interim government is sworn in and a UN-led stabilisation force is deployed
*c.*1490	1791	1915	1956-85	1994	2010
1697	1804	1934	1990	2004	
Hispaniola visited by Columbus and colonised by the Spanish	Slave rebellion expels French from the northen region; a long war between freed slaves and colonists begins	Ongoing political disorder leads to USA occupation	Duvalier family dictatorial rule	Aristide restored to power after 1991 military coup	Earthquake leaves 230,000 dead and 1.2 million homeless

BALANCE OF PAYMENTS
Trade – US$3,100m deficit (2017)
Current Account – US$72m surplus (2019)

Trade with UK	2018	2019
Imports from UK	£11,038,339	£9,769,492
Exports to UK	£4,840,607	£6,532,819

COMMUNICATIONS
Airports and waterways – Four; the international airports and main ports are at Port-au-Prince and Cap-Haïtien
Roadways – There are 768km of paved roads
Telecommunications – 5,922 fixed lines and 6.4 million mobile subscriptions (2018); there were 3.5 million internet users in 2018
Internet code and IDD – ht; 509 (from UK), 44 (to UK)
Major broadcasters – The government-owned Television Nationale d'Haiti broadcasts in Creole, French and Spanish
Press – There are two daily newspapers, *Le Matin* and *Le Nouvelliste*
WPFI score – 30.20 (83)

HONDURAS

República de Honduras – Republic of Honduras

Area – 112,090 sq. km
Capital – Tegucigalpa; population, 1,444,000 (2020 est)
Major cities – Choloma, El Progreso, La Ceiba, San Pedro Sula
Currency – Lempira of 100 centavos
Population – 9,235,340 rising at 1.27 per cent a year (2020 est)
Religion – Christian (Roman Catholic 46 per cent, Protestant 41 per cent) (est)
Language – Spanish (official), Amerindian dialects
Population density – 86 per sq. km (2019)
Urban population – 57.7 per cent (2019 est)
Median age (years) – 24.4 (2020 est)
National anthem – 'Himno Nacional de Honduras' 'National Anthem of Honduras'
National day – 15 September (Independence Day)
Death penalty – Abolished for all crimes (since 1956)
CPI score – 26 (146)
Military expenditure – US$410m (2018 est)

CLIMATE AND TERRAIN
Honduras has a mountainous interior, falling to narrow coastal plains. Elevation extremes range from 2,870m (Cerro Las Minas) to 0m (Caribbean Sea). The climate is subtropical in the lowlands and temperate in the mountains. The average temperature is 24.4°C.

HISTORY AND POLITICS
Honduras was home to part of the Mayan civilisation between the fourth and ninth centuries AD. Christopher Columbus first set foot on the American mainland at Trujillo in Honduras in 1502, but it was 1525 before Spanish colonisation began. In 1821, the country gained independence from Spain, and it was part of a Central American federation of former Spanish colonies from 1823 until it became fully independent in 1839. Thereafter the country underwent periods of political instability interspersed with military rule until 1982, when a civilian government took office. During the civil wars in Nicaragua and El Salvador, Honduras acted as a base for US forces and anti-Sandinista Contras, and there was a marked decline in its respect for human rights. The end of the civil wars led to a decline in the power of the army, which was brought under civilian control in 1999, but there are still very high levels of violent crime. In 2011 congress voted to allow troops to take on police responsibilities in an attempt to curb the high murder rate.

In November 2013, Juan Orlando Hernández was declared the winner of the presidential election, and was re-elected in November 2017. Hernández claimed a 2015 court ruling allowed him to stand for re-election despite a prohibition in the constitution, thus ending presidential term limits. His right-wing National Party remained the largest party in Congress in simultaneous legislative elections, despite international pressure for a fresh vote over allegations of corruption, fraud and state-sponsored killings.

Under the 1982 constitution, the executive president is directly elected for a four-year term, and appoints the government. The unicameral National Congress has 128 members, directly elected by proportional representation for a four-year term.

HEAD OF STATE
President, Juan Orlando Hernández, *elected* 24 November 2013, *took office* 27 January 2014, *re-elected* 26 November 2017
First Vice-President, Ricardo Antonio Alvarez

SELECTED GOVERNMENT MEMBERS *AS AT NOVEMBER 2020*
Economy and Finance, Arnaldo Castillo
Foreign Relations, Lisandro Rosales

EMBASSY OF HONDURAS
4th Floor, 136 Baker Street, London W1U 6UD
T 020-7486 4880 **E** hondurasuk@lineone.net
W www.honduras.embassyhomepage.com/
Ambassador Extraordinary and Plenipotentiary, HE Ivan Romero-Martinez, *apptd* 2008

BRITISH AMBASSADOR
HE Nicholas Whittingham, *apptd* 2019, resident at Guatemala City, Guatemala

ECONOMY AND TRADE
The country has a huge imbalance in wealth and high levels of corruption and violent crime, often connected with drug-trafficking. Nearly 65 per cent live in poverty and remittances from expatriate workers are a significant source of GDP. Economic activity is heavily dependent on the USA; a drop in exports and remittances due to the global economic downturn contributed to the economy's contraction in 2009. Economic difficulties led to government workers and suppliers going without pay in the winter of 2012. In 2014, the IMF agreed to provide the government with loans totalling US$189m (£120.7m) in order to pay off increasing government debt,

and prior to 2020 the debt-to-GDP ratio had been falling. Investor confidence had been growing and the economy outperformed expectations between 2010 and 2018, but is likely to contract by around 6.6 per cent in 2020.

Although still dependent on agriculture, fishing and forestry, whose products form the basis of industrial activity and are the main exports, the economy is gradually diversifying into offshore assembly for re-export and tourism. Agriculture employs 39.2 per cent of the workforce and contributes 14.2 per cent of GDP. Industry accounts for 28.8 per cent of GDP and 20.9 per cent of employment, and the services sector for 57 per cent of GDP and 39.8 per cent of employment.

The main trading partner is the USA, which receives 34.5 per cent of exports and provides 40.3 per cent of imports. Principal exports are garments, coffee, shrimp, wire harnessing, cigars, bananas, gold, palm oil, fruit, lobster and timber. The main imports are machinery and transport equipment, industrial raw materials, chemical products, fuels and foodstuffs.

GNI – US$23.3bn; US$2,390 per capita (2019)
Annual average growth of GDP – 4.8 per cent (2017 est)
Inflation rate – 3.9 per cent (2017 est)
Unemployment – 5.6 per cent (2017 est)
Population below poverty line – 29.6 per cent (2014 est)
Total external debt – US$8.625bn (2017 est)
Imports – US$10,700m (2017)
Exports – US$7,362m (2017)

BALANCE OF PAYMENTS
Trade – US$3,337m deficit (2017)
Current Account – US$346m deficit (2019)

Trade with UK	2018	2019
Imports from UK	£11,511,857	£10,307,087
Exports to UK	£126,596,350	£131,037,264

COMMUNICATIONS
Airports – 13; the principal airports are at Tegucigalpa, La Ceiba and San Pedro Sula
Waterways – Honduras has ports on its Caribbean (Puerto Castilla, Puerto Cortes, Tela) and Pacific (San Lorenzo) coasts, and 465km of navigable waterways (mostly by small boats)
Roadways and railways – There are 3,367km of paved roads; 699km of railways
Telecommunications – 532,004 fixed lines and 7.6 million mobile subscriptions (2018); there were 2.9 million internet users in 2018
Internet code and IDD – hn; 504 (from UK), 44 (to UK)
Major broadcasters – Televicentro operates several channels throughout the country; CBC Canal 6, Vica TV and Sotel Canal 11 are all private broadcasters; private radio stations include Radio America and Radio HRN
Press – There are four private daily newspapers, including *El Heraldo* and *La Prensa*
WPFI score – 48.20 (148)

EDUCATION AND HEALTH
Primary and secondary education is free of charge; primary education is compulsory between the ages of six and 11.
Literacy rate – 87.2 per cent (2018 est)
Gross enrolment ratio (percentage of relevant age group) – primary 91.5 per cent, secondary 66.2 per cent (2019 est); tertiary 26.2 per cent (2018 est)
Health expenditure (per capita) – US$196 (2017)
Hospital beds (per 1,000 people) – 0.7 (2014)
Life expectancy (years) – 74.6 (2020 est)
Mortality rate – 4.7 (2020 est)

Birth rate – 18.5 (2020 est)
Infant mortality rate – 14.6 (2020 est)
HIV/AIDS adult prevalence – 0.3 per cent (2019 est)

HUNGARY

Magyarorszag – Republic of Hungary

Area – 93,028 sq. km
Capital – Budapest; population, 1,768,000 (2020 est)
Major cities – Debrecen, Gyor, Miskolc, Pecs, Szeged
Currency – Forint of 100 filler
Population – 9,771,827 falling at 0.28 per cent a year (2020 est)
Religion – Christian (Roman Catholic 37.2 per cent, Calvinist 11.6 per cent, Lutheran 2.2 per cent) (est)
Language – Hungarian (official), English, German, Russian, Romanian, French
Population density – 108 per sq. km (2019)
Urban population – 71.6 per cent (2019 est)
Median age (years) – 43.6 (2020 est)
National anthem – 'Himnusz' 'Hymn'
National day – 20 August (St Stephen's Day)
Death penalty – Abolished for all crimes (since 1990)
CPI score – 44 (76)
Military expenditure – US$1,642m (2018)

CLIMATE AND TERRAIN
Hungary lies mostly on the vast plain created by the Danube and Tisza rivers, with hills and mountains along the northern border. Elevation extremes range from 1,014m (Mt Kekes) to 78m (river Tisza). Lake Balaton lies in the west. Average temperatures range from −0.6°C in January to 21.1°C in July.

POLITICS
The 1949 constitution was superseded in 2012 by a new constitution approved by the legislature in April 2011. Parliament has since acted to limit the powers of the constitutional court following clashes, notably on electoral law. The president is elected by the legislature for a five-year term, renewable once; under the new constitution, the president nominates the prime minister who is then elected by parliament. The unicameral National Assembly has 199 members directly elected for a four-year term.

The 2010 legislative election was won by the opposition Fidesz and Christian Democratic People's Party bloc and it formed a government under Viktor Orban (prime minister 1998–2002), who was re-elected in 2014 and 2018 on an anti-immigration platform. Orban's right-wing populism has been marked by national conservatism and euroscepticism, as he has sought to form an 'illiberal' polity. Fidesz regained its two-thirds 'super majority' in the April 2018 elections, the first time since 2015. The 2010 presidential election was won outright at the first vote by Pal Schmitt of the Fidesz party,

Most of kingdom conquered by Ottoman Turks — Dual monarchy created between Austrian and Hungarian crowns; period of economic success — Austro-Hungarian Empire defeated in the First World War — Joins Axis powers in the Second World War — Opens border with Austria, indirectly triggering the fall of communism throughout eastern Europe; communist rule ends soon after

c.1000   1526   1699   1867   1918   1920   1941   1944   1949   1989   1999   2004

Settled by Magyar tribes, becomes a Christian kingdom under St Stephen — Turks expelled by Habsburgs; country becomes a province in dynasty's central European empire — Becomes a kingdom with Admiral Horthy as regent — Horthy deposed after seeking armistice with USSR — Becomes a communist state aligned with the Soviet Union — Joins NATO — Joins the EU

who subsequently resigned from office in April 2012 after admitting he had plagiarised much of his doctoral thesis; the Fidesz party elected Janos Ader as his replacement, and Ader was re-elected in 2017.

HEAD OF STATE
President, Janos Ader, *elected* 2 May 2012, *sworn in* 10 May 2012, *re-elected* 13 March 2017

SELECTED GOVERNMENT MEMBERS *AS AT NOVEMBER 2020*
Prime Minister, Viktor Orban
Deputy Prime Ministers, Mihaly Varga *(Economy)*; Sandor Pinter *(Interior)*; Zsolt Semjen
Defence, Tibor Benko
Foreign Affairs, Peter Szijjarto

EMBASSY OF THE REPUBLIC OF HUNGARY
35 Eaton Place, London SW1X 8BY
T 020-7201 3440 E mission.lon@mfa.gov.hu W www.london.gov.hu
Ambassador Extraordinary and Plenipotentiary, HE Ferenc Kumin, apptd 2020

BRITISH EMBASSY
Harmincad Utca 6, 1051 Budapest
T (+36) (1) 266 2888 W www.gov.uk/government/world/hungary
Ambassador Extraordinary and Plenipotentiary, HE Iain Lindsay, OBE, apptd 2016

ECONOMY AND TRADE
Hungary made a successful transition to a market economy after 1989, attracting high levels of foreign direct investment. Largely dependent on the export market, since 2010 the government has increased its management of the economy. Strong economic growth started to slow in 2006–7, partly as a result of a government austerity programme intended to reduce the budget deficit and public debt. The global economic downturn left Hungary struggling to service both state and private debt in the face of rising interest rates and falling export demand, and the government had to obtain international assistance in 2008. By 2013, Hungary had cut its deficit to under 3 per cent of GDP, allowing the country to exit the EU's Excessive Deficit Procedure. Increases in tourism, household spending, car manufacturing and EU funding contributed to stronger growth between 2014 and 2019, but entered recession in 2020 due to the coronavirus pandemic.

Nearly half the land is under cultivation, but agriculture accounts for only 3.9 per cent of GDP; the main crops are cereals, sunflower seeds, vegetables, livestock and dairy products. Industry contributes 31.3 per cent of GDP; the main activities include mining, metallurgy, food processing, and the production of construction materials, textiles, chemicals (especially pharmaceuticals) and motor vehicles. The main trading partners are Germany, Austria, Slovakia and Romania. Machinery and manufactured goods account for 88.5 per cent

of exports and 79.7 per cent of imports. The country is a net importer of fuels and electricity.
GNI – US$157.7bn; US$16,140 per capita (2019)
Annual average growth of GDP – 4.58 per cent (2019 est)
Inflation rate – 2.4 per cent (2017 est)
Unemployment – 3.45 per cent (2019 est)
Population below poverty line –14.9 per cent (2015)
Total external debt – US$138.1bn (2017 est)
Imports – US$112,327m (2017)
Exports – US$122,639m (2017)

BALANCE OF PAYMENTS
Trade – US$10,311m surplus (2017)
Current Account – US$325m deficit (2019)

Trade with UK	2018	2019
Imports from UK	£1,457,871,019	£1,336,055,031
Exports to UK	£2,804,746,413	£3,065,125,154

COMMUNICATIONS
Airports and waterways – 20, with the principal airport at Budapest; there are 1,622km of permanently navigable waterways, mainly on the river Danube, which has several major river ports and harbours including Budapest
Roadways and railways – There are 77,087km of surfaced roads and 8,057km of railways (including a cross-border line to Austria jointly managed by the two countries)
Telecommunications – 3 million fixed lines and 10 million mobile subscriptions (2018); there were 7.5 million internet users in 2018
Internet code and IDD – hu; 36 (from UK), 44 (to UK)
Major broadcasters – Mixed system of state-supported public service broadcast media and private broadcasters; Magyar Televizio operates two public channels alongside private channels TV2 and RTL Klub; Duna TV operates satellite channels for Hungarian minorities living in neighbouring states
Press – There are four daily newspapers, including Nepszabadsag, Magyar Hirlap and Magyar Nemzet
WPFI score –30.84 (89)

EDUCATION AND HEALTH
Hungarians have ten years of compulsory education until age 16; a further two years at secondary level is optional.
Literacy rate – 98.8 per cent (2015 est)
Gross enrolment ratio (percentage of relevant age group) – primary 96.8 per cent, secondary 103.9 per cent, tertiary 50.3 per cent (2018 est)
Health expenditure (per capita) – US$981 (2017)
Hospital beds (per 1,000 people) – 7 (2013)
Life expectancy (years) – 76.7 (2020 est)
Mortality rate – 12.9 (2020 est)
Birth rate – 8.8 (2020 est)
Infant mortality rate – 4.7 (2020 est)

ICELAND

Lydveldid Island – Republic of Iceland

Area – 103,000 sq. km
Capital – Reykjavik; population, 216,000 (2018 est)
Major towns – Hafnarfjordur, Kopavogur
Currency – Icelandic kronur (Kr) of 100 aurar
Population – 350,734 rising at 1.02 per cent a year (2020 est)
Religion – Christian (officially Lutheran 67.2 per cent, Roman Catholic 3.9 per cent, other Christian 6.9 per cent) (est)
Language – Icelandic (official), English, German
Population density – 4 per sq. km (2019)
Urban population – 93.9 per cent (2019 est)
Median age (years) – 37.1 (2020 est)
National anthem – 'Lofsongur' 'Hymn'
National day – 17 June (Independence Day)
Death penalty – Abolished for all crimes (since 1928)
CPI score – 78 (11)
Gross enrolment ratio (percentage of relevant age group) – primary 100.4 per cent, secondary 118 per cent, tertiary 73.1 per cent (2018 est)
Health expenditure (per capita) – US$6,086 (2017)
Life expectancy (years) – 83.3 (2020 est)
Mortality rate – 6.6 (2020 est)
Birth rate – 13.3 (2020 est)
Infant mortality rate – 2.1 (2020 est)

CLIMATE AND TERRAIN

Iceland is a volcanic island in the North Atlantic Ocean, to the east of Greenland and to the west of Norway, and its northernmost point reaches the Arctic Circle. Some parts of the coastline have narrow strips of low-lying land; others are sheer cliffs. An inland plateau of glaciers, lakes and lava fields covers most of the interior, with mountainous areas in the north and at the four glaciers in the centre and south. Elevation extremes range from 2,110m (Hvannadalshnukur, on the Oraefajokull volcano) to 0m (North Atlantic Ocean). There are geysers and hot springs owing to the numerous active volcanoes, which can create new islands, such as Surtsey in 1963; the volcano under the Eyjafjallajokull glacier has been active since March 2010 after nearly 190 years of inactivity. It is estimated that over the past 500 years, Iceland has emitted one-third of the Earth's total lava flow. The climate is influenced by the Gulf Stream; average temperatures range from −1.7°C in January to 9.3°C in July.

HISTORY AND POLITICS

The first major settlement occurred from around AD 870 onwards, as turmoil in Scandinavia drove migrants to seek new homelands. Iceland hosted a flourishing Viking culture in the ninth and tenth centuries, becoming a fully Christian country in 1000. Iceland recognised Norwegian sovereignty in 1263 and, with Norway, came under Danish rule in 1397. When Norway was ceded to Sweden in 1814, Iceland remained Danish territory, achieving autonomy in domestic affairs in

1874. Although it became an independent state with the same sovereign as Denmark in 1918, Copenhagen continued to control its foreign policy and defence. The treaty of union with Denmark expired in 1943, while Denmark was under German occupation, and in a referendum Icelanders voted to become a fully independent republic, proclaimed on 17 June 1944.

The country's dependence on the fishing industry has led occasionally to fraught foreign relations. The introduction and extensions of an exclusive fishing limit around Iceland in 1958, 1972 and 1975 caused the so-called 'Cod War' disputes with the UK.

Post-independence politics was dominated by the conservative Independence Party (SSF) until January 2009, when the country's economic crisis forced the government first to call an early election, then to resign with immediate effect. The Progressive and Independence parties won the April 2013 parliamentary elections with 19 seats each and formed a coalition government in May. In 2015, Iceland announced that it would withdraw its EU accession bid, having been a candidate country since 2010. Following snap elections in October 2016 in which no single party gained a majority, it took three months to form a government of the Independence, Bright Future and Reform parties but this collapsed within the year. Following elections in October 2017, Katrin Jakobsdottir, the leader of the Left-Green Movement, was asked to form a new government, at the head of another three-party coalition. History professor and independent Gudni Johannesson was elected president in 2016 and re-elected in June 2020 with 92 per cent of the vote.

Under the 1944 constitution, the head of state is the president, who is directly elected for a four-year term with no term limits. The unicameral legislature, the *Althing*, has 63 members, who are directly elected for a four-year term. Founded in AD 930, the *Althing* is the world's oldest functioning parliament.

HEAD OF STATE

President, Gudni Johannesson, *elected* 26 June 2016, *sworn in* 1 August 2016, *re-elected* 27 June 2020

SELECTED GOVERNMENT MEMBERS *AS AT NOVEMBER 2020*
Prime Minister, Katrin Jakobsdottir
Finance, Bjarni Benediktsson
Foreign Affairs, Gudlaugur Thor Thordarson

EMBASSY OF ICELAND
2A Hans Street, London SW1X 0JE
T 020-7259 3999 E emb.london@mfa.is W www.iceland.is/uk
Ambassador Extraordinary and Plenipotentiary, HE Stefan Haukur Johannesson, *apptd* 2017

BRITISH EMBASSY
Laufasvegur 31, 101 Reykjavík
T (+354) 550 5100 E info@britishembassy.is
W www.gov.uk/government/world/iceland
Ambassador Extraordinary and Plenipotentiary, HE Michael Nevin, *apptd* 2016

ECONOMY AND TRADE

Iceland has a market economy with an extensive welfare system. While it remains heavily dependent on the fishing industry, tourism is now its major industry accounting for 10 per cent of GDP and 40 per cent of total exports of merchandise and services. There has also been a recent diversification into aluminium smelting, ferrosilicon production, software production and biotechnology, its reliance on tourism means the economy if volatile. A major area of diversification was banking, but aggressive expansion in the 2000s led to over-exposure in foreign markets. In the 2008 global financial crisis, the three largest banks collapsed and the government required over US$10bn (£6.3bn) in loans to stabilise its currency and financial system. The economy contracted sharply, causing widespread unemployment and rapid inflation; however, the economy generally grew 2011–19 and the country compensated payments to international claimants of failed Icelandic banks. In January 2013, Iceland awarded licences for oil and gas exploration and production in the waters off its north-east coast to Faroe Petroleum and Valiant Petroleum; Norway took a 25 per cent stake in both. Iceland withdrew its candidacy to the EU in 2015 over concerns about loss of control of the fishing industry and the eurozone's financial troubles. In March 2017 capital controls were lifted, opening up new opportunities for foreign investment, but the collapse of Icelandic airline WOW in March 2019 and the coronavirus pandemic both led to a sharp fall in tourists. The economy is expected to contract by 7.2 per cent in 2020.

The main trading partners are the Netherlands, Germany and the UK. Principal exports are fish and fish products, aluminium, medicines and ferrosilicon. The main imports are machinery, petroleum products, foodstuffs and textiles.

GNI – US$26.3bn; US$72,850 per capita (2019)
Annual average growth of GDP – 1.94 per cent (2019 est)
Inflation rate – 1.8 per cent (2017 est)
Unemployment – 3.62 per cent (2017 est)
Total external debt – US$21.7bn (2017 est)
Imports – US$10,244m (2017)
Exports – US$11,304m (2017)

BALANCE OF PAYMENTS
Trade – US$1,060m surplus (2017)
Current Account – US$1,568m surplus (2019)

Trade with UK	2018	2019
Imports from UK	£321,465,57	£302,204,936
Exports to UK	£476,810,025	£478,432,821

COMMUNICATIONS
Airports – Seven, with the principal airports at Keflavik, near Reykjavik, in the south, and Akureyri in the north
Roadways – There are 5,647km of paved and oiled gravel roads
Telecommunications – 136,713 fixed lines and 424,720 mobile subscriptions (2018); there were 340,117 internet users in 2018
Internet code and IDD – is; 354 (from UK), 44 (to UK)
Major broadcasters – Icelandic National Broadcasting Service operates radio and television services across the country
Press – There are three major daily newspapers: *Frettabladid, Morgunbladid* and *DV*
WPFI score – 15.12 (15)

INDIA

Bharatiya Ganarajya – Republic of India

Area – 3,287,263 sq. km
Capital – New Delhi; population, 30,291,000 (2020 est)

Major cities – Ahmadabad, Bengaluru (Bangalore), Chennai (Madras), Hyderabad, Jaipur, Kanpur, Kolkata (Calcutta), Mumbai (Bombay), Pune, Surat
Currency – Indian rupee (Rs) of 100 paise
Population – 1,326,093,247 rising at 1.1 per cent a year (2020 est); Indo-Aryan (72 per cent), Dravidian (25 per cent) (est)
Religion – Hindu 79.8 per cent, Muslim 14.2 per cent, Christian 2.3 per cent, Sikh 1.7 per cent (est)
Language – Hindi, Bengali, Marathi, Telugu, Tamil, Gujarati, Urdu, Kannada, Odia, Malayalam, Punjabi, Assamese, Maithili, English (official subsidiary language)
Population density – 455 per sq. km (2019)
Urban population – 34.5 per cent (2019 est)
Median age (years) – 28.7 (2020 est)
National anthem – 'Jana-Gana-Mana' 'Thou Art the Ruler of the Minds of all People'
National day – 26 January (Republic Day)
Death penalty – Retained
CPI score – 41 (80)
Military expenditure – US$66,510m (2018)

CLIMATE AND TERRAIN
India has three well-defined regions: the mountain range of the Himalayas, the Indo-Gangetic plain and the southern peninsula. The Himalayas along the northern border reach 8,598m (Kangchenjunga), then drop to the northern plains formed by the basins of the Indus, Ganges and Brahmaputra rivers before rising to low hills running east to west that mark the division with the southern Deccan peninsula. The peninsula has narrow coastal plains rising to a central plateau, with the Western Ghats and Eastern Ghats ranges of hills lying along the west and east coasts respectively. The Thar Desert lies in the north-west. The climate varies from tropical in the south to temperate in the north. It is influenced by the south-west monsoon; the main rainy season is June to October. During the drier season from December to May, the weather is cooler until February and then becomes increasingly hot until the monsoon breaks. The average temperature in New Delhi ranges from 13.8°C in January to 34°C in June.

POLITICS
Under the 1950 constitution, the president is elected for a five-year term by an electoral college consisting of members of both chambers of the legislature, with no term limits. The president appoints the prime minister, who is responsible to the legislature. The vice-president, who is elected by both chambers for a five-year term, is *ex-officio* chair of the upper chamber. The legislature, the *Sansad,* consists of two chambers. The upper chamber, the Council of States *(Rajya Sabha),* has up to 245 members, who serve a six-year term; up to 233 members are elected by the state legislative assemblies as individual terms expire, and 12 are nominated by the president. The House of the People *(Lok Sabha)* has 545 members; 543 are directly elected for a five-year term, and two representatives of the Anglo-Indian community are nominated by the president.

There are 29 states and seven union territories (including the national capital territory). Each state has its own executive, comprising a governor, who is appointed by the president for a five-year term, and a council of ministers. All states have a legislative assembly, and some also have a legislative council, elected directly for a maximum period of five years. The states have considerable autonomy, although the union government controls such matters as foreign policy, defence and external trade. The union territories are administered, except where otherwise provided by parliament, by a lieutenant-governor or an administrator appointed by the president.

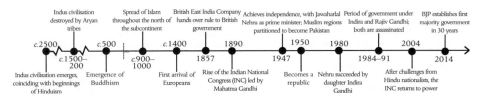

Indus civilisation destroyed by Aryan tribes — Spread of Islam throughout the north of the subcontinent — British East India Company hands over rule to British government — Achieves independence, with Jawaharlal Nehru as prime minister; Muslim regions partitioned to become Pakistan — Period of government under Indira and Rajiv Gandhi; both are assassinated — BJP establishes first majority government in 30 years

*c.*2500   *c.*500   *c.*1400   1890   1950   1980   2004

*c.*1500–200   *c.*900–1000   1857   1947   1984–91   2014

Indus civilisation emerges, coinciding with beginnings of Hinduism — Emergence of Buddhism — First arrival of Europeans — Rise of the Indian National Congress (INC) led by Mahatma Gandhi — Becomes a republic — Nehru succeeded by daughter Indira Gandhi — After challenges from Hindu nationalists, the INC returns to power

In the legislative elections held in May 2014, the right-wing Hindu-nationalist Bharatiya Janata Party (BJP) won a landslide victory against the incumbent centre-left India National Congress and its coalition partners, establishing India's first majority government since 1984 with 282 seats in the *Lok Sabha*. The BJP unexpectedly extended its majority to 303 seats in the May 2019 elections. The 2019 legislative election saw the largest turnout for a democratic election in history, with over 580 million votes cast. The 2017 presidential election was won by Ram Nath Kovind, who was backed by the ruling BJP.

HEAD OF STATE
President, Ram Nath Kovind, *elected* 17 July 2017, *took office* 25 July 2017
Vice-President, M. Venkaiah Naidu

SELECTED GOVERNMENT MEMBERS *AS AT NOVEMBER 2020*
Prime Minister, Narendra Modi
Defence, Raj Nath Singh
Finance, Nirmala Sitharaman
Home Affairs, G. Kishan Reddy

OFFICE OF THE HIGH COMMISSIONER FOR INDIA
India House, Aldwych, London WC2B 4NA
T 020-7836 8484 **E** info.london@hcilondon.in **W** www.hcilondon.in
High Commissioner, HE Gaitri Issar Kumar, *apptd* 2020

BRITISH HIGH COMMISSION
Shantipath, Chanakyapuri, New Delhi 110021
T (+91) (11) 2419 2100 **E** web.newdelhi@fco.gov.uk
W www.gov.uk/government/world/india
High Commissioner, Sir Dominic Asquith, KCMG, *apptd* 2016

FOREIGN RELATIONS
Since partition, India and Pakistan have disputed sovereignty over the predominantly Muslim state of Jammu and Kashmir. A short war in 1947–8 resulted in the state being partitioned between the two countries, and its status remained unresolved despite further outbreaks of war in 1965 and 1971, low-level conflict for control of the Siachen glacier since 1985 and occasional increases in military exchanges, most recently in 1999–2002, 2003 and 2016–17. Both countries' acquisition of nuclear weapons has spurred efforts to reach a settlement. Peace talks began in 2003 when diplomatic missions were reopened and the resumption of transport links was initiated. Formal diplomatic talks began in 2004 and have achieved several accords intended to calm relations between the two countries. Talks were temporarily suspended by the Indian government after the 2008 terrorist attacks on Mumbai, but were resumed in 2010 despite heightened tensions along Kashmir's Line of Control in late 2016 to 2017.

Tensions flared in February 2019 after a suicide car bombing that killed dozens of Indian police was blamed on Pakistani-backed Muslim militants, and India responded with air strikes and tariff hikes. Pakistan's support for the Muslim insurgency in the Indian part of the state, which began in the late 1980s and has included terrorist attacks in Indian cities, has strained relations but Pakistan distanced itself from the insurgents in early 2019 in an effort to defuse tensions. In August, the Indian government stripped Jammu and Kashmir of their semi-autonomous status and imposed a military crackdown.

In the Sino-Indian war in 1962, India lost territory to China. In addition, China claims Arunachal Pradesh and does not recognise Indian sovereignty over Sikkim. Talks between India and China in 2003 resulted in India's formal recognition of the Tibetan Autonomous Region as a part of China and a cross-border trade agreement on Sikkim. In May and June 2020 a series of military skirmishes and standoffs between Chinese and Indian troops along this part of the border resulted in a few dozen deaths, before diplomacy de-escalated the situation by October.

ECONOMY AND TRADE
The economy was closed for several decades after independence, with high import tariffs and limits on foreign investment intended to stimulate domestic growth industry. Since 1991, economic liberalisation and increased foreign investment have generated rapid expansion, with GDP growing by an average 7 per cent a year since 1997. Following a brief contraction in 2008–9 during the global economic downturn, growth exceeded 8 per cent in 2010, slowed to a ten-year low in 2013 and accelerated up to 2018. In 2019 the economy grew by 4.2 per cent, but is expected to contract by 10.3 per cent in 2020 due to the coronavirus pandemic, where it experienced the world's second-highest number of cases and deaths.

India's large skilled workforce has enabled it to develop knowledge-based industries and become a global centre for manufacturing and services. Other areas of growth are pharmaceuticals, tourism and the provision of services to the burgeoning urban middle class. The rapidly growing service sector now accounts for 61.5 per cent of GDP and industry for 23 per cent, employing 31 per cent and 22 per cent of the workforce respectively.

Although about 1 per cent of the population has been lifted out of poverty each year since 1997, rural areas have benefited disproportionately little from the economic growth. Agriculture, forestry and fishing support 47 per cent of the population and contribute 15.4 per cent of GDP. The main food crops are rice, cereals (principally wheat) and pulses. The major cash crops include cotton, jute, tea and sugar cane. Agriculture and forestry are threatened by climate change, deforestation, soil erosion, over-grazing and desertification.

Despite recent advances, the economy faces a number of problems, chiefly underinvestment in infrastructure and discrimination against women and girls. Economic constraints also include shortfalls in energy generation, limited educational provision, high youth unemployment, the pressures of rapid urbanisation and corruption; in 2016, investors shifted capital away from India, which caused a sharp decline in the rupee's value. Almost 200 million Indians took part in a strike in January 2019 to protest against the government's handling of the economy.

The main trading partners are the USA, the UAE and China. Principal exports include petroleum products, precious stones,

machinery, iron and steel, chemicals, vehicles and pharmaceuticals. Its main imports are crude oil, precious stones, machinery, fertiliser, iron and steel, and chemicals.
GNI – US$2,910.8bn; US$2,130 per capita (2019)
Annual average growth of GDP – 4.86 per cent (2019 est)
Inflation rate – 3.6 per cent (2017 est)
Population below poverty line – 21.9 per cent (2011 est)
Unemployment – 8.5 per cent (2017 est)
Total external debt – US$501.6bn (2017 est)
Imports – US$606,067m (2017)
Exports – US$488,145m (2017)

BALANCE OF PAYMENTS
Trade – US$117,922m deficit (2017)
Current Account – US$29,762m deficit (2019)

Trade with UK	2018	2019
Imports from UK	£4,953,960,805	£4,602,958,335
Exports to UK	£7,362,619,990	£7,901,327,220

COMMUNICATIONS
Airports – 253 airports with paved runways, principally at Delhi, Mumbai, Chennai and Kolkata
Waterways – The chief seaports are Mumbai, Kolkata, Haldia, Chennai, Cochin, Visakhapatnam, Mangalore and Tuticorin; there are 340 ships of over 1,000 tonnes in the merchant fleet. There are 485km of canals and the great rivers provide around 5,200km of navigable waterways
Roadways and railways – 4,699,024km; 68,525km
Telecommunications – 21.8 million fixed lines and 1.2 billion mobile subscriptions (2018); there were 447 million internet users in 2018
Internet code and IDD – in; 91 (from UK), 44 (to UK)
Major broadcasters – The public-owned Doordarshan network operates several national, regional and local services, and All India Radio is the country's largest radio broadcaster
Press – Eight major daily newspapers, including *The Times of India, The Hindu* and *India Today*
WPFI score – 45.33 (142)

EDUCATION AND HEALTH
Education is free and compulsory from age six to 14.
Literacy rate – 74.4 per cent (2018 est)
Gross enrolment ratio (percentage of relevant age group) – primary 96.8 per cent, secondary 73.8 per cent, tertiary 28.6 per cent (2019 est)
Health expenditure (per capita) – US$69 (2017)
Hospital beds (per 1,000 people) – 0.7 (2011)
Life expectancy (years) – 69.7 (2020 est)
Mortality rate – 7.3 (2020 est)
Birth rate – 18.2 (2020 est)
Infant mortality rate – 35.4 (2020 est)
HIV/AIDS adult prevalence – 0.3 per cent (2016 est)

INDONESIA
Republik Indonesia – Republic of Indonesia

Area – 1,904,569 sq. km
Capital – Jakarta; population, 10,770,000 (2020 est)
Major cities – Bandung, Bekasi, Depok, Makasar, Medan, Palembang, Semarang, Surabaya, Tangerang

Currency – Rupiah (Rp) of 100 sen
Population – 267,026,366 rising at 0.79 per cent a year (2020 est); Javanese (40.1 per cent), Sundanese (15.5 per cent), Malay (3.7 per cent), Batak (3.6 per cent) (est)
Religion – Muslim 87.2 per cent (predominantly Sunni), Christian (Protestant 7 per cent, Roman Catholic 2.9 per cent), Hindu 1.7 per cent (est)
Language – Bahasa Indonesia (official), English, Dutch, Javanese, over 580 languages and dialects
Population density – 148 per sq. km (2019)
Urban population – 56 per cent (2019 est)
Median age (years) – 31.1 (2019 est)
National anthem – 'Indonesia Raya' 'Great Indonesia'
National day – 17 August (Independence Day)
Death penalty – Retained
CPI score – 40 (85)
Military expenditure – US$7,437m (2018)
Conscription – 18–45 years of age; 24 months (selective)
Literacy rate – 95.7 per cent (2018 est)
Gross enrolment ratio (percentage of relevant age group) – primary 106.4 per cent, secondary 88.9 per cent, tertiary 36.3 per cent (2018 est)
Health expenditure (per capita) – US$115 (2017)
Hospital beds (per 1,000 people) – 1.2 (2015)
Life expectancy (years) – 73.7 (2020 est)
Mortality rate – 6.6 (2020 est)
Birth rate – 15.4 (2020 est)
Infant mortality rate – 20.4 (2020 est)
HIV/AIDS adult prevalence – 0.4 per cent (2016 est)

CLIMATE AND TERRAIN
Indonesia is an archipelago of over 17,500 islands, of which about 6,000 are inhabited. They include the islands of Sumatra, Java, Madura, Bali, Lombok, Sumbawa, Sumba, Flores, the Riouw-Lingga archipelago, Bangka and Billiton, part of the island of Borneo (Kalimantan), Sulawesi (formerly Celebes), the Maluku (formerly Moluccas) archipelago and others comprising the provinces of East and West Nusa Tenggara, and the western halves of the islands of New Guinea (Papua; formerly Irian Jaya) and Timor. Many of the islands have narrow coastal plains with hilly or mountainous interiors, and around half of the country is covered by tropical rainforest. Elevation extremes range from 4,884m (Puncak Jaya, in Papua) to 0m (Indian Ocean). The climate is tropical; the average temperature is 26.2°C and rainfall peaks in January and February, and is lowest in August.
The country is located near to an intersection of tectonic plates, making it susceptible to seismic activity such as earthquakes and volcanic eruptions; in January 2014 the eruption of Mt Kelud caused mass evacuations in East Java. Indonesia's weather patterns are being affected by climate change. In November 2017, Mount Agung volcano on the island of Bali erupted five times, causing thousands to evacuate, disrupting travel and causing significant environmental damage.

HISTORY AND POLITICS
Hindu and Buddhist kingdoms existed in some parts of the Indonesian islands until the 14th century. Islam was introduced in the 13th century and spread over the next three centuries. Trading by the Portuguese began in the 16th century, but the Portuguese were displaced by the Dutch who, lured by the rich spice trade, came to dominate Indonesia by the early 20th century. Opposition to Dutch rule grew in the 1920s and the Japanese occupation of Indonesia during the Second World War strengthened nationalism, leading to a declaration of independence after liberation in 1945. This was not recognised by the Dutch, but after four years of guerrilla

warfare they granted independence to the Netherlands Indies in 1949. Irian Jaya (now Papua) was annexed in 1963. Timor–Leste was invaded and annexed in 1975 but gained its independence in 2002.

Achmed Soekarno, the foremost proponent of self-rule since the 1920s, became president in 1949 but was deposed in 1966 in a military coup suppressed by General Suharto, who subsequently became president. Suharto remained in power until 1998 when, amid economic and social upheaval, he was succeeded by his deputy B. J. Habibie. Habibie was defeated in 1999 by Abdurrahman Wahid in the first democratic elections for 44 years. President Wahid was impeached for alleged financial corruption and in 2001 the legislature appointed Megawati Soekarnoputri (daughter of Achmed Soekarno) to replace him.

The April 2014 legislative elections were won by the ruling Democratic Party and the July 2014 presidential election by their candidate, Joko Widodo. The results were subsequently challenged by his opponent Prabowo Subianto who alleged that widespread electoral fraud had taken place, but the constitutional court rejected the claims. Widodo was re-elected in April 2019, and the result was again challenged by Subianto and upheld by the constitutional court.

The 1959 constitution was amended in 2001 to provide for the establishment of the upper chamber of the legislature, and in 2002 to provide for the direct election of the president and the abolition of parliamentary seats reserved for the armed forces.

The executive president is directly elected for a five-year term, renewable once, and appoints the cabinet. The bicameral People's Consultative Assembly comprises the House of Representatives, which has 560 members directly elected for a five-year term, and the Regional Representative Council, which has 132 members, four for each province, directly elected on a non-partisan basis for a five-year term.

HEAD OF STATE

President, Joko Widodo, *elected* 22 July 2014, *re-elected* 17 April 2019
Vice-President, Musuf Amin

SELECTED GOVERNMENT MEMBERS *AS AT NOVEMBER 2020*

Defence, Prabowo Subianto
Finance, Sri Mulyani Indrawati
Foreign Affairs, Retno Lestari Priansari Marsudi

EMBASSY OF THE REPUBLIC OF INDONESIA

30 Great Peter Street, London SW1P 2BU
T 020-7499 7661 **E** kbri@btconnect.com
W www.indonesianembassy.org.uk
Ambassador Extraordinary and Plenipotentiary, HE Dr Rizal Sukma, *apptd* 2016

BRITISH EMBASSY

Jl Patra Kuningan Raya Blok L5-6, Jakarta 12950
T (+62) (21) 2356 5200 **E** jakarta.mcs@fco.gov.uk
W http://ukinindonesia.fco.gov.uk
Ambassador Extraordinary and Plenipotentiary, HE Owen Jenkins, *apptd* 2019

INSURGENCIES

Separatist movements developed in several parts of Indonesia after independence, including Maluku, which fought an unsuccessful separatist war in the 1950s; Irian Jaya (now Papua), which was granted greater autonomy in 2002, although separatist agitation continues; Timor–Leste, from its annexation in 1975 until independence in 2002; and Aceh province in Sumatra, which was granted a degree of autonomy in 2005.

Since the fall of Suharto in 1998, tensions between different ethnic and religious groups have surfaced, and there has been intercommunal violence in Kalimantan (1996–7, 1999, 2001), Sulawesi (1998–2000, 2001, 2005) and Maluku (1999–2002, 2004).

Muslim extremist groups that claim links with al-Qaida have been held responsible for bombings in Bali in 2002 and 2005, and Jakarta in 2003, 2004 and 2009, while groups with links to IS have been blamed for attacks in Jakarta in 2016–17 and Surabaya in 2018.

ECONOMY AND TRADE

The largest economy in south-east Asia, it struggled from the late 1990s until recent years as it was hit in succession by the Asian financial crisis, the political turmoil following the fall of Suharto, and a downturn in tourism following the Bali and Jakarta bombings. A number of natural disasters since 2004 have also disrupted the economy, especially tourism, including widespread damage caused by major earthquakes. A tsunami that struck Sulawesi in September 2018 devastated the capital, Pula, killing more than 2,000 people and destroying 68,000 homes. Soon after, in December 2018, another tsunami hit the coastlines of Java and Sumatra, killing at least 430 people.

Significant economic reforms in 2004–8 reduced debt, unemployment and inflation, and boosted growth. Although growth slowed in 2008, government stimulus measures countered the effect of the global downturn in 2009 and by 2011 Indonesia's credit rating was raised to investment grade due mainly to its low rates of inflation and small current account surplus. The economy slowed for a fourth consecutive year in 2014 and thereafter grew by around 5 per cent each year until 2020, when it entered recession for the first time since 1998. Indonesia became a member of the Asian Economic Community on 31 December 2015, although economic integration has been slow to materialise and trade tensions with the USA and China is ongoing.

Natural resources include oil, tin, natural gas, nickel, timber, bauxite, copper, coal, gold and silver. However, a lack of investment in prospecting for new sources has led to a decline in oil production and Indonesia has been a net importer since 2004. The exploitation and processing of mineral assets, production of textiles, clothing, cement, fertilisers, plywood and rubber, and tourism are the main industrial activities; industry accounts for 41 per cent of GDP and services 45.4 per cent, employing 21 per cent and 47 per cent of the workforce respectively. Agriculture contributes 13.7 per cent of GDP but employs 32 per cent of the workforce. The main crops are rubber, rice, cassava, peanuts, cocoa, coffee, palm oil, copra and livestock products.

The main trading partners are Singapore, Japan, China, the USA, South Korea and India. Principal exports are mineral fuels, animal and vegetable fats, electrical appliances, rubber and machinery. The main imports are fuel, machinery, and foodstuffs.

GNI – US$1,026.8bn; US$3,840 per capita (2018)
Annual average growth of GDP – 5.2 per cent (2017 est)
Inflation rate – 4.0 per cent (2017 est)
Population below poverty line – 10.9 per cent (2016)
Unemployment – 5.4 per cent (2017 est)
Total external debt – US$322.6bn (2017 est)
Imports – US$182,600m (2017)
Exports – US$193,522m (2017)

BALANCE OF PAYMENTS

Trade – US$10,921m surplus (2017)
Current Account – US$68,453m deficit (2018)

Trade with UK	2018	2019
Imports from UK	£701,058,567	£682,008,025
Exports to UK	£1,153,884,633	£1,199,514,028

COMMUNICATIONS

Airports – 186; each of the main islands has a major airport, with most capable of accepting international flights
Waterways – There are nine major ports, usually the chief towns of the major islands, and the merchant fleet contains 1,340 ships of over 1,000 tonnes
Roadways and railways – 283,102km; 8,159km
Telecommunications – 8.3 million fixed lines and 319.4 million mobile subscriptions (2018); there were 104.5 million internet users in 2018
Internet code and IDD – id; 62 (from UK), 1 44/8 44 (to UK)
Major broadcasters – Radio and Televisi Republik Indonesia, the country's principal broadcaster, operates six television and two radio networks
Press – *The Jakarta Post* and *The Jakarta Globe* dominate a competitive market that includes eight other dailies
WPFI score – 36.82 (119)

IRAN

Jomhuri-ye Eslami-ye Iran – *Islamic Republic of Iran*

Area – 1,648,195 sq. km
Capital – Tehran; population, 9,135,000 (2020 est)
Major cities – Ahvaz, Esfahan, Karaj, Mashhad, Qom, Shiraz, Tabriz
Currency – Iranian rial of 100 dinar
Population – 84,923,314 rising at 1.1 per cent a year (2020 est); Persian, Azeri, Kurd, Lur, Baloch, Arab, Turkmen and Turkic tribes
Religion – Muslim (official) 99.4 per cent (Shia 90–95 per cent, Sunni 5–10 per cent) (est)
Language – Persian (official), Turkic, Kurdish, Gilaki and Mazandarani, Luri, Balochi, Arabic
Population density – 50 per sq. km (2019)
Urban population – 75.4 per cent (2019 est)
Median age (years) – 31.7 (2020 est)
National anthem – 'Sorud-e Melli-ye Jomhouri-ye Eslami-ye Iran' 'National Anthem of the Islamic Republic of Iran'
National day – 1 April (Republic Day)
Death penalty – Retained
CPI score – 26 (146)
Military expenditure – US$13,194m (2018)
Conscription – 18 years of age, male only; 18–24 months

CLIMATE AND TERRAIN

Apart from narrow coastal plains on the Gulf coasts and the shores of the Caspian Sea, the interior is a plateau consisting of barren desert in the centre and east. This is enclosed by high mountains in the west and north, with smaller ranges on the eastern border and the southern coast. Elevation extremes range from 5,671m (Kuh-e Damavand) to −28m (Caspian

Sea). Earthquakes are frequent. The climate is arid or semi-arid in the interior, and subtropical on the Caspian shores. Average temperatures are 5.2°C in January and 29.8°C in July.

POLITICS

Under the 1979 constitution, overall authority rests with the spiritual leader of the republic, who is appointed for life by the Assembly of Experts; this consists of 83 clerics who are directly elected and decide religious and spiritual matters. The executive president is directly elected for a four-year term, renewable once. Ministers are nominated by the president but must be approved by the legislature. The unicameral Consultative Assembly *(Majles-e Shura-ye Eslami)* has 290 members who are directly elected for a four-year term on a non-party basis; five seats are reserved for religious minorities. Laws passed by the legislature must be approved by the Council of Guardians of the Constitution, six theologians appointed by the spiritual leader and six jurists nominated by the judiciary and approved by the legislature; it also has a supervisory role in elections. In 1997, the Constitutional Surveillance Council, a five-member body, was established to supervise the proper application of constitutional laws.

Mahmoud Ahmadinejad won the presidential election in 2005 and 2009. The results of the 2009 election were challenged by the other candidates, who alleged electoral fraud. Following massive protest rallies, the Council of Guardians confirmed Ahmadinejad's victory and ruled out an annulment; further popular protests were suppressed. After the protests in summer 2009, Ahmadinejad's government ruthlessly suppressed the opposition (the Green Movement) and purged liberals from official positions. In the June 2013 presidential election, moderate candidate Hassan Rouhani defeated the conservative mayor of Tehran, Mohammed Baqer Qaliaf. Legislative elections in February 2016 consolidated President Rouhani's position, with wins for moderate and reformist candidates, but conservatives overwhelmingly won the 2020 elections in which dozens of reformist candidates were disqualified; he was re-elected president in May 2017, winning 59 per cent of the vote. Amnesty International estimated 7,000 dissidents had been detained by 2018 following protests against economic hardship and theocratic rule, and were subjected to human rights violations including torture.

Spiritual Leader of the Islamic Republic and C.-in-C. of Armed Forces, Ayatollah Seyed Ali Khamenei, *apptd* June 1989
President, Hassan Rouhani, *elected* 15 June 2013, *re-elected* 19 May 2017
First Vice-President, Es'haq Jahangiri

SELECTED GOVERNMENT MEMBERS *AS AT NOVEMBER 2020*
Defence, Brig.-Gen. Amir Hatami
Economic Affairs, Mohammad Nahavandian
Foreign Affairs, Mohammad Javad Zarif

EMBASSY OF THE ISLAMIC REPUBLIC OF IRAN
16 Prince's Gate, London SW7 1PT
T 020-7225 4208 **W** london.mfa.ir
Ambassador Extraordinary and Plenipotentiary, HE Hamid Baeidinejad, *apptd* 2016

BRITISH EMBASSY
198 Ferdowsi Avenue, 11316–91144, Tehran
T (+44) 19 0851 6666 **W** www.gov.uk/government/world/iran
Ambassador Extraordinary and Plenipotentiary, HE Robert Macaire, CMG, *apptd* 2018

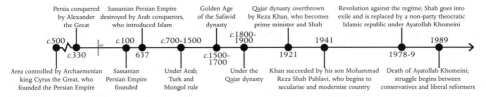

Persia conquered by Alexander the Great — Sassanian Persian Empire destroyed by Arab conquerors, who introduced Islam — Golden Age of the Safavid dynasty — Qajar dynasty overthrown by Reza Khan, who becomes prime minister and Shah — Revolution against the regime; Shah goes into exile and is replaced by a non-party theocratic Islamic republic under Ayatollah Khomeini

c.500   AD   c.100   c.700-1500   c.1800-1900   1941   1989

c.330   637   c.1500-1700   1921   1978-9

Area controlled by Archaemenian king Cyrus the Great, who founded the Persian Empire — Sassanian Persian Empire founded — Under Arab, Turk and Mongol rule — Under the Qajar dynasty — Khan succeeded by his son Mohammad Reza Shah Pahlavi, who begins to secularise and modernise country — Death of Ayatollah Khomeini; struggle begins between conservatives and liberal reformers

FOREIGN RELATIONS

Between 1980 and 1988, Iran was engaged in a bitter war with Iraq over the Shatt-al-Arab waterway. Iran remained neutral in the Gulf War (1991) and the Iraq War (2003), but it has been accused since of subverting reconstruction in Iraq by arming Shia insurgents.

Since the 1978 revolution, Iran's relations with the West, and especially the USA and the UK, have been strained. It has not cooperated with international efforts to achieve peace in the Middle East, and has long been suspected of sponsoring terrorism by Islamic fundamentalists, especially in Lebanon and Palestine, as well as supporting the regime in Syria. Increasing Iranian involvement in the Syrian civil war escalated Iran's proxy war with Israel into direct confrontation in 2018; the two nations have since sporadically exchanged missile fire in Syria.

Since 2002 international relations deteriorated further because of concerns over Iran's nuclear and ballistic missile programmes, especially its acquisition of the ability to enrich uranium. The UN passed six resolutions from 2006 to 2010 calling on Iran to suspend uranium enrichment and reprocessing, and to comply with its IAEA obligations and responsibilities; four of the resolutions imposed or extended sanctions on trade and travel. In an escalation of the nuclear row, the EU imposed an oil embargo on Iran in January 2012, after the country reportedly began to enrich uranium at its underground plant in Fordo. In July 2015, Iran accepted strict limits on its nuclear programme in exchange for the lifting of sanctions. The country pledged to reduce the number of gas centrifuges by two-thirds, engage solely in non-military research at Fordo and reduce its stockpile of enriched uranium by 98 per cent. However, the deal was undermined following the withdrawal of the USA in May 2018, and international efforts to salvage the agreement, especially by European leaders, have been unsuccessful.

In 2019 tensions with the USA intensified after Iran was accused of attacking oil tankers in the Gulf of Oman. Outright war was narrowly avoided after Iran downed an unmanned US drone, and US sanctions were subsequently strengthened. War was closely avoided again in January 2020 when a US air strike killed leading miliary figures including Maj.-Gen. Quasem Soleimani, after which Iran retaliated by launching missiles against US bases in Iraq. In July 2019, Iran twice broke the 2015 nuclear agreement by stockpiling uranium and surpassing enrichment thresholds, and in January 2020 withdrew entirely from the agreement.

Following an attack on the British embassy in November 2011, Britain closed its embassy in Tehran and expelled all Iranian diplomats from London, but the embassy reopened in August 2015.

ECONOMY AND TRADE

Iran was one of the best-performing economies in the Middle East owing to its vast reserves of oil and natural gas, but its performance has been deteriorating; the predominantly state-controlled economy is inefficient, with little diversification and only a limited, small-scale private sector. Unemployment and underemployment are serious problems, and there is a flourishing unofficial economy. The election of the reformer

Hassan Rouhani coincided with a strengthened national currency and an increase in the value of the Tehran stock exchange, but UN sanctions have increased Iran's economic problems. The economy left recession in 2014 and benefited from opportunities for foreign investment following the 2015 nuclear deal, however since the US withdrawal from the nuclear agreement in 2018, and the subsequent extension of US sanctions, conditions have deteriorated. There has been frequent public protests over the state of the economy and the government's response to flooding in early 2019, which left an estimated 2 million people in need of aid. Increasing economic integration with China and Russia, including a planned 25-year $400bn investment agreement reached with the former in 2016, may generate long-term growth and stability, but the coronavirus pandemic pushed the economy into recession in 2020.

Oil and gas extraction and processing dominate the economy, but other industries include petrochemicals, textiles, construction materials, food processing, metal fabrication and armaments. Agricultural production includes wheat, rice, other grains, sugar beet and sugar cane, fruit, nuts, cotton, dairy products, wool and caviar.

The main trading partners are China, the UAE, Turkey, India and South Korea. Principal exports are petroleum (60 per cent), chemical and petrochemical products, fruit and nuts, carpets and cement. The main imports are industrial raw materials and intermediate goods, capital goods, foodstuffs, consumer goods and technical services.

GNI – US$441bn; US$5,470 per capita (2018)
Annual average growth of GDP – 3.7 per cent (2017 est)
Inflation rate – 9.6 per cent (2017 est)
Population below poverty line – 18.7 per cent (2007 est)
Unemployment – 11.8 per cent (2017 est)
Total external debt – US$7.995bn (2017 est)
Imports – US$96,821m (2017)
Exports – US$119,116m (2017)

BALANCE OF PAYMENTS

Trade – US$22,295m surplus (2017)
Current Account – US$3,106m deficit (2018)

Trade with UK	2018	2019
Imports from UK	£165,247,241	£82,189,106
Exports to UK	£26,767,801	£17,530,075

COMMUNICATIONS

Airports and waterways – 140; the principal airports are at Tehran and Shiraz; Iran's seaports include Asaluyeh, Bushehr and Abadan on the Persian Gulf, and Bandar Abbas on the Strait of Hormuz
Roadways and railways – 223,485km; 8,484km
Telecommunications – 30.4 million fixed lines and 88.7 million mobile subscriptions (2018); there were 58.1 million internet users in 2019
Internet code and IDD – ir; 98 (from UK), 44 (to UK)
Major broadcasters – Islamic Republic of Iran Broadcasting is the state-run broadcast media with approximately 50

channels, including news, and 16 radio channels; no private, independent broadcasters
Press – Major daily newspapers include the English-language daily *Tehran Times,* the conservative *Kayhan* and reformist *Sharq*
WPFI score – 64.81 (173)

EDUCATION AND HEALTH
Primary education, between the ages of six and 14, is compulsory and free.
Literacy rate – 85.5 per cent (2016 est)
Gross enrolment ratio (percentage of relevant age group) – primary 110.7 per cent, secondary 86.3 per cent (2017 est); tertiary 62.8 per cent (2018 est)
Health expenditure (per capita) – US$475 (2017)
Hospital beds (per 1,000 people) – 0.2 (2014)
Life expectancy (years) – 74.5 (2020 est)
Mortality rate – 5.3 (2020 est)
Birth rate – 16.3 (2020 est)
Infant mortality rate – 14.9 (2020 est)
HIV/AIDS adult prevalence – 0.1 per cent (2019 est)

IRAQ
Jumhuriyat al-Iraq/Komar-i Eraq – *Republic of Iraq*

Area – 438,317 sq. km
Capital – Baghdad; population, 7,144,000 (2020 est)
Major cities – Arbil, Basra, Karbala, Kirkuk, Mosul, Najaf, Sulaymaniyah
Currency – Iraqi dinar (NID) of 1,000 fils
Population – 38,872,655 rising at 2.16 per cent a year (2020 est); Arab (75–80 per cent), Kurdish (15–20 per cent) (est)
Religion – Muslim (official) 95–8 per cent (Shia 64–9 per cent, Sunni 29–34 per cent), Christian 1 per cent (est)
Language – Arabic, Kurdish (both official), Turkmen, Syriac, Aremenian
Population density – 89 per sq. km (2019)
Urban population – 70.7 per cent (2019 est)
Median age (years) – 21.2 (2020 est)
National anthem – 'Mawtini' 'My Homeland'
National day – 14 July (Republic Day)
Death penalty – Retained
CPI score – 20 (162)
Military expenditure – US$6,318m (2018 highly uncertain figure)

CLIMATE AND TERRAIN
The north-west and south of Iraq consist of an almost barren desert plain. The area between the Euphrates and Tigris rivers, which run across the country from north-west to south-east, is fertile, irrigated and heavily cultivated. The rivers run through marshland to their outflow in the Persian Gulf, on which Iraq has a 58km coastline. In the north-east the land rises to the Kurdistan mountains. Elevation extremes range from 3,611m (Cheekha Dar) to 0m (Persian Gulf). The climate is mostly desert, though colder and wetter in the mountains. Average temperatures range from 8.9°C in January to 33.9°C in July and August.

POLITICS
Under the 2005 constitution, the president is elected by the legislature for a four-year term, renewable once. The president nominates the prime minister, subject to the approval of the legislature. The unicameral Council of Representatives *(Majlis al-Nuwab)* has 329 members, with nine seats reserved for minority groups; members are directly elected for a four-year term.

After several months of negotiations following the March 2010 elections, the Iraqi National Movement (al-Iraqiya), SL and Kurdistan Alliance (KA) blocs agreed to form a coalition government under Nouri al-Maliki, and this was sworn in on 21 December. Jalal Talabani (1933–2017), the Kurdish president of the interim government in 2005 and re-elected to the office in 2006, was re-elected for a second term in November 2010. In the April 2014 legislative elections al-Maliki's coalition remained the largest political grouping and Fouad Massoum was elected president in July. The military victories of Islamic State (IS) in the north of the country resulted in al-Maliki's resignation as prime minister in August in favour of an inclusive government. Legislative elections in May 2018 were followed by a lengthy recount and five months of political deadlock as competing blocs claimed victory, amid violent protests over unemployment and poor public services. Negotiations ended in October, with veteran Kurdish politician Barham Salih elected head of another nonsectarian government.

HEAD OF STATE
President, Barham Salih, *elected* 2 October 2018

SELECTED GOVERNMENT MEMBERS *AS AT MAY 2019*
Prime Minister, Mustafa al-Kadhimi
Finance, Abdul Amir Allawi
Foreign Affairs, Fuad Hussein

EMBASSY OF THE REPUBLIC OF IRAQ
21 Queens Gate, London SW7 5JE
T 020-7590 7650 E lonemb@mofaml.gov.iq
W www.iraqembassy.org.uk
Ambassador Extraordinary and Plenipotentiary, HE Mohammad Jaafar Bakr Haidar Al-Sadir, *Sadr, apptd* 2019

BRITISH EMBASSY
International Zone, Baghdad
T (+964) 790 192 6280 E baghdad.consularenquiries@fco.gov.uk
W www.gov.uk/government/world/iraq
Ambassador Extraordinary and Plenipotentiary, HE Stephen Hickey, *apptd* 2019

INTERNAL UNREST
There are about 4 million Kurds in north-east Iraq, in areas adjoining the predominantly Kurdish areas in Iran and Turkey. Iraq's Kurdish nationalists have demanded an autonomous homeland, Kurdistan, since the 1960s, and turned to militant tactics in the 1970s. Their demands were opposed by Saddam Hussein's regime with great brutality. An uprising after the Gulf War (1991) was suppressed by Iraqi troops, prompting the creation of UN safe havens, which enabled the Kurds to set up a semi-autonomous region in the north. An air exclusion zone was also established, but there was further conflict with Iraqi forces and between the two main Kurdish parties in the 1990s. During the war in 2003,

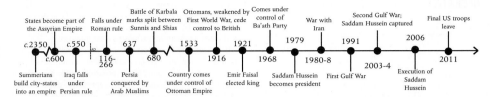

States become part of the Assyrian Empire — *c.*2350

Summerians build city-states into an empire — *c.*2350

Iraq falls under Persian rule — *c.*600

Falls under Roman rule — *c.*550

116-266

Battle of Karbala marks split between Sunnis and Shias — 637

Persia conquered by Arab Muslims — 680

Ottomans, weakened by First World War, cede control to British — 1533

Country comes under control of Ottoman Empire — 1916

Comes under control of Ba'ath Party — 1921

Emir Faisal elected king — 1968

War with Iran — 1979

Saddam Hussein becomes president — 1980-8

Second Gulf War; Saddam Hussein captured — 1991

First Gulf War — 2003-4

Execution of Saddam Hussein — 2006

Final US troops leave — 2011

Kurdish fighters fought alongside US troops in the north, taking control of the northern cities and establishing an administration in the area, which is now autonomous.

The Shias in southern Iraq also rebelled after the Gulf War and were brutally suppressed. The UN established an air exclusion zone over southern Iraq in 1992 to protect the population, but persecution continued until 2003.

After May 2003, there was insurgent activity throughout the country, particularly in the Baghdad area, the predominantly Sunni-populated towns in the centre and west of the country, and in and around Mosul. The level of violence dropped after 2007 because of the US military 'surge', a ceasefire by one of the main militias, the Mahdi Army, from August 2007, and a key Sunni militia, the Awakening movement, turning against al-Qaida. There was an upsurge of violence in 2008 as the government mounted offensives against militias in Basra, Mosul and parts of Baghdad, and another upsurge in 2009–10 in the run-up to the legislative election and in the months following its inconclusive result. The approximate number of deaths as at December 2010 was: Iraqi civilians 99,000–108,000; US troops 4,400; and other coalition troops 318. Sectarian violence has continued following the withdrawal of coalition troops; in 2012 Shia areas were targeted with numerous bomb and gun attacks. In 2013 a series of deadly bomb attacks marked the ten-year anniversary of the US-led invasion.

In January 2014, after seizing territory in the east of Syria, IS captured the Iraqi cities of Fallujah and Ramadi. Mosul, Iraq's second largest city, Tikrit and the Kurdish city of Kirkuk were captured in June. Iraqi forces reclaimed Ramadi with US support in December 2015 but the local Anbar government warned civilians not to return to the city due to unexploded munitions. In June 2016 government forces entered the centre of Fallujah while Mosul was recaptured in July 2017. The government declared victory over IS in December 2017.

ECONOMY AND TRADE

The economy suffered three decades of state intervention, mismanagement, corruption, militarisation, war and international sanctions as well as the looting, insurgency and sabotage that followed the 2003 allied invasion. With the improvement in the security situation, economic activity had increased and a debt-reduction programme had been arranged. However, civil conflict, political upheaval and low oil prices caused the economy to contract in 2017, with corruption and a lack of economic and legal reforms further deterring foreign investment. The decline of IS, a rise in oil prices and economic restructuring meant the economy returned to growth in 2019, but contracted sharply in 2020 due to the coronavirus pandemic. GDP is expected to fall by 12.1 per cent in 2020.

Oil is the main resource and export, providing more than 85 per cent of government revenue. Other industries include chemicals, textiles, construction materials, food processing and metal fabrication.

The main trading partners are Turkey, China, India and the USA. Principal exports are crude oil (99 per cent), other crude materials, food and livestock. The main imports are food, medicine and manufactured goods.

GNI – US$225.7bn; US$5,740 per capita (2019)
Annual average growth of GDP – −2.1 per cent (2017 est)
Inflation rate – 0.1 per cent (2017 est)
Population below poverty line – 23 per cent (2014 est)
Unemployment – 16 per cent (2012 est)
Total external debt – US$73.02bn (2017 est)
Imports – US$29,612m (2017)
Exports – US$33,194m (2017)

BALANCE OF PAYMENTS

Trade – US$3,582m surplus (2016)
Current Account – US$15,762m surplus (2019)

Trade with UK	2018	2019
Imports from UK	£354,927,689	£393,879,693
Exports to UK	£3,621,911	£2,791,718

COMMUNICATIONS

Airports and waterways – 72; the main international airport is at Baghdad; the 5,279km of waterways are primarily on the Tigris and Euphrates rivers
Roadways and railways – 59,623km; 2,370km
Telecommunications – 2.7 million fixed lines and 36.5 million mobile subscriptions (2018); there were 18.4 million internet users in 2018
Internet code and IDD – iq; 964 (from UK), 44 (to UK)
Major broadcasters – State-run services include Al-Iraqiya (TV) and Republic of Iraq Radio; there are several private radio and television broadcasters
Press – There are more than 100 newspapers and periodicals, many with an ethnic or religious affiliation; publications include the state-run *Al-Sabah*, the private *Al-Mada* and the London-based *Al-Zaman*
WPFI score – 55.37 (162)

EDUCATION AND HEALTH

Since 2003 the country's education system has been reviewed and over 2,500 schools have been refurbished. Primary education is compulsory.

Literacy rate – 85.6 per cent (2017 est)
Health expenditure (per capita) – US$210 (2017)
Hospital beds (per 1,000 people) – 1.4 (2014)
Life expectancy (years) – 72.6 (2020 est)
Mortality rate – 3.9 (2020 est)
Birth rate – 25.7 (2020 est)
Infant mortality rate – 19.5 (2020 est)

IRELAND

Eire – Ireland

Area – 70,273 sq. km

Capital – Dublin *(Baile Atha Cliath);* population, 1,228,000 (2020 est)

Major cities – Cork (Corcaigh), Donegal (Dun na nGall), Galway (Gaillimh), Limerick (Liumneach), Swords (Sord Cholm Cille), Waterford (Port Lairge)

Currency – Euro (€) of 100 cents

Population – 5,176,569 rising at 1.04 per cent a year (2020 est)

Religion – Christian (Roman Catholic 78.3 per cent, Church of Ireland 2.7 per cent, other Christian 2.9 per cent), Muslim 1.3 per cent (est)

Language – English, Irish (Gaelic) (both official)

Population density – 71 per sq. km (2019)

Urban population – 63.4 per cent (2019 est)

Median age (years) – 37.8 (2020 est)

National anthem – 'Amhran na bhFiann' 'The Soldier's Song'

National day – 17 March (St Patrick's Day)

Death penalty – Abolished for all crimes (since 1990)

CPI score – 74 (18)

Military expenditure – US$1,208m (2018)

CLIMATE AND TERRAIN

The greatest length of the island of Ireland is 486km, from Torr Head in the north-east to Mizen Head in the south-west, and the greatest breadth is 280km, from Dundrum Bay in the east to Annagh Head in the west. Northern Ireland, in the north-east, is part of the UK. The republic has a central plain broken by hills and numerous lakes and bogs. It is surrounded by low mountains, including the Wicklow, Knockmealdown, Galty and Boggeragh mountains, and drained by the principal river, the Shannon (386km), which flows into the Atlantic Ocean. On the north coast of Achill Island (Co. Mayo) are the highest cliffs in the British Isles, 609m above sea level. Elevation extremes range from 1,041m (Carrauntoohil, Co. Kerry) to 0m (Atlantic Ocean).

POLITICS

Under the 1937 constitution, the president *(Uachtaran na Eireann)* is directly elected for a seven-year term, renewable once. The bicameral National Parliament *(Oireachtas)* consists of the House of Representatives *(Dail Eireann)* and the senate *(Seanad Eireann).* The *Dail* has 158 members, elected for a five-year term by proportional representation. The *Seanad* has 60 members, who serve a five-year term; of these, 11 are nominated by the prime minister *(Taoiseach)* and 49 are elected, six by the universities and 43 from panels of candidates representing various sectoral interests.

The *Taoiseach* is appointed by the president on the nomination of the *Dail,* while other members of the government are appointed by the president on the nomination of the *Taoiseach* with the previous approval of the *Dail.* The *Taoiseach* appoints a member of the government to be the deputy prime minister *(Tanaiste).*

Support for the Labour-Fine Gail (FG) government slumped at the February 2016 election despite a strong economy. In late April, FG leader Enda Kenny formed a minority government after the opposition, Fianna Fail (FF), pledged its support for two years in an unprecedented deal. Leo Varadkar was elected *Taoiseach* in June 2017 following Kenny's retirement. The February 2020 election resulted in a three-way split, with Sinn Fein recording its best results in decades and breaking the previously stable two-party system. A coalition was formed in June from FG, FF and the Green Party, with FF's Michael Martin appointed *Taoiseach.* Following the introduction of same-sex marriage in 2015, a referendum in May 2018 on the nation's strict abortion laws resulted overwhelmingly in support for their relaxation.

Labour Party candidate Michael D. Higgins won the 2011 presidential election and was re-elected in October 2018.

HEAD OF STATE

President, Michael D. Higgins, *elected* 27 October 2011, *sworn in* 11 November 2011, *re-elected* 26 October 2018

SELECTED GOVERNMENT MEMBERS *AS AT NOVEMBER 2020*

Taoiseach (Prime Minister), Defence, Michael Martin

Tanaiste (Deputy Prime Minister), Foreign Affairs, Trade, Leo Varadkar

Finance, Paschal Donohoe

EMBASSY OF IRELAND

17 Grosvenor Place, London SW1X 7HR

T 020-7235 2171 **E** londonembassymail@dfa.ie

W www.embassyofireland.co.uk

Ambassador Extraordinary and Plenipotentiary, HE Adrian O'Neill, *apptd* 2017

BRITISH EMBASSY

29 Merrion Road, Ballsbridge, Dublin 4

T (+353) (1) 205 3700 **W** www.gov.uk/government/world/ireland

Ambassador Extraordinary and Plenipotentiary, HE Robin Barnett, CMG, *apptd* 2016

ECONOMY AND TRADE

Since the 1980s Ireland's economy has been transformed from a mainly agricultural to a modern, export-led economy that experienced strong growth from the mid-1990s. But an over-inflated property sector and high levels of personal debt left the economy exposed in the 2008 global financial crisis, causing it to go into a deep recession. Despite passing austerity budgets in 2009 and 2010, in November 2010 the

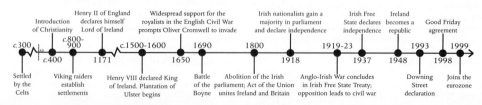

government agreed loan packages with the IMF and EU to avoid defaulting on its sovereign debt. In 2011, austerity measures increased in order to reach Ireland's EU-IMF deficit targets, and towards the end of 2013 Ireland exited its EU-IMF bailout program after meeting deficit reduction targets and reducing banking debt. Ireland was the fastest-growing economy in the eurozone between 2014 and 2018, but decelerated in 2019 ahead of the UK's withdrawal from the EU. It entered recession in 2020 due to the coronavirus pandemic and is highly vulnerable to a 'hard Brexit', as the UK is its second-largest trading partner. Loose tax laws have made Ireland desirable for many multinational firms seeking to pay less tax, but these loopholes have gradually been closed since 2014.

Agriculture now accounts for 1.2 per cent of GDP and 5 per cent of employment; services contribute 60.2 per cent and industry 38.6 per cent of GDP, and these sectors account for 84 per cent and 11 per cent of employment respectively. Major industries include pharmaceuticals and medical devices, chemicals, computer hardware and software, food and drink production, and tourism. The Kinsale gas field off the south coast meets some of Ireland's gas needs, and hydroelectric power is generated from the Shannon barrage and other schemes; as of 2017 the country was a net exporter of energy. The introduction of charges for domestic water in 2014, a measure that was part of Ireland's bailout agreement with EU and IMF, was met with protests.

The main trading partners are the UK, other EU countries and the USA. Principal exports are machinery, computers, chemicals, pharmaceuticals, livestock and animal products. The main imports are data processing equipment, other machinery, chemicals, petroleum and petroleum products, textiles and clothing.

GNI – US$307.4bn; US$62,210 per capita (2019)
Annual average growth of GDP – 5.86 per cent (2019 est)
Inflation rate – 0.3 per cent (2017 est)
Population below poverty line – 8.2 per cent (2013 est)
Unemployment – 4.98 per cent (2019 est)
Total external debt – US$2.47 trillion (2016 est)
Imports – US$294,946m (2017)
Exports – US$403,887m (2017)

BALANCE OF PAYMENTS
Trade – US$108,941m surplus (2017)
Current Account – US$44,933m deficit (2019)

Trade with UK	2018	2019
Imports from UK	£21,178,906,885	£21,922,472,403
Exports to UK	£13,698,915,031	£13,925,945,573

COMMUNICATIONS
Airports – The principal airport is at Dublin, with others at Shannon, Waterford, Cork, Killarney, Galway and Knock
Waterways – There are 956km of waterways, although these are used only by leisure craft; the main ports are Cork, Dun Laoghaire, Galway, Limerick and Waterford
Roadways and railways – 99,830km; 3,237km
Telecommunications – 1.8 million fixed lines and 5 million mobile subscriptions (2018); there were 4.3 million internet users in 2018
Internet code and IDD – ie; 353 (from UK), 44 or 048 for Northern Ireland (to UK)
Major broadcasters – The main radio and television broadcaster is the state-run Raidio Telefis Eireann (RTE), whose competitors include a handful of Irish commercial stations and British terrestrial and satellite services

Press – There are three national newspapers: *The Irish Times, Irish Independent* and *Irish Examiner*
WPFI score – 12.6 (13)

EDUCATION AND HEALTH
Primary education is directed by the state and education is compulsory until age 16.
Gross enrolment ratio (percentage of relevant age group) – primary 101 per cent, secondary 155 per cent, tertiary 77.3 per cent (2018 est)
Health expenditure (per capita) – US$4,239 (2014)
Hospital beds (per 1,000 people) – 2.8 (2013)
Life expectancy (years) – 81.2 (2020 est)
Mortality rate – 6.8 (2020 est)
Birth rate – 13.0 (2020 est)
Infant mortality rate – 3.6 (2020 est)
HIV/AIDS adult prevalence – 0.2 per cent (2019 est)

ISRAEL AND PALESTINIAN TERRITORIES
Medinat Yisra'el/Dawlat Isra'il – State of Israel

Area – 20,770 sq. km (includes Jerusalem and the Golan Heights)
Capital – The legislature and most government departments are in Jerusalem; population, 932,000 (2020 est). A resolution proclaiming Jerusalem as the capital of Israel was adopted by the *Knesset* in 1950. It is not, however, recognised as the capital by the UN because East Jerusalem is part of the Occupied Territories captured in 1967; the UN and international law consider Tel Aviv (2018 population, 4,011,000) to be the capital
Major cities – Bethlehem, Eilat, Haifa, Rishon Le'Zion
Currency – New Israeli Shekel (NIS) of 100 agora
Population – 8,675,475 rising at 1.46 per cent a year (2020 est); Jewish (74.4 per cent, of which Israel-born (76.9 per cent), Europe/America/Oceania-born (15.9 per cent), African-born (4.6 per cent)), Arab (20.9 per cent) (est)
Religion – Jewish 74.3 per cent, Muslim 17.8 per cent (predominantly Sunni, Druze 2 per cent), Christian 2 per cent (predominantly Eastern Orthodox) (est)
Language – Hebrew, Arabic (both official), English
Population density – 410 per sq. km (2019)
Urban population – 92.5 per cent (2019 est)
Median age (years) – 30.4 (2020 est)
National anthem – 'Hatikvah' 'The Hope'
National day – Fifth day of Jewish month of Iyar (anniversary of Independence Day, 1948)
Death penalty – Retained for certain crimes (last used 1962)
CPI score – 60 (35)
Military expenditure – US$15,947m (2018)
Conscription – 18 years of age (Jews and Druze only; Christians, Circassians and Muslims may volunteer); 24 months (women), 32 months (men), 48 months (officers only)

CLIMATE AND TERRAIN

Israel comprises the partly forested hill country of Galilee and parts of Judea and Samaria, the coastal plain from the Gaza Strip to north of Acre (including the plain of Esdraelon running from Haifa Bay to the south-east); the Negev, a triangular rocky desert in the south; and parts of the Jordan valley, including the Hula region, Lake Tiberias and the southwestern part of the Dead Sea. Elevation extremes range from 1,208m (Har Meron) to −408m (Dead Sea), which is the Earth's deepest depression. The climate is temperate, with hotter, drier conditions in the south and east. Average temperatures range from 11.8°C in January to 27.8°C in August.

POLITICS

Israel has no written constitution; most constitutional provision is set out in the basic law on government. The head of state is the president, elected by the legislature for a seven-year term, which is not renewable. The unicameral *Knesset* has 120 members elected by proportional representation for a four-year term. The prime minister is responsible to the *Knesset*, and appoints the cabinet, subject to the approval of the *Knesset*.

Following the March 2015 parliamentary election the Likud party formed a coalition government with the centre-right Kulanu, the pro-settler Habayit Hayehudi, the ultra-orthodox Shas and Yahadut Hatorah parties, with incumbent Benjamin Netanyahu (Likud) appointed prime minister. Right-wing parties continued to dominate the April 2019 election but coalition talks failed and the *Knesset* voted to dissolve itself for the first time in Israel's history. Another political deadlock following this election, held in September 2019, and a third was held in March 2020. A coalition between Likud and the centrist Blue and White party was finally agree in May, in which Netanyahu continued as prime minister and Benny Gantz was appointed alternate prime minister. The 2014 presidential election was won by Reuven Rivlin.

Tensions with Iran have heightened in recent years as the civil war in Syria eased and Iran's military presence in the country increased. Israeli forces have intermittently bombed Iranian military infrastructure in Syria, and acts of sabotage have been committed on both sides.

HEAD OF STATE
President, Reuven Rivlin, *elected* 10 June 2014, *sworn in* 27 July 2014

SELECTED GOVERNMENT MEMBERS *AS AT NOVEMBER 2020*
Prime Ministe, Benjamin Netanyahu
Alternate Prime Minister, Defence, Benny Gantz
Finance, Yisrael Katz
Foreign Affairs, Gavriel Ashkenazi
Internal Affairs, Aryeh Deri

EMBASSY OF ISRAEL
2 Palace Green, London W8 4QB
T 020-7957 9500 E info@london.mfa.gov.il
W http://embassies.gov.il/london/Pages/default.aspx

Ambassador Extraordinary and Plenipotentiary, HE Mark Regev, *apptd* 2016

BRITISH EMBASSY
192 Hayarkon Street, Tel Aviv 6340502
T (+972) (3) 725 1222 E webmaster.telaviv@fco.gov.uk
W www.gov.uk/government/world/israel
Ambassador Extraordinary and Plenipotentiary, HE Neil Wigan, OBE, *apptd* 2019

ECONOMY AND TRADE

Israel has a technically advanced market economy, having developed its agriculture and industry intensively since the 1970s despite limited natural resources. After a short recession in the early 2000s, structural reforms and tighter fiscal control were implemented, resulting in steady growth from 2003 to 2013 – although it contracted slightly in 2008–9 – as well as increased foreign investment and a rising demand for exports. Despite the high level of external debt, the economy proved resilient in the global downturn and the 2011 Arab Spring. Growth slowed between 2014 and 2016, but rebounded strongly before 2020 thanks to domestic demand. Geopolitical tensions and the effects of the coronavirus pandemic brought about recession in 2020, with the economy likely to contract by 6 per cent. Its debt and deficits, which have been falling, are covered by foreign aid and loans; the USA is the main source of economic and military aid and is Israel's main creditor, owed about half of its external debt. Israel's income inequality and poverty rates are among the highest of any developed nation. The country is increasingly exploiting natural gas, with production likely stimulating growth.

Israel has developed a strong technology sector, central to which are the aviation, electronics, biotechnology, communications and software industries. Other important industries include timber and paper, mineral and metal products, cement, chemicals, plastics, textiles, diamond cutting and tourism, which is reviving. The country is also an important producer of citrus fruits, vegetables, cotton, beef, poultry and dairy products. Service industries account for 69.5 per cent of GDP, industry for 26.5 per cent and agriculture for 2.4 per cent.

The main trading partners are the USA, China, the UK and other EU states. Principal exports are high-technology machinery and equipment, software, cut diamonds, agricultural products, chemicals, textiles and clothing. The main imports are raw materials, military equipment, investment goods, rough diamonds, fuels, grain and consumer goods.
GNI – US$391.9bn; US$43,290 per capita (2019)
Annual average growth of GDP – 3.28 per cent (2019 est)
Inflation rate – 0.2 per cent (2017 est)
Population below poverty line – 22 per cent (2014)
Unemployment – 3.81 per cent (2019 est)
Total external debt – US$88.66bn (2017 est)
Imports – US$97,735m (2017)
Exports – US$102,988m (2017)

Conquered by Muslim Arabs	Part of the Ottoman Empire	Zionist settlement begins	British Mandate withdraws; UN's partitioned state rejected by Arabs; State of Israel created	The Palestine Liberation Organisation begins terrorist campaign against Israel	Yom Kippur War	Signing of the Oslo Accords ends *intifada*	UN proposes two-state 'road map' for peace
c.500-100	c.1000-1300	1917	1956	1967	1987-93	2000-2	2014
c.600	c.1500	c.1880	1948	c.1960	1973	1993	2003
Conquered by Babylon, Greece and Rome	Contested by Muslims during Crusades	British capture region from Ottomans; establish Palestine	Ten-Month War against Arab states	Suez War between Israel and Egypt	Israel gains control of Gaza Strip in Six-Day War	Uprising (*intifada*) begins in West Bank and Gaza Strip	Breakdown of Oslo Accords	Seven-week conflict in Gaza against Hamas

BALANCE OF PAYMENTS
Trade – US$5,253m deficit (2017)
Current Account – US$13,135m surplus (2019)

Trade with UK	2018	2019
Imports from UK	£1,092,378,732	£1,464,676,966
Exports to UK	£1,116,380,285	£1,238,250,080

COMMUNICATIONS
Airports and waterways – 33, with the chief international airport Ben Gurion, between Tel Aviv and Jerusalem; the chief seaports are Haifa and Ashdod on the Mediterranean, and Eilat on the Red Sea
Roadways and railways – There are 19,555km of roadways; 1,384km
Telecommunications – 3.2 million fixed lines and 10.7 million mobile subscriptions (2018); there were 6.8 million internet users in 2018
Internet code and IDD – il; 972 (from UK), 44/012/013/014 (to UK)
Major broadcasters – The Israel Broadcasting Authority, which operated public television and radio services across the country, was abruptly dissolved in May 2017 after nearly 70 years and replaced by the Israeli Public Broadcasting Corporation, known as KAN; Galei Zahal Israel Defence Force (IDF) radio broadcasts to a mostly civilian audience
Press – Daily newspapers include *Yediot Aharonot*, *Ha'aretz* and *Jerusalem Post*
WPFI score – 30.84 (88)

EDUCATION AND HEALTH
Education is free and is compulsory between the ages of five and 16.
Literacy rate – 97.8 per cent (2011 est)
Gross enrolment ratio (percentage of relevant age group) – primary 104.7 per cent, secondary 105.6 per cent, tertiary 61.5 per cent (2018 est)
Health expenditure (per capita) – US$3,145 (2017)
Hospital beds (per 1,000 people) – 3.4 (2012)
Life expectancy (years) – 83 (2020 est)
Mortality rate – 5.3 (2020 est)
Birth rate – 17.6 (2020 est)
Infant mortality rate – 3.3 (2020 est)

PALESTINIAN AUTONOMOUS AREAS
Area – The total area is 6,231 sq. km. The area which is fully autonomous is 412 sq. km and the Gaza Strip is 360 sq. km
Capital – Although Palestinians claim East Jerusalem as their capital, the administrative capital was established in 1994 in Gaza City; population, 479,400 (2005 est); since 2007 the president and transitional government have been located in Ramallah, on the West Bank; population, 69,479 (2009 est)
Major towns – Jabalia, Khan Yunis, Rafah in the Gaza Strip; Hebron, Jericho, Nablus and Ramallah on the West Bank
Population – 4,818,255 (Gaza Strip – 1,918,221 rising at 2.13 per cent (2020 est); West Bank – 2,900,034 (2020 est) rising at 1.77 per cent (2020 est))
Religion – Muslim 98 per cent (Sunni) (est)
Population density – 759 per sq. km (2019)
Urban population – 76.4 (2019 est)
Median age (years) – Gaza Strip 18; West Bank 21.9 (2020 est)
National anthem – 'Fidai, Fidai' 'Freedom Fighter, Freedom Fighter'
Death penalty – Retained

Literacy rate – 97.2 per cent (2018 est)
WPFI score – 44,68 (137)

POLITICS
The Interim Agreement of 1995, amended several times, invested the Palestinian Authority with executive, legislative and judicial authority, but not sovereignty, in the autonomous areas. Large, violent demonstrations began on the Gaza–Israel border in March 2019 against Israeli occupation and intermittently continued throughout the year. Rocket fire and air strikes were periodically exchanged between Israeli forces and Hamas.

The executive president is directly elected for a four-year term, renewable once. The unicameral Palestinian Legislative Council *(Majlis al-Tashri'i)* has one seat reserved for the president and 132 seats for members elected from party lists for a four-year term. The president appoints the prime minister, who appoints the council of ministers, which must be approved by the legislature. In April 2019, Mohammad Shtayyeh was appointed prime minister.

SELECTED GOVERNMENT MEMBERS *AS AT NOVEMBER 2020*
President, Mahmoud Abbas, *elected* 9 January 2005
Prime Minister, Interior, Mohammad Shtayyeh
Foreign Affairs, Riyad Najib Abd-al-Rahman al-Maliki

PALESTINIAN MISSION TO THE UK
5 Galena Road, London W6 0LT
T 020-8563 0008 **W** http://palmissionuk.org/
Head of Mission, Prof. Manuel Hassassian

BRITISH CONSULATE-GENERAL
PO Box 19690, 15 Nashashibi Street, Sheikh Jarrah Quarter, East Jerusalem 97200
T (+972) (2) 541 4100
W www.gov.uk/government/world/the-occupied-palestinian-territories
Consul-General, Philip Hall, OBE, *apptd* 2017

ECONOMY AND TRADE
The *intifada,* and Israeli security restrictions in response to it, have damaged infrastructure and severely constrained economic activity in the Palestinian areas and external trade since 2000. Incomes had dropped and poverty risen sharply even before 2006, when the policies of the new Hamas government led to an embargo by international funding providers, and Israel stopped remitting customs dues collected on behalf of the Palestinian Authority. Emergency aid, provided through channels that bypass the Hamas government, was resumed in late 2006. The effects were most severe in Gaza, where the population is dependent on food aid. Public sector salary cuts and restrictions on aid in 2017, coupled with Egypt's ongoing crackdown on smuggling networks, have exacerbated shortages and tensions with Israel. The 2014 conflict in Gaza caused an estimated US$2.8bn (£1.8bn) worth of damage. On the West Bank, some Israeli restrictions have been eased since 2007 and economic reforms made since 2008, underpinned by foreign aid donors, have stimulated economic development. Nonetheless, unemployment, poverty and restrictions on access to foreign markets persist in both Palestinian areas, the former two exacerbated by the coronavirus pandemic.

Most economic activity consists of small family businesses engaged in farming, quarrying and small-scale manufacturing of construction materials and textiles, metal goods, handicrafts and agricultural processing. The main exports are fruit, fish, olives, vegetables and flowers, and the main trading partners are Israel, Jordan and Egypt.

Frustration at occupation leads to popular uprising — 1967

Creation of the Palestinian National Authority (PNA) — 1993

Oslo Accords talks break down; second uprising begins — 1995

— 2003

Death of PNA president Yasser Arafat; talks with Israel resume but are hindered by violence of Palestinian extremists — 2005

Victory in the legislative election for the anti-Israeli party Hamas — 2007

Confrontation leads to military invasion from Israel

Gaza Strip and West Bank under Israeli occupation — 1987

Signing of Oslo Accords — 1994

Six West Bank towns and Hebron returned to PNA — 2000-2

UN 'road map' peace plan proposed — 2004

Establishment of autonomous Palestinian state; presidential election won by Fatah candidate Mahmoud Abbas — 2006

Conflict between Hamas and Fatah movements; Abbas declares state of emergency and dissolves government — 2008-9

GNI – US$16.8bn; US$3,710 per capita (2017)
Annual average growth of GDP – West Bank -5.3 per cent; Gaza Strip -15.2 per cent (2014 est)
Inflation rate – West Bank 0.2 per cent; Gaza Strip 0.2 per cent (2017 est)
Population below poverty line – West Bank 18 per cent; Gaza Strip 30 per cent (2011 est)
Unemployment – West Bank 27.9 per cent; Gaza Strip 27.9 per cent (2017 est)
Imports – US$5,058m (2016)
Exports – US$929m (2016)

BALANCE OF PAYMENTS
Trade – US$4,128m deficit (2016)
Current Account – US$1,833m deficit (2019)

Trade with UK	2016	2017
Imports from UK	£7,496,929	£5,635,012
Exports to UK	£1,179,430	£1,246,795

ITALY
Repubblica Italiana – Italian Republic

Area – 301,340 sq. km
Capital – Rome; population, 4,257,000 (2020 est)
Major cities – Bari, Bologna, Florence, Genoa, Milan, Naples, Turin, Venice, Verona. The chief towns of Sicily and Sardinia are Palermo and Cagliari respectively
Currency – Euro (€) of 100 cents
Population – 62,402,659 rising at 0.11 per cent a year (2020 est)
Religion – Christian 83.3 per cent (predominantly Roman Catholic with small Protestant and Jehovah's Witness minorities) (est)
Language – Italian (official), German, French, Slovene
Population density – 205 per sq. km (2019)
Urban population – 70.7 per cent (2019 est)
Median age (years) – 46.5 (2020 est)
National anthem – 'Il Canto degli Italiani' 'The Song of the Italians'
National day – 2 June (Republic Day)
Death penalty – Abolished for all crimes (since 1994)

CPI score – 53 (51)
Military expenditure – US$27,808m (2018)

CLIMATE AND TERRAIN
Italy consists of a peninsula, the islands of Sicily, Sardinia, Elba and about 70 smaller islands. The smaller islands include Pantelleria, the Pelagian islands, the Aeolian islands, Capri, the Flegrean islands, the Pontine archipelago, the Tremiti islands and the Tuscan archipelago. Most of the islands are mountainous.

The peninsula is also largely mountainous, but between the spine of the Apennines and the eastern coastline are two large fertile plains: Emilia-Romagna in the north and Apulia in the south. Italy is divided from France and Switzerland by the Alps, and from Austria and Slovenia by both the Alps and the Dolomites. Three volcanoes, Vesuvius, Etna and Stromboli, are still active. Elevation extremes range from 4,748m (Mt Bianco di Courmayeur) to 0m (Mediterranean Sea). At the foot of the Alps lie the great lakes of Como, Maggiore and Garda. The chief rivers are the Po (651km) and the Adige, flowing through the northern plain to the Adriatic Sea, and the Arno (Florentine plain) and the Tiber (flowing through Rome to Ostia), which flow to the west coast. The climate is Mediterranean, with warm dry summers and mild winters.

POLITICS
The 1948 constitution has been amended several times, notably in 2001 to provide greater autonomy for the 20 regions in tax, education and environment matters. The president, who must be over 50 years of age, is elected for a seven-year term by an electoral college consisting of both chambers of the legislature and 58 regional representatives, with no term limits. The bicameral *Parlamento* comprises a 630-member Chamber of Deputies and a senate with 315 members directly elected on a regional basis and a variable number of life senators, who are past presidents and senators appointed by incumbent presidents. Elected members of both chambers serve a five-year term. In 2015, parliament passed new legislation to ensure that the party that wins the most votes in a legislative election will be allocated a majority of seats. Any party that wins more than 40 per cent of the national vote will be awarded 340 seats. If no party reaches the threshold, there is a second-place run-off between the two parties with the most votes.

Having been elected the leader of the centre-left Democratic Party (PD) in December 2013, Matteo Renzi succeeded Enrico Letta as prime minister in February 2014. Renzi resigned in December 2016, following defeat in a referendum to change the constitution, and was replaced by Paolo Gentiloni. Legislative elections in March 2018 were marked by the success of two populist parties, which formed a coalition government in June, the anti-establishment Five Star Movement and far-right League. They appointed compromise candidate and political novice Giuseppe Conte as prime minister, the country's fifth unelected head of government in a row; Conte resigned in August 2019, blaming interior minister and deputy prime minister Matteo Salvini for causing a government crisis, and in doing so triggered a new round of coalition talks. In September, the Five Star Movement and PD

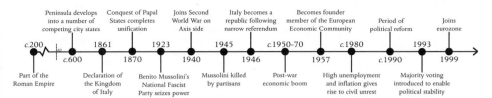

Peninsula develops into a number of competing city states	Conquest of Papal States completes unification	Joins Second World War on Axis side	Italy becomes a republic following narrow referendum	Becomes founder member of the European Economic Community	Period of political reform	Joins eurozone

*c.*200   1861   1923   1945   *c.*1950-70   *c.*1980   1993

*c.*600   1870   1940   1946   1957   *c.*1990   1999

| Part of the Roman Empire | Declaration of the Kingdom of Italy | Benito Mussolini's National Fascist Party seizes power | Mussolini killed by partisans | Post-war economic boom | High unemployment and inflation gives rise to civil unrest | Majority voting introduced to enable political stability |

formed a new coalition with Conte reinstated as prime minister. In January 2015, PD's Sergio Mattarella was elected president by parliament following the resignation of Georgio Napolitano due to ill health.

HEAD OF STATE
President, Sergio Mattarella, *elected* 31 January 2015, *sworn in* 4 February 2015

SELECTED GOVERNMENT MEMBERS *AS AT NOVEMBER 2020*
Prime Minister, Giuseppe Conte
Defence, Lorenzo Guerini
Foreign Affairs, Luigi Di Maio
Interior, Luciana Lamorgese

ITALIAN EMBASSY
14 Three Kings Yard, Davies Street, London W1K 4EH
T 020-7312 2200 **E** ambasciata.londra@esteri.it
W www.amblondra.esteri.it
Ambassador Extraordinary and Plenipotentiary, HE Raffaele Trombetta, *apptd* 2018

BRITISH EMBASSY
Via XX Settembre 80A, 00187 Rome
T (+39) (06) 4220 0001 **W** www.gov.uk/government/world/italy
Ambassador Extraordinary and Plenipotentiary, HE Jill Morris, CMG, *apptd* 2016

ECONOMY AND TRADE
Economically, Italy is divided between a prosperous and industrially developed north and a largely agricultural and welfare-dependent south that has high unemployment levels. There is a large unofficial economy that is estimated to be worth possibly 17 per cent of GDP, but measures to tackle this and wider structural reforms have made slow progress because of political opposition and sluggish economic performance. Unemployment fell to 10 per cent in 2019, but youth unemployment remained high at 25.7 per cent. The economy grew in 2014 for the first time in three years and this continued, albeit only slightly, until 2020. The coronavirus outbreak was particularly extensive in Italy, recording the fourth highest number of cases in the world to November, and the economy is set to contract by 10.6 per cent in 2020. This will only exacerbate its public debt problem, which stood at 133.2 per cent of GDP in 2019

Tourism is the largest industry. Other major industries include precision machinery, iron and steel, chemicals, food processing, textiles, motor vehicles, fashion, footwear, and ceramics. The services sector contributes 73.9 per cent of GDP, industry 23.9 per cent and agriculture 2.1 per cent. The main trading partners are other EU states, especially Germany and France. Principal exports are the products of the main industries, plus food, beverages, minerals and non-ferrous metals. The main imports are engineering and energy products, industrial raw materials, transport equipment and consumer goods.
GNI – US$2,077.7bn; US$34,460 per capita (2019)
Annual average growth of GDP – 0.34 per cent (2019 est)

Inflation rate – 1.3 per cent (2017 est)
Population below poverty line – 29.9 per cent (2012 est)
Unemployment – 9.88 per cent (2019 est)
Total external debt – US$2.444 trillion (2016 est)
Imports – US$547,188m (2017)
Exports – US$605,885m (2017)

BALANCE OF PAYMENTS
Trade – US$58,696m surplus (2017)
Current Account – US$59,157m surplus (2019)

Trade with UK	2018	2019
Imports from UK	£10,468,179,459	£9,992,135,950
Exports to UK	£19,448,399,626	£20,279,371,721

COMMUNICATIONS
Airports and waterways – 98, including major airports at Rome, Milan, Naples and Venice, Palermo and Catania (Sicily), and Cagliari (Sardinia); the main seaports are Naples, Genoa, Livorno, Trieste, Venice, Palermo and Catania
Roadways – 487,700km, including a 6,700km network of motorways *(autostrade)*
Railways – There are 20,182km of railways (2014); the main railway system is run by the state-owned *Ferrovia dello Stato.* In February 2015 it was agreed a new high-speed rail link between Lyon and Turin worth €26bn (£18bn) would be built by 2020, including a 57km tunnel through the Alps
Telecommunications – 20.4 million fixed lines and 83.3 million mobile subscriptions (2018); there were 46.3 million internet users in 2018
Internet code and IDD – it; 39 (from UK), 44 (to UK)
Major broadcasters – Rai is Italy's public radio and television broadcaster and competes with a number of private television broadcasters, the leading one being Mediaset, part of the media empire of former prime minister Silvio Berlusconi
Press – The press is highly regionalised; daily newspapers include *La Stampa* (Turin-based), *La Repubblica* (Rome) and *Corriere della Sera* (Milan)
WPFI score – 23.69 (41)

EDUCATION AND HEALTH
Education is free and compulsory between the ages of six and 16.
Literacy rate – 99.2 per cent (2018 est)
Gross enrolment ratio (percentage of relevant age group) – primary 101.2 per cent, secondary 101.4 per cent, tertiary 64.3 per cent (2018 est)
Health expenditure (per capita) – US$2,840 (2017)
Hospital beds (per 1,000 people) – 3.4 (2012)
Life expectancy (years) – 82.5 (2020 est)
Mortality rate – 10.7 (2020 est)
Birth rate – 8.4 (2020 est)
Infant mortality rate – 3.2 (2020 est)
HIV/AIDS adult prevalence – 0.2 per cent (2019 est)

JAMAICA

Caribbean Sea

NORTH AMERICA

SOUTH AMERICA

Montego Bay

JAMAICA

■Kingston

Area – 10,991 sq. km
Capital – Kingston; population, 591,000 (2020)
Major towns – Montego Bay, Portmore, Spanish Town
Currency – Jamaican dollar (J$) of 100 cents
Population – 2,808,570 falling at 0.07 per cent a year (2020 est)
Religion – Christian (Protestant 64.8 per cent, Roman Catholic 2.2 per cent), Rastafarian 1.1 per cent (est)
Language – English (official), Jamaican patois
Population density – 271 per sq. km (2019)
Urban population – 56 per cent (2019 est)
Median age (years) – 29.4 (2020 est)
National anthem – 'Jamaica, Land We Love'
National day – 6 August (Independence Day)
Death penalty – Retained
CPI score – 43 (74)
Military expenditure – US$208m (2018)

CLIMATE AND TERRAIN
An island in the Caribbean Sea, south of Cuba and west of Hispaniola, Jamaica is mostly mountainous and forested, with a narrow coastal plain. Elevation extremes range from 2,256m (Blue Mountain Peak) to 0m (Caribbean Sea). The climate is tropical, although more temperate inland. The average temperature in Jamaica is 25.6°C.

HISTORY AND POLITICS
Jamaica was visited by Columbus in 1494 and settled by the Spanish from 1509. Captured by the British in 1655, it became a crown colony in 1865. Jamaica became internally self-governing in 1959 and independent in 1962.

Post-independence politics has been dominated by the conservative Jamaican Labour Party (JLP) and social-democratic People's National Party (PNP). Relations between the two parties, often fraught, degenerated in the 1970s into violence that marred elections and political life for some years. Despite the current political stability, there is still widespread lawlessness often connected to drug-trafficking.

In the 2016 legislative election, the JLP narrowly defeated the PNP to secure a 32–31 seat majority. The JLP extended its mandate in an early election held in September 2020, in which the party won 49 seats.

Under the 1962 constitution, the head of state is Queen Elizabeth II, represented locally by a governor-general. The bicameral parliament consists of the House of Representatives, with 63 directly elected members, and the senate of 21 appointed members, 13 nominated by the prime minister and eight by the leader of the opposition; both chambers serve five-year terms. The prime minister is the leader of the majority party in the elected chamber.

Governor-General, HE Sir Patrick Allen, GCMG, *apptd* 2009

SELECTED GOVERNMENT MEMBERS *AS AT NOVEMBER 2020*
Prime Minister, Defence, Andrew Holness
Deputy Prime Minister,National Security, Horace Chang
Finance, Nigel Clarke
Foreign Affairs, Kamina Johnson-Smith

JAMAICAN HIGH COMMISSION
1–2 Prince Consort Road, London SW7 2BZ
T 020-7823 9911 **E** jamhigh@jhcuk.com **W** www.jhcuk.org
High Commissioner, HE Seth George Ramocan, *apptd* 2016

BRITISH HIGH COMMISSION
PO Box 575, 28 Trafalgar Road, Kingston 10
T (+1) (876) 936 0700 **E** ppa.kingston@fco.gov.uk
W www.gov.uk/government/world/jamaica
High Commissioner, HE Asif Ahmad, *apptd* 2017

ECONOMY AND TRADE
The economy is struggling owing to increased foreign competition, high unemployment and crime rates, internal and external debt, and hurricane and storm damage in 2004, 2007, 2008 and 2017. Following the global financial crisis, Jamaica turned to the IMF for support in 2010 and again in 2013; to secure about US$1bn in funds, the government pledged to reduce its debt below 60 per cent of GDP by 2025. In 2014 the figure stood at 132.7 per cent, but in 2019 it had fallen 93.5 per cent. Poverty and unemployment have been falling in recent years, and living standards improving, but the coronavirus pandemic is expected to contract the economy by 8.6 per cent in 2020. Tourism and remittances from expatriates account for 34 per cent of GDP. Economic growth is hampered by weak domestic demand, and growth has been sluggish for several years.

The economy is dominated by the service sector, primarily tourism, which makes up 71.9 per cent of GDP; industry accounts for 21.1 per cent, and agriculture for 7 per cent. Industries include alumina and bauxite extraction, processing agricultural produce and light manufacturing.

The main trading partners are the USA (39.1 per cent of exports and 40.6 per cent of imports), the Netherlands and Canada. Principal exports are alumina, bauxite, sugar, coffee, yams, beverages, clothing and scrap metal. The main imports are food, consumer goods, industrial supplies, fuel, and parts and accessories for capital goods.

GNI – US$15.5bn; US$5,250 per capita (2019)
Annual average growth of GDP – 0.7 per cent (2017 est)
Inflation rate – 4.4 per cent (2017 est)
Population below poverty line – 17.1 per cent (2016 est)
Unemployment – 7.72 per cent (2019 est)
Total external debt – US$14.94bn (2017 est)
Imports – US$7,457m (2017)
Exports – US$4,771m (2017)

BALANCE OF PAYMENTS
Trade – US$2,685m deficit (2017)
Current Account – US$287m deficit (2018)

Trade with UK	2018	2019
Imports from UK	£50,405,542	£55,522,367
Exports to UK	£40,267,287	£40,075,981

COMMUNICATIONS
Airports and waterways – The principal airports are at Kingston and Montego Bay; there are several harbours, Kingston being the main seaport
Roadways and railways – The island has 22,121km of roadways; the rail network is no longer in use
Telecommunications – 393,820 fixed lines and 2.9 million mobile telephone subscriptions (2018); there were 1.5 million internet users in 2018

Internet code and IDD – jm; 1 876 (from UK), 011 44 (to UK)
Major broadcasters – The state broadcaster was privatised in 1997 and now operates as Television Jamaica Ltd; Radio Jamaica Ltd (RJR) operates a number of stations
Press – There are three main daily newspapers: *The Jamaica Gleaner*, *The Jamaica Star* and the *Jamaica Observer*
WPFI score – 10.51 (6)

EDUCATION AND HEALTH
In 2010 the Inter-American Development Bank provided US$45m in funding to enable the government to make improvements to the education system and expand compulsory schooling from age 16 to 18.
Literacy rate – 88.7 per cent (2015 est)
Gross enrolment ratio (percentage of relevant age group) – primary 85.1 per cent, secondary 85.4 per cent (2019 est); tertiary 27.1 per cent (2015 est)
Health expenditure (per capita) – US$307 (2017)
Hospital beds (per 1,000 people) – 1.7 (2013)
Life expectancy (years) – 75.2 (2020 est)
Mortality rate – 7.5 (2020 est)
Birth rate – 16.1 (2020 est)
Infant mortality rate – 11.6 (2020 est)
HIV/AIDS adult prevalence – 1.4 per cent (2019 est)

JAPAN
Nihon-koku/Nippon-koku – *Japan*

Area – 377,915 sq. km
Capital – Tokyo; population, 37,393,000 (2020 est)
Major cities – Fukuoka, Hiroshima, Kawasaki, Kobe, Kyoto (the ancient capital), Nagoya, Osaka, Saitama, Sapporo, Yokohama
Currency – Yen of 100 sen
Population – 125,507,472 falling at 0.27 per cent a year (2020 est)
Religion – Shinto 70.4 per cent, Buddhist 69.8 per cent, Christian 1.5 per cent (est); much of the population adheres to more than one religion, most commonly combining Shinto and Buddhist beliefs
Language – Japanese (official)
Population density – 347 per sq. km (2019)
Urban population – 91.9 per cent (2019 est)
Median age (years) – 48.6 (2020 est)
National anthem – 'Kimigayo' 'The Emperor's Reign'
National day – 23 December (Birthday of Emperor Akihito)
Death penalty – Retained
CPI score – 73 (20)
Military expenditure – US$46,618m (2018)

CLIMATE AND TERRAIN
Japan consists of four large islands: Honshu (or Mainland), Shikoku, Kyushu and Hokkaido, and many smaller islands. Typically, the islands have coastal plains and wooded, mountainous interiors; 67 per cent of Japan's land area is forested. The mountains running across the mainland from the Sea of Japan to the Pacific Ocean include a number of volcanoes, mainly extinct or dormant. Elevation extremes range from 3,776m (Mt Fuji) to −4m (Hachiro-gata). The climate varies from temperate in the north to tropical in the south. Average temperatures range from 1°C in January to 23.7°C in August.

The islands are located at the intersection of three tectonic plates and are prone to seismic activity; 20 per cent of the world's major earthquakes occur in this area. A magnitude-9 earthquake and the ensuing tsunami devastated the north-east of Honshu in March 2011.

POLITICS
The 1947 constitution established Japan as a constitutional monarchy with a hereditary emperor as head of state. The bicameral Diet comprises the House of Representatives (the lower house) and the House of Councillors. The House of Representatives has 465 members directly elected for a four-year term, including 176 by proportional representation. The House of Councillors has 242 members, including 96 elected by proportional representation, who serve six-year terms, with half elected every three years; unlike the lower house, it cannot be dissolved by the prime minister. The prime minister is formally elected by the House of Representatives and appoints the cabinet.

The Liberal Democrat Party (LDP) has dominated post-war politics, holding power continuously from 1955 to 1993, and then – usually as the main party in coalition governments – from 1994 to 2009. In 2010, it regained control of the upper house of the legislature from the Democratic Party of Japan. The LDP returned to power in the 2012 parliamentary election and Shinzo Abe once again took the position of prime minister. Snap legislative elections in December 2014 and October 2017 resulted in majorities for the the LDP and its coalition allies. The coalition lost its two-thirds majority in the House of Councillors in the July 2019 elections, but maintained its majority. In September 2020 Abe resigned for health reasons and was replaced by Yoshihide Suga; he was Japan's the longest serving prime minster. Emperor Akihito became the first monarch to abdicate in over two centuries in April 2019 and was replaced by his son Naruhito, marking the start of the Reiwa era.

HEAD OF STATE
HIM The Emperor of Japan, Naruhito, *born* 23 February 1960, *succeeded* 1 May 2019, *enthroned* 22 October 2019
Heir, HRH Crown Prince Fumihito, *born* 30 November 1965

SELECTED GOVERNMENT MEMBERS *AS AT NOVEMBER 2020*
Prime Minister, Yoshihide Suga
Deputy Prime Minister, Finance, Taro Aso
Foreign Affairs, Toshimitsu Motegi

EMBASSY OF JAPAN
101–104 Piccadilly, London W1J 7JT
T 020-7465 6500 **E** info@ld.mofa.go.jp **W** www.uk.emb-japan.go.jp
Ambassador Extraordinary and Plenipotentiary, HE Yasumasa Magamine, *apptd* 2016

BRITISH EMBASSY
No. 1 Ichiban-cho, Chiyoda-ku, Tokyo 102–8381
T (+81) (3) 5211 1100 **E** public-enquiries.tokyo@fco.gov.uk
W www.gov.uk/government/world/japan
Ambassador Extraordinary and Plenipotentiary, HE Paul Madden, CMG, *apptd* 2017

Period of conflict between *samurai* families and successive dynasties of *shoguns*

Imperial control re-established

Defeated Russia in the Russo-Japanese War

Enters into Second World War alongside Germany and Italy; Japanese attack on Pearl Harbor

Independence restored

Kobe earthquake

*c.*600 | 1852-4 | 1889 | 1910-31 | 1945 | 1989 | 2011

*c.*1100-1800 | 1868 | 1904-5 | 1941 | 1952 | 1995

Centralised state established

Commodore Perry visits Japan, precipitating first trade with the west

Adopts western-style constitution

Annexation of Korea and Manchuria

Surrenders after atomic bombing of Hiroshima and Nagasaki; Allied occupation begins

Death of Emperor Hirohito

Fukushima nuclear disaster

ECONOMY AND TRADE

Japan has the third-largest economy in the world after China and the USA. Its rapid post-war economic growth, based largely on car and consumer electronics manufacturing, experienced a marked contraction from 1990 ('The Lost Decade') which was exacerbated by the 1997 Asian economic crisis. Reforms introduced from 2001, particularly to the corporate and public sectors, improved economic growth from 2002 to 2007, but the economy has fallen into recession five times since 2008 owing to the global downturn and, latterly, the coronavirus pandemic. In 2020 it recorded its biggest fall in GDP on record, and is expected to contract by around 5.3 per cent. The country's reliance on exports make it particularly vulnerable, which have been negatively impacted by the US-China trade war since 2018, and its aging population and declining birthrate are also serious long-term issues.

Following the 2011 earthquake and tsunami there was a drop in production; the economy largely recovered in the following two years, but was less complete in the Tohoku region. Since 2011, energy needs have been met by foreign fuel imports. Though the economy has benefited from declining oil prices and a weak yen, a series of tax rises and high public debt, which was 237 per cent of GDP in 2019 and is still the highest debt-to-GDP ratio in the world, have limited growth. Japan was one of 11 trading partners to sign the Trans-Pacific Partnership in November 2017, and in 2018 also signed an Economic Partnership Agreement with the EU, allowing for reduced trade barriers, which are likely to improve the country's economic outlook.

High-technology industries remain the mainstay of the economy, producing vehicles, electronic equipment, machine tools, steel and other metals, ships, chemicals, textiles and processed food. Financial services are also a major sector, supplying a global market. Agriculture is constrained by the mountainous terrain but intensive cultivation produces high yields, and there is a large fishing industry. The service sector contributes 68.7 per cent of GDP, industry 30.1 per cent and agriculture 1.1 per cent.

The main trading partners are China, the USA and other Pacific Rim countries. Principal exports include transport vehicles, semiconductors, and electrical machinery. The main imports are machinery and equipment, fuels, clothing, chemicals and raw materials.

GNI – US$5,263.5bn; US$41,690 per capita (2019)
Annual average growth of GDP – 0.7 per cent (2019 est)
Inflation rate – 0.5 per cent (2017 est)
Population below poverty line – 16.1 per cent (2013 est)
Unemployment – 2.36 per cent (2019 est)
Total external debt – US$3.24 trillion (2016 est)
Imports – US$835,640m (2017)
Exports – US$873,694m (2017)

BALANCE OF PAYMENTS
Trade – US$38,053m surplus (2017)
Current Account – US$184,539m surplus (2019)

Trade with UK	2018	2019
Imports from UK	£6,276,264,728	£6,527,406,910
Exports to UK	£9,945,968,440	£10,351,748,090

COMMUNICATIONS

Airports – 142; the principal airports include Haneda (Tokyo), Narita, Kansai and Chubu
Waterways – Japan has a large merchant fleet; the main seaports are Tokyo, Osaka, Nagoya, Yokohama, Kobe and Kawasaki
Roadways and railways – 1,218,772km; 27,311km
Telecommunications – 63.5 million fixed lines and 179.8 million mobile subscriptions (2018); there were 106.7 million internet users in 2018
Internet code and IDD – jp; 81 (from UK), 1 44/010 44/41 44/61 44 (to UK)
Major broadcasters – A public broadcaster, NHK, provides radio and television services; satellite and cable television is widespread and digital broadcasting is expanding
Press – Around 80 per cent of the population reads a daily newspaper, creating huge markets for publications such as *Asahi Shimbun* and English-language title *The Japan Times*
WPFI score – 28.86 (66)

EDUCATION AND HEALTH

Elementary education is free and compulsory at elementary level (six-year course) and lower secondary (three-year course).
Gross enrolment ratio (percentage of relevant age group) – primary 101.2 per cent, secondary 101.7 per cent, tertiary 63.4 per cent (2014 est)
Health expenditure (per capita) – US$4,169 (2017)
Hospital beds (per 1,000 people) – 13.4 (2012)
Life expectancy (years) – 86 (2020 est)
Mortality rate – 10.2 (2020 est)
Birth rate – 7.3 (2020 est)
Infant mortality rate – 1.9 (2020 est)

JORDAN

Al-Mamlakah al-Urduniyah al-Hashimiyah – Hashemite Kingdom of Jordan

Area – 89,342 sq. km
Capital – Amman; population, 2,148,000 (2020 est)
Major cities – Aqaba, Az Zarqa, Irbid
Currency – Jordanian dinar (JD) of 10 dirhams

Population – 10,820,644 rising at 1.4 per cent a year (2020 est); Jordanian (69.3 per cent), Syrian (13.3 per cent), Egyptian (6.7 per cent), Palestinian (6.7 per cent)
Religion – Muslim (official; predominately Sunni) 97.2 per cent, Christian 2.2 per cent (est)
Language – Arabic (official), English
Population density – 112 per sq. km (2019)
Urban population – 91.2 per cent (2019 est)
Median age (years) – 23.5 (2020 est)
National anthem – 'As-Salam al-Malaki al-Urdoni' 'Long Live the King of Jordan'
National day – 25 May (Independence Day)
Death penalty – Retained
CPI score – 48 (60)
Military expenditure – US$1,958m (2018)

CLIMATE AND TERRAIN

Most of the country is a desert plateau, with the valley of the Jordan river and the Dead Sea in the west marking the border with Israel. The Jordan valley and its extension from the Dead Sea to the Gulf of Aqaba are part of the Great Rift valley in Africa. The only hills lie in the south, along the edge of the Great Rift valley, although there is a hilly outcrop in the centre of the desert. Elevation extremes range from 1,854m (Jabal Umm ad Dami) to −408m (Dead Sea). The climate is arid, but with a rainy season in the west from November to April. Average daily temperatures range from 8.8°C in January to 28.3°C in August. Winters can be cold, with frost and snow on the plateau.

POLITICS

The 1952 constitution provides for a monarchy with a hereditary king as head of state. The bicameral National Assembly comprises a House of Deputies and a senate or House of Notables. The House of Deputies has 130 members, directly elected for a four-year term; 15 seats are reserved for women and 12 to represent minorities. The senate has 65 members, who are appointed by the king for a four-year term. The king appoints the prime minister, who chooses the council of ministers.

After the 2010 legislative election, over 85 per cent of seats were won by pro-government candidates; the announcement of this result led to rioting. From January 2011, Jordan experienced demonstrations similar to those elsewhere in the Arab world, with protestors demanding political reform, lower food prices and measures to tackle unemployment. This led to the king dismissing the government in February 2011 and to the appointment of four prime ministers in 14 months. Interim prime minister Hani Mulki was appointed to the post following legislative elections in September 2016, when voter turnout was just 37 per cent, but resigned in July 2018 following mass protests over plans to raise taxes. He was replaced by former World Bank economist Omar Razzaz, who resigned in October 2020 and was replaced by Bisher Al Khasawneh.

HEAD OF STATE

HM The King of Jordan, Abdullah II bin al-Hussein, *born* 30 January 1962, *succeeded* 7 February 1999

Heir, HRH Crown Prince Hussein bin al-Abdullah, *born* 29 March 1982

SELECTED GOVERNMENT MEMBERS *AS AT NOVEMBER 2020*
Prime Minister, Defence, Bisher Al Khasawneh
Deputy Prime Minister, Tawiq Kreishan
Finance, Mohamad al-Ississ
Interior, Tawiq Halalmeh

EMBASSY OF THE HASHEMITE KINGDOM OF JORDAN
6 Upper Phillimore Gardens, London W8 7HA
T 020-7937 3685 **E** london@fm.gov.jo
W www.jordanembassy.org.uk
Ambassador Extraordinary and Plenipotentiary, HE Omar B. Al-Nahar, *apptd* 2017

BRITISH EMBASSY
PO Box 87, Abdoun, Amman 11118
T (+962) (6) 590 9200 **E** amman.enquiries@fco.gov.uk
W www.gov.uk/government/world/jordan
Ambassador Extraordinary and Plenipotentiary, HE Bridget Brind, OBE, *apptd* 2015

ECONOMY AND TRADE

Jordan's economic development has been hindered by its lack of natural resources, influxes of refugees from the West Bank in 1967, Iraq since 2003, and 1.3 million from Syria since 2013, and the impact of conflict on its trade with Israel and Iraq. High levels of poverty, unemployment and government debt are long-term problems. Since 1999, King Abdullah has implemented economic reforms, and these measures have increased productivity and exports, begun to attract foreign direct investment, and won agreement from international donors to reschedule debt. Even so, the economy is still dependent on foreign aid, of which the USA is the largest provider, and in 2016 Jordan began a second IMF funding package aimed at reducing government spending and debt. Between 2010 and 2019 GDP grew slowly, at an average of 2.5 per cent per year, but is expected to contract by 5 per cent in 2020.

Jordan has abundant but unexploited oil reserves and few water resources. Renewable and nuclear energy sources are being explored by the government to diversify its energy mix, as nearly all energy needs are met through the importation of natural gas. It aims to become a net exporter of electricity via its national grid's links with those of Syria and Egypt. Jordan has also begun joint ventures with Israel and Syria to guarantee water supplies.

The service sector, including tourism, accounts for 66.6 per cent of GDP. Industry generates 28.8 per cent, from activities that include information technology, garment manufacturing, fertilisers, potash and phosphate mining, pharmaceuticals, oil refining, cement, inorganic chemicals and light manufacturing. Agriculture, which accounts for 4.5 per cent of GDP, produces citrus and stone fruits, tomatoes, cucumbers, olives, sheep, poultry and dairy products.

The main trade partners are the USA, India, China and Saudi Arabia. Principal exports are clothing, fertilisers, potash,

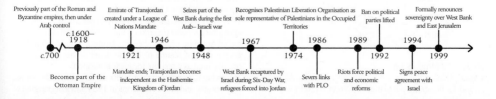

Previously part of the Roman and Byzantine empires, then under Arab control	Emirate of Transjordan created under a League of Nations Mandate	Seizes part of the West Bank during the first Arab–Israeli war	Recognises Palestinian Liberation Organisation as sole representative of Palestinians in the Occupied Territories	Ban on political parties lifted	Formally renounces sovereignty over West Bank and East Jerusalem
c.1600–1918	1946	1967	1986	1989	1994
c.700	1921	1948	1974	1992	1999
Becomes part of the Ottoman Empire	Mandate ends; Transjordan becomes independent as the Hashemite Kingdom of Jordan	West Bank recaptured by Israel during Six-Day War, refugees forced into Jordan	Severs links with PLO	Riots force political and economic reforms	Signs peace agreement with Israel

phosphates, vegetables and pharmaceuticals. The main imports are crude oil, machinery, transport equipment, iron and cereals.
GNI – US$43.5bn; US$4,300 per capita (2019)
Annual average growth of GDP – 2.0 per cent (2019 est)
Inflation rate – 3.3 per cent (2017 est)
Unemployment – 19.1 per cent (2019 est)
Total external debt – US$29.34bn (2017 est)
Imports – US$22,364m (2017)
Exports – US$14,184m (2017)

BALANCE OF PAYMENTS
Trade – US$8,180m deficit (2017)
Current Account – US$1,003m deficit (2019)

Trade with UK	2018	2019
Imports from UK	£245,368,790	£279,268,053
Exports to UK	£32,943,174	£34,242,078

COMMUNICATIONS
Airports – 16; the largest airports are at Amman and Aqaba
Waterways – Amman is linked to Jordan's seaport at Aqaba, the Saudi Arabian port of Jeddah, and the Syrian and Iraqi capitals by roads, which are of considerable importance in the overland trade of the Middle East
Roadways and railways – 7,203km; 509km
Telecommunications – 396,145 fixed lines and 8.7 million mobile subscriptions (2018); there were 7 million internet users in 2018
Internet code and IDD – jo; 962 (from UK), 44 (to UK)
Major broadcasters – Jordan Radio and Television, the state-run broadcaster, operates three terrestrial television channels and a satellite channel as well as radio services in Arabic, English and French
Press – Major daily newspapers include *Ad Dustour, Al Ra'y* and *Al Ghadd*
WPFI score – 42.08 (128)

EDUCATION AND HEALTH
Literacy rate – 98.2 per cent (2018 est)
Gross enrolment ratio (percentage of relevant age group) – primary 81.8 per cent, secondary 65.2 per cent (2019 est); tertiary 34.4 per cent (2018 est)
Health expenditure (per capita) – US$341 (2017)
Hospital beds (per 1,000 people) – 1.4 (2015)
Life expectancy (years) – 75.5 (2020 est)
Mortality rate – 3.4 (2020 est)
Birth rate – 23 (2020 est)
Infant mortality rate – 12.8 (2020 est)

KAZAKHSTAN
Qazaqstan Respublikasy – Republic of Kazakhstan

Area – 2,724,900 sq. km
Capital – Nur-Sultan (previously known as Astana, Akmola and Tselinograd); population, 1,896,000 (2020 est)

Major cities – Almaty (the former capital), Oskemen, Pavlodar, Qaraghandy, Semey, Shymkent, Taraz
Currency – Tenge of 100 tiyn
Population – 19,091,949 rising at 0.89 per cent a year (2020 est); Kazakh (68 per cent), Russian (19.3 per cent). The Russian population is concentrated in the north of Kazahkstan, where it forms a significant majority, and in Almaty
Religion – Muslim 70.2 per cent (predominantly Sunni), Christian 26.2 per cent (mostly Russian Orthodox) (est)
Language – Kazakh, Russian (both official)
Population density – 7 per sq. km (2019)
Urban population – 57.5 per cent (2019 est)
Median age (years) – 31.6 (2020 est)
National anthem – 'Menin Qazaqstanim' 'My Kazakhstan'
National day – 16 December (Independence Day)
Death penalty – Retained for certain crimes
CPI score – 34 (113)
Military expenditure – US$1,614m (2018)
Conscription – 18 years of age; 24 months
Literacy rate – 99.8 per cent (2018 est)
Gross enrolment ratio (percentage of relevant age group) – primary 104.4 per cent, secondary 113.2 per cent, tertiary 61.7 per cent (2019 est)
Health expenditure (per capita) – US$280 (2017)
Hospital beds (per 1,000 people) – 6.7 (2013)
Life expectancy (years) – 72 (2020 est)
Mortality rate – 8.2 (2020 est)
Birth rate – 16.4 (2020 est)
Infant mortality rate – 17.9 (2020 est)
HIV/AIDS adult prevalence – 0.3 per cent (2019 est)

CLIMATE AND TERRAIN
Kazakhstan stretches from the basin of the river Volga and the Caspian Sea in the west to the Altai and Tien Shan mountains in the east. The terrain consists of arid steppes and semi-deserts; it is flat in the west, hilly in the east and mountainous in the south-east. Elevation extremes range from 6,995m (Khan Tangiri Shyngy) to −132m (Vpadina Kaundy). The country contains the northern part of the Aral Sea in the south-west, and Lake Balkhash and Lake Zaysan in the east. The Aral Sea has suffered significant pollution and desertification since the 1960s, creating the Aralkum desert. The climate is continental, and while arid in much of the country, it can be Siberian in the north. Average yearly temperatures in Nur-Sultan range from −11.3°C in January to 23.1°C in July.

HISTORY AND POLITICS
Kazakhstan was inhabited by nomadic tribes before being invaded by Genghis Khan and incorporated into his empire in 1218. After this empire disintegrated, feudal towns emerged based on large oases and the nomadic tribes formed federations led by khans. The towns affiliated in the late 15th century and established a Kazakh state, which engaged in almost continuous warfare with the marauding khanates on its southern border. After turning to Russia for protection in the 1730s, the Kazakh khanates were formally incorporated into the Russian Empire in the early 19th century.
   The 1917 Bolshevik revolution in Russia was followed by civil war in Kazakhstan, which became an autonomous republic within the USSR in 1920 and a full union republic in 1936. Kazakhstan suffered severely under Stalin's policies of agricultural collectivisation and 'sedentarisation', which forced nomadic tribes to become farmers; around 1.5 million people died of famine or disease. Later Soviet rule saw the country used as a test site for nuclear weapons.
   Growing nationalism in the 1980s and a reformist leader led to economic and cultural reforms in 1989 and a declaration of

sovereignty in 1990. Kazakhstan declared its independence in December 1991, and became a founding member of the Commonwealth of Independent States (CIS). It entered an economic, social and military union with Kyrgyzstan and Uzbekistan in 1994, and an economic and military pact with Russia in 1995, when it achieved nuclear-free status.

Nursultan Nazarbayev, the reformist communist leader of 1989, became head of state in 1990 and was re-elected in 1991, 1999, 2005 and 2011; the April 2011 election, in which he received 95 per cent of the vote, was criticised by international observers. A 2007 constitutional reform allows him to serve for an unlimited number of terms. Nazarbayev was re-elected in the April 2015 presidential election and claimed to have won over 97 per cent of the popular vote, easily defeating his pro-government opponents. The elections were judged to be unsound by a number of human rights groups. Nazarbayev unexpectedly retired in March 2019 after three decades in power, and was replaced by appointed heir and former prime minister Kasymzhomart Tokayev, although Nazarbayev retained key civil and military positions. Tokayev's premiership was confirmed by popular vote in June, in an election once again condemned by international observers. The capital Astana was renamed Nur-Sultan for its outgoing leader in March 2019.

In 2006, three pro-government parties merged with Nazarbayev's Fatherland Republican Party (Otan), which subsequently changed its name to Nur-Otan. Nur-Otan won every seat in the lower legislative chamber in the 2007 legislative elections and retained 83 seats in the 2012 elections; in March 2016 legislative elections, the party won 82 per cent of the vote. Before resigning, Nazarbayev sacked the government in February 2019 and appointed Askar Mamin as prime minister.

The president is directly elected; in 2007 the constitution was amended to reduce the presidential term from seven to five years, renewable once, although Nazarbayev was exempt from this restriction. The bicameral parliament is composed of the assembly *(Majlis)* and the senate. The assembly has 107 members, 98 directly elected on a single constituency basis and nine seats reserved for ethnic groups; all serve a five-year term. The senate has 47 members, of whom 32 are indirectly elected and 15 are appointed by the president for a six-year term, with half elected every three years. The president appoints the prime minister and other senior ministers.

HEAD OF STATE
Interim President, C-in-C of the Armed Forces, Kasymzhomart
    Tokayev, *appointed* 20 March 2019, *elected* 9 June 2019

SELECTED GOVERNMENT MEMBERS *AS AT*
NOVEMBER 2020
Prime Minister, Askar Mamin
First Deputy Prime Minister, Alikhan Smailov
Foreign Affairs, Mukhtar Tleuberdi
Internal Affairs, Yerlan Turgumbayev

EMBASSY OF THE REPUBLIC OF KAZAKHSTAN
125 Pall Mall, London SW1Y 5EA
T 020-7925 1757 **E** london@mfa.kz **W** www.kazembassy.org.uk
Ambassador Extraordinary and Plenipotentiary, HE Erlan
    Idrissov, *apptd* 2017

BRITISH EMBASSY
62 Kosmonavtov Street, Nur-Sultan
T (+7) (717) 255 6200 **E** ukinkz@fco.gov.uk
W www.gov.uk/government/world/kazakhstan
Ambassador Extraordinary and Plenipotentiary, HE Michael
    Gifford, *apptd* 2018

ECONOMY AND TRADE

Economic reforms and privatisation in the 1990s enabled GDP to grow by at least 8 per cent a year from 2002 to 2007, although lower commodity prices and banking sector problems caused the economy to contract briefly in 2008–9. Growth has largely been achieved through exploitation of vast oil and natural gas reserves (75 per cent of exports), particularly since the opening of export pipelines to Black Sea ports (in 2001) and China (2005), Kazakhstan's use of the Azerbaijan–Turkey pipeline (from 2008), and the exploitation of the giant Kashagan field since October 2016. The nation's oil production rose by 10.5 per cent in 2017, and significant further extraction in the Tengiz field is due for completion in 2022. As a result of the boom, the government has tried to eliminate the budget deficit, but it is also trying to stimulate growth in other industries, especially mining, to reduce dependency on oil. Kazakhstan has been badly affected by weaknesses in the Russian economy and by falling commodity prices, with a stimulus package consequently introduced in December 2014, but growth returned prior to the 2020 coronavirus pandemic thanks to higher domestic demand and a construction boom.

Other mineral resources are considerable and there is a significant mining industry exploiting coal, iron ore, manganese, chrome, lead, zinc, copper, titanium, bauxite, silver, gold, phosphate and uranium deposits. A large and well-developed agricultural sector produces grain, wool, cotton and livestock as cash crops. The main industries are mineral extraction and processing, and machine building, especially agricultural machinery and electric motors. Services contribute 61.2 per cent of GDP, industry 34.1 per cent and agriculture 4.7 per cent.

The main trading partners are China, Russia and EU states. Principal exports are oil and oil products, natural gas, ferrous metals, chemicals, machinery, grain, wool, meat and coal. The main imports are machinery and equipment, metal products and foodstuffs. Kazakhstan became a founding member of the Eurasian Economic Union (EEU) in 2015, a customs union with Russia and Belarus that stimulated sharp increases in trade between these nations.

GNI – US$163.1bn; US$8,810 per capita (2019)
Annual average growth of GDP – 6.13 per cent (2019 est)
Inflation rate – 7.4 per cent (2017 est)
Population below poverty line – 2.6 per cent (2016 est)
Unemployment – 4.8 per cent (2019 est)
Total external debt – US$167.5bn (2017 est)
Imports – US$42,927m (2017)
Exports – US$55,849m (2017)

BALANCE OF PAYMENTS
Trade – US$12,922m surplus (2017)
Current Account – US$7,206m deficit (2019)

Trade with UK	2018	2019
Imports from UK	£300,516,791	£360,057,883
Exports to UK	£349,000,490	£362,096,038

COMMUNICATIONS

Airports – 63; the largest airports are at Nur-Sultan, Almaty and Atyrau
Waterways – There are ports on the Caspian and Aral seas, which permit international trade; the Syr Darya and Irtysh rivers provide 4,000km of navigable waterways
Roadways and railways – 81,814km of paved roads; 16,614km
Telecommunications – 3.4 million fixed lines and 26.1 million mobile subscriptions (2018); there were 14.8 million internet users in 2018

Internet code and IDD – kz; 7 (from UK), 810 44 (to UK)
Major broadcasters – There are 250 television and radio stations according to official statistics; the influential Khabar Agency, founded by the president's eldest daughter, Dariga Nazarbayeva, operates channels in both Russian and Kazakh
Press – Major newspapers include the government-backed Russian-language *Kazakhstanskaya Pravda* and the Kazakh-language *Yegemen Qazaqstan*
WPFI score – 54.11 (157)

KENYA

Jamhuri ya Kenya – Republic of Kenya

Area – 580,367 sq. km
Capital – Nairobi; population, 4,735,000 (2020 est)
Major cities – Eldoret, Kisumu, Mombasa, Nakuru
Currency – Kenyan shilling (Ksh) of 100 cents
Population – 53,527,936 rising at 2.2 per cent a year (2020 est); Kikuyu (17.1 per cent), Luhya (14.3 per cent), Kalenjin (13.4 per cent), Luo (10.7 per cent), Kamba (9.8 per cent), Somali (5.8 per cent), Kisii (5.7 per cent), Mijikenda (5.2 per cent) (est)
Religion – Christian 85.5 per cent (Protestant 33.4 per cent, Roman Catholic 20.6 per cent, other Christian 11.1 per cent), Muslim 11.2 per cent (est)
Language – English, Swahili (both official), indigenous languages
Population density – 90 per sq. km (2019)
Urban population – 27.5 per cent (2019 est)
Median age (years) – 20 (2020 est)
National anthem – 'Ee Mungu Nguvu Yetu' 'Oh God of All Creation'
National day – 12 December (Independence Day)
Death penalty – Retained (last used 1987)
CPI score – 28 (137)
Military expenditure – US$1,097m (2018)

CLIMATE AND TERRAIN
The coastal plain and semi-desert plains in the east rise to mountainous highlands in the centre and west that are divided by the Great Rift valley. Elevation extremes range from 5,199m (Mt Kenya) to 0m (Indian Ocean). The country includes part of Lake Victoria in the south-west and most of Lake Turkana (Rudolph) in the north. Kenya is an equatorial country; the climate is tropical on the coast and arid in the interior, tempered by altitude. The average temperature is 25°C.

HISTORY AND POLITICS
Fossils of early hominids found in the Lake Turkana region suggest that the area was inhabited some 2.6 million years ago. Arabs and Persians settled on the Kenyan coast from the eighth century AD. The Portuguese gained control of coastal areas in the 16th century but Arab overlordship was reasserted in the 18th century.

European exploration of the interior began in the 19th century and in 1895, Kenya became part of Britain's East African Protectorate, becoming a colony in 1920. Demands for internal self-government by white settlers were rejected in 1923, but from 1944 a nationalist group, the Kenya African Union (KAU), was founded to campaign for African rights. The Mau Mau rebellion of 1952–6, intended to drive white settlers from African tribal lands, resulted in a state of emergency that lasted until 1960, when preparations for majority African rule began. Kenya became independent in 1963, and a republic in 1964. President Jomo Kenyatta's death in 1978 brought Daniel arap Moi to power, and he remained president until 2002, when he was barred from standing for re-election.

Kenya was a one-party state ruled by the Kenya African National Union (KANU) between 1964 and 1991. A multiparty system was reintroduced after violent agitation and international pressure in the early 1990s but KANU maintained its grip on power until the 2002 elections, which were won by the National Rainbow Coalition (NARC). Despite the NARC's anti-corruption electoral platform, once in government it made little headway against endemic corruption, and government ministers were implicated in corruption scandals in 2005 and 2006. It is estimated that up to US$1,000m (£650m) of official funds were misappropriated in 2002–7.

After decades of stability, intercommunal violence and conflict over land and water rights have become more frequent since the 1990s, exacerbated by a rural food crisis since 2004 following persistent drought and crop failures. In 2018, the Patel Dam burst causing widespread devastation and displacing over 220,000 people.

The president is directly elected for a five-year term, renewable once. The bicameral parliament as defined in the 2010 constitution was first elected in 2013; members of both houses serve five-year terms. The lower chamber, the National Assembly, has 350 members, of whom 290 are directly elected; 47 seats are reserved for women, directly elected from each county, 12 members are nominated pro rata by political parties to represent special interests including youth, persons with disabilities and workers, and the speaker is a member *ex officio*. The upper chamber, the senate, has 68 members: 47 are directly elected from each county, 16 seats are reserved for women, nominated pro rata by political parties, and four members are nominated to represent youth and persons with disabilities; the speaker is a member *ex officio*.

The 2007 legislative elections were won by the Orange Democratic Movement (ODM), led by Raila Odinga. The announcement that President Kibaki had won the simultaneous presidential election triggered weeks of serious rioting; this developed into ethnic violence that left over 1,000 dead and 600,000 displaced. After international mediation, a power-sharing agreement was signed in February 2008; under this, Kibaki remained president and the post of prime minister was created for Raila Odinga, although this post was abolished in 2013.

In March 2013 Uhuru Kenyatta, the son of Kenya's first president, was elected president with 50.5 per cent of the vote; his Jubilee coalition became the largest bloc in both houses in the legislative elections. In March 2015 International Criminal Court judges terminated charges against Uhuru Kenyatta relating to 2007's post-election violence, citing lack of adequate evidence. President Kenyatta was re-elected in August 2017, although the result was contested by opposition leader Raila Odinga and was nullified in September 2017. In October, President Kenyatta won fresh elections that had been boycotted by the opposition.

In recent years Kenya has suffered a number of terrorist attacks linked to Islamism, with the Somalian group al-

Shabab attacking US, Israeli and Kenyan targets within the country. In September 2013, al-Shabab gunmen killed at least 62 people in the Westgate shopping mall in Nairobi; in April 2015, 148 people at Garissa University College; and in January 2019, 21 people at a luxury hotel in Nairobi.

HEAD OF STATE
President, C-in-C of the Armed Forces, Uhuru Kenyatta, *elected* 4 March 2013, *took office* 9 April 2013, *re-elected* 8 August 2017
Vice-President, William Ruto

SELECTED GOVERNMENT MEMBERS *AS AT NOVEMBER 2020*
Defence, Monica Juma
Foreign Affairs, Raychelle Omamo
Interior, Fred Okengo Matiang'i

KENYA HIGH COMMISSION
45 Portland Place, London W1B 1AS
T 020-7636 2371 **E** info@kenyahighcom.org.uk
W www.kenyahighcom.org.uk
High Commissioner, HE Manoah Esipisu, *apptd* 2018

BRITISH HIGH COMMISSION
PO Box 30465, Upper Hill Road, 00100 Nairobi
T (+254) (20) 284 4000 **E** nairobi.enquiries@fco.gov.uk
W www.gov.uk/government/world/kenya
High Commissioner, HE Jane Marriott, OBE, *apptd* 2019

ECONOMY AND TRADE
Kenya acts as a regional trade and finance hub for its landlocked neighbours. However, its own economy is weak owing to endemic corruption, low commodity prices, low investor confidence and the frequent suspension of international aid because of successive governments' failure to tackle corruption. These problems are exacerbated by terrorist attacks, political instability, unemployment and the occasional severe drought. The lengthy election campaign of 2017 drained government resources and combined with drought-like conditions to slow growth; nonetheless, peaceful elections, infrastructure investment (mainly from China) and rising tourism has resulted in strong economic growth over the past decade and in 2016 its was categorised as a middle-income country..

The country is overwhelmingly agricultural, with about 61.1 per cent of the population engaged in agricultural and horticultural production; this sector contributes 34.5 per cent of GDP. The world's third-largest producer of tea, Kenya also grows coffee, maize, wheat, sugar cane, fruit and vegetables. Natural resources include gold, limestone, soda ash, salt, rubies, garnets and hydroelectric power, which makes it self-sufficient in energy.

The industrial sector has grown over the past two decades, developing a manufacturing base in consumer goods (such as clothing and furniture) and agricultural products (such as dehydrated vegetables), as well as oil refining, commercial ship repair and the production of steel, aluminium, lead and cement. Tourism is an important source of income and is growing, though it is threatened by terrorism. Industry contributes 17.8 per cent to GDP and the service sector 47.5 per cent.

The main export markets are Uganda, the USA and Pakistan, while imports come mainly from India, China and the UAE. Principal exports are tea, horticultural products, coffee, petroleum products, fish, clothing and cement. The main imports are machinery and transport equipment, petroleum products, iron and steel, resins and plastics.
GNI – US$91.8bn; US$1,750 per capita (2019)
Annual average growth of GDP – 5.39 per cent (2019 est)

Inflation rate – 8.0 per cent (2017 est)
Population below poverty line – 36.1 per cent (2016 est)
Unemployment – 40 per cent (2013 est)
Total external debt – US$27.59bn (2017 est)
Imports – US$19,315m (2017)
Exports – US$10,737m (2017)

BALANCE OF PAYMENTS
Trade – US$8,577m deficit (2017)
Current Account – US$5,559m deficit (2019)

Trade with UK	2018	2019
Imports from UK	£384,045,622	£337,994,615
Exports to UK	£435,354,232	£317,036,043

COMMUNICATIONS
Airports – 16; the largest airports are at Nairobi, Mombasa and Eldoret
Waterways – The only significant inland waterway is the Kenyan portion of Lake Victoria; Kisumu is the main port
Roadways and railways – There are 117,800km of roadways, of which only 14,420 are paved; 3,819km
Telecommunications – 65,644 fixed lines and 49 million mobile subscriptions (2018); there were 9.1 million internet users in 2018
Internet code and IDD – ke; 254 (from UK), 0 44 (to UK)
Major broadcasters – The state-run Kenya Broadcasting Corporation (KBC) competes with a range of commercial television and radio stations
Press – Daily newspapers include the English-language *Daily Nation* and *The Standard,* and *Taifa Leo* (Swahili)
WPFI score – 33.72 (103)

EDUCATION AND HEALTH
The state provides eight years of free primary education.
Literacy rate – 81.5 per cent (2018 est)
Gross enrolment ratio (percentage of relevant age group) – primary 103.2 per cent (2016 est); secondary 68 per cent (2012 est)
Health expenditure (per capita) – US$77 (2017)
Hospital beds (per 1,000 people) – 1.4 (2010)
Life expectancy (years) – 69 (2020 est)
Mortality rate – 5.2 (2020 est)
Birth rate – 27.2 (2020 est)
Infant mortality rate – 29.8 (2020 est)
HIV/AIDS adult prevalence – 4.5 per cent (2019 est)

KIRIBATI
Republic of Kiribati

Area – 811 sq. km
Capital – Tarawa, on Bairiki; population, 64,000 (2018)
Currency – Australian dollar ($A) of 100 cents
Population – 111,796 rising at 1.09 per cent a year (2020 est)
Religion – Christian (Roman Catholic 57.3 per cent, Kiribati Uniting Church 31.3 per cent, Mormon 5.3 per cent), Baha'i 2.1 per cent (est)

Language – English, Kiribati (Gilbertese) (both official)
Population density – 143 per sq. km (2019)
Urban population – 54.8 per cent (2019 est)
Median age (years) – 25.7 (2020 est)
National anthem – 'Teirake Kaini Kiribati' 'Stand up, Kiribati'
National day – 12 July (Independence Day)
Death penalty – Not since independence
Gross enrolment ratio (percentage of relevant age group) – primary
    101.3 per cent (2017 est); secondary 86 per cent (2011
    est)
Health expenditure (per capita) – US$171 (2017)
Life expectancy (years) – 67.5 (2020 est)
Mortality rate – 6.9 (2020 est)
Birth rate – 20.5 (2020 est)
Infant mortality rate – 29.2 (2020 est)

CLIMATE AND TERRAIN

Kiribati (pronounced Kiri-bas) comprises 32 atolls and one island. About 20 are inhabited: Banaba island; the Kiribati (Gilbert) group (17); the Rawaki (Phoenix) Islands (8); and some of the Line Islands (11), including Kiritimati (Christmas Island). They are situated in the southern central Pacific Ocean, crossed by the equator; the area was also crossed by the international date line until 1995, when the government unilaterally moved the date line eastwards so that the whole country shared the same day. Few of the atolls are more than 800m wide or more than 3m high, making the country particularly vulnerable to rising sea levels. The highest point is 81m (on Banaba) and the lowest is 0m (Pacific Ocean). The climate is tropical.

HISTORY AND POLITICS

The islands were settled by Austronesian-speaking peoples in the first millennium BC, and Samoans, Fijians and Tongans migrated there in the 11th to 14th centuries. British settlers arrived in the islands in the early 19th century. In 1892, the Gilbert (Kiribati) and Ellice (Tuvalu) islands were proclaimed a British protectorate and in 1916 became a British colony that subsequently incorporated the Line Islands and Phoenix Islands. During the Second World War, Banaba and the Gilbert islands were occupied by the Japanese and were the scene of fierce fighting between Japanese and US troops. Some of the Line Islands were used for British nuclear weapons tests in the 1950s and 1960s. In 1975, the territories separated and the Gilbert, Phoenix and Line Islands became independent as the Republic of Kiribati in 1979.

Open-cast phosphate mining left Banaba unfit for human habitation and the population was evacuated in 1945, to be relocated to a northern island of Fiji. Overcrowding and lack of infrastructure have caused more general environmental degradation, especially in urban areas. However, the main problem is the rise in the sea level due to global warming; salination is already contaminating water supplies and agricultural land, causing villages to be relocated, and Kiribati is expected to be the first state to lose territory. The government is seeking permanent refugee status for its citizens in neighbouring countries.

Political parties are primarily divided by their allegiance to China or Taiwan. In the 2020 legislative elections, the pro-China Tobwaan Kiribati Party (TKP) lost its majority as the House of Assembly was split, with 22 seats on either side. TKP's Taneti Maamau was elected president in 2016 after Anote Tong reached his three-term limit, and was re-elected in June 2020.

Under the 1979 constitution, the executive president is directly elected for a four-year term, with a maximum of three terms; presidential candidates are selected by and from members of the legislature. The unicameral legislature, the House of Assembly, has 46 members: 44 members directly elected for a four-year term, an appointed representative of the Banaban community in Fiji and the attorney-general. There were no formal political parties, but since the 1980s associations of politicians formed for elections have proved durable enough to be given names.

HEAD OF STATE

President, Taneti Maamau, *elected* 9 March 2016, *sworn in* 11
    March 2016 *re-elected,* 22 June 2020
Vice-President, Finance, Teuea Toatu

SELECTED GOVERNMENT MEMBERS *AS AT NOVEMBER 2020*

Commerce, Industry and Co-Operatives, Booti Nauan
Internal, Boutu Bateriki

KIRIBATI HONORARY CONSULATE

The Great House, Llanddewi Rhydderich, Monmouthshire NP7 9UY
Honorary Consul, Michael Walsh

BRITISH HIGH COMMISSIONER

HE Melanie Hopkins, *apptd* 2016, resident at Suva, Fiji

ECONOMY AND TRADE

Since the phosphate deposits on Banaba ran out in 1979, the economy has been weak and has few natural resources. The country is dependent on coconuts, fish and tourism as the main economic activities; development is hampered by remoteness, poor transport connections and the lack of funding, infrastructure and skills. A large portion of GDP comes from international aid (around 32.7 per cent of government revenue in 2016), the sale of fishing licences, remittances from expatriates and monies from the trust fund established with phosphate mining revenues. A financial sector is being developed. The main trading partners are Pacific Rim countries. The principal exports are coconuts and fish. The principal imports are foodstuffs, machinery and transport equipment, manufactured goods and fuel.
GNI – US$0.4bn; US$3,350 per capita (2019)
Annual average growth of GDP – 3.1 per cent (2017 est)
Inflation rate – 0.4 per cent (2017 est)
Total external debt – US$40.9m (2016 est)
Imports – US$173m (2016)
Exports – US$20m (2016)

BALANCE OF PAYMENTS

Trade – US$153m deficit (2016)
Current Account – US$76m surplus (2018)

Trade with UK	2018	2019
Imports from UK	£268,957	£44,548
Exports to UK	£3,206	£0

COMMUNICATIONS

Airports and waterways – Four, with the main international airport on Tarawa, while another on Kiritimati operates regular services to Fiji and Hawaii; the main seaport is Betio, on Tarawa
Roadways – 670km
Telecommunications – 765 fixed lines (2017) and 58,838 mobile subscriptions (2018); there were 15,946 internet users in 2018
Internet code and IDD – ki; 686 (from UK), 44 (to UK)
Media – The government-run newspaper and radio stations offer a diverse range of views; *Te Uekera* is the principal weekly newspaper

DEMOCRATIC PEOPLE'S REPUBLIC OF KOREA

Choson-minjujuui-inmin-konghwaguk – Democratic People's Republic of Korea

Area – 120,538 sq. km
Capital – Pyongyang; population, 3,084,000 (2020 est)
Major cities – Chongjin, Hamhung, Hungnam, Kaesong, Nampo, Wonsan
Currency – North Korean won of 100 chon
Population – 25,643,466 rising at 0.51 per cent a year (2020 est)
Religion – Religious activity is almost non-existent outside government-sponsored religious groups, although many believers are thought to worship in private. Historically, the main religions were Buddhism and Confucianism; Buddhism, Christianity and Chondo (a syncretic religion) are officially recognised
Language – Korean (official)
Population density – 212 per sq. km (2019)
Urban population – 62.1 per cent (2019 est)
Median age (years) – 34.6 (2020 est)
National anthem – 'Aegukka' 'Patriotic Song'
National day – 9 September (Founding of the Democratic People's Republic of Korea, 1948)
Death penalty – Retained
CPI score – 17 (172)
Conscription – 17 years of age; 10 years for men, to age 23 for women
Literacy rate – 100 per cent (2015 est)
Gross enrolment ratio (percentage of relevant age group) – primary 89.3 per cent (2018 est); secondary 92.3 per cent (2015 est); tertiary 26.8 per cent (2018 est)
Health expenditure (per capita) – $22 (2007)
Life expectancy (years) – 71.6 (2020 est)
Mortality rate – 9.4 (2020 est)
Birth rate – 14.5 (2020 est)
Infant mortality rate – 20 (2020 est)

CLIMATE AND TERRAIN
The republic occupies the northern half of the Korean peninsula. The land rises from coastal plains in the west to mountains and hills that occupy 80 per cent of the land area. Elevation extremes range from 2,744m (Paektu-san) to 0m (Sea of Japan). The climate is temperate, though more extreme than in South Korea. Average temperatures range from −10.5°C in January to 21.3°C in July and August.

POLITICS
After the Korean war ended in 1953, Kim Il-sung continued the process of Soviet-style reform begun in 1946. He also developed *Juche* (self-reliance), an ideology demanding total economic independence. North Korea pursued an isolationist foreign policy for several decades, only signing a mutual assistance treaty with China in 1961 and improving relations with the USSR in 1985. It established diplomatic contacts with South Korea and Japan in 1990, raising hopes that it was abandoning its isolationism, but it remains a secretive, closed country under rigid state control.

Kim Il-sung died in 1994. His son Kim Jong-il became chairman of the National Defence Commission, designated as the highest post of the state, and general secretary of the Korean Workers' Party in 1997. In September 2010 the Korean Workers' Party congress (the first for 44 years) renewed the top party leadership; Kim Jong-il's third son, Kim Jong-un, was appointed to senior political and military posts, before ascending to supreme leader following the death of Kim Jong-il in December 2012. In December 2013 Kim Jong-un's uncle, Chang Song-thaek, was executed in a move seen by observers as an attempt to consolidate Kim's regime. In October 2020 Kim Jong-un apologised to the nation for his poor leadership during the coronavirus outbreak, which saw the economy spiral even further.

The communist Korean Workers' Party, founded in 1946 by Kim Il-sung, is the only permitted political party. However, political control and leadership is maintained by the cult of personality created by Kim Il-sung and continued by his successors Kim Jong-il and Kim Jong-un. Elections to the Supreme People's Assembly last took place in March 2019.

The 1972 constitution was amended in 1998 to designate leading state posts; it made Kim Il-sung the Eternal President and the chairmanship of the National Defence Commission (NDC), held by Kim Jong-il, the highest post in the state, while providing that the chairman of the Presidium of the Supreme People's Assembly would represent the state on formal occasions. A further amendment in 2009 named the NDC chairman as the 'supreme leader of the state'; it also removed all references to communism, and established the *songun* principle of military responsibility for all internal affairs.

There is a unicameral legislature, the Supreme People's Assembly, which has 687 members directly elected from a single list of candidates for a five-year term. The assembly elects a presidium and the premier, appointing the government on the recommendation of the premier. The Central People's Committee, which is also elected by the assembly, directs the administrative council (government), which implements the policy formulated by the committee.

HEAD OF STATE
Eternal President, Kim Il-sung (deceased)
Eternal General Secretary, Kim Jong-il (deceased)
Supreme Leader, Kim Jong-un
President of the Presidium of the Supreme People's Assembly, Choe Ryong-hae

SELECTED GOVERNMENT MEMBERS *AS AT NOVEMBER 2020*
Premier, Kim Tok-hun
Deputy Premiers, Im Chol-ung; Ru Ju-o; Jon Kwang-ho; Tong Jong-ho; Ko In-ho; Ri Ryong-nam; Kim Il-Chol; Yang Sung-ho
Finance, Ki Kwang-ho
Foreign Affairs, Ri Son-Gwon

EMBASSY OF THE DEMOCRATIC PEOPLE'S REPUBLIC OF KOREA
73 Gunnersbury Avenue, London W5 4LP
T 020-8992 4965 **E** prkinfo@yahoo.com
Ambassador Extraordinary and Plenipotentiary, HE Il Choe, *apptd* 2016

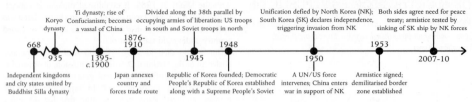

BRITISH EMBASSY

Munsu Dong compound, Pyongyang

T (+850) (2) 381 7980 **E** pyongyang.enquiries@fco.gov.uk

W www.gov.uk/government/world/north-korea

Ambassador Extraordinary and Plenipotentiary, HE Colin
Crooks, LVO, *apptd* 2018

INTERNATIONAL RELATIONS

The D. P. R. K's relations with other countries have been erratic over the past 20 years, largely owing to its nuclear ambitions and international reaction to these. It first agreed to freeze its nuclear development programme in return for fuel and development aid in 1994, only to restart the programme in 2002, claiming that other parties to the agreement had reneged on it. This pattern has been repeated several times, with the regime using the discontinuation of its nuclear and missile development programmes to bargain for aid from international agencies, the lifting of sanctions and regional powers. Six-nation talks to resolve the nuclear issues began in 2003 after North Korea withdrew from the Nuclear Non-Proliferation Treaty, but North Korea has never fully complied with any of the agreements concluded at the talks. The consequent suspension of aid by other nations, and UN censure and sanctions following regular testing of ballistic missiles and nuclear devices since 2006, had been interpreted as acts of aggression by North Korea and was met with a bellicose response from the regime.

Tensions with the USA and its allies heightened in August 2017, but renewed demilitarisation and denuclearisation talks were held with China and South Korea in early 2018. These discussions culminated in a summit between Kim Jong-un and US President Donald Trump in June 2018, the first meeting between leaders of the two nations. However, a second summit in February 2019 broke down and further missile tests soon followed, and little further progress was made in 2020.

ECONOMY AND TRADE

Although North Korea is rich in natural resources and had developed a heavy industry base in the first half of the 20th century, the economy is stagnant after decades of mismanagement, underinvestment, low export levels and the diversion of resources to military expenditure. Its long decline was compounded by the loss of Soviet support from 1991.

A series of natural disasters in the 1990s caused severe famine, obliging the government to request international aid. It is estimated that 3 million people have died since the 1990s as a result of the acute food shortages, which continue despite international food and fuel aid.

A redenomination of North Korea's currency in 2009 wiped out many people's savings, disrupted the nascent private sector, triggered rapid inflation and was met with unprecedented public protests that lasted some weeks. The country continues to develop special economic zones with China and South Korea.

Industrial output is centred on mining, metallurgy, chemicals, machine building and military products, but antiquated machinery and fuel shortages have limited output to a fraction of pre-1990 levels. Agriculture is in an equally perilous state; lack of arable land and chronic shortages of fertilisers and agricultural machinery prevent the country from producing enough to feed its population. North Korea has been dependent on massive amounts of food aid since the mid-1990s to avert a repeat of the 1995 famine, but chronic malnutrition is widespread. A relaxation of restrictions on private farming and markets in 2003 was partially rescinded in 2005 and a centralised rationing system was reinstated. South Korean assistance in developing infrastructure, industry, the Kaesong Industrial Zone (closed in 2016 after nuclear tests) and tourism have been limited by South Korean sanctions imposed on the North in 2010, and following missile tests the strengthening of UN sanctions in 2016 and 2017. These sanctions resulted in a sharp contraction of the economy in 2017 and 2018, even before the coronavirus pandemic caused a considerable fall in trade with China in 2020. Kim Jong-un has maintained the price for partial denuclearisation is a lifting of all major sanctions.

The main imports are petroleum, coal, machinery and equipment, textiles and grain. Principal exports are minerals, metallurgical products, armaments, textiles, and agricultural and fish products. Nearly all trade is done with China.

Annual average growth of GDP – –1.1 per cent (2015 est)
Unemployment – 25.6 per cent (2013 est)
Total external debt – US$5bn (2013 est)
Imports – US$2,460m (2014)
Exports – US$965m (2014)

Trade with UK	2018	2019
Imports from UK	£166,218	£19,800
Exports to UK	£36,870	£54,653

COMMUNICATIONS

Airports and waterways – There are 39 airports, the largest of which is at Pyongyang. There are some 2,250km of waterways but these are navigable only by small craft; the main seaports are Chongjin, Nampo and Wonsan

Roadways and railways – There are 724km of paved roadways and 7,435km of railways

Telecommunications – 1.2 million fixed lines and 3.6 million mobile subscriptions (2016)

Internet code and IDD – kp; 850 (from UK), 44 (to UK)

Media – There are no independent media outlets in North Korea; all television, radios and national newspapers are government organs. There are 12 principal newspapers and 20 major periodicals, some of which are published in English

WPFI score – 85.82 (180)

REPUBLIC OF KOREA

Taehan-min'guk – Republic of Korea

Area – 99,720 sq. km

Capital – Seoul; population, 9,963,000 (2018 est)

Major cities – Busan, Changwon, Daegu, Daejon, Gwangju, Incheon, Kwangju, Suwon, Taejon, Urusan

Currency – South Korean won of 100 jeon

Population – 51,835,110 rising at 0.39 per cent a year (2020 est)

Religion – Christian (Protestant 19.7 per cent, Roman Catholic 7.9 per cent), Buddhist 15.5 per cent (predominantly the Jogye order of the Seon (Zen) school) (est)

Language – Korean (official), English

Population density – 529 per sq. km (2019)

Urban population – 81.4 per cent (2019 est)

Median age (years) – 43.2 (2020 est)

National anthem – 'Aegukga' 'Patriotic Song'

National day – 15 August (Liberation Day)

Death penalty – Retained (last used 1997)

CPI score – 59 (39)

Military expenditure – US$43,070m (2018)

Conscription – 20–30 years of age; 21–24 months (selective)

CLIMATE AND TERRAIN

The country occupies the southern part of the mountainous Korean peninsula, with highlands and mountains accounting for around 70 per cent of the land area. Elevation extremes range from 1,950m (Halla-san) to 0m (Sea of Japan). The climate is temperate, although winters are very cold for the latitude. Average temperatures range from −2.5°C in January to 24.3°C in August. The rainy season lasts from June to September.

HISTORY AND POLITICS

From 1948, South Korea experienced over 40 years of mostly authoritarian, often military, rule and great industrial development. Syngman Rhee, president from 1948, resigned in 1960 in the face of popular protests at corruption and electoral fraud. A military coup in 1961 brought General Park Chung-hee to power and he instigated a programme of industrial development; by the time of his assassination in 1979, Korea was a leading shipbuilding nation and producer of electronic goods.

Following riots against the interim government, General Chun Do-hwan assumed power in 1980 after martial law was declared. Pro-democracy agitation in the mid-1980s led to constitutional changes in 1987 and the first multiparty legislative elections in 1988, but despite subsequent anti-corruption campaigns, politics has continued to be plagued by allegations of corruption and fraud, and has been subject to military influence. The first civilian president and the first

wholly civilian government since 1961 were appointed in 1993.

In December 2012, Park Geun-hye was elected South Korea's first woman president and assumed office in February 2013. In April 2016 legislative election, Park's ruling, centre-right party Saenuri (formerly the Grand National Party) lost the majority it had held for 16 years by one seat to the newly formed Minjoo opposition. In March 2017, Park became the country's first democratically elected leader to be forced from office for corruption when the constitutional court upheld her impeachment, and she was sentenced to 24 years in prison in April 2018. Moon Jae-in of the centrist Democratic Party won the May 2017 presidential election; he has promised rapprochement with North Korea, and despite heightened tensions in late 2017, cooperation between the two nations has slowly progressed. The April 2020 legislative election was won by the Democratic Party and its allies who claimed 180 seats, the largest majority since 1987.

The 1948 constitution was heavily amended when the Sixth Republic was inaugurated in 1988. Under this, the president is directly elected for a single five-year term. The president appoints the prime minister with the approval of the legislature, and members of the state council (cabinet) on the recommendation of the prime minister. The president is also empowered to take wide-ranging measures in an emergency, but must obtain the agreement of the legislature. The unicameral National Assembly has 300 members who are directly elected for a four-year term.

HEAD OF STATE

President, Moon Jae-in, *elected* 9 May 2017

SELECTED GOVERNMENT MEMBERS *AS AT NOVEMBER 2020*

Prime Minister, Chung Sye-kyun

Deputy Prime Ministers, Hong Nam-ki *(Economy)*; Ryu Eun-he

Defence, Gen. Suh Wook

Foreign Affairs, Kang Kyung-wha

EMBASSY OF THE REPUBLIC OF KOREA

60 Buckingham Gate, London SW1E 6AJ

T 020-7227 5500 **E** koreanembinuk@mofat.go.kr

W www.gbr.mofat.go.kr

Ambassador Extraordinary and Plenipotentiary, HE Park Enna, *apptd* 2018

BRITISH EMBASSY

Sejong-daero 19-gil 24, Jung-gu, Seoul 100–120

T (+82) (2) 3210 5500 **E** enquiry.seoul@fco.gov.uk

W www.gov.uk/government/world/south-korea

Ambassador Extraordinary and Plenipotentiary, HE Simon Smith, CMG, *apptd* 2018

ECONOMY AND TRADE

Industrialisation from the 1960s transformed South Korea from a predominantly agrarian country into one of the Asian 'miracle' economies by the 1980s. Initially based on shipbuilding and electrical goods, production shifted towards electronics and IT goods in the 1980s. By 1997, South Korea was the world's 11th-largest economy, with an annual GDP growth rate of 8 per cent. However, the dominating conglomerates *(chaebols)* were experiencing difficulties which, exacerbated by the Asian financial crisis in 1997, caused a number to collapse in the late 1990s and the economy to contract sharply. Corporate and financial reforms were introduced and GDP growth resumed from the early 2000s. Slow growth in Europe, the USA and China has reduced growth in recent years, which has plateaued at 2–3 per cent. Although the country's handling of COVID-19 was widely praised, the economy is expected to contract by 1.9 per cent in 2020, partly owing to a slowdown in the Chinese economy and the US-China trade dispute. Moreover, a diplomatic dispute with Japan over Second World War reparations resulted in Japan imposing controls on three chemicals crucial to South Korea's semiconductor industry in July 2019, which threatens to curtail the important industry. Long-term challenges include an aging population, reliance on a small number of large companies and a dependence on exports.

Services contribute 58.3 per cent to GDP, industry 39.3 per cent and agriculture 2.2 per cent. Major manufacturing industries include electronics, telecommunications, motor vehicles, chemicals, shipbuilding and steel. Tourism is of growing importance.

The main trading partners are China, Japan and the USA (the US–South Korea Trade Agreement was first signed in 2007 and ratified in 2011). Principal exports are semiconductors, petrochemicals, telecommunications equipment, motor vehicles, electronics, steel and ships. The main imports are oil, gas, electronics and electronic equipment, steel, communication equipment, organic chemicals and textiles.

GNI – US$1,743.7bn; US$33,720 per capita (2019)
Annual average growth of GDP – 2.04 per cent (2019 est)
Inflation rate – 1.9 per cent (2017 est)
Population below poverty line – 14.4 per cent (2016 est)
Unemployment – 3.76 per cent (2019 est)
Total external debt – US$384.6bn (2017 est)
Imports – US$579,461m (2017)
Exports – US$664,878m (2017)

BALANCE OF PAYMENTS
Trade – US$85,416m surplus (2017)
Current Account – US$59,971m surplus (2019)

Trade with UK	2018	2019
Imports from UK	£5,838,777,083	£3,760,984,639
Exports to UK	£4,108,412,422	£4,105,713,416

COMMUNICATIONS
Airports and waterways – 71, including international airports at Seoul (Kimpo), Kimhae (near Busan), Daegu, Cheju city and Incheon; Busan, Incheon and Pohang are the major ports, although development and operations at Incheon are hampered by tidal variations of 9–10m
Roadways and railways – There are 92,795km of paved roadways; 3,397km
Telecommunications – 25.9 million fixed lines and 66.4 million mobile telephone subscriptions (2018); there were 49.3 million internet users in 2018
Internet code and IDD – kr; 82 (from UK), 1 44/2 44 (to UK)
Major broadcasters – Korea has a number of public radio and television broadcasters, including Korea Broadcasting System (KBS) and Munhwa Broadcasting Corporation (MBC), as well as a diversified commercial sector
Press – Major newspapers include *Chosun Ilbo, Korea Daily* and English-language daily *Korea Herald*
WPFI score – 23.70 (42)

EDUCATION AND HEALTH
Primary education is free and compulsory for nine years from the age of six.
Gross enrolment ratio (percentage of relevant age group) – primary 99.6 per cent, secondary 98.5 per cent, tertiary 95.9 per cent (2018 est)
Health expenditure (per capita) – US$2,283 (2017)
Hospital beds (per 1,000 people) – 11.5 (2015)
Life expectancy (years) – 82.6 (2020 est)

Mortality rate – 6.8 (2020 est)
Birth rate – 8.2 (2020 est)
Infant mortality rate – 3 (2020 est)

KOSOVO

Republika e Kosoves – Republic of Kosovo

Area – 10,887 sq. km
Capital – Pristina; population, 214,688 (2018 est)
Major towns – Mitrovica, Pec, Prizren
Currency – Euro (€) of 100 cents; the Serbian dinar is also in circulation
Population – 1,932,774 rising at 0.66 per cent a year (2018 est)
Religion – Muslim 95.6 per cent, Roman Catholic 2.2 per cent, Orthodox 1.5 per cent (est)
Language – Albanian, Serbian (both official), Bosnian, Turkish, Romani
Population density – 165 per sq. km (2019)
Median age (years) – 30.5 (2020 est)
National anthem – 'Europe'
National day – 17 February (Independence Day)
Death penalty – Not since independence
CPI score – 36 (101)
Military expenditure – US$63.3m (2018)

CLIMATE AND TERRAIN
Kosovo has a hilly central region that divides plains in the east and west. Mountains lie along the borders with Albania, Macedonia and Montenegro, and along much of the border with Serbia. Elevation extremes range from 2,656m (Gjeravica) to 297m (Drini i Bardhe river). The main rivers are the Drini i Bardhe in the west and the Iberi in the north. The climate is continental.

POLITICS
Under the 2008 constitution, the president is elected by the legislature for a five-year term and can be re-elected once. The unicameral legislature, the Assembly of Kosovo, has 120 members, elected for a four-year term; 100 seats have directly elected members, ten seats are reserved for Serbs and ten for other minorities. The majority party or coalition nominates the prime minister, who is appointed by the president. Both the prime minister and the government must be approved by the legislature. Prime Minister Ramush Haradinaj resigned in July 2019 after a war crimes court in The Hague summoned him for questioning.

Following the October 2019 legislative elections, the ruling Democratic Party of Kosovo-led coalition was initially replaced by a centrist coalition led by Albin Kurti. Kurti quit as prime minister in June 2020 as a result of disagreements over the handling of the coronavirus pandemic. A new coalition was later formed and led by the pro-European, centre-right Democratic League of Kosovo. The Democratic

Serbia regains control after First Balkan War; becomes province of Serbia, then part of Yugoslavia

Stripped of its autonomy by Serbian government and Albanian majority; gradually excluded from public life

Insurgency by the Kosovan Liberation Army provokes Serbian military reprisals

NATO intervention; Serbia signs peace plan and withdraws forces

International Court of Justice rules declaration legal; it is accepted by UN but refused by Serbia

1389 1945 1991 1998 2008

1913 1989 c.1995 1999 2010

Battle of Kosovo; Serbian principalities become part of the Ottoman Empire

Becomes an autonomous republic within Serbia

Vote of independence declared illegal by Serbian government

Serbia begins systematic ethnic cleansing of country

Kosovan government declares independence; it goes unrecognised by the UN

Party's Hashim Thaci was elected president in the third round of voting, in February 2016, succeeding Atifete Jahjaga.

HEAD OF STATE
President, Hashim Thaci, *elected* 26 February 2016

SELECTED GOVERNMENT MEMBERS *AS AT NOVEMBER 2020*
Prime Minister, Avdullah Hoti
Finance, Hykmete Bajrami
Foreign Affairs, Meliza Hardadinaj
Internal Affairs, Agrim Veliu

EMBASSY OF THE REPUBLIC OF KOSOVO
8 John Street, London WC1N 2ES
T 020-3585 4167 **E** embassy.uk@rks-gov.net
W www.kosovoembassy.org.uk
Ambassador Extraordinary and Plenipotentiary, vacant

BRITISH EMBASSY
Ismail Qemali 6, Arberi, Dragodan, Pristina
T (+381) 3825 4700 **E** britishembassy.pristina@fco.gov.uk
W www.gov.uk/government/world/kosovo
Ambassador Extraordinary and Plenipotentiary, HE Nicholas Abbott, *apptd* 2019

ECONOMY AND TRADE
Under UN administration Kosovo began the transition to a market economy, and over half of state-owned businesses have been privatised. However, income levels are the second-lowest in Europe, and the economy is dependent on international and foreign aid and the remittances of expatriates, worth about 10 per cent and 16 per cent of GDP respectively. Agriculture is close to subsistence level and inefficient; industrial output has declined because of insufficient investment and an unemployment level of over 30 per cent encourages emigration. International agencies and foreign governments are working with the Kosovan government to stimulate economic growth, attract investment and reduce unemployment. Prior to the coronavirus pandemic the economy was performing well, growing on average 4–5 per cent between 2015 and 2019.

Kosovo joined the Central Europe Free Trade Area (CEFTA) in 2006, and its members are the main markets for exports of minerals and processed metal products, scrap metals, leather goods, machinery and appliances. Imports of foodstuffs, wood, fuels, chemicals, machinery and textiles come mainly from EU and neighbouring countries. In 2011, Serbia and Bosnia resumed trade with Kosovo, while a free trade agreement was signed with Turkey in 2013. The country continues to negotiate trade liberalisation with the EU.
GNI – US$8.3bn; US$4,640 per capita (2019)
Annual average growth of GDP – 3.7 per cent (2017 est)
Inflation rate – 1.5 per cent (2017 est)
Population below poverty line – 17.6 per cent (2015 est)
Unemployment – 30.5 per cent (2017 est)
Total external debt – US$506m (2017 est)
Imports – US$2,687m (2014 est)
Exports – US$349m (2014 est)

BALANCE OF PAYMENTS
Current Account – US$447m deficit (2019)

Trade with UK	2018	2019
Imports from UK	£6,415,196	£7,814,294
Exports to UK	£913,851	£1,351,906

COMMUNICATIONS
Airports – Three; the principal international terminal is at Pristina
Roadways and railways – 2,012km; 333km
Telecommunications – 831,470 fixed lines and 562,000 mobile telephone subscriptions (2016); there were 1.7 million internet users in 2018
Internet code and IDD – kv; 381 (from UK), 44 (to UK)
Major broadcasters – Kosovo Radio-Television is the country's public broadcaster
Press – Leading dailies include *Koha Ditore, Bota Sot* and *Kosova Sot*
WPFI score – 29.33 (70)

KUWAIT
Dawlat al-Kuwayt – State of Kuwait

Area – 17,818 sq. km
Capital – Kuwait City (al-Kuwayt); population, 3,115,000 (2020 est)
Major cities – Al-Ahmadi, As Salimiyah, Hawalli
Currency – Kuwaiti dinar (KD) of 1,000 fils
Population – 2,993,706 rising at 1.27 per cent a year (2020 est); Asian (40.3 per cent), Kuwaiti (30.4 per cent), other Arab (27.4 per cent) (est)
Religion – Muslim (official) 74.6 per cent, Christian 18.2 per cent (est); Hindu and Parsi minorities, mostly expatriates
Language – Arabic (official), English
Population density – 232 per sq. km (2019)
Urban population – 100 per cent (2019 est)
Median age (years) – 29.7 (2020 est)
National anthem – 'Al-Nasheed al-Watani' 'National Anthem'
National day – 25 February
Death penalty – Retained
CPI score – 40 (85)
Military expenditure – US$7,296m (2018)

CLIMATE AND TERRAIN
Kuwait is an almost entirely flat desert plain, with elevation extremes ranging from 306m to 0m (Persian Gulf). Its territory includes the island of Bubiyan and others at the head of the Persian Gulf. The climate is arid, with little rainfall but high levels of humidity. Average temperatures range from 12.5°C in January to 37°C in July and August.

HISTORY AND POLITICS
The area was under the nominal control of the Ottoman Empire from the late 16th century, but in 1756 an autonomous sheikhdom was founded that has been ruled by the al-Sabah family ever since. Kuwait entered into a treaty of friendship with Britain in 1899, in order to protect itself from Ottoman and Saudi domination, and it became a British protectorate in 1914. The borders with Saudi Arabia and Iraq were agreed between 1922 and 1933. Full independence was achieved in 1961, although Britain retained a military presence in the country until 1971.

An attempted Iraqi invasion shortly after independence in 1961 was discouraged by British troops in the Gulf. However, in August 1990 Iraq invaded and occupied Kuwait, proclaiming it a province of Iraq. In 1991, a short military campaign by a US-led alliance expelled the Iraqi forces, although there were further Iraqi incursions in 1993 before Iraq renounced its claim and recognised the new UN-demarcated border in 1994. Extensive damage was caused to the country's infrastructure and environment during the Iraqi occupation and reconstruction was a priority throughout the 1990s; in 2003, Kuwait was a base for forces involved in the Iraq War.

In recent years, there have been clashes between security forces and militant Islamists, some of whom are alleged to have links to al-Qaida.

Although Kuwait was the first Arab country in the Gulf to have an elected legislature, this was suspended from 1977–81, 1986–92, and in 1999, 2012 and 2013. The political system is subject to instability, with electoral boycotts by Islamist and liberal parties common; two elections were held in 12 months in 2008–9 owing to the legislature's efforts to subject the government to parliamentary scrutiny. Pro-reform demonstrations took place in spring 2011, forcing Sheikh Nasser al-Muhammad al-Ahmed al-Sabeh's government to resign from office. The last legislative elections took place in 2016 and gave opposition politicians and independents a slim majority.

The 1962 constitution was amended in 2005 to extend the franchise to women. The head of state is the emir, chosen from among the ruling family and confirmed by the National Assembly. He exercises executive power through the council of ministers; in 2003, the post of prime minister was separated from the role of heir to the throne for the first time. The unicameral National Assembly has 65 members who serve four-year terms; 50 are directly elected and 15 *ex-officio* members are appointed by the prime minister to serve in the cabinet. There are no formal political parties.

The country is divided into six governorates: Capital, Hawalli, al-Ahmadi, al-Jahrah, al-Farwaniya and Mubarak al-Kabeer.

HEAD OF STATE
HH The Emir of Kuwait, Sheikh Nawaf al-Ahmad al-Jaber al-Sabah, *born* 1937, *acceded* 30 September 2030
Crown Prince, HH Sheikh Meshal al-Ahmad al-Jaber al-Shabah

SELECTED GOVERNMENT MEMBERS *AS AT NOVEMBER 2020*
Prime Minister, Sheikh Saber al-Khalid al-Hamad al-Sabah
First Deputy Prime Minister, Defence, Sheikh Ahmad Mansour al-Ahmad al-Sabah
Deputy Prime Minister, Interior, Sheikh Khaled Nasser al-Seleh
Foreign Affairs, Sheikh Ahmad Nasser Al-Mohammad al-Sabah

EMBASSY OF THE STATE OF KUWAIT
2 Albert Gate, London SW1X 7JU
T 020-7590 3400 **E** kuwait@dircon.co.uk
Ambassador Extraordinary and Plenipotentiary, HE Khaled al-Duwaisan, GCVO, *apptd* 1993

BRITISH EMBASSY
PO Box 2, Arabian Gulf Street, Safat 13001
T (+965) 2259 4320 **E** kuwait.generalenquiries@fco.gov.uk
W www.gov.uk/government/world/kuwait
Ambassador Extraordinary and Plenipotentiary, HE Michael Davenport, MBE, *apptd* 2017

ECONOMY AND TRADE
Oil was discovered in 1938 and the development of the oil industry after 1945 transformed the country from one of the poorest in the world to one of the richest. Petroleum accounts for 92 per cent of export revenues and 90 per cent of government income, and extraction is set to increase. Income from foreign reserves and investment is also high, cushioning the economy from the effects of dependency on oil. Economic reform is slow owing to the tensions between the government and legislature; a diversification fund worth US$104bn was established in 2010, though much of this money has yet to be spent. Kuwait has a rich sovereign wealth fund, worth as much as US$600bn (£417bn) according to some estimates, but in 2016 it ran its first current-account deficit since 1992 due to falling oil prices. Low oil prices and output decelerated growth in 2019, before the 2020 coronavirus pandemic further reduced global prices and pushed the economy into recession.

The climate and terrain limit agriculture and, with the exception of fish, all food is imported; the agriculture sector contributes only 0.4 per cent of GDP. Services account for 40.9 per cent of GDP and industry for 58.7 per cent. Apart from the oil and petrochemical industries, activities include the production of cement and construction materials, shipbuilding and repair, water desalination and food processing.

The main export markets are South Korea, China, Japan, India and Singapore, and the main sources of imports are China, the USA, the UAE, Saudi Arabia and Germany. Principal exports are oil and refined products, and fertilisers. The main imports are food, construction materials, vehicles and vehicle parts, and clothing.

GNI – US$141.9bn; US$34,290 per capita (2018)
Annual average growth of GDP – −3.3 per cent (2017 est)
Inflation rate – 1.5 per cent (2017 est)
Unemployment – 1.1 per cent (2017 est)
Total external debt – US$47.24bn (2017 est)
Imports – US$58,093m (2017)
Exports – US$60,337m (2017)

BALANCE OF PAYMENTS
Trade – US$2,244m surplus (2017)
Current Account – US$33,810m surplus (2019)

Trade with UK	2018	2019
Imports from UK	£547,671,677	£538,442,857
Exports to UK	£539,789,448	£582,917,316

COMMUNICATIONS

Airports and waterways – Four, with an international airport at Kuwait City; the main seaports are Ash Shu'aybah and Ash Shuwaykh

Roadways – 5,749km

Telecommunications – 515,542 fixed lines and 7.1 million mobile subscriptions (2018); there were 2.9 million internet users in 2018

Internet code and IDD – kw; 965 (from UK), 44 (to UK)

Major broadcasters – Kuwaiti TV and Radio Kuwait are the public broadcasters and compete with commercial stations; satellite television is also widely watched

Press – Major dailies include *Al-Watan*, *Al-Qabas* and the *Kuwait Times*

WPFI score – 34.30 (109)

EDUCATION AND HEALTH

Education is free and compulsory from six to 14 years.

Literacy rate – 96.1 per cent (2018 est)

Gross enrolment ratio (percentage of relevant age group) – primary 88 per cent (2019 est); secondary 97.8 per cent (2015 est); tertiary 55.3 per cent (2019 est)

Health expenditure (per capita) – US$1,529 (2017)

Hospital beds (per 1,000 people) – 2 (2014)

Life expectancy (years) – 78.6 (2020 est)

Mortality rate – 2.3 (2020 est)

Birth rate – 18 (2020 est)

Infant mortality rate – 6.5 (2020 est)

KYRGYZSTAN

Kyrgyz Respublikasy – Kyrgyz Republic

Area – 199,951 sq. km

Capital – Bishkek; population, 1,038,000 (2020 est)

Major city – Osh

Currency – Som of 100 tyiyn

Population – 5,964,897 rising at 0.96 per cent a year (2020 est); Kyrgyz (73.5 per cent), Uzbek (14.7 per cent), Russian (5.5 per cent) (est)

Religion – Muslim 90 per cent (predominantly Sunni), Christian 7 per cent (predominantly Russian Orthodox), other 3 per cent (including Jewish, Buddhist and Baha'i) (est)

Language – Kyrgyz, Russian (both official), Uzbek

Population density – 33 per sq. km (2019)

Urban population – 36.6 per cent (2019 est)

Median age (years) – 27.3 (2020 est)

National anthem – 'Kyrgyz Respublikasynyn Mamlekettik Gimni' 'National Anthem of the Kyrgyz Republic'

National day – 31 August (Independence Day)

Death penalty – Abolished for all crimes (since 2007)

CPI score – 30 (126)

Military expenditure – US$121m (2018 est)

Conscription – 18–27 years of age, male only; 12 months

Literacy rate – 99.9 per cent (2018 est)

Gross enrolment ratio (percentage of relevant age group) – primary 106 per cent, secondary 96.3 per cent, tertiary 42.3 per cent (2019 est)

Health expenditure (per capita) – US$79 (2017)

Hospital beds (per 1,000 people) – 4.5 (2013)

Life expectancy (years) – 71.8 (2020 est)

Mortality rate – 6.3 (2020 est)

Birth rate – 20.6 (2020 est)

Infant mortality rate – 23.3 (2020 est)

HIV/AIDS adult prevalence – 0.2 per cent (2019 est)

CLIMATE AND TERRAIN

Kyrgyzstan is a landlocked and mountainous country lying in the Tien Shan mountain range, with the Pamir mountains in the extreme south. Elevations range from 7,439m (Jengish Chokusu) to 132m (Kara-Darya), though most of the country lies at over 1,000m. The principal rivers are the Naryn and the Chu, and the vast Issyk-Kul lake lies in the north-east. The climate is continental but with temperatures and humidity moderated by the altitude; typical temperatures range from −12.6°C in January to 15.2°C in July. Rainfall is low for the altitude, owing to Kyrgyzstan's distance from the sea and the rain-shadow effect of the Himalayan and Pamir ranges.

HISTORY AND POLITICS

After centuries of Turkic, Mongol and Chinese rule, the Kyrgyz became part of the Russian Empire in the 1860s and 1870s. After the October 1917 revolution in Russia, the area became part of the Turkestan autonomous republic within the USSR until 1924, when the Kirgiz Autonomous Region was formed. Soviet rule brought land reforms in the 1920s that resulted in the settlement of many of the nomadic Kyrgyz. Kyrgyzstan became an autonomous republic in 1926 and a constituent republic of the USSR in 1936.

Reform in the USSR in the 1980s provoked an upsurge in nationalism in Kyrgyzstan and agitation for independence. Following the attempted coup in Moscow in 1991, Kyrgyzstan became an independent republic and joined the Commonwealth of Independent States.

Since independence, there has been tension between the Kyrgyz and ethnic Uzbeks, concentrated around Osh, and between the Kyrgyz and Dungans (ethnic Chinese) near Bishkek. There have also been clashes between security forces and militant Islamists, active near the border with Tajikistan.

Askar Akayev, a pro-reform communist, was president from 1990 until he was deposed in March 2005 in a popular uprising over alleged electoral fraud; the uprising was also fuelled by years of unrest over the dire economic situation, corruption, nepotism and crime. The opposition leader Kurmanbek Bakiyev was elected president in July 2005 and re-elected in 2009, but forced from office in April 2010 after attempts to suppress anti-government demonstrations left over 80 protestors dead. An interim government was formed, but intercommunal violence between Kyrgyz and Uzbeks erupted in June 2010, spreading to Jalalabad; a referendum held in the same month approved a draft constitution granting greater powers to parliament at the expense of the president.

Following the October 2020 legislative election, in which pro-government parties were awarded a super majority, violent protests erupted against alleged vote rigging and political repression. The results were quickly annulled and President Sooronbay Jeenbekov resigned, and was replaced by Sadyr Japarov as interim president and prime minister.

Under the 2010 constitution, the president is directly elected for a six-year term, which is not renewable. The unicameral Supreme Council has 120 members directly elected for a five-year term. The largest party in the legislature nominates the prime minister, and the president appoints the cabinet; the appointments are subject to the approval of the Supreme Council.

HEAD OF STATE
President (Interim), Prime Minister (Interim), Sadyr Japarov, *assumed office* 15 November 2020

SELECTED GOVERNMENT MEMBERS *AS AT NOVEMBER 2020*
First Deputy Prime Minister, Artem Novikov
Foreign Affairs, Ruslan Kazakbaev
Internal Affairs, Ulan Niyazbekov

EMBASSY OF THE KYRGYZ REPUBLIC
Ascot House, 119 Crawford Street, London W1U 6BJ
T 020-7935 1462 **E** mail@kyrgyz-embassy.org.uk
W www.kyrgyz-embassy.org.uk
Ambassador Extraordinary and Plenipotentiary, HE Edil Baisalov, *apptd* 2019

BRITISH EMBASSY
21 Erkindik Boulevard, Office 404, Bishkek, 720040, Kyrgyzstan
T (+996) 312 303 637 **E** ukinkyrgyzrepublic@fco.gov.uk
W www.gov.uk/government/world/kyrgyzstan
Ambassador Extraordinary and Plenipotentiary, HE Charles Garrett, MVO, *apptd* 2019

ECONOMY AND TRADE
Economic reforms in the early 1990s caused severe hardship, and although productivity and exports have grown since the late 1990s, poverty is widespread. The economy, which is heavily dependent on gold exports, contracted in 2009 owing to the global downturn, and production and trade were reduced further by the political violence and disruption of 2010. Despite such damage to the infrastructure, the economy grew to 17.4 per cent in 2013, and has experienced steady growth since. The government, with international support, is pursuing poverty-reduction and economic-growth programmes, but the greater foreign direct investment that these require may be deterred by political volatility, lack of transparency and the high level of organised crime. Kyrgyzstan became the fifth member of the Eurasian Economic Union (EEU) in May 2015 and while membership was expected to boost trade, economic growth was hit by slowing economies in Russia and China, coupled with low commodity prices. Remittances from migrant workers located mainly in Russia are equal to over a quarter of GDP, and foreign donor support is needed to finance government spending.

The economy is predominantly agrarian, with agriculture accounting for 14.3 per cent of GDP and employing 48 per cent of the workforce. There are deposits of gold, uranium, mercury and natural gas. Apart from mining, industry consists of hydroelectric power generation and light manufacturing, contributing 31.2 per cent of GDP; services account for 54.2 per cent.

The main trading partners are Switzerland (59.1 per cent of exports), Kazakhstan, Russia and China. Principal exports are gold, cotton, wool, meat, tobacco, mercury, uranium, electricity, machinery and shoes. The main imports are oil, gas, machinery and equipment, chemicals and foodstuffs.
GNI – US$8.0bn; US$1,240 per capita (2019)
Annual average growth of GDP – 4.6 per cent (2017 est)
Inflation rate – 3.2 per cent (2017 est)
Population below poverty line – 32.1 per cent (2015 est)
Unemployment – 3.18 per cent (2019 est)
Total external debt – US$8.164bn (2017 est)

Imports – US$4,969m (2017)
Exports – US$2,660m (2017)

BALANCE OF PAYMENTS
Trade – US$2,309m deficit (2017)
Current Account – US$1,091m deficit (2019)

Trade with UK	2018	2019
Imports from UK	£4,046,007	£3,993,349
Exports to UK	£503,478,690	£651,571,582

COMMUNICATIONS
Airports and waterways – 18, with an international airport outside Bishkek; there are 600km of waterways
Roadways and railways – 34,000km; 424km
Telecommunications – 331,140 fixed lines and 8.7 million mobile subscriptions (2018); there were 2.2 million internet users in 2018
Internet code and IDD – kg; 996 (from UK), 44 (to UK)
Major broadcasters – Kyrgyz National TV and Radio Broadcasting Corporation runs various networks alongside a number of private broadcasters
Press – Major newspapers include the government-owned *Slovo Kyrgyzstana Plus* and the private *Vecherniy Bishkek*
WPFI score – 30.19 (82)

LAOS

Sathalanalat Paxathipatai Paxaxon Lao – Lao People's Democratic Republic

Area – 236,800 sq. km
Capital – Vientiane; population, 683,000 (2020 est)
Major towns – Luang Prabang, Pakse, Savannakhet
Currency – Kip (K) of 100 att
Population – 7,447,396 rising at 1.44 per cent a year (2020 est); there are 49 ethnic groups, including Lao (53.2 per cent), Khmou (11 per cent), Hmong (9.2 per cent) (est)
Religion – Buddhist 64.7 per cent (predominantly Theravada), Christian 1.7 per cent (est)
Language – Lao (official), French, English, ethnic languages
Population density – 31 per sq. km (2019)
Urban population – 35.6 per cent (2019 est)
Median age (years) – 24 (2020 est)
National anthem – 'Pheng Xat Lao' 'Hymn of the Lao People'
National day – 2 December (Republic Day)
Death penalty – Retained (last used 1989)
CPI score – 29 (130)
Military expenditure – US$23.3m (2013)
Conscription – 18 years of age; 18 months
Literacy rate – 84.7 per cent (2015 est)

Gross enrolment ratio (percentage of age group) – primary 100 per cent, secondary 65.8 per cent, tertiary 14.5 per cent (2019 est)
Health expenditure (per capita) – US$62 (2017)
Hospital beds (per 1,000 people) – 1.5 (2012)
Life expectancy (years) – 65.7 (2020 est)
Mortality rate – 7.2 (2020 est)
Birth rate – 22.4 (2020 est)
Infant mortality rate – 45.6 (2020 est)
HIV / AIDS adult prevalence – 0.3 per cent (2019 est)

CLIMATE AND TERRAIN
Laos is mostly mountainous, the land rising from the Mekong river basin in the west to mountains in the north and east. Elevation extremes range from 2,817m (Phou Bia) to 70m (Mekong river). Much of the land is covered by rainforest. The climate is tropical, with a wet season from May to October, during which humidity levels are very high. Average temperatures in Vientiane range from 19.9°C in January to 26.3°C in June.

HISTORY AND POLITICS
From the ninth to the 13th centuries, Laos was part of the Khmer Empire centred on Angkor in Cambodia. Small principalities developed from the 12th century and were united in the 14th century into the Lao kingdom of Lan Xang ('the land of a million elephants'), which dominated until 1713, when it split into the separate kingdoms of Luang Prabang, Vientiane and Champassac, which became tributaries of Siam (Thailand) in the late 18th century and then a protectorate of France from 1893.

Japanese occupation during the Second World War inspired a Lao nationalist movement, which proclaimed independence in 1945, but the French regained control of the country in 1946. Independence as a constitutional monarchy was granted in 1953, but much of the following 20 years was spent in civil war between the communist Pathet Lao movement, backed first by China and then by North Vietnam, and royalists, who attracted US and Thai support from the early 1960s. A ceasefire in 1973 partitioned the country between the two sides, but in 1975 the Pathet Lao seized power in the rest of the country and proclaimed a republic, introducing a one-party state and initiating socialist policies. Greater economic liberalisation was introduced from the mid-1980s, and the first legislative elections since 1975 were held in 1989.

Ethnic Hmong minority groups have maintained a low-level insurgency against the communist regime since 1975. In 2000 and 2004, Laos suffered serious civil disturbances, including bombings and armed attacks on buses. These were variously attributed to Hmong insurgents and anti-government groups based abroad.

In the March 2016 legislative election, Lao People's Revolutionary Party (LPRP) candidates won all but five of the seats, the remaining seats being taken by approved independent candidates. The legislature elected former vice-president Bounnhang Vorachit as president in April and approved a reshuffled council of ministers.

Under the 1991 constitution, the head of state is a president elected by the legislature for a five-year term, with no term limits. The unicameral National Assembly has 149 members, who are party-approved candidates directly elected for a five-year term. The LPRP is the only legal political party, although it has given approval to non-partisan candidates for legislative seats. Party congresses are held every five years.

HEAD OF STATE
President, Bounnhang Vorachit, *elected* 20 April 2016
Vice-President, Phankham Viphavanh

SELECTED GOVERNMENT MEMBERS *AS AT NOVEMBER 2020*
Prime Minister, Thongloun Sisoulith
Deputy Prime Ministers, Somdy Douangdy *(Finance);* Bounpone Bouttanavong; Bounthong Chitmany; Sonexay Siphandone
Foreign Affairs, Saleumxay Kommasith
National Defence, Lt.-Gen. Chansamone Chanyalath

EMBASSY OF THE LAO PEOPLE'S DEMOCRATIC REPUBLIC
49 Porchester Terrace, London W2 3TS
T 020-7402 3770 **E** laosemblondon@gmail.com
Ambassador Extraordinary and Plenipotentiary, HE Phongsavanh Sisoulath, *apptd* 2019

BRITISH EMBASSY
Rue J. Nehru, Phonexay, Saysettha District, Vientiane
T (+856) 030 770 0000 **E** britishembassy.vientiane@fco.gov.uk
W www.gov.uk/government/world/organisations/british-embassy-vientiane
Ambassador Extraordinary and Plenipotentiary, HE John Pearson, *apptd* 2019

ECONOMY AND TRADE
Economic liberalisation and a measure of private enterprise were introduced from 1986, producing growth averaging over 6 per cent a year between 1988 and 2008 (except during the 1997 Asian financial crisis) and over 7 per cent between 2008 and 2019, making Laos' one of the fastest-growing economies in Asia. Recent economic growth has been driven by foreign investment in dam and transport construction projects, hydroelectric power and mining; but corruption, a small domestic market and a limited labour pool are deterrents. The country remains very poor, with a rudimentary although steadily improving infrastructure, and is dependent on international aid and investment. Laos was admitted to the World Trade Organization in 2013.

Subsistence agriculture, principally rice, accounts for 20.9 per cent of GDP and 73.1 per cent of employment. Deposits of copper, tin, gold and gypsum are exploited, as is the abundance of timber in the rainforests. Other activities include food processing, rubber production, and tourism. A hydroelectric dam on the Mekong river exports electricity to Thailand.

The main trading partners are Thailand (42.6 per cent of exports; 59.1 per cent of imports), Vietnam and China. Principal exports are timber products, coffee, electricity, tin, copper and gold. The main imports are machinery and equipment, vehicles, fuel and consumer goods.
GNI – US$18.4bn; US$2,570 per capita (2019)
Annual average growth of GDP – 6.9 per cent (2017 est)
Inflation rate – 0.8 per cent (2017 est)
Population below poverty line – 22 per cent (2013 est)
Unemployment – 0.7 per cent (2017 est)
Total external debt – US$14.9bn (2017 est)
Imports – US$5,927m (2016)
Exports – US$4,945m (2016)

BALANCE OF PAYMENTS
Trade – US$981m deficit (2016)
Current Account – US$947m deficit (2019)

Trade with UK	2018	2019
Imports from UK	£8,716,226	£10,991,744
Exports to UK	£10,702,214	£14,866,425

COMMUNICATIONS

Airports and waterways – Eight, with the largest airports at Vientiane and Luang Prabang; there are around 4,600km of navigable waterways, principally on the Mekong and its tributaries, although some are not passable in the dry season

Roadways and railways – There are 5,415km of paved roadways; the Friendship Bridge over the Mekong river connects with Thailand, and links up road routes from Singapore to China. A rail track across the bridge links the Thai and Laotian rail systems

Telecommunications – 1.5 million fixed lines and 3.7 million mobile subscriptions (2018); there were 1.8 million internet users in 2018

Internet code and IDD – la; 856 (from UK), 44 (to UK)

Major broadcasters – The state-run Lao National TV is the country's principal broadcaster

Press – There are three state-run news publications, including the *Vientiane Mai*

WPFI score – 64.28 (172)

LATVIA

Latvijas Republika – Republic of Latvia

Area – 64,589 sq. km

Capital – Riga; population, 631,000 (2020 est)

Major cities – Daugavpils, Jelgava, Liepaja

Currency – Euro (€) of 100 cents

Population – 1,881,232 falling at 1.12 per cent a year (2020 est); Latvian (62.2 per cent), Russian (25.2 per cent) (est)

Religion – Christian (Lutheran 36.2 per cent, Orthodox 19.1 per cent, other Christian 1.6 per cent) (est)

Language – Latvian (official), Russian

Population density – 31 per sq. km (2019)

Urban population – 68.2 per cent (2019 est)

Median age (years) – 44.4 (2020 est)

National anthem – 'Dievs, Sveti Latviju' 'God Bless Latvia'

National day – 18 November (Independence Day)

Death penalty – Abolished for all crimes (since 2012)

CPI score – 56 (44)

Military expenditure – US$425m (2016)

CLIMATE AND TERRAIN

Latvia is a flat, low-lying country on the eastern shore of the Baltic Sea, with low hills and many lakes in the south-east. Elevation extremes range from 312m (Gaizinkalns) to 0m (Baltic Sea). The climate is temperate, and average temperatures range from −3.2°C in February to 17.9°C in July.

HISTORY AND POLITICS

Conquered and Christianised in the 13th century by the Teutonic Knights, Latvia was successively under Polish, Lithuanian and Swedish rule in the 16th and 17th centuries until it was incorporated into the Russian Empire in 1721. Under partial German occupation during the First World War, it declared its independence in 1918 and successfully defended this against the Bolsheviks in 1918–20. A dictatorship was established in 1934 following a period of political instability and economic depression. The USSR invaded and annexed Latvia in 1940, and regained control in 1944 after ousting the German forces that had invaded in 1941. Latvia suffered huge civilian losses during the Second World War, including the destruction of its large Jewish community. Many more Latvians died after the war in purges and deportations ordered by Stalin.

Agitation by nationalist groups grew from the mid-1980s. In May 1990 the legislature declared independence. The last Russian troops left in 1994 but a large Russian minority remains and there are intercommunal tensions. Latvia joined NATO and the EU in 2004.

No single party has ever secured a majority in parliament. In the October 2014 legislative election, the ruling coalition, led by the centre-right Unity party, retained its majority, despite the pro-Russian Harmony Centre remaining the largest single party. Laimdota Straujuma resigned as prime minister in December 2015 following disputes within the coalition and in February 2016 she was replaced by Maris Kucinskis. A centre-right coalition of five parties took power in January 2019 after four months of negotiations and Krisjanis Karins of the Unity party was appointed prime minister. Egils Levits was elected president in May 2019.

The 1922 constitution was restored in 1993. The head of state is a president, who is elected by the legislature for a four-year term which may be renewed once. The president appoints the prime minister, who appoints the cabinet subject to approval by the legislature. The unicameral *Saeima* has 100 deputies who are directly elected for a four-year term.

HEAD OF STATE

President, Egils Levits, *elected* 29 May 2019, *sworn in* 8 July 2019

SELECTED GOVERNMENT MEMBERS *AS AT NOVEMBER 2020*

Prime Minister, Krisjanis Karins

Economics, Janis Vitenbergs

Finance, Janis Reirs

Foreign Affairs, Edgars Rinkevics

EMBASSY OF THE REPUBLIC OF LATVIA

45 Nottingham Place, London W1U 5LY

T 020-7312 0041 **E** embassy.uk@mfa.gov.lv

W www.mfa.gov.lv/london

Ambassador Extraordinary and Plenipotentiary, HE Ivita Burmistre, *apptd* 2016

BRITISH EMBASSY

5 J. Alunana iela, Riga LV1010

T (+371) 6777 4700 **E** britishembassy.riga@fco.gov.uk

W www.gov.uk/government/world/latvia

Ambassador Extraordinary and Plenipotentiary, HE Keith Shannon, *apptd* 2017

ECONOMY AND TRADE

The country made the transition from a planned to a market economy in the decade after independence, with some large enterprises remaining in state ownership. The economy grew rapidly from 2004 to 2007, but was severely affected by the global economic downturn because of its large current account deficit and private-sector debt. The economy contracted by 14 per cent in 2009 and was slow to return to growth. The IMF, the World Bank and the EU provided aid in 2008–9 to avoid devaluation in return for a 40 per cent cut in public spending. The IMF programme was successfully concluded in December 2011 and Latvia joined the eurozone in 2014 and the OEDC in 2016. In 2017 Latvia returned to pre-crisis levels of growth, which was sustained thanks to rising domestic demand and a €4.5bn EU investment fund that concluded in 2020; however, it entered recession in 2020 due to the coronavirus pandemic. Long-term impediments include corruption and a decreasing population, the latter due largely to the exodus of skilled workers.

The economy has shifted towards service industries since independence. Services, especially transit services and banking, is the largest sector, contributing 73.7 per cent of GDP. Industry contributes 22.4 per cent of GDP and includes food processing and the manufacture of processed wood products, textiles, processed metals, pharmaceuticals, rail transport vehicles, synthetic fibres and electronics. The agricultural sector accounts for 3.9 per cent of GDP, employs 7.7 per cent of the workforce and specialises in rearing livestock, dairy farming and crops including grain, rapeseed, potatoes and other vegetables.

The main trading partners are other EU states and Russia, with exports contributing more than half of GDP. Principal exports are food products, timber and wood products, metals, machinery and equipment, and textiles. The main imports are machinery and equipment, consumer goods, chemicals, fuel and vehicles.

GNI – US$33.9bn; US$17,730 per capita (2019)
Annual average growth of GDP – 2.08 per cent (2019 est)
Inflation rate – 2.9 per cent (2017 est)
Population below poverty line – 25.5 per cent (2015 est)
Unemployment – 6.14 per cent (2019 est)
Total external debt – US$40.02bn (2016 est)
Imports – US$18,601m (2017)
Exports – US$18,539m (2017)

BALANCE OF PAYMENTS
Trade – US$61m deficit (2017)
Current Account – US$221m deficit (2019)

Trade with UK	2018	2019
Imports from UK	£388,703,486	£391,031,348
Exports to UK	£767,308,975	£769,031,348

COMMUNICATIONS
Airports and waterways – There are 18 airports with the largest at Riga, Ventspils and Liepaja; there are major ports at Riga and Ventspils
Roadways and railways – 15,158km; 1,860km
Telecommunications – 266,214 fixed lines and 2.1 million mobile subscriptions (2018); there were 1.6 million internet users in 2018
Internet code and IDD – lv; 371 (from UK), 44 (to UK)
Major broadcasters – Latvian Television (LTV) and Latvian Radio are the state broadcasters
Press – Prominent daily newspapers include *Diena, Neatkariga Rita Avize* (both Latvian language) and *Telegraf* (mainly Russian)
WPFI score – 18.56 (22)

EDUCATION AND HEALTH
Education is compulsory from age of seven to 16, after which there is the option for a further three years of either secondary or vocational study.
Literacy rate – 99.9 per cent (2018 est)
Gross enrolment ratio (percentage of relevant age group) – primary 99.6 per cent, secondary 109.2 per cent, tertiary 93 per cent (2018 est)
Health expenditure (per capita) – US$930 (2017)
Hospital beds (per 1,000 people) – 5.8 (2013)

Life expectancy (years) – 75.4 (2020 est)
Mortality rate – 14.6 (2020 est)
Birth rate – 9.2 (2020 est)
Infant mortality rate – 5 (2020 est)
HIV/AIDS adult prevalence – 0.5 per cent (2019 est)

LEBANON

Al-Jumhuriyah al-Lubnaniyah – Lebanese Republic

Area – 10,400 sq. km
Capital – Beirut (Bayrut); population, 2,424,000 (2020 est)
Major cities – Sidon, Tripoli (Tarabulus)
Currency – Lebanese pound (L£) of 100 piastres
Population – 5,469,612 falling at 6.68 per cent a year (2020 est)
Religion – Muslim 61.1 per cent (Sunni 30.6 per cent, Shia 30.5 per cent), Christian 33.7 per cent (predominantly Maronite Catholic), Druze 5.2 per cent (est)
Language – Arabic (official), French, English, Armenian
Population density – 669 per sq. km (2019)
Urban population – 88.8 per cent (2019 est)
Median age (years) – 33.7 (2020 est)
National anthem – 'Kulluna lil-watan' 'All of Us, For Our Country'
National day – 22 November (Independence Day)
Death penalty – Retained
CPI score – 28 (137)
Military expenditure – US$2,776m (2018 est)

CLIMATE AND TERRAIN
A narrow plain along the Mediterranean Sea coast is backed by the Lebanon mountains, along which the Anti-Lebanon range runs parallel, forming the border with Syria. Between the two ranges lies the fertile Bekaa valley, the northern extremity of Africa's Great Rift valley. Elevations range from 3,088m (Qurnat as Sawda') to 0m (Mediterranean Sea). The climate is Mediterranean, although the mountains usually receive snow in winter. Average temperatures in Beirut are 7.4°C in January and 25.3°C in August.

POLITICS
The constitution dates from 1926 but has been heavily amended, most significantly in 1943, when the National Covenant set out the division of power between the religious communities, and in 1990 to incorporate the provisions of the Ta'if accord. By convention, the presidency is held by a Maronite Christian, the prime minister is a Sunni Muslim and the speaker is a Shia Muslim.

The president is elected by the legislature for a six-year term, which is not renewable consecutively. The unicameral National Assembly has 128 members, directly elected for a four-year term by proportional representation; seats are divided equally between Christians and Muslims, whose

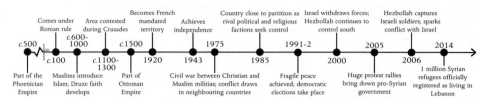

Comes under Roman rule c.500 | Area contested during Crusades c.600–1000 | Becomes French mandated territory c.1500 | Achieves independence 1975 | Country close to partition as rival political and religious factions seek control 1991-2 | Israel withdraws forces; Hezbollah continues to control south 2005 | Hezbollah captures Israeli soldiers; sparks conflict with Israel 2014

c.100 | c.1100–1300 | 1920 | 1943 | 1985 | 2000 | 2006

Part of the Phoenician Empire | Muslims introduce Islam; Druze faith develops | Part of Ottoman Empire | Civil war between Christian and Muslim militias; conflict draws in neighbouring countries | Fragile peace achieved; democratic elections take place | Huge protest rallies bring down pro-Syrian government | 1 million Syrian refugees officially registered as living in Lebanon

quotas are subdivided by religious 'confession' according to the distribution formalised in the 2008 election law. The prime minister is appointed by the president following consultation with the legislature.

New legislative elections, originally due to take place in 2014, were first delayed until June 2017 due to security concerns related to the conflict in Syria and then to May 2018 after politicians approved a new draft electoral law. Pro-Iran parties performed well but the elections resulted in no change in the country's political leadership. However, after 2,750 tonnes of ammonium nitrate exploded in Beirut in August 2020, which had been improperly stored on an abandoned ship for six years, large demonstrations forced the cabinet to resign. The explosion killed over 200 people, left 300,000 homeless and caused more than £2.3bn of damage.

In October 2016, Michel Aoun was confirmed as president after two years of political deadlock.

HEAD OF STATE
President, Michel Aoun, *apptd* 31 October 2016

SELECTED GOVERNMENT MEMBERS *AS AT NOVEMBER 2020*
Prime Minister, vacant
Deputy Prime Minister, Zeina Akar
Finance, vacant

EMBASSY OF LEBANON
15 Palace Gardens Mews, London W8 4RB
T 020-7229 7265 **E** lebanonconsulate@btconnect.com
W http://london.mfa.gov.lb/britain/english/home
Ambassador Extraordinary and Plenipotentiary, HE Rami Mortada, *apptd* 2017

BRITISH EMBASSY
PO Box 11–471, Serail Hill, Beirut Central District, Beirut
T (+961) (1) 960 800 **E** www.gov.uk/government/world/lebanon
Ambassador Extraordinary and Plenipotentiary, HE Christopher Rampling, MBE, *apptd* 2018

ECONOMY AND TRADE
The civil war seriously damaged Lebanon's strong commercial economy and infrastructure, as well as its role as an entrepôt and financial services centre for the region. Reconstruction was almost complete when the Israeli attacks in 2006 caused an estimated US$3.6bn (£2.1bn) of infrastructure damage. Recovery was hindered by internal instability, which also postponed the introduction of the economic reforms that were a condition of international funding for reconstruction. The mass migration of refugees from Syria since 2011 has seriously increased income inequality, social tensions and unemployment, with anywhere up to 2 million refugees estimated to be in the country. The Beirut explosion, coupled with the coronavirus pandemic, has severely impacted an economy that was already contracting significantly before 2020, and according to the IMF may result in a 25 per cent fall in GDP.

The service sector contributes 83 per cent of GDP, largely through banking and tourism, which are the two main economic activities. Industry accounts for 13.1 per cent, through food processing, wine production and the manufacture of jewellery, cement, textiles, mineral and chemical products, timber and furniture, oil refining and metal fabrication. Agriculture contributes 3.9 per cent of GDP, producing fruit, vegetables, tobacco and livestock.

The main export markets are China, the UAE, South Africa and Saudi Arabia, while imports come mainly from China, Italy, Greece and Germany. Principal exports include jewellery, base metals, chemicals, consumer goods, fruit, vegetables, tobacco and construction materials. The main imports are petroleum products, vehicles, medicines, clothing, meat, livestock and consumer goods.

GNI – US$52.1bn; US$7,600 per capita (2019)
Annual average growth of GDP – 1.5 per cent (2017 est)
Inflation rate – 4.5 per cent (2017 est)
Total external debt – US$39.3bn (2017 est)
Imports – US$30,839m (2017)
Exports – US$19,870m (2017)

BALANCE OF PAYMENTS
Trade – US$10,968m deficit (2017)
Current Account – US$11,539m deficit (2019)

Trade with UK	2018	2019
Imports from UK	£346,426,614	£305,733,441
Exports to UK	£31,455,002	£39,106,727

COMMUNICATIONS
Airports and waterways – There are five airports, including the international airport at Beirut; the principal seaports are Beirut and Tripoli
Roadways and railways –21,705km; 401km
Telecommunications – 893,529 million fixed lines and 4.4 million mobile subscriptions (2018); there were 4.8 million internet users in 2018
Internet code and IDD – lb; 961 (from UK), 44 (to UK)
Major broadcasters – Télé-Liban is the state-run broadcaster and competes with several commercial stations, including pro-Hezbollah al-Manar TV and the market-leading Lebanese Broadcasting Corporation and Future TV
Press – Leading dailies include *An-Nahar, Al-Safir* (both Arabic language) and *L'Orient-Le Jour* (French)
WPFI score – 33.19 (102)

EDUCATION AND HEALTH
There are nine years of compulsory education.
Literacy rate – 95.1 per cent (2018 est)
Gross enrolment ratio (percentage of relevant age group) – primary 89 per cent, secondary 60 per cent, tertiary 38 per cent (2016 est)
Health expenditure (per capita) – US$719 (2017)
Hospital beds (per 1,000 people) – 2.9 (2014)
Life expectancy (years) – 78.3 (2020 est)
Mortality rate – 5.4 (2020 est)
Birth rate – 13.6 (2020 est)
Infant mortality rate – 6.8 (2020 est)
HIV/AIDS adult prevalence – 0.1 per cent (2019 est)

LESOTHO

Kingdom of Lesotho

Area – 30,355 sq. km
Capital – Maseru; population, 202,000 (2018)
Major cities – Leribe, Mafeteng, Quthing
Currency – Loti (M) of 100 lisente; the South African rand is
    also legal tender
Population – 1,969,334 rising at 0.16 per cent a year (2020
    est)
Religion – Christian (Protestant 47.8 per cent, Roman
    Catholic 39.3 per cent, other Christian 9.1 per cent) (est)
Language – English, Sesotho (both official), Zulu, Xhosa
Population density – 69 per sq. km (2019)
Urban population – 28.6 per cent (2019 est)
Median age (years) – 24.7 (2020 est)
National anthem – 'Lesotho Fatse la Bo Ntat'a Rona' 'Lesotho,
    Land of Our Fathers'
National day – 4 October (Independence Day)
Death penalty – Retained
CPI score – 40 (85)
Military expenditure – US$51.1m (2018)

CLIMATE AND TERRAIN
Lesotho consists of a highland plateau with mountains in the
east. The lower land in the west contains most of the arable
land and 70 per cent of the population. Elevation extremes
range from 3,482m (Thabana Ntlenyana) to 1,400m (the
junction of the Orange and Makhaleng rivers). As 80 per cent
of the country lies above 1,800m, the climate is temperate, with
snow in the highlands in winter. Temperatures average 18.3°C
in January and 7°C in June.

HISTORY AND POLITICS
The area was organised into a single territory by Moshoeshoe
the Great from the 1820s as the Sotho people came under
pressure from both the expanding Zulu nation and the Boers.
In 1868, after fighting two wars with the Boers, Moshoeshoe
sought protection from the British government, and
Basutoland became first a British territory (1868) and then a
crown colony (1884).
    The country gained independence in 1966 as the kingdom
of Lesotho, under Moshoeshoe II and with Chief Lebua
Jonathan as prime minister. Chief Jonathan was overthrown in
a military coup in 1986; military rule ended with multiparty
elections in 1993 and democratic rule was restored in 1994.
The 1998 elections were also followed by severe disturbances,
which were quelled by an intervention force from
neighbouring countries. King Moshoeshoe II, deposed in
1990, was reinstated in 1995 but died in 1996; he was
succeeded by King Letsie III, who had been king during his
father's exile.
    In the 2012 legislative election, the Democratic Congress
(DC) party won the largest number of seats but did not gain a
majority, and Motsoahae Tom Thabane of the All Basotho

Convention (ABC) party was appointed prime minister. In
August 2014, an attempted military coup caused Thabane to
briefly flee to South Africa. After the coup attempt, early
elections were held in 2015 in an attempt to create a stable
government. The DC, under Bethuel Pakalitha Mosisili,
emerged again as the largest single party and was able to form
a governing coalition. However, in February 2017 Mosisili lost
a parliamentary vote of no confidence and Thabane was re-
elected prime minister following new elections in June. In May
2020 Thabane resigned after he was alleged to have arranged
his ex-wife's murder, and was replaced by finance minister
Moeketsi Majoro.
    Under the 1993 constitution, subsequently amended, the
head of state is a hereditary monarch, with ceremonial duties
but no executive or legislative powers. The bicameral
parliament comprises the National Assembly, with 120
members elected for a five-year term, one-third by
proportional representation, and the senate, whose 33
members comprise 22 principal chiefs and 11 members
nominated by the king. The prime minister is the leader of the
majority party in the legislature and appoints the council of
ministers.

HEAD OF STATE
HM The King of Lesotho, King Letsie III, *acceded* 7 February
    1996, *crowned* 31 October 1997
Heir, HRH Crown Prince Lerothi Seeiso

SELECTED GOVERNMENT MEMBERS *AS AT*
NOVEMBER 2020
Prime Minister, Moeketsi Majoro
Deputy Prime Minister, Mathibeli Mokhothu
Finance, Thabo Sofonea

HIGH COMMISSION OF THE KINGDOM OF LESOTHO
7 Chesham Place, London SW1X 8HN
T 020-7235 5686 **E** hicom@lesotholondon.org.uk
W www.lesotholondon.org.uk
High Commissioner, HE Rethabile Mahlompho Mokaeane,
    apptd 2019

BRITISH HIGH COMMISSION
HE Anne Macro, CMG, MVO, *apptd* 2019, resident at
    Pretoria (Tshwane), South Africa

ECONOMY AND TRADE
The country is one of the poorest in the world, with around
57 per cent of the population living below the poverty line.
With few natural resources apart from water, the main sources
of government revenue are customs dues from the South
African customs union and, since 1998, the export of water and
electricity to South Africa from the hydroelectric facilities
created by the Lesotho Highlands Water Project. The
economic situation worsened in the early 2000s due to a series
of severe droughts and declining demand for mineworkers in
South Africa.
    This decline has been partially compensated for by the
resumption of diamond mining in 2003, and the development
of a small manufacturing base processing agricultural products,
producing textiles and assembling garments, coupled with
tourism, especially in the highlands. Lesotho's economy
recovered well from the global economic crisis in 2008–9 with
growth averaging nearly 5 per cent between 2010 and 2014,
but subsequently decelerated up to 2019 and is expected to
decline by 5.2 per cent in 2020. The economy is heavily reliant
on government consumption, which accounts for roughly 26
per cent of GDP; diamond mining, which accounts for around
35 per cent of total exports; and remittances supplied by
migrants to South Africa. Unemployment remains high, at over
25 per cent.

Subsistence agriculture employs about three-quarters of the population, although the nation produces less than one-fifth of food demand. Principal exports are clothing, footwear, wool and mohair, food and livestock. The main imports, 87.2 per cent of which come from South Africa, are food, construction materials, vehicles, machinery, medicines and petroleum products.

GNI – US$2.9bn; US$1,360 per capita (2019)
Annual average growth of GDP – -1.6 per cent (2017 est)
Inflation rate – 5.3 per cent (2017 est)
Population below poverty line – 57 per cent (2016 est)
Unemployment – 28.1 per cent (2014)
Total external debt – US$934.6m (2017 est)
Imports – US$2,180m (2017)
Exports – US$1,053m (2017)

BALANCE OF PAYMENTS
Trade – US$1,126m deficit (2017)
Current Account – US$98m deficit (2019)

Trade with UK	2018	2019
Imports from UK	£1,487,418	£1,073,397
Exports to UK	£259,833	£354,417

COMMUNICATIONS
Airports – There are three airports; the international airport is at Maseru
Roadways – There are 1,069km of paved roads
Telecommunications – 8,328 fixed lines (2018) and 2.4 million mobile subscriptions (2017); there were 570,000 internet users in 2018
Internet code and IDD – ls; 266 (from UK), 44 (to UK)
Major broadcasters – Radio is the most important medium, although only the state-run Radio Lesotho has national coverage; Lesotho Television, also state-run, is the only television station, but South African broadcasts can be received
Press – A number of weekly newspapers are published in English and Sesotho
WPFI score – 30.45 (86)

EDUCATION AND HEALTH
Literacy rate – 85.1 per cent (2017)
Gross enrolment ratio (percentage of relevant age group) – primary 120.9 per cent, secondary 62 per cent (2017 est); tertiary 10.1 per cent (2018 est)
Health expenditure (per capita) – US$105 (2017)
Life expectancy (years) – 53 (2020 est)
Mortality rate – 15.4 (2020 est)
Birth rate – 23.2 (2020 est)
Infant mortality rate – 41.5 (2020 est)
HIV/AIDS adult prevalence – 22.8 per cent (2019 est)

LIBERIA
Republic of Liberia

Area – 111,369 sq. km
Capital – Monrovia; population, 1,517,000 (2020 est)

Currency – Liberian dollar (L$) of 100 cents
Population – 5,073,296 rising at 2.71 per cent a year (2020 est); Kpelle (20.3 per cent), Bassa (13.4 per cent), Grebo (10 per cent), Gio (8 per cent), Mano (7.9 per cent) (est)
Religion – Christian 85.6 per cent, Muslim 12.2 per cent (est)
Language – English (official), about 20 ethnic languages
Population density – 50 per sq. km (2018)
Urban population – 51.2 per cent (2018 est)
Median age (years) – 18 (2020 est)
National anthem – 'All Hail, Liberia, Hail!'
National day – 26 July (Independence Day)
Death penalty – Retained (last used 2000)
CPI score – 28 (137)
Military expenditure – US$15.8m (2018)
Literacy rate – 48.3 per cent (2017 est)
Gross enrolment ratio (percentage of relevant age group) – primary 85.1 per cent (2017 est); secondary 37.9 per cent (2015 est); tertiary 12 per cent (2012 est)
Health expenditure (per capita) – US$57 (2017)
Hospital beds (per 1,000 people) – 0.8 (2010)
Life expectancy (years) – 64.7 (2020 est)
Mortality rate – 7.0 (2020 est)
Birth rate – 37.3 (2020 est)
Infant mortality rate – 47.4 (2020 est)
HIV/AIDS adult prevalence – 1.5 per cent (2019 est)

CLIMATE AND TERRAIN
Liberia lies on the west African coast, just north of the equator. There are forested highlands and grassy plateaux in the interior and swampy plains on the coast, where several rivers enter the ocean. Elevation extremes range from 1,380m (Mt Wuteve) to 0m (Atlantic Ocean). The climate is tropical, with very high rainfall.

HISTORY AND POLITICS
The land was purchased by the American Colonisation Society in 1821 and turned into a settlement for liberated black slaves from the USA, gaining recognition as an independent state in 1847.

In the first century of statehood, politics was dominated by the True Whig Party of the Americo-Liberian minority. Political stability ended in 1980 when a coup installed a military government under Samuel Doe. When civilian rule was restored in 1985, Doe became president, but his regime's arbitrary, corrupt rule combined with an economic collapse led to a revolt in 1989 by Charles Taylor's National Patriotic Forces of Liberia (NPFL) and the Armed Forces of Liberia (AFL). The country descended into a civil war that, apart from a respite in 1996–9, lasted until 2003. Around 250,000 people were killed and thousands were displaced. Following mediation by a number of African and European countries, all factions in the conflict signed a peace agreement in 2003 and a UN peacekeeping force was deployed. The disarming of militias was completed in 2005, and a truth and reconciliation commission was set up in 2006 and reported in 2009. In 2012, Taylor was found guilty of war crimes and sentenced to 50 years in jail to be served in a British prison.

After a period of transitional government, presidential and legislative elections were held in late 2005. In the legislative election, the Congress for Democratic Change (CDC) won the most seats but without an overall majority. The Unity Party leader, Ellen Johnson Sirleaf, was elected president in the second round of voting and took office in January 2006. Sirleaf regained the presidential nomination in the 2011 election, picking up 43.9 per cent of the overall vote. The Unity Party gained the most votes in the 2011 and 2014 legislative elections but lost control of the senate. After irregularities were alleged to have taken place in the October

2017 presidential elections, former footballer George Weah won a run-off vote in December 2017 on an anti-corruption platform.

Under the 1986 constitution, the head of state is an executive president who is directly elected for a six-year term, renewable once. There is a bicameral National Assembly, consisting of the House of Representatives, with 73 members directly elected for a six-year term, and a senate, with 30 members (two from each of the 15 counties) elected for nine-year staggered terms. The president appoints the cabinet, which must be approved by the legislature.

HEAD OF STATE
President, George Weah, *elected* 26 December 2017, *sworn in* 22 January 2018
Vice-President, Jewel Taylor

SELECTED GOVERNMENT MEMBERS, *AS AT NOVEMBER 2020*
Defence, Maj.-Gen. (retd) Daniel Dee Ziankahn
Finance, Samuel Tweah
Foreign Affairs, Dee-Maxwell Kemayah

EMBASSY OF THE REPUBLIC OF LIBERIA
23 Fitzroy Square, London W1T 6EW
T 020-7388 5489 E info@embassyofliberia.org.uk
W www.embassyofliberia.org.uk
Ambassador Extraordinary and Plenipotentiary, Gurly Gibson, *apptd* 2019

BRITISH AMBASSADOR
Leone Compound, 12th Street Beach-side, Sinkor, Monrovia
T (+231) (0)77530320 E monrovia.generalenquiries@fco.gov.uk
W www.gov.uk/government/world/liberia
Ambassador Extraordinary and Plenipotentiary, HE David Belgrove, OBE, *apptd* 2015

ECONOMY AND TRADE
The civil war devastated an economy already weakened by government mismanagement and corruption, and drove those with expertise and capital into exile. Remittances are now an important sources of national income. Since the war ended, foreign aid has been received to finance reconstruction, conditional on the adoption of anti-corruption measures, and economic activity has revived. Growth since 2006 has been driven by donor aid and exports, particularly of rubber and, since UN sanctions were lifted in 2006 and 2007 respectively, timber and diamonds. The country also benefited from substantial debt relief in 2010, a 2011 African Development Bank a grant of US$48m, and US$213.6m extended credit facility from the IMF in December 2019. Economic growth partially recovered after the 2014 Ebola outbreak that collapsed 90 per cent of the economy, with the rehabilitation of Mount Coffee Hydroelectric Dam and the opening of new gold and iron ore mines, but the economy contracted in 2019 and this is expected to continue in 2020.

Agriculture was the main economic activity during the civil war but its contribution to GDP and its share of the labour market has declined as the industrial and service sectors have revived. Industry centres on the processing of rubber and palm oil, forestry and mining (diamonds, gold and iron ore).

The main export markets are the UAE and EU countries, while imports come mainly from Singapore, South Korea, China and Japan. Principal exports are rubber, timber, iron, diamonds, cocoa and coffee. The main imports are fuels, chemicals, machinery, transport equipment, manufactured goods and foodstuffs.
GNI – US$2.9bn; US$580 per capita (2019)
Annual average growth of GDP – 2.5 per cent (2017 est)

Inflation rate – 12.4 per cent (2017 est)
Population below poverty line – 54.1 per cent (2014 est)
Total external debt – US$1.036bn (2017 est)
Import – US$1,857m (2016)
Export – US$345m (2016)

BALANCE OF PAYMENTS
Trade – US$1,511m deficit (2016)
Current Account – US$653m deficit (2019)

Trade with UK	2018	2019
Imports from UK	£13,624,497	£8,230,678
Exports to UK	£7,296,577	£1,681,124

COMMUNICATIONS
Airports and waterways – There are two international airports, Robertsfield and Spriggs Payne, in Monrovia; the main seaports are Monrovia and Buchanan, and there is a merchant fleet of 2,771 ships of over 1,000 tonnes, including 2,581 foreign-owned ships registered in Liberia
Roadways and railways – There are 657km of paved roadways; due to war damage, little of the 429km of railway track is operational, although reconstruction is underway
Telecommunications – 8,000 fixed lines and 3.1 million mobile subscriptions (2016); there were 383,819 internet users in 2018
Internet code and IDD – lr; 231 (from UK), 44 (to UK)
Major broadcasters – Media are largely privately owned, although the state-run Liberian Broadcasting System operates Radio Liberia; television broadcasters include Clar TV and Power TV
Press – There are two major daily newspapers, *The Inquirer* and *The New Dawn,* both privately owned
WPFI score – 32.25 (95)

LIBYA

Dawlat Libya – State of Libya

Area – 1,759,540 sq. km
Capital – Tripoli (Tarabulus); population, 1,165,000 (2020)
Major cities – al-Hums, az-Zawiyah, Benghazi, Misratah, Tarhunah, Zuwarah
Currency – Libyan dinar (LD) of 1,000 dirhams
Population – 6,890,535 rising at 1.94 per cent a year (2020 est)
Religion – Muslim (official; predominantly Sunni) 96.6 per cent, Christian 2.7 per cent (est)
Language – Arabic (official), Italian, English, Berber dialects
Population density – 4 per sq. km (2019)
Urban population – 80.4 per cent (2019 est)
Median age (years) – 25.8 (2020 est)
National anthem – 'Libya, Libya, Libya'

National day – 23 October (Liberation Day)
Death penalty – Retained
CPI score – 18 (168)
Military expenditure – US$6,320m (2014)
Conscription – 18 years of age for mandatory or voluntary service

CLIMATE AND TERRAIN

Apart from hills on the north-west and north-east coasts and in the far south, the country is made up of plains and plateaux, with some depressions; 90 per cent is desert or semi-desert. Elevation extremes range from 2,267m (Bikku Bitti) to −47m (Sabkhat Ghuzayyil). The climate is Mediterranean on the coast, and arid desert in the interior. Average temperatures in Tripoli range from 12.9°C in January to 30.4°C in July.

POLITICS

Following the overthrow of the 'Leader of the Revolution', Col. Muammar al-Gaddafi, the National Transitional Council (NTC) set out plans for a 'political democratic regime to be based upon the political multitude and multi-party system'.

In July 2012, the General National Congress was elected and power was handed over from the transitional government in August; Mohammed Magarief was elected interim head of state. In October 2012, prime minister-elect Mustafa Abu Shagur failed in two attempts to gain parliamentary approval for his government; the national congress elected Ali Zidan prime minister in his place. In May 2014 businessman Ahmed Maiteg was elected prime minister but stood down one month later, when the Supreme Court ruled his election unconstitutional.

Abdullah al-Thinni was appointed Libya's acting prime minister in June 2014. In August, the House of Representatives replaced the General National Congress as the legislative body and its president, Akila Issa, became the new head of state. Continuing political chaos saw the former legislative body, the General National Congress, appoint their own prime minister, Islamist Omar al-Hassi, on 25 August, resulting in two rival governments. Al-Thinni's government resigned on 29 August in order to allow for the formation of a national unity government; however, al-Thinni was reappointed in September after Tripoli was captured by rebel groups, forcing the government to relocate to Tobruk. Talks between the two rival administrations, held in Morocco in June 2015, failed to result in the formation of a new national unity government. A new UN-backed government was announced in January 2016, led by Prime Minister Fayez Sarraj.

A multi-sided civil war has developed with pockets of Islamist militants in the north, Tuareg militias in the south, the UN-backed government holding Tripoli and western regions, and the rival Tobruk-based government occupying the north-east. The fighting has contributed to a refugee crisis, which has seen tens of thousands attempting to cross the Mediterranean Sea every year. Following a summit in Paris, leaders agreed to hold fair elections in December 2018, but they were delayed, and in April 2019 Khalifa Haftar's Tobruk-based National Liberation Army, which controlled two-thirds of the country, began an assault on the UN-backed government in Tripoli. In July 2019, after three months of fighting, the conflict had claimed nearly 1,000 lives and displaced over 100,000. Haftar received international support from Egypt, France, Saudi Arabia, Russia and the UAE, meaning both EU and UN resolutions condemning Haftar's assault failed. A ceasefire and roadmap to elections were agreed in late 2020, amid nationwide protests against both regimes.

UN-RECOGNISED GOVERNMENT

HEAD OF STATE
Prime Minister, Fayez al-Sarraj

SELECTED GOVERNMENT MEMBERS *AS AT NOVEMBER 2020*
Deputy Prime Ministers, Ahmed Meitig; Abdelsalam Saad Husayn Kajman
Finance, Faraj Bumatari
Foreign Relations, Mohamed Taha Siala

EMBASSY OF LIBYA
15 Knightsbridge, London SW1X 7LY
T 020-7201 8280 **W** http://english.libyanembassy.org
Ambassador Extraordinary and Plenipotentiary, vacant

BRITISH AMBASSADOR
24th Floor, Tripoli Towers, PO Box 4206, Tripoli
T (+218) 21335108 **E** tripoliconsular@fco.gov.uk
W www.gov.uk/government/world/libya
Ambassador Extraordinary and Plenipotentiary, HE Nicholas Hopton, *apptd* 2019

ECONOMY AND TRADE

Oil and gas exports dominate the economy, although production has become erratic since the start of the civil war in 2011, and many oil wells are now controlled by the rival Tobruk-based government or anti-government militias. The end of unilateral US sanctions in 2006 had dramatically increased foreign investment in the energy and banking sectors, but since 2014 further instability, low oil prices and disrupted production have reversed these gains and helped foster a thriving black market. Widespread power outages, high levels of inflation and a lack of everyday necessities has added further strain to the embattled economy. The economic situation is very volatile. Huge growth in 2017 of 64 per cent was followed by continued improvements until 2020, where the coronavirus pandemic is expected to contract the economy by 66.7 per cent.

Industries include the production of petrochemicals, iron, steel and aluminium in addition to food processing and textiles. Owing to the terrain and climate, agriculture is a small sector, contributing only 1.3 per cent of GDP.

The main trading partners are Italy, other EU countries, China and Turkey. Principal exports are crude oil, refined petroleum products, natural gas and chemicals. The main imports are machinery, semi-finished goods, food, transport equipment and consumer products.

GNI – US$51.8bn; US$7,640 per capita (2019)
Annual average growth of GDP – 64 per cent (2017 est)

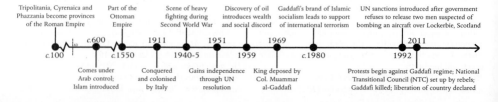

Tripolitania, Cyrenaica and Phazzania become provinces of the Roman Empire | Part of the Ottoman Empire | Scene of heavy fighting during Second World War | Discovery of oil introduces wealth and social discord | Gaddafi's brand of Islamic socialism leads to support of international terrorism | UN sanctions introduced after government refuses to release two men suspected of bombing an aircraft over Lockerbie, Scotland

*c.*600   1911   1951   1969   2011
*c.*100   *c.*1550   1940–5   1959   *c.*1980   1992

Comes under Arab control; Islam introduced | Conquered and colonised by Italy | Gains independence through UN resolution | King deposed by Col. Muammar al-Gaddafi | Protests begin against Gaddafi regime; National Transitional Council (NTC) set up by rebels; Gaddafi killed; liberation of country declared

Inflation rate – 28.5 per cent (2017 est)
Total external debt – US$3.02bn (2017 est)
Imports – US$11,550m (2016)
Exports – US$6,89m (2016)

BALANCE OF PAYMENTS
Trade – US$4,700m deficit (2016)
Current Account – US$11,276m surplus (2018)

Trade with UK	2018	2019
Imports from UK	£126,862,617	£157,730,073
Exports to UK	£625,481,066	£198,659,728

COMMUNICATIONS
Airports and waterways – There are 68 airports; the principal airports are at Tripoli, Benghazi and Sebha, while the main seaports are Benghazi, Tripoli and Tobruk
Roadways – 37,000km
Telecommunications – 1.6 million fixed lines and 6 million mobile subscriptions (2017); there were 1.4 million internet users in 2018
Internet code and IDD – ly; 218 (from UK), 44 (to UK)
Major broadcasters – Launched in April 2011 following the uprising, Libyan Radio and TV (LRT) has been joined by more than 20, mainly privately owned, TV and radio stations
Press – Major dailies include *February* and *New Quryna* (Arabic language) and *The Tripoli Post* (English language)
WPFI score – 55.77 (164)

EDUCATION AND HEALTH
There are six years of primary education and six of secondary, nine of which are compulsory.
Literacy rate – 100 per cent (2015 est)
Health expenditure (per capita) – US$372 (2014)
Hospital beds (per 1,000 people) – 3.7 (2014)
Life expectancy (years) – 76.7 (2020 est)
Mortality rate – 3.5 (2020 est)
Birth rate – 23 (2020 est)
Infant mortality rate – 11.5 (2020 est)
HIV/AIDS adult prevalence – 0.2 (2019 est)

LIECHTENSTEIN

Fürstentum Liechtenstein – Principality of Liechtenstein

Area – 160 sq. km
Capital – Vaduz; population, 5,000 (2018)
Major town – Schaan
Currency – Swiss franc of 100 rappen (or centimes)
Population – 39,137 rising at 0.75 per cent a year (2020 est); Liechtensteiner (66 per cent), Swiss (9.6 per cent) (est)

Religion – Christian (officially Roman Catholic 73.4 per cent, Protestant Reformed 6.3 per cent, Christian Orthodox 1.3 per cent, Lutheran 1.2 per cent), Muslim 5.9 per cent (est)
Language – German (official; Alemannic is the main dialect), Italian, Turkish, Portuguese
Population density – 237 per sq. km (2019)
Urban population – 14.4 per cent (2019 est)
Median age (years) – 43.7 (2020 est)
National anthem – 'Oben am Jungen Rhein' 'High Above the Young Rhine'
National day – 15 August (Feast of the Assumption)
Death penalty – Abolished for all crimes (since 1987)
Gross enrolment ratio (percentage of relevant age group) – primary 106.3 per cent, secondary 112 per cent, tertiary 38.3 per cent (2018 est)
Life expectancy (years) – 82.2 (2020 est)
Mortality rate – 7.8 (2020 est)
Birth rate – 10.4 (2020 est)
Infant mortality rate – 4.2 (2020 est)

CLIMATE AND TERRAIN
Liechtenstein is a small, mountainous landlocked principality in the Alps. The land falls in the west, in the valley of the river Rhine, which forms the western border. Elevation extremes range from 2,599m (Grauspitz) to 430m (Ruggeller Riet). The climate is continental, with heavy snowfall in winter; average temperatures range from −0.8°C in January to 16.2°C in July and August.

HISTORY AND POLITICS
Although there was a sovereign state within the present boundaries from the 14th century, the present state of Liechtenstein was formed from the lordships of Schellenberg and Vaduz in 1719. Part of the Holy Roman Empire, the principality became a member of the Confederation of the Rhine that succeeded the Empire in 1806, and then of the German Confederation from 1815 until 1866. It was the only German principality to remain outside the German Empire formed in 1871. The country abolished its armed forces and declared permanent neutrality in 1868. This was maintained in both world wars.

Economic decline in the years following the First World War led Liechtenstein to adopt the Swiss currency in 1921 and to enter into a Swiss customs union in 1923. The country became extremely prosperous as an international finance centre after the Second World War. Since 2000 it has tightened its laws to prevent money laundering, and since 2008 it has started to meet international financial transparency standards.

Governments in the 20th and 21st centuries have been formed by the two main parties, the northern-based Progressive Citizens' Party (FBP) and the southern-based Fatherland Union (VU). Usually they have formed a coalition government, although the FBP formed a single-party government from 2001 to 2005. However, the government's power is limited by that of the monarchy, whose authority over the government and judiciary was increased by a 2003 referendum. Prince Hans Adam II remains head of state but in 2004 he handed over day-to-day responsibility for government to his son, Prince Alois.

The VU won an overall majority in the 2009 election. The coalition government formed with the FBP in 2005 continued, although the premiership passed from the FBP to the VU. After the 2013 legislative elections the FBP became the dominant coalition partner, and this continued following the 2017 elections.

Under the 1921 constitution, Liechtenstein is a constitutional monarchy, with the hereditary prince as head of state. The unicameral legislature, the *Landtag*, has 25 members directly elected for a four-year term. The cabinet is appointed by the prince on the advice of the *Landtag* and consists of the head of government and four ministers.

HEAD OF STATE
HSH The Prince of Liechtenstein, Hans-Adam II, *born* 14 February 1945, *succeeded* 13 November 1989
Heir, HSH Crown Prince Alois, *born* 11 June 1968

SELECTED GOVERNMENT MEMBERS *AS AT NOVEMBER 2020*
Prime Minister, Finance, Adrian Hasler
Deputy Prime Minister, Economy, Daniel Risch
Foreign Affairs, Katrin Eggenberger

BRITISH AMBASSADOR
HE Jane Owen, *apptd* 2018, resident at Bern, Switzerland

ECONOMY AND TRADE
Liechtenstein has a prosperous, highly industrialised and diversified economy, boasting the highest GDP per capita in the world. Its mainstay is the financial services sector, which, with other service industries such as tourism, employs over half of the workforce. A light industrial base produces electronics, metal manufactures, dental products, ceramics, pharmaceuticals, food products, precision and optical instruments, and employs 41 per cent of the workforce. Over half the workforce commutes daily from Austria, Switzerland and Germany.
  Liechtenstein became a member of the European Free Trade Association in 1991, and of the European Economic Area in 1995. After combating its reputation as a tax haven and working with the EU to tackle international tax fraud and evasion, in October 2018 Liechtenstein was removed from the OECD's 'grey list' of countries that have not implemented the organisation's model tax convention. In 2011, Liechtenstein joined the Schengen area. Most of its trade is with EU countries and Switzerland. The principal exports are its industrial products. The main imports are agricultural and energy products, raw materials, machinery, metal goods, textiles, foodstuffs and vehicles.
GNI – US$4,816m; US$136,770 per capita (2009)
Annual average growth of GDP – 1.8 per cent (2012)
Inflation rate – −0.4 per cent (2016 est)
Unemployment – 2.4 per cent (2015)

Trade with UK	2018	2019
Imports from UK	£18,071,889	£20,186,479
Exports to UK	£4,559,940	£5,247,860

COMMUNICATIONS
Transport – Liechtenstein has no airports and only 630km of roads, 28km of waterways and 9km of rail track, which is part of the Austrian system connecting Austria and Switzerland
Telecommunications – 15,243 fixed lines and 47,272 mobile subscriptions (2018); there were 47,272 internet users in 2018
Internet code and IDD – li; 423 (from UK), 44 (to UK)
Media – The country has a very small media sector; its citizens rely on foreign broadcasters for most television and radio services. News publications include *Liechtensteiner Vaterland* and *Liechtensteiner Volksblatt*
WPFI score – 19.52 (24)

LITHUANIA
Lietuvos Respublika – Republic of Lithuania

Area – 65,300 sq. km
Capital – Vilnius; population, 539,000 (2020 est)
Major cities – Kaunas, Klaipeda, Siauliai
Currency – Euro (€) of 100 cents
Population – 2,731,464 falling at 1.13 per cent a year (2020 est); Lithuanian (84.1 per cent), Polish (6.6 per cent), Russian (5.8 per cent) (est)
Religion – Christian (Roman Catholic 77.2 per cent, Orthodox 4.1 per cent) (est)
Language – Lithuanian (official), Russian, Polish
Population density – 45 per sq. km (2019)
Urban population – 67.9 per cent (2019 est)
Median age (years) – 44.5 (2020 est)
National anthem – 'Tautiska Giesme' 'The National Song'
National day – 16 February (Independence Day)
Death penalty – Abolished for all crimes (since 1998)
CPI score – 60 (35)
Military expenditure – US$1,030m (2018)
Conscription – 18 years of age; 9 months

CLIMATE AND TERRAIN
Lithuania is a low-lying country with low hills in the west and south-east. It contains around 6,000 lakes and lagoons – over 2,800 of them sizeable – mostly lying in the east, although the Courland lagoon on the west coast is a major feature. Elevation extremes range from 294m (Aukstojas Hill) to 0m (Baltic Sea). The climate is mainly continental, and average temperatures range from −2.6°C in January to 18.1°C in July.

HISTORY AND POLITICS
Lithuania became a nation in the 13th century. It remained pagan for far longer than the rest of Europe, only becoming fully Christian in the 15th century when the Samogitians and the Aukstaitiai, the two main ethnic groups in the region, were converted. In the 14th century, a grand duchy was formed that stretched from the Baltic to the Black Sea and eastwards almost as far as Moscow. It confederated with Poland in the 16th century, before coming under Russian rule in 1795. The country joined Poland in rebelling against Russian domination twice in the 19th century.
  Occupied by Germany during the First World War, Lithuania declared its independence in 1918 and successfully defended its autonomy against the Bolsheviks in 1918–19. However, the province and city of Vilnius were occupied by the newly independent Poland from 1920 until 1939. The USSR invaded and annexed Lithuania in 1940, but the country revolted in 1941 and briefly established its own government before being invaded and occupied by the Germans in their 1941 offensive against the USSR. Around 210,000 Lithuanians, mainly Jews, were killed during the German occupation. Soviet troops ousted the Germans in

1944 and re-established Soviet control, against which Lithuanians carried on a guerrilla war until 1952.

Growing nationalist sentiment led to the formation of the pro-democracy *Sajudis* ('The Movement') in 1988 to campaign for greater autonomy. A unilateral declaration of independence in 1990 was blocked by the USSR but following the failed coup in Moscow in 1991, Lithuania declared its independence a second time, and this was internationally recognised. The last Russian troops left the country in 1993. Lithuania joined NATO and the EU in 2004.

In the October 2020 legislative elections, the centre-right Homeland Union won the largest number of seats and formed a three-party coalition with the Liberal Movement and Freedom Party, and elected Ingrid Simonyte as prime minister. Independent, centre-right candidate Gitanas Nauseda won the 2019 presidential election.

Under the 1992 constitution, the head of state is a president, who is directly elected for a five-year term, renewable once. The unicameral *Seimas* has 141 members who are directly elected for a four-year term; 71 members are elected in first-past-the-post constituencies and 70 by proportional representation. The prime minister is appointed by the president with the approval of the *Seimas,* and ministers are appointed upon the recommendation of the prime minister.

HEAD OF STATE
President, Gitanas Nauseda, *elected* 26 May 2019, *sworn in* 12 July 2019

SELECTED GOVERNMENT MEMBERS *AS AT NOVEMBER 2020*
Prime Minister-designate, Ingrid Simonyte
Defence, Raimundas Karoblis
Foreign Affairs, Linas Antanas Linkevicius
Interior, Rita Tamasuniene

EMBASSY OF THE REPUBLIC OF LITHUANIA
Lithuania House, 2 Bessborough Gardens, London SW1V 2JE
T 020-7592 2840 **E** amb.uk@urm.lt
W www.lithuanianembassy.co.uk/
Ambassador Extraordinary and Plenipotentiary, HE Renatas Norkus, *apptd* 2017

BRITISH EMBASSY
2 Antakalnio, Vilnius LT-10308
T (+370) (5) 246 2900 **E** consular.vilnius@fco.gov.uk
W www.gov.uk/government/world/lithuania
Ambassador Extraordinary and Plenipotentiary, HE Brian Olley, *apptd* 2019

ECONOMY AND TRADE
Lithuania's transition to a market economy is nearly complete, with the private sector now accounting for about 80 per cent of GDP. The transition initially caused a recession, but the economy recovered and grew steadily from 2004 to 2008 before being plunged into a deep recession, along with the other Baltic states, by the global economic downturn. Drastic government cuts in public spending and the halving of imports in 2009 restored the budget deficit to a surplus. The economy returned to growth in 2010 and exports, investment and wages subsequently increased steadily, while unemployment and public debt fell; however, the economy is expected to slightly contract in 2020 owing to the coronavirus pandemic. Domestic extraction of gas since 2015 has significantly reduce the nation's dependence on Russian imports. The country

joined the EU in 2004, the eurozone in 2015 and the OEDC in 2018.

The economy is diverse, and industries include metal-cutting machine tools, electric motors, domestic appliances, oil refining, shipbuilding, furniture making, textiles and amber extraction and jewellery making. Industry contributes 29.4 per cent to GDP, services 67.2 per cent and agriculture 3.5 per cent.

The main trading partners are Russia and other EU countries. Principal exports are refined fuel, machinery and equipment, chemicals, textiles, foodstuffs and plastics. The main imports are oil, gas, machinery, transport equipment, chemicals, textiles, clothing and metals.

GNI – US$52.9bn; US$18,990 per capita (2019)
Annual average growth of GDP – 4.33 per cent (2019 est)
Inflation rate – 3.7 per cent (2017 est)
Population below poverty line – 22.2 per cent (2015 est)
Unemployment – 8.4 per cent (2019 est)
Total external debt – US$34.48bn (2016 est)
Imports – US$37,169m (2017)
Exports – US$38,486m (2017)

BALANCE OF PAYMENTS
Trade – US$1,317m surplus (2017)
Current Account – US$1,816m surplus (2019)

Trade with UK	2018	2019
Imports from UK	£473,662,804	£527,973,528
Exports to UK	£844,965,875	£850,017,427

COMMUNICATIONS
Airports and waterways – There are 22 airports, with the largest at Vilnius, Kaunas and Palanga; the main seaport is at Klaipeda
Roadways and railways – 84,166km; a railway system of 1,768km links the major towns with Vilnius and Klaipeda
Telecommunications – 427,066 fixed lines and 4.6 million mobile subscriptions (2018); there were 2.2 million internet users in 2018
Internet code and IDD – lt; 370 (from UK), 44 (to UK)
Major broadcasters – Lithuania Radio and TV is the public broadcaster
Press – Major dailies include *Lietuvos Rytas, Respublika* and *Vakaro Zinios*
WPFI score – 21.19 (28)

EDUCATION AND HEALTH
Education is free and compulsory from seven to 16 years, with the system comprising primary school (four years), lower secondary school (six years) and upper secondary education (two years).
Literacy rate – 99.9 per cent (2015 est)
Gross enrolment ratio (percentage of relevant age group) – primary 104.2 per cent, secondary 108.2 per cent, tertiary 73.7 per cent (2018 est)
Health expenditure (per capita) – US$1,078 (2017)
Hospital beds (per 1,000 people) – 7.3 (2013)
Life expectancy (years) – 75.5 (2020 est)
Mortality rate – 15 (2020 est)
Birth rate – 9.5 (2020 est)
Infant mortality rate – 3.8 (2020 est)

LUXEMBOURG

Groussherzogtom Lëtzebuerg/Grand-Duché de Luxembourg/
Großherzogtum Luxembourg – Grand Duchy of Luxembourg

Area – 2,586 sq. km
Capital – Luxembourg; population, 120,000 (2018)
Major towns – Dudelange, Esch-sur-Alzette
Currency – Euro (€) of 100 cents
Population – 628,381 rising at 1.8 per cent a year (2020 est);
    Luxembourger (51.1 per cent), Portuguese (15.7 per cent),
    French (7.5 per cent) (est)
Religion – Christian (predominantly Roman Catholic 70.4
    per cent), Muslim 2.3 per cent (est)
Language – Luxembourgish, French, German (all official),
    Portuguese, Italian, English
Population density – 250 per sq. km (2019)
Urban population – 91.2 per cent (2019 est)
Median age (years) – 39.5 (2020 est)
National anthem – 'Ons Heemecht' 'Our Homeland'
National day – 23 June (official birthday of Grand Duchess
    Charlotte)
Death penalty – Abolished for all crimes (since 1979)
CPI score – 80 (9)
Military expenditure – US$419m (2018 est)
Gross enrolment ratio (percentage of relevant age group) – primary
    103.2 per cent, secondary 104.3 per cent, tertiary 18.6
    per cent (2018 est)
Health expenditure (per capita) – US$5,783 (2017)
Hospital beds (per 1,000 people) – 4.9 (2014)
Life expectancy (years) – 82.6 (2020 est)
Mortality rate – 7.3 (2020 est)
Birth rate – 11.6 (2020 est)
Infant mortality rate – 3.3 (2020 est)

CLIMATE AND TERRAIN

Luxembourg has the forested plateau of the Ardennes in the
north, forming part of the Natural Germano-Luxembourg
Park, which extends east into Germany. The south of the
country is mainly fertile farmland, and in the east is the wine-
growing region of the Moselle valley. Elevation extremes
range from 559m (Buurgplaatz) to 133m (Moselle river). The
climate is modified continental, and average temperatures
range from 2°C in January to 18.6°C in July.

HISTORY AND POLITICS

The area was part of the Roman Empire and then became part
of the Frankish Empire in the fifth century AD. It became
autonomous within the Holy Roman Empire under Siegfried,
Count of Ardennes, and was given the status of a duchy in
1354. Controlled by a succession of European powers after
1437 (when the House of Luxembourg died out), it was made
a grand duchy under Dutch rule after the Napoleonic wars.
  Much of Luxembourg joined the Belgians in their revolt
against the Netherlands in 1830; in 1838 the western,

French-speaking region was assigned to Belgium, and the
remainder became an independent grand duchy in 1839.
The Treaty of London in 1867 confirmed its independence
and neutrality. Occupation by Germany in both world wars
prompted Luxembourg to give up its neutrality and it was a
founding member of NATO in 1949.
  Luxembourg entered into economic union with Belgium in
1921 and joined the Benelux economic union in 1948. It was
a founder member of the EEC in 1958 and joined the
eurozone in 1999.
  Following a snap election in October 2013, the liberal
Democratic Party (DP) formed a coalition with the
Luxembourg Socialist Workers' Party and The Greens. The
elections were called after prime minister Jean-Claude Juncker
of the Christian Social Party (CSV) stood down following
revelations that his administration failed to prevent corruption
within the security services. The coalition narrowly
maintained power in the October 2018 general election.
  Under the 1868 constitution, the head of state is a hereditary
grand duke, whose role is now largely ceremonial. The
unicameral legislature, the Chamber of Deputies, has 60
members directly elected for a five-year term. There is also a
Council of State, which has 21 members nominated by the
grand duke; this acts as the supreme administrative tribunal
and has some legislative functions. The prime minister is
appointed by the grand duke on the basis of the election
results and appoints the cabinet.

HEAD OF STATE
HRH The Grand Duke of Luxembourg, Grand Duke Henri,
    born 16 April 1955, *succeeded* 7 October 2000
Heir, HRH Prince Guillaume, *born* 11 November 1981

SELECTED GOVERNMENT MEMBERS *AS AT*
NOVEMBER 2020
Prime Minister, Xavier Bettel
Deputy Prime Ministers, Dan Kersch *(Economy);* Francois
    Bausch *(Defence)*
Finance, Pierre Gramegna
Foreign Affairs, Jean Asselborn

EMBASSY OF LUXEMBOURG
27 Wilton Crescent, London SW1X 8SD
T 020-7235 6961 **E** londres.amb@mae.etat.lu
W http://londres.mae.lu
Ambassador Extraordinary and Plenipotentiary, HE Jean Olinger,
    apptd 2017

BRITISH EMBASSY
5 Boulevard Joseph II, L-1840, Luxembourg
T (+352) 229 864 **E** britemb@internet.lu
W www.gov.uk/government/world/luxembourg
Ambassador Extraordinary and Plenipotentiary, HE John
    Marshall, *apptd* 2016

ECONOMY AND TRADE

The economy is stable, with high growth, low public debt,
high levels of employment and low inflation providing an
exceptionally high standard of living and the third-highest
GDP per capita in the world. The government offset the
contraction in the economy in 2008–9 with economic
stimulus measures, which led to a budget deficit in 2009, but
growth resumed in 2010. Banking and financial services are
the dominant sector, contributing over 35 per cent of GDP,
but since 2015 EU legislation has tackled secrecy laws and
constricted banking activity. Steel production used to
dominate the industrial sector, but this has diversified to
include IT, telecommunications, freight transport, food
processing, chemicals, metal products and construction. The

small agricultural sector consists mainly of family-owned farms. Services account for 86.9 per cent of GDP, industry for 12.8 per cent and agriculture for 0.3 per cent. Over half the workforce commutes daily from France, Belgium and Germany. Banking sector reform in 2015 ended Luxembourg's culture of financial secrecy.

The main trading partners are other EU countries. Principal exports are the products of industrial activities. The main imports are commercial aircraft, minerals, metals, foodstuffs and luxury consumer goods.

GNI – US$45.8bn; US$73,910 per capita (2019)
Annual average growth of GDP – 2.31 per cent (2019 est)
Inflation rate – 2.1 per cent (2017 est)
Unemployment – 5.36 per cent (2019 est)
Total external debt – US$3.781 trillion (2016 est)
Imports – US$100,024m (2017)
Exports – US$122,634m (2017)

BALANCE OF PAYMENTS
Trade – US$22,610m deficit (2017)
Current Account – US$3,095m surplus (2019)

Trade with UK	2018	2019
Imports from UK	£241,049,102	£240,334,686
Exports to UK	£414,085,150	£603,801,435

COMMUNICATIONS
Transport – Luxembourg has one airport with paved runways; there are 2,899km of road (including 152km of motorways), and 275km of railway. The Moselle river provides 37km of navigable waterway
Telecommunications – 273,530 fixed lines and 798,600 mobile subscriptions (2018); there were 587,955 internet users in 2018
Internet code and IDD – lu; 352 (from UK), 44 (to UK)
Major broadcasters – Luxembourg is the headquarters of the Société Européenne des Satellites (SES), which operates Europe's largest satellite operation; RTL Tele Letzebuerg and RTL Radio Letzebuerg are the public broadcasters
Press – Leading dailies include *Letzebuerger Journal*, *Luxemburger Wort* and *Tageblatt* (all German language)
WPFI score – 15.46 (17)

MADAGASCAR
Repoblikan'i Madagasikara/République de Madagascar – Republic of Madagascar

Area – 587,041 sq. km
Capital – Antananarivo; population, 3,369,000 (2020 est)
Major cities – Antsirabe, Antsiranana, Fianarantsoa, Mahajanga, Toamasina

Currency – Ariary (MGA) of five iraimbilanja
Population – 26,955,737 rising at 2.39 per cent a year (2020 est); the population is made up of mixed Malayo-Indonesian, Arab and African origin. There are sizeable French, Chinese and Indian communities
Religion – Christian, indigenous, Muslim
Language – Malagasy, French (both official), English
Population density – 45 per sq. km (2019)
Urban population – 37.9 per cent (2019 est)
Median age (years) – 20.3 (2020 est)
National anthem – 'Ry Tanindrazanay malala ô' 'Oh, Our Beloved Land'
National day – 26 June (Independence Day)
Death penalty – Abolished for all crimes (since 2015)
CPI score – 24 (158)
Military expenditure – US$73.3m (2018)

CLIMATE AND TERRAIN
Madagascar, the fourth-largest island in the world, lies 386km off the south-east coast of Africa, from which it is separated by the Mozambique Channel. Coastal plains rise to a central plateau and mountains indented with river valleys. Elevation extremes range from 2,876m (Maromokotro) to 0m (Indian Ocean).

The climate is tropical on the coast, temperate in the interior and arid in the south; average temperatures range from 19.6°C in July to 24.9°C in December. Madagascar is subject to tropical cyclones, which cause flooding and wind damage, particularly on the coast.

HISTORY AND POLITICS
The island was settled by peoples from south-east Asia and East Africa from around the first century AD. Although first visited by Europeans c.1500, local kingdoms ruled until the early 19th century, when the Merina kingdom conquered the island. France made the island a protectorate in 1895 after the last indigenous resistance was defeated. During the Second World War, the British invaded in order to replace the pro-Vichy government with a Free French government. At the end of the war Madagascar was returned to France, which suppressed a nationalist uprising in 1947–8. Nationalist agitation continued throughout the 1950s and resulted in independence in 1960.

The military took control in 1972 following civil disturbances, and in 1975 martial law was imposed after a coup. A Marxist one-party state was created with Lt.-Cdr. Didier Ratsiraka as president. Marxism was abandoned in 1980 and a new constitution introduced parliamentary democracy in 1992.

Didier Ratsiraka was defeated in the 1993 presidential elections but returned to office in 1997 after winning the 1996 election. He refused to accept his defeat in the 2001 presidential election and the six-month struggle between his supporters and those of Marc Ravalomanana, the successful candidate, brought the country close to civil war until, in July 2002, Ratsiraka went into exile and his supporters surrendered. Ravalomanana was re-elected in 2006 and his I Love Madagascar party (TIM) retained its large majority in the 2007 legislative election.

A power struggle between Ravalomanana and opposition leader Andry Rajoelina began in December 2008. Following an army mutiny and Ravalomanana's resignation, Rajoelina assumed power in March 2009 with the backing of the military and the high court, but the takeover provoked continued demonstrations and widespread international condemnation. The December 2013 presidential election was won by Hery Rajaonarimampianina, while Miaraka Amin'ny Prézidà Andry Rajoelina (MAPAR) emerged as the single largest party in the simultaneous legislative elections. In May 2015, parliament voted to impeach President Rajaonarimampianina amid claims that he had failed to enact promised political reforms; the supreme court annulled the decision on legal grounds in June. Rajoelina reclaimed power in the presidential election of November 2018, beating Rajaonarimampianina and Ravalomanana. A coalition of parties headed by Rajoelina secured the majority of National Assembly seats in the May 2019 elections. Olivier Solonandrasana was replaced as prime minister by independent Christian Ntsay in June 2018 after widespread violent protests over proposed electoral changes.

Under the 2010 constitution, since amended, the president is directly elected and serves a five-year term, renewable once; the minimum age requirement for presidential candidates was lowered in 2010 to 35. The legislature is bicameral, comprising the National Assembly, which has 151 members directly elected for a four-year term, and the senate, which has 63 members, of whom two-thirds are appointed by the regional assemblies and one-third by the president; they serve a six-year term. The senate was dissolved following the 2009 coup and re-established in December 2015.

HEAD OF STATE
President, Andry Rajoelina, *sworn in* 19 January 2019

SELECTED GOVERNMENT MEMBERS *AS AT NOVEMBER 2020*
Prime Minister, Christian Ntsay
Finance, Richard Randriamandrato
Foreign Affairs, Djacoba Tehindrazanarivelo

EMBASSY OF THE REPUBLIC OF MADAGASCAR
5th Floor, One Knightsbridge Green, London SW1X 7NE
T (+32) (0) 2770 1726 **E** info@madagascar-embassy.eu
W www.madagascar-embassy.eu
Ambassador Extraordinary and Plenipotentiary, vacant

BRITISH EMBASSY
9th Floor, Tour Zital, Ravoninahitriniarivo Street, Antananarivo 101
T (+261) (20) 223 3053 **E** BEAntananarivo@moov.mg
W www.gov.uk/government/world/madagascar
Ambassador Extraordinary and Plenipotentiary, HE Dr Philip
   Boyle, *apptd* 2017

ECONOMY AND TRADE
Economic liberalisation and privatisation since the mid-1990s have resulted in slow but steady growth, although recent political disturbances and cyclone devastation in 2000 and 2004 have been serious setbacks. While the nation has an abundance of natural resources, most remain unexploited and it is heavily reliant on vanilla exports, which are vulnerable to price fluctuations. A largely unregulated economy, ineffective law enforcement, ecological destruction, and widespread corruption restricts further development, and while IMF measures aim to strengthen the economy reforms have been modest. Around 75 per cent live below the international poverty line.

President Ravalomanana's reforms and anti-corruption measures attracted increased international aid, and in 2004 half of the country's foreign debt was written off. International aid was suspended in 2010 following the 2009 coup; the country began to receive limited amounts of aid after a new government was appointed in 2014.

Agriculture, fishing and forestry are the mainstays of the economy, accounting for 24 per cent of GDP and employing around 80 per cent of the workforce. The main cash crops include coffee, vanilla, fish, sugar cane, cocoa, cloves and cotton. The industrial sector contributes 19.5 per cent of GDP, through processing meat, fish and other agricultural products, manufacturing (textiles, paper, cement, chemicals), car

assembly and mining (chromite, graphite, sapphires). Tourism is of growing importance.

The main trading partners are France, China, the USA and India. Principal exports are agricultural products, textiles, chromite, petroleum products, metals and gems. The main imports are capital goods, petroleum, consumer goods and food.

GNI – US$14.1bn; US$520 per capita (2019)
Annual average growth of GDP – 4.2 per cent (2017 est)
Inflation rate – 8.3 per cent (2017 est)
Population below poverty line – 70.7 per cent (2012 est)
Unemployment – 1.8 per cent (2017 est)
Total external debt – US$4.089bn (2017 est)
Imports – US$3,498m (2016)
Exports – US$3,346m (2016)

BALANCE OF PAYMENTS
Trade – US$151m deficit (2016)
Current Account – US$330m deficit (2019)

Trade with UK	2018	2019
Imports from UK	£10,340,463	£10,706,910
Exports to UK	£31,005,964	£33,749,544

COMMUNICATIONS
Airports and waterways – There are 26 airports, with the largest at Antananarivo and Mahajanga; there are 432km of navigable waterways
Roadways and railways – There are 31,640km of roadways, of which most are unpaved, and 836km of railways
Telecommunications – 69,000 fixed lines and 10.7 million mobile subscriptions (2018); there were 2.5 million internet users in 2018
Internet code and IDD – mg; 261 (from UK), 44 (to UK)
Major broadcasters – Television Malagasy (TVM) and Malagasy National Radio (RNM) are the state broadcasters and have a monopoly on national broadcasting; there are hundreds of private local radio and TV stations
Press – Daily titles include *Midi-Madagasikara, Madagascar-Tribune* and *La Gazette de la Grande Ile* (all French language)
WPFI score – 27.68 (54)

EDUCATION AND HEALTH
Education is free and compulsory for nine years, but attendance is variable.
Literacy rate – 74.8 per cent (2018)
Gross enrolment ratio (percentage of relevant age group) – primary 134 per cent, secondary 34.6 per cent (2019); tertiary 5.4 per cent (2018 est)
Health expenditure (per capita) – US$25 (2017)
Life expectancy (years) – 67.3 (2020 est)
Mortality rate – 6.2 (2020 est)
Birth rate – 29.9 (2020 est)
Infant mortality rate – 37.8 (2020 est)
HIV/AIDS adult prevalence – 0.3 per cent (2019 est)

MALAWI

Dziko la Malawi – Republic of Malawi

Area – 118,484 sq. km
Capital – Lilongwe; population, 1,122,000 (2020 est)
Major cities – Blantyre, the commercial and industrial centre; Mzuzu; Zomba, the former capital
Currency – Kwacha (K) of 100 tambala
Population – 21,196,629 rising at 3.3 per cent a year (2020 est); Chewa (34.3 per cent), Lomwe (18.8 per cent), Yao (13.2 per cent), Ngoni (10.4 per cent), Tumbuka (9.2 per cent) (est)
Religion – Christian (Protestant 33.5 per cent, Catholic 17.2 per cent), Muslim 13.8 per cent (est)
Language – English (official), Chichewa, Chinyanja, Chiyao, Chitumbuka
Population density – 192 per sq. km (2019)
Urban population – 17.2 per cent (2019 est)
Median age (years) – 16.8 (2020 est)
National anthem – 'Mulungu dalitsa Malawi' 'Oh God Bless Malawi'
National day – 6 July (Independence Day)
Death penalty – Retained (last used 1992)
CPI score – 31 (123)
Military expenditure – US$58.4m (2018)

CLIMATE AND TERRAIN
The landlocked state lies along the western and southern shores of Lake Malawi (Nyasa). The northern and central regions are plateaux with rolling terrain, while the south is mainly hills and mountains. Elevation extremes range from 3,002m (Sapitwa) to 37m (junction of Shire river and Mozambique border). The climate is subtropical, with a wet season from November to April; average temperatures in Lilongwe range from 18.1°C in July to 25.2°C in November.

HISTORY AND POLITICS
Until contact was made with European missionaries in the 19th century, Malawi was dominated by a succession of powerful tribes that included the Maravi, the Yao and the Nguni. The missionaries campaigned for official intervention to end the east-coast slave trade, which had begun in the early 19th century, and in 1891 Britain established the Nyasaland and District Protectorate over the area. Renamed the British Central Africa Protectorate in 1893, it became the British colony of Nyasaland in 1907. The country was joined with Northern and Southern Rhodesia (now Zambia and Zimbabwe) between 1953 and 1963. It became independent, as Malawi, in 1964, with Dr Hastings Banda as prime minister.

In 1966, the country became a one-party state ruled by the Malawi Congress Party (MCP) and Dr Banda became president, declaring himself president for life in 1971. In the early 1990s, increasing pro-democracy agitation and international pressure forced Banda to introduce multiparty democracy in 1994.

In 2005, President Bingu wa Mutharika resigned from the ruling United Democratic Front party over the hostility of the party to his anti-corruption campaign and founded a new party, the Democratic Progressive Party (DPP). The 2009 legislative election was won by the DPP and President Mutharika was re-elected; Joyce Banda was appointed interim president following Mutharika's death in April 2012. The DPP retained power in the May 2014 and May 2019 legislative elections. In both elections opposition parties claimed widespread electoral fraud occurred but the results were upheld by Malawi's electoral commission. Peter Mutharika, Bingu wa's younger brother, was elected president in 2014 and was narrowly re-elected in 2019, but the latter vote was annulled in March 2020 due to evidence of irregularities. The re-run took place in June 2020, which anti-corruption candidate Lazarus Chakwera of the Malawi Congress Party won with 59 per cent of the vote.

Under the 1995 constitution, the executive president is directly elected for a five-year term, renewable once. The unicameral National Assembly consists of 193 members, who are directly elected for a five-year term.

HEAD OF STATE
President, C-in-C of the Armed Forces, Defence, Lazarus Chakwera *elected* 23 July 2020, *re-elected* 28 June 2020
Vice-President, Saulos Klaus Chilima

SELECTED GOVERNMENT MEMBERS *AS AT NOVEMBER 2020*
Finance, Felix Mlusu
Foreign Affairs, Eisenhower Mkaka
Homeland Security, Richard Banda

HIGH COMMISSION OF THE REPUBLIC OF MALAWI
36 John Street, London WC1N 2AT
T 020-7421 6010 **E** malawihighcommission@btconnect.com
W www.malawihighcommission.co.uk
High Commissioner, HE Kenna Mphonda, *apptd* 2015

BRITISH HIGH COMMISSION
Off Convention Drive, PO Box 30042, Lilongwe 3
T (+265) (1) 772 400 **E** bhclilongwe@fco.gov.uk
W www.gov.uk/government/world/malawi
High Commissioner, HE Holly Tett, *apptd* 2017

ECONOMY AND TRADE
Malawi is one of the poorest countries in Africa. It has few natural resources and its agricultural land is under pressure because of population growth. It also experienced years of mismanagement under earlier governments, and corruption remains a problem despite the government's determination to eliminate it. These factors, high HIV/AIDS rates and the vulnerability of agricultural production to both drought and severe flooding make the country heavily dependent on food and economic aid from international agencies and donor nations, although international aid was suspended from 2013 until May 2017 following a major corruption scandal. Diversification away from agricultural exports is being pursued.

The economy is primarily agricultural, with 76.9 per cent of the workforce engaged in agriculture, which accounts for 28.6 per cent of GDP and 80 per cent of export revenue. Tobacco is the most important cash crop, followed by dried legumes, tea, sugar, cotton, coffee, soy and peanuts, all of which are the nation's main exports. The chief industrial activities are agricultural processing, sawmill products, cement and consumer goods, now supplemented by mining uranium, of which exports began in 2009.

The main export markets are Zimbabwe, Mozambique, Belgium and South Africa; imports come mainly from South Africa, China, India and the UAE. The main imports are food, fuels, semi-manufactures, consumer goods and transport equipment.

GNI – US$7.2bn; US$380 per capita (2019)
Annual average growth of GDP – 4.0 per cent (2017 est)
Inflation rate – 12.2 per cent (2017 est)
Population below poverty line – 50.7 per cent (2014 est)
Total external debt – US$2.102bn (2017 est)
Imports – US$2,373m (2016)
Exports – US$1,216m (2016)

BALANCE OF PAYMENTS
Trade – US$1,156m deficit (2016)
Current Account – US$1,837m deficit (2019)

Trade with UK	2018	2019
Imports from UK	£14,873,384	£15,541,675
Exports to UK	£13,519,832	£16,485,391

COMMUNICATIONS
Airports and waterways – The main airports are at Blantyre and Lilongwe, with five smaller airports around the country; there are 700km of navigable waterways on Lake Malawi (Nyasa) and the Shire river
Roadways and railways – 15,452km; 767km of railways, including a line linking the Zambian town of Chipata to the Indian Ocean coast at Nacala in Mozambique
Telecommunications – 15,000 fixed lines and 7.1 million mobile subscriptions (2018); there were 2.7 million internet users in 2018
Internet code and IDD – mw; 265 (from UK), 44 (to UK)
Major broadcasters – Television Malawi (TVM) and Malawi Broadcasting Corporation (radio) are the state broadcasters
Press – *The Nation* and *The Daily Times* are the only daily national newspapers
WPFI score – 29.32 (69)

EDUCATION AND HEALTH
The government is responsible for primary and secondary schools, technical education and primary teacher training.
Literacy rate – 62.1 per cent (2015 est)
Gross enrolment ratio (percentage of relevant age group) – primary 144.8 per cent, secondary 37 per cent (2019 est); tertiary 1 per cent (2011 est)
Health expenditure (per capita) – US$32 (2017)
Hospital beds (per 1,000 people) – 1.3 (2011)
Life expectancy (years) – 63.2 (2020 est)
Mortality rate – 7.2 (2020 est)
Birth rate – 40.1 (2020 est)
Infant mortality rate – 39.5 (2020 est)
HIV/AIDS adult prevalence – 8.9 per cent (2019 est)

MALAYSIA

Area – 329,847 sq. km
Capital – Kuala Lumpur; population, 7,997,000 (2020 est); Putrajaya is the administrative capital

Major cities – Ampang Jaya, George Town, Ipoh, Johor Bahru, Klang, Kota Kinabalu, Kuantan, Kuching, Petaling Jaya, Shah Alam
Currency – Malaysian ringgit (RM) of 100 sen; also known as Malaysian dollar
Population – 32,652,083 rising at 1.29 per cent a year (2020 est); Bumiputera (Malay and indigenous peoples) (62 per cent), Chinese (20.6 per cent) (est)
Religion – Muslim (official) 61.3 per cent, Buddhist 19.8 per cent, Christian 9.2 per cent, Hindu 6.3 per cent, Chinese traditional religions (including Confucianism and Taoism) 1.3 per cent (est)
Language – Bahasa Malaysia (Malay) (official), English, Cantonese, Mandarin, Tamil, Telugu, Malayalam, Punjabi, Thai
Population density – 96 per sq. km (2019)
Urban population – 76.6 per cent (2019 est)
Median age (years) – 29.2 (2020 est)
National anthem – 'Negaraku' 'My Country'
National day – 31 August (Independence Day)
Death penalty – Retained
CPI score – 53 (51)
Military expenditure – US$3,470m (2018)

CLIMATE AND TERRAIN
Malaysia comprises the 11 states of peninsular Malaya plus the states of Sabah and Sarawak on the island of Borneo. The Malay peninsula, which extends from the isthmus of Kra to the Singapore Strait, is a plain with two highland areas in the north. The Malaysian part of Borneo is mostly high plateau, rising to mountains in western Sabah and eastern Sarawak, while Sarawak also has lower-lying land along the coast and in the Rajang valley; both states are densely forested. Elevation extremes range from 4,100m (Gunung Kinabalu, Sabah) to 0m (Indian Ocean). The climate is tropical, experiencing the south-west monsoon from May to September and the north-east monsoon from November to March. The average daily temperature is 25.9°C.

POLITICS
The federal *Parlimen* has two houses, the House of Representatives and the senate. The former is the lower house and has 222 members, directly elected for a five-year term. The senate has 70 members who serve a three-year term; the legislative assembly of each state elects two members, and 44 are nominated by the head of state.

The 1957 constitution provides for a federal government and a degree of autonomy for the state governments. Each of the 13 states has its own constitution, which must not be inconsistent with the federal constitution. The Malay rulers are either chosen or succeed to their position in accordance with the custom of their particular state; in other states of Malaysia, choice of the head of state is at the discretion of the *Yang di-Pertuan Agong* after consultation with the chief minister of the state. The ruler or governor acts on the advice of an executive council appointed on the advice of the chief minister and a single-chamber legislative assembly. The legislative assemblies are elected on the same basis as the lower chamber of the federal legislature.

The Barisan Nasional (BN) coalition maintained power for 60 years before being replaced in the 2018 legislative elections by the centre-left People's Alliance, led by 92-year-old former prime minister Mahathir bin Mohamad. Mohamad replaced former protégé and long-term ally Najib Razak as prime minister, who in July 2020 was found guilty of seven counts of abuse of power, money laundering and corruption.

The supreme head of state, a largely ceremonial role, is elected by the nine hereditary rulers of the peninsular states

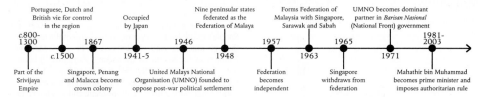

Timeline:

Portuguese, Dutch and British vie for control in the region — c.800–1300

Occupied by Japan — 1867

Nine peninsular states federated as the Federation of Malaya — 1946

Forms Federation of Malaysia with Singapore, Sarawak and Sabah — 1957

UMNO becomes dominant partner in *Barisan Nasional* (National Front) government — 1981–2003

c.1500 — 1941-5 — 1948 — 1963 — 1965 — 1971

Part of the Srivijaya Empire

Singapore, Penang and Malacca become crown colony

United Malays National Organisation (UMNO) founded to oppose post-war political settlement

Federation becomes independent

Singapore withdraws from federation

Mahathir bin Muhammad becomes prime minister and imposes authoritarian rule

from among their number and serves a five-year term. Sultan Muhammad V unexpectedly became the first monarch to abdicate in January 2019.

HEAD OF STATE
Supreme Head of State, Sultan of Pahang, HM Sultan Abdullah Sultan Ahmad Shah, *appointed* 24 January 2019
Deputy Head of State, Sultan of Perak, HM Sultan Nazrin Muizzuddin Shah

SELECTED GOVERNMENT MEMBERS *AS AT NOVEMBER 2020*
Prime Minister, Muhyiddin bin Haji Mohamad Yassin
Defence, Ismail Sabri bin Yaakob
Economy, Mohamed Azmin Ali
Home Affairs, Hamzah bin Zainuddin

MALAYSIAN HIGH COMMISSION
45–46 Belgrave Square, London SW1X 8QT
T 020-3931 6189 **E** asst1@btconnect.com **W** www.jimlondon.net
High Commissioner, HE Datuk Mohamad Sadik Kethergany, *apptd* 2019

BRITISH HIGH COMMISSION
Level 27 Menara Binjai, 2 Jalan Binjai, Kuala Lumpur 50450
T (+60) (3) 2170 2200 **E** consular.kualalumpur@fco.gov.uk
W www.gov.uk/government/world/malaysia
High Commissioner, HE Charles Hay, MVO, *apptd* 2019

ECONOMY AND TRADE
The economy has grown vigorously since the 1970s, transforming the country into a diversified emerging economy. The government's goal is to achieve developed nation status by 2024. To this end, it has encouraged investment in high-technology industries, medical technology and pharmaceuticals, and growth as a regional financial hub, especially for Islamic finance. Despite falling oil prices, high domestic consumption and an increasing range of exports fuelled steady growth in recent years, prior to a contraction during the 2020 coronavirus pandemic. Malaysia formed a common market with the other members of the Association of Southeast Asian Nations (ASEAN) in 2015.

The agricultural sector produces the raw materials for its highly developed industries. Industrial production includes rubber manufacturing, palm oil processing, light manufacturing, electronics, natural gas, and timber processing; in addition, oil is produced in Sabah and Sarawak, and refined in Sarawak. Tourism is a major industry. The services sector contributes 53.6 per cent of GDP, industry 37.6 per cent and agriculture 8.8 per cent.

The main trading partners are China, Singapore, Japan, the USA and other south-east Asian countries. Principal exports are electronic equipment, petroleum and liquefied natural gas, timber and wood products, palm oil, rubber, textiles and chemicals. The main imports are electronics, machinery, petroleum products, plastics, vehicles, iron and steel products, and chemicals.

GNI – US$358bn; US$11,200 per capita (2019)
Annual average growth of GDP – 4.31 per cent (2019)
Inflation rate – 3.8 per cent (2017 est)
Unemployment – 3.3 per cent (2019 est)
Total external debt – US$217.2bn (2017 est)
Imports – US$200,139m (2017)
Exports – US$224,492m (2017)

BALANCE OF PAYMENTS
Trade – US$24,352m surplus (2017)
Current Account – US$12,296m surplus (2019)

Trade with UK	2018	2019
Imports from UK	£1,304,678,841	£1,356,486,196
Exports to UK	£2,000,968,154	£2,002,048,182

COMMUNICATIONS
Airports – There are 39 airports; the main international airports are at Kuala Lumpur, Kota Kinabalu, Kuching and Penang
Waterways – There are six main seaports in peninsular Malaysia, plus Kota Kinabalu (Sabah) and Kuching (Sarawak), and a merchant fleet of 315 ships of more than 1,000 tonnes; there are 7,200km of navigable waterways
Roadways and railways – 144,403km (excluding local roads); 1,851km
Telecommunications – 6.4 million fixed lines and 42.4 million mobile subscriptions (2018); there were 25.9 million internet users in 2018
Internet country code and IDD – my; 60 (from UK), 44 (to UK)
Major broadcasters – The state-run Radio Television Malaysia provides services in competition with commercial operators, which broadcast in Malay, Tamil, Chinese and English
Press – The four main national daily newspapers are in English: *The Star, The Sun, New Straits Times* and *The Malay Mail*
WPFI score – 33.12 (101)

EDUCATION AND HEALTH
There are six years of compulsory education.
Literacy rate – 94.9 per cent (2018 est)
Gross enrolment ratio (percentage of relevant age group) – primary 105.3 per cent (2017 est); secondary 83.7 per cent, tertiary 43.1 per cent (2019 est)
Health expenditure (per capita) – US$384 (2017)
Hospital beds (per 1,000 people) – 1.9 (2015)
Life expectancy (years) – 75.9 (2020 est)
Mortality rate – 5.3 (2020 est)
Birth rate – 18.3 (2020 est)
Infant mortality rate – 11.4 (2020 est)
HIV/AIDS adult prevalence – 0.4 per cent (2019 est)

MALDIVES

Dhivehi Raajjeyge Jumhooriyyaa – Republic of Maldives

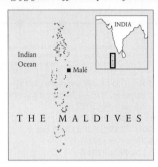

Area – 298 sq. km
Capital – Malé; population, 177,000 (2018)
Currency – Rufiyaa of 100 laarees
Population – 391,904 falling at 0.08 per cent a year (2020 est)
Religion – Sunni Muslim (official); public practice of other religions is illegal
Language – Dhivehi (official), English
Population density – 1,719 per sq. km (2019)
Urban population – 30.2 per cent (2019 est)
Median age (years) – 29.5 (2020 est)
National anthem – 'Gaumii Salaam' 'National Salute'
National day – 26 July (Independence Day)
Death penalty – Retained (last used 1954)
CPI score – 29 (130)
Literacy rate – 97.7 per cent (2016 est)
Gross enrolment ratio (percentage of relevant age group) – primary 98 per cent, secondary 81.3 per cent (2019 est); tertiary 31.2 per cent (2017 est)
Health expenditure (per capita) – US$1,007 (2017)
Life expectancy (years) – 76.4 (2020 est)
Mortality rate – 4.1 (2020 est)
Birth rate – 16 (2020 est)
Infant mortality rate – 19.8 (2020 est)

CLIMATE AND TERRAIN
The republic is an archipelago of atolls in the Indian Ocean, 643km to the south-west of Sri Lanka. There are about 1,190 coral islands grouped into 26 clusters of atolls, about 200 of which are inhabited. The islands are all flat and low-lying; none is more than 2.4m above sea level, making them vulnerable to rising sea levels caused by climate change. The climate is tropical, affected by the dry north-east monsoon (January–March) and the wet south-west monsoon (May–November).

HISTORY AND POLITICS
The Maldives were an independent sultanate from the mid-12th century. The sultan was overthrown by the Portuguese in 1558 but they were driven out in 1573 and the sultanate was re-established. In 1645, the islands became a dependency of Ceylon, which was under Dutch and then British rule. In 1887 they became an internally self-governing British protectorate. Independence was achieved in 1965, and in 1968 the Maldives became a republic under President Ibrahim Nasir.

The autocratic Nasir retired in 1978 and was succeeded by Maumoon Abdul Gayoom. His 30-year tenure, although equally autocratic, maintained political stability and economic development. However, unprecedented violence during anti-government demonstrations in 2003 and 2004 led to the legalising of political parties in 2005.

In the first multi-party legislative elections in 2009, the People's Party, led by Gayoom, won control of the legislature through alliances with smaller parties. In 2008 Mohamed Nasheed of the Maldivian Democratic Party (MDP) became the first democratically elected president, but was subsequently jailed for 13 years for ordering the arrest of a senior judge during his time as president, and was forced into exile. In the presidential election of 2018, Ibrahim Mohamed Solih (MDP) was elected and replaced Abdulla Gayoom, half-brother of former dictator Maumoon Abdul Gayoom. A state of emergency was declared in February 2018 after the government refused to release political opponents, and subsequently many opposition MPs were arrested on corruption charges. The MDP won a landslide victory in the April 2019 elections.

Under the 2008 constitution, the executive president is directly elected for a five-year term, renewable once. The unicameral People's Assembly *(Majlis)* has 87 members, who are directly elected for a five-year term.

HEAD OF STATE
President, Ibrahim Mohamed Solih, *sworn in* 17 November 2018
Vice-President, Faisal Naseem

SELECTED GOVERNMENT MEMBERS *AS AT NOVEMBER 2020*
Defence, Mariya Ahmed Didi
Finance, Ibrahim Ameer
Foreign Affairs, Abdulla Shahid

MALDIVES HIGH COMMISSION
22 Nottingham Place, London W1U 5NJ
T 020-7224 2135 **E** info@maldivesembassy.uk
W www.maldivesembassy.uk
High Commissioner, HE Farahanaz Faizal, *apptd* 2019

BRITISH HIGH COMMISSION
High Commissioner, HE Caron Röhsler, *apptd* 2019

ECONOMY AND TRADE
Political stability and economic liberalisation have produced steady economic growth since the 1980s. However, economic performance is tied to tourism and this has been disrupted several times: in 2005 owing to the devastation caused by the 2004 tsunami, in 2009 due to the global economic downturn, and in 2020 during the coronavirus pandemic. Balance of payments difficulties forced the government to seek IMF standby funding in 2009. The government has created a number of special economic zones to increase foreign investment and diversify away the economy. Agriculture and manufacturing are constrained by a shortage of cultivable land and domestic labour, so most food is imported. Industry is concentrated on fish processing, boat-building and shipping.

The main export markets are Thailand, Sri Lanka and Bangladesh. The only significant export is fish. Imports include petroleum products, clothing and capital goods, and are provided mainly by the UAE, India, Singapore and China.
GNI – US$5.1bn; US$9,650 per capita (2019)
Annual average growth of GDP – 4.8 per cent (2017)
Inflation rate – 2.3 per cent (2017 est)
Population below poverty line – 15 per cent (2009 est)
Unemployment – 2.9 per cent (2017 est)
Total external debt – US$848.8m (2017 est)
Imports – US$3,521m (2017)
Exports – US$3,467m (2017)

BALANCE OF PAYMENTS
Trade – US$53m deficit (2017)
Current Account – US$1,513m deficit (2019)

Trade with UK	2018	2019
Imports from UK	£16,472,200	£24,887,901
Exports to UK	£14,131,449	£9,713,913

COMMUNICATIONS
Transport – The country has seven airports, two of which handle international traffic; the main port is Malé and there are 93km of roads
Telecommunications – 12,316 fixed lines and 611,622 mobile subscriptions (2019); there were 248,004 internet users in 2018
Internet code and IDD – mv; 960 (from UK), to UK (44)
Major broadcasters – The state broadcaster Maldives National Broadcasting Corporation operates radio and TV stations; a small number of private broadcasters are permitted to operate
Press – Daily newspapers include *Miadhu News* and *Haveeru Daily*. The crackdown on press freedom is gradually being lifted by President Solih
WPFI score – 29.93 (79)

MALI

République de Mali – Republic of Mali

Area – 1,240,192 sq. km
Capital – Bamako; population, 2,618,000 (2020 est)
Major cities – Kayes, Koutiala, Mopti, Ségou, Sikasso, Timbuktu
Currency – Franc CFA of 100 centimes
Population – 19,553,397 rising at 2.95 per cent a year (2020 est); Bambara (33.3 per cent), Fulani (13.3 per cent), Sarakole (9.8 per cent), Senufo (9.6 per cent), Dogon (8.7 per cent), Malinke (6.0 per cent) (est)
Religion – Muslim 93.9 per cent, Christian 2.8 per cent, animist 2 per cent (est)
Language – French (official), Bambara, other African languages
Population density – 16 per sq. km (2019)
Urban population – 43.1 per cent (2019 est)
Median age (years) – 16 (2020 est)
National anthem – 'Le Mali' 'Mali'
National day – 22 September (Independence Day)
Death penalty – Retained (last used 1980)
CPI score – 29 (130)
Military expenditure – US$495m (2018)
Conscription – 18 years of age; 24 months (selective)

CLIMATE AND TERRAIN
The west African state is mainly savannah in the south and desert plains in the north, with some hills in the north-east; over 60 per cent is desert or semi-desert. The centre is drained by the Niger river and the south-west by the Senegal river. Elevation extremes range from 1,155m (Hombori Tondo) to 23m (Senegal river). The climate is subtropical in the south with a rainy season from June to November, and arid in the north. Average temperatures range from 21.4°C in January to 33.9°C in June.

HISTORY AND POLITICS
Mali was successively part of the empire of the Malinke people from the 13th to 15th centuries, and of the Songhai Empire in the 15th to 16th centuries. With the fall of the Songhai Empire, it was divided between the Tuareg and the Fulani and Bambara kingdoms, and then the Tukolor and Samori kingdoms. It was conquered by the French in 1880–95 and became a French colony. In 1959, it formed the Federation of Mali with Senegal before becoming a separate independent state in 1960 under a one-party socialist regime.

In 1968, a military coup led by Lt. Moussa Traoré resulted in 23 years of oppressive military rule. Traoré was ousted as president in a military coup led by Gen. Amadou Toumani Touré in 1991. Multiparty elections were held in 1992, returning the country to civilian government.

A degree of decentralisation was introduced in 1999, partly in response to rebellions in the north by the Tuareg over land and cultural rights. Another rebellion in 2006 by Tuareg seeking greater autonomy for their region was settled within a few months, but a more militant faction carried on an insurrection from 2007 to 2009. In May 2014 Tuareg separatists occupied several northern towns.

Islamist extremists took control of the country's desert north in early 2012, but were largely driven out by a French-led military operation in January 2013. A 2015 peace agreement with some armed groups that sought to end the Islamist threat helped calm tensions, but large areas still remain lawless. Around 5,000 French troops were stationed in the country in 2020, and fighting is ongoing. Ethnic conflicts have increased in the central Mopti region in recent years, with hundreds of deaths reported and thousands displaced in 2018 and 2019.

In the 2007 legislative elections, the Alliance for Democracy in Mali (ADEMA), which had dominated government coalitions since 1992, won the largest number of seats and formed another coalition government. A military coup overthrew Touré's government in March 2012, claiming that the government had not supported the country's army against the advancing Tuareg-led rebellion. Cissé Mariam Kaidama Sidibé, the country's first woman prime minister, was arrested shortly after the coup. In the subsequent 2013 presidential elections, former prime minister Ibrahim Boubacar Keita comfortably defeated rival candidate Soumaila Cissé and was re-elected in August 2018. Ethnic violence and instability resulted in series of different prime ministers prior to the April 2020 legislative elections, which were due to take place in November 2018 and were marred by violence and kidnappings. A series of large protests followed the election, which contained irregularities and handed victory to Keita's ADEMA, calling for Keita's resignation. In July the protests escalated into violence, and in August soldiers detained Keita and key government figures, who later fled the country. The military established an 18-month transitional government in September, before fresh elections can be held.

Under the 1992 constitution, the president is directly elected for a five-year term, which is renewable once. The unicameral National Assembly has 147 members directly elected for a maximum of two terms, with 13 reserved to represent Malians abroad; all serve a five-year term. The president appoints the prime minister, who appoints the cabinet.

HEAD OF STATE
Transitional President, Col. (retd) Ba N'Daou, *assumed office* 25 September 2020
Transitional Vice-President, Assimi Goïti

SELECTED GOVERNMENT MEMBERS *AS AT NOVEMBER 2020*
Prime Minister, Moctar Ouane
Defence, Col. Sadio Camara
Foreign Affairs, Zeyni Moulaye

EMBASSY OF THE REPUBLIC OF MALI
Avenue Molière 487, 1050 Brussels, Belgium
T (+32) (2) 345 7432 **E** info@amba-mali.be **W** www.amba-mali.be
Ambassador Extraordinary and Plenipotentiary, vacant

BRITISH AMBASSADOR
Immeuble Semega, Route de Koulikoro, Hippodrome, BP 2069, Bamako
T (+223) 2021 3412 **W** www.gov.uk/government/world/mali
Ambassador Extraordinary and Plenipotentiary, HE Guy Warrington, *apptd* 2020

ECONOMY AND TRADE
Despite the internal conflict economic reform since the mid-1990s has produced steady growth, although Mali is heavily dependent on foreign aid and remittances from expatriates. Good harvests and the performance of the service sector have helped the economy grow by around 5 per cent in recent years, but security concerns, political instability, corruption, poor infrastructure, high public debt and vulnerability to commodity fluctuations constraints development. Almost 43 per cent of the population live in extreme poverty, largely in rural areas.

The economy is based primarily on subsistence farming and animal husbandry, which generates 41.8 per cent of GDP, employs roughly 80 per cent of the workforce and provides 80 per cent of export earnings. Gold, phosphate and iron-ore mining, and cotton and food processing are the main activities in Mali's industrial sector, which accounts for 18.1 per cent of GDP. Export of hydroelectric power is expected to contribute to future earnings.

The main export markets are Switzerland, the UAE and Burkina Faso; imports come mainly from Senegal, China and Côte d'Ivoire. Principal exports are cotton, gold and livestock. The main imports are fuel, machinery and equipment, construction materials, foodstuffs and textiles.

GNI – US$17.3bn; US$880 per capita (2019)
Annual average growth of GDP – 5.4 per cent (2017 est)
Inflation rate – 1.8 per cent (2017 est)
Population below poverty line – 36.1 per cent (2005 est)
Unemployment – 7.9 per cent (2017 est)
Total external debt – US$4.192bn (2017 est)
Imports – US$5,651m (2016)
Exports – US$3,285m (2016)

BALANCE OF PAYMENTS
Trade – US$2,365m deficit (2016)
Current Account – US$835m deficit (2018)

Trade with UK	2018	2019
Imports from UK	£52,610,040	£36,455,545
Exports to UK	£1,071,555	£64,323,388

COMMUNICATIONS
Airports and waterways – There are eight airports, with the largest at Bamako; the main port is Koulikoro on the Niger river
Roadways and railways – 139,107km (including paved, unpaved and local roads); 593km
Telecommunications – 227,831 fixed lines and 21.8 million mobile subscriptions (2019); there were 2.4 million internet users in 2018
Internet code and IDD – ml; 223 (from UK), 44 (to UK)
Major broadcasters – The public Office de la Radiodiffusion Télévision du Mali operates a number of radio and television channels in French and local vernacular languages
Press – There are five main daily newspapers, including *L'Essor,* the state-owned national daily
WPFI score – 34.12 (108)

EDUCATION AND HEALTH
There are nine years of free, compulsory education beginning at age seven.
Literacy rate – 35.5 per cent (2018 est)
Gross enrolment ratio (percentage of relevant age group) – primary 75.6 per cent, secondary 41 per cent (2018 est); tertiary 5.5 per cent (2015 est)
Health expenditure (per capita) – US$31 (2017)
Hospital beds (per 1,000 people) – 0.1 (2010)
Life expectancy (years) – 61.6 (2020 est)
Mortality rate – 9 (2020 est)
Birth rate – 42.2 (2020 est)
Infant mortality rate – 64 (2020 est)
HIV/AIDS adult prevalence – 1.2 per cent (2019 est)

MALTA
Repubblika ta' Malta – Republic of Malta

Area – 316 sq. km
Capital – Valletta; population, 213,000 (2018)
Major towns – Birkirkara, Mosta, Qormi, Saint Paul's Bay (San Pawl il-Bahar), Victoria
Currency – Euro (€) of 100 cents
Population – 457,267 rising at 0.87 per cent a year (2020 est)
Religion – Christian (officially Roman Catholic 90 per cent) (est)
Language – Maltese, English (both official)
Population density – 1,5114 per sq. km (2019)
Urban population – 94.7 per cent (2019 est)
Median age (years) – 42.3 (2020 est)
National anthem – 'L-Innu Malti' 'Hymn of Malta'
National day – 21 September (Independence Day)
Death penalty – Abolished for all crimes (since 2000)
CPI score – 54 (50)
Military expenditure – US$69.3m (2018)

CLIMATE AND TERRAIN

Malta is an archipelago of six islands in the Mediterranean Sea; Malta, Gozo and Comino are the largest. The island of Malta has a coastal plain in the north-east, rising to low hills in the south-west. Elevation extremes range from 253m (Ta'Dmejrek) to 0m (Mediterranean Sea). Average temperatures range from 12.7°C in February to 27.2°C in August.

HISTORY AND POLITICS

The islands were ruled successively by the Phoenicians, Greeks, Carthaginians, Romans, Arabs, Spanish and the Sovereign Military Order of Malta (known as the Knights of St John), which held them from 1530 until a French invasion in 1798. Liberated from French rule with British naval support in 1800, the island of Malta became a British colony in 1814, and was developed into a substantial naval base and dockyard. Malta was strategically important in both world wars, but particularly the second, when it was blockaded and subjected to aerial bombardment for five months. Its resistance led to the people of Malta being awarded the George Cross, the UK's highest award for civilian bravery, in 1942.

Malta gained its independence in 1964 and became a republic in 1974. In the 1970s it developed close links with communist and Arab states, but more pro-European and pro-US policies were adopted after the election of the Nationalist Party in 1987. Malta became a member of the EU in 2004, and adopted the euro in 2008. Since joining the EU, Malta has experienced a marked increase in illegal immigration from northern Africa.

The Labour Party was returned to power in legislative elections in 2013. Party leader Marie-Louise Coleiro Preca was confirmed as president in April 2014, and was replaced by former minister for foreign affairs George Vella in April 2019. The murder of investigative journalist Daphne Caruana Galizia in October 2017 attracted international attention over alleged corruption in the country, and resulted in an early election in June 2017, which the Labour Party won. Former prime minister Joseph Muscat, who is alleged to have ties to the murder, stood down in January 2020.

Under the 1974 constitution, the president is elected by the legislature for a five-year term, renewable once. The unicameral legislature, the House of Representatives, has 65 members directly elected for a five-year term; if a party wins the majority of votes in a general election without winning a majority of seats, new seats are created until that party holds a majority of one seat. The prime minister is appointed by the president and nominates the other ministers.

HEAD OF STATE
President, George Vella, *took office* 4 April 2019

SELECTED GOVERNMENT MEMBERS *AS AT NOVEMBER 2020*
Prime Minister, Robert Abela
Economy, Silvio Schembri
Finance, Edward Scicluna
Foreign Affairs, Evarist Bartolo

MALTA HIGH COMMISSION
Malta House, 36–38 Piccadilly, London W1J 0LE
T 020-7292 4800 **E** maltahighcommission.london@gov.mt
W www.foreign.gov.mt/uk
High Commissioner, HE Joseph Cole, *apptd* 2018

BRITISH HIGH COMMISSION
Whitehall Mansions, Ta' Xbiex Seafront, Ta' Xbiex XBX 1026
T (+356) 2323 0000 **E** bhcvalletta@fco.gov.uk

W www.gov.uk/government/world/malta
High Commissioner, HE Stuart Gill, OBE, *apptd* 2016

ECONOMY AND TRADE

The mainstay of the economy for over a century was the dockyard, and while shipbuilding and ship repairs remain significant industries, since the 1980s Malta has developed into a tourist destination, financial services centre and freight trans-shipment point. Tourism is now the main source of income, followed by foreign trade and manufacturing, especially of electronics and pharmaceuticals. All were adversely affected by the global downturn in 2009, but Malta's low levels of public debt and buoyant tourism allowed it to weather the downturn better than other eurozone states. Prior to the coronavirus pandemic the economy performed strongly, recording high levels of growth and employment, but the loss of tourism is expected to contribute to a contraction of 7.9 per cent in 2020. The service sector accounts for 88.7 per cent of GDP, industry for 10.2 per cent and agriculture for 1.1 per cent.

The main trading partners are other EU states. Principal exports are electrical machinery, mechanical appliances, mineral fuels, oil and petroleum products, and pharmaceuticals. The main imports are mineral fuels and oil, machinery, aircraft and other transport equipment, and food.
GNI – US$13.7bn; US$27,290 per capita (2019)
Annual average growth of GDP – 4.94 per cent (2019 est)
Inflation rate – 1.3 per cent (2017 est)
Population below poverty line – 16.3 per cent (2015 est)
Unemployment – 0.78 per cent (2019 est)
Total external debt – US$90.98bn (2016 est)
Imports – US$14,580m (2017)
Exports – US$16,943m (2017)

BALANCE OF PAYMENTS
Trade – US$2,363m surplus (2017)
Current Account – US$717m surplus (2019)

Trade with UK	2018	2019
Imports from UK	£638,488,724	£1,380,214,174
Exports to UK	£101,014,211	£84,854,355

COMMUNICATIONS

Airports and waterways – The international airport is at Luqa, south-west of Valletta; the main ports are Marsaxlokk (Malta's freeport) and Valletta, and there is a large merchant fleet of 1,650 ships of over 1,000 tonnes
Roadways – 2,704km
Telecommunications – 264,557 fixed lines and 653,414 mobile subscriptions (2019); there were 365,521 internet users in 2018
Internet code and IDD – mt; 356 (from UK), 44 (to UK)
Major broadcasters – Television Malta (TVM) and Radio Malta are the public broadcasters
Press – Daily national newspapers include *Times of Malta, Malta Independent* (both English language) and *L-Orizzont* (Maltese)
WPFI score – 30.16 (81)

EDUCATION AND HEALTH

Education is free at all levels and compulsory between the ages of five and 16.
Literacy rate – 94.5 per cent (2018 est)
Gross enrolment ratio (percentage of relevant age group) – primary 106.7 per cent, secondary 107.3 per cent, tertiary 59.3 per cent (2018 est)
Health expenditure (per capita) – US$2,586 (2017)
Life expectancy (years) – 82.8 (2020 est)

Mortality rate – 8.3 (2020 est)
Birth rate – 9.9 (2020 est)
Infant mortality rate – 4.6 (2020 est)

MARSHALL ISLANDS

Republic of the Marshall Islands
Area – 181 sq. km (plus 11,673 sq. km of lagoon waters)
Capital – Majuro; population, 31,000 (2018)
Major towns – Ebeye, Rita
Currency – US dollar (US$) of 100 cents
Population – 77,917 rising at 1.43 per cent a year (2020 est)
Religion – Christian (Protestant 80.5 per cent, Roman
    Catholic 8.5 per cent, Mormon 7 per cent) (est)
Language – Marshallese, English (both official)
Population density – 325 per sq. km (2019)
Urban population – 77.4 per cent (2019 est)
Median age (years) – 23.8 (2020 est)
National anthem – 'Forever Marshall Islands'
National day – 1 May (Constitution Day)
Death penalty – Not since independence
Gross enrolment ratio (percentage of relevant age group) – primary
    79.6 per cent, secondary 64 per cent, tertiary 25.8 per
    cent (2019 est)
Health expenditure (per capita) – US$642 (2014)
Life expectancy (years) – 74.1 (2020 est)
Mortality rate – 4.3 (2020 est)
Birth rate – 22.8 (2020 est)
Infant mortality rate – 17.4 (2020 est)

CLIMATE AND TERRAIN
The republic consists of two chains of 29 atolls, five islands
and over 1,000 islets in the western Pacific Ocean. All of the
islands are low-lying (the highest point is 10m) and
vulnerable to rising sea levels, which could submerge them by
the mid-21st century. The climate is tropical, with a wet
season from June to November.

HISTORY AND POLITICS
The Marshall Islands were first claimed by Spain in 1592 but
were left largely undisturbed. Subsequently they were seized
by Germany and formally became a protectorate in 1886.
Japan took control of the islands in 1914 on behalf of the
Allied powers and administered them from 1920 until 1944,
when they were captured by US forces. In 1947 the islands
became part of the UN Trust Territory of the Pacific Islands,
administered by the USA. Between 1946 and 1958, US
nuclear weapons were tested on Bikini and Enewetak atolls.
Enewetak has been partially decontaminated but Bikini is
uninhabitable; the USA paid compensation to the test victims
in the 1980s but the government is seeking further
compensation to cover the medical care of radiation victims
and rectify environmental damage.

The islands became internally self-governing in 1979, and
US administration ended in 1986, when a compact of free
association between the Republic of the Marshall Islands and
the USA came into effect. Under this agreement, the USA
recognised the republic as a sovereign and independent state
but retained responsibility for external security and defence as
well as giving financial help. UN trust territory status was
terminated in 1990 and full independence was granted in
December 1990. A renegotiated compact with the USA was
signed in 2003. The USA retains control of the Kwajalein
atoll, where it has a military base and missile tracking station.

Candidates in the legislative elections, last held in November
2019, are not listed by party but by name alone. David Kabua
was elected president in January 2020.

Under the 1979 constitution, the executive president is
elected by the legislature from among its members to serve a
four-year term, with no term limits. The bicameral legislature
if formed of the directly elected 33-member *Nitijela,* which
serves four-year terms, and the 12-member Council of Iroij
made up of tribal chiefs as an advisory body. There are no
formal political parties, although groupings of like-minded
independents have emerged in recent years.

HEAD OF STATE
President, David Kabua, *elected* 6 January 2020, *sworn in* 13
    January 2020

SELECTED GOVERNMENT MEMBERS *AS AT*
NOVEMBER 2020
Environment, Chris Loeak
Finance, Alfred Alfred
Foreign Affairs, Casten Menra

BRITISH AMBASSADOR
Ambassador, HE Melanie Hopkins, *apptd* 2016, resident at
    Suva, Fiji

ECONOMY AND TRADE
The islands have few natural resources, apart from possible
seabed mineral deposits, and the economy is dependent on aid
from the USA and lease payments for the use of Kwajalein
Atoll as a US military base, supplemented by ship registration
fees and the sale of fishing licences. Most islanders live by
subsistence farming and fishing, with coconuts, tomatoes and
fish the main commercial crops. The islands are particularly
vulnerable to rising sea levels and climate change. A small-
scale industrial sector produces copra and handicrafts and
processes tuna. Tourism is being encouraged but has declined
recently, which, with a similar decline in fishing licence sales,
has limited economic growth. The government is the largest
employer. Principal exports are copra and coconut products,
handicrafts and fish. Main imports include food and fuel.
GNI – US$0.3bn; US$4,860 per capita (2018)
Annual average growth of GDP – 2.5 per cent (2017 est)
Inflation rate – 0.7 per cent (2017 est)
Total external debt – US$97.96m (2013 est)
Imports – US$82,829m (2014)
Exports – US$23,373m (2014)

BALANCE OF PAYMENTS
Current Account – US$53m surplus (2018)

Trade with UK	2018	2019
Imports from UK	£2,645,450	£2,548,965
Exports to UK	£1,360,478	£2,326,931

COMMUNICATIONS
Airports and waterways – There are four airports throughout the
islands; Majuro is the main airport as well as the main port,
with a merchant fleet of 1,593 ships of over 1,000 tonnes,
1,468 of which are foreign-owned
Roadways – 2,028km
Telecommunications – 3,172 fixed lines and 21,169 mobile
subscriptions (2019); there were 29,290 internet users in
2018
Internet code and IDD – mh; 692 (from UK), 011 44 (to UK)
Media – MBC TV is the state-run broadcaster; the English and
Marshallese-language *Marshall Islands Journal* is published on
a weekly basis

MAURITANIA

Al-Jumhuriyah al-Islamiyah al-Muritaniyah – Islamic Republic of Mauritania

Area – 1,030,700 sq. km

Capital – Nouakchott; population, 1,315,000 (2020 est)

Major towns – Kaedi, Kiffa, Nouadhibou, Rosso, Zuwarat

Currency – Ouguiya (UM) of 5 khoums

Population – 4,005,475 rising at 2.09 per cent a year (2020 est)

Religion – Muslim (official; predominantly Sunni) 100 per cent

Language – Arabic (official), Pulaar, Soninke, Wolof, French

Population density – 4 per sq. km (2019)

Urban population – 54.5 per cent (2019 est)

Median age (years) – 21 (2020 est)

National anthem – 'Hymne National de la Republique Islamique de Mauritanie' 'National Anthem of the Islamic Republic of Mauritania'

National day – 28 November (Independence Day)

Death penalty – Retained (last used 1987)

CPI score – 28 (137)

Military expenditure – US$159m (2018)

Literacy rate – 53.5 per cent (2017 est)

Gross enrolment ratio (percentage of relevant age group) – primary 100.4 per cent, secondary 39.4 per cent, tertiary 5.8 per cent (2019 est)

Health expenditure (per capita) – US$49 (2017)

Life expectancy (years) – 64.5 (2020 est)

Mortality rate – 7.5 (2020 est)

Birth rate – 29 (2020 est)

Infant mortality rate – 47.9 (2020 est)

HIV/AIDS adult prevalence – 0.2 per cent (2019 est)

CLIMATE AND TERRAIN

About 60 per cent of the country is covered by the plains of the Sahara Desert, with some hills in the centre. The terrain is arid, apart from in the Senegal river valley on the southern border; most of the population lives there or on the coast at Nouakchott and Nouadhibou. Elevation extremes range from Kediet Ijill (915m) to −5m (Sebkhet Te-n-Dghamcha). There is a desert climate; the north of the country is virtually rainless, while the south receives some unreliable rainfall between June and October. Humidity can be high in the wet season, especially on the coast. Average temperatures range from 20.3°C in January to 33.9°C in June.

HISTORY AND POLITICS

Eastern Mauritania was part of the Ghana Empire and then the Muslim Almoravid and Almohad empires from the 11th to the 13th century. The area became part of the French West Africa protectorate in 1903 and then a colony in 1920. The country became independent as the Islamic Republic of Mauritania on 28 November 1960.

Mauritania has experienced several military coups and periods of military rule since independence. The 1984 coup brought to power Col. Maaouya ould Sid Ahmed Taya, who restored civilian rule in 1992 with multiparty elections in which he was elected president. President Taya was deposed in a military coup in 2005 and after a period of transitional government, elections were held in late 2006 and early 2007.

The 2007 presidential election was won by Sidi ould Cheikh Abdallahi who was subsequently overthrown in a military coup after attempting to sack four military leaders. Democracy was restored with the 2009 presidential election, which was won by General Mohamed ould Abdelaziz, who had led the 2008 coup, but the 2011 legislative elections were postponed. In December 2013 Abdelaziz's Union for the Republic party (UPR) won a majority in the first legislative elections since 2006, although the polls were widely boycotted by opposition parties. UPR maintained its grip on power during peaceful legislative elections in September 2018, which included broad participation from opposition parties. President Abdelaziz was elected for a further five-year term in June 2014, and was replaced by fellow UPR candidate and high-ranking military figure Mohamed ould Ghazouani following the June 2019 presidential elections; opposition parties rejected the results of the vote. It was the first democratic transition of power since achieving independence.

The 1991 constitution was amended in 2007 to reduce the term of the president, who is directly elected, to five years, renewable once. A referendum in August 2017 approved a constitutional amendment which altered the parliamentary structure from bicameral to unicameral by abolishing the senate and establishing regional councils. The National Assembly has 157 members who are directly elected for a five-year term: 113 in single- or two-seat constituencies by absolute majority, 40 by proportional representation in constituencies with three or more seats, and four members to represent Mauritanians overseas.

HEAD OF STATE

President, Gen. Mohamed ould Ghazouani, *elected* 22 June 2019, *sworn in* 1 August 2019

SELECTED GOVERNMENT MEMBERS *AS AT NOVEMBER 2020*

Prime Minister, Mohamed ould Bilal

Finance, Mohamed Lemine ould Dhehbi

Foreign Affairs, Ismail ould Cheikh Ahmed

Interior, Mohamed Salem ould Merzoug

EMBASSY OF THE ISLAMIC REPUBLIC OF MAURITANIA

Carlyle House, 235 Vauxhall Bridge Road, London SW1V 1EJ

T 020-7233 6158 E info@mauritanianembassy.org.uk

W www.mauritanianembassy.org.uk

Ambassador Extraordinary and Plenipotentiary, HE Sidya ould Elhadji, *apptd* 2020

BRITISH AMBASSADOR

Ambassador Extraordinary and Plenipotentiary, HE Simon Boyden, *apptd* 2019

ECONOMY AND TRADE

Mauritania is one of the poorer countries in the region, with around 31 per cent of the population living below the poverty line and unemployment at roughly 10 per cent. Past economic mismanagement and droughts created a huge foreign debt, although the country has benefited from debt cancellation since 2000. Despite a drought in 2017, strong growth was recorded until 2020 thanks to external investment in the oil and mining sectors, and favourable trading conditions. In

December 2017, Mauritania and the IMF agreed a three-year Extended Credit Facility to encourage infrastructure investment and economic stability.

Natural resources include iron ore, copper, gold, gypsum, oil and rich fishing waters, although the latter are threatened by over-exploitation and gypsum deposits have yet to be exploited. Potential deposits of natural gas and rare metals are also being explored. Agriculture and animal husbandry, mainly at subsistence level, are the mainstay of the economy, accounting for 27.8 per cent of GDP and engaging 50 per cent of the population. The main industries are fish processing, oil production and refining, and mining.

The main trading partners are China, the UAE, Switzerland and EU countries. Principal exports are iron ore, fish and fish products, livestock, gold, copper and oil. The main imports are machinery, petroleum products, capital goods, food and consumer goods.

GNI – US$7.5bn; US$1,660 per capita (2019)
Annual average growth of GDP – 3.5 per cent (2017 est)
Inflation rate – 2.3 per cent (2017 est)
Population below poverty line – 31 per cent (2014 est)
Unemployment – 10.2 per cent (2017 est)
Total external debt – $4.15bn (2017 est)
Imports – US$2,505m (2016)
Exports – US$1,382m (2016)

BALANCE OF PAYMENTS
Trade – US$1,123m deficit (2016)
Current Account – US$831m deficit (2019)

Trade with UK	2018	2019
Imports from UK	£7,210,473	£23,936,674
Exports to UK	£1,865,283	£2,729,631

COMMUNICATIONS
Transport – There are nine airports; the main seaports are Nouakchott and Nouadhibou; there are 3,988km of paved roadways and 728km of railways
Telecommunications – 53,742 fixed lines and 4.1 million mobile subscriptions (2019); there were 798,809 internet users in 2018
Internet code and IDD – mr; 222 (from UK), 44 (to UK)
Major broadcasters – Télévision de Mauritanie and Radio Mauritanie are the public broadcasters and offer programmes in Arabic and French; private broadcast media have been allowed to operate since 2011
Press – Major daily newspapers include the Arabic-language *Al-Sha'b* and the French-language *Horizons* (both state-run)
WPFI score – 32.54 (97)

MAURITIUS

Republic of Mauritius

Area – 2,040 sq. km (includes Rodrigues and other islands)
Capital – Port Louis; population, 149,000 (2018)

Major towns – Beau-Bassin Rose-Hill, Curepipe, Quatre Bornes, Vacoas-Phoenix
Currency – Mauritius rupee of 100 cents
Population – 1,379,365 rising at 0.54 per cent a year (2020 est)
Religion – Hindu 48.5 per cent, Christian (Roman Catholic 26.3 per cent, other Christian 6.4 per cent), Muslim 17.3 per cent (est)
Language – English (official), Creole, French, Bhojpuri
Population density – 623 per sq. km (2019)
Urban population – 40.8 per cent (2019 est)
Median age (years) – 36.3 (2020 est)
National anthem – 'Motherland'
National day – 12 March (Independence Day)
Death penalty – Abolished for all crimes (since 1995)
CPI score – 52 (56)
Military expenditure – US$23.2m (2018)

CLIMATE AND TERRAIN
The republic is an island group in the Indian Ocean, approximately 885km east of Madagascar. The volcanic island of Mauritius rises from narrow coastal plains to a central plateau ringed by mountains. Elevation extremes range from 828m (Mt Piton) to 0m (Indian Ocean). The island of Rodrigues, formerly a dependency but now part of Mauritius, is about 563km east of Mauritius, with an area of 109 sq. km; the population is 37,922 (2011). The islands of Agalega and St Brandon are dependencies of Mauritius; their total population is about 350 (2011).

There is a tropical climate, modified by south-east trade winds, and little variation in temperature throughout the year. The cyclone season (December–April) brings rain but cyclones usually miss the islands.

HISTORY AND POLITICS
The islands were first visited in the tenth century, but were settled only after 1638 by the Dutch, who introduced sugar cane cultivation; the colonists withdrew in 1710. A decade later they were replaced by the French, who established plantations that were worked by African slaves. In 1814 Mauritius was ceded to the British, who had occupied it in 1810. The British abolished slavery in 1834 and imported indentured Indian and Chinese labourers to work on the plantations. Independence was achieved on 12 March 1968 and the state became a republic in 1992.

The Militant Socialist Movement (MSM) under Sir Anerood Jugnauth held power from 1983 until 1995, and then returned to power in 2000 in coalition with the Mauritian Militant Movement (MMM). Jugnauth stood down as party leader and prime minister in 2003; he was elected president later that year and again in 2008. The MSM-MMM coalition lost the 2005 election to the opposition Socialist Alliance, but the MSM returned to power in 2010 and have continued to govern by forming coalitions after the 2014 and 2019 elections. President Rajkeswur Purryag resigned from office in May 2015 and, in June, Ameenah Gurib-Fakim was elected in his place, becoming the country's first woman president. However she was forced to resign from the largely ceremonial position in March 2018 following a financial scandal. MSM's Pradeep Roopun was elected as president in December 2019.

The 1968 constitution was amended in 1992 to introduce a republican form of government, and in 2001 to give the island of Rodrigues a degree of autonomy.

The president is elected by the legislature for a five-year term, renewable once. The unicameral National Assembly has 62 elected members (including two representing Rodrigues) and eight appointed members, all of whom serve a five-year term; the electoral commission allocates the appointed seats

United Kingdom & Ireland

ATLANTIC OCEAN

North Sea

Shetland Islands
Lerwick

Fair Isle

Orkney Islands
Kirkwall

Cape Wrath
Pentland Firth
Thurso · Duncansby Head
Wick

North West Highlands

Lewis
Stornoway

Outer Hebrides

Harris

N. Uist

S. Uist

Skye
Kyle of Lochalsh

Ullapool

Dornoch
Dingwall
Moray Firth
Elgin
Fraserburgh
Inverness
Spey
Peterhead
Loch Ness
Cairngorms
Ben Macdhui 1309
Aberdeen
Stonehaven

SCOTLAND

Grampian Mts.

Mallaig

Fort William
Ben Nevis 1345

Mull

Oban

Loch Lomond

Perth
Dundee
St. Andrews
Fife Ness

Stirling
Kirkcaldy
Dunfermline
Firth of Forth
Falkirk
Greenock
Edinburgh
Paisley
Glasgow
Kilmarnock
Peebles
Galashiels
Berwick-upon-Tweed

Arran
Ayr
Nith
Tweed
Jedburgh
Cheviot Hills
Alnwick

Southern Uplands

Malin Head

Bloody Foreland
Londonderry
Coleraine
Dumfries
Blyth
Newcastle upon Tyne

Malinmore Head
Donegal
Strabane
Ballymena
Larne
Stranraer
Wigtown
Kirkcudbright
Solway Firth
Carlisle
Consett
Durham
Sunderland
Hartlepool

Donegal Bay
Lough Erne
Omagh
Lough Neagh
NORTHERN
IRELAND
Belfast
Bangor
Workington
Keswick
Penrith
Eden
Darlington
Middlesbrough

Sligo
Enniskillen
Portadown
Armagh
Lurgan
Strangford Lough
Downpatrick
Lake District
Kendal
Scarborough

Ballina
Lough Conn
Carrick on Shannon
Newry
Mourne Mts.
Isle of Man
Douglas
Windermere
Lancaster
Bridlington

Clew Bay
Westport
Roscommon
Longford
Dundalk
Drogheda
Barrow-in-Furness
Harrogate
York
Kingston upon Hull

Castlebar
Mask
REPUBLIC
Nenagh
Irish
Blackpool
Ribble
Leeds
Spurn Head

Clifden
Corrib
Athlone
Lough Ree
Mullingar
Sea
Preston
Bradford
Grimsby

Galway Bay
Galway
OF
Tullamore
Dublin
Liverpool
Manchester
Sheffield

Midtown Malbay
Ennis
Lough Derg
Port Laoise
Dun Laoghaire
Anglesey
Holyhead
Birkenhead
Peak District
Chesterfield
Lincoln
Skegness

Kilrush
IRELAND
Liffey
Kildare
Holyhead
Llandudno
Chester
Crewe
Nottingham
Boston
The Wash

Limerick
Kilkenny
Carlow
Wicklow Mts.
Wicklow
Caernarfon
Denbigh
Stoke-on-Trent
Derby
Grantham
Kings Lynn
Norfolk Broads
Great Yarmouth

Dingle
Tralee
Tipperary
Clonmel
Enniscorthy
Arklow
Snowdon 1085
Wrexham
Leicester
Peterborough
Norwich

Valentia
Killarney
Mallow
Suir
Waterford
Wexford
Rosslare
Dolgellau
Shrewsbury
Montgomery
ENGLAND
Waveney

Cork
Youghal
Dungarvan
Mine Head
St. George's Channel
Fishguard
Cardigan Bay
Aberystwyth
Llandrindod Wells
Wolverhampton
Birmingham
Coventry
Rugby
Northampton
Cambridge
Ipswich

Cape Clear
Bantry
Kenmare
Cardigan
Teifi
WALES
Worcester
Bedford
Luton
Hel'wich
The Naze

Carmarthen
Gloucester
Cotswolds
Oxford
LONDON
Colchester

Llanelli
Ebbw Vale
Severn
Chiltern Hills
Thames
Southend-on-Sea

Milford Haven
Swansea
Port Talbot
Newport
Bristol
Swindon
Reading
Maidstone
Margate
Canterbury

St. David's Head
Cardiff
Bath
Salisbury Plain
Guildford
Dover
Calais
Strait of Dover

Bristol Channel
Exmoor
Taunton
Salisbury
Winchester
The Weald
Folkestone

Hartland Point
Barnstaple
Yeovil
Southampton
Portsmouth
Brighton
Hastings
Boulogne
Le Touquet

Bude
Poole
Isle of Wight

Dartmoor
Exeter
Weymouth
Bournemouth

Bodmin
Tavistock
Portland Bill

Plymouth
Torquay

Penzance
Land's End
Falmouth
Start Point

Isles of Scilly
Lizard Point

English Channel

Alderney
Cherbourg
Baie de la Seine
Dieppe
FRANCE
Abbeville

Guernsey
Sark
Le Havre
Rouen
Seine

Jersey
Caen
Collines de Normandie

Scale

0	25	50	75	100 Miles
0	50	100	150 Kms	

Conical Orthomorphic Projection

60°N · 55°N · 50°N

10°W · 5°W · 0°

Europe

ICELAND

Arctic Circle

Reykjavik

Norwegian

Sea

0   100   200   300   400 Miles
0   100   200   300   400   500   600 Kms

Conical Orthomorphic Projection

© Oxford Cartographers, 98687
+44 (0)1993 705 394
E & OE

Faroe Is.
(Denmark)

Trondheim

Bergen

Shetland Is.

Tromsø

Bodø

N
O
R
W
A
Y

S
W
E
D

Stavanger

Oslo

Uppsala
Vasteras
Stockholm
Orebro
Norrkop
Linkopi
Jonkoping
Gothenburg

Kristiansand

Helsingborg
DENMARK   **Copenhagen**
Odense   Malmo
Bornho
(Den.)

A
T
L
A
N
T
I
C

O
C
E
A
N

Hebrides

Inverness

Glasgow
Edinburgh

Londonderry

Belfast

Galway   **Dublin**

REP. OF
IRELAND

Cork

Orkney Is.

Aberdeen

Dundee

UNITED

KINGDOM
Newcastle
upon Tyne

North

Sea

Liverpool   Leeds
Manchester
Sheffield
Stoke-
on-Trent   Norwich
Swansea   **Birmingham**
Cardiff
Bristol

Plymouth
Southampton

Alborg
Arhus
Kiel
Rostock
Koszalin
Hamburg   Szczecin
Bremen
Hanover   **Berlin**

P
Po.
Wrocla

English Channel
Cherbourg
Le Havre   Lille
Caen
Brest
Rennes
Nantes   *Loire*

Amsterdam
NETHERLANDS
Rotterdam
Antwerp
Brussels
BELGIUM
LUX.
Luxembourg
Amiens
Rouen   Reims
Seine   **Paris**
Orléans
Tours

Essen
Münster   Osnabrück
Dortmund
Düsseldorf
Cologne   Leipzig   Dresden
Frankfurt   Chemnitz
Mannheim   Nuremberg
Metz
Strasbourg   Stuttgart   *Danube*
Nancy
Dijon

Regensburg   Brno
Munich   Salzburg   **Vienna**
LIECH.   Innsbruck   **AUSTRIA**
Graz

Plzen   **Prague**
CZECHIA
Bratisla

Bay of

Biscay

La Coruña
Vigo

Gijón
León   Bilbao
Valladolid
Burgos
Salamanca

Bordeaux

F R A N C E

Limoges
Clermont-
Ferrand
Lyon

Rhône
Grenoble

Mt. Blanc
4808

Bern
SWITZERLAND
Zurich
Geneva

Milan

Trento
Verona
Parma
Turin   *Po*   Venice
Genoa

Bologne

Triests

SLOV.
Ljubljana   Zag
Rijeka   Ban
Lu

CROATIA

Adriat

PORTUGAL

Oporto
Douro
Coimbra
Amadora
Lisbon
Tagus
Setubal
Badajoz

Faro

Pamplona
San Sebastian
S P A I N
Zaragoza
Lerida
Madrid

Barcelona

Montpellier
Toulouse
Pyrenees
ANDORRA

Nimes
Nice
Marseille   **MONACO**
La Spezia   Livorno

Florence
SAN
MARINO
Ancona

Pescara

I T A L Y
Apennines
Rome

Fo

Córdoba
Huelva
Seville
Cadiz
Gibraltar(U.K.)
Tangier   Ceuta(Sp.)
Tetouan

Granada
Murcia
Malaga   Almeria
Cartagena

Valencia
Balearic Is.
(Sp.)
Palma
Mallorca

Corsica
(Fr.)   Ajaccio

Sardinia
(It.)
Sassari

Cagliari

Naples   Salerno

Palermo   Messina
Reg
Cala
Sicily

Syrac

M e d i t e r r a n e a

Rabat
Casablanca

Melilla(Sp.)   Oran
Fes
Meknes
Oujda   Sidi Bel Abbes

Algiers
Blida   Skikda   Annaba
Bejaia
Constantine   Ariana   **Tunis**

Sousse

M O R O C C O   *Mountains*

Atlas

A L G E R I A

TUNISIA

Valletta
MALTA

Sfax

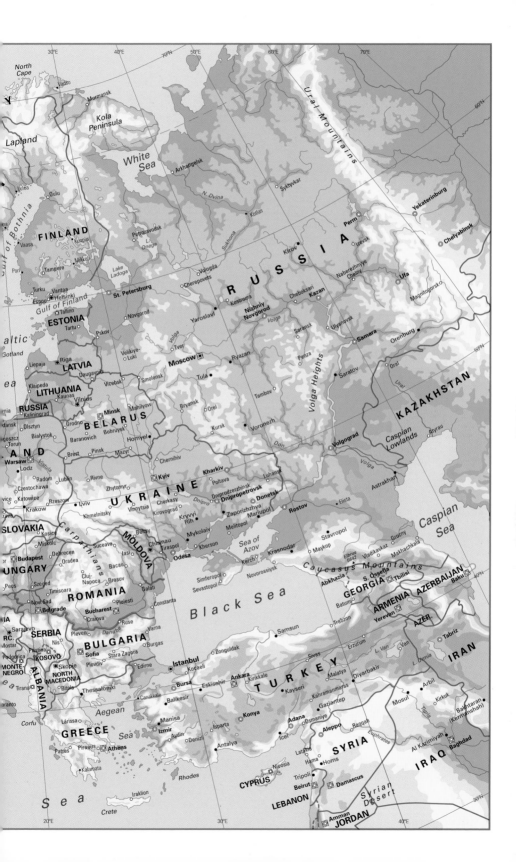

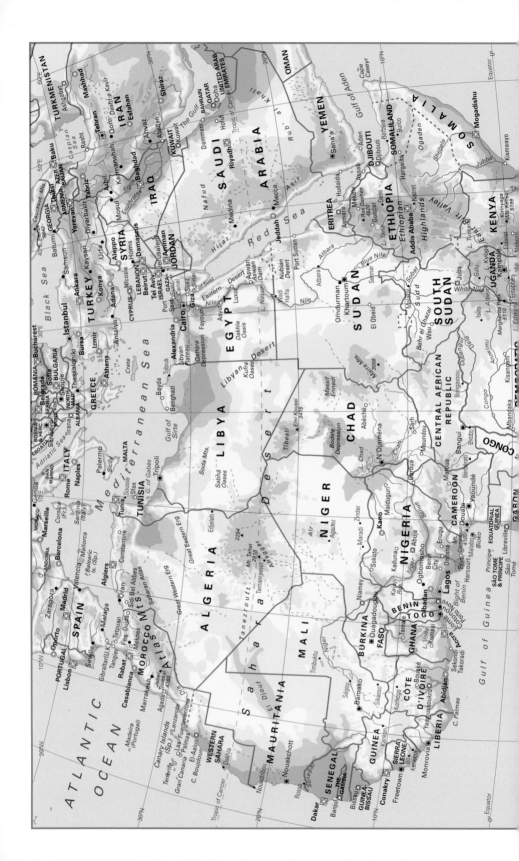

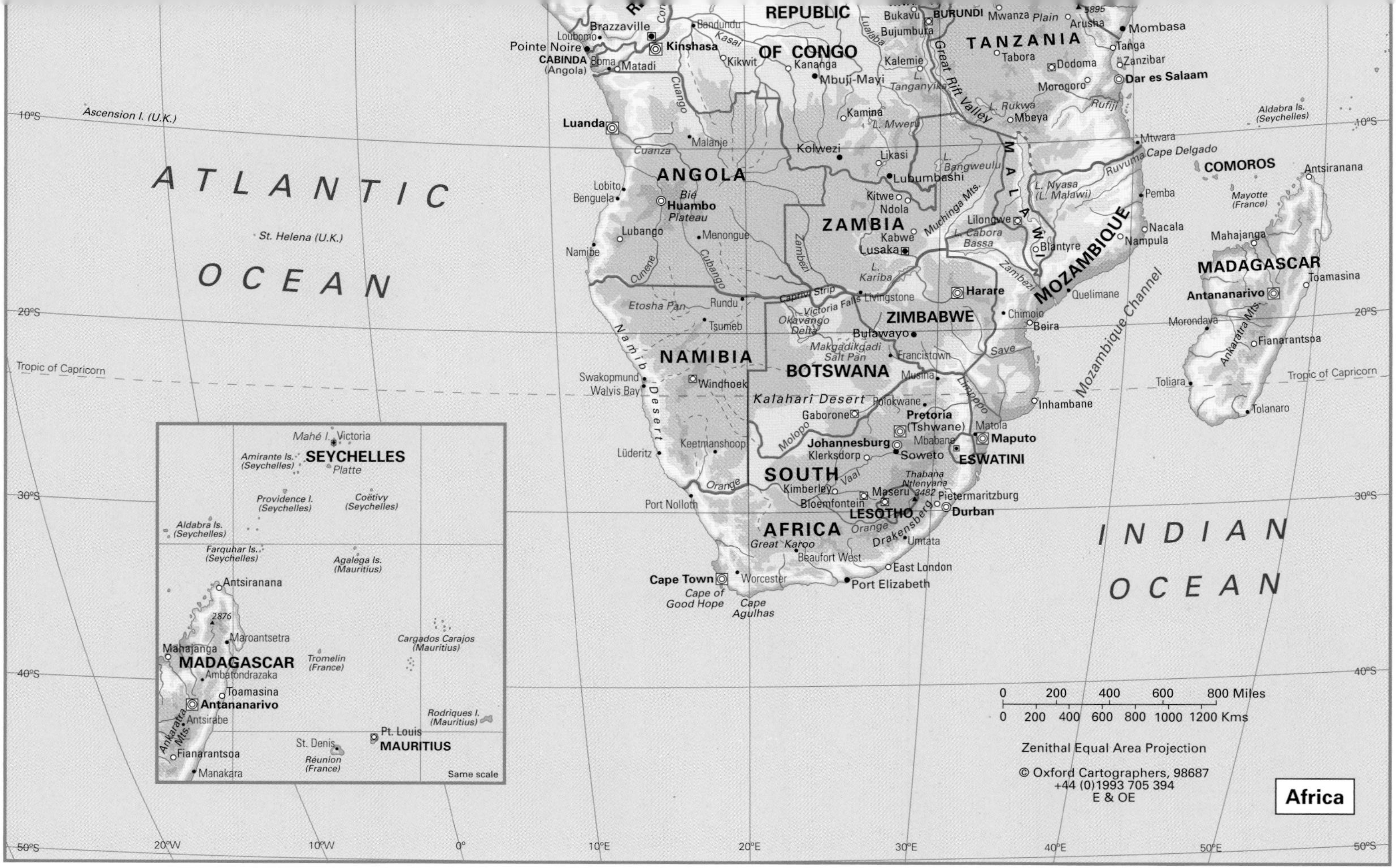

ATLANTIC
OCEAN
INDIAN
OCEAN
Ascension I. (U.K.)
St. Helena (U.K.)
Tropic of Capricorn
REPUBLIC
OF CONGO
TANZANIA
BURUNDI
ANGOLA
ZAMBIA
MALAWI
MOZAMBIQUE
COMOROS
Mayotte (France)
MADAGASCAR
ZIMBABWE
NAMIBIA
BOTSWANA
SOUTH
AFRICA
LESOTHO
ESWATINI
CABINDA (Angola)
Brazzaville
Loubomo
Pointe Noire
Boma
Matadi
Kinshasa
Bandundu
Kasai
Kikwit
Kananga
Mbuji-Mayi
Lualaba
Bukavu
Bujumbura
Kalemie
L. Tanganyika
Great Rift Valley
Mwanza
Plain
Arusha
5895
Mombasa
Tanga
Zanzibar
Tabora
Dodoma
Dar es Salaam
Morogoro
Rufiji
L. Rukwa
Mbeya
Aldabra Is. (Seychelles)
Luanda
Cuango
Malanje
Cuanza
Kamina
L. Mweru
Kolwezi
Likasi
L. Bangweulu
Lubumbashi
Mtwara
Cape Delgado
Ruvuma
Antsiranana
Lobito
Benguela
Bié
Huambo
Plateau
Lubango
Menongue
Namibe
Cunene
Cubango
Kitwe
Ndola
Muchinga Mts.
Lilongwe
L. Nyasa (L. Malawi)
Pemba
Nacala
Nampula
Mahajanga
L. Cabora Bassa
Kabwe
Lusaka
Zambezi
L. Kariba
Blantyre
Zambezi
Quelimane
Toamasina
Antananarivo
Harare
Etosha Pan
Rundu
Caprivi Strip
Victoria Falls
Livingstone
Okavango Delta
Tsumeb
Chimoio
Beira
Mozambique Channel
Morondava
Ankaratra Mts.
Fianarantsoa
Bulawayo
Makgadikgadi Salt Pan
Francistown
Save
Namib Desert
Swakopmund
Walvis Bay
Windhoek
Musina
Limpopo
Toliara
Tolanaro
Kalahari Desert
Polokwane
Inhambane
Gaborone
Pretoria (Tshwane)
Matola
Maputo
Molopo
Keetmanshoop
Johannesburg
Mbabane
Klerksdorp
Soweto
Lüderitz
Vaal
Thabana Ntlenyana 3482
Orange
Kimberley
Maseru
Pietermaritzburg
Port Nolloth
Bloemfontein
Durban
Orange
Drakensberg
Great Karoo
Umtata
Beaufort West
East London
Cape Town
Worcester
Port Elizabeth
Cape of Good Hope
Cape Agulhas
Mahé I.
Victoria
Amirante Is. (Seychelles)
SEYCHELLES
Platte
Providence I. (Seychelles)
Coëtivy (Seychelles)
Aldabra Is. (Seychelles)
Farquhar Is. (Seychelles)
Agalega Is. (Mauritius)
Antsiranana
2876
Maroantsetra
Cargados Carajos (Mauritius)
Mahajanga
MADAGASCAR
Tromelin (France)
Ambatondrazaka
Toamasina
Antananarivo
Antsirabe
Ankaratra Mts.
Rodriques I. (Mauritius)
Pt. Louis
MAURITIUS
St. Denis
Réunion (France)
Fianarantsoa
Manakara
Same scale
10°S
20°S
30°S
40°S
50°S
20°W
10°W
0°
10°E
20°E
30°E
40°E
50°E
0 200 400 600 800 Miles
0 200 400 600 800 1000 1200 Kms
Zenithal Equal Area Projection
© Oxford Cartographers, 98687
+44 (0)1993 705 394
E & OE
Africa

North America

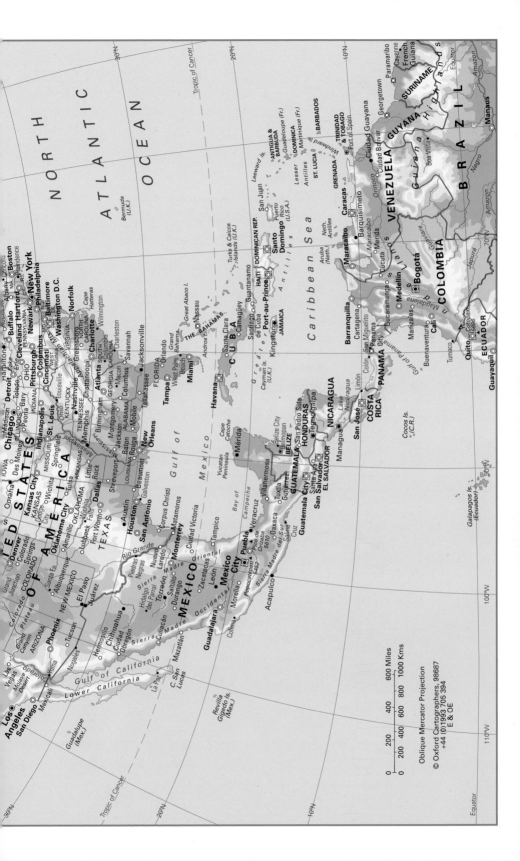

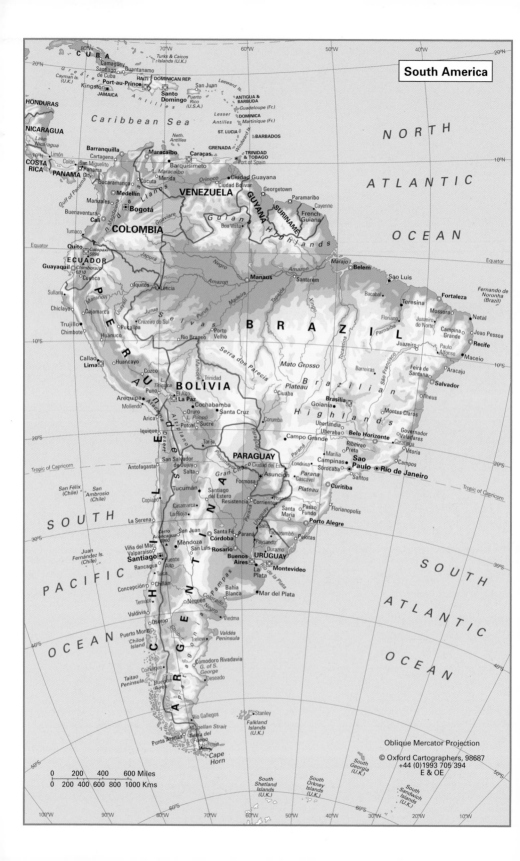

South America

NORTH

ATLANTIC

OCEAN

Caribbean Sea

CUBA
Camagüey
Santiago de Cuba
Guantanamo
Turks & Caicos Islands (U.K.)
Cayman Is. (U.K.)
Kingston
Port-au-Prince
HAITI
DOMINICAN REP.
Santo Domingo
San Juan
Puerto Rico (U.S.A.)
Leeward Is.
ANTIGUA & BARBUDA
Guadeloupe (Fr.)
DOMINICA
Martinique (Fr.)
ST. LUCIA
BARBADOS
GRENADA
Neth. Antilles
Lesser Antilles
JAMAICA

HONDURAS
NICARAGUA
Lake Nicaragua
Limón
COSTA RICA
Colón
San Miguelito
Panama City
PANAMA
Gulf of Panama
Buenaventura

Barranquilla
Cartagena
Maracaibo
Maracaibo
Caracas
Barquisimeto
TRINIDAD & TOBAGO
Port of Spain
Bucaramanga
Cúcuta
Merida
Orinoco
Ciudad Guayana
Ciudad Bolívar
Georgetown
Paramaribo
Cayenne
French Guiana
Medellín
VENEZUELA
Manizales
Bogotá
Cali
Boa Vista
GUYANA
SURINAME
Guiana Highlands
COLOMBIA
Tumaco
Quito
Cotopaxi 5896
ECUADOR
Chimborazo 6310
Guayaquil
Cuenca
Iquitos
Leticia
Napo
Negro
Amazon
Manaus
Santarem
Belem
Sao Luis
Fortaleza
Fernando de Noronha (Brazil)
Sullana
Chiclayo
Marañón
Cajamarca
Cruzeiro do Sul
Selvas
Purus
Madeira
Tapajos
Xingu
Bacabal
Teresina
Mossoró
Natal
Joao Pessoa
Recife
Trujillo
Chimbote
Huánuco
Pucallpa
Porto Velho
Rio Branco
BRAZIL
Floriano
Parnaiba
Juazeiro do Norte
Campina Grande
PERU
Callao
Lima
Cuzco
Huancayo
Serra dos Parecis
Mato Grosso
Juazeiro
Sao Paulo
Alfonso
Maceio
Barreiras
Sao Francisco
Titicaca
Puno
El Alto
BOLIVIA
La Paz
Cochabamba
Santa Cruz
Trinidad
Brazilian
Brasília
Goiânia
Feira de Santana
Salvador
Ilheus
Arica
Oruro
Sucre
Potosí
Ciuaba
Plateau
Highlands
Montes Claros
Arequipa
Mollendo
Corumba
Uberlândia
Uberaba
Belo Horizonte
Governador Valadares
Caratinga
Iquique
Altiplano
Tarija
Campo Grande
Ribeirao Preto
Vitoria
Antofagasta
San Salvador de Jujuy
Salta
PARAGUAY
Gran Chaco
Ciudad del Este
Asunción
Marilia
Campinas
Londrina
Parana
Sorocaba
Sao Paulo
Campos
Rio de Janeiro
Santos
Tucumán
Santiago del Estero
Formosa
Posadas
Curitiba
Copiapo
Catamarca
La Rioja
Resistencia
Corrientes
Parana
Santa Maria
Passo Fundo
Florianopolis
San Félix (Chile)
San Ambrosio (Chile)
La Serena
Cerro Aconcagua 6960
San Juan
Santa Fe
Paraná
Salto
Tacuarembó
Porto Alegre
Pelotas
Juan Fernández Is. (Chile)
Viña del Mar
Valparaíso
Santiago
Mendoza
Córdoba
San Luis
Rosario
Paysandu
Duramo
Uruguay
URUGUAY
Rancagua
Puente Alto
Talca
Buenos Aires
Montevideo
Concepción
Chillán
La Plata
Mar del Plata
Bahia Blanca
Pampas
Temuco
Neuquen
Valdivia
Colorado
Negro
Osorno
Viedma
Puerto Montt
Chiloé Island
Trelew
Valdés Peninsula
ARGENTINA
Comodoro Rivadavia
G. of S. George
Deseado
Taitao Peninsula
Coihaique
Puerto Aisen
PACIFIC
OCEAN
Rio Gallegos
Stanley
Falkland Islands (U.K.)
Punta Arenas
Magellan Strait
Tierra del Fuego
Ushuaia
Cape Horn

Equator

Equator

10°S

10°S

Tropic of Capricorn

Tropic of Capricorn

SOUTH

ATLANTIC

OCEAN

SOUTH

PACIFIC

OCEAN

20°N

10°N

10°S

20°S

30°S

40°S

50°S

100°W 90°W 80°W 70°W 60°W 50°W 40°W 30°W 20°W 10°W

80°W 70°W 60°W 50°W 40°W

South Georgia (U.K.)
South Shetland Islands (U.K.)
South Orkney Islands (U.K.)
South Sandwich Islands (U.K.)

Oblique Mercator Projection

© Oxford Cartographers, 98687
+44 (0)1993 705 394
E & OE

0   200   400   600 Miles
0 200 400 600 800 1000 Kms

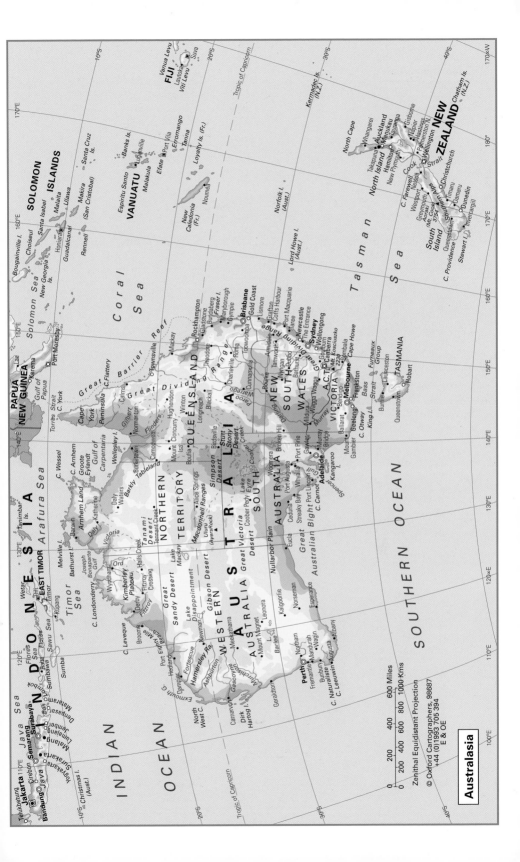

Australasia

© Oxford Cartographers, 98687
+44 (0)1993 705 394
E & OE
Zenithal Equidistant Projection

0   200   400   600 Miles
0   200 400 600 800 1000 Kms

INDONESIA

Java Sea
Telukbetung
Jakarta
Bandung   Java
Surakarta
Yogyakarta
Semarang   Cirebon
Surabaya
Malang
Jember   Lumajang
Bali
Denpasar
Lombok
Sumbawa
Mataram
Flores
Sumba
Sawu Sea
Timor Sea
Kupang
Timor
EAST TIMOR
Wetar
Tanimbar
Is.
Arafura Sea

Christmas I.
(Aust.)

PAPUA
NEW GUINEA
Lae
Kerema
Port Moresby
Gulf of
Papua
Torres Strait

SOLOMON
ISLANDS
Bougainville I.
Choiseul
Santa Isabel
New Georgia
Is.
Honiara
Guadalcanal
Malaita
Ulawa
Makira
(San Cristobal)
Rennell
Solomon Sea

Santa Cruz
Is.

VANUATU
Espiritu Santo
Malakula
Efate
Port Vila
Erromango
Tanna
Banks Is.
Loyalty Is. (Fr.)
Lifou

New
Caledonia
(Fr.)
Nouméa

FIJI
Vanua Levu
Lautoka
Viti Levu
Suva

Coral
Sea

Tropic of Capricorn

Norfolk I.
(Aust.)

Lord Howe I.
(Aust.)

NEW
ZEALAND
North Cape
Whangarei
Auckland
Manukau
Hamilton
Tauranga
New Plymouth
Gisborne
Napier
Hastings
Palmerston
North
Wellington
Tatapauri
Nelson
Westport
Greymouth
Mt. Cook
3754
Southern Alps
Christchurch
Timaru
Oamaru
Dunedin
Invercargill
Queenstown
C. Farewell
North Island
South Island
Cook Strait
Stewart I.
C. Providence

Chatham Is.
(N.Z.)

Tasman
Sea

Kermadec Is.
(N.Z.)

INDIAN
OCEAN

SOUTHERN OCEAN

AUSTRALIA

WESTERN AUSTRALIA
Exmouth G.
North West C.
Camarvon
Dirk Hartog I.
C. Leeuwin
C. Naturaliste
Bunbury
Fremantle
Perth
Mandurah
Northam
Wagin
Katanning
Mount Magnet
Meekatharra
Newman
Leonora
Leinster
Kalgoorlie
Coolgardie
Norseman
Esperance
Geraldton
Hamersley Ra.
Fortescue
Ashburton
Gascoyne
Murchison
Dampier
Port Hedland
Broome
C. Leveque
Derby
Fitzroy
Fitzroy
Crossing
Halls Creek
Great
Sandy Desert
Lake
Disappointment
Gibson Desert
Great Victoria Desert
Nullarbor Plain
Great Australian Bight

Kimberley
Plateau
Wyndham
Joseph
Bonaparte
Gulf
C. Londonderry
Ord
Kununurra
Tanami
Desert

NORTHERN
TERRITORY
Darwin
Katherine
Daly Waters
Tennant Creek
Daly
Victoria
Alice Springs
MacDonnell Ranges
Uluru
(Ayers Rock)
Tanami
Desert
Mackay
Simpson
Desert
Melville I.
Bathurst I.
C. Arnhem
Arnhem Land
Groote
Eylandt
Gulf of
Carpentaria
Wellesley I.
Burketown
Normanton
Cloncurry
Mount Isa
Camooweal
Barkly Tableland

QUEENSLAND
C. York
Cape York
Peninsula
C. Flattery
Cairns
Townsville
Great Barrier Reef
Mackay
Rockhampton
Gladstone
Bundaberg
Maryborough
Fraser I.
Gympie
Brisbane
Gold Coast
Charleville
Roma
Toowoomba
Longreach
Blackall
Winton
Hughenden
Thargomindah
Birdsville
Great Dividing Range
Flinders
Gilbert
Georgina
Diamantina
Cooper Creek
Sturt
Stony
Desert

SOUTH
AUSTRALIA
Lake Eyre
Coober Pedy
Woomera
Port Augusta
Whyalla
Port Pirie
Port Lincoln
Spencer
Gulf
Adelaide
Murray Bridge
Kangaroo I.
Ceduna
Streaky Bay
C. Carnot
Eucla
Lake
Torrens
Lake
Gairdner
Broken Hill

NEW
SOUTH
WALES
Darling
Bourke
Dubbo
Bathurst
Wagga Wagga
Broken Hill
Wilcannia
Cobar
Tamworth
Armidale
Grafton
Lismore
Coffs Harbour
Port Macquarie
Taree
Newcastle
Sydney
Wollongong
Mt. Kosciuszko
2230
Mildura
Griffith
Murrumbidgee
Murray
Deniliquin

A.C.T.
Canberra

VICTORIA
Mildura
Swan Hill
Bendigo
Ballarat
Geelong
Melbourne
Frankston
Warrnambool
Hamilton
Horsham
C. Otway
King I.

Bass
Strait
Cape Howe
Furneaux
Group

TASMANIA
Burnie
Launceston
Queenstown
Hobart

Murray
Lake
Mackay

Tropic of Capricorn

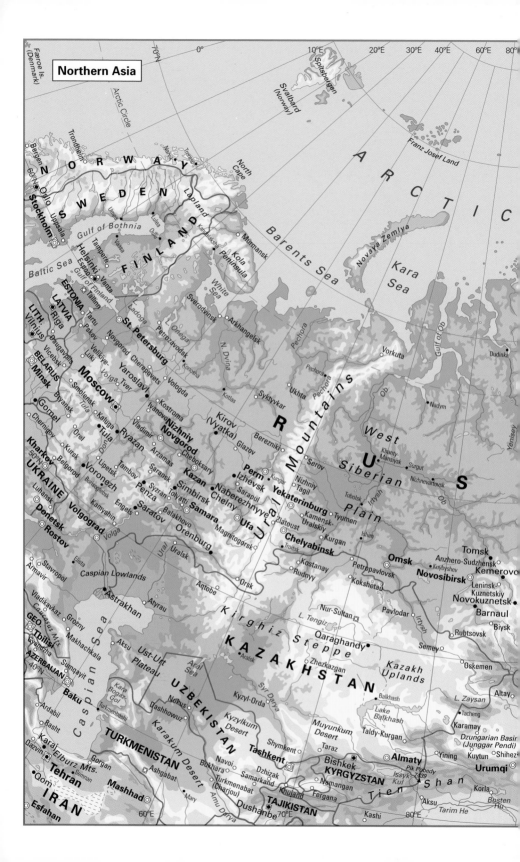

Northern Asia

Faroe Is. (Denmark)

0° 10°E 20°E 30°E 40°E 60°E 80°E

70°N

Spitsbergen

Svalbard (Norway)

Arctic Circle

North Cape

Franz Josef Land

A R C T I C

Trondheim

Tromsø

Narvik

N O R W A Y

Bergen

Oslo

60°N

Uppsala

Stockholm

S W E D E N

Lapland

Umeå

Luleå

Gulf of Bothnia

Vaasa

Tampere

Kandalaksha

Murmansk

Kola Peninsula

Barents Sea

Novaya Zemlya

Kara Sea

Gulf of Ob

Dudinka

Helsinki

Vanta

F I N L A N D

Baltic Sea

Gulf of Finland

Espoo

Tallinn

White Sea

Sverdlovsk

Arkhangelsk

N. Dvina

Pechora

Vorkuta

Nadym

ESTONIA

LATVIA

Tartu

Pärnu

Pskov

L. Ladoga

Petrozavodsk

L. Onega

Kotlas

Syktyvkar

Ukhta

Pechora

Ob

Surgut

Nizhnevartovsk

Yenisey

Riga

LITH.

Vilnius

Panevėžys

Velikiye Luki

Cherepovets

St. Petersburg

Novgorod

Vologda

U

r

a

l

Khanty-Mansiysk

BELARUS

Minsk

Vitebsk

Smolensk

Tver

Yaroslavl

Volga

Ivanovo

Kostroma

Kirov (Vyatka)

Berezniki

M

o

u

n

t

a

i

n

s

West

Minsk

Moscow

Kaluga

Vladimir

Nizhniy Novgorod

Glazov

Serov

Siberian

Gomel

Bryansk

Tula

Ryazan

Arzamas

Cheboksary

Perm

Nizhniy Tagil

R

U

S

Chernigov

Orel

Lipetsk

Tambov

Saransk

Kazan

Izhevsk

Yekaterinburg

Tyumen

Plain

Kharkov

50°N

Kursk

Belgorod

Voronezh

Penza

Simbirsk

Naberezhnye Chelny

Sarapul

Kungur

Tobolsk

Irtysh

Ob

UKRAINE

Borisoglebsk

Syzran

Tolyatti

Samara

Ufa

Zlatoust

Kamensk-Uralskiy

Ishim

Luhansk

Kamyshin

Saratov

Balakhovo

Magnitogorsk

Chelyabinsk

Kurgan

Donetsk

Engels

Volgograd

Orenburg

Troitsk

Omsk

Tomsk

Rostov

Volga

Ural

Uralsk

Orsk

Kostanay

Petropavlovsk

Anzhero-Sudzhensk

Kemerovo

Elista

Uralsk

Aqtobe

Rudnyy

Kokshetau

Kuybyshev

Novosibirsk

Leninsk-Kuznetskiy

Stavropol

Caspian Lowlands

Atyrau

Pavlodar

Novokuznetsk

Armavir

Astrakhan

K i r g h i z

Nur-Sultan

Semey

Barnaul

Vladikavkaz

Grozny

Makhachkala

S t e p p e

L. Tengiz

Qaraghandy

Biysk

Rubtsovsk

GEO.

Caucasus Mts.

Tbilisi

Alanzha

Aksu

Ust-Urt Plateau

K A Z A K H S T A N

Zhezkazgan

Kazakh Uplands

Oskemen

Altay

AZERBAIJAN

Sumqayit

40°N

Aral Sea

Aralsk

Balkhash

L. Zaysan

Baku

Kara Bogaz Gol

Turkmenbashi

Syr Darya

Lake Balkhash

Tacheng

Karamay

Ardabil

Rasht

TURKMENISTAN

Karakum Desert

U Z B E K I S T A N

Nukus

Dashhowuz

Kyzyl-Orda

Kyzylkum Desert

Muyunkum Desert

Taldy-Kurgan

Dzungarian Basin (Junggar Pendi)

Yining

Kuytun

Shihezi

Karaj

Qazvin

Elburz Mts.

Gorgan

Serakhs

Ashgabat

Turkmenabat (Charjou)

Bukhara

Navoi

Dzhizak

Samarkand

Shymkent

Taraz

Almaty

Pik Pobedy 7439

KYRGYZSTAN

Bishkek

Issyk Kul

Urumqi

Tehran

Mashhad

Mary

Amu Darya

Turkmenbashi

Namangan

Fergana

Khujand

TAJIKISTAN

Dushanbe

70°E

Tashkent

T i e n

S h a n

Korla

Aksu

Bosten Hu

Qom

IRAN

Esfahan

60°E

Ashgabat

Dushanbe

Kashi

Tarim He

80°E

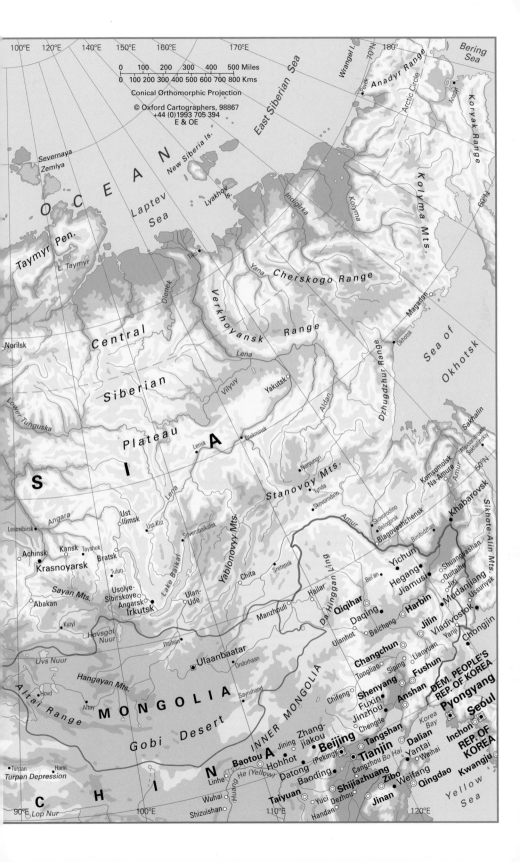

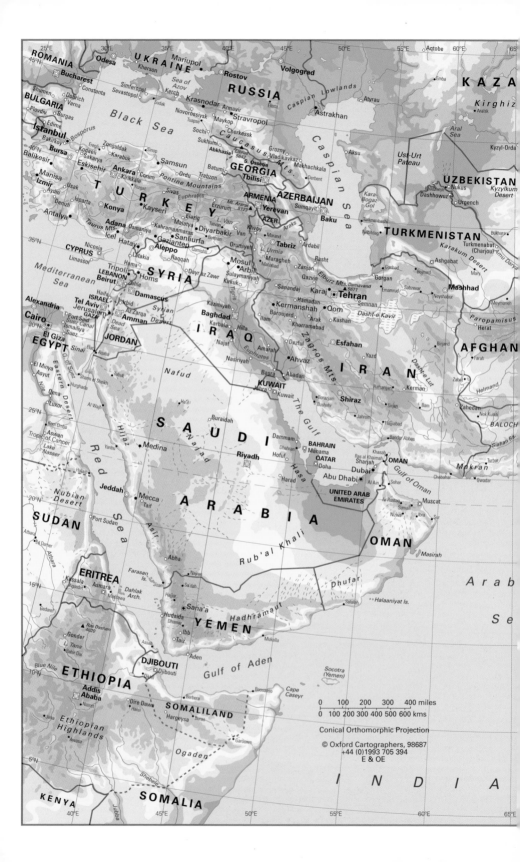

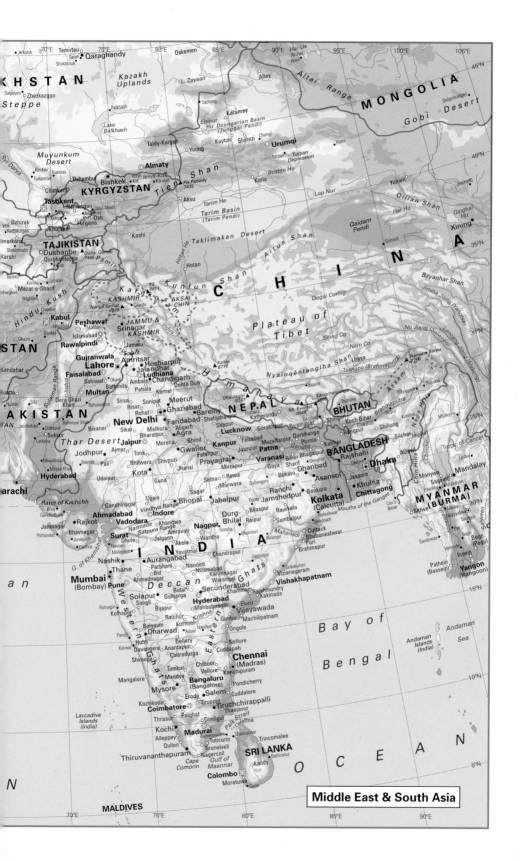

Middle East & South Asia

Pacific

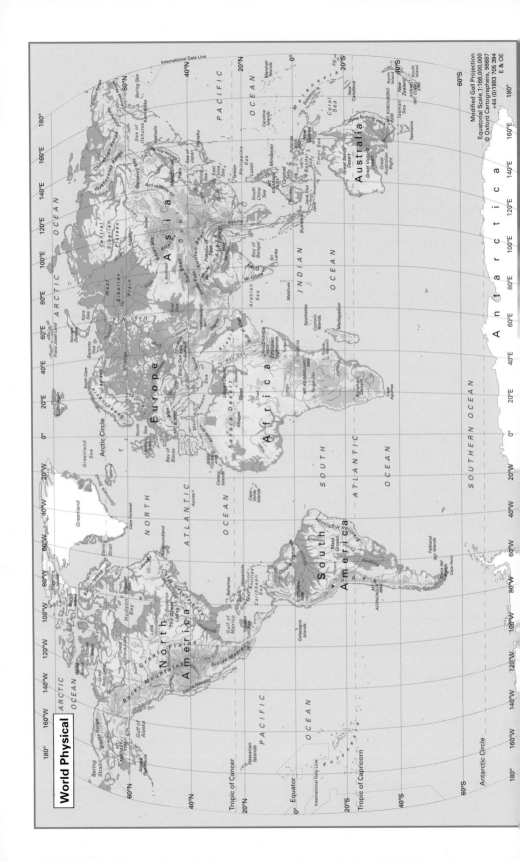

World Physical

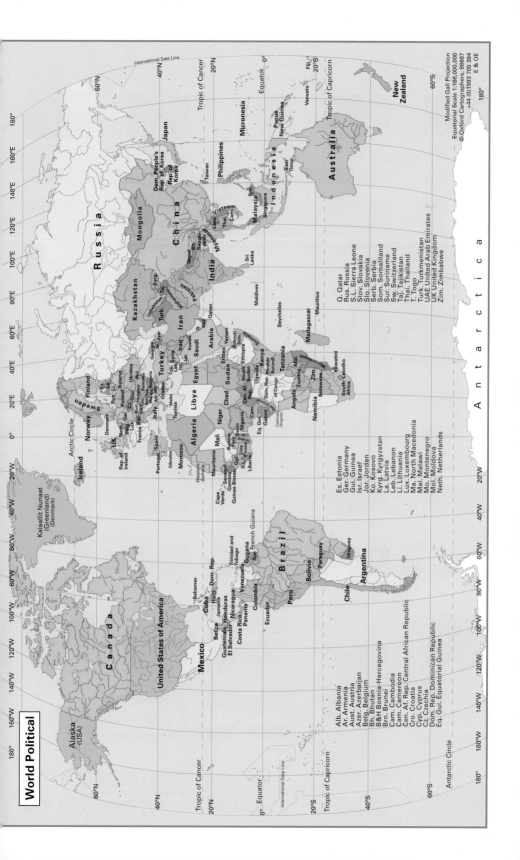

World Political

Alaska (USA)

Kalaallit Nunaat (Greenland) (Denmark)

Iceland

C a n a d a

United States of America

Mexico

Belize
Guatemala Honduras
El Salvador Nicaragua
Costa Rica
Panama

Bahamas
Cuba
Haiti Dom. Rep.
Jamaica
Trinidad and
Tobago

Venezuela
Colombia
Ecuador
Peru
B r a z i l
Bolivia
Paraguay
Chile
Argentina
Uruguay

Guyana
Suriname
French Guiana

Norway
Sweden
Finland

Rep. of Ireland
UK
Denmark

Portugal Spain

Morocco
Western Sahara
Mauritania
Cape Verde
Senegal
Gambia
Guinea Bissau

Algeria
Mali
Niger

L i b y a

Chad

Mauritania

Nigeria

Tunisia

Egypt

Sudan
South Sudan
Ethiopia
Somalia
Kenya
Uganda
Tanzania
Angola
Zambia
Zimbabwe
Namibia
Botswana
South Africa
Lesotho
Madagascar
Mauritius
Seychelles
Maldives

R u s s i a

Kazakhstan
Mongolia
C h i n a
Japan
Dem. People's Rep. of Korea
Rep. of Korea
Taiwan

I n d i a
Nepal
Sri Lanka
Myanmar
Laos
Vietnam
Thai.
Camb.
Philippines
Malaysia
Singapore
I n d o n e s i a
East Timor
Brunei

Turkey
Iran
Saudi Arabia
Yemen
Oman
Iraq

Papua New Guinea
Micronesia

Australia

New Zealand

Fiji
Vanuatu

A n t a r c t i c a

Alb. Albania
Ar. Armenia
Aust. Austria
Azer. Azerbaijan
Belg. Belgium
Bh. Bhutan
B&H Bosnia-Hercegovina
Brn. Brunei
Cam. Cambodia
Cam. Cameroon
Cen. Af. Rep. Central African Republic
Cro. Croatia
Cz. Czechia
Cyp. Cyprus
Dom. Rep. Dominican Republic
Eq. Gui. Equatorial Guinea

Es. Estonia
Ger. Germany
Gui. Guinea
Isr. Israel
Jor. Jordan
Ko. Kosovo
Kyrg. Kyrgyzstan
La. Latvia
Leb. Lebanon
Li. Lithuania
Lux. Luxembourg
Ma. North Macedonia
Mal. Malawi
Mo. Montenegro
Mol. Moldova
Neth. Netherlands

Q. Qatar
Rus. Russia
S.L. Sierra Leone
Slov. Slovakia
Slo. Slovenia
Serb. Serbia
Som. Somaliland
Sur. Suriname
Sw. Switzerland
Taj. Tajikistan
Thai. Thailand
T. Togo
Turk. Turkmenistan
UAE United Arab Emirates
UK United Kingdom
Zim. Zimbabwe

International Date Line
Arctic Circle
Tropic of Cancer
Equator
Tropic of Capricorn
Antarctic Circle

Modified Gall Projection
Equatorial Scale 1:166,000,000
© Oxford Cartographers, 99687
+44 (0)1993 705 394
E & OE

FLAGS OF THE WORLD

The following four pages show the national flag of each country, as it is used for international purposes. In some cases this means that the state flag is shown. Where this is the case the country name is marked (†).

AFGHANISTAN

ALBANIA

ALGERIA

ANDORRA

ANGOLA

ANTIGUA AND BARBUDA

ARGENTINA

ARMENIA

AUSTRALIA

AUSTRIA

AZERBAIJAN

THE BAHAMAS

BAHRAIN

BANGLADESH

BARBADOS

BELARUS

BELGIUM

BELIZE

BENIN

BHUTAN

BOLIVIA†

BOSNIA AND HERCEGOVINA

BOTSWANA

BRAZIL

BRUNEI

BULGARIA

BURKINA FASO

BURUNDI

CAMBODIA

CAMEROON

CANADA

CAPE VERDE

CENTRAL AFRICAN REPUBLIC

CHAD

CHILE

CHINA

COLOMBIA

THE COMOROS

DEM. REPUBLIC OF THE CONGO

REPUBLIC OF THE CONGO

COSTA RICA

CÔTE D'IVOIRE

CROATIA

CUBA

CYPRUS

CZECH REPUBLIC

DENMARK

DJIBOUTI

DOMINICA

DOMINICAN REPUBLIC

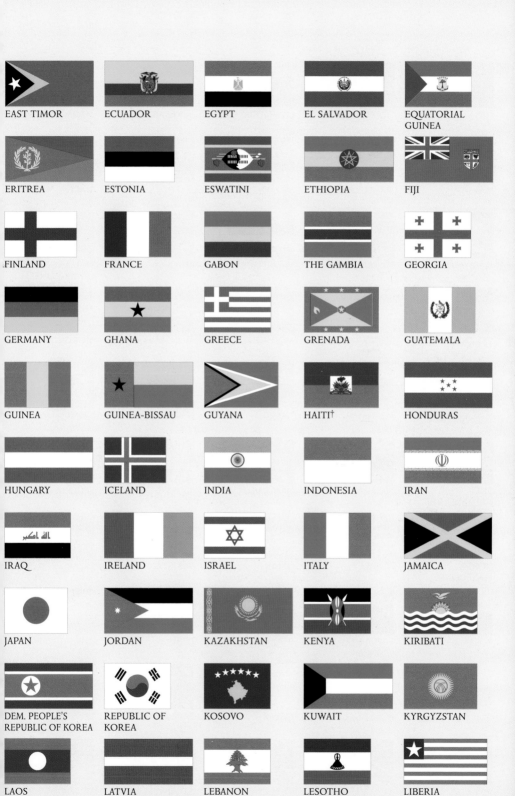

EAST TIMOR

ECUADOR

EGYPT

EL SALVADOR

EQUATORIAL GUINEA

ERITREA

ESTONIA

ESWATINI

ETHIOPIA

FIJI

FINLAND

FRANCE

GABON

THE GAMBIA

GEORGIA

GERMANY

GHANA

GREECE

GRENADA

GUATEMALA

GUINEA

GUINEA-BISSAU

GUYANA

HAITI†

HONDURAS

HUNGARY

ICELAND

INDIA

INDONESIA

IRAN

IRAQ

IRELAND

ISRAEL

ITALY

JAMAICA

JAPAN

JORDAN

KAZAKHSTAN

KENYA

KIRIBATI

DEM. PEOPLE'S REPUBLIC OF KOREA

REPUBLIC OF KOREA

KOSOVO

KUWAIT

KYRGYZSTAN

LAOS

LATVIA

LEBANON

LESOTHO

LIBERIA

LIBYA

LIECHTENSTEIN

LITHUANIA

LUXEMBOURG

MADAGASCAR

MALAWI

MALAYSIA

MALDIVES

MALI

MALTA

MARSHALL
ISLANDS

MAURITANIA

MAURITIUS

MEXICO

FEDERATED STATES
OF MICRONESIA

MOLDOVA

MONACO

MONGOLIA

MONTENEGRO

MOROCCO

MOZAMBIQUE

MYANMAR

NAMIBIA

NAURU

NEPAL

THE
NETHERLANDS

NEW ZEALAND

NICARAGUA

NIGER

NIGERIA

NORTH
MACEDONIA

NORWAY

OMAN

PAKISTAN

PALAU

PANAMA

PAPUA NEW
GUINEA

PARAGUAY

PERU

THE PHILIPPINES

POLAND

PORTUGAL

QATAR

ROMANIA

RUSSIAN
FEDERATION

RWANDA

ST CHRISTOPHER
AND NEVIS

ST LUCIA

ST VINCENT AND
THE GRENADINES

SAMOA

SAN MARINO†

 SAO TOME AND PRINCIPE

 SAUDI ARABIA

 SENEGAL

 SERBIA†

 SEYCHELLES

 SIERRA LEONE

 SINGAPORE

 SLOVAKIA

 SLOVENIA

 SOLOMON ISLANDS

 SOMALIA

 SOUTH AFRICA

 SOUTH SUDAN

 SPAIN

 SRI LANKA

 SUDAN

 SURINAME

 SWEDEN

 SWITZERLAND

 SYRIA

 TAIWAN

 TAJIKISTAN

 TANZANIA

 THAILAND

 TOGO

 TONGA

 TRINIDAD AND TOBAGO

 TUNISIA

 TURKEY

 TURKMENISTAN

 TUVALU

 UGANDA

 UKRAINE

 UNITED ARAB EMIRATES

 UNITED KINGDOM

 UNITED STATES OF AMERICA

 URUGUAY

 UZBEKISTAN

 VANUATU

 VATICAN CITY STATE

 VENEZUELA

 VIETNAM

 YEMEN

 ZAMBIA

ZIMBABWE

WORLD PRESS FREEDOM INDEX, 2019

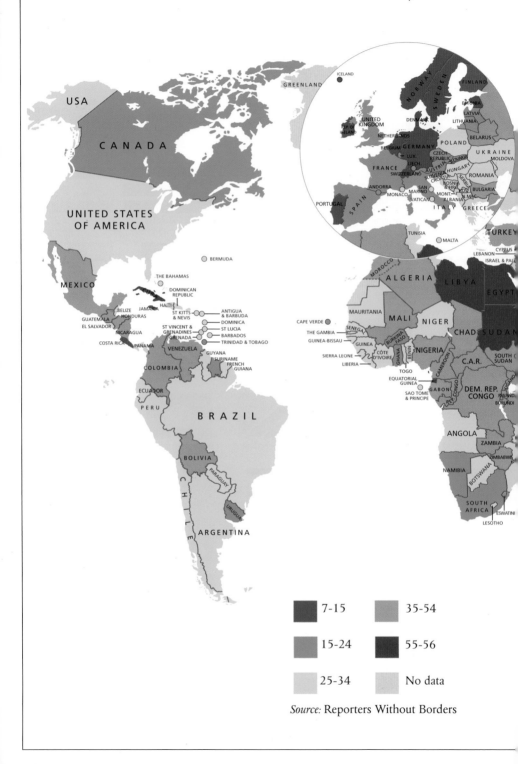

■ 7-15	■ 35-54
■ 15-24	■ 55-56
■ 25-34	□ No data

Source: Reporters Without Borders

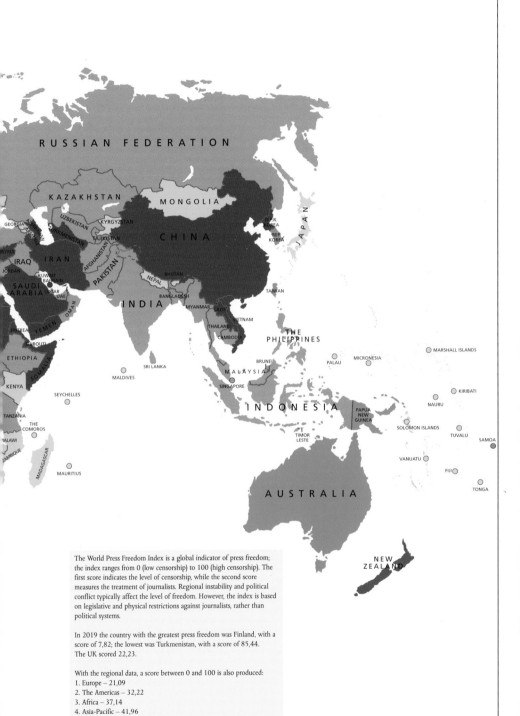

RUSSIAN FEDERATION

KAZAKHSTAN

MONGOLIA

GEORGIA

UZBEKISTAN

KYRGYZSTAN

TURKMENISTAN

TAJIKISTAN

D.P.R. KOREA

REP. KOREA

JAPAN

SYRIA

IRAQ

JORDAN

IRAN

KUWAIT

BAHRAIN

AFGHANISTAN

PAKISTAN

CHINA

SAUDI ARABIA

QATAR

UAE

OMAN

NEPAL

BHUTAN

INDIA

BANGLADESH

MYANMAR

LAOS

TAIWAN

ERITREA

YEMEN

VIETNAM

THAILAND

DJIBOUTI

CAMBODIA

THE PHILIPPINES

MARSHALL ISLANDS

ETHIOPIA

SOMALIA

SRI LANKA

BRUNEI

PALAU

MICRONESIA

KENYA

SEYCHELLES

MALDIVES

MALAYSIA

SINGAPORE

KIRIBATI

NAURU

TANZANIA

THE COMOROS

INDONESIA

PAPUA NEW GUINEA

SOLOMON ISLANDS

TUVALU

MALAWI

SAMOA

ZAMBIQUE

MADAGASCAR

TIMOR LESTE

VANUATU

FIJI

MAURITIUS

TONGA

AUSTRALIA

NEW ZEALAND

The World Press Freedom Index is a global indicator of press freedom;
the index ranges from 0 (low censorship) to 100 (high censorship). The
first score indicates the level of censorship, while the second score
measures the treatment of journalists. Regional instability and political
conflict typically affect the level of freedom. However, the index is based
on legislative and physical restrictions against journalists, rather than
political systems.

In 2019 the country with the greatest press freedom was Finland, with a
score of 7,82; the lowest was Turkmenistan, with a score of 85,44.
The UK scored 22,23.

With the regional data, a score between 0 and 100 is also produced:
1. Europe – 21,09
2. The Americas – 32,22
3. Africa – 37,14
4. Asia-Pacific – 41,96
5. Eastern Europe and Central Asia – 48,03
6. The Middle East and North Africa – 50,26

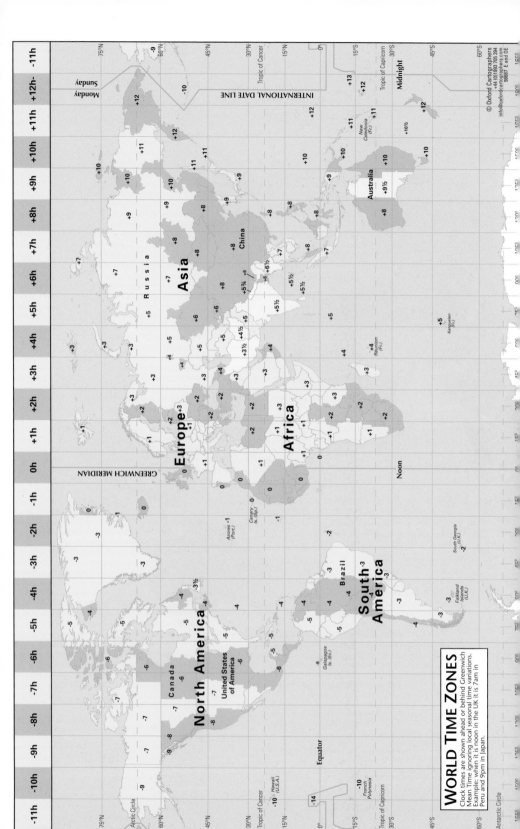

WORLD TIME ZONES

Clock times are shown ahead or behind Greenwich
Mean Time ignoring local seasonal time variations.
Example: when it is noon in the UK it is 7am in
Peru and 9pm in Japan.

© Oxford Cartographers
+44 (0)1993 705 394
info@oxfordcartographers.com
98687 E and OE

on a 'best loser' basis to give more equitable representation to ethnic minorities. The prime minister is the leader of the majority party in the legislature.

Rodrigues has had an 18-member regional assembly, a chief commissioner and a chief executive since 2002.

HEAD OF STATE
President, Prithvirajsing 'Pradeep' Roopun, *elected and sworn in* 2 December 2019

SELECTED GOVERNMENT MEMBERS *AS AT NOVEMBER 2020*
Prime Minister, Finance, Home Affairs, Pravind Jugnauth
Deputy Prime Minister, Ivan Collendavelloo
Vice-Prime Ministers, Leela Dookun-Luchoomun; Mohammad Husnoo
Foreign Affairs, Nandcoomar Bodha

MAURITIUS HIGH COMMISSION
32–33 Elvaston Place, London SW7 5NW
T 020-7581 0294 **E** londonhc@govmu.org
W london.mauritius.gov.mu
High Commissioner, HE Girish Nunkoo, *apptd* 2015

BRITISH HIGH COMMISSION
7th floor, Cascades Building, Edith Cavell Street, PO Box 1063, Port Louis
T (+230) 202 9400 **E** bhc@intnet.mu
W www.gov.uk/government/world/mauritius
High Commissioner, HE Keith Allan, *apptd* 2017

ECONOMY AND TRADE
Since independence Mauritius has developed from an economy dependent on agriculture to one with prospering tourist, manufacturing (primarily of textiles and garments) and financial sectors. Although sugar remains an important commodity (sugar cane is grown on 90 per cent of cultivated land), both the sugar and textile industries are beginning to decline. Diversification into fish processing, information and communications technology, banking, hospitality and property development is being encouraged. The island's attractive business environment has attracted a significant number of offshore businesses with commerce in India, South Africa and China; financial services accounts for 76 per cent of GDP.

The services sector accounts for 74.1 per cent of GDP, industry for 21.8 per cent and agriculture for 4 per cent. The main trading partners are India, the UK, the USA and France. Principal exports are clothing, textiles, sugar, cut flowers, molasses and fish. The main imports are manufactured goods, capital equipment, food, fuels and chemicals.
GNI – US$16.1bn; US$12,740 per capita (2019)
Annual average growth of GDP – 3.8 per cent (2017 est)
Inflation rate – 3.7 per cent (2017 est)
Unemployment – 6.65 per cent (2017 est)
Total external debt – US$19.99bn (2017 est)
Imports – US$7,125m (2017)
Exports – US$5,374m (2017)

BALANCE OF PAYMENTS
Trade – US$1,860m deficit (2017)
Current Account – US$761m deficit (2019)

Trade with UK	2018	2019
Imports from UK	£77,222,655	£78,146,920
Exports to UK	£141,436,965	£124,744,023

COMMUNICATIONS
Airports and waterways – The international airport and the main port are at Port Louis
Roadways – 2,428km, including 99km of motorways
Telecommunications – 470,166 fixed lines and 2.1 million mobile subscriptions (2019); there were 799,470 internet users in 2018
Internet code and IDD – mu; 230 (from UK), 44 (to UK)
Major broadcasters – The state-owned Mauritius Broadcasting Corporation runs television and radio services funded through advertising and a licence fee
Press – Leading dailies include *L'Express, Le Mauricien* and *Le Matinal*
WPFI score – 28.00 (56)

EDUCATION AND HEALTH
Twelve years of education are free and compulsory.
Literacy rate – 91.3 per cent (2018 est)
Gross enrolment ratio (percentage of relevant age group) – primary 99.5 per cent, secondary 97.1 per cent (2019 est); tertiary 40.6 per cent (2017 est)
Health expenditure (per capita) – US$600 (2017)
Hospital beds (per 1,000 people) – 3.59 (2016)
Life expectancy (years) – 76.5 (2020 est)
Mortality rate – 7.3 (2020 est)
Birth rate – 12.6 (2020 est)
Infant mortality rate – 9 (2020 est)
HIV/AIDS adult prevalence – 1.2 per cent (2019 est)

MEXICO

Estados Unidos Mexicanos – United Mexican States

Area – 1,964,375 sq. km
Capital – Mexico City; population, 21,782,000 (2020 est)
Major cities – Ciudad Juárez, Ecatepec, Guadalajara, León, Monterrey, Puebla, Tijuana
Currency – Peso of 100 centavos
Population – 128,649,565 rising at 1.04 per cent a year (2020 est)
Religion – Christian (Roman Catholic 82.7 per cent, Evangelical 8 per cent) (est)
Language – Spanish (official), indigenous languages including dialects of Mayan and Nahuatl
Population density – 65 per sq. km (2019)
Urban population – 80.4 per cent (2019 est)
Median age (years) – 28.6 (2020 est)
National anthem – 'Himno Nacional Mexicano' 'Mexican National Anthem'
National day – 16 September (Independence Day)
Death penalty – Abolished for all crimes (since 2005)
CPI score – 29 (130)
Military expenditure – US$6,568m (2018)
Conscription – 18 years of age; 12 months

CLIMATE AND TERRAIN

The Rio Grande river forms the eastern part of the border with the USA. South of this, coastal plains rise to a central plateau that lies between two spines of high mountains, the Western and the Eastern Sierra Madre, running from the north-west to south-east. The mountains include volcanoes such as Popocatepetl, and in the south are covered with dense jungle. The Yucatán peninsula in the south-east is low-lying, and marshy on the coast. The narrow Baja California peninsula, separated from the rest of the country by the Gulf of California, has a range of hills running along it. Elevation extremes range from 5,700m (Volcan Pico de Orizaba) to −10m (Laguna Salada). The north has a desert climate, while the south is tropical. The average temperature ranges from 16.1°C in January to 25.9°C in June and July.

POLITICS

Under the 1917 constitution, the federal republic consists of 31 states and the federal capital. The head of state is an executive president, directly elected for a single six-year term. The bicameral legislature is the Congress of the Union: the lower house, the Chamber of Deputies, has 500 members, directly elected for a three-year term, and the senate has 128 members, directly elected for a six-year term. The president appoints the cabinet.

Each of the states has its own constitution and is administered by a governor, elected for a six-year term, and a state chamber of deputies, elected for a three-year term.

The Institutional Revolutionary Party's (PRI) political dominance ended at the 1997 election, when it lost its absolute majority in the lower house of the legislature, although it continued in government until 2000 and was again in power from 2003 until 2006. The presidential elections were won by Felipe Calderón of the Partido Accion Nacional (PAN) in 2006 and by the PRI's Enrique Peña Nieto in 2012. The PRI became the largest party in the Chamber of Deputies in the 2012 legislative election, and along with its allies the Green Party and New Alliance Party, increased its majority in the 2015 elections. The three-party *Juntos Haremos Historia* coalition, led by the left-wing National Regeneration Movement party (MORENA), won large majorities in both houses in the July 2018 election. MORENA was founded in 2014 by populist veteran Andrés López Obrador, who won the simultaneous presidential elections on an anti-corruption platform.

Mexico's war on drugs, and cartel-related crime, has continued to shape domestic polities in recent years; in 2019 the national murder rate was nearly 35,000, the highest since 1997.

HEAD OF STATE
President, Andrés López Obrador, *elected* 1 July 2018, *sworn in* 1 December 2018

SELECTED GOVERNMENT MEMBERS *AS AT NOVEMBER 2020*
Defence, Luis Crescencio Sandoval
Economy, Graciela Marquez Colin
Foreign Affairs, Marcelo Ebrard Casaubon
Interior, Olga Sanchez Cordero

EMBASSY OF MEXICO
16 St George Street, London W1S 1FD
T 020-7499 8586 **E** mexuk@sre.gob.mx
W www.sre.gob.mx/reinounido
Ambassador Extraordinary and Plenipotentiary, vacant

BRITISH EMBASSY
Río Lerma 71, Col. Cuauhtémoc, 06500 Mexico City
T (+52) (55) 1670 3200 **E** ukinmexico@fco.gov.uk
W www.gov.uk/government/world/mexico
Ambassador Extraordinary and Plenipotentiary, HE Corin Robertson, *apptd* 2018

ECONOMY AND TRADE

Mexico had a relatively closed economy until the mid-1980s, but increased trade and domestic liberalisation in the 1990s stimulated economic growth and development, particularly in the industrial sector. However, although it has free trade agreements with 46 countries, its economy is still closely tied to that of the USA and experienced a deep recession in 2009 as the global downturn affected its main export market. Since 2013 growth has been incremental, partly due to low global oil prices and the persistence of issues such as high levels of inequality and organised crime. The election of President Trump in the USA had adversely affected the value of the peso and the Mexican economy, especially after fears tariffs would be introduced, but a new trade deal between the two countries was agreed in August 2018. Exports accounts for over 75 per cent of GDP, which declined during the coronavirus pandemic. It is estimated the economy will contract by 9 per cent in 2020.

Agriculture is diverse and productive; major crops include maize, wheat, soya beans, rice, beans, cotton, coffee, fruit, tomatoes, beef, poultry and dairy products. Agriculture accounts for 3.6 per cent of GDP and around 13 per cent of employment. The main industries include production of food, beverages, tobacco, chemicals, iron and steel, textiles, clothing, motor vehicles, consumer durables, oil production, mining and tourism. The services sector accounts for 64.5 per cent of GDP and industry for 31.9 per cent.

The main trading partner is the USA (79.9 per cent of exports; 46.4 per cent of imports). Canada is the other main export market, and China and Japan the other main source of imports. Principal exports include manufactured goods, electronics, oil and oil products, silver, vehicles, and agricultural products. The main imports include metalworking machines, steel mill products, agricultural machinery, electronics, car parts for assembly, vehicle repair parts, aircraft and aircraft parts.

GNI – US$1,203.6bn; US$9,430 per capita (2019)
Annual average growth of GDP – -0.3 per cent (2019 est)
Inflation rate – 6 per cent (2017 est)
Population below poverty line – 46.2 per cent (2014 est)
Unemployment – 3.49 per cent (2019 est)
Total external debt – US$445.8bn (2017 est)
Imports – US$457,632m (2017)
Exports – US$436,846m (2017)

BALANCE OF PAYMENTS
Trade – US$20,786m deficit (2017)
Current Account – US$4,363m deficit (2019)

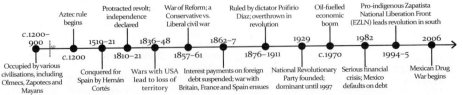

Trade with UK	2018	2019
Imports from UK	£1,509,758,553	£1,413,032,052
Exports to UK	£1,669,537,663	£2,200,075,043

COMMUNICATIONS

Airports – The main international airport is at Mexico City, with 242 others around the country
Waterways – Veracruz, Tampico and Coatzacoalcos are the chief seaports on the east coast, and Guaymas, Mazatlán, Lázaro Cárdenas and Salina Cruz on the Pacific; there are 2,900km of navigable rivers and coastal canals
Roadways and railways – There are 398,148km of roadways, of which 174,191 are paved; 20,825km
Telecommunications – 22.5 million fixed lines and 121.1 million mobile subscriptions (2019); there were 82.8 million internet users in 2018
Internet code and IDD – mx; 52 (from UK), 44 (to UK)
Major broadcasters – The Televisa group used to dominate broadcasting but now competes with other television channels and a huge number of independent radio stations
Press – Leading dailies include *Excelsior, La Jornada* and *Reforma*
WPFI score – 45.45 (143)

EDUCATION AND HEALTH

Education is compulsory in Mexico for ten years from age six, although attainment varies among states.
Literacy rate – 95.4 per cent (2018 est)
Gross enrolment ratio (percentage of relevant age group) – primary 105 per cent, secondary 105.1per cent, tertiary 41.5 per cent (2018 est)
Health expenditure (per capita) – US$495 (2017)
Hospital beds (per 1,000 people) – 1.5 (2015)
Life expectancy (years) – 76.7 (2020 est)
Mortality rate – 5.4 (2020 est)
Birth rate – 17.6 (2020 est)
Infant mortality rate – 10.7 (2020 est)
HIV/AIDS adult prevalence – 0.3 per cent (2016 est)

FEDERATED STATES OF MICRONESIA

Area – 702 sq. km
Capital – Palikir, on Pohnpei; population, 7,000 (2018)
Major towns – Kolonia, Weno
Currency – US dollar (US$) of 100 cents
Population – 102,436 falling at 0.6 per cent a year (2020 est); Chuukese (49.3 per cent), Pohnpeian (29.8 per cent), Kosraen (6.3 per cent), Yapese (5.7 per cent), Yap outer islanders (5.1 per cent) (est)
Religion – Christian (Roman Catholic 54.7 per cent, Protestant 41.1 per cent, Mormon 1.5 per cent) (est)
Language – English (official), Chuukese, Kosraen, Pohnpeian, Yapese, Ulithian, Woleaian, Nukuoro, Kapingamarangi
Population density – 161 per sq. km (2019)
Urban population – 22.8 per cent (2019 est)

Median age (years) – 26.3 (2020 est)
National anthem – 'Patriots of Micronesia'
National day – 10 May (Constitution Day)
Death penalty – Not since independence
Gross enrolment ratio (percentage of relevant age group) – primary 96.8 per cent (2018 est)
Health expenditure (per capita) – US$425 (2017 est)
Life expectancy (years) – 73.9 (2020 est)
Mortality rate – 4.3 (2020 est)
Birth rate – 18.9 (2020 est)
Infant mortality rate – 17.8 (2020 est)

CLIMATE AND TERRAIN

The republic consists of four major island groups totalling over 600 mountainous volcanic islands and low-lying atolls, extending over 2,900 sq. km of the western Pacific Ocean. Elevation extremes range from 791m (Dolohmwar) to 0m (Pacific Ocean). The climate is tropical, with only slight seasonal variations in temperatures; there is a stormy season between July and November. The islands are vulnerable to the effects of global warming, particularly an increase in the frequency and intensity of cyclones in the region.

HISTORY AND POLITICS

Inhabited since around 4,000 BC by migrants from the Philippines and Indonesia, Micronesia experienced contact with Europeans from the 1520s, and the islands were colonised by Spain from the 16th century. German encroachment in the 1870s and 1880s was resisted until 1899, when Germany purchased the islands from Spain. The islands were occupied by Japan on behalf of the Allies during the First World War, and administered as a League of Nations mandated territory by Japan from 1920 until the Japanese defeat in the Second World War. In 1947 the islands became part of the UN Trust Territory of the Pacific, administered by the USA.

A constitution was adopted in 1979 and the islands became independent in 1986 under a compact of free association with the USA, by which the USA retains responsibility for defence and provides substantial financial aid; a renegotiated agreement came into force in 2004. The UN trusteeship was formally terminated in 1990.

Peter Christian was elected president in March 2015, but his term in office was marred by a bribery scandal and he lost his seat in the March 2019 legislative elections. Christian was replaced by David Panuelo in May.

The 1979 constitution established a federal republic of four states: Chuuk, Kosrae, Pohnpei and Yap. The federal head of state is an executive president, who is elected by the federal legislature for a four-year term, renewable once. The unicameral congress has 14 members, ten senators directly elected for a two-year term and four senators 'at large' (one from each state) elected for a four-year term; the president and vice-president must be selected from among the 'at large' senators. The federal cabinet is appointed by the president and approved by the congress. There are no formal political parties.

Each state has its own constitution, legislature and government.

HEAD OF STATE

President, David Panuelo, *elected and sworn in* 11 May 2019
Vice-President, Yosiwo George

SELECTED GOVERNMENT MEMBERS *AS AT*
NOVEMBER 2020
Finance, Eugene Amor
Foreign Affairs, Kandhi Elieisar
Justice, Joses Gallen

BRITISH AMBASSADOR
HE Melanie Hopkins, *apptd* 2016, resident at Suva, Fiji

ECONOMY AND TRADE

Micronesia has few natural resources apart from phosphate, which is not exploited, and is highly dependent on aid from the USA, which constitutes 40 per cent of government revenue. These subsidies are scheduled to end in 2023, and the government is looking to China for future support. The main economic activities are subsistence farming and fishing, which account for 26.3 per cent of GDP, but both are threatened by climate change and over-fishing. The islands' remoteness and lack of facilities has constrained the development of tourism, the main industry; other industries include construction, fish processing, specialised aquaculture and handicrafts. Two-thirds of the workforce is employed by the government. The main trading partners are the USA and Japan. Principal exports are fish, kava, betel nuts and black pepper. The main imports are food, manufactured goods and clothing.
GNI – US$0.4bn; US$3,400 per capita (2018)
Annual average growth of GDP – 2.0 per cent (2017 est)
Inflation rate – 0.5 per cent (2017 est)
Total external debt – US$93.6m (2013 est)
Imports – US$117m (2014)
Exports – US$19m (2014)

BALANCE OF PAYMENTS
Current Account – US$22,186m deficit (2018)

Trade with UK	2018	2019
Imports from UK	£82,234	£106,889
Exports to UK	–	£12,600

COMMUNICATIONS

Transport – There are six airports, including major airports on the four main islands; the main seaports are Colonia (Yap), Kolonia (Pohnpei), Lele and Moen; most interior roads are unpaved
Telecommunications – 6,420 fixed lines and 21,374 mobile subscriptions (2019); there were 36,586 internet users in 2018
Internet code and IDD – fm; 691 (from UK), 011 44 (to UK)
Media – The federal government produces a fortnightly information bulletin and state governments produce weekly news publications; the majority of television programming is imported

MOLDOVA

Republica Moldova – Republic of Moldova

Area – 33,851 sq. km
Capital – Chisinau; population, 499,000 (2020 est)

Major towns – Balti, Tighina, Tiraspol
Currency – Moldovan leu (plural lei) of 100 bani
Population – 3,364,496 falling at 1.08 per cent a year (2020 est); Moldovan (75.1 per cent), Romanian (7.0 per cent), Ukrainian (6.6 per cent), Gagauz (4.6 per cent), Russian (4.1 per cent), Bulgarian (1.9 per cent) (est)
Religion – Christian (Orthodox 90.1 per cent, other Christian 2.6 per cent) (est)
Language – Moldovan (official; linguistically identical to Romanian), Russian, Gagauz, Ukrainian, Bulgarian, Romani
Population density – 94 per sq. km (2019)
Urban population – 42.7 per cent (2019 est)
Median age (years) – 37.7 (2020 est)
National anthem – 'Limba Noastra' 'Our Language'
National day – 27 August (Independence Day)
Death penalty – Abolished for all crimes (since 1995)
CPI score – 32 (126)
Military expenditure – US$34m (2018)
Conscription – 18 years of age; 12 months

CLIMATE AND TERRAIN

The landlocked country consists of rolling steppe lying mostly between the Prut and Dniester rivers. Elevation extremes range from 430m (Dealul Balanesti) at the highest point to 2m (river Dniester) at the lowest. The climate is continental, and average temperatures range from −1.5°C in January to 22.4°C in July.

POLITICS

The 1997 constitution was amended in 2000 to increase the powers of the legislature and the executive. The head of state is the president who, following a ruling in 2016, is now directly elected for a four-year term, renewable once. The unicameral legislature, the *Parlamentul,* has 101 members, who are directly elected for a four-year term. The prime minister is nominated by the president.

The governments in the first decade after independence were made up of moderate reformists, but there was a resurgence in support for the Communist Party of Moldova (PCM), which won the majority of seats in the 1998, 2001, 2005, 2009 (April and July) and 2010 legislative elections, forming the government from 2005 to 2009. Pro-Western parties formed coalition governments after legislative elections in 2010 and 2014, despite the PCM emerging as the single largest party in both elections. However, in the 2019 elections the PCM lost all its seats.

Pro-Moscow candidate Igor Dodon was elected president in November 2016, and has since been temporarily suspended three times for clashing with the Moldovan Constitutional Court after rejecting ministerial appointments and refusing to sign laws. Four months of talks followed the February 2019 legislative elections and resulted in an unlikely coalition between the pro-Russian Party of Socialists and the pro-European ACUM party, but the constitutional court declared the government invalid after just one day, suspended Dodon's presidential powers and transferred them to incumbent prime minister Pavel Filip. Filip subsequently dissolved parliament and called for early elections, but this was rejected by the opposition and two rival governments were formed. Under international pressure to end the crisis, Filip and the Democratic Party resigned and the coalition took power in June, only to collapse in November. It was replaced by a pro-Russian minority government led by Ion Chicu and other Dodon allies.

HEAD OF STATE
President, Igor Dodon, *sworn in* 23 December 2016

Becomes part of a larger Moldovan kingdom | Bessarabia granted to Russia | Area returned to USSR; becomes the Moldavian Soviet Socialist Republic | Recaptured by USSR | Joins Commonwealth of Independent States following collapse of USSR

106 — 1350 — 1500-1800 — 1812 — 1918 — 1940 — 1941 — 1944 — 1990 — 1991 — 1994

Part of the Roman province of Dacia (known as Bessarabia) | Territory contested by Ottoman and Russian empires | Becomes province of Romania following Russian Revolution | Area retaken by Romania | Parliament asserts its political and economic sovereignty | Referendum endorses independence

SELECTED GOVERNMENT MEMBERS *AS AT NOVEMBER 2020*
Prime Minister, Ion Chicu
Deputy Prime Ministers, Sergiu Puscuta *(Finance)*; Christina Lesnic
Defence, Alexandru Pinzari
Economy, Sergiu Railean

EMBASSY OF THE REPUBLIC OF MOLDOVA
5 Dolphin Square, Edensor Road, London W4 2ST
T 020-8995 6818 **E** embassy.london@mfa.md
W www.britania.mfa.gov.md
Ambassador Extraordinary and Plenipotentiary, Angela Ponomariov, *appt* 2018

BRITISH EMBASSY
18/1 Nicolae Iorga Str., Chisinau, MD-2012
T (+373) 222 225902 **E** enquiries.chisinau@fco.gov.uk
W www.gov.uk/government/world/moldova
Ambassador Extraordinary and Plenipotentiary, HE Steven Fisher, *apptd* 2019

SECESSION
Moldovan nationalism in the late 1980s and possible reunification with Romania alarmed the republic's Russian and Ukrainian ethnic minorities in the Transdniestria region (east of the Dniester) and the Gagauz (Turkish-speaking Christians) in the south-west. Both areas declared independence unilaterally in 1990, though this was not recognised. The regions were granted a special status by the 1994 constitution, and the Gagauz have since exercised a degree of autonomy over their political, economic and cultural affairs.

In response to the Russian takeover of Crimea, in March 2014 then-president Nicolae Timofti warned Russia against trying to annex Transdniestria while also calling on the EU to fast-track Moldova's entry into the organisation in order to deter invasion.

ECONOMY AND TRADE
Moldova is one of the poorest countries in Europe, despite moves towards a market economy since independence. With few natural resources and most industry lying in the breakaway Transdniestria region, the economy is dependent on agriculture and remittances from around 1 million expatriate workers (roughly 15 per cent of GDP), and the country remains one of the poorest in Europe despite declining poverty levels. Following the global downturn, the economy recovered in 2011, but a £700m bank heist in November 2014 robbed the country of one-eighth of its GDP and had ongoing political and economic repercussions, pushing the economy into recession from mid-2015. An IMF loan was approved in November 2016, easing public finances and contributing to better-than-expected growth in recent years, but the coronavirus pandemic is expected to contract the economy by 4.5 per cent in 2020. Moldova heavily depends on imported natural gas from Russia, to which it is indebted, but economic growth since 2014 has been fuelled by a comprehensive free trade agreement with the EU.

The agricultural sector accounts for 17.7 per cent of GDP. Principal crops include vegetables, fruit, wine, grain, sugar beet, sunflower seeds, tobacco, beef and milk. Major industrial activities include food processing and production of sugar, vegetable oil, agricultural machinery, foundry equipment, domestic appliances, footwear and textiles. Industry accounts for 20.3 per cent of GDP and services for 62 per cent.

The main trading partners are Russia, Romania and EU nations. Principal exports are foodstuffs, textiles and machinery. The main imports are mineral products and fuel, machinery and equipment, chemicals and textiles.
GNI – US$10.6bn; US$3,930 per capita (2018)
Annual average growth of GDP – 4.5 per cent (2017 est)
Inflation rate – 6.6 per cent (2017 est)
Population below poverty line – 9.6 per cent (2015 est)
Unemployment – 6.99 per cent (2019 est)
Total external debt – US$6.549bn (2017 est)
Imports – US$5,364m (2017)
Exports – US$3,114m (2017)

BALANCE OF PAYMENTS
Trade – US$2,249m deficit (2017)
Current Account – US$1,11980m deficit (2019)

Trade with UK	2018	2019
Imports from UK	£39,167,002	£23,947,806
Exports to UK	£43,924,194	£33,791,462

COMMUNICATIONS
Airports and waterways – There are five airports, including the principal airport at Chisinau; there are 558km of navigable waterways on the Prut, Dniester and Danube rivers
Roadways and railways – 9,352km; 1,190km
Telecommunications – 901,317 million fixed lines and 3 million mobile subscriptions (2019); there were 2.6 million internet users in 2018
Internet code and IDD – md; 373 (from UK), 44 (to UK)
Major broadcasters – Public networks Moldova One (TV) and Radio Moldova broadcasts nationally alongside Russian and Romanian stations
Press – Major daily newspapers include *Timpul, Flux* (both in Moldovan) and *Kommersant Moldoviy* (Russian language)
WPFI score – 31.16 (91)

EDUCATION AND HEALTH
Literacy rate – 100 per cent (2015 est)
Gross enrolment ratio (percentage of relevant age group) – primary 89.5 per cent, secondary 86.4 per cent, tertiary 39.2 per cent (2019 est)
Health expenditure (per capita) – US$191 (2017)
Hospital beds (per 1,000 people) – 5.8 (2013)
Life expectancy (years) – 71.9 (2020 est)
Mortality rate – 12.6 (2020 est)
Birth rate – 10.7 (2020 est)
Infant mortality rate – 11.1 (2020 est)
HIV/AIDS adult prevalence – 0.7 per cent (2019 est)

MONACO

Principauté de Monaco – Principality of Monaco

Area – 2 sq. km
Capital – Monaco; population, 39,000 (2018 est)
Major town – Monte Carlo
Currency – Euro (€) of 100 cents
Population – 39,000 growing at 0.37 per cent a year (2020 est); Monegasque (32.1 per cent), French (19.9 per cent), Italian (15.3 per cent) (est)
Religion – Christian (officially Roman Catholic 90 per cent), other 10 per cent (est)
Language – French (official), English, Italian, Monegasque
Population density – 19,196 per sq. km (2019)
Urban population – 100 per cent (2019 est)
Median age (years) – 55.4 (2020 est)
National anthem – 'Hymne Monegasque' 'Hymn of Monaco'
National day – 19 November (St Rainier's Day)
Death penalty – Abolished for all crimes (since 1962)
Health expenditure (per capita) – US$2,932 (2017)
Life expectancy (years) – 89.3 (2020 est)
Mortality rate – 10.8 (2020 est)
Birth rate – 6.4 (2020 est)
Infant mortality rate – 1.9 (2020 est)

CLIMATE AND TERRAIN

Monaco lies on 4km of steep, rugged coastline. It has been expanded by 0.3 sq. km with land reclaimed from the sea by infilling. Elevation extremes range from 140m (Mt Agel) to 0m (Mediterranean Sea). The climate is Mediterranean, with average temperatures ranging from 6.6°C in January to 22°C in August.

HISTORY AND POLITICS

Monaco has been ruled by the Grimaldi family since the 13th century. Monarchical France recognised Monaco's independence in the 15th century, but Revolutionary France annexed it in 1793. Although the prince was restored to power in 1814, Monaco did not regain its independence until 1861. It was occupied by the Italians and subsequently by the Germans in the Second World War. The principality's foreign relations and security have been aligned to those of France since 1861 by various treaties; the terms were changed in 2005 to allow Monaco greater control over its foreign relations and internal administration.

The 1962 constitution was amended in 2002 to allow the throne to pass through the female line in the absence of male heirs. Legislative power is held jointly by the prince and a 24-member National Council, which is directly elected for a five-year term. Executive power is exercised by the prince and a six-member Council of Government, headed by a minister of state who is nominated by the prince and approved by the French government. The judicial code is based on that of France.

In the 2018 legislative election, the Priority Party won 21 seats and reduced the previously dominant Horizon Monaco Party's 20 seats to just two. Serge Telle replaced Michel Roger as head of the government in February 2016.

HEAD OF STATE
HSH The Prince of Monaco, Prince Albert II (Alexandre Louis Pierre), *born* 14 March 1958, *succeeded* 6 April 2005
Heir, HSH Prince Jaques (Crown Prince), *born* 10 December 2014

SELECTED GOVERNMENT MEMBERS *AS AT NOVEMBER 2020*
Minister of State, Pierre Dartout
Finance and Economy, Jean Castellini
Foreign Affairs, Laurent Anselmi

EMBASSY OF THE PRINCIPALITY OF MONACO
7 Upper Grosvenor Street, London W1K 2LX
T 020-7318 1078 **E** embassy.uk@gouv.mc
W www.monaco-embassy-uk.gouv.mc
Ambassador Extraordinary and Plenipotentiary, HE Evelyne Genta, *apptd* 2010

BRITISH HONORARY CONSULATE
Contact British Consulate Marseille, 24 Avenue du Prado, 13006 Marseille
T (+33) (0) 4 9115 7210

ECONOMY AND TRADE

The economy has diversified away from its historic dependence on tourism and gambling, and over half its revenue now comes from financial services, retail, real estate, construction and light industry (chemicals, pharmaceuticals, cosmetics, medical devices, plastics, electronics).

As the state collects no taxes from individuals and little from businesses, it has become a tax haven for wealthy expatriates and foreign companies. However, in 2016 the nation joined the OECD's multilateral efforts to tackle tax avoidance and evasion. The state retains monopolies in a number of sectors, including tobacco, the telephone network and the postal service. Since 1963 Monaco has been in a customs union with France, and through this it participates in the EU market. Over half its trade is with EU countries, particularly France and Italy.

GNI – US$6,075m; US$167,021 per capita (2011)
Annual average growth of GDP – 5.4 per cent (2015 est)
Unemployment – 2 per cent (2012)

COMMUNICATIONS

Transport – The nearest international airport is the Côte d'Azur airport in Nice, France; the installation of a large floating jetty in 2002 doubled the port of Monaco's capacity to handle cruise ships; there are 77km of roads and a single railway station, Monaco-Monte Carlo
Telecommunications – 34,903 fixed lines and 26,725 mobile subscriptions (2019); there were 29,821 internet users in 2018
Internet code and IDD – mc; 377 (from UK), 44 (to UK)
Media – Monaco has one television station and the principality's news is covered by the French press

MONGOLIA

Mongol Uls – Mongolia

Area – 1,564,116 sq. km
Capital – Ulaanbaatar; population, 1,584,000 (2020 est)
Major towns – Darhan, Erdenet
Currency – Tugrik of 100 mongo
Population – 3,168,026 rising at 0.99 per cent a year (2020 est); Khalkh (84.5 per cent), Kazakh (3.9 per cent), Dorvod (2.4 per cent) (est)
Religion – Buddhist 53 per cent, Muslim 3 per cent, Shamanist 2.9 per cent, Christian 2.2 per cent (est)
Language – Khalkha Mongol (official), Turkic, Russian
Population density – 2 per sq. km (2019)
Urban population – 68.5 per cent (2019 est)
Median age (years) – 29.8 (2020 est)
National anthem – 'Mongol ulsyn toriin duulal' 'National Anthem of Mongolia'
National day – 11–15 July (Revolution Day)
Death penalty – Abolished for all crimes (since 2017)
CPI score – 35 (106)
Military expenditure – US$96m (2018)
Conscription – 18–27 years of age, male only; 12 months
Literacy rate – 98.4 per cent (2018 est)
Gross enrolment ratio (percentage of relevant age group) – primary 104 per cent (2018 est); secondary 91.5 per cent (2015 est); tertiary 65.6 per cent (2018 est)
Health expenditure (per capita) – US$149 (2017)
Hospital beds (per 1,000 people) – 7 (2012)
Life expectancy (years) – 70.8 (2020 est)
Mortality rate – 6.3 (2020 est)
Birth rate – 16.6 (2020 est)
Infant mortality rate – 19.2 (2020 est)
HIV/AIDS adult prevalence – 0.1 per cent (2019 est)

CLIMATE AND TERRAIN

The eastern part of Mongolia lies on a semi-desert plateau, with steppes rising to the Mongolian Altai and Hangai mountain ranges in the west. The Gobi desert covers the southern third of the country. Elevation extremes range from 4,374m (Nayramadlin Orgil) to 560m (Hoh Nuur). The country has long, cold winters, which quickly turn into short and warm summers. The wet season runs from June to September. Average temperatures range from −20.1°C in January to 18.5°C in July.

POLITICS

The 1992 constitution was amended in 2000 to give the president the right to dissolve the legislature if it is unable to reach agreement on appointing a prime minister. The president is directly elected for a four-year term, which is renewable once. The unicameral State Great Hural has 76 members who are directly elected for a four-year term. The prime minister is elected by the legislature and appoints the cabinet.

The opposition Mongolian People's Party (MPP) swept back to power with a landslide in legislative elections in June 2016, winning 65 seats in parliament, and maintained its majority in the June 2020 elections. Jargaltulga Erdenebat was appointed prime minister in July but was voted out of office over allegations of corruption in September 2017, being replaced by Ukhnaa Khurelsukh. The 2017 presidential election was won in the second round by Khaltmaa Battulga, who replaced Tsakhiagiin Elbegdorj (prime minister 1998, 2004–6; president 2009–17).

HEAD OF STATE

President, Khaltmaa Battulga, *elected* 7 July 2017, *sworn in* 10 July 2017

SELECTED GOVERNMENT MEMBERS *AS AT NOVEMBER 2020*
Prime Minister, Ukhnaa Khurelsukh
Deputy Prime Minister, Yangug Sodbaatar
Defence, Gursed Saikhanbayar
Foreign Affairs, Nyamtseren Enkhtaivan

EMBASSY OF MONGOLIA
7–8 Kensington Court, London W8 5DL
T 020-7937 0150 **E** office@embassyofmongolia.co.uk
W www.embassyofmongolia.co.uk
Ambassador Extraordinary and Plenipotentiary, HE Tulga Narkhuu, *apptd* 2018

BRITISH EMBASSY
Peace Avenue 30, Bayanzurkh District, Ulaanbaatar 13381
T (+976) (11) 458 133 **E** enquiries.mongolia@fco.gov.uk
W www.gov.uk/government/world/mongolia
Ambassador Extraordinary and Plenipotentiary, HE Philip Malone, LVO, *apptd* 2018

ECONOMY AND TRADE

The economy suffered during the transition to a market economy but recovered before the global economic downturn in 2008. Declining commodity prices and export demand, and soaring inflation, caused difficulties that forced the government to seek an IMF loan in spring 2009. Mongolia has attracted foreign investment, particularly in mining, agricultural processing and infrastructure, but administrative corruption, dependency on imported energy supplies (mostly from Russia) and the vulnerability of the agrarian sector to climate extremes continue to hinder growth. In 2017 the IMF agreed a US$440m loan as part of a US$5.5bn bailout package that, alongside expansion of the Oyu Tolgoi copper and gold mine in the Gobi desert and rising commodity

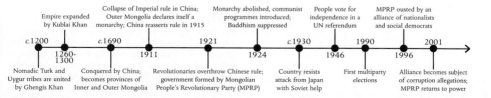

Empire expanded by Kublai Khan — c.1200

1260-1300 — Nomadic Turk and Uygur tribes are united by Ghengis Khan

Collapse of Imperial rule in China; Outer Mongolia declares itself a monarchy; China reasserts rule in 1915 — c.1690

1911 — Conquered by China; becomes provinces of Inner and Outer Mongolia

1921 — Revolutionaries overthrow Chinese rule; government formed by Mongolian People's Revolutionary Party (MPRP)

Monarchy abolished, communist programmes introduced; Buddhism suppressed — 1924

c.1930 — Country resists attack from Japan with Soviet help

People vote for independence in a UN referendum — 1946

1990 — First multiparty elections

MPRP ousted by an alliance of nationalists and social democrats — 1996

2001 — Alliance becomes subject of corruption allegations; MPRP returns to power

prices, significantly boosted GDP growth in recent years. With GDP per capita having tripled in the past 25 years, poverty has fallen (around one third live below the poverty line) and educational opportunities greatly improved.

Deposits of copper, coal, molybdenum, fluorspar, tin, tungsten, uranium, gold and oil are being exploited; copper and gold sales are major drivers of recent economic growth. The agrarian sector, which makes up 12.1 per cent of GDP, engages 31.1 per cent of the workforce in agriculture and herding. The main products are grains, vegetables, forage crops, sheep, goats and other livestock. The main industries are construction, mining, processing animal products, and the production of oil, food and beverages, cashmere and natural yarns.

The main export markets are China (85 per cent) and the UK; the main import providers are China (32.6 per cent) and Russia (28.1 per cent). Exports, which account for over 40 per cent of GDP, include copper, clothing, livestock, animal products, cashmere, wool, hides, fluorspar, metals and coal. The main imports are machinery and equipment, fuels, cars, foodstuffs, industrial consumer goods, chemicals and construction materials.

GNI – US$12.2bn; US$3,780 per capita (2019)
Annual average growth of GDP – 5.1 per cent (2017 est)
Inflation rate – 4.6 per cent (2017 est)
Population below poverty line – 29.6 per cent (2016 est)
Unemployment – 8 per cent (2017 est)
Total external debt – US$25.33bn (2017 est)
Imports – US$6,546m (2017)
Exports – US$6,244m (2017)

BALANCE OF PAYMENTS
Trade – US$301m deficit (2017)
Current Account – US$2,161m deficit (2019)

Trade with UK	2018	2019
Imports from UK	£19,432,617	£18,255,382
Exports to UK	£5,729,681	£8,767,252

COMMUNICATIONS

Airports and waterways – The main airport is at Ulaanbaatar – there are 14 other airports around the country; the 580km of waterways are navigable in the summer months although Lake Hovsgol near the Russian border is the only waterway in commercial operation
Roadways and railways – 10,600km of paved roads; 1,815km
Telecommunications – 385,191 fixed lines and 4.3 million mobile subscriptions (2019); there were 735,823 internet users in 2018
Internet code and IDD – mn; 976 (from UK), 1 44 (to UK)
Major broadcasters – Mongolian National Broadcaster (MNB) is the state-owned national television broadcaster; the publicly owned Mongolian Radio is the only radio station with national coverage
Press – Major national dailies include *Onoodor,* which has the biggest circulation, and *Unen* (Truth), the organ of the MPRP and the country's oldest newspaper
WPFI score – 29.61 (73)

MONTENEGRO

Crna Gora – Montenegro

Area – 13,812 sq. km
Capital – Podgorica; population, 177,000 (2018)
Major cities – Cetinje (historic and cultural capital), Niksic, Pljevlja
Currency – Euro (€) of 100 cents
Population – 609,859 falling at 0.37 per cent a year (2020 est); Montenegrin (45 per cent), Serbian (28.7 per cent), Bosniak (8.7 per cent), Albanian (4.9 per cent) (est)
Religion – Christian (Orthodox 72.1 per cent, Roman Catholic 3.4 per cent), Muslim 19.1 per cent (est)
Language – Montenegrin (a version of Serbo-Croat) (official), Serbian, Bosnian, Albanian, Croatian
Population density – 46 per sq. km (2019)
Urban population – 67.2 per cent (2019 est)
Median age (years) – 39.6 (2020 est)
National anthem – 'Oj, Svijetla Majska Zoro' 'Oh, Bright Dawn of May'
National day – 13 July (Statehood Day)
Death penalty – Abolished for all crimes (since 2002)
CPI score – 45 (66)
Military expenditure – US$83.8m (2018)
Literacy rate – 98.8 per cent (2018 est)
Gross enrolment ratio (percentage of relevant age group) – primary 100.6 per cent, secondary 90.1 per cent, tertiary 54.2 per cent (2019 est)
Health expenditure (per capita) – US$458 (2014)
Life expectancy (years) – 77.3 (2020 est)
Mortality rate – 10.4 (2020 est)
Birth rate – 11.5 (2020 est)
Infant mortality rate – 3.4 (2020 est)
HIV/AIDS adult prevalence – 0.1 (2019 est)

CLIMATE AND TERRAIN

The terrain is mountainous in the north and centre of the country, intersected by deep canyons and river valleys, and falls to a narrow plain on the highly indented Adriatic coast. About 40 per cent of the country is forested. Elevation extremes range from 2,522m (Bobotov Kuk) to 0m (Adriatic Sea). The main rivers are the Piva (Drina), the Tara and the Lim. Lake Skadarsko straddles the border with Albania. The climate is Mediterranean on the coast, but more continental inland. Average temperatures in Podgorica range from 0.1°C in January to 20.2°C in July and August.

HISTORY AND POLITICS

The area was part of the Roman province of Illyria, and then was settled by Slavs in the seventh century. In the late 12th century it was incorporated into the medieval kingdom of Serbia and so became part of the Ottoman Empire after Serbia's defeat by the Turks in 1389. When Serbia became independent in 1878, Montenegro followed and remained an independent monarchy until the end of the First World War. In 1918, Montenegro joined with Serbia and the former Austro-Hungarian provinces of Slovenia, Croatia and Bosnia-Hercegovina to form the Kingdom of Serbs, Croats and Slovenes, which was renamed Yugoslavia in 1929. Yugoslavia was occupied by Axis forces in 1941, and after liberation it reformed as a communist federal republic in 1945. When the federation disintegrated in 1991, Serbia and Montenegro formed the Federal Republic of Yugoslavia, declared on 27 April 1992.

Montenegro's desire for independence led in 2002 to an EU-brokered agreement between the leaders of Serbia, Montenegro and the Federal Republic of Yugoslavia that restructured the republic into a union of two semi-independent states, named Serbia and Montenegro, with effect from March 2003. The agreement provided for the two republics to hold referendums on whether to retain or end the union after a minimum of three years. In a referendum held in Montenegro on 21 May 2006, 55.5 per cent voted in favour of independence, which was declared on 3 June and acknowledged by Serbia on 5 June. Montenegro joined the UN in June 2006, and formally applied for EU membership in 2008.

In December 2012, Milo Djukanovic became prime minister for the seventh time. He claimed victory in the October 2016 legislative election but resigned nine days later, alleging a foreign power had been involved in a plot to seize power on election day, and returned to win the 2018 presidential election on a pro-EU platform. Large anti-government protests in 2019 against corruption resulted in victory for opposition parties in the August 2020 parliamentary election. A 'pro-European and pro-Western' coalition will take power in November, formed of three parties.

Under the 2007 constitution, the president is directly elected for a five-year term, which is renewable once. The unicameral Assembly of the Republic of Montenegro has 81 members directly elected for a four-year term; five members are elected from the ethnic Albanian community. The prime minister appoints the cabinet, subject to the approval of the assembly.

HEAD OF STATE
President, Milo Djukanovic, *elected* 15 April 2018, *sworn in* 20 May 2018

SELECTED GOVERNMENT MEMBERS *AS AT OCTOBER 2020*
Prime Minister, Dusko Markovic
Deputy Prime Ministers, Zoran Pazin *(Justice);* Rafet Husovic; Milutin Simovic
Defence, Predrag Boskovic
Foreign Affairs, Srdan Darmanovic

EMBASSY OF MONTENEGRO
47 De Vere Gardens, London W8 5AW
T 020-3302 7227 **E** unitedkingdom@mfa.gov.me
Ambassador Extraordinary and Plenipotentiary, vacnt

BRITISH EMBASSY
Ulcinjska 8, Gorica C, 81000 Podgorica
T (+382) (20) 618 010 **E** podgorica@fco.gov.uk
W www.gov.uk/government/world/montenegro
Ambassador Extraordinary and Plenipotentiary, HE Alison Kemp, apptd 2017

ECONOMY AND TRADE

Montenegro achieved fiscal autonomy from the Yugoslav federation in the 1990s. However, it faced the same problems as Serbia – slow growth, foreign debt, lack of foreign investment, high unemployment, corruption and organised crime – as well as having more limited health and education facilities, and a poor administrative capacity. Since independence, it has pursued international integration and privatisation, prioritising in particular its bid for EU membership. Negotiations for membership began in 2012, and although it uses the euro as its domestic currency, it is not officially a member of the eurozone. It has privatised roughly 90 per cent of state-owned companies, and in recent years has invested in hydropower generation with the aim of becoming a net exporter of energy. The construction of several luxury tourism complexes has contributed to rising numbers of visitors, at around three times the population and accounting for over 20 per cent of GDP, but the coronavirus pandemic has negatively impacted this industry and the economy is expected to contract by 12 per cent in 2020. Rising public debt, a result of major infrastructure spending, has been partly offset by significant direct foreign investment, which per capita is one of the highest in Europe.

The main agricultural products are tobacco, potatoes, citrus fruits and olives. Major industrial activities include production of steel, aluminium and consumer goods, processing of agricultural products and tourism. The main trading partners are EU and other Balkan countries.
GNI – US$11.4bn; US$8,400 per capita (2018)
Annual average growth of GDP – 3.0 per cent (2017 est)
Inflation rate – 2.1 per cent (2017 est)
Population below poverty line – 8.6 per cent (2013 est)
Unemployment – 17.1 per cent (2016 est)
Total external debt – US$1.576bn (2014 est)
Imports – US$3,138m (2017)
Exports – US$2,005m (2017)

BALANCE OF PAYMENTS
Trade – US$1,132m deficit (2017)
Current Account – US$1,902m deficit (2018)

Trade with UK	2018	2019
Imports from UK	£16,049,999	£41,703,403
Exports to UK	£6,122,639	£6,733,471

COMMUNICATIONS

Airports and waterways – There are five airports, including international airports at Podgorica and Tivat; the major seaport is located at Bar
Roadways and railways – 7,762km of roadways; 250km of railway track linking the Adriatic port of Bar with Belgrade, via Podgorica
Telecommunications – 183,387 fixed lines and 1.1 million mobile subscriptions (2019); there were 439,311 internet users in 2018
Internet code and IDD – me; 382 (from UK), 44 (to UK)
Major broadcasters – The state-funded TV Montenegro and Radio Montenegro operate national stations
Press – Leading national papers include *Vijesti, Pobjeda, Republika* and *Dan*
WPFI score – 33.83 (105)

MOROCCO

Al-Mamlakah al-Maghribiyah – Kingdom of Morocco

Area – 446,550 sq. km
Capital – Rabat; population, 1,885,000 (2020 est)
Major cities – Agadir, Casablanca, Fez, Marrakesh, Meknes, Tangier
Currency – Dirham (DH) of 100 centimes
Population – 35,561,654 rising at 0.96 per cent a year (2020 est)
Religion – Muslim (official; predominantly Sunni) 99 per cent (est)
Language – Arabic (official), French, Berber dialects
Population density – 81 per sq. km (2019)
Urban population – 63 per cent (2019 est)
Median age (years) – 29.1 (2020 est)
National anthem – 'Hymne Chérifien' 'Hymn of the Sharif'
National day – 30 July (Throne Day)
Death penalty – Retained (last used 1993)
CPI score – 41 (80)
Military expenditure – US$3,697m (2018)
Conscription – 19 years of age; 12 months

CLIMATE AND TERRAIN

Fertile coastal plains in the west rise to a mountainous centre, with ranges, including the Atlas range, running north-east to south-west. The Rif mountains lie along the northern, Mediterranean coast. Elevation extremes range from 4,165m (Jebel Toubkal) to −55m (Sebkha Tah). The climate is Mediterranean, becoming more extreme in the interior. Average temperatures range from 9.9°C in January to 26.8°C in July, although summer temperatures in the desert can reach over 40°C.

HISTORY AND POLITICS

From the tenth century BC, the northern coast was settled by the Phoenicians. Morocco was part of the Roman Empire from the first century AD until it was invaded by first the Vandals and then the Visigoths in the fifth and sixth centuries. Arab conquest of the area began in the seventh century but Morocco was independent from about the ninth century, successfully resisting inclusion in the Ottoman Empire in the 16th century. The current Alawite dynasty was founded in the mid-17th century. Morocco remained isolated until the mid-19th century, when the country opened up to European trade. The subsequent growth in Spanish and French influence resulted in its partition into two protectorates from 1912. In the Second World War, Morocco was a base for the Allied offensives that drove German forces out of North Africa.

Nationalist campaigning for independence began in the 1940s. French and Spanish forces withdrew in 1956, leaving Morocco independent under Sultan Mohammed V, who adopted the title of king in 1957; the coastal towns of Ceuta and Melilla remain under Spanish control. King Hassan II,

who ruled from 1961 to 1999, annexed the mineral-rich Western Sahara region in 1975.

Since the accession of King Mohammed VI in 1999, Morocco has been moving away from absolute monarchy, increasing civil liberties and addressing human rights issues. Pro-reform demonstrations in spring 2011 led to a referendum in July in which an overwhelming majority voted in favour of constitutional changes that would make the prime minister, rather than the king, the head of government.

In the October 2016 legislative election the Justice and Development Party (PJD) remained the largest party in the House of Representatives, but was unable to secure a ruling coalition with other parties. In March 2017 after five months of deadlock, the king replaced Prime Minister Abdelilah Benkirane and asked Saad-Eddine El Othmani, also of the PJD, to form a government.

The head of state is a hereditary constitutional monarch. The king appoints the prime minister, who appoints the members of the council of ministers. There is a bicameral legislature; the lower house, the House of Representatives *(Majlis al-Nuwab)* has 395 members who are directly elected for a five-year term, with 60 seats reserved for women. The House of Councillors *(Majlis al-Mustasharin)* has 120 members, elected by local councils, professional organisations and labour unions to serve a six-year term.

HEAD OF STATE
HM The King of Morocco, King Mohammed VI (Sidi Mohammed Ben Hassan), *born* 21 August 1963, *acceded* 23 July 1999, *crowned* 30 July 1999
Heir, HRH Crown Prince Moulay Hassan, *born* 2003

SELECTED GOVERNMENT MEMBERS *AS AT NOVEMBER 2020*
Prime Minister, Saad-Eddine El Othmani
Economy and Finance, Mohamed Benchaaboun
Foreign Affairs, Nasser Bourita
Interior, Abdelouafi Laftit

EMBASSY OF THE KINGDOM OF MOROCCO
49 Queen's Gate Gardens, London SW7 5NE
T 020-7581 5001 **E** ambalondres@maec.gov.ma
W www.moroccanembassylondon.org.uk
Ambassador Extraordinary and Plenipotentiary, HE Abdesselam Aboudrar, *apptd* 2016

BRITISH EMBASSY
28 Avenue SAR Sidi Mohammed, Souissi 10105 (BP45), Rabat
T (+212) (0) 537 633 333 **E** rabat.consular@fco.gov.uk
W www.gov.uk/government/world/morocco
Ambassador Extraordinary and Plenipotentiary, HE Simon Martin, CMG, *apptd* 2020

ECONOMY AND TRADE

Economic liberalisation since 1999 has attracted foreign direct investment, and the industrial and service sectors are being developed. Despite steady growth and low inflation Morocco remains a poor country, with unemployment at around 10 per cent prior to the coronavirus pandemic, and 15 per cent of people living in poverty. The remittances of expatriate workers are crucial to the domestic economy but these, along with tourism and export demand, declined in 2008–9 owing to the global downturn. Unemployment, poverty and illiteracy remain high in rural areas. The government has stabilised the country's finances by decreasing debt and reducing fuel subsidies. Investment in new ports and industrial infrastructure are improving the nation's competitiveness, while expanding renewable energy production is a government priority.

The large agrarian sector generates 14 per cent of GDP and engages 39.1 per cent of the workforce, producing cereals, citrus fruits, vegetables, wine, olives and livestock. It faces environmental problems such as desertification and soil erosion. Another major sector is the exploitation of mineral reserves, especially phosphate. Other industries include food processing, automotive parts, aerospace, textiles, leather goods and tourism. Industry accounts for 29.5 per cent of GDP and services for 56.5 per cent.

The main trading partners are EU countries, especially France and Spain. Principal exports are textiles, automobiles, electrical components, inorganic chemicals, transistors, crude minerals, fertilisers, petroleum products, fruit and vegetables. The main imports are crude petroleum, fabrics, telecommunications equipment, wheat, gas and electricity.

GNI – US$118bn; US$3,190 per capita (2019)
Annual average growth of GDP – 2.5 per cent (2019 est)
Inflation rate – 0.8 per cent (2017 est)
Population below poverty line – 15 per cent (2007 est)
Unemployment – 9.23 per cent (2019 est)
Total external debt – US$51.48bn (2017 est)
Imports – US$49,446m (2017)
Exports – US$38,684m (2017)

BALANCE OF PAYMENTS
Trade – US$10,762m deficit (2017)
Current Account – US$4,915m deficit (2019)

Trade with UK	2018	2019
Imports from UK	£684,821,480	£635,655,161
Exports to UK	£683,208,523	£653,649,304

COMMUNICATIONS
Airports and waterways – The principal airports are at Rabat, Agadir, Casablanca and Marrakesh; the main ports are Tangier, Casablanca and Agadir, on the Atlantic coast
Roadways and railways – There are 41,116km of roadways, including 1,080km of motorways, and 2,067km of railways
Telecommunications – 1.9 million fixed lines and 45 million mobile subscriptions (2019); there were 22.6 million internet users in 2018
Internet code and IDD – ma; 212 (from UK), 44 (to UK)
Major broadcasters – The government owns Radio-Télévision Marocaine and has a stake in 2M, the other main television network
Press – There are a number of daily newspapers, including the semi-official *Le Matin* (French language), *Al-Massae* and *Assabah* (both Arabic language)
WPFI score – 42.88 (133)

EDUCATION AND HEALTH
Education is compulsory between the ages of six and 15.
Literacy rate – 73.8 per cent (2018 est)
Gross enrolment ratio (percentage of relevant age group) – primary 114.8 per cent, secondary 81.2 per cent, tertiary 38.5 per cent (2019 est)
Health expenditure (per capita) – US$161 (2017)
Hospital beds (per 1,000 people) – 1.1 (2014)
Life expectancy (years) – 77.7 (2020 est)
Mortality rate – 6.6 (2020 est)
Birth rate – 17.9 (2020 est)
Infant mortality rate – 18.2 (2020 est)
HIV/AIDS adult prevalence – 0.1 per cent (2019 est)

WESTERN SAHARA

Al-Jumhuriyya al-'Arabiyya as-Sahrawiyya ad-Dimuqratiyya – Sahrawi Arab Democratic Republic
Area – 266,000 sq. km. Neighbours: Morocco (north), Algeria (north-east), Mauritania (east and south)
Administrative centre – El-Aaiun (Laayoune); population, 232,000 (2018)
Population – 619,551 rising at 2.64 per cent a year (2018 est)
Religion – Muslim (99 per cent) (est)
Language – Hassaniyya Arabic, Moroccan Arabic
Urban population – 86.6 per cent (2019 est)
Median age (years) – 21.5 (2018 est)
Flag – Three horizontal stripes of black, white and green with a red crescent and a five-pointed star in the centre and a red triangle based on the hoist

Western Sahara came under Spanish rule in 1884, and became a province in 1934. Following Spain's withdrawal in 1976, Morocco and Mauritania annexed the territory and divided it between them. The Polisario Front declared Western Sahara's independence as the Sahrawi Arab Democratic Republic in 1976, and began a guerrilla war to win the territory, setting up a government in exile. In 1979, Mauritania withdrew from its part of the territory, which was annexed by Morocco.

A ceasefire was established in 1991 following both sides' agreement in 1988 to UN proposals for a peace settlement, which included holding a referendum on the future status of Western Sahara. But the precise terms of the referendum have proved a sticking point and an impasse was reached that has still not been overcome, despite further negotiations in 2001–4; Polisario agreed to a referendum offering the options of independence, semi-autonomy or integration for Western Sahara, but Morocco is only prepared to accept semi-autonomy or integration. Talks have taken place intermittently since 2007 but have made no progress; in March 2017, UN Secretary-General António Guterres called for the resumption of discussions.

MOZAMBIQUE

Republica de Mocambique – Republic of Mozambique

Area – 799,380 sq. km
Capital – Maputo; population, 1,110,000 (2020 est)
Major cities – Beira, Chimoio, Matola, Nampula
Currency – New metical (MT) of 100 centavos
Population – 30,098,197 rising at 2.62 per cent a year (2020 est)
Religion – Christian (Roman Catholic 27.2 per cent, Zionist Christian 15.6 per cent, Evangelical and Pentecostal 15.3 per cent, Anglican 1.7 per cent), Muslim 18.9 per cent, other 4.8 per cent (est)
Language – Portuguese (official), Emakhuwa, Xichangana, Elomwe, Cisena, Echuwabo

Population density – 38 per sq. km (2020)
Urban population – 36.5 per cent (2020 est)
Median age (years) – 17 (2020)
National anthem – 'Patria Amada' 'Beloved Fatherland'
National day – 25 June (Independence Day)
Death penalty – Abolished for all crimes (since 1990)
CPI score – 26 (146)
Military expenditure – US$145m (2018)
Conscription – 18–35 years of age; 24 months (selective)
Literacy rate – 60.7 per cent (2017 est)
Gross enrolment ratio (percentage of relevant age group) – primary 107.8 per cent, secondary 35.4 per cent, tertiary 7.1 per cent (2017 est)
Health expenditure (per capita) – US$21 (2017)
Hospital beds (per 1,000 people) – 0.7 (2011)
Life expectancy (years) – 55.9 (2020 est)
Mortality rate – 11 (2020 est)
Birth rate – 38.6 (2020 est)
Infant mortality rate – 64.7 (2020 est)
HIV/AIDS adult prevalence – 12.4 per cent (2019 est)

CLIMATE AND TERRAIN
Coastal plains rise to plateaux in the centre and west, with mountains on the western borders. Elevation extremes range from 2,436m (Mt Binga) to 0m (Indian Ocean). A number of rivers run from the western highlands to the Indian Ocean coast, including the Zambezi, Limpopo, Save and Ruvuma. The climate is tropical, with average temperatures in Maputo ranging from 19.9°C in July to 26.6°C in November.

HISTORY AND POLITICS
Between the first and fourth centuries Mozambique was settled by Bantu peoples. Trade with India and the Arabian peninsula grew and migrants from both these regions settled in the coastal areas. From the 16th century the Portuguese established settlements on the coast and along the Zambezi, trading in gold, ivory, spices and slaves, and in the late 19th century they succeeded in conquering the interior. The area was administered as part of Portuguese India from 1751, becoming a separate colony in the late 19th century and an overseas province of Portugal in 1951. Concessions to private companies that had operated as *de facto* rulers over much of the country were ended in 1930.

The *Frente de Libertacao de Mocambique* (Frelimo) was founded in 1962 to fight for independence, and a ten-year guerrilla war against Portuguese forces began in 1964. Independence was achieved in 1975, when a one-party socialist republic was set up. Opposition to this was led from 1977 by the *Resistencia Nacional de Mocambique* (Renamo) and a brutal civil war broke out that lasted until 1992. Mozambique joined the Commonwealth in 1995; although it had never been under British rule, it has close relationships and a shared experience with its neighbours, all former British colonies. Reconstruction of the economy and infrastructure progressed quickly after the civil war, although a series of natural catastrophes since 2000, high HIV/AIDS infection rates and remaining civil war landmines have slowed progress. Cyclone Idai resulted in widespread flooding in March 2019, causing the destruction of nearly 250,000 homes and killing at least 602 people.

In 1990 Frelimo abandoned Marxist-Leninism and ended one-party rule, introducing a multiparty system. The first elections under the new constitution were held in 1994 and won by Frelimo. Frelimo retained power in the 1999, 2004 and 2009 elections, prompting allegations of vote-rigging by Renamo. The October 2014 and October 2019 presidential elections were won by Filipe Nyusi of the Frelimo party, and Frelimo retained an overall majority in both simultaneous legislative elections. Opposition groups claimed the elections were fraudulent and intimidation tactics were widely used.

Under the 2004 constitution, the executive president is directly elected for a five-year term, renewable once. The unicameral Assembly of the Republic has 250 members, who are directly elected for a five-year term. The president appoints the prime minister and the council of ministers.

HEAD OF STATE
President, C-in-C of the Armed Forces, Filipe Jacinto Nyusi, *elected* 24 October 2014, *sworn in* 15 January 2015, *re-elected* 15 October 2020

SELECTED GOVERNMENT MEMBERS *AS AT NOVEMBER* 2020
Prime Minister, Carlos Agostinho Do Rosario
Economy and Finance, Adriano Afonso Maleiane
Foreign Affairs, Veronica Macamo
Interior, Armade Miquidade

HIGH COMMISSION FOR THE REPUBLIC OF MOZAMBIQUE
21 Fitzroy Square, London W1T 6EL
T 020-7383 3800 **E** sectorconsular@mozambiquehc.co.uk
W www.mozambiquehighcommission.org.uk
High Commissioner, HE Filipe Chidumo, *apptd* 2015

BRITISH HIGH COMMISSION
Avenida Vladmir Lenine, 310 Maputo City, Maputo, PO Box 55
T (+258) (21) 356 000 **E** maputo.consularenquiries@fco.gov.uk
W www.gov.uk/government/world/mozambique
High Commissioner, HE NneNne Iwuji-Eme, *apptd* 2018

ECONOMY AND TRADE
Political stability and economic liberalisation have attracted foreign direct investment and donor support, and achieved economic growth despite setbacks from devastating flooding (2000, 2001, 2007, 2008, 2010, 2015, 2019), droughts (2002, 2003, 2009, 2010, 2016) and an earthquake (2006). But the country remains dependent on foreign aid, with almost half of the population living below the poverty line. The huge foreign debt has been reduced to a more manageable size by debt cancellation and rescheduling, but there is a substantial ongoing trade imbalance. Growth slowed in 2016 and Mozambique defaulted on its sovereign bond repayment in January 2017; the IMF halted direct budget support in 2016 because of a scandal involving the misuse of funds, but assistance continued in the wake of Cyclone Idai in 2019.

Agriculture and forestry are the mainstays of the economy, accounting for 23.9 per cent of GDP and engaging about 74.4 per cent of the workforce; shellfish, cashew nuts, cotton, sugar, citrus fruits and timber are important exports. There are considerable oil, gas, mineral and hydroelectric power resources, which are increasingly being exploited. Industries include aluminium, titanium, petroleum products, natural gas extraction, chemicals, food processing, cement, glass and textiles. Exploitation of natural gas reserves by international consortiums is expected to generate billions for government revenue after 2022. Industry generates 19.3 per cent of GDP and services 56.8 per cent.

The main trading partners are South Africa, India and the Netherlands. The country also benefits from trade with its landlocked neighbours. Principal exports are aluminium, agricultural products, timber and electricity. The main imports are machinery, vehicles, fuel, chemicals, metal products, foodstuffs and textiles.

GNI – US$14.5bn; US$480 per capita (2019)
Annual average growth of GDP – 3.11 per cent (2018 est)

Inflation rate – 15.3 per cent (2017 est)
Population below poverty line – 46.1 per cent (2015 est)
Total external debt – US$10.91bn (2017 est)
Imports – US$8,294m (2017)
Exports – US$5,375m (2017)

BALANCE OF PAYMENTS
Trade – US$2,918m deficit (2017)
Current Account – US$3,024m deficit (2019)

Trade with UK	2018	2019
Imports from UK	£23,760,609	£107,353,575
Exports to UK	£104,953,384	£29,805,258

COMMUNICATIONS

Airports and waterways – The principal airports are at Maputo and Beira, with 19 other airports around the country; the main seaports are Maputo, Beira and Nacala, which also handle trade for neighbouring countries
Roadways and railways – 7,365km of paved roadways; 4,787km
Telecommunications – 61,575 fixed lines and 14 million mobile subscriptions (2019); there were 2.9 million internet users in 2018
Internet code and IDD – mz; 258 (from UK), 44 (to UK)
Major broadcasters – Televisao de Mozambique (TVM) is the state-run television broadcaster; Radio Mozambique and Radio Cidade are the public radio broadcasters
Press – Leading national dailies include *Diario de Mocambique, O Pais* and *Noticias* (partly state owned)
WPFI score – 33.79 (104)

MYANMAR

Pyidaungzu Thammada Myanma Naingngandaw – Republic of the Union of Myanmar

Area – 676,578 sq. km
Capital – Yangon (Rangoon); population, 5,332,000 (2020 est)
Major cities – Bago, Mandalay, Mawlamyine (Moulmein), Pathein (Bassein)
Currency – Kyat (K) of 100 pyas
Population – 56,590,071 rising at 0.85 per cent a year (2020 est); there are 135 indigenous ethnic groups, of which Burman (68 per cent), Shan (9 per cent), Karen (7 per cent) are the largest (est)
Religion – Buddhist 87.9 per cent, Christian 6.2 per cent, Muslim 4.3 per cent (est)
Language – Burmese (official), numerous ethnic languages
Population density – 82 per sq. km (2019)
Urban population – 30.9 per cent (2019 est)
Median age (years) – 29.2 (2020 est)

National anthem – 'Kaba Ma Kyei' 'Till the End of the World, Myanmar'
National day – 4 January (Independence Day)
Death penalty – Retained (last used 1988)
CPI score – 29 (130)
Military expenditure – US$716m (2005)

CLIMATE AND TERRAIN

Central lowlands are ringed by mountains in the west, north (part of the foothills of the Himalayas) and east. The eastern range extends down the Kra isthmus that Myanmar shares with Thailand, forming a natural border. Elevation extremes range from 5,870m (Gamlang Razi) to 0m (Andaman Sea). The lowlands are drained by the Irrawaddy river and its chief tributary, the Chindwin, and the eastern mountains by the Salween. The Irrawaddy has a large delta on the Andaman coast. The climate is tropical, with a wet season from May to September. Average temperatures in Mandalay, representative of the interior lowlands, range from 18.4°C in January to 25.2°C in April and May, although temperatures in the interior can reach 44°C in May.

POLITICS

Under the 2010 constitution, the head of state is a president elected by the legislature for a five-year term, renewable once. The president is also head of government and appoints ministers with the approval of the legislature. The bicameral People's Assembly comprises the 440-member House of Representatives, the lower chamber, and the 224-member House of Nationalities. In each chamber, 25 per cent of seats are reserved for the military and the rest are directly elected; both chambers serve a five-year term. Constitutional changes require approval by a 75 per cent majority.

In preparation for legislative elections in late 2010, several electoral laws were introduced in March 2010; these excluded many political activists, such as Aung San Suu Kyi, from participation in the elections, set restrictive conditions for party registration, and tightly regulated campaigning and funding; the National League for Democracy (NLD) announced a boycott of the elections. Several members of the government resigned their military commissions to contest the elections as civilians, registering a new political party, the Union Solidarity and Development Party (USDP).

In November 2010, the USDP won majorities in both chambers in an election that opposition groups claimed was fraudulent and was condemned internationally as a sham. The new legislature convened in January 2011 and a new, nominally civilian government was sworn in in March, and the dissolution of the State Peace and Development Council was announced. In 2012 the NLD, led by Aung San Suu Kyi, contested 44 of the 46 seats in the lower house by-elections, winning 43 of them. In the November 2015 general election, the NLD won a landslide 135 seats in the upper house and 255 seats in the lower house, and this large mandate was extended in the the November 2020 election. Ethnic minorities, including the Rohingya, were excluded from voting. Suu Kyi was ineligible to run for the presidency as both her sons have British nationality; while Win Myint, an ally of Suu Kyi, was appointed president in March 2018. In April 2016, Suu Kyi freed 113 political prisoners in her first act as 'state counsellor', a position comparable to prime minister, but her subsequent refusal to condemn the violence against the Rohingya alienated most of her western supporters.

HEAD OF STATE
President, Chair of National Defence and Security Council, Win Myint *sworn in* 30 March 2018

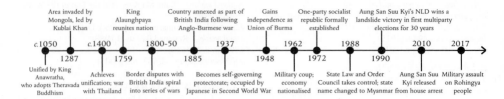

Area invaded by Mongols, led by Kublai Khan	King Alaungphaya reunites nation	Country annexed as part of British India following Anglo-Burmese war	Gains independence in Union of Burma	One-party socialist republic formally established	Aung San Suu Kyi's NLD wins a landslide victory in first multiparty elections for 30 years
c.1050	c.1400	1800-50	1937	1962	1988	2010	2017
1287	1759	1885	1948	1972	1990
Unified by King Anawratha, who adopts Theravada Buddhism	Achieves unification; war with Thailand	Border disputes with British India spiral into series of wars	Becomes self-governing protectorate; occupied by Japanese in Second World War	Military coup; economy nationalised	State Law and Order Council takes control; state name changed to Myanmar	Aung San Suu Kyi released from house arrest	Military assault on Rohingya people

First Vice-President, Lt.-Gen. (retd) Myint Swe
Second Vice-President, Maj. (retd) Henry Van Thio

SELECTED GOVERNMENT MEMBERS *AS AT NOVEMBER 2020*
State Counsellor, Foreign Affairs, Aung San Suu Kyi
Defence, Lt.-Gen. Sein Win
Home Affairs, Lt.-Gen. Soe Htut

EMBASSY OF THE REPUBLIC OF THE UNION OF MYANMAR
19A Charles Street, London W1J 5DX
T 020-7499 4340
E ambassadoroffice@myanmarembassylondon.com
W www.myanmarembassylondon.com
Ambassador Extraordinary and Plenipotentiary, HE Kyaw Zwar Minn, *apptd* 2013

BRITISH EMBASSY
80 Strand Road (Box 638), Rangoon
T (+95) (1) 370 865 **E** be.rangoon@fco.gov.uk
W www.gov.uk/government/world/burma
Ambassador Extraordinary and Plenipotentiary, HE Daniel Chugg, *apptd* 2018

INSURGENCIES
Since independence in 1948 there have been various insurgencies, mostly by ethnic groups. These have included the Kachin, Kayin (Karen), Karenni, Wa, Shan, Mon, Arakan Chin and Kokang ethnic minorities. Since 1992, 18 ethnic groups have signed ceasefire agreements; the government is accused of breaking four of these since the November 2010 election. Some groups have achieved a degree of autonomy in their region; others have splintered, creating intra-ethnic tension. In October 2015 the government signed a ceasefire agreement with eight rebel groups, though seven other major insurgent groups refused to sign. The country's ethnic minorities are believed to bear the brunt of the government's human rights abuses, with the Muslim Rohingya of western Burma considered one of the most oppressed peoples in the world.

Since August 2017, following clashes between the military and Rohingya militants, an estimated 745,000 Rohingya have fled Rakhine province into neighbouring Bangladesh and an estimated 25,000 people have been killed in what the UN described as a genocide and 'a textbook example of ethnic cleansing'. Myanmar's military denied targeting civilians, while Suu Kyi rejected the UN analysis and defended the jailing of journalists amid claims of a crackdown on the freedom of expression. An agreement with Bangladesh to involuntarily repatriate refugees from November 2018 was abandoned due to Rohingya and international opposition, but remains a long-term goal. In July 2019, the UN estimated over 120,000 Rohingya in Myanmar were living in conditions akin to concentration camps.

ECONOMY AND TRADE
Myanmar has fertile soil, occupies strategic trade routes between India, China and south-east Asia, and has an abundance of natural resources such as natural gas (one of Asia's largest exporters), timber (the world's largest exporter of teak), precious gems (jade, pearls, rubies and sapphires) and oil, but the economy is characterised by mismanagement and corruption. The country became increasingly poverty-stricken under military rule and over a quarter of people live below the poverty line. The economy suffers from unpredictable policies, market distortions, insurgencies and ethnic violence, and inadequate commercial, transport and energy infrastructure. The regime's repressiveness lost it development aid and attracted economic and trade sanctions, but since the transition to a civil-led government in 2011 the nation has sought global economic reintegration. Myanmar formed a common market with the other members of the Association of Southeast Asian Nations (ASEAN) in 2015. Sanctions imposed by the US were lifted in 2016 and subsequent reforms have intended to make foreign investment easier, while Aung San Suu Kyi has attempted to modernise the nation's agriculture, banking and energy. Around a quarter of the population live in poverty. There is a large grey economy and considerable unofficial cross-border trade.

Agriculture is the dominant economic activity, accounting for 24.1 per cent of GDP and engaging roughly 70 per cent of the workforce; the most important export crops are rice, pulses, beans and fish. The main industries are forestry, mining, and oil and gas extraction, and these have attracted some foreign investment; manufacturing and services are struggling, but the growing tourist industry has not yet declined despite the Rohingya humanitarian crisis. Industry contributes 35.6 per cent of GDP and services 40.3 per cent.

The main trading partners are China (36.5 per cent of exports; 31.4 per cent of imports), Thailand, Singapore and India. Principal exports are natural gas, wood products, agricultural produce, clothing and gems. The main imports are fabric, petroleum products, fertiliser, plastics, machinery, transport equipment, construction materials and food.

GNI – US$75.2bn; US$1,390 per capita (2019)
Annual average growth of GDP – 6.8 per cent (2017)
Inflation rate – 4 per cent (2017 est)
Population below poverty line – 25.6 per cent (2016 est)
Unemployment – 4 per cent (2017 est)
Total external debt – US$6.594bn (2017 est)
Imports – US$15,710m (2016)
Exports – US$13,025m (2016)

BALANCE OF PAYMENTS
Trade – US$2,684m deficit (2016)
Current Account – US$240m surplus (2019)

Trade with UK	2018	2019
Imports from UK	£38,342,007	£32,456,260
Exports to UK	£267,835,943	£330,497,749

COMMUNICATIONS

Airports and waterways – The main airports are at Yangon and Mandalay; the 12,800km of navigable waterways include the Irrawaddy and Chindwin rivers, and the chief seaports are Yangon (Rangoon), Mawlamyine (Moulmein) and Akyab (Sittwe)

Roadways and railways – 34,700km; 5,031km

Telecommunications – 544,283 fixed lines and 63.9 million mobile subscriptions (2019); there were 17.1 million internet users in 2018

Internet code and IDD – mm; 95 (from UK), 44 (to UK)

Major broadcasters – Democratic Voice of Burma, an opposition radio station broadcasting via short-wave from Norway, and foreign services such as the BBC and Voice of America, are key sources of information for the population; TV Myanmar is the state-run national broadcaster

Press – Leading dailies include the state-run *Kyehmon* and *Myanmar Alin;* legislation increasing journalistic freedom was passed in 2014

WPFI score – 44.77 (139)

EDUCATION AND HEALTH

Literacy rate – 75.6per cent (2016 est)

Gross enrolment ratio (percentage of relevant age group) – primary 112.3 per cent, secondary 68.4 per cent, tertiary 18.8 per cent (2018 est)

Health expenditure (per capita) – US$58 (2017)

Hospital beds (per 1,000 people) – 0.9 (2012)

Life expectancy (years) – 60.3 (2020 est)

Mortality rate – 7.2 (2020 est)

Birth rate – 17 (2020 est)

Infant mortality rate – 31.7 (2020 est)

HIV/AIDS adult prevalence – 0.7 per cent (2019 est)

NAMIBIA

Republic of Namibia

Area – 824,292 sq. km

Capital – Windhoek; population, 431,000 (2020 est)

Major towns – Oshakati, Rundu, Walvis Bay

Currency – Namibian dollar of 100 cents, at parity with South African rand

Population – 2,630,073 rising at 1.86 per cent a year (2020 est); Ovambo (50 per cent), Kavangos (9 per cent), Damara (7 per cent), Nama (5 per cent) (est)

Religion – Christian 80–90 per cent (at least 50 per cent Lutheran), indigenous beliefs 10–20 per cent (est)

Language – English (official), Afrikaans (lingua franca), Oshiwambo, Herero, Nama, other indigenous languages

Population density – 3 per sq. km (2019)

Urban population – 51 per cent (2019 est)

Median age (years) – 21.8 (2020 est)

National anthem – 'Namibia, Land of the Brave'

National day – 21 March (Independence Day)

Death penalty – Abolished for all crimes (since 1990)

CPI score – 52 (56)

Military expenditure – US$452m (2018 est)

Literacy rate – 91.5 per cent (2018 est)

Gross enrolment ratio (percentage of relevant age group) – primary 124.2 per cent (2018 est)

Health expenditure (per capita) – US$447 (2017)

Hospital beds (per 1,000 people) – 2.7 (2009)

Life expectancy (years) – 65.3 (2020 est)

Mortality rate – 7.3 (2020 est)

Birth rate – 25.7 (2020 est)

Infant mortality rate – 31.4 (2020 est)

HIV/AIDS adult prevalence – 11.5 per cent (2019)

CLIMATE AND TERRAIN

The Namib desert runs along the Atlantic coast and is separated by a line of hills and high veldt from the Kalahari desert in the interior. Elevation extremes range from 2,606m (Konigstein) to 0m (Atlantic Ocean). Major rivers include the Orange, which forms the southern border with South Africa, and the Zambezi, which runs through the Caprivi Strip in the extreme north-east of the country. The climate is arid in the west and semi-arid in the centre and north-east; rainfall is sparse and droughts are frequent. The coast is cooler and frequently foggy. Average temperatures range from 14.9°C in July to 24.4°C in January.

HISTORY AND POLITICS

Pre-colonial Namibia was inhabited by San and then by Bantu tribes. It was annexed by Germany in 1884 and named South West Africa. Indigenous uprisings against colonial settlement in the early 20th century were brutally suppressed, with some tribes suffering severe losses; the Herero and Nama were nearly wiped out. The territory was occupied by South Africa on behalf of the Allies in 1915 and after the First World War it became a League of Nations mandated territory, administered by South Africa.

The arrangement continued under the UN after the Second World War, but South Africa exceeded its mandate by effectively annexing the country, extending representation in the South African parliament to the white population in 1949, and applying apartheid in 1966. These actions were taken despite the UN's refusal to permit the country's incorporation into South Africa in 1946 and its termination of the mandate in 1966. In 1968, the UN changed the country's name to Namibia, and the South West Africa People's Organisation (SWAPO), which had campaigned for racial equality and independence since 1960, began a guerrilla war against South Africa.

South Africa's peace talks with Angola in 1988 led to agreement on independence for Namibia, and this was achieved on 21 March 1990; South Africa's Walvis Bay enclave was returned to Namibia in 1994.

The country has enjoyed stability since independence, apart from a brief period of secessionist violence in the Caprivi Strip in the late 1990s, and has been recognised by observers as having one of the freest media industries in Africa. Following agitation for an acceleration of land reform, the government programme moved from voluntary sales to expropriation of white-owned farms in 2005. The country's main problems arise from the demographic, economic and social impact of the high level of HIV/AIDS infection among the population.

SWAPO has been the dominant party since independence, holding the presidency and commanding a parliamentary majority without interruption. The November 2014 presidential election was won by Hage Geingob of SWAPO, who collected 86.7 per cent of the vote, and he was re-elected in November 2019. SWAPO retained its majority in the November 2019 election, but lost its super majority that it had held since 1994.

Under the 1990 constitution, the executive president is directly elected for a five-year term, renewable once. There is a bicameral parliament consisting of a National Assembly, with 96 members directly elected for a five-year term and eight additional non-voting members appointed by the president, and a National Council, whose 42 members are elected by the regional councils from among their own members for a five-year term; the latter's main function is to review and consider legislation from the lower chamber. The president appoints the prime minister and the other ministers.

HEAD OF STATE
President, Hage Geingob, *elected* 28 November 2014, *sworn in* 21 March 2015, *re-elected* 27 November 2019
Vice-President, Nangolo Mbumba

SELECTED GOVERNMENT MEMBERS *AS AT NOVEMBER 2020*
Prime Minister, Saara Kuugongelwa-Amadhila
Deputy Prime Minister, Netumbo Nandi-Ndaitwah
Defence, Peter Vilho
Finance, Iipumbu Shiimi

HIGH COMMISSION FOR THE REPUBLIC OF NAMIBIA
6 Chandos Street, London W1G 9LU
T 020-7636 6244 **E** info@namibiahc.org.uk
W www.namibiahc.org.uk
High Commissioner, HE Linda Scott, *apptd* 2019

BRITISH HIGH COMMISSION
116 Robert Mugabe Avenue, PO Box 22202, Windhoek
T (+264) (61) 274 800 **E** general.windhoek@fco.gov.uk
W www.gov.uk/government/world/namibia
High Commissioner, HE Kate Airey, OBE, *apptd* 2018

ECONOMY AND TRADE
Despite a high GDP per capita, Namibia has high levels of poverty and inequality, and very high unemployment. Its arid terrain limits agriculture, but the emphasis on environmental protection (enshrined in the constitution) has helped the development of tourism. The country has rich mineral deposits; extraction of these is the main industrial activity and minerals account for over 50 per cent of foreign exchange earnings. However, a drop in export sales and a drought in 2019 meant the economy contracted, before the coronavirus pandemic exacerbated this decline. It is one of the world's largest producers of uranium, and also extracts large amounts of Zinc and smaller quantities of other minerals. This leaves the economy vulnerable to global price fluctuations, and the government is encouraging foreign investment to help diversification. Other industries process the products of the farming and fisheries sectors. Agriculture operates mostly at subsistence level, accounting for 6.7 per cent of GDP and engages 31 per cent of the workforce.

The main trading partners are South Africa (27.1 per cent of exports and 61.4 per cent of imports), Botswana and Switzerland. Principal exports are diamonds, copper, gold, zinc, lead, uranium and fish. The main imports are foodstuffs (particularly grain), petroleum products and fuel, machinery and equipment, and chemicals.
GNI – US$12.6bn; US$5,060 per capita (2019)
Annual average growth of GDP – –1.56 per cent (2019 est)
Inflation rate – 6.1 per cent (2017 est)
Population below poverty line – 28.7 per cent (2010 est)
Unemployment – 34 per cent (2016 est)
Total external debt – US$7.969bn (2017 est)

Imports – US$5,954m (2017)
Exports – US$4,057m (2017)

BALANCE OF PAYMENTS
Trade – US$1,896m deficit (2017)
Current Account – US$215m deficit (2019)

Trade with UK	2018	2019
Imports from UK	£43,632,993	£40,963,197
Exports to UK	£26,754,557	£31,171,424

COMMUNICATIONS
Airports and waterways – The main airports are at Windhoek and Odangwa, with 17 smaller airports around the country; the two main seaports are Walvis Bay and Luderitz
Roadways and railways – 7,893km; 2,628km
Telecommunications – 144,575 fixed lines and 2.9 million mobile subscriptions (2019); there were 1.3 million internet users in 2018
Internet code and IDD – na; 264 (from UK), 44 (to UK)
Major broadcasters – The Namibian Broadcasting Corporation (NBC) is publicly owned and operates television and radio stations
Press – There are five national daily newspapers including *The Namibian* (English and Oshiwambo language), *Die Republikein* (Afrikaans) and the state-owned *New Era*
WPFI score – 19.25 (23)

NAURU

Republic of Nauru

Area – 21 sq. km
Capital – Yaren (unofficial)
Currency – Australian dollar (A$) of 100 cents
Population – 11,000 rising at 0.46 per cent a year (2020 est)
Religion – Christian (Protestant 60.4 per cent, Roman Catholic 33 per cent), other 3.7 per cent (est)
Language – Nauruan (official), English
Population density – 635 per sq. km (2019)
Urban population – 100 per cent (2019 est)
Median age (years) – 27 (2020 est)
National anthem – 'Nauru Bwiema' 'Song of Nauru'
National day – 31 January (Independence Day)
Death penalty – Abolished for all crimes (since 2016)
Life expectancy (years) – 68.4 (2020 est)
Mortality rate – 6 (2020 est)
Birth rate – 21.9 (2020 est)
Infant mortality rate – 7.4 (2020 est)

CLIMATE AND TERRAIN

Nauru is a low-lying island in the southern Pacific Ocean, 42km south of the equator and 4,000km north-east of Sydney, Australia. There is a fertile coastal plain but about 60 per cent of the land area consists of the central plateau, formed of phosphate, which has been extensively mined. The plateau rim is the highest point, at 61m; the lowest is 0m at sea level. The climate is tropical, with a rainy season from November to February.

HISTORY AND POLITICS

Nauru was first settled by Polynesian and Melanesian groups. The first Europeans to visit the island were British whalers in 1798, and by 1888 Nauru was annexed by Germany. At the outbreak of the First World War, Nauru was occupied by Australia, which continued to administer the island under a League of Nations mandate from 1920. The island was occupied by the Japanese in 1942–3, but in 1947 UN trusteeship status superseded the mandate and Nauru continued to be administered by Australia until it became independent on 31 January 1968. A detention centre, established in partnership with Australia to house asylum seekers headed towards that country, has attracted controversy for its allegedly harsh conditions.

A financial crisis in 2003 caused some political instability, though a more stable period during Ludwig Scotty's second presidency (2004–7) saw the introduction of austerity measures and public sector reform. Scotty lost a vote of confidence in December 2007 and was replaced by Marcus Stephen. President Stephen resigned in 2011 amid allegations of corruption and was replaced first by Frederick Pitcherr, then Sprent Dabwido, and finally Baron Waqa (2013–20). Former human rights lawyer Lionel Aingimea was appointed president in August 2020.

Under the 1968 constitution, the executive president is elected by the legislature from among its members for a three-year term, renewable once. The unicameral parliament has 19 members, who are directly elected for a three-year term. The president appoints the cabinet. Although there are active political parties, most parliamentary candidates stand as independents.

HEAD OF STATE

President, Foreign Affairs, Lionel Aingimea, *elected* 27 August 2020

SELECTED GOVERNMENT MEMBERS *AS AT NOVEMBER 2020*

Finance, Martin Hunt
Home Affairs, Isabella Dageago

HONORARY CONSULATE

Romshed Courtyard, Underriver, Sevenoaks, Kent TN15 0SD
T 01732-746061 **E** nauru@weald.co.uk
Honorary Consul, Martin Weston

BRITISH HIGH COMMISSIONER

HE Dr Brian Jones, *apptd* 2019, resident at Honiara, Solomon Islands

ECONOMY AND TRADE

Phosphate is the only resource and its extraction is the dominant industry, but reserves will be exhausted in 30 years. Profits derived from the mining industry were invested in trust funds to provide for the post-mining future, but heavy spending from the funds has left the country virtually bankrupt, causing it to default on loans and have assets seized in 2004. The economy is dependent on international aid

(principally from Australia) and revenue from the sale of fishing licences, but diversification efforts include offshore banking, small-scale tourism, and the Australian Regional Processing Centre opened in 2012.

The main trading partners are Australia and Nigeria. The only export is phosphate. All food, fuel, manufactured goods, machinery and construction materials are imported.
GNI – US$0.1bn; US$14,230 per capita (2019)
Annual average growth of GDP – 4.0 per cent (2017 est)
Inflation rate – 5.1 per cent (2017 est)
Imports – US$40m (2014)
Exports – US$34m (2014)

BALANCE OF PAYMENTS
Current Account – US$590m deficit (2018)

Trade with UK	2018	2019
Imports from UK	£23,889	£280,234
Exports to UK	£9,647	£3,028

COMMUNICATION

Transport – The island has one international airport and 30km of roadways
Telecommunications – 1,900 fixed lines (2016) and 9,212 mobile phone subscriptions (2019); there were 5,524 internet users in 2018
Internet code and IDD – nr; 674 (from UK), 44 (to UK)
Media – The government-owned Nauru Television and Radio Nauru are the island's principal broadcasters; there are no daily newspapers

NEPAL

Sanghiya Loktantrik Ganatantra Nepal – Federal Democratic Republic of Nepal

Area – 147,181 sq. km
Capital – Kathmandu; population, 1,424,000 (2020 est)
Major cities – Biratnagar, Lalitpur, Lumbini, Pokhara
Currency – Nepalese rupee (Rs) of 100 paisa
Population – 30,327,877 rising at 0.98 per cent a year (2020 est); there are 125 ethnic groups, of which Chhetri (16.6 per cent), Brahman-Hill (12.2 per cent), Magar (7.1 per cent), Tharu (6.6 per cent) and Tamang (5.8 per cent) are the largest (est)
Religion – Hindu 81.3 per cent, Buddhist 9 per cent, Muslim 4.4 per cent, Kirant 3.1 per cent (practised by a large proportion of Nepal's Kirati population), Christian 1.4 per cent (est)
Language – Nepali (official); 123 other languages including English
Population density – 196 per sq. km (2019)
Urban population – 20.2 per cent (2019 est)
Median age (years) – 25.3 (2020 est)

National anthem – 'Sayaun Thunga Phool Ka' 'Hundreds of Flowers'
National day – 29 May (Republic Day)
Death penalty – Abolished for all crimes (since 1997)
CPI score – 34 (113)
Military expenditure – US$399m (2018)

CLIMATE AND TERRAIN
The north of Nepal lies in the Himalayas, with the snowline at about 4,880m. The terrain descends from the mountains through a hilly central region with fertile valleys to the southern plains, the Terai, that lie in the valley of the Ganges. Elevation extremes range from 8,850m (Mt Everest) to 70m (Kanchan Kalan). The climate varies from subtropical in the south to much cooler with severe winters in the north. Average temperatures range from 4.8°C in January to 19.1°C in June and July. The rainy season lasts from June to September.

HISTORY AND POLITICS
Modern Nepal was formed from a number of small states that were conquered and unified in the 18th century by the Gurkha ruler Prithvi Naryan Shah. After war with the British in 1815–16, Nepal became a British-dependent buffer state; its independence was formally recognised in 1923.

Power was seized by Jung Bahdur in 1846. He assumed the title Rana and his family became hereditary chief ministers, reducing the monarchy to a purely ceremonial role and keeping the country isolated. In 1950–1, the Ranas were overthrown and the monarchy was restored to power. Apart from 1959–60, when a parliamentary system of government was in place, the kings ruled as absolute monarchs until 1990, when a new constitution was introduced that made the country a constitutional monarchy and multiparty parliamentary democracy.

However, factionalism led to frequent changes of government, causing political and social instability, which was exacerbated from 1996 by a Maoist insurgency led by the Nepal Communist Party. The insurgency began in the west and spread quickly. By 2006 the insurgents controlled 80 per cent of the country.

King Gyanendra's assumption of direct rule in 2005 led politicians to ally themselves with the Maoists to achieve the restoration of democracy, and in April 2006 the king reinstated the legislature after three months of violent pro-democracy protests. In November 2006 a peace accord was signed, an interim legislature was established in January 2007 and a multiparty government took office in April.

Elections to the constituent assembly took place in April 2008; the Communist Party of Nepal–Maoists (CPN-M) won the most seats and abolished the monarchy on 28 May 2008. The assembly elected Ram Baran Yadav of the Nepali Congress party as the country's first president in July. In legislative elections in November 2013, the social-democratic Nepali Congress party became the largest party; its leader Sushil Koirala was elected prime minister by parliament but had to step down in October 2015 under the new constitution. K. P. Sharma Oli of the Communist Party of Nepal (Unified Marxist Leninist) was then elected prime minister and women's rights campaigner Bidha Devi Bhandari, vice-chair of the same political party, became the country's second president and its first woman president. Oli resigned in July 2016 just hours before a vote of no confidence in parliament and was replaced by former rebel leader Pushpa Kamal Dahal in August, but was reinstated in February 2018. Bhandari was re-elected in March 2018.

The monarchy was abolished in May 2008 and the country declared a republic; on 20 September 2015 a new constitution was adopted that divided the country into seven federal provinces. The head of state is the president, who is elected by parliament and state assemblies for a five-year term, renewable once. The bicameral Federal Parliament consists of 275 directly elected members who serve five-year terms, and 59 National Assembly members serving six-year terms; 56 are indirectly elected by an electoral college of state and municipal government leaders, and three appointed by the government.

The prime minister is appointed by consensus among the political parties or elected by a two-thirds majority of the assembly. The council of ministers is appointed by the prime minister.

HEAD OF STATE
President, Bidha Devi Bhandari, *elected* 28 October 2015, *sworn in* 29 October 2015, *re-elected* 13 March 2018
Vice-President, Nanda Kishor Pun

SELECTED GOVERNMENT MEMBERS *AS AT NOVEMBER 2020*
Prime Minister, Khadga Prasad Sharma Oli
Deputy Prime Minister, Ishwor Pokharel
Finance, Bishnu Paudel
Foreign Affairs, Pradeep Kumar Gyawali

EMBASSY OF NEPAL
12A Kensington Palace Gardens, London W8 4QU
T 020-7229 1594 **E** eon@nepembassy.org.uk
W www.nepembassy.org.uk
Ambassador Extraordinary and Plenipotentiary, HE Dr Durga Bahadur Subedi, *apptd* 2016

BRITISH EMBASSY
PO Box 106, Lainchaur, Kathmandu
T (+977) (1) 441 0583 **E** bekathmandu@fco.gov.uk
W www.gov.uk/government/world/nepal
Ambassador Extraordinary and Plenipotentiary, HE Nicola Pollitt, *apptd* 2019

ECONOMY AND TRADE
The country is one of the poorest in Asia, and the economy is dependent on foreign aid, remittances (30 per cent of GDP) and trade with India. Tourism and hydroelectric power have potential for development, although this might compound growing environmental problems. Investment agreements have been signed with India, China and the US, focusing on electricity generation and infrastructure. A cross-border oil pipeline – the first in South Asia – opened with India in September 2019. Greater political stability resulted in strong growth between 2016 and 2019.

Agriculture is the main economic sector, generating 27 per cent of GDP and engaging about 69 per cent of the workforce; principal crops are pulses, rice, maize, wheat, sugar cane, jute, root crops, milk and meat. Industries other than tourism include carpets, textiles, cigarettes, cement and bricks, and the processing agricultural products. Industry accounts for 13.5 per cent of GDP and services for 59.5 per cent. The April 2015 earthquake severely damaged the economy, with reconstruction costs estimated at roughly US$10bn (£6.5bn), around 50 per cent of Nepal's GDP.

The main export market is India (53.1 per cent); the main import providers are India (70.2 per cent) and China. Principal exports are clothing, pulses, carpets, textiles, juice and jute goods. The main imports are petroleum products, machinery, gold, electrical goods and medicine.
GNI – US$31bn; US$1,090 per capita (2019)
Annual average growth of GDP – 7.9 per cent (2017 est)
Inflation rate – 4.5 per cent (2017 est)

Population below poverty line – 25.2 per cent (2011)
Unemployment rate – 3 per cent (2017 est)
Total external debt – US$5.849bn (2017 est)
Imports – US$11,617m (2017)
Exports – US$2,434m (2017)

BALANCE OF PAYMENTS
Trade – US$9,182m deficit (2017)
Current Account – US$9m deficit (2018)

Trade with UK	2018	2019
Imports from UK	£11,827,388	£16,759,379
Exports to UK	£19,046,181	£16,242,854

COMMUNICATIONS

Airports – The principal airport is at Kathmandu, and there are ten smaller airports around the country
Roadways and railways – 27,990km; 59km
Telecommunications – 855,926 fixed lines and 41.9 million mobile subscriptions (2019); there were 10.1 million internet users in 2018
Internet code and IDD – np; 977 (from UK), 44 (to UK)
Major broadcasters – The state-run Nepal Television Corporation operates various channels across the country alongside numerous private operators
Press – Dailies include the semi-official *Gorkhapatra,* Nepal's oldest newspaper, and *The Rising Nepal,* plus the private *The Kathmandu Post*
WPFI score – 35.10 (112)

EDUCATION AND HEALTH

Literacy rate – 68 per cent (2018 est)
Gross enrolment ratio (percentage of relevant age group) – primary 142.1 per cent, secondary 80.1 per cent, tertiary 13.3 per cent (2019 est)
Health expenditure (per capita) – US$48 (2017)
Hospital beds (per 1,000 people) – 3 (2012)
Life expectancy (years) – 71.8 (2020 est)
Mortality rate – 5.7 (2020 est)
Birth rate – 18.1 (2020 est)
Infant mortality rate – 25.1 (2020 est)
HIV/AIDS adult prevalence – 0.1 per cent (2019 est)

THE NETHERLANDS

Koninkrijk der Nederlanden – *Kingdom of the Netherlands*

Area – 41,543 sq. km
Capital – Amsterdam; population, 1,149,000 (2020 est)
Seat of government – The Hague (Den Haag or, in full, 's-Gravenhage); population, 629,000 (2009 est)
Major cities – Almere, Eindhoven, Haarlem, Groningen, Rotterdam, Tilburg, Utrecht

Currency – Euro (€) of 100 cents
Population – 17,280,397 rising at 0.37 per cent a year (2020 est); Dutch (76.9 per cent), Turkish (2.4 per cent), Moroccan (2.3 per cent)
Religion – Christian (Roman Catholic 23.6 per cent, Protestant 14.9 per cent), Muslim 5.1 per cent, other (including Hindu, Buddhist, Jewish) 5.6 per cent (est)
Language – Dutch (official), Frisian, Low Saxon, and Limburgish (official regional languages); English is widely spoken
Population density – 511 per sq. km (2019)
Urban population – 91.9 per cent (2019 est)
Median age (years) – 42.8 (2020 est)
National anthem – 'Het Wilhelmus' 'The William'
National day – 27 April (King's Day)
Death penalty – Abolished for all crimes (since 1982)
CPI score – 82 (8)
Military expenditure – US$11,243m (2018)

CLIMATE AND TERRAIN

The Netherlands is a low-lying country; about a quarter is below sea level, making it susceptible to flooding despite the coastal defences and a network of dykes and canals. Its land area has been extended over the centuries by land reclamation (polders), found especially in the west around the huge freshwater lake of Yssel, created in the 1930s by damming the Zuider Zee. The country is crossed by three major European rivers, the Rhine, Maas (Meuse) and Scheldt, whose estuaries are in the south-west. Mt Scenery (862m), on the Caribbean island of Saba, is considered the highest point of the Kingdom of the Netherlands. Elevation extremes in the Netherlands itself range from 322m (Vaalserberg) to −7m (Zuidplaspolder). The climate is temperate, with average temperatures ranging from 3.5°C in January to 18°C in August.

POLITICS

Under the 1983 constitution, the head of state is a hereditary constitutional monarch. The States-General *(Staten-Generaal)* consists of the First Chamber *(Eerste Kamer)* of 75 members, elected for a four-year term by the Provincial States; and the Second Chamber *(Tweede Kamer)* of 150 members, directly elected for a four-year term. The head of government is the prime minister, who is responsible to the legislature.

Although it is a stable democracy, one party has rarely commanded a sufficient parliamentary majority to govern alone in the post-war period; governments have usually been coalitions of two or more parties. In the May 2015 election to the First Chamber, the People's Party for Freedom and Democracy (VVD) led by Mark Rutte retained its position as the largest party; since 2012 the VVD has been the largest party in the Second Chamber, elections for which were held most recently in March 2017. Following those elections, it took Prime Minister Mark Rutte 225 days to form a new government – the longest coalition talks in the Netherlands' history. In March 2019, Dutch politics was fragmented further after the VVD was replaced as the largest party in the First Chamber by the anti-immigration Forum for Democracy. In April 2013, Queen Beatrix abdicated in favour of Willem-Alexander, her eldest son.

HEAD OF STATE
The King of the Netherlands, HM King Willem-Alexander, *born* 27 April 1967, *succeeded* 30 April 2013
Heir, Princess of Orange (Crown Princess), HRH Catharina-Amalia, *born* 7 December 2003

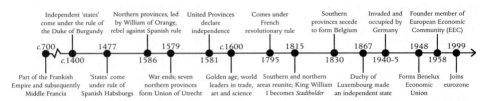

Independent 'states' come under the rule of the Duke of Burgundy	Northern provinces, led by William of Orange, rebel against Spanish rule	United Provinces declare independence	Comes under French revolutionary rule		Southern provinces secede to form Belgium	Invaded and occupied by Germany	Founder member of European Economic Community (EEC)	

c.700   1477   1579   c.1600   1815   1867   1948   1999
c.1400   1586   1581   1795   1830   1940-5   1958

Part of the Frankish Empire and subsequently Middle Francia | 'States' come under rule of Spanish Habsburgs | War ends; seven northern provinces form Union of Utrecht | Golden age; world leaders in trade, art and science | Southern and northern areas reunite; King William I becomes *Stadtholder* | Duchy of Luxembourg made an independent state | Forms Benelux Economic Union | Joins eurozone

SELECTED GOVERNMENT MEMBERS *AS AT NOVEMBER 2020*

Prime Minister, Mark Rutte
Deputy Prime Ministers, Hugo de Jonge; Carola Schouten; Wouter Koolmees
Defence, Ank Bijleveld-Schouten
Foreign Affairs, Stefan Blok

EMBASSY OF THE KINGDOM OF THE NETHERLANDS
38 Hyde Park Gate, London SW7 5DP
T 020-7590 3200 **E** lon@minbuza.nl **W** www.dutchembassyuk.org
Ambassador Extraordinary and Plenipotentiary, HE Simon Smits, *apptd* 2015

BRITISH EMBASSY
Lange Voorhout 10, The Hague, 2514 ED
T (+31) (70) 427 0427 **E** ukinnl@fco.gov.uk
W www.gov.uk/government/world/netherlands
Ambassador Extraordinary and Plenipotentiary, HE Peter Wilson, CMG, *apptd* 2017

ECONOMY AND TRADE
The Netherlands has a highly industrialised and diversified market economy, and is a major European transportation hub. The economy depends heavily on foreign trade and financial services, and contracted sharply in 2009 as exports fell by almost 25 per cent in the global economic downturn. The government nationalised two banks to stabilise the financial sector and introduced stimulus and austerity measures. The economy started growing again in 2014, and in 2017 the government recorded its first budget surplus since the crisis as GDP per capita also overtook pre-2008 levels. Growth was strong in subsequent years, but is expected to contract by 5.4 per cent in 2020 owing to the coronavirus pandemic.

The highly mechanised agricultural sector employs only 1.2 per cent of the workforce but output supplies the food processing industries and the export as well as the domestic market. Flower bulbs and cut flowers are a major contributor to this sector, as are fishing and livestock. The industrial sector contributes 17.9 per cent of GDP; major industries include food processing, and the manufacture of metal and engineering products, electrical machinery and equipment, chemicals, oil refining, construction and micro-electronics. The service industries represent 70.2 per cent of the economy. Other EU countries, China and the USA account for most overseas trade. Principal exports are machinery and equipment, chemicals, manufactured goods, fuels and foodstuffs. The main imports are machinery and transport equipment, chemicals, fuels, foodstuffs and clothing.
GNI – US$922.1bn; US$53,200 per capita (2019)
Annual average growth of GDP – 1.63 per cent (2019)
Inflation rate – 1.3 per cent (2017 est)
Population below poverty line – 8.8 per cent (2015 est)
Unemployment – 3.41 per cent (2019 est)
Total external debt – US$4.063 trillion (2016 est)
Imports – US$651,733m (2017)
Exports – US$739,098m (2017)

BALANCE OF PAYMENTS
Trade – US$87,365m surplus (2017)
Current Account – US$90,206m surplus (2019)

Trade with UK	2018	2019
Imports from UK	£25,771,513,485	£23,843,574,316
Exports to UK	£41,821,985,949	£42,534,060,763

COMMUNICATIONS
Airports – The principal airports are at Amsterdam, Rotterdam, Eindhoven and Maastricht, with a further 19 airports around the country
Waterways – The main seaport is Rotterdam, although there are a number of other ports on river estuaries or linked to the coast by the canals; 6,237km of inland waterways are navigable by ships of up to 50 tonnes. The large merchant fleet includes 744 ships of over 1,000 tonnes
Roadways and railways – 139,124km; 3,058km
Telecommunications – 5.6 million fixed lines and 21.9 million mobile subscriptions (2019); there were 16.2 million internet users in 2018
Internet code and IDD – nl; 31 (from UK), 44 (to UK)
Major broadcasters – A competitive broadcasting sector includes Nederlandse Omroep Stichting (NOS), which operates public radio and television stations
Press – Leading dailies include *Algemeen Dagblad, NRC Handelsblad* and *De Telegraaf*
WPFI score – 9.96 (5)

EDUCATION AND HEALTH
Education is free and compulsory for 13 years.
Gross enrolment ratio (percentage of relevant age group) – primary 105.2 per cent, secondary 134.3 per cent, tertiary 87.1 per cent (2018 est)
Health expenditure (per capita) – US$4,911 (2017)
Hospital beds (per 1,000 people) – 4.7 (2009)
Life expectancy (years) – 81.7 (2020 est)
Mortality rate – 9.2 (2020 est)
Birth rate – 11 (2020 est)
Infant mortality rate – 3.5 (2020 est)

OVERSEAS TERRITORIES
The Kingdom of the Netherlands consists of four autonomous elements: the Netherlands (European and Caribbean Netherlands), Aruba, Curacao and St Maarten; the latter two were part of the Netherlands Antilles until its dissolution on 10 October 2010. The other three islands of the Netherlands Antilles, the 'Caribbean Netherlands', comprising Bonaire, St Eustatius and Saba, are now autonomous special municipalities of the Netherlands.

ARUBA
Area – 180 sq. km
Capital – Oranjestad; population, 30,000 (2018)
Currency – Aruban florin of 100 cents
Population – 119,428 rising at 1.19 per cent a year (2020 est)
Religion – Christian (Roman Catholic 75.3 per cent, Protestant 4.9 per cent) (2010 est)
Language – Dutch (official), Papiamento, Spanish, English
Population density – 588 per sq. km (2018)
Urban population – 43.5 per cent (2018 est)

Median age (years) – 39.9 (2020 est)
National Day – 18 March (Flag Day)
The Caribbean island was colonised by the Dutch in the 17th century. It was part of the Netherlands Antilles until 1986, when it became a separate, autonomous territory. The Dutch government is responsible for external affairs and represented by a resident governor. Internal government is in the hands of the prime minister and council of ministers, *who are* responsible to the 21-member unicameral legislature *(Staten),* directly elected for a four-year term.

The principal economic activities are tourism and offshore financial services.

Governor, Alfonso Boekhoudt, *apptd* 2017
Prime Minister, Evelyn Wever-Croes, *elected* 2017

CURACAO
Area – 444 sq. km
Capital – Willemstad; population, 144,000 (2018)
Currency – Caribbean guilder of 100 cents
Population – 151,345 rising at 0.35 per cent a year (2020 est)
Religion – Christian (Roman Catholic 89.1 per cent, Pentecostal 6.6 per cent, Protestant 3.2 per cent) (2011 est)
Language – Dutch (official), Papiamento, English, Spanish
Population density – 109 per sq. km (2019)
Urban population – 89.1 per cent (2019 est)
Median age (years) – 36.7 (2020 est)
The island was colonised by the Dutch in the 17th century and was part of the Netherlands Antilles from 1954 until 10 October 2010, when it became a separate, autonomous territory. The Dutch government is responsible for external affairs and represented by a resident governor. Internal affairs are in the hands of a prime minister and council of ministers, who are responsible to the 21-member directly elected unicameral legislature *(Staten),* which serves a four-year term.

The principal economic activities are tourism, oil refining and offshore financial services.

Governor, Lucille George-Wout, *apptd* 2013
Prime Minister, Eugene Rhuggenaath, *took office* 2017

ST MAARTEN
Area – 34 sq. km
Capital – Philipsburg; population, 1,327 (est)
Currency – Caribbean guilder of 100 cents
Population – 43,847 rising at 1.34 per cent (2020 est)
Religion – Christian (Protestant 41.9 per cent, Roman Catholic 33.1 per cent), Hindu 5.2 per cent (2011 est)
Language – Dutch, English (official), Spanish, Creole
Population density – 1,193 per sq. km (2017)
Median age (years) – 41.1 (2020 est)
The territory forms the southern part of the island of St Martin in the Caribbean; the north is French territory. Possession of the island was disputed between the Dutch and the Spanish until 1648, when the Spanish relinquished it to the Dutch and French, who divided it between them. The Dutch territory was part of the Netherlands Antilles from 1954 until 10 October 2010, when it became a separate, autonomous territory. The Dutch government is responsible for external affairs and represented by a governor. Internal affairs are in the hands of a prime minister and council of ministers, who are responsible to the directly elected 15-member unicameral legislature *(Staten),* which serves a four-year term.

The principal economic activities are tourism and sugar production.

Governor, Eugene Holiday, *apptd* 2010
Prime Minister, Silveria Jacobs, *apptd* 2019

NEW ZEALAND
Aotearoa – *New Zealand*

Area – 268,838 sq. km (includes outlying islands)
Capital – Wellington; population, 415,000 (2020 est)
Major cities – Auckland, Christchurch, Dunedin, Hamilton, Manakau, North Shore, Tauranga, Waitakere
Currency – New Zealand dollar (NZ$) of 100 cents
Population – 4,925,477 rising at 1.44 per cent a year (2020 est); European (64.1 per cent), Maori (16.5 per cent), Asian (11.3 per cent), Pacific Islander (7.6 per cent) (est)
Religion – Christian 37.3 per cent, Hindu 2.7 per cent, Buddhist 1.1 per cent, Muslim 1.3 per cent, other (including Jewish, Spiritualist, Baha'i) 1.6 per cent (est)
Language – English, Maori, New Zealand Sign Language (all official), Samoan, Hindi, French, Northern Chinese, Yue
Population density – 18 per sq. km (2019)
Urban population – 86.6 per cent (2019 est)
Median age (years) – 37.2 (2020 est)
National anthems – 'God Defend New Zealand'
National day – 6 February (Waitangi Day)
Death penalty – Abolished for all crimes (since 1989)
CPI score – 87 (1)
Military expenditure – US$2,263m (2018)

CLIMATE AND TERRAIN
New Zealand consists of North Island, South Island and neighbouring coastal islands such as Stewart Island, and outlying islands that include the Chatham, Kermadec, Three Kings, Bounty, Antipodes, Snares, Auckland and Campbell groups in the South Pacific Ocean. The two larger islands, North Island and South Island, are separated by the relatively narrow Cook Strait. The island groups are much smaller and more widely dispersed.

Much of the North and South Islands is mountainous. The North Island mountains include several volcanoes, three of which are active. The principal range is the Southern Alps, extending the entire length of South Island to the west of the Canterbury Plains. There are geysers and hot springs in the Rotorua district and glaciers in the Southern Alps. Elevation extremes range from 3,754m (Aoraki/Mt Cook) to 0m (Pacific Ocean). The climate is temperate, though with marked regional variations; average temperatures range from 5.5°C in July to 15.5°C in February. The country is subject to seismic activity; a major earthquake devastated Christchurch in February 2011.

HISTORY AND POLITICS
Settled by Polynesian tribes, the ancestors of the Maori, from about the tenth century, New Zealand was sighted by the Dutch navigator Abel Tasman in 1642 but he did not land. The British explorer James Cook surveyed the coastline in 1769, the year in which the islands were claimed by the British. The Maori accepted British sovereignty in 1840,

under the Treaty of Waitangi, in return for land rights and the rights of British subjects. Large-scale European immigration and the 1860s gold rush led to encroachment by settlers and 'land wars' with the Maori in 1860 and 1872; Maori resistance was defeated but concessions such as parliamentary representation were won. A tribunal was set up in 1975 to consider grievances caused by breaches of the Waitangi Treaty, and in the 1990s the Maori were compensated for land lost to European settlers.

New Zealand was administered as part of Britain's New South Wales colony until 1841, when it became a separate colony. In 1907 it was granted dominion status; in 1931 the Statute of Westminster tacitly acknowledged its independence, which was formally confirmed in 1947.

New Zealand forces took part in the Boer War, both world wars, the Korean War and the Vietnam War. Since the UK's entry into the EEC in 1973, the focus of New Zealand's foreign and trade policies has shifted to Asia and the Pacific region.

Post-war politics has been dominated by the National Party and the Labour Party, either forming governments on their own or in coalition with smaller parties; coalitions have been the norm since a proportional representation voting system was introduced in 1996. After inconclusive legislative elections in September 2017, the Labour Party (LP), led by Jacinda Ardern, 37, formed a government with the New Zealand First Party in October; in the process, Ardern became the country's youngest prime minister since 1856. In the October 2020 elections the LP won by a landslide, the first time a single party had won a majority since the introduction of proportional representation. A 2016 referendum voted by a margin of more than 10 per cent to retain the country's flag, which features the Union Flag, as opposed to a design bearing a silver fern.

There is no written constitution. The head of state is Queen Elizabeth II, represented by the governor-general, who is appointed on the advice of the New Zealand government. The unicameral House of Representatives usually has 120 members elected for a three-year term; there are 71 members from single-member constituencies, which includes seven Maori constituencies, and 49 by proportional representation; if a party wins a significantly larger proportion of constituency seats relative to their party list vote, this can result in an 'overhang' of extra seats. The prime minister and cabinet are appointed by the governor-general on the advice of the legislature.

GOVERNOR-GENERAL
Governor-General, HE Dame Patricia Reddy, DNZM, *sworn in* September 2016

SELECTED GOVERNMENT MEMBERS *AS AT NOVEMBER 2020*
Prime Minister, Jacinda Ardern
Deputy Prime Minister, Finance, Grant Robertson
Foreign Affairs, Nania Mahuta

NEW ZEALAND HIGH COMMISSION
New Zealand House, 80 Haymarket, London SW1Y 4TQ
T 020-7930 8422 **E** aboutnz@newzealandhc.org.uk
W www.nzembassy.com/uk
High Commissioner, HE Bede Gilbert Corry, *apptd* 2017

BRITISH HIGH COMMISSION
44 Hill Street, Thorndon, Wellington 6011
T (+64) (4) 924 2888 **E** consularmail.wellington@fco.gov.uk
W www.gov.uk/government/world/new-zealand
High Commissioner, HE Laura Clarke, *apptd* 2018

ECONOMY AND TRADE
Since the 1980s industrial and service sectors have superseded the large, efficient agricultural sector. Growth has been driven by trade, particularly in agricultural products, but various factors had pushed the economy into recession in 2008 before the global downturn. The government managed to return a surplus in 2014–15, and have prioritised free trade agreements with many nations in recent years, especially China. Growth was maintained prior to the coronavirus pandemic in 2020. Although the government's handling of the virus was internationally praised, the economy is nonetheless expected to shrink by 6.1 per cent in 2020.

The agricultural sector contributes 5.7 per cent of GDP and employs 6.6 per cent of the workforce. The main products are dairy products, meat, cereals, pulses, fruit, vegetables, wool and fish. The major industries are food processing, wood and paper products, manufacturing, financial services, mining, and tourism, which is overtaking agriculture as the main source of foreign exchange revenue. Non-metallic minerals such as coal, limestone and dolomite are heavily exploited, and gold and iron production is economically important. Natural gas deposits in offshore and onshore fields are used for electricity generation, though a significant amount of the country's energy is derived from sustainable sources such as hydroelectric power. Industry contributes 21.5 per cent of GDP and services 72.8 per cent.

The main trading partners are China, Australia, the USA and Japan. Principal exports are dairy products, meat, wood, fruit, fish, crude oil and wine. The main imports are machinery and equipment, vehicles and aircraft, petroleum, electronics and textiles.

GNI – US$209.8bn; US$42,670 per capita (2019)
Annual average growth of GDP – 2.22 per cent (2019 est)
Inflation rate – 1.9 per cent (2017 est)
Unemployment – 4.13 per cent (2019 est)
Total external debt – US$91.62bn (2017 est)
Imports – US$52,685m (2018)
Exports – US$54,342m (2018)

BALANCE OF PAYMENTS
Trade – US$1,656m surplus (2017)
Current Account – US$6,842m deficit (2019)

Trade with UK	2018	2019
Imports from UK	£904,982,339	£839,145,425
Exports to UK	£893,035,130	£868,325,820

Figures include Cook Islands and Niue

COMMUNICATIONS
Airports and waterways – The principal airports are at Auckland, Wellington (North Island), Christchurch and Dunedin (South Island) and there are 35 smaller airports around the country; Tauranga, Christchurch, New Plymouth, Auckland and Napier are the main seaports
Roadways and railways – 94,000km; 4,128km
Telecommunications – 1.8 million fixed lines and 6.6 million mobile subscriptions (2019); there were 4.3 million internet users in 2018
Internet code and IDD – nz; 64 (from UK), 44 (to UK)
Major broadcasters – The state-owned Television New Zealand and Radio New Zealand operate nationally; Niu FM is the national government-funded station for the Pacific island communities
Press – The Auckland-based *New Zealand Herald* has the largest circulation, alongside Wellington-based *Dominion Post* and Christchurch-based *The Press*
WPFI score – 10.69 (9)

EDUCATION AND HEALTH

Education is free of charge and compulsory between the ages of 5 and 16.

Gross enrolment ratio (percentage of relevant age group) – primary 101.1 per cent, secondary 114.6 per cent, tertiary 83 per cent (2018 est)
Health expenditure (per capita) – US$3,937 (2017)
Hospital beds (per 1,000 people) – 2.8 (2013)
Life expectancy (years) – 82.1 (2020 est)
Mortality rate – 6.9 (2020 est)
Birth rate – 12.8 (2020 est)
Infant mortality rate – 3.5 (2020 est)

TERRITORIES

TOKELAU

Area – 12 sq. km
Population – 1,647 (2019 est) falling at 0.01 per cent a year (2014 est)

Tokelau consists of three atolls, Fakaofo, Nukunonu and Atafu, in the southern Pacific Ocean. Formerly part of Britain's Gilbert and Ellice Islands colony, Tokelau was transferred to New Zealand administration in 1926 and proclaimed part of New Zealand in 1949.

The territory is self-administering, but has rejected greater autonomy in two referendums (2006 and 2007). The Council for the Ongoing Government (cabinet) comprises three *Faipule* (village leaders) and three *Pulenuku* (village mayors), one from each atoll; the position of *Ulu-o-Tokelau* (leader) is rotated among the three *Faipule* members annually. The *General Fono*, which has 20 members elected for a three-year term, has legislative powers. Each atoll has a *Taupulega* (council of elders).

The economy is heavily dependent on New Zealand budgetary aid, with some revenue derived from remittances and the sale of fishing rights, stamps, coins and the use of its internet suffix. The main activities are subsistence farming, copra production and handicrafts. In 2011 Tokelau changed its position within the international dateline in order to improve trade links with Australia and New Zealand.
Administrator, Ross Adern, *apptd* 2018

THE ROSS DEPENDENCY

New Zealand has administrative responsibility for the Ross Dependency. This is defined as all the Antarctic islands and territories between 160° E. and 150° W. longitude that are situated south of the 60° S. parallel, including Edward VII Land and portions of Victoria Land (*see also* The North and South Poles).

ASSOCIATED STATES

COOK ISLANDS

Area – 236 sq. km
Population – 8,574 falling at 2.59 per cent a year (2020 est)
Capital – Avarua, on Rarotonga
Religion – Christian (Protestant 62.8 per cent, Roman Catholic 17 per cent, Mormon 4.4 per cent), other 8 per cent (est)
Urban population – 75.3 per cent (2019 est)

The Cook Islands consist of 15 volcanic islands and coral atolls in the southern Pacific Ocean. A former British protectorate, since 1965 the islands have been self-governing in free association with New Zealand.

Queen Elizabeth II has a representative on the islands, and the New Zealand government is represented by a high commissioner. There is a 24-member legislative assembly, and the House of Ariki, made up of 15 traditional leaders who advise on traditional matters. Executive power is exercised by a prime minister and a cabinet responsible to the legislature.

The main economic activities are tourism, offshore banking, agriculture (especially tropical fruits), fruit processing, fishing, garment manufacturing, handicrafts and pearl-farming; black pearls are the main export.
HM Representative, HE Sir Tom Marsters, KBE *apptd* 2013
Prime Minister, Mark Brown, *apptd* 2020

NIUE

Area – 260 sq. km
Population – 2,000 (2019 est) falling at 0.03 per cent a year (2014 est)
Capital – Alofi; population 1,000 (2014 est)
Religion – Christian (Ekalesia Niue 67 per cent, Mormon 10 per cent, Roman Catholic 10 per cent, Jehovah's Witness 2 per cent) (est)
Urban population – 45.5 per cent (2019 est)

Although part of the Cook Islands group, Niue was administered separately after 1903. Since 1974 the island has been self-governing in free association with New Zealand.

A New Zealand high commissioner represents both the Queen and the New Zealand government. There is a 20-member legislative assembly; executive power is exercised by a prime minister and a three-member cabinet drawn from the assembly's members.

The principal economic activities are agriculture, fishing, tourism, handicrafts, food processing and the sale of postage stamps and the use of its internet suffix.
New Zealand High Commissioner, Fisu Pihigia, *apptd* 2017
Premier, Toke Talagi, *apptd* 2008

NICARAGUA

República de Nicaragua – Republic of Nicaragua

Area – 130,370 sq. km
Capital – Managua; population, 1,064,000 (2020 est)
Major cities – Chinandega, León, Masaya, Tipitapa
Currency – Córdoba (C$) of 100 centavos
Population – 6,203,441 rising at 0.96 per cent a year (2020 est)
Religion – Christian (Roman Catholic 50 per cent, Evangelical 33.2 per cent) (est)
Language – Spanish (official), English, Miskito
Population density – 54 per sq. km (2019)
Urban population – 58.8 per cent (2019 est)
Median age (years) – 27.3 (2020 est)
National anthem – 'Salve a ti, Nicaragua' 'Hail to Thee, Nicaragua'
National day – 15 September (Independence Day)
Death penalty – Abolished for all crimes (since 1979)
CPI score – 22 (161)
Military expenditure – US$81.6m (2018)

CLIMATE AND TERRAIN

The narrow Pacific coastal plain is broken by active volcanoes and lakes Managua and Nicaragua. A mountainous central region separates it from the broad Atlantic coastal plain, which constitutes 60 per cent of the country and is covered by tropical rainforest. Elevation extremes range from 2,438m (Mogoton) to 0m (Pacific Ocean). The climate is generally tropical on the plains but cooler at altitude; the average temperature is 25.6°C. The country is subject to frequent earthquakes.

HISTORY AND POLITICS

Nicaragua was originally populated by tribes related to the Aztec, Maya and other indigenous people. Fossilised footprints, the oldest in South America, indicate a human presence in Nicaragua dating back 6,000 years. Spanish colonisation began in 1523 but in the 17th and 18th centuries the British were the dominant presence on the Caribbean coast, with the Spanish controlling the Pacific plain. Independence from Spain was achieved in 1821 and the area was initially incorporated into Mexico. In 1823 it became part of a Central American federation of former Spanish provinces but seceded and became fully independent in 1838. British control of the Caribbean coast was ceded to Nicaragua in 1860.

In 1893, General José Santos Zelaya established a dictatorship that lasted until 1909, when he was overthrown by US troops. General Anastasio Somoza established a dictatorship in 1938 and ruled until his assassination in 1956, when he was succeeded as president by his sons Luis (1956–67) and Anastasio (1967–79). After 44 years in power, the family was overthrown in 1979 in a popular revolt led by the *Frente Sandinista de Liberación Nacional* (FSLN), popularly known as the *Sandinistas*.

The Sandinistas' socialist government redistributed land and promoted education and health services, but was opposed by US-backed right-wing guerrillas (the Contras). The civil war lasted from 1982 until 1990 (although there was a ceasefire from 1988), when the Sandinistas were unexpectedly defeated in elections by a coalition of opposition parties.

From 1990 to 2006, governments were liberal or liberal-dominated coalitions, keeping the FSLN from power even though it was often the largest party in the legislature. However, in the 2006 presidential and legislative elections, the FSLN candidate, Daniel Ortega (president 1984–90), was elected president and the FSLN was returned to government.

In 2009 the Supreme Court lifted the ban on a president serving two consecutive terms and in 2014 the National Assembly eliminated constitutional term limits for the presidency altogether, allowing President Ortega to run for re-election in 2011 and again in November 2016. Opposition parties called the changes undemocratic and labelled as flawed the 2016 election, which President Ortega won with a landslide. His FSLN party also won over 65 per cent of the 2016 vote for the National Assembly. Prompted by cuts to social security, nationwide anti-government protests began in April 2018 and were violently suppressed by police forces and militias of Ortega supporters. Around 300 people were killed and an estimated 100,000 Nicaraguans have fled the country since.

The unicameral National Assembly has 90 members directly elected for a five-year term, plus unsuccessful presidential and vice-presidential candidates may be awarded a seat if they receive more than the average percentage of the vote in each electoral district. The cabinet is appointed by the president.

HEAD OF STATE

President, Daniel Ortega, *elected* 5 November 2006, *sworn in* 10 January 2007, *re-elected* 2011, 2016
Vice-President, Rosaria Murillo

SELECTED GOVERNMENT MEMBERS *AS AT NOVEMBER 2020*

Defence, Martha Elena Ruiz Sevilla
Finance, Ivan Acosta Montalvan
Foreign Affairs, Dennis Moncada Colindres
Interior, Maria Amelia Coronel Kinloch

EMBASSY OF NICARAGUA

Suite 2, Vicarage House, 58–60 Kensington Church Street, London W8 4DP
T 020-7938 2373
Ambassador Extraordinary and Plenipotentiary, HE Guisell Morales-Echaverry, *apptd* 2015

BRITISH AMBASSADOR

HE Ross Denny, *apptd* 2015, resident at San José, Costa Rica

ECONOMY AND TRADE

Progress towards economic recovery and reconstruction after the civil war has been slow and the country remains the poorest in Central America. The economy contracted in 2009 as the global downturn reduced key commodity prices, export demand and remittances. Although almost 80 per cent of debt was cancelled in 2004 and 2006, the government is dependent on foreign aid and 29.6 per cent of the population live below the poverty line. A Chinese-led US$50bn inter-oceanic canal project agreed in 2013 has yet to begin construction. The economy contracted by 4 per cent in 2018, its worst performance since the civil war of the 1980s, and has also suffered because of sustained nationwide opposition to President Ortega's rule. This trend has continued, with a contraction of 3.9 per cent in 2019 and an expected fall of 5.5 per cent in 2020, partly due to the coronavirus pandemic.

Agriculture is the mainstay of the economy, accounting for 15.5 per cent of GDP and roughly 31 per cent of employment. The main commercial crops are coffee, bananas, sugar cane, beef, shellfish, tobacco and peanuts. Industry includes food and timber processing, mining, the manufacture of chemicals, machinery, metal products, clothing and footwear, oil refining and wood. Industry contributes 24.4 per cent of GDP and services 60 per cent.

The main trading partners are the USA, and other Central and South American countries. Principal exports are the main commercial crops and gold. The main imports are consumer goods, machinery and equipment, raw materials and petroleum products.

GNI – US$12.5bn; US$1,910 per capita (2019)
Annual average growth of GDP – 4.9 per cent (2017 est)
Inflation rate – 3.9 per cent (2017 est)
Population below poverty line – 29.6 per cent (2015 est)
Unemployment – 6.4 per cent (2017 est)
Total external debt – US$11.31bn (2017 est)
Imports – US$7,656m (2017)
Exports – US$5,372m (2017)

BALANCE OF PAYMENTS

Trade – US$2,283m deficit (2017)
Current Account – US$755m surplus (2019)

Trade with UK	2018	2019
Imports from UK	£5,397,393	£4,442,153
Exports to UK	£42,194,841	£40,408,455

COMMUNICATIONS

Airports – The main airport is at Managua, and there are a further 11 airports around the country
Waterways – The chief ports are Corinto (Pacific) and Bluefields and El Bluff (Caribbean); there are 2,220km of inland waterways, mostly on lakes Managua and Nicaragua
Roadways – 3,346km; the Inter-American Highway runs between Nicaragua's Honduran and Costa Rican borders, and

the Inter-Oceanic Highway runs from Corinto on the Pacific coast via Managua to Rama, where there is a natural waterway to Bluefields on the Caribbean
Telecommunications – 215,055 fixed lines and 5.4 million mobile subscriptions (2018); there were 1.7 million internet users in 2018
Internet code and IDD – ni; 505 (from UK), 44 (to UK)
Major broadcasters – There are several commercial television and radio broadcasters, including Nicavision Canal 12; Radio Nicaragua is publicly owned
Press – *La Prensa* and *El Nuevo Diario* are the country's two principal daily newspapers
WPFI score – 35.81 (117)

EDUCATION AND HEALTH
Literacy rate – 82.6 per cent (2015 est)
Gross enrolment ratio (percentage of relevant age group) – primary 117 per cent, secondary 69 per cent (2010 est)
Health expenditure (per capita) – US$192 (2017)
Hospital beds (per 1,000 people) – 0.9 (2014)
Life expectancy (years) – 74.2 (2020 est)
Mortality rate – 5.2 (2020 est)
Birth rate – 17.1 (2020 est)
Infant mortality rate – 16.5 (2020 est)
HIV/AIDS adult prevalence – 0.2 per cent (2016 est)

NIGER

République du Niger – *Republic of Niger*

Area – 1,267,000 sq. km
Capital – Niamey; population, 1,292,000 (2020 est)
Major cities – Agadez, Maradi, Zinder
Currency – Franc CFA of 100 centimes
Population – 22,772,361 rising at 3.66 per cent a year (2020 est); Hausa (53.1 per cent), Zarma/Songhai (21.2 per cent), Tuareg (11 per cent), Fulani (6.5 per cent), Kanouri (5.9 per cent) (est)
Religion – Muslim 99.3 per cent (est)
Language – French (official), Hausa, Djerma
Population density – 18 per sq. km (2019)
Urban population – 16.5 per cent (2019 est)
Median age (years) – 14.8 (2020 est)
National anthem – 'La Nigérienne' 'The Nigerian'
National day – 18 December (Republic Day)
Death penalty – Retained (no known use since 1976)
CPI score – 32 (120)
Military expenditure – US$230m (2018 est)
Conscription – 18 years of age; 24 months (selective)
Literacy rate – 35.0 per cent (2018 est)
Gross enrolment ratio (percentage of relevant age group) – primary 66.4 per cent (2019 est); secondary 24.3 per cent (2017 est); tertiary 4.2 per cent (2019 est)
Health expenditure (per capita) – US$29 (2017)

Life expectancy (years) – 53.9 (2020 est)
Mortality rate – 10.2 (2020 est)
Birth rate – 47.5 (2020 est)
Infant mortality rate – 67.7 (2020 est)
HIV/AIDS adult prevalence – 0.2 per cent (2019 est)

CLIMATE AND TERRAIN
Niger is mostly desert, with low hills in the north and savannah in the south. Elevation extremes range from 2,022m (Mt Idoukal-n-Taghes/Bagzane) to 200m (Niger river). The Niger valley in the south-west is the only well-watered area. There is a desert climate, except in the extreme south, which is subtropical. Average temperatures range from 19.3°C in January to 33.3°C in June.

HISTORY AND POLITICS
The area was divided between several kingdoms formed by different tribes (Tuareg, Songhai, Hausa, Fulani) from the tenth to 19th centuries. French colonial expansion from the 1880s brought the whole area under its control in 1898 and in 1904 it became part of French West Africa. The country became autonomous in 1958 and achieved full independence in 1960.

The first president introduced a one-party regime, which continued under the military government installed after a coup in 1974. Following popular agitation, civilian government was reintroduced in 1989, other parties were legalised in 1990, and multi-party elections held in 1993. This political liberalisation was reversed following a military coup in 1996 led by Brig. Ibrahim Barre Mainassara. He was assassinated in 1999 by the military, who restored political pluralism.

From 1990 there was a rebellion in the north by Tuareg seeking greater social equality and political representation. Peace agreements with rebel groups in 1995 and 1997 brought calm until 2007, when a new rebel group emerged, seeking greater autonomy and access to mining revenue; this group signed a ceasefire with the government in 2009. Boko Haram militants have posed an increasing threat to civilian life in recent years, especially in the country's south-east.

After seeking to increase his powers in 2009, President Mamadou Tandja (first elected in 1999) was deposed in February 2010 by the military. A referendum on a new constitution was held in October 2010, and presidential and legislative elections were held in January 2011. The Nigerien Party for Democracy and Socialism (PNDS-Tarayya) won the most seats, but without a majority; in August 2013 a unity government was declared under Prime Minister Brigi Rafini. PNDS-Tarayya retained control of the legislature in the February 2016 general elections and the party's leader, Mahamadou Issoufou, was re-elected president in the second round of voting a month later, having assumed the role in 2011.

The 2010 constitution, amended in 2016, reduced the president's powers and restored the limit on presidential terms. The executive president is directly elected for a five-year term, renewable once. The unicameral National Assembly has 171 members directly elected for a five-year term; eight seats are reserved for minorities and five for Nigeriens living abroad. The prime minister is appointed by the president.

HEAD OF STATE
President, Mahamadou Issoufou, *elected* 12 March 2011, *took office* 7 April 2011, *re-elected* 20 March 2016

SELECTED GOVERNMENT MEMBERS *AS AT NOVEMBER 2020*
Prime Minister, Brigi Rafini
Finance, Mamadou Diop

Foreign Affairs, Kalla Hankouraou
Interior, Alkache Alhada

EMBASSY OF REPUBLIC OF NIGER
154 Rue de Longchamp, 75116 Paris, France
T (00) 331 4504 8060
Ambassador Extraordinary and Plenipotentiary, HE Ado Elhadji
  Abou, *apptd* 2018

BRITISH AMBASSADOR
Ambassador Extraordinary and Plenipotentiary, HE Guy
  Warrington, *apptd* 2020, resident at Bamako, Mali

ECONOMY AND TRADE

Niger is considered the least developed country in the world, with almost half of the population living below the poverty line. Economic progress has been hampered by terrorist activity, political instability, food insecurity caused by recurrent droughts, desertification and over-grazing, and rapid population growth. The country is dependent on foreign aid, which makes up a large proportion of government revenue. Its huge foreign debt burden was much reduced by debt relief and cancellation in 2000 and 2005, but public debt has been growing since 2011 as spending on infrastructure and security has increased. While the country negotiated an extended credit facility agreement with the IMF in 2012–16 and for 2017–20, and in June 2017 agreed a three-year $1bn (£775m) grant with the World Bank to boost climate-resilient agricultural production and alleviate poverty, Niger suffers from fluctuations in the price of its exports and has struggled to diversify its economy.

The mainstay of the economy is currently subsistence agriculture and herding, which accounts for 41.6 per cent of GDP and engages 79.2 per cent of the population; the main cash crops are cowpeas, cotton, vegetables, peanuts and livestock. The most significant export is uranium, making the economy vulnerable to fluctuations in global prices; efforts are being made to diversify into exploitation of other mineral resources, including gold and oil. The other industries include processing agricultural products and manufacturing cement, bricks, soap, textiles and chemicals. Industry contributes 19.5 per cent of GDP and services 41.6 per cent.

The main trading partners are France, Thailand and China. Principal exports are uranium ore, livestock, cowpeas and onions. The main imports are foodstuffs, machinery, vehicles and parts, petroleum and cereals.

GNI – US$13.1bn; US$560 per capita (2019)
Annual average growth of GDP – 4.9 per cent (2017 est)
Inflation rate – 2.4 per cent (2017 est)
Population below poverty line – 45.4 per cent (2014 est)
Unemployment – 0.3 per cent (2017 est)
Total external debt – US$3.728bn (2017 est)
Imports – US$2,525m (2016)
Exports – US$1,188m (2016)

BALANCE OF PAYMENTS
Trade – US$1,337m deficit (2016)
Current Account – US$1,625m deficit (2018)

Trade with UK	2018	2019
Imports from UK	£2,483,205	£4,148,983
Exports to UK	£1,664,331	£543,852

COMMUNICATIONS

Airports and waterways – The principal airport is at Niamey and there are a further nine airports; the river Niger is navigable between September and March for 300km from Niamey to the Benin frontier
Roadways – 3,912km
Telecommunications – 116,352 fixed lines and 8.9 million mobile subscriptions (2019); there were 1.1 million internet users in 2018
Internet code and IDD – ne; 227 (from UK), 44 (to UK)
Major broadcasters – The government-owned Télé-Sahel (TV) competes with a number of commercial stations; state-run La Voix du Sahel is the only radio station offering national coverage
Press – The state-run *Le Sahel* is the only national daily
WPFI score – 28.25 (57)

NIGERIA

Federal Republic of Nigeria

Area – 923,768 sq. km
Capital – Abuja (since 1991); population, 3,278,000 (2020 est)
Major cities – Aba, Benin City, Ibadan, Ilorin, Kaduna, Kano, Lagos (the former capital), Port Harcourt, Warri, Zaria
Currency – Naira (N) of 100 kobo
Population – 214,028,302 rising at 2.53 per cent a year (2020 est); Hausa (30 per cent), Yoruba (15.5 per cent), Igbo (15.2 per cent), Fulani (6 per cent) (est)
Religion – Muslim 53.5 per cent, Christian 45.9 per cent (est)
Language – English (official), Hausa, Yoruba, Igbo, Fulani, over 500 other languages
Population density – 215 per sq. km (2019)
Urban population – 51.2 per cent (2019 est)
Median age (years) – 18.6 (2020 est)
National anthem – 'Arise O Compatriots, Nigeria's Call Obey'
National day – 1 October (Independence Day)
Death penalty – Retained
CPI score – 26 (146)
Military expenditure – US$2,043m (2018)

CLIMATE AND TERRAIN

The north is arid savannah and semi-desert plains, which rise to central hills and plateaux. There are mountains along the southeastern border, but the south is generally low-lying and covered in tropical rainforest, with mangrove swamps along the coast and hills in the south-east. Elevation extremes range from 2,419m (Chappal Waddi) to 0m (Atlantic Ocean). The river Niger flows across the country from the north-west to the south coast, where it forms a broad delta on the Gulf of

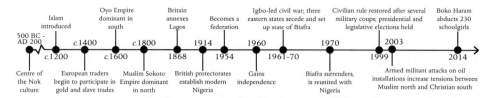

Timeline:

500 BC – AD 200 — Centre of the Nok culture
c.1200 — European traders begin to participate in gold and slave trades
c.1400 — Islam introduced
c.1600 — Muslim Sokoto Empire dominant in north
Oyo Empire dominant in south
c.1800
1868 — British protectorates establish modern Nigeria
Britain annexes Lagos
1914
1954 — Becomes a federation
1960 — Gains independence
Igbo-led civil war; three eastern states secede and set up state of Biafra
1961-70
1970 — Biafra surrenders, is reunited with Nigeria
Civilian rule restored after several military coups; presidential and legislative elections held
1999
2003 — Armed militant attacks on oil installations increase tensions between Muslim north and Christian south
Boko Haram abducts 230 schoolgirls
2014

Guinea. The climate is equatorial in the south, tropical in the centre and arid in the north. The north has one rainy season (June to September), while the south has two (March–July, September–October); average national temperatures range from 24.9°C in January to 30.4°C in April.

POLITICS

The country is a federal democratic republic. Under the 1999 constitution, the executive president is directly elected for a four-year term, renewable once. The president appoints the federal executive council, which must be approved by the senate. The bicameral National Assembly comprises the 360-member House of Representatives and the 109-member senate, both elected for a four-year term.

The March 2015 presidential election was won by former military ruler Muhammadu Buhari of the All Progressives Congress (APC) – the first time an opposition candidate has unseated the incumbent at the ballot box. The APC also secured a majority in both houses during the simultaneous legislative elections. Despite some allegations of fraud, the elections were described as largely fair by the majority of observers. Buhari was re-elected in February 2019 in an election marked by low voter turnout; opposition candidate Atiku Abubakar publicly and legally challenged the results. Buhari's APC retained its majority in both houses. Protests erupted in October 2020 against police brutality, which were met with violence by authorities and resulted in the deaths of at least 12 protesters.

Ethnic and religious violence was still commonplace in 2018–19: it was believed the Boko Haram insurgency had displaced almost 2.4 million people by December 2018. As at June 2018, the country was estimated to contain the largest concentration of people living in extreme poverty in the world, at nearly 87 million.

HEAD OF STATE

President, C-in-C of the Armed Forces, Muhammadu Buhari, *elected* 31 March 2015, *sworn in* 5 May 2015, *re-elected* 23 February 2019
Vice-President, Yemi Osinbajo

SELECTED GOVERNMENT MEMBERS *AS AT NOVEMBER 2020*

Finance, Zainab Ahmed
Foreign Affairs, Geoffrey Onyeama
Interior, Rauf Aregbesola

HIGH COMMISSION FOR THE FEDERAL REPUBLIC OF NIGERIA

Nigeria House, 9 Northumberland Avenue, London WC2N 5BX
T 020-7839 1244 **E** information@nigeriahc.org.uk
W www.nigeriahc.org.uk
High Commissioner, HE George Oguntade, *apptd* 2017

BRITISH HIGH COMMISSION

19 Torrens Close, Mississippi, Maitama, Abuja
T (+234) (9) 462 2200 **E** ppainformation.abuja@fco.gov.uk
W www.gov.uk/government/world/nigeria
High Commissioner, HE Catriona Laing, *apptd* 2018

FEDERAL STRUCTURE

The federal republic is divided into 36 states and the Federal Capital Territory: Abia, Adamawa, Akwa Ibom, Anambra, Bauchi, Bayelsa, Benue, Borno, Cross River, Delta, Ebonyi, Edo, Ekiti, Enugu, Gombe, Imo, Jigawa, Kaduna, Kano, Katsina, Kebbi, Kogi, Kwara, Lagos, Nassarawa, Niger, Ogun, Ondo, Osun, Oyo, Plateau, Rivers, Sokoto, Taraba, Yobe and Zamfara. Each state has an elected governor and legislature.

ECONOMY AND TRADE

In April 2014 a statistical 'revaluation' of the economy by the Nigerian government increased its size by 89 per cent overnight, and Nigeria has now emerged as Africa's largest economy. Nonetheless, half the population (100 million people) live in poverty. The country is the largest sub-Saharan oil producer, enjoying an oil boom in the 1970s, however, mismanagement and corruption mean the majority of the population has yet to derive much benefit, and oil production has been declining since 2012 partly because of militant attacks on pipelines. Since 2008 economic reforms have been introduced to improve fiscal and monetary management, curb inflation and address regional agitation for wider distribution of oil revenues. Factors such as security and inadequate infrastructure, especially electricity supply and roads, remain obstacles to growth. Low oil prices coupled with the impact of foreign-exchange controls meant the country entered recession in 2016, but returned to growth in 2017–19; it is expected to contract by 4.3 per cent in 2020. As a result of Boko Haram's terror campaign in the north-east, internal displacement, underinvestment and difficulties in supplying aid, Nigeria faces one of the world's largest humanitarian crises, with an estimated 10.6 million people in need of urgent assistance in 2020.

Agriculture, mostly at subsistence level, generates 21.1 per cent of GDP and engages about 70 per cent of the labour force. The main crops include cocoa, peanuts, cotton, palm oil, maize, rice, sorghum, millet and rubber. However, agricultural output has failed to keep pace with rapid population growth, changing Nigeria from a net food exporter to a food importer. Industrial activities include oil and natural gas production, mining (coal, tin, columbite), processing agricultural products, textiles, cement and other construction materials and footwear. Industry contributes 22.5 per cent of GDP and services 56.4 per cent.

The main trading partners are China, India, the USA, and EU nations. Exports are almost entirely oil and oil products. The main imports are machinery, chemicals, transport equipment, manufactured goods, food and live animals.

GNI – US$408bn; US$2,030 per capita (2019)
Annual average growth of GDP – 0.8 per cent (2017 est)
Inflation rate – 16.5 per cent (2017 est)
Population below poverty line – 70 per cent (2010 est)
Unemployment – 16.5 per cent (2017 est)
Total external debt – US$40.96bn (2017 est)
Imports – US$50,850m (2017)
Exports – US$50,764m (2017)

BALANCE OF PAYMENTS

Trade – US$86m deficit (2017)
Current Account – US$17,016m deficit (2019)

Trade with UK	2018	2019
Imports from UK	£1,324,467,847	£1,307,541,584
Exports to UK	£2,409,168,438	£1,421,643,892

COMMUNICATIONS

Airports and waterways – There are 40 airports, including the principal airports at Lagos, Abuja, Kano and Port Harcourt; there are 8,600km of waterways, mostly on the Niger and Benue rivers; the main seaports are Lagos, Port Harcourt, Warri and Calabar

Roadways and railways – 195,000km; the Nigerian railway network, which is in a severe state of disrepair, has 3,798km of track

Telecommunications – 146,075 fixed lines and 184 million mobile subscriptions (2018); there were 85.5 million internet users in 2016

Internet code and IDD – ng; 234 (from UK), 9 44 (to UK)

Major broadcasters – The Nigerian Television Authority (NTA) and Federal Radio Corporation of Nigeria (FRCN) are the public broadcasters

Press – *The Guardian* is one of the most influential news publications in the country

WPFI score – 36.63 (115)

EDUCATION AND HEALTH

Literacy rate – 62 per cent (2018 est)

Gross enrolment ratio (percentage of relevant age group) – primary 84.7 per cent, secondary 42 per cent (2016 est)

Health expenditure (per capita) – US$74 (2017)

Hospital beds (per 1,000 people) – 0.5 (2004–9)

Life expectancy (years) – 60.4 (2020 est)

Mortality rate – 9.1 (2020 est)

Birth rate – 34.6 (2020 est)

Infant mortality rate – 59.8 (2020 est)

HIV/AIDS adult prevalence – 1.3 per cent (2019 est)

NORTH MACEDONIA

Republika Severna Makedonija – Republic of North Macedonia

Area – 25,713 sq. km

Capital – Skopje; population, 595,000 (2020 est)

Major cities – Bitola, Kumanovo

Currency – Denar of 100 deni

Population – 2,125,971 rising at 0.15 per cent a year (2020 est); Macedonian (64.2 per cent), Albanian (25.2 per cent) (est). Romani populations are usually underestimated and may represent 6.5–13 per cent of the population

Religion – Christian (Orthodox 64.8 per cent), Muslim 33.3 per cent (est)

Language – Macedonian (official), Albanian, Turkish, Romani, Serbian (all official in different regions)

Population density – 83 per sq. km (2019)

Urban population – 58.2 per cent (2019 est)

Median age (years) – 39 (2020 est)

National anthem – 'Denes Nad Makedonija' 'Today Over Macedonia'

National day – 8 September (Independence Day)

Death penalty – Abolished for all crimes (since 1991)

CPI score – 35 (106)

Military expenditure – US$117m (2018)

Literacy rate – 97.8 per cent (2014 est)

Gross enrolment ratio (percentage of relevant age group) – primary 98.2 per cent, secondary 80 per cent, tertiary 43.1 per cent (2018 est)

Health expenditure (per capita) – US$328 (2017)

Hospital beds (per 1,000 people) – 4.4 (2013)

Life expectancy (years) – 76.3 (2020 est)

Mortality rate – 9.6 (2020 est)

Birth rate – 10.7 (2020 est)

Infant mortality rate – 7.4 (2020 est)

CLIMATE AND TERRAIN

The landlocked country is a mountainous plateau divided by deep river valleys and basins, including the valleys of the Vardar river and its tributaries. Elevation extremes range from 2,764m (Golem Korab) to 50m (Vardar river). Lakes Ohrid and Prespa straddle the border with Albania, and Lake Doiran the border with Greece. The climate is continental, with average temperatures ranging from −0.7°C in January to 20.6°C in July and August.

HISTORY AND POLITICS

The area of present-day North Macedonia was part of the ancient Macedonian kingdom, which also included northern Greece and south-west Bulgaria, in the fourth century BC. The Macedonian kingdom became a province of the Roman Empire in the second century BC, coming under the control of the Byzantine Empire from the fourth century AD. Slav peoples settled the area in the seventh century and mixed with the Greek, Illyrian, Thracian, Scythian and Turkish peoples.

From the ninth to the 14th centuries the area was under the rule successively of the Bulgars, Byzantium and the Serbs, and became part of the Ottoman Empire in the late 14th century. Following the Balkan wars of 1912 and 1913 the region was divided between Bulgaria, Serbia and Greece. After the First World War, the Serbian part was awarded to the newly created state that became Yugoslavia. During the Second World War, this area was occupied by Bulgaria from 1941 to 1944, and after liberation became a republic within the communist Federal Republic of Yugoslavia.

Nationalist sentiment grew throughout the 1980s, and in 1991 North Macedonia declared its independence, which Yugoslavia recognised in 1992. International recognition was initially delayed by Greece's objection to the republic's name (Greece claimed that its region of Macedonia is the only one entitled to the name), but the country joined the UN in 1993 as the Former Yugoslav Republic of Macedonia; Greece recognised it under this name and lifted its trade blockade in 1995, but in 2008 blocked the republic's membership of NATO. In June 2018, a deal was agreed to rename the nation the Republic of North Macedonia and end the 27-year dispute, paving the way for NATO and EU membership. A constitutional amendment was passed on 11 January 2019, and confirmed on 12 February 2019 following ratification by the Greek parliament.

Throughout the 1990s there was tension and sporadic violence with the large ethnic Albanian minority, aggrieved at their lack of civil rights. Instability in neighbouring Kosovo spilled over into Macedonia in 2001, sparking a two-month uprising by ethnic Albanian separatists. Peace talks facilitated by international bodies resulted in the Ohrid framework agreement, giving Albanians greater recognition within North Macedonia and making Albanian an official language.

North Macedonia experienced instability in 2015, following allegations that the government had illegally tapped the phones of 20,000 people, including politicians, journalists and judges. The accusations led to large protests both against and for the government, and the resignation of two ministers and a number of intelligence officers. Ethnic Albanian groups were targeted in anti-terrorism raids.

In the legislative election in December 2016, the VMRO-DPMNE gained two more seats than the opposition Social Democrats but was unable to form a coalition. In May 2017, Zoran Zaev was narrowly elected prime minister by parliament, heading a coalition of the Social Democrats and ethnic Albanian parties. A snap election was held in July 2020, preceding EU accession talks, which the pro-western Social Democrats emerged as the largest party. As of November 2020, no coalition had been formed. In May 2019 Social Democrat Stevo Pendarovski was elected as the nation's fifth president.

The 1991 constitution was amended in 2001 to incorporate provisions of the Ohrid agreement relating to ethnic Albanian rights, and several times since, most notably in 2004 to give ethnic Albanians greater local autonomy in areas where they predominate.

The head of state is a president, who is directly elected for a five-year term, renewable once. The unicameral legislature, the *Sobranie,* has between 120 and 140 members directly elected for a four-year term. The prime minister is appointed by the president. Government ministers are elected by the assembly but are not members of it.

HEAD OF STATE
President, Stevo Pendarovski, *elected* 5 May 2019, *sworn in* 12 May 2019

SELECTED GOVERNMENT MEMBERS *AS AT NOVEMBER 2020*
Prime Minister, Zoran Zaev
Deputy Prime Ministers, Artan Grubi; Ljupcho Nikolovski; Fatmir Bytyqi *(Economy);* Nikola Dimitrov
Foreign Affairs, Bujar Osmani
Interior, Oliver Spasovski

EMBASSY OF THE REPUBLIC OF NORTH MACEDONIA
Suites 2.1/2.2, Buckingham Court, 75–83 Buckingham Gate, London SW1E 6PE
T 020-7976 0535 **E** london@mfa.gov.mk
W www.missions.gov.mk/london
Ambassador Extraordinary and Plenipotentiary, Aleksandra Miovska, *apptd* 2018

BRITISH EMBASSY
Todor Aleksandrov 165, Skopje 1000
T (+389) (2) 329 9299 **E** britishembassyskopje@fco.gov.uk
W www.gov.uk/government/world/macedonia
Ambassador Extraordinary and Plenipotentiary, HE Rachel Galloway, *apptd* 2018

ECONOMY AND TRADE
Macedonia was the least developed republic in the former Yugoslavia before 1991, and economic growth was initially hindered by the trade embargo by Greece (1993–5) and the 2001 ethnic Albanian uprising. Liberalisation has since brought foreign investment, and economic growth was steady from 2003 to 2008, although the economy contracted briefly in 2009 owing to the global downturn. A decade of growth has significantly improved the economy, and although

joblessness remains high figures may be overstated because of the size of the grey economy, estimated to be between 20 and 45 per cent of GDP.

Services contribute roughly 62.5 per cent of GDP, industry 26.6 per cent and agriculture 10.9 per cent. Food processing and winemaking are major industries, along with textiles, chemicals, iron, steel, cement, energy, pharmaceuticals and vehicle parts. The main trading partners are Germany, the UK, Greece and other Balkan states. Principal exports are food, wine, tobacco, textiles, manufactured goods, iron and steel. The main imports are machinery and equipment, vehicles, chemicals, fuels and food.

GNI – US$12.3bn; US$5,910 per capita (2019)
Annual average growth of GDP – 0.0 per cent (2017)
Inflation rate – 1.4 per cent (2017 est)
Population below poverty line – 21.5 per cent (2015 est)
Unemployment – 17.29 per cent (2019 est)
Total external debt – US$8.79bn (2017 est)
Imports – US$7,832m (2017)
Exports – US$6,205m (2017)

BALANCE OF PAYMENTS
Trade – US$1,627m deficit (2017)
Current Account – US$418m deficit (2019)

Trade with UK	2018	2019
Imports from UK	£841,488,826	£1,202,349,509
Exports to UK	£82,598,334	£114.848.369

COMMUNICATIONS
Airports – The principal airports are at Skopje and Ohrid, and there are a further six airports around the country
Roadways and railways – 14,182km; 925km
Telecommunications – 402,250 fixed lines and 2.1 million mobile subscriptions (2019); there were 1.7 million internet users in 2018
Internet code and IDD – mk; 389 (from UK), 44 (to UK)
Major broadcasters – MTV and Macedonian Radio are the public broadcasters
Media – Leading dailies include *Nova Makedonija* (state subsidised), *Utrinski Vesnik* and *Dnevnik*
WPFI score – 31.28 (92)

NORWAY

Kongeriket Norge – Kingdom of Norway

Area – 323,802 sq. km
Capital – Oslo; population, 1,041,000 (2020 est)
Major cities – Bergen, Stavanger, Trondheim
Currency – Krone of 100 ore
Population – 5,467,439 rising at 0.85 per cent a year (2020 est)

Religion – Christian (Church of Norway, Evangelical Lutheran (official) 70.6 per cent, other Christian 6.7 per cent), Muslim 3.2 per cent (est)
Language – Bokmal and Nynorsk Norwegian (both official), Finnish, Sami (official in six municipalities)
Population density – 15 per sq. km (2019)
Urban population – 82.6 per cent (2019 est)
Median age (years) – 39.5 (2020 est)
National anthem – 'Ja, Vi Elsker Dette Landet' 'Yes, We Love This Country'
National day – 17 May (Constitution Day)
Death penalty – Abolished for all crimes (since 1979)
CPI score – 84 (7)
Military expenditure – US$7,067m (2018)
Conscription – 19–35 years of age; 19 months

CLIMATE AND TERRAIN

The terrain is mostly mountainous, with elevated, barren plateaux separated by deep, narrow valleys; the north is arctic tundra. The coastline is deeply indented with numerous fjords and fringed with thousands of rocky islands and islets; Geirangerfjord and Naeroyfjord are UNESCO World Heritage Sites. Elevation extremes range from 2,469m (Galdhopiggen) to 0m (Norwegian Sea).

Nearly half of the country lies north of the Arctic Circle, and at North Cape the sun does not appear to set between about 14 May and 29 July, causing the phenomenon known as the midnight sun; conversely, there is no apparent sunrise from about 18 November to 24 January. The climate is temperate on the coast but colder and wetter inland; average temperatures range from −6.6°C in January to 12.6°C in July, but winter temperatures in parts of the north can drop to −40°C.

HISTORY AND POLITICS

Norway became a unified country under the rule of King Harald Fairhair in *c*.900 but dissolved after his death and was reunified by Olav II in *c*.1016–28. Canute brought Norway under Danish rule in 1028 but the throne reverted on his death to Magnus I. When the royal house died out in the 14th century, the Danish monarch was the nearest heir and in 1397 Norway, Denmark and Sweden were united under a single monarch in the Kalmar Union. Sweden seceded from the union in 1523, but Norway continued to be ruled by the Danish crown until 1814, when it was ceded to Sweden.

Although internal self-government was established in 1814, growing tension over constraints on the Norwegian government led to the union being dissolved, and Norway became independent in 1905. The first king of the newly independent country was a Danish prince, who took the throne as King Haakon VII.

The country was neutral in the First World War, but in the Second World War Norway was invaded and occupied by Germany from 1940 until 1945. Norway joined NATO in 1949 and was a founder member of the European Free Trade Association in 1960. Membership of the EU was rejected in referendums in 1972 and 1994.

After 1945, governments pursued policies of economic planning and an extensive welfare state. The Labour Party dominated politics from the 1930s to the early 1980s, governing either on its own or in coalition with smaller parties. It was returned to power in 2005. After legislative elections in 2013 and 2017, the Conservative Party formed a minority government with the right-wing Progress Party, despite the Labour Party remaining the largest single party in the legislature.

Norway is a constitutional monarchy with a hereditary monarch as head of state. Under the 1814 constitution, amended over 400 times, the unicameral *Storting* has 169 members who are directly elected for a four-year term; a 2007 constitutional amendment abolished a bicameral division within the *Storting*, which took effect from the 2009 election. The prime minister, who is responsible to parliament, appoints the cabinet.

HEAD OF STATE

HM The King of Norway, King Harald V, KG, GCVO, *born* 21 February 1937, *succeeded* 17 January 1991
Heir, HRH Crown Prince Haakon Magnus, *born* 20 July 1973

SELECTED GOVERNMENT MEMBERS *AS AT NOVEMBER 2020*

Prime Minister, Erna Solberg
Defence, Frank Bakke-Jensen
Finance, Jan Sanner
Foreign Affairs, Ine Marie Eriksen Soreide

ROYAL NORWEGIAN EMBASSY

25 Belgrave Square, London SW1X 8QD
T 020-7591 5500 **E** emb.london@mfa.no **W** www.norway.org.uk
Ambassador Extraordinary and Plenipotentiary, HE Wegger Strommen, *apptd* 2019

BRITISH EMBASSY

Thomas Heftyes Gate 8, 0244 Oslo
T (+47) 2313 2700 **E** britemb@online.no
W www.gov.uk/government/world/norway
Ambassador Extraordinary and Plenipotentiary, HE Richard Wood, *apptd* 2018

ECONOMY AND TRADE

Norway's prosperity depends primarily upon oil and gas extraction, which accounts for nearly half of exports, and its fisheries. Oil production is declining, but oil and gas deposits in the Barents Sea and other areas are becoming more accessible as the Arctic ice cap retreats. Norway has planned for the time when reserves are exhausted by investing revenue from this sector in the world's largest sovereign wealth fund, valued at over US$1.14 trillion in 2019. The state retains a majority share in key enterprises, including the oil industry. While the economy contracted in 2009, it grew modestly over the past decade, but occasionally contracted owing to low oil and gas prices. It is expected to contract by 2.8 per cent in 2020.

The nature of the terrain restricts agriculture, which generates 2.3 per cent of GDP. The main industries apart from oil and gas are fishing (the world's second-largest exporter), forestry, food processing, shipbuilding, pulp and paper products, metals, chemicals, mining and textiles. Shipping freight services are also significant, with Norway ranked as the fifth-largest shipping nation by fleet value. Industry contributes 33.7 per cent of GDP and services 64 per cent.

The main trading partners are the UK (21.1 per cent of exports), other EU countries, the USA and China. Principal exports are oil and petroleum products, machinery and equipment, metals, chemicals, ships and fish. The main imports are machinery and equipment, chemicals, metals and foodstuffs.

GNI – US$441.2bn; US$82,500 per capita (2019)
Annual average growth of GDP – 0.86 per cent (2019 est)
Inflation rate – 1.9 per cent (2017 est)
Unemployment – 3.72 per cent (2019 est)
Total external debt – US$642.3bn (2016 est)
Imports – US$130,585m (2017)
Exports – US$140,360m (2017)

BALANCE OF PAYMENTS
Trade – US$9,775m surplus (2017)
Current Account – US$16,654m surplus (2019)

Trade with UK	2018	2019
Imports from UK	£3,374,443,863	£3,445,060,890
Exports to UK	£20,103,734,724	£15,860,941,588

COMMUNICATIONS
Airports and waterways – There are 67 airports, including the principal airports at Oslo, Bergen, Stavanger and Trondheim; the main ports are Oslo, Bergen, Kristiansand, Tonsberg, Stavanger and Narvik, and there is a large merchant fleet, with 585 ships of over 1,000 tonnes registered in Norway and 974 registered abroad
Roadways and railways – 94,902km; 4,200km
Telecommunications – 571,958 million fixed lines and 5.8 million mobile subscriptions (2019); there were 5.2 million internet users in 2018
Internet code and IDD – no; 47 (from UK), 44 20 (to UK)
Major broadcasters – The public broadcaster NRK operates radio and television channels, in competition with a number of commercial rivals
Press – *VG* has the largest circulation among the country's daily news publications; other newspapers include *The Norway Post* and *Dagbladet*
WPFI score – 7.84 (1)

EDUCATION AND HEALTH
Education from six to 16 is free and compulsory in the basic schools, and free from 16 to 19 years.
Gross enrolment ratio (percentage of relevant age group) – primary 100.1 per cent, secondary 117.5 per cent, tertiary 83 per cent (2018 est)
Health expenditure (per capita) – US$7,936 (2017)
Hospital beds (per 1,000 people) – 3.8 (2015)
Life expectancy (years) – 82.1 (2020 est)
Mortality rate – 8.1 (2020 est)
Birth rate – 12.2 (2020 est)
Infant mortality rate – 2.5 (2020 est)
HIV/AIDS adult prevalence – 0.15 per cent (2014 est)

TERRITORIES

JAN MAYEN ISLAND
Area – 377 sq. km
Population – The only residents are the staff of the radio and meteorological stations
The island is barren, volcanic and partially covered by glaciers, with no exploitable natural resources. It lies in the North Atlantic Ocean about 950km west of Norway and is home to the Beerenberg volcano, the northernmost active volcano on Earth. It was annexed by Norway in 1922 and integrated into the kingdom in 1930; since 1995 it has been administered by the governor of Nordland county.

SVALBARD
Area – 62,045 sq. km
Population – 2,926 (2019 est) falling at 0.03 per cent a year (2014 est); Norwegian 58 per cent, Russian and Ukrainian 42 per cent
The Svalbard archipelago consists of Spitsbergen, North East Land, the Wiche Islands, Barents Island, Edge Island, Prince Charles Foreland, Hope Island and Bear Island. It lies north of the Arctic Circle, and glaciers and snow cover around 60 per cent of the area, although the west coast is ice-free for about half the year. Some 65 per cent of the Svalbard archipelago is

protected to ensure biodiversity; there are seven national parks, six large nature reserves, 15 bird sanctuaries and one geotopic protected area. A global seed repository has been established on Spitsbergen. Norway's sovereignty was recognised by treaty in 1920 but the other signatories were granted equal rights to exploit mineral deposits, although this right is now only exercised by Russia. The territory is administered by a governor, who is responsible to the Ministry of Justice and Police. The main economic activities are coal mining, tourism, and research and education.

NORWEGIAN ANTARCTIC TERRITORY
The Norwegian Antarctic Territory consists of Queen Maud Land, Bouvet Island and Peter the First Island. Claimed in 1938, Queen Maud Land is a sector of the Antarctic continent that extends from 45° E. to 20° E. Peter the First Island was formally claimed in 1931 and is the only claimed area covered under the Antarctic Treaty that is not part of the main landmass. Bouvet Island was claimed in 1930 (*see also* The North and South Poles).

OMAN
Saltanat Uman – *Sultanate of Oman*

Area – 309,500 sq. km
Capital – Muscat (Masqat); population, 1,550,000 (2020 est)
Major cities – Ibri, Salalah, Suhar, as-Suwayq
Currency – Omani Rial (OR) of 1,000 baisas
Population – 4,664,844 (2019 est) rising at 1.96 per cent a year (2020 est); Arab, Baluchi, Indian, Pakistani, Sri Lankan, Bangladeshi, African
Religion – Muslim 85.9 per cent (majority are Ibadhi, lesser numbers of Sunni and Shia), Christian 6.5 per cent, Hindu 5.5 per cent (est)
Language – Arabic (official), English, Baluchi, Swahili, Urdu, Indian dialects
Population density – 16 per sq. km (2019)
Urban population – 85.4 per cent (2019 est)
Median age (years) – 26.2 (2020 est)
National anthem – 'Nashid as-Salaam as-Sultani' 'The Sultan's Anthem'
National day – 18 November (Birthday of Sultan Qaboos, 1940)
Death penalty – Retained
CPI score – 52 (56)
Military expenditure – US$7,739m (2015)

CLIMATE AND TERRAIN
Oman lies at the southeastern corner of the Arabian peninsula and includes territory at the tip of the Musandam peninsula, which is separated from the rest of the country by the UAE. There are mountains in the north and the south-west of the country, divided by a high desert plateau; over 80 per cent of the country is desert. The plateau descends to a fertile plain on

the Arabian Sea coast. Elevation extremes range from 2,980m (Jabal Shams) to 0m (Arabian Sea). The climate is arid, with high temperatures and humidity throughout the year; temperatures are lower on the coast, but the high humidity often makes coastal areas the most inhospitable. Average temperatures range from 20.4°C in January to 30.4°C in June.

HISTORY AND POLITICS
Oman began to build an empire in the Middle East from the eighth century AD and remained largely unchallenged until the arrival in 1506 of the Portuguese, who were ousted in 1650. An independent sultanate was established in 1749 by the founder of the dynasty that still rules the country. By the early 19th century, Omani rule extended to the east African coast and parts of Persia and Balochistan (in modern Pakistan). The kingdom came under British influence from the late 19th century until 1951.

The country was divided from 1913, with religious leaders in control of the interior and the sultan of the coastal regions. The interior's attempts to assert its independence led to clashes in the 1950s, but by 1959 the sultan had established control over the whole country. An insurrection in the south by left-wing rebels supported by South Yemen began in 1965 and was defeated with British military assistance in 1975. The discovery and subsequent exploitation of oil in the mid-1960s led to the steady economic transformation of Oman, and in 1970 the sultan was overthrown in a bloodless coup by his son, Sultan Qaboos bin Said al-Said, who initiated a modernisation programme. Former minister of national culture Haitham bin Tariq al-Said succeeded Sultan Qaboos following his cousin's death in January 2020.

The country is still essentially an absolute monarchy, although a degree of political liberalisation has occurred in the past 20 years. In 1996 the sultan issued a Basic Statute that is in effect a constitution; it established a succession mechanism, codified the system of government and set up a bicameral legislature. The first direct election to the consultative council was held in 2000 and the first by universal adult suffrage in 2003. Pro-reform demonstrations occurred prior to the October 2011 elections, and nationwide demonstrations against inequality and unemployment have also taken place in recent years. The last elections took place in 2019, and organised political parties are illegal.

At present, legislation is proposed by the sultan and passed by decree. The sultan is advised by the bicameral Council of Oman, comprising the Consultative Council *(Majlis al-Shura)*, which has 85 members directly elected for a four-year term, and the Council of State *(Majlis al-Dawlah)*, which has 85 members appointed by the sultan for a four-year term. The Consultative Council has the right to review legislation, question ministers and make policy proposals. The Council of State is intended to facilitate 'constructive cooperation between the government and the citizens'.

HEAD OF STATE
HM The Sultan of Oman, Prime Minister, C-in-C of the Armed Forces, Sultan Qaboos bin Said al-Said, *succeeded,* 11 January 2020

SELECTED GOVERNMENT MEMBERS *AS AT NOVEMBER 2020*
Deputy Prime Ministers, Fahd bin Mamud al-Said; Shihab bin Tariq bin Taimour al-Said *(Defence)*
Foreign Affairs, Badr bin Hamad bin Hamoud al-Busaidi
Interior, Hamoud bin Faisal al-Busaidi

EMBASSY OF THE SULTANATE OF OMAN
167 Queen's Gate, London SW7 5HE
T 020-7225 0001

Ambassador Extraordinary and Plenipotentiary, HE Abdul Aziz al-Hinai, *apptd* 2009

BRITISH EMBASSY
PO Box 185, Mina al-Fahal, 116 Muscat
T (+968) (24) 609 000 **E** muscat.enquiries@fco.gov.uk
W www.gov.uk/government/world/oman
Ambassador Extraordinary and Plenipotentiary, HE Hamish Cowell, CMG, *apptd* 2017

ECONOMY AND TRADE
Although its production is more modest than other Gulf states, oil and gas are the mainstay of Oman's economy and provide the majority of government revenue. Oil reserves are dwindling and development plans centre on diversification, industrialisation and privatisation, with the aim of reducing the oil sector's contribution to GDP. Industrial development is focused on natural gas production, metal manufacturing, petrochemicals and trans-shipment ports, with plans also to develop tourism and communication technology industries. Improved training, especially in IT and business skills, is intended to enable the local population to replace expatriate workers. The economy decelerated in 2019 due to lower domestic demand, and is expected to contract by 10 per cent in 2020.

Agriculture and fishing account for 1.8 per cent of GDP, producing dates, limes, bananas, alfalfa and vegetables as well as fish. The main industries apart from oil and natural gas extraction are oil refining, liquefied natural gas production, construction and production of cement, copper, steel, chemicals and optic fibre. Industry accounts for 46.4 per cent of GDP and services 51.8 per cent.

The main trading partners are China, the UAE, the USA and South Korea. Principal exports are petroleum, re-exports, fish, metals and textiles. The main imports are machinery, transport equipment, manufactured goods, food and livestock.
GNI – US$76.3bn; US$15,330 per capita (2019)
Annual average growth of GDP – −0.9 per cent (2017 est)
Inflation rate – 1.6 per cent (2017 est)
Total external debt – US$46.27bn (2017 est)
Imports – US$31,232m (2016)
Exports – US$31,148m (2016)

BALANCE OF PAYMENTS
Trade – US$83m deficit (2016)
Current Account – US$4,140m deficit (2019)

Trade with UK	2018	2019
Imports from UK	£1,012,256,852	£544,169,038
Exports to UK	£186,574,899	£234,286,120

COMMUNICATIONS
Airports and waterways – The main airports are at Muscat and Salalah; the main ports are Salalah and Port Qaboos at Mutrah, which has eight deep-water berths
Roadways – There are 29,685km of roadways, including 1,943km of motorways
Telecommunications – 456,940 fixed lines and 4.9 million mobile telephone subscriptions (2019); there were 2.8 million internet users in 2018
Internet code and IDD – om; 968 (from UK), 44 (to UK)
Media – Oman TV and Radio Oman are the state-run broadcasters; *Al-Watan* and the *Oman Daily* are the principal daily newspapers
WPFI score – 43.42 (135)

EDUCATION AND HEALTH

Literacy rate – 95.7 per cent (2018 est)
Gross enrolment ratio (percentage of relevant age group) – primary 103 per cent, secondary 107.1 per cent, tertiary 40.4 per cent (2019 est)
Health expenditure (per capita) – US$588 (2017)
Hospital beds (per 1,000 people) – 1.6 (2014)
Life expectancy (years) – 76.3 (2020 est)
Mortality rate – 3.3 (2020 est)
Birth rate – 23.1 (2020 est)
Infant mortality rate – 11.7 (2020 est)
HIV/AIDS adult prevalence – 0.1 per cent (2019 est)

PAKISTAN

Jamhuryat Islami Pakistan – *Islamic Republic of Pakistan*

Area – 796,095 sq. km
Capital – Islamabad; population, 1,129,000 (2020 est)
Major cities – Faisalabad, Gujranwala, Hyderabad, Karachi, Lahore, Multan, Peshawar, Quetta, Rawalpindi
Currency – Pakistan rupee of 100 paisa
Population – 233,500,636 rising at 2.07 per cent a year (2020 est); Punjabi (44.7 per cent), Pashtun (15.4 per cent), Sindhi (14.1 per cent), Sariaki (8.4 per cent), Muhajirs (7.6 per cent), Balochi (3.6 per cent) (est)
Religion – Muslim (official) 96.4 per cent (Sunni 85–90 per cent, Shia 10–15 per cent), other (includes Christian and Hindu) 3.6 per cent; Islam is the state religion
Language – English, Urdu (both official), Balochi, Brahui, Burushaski, Hindko, Pashto, Punjabi, Sindhi, Saraiki
Population density – 275 per sq. km (2019)
Urban population – 36.9 per cent (2019 est)
Median age (years) – 22 (2020 est)
National anthem – 'Qaumi Tarana' 'The Sacred Land'
National day – 23 March (Republic Day)
Death penalty – Retained
CPI score – 32 (120)
Military expenditure – US$11,376m (2018)

CLIMATE AND TERRAIN

The arid Thar desert in the east gives way to the fertile Indus valley in the centre of the country. The terrain then rises to the Makran, Kirthar and Sulaiman mountain ranges in the west and the Karakoram and Himalayan ranges in the north. Elevation extremes range from 8,611m (K2) to 0m (Indian Ocean). The climate varies greatly across the country. For most areas, the rainy season runs from July to September and is accompanied by very high humidity. Average temperatures range from 8.8°C in January to 28.6°C in June. Pakistan is prone to earthquakes – the most recent major occurrences were in 2008, 2013 and 2015 – and flooding; following heavy monsoon rains in 2010 the entire length of the Indus valley was flooded, displacing millions of people.

POLITICS

Pakistan is a federal republic. The 1973 constitution has been suspended, restored and amended several times, and in 2010 was reinstated in its original form, returning some of the president's powers to the prime minister.

The president is elected by the legislature for a five-year term, renewable once. The parliament *(Majlis as-Shura)* comprises a lower house, the National Assembly and the senate. The National Assembly has 342 seats, of which 60 are reserved for women and ten are elected by non-Muslim minorities; members serve a five-year term. The senate has 104 members indirectly elected by provincial assemblies; they serve a six-year term, with half elected every three years. The prime minister is nominated by and is responsible to the legislature.

There are four provinces: Balochistan, Khyber Pukhtoonkhwa (formerly North-West Frontier Province), Punjab and Sindh. Each has a provincial assembly and government. In addition, there are the Federally Administered Tribal Areas and the Islamabad Capital Territory.

The legislative elections originally scheduled for January 2008 were postponed to February after the assassination of Benazir Bhutto in December 2007. The two main opposition parties, Bhutto's Pakistan People's Party (PPP) and the Pakistan Muslim League–Nawaz Sharif (PML-N), won the most seats and formed a coalition government with two smaller parties; the PML-N withdrew from the coalition government in August 2008. The presidential election in July 2013 was won by Mamnoon Hussain, the first instance in Pakistan's history in which one elected civilian president was replaced by another. Nawaz Sharif was elected prime minister in June 2013, but in July 2017 was removed from office by the supreme court over corruption allegations and was later sentenced to ten years in prison. The PML-N subsequently lost the 2018 elections to the centrist Pakistan Movement for Justice (PTI), founded by former cricketer Imran Kahn in 1996, in an election marred by violent IS attacks. Kahn was later named prime minister, and PTI's Arif Alvi elected president.

HEAD OF STATE
President, Arif Alvi, *elected* 4 September 2018, *sworn in* 9 September 2018

SELECTED GOVERNMENT MEMBERS *AS AT NOVEMBER 2020*
Prime Minister, Finance, Imran Kahn
Defence, Pervez Khattak
Foreign Affairs, Mahmood Qureshi
Interior, Ijaz Ahmed Shah

HIGH COMMISSION FOR THE ISLAMIC REPUBLIC OF PAKISTAN
35–36 Lowndes Square, London SW1X 9JN
T 020-7664 924 **E** poldiv@phclondon.org **W** www.phclondon.org

High Commissioner, HE Mohammad Nafees Zakaria, *apptd* 2019

BRITISH HIGH COMMISSION
Diplomatic Enclave, Ramna 5, PO Box 1122, Islamabad
T (+92) (51) 201 2000 **E** islamabad-general.enquiries@fco.gov.uk
W www.gov.uk/government/world/pakistan
High Commissioner, HE Christian Turner, CMG, *apptd* 2019

INSURGENCIES
Balochistan, Punjab and Sindh provinces have all been affected since the 1980s by conflict between Shia and Sunni fundamentalists. Balochistan and, since the early 1990s, Sindh (especially Karachi) have experienced violence by armed militants seeking greater autonomy for each province.

Civil order has always been harder to maintain in Pukhtoonkhwa and the federally administered tribal areas than in the rest of the country. These areas became havens for the Taliban and al-Qaida fleeing Afghanistan after 2001, radicalising and destabilising increasingly wide areas. Government military and security forces are struggling to maintain control in over half of these areas. The government conceded the imposition of Shari'ah law in the Swat valley as part of a ceasefire agreement with the Taliban in early 2009, but when the Taliban attempted to extend its influence further into the country, the army began a counter-insurgency offensive to retake the area in April 2009, subsequently moving against the Taliban in other strongholds such as South Waziristan. An increase in militant attacks in the major cities led to the resumption of peace talks with the Taliban in March 2014. Nevertheless, attacks on civilian targets continue: in October 2014 Malala Yousafzai was shot in the head in an attack on a school bus in Swat; in December 2015, 150 people, predominantly children, were killed in a Taliban attack on an army-run school in Peshawar; and in March 2016, more than 70 people were killed when suicide bombers targeted Christian families celebrating Easter at a park in Lahore. A moratorium on the death penalty was lifted following the attack in Peshawar.

FOREIGN RELATIONS
Since partition, India and Pakistan have disputed sovereignty over the predominantly Muslim state of Jammu and Kashmir. A short war in 1947–8 resulted in the state being partitioned between the two countries, and its status remained unresolved despite further outbreaks of war in 1965 and 1971, low-level conflict for control of the Siachen glacier since 1985 and occasional increases in military exchanges, most recently in 1999–2002, 2003 and 2016–17. Both countries' acquisition of nuclear weapons has spurred efforts to reach a settlement. Peace talks began in 2003 when diplomatic missions were reopened and the resumption of transport links was initiated. Formal diplomatic talks began in 2004 and have achieved several accords intended to calm relations between the two countries. Talks were temporarily suspended by the Indian government after the 2008 terrorist attacks on Mumbai, but were resumed in 2010 despite heightened tensions along Kashmir's Line of Control in late 2016 to 2017.

Tensions flared in February 2019 after a suicide car bombing that killed dozens of Indian police was blamed on Pakistani-backed Muslim militants, and India responded with air strikes and tariff hikes. Pakistan's support for the Muslim insurgency in the Indian part of the state, which began in the late 1980s and has included terrorist attacks in Indian cities, has strained relations but Pakistan distanced itself from the insurgents in early 2019 in an effort to defuse tensions. In August, the Indian government stripped Jammu and Kashmir of their semi-autonomous status and imposed a military crackdown.

ECONOMY AND TRADE
Decades of political instability, inefficiency, corruption and high military expenditure have left Pakistan an underdeveloped country, averaging poor economic growth between 2008 and 2012, although this improved between 2013 and 2019. In the 2000s economic reforms, international aid and greater foreign investment produced steady growth of 5–8 per cent a year until 2008, notably in the industrial and service sectors, and reduced poverty levels by 10 per cent between 2001 and 2007. However, slower growth in 2008 caused budget and fiscal deficits that forced Pakistan to seek IMF assistance in 2013. These problems were exacerbated by the 2010 floods, which left millions homeless, destroyed crops and damaged infrastructure. A large proportion of the country's labour force works abroad, especially in the Middle East, providing valuable remittances but also causing the use of child labour within Pakistan. The informal economy is widespread and underemployment is high. The Sharif government (2013–17) implemented fiscal and energy reforms, bolstered by implementation of the China–Pakistan Economic Corridor. Further loans were approved by the IMF in 2019 and 2020 to shore up its dwindling foreign exchange reserves. Nevertheless, security and political instability remain significant threats to further development, as well as underinvestment in education, sanitation and healthcare.

Agriculture employs 42.3 per cent of the workforce, producing cotton, wheat, rice, sugar cane, fruits, vegetables, milk, meat and eggs, and contributes 24.4 per cent of GDP. Significant manufacturing industries include textiles and clothing, food processing, pharmaceuticals, surgical equipment, construction materials, paper products, fertiliser and seafood. Industry accounts for 19.1 per cent of GDP and services for 56.5 per cent.

The main trading partners are China, the USA, the UAE, the UK and Germany. Principal exports are textiles (clothing, bed linen, cotton cloth and yarn), rice, leather goods, sports goods, chemicals, surgical equipment, carpets and rugs. The main imports are petroleum, machinery, plastics, transport equipment, edible oils, paper, iron, steel and tea.

GNI – US$331.6bn; US$1,530 per capita (2019)
Annual average growth of GDP – 5.4 per cent (2017 est)
Inflation rate – 4.1 per cent (2017 est)
Population below poverty line – 29.5 per cent (2013 est)
Unemployment – 6 per cent (2017 est)
Total external debt – US$82.19bn (2017 est)
Imports – US$62,973m (2017)
Exports – US$28,869m (2017)

BALANCE OF PAYMENTS
Trade – US$34,103m deficit (2017)
Current Account – US$7,143m deficit (2019)

Trade with UK	2018	2019
Imports from UK	£746,215,502	£732,082,151
Exports to UK	£1,270,390,667	£1,311,325,778

COMMUNICATIONS
Airports and waterways – The principal airports are at Karachi, Islamabad, Lahore, Peshawar and Sialkot, and 103 other airports; the main seaports are Karachi and Port Muhammad bin Qasim, and there is a deep-water port at Gwadar
Roadways and railways – 185,063km, including 708km of motorways; 11,881km
Telecommunications – 2.6 million fixed lines and 174.7 million mobile subscriptions (2019); there were 34.7 million internet users in 2018
Internet code and IDD – pk; 92 (from UK), 44 (to UK)

Major broadcasters – Radio Pakistan and Pakistan Television Corporation Ltd are the principal state broadcasters
Press – Leading dailies include *Daily Jang* (Urdu language), *Dawn* and *The Nation* (both English language)
WPFI score – 45.52 (145)

EDUCATION AND HEALTH

Education is free to upper secondary level.
Literacy rate – 59.1 per cent (2017)
Gross enrolment ratio (percentage of relevant age group) – primary 95.4 per cent, secondary 43.8 per cent (2019 est); tertiary 9 per cent (2017 est)
Health expenditure (per capita) – US$45 (2017)
Hospital beds (per 1,000 people) – 0.6 (2014)
Life expectancy (years) – 69.2 (2020 est)
Mortality rate – 6.2 (2020 est)
Birth rate – 27.4 (2020 est)
Infant mortality rate – 52.3 (2020 est)
HIV/AIDS adult prevalence – 0.1 per cent (2019 est)

PALAU

Beluu er a Belau – Republic of Palau

Area – 459 sq. km
Capital – Ngerulmud, on Babeldaob; population, 277 (2018)
Major town – Koror
Currency – US dollar (US$) of 100 cents
Population – 21,685 rising at 0.39 per cent a year (2020 est); Palauan (73 per cent), Asian (21.7 per cent) (est)
Religion – Christian (Roman Catholic 45.3 per cent, Protestant 34.9 per cent, Modekngei 5.7 per cent (indigenous to Palau; combines animism and Christianity), Muslim 3 per cent, other 9.7 per cent (est)
Language – Palauan (official on most islands), English (official), other Micronesian, Filipino, Chinese
Population density – 39 per sq. km (2019)
Urban population – 80.5 per cent (2019 est)
Median age (years) – 33.9 (2020 est)
National anthem – 'Belau rekid' 'Our Palau'
National day – 9 July (Constitution Day)
Death penalty – Abolished for all crimes (since 1994)
Literacy rate – 96.6 per cent (2015 est)
Gross enrolment ratio (percentage of relevant age group) – primary 112.6 per cent, secondary 116.5 per cent (2014 est); tertiary 54.7 (2013 est)
Health expenditure (per capita) – US$1,596 (2017)
Life expectancy (years) – 74.1 (2020 est)
Mortality rate – 8.3 (2020 est)
Birth rate – 11.3 (2020 est)
Infant mortality rate – 9.8 (2020 est)

CLIMATE AND TERRAIN

The republic consists of six island groups in the western Pacific Ocean; these comprise eight large islands and over 300 smaller islands or islets that are either volcanic and mountainous or coral and low-lying. Elevation extremes range from 242m (Mt Ngerchelchuus) to 0m (Pacific Ocean). The climate is tropical, with a wet season from May to November. The average temperature is 27.8°C.

HISTORY AND POLITICS

Palau has been inhabited since the first millennium BC. In the 19th century, Spain and Germany vied for possession until 1889, when Spain sold the islands to Germany, which exploited the phosphate deposits and developed coconut plantations. Japan occupied the islands on behalf of the Allies in 1914 and administered them after the First World War under a League of Nations mandate. Japanese forces were ousted by US troops during the Second World War.

In 1947 the islands became part of the UN Trust Territory of the Pacific, administered by the USA. In 1982 a compact of free association was signed with the USA under which the USA retained responsibility for defence and foreign policy in return for providing economic aid; the compact was ratified in 1993 and entered into force when Palau became independent on 1 October 1994.

The latest presidential and legislative elections were held in November 2020; Surangel Whipps Jr was elected president.

Under the 1981 constitution, the executive president is directly elected for a four-year term, renewable once. The president appoints the cabinet. The bicameral National Congress comprises the House of Delegates, which has 16 members (one from each state), and the 13-member senate; members of both chambers stand for election as independents and serve a four-year term. A council of indigenous chiefs, composed of the paramount chief from each of the 16 states, acts as an advisory body to the president on matters concerning traditional law and customs.

Each of the 16 constituent states has its own governor and legislature.

HEAD OF STATE
President-elect, Tommy Remengesau Jr, *elected* 3 November 2020, *assuming office* 17 January 2021

SELECTED GOVERNMENT MEMBERS *AS AT NOVEMBER 2020*
Finance, Elbuchel Sadang
Minister of State, Faustina Rehuher-Marugg

HONORARY CONSULATE OF THE REPUBLIC OF PALAU
Bankfoot Square, Bankfoot Street, Batley WF17 5LH
T 01924-470786 W www.palauconsulate.org.uk

BRITISH AMBASSADOR
HE Daniel Pruce, *apptd* 2017, resident at Manila, Philippines

ECONOMY AND TRADE

The economy is reliant on economic aid from the USA and the government is keen to diversify. Tourism is now the main industry, catering for over 130,000 people a year and fuelled by prosperity in East Asia. It enjoys a per capita income double that of the Philippines. The other main industry is fishing, which it the nation's only significant export. Subsistence agriculture engages 1.2 per cent of the workforce and produces crops such as coconuts, copra, cassava and sweet potatoes. Revenue is also derived from the sale of licences to foreign fishing fleets. In September 2020 Palau urged the

USA to build a military base on the island to counter the growing influence of China in the region, which would generate significant revenue.

The main trading partners are Japan (over half of all exports), the USA, India, China and Guam. The main imports are machinery and equipment, fuels, metals and foodstuffs.
GNI – US$0.3bn; US$17,280 per capita (2018)
Annual average growth of GDP – -3.7 per cent (2017 est)
Inflation rate – 0.9 per cent (2017 est)
Total external debt – US$18.38m (2014 est)
Imports – US$177m (2015)
Exports – US$15m (2015)

BALANCE OF PAYMENTS
Trade – US$162m deficit (2015)
Current Account – US$18,989m deficit (2018)

Trade with UK	2018	2019
Imports from UK	£76,619	£21,981
Exports to UK	£29,445	£3,079,497

COMMUNICATIONS
Airports and waterways – There are three airports, on Koror, Peleliu and Angaur, which receive international flights from Guam, Japan, the Philippines and Taiwan; Koror is also the main seaport
Roadways – 125km
Telecommunications – 8,808 fixed lines and 29,033 mobile subscriptions (2019); there were 7,650 internet users in 2016
Internet code and IDD – pw; 680 (from UK), 0 11 44 (to UK)
Media – T8AA Eco Paradise (radio) is the public broadcaster; there are no TV stations based in Palau or daily newspapers

PANAMA

República de Panamá – Republic of Panama

Area – 75,420 sq. km
Capital – Panama City; population, 1,860,000 (2020 est)
Major cities – Colón, David, San Miguelito
Currency – Balboa of 100 centésimos; at parity with the US dollar, which is used as paper currency. Both Panamanian and US coins are used
Population – 3,894,081 rising at 1.2 per cent a year (2020 est)
Religion – Christian (Roman Catholic 85 per cent, Protestant 15 per cent) (est)
Language – Spanish (official), English, Chinese, Arabic, French Creole, indigenous languages, Yiddish, Hebrew, Korean, Japanese
Population density – 56 per sq. km (2019)
Urban population – 68.1 per cent (2019 est)
Median age (years) – 30.1 (2020 est)

National anthem – 'Himno Istmeño' 'Hymn of the Isthmus'
National day – 3 November (Independence Day)
Death penalty – Abolished for all crimes (since 1922)
CPI score – 36 (101)

CLIMATE AND TERRAIN
Panama lies on the isthmus connecting North and South America. A mountain range runs along the centre, falling to coastal plains on both coasts. There is dense tropical rainforest in the east. Elevation extremes range from 3,475m (Volcan Baru) to 0m (Pacific Ocean). The climate is tropical, with a prolonged wet season from May to January. The average temperature is 23.8°C.

HISTORY AND POLITICS
Panama was visited by Spanish explorers from 1502, and in 1519 became part of the Viceroyalty of New Andalucia, later New Grenada. When it gained its independence from Spain in 1821, Panama joined the confederacy of Gran Colombia (comprising Colombia, Venezuela, Ecuador, Peru and Bolivia). The confederacy split up in 1830 and Panama became part of Colombia until 1903, when it achieved its independence.

In the 1880s, the French attempted to construct a canal across Panama to link the Atlantic and Pacific oceans. In 1903 the USA bought the rights to build the canal, which was completed in 1914 and opened in 1919. The USA was also given control of the canal and land to either side of it, known as the Canal Zone, in perpetuity but, under a 1977 agreement, sovereignty over the Canal Zone was transferred to Panama on 31 December 1999.

Panama was under the military rule of General Omar Torrijos from 1968 until his death in 1981. In 1983, General Manuel Noriega seized power and instigated a period of military rule, supported by the USA until 1987. An internal coup to unseat Noriega was unsuccessful in 1988, but in 1989 US forces invaded and deposed him. Noriega surrendered in 1990 and in 1992 was tried and sentenced in the USA on drug-trafficking and money-laundering charges. He was extradited to Panama in 2011 where he was imprisoned until he died in May 2017.

Juan Carlos Varela of the right-wing Panamenista party was replaced as president by centrist Laurentino Cortizo following the May 2019 elections. In the simultaneous legislative election Cortizo's Democratic Revolutionary Change party won 35 seats.

Under the 1972 constitution, as amended in 1983, the executive president is directly elected for a five-year term, which is not renewable. The unicameral National Assembly has 71 members, who are directly elected for a five-year term. The president, who is responsible to the legislature, appoints the cabinet.

HEAD OF STATE
President, Laurentino Cortizo *elected* 5 May 2019, *sworn in* 1 July 2019
Vice-President, Foreign Affairs, Jose Gabriel Carrizo

SELECTED GOVERNMENT MEMBERS *AS AT NOVEMBER 2020*
Economy and Finance, Hector Alexander
Security, Juan Pino

EMBASSY OF PANAMA
40 Hertford Street, London W1J 7SH
T 020-7493 4646 **E** panama1@btconnect.com
W www.panamaconsul.co.uk
Ambassador Extraordinary and Plenipotentiary, Natalia Royo, apptd 2019

BRITISH EMBASSY
Humboldt Tower, 4th Floor, Calle 53, Marbella, PO Box 0816-07946, Panama City
T (+507) 297 6550 **W** www.gov.uk/government/world/panama
Ambassador Extraordinary and Plenipotentiary, HE Damion Potter, *apptd* 2017

ECONOMY AND TRADE

The economy is based on a large service sector and experienced steady growth prior to 2020. However, the distribution of wealth is uneven: almost one-quarter of the population live below the poverty line despite high levels of employment. The economy has grown quickly since 2009, and has been boosted by the completion of the expanded Panama Canal in 2016, which more than doubled the canal's capacity but significantly added to public debt.

The service sector accounts for 82 per cent of GDP, derived from the operation of the Panama Canal and the Colón free trade zone, offshore banking and financial services, container ports, ship registry and tourism. Industry, which contributes 15.7 per cent of GDP, includes construction, brewing, sugar refining and the manufacture of cement and other construction materials. Agriculture, which accounts for 2.4 per cent of GDP, is centred on bananas, rice, maize, coffee, sugar cane, vegetables, livestock and shrimp.

The main trading partners are the USA, China, the Netherlands and Mexico. Principal exports are fish, fruit, nuts, iron and steel waste, and wood. The main imports are fuel products, machinery, vehicles, iron and steel rods, and pharmaceuticals.

GNI – US$63.5bn; US$14,950 per capita (2019)
Annual average growth of GDP – 5.4 per cent (2017 est)
Inflation rate – 0.9 per cent (2017 est)
Population below poverty line – 23 per cent (2015 est)
Unemployment – 6.14 per cent (2018 est)
Total external debt – US$91.53bn (2017 est)
Imports – US$26,597m (2017)
Exports – US$28,788m (2017)

BALANCE OF PAYMENTS
Trade – US$2,191m deficit (2017)
Current Account – US$3,500m deficit (2019)

Trade with UK	2018	2019
Imports from UK	£166,469,430	£164,923,825
Exports to UK	£26,905,089	£32,694,086

COMMUNICATIONS

Airports – There are 57 airports; the principal airport is at Panama City
Waterways – The Panama Canal connects the Pacific and Atlantic oceans. Each year the canal handles about 5 per cent of world trade and over 40 per cent of trade between Asia and the east coast of the USA. The chief ports are Colón, Cristóbal and Balboa, at either end of the canal. Because of its role as a ship registry, there were 6,413 Panamanian- and 5,162 foreign-owned ships of over 1,000 tonnes registered under its flag in 2011
Roadways and railways – 6,351km (including paved, unpaved and local roads); 77km
Telecommunications – 671,799 fixed lines and 5.1 million mobile subscriptions (2019); there were 2.2 million internet users in 2018
Internet code and IDD – pa; 507 (from UK), 44 (to UK)
Major broadcasters – The sector is dominated by private firms, including Telemetro (TV) and RPC Radio

Press – *La Prensa, The Panama News* and *El Siglo* are among the leading daily newspapers
WPFI score – 29.78 (76)

EDUCATION AND HEALTH

There are nine years of compulsory education.
Literacy rate – 95.4 per cent (2018 est)
Gross enrolment ratio (percentage of relevant age group) – primary 94.4 per cent, secondary 76.1 per cent (2017 est); tertiary 47.8 per cent (2016 est)
Health expenditure (per capita) – US$1,112 (2017)
Hospital beds (per 1,000 people) – 2.3 (2013)
Life expectancy (years) – 79.2 (2020 est)
Mortality rate – 5.1 (2020 est)
Birth rate – 17.1 (2020 est)
Infant mortality rate – 9.1 (2020 est)
HIV/AIDS adult prevalence – 0.8 per cent (2016 est)

PAPUA NEW GUINEA

Gau Hedinarai ai Papua-Matamata Guinea – Independent State of Papua New Guinea

Area – 462,840 sq. km
Capital – Port Moresby; population, 383,000 (2020 est)
Major town – Arawa, Lae
Currency – Kina (K) of 100 toea
Population – 7,259,456 rising at 1.6 per cent a year (2020 est)
Religion – Christian (Protestant 64.3 per cent, Roman Catholic 26 per cent), indigenous beliefs and other 3.1 per cent (est)
Language – English, Tok Pisin, Hiri Motu (all official), Motu; 836 indigenous languages are spoken, representing over 12 per cent of the world total
Population density – 19 per sq. km (2019)
Urban population – 13.3 per cent (2019 est)
Median age (years) – 24 (2020 est)
National anthem – 'O Arise, All You Sons'
National day – 16 September (Independence Day)
Death penalty – Retained (last used 1950)
CPI score – 28 (137)
Military expenditure – US$60.6m (2018)

CLIMATE AND TERRAIN

Papua New Guinea lies in the southwestern Pacific Ocean and consists of the eastern half of the island of New Guinea, the islands of Bougainville, New Britain and New Ireland, the Admiralty Islands, the D'Entrecasteaux Islands and the Louisiade archipelago. A range of densely forested mountains runs across the centre of the Papuan part of New Guinea, descending to coastal plains and swamps, and coral reefs. Elevation extremes range from 4,509m (Mt Wilhelm) to 0m (Pacific Ocean). There are a number of active volcanoes and

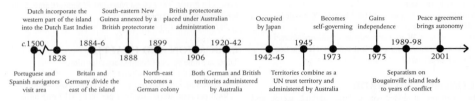

Dutch incorporate the western part of the island into the Dutch East Indies | South-eastern New Guinea annexed by a British protectorate | British protectorate placed under Australian administration | Occupied by Japan | Becomes self-governing | Gains independence | Peace agreement brings autonomy

c.1500 | 1884–6 | 1899 | 1920–42 | 1945 | 1989–98

1828 | 1888 | 1906 | 1942–45 | 1973 | 1975 | 2001

Portuguese and Spanish navigators visit area | Britain and Germany divide the east of the island | North-east becomes a German colony | Both German and British territories administered by Australia | Territories combine as a UN trust territory and administered by Australia | Separatism on Bougainville island leads to years of conflict

the country is subject to frequent eruptions and earthquakes. Over 50 per cent of the country is forested, and 20 per cent is permanently or seasonally flooded. The climate is tropical and subject to the north-west monsoon (December–March) and south-east monsoon (May–October).

POLITICS

The 1975 constitution was amended in 1998 to grant greater autonomy to Bougainville, and in March 2010 to expand the maximum number of cabinet ministers from 28 to 31. The head of state is Queen Elizabeth II, represented by a governor-general who is elected by the legislature for a six-year term. The unicameral National Parliament has a maximum of 126 members (currently 111), 20 from provincial electorates and the remainder from open electorates, who are directly elected for a five-year term. The prime minister is nominated by the legislature and appointed by the governor-general. In 2019, Bougainville voted overwhelmingly for independence in a non-binding referendum.

Factionalism and shifting alliances have caused political instability since independence, and a proportional representation element was introduced into the voting system in 2007 to try to increase the stability of governments. Following the 2007 legislative election, the National Alliance Party (NAP) leader, Sir Michael Somare, was elected prime minister for the fourth time, forming a new coalition government. Somare was convicted of financial irregularities in March 2011 and suspended for 14 days; former transport minister Peter O'Neill was elected as prime minister in August 2011. Legislative elections in 2012 saw the People's National Congress Party (PNC) gain the most seats but without a majority. The 2017 legislative elections were marked by official irregularities, alleged voter intimidation, and illicit, stolen or destroyed ballots. The PNC again gained the most seats but did not win a majority. O'Neill was forced to resign in May 2018 due to public pressure over a controversy involving a multi-billion-dollar gas deal, and was replaced by former finance minister James Marape.

Governor-General, HE Sir Robert Dadae, *sworn in* 28 February 2017

SELECTED GOVERNMENT MEMBERS *AS AT NOVEMBER 2020*
Prime Minister, James Marape
Deputy Prime Minister, Sam Basil
Foreign Affairs, Patrick Pruaitch

PAPUA NEW GUINEA HIGH COMMISSION
3rd Floor, 14 Waterloo Place, London SW1Y 4AR
T 020-7930 0922 E info@pnghighcomm.org.uk
W www.pnghighcomm.org.uk
High Commissioner, HE Winnie Kiap, *apptd* 2011

BRITISH HIGH COMMISSION
Sec 411 Lot 1 & 2, Kiroki Street, Waigani, National Capital District, Port Moresby
T (+675) 325 1677 E uk.inpng@fco.gov.uk
W www.gov.uk/government/world/papua-new-guinea

High Commissioner, HE Keith Scott, *apptd* 2018

ECONOMY AND TRADE

Political instability, corruption, a weak economy and high unemployment and crime levels brought the country to the brink of economic and social collapse in 2004. The economy subsequently achieved 13 years of continuous growth owing to higher commodity prices, but a fall in export prices resulted in a contraction in 2018. The country remains poor and underdeveloped, but is actively seeking new trade agreements. Foreign investment in oil and liquid natural gas extraction since 2004 has boosted economic growth; the export of liquefied natural gas to Asian economies began in March 2014, and its success has raised the possibility of similar projects as the government seeks further investment and trade.

About 85 per cent of the population practises subsistence farming, including some tribes in the interior so isolated that their economy is not monetised. Mineral deposits, including copper, gold, silver, nickel, oil and natural gas, are abundant and constitute the main sources of revenue, although exploitation is forced to overcome difficult terrain and poor infrastructure. This has been addressed by the government, which passed legislation in 2011 for an offshore sovereign wealth fund to manage government surpluses from mineral, oil and natural gas projects. The main industries are mining, oil extraction and refining, forestry, processing of agricultural and forestry products, construction and tourism. Industry contributes 42.9 per cent of GDP and services 35 per cent.

The main trading partners are Australia, China and Singapore. Principal exports are liquefied natural gas, oil, gold, copper ore, nickel, palm oil, cobalt, coffee, cocoa and shellfish. The main imports are machinery and transport equipment, manufactured goods, food, fuels and chemicals.

GNI – US$24.4bn; US$2,780 per capita (2019)
Annual average growth of GDP – 2.5 per cent (2017 est)
Inflation rate – 5.4er cent (2017 est)
Population below poverty line – 37 per cent (2002 est)
Unemployment – 2.5 per cent (2017 est)
Total external debt – US$17.94bn (2017 est)
Imports – US$3,977m (2017)
Exports – US$10,255m (2017)

BALANCE OF PAYMENTS
Trade – US$6,277m surplus (2017)
Current Account – US$5,450m surplus (2018)

Trade with UK	2018	2019
Imports from UK	£8,796,201	£11,941,358
Exports to UK	£76,083,657	£75,780,401

COMMUNICATIONS

Airports and waterways – 21, the principal airports being at Port Moresby, Lae and Rabaul; there are 11,000km of navigable waterways
Roadways – 3,000km
Telecommunications – 133,593 fixed lines and 3.4 million mobile subscriptions (2019); there were 787,764 internet users in 2018

Internet code and IDD – pg; 675 (from UK), 44 (to UK)
Major broadcasters – The National Television Service and National Broadcasting Corporation (radio) are the public broadcasters
Press – There are two foreign-owned daily newspapers: *The National* (Australia) and *The Post-Courier* (Malaysia)
WPFI score – 23.93 (46)

EDUCATION AND HEALTH
Literacy rate – 72.4 per cent (2015 est)
Health expenditure (per capita) – US$61 (2017)
Life expectancy (years) – 67.8 (2020 est)
Mortality rate – 6.7 (2020 est)
Birth rate – 22.5 (2020 est)
Infant mortality rate – 33.2 (2020 est)
HIV/AIDS adult prevalence rate – 0.9 per cent (2019 est)

PARAGUAY

República del Paraguay – Republic of Paraguay

Area – 406,752 sq. km
Capital – Asunción; population, 3,337,000 (2020 est)
Major cities – Ciudad del Este, Concepción, Lambaré, Limpio, San Lorenzo
Currency – Guaraní (Gs) of 100 céntimos
Population – 7,191,685 rising at 1.16 per cent a year (2020 est)
Religion – Christian (Roman Catholic 89.6 per cent, Protestant 6.2 per cent) (est)
Language – Spanish, Guaraní (both official), Portuguese, German
Population density – 18 per sq. km (2019)
Urban population – 61.7 per cent (2019 est)
Median age (years) – 29.7 (2020 est)
National anthem – 'Paraguayos, República o Muerte'
'Paraguayans, the Republic or Death'
National day – 15 May (Independence Day)
Death penalty – Abolished for all crimes (since 1992)
CPI score – 28 (137)
Military expenditure – US$387m (2018)
Conscription – 18 years of age; 12–24 months (selective)

CLIMATE AND TERRAIN
The country is divided by the river Paraguay into two distinct regions. The area east of the Paraguay is a fertile, grassy plateau where most of the population lives. The area to the west, the Gran Chaco, consists of a grassy and occasionally marshy plain that extends into neighbouring countries. Elevation extremes range from 842m (Cerro Pero) to 46m (the junction of the Paraguay and Paraná rivers). The climate varies from subtropical to temperate, with higher rainfall in the east and semi-arid conditions in the west. Average temperatures range from 18.2°C in July to 27.6°C in January.

HISTORY AND POLITICS
Spanish colonisation of Paraguay began in the early 16th century and Asunción was founded in 1537. Paraguay became independent from Spain in 1811 under the dictator José Gaspar Rodriguez de Francia, who ruled until his death in 1840. His successors instigated a period of reform and modernisation, which ended in 1865–70 with the catastrophic War of the Triple Alliance against Brazil, Uruguay and Argentina over access to the sea. The war resulted in the loss of over half the population as well as 150,000 sq. km of territory, and initiated a period of political instability that lasted until 1912. In the Chaco War of 1932–5, Paraguay gained territory in the west from Bolivia in a conflict that killed 100,000 people.

Political instability and conflict in the late 1940s ended with a coup in 1954 in which General Alfredo Stroessner seized power. His rule was autocratic and increasingly repressive, marked by corruption and human rights abuses. He was ousted in a coup in 1989 that paved the way for free multiparty elections to the presidency and legislature in 1993. These were won by the National Republican Association-Colorado Party (ANR-PC) and its presidential candidate, and the ANR-PC won all subsequent elections until 2008. Instability has prevailed since the 1990s, however, with the assassination of a vice-president, an attempted coup, widespread corruption and the growth of drug-trafficking, money-laundering and organised crime.

The 2008 presidential election was won by Fernando Lugo of the Patriotic Alliance for Change coalition (APC), the first president from outside the ANR-PC in 61 years; Lugo, however, was removed from office by impeachment of the senate in June 2012 for failing to manage fatal clashes over land evictions. The 2013 presidential and legislative elections were both won by the ANR-RC. In March 2017 president Horacio Cartes of the ANR-PC attempted to amend the constitution to allow him to stand for re-election in 2018, provoking violent protests. The 2018 presidential election was again won by an ANR-RC candidate, Mario Abdo Benítez, and in the simultaneous legislative elections the party lost ground but remained the largest party in both houses.

Under the 1992 constitution, the executive president is directly elected for a five-year term, which is not renewable. The bicameral Congress consists of a 45-member senate and an 80-member Chamber of Deputies, both directly elected for a five-year term. The president, who is responsible to the legislature, appoints the council of ministers.

HEAD OF STATE
President, Mario Abdo Benítez, *elected* 23 April 2018, *sworn in* 16 August 2018
Vice-President, Hugo Velazquez

SELECTED GOVERNMENT MEMBERS *AS AT NOVEMBER 2020*
Defence, Gen. (retd) Bernardino Soto Estigarribia
Foreign Affairs, Frederico Gonzalez
Interior, Eucildes Acevedo

EMBASSY OF THE REPUBLIC OF PARAGUAY
3rd Floor, 344 Kensington High Street, London W14 8NS
T 020-7610 4180 **E** embapar@btconnect.com
W www.paraguayembassy.co.uk
Ambassador Extraordinary and Plenipotentiary, HE Genaro Vicente Pappalardo Ayala, *apptd* 2017

BRITISH EMBASSY
Edificio Citicenter, Piso 5, Av. Mariscal López y Cruz del Chaco, Asunción
T (595) (21) 614 588 **E** BE-Asuncion.Enquiries@fco.gov.uk

W www.gov.uk/government/world/paraguay
Ambassador Extraordinary and Plenipotentiary, HE Ramin Navai, apptd 2020

ECONOMY AND TRADE
Paraguay's economy features a large informal sector and benefits from the proceeds of re-exporting to neighbouring countries. The economy started to slow in 2008, when drought reduced production of key exports, and went into recession in 2009, when the global downturn reduced export demand and commodity prices. Growth resumed in 2014 and averaged 5 per cent annually until 2019, but in the longer term the economy is hampered by political instability, corruption, national and foreign debt, inadequate infrastructure and high crime levels. The economy sharply decelerated in 2019 and is expected to contract by 4 per cent in 2020 owing to the coronavirus pandemic. Over one-quarter of the population lives below the poverty line and a high percentage of the rural population are landless, which has resulted in significant migration to urban centres due to the commercialisation of agriculture and forest clearances. Real incomes have steadily grown, however, as demand for Paraguay's highly priced commodities have risen, and low labour costs have helped triple the number of factories in the country since 2014.

The country has few mineral resources although exploration for oil and gas is underway. The economy is largely agricultural, much of it at subsistence level. Agricultural production, which accounts for 17.9 per cent of GDP and engages roughly a quarter of the workforce, is centred on cotton, sugar cane, soya beans, maize, wheat, tobacco, cassava, fruit, vegetables and livestock products. The main industries are sugar refining, forestry, manufacturing (cement, textiles, beverages, wood products, steel) and hydroelectric power generation. Industry accounts for 27.7 per cent of GDP and services for 54.5 per cent.

The main trading partners are Brazil, China, Argentina, Chile and the USA. Principal exports are soya beans, feed, cotton, meat, edible oils, timber, gold and leather. The main imports are road vehicles, consumer goods, tobacco, petroleum products, chemicals and electrical machinery.

GNI – US$38.8bn; US$5,510 per capita (2019)
Annual average growth of GDP – 4.8 per cent (2017 est)
Inflation rate – 3.6 per cent (2017 est)
Population below poverty line – 22.2 per cent (2015 est)
Unemployment – 5.7 per cent (2017 est)
Total external debt – US$17.7bn (2017 est)
Imports – US$12,498m (2017)
Exports – US$14,247m (2017)

BALANCE OF PAYMENTS
Trade – US$1,749m surplus (2017)
Current Account – US$385m deficit (2019)

Trade with UK	2018	2019
Imports from UK	£37,094,787	£32,226,630
Exports to UK	£24,029,081	£25,474,543

COMMUNICATIONS
Airports and waterways – 15, including the principal airport at Asunción; and around 3,100km of navigable waterways around the country
Roadways and railways – 6,167km; 36km
Telecommunications – 309,221 fixed lines and 7.6 million mobile subscriptions (2019); there were 4.6 million internet users in 2018
Internet code and IDD – py; 595 (from UK), 44 (to UK)

Major broadcasters – The state-owned Radio Nacional del Paraguay and TV Publica operate alongside a wealth of private broadcasters
Press – Major daily newspapers include *ABC Color, La Nación* and *Ultima Hora*
WPFI score – 32.97 (100)

EDUCATION AND HEALTH
Basic education is free and compulsory for nine years.
Literacy rate – 94 per cent (2018 est)
Gross enrolment ratio (percentage of relevant age group) – primary 104.4 per cent, secondary 76 per cent (2012 est); tertiary 35 per cent (2010 est)
Health expenditure (per capita) – US$381 (2017)
Hospital beds (per 1,000 people) – 1.3 (2011)
Life expectancy (years) – 77.9 (2020 est)
Mortality rate – 4.9 (2020 est)
Birth rate – 16.6 (2020 est)
Infant mortality rate – 16.9 (2020 est)
HIV/AIDS adult prevalence – 0.5 per cent (2019 est)

PERU
República del Perú – Republic of Peru

Area – 1,285,216 sq. km
Capital – Lima; population, 10,719,000 (2020 est)
Major cities – Arequipa, Chiclayo, Cuzco, Iquitos, Piura, Trujillo
Currency – Nuevo sol of 100 centimos
Population – 31,914,989 rising at 0.92 per cent a year (2020 est)
Religion – Christian (Roman Catholic 60 per cent, Evangelical 11.1 per cent, other Christian 3.5 per cent) (est)
Language – Spanish, Quechua, Aymara (all official), other Amerindian languages
Population density – 25 per sq. km (2019)
Urban population – 78.1 per cent (2019 est)
Median age (years) – 29.1 (2020 est)
National anthem – 'Himno Nacional del Perú' 'National Anthem of Peru'
National day – 28 July (Independence Day)
Death penalty – Retained for certain crimes (last used 1979)
CPI score – 36 (101)
Military expenditure – US$2,709m (2018)

CLIMATE AND TERRAIN
Peru has three main regions: the Costa, the coastal desert plain west of the Andes; the Sierra (mountain range) of the Andes, which runs parallel to the Pacific coast; and the Montaña (or Selva), a vast area of jungle stretching from the eastern foothills of the Andes to the country's eastern and north-eastern borders. Elevation extremes range from 6,768m

(Nevado Huascaran) to 0m (Pacific Ocean). The climate is arid in the west, temperate in the mountains and tropical in the east. Occasionally, due to the El Niño weather system, the northern districts experience a period of higher temperatures accompanied by torrential rain. The average temperature is 19.9°C.

HISTORY AND POLITICS

The Inca Empire centred on Cuzco superseded earlier civilisations in Peru and flourished from the 13th to the 15th century, when the empire reached its zenith before falling to Spanish conquistadores led by Francisco Pizarro in 1532–3. The territory formed the Viceroyalty of Peru and its gold and silver mines made Peru the principal source of wealth in Spain's American empire. After 1810, Peru became the centre of Spanish colonial government as its other colonies rebelled. Although Peru declared its independence in 1821, this was achieved only with the final defeat of Spanish forces in 1824.

Peru entered into several border disputes with its neighbours in the 19th and 20th centuries, including the Pacific War (1879–83) in which it lost three southern coastal provinces to Chile. A border dispute with Ecuador was renewed in 1981, leading to a short, inconclusive war in 1995, but was resolved in 1998 following adjudication. A border dispute with Chile ended in 1999 with the implementation of accords first agreed in 1929.

Following independence, Peru alternated between periods of military dictatorship and democratic rule. Two left-wing insurgencies, by the Maoist *Sendero Luminoso* (Shining Path) and the *Movimento Revolucionario Tupac Amaru* (MRTA), began in the 1980s. The conflict caused about 69,000 deaths and saw human rights abuses by both the security forces and the guerrillas. By the late 1990s both insurgencies had been overcome, although a few Maoists remain active. The conflict has left a legacy of criminal violence, much of it related to drug production and trafficking.

Alberto Fujimori, elected president in 1990 on a platform of economic reform, subverted democratic institutions in Peru during his decade in power, suspending the legislature for three years, sacking judges and imposing order through an 'emergency national reconstruction government'. He fled to Japan in 2000 to escape corruption charges, but was extradited and convicted in 2007 of abuse of power and in 2009 of human rights abuses.

Former World Bank economist Pedro Pablo Kuczynski narrowly won the June 2016 presidential election, but was forced to resign in March 2018 following a corruption scandal. He was replaced by Vice-President Martín Vizcarra. In December 2018, the public strongly supported measures to tackle corruption, which included establishing an elected judiciary and regulating the finances of political organisations. Snap elections to push through these reforms in January 2020 produced no outright majority, although indicated support for Vizcarra's agenda, but in November 2020 Vizcarra was impeached over bribery allegations and was replaced by speaker of Congress Manuel Merino. Supporters of Vizcarra labelled this a parliamentary coup and violent protests resulted in Merino's resignation after less than a week.

Under the 1993 constitution, the executive president is directly elected for a five-year term, renewable once. The unicameral legislature, the Congress of the Republic, has 130 members, directly elected for a five-year term. The president, who is responsible to the legislature, appoints the council of ministers.

HEAD OF STATE
President, vacant

SELECTED GOVERNMENT MEMBERS *AS AT NOVEMBER 2020*
Prime Minister, Gen. (retd) Walter Martos
Defence, Gen. Jorge Chavez
Economy and Finance, Maria Alva
Foreign Affairs, Mario Lopez

EMBASSY OF PERU
52 Sloane Street, London SW1X 9SP
T 020-7235 3802 **E** postmaster@peruembassy-uk.com
W www.peruembassy-uk.com
Ambassador Extraordinary and Plenipotentiary, HE Juan Carlos Gamarra, *apptd* 2018

BRITISH EMBASSY
Torre Parque Mar, Avenida José Larco 1301, Lima
T (+51) (1) 617 3000 **E** belima@fco.gov.uk
W www.gov.uk/government/world/peru
Ambassador Extraordinary and Plenipotentiary, HE Kate Harrisson, *apptd* 2018

ECONOMY AND TRADE

The Peruvian economy grew by an average of 6 per cent between 2004 and 2012, and 5.6 per cent from 2009 to 2013, which made it one of the fastest growing economies in Latin America. However, since 2015 the economy has decelerated and is expected to contract by 13.9 per cent in 2020, owing to the coronavirus pandemic, political instability, and lower export prices. The economy is largely driven by exports of silver, copper, and other metal and mineral products, which accounts for 55 per cent of total exports. Tourism, agricultural produce and fishing has also driven growth. Poverty remains widespread, but the benefits of economic growth are starting to be felt in the poorer regions and the poverty rate has declined by 35 per cent since 2002. The dependence on metal exports and imported foodstuffs makes the economy vulnerable to fluctuations in world prices. Successive governments' free trade policies have contributed to greater international investment and mining output, but development has been hindered by corruption scandals, flooding and project delays in recent years.

Mineral resources, including copper, gold, silver, zinc, oil and natural gas, are abundant, and extracting and refining these is the mainstay of the economy. Other industries include steel and metal fabrication, fishing and fish processing, textiles and clothes manufacture and food processing. Agriculture is centred on avocado and other fruits, coffee, cocoa, cotton, sugar cane, rice, cereals, vegetables, coca, medicinal plants, meat and dairy products. Services contribute 59.9 per cent to GDP, industry 32.7 per cent and agriculture 7.6 per cent.

The main trading partners are China, the USA, Brazil, Switzerland and Mexico. Principal exports are mining and mineral products, crude oil and petroleum products, natural gas, coffee, vegetables, fruit, fish, textiles and chemicals. The main imports are oil and petroleum products, chemicals, plastics, machinery, vehicles, telecommunications equipment, iron and steel, and food.

GNI – US$219.1bn; US$6,740 per capita (2019)
Annual average growth of GDP – 2.18 per cent (2019 est)
Inflation rate – 2.8 per cent (2017 est)
Population below poverty line – 22.7 per cent (2014 est)
Unemployment – 6.58 per cent (2019 est)
Total external debt – US$66.25bn (2017 est)
Imports – US$47,093m (2017)
Exports – US$52,312m (2017)

BALANCE OF PAYMENTS
Trade – US$5,219m surplus (2017)
Current Account – US$3,531m deficit (2019)

Trade with UK	2018	2019
Imports from UK	£173,287,379	£164,536,694
Exports to UK	£391,474,501	£464,523,459

COMMUNICATIONS

Airports and waterways – There are 59 airports, including the international airport at Lima; there are 8,808km of inland waterways, and the main seaports are Callao and Matarani
Roadways and railways – There are 18,699km of paved roadways; the state-run railways have 1,907km of track
Telecommunications – 3.1 million fixed lines and 39.1 million mobile subscriptions (2019); there were 16.5 million internet users in 2018
Internet code and IDD – pe; 51 (from UK), 44 (to UK)
Major broadcasters – The state-owned TV Peru and Radio Nacional operate alongside a number of private broadcasters
Press – Major daily newspapers include *El Bocón*, *La República* and *Ojo*
WPFI score – 30.94 (90)

EDUCATION AND HEALTH

Education is free and compulsory for 11 years.
Literacy rate – 94.4 per cent (2018 est)
Gross enrolment ratio (percentage of relevant age group) – primary 113.5 per cent, secondary 108.8 per cent (2019 est); tertiary 70.7 per cent (2017 est)
Health expenditure (per capita) – US$333 (2017)
Hospital beds (per 1,000 people) – 1.6 (2014)
Life expectancy (years) – 74.2 (2020 est)
Mortality rate – 6.1 (2020 est)
Birth rate – 7.6 (2020 est)
Infant mortality rate – 17.8 (2020 est)
HIV/AIDS adult prevalence – 0.3 per cent (2019 est)

THE PHILIPPINES

Republika ng Pilipinas – Republic of the Philippines

Area – 300,000 sq. km
Capital – Manila; population (Metro Manila, including Quezon City), 13,923,000 (2020 est)
Major cities – Bacolod, Cagayan de Oro, Cebu, Davao, General Santos (Dadiangas), Iloilo, Laoag, Zamboanga
Currency – Philippine peso (P) of 100 centavos
Population – 109,180,815 rising at 1.52 per cent a year (2020 est); Tagalog (24.4 per cent), Bisaya (11.4 per cent), Cebuano (9.9 per cent), Ilocano (8.4 per cent), Hiligaynon (8.4 per cent), Bikol (6.8 per cent) (est)
Religion – Christian (Roman Catholic 80.6 per cent, Protestant 8.2 per cent), Muslim 5.6 per cent (est)
Language – Filipino, English (both official), Tagalog, Cebuano, Ilocano, Hiligaynon, Bicol, Waray, Pampango, Pangasinan

Population density – 358 per sq. km (2019)
Urban population – 47.1 per cent (2019 est)
Median age (years) – 24.1 (2020 est)
National anthem – 'Lupang Hinirang' 'Chosen Land'
National day – 12 June (Independence Day)
Death penalty – Abolished for all crimes (since 2006)
CPI score – 34 (114)
Military expenditure – US$3,770m (2018 est)

CLIMATE AND TERRAIN

The Philippines comprises over 7,100 islands in the western Pacific Ocean. The principal islands are Luzon, Mindanao, Mindoro, Samar, Negros, Palawan, Panay and Leyte; other groups include the Sulu islands, Babuyanes and Batanes, Calamian and Kalayaan islands. The islands mostly have mountainous interiors and narrow coastal plains. The mountain ranges are volcanic, and some volcanoes are still active. Elevation extremes range from 2,954m (Mt Apo) to 0m (Philippine Sea). The climate is tropical; the average temperature is 26.2°C, and relative humidity is high. The country is affected by the monsoons, which cause the rainy season between July and October. During this period the country is also susceptible to typhoons, which frequently cause widespread damage and loss of life.

HISTORY AND POLITICS

The Philippine islands were settled first by Malays, then by Chinese, Indonesian and Arab traders. Islam was introduced in the 14th century and became the dominant religion in the south. The islands were discovered by Spain and then settled from 1565 by the Spanish, who introduced Roman Catholicism. Colonial rule lasted until 1898, when Spain ceded the colony to the USA following the Spanish-American War. The country became internally self-governing in 1935, was occupied by Japan from 1942 to 1944, and achieved independence from the USA in 1946.

Ferdinand Marcos was elected president in 1965, imposing martial law in 1972. His regime became increasingly repressive, corrupt and violent, and when he falsified election results in 1986 to prevent Corazon Aquino from taking office as president, a popular uprising forced him to flee the country. Aquino survived political unrest and ten attempted military coups to introduce a new constitution and entrench democratic politics.

Fidel Ramos, Aquino's successor in 1992, built on her work, raised the country's international profile and instigated peace talks with insurgents (*see* below). Joseph Estrada, elected president in 1998, was overthrown in 2001 in a popular uprising; his term was completed by Vice-President Gloria Arroyo. President Arroyo retained the presidency in the 2004 presidential election, but her popularity plummeted and her anti-corruption measures and economic reforms were undermined by corruption scandals and impeachment attempts.

In the May 2013 legislative elections, the Liberal Party (LP) won the most seats in the house of representatives but without a majority. The 2016 presidential election was won by Rodrigo Duterte, the former mayor of Davao City, known as 'Duterte Harry' for his support of capital punishment and backing of extrajudicial killings. He initiated a brutal crackdown on drug cartels, which Human Rights Watch claimed to have resulted in over 26,000 deaths by September 2020. Duterte's hold on Congress was strengthened following midterm elections in May 2019.

Under the 1987 constitution, the executive president is directly elected for a six-year term, which is not renewable. There is a bicameral Congress. The lower house, the House of Representatives, has up to 238 directly elected members, plus

59 members appointed from party and minority group lists; all serve a three-year term. The senate has 24 members directly elected for a six-year term, with half re-elected every three years.

The Autonomous Region of Muslim Mindanao comprises the provinces of Lanao del Sur and Maguindanao on Mindanao and the island provinces of Sulu, Tawi-Tawi and Basilan. It has a 24-member regional assembly and a governor.

HEAD OF STATE
President, Rodrigo Duterte, *elected* 9 May 2016, *sworn in* 30 June 2016
Vice-President, Leni Robredo

SELECTED GOVERNMENT MEMBERS *AS AT NOVEMBER 2020*
Defence, Delfin Lorenzana
Finance, Carlos Dominguez
Foreign Affairs, Teodoro Locsin

EMBASSY OF THE REPUBLIC OF THE PHILIPPINES
6–11 Suffolk Street, London SW1Y 4HG
T 020-7451 1780 **E** embassy@philemb.co.uk
W www.philembassy-uk.org
Ambassador Extraordinary and Plenipotentiary, HE Antonio Manuel Lagdameo, *apptd* 2017

BRITISH EMBASSY
120 Upper McKinley Road, McKinley Hill, Taguig City 1634, Manila
T (+63) (2) 858 2200 **E** ukinthephilippines@fco.gov.uk
W www.gov.uk/government/world/philippines
Ambassador Extraordinary and Plenipotentiary, HE Daniel Pruce, *apptd* 2017

INSURGENCIES
A communist insurgency by the New People's Army (NPA) began in the late 1960s. The NPA is based in Mindanao but has groups in rural areas throughout the country. Peace talks between the government and the NPA's political front, the National Democratic Front, stalled in 2004 and were resumed in early 2011, but were abandoned following the election of the belligerent President Duterte in 2016. In April 2017, a temporary ceasefire was agreed but fighting resumed in December that year.

There has been a Muslim (Moro) insurgency in the southern islands, particularly Mindanao, since the 1970s. The Moro National Liberation Front (MNLF) concluded a peace agreement with the government in 1996 that ended its insurgency and established the Autonomous Region of Muslim Mindanao (ARMM). The Moro Islamic Liberation Front (MILF) agreed a ceasefire with the government in 2003, but negotiations over a Muslim 'homeland' broke down in 2008; a resumption of violence in 2009 displaced over 300,000 people until another ceasefire was agreed and peace talks resumed in late 2009. Talks broke down in October 2011, however, after air strikes on MILF areas in Zamboanga left 35 people dead. In January 2014, the government agreed to create a new Muslim autonomous area called Bangsamoro in the south of the Philippines by 2016 in return for the disbanding of the MILF. Despite the agreement, MILF members are believed to have been involved in an attack that killed more than 40 Filipino police officers in January 2015. Subsequently the proposed Bangsamoro Organic Law that would have led to the creation of the autonomous region was shelved, but on 21 January 2019 the region overwhelmingly voted to support the law in a referendum, and its implementation began soon after.

The radical Muslim separatist group Abu Sayyaf, based on Jolo and Basilan, is viewed as a terrorist organisation and the government refuses to negotiate with it. It pledged allegiance to Islamic State (IS) in October 2014. In May 2017, the radical Islamist Maute group took control of Marawi in the southern Philippines, apparently after the government launched a raid to capture Abu Sayyaf leader Isnilon Hapilon, who was rumoured to be in the city; as a result, martial law was declared on the island of Mindanao and thousands died or were displaced in the subsequent fighting.

ECONOMY AND TRADE
The economy has survived the 2009 recession better than other Asian economies thanks to low dependence on exports, robust domestic consumption and remittances from roughly 10 million overseas workers. Despite this, poverty remains high, especially in rural areas, as economic expansion struggles to offset the high rate of population growth; one third of the population lives below the poverty line. Growth averaged over 6 per cent annually during 2011–19, largely thanks to strong domestic demand. During 2017, significant infrastructure spending was coupled with record levels of foreign investment, but underemployment, inequality and a significant informal sector continue to limit economic potential. The coronavirus pandemic is expected to cause a contraction in the economy in 2020 by around 8.3 per cent. The Philippines formed a common market with the other members of the Association of Southeast Asian Nations (ASEAN) in 2015.

Major industries include electronics assembly, manufacture of clothing, business process outsourcing, pharmaceuticals, chemicals and wood products, food processing and fishing. The large agricultural sector employs 25.4 per cent of the workforce, producing sugar cane, coconuts, rice, maize, tropical fruits and livestock products. Agriculture accounts for 9.6 per cent of GDP, industry for 30.6 per cent and services for 59.8 per cent.

The main trading partners are Japan, the USA, China, South Korea and other Asian states. Principal exports are semiconductors and electronic products, machinery, clothing, wood manufactures, chemicals and processed food and beverages. The main imports are electronic products, fuels, machinery and transport equipment, iron and steel, fabrics, grains, chemicals and plastics.

GNI – US$415.7bn; US$3,850 per capita (2019)
Annual average growth of GDP – 6.04 per cent (2019 est)
Inflation rate – 2.9 per cent (2017 est)
Population below poverty line – 21.6 per cent (2017 est)
Unemployment – 5.11 per cent (2019 est)
Total external debt – US$76.18bn (2017 est)
Imports – US$118,478m (2017)
Exports – US$86,318m (2017)

BALANCE OF PAYMENTS
Trade – US$32,159m deficit (2017)
Current Account – US$3,386m deficit (2019)

Trade with UK	2018	2019
Imports from UK	£542,552,143	£696,205,260
Exports to UK	£576,619,783	£507,738,037

COMMUNICATIONS
Airports and waterways – There are 89 airports; the main ports are Manila (Luzon), Cebu, Davao, Subic Bay, Batangas and Iloilo, and there are 3,219km of waterways
Roadways and railways – 61,093km of paved roads; 77km
Telecommunications – 4.1 million fixed lines and 166.4 million mobile subscriptions (2019); there were 63.6 million internet users in 2018

Internet code and IDD – ph; 63 (from UK), 44 (to UK)
Major broadcasters – The government-owned People's Television and Philippine Broadcasting Service (radio) compete with two major commercial broadcasters and over 600 radio stations
Press – Daily newspapers include the *Daily Tribune, Malaya* and *Philippine Star*
WPFI score – 43.54 (136)

EDUCATION AND HEALTH

There are seven years of free and compulsory primary education, followed by three years of free but non-compulsory secondary education.
Literacy rate – 98.2 per cent (2015 est)
Gross enrolment ratio (percentage of relevant age group) – primary 101.9 per cent, secondary 84.0 per cent (2018 est); tertiary 35.5 per cent (2017 est)
Health expenditure (per capita) – US$133 (2014)
Hospital beds (per 1,000 people) – 1 (2011)
Life expectancy (years) – 70 (2020 est)
Mortality rate – 6 (2020 est)
Birth rate – 22.9 (2020 est)
Infant mortality rate – 20 (2020 est)
HIV/AIDS adult prevalence – 0.2 per cent (2019 est)

POLAND

Rzeczpospolita Polska – Republic of Poland

Area – 312,685 sq. km
Capital – Warsaw; population, 1,783,000 (2020 est)
Major cities – Bydgoszcz, Gdansk, Katowice, Krakow, Lodz, Lublin, Poznan, Szczecin, Wroclaw
Currency – Zloty of 100 groszy
Population – 38,282,325 falling at 0.19 per cent a year (2020 est)
Religion – Christian (Roman Catholic 87.2 per cent, Orthodox 1.3 per cent) (est)
Language – Polish (official)
Population density – 124 per sq. km (2019)
Urban population – 60.0 per cent (2019 est)
Median age (years) – 41.9 (2020 est)
National anthem – 'Mazurek Dabrowskiego' 'Dabrowski's Mazurka'
National day – 3 May (Constitution Day)
Death penalty – Abolished for all crimes (since 1997)
CPI score – 58 (41)
Military expenditure – US$11,596m (2018)

CLIMATE AND TERRAIN

Poland lies mostly in a great plain crossed by the Oder, Neisse and Vistula rivers. The land rises to the Carpathian, Tatra and Sudeten mountains along the southern border. Elevation extremes range from 2,499m (Rysy) to −2m (Raczki Elblaskie). The climate is continental, and average temperatures range from −1.3°C in January to 18.5°C in July.

POLITICS

Under the 1997 constitution, the head of state is the president, who is directly elected for a five-year term, renewable once. The president nominates the prime minister and has the right to be consulted over the appointment of the foreign, defence and interior ministers. The National Assembly is bicameral; the lower house, the Diet *(Sejm)*, has 460 members elected by proportional representation for a four-year term. The senate has 100 members elected on a provincial basis for a four-year term.

The right-wing Law and Justice party (PiS) won the legislative elections in October 2015, securing more than one-third of the vote. Andrzej Duda of the PiS was elected president in May 2015, and was re-elected in the delayed July 2020 elections in the second round. In July 2017, the PiS provoked international condemnation when it pushed through legal reforms that critics said threatened the independence of the judiciary; the ruling party has also attracted criticism for changes that undermine women's rights and for criminalising accusations of national complicity in crimes committed by Nazi Germany. The PiS lost its majority in the senate in the October 2019 parliamentary election, but retained its majority in the *Sejm*.

HEAD OF STATE
President, Andrzej Duda, *elected* 26 May 2015, *sworn in* 6 August 2015, *re-elected* 12 July 2020

SELECTED GOVERNMENT MEMBERS *AS AT NOVEMBER 2020*
Prime Minister, Mateusz Morawiecki
Deputy Prime Ministers, Piotr Glinski; Jaroslaw Gowin; Jacek Sasin
Defence, Mariusz Blaszczak
Foreign Affairs, Zbigniew Rau

EMBASSY OF THE REPUBLIC OF POLAND
47 Portland Place, London W1B 1JH
T 020-7291 3520 **E** london@msz.gov.pl **W** www.london.polemb.net
Ambassador Extraordinary and Plenipotentiary, HE Prof. Arkady Rzegocki, *apptd* 2016

BRITISH EMBASSY
Ul. Kawalerii 12, 00-468 Warsaw
T (+48) (22) 311 0000 **E** info@britishembassy.pl
W www.gov.uk/government/world/poland
Ambassador Extraordinary and Plenipotentiary, HE Anna Clunes, OBE, *apptd* 2020

ECONOMY AND TRADE

Poland's successful transition to a market economy in the 1990s came at the cost of high levels of public debt, unemployment and inflation, which were reduced by subsequent governments. The economy has grown steadily since 1992 and particularly since accession to the EU in 2004, and Poland was the only EU nation to avoid recession in 2008–9. The largest recipient of EU development funds, GDP grew steadily between 2014 and 2019, but is expected to contract by 3.6 per cent on 2020 owing to the coronavirus pandemic.

Poland has vast mineral resources, especially coal, and nearly half its area is fertile arable land. The large agricultural sector has been modernised but remains inefficient; it employs 11.5 per cent of the workforce but contributes only 2.4 per cent of GDP. The agricultural products are potatoes, vegetables, fruit, wheat, meat, eggs and dairy products. The main industries are machine building, iron and steel production, coal mining, chemicals, shipbuilding, food processing, glass, beverages and textiles. Industry accounts for 40.2 per cent of GDP.

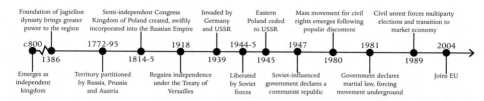

| Foundation of Jagiellon dynasty brings greater power to the region | Semi-independent Congress Kingdom of Poland created, swiftly incorporated into the Russian Empire | Invaded by Germany and USSR | Eastern Poland ceded to USSR | Mass movement for civil rights emerges following popular discontent | Civil unrest forces multiparty elections and transition to market economy |

c.800 — 1386 — 1772-95 — 1814-5 — 1918 — 1939 — 1944-5 — 1945 — 1947 — 1980 — 1981 — 1989 — 2004

| Emerges as independent kingdom | Territory partitioned by Russia, Prussia and Austria | Regains independence under the Treaty of Versailles | Liberated by Soviet forces | Soviet-influenced government declares a communist republic | Government declares martial law, forcing movement underground | Joins EU |

The main trading partners are other EU countries (especially Germany), China and Russia. Principal exports include machinery and vehicles, manufactured and semi-manufactured goods, food and livestock. The main imports are machinery and vehicles, semi-manufactured goods, chemicals, minerals, fuels and lubricants.
GNI – US$577.3bn; US$15,200 per capita (2019)
Annual average growth of GDP – 4.55 per cent (2019 est)
Inflation rate – 2.0 per cent (2017 est)
Population below poverty line – 17.6 per cent (2015 est)
Unemployment – 5.43 per cent (2019 est)
Total external debt – US$241bn (2017 est)
Imports – US$264,157m (2017)
Exports – US$286,798m (2017)

BALANCE OF PAYMENTS
Trade – US$22,641m surplus (2017)
Current Account – US$2,931m surplus (2019)

Trade with UK	2018	2019
Imports from UK	£5,267,623,829	£5,338,819,951
Exports to UK	£10,784,801,542	£11,246,793,672

COMMUNICATIONS
Airports and waterways – The principal airports are at Warsaw, Krakow, Katowice and Wroclaw, and there are 83 smaller airports; the principal seaports are Gdansk, Gdynia, Swinoujscie and Szczecin, and there are 3,997km of navigable rivers and canals
Roadways and railways – 420,000km; 19,321km
Telecommunications – 6.9 million fixed lines and 52.9 million mobile subscriptions (2019); there were 29.8 million internet users in 2018
Internet code and IDD – pl; 48 (from UK), 44 (to UK)
Major broadcasters – Telewizja Polska (TVP) and Polish Radio are the principal state broadcasters
Press – *Gazeta Wyborcza*, *Fakt* and *Rzeczpospolita* are the principal mass-circulation dailies
WPFI score – 28.65 (62)

EDUCATION AND HEALTH
Elementary education (ages seven to 15) is free and compulsory. Secondary education is also free, but optional.
Literacy rate – 100 per cent (2015 est)
Gross enrolment ratio (percentage of relevant age group) – primary 96.9 per cent, secondary 112 per cent, tertiary 68.6 per cent (2018 est)
Health expenditure (per capita) – US$907 (2017)
Hospital beds (per 1,000 people) – 6.5 (2011)
Life expectancy (years) – 78.3 (2020 est)
Mortality rate – 10.6 (2020 est)
Birth rate – 8.9 (2020 est)
Infant mortality rate – 4.3 (2020 est)

PORTUGAL
República Portuguesa – Portuguese Republic

Area – 92,090 sq. km
Capital – Lisbon; population, 2,957,000 (2020 est)
Major cities – Coimbra, Faro, Oporto, Setubal
Currency – Euro (€) of 100 cents
Population – 10,302,674 falling at 0.25 per cent a year (2020 est)
Religion – Christian (Roman Catholic 81 per cent, other Christian 3.3 per cent) (est)
Language – Portuguese, Mirandese (both official)
Population density – 112 per sq. km (2019)
Urban population – 65.8 per cent (2019 est)
Median age (years) – 44.6 (2020 est)
National anthem – 'A Portuguesa' 'The Portuguese'
National day – 10 June (Portugal Day)
Death penalty – Abolished for all crimes (since 1976)
CPI score – 62 (30)
Military expenditure – US$4,248m (2018)

CLIMATE AND TERRAIN
The terrain is mountainous north of the river Tagus, with rolling hills and plains in the south. Elevation extremes range from 2,351m (Ponta do Pico, Azores) to 0m (Atlantic Ocean). Forests of pine, cork oak and eucalyptus cover about 38 per cent of the country. The climate is temperate, with average temperatures ranging from 9.7°C in January to 22.5°C in August.

HISTORY AND POLITICS
Part of the Roman Empire from the second century BC, the country was overrun by Vandals and Visigoths in the fifth century AD. The Visigoths were ousted by Muslims from north Africa in the eighth century, but Christian reconquest began in the tenth century and an independent Christian kingdom was established in the 12th century.
Portuguese navigators led the 15th-century European age of exploration and the country soon became a major commercial and colonial power, its empire expanding to include Brazil, parts of China and large areas of Africa. In 1807 Portugal was invaded by Napoleonic France and then became the base from which Allied forces liberated Portugal and Spain in the Peninsular War. The 19th century was politically turbulent,

with power struggles between conservative and liberal politicians, and within different factions of the royal family. In 1910 an armed uprising in Lisbon drove King Manuel II into exile and a republic was declared.

A period of political instability ensued until the military intervened in 1926. The constitution of 1933 gave formal expression to the authoritarian *Estado Novo* (New State) introduced by Dr Antonio Salazar, prime minister from 1932 until 1968. Marcello Caetano succeeded Salazar in 1968 but the regime's failure to liberalise at home or to conclude wars in the African colonies resulted in the government's overthrow in a military coup in 1974. Great political turmoil followed in 1974–5, a period in which most of the country's colonies gained their independence. Elections in 1976 stabilised the situation and full civilian government was restored in 1982. Portugal joined the EEC in 1986 and adopted the euro in 2002.

The centre-right Portugal Ahead coalition won the most seats in legislative elections in October 2015 but lost the majority it had held since 2011. However, Socialist Party (SP) leader Antonio Costa became prime minister in November following an alliance with Communist, Green and Left Bloc parties, which toppled conservative Pedro Passos Coelho's 11-day-old government in a parliamentary vote – the shortest administration in Portuguese history. The SP increased its number of seats in the October 2019 election and Costa continued as prime minister of a minority government, but with bill-by-bill support from other left-wing parties. The centre-right candidate Marcelo Rebelo de Sousa won the presidential election in January 2016 with 52 per cent of the vote.

Under the 1976 constitution, amended in 1982 and 1989, the head of state is a president who is directly elected for a five-year term, renewable once. The unicameral Assembly of the Republic has 230 members, directly elected by proportional representation for a four-year term. The prime minister, appointed by the president, is usually the leader of the largest party in the assembly.

HEAD OF STATE
President of the Republic, Marcelo Rebelo de Sousa, *elected* 24 January 2016, *sworn in* 9 March 2016

SELECTED GOVERNMENT MEMBERS *AS AT NOVEMBER 2020*
Prime Minister, Antonio Costa
Finance, Joao Leao
Internal Administration, Eduardo Cabrita

EMBASSY OF PORTUGAL
11 Belgrave Square, London SW1X 8PP
T 020-7235 5331 **E** londres@mne.pt
W www.portuguese-embassy.co.uk
Ambassador Extraordinary and Plenipotentiary, HE Manuel Lobo Antunes, *apptd* 2016

BRITISH EMBASSY
Rua de Sao Bernardo 33, 1249-082 Lisbon
T (+351) (21) 392 4000 **E** portugal.consulate@fco.gov.uk
W www.gov.uk/government/world/portugal
Ambassador Extraordinary and Plenipotentiary, HE Christopher Sainty, *apptd* 2018

ECONOMY AND TRADE
Portugal's economy was transformed after it joined the EU in 1986 into a diversified and increasingly service-based economy. The rapid growth of the 1990s slowed in 2001–8, and the global downturn pushed the economy into recession in 2009. Despite government austerity measures, a budget deficit treble the eurozone limit led to the country to obtain EU financial support in 2011. GDP fell in 2012 and 2013, as the government cut spending and increased tax to comply with the conditions of an EU-IMF financial rescue package. Portugal's economic recovery quickened after 2014 and it exited the EU's excessive deficit programme in 2017, posting its strongest growth in a century. Unemployment and public debt also fell, but the impact of the coronavirus pandemic (particularly to tourism) is expected to result in negative growth of 10 per cent in 2020. The government has promised a socialist programme allowing for a 'sustainable reduction in deficits and debt', and has boosted confidence by repaying its IMF loan ahead of schedule.

Around 8.6 per cent of the workforce is engaged in agriculture, contributing 2.2 per cent of GDP. The chief products are grain, fruit and vegetables, livestock, fish, dairy products, timber and cork. The main industries are tourism, manufacturing (textiles, footwear, cork, pulp and paper, chemicals, motor vehicle components), metalworking, winemaking, oil refining, and shipbuilding and repair. Natural resources are being exploited to generate electricity from hydroelectric and solar sources, to reduce dependence on imported fuel and energy. Industry accounts for 22.1 per cent of GDP and services for 75.7 per cent.

The main trading partners are other EU countries, particularly Spain. Principal exports are agricultural products, food, wine, oil products, wood products, other industrial products, machinery and tools. The main imports include agricultural products, chemicals, vehicles, optical and precision instruments, and computer and IT components.
GNI – US$237bn; US$23,080 per capita (2019)
Annual average growth of GDP – 2.24 per cent (2019 est)
Inflation rate – 1.6 per cent (2017 est)
Population below poverty line – 19 per cent (2015)
Unemployment – 6.55 per cent (2019 est)
Total external debt – US$449bn (2016 est)
Imports – US$90,907m (2017)
Exports – US$95,200m (2017)

BALANCE OF PAYMENTS
Trade – US$4,293m surplus (2017)
Current Account – US$235m deficit (2019)

Trade with UK	2018	2019
Imports from UK	£1,579,547,888	£1,582,360,072
Exports to UK	£3,100,547,582	£3,204,853,205

COMMUNICATIONS
Airports and waterways – There are 43 airports, including international airports at Lisbon, Oporto, Faro, Santa Maria (Azores) and Funchal (Madeira); the main ports are Aveiro, Figueira da Foz, Leixoes, Lisbon, Setubal and Sines
Roadways and railways – 82,900km; 3,319km
Telecommunications – 5.2 million fixed lines and 12 million mobile subscriptions (2019); there were 7.7 million internet users in 2018
Internet code and IDD – pt; 351 (from UK), 44 (to UK)
Major broadcasters – The monopoly of the public broadcaster RTP (TV) and RDP (radio) ended in 1992, and commercial stations now dominate the market
Press – Principal national newspapers include the daily titles *Diario de Noticias, Correio da Manha* and *Jornal de Noticias*
WPFI score – 11.83 (10)

EDUCATION AND HEALTH
Education is free and compulsory for nine years from the age of six. The university at Coimbra was founded in 1290.
Literacy rate – 96.1 per cent (2018 est)
Gross enrolment ratio (percentage of relevant age group) – primary 106.8 per cent, secondary 120.8 per cent, tertiary 65.7 per cent (2018 est)

Health expenditure (per capita) – US$1,908 (2017)
Hospital beds (per 1,000 people) – 3.4 (2013)
Life expectancy (years) – 81.1 (2020 est)
Mortality rate – 10.8 (2020 est)
Birth rate – 8.1 (2020 est)
Infant mortality rate – 2.6 (2020 est)

AUTONOMOUS REGIONS

Madeira and the Azores are both autonomous regions, each with its own locally elected assembly and government.
MADEIRA is a group of islands in the Atlantic Ocean about 990km south-west of Lisbon, and consists of Madeira, Porto Santo and three uninhabited islands. Total area is 801 sq. km; population, 253,945 (2019 est). Funchal on Madeira, the largest island, is the capital.
THE AZORES is an archipelago of nine islands in the Atlantic Ocean 1,400–1,800km west of Lisbon, and consists of Flores, Corvo, Terceira, Sao Jorge, Pico, Faial, Graciosa, Sao Miguel and Santa Maria. Total area is 2,322 sq. km; population, 245,766 (2016). Ponta Delgada, on Sao Miguel, is the capital.

QATAR

Dawlat Qatar – State of Qatar

Area – 11,586 sq. km
Capital – Doha; population, 641,000 (2020 est)
Major cities – Ar Rayyan, al-Wakrah
Currency – Qatar riyal of 100 dirhams
Population – 2,444,174 rising at 1.55 per cent a year (2020 est); non-Qatari (88.4 per cent), Qatari (11.6 per cent) (est)
Religion – Muslim 67.7 per cent (predominantly Sunni), Christian 13.8 per cent, Hindu 13.8 per cent, Buddhist 3.1 per cent (est)
Language – Arabic (official), English
Population density – 240 per sq. km (2019)
Urban population – 99.2 per cent (2019 est)
Median age (years) – 33.7 (2020 est)
National anthem – 'As-Salam Al-Amiri' 'Peace to the Amir'
National day – 18 December
Death penalty – Retained
CPI score – 62 (30)
Military expenditure – US$2,174m (2010)
Conscription – 18–35 years of age, male only; 4–12 months (selective)
Literacy rate – 93.5 per cent (2017 est)
Gross enrolment ratio (percentage of relevant age group) – primary 103.5 per cent (2019 est); secondary 93 per cent (2016 est); tertiary 18.9 per cent (2019 est)
Health expenditure (per capita) – US$1,649 (2017)
Life expectancy (years) – 79.4 (2020 est)
Mortality rate – 1.6 (2020 est)
Birth rate – 9.3 (2020 est)
Infant mortality rate – 5.7 (2020 est)

CLIMATE AND TERRAIN

Qatar occupies a peninsula in the Persian Gulf and is mostly a low-lying desert plain, with sand dunes in the south. Elevation extremes range from 103m (Tuwayyir al-Hamir) to 0m (Persian Gulf). The country has a desert climate, with low rainfall and average temperatures ranging from 17.1°C in January to 36.6°C in July. Humidity along the coast often reaches 90 per cent in summer.

HISTORY AND POLITICS

Towns on the Qatari coast developed into important trading centres from the 18th century. Persian rule of the area ended in the mid-18th century and after a period of conflict, the peninsula became a dependency of Bahrain in the 1850s. A revolt against Bahraini rule in the 1860s was suppressed, but Britain intervened in 1867, recognising the dependency as a separate entity. Nominally under the rule of the Ottoman Empire from 1871 until the outbreak of the First World War, Qatar became a British protectorate in 1916, when the al-Thani family was recognised as the ruling house. It became independent in 1971.
In 1972 Sheikh Ahmad was overthrown by the crown prince and prime minister, Sheikh Khalifa. Sheikh Khalifa was overthrown in 1995 by his son and heir, Sheikh Hamad, who has since introduced liberal reforms. Municipal elections, the first democratic polls since independence, were held in 1999. A referendum in 2003 approved a new constitution, which came into force in 2005. Elections to the partially elected consultative council established by the constitution have yet to take place. In June 2013 Sheikh Tamim bin Hamad al-Thani took over as emir after his father abdicated.
In June 2017, the state was isolated by other Arab nations, including Saudi Arabia, Egypt, Bahrain and the UAE, apparently over its links with Iran and Islamist groups such as the Muslim Brotherhood. An economic blockade was put in place, alongside a denial of airspace, severing of diplomatic ties and the expulsion of Qatari nationals from neighbouring countries at short notice. The blockade has remained in place as Qatar has pursued a legal resolution through the International Court of Justice; regional support has come from Iran and Turkey.
A new constitution came into force in 2005. The head of state is a hereditary absolute monarch, the emir. There is no legislature at present, although the 2005 constitution provides for an advisory legislative council with 45 members, 30 directly elected and 15 appointed by the emir. Elections were planned for 2007 but have been repeatedly extended. At present there is an advisory council with 35 members appointed by the emir. There are no political parties. Women have been permitted to vote and stand for election since 1999.

HEAD OF STATE
HH Emir of Qatar, Defence, Sheikh Tamim bin Hamad al-Thani, assumed power 25 June 2013
Crown Prince, HE Sheikh Abdullah bin Hamad al-Thani

SELECTED GOVERNMENT MEMBERS AS AT NOVEMBER 2020
Prime Minister, Interior, HE Sheikh Khalid bin Khalifa bin Abdulaziz al-Thani
Deputy Prime Ministers, Khalid bin Mohammed al-Attiyah (Defence); HE Sheikh Mohamed bin Abdulrahman al-Thani (Foreign Affairs)
Finance, Ali bin Sherif al-Emadi

EMBASSY OF THE STATE OF QATAR
1 South Audley Street, London W1K 1NB
T 020-7493 2200 E amb@qatarembassy.org.uk
W www.qatarembassy.info

Ambassador Extraordinary and Plenipotentiary, HE Yousef Ali al-Khater, *apptd* 2014

BRITISH EMBASSY
West Bay, PO Box 3, Off Wahda Street near Rainbow Roundabout, Doha
T (+974) 4496 2000 **E** embassy.qatar@fco.gov.uk
W www.gov.uk/government/world/qatar
Ambassador Extraordinary and Plenipotentiary, HE Ajay Sharma, CMG, *apptd* 2015

ECONOMY AND TRADE
The economy is based largely on the production of oil and gas, which made Qatar the world's highest per-capita income country in 2018. The state-owned Qatar General Petroleum Corporation controls the industry, and is responsible for oil production onshore and offshore. There has been substantial foreign investment in exploitation of Qatar's gas fields, and the country is now the second-largest exporter of natural gas, which now accounts for two-thirds of its GDP. Trade restrictions imposed in 2017 by neighbouring countries, low oil prices and construction costs (particularly for the FIFA World Cup in 2022) have resulted in efforts to curtail its budget deficit. The economy has achieved small but steady growth since 2015, but is expected to contract by 4.5 per cent in 2020.

Other industries, which are actively sought for economic diversification, include oil refining, production of ammonia, fertilisers, petrochemicals, steel and cement, and ship repairing. Industry contributes 50.3 per cent of GDP and services 49.5 per cent.

The main export markets are Japan, South Korea and India; the chief sources of imports are China, the USA, and EU states. Principal exports are liquefied natural gas, petroleum products, fertilisers and steel. The main imports are machinery and transport equipment, food and chemicals.
GNI – US$179.6m; US$63,410 per capita (2019)
Annual average growth of GDP – 1.6 per cent (2017 est)
Inflation rate – 0.4 per cent (2017 est)
Unemployment – 8.9 per cent (2017 est)
Total external debt – US$167.8bn (2017 est)
Imports – US$62,192m (2017)
Exports – US$85,204m (2017)

BALANCE OF PAYMENTS
Trade – US$23,011m surplus (2017)
Current Account – US$4,259m surplus (2019)

Trade with UK	2018	2019
Imports from UK	£2,307,098,358	£2,552,735,623
Exports to UK	£1,335,612,804	£2,187,810,005

COMMUNICATIONS
Airports and waterways – Doha is the principal airport and also the main seaport
Roadways – 7,039km
Telecommunications – 392,048 fixed lines and 3.3 million mobile subscriptions (2019); there were 2.35 million internet users in 2018
Internet code and IDD – qa; 974 (from UK), 44 (to UK)
Major broadcasters – The country hosts the government-owned Al-Jazeera (TV), which broadcasts internationally in English and Arabic; Qatar TV and Qatar Broadcasting Service (QBS) are also public broadcasters
Press – *Al-Watan, Al-Rayah* and *Al-Sharq* are leading daily newspapers
WPFI score – 42.51 (129)

ROMANIA

Area – 238,391 sq. km
Capital – Bucharest; population, 1,803,000 (2018 est)
Major cities – Brasov, Cluj-Napoca, Constanta, Craiova, Galati, Iasi, Timisoara
Currency – New leu (plural lei) of 100 bani
Population – 21,302,893 falling at 0.37 per cent a year (2020 est); Romanian (83.4 per cent), Hungarian (6.1 per cent), Romani (3.1 per cent). Romani populations are usually underestimated and may represent 5–11 per cent of the population (est)
Religion – Christian (Orthodox 81.9 per cent, Protestant 6.4 per cent, Roman Catholic 4.3 per cent) (est)
Language – Romanian (official), Hungarian, Romani
Population density – 85 per sq. km (2019)
Urban population – 54.1 per cent (2019 est)
Median age (years) – 42.5 (2020 est)
National anthem – 'Desteapta-te, Romane' 'Wake Up, Romanian'
National day – 1 December (Unification Day)
Death penalty – Abolished for all crimes (since 1989)
CPI score – 44 (70)
Military expenditure – US$4,609m (2018)

CLIMATE AND TERRAIN
The Carpathian mountain range runs south from the Ukrainian border into the centre of the country and then turns west (the Transylvanian Alps) and north. The mountains enclose the central Transylvanian plateau and divide it from the southern Wallachian plain, part of the basin of the river Danube, which runs along most of the southern border, and the eastern Moldavian plateau, through which the river Siret flows, and the Black Sea coast. The mountains are thickly forested. Elevation extremes range from 2,544m (Moldoveanu) to 0m (Black Sea). The climate is continental, with average temperatures ranging from −1.9°C in January to 20.9°C in July.

POLITICS
The 1991 constitution was amended in 2003 to bring it into line with EU requirements. The president is directly elected for a five-year term, renewable once. The bicameral parliament comprises the Chamber of Deputies with 329 seats, of which 17 are reserved for ethnic minorities, and the senate with 136 seats. Both houses are directly elected for a four-year term by proportional representation. The prime minister is appointed by the president.

In the 2012 legislative elections, the four-party Social Liberal Union won a significant majority in both chambers and the leader of the Social Democratic Party (PSD), Victor Ponta, was reappointed prime minister, but his government resigned in November 2015 following anti-corruption protests prompted by a nightclub fire in Bucharest in October

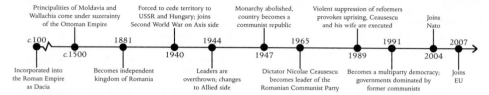

Principalities of Moldavia and Wallachia come under suzerainty of the Ottoman Empire	Forced to cede territory to USSR and Hungary; joins Second World War on Axis side	Monarchy abolished, country becomes a communist republic	Violent suppression of reformers provokes uprising, Ceausescu and his wife are executed	Joins Nato			

(Timeline)

c.100 — 1881 — 1944 — 1965 — 1991 — 2007
c.1500 — 1940 — 1947 — 1989 — 2004

Incorporated into the Roman Empire as Dacia | Becomes independent kingdom of Romania | Leaders are overthrown; changes to Allied side | Dictator Nicolae Ceausescu becomes leader of the Romanian Communist Party | Becomes a multiparty democracy; governments dominated by former communists | Joins EU

2015 that left 48 people dead. The Social Democrats clinched the December 2016 legislative elections with 46 per cent of the vote, and Sorin Grindeanu was appointed prime minister. In June 2017, Grindeanu lost a vote of no confidence and was initially replaced by Mihai Tudose, who was succeeded by Vasilica-Viorica Dancila in January 2018 as the first woman premier. Dancila was ousted by a vote of no confidence in October 2019 and replaced by a minority government led by Ludovic Orban, the leader of the centre-right National Liberal Party (PNL) and the fifth head of government since January 2017. The 2014 presidential election was won by PNL candidate Klaus Iohannis; he was re-elected in November 2019 in the second round of voting.

HEAD OF STATE

President of the Republic, Klaus Iohannis, *elected* 16 November 2014, *sworn in* 21 December 2014, *re-elected* 24 November 2019

SELECTED GOVERNMENT MEMBERS *AS AT NOVEMBER 2020*
Prime Minister, Ludovic Orban
Deputy Prime Minister, Raluca Turcan
Finance, Vasile-Florin Citu
Foreign Affairs, Bogdan Lucian Aurescu

EMBASSY OF ROMANIA
Arundel House, 4 Palace Green, London W8 4QD
T 020-7937 9666 **E** londra@mae.ro **W** www.londra.mae.ro
Ambassador Extraordinary and Plenipotentiary, HE Sorin-Dan Mihalache, *apptd* 2016

BRITISH EMBASSY
24 Strada Jules Michelet, 010463 Bucharest
T (+40) (21) 201 7200 **E** Press.Bucharest@fco.gov.uk
W www.gov.uk/government/world/romania
Ambassador Extraordinary and Plenipotentiary, HE Andrew Noble, LVO, *apptd* 2018

ECONOMY AND TRADE
Transition to a market economy made sluggish progress until 2000, accelerating after 2004 in order to meet the requirements for EU accession. Although the economy grew steadily from 2000 to 2008, it was from a low base and poverty is still widespread. The economy contracted sharply in 2009 owing to the global downturn, and the government sought IMF and EU funding. The economy returned to positive growth in 2011 and performed strongly between 2013 and 2019, driven by industrial exports, healthy agricultural harvests and rising domestic demand. The impact of the coronavirus pandemic is expected to contract the economy by 4.8 per cent in 2020. Corruption, an aging population and considerable tax evasion are long-term issues.

Agriculture remains inefficient, employing 28.3 per cent of the workforce but contributing only 4.2 per cent of GDP. The principal crops are grains, sugar beet, sunflower seeds, vegetables and livestock products. Vines and fruit are grown, and extensive forests support an important timber industry. There are reserves of natural gas and oil, but Romania is a net importer of fossil fuels, although it exports electricity. Mineral deposits, including coal, iron ore, bauxite, chromium and uranium support a mining industry. Other industries include manufacturing, electrical and light machinery and car assembly, metallurgy, food processing and textiles.

The main trading partners are EU states (especially Italy and Germany) and China. Principal exports include machinery and equipment, textiles, footwear, metals and metal products, minerals and fuels, chemicals and agricultural products. The main imports are machines and equipment, fuels, minerals, chemicals, base metals and agricultural products.
GNI – US$244.5bn; US$12,630 per capita (2019)
Annual average growth of GDP – 4.2 per cent (2019 est)
Inflation rate – 1.3 per cent (2017 est)
Population below poverty line – 22.4 per cent (2012 est)
Unemployment – 3.06 per cent (2019 est)
Total external debt – US$95.97bn (2017 est)
Imports – US$92,285m (2017)
Exports – US$87,823m (2017)

BALANCE OF PAYMENTS
Trade – US$4,462m deficit (2017)
Current Account – US$11,707m deficit (2019)

Trade with UK	2018	2019
Imports from UK	£1,305,665,516	£1,279,975,589
Exports to UK	£2,410,600,723	£2,037,671,595

COMMUNICATIONS
Airports and waterways – The main airports are at Bucharest and Timisoara; the main ports are Braila, Constanta, Galati and Tulcea, with 1,599km of navigable waterways on the river Danube and its tributaries and 132km of canals
Roadways and railways – 84,185km; 11,268km
Telecommunications – 3.7 million fixed lines and 25 million mobile subscriptions (2019); there were 15.2 million internet users in 2018
Internet code and IDD – ro; 40 (from UK), 44 (to UK)
Major broadcasters – The state-owned Televiziunea (TVR) and Radio Romania are the country's principal broadcasters
Press – There are several daily newspapers, including *Adevarul, Libertatea* and *Evenimentul Zilei*
WPFI score – 25.91 (48)

EDUCATION AND HEALTH
Primary and secondary education is free and compulsory for ten years.
Literacy rate – 98.8 per cent (2018 est)
Gross enrolment ratio (percentage of relevant age group) – primary 87.3 per cent, secondary 89.1 per cent, tertiary 51 per cent (2018 est)
Health expenditure (per capita) – US$555 (2017)
Hospital beds (per 1,000 people) – 6.3 (2013)
Life expectancy (years) – 76 (2020 est)
Mortality rate – 12 (2020 est)
Birth rate – 8.5 (2020 est)
Infant mortality rate – 8.7 (2020 est)
HIV/AIDS adult prevalence – 0.1 per cent (2019 est)

RUSSIA

Rossiyskaya Federatsiya – Russian Federation

Area – 17,098,242 sq. km. Includes the Kaliningrad exclave, between Lithuania and Poland. Neighbours: Norway, Finland, Estonia, Latvia, Belarus, Ukraine (west), Georgia, Azerbaijan, Kazakhstan, China, Mongolia, North Korea (south)

Capital – Moscow; population, 12,538,000 (2020 est). Founded in around 1147, it became the centre of the rising Moscow principality and in the 15th century the capital of the whole of Russia (Muscovy). In 1703 Peter the Great transferred the capital to St Petersburg, but Moscow became the capital again in 1918

Major cities – Chelyabinsk, Kazan, Nizhny Novgorod (Gorky 1932–90), Novosibirsk (Novonikolayevsk until 1926), Omsk, Perm, Rostov, St Petersburg (Petrograd 1914–24; Leningrad 1924–91), Samara (Kuibyshev 1935–90), Ufa, Vladivostok, Volgograd (Stalingrad 1925–61), Yekaterinburg (Sverdlovsk 1924–91)

Currency – Rouble of 100 kopeks

Population – 141,722,205 falling at 0.16 per cent a year (2020 est); there are nearly 200 recognised ethnic groups, of which Russian (77.7 per cent) is the largest. Tatar (3.7 per cent), Ukrainian (1.4 per cent), Bashkir (1.1 per cent) and Chuvash (1.1 per cent) also have sizeable populations

Religion – Russian Orthodox 15–20 per cent, Muslim 10–15 per cent (est)

Language – Russian (official); many minority languages

Population density – 9 per sq. km (2019)

Urban population – 74.6 per cent (2019 est)

Median age (years) – 40.3 (2020 est)

National anthem – 'Gosudarstvenny Gimn Rossiyskoy Federatsii' 'State Anthem of the Russian Federation'

National day – 12 June (Russia Day)

Death penalty – Retained (last used 1999)

CPI score – 28 (137)

Military expenditure – US$61,388m (2018)

Conscription – 18–27 years of age; 12 months

CLIMATE AND TERRAIN

Russia includes the easternmost areas of Europe and the whole of northern Asia. It lies mostly on plains that extend eastwards to the Ural mountains and then from the Urals to the Yenesei river. To the east of the Yenesei are plateaux, with lowlands in northern Siberia. Mountainous areas lie along the southern borders, in eastern Siberia and the Kamchatka peninsula. The terrain varies from the tundra of the Arctic region, through the taiga (the largest zone) of the north and centre, to the grassy plains (steppe) between the forests and the mountains. Elevation extremes range from 5,633m (Mt Elbrus, Caucasus)

to −28m (Caspian Sea). Russia has the longest Arctic coastline in the world (over 27,000km); it also has Baltic, Black Sea and Pacific coastlines.

The most important rivers are the Volga, the Northern Dvina, the Neva, the Don and the Kuban in the European part, and in the Asiatic part the Ob, the Irtysh, the Yenisei, the Lena, the Amur and, further north, the Khatanga, Olenek, Yana, Indigirka and Kolyma. Lake Baikal in eastern Siberia is the deepest lake in the world. Part of the Caspian Sea lies within Russia.

The climate is mostly continental, but varies with latitude and terrain, from arctic conditions in the north to subtropical in the far east and on the Black Sea coast. Average national temperatures range from −25.2°C in January to 14.9°C in July. Rainfall is low to moderate in most of the country.

POLITICS

The 1993 constitution introduced multiparty democracy and enshrines various human rights and civil liberties; amendments in 2008 extended the terms of office for the presidency and the State *Duma* from the 2012 elections. The head of state is a president, who is directly elected for a six-year term, renewable once consecutively. The bicameral Federal Assembly comprises the State *Duma* (lower house) of 450 members, all elected by proportional representation for a five-year term, and the Council of the Federation, which has 170 members (two from each member of the federation and two from Ukraine's autonomous Republic of Crimea, which Russia annexed in 2014), appointed for four-year terms. The president appoints the chair of the council of ministers (prime minister), subject to the approval of the legislature, but is also entitled to chair sessions of the council.

In the September 2016 legislative elections, the pro-Vladimir Putin United Russia party retained its majority in the *Duma* winning 76.7 per cent of the vote. Putin (president between 2000 and 2008) was elected president once more in March 2012 and re-elected in 2018, picking up 76.7 per cent of the overall vote amid allegations of ballot stuffing. He was inaugurated as president in May 2012 and duly appointed former president Dmitry Medvedev as Chair of the Council of Ministers. Opposition figures are regularly arrested and targeted by authorities; in August 2020, leading opposition figure Alexei Nalvany was hospitalised with Novichok poisoning, resulting in further sanctions from the EU and UK.

HEAD OF STATE

President, Vladimir Putin, *elected* 4 March 2012, *took office* 7 May 2012, *re-elected* 18 March 2018

SELECTED GOVERNMENT MEMBERS *AS AT NOVEMBER 2020*

Chair of the Council of Ministers, Mikhail Mishustin

First Deputy Prime Minister, Finance, Andrei Belousov

Deputy Prime Ministers, Dmitry Grogorenko; Viktoria Abramchanko; Yury Borisov; Konstantin Chuichenko; Tatyana Golikova; Alexei Overchuk; Yury Trutnev; Marat Khusnullin

Foreign Affairs, Sergei Lavrov

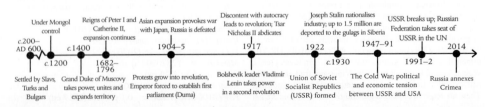

Under Mongol control
c.200–AD 600

c.1200
Settled by Slavs, Turks and Bulgars

c.1400
Grand Duke of Muscovy takes power, unites and expands territory

Reigns of Peter I and Catherine II, expansion continues
1682–1796
Protests grow into revolution, Emperor forced to establish first parliament (Duma)

Asian expansion provokes war with Japan, Russia is defeated
1904–5

Discontent with autocracy leads to revolution; Tsar Nicholas II abdicates
1917
Bolshevik leader Vladimir Lenin takes power in a second revolution

Union of Soviet Socialist Republics (USSR) formed
1922

Joseph Stalin nationalises industry; up to 1.5 million are deported to the gulags in Siberia
c.1930

1947–91
The Cold War; political and economic tension between USSR and USA

USSR breaks up; Russian Federation takes seat of USSR in the UN
1991–2

Russia annexes Crimea
2014

EMBASSY OF THE RUSSIAN FEDERATION
13 Kensington Palace Gardens, London W8 4QX
T 020-7229 3620 **E** info@rusemb.org.uk **W** www.rusemb.org.uk
Ambassador Extraordinary and Plenipotentiary, HE Andrei Kelin,
apptd 2019

BRITISH EMBASSY
Smolenskaya Naberezhnaya 10, 121099 Moscow
T (+7) (495) 956 7200 **E** enquiriesukinrussia@fco.gov.uk
W www.gov.uk/government/world/russia
Ambassador Extraordinary and Plenipotentiary, HE Deborah
Bronnert, CMG, apptd 2020

INSURGENCIES
Chechnya occupies an area that is strategically important to
Russia because routes from central Russia to the Black Sea and
Caspian Sea, and oil and gas pipelines from neighbouring
countries, pass through it. The republic declared itself
independent in 1991 but its attempts to assert its
independence led to two wars with the federal government.
The first of these, in 1994–6, resulted in the signing of the
Khasavyurt accords. After the peace broke down and Russia
invaded Chechnya again in 1999, President Putin refused
negotiations and imposed direct rule from Moscow in 2000.
Rebels continued with terrorist attacks, although these have
decreased since 2007. Russia announced the end of counter-
terrorism operations in Chechnya in 2009, but has had to
reinstate these in some areas where rebels remain active.
The conflict in Chechnya has destabilised the whole of the
northern Caucasus, especially Ingushetia and Dagestan, where
violence has increased in recent years. The violence has also
affected other parts of Russia, where extremists linked to
Chechen separatists have carried out suicide bombings and
attacks such as the Moscow theatre siege in 2002, the Beslan
school siege in 2004 and the bombing of Moscow's metro
system in 2010. A suicide bomb attack on St Petersburg's
underground in April 2017 killed 14 people; a group affiliated
to al-Qaida later claimed responsibility.

FEDERAL STRUCTURE
Following the break-up of the USSR in 1991, a new federal
treaty was signed in 1992 between the central government
and the autonomous republics of the Russian Federation.
Tatarstan and Bashkortostan signed the treaty in 1994 after
securing considerable legislative and economic autonomy.
The Russian Federation comprises 46 *oblasti* (regions), nine
krai (autonomous territories), 21 *respubliki* (autonomous
republics), four *okrugi* (autonomous areas), two cities with
federal status (Moscow and St Petersburg) and one
autonomous Jewish *oblast,* Yevrey. The *oblasti* are Amur,
Arkhangelsk, Astrakhan, Belgorod, Bryansk, Chelyabinsk,
Irkutsk, Ivanovo, Kaliningrad, Kaluga, Kemerovo, Kirov,
Kostroma, Kurgan, Kursk, Leningrad, Lipetsk, Magadan,
Moscow, Murmansk, Nizhny Novgorod, Novgorod,
Novosibirsk, Omsk, Orel, Orenburg, Penza, Pskov, Rostov,
Ryazan, Sakhalin, Samara, Saratov, Smolensk, Sverdlovsk,
Tambov, Tomsk, Tula, Tver, Tyumen, Ulyanovsk, Vladimir,
Volgograd, Vologda, Voronezh and Yaroslavl. The *krai* are
Altai, Kamchatka, Khabarovsk, Krasnodar, Krasnoyarsk,
Perm, Primorski, Stavropol and Zabaykalsk. The *respubliki* are
Adygeia, Altai, Bashkortostan, Buryatia, Chechnya,
Chuvashia, Dagestan, Ingushetia, Kabardino-Balkaria,
Kalmykiya, Karachayevo-Cherkessia, Karelia, Khakassia,
Komi, Mari-El, Mordovia, North Ossetia, Sakha, Tatarstan,
Tuva and Udmurtia. The *okrugi* are Chukotka, Khanty-Mansi,
Nenets and Yamalo-Nenets. In April 2014, Russia recognised
Crimea as a *respublika* and Sevastopol as a federal city,
following the annexation of the territory from Ukraine. The
USA and EU do not recognise the region as part of Russia.

ECONOMY AND TRADE
Under the Soviet regime, an essentially agrarian economy in
1917 was transformed by the early 1960s into the second-
greatest industrial power in the world. However, by the early
1970s the concentration of resources on the military-
industrial complex had caused stagnation in the civilian
economy. Economic reforms were introduced by President
Gorbachev, including the legalisation of small private
businesses, the reduction of state control over the economy,
and denationalisation and privatisation. Mass privatisation of
state industries began in 1992, and 80 per cent of the
economy had been privatised by 1996. The largest and most
economically significant industries, oil and gas, were partially
renationalised from 2004.
The transition to a market economy caused severe economic
crises in 1993 and 1998, but from 1999 to 2008 the
economy sustained growth averaging 7 per cent a year.
Political and economic uncertainties, corruption, excessive red
tape and a lack of trust in institutions continue to inhibit
growth however. Other problems include the economy's
vulnerability to fluctuations in global prices of key
commodities, a dilapidated infrastructure and international
sanctions. Some of these factors exacerbated the impact on
Russia of the global financial crisis in autumn 2008, when a
sharp fall in oil prices coincided with turmoil in the banking
system and a 70 per cent drop in the stock market. Credit
problems, a severe drop in production and rising
unemployment caused a sharp contraction in the economy
until late 2009, before high oil prices boosted economic
growth in 2011–12. Russia joined the World Trade
Organization in 2012, providing greater access to foreign
markets. Russia's involvement in the Ukraine crisis caused a
number of nations to impose economic sanctions, including
the US, the EU and Japan. Subsequent sanctions since 2014
have primarily targeted the energy, financial and military
sectors of the economy and contributed to a deep recession
between 2014 and 2017, caused by capital flight, falling oil
prices and the collapse of the rouble. Real growth returned in
2017–19, but the coronavirus pandemic pushed the economy
back into recession.
Russia has some of the world's richest natural resources,
especially mineral deposits and timber. Growth in the
economy is reliant on the exploitation and export of its oil and
natural gas reserves. Russia is the world's third-largest oil
producer (recently surpassed by the USA and Saudi Arabia)
and leading exporter of hydrocarbons, and a leading supplier
to European countries and China, a position that has led the
country into disputes with some of its neighbours; Ukraine,
Georgia, Lithuania, Czechia, Armenia, Azerbaijan, Poland and
Belarus have all had gas or oil supplies cut for short periods
during price negotiations.
Mining (coal, iron ore, aluminium and other non-ferrous
metals) and oil and natural gas extraction are concentrated in
the region south of Moscow, the Volga valley, the northern
Caucasus, the Urals, Siberia, and the far east and north. Russia
is also keen to exploit the shrinking of the Arctic ice cap to
prospect for previously inaccessible deposits under the Arctic
Sea. The main industries are extracting and processing oil, gas
and minerals, forestry, all forms of machine building
(including transport, communications, agricultural,
construction, and power generating and transmitting
equipment), defence industries, shipbuilding, medical and
scientific instruments, consumer durables, textiles and food
processing.
The vast area and the great variety in climatic conditions are
reflected in the structure of agriculture. In the far north, only
reindeer breeding, hunting and fishing are possible; further
south, forestry is combined with grain growing. In the
southern half of the forest zone and in the adjacent forest-

steppe zone, the acreage under grain crops is larger and agriculture more complex. The southern part of the Western Siberian plain is an important grain-growing and stock-breeding area. In the extreme south, cotton is cultivated. Vine, tobacco and other southern crops are grown on the Black Sea shore of the Caucasus.

The service sector is the largest, accounting for 62.3 per cent of GDP and employing 63 per cent of the workforce; industry contributes 32.4 per cent of GDP and employs 27.6 per cent of the workforce; and agriculture accounts for 4.7 per cent of GDP and 9.4 per cent of employment.

Russia's main trading partners are China, EU countries (especially Germany) and the USA. Principal exports are oil and petroleum products, natural gas, metals, timber and wood products, chemicals, manufactured goods, military vehicles and defence equipment. The main imports are machinery, vehicles, pharmaceuticals, plastics, semi-finished metal products, meat, fruits and nuts, optical and medical equipment, iron and steel.

GNI – US$1,651.6bn; US$11,260 per capita (2019)
Annual average growth of GDP – 1.34 per cent (2019 est)
Inflation rate – 3.7 per cent (2017 est)
Population below poverty line – 13.3 per cent (2015)
Unemployment – 4.6 per cent (2019 est)
Total external debt – US$539.6bn (2017 est)
Imports – US$326,772m (2017)
Exports – US$411,375m (2017)

BALANCE OF PAYMENTS
Trade – US$84,603m surplus (2017)
Current Account – US$65,337m surplus (2019)

Trade with UK	2018	2019
Imports from UK	£2,483,421,324	£2,643,340,766
Exports to UK	£7,180,227,554	£11,169,479,739

COMMUNICATIONS
Airports – There are 594 airports; the principal international airports are at Moscow, St Petersburg and Novosibirsk
Waterways – Major ports include Kaliningrad on the Baltic Sea and Novorossiysk on the Black Sea. Two of the three northern ports, St Petersburg and Arkhangelsk, are icebound during winter; only Murmansk is accessible. There is a large merchant fleet of 1,143 ships of 1,000 tonnes and over, with a further 439 ships registered in other countries. There are 102,000km of waterways, supplemented by a 72,000km system of canals, which provides a through route between the White Sea and Baltic Sea in the north and the Black Sea, Caspian Sea and the Sea of Azov in the south
Roadways – 927,721km of paved roads
Railways – The railways are state-run, with 87,157km of the network used for passenger transport plus 30,000km by industry
Telecommunications – 31.2 million fixed lines and 233.3 million mobile subscriptions (2019); there were 114.9 million internet users in 2018
Internet code and IDD – ru; 7 (from UK), 810 44 (to UK)
Major broadcasters – Broadcasting is dominated by the Russian State Television and Radio Broadcasting Company (VGTRK) and stations part-owned by the government or whose owners have close ties to it
Press – There are over 400 major newspapers printed every week, including *Komsomolskaya Pravda, Moskovsky Komsomolets* and *Izvestia*
WPFI score – 48.92 (149)

EDUCATION AND HEALTH
There are 11 years of compulsory education: nine at basic school level and a further two at senior secondary level.
Literacy rate – 99.7 per cent (2018 est)
Gross enrolment ratio (percentage of relevant age group) – primary 104.7 per cent, secondary 103.8 per cent, tertiary 84.6 per cent (2018 est)
Health expenditure (per capita) – US$586 (2017)
Hospital beds (per 1,000 people) – 8.2 (2013)
Life expectancy (years) – 71.9 (2020 est)
Mortality rate – 13.4 (2020 est)
Birth rate – 10 (2020 est)
Infant mortality rate – 6.5 (2020 est)
HIV/AIDS adult prevalence – 1 per cent (2009 est)

RWANDA

Republika y'u Rwanda/République du Rwanda – Republic of Rwanda

Area – 26,338 sq. km
Capital – Kigali; population, 1,132,000 (2020 est)
Major towns – Butare, Gisenyi, Gitarama, Ruhengeri
Currency – Rwanda franc of 100 centimes
Population – 12,712,431 rising at 2 per cent a year (2020 est); Hutu, Tutsi, Twa
Religion – Christian (Protestant 49.5 per cent, Roman Catholic 43.7 per cent), Muslim 2 per cent (est)
Language – Kinyarwanda, French, English, Swahili (all official)
Population density – 499 per sq. km (2019)
Urban population – 17.3 per cent (2019 est)
Median age (years) – 19.7 (2020 est)
National anthem – 'Rwanda Nziza' 'Rwanda, Our Beautiful Country'
National day – 1 July (Independence Day)
Death penalty – Abolished for all crimes (since 2007)
CPI score – 53 (51)
Military expenditure – US$119m (2018)
Literacy rate – 73.2 per cent (2018 est)
Gross enrolment ratio (percentage of relevant age group) – primary 131.3 per cent, secondary 44.3 per cent, tertiary 6.2 per cent (2019 est)
Health expenditure (per capita) – US$49 (2017)
Hospital beds (per 1,000 people) – 1.6 (2007)
Life expectancy (years) – 65.1 (2020 est)
Mortality rate – 6.1 (2020 est)
Birth rate – 27.9 (2020 est)
Infant mortality rate – 28 (2020 est)
HIV/AIDS adult prevalence – 2.6 per cent (2020 est)

CLIMATE AND TERRAIN

Landlocked Rwanda's terrain is mostly savannah uplands and mountains, including the volcanic Virunga range in the northwest. Elevation extremes range from 4,519m (Volcan Karisimbi) to 950m (Rusizi River). Rwanda's western border runs through Lake Kivu. The climate is temperate, with a wet season from October to May. The average temperature in Rwanda is 19.4°C.

POLITICS

The Rwandan Patriotic Front (FPR) won the 2003 legislative elections and has retained power since, aided by a number of small independent coalition partners. The coalition won roughly three-quarters of votes in the September 2018 legislative elections. FPR leader Paul Kagame became president in 2000; he was elected president under a new constitution in 2003, and re-elected in 2010 and 2017. Edouard Ngirente became prime minister in August 2017, replacing Anastase Murekezi, who held the position for three years.

Under the 2003 constitution, amended multiple times, the president is directly elected for a five-year term, renewable once. In December 2016 a constitutional amendment reduced this term from seven to five years but included an exception that allowed Kagame to serve another seven-year term in 2017. The bicameral parliament consists of the Chamber of Deputies (the lower house) and the senate. The Chamber of Deputies has 80 members, of whom 53 are directly elected, 24 are women members elected by the provinces, two represent youth organisations and one represents organisations of disabled people; all serve a five-year term. The senate has 26 members indirectly elected for an eight-year term. Political parties are barred from organising on an ethnic, regional or religious basis.

In 2006 the 12 provinces were replaced by five provinces: North, East, South, West and Kigali, with the aim of creating more ethnically diverse administrative areas.

HEAD OF STATE

President, Maj.-Gen. Paul Kagame, *apptd* 17 April 2000, *sworn in* 22 April 2000, *elected* 25 August 2003, *re-elected* 2010, 2017

SELECTED GOVERNMENT MEMBERS *AS AT NOVEMBER 2020*

Prime Minister, Edouard Ngirente
Defence, Maj.-Gen. Albert Murasira
Finance and Economic Planning, Uzziel Ndagijmana
Foreign Affairs, Vincent Biruta

HIGH COMMISSION OF THE REPUBLIC OF RWANDA

120–122 Seymour Place, London W1H 1NR
T 020-7224 9832 **E** uk@rwandahc.org **W** www.rwandahc.org
High Commissioner, HE Yamina Karitanyi, *apptd* 2016

BRITISH HIGH COMMISSION

Parcelle No. 1131, Blvd de l'Umuganda, Kacyira-Sud, BP 576 Kigali
T (+250) 252 556 000 **E** BHC.Kigali@fco.gov.uk
W www.gov.uk/government/world/rwanda
High Commissioner, HE Joanne Lomas, *apptd* 2018

ECONOMY AND TRADE

Rwanda is the most densely populated country in Africa, with few natural resources and minimal industry. Nearly 40 per cent of the population lives below the poverty line, although this is declining, and economic growth, especially in food production, struggles to keep up with population growth. It is dependent on international aid but the demands of its high foreign debt have been reduced by debt relief. Regional instability, inadequate transport links with other countries and energy shortages hamper development, although electricity supply is expected to become more reliable when methane from Lake Kivu starts to be tapped. Rwanda has actively sought foreign investment and diversification, and infrastructure spending and good harvests have helped the economy grow significantly 2017–19.

The economic base of the country has significantly improved since the genocide in 1994, which alienated private and external investment and impoverished the population, and has experienced annual average growth of 6–8 per cent since 2003 with inflation reduced to single digits. Nonetheless, around 63 per cent of export earnings are derived from agricultural products.

Around 75.3 per cent of the population is engaged in agriculture, which is mainly at subsistence level and contributes 30.9 per cent of GDP. The main industries are mining, processing agricultural products and small-scale manufacturing, cement and tourism.

The main trading partners are China, Uganda and the UAE. The main exports are coffee, tea, hides and tin ore. The principal imports are foodstuffs, machinery and equipment, steel, petroleum products and construction materials.

GNI – US$10.4bn; US$820 per capita (2018)
Annual average growth of GDP – 6.1 per cent (2017 est)
Inflation rate – 4.8 per cent (2017 est)
Population below poverty line – 39.1 per cent (2015 est)
Total external debt – US$3.258bn (2017 est)
Imports – US$2,949m (2017)
Exports – US$2,048m (2017)

BALANCE OF PAYMENTS

Trade – US$901m deficit (2017)
Current Account – US$114,900m surplus (2018)

Trade with UK	2018	2019
Imports from UK	£13,132,447	£13,777,929
Exports to UK	£6,110,739	£6,609,238

COMMUNICATIONS

Airports and waterways – The principal airport is at Kigali; Lake Kivu is navigable by shallow boats and provides access to the Democratic Republic of the Congo
Roadways – There are 1,207km of paved roads that link with those of neighbouring countries to provide access to Kenyan and Tanzanian ports
Telecommunications – 11,215 fixed lines and 9.5 million mobile subscriptions (2019); there were 2.7 million internet users in 2018
Internet code and IDD – rw; 250 (from UK), 44 (to UK)

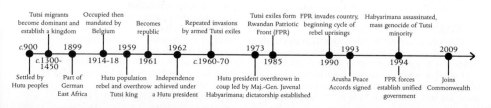

Tutsi migrants become dominant and establish a kingdom	Occupied then mandated by Belgium	Becomes republic	Repeated invasions by armed Tutsi exiles	Tutsi exiles form Rwandan Patriotic Front (FPR)	FPR invades country, beginning cycle of rebel uprisings	Habyarimana assassinated, mass genocide of Tutsi minority	
c.900	1899	1959	1962	1973	1993		2009
c.1300-1450	1914-18	1961	c.1960-70	1985	1990	1994	
Settled by Hutu peoples	Part of German East Africa	Hutu population rebel and overthrow Tutsi king	Independence achieved under a Hutu president	Hutu president overthrown in coup led by Maj.-Gen. Juvenal Habyarimana; dictatorship established	Arusha Peace Accords signed	FPR forces establish unified government	Joins Commonwealth

Major broadcasters – The state-owned Rwanda Broadcasting Agency operates Rwanda TV and Radio Rwanda, which broadcasts in English, French, Kinyarwanda and Swahili
Press – Leading newspapers include *The New Times* and *Rwanda Herald*
WPFI score – 50.34 (155)

ST KITTS AND NEVIS

Federation of St Christopher and Nevis (Federation of St Kitts and Nevis)

Area – 261 sq. km
Capital – Basseterre; population, 14,000 (2018)
Major town – Charlestown, the chief town of Nevis
Currency – East Caribbean dollar (EC$) of 100 cents
Population – 53,821 rising at 0.67 per cent a year (2020 est)
Religion – Christian (Protestant 74.4 per cent, Roman Catholic 6.7 per cent), Rastafarian 1.7 per cent, other 7.6 per cent (est)
Language – English (official)
Population density – 202 per sq. km (2019)
Urban population – 30.8 per cent (2019 est)
Median age (years) – 36.5 (2020 est)
National anthem – 'Oh Land of Beauty!'
National day – 19 September (Independence Day)
Death penalty – Retained
Gross enrolment ratio (percentage of relevant age group) – primary 108.7 per cent, secondary 106.9 per cent (2016 est); tertiary 79.6 per cent (2015 est)
Health expenditure (per capita) – US$903 (2017)
Life expectancy (years) – 76.6 (2020 est)
Mortality rate – 7.3 (2020 est)
Birth rate – 12.6 (2020 est)
Infant mortality rate – 7.8 (2020 est)

CLIMATE AND TERRAIN

The volcanic islands of St Kitts (St Christopher) (168 sq. km) and Nevis (93 sq. km) are part of the Leeward group in the eastern Caribbean Sea. The centre of St Kitts is forest-clad and mountainous, with the Great Salt Pond occupying the tip of its southern peninsula; elevation extremes range from 1,156m (Mt Liamuiga) to 0m (Caribbean Sea). Nevis, separated from the southern tip of St Kitts by a strait 3km wide, is dominated by Nevis Peak (985m). The climate is tropical, moderated by north-east trade winds, and a wet season occurs from May to September. The islands are in the hurricane belt.

HISTORY AND POLITICS

The islands were inhabited by Carib, or Kalinago, people when discovered in 1493 by Christopher Columbus, who gave St Christopher its name. Colonisation by the British began in 1623–4, when St Kitts became the first British colony in the West Indies, and French settlement began shortly after. The island was held jointly from 1628 to 1713, although there

were skirmishes between the British and French settlers in the 17th century; France dropped its claims after 1783. Nevis was settled by the British from 1628. The two islands were part of the Leeward Islands colony from 1871 to 1956, and then of the West Indies Federation from 1958 to 1962. They achieved internal self-government in 1967 and became independent in September 1983.

The Labour Party, which had been in power since 1995, lost the 2015 National Assembly election to the Team Unity coalition, which won seven of the 11 elected seats. The coalition's majority was extended to nine seats in the June 2020 election. Timothy Harris of the People's Labour Party was appointed prime minister.

Under the 1983 constitution, the head of state is Queen Elizabeth II, represented by a governor-general appointed on the advice of the prime minister. The unicameral National Assembly has 15 members: 11 directly elected for a five-year term, a speaker, and three appointed by the governor-general on the advice of the prime minister and the leader of the opposition. The prime minister, who is responsible to the legislature, and the cabinet are appointed by the governor-general.

Nevis is responsible for its own internal affairs. It has an eight-member Nevis Island assembly and is governed by the Nevis Island administration, headed by the premier.

Governor-General, HE Sir Samuel Seaton, GCMG, CVO, *apptd* 2015

SELECTED GOVERNMENT MEMBERS *AS AT NOVEMBER 2020*
Prime Minister, Finance, Timothy Harris
Deputy Prime Minister, Shawn Richards
Foreign Affairs, Mark Brantley

HIGH COMMISSION FOR ST KITTS AND NEVIS
10 Kensington Court, London W8 5DL
T 020-7937 9718 **E** info@sknhc.co.uk **W** www.stkittsnevisuk.com/
High Commissioner, HE Kevin Isaac, *apptd* 2011

BRITISH HIGH COMMISSIONER
HE Janet Douglas, CMG, *apptd* 2017, resident at Bridgetown, Barbados

ECONOMY AND TRADE

The sugar industry was the mainstay of the economy for over 300 years but was closed down in 2005 after decades of operating at a loss. Tourism (the chief source of foreign exchange revenue), offshore financial services and manufacturing, especially distilling, food processing, clothing and electronics are being developed. Services now account for 68.9 per cent of GDP, industry for 30 per cent and agriculture for 1.1 per cent. The economy of Nevis relies on farming, but a sea-island cotton industry is being developed for export. The economy was restricted by one of the world's highest public debt burdens, but after peaking at 154 per cent of GDP in 2011 debt has steadily fallen, and stood at 62.9 per cent of GDP in 2017. The global downturn impacted negatively on tourism and the economy contracted between 2009 and 2013, and in 2020 owing to the coronavirus pandemic. The country remains vulnerable to costly damage from natural disasters and shifts in demand from tourism.

The main trading partners are the USA, Poland and Trinidad and Turkey. Principal exports are machinery, food, electronics, beverages and tobacco. The main imports are machinery, manufactured goods, food and fuels.

GNI – US$1bn; US$19,030 per capita (2019)
Annual average growth of GDP – 2.1 per cent (2017 est)
Inflation rate – 0.0 per cent (2017 est)
Total external debt – US$201.8m (2017 est)

Imports – US$540m (2016)
Exports – US$518m (2016)

BALANCE OF PAYMENTS
Trade – US$22m deficit (2016)
Current Account – US$73m deficit (2018)

Trade with UK	2018	2019
Imports from UK	£5,325,308	£8,039,830
Exports to UK	£759,309	£257,138

COMMUNICATIONS
Airports – There are two airports; the one on St Kitts can take most large jet aircraft
Waterways – Basseterre is a port of registry and has deep-water harbour facilities; there are regular ferries between Basseterre and Charlestown
Roadways and railways – The islands have 383km of roadways, and 50km of narrow-gauge railways on St Kitts
Telecommunications – 17,766 fixed lines and 78,970 mobile subscriptions (2019); there were 42,852 internet users in 2018
Internet code and IDD – kn; 1 869 (from UK), 011 44 (to UK)
Media – The government-owned broadcaster ZIZ operates national television and radio networks; *The Sun* is the sole daily newspaper
WPFI Score – 23.78 (44)

ST LUCIA

Area – 616 sq. km
Capital – Castries; population, 22,000 (2018)
Major town – Soufrière
Currency – East Caribbean dollar (EC$) of 100 cents
Population – 166,487 rising at 0.29 per cent a year (2020 est)
Religion – Christian (Roman Catholic 61.5 per cent, Protestant 25.5 per cent, other Christian 3.4 per cent), Rastafarian 1.9 per cent (est)
Language – English (official), French patois
Population density – 298 per sq. km (2019)
Urban population – 18.8 per cent (2019 est)
Median age (years) – 36.9 (2020 est)
National anthem – 'Sons and Daughters of Saint Lucia'
National day – 22 February (Independence Day)
Death penalty – Retained
CPI score – 55 (48)
Gross enrolment ratio (percentage of relevant age group) – primary 102.3 per cent, secondary 89.9 per cent, tertiary 15.4 per cent (2019 est)
Health expenditure (per capita) – US$460 (2017)
Life expectancy (years) – 78.5 (2020 est)

Mortality rate – 8.1 (2020 est)
Birth rate – 12.5 (2020 est)
Infant mortality rate – 10.1 (2020 est)

CLIMATE AND TERRAIN
St Lucia is the second-largest island in the Windward group. The interior is mountainous and densely forested, with elevation extremes ranging from 950m (Mt Gimie) to 0m (Caribbean Sea). The area around the volcanic peaks of Gros Piton and Petit Piton is a UNESCO World Heritage Site. The climate is tropical, moderated by trade winds and with a wet season from July to November. The island is in the hurricane belt.

HISTORY AND POLITICS
The original Arawak settlers were superseded by Caribs by AD 800. The island was sighted by Columbus in 1502 and European settlement began in the 1550s. Control was disputed between France and Britain from the mid-17th century until 1814, when the island was ceded to Britain. It achieved internal self-government in 1967 and became independent in 1979.

The United Workers' Party (UWP) won the 2016 legislative election, defeating the incumbent St Lucia Labour Party, winning 11 assembly seats to the latter's six. Allen Chastanet of the UWP was sworn in as prime minister in June.

Under the 1979 constitution, the head of state is Queen Elizabeth II, represented by a governor-general appointed on the advice of the prime minister. The bicameral parliament consists of the house of assembly and the senate. The senate has 11 members, six nominated by the government, three by the opposition and two by the governor-general. The House of Assembly has 17 elected members and an appointed speaker who serve a five-year term. The prime minister, who is responsible to the legislature, and the cabinet are appointed by the governor-general.
Governor-General, HE Sir Neville Cenac, GCMG, *apptd* 2018

SELECTED GOVERNMENT MEMBERS *AS AT NOVEMBER 2020*
Prime Minister, External Affairs, Finance, Allen Chastanet
Agriculture, Fisheries, Ezechiel Joseph
Home Affairs, Hermangild Francis

HIGH COMMISSION FOR ST LUCIA
1 Collingham Gardens, London SW5 0HW
T 020-7370 7123 **E** enquiries@stluciahcuk.org
W www.stluciahcuk.org
High Commissioner, HE Guy Mayers, *apptd* 2016

BRITISH HIGH COMMISSIONER
HE Janet Douglas, CMG, *apptd* 2017, resident at
   Bridgetown, Barbados

ECONOMY AND TRADE
The economy was dependent on bananas, but has diversified since preferential access to EU markets ended in 1999. Tourism is the main source of jobs, foreign exchange earnings and GDP, but has struggled since airlines cut services in 2012, and growth has since been minimal. Offshore financial services have also been developed, and the manufacturing sector is the most diverse in the eastern Caribbean, processing agricultural products, assembling electronic components and producing clothing, beverages and corrugated cardboard boxes. Services account for 82.8 per cent of GDP, industry for 14.2 per cent and agriculture for 2.9 per cent.

The main trading partners are the USA (67.6 per cent of exports and 53.3 per cent of imports), the UK, and Trinidad

and Tobago. Principal exports are bananas, clothing, cocoa, fruit and coconut oil. The main imports are food, manufactured goods, machinery and transport equipment, chemicals and fuels.
GNI – US$2bn; US$11,020 per capita (2019)
Annual average growth of GDP – 3.0 per cent (2017 est)
Inflation rate – 0.1 per cent (2017 est)
Total external debt – US$570.6m (2017 est)
Imports – US$895m (2016)
Exports – US$935m (2016)

BALANCE OF PAYMENTS
Trade – US$39m surplus (2016)
Current Account – US$102m surplus (2018)

Trade with UK	2018	2019
Imports from UK	£19,104,624	£19,681,127
Exports to UK	£5,442,485	£5,388,130

COMMUNICATIONS
Airports and waterways – There are two airports in Castries and Vieux Fort; Castries also has a deep-water harbour
Roadways – 1,210km
Telecommunications – 33,285 fixed lines and 168,797 mobile subscriptions (2019); there were 84,112 internet users in 2018
Internet code and IDD – lc; 1-758 (from UK), 011 44 (to UK)
Media – Television stations are privately owned and Radio Saint Lucia (RSL) is the state broadcaster; there are several newspapers but none daily
WPFI Score – 23.78 (44)

ST VINCENT AND THE GRENADINES

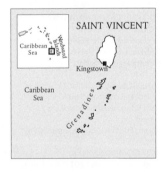

Area – 389 sq. km
Capital – Kingstown; population, 27,000 (2018)
Currency – East Caribbean dollar (EC$) of 100 cents
Population – 101,390 falling at 0.22 per cent a year (2020 est)
Religion – Christian (Protestant 75 per cent, Roman Catholic 6.3 per cent, Evangelical 3.8 per cent), Rastafarian 1.1 per cent, other 4.7 per cent (est)
Language – English (official), French patois
Population density – 283 per sq. km (2019)
Urban population – 52.6 per cent (2019 est)
Median age (years) – 35. (2020)
National anthem – 'St Vincent! Land So Beautiful'
National day – 27 October (Independence Day)
Death penalty – Retained
CPI score – 54 (39)

Gross enrolment ratio (percentage of relevant age group) – primary 113.4 per cent, secondary 107.2 per cent (2018 est); tertiary 23.7 per cent (2015 est)
Health expenditure (per capita) – US$321 (2017)
Life expectancy (years) – 75.8 (2020 est)
Mortality rate – 7.4 (2020 est)
Birth rate – 13 (2020 est)
Infant mortality rate – 11.7 (2020 est)

CLIMATE AND TERRAIN
The state, which lies in the Windward group, consists of St Vincent and the 32 small islands and cays of the northern Grenadines, a chain stretching 64km across the eastern Caribbean Sea between St Vincent and Grenada. St Vincent itself is a mountainous and densely forested volcanic island. The Grenadines, of which the largest are Bequia, Canouan, Mayreau, Mustique and Union Island, are low-lying coral islands. Elevation extremes range from 1,234m (La Soufrière volcano, St Vincent) to 0m (Caribbean Sea). The climate is tropical, with a rainy season from May to November. The islands lie in the hurricane belt.

HISTORY AND POLITICS
Settled successively by the Ciboney people, the Arawaks and the Caribs, St Vincent was sighted by Christopher Columbus in 1498. Although granted by Charles I to the Earl of Carlisle in 1627, control was disputed between the British and the French until the islands were ceded to Britain in 1783. Internal self-government was granted in 1969, and independence as St Vincent and the Grenadines was achieved in 1979.

The Unity Labour Party, under the leadership of Ralph Gonsalves, has governed since 2001. In the November 2020 elections it won nine seats. A referendum in 2009 rejected a draft constitution that proposed to replace the monarchy with a republic.

Under the 1979 constitution, the head of state is Queen Elizabeth II, represented by a governor-general appointed on the advice of the prime minister. The unicameral House of Assembly has 23 members: 15 directly elected for a five-year term, six senators appointed by the governor-general and two *ex officio* members in the speaker and attorney general. The prime minister, who is responsible to the legislature, and the cabinet are appointed by the governor-general.
Governor-General, Susan Dougan, GCMG, OBE, *apptd* 2019

SELECTED GOVERNMENT MEMBERS *AS AT NOVEMBER 2020*
Prime Minister, National Security, Ralph Gonsalves
Deputy Prime Minister, Foreign Affairs, Sir Louis Straker, KCMG
Attorney-General, Jaundy Martin

HIGH COMMISSION FOR ST VINCENT AND THE GRENADINES
10 Kensington Court, London W8 5DL
T 020-7565 2874 **E** info@svghighcom.co.uk
W www.svghighcom.co.uk
High Commissioner, HE Cenio E. Lewis, *apptd* 2001

BRITISH HIGH COMMISSIONER
HE Janet Douglas, CMG, *apptd* 2017, resident at Bridgetown, Barbados

ECONOMY AND TRADE
Tourism, the development of which has been hampered by drug-related crime, has been increasing and was boosted by the opening of an international airport in 2017. Manufacturing and offshore banking services have all expanded, and while the economy contracted in 2009 it gradually recovered despite a high public debt burden.

Services account for 75.5 per cent of GDP, industry for 17.4 per cent and agriculture for 7.1 per cent. Floods and mudslides caused by heavy rainfall in 2013 resulted in US$112m (£71.2m) worth of damage.

The main export markets are Jordan, France and neighbouring island nations. Imports come mostly from the USA, Trinidad and Tobago, and the UK. Principal exports are bananas, vegetables, starch and tennis racquets. The main imports are foodstuffs, machinery and equipment, chemicals, fertilisers, minerals and fuel.

GNI – US$0.8bn; US$7,460 per capita (2019)
Annual average growth of GDP – 0.7 per cent (2017 est)
Inflation rate – 2.2 per cent (2017 est)
Total external debt – US$362.2m (2017 est)
Imports – US$413m (2016)
Exports – US$282m (2016)

BALANCE OF PAYMENTS
Trade – US$131m deficit (2016)
Current Account – US$99m deficit (2018)

Trade with UK	2018	2019
Imports from UK	£13,065,109	£14,043,827
Exports to UK	£863,037	£703,177

COMMUNICATIONS
Airports and waterways – There are five airports; one, Argyle, close to the capital Kingstown, can handle international flights and was completed in February 2017
Roadways – 580km are surfaced
Telecommunications – 11,889 fixed lines and 94,367 mobile subscriptions (2019); there were 22,803 internet users in 2018
Internet code and IDD – vc; 1 784 (from UK), 011 44 (to UK)
Media – Television broadcasting is operated by the St Vincent and the Grenadines Broadcasting Corporation, and NBC Radio is partly government funded; there is one daily newspaper, *The Herald*

SAMOA

Malo Sa'oloto Tuto'atasi o Samoa – Independent State of Samoa

Area – 2,831 sq. km
Capital – Apia, on Upolu; population, 36,000 (2018)
Major town – Fagamalo, on Savai'i
Currency – Tala (S$) of 100 sene
Population – 203,774 rising at 0.61 per cent a year (2020 est)
Religion – Christian (Protestant 54.9 per cent, Roman Catholic 18.8 per cent, Mormon 16.9 per cent, Worship Centre 2.8 per cent, other Christian 3.6 per cent), other 2.9 per cent (including Baha'i and Muslim) (est)

Language – Samoan, English (both official)
Population density – 69 per sq. km (2019)
Urban population – 18.1 per cent (2019 est)
Median age (years) – 25.6 (2020 est)
National anthem – 'O le Fu'a o le Sa'olotoga o Samoa' 'The Banner of Freedom'
National day – 1 June (Independence Day celebration; independence was achieved on 1 January 1962)
Death penalty – Abolished for all crimes (since 2004)
Literacy rate – 99.1 per cent (2018 est)
Gross enrolment ratio (percentage of relevant age group) – primary 115.1 per cent (2019 est); secondary 93.2 per cent (2016 est); tertiary 14.6 per cent (2018 est)
Health expenditure (per capita) – US$233 (2017)
Life expectancy (years) – 74.7 (2020 est)
Mortality rate – 5.4 (2020 est)
Birth rate – 19.6 (2020 est)
Infant mortality rate – 17 (2020 est)

CLIMATE AND TERRAIN
Samoa consists of the islands of Savai'i, Upolu, Apolima, Manono, Fanuatapu, Namua, Nu'utele, Nu'ulua and Nu'usafe'e in the south Pacific Ocean. All the islands are volcanic in origin, with narrow coastal plains and mountainous, densely forested interiors. Elevation extremes range from 1,857m (Mauga Silisili, Savai'i) to 0m (Pacific Ocean). The climate is tropical, with a wet season from November to April; the average temperature is 27.6°C. The islands are vulnerable to cyclones and tsunamis.

HISTORY AND POLITICS
Inhabited since *c*.1000 BC, Samoa was visited by European traders, explorers and missionaries from the 18th century. Germany, the UK and the USA disputed control of the islands until 1899, when the nine western islands (Western Samoa) became a German colony and the eastern islands American Samoa. Western Samoa was occupied by New Zealand on the outbreak of the First World War and became a mandated territory administered by New Zealand from 1920. Internal self-government was granted in 1959, and Western Samoa became independent on 1 June 1962. The state was treated as a member country of the Commonwealth until its formal admission in 1970. In 1997 the state dropped 'Western' from its name.

Former prime minister Tuiatua Tupua Tamasese Efi was elected head of state in June 2007 and re-elected unopposed in July 2012. He was replaced by independent Tuimaleali'ifano Va'aletoa Sualauvi II in July 2017 after deciding to step down. The Human Rights Protection Party, which has been in power since 1981, remained by far the largest party in the legislature after the March 2016 election, which it won with a landslide.

Under the 1962 constitution, the head of state is elected and has functions analogous to those of a constitutional monarch. Initially an office held for life, but is now elected by the legislature for a five-year term, renewable once. The unicameral legislative assembly *(Fono)* has 50 members elected for a five-year term, with at least five women representatives; only members of the *Matai* (elected clan leaders) may stand for election except for two seats reserved for citizens without affiliation to a traditional village. The prime minister is appointed by the head of state on the recommendation of the legislature and appoints the cabinet.

HEAD OF STATE
Head of State, Tuimaleali'ifano Va'aletoa Sualauvi II, *elected* 7 July 2017

SELECTED GOVERNMENT MEMBERS *AS AT NOVEMBER 2020*
Prime Minister, Foreign Affairs, Tuilaepa Sailele Malielegaoi
Finance, Sili Epa Tuioti

EMBASSY OF SAMOA
20 avenue de l'Oree, 1000 Brussels, Belgium
T (+32) (2) 660 8454 **E** samoanembassy@skynet.be
W www.samoaembassybelgium.com
High Commissioner, HE Dr Fatumanava Pa'olelei Luteru, *apptd* 2012

BRITISH HIGH COMMISSION
Cross Island Road, Apia, Samoa
T (+64) 04 924 24888
W www.gov.uk/world/organisations/british-high-commission-apia
High Commissioner, HE David Ward, *apptd* 2019

ECONOMY AND TRADE

The economy is underdeveloped (until 2014, considered the least developed in the world) but has grown steadily in the past decade, diversifying away from its traditional dependence on fishing, agriculture, remittances from migrant workers and international aid. Economic strengths include a flexible labour market, stable external debt and low inflation. Agriculture and fishing generate 10.4 per cent of GDP, employing almost two-thirds of the labour force and supplying about 90 per cent of exports. Manufacturing is branching out from small-scale processing of agricultural products into light manufacturing (particularly of motor vehicle components) and building materials, and offshore financial services are being developed. Tourism has grown rapidly and accounts for about 25 per cent of GDP. Public finances were weakened by a tsunami in 2009 and a tropical cyclone in 2012, both of which caused severe damage; the conoravirus pandemic restricted tourism and growth in 2020.

The main trading partners are American Samoa, New Zealand, the USA, Australia and China. Principal exports are fish, coconut oil and cream, copra, taro, vehicle parts, garments and beer. The main imports are machinery and equipment, industrial supplies and foodstuffs.

GNI – US$0.8bn; US$4,180 per capita (2019)
Annual average growth of GDP – 2.5 per cent (2017 est)
Inflation rate – 1.3 per cent (2017 est)
Total external debt – US$447.2m (2013 est)
Imports – US$413m (2017)
Exports – US$285m (2017)

BALANCE OF PAYMENTS
Trade – US$127m deficit (2017)
Current Account – US$20m surplus (2018)

Trade with UK	2018	2019
Imports from UK	£179,284	£717,195
Exports to UK	£433,647	£7,295,284

COMMUNICATIONS

Airports and waterways – There is one international airport on Upolu; the southern island also contains the harbours of Apia and Mulifanua, and Salelologa, the harbour of Savai'i
Roadways – 1,150km
Telecommunications – 8,770 fixed lines and 128,776 mobile subscriptions (2019); there were 67,662 internet users in 2018
Internet code and IDD – ws; 685 (from UK), 044 (to UK)
Media – The Samoa Broadcasting Corporation (TV) and National Radio 2AP are the state broadcasters; the *Samoa Observer* and *Samoa Times* are the only daily newspapers
WPFI score – 18.25 (21)

SAN MARINO

Repubblica di San Marino – Republic of San Marino

Area – 61 sq. km
Capital – San Marino; population, 4,000 (2018 est)
Currency – Euro (€) of 100 cents
Population – 34,232 rising at 0.65 per cent a year (2020 est)
Religion – Christian (predominantly Roman Catholic)
Language – Italian
Population density – 563 per sq. km (2019)
Urban population – 97.4 per cent (2019 est)
Median age (years) – 45.2 (2020 est)
National anthem – 'Inno Nazionale della Repubblica' 'National Anthem of the Republic'
National day – 3 September (Republic Day)
Death penalty – Abolished for all crimes (since 1865)
Literacy rate – 99.9 per cent (2018 est)
Gross enrolment ratio (percentage of relevant age group) – primary 104.4 per cent, secondary 68 per cent, tertiary 51.2 per cent (2019 est)
Health expenditure (per capita) – US$3,362 (2017)
Life expectancy (years) – 83.5 (2020 est)
Mortality rate – 9 (2020 est)
Birth rate – 8.8 (2020 est)
Infant mortality rate – 4.2 (2020 est)

CLIMATE AND TERRAIN

A landlocked enclave in central Italy, the republic lies in the foothills of the Apennines, 20km from the Adriatic Sea. Elevation extremes range from 755m (Mt Titano) to 55m (Torrente Ausa). The climate is Mediterranean, with an average annual rainfall of 836mm.

HISTORY AND POLITICS

The republic is said to have been founded in the fourth century by a Christian stonecutter seeking refuge from religious persecution. By the 12th century a self-governing commune was established, and a parliamentary constitution was adopted in 1600. The republic resisted papal claims and those of neighbouring dukedoms from the 15th to 18th centuries, and the papacy recognised its independence in 1631. In 1862 it signed a treaty with the newly united kingdom of Italy, which recognised its integrity and sovereignty and accorded it the protection of Italy. San Marino became a member of the UN in 1992. A 2013 poll supported moves to join the EU, but the number of voters did not exceed the minimum 32 per cent of the electorate needed to enact the measure.

The Sammarinese Christian Democratic Party won the most seats in the December 2019 legislative election, and formed a coalition with two other parties.

The 1600 constitution has been amended several times, operating alongside the Declaration of Citizen Rights, which was passed in 1974. The joint heads of state are two captains-regent who are elected at six-monthly intervals (March and September) by the legislature, taking office the month after the election. Executive power is vested in the captains-regent and the Congress of State (cabinet), which is also elected by the legislature. The unicameral legislature, the Great and General Council, has 60 members, who are directly elected for a five-year term.

HEADS OF STATE
Captains-Regent, Alessandro Cardelli; Mirko Dolcini

SELECTED GOVERNMENT MEMBERS *AS AT NOVEMBER 2020*
Finance, Marco Gatti
Foreign Affairs, Luca Beccari
Internal Affairs, Matteo Zeppa

EMBASSY OF THE REPUBLIC OF SAN MARINO
c/o Department of Foreign Affairs, Palazzo Begni – Contrado Ormerelli, 47890 San Marino
T 378 (0549) 88 2422 **E** dipartimentoaffariesteri@pa.sm
Ambassador Extraordinary and Plenipotentiary, HE Silvia Marchetti, *apptd* 2018

BRITISH AMBASSADOR
HE Jill Morris, CMG, *apptd* 2016, resident at Rome, Italy

ECONOMY AND TRADE
Tourism and banking are the basis of the economy, and the service sector contributes 60.7 per cent of GDP. In 2009, investment outflows following Italy's tax amnesty, a money-laundering scandal at its largest bank and the global downturn contributed to a deep recession that it never fully recovered from prior to the 2020 coronavirus pandemic. The government is working to improve standards of financial transparency.

The principal agricultural products are grains, grapes, olives, livestock and hides. The main industries, apart from tourism and banking, are winemaking, clothing, cement, electronics and ceramics. Sales of postage stamps and coins also generate significant revenue. San Marino is in a customs union with the EU but is not a full member.
GNI – US$1,572m; US$51,470 per capita (2008)
Annual average growth of GDP – 1.9 per cent (2017 est)
Inflation rate – 1 per cent (2017 est)
Unemployment – 8.1 per cent (2017 est)

Trade with UK	2018	2019
Imports from UK	£8,025,362	£5,415,789
Exports to UK	£4,188,696	£4,477,513

COMMUNICATIONS
Roadways – 292km
Telecommunications – 16,070 fixed lines and 38,921 mobile subscriptions (2019); there were 20,328 internet users in 2018
Internet code and IDD – sm; 378 (from UK), 44 (to UK)
Media – Broadcasting services are state-run; daily newspapers include *La Tribuna Sammarinese*

SAO TOME AND PRINCIPE
Republica Democratica de Sao Tome e Principe – Democratic Republic of Sao Tome and Principe

Area – 964 sq. km
Capital – Sao Tome; population, 80,000 (2018)
Major Town – Santo Antonio, on Principe
Currency – Dobra of 100 centimos
Population – 211,122 rising at 1.58 per cent a year (2020 est)
Religion – Christian (Roman Catholic 55.7 per cent, Adventist 4.1 per cent, Assembly of God 3.4 per cent, New Apostolic 2.9 per cent) (est)
Language – Portuguese (official), Creole dialects, French, English
Population density – 220 per sq. km (2019)
Urban population – 73.6 per cent (2019 est)
Median age (years) – 19.3 (2020 est)
National anthem – 'Independencia total' 'Total Independence'
National day – 12 July (Independence Day)
Death penalty – Abolished for all crimes (since 1990)
CPI score – 46 (64)
Conscription – 18 years of age
Literacy rate – 92.8 per cent (2018 est)
Gross enrolment ratio (percentage of relevant age group) – primary 106.8 per cent, secondary 89.3 per cent (2017 est); tertiary 13.4 per cent (2015 est)
Health expenditure (per capita) – US$120 (2017)
Life expectancy (years) – 66.3 (2020 est)
Mortality rate – 6.3 (2020 est)
Birth rate – 29.7 (2020 est)
Infant mortality rate – 41.7 (2020 est)
HIV/AIDS adult prevalence – 0.79 per cent (2014 est)

CLIMATE AND TERRAIN
The republic consists of the islands of Sao Tome, Principe and several uninhabited islets off the west coast of Africa. The islands, which are volcanic in origin, are mountainous and thickly forested. Elevation extremes range from 2,024m (Pico de Sao Tome) to 0m (Atlantic Ocean). The climate is tropical, with a wet season from October to May. The average temperature is 24.1°C.

HISTORY AND POLITICS
The uninhabited islands were discovered by the Portuguese between 1469 and 1472, and settlement began in 1493. Agitation against Portuguese rule began in the late 1950s. The islands gained independence from Portugal in 1975 and became a one-party state under the rule of the Movement for the Liberation of Sao Tome and Principe (MLSTP). Close links with the communist bloc were scaled down in the 1980s as the economy deteriorated, and in 1990 the MLSTP abandoned Marxism and introduced political pluralism and

economic liberalisation. The first multiparty elections were held in 1991.

The Independent Democratic Action (ADI) party maintained a majority in the legislature at the 2018 elections and Jorge Bom Jesus of the Social Democratic Party was appointed prime minister in December. Evaristo Carvalho of the ADI was elected president in August 2016, defeating incumbent Manuel Pinto da Costa, who had been the country's first post-independence president. Da Costa pulled out of the second round of voting citing electoral fraud, so Carvalho was elected unopposed.

Under the 1990 constitution, the president is directly elected for a five-year term, renewable once. The unicameral National Assembly has 55 members, directly elected for a four-year term. The prime minister is appointed by the president and nominates the cabinet.

Since 1995 Principe has been internally self-governing, with an eight-member regional council.

HEAD OF STATE
President, C-in-C of the Armed Forces, Evaristo Carvalho, *elected* 7 August 2016, *sworn in* 3 September 2016

SELECTED GOVERNMENT MEMBERS *AS AT NOVEMBER 2020*
Prime Minister, Jorge Bom Jesus
Defence, Oscar Aguiar Sacramento e Sousa
Finance, Osvaldo Tavares dos Santos Vas
Foreign Affairs, Edite dos Ramos Ten Jua

EMBASSY OF SAO TOME AND PRINCIPE
175 avenue de Tervueren, 1150 Brussels, Belgium
T (+32) (2) 734 8966 E ambassade@saotomeprincipe.be
Ambassador Extraordinary and Plenipotentiary, vacant

BRITISH AMBASSADOR
HE Jessica Hand, *apptd* 2018, resident at Luanda, Angola

ECONOMY AND TRADE
The economy has benefited from cancellation of about 90 per cent of the country's external debt over the past decade. It is largely dependent on cocoa, which has declined in recent years due to mismanagement and drought, but tourism is being encouraged in an attempt to diversify. A major economic shift will begin with the start of oil production from offshore reserves in the Gulf of Guinea, which are being developed jointly with Nigeria, and Sao Tome and Principe will receive 40 per cent of the revenue. Most of the population is engaged in subsistence farming and fishing. Chinese investment is set to significantly increase following a mutual cooperation agreement signed in 2017, lasting over five years.

The principal export markets are Guyana (43.7 per cent) and Germany (23.6 per cent), and the main source of imports is Portugal (54.7 per cent). Principal exports are cocoa (68 per cent), copra, coffee and palm oil. The main imports are machinery and electrical equipment, foodstuffs and petroleum products.

GNI – US$0.4bn; US$1,96 per capita (2019)
Annual average growth of GDP – 3.9 per cent (2017 est)
Inflation rate – 5.7 per cent (2017 est)
Population below poverty line – 66.2 per cent (2009 est)
Unemployment – 12.2 per cent (2017 est)
Total external debt – US$292.9m (2017 est)
Imports – US$193m (2017)
Exports – US$92m (2017)

BALANCE OF PAYMENTS
Trade – US$101m deficit (2017)
Current Account – US$89m deficit (2019)

Trade with UK	2018	2019
Imports from UK	£314,553	£141,813
Exports to UK	£1,003	£7,004

COMMUNICATIONS
Airports and waterways – There are two airports; the ports are Santo Antonio, on Principe, and Sao Tome
Roadways – 230km of paved roads
Telecommunications – 4,614 fixed lines and 160,189 mobile subscriptions (2019); there were 61,193 internet users in 2018
Internet code and IDD – st; 239 (from UK), 44 (to UK)
Media – Televisao Saotomense and Radio Nacional de Sao Tome e Principe are the state broadcasters; *Téla Nón Diario de Sao Tome e Principe* is the only daily newspaper

SAUDI ARABIA
Al-Mamlakah al-Arabiyah as-Suudiyah – Kingdom of Saudi Arabia

Area – 2,149,690 sq. km
Capital – Riyadh; population, 7,231,000 (2020 est)
Major cities – At Taif, Dammam, Jeddah, Mecca, Medina, Tabuk
Currency – Saudi riyal (SR) of 100 halalas
Population – 34,173,498 rising at 1.6 per cent a year (2020 est); includes 37 per cent non-nationals (2017 est)
Religion – Muslim (official) (Sunni 85–90 per cent, predominantly Wahhabi; Shia 10–15 per cent) (est); public practice of other religions is restricted
Language – Arabic (official)
Population density – 16 per sq. km (2019)
Urban population – 84.1 per cent (2019 est)
Median age (years) – 30.8 (2020)
National anthem – 'As-Salaam al-Malaki' 'The Royal Salute'
National day – 23 September (Unification Day)
Death penalty – Retained
CPI score – 43 (51)
Military expenditure – US$67,555m (2018 est)

CLIMATE AND TERRAIN
Saudi Arabia comprises about 80 per cent of the Arabian peninsula. The Hejaz region (north-west) runs along the northern Red Sea coast to the Asir and contains the holy cities of Mecca and Medina. The mountainous Asir (south-west) and the coastal plain of the Tihama lie along the southern Red Sea coast from the Hejaz to the border with Yemen. The Nejd plateau extends over the centre, including the Nafud and Dahna deserts. The Hasa (east) is low-lying and largely desert. The Empty Quarter (south) is the world's largest sand desert. Elevation extremes range from 3,133m (Jabal Sawda) to 0m (Persian Gulf). There is a desert climate, with extremes of temperature in the interior; coastal areas are more temperate but extremely humid. Average temperatures range from 15.7°C in January to 32.9°C in August.

HISTORY AND POLITICS

The Arabian peninsula was the birthplace of the Muslim faith in the seventh century and the base from which the religion and four Islamic Caliphates, the Rashidun, Umayyad, Abbasid and Fatimid, emerged. When the Fatimid empire declined in the 12th century, Arabia became isolated and internally divided. The rise of the al-Saud family began in the 18th century, when it united the Nejd in support of the Wahhabi religious movement. The modern state was the culmination of a 30-year campaign by Abd-al Aziz al-Saud (often known as Ibn Saud) to unite the four tribal regions of the Hejaz, Asir, Najd and Hasa; the Kingdom of Saudi Arabia was proclaimed on 23 September 1932.

The ruling family preserved stability for many years by suppressing dissent and resisting calls for greater democracy. Since 2003 demand for political reform has grown and become more militant. In 2005, the country's first nationwide elections were held for half the seats on municipal councils, with voting by universal male suffrage. Women's rights have slowly advanced in recent years with municipal voting rights introduced (2011) and, in June 2018, the right to drive a vehicle.

Following the death of King Abdullah in January 2015, his half-brother, King Salman, acceded to the throne. In June 2017, his son Mohammed bin Salman was appointed crown prince and took a leading role in government. Although initially welcomed by western allies as a reformer, his alleged involvement in the assassination of dissident journalist Jamal Khashoggi in October 2018, and Saudi Arabia's continued human rights abuses, have alienated many of his international supporters.

There is no written constitution; constitutional practice is provided for by articles of government based on the Qur'an and the teachings and sayings of the Prophet Muhammad *(Sunnah)* and issued by royal decree.

Saudi Arabia is a hereditary monarchy. The king is head of government and appoints the council of ministers (established in 1953), whose term of office was fixed in 1993 at four years.

There is no legislature; the Consultative Council *(Majlis-al-Shura)* debates policy, proposes legislation in certain areas and makes recommendations to the king. The council's 150 members are appointed by the king and serve a four-year term. As of 2013, 30 seats are reserved for women. Its decisions are taken by majority vote, and there are no political parties.

Each of the 13 provinces has a governor appointed by the king and a council of prominent local citizens to advise the governor on local government, budgetary and planning issues.

HEAD OF STATE

The King of Saudi Arabia, Custodian of the Two Holy Mosques, Prime Minister, King Salman bin Abdul Aziz al-Saud, *born* 31 December 1935, *succeeded* 23 January 2015
Crown Prince, Deputy Prime Minister, Defence, Mohammad bin Salman bin Abdul Aziz al-Saud

SELECTED GOVERNMENT MEMBERS *AS AT NOVEMBER 2020*

Economy, Mohammed bin Abdullah bin Abdulaziz al-Jadaan
Foreign Affairs, Faisel bin Farnhan al-Saud
Interior, Abdul Aziz bin Saud bin Nayef bin Adbul Aziz al-Saud

ROYAL EMBASSY OF SAUDI ARABIA

30 Charles Street, London W1J 5DZ
T 020-7917 3000 E ukemb@mofa.gov.sa
W www.saudiembassy.org.uk
Ambassador Extraordinary and Plenipotentiary, HE Prince Khalid bin Bandar bin Sultan al-Saud, *apptd* 2019

BRITISH EMBASSY

PO Box 94351, Diplomatic Quarter, Riyadh 11693
T (+966) (0) 11 4819 100 E consular.riyadh@fco.gov.uk
W www.gov.uk/government/world/saudi-arabia
Ambassador Extraordinary and Plenipotentiary, HE Neil Crompton, *apptd* 2020

ECONOMY AND TRADE

The largest economy in the Middle East, Saudi Arabia's wealth is based on oil extraction and processing, although since 1970 the government has used five-year development plans to encourage diversification. Recent development plans aimed to increase natural gas production and to promote the growth of small- and medium-sized businesses, partly through further privatisation; it also partially opened the Saudi stock market to foreign investors. Nonetheless, oil still accounts for 42 per cent of GDP and a downturn in 2019, coupled with the sabotage of an oil refinery, resulted in just 0.3 per cent growth in 2020. In 2019, the government raised £19.4bn through the initial public offering of state-owned Saudi Aramco, reportedly the most profitable company in the world. The economy is set to contract by 5.4 per cent in 2020.

Oil extraction since the 1940s has brought great wealth. Saudi Arabia has the second-largest proven reserves of oil in the world (about 16 per cent of the world total) and the fifth-largest reserves of recoverable gas.

The main industries, apart from oil extraction and refining, include production of petrochemicals, ammonia, industrial gases, caustic soda, cement, fertiliser, plastics and metals, commercial ship and aircraft repair and construction. Industry accounts for 44.2 per cent of GDP and the service sector for 53.2 per cent. Agriculture contributes 2.6 per cent but is limited by the terrain, although productivity has been increased by extensive irrigation, desalination and the use of aquifers. The main products are grains, fruit, meat and dairy.

The main trading partners are China, the USA, Japan, India and South Korea. Oil and petroleum products constitute 90 per cent of exports. The principal imports are machinery and equipment, foodstuffs, chemicals, motor vehicles and textiles.
GNI – US$782.9bn; US$22,850 per capita (2019)
Annual average growth of GDP – –0.9 per cent (2017 est)
Inflation rate – –0.9 per cent (2017 est)
Unemployment – 6 per cent (2017 est)
Total external debt – US$205.1bn (2017 est)
Imports – US$200,218m (2017)
Exports – US$239,882m (2017)

BALANCE OF PAYMENTS

Trade – US$39,664m surplus (2017)
Current Account – US$38,229m surplus (2019)

Trade with UK	2018	2019
Imports from UK	£3,675,266,168	£3,263,193,443
Exports to UK	£2,562,057,467	£2,593,422,290

COMMUNICATIONS

Airports – There are 82 airports; the three international airports are at Riyadh, Jeddah (serving Mecca) and Dammam
Waterways – The main cargo ports are Jeddah on the Red Sea coast and Dammam on the Gulf coast; the main oil port (the world's largest) is Ras Tanura
Roadways and railways – The surfaced network totals 47,529km, including a 3,891km motorway system; 5,410km
Telecommunications – 5.2 million fixed lines and 40.5 million mobile subscriptions (2019); there were 30.9 million internet users in 2018
Internet code and IDD – sa; 966 (from UK), 44 (to UK)

Major broadcasters – Saudi TV and Saudi Radio are the state-run broadcasters
Press – Leading daily newspapers include *Al-Riyadh, Al-Watan* and the English-language *Arab News*
WPFI score – 62.14 (170)

EDUCATION AND HEALTH
With the exception of a few schools for expatriate children, all schools are segregated and supervised by the government.
Literacy rate – 95.3 per cent (2017 est)
Gross enrolment ratio (percentage of relevant age group) – primary 100.7 per cent, secondary 111.8 per cent, tertiary 70.9 per cent (2019 est)
Health expenditure (per capita) – US$1,093 (2017)
Hospital beds (per 1,000 people) – 2.7 (2014)
Life expectancy (years) – 76.2 (2020 est)
Mortality rate – 3.4 (2020 est)
Birth rate – 14.7 (2020 est)
Infant mortality rate – 11.3 (2020 est)

SENEGAL

République du Sénégal – Republic of Senegal

Area – 196,722 sq. km
Capital – Dakar; population, 3,140,000 (2020 est)
Major cities – Kaolack, Mbour, Saint-Louis, Thiès, Touba, Ziguinchor
Currency – Franc CFA of 100 centimes
Population – 15,736,368 rising at 2.31 per cent a year (2020 est); Wolof (37.1 per cent), Pular (26.2 per cent), Serer (17 per cent) (est)
Religion – Muslim 95.9 per cent, Christian 4.1 per cent (predominantly Roman Catholic) (est); most incorporate indigenous beliefs into their worship
Language – French (official), Wolof, Pular, Jola, Mandinka, Serer, Soninke
Population density – 82 per sq. km (2019)
Urban population – 47.7 per cent (2019 est)
Median age (years) – 19.4 (2020 est)
National anthem – 'Pincez Tous vos Koras, Frappez les Balafons' 'All Pluck Your Koras, Strike the Balafons'
National day – 4 April (Independence Day)
Death penalty – Abolished for all crimes (since 2004)
CPI score – 45 (66)
Military expenditure – US$347m (2018)
Conscription – 20 years of age; 24 months (selective)

CLIMATE AND TERRAIN
The terrain is generally low and rolling, with plains rising to hills in the south-east. There is desert in the north, savannah in the centre and tropical forest in the south. Elevation extremes range from 581m (near Nepen Diakha) to 0m (Atlantic Ocean). There are three rivers: the Senegal on the northern border, and the Gambia and the Casamance in the

south. The climate is tropical, with a wet season from June to September; the average temperature is 28.4°C.

HISTORY AND POLITICS
Senegal was part of the Mali Empire in the 14th to 15th centuries. The first European visitors were the Portuguese in 1445. The interior was colonised by the French in the mid-19th century and the territory became part of French West Africa in 1902. It became an autonomous state in 1958 and achieved independence as part of the Federation of Mali in June 1960, seceding to form the Republic of Senegal in August 1960. From 1966 to 1978, the country was a one-party state under the rule of the Senegalese Progressive Union (UPS), which changed its name to the Socialist Party (PS) in 1976.

In the early 1980s a separatist insurgency led by the Movement of Democratic Forces of Casamance (MFDC) began in the impoverished Casamance region south of the river Gambia. Splits and leadership changes among the separatists have prevented the implementation of peace agreements in 2001 and 2004, and clashes continue between government troops and rebels.

The Socialist Party's 40 years of political domination ended in 2000 with the election of Abdoulaye Wade, leader of the Senegalese Democratic Party (PDS), as president. President Wade lost the 2012 presidential election to the Alliance for the Republic–Yakaar (BBY) leader Macky Sall, who picked up 65 per cent of the overall vote in the second round. The liberal BBY claimed a large parliamentary majority in the 2017 elections. Neither the PDS nor PS fielded a candidate in the February 2019 presidential election due to corruption convictions for both parties' leading politicians, and Sall comfortably won a second term with over 58 per cent of the first-round vote.

The 2001 constitution was amended in 2007 to re-establish the senate as the upper chamber of a bicameral legislature, but this was abolished in 2012 by the National Assembly. The National Assembly has 165 members, directly elected for a five-year term; 105 are elected by majority in single member constituencies and 60 are elected by proportional representation. A referendum in 2016 cut presidential terms from seven to five years, renewable once, which will be introduced from 2019. The president is directly elected and appoints the prime minister, who nominates the other ministers.

HEAD OF STATE
President, C-in-C of the Armed Forces, Macky Sall, *elected* 18 March 2012, *sworn in* 2 April 2012, *re-elected* 24 February 2019

SELECTED GOVERNMENT MEMBERS *AS AT NOVEMBER 2020*
Prime Minister, Oumaar Ba
Finance, Abdoulaye Diallo
Foreign Affairs, Aissata Tall Sall
Interior, Antoine Diome

EMBASSY OF THE REPUBLIC OF SENEGAL
39 Marloes Road, London W8 6LA
T 020-7938 4048
Ambassador Extraordinary and Plenipotentiary, HE Fatimata Dia, *apptd* 2019

BRITISH EMBASSY
PO Box 6025, 20 rue du Docteur Guillet, Dakar
T (+221) 823 7392 E dakar.consularenquiries@fco.gov.uk
W www.gov.uk/government/world/senegal
Ambassador Extraordinary and Plenipotentiary, HE George Hodgson, *apptd* 2020

ECONOMY AND TRADE

Despite steady growth since the mid-1990s and the cancellation of two-thirds of its foreign debt in recent years, Senegal remains poor. The country is heavily dependent on foreign aid and remittances from expatriate workers, but infrastructure projects and the development of the textiles, information technology, oil and gas extraction, telecommunications services and tourism industries are government priorities. The government has announced a set of economic policies known as the Emerging Senegal Plan (ESP), which aims to turn Senegal into an emerging economy by 2035. Financial markets have shown increasing confidence in the economy in recent years, and 2017 was marked by the opening of a new international airport.

Agriculture and fishing are the mainstays of the economy, engaging around three-quarters of the workforce and contributing 16.9 per cent of GDP. The main industries are food and fish processing, mining (phosphate, iron, zircon, gold), oil refining, the production of fertiliser and construction materials, ship construction and tourism. Industry accounts for 24.3 per cent of GDP and services for 58.8 per cent.

The main trading partners are France, Mali, Nigeria, China and Switzerland. The principal exports are fish, peanuts, petroleum products, phosphates and cotton. Principal imports are food, beverages, capital goods and fuels.

GNI – US$23.6bn; US$1,450 per capita (2019)
Annual average growth of GDP – 7.2 per cent (2017 est)
Inflation rate – 1.3 per cent (2017 est)
Population below poverty line – 46.7 per cent (2011 est)
Total external debt – US$8.571bn (2017 est)
Imports – US$1,616m (2016)
Exports – US$4,118m (2016)

BALANCE OF PAYMENTS

Trade – US$2,042m deficit (2016)
Current Account – US$2,215m deficit (2018)

Trade with UK	2018	2019
Imports from UK	£168,506,883	£174,746,527
Exports to UK	£41,717,144	£44,403,683

COMMUNICATIONS

Airports and waterways – Dakar is the main port and the location of the principal airport (there are nine airports in total); seaport facilities are being modernised and there are 1,000km of navigable waterways, mainly on the Senegal, Saloum and Casamance rivers
Roadways and railways – 6,126km of paved roadways; 906km
Telecommunications – 195,288 fixed lines and 16.9 million mobile subscriptions (2019); there were 6.9 million internet users in 2018
Internet code and IDD – sn; 221 (from UK), 44 (to UK)
Major broadcasters – State-run Radiodiffusion Television Senegalaise operates the only free television channels and the main national and regional radio networks
Press – Leading daily newspapers include the French-language Le Quotidien, L'Observateur and Sud Quotidien
WPFI score – 23.99 (47)

EDUCATION AND HEALTH

Literacy rate – 6273.1 per cent (2017)
Gross enrolment ratio (percentage of relevant age group) – primary 82.1 per cent, secondary 46.2 per cent, tertiary 13.1 per cent (2019 est)
Health expenditure (per capita) – US$55 (2017)
Hospital beds (per 1,000 people) – 0.3 (2009)
Life expectancy (years) – 63.2 (2020 est)

Mortality rate – 7.6 (2020 est)
Birth rate – 31.8 (2020 est)
Infant mortality rate – 45.7 (2020 est)
HIV/AIDS adult prevalence – 0.4 per cent (2019 est)

SERBIA

Republika Srbija – Republic of Serbia

Area – 77,474 sq. km
Capital – Belgrade; population, 1,398,000 (2020 est)
Major cities – Kragujevac, Nis, Novi Sad
Currency – Serbian dinar of 100 paras
Population – 7,012,165 falling at 0.47 per year (2020 est); Serb (83.3 per cent), Hungarian (3.5 per cent), Romani (2.1 per cent), Bosniak (2 per cent) (est); Albanian and Romani populations are usually underestimated
Religion – Christian (Orthodox 84.6 per cent, Catholic 5 per cent, Protestant 1 per cent), Muslim 3.1 per cent (est)
Language – Serbian (official), Hungarian, Bosnian, Romani, Romanian, Croatian, Ruthenian (all official in Vojvodina)
Population density – 80 per sq. km (2019)
Urban population – 56.3 per cent (2019 est)
Median age (years) – 43.4 (2020 est)
National anthem – 'Boze Pravde' 'God of Justice'
National day – 15 February (Constitution Day)
Death penalty – Abolished for all crimes (since 2002)
CPI score – 39 (91)
Military expenditure – US$904m (2018 est)
Literacy rate – 98.8 per cent (2016 est)
Gross enrolment ratio (percentage of relevant age group) – primary 99.6 per cent, secondary 94.4 per cent, tertiary 67.8 per cent (2019 est)
Health expenditure (per capita) – US$529 (2017)
Hospital beds (per 1,000 people) – 5.7 (2012)
Life expectancy (years) – 76.3 (2020 est)
Mortality rate – 13.5 (2020 est)
Birth rate – 8.8 (2020 est)
Infant mortality rate – 5.6 (2020 est)

CLIMATE AND TERRAIN

The landlocked country is mountainous in the south, while the north is dominated by the low-lying plains of the Danube and its major tributaries, the Sava, the Tisa and the Morava. Its highest point is 2,169m (Midzor) and its lowest is 35m (the confluence of the Danube and Timok rivers). The climate is continental; average temperatures range from −0.5°C in January to 21.5°C in July and August.

POLITICS

Under the 2006 constitution, the president is directly elected for a five-year term, renewable once. The unicameral National Assembly has 250 members, directly elected for a four-year term. The prime minister is appointed by the president.

A coalition led by the Serbian Progressive Party (SNS) formed a government following the 2014 legislative election,

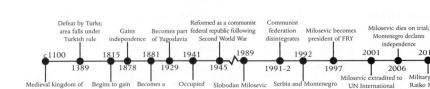

Defeat by Turks; area falls under Turkish rule c1100 — Medieval kingdom of Serbia emerges as large state in Balkans

1389

Begins to gain autonomy from Ottoman Empire 1878

Gains independence 1815

Becomes a kingdom 1881

Becomes part of Yugoslavia 1929

Occupied by Axis powers 1941

Reformed as a communist federal republic following Second World War 1945

Slobodan Milosevic becomes president 1989

Communist federation disintegrates 1991-2

Serbia and Montenegro form Federal Republic of Yugoslavia (FRY) 1992

Milosevic becomes president of FRY 1997 — Milosevic extradited to UN International Criminal Tribunal after violent 'ethnic cleansing'

Milosevic dies on trial; Montenegro declares independence 2001

2006 — Military leader Ratko Mladic arrested

Begins EU accession negotiations 2011

2014

and kept power in the 2016 election. The June 2020 elections were boycotted by the main opposition coalition, which alleged they were neither free nor fair, and the SNS retained its majority in an election with the lowest ever turnout. In April 2017, pro-EU Aleksandar Vucic won the presidential election in the first round, and he nominated Ana Brnabic as the country's first woman prime minister. Nonviolent protests calling for Vucic's resignation, greater media freedom and free elections began in December 2018 and continued until April 2019.

HEAD OF STATE
President, Aleksandar Vucic, *elected* 2 April 2017, *sworn in* 31 May 2017

SELECTED GOVERNMENT MEMBERS *AS AT NOVEMBER 2020*
Prime Minister, Ana Brnabic
First Deputy Prime Minister, Branko Ruzic
Finance, Sinisa Mali
Foreign Affairs, Nikola Selakovic

EMBASSY OF THE REPUBLIC OF SERBIA
28 Belgrave Square, London SW1X 8QB
T 020-7235 9049 **E** london@serbianembassy.org.uk
W www.serbianembassy.org.uk
Ambassador Extraordinary and Plenipotentiary, HE Aleksandra Joksimovic, *apptd* 2018

BRITISH EMBASSY
Resavska 46, 11000 Belgrade
T (+381) (11) 306 0900 **E** belgrade.PPD@fco.gov.uk
W www.gov.uk/government/world/serbia
Ambassador Extraordinary and Plenipotentiary, HE Sian MacLeod, OBE, *apptd* 2019

ECONOMY AND TRADE
Economic mismanagement, UN sanctions in the 1990s along with damage to infrastructure and industry from NATO bombing in 1999 reduced the economy by about 50 per cent between 1990 and 1999. Since 2000, governments have pursued economic reforms and international reintegration, obtained overseas support for economic restructuring, rescheduled payments and received debt relief on much of its foreign debt. Most of the economy is now privatised. Economic liberalisation policies continue to be a priority, but Serbia's GDP is still sizably smaller than it was three decades ago.

Economic growth averaged 6 per cent until 2008 when it was severely affected by the global economic downturn. The government sought external fiscal support in 2008 and signed a standby agreement with the IMF in 2012, which was frozen after the country's 2012 budget deviated from the programme framework. Serbia gained EU candidate status in March 2012 and began accession negotiations in January 2014. After GDP contracted in 2014, the government accepted a three-year €1.3bn (£795m) stand-by loan from the IMF in February 2015 after agreeing to implement a programme of spending cuts. Strong subsequent growth ended in 2020 due to the coronavirus pandemic; the economy is expected to contract by 2.5 per cent.

Agriculture accounts for 9.8 per cent of GDP and employs 19.4 per cent of the workforce. The main agricultural products are wheat, maize, sugar beet, sunflowers, fruit, vegetables, meat and milk. Industry includes food processing and production of base metals, vehicles, furniture, machinery, chemicals, sugar, tyres, clothing and pharmaceuticals. Industry contributes 41.1 per cent of GDP and services 49.1 per cent.

The main trading partners are the EU, Russia, and Bosnia and Hercegovina. Principal exports are vehicles, iron and steel, rubber, clothing, wheat, fruit, vegetables and non-ferrous metals.

GNI – US$48.8bn; US$7,020 per capita (2019)
Annual average growth of GDP – 4.18 per cent (2019 est)
Inflation rate – 3.1 per cent (2017 est)
Population below poverty line – 8.9 per cent (2014 est)
Unemployment – 14.4 per cent (2017 est)
Total external debt – US$29.5bn (2017 est)
Imports – US$25,873m (2017)
Exports – US$23,367m (2017)

BALANCE OF PAYMENTS
Trade – US$2,506m deficit (2017)
Current Account – US$3,535m deficit (2019)

Trade with UK	2018	2019
Imports from UK	£176,215,175	£159,625,761
Exports to UK	£233,956,683	£277,176,033

COMMUNICATIONS
Airports and waterways – The main international airport is at Belgrade (there are ten airports in total); there are 587km of navigable waterways, and principal ports include Belgrade and Novi Sad on the Danube
Roadways and railways – 28,000km; 3,809km
Telecommunications – 2.1 million fixed lines and 6.8 million mobile subscriptions (2019); there were 5.2 million internet users in 2018
Internet code and IDD – rs; 381 (from UK), 44 (to UK)
Major broadcasters – Radio-Television Serbia (RTS) is the state-operated broadcaster
Press – National daily newspapers include *Blic, Danas* and *Politika*
WPFI score – 31.62 (93)

SEYCHELLES

République des Seychelles/Repiblik Sesel – Republic of Seychelles

Area – 455 sq. km
Capital – Victoria, on Mahé; population, 28,000 (2018)
Major town – Anse Boileau, on Mahé
Currency – Seychelles rupee of 100 cents
Population – 95,981 rising at 0.69 per cent a year (2020 est);
   predominantly Creole, with French, Indian, Chinese and
   Arab populations
Religion – Christian (Roman Catholic 76.2 per cent,
   Protestant 10.5 per cent, other Christian 2.4 per cent),
   Hindu 2.4 per cent, Muslim 1.6 per cent (est)
Language – Seychellois Creole, English, French (all official)
Population density – 210 per sq. km (2019)
Urban population – 57.1 per cent (2019 est)
Median age (years) – 36.8 (2020 est)
National anthem – 'Koste Seselwa' 'Seychellois Unite'
National day – 18 June (Constitution Day)
Death penalty – Abolished for all crimes (since 1993)
CPI score – 66 (27)
Military expenditure – US$22.8m (2018)
Literacy rate – 95.9 per cent (2018 est)
Gross enrolment ratio (percentage of relevant age group) – primary
   100.4 per cent, secondary 78.6 per cent, tertiary 19.2 per
   cent (2019 est)
Health expenditure (per capita) – US$792 (2017)
Life expectancy (years) – 75.6 (2020 est)
Mortality rate – 7.1 (2020 est)
Birth rate – 12.8 (2020 est)
Infant mortality rate – 9.3 (2020 est)

CLIMATE AND TERRAIN

Seychelles consists of 115 islands spread over 643,737 sq. km
of the south-west Indian Ocean, north of Madagascar. There
is a relatively compact granitic group of 32 islands, with high
hills and mountains, of which Mahé is the largest and most
populated (about 90 per cent of the population lives on
Mahé), and an outlying coralline group, for the most part only
slightly above sea level. Elevation extremes range from 905m
(Morne Seychellois) to 0m (Indian Ocean). The climate is
tropical, with an average temperature of 27.3°C, and a wet
season from November to March.

HISTORY AND POLITICS

The uninhabited islands were proclaimed French territory in
1756, but settlement of the Mahé group began only in 1770.
The group was a dependency of Mauritius, and was ceded to
Britain with Mauritius in 1814. In 1903 these islands,
together with the coralline group, were formed into a colony
separate from Mauritius. On 29 June 1976, the islands became
an independent republic.

Following a coup d'état in 1977, when France-Albert René
became president, Seychelles became a one-party state ruled
by the Seychelles People's Progressive Front (SPPF) in 1979.
Opposition parties were permitted from 1991 and in 1993 a
multiparty constitution was reintroduced. In 2009 the SPPF
was renamed the People's Party (PL).

In the September 2016 legislative election, the PL was
narrowly beaten by the opposition Linyon Demokratik
Seselwa alliance (LDS); it was the first time the PL had not
won a majority since 1979. The LDS extended its majority in
the October 2020 election, and LDS candidate Wavel
Ramkalawan won the simultaneous presidential election.

Under the 1993 constitution, the executive president is
directly elected for a five-year term. In 2016, the country
voted to reduce presidential limits from three to two
consecutive terms. The unicameral National Assembly has up
to 35 members: 25 directly elected by constituencies and up
to ten allocated by proportional representation; members
serve a five-year term. The council of ministers is appointed by
the president.

HEAD OF STATE
President, Defence, Foreign Affairs, Wavel Ramkalawan, *took
   office* 26 October 2020
Vice-President, Ahmed Afif

SELECTED GOVERNMENT MEMBERS *AS AT
NOVEMBER 2020*
Finance, vacant
Home Affairs, vacant

THE HIGH COMMISSION OF THE REPUBLIC OF
SEYCHELLES
130-132 Buckingham Palace Road, London SW1W 9SA
T 020-7730 2046 **E** seyhc.london@btconnect.com
High Commissioner, HE Derick Ally, *apptd* 2017

BRITISH HIGH COMMISSION
PO Box 161, Oliaji Trade Centre, Victoria, Mahé
T (+248) 283 666 **E** bhcvictoria@fco.gov.uk
W www.gov.uk/government/world/seychelles
High Commissioner, HE Patrick Lynch, *apptd* 2019

ECONOMY AND TRADE

Seychelles prospered after independence owing to the
development of tuna fishing and tourism; the latter employs
about 26 per cent of the workforce and accounts for over 55
per cent of GDP. The economy struggled in 2008–9 owing
to external debt, high deficits, food and oil price rises, and the
global recession, but recovered in 2010–11. In January 2017
it gained developed country status, and subsequent growth to
2020 was strong due to rising tourism, but high inequality,
vulnerability to changes in world markets and climate change
are long-term challenges. The sharp reduction in tourists in
2020, due to the coronavirus pandemic, is expected to
contract the economy by 13.8 per cent.

Agriculture, small-scale manufacturing and offshore financial
services are being developed to diversify the economy. Apart
from fishing and tourism, the main industries involve
processing fish, coconuts and vanilla, and producing
beverages.

The main trading partners are the UAE, and EU countries.
The principal exports are canned tuna, frozen fish, and re-
exports of petroleum products. The principal imports are
machinery and equipment, foodstuffs, petroleum products,
chemicals and manufactured goods.

GNI – US$1.6bn; US$16,870 per capita (2019)
Annual average growth of GDP – 5.3 per cent (2017 est)
Inflation rate – 2.9 per cent (2017 est)
Population below poverty line – 39.3 per cent (2013 est)
Unemployment – 3 per cent (2017 est)

Total external debt – US$2.559bn (2017 est)
Imports – US$1,706m (2017)
Exports – US$1,562m (2017)

BALANCE OF PAYMENTS
Trade – US$143m deficit (2017)
Current Account – US$270m deficit (2019)

Trade with UK	2018	2019
Imports from UK	£61,666,655	£26,555,838
Exports to UK	£67,135,925	£63,275,691

COMMUNICATIONS

Airports and waterways – The principal airport is at Mahé (there are seven airports in total); the main port is Victoria, and ferries run regularly between Mahé, Praslin and La Digue
Roadways – 526km
Telecommunications – 19,627 fixed lines and 188,879 mobile subscriptions (2019); there were 55,616 internet users in 2018
Internet code and IDD – sc; 248 (from UK), 44 (to UK)
Media – The state-run Seychelles Broadcasting Corporation operates various channels across the country; daily newspapers include *The Rising Sun* and the government-owned *Seychelles Nation*
WPFI score – 28.66 (63)

SIERRA LEONE

Republic of Sierra Leone

Area – 71,740 sq. km
Capital – Freetown; population, 1,202,000 (2020 est)
Major towns – Bo, Kenema
Currency – Leone (Le) of 100 cents
Population – 6,624,933 rising at 2.43 per cent a year (2020 est); 20 ethnic groups, of which the largest are Temne (35.5 per cent), Mende (33.2 per cent) and Limba (6.4 per cent) (est)
Religion – Muslim 78.6 per cent, Christian 20.8 per cent (est)
Language – English (official), Mende, Temne, Krio (English-based Creole)
Population density – 106 per sq. km (2019)
Urban population – 42.5 per cent (2019 est)
Median age (years) – 19.1 (2020 est)
National anthem – 'High We Exalt Thee, Realm of the Free'
National day – 27 April (Independence Day)
Death penalty – Retained (last used 1998)
CPI score – 33 (119)
Military expenditure – US$29.6m (2018 est)

CLIMATE AND TERRAIN

The land rises from mangrove swamps along the coast, to low-lying wooded country, and then to a mountainous plateau in the east. Elevation extremes range from 1,948m (Loma Mansa) to 0m (Atlantic Ocean). The climate is tropical, with a rainy season from May to November; rainfall peaks in July and August, and is particularly heavy on the coast. The average temperature is 26.4°C.

HISTORY AND POLITICS

In 1787 British philanthropists and abolitionists established a settlement for repatriated former slaves from Britain and its colonies on the Freetown peninsula. In 1808 the settlement was declared a crown colony and became the main base in west Africa for enforcing the 1807 Act outlawing the slave trade. In 1896 a protectorate was declared over the hinterland. The Freetown colony and the protectorate were united in 1951, and in 1961 Sierra Leone became independent.

The country became a republic in 1971 and a one-party state in 1978. Transition to a multiparty democracy began in 1991 but was aborted by a military coup in 1992. Civilian rule was restored with the 1996 elections. Another coup in May 1997 was short-lived, and the government was reinstated in March 1998 with the assistance of Economic Community of West African States (ECOWAS) troops.

The transition to multiparty and civilian rule was complicated by the civil war with the Revolutionary United Front (RUF), which began in 1991. Fighting continued until 2001, when a lasting ceasefire was agreed, and the war was declared over in 2002. An estimated 50,000 people were killed, 30,000 mutilated and a third of the population displaced between 1991 and 2002. A truth and reconciliation commission and a UN-supported war crimes tribunal were set up in 2002.

The 2018 presidential election was won by Sierra Leone People's Party candidate and former military ruler Julius Maada Bio, following ten years of rule by Ernest Bai Koroma of the All People's Congress (APC). The APC won a majority of seats in the simultaneous legislative election.

Under the 1991 constitution, the executive president is directly elected for a five-year term, renewable once. The unicameral parliament has 146 members elected for a five-year term: 132 directly elected, and 14 indirectly elected to serve as non-partisan 'Paramount Chiefs'. The president, who is responsible to the legislature, appoints and chairs the cabinet.

HEAD OF STATE
President, Julius Maada Bio, *sworn in* 4 April 2018
Vice-President, Mohamed Juldeh Jalloh

SELECTED GOVERNMENT MEMBERS *AS AT NOVEMBER 2020*
Chief Minister, David Francis
Finance, Jacob Jusu Saffa
Internal Affairs, Maurice Panda-Noah

SIERRA LEONE HIGH COMMISSION
41 Eagle Street, London WC1R 4TL
T 020-7404 0140 **E** info@slhc-uk.org **W** www.slhc-uk.org
High Commissioner, HE Morie Komba Manyeh, *apptd* 2019F

BRITISH HIGH COMMISSION
6 Spur Road, Freetown
T (+232) (0) 76 541 386 **E** freetown.general.enquiries@fco.gov.uk
W www.gov.uk/government/world/sierra-leone
High Commissioner, HE Simon Mustard, *apptd* 2019

ECONOMY AND TRADE

The country was devastated by a decade of civil war, and unemployment increased with the demobilisation of former combatants. Economic activity has grown since the end of the war but the country remains extremely poor, dependent on foreign aid and expatriates' remittances, although since 2014 has achieved more independence. It benefited from having around 90 per cent of its foreign debt written off in 2006.

There are significant mineral deposits and agricultural and fishery resources, although the lack of infrastructure hampers development. Diamonds and iron ore generate most export earnings, but 60.7 per cent of GDP is generated by agriculture, much of which is at subsistence level. Industry consists mainly of mining (diamonds, rutile, iron ore, bauxite), processing agricultural products and light manufacturing for the domestic market. Economic output was severely effected by the 2014–15 Ebola outbreak and falling export prices, and although growth returned 2017–19 with an increase of iron ore extraction, it is expected to contract by 3.1 per cent in 2020.

The main export markets are Côte d'Ivoire, Belgium, the USA and China; the chief import suppliers are China, the USA, Belgium and the UAE. Principal exports are iron ore, diamonds, rutile, cocoa, coffee and fish. The main imports are foodstuffs, machinery and equipment, fuels and lubricants, and chemicals.

GNI – US$3.9bn; US$500 per capita (2019)
Annual average growth of GDP – 3.7 per cent (2017 est)
Inflation rate – 18.2 per cent (2017 est)
Population below poverty line – 52.9 per cent (2011 est)
Unemployment – 15 per cent (2017 est)
Total external debt – US$1.615bn (2017 est)
Imports – US$1,423m (2016)
Exports – US$926m (2016)

BALANCE OF PAYMENTS
Trade – US$746m deficit (2015)
Current Account – US$646m deficit (2018)

Trade with UK	2018	2019
Imports from UK	£30,789,036	£34,396,849
Exports to UK	£1,495,035	£1,358,199

COMMUNICATIONS

Airports and waterways – There is an international airport at Freetown; Freetown, which has one of the world's largest natural harbours, is the main port and there are smaller ports at Pepel and Sherbro
Roadways – 1,501km of paved roadways
Telecommunications – 2,586 fixed lines and 5.6 million mobile subscriptions (2019); there were 568,099 internet users in 2018
Internet code and IDD – sl; 232 (from UK), 44 (to UK)
Media – The Sierra Leone Broadcasting Corporation was formed in 2010 and is the country's principal TV and radio broadcaster; newspapers include *Awoko* and the *Standard Times*
WPFI score – 30.28 (85)

EDUCATION AND HEALTH

The public University of Sierra Leone incorporates several campuses in Freetown, and Njala University was established in Bo in 2005; there are a number of other technical and teacher-training institutes throughout the country.
Literacy rate – 43.2 per cent (2018 est)
Gross enrolment ratio (percentage of relevant age group) – primary 124.5 per cent, secondary 41.8 per cent (2017 est)
Health expenditure (per capita) – US$66 (2017)

Hospital beds (per 1,000 people) – 0.4 (2006)
Life expectancy (years) – 59.8 (2020 est)
Mortality rate – 9.8 (2020 est)
Birth rate – 35.4 (2020 est)
Infant mortality rate – 63.6 (2020 est)
HIV / AIDS adult prevalence – 1.6 per cent (2019 est)

SINGAPORE

Xinjiapo Gongheguo / Republik Singapura / Cinkappur Kutiyaracu – Republic of Singapore

Area – 719.2 sq. km
Capital – Singapore; population, 5,935,000 (2020 est)
Currency – Singapore dollar (S$) of 100 cents
Population – 6,209,660 rising at 1.73 per cent a year (2020 est); Chinese (74.3 per cent), Malay (13.4 per cent), Indian (9 per cent) (est)
Religion – Buddhist 33.2 per cent, Christian 18.8 per cent, Muslim 14 per cent, Taoist 10 per cent, Hindu 5 per cent (est)
Language – Mandarin, English, Malay, Tamil (all official), Hokkien, Cantonese, Teochew
Population density – 7,953 per sq. km (2019)
Urban population – 100 per cent (2019 est)
Median age (years) – 35.6 (2020 est)
National anthem – 'Majulah Singapura' 'Onward, Singapore'
National day – 9 August (Independence Day)
Death penalty – Retained
CPI score – 85 (4)
Military expenditure – US$10,841m (2018)
Conscription – 18–21 years of age, male only; 24 months
Literacy rate – 97.3 per cent (2018)
Gross enrolment ratio (percentage of relevant age group) – primary 100.3 per cent, secondary 105.8 per cent, tertiary 88.9 per cent (2018 est)
Health expenditure (per capita) – US$2,619 (2017)
Hospital beds (per 1,000 people) – 2.4 (2015)
Life expectancy (years) – 86 (2020 est)
Mortality rate – 3.6 (2020 est)
Birth rate – 8.9 (2020 est)
Infant mortality rate – 2.3 (2020 est)

CLIMATE AND TERRAIN

Singapore consists of the island of Singapore and 63 islets situated off the southern extremity of the Malay peninsula, from which it is separated by the Straits of Johor. The land rises from the shore to a low, undulating central plateau. Elevation extremes range from 166m (Bukit Timah) to 0m (Singapore Strait). The state is just north of the equator and the climate is tropical, subject to monsoons in June to September and December to March. The average temperature is 27.6°C, and there is frequent rain and high humidity.

HISTORY AND POLITICS

Singapore, a trading site since the 13th century, was established as a British trading post by Sir Stamford Raffles in 1819 and was ceded to Britain in perpetuity in 1824. In 1826 it was incorporated with Penang and Malacca to form the Straits Settlements and they became a crown colony in 1867. Singapore became the commercial and financial hub of southeast Asia in the 19th century, and the principal British military base in the Far East in the 1920s. In 1942, during the Second World War, it fell to Japanese forces. Liberated in 1945, it became a separate colony in 1946, and internal self-government was introduced in 1959. It became part of the Federation of Malaysia in 1963, before withdrawing to become an independent sovereign state in 1965.

Although Singapore is a multiparty state, the People's Action Party (PAP) has dominated politics since 1959; opposition candidates were elected to parliament for the first time in 1981.

Independent candidate Tony Tan was elected president in 2011, replacing PAP's Sellapan Rama Nathan. In September 2017, PAP candidate Halimah Yacob was elected as the first female president, being the only eligible candidate. In the 2019 general election, PAP retained its large majority and secured a fifteenth consecutive term in office. Lee Hsien Loong continued in office as prime minister, a post he has held since 2004.

The 1959 constitution was amended in 1965 to end the affiliation with Malaysia and make Singapore a republic, and in 1991 to make the presidency directly elected. The president is directly elected for a six-year term, with no term limits; the president appoints the prime minister and the members of the cabinet. There is a unicameral parliament with 89 directly elected members, up to nine additional opposition members nominated by a parliamentary select committee and appointed by the president, and up to nine extra members from opposition parties (NCMPs) (currently three), depending on their share of the vote; all members serve a five-year term.

HEAD OF STATE

President, Halimah Yacob, *took office* 14 September 2017

SELECTED GOVERNMENT MEMBERS *AS AT NOVEMBER 2020*

Prime Minister, Lee Hsien Loong
Deputy Prime Minister, Finance, Tharman Shanmugaratnam
Foreign Affairs, Vivian Balakrishnan
Home Affairs, Kasiviswanathan Shanmugam

HIGH COMMISSION FOR THE REPUBLIC OF SINGAPORE

9 Wilton Crescent, London SW1X 8SP
T 020-7235 8315 **E** singhc_lon@sgmfa.gov.sg
W www.mfa.gov.sg/london
High Commissioner, HE Thuan Kulan Lim, *apptd* 2020

BRITISH HIGH COMMISSION

100 Tanglin Road, Singapore 247919
T (+65) 6424 4200 **E** consular.singapore@fco.gov.uk
W www.gov.uk/government/world/organisations/british-high-commission-singapore
High Commissioner, HE Kara Owen, CMG, *apptd* 2019

ECONOMY AND TRADE

Historically based on trade in raw materials from surrounding countries and on trade in finished products, the economy industrialised rapidly after independence and diversified, becoming a regional financial and technology centre, and a tourist destination. Economic growth has rarely flagged since 1965; although the global economic downturn pushed the economy into recession in 2008. However, the country is highly dependent on international trade and the trade conflict between China and the USA resulted in only 0.9 per cent growth in 2019; the economy is expected to contract by 6 per cent in 2020. Singapore joined a common market with the other members of the Association of Southeast Asian Nations (ASEAN) in 2015. With low unemployment, high incomes and little corruption, Singapore enjoys one of the highest per capita GDP levels in the world.

Agriculture is limited and contributes little to GDP. Industries include manufacturing (especially consumer electronics, information technology products, biomedical sciences, pharmaceuticals and chemicals), engineering, oil refining, food processing and ship repair; industry contributes 24.8 per cent of GDP. The service sector (financial and business services, entrepôt trade, tourism) accounts for 75.2 per cent of GDP and employs 73.7 per cent of the native workforce.

The main trading partners are Malaysia, China, Hong Kong and the USA. Principal exports are machinery and equipment (especially electronic), consumer goods, pharmaceuticals and other chemicals and mineral fuels. The main imports are machinery and equipment, mineral fuels, chemicals, food and consumer goods.

GNI – US$339.9bn; US$59,590 per capita (2019)
Annual average growth of GDP – 0.73 per cent (2019 est)
Inflation rate – 0.6 per cent (2017 est)
Unemployment – 2.25 per cent (2019 est)
Total external debt – US$566.1bn (2017 est)
Imports – US$482,881m (2017)
Exports – US$561,467m (2017)

BALANCE OF PAYMENTS

Trade – US$78,585m surplus (2017)
Current Account – US$63,139m surplus (2019)

Trade with UK	2018	2019
Imports from UK	£5,150,568,928	£5,384,619,919
Exports to UK	£2,274,278,226	£3,342,785,840

COMMUNICATIONS

Airports and waterways – There is one international airport, at Changi. Singapore is one of the busiest seaports in the world, although there is a high risk of piracy in the South China Sea; it has a large merchant fleet of 1,599 ships of over 1,000 tonnes, with 344 registered in other countries, while 966 foreign-owned ships are registered in Singapore
Roadways and railways – There are 3,500m of roadways and an extensive light rail system on the island
Telecommunications – 2 million fixed lines and 9.5 million mobile subscriptions (2019); there were 5.3 million internet users in 2018
Internet code and IDD – sg; 65 (from UK), 1/2/8 44 (to UK)
Major broadcasters – TV and radio broadcasting is dominated by MediaCorp, owned by a state investment agency
Press – Singapore Press Holdings, which has close links to the ruling party, has a virtual monopoly on the newspaper industry and publishes 15 newspapers
WPFI score – 55.23 (158)

SLOVAKIA

Slovenska republika – Slovak Republic

Area – 49,035 sq. km
Capital – Bratislava; population, 435,000 (2020 est)
Major city – Kosice
Currency – Euro (€) of 100 cents
Population – 5,440,602 falling at 0.05 per cent a year (2020 est); Slovak (80.7 per cent), Hungarian (8.5 per cent), Romani (2 per cent). Romani populations are usually underestimated and may represent 7–11 per cent of the population (est)
Religion – Christian (Roman Catholic 62 per cent, Protestant 8.2 per cent, Greek Catholic 3.8 per cent) (est)
Language – Slovak (official), Hungarian, Roma, Ruthenian
Population density – 113 per sq. km (2019)
Urban population – 53.7 per cent (2019 est)
Median age (years) – 41.8 (2020 est)
National anthem – 'Nad Tatrou sa blýska' 'Lightning Over the Tatras'
National day – 1 September (Constitution Day)
Death penalty – Abolished for all crimes (since 1990)
CPI score – 50 (59)
Military expenditure – US$1,281m (2018)
Literacy rate – 99.45 per cent (2015)
Gross enrolment ratio (percentage of relevant age group) – primary 99.7 per cent, secondary 91.4 per cent, tertiary 45.4 per cent (2018 est)
Health expenditure (per capita) – US$1,186 (2017)
Hospital beds (per 1,000 people) – 5.8 (2015)
Life expectancy (years) – 77.8 (2020 est)
Mortality rate – 10.1 (2020 est)
Birth rate – 9.3 (2020 est)
Infant mortality rate – 4.9 (2020 est)

CLIMATE AND TERRAIN

Slovakia is landlocked and mountainous, lying in the western Carpathian range, which includes the Tatra and Beskid mountains to the north. The mountains fall to plains in the south-east and south-west; the latter is the plain of the river Danube and its tributary the Vah, which rises in the Tatras. Elevation extremes range from 2,655m (Gerlachovsky stit) to 94m (Bodrog river). The climate is temperate, with warm humid summers and cold dry winters. Average temperatures range from −2.4°C in January to 18.5°C in July.

POLITICS

The 1993 constitution has been amended several times, most significantly in 1999 to allow direct elections to the presidency. The president is directly elected for a five-year term, renewable once. The unicameral National Council has 150 members, who are directly elected for a four-year term by proportional representation. The prime minister, who is appointed by the president, nominates the cabinet.

The centre-left Direction-Social Democracy (Smer-SD) remained the largest party after the March 2016 legislative election, but lost its parliamentary majority. Prime Minister Robert Fico formed a coalition government but resigned in 2018 following popular anti-corruption protests sparked by the death of a journalist, Jan Kuciak, investigating links between the mafia and Fico's close advisers. Smer-SD subsequently lost the February 2020 elections to a coalition of right-wing parties let by anti-corruption party Ordinary People. The Andrej Kiska was replaced as president in July 2019 by political outsider, anti-corruption campaigner and independent Zuzana Caputova, Slovakia's first woman head of state.

HEAD OF STATE
President, Zuzana Caputova, *elected* 30 March 2019, *sworn in* 15 June 2019

SELECTED GOVERNMENT MEMBERS *AS AT NOVEMBER 2020*
Prime Minister, Igor Matovic
Deputy Prime Ministers, Richard Sulik *(Economy, Foreign Affairs),* Veronika Remisova; Stefan Holy; Eduard Heger *(Finance)*
Defence, Jaroslav Nad
Interior, Roman Mikulec

EMBASSY OF THE SLOVAK REPUBLIC
25 Kensington Palace Gardens, London W8 4QY
T 020-7313 6470 E emb.london@mzv.sk W www.mzv.sk/londyn
Ambassador Extraordinary and Plenipotentiary, HE Lubomir Rehak, *apptd* 2015

BRITISH EMBASSY
Panska 16, Bratislava 811 01
T (+421) (2) 5998 2000 E bebra@internet.sk
W www.gov.uk/government/world/slovakia
Ambassador Extraordinary and Plenipotentiary, HE Nigel Baker, OBE, *apptd* 2020

ECONOMY AND TRADE

Slovakia has almost completely transitioned from a centrally planned to a free-market economy, following structural reforms and privatisation begun after 1998. As a result, foreign investment has risen, especially in the vehicle and electronics industries, and GDP grew steadily between 2000 and 2008. The economy contracted in 2009 because of the global economic downturn, recovering in 2010. The economy has been affected by EU economic sanctions against Russia since 2014, but rebounded 2017–19 thanks to foreign investment, rising domestic consumption and record low levels of unemployment. However, it is expected to contract by 7.1 per cent in 2020.

Slovakia's open economy, which joined the EU in 2004 and eurozone in 2009, is fuelled by vehicle and electronic exports, which account for over 80 per cent of GDP. Natural resources include brown coal and lignite, natural gas, oil, iron ore, copper and manganese. Major industries include production of vehicles, metal and metal products, food and beverages, fuel and energy (electricity, gas, coke, oil and nuclear), chemicals and synthetic fibres, machinery, wood and paper products, ceramics, textiles and electrical and optical equipment. Slovakia's growing industrial sector accounts for 35 per cent of GDP, services 61.2 per cent and agriculture 3.8 per cent.

The main trading partners are other EU countries, especially Germany and Czechia. Principal exports are machinery and electrical equipment, vehicles, nuclear reactors and furnaces, base metals, minerals and fuels. The main imports are machinery and transport equipment, mineral products, vehicles, nuclear reactors and fuel.

GNI – US$105.3bn; US$19,320 per capita (2019)
Annual average growth of GDP – 2.4 per cent (2019 est)
Inflation rate – 1.3 per cent (2017 est)
Population below poverty line – 12.3 per cent (2015 est)
Unemployment – 5 per cent (2017 est)
Total external debt – US$75.04bn (2016 est)
Imports – US$88,494m (2017)
Exports – US$90,331m (2017)

BALANCE OF PAYMENTS
Trade – US$1,836m surplus (2017)
Current Account – US$2,842m deficit (2019)

Trade with UK	2018	2019
Imports from UK	£608,575,349	£1,085,554,129
Exports to UK	£2,351,711,149	£2,589,768,751

COMMUNICATIONS
Airports and waterways – The principal airport is at Bratislava and the main Danube ports are Bratislava and Komarno
Roadways and railways – 56,926km, including 464km of motorways; 3,580km of railways
Telecommunications – 673,341 fixed lines and 7.4 million mobile subscriptions (2019); there were 4.4 million internet users in 2018
Internet code and IDD – sk; 421 (from UK), 44 (to UK)
Major broadcasters – The public broadcasters Slovak TV and Slovak Radio operate national networks in competition with private companies
Press – The major daily newspapers, including *Pravda, Sme* and *Novy Cas,* are all privately owned
WPFI score – 22.67 (33)

SLOVENIA
Republika Slovenija – Republic of Slovenia

Area – 20,273 sq. km
Capital – Ljubljana; population, 286,000 (2018)

Major city – Maribor
Currency – Euro (€) of 100 cents
Population – 2,102,678 rising at 0.01 per cent a year (2020 est); Slovene (83.1 per cent), Serb (2 per cent), Croat (1.8 per cent), Bosniak (1.1 per cent) (est)
Religion – Christian (Catholic 57.8 per cent, Orthodox 2.3 per cent), Muslim 2.4 per cent (est)
Language – Slovene (official), Serbo-Croatian; Hungarian and Italian are also official in designated municipalities
Population density – 103 per sq. km (2019)
Urban population – 54.5 per cent (2019 est)
Median age (years) – 44.9 (2020 est)
National anthem – 'Zdravljica' 'A Toast'
National day – 25 June (Statehood Day)
Death penalty – Abolished for all crimes (since 1989)
CPI score – 60 (35)
Military expenditure – US$529m (2018)

CLIMATE AND TERRAIN
The Alps cover 42 per cent of the country, towards the north, and the south lies on the high Karst plateau. The only low-lying areas are the Pannonian plain in the east and north-east, and the short (47km) narrow coastal belt on the Adriatic Sea. Elevation extremes range from 2,864m (Triglav) to 0m (Adriatic Sea). The climate is continental in most of the country but Mediterranean on the coast. Average temperatures range from 0.3°C in January to 19.7°C in July.

POLITICS
Under the 1991 constitution, the president is directly elected for a five-year term, renewable once. The bicameral National Assembly consists of the 90-member National Assembly, which is directly elected for a four-year term, and the National Council which has 40 members indirectly elected for a five-year term as a largely advisory body. The prime minister, who is nominated by the president and elected by the legislature, appoints the cabinet.

The anti-immigration Slovenian Democratic Party (SD) won the largest number of seats in the June 2018 parliamentary election, but following three months of political deadlock a centre-left minority coalition was formed led by the newly-established List of Marjan Sarec party (LMS). This government collapsed due to internal disagreements in January 2020 and was replaced by an SDP-led coalition, with Janez Jansa appointed as prime minister. Borut Pahor (SD) was elected president in December 2012, defeating the incumbent Danilo Turk, and was re-elected in November 2017.

HEAD OF STATE
President, Borut Pahor, *elected* 2 December 2012, *sworn in* 22 December 2012, *re-elected* 12 November 2017

SELECTED GOVERNMENT MEMBERS *AS AT NOVEMBER 2020*
Prime Minister, Janez Jansa
Finance, Andrej Sircelj
Foreign Affairs, Anze Logar

EMBASSY OF THE REPUBLIC OF SLOVENIA
17 Dartmouth Street, London SW1H 9BL
T 020-7222 5700 **E** vlo@gov.si
W http://london.embassy.si
Ambassador Extraordinary and Plenipotentiary, HE Tadej Rupel, *apptd* 2014

BRITISH EMBASSY
4th Floor, Trg Republike 3, 1000 Ljubljana
T (+386) (1) 200 3910 **E** info@british-embassy.si
W www.gov.uk/government/world/slovenia

Ambassador Extraordinary and Plenipotentiary, HE Tiffany
Sadler, *apptd* 2020

ECONOMY AND TRADE
Always the most prosperous republic of the former
Yugoslavia, Slovenia's transition to a market economy was
smoothed by good infrastructure and a well-educated
workforce. Much of the economy remains in state ownership
and taxes are high. In 2014, Slovenia became the first
transition country to progress from borrower status at the
World Bank to donor partner; it joined the EU in 2004 and
eurozone in 2007. The economy contracted sharply in 2009
owing to the global downturn and again experienced
recession in 2012 and 2013, but recorded stronger growth
2017-18. Growth decelerated in 2019 due to weaker export
demand, and the economy is expected to contract by 6.7 per
cent in 2020 due to the coronavirus pandemic.

Industry contributes 32.2 per cent of GDP, the service sector
65.9 per cent and agriculture 1.8 per cent. The main
agricultural products are hops, wheat, coffee, maize, apples,
pears and livestock. Industries include mining and mineral
processing (iron ore, aluminium, lead, zinc), electronics
(including for military purposes), vehicles, electric power
equipment, wood products, textiles, chemicals and machine
tools.

The main trading partners are other EU countries
(particularly Germany, Austria and Italy) and Turkey.
Principal exports are manufactured goods, machinery and
transport equipment, chemicals and food. These items, along
with fuels and lubricants, are also the main imports.
GNI – US$53.8bn; US$25,750 per capita (2019)
Annual average growth of GDP – 2.4 per cent (2019 est)
Inflation rate – 1.4 per cent (2017 est)
Population below the poverty line – 13.9 per cent (2016 est)
Unemployment – 7.64 per cent (2019 est)
Total external debt – US$46.3bn (2017 est)
Imports – US$35,522m (2017)
Exports – US$40,178m (2017)

BALANCE OF PAYMENTS
Trade – US$4,656m surplus (2017)
Current Account – US$3,049m surplus (2019)

Trade with UK	2018	2019
Imports from UK	£328,288,729	£281,148,702
Exports to UK	£422,561,962	£441,178,011

COMMUNICATIONS
Airports and waterways – The international airports are at
Ljubljana, Maribor and Portoroz; Koper is the main port
Roadways and railways – 38,985km; 1,229km
Telecommunications – 715,283 fixed lines and 2.5 million
mobile subscriptions (2019); there were 1.7 million internet
users in 2018
Internet code and IDD – si; 386 (from UK), 44 (to UK)
Media – The public broadcaster RTV Slovenia operates TV
and radio stations; daily newspapers include *Delo, Dnevnik* and
Slovenske Novice
WPFI score – 22.64 (32)

EDUCATION AND HEALTH
Education is free and compulsory between the ages of six and
15.
Literacy rate – 99.9 per cent (2015)
Gross enrolment ratio (percentage of relevant age group) – primary
102.1 per cent, secondary 114.5 per cent, tertiary 77.1
per cent (2018 est)

Health expenditure (per capita) – US$21,920 (2017)
Hospital beds (per 1,000 people) – 4.6 (2013)
Life expectancy (years) – 81.4 (2020 est)
Mortality rate – 10.3 (2020 est)
Birth rate – 8.7 (2020 est)
Infant mortality rate – 1.7 (2020 est)

SOLOMON ISLANDS

Area – 28,896 sq. km
Capital – Honiara, on Guadalcanal; population, 82,000
(2018)
Major town – Kirakira, on Makira
Currency – Solomon Islands dollar (SI$) of 100 cents
Population – 685,097 rising at 1.84 per cent a year (2020
est); Melanesian (95.3 per cent), Polynesian (3.1 per cent),
Micronesian (1.2 per cent) (est)
Religion – Christian (Protestant 73.4 per cent, Roman
Catholic 19.6 per cent, other Christian 2.9 per cent),
other 4 per cent (est)
Language – English (official), Melanesian Pidgin (lingua
franca); around 120 indigenous languages exist
Population density – 23 per sq. km (2019)
Urban population – 24.2 per cent (2019 est)
Median age (years) – 23.5 (2020 est)
National anthem – 'God Save Our Solomon Islands'
National day – 7 July (Independence Day)
Death penalty – Retained for certain crimes (not used since
independence)
CPI score – 42 (77)
Gross enrolment ratio (percentage of relevant age group) – primary
106.2 per cent (2018 est)
Health expenditure (per capita) – US$101 (2017)
Life expectancy (years) – 76.2 (2020 est)
Mortality rate – 3.8 (2020 est)
Birth rate – 23.6 (2020 est)
Infant mortality rate – 13.4 (2020 est)

CLIMATE AND TERRAIN
Forming a scattered archipelago of mountainous islands and
low-lying coral atolls in the south-west Pacific Ocean, the
Solomon Islands stretch about 1,448km in a south-easterly
direction from the Shortland Islands to the Santa Cruz islands.
The six biggest islands are Choiseul, New Georgia, Santa
Isabel, Guadalcanal, Malaita and Makira (San Cristobal). They
are characterised by thickly forested mountain ranges
intersected by deep, narrow valleys. Elevation extremes range
from 2,310m (Mt Popomanaseu) to 0m (Pacific Ocean). The
climate is tropical, with little variation in temperature, and a
wet season between November and April. The islands are
prone to seismic activity and tsunamis.

HISTORY AND POLITICS

The islands were colonised by Austronesian people 30,000 years ago. Spanish explorers reached the islands in 1568 and the area continued to be visited by Europeans intermittently for about 300 years. Following the arrival of missionaries and traders, Britain declared a protectorate in 1893 over the southern islands; the northern islands were ceded to Britain by Germany in 1899. After the Second World War, campaigns began for self-government, which was achieved in 1976; independence followed in 1978.

Ethnic tension on Guadalcanal between the indigenous Isatabus and migrants from the island of Malaita escalated from 1998 into conflict between militant factions. Despite a fragile peace following a ceasefire agreement signed in October 2000, and elections in 2001, lawlessness and corruption pervaded the country. An Australian-led regional assistance mission restored public order and disarmed the militias by late 2003.

Following the April 2019 general election, Manasseh Sogavare was appointed prime minister, having previously served in this role three times. The move was boycotted by his opponents and sparked riots in Honiara. Like other pacific islands, the political landscape has been divided by the influence of China in recent years; in September 2020 the pro-Taiwan provincial government on the island of Malaita announced plans for an independence referendum.

Under the 1978 constitution, the Solomon Islands is a constitutional monarchy. The head of state is Queen Elizabeth II, represented by a governor-general, who is chosen by the legislature. The unicameral National Parliament has 50 members who are directly elected for a four-year term. The prime minister is elected by the legislature from among its members, and nominates the cabinet, which is formally appointed by the governor-general.

Governor-General, HE Sir David Vunagi, GCMG, *apptd* 2019

SELECTED GOVERNMENT MEMBERS *AS AT NOVEMBER 2020*
Prime Minister, Manasseh Sogavare
Deputy Prime Minister, Nestor Ghiro
Foreign Affairs, Jeremiah Manele

HIGH COMMISSION FOR THE SOLOMON ISLANDS
Room 1819 Portland House, Bressenden Place, London SW1E 5RS
E siembassy@compuserve.com
High Commissioner, HE Eliam Tangirongo, *apptd* 2018

BRITISH HIGH COMMISSION
PO Box 676, Tanuli Ridge, Honiara
T (+677) 21705 **E** bhc@solomon.com.sb
W www.gov.uk/government/world/solomon-islands
High Commissioner, HE David Ward, *apptd* 2016

ECONOMY AND TRADE

The civil unrest of 1998–2003 left the country virtually bankrupt but the restoration of law and order enabled the economy to recover until its modest but steady growth was curtailed by the global downturn and natural disasters in 2009 and 2010. The country's greater dependency since 2003 on foreign aid, principally from Australia, increased as the downturn reduced government revenues. A regional assistance programme, which ended in June 2017, helped the economy return to modest growth. In February 2019, a bulk carrier ran aground on a coral reef and spilled 80 tonnes of oil, creating the worst environmental disaster in the nation's history.

Agriculture, much at subsistence level, is the largest economic sector, accounting for 34.3 per cent of GDP and engaging about 75 per cent of the population. Abundant mineral resources are largely undeveloped, although there are plans to better exploit them. The main industries are fishing, mining and forestry; industry contributes 7.6 per cent of GDP.

The main trade partners are China, Australia and Malaysia. Principal exports are timber, fish, copra, cocoa, palm and coconut oil. The main imports are food, machinery and equipment, manufactured goods, fuels and chemicals.
GNI – US$1.4bn; US$2,050 per capita (2019)
Annual average growth of GDP – 3.5 per cent (2017 est)
Inflation rate – 0.5 per cent (2017 est)
Total external debt – US$757m (2017 est)
Imports – US$678m (2017)
Exports – US$590m (2017)

BALANCE OF PAYMENTS
Trade – US$88m deficit (2017)
Current Account – US$154m deficit (2019)

Trade with UK	2018	2019
Imports from UK	£1,196,164	£666,793
Exports to UK	£598,747	£605,925

COMMUNICATIONS

Airports and waterways – Air Niugini flies from Papua New Guinea to Honiara; the main ports are Honiara and Viru
Roadways – 1,390km
Telecommunications – 7,130 fixed lines and 480,124 mobile subscriptions (2019); there were 78,686 internet users in 2018
Internet code and IDD – sb; 677 (from UK), 44 (to UK)
Media – The Solomon Islands Broadcasting Corporation (SIBC) operates public radio services and One Television provides television programmes; the *Solomon Star* is the single daily newspaper

SOMALIA

Jamhuuriyadda Federaalkaa Soomaaliya – Federal Republic of Somalia

Area – 637,657 sq. km
Capital – Mogadishu; population, 2,282,000 (2020)
Major cities – Baidoa, Berbera, Burao, Hargeisa, Kismayu
Currency – Somali shilling of 100 cents; other currencies are also in circulation
Population – 11,757,124 rising at 2.21 per cent a year (2020 est); Somali (85 per cent), Bantu and other non-Somali (15 per cent), including 30,000 Arabs (est)
Religion – Muslim (official; predominantly Sunni)
Language – Somali, Arabic (both official), Italian, English
Population density – 24 per sq. km (2019)
Urban population – 45.6 per cent (2019 est)

Median age (years) – 18.5 (2020 est)
National anthem – 'Qolobaa Calankeed' 'Every Nation Has its Own Flag'
National day – 1 July (Foundation Day)
Death penalty – Retained
CPI score – 9 (180)
Military expenditure – $62m (2018 est)
Conscription – 18 years of age
Life expectancy (years) – 54 (2020 est)
Mortality rate – 12.4 (2020 est)
Birth rate – 38.7 (2020 est)
Infant mortality rate – 89.5 (2020 est)
HIV/AIDS adult prevalence – 0.1 per cent (2019 est)

CLIMATE AND TERRAIN

The country is mostly an arid and flat or undulating plateau, rising to hills in the north. Elevation extremes range from 2,416m (Shimbiris) to 0m (Indian Ocean). The climate is tropical, influenced by the north-east and south-west monsoons. Rainfall is greater in the south than the north, but is low and irregular throughout the country, leading to frequent droughts. The average temperature is 27.1°C.

POLITICS

Due to a lack of security, legislative elections could not be held in 2012; initial members of the parliament were chosen by 135 clan elders, themselves selected by the outgoing constituent assembly. Indirect legislative elections were held from October to November 2017, with 14,025 delegates, themselves appointed by clan elders, voting due to the ongoing civil war. Former prime minister Mohamed Abdullahi Mohamed was elected president in February 2017. It was hoped the first universal elections since 1969 would take place in 2020, but the failure to hold these resulted in the near-unanimous removal of Hassan Ali Khaire as prime minister in July 2020 by parliament.

Under the 2012 provisional constitution the president is elected by the legislature for a four-year term. The president appoints the prime minister, who names the cabinet. The bicameral parliament has 275 directly elected members in the House of the People, who serve a four-year term; the Upper House has a maximum of 54 members, serving a four-year term and directly elected from the 18 regions of Somalia.

Most of Somalia's territory is under government control, but guerrilla-style attacks from the Islamist militia al-Shabab are frequent; the group was blamed for the killing of at least 500 people in Mogadishu in October 2017 and 53 in two separate attacks in early 2019.

HEAD OF STATE
President, Mohamed Abdullahi Mohamed, *elected* 7 February 2017

SELECTED GOVERNMENT MEMBERS *AS AT NOVEMBER 2020*
Prime Minister, Mohamed Hussein Robel
Deputy Prime Minister, Mahdi Ahmed Guled
Finance, Abdirahman Dualle Beyle
Foreign Affairs, Ahmed Isse Awad
Interior, Gen. Mukhtar Hussein Afrah

BRITISH AMBASSADOR
Ambassador Extraordinary and Plenipotentiary, HE Benjamin Fender, OBE, *apptd* 2019

REPUBLIC OF SOMALILAND
In the north-east of the country, the Republic of Somaliland proclaimed independence in May 1991 from Somalia's dictator Siad Barre. While a functioning political system with its own government, currency and police force, it is not recognised by the UN or any government. The region has its own constitutional democracy, including regular municipal, parliamentary and presidential elections; the former British protectorate has largely escaped the instability and violence Somalia has experienced in recent decades. Muse Bihi Abdi was elected president in November 2017, succeeding incumbent Ahmed Silanyo.

HEAD OF STATE
President, Muse Bihi Abdi, *elected* 13 December 2017
Vice-President, Abdirahman Saylici

SELECTED GOVERNMENT MEMBERS *AS AT NOVEMBER 2020*
Foreign Affairs, Yasin Haji Mohamoud
Interior, Mohamed Kahin Ahmed

ECONOMY AND TRADE

The lack of central government before 2012 prevented broad-based economic development or assistance from international donors. Natural resources are not exploited and industry is virtually non-existent, but the lack of regulation led to a thriving and relatively sophisticated informal entrepreneurial economy, especially in livestock, remittance/money transfer services (in the absence of a banking sector) and telecommunications. Infrastructure has been developed by commercial concerns, with businesses building small airfields and using natural harbours for overseas trade, and the three main telecommunications companies jointly funding internet infrastructure. The formal economy has grown in recent years but has failed to spread beyond Mogadishu, and the small industrial secor has largely been looted. Since the election of Mohamed Abdullahi Mohamed in 2017, there has been record levels of foreign aid and investment.

Agriculture, primarily livestock-raising by nomads or semi-nomads, is the most important economic sector. It accounts for about 60.2 per cent of GDP and over half of export earnings, but is vulnerable to drought. In March 2017, following a two-year drought, the UN warned that Somalia and three other countries face the world's largest humanitarian crisis since 1945; 2.9 million people are at risk of famine in the country. Similar warnings were repeated in June 2019 after another drought placed an estimated 5.4 million at risk of starvation.

The main export markets are Oman, Saudi Arabia and the UAE; imports come mainly from China and India. Principal exports are livestock, bananas, hides, fish, charcoal and scrap metal. The main imports are manufactured goods, petroleum products, foodstuffs, construction materials and khat.
Annual average growth of GDP – 2.3 per cent (2017 est)
Inflation rate – 1.5 per cent (2017 est)

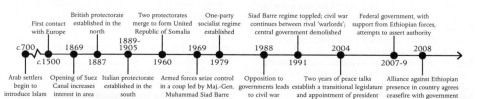

		British protectorate established in the north	Two protectorates merge to form United Republic of Somalia	One-party socialist regime established	Siad Barre regime toppled; civil war continues between rival 'warlords'; central government demolished	Federal government, with support from Ethiopian forces, attempts to assert authority
First contact with Europe			1889-1905			
*c.*700	1869			1969	1988	2004	2008
	*c.*1500	1887	1960	1979	1991	2007-9
Arab settlers begin to introduce Islam	Opening of Suez Canal increases interest in area	Italian protectorate established in the south	Armed forces seize control in a coup led by Maj.-Gen. Muhammad Siad Barre	Opposition to governments leads to civil war	Two years of peace talks establish a transitional legislature and appointment of president	Alliance against Ethiopian presence in country agrees ceasefire with government

Total external debt – US$5.3bn (2014 est)
Imports – US$2,512m (2017)
Exports – US$823m (2017)

BALANCE OF PAYMENTS
Trade – US$1,689m deficit (2017)
Current Account – US$92m deficit (2018)

Trade with UK	2018	2019
Imports from UK	£13,876,481	£12,639,730
Exports to UK	£496,326	£588,706

COMMUNICATIONS

Airports and waterways – The international airports are at Mogadishu and Hargeisa; the main ports are Mogadishu, Kismayu and Merca in the south, and Berbera in the north. Increased security has led to a significant drop in piracy and armed robbery against ships in the Gulf of Aden and Indian Ocean since 2012
Roadways – 2,608km are surfaced
Telecommunications – 74,800 fixed lines and 5.6 million mobile subscriptions (2019); there were 225,181 internet users in 2018
Internet code and IDD – so; 252 (from UK), 44 (to UK)
Broadcasters – There is one state-operated TV station and two private broadcasters, with a number of radio stations operating on a regional basis
Press – There are various Mogadishu-based newspapers and an English-language weekly, *Somaliland Times*, but journalists are routinely threatened
WPFI score – 55.45 (163)

SOUTH AFRICA

Republic of South Africa

Area – 1,219,090 sq. km
Capital – The seat of government is Pretoria (Tshwane): population, 2,566,000 (2020 est); the seat of the legislature is Cape Town: population, 4,618,000 (2020 est); and the seat of the judiciary is Bloemfontein: population, 496,000 (2014 est)
Major cities – Durban, Johannesburg, Port Elizabeth
Currency – Rand (R) of 100 cents
Population – 56,463,617 rising at 0.97 per cent a year (2020 est)
Religion – Christian 86 per cent, other 6.9 per cent (including ancestral, tribal, animist and other traditional African religions), Muslim 1.9 per cent (est)
Language – isiZulu, isiXhosa, Afrikaans, Sepedi, Setswana, English, Sesotho, Xitsonga, siSwati, Tshivenda, isiNdebele (all official)
Population density – 48 per sq. km (2019)

Urban population – 66.9 per cent (2019 est)
Median age (years) – 28 (2020 est)
National anthems – 'Nkosi Sikelel' iAfrika' 'God Bless Africa', incorporating 'Die Stem van Suid Afrika' 'The Call of South Africa'
National day – 27 April (Freedom Day)
Death penalty – Abolished for all crimes (since 1997)
CPI score – 44 (70)
Military expenditure – US$3,640m (2018)

CLIMATE AND TERRAIN

South Africa occupies the southernmost part of the African continent, with the exception of eSwatini and Lesotho. Its territory includes Prince Edward and Marion Islands, 1,920km to the south-east of Cape Town. The narrow coastal plain is separated by a mountainous escarpment, including the Drakensberg range, from a high inland plateau (the Great Karoo and the Highveld), an area of semi-arid scrubland in the west merging into grasslands or savannah in the centre and east. Elevation extremes range from 3,408m (Njesuthi) to 0m (Atlantic Ocean). The main rivers are the Orange and the Limpopo and their tributaries. The country lies at the convergence of the Atlantic and Indian oceans, and the climate is influenced by the cold Benguela current along the west coast and the warm Agulhas current along the east, as well as by the altitude of the interior. These influences cause cooler, drier conditions in the west and almost subtropical warmth and rainfall in the east. Average temperatures range from 11.8°C in July to 23.4°C in January and February.

POLITICS

Under the 1997 constitution, the executive president is elected by the National Assembly for a five-year term, renewable once. The president, who is responsible to the legislature, appoints the cabinet. The bicameral parliament consists of the National Assembly, the lower house and the National Council of Provinces. The National Assembly has 400 members directly elected by proportional representation for a five-year term. The National Council of Provinces has 90 members, ten for each province, selected by the provincial legislatures for a five-year term.

South Africa is divided into nine provinces: Eastern Cape, Free State, Gauteng, KwaZulu-Natal, Limpopo, Mpumalanga, Northern Cape, North-West and Western Cape. Each province has its own premier, legislature and constitution.

The African National Congress (ANC) has won all the legislative elections since 1994, but is increasingly racked by internal tensions and tainted by corruption allegations. In the May 2014 legislative elections, the ANC received 62.2 per cent of the vote and its leader Jacob Zuma was elected president for the second time. In February 2018, Zuma was forced to resign over corruption allegations, and was replaced by ANC leader Cyril Ramaphosa. Ramaphosa led the ANC to another electoral victory in May 2019 against a background of sluggish economic growth and high levels of unemployment; the party retained over 57 per cent of the electoral vote, which was its lowest share since free polls started in 1994.

HEAD OF STATE
President, C-in-C of the Armed Forces, Cyril Ramaphosa, *sworn in* 15 February 2018, *re-elected* 22 May 2019
Deputy President, David Mabuza

SELECTED GOVERNMENT MEMBERS *AS AT NOVEMBER 2020*
Defence, Nosiviwe Noluthando Mapisa-Nqakula
Finance, Tito Mboweni
Home Affairs, Pakishe Aaron Motsoaledi

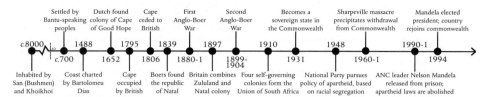

Settled by Bantu-speaking peoples — 1488 — **Dutch found colony of Cape of Good Hope** — 1795 — **Cape ceded to British** — 1839 — **First Anglo-Boer War** — 1897 — **Second Anglo-Boer War** — 1910 — **Becomes a sovereign state in the Commonwealth** — 1948 — **Sharpeville massacre precipitates withdrawal from Commonwealth** — 1990-1 — **Mandela elected president; country rejoins commonwealth**

c.8000 AD / c.700 — 1652 — 1806 — 1880-1 — 1899-1904 — 1931 — 1960-1 — 1994

Inhabited by San (Bushmen) and Khoikhoi — **Coast charted by Bartolomeu Dias** — **Cape occupied by British** — **Boers found the republic of Natal** — **Britain combines Zululand and Natal colony** — **Four self-governing colonies form the Union of South Africa** — **National Party pursues policy of apartheid, based on racial segregation** — **ANC leader Nelson Mandela released from prison; apartheid laws are abolished**

SOUTH AFRICAN HIGH COMMISSION
South Africa House, Trafalgar Square, London WC2N 5DP
T 020-7451 7299 **W** www.southafricahouseuk.com
High Commissioner, HE Nomatemba Tambo, *apptd* 2018

Trade with UK	2018	2019
Imports from UK	£1,934,613,774	£1,839,684,307
Exports to UK	£6,040,809,674	£6,499,762,069

BRITISH HIGH COMMISSION
255 Hill Street, Arcadia 0028, Pretoria (Tshwane)
T (+27)(12) 421 7500 **E** pta.assistanceforbritishnationals@fco.gov.uk
W www.gov.uk/government/world/south-africa
High Commissioner, HE Nigel Casey, CMG, MVO, *apptd* 2017

ECONOMY AND TRADE
The economy varies between the sophisticated and well-developed, based on manufacturing, mining and financial services; the living eked out by the very poor, mostly through subsistence agriculture; and a large informal sector. Growth was strong until 2008, when the global economic downturn caused a contraction in the economy. Recovery was slow, hindered by some of the highest levels of inequality and unemployment in the world. The economy is expected to contract by 8 per cent in 2020 due to the coronavirus pandemic. Economic development has been constrained by an outdated infrastructure, power cuts, a skills shortage, labour unrest, corruption, political instability and high levels of public debt.

Agriculture, forestry and fishing account for 2.8 per cent of GDP and employ 4.6 per cent of the workforce. Principal crops are maize, wheat, sugar cane, fruit and vegetables. Livestock farming, wool and viticulture are also widespread.

The largest industry is mining; South Africa is the world's largest producer of gold, platinum and chromium, as well as producing diamonds, manganese, coal, copper, iron ore, tin, uranium and titanium. Other industries include car assembly, metalworking, food processing, ship repair and production of machinery, textiles, iron and steel, chemicals and fertiliser; manufacturing is concentrated most heavily around Johannesburg, Pretoria (Tshwane) and the major ports. Tourism is a significant industry, and South Africa is a major transit point for its landlocked neighbours. Industry contributes 29.7 per cent of GDP and services 67.5 per cent.

Fossil-fuel based electricity generation is being supplemented by nuclear power; one nuclear power station is in operation and two others are planned. Water resources are inadequate to meet demand, so water is imported from the highlands of Lesotho.

The main trading partners are China, Germany, Japan and the USA. Principal exports are gold, diamonds, platinum, other metals and minerals, and machinery and equipment. Principal imports are machinery and equipment, chemicals, petroleum products, scientific instruments and foodstuffs.
GNI – US$353.5bn; US$6,040 per capita (2019)
Annual average growth of GDP – 0.06 per cent (2019 est)
Inflation rate – 5.3 per cent (2017 est)
Unemployment – 28.53 per cent (2019 est)
Population below poverty line – 16.6 per cent (2016 est)
Total external debt – US$156.3bn (2017 est)
Imports – US$98,816m (2017)
Exports – US$103,863m (2017)

BALANCE OF PAYMENTS
Trade – US$5,047m surplus (2017)
Current Account – US$10,666m deficit (2019)

COMMUNICATIONS
Airports and waterways – 144 airports, with international airports at Johannesburg, Durban and Cape Town; Durban is the largest seaport, while other major ports are Cape Town, Port Elizabeth, East London, Saldanha, Mossel Bay and Richards Bay
Roadways and railways – There are 158,952km of surfaced roadways and 20,986km of railways, including the high-speed Gautrain, which links Johannesburg's main international airport and Pretoria
Telecommunications – 1.9 million fixed lines and 92.6 million mobile subscriptions (2019); there were 31.1 million internet users in 2018
Internet code and IDD – za; 27 (from UK), 44 (to UK)
Major broadcasters – The South African Broadcasting Corporation (SABC) is the country's major, state-owned television and radio broadcaster
Press – *The Star* is Johannesburg's oldest daily newspaper, while the *Sunday Times* is the longest running weekly title; *Beeld* is a popular Afrikaans daily title
WPFI score – 22.41 (31)

EDUCATION AND HEALTH
Education is compulsory between the ages of seven and 15.
Literacy rate – 87.0 per cent (2017 est)
Gross enrolment ratio (percentage of relevant age group) – primary 98.5 per cent, secondary 100.5 per cent, tertiary 23.8 (2018 est)
Health expenditure (per capita) – US$499 (2017)
Hospital beds (per 1,000 people) – 2.8 (2004–9)
Life expectancy (years) – 64.8 (2020 est)
Mortality rate – 9.3 (2020 est)
Birth rate – 19.2 (2020 est)
Infant mortality rate – 27.8 (2020 est)
HIV/AIDS adult prevalence – 19 per cent (2019 est)

SOUTH SUDAN
Republic of South Sudan

Area – 644,329 sq. km
Capital – Juba; population, 403,000 (2020 est)

Major cities – Malakal, Wau
Currency – South Sudanese pound (SSDP) of 100 piastres
Population – 10,561,244 rising at 2.47 per cent a year (2020
   est); Dinka (35.8 per cent), Nuer (15.6 per cent) (est)
Religion – Christian, animist (many animists also follow
   Christian practices)
Language – English (official), Arabic, indigenous languages
Urban population – 19.9 per cent (2019 est)
Median age (years) – 18.6 (2020 est)
National anthem – 'South Sudan Oyee!' 'Hooray!'
National day – 9 July (Independence Day)
Death penalty – Retained
CPI score – 12 (179)
Military expenditure – US$59m (2018)
Conscription – 18 years of age; 19,000 child soldiers are still
   used in the country's civil war (2018 est)
Literacy rate – 34.5 per cent (2018)
Gross enrolment ratio (percentage of relevant age group) – primary
   73 per cent, secondary 11.0 per cent (2015 est)
Health expenditure (per capita) – US$23 (2017)
Life expectancy (years) – 55.5 (2020 est)
Mortality rate – 11.4 (2020 est)
Birth rate – 38.8 (2020 est)
Infant mortality rate – 69.9 (2020 est)
HIV/AIDS adult prevalence – 2.5 per cent (2019 est)

CLIMATE AND TERRAIN
The White Nile, flowing north out of the uplands of central
Africa, is the principal feature of the country, and formed part
of the Sudd, a vast swamp of more than 100,000 sq. km.
Divided by the river, the terrain rises from the plains on the
northern border to wet southern highlands along the Kenya–
Uganda divide to a maximum height of 3,187m (Mt Kinyeti).
The climate is hot with seasonal rainfall and the average
annual temperature is 27.7°C.

HISTORY AND POLITICS
The history of the area is largely unrecorded until the early
19th century, as natural barriers prevented the invasions and
occupations affecting northern Sudan. In the 19th century,
Egypt attempted to extend its influence in the region but the
south was only joined with the north with the arrival of the
British in the late 19th century, becoming part of a joint
Anglo-Egyptian condominium from 1899. Following the
independence of Sudan in 1955, tensions between the
dominant Arab, Muslim north and the black African,
Christian and animist south led to civil war from 1955 to
1972, and again in 1983. A peace process began in 2000 and
the parties to it – the government, the Sudan People's
Liberation Army/Movement (SPLA/M) and the southern
National Democratic Alliance – finalised a peace agreement in
2004. Under this, the southern parties joined a national unity
government, a largely autonomous administration was set up
in the south in October 2005 and a referendum on
independence for the south was held after six years.

In the referendum in January 2011, the south voted
overwhelmingly to separate from the north. In the run-up to
independence on 9 July, disputes led to a deteriorating
security situation in border areas, particularly over control of
the oil-rich territory of Abyei.

In December 2013, fighting broke out between political
factions after the finance minister was dismissed following
corruption allegations in July. Although President Salva Kiir
signed a peace treaty with rebel groups in August 2015,
officially ending the conflict, in July 2016 hundreds of people
were killed in renewed fighting between forces loyal to
President Kiir and Vice-President Riek Machar, and the latter
was replaced by Taban Deng Gai. When peace was again

declared 31 October 2018, it was estimated the five-year
conflict had claimed the lives of 400,000 people and
displaced 4 million. Legislative elections originally due to take
place in 2015 were delayed by the civil war and were due to
take place in 2018, when they were again delayed until 2021
after parliament voted to extend Kiir's presidential term.

The transitional constitution came into effect at
independence and will remain in force until a permanent
constitution is adopted. It provides for the current president of
the government of South Sudan to become president of the
independent republic, and for the National Legislative
Assembly (comprising 170 members of the former South
Sudan Legislative Assembly, plus 96 South Sudanese former
members of the National Assembly to the Republic of Sudan;
both these groups were directly elected in 2010) and the
Council of States (comprising 20 former South Sudan
members of the Council of States of the Republic of Sudan,
plus 30 representatives appointed by the president). An
agreement in August 2016 led to the appointment of 68
additional National Assembly members, which is expected to
reach 550 members after full elections take place.

HEAD OF STATE
President, C-in-C of the Armed Forces, Salva Kiir, *sworn in under
   draft constitution* 9 July 2011
First Vice-President, Riek Machar
Second Vice-President, James Wani

SELECTED GOVERNMENT MINISTERS *AS AT
NOVEMBER 2020*
Defence, Angelina Teny
Finance, Athian Diing Athian
Foreign Affairs, Beatrice Kamisa

EMBASSY OF THE REPUBLIC OF SOUTH SUDAN
22–25 Portman Close, London W1H 6BS
T 020-368 72366 **E** info@embrss.org.uk **W** www.embrss.org.uk
Ambassador Extraordinary and Plenipotentiary, vacant

BRITISH EMBASSY
EU Compound, Kololo Road, Thom Ping, Juba
T (+211) (0) 912 323 712 **E** ukin.southsudan@fco.gov.uk
W www.gov.uk/government/world/south-sudan
Ambassador Extraordinary and Plenipotentiary, HE Christopher
   Trott, *apptd* 2019

ECONOMY AND TRADE
The troubled South Sudan economy, hindered by decades of
civil war with the north, is based on subsistence agriculture,
which provides a living for the majority of the population.
This is of one of the richest agricultural areas in Africa with
fertile soils and excellent water supplies, but a lack of industry
and infrastructure has forced the reliance on imports of goods
and services from the neighbouring countries. Just 2 per cent
of roads are paved and less than 2 per cent of the population
has access to electricity. Hugely oil-dependent, the
government derives 98 per cent of its budget from oil
revenues and consequently economic development has been
hit by falling oil prices and production cuts, as well as the
country's internal conflict.

South Sudan faces tough economic challenges and has
received more than US$11bn in foreign aid since 2005,
mainly from the UK, the USA and the EU, while Chinese
investment is rising. Annual inflation rose to 800 per cent in
October 2016 and remains high, as continuing civil conflict
has had a seriously deleterious effect on the economy. In
October 2020, the UN estimated 7.5 million people were in
need of humanitarian aid in the country, and 1.6 million had
been internally displaced.

Subsistence crops include sorghum, maize, rice millet, wheat, sugar cane, papayas, bananas and mangoes.
GNI – US$5bn; US$460 per capita (2018)
Annual average growth of GDP – –5.2 (2017 est)
Inflation rate – 187.9 per cent (2017 est)
Population below the poverty line – 66 per cent (2015 est)
Imports – US$4,164m (2017)
Exports – US$2,373m (2017)

BALANCE OF PAYMENTS
Current Account – US$256m surplus (2019)

Trade with UK	2018	2019
Imports from UK	£2,038,487	£6,115,298
Exports to UK	£15,550	£55,709

COMMUNICATIONS
Airports – There are three airports including an international terminal in Juba
Roadways and railways – There are 90,200km of mainly unpaved roadways in poor condition and 248km of railways
Internet code and IDD – ss; 211 (from UK), 44 (to UK)
Media – The country's fledgling media network faces political, social and logistical challenges; the government-run Southern Sudan TV and Radio is the country's sole network; *The Citizen* and *Juba Monitor* (both English language), and *Al-Masir* (Arabic) are the major daily newspapers
WPFI score – 44.49 (138)

SPAIN

Reino de España – Kingdom of Spain

Area – 505,370 sq. km
Capital – Madrid; population, 6,618,000 (2020 est)
Major cities – Barcelona, Bilbao, Las Palmas (Gran Canaria), Málaga, Murcia, Palma (Majorca/ Mallorca), Seville, Valencia, Zaragoza
Currency – Euro (€) of 100 cents
Population – 50,015,792 rising at 0.67 per cent a year (2020 est)
Religion – Christian (Roman Catholic 68.9 per cent) (est)
Language – Castilian (Spanish) (official), Catalan, Galician, Basque, Aranese (all official in certain regions)
Population density – 94 per sq. km (2019)
Urban population – 80.6 per cent (2019 est)
Median age (years) – 43.9 (2020 est)
National anthem – 'Himno Nacional Espanol' 'National Anthem of Spain'
National day – 12 October (marks Columbus's arrival in the Americas)
Death penalty – Abolished for all crimes (since 1995)

CPI score – 62 (30)
Military expenditure – US$18,248m (2018)

CLIMATE AND TERRAIN
Spain occupies over 80 per cent of the Iberian peninsula, and includes two archipelagos and territories on or just off the Moroccan coast. The interior consists of an elevated plateau surrounded and traversed by mountain ranges: the Pyrenees on the border with France, the Cantabrian mountains (north-west), the Sierra de Guadarrama, Sierra Morena, Montes de Toledo (centre) and the Sierra Nevada (south). Elevation extremes range from 3,718m (Pico de Teide, Tenerife, Canary Islands) to 0m (Mediterranean Sea). The principal rivers are the Duero, the Tajo (Tagus), the Guadiana, the Guadalquivir, the Ebro and the Miño. The climate is Mediterranean in the southern and eastern coastal areas, and temperate further inland and at altitude. Average temperatures range from 7°C in January to 23.1°C in July.

POLITICS
The 1978 constitution has been amended at various times to devolve powers to the 19 autonomous regions. The head of state is a hereditary constitutional monarch. There is a bicameral legislature, the *Cortes Generales,* comprising a 350-member Congress of Deputies directly elected for a four-year term, and a senate with 266 members, 208 directly elected and 58 appointed by the assemblies of the autonomous regions, for a four-year term.

There are 19 autonomous regions: Andalucía, Aragón, Asturias, Balearic Islands, the Basque Country, Canary Islands, Cantabria, Castilla-La Mancha, Castilla y León, Catalonia, Ceuta, Extremadura, Galicia, La Rioja, Madrid, Melilla, Murcia, Navarre and Valencia. Each has its own elected legislature and government.

In 2006 a referendum endorsed the *Cortes'* approval of greater autonomy for Catalonia. Unofficial independence referendums, rallies and declarations of sovereignty have augmented the independence movement since 2009, resulting in the exile of pro-independence Catalonian president Carles Puigdemont in November 2017 following a declaration of independence.

The ruling Popular Party (PP) won the December 2015 and June 2016 legislative elections but failed to secure a majority; in October 2016, Mariano Rajoy was re-elected prime minister at the head of a minority government. In June 2018 Rajoy lost a no-confidence vote following a corruption scandal and was replaced by Socialist Workers' Party leader Pedro Sánchez. The ruling socialists emerged as the largest party in snap elections held in April 2018, but fell short of a majority, while the far-right Vox party made significant ground as PP support fell sharply. Months of coalitions failed to produce a coalition government, and a fourth election in four years was held in November 2019 that once again failed to produce a majority. However, a coalition government, the first in 80 years, was agreed between the socialists and the anti-austerity Unidas Podemos alliance in January 2020.

HEAD OF STATE
HM The King of Spain, King Felipe VI de Borbon y Grecia, born 30 January 1968, *acceded to the throne* 19 June 2014
Heir, HRH The Princess of the Asturias, Leonor de Borbon y Ortiz, *born* 31 October 2005

SELECTED GOVERNMENT MEMBERS *AS AT NOVEMBER 2020*
Prime Minister, Pedro Sánchez
First Vice-President, María del Carmen Calvo
Finance, Maria Jesús Montero

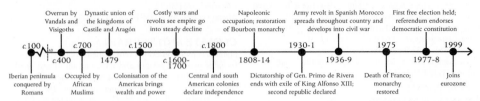

Timeline:

- Overrun by Vandals and Visigoths
- Dynastic union of the kingdoms of Castile and Aragón
- Costly wars and revolts see empire go into steady decline
- Napoleonic occupation; restoration of Bourbon monarchy
- Army revolt in Spanish Morocco spreads throughout country and develops into civil war
- First free election held; referendum endorses democratic constitution

- c.100 AD
- c.700
- c.1500
- c.1800
- 1930–1
- 1975
- 1999

- c.400
- 1479
- c.1600–1700
- 1808–14
- 1936–9
- 1977–8

- Iberian peninsula conquered by Romans
- Occupied by African Muslims
- Colonisation of the Americas brings wealth and power
- Central and south American colonies declare independence
- Dictatorship of Gen. Primo de Rivera ends with exile of King Alfonso XIII; second republic declared
- Death of Franco; monarchy restored
- Joins eurozone

Foreign Affairs, Arancha Gonzalez

EMBASSY OF SPAIN
39 Chesham Place, London SW1X 8SB
T 020-7235 5555 E emb.londres@maec.es
W www.exteriores.gob.es/embajadas/londres
Ambassador Extraordinary and Plenipotentiary, HE Carlos Bastarreche, *apptd* 2017

BRITISH EMBASSY
Torre Espacio, Paseo de la Castellana 259D, 28046 Madrid
T (+34) (91) 714 6300 E spain.consulate@fco.gov.uk
W www.gov.uk/government/world/spain
Ambassador Extraordinary and Plenipotentiary, HE Hugh Elliott, *apptd* 2019

INSURGENCIES
The Basque separatist organisation ETA (*Euzkadi ta Azkatasuna* – Basque Nation and Liberty), formed in 1959, began a terrorist campaign of bombings, shootings and kidnappings in 1961 in an attempt to gain independence for the Basque country. ETA rejected regional autonomy for the Basque country in 1979 as insufficient and continued its campaign, but was greatly weakened in the early 1990s by increased cooperation between Spanish security forces and their European counterparts. ETA announced a permanent ceasefire in January 2011; in March 2017 the group announced it was laying down its arms and handed over an inventory of weapons caches in early April.

ECONOMY AND TRADE
Economic protectionism and isolation held back economic development until the mid-20th century, but the economy improved from the 1950s with industrialisation and the development of tourism. The mixed capitalist economy showed above-average growth, stimulated by liberalisation, privatisation and deregulation from the mid-1990s until 2008, when it entered a severe recession because of the global economic crisis.

The downturn in construction and the property market left many banks struggling in 2010, and rising public-sector debt led to Spain's international credit rating being downgraded; the government introduced austerity measures in response alongside labour reforms. The government shored up struggling banks exposed to Spain's depressed domestic construction and real estate sectors by completing an EU-funded restructuring and recapitalisation programme in December 2013. Growth returned in 2014–19, but unemployment and public debt remained high. The economy suffered badly during the coronavirus pandemic, not least from a sharp fall in tourism, and is forecast to contract by 12.8 per cent in 2020; unemployment is expected to reach 20.8 per cent of the labour force.

The generally fertile country produces grains, vegetables, olives, sugar beets, citrus and other fruits, meat and dairy products. Viticulture is widespread. Spain also has one of Europe's largest fishing industries. The agricultural sector contributes 2.6 per cent of GDP and employs 4.2 per cent of the workforce. Abundant mineral resources include coal, iron ore, copper, zinc, lead, uranium and tungsten. Metal extraction and the manufacture of metal products, including steel, are major industries. A diverse industrial sector includes manufacturing (principally textiles, clothing, footwear, beverages, chemicals, cars, machine tools, clay products, pharmaceuticals and medical equipment), food processing, shipbuilding and tourism. Industry accounts for 23.2 per cent of GDP and the service sector for 74.2 per cent.

The main trading partners are other EU countries, especially France and Germany. Principal exports include machinery, vehicles, foodstuffs, pharmaceuticals, medicines and other consumer goods. The main imports are machinery and equipment, fuels, chemicals, semi-finished goods, foodstuffs, consumer goods, and measuring and medical control instruments.

GNI – US$1,430.8bn; US$30,390 per capita (2019)
Annual average growth of GDP – 1.95 per cent (2019 est)
Inflation rate – 2 per cent (2017 est)
Population below the poverty line – 21.1 per cent (2012 est)
Unemployment – 14.13 per cent (2019 est)
Total external debt – US$2.094 trillion (2016 est)
Imports – US$414,146m (2017)
Exports – US$452310m (2017)

BALANCE OF PAYMENTS
Trade – US$38,163m surplus (2017)
Current Account – US$29,606m surplus (2019)

Trade with UK	2018	2019
Imports from UK	£10,467,590,152	£10,741,442,914
Exports to UK	£15,746,792,328	£16,752,193,204

COMMUNICATIONS
Airports – Of the 102 airports, the principal terminals are at Madrid, Barcelona, Alicante, Málaga, Valencia and Bilbao
Waterways – The main ports are Algeciras, Alicante, Barcelona, Bilbao, Cádiz, Santander and Valencia, and Las Palmas in the Canary Islands; there are also 1,000km of navigable inland waterways
Roadways and railways – 683,175km; 15,333km
Telecommunications – 21.1 million fixed lines and 58.8 million mobile subscriptions (2019); there were 42.5 million internet users in 2018
Internet code and IDD – es; 34 (from UK), 44 (to UK)
Major broadcasters – Public radio and television services are run by Radio Television Espanola (RTVE), which is funded by advertising and state subsidies
Press – Popular newspaper titles include *El Mundo, ABC, El País* and *El Periodico de Catalunya*
WPFI score – 22.16 (29)

EDUCATION AND HEALTH
Education is free from age six to 18, and compulsory to the age of 16.
Literacy rate – 98.4 per cent (2018)
Gross enrolment ratio (percentage of relevant age group) – primary 102 per cent, secondary 126.2 per cent, tertiary 91.1 per cent (2018 est)

Health expenditure (per capita) – US$2,506 (2017)
Hospital beds (per 1,000 people) – 3 (2013)
Life expectancy (years) – 82 (2020 est)
Mortality rate – 9.3 (2020 est)
Birth rate – 8.7 (2020 est)
Infant mortality rate – 3.2 (2020 est)
HIV/AIDS prevalence – 0.4 per cent (2019 est)

ISLANDS AND ENCLAVES

THE BALEARIC ISLES form an archipelago off the east coast of Spain. There are four large islands (Majorca/ Mallorca, Minorca, Ibiza and Formentera) and seven smaller ones (Aire, Aucanada, Botafoch, Cabrera, Dragonera, Pinto and El Rey). Area 4,992 sq. km; population 1,107,000 (2016 est). The archipelago forms a province of Spain. The capital is Palma, on Majorca.

THE CANARY ISLANDS are an archipelago in the Atlantic off the African coast, consisting of seven islands and six islets. Area 7,447 sq. km; population 2,207,000 (2019 est). The Canary Islands form two provinces of Spain: Las Palmas, comprising Gran Canaria, Lanzarote, Fuerteventura and six islets, with the seat of administration at Las Palmas, in Gran Canaria; and Santa Cruz de Tenerife, comprising Tenerife, La Palma, La Gomera and El Hierro, with the seat of administration at Santa Cruz, in Tenerife.

CEUTA is a fortified post on the Moroccan coast, opposite Gibraltar. Area 19 sq. km; population 85,144 (2018 est). Ceuta is an autonomous city of Spain.

ISLA DE FAISANES an uninhabited Franco-Spanish condominium, at the mouth of the Bidassoa in La Higuera bay.

MELILLA is a town on a rocky promontory of the Moroccan coast, connected with the mainland by a narrow isthmus. Area 13 sq. km; population 84,689 (2019 est). Melilla is an autonomous city of Spain.

OVERSEAS TERRITORIES

The following territories, which are Spanish settlements on the Moroccan seaboard, come under direct Spanish administration. They are uninhabited other than by military personnel.

PENON DE ALHUCEMAS is a bay including six islands.

PENON DE LA GOMERA (or Peñón de Velez) is a fortified rocky islet.

THE CHAFFARINAS (or Zaffarines) is a group of three islands near the Algerian frontier.

SRI LANKA

Shri Lanka Prajatantrika Samajavadi Janarajaya/Ilankai Jananayaka Choshalichak Kutiyarachu – Democratic Socialist Republic of Sri Lanka

Area – 65,610 sq. km
Capital – Colombo; population, 613,000 (2020 est); the administrative capital is Sri Jayewardenepura Kotte; population, 103,000 (2020 est)

Major cities – Dehiwala-Mount Lavinia, Jaffna, Kalmunai, Kandy, Moratuwa, Negombo, Trincomalee, Vavuniya
Currency – Sri Lankan rupee of 100 cents
Population – 22,889,201 rising at 0.67 per cent a year (2020 est); Sinhalese (74.9 per cent), Sri Lankan Tamil (11.2 per cent), Sri Lankan Moors (9.2 per cent), Indian Tamil (4.2 per cent) (est)
Religion – Buddhist (official) 70.2 per cent (predominantly Theravada), Hindu 12.6 per cent, Muslim 9.7 per cent, Christian 7.4 per cent (predominantly Roman Catholic) (est)
Language – Sinhala, Tamil (both official), English
Population density – 346 per sq. km (2019)
Urban population – 18.6 per cent (2019 est)
Median age (years) – 33.7 (2020 est)
National anthem – 'Sri Lanka Matha' 'Mother Sri Lanka'
National day – 4 February (Independence Day)
Death penalty – Retained (last used 1976)
CPI score – 38 (93)
Military expenditure – US$1,681m (2018)
Literacy rate – 91.7 per cent (2018 est)
Gross enrolment ratio (percentage of relevant age group) – primary 100.2 per cent, secondary 100.3 per cent, tertiary 19.6 per cent (2018 est)
Health expenditure (per capita) – US$159 (2017)
Hospital beds (per 1,000 people) – 3.6 (2012)
Life expectancy (years) – 77.5 (2020 est)
Mortality rate – 6.5 (2020 est)
Birth rate – 14.2 (2020 est)
Infant mortality rate – 7.8 (2020 est)
HIV/AIDS adult prevalence – 0.1 per cent (2019 est)

CLIMATE AND TERRAIN

Sri Lanka (formerly Ceylon) is an island in the Indian Ocean, separated from India by the narrow Palk Strait. The land is low-lying in the north and along the coasts, rising to a central massif with hills and mountains in the south and centre. Forests, jungle and scrub cover the greater part of the island. In areas over 600m above sea level, grasslands *(patanas* or *talawas)* are found. Elevation extremes range from 2,524m (Pidurutalagala) to 0m (Indian Ocean). The climate is tropical with little seasonal variation in conditions and humidity, which often reaches around 90 per cent. The island experiences the south-west monsoon from May to September and the north-east monsoon from October to January.

POLITICS

The Rajapaksa brothers, Mahinda and Gotabaya, have dominated Sri Lankan politics for the past two decades. In October 2018, President Sirisena dissolved parliament, sacked Prime Minister Ranil Wickremesinghe and appointed former president Mahinda Rajapaksa to the post, resulting in a constitutional crisis. Following civil unrest and parliamentary opposition, Wickremesinghe was reinstated in December 2018. Sirisena was unable to contest the November 2019 presidential election, which Mahinda's younger brother Gotabaya Rajapaksa won. The August parliamentary election was comprehensively won by the Rajapaksa brothers' left-wing Sri Lanka People's Freedom Alliance, and Mahinda was installed as prime minister.

The 1978 constitution was amended in 1983 to ban parties advocating separatism, in 1987 to create provincial councils, and in 2010 to remove the limit on presidential terms. The executive president is directly elected for a five-year term, which may be renewed. The unicameral parliament has 225 members directly elected by proportional representation for a five-year term. The president appoints the prime minister and cabinet. The Northern and Eastern provinces were merged into one from 1988 to 2006.

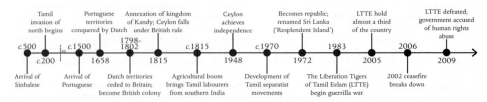

Tamil invasion of north begins — Portuguese territories conquered by Dutch — Annexation of kingdom of Kandy; Ceylon falls under British rule — Ceylon achieves independence — Becomes republic; renamed Sri Lanka ('Resplendent Island') — LTTE hold almost a third of the country — LTTE defeated; government accused of human rights abuse

c.500 | c.1500 | 1798–1802 | c.1815 | c.1970 | 1983 | 2006

c.200 | 1658 | 1815 | 1948 | 1972 | 2005 | 2009

Arrival of Sinhalese — Arrival of Portuguese — Dutch territories ceded to Britain; become British colony — Agricultural boom brings Tamil labourers from southern India — Development of Tamil separatist movements — The Liberation Tigers of Tamil Eelam (LTTE) begin guerrilla war — 2002 ceasefire breaks down

Elected councils were set up in the nine provinces in 1987 in an attempt to defuse ethnic tensions between Sinhalese Buddhists and Muslims, but tensions still flare occasionally. In recent years, the threat from Islamists has grown. In April 2019, a series of coordinated suicide bombings targeting luxury hotels and churches on Easter Sunday killed over 250 people was blamed on the IS-inspired National Thowheeth Jama'ath, and sparked anti-Muslim riots.

HEAD OF STATE
President, Defence, Gotabaya Rajapaksa, *elected* 16 November 2019, *sworn in* 18 November 2019

SELECTED GOVERNMENT MEMBERS *AS AT NOVEMBER 2020*
Prime Minister, Economy, Mahinda Rajapaksa
Foreign Affairs, Dinesh Gunawardena
Justice, Ali Sabry

HIGH COMMISSION OF THE DEMOCRATIC SOCIALIST REPUBLIC OF SRI LANKA
13 Hyde Park Gardens, London W2 2LU
T 020-7262 1841 **E** mail@slhc-london.co.uk **W** www.srilankahc.uk
High Commissioner, HE Saroja Sirisena, *apptd* 2020

BRITISH HIGH COMMISSION
389 Bauddhaloka Mawatha, Colombo 7
T (+94) (11) 539 0639 **E** colombo.general@fco.gov.uk
W www.gov.uk/government/world/sri-lanka
High Commissioner, Sarah Hulton, OBE, *apptd* 2019

ECONOMY AND TRADE
Despite the 26-year civil war and the 2004 Indian Ocean tsunami, which destroyed tourist resorts and the fishing industry, the economy saw sustained growth throughout the 2000s. The 2008–9 global downturn affected productivity only slightly, but high public debt and budget deficits obliged the government to seek an IMF loan in 2016. Improved trade relations with the EU and rising tourism boosted growth until 2020, and progress was made with international bodies on the issues of money laundering and terrorist financing. The once predominantly agricultural economy has become increasingly industrialised and diversified. Remittances from expatriate workers are also economically significant. Government debt of around 83 per cent of GDP in 2019 is among the highest of developing nations and is set to significantly increase owing to the coronavirus pandemic; the economy is set to contract by 4.6 per cent in 2020.

Agriculture accounts for 7.8 per cent of GDP and 27 per cent of employment. The main crops are rice, sugar cane, grains, pulses, oilseed, spices, vegetables, fruit, tea, rubber, coconuts, livestock products and fish. Manufacturing is based on processing the main cash crops of rubber, tea, coconuts, tobacco and other commodities, and production of textiles, clothing, beverages and cement; other industries include oil refining and mining gemstones. Service industries such as telecommunications, banking and insurance, information technology services and tourism are also important. The service sector accounts for 61.7 per cent of GDP and industry for 30.5 per cent.

The main trading partners are India, the USA, China, Singapore and the UK. Principal exports are textiles and clothing, tea, rubber manufactures, spices, diamonds, emeralds, rubies, coconut products and fish. The main imports are oil, textile fabrics, machinery, transport equipment, building materials, mineral products and foodstuffs.
GNI – US$87.9bn; US$4,060 per capita (2018)
Annual average growth of GDP – 2.29 per cent (2019 est)
Inflation rate – 6.5 per cent (2017 est)
Population below poverty line – 6.7 per cent (2012 est)
Unemployment – 4.83 per cent (2019 est)
Total external debt – US$51.72bn (2017 est)
Imports – US$26,858m (2017)
Exports – US$18,794m (2017)

BALANCE OF PAYMENTS
Trade – US$8,063m deficit (2017)
Current Account – US$1,808m deficit (2019)

Trade with UK	2018	2019
Imports from UK	£293,199,487	£272,189,401
Exports to UK	£696,658,932	£748,369,347

COMMUNICATIONS
Airports and waterways – The principal airport is Bandaranaike International, to the north of the capital; Colombo is the main port although the first phase of a deep-water container port opened in 2010 at Hambantota
Roadways and railways – 16,977km; 1,562km
Telecommunications – 2.6 million fixed lines and 26.2 million subscriptions (2019); there were 7.7 million internet users in 2018
Internet code and IDD – lk; 94 (from UK), 44 (to UK)
Media – The state-owned Sri Lanka Rupavahini Corporation operates TV and radio stations; daily newspapers include *The Island* (English language), *Dinamina* (Sinhala) and *Virakesari* (Tamil)
WPFI score – 41.94 (127)

SUDAN

Jumhuriyat as-Sudan – Republic of the Sudan

Area – 1,861,484 sq. km
Capital – Khartoum; population, 5,829,000 (2020 est)
Major cities – El Obeid, Kassala, Kusti, Nyala, Port Sudan
Currency – Sudanese pound (SDP) of 100 piastres

Population – 45,561,556 rising at 2.69 per cent a year (2020 est); Sudanese Arab (70 per cent) (est), Fur, Beja, Nuba, Fallata

Religion – Muslim (predominantly Sunni), small Christian minority (est)

Language – Arabic, English (both official), Nubian, Ta Bedawie, Fur

Population density – 23 per sq. km (2019)

Urban population – 34.9 per cent (2019 est)

Median age (years) – 18.3 (2020 est)

National anthem – 'Nahnu Djund Allah Djund al-Watan' 'We Are the Army of God and of Our Land'

National day – 1 January (Independence Day)

Death penalty – Retained

CPI score – 16 (173)

Military expenditure – US$1,048m (2018)

Conscription – 18–33 years of age; 12–24 months

CLIMATE AND TERRAIN

Sudan is predominantly desert; the Libyan Desert in the west is separated from the rocky Nubian Desert in the east by the fertile valley of the Nile and its tributaries. There are mountains in the west and the south, and along the Red Sea coast. Elevation extremes range from 3,071m (Jabal Marrah) to 0m (Red Sea). The climate is arid on the desert plains, tropical in the south and cooler at altitude. There is a rainy season from April to October. Average temperatures range from 22.7°C in January to 31°C in May.

POLITICS

Under the 2005 constitution, the executive president is directly elected for a five-year term. The bicameral National Legislature comprises a National Assembly *(Majlis Watani)* with 426 members, including 128 seats reserved for women, and a Council of States *(Majlis al-Wilayat)* with 54 members indirectly elected by state legislatures. All members serve six-year terms. The president appoints the cabinet.

Former president al-Bashir, having assumed power through a military coup in 1989, was re-elected following the April 2015 presidential election, having claimed 95 per cent of the popular vote, while al-Bashir's National Congress party won the simultaneous legislative elections; opposition groups alleged widespread vote-rigging had taken place.

Anti-government protests calling for an end to al-Bashir's autocratic rule began in December 2018 and were violently suppressed. In February 2019, the president declared a national state of emergency and dismissed the government, but the military arrested al-Bashir in April, charged him over the killing of protesters in May and established a military council. Negotiations with protesters over a transition to civilian rule broke down in June, when military leaders reneged on promises and security forces killed more than 100 people camped outside the military headquarters in Khartoum. In August, a power-sharing deal was brokered in which a transitional sovereign council of civilian leaders and military officials would govern until elections took place in 2022, with the head of state regularly rotating between a civilian and military ruler. In September, the 18-member cabinet was sworn

in, which included four women, and ended 30 years of full military control.

SELECTED GOVERNMENT MEMBERS *AS AT NOVEMBER 2020*
Sovereign Council Leader, Gen. Abdel Fattah Burhan
Prime Minister, Abdalla Hamdok
Foreign Affairs (acting), Omar Gamareldin
Interior, Gen. El Tereifi Idris

EMBASSY OF THE REPUBLIC OF THE SUDAN
3 Cleveland Row, London SW1A 1DD
T 020-7839 8080 **E** admin@sudanembassy.co.uk
W www.sudan-embassy.co.uk
Ambassador Extraordinary and Plenipotentiary, HE Mohammed Abdalla Adris Mohamed, *apptd* 2019

BRITISH EMBASSY
PO Box 801, Off Sharia Al Baladiya, Khartoum East
T (+249) (1) 8377 7105 **E** consular.khartoum@fco.gov.uk
W www.gov.uk/government/world/sudan
Ambassador Extraordinary and Plenipotentiary, HE Irfan Siddiq, OBE, *apptd* 2018

INSURGENCIES

In the western region of Darfur, tension between nomadic Arab livestock herders and black African farmers over land and grazing rights led to a rise in intercommunal violence in the 1990s. Between 2002 and 2009 black African rebels were ruthlessly suppressed by government forces, often operating through Arab militia *(Janjaweed)*, which carried out mass executions and forcible depopulation. The UN estimated that between 2003 and 2019 the ongoing war in Darfur had killed 300,000 people.

Two of the main rebel groups in Darfur signed peace agreements with the government, one in 2006 and the other in 2009. The International Criminal Court issued a warrant for the arrest of former president al-Bashir for war crimes and crimes against humanity in 2009, and for genocide in 2010. In 2011, a related ethnic conflict broke out in the southern provinces of South Kordofan and the Blue Nile; fighting here intensified in 2015 as the government looked to make territorial gains before elections.

As of January 2020, an estimated 9.3 million people (23 per cent of the population) were still in need of humanitarian assistance and over 1 million Sudanese were thought to be refugees.

ECONOMY AND TRADE

Since 1997 Sudan has worked with the IMF to implement economic reforms which, despite the country's political instability and vulnerability to drought, have stabilised the economy. In 1999 Sudan began exporting oil, and the economy boomed as a result until the civil war in 2011, when it lost three-quarters of production owing to the secession of South Sudan. The country has struggled to make up this lost revenue and also suffers from a poor infrastructure, high inflation, civil conflict and widespread poverty. The economy has, however, benefited from recent diversification into gold

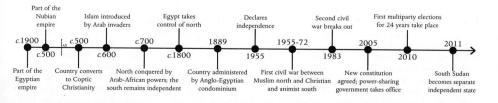

Part of the Nubian empire | Islam introduced by Arab invaders | Egypt takes control of north | Declares independence | Second civil war breaks out | First multiparty elections for 24 years take place
c.1900 | c.500 | c.700 | 1889 | 1955-72 | 2005 | 2011
c.500 | c.600 | c.1800 | 1955 | 1983 | 2010
Part of the Egyptian empire | Country converts to Coptic Christianity | North conquered by Arab-African powers; the south remains independent | Country administered by Anglo-Egyptian condominium | First civil war between Muslim north and Christian and animist south | New constitution agreed; power-sharing government takes office | South Sudan becomes separate independent state

mining and the lifting of US sanctions in October 2017. Almost half the population live below the poverty line.

Agriculture, much at subsistence level, provides employment for around 80 per cent of the workforce and contributes 39.6 per cent of GDP. Mechanised and traditional agriculture is practised in areas with sufficient rainfall and irrigation. The principal crops include cotton, peanuts, sorghum, millet, wheat, sugar cane, tropical fruits and livestock. The country exports 75–80 per cent of the world's gum arabic. Industry consists of oil extraction and refining, cotton ginning, manufacture of textiles, cement, edible oils, sugar, soap, shoes, pharmaceuticals, armaments and vehicle assembly. Industry contributes just 2.6 per cent of GDP and services 57.8 per cent.

The main trading partners are the UAE, Egypt and Saudi Arabia. Principal exports are gold, oil and petroleum products, cotton, sesame, livestock, peanuts, gum arabic and sugar. The main imports are foodstuffs, manufactured goods, refinery and transport equipment, medicines, chemicals, textiles and wheat.

GNI – US$25.5bn; US$590 per capita (2019)
Annual average growth of GDP – 1.4 per cent (2017 est)
Inflation rate – 32.4 per cent (2017 est)
Population below poverty line – 46.5 per cent (2015 est)
Unemployment – 19.6 per cent (2017 est)
Total external debt – US$56.05bn (2017 est)
Imports – US$10,126m (2017)
Exports – US$5,577m (2017)

BALANCE OF PAYMENTS
Trade – US$4,548m deficit (2017)
Current Account – US$5,215m deficit (2019)

Trade with UK	2018	2019
Imports from UK	£70,468,660	£81,373,542
Exports to UK	£9,041,307	£15,303,094

COMMUNICATIONS
Airports and waterways – There are 17 airports, with the principal terminal at Khartoum; there are 4,068km of navigable waterways, including 1,723km on the White and Blue Nile rivers
Roadways and railways – 8,000km of paved roadways; 7,251km
Telecommunications – 141,922 fixed lines and 34.2 million mobile subscriptions (2019); there were 13.3 million internet users in 2018
Internet and IDD – sd; 249 (from UK), 44 (to UK)
Media – Sudan TV and Sudan Radio are the government-operated broadcasters; leading daily newspapers include *Al-Ra'y al-Amm*, *Al-Ayam* and *Al-Jareeda* (all Arabic-language)
WPFI score – 55.33 (159)

EDUCATION AND HEALTH
Education is free of charge for most children, and compulsory for eight years; six years of primary education is followed by at least two years of secondary education.
Literacy rate – 60.7 per cent (2018 est)
Gross enrolment ratio (percentage of relevant age group) – primary 76.8 per cent, secondary 46.6 per cent (2017 est); tertiary 16.9 per cent (2015 est)
Health expenditure (per capita) – US$194 (2017)
Hospital beds (per 1,000 people) – 0.8 (2013)
Life expectancy (years) – 66.5 (2020 est)
Mortality rate – 6.5 (2020 est)
Birth rate – 33.8 (2020 est)
Infant mortality rate – 41.8 (2020 est)
HIV/AIDS adult prevalence – 0.2 per cent (2019 est)

SURINAME
Republiek Suriname – Republic of Suriname

Area – 163,820 sq. km
Capital – Paramaribo; population, 239,000 (2018)
Major towns – Lelydorp, Nieuw Nickerie
Currency – Suriname dollar of 100 cents
Population – 609,569 rising at 0.95 per cent a year (2020 est); Hindustani (27.4 per cent), Maroon (21.7 per cent), Creole (15.7 per cent), Javanese (13.7 per cent) (est)
Religion – Christian (Protestant 23.6 per cent, Roman Catholic 21.6 per cent, other Christian 3.2 per cent), Hindu 22.3 per cent, Muslim 13.8 per cent (est)
Language – Dutch (official), English, Surinamese (Sranang Tongo), Caribbean Hindustani (a dialect of Hindi), Javanese
Population density – 4 per sq. km (2019)
Urban population – 66.1 per cent (2019 est)
Median age (years) – 31 (2020 est)
National anthem – 'God zij met ons Suriname' 'God Be With Our Suriname'
National day – 25 November (Independence Day)
Death penalty – Abolished for all crimes (since 2015)
CPI score – 44 (70)
Literacy rate – 94.4 per cent (2018 est)
Gross enrolment ratio (percentage of relevant age group) – primary 109.2 per cent (2019 est); secondary 82.3 per cent (2018 est)
Health expenditure (per capita) – US$339 (2017 est)
Life expectancy (years) – 73.3 (2020 est)
Mortality rate – 6.2 (2020 est)
Birth rate – 15.6 (2020 est)
Infant mortality rate – 14.9 (2020 est)
HIV/AIDS adult prevalence – 22.2 per cent (2019 est)

CLIMATE AND TERRAIN
The narrow, swampy coastal plain is home to about 90 per cent of the population. From the coastal belt, the land rises to a hilly interior covered by tropical rainforest and savannah; the rainforest contains a great diversity of flora and fauna. Elevation extremes range from 1,230m (Juliana Top) to −2m (coastal plain). The land is drained by several rivers, some of which have been dammed to create large artificial lakes used to generate hydroelectric power. The climate is tropical, moderated by the north-east trade winds. There are two wet seasons, from April to August and November to February.

HISTORY AND POLITICS
Originally settled by Arawak and Carib peoples, the area was visited by Spanish explorers in 1593. Early European settlements failed, until a British colony was founded in 1651. The colony was ceded to the Dutch in 1667. Dutch rule was interrupted by British occupation during the French Revolutionary and Napoleonic wars, but was restored in

1816. The colony, known as Dutch Guiana, became autonomous in 1954, and achieved independence in 1975 as Suriname.

The early years of independence were politically unstable, with a period of military rule under Desi Bouterse following a coup in 1980. Democratic, civilian rule was restored with elections in 1987, but the military overthrew the government in 1990 in a coup engineered by Bouterse. Democratic elections in 1991 were won by the New Front for Democracy and Development alliance, led by Ronald Venetiaan, who became president. President Venetiaan introduced an unpopular austerity programme, which improved the economy but lost him the 1996 election.

After the 2010 legislative election, the Mega Combination bloc, dominated by Desi Bouterse's National Democratic Party (NDP), held the most seats in the legislature and formed a coalition government. Bouterse was subsequently elected president by parliament. In the May 2015 legislative elections, the NDP emerged as the largest single party, and re-elected Bouterse as president. In November 2019 Bouterse was found guilty of the execution of 15 political opponents in 1982 and sentenced to 20 years in prison. Support for the NDP significantly fell in the May 2020 election in favour of the Progressive Reform Party (VHP), which formed a coalition government soon after. VHP leader Chan Santokhi was subsequently elected president.

Under the 1987 constitution, the executive president is elected for a five-year term by a two-thirds majority in the legislature or, if the required majority cannot be achieved, by a specially convened United People's Assembly including district and local council representatives. The vice-president is elected in the same way, and neither have term limits. The unicameral National Assembly has 51 members directly elected for a five-year term. The council of ministers is appointed by the president and chaired by the vice-president.

HEAD OF STATE

President, Chan Santokhi, *elected* 25 May 2020, *sworn in* 16 July 2020
Vice-President, Ronnie Brunswijk

SELECTED GOVERNMENT MEMBERS *AS AT NOVEMBER 2020*
Defence, Krishna Mathoera
Foreign Affairs, Albert Ramdin
Internal Affairs, Broto Somohardjo

HONORARY CONSULATE OF THE REPUBLIC OF SURINAME
127 Pier House, 31 Cheyne Walk, London SW3 5HN
T 07768-196 326 **E** ajethu@honoraryconsul.info
W www.honoraryconsul.info
Ambassador Extraordinary and Plenipotentiary, HE Reggy Nelson, *apptd* 2019

BRITISH AMBASSADOR
Ambassador Extraordinary and Plenipotentiary, HE Gregory Quinn, *apptd* 2015, resident at Georgetown, Guyana

ECONOMY AND TRADE

Former president Venetiaan introduced policies that contained rampant inflation and other economic problems, and produced steady growth for a few years before the global downturn, which caused the economy to contract owing to reduced global prices for key commodities. The economy contracted in 2015 and 2016, partly due to the withdrawal of a US mining company and a sharp depreciation in the Suriname dollar, but growth returned in 2017–19. The economy is expected to significantly contract in 2020 owing to the coronavirus pandemic, by an estimated 13.1 per cent.

The mainstays of the economy are mining, especially bauxite and gold, and oil and alumina production; these account for 85 per cent of exports and 27 per cent of government revenues, making the economy vulnerable to global price fluctuations. Bauxite reserves are declining, but oil production is increasing from existing offshore fields and onshore exploration has begun. Other industries include forestry, food processing and fishing. Industry accounts for 31.1 per cent of GDP and services for 57.4 per cent. Agriculture employs 11.2 per cent of the population and produces 11.6 per cent of GDP.

The main trading partners are the USA, Switzerland, the Netherlands and Hong Kong. Principal exports are alumina, gold, crude oil, timber, fish and shrimps, rice and bananas. The main imports are capital equipment, petroleum, foodstuffs, cotton and consumer goods.

GNI – US$3.2bn; US$5,540 per capita (2019)
Annual average growth of GDP – 1.9 per cent (2017 est)
Inflation rate – 22.0 per cent (2017 est)
Unemployment – 8.9 per cent (2017 est)
Total external debt – US$1.7bn (2017 est)
Imports – US$1,702m (2017)
Exports – US$2,277m (2017)

BALANCE OF PAYMENTS
Trade – US$574m surplus (2017)
Current Account – US$420m deficit (2019)

Trade with UK	2018	2019
Imports from UK	£7,112,764	£12,162,297
Exports to UK	£1,278,017	£696,101

COMMUNICATIONS

Airports and waterways – The principal airport and seaport is at Paramaribo
Roadways – 4,304km
Telecommunications – 96,310 fixed lines and 845,292 mobile subscriptions (2019); there were 292,685 internet users in 2018
Internet code and IDD – sr; 597 (from UK), 44 (to UK)
Media – The government operates Radio SRS Suriname and two TV stations, Algemene Televisie Verzorging and Surinaamse Televisie Stichting; there are two privately owned daily newspapers, *De West* and *De Ware Tijd*
WPFI score – 17.50 (20)

SWEDEN

Konungariket Sverige – Kingdom of Sweden

Area – 450,295 sq. km
Capital – Stockholm; population, 1,633,000 (2020 est)
Major cities – Gothenburg, Malmo, Uppsala
Currency – Swedish krona of 100 ore

Population – 10,202,491 rising at 0.79 per cent a year (2020 est)
Religion – Christian (Lutheran 60.2 per cent), other 8.5 per cent (including other Christian, Muslim, Jewish and Buddhist) (est)
Language – Swedish (official), Finnish, Sami, Romani, Yiddish, Meankieli (all official minority languages)
Population density – 25 per sq. km (2019)
Urban population – 87.7 per cent (2019 est)
Median age (years) – 41.1 (2020 est)
National anthem – 'Du Gamla, Du Fria' 'Thou Ancient, Thou Free'
National day – 6 June
Death penalty – Abolished for all crimes (since 1972)
CPI score – 85 (4)
Military expenditure – US$5,755m (2018)
Conscription – 18-47 years of age; 7–15 months (abolished in 2010, reinstated in 2018)

CLIMATE AND TERRAIN

The terrain is mostly flat or rolling lowlands in the south and along the east coast, with mountains in the west. Elevation extremes range from 2,111m (Kebnekaise) to −2.4m (reclaimed bay of Lake Hammarsjon). There are many lakes, including Vanern, Vattern, Malaren and Hjalmaren in the south, and over 20,000 islands off the coast near Stockholm. The climate is temperate in the south and subarctic in the north; average temperatures range from −7°C in January and February to 14.5°C in July.

POLITICS

Sweden is a hereditary constitutional monarchy. The 1975 constitution was amended in 1979 to vest the succession in the monarch's eldest child irrespective of gender. The unicameral legislature, the *Riksdag*, has 349 members directly elected by proportional representation for a four-year term. The prime minister appoints the council of ministers. Sweden is divided into 21 counties *(lan)* and 290 municipalities *(kommun)*.

Legislative elections in September 2014 saw the Social Democrats remain the largest party in the *Riksdag* and form a minority government with support from the Green Party. However, following budget disputes a new agreement was reached with the opposition centre-right Alliance coalition that allowed the government to continue to operate without holding early elections. The September 2018 legislative elections resulted in over four months of deadlock, due in part to the growth of the far-right Sweden Democrats, before incumbent Stefan Lofven continued as the head of a centre-left minority coalition.

HEAD OF STATE
HM The King of Sweden, King Carl XVI Gustaf, KG, *born* 30 April 1946, *succeeded* 15 September 1973
Heir, HRH Crown Princess Victoria, Duchess of Vastergotland, *born* 14 July 1977

SELECTED GOVERNMENT MEMBERS *AS AT NOVEMBER 2020*
Prime Minister, Stefan Lofven
Deputy Prime Minister, Isabella Lovin

Defence, Peter Hultqvist
Finance, Magdalena Andersson

EMBASSY OF SWEDEN
11 Montagu Place, London W1H 2AL
T 020-7917 6400 E ambassaden.london@gov.se
W www.swedenabroad.com/london
Ambassador Extraordinary and Plenipotentiary, HE Torbjorn Sohlstrom, *apptd* 2016

BRITISH EMBASSY
PO Box 27819, Skarpogatan 6–8, 115 93 Stockholm
T (+46) (8) 671 3000 E info@britishembassy.se
W www.gov.uk/government/world/sweden
Ambassador Extraordinary and Plenipotentiary, HE Judith Gough, CMG, *apptd* 2019

ECONOMY AND TRADE

Sweden developed from an agricultural to an industrial economy in the early 20th century. The prosperity that had funded the generous welfare state after 1946 ended in the early 1990s, when Sweden experienced a deep recession. It recovered to experience strong growth before briefly entering recession again in 2008–9 as a result of the global downturn. Sweden subsequently experienced strong growth thanks to investment in the construction sector but weaker global demand during 2020, in part due to the coronavirus pandemic, is expected to contract the economy by 4.7 per cent.

The Swedish economy relies heavily on exports, which are primarily found in the engineering and high-tech manufacturing industries, mining and forestry. Mineral resources include iron ore, copper, lead, zinc, sulphur, granite, marble, precious and heavy metals (the latter not exploited) and extensive deposits of low-grade uranium ore. The engineering sector is a key industry, particularly specialised machinery and systems such as electrical and electronic equipment and armaments, hydropower, motor vehicles and aircraft; other industries produce pharmaceuticals, plastics and chemicals.

Agriculture contributes 1.6 per cent of GDP, industry 33 per cent and services 65.4 per cent.

The main trading partners are other EU states, Norway and the USA. Principal exports include machinery, vehicles, paper products, pulp and wood, iron and steel products, and chemicals. The main imports are machinery, oil and petroleum products, chemicals, vehicles, iron and steel, foodstuffs and clothing.

GNI – US$574.3bn; US$55,840 per capita (2019)
Annual average growth of GDP – 1.29 per cent (2019 est)
Inflation rate – 1.9 per cent (2017 est)
Population below poverty line – 15 per cent (2014 est)
Unemployment – 6.78 per cent (2019 est)
Total external debt – US$939.9bn (2017 est)
Imports – US$221,100m (2017)
Exports – US$238,211m (2017)

BALANCE OF PAYMENTS
Trade – US$17,111m surplus (2017)
Current Account – US$22,345bn deficit (2019)

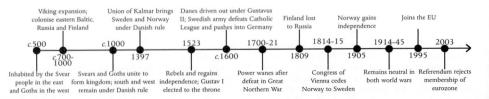

Trade with UK	2018	2019
Imports from UK	£5,510,742,032	£5,007,434,152
Exports to UK	£7,128,633,681	£6,527,467,617

COMMUNICATIONS

Airports and waterways – The principal airports are at Stockholm, Gothenburg, Lulea, Malmo and Umea; the main ports are Gothenburg, Helsingborg, Malmo and Stockholm
Roadways and railways – 573,134km, including 2,050km of motorways; 14,127km
Telecommunications – 1.9 million fixed lines and 12.8 million mobile subscriptions (2019); there were 9.3 million internet users in 2018
Internet code and IDD – se; 46 (from UK), 44 (to UK)
Major broadcasters – The public broadcasters are Sveriges Television (SVT) and Sveriges Radio
Press – Major daily newspapers include *Aftonbladet, Dagens Nyheter* and *Goteborgs Posten*
WPFI score – 9.25 (4)

EDUCATION AND HEALTH

The state education system provides nine years of free and compulsory schooling from the age of seven to 16 in the comprehensive elementary schools.
Gross enrolment ratio (percentage of relevant age group) – primary 128.6 per cent, secondary 151.7 per cent, tertiary 72.5 per cent (2018 est)
Health expenditure (per capita) – US$5,905 (2017)
Hospital beds (per 1,000 people) – 2.7 (2011)
Life expectancy (years) – 82.4 (2020 est)
Mortality rate – 9.4 (2020 est)
Birth rate – 12.1 (2020 est)
Infant mortality rate – 2.6 (2020 est)
HIV/AIDS adult prevalence – 0.18 per cent (2014 est)

SWITZERLAND

Schweizerische	Eidgenossenschaft/Confédération	suisse/
Confederazione	Svizzera/Confederaziun svizra	– Swiss
Confederation		

Area – 41,277 sq. km
Capital – Bern; population, 1,395,000 (2020)
Major cities – Basel, Geneva, Lausanne, Zurich
Currency – Swiss franc of 100 rappen (or centimes)
Population – 8,403,994 rising at 0.66 per cent a year (2020 est)
Religion – Christian (Roman Catholic 35.9 per cent, Protestant 23.8 per cent, other Christian 5.9 per cent), Muslim 5.4 per cent (est)
Language – German, French, Italian, Romansch (all official), Albanian, English, Portuguese, Serbo-Croatian, Spanish
Population density – 215 per sq. km (2019)

Urban population – 73.8 per cent (2019 est)
Median age (years) – 42.7 (2020 est)
National anthem – 'Schweizerpsalm'/'Cantique suisse'/'Salmo svizzero'/'Psalm svizzer' 'Swiss Psalm'
National day – 1 August (Confederation Day)
Death penalty – Abolished for all crimes (since 1992)
CPI score – 85 (4)
Military expenditure – US$4,796m (2018)
Conscription – 8–30, male only; 18 weeks mandatory training, then intermittent three-week refresher courses for the next 10 years

CLIMATE AND TERRAIN

Switzerland is the most mountainous country in Europe. The central plateau of hills, plains and over 1,500 lakes is enclosed by mountains. The Jura mountains lie in the north-west and the Alps, which cover two-thirds of the country, occupy the south and east. Elevation extremes range from 4,634m (Dufourspitze, Alps) to 195m (Lake Maggiore). Lakes Neuchâtel, Lucerne and Zurich lie wholly within the country, but Lake Maggiore is shared with Italy, Lake Geneva with France and Lake Constance with Germany and Austria. The Rhine, Rhône and Inn rivers all rise in the Alps. The climate is temperate, with conditions that vary with altitude. Average temperatures range from −1.5°C in January to 15.2°C in July.

HISTORY AND POLITICS

The area was conquered by the Romans in 58 BC and then overrun by Germanic tribes in the fourth century AD. It was a province of the medieval Holy Roman Empire from 1033. The Swiss confederation began in 1291 as a defensive alliance of three cantons to protect their autonomy, and expanded during the following centuries, becoming independent of the Habsburgs in the 14th century. Its independence was recognised by the Treaty of Westphalia in 1648. French revolutionary forces captured Switzerland in 1789 and named it the Helvetic Republic. Independence was restored in 1814, and the congress of Vienna (1815) joined Geneva, Neuchatel and Valais to the confederation and recognised the country's perpetual neutrality in international affairs.
Many policy decisions are submitted to national referendums. Although the federal government has pursued a policy of gradual integration with the EU and applied for membership in 1992, referendums have rejected membership of the European Economic Area (1992), approved bilateral trade agreements with the EU (2000) and rejected EU membership (2001).
Proportional representation, introduced in 1919, resulted in coalition governments throughout the 20th and into the 21st century. Since 1959 the federal government has primarily consisted of a coalition between the four largest parties: the Swiss People's Party (SVP), the Social Democratic Party (SP), the Christian Democratic People's Party (CVP) and the Free Democratic Party (FDP). The SVP remained the largest party in the National Council in the October 2015 and October 2019 legislative elections, but this state of affairs ended in the latter election due to a 'green wave' which saw large gains for the Green Party and Green Liberal Party.
Under the 1998 constitution, the head of state is a president elected annually (along with the vice-president) for a one-year term by the federal legislature from the members of the Federal Council; consecutive terms may not be served. The bicameral legislature, the Federal Assembly, has two chambers: the National Council has 200 members, directly elected for a four-year term; the Council of States has 46 members (two from each canton and one from each half-canton) directly elected within each canton for a four-year term.

Executive power is in the hands of a Federal Council of seven members, elected for a four-year term by the Federal Assembly after every legislative election. The Federal Council is chaired by the president. Not more than one person from the same canton may be elected a member of the Council; however, there is a tradition that Italian- and French-speaking areas should between them be represented on the council by at least two members.

HEAD OF STATE
President of the Swiss Confederation, Simonetta Sommaruga, *sworn in* 1 January 2020
Vice-President, Guy Parmelin

SELECTED GOVERNMENT MEMBERS *AS AT NOVEMBER 2020*
Economy, Guy Parmelin
Foreign Affairs, Ignazio Cassis

EMBASSY OF SWITZERLAND
16–18 Montagu Place, London W1H 2BQ
T 020-7616 6000 **E** lon.swissembassy@eda.admin.ch
W www.eda.admin.ch/london
Ambassador Extraordinary and Plenipotentiary, HE Alexandre Fasel, *apptd* 2017

BRITISH EMBASSY
Thunstrasse 50, 3005 Bern
T (+41) (31) 359 7700 **E** info.berne@fco.gsi.gov.uk
W www.gov.uk/government/world/switzerland
Ambassador Extraordinary and Plenipotentiary, HE Jane Owen, *apptd* 2018

CONFEDERAL STRUCTURE
There are 23 cantons, three of which are subdivided, making 20 cantons and six half-cantons, or 26 in all. Each canton and half-canton has its own government and a substantial degree of autonomy. The main language in 19 of the cantons is German; in six others it is French and one Italian.

ECONOMY AND TRADE
Switzerland has a prosperous and stable market economy with low unemployment and a highly skilled labour force. Its prosperity is based on banking, financial services and export-orientated industrial manufacturing. The economy went into recession in 2009 owing to slower export demand and the impact on the banking sector during the 2008 global financial crisis. Growth was slow 2013–19 due to the poor performance of the eurozone and the strength of the Swiss Franc, which made exports less competitive. In 2015 the Swiss National Bank actively sought to weaken the currency by unpegging it to the euro. Although not an EU member, Switzerland has brought many practices in line with the EU to maintain competitiveness, and has adopted OECD standards on tax administration and transparency owing to international pressure. The economy is expected to contract by 5.3 per cent in 2020 due to the coronavirus pandemic.

Agriculture is practised in the mountain valleys and the central plateau, where grains, fruits and vegetables are grown. Dairy farming and stock-raising are also important. The industrial sector is noted for precision, electrical and mechanical engineering, pharmaceuticals, chemicals, luxury consumer goods and textiles. Banking, insurance and tourism are the major service industries. Agriculture contributes 0.7 per cent of GDP, industry 25.6 per cent and services 73.7 per cent.

The main trading partners are EU countries (especially Germany) and the USA. Principal exports are machinery, chemicals, metals, watches and agricultural products. The main imports are machinery, chemicals, vehicles, metals, agricultural products and textiles.

GNI – US$773.1bn; US$85,500 per capita (2019)
Annual average growth of GDP – 1.11 per cent (2019 est)
Inflation rate – 0.5 per cent (2017 est)
Population below poverty line – 6.6 per cent (2014 est)
Unemployment – 2.31 per cent (2019 est)
Total external debt – US$1.664 trillion (2016 est)
Imports – US$367,300m (2017)
Exports – US$436,491m (2017)

BALANCE OF PAYMENTS
Trade – US$69,191m surplus (2017)
Current Account – US$79,941m surplus (2019)

Trade with UK	2018	2019
Imports from UK	£19,149,758,089	£12,074,141,631
Exports to UK	£6,821,229,875	£20,587,711,914

COMMUNICATIONS
Airports and waterways – The principal airports are at Zurich, Basel, Bern and Geneva; the Rhine carries commercial shipping on the 65km stretch from Basel–Rheinfelden and Schaffhausen–Bodensee, and there are 12 navigable lakes
Roadways and railways – 71,557km; 5,690km
Telecommunications – 3 million fixed lines and 10.6 million mobile subscriptions (2019); there were 7.4 million internet users in 2018
Internet code and IDD – ch; 41 (from UK), 44 (to UK)
Major broadcasters – The public-service Swiss Broadcasting Corporation (SRG/SSR), which is funded mainly through licence fees, dominates broadcasting
Press – Newspapers tend to be regional, reflecting linguistic divisions: major titles include *Neue Zürcher Zeitung* (Zurich based), *Le Temps* (Geneva) and *Corriere del Ticino* (Lugano)
WPFI score – 10.62 (8)

EDUCATION AND HEALTH
Education is controlled by cantonal and communal authorities and is free and compulsory from age seven to 16.
Gross enrolment ratio (percentage of relevant age group) – primary 105.5 per cent, secondary 102.6 per cent, tertiary 61.4 per cent (2018 est)
Health expenditure (per capita) – US$9,956 (2017)
Hospital beds (per 1,000 people) – 5.0 (2011)
Life expectancy (years) – 82.8 (2020 est)
Mortality rate – 8.5 (2020 est)
Birth rate – 10.5 (2020 est)
Infant mortality rate – 3.5 (2020 est)
HIV/AIDS adult prevalence – 0.2 per cent (2019 est)

SYRIA

Al-Jumhuriyah al-Arabiyah as-Suriyah – Syrian Arab Republic

Area – 185,180 sq. km
Capital – Damascus; population, 2,392,000 (2020 est)

Major cities – Aleppo (Halab), Hama (Hamah), Homs (Hims), Latakia (al-Ladhiqiyah)
Currency – Syrian pound (S£) of 100 piastres
Population – 19,398,448 rising at 4.25 per cent (2020 est); Arab (50 per cent), Alawite (15 per cent), Kurd (10 per cent), Levantine (10 per cent), other, including Druze, Ismaili, Imami, Nusairi, Assyrian, Turkoman and Armenian (15 per cent) (est)
Religion – Muslim (official) 87 per cent (Sunni 74 per cent, Alawi, Ismaili and Shia 13 per cent), Christian 10 per cent, Druze 3 per cent (est)
Language – Arabic (official), Kurdish, Armenian, Aramaic, Circassian, French, English
Population density – 92 per sq. km (2019)
Urban population – 54.8 per cent (2019 est)
Median age (years) – 23.5 (2020 est)
National anthem – 'Homat al-Diyar' 'Guardians of the Homeland'
National day – 17 April (Independence Day)
Death penalty – Retained
CPI score – 13 (178)
Conscription – 18, male only; 18 months

CLIMATE AND TERRAIN
There is a narrow coastal plain and ranges of mountains in the west, and the fertile basin of the river Euphrates in the north-east. The centre and south of the interior consist of semi-arid and desert plateaux. Elevation extremes range from 2,814m (Mt Hermon) to −200m (unnamed location near Lake Tiberias). There is a desert climate in much of the country, moderated by altitude in the mountains, and a Mediterranean climate on the coast. Average temperatures range from 6.4°C in January to 29.6°C in July.

POLITICS
In March 2011, protests against the ruling Assad regime broke out in a number of cities, including Damascus and Deraa. In May, the army was used to restore order in a number of towns. Many soldiers and commanders unwilling to use force against civilians broke away from the government, forming the Free Syrian Army, which began fighting against the administration. Mounting civilian casualties escalated the conflict, leading to the involvement of a number of different anti-Assad groups, including the Kurdish People's Protection Units (YPG) operating in the north-east of the country, Islamist groups and Hezbollah fighters from neighbouring Lebanon.

Following a chemical attack on the town of Ghouta by the Syrian air force in August 2013, the Syrian government came under sustained international pressure to abandon its stockpile of chemical weapons. In April 2014, 92.5 per cent of the country's chemical weapons were confirmed to have been removed or destroyed by UN observers. The government continued to cede control of its territory in 2015, losing control of Idlib province to Islamists in March, the Jordanian and Iraqi borders to secular and Islamist groups in March and June, and control of the eastern areas of the country to Kurdish fighters in June. In September, Russia entered the conflict in support of government forces; the Kremlin said its air strikes targeted Islamic State (IS) fighters, but many Western observers and the Syrian opposition claimed the attacks hit anti-Assad rebels. In December, the Syrian Army retook Homs after four years of fighting.

A partial ceasefire between the army and major rebel forces came into effect in February 2016, although it did not include IS fighters. In March, government forces retook Palmyra with Russian air support and in May the ceasefire was extended to Aleppo. In April 2017, the government was accused of killing

at least 74 people in a sarin gas attack on Khan Shaykhun, Idlib province, provoking an aerial response from the US. Following another suspected chemical attack in Douma in April 2018, chemical weapons storage facilities were targeted by US, UK and French air strikes. In January 2018, Turkish forces attacked Kurdish militias in northern Syria, and occupied northwestern Syria. IS, which held large areas of Iraq and Syria governing 10 million people in 2015, was destroyed as a landholding force in March 2019 by Kurdish and Western forces. Formerly rebel-held provinces were captured by al-Qaida-linked jihadist groups in early 2019. As the numerous factions reached a relative stalemate by the end of 2018, the Assad regime vowed to end the 'frozen conflict' in April 2019 and began an assault, with Russian assistance, on the rebel-held province of Idlib, during which the government was again accused of using chemical weapons. This assault continued into 2020, including clashes between advancing Syrian and Turkish forces prior to a ceasefire agreement signed in March. As of late November 2020, Idlib remained contested territory as Syrian, Turkish, Kurdish, Russian, Jihadist and US forces occupied territory, as well as Syrian rebels and Turkish-backed Syrian rebels.

By March 2020, the Syrian Observatory for Human Rights estimated up to 586,100 people may have been killed in the multi-sided civil war, more than 1 million had been injured and over 12 million (half the country's pre-war population) had been displaced.

In February 2012, a new constitution providing for multiparty elections was approved via a referendum. The majority of countries refused to recognise the outcome of the poll; exceptions included Russia and China.

HEAD OF STATE
President, Lt.-Gen. Bashar al-Assad, *elected* 27 June 2000, *confirmed by referendum* 10 July 2000, *re-elected* 2007, 2014
Vice-President, Najah al-Attar

SELECTED GOVERNMENT MEMBERS *AS AT NOVEMBER 2020*
Prime Minister, Hussein Arnous
Deputy Prime Minister, Defence, Maj.-Gen. Ali Abdullah Ayoub
Finance, Kinan Yaghi

EMBASSY OF THE SYRIAN ARAB REPUBLIC
8 Belgrave Square, London SW1X 8PH
T 020-7245 9012 **W** www.syremb.com
Closed due to the conflict

ECONOMY AND TRADE
Since the start of the civil war in 2011, the economy has declined by over 70 per cent thanks to widespread disruption and damage, international sanctions, migration, high inflation, low domestic demand, a depreciating currency and rising budgets. As government control has consolidated, some economic indicators have stabilised since 2017, including inflation. The humanitarian crisis continued in 2020, with more than 11 million Syrians believed to be in need of aid, 6.2 million said to be internally displaced and an estimated 5.7 million having fled to neighbouring countries; the situation has been further negatively impacted by the coronavirus pandemic.

Before the conflict, the economy was state-controlled and predominantly state-owned, but liberalising policies were being pursued. Oil and agriculture accounted for nearly half of GDP, although other activities, such as financial services, telecommunications, tourism and non-oil industry and trade, were becoming increasingly important.
GNI – US$70,501m; US$2,610 per capita (2010)
Annual average growth of GDP – −9.9 per cent (2015 est)
Inflation rate – 28.1 per cent (2017 est)

Conquered by the Turks	Becomes French-mandated territory	First war with Israel	Ba'ath Party becomes ruling party	Hafez al-Assad seizes power in a coup and is elected president	Death of al-Assad; Bashar al-Assad succeeds his father	Spread of pro-democracy protests triggers violent military crackdowns

Top timeline dates: c.600 | 1516 | 1946 | 1958–61 | 1967 | 1976 | 2005 | 2013

Bottom timeline dates: c.1000 | 1920 | 1948 | 1963 | 1970–1 | 2000 | 2011

| Conquered by Muslim Arabs | Becomes part of the Ottoman Empire | Gains independence | Forms part of the United Arab Republic with Egypt | Second war; loses Golan Heights to Israel | Begins intervention in Lebanon | Syria withdraws troops from Lebanon | ISIS formed; seizes territory in the east |

Population below poverty line – 82.5 per cent (2014 est)
Unemployment – 50 per cent (2017 est)
Total external debt – US$4.989bn (2017 est)
Imports – US$4,313m (2014)
Exports – US$2,250m (2014)

BALANCE OF PAYMENTS
Trade – US$2,800m deficit (2013)
Current Account – US$68,833m surplus (2018)

Trade with UK	2018	2019
Imports from UK	£10,777,820	£11,799,929
Exports to UK	£5,344,335	£5,179,141

COMMUNICATIONS
Airports and waterways – The principal airport is at Damascus; the main port is Latakia
Roadways and railways – 69,873km; 2,052km (2014)
Telecommunications – 3.1 million fixed lines and 21.1 million mobile subscriptions (2019); there were 6.1 million internet users in 2018
Internet code and IDD – sy; 963 (from UK), 44 (to UK)
Major broadcasters – Syrian Arab Republic Radio and Syrian TV are the public broadcasters; opposition groups operate TV and radio stations, including Al-Ghad (TV) and the Syrian Radio Network
Press – Only government-owned newspapers publish daily; leading titles include Al-Baath, Al-Thawra and Tishrin
WPFI score – 72.57 (174)

EDUCATION AND HEALTH
Education is under state control. Elementary education is free at state schools and is compulsory from the age of seven.
Literacy rate – 96.4 per cent (2015 est)
Gross enrolment ratio (percentage of relevant age group) – primary 80.1 per cent, secondary 50.5 per cent (2013 est); tertiary 39 per cent (2016 est)
Health expenditure (per capita) – US$66 (2014)
Hospital beds (per 1,000 people) – 1.5 (2014)
Life expectancy (years) – 73.7 (2020 est)
Mortality rate – 4.5 (2020 est)
Birth rate – 23.8 (2020 est)
Infant mortality rate – 16.5 (2020 est)
HIV/AIDS adult prevalence – 0.1 per cent (2019 est)

TAIWAN

T'ai-wan – Taiwan (Republic of China)

Area – 35,980 sq. km
Capital – Taipei; population, 2,721,000 (2020 est)
Major cities – Kaohsiung, Taichung, Tainan
Currency – New Taiwan dollar (NT$) of 100 cents
Population – 23,603,049 rising at 0.11 per cent a year (2020 est); Han Chinese (95 per cent), indigenous Malayo-Polynesian (2.3 per cent) (est)
Religion – Buddhist 35.3 per cent, Taoist 33.2 per cent, Christian 3.9 per cent, folk religions (including Confucian) 10 per cent (est)
Language – Mandarin (official), Taiwanese (Min), Hakka dialects
Population density – 618 per sq. km (2001)
Urban population – 81.1 (2019 est)
Median age (years) – 42.3 (2020 est)
National anthem – 'San Min Chu I' 'Three Principles of the People'
National day – 10 October (Republic Day)
Death penalty – Retained
CPI score – 68 (28)
Military expenditure – US$10,714m (2018)
Conscription – 18–36 years of age; 4–12 months
Life expectancy (years) – 80.6 (2020 est)
Mortality rate – 7.9 (2020 est)
Birth rate – 8 (2020 est)
Infant mortality rate – 4.2 (2020 est)

CLIMATE AND TERRAIN
The island of Taiwan (formerly Formosa) lies 145km east of the Chinese mainland. Mountains run the length of the island, covering over half the terrain, with lowlands in the west. Elevation extremes range from 3,952m (Yu Shan) to 0m (South China Sea). Taiwan shares the tropical monsoon climate of southern China, with large seasonal variations in temperature, dry winters and wet summers. The typhoon season lasts from May to November, with particularly high humidity between July and September. Average temperatures in Taipei range from 16°C in January and February and 29°C in July and August.

Territories include the Penghu (Pescadores) islands (80.47 sq. km), some 56km west of Taiwan, as well as Kinmen (Quemoy) (109 sq. km) and Matsu (7 sq. km), which are only a few kilometres from mainland China.

HISTORY AND POLITICS

Originally settled by Austronesian people 8,000 years ago, Chinese colonists arrived on the island from around the 12th century. The island was annexed by China in the 17th century, and ceded to Japan in 1895 at the end of the Sino-Japanese War. It was returned to China after Japan's defeat in the Second World War. The Kuomintang (KMT) government, led by Gen. Chiang Kai-shek, withdrew to Taiwan in 1949 after being defeated by the communists in mainland China. The territory remained under Chiang Kai-shek's presidency until his death in 1975. He was succeeded as president by his son, Gen. Chiang Ching-kuo, who ruled until his death in 1988. Martial law was lifted in 1987 after 38 years. In 1991 the Taiwanese government declared an end to the state of war with China, officially recognising the People's Republic of China for the first time, and ended emergency measures that had frozen political life in Taiwan since 1949.

Democratisation of the authoritarian one-party state began in the 1980s and led to the first multiparty elections in 1992. The 'Senior Parliamentarians' who had retained their seats since being elected on the mainland in 1948 were forcibly retired in 1991–2. From this point, power shifted away from the mainlanders to the native Taiwanese, and 50 years of KMT rule ended when the Democratic Progressive Party (DPP), which favours self-determination, won the presidency in 2000 and the 2001 legislative election.

The DPP retained the presidency and continued in government after the 2004 elections. However, in the 2008 elections the KMT returned to power, and the KMT candidate, Ma Ying-jeou, was elected president. The KMT retained its majority in the 2012 legislative election and Ma Ying-jeou was re-elected. The government resigned in November 2014 following poor local election results and in January 2016 Tsai Ing-wen of the DPP won the presidential election, becoming the country's first woman leader, while her party won 68 seats in the simultaneous legislative election. President Tsai Ing-wen was re-elected in January 2020 with 57 per cent of the vote; the DPP lost the seven seats in the simultaneous legislative election it retained its majority.

Most nations acknowledge the position of the Chinese government that Taiwan is a province of the People's Republic of China, and as a result Taiwan has formal diplomatic relations with only 15 countries and no seat at the UN. China has sanctioned the use of force to prevent Taiwan declaring itself independent.

Contacts between Taiwan and China began in the 1980s and have led to a gradual relaxation of restrictions on direct economic, trade and transport links, and on travel and tourism. After the KMT returned to power in 2008, Taiwan sought greater economic cooperation and integration with the mainland, but relations have deteriorated since President Tsai's election.

The 1947 constitution (which originally applied to the whole of China) has been amended a number of times since 1991. In 2004 an amendment provided for future proposed constitutional changes to be put to a referendum instead of the National Assembly (formerly the upper house of the legislature), which was disbanded under 2005 provisions that also reduced the number of legislative seats with effect from the 2008 election.

The president is directly elected for a four-year term, renewable once. The unicameral Legislative Yuan has 113 members: 73 directly elected, 34 elected proportionately by party and six elected by indigenous peoples in two constituencies; all serve a four-year term. The president appoints the premier and, on the premier's advice, the cabinet.

HEAD OF STATE

President, Tsai Ing-wen, *elected* 17 January 2016, *sworn in* 20 May 2016
Vice-President, William Lai

SELECTED GOVERNMENT MEMBERS *AS AT NOVEMBER 2020*
Premier, Su Tseng-chang
Defence, Gen. (retd) Yen De-fa
Finance, Su Jain-rong
Foreign Affairs, Joseph Wu Jau-shieh

ECONOMY AND TRADE

Since the 1950s Taiwan has transformed itself from a mainly agricultural country into a highly developed industrial economy. This transition was driven by exports. There has been a gradual shift away from state domination of the economy, with a reduction in government influence on investment and foreign trade, and privatisation in the financial and industrial sectors. Taiwan's export markets suffered severely in the global economic downturn and the economy contracted sharply in 2008–9. After achieving double-digit growth in 2010, the economy slowed in 2011–16 before rising to 2 per cent in 2017 and further accelerating 2018–19, thanks to increased exports. The new government has shifted trade towards south and south-east Asia, and has also benefited from trade deals signed with China (2010), New Zealand (2013) and Singapore (2013) and the USA. However, little has been done to tackle domestic concerns including youth unemployment, affordable housing, diplomatic isolation, stagnant wages and a rapidly aging population.

Only a quarter of the land area is suitable for agriculture but the soil is very fertile, producing rice, vegetables, fruit, tea, flowers, meat and dairy products. The industrial base includes electronics, communications and information technology products, oil refining, chemicals, textiles, iron and steel, machinery, cement, food processing, vehicles, consumer goods, pharmaceuticals and fishing. Agriculture contributes 1.8 per cent of GDP, industry 36 per cent and services 62.1 per cent.

The main trading partners are China, Japan, the USA and Hong Kong. Principal exports are electronic and computer equipment, flat panel displays, petrochemicals, vehicles, metals, plastics, ships and precision instruments. The main imports are electronic and electrical equipment, machinery, crude oil and natural gas.

Average annual growth of GDP – 2 per cent (2017 est)
Inflation rate – 1.1 per cent (2017 est)
Population below poverty line – 1.5 per cent (2012 est)
Unemployment – 3.73 per cent (2019 est)
Total external debt – US$181.9bn (2017 est)
Imports – US$322,224m (2017)
Exports – US$394,879m (2017)

BALANCE OF PAYMENTS

Trade – US$72,655m surplus (2017)
Current Account – US$48m deficit (2018)

Trade with UK	2018	2019
Imports from UK	£1,312,372,691	£1,463,677,968
Exports to UK	£3,456,398,159	£3,546,000,177

COMMUNICATIONS

Airports and waterways – There are international airports at Taoyuan (near Taipei), Kaohsiung and Taichung; the main ports are Keelung, Kaohsiung and Taichung
Roadways and railways – 43,206km; 1,613km
Telecommunications – 12.9 million fixed lines and 29 million mobile subscriptions (2019); there were 21.8 million internet users in 2018
Internet code and IDD – tw; 886 (from UK), 2 44 (to UK)

Broadcasters – The government runs two non-profit public broadcasters, Public Television Service and CBS-Radio Taiwan International
Press – Major daily newspapers include *United Daily News, China Times* (both Chinese language) and *The China Post* (English)
WPFI score – 23.76 (43)

TAJIKISTAN

Jumhurii Tojikiston – Republic of Tajikistan

Area – 144,100 sq. km
Capital – Dushanbe; population, 916,000 (2018 est)
Major towns – Khujand, Kulob
Currency – Somoni of 100 dirams
Population – 8,873,669 rising at 1.52 per cent a year (2020 est); Tajik (84.3 per cent), Uzbek (13.8 per cent) (est)
Religion – Muslim 98 per cent (Sunni 95 per cent, Shia 3 per cent) (est)
Language – Tajik (official), Uzbek, Kyrgyz, Russian (widely used in government and business)
Population density – 66 per sq. km (2019)
Urban population – 27.3 per cent (2019 est)
Median age (years) – 25.3 (2020 est)
National anthem – 'Surudi Milli' 'National Anthem'
National day – 9 September (Independence Day)
Death penalty – Retained (last used 2004)
CPI score – 25 (153)
Military expenditure – US$79.7m (2015)
Conscription – 18–27 years of age; 24 months
Literacy rate – 99.9 per cent (2015 est)
Gross enrolment ratio (percentage of relevant age group) – primary 100.9 per cent (2017 est); secondary 88.5 per cent (2013 est); tertiary 31.3 per cent (2017 est)
Health expenditure (per capita) – US$58 (2017)
Hospital beds (per 1,000 people) – 4.8 (2013)
Life expectancy (years) – 69 (2020 est)
Mortality rate – 5.8 (2020 est)
Birth rate – 21.8 (2020 est)
Infant mortality rate – 28.8 (2020 est)
HIV/AIDS adult prevalence – 0.2 per cent (2019 est)

CLIMATE AND TERRAIN
Tajikistan is mountainous, with the Pamir highlands in the east and the high ridges of the Pamir-Altai ranges in the centre. More than half of the country lies above 3,000m. Elevation extremes range from 7,495m (Qullai Ismoili Somoni) to 300m (Syr Darya river). The main rivers are the Syr Darya, flowing through the Fergana valley in the north, and the Amu Darya and its tributaries in the west and south. Most of the population lives on the fertile plains formed by these rivers. The climate is continental; average temperatures range from −8.6°C in January to 16.5°C in July.

HISTORY AND POLITICS
The area that is now Tajikistan was first settled by Iranian peoples 3,000 years ago and was conquered by Alexander the Great in the fourth century BC, remaining under Greek and Greco-Persian rule for 200 years until the kingdom of Kushan was established throughout the Bactria region.

Tajikistan was invaded by Muslim Arabs in the eighth century AD, and Islam was the prevalent religion by the time of the Samanid Persian conquest in the ninth century. In 1868, the northern part was subsumed within the Russian Empire, while the south was annexed by the Bukhara khanate. At the time of the Russian revolution in 1917 the Central Asian territories attempted to establish their independence, but Bolshevik power was consolidated in the north by April 1918, and in the rest of Tajikistan by 1920. In 1924 the Tajikistan Autonomous Soviet Socialist Republic was formed as part of the Uzbek Republic, before Tajikistan was given the status of a full republic within the USSR in 1929.

Tajikistan declared its independence on 9 September 1991. In 1992, anti-government demonstrations escalated into a five-year civil war between government forces and Islamic and pro-democracy groups. A peace accord signed in 1997 was implemented by 2000. Political assassinations and bombings occurred after the end of the civil war, but the level of violence has dropped since 2002.

Former communists have dominated politics since 1991 and power is concentrated in the president's hands. Opposition parties are weak and face harassment; a number of opposition leaders have been arrested on criminal charges, moves that their supporters claim are politically motivated.

President Rakhmon has served as head of state since 1992, and was re-elected for a fifth term in 2020. The October 2020 legislative election was again won by the incumbent (former communist) People's Democratic Party of Tajikistan; the only opposition party officially won just 0.3 per cent of the vote and no seats.

The 1994 constitution has been amended multiple times, following referendums, to introduce changes to the presidential term of office and the legislative structure. The executive president is directly elected for a seven-year term, renewable once. However, the 2003 amendment permitted the current incumbent to stand for two further terms, and a 2016 referendum allowed President Rakhmon an unlimited number of terms as the 'Leader of the Nation'. The bicameral parliament consists of the Assembly of Representatives *(Majlisi Namoyandogan)*, which has 63 members directly elected for a five-year term, and the Supreme Assembly *(Majlisi Milli)*, which has 33 members plus any living former president, 25 elected by five regional assemblies and eight appointed by the president. Administratively, Tajikistan is divided into two provinces, one capital region and the Gorno-Badakhshan autonomous region.

HEAD OF STATE
President, Emomali Rakhmon, *elected by Supreme Soviet*
    19 November 1992, *elected* 6 November 1994, *re-elected*
    1999, 2006, 2013, 2020

SELECTED GOVERNMENT MEMBERS *AS AT*
NOVEMBER 2020
Prime Minister, Qohir Rasulzoda
First Deputy Prime Minister, Davlatali Saidov
Deputy Prime Ministers, Yunusal Usmonzoda; Matlubakhon Sattoriyon
Defence, Col.-Gen. Sherali Mirzo

EMBASSY OF THE REPUBLIC OF TAJIKISTAN
FM House, 110 Clarendon Road, London W11 2HR
T 020-3609 8788 **E** info@tajembassy.org.uk
W www.tajembassy.org.uk

Ambassador Extraordinary and Plenipotentiary. Masud Khalifazoda, *apptd* 2018

BRITISH EMBASSY
65 Mirzo Tursunzoda Street, Dushanbe 734002
T (+992) 372 42221 **E** dushanbe.reception@fco.gov.uk
W www.gov.uk/government/world/tajikistan
Ambassador Extraordinary and Plenipotentiary, HE Matthew Lawson, *apptd* 2019

ECONOMY AND TRADE
Since the civil war, there has been steady economic growth but the economy remains fragile owing to the inconsistent implementation of structural reforms, corruption, poor industrial and transport infrastructure, energy shortages and high foreign debt. The country has benefited from debt cancellation and is receiving substantial aid, primarily to develop industrial and transport infrastructure. The economy is dependent on remittances, with around 90 per cent of the country's migrant workers residing in Russia; it is the poorest of the former Soviet republics. However, between 2000 and 2016 the population living in poverty declined from 83 per cent to 21 per cent. A thriving informal narcotics trade, an unstable banking sector and currency devaluations are significant problems, but foreign investment in hydropower could prove a vital revenue stream once the Roghun dam is finished around 2029.

Agriculture accounts for 28.6 per cent of GDP but 43 per cent of employment. Cattle-raising and cotton-growing predominate; other crops are grain, fruit, grapes and vegetables. Abundant mineral deposits are not fully exploited. Industry consists of aluminium and hydroelectric power production, mining (aluminium, antimony, gold, silver, tungsten and uranium) and production of cement, textiles and vegetable oil. Industry contributes 25.5 per cent of GDP and employs 10.6 per cent of the workforce. The services sector contributes the most to GDP at 45.9 per cent and employs 46.4 per cent of the workforce.

The main trading partners are China, Turkey and Russia. Principal exports are aluminium, electricity, cotton, fruit, vegetable oil and textiles. The main imports are petroleum products, aluminium oxide, machinery and equipment, and foodstuffs.

GNI – US$9.6bn; US$1,030 per capita (2019)
Annual average growth of GDP – 7.1 per cent (2017 est)
Inflation rate – 7.3 per cent (2017 est)
Population below poverty line – 31.5 per cent (2016 est)
Unemployment – 2.4 per cent (2016 est)
Total external debt – US$5.75bn (2017 est)
Imports – US$2,928m (2017)
Exports – US$1,307m (2017)

BALANCE OF PAYMENTS
Trade – US$1,891m deficit (2017)
Current Account – US$185m deficit (2019)

Trade with UK	2018	2019
Imports from UK	£2,330,909	£3,989,299
Exports to UK	£1,055,753	£1,320,090

COMMUNICATIONS
Airports and waterways – The main airport is at Dushanbe and there are 16 others around the country; 200km of the river Vakhsh is navigable
Roadways and railways – 30,000km; 680km
Telecommunications – 471,000 fixed lines and 9.7 million mobile subscriptions (2019); there were 1.9 internet users in 2018

Internet code and IDD – tj; 992 (from UK), 810 44 (to UK)
Media – The state-run Tajik TV and Tajik Radio are the state broadcasters; major newspapers include the government-owned *Jumhuriyat* (Tajik language) and *Khalq Ovozi* (Uzbek)
WPFI score – 55.34 (161)

TANZANIA
Jamhuri ya Muungano wa Tanzania – United Republic of Tanzania

Area – 947,300 sq. km
Capital – Dodoma (legislative capital); population, 262,000 (2018 est); Dar es Salaam (administrative capital); population, 6,048,000 (2018 est)
Major cities – Arusha, Mbeya, Mwanza, Zanzibar
Currency – Tanzanian shilling of 100 cents
Population – 58,552,845 rising at 2.71 per cent a year (2020 est); over 130 African ethnic groups on the mainland, of which Bantu (95 per cent) is the largest (est); Arab and African on Zanzibar
Religion – Christian 61.4 per cent, Muslim 35.2 per cent, folk religions 1.8 per cent (est); Zanzibar is predominantly Muslim
Language – Swahili, English (both official), Arabic (especially on Zanzibar)
Population density – 64 per sq. km (2019)
Urban population – 34.5 per cent (2019 est)
Median age (years) – 18.2 (2020 est)
National anthem – 'Mungu ibariki Afrika' 'God Bless Africa'
National day – 26 April (Union Day)
Death penalty – Retained (last used 1995)
CPI score – 37 (96)
Military expenditure – US$675m (2018)

CLIMATE AND TERRAIN
Tanzania comprises the former Tanganyika, on the mainland of east Africa, and the islands of Zanzibar, Pemba and Mafia. Most of the country lies on the central African plateau, from which rise mountains that run across the centre of the country from north-east to south-west. Peaks include Mt Kilimanjaro (5,895m), the highest point on the continent of Africa; the lowest point is 0m (Indian Ocean). Large areas of lakes Victoria, Tanganyika and Malawi (Nyasa) lie on the northern and western borders, and there are smaller lakes in the north-east and south-west. The Serengeti National Park covers an area of 9,656 sq. km in the north of the country. The climate is tropical, modified by altitude, with a rainy season from November to April except in coastal regions, which get most rain between March and May; rainfall is sporadic in the interior but more reliable and heavier on the coast.

POLITICS
The 1977 constitution was amended in 1992 to introduce multiparty elections, and in 2000 to allow the president to nominate up to ten members of parliament. The executive president is directly elected for a five-year term, renewable once. The president is always from Tanganyika and the vice-president is always from Zanzibar. The unicameral National

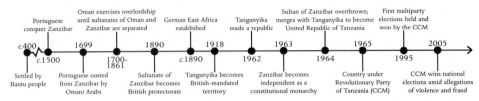

Portuguese conquer Zanzibar — c.400
Oman exercises overlordship until sultanates of Oman and Zanzibar are separated — 1699
German East Africa established — 1890
Tanganyika made a republic — 1918
Sultan of Zanzibar overthrown; merges with Tanganyika to become United Republic of Tanzania — 1963
First multiparty elections held and won by the CCM — 1965
— 2005

c.1500 — Settled by Bantu people
1700–1861 — Portuguese ousted from Zanzibar by Omani Arabs
c.1890 — Sultanate of Zanzibar becomes British protectorate
1962 — Tanganyika becomes British-mandated territory
1964 — Zanzibar becomes independent as a constitutional monarchy
1995 — Country under Revolutionary Party of Tanzania (CCM)
— CCM wins national elections amid allegations of violence and fraud

Assembly *(Bunge)* has 393 members: 264 directly elected, 113 seats reserved for women, ten appointed by the president (including five women), five chosen by Zanzibar's legislature, and the attorney general. All serve a five-year term. The *Bunge* enacts laws that apply to the whole of Tanzania and laws that apply only to the mainland; laws that apply specifically to Zanzibar are enacted by the island's own legislature, the 82-member House of Representatives. Zanzibar also has its own directly elected president (who is a member of the Union government) and legislature.

In the October 2015 national elections, John 'Bulldozer' Magufuli was elected president, while his Revolutionary Party of Tanzania (CCM) retained its overwhelming majority in the legislature. Magufuli was accused of overseeing a sharp crackdown on press freedom and political opposition, and was re-elected in October 2020 in an election the opposition labelled fraudulent. Hussein Mwinya was elected president of Zanzibar in simultaneous elections.

HEAD OF STATE
President of the United Republic, C-in-C of the Armed Forces, John Magufuli, *elected* 25 October 2015, *took office* 4 November 2015, *re-elected* 28 October 2020
Vice-President, Samia Suluhu Hassan
President of Zanzibar, Hussein Mwinya

SELECTED GOVERNMENT MEMBERS *AS AT NOVEMBER 2020*
Prime Minister, Kassim Majaliwa Majaliwa
Finance, Philip Mpango

HIGH COMMISSION OF THE UNITED REPUBLIC OF TANZANIA
3 Stratford Place, London W1C 1AS
T 020-7569 1470 E balozi@tanzania-online.gov.uk
W www.tanzania-online.gov.uk
High Commissioner, HE Asha-Rose Migiro, *apptd* 2016

BRITISH HIGH COMMISSION
PO Box 9200, Umoja House, Garden Avenue, Dar es Salaam
T (+255) (22) 229 0000 E bhc.dar@fco.gov.uk
W www.gov.uk/government/world/tanzania
High Commissioner, HE David Concar, *apptd* 2020

ECONOMY AND TRADE
State control has been dismantled gradually since the mid-1980s. Liberalisation and modernisation policies, supported by the World Bank, IMF and aid donors, have increased private-sector growth and investment. Between 2009 and 2019 annual growth averaged almost 7 per cent, however 26.4 per cent of the population still live below the poverty line. The expansion of foreign banking, increased gold production, infrastructure investment and improvements in education have all strengthened the economy in recent years.

Agriculture is the mainstay of the economy, accounting for 23.4 per cent of GDP, 66.9 per cent of employment and the majority of exports. It provides coffee, tea, cotton, pyrethrum, cashew nuts, grains, fruit and vegetables as well as the raw materials for industries producing sugar, beer, cigarettes and sisal twine. Zanzibar and Pemba produce cloves and clove oil, and coconuts and their derivatives. Increased output of minerals (chiefly diamonds, gold and iron) has driven recent economic growth, and salt, soda ash, cement, petroleum products, footwear, clothing, wood products and fertiliser are also produced. Tourism is a major source of revenue, especially for Zanzibar. Industry accounts for 28.6 per cent of GDP and services for 47.6 per cent.

The main trading partners are China, India, South Africa and Kenya. Principal exports are gold, coffee, cashew nuts, manufactures (especially clothing) and cotton. The main imports are consumer goods, machinery and transport equipment, industrial raw materials and crude oil.
GNI – US$60.8bn; US$1,080 per capita (2019)
Annual average growth of GDP – 6.98 per cent (2019 est)
Inflation rate – 5.3 per cent (2017 est)
Population below poverty line – 22.8 per cent (2015 est)
Total external debt – US$17.66bn (2017 est)
Imports – US$8,641m (2017)
Exports – US$8,683m (2017)

BALANCE OF PAYMENTS
Trade – US$42m surplus (2017)
Current Account – US$1,890m deficit (2019)

Trade with UK	2018	2019
Imports from UK	£110,191,477	£112,612,670
Exports to UK	£15,500,219	£17,160,348

COMMUNICATIONS
Airports – The principal international airports are at Dar es Salaam, Kilimanjaro and Zanzibar
Waterways – The three great lakes (Tanganyika, Victoria and Nyasa) are the principal trade routes with neighbouring countries; the main seaports are Dar es Salaam, Tanga, Mtwara, Zanzibar, Mkoani and Wete (Pemba)
Roadways and railways – 10,025km of paved roadways; 4,567km
Telecommunications – 74,081 fixed lines and 46.8 million mobile subscriptions (2019); there were 13.8 internet users in 2018
Internet code and IDD – tz; 255 (from UK), 44 (to UK)
Major broadcasters – The state-run Tanzania Broadcasting Corporation operates TV and radio stations
Press – Newspapers include the government-owned *Daily News* (English language), and Swahili *Habari Leo* and *Uhuru*
WPFI score – 40.25 (124)

EDUCATION AND HEALTH
Education is compulsory for seven years.
Literacy rate – 77.9 per cent (2015 est)
Gross enrolment ratio (percentage of relevant age group) – primary 98.8 per cent, secondary 32 per cent, tertiary 3.1 per cent (2019 est)
Health expenditure (per capita) – US$34 (2017)
Hospital beds (per 1,000 people) – 0.7 (2010)
Life expectancy (years) – 63.9 (2020 est)
Mortality rate – 7.1 (2020 est)

Birth rate – 34.6 (2020 est)
Infant mortality rate – 36.4 (2020 est)
HIV / AIDS adult prevalence – 4.8 per cent (2019 est)

THAILAND

Ratcha Anachak Thai – Kingdom of Thailand

Area – 513,120 sq. km
Capital – Bangkok (Krung Thep); population, 10,539,000 (2020 est)
Major cities – Chon Buri, Nonthaburi, Samut Prakan, Udon Thani
Currency – Baht of 100 satang
Population – 68,977,400 rising at 0.25 per cent a year (2020 est)
Religion – Buddhist 94.6 per cent, Muslim 4.3 per cent, Christian 1 per cent (est)
Language – Thai (official), Malay, Burmese; English is widely spoken as a second language
Population density – 136 per sq. km (2019)
Urban population – 50.7 per cent (2019 est)
Median age (years) – 39 (2020 est)
National anthem – 'Phleng Chat Thai' 'National Anthem of Thailand'
National day – 28 July (Birthday of the King)
Death penalty – Retained
CPI score – 36 (101)
Military expenditure – US$6,829m (2018)
Conscription – 21 years of age; 24 months

CLIMATE AND TERRAIN
Thailand is divided geographically into four regions: the north is mountainous and forested; to the north-east is the semi-arid Korat plateau; the centre is a fertile plain lying in the Chao Phraya basin; and the south is the narrow, mountainous isthmus of Kra. Extremes of elevation range from 2,576m (Doi Inthanon) to 0m (Gulf of Thailand). The principal rivers are the Chao Phraya and its tributaries in the central plains and the Mekong on the northern and eastern borders. The climate is tropical, with a monsoon season from June to October and high humidity.

POLITICS
On 22 May 2014, the Royal Thai Armed Forces conducted a military coup after months of political tension between the ruling Pheu Thai Party and the opposition People's Democratic Reform Committee. Following the successful corruption proceedings filed against Prime Minister Yingluck and her subsequent removal from office on 7 May, martial law was declared by the military on 20 May before a new military government. styled the National Council for Peace and Order, was established. The military government announced the end of martial law in March 2015 and a new constitution backed by the military was approved in an August 2016 referendum.
Thailand is a constitutional monarchy with a hereditary monarch as head of state. The bicameral National Assembly was re-established under the 2017 constitution, comprising a 250-member military-appointed senate, with senators serving five-year terms, and a 500-member house of representatives, elected for a four-year term. The first elections since the coup took place in March 2019, and were promised to restore democracy to the country but were marred by delays and irregularities. The military-backed coalition were victorious, with former army chief and leader of the 2014 coup Prayuth Chan-ocha continuing as head of the government.

HEAD OF STATE
HM The King of Thailand, King Maha Vajiralongkorn Bodindradebayavarangkun (Rama X), *born* 28 July 1952, *succeeded* 13 October 2016, *enthroned* 6 May 2019

SELECTED GOVERNMENT MEMBERS *AS AT NOVEMBER 2020*
Prime Minister, Defence, Gen. (retd) Prayuth Chan-ocha
Deputy Prime Ministers, Prawit Wongsuwan; Wissanu Kreangam; Jurin Laksanawisit; Anutin Charnvirakul; Don Pramudwinai *(Foreign Affairs)*
Finance, Arkhom Termpittayapaisith

ROYAL THAI EMBASSY
29–30 Queen's Gate, London SW7 5JB
T 020-789 2944 **E** csinfo@thaiembassyuk.org.uk
W www.thaiembassyuk.org.uk
Ambassador Extraordinary and Plenipotentiary, HE Pisanu Suvanajata, *apptd* 2017

BRITISH EMBASSY
14 Wireless Road, Bangkok 10330
T (+66) (0) 2 305 8333 **E** info.bangkok@fco.gov.uk
W www.gov.uk/government/world/thailand
Ambassador Extraordinary and Plenipotentiary, HE Brian Davidson, *apptd* 2016

FOREIGN RELATIONS
Sovereignty over border territory around the Hindu temple complex at Preah Vihear has been disputed with Cambodia for over a century. Although the temple complex was awarded to Cambodia in 1962, the status of adjacent territory remains unsettled. Tensions increased in 2008, when Cambodia had the temple listed as a UNESCO World Heritage Site, and there has been frequent sporadic fighting in the area between

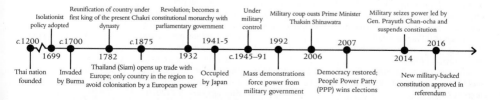

	Reunification of country under	Revolution; becomes a	Under	Military coup ousts Prime Minister	Military seizes power led by
Isolationist	first king of the present Chakri	constitutional monarchy with	military	Thaksin Shinawatra	Gen. Prayuth Chan-ocha and
policy adopted	dynasty	parliamentary government	control		suspends constitution

c.1200 — c.1700 — c.1875 — 1941-5 — 1992 — 2007 — 2016
1699 — 1782 — 1932 — c.1945–91 — 2006 — 2014

Thai nation	Invaded	Thailand (Siam) opens up trade with	Occupied	Mass demonstrations	Democracy restored;	New military-backed
founded	by Burma	Europe; only country in the region to	by Japan	force power from	People Power Party	constitution approved in
		avoid colonisation by a European power		military government	(PPP) wins elections	referendum

the countries' troops. Both nations agreed to withdraw their troops from the disputed border area in 2011, and in 2013 the International Court of Justice upheld the 1962 ruling and obliged Thailand to withdraw any armed forces stationed in the area.

ECONOMY AND TRADE

Thailand was transformed from an agricultural to an export-orientated industrial economy in the last quarter of the 20th century, sustaining steady growth after its quick recovery from the 1997 economic crisis. Poverty has significantly fallen in this period, afflicting 9.8 per cent of the population in 2018. The 2008 global economic downturn caused the export-dependent economy to contract sharply, and flooding reduced growth to only 0.1 per cent in 2011. Growth increased to 5.5 per cent in 2012, but the tourism sector initially contracted following the 2014 military coup before slowly recovering, helped by greater infrastructure spending. Growth since then has been hampered by the China-USA trade dispute, and the economy is expected to contract by 7.1 per cent in 2020.

The agricultural sector generates 8.2 per cent of GDP and employs 31.8 per cent of the workforce. The main crops are rice, cassava, rubber, maize, sugar cane, coconuts and palm oil. In recent years fishing and livestock production have grown in importance. There are reserves of natural gas, lignite and lead; Thailand is the world's second-largest producer of tungsten and third-largest producer of tin.

Other industries include textiles and clothing, agricultural processing, beverages, tobacco, cement, mining and light manufacturing (jewellery, electrical appliances, computers and parts), furniture, plastics and cars, and vehicle parts. A major industry is tourism, which has been a significant foreign exchange earner since the 1980s. Industry contributes 36.2 per cent of GDP and services 55.6 per cent.

The main trading partners are China, Japan, the USA and Malaysia. Principal exports are vehicles and vehicle parts, textiles and footwear, fish products, fuels, chemicals, rice, rubber, sugar, jewellery, computers and electrical appliances. The main imports are capital goods, intermediate goods and raw materials, consumer goods and fuels.

GNI – US$505.2bn; US$7,260 per capita (2019)
Annual average growth of GDP – 2.62 per cent (2019 est)
Inflation rate – 0.7 per cent (2017 est)
Population below poverty line – 7.2 per cent (2015 est)
Unemployment – 0.99 per cent (2019 est)
Total external debt – US$132bn (2017 est)
Imports – US$236,996m (2017)
Exports – US$305,111m (2017)

BALANCE OF PAYMENTS

Trade – US$68,115m surplus (2017)
Current Account – US$37,033m surplus (2019)

Trade with UK	2018	2019
Imports from UK	£1,475,634,476	£1,220,489,120
Exports to UK	£3,014,691,048	£2,999,371,574

COMMUNICATIONS

Airports and waterways – Bangkok is the main international airport and the main seaports are located in Bangkok and Sattahip; there are also 3,701km of navigable inland waterways (4,000km in total)
Roadways and railways – 180,053km, including 450km of motorways; 4,127km
Telecommunications – 2.6 million fixed lines and 128.1 million mobile subscriptions (2019); there were 39 million internet users in 2018

Internet and IDD – th; 66 (from UK), 1 44 (to UK)
Major broadcasters – The government and military both operate a number of TV and radio stations, including Thai TV3 and Radio Thailand
Press – Leading daily newspapers include the *Bangkok Post* and *The Nation* (both English language), and the *Daily News* (Thai)
WPFI score – 44.94 (140)

EDUCATION AND HEALTH

Primary and lower secondary education is compulsory and free, and upper secondary education is free in government schools.
Literacy rate – 93.8 per cent (2018 est)
Gross enrolment ratio (percentage of relevant age group) – primary 101.1 per cent; secondary 115.2 per cent (2019 est); tertiary 49.3 per cent (2016 est)
Health expenditure (per capita) – US$247 (2017)
Life expectancy (years) – 75.6 (2020 est)
Mortality rate – 8.3 (2020 est)
Birth rate – 10.7 (2020 est)
Infant mortality rate – 8.6 (2020 est)
HIV/AIDS adult prevalence – 0.1 per cent (2019 est)

TIMOR–LESTE

Republika Demokratika Timor Lorosa'e / Republica Democratica de Timor-Leste – Democratic Republic of Timor-Leste

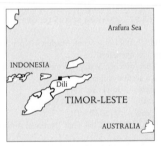

Area – 14,874 sq. km; includes the enclave of Oecussi
Capital – Dili; population, 281,000 (2018)
Major towns – Baucau, Los Palos, Maliana, Pantemakassar (Oecussi), Same
Currency – US dollar (US$) of 100 cents
Population – 1,383,723 rising at 2.27 per cent a year (2020 est); predominantly Malayo-Polynesian and Melanesian-Papuan. There is a small Chinese minority
Religion – Christian (Roman Catholic 97.6 per cent, Protestant 2 per cent) (est)
Language – Tetum, Portuguese (both official), Indonesian, English, around 32 indigenous languages
Population density – 85 per sq. km (2019)
Urban population – 30.9 per cent (2019 est)
Median age (years) – 19.6 (2020 est)
National anthem – 'Patria' 'Fatherland'
National day – 28 November (Independence Day)
Death penalty – Abolished for all crimes (since 1999)
CPI score – 38 (93)
Military expenditure – US$20.6m (2018)
Literacy rate – 68.1 per cent (2018 est)
Gross enrolment ratio (percentage of relevant age group) – primary 112.5 per cent, secondary 86.5 per cent (2019 est); tertiary 16.7 per cent (2011 est)
Health expenditure (per capita) – US$83 (2017)
Life expectancy (years) – 69.3 (2020 est)
Mortality rate – 5.7 (2020 est)

Birth rate – 32 (2020 est)
Infant mortality rate – 31.7 (2020 est)

CLIMATE AND TERRAIN

The republic comprises the eastern half of the island of Timor, plus the enclave of Oecussi, which lies on the northern coast, separated from the rest of the country by the Indonesian province of West Timor. The island, about 296km long and 72km wide, lies at the eastern end of the Malay archipelago and is the largest of the Lesser Sunda Islands. The interior is covered in forests and mountains. Elevation extremes range from 2,963m (Mt Tatamailau) to 0m (Timor Sea). The climate is tropical.

POLITICS

The 2002 constitution established a parliamentary democracy. The president, who holds extensive powers, is directly elected for a five-year term, renewable once. The unicameral National Parliament has 65 members, directly elected for a five-year term. The council of ministers is nominated by the prime minister, who is appointed by the president.

The 2017 presidential election was won in the first round by former guerilla fighter Francisco Guterres of the left-wing Fretilin party. In the 2012 legislative election, the National Congress for Timorese Reconstruction party (CNRT) emerged as the single largest party. Freitlin and the CNRT won the largest share of the votes in the July 2017 legislative election, but after parliament was dissolved in January 2018 fresh elections resulted in victory for the CNRT-led coalition, the Change for Progressive Alliance.

HEAD OF STATE
President, Francisco Guterres, *elected* 20 April 2017, *took office*
    20 May 2017

SELECTED GOVERNMENT MEMBERS *AS AT*
NOVEMBER 2020
Prime Minister, Interior, Taur Matan Rauk
Deputy Prime Ministers, Armanda Dos Santos; Jose Dos Reis
Defence, Filomeno Tirocinado da Paixao
Foreign Affairs, Adaljiza Magno

EMBASSY OF THE DEMOCRATIC REPUBLIC OF
TIMOR-LESTE
83 Victoria Street, London SW1H 0HW
T 020-3440 9025
Ambassador Extraordinary and Plenipotentiary, HE Gil Da Costa,
    apptd 2020

BRITISH EMBASSY
HE Moazzam Malik, CMG, *apptd* 2020, resident at Jakarta,
    Indonesia

ECONOMY AND TRADE

An internationally funded programme in 2002–5 achieved substantial reconstruction of the infrastructure destroyed in the 1999 post-referendum violence, but civil unrest in 2006 caused further damage and disrupted economic activity. Economic growth since independence is largely down to the exploitation of offshore oil and gas deposits, which has boosted government revenue but has had little impact on unemployment levels; there are no domestic production facilities so oil and gas are piped to Australia for processing. Poverty afflicts over 40 per cent of the population, and coupled with weak civil administration, a low skills base and inadequate infrastructure, economic development has been impeded. Dependence on oil, which accounts for 95 per cent of export revenues, has meant the economy is highly vulnerable to price fluctuations.

Industry contributes 56.7 per cent of GDP, services 34.4 per cent and agriculture 9.1 per cent, although it engages 41 per cent of the population. The main commercial crops are coffee, rice, maize, vegetables, tropical fruits, soya beans and vanilla. The main trading partners are Australia, Thailand, the USA and EU countries. Principal exports are coffee, oil, sandalwood and marble. The main imports are food, fuels and machinery.
GNI – US$2.4bn; US$1,890 per capita (2019)
Annual average growth of GDP – −4.6 per cent (2017 est)
Inflation rate – 0.6 per cent (2017 est)
Population below poverty line – 41.8 per cent (2014 est)
Unemployment – 4.4 per cent (2014 est)
Total external debt – US$311.5m (2014 est)
Imports – US$1,122m (2017)
Exports – US$109m (2017)

BALANCE OF PAYMENTS
Trade – US$1,012 deficit (2017)
Current Account – US$133m surplus (2019)

Trade with UK	2018	2019
Imports from UK	£266,130	£471,453
Exports to UK	£89,459	£155,864

COMMUNICATIONS

Airports and waterways – The international airport and seaport are at Dili
Roadways – There are 2,600km of paved roads, including one major road linking the main townships on the northern coast
Telecommunications – 2,164 fixed lines and 1.5 million mobile subscriptions (2019); there were 363,398 internet users in 2018
Internet code and IDD – tl; 670 (from UK), 44 (to UK)
Major broadcasters – Televisao de Timor-Leste and Radio Timor-Leste are the state-owned broadcasters
Press – Major daily newspapers include *Suara Timor Lorosae* (Tetum language), *Diario Nacional* (Portuguese) and the *Timor Post* (English)
WPFI score – 29.90 (78)

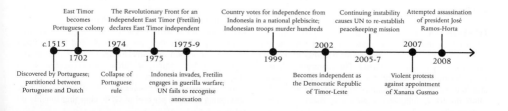

East Timor becomes Portuguese colony	The Revolutionary Front for an Independent East Timor (Fretilin) declares East Timor independent		Country votes for independence from Indonesia in a national plebiscite; Indonesian troops murder hundreds		Continuing instability causes UN to re-establish peacekeeping mission	Attempted assassination of president José Ramos-Horta
*c.*1515	1974	1975-9		2002		2007
1702		1975	1999		2005-7	2008
Discovered by Portuguese; partitioned between Portuguese and Dutch	Collapse of Portuguese rule	Indonesia invades, Fretilin engages in guerilla warfare; UN fails to recognise annexation		Becomes independent as the Democratic Republic of Timor-Leste		Violent protests against appointment of Xanana Gusmao

TOGO

République togolaise – Togolese Republic

Area – 56,785 sq. km
Capital – Lomé; population, 1,828,000 (2018)
Major cities – Atakpamé, Kara, Sokodé
Currency – Franc CFA of 100 centimes
Population – 8,608,444 rising at 2.56 per cent a year (2020 est); there are 37 ethnic groups, of which Adja-Ewe (42.4 per cent), Kabye (25.9 per cent) and Para-Gourma (17.1 per cent) are the largest (est)
Religion – Indigenous beliefs 51 per cent, Christian 29 per cent, Muslim 20 per cent (est)
Language – French (official), Ewe and Mina (in the south), Kabye and Dagomba (in the north)
Population density – 145 per sq. km (2019)
Urban population – 42.2 per cent (2019 est)
Median age (years) – 20 (2020 est)
National anthem – 'Salut à toi, pays de nos aïeux' 'Hail to Thee, Land of Our Forefathers'
National day – 27 April (Independence Day)
Death penalty – Abolished for all crimes (since 2009)
CPI score – 29 (130)
Military expenditure – US$104.4m (2018)
Conscription – 18 years of age; 24 months
Literacy rate – 63.7 per cent (2015 est)
Gross enrolment ratio (percentage of relevant age group) – primary 124.3 per cent (2019 est); secondary 61.8 per cent (2017 est); tertiary 14 per cent (2019 est)
Health expenditure (per capita) – US$38 (2017)
Hospital beds (per 1,000 people) – 0.7 (2011)
Life expectancy (years) – 66.6 (2020 est)
Mortality rate – 6.5 (2020 est)
Birth rate – 32 (2020 est)
Infant mortality rate – 38.5 (2020 est)
HIV/AIDS adult prevalence – 2.2 per cent (2019 est)

CLIMATE AND TERRAIN

From hills in the centre of the country, the terrain declines to savannah in the north and in the south to a plateau that leads to a coastal plain with marshes and lagoons. Elevation extremes range from 986m (Mt Agou) to 0m (Atlantic Ocean). The climate in the south is tropical with two wet seasons (March to July and September to November). In the north it is semi-arid with one wet season (May to September). The average temperature is 27.4°C.

HISTORY AND POLITICS

Germany established a protectorate, Togoland, over the area in 1884, and this was occupied on the outbreak of the First World War by Britain and France. The country was divided between Britain and France as a League of Nations mandate after the war and the mandate was renewed by the UN in 1946. In 1957, following a plebiscite, British Togoland

integrated with Ghana when it became independent. French Togoland achieved independence as the Republic of Togo in 1960.

There was a military coup in 1963 led by Gnassingbé Eyadéma, who installed a civilian president. In 1967 Eyadéma overthrew the government and became president himself, introducing a one-party state under his *Rassemblement du peuple togolais* (RPT). Violent demonstrations in 1990 forced the government to introduce a multiparty constitution in 1992. Eyadéma and the RPT were returned to power in the first multiparty elections in 1993 and in two subsequent elections.

After President Eyadéma's death in February 2005, the military attempted to install his son, Faure Gnassingbé, who resigned as acting president following widespread condemnation of the move, only to be elected to the presidency in April 2005. Following reconciliation talks in 2006, the government and opposition leaders signed an accord providing for the participation of opposition parties, and a national unity government was appointed until a legislative election was held in 2007. The election was nevertheless won by the RPT. Following the RPT's dissolution in 2012, the 2013 election was won by its successor party, the Union for the Republic (UNIR), led by President Gnassingbé. Popular and violent protests against Gnassingbé's rule in 2017 failed to prevent the UNIR winning the December 2018 legislative elections, which were boycotted by all major opposition parties, who claimed they were fraudulent. Gnassingbé won the February 2020 presidential election and was re-elected for a fourth term; opposition parties claimed irregularities occurred.

Under the 1992 constitution, the president is directly elected for a five-year term with no term limits. The unicameral National Assembly has 91 members, who are directly elected for a five-year term. The prime minister is appointed by the president and appoints the cabinet in consultation with the president.

HEAD OF STATE
President, Defence, Faure Gnassingbé, *elected* 24 April 2005, *sworn in* 4 May 2005, *re-elected* 2010, 2015, 2020

SELECTED GOVERNMENT MEMBERS *AS AT NOVEMBER* 2020
Prime Minister, Victorie Tomégah-Bogbé
Economy and Finance, Sani Yaya
Foreign Affairs, Robert Dussey

EMBASSY OF THE REPUBLIC OF TOGO
Unit 3, 7 and 8, Lysander Mews, Lysander Grove, London N19 3QP
T 020-7263 7522
Ambassador Extraordinary and Plenipotentiary, vacant

BRITISH AMBASSADOR
HE Iain Walker, *apptd* 2017, resident in Accra, Ghana

ECONOMY AND TRADE

Progress on economic reform, intended to attract foreign investment and balance the budget, has been slow, lacking impetus on privatisation and financial transparency. Resumption of aid to Togo, mostly suspended in the 1990s because of its human rights record, has increased since the 2007 election, and the country had 95 per cent of its external debt written off in 2010. Subsequent steady growth has been assisted by infrastructure spending, including a new airport terminal and seaport, and direct foreign investment. In January 2017, the IMF agreed a further loan package worth US$238m over three years.

The economy is predominantly based on agriculture, accounting for 28.8 per cent of GDP, engaging roughly 60 per cent of the workforce and providing most of the country's exports as well as the raw materials for industry. Industrial activity centres on phosphate mining, agricultural processing and manufacture of cement, handicrafts, textiles and beverages. Industry accounts for 21.8 per cent of GDP and 5 per cent of employment. The service sector accounts for 49.8 per cent of GDP.

The main export markets are Benin, Burkina Faso, Niger and India; imports come mainly from China and EU states. Principal exports are re-exports, cotton, phosphates, coffee and cocoa. The main imports are machinery and equipment, foodstuffs and petroleum products.

GNI – US$5.6bn; US$690 per capita (2019)
Annual average growth of GDP – 4.4 per cent (2017 est)
Inflation rate – -0.7 per cent (2017 est)
Population below poverty line – 55.1 per cent (2015 est)
Total external debt – US$1.442bn (2017 est)
Imports – US$2,377m (2016)
Exports – US$1,533m (2016)

BALANCE OF PAYMENTS
Trade – US$843m deficit (2016)
Current Account – US$184m deficit (2018)

Trade with UK	2018	2019
Imports from UK	£54,796,759	£21,727,912
Exports to UK	£3,402,573	£1,299,882

COMMUNICATIONS
Airports – The principal airport is at Lomé
Roadways and railways – 1,794km of paved roadways; 568km
Telecommunications – 45,311 fixed lines in use and 6.5 million mobile subscriptions (20119); there were 1 million internet users in 2016
Internet code and IDD – tg; 228 (from UK), 44 (to UK)
Major broadcasters – Public broadcasting is provided by Radio Togolaise, Television Togolaise and Telesports TV
Press – Major daily newspapers include *Togo-Presse, Liberté* and *Forum de la Semaine* (all French language)
WPFI score – 29.33 (71)

TONGA
Pule'anga Tonga – Kingdom of Tonga

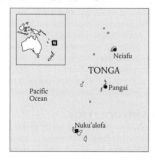

Area – 747 sq. km
Capital – Nuku'alofa, on Tongatapu; population, 23,000 (2018 est)
Major towns – Neiafu, on Vava'u, Pangai, on Lifuka
Currency – Pa'anga (T$) of 100 seniti
Population – 106,095 falling at 0.16 per cent a year (2020 est)

Religion – Christian (Protestant 64.1 per cent, Mormon 18.6 per cent, Roman Catholic 14.2 per cent), other 2.4 per cent (est)
Language – English, Tongan (both official)
Population density – 143 per sq. km (2019)
Urban population – 23.1 per cent (2019 est)
Median age (years) – 24.1 (2020 est)
National anthem – 'Koe Fasi Oe Tu'i Oe Otu Tonga' 'Song of the King of the Tonga Islands'
National day – 4 November (Constitution Day)
Death penalty – Retained (last used 1982)
Literacy rate – 99.4 per cent (2018 est)
Gross enrolment ratio (percentage of relevant age group) – primary 116.3 per cent, secondary 100.9 per cent (2015 est)
Health expenditure (per capita) – US$222 (2017)
Life expectancy (years) – 77 (2020 est)
Mortality rate – 4.9 (2020 est)
Birth rate – 21 (2020 est)
Infant mortality rate – 10.3 (2020 est)

CLIMATE AND TERRAIN
Tonga comprises over 170 islands in three groups, situated in the south Pacific Ocean some 724km east-south-east of Fiji. Most of the islands are of coral formation, but some are volcanic (Tofua, Kao and Niuafo'ou or 'Tin Can' Island). Elevation extremes range from 1,033m (on Kao Island) to 0m (Pacific Ocean). The climate is tropical, moderated by trade winds, with an average temperature of 25.4°C.

HISTORY AND POLITICS
The islands were settled by Polynesians from *c.* AD 1000. They were visited by European explorers from the 17th century. The country was reunited in 1845 after a civil war, and a modern constitution adopted in 1875. Tonga became a British protectorate in 1900, and regained full independence on 4 June 1970.

A pro-democracy movement began in 1992 and gathered momentum throughout the 1990s, with the first political party being established in 1994. Following consultation on political and constitutional reform in 2005 and negotiations in 2007, a commission reported in 2009, recommending reducing the monarchy to a ceremonial role and introducing a popularly elected legislature. These constitutional changes took effect with the 2010 legislative election.

In the 2017 legislative election, the Democratic Party of the Friendly Islands (DPFI) maintained power and extended its control over the Legislative Assembly.

The 1875 constitution was amended in 2003 to give greater powers to the king; the present king relinquished some of his executive powers in 2008 and most of the remainder in 2010, when the new constitutional arrangements came into effect. The unicameral Legislative Assembly *(Fale Alea)* has 26 members: nine hereditary nobles elected by their peers, and 17 popularly elected representatives who serve a three-year term. The 14-member privy council acts as a cabinet. The prime minister is elected by the legislature and appointed by the king.

HEAD OF STATE
HM The King of Tonga, King Tupou VI, *born* 12 July 1959, *acceded* 18 March 2012
Heir, HM Crown Prince of Tonga Tupouto'a 'Ulukalala, *born* 17 September 1985

SELECTED GOVERNMENT MEMBERS *AS AT*
NOVEMBER 2020
Prime Minister, Pohiva Tu'i'onetoa
Deputy Prime Minister, Sione Fa'otusia

Finance, Tevita Lavemaau

TONGA HIGH COMMISSION
36 Molyneux Street, London W1H 5BQ
T 020-7724 5828 **E** office@tongahighcom.co.uk
High Commissioner, Titilupe Tuivakano, *appt* 2018

BRITISH HIGH COMMISSIONER
HE Lucy Joyce, OBE, *apptd* 2020, resident at Suva, Fiji

ECONOMY AND TRADE
There are few natural resources and the country is dependent on foreign aid and remittances from Tongans working abroad. The government is encouraging the development of a private sector and committing increased funds towards education and health, while deep-sea mining and renewable energy offer investment opportunities. The island was badly damaged by Cyclone Gita in February 2018.

The main economic activities are agriculture, fishing and tourism; the latter is the second-largest source of foreign exchange revenue after remittances. The main crops are squashes, coconuts, bananas, vanilla beans, cocoa, coffee, sweet potatoes and cassava, but a large proportion of food is imported. Fish is an important export. A small light industry sector processes agricultural produce.

The main export markets are Hong Kong, the USA and New Zealand; imports come chiefly from Fiji, New Zealand and the USA. Principal exports are squashes, fish, vanilla beans and root crops. The main imports are foodstuffs, machinery and transport equipment, fuels and chemicals.

GNI – US$0.4bn; US$4,300 per capita (2018)
Annual average growth of GDP – 2.5 per cent (2017 est)
Inflation rate – 7.4 per cent (2017 est)
Population below poverty line – 22.5 per cent (2004)
Total external debt – US$189.9m (2017 est)
Imports – US$299m (2017)
Exports – US$114m (2017)

BALANCE OF PAYMENTS
Trade – US$185m deficit (2017)
Current Account – US$4.21m deficit (2019)

Trade with UK	2018	2019
Imports from UK	£416,826	£1,365,641
Exports to UK	£233,344	£240,411

COMMUNICATIONS
Airports and waterways – There is one airport; the principal port is Nuku'alofa
Roadways – 680km, of which 184km are paved
Telecommunications – 6,748 fixed lines and 63,156 mobile subscriptions (2019); there were 43,889 internet users in 2018
Internet code and IDD – to; 676 (from UK), 44 (to UK)
Media – The government-run Tonga Broadcasting Commission operates TV and radio stations; there are no daily newspapers
WPFI score – 27.27 (50)

TRINIDAD AND TOBAGO
Republic of Trinidad and Tobago

Area – 5,128 sq. km
Capital – Port of Spain, on Trinidad; population, 544,000 (2020)
Major towns – Chaguanas, San Fernando (Trinidad), Scarborough (Tobago)
Currency – Trinidad and Tobago dollar (T$) of 100 cents
Population – 1,208,789 falling at 0.3 per cent a year (2020 est)
Religion – Christian (Protestant 32.1 per cent, Roman Catholic 21.6 per cent), Hindu 18.2 per cent, Muslim 5 per cent, Jehovah's Witnesses 1.5 per cent (est)
Language – English (official), Trinidadian Creole English, Tabagonian Creole English, Caribbean Hindustani, Trinidadian Creole French, Spanish, Chinese
Population density – 271 per sq. km (2019)
Urban population – 53.2 per cent (2019 est)
Median age (years) – 37.8 (2020 est)
National anthem – 'Forged from the Love of Liberty'
National day – 31 August (Independence Day)
Death penalty – Retained
CPI score – 40 (85)
Military expenditure – US$169m (2018)

CLIMATE AND TERRAIN
Trinidad, the most southerly of the West Indian islands, lies 11km off the north coast of Venezuela. The island is mostly flat, with low mountains, the Northern Range, across almost its entire northern width and some low hills in the centre. Elevation extremes range from 940m (Mt Aripo) to 0m (Caribbean Sea). Pitch Lake, on the south-west coast, is the world's largest natural source of asphalt.

Tobago lies 30km north-east of Trinidad. The island has a range of hills, Main Ridge, running along its length; the highest point is 549m. Several islands, mainly, Chacachacare, Huevos, Monos and Gaspar Grande, lie west of Corozal Point, the north-west extremity of Trinidad.

The climate is tropical, with a wet season from June to December. Temperatures are constant all year round.

HISTORY AND POLITICS
Trinidad is believed to be the oldest site of human habitation in the Caribbean archipelago, with excavated human remains dating back 7,200 years. The islands were home to a number of indigenous peoples, including the Nepuyo, Yaio and Caribs.

Trinidad and Tobago were discovered by Columbus in 1498. Trinidad was colonised in 1532 by Spain, capitulated to the British in 1797 and was ceded to Britain in 1802. Tobago was colonised by the Dutch from the 1630s but subsequently changed hands numerous times until it was ceded to Britain by France in 1814. The two islands were amalgamated into a single British colony in 1889. Internal self-government was granted in 1959 and independence was attained in 1962; the country became a republic in 1976.

The People's National Movement (PNM) has dominated post-independence politics, only out of office in 1986–91, 1995–2001 and 2010–15. The PNM lost the early general election in 2010 to the People's Partnership coalition, which took office under Kamla Persad-Bissessar, the country's first female prime minister. The PNM reclaimed control of the House of Representatives the 2015 legislative election, with Keith Rowley becoming prime minister, and maintained a slim majority in the August 2020 election. Independent candidate Anthony Carmona was replaced by Paula-Mae Weekes unopposed in March 2018, another independent and the nation's first woman president.

Under the 1976 constitution, the president is elected for a five-year term by an electoral college consisting of both houses of the legislature, renewable once. The bicameral parliament comprises the House of Representatives and the senate. The former has 41 members directly elected for a five-year term plus the house speaker, who is usually designated from outside parliament. The senate has 31 members, of whom 16 are appointed on the advice of the prime minister, six on the advice of the leader of the opposition and nine at the discretion of the president, to serve a five-year term.

Since 1980 Tobago has had internal self-government through its House of Assembly, which has 16 members, 12 directly elected and four appointed, who serve a four-year term.

HEAD OF STATE
President, Paula-Mae Weekes, *took office* 19 March 2018

SELECTED GOVERNMENT MEMBERS *AS AT JUNE 2019*
Prime Minister, Keith Rowley
Attorney-General, Faris al-Rawi
Foreign Affairs, Amery Browne

HIGH COMMISSION OF THE REPUBLIC OF TRINIDAD AND TOBAGO
42 Belgrave Square, London SW1X 8NT
T 020-7245 9351 **W** www.tthighcommission.co.uk
High Commissioner, HE Orville London, *apptd* 2017

BRITISH HIGH COMMISSION
PO Box 778, 19 St Clair Avenue, St Clair, Port of Spain
T (+868) 350 0444
W www.gov.uk/government/world/trinidad-and-tobago
High Commissioner, HE Tim Stew, MBE, *apptd* 2015

ECONOMY AND TRADE
The country is the most prosperous in the Caribbean, owing largely to its oil and natural gas reserves, but the government has encouraged diversification into petrochemicals, aluminium, plastics, financial services and tourism to reduce its dependence on the energy sector. After years of strong growth, the economy contracted 2009–12 as export demand and oil prices declined, fell into recession again between 2014 and 2018, and reported nil growth in 2019. Crime and bureaucracy deter greater foreign investment.

The agricultural sector is small, accounting for 0.4 per cent of GDP; the main products are cocoa, rice, citrus fruits, coconut water, vegetables and poultry. Apart from oil and gas extraction and processing, the main industries are tourism, food processing, steel products, cement, beverages and cotton textiles.

The main trading partners are the USA, Russia, Argentina and Colombia. Principal exports are oil and petroleum products, liquefied natural gas, chemicals, steel products, beverages, cereals and cereal products, cocoa, fish, citrus fruits, cosmetics and plastic packaging. The main imports are fuels,

lubricants, machinery, transport equipment, manufactured goods, food, chemicals and livestock.
GNI – US$23.6bn; US$16,890 per capita (2019)
Annual average growth of GDP – –2.6 per cent (2017 est)
Inflation rate – 1.9 per cent (2017 est)
Population below poverty line – 20 per cent (2014 est)
Unemployment – 4.9 per cent (2017 est)
Total external debt – US$8.238bn (2017 est)
Imports – US$8,995m (2017)
Exports – US$11,059m (2017)

BALANCE OF PAYMENTS
Trade – US$2,063m surplus (2017)
Current Account – US$1,023m deficit (2019)

Trade with UK	2018	2019
Imports from UK	£134,555,382	£106,922,870
Exports to UK	£159,123,498	£103,094,648

COMMUNICATIONS
Airports and waterways – The international airport is at Port of Spain on Trinidad, and Tobago is served by Crown Point airport; the three main ports are Scarborough (Tobago), Port of Spain and Point Lisas
Roadways – 4,252km
Telecommunications – 298,493 fixed lines and 1.9 million mobile subscriptions (2019); there were 940,000 internet users in 2018
Internet code and IDD – tt; 1 868 (from UK), 011 44 (to UK)
Media – CTV and Talk City 91.1 (radio) are the state broadcasters; leading daily newspapers include *Newsday, Trinidad Guardian* and *Trinidad and Tobago Express*
WPFI score – 23.22 (36)

EDUCATION AND HEALTH
Education is free at all state-owned and government-assisted denominational schools, and at certain faculties at the University of the West Indies.
Literacy rate – 99.6 per cent (2015 est)
Gross enrolment ratio (percentage of relevant age group) – primary 106 per cent (2010 est); secondary 90 per cent (2011 est)
Health expenditure (per capita) – US$1,124 (2017)
Hospital beds (per 1,000 people) – 3 (2014)
Life expectancy (years) – 73.9 (2020 est)
Mortality rate – 9.1 (2020 est)
Birth rate – 11.4 (2020 est)
Infant mortality rate – 20.1 (2020 est)
HIV/AIDS adult prevalence – 0.7 (2019 est)

TUNISIA

Al-Jumhuriyah at-Tunisiyah – *Tunisian Republic*

Area – 163,610 sq. km
Capital – Tunis; population, 2,365,000 (2020 est)

Major cities – Sfax, Sousse
Currency – Tunisian dinar of 1,000 millimes
Population – 11,712,177 rising at 0.85 per cent a year (2020 est)
Religion – Muslim 99.1 per cent (official; predominantly Sunni) (est); small minorities of Christians and Jews
Language – Arabic (official), French, Berber
Population density – 74 per sq. km (2019)
Urban population – 69.3 per cent (2019 est)
Median age (years) – 32.7 (2020 est)
National anthem – 'Humat al-Hima' 'Defenders of the Homeland'
National day – 20 March (Independence Day)
Death penalty – Retained (last used 1991)
CPI score – 43 (74)
Military expenditure – US$844m (2018)
Conscription – 20–23 years of age; 12 months

CLIMATE AND TERRAIN

A central plain rises to mountains in the north, and in the semi-arid south merges into the Sahara desert. There are salt lakes in the west. Elevation extremes range from 1,544m (Jebel ech Chambi) to −17m (Shatt al Gharsah). The northern and coastal regions have a Mediterranean climate, while there is a desert climate in the south. Average temperatures range from 10.9°C in January to 30°C in August.

HISTORY AND POLITICS

The area was ruled successively by the Phoenicians, Carthaginians, Romans, Byzantines and Arabs before becoming a largely autonomous part of the Ottoman Empire in the 16th century. In the 19th century French influence grew and it was formally declared a French protectorate in 1883. It was briefly occupied by Germany during the Second World War (1942–3), and became independent as a monarchy under the bey, or governor, in 1956. In 1957 the bey was deposed and the country became a republic under one-party rule, with Habib Bourguiba as president.

Multiparty legislative elections were held in 1981, but the ruling party, the Constitutional Democratic Rally (RCD), retained its grip on power until 2011. Although proclaimed president for life in 1975, President Bourguiba was deposed in 1987 on the grounds of senility by the prime minister Zine el-Abidine Ben Ali. Ben Ali was subsequently elected president in unopposed elections in 1989 and 1994, and in multiparty elections in 1999, 2004 and 2009.

Nationwide protests against Ben Ali's authoritarian regime and unemployment broke out in December 2010, forcing him to leave office and flee the country in January 2011. Moncef Marzouki was elected interim president by the new Constituent Assembly in December 2011; his nomination followed legislative elections in which the former opposition party al-Nahda won the most seats but not an overall majority. Attempts to implement some Islamic reforms by the moderate Islamist government resulted in protests by supporters of secularism and more violent demonstrations from Salafi Islamists.

In July 2013, the assassination of the Arab nationalist politician Mohamed Brahmi caused a general strike and calls for the government to resign. An interim government was created in December 2013, with new electoral laws approved in May 2014. In the October 2014 legislative elections, the secular Nidaa Tounes emerged as the single largest party, winning 85 seats, and formed a coalition in February 2015. Nidaa Tounes lost significant support in the October 2019 parliamentary election, in which no one party gained a majority. After months of negotiations a coalition was formed led by the largest party in February 2020, the Ennahda

Movement, as the economic situation continued to deteriorate. Following the death of President Beji Caid Essebsi in July 2019, independent candidate Kais Saied was elected as his successor in October 2019.

The new constitution was implemented on 26 January 2014. The president is directly elected by absolute majority popular vote for a five-year term, renewable once. The legislature, the Assembly of People's Representatives *(Majlis Nuwab al-Shab)*, is unicameral and directly elected for a five-year term. It has 217 seats, 18 of which are reserved for Tunisians abroad.

HEAD OF STATE

President, Kais Saied, *elected* 13 October 2019, *sworn in* 23 October 2019

SELECTED GOVERNMENT MEMBERS *AS AT NOVEMBER 2020*
Prime Minister, Hichem Mechichi
Finance, Ali Kooli
Foreign Affairs, Othman Jerandi
Interior, Taoufik Charfeddine

EMBASSY OF TUNISIA
29 Prince's Gate, London SW7 1QG
T 020-7584 8117 **E** london@tunisianembassy.co.uk
W www.at-londres.diplomatie.gov.tn
Ambassador Extraordinary and Plenipotentiary, HE Nabil Ben Khedher, *apptd* 2017

BRITISH EMBASSY
Rue du Lac Windermere, Les Berges du Lac, 1053 Tunis
T (+216) (71) 108 700 **E** britishembassytunis@fco.gov.uk
W www.gov.uk/government/world/tunisia
Ambassador Extraordinary and Plenipotentiary, HE Louise de Sousa, *apptd* 2016

ECONOMY AND TRADE

The economy is diverse and an increasing proportion is in private ownership, but limited by corruption, inequality and a depleted tourism industry. Growth was steady from the late 1990s until 2008, although the economy contracted in 2009 as export demand dropped. The 2011 Arab Spring led to years of economic neglect amid political instability that resulted in several credit rating downgrades. The economy suffered further due to terrorist attacks on tourist sites in 2015, in which nearly 60 people were killed, coupled with unrest in 2016 provoked by high unemployment. A sizeable informal economy, high levels of joblessness especially among youth, economic disparities between the more developed coastal region and the impoverished interior, and strikes in the phosphate sector have also slowed economic growth. The economy remains fragile, and is expected to contract by 7 per cent in 2020 owing to the coronavirus pandemic.

Agriculture and fisheries account for 10.1 per cent of GDP; the main products are olives, grain, tomatoes, citrus fruits, sugar beets, dates, almonds, meat and dairy products. The main industries are oil production, mining (principally phosphates and iron ore), tourism, processing agricultural products and manufacture of textiles, footwear and beverages.

The main trading partners are EU countries, especially France and Italy. Principal exports are clothing, semi-finished goods and textiles, agricultural products, mechanical goods, phosphates and chemicals, hydrocarbons and electrical equipment. The main imports are textiles, machinery and equipment, hydrocarbons, chemicals and foodstuffs.

GNI – US$39.3bn; US$3,360 per capita (2019)
Annual average growth of GDP – 2 per cent (2017 est)
Inflation rate – 5.3 per cent (2017 est)
Population below poverty line – 15.5 per cent (2010 est)

Unemployment – 15.5 per cent (2017 est)
Total external debt – US$30.19bn (2017 est)
Imports – US$22,498m (2017)
Exports – US$17,489m (2017)

BALANCE OF PAYMENTS
Trade – US$5,009m deficit (2017)
Current Account – US$3,284m deficit (2019)

Trade with UK	2018	2019
Imports from UK	£160,245,910	£172,615,567
Exports to UK	£158,360,400	£189,468,461

COMMUNICATIONS
Airports and waterways – The principal airports are at Tunis, Monastir and Djerba, and the main ports include Bizerte, Sfax and Rades
Roadways and railways – 20,000km; 2,173km
Telecommunications – 1.4 million fixed lines and 14.7 million mobile subscriptions (2019); there were 7.4 million internet users in 2018
Internet code and IDD – tn; 216 (from UK), 44 (to UK)
Major broadcasters – Al-Watania (TV) and Tunisian Radio are the state broadcasters
Press – Major daily newspapers include *La Presse* (French language), and *Esshafa* and *Assabah* (both Arabic)
WPFI score – 29.45 (72)

EDUCATION AND HEALTH
There are 11 years of free and compulsory education.
Literacy rate – 98.1 per cent (2015 est)
Gross enrolment ratio (percentage of relevant age group) – primary 115.4 per cent (2018 est); secondary 92.9 per cent (2016 est); tertiary 31.8 per cent (2019 est)
Health expenditure (per capita) – US$251 (2017)
Hospital beds (per 1,000 people) – 2.2 (2014)
Life expectancy (years) – 76.3 (2020 est)
Mortality rate – 6.4 (2020 est)
Birth rate – 15.9 (2020 est)
Infant mortality rate – 11 (2020 est)
HIV/AIDS adult prevalence – 0.1 per cent (2019 est)

TURKEY

Turkiye Cumhuriyeti – Republic of Turkey

Area – 783,562 sq. km
Capital – Ankara (Angora), in Asia; population, 5,118,000 (2020 est)
Major cities – Adana, Antalya, Bursa, Gaziantep, Istanbul, Izmir, Konya
Currency – Turkish lira (TL) of 100 kurus

Population – 82,017,514 rising at 0.45 per cent a year (2020 est); Turkish (70–75 per cent), Kurdish (19 per cent) (est)
Religion – Muslim (predominantly Sunni) 99.8 per cent (est); small minorities of Christians and Jews
Language – Turkish (official), Kurdish
Population density – 107 per sq. km (2019)
Urban population – 75.6 per cent (2019 est)
Median age (years) – 32.2 (2020 est)
National anthem – 'Istiklal Marsi' 'The Independence March'
National day – 29 October (Republic Day)
Death penalty – Abolished for all crimes (since 2004)
CPI score – 39 (91)
Military expenditure – US$18,967m (2018)
Conscription – 21–41 years of age, male only; 12 months (selective); expected to implement a new five-tier conscription system at the end of 2019

CLIMATE AND TERRAIN
Turkey in Europe consists of the relatively low-lying area of Eastern Thrace, including the cities of Istanbul and Edirne, and is separated from Asia by the Bosporus at Istanbul and by the Sea of Marmara and the Dardanelles (a strait about 64km in length, with a width varying from 1.6km to 6.4km).
Turkey in Asia comprises the whole of Asia Minor or Anatolia. Western Anatolia consists of a high central plateau with narrow coastal plains fringed by mountains in the north and south. Eastern Anatolia is mountainous, the land falling to a plateau between the mountains and the Syrian border. Elevation extremes range from 5,166m (Mt Ararat) to 0m (Mediterranean Sea). The Euphrates and Tigris rivers rise in the eastern mountains, which also contain many lakes, including Lake Van. Anatolia is prone to earthquakes.
The climate is temperate, but more extreme in the interior. Average temperatures range from 0.2°C in January to 23.1°C in August.

POLITICS
The 1982 constitution has been amended several times, significantly in 2010 when parliamentary control over the judiciary and the military was increased, and to strengthen executive power following a failed military coup in July 2016. Since June 2018, the president is directly elected for a five-year term, renewable once. The unicameral Turkish Grand National Assembly has 600 members who are directly elected for a five-year term. The office of prime minister was abolished in 2018 to consolidate presidential power, and the post of vice-president was introduced.
Tension between secularists and Islamists has grown in recent years, particularly since the Islamic-based Justice and Development Party (AKP), led by Recep Tayyip Erdogan, came to power in 2002. Secularists' concerns about the AKP's agenda caused a four-month political crisis in 2007, preventing the election of a new president and leading outgoing President Sezer to refuse approval of constitutional amendments. The impasse was ended by early legislative elections in July 2007, in which the AKP-led coalition won a greatly increased majority.
The AKP-led coalition retained power following the June 2018 legislative elections, securing 344 seats. The pro-Kurdish People's Democratic Party (HDP) won 67 seats, while an alliance of three opposition parties opposed to Erdogan's presidential reforms won 189 seats. In simultaneous presidential elections President Erdogan consolidated his grip on the country following the 2016 attempted military coup. Constitutional amendments paving the way for an executive presidency were approved in April 2017, and potentially allow Erdogan to rule until 2032. President Erdogan's rule in recent years has been

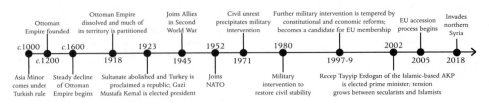

Timeline:

Ottoman Empire founded	Ottoman Empire dissolved and much of its territory is partitioned	Joins Allies in Second World War	Civil unrest precipitates military intervention	Further military intervention is tempered by constitutional and economic reforms; becomes a candidate for EU membership	EU accession process begins	Invades northern Syria

c.1000   c.1600   1923   1952   1980   2002
c.1200   1918   1945   1971   1997-9   2005   2018

Asia Minor comes under Turkish rule | Steady decline of Ottoman Empire begins | Sultanate abolished and Turkey is proclaimed a republic; Gazi Mustafa Kemal is elected president | Joins NATO | Military intervention to restore civil stability | Recep Tayyip Erdogan of the Islamic-based AKP is elected prime minister; tension grows between secularists and Islamists

characterised by democratic backsliding, a crackdown on media freedom and a more expansionist foreign policy.

HEAD OF STATE

President, Recep Tayyip Erdogan, *elected* 10 August 2014, *sworn in* 28 August 2014, *re-elected* 24 June 2018
Vice-President, Fuat Oktay

SELECTED GOVERNMENT MEMBERS *AS AT NOVEMBER 2020*

Defence, Hulusi Akar
Finance, Lutfi Elvan
Foreign Affairs, Mevlut Cavusoglu

EMBASSY OF THE REPUBLIC OF TURKEY

43 Belgrave Square, London SW1X 8PA
T 020-7393 0202 **E** embassy.london@mfa.gov.tr
W www.london.emb.mfa.gov.tr
Ambassador Extraordinary and Plenipotentiary, HE Umit Yalcin, *apptd* 2018

BRITISH EMBASSY

Sehit Ersan Caddesi 46/A, Cankaya, Ankara
T (+90) (312) 455 3344 **E** info.officer@fco.gov.uk
W www.gov.uk/government/world/turkey
Ambassador Extraordinary and Plenipotentiary, HE Sir Dominick Chilcott, KCMG, *apptd* 2018

INSURGENCIES

Turkey's 12 million Kurds are the majority population in the south-east of the country, and have sought greater political and cultural rights for many years. The Kurdistan Workers' Party (PKK) has fought a guerrilla war for an ethnic homeland in the south-east since 1984 and has been blamed for bombings in other parts of Turkey. Conflict on the Turkey–Iraq border has caused tension in relations with Iraq, especially in 2008 after Turkish military incursions into the autonomous Kurdish area in northern Iraq. The government started to seek a political solution to the violence in 2009, introducing measures to increase Kurdish language rights and reduce the military presence in the south-east.

Following a statement requesting a ceasefire by jailed PKK leader Abdullah Ocalan, Kurdish fighters withdrew from Turkey in 2013. In July 2015, the Turkish Air Force bombed PKK bases in Iraq following an apparent attack by the PKK near the Turkish town of Diyarbakir that killed two soldiers. In early 2016, a hardline faction of the PKK called the Kurdistan Freedom Hawks (TAK) claimed responsibility for at least two bomb attacks in Ankara that killed 75 people in total. In January 2018, Turkish forces began an invasion of Kurdish-held territory in northern Syria (*see* Syria), which included attacking the USA's Kurdish allies, causing hundreds of thousands to flee the region. After President Trump ordered the withdrawal of US troops in October 2019, a week-long assault by Turkish forces displaced 200,000 people before a ceasefire was brokered. Amnesty International claimed the Turkish military committed war crimes, including summary executions and the indiscriminate killing of civilians.

ECONOMY AND TRADE

The economy combines modern industry and commerce with a traditional agriculture sector. The private sector is growing steadily following large-scale privatisations of basic industry, banking, transport and communications. Since 2016 the economy has relied on external investment to finance growth, meaning recent government interference to target political opponents has shaken confidence. Financial and fiscal reforms from 2002 achieved economic growth, but continued violence – notably a terror attack on Istanbul's Ataturk airport in June 2016 – means that political instability and security concerns remain. Sanctions imposed by the US in 2018 over diplomatic disputes, including Turkish aggression against US allies in Syria, resulted in the lira plummeting 34 per cent against the US dollar in the first seven months of the year, hitting a record low in August 2018. A small recovery in 2019 was followed by a contraction in 2020 due to the coronavirus pandemic; the economy is expected to contract by 5 per cent in 2020. Declining oil export revenues, rising unemployment and inflation, and a large government deficit have limited investor confidence.

The agricultural sector accounts for 6.8 per cent of GDP and employs 18.4 per cent of the workforce. The principal crops are tobacco, cotton, grain, olives, sugar beets, pulses, nuts, citrus and other fruits, and livestock products. A diverse industrial sector is dominated by textiles and clothing, but the automotive, electronics and petrochemical sectors have recently overtaken the former in exports. Food processing, mining, iron and steel, construction, timber and paper are also important industries. Turkey is also a destination and a transit route for oil and gas from central Asian countries. Tourism is a major industry and source of foreign revenue. Industry contributes 32.3 per cent of GDP and services 60.7 per cent.

The main trading partners are EU countries (especially Germany), Russia, China and the UAE. Principal exports are clothing, foodstuffs, textiles, metal manufactures and transport equipment. The main imports are machinery, chemicals, semi-finished manufactures, fuels and transport equipment.

GNI – US$801.4bn; US$9,610 per capita (2019)
Annual average growth of GDP – 0.98 per cent (2019 est)
Inflation rate – 11.1 per cent (2017 est)
Population below poverty line – 21.9 per cent (2015 est)
Unemployment – 13.68 per cent (2019 est)
Total external debt – US$452.4bn (2017 est)
Imports – US$249,169m (2017)
Exports – US$210,163m (2017)

BALANCE OF PAYMENTS

Trade – US$39,006m deficit (2017)
Current Account – US$6,909m surplus (2019)

Trade with UK	2018	2019
Imports from UK	£7,044,451,167	£5,023,297,519
Exports to UK	£8,944,080,236	£9,664,414,125

COMMUNICATIONS

Airports and waterways – The principal airports are at Istanbul and Ankara, and the main ports are at Istanbul (Europe) and Izmir (Asia)

Roadways and railways – 24,082km, including 2,159km of motorways; 12,710km

Telecommunications – 11.3 million fixed lines and 79.1 million mobile subscriptions (2019); there were 57.7 million internet users in 2018

Internet code and IDD – tr; 90 (from UK), 44 (to UK)

Major broadcasters – Turkish Radio Television (TRT) is the country's public broadcaster, and the country has over 300 private television channels and more than 1,000 private radio stations

Press – Major national daily newspapers include *Hurriyet, Milliyet* and *Cumhuriyet*

WPFI score – 50.02 (154)

EDUCATION AND HEALTH

Education is free and compulsory from the ages of six to 14.

Literacy rate – 96.2 per cent (2017 est)

Gross enrolment ratio (percentage of relevant age group) – primary 94.9 per cent, secondary 104.5 per cent, tertiary 113.2 per cent (2018 est)

Health expenditure (per capita) – US$445 (2017)

Hospital beds (per 1,000 people) – 2.7 (2013)

Life expectancy (years) – 75.7 (2020 est)

Mortality rate – 6.1 (2020 est)

Birth rate – 14.8 (2020 est)

Infant mortality rate – 15.8 (2020 est)

TURKMENISTAN

Area – 488,100 sq. km

Capital – Ashgabat; population, 846,000 (2018)

Major cities – Dashoguz, Turkmenabat

Currency – Manat of 100 tennesi

Population – 5,528,627 rising at 1.06 per cent a year (2020 est); Turkmen (85 per cent), Uzbek (5 per cent), Russian (4 per cent) (est)

Religion – Muslim 89 per cent, Christian 9 per cent (Orthodox) (est)

Language – Turkmen (official), Russian, Uzbek

Population density – 12 per sq. km (2019)

Urban population – 52 per cent (2019 est)

Median age (years) – 29.2 (2020 est)

National anthem – 'Garassyz, Bitarap Turkmenistanyn Dowlet Gimni' 'National Anthem of Independent, Neutral Turkmenistan'

National day – 27 October (Independence Day, 1991)

Death penalty – Abolished for all crimes (since 1999)

CPI score – 19 (165)

Conscription – 18–27 years of age; 24 months

Literacy rate – 99.7 per cent (2014 est)

Health expenditure (per capita) – US$456 (2017)

Hospital beds (per 1,000 people) – 7.4 (2013)

Life expectancy (years) – 71.3 (2020 est)

Mortality rate – 6.1 (2020 est)

Birth rate – 18.3 (2020 est)

Infant mortality rate – 30.8 (2020 est)

CLIMATE AND TERRAIN

Over 80 per cent of the country is taken up by the Kara Kum (Black Sands) desert. There are mountains in the south and along the Iranian border, and areas below sea level along the edges of the Caspian Sea. Elevation extremes range from 3,139m (Gora Ayribaba) to −81m (Vpadina Akchanaya, although Lake Sarygamysh sometimes has a lower elevation because of fluctuations in its water level). There is a subtropical desert climate. Average temperatures range from 1.8°C in January to 29.7°C in July.

HISTORY AND POLITICS

Turkmenistan was conquered successively by the Persians, Greeks (under Alexander the Great), Parthians, Arabs and Mongols from the sixth century BC. From the early 19th century Turkmenistan was gradually incorporated into the Russian Empire. A Turkmen revolt against Russian rule in 1916 brought a period of autonomy until 1921, when Soviet control over Turkmenistan was established and it became an Autonomous Soviet Socialist Republic. Turkmenistan became a full republic of the USSR in 1925. It declared its independence from the USSR on 27 October 1991.

Saparmurat Niyazov became leader of the Turkmen Communist Party in 1985, and was elected president in 1990, becoming president for life in 2004. His autocratic regime, through harassment and authoritarianism, prevented the development of any effective political opposition or press freedom, rejecting political pluralism in favour of a cult of personality. After President Niyazov's death in 2006, Gurbanguly Berdimuhammedov was elected president, and was re-elected with a huge majority in both 2012 and 2017. Parties supportive of the president won overwhelmingly in the 2013 and 2018 legislative elections.

The 1992 constitution was amended in 2008 to encourage multiparty politics and economic liberalisation, and also abolished the People's Council and increased the powers of the enlarged legislature. It was amended again in 2016 to increase presidential terms from five to seven years, and remove the 70-year age restriction to allow Berdimuhammedov to potentially rule for life. There are no presidential term limits. The unicameral parliament *(Majlis)* has 125 members directly elected for a five-year term.

The country is divided into five provinces (Ahal, Balkan, Dashhowuz, Lebap and Mary) and the city of Ashgabat.

HEAD OF STATE

President, Chair of the Council of Ministers, Gurbanguly Berdimuhammedov, *elected* 14 February 2007, *re-elected* 2012, 2017

SELECTED GOVERNMENT MEMBERS *AS AT NOVEMBER 2020*

Defence, Maj.-Gen. Begench Gundogdyev

Economy and Finance, Gadyrgeldy Mushshikov

Foreign Affairs, Rashid Meredov

EMBASSY OF TURKMENISTAN

131 Holland Park Avenue, London W11 4UT

T 020-7610 5239 **E** tkm-embassy-uk@btconnect.com

Ambassador Extraordinary and Plenipotentiary, HE Yazmurad Seryayev, *apptd* 2003

BRITISH EMBASSY
Third Floor Office Building, Four Points Ak Altin Hotel, 744001
Ashgabat
T (+993) (12) 363 462 **E** beasb@online.tm
W www.gov.uk/government/world/turkmenistan
Ambassador Extraordinary and Plenipotentiary, HE Hugh
Philpott, OBE, *apptd* 2019

ECONOMY AND TRADE
Turkmenistan has large reserves of natural gas and some oil,
but exports were restricted by a lack of export routes until
2009–10, when existing pipelines to Russia and Iran were
supplemented by a new gas pipeline to China and a second
pipeline to Iran; a trans-Caspian route to European markets
and a pipeline to India are also under exploration. Attempts to
privatise the primarily state-run economy have been made
since 2012, but implementation has been slow. Autocratic
control, corruption and isolationism have limited foreign
investment, resulting in economic stagnation and currency
devaluation. Falling oil prices caused the government to
devalue the manat by nearly 20 per cent in 2014 in a bid to
increase exports. The economy grew by 6.3 per cent in 2019,
and is expected to decelerate to 1.8 per cent in 2020.

Agriculture is intensive around the irrigated oases, with half
the irrigated land used to grow cotton. Agriculture accounts
for 7.5 per cent of GDP and almost half of employment; grain
and livestock are the other main products. The principal
industries are gas and oil production, petroleum products,
textiles (including silk) and food processing. Industry
contributes 44.9 per cent of GDP.

The main trading partners are China (83.7 per cent of
exports), Turkey, Algeria, Russia and EU countries. Principal
exports are gas, crude oil, petrochemicals, textiles and cotton
fibre. The main imports are machinery and equipment,
chemicals and foodstuffs.

GNI – US$39.4bn; US$6,740 per capita (2018)
Annual average growth of GDP – 6.5 per cent (2017 est)
Inflation rate – 8 per cent (2017 est)
Population below poverty line – 0.2 per cent (2012 est)
Unemployment – 11 per cent (2014 est)
Total external debt – US$539.4m (2017 est)
Imports – US$2,556m (2014)
Exports – US$3,600m (2014)

BALANCE OF PAYMENTS
Current Account – US$27m deficit (2018)

Trade with UK	2018	2019
Imports from UK	£27,483,872	£14,895,533
Exports to UK	£3,581,217	£1,923,596

COMMUNICATIONS
Airports and waterways – The main airport is at Ashgabat; there
are two important waterways, the Amu Darya river in the
north-east and the Niyazov (formerly Kara Kum) canal, and
the main port is Turkmenbashi, on the Caspian Sea
Roadways and railways – 58,592km; 5,113km
Telecommunications – 648,223 fixed lines and 8.9 million
mobile subscriptions (2019); there were 1.1 million internet
users in 2018
Internet code and IDD – tm; 993 (from UK), 810 44 (to UK)
Media – The country's public broadcasters are Turkmen TV
and Turkmen Radio; leading daily newspapers include
Neytralnyy Turkmenistan (Russian language), and *Turkmenistan*
and *Watan* (both Turkmen)
WPFI score – 85.44 (179)

TUVALU

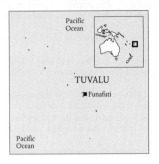

Area – 26 sq. km
Capital – Funafuti; population, 7,000 (2018 est)
Currency – The Australian dollar (A$) of 100 cents is legal
tender; in addition there are Tuvalu dollar and cent coins
in circulation
Population – 11,342 rising at 0.87 per cent a year (2020 est)
Religion – Christian (Protestant 92.4 per cent, Jehovah's
Witness 1.3 per cent, Mormon 1 per cent), Baha'i 2 per
cent (est)
Language – English, Tuvaluan (both official), Samoan, Kiribati
(on Nui)
Population density – 384 per sq. km (2019)
Urban population – 63.2 per cent (2019 est)
Median age (years) – 26.6 (2020 est)
National anthem – 'Tuvalu mo te Atua' 'Tuvalu for the
Almighty'
National day – 1 October (Independence Day)
Death penalty – Not since independence
Gross enrolment ratio (percentage of relevant age group) – primary
108.8 per cent, secondary 41.1 per cent (2019 est)
Health expenditure (per capita) – US$622 (2017)
Life expectancy (years) – 67.9 (2020 est)
Mortality rate – 8.2 (2020 est)
Birth rate – 23.4 (2020 est)
Infant mortality rate – 26.6 (2020 est)

CLIMATE AND TERRAIN
Tuvalu comprises nine low-lying coral islands and atolls in the
south-west Pacific Ocean. The highest elevation is 5m and the
lowest is 0m (Pacific Ocean). The climate is tropical, with an
average temperature of 28.4°C.

HISTORY AND POLITICS
The islands were settled by Polynesians from Tonga 2,000
years ago. Europeans arrived in the 18th century and, as the
Ellice Islands, Tuvalu came under the control of the British in
1877. They formed part of the Gilbert and Ellice Islands
protectorate (later a colony) from 1892, but were granted
separate status from the Gilbert Islands in 1975. The islands
became independent as Tuvalu on 1 October 1978. The
country is seriously affected by rising sea levels, which are
threatening its economic viability.

There are no political parties; allegiances are influenced by
personal and island loyalties. Politically stable as a democracy,
there are frequent changes in government as support in
parliament shifts.

Under the 1978 constitution, Tuvalu is a constitutional
monarchy with Queen Elizabeth II as head of state,
represented by a governor-general who is appointed on the
advice of the prime minister. The unicameral legislature, the
Parliament of Tuvalu, has 15 members who are directly
elected for a four-year term. The prime minister is elected by

the legislature from among its members, and appoints the cabinet, who must be members of parliament. Local government services are provided by elected island councils.
Governor-General, HE Teniku Talesi, *apptd* 2013

SELECTED GOVERNMENT MEMBERS *AS AT NOVEMBER 2020*
Prime Minister, Kausea Natano
Deputy Prime Minister, Minute Taupo
Foreign Affairs, Simon Kofe

HONORARY CONSULATE OF TUVALU
Tuvalu House, 230 Worple Road, London SW20 8RH
T 020-8879 0985 **E** tuvaluconsulate@netscape.net
Honorary Consul, Sir Iftikhar Ayaz, KBE

BRITISH HIGH COMMISSIONER
HE Melanie Hopkins, *apptd* 2016, resident at Suva, Fiji

ECONOMY AND TRADE
The main economic activities are subsistence agriculture and fishing, although agricultural productivity is threatened by the increasing salinity of the soil as the sea level rises; the only cash crop is coconuts. Tourism is limited by the state's remoteness, and the economy is almost entirely dependent on imports of food and fuel. Most employment is in the public sector or abroad, often as merchant seamen; many families rely on remittances from expatriate workers. The government receives substantial annual income from a trust fund set up in 1987, and raises revenue through the sale of fishing licences, postage stamps and coins, and the leasing of its telephone code and internet suffix.

The main trading partners are Singapore, the USA, Fiji and Australia. The only exports are copra and fish. The main imports are food, livestock, fuels, machinery and manufactured goods.
GNI – US$0.6bn; US$5,620 per capita (2019)
Annual average growth of GDP – 3.2 per cent (2017 est)
Population below poverty line – 26.3 per cent (2010 est)
Inflation rate – 2.9 per cent (2017 est)
Imports – US$40m (2017)
Exports – US$18 m (2017)

BALANCE OF PAYMENTS
Trade – US$22m deficit (2017)
Current Account – US$1,388m surplus (2018)

Trade with UK	2018	2019
Imports from UK	£191,235	£58,783
Exports to UK	£33,751	£23,125

COMMUNICATIONS
Airports and waterways – Funafuti has an airfield, from which a regular service operates to Fiji and Kiribati, and it is also the main port
Roadways – 8km
Telecommunications – 2,000 fixed lines and 7,900 mobile subscriptions (2019); there were 5,500 internet users in 2018
Internet code and IDD – tv; 688 (from UK), 44 (to UK)
Media – The state-owned Tuvalu Media Corporation publishes a fortnightly newspaper and runs Radio Tuvalu, the main information source for islanders

UGANDA
Republic of Uganda

Area – 241,038 sq. km
Capital – Kampala; population, 3,298,000 (2020 est)
Major towns – Entebbe, Gulu, Lira, Mbale
Currency – Uganda shilling of 100 cents
Population – 43,252,966 rising at 3.34 per cent a year (2020 est); Baganda (16.5 per cent), Banyakole (9.6 per cent), Basoga (8.8 per cent), Bakiga (7.1 per cent), Iteso (7 per cent), Langi (6.3 per cent), Bagisu (4.9 per cent), Acholi (4.4 per cent), Lugbara (3.3 per cent) (est)
Religion – Christian (Protestant 45.1 per cent, Roman Catholic 39.3 per cent), Muslim 13.7 per cent (est)
Language – English, Swahili (both official), Luganda, Niger-Congo languages, Nilo-Saharan languages, Arabic
Population density – 213 per sq. km (2019)
Urban population – 24.4 per cent (2019 est)
Median age (years) – 15.7 (2020 est)
National anthem – 'O Uganda, Land of Beauty!'
National day – 9 October (Independence Day)
Death penalty – Retained
CPI score – 28 (137)
Military expenditure – US$408m (2018 est)

CLIMATE AND TERRAIN
Uganda lies on a high plateau with mountain ranges in the west, south-west and north-east. Elevation extremes range from 5,110m (Mt Stanley) to 621m (Lake Albert). Nearly 20 per cent of the country is covered by lakes, rivers and wetlands, and it contains about half of lakes Victoria, Edward and Albert (Mobuto), as well as lakes Kyoga, Kwania, George and Bisina (formerly Salisbury) and the course of the Nile from its outlet from Lake Victoria to the South Sudan border at Nimule. The climate is tropical, moderated by the altitude. There are two rainy seasons (March–May, October–December) in the south; the north is drier, semi-arid in places, with a single, longer rainy season.

HISTORY AND POLITICS
Indigenous people had formed several kingdoms in the area by the 14th century. A British protectorate was established over the kingdom of Buganda in 1894 and gradually extended to other territory by 1914. Uganda became independent on 9 October 1962 as a federation of the kingdoms of Ankole, Buganda, Bunyoro, Busoga and Toro.

In 1963 Uganda was proclaimed a federal republic but in 1966 Prime Minister Milton Obote overthrew the president, ended the federal status and became executive president. In 1971 President Obote was deposed in an army coup led by Maj.-Gen. Idi Amin, who proclaimed himself head of state.

His brutal dictatorship was overthrown in 1979 with military assistance from Tanzania.

Milton Obote was re-elected president in 1980 but political instability and human rights abuses continued. He was ousted by a military coup in 1985 amid a civil war with the rebel National Resistance Army (NRA) led by Yoweri Museveni. A military council was installed but the NRA captured Kampala in January 1986, securing control of the rest of the country in the following few months.

Museveni's 'Movement' system of government, under which political parties were allowed to exist but not to contest elections, was in place from 1986 until a 2005 referendum resulted in a return to multiparty politics. In February 2016 elections, President Museveni was re-elected for a fifth term and the National Resistance Movement retained its majority in parliament, although domestic and international observers criticised the fairness and transparency of the electoral process.

The Lord's Resistance Army (LRA), whose stated goals have proved inconsistent, began a low-level insurgency in northern Uganda in the late 1980s. Its activities have spread into northeastern Congo (where most of the LRA is now located), southern Sudan, the Central African Republic and Kenya, despite offensives against LRA bases by Ugandan, Sudanese and Congolese forces since 2008. In Uganda, thousands have been massacred or mutilated, an estimated 20,000 children abducted to serve in its forces and 1.7 million people displaced into camps.

Terrorist attacks by Islamic extremists have begun in recent years. Some were carried out by Somalian Islamists, as African Union peacekeepers (predominantly Ugandan) have prevented them establishing complete control of the Somalian capital, but other attacks were the work of the Allied Democratic Forces, based in the Democratic Republic of the Congo, which seeks to create an Islamic state in Uganda.

The 1995 constitution was amended in 2005 to allow multiparty elections. The president is directly elected for a five-year term; the two-term limit was abolished in 2005. The 445-seat unicameral parliament has 290 directly elected members, 137 (including 112 women) elected indirectly to represent particular groups and 18 *ex officio* members appointed by the president; all serve a five-year term. The prime minister is appointed by the president, subject to the approval of parliament.

HEAD OF STATE
President, C-in-C of the Armed Forces, Yoweri Museveni, *sworn in* 29 January 1986, *elected* 9 May 1996, *re-elected* 2001, 2006, 2011, 2016
Vice-President, Edward Kiwanuka Ssekandi

SELECTED GOVERNMENT MEMBERS *AS AT NOVEMBER 2020*
Prime Minister, Ruhakana Rugunda
First Deputy Prime Minister, Gen. Moses Ali
Defence, Adolf Mwesige
Finance, Matia Kasaija

UGANDA HIGH COMMISSION
Uganda House, 58–59 Trafalgar Square, London WC2N 5DX
T 020-7839 5783 **E** info@ugandahighcommission.co.uk
W www.ugandahighcommission.co.uk
High Commissioner, HE Julius Moto, *apptd* 2017

BRITISH HIGH COMMISSION
PO Box 7070, 4 Windsor Loop, Kampala
T (+256) (31) 231 2000 **E** bhcinfo@starcom.co.ug
W www.gov.uk/government/world/uganda
High Commissioner, HE Peter West, CMG, *apptd* 2016

ECONOMY AND TRADE
Economic reforms adopted since 1986 have produced steady economic growth, which was only slightly affected by the global downturn and the conflict in South Sudan; between 1992 and 2010 the poverty was halved and GDP per capita tripled. However, there has been little industrialisation so the economy is vulnerable to fluctuations in global commodity prices, especially that of coffee, its main export. Uganda's debt burden has been reduced by debt relief since 2000 but it is still dependent on foreign aid. Good harvests, increasing gold exports and significant foreign investment in oil production sustained strong growth until 2020.

Agriculture is the most important economic sector, contributing 28.2 per cent of GDP and engaging about 71 per cent of the workforce. The principal crops are coffee, tea, cotton, tobacco, cassava, potatoes, maize, millet, pulses, cut flowers and livestock products. Industrial activity centres on production of sugar, tobacco, cotton textiles, cement and steel, brewing and fishing. Tourism is growing, and oil has been discovered but production is years from completion.

The main export markets are neighbouring countries, the UAE and the EU; imports come chiefly from China, India, the UAE and Kenya. Principal exports are coffee, fish and fish products, tea, cotton, cut flowers, horticultural products and gold. Electricity is exported although less than a quarter of Ugandans have access to it. The main imports are capital equipment, vehicles, petroleum, medical supplies and cereals.

GNI – US$34.5bn; US$780 per capita (2019)
Annual average growth of GDP – 4.8 per cent (2017 est)
Inflation rate – 5.6 per cent (2017 est)
Population below poverty line – 21.4 per cent (2017 est)
Unemployment – 9.4 per cent (2014 est)
Total external debt – US$10.8bn (2018 est)
Imports – US$6,832m (2017)
Exports – US$4,640m (2017)

BALANCE OF PAYMENTS
Trade – US$2,191m deficit (2017)
Current Account – US$2,332m deficit (2019)

Trade with UK	2018	2019
Imports from UK	£39,812,672	£38,757,530
Exports to UK	£12,205,809	£12,727,599

COMMUNICATIONS
Airports and waterways – There is an international airport at Entebbe; some of the lakes and parts of the river Nile provide navigable routes internally
Roadways and railways – 20,544km; 1,244km
Telecommunications – 184,065 fixed lines and 23.9 million mobile subscriptions (2019); there were 9.6 million internet users in 2018
Internet code and IDD – ug; 256 (from UK), 0 44 (to UK)
Media – The Uganda Broadcasting Company is the main public-run broadcaster; major newspapers include the state-owned *New Vision,* as well as the privately owned *The Monitor* and *The Observer*
WPFI score – 40.95 (125)

EDUCATION AND HEALTH
Education is a joint undertaking by the government, local authorities and voluntary agencies.
Literacy rate – 76.5 per cent (2018 est)
Gross enrolment ratio (percentage of relevant age group) – primary 102.7 per cent (2017 est); secondary 26.1 per cent (2014 est); tertiary 4 per cent (2011 est)
Health expenditure (per capita) – US$38 (2017)

Hospital beds (per 1,000 people) – 0.5 (2010)
Life expectancy (years) – 68.2 (2020 est)
Mortality rate – 5.3 (2020 est)
Birth rate – 42.3 (2020 est)
Infant mortality rate – 32.6 (2020 est)
HIV/AIDS adult prevalence – 5.8 per cent (2019 est)

UKRAINE

Ukrayina – Ukraine

Area – 603,550 sq. km
Capital – Kiev (Kyiv); population, 2,988,000 (2020 est)
Major cities – Dnipropetrovsk, Donetsk, Kharkiv, L'viv, Odesa, Sevastopol, Zaporizhzhya
Currency – Hryvnia of 100 kopiykas
Population – 43,922,939 falling at 0.1 per cent a year (2020 est); Ukrainian (77.8 per cent), Russian (17.3 per cent) (est)
Religion – Christian (including Orthodox 65 per cent, Ukrainian Orthodox 25 per cent, Ukrainian Greek Catholic 8–10 per cent) (est); small Muslim and Jewish minorities
Language – Ukrainian (official), Russian
Population density – 77 per sq. km (2019)
Urban population – 69.5 per cent (2019 est)
Median age (years) – 41.2 (2020 est)
National anthem – 'Shche ne vmerla, Ukraina' 'Ukraine Has Not Yet Perished'
National day – 24 August (Independence Day)
Death penalty – Abolished for all crimes (since 1999)
CPI score – 30 (126)
Military expenditure – US$4,750m (2018 est)
Conscription – 20–27 years of age; 12 months

CLIMATE AND TERRAIN

Much of the country lies in a plain (steppe), with the Carpathian mountains in the west and mountains in the south of the Crimean peninsula. Elevation extremes range from 2,061m (Hora Hoverla) to 0m (Black Sea). The main rivers are the Dnieper, which runs through the centre of the country, the Dniester in the west, the Southern Buh and the Northern Donets (a tributary of the Don). The climate is continental, and Mediterranean in the southern Crimea. Average temperatures range from −2.9°C in January to 21.2°C in July.

POLITICS

The 1996 constitution was amended in 2004 to transfer some powers from the president to the legislature *(Verkhovna Rada)*; the constitutional court returned these powers to the president in late 2010 although in February 2014 the 2004 constitutional amendments were reinstated. The president is directly elected for a five-year term, renewable once. The unicameral Supreme Council has 450 members, who are directly elected for a five-year term. The prime minister is appointed by the president, subject to the legislature's approval.

Following the decision of Viktor Yanukovych's government to abandon plans for an association agreement with the EU in November 2013, tens of thousands of pro-EU demonstrators protested in Kiev and other cities. The widespread and sometimes violent demonstrations, which left at least 77 protestors dead in Kiev, resulted in President Yanukovych leaving Ukraine and seeking asylum in Russia, causing opposition parties to form an interim government.

In August 2015, parliament voted to provide greater autonomy to areas in the east of the country controlled by pro-Russian separatists. Prime Minister Yatsenyuk stepped down in April 2016 amid accusations of corruption levelled at his government, coupled with frustration at the slow pace of reforms, to be replaced by Volodymyr Groysman.

The speaker of the parliament, Oleksandr Turchynov, was appointed interim president in February 2014 and replaced by Arseniy Yatsenyuk of the Fatherland party soon after, as head of a national unity government. In May 2014, long-serving politician Petro Poroshenko was elected as Ukraine's fifth president, but was defeated in the second round of voting in April 2019 by comedian and actor Volodymyr Zelensky, who had no political experience. Zelensky, running on an anti-corruption platform, immediately called a snap parliamentary election for July 2019. Zelensky's party, Servant of the People (named after his television show), won the first overall majority in parliament since 1991.

HEAD OF STATE
President, Volodymyr Zelensky, *elected* 21 April 2019, *sworn in* 20 May 2019

SELECTED GOVERNMENT MEMBERS *AS AT NOVEMBER 2020*
Prime Minister, Danys Shmyhal
Deputy Prime Ministers, Olha Stefanishyna; Mykhailo Fedrova; Oleksiy Rezinkov; Oleh Urusky
Foreign Affairs, Dmytro Kuleba
Internal, Arsen Avakov

EMBASSY OF UKRAINE
60 Holland Park, London W11 3SJ
T 020-7727 6312 E emb_gb@mfa.gov.ua W www.ukremb.org.uk
Ambassador Extraordinary and Plenipotentiary, HE Vadym Prystaiko, *apptd* 2020

BRITISH EMBASSY
Desyatynna 9, Kiev 01025
T (+380) (44) 490 3660 E ukembinf@gmail.com

W www.gov.uk/government/world/ukraine
Ambassador Extraordinary and Plenipotentiary, HE Melinda
   Simmons, *apptd* 2019

FOREIGN RELATIONS

Following the disintegration of the USSR in 1991, relations between Ukraine and Russia were strained by disputes over the Black Sea fleet and the status of Crimea, a self-administered republic within Ukraine, which had been part of Russia until 1954; these disputes often came to a head when Russia suspended gas supplies to Ukraine. However, in February 2014 armed pro-Russian groups seized government buildings in Crimea. The region was formally annexed by the Russian government on the 18 March 2014 after a controversial independence vote in the Crimean parliament. Ukraine and a majority of UN member states do not accept the status of Crimea and Sevastopol as federal subjects of the Russian Federation.

From April, pro-Russian groups in the east of Ukraine seized government buildings and two self-proclaimed pro-Russian states were established in the east of the country: the Donetsk People's Republic and the Luhansk People's Republic. Independence referendums were held on 11 May in both territories, with administrators claiming very large wins for supporters of independence. Both republics merged on 24 May to form The Federal State of Novorossiya. The breakaway states have not been recognised by Russia, Ukraine or the wider international community. While political tensions eased when the Russian government advised it would be pulling troops away from the Ukrainian border, violence between the Ukrainian army and separatist militias continued to occur.

Tensions were reignited by the downing of Malaysia Airlines flight MH17 over Ukrainian soil on 17 July 2014, apparently by pro-Russian separatists. In September, a ceasefire was agreed between the government and separatists, though it soon broke down and a new agreement was brokered in February 2015 after rebel forces captured the strategically important town of Debaltseve. Tensions were reignited in January–February 2017 with claims of shelling in Donetsk and Avdiyivka. Between April 2014 and February 2020 an estimated 13,000 people had been killed in the conflict, including more than 3,300 civilian deaths.

ECONOMY AND TRADE

The first decade of independence was characterised by economic mismanagement and opposition to economic restructuring. When reform began in the late 1990s, it brought economic growth, with rises in output and exports and a reduction in inflation. However, slow progress has been a drag on the economy, leaving it vulnerable to external factors such as the global economic downturn; it was heavily affected in 2009 as the economy contracted by 15 per cent. Slow economic growth between 2010 and 2013 was marred by allegations that the Yanukovych regime misappropriated billions of dollars during its time in power. A trade war with Moscow, ongoing fighting in the east and the annexation of Crimea (and the heavily industrialised Donbass region) resulted in a sharp loss of GDP and high inflation in 2014 and 2015.

After incurring debts worth US$1.9bn with state-run Russian energy firm Gazprom, Russia ended its practice of supplying Ukraine with subsidised fossil fuels, greatly increasing domestic prices. In March 2015, the IMF approved a US$17.5bn (£11.28bn) loan to Ukraine in order to prevent the country from defaulting. Ukraine's free-trade agreement with the EU came into force at the start of 2016, deepening tensions with Russia as trade activity shifted west, but nonetheless the economy grew between 2016 and 2019.

The agricultural sector is large and productive, with over half the land under cultivation. The main crops are grain, sugar beet, sunflower seeds and vegetables; stock-raising and dairy farming are also important. Agriculture accounts for 1 per cent of GDP and 5.8 per cent of employment. There are large deposits of coal, iron ore and other minerals. The main industrial activities are mining and metal processing, manufacture of machinery and transport equipment and chemicals, electricity generation and food processing, especially sugar. Ukraine imports three-quarters of its oil and gas, principally from Russia; supplies have been suspended on occasion due to price disputes.

The main trading partners are Russia, China, Germany and Turkey. Principal exports are ferrous and non-ferrous metals (especially steel), fuel and petroleum products, chemicals, machinery and transport equipment, and foodstuffs. The main imports are energy (primarily gas), machinery and equipment, and chemicals.

GNI – US$141.6bn; US$3,370 per capita (2019)
Annual average growth of GDP – 3.24 per cent (2019 est)
Inflation rate – 14.4 per cent (2017 est)
Population below poverty line – 3.8 per cent (2016)
Unemployment – 8.89 per cent (2019 est)
Total external debt – US$130bn (2017 est)
Imports – US$62,689m (2017)
Exports – US$53,788m (2017)

BALANCE OF PAYMENTS
Trade – US$8,901m deficit (2017)
Current Account – US$4,124m deficit (2019)

Trade with UK	2018	2019
Imports from UK	£516,366,058	£515,274,633
Exports to UK	£524,247,478	£602,685,987

COMMUNICATIONS

Airports and waterways – The principal airports are at Kiev and Odesa; the main seaports are Mariupol on the Sea of Azov, and Kherson, Mykolayiv and Odesa on the Black Sea
Roadways and railways – 169,694km; 21,733km
Telecommunications – 4.4 million fixed lines and 57.4 million mobile subscriptions (2019); there were 25.9 million internet users in 2018
Internet code and IDD – ua; 380 (from UK), 44 (to UK)
Major broadcasters – The National TV Company of Ukraine and the National Radio Company of Ukraine are the principal public broadcasters
Press – Major dailies include *Fakty i Kommentari* (Ukrainian language), and *Silski Visti* and *Segodnya* (both Russian language)
WPFI score – 32.52 (96)

EDUCATION AND HEALTH

Literacy rate – 99.8 per cent (2015)
Gross enrolment ratio (percentage of relevant age group) – primary 99 per cent, secondary 96 per cent, tertiary 82.6 per cent (2014 est)
Health expenditure (per capita) – US$177 (2017)
Hospital beds (per 1,000 people) – 8.8 (2013)
Life expectancy (years) – 72.9 (2020 est)
Mortality rate – 14 (2020 est)
Birth rate – 9.6 (2020 est)
Infant mortality rate – 7.4 (2020 est)
HIV/AIDS adult prevalence – 1 per cent (2019 est)

UNITED ARAB EMIRATES

Al-Imarat al-Arabiyah al-Muttahidah – United Arab Emirates

Area – 83,600 sq. km
Capital – Abu Dhabi; population, 1,483,000 (2018 est)
Major cities – Ajman, Al-Ain, Dubai, Sharjah
Currency – UAE dirham (Dh) of 100 fils
Population – 9,992,083 rising at 1.49 per cent a year (2020
    est); Indian (38.2 per cent), Emirati (11.6 per cent),
    Egyptian (10.2 per cent), Bangladeshi (9.5 per cent),
    Pakistani (9.4 per cent), Filipino (6.1 per cent) (est)
Religion – Muslim (official) 76 per cent, Christian 9 per cent,
    other (including Hindu and Buddhist) 15 per cent (est)
Language – Arabic (official), English, Hindi, Malyam, Urdu,
    Pashto, Tagalog, Persian
Population density – 136 per sq. km (2019)
Urban population – 86.8 per cent (2019 est)
Median age (years) – 38.4 (2020 est)
National anthem – 'Nashid al-watani al-imarati' 'National
    Anthem of the UAE'
National day – 2 December (Independence Day)
Death penalty – Retained
CPI score – 71 (21)
Military expenditure – US$24,601m (2014 est)
Conscription – 18–30, male only; 12–24 months (selective)

CLIMATE AND TERRAIN

The United Arab Emirates (UAE) is situated in the south-east
of the Arabian peninsula. Six of the emirates lie on the shore
of the Gulf, between the Musandam peninsula in the east and
the Qatar peninsula in the west, while the seventh, Fujairah,
lies on the Gulf of Oman. A flat coastal plain merges into the
desert of the interior, and there are mountains in the east.
Elevation extremes range from 1,527m (Jabal Yibir) to 0m
(Persian Gulf). There is a desert climate, although it is cooler
in the mountains, with high humidity on the coast. Average
temperatures range from 18.5°C in January to 34.4°C in July.

HISTORY AND POLITICS

The United Arab Emirates (formerly the Trucial States) is
composed of seven emirates. Six of these came together as an
independent state on 2 December 1971 when they ended their
individual special treaty relationships with the British
government, and they were joined by Ras al-Khaimah on 10
February 1972.

Sheikh Zayed of Abu Dhabi was president from
independence until his death in 2004. He was succeeded as
Sultan of Abu Dhabi by his son, Sheikh Khalifa, who was also
elected president of the UAE. The first national elections were
held in 2006, when half the members of the Federal National
Council (FNC) were elected by a small electoral college of
6,600 voters. The size of the electoral college has increased
significantly in recent elections, to 337,738 voters (women
comprised over half of this total), in the most recent legislative

election held in October 2019. President al-Nahyan has ruled
since 2004.

The 1971 provisional constitution, approved in 1996, was
amended in 2008 to convert the FNC from a consultative into
a legislative body and to extend its original two-year term to
2011. Overall authority lies with the Supreme Council,
comprising the hereditary rulers of the seven emirates, each of
whom also governs in his own territory. The president is
elected every five years by the Supreme Council from among
its members, but is *de facto* hereditary. The president appoints
the prime minister and the council of ministers. The unicameral
FNC has 40 members, eight members each from Abu Dhabi
and Dubai, six each from Sharjah and Ras al-Khaimah and four
each for Ajman, Fujairah and Umm al-Qaiwain; half are elected
by an electoral college and half are appointed by the rulers of
each emirate.

HEAD OF STATE
President, HH Sheikh Khalifa bin Zayed al-Nahyan *(Abu
    Dhabi), elected* 3 November 2004, *re-elected* 2009, 2014,
    2019
Vice-President, Prime Minister, Defence, HH Sheikh Mohammed
    bin Rashid al-Maktoum *(Dubai)*

SELECTED GOVERNMENT MEMBERS *AS AT
NOVEMBER 2020*
Deputy Prime Ministers, Lt.-Gen. Sheikh Saif bin Zayed al-
    Nahyan *(Interior);* Sheikh Mansour bin Zayed al-Nahyan
Finance, HH Sheikh Hamdan bin Rashid al-Maktoum
Foreign Affairs, Sheikh Abdullah bin Zayed al-Nahyan

EMBASSY OF THE UNITED ARAB EMIRATES
1–2 Grosvenor Crescent, London SW1X 7EE
T 020-7581 1281 **E** informationuk@mofa.gov.ae
W www.uae-embassy.ae/uk
Ambassador Extraordinary and Plenipotentiary, HE Mansoor
    Abulhoul, *apptd* 2019

BRITISH EMBASSY
PO Box 248, Khalid bin al-Waleed Street (Street 22), Abu Dhabi
T (+971) (2) 610 1100 **E** consular.UAE@fco.gov.uk
W www.gov.uk/government/world/united-arab-emirates
Ambassador Extraordinary and Plenipotentiary, HE Patrick
    Moody, *apptd* 2018

FEDERAL STRUCTURE
The emirates are: Abu Dhabi, Ajman, Dubai, Fujairah, Ras al-
Khaimah, Sharjah and Umm al-Qaiwain. Each emirate has its
own government, judicial system and penal code. Abu Dhabi
has an executive council chaired by the crown prince.

ECONOMY AND TRADE

Exploitation of the territories' oil reserves began in the 1960s
and transformed the UAE from poor rural principalities into
modern states with a high standard of living. Oil and gas
production dominate the economy, although diversification
efforts mean that output now accounts for only 30 per cent of
GDP, and it is one of the most diversified of the Gulf states.
The economy is also dependent on foreign workers, but the
government aims to increase opportunities for its citizens
through improved education and expansion of the private
sector. The economy was badly hit by the global downturn,
but its debt crisis has been alleviated by loans from federal and
Abu Dhabi institutions. Low oil prices led to cuts in
government expenditure and the introduction of excise taxes
in 2017 and value added tax in 2018. A fall in oil demand and
tourism is expected to contract the economy by 6.6 per cent in
2020.

Agriculture is limited by the terrain but the area under cultivation has been extended by irrigation and water desalination projects. The main products are dates, vegetables, watermelons, poultry, eggs and dairy products. Non-hydrocarbon industries include fishing, aluminium, cement, petrochemicals, fertilisers, commercial ship repair, construction materials, handicrafts, textiles, boat-building, financial services and tourism. Several free-trade, zero-tax zones attract foreign investment.

The main export markets are India, Iran and Japan; imports come chiefly from China, the USA and India. Principal exports are crude oil (45 per cent), natural gas, re-exports, dried fish and dates. The main imports are machinery and transport equipment, chemicals and food.

GNI – US$424.8bn; US$43,470 per capita (2019)
Annual average growth of GDP – 0.8 per cent (2017 est)
Inflation rate – 2 per cent (2017 est)
Population below poverty line – 19.5 per cent (2003)
Total external debt – US$237.6bn (2017 est)
Imports – US$318,148m (2017)
Exports – US$384,043m (2017)

BALANCE OF PAYMENTS
Trade – US$65,895m surplus (2017)
Current Account – US$4,659m deficit (2018)

Trade with UK	2018	2019
Imports from UK	£7,563,892,011	£7,776,098,705
Exports to UK	£3,417,123,300	£2,766,046,654

COMMUNICATIONS
Airports and waterways – There is an international airport in every emirate except Ajman, and significant ports in Jebel Ali, Khor Fakkan, Mina Khalid, Mina Rashid, Mina Saqr, Mina Khalid and Mina Zayed
Roadways – 4,080km
Telecommunications – 2.4 million fixed lines and 19.8 million mobile subscriptions (2019); there were 9.5 million internet users in 2018
Internet code and IDD – ae; 971 (from UK), 44 (to UK)
Media – Dubai Media Incorporated (TV) is the government-owned broadcaster; major newspapers include *Al-Bayan*, the *Khaleej Times* and *Gulf News*
WPFI score – 42.69 (131)

EDUCATION AND HEALTH
Education is free in state schools and compulsory from age six to 14.
Literacy rate – 93.2 per cent (2015 est)
Gross enrolment ratio (percentage of relevant age group) – primary 108.4 per cent, secondary 104.9 per cent (2017 est); tertiary 37 per cent (2016 est)
Health expenditure (per capita) – US$1,357 (2017)
Hospital beds (per 1,000 people) – 1.2 (2013)
Life expectancy (years) – 79 (2020 est)
Mortality rate – 2 (2020 est)
Birth rate – 9.5 (2020 est)
Infant mortality rate – 5.3 (2020 est)

UNITED KINGDOM
United Kingdom of Great Britain and Northern Ireland

Area – 243,610 sq. km
Capital – London; population, 9,304,000 (2020 est)
Major cities – Belfast, Birmingham, Cardiff, Edinburgh, Glasgow, Leeds, Liverpool, Manchester
Currency – Pound sterling (£) of 100 pence
Population – 65,761,117 rising at 0.49 per cent a year (2020 est)
Religion – Christian 59.5 per cent, Muslim 4.4 per cent, Hindu 1.3 per cent (est)
Language – English, Scottish Gaelic, Welsh, Irish, Cornish, Scots (regional language)
Population density – 275 per sq. km (2018)
Urban population – 83.7 per cent (2018 est)
Median age (years) – 40.6 (2020 est)
National anthem – 'God Save the Queen'
Death penalty – Abolished for all crimes (since 1998)
CPI score – 77 (12)
Military expenditure – US$49,997m (2018)

CLIMATE AND TERRAIN
The terrain of Great Britain is higher in the north and west, with low mountains and rugged hills in Scotland, northern England and Wales; the land declines towards the south and east, with its lowest points in the south-east. Northern Ireland is more low-lying, with low mountains in the north and east. The heavily indented coastline varies in height between high cliffs and sea level. Elevation extremes range from 1,345m (Ben Nevis, Scotland) to −4m (the Fens, eastern England). Although Scotland contains numerous large lochs and northern England includes an area known as the Lake District, the largest freshwater lake is Lough Neagh in Northern Ireland. The main rivers are the Thames, the Severn and the Trent in England and Wales, and the Tay in Scotland. The climate is temperate and extremes are rare, but the convergence of Atlantic, Arctic and European weather systems produces unusually changeable weather conditions. Average temperatures range from 4.4°C in January and December to 15.1°C in August.

POLITICS
There is no written constitution. The head of state is a hereditary constitutional monarch. The bicameral parliament consists of the House of Commons, the lower house, and the House of Lords. The House of Commons has 650 seats, directly elected for a five-year term. The House of Lords is appointed and numbers vary; in May 2018 it had 780 members, comprising 26 archbishops and bishops of the Church of England, 664 life peers and 90 hereditary peers. The prime minister is the leader of the majority party or coalition in the House of Commons.

Powers over certain internal matters were devolved in 1999 to Scotland, Wales and Northern Ireland, each of which has

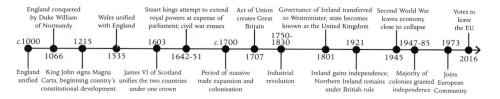

England conquered by Duke William of Normandy — *c.*1000

Wales unified with England — 1215

Stuart kings attempt to extend royal powers at expense of parliament; civil war ensues — 1603

Act of Union creates Great Britain — *c.*1700

Governance of Ireland transferred to Westminister; state becomes known as the United Kingdom — 1750-1830

Second World War leaves economy close to collapse — 1921

Votes to leave the EU — 1947-85 / 1973

England unified — 1066

King John signs Magna Carta, beginning country's constitutional development — 1535

James VI of Scotland unifies the two countries under one crown — 1642-51

Period of massive trade expansion and colonisation — 1707

Industrial revolution — 1801

Ireland gains independence; Northern Ireland remains under British rule — 1945

Majority of colonies granted independence — 1973

Joins European Community — 2016

its own legislature and government; devolution was suspended in Northern Ireland several times between 2000 and 2007 owing to the breakdown of power-sharing arrangements.

The Labour government elected in 1945 pursued socialist economic and welfare policies, nationalising key industries, setting up the National Health Service and expanding the social security system. State involvement in the economy was reduced in the 1980s by the Conservative government led by Margaret Thatcher, the country's first woman prime minister. Her administration privatised industries, opened up welfare services to market forces and reduced the role of local government, polarising politics and public opinion. She also established a close relationship with the USA and was supportive of its foreign policy. This has been continued by her successors, notably in the support for the US 'war on terror' and the deployment of British forces in Afghanistan from 2001, Iraq from 2003 to 2009, and in Libyan air space in 2011.

At the 2015 legislative election, the Conservative party won its first outright majority since 1996 while the Scottish Nationalist Party won 56 of the 59 seats contested in Scotland. A snap election in June 2017 intended to strengthen the Conservative mandate resulted in the party losing its majority and establishing a 'confidence and supply' agreement with the Democratic Unionist Party. Divisions on Britain's withdrawn from the EU, which 52 per cent of voters supported in a 2016 referendum, resulted in a second second snap election in December 2019 which the Conservatives won with a large majority.

The formal process to exit the EU was triggered on 29 March 2017, but the intended leave date of 29 March 2019 was extended numerous times by the EU after the government's withdrawal agreement was heavily defeated three times in parliament. Prime Minister Theresa May resigned soon after these defeats on 7 June 2019 and was replaced by Boris Johnson. The UK formally withdrew on 31 January 2020, triggering an 11-month transitional period needed to negotiate future trading arrangements.

HEAD OF STATE

HM The Queen of the United Kingdom of Great Britain and Northern Ireland, Queen Elizabeth II, *born* 21 April 1926, *succeeded* 6 February 1952, *crowned* 2 June 1953
Heir, HRH The Prince of Wales (Prince Charles Philip Arthur George), *born* 14 November 1948

SELECTED GOVERNMENT MEMBERS *AS AT NOVEMBER 2020*

Prime Minister, First Lord of the Treasury, Civil Service, Boris Johnson
Chancellor of the Exchequer, Rishi Sunak
Defence, Ben Wallace
Foreign and Commonwealth Affairs, Dominic Raab
Home Affairs, Priti Patel
Justice, Lord Chancellor, Robert Buckland

ECONOMY AND TRADE

The UK has a highly developed and technologically advanced economy, that is now dominated by services and trade. It was the first industrialised nation, developing an economy in the 19th century based on heavy industry, mass manufacturing and global trade. It became less predominant as industrialisation spread to other countries, and emerged as a service economy. In the 1980s, privatisation of state industries, constraints on public spending and an oil boom improved government finances. After emerging from recession in the early 1990s, the economy experienced its longest-recorded period of expansion, outperforming the rest of the EU states, until 2008. The global economic downturn, tight credit and the end of the property boom caused the economy to go into recession from early 2008 until late 2009 and again at the start of 2012. The banking sector in particular was badly affected by the global financial crisis in 2008 and government intervention was necessary to stabilise the financial system, including nationalising or part-nationalising major banks. These measures left the government with a large public-sector debt to service, and the coalition government announced tight constraints on public spending from 2010. The budget deficit was persistently high, at around at 3.6 per cent in 2017, but fell to 1.2 per cent in March 2019. Austerity measures restricted growth and increased poverty, which was estimated at over 20 per cent of the population in February 2020. Since deciding to leave the EU in June 2016, growth has slowed and the pound has depreciated, resulting in lower consumer spending but no significant increase in exports due to uncertainty over the UK's future trading relations. Prior to 2020 the economy recorded incremental growth in 2018 and 2019, but sharply contracted in 2020 owing to the coronavirus pandemic, which killed over 50,000 people up to November 2020, and continued Brexit uncertainty; the economy is expected to contract by 9.8 per cent in 2020.

The service sector, especially banking, insurance and business services, electronics, telecommunications and tourism, contributes 79.2 per cent of GDP and employs 83.5 per cent of the workforce. Agriculture is intensive, highly mechanised and efficient, employing just 1.3 per cent of the workforce but providing about 60 per cent of food needs. The UK has large but declining reserves of oil, gas and coal, and the country became a net importer of energy in 2005. Other industrial output is mostly manufactured goods, including machine tools, electrical power equipment, automation and transport equipment, aircraft, ships, motor vehicles and parts, electronics and communications equipment, metals, chemicals, paper and paper products, food processing, textiles, clothing and other consumer goods. Manufacturing has declined in importance but still accounts for 20.2 per cent of GDP.

The main trading partners are EU countries, the USA and China. The principal exports are manufactured goods, fuels, chemicals, food, beverages and tobacco. The main imports are manufactured goods, machinery, fuels and foodstuffs.
GNI – US$2,831.8bn; US$42,370 per capita (2019)
Annual average growth of GDP – 1.26 per cent (2019 est)
Inflation rate – 2.7 per cent (2017 est)
Population below poverty line – 15 per cent (2013 est)

Unemployment – 3.17 per cent (2019 est)
Total external debt – US$8.126 trillion (2016 est)
Imports – US$826,657m (2017)
Exports – US$786,259m (2017)

BALANCE OF PAYMENTS
Trade – US$40,397m deficit (2017)
Current Account – US$121,625m deficit (2019)

COMMUNICATIONS
Airports – There are 271 licensed civil airports, of which Heathrow (the world's fifth busiest international airport), Gatwick, Stansted and Manchester handle the highest volume of passengers
Waterways – Traditionally a seafaring nation, the UK has a large merchant navy, with 504 ships of over 1,000 tonnes registered in the UK and 308 ships registered overseas. The main ports are at Grimsby and Immingham, London, Milford Haven, Southampton, Tees and Hartlepool, Liverpool, Felixstowe, Forth, Dover and Belfast
Roadways and Railways – There are 394,428km of roadways, including 3,617km of motorways; 16,454km
Telecommunications – 31.1 million fixed lines and 76.9 million mobile subscriptions (2019); there were 61.8 million internet users in 2018
Major broadcasters – The British Broadcasting Corporation is a public service broadcaster and provides radio and television programmes, in competition with several commercial radio and television stations, including cable and satellite services
Press – The lively and occasionally controversial newspaper press publishes around ten newspapers daily, including *The Times, The Guardian* and *The Sun*
WPFI score – 22.93 (35)

EDUCATION AND HEALTH
Full-time education is compulsory between the ages of five and 16 in Wales and Scotland and four and 16 in Northern Ireland. In England, full-time education is compulsory between the age of five until the end of the academic year of the pupil's 17th birthday.
Gross enrolment ratio (percentage of relevant age group) – primary 101 per cent, secondary 120.8 per cent, tertiary 61.4 per cent (2018 est)
Health expenditure (per capita) – US$3,859 (2017)
Hospital beds (per 1,000 people) – 2.8 (2013)
Life expectancy (years) – 81.1 (2020 est)
Mortality rate – 9.5 (2020 est)
Birth rate – 11.9 (2020 est)
Infant mortality rate – 4.1 (2020 est)
HIV/AIDS adult prevalence – 0.33 per cent (2013 est)

OVERSEAS TERRITORIES
See UK Overseas Territories

UNITED STATES OF AMERICA

Area – 9,833,517 sq. km
Capital – Washington, District of Columbia; population, 5,322,000 (2020)
Major cities – Boston, Chicago, Dallas, Houston, Los Angeles, Miami, New York, Philadelphia, Phoenix, San Antonio, San Diego, San Francisco, San Jose
Currency – US dollar (US$) of 100 cents
Population – 332,639,102 rising at 0.72 per cent a year (2020 est)
Religion – Christian (Protestant 46.5 per cent, Roman Catholic 20.8 per cent, Mormon 1.6 per cent), Jewish 1.9 per cent (est)
Language – English, Spanish, Chinese, Hawaiian (official language in Hawaii), 20 indigenous languages (official in Alaska)
Population density – 36 per sq. km (2019)
Urban population – 82.5 per cent (2019 est)
Median age (years) – 38.5 (2020 est)
National anthem – 'The Star-Spangled Banner'
National day – 4 July (Independence Day)
Death penalty – Abolished in 22 states, District of Columbia and US insular territories
CPI score – 69 (23)
Military expenditure – US$648,798m (2018)

CLIMATE AND TERRAIN
The coastline has a length of about 3,329km on the Atlantic Ocean, 12,268km on the Pacific, 1,705km on the Arctic and 2,624km on the Gulf of Mexico. The principal river is the Mississippi-Missouri-Red (5,970km long), traversing the whole country from Montana to its mouth in the Gulf of Mexico. The Rocky mountains range runs the length of the western portion of the country. West of this, bordering the Pacific coast, the Cascade mountains and Sierra Nevada form the outer edge of a high tableland, consisting partly of stony and sandy desert and partly of grazing land and forested mountains, and including the Great Salt Lake, which extends to the Rocky mountains. A vast central plain lies between the Rockies and the hills and low mountains of the eastern states, where large forests still exist, remnants of the forests that formerly extended over the entire Atlantic slope. Elevation extremes range from 6,190m (Denali, Alaska) to −86m (Death Valley, California). The climate varies with latitude but is mostly temperate, with semi-arid conditions on the Great Plains and arid in the south-west. Average temperatures range from −4.8°C in January to 20°C in July.

Two states are detached: Alaska and Hawaii. Alaska occupies the north-western extremity of North America, separated from the rest of the USA by the Canadian province of British Columbia. The terrain is arctic tundra with mountain ranges, and the climate is arctic. The state of Hawaii is a chain of about 20 mountainous volcanic islands in the north Pacific

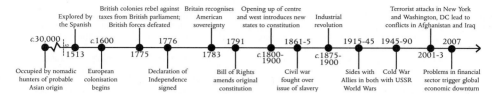

Timeline:

- c.30,000 — Occupied by nomadic hunters of probable Asian origin
- 1513 — Explored by the Spanish
- c.1600 — European colonisation begins
- 1775 — British colonies rebel against taxes from British parliament; British forces defeated
- 1776 — Declaration of Independence signed
- 1783 — Britain recognises American sovereignty
- 1791 — Bill of Rights amends original constitution
- c.1800–1900 — Opening up of centre and west introduces new states to constitution
- 1861–5 — Civil war fought over issue of slavery
- c.1875–1900 — Industrial revolution
- 1915–45 — Sides with Allies in both World Wars
- 1945–90 — Cold War in both with USSR
- 2001–3 — Terrorist attacks in New York and Washington, DC lead to conflicts in Afghanistan and Iraq
- 2007 — Problems in financial sector trigger global economic downturn

Ocean, of which the chief islands are Hawaii, Maui, Oahu, Kauai and Molokai. The climate is tropical.

The Pacific coast and Hawaii are prone to seismic activity. The Atlantic and Gulf of Mexico coasts frequently experience hurricanes.

POLITICS

By the constitution of 17 September 1787 (which has been amended 15 times, most recently in 1992), the government of the USA is entrusted to three separate authorities: the federal executive (the president and cabinet), the legislature (Congress, which consists of a senate and a House of Representatives) and the judicature. The president is indirectly elected by an electoral college to serve a four-year term, and may serve a maximum of two consecutive terms. If a president dies in office, the vice-president serves the remainder of the term. The president appoints the cabinet officers and all the chief officials, subject to confirmation by the senate. They makes recommendations of a general nature to Congress, and when laws are passed, they can return them to Congress with a veto. But, if a measure so vetoed is again passed by both houses by a two-thirds majority in each house, it becomes law, notwithstanding the objection of the president.

Each of the 50 states has its own executive, legislature and judiciary. In theory, they are sovereign, but in practice their autonomy is increasingly circumscribed.

Barack Obama's two terms as president were characterised domestically by healthcare reform and tighter financial regulations following the 2007–8 global financial crisis. Internationally, Obama expanded the use of military air strikes and special forces in dealing with global terrorism, and took measures to combat climate change which culminated in the 2016 Paris Agreement. Upon taking office in November 2016, President Donald Trump oversaw efforts to counteract the Paris Agreement domestically, alongside anti-immigration measures and tax cuts. Trump's international aims focused on denuclearising the Korean peninsular and tackling perceived Iranian aggression. President Trump was impeached in December 2019 on charges of abuse of power and obstruction of congress, over claims he withheld military aid in an effort to pressure Ukraine into announcing an investigation into Democratic rival Joe Biden's son; he became the third US president to have been impeached. Trump was acquitted by the senate in February 2020.

PRESIDENTIAL ELECTIONS

Candidates for the presidency must be at least 35 years of age and a native citizen of the USA. The electoral college for each state is directly elected by universal adult suffrage in the November preceding the January in which the presidential term expires. The number of members of the electoral college is equal to the whole number of senators and representatives to which the state is entitled in the national congress. The electoral college for each state meets in its state in December and each member votes for a presidential candidate by ballot. The ballots are sent to Washington, DC, and opened on 6 January by the president of the senate in the presence of Congress. The candidate who has received a majority of the whole number of electoral votes cast is declared president for

the ensuing term. If no one has a majority, then from the highest on the list (not exceeding three) the House of Representatives elects a president, the votes being taken by states, the representation from each state having one vote. A presidential term begins at noon on 20 January.

The 2008 presidential election was won by the Democrat candidate Barack Obama, the first African-American to hold the office; he was re-elected in November 2012. The November 2016 presidential election was won by the Republican candidate, Donald Trump. Democrat and former vice-president Joe Biden won the November 2020 election, the results of which were challenged by President Trump; with over 81.2 million votes, Biden received the highest number of votes of any presidential candidate in US history. Kamala Harris became the first woman and first person of colour to be appointed vice-president.

HEAD OF STATE

President, Donald J. Trump, *elected* 2016, *sworn in* 20 January 2017
Vice-President, Mike Pence
President-elect, Joe Biden
Vice-President-elect, Kamala Harris

SELECTED GOVERNMENT MEMBERS *AS AT DECEMBER 2020*

Defense, Christopher Milles *(acting)*
Interior, David Bernhardt
Secretary for Homeland Security, Chad Wolf *(acting)*
Secretary of State, Mike Pompeo
Treasury, Steven T. Mnuchin

THE CONGRESS

Legislative power is vested in the bicameral Congress, comprising the senate and the House of Representatives. The senate has 100 members, two from each state, elected for a six-year term, with one-third elected every two years. The House of Representatives has 435 members directly elected in each state for a two-year term; a resident commissioner from Puerto Rico and a delegate each from American Samoa, the District of Columbia, Guam, the Northern Mariana Islands and the Virgin Islands serve as non-voting members of the house.

In the 2018 legislative elections, the Republican Party lost its majority in the House of Representatives to the Democratic Party but retained control of the senate. The Democrats maintained their lower-house majority in the November 2020 elections; the balance of power in the senate will be decided via a runoff election in Georgia in January 2021. Members of the 117th Congress were elected on 3 November 2020 and were sworn into office on 3 January 2021. As at December 2020, Congress is constituted as follows:
Senate: Republicans 53; Democrats 45; Independents 2
House of Representatives: Democrats 233; Republicans 196; Libertarian 1
President of the Senate, The Vice-President
Senate majority leader, Mitch McConnell *(R), Kentucky*
Speaker of the House of Representatives, Nancy Pelosi *(D), California*
House majority leader, Steny Hoyer *(D), Maryland*

THE JUDICATURE

The federal judiciary consists of three sets of federal courts: the Supreme Court at Washington, DC, consisting of a Chief Justice and eight Associate Justices; the US court of appeals, consisting of 179 circuit judges within 12 regional circuits and one federal circuit; and the 94 US district courts served by 678 district court judges.

THE SUPREME COURT

US Supreme Court Building, Washington, DC 20543
Chief Justice, John Roberts Jr., *apptd* 2005

UNITED STATES EMBASSY

33 Nine Elms Lane, London SW11 7US
T 020-7499 9000 **W** http://london.usembassy.gov
Ambassador Extraordinary and Plenipotentiary, HE Robert Wood Johnson IV, *apptd* 2017

BRITISH EMBASSY

3100 Massachusetts Avenue NW, Washington, DC 20008
T (+1) (202) 588 6500 **E** washi@fco.gov.uk
W www.gov.uk/government/world/usa
Ambassador Extraordinary and Plenipotentiary, Karen Pierce, DCMG

ECONOMY AND TRADE

The USA is one of the world's leading industrial nations, with a sophisticated market economy that saw huge growth during the 20th century. Economic development was due in part to the mechanisation of the agrarian economy, the expansion of the transport infrastructure and large amounts of relatively cheap migrant labour; more recently it has been driven by rapid advances in technology. In the late 20th century, the economy shifted emphasis from industry to services, and government involvement in the economy was steadily reduced.

The US sub-prime mortgage crisis in 2007 triggered a global economic downturn, and falling property prices and tight credit pushed the domestic economy into recession by mid-2008. Following the failure of several investment banks, Congress passed a US$700bn relief programme to stabilise the financial markets in October 2008, a US$787bn fiscal stimulus package in spring 2009 and a record US$3.6 trillion budget in 2010. Despite these measures, the economy still experienced the collapse of key industries (such as vehicle manufacturing), and rising unemployment and inflation before growth restarted in late 2009 after the USA's longest and deepest recession since the 1930s, and grew steadily during 2009–19. By 2018, the wars in Iraq and Afghanistan had cost the treasury an estimated US$1.9 trillion. President Trump's corporate and individual tax cuts introduced in January 2018 strengthened private spending but increased the federal deficit, which was exacerbated by the coronavirus pandemic in 2020, while he also pursued a trade standoff with China that slowed growth globally. However the coronavirus pandemic heavily impacted the country, causing over 300,000 deaths as at December 2020 and resulting in an estimated economic contraction of 4.3 per cent in 2020. Rising inequality, an aging population, stagnating lower and middle-income wages, and a deteriorating infrastructure pose long-term challenges.

Agriculture is a major industry in the USA; principal crops are wheat, maize, other grains, fruit, vegetables, cotton, meat and dairy products. Agriculture, fishing and forestry contribute 0.9 per cent of GDP and employ 0.7 per cent of the workforce.

Mining and extraction are important to the economy. Large quantities of coal, iron ore, phosphate rock, copper, zinc and lead are mined. Over one-half of the country's oil requirements are imported, with global prices acting as a major determinant of the health of the economy. Natural gas is also produced. Despite its domestic oil and natural gas resources and its electricity generating capacity, the USA is a net importer of energy.

The industrial sector is highly diversified and technologically advanced. The main manufacturing industries produce steel, vehicles, aircraft and aerospace equipment, telecommunications equipment, chemicals, electronic equipment and consumer goods, and process food. Industry contributes 19.1 per cent of GDP and services account for 80 per cent of GDP.

The main trading partners are Canada, China, Mexico, Japan and Germany. Principal exports are capital goods (chiefly transistors, aircraft, vehicle parts, computers, telecommunications equipment), industrial supplies, consumer goods (cars, medicines) and agricultural produce (soya beans, fruit, maize). The main imports are industrial goods (especially crude oil), consumer goods (cars, clothing, medicines, furniture, toys), capital goods (computers, telecommunications equipment, vehicle parts, office machines, electric power machinery) and agricultural products.

GNI – US$21,584.4bn; US$65,760 per capita (2019)
Annual average growth of GDP – 2.16 per cent (2019 est)
Inflation rate – 2.1 per cent (2017 est)
Population below poverty line – 15.1 per cent (2010 est)
Unemployment – 3.894 per cent (2018 est)
Total external debt – US$17.91 trillion (2016 est)
Imports – US$2,898,989m (2017)
Exports – US$2,334,257m (2017)

BALANCE OF PAYMENTS

Trade – US$564,731m deficit (2017)
Current Account – US$480,228m deficit (2019)

Trade with UK	2018	2019
Imports from UK	£48,829,413,959	£57,392,343,840
Exports to UK	£44,466,459,174	£51,065,969,610

COMMUNICATIONS

Airports – There are 5,054 airports; nearly 200 are capable of handling international flights, the rest cater for the high domestic demand
Waterways – The main seaports are at Baton Rouge, Corpus Christi, Hampton Roads, Houston, Long Beach, Los Angeles, Miami, New Orleans, New York, Oaklands, Plaquemines, Port Canaveral, Port Everglades, Savannah, Seattle, Tampa and Texas City
Roadways and railways – 6,586,610km; 293,564km
Telecommunications – 107.7 million fixed lines and 408.5 million mobile subscriptions (2019); there were 285.5 million internet users in 2018
Internet code and IDD – us; 1 (from UK), 011 44 (to UK)
Major broadcasters – The major television networks are ABC, CBS, NBC, CNN, Fox, MTV, HBO and the Public Broadcasting System, which serves around 350 local member stations and is partially funded by the government and private grants
Press – There are more than 1,500 daily newspapers, including *The Wall Street Journal, USA Today, The Washington Post* and *The New York Times*
WPFI score – 23.85 (45)

EDUCATION AND HEALTH

All the states have compulsory school attendance laws. In general, children are obliged to attend school from seven to 16 years of age.
Gross enrolment ratio (percentage of relevant age group) – primary 101.3 per cent, secondary 99.3 per cent; tertiary 88.3 per cent (2018 est)

THE STATES OF THE UNION

The USA is a federal republic consisting of 50 states and the federal District of Columbia, and also of organised territories. Of the present 50 states, 13 are original states, seven were admitted without previous organisation as territories, and 30 were admitted after such organisation.

§ The 13 original states

(D) Democratic Party; (I) Independent; (R) Republican Party; New Progressive Party (NPP)

State (date and order of admission)	Capital	Governor (end of term in office)	Area (sq. km)	Pop.*
Alabama (AL) (1819, 22)	Montgomery	Kay Ivey (R), Jan. 2021	135,767	4,903,185
Alaska (AK) (1959, 49)	Juneau	Mike Dunleavy (R), Dec. 2022	1,723,337	731,545
Arizona (AZ) (1912, 48)	Phoenix	Doug Ducey (R), Jan 2023	295,234	7,278,717
Arkansas (AR) (1836, 25)	Little Rock	Asa Hutchinson (R), Jan. 2023	137,732	3,017,804
California (CA) (1850, 31)	Sacramento	Gavin Newsom (D), Jan. 2023	423,967	39,512,223
Colorado (CO) (1876, 38)	Denver	Jared Polis (D), Jan. 2023	269,601	5,758,736
Connecticut (CT) § (1788, 5)	Hartford	Ned Lamont (D), Jan. 2023	14,357	3,565,287
Delaware (DE) § (1787,1)	Dover	John Carney (D), Jan. 2021	6,446	973,764
Florida (FL) (1845, 27)	Tallahassee	Ron DeSantis (R), Jan. 2023	170,312	21,477,737
Georgia (GA) § (1788, 4)	Atlanta	Brian Kemp (R), Jan. 2023	153,910	10,617,423
Hawaii (HI) (1959, 50)	Honolulu	David Ige (D), Dec. 2022	28,313	1,415,872
Idaho (ID) (1890, 43)	Boise	Brad Little (R), Jan. 2023	216,443	1,787,065
Illinois (IL) (1818, 21)	Springfield	JB Pritzker (D), Jan. 2023	149,995	12,671,821
Indiana (IN) (1816, 19)	Indianapolis	Eric Holcomb (R), Jan. 2021	94,326	6,732,219
Iowa (IA) (1846, 29)	Des Moines	Kim Reynolds (R), Jan. 2021	145,746	3,155,070
Kansas (KS) (1861, 34)	Topeka	Laura Kelly (D), Jan. 2023	213,100	2,913,314
Kentucky (KY) (1792, 15)	Frankfort	Andy Beshear, (D), Dec. 2023	104,656	4,467,673
Louisiana (LA) (1812, 18)	Baton Rouge	John Bel Edwards (D), Jan. 2020	135,659	4,648,794
Maine (ME) (1820, 23)	Augusta	Janet Mills (D), Jan. 2023	91,633	1,344,212
Maryland (MD) § (1788, 7)	Annapolis	Larry Hogan (R), Jan. 2023	32,131	6,045,680
Massachusetts (MA) § (1788, 6)	Boston	Charlie Baker (R), Jan. 2023	27,336	6,892,503
Michigan (MI) (1837, 26)	Lansing	Gretchen Whitmer (D), Jan. 2023	250,487	9,986,857
Minnesota (MN) (1858, 32)	St Paul	Tim Walz (D), Jan. 2023	225,163	5,639,632
Mississippi (MS) (1817, 20)	Jackson	Tate Reeves (R), Jan 2024	125,438	2,976,149
Missouri (MO) (1821, 24)	Jefferson City	Mike Parson (R), Jan. 2021	180,540	6,137,428
Montana (MT) (1889, 41)	Helena	Steve Bullock (D), Jan. 2021	380,831	1,068,778
Nebraska (NE) (1867, 37)	Lincoln	Pete Ricketts (R), Jan. 2023	200,330	1,934,408
Nevada (NV) (1864, 36)	Carson City	Steve Sisolak (D), Jan. 2023	286,380	3,080,156
New Hampshire (NH) § (1788, 9)	Concord	Chris Sununu (R), Jan. 2023	24,214	1,359,711
New Jersey (NJ) § (1787, 3)	Trenton	Phil Murphy (D), Jan. 2022	22,591	8,882,190
New Mexico (NM) (1912, 47)	Santa Fe	Michelle L Grisham (R), Jan. 2023	314,917	2,096,829
New York (NY) § (1788, 11)	Albany	Andrew Cuomo (D), Jan. 2023	141,297	19,453,561
North Carolina (NC) § (1789, 12)	Raleigh	Roy Cooper (D), Jan. 2021	139,391	10,488,084
North Dakota (ND) (1889, 39)	Bismarck	Doug Burgum (R), Dec. 2020	183,108	762,062
Ohio (OH) (1803, 17)	Columbus	Mike DeWine (R), Jan. 2023	116,098	11,689,100
Oklahoma (OK) (1803, 17)	Oklahoma City	Kevin Stitt (R), Jan. 2023	181,037	3,956,971
Oregon (OR) (1859, 33)	Salem	Kate Brown (D), Jan. 2023	254,799	4,217,737
Pennsylvania (PA) § (1787, 2)	Harrisburg	Tom Wolf (D), Jan. 2023	119,280	12,801,989
Rhode Island (RI) § (1790, 13)	Providence	Gina Raimondo (D), Jan. 2023	4,001	1,059,361
South Carolina (SC) § (1788, 8)	Columbia	Henry McMaster (R), Jan. 2021	82,933	5,148,714
South Dakota (SD) (1889, 40)	Pierre	Kristi Noem (R), Jan. 2023	199,729	884,659
Tennessee (TN) (1796, 16)	Nashville	Bill Lee (R), Jan. 2023	109,153	6,829,174
Texas (TX) (1845, 28)	Austin	Greg Abbott (R), Jan. 2023	695,662	28,995,881
Utah (UT) (1896, 45)	Salt Lake City	Gary Herbert (R), Jan. 2021	219,882	3,205,959
Vermont (VT) (1791, 14)	Montpelier	Phil Scott (R), Jan. 2021	24,906	623,989
Virginia (VA) § (1788, 10)	Richmond	Ralph Northam (D), Jan. 2022	110,787	8,535,519
Washington (WA) (1889, 42)	Olympia	Jay Inslee (D), Jan. 2021	184,661	7,614,893
West Virginia (WV) (1863, 35)	Charleston	Jim Justice (D), Jan. 2021	62,756	1,792,147
Wisconsin (WI) (1848, 30)	Madison	Tony Evers (D), Jan. 2023	169,635	5,822,434
Wyoming (WY) (1890, 44)	Cheyenne	Mark Gordon (R), Jan. 2023	253,335	578,759
Dist. of Columbia (DC) (1791)	–	Muriel Bowser (D), Jan. 2022 *(Mayor)*	177	705,749

OUTLYING TERRITORIES AND POSSESSIONS

American Samoa	Pago Pago	Lolo Matalasi Moliga (I), Jan. 2021	199	58,500
Guam	Hagatna	Lou Leon Guerrero (D), Jan. 2023	544	167,294
Northern Mariana Islands	Saipan	Ralph Torres (R), Dec. 2019	464	57,216
Puerto Rico	San Juan	Wanda Garced (NPP), Jan. 2021	13,790	3,193,694
US Virgin Islands	Charlotte Amalie	Albert Bryan (D), Jan. 2023	1,910	104,578

* States 2019 estimate; outlying territories 2019 estimate

Health expenditure (per capita) – US$10,246 (2017)
Hospital beds (per 1,000 people) – 2.9 (2013)
Life expectancy (years) – 80.3 (2020 est)
Mortality rate – 8.3 (2020 est)
Birth rate – 12.4 (2020 est)
Infant mortality rate – 5.3 (2020 est)

US TERRITORIES ETC

US insular areas are territories that are not part of one of the 50 US states or a federal district. The US Department of the Interior's Office of Insular Affairs has jurisdiction over American Samoa, Guam, the Northern Mariana Islands, the US Virgin Islands, part of Palmyra Atoll (4 sq. km) and Wake Atoll (6.4 sq. km), the latter shared with the US army's Space and Strategic Defence Command. The US Fish and Wildlife Service has jurisdiction over Baker Island (1.5 sq. km), Howland Island (2.5 sq. km), Jarvis Island (4.2 sq. km), Johnston Atoll (2.5 sq. km, shared with the Defence Threat Reduction Agency), Midway Atoll (5.2 sq. km), Navassa Island (7.8 sq. km), Kingman Reef and part of Palmyra Atoll. The Aleutian Islands (17,666 sq. km) form part of the Alaskan archipelago.

AMERICAN SAMOA
Territory of American Samoa
Area – 199 sq. km
Capital – Pago Pago; population, 49,000 (2018 est)
Population – 49,437 falling at 1.4 per cent a year (2020 est)
Population density – 277 per sq. km (2019)
Urban population – 87.1 per cent (2019 est)
Median age (years) – 27.2 (2020 est)
National day – 17 April (Flag Day)
American Samoa consists of the islands of Tutuila, Aunu'u, Ofu, Olosega, Ta'u, Rose Island and Swains Island. The islands were discovered by Europeans in the 18th century and the USA took possession in 1900. Those born in American Samoa are US non-citizen nationals, although some have acquired citizenship through service in the US armed forces or other naturalisation procedures. American Samoa is represented in Congress by a non-voting delegate, who is directly elected for a two-year term. Under the 1966 constitution, American Samoa has a measure of self-government, with certain powers reserved to the US Secretary of the Interior. The governor and deputy governor are directly elected for a four-year term. The bicameral legislative assembly comprises a 21-member House of Representatives (one appointed member and 20 members directly elected for a two-year term) and an 18-seat senate with members elected from among the traditional chiefs for a four-year term. Tuna fishing and canning are the principal economic activities.
Governor, Lemanu Palepoi Mauga (I)

GUAM
Guåhan – Territory of Guam
Area – 544 sq. km
Capital – Hagåtña (also known as Agana); population, 147,000 (2018 est)
Population – 168,485 rising at 0.2 per cent a year (2020 est); Chamorro (37.3 per cent), Filipino (26.3 per cent) (est).The official languages are Chamorro (a language of the Malayo-Polynesian family with Spanish) and English; most Chamorro residents are bilingual
Religion – Roman Catholic 85 per cent (est)
Population density – 307 per sq. km (2019)
Urban population – 94.9 per cent (2019 est)
Median age (years) – 29.4 (2020 est)
National day – first Monday in March (Discovery Day)
Guam is the largest of the Mariana Islands, in the north Pacific Ocean. A Spanish colony for centuries, it was ceded to the USA in 1898 after the Spanish–American War. Guam was occupied

by the Japanese in 1941 but was recaptured by US forces in 1944. Any person born in Guam is a US citizen. Guam is represented in Congress by a non-voting delegate, who is directly elected for a two-year term. Under the Organic Act of Guam 1950, Guam has statutory powers of self-government. The governor and lieutenant-governor are directly elected for a four-year term, renewable once. The 15-member unicameral legislature is directly elected every two years; the November 2020 election returned eight Democrats and seven Republicans. The main sources of revenue are tourism (particularly from Japan) and US military spending; the military installation is one of the most strategically important US bases in the Pacific.
Governor, Lourdes Leon Guerrero (D)
Imports – US$707m (2014)
Exports – US$41m (2014)

Trade with UK	2018	2019
Imports from UK	£3,151,911	£2,805,717
Exports to UK	£291,187	£681,578

NORTHERN MARIANA ISLANDS
Commonwealth of the Northern Mariana Islands
Area – 464 sq. km
Seat of government – Saipan; population, 51,000 (2018 est)
Population – 51,433 falling at 0.55 per cent a year (2020 est); Asian (predominantly Filipino and Chinese) (50 per cent), Native Hawaiian or Pacific Islander (34.9 per cent) (est)
Population density – 124 per sq. km (2019)
Urban population – 91.7 per cent (2019 est)
Median age (years) – 32.8 (2020 est)
National day – 8 January (Commonwealth Day)
The USA administered the Northern Mariana Islands, a group of 14 islands in the north-west Pacific Ocean, as part of a UN trusteeship until the trusteeship agreement was terminated in 1986, when the islands became a commonwealth under US sovereignty. Those resident in 1976 or subsequently born in the islands are US citizens. The islands are represented in Congress by a non-voting representative, who is directly elected for a two-year term. Under the 1978 constitution, the islands are self-governing. The governor and lieutenant-governor are directly elected for a four-year term. The bicameral legislature comprises a 20-member House of Representatives and a nine-member senate; members are directly elected, representatives for two years and senators for four years. Tourism and manufacturing, especially of clothing, are the main industries.
Governor, Ralph Deleon Guerrero Torres (R)

PUERTO RICO
Commonwealth of Puerto Rico
Area – 13,791 sq. km
Capital – San Juan; population, 2,448,000 (2020 est). Other major towns are Bayamón, Carolina, Poncel
Population – 3,189,068 falling at 1.59 per cent a year (2020 est)
Religion – Christian (Roman Catholic 85 per cent, Protestant and other 15 per cent) (est)
Population density – 360 per sq. km (2019)
Urban population – 93.6 per cent (2019 est)
Median age (years) – 43.6 (2020 est)
National day – 25 July (Constitution Day)
GNI – US$70.2bn; US$21,970 per capita (2019)
Annual average growth of GDP – −2.4 per cent (2017 est)
Puerto Rico (Rich Port) is an island of the Greater Antilles group in the Caribbean Sea and was discovered in 1493 by Columbus. It was a Spanish possession until 1898, when it

was ceded to the USA after the Spanish–American War. Residents have been US citizens since 1917, and Puerto Rico is represented in Congress by a non-voting resident commissioner, who is directly elected for a four-year term. Under its 1952 constitution, Puerto Rico is a self-governing commonwealth. The governor is directly elected for a four-year term. Ricardo Rosselló resigned as governor in July 2019 after leaked text messaged showed him using homophobic and misogynistic language, which provoked widespread protests. The bicameral legislative assembly consists of a 27-member senate and a 51-member House of Representatives, whose members serve four-year terms. Tourism, pharmaceuticals, electronics, clothing and food processing are the main economic activities. In May 2017, Puerto Rico filed for the largest municipal bankruptcy in US history having accrued a US$70bn debt over ten years of recession, while an overwhelming majority of voters backed a plebiscite in June to become a fully fledged US state. Growth has been negative since 2006. Following Hurricane Maria in September 2017, the island was declared a federal disaster zone.

Governor, Pedro Pierluisi Urrutia (NPP)

THE UNITED STATES VIRGIN ISLANDS
Area – 1,910 sq. km
Capital – Charlotte Amalie, on St Thomas; population, 52,000 (2018 est)
Population – 106,235 falling at 0.37 per cent a year (2020 est)
Religion – Christian (Protestant 59 per cent, Roman Catholic 34 per cent) (est)
Population density – 306 per sq. km (2019)
Urban population – 95.8 per cent (2019 est)
Median age (years) – 41.8 (2020 est)
National day – 31 March (Transfer Day)
There are three main islands, St Thomas, St Croix and St John, and about 50 small islets or cays. These constituted the Danish part of the Virgin Islands from the 17th century until purchased by the USA in 1917. Those born in the US Virgin Islands are US nationals. The Virgin Islands are represented in Congress by a non-voting representative, who is directly elected for a two-year term. Under the provisions of the Revised Organic Act of 1954, the islands have powers of self-government. The governor and lieutenant-governor are directly elected for a four-year term. The unicameral senate has 15 members directly elected for a two-year term. Tourism, rum and manufacturing are the main industries.

Governor, Albert Bryan (D)

URUGUAY

República Oriental del Uruguay – Oriental Republic of Uruguay

Area – 176,215 sq. km
Capital – Montevideo; population, 1,752,000 (2020 est)
Major towns – Ciudad de la Costa, Salto
Currency – Uruguayan peso of 100 centésimos

Population – 3,387,605 rising at 0.27 per cent a year (2020 est)
Religion – Christian (Roman Catholic 47.1 per cent, non-Catholic Christians 11.1 per cent) (est)
Language – Spanish (official)
Population density – 20 per sq. km (2019)
Urban population – 95.4 per cent (2019 est)
Median age (years) – 35.5 (2020 est)
National anthem – 'Himno Nacional' 'National Anthem'
National day – 25 August (Independence Day)
Death penalty – Abolished for all crimes (since 1907)
CPI score – 71 (21)
Military expenditure – US$1,168m (2018)

CLIMATE AND TERRAIN
The country consists mainly of undulating grassy plains, with low hills. Elevation extremes range from 514m (Cerro Catedral) to 0m (Atlantic Ocean). The principal river is the Rio Negro (with its tributary, the Yi), flowing from north-east to south-west into the Rio Uruguay; damming of the Negro has created a reservoir that is the largest artificial lake in South America. The climate is warm temperate, with occasional cold and strong winds. Average temperatures range from 11.5°C in July to 24.1°C in January.

HISTORY AND POLITICS
The hostility of the indigenous Charrúa Amerindians when the Rio de la Plata was first explored by the Spanish in 1516 discouraged colonisation until the 17th century. Although initially settled by the Portuguese, the *Banda Oriental,* as the territory lying on the eastern bank of the river Uruguay was then called, was disputed between the Portuguese and the Spanish until the late 18th century and then between Brazil and Argentina after Spanish rule was overthrown. Uruguay's independence was recognised in 1828 and a republic was inaugurated in 1830. In the mid-19th century there was a power struggle between the conservatives *(Blancos)* and liberals *(Colorados),* which descended into civil war. From 1904 until the 1960s the country experienced political stability and prosperity.

The period from 1962 to 1973 saw economic decline and turmoil caused by the Marxist Tupamaros guerrillas. They were crushed by a military dictatorship that held power from 1973 until 1985, when a return to civilian rule was agreed after violent anti-government protests at the regime's repressive rule and the deteriorating economy.

The Colorado and National *(Blanco)* parties occupy the centre ground, but their dominance has been eroded by left-wing parties such as New Space and coalitions such as Broad Front (BF). The BF lost support in the October 2019 general election but remained the largest bloc in both chambers. The centre-right candidate Luis Lacalle Pou won the November 2019 presidential runoff, ending 15 years of BF rule.

Under the 1997 constitution, the executive president is directly elected for a five-year term, which is not consecutively renewable. The president, who appoints the council of ministers, is responsible to the legislature. The bicameral general assembly consists of a Chamber of Representatives, with 99 members directly elected for a five-year term, and the Chamber of Senators, which has 31 members, 30 directly elected for a five-year term and the vice-president as an *ex officio* member.

The republic is divided into 19 departments, each with an elected governor and legislature.

HEAD OF STATE
President, Luis Lacalle Pou, *elected* 24 November 2020, *sworn in* 1 March 2020
Vice-President, Beatrice Argimom Cedeira

SELECTED GOVERNMENT MEMBERS *AS AT NOVEMBER 2020*
Defence, Javier García
Economy and Finance, Azucena Arbeleche
Foreign Affairs, Francisco Bustillo Bonasso
Interior, Jorge Larrañaga

EMBASSY OF URUGUAY
150 Brompton Road, London SW3 1HX
T 020-7584 2947 E cdlondres@mrree.gub.uy
Ambassador Extraordinary and Plenipotentiary, vacant

BRITISH EMBASSY
PO Box 16024, Calle Marco Bruto 1073, 11300 Montevideo
T (+598) (2) 622 3630 E ukinuruguay@adinet.com.uy
W www.gov.uk/government/world/uruguay
Ambassador Extraordinary and Plenipotentiary, HE Fay
    O'Connor, *apptd* 2020

ECONOMY AND TRADE

After years of steady growth, Uruguay's free market, export-oriented economy suffered a severe recession from 1998, largely owing to the economic problems of Brazil and Argentina, its main markets and sources of tourists. The recession culminated in a banking crisis in 2002; IMF loans, the rescheduling of foreign debt repayments and the government's emergency measures achieved a recovery and the economy grew strongly from 2004 to 2008. The 2008 global downturn slowed economic growth in 2009, but Uruguay avoided recession, mainly through increased public expenditure. The economy decelerated between 2012 and 2016, before improving in 2017 and 2018. Weak growth in 2019, due to a slowdown in Brazil, was followed by contraction in 2020 by an estimated 4.5 per cent.

Ranching and livestock products (beef, mutton, wool) have been the mainstay of the economy since the mid-19th century, generating the prosperity that enabled Uruguay to develop an extensive welfare system in the early 20th century, although dependence on these products leaves the economy vulnerable to price fluctuations. Other crops include rice, grains, soya beans, wine grapes, linseed and sunflower seed. Agricultural produce is the basis of the food processing and beverage industries. Other industries include fishing, forestry and the manufacture of electrical machinery, transport equipment, petroleum products, textiles and chemicals. Exploited minerals include clinker, dolomite, marble and granite. Tourism and offshore financial services also contribute substantially to revenue. Agriculture contributes 6.2 per cent of GDP, industry 24.1 per cent and services 69.7 per cent.

The main trading partners are China, Brazil, Argentina and the USA. Principal exports are meat, soya beans, cellulose, rice, wheat, timber, dairy products and wool. The main imports are crude and refined oil, vehicles and vehicle parts, and mobile phones.

GNI – US$56.2bn; US$16,230 per capita (2019)
Annual average growth of GDP – 2.7 per cent (2017 est)
Inflation rate – 6.2 per cent (2017 est)
Population below poverty line – 9.7 per cent (2015 est)
Unemployment – 7.6 per cent (2017 est)
Total external debt – US$28.37bn (2017 est)
Imports – US$12,218m (2017)
Exports – US$14,783m (2017)

BALANCE OF PAYMENTS
Trade – US$2,565m surplus (2017)
Current Account – US$743m surplus (2019)

Trade with UK	2018	2019
Imports from UK	£134,806,741	£136,507,184
Exports to UK	£59,649,519	£50,743,661

COMMUNICATIONS

Airports and waterways – There are 11 airports, including an international airport near Montevideo; there are 1,600km of navigable waterways, mainly on the Uruguay and Negro rivers, and the main ports are located in Montevideo, Colonia, Fray Bentos and Paysandú
Roadways and railways – 7,732km of paved roadways; 1,673km
Telecommunications – 1.1 million fixed lines in use and 4.7 million mobile subscriptions (2019); there were 2.3 million internet users in 2018
Internet code and IDD – uy; 598 (from UK), 44 (to UK)
Major broadcasters – State-run television and radio are operated by SODRE, the official broadcasting service
Press – Major daily newspapers include *El Pais, El Observador* and *El Telegrafo*
WPFI score – 15.79 (19)

EDUCATION AND HEALTH

Primary and secondary education is compulsory and free, and technical and trade schools and evening courses for adult education are state-run.

Literacy rate – 98.7 per cent (2018 est)
Gross enrolment ratio (percentage of relevant age group) – primary 106 per cent, secondary 121.2 per cent (2018 est); tertiary 63.1 per cent (2017 est)
Health expenditure (per capita) – US$1,592 (2017)
Hospital beds (per 1,000 people) – 2.8 (2014)
Life expectancy (years) – 77.9 (2020 est)
Mortality rate – 9.3 (2020 est)
Birth rate – 12.9 (2020 est)
Infant mortality rate – 7.8 (2020 est)
HIV/AIDS adult prevalence – 0.6 per cent (2016 est)

UZBEKISTAN

O'zbekiston Respublikasi – Republic of Uzbekistan

Area – 447,400 sq. km
Capital – Tashkent; population, 2,517,000 (2020 est)
Major cities – Andijan, Bukhara, Karsi, Namangan, Nukus, Samarkand
Currency – Som of 100 tiyins
Population – 30,565,411 rising at 0.88 per cent a year (2020 est); Uzbek (83.8 per cent) (est). Other minority populations including Tajik, Kazakh, Russian, Karakalpak and Tatar
Religion – Muslim 88 per cent (predominantly Sunni), Eastern Orthodox 9 per cent (est)
Language – Uzbek (official), Russian, Tajik
Population density – 77 per sq. km (2019)
Urban population – 50.4 per cent (2019 est)
Median age (years) – 35.5 (2020 est)

National anthem – 'O'zbekiston Respublikasining Davlat Madhiyasi' 'National Anthem of the Republic of Uzbekistan'
National day – 1 September (Independence Day, 1991)
Death penalty – Abolished for all crimes (since 2008)
CPI score – 25 (153)
Conscription – 18 years of age; 1–12 months (selective)

CLIMATE AND TERRAIN
Landlocked Uzbekistan has four regions: the Ustyurt plateau and Amu Darya delta in the west; the Kyzyl Kum desert east of the Aral Sea; the Tien Shan and Pamir mountains in the east and south-east; and the fertile Fergana valley in the east, crossed by the Syr Darya river. Elevation extremes range from 4,301m (Adelunga Toghi) to −12m (Sariqarnish Kuli). The country includes the southern part of the Aral Sea. There is a semi-arid desert climate, although it is colder in the mountains. Average temperatures range from −2.6°C in January to 27.3°C in July.

HISTORY AND POLITICS
Settlements in the south developed as important transit points on the ancient 'Silk Road' in the first century BC. Bukhara and Samarkand became two of the most important cultural and academic centres in the Islamic world after the religion was introduced in the eighth century. In the 13th century the area became part of the Mongol Empire, with Samarkand as its capital during the reign of Amir Timur (Tamerlane). As the empire declined, independent principalities emerged. The three khanates in what is now Uzbekistan, Khiva, Kokand and Bukhara, were annexed by the Russian Empire in the second half of the 19th century. In 1917 a Bolshevik revolution broke out in Tashkent and by 1921 all of Uzbekistan had been absorbed into the USSR.

Uzbekistan declared its independence from the USSR on 1 September 1991 but post-independence political life has been dominated by the former communists. The main opposition parties, *Erk* (Freedom) and *Birlik* (Unity), were banned in 1992 and have since become inactive. The former communist leader Islam Karimov, who came to power in 1990, was elected president in 1991 and retained the presidency, in unopposed elections or through the extension of his term of office in referendums, until his death in September 2016. Interim leader Shavkat Mirziyoev overwhelmingly won the December 2016 presidential election and Abdulla Aripov was nominated as prime minister.

All legislative elections since independence have been won by the People's Democratic Party (the former Communist Party) or its allies; opposition parties are barred from contesting elections.

The Islamic Movement of Uzbekistan (IMU), founded in 1996, has carried out armed attacks and bombings sporadically since 1999, but has little support. However, its activities have provided the government with an excuse to curtail human rights and suppress political opposition and protests.

The 1992 constitution was amended in 2002 to create a bicameral legislature and extend the president's term of office. In 2011 it was amended to make the prime minister responsible to the legislature and reduce presidential terms back to five years, after they were raised to seven years in 2002. The president is directly elected and terms are renewable only once. The legislature, the Supreme Assembly, became bicameral after the 2004–5 elections. The Legislative Chamber has 150 directly elected members. The senate has 100 members, 16 appointed by the president and 84 elected by regional deputies to represent the regions and the capital. Members of both houses serve a five-year term. The president appoints the cabinet, which is chaired by the prime minister.

The country is divided into 12 provinces, the autonomous republic of Karakalpakstan, and the city of Tashkent.

HEAD OF STATE
President, Shavkat Mirziyoev, *sworn in* 8 September 2016, *elected* 2 December 2016

SELECTED GOVERNMENT MEMBERS *AS AT NOVEMBER 2020*
Prime Minister, Abdulla Aripov
First Deputy Prime Minister, Achilbay Ramatov
Deputy Prime Ministers, Jamshid Kuchkarov *(Finance);* Aziz Abdukhakimov; Elmira Basitkhanova
Foreign Affairs, Abdulaziz Kamilov

EMBASSY OF THE REPUBLIC OF UZBEKISTAN
41 Holland Park, London W11 3RP
T 020-7229 7679 **E** info@uzbekembassy.org
W www.uzbekembassy.org
Ambassador Extraordinary and Plenipotentiary, HE Said Rusamov, *apptd* 2019

BRITISH EMBASSY
Ul. Gulyamova 67, Tashkent 100000
T (+998) (71) 120 1500 **E** ukin.uzbekistan@fco.gov.uk
W www.gov.uk/government/world/uzbekistan
Ambassador Extraordinary and Plenipotentiary, HE Timothy Torlot, *apptd* 2019

ECONOMY AND TRADE
The economy remains centrally planned, but under President Mirziyoev's reforms the private sector has expanded. Economic growth and living standards are among the worst in the former Soviet republics, and there is a large informal economy. The 2008 global downturn had little impact owing to the country's relative economic isolation, and the government has since sought foreign investment by devaluing the official currency by 50 per cent in September 2017 and loosening currency restrictions. Economic performance is closely tied to the Chinese and Russian economies, with strong growth reported in 2018 and 2019 prior to the coronavirus pandemic.

The economy is based on intensive agricultural production, particularly of cotton, made possible by extensive irrigation schemes. Vegetables, fruit, grain and livestock are also produced. The main industries are textile manufacture, food processing, machine building, metallurgy, mining (especially for gold), oil and natural gas production and chemicals. Oil and gas exports offer potential for greater economic growth and have attracted foreign interest, notably from Russia and China, but exploitation is hampered by a lack of modern oil pipelines and basic infrastructure. Agriculture contributes 17.9 per cent of GDP, industry 33.7 per cent and services 48.5 per cent.

The main trading partners are Russia, China, Switzerland, Kazakhstan and South Korea. Principal exports are oil and natural gas, cotton, gold, mineral fertilisers, metals, textiles, food products, machinery and motor vehicles. The main imports are machinery and equipment, foodstuffs, chemicals and metals.

GNI – US$60.4bn; US$1,800 per capita (2019)
Annual average growth of GDP – 5.3 per cent (2017 est)
Inflation rate – 12.5 per cent (2017 est)
Population below poverty line – 14 per cent (2016 est)
Unemployment – 5 per cent (2017 est)
Total external debt – US$16.9bn (2017 est)
Imports – US$13,013m (2017)
Exports – US$13,893m (2017)

BALANCE OF PAYMENTS
Trade – US$880m surplus (2017)
Current Account – US$3,360m deficit (2019)

Trade with UK	2018	2019
Imports from UK	£30,945,046	£40,840,383
Exports to UK	£1,639,190	£1,872,955,087

COMMUNICATIONS
Airports and waterways – The principal airport is at Tashkent and there are 1,100km of waterways
Roadways and railways – 86,496km; 4,642km
Telecommunications – 3.3 million fixed lines and 30.6 million mobile subscriptions (2019); there were 15.7 million internet users in 2018
Major broadcasters – The National Television and Radio Company is the state-operated broadcaster
Press – Leading dailies include *Khalq Sozi* (Uzbek language), and *Narodnoye Slovo* and *Pravda Vostoka* (both Russian language)
WPFI score – 53.07 (156)

EDUCATION AND HEALTH
Literacy rate – 100 per cent (2018 est)
Gross enrolment ratio (percentage of relevant age group) – primary 102.2 per cent, secondary 97.4 per cent, tertiary 12.6 per cent (2019 est)
Health expenditure (per capita) – US$99 (2017)
Hospital beds (per 1,000 people) – 4 (2013)
Life expectancy (years) – 74.8 (2020 est)
Mortality rate – 5.4 (2020 est)
Birth rate – 16.1 (2020 est)
Infant mortality rate – 16.3 (2020 est)
HIV/AIDS adult prevalence – 0.2 per cent (2019 est)

VANUATU

Ripablik blong Vanuatu/République de Vanuatu – Republic of Vanuatu

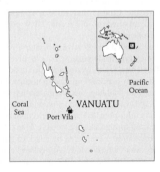

Area – 12,189 sq. km
Capital – Port Vila, on Efaté; population, 53,000 (2018 est)
Major town – Luganville, on Espiritu Santo
Currency – Vatu
Population – 298,333 rising at 1.73 per cent a year (2020 est); Melanesian (99.2 per cent) (est)
Religion – Christian (Protestant 70 per cent, Roman Catholic 12.4 per cent), other 12.9 per cent (est)
Language – Bislama, English, French (all official); over 100 local languages exist
Population density – 24 per sq. km (2019)
Urban population – 25.4 per cent (2019 est)
Median age (years) – 23 (2020 est)
National anthem – 'Yumi, Yumi, Yumi' 'We, We, We'
National day – 30 July (Independence Day)

Death penalty – Not since independence
CPI score – 46 (64)
Literacy rate – 87.5 per cent (2018 est)
Gross enrolment ratio (percentage of relevant age group) – primary 109.3 per cent, secondary 54.2 (2013 est)
Health expenditure (per capita) – US$166 (2017)
Life expectancy (years) – 74.6 (2020 est)
Mortality rate – 4 (2020 est)
Birth rate – 22.4 (2020 est)
Infant mortality rate – 12.7 (2020 est)

CLIMATE AND TERRAIN
Situated in the south Pacific Ocean, Vanuatu comprises 13 large and some 70 small islands, of either coral or volcanic origin, including the Banks Islands and Torres Islands in the north. The principal islands are Vanua Lava, Espiritu Santo, Maewo, Pentecost, Ambae, Malekula, Ambrym, Epi, Efaté, Erromango, Tanna and Aneityum. Most islands are mountainous and covered with dense rainforest. Elevation extremes range from 1,877m (Tabwemasana) to 0m (Pacific Ocean). The climate varies from tropical in the north of the archipelago to subtropical in the south, and all the islands experience cyclones. In 2018, a volcanic eruption on Ambae island forced the evacuation of all 11,000 inhabitants.

HISTORY AND POLITICS
Some of the islands of Vanuatu have been inhabited for over 4,000 years. Europeans first visited in the early 17th century, and Captain Cook named the islands the New Hebrides in 1774. In the 19th century, the British and the French established plantations, and from 1906 jointly administered the islands as the Condominium of the New Hebrides. This became independent as the Republic of Vanuatu in 1980.

Vanuatu has a history of producing unstable governments and three prime ministers have been deposed by parliamentary votes of no confidence since the 2012 elections: Sato Kilman in March 2013, Mona Kalosil in May 2014 and Joe Natuman in June 2015. Parliament was dissolved in November 2015 after 14 MPs were convicted of bribery. In the January 2016 legislative election no single party had a parliamentary majority and 11 political groupings formed the government; the March 2020 election also resulted in a coalition, this time of seven parties. Independent candidate Baldwin Lonsdale won the presidency in 2014 following eight rounds of voting, but was replaced by Tallis Obed Moses in July 2017 after his sudden death.

Under the 1980 constitution, the head of state is a president who is elected for a five-year term by an electoral college consisting of the members of the legislature and the presidents of the six provincial governments. The unicameral parliament has 52 members, directly elected for a four-year term. The prime minister is elected by parliament from among its members, and appoints the council of ministers. The National Council of Chiefs advises on matters of custom.

HEAD OF STATE
President, Tallis Obed Moses, *elected* 6 July 2017

SELECTED GOVERNMENT MEMBERS *AS AT NOVEMBER 2020*
Prime Minister, Bob Loughman
Deputy Prime Minister, Internal Affairs, Ishmael Kalsakau
Finance, Johnny Konapo

EMBASSY OF VANUATU
Avenue de Tervueren 380, Chemin de Ronde 1150, Brussels
T (+32) (2) 771 7494 **E** info@vanuataembassy.be
High Commissioner, HE Roy Mickey Joy, *apptd* 2011

BRITISH HIGH COMMISSION
La Casa D'Andrea E Luciano, Rue Pierre Lamy, Port Vila
T (+61) (02) 6270 6666
High Commissioner, HE Karen Bell, *apptd* 2019

ECONOMY AND TRADE

The economy is based on small-scale agriculture and fishing; around two-thirds of the population is employed on plantations or in subsistence agriculture, although the sector was devastated by Cyclone Pam in March 2015. Subsistence crops include yams, taro, fruit and vegetables; the principal cash crops are coconuts, cocoa and coffee. Cattle are kept on the plantations. There is a small light industrial sector producing frozen food, fish and canned meat, and processing wood. Eco-tourism and offshore financial services are of growing importance. While Australia and New Zealand supply revenue via aid, tourism from those countries was hit in 2016 when three major carriers suspended flights due to the poor runway conditions. Tourism has since improved and accounted for 40 per cent of GDP in 2019.

The main export markets are the Philippines, Australia and the USA; imports come chiefly from Russia, Australia, Japan and New Zealand. Principal exports are copra, beef, cocoa, timber, kava, coffee, coconut products and fish. The main imports are machinery and equipment, foodstuffs and fuels.

GNI – US$0.9bn; US$3,170 per capita (2019)
Annual average growth of GDP – 4.2 per cent (2017 est)
Inflation rate – 3.1 per cent (2017 est)
Total external debt – US$200.5m (2017 est)
Imports – US$411m (2017)
Exports – US$384m (2017)

BALANCE OF PAYMENTS
Trade – US$27m deficit (2017)
Current Account – US$85m surplus (2018)

Trade with UK	2018	2019
Imports from UK	£1,438,510	£433,916
Exports to UK	£797,742	£108,821

COMMUNICATIONS

Airports and waterways – The main international airport is at Port Vila and the main ports are located in Forari, Port Vila and Santo
Roadways – 1,070km
Telecommunications – 3,724 main fixed lines and 259,317 mobile subscriptions (2019); there were 74,083 internet users in 2016
Media – Vanuatu Broadcasting and Television Corporation operates Television Blong Vanuatu

VATICAN CITY STATE

Status Civitatis Vaticanae or Sancta Sedes/Stato della Città del Vaticano or Santa Sede – *State of the Vatican City*

Area – 0.44 sq. km (enclave only)
Capital – Vatican City; population 1,000 (2018 est)

Currency – Euro (€) of 100 cents
Population – 1,000 (2019 est)
Religion – Christian (Roman Catholic)
Language – Italian, Latin, French
National anthem – 'Inno e Marcia Pontificale' 'Hymn and Pontifical March'
National day – 13 March (election of Pope Francis)
Death penalty – Abolished for all crimes (since 1969)

HISTORY AND POLITICS

The Vatican City State is an independent sovereign state that consists of an enclave within the city of Rome and extraterritorial areas including offices and basilicas in Rome, the pope's summer residence and the location of Vatican Radio's transmitter. The Holy See, which comprises the pope and the departments that carry out the government of the Roman Catholic Church worldwide, has sovereign authority over the Vatican City State's territory, providing its government and diplomatic representation overseas.

The head of the Roman Catholic Church became a temporal ruler in the eighth century, holding territory in central Italy. The Papal States were annexed in 1860 by the newly unified kingdom of Italy, and Rome was captured by Italian troops in 1870–1, when the pope withdrew into the Vatican palace. In the Lateran treaties (1929), Italy recognised the pope's sovereignty over the city of the Vatican, and declared the state to be neutral and inviolable territory. The Vatican City State has special observer status at the United Nations.

The pope, the Sovereign Pontiff, is the head of state of the Vatican City, which is governed as an absolute monarchy. He is elected for life by a conclave consisting of those members of the Sacred College of Cardinals who are under the age of 80. Administration of the state is carried out by the Pontifical Commission and the Secretariat of State, which are appointed by the pope. All Vatican officials vacate their offices on the death of a pope. Pope Benedict XVI confirmed in office the president of the Pontifical Commission and the members of the Secretariat of State after his election. Pope Benedict XVI resigned in February 2013 and was succeeded by Pope Francis.

Sovereign Pontiff, His Holiness Pope Francis (Jorge Mario Bergoglio), *born* 17 December 1936, *elected* 13 March 2013, *inaugurated* 19 March 2013

SECRETARIAT OF STATE *AS AT NOVEMBER 2020*
Secretary of State, Cardinal Pietro Parolin
Substitute for General Affairs, Archbishop Edgar Peña Parra
Secretary for Relations with States, Archbishop Paul Gallagher

PONTIFICAL COMMISSION
President, Cardinal Giuseppe Bertello

APOSTOLIC NUNCIATURE
54 Parkside, London SW19 5NE
T 020-8944 7189
Apostolic Nuncio, vacant

BRITISH EMBASSY TO THE HOLY SEE
Via XX Settembre 80/A, 00187 Rome
T (+39) (6) 4220 4000 E holysee@fco.gov.uk
W www.gov.uk/government/world/holy-see
Ambassador Extraordinary and Plenipotentiary, HE Sally Axworthy, MBE, *apptd* 2016

ECONOMY

The Vatican City budget is separate from that of the Holy See. The City's revenue is generated by museum admission charges and the sale of postage stamps, coins, medals, souvenirs and publications. The Holy See derives its income from investments, property, global banking and financial services, and donations from Roman Catholics worldwide. Pope Francis began a process of reforming the Vatican Bank in 2014 following a number of scandals and several budget deficits. The annual collections known as Peter's Pence are used for charitable and overseas aid work and disaster relief.

VENEZUELA

República Bolivariana de Venezuela – Bolivarian Republic of Venezuela

Area – 912,050 sq. km
Capital – Caracas; population, 2,939,000 (2020 est)
Major cities – Barquisimeto, Ciudad Guayana, Maracaibo, Valencia
Currency – Bolívar fuerte (Bs. F) of 100 céntimos
Population – 28,644,603 falling at 0.18 per cent a year (2020 est)
Religion – Christian (nominally Roman Catholic 96 per cent, Protestant 2 per cent) (est)
Language – Spanish (official), several indigenous languages
Population density – 33 per sq. km (2019)
Urban population – 88.2 per cent (2019 est)
Median age (years) – 30 (2020 est)
National anthem – 'Gloria al Bravo Pueblo' 'Glory to the Brave People'
National day – 5 July (Independence Day)
Death penalty – Abolished for all crimes (since 1863)
CPI score – 16 (173)
Military expenditure – US$954m (2014)
Conscription – 18–60 years of age; 12 months

CLIMATE AND TERRAIN

The Andean mountains, of which the main range is the Sierra Nevada de Mérida, run across the north-west of the country, separating the northern coast from the central plains *(llanos)*. The Guiana Highlands occupy the south-east of the country. Elevation extremes range from 5,007m (Pico Bolivar) to 0m (Caribbean Sea). The Orinoco flows across the centre of the country to its delta on the Atlantic coast. Its upper waters are united with those of the Rio Negro (a Brazilian tributary of the Amazon) by a natural river or canal, known as the Brazo Casiquiare. The coastal lowlands contain many lagoons and lakes, including Lake Maracaibo (area 13,351 sq. km), the largest lake in South America. The climate varies from tropical to alpine, depending on altitude, and most areas experience a wet season from May to November. The average temperature is 25.8°C.

HISTORY AND POLITICS

Columbus landed on the coast in 1498, and the first Spanish settlement was established at Cumaná in 1520. Venezuela became part of the Viceroyalty of New Granada in the early 18th century. There were several revolts against Spanish colonial rule, and a declaration of independence in 1811 was followed by several years of struggle until troops led by Simón

Bolivar defeated the Spanish at the battle of Carabobo in 1821. Venezuela became part of Gran Colombia (with Colombia, Ecuador and Panama), and then an independent republic in 1830 under the first of a series of *caudillos* (military leaders). The first truly democratic elections were held in 1947 but the government was overthrown by the military within months. An enduring civilian democracy was established in 1958.

Oil revenues supported a buoyant economy in the 1970s but a price collapse in the mid-1980s led to economic difficulties and a number of attempted coups. After he came to power in 1998, President Hugo Chávez's economic and social reforms, and his authoritarian style, polarised domestic opinion, provoking strikes and demonstrations, an attempted military coup in 2002 and a recall referendum in 2004, which he won.

President Hugo Chávez was re-elected in 2006. Despite re-election in October 2012, the president was too ill to be re-inaugurated and died on 5 March 2013. Nicolas Maduro, also of the United Socialist Party of Venezuela (PSUV), was elected to succeed him in April 2013. The opposition Democratic Unity alliance (MUD) won 112 seats in the December 2015 legislative election to the PSUV's 55, threatening President Maduro's position.

Rising authoritarianism and a failing economy have been the focus of demonstrations since April 2017, some of which have resulted in violence and deaths. Opposition candidates boycotted the May 2018 presidential elections, handing Maduro a second term but claiming widespread electoral fraud. In January 2019, opposition leader Juan Guaidó declared himself interim president in order to oust Maduro and quickly received international backing, especially from the USA. Guaidó attempted a popular uprising the following April but it was swiftly suppressed. Continued military support for Maduro, aided by Russia, nonetheless kept him in power despite diplomatic isolation, US sanctions, a deteriorating economy and internal unrest.

Under the 1999 constitution, the executive president is directly elected for a six-year term; the limit on the number of successive terms was abolished in 2009. The unicameral National Assembly has 167 members, 164 directly elected and three representing indigenous people, who serve a five-year term. The president appoints the vice-president and the council of ministers.

The country is divided into 23 states, one capital district and one federal dependency composed of 11 island groups (72 individual islands). The states have considerable autonomy and each has its own legislature and elected governor.

HEAD OF STATE
President, Nicolas Maduro, *elected* 14 April 2013, *sworn in* 19 April 2013, *re-elected* 20 May 2018
Executive Vice-Presidents, Delcy Rodriguez; Aristobulo isuriz; Tareck El Aissami *(Economy)*; Ricardo Menendez; Vladimir Padrino *(Defence)*

SELECTED GOVERNMENT MEMBERS *AS AT NOVEMBER 2020*
Foreign Relations, Jorge Arreaza

EMBASSY OF THE BOLIVARIAN REPUBLIC OF VENEZUELA
1 Cromwell Road, London SW7 2HW
T 020-7584 4206 **E** embavenezuk@venezlon.co.uk
W http://reinounido.embajada.gob.ve
Ambassador Extraordinary and Plenipotentiary, HE Rocio Maneiro, *apptd* 2014

BRITISH EMBASSY
Edificio Torre la Castellana, Piso 11, Avenida la Principal de la Castellana, Caracas 1601

T (+58) (212) 263 8411 **E** ukinvenezuela@fco.gov.uk
W www.gov.uk/government/world/venezuela
Ambassador Extraordinary and Plenipotentiary, HE Andrew
Soper, *apptd* 2017

ECONOMY AND TRADE

Much of industry is state-owned; after the Chávez regime came to power a large proportion of the private sector, some foreign-owned, was nationalised, including oil, electricity, financial, steel, construction and agribusiness companies. Laws passed in December 2010 aimed to increase government control of the economy, which struggled because of imbalances, high inflation and electricity shortages caused by a severe drought in 2009–10 that left hydroelectric plants inoperable. Low oil prices and political instability have helped fuel hyperinflation, a large black market and little external investment in recent years have caused widespread shortages and a migration crisis. It is estimated around 4 million people left the country between 2014 and June 2018. Political unrest in 2019 exacerbated these economic woes, resulting in rolling blackouts, water shortages and a 35 per cent decline in GDP that year. The coronavirus pandemic negated the improved political situation in 2020, and the economy is expected to contract by a further 25 per cent.

Oil and gas are the mainstays of the economy; other major industries are mining (coal, iron ore, bauxite, gold), production of construction materials, medical equipment, chemicals, steel and aluminium, pharmaceuticals and food processing. Industry contributes 40.4 per cent of GDP and services 57.9 per cent.

Agriculture comprises large-scale commercial farms and subsistence farming. Land distribution is uneven, but redistribution to the rural poor by breaking up larger estates has begun. Agricultural products include maize, sorghum, sugar cane, rice, bananas, vegetables and coffee. There is an extensive beef and dairy farming industry. Agriculture provides 4.7 per cent of GDP and engages 7.3 per cent of the workforce.

The main trading partners are the USA, China and India. Principal exports are oil, bauxite and aluminium, minerals, chemicals, and agricultural products. The main imports are agricultural products, raw materials, machinery, transport equipment, construction materials and medical products.
GNI – US$356,678m (2015 est); US$11,780 per capita (2013)
Annual average growth of GDP – –19.67 per cent (2018 est)
Inflation rate – 1,087.5 per cent (2017 est)
Population below poverty line – 19.7 per cent (2015 est)
Unemployment – 6.9 per cent (2018 est)
Total external debt – US$100.3bn (2017 est)
Imports – US$25,810m (2016)
Exports – US$28,405m (2016)

BALANCE OF PAYMENTS
Trade – US$2,595m deficit (2016)
Current Account – US$64m deficit (2018)

Trade with UK	2018	2019
Imports from UK	£21,009,970	£22,905,251
Exports to UK	£38,849,728	£45,971,777

COMMUNICATIONS

Airports and waterways – There are 127 airports, the principal terminals being at Caracas and Maracaibo; the main ports are Maracaibo, Puerto Cabello and Caracas-La Guaira
Roadways and railways – 96,189km; 447km
Telecommunications – 5.5 million fixed lines in use and 16.7 million mobile subscriptions (2019); there were 21.4 million internet users in 2018

Internet code and IDD – ve; 58 (from UK), 44 (to UK)
Major broadcasters – Venezolana de Television and Radio Nacional de Venezuela are the state broadcasters
Press – Major daily newspapers include *El Mundo, El Nacional* and *Ultimas Noticias*
WPFI score – 45.66 (147)

EDUCATION AND HEALTH

There are nine years of compulsory education.
Literacy rate – 97.1 per cent (2016 est)
Gross enrolment ratio (percentage of relevant age group) – primary 97.2 per cent, secondary 88.1 per cent (2017 est); tertiary 78 per cent (2013 est)
Health expenditure (per capita) – US$94 (2017)
Hospital beds (per 1,000 people) – 0.8 (2014)
Life expectancy (years) – 71 (2020 est)
Mortality rate – 7.5 (2020 est)
Birth rate – 17.9 (2020 est)
Infant mortality rate – 27.9 (2020 est)
HIV/AIDS adult prevalence – 0.6 per cent (2019 est)

VIETNAM

Cong Hoa Xa Hoi Chu Nghia Viet Nam – Socialist Republic of Vietnam

Area – 331,210 sq. km
Capital – Hanoi; population, 4,678,000 (2020 est)
Major cities – Bien Hoa, Da Nang, Haiphong, Ho Chi Minh City (Saigon)
Currency – Dong of 10 ho or 100 xu
Population – 98,721,275 rising at 0.84 per cent a year (2020 est); there are 54 ethnic groups, of which Kinh (85.7 per cent) is the largest (est)
Religion – Buddhist 7.9 per cent, Christian (Roman Catholic) 6.6 per cent, Hoa Hao (Buddhist) 1.7 per cent, Cao Dai (syncretistic religion) 0.9 per cent (est)
Language – Vietnamese (official), English, French, Chinese, Khmer; Mon-Khmer and Malayo-Polynesian are spoken in mountain areas
Population density – 308 per sq. km (2019)
Urban population – 36.6 per cent (2019 est)
Median age (years) – 31.9 (2020 est)
National anthem – 'Tien Quan Ca' 'The Marching Song'
National day – 2 September (Independence Day)
Death penalty – Retained
CPI score – 37 (96)
Military expenditure – US$3,233m (2011)
Conscription – 18–25, male only; 18–24 months

CLIMATE AND TERRAIN

The country is mostly mountainous, apart from the densely populated fertile plains around the deltas of the Hong (Red river) in the north and the Mekong in the south. Elevation extremes range from 3,144m (Fan Si Pan) to 0m (South China Sea). The climate is tropical and affected by the monsoon cycle. The wet season lasts from May to September, although

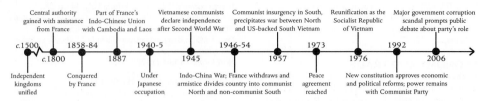

Central authority gained with assistance from France — Part of France's Indo-Chinese Union with Cambodia and Laos — Vietnamese communists declare independence after Second World War — Communist insurgency in South, precipitates war between North and US-backed South Vietnam — Reunification as the Socialist Republic of Vietnam — Major government corruption scandal prompts public debate about party's role

c.1500   1858–84   1940-5   1946-54   1973   1992
c.1800   1887   1945   1957   1976   2006

Independent kingdoms unified — Conquered by France — Under Japanese occupation — Indo-China War; France withdraws and armistice divides country into communist North and non-communist South — Peace agreement reached — New constitution approves economic and political reforms; power remains with Communist Party

the coast, being affected by typhoons and tropical storms, receives most rain between September and January.

POLITICS

The 1992 constitution was amended in 2001 to allow small-scale capitalism greater freedom. The president is elected by the legislature to serve a single five-year term. The unicameral National Assembly *(Quoc-Hoi)* has 500 members, who are directly elected for a five-year term. The head of government is the prime minister, who is responsible to the National Assembly, which appoints the council of ministers. However, effective power lies with the Communist Party of Vietnam. Its highest executive body is the Central Committee, elected by the national party congress held every five years. The politburo and the secretariat of the central committee, which exercise the real power, are elected at the party congress.

After the 2006 Communist Party Congress, the president and prime minister resigned to allow a younger leadership to be appointed. In April 2016, Tran Dai Quang was elected president and Nguyen Xuan Phuc became prime minister. Following the death of President Quang in September 2018, Nguyen Phu Trong was elected chief of state. In the May 2016 legislative election, 494 candidates secured enough votes to be elected to the National Assembly, including 475 members of the Communist Party, the highest proportion ever.

HEAD OF STATE

President, Nguyen Phu Trong, *elected* 23 October 2018
Vice-President, Dang Thi Ngoc Thinh

SELECTED GOVERNMENT MEMBERS *AS AT NOVEMBER 2020*

Prime Minister, Nguyen Xuan Phuc
Deputy Prime Ministers, Pham Binh Minh *(Foreign Affairs);* Truong Hoa Binh; Vu Duc Dam; Trinh Dinh Dung; Vuong Dinh Hue
Defence, Gen. Ngo Xuan Lich
Finance, Dinh Tien Dung

EMBASSY OF THE SOCIALIST REPUBLIC OF VIETNAM

12–14 Victoria Road, London W8 5RD
T 020-7937 1912 E vanphong@vietnamembassy.org.uk
W www.vietnamembassy.org.uk
Ambassador Extraordinary and Plenipotentiary, HE An Ngoc Tran, *apptd* 2017

BRITISH EMBASSY

Central Building, 31 Hai Ba Trung, Hanoi
T (+84) (4) 3936 0500 E consularenquiries.vietnam@fco.gov.uk
W www.gov.uk/government/world/vietnam
Ambassador Extraordinary and Plenipotentiary, HE Gareth Ward, *apptd* 2018

ECONOMY AND TRADE

The economy struggled for a decade after 1975 owing to the devastation of war and the imposition of a centrally planned economy. Since economic liberalisation and international integration were adopted in 1986, the economy has grown substantially, albeit from a low base, and export-driven industries are being developed. The global downturn reduced economic growth in 2008–9, and in early 2012 the government introduced a three-fold economic reform programme, proposing a restructuring of the banking sector, public spending and state-owned enterprises. Vietnam formed a common market with the other members of the Association of Southeast Asian Nations (ASEAN) in 2015 and in 2017 exceeded growth predictions thanks to domestic demand and rising manufacturing exports. Previously one of the fastest growing economies in the world, environmental destruction and the coronavirus pandemic in 2020 is expected to decelerate growth to 1.6 per cent.

Agriculture's contribution is gradually shrinking, but still accounts for 15.3 per cent of GDP and employs 40.3 per cent of the workforce. The main industries are food processing, clothing and footwear, machine building, coal mining, steel, cement, chemical fertiliser, glass, tyres and mobile phone production, and oil and gas production from large offshore reserves. Tourism is also a growing sector. Industry contributes one-third of GDP and services 51.3 per cent.

The main trading partners are China, Japan, South Korea and the USA. Principal exports are clothing, footwear, electronics, seafood, crude oil, wood products, rice and machinery. The main imports are machinery and equipment, petroleum products, steel products, raw materials, electronics, plastics and vehicles.

GNI – US$244.9bn; US$2,540 per capita (2019)
Annual average growth of GDP – 6.8 per cent (2017 est)
Inflation rate – 3.5 per cent (2017 est)
Population below poverty line – 8 per cent (2017 est)
Unemployment – 3.11 per cent (2018 est)
Total external debt – US$96.58bn (2017 est)
Imports – US$219,640m (2017)
Exports – US$227,281m (2017)

BALANCE OF PAYMENTS

Trade – US$7,641m surplus (2017)
Current Account – US$13,101m surplus (2019)

Trade with UK	2018	2019
Imports from UK	£628,876,701	£607,966,485
Exports to UK	£4,358,635,663	£4,590,099,851

COMMUNICATIONS

Airports and waterways – The principal airports and ports are at Ho Chi Minh City, Hanoi and Da Nang
Roadways and railways – 195,468km; 2,632km
Telecommunications – 3.7 million fixed lines and 138.3 million mobile subscriptions (2019); there were 68.2 million internet users in 2018
Internet code and IDD – vn; 84 (from UK), 44 (to UK)
Major broadcasters – Vietnam Television (VTV) and Voice of Vietnam (radio) are the state-run broadcasters
Press – Leading newspapers include the Communist Party daily *Nhan Dahn, Vietnam Economic Times* and *Le Courrier du Vietnam*
WPFI score – 74.71 (175)

EDUCATION AND HEALTH

Literacy rate – 95 per cent (2018 est)
Gross enrolment ratio (percentage of relevant age group) – primary 115.4 per cent (2019 est); secondary 77 per cent (2011 est); tertiary 28.6 per cent (2019 est)
Health expenditure (per capita) – US$130 (2017)
Hospital beds (per 1,000 people) – 2.6 (2013)
Life expectancy (years) – 74.4 (2020 est)
Mortality rate – 6 (2020 est)
Birth rate – 14.5 (2020 est)
Infant mortality rate – 15.7 (2020 est)
HIV/AIDS adult prevalence – 0.3 per cent (2019 est)

YEMEN

Al-Jumhuriyah al-Yamaniyah – Republic of Yemen

Area – 527,968 sq. km
Capital – Sana'a; population, 2,973,000 (2020 est)
Major cities – Aden (the former capital of South Yemen), Hudaida (al-Hudaydah), Ibb, al-Mukalla, Taiz
Currency – Riyal of 100 fils
Population – 29,884,405 rising at 2.04 per cent a year (2020 est)
Religion – Muslim (official) 99.1 per cent (Sunni 65 per cent, Shia 35 per cent) (est)
Language – Arabic (official)
Population density – 54 per sq. km (2019)
Urban population – 37.3 per cent (2019 est)
Median age (years) – 19.8 (2020 est)
National anthem – 'Al-Jumhuriyah al-Muttahida' 'United Republic'
National day – 22 May (Unification Day)
Death penalty – Retained
CPI score – 15 (177)
Military expenditure – US$2,093m (2014)

CLIMATE AND TERRAIN

A mountainous region in the west and south divides the desert plains of the interior from the narrow coastal plains. Elevation extremes range from 3,760m (Jabal an Nabi Shu'ayb) to 0m (Arabian Sea). There is a desert climate, which is particularly harsh in the east, but moderated in the western mountains by the monsoon. The coast experiences high humidity and the average temperature is 24.4°C.

The islands of Perim and Kamaran in the Red Sea, and Suqutra in the Gulf of Aden, are Yemeni territory. The border with Saudi Arabia, except for the north-west corner, is unclear and is being delineated following an agreement between the two countries.

POLITICS

After rising political tensions and violence in 2013 and 2014, in September 2014 Houthi rebels took control of most of the capital, Sana'a, when the government failed to acquiesce to their demands for reform. In January 2015 the rebels rejected proposals for a new constitution and in February, President Hadi fled to Aden. In March, the group looked to annex territory in southern Yemen and were attacked by both IS suicide bombers, who targeted Shia mosques, and Saudi Arabian air strikes. Saudi-backed forces began to recapture territory from the Houthis in September. UN-sponsored peace talks commenced in April 2016 but attacks continued on the military, rebels and civilians, as Saudi Arabia and the USA continued to carry out air strikes. In June 2018, the Saudi-led coalition launched an offensive to retake the port of Hodeidah, sparking the largest battle of the war. A ceasefire was agreed in December 2018 but fighting continued; a planned Houthi withdrawal in May 2019 intended to propel the peace process led to renewed fighting. Saudi Arabia has blamed Iran for supporting and financing the Houthi insurgency.

A Saudi Arabian and US blockade of the country, which started in 2015, contributed to the worst humanitarian crisis in the world, according to the UN. Hunger and malnutrition is widespread, and in November 2020 it was estimated 24 million people (80 per cent of the population) were in need of humanitarian assistance. The situation has been compounded by large outbreaks of cholera and COVID-19. In December 2019 it was estimated over 233,000 people had died in the civil war.

The president announced in March 2011 the drafting of a new constitution transferring powers from the presidency to the legislature. Under the 1991 constitution, the president is directly elected for a seven-year term, renewable once. The bicameral parliament consists of the House of Representatives *(Majlis al-Nuwaab)*, which has 301 members directly elected for a six-year term, and 111 members in the Shura Council *(Majilis Ashoora)*, directly appointed by the president, who also appoints the prime minister.

In the 2003 legislative election, the ruling General People's Congress (GPC) won 238 seats and formed a coalition government with the Yemeni Alliance for Reform (YAR or al-Islah). Lt.-Gen. Ali Abdullah Saleh, president of North Yemen from 1978 and president of the united country since 1990, was forced to resign in December 2011 following sustained protests. He was replaced by former vice-president Abd-Rabbu Mansour Hadi after transitional presidential elections in 2012. Parliamentary elections scheduled for 2009 have been repeatedly postponed due to the ongoing conflict.

HEAD OF STATE
President, Gen. Abd-Rabbu Mansour Hadi, *elected* 21 February 2012

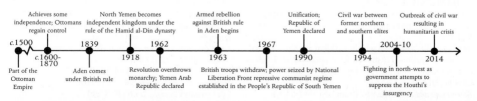

Vice-President, Maj.-Gen. Ali Mohsin al-Ahmar

SELECTED GOVERNMENT MEMBERS *AS AT*
NOVEMBER 2020
Prime Minister, Maeen Abdulmalik Saeed
Deputy Prime Minister, Interior, Ahmed bin Ahmed al-Maysari
Defence, Mohammed al-Maqdishi

EMBASSY OF THE REPUBLIC OF YEMEN
57 Cromwell Road, London SW7 2ED
T 020-7584 6607 **E** yemen.embassy@btconnect.com
W www.yemenembassy.co.uk
Ambassador Extraordinary and Plenipotentiary, HE Yassin Saeed
Ahmed, *apptd* 2015

BRITISH EMBASSY
Suspended since February 2015. **W** www.gov.uk/government/
world/yemen
Ambassador Extraordinary and Plenipotentiary, HE Michael
Aron, *apptd* 2018

ECONOMY AND TRADE

The war has prevented almost all exports, primarily oil which
is the mainstay of the economy. Yemen is one of the poorest
countries in the Arab world. The government began an IMF
restructuring programme in 2006 that aimed to diversify the
economy and attract foreign investment, but the economy has
been devastated since the outbreak of war in 2014 and the
Saudi-led blockade from 2015, which has contributed to the
ongoing humanitarian crisis.

Agriculture is largely of a subsistence nature and, with
herding and fishing, engages the majority of the population.
Apart from oil and natural gas extraction and oil refining,
industry consists of small-scale manufacturing of cotton
textiles, leather goods, handicrafts, aluminium products,
cement, food processing and ship repair.

The main trading partners are Egypt, the UAE, China and
Thailand. Principal exports are crude oil, coffee, dried and
salted fish, and liquefied natural gas. The main imports are
food, livestock, machinery and equipment, and chemicals.
GNI – US$27.4bn; US$960 per capita (2018)
Annual average growth of GDP – –5.9 per cent (2017 est)
Inflation rate – 24.7 per cent (2017 est)
Population below poverty line – 54 per cent (2014 est)
Unemployment – 27 per cent (2014 est)
Total external debt – US$7.068bn (2017 est)
Imports – US$13,048m (2014)
Exports – US$10,555m (2014)

BALANCE OF PAYMENTS
Trade – US$3,000m deficit (2013)
Current Account – US$7,309m surplus (2018)

Trade with UK	2018	2019
Imports from UK	£37,160,285	£45,530,222
Exports to UK	£786,417	£445,623

COMMUNICATIONS

Airports and waterways – Principal airports are at Sana'a and
Aden, and the main ports are at Aden, Hudaida and al-
Mukalla
Roadways – 71,300km, of which 6,200km are paved (2005)
Telecommunications – 1.3 million fixed lines and 16.2 million
mobile subscriptions (2019); there were 7.7 million internet
users in 2018
Internet code and IDD – ye; 967 (from UK), 44 (to UK)

Media – Republic of Yemen Television and Republic of
Yemen Radio are the state-run broadcasters; leading daily
newspapers include *Al-Thawra* (Arabic language), and the
Yemen Post (English language)
WPFI score – 58.25 (167)

EDUCATION AND HEALTH

Literacy rate – 90.2 per cent (2015 est)
Gross enrolment ratio (percentage of relevant age group) – primary
92 per cent, secondary 51 per cent (2016 est)
Health expenditure (per capita) – US$72 (2015)
Hospital beds (per 1,000 people) – 0.7 (2014)
Life expectancy (years) – 66.9 (2020 est)
Mortality rate – 5.6 (2020 est)
Birth rate – 25.8 (2020 est)
Infant mortality rate – 41.9 (2020 est)
HIV/AIDS adult prevalence – 0.1 per cent (2019 est)

ZAMBIA

Republic of Zambia

Area – 752,618 sq. km
Capital – Lusaka; population, 2,774,000 (2020)
Major cities – Kitwe, Ndola
Currency – Kwacha (K) of 100 ngwee
Population – 17,426,623 rising at 2.89 per cent a year (2020
est); Bemba (21 per cent), Tonga (13.6 per cent), Chewa
(7.4 per cent), Lozi (5.7 per cent), Nsenga (5.3 per cent)
(est)
Religion – Christian (Protestant 75.3 per cent, Roman
Catholic 20.2 per cent), other (including Muslim,
Buddhist, Hindu and Baha'i) 2.7 per cent (est)
Language – English (official), Bemba, Nyanja, Tonga, Lozi,
Chewa, Nsenga, Tumbuka, Lunda, Kaonde, Lala, Lamba,
Luvale, Mambwe, Namwanga, Lenje, Busa; Zambia has
over 70 known languages
Population density – 23 per sq. km (2019)
Urban population – 44.1 per cent (2019 est)
Median age (years) – 16.9 (2020 est)
National anthem – 'Lumbanyeni Zambia' 'Stand and Sing of
Zambia, Proud and Free'
National day – 24 October (Independence Day)
Death penalty – Retained (not used since 1997)
CPI score – 34 (113)
Military expenditure – US$378m (2018)
Conscription – National registration required at 16; 18–25
years of age for male and female voluntary military service
Literacy rate – 86.7 per cent (2018 est)
Gross enrolment ratio (percentage of relevant age group) – primary
98.7 per cent (2017 est)
Health expenditure (per capita) – US$68 (2017)
Hospital beds (per 1,000 people) – 2 (2010)
Life expectancy (years) – 53.6 (2020 est)

Mortality rate – 11.6 (2020 est)
Birth rate – 40.4 (2020 est)
Infant mortality rate – 56 (2020 est)
HIV/AIDS adult prevalence – 11.5 per cent (2016 est)

CLIMATE AND TERRAIN

Landlocked Zambia lies on a forested plateau cut through by river valleys and with higher land in the north and north-east. Elevation extremes range from 2,301m (in the Mafinga Hills) to 329m (Zambezi river). The Zambezi and its tributaries are the main rivers. Lake Bangweulu and parts of Lakes Tanganyika, Mweru and Kariba lie within its boundaries. The climate is tropical, moderated by altitude, with a rainy season from October to April.

HISTORY AND POLITICS

Most of the ethnic groups in Zambia migrated there between the 16th and the 18th centuries. Portuguese explorers arrived in the late 18th century and, with Arab traders, began slave-trading in the 19th century. The area came under British administration in 1889, was named Northern Rhodesia in 1911 and became a British protectorate in 1924. It was part of the Central African Federation with South Rhodesia (Zimbabwe) and Nyasaland (Malawi) from 1953 to 1963, when the federation was dissolved and Northern Rhodesia achieved internal self-government. It became an independent republic in 1964 under the name of Zambia.

Kenneth Kaunda of the United National Independence Party (UNIP) became president at independence and remained in power until 1991. Zambia was a one-party state ruled by the UNIP from 1972 until 1990, when pressure from opposition groups led to a new constitution, under which multiparty legislative and presidential elections were held in 1991.

The Patriotic Front (PF) won the 2011 legislative election, gaining enough seats for a small majority in the National Assembly, which it built on in 2016. The PF's leader, Michael Sata, won the 2011 presidential election. After the death of President Sata in October 2014 following an illness, Edgar Lungu of the PF won the January 2015 presidential elections, and was re-elected in August 2016 in polls rejected by the main opposition party.

Under the 1991 constitution, the executive president is directly elected for a five-year term, renewable once. The unicameral National Assembly has 164 members: 156 directly elected and up to eight nominated by the president; all serve a five-year term. The president appoints the cabinet.

HEAD OF STATE

President, Edgar Lungu, *elected* 24 January 2015, *sworn in* 25 January 2015, *re-elected* 2016
Vice-President, Inonge Wina

SELECTED GOVERNMENT MEMBERS *AS AT NOVEMBER 2020*
Finance, Bwalya Ng'andu
Foreign Affairs, Joel Malanji
Home Affairs, Steven Kampyongo

HIGH COMMISSION FOR THE REPUBLIC OF ZAMBIA
Zambia House, 2 Palace Gate, London W8 5NG
T 020-7589 6655 **E** info@zambiahc.org.uk **W** www.zambiahc.org.uk
High Commissioner, HE Le.-Gen. Paul Mihova, *apptd* 2019

BRITISH HIGH COMMISSION
PO Box 5005, 5210 Independence Avenue, 15101 Ridgeway, Lusaka
T (+260) (21) 1423 2001251 133
E lusakageneralenquiries@fco.gov.uk
W www.gov.uk/government/world/zambia
High Commissioner, HE Nicholas Woolley, *apptd* 2019

ECONOMY AND TRADE

The transition since the 1990s from a state-controlled to a free-market economy has improved productivity, especially in the now-privatised copper industry. One of the world's fastest growing economies between 2004 and 2014, growth decelerated in 2015–16 due to low copper prices, but the economy improved in 2017 and 2018 as prices rose. Growth slowed again in 2019, and the economy is expected to contract by 4.8 per cent in 2020. Significant international investment since 2012, including Chinese-financed infrastructure projects, has failed to significantly combat high unemployment, debt and extreme poverty.

Copper is the main source of foreign earnings and increased demand in recent years for electronics has spurred investment and greater output, although weakening global copper prices caused a rapid depreciation of the kwacha in 2014. However, 54.8 per cent of the workforce remains engaged in agriculture, mostly at subsistence level, which accounts for 7.5 per cent of GDP. The main industries are copper and cobalt mining and processing, construction, food processing, emerald mining, beverages, chemicals, textiles, fertiliser and horticulture. Hydroelectric power generation and tourism are also important sectors.

The main trading partners are South Africa, Switzerland, China and the Democratic Republic of the Congo. Principal exports are copper, cobalt, electricity, tobacco, cut flowers and cotton. The main imports are machinery, transport equipment, petroleum products, electricity, fertiliser, foodstuffs and clothing.

GNI – US$25.9bn; US$1,450 per capita (2019)
Annual average growth of GDP – 3.4 per cent (2017 est)
Inflation rate – 6.6 per cent (2017 est)
Population below poverty line – 54.4 per cent (2015 est)
Total external debt – US$11.66bn (2017 est)
Imports – US$9,376m (2017)
Exports – US$8,924m (2017)

BALANCE OF PAYMENTS
Trade – US$451m deficit (2017)
Current Account – US$146m surplus (2019)

Trade with UK	2018	2019
Imports from UK	£76,615,405	£66,028,047
Exports to UK	£5,737,727	£4,260,9097

COMMUNICATIONS

Airports and waterways – There are eight airports and 2,250km of navigable waterways on Lake Tanganyika and the Zambezi and Luapula rivers
Roadways and railways – 14,888km of paved roadways; 3,126km
Telecommunications – 91,422 fixed lines and 16.3 million mobile subscriptions (2019); there were 2.4 million internet users in 2018
Internet code and IDD – zm; 260 (from UK), 44 (to UK)
Media – The state-run Zambia National Broadcasting Association operates TV and radio stations; major daily newspapers include the *Zambia Daily Mail, Times of Zambia* (both state-owned) and *The Post* (privately owned)
WPFI score – 37.00 (120)

ZIMBABWE

Republic of Zimbabwe

Area – 390,757 sq. km
Capital – Harare; population, 1,530,000 (2020)
Major cities – Bulawayo, Chitungwiza, Gweru, Mutare
Currency – US dollars; other currencies, including the South African rand, are in use
Population – 14,546,314 rising at 1.87 per cent a year (2020 est); predominantly Shona and Ndebele
Religion – Christian (Protestant 74.8 per cent, Roman Catholic 7.3 per cent, other Christian 5.3 per cent), traditional religions 1.5 per cent (est)
Language – Shona, Ndebele, English (all official); 13 minority languages
Population density – 37 per sq. km (2019)
Urban population – 32.2 per cent (2019 est)
Median age (years) – 20.5 (2020 est)
National anthem – 'Simudzai Mureza wedu WeZimbabwe' 'Blessed be the Land of Zimbabwe'
National day – 18 April (Independence Day)
Death penalty – Retained
CPI score – 24 (158)
Military expenditure – US$420m (2018)

CLIMATE AND TERRAIN

Zimbabwe lies mainly on a high plateau with a central high veld and mountains in the east. Elevation extremes range from 2,592m (Inyangani) to 162m (confluence of the Runde and Save rivers). The climate is tropical, moderated by altitude, with a wet season from November to March. Average temperatures range from 16.5°C in July to 25.4°C in November.

POLITICS

Under the 2013 constitution, the term of the executive president was reduced from six years to five and is renewable once, however this did not apply retrospectively to former president Robert Mugabe (1924–2019). The bicameral parliament comprises the National Assembly and the senate. The former has 210 members directly elected for a five-year term plus 60 seats reserved for women. The senate has 80 members, who serve a five-year term: 60 directly elected (six from each of the ten provinces), 16 indirectly elected by

regional councils, two traditional chiefs and two reserved for disabled candidates.

The country is divided into eight provinces and two cities (Bulawayo and Harare) with provincial status. The provinces are: Manicaland, Mashonaland Central, Mashonaland East, Mashonaland West, Masvingo, Matabeleland North, Matabeleland South and Midlands.

An internationally brokered power-sharing arrangement was agreed between the Zimbabwe African National Union-Patriotic Front (ZANU-PF) and the Movement for Democratic Change (MDC) in 2008 and lasted until 2013, when Mugabe was re-elected president and ZANU-PF won the legislative election. The office of prime minister was abolished under the 2013 constitution. The army ousted President Mugabe in November 2017 and he was replaced by former vice-president Emmerson Mnangagwa. Mnangagwa and ZANU-PF overwhelmingly won simultaneous presidential and parliamentary elections in 2018, which the MDC claimed were rigged and resulted in months of post-election violence. A general strike was called in January 2019 in response to food and fuel shortages, which led to a violent military crackdown, and subsequent protests which continued into 2020 were also met with repressive measures.

HEAD OF STATE
President, C-in-C of the Armed Forces, Emmerson Mnangagwa, *sworn in* 24 November 2017, *elected* 30 July 2018
Vice-Presidents, Gen. (retd) Constantino Chiwenga; Kembo Mohadi

SELECTED GOVERNMENT MEMBERS *AS AT NOVEMBER 2020*
Defence, Oppah Muchinguri-Kashiri
Finance, Mthuli Ncube
Foreign Affairs, Lt.-Gen. (retd) Sibusiso Moyo

EMBASSY OF THE REPUBLIC OF ZIMBABWE
Zimbabwe House, 429 Strand, London WC2R 0JR
T 020-7836 7755 **E** zimlondon@zimfa.gov.zw
W www.zimlondon.gov.zw
Ambassador Extraordinary and Plenipotentiary, HE Col. (retd) Christian Katsande, *apptd* 2018

BRITISH EMBASSY
PO Box 4490, 3 Norfolk Road, Mount Pleasant, Harare
T (+263) (4) 8585 5200 **E** ukinfo.harare@fco.gov.uk
W www.gov.uk/government/world/zimbabwe
Ambassador Extraordinary and Plenipotentiary, HE Melanie Robinson, *apptd* 2019

ECONOMY AND TRADE

Poor governance, and in particular the seizure of almost all the white-owned commercial farms, caused a rapid contraction in the agriculture-based economy in the decade from the late 1990s; agricultural output and GDP halved, international aid was suspended because of the government's outstanding arrears on past loans, and the migration of professional and skilled labour, and high levels of HIV/AIDS infection, depleted the workforce. After the national unity government

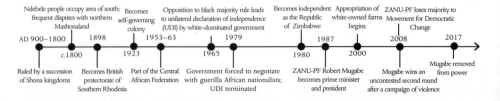

		Opposition to black majority rule leads		Becomes independent	Appropriation of	ZANU-PF loses majority to
Ndebele people occupy area of south;	Becomes	to unilateral declaration of independence		as the Republic	white-owned farms	Movement for Democratic
frequent disputes with northern	self-governing	(UDI) by white-dominated government		of Zimbabwe	begins	Change
Mashonaland	colony					
AD 900–1800	1898	1953–63	1979		1987	2008	2017
*c.*1800	1923	1965		1980	2000	
						Mugabe removed
Ruled by a succession	Becomes British	Part of the Central	Government forced to negotiate	ZANU-PF Robert Mugabe	Mugabe wins an	from power
of Shona kingdoms	protectorate of	African Federation	with guerilla African nationalists;	becomes prime minister	uncontested second round	
	Southern Rhodesia		UDI terminated	and president	after a campaign of violence	

took office, the US dollar was adopted in 2009 and the Zimbabwe dollar phased out by late 2015, following years of rampant hyperinflation. Other currencies were also accepted before the reintroduction of the Zimbabwe dollar in June 2019, which failed to prevent spiralling inflation. Acute shortages of fuel and rolling power cuts crippled the economy, and by 2020 it was estimated 7.7 million people were in need of food aid. The country is vulnerable to natural disasters; in March 2019, tens of thousands of homes were destroyed and at least 344 people were killed by Cyclone Idai. The economy contracted by 6.5 per cent in 2019, and this is expected to accelerate in 2020. Almost three-quarters of the population lives below the poverty line.

Agriculture accounts for 12.5 per cent of GDP and engages over two-thirds of the workforce. The most important crops are cotton and tobacco for export and maize for domestic consumption. Other crops include wheat, coffee, sugar cane, peanuts and livestock.

The mining sector is important to the economy as a foreign exchange earner. Almost all mineral production is exported. Gold is the most important product; others are coal, platinum, copper, nickel, tin, diamonds, iron ore and other metal and non-metal ores. Mining is the largest industrial activity and supports a ferro-alloy industry and a steel works. Manufacturing, traditionally highly dependent on the agricultural sector for raw materials, produces wood products, cement, chemicals, fertiliser, clothing, footwear, foodstuffs and beverages; output has dropped in some industries because of transport difficulties and power rationing. Industry generates 26.9 per cent of GDP and services 60.6 per cent.

The main trading partners are South Africa, China, Zambia and Mozambique. Principal exports are platinum, cotton, tobacco, gold, ferro-alloys, textiles and clothing. The main imports are machinery and transport equipment, other manufactures, chemicals, fuels and food.

GNI – US$20.4bn; US$1,390 per capita (2019)
Annual average growth of GDP – 3.7 per cent (2017 est)
Inflation rate – 0.9 per cent (2017 est)
Population below poverty line – 72.3 per cent (2012 est)
Total external debt – US$9.357m (2017 est)
Imports – US$6,426m (2016)
Exports – US$4,059m (2016)

BALANCE OF PAYMENTS
Trade – US$2,367m deficit (2016)
Current Account – US$1,260m deficit (2018)

Trade with UK	2018	2019
Imports from UK	£45,307,225	£39,123,708
Exports to UK	£73,700,613	£64,179,202

COMMUNICATIONS

Airports – The main airports are at Harare and Bulawayo, and there are 15 others
Roadways and railways – 18,481km of paved roadways; 3,427km
Telecommunications – 258,419 fixed lines and 12.8 million mobile subscriptions (2019); there were 3.8 million internet users in 2018
Internet code and IDD – zw; 263 (from UK), 44 (to UK)
Major broadcasters – The Zimbabwe Broadcasting Corporation operates the only official TV and radio stations; opposition groups operate a number of illegal radio stations, such as Voice of the People and Radio Dialogue from abroad
Press – The government publishes the only daily newspapers, *The Herald* and *The Chronicle*
WPFI score – 40.95 (126)

EDUCATION AND HEALTH

Education is compulsory at primary level, and the language of instruction is English.
Literacy rate – 91.7 per cent (2015 est)
Gross enrolment ratio (percentage of relevant age group) – primary 99.9 per cent, secondary 47.6 per cent (2013 est); tertiary 8.4 per cent (2015 est)
Health expenditure (per capita) – US$110 (2017)
Hospital beds (per 1,000 people) – 1.7 (2011)
Life expectancy (years) – 62.3 (2020 est)
Mortality rate – 9.3 (2020 est)
Birth rate – 33.6 (2020 est)
Infant mortality rate – 30.3 (2020 est)
HIV/AIDS adult prevalence – 12.8 per cent (2019 est)

UK OVERSEAS TERRITORIES

ANGUILLA

Area – 91 sq. km
Capital – The Valley; population, 1,000 (2018 est)
Currency – East Caribbean dollar (EC$) of 100 cents
Population – 17,422 rising at 1.92 per cent a year (2018 est)
Religion – Christian (Protestant 73.2 per cent, Roman
    Catholic 6.8 per cent) (est)
Language – English (official)
Flag – British blue ensign with the coat of arms and three
    dolphins in the fly
National day – 30 May (Anguilla Day)
Median age (years) – 35.1 (2018 est)
Life expectancy (years) – 81.6 (2018 est)
Mortality rate – 4.7 (2018 est)
Birth rate – 12.4 (2018 est)
Infant mortality rate – 3.3 (2018 est)
WPFI score – 23,78 (44)

CLIMATE AND TERRAIN

Anguilla is a flat coralline island in the eastern Caribbean and
one of the most northerly of the Leeward Islands. Elevation
extremes range from 65m (Crocus Hill) to 0m (Caribbean Sea).
The climate is tropical, modified by north-east trade winds,
with temperatures ranging from 24.7°C in January to 27.4°C
in August.

HISTORY AND POLITICS

Anguilla has been a British colony since 1650. For much of its
history it was linked administratively with St Kitts, but three
months after the Associated State of Saint Christopher (St
Kitts)-Nevis-Anguilla came into being in 1967, the Anguillans
repudiated government from St Kitts. Final separation from St
Kitts and Nevis was effected in December 1980 and Anguilla
reverted to a British dependency.

   The 1982 constitution (amended in 1990) provides for a
governor, an executive council comprising four of the elected
assembly members and two *ex-officio* members (the attorney-
general and deputy governor), and an 11-member House of
Assembly, consisting of a speaker, seven elected members, two
nominated members and two *ex-officio* members (the attorney-
general and deputy governor). The 2015 general election was
won by the Anguilla United Front with six seats. In September
2017 the island was badly damaged by Hurricane Irma.
Governor, Tim Foy, *apptd* 2017
Premier, Ellis Webster

ECONOMY

With few natural resources, the main economic activities are
luxury tourism and offshore banking. Lobster fishing and
expatriates' remittances are also important. Export earnings are
mainly from sales of lobster, fish, livestock, salt, concrete
blocks and rum.
Imports – US$274m (2016)
Exports – US$198m (2016)

BALANCE OF PAYMENTS
Trade – US$76m deficit (2016)
Current Account – US$99.2m deficit (2016)

Trade with UK	2018	2019
Imports from UK	£969,685	£965,917
Exports to UK	£621,934	£1,462,432

COMMUNICATIONS

Some 82km of the road network are paved. The main ports
are Blowing Point ferry terminal and Clayton J. Lloyd
(formerly Wallblake) airport, near The Valley.

BERMUDA

Area – 54 sq. km
Capital – Hamilton, on Main Island; population, 10,000
    (2018 est)
Currency – Bermudian dollar (BD$) of 100 cents
Population – 71,176 rising at 0.43 per cent a year (2018 est)
Religion – Christian (Protestant 46.2 per cent, Roman
    Catholic 14.5 per cent) (est)
Language – English (official), Portuguese
Population density – 1,185 per sq. km (2018 est)
Flag – British red ensign with the coat of arms in the fly
National day – 24 May (Bermuda Day)
Median age (years) – 43.5 (2018 est)
Life expectancy (years) – 81.5 (2018 est)
Mortality rate – 8.7 (2018 est)
Birth rate – 11.3 (2018 est)
Infant mortality rate – 2.5 (2018 est)

CLIMATE AND TERRAIN

Bermuda is a group of over 130 small islands, of which about
20 are inhabited, in the North Atlantic Ocean. All the islands
are volcanic in origin, with hilly interiors, surrounded by coral
reefs. Elevation extremes range from 76m (Town Hill) to 0m
(Atlantic Ocean). The climate is subtropical, regulated by the
Gulf Stream, with average temperatures ranging from 16.7°C
in February to 26.3°C in August.

HISTORY AND POLITICS

Bermuda was discovered by the Spanish in 1503 but colonised by the British from the early 17th century, becoming a colony in 1684. Independence from the UK was rejected in a 1995 referendum.

Internal self-government was introduced in 1968. The governor is responsible for external affairs, defence, internal security and the police, although administrative matters for the police service have been delegated to the minister of labour, home affairs and public safety. The cabinet comprises the premier and six elected assembly members. The legislature consists of the senate of 11 appointed members and the House of Assembly with 36 members elected for a five-year term. At the 2012 election, centre-left opposition party One Bermuda Alliance ousted the ruling Progressive Labour Party (PLP) for the first time in 14 years, but the PLP won strong majorities in the July 2017 and October 2020 elections. In February 2018, Bermuda became the first jurisdiction to legalise and then repeal same-sex marriage.

Governor, HE Rena Lalgie, *apptd* 2020
Premier, Hon. David Burt

ECONOMY

The main economic activity is international financial services, accounting for about 85 per cent of GPD, and it means the island boasts one of the highest per capita incomes in the world. Tourism claims just 5 per cent of GDP but is the largest employer. High unemployment and rising public debt have been, and remain, significant issues since the global downturn. Trade is dominated by re-exporting pharmaceuticals, while almost everything is imported.

Total external debt – US$2,515bn (2017 est)
Imports – US$2,158m (2017)
Exports – US$1,416m (2017)

BALANCE OF PAYMENTS
Trade – US$742m deficit (2017)
Current Account – US$766m surplus (2016)

Trade with UK	2018	2019
Imports from UK	£57,946,300	£28,697,710
Exports to UK	£57,946,300	£5,218,503

COMMUNICATIONS

The main islands are connected by a series of bridges and causeways. There are 447km of roads, all of which are paved but only around half of which are public, and one airport, near Ferry Reach on St David's Island. The main ports are at Hamilton, Freeport and St George.

BRITISH ANTARCTIC TERRITORY

See also The North and South Poles
Area – 1,709,400 sq. km. This area is overlapped by territorial claims from Chile and Argentina. However, no claims are recognised internationally under the Antarctic Treaty of 1961
Population – There is no indigenous population. The British Antarctic Survey maintains two permanently staffed research stations, at Halley and Rothera; one part-time (summer-only) station at Signy (South Orkney Islands); and two summer-only logistics facilities, at Fossil Bluff (Alexander Island) and Sky Blu (Eastern Ellsworth Land). Several other countries maintain research stations in the territory
Flag – British white ensign, without the cross of St George, with the territory's coat of arms in the fly

CLIMATE AND TERRAIN

The British Antarctic Territory (BAT) consists of the areas south of 60°S. latitude, between longitudes 20°W. and 80°W. The territory includes the South Orkney Islands, the South Shetland Islands, the mountainous Antarctic Peninsula and all adjacent islands, and the land mass extending to the South Pole. The highest point of the territory is 3,184m (Mt Jackson).

Only around 0.7 per cent of the territory remains ice-free, and the permanent ice-sheet that covers the remainder is, in places, nearly 5km thick. The climate is polar desert with very little precipitation, and the annual average temperature at the South Pole is −48°C.

HISTORY AND POLITICS

Britain made its first territorial claim to part of the Antarctic in 1908. Since 1943, a permanent presence has been maintained, which became the British Antarctic Survey (BAS) in 1962. In the same year, the territory, originally a Dependency of the Falkland Islands, became a UK overseas territory in its own right, although it continued to be administered from the Falkland Islands until 1989 when the role of Commissioner of the British Antarctic Territory was created.

The BAT is the UK's largest overseas territory and is administered by the Foreign and Commonwealth Office. It has a full suite of laws, legal and postal administrations. All activities are governed by the Antarctic Treaty of 1961, which has the objectives of keeping Antarctica demilitarised and promoting international scientific cooperation. The territory is self-financing from income-tax revenue and the sale of postage stamps and coins.

GOVERNMENT OF THE BRITISH ANTARCTIC TERRITORY
Polar Regions Department, Overseas Territories Directorate, Room 2/135, Old Admiralty Building, London SW1A 2AH
T 020-7008 1639 **E** polarregions@fco.gov.uk
Commissioner (non-resident), Ben Merrick, *apptd* 2017

BRITISH INDIAN OCEAN TERRITORY

Area – 54,400 sq. km, of which 60 sq. km is land
Currency – US dollar (US$) of 100 cents
Population – No indigenous population now lives in the archipelago; around 3,000 military personnel and civilian contract employees are based at the joint UK–US naval support facility on Diego Garcia
Flag – Divided horizontally into blue and white wavy stripes, with the Union Flag in the canton and a crowned palm tree over all in the fly

CLIMATE AND TERRAIN
The British Indian Ocean Territory (BIOT) comprises the Chagos Archipelago of 55 islands in six main groups, situated on the Great Chagos Bank in the Indian Ocean. The largest and most southerly of the islands is Diego Garcia, a sand cay with an area of about 44 sq. km. The main island groups are Peros Banhos (29 islands with a total land area of 6.5 sq. km) and Salomon (11 islands with a total land area of 3.2 sq. km). The flat and low terrain rarely rises more than 2m above sea level, being only 15m at its highest point. The climate is hot and humid, although moderated by trade winds.

HISTORY AND POLITICS
The Chagos Archipelago, originally colonised by the French, was one of the dependencies of Mauritius ceded to Britain in 1814 and was administered from Mauritius until 1965, when the BIOT was established. The islands of Farquhar, Desroches and Aldabra became part of the Seychelles when it became independent in 1976. Since the 1980s, successive Mauritian governments have claimed sovereignty over the remaining Chagos islands, arguing that they were annexed illegally.
Diego Garcia is used as a joint naval support facility by Britain and the USA. The islands' former inhabitants were forcibly relocated between 1967 and 1973 to allow for the construction of the naval base, most being resettled in Mauritius and the Seychelles. Since the 1990s they have taken legal action to obtain the right to return to and settle in the islands. In 2006, the Chagossians won a High Court case allowing them to return to the archipelago, but not to Diego Garcia. The House of Lords overturned this ruling on appeal in 2008; a case before the European Court of Human Rights was ruled inadmissable in December 2012 as the islanders had previously accepted financial compensation. The British government unilaterally, and controversially, declared the Chagos Archipelago a marine-protected area (MPA) in April 2010, a decision that was upheld by the High Court in 2013. In March 2015, a UN tribunal declared the creation of the MPA illegal, and ordered the UK and Mauritius governments to renegotiate sovereignty of the area. In November 2016, the British Foreign Office announced that the islanders would not be allowed to return to their home. However, in June 2017, the UN general assembly ruled the sovereignty dispute should be referred to the International Court of Justice. In February 2019 the court issued an advisory ruling against the British government and it was ordered to return the islands to Mauritius 'as rapidly as possible'.
Commissioner (non-resident), Ben Merrick, *apptd* 2017
Deputy Commissioner (non-resident), Stephen Hilton

BRITISH VIRGIN ISLANDS

Area – 151 sq. km
Capital – Road Town, on Tortola; population, 15,000 (2018 est)
Currency – US dollar (US$) of 100 cents
Population – 35,802 rising at 2.2 per cent a year (2018 est)

Religion – Christian (Protestant 70.2 per cent, Roman Catholic 8.9 per cent), Hindu 1.9 per cent (est)
Language – English (official)
Population density – 199 per sq. km (2018)
Flag – British blue ensign with the coat of arms in the fly
National day – 1 July (Territory Day)
Median age (years) – 36.7 (2018 est)
Life expectancy (years) – 78.9 (2017 est)
Mortality rate – 5.2 (2018 est)
Birth rate – 11.1 (2018 est)
Infant mortality rate – 11.7 (2018 est)
WPFI score – 23,78 (44)

CLIMATE AND TERRAIN
The easternmost part of the Virgin Islands archipelago in the Caribbean Sea, the British Virgin Islands comprise Tortola, Anegada, Virgin Gorda, Jost Van Dyke and about 40 islets and cays; 16 of the islands are inhabited. Apart from Anegada, which is flat, the British Virgin Islands are hilly with coral reefs offshore. The highest point of elevation is 521m (Mt Sage, on Tortola). The climate is subtropical, with little variation in average temperatures, which typically range between 23.4°C in January and February and 26.4°C in August and September. The hurricane season is from June to November.

HISTORY AND POLITICS
Initially settled by Arawak Indians, the islands were named by Christopher Columbus in 1493 and colonised by the Dutch in the early 17th century. Annexed by the British in 1672, the islands were part of the Leeward Islands colony from 1872 to 1960. After a period of direct rule, a measure of self-government was introduced by the 1977 constitution and extended in 2000.
Under the 2007 constitution, the governor, appointed by the crown, retains responsibility for defence, security, external affairs and the civil service. The executive council comprises the premier, four other elected assembly members and the attorney-general. The House of Assembly consists of a speaker, one *ex-officio* member (the attorney-general) and 13 members elected for a four-year term.
The National Democratic Party won the 2011 and 2015 elections, but was defeated by the Virgin Islands Party in the February 2019 election. Andrew Fahie subsequently replaced Orlando Smith as premier.
Governor, HE Augustus Jaspert, *apptd* 2017
Premier, Hon. Andrew Fahie

ECONOMY
One of the most stable and prosperous Caribbean islands, tourism generates about 45 per cent of GDP and has started to recover since the devastation caused by Hurricane Irma in September 2017. Alongside offshore financial services, other industries include construction and light manufacturing. The major exports are rum, fresh fish, fruit, livestock, gravel and sand. Chief imports are building materials, vehicles, foodstuffs and machinery.

Trade with UK	2018	2019
Imports from UK	£17,639,910	£12,980,648
Exports to UK	£10,865,931	£11,068,188

COMMUNICATIONS
The principal airport is on Beef Island, linked by bridge to Tortola, and there are also airfields on Anegada and Virgin Gorda. Road Harbour, at Road Town, is the main port, and ferry services connect the main islands. Much of the 200km of road is steep and narrow.

CAYMAN ISLANDS

Area – 264 sq. km
Capital – George Town, on Grand Cayman; population, 35,000 (2018 est)
Currency – Caymanian dollar (CI$) of 100 cents
Population – 59,613 rising at 1.96 per cent a year (2018 est)
Religion – Christian (Protestant 67.8 per cent, Roman Catholic 14.1 per cent) (est)
Language – English (official), Spanish
Population density – 267 per sq. km (2018 est)
Flag – British blue ensign with the coat of arms in the fly
National day – First Monday in July (Constitution Day)
Median age (years) – 40.2 (2018 est)
Life expectancy (years) – 81.4 (2018 est)
Mortality rate – 5.9 (2018 est)
Birth rate – 12 (2018 est)
Infant mortality rate – 5.7 (2018 est)
Annual average growth of GDP – 2 per cent (2017)

CLIMATE AND TERRAIN
The Cayman Islands comprise Grand Cayman, Cayman Brac and Little Cayman. Situated around 240km south of Cuba, the low-lying islands are divided from Jamaica, 268km to the south-east, by the Cayman Trench, the deepest part of the Caribbean Sea. The average temperature is 27°C. Hurricane season is from July to November.

HISTORY AND POLITICS
The territory derives its name from the Carib word *caymanas* (crocodile). The islands were ceded to Britain by Spain in 1670, and permanent settlement began in the 1730s. A dependency of Jamaica from 1863, the islands came under direct rule after 1962, and a measure of self-government was granted in 1972.

The 1972 constitution (revised in 1994 and 2009) provides for a governor, a legislative assembly and a cabinet. The governor is responsible for the police, civil service, internal security, defence, external affairs, and chairs the cabinet. The cabinet comprises two appointed official members (the deputy governor and attorney-general) and five of the assembly's elected members. The Legislative Assembly has 21 members elected for a four-year term and the two appointed official members of the cabinet, as well as a speaker. In September 2017 the islands were badly damaged by Hurricane Irma.
Acting Governor, Martyn Roper, *apptd* 2018
Premier, Hon. Alden McLaughlin, MBE

CAYMAN ISLANDS GOVERNMENT OFFICE
6 Arlington Street, London SW1A 1RE **T** 020-7491 7772
W www.gov.ky

ECONOMY
The mainstays of the economy are offshore financial services (largely owing to the absence of direct taxation) and tourism; the latter accounts for around 70 per cent of GDP. Government revenue is derived from fees and duties. The island experienced rapid economic growth in the past two decades

Imports – US$2,309m (2016)
Exports – US$2,467m (2016)

BALANCE OF PAYMENTS
Trade – US$159m surplus (2016)

Trade with UK	2018	2019
Imports from UK	£16,107,012	£19,561,749
Exports to UK	£700,586	£1,320,758

COMMUNICATIONS
The islands are served by airports at George Town and on Cayman Brac and by an airfield on Little Cayman. George Town is the main port. There are 785km of surfaced roads.

FALKLAND ISLANDS

Area – 12,173 sq. km
Capital – Stanley, on East Falkland; population, 2,000 (2018 est)
Currency – Falkland Island pound (FK£) of 100 pence
Population – 3,198 (2016 est) rising at 0.01 per cent a year (2018 est)
Religion – Christian 57.1 per cent, other 1.6 per cent (est)
Language – English
Urban population – 77.7 per cent (2018 est)
Flag – British blue ensign with coat of arms centred in the fly
National day – 14 June (Liberation Day)

CLIMATE AND TERRAIN
The Falkland Islands consist of East Falkland (6,759 sq. km), West Falkland (5,413 sq. km) and around 700 small islands. Elevation extremes range from 705m (Mt Usbourne) to 0m (Atlantic Ocean). Average temperatures range from 1.3°C in July to 8°C in January, and annual rainfall is low (around 543.3mm per year).

HISTORY AND POLITICS
The Falkland Islands have a long history of occupation by European countries, including France, Spain and the UK, which claimed sovereignty in 1765 and established its first settlement in 1766.

In 1820 the Falklands were claimed for the newly independent Argentina and a settlement was founded in 1826, but this was destroyed by the USA in 1831. In 1833 occupation was resumed by the British, and the islands were permanently colonised. Argentina continued to claim sovereignty over the islands (known to them as *las Islas Malvinas),* and invaded the islands on 2 April 1982. A British naval and military task force recaptured the islands on 14 June 1982. A small naval and military garrison remains in the islands. Argentina has reasserted its claims of sovereignty since 2007, and political tensions with the UK remain high. In a referendum in March 2013, the islanders voted overwhelmingly to remain a UK overseas territory; on a turnout of more than 90 per cent, 1,513 votes were cast in favour, with three against.

Under the 2009 constitution, the governor chairs an executive council consisting of three of the elected members of the legislative assembly and two *ex-officio* members, the chief executive and the financial secretary. The legislative assembly consists of eight members elected for a four-year term, the same two *ex-officio* members and a speaker. The last election was held in 2017. There are no political parties and all members sit as independents.

Governor, HE Nigel Phillips, CBE *apptd* 2017
Chief Executive, Barry Rowland

FALKLAND ISLANDS GOVERNMENT OFFICE
Falkland House, 14 Broadway, London SW1H 0BH
T 020-7222 2542 **W** www.falklands.gov.fk

ECONOMY
Since the establishment of a conservation and managed fishing zone around the islands in 1987, the economy has been transformed, with revenue from fishing (mainly squid) and related activities overtaking sheep-farming as the main industry. Fishing licence fees now provide about half of government revenue, making the islands self-supporting in all but defence costs. Tourism, especially wildlife tourism, has grown rapidly, with roughly 69,000 people visiting each year. Fish, meat, wool and hides are the principal exports. Chief imports are fuel, food and drink, construction materials and clothing.

There are believed to be substantial reserves of oil and gas offshore and the Falkland Islands government has licensed exploration for exploitable sites; in late 2015, two exploration firms announced plans to combine their efforts to commence oil production.

Trade with UK	2018	2019
Imports from UK	£52,236,845	£60,596,876
Exports to UK	£7,470,397	£5,855,540

COMMUNICATIONS
There is an international airport at Mt Pleasant, served by military flights to the UK and by commercial flights to Chile. The main port is Stanley Harbour and a regular shipping service operates to the UK. The road network is gradually expanding but only roads in and around Stanley are paved, and most longer internal journeys are by light aircraft. International telecommunications are possible through a satellite link, and the majority of households have internet access.

GIBRALTAR

Area – 6.5 sq. km
Capital – Gibraltar, population, 35,000 (2018)

Currency – Gibraltar pound of 100 pence
Population – 29,461 rising at 0.21 per cent a year (2018 est)
Religion – Christian (Roman Catholic 72.1 per cent, Church of England 7.7 per cent), Muslim 3.6 per cent, Jewish 2.4 per cent, Hindu 2 per cent (est)
Language – English (official), Spanish, Italian, Portuguese
Population density – 3,372 per sq. km (2018)
Flag – White with a red stripe along the lower edge; over all a red castle with a key hanging from its gateway
National day – 10 September
Median age (years) – 35 (2018 est)
Life expectancy (years) – 79.7 (2018 est)
Mortality rate – 8.5 (2018 est)
Birth rate – 13.9 (2018 est)
Infant mortality rate – 5.8 (2018 est)

CLIMATE AND TERRAIN
Gibraltar is a rocky promontory, 426m at its highest point, that juts southwards from the south-east coast of Spain, with which it is connected by a low isthmus. It is about 32km from the coast of Africa, across the Strait of Gibraltar.

HISTORY AND POLITICS
Gibraltar was captured in 1704, during the War of the Spanish Succession, by a combined Dutch and English force, and was ceded to Britain in the Treaty of Utrecht (1713).

Spanish claims to the territory continue to be a source of tension, but after the overwhelming rejection of a joint sovereignty arrangement in a referendum in 2002, Spain moderated its attitude and the previously bilateral Anglo-Spanish talks about the territory became tripartite with the inclusion of Gibraltar from 2006.

Gibraltar is part of the EU (with the UK government responsible for enforcing EU directives affecting Gibraltar), but is not a full member and is exempt from the common policies on customs, commerce, agriculture, fisheries and VAT. Gibraltarians have voted in EU elections since 2004, but its future relationship is in doubt as the UK negotiates its withdrawal from the EU.

The 1969 constitution made provision for self-government in respect of certain domestic matters, but full internal autonomy came into effect with the 2006 constitution. This limited the governor's responsibilities to external affairs, defence, internal security and public service. The House of Assembly was restyled the Gibraltar Parliament, and may determine its own size; at present, it consists of an appointed speaker and 17 members elected for a four-year term. The government is formed by the chief minister (who is the leader of the majority party) and ministers from among the elected members of parliament.

The October 2019 election was won by Chief Minister Fabian Picardo's Gibraltar Socialist Labour Party.

Governor, HE Vice-Adm. David Steel, KBE, DL, *apptd* 2020
Chief Minister, Hon. Fabian Picardo

GOVERNMENT OF GIBRALTAR
150 Strand, London WC2R 1JA **T** 020-7836 0777
W www.gibraltar.gov.uk

ECONOMY
The economy is dominated by tourism (especially retail for day visitors), offshore financial services and shipping, and these three sectors account for about 85 per cent of GDP. Diversification efforts have encouraged telecommunications in particular and Gibraltar has become a centre for internet businesses, especially online gambling and gaming. A shift from a predominantly public-sector to a private-sector economy has occurred in recent years, although government spending still has a significant impact on the local economy. The chief sources of government revenue are port dues, the

rent of the Crown Estate in the town and duties on consumer items (although VAT is not applied in the territory).

Trade with UK	2018	2019
Imports from UK	£361,346,187	£434,020,327
Exports to UK	£15,911,069	£6,687,197

COMMUNICATIONS
Gibraltar has one international airport. The 29km road network is all surfaced; road links to Spain reopened in the 1980s. The port services the large shipping industry, cruise liners and a regular ferry service to Tangiers (Morocco).

MONTSERRAT

Area – 102 sq. km
Capital – Plymouth (abandoned 1997); the seat of government is now at Brades, in the north, population, 391 (2016 est); a new capital is under construction at nearby Little Bay
Currency – East Caribbean dollar (EC$) of 100 cents
Population – 5,315 rising at 0.43 per cent a year (2018 est)
Religion – Christian (Protestant 67.1 per cent, Roman Catholic 11.6 per cent, Rastafarian 1.4 per cent (est)
Language – English (official)
Flag – British blue ensign with the coat of arms in the fly
National day – Second Saturday in June (birthday of Queen Elizabeth II)
Median age (years) – 33.8 (2018 est)
Life expectancy (years) – 74.8 (2018 est)
Mortality rate – 6.2 (2018 est)
Birth rate – 10.5 (2018 est)
Infant mortality rate – 11.9 (2018 est)
WPFI score – 23,78 (44)

CLIMATE AND TERRAIN
Montserrat is a mountainous volcanic island in the Leeward group in the Caribbean Sea. Its lowest point of elevation is 0m (Caribbean Sea); its highest point was 914m (Chances Peak), although a lava dome in a crater in the Soufrière Hills volcano is estimated to be over 930m. Volcanic activity since 1995 has left over half of the island devastated by lava flows and ash. The climate is tropical and the average temperature is 25.9°C.

HISTORY AND POLITICS
Discovered by Columbus in 1493, Montserrat became a British colony in 1632. It was fought over by the French and British throughout the 17th and 18th centuries, before being finally restored to Britain in 1783.

Continual volcanic activity by the Soufrière Hills volcano between 1995 and 2014 has left over half of the island uninhabitable, and prompted the migration of two-thirds of the population in the late 1990s. An 'exclusion zone', to which access is restricted, covers two-thirds of the island and

two maritime exclusion zones extend between 2km and 4km offshore.

The 1990 constitution was amended in 1999 after more than half of the constituencies were made uninhabitable by volcanic activity. Following modernisation talks, a new constitution came into force in September 2011, which established a new National Advisory Council to enhance democracy and governance. Under the new constitution, the cabinet is chaired by the governor and comprises the premier, three other elected members and two *ex-officio* members (the attorney-general and the financial secretary). The legislative assembly consists of nine members elected for a five-year term and two *ex-officio* members. In the 2019 general election the People's Democratic Movement won the most seats.
Governor, HE Andrew Pearce, OBE, *apptd* 2018
Premier, Hon. Donaldson Romeo

GOVERNMENT OF MONTSERRAT
180–186 Kings Cross Road, London WC1X 9DE
T 020-7520 2622

ECONOMY
Continuing volcanic activity has restricted economic activity to the northern third of the island and considerably impacted the agricultural sector. Activity includes mining and quarrying, construction (mostly public sector), financial and professional services, and tourism. In January 2013 the EU granted a £33.4m aid package to bolster recovery; Montserrat will maintain a direct agreement with the EU despite the UK's withdrawal. Communications improved with the opening of Gerald's Airport in the north in 2005, allowing regular commercial air services to resume. There are port facilities at Little Bay, and a ferry service to and from Antigua.
Imports – US$55m (2016)
Exports – US$21m (2016)

BALANCE OF PAYMENTS
Trade – US$34m deficit (2016)
Current Account – US$8.8m deficit (2016)

Trade with UK	2018	2019
Imports from UK	£1,682,753	£844,707
Exports to UK	£143,016	£37,174

PITCAIRN ISLANDS

Pitcairn, Henderson, Ducie and Oeno Islands

Area – 47 sq. km
Capital – Adamstown, on Pitcairn Island
Currency – New Zealand dollar (NZ$) of 100 cents
Population – 54 (2016 est)
Religion – Christian (Seventh-day Adventist)
Language – English, Pitkern (both official)
Flag – British blue ensign with the coat of arms in the fly

National day – 23 January (Bounty Day)

CLIMATE AND TERRAIN

Pitcairn is the chief of a group of rugged islands situated in the South Pacific Ocean. The other main islands of the group are Henderson, lying 168km north-east of Pitcairn; Oeno, lying 120km north-west; and Ducie, lying 470km east. These are uninhabited. Henderson Island is a UNESCO World Heritage Site. The climate is tropical with an average temperature of 20.8°C.

HISTORY AND POLITICS

Pitcairn was settled in 1790 by mutineers from the *Bounty* and their Tahitian companions. It became a British settlement under the British Settlements Act 1887.

Under the 2010 constitutional arrangements, the islands are administered by the governor (usually the British High Commissioner to New Zealand), in consultation with the island council, which manages internal affairs. The commissioner liaises between the governor and the council. The island council comprises ten members: the governor; two members appointed by the governor; one member appointed by the council itself; and six, including the mayor, who are elected. The mayor is elected every three years; elections for other council members are held every year in December.

Governor (non-resident), HE Laura Clarke, *apptd* 2018 *(British High Commissioner to New Zealand)*

Mayor, Charlene Warren-Peu

ECONOMY

The islanders live by subsistence fishing and horticulture, and the sale of honey and handicrafts, although tourism is being promoted. Apart from small fees charged for licences there are no taxes and government revenue is derived almost solely from the sale of postage stamps and .pn internet domain names, and income from investments. Since financial reserves became exhausted a few years ago the islands have received budgetary aid from the UK.

Trade with UK	2018	2019
Imports from UK	£399,349	£155,529
Exports to UK	£15,583	£19,664

COMMUNICATIONS

There is no airfield and the only means of access is by sea; cruise and container ships stop irregularly but a regular shipping supply route to French Polynesia was established in 2006. There are about 6km of dirt roads on the islands. Broadband is available in all homes.

ST HELENA, ASCENSION AND TRISTAN DA CUNHA

Area – 308 sq. km
Population – 7,841 rising at 0.18 per cent (2018 est)
Religion – Christian (Protestant 75.9 per cent, Roman Catholic 1.2 per cent) (est)
Language – English (official)

National day – Second Saturday in June (birthday of Queen Elizabeth II)
Median age (years) – 42.4 (2018 est)
Life expectancy (years) – 79.8 (2018 est)
Mortality rate – 8 (2018 est)
Birth rate – 9.4 (2018 est)
Infant mortality rate – 12.8 (2017 est)

ST HELENA

Area – 122 sq. km
Capital – Jamestown; population, 1,000 (2018 est)
Currency – St Helena pound (£) of 100 pence
Population – 5,901 (2016 est)
Flag – British blue ensign with the coat of arms in the fly

CLIMATE AND TERRAIN

St Helena is a rugged and volcanic island, with sheer cliffs rising to a central plateau. Mt Actaeon, at 818m, is the highest elevation. The climate is tropical but mild, tempered by trade winds, and the average temperature is 18.1°C.

HISTORY AND POLITICS

St Helena is believed to have been discovered by the Portuguese navigator Joao da Nova in 1502. It was used as a port of call for vessels of all nations trading to the East until the late 19th century. From 1815 to 1821 the island was lent to the British government as a place of exile for Napoléon Bonaparte, who died there on 5 May 1821, and in 1834 it was annexed to the British crown. The Zulu chief Dinizulu was exiled to the island in 1890, and up to 6,000 Boer prisoners were held there between 1900 and 1903.

Under the 2009 constitution, government is administered by a governor, advised by an executive council comprising three *ex-officio* members (the chief secretary, financial secretary and attorney-general) and five elected members of the legislative council. The legislative council consists of 12 members elected for a four-year term, the three *ex-officio* members of the executive council, the speaker and the deputy speaker.

Governor, HE Dr Philip Rushbrook, *apptd* 2019

GOVERNMENT OF ST HELENA
16 Old Queen Street, London SW1H 9HP
T 020-3170 8705

ECONOMY AND TRADE

The island has few natural resources and its economy is dependent on an annual grant from the UK. The main economic activities are agriculture, the sale of fishing licences, fish processing and tourism. The only significant exports are coffee and frozen, canned and dried fish.

Trade with UK	2017	2018
Imports from UK	£15,699,045	£16,966,186
Exports to UK	£363,290	£999,318

COMMUNICATIONS

Access is predominantly by sea to Jamestown port, provided by a regular supply ship. The first scheduled commercial flight landed at the island's £285 million airport in October 2017. There are 118km of paved roads on the island. There are two local radio stations and two weekly newspapers.

ASCENSION ISLAND

Area – 88 sq. km
Capital – Georgetown
Currency – St Helena pound (£) of 100 pence
Population – 806 (2016 est)

CLIMATE AND TERRAIN
The island is a rocky volcanic peak that lies in the South Atlantic Ocean some 1,200km north-west of St Helena. The highest point (Green Mountain, 859m) is covered with lush vegetation. It is an important breeding place for the green turtle and a number of seabird species.

HISTORY AND POLITICS
Ascension is said to have been discovered by Joao da Nova in 1501 and two years later it was visited on Ascension Day by Alphonse d'Albuquerque, who gave the island its present name. The island was an important logistical centre in both world wars and during the Falklands conflict, and it has a continuing role as a military air base and in broadcasting, telecommunications and satellite tracking.

In 2002 new constitutional arrangements introduced a measure of self-government, and in 2009 Ascension ceased to be a dependency of St Helena. The governor, who is resident in St Helena, retains responsibility for defence, external affairs, internal security and public services. The governor, represented locally by the island administrator, chairs the island council, which consists of five elected members and two ex-officio members (the director of resources and the attorney-general).

Administrator, Sean Burns, *apptd* 2020

ECONOMY
Before 2002 the island was administered and financed by commercial operators, including the BBC and Cable and Wireless, and the military. With the change in governance in 2002, a fiscal regime was introduced to finance public services through taxation. A private sector is developing following the sale of government-owned concerns to commercial operators and the establishment of a sports fishing industry.

COMMUNICATIONS
Georgetown is the only port, but regular air links to the UK and the USA have been limited by the poor state of the runway. Ascension has 40km of roads. Telecommunication services are provided via satellite links. There is a local radio station and a weekly newspaper.

TRISTAN DA CUNHA
Area – 98 sq. km
Capital – Edinburgh of the Seven Seas
Currency – Pound sterling (£) of 100 pence
Population – 262 (2017 est)
Flag – British blue ensign with the coat of arms in the fly

CLIMATE AND TERRAIN
Tristan da Cunha is the chief of a group of islands in the South Atlantic Ocean which lie some 2,333km south-west of St Helena. All of the islands are volcanic and steep-sided with cliffs or narrow beaches. The island is home to the highest peak in the South Atlantic, Queens Mary's Peak, which rises to 2,060m above sea level. Gough and Inaccessible Islands are UNESCO World Heritage Sites.

HISTORY AND POLITICS
Tristan da Cunha was discovered in 1506 by the Portuguese navigator Tristao da Cunha. In 1816 the group was annexed to the British crown and a garrison was placed on Tristan da Cunha. When this force was withdrawn in 1817, four adults and two children remained at their own request and formed a settlement, which was joined in 1827 by five women from St Helena and afterwards by others from Cape Colony. Owing to its position on a major sea route the colony thrived, with an economy based on trade with passing ships, until the late 19th century, when the opening of the Suez Canal led to decline.

Tristan da Cunha and Inaccessible, Nightingale and Gough Islands were dependencies of St Helena from 1938 to 2009. They are administered by the governor of St Helena through a resident administrator, who is advised by an island council. This consists of eight members elected for a three-year term, of whom one must be a woman, and three appointed members.

Administrators, Fiona Kilpatrick; Steve Townsend, *apptd* 2020

ECONOMY
The island is almost financially self-sufficient; UK government aid finances training scholarships and a resident medical officer at the hospital. The main activities are crayfish fishing, fish processing, agriculture and the sale of postage stamps and coins.

COMMUNICATIONS
Communications with the outside world are by sea as there is no airport. Scheduled visits to the island are limited to about nine calls a year by fishing vessels from Cape Town and annual calls by a South African research vessel. Tristan da Cunha has 20km of roads, half of which are paved. There is a local radio station and a newspaper.

SOUTH GEORGIA AND THE SOUTH SANDWICH ISLANDS

For map *see* Falkland Islands entry.
Area – 3,903 sq. km
Capital – King Edward Point (administrative centre), on South Georgia
Currency – Pound sterling (£) of 100 pence
Population – There is no indigenous population. The British Antarctic Survey maintains two permanently staffed research stations, at King Edward Point and on Bird Island, to the north-west of South Georgia; in addition, there are the government officers at King Edward Point; population, 268 (2015 est) and the curators of the museum at Grytviken, South Georgia
Flag – British blue ensign, with the coat of arms in the fly

CLIMATE AND TERRAIN
Over half of South Georgia is permanently ice-covered, with many large glaciers. The main mountain range is the Allardyce, and elevation extremes range from 2,934m (Mt Paget) to 0m (Atlantic Ocean). The South Sandwich Islands are a chain of 11 uninhabited volcanic islands some 350km long.

HISTORY AND POLITICS
South Georgia was used by whalers and sealers of many nationalities following its discovery by Captain Cook in 1775. Britain annexed South Georgia and the South Sandwich Islands in 1908 and since then they have been under continuous British occupation, apart from a brief period during the Falklands conflict in 1982; Argentina claims sovereignty over the territory. A small British army garrison was maintained on South Georgia until 2001, before being replaced by scientists from the British Antarctic Survey.

Under the present constitution, which came into effect in 1985, the commissioner is concurrently the governor of the Falkland Islands. A chief executive officer, also based in the Falkland Islands, is responsible for administration. Government officers are based in South Georgia.

Commissioner (non-resident), HE Nigel Phillips, CBE, *apptd* 2017
Chief Executive (non-resident), Helen Havercroft, *apptd* 2018

ECONOMY

A conservation and management fishing zone was established around the islands in 1993 and a licensing regime introduced for fishing vessels. Sale of fishing licences, passenger landing fees, harbour dues, and the sale of postage stamps and commemorative coins are the main sources of revenue. Tourism, especially wildlife tourism, is growing quickly, but prior permission to land on the islands must be sought.

TURKS AND CAICOS ISLANDS

Area – 948 sq. km

Capital – Cockburn Town, on Grand Turk; population, 5,000 (2018 est)

Currency – US dollar (US$) of 100 cents

Population – 53,701 rising at 2.09 per cent a year (2018 est)

Religion – Christian (Protestant 72.8 per cent, Roman Catholic 11.4 per cent) (est)

Language – English (official)

Population density – 37 per sq. km (2017)

Flag – British blue ensign with the coat of arms in the fly

National day – 30 August (Constitution Day)

Median age (years) – 33.8 (2018 est)

Life expectancy (years) – 80.1 (2018 est)

Mortality rate – 3.3 (2018 est)

Birth rate – 14.9 (2018 est)

Infant mortality rate – 9.8 (2018 est)

CLIMATE AND TERRAIN

Around 40 islands and cays make up the the Turks and Caicos Islands, of which eight are permanently inhabited. The climate is marine tropical, moderated by trade winds; the average annual temperature is 26°C. Flamingo Hill on East Caicos is the highest elevation, at 48m.

HISTORY AND POLITICS

The islands changed hands several times between the French, Spanish and British after their discovery in 1512 and before the arrival of the first settlers, a group of Bermudans, in the 1670s. They achieved separate colonial status under the administration of the Bahamas in 1848, and since 1973 the territory has had its own governor and internal self-government.

The constitution implemented in 2012 re-established home rule after the House of Assembly and 2006 constitution were suspended in 2009 following a corruption scandal. The constitution provides for a legislature consisting of 15 elected members and four members appointed by the governor. The UK remains responsible for defence, external affairs and international and offshore financial relations. The People's Democratic Movement (PDM) won elections held in December 2016, garnering ten seats to the ruling Progressive National Party's (PNP) five, prompting the resignation of premier Rufus Ewing. In September 2017 the islands were badly damaged by Hurricane Irma and Hurricane Maria.

Governor, HE Nigel Dakin, *apptd* 2019

Premier, Hon. Sharlene Cartwright-Robinson

ECONOMY

The main industries are offshore financial services, fishing and tourism, with over 1 million people visiting the island annually – mainly from the USA.

Imports – US$389m (2016)

Exports – US$4m (2016)

BALANCE OF PAYMENTS

Trade – US$385m deficit (2016)

Trade with UK	2018	2019
Imports from UK	£4,920,343	£4,231,195
Exports to UK	£2,186,800	£361,275

COMMUNICATIONS

The principal airports are on the islands of Grand Turk and Providenciales and provide international air links; the main seaports are on Grand Turk and Providenciales. The islands have about 24km of surfaced roads.

THE NORTH AND SOUTH POLES

THE ARCTIC

The Arctic is the region around the Earth's north pole. It includes the ice-covered Arctic Ocean, parts of Canada, the USA, Greenland, Iceland, Finland, Norway, Sweden and Russia. The area is commonly defined as lying north of the line of latitude known as the Arctic Circle (running at 66° 34' N.) or inside the 10°C July isotherm.

The climate is harsh, particularly during winter (October–March) when the Arctic receives little sunlight; the average monthly temperature in December–February is around −10 to −15°C. Continental areas, including Northern Canada and Alaska, can experience lows of −60°C in winter. In summer, the interior of Greenland remains subzero, while more southerly regions such as the Siberian tundra, can rise to 30°C; a record high of 38°C was recorded in June 2020 in Verkhoyansk, Russia. Coastal areas, including Iceland and Northern Scandinavia, have a milder, maritime climate with an average yearly temperature of 10°C. The Arctic is rarely as cold as the Antarctic since there is water, not land, underneath the Arctic ice. The water is warmer than the air above it, causing heat to rise and moderate the cold.

The polar bear is the region's apex predator. Other native species include varieties of caribou, lemming, wolf, hare and fox; around 200 bird species migrate to tundra areas in summer. Until recently, vegetation was limited to Arctic tundra, a biome consisting of around 1,700 species of low-lying shrubs, grasses, sedges, lichens and mosses. However, this tundra is slowly being replaced with flora typical of more southern locations, such as trees and evergreen shrubs. In 2013, a comprehensive study of these changes, the Arctic Biodiversity Assessment (ABA) (**W** www.arcticbiodiversity.is), concluded that climate change and the effects of collective industrial development were degrading arctic biodiversity. Following this, the *Actions for Arctic Biodiversity, 2013–21* plan was established to implement recommendations made in the ABA, it is revised and updated biannually with a final report due in 2021.

ARCTIC SEA ROUTES

In 1906 Norwegian explorer Roald Amundsen first successfully navigated the Northwest Passage, but the shallow waterways he encountered ensured that the route held little commercial potential until recently. Similarly, the Northern Sea Route (formerly the Northeast Passage) linking the Atlantic and Pacific oceans around Russia's Arctic coast, was first navigated by Finnish-Swedish explorer Adolf Erik Nordenskjold in 1878–9, but thereafter only icebreakers and Russian submarines regularly traversed it.

In summer 2007, the Northwest Passage was declared open for the first time since records began in late 1978; the first commercial ship travelled through it in September 2008. In August 2008 the Northwest Passage and the Northern Sea Route were open simultaneously for the first time, making the Arctic circumnavigable. Two German cargo vessels became the first to navigate the Northern Sea Route in September 2009 and in August 2012 *The World* became the largest passenger ship to navigate the Northwest Passage, following Amundsen's route. In February 2018 a commercial ship became the first to travel the Northern Sea Route in winter without an icebreaker vessel.

CLIMATE CHANGE

The extent of ice in the Arctic has become a key measure of global climate change. The rate at which the ice melts grows exponentially: whereas the white ice reflects sunlight back into space, the darker seas absorb its heat, and the rising sea temperature melts the surrounding ice. The area of the sea ice reaches its greatest extent in March and retreats to its lowest point in September. The maximum ice extent in March 2020 was recorded as 15.05 million km² (5.81 million miles²); the eleventh lowest in the 42-year satellite record and 590,000km² (227,800 miles²) below the 1981 to 2010 average maximum. The minimum ice extent – measured on 10 September 2019 – was recorded as 4.19 million km² (1.62 million miles²). The 2019 minimum is the second lowest on record, tied with 2008 and 2016. Estimates of sea ice volume have been obtained via the University of Washington Polar Science Center's PIOMAS. For 2020, PIOMAS calculated an annual average sea ice volume of 13,500km³ (3,238 miles³), the third lowest on record. It was only a 700km³ gain over 2017 which was the lowest annual average volume of sea ice yet recorded; it is estimated that in 1979, the annual average was around 25,430km³ (6,100 miles³).

NATURAL RESOURCES

The Arctic's receding ice presents opportunities for national governments to lay claim to a wealth of hydrocarbon and mineral deposits. In 2008 the US Geological Survey estimated that 20 per cent of the world's undiscovered oil and gas reserves – as much as 90 billion barrels of oil, 44 billion barrels of natural gas liquids and 1,670 trillion cubic feet of natural gas – are located within the Arctic Circle. In December 2016 the USA and Canada introduced bans on offshore drilling covering large portions of the Arctic. Under the 1982 UN Convention on the Law of the Sea, no state owns the pole or the ocean surrounding it: the five countries that border the Arctic Ocean – Canada, Denmark, Norway, Russia and USA (a non-signatory) – are limited to an economic zone of 200 nautical miles from their coastline, unless able to prove that their continental shelf extends beyond that limit. Under the convention the countries have ten years from their date of ratification to assert a claim that their continental shelf extends into arctic territory. In August 2007, Russia planted a flag in the seabed below the pole, on the Lomonosov Ridge which spans much of the Arctic, and which Russia claims is an extension of the Eurasian continent and therefore part of its territory. However, Canada asserts that Lomonosov is an extension of the North American continent, and therefore falls under their jurisdiction. In December 2014 Denmark followed Canada, Norway and Russia in submitting a claim under UNCLOS, arguing that the Lomonosov Ridge is part of Greenland's continental shelf. Russia resubmitted its bid in August 2015, laying claim to 1.2 million km² of the shelf.

THE ANTARCTIC

The Antarctic is generally defined as the area lying within the Antarctic Convergence, the zone where cold northward-flowing Antarctic sea water sinks below warmer southward-flowing water. This zone fluctuates unevenly between the latitudes of 48° S. and 61° S., typically extending further north in the Atlantic Ocean than in the Pacific. The continent itself lies almost entirely within the Antarctic Circle; it has an area of around 14 million km², 98 per cent of which is permanently ice-covered. In 2013 the international project Bedmap2 found that the mean thickness of ice, excluding ice shelves, is 2,126m, with the thickest ice depth located in the Astrolabe Subglacial Basin at 4,897m; the total ice volume amounts to some 26.5 million km³, and represents around 60 per cent of the world's fresh water and 91 per cent of the world's glacier ice. Much of the sea freezes in winter, forming fast ice which breaks free of the coast in summer and drifts north as pack ice.

CLIMATE AND TERRAIN

Antarctica is the highest, coldest and driest continent on Earth, with average coastal temperatures ranging from just above freezing in the summer (December–February) to −30°C in winter. Conditions on the interior plateau are more severe, with katabatic (gravity-driven) winds and frequent cyclonic storms reducing average winter temperatures to −65°C. The lowest surface temperature on Earth was recorded as −89.2°C at the Vostok research station in 1983. Elevation extremes range from 4,892m (Vinson Massif) at the highest point to more than −2,540m (Bentley Subglacial Trench) at the lowest. The Transantarctic Mountains bisect the continent north–south, dividing the west Antarctic ice-sheet, an ice-filled marine basin, from the significantly larger and more elevated east sheet. Precipitation levels range from less than 50mm a year inland to around 400mm in some coastal areas. With average precipitation of 140mm a year, Antarctica is considered a desert.

CLIMATE CHANGE

While the recent decline in ice levels in the Arctic has been clear, concurrent changes in the Antarctic have been more complex. Despite reports of a recent thickening of the interior of the east ice-sheet due to increased snowfall, studies of data produced by the European Space Agency's Cryosat satellite indicate that, due to melt, the Antarctic ice-sheet is losing 159 billion tonnes of ice yearly. The melt from the ice-sheet alone is enough to raise global sea levels by 0.45mm each year. On 2 October 2018 the maximum sea ice extent reached 18.15 million km² (7.01 million miles²), the fourth lowest recorded. The US National Snow and Ice Data Center recorded the 2019 minimum sea ice extent for the year on both 28 February and 1 March at 2.47 million km² (954,000 miles²), the seventh lowest in satellite record. The annual average sea ice extent for 2018 was the second smallest on record at 10.88 million km² (4.20 million miles²); 199,429km² (77,000 miles²) larger than the smallest annually averaged extent recorded in 2017.

The British Antarctic Survey has found that the Antarctic Peninsula west coast has become one of the fastest-warming areas on the planet, with annual mean temperatures rising by 3.2°C over the past 60 years. In March 2015 the Esperanza research station recorded a record high of 17.5°C on the western peninsula. In 2009, a group of British geophysicists found that the retreat of the Pine Island Glacier in the Western Antarctic had quadrupled between 1995 and 2006. However, the temperatures recorded by the Amundsen-Scott station at the South Pole show a recent cooling, as do some studies of east Antarctica. It was determined that these falling temperatures have been caused by the thinning of Antarctica's ozone layer that has in turn cooled the stratosphere above the continent. The historical use of chlorofluorocarbons (CFCs) by humans has contributed to the destruction of Antarctica's ozone layer, as the clouds that form in the winter polar vortex – an area of very cold air above the continent – react with these CFCs to release chlorine which destroys ozone. These chemicals were internationally banned in the 1980s and a study released by NASA in 2018 was the first to show that the decline in chlorine as a result of the CFC ban had resulted in less ozone depletion. The Antarctic ozone hole is expected to largely recover by 2060–80.

HISTORY AND DISCOVERY

The idea of Antarctica is much older than proof of the continent's existence. The notion of *Terra Australis*, a vast southern continent which counterbalanced the northern lands of Europe, Asia and North Africa, originated with Aristotle, and was depicted on a world map in 1531. The supposed size of this land was amended over the course of 16th-century exploration and further corrected after James Cook's 1774 circumnavigation of the globe. His journey from New Zealand to the Cape of Good Hope (via Tierra del Fuego), travelling at a high southern latitude (between 53° and 60°), confirmed that any land mass must be confined to the polar region.

The date of the first sighting of Antarctica is unclear. In 1820 three separate expeditions, from the UK, the USA and Russia, each claimed to have seen the continent within days of each other, and the argument has never been settled. The golden age of Antarctic exploration was prompted by the discovery of the magnetic North Pole in 1831, but it was not until the beginning of the 20th century that real progress was made. James Clark Ross was the first to identify the approximate location of the South Pole, but was unable to reach it. British explorers Robert Scott in 1901–4 and Ernest Shackleton in 1907–9 got closer, but it was not until Norwegian adventurer Roald Amundsen pioneered a new route, through the Axel Heiberg Glacier, that the pole was reached in December 1911. Scott's second attempt was also successful, but he arrived a month later and perished with his team on the return journey.

FLORA AND FAUNA

The only land animals to survive on the Antarctic continent are tiny invertebrates, including microscopic mites, lice, ticks, nematodes, rotifers and tardigrades. The largest land animal is the *Belgica antarctica*, a flightless midge just 2–6mm in size. The snow petrel, one of only three birds that breed exclusively in Antarctica, has been spotted at the South Pole. Large numbers of seals, penguins and other seabirds go ashore to breed in the summer; the emperor penguin is the only species that breeds ashore throughout the winter. Four species of albatross breed in South Georgia during the summer, but their numbers are in serious decline owing to the effects of longline fishing in the Southern Ocean region. Recent climate change has also affected the continent's wildlife, with the number of Adélie penguins falling significantly, as open-water species such as the chinstrap and gentoo penguins invade its Antarctic Peninsula habitat to take advantage of the warming temperatures.

By contrast, the Antarctic seas abound with life; recent expeditions identified over 700 previously unknown species. Krill, which congregate in large schools, is crucial to the ecosystem and provides a diet for migratory whales (including killer, humpback and blue whales), a number of species of seal, penguin, albatross and other, smaller birds. Each of these species is threatened by an 80 per cent fall in recorded levels of krill since the 1970s, thought to be caused by warmer sea water and, paradoxically, the decimation of the blue whale through hunting in the first half of the 20th century: although whales eat krill, the iron in whale excrement is essential to the algae on which the krill feed. In 2010 a group of research bodies completed the Census of Antarctic Marine Life, an inventory of over 16,000 marine species compiled from 19 expeditions; scientists estimate that 39–58 per cent of the Antarctic's marine species are yet to be described.

With almost all of the Antarctic continent permanently covered in ice, only a small number of flowering plants, ferns and club mosses survive. Most of these are found on the sub-Antarctic islands, while only two species (a grass and a pearlwort) extend south of 60° S. Antarctic vegetation is dominated by lichens and mosses, with a few liverworts, algae and fungi surviving in the cracks and pore spaces of sandstone and granite rocks.

SCIENTIFIC RESEARCH

As at May 2019 there were 20 nations with open year-round, permanently manned, research stations in Antarctica:

Country	Number of research stations
Argentina	6
Russia	5
Chile	4
Australia	3
USA	3
China	2
France	*2
India	2
South Korea	2
UK	†2

Brazil, Italy (*shared with France), Japan, New Zealand, Norway, Poland, South Africa, Ukraine and Uruguay each have a single station. Germany has Neumeyer III and also operates the Antarctic Receiving Station (GARS) at the Chilean O'Higgins base.

The British Antarctic Survey's (BAS) Halley research station (†), normally a year-round research facility, is temporarily operating as a seasonal facility, closing for the Antarctic winters. A series of remote monitoring systems have been set up to allow the facility to run autonomous experiments so that data collection is not interrupted while the station is unmanned. The seasonal status of the station is due to the discovery of a crack in the Brunt Ice Shelf, which originally forced the station to relocate 23km (14.3 miles) inland in March 2017. Until it is established that the shelf is safe for year-round occupation, BAS will not over-winter at Halley. The station was due to reopen in November 2019, however it

was only operational on a temporary basis due to a combination of safety concerns and inability to travel because of the COVID-19 pandemic.

ANTARCTIC LAW

The Antarctic Treaty was signed on 1 December 1959 when 12 states (Argentina, Australia, Belgium, Chile, France, Japan, New Zealand, Norway, Russia, South Africa, the UK and the USA) pledged to promote scientific and technical cooperation unhampered by politics. The signatories agreed to establish free use of the Antarctic continent for peaceful scientific purposes; freeze all territorial claims and disputes in the Antarctic; ban all military activities in the area; and prohibit nuclear explosions and the disposal of radioactive waste. The Antarctic Treaty was defined as covering areas south of latitude 60° S., excluding the high seas but including the ice shelves, and came into force in 1961. The treaty provides that any member of the UN can accede to it and, to date, has since been signed by a further 42 states. In 1998 an extension to the treaty came into effect, placing a 50-year ban on mining, oil exploration and mineral extraction in Antarctica, and stipulating that all tourists, explorers and expeditions now require permission to enter the Antarctic from a relevant national authority. In recent years the region's coastal states have asserted often conflicting claims to oil- and gas-rich territory on the Antarctic seabed. Under the terms of the UN Convention on the Law of the Sea, each nation's sovereignty over its continental shelf extends up to 350 nautical miles beyond its territorial coasts; the UN Commission on the Limits of the Continental Shelf is examining evidence submitted in support of these claims.

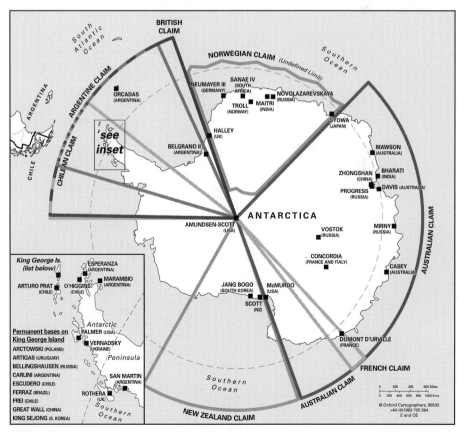

POPULATION AND TOURISM

Antarctica has no indigenous inhabitants, although the continent maintains a population of scientists and research workers which peaks in the summer months at over 4,400.

Antarctic tourism is a growth industry. The first *Lonely Planet* guide to Antarctica was published in 1996, and ship-borne cruises typically depart from Argentina, Chile and the Falkland Islands. The continent has also become a popular venue for extreme sports enthusiasts: it is now possible to sky-dive, ski, ride a motorbike and fly a helicopter across the continent, and the Vinson Massif and other peaks have become desirable destinations for mountaineers. The huts built by Scott and Shackleton are also popular attractions. In 1991 the International Association of Antarctica Tour Operators (IAATO) was founded with the objective of providing a self-regulating code of conduct for all operators to follow, but membership is voluntary, and fears remain regarding tourism-related environmental damage. IAATO recorded 6,704 tourists in the 1992–3 summer season, rising to more than 46,000 in 2007–8 and again to nearly 74,000 in 2019–20.

THE BRITISH ANTARCTIC SURVEY

The British Antarctic Survey (BAS) is part of the Natural Environment Research Council and carries out the majority of Britain's scientific research in Antarctica. Over 500 staff are employed by BAS and the organisation supports five research stations, four of which are staffed throughout the winter months (two in South Georgia and two in Antarctica). An unmanned submersible, named Boaty McBoatface in a public competition, embarked on its first Antarctic research mission in March 2017 aboard the BAS ship RRS *James Clark Ross* as part of a seven-week expedition. Boaty McBoatface completed three missions during the expedition, capturing unprecedented data at the Orkney Passage in the Antarctic Bottom Water, some of the coldest waters on earth. This data is the first of its kind and it may be years before detailed reports are published. *See* the BAS website (**W** www.antarctica.ac.uk) for further information.

THE YEAR 2019–20

The year under review covers the period from 1 August 2019 to 31 December 2020

A CENTURY AGO IN WHITAKER'S

EVENTS OF THE YEAR 1919–20

The following constitutes selected extracts from the Events of the Year chapter as recorded in the 1919 and 1920 editions of *Whitaker's Almanack*, published a century ago. The text has been reproduced in its original form, along with its idiosyncrasies of style and archaic spellings of names. The information in parentheses following the date is the name of the sub-section the extract was taken from.

NOVEMBER 1919
11. (The King and Court) At the call of the King the Empire rendered homage to the Glorious Dead on the anniversary of Armistice Day by suspending all business for two minutes at 11 a.m. **12. (Aviation)** Capt. Boss M. Smith and his brother left Hounslow in Vickers-Vimy on attempt to fly to Australia. **14. (United States)** Senate passed Reservation to Article X of League of Nations Covenant, amounting to rejection of Peace Treaty. **18. (Imperial Dominions)** Officially announced that the Milner Commission was to draw up a Constitution for Egypt, giving Egyptians increasing share in Government, but preserving the autonomy.

DECEMBER 1919
1. (Imperial Politics) Viscountess Astor, M.P., took her seat in House of Commons, being first woman to do so. **10. (Aviation)** Capt. Ross Smith and his brother, Lieut. Keith Smith, with two sergeants, arrived at Port Darwin, Australia, and won the Australian Government's prize of £10,000 having covered 11,294 miles in just under 23 days in their Vickers-Vimy. They both received the K. B.E. from the King. **18. (Educational)** Two women were among successful candidates for Beit Fellowships. **18 (Naval)** In its trials new destroyer Tyrian attained record speed of over 45 miles an hour in deep water.

JANUARY 1920
IO. (France) The protocol relating to reparation was signed in Paris, and the Treaty of Versailles came into force, peace between the Allies and Germany being restored. **12. (Accidents at Sea)** French liner L'Afrique, with 465 passengers on board, went down 50 miles from La Rochelle, many lives being lost. **16. (League of Nations)** The first meeting of the Council was held in Paris at the Quai d'Orsay, M. Leon Bourgeois presiding. Earl Curzon was the chief British representative.

FEBRUARY 1920
4. (Aviation) In another Vickers-Vimy aeroplane, the "Silver Queen," Lieut.-Col. Van Ryneveld and Flight-Lieut. Brand, South Africans, left Brooklands for the Cape. **IO. (Aviation)** "Silver Queen" arrived at Cairo. **11. (Aviation)** It crashed at Korosko. **22. (Aviation)** Ryneveld and Brand left Cairo in "Silver Queen II."

MARCH 1920
2. (Educational) Convocation at Oxford passed a statute making Greek no longer compulsory subject for the Responsions examination. **6. (Aviation)** The "Silver Queen II." crashed at Bulawayo, after covering 3.880 miles from Cairo; airmen unhurt. **17. (Aviation)** Van Ryneveld and Brand left Buluwayo in another aeroplane supplied by Union Government. **19. (United States)** Senate again declined to ratify the Peace Treaty, two-thirds majority not being obtained. **20. (Aviation)** They reached Cape Town and were awarded £5,000 by Union Government to mark their achievement. King appointed each a K.B.E. **22. (The King and Court)** His Majesty held a levee at St. James's Palace, the first since 1914.

APRIL 1920
9. (United States) House of Representatives, by 242 to 150, passed peace resolution terminating state of war with Germany. **11. (United States)** An Englishman named Stephens was killed in attempting to go over Niagara Falls in a barrel. **13. (Legal)** Four women were successful in Easter Bar examination. **24. (Germany)** Allied Council at San Remo agreed to issue Franco-British manifesto insisting on the Treaty and disarmament of Germany.

MAY 1920
11. (Educational) Statute providing that women may be admitted to degrees at Oxford passed by Convocation. **14. (Imperial Politics)** British and French Premiers met at Hythe and decided on Spa Conference with Germans, and that Peace Treaty should be enforced in all its details. **15. (United States)** Senate passed resolution declaring war with Germany and Austria at an end. **19. (Educational)** Announced that University of London had been offered by Government site behind British Museum for new headquarters of University. **28. (The King and Court)** The King, accompanied by the Queen, laid foundation stone of new building of London School of Economics.

JUNE 1920
1. (Ireland) Office of Registrar of Deeds, Dublin, was raided, and guns and ammunition taken from soldiers. **7. (United States)** Supreme Court declared Federal Prohibition Amendment and Volstead Enforcement Bill constitutional. **IO. (The King and Court)** The King opened the Imperial War Museum at the Crystal Palace. Their Majesties held their first Court since 1914 at Buckingham Palace. **23. (Ireland)** In street fighting in Londonderry 17 men were killed. **28. (Ecclesiastical)** Dean of Westminster issued appeal for £250,000 for preservation of Westminster Abbey.

JULY 1920
6. (The King and Court) His Majesty laid foundation stone of new building of Edinburgh University, and Queen was given honorary degree. **8. (Imperial Dominions)** Annexation of East Africa Protectorate under name of Kenya Colony announced. **9. (Germany)** Germans signed document containing Allies' disarmament conditions. **15. (Accidents, General)** Tent in which Sanger's Circus was performing at Taunton caught fire, many people being burnt or injured in the stampede, three children and a woman fatally. **27. (International Courtesies)** The St. Gaudens statue of Abraham Lincoln, America's gift, was unveiled at Westminster by Duke of Connaught.

AUGUST 1920
13. (United States) Woman suffrage became law. **27. (Aviation)** Sadi Lecointe won Gordon Bennett air race near Etampes, covering 188 miles in 66 mins. 8 secs.

SEPTEMBER 1920
7. (Other Countries) Considerable damage done by severe earthquake shocks in Tuscany, over 300 lives being lost.

OCTOBER 1920
7. (Educational) The first women undergraduates were admitted to Oxford University. **18. (Labour)** Riots in Downing Street followed unemployed demonstration. Prime Minister told London Mayors elaborate schemes were in preparation for winter, Government to pay half cost. **20. (Educational)** Senate of London University decided to accept the Bloomsbury site offered by Government. **27. (League of Nations)** Headquarters of League removed from London to Geneva. The Council met at Brussels and condemned poison gas.

EVENTS OF THE YEAR 2019–20

UK AFFAIRS

AUGUST 2019

1. Parts of the Derbyshire towns of Whaley Bridge, Furness Vale and New Mills were evacuated after concrete slabs on the dam spillway of the Toddbrook Reservoir partially collapsed. **5.** The historic shipyard Harland and Wolff, which built the *RMS Titanic*, ceased trading. **9.** A power blackout hit parts of England and Wales, affecting nearly a million people and causing widespread travel disruption. **10.** Richard Braine was elected as leader of the UK Independence Party, succeeding Gerard Batten. **15.** The former Conservative and Change UK MP Sarah Wollaston joined the Liberal Democrats, saying she felt it was the best way for her to fight to keep Britain in the European Union. **18.** More than 100 MPs wrote to Prime Minister Boris Johnson calling for a recall of Parliament to debate concerns that the UK was facing a national emergency over Brexit. **22.** Boris Johnson met French President Emmanuel Macron in Paris where they discussed Brexit; Johnson insisting that the Brexit impasse could be broken with energy and creativity. Macron reiterated that the Republic of Ireland–Northern Ireland backstop plan was indispensable to preserving political stability and the single market. **23.** Boris Johnson and Jeremy Corbyn express concern over major fires in the Amazon rainforest, ahead of the latest G7 summit. **24.** Prince Andrew defended his former friendship with the convicted sex offender Jeffrey Epstein's after video footage emerged of himself at Jeffrey Epstein's mansion in 2010. **25.** The UK experienced its hottest late August bank holiday weekend on record, with temperatures reaching 33.3 °C in west London. **26.** The UK's biggest ever fracking-related tremor was recorded at a Cuadrilla site near Blackpool, with a magnitude of 2.9. **27.** Greater Manchester-based club Bury FC were expelled from the English Football League after a takeover bid collapsed. **28.** Boris Johnson asked the Queen to suspend Parliament from early September until 14 October; following precedent, she approved the request. While many Brexit supporters welcomed the move, the action receives widespread condemnation from those in favour of the UK remaining in the EU. **29.** Ruth Davidson resigned as leader of the Scottish Conservatives. **31.** Demonstrations were held across the UK in protest at Boris Johnson's decision to suspend parliament (*see* 28 August).

SEPTEMBER 2019

2. Giving a speech outside 10 Downing Street, Boris Johnson stated his opposition to calling a general election and urged MPs not to vote for another delay to Brexit. **3.** The government lost its majority in the House of Commons after Conservative MP Phillip Lee crossed the floor to join the Liberal Democrats, and MPs opposed to a no-deal Brexit took control of the House of Commons business by 328 votes to 301; Johnson responded by telling MPs he would seek an October general election. The prime minister withdrew the whip from 21 Conservative MPs who voted against the government, including several former cabinet ministers such as Ken Clarke, who had served as an MP since 1970, and Sir Nicholas Soames, the grandson of former prime minister Winston Churchill. **4.** A bill intended to block the possibility of the UK leaving the EU without a deal passed its first commons vote by 329 to 300, and MPs rejected Boris Johnson's motion to call a snap general election for October; Labour MPs abstain from the vote. **5.** The former Labour and Change UK MP Luciana Berger joined the Liberal Democrats. **6.** The bill designed to prevent a no-deal Brexit was passed by the House of Lords. **7.** Work and Pensions Secretary Amber Rudd resigned from the cabinet and surrendered the Conservative Party whip, in support of the Conservatives that has been expelled (*see* 3 September). **9.** John Bercow announced that he would stand down as Speaker of the House of Commons on 31

October, or at the next general election, depending on which came first. The Benn bill, intended to stop Britain leaving the EU without a deal, was granted royal assent and a motion calling for the publication of all government communications relating to no-deal Brexit planning and the suspension of Parliament passed by a vote of 311 to 302. A second government motion calling for an early general election failed to achieve the required super-majority, with 293 MPs voting in favour of it (*see* 4 September). **10.** Parliament was prorogued amid significant protests in the House of Commons from opposition MPs, with some holding up signs saying 'silenced'. **11.** Three judges at Scotland's highest civil court ruled that the government's prorogation of the UK Parliament was unlawful 'and is thus null and of no effect'; approximately 40 MPs returned to work in Parliament, protesting at its suspension and to show their support for the court ruling. **12.** The High Court in Belfast rejected a legal challenge against a no-deal Brexit that was brought on the argument it breached the Good Friday Agreement. **13.** The former English Defence League leader, Tommy Robinson, was released from prison after nine weeks. **14.** Ex-Conservative MP Sam Gyimah, one of the 21 rebels who had the whip removed on 3 September, joined the Liberal Democrats. **20.** Some of the largest climate change protests ever seen in the UK were held in towns and cities across the country as part of a worldwide day of strikes and protests, demanding action on carbon emissions. An American woman, Virginia Giuffre (*née* Roberts), said she had sex with Prince Andrew as a 17-year-old and was 'trafficked' to the prince; the Duke of York denied having any relationship with her. **22.** An article in the *Sunday Times* accused Prime Minister Boris Johnson of misconduct in office while Mayor of London, alleging that US businesswoman Jennifer Arcuri received favourable treatment with the awarding of grants to her company because of her friendship with Johnson. **23.** The travel company Thomas Cook collapsed after 178 years in business, triggering the largest ever peacetime repatriation process with an estimated 150,000 holidaymakers left stranded abroad. **24.** The 11 justices of the Supreme Court ruled unanimously that the prorogation brought forward by Boris Johnson was both justiciable and unlawful, and therefore null and of no effect (*see* 11 September). **25.** MPs returned to Parliament after the ending of prorogation; amid furious scenes in the commons, opposition politicians accused Prime Minister Boris Johnson of using inflammatory language. Johnson, who described the law seeking to block a no-deal Brexit as 'the surrender bill', defended his actions. **26.** A 36-year-old man was arrested outside the office of Labour MP Jess Phillips after she tabled an urgent question in the commons on inflammatory language; the man was alleged to have tried to smash windows and kick a door open while shouting insults. Buckingham Palace announced the engagement of Princess Beatrice and Edoardo Mapelli Mozzi. **27.** Prime Minister Boris Johnson was referred to the Independent Office for Police Conduct (IOPC), having been accused of misconduct in office while Mayor of London (*see* 22 September). **28.** Downing Street dismissed Johnson's IOPC referral as being politically motivated. **29.** *Sunday Times* carried fresh allegations about the relationship between Boris Johnson and Jennifer Arcuri, alleging the two were engaged in an affair; Johnson denied any conflict of interest.

OCTOBER 2019

1. Torrential rain brought flooding to many parts of the UK with dozens of warnings issued by the Environment Agency. Some areas in the Midlands, Wales and southern England were hit by a week's rain in just one hour. Following a report from the Oil and Gas Authority, the government called a halt to all fracking in the UK with immediate effect and warned shale gas companies that it would not support future projects (*see* 16 August). **2.** Boris Johnson published his Brexit plan, which included proposals to replace the

Irish backstop meaning Northern Ireland would essentially stay in the European Single Market for agricultural and industrial goods. The government announced fresh plans to prorogue parliament, from 8–14 October to allow it to bring the current parliamentary session to an end and introduce a new Queen's Speech. **4.** The government assured the highest civil court in Scotland that the Prime Minister would send a letter to the EU seeking an extension to Article 50 as required by the Benn Act. Prince Harry began legal action against the owners of *The Sun* and the *Daily Mirror*, in relation to alleged phone-hacking. **5.** More than fifty people were injured after a double-decker bus crashed and overturned on the A385 Berry Pomeroy, between Totnes and Paignton in Devon, England. Lucia Lucas became the first transgender singer to perform with the English National Opera in London. Foreign Secretary Dominic Raab said he had called the US ambassador to the United Kingdom to express his disappointment that a US diplomat's wife who was the subject of a police investigation following a fatal road crash had left the UK. **6.** Flights repatriating the final 4,800 Thomas Cook holidaymakers stranded abroad following the company's collapse took off, bringing to an end Operation Matterhorn, the largest peacetime repatriation operation in history (*see* 23 September). Parliament was prorogued until 14 October. **8–9.** Storm Ciara hit the UK, bringing winds of up to 130 Km an hour. **9.** A British Airways Boeing 747 aircraft made the fastest ever subsonic New York JFK to London Heathrow crossing, lasting in 4 hours 56 minutes; it reached ground speeds of up to 825mph by riding the jet stream bringing Storm Ciara to the UK. **10.** The British government confirmed it had begun to study the feasibility of a Scotland-Northern Ireland bridge, with project costs estimated at £15–20bn. **11.** The Arndale Centre in Manchester was evacuated after a number of stabbings, in which four people were injured. A man in his 40s was arrested on suspicion of planning an act of terrorism. **13.** The canonisation of Cardinal John Henry Newman (*d.* 1890) by Pope Francis in St. Peter's Square, Vatican City, in the presence of Prince Charles and representatives of the Anglican church, made Newman the first English person who has lived since the 17th century to be recognised officially as a saint by the Roman Catholic Church. **16.** Storm Dennis caused a record high number of flood warnings to be declared over England, with 600 in place by the evening; police declared major incidents in a number of regions, including South Wales, after towns and villages north of Cardiff receive more than a month's worth of rainfall in 24 hours. **17.** The UK and EU agreed a new Brexit withdrawal agreement, with the DUP confirming they would not support its passage through Parliament. **18.** Sainsbury's became the first major supermarket to stop selling fireworks at its 2,300 stores across the UK. **19.** A special Saturday sitting of Parliament was held to debate the revised EU withdrawal agreement and MPs passed amendments 322 to 306 that withheld Parliament's approval until legislation implementing the deal had been passed, and forced the government to request a delay to Brexit until 31 January 2020. **20.** Downing Street confirmed that Boris Johnson would send a letter to the EU requesting an extension to Article 50, but would not sign it; EU Council President Donald Tusk subsequently confirmed receipt of the letter. Johnson sent a second letter describing any further delay to Brexit as a mistake. Another People's Vote march was held in London. **21.** Speaker of the House John Bercow refused to allow a 'meaningful vote' on the latest Brexit deal, stating that 'the motion would not be debated today as it would be repetitive and disorderly to do so.' **22.** MPs allowed the government's new withdrawal agreement bill to pass to the next stage of the parliamentary process, by 329 votes to 299, but rejected the proposed timetable of three days. Abortion was decriminalised in Northern Ireland. **23.** The bodies of 38 adults and a teenager were found in a lorry container in Essex; a 25-year-old man from Northern Ireland was arrested on suspicion of murder. **28.** MPs rejected a motion for a 12 December general election, with only 299 votes in favour, which was 135 votes short of the two-thirds majority needed; Boris Johnson said he would table a new bill after losing this motion. **29.** Labour leader Jeremy Corbyn announced that he and his party would now support

a general election; MPs voted by 438 to 20 in favour of a general election, scheduled for Thursday 12 December 2019, by passing the Early Parliamentary General Election Bill. **30.** Survivors and bereaved relatives of the Grenfell Tower fire called for London Fire Brigade chief Dany Cotton to resign, after a highly critical report from the inquiry into the blaze.

NOVEMBER 2019

4. The UK terrorism threat level was reduced from 'severe' to 'substantial' for the first time since 2014. Sir Lindsay Hoyle, Member of Parliament for Chorley, was elected Speaker of the House, replacing John Bercow who stepped down after ten years. **5.** Retailer Mothercare collapsed into administration, putting 2,500 UK jobs at risk. **6.** The 57th parliament was dissolved in preparation for the general election on 12 December 2019. **7.** *The Times* reported that Downing Street was suspected by unnamed sources of suppressing a parliamentary report into Russian interference because it contained 'embarrassing' disclosures about the Kremlin links of wealthy Russian donors to the Conservative Party. **8.** More than 100 flood warnings were issued across the Midlands and northern England, with some areas receiving a month's worth of rainfall in 24 hours; the torrential downpours led to the death of a former Derbyshire High Sheriff, Annie Hall. **16.** In a BBC interview with Emily Maitlis, Prince Andrew, Duke of York, denied having sex with Virginia Giuffre (*née* Roberts), when she was a teenager, and expresses regret at having met convicted child sex offender Jeffrey Epstein in 2010; he was widely criticised for the interview. **19.** Boris Johnson and Jeremy Corbyn appeared on ITV in a head-to-head election debate. **20.** Prince Andrew announced he was stepping down from public duties for the foreseeable future after being engulfed in the Jeffrey Epstein scandal (*see* 16 November). **23.** Five teenagers, including a 13-year-old girl, were arrested following a brawl at Vue Cinema in the Star City complex in Birmingham, before the screening of the film *Blue Story*; it was reported that the arrested were armed with machetes and the police had to draw tasers. **28.** Former South Yorkshire police chief, David Duckenfield, was found not guilty of manslaughter in the Hillsborough disaster trial. **29.** A mass stabbing at a London Bridge venue resulted in two victims killed and at least five people injured; the suspect, wearing a hoax explosive device, was shot by police and died at the scene.

DECEMBER 2019

7. Virgin Trains ceased operations on the West Coast Main Line after running trains since 9 March 1997; they were replaced the following day by Avanti West Coast. **12.** In the general election, the Conservative Party, led by Boris Johnson, achieved a majority of 80 seats in the House of Commons, while the Labour Party, led by Jeremy Corbyn, suffered major losses resulting in their lowest proportion of seats since 1935. The Scottish National Party won a landslide in Scotland, winning 48 of the 59 seats. **13.** Jeremy Corbyn announced he would not lead Labour into a future general election. **17.** Boris Johnson announced his plans to rule out (legally) any extension to the transition period after the UK leaves the EU. **19.** The British High Court ruled that the Home Office's £1,012 child citizenship fee was unlawful. **20.** MPs voted in favour of the Brexit withdrawal agreement by 358 to 234, creating a path for the UK's exit from the EU on 31 January 2020. Andrew Bailey was appointed as Governor of the Bank of England, effective from February 2020. **22.** Supermarket chain Tesco halted production of Christmas cards made in China after a girl in south London found a card with a hand-written note asking for help; the author claimed to be a prisoner being forced to work. **26.** The RSPCA began an investigation after a prominent lawyer, Jolyon Maugham, said that he killed an urban fox with a baseball bat. **28.** The Cabinet Office apologised after the addresses of more than 1,000 2020 New Year Honours recipients, including senior police and political figures, were accidentally published online. **31.** The first opposite-sex couples were granted civil partnerships in England and Wales by amended legislation under the Civil Partnerships, Marriages and Deaths (Registration etc.) Act of 26 March 2019.

JANUARY 2020

4. The Foreign Office warned British nationals against all but essential travel to Iran and Iraq, following a US airstrike in Baghdad the previous day in which Iranian general Qasem Soleimani was killed. **6.** Downing Street stated that Britain would not support US President Donald Trump's threat to bomb Iranian cultural and heritage sites. **7.** The Labour Party leadership election formally began, with the new leader scheduled to be announced on 4 April 2020. **8.** The Duke and Duchess of Sussex announced that they planned to step back as senior members of the Royal Family, and divide their time between the UK and North America. **9.** The House of Commons gave its third and final backing to the Withdrawal Agreement Bill, voting 330 to 231 in favour (*see* 20 December 2019); the bill passed to the House of Lords for scrutiny. **12.** The Terrorist Offenders Bill, designed to end the early release of prisoners convicted of terrorist offences, passed unopposed through the House of Commons to complete the first stage of the process to becoming law. **13.** The Queen agreed to a period of transition, during which the Duke and Duchess of Sussex would spend time in Canada and the UK (*see* 8 January). **14.** Boris Johnson formally rejected Scottish First Minister Nicola Sturgeon's request for a second independence referendum for Scotland. **16.** Legislation was drafted for Parliament to allow the use of television cameras during trials at Crown Courts in England and Wales; the major detail being that only the judges would be filmed. **18.** Buckingham Palace confirmed that from spring 2020 the Duke and Duchess of Sussex would no longer use their royal titles and would no longer receive public funds for their royal duties. **21.** The Office of Rail and Road announced that Network Rail was being investigated over its poor performance on routes used by train operators Arriva Rail North and the TransPennine Express. **22.** The EU withdrawal deal successfully completed its passage through parliament, with the EU Withdrawal Agreement Bill being voted through without change (several amendments proposed by the House of Lords were rejected, *see* 9 January). **24.** The EU withdrawal agreement was signed by both parties: in Brussels by European Council President Charles Michel and European Commission President Ursula von der Leyen for the EU, and in London by Prime Minister Boris Johnson. **27.** The UK Health Secretary, Matt Hancock, told the House of Commons that 200 British citizens trapped in Wuhan, China, would be offered repatriation to the UK in light of the emerging COVID-19 outbreak in Hubei province. **28.** Boris Johnson approved a limited role for China's Huawei in Britain's 5G mobile network, despite US pressure to exclude the company. **29.** Transport Secretary Grant Shapps announced that train operator Arriva Rail North would be brought under government control from 1 March 2020 following a prolonged period of poor performance. British Airways suspended all flights to and from mainland China with immediate effect, due to the COVID-19 outbreak. **31.** The first two cases of COVID-19 were discovered and confirmed in the UK.

FEBRUARY 2020

6. A third case of COVID-19 was detected in the UK. **7.** Buckingham Palace announced that the wedding of Princess Beatrice of York and Edoardo Mapelli Mozzi would take place on 29 May (later postponed to 17 July). **10.** A sample taken from a 75-year-old woman from Nottinghamshire was later identified as the earliest person known to have been infected by severe acute respiratory syndrome COVID-19 (SARS-CoV-2) in the UK; the sample tested positive when examined months later in August. She was thought to be the first person in the UK to die with coronavirus disease in 2019. **12.** The government announced plans to extend the remit of the media regulator Ofcom to include internet and social media content in the UK. **13.** Boris Johnson carried out a cabinet reshuffle and Sajid Javid resigned as Chancellor of the Exchequer; he was succeeded by Rishi Sunak. **20.** A new pound sterling £20 polymer banknote entered circulation; it featured the face of artist JMW Turner and joined the updated and more secure pound sterling £5 and £10 banknotes that were introduced in 2016 and 2017, respectively. **28.** The first British death from coronavirus

disease in 2019 was reported; COVID-19 was confirmed aboard the *Diamond Princess* cruise ship by the Japanese Health Ministry, and a British man was quarantined on the ship. **29.** The UK Home Office's top civil servant, Sir Philip Rutnam, resigned and announced he planned to claim constructive dismissal by the government following a series of clashes with Home Secretary Priti Patel. Boris Johnson announced that he and his partner, Carrie Symonds, were expecting a baby in the summer, and that they were engaged.

MARCH 2020

2. The UK government held a COBRA meeting to discuss its preparations and response to the COVID-19 outbreak, as the number of British cases jumped to 36. **3.** The government published its action plan for dealing with the COVID-19 pandemic; it included scenarios ranging from a milder pandemic to a 'severe prolonged pandemic as experienced in 1918' and warned that a fifth of the national workforce could be absent from work during the infection's peak. **5.** The number of COVID-19 cases reached 115; England's Chief Medical Officer Chris Whitty told MPs that the UK had now moved to the second stage of dealing with COVID-19 from 'containment' to the 'delay' phase. **6.** The Prime Minister announced £46m in funding for research into a COVID-19 vaccine and rapid COVID-19 testing. **8.** A third death from COVID-19 was reported, at North Manchester General Hospital. **11.** The Bank of England cut its baseline interest rate from 0.75 per cent to 0.25 per cent, back down to the lowest level in history. Chancellor of the Exchequer Rishi Sunak presented the new government's first budget, which includes £30bn in measures to protect the economy from the effects of the pandemic. **12.** Following a series of recent major falls the FTSE 100 plunged again, this time by over 10 per cent, its biggest drop since 1987, while other markets around the world were similarly affected by ongoing economic turmoil. **13.** The football Premier League 2019–20 season was suspended, amid a growing list of worldwide sporting cancellations and postponements due to COVID-19. Elections, including the English local elections, London mayoral election and police and crime commissioner elections, scheduled for May 2020, were postponed for a year. **14.** A further ten people were reported to have died from COVID-19, almost doubling the British death toll from 11 to 21. In the USA, Vice President Mike Pence announced the US was to extend its European travel ban to include the UK from 16 March. **15.** The Foreign Office advised against 'all but essential travel' to the US, and Health Secretary Matt Hancock said that within the coming weeks every British resident over the age of 70 would be told to self-isolate for 'a very long time' to shield them from COVID-19. **16.** The British death toll from COVID-19 reached 55, with the number of cases of the illness passing the 1,500 mark; Prime Minister Boris Johnson advised everyone in the UK against non-essential travel and contact with others to curb transmission of the virus, as well as suggesting people should avoid pubs, clubs and theatres, and work from home if possible. The BBC delayed its planned changes to TV licences for the over-75s from June to August because of the pandemic. **17.** Hashem Abedi, brother of Manchester Arena bomber Salman Abedi, was found guilty of murdering 22 people in 2017. NHS England announced that all non-urgent operations in England would be postponed from 15 April to free up 30,000 beds to accommodate COVID-19 patients; the Chancellor of the Exchequer Rishi Sunak announced that £330bn would be made available in loan guarantees for businesses affected by the government's response to the COVID-19 pandemic. **18.** Pound sterling fell below $1.18, its lowest level since 1985. The UK government advised that schools in all four countries would shut from the afternoon of Friday 20 March, except for those looking after the children of keyworkers and vulnerable children, and no exams would take place in England and Wales that academic year; the government also announced emergency legislation to impose a complete ban on new evictions for three months as part of measures to help protect renters in social and private rented accommodation. The 50th anniversary Glastonbury Festival was cancelled as a result of the pandemic. **19.** The Bank of England cuts interest rates again from 0. 25 per cent to 0.1 per cent, the lowest in the Bank's 325-year history. **20.** Chancellor Rishi Sunak announced that the UK government would pay 80 per cent of wages for employees not working, up to £2,500 a month, as part of measures to protect people's jobs; Prime Minister Boris Johnson ordered all cafes, pubs and restaurants to close from the evening of 20 March, except for take-away food, to promote social distancing. All nightclubs, theatres, cinemas, gyms and leisure centres were also told to close as soon as they reasonably could. **22.** The UK Nursing and Midwifery Council announced that more than 5,600 former nurses had registered to offer their services in the pandemic, as Boris Johnson warned that tougher measures were possible if people did not follow government advice on social distancing. **23.** The government announced emergency measures to safeguard rail transport, with season ticket holders given refunds if working from home, and rail franchise agreements nationalised for at least six months to prevent rail companies from collapsing. In a televised address, Boris Johnson announced a UK-wide lockdown with immediate effect, to contain the spread of COVID-19: people were able to leave their homes only for 'very limited purposes', including shopping for basic necessities; for one form of exercise a day; for any medical need; and to travel to and from work when 'absolutely necessary'. A number of other restrictions were imposed, with police given powers to enforce the measures, including the use of fines. **24.** The highest number of COVID-19 deaths in one day were recorded, after another 87 people died across the country, bringing the total to 422. For the first time, all of the UK's mobile networks sent out a government text alert, ordering people to stay at home. **25.** Prince Charles tested positive for COVID-19, Parliament was closed for a month and the British Transport Police deployed 500 officers to patrol the rail network in an effort to discourage non-essential journeys. **26.** The government announced that the self-employed would be paid 80 per cent of profits, up to £2,500 a month, to help them cope during the economic crisis triggered by COVID-19 and at 8pm, millions of people around the country took part in a 'Clap for Our Carers' tribute, applauding the NHS and other care workers (the gesture was repeated every Thursday for ten weeks). **27.** Prime Minister Boris Johnson tested positive for COVID-19, and announced he would self-isolate at 10 Downing Street; Health Secretary Matt Hancock also tested positive for COVID-19 and reported that he would be working from home and self-isolating.

APRIL 2020

1. The contactless payment limit for in-store spending was raised from £30 to £45 and the National Living Wage rose from £8.21 to £8.72, an increase of 6.2 per cent. The 26th session of the Conference of the Parties (COP26) was once again postponed, this time until 2021, due to the COVID-19 pandemic. **3.** The NHS Nightingale Hospital London, the first temporary critical care hospital to treat COVID-19 patients, opened at the ExCel centre in East London, employing NHS staff and military personnel, with a bed capacity of up to 4,000; it was the first of several temporary critical care hospitals planned and opened across the UK. **4.** The results of the 2020 Labour Party leadership election and the 2020 Labour Party deputy leadership election were announced, in which Sir Keir Starmer was elected as the leader of the Labour Party, succeeding Jeremy Corbyn, and Angela Rayner was elected as deputy leader of the party. **5.** Queen Elizabeth II made a rare broadcast to the UK and the wider Commonwealth, something she has done on only four previous occasions; she thanked people for following the government's social distancing rules and paid tribute to key workers. Prime Minister Boris Johnson was admitted to hospital for tests after testing positive for COVID-19 ten days earlier. **6.** Debenhams, one of the UK's largest and oldest department store retail chains, went into administration for the second time in 12 months. The COVID-19 death toll exceeded 5,000, with the total number of reported cases at nearly 52,000. Prime Minister Boris Johnson was taken into intensive care (*see* 5 April); it was announced that First Secretary of State Dominic Raab

would deputise for him. **8.** The Resolution Foundation, using figures from the British Chambers of Commerce, reported that more than nine million workers were expected to be furloughed under the government's job retention scheme, with an estimated cost to the taxpayer of between £30 and £40bn. **9.** Foreign Secretary Dominic Raab acknowledged that people in the UK were starting to see the impact of the restrictions but that it was too early to lift them, and urged people to stay indoors over the Easter weekend. Prime Minister Boris Johnson was moved out of intensive care, but remained in hospital (*see* 6 April). **11.** Queen Elizabeth II made her first ever Easter message to the nation, offering hope for the nation during the pandemic. **12.** Prime Minister Boris Johnson was discharged from hospital after being treated for COVID-19 (*see* 9 April). **16.** The 99-year-old war veteran Captain Tom Moore raised over £13m (subsequently over £30m) for NHS Charities Together after walking more than 100 laps of his garden, with hundreds of thousands (subsequently over a million) of people donating to his JustGiving page. Foreign Secretary Dominic Raab announced a three-week extension to the nationwide lockdown measures as the number of confirmed COVID-19 cases in the UK surpassed 100,000. **19.** Michael Gove gave a BBC interview with Andrew Marr and confirmed that the prime minister had missed five COBRA meetings in the early stages of the viral outbreak, and that the UK shipped personal protective equipment to China in February. **22.** MPs took part in the first 'virtual' Prime Minister's Questions, via Zoom. **23.** The first human trial in Europe of a COVID-19 vaccine, AZD1222, began in Oxford. **24.** The UK government launched a website for key workers to apply for COVID-19 tests at drive-through centres and for home delivery. **27.** Prime Minister Boris Johnson returned to work after three weeks of illness; in his first speech outside 10 Downing Street since recovering from COVID-19, he urged the public not to lose patience with the lockdown and warned that the UK was at the moment of 'maximum risk'. **28.** A minute's silence was held across the UK to commemorate the key workers who had died from COVID-19. **29.** Prime Minister Boris Johnson and his fiancée, Carrie Symonds, announced that she had given birth to Wilfred Lawrie Nicholas Johnson in the early hours of the morning. **30.** UK clothing companies Oasis and Warehouse closed with the loss of 1,800 jobs after going into administration in mid-April.

MAY 2020

4. Conor Burns resigned as Minister of State for Trade Policy after a report found he used his position as an MP to intimidate a member of the public. **5.** The UK death toll from COVID-19 was reported as the highest in Europe, at 32,313 (including suspected cases), after exceeding the death toll of 29,029 (excluding suspected cases) in Italy. **6.** The National Assembly for Wales became the Senedd Cymru, or Welsh Parliament. **7.** The government confirmed that 400,000 gowns ordered from Turkey to protect NHS staff from COVID-19 had been impounded, after failing to meet the required safety standards. **10.** The government revealed that its lockdown slogan 'Stay Home. Protect the NHS. Save Lives.' was to be replaced, in England, with the new message, 'Stay alert. Control the virus. Save lives', while Scotland, Wales and Northern Ireland continued with 'stay at home'. A new alert scale system for England was announced, ranging from green (level one) to red (level five). **12.** The UK official death toll from COVID-19 exceeded 40,000, including almost 10,000 care home residents, and the furlough scheme was extended until October 2020, with employees continuing to receive 80 per cent of their monthly wages up to £2,500. A quarter of the workforce, some 7.5 million people, were covered by the scheme, which cost £14bn a month. **14.** The Northern Ireland First Minister Arlene Foster announced that scientific data was sufficiently encouraging to begin the executive's policy for easing lockdown on the 18 May. **18.** Loss of smell and taste were added to the UK's official list of symptoms of COVID-19 that people should look out for and self-isolate if experienced. First minister of Scotland Nicola Sturgeon announced that lockdown restrictions in Scotland would be eased from 28 May. **19.** It was announced that Captain Tom Moore, who by this time had raised £32m for NHS charities, was to be knighted for his fundraising efforts following a special nomination from Prime Minister Boris Johnson. **20.** Rolls-Royce announced plans to cut 9,000 jobs as a result of the pandemic, predominantly affecting its operations at Derby, warning that it could take years for the airline industry to recover. **21.** Antibody tests to check if someone has had a COVID-19 infection would be made available on the NHS following an agreement between the government and the pharmaceutical company Roche. **22.** The Office for National Statistics reported that government borrowing rose to £62bn in April, the highest monthly figure on record. **23.** Dominic Cummings, Boris Johnson's senior adviser, faced calls to resign after a joint investigation by the *Daily Mirror* and *The Guardian* alleged he had travelled 260 miles from London to his parents' home in Durham while he was displaying COVID-19 symptoms, during lockdown. **24.** Following further print news articles by *The Observer* and the *Sunday Mirror* with allegations that Dominic Cummings made a second trip to the North East during lockdown, Boris Johnson expressed his support for his senior adviser during the government's coronavirus daily briefing. **25.** Dominic Cummings addressed criticism for his actions in an unprecedented public statement from a senior adviser in the 10 Downing Street Rose Garden, where he offered little remorse for his actions. **26.** Junior minister Douglas Ross resigned, giving Dominic Cummings' view on lockdown guidance as the reason. **27.** Boris Johnson appeared before the House of Commons Liaison Committee for the first time, during which he ruled out an inquiry into Dominic Cummings' actions during lockdown. **28.** First Minister Nicola Sturgeon announced an easing of the lockdown in Scotland from the following day with people able to meet friends and family outside in groups of no more than eight, but keeping two metres apart. EasyJet announced plans to cut up to 4,500 jobs as it struggled with a collapse in air travel caused by the pandemic, and the British government approved Cleve Hill Solar Park on the north Kent coast, the UK's biggest ever solar farm at 900 acres in size and 350MW of capacity, enough to power over 91,000 homes. The Dominic Cummings scandal continued, with Durham Constabulary concluding that no offence had been committed by Cummings in travelling from London to Durham during the lockdown, but also said that a minor breach of the lockdown rules might have occurred at Barnard Castle, but because there was no apparent breach of the social distancing rules, no further action would be taken. **29.** Chancellor Rishi Sunak confirmed that the Coronavirus Job Retention Scheme would end at the end of October, with employers having to pay National Insurance and pension contributions from August, 10 per cent of pay from September, and then 20 per cent in October. First Minister of Wales Mark Drakeford announced an easing of lockdown restrictions in Wales from 1 June, allowing people from two different households to meet outdoors while socially distancing. **30.** Boris Johnson announced a relaxing of restrictions in England for the 2.2 million vulnerable individuals who had been 'shielding' in their homes, allowing them to spend time outdoors for the first time in ten weeks from 1 June. **31.** Thousands of people gathered in London, Manchester and Cardiff to protest against the killing of George Floyd, an unarmed black man who died while being arrested by police in Minneapolis, USA.

JUNE 2020

1. Some primary schools in England reopened to more pupils from Reception, Year One and Year Six. **2.** *The Guardian* calculated the death toll from COVID-19 was 50,032; Reuters gave the figure as 49,646. 'Black Out Tuesday' was held to highlight racial injustice and anti-racism in response to the killing of George Floyd. **3.** Home Secretary Priti Patel confirmed plans to force almost all arrivals to the UK to self-isolate for 14 days from 8 June; failure to adhere to quarantine conditions in England could result in a £1,000 fine or prosecution. **4.** Transport Secretary Grant Shapps announced that wearing face coverings would be made compulsory on public transport in England from 15 June. **5.** The BBC announced Tim Davie as its new Director-General, effective from 1 September

2020. **6.** Thousands turned out for anti-racism protests across the UK in London, Manchester, Cardiff, Leicester and Sheffield following the killing of George Floyd, despite calls from Health Secretary Matt Hancock for people not to attend mass demonstrations in breach of lockdown rules. **7.** A statue of 17th century merchant, slave trader, MP and philanthropist Edward Colston was pulled down by anti-racism protesters in Bristol. **8.** BP announced plans to cut 10,000 jobs following a global drop in demand for oil. **9.** Education Secretary Gavin Williamson dropped plans for all primary school children in England to return to school before the end of the summer term. **11.** Centrica, the owner of British Gas, announced plans to cut 5,000 jobs by the end of 2020 in order to 'arrest the decline' of the company. **12.** Figures released by the Office for National Statistics showed that the British economy shrunk by 20.4 per cent in April, the largest monthly contraction on record. **13.** Large crowds, including far-right protesters, clashed with police in central London in response to recent anti-racism rallies and the tearing down of statues. **15.** Long queues of shoppers were reported across England as all non-essential retailers were allowed to reopen. **16.** The University of Oxford reported that a major trial of dexamethasonea, a cheap, widely available corticosteroid medication, showed it could significantly reduce mortality in COVID-19 patients. **19.** The UK's epidemic alert level was downgraded from four to three (out of five possible levels), meaning the virus remained in general circulation but transmission was no longer 'high or rising exponentially.' **23.** Boris Johnson announced an easing of the two-metre rule in England in favour of a 'one-metre-plus' approach so two different households would be able to eat, drink or dine together from 4 July as long as they maintained physical-distancing guidelines; households would also be able to visit each other, including staying overnight. **25.** A major incident was declared by Bournemouth, Christchurch and Poole Council after thousands of people arrived on beaches and other stretches of the Dorset coast, ignoring requests to stay away. The UK experienced its hottest day of the year so far, with temperatures reaching as high as 33.3°C. Liverpool FC were confirmed as champions of the 2019–20 Premier League after Manchester City lost to Chelsea FC, meaning that Liverpool had an unassailable 23-point lead with 7 matches left to play; it was the club's first league title for 30 years, and first Premier League title. **26.** Jonty Bravery, 18, was jailed for 15 years after throwing a six-year-old boy off a 200ft balcony at London's Tate Modern gallery, leaving him with a bleed to the brain and life-changing injuries. **27.** Kate Green was appointed by Sir Keir Starmer as Shadow Secretary of State for Education, replacing Rebecca Long-Bailey. **29.** Following a spike in COVID-19 cases in Leicester, the UK's first full local lockdown was introduced in the city, with non-essential retailers told to shut from the following day and schools close from 2 July.

JULY 2020

1. Prime Minister Boris Johnson denounced China's imposition of a controversial national security law on Hong Kong as a violation of its treaty with the UK, and announced plans to extend the British National (Overseas) rights of up to three million Hong Kong residents born under British rule and open a route for them to become British citizens. **2.** The UK National Crime Agency reported that a Europe-wide operation lasting over three months, which involved the interception of messages on EncroChat, resulted in the arrests of more than 800 people, including major crime figures, and the seizure of over two tonnes of drugs, several dozen guns and £54m in cash. **4.** A major easing of the lockdown in England, subject to modified physical distancing conditions, allowed the reopening of bingo halls, cinemas, galleries, hairdressers, hotels, pubs, restaurants and theme parks. **6.** The government announced a £1.57bn support package to help British theatres, galleries, museums and other arts and cultural venues during the economic downturn. The UK was warned by China not to interfere with its new Hong Kong national security law and to stop 'making irresponsible remarks on Hong Kong affairs' (*see* 1 July). **7.** The British government announced that it would resume arms sales to Saudi Arabia after a review found 'no clear risk' that they would be used in violation of international humanitarian law; sales had been suspended in 2019 after a legal challenge by campaigners. **8.** Chancellor Rishi Sunak unveiled a £30bn spending package aimed at mitigating the economic impact of the COVID-19 pandemic, including a temporary reduction in VAT for the hospitality sector, a scheme to pay firms £1,000 for each employee brought back from furlough, a scheme to get young people into employment, and a temporary rise in the stamp duty threshold. **9.** UK retailers Boots and John Lewis announced job losses as a result of the pandemic, with Boots cutting 4,000 jobs and John Lewis saying it was shutting down eight of its stores, putting 1,300 jobs at risk. **10.** Face coverings in shops and supermarkets became mandatory in Scotland. **11.** Further easing of the lockdown was introduced in England, with outdoor pools and water parks allowed to reopen, while indoor gyms, pools and leisure centres could reopen from 25 July. **13.** The remainder of The Health Protection (Coronavirus, Restrictions) (No. 2) (England) Regulations 2020 came into effect, which allowed the re-opening of nail bars and salons, spas and beauty salons, massage parlours, tattoo parlours, and body and skin piercing services. **14.** British mobile providers were ordered to remove 5G equipment by Chinese firm Huawei from networks by 2027, over security fears. **15.** The UK government announced that citizens of the EU living in England would be able to vote in the 2021 local elections (*see* 13 March). **17.** Boris Johnson announced further easing of lockdown restrictions, with plans for a 'significant return to normality' by Christmas; the new rules allowed people to use public transport for non-essential journeys with immediate effect, while employers would have more discretion over their workplaces from 1 August; from 18 July, local authorities would have the power to enforce local lockdowns. Princess Beatrice married Edoardo Mapelli Mozzi at a private ceremony at the Royal Chapel of All Saints, the service having been previously delayed by the pandemic. **20.** Clinical trials of the vaccine being developed by the Jenner Institute and Oxford Vaccine Group at the University of Oxford on 1,077 patients showed that it appears to be safe, and trained the immune system to produce COVID-19 antibodies. Foreign Secretary Dominic Raab announced that the government would suspend its extradition treaty with Hong Kong 'immediately and indefinitely' over the controversial national security law (*see* 1 July). **21.** The Intelligence and Security Committee published a long-delayed report on Russian influence in British politics; it showed that the government and intelligence agencies both failed to prepare or conduct any proper assessment of Kremlin attempts to interfere with the 2016 Brexit referendum. **22.** The UK and US agreed to amend an 'anomaly' that allowed Harry Dunn death suspect Anne Sacoolas to claim diplomatic immunity (*see* 5 October). **24.** Face coverings in shops and supermarkets become mandatory in England. **25.** Following a rise in COVID-19 cases in Spain, and concerns of a second wave of the virus, the UK government and the governments of Scotland, Wales and Northern Ireland announced that travellers returning from Spain would be required to quarantine for 14 days from 26 July. **27.** The UK's Chief Veterinary Officer confirmed that COVID-19 had been detected in a pet cat, the first known case of infection in an animal in the UK. The government announced a ban on junk food advertising before 9pm for the whole UK, restrictions in England on how foods high in fat and sugar can be promoted in-store, and new rules for displaying calories on menus. **29.** The government signs a deal with GSK and Sanofi to provide 60 million doses of their potential COVID-19 vaccine; this followed three previous deals with other companies, taking the UK's potential vaccine availability to 250 million doses. **30.** UK retailer Argos announced an end to its printed catalogue after almost 50 years of publication. **31.** A further easing of the lockdown in England, which was due to begin on 1 August, was postponed for at least two weeks because of an increase in COVID-19.

AUGUST 2020

1. The BBC ended free television licensing for the over-75s. **7.** The UK had its hottest August day in 17 years, with temperatures surpassing 36°C in south-east England. **12.** The Office for National Statistics reported that Britain's GDP fell by 20.4 per cent in the second quarter of 2020, the biggest quarterly decline since records began in 1955, and the worst economic figure of any G7 nation. A train derailment killed three people near Stonehaven in Aberdeenshire, caused by heavy rain triggering a landslide. **13.** A-level results were published in England, Northern Ireland and Wales; the year's exams were cancelled due to the COVID-19 epidemic, so results were calculated using predictions submitted by teachers. The predictions were then moderated by the regulator, Ofqual, using an algorithm designed to eliminate grade inflation, however, following concerns that 39 per cent of results predicted by teachers in England were downgraded by the moderation process, Ofqual accused some teachers of submitting 'implausibly high' predictions. **16.** The 2020 World Snooker Championship concluded with Ronnie O'Sullivan defeating Kyren Wilson 18–8 in the final to win his sixth world title. **17.** In a reversal of previous government decision (*see* 13 August), A-levels and GCSE grades in England reverted to unmoderated teacher predictions; similar reversals were also made in Wales and Northern Ireland. **20.** 22-year-old Hashem Abedi was jailed for a minimum of 55 years for his part in the Manchester Arena bombing. **21.** UK government debt was reported to be over £2 trillion for the first time. **25.** Scientists identified the earliest person known to have been infected by COVID-19 in the UK; a 75-year-old woman from Nottinghamshire who tested positive on 21 February. **26.** A significant fall in wheat production was reported due to extreme weather, with yields expected to be 40 per cent lower, the worst British harvest in 40 years. **27.** Sir Ed Davey was elected as the next leader of the Liberal Democrats.

SEPTEMBER 2020

1. Most schools in England, Wales and Northern Ireland reopened at full capacity early in September, following those in Scotland that did so in August, ending almost half a year of closures due to the COVID-19 pandemic. **4.** Construction work officially began on the HS2 high-speed rail network. **5.** Extinction Rebellion activists blocked access to three printing presses owned by Rupert Murdoch, delaying the publication of several national newspapers; police arrested 63 people. **6.** Almost 3,000 people in the UK test positive for COVID-19, a 50 per cent increase in a single day and the highest daily total since May. **8.** Sir Jonathan Jones, Head of the Government Legal Profession, resigned in protest at the government's reported plans to make changes to the Brexit withdrawal agreement, becoming the sixth senior civil servant to stand down in 2020. **9.** Siân Berry and Jonathan Bartley were re-elected as co-leaders of the Green Party. **11.** The COVID-19 reproduction number ('R number') increased to between 1.0 and 1.2 for the first time since March. **12.** Sir Mark Walport, former chief scientific adviser and member of SAGE, warned that the UK was 'on the edge of losing control' as recorded cases of COVID-19 exceeded 3,000 for the second day in a row. **14.** The new 'rule of six' law came into force: in England, unless participating in organised team sports including sailing, angling, shooting, polo, dodgeball, floorball and goalball, the law provided authorities to limit the number of persons in a gathering to no more than six. Equivalent rules were also adopted in Wales and Scotland, with some differences including exemptions for children beneath the ages of 11 and 12, respectively. **15.** Former Conservative MP Charlie Elphicke was jailed for two years for sexually assaulting two women, in 2007 and 2016. **16.** The UK returned three antique bronze sculptures to India more than 40 years after they were stolen from a Hindu temple in Tamil Nadu; they were found in London after one was offered for sale in 2019. **18.** With the R number (*see* 11 September) between 1.1 to 1.4 and cases rising around the country among all age groups, Prime Minister Boris Johnson declared the UK was experiencing a second wave of COVID-19. **21.** The Joint Biosecurity Centre recommended that the COVID-19 alert level for the UK should be increased to Level 4, meaning that transmission of the virus was 'high or rising exponentially.' **22.** Michael Gove recommended that employees should work from home if able to do so. **24.** The UK recorded 6,634 new positive tests for COVID-19, the highest daily figure since mass testing began. **25.** Sgt Matiu Ratana, a long serving police officer with the Metropolitan Police, was shot dead during an incident at a custody centre in Croydon, London.

OCTOBER 2020

1. Margret Ferrier, MP for Rutherglen and Hamilton West, was suspended from the Scottish National Party after travelling from London to Scotland after being confirmed positive for COVID-19. **2.** Cumbria County Council approved the first new deep coalmine for 30 years, voting 12–3 in favour; opponents, which included Extinction Rebellion, argued that it contradicted the UK's pledge to be carbon neutral by 2050. **3.** The UK recorded its wettest day on record, with an average of 31.7mm of rain across the entire country. **7.** British Airways' last two Heathrow-based Boeing 747 planes departed on their final flight. **9.** A report from the ONS stated that COVID-19 infections in England had 'increased rapidly' with one in 240 people infected; science advisers warned that hospital admissions were approaching levels seen at the start of the crisis in early March 2020. Chancellor Rishi Sunak announced that workers would get two-thirds of their wages paid for by the government if their employer was forced to shut because of the government's response to the COVID-19 pandemic. **11.** At the 2020 Eifel Grand Prix, Lewis Hamilton equalled Michael Schumacher's record of 91 for the most Formula One Grand Prix wins. **12.** Boris Johnson informed Parliament that there would be a new three-tier alert system for local authorities in England; the tiers were medium (Tier 1), high (Tier 2), and very high (Tier 3). **16.** Prime Minister Johnson suggested that trade talks with the EU were effectively over and that the UK should prepare for a trading relationship with the EU similar to Australia's. Greater Manchester mayor Andy Burnham refused to accept further COVID-19 restrictions from the government without further financial support, with Boris Johnson warning he may 'need to intervene' if new measures cannot be agreed. **23.** Nicola Sturgeon announced that Scotland was to enter a new five-level system of social distancing restrictions. **25.** An oil tanker south-east of the Isle of Wight, suspected to have been hijacked by Nigerian stowaways, was stormed by the Special Boat Service; seven people believed to be Nigerians seeking British asylum were handed over to Hampshire Police. **29.** A major study by Imperial College London suggested that nearly 100,000 people were catching the virus every day in England, a figure then doubling every nine days. The Labour Party suspended former party leader Jeremy Corbyn over his reaction to a report into anti-Semitism. **31.** The UK exceeded 1 million COVID-19 cases; in a televised address, Prime Minister Johnson announced a new four-week lockdown for England, to be enforced from 5 November until 2 December.

NOVERMBER 2020

3. The UK terror threat level was raised from 'substantial' to 'severe', following Islamist attacks in France and Austria. **5.** Chancellor Rishi Sunak extended the UK government's furlough scheme to the end of March 2021. Dominic Chappell, the former owner of retail chain BHS, was sentenced to six years in jail for tax evasion. **7.** The Scottish and UK governments imposes a ban on non-British citizens arriving from Denmark after a new COVID-19 variant, Cluster 5, was spread from mink to humans in mink farms. **10.** A record high level of redundancies was reported by the Office For National Statistics, approximating 314,000 people were made redundant in the three months leading to September, more than during the peak of the Great Recession. Following the first successful phase III trial of a COVID-19 vaccine, Health Secretary Matt Hancock stated that the NHS was ready to start providing doses in the UK soon, with a mass roll-out expected in the first quarter of 2021. **13.** Lee Cain, director of communications at Downing Street, announced his intention to stand down at the end of the year after reports of infighting in Number 10. Dominic Cummings, Boris Johnson's chief adviser, resigned shortly after. **14.** The government commissioned research into space-based solar

power. **15.** Lewis Hamilton wons a seventh Formula One title, equalling the record of Michael Schumacher. **16.** The government ordered five million doses of a new COVID-19 vaccine from American biotech company Moderna, after a phase III trial showed it to have almost 95 per cent efficacy. **17.** Labour readmitted Jeremy Corbyn following his suspension over antisemitism (*see* 29 October); Sir Keir Starmer subsequently decided not to restore Corbyn's party whip. **19.** The UK government announced an extra £16.5bn in defence spending over the next four years to 'extend British influence'. The PlayStation 5 was released in the UK; delivery problems were reported due to huge demand. **23.** Boris Johnson confirmed that the lockdown in England would end on 2 December, with 'tougher' three-tiered regional measures being introduced until March 2021. AstraZeneca's COVID-19 vaccine, developed in collaboration with the University of Oxford's Jenner Institute and the Oxford Vaccine Group, was shown to be 70 per cent effective in protecting against COVID-19 and that the efficacy could be raised to 90 per cent if an initial half dose was followed by a full dose a month later, based on interim data. **24.** Harry Dunn's parents lost a high court battle against the Foreign Office over whether their son's alleged killer, Anne Sacoolas, had diplomatic immunity at the time of the road traffic collision in 2019 (*see* 22 July). The leaders of the three devolved nations of the UK agreed with the prime minister plans that would permit up to three households to form a 'Christmas bubble' during a five-day period from 23–27 December, allowing them to mix in homes, places of worship, and outdoor spaces. **25.** Chancellor Rishi Sunak said that the 'economic emergency' caused by COVID-19 had 'only just begun' during his spending review announcement to the House of Commons, as figures from the Office for Budget Responsibility showed that the economy was forecasted to shrink by 11.3 per cent in 2020, the UK's biggest economic decline in 300 years. The Duchess of Sussex, Meghan Markle, revealed to *The New York Times* that she had a miscarriage in July 2020, which caused her 'almost unbearable grief'. **26.** Boris Johnson appointed Dan Rosenfield as his new Downing Street Chief of Staff, effective from 1 January 2021. **27.** Following three weeks of lockdown in England, the R number for COVID-19 in the UK was reported to have fallen to between 0.9 and 1 for the first time since mid-August. **30.** Retail group Arcadia, whose operations included Topshop, Burton and Dorothy Perkins, went into administration, threatening 13,000 jobs. Protein folding, one of the biggest mysteries in biology, was solved by London-based AI company DeepMind.

DECEMBER 2020

1. MPs voted 291–78 in favour of introducing England's new COVID-19 tier system with The Health Protection (Coronavirus, Restrictions) (All Tiers) (England) Regulations 2020; 55 backbench Conservatives voted against the government, while another 16 abstained. Debenhams stores were set to close with the loss of 12,000 jobs after attempts to find a buyer for the retailer fell through when JD Sports pulled out of negotiations. **2.** The UK became the first country to approve the new Pfizer/BioNTech vaccine; 800,000 doses were planned for arrival in the following days, with a further 40 million in 2021, enough to vaccinate 20 million people. The BBC reported that what became known as the 'jab' was 'the fastest vaccine to go from concept to reality, taking only ten months to follow the same steps that normally span ten years. **3.** Four people were killed after a large explosion at a waste water treatment works in Avonmouth, Bristol. The first batch of the Pfizer/BioNTech vaccine arrived in the UK, and was stored at an undisclosed location ready for distribution to hospital vaccination centres around the country. **4.** Liverpool mayor Joe Anderson was arrested, along with four others, on suspicion of conspiracy to commit bribery and witness intimidation, related to the awarding of building contracts in the city. **7.** MPs voted by 357–268 to reinstate controversial sections of the Internal Market Bill linked to the Northern Ireland protocol, which the EU continued to oppose. **8.** A 90-year-old British woman, Margaret Keenan, became the first person in the world to receive the Pfizer/BioNTech COVID-19 injection as part of a mass vaccination programme; the injection was the first of 800,000 doses to be offered to people in the UK in the first wave of vaccinations. A group of former rugby players, including Rugby World Cup winner Steve Thompson, began a claim against the game's authorities after being diagnosed with early signs of dementia, saying that repeated blows to the head from playing the sport were to blame. **12.** Silverstone Circuit announced the renaming of the 'International Pits Straight' the 'Lewis Hamilton Straight' after he won his seventh world title and broke the record for most wins. **14.** Health Secretary Matt Hancock informed MPs that a new variant of COVID-19 had been identified which was spreading faster in some areas of the country; the variant showed changes to the spike protein which could make the virus more infectious. **16.** London was one of several areas in the South East of England placed into tier 3 of the country's COVID-19 tier system, following a sharp rise of infections in the capital. The Supreme Court overruled the Court of Appeal ban on the development of a third runway at Heathrow Airport, allowing a planning application to go ahead. **18.** The New and Emerging Respiratory Virus Threats Advisory Group and the government were informed of evidence of increased transmissibility of the COVID-19 variant. **19.** Boris Johnson announced a new 'tier 4' lockdown for London and much of South East England from midnight that day, as the variant was identified with a 70 per cent higher transmission rate. Nicola Sturgeon announced 'firm preventative action' including a ban on travel to the rest of the UK over the festive period; the relaxation of rules on meeting households indoors would only apply on Christmas Day and all of mainland Scotland would move into the toughest level four from 26 December. **20.** Austria, Belgium, Bulgaria, France, Germany, Ireland, Italy and the Netherlands announced the banning of flights from the UK, in response to COVID-19 variant; a new record high daily case figure was reported in the UK, with 35,928 new infections, double the number of the previous Sunday. France announced it would stop freight lorry movements from the UK for 48 hours because of the spread of variant in the UK. **21.** The number of countries halting travel from the UK exceeded 40. **22.** The UK and France reached an agreement to reopen their border the following day, allowing freight drivers and EU citizens to travel between the two countries, subject to a recent negative COVID-19 test. Tesco reintroduced a purchasing limit on some items, including eggs, rice, soap and toilet rolls to ensure there was no shortage of products due to panic buying. A new mineral, dark green in colour and named kernowite, was discovered in Cornwall. **23.** Another record high daily case figure was reported, with 39,237 new infections; Tier 4 restrictions were announced for more areas in England from Boxing Day. A new highly infectious strain, originating from South Africa, was also confirmed to be present in London and the North West of England. **24.** The government suspended travel from South Africa due to the new COVID-19 variant. The government and the EU agreed to a free trade agreement prior to the end of the transition period. **25.** The United States became the latest country to impose travel restrictions on the UK in response to COVID-19 variant, forcing all passengers travelling to the US to produce a negative COVID-19 test before being allowed to travel. Channel 4 aired a 'deepfake' video of the Queen's speech, to offer 'a stark warning about the advanced technology that is enabling the proliferation of misinformation and fake news in a digital age.' YouTube star LadBaby became only the third act in UK chart history to achieve three consecutive Christmas number one singles with his novelty version of Journey's 'Don't Stop Believin'. **26.** Bryony Frost became the first female jockey to win the King George VI Chase at Kempton Park. **28.** Another record high daily case figure of COVID-19 was reported, with 41,385 new infections and the number of patients with the virus in hospitals exceeded 20,000, surpassing the peak of the first wave in April; a day later 53,135 new infections were reported. **30.** The UK approved its second vaccine against COVID-19, developed by Oxford-AstraZeneca. The post-Brexit trade agreement with the EU was passed in the House of Commons by 521 votes to 73. **31.** Another record high daily COVID-19 case figure was reported,

with 55,892 new infections. The government approved planning consent for the 2.4GW Hornsea Project Three wind farm; concerns were raised over the impact on bird colonies in the region. The transition period expired at 11pm GMT and the UK completed its final separation from the EU, four and a half years after the referendum.

INTERNATIONAL AFFAIRS

AUGUST 2019

2. (Americas) The USA formally withdrew from the intermediate-range nuclear forces treaty after suspending compliance in February, citing Russian violations including the failure to destroy a missile developed in secret. **(Middle East)** In a partial dismantling of guardianship laws that confined women in Saudi Arabia to narrow gender roles and marginalised their role in society, new laws were introduced allowing Saudi women to travel, divorce and apply for official documents without needing permission from a male guardian. **4. (Europe)** French inventor Franky Zapata crossed the 22-mile English Channel on a jet-powered hoverboard. **5. (Asia)** Hong Kong experienced its first general strike for more than 50 years as pro-democracy protests failed to abate, despite obstinacy and repressive tactics from authorities including the use of teargas, rubber bullets and sponge grenades. **7. (Africa)** The UN described an outbreak of malaria in Burundi as an 'epidemic', estimating it had infected almost half the population (nearly 6 million people) since January and killed about 1,800 people; the government refused to declare the situation as an emergency. **8. (Asia)** The former president of Kyrgyzstan, Kremlin-backed Almazbek Atambayev, was arrested for murder following several violent clashes between his supporters and police officers that caused one fatality; there had been two revolutions in the country since 2005. **(Middle East)** *The Times* reported Israel 'almost certain[ly]' bombed Iranian-backed Shia militia bases in Iraq in July, the first time Israel had bombed Iraq since 1981. **11.** (Europe) In the fifth consecutive weekend of demonstrations, an estimated 60,000 people marched through Moscow, Russia, protesting against President Vladimir Putin's rule. **16. (Africa)** Riot police in Harare, Zimbabwe, violently suppressed anti-government protesters in a wider crackdown on dissent in the country, which included allegations of state kidnappings and torture, as its economy continued to deteriorate. **(Asia)** North Korea fired at least two missiles into the sea off its east coast soon after denouncing South Korea's military drills with the USA, and declared an end to inter-Korean talks. **(Europe)** Greenland, a largely autonomous country of the kingdom of Denmark, declared it was not for sale after reports emerged US President Donald Trump wished to buy the island; the reports were later confirmed, and Trump subsequently cancelled his planned trip to Denmark, labelling the country's prime minister as 'nasty'. **18. (Asia)** Pro-democracy protests in Hong Kong entered their eleventh week, as an estimated 1.7 million people (or a quarter of the population of Hong Kong) staged a peaceful march through the city; however, chief executive Carrie Lam refused to offer further political concessions. **20. (Americas)** Russia and China accused the USA of stoking a new arms race after it tested a cruise missile (*see* 2 August). **22. (Asia)** A second attempt to repatriate thousands of Rohingya Muslims who fled from Myanmar to Bangladesh failed, as the refugees refused to accept they would be safe upon their return; on the 25th, around 200,000 of the nearly one million Rohingya refugees in Bangladesh held a rally to mark two years since they fled the violent crackdown in Myanmar. **(Australia and the Pacific)** After days of popular protests and rioting in the Indonesian province of West Papua by separatist supporters, which resulted in one death and hundreds of injuries, the government cut internet access and deployed 1,000 security personnel to the quell the protests. **23. (Americas)** Leaders of the world's major democracies threatened to block a trade agreement between the EU and South America if Jair Bolsonaro, president of Brazil, failed to stop the deforestation of the Amazon caused by wildfires; Bolsonaro's claims that the fires were started by environmental groups were dismissed as 'Orwellian'.

SEPTEMBER 2019

5. (Africa) Thousands of South African women protested in Cape Town against the government's failure to tackle rising violence against women; around 137 sexual offences, mainly against women, were committed every day in South Africa, and August was the most deadly month for violent attacks on women ever recorded. **(Europe)** The Ukrainian government was criticised after a court ordered the release of Vladimir Tsemakh, a separatist from eastern Ukraine accused of being behind the downing of Malaysian Airlines flight MH17 in July 2014 that killed 298 people; Russia's President Putin confirmed the two countries were working on a deal to swap prisoners. **8. (Middle East)** Air strikes in eastern Syria, which were suspected to have been conducted by Israel, killed 18 Iranian or pro-Iran fighters near the town of Abu Kamal; a day later, Israel's Prime Minister Benjamin Netanyahu claimed Iran had dismantled a secret nuclear weapons facility to hide the evidence. **9. (Middle East)** Sahar Khodayari, an Iranian woman caught attempting to enter a football stadium dressed as a man, killed herself by self-immolation in front of a Tehran court upon learning she could have been imprisoned for six months. **12. (Americas)** The maker of OxyContin, Purdue Pharma, and the family that owned it, the Sacklers, reached a tentative settlement with over 20 US states and thousands of local governments worth an estimated £9.7bn; the painkiller OxyContin helped fuel the opioid epidemic in the USA that was believed to have claimed the lives of 130 US citizens every day. **(Europe)** Russian state security services carried out over 200 raids targeting offices and individuals allied to opposition leader Alexei Navalny, four days after pro-Putin candidates suffered significant losses in Moscow city assembly elections. **13. (Americas)** A senior Canadian federal intelligence official was charged with leaking covert information in what security experts believed could have been the biggest security breach in the country's history. **16. (Europe)** Prime Minister Xavier Bettel of Luxembourg refused to change the location of a press conference with Boris Johnson because of disruptive anti-Brexit protesters; in a break with protocol Bettel proceeded without Johnson and left his podium empty whilst criticising the UK's plans to leave the EU. **17. (Middle East)** In the run up to elections and peace talks with the USA, Taliban suicide bombers killed at least 48 people in Afghanistan in two separate attacks, one near the US embassy in Kabul and the other near where a rally was being held by President Ashraf Ghani in Parwan province; two days later, a suicide bomber driving a lorry packed with explosives killed 20 people outside a hospital in Qalat city, as the USA announced plans to significantly cut funding to the Afghan government over corruption allegations. **20. (Americas)** Following an anonymous whistleblower complaint that President Trump may have used his office to pressure Ukraine's President Volodymyr Zelensky to investigate Hunter Biden, the son of former vice-president Joe Biden and political opponent for the 2020 presidential election. Trump denied the accusation; on the 26th, it emerged the whistleblower accused Trump of attempting to hide evidence of the call and that he posed a risk to national security. Later, House of Representatives speaker, Nancy Pelosi, announced an official impeachment inquiry into Trump's actions. **(Europe)** Protesters took to the streets of more than 250 towns and cities across Spain to declare a 'feminist emergency' after several high-profile rape cases, a rise in the number of women murdered and a scandal earlier in the year involving the lenient sentencing of five men, who labelled themselves the 'wolf pack', for a gang rape in Pamplona in 2016. **22. (Asia)** Violence in Hong Kong escalated as pro-democracy protests entered their 16th consecutive weekend, in the lead up to the 70th anniversary of the founding of the People's Republic of China on 1 October. **23. (Americas)** Three days after millions of people took to the streets worldwide to demand emergency government action to tackle the climate crisis, leading environmental activist, 16-year-old Greta Thunberg, excoriated world leaders at a UN summit in New York for their 'betrayal' of young people as nations outlined their environmental policies, most of which disappointed environmentalists in their lack of immediacy

or magnitude. **(Europe)** A landmark trial for manslaughter, fraud and deceit began in Paris concerning a weight-loss drug produced by one of France's largest pharmaceutical laboratories, Servier, that had been linked to the deaths of up to 2,000 people in France since 1976. **25. (Australia and the Pacific)** Saudi Arabia accused the Australian government of racism and of supporting anti-Islamic terrorists – like Brenton Tarrant, the alleged terrorist who killed 51 people at a mosque in Christchurch, New Zealand, on 15 March 2019 – after Australia's ambassador to the UN led a coalition of 24 countries condemning Saudi Arabia over its human rights record. **29. (Asia)** Pakistan's prime minister, cricket legend Imran Khan, warned the UN general assembly in New York that India's actions in Kashmir could provoke a war between the two nuclear-armed countries; Pakistani officials estimated 10,000 people had been detained by Indian security forces in the region, and some had been tortured.

OCTOBER 2019

1. (Americas) Peruvian interim President Araoz announced her resignation following the dissolution of the Congress of Peru by President Martin Vizcarra the day before, starting a constitutional crisis in Peru. **2. (Americas)** California becomes the second US state, after North Dakota, to permit the establishment of public banks as an alternative to commercial banks. **3. (Europe)** Finland agreed to return the remains of Native Americans, and other stolen artifacts from 1891, to the Mesa Verde National Park in Colorado, USA. **(Europe)** The European Court of Justice ruled that the social media company Facebook had to remove a defamatory and insulting post about Austrian politician Eva Glawischnig-Piesczek; it was ruled that the post must be removed globally. **4. (Middle East)** Microsoft claimed the Iranian government-linked group *Phosphorus* attempted to hack the accounts of American journalists, former government officials and the accounts of prominent Iranians living outside Iran. **7-14. (Global)** Climate change protests linked to the global environmental movement Extinction Rebellion took place in cities around the world; hundreds of scientists supported mass 'civil disobedience' as a way of protesting government inaction against climate change. **18. (Americas)** The first all-female spacewalk outside the International Space Station was conducting by NASA astronauts Jessica Meir and Christina Koch. **23. (Africa)** A Tanzanian court overturned a law that permitted children to enter into marriage from age 15. **25. (Australia and the Pacific)** Tourists visited the summit of Uluru (Ayers Rock) for the last time as a ban on climbing the Aboriginal people's sacred landmark came into effect. **28. (Americas)** Claudia Lopez Hernandez was elected mayor of Bogota, Colombia and became the first woman and the first lesbian to hold the office. **30. (Global)** Social Media company Twitter banned all political advertising worldwide. **31. (Asia)** A fire started in the 500-year-old Japanese Shuri Castle, destroying much of the UNESCO World Heritage Site.

NOVEMBER 2019

5. (Global) 11,000 scientists from around the world published a study in the scientific journal *BioScience*, warning that 'clearly and unequivocally planet Earth is facing a climate emergency.' **7. (Africa)** Bosco Ntaganda, a former Congolese rebel leader, was sentenced to 30 years in prison for war crimes and crimes against humanity; it was the longest sentence ever handed down by the International Criminal Court. **12. (Europe)** Venice Mayor Luigi Brugnaro announced that historic flooding in Venice was due to climate change. **13. (Americas)** The public impeachment hearings against US President Donald Trump began in the House of Representatives. **16. (Asia)** Leaked documents reported by *The New York Times* showed that over the course of the previous three years, more than one million Muslims had been arrested and imprisoned in the Xinjiang Uygur Autonomous Region in China. **16. (Europe)** One day before the 30th anniversary of the Velvet Revolution, hundreds of thousands of demonstrators marched in Prague, Czech Republic to protest against Prime Minister Angrej Babis for collaborating with the StB, the communist-era Secret Police. **19.**

(Americas) Google launched cloud gaming service *Stadia*, officially entering the company into the gaming market. 23. (Asia) The last known Sumatran rhinoceros in Malaysia died. (Australia and the Pacific) Papua New Guinea held an independence referendum, voters overwhelmingly voted for independence. 25. (Global) The World Meteorological Organisation reported that levels of heat-trapping greenhouse gases in the atmosphere had reached a record high of 407.8 parts per million, with 'no sign of a slowdown, let alone a decline.' 26. (Europe) The world's deadliest earthquake of 2019 struck in Albania, killing 51 people and injuring 2,000; the 6.4 magnitude earthquake was the strongest to hit Albania in more than 40 years.

DECEMBER 2019

1. (Americas) President Jair Bolsonaro of Brazil blamed Leonardo DiCaprio, the American actor and environmentalist, for the 2019 Amazon rainforest wildfires; DiCaprio, the Global Wildlife Conservation, and the IUCN Special Survival Commission condemned Bolsonaro's accusations. (Asia) The world's first known human case of the coronavirus disease 2019, later called COVID-19, was identified in a patient in Wuhan, China. 2-13. (Europe) Madrid, Spain hosts the 2019 UN Climate Change Conference after Chile announced it could not host due to political unrest in the country. 8. (Asia) A factory fire in Delhi, India, killed 43 people and injured at least 50. 10. (Europe) Sanna Marin, at 34-years-old, was selected to lead Finland's Social Democratic Party, becoming the world's youngest serving prime minister. 11. (Americas) After the US blocked the appointment of new panel members to the World Trade Organization, the WTO was left unable to intervene in trade disputes. 18. (Americas) The US House of Representatives approved two articles of impeachment against President Donald Trump, making him the third-ever US president to be impeached. 19. (Africa) In Ethiopia and Somalia, 70,000 hectares of crop and grazing lands were destroyed by a locust plague. 20. (Americas) The US established the United States Space Force, a US Armed Forced branch dedicated to space warfare. 21. (Australia and the Pacific) The New Zealand government announced that its gun buy-back program, launched in March 2019, had collected 51,000 guns from 33,000 owners across the state. 23. (Middle East) For the death of *The Washington Post* journalist Jamal Khashoggi, the Saudi Arabian government executed five officials and sentenced three others to prison. 31. (Asia) The first widely circulated reports of an outbreak of a novel coronavirus in Wuhan, China began to be reported outside China.

JANUARY 2020

3. (Americas) Iranian general Qasem Soleimani and Iraqi paramilitary leader Abu Mahdi al-Muhandis were killed in an US drone strike. 4. (Australia and the Pacific) Penrith, New South Wales recorded temperatures of 48.9&ringwhich made it the hottest location on Earth at the time of the recording. 8. (Middle East) Iran launched ballistic missiles at two Iraqi military bases where American soldiers were stationed. (Middle East) A Boeing 737 was shot down shortly after take off from Tehran's Imam Khomeini International Airport, all 176 passengers and crew were killed. 9. (Americas) The impeachment trial of President Trump began. (Asia) A 61-year-old man from Wuhan became the world's first person to die from COVID-19. 11. (Middle East) Iran announced that the Boeing 737 (*see* 8 January) had been unintentionally shot down by the Iranian military, which occurred shortly after Iran had launched a barrage of missiles as US forces. 25. (Australia and the Pacific) The first case of COVID-19 case was confirmed in Australia; he was a traveller who had who had recently been in Wuhan. 29. (Americas) President Trump signed the paperwork to replace the NAFTA trade agreement with the United States-Mexico-Canada Agreement. 30. (Asia) The first case of COVID19 was confirmed in Kerala, India. 31. (Europe) The first COVID-19 case was confirmed in Italy. 31. (Global) The World Health Organization declared an international public health emergency over the spread of COVID-19.

FEBRUARY 2020

9. (Asia) South Korea's Bong Joon Ho's film, Parasite, won four Academy Awards and marked the first time a non-English-language film won Best Picture. 11. (Global) The World Health Organization formally named the novel coronavirus 'COVID-19'. 12. (Americas) The first community transmission of COVID-19 was detected in the USA. 18. (Americas) Guatemala began a campaign to reunite families who were separated because of kidnapping or irregular adoption during the Guatemalan Civil War of 1960–96. 23. (Asia) The North East Delhi riots began between the Hindu and Muslim communities; 53 people were reported to have died. 23. (Europe) Small towns in northern Italy were placed under quarantine, and large celebrations and gatherings were cancelled across the state due to COVID-19. (Middle East) A 5.8 magnitude earthquake hit the Iranian-Turkish border near Khoy, killing nine people. 25. (Americas) Hollywood's Harvey Weinstein was found guilty of rape and sexual assault by a jury in New York. 27.(Middle East) An airstrike by pro-Syrian government forces killed 33 Turkish soldiers. 29. (Asia) The USA and the Taliban signed a conditional peace agreement in Doha, Qatar.

MARCH 2020

2. (Australia and the Pacific) New South Wales Rural Fire Service announced that, for the first time in more than 240 days, there were no active bush or grass fires burning; more than 42,000 square miles had been burned across the country. 5. (Middle East) The Afghanistan war crimes inquiry was authorised by the International Criminal Court, which allowed US citizens to be investigated. 9. (Europe) In Italy, a nation-wide lockdown was introduced to halt the spread of COVID-19; by 21 March 2020, 4,825 people had died in the country. 12. (Australia and the Pacific) US actor Tom Hanks and wife Rita tested positive for COVID-19 while filming in Australia, and are hospitalised and quarantined for two weeks. 13. (Asia) Mount Everest was closed to climbers for the rest of the season by the Nepali government due to concerns over COVID-19. 16. (Americas) The Dow Jones fell by nearly 3,000 points in the large single point drop in history. 18. (Europe) The Eurovision Song Contest 2020 was cancelled for the first time ever due to the spread of COVID-19. 24. (Asia) The Tokyo Olympic and Paralympic Games 2020were postponed until 2021.

APRIL 2020

1. (Asia) China reported 130 asymptomatic cases of COVID-19. The Myanmar military extended a unilateral ceasefire with major ethic armed groups as clashes continued across the state. 4. (Europe) A terror attack in Romans-sur-Isére, France killed two and wounded five others; the attacker was arrested and charged with terrorist crimes. 8. (Asia) A Saudi Arabian coalition declared a ceasefire with Yemen-based Houthi forces. 14.(Global) The IMF announced that it expected the global economy to shrink by 3 per cent in 2020, the largest fall since the Great Depression. 15. (Europe) Due to COVID-19, the Tour de France was delayed until August 2020. 18. (Africa) In a prison in Chad, 44 Boko Haram militants were found dead and it is suspected they were poisoned. 19. (Asia) Vietnam condemned China's decision to establish administrative districts in the disputed areas of the Paracel Islands and the Spratly Islands. 19. (Australia and the Pacific) Australia's Competition and Consumer Commission outlined a mandatory code of conduct for Facebook, Google, and other tech companies that required them to pay news outlets when they used their content. 20. (Americas) In Nova Scotia, Canada a mass-shooting resulted in the deaths of 22 people. 20. (Americas) The West Texas Intermediate crude oil price fell to negative US$37.63. 23. (Middle East) The Ramadan night-time curfew was shortened by one hour and ran from 9pm to 6am. 24. (Australia and the Pacific) Australia's Perth Airport used bulldozers to block an airport runway to pressure Virgin Australia Airlines to pay AUD$16m debt. 26. (Middle East) In Saudi Arabia, a royal decree was announced stating that the country would no longer execute

individuals for crimes committed as a minor. **27. (Americas)** The Pentagon formally released video footage of US Navy pilots encountering 'unidentified aerial phenomena', thought by many to be UFOs.

MAY 2020

2. (Americas) Asian Giant Hornets, dubbed 'Murder Hornets', were first spotted in the USA. **3. (Middle East)** Amnesty International reported that over the last four years, journalism in Egypt had 'effectively become a crime.' **4. (Africa)** Kenyan and British scientists announced the discovery of a parasitic microbe that prevented mosquitoes from carrying malaria. **5. (Asia)** One hundred and fifty Indian and Chinese soldiers clashed at the Nathu La crossing. **22. (Americas)** South America became the new global epicentre for COVID-19, with Brazil confirming more cases than any other South American country. **25. (Americas)** A US Minneapolis police officer knelt on the neck of African American George Floyd for eight minutes, eventually killing him and sparking national and international Black Lives Matter protests. **26. (Americas)** Costa Rica became the first Central American country to legalise same-sex marriage. **27. (Australia and the Pacific)** Australian mining company Rio Tinto destroyed a 46,000-year-old Aboriginal heritage site in a mining blast. **29. (Europe)** A Russian diesel oil tank collapsed, spilling 21,000 tons of oils into Arctic waterways. **30. (Americas)** Elon Musk's SpaceX and NASA launched two astronauts to the International Space Station, the first time humans had been launched into space from US soil in nearly a decade.

JUNE 2020

1-5. (Global) Protests and marches against the killing of George Floyd in the US (*see* 25 May) and other instances of police brutality extended to hundreds of cities in at least 40 countries around the world. **1. (Africa)** The Democratic Republic of the Congo announced that a new Ebola virus outbreak was occurring in the Wangata health zone. **(Americas)** The US government cleared peaceful Black Lives Matter protestors from Lafayette Square using tear gas and riot control tactics to allow President Trump to pose with a bible outside St. John's Episcopal Church. **3. (Europe)** President Vladimir Putin of Russia declared a state of emergency after a large oil spill within the Arctic Circle (*see* 29 May). **5. (Africa)** The Malian protests, also known as the June 5 Movement, began when protestors in Bamako, Mali called for President Ibrahim Boubacar Keïta to resign. **8. (Global)** The number of confirmed COVID-19 cases reached 7m worldwide. **9. (Americas)** A study from Harvard University in the USA suggests that COVID-19 may have been spreading throughout China as early at August 2019. **15. (Asia)** A clash on the Indian-Chinese border in the Ladakh region resulted in the deaths of at least 25 Indian soldiers and 40 Chinese soldiers. **16. (Asia)** The Inter-Korean Liaison Office in Kaesong, which was established in 2018 to improve relations between the Koreas, was demolished by the North Korean government. **17. (Asia)** During the 2020 UN Security Council Elections, India won a two-year seat on the council. **20. (Africa)** Economic Community of West African States (ECOWAS) called for new elections to be held due to the disputes regarding the 2020 Malian parliamentary election legitimacy (*see* 5 June). **23. (Americas)** In Oaxaca, Mexico, a 7.5 magnitude earthquake killed four people; tremors are felts up to 630km (400m) away. **27. (Australia and the Pacific)** New Zealand lifted all COVID-19 restrictions, declaring the nation coronavirus-free; the country was placed back into lockdown periodically throughout the year but regular life largely resumed for New Zealanders. **28. (Global)** The number of confirmed COVID-19 cases reached 10m worldwide; the US reported the highest number of cases, totalling roughly one-quarter of all cases globally. **30. (Asia)** The 'Hong Kong national security law' was passed in China, allowing Chinese authorities to crack down on opposition to Beijing at home and abroad.

JULY 2020

6. (Middle East) Several doctors and medical workers who criticized the Egyptian government's handling of COVID-19 were arrested. **(Asia)** A suspected case of bubonic plague was found in Mongolia; the city of Bayannur was put on a 'Level 3' plague prevention warning. **8. (Americas)** Paintings by Frida Kahlo and Rufino Tamayo were reported as stolen from a private collection in Mexico City. **(Australia and the Pacific)** New genetic research suggested contact was made between ancient Polynesians and South American peoples. **11. (Middle East)** Turkish President Recep Tayyip Erdo&gbreve ordered the Hagia Sophia in Istanbul to be reverted to a mosque following a supreme court annulment of a 1934 presidential decree that declared it a museum. **16. (Africa)** Satellite measurements were used over the Danakil Desert in Ethiopia to study Africa's tectonic plates, as the continent shifted and was slowly torn apart; it was predicted that in millions of years a new ocean would likely appear there. **19. (Asia)** Vidisha Baliyan became the first Indian Miss Deaf World. **21. (Europe)** European Union leaders agreed to a €750bn recovery fund to help rebuild EU economies impacted by the COVID-19 pandemic. **28. (Global)** The number of confirmed COVID-19 cases reached 15m worldwide. **30. (Americas)** NASA launched the Mars 2020 rover to search for signs of ancient life and collect samples from the planet before returning to Earth; the mission was partly an experiment to prepare for future human-led missions to Mars.

AUGUST 2020

(Middle East) A series of flash floods in Afghanistan throughout the month of August killed at least 190 people across the state and damaged several UNESCO world heritage sites. **4. (Australia and the Pacific)** Three Micronesian men were rescued from a remote Pacific island after they wrote 'SOS' in the sand. **(Middle East)** An explosion in the port of Beirut killed 220 people, caused by ammonium nitrate that was unsafely stored. **5. (Asia)** The foundation stone of the Ram Temple at Ayodhya, India was installed. **10. (Middle East)** Lebanon Prime Minister Hassan Diab announced his resignation and that of his entire cabinet following the explosion in Beirut (*see* 4 August). **11. (Europe)** Russia announced that it had approved the world's first COVID-19 vaccine, Sputnik V. **15. (Africa)** The Japanese bulk carrier Wakashio broke in half after being stranded on a reef off the coast of Mauritius and spilt 1,000 tonnes of oil into the ocean. **25. (Africa)** Africa eradicated all 'wild' polio cases. **30. (Global)** The number of confirmed COVID-19 cases reached 25m worldwide. **(Americas)** Argentina launched its Earth observation satellite SAOCOM 1B from USA's Cape Canaveral launch site. **31. (Middle East)** The Sudanese Peace Agreement was signed between the Sudanese government and several Sudanese rebel groups, bringing an end to decades-long conflict that killed more than 300,000 people.

SEPTEMBER 2020

3. (Americas) Around 200 mammoth skeletons and 30 more animal remains were unearthed at a construction site near Mexico City, in the largest find of mammoth bones to date. **4. (Americas)** The longest road tunnel in South America, the La Linea highway tunnel, opened in Colombia. **4. (Europe)** Pope Benedict XVI became oldest living pope at 93 years, four months, and 16 days. **10. (Africa)** The African Sahel region experienced record levels of rains; subsequent floods displaced thousands of people. **14. (Europe)** The Royal Astronomical Society detected phosphine in Venus's atmosphere, a predictor of microbial life. **14. (Europe)** The remains of a perfectly preserved cave bear was discovered in Siberian permafrost, it was estimated to be between 22,000 and 39,500 years old. **16. (Americas)** The UN Human Rights Council accused the Venezuelan government, including President Nicolás Maduro and other senior officials, of crimes against humanity. **18. (Americas)** US Supreme Court Justice Ruth Bader Ginsburg died. **19. (Europe)** A copy of *The Two Noble Kinsmen* by William Shakespeare was found at the Royal Scots College in Spain, the edition dates from 1634 and was believed to be the oldest copy of any of the poet's works in the country. **21. (Global)** More than 160 world leaders asked the UK to release Julian Assange, WikiLeaks founder, and not to extradite him to the USA. **25.**

(Europe) A terror attack outside the offices of satirical magazine *Charlie Hebdo* in Paris, France resulted in the deaths of two people. 27. (Europe) Fighting broke out between Azerbaijan and Armenia over the disputed region of Nagorno-Karabakh. 29. (Global) The global death toll from COVID-19 surpassed 1 million.

OCTOBER 2020

8. (Americas) The FIFA World Cup 2022 World Qualifiers were held in Colombia amid the COVID-19 pandemic, with no fans permitted in the stadium. 15. (Asia) Thailand declared a severe state of emergency following anti-government protests, banning gatherings of five or more people, and enforcing media censorship. 17. (Australia and the Pacific) In the 2020 New Zealand general election, incumbent Jacinda Ardern's Labour party won a second term in a landslide victory. 19. (Global) The number of confirmed COVID-19 cases reached 40m worldwide. 20. (Middle East) The 2020 World Exposition, meant to begin on 20 October 2020, was postponed until October 2021; this was the first time the World Exposition was delayed, rather than cancelled outright. 23. (Americas) After more than a decade removing land mines from the Falkland Islands, the archipelago was declared mine-free. (Middle East) Israel and Sudan agreed to the fifth Israel-Arab peace deal. 26. (Americas) NASA announced that it has found molecular water on the moon. (Australia and the Pacific) A lightening bolt that hit the Gospers Mountain, New South Wales, sparked a mega fire that eventually destroyed 444,000 hectares. 29. (Africa) In the deadliest shipwreck of 2020, 140 lives were lost when a ship carrying migrants to the Canary Islands capsized. 30. (Africa) Africa's largest hackathon, NaijaHacks, hosted the 'NaijaHacks from Home' 2020 Hackathon. (Europe) A 7.0 magnitude earthquake off the Aegean coast of Turkey caused a Tsunami that hits the Greek island of Samos and the Aegean coast of the Turkish Izmir region, killing at least 81 people. 31. (Australia and the Pacific) The strongest tropical cyclone in history to make landfall, Typhoon Goni, hit the Philippines, killing dozens and displacing thousands of people.

NOVEMBER 2020

1. (Europe) Moldova elected Maia Sandu, former prime minister, as its president the first woman to ever hold the office. 3-7. (Americas) Former Vice-President Joe Biden was elected president of the USA; his vice-president, Kamala Harris, became the first woman, first African American and first Asian American to ever hold the office. 4. (Americas) The USA formally exited the Paris Climate Agreement. 9. (Global) American pharmaceutical company Pfizer and German pharmaceutical company BioNTech announced the first successful phase III trial of a COVID-19 vaccine. 9. (Europe) The 2020 Nagorno-Karabakh ceasefire agreement was signed by President Ilham Aliyev of Azerbaijan, and the Prime Minister Nikol Pashintan of Armenia, overseen by Russia President Vladimir Putin (*see* 27 September). 11. (Russia) Russia's Sputnik V COVID-19 vaccine was reported to be 92 per cent effective against COVID-19 in trial results. 12. (Asia) Pro-democracy lawmakers resigned *en masse* after the government disqualified four lawmakers. 15. (Australia and the Pacific) Asia-Pacific countries signed the Regional Comprehensive Economic

Partnership (RCEP), creating the largest free-trade bloc in the world. 16. (Americas) Drug company Moderna announced their mRNA vaccine as 94.5 per cent effective against COVID-19 based on trial results. 18. (Americas) The first of three metal monoliths appeared in Utah, followed shortly by one in California and then one in Romania; by 6 December monoliths were 'found' and 'installed' all over the world as part of publicity stunts and art installations. 19. (Americas) Mexico's senate approved a cannabis legalisation bill that created the world's largest legal marijuana market. 22. (Americas) Outgoing President Donald Trump withdrew the USA from the Treaty on Open Skies. 30. (Americas) A Google-developed artificial intelligence program solved the biological mystery 'protein folding', using an algorithm developed by DeepMind, a British artificial intelligence lab that was acquired by Google in 2014. (Americas) Moderna filed for an Emergency Use Authorization application for use of its COVID-19 vaccine in the USA.

DECEMBER 2020

1. (Europe) Pfizer and BioNTech filed for an Emergency Use Authorization application with the European Medicines Agency. 5. (Europe) Russia began a mass vaccination program against COVID-19 virus using the Sputnik V vaccine. 8. (Asia) An agreement was reached between Nepal and China on Mount Everest's official height: 8,848.86ft. 11. (Europe) The EU agreed to reduce greenhouse gas emissions by 55 per cent over the next ten years. 13. (Africa) Eswatini Prime Minister Ambrose Dlamini became the first world leader to die from COVID-19. 14. (Americas) Argentina and Chile experience a total solar eclipse. 15. (Australia and the Pacific) An unmanned boat loaded with 649kg of cocaine washed up on the shores of the Ailuk Atoll Beach in the Marshall Islands. 18. (Global) Reports surface that a 'Breakthrough Listen Initiative' had detected radio signals coming from Proxima Centauri, the closet star to the sun, that were considered one of the strongest candidates for a radio signal received from extraterrestrial intelligence ever discovered. (Africa) The South African Health Department reported a 'South African COVID-19 variant' had been discovered; it was a new, more highly transmissible strain of the virus. 19. (Australia and the Pacific) Hurricane Yasa made landfall in Vanua Levu, killing at least four people and displacing thousands. 21. (Americas) The Antarctic Base General Bernardo O'Higgins Riquelme reported 36 cases of COVID-19, making Antarctica the last continent to report positive cases of the virus. 24. (Americas) Chile became the first country in South America to begin COVID-19 vaccinations. 24. (Europe) Russian authorities admitted that the Norilsk diesel oil spill (*see* 29 May) was the second-largest largest oil spill in world history. 26. (Africa) The UN recognised Kenyan woman Nzambi Matee as one of seven Young Champions of the Earth for 2020, for their recycling innovation that turned discarded plastic into paving stones for construction projects. 29. (Global) The number of confirmed COVID-19 cases reached 80m worldwide. 30. (Americas) Argentina legalised abortion. 31. (Africa) Soliyanan Dizaw from Ethiopia, a ten-year-old child, won the 2020 African Code Challenge with her SRATCH-based game, 'Mathstainment'.

OBITUARIES 2019–20

A selection of obituaries from August 2019.

Adams, Fiona, photographer, *b.* 26 September 1935; *d.* 26 June 2020

Alonso, Alicia (full name Alicia Ernestina de la Caridad del Cobre Martínez y del Hoyo), ballerina, ballet director and choreographer, *b.* 21 December 1920; *d.* 17 October 2019

Armstrong of Ilminster, Lord, civil servant, *b.* 30 March 1927; *d.* 3 April 2020

Ashton, Chrystal Heather, psychopharmacologist, writer, *b.* 11 July 1929; *d.* 15 September 2019

Ashton, Joseph William, OBE, Labour Party politician, *b.* 9 October 1933; *d.* 30 March 2020

Baker, Peter Edward 'Ginger', drummer for the band Cream, *b.* 19 August 1939; *d.* 6 October 2019

Ball, Bobby (*b.* Robert Harper), comedian and actor, *b.* 28 January 1944; *d.* 28 October 2020

Beeny, Christopher Winton, actor, *b.* 7 July 1941; *d.* 3 January 2020

Bellamy, David James, OBE, botanist, environmentalist, broadcaster and writer, *b.* 18 January 1933; *d.* 11 December 2019

Blackman, Honor, actor, *b.* 22 August 1925; *d.* 5 April 2020

Boseman, Chadwick Aaron, actor and playwright, *b.* 29 November 1976; *d.* 28 August 2020

Boston, Mary, child psychotherapist, author, *b.* 27 May 1923; *d.* 14 January 2020

Bramall, Lord, Field Marshal, army officer, *b.* 18 December 1923; *d.* 12 November 2019

Brathwaite, Edward Kamau, CHB, poet, academic and historian, *b.* 11 May 1930; *d.* 4 February 2020

Britton, Anthony Edward Lowry, actor, *b.* 9 June 1924; *d.* 22 December 2019

Brooke-Taylor, Timothy Julian, OBE, actor and writer, *b.* 17 July 1940; *d.* 12 April 2020

Brooker, Ralph Anthony, computer scientist and educationist, inventor of the first practical computer programming language, *b.* 22 September 1925; *d.* 20 November 2019

Bryan, Felicity Anne, MBE, literary agent, *b.* 16 October 1945; *d.* 21 June 2020

Burl, Harry Aubrey Woodruff, FSA, writer and archaeologist, *b.* 24 September 1926; *d.* 8 April 2020

Burnyeat, Myles Fredric, CBE, FBA, philosopher and classicist, president of the Mind Association, *b.* 1 January 1939; *d.* 20 September 2019

Camp, Jeffery, RA, artist, teacher and writer, *b.* 17 April 1923; *d.* 5 April 2020

Capel, David John, cricketer, *b.* 6 February 1963; *d.* 2 September 2020

Cardinal, Roger, art historian, author of *Outsider Art*, *b.* 27 February 1940; *d.* 1 November 2019

Carr, Janet Gould, OBE, clinical psychologist, *b.* 31 March 1927; *d.* 17 March 2020

Carson, Ciaran, poet, winner of the TS Eliot prize, the Irish Times Irish Literature prize, the Cholmondeley award and the Forward prize, first director of the Seamus Heaney Centre for Poetry at Queen's *b.* 9 October 1948; *d.* 6 October 2019

Cave, Julia, television director and producer, filmmaker, *b.* 1 June 1937; *d.* 21 October 2019

Chalfont, Lord, OBE, PC, British Army officer, politician and journalist, *b.* 5 December 1919; *d.* 10 January 2020

Chase, Malcolm Sherwin, historian, *b.* 3 February 1957; *d.* 29 February 2020

Chirac, Jacques René, former President of France and Mayor of Paris, statesman, *b.* 29 November 1932, *d.* 26 September 2019

Clark, Leonard Joseph John, civil servant and countryside campaigner, *b.* 19 August 1916; *d.* 11 September 2019

Coe, Michael Douglas, archaeologist and author specialising in the early civilizations of Mexico and Central America, *b.* 14 May 1929, *d.* 25 September 2019

Collings, David Cressy, actor, *b.* 4 June 1940; *d.* 23 March 2020

Connery, Sir Thomas Sean, actor, Academy Award winner, most notable for playing James Bond, *b.* 25 August 1930; death announced 31 October 2020

Cullinan, Edward Horder, CBE, architect, *b.* 17 July 1931; *d.* 11 November 2019

Cummings, Elijah Eugene, politician, US Democratic congressman, *b.* 18 January 1951; *d.* 17 October 2019

Cussler, Clive Eric, bestselling novelists and writer, *b.* 15 July 1931; *d.* 24 February 2020

Cuthbert, Sir Ian Holm, CBE, actor, *b.* 12 September 1931; *d.* 19 June 2020

Davis, Peter Edward, MBE, ornithologist and conservationist, credited as the driving force behind saving the red kite, one of Britain's most charismatic birds of prey, *b.* 8 October 1928; *d.* 28 October 2019

Dennehy, Brian Manion, award winning actor, *b.* 9 July 1938; *d.* 15 April 2020

Dicks, Terence Patrick, Conservative Party politician, *b.* 17 March 1937; *d.* 17 June 2020

Dicks, Terrance William, writer, producer and script editor, known for his extensive work on the Doctor Who franchise, *b.* 14 April 1935; *d.* 29 August 2019

Dobson, Sir Christopher Martin, Kt, chemist, master of St John's College, Cambridge, *b.* 8 October 1949 *d.* 8 September 2019

Dobson, Frank Gordon, Labour Party politician, former health secretary, *b.* 15 March 1940; *d.* 11 November 2019

Drake, Christopher Hallam Mylverton, BBC broadcaster, founder of Nicosia, *b.* 29 April 1942; *d.* 28 August 2019

Dyson, Freeman John, FRS, mathematician and physicist, *b.* 15 December 1923; *d.* 28 February 2020

Edwardes, Sir Michael Owen, Kt, businessman, former chairman and chief executive of British Leyland, *b.* 11 October 1930, *d.* 15 September 2019

Elliott, Anthony Michael Manton, CBE, publisher, *b.* 7 January 1947; *d.* 17 July 2020

Fay, Stephen Francis John, writer and journalist, *b.* 14 August 1938; *d.* 12 May 2020

Feinstein, Elaine Barbara, RSL, poet, novelists and biographer, *b.* 24 October 1930, *d.* 23 September 2019

Fergusson, Jean Mitchell, actor, *b.* 30 December 1944; *d.* 14 November 2019

Figes, Kate, author and journalist, *b.* 6 November 1957; *d.* 7 December 2019

Fowlds, Derek James, actor, known for *Yes Minister* and *Yes Prime Minister*, *The Basil Brush Show*, *Heartbeat* and many more, *b.* 2 September 1937; *d.* 17 January 2020

Frank, Robert Louis, photographer and film-maker, author of *The Americans*, *b.* 9 November 1924; *d.* 9 September 2019

Frankland, Alfred William, MBE, immunologist, *b.* 19 March 1912; *d.* 2 April 2020

Freeman, Catherine, television producer, *b.* 10 August 1931; *d.* 15 July 2020

Freeman, Robert Grahame, photographer and film director, best known for his covers of several Beatles albums, *b.* 5 December 1936; *d.* 6 November 2019

Friedeberger, Klaus, artist and designer, *b.* 23 August 1922; *d.* 19 September 2019

Freni, Mirella, celebrated soprano, *b.* 27 February 1935; *d.* 9 February 2020

Garnett, Henrietta Catherine, writer, *b.* 15 May 1945; *d.* 4 September 2019

Garnett, Tony (*b.* Anthony Edward Lewis), producer, writer and director, known of *Kes*, *This Life*, *Cathy Come Home*, *Ballykissangel* and more, *b.* 3 April 1936; *d.* 12 January 2020

Ginsburg, Joan Ruth Bader, American lawyer and jurist, associate Justice of the Supreme Court of the United States, *b.* 15 March 1933; *d.* 18 September 2020

Gordon of Strathblane, Lord, broadcaster, businessman and politician, *b.* 17 May 1936; *d.* 1 April 2020

Graham of Edmonton, Lord, politician, *b.* 26 March 1925; *d.* 21 March 2020

Gray, Alasdair, Scottish novelist, playwright, academic and artist, famous for his novel, *Lanark*, *b.* 28 December 1934; *d.* 29 December 2019

Hain, Adelaine Florence, political activist, *b.* 16 February 1927; *d.* 8 September 2019

Houghton, John Theodore, CBE, atmospheric physicist, *b.* 30 December 1931; *d.* 15 April 2020

Howard, Sir Michael Eliot, OM, CH, CBE, military historian, described in the *Financial Times* as 'Britain's greatest living historian', *b.* 29 November 1922; *d.* 30 November 2019

James, Clive Vivian Leopold, CBE, poet, writer and television presenter, winner of the George Orwell Special Prize, *b.* 7 October 1939; *d.* 24 November 2019

Jencks, Charles Alexander, architectural historian, landscape architect, designer and writer, known for Northumberlandia (a.k.a. the Lady of the North) *b.* 21 June 1939; *d.* 13 October 2019

Johnson, Derek Francis (known professionally as Derek Acorah), footballer, spiritual medium, broadcaster and writer, *b.* 27 January 1950; *d.* 4 January 2020

Johnston, Daniel Dale, singer, songwriter and artist, *b.* 22 January 1961; *d.* 10 September 2019

Jones, Terence Graham Parry, writer, poet, Python, actor and director, *b.* 1 February 1942; *d.* 21 January 2020

Kancheli, Giya Alexandrovich, composer, honoured as a People's Artist of the USSR, *b.* 10 August 1935; *d.* 2 October 2019

Kapoor, Rishi Raj, award-winning actor, *b.* 4 September 1952; *d.* 30 April 2020

Khan, Abdul Qadir, cricketer, *b.* 15 September 1955; *d.* 6 September 2019

Killip, Christopher David, photographer and author, *b.* 11 July 1946; *d.* 13 October 2020

Kupfer, Harry Alfred Robert, opera director, *b.* 12 August 1935; *d.* 30 December 2019

Le Mesurier, James, OBE, soldier and humanitarian worker, *b.* 25 May 1971; *d.* 11 November 2019

Lewis, John Robert, US politician and civil rights leader, *b.* 21 February 1940; *d.* 17 July 2020

Lynn, Vera (*b.* Vera Margaret Welch), CH, DBE, singer, songwriter and entertainer, *b.* 20 March 1917; *d.* 18 June 2020

MacCarthy, Fiona, OBE, biographer, cultural historian and journalist, *b.* 23 January 1940; *d.* 29 February 2020

Macdonald, Ian Alexander, barrister, immigration and human rights lawyer, *b.* 12 January 1939; *d.* 12 November 2019

McGinnis, Edward Hugh, best known by his stage name, Eddie Large, comedian, *b.* 25 June 1941; *d.* 2 April 2020

Martínez, Ernesto Cardenal, priest, poet and politician, *b.* 20 January 1925; *d.* 1 March 2020

Maschler, Thomas Michael, publisher and founder of the Booker Prize, *b.* 16 August 1933; *d.* 15 October 2020

Mawhinney, Lord, politician, *b.* 26 July 1940; *d.* 9 November 2019

Mitchell, Ann Katherine, Bletchley Park codebreaker and social scientist, *b.* 19 November 1922; *d.* 11 May 2020

Moore, Stephen Vincent, actor, known for *The Hitchhiker's Guide to the Galaxy* radio series, television and theatre, *b.* 11 December 1937; *d.* 4 October 2019

Moseley, Rev. David John Reading, clergyman and crossword setter, *b.* 24 September 1930; *d.* 26 February 2020

Norman, Jessye, operatic soprano and winner of the 1968 Munich International music competition, *b.* 15 September 1945; *d.* 30 September 2019

Ogata, Sadako, diplomat, the first female head of UNHCR, *b.* 16 September 1927; *d.* 22 October 2019

Orr, Deborah Jane, journalist, writer, editor, *b.* 23 September 1962; *d.* 19 October 2019

Parker, Alan William, CBE, film director, producer and writer, *b.* 14 February 1944; *d.* 31 July 2020

Peacock, Ian Michael, OBE, broadcasting executive, led the launch of BBC Two, *b.* 14 September 1929; *d.* 6 December 2019

Peters, Martin, MBE, footballer and manager, *b.* 8 November 1943; *d.* 21 December 2019

Ponsonby, Robert Noel, arts administrator, director of the Edinburgh festival, artistic director of the Canterbury festival, *b.* 19 December 1926; *d.* 3 November 2019

Powell, Nik, film producer and businessman, chaired the European Film Academy from 1996 to 2003, director of the National Film and Television School, *b.* 4 November 1950; *d.* 7 November 2019

Quayle, Anne Veronica Maria, actor known for *Chitty Chitty Bang Bang, Grange Hill* and more, *b.* 6 October 1932; *d.* 16 August 2019

Renton of Mount Harry, Lord, politician, *b.* 28 May 1932; *d.* 25 August 2020

Rhodes, Gary, OBE, chef, writer and TV presenter, *b.* 22 April 1960; *d.* 26 November 2019

Rigg, Dame Enid Diana Elizabeth, DBE, actor, *b.* 20 July 1938; *d.* 10 September 2020

Rogers, Kenny (Kenneth Ray), writer, singer and musician, b. 21 August 1938; d. 20 March 2020

Russell, Diana Elizabeth Hamilton, feminist activist, scholar and writer, *b.* 6 November 1938; *d.* 28 July 2020

Sai, Frederick Torgbor, community health physician and reproductive rights advocate, author, *b.* 23 June 1924; *d.* 17 September 2019

Shaw, Susan, publisher and founder of the Type Museum in London, *b.* 12 August 1932, *d.* 13 June 2020

Sheldon, Lord, PC, Labour Party politician, *b.* 13 September 1923; *d.* 2 February 2020

Shrapnel, John Morley, actor, known for his stage work with the RSC and National Theatre in the United Kingdom, and his many television roles, *b.* 27 April 1942; *d.* 14 February 2020

Singer, Harold Joseph, jazz saxophonist and bandleader, *b.* 8 October 1919; *d.* 18 August 2020

Sissons, Peter George, newscaster and TV presenter with ITN, Channel Four and the BBC, *b.* 17 July 1942, *d.* 1 October 2019

Smirnov, Dmitri, composer and translator, b. 2 November 1948; d. 9 April 2020

Smith, Alex Duval, journalist and foreign correspondent, worked for *The Guardian, The Independent* and the BBC, b. 28 October 1964; d. 7 December 2019

Snell, Sir Peter George, athlete, Olympic gold medal winner, *b.* 17 December 1938; *d.* 13 December 2019

Spencer, Margaret Meek, educationist and writer, *b.* 14 January 1925; *d.* 4 May 2020

Stanley, Richard Mark, film-maker and road safety campaigner, *b.* 27 April 1948; *d.* 25 October 2019

Steiner, Zara Alice, historian and academic, *b.* 6 November 1928; *d.* 13 February 2020

Sydow, Max von (b. Carl Adolf von Sydow), celebrated Academy, Golden Globe and Emmy Award-nominated actor; *b.* 10 April 1929; *d.* 8 March 2020

Thynn, Alexander George, 7th Marquess of Bath, owner of the Longleat estate, *b.* 6 May 1932; *d.* 4 April 2020

Tolkien, Christopher Reuel, Royal Air Force officer, editor, illustrator and scholar, son of J. R. R. Tolkien, winner of the Bodley Medal, *b.* 21 November 1924; *d.* 16 January 2020

Tombs, Lord, engineer and industrialist, *b.* 17 May 1924; *d.* 11 April 2020

Welch, Robin, potter and painter, his work is held by the Victoria and Albert Museum, *b.* 23 July 1936; *d.* 5 December 2019

Williams, Betty (Elizabeth), peace campaigner, Nobel Peace Prize recipient, *b.* 22 May 1943; *d.* 17 March 2020

Willis, Robert George Dylan, cricketer, former England cricket captain, broadcaster, *b.* 30 May 1949; *d.* 4 December 2019

Withers, Bill (William Harrison Withers Jr), singer and songwriter, *b.* 4 July 1938; *d.* 30 March 2020

Wood, Charles Gerald, soldier, playwright and screenwriter, *b.* 6 August 1932; *d.* 1 February 2020

Wood, Lynn Faulds, journalist and TV presenter, *b.* 25 March 1948; *d.* 24 April 2020

Woodley, Leonard Gaston, QC, barrister, the first person in Britain of Afro-Caribbean heritage to become a Queen's Counsel, *b.* 13 September 1927; *d.* 19 January 2020

Wurtzel, Elizabeth Lee, lawyer, writer and author of *Prozac Nation, b.* 31 July 1967; *d.* 7 January 2020

Zafón, Carlos Ruiz, novelist, *b.* 25 September 1964; *d.* 19 June 2020

ARCHAEOLOGY

Andrew Earnshaw

ALL IS REVEALED

Archaeology is a discipline which is forever changing as new discoveries come to the fore, either from beneath the ground or in labs and libraries around the world. This has been especially true of 2020, a year filled with surprising discoveries by amateurs and professionals alike. Such revelations have again shown that archaeology uncovers fundamental parts of the human experience, including physical things, like children's toys and love letters, but also emotions and concepts like home, family, mourning, gift giving, or simply connecting with the natural world. Such discoveries remind us that the strife facing us right now is not unique to us and that good things will return.

2020 both revealed plenty of such discoveries and has shown the world anew that the modern context in which archaeology is uncovered is as important as the ancient world in which much of this archaeology first existed. While archaeology is undoubtedly scientific, it doesn't produce unqualified, unquestionable facts. Instead, archaeology finds the scraps of an atomised jigsaw puzzle that can only be completed by the imaginations of those in the modern day. That is the joy of archaeology, but also a danger. It is easy for archaeological narratives to be over-simplified or misused to fit particular narratives. Archaeology benefits from a lot of people, from diverse backgrounds, working together to try and understand the past. Therefore, beyond introducing many great discoveries, it is worthwhile considering the context in which much archaeological excavation is conducted, the contribution of enthusiasts, amateurs and members of the public and also the presence of archaeology in today's media.

MAJOR FIELDWORK

For those who are fans of the Dark Ages, or enjoy television shows like *Vikings* or *The Last Kingdom*, 2019-20 has been full of excitement. In December 2020 results of radiocarbon dating of organic material found in the bottom of a mosaic's construction trench at Chedworth Roman villa, as reported in *Current Archaeology* 371, placed the building date of this mosaic after AD 424, and probably around the middle part of the fifth century AD. This is Britain's first fifth century mosaic and demonstrates that new mosaics were being created in Britain well after the Romans left in AD 410. This fits with a developing picture of the immediate post-Roman period that is by all accounts far more complicated, nuanced and interesting than the traditional story of scared Britons hiding in their villas or running to the west as Saxons rampaged across the country. Instead, what is being shown is that a lot of Romano-British culture continued after the Romans left and while German immigrants arrived on the east coast. The 'Anglo-Saxon' culture which emerged in the 500s may, therefore, be less a direct European import but a result of a blend between native Briton (or Celtic) populations, Romans and Germanic immigrants, creating something unique to Britain. This fits with the work suggested in a recent article by Dr Toby Martin published this year in the *Journal of Archaeological Method and Theory*, which argues that while Anglo Saxon brooch styles in the sixth and seventh century had strong influences from Frankia (France and Germany) and Scandinavia, there is a clearly defined style unique to Britain. We can see this transition at Chedworth, the inhabitants of this grand villa continued to live in style in the Cotswold Hills above Cirencester for a long time after Roman administration fell away. That said, while the ability to create mosaics

remained, some secrets, like underfloor heating, do appear to have been forgotten; Chedworth's best mosaics are scarred by fifth century braziers used to heat the grand dining rooms after the hypocausts – Roman underfloor heating – fell into disuse.

There's more to report from the Early Medieval period (AD 410–1066). On top of a gentle hill, now filled with wheat, which overlooks the river Thames near Marlow, Buckinghamshire, a very special Anglo-Saxon burial has been uncovered. This burial, as reported in *Current Archaeology* 369, is very rich, containing two bronze bowls, two spearheads, a sword with a well-preserved scabbard of wood and leather, a glass vessel, dress fittings and other personal items. Gifts of weapons, jewellery and rare items like glass were a core part of Anglo-Saxon culture as kings and warlords used such wealth to maintain small groups of warriors to protect themselves and express their own power. Such 'psychopathic peacocks' as described by the *British History Podcast*, were some of the richest men in the country and it appears that this 'Marlow Warrior' might be such a man who lived during a time when Buckinghamshire was being fought over by the kingdoms of Kent, Wessex and Mercia.

To continue the rich vein of Early Medieval discoveries, as reported in *The Independent* and *Current Archaeology* 362, scientists working with Folkestone museum have analysed the bones widely claimed to belong to St Eanswythe. Eanswythe was born in the 640s to the royal family of Kent and, as a teenager, became a nun, founding one of England's first nunneries at Folkestone, Kent before dying sometime in the AD 660s. Eanswythe was something of a trendsetter, as joining a nunnery became a common life choice for many female nobles in this period, either due to ambition, piety or an unwillingness to be married as part of a political alliance. Some of these women ended up becoming incredibly powerful and much loved. Eanswythe was revered, her bones were kept at the monastery and moved to Folkestone church in 1138, where they were at the centre of an active shrine until the Reformation under Henry VIII in the 1530s. Eanswythe's bones were assumed to have been destroyed during the Reformation but in 1885 they were found in a lead container hidden in one of the church's walls. The bones have been analysed before in 1980 when they were confirmed as female, but the Finding Eanswythe project wanted to better understand her. To do this, they set up a lab within the church of St Mary & St Eanswythe so the bones did not have to risk travel, save for some small samples sent for more specialist analysis. The radiocarbon dating, and rigorous osteological analysis have shown the bones belonged to a young woman, who was 17 to 20-years-old when she died between AD 649–684. Further DNA analysis is being conducted, but it is expected that such analysis will confirm that this is St Eanswythe, making her the earliest confirmed saint in England and the earliest identified relative of Queen Elizabeth II.

Nor have royal discoveries from this period been confined to Britain. Across the waves in Norway, excavations began at the site of Gjellestad on the largest Viking-age boat discovered since the Oseberg ship in 1904. Archaeologists have had their suspicions about this site for a long time as it is home to the Jell Mound, the second largest early medieval mound in Norway. Ground penetrating radar has allowed archaeologists to quickly and relatively cheaply survey the burial mounds and *Heritage Daily* reported that Mound 13 has a suspiciously ship-shaped anomaly within. These ship burials were reserved for the most powerful of kings, and so generate excitement and intrigue that lasts for generations. Britain's best parallel to Gjellestad and Oseburg – Sutton Hoo – is still attracting attention 80 years after its discovery. Ralph Fiennes will star in *The Dig*, a romanticised account of the very true story of a gardener moonlighting as an archaeologist and discovering Britain's richest burial. Most believe that Sutton Hoo was the final resting place of Raedwald, the pagan king of East Anglia who died six years before St Eanswythe was born in Kent.

Returning to the Vikings, *Current Archaeology* 367 reports the results of a project using remote sensing geophysical analysis and sediment sampling, which identified a series of shallow, man-made water channels cutting across Mainland, Orkney – connecting the Atlantic Ocean with Scapa Flow, probably made by the Vikings. Ships were vital to the Viking way of life and presumably such waterways allowed the islands to be crossed without having to drag the boats across land as was the case in other Norse colonies, like those on the Danube. Especially on Orkney, famous for its dangerous waters, such routes may have also allowed ocean traffic to flow across the island without risking the storms and tides that surround them. Such work is also a reminder of how much fieldwork can be achieved using survey techniques, which allows much larger sites to be identified, like the recent discovery of another Nazca Line, in Peru. The Nazca lines are geoglyphs, images created by digging narrow channels into the earth to reveal the lighter soil beneath. These works are 1500–2500 years old and are often vast, some stretching for over 1km and are best seen from the air, suggesting these were built to be visible to the gods and gods alone. This geoglyph, as reported by the BBC, is of a relaxing cat carved into a hill face and was discovered by drones flying over the landscape ahead of building vantage points for tourists to view these enigmatic works.

Finally, Aberdeen University released a press release in May 2020 confirming that they had discovered one of the largest ancient settlements ever discovered in Scotland at Tap O'Noth. This hillfort in Aberdeenshire covers an area of 17 acres, or nine and a half football fields. Over 400 huts discovered so far could have supported a population of over 8000 people. The site dates back as early as the third century AD and lasted until the 500s, meaning it was almost certainly a Pictish settlement. The Picts, a term that covers the people living in Scotland during the Iron Age, Roman Period and the Early Medieval until the arrival of the Scotti from Ireland, remain a mysterious people. They left scant documentary evidence and there is also relatively little archaeology confidently associated with the Picts, so such a large site has the potential to contribute a lot to the understanding of this imagination-grabbing culture.

ARCHAEOLOGY IN THE MEDIA

There has been much debate in the media surrounding the proposal to put the A303 road, near Stonehenge, underground. This road runs from London to Devon, following an ancient trackway that cuts through the Stonehenge World Heritage site, as well as coming within 200m of Stonehenge itself. This busy route has regular traffic jams next to Stonehenge and there have been calls for decades to turn the road into a dual carriageway in a way that doesn't damage the archaeology and improves the visitor experience to the site. As reported by the BBC, the UK government has approved a £1.7bn plan that would see a tunnel being created by digging a large hole before being covered back up once the road was complete. The Stonehenge tunnel would allow all of Stonehenge's immediate environment to be turned into chalk grasslands and the full landscape opened up to visitors, however, many are concerned by the potential environmental impact of such a large road project and others have pointed out that it poses a significant risk to much of the archaeology yet to be discovered at Stonehenge. The fact that such a well-studied landscape is still packed with archaeological secrets to uncover has been amply

demonstrated this year with the discovery of Durrington Shafts and the 'city' at Blick Mead. As reported in *Current Archaeology* 366, Durrington Shafts are a series of giant pits (10m across and 5m deep) surrounding Britain's largest henge – Durrington Walls. These shafts end only 800m from Stonehenge and are linked with other features, like the Larkhill Causewayed Enclosure. They appear to have been part of an enormous, continuous circle of pits surrounding the already massive Durrington Walls and further linking the Durrington Walls landscape with the Stonehenge landscape.

Durrington Shafts are contemporary with the 'Classic' period of Stonehenge when the great sarsen stones were raised around 2500 BC. Stonehenge's history, however, goes much further back in time, as is being revealed at Blick Mead. *The Telegraph* describes a site that may have been an occasional home to the people who began to turn Stonehenge's corner of Salisbury Plain into such a vital ritual landscape. Blick Mead is a spring, a mile from Stonehenge, which has a constant temperature of 11°C and never freezes. Around this spring, intermittent excavations heavily reliant on volunteers has revealed human habitation going back 10,000 years, the same time the earliest monuments were being raised at Stonehenge – giant, wooden poles not dissimilar to totem poles. Not only does Blick Mead potentially reveal the first people who began building Stonehenge, but it might also reveal why this site was deemed so special. A rare alga lives in the Blick Mead spring which turns stone bright red in a matter of hours upon exposure to air. The speed and bright colour of this change, as well as the constant source of fresh water may have made this place very important both economically and ritually to the hunter-gatherers of the area, especially during winter when the unfrozen, clean water would have been important to survival. Both Durrington Shafts and Blick Mead are not yet fully understood but they demonstrate that the Stonehenge landscape has far more to teach archaeology.

High Speed 2 (HS2), Europe's largest infrastructure project, has demonstrated amply how much archaeology remains to be uncovered in Britain. HS2 is a controversial project to better connect Britain's major cities by building a high-speed rail network initially from London to Birmingham, and then expanding to both Leeds and Manchester. HS1 was the Channel Tunnel. One of many potential examples of archaeological discoveries due to this program is in Birmingham, the terminus for the first part of HS2. In April, *Current Archaeology* 362 reported on the intriguing finds at the Curzon Street station, originally built in the 1830s. It is full of Victoriana, particularly the old roundhouse. These roundhouses were circular or semicircular steam-powered turntables which turned the locomotives around when they reached Birmingham, so they could complete their return journey. This roundhouse, the earliest of its type, was designed by Robert Stephenson, son of George Stephenson, the 'father' of the railways', who among other things, set the standard gauge for most of the modern world's railways. When working, this roundhouse could accommodate 32 locomotives and there are records of a vast vault beneath the roundhouse, a cavernous arcade 20ft deep, 300ft long and 40ft wide. This vault would have stored coal, which was turned into coke at Curzon Street to fuel the locomotives. Other notable discoveries during preparatory work for HS2 include the discovery at Wellwick farm of an Iron Age execution victim. He was found lying face down in a ditch with his hands beneath his body over his pelvis, suggesting his hands had been bound in front of him before he was executed. Further work is ongoing to identify the cause of death.

There have also been some excellent discoveries not from infrastructure projects. Indeed, some of Britain's most important places have had new chapters added to their stories through archaeological excavation, namely Westminster Abbey. Pre-Construct Archaeology Ltd. were hired by Westminster abbey in January 2020 to excavate the abbey's sacristy, and have already had impressive results. So far, along with uncovering the superstructure of the sacristy, hundreds of burials have been revealed. Since the abbey's foundations in the 11th century, thousands have been buried as close as possible to the abbey and more burials are expected to be discovered. This part of the abbey was built in the 1250s on the orders of Henry III, during his work to completely reconstruct Edward the Confessor's original church. The sacristy is a space for storing vestments and other items associated with mass and, after the dissolution it was used as a house before being demolished in 1740, having fallen into a bad state of repair and consequently preventing necessary repairs to the main building. The narrow internal wall means that part of the building may have been part-timbered, and the internal walls would have been brightly painted with red, white and black flowers. Avid fans of Channel Four's *Time Team*, may remember that the show conducted initial investigations of the sacristy in Series 17, Episode 1. The excavations this year confirm the layout *Time Team* proposed and uncovered many of the burials they had been expecting to find. The television show ended in 2014, but ever since its end the team behind the show have been trying to find new ways to continue the program. They have announced that they believe it to be time for *Time Team* to make a return to our screens, though initially via YouTube, rather than on television.

ARCHAEOLOGY DURING THE LOCKDOWN

Archaeological fieldwork has both struggled and thrived amidst the challenges posed by COVID-19. On one hand, traditional archaeological fieldwork, whether research excavations or ahead of development, has either been limited due to travel and social restrictions or made extremely difficult by asking people to spend all day swinging mattocks and heaving wheelbarrows while wearing masks and maintaining social distance. On the other hand, far more people have been spending time in their gardens, while others have been taking up new hobbies well suited to being outside and socially distanced, like metal detecting; both of which have resulted in some spectacular discoveries. *The New York Times*, on 9 December reported that over 47,000 archaeological finds were reported in Britain during 2020, far more than previous years. Two notable discoveries were found in British gardens, the first a hoard of 50 solid gold Krugerrand, from Apartheid era South Africa discovered in Milton Keynes. The second is a hoard discovered in Hampshire consisting of 63 gold coins and one silver coin dating from the time of Henry VIII, with four being inscribed with the initials of either Catherine of Aragon, Anne Boleyn or Jane Seymour, who together make up the first half of the famous mnemonic to remember the fate of Henry's six wives (divorced, beheaded, died respectively). Hoards like these are amongst the more spectacular things one can find in Britain's earth, and they do prompt important questions which archaeologists are only just beginning to grapple with like, why were they buried and is there a pattern to where hoards are buried that might tell us more about how people in the past thought about the world and these artefacts?

Metal detectorists also got into the news multiple times this year. It was a metal detectorist (Sue Washington) who discovered the Marlow Warrior and a Polish immigrant called Mariusz Stepien uncovered the Peebles Hoard, an extremely rare Bronze Age hoard found near Edinburgh. Mariusz contacted archaeologists immediately upon discovering the hoard and his quick thinking allowed the site to be excavated correctly, meaning the horse harness which was recovered still contains some of the original leather, so well-preserved that the tooling marks are still visible, despite being over 3000 years old. Such discoveries, excavated properly, are vital to developing our understanding of how textiles developed and helping archaeologists understand the development of horse-riding, as well as improving the accuracy of visual recreations of the past.

Heritage organisations have also aimed to keep projects running if at all possible. One pleasantly surprising example is the New Forest Graffiti Project. As reported by *The Guardian*, the National Park Authority has asked people walking in the New Forest to send them examples of graffiti carved into the bark of the trees. There is an increasing awareness of the importance of small, personal and individual interactions with the environment and what is now the archaeological record but used to just be the things of everyday life. While the over 100 individual pieces of graffiti recorded by August were primarily lovers' initials, dotted among the assemblage were glimpses of the life witnessed by the New Forest going back hundreds of years. One example is the numerous 'king's marks' recorded. These are scratches into the bark noting that the tree was set to be felled to build ships for the Royal Navy, a reminder that the term 'forest' might mean a lot of trees nowadays, but used to mean an area of land set aside for the use of the king. Other marks are more recent, with there bring numerous initials and dates relating to the US servicemen based at nearby RAF Stoney Cross during the Second World War and a highly ornate mark spelling out 'Summer of Love, 1967'. There are also many 'witch marks', not made by witches but by people attempting to ward off those who may bring evil with them. Projects like that in the New Forest happen all over the country and are wonderful ways of adding interest and intrigue to government-mandated exercise or simply a way to contribute to the understanding of Britain's past.

Nor has it only been amateurs who have made unexpected discoveries during the lockdown. The team at Vindolanda, a large Roman auxiliary fort associated with Hadrian's Wall, have being using the site's closure due to Coronavirus to explore their records and, in their archives, they uncovered a previously unreported leather toy mouse, as reported by the Vindolanda Trust in May 2020. In Britain, organic materials like wood, leather and cloth don't survive well due to our very wet climate. Vindolanda, however, is so very wet that the soils are waterlogged, meaning there is not enough oxygen for bacteria to survive, which greatly hinders decomposition. When the site was first excavated, thin sheets of wood and papyrus were found so well preserved that the writing on the documents could be read, revealing a world of organisation, parties and gossip. This leather toy mouse equally adds colour to our image of the Romans, reminding the world that even austere men like Julius Caesar were children once, who played with small and simple toys like this little leather mouse.

NEW ARCHAEOLOGICAL IDEAS

Archaeology is a vibrant discipline taking place in labs and libraries as well as the field and, despite those labs and libraries being closed for large swathes of this year, some exciting archaeology away from the field has been completed. For example, Chris Gosden released his first non-academic book *A History of Magic* (Viking/Penguin). In this book, which is a survey of magical artefacts from the Ice Age to modern day, Gosden argues that magic is as important to human interaction with the world as religion and science and that, if science seeks to understand the universe and religion seeks to explain that universe, then magic is the way humans aim to manipulate or affect the universe. This fits with a wider recognition in academic archaeology that artefacts are far more than the results of society but are instead a vital part in creating the world and changing the way humans think about themselves and the society in which they live.

Archaeology is not isolated from the world in which it exists and the protests against racism sparked by the death of George Floyd affected archaeology as well. Most notably, the dumping of the statue of Edward Colston into the Bristol harbour brought to the fore the contemporary political relevance of much of Britain's heritage industry. Dan Hicks has released a timely book wittily called *The Brutish Museums* (Pluto Press) which explores the history of many of the collections in Britain's museums and provides an academic argument to the call for the restitution of many of the artefacts held in British museums to the countries from which they were taken, particularly the Benin Bronzes. This is far from the final word in a debate that seems set to continue for many years within museums in the global north.

To close, one book about archaeology has aimed to capture the joy of discovery and engaging with the past. *Surfacing* by Kathleen Jamie (Sort of Books) was published in paperback and won the 2019 Highland Book prize. This book, a collection of essays by Jamie, brings together archaeology, nature writing and personal reflection in a book which reminds the reader that while archaeology is an exciting and necessary subject if humans are to better understand themselves, the true beauty and wonder of the discipline is its inherent romance which connects us to our childhood, the people around us and all those who have come before.

BUSINESS AND FINANCE

Lisa Carden

It's almost impossible to know where – and how – to begin. 2020 was a brutal year for the UK. Tens of thousands of people have fallen victim to the COVID-19 pandemic, despite the best efforts of a committed and courageous NHS, and what most of us regarded as 'normal' life has been put on hold. Many of the restrictions instituted by the government in order to suppress the spread of the coronavirus will have affected us both as employees, employers, and consumers. So, what are the main talking points?

BREXIT: THE NEVER-ENDING STORY
Almost implausibly, a trade deal had still not been done as of early December 2020. More than four years after the UK's first vote to leave the EU – and subsequently reinforced by two general elections – discussions went down to the very wire. Fishing rights – in terms of both access and quotas – remained a principal sticking point, as did the concept of a 'level playing field' in business competition, and dispute resolution. At last, an early Christmas miracle occurred when an agreement was finally reached on 24 December, but it will be months before the real-life consequences of the deal are apparent to all.

What *is* already clear, however, is the sheer amount of paperwork involved in the UK's final break with the EU is enormous: Jim Harra, chief executive of HM Revenue and Customs, said in December 2020 that the 'administrative burden' of filling in customs forms once the transition is over would be £7.5bn per year (this figure was first mooted in 2018, and according to Mr Harra, still stands). The whole issue of customs was an extremely fraught one as 2020 wound to a close: freight was getting stuck in UK ports as a result of delays linked to the impact of the coronavirus and pre-Brexit stock movement, so much so that Honda had to pause production at its Swindon plant due to a parts shortage. Builders were also reporting problems in accessing timber, roof tiles, power tools, and even screws, and they weren't alone in experiencing supply-chain issues. (It should be noted that the UK was just one of numerous countries suffering freight woes, and ports were congested around the world: for example, at one point in late November, the *LA Times* reported that twelve cargo ships were anchored south of Los Angeles waiting for a berth, while the ports of Los Angeles and Long Beach were already full to capacity.)

While it had always been suspected that negotiations between the UK and EU would come down the last possible minute, what transpired was *so* last minute that British retailers, exporters, and suppliers were left desperately trying to prepare – at the government's request – for a future about which they had been given no details. Key questions about vital issues such as tariffs, fees, stock movements, pre-existing contracts, and future work prospects were left unanswered. The official slogan of 'Check, Change, Go' belied the enormity of the situation. In the face of this, the news that the multinational INEOS, owned by Brexit supporter Jim Radcliffe, announced that it would be building a manufacturing plant for its Grenadier off-road vehicle on the French/German border rather than in Bridgend, as had been suggested, was particularly poorly timed.

LOCKDOWN BLUES
On the evening of 23 March 2020, the prime minister addressed the UK. He explained that (and as had widely been expected) in order to stop the spread of the coronavirus, the nation should work from home wherever possible, reduce social contact with others and shop only for essentials. To that end, supermarkets would remain open (with social distancing procedures in place), along with pharmacists and a handful of other outlets, but pretty much everything was closed. The hospitality and travel industries shut their doors and the country fell quiet.

Many white-collar office-based businesses and organisations would continue to function (after a fashion) thanks to a range of 'virtual' meetings solutions (see below), but what of those that relied on people crossing the threshold? The very backbone of British high streets – from pubs to bookshops, cafes to hairdressers – was gone in the blink of an eye. How could these businesses keep going? The government stepped in, offering a Coronavirus Job Retention Scheme (more commonly referred to as 'furlough') that would, in effect, pay a large proportion (80 per cent) of employees' wages for a specified time period (furlough has now been extended several times and at the time of writing will be in place until April 2021). Grants and loans were also made available throughout the year (some during the first, national lockdown and others later in the year during the local restrictions). Assistance for the self-employed came in the form of the Self-Employed Income Support Scheme, which offered a grant to those businesses that had seen a dramatic fall in demand due to the impact of the pandemic or had been forced to close temporarily because of it). In all, the government claimed it had offered an 'unprecedented' financial aid package of over £200m, saving 9 million jobs in the process. And it is certainly true that the support was welcome.

There were, however, some gaps in the coverage, and the self-employed were at a particular disadvantage if: a) their business was relatively new, and thus had no 'track record' to be judged on; b) they had been in effect, too successful, having an average trading profit of over £50,000 for the three tax years immediately prior to the pandemic; or c) owners (perfectly legally) paid themselves a salary and dividends through their company. In such situations, they did not qualify for government assistance. According to the Institute of Fiscal Studies, almost a fifth (18 per cent) of those for whom self-employment accounts for the bulk of their income were left out in the cold.

Despite the government's efforts, and although many businesses took advantage of an online presence to keep trading during both the initial lockdown and the subsequent local restrictions, a good number of the UK's most famous and best-loved trading names did not survived COVID-19. In the space of 24 hours during early December, 25,000 jobs were put at risk when Sir Philip Green's Arcadia Group – which includes brands such as Topshop, Dorothy Perkins and Burton – went into administration, and Debenhams, which first opened in 1813, went into liquidation (it had been in trouble for some time). Even John Lewis was not immune: in August 2020, it announced plans to close eight stores, some of which were relatively small but one – in Birmingham – was opened only in 2015 as part of an enormously expensive regeneration project near to the city's New Street Station. And these were just a handful of the famous retail names that fell by the wayside over the twelve months. Worryingly, the immediate future does not look brighter: in November 2020, the chief executive of Fortnum & Mason, Ewan Venters, said in an interview with Radio 4's *Today* programme that he expected a third of leading retail brands to have vanished by the end of March 2021.

For hospitality and personal care businesses, the on/off nature of the restrictions was particularly problematic. Even though many were able to trade throughout July, August, and even September (once appropriately covid-secure), the regional lockdowns that were rolled out during the late autumn meant that it simply wasn't worth opening up again until 2021. This is certainly the case in Wales, which had a 'firebreak' lockdown from 23 October to 9 November, swiftly followed by further restrictions less than a month later, as part of which pubs were not allowed to serve alcohol. The country's largest Welsh-owned brewery, Brains, said it would shut 100 of its pubs until the New Year and estimated that the firebreak had cost the company over £1.5m. Both England and Scotland implemented (slightly different) tier systems, under which pubs could open in the less severely-hit areas, while the situation in Northern Ireland remained unpredictable: a 'circuit-breaker' lockdown that was due to end in late November was extended at very short notice for a further two weeks, leaving both retail and hospitality in the region in disarray.

The overall effects of the pandemic on jobs and the UK's longer-term economic future are staggering. In his Spending Review in late November 2020, Rishi Sunak, Chancellor of the Exchequer, warned that the UK's economic emergency had 'only just begun'. Government borrowing was expected to exceed £390bn in 2020 alone, while expenditure on tackling COVID-19 would be in the region of £280bn. Unemployment figures had risen by 300,000 on 2019, up to 1.62m. Winter was coming, in every sense.

PARADIGM SHIFTS

There were, however, some pockets of good news. For obvious reasons, the demand for online food shopping soared during 2020, and although access to those services was problematic during the spring lockdown, things evened out in time for the subsequent autumn restrictions (which varied in duration and detail across the UK). While nearly all of the UK's supermarkets had an online operation too, Ocado was the only one that was digital-only. It had been popular for some time but – famously – had only made a profit in three of the twenty years it has been operational. The game certainly changed during 2020, despite a challenging start when an extensive warehouse fire in February cost the business over £200m. In July, however, its chief executive and co-founder, Tim Steiner, announced that half-year sales had reached £1bn, a rise of over 25 per cent in retail revenues. By early November 2020, share price rises meant that Ocado was worth £18bn – almost on a par with Tesco. Groceries aside – these are now, in fact, part of a jointly owned business with Marks & Spencer, whose products Ocado has stocked since September 2020 following the end of its previous deal with Waitrose – Ocado's tech solutions may prove to be a longer-term source of revenue. As a *Guardian* article reported in November 2020, Ocado had licensed its software and picking robots to supermarkets around the world and in so doing hoped to make further inroads into a market estimated to be worth over £7.5 *trillion*.

One of the unexpected trends of the pandemic has perhaps been an acceleration of change. During the spring restrictions, many workplaces closed. All over the country, people speedily carved out 'offices' in their homes and got used to 'Zooming' – that is, holding meetings over the eponymous online video-conferencing service. Formed in California in 2011, Zoom allowed people to (just about) go about their day jobs by seeing and speaking to colleagues, clients, suppliers and so on. A host of other options were available, of course, many of which (such as Microsoft Teams and Google Classroom) were adopted by UK schools as they attempted to maintain their pupils' education and motivation, but Zoom became emblematic of the nation's attempts to remain engaged and productive. The company's worth leapt as a result: in August 2020, the BBC reported that revenues had rocketed by more than 300 per cent for the three months to end of July, reaching over $660m (£450m), while profits jumped to $186m. Although growth will probably be less marked in the years ahead, demand is likely to remain high for the first quarter of 2021, with many offices not expected to open up fully before late spring.

Other industries – traditional and otherwise – also saw some positive effects from a hugely challenging time. Publishing is just one of the creative industries of which the UK can be rightly proud, and books continued to be a source of solace for many during 2020. Audiobooks have been increasingly popular over recent years – a report published by Deloitte Insights in December 2019 estimated that the global audiobook market would be worth $3.5bn during 2020, a jump of 25 per cent – but the pandemic was an extra catalyst to an established trend. Ebooks also benefited: after their heyday about a decade ago – when it was suggested that they were the future of books full stop – digital versions of books had remained relatively popular (arguably thanks to Amazon's Kindle device) but were no longer setting the world on fire. Given that only 'essential shops' were open for most of the spring, though, and that Amazon de-prioritised book deliveries for a time, their speed of delivery and ease of use meant that ebooks became popular again. According to a *Guardian* story in November 2020, sales were up 17 per cent on the previous year, and ebooks were on track to have their best year since 2015. (The government's removal of VAT on them was also a boon.) Even though print books were harder to come by than normal during the spring, some publishers had a good year overall. Bloomsbury, for example, had its highest first half results since 2008, and was able to repay roughly £700,000 to members of staff who took a pay cut to see the firm through the early phase of the pandemic. The end of the autumn restrictions in England did bring good news for booksellers, though: *The Bookseller* magazine reported a 'pre-Christmas bonanza' as more shops re-opened and shoppers emerged.

The other creative industries, however, took a battering. Cinemas and theatres alike had to shut in the spring and while some cinemas were able to reopen briefly over the summer, the autumn COVID-19 restrictions were an unfortunate end to a bad year. It is likely some will not open up again, although there was some good news in December 2020 for those towns and cities with Cineworld venues: it was announced that these would reopen in the UK in March 2021, earlier than anticipated when in October 2020 it was announced that they would all close temporarily.

One of the biggest unknowns going forward will be the impact of home screening options, which allow us to watch films at home via the TV or on computer. Prior to the pandemic, services such as Netflix, Amazon Prime, and Sky Box Office had (broadly speaking) co-existed with standard cinema offerings, although the more traditional film establishment had been rather lukewarm towards Netflix-originated films when it came to awards season (see the reaction to Alfonso Cuarón's 2019 film, *Roma*, often because such productions aired on the TV at the same time as they were released into cinemas, thereby reducing revenue. Again, restrictions imposed due to the pandemic sped up the pace of change. Although some box office blockbusters were been held back so that they could appear on (literal) big screens first – most notably *No Time to Die*, Daniel Craig's final outing as James Bond, which is now expected to appear in October 2021 (and the postponement of which forced Cineworld's hand in the same month of 2020) – many were just being streamed first (as was the case with Disney's reboot of *Mulan*). More worryingly for cinema chains, in early December 2020, HBO Max in the US announced that it would stream many of Warner Bros'. 2021 titles at no extra cost to existing subscribers for one month: given that these films include a raft of productions that could well be the highlight of any other year by themselves – such as *Wonder Woman 1984*, *Matrix 4* and *Dune* – cinema chains have every right to be worried. At the time of writing, it is probable that these films will be streamed in the UK at the same time.

Exercising at home was another area of growth in 2020, given the complex patchwork of closures and reopenings of gyms and recreational facilities across the UK since March, not to mention concerns about social distancing and hygiene precautions. Classes of all types switched to Zoom, free sessions were available on YouTube and sales of equipment soared. As a BBC article explained, road bikes and exercise bikes enjoyed a healthy uplift in sales during the spring. Perhaps one of the highest-profile home exercise regimes was Peloton, which offered a range of live-streamed or on-demand classes, some using a branded stationary bike or treadmill. Peloton is, to put it bluntly, not cheap: at the time of writing, the 'original' bike costs £1,750 alone, and then users need to factor in £39 per month for classes (cheaper alternatives, not including the bike, are also available). The cost didn't seem to put people off, however: in September 2020, the company announced that it had doubled its membership numbers at the end of June, and now had over 3 million – twice as many as the same time in 2019. The increase in subscribers meant that revenue was now in excess of $600m (over £400m), and the company was on track to make a profit for the first time. Supply-chain issues meant there was a backlog in getting some hardware to new customers, but as a long winter beckoned, exercising at home is an attractive option for many at the moment.

The popularity of meal kits also soared during 2020, as people's shopping and eating habits changed. Hello Fresh was a key player in this market: customers could buy ingredients and a set of cooking instructions for meals of varying sizes and types (to suit their household), all of which was delivered to their home. As *The Financial Times* reported in November 2020, Hello Fresh doubled its revenues between July and September 2020: demand was up 120 per cent on the same time last year, and the German-owned company's sales reached €970m.

Competitors of all sizes were eager to take a bite of this particular cherry, however: the giant conglomerate Nestlé sank $950m into its acquisition of the US pre-prepared food chain, Freshly, while in the UK, the start-up Gousto went from strength to strength. In the first six months of 2020 it more than matched its 2019 total revenues of £83m, it announced plans to double its workforce to 2,000 by 2022 and secured another £25m of investment from some of its existing backers, bringing the total investment in the business to £155m.

Perhaps the most surprising trend of the spring restrictions across the UK was that alcohol sales *fell*: according to a report released by Nielsen Datatrack in September 2020, volume fell from 2 billion litres in 2019 for the seventeen weeks up to 11 July to 1.3 billion in 2020. Clearly much of this can be ascribed to licensed premises having to close their doors during that time. People were very much at liberty to drink at home, though, and supermarket alcohol sales during this period were in excess of £7.5bn. Beer, cider, wine and spirits all rose in popularity during the first lockdown but it will probably come as no surprise that Champagne sales were lacking in fizz, tumbling by £9m on last year.

In the spirit of necessity being the mother of invention, some of the UK's independent brewers and distillers diversified when lockdown hit. Aberdeen-based Brewdog, for example, started making hand sanitiser when national stocks ran low during the first wave of the pandemic; not to be outdone, a number of gin distilleries rallied to the cause and – from the Isle of Harris to West London – put their production facilities to a different use.

STRAPPED FOR CASH?

Paying by card became the norm in 2020. The news in early December that the Bank of England was rather hazy about the whereabouts of £50bn worth of banknotes, however, seemed to be taking this new approach to its very limits. (A vivid example in a *Guardian* article on this issue explained that the money was equivalent to an 800-mile-high stack of £5 notes.) The Public Accounts Committee at the House of Commons took a dim view, with its chair, Meg Hillier (MP for Hackney South and Shoreditch) saying that the Bank of England: '[needs] to be more concerned about where the missing £50bn is. Depending where it is and what it's being used for, that amount of money could have material implications for public policy and the public purse. The Bank needs to get a better handle on the national currency it controls.' The Bank replied that it was not the public's responsibility to explain where they stored or used their notes – at home, abroad or (probably the key issue) for illicit purposes – and thus the notes were not 'lost' at all.

Perhaps the wider issue here was access to cash. Even with a shift to digital payments, elderly people or those in more rural locations and on low incomes do still need to be able to withdraw money – many small businesses still trade in cash too – but the number of free cashpoints is falling. According to Which?, both NatWest and Barclays have each closed 500 branches since 2015, and TSB is expected to shut over 150 in 2021. By contrast, the number of cashpoints charging a fee rose by over 4,000, according to the Public Accounts Committee. The Treasury has published a report on expanding cash access and has committed to introduce legislation on this issue.

A WINTER'S TALE

As 2020 stumbled to a close, there was at last some good news in the form of three potential vaccines for coronavirus. Work began on them in the spring, and partly thanks to the fact crucial testing phases ran in parallel rather than sequentially it meant they were able to get to market in ten months rather than ten years. The first out of the blocks was created by Pfizer and the German company BioNTech: the UK was the first country in the world to approve its use, and vaccinations began on 8 December 2020: rather splendidly, the second person to receive the vaccine – following 91-year-old Margaret Keenan, at University Hospital, Coventry – shared a name with that icon of the Midlands, William Shakespeare. Also, under consideration by the Medicines and Healthcare products Regulatory Agency (MHRA) was a vaccine produced by the US firm Moderna, and one produced in a joint effort between Oxford University and AstraZeneca. While BioNTech was first, the Oxford option has attracted a good deal of attention in the UK, quite understandably, although there has been some confusion about its efficacy and correct dosing requirements. From a business perspective, AstraZeneca won plaudits for saying it would not make a profit on the vaccine while the pandemic lasted, although it is not yet known how that would be quantified.

AstraZeneca is a British/Swedish multinational company, its UK roots stretching back to the world's first chemical company, ICI. It is a key player in an important industry both nationally and globally: while recent UK figures are hard to come by – even the facts and figures featured on the website Association of the British Pharmaceutical Industry only go up to 2016/17 – the global statistics are staggering. Projected global spending on medicines by 2024 was $1.6 trillion, while the projected 2019 revenue for just one drug – Opdivo, manufactured by Bristol–Myers Squibb – was $3.6bn.

Given these numbers, 'Big Pharma' is a commonly used pejorative group name for these huge businesses, and there have certainly been instances in the past where outcomes have been very far from ideal. However, the way in which the industry – and its collaborators in academia – have pulled together in the face of threat to life as we know it, has been nothing short of jaw-dropping. If the biggest lesson we can take from 2020 is that knowledge, expertise and collaboration can make a genuine difference, then perhaps the year won't have been in vain after all.

CLASSICAL MUSIC AND OPERA
Leonora Dawson-Bowling

The classical 2019–20 season was one of two halves: the first half rich with musical events and then all venues suddenly closing in mid-March as a result of COVID-19 and related restrictions. By July and the end of the season, some organisations were just starting to reassemble in small ways to put on outdoor or streamed performances.

ANNIVERSARIES
The season saw continued celebrations of the 150th anniversary of Berlioz's death along with significant anniversaries of Barbara Strozzi, Jacques Offenbach and Clara Schumann. Mieczysław Weinberg's centenary continued to be observed with BBC Proms performances of his String Quartet No. 7 along with the London premieres of his Cello Concerto and Symphony No. 3, and Wigmore Hall launched a cycle of his 17 string quartets, programmed alongside works by Shostakovich.

With 2020 came the 250th anniversary of Beethoven's birth, which brought about a vast number of concerts and series from all the major venues, orchestras, choirs and opera companies: everything from symphony cycles and concertos to stagings and concert performances of his opera *Fidelio*, to intimate chamber concerts and vocal works, as well as a several exhibitions and talks. Of particular note was a complete symphonic cycle weekend at the Barbican and then at the Sage Gateshead, a collaboration between five major UK orchestras. Beethoven's rarely performed oratorio *Christ on the Mount of Olives* was also programmed (separately) by the London Symphony Orchestra, Royal Northern Sinfonia and the Hallé. In London the Philharmonia and in Cardiff the BBC National Orchestra of Wales combined with the Welsh National Opera Orchestra replicated Beethoven's 1808 four-hour epic 'Akademie' concert, which included his fifth and sixth symphonies, *Piano Concerto No. 4* and *Choral Fantasy*. The Royal Scottish National Orchestra's 'Beethoven Revolution' programmed a number of 'era-defining' Beethoven symphonies, concertos, chamber and solo works alongside music by later composers who created musical revolutions in their own right. The London Symphony Orchestra also paired Beethoven works with those of Berg and Tippett.

The Academy of St Martin-in-the-Fields celebrated its 60th birthday with a gala concert at the Queen Elizabeth Hall. The Philharmonia started its 75th birthday celebrations with a programme of music from its founding year (1945) and the CBSO embarked on the first season of its two-year-long centenary celebrations.

OTHER HIGHLIGHTS
Wigmore Hall's season focused on Haydn's quartets, piano works, chamber music and songs as well as 'three Bs': Beethoven, Brahms and Britten. The Barbican's 'Bach: A Beautiful Mind' also explored the genius of Bach in a weekend featuring talks along with performances of *The Musical Offering*, *The Art of Fugue* and his solo cantatas.

The City of Birmingham Symphony Orchestra set out to perform a number of the choral masterpieces associated with Birmingham (although many were cancelled after lockdown was introduced in March) and the London Philharmonic also presented a rich seam of choral works including Verdi's *Requiem*, Elgar's *The Apostles*, Mahler's *'Resurrection' Symphony*, Walton's *Belshazzar's Feast* and Fauré's *Requiem*.

The Philharmonia's Russian theme was led by Principal Guest Conductor Santtu-Matias Rouvali who conducted works by Tchaikovsky, Prokofiev, Stravinsky and Rachmaninov while the London Symphony Orchestra's Principal Guest Conductor Gianandrea Noseda delved further into Russian identity with works by Mussorgsky, Prokofiev, Rimsky-Korsakov and Tchaikovsky, and continued his Shostakovich symphony cycle. Shostakovich's symphonic output was also taken up by the Royal Scottish National Orchestra along with that of Rachmaninov.

The London Symphony Orchestra presented many of Béla Bartók's works 75 years on from his death. The orchestra's Principal Guest Conductor François-Xavier Roth paired ballet works with contrasting pieces by the composer's contemporaries. And although Sir Simon Rattle's major Bartók concerts were cancelled due to coronavirus, LSO St Luke's had earlier played host to a number of Bartók string quartet performances. The LSO under Sir John Eliot Gardiner also investigated Czech roots with two concerts that brought together works by composers who defined the 'Czech sound' and drew their material from their country's history, legends and landscapes: Janáček, Dvořák and Suk.

The LSO's exploration of British identity and origins, in programmes pairing Vaughan Williams symphonies with Tippett, Britten and Elgar led by Sir Mark Elder and Sir Antonio Pappano, were also cut short by COVID-19 restrictions. However, the London Philharmonic Orchestra did complete their 2019 'Isle of Noises' celebration of works inspired by the British Isles including 'the first great English opera' Purcell's *Dido and Aeneas*, Elgar's *Cello Concerto*, rarely performed pieces such as Alwyn's harp concerto *Lyra Angelica* and Foulds' piano concerto *Dynamic Triptych*, British film music, and works by Bax, Britten, Butterworth, Handel, Holst, Vaughan Williams and Walton.

The Philharmonia's Mahler focus was also obliterated by COVID-19 restrictions but not before a compelling performance of *Symphony No. 2* ('The Resurrection' symphony) under Principal Guest Conductor Jakub Hrůša. The Royal Liverpool Philharmonic Orchestra likewise had the conclusion of their Mahler symphony cycle under Vasily Petrenko cut somewhat short but Mahler also featured in the Royal Scottish National Orchestra's 'The Golden Age of Vienna' thread which saw his works paired with Richard Strauss tone poems under Music Director Thomas Søndergård.

One Bournemouth Symphony Orchestra highlight was a mixed-media performance, 'Weimar Connections', which featured the UK premiere of Liszt's rarely performed *Vor hundert Jahren* (originally written for a Schiller festival in Weimar) alongside works by Hummel and Richard Strauss, who also had strong associations with the German city. Esa-Pekka Salonen and the Philharmonia's 'Weimar Berlin: Bittersweet Metropolis' series explored the music, culture and politics of Germany during the Weimar Republic, a politically turbulent and explosively creative period, with performances of Weill, Hindemith and Berg, a concert of cabaret songs and a screening of 1927 expressionist film *Metropolis* with live orchestral accompaniment.

The 'roaring twenties' featured for the Royal Northern Sinfonia who performed works by Barber, Copland, Milhaud, Martinů, Gershwin, Korngold, Beach and Walton, and likewise for the City of Birmingham Symphony Orchestra as part their centenary celebrations. Meanwhile the London Philharmonic Orchestra's '2020 Vision' series explored works that have defined the sound of the 21st century paired with influential works composed exactly 100 or 200 years earlier, and the London Sinfonietta's parallel 'Sound across a Century' series explored the influence of the 20th century's fast-changing culture on 21st-century composition. The London Symphony Orchestra also introduced an exploration of significant works from the latter half of the 20th century to the present day, programming works by Berio, Ligeti, Lera Auerbach, Sofia Gubaidulina, Elizabeth Ogonek, Kaija Saariaho, Michael Tilson Thomas and Jörg Widmann, with a particular focus on Michael Tippett's post-war works. The opening nights featured Colin Matthews' *Violin Concerto*, Walton's *Symphony No. 1*, Messiaen's *Éclairs sur l'Au-delà*, a work for over 120 musicians which melded together the composer's fascination with Roman Catholic theology and ornithology, and the world premiere of *Antisphere* by Emily Howard, whose influences include geometry, magnetism and the brain's neural networks. This performance also formed part of the Barbican's 'Life Rewired' season which featured several other Barbican-commissioned works performed by the Britten Sinfonia and BBC Symphony Orchestra.

The Barbican also mounted two 'Total Immersion' days into the works of contemporary German composer Detlev Glanert and Swedish composer Anders Hillborg, and Wigmore Hall celebrated the 70th birthday of South African composer Kevin Volans with a concert and a study day. The Southbank Centre partnered with BBC Radio 3 for several 'Unclassified Live' concerts, traversing a range of eclectic sounds, from ambient soundscapes to contemporary compositions and experimental electronic music, also forming part of the Southbank's 'Contemporary Edit' thread. The Southbank also hosted four performances by the Colin Currie Group of Steve Reich's *Drumming* in the Hayward Gallery, the site of its European premiere in 1972. And the BBC National Orchestra of Wales presented a new strand of concerts, 'CoLaboratory', exploring surprising and experimental collaborations, fusing the musical worlds of American rap and Australian didgeridoo, among others, with the sound of the orchestra.

Performers and venues continued to look for opportunities to engage with new audiences. The BBC Symphony Orchestra presented its first ever 'Family Total Immersion', inspired by the 50th anniversary of the Moon landing. The City of Birmingham Symphony Orchestra programmed 30 concerts for children and young people, along with extensive education and community plans, and discounted concert tickets from £6. The Young Barbican scheme likewise offered thousands of discounted tickets to 14–25-year-olds. London Sinfonietta continued its ongoing learning project exploring the basics of how to compose, perform and listen to new music in the classroom, and its 'Sound Out 2020' concert was the culmination of a season of collaborations with schools and music hubs. The BBC Scottish Symphony Orchestra brought back its flagship classical music education project 'BBC Ten Pieces' which included interactive jam sessions for early years and primary school children, orchestral coaching for young musicians, accessible introductions to classical pieces and teacher CPDs based on delivering 'BBC Ten Pieces' resources in classrooms. The London Philharmonic launched a series of free concerts featuring the 'talent of tomorrow' including musicians and composers nurtured through LPO's Education and Community programmes. The Southbank Centre's new 'Encounters' initiative also offered free tickets to classical newcomers and the opportunity to attend concerts with famous musicians.

FESTIVALS

The 2019 BBC Proms played host to more than 90 concerts in eight weeks. The festival celebrated 50 years since Apollo 11 landed on the Moon with works imagining and creating the sound of space including Holst's *The Planets*, the UK premiere of Anna Thorvaldsdottir's *Metacosmos* – a musical

metaphor for falling into a black hole, the world premiere of Zosha Di Castri's *Long Is The Journey, Short Is The Memory* along with the orchestration of Public Service Broadcasting's concept album *The Race For Space* – a mix of music and broadcast recordings portraying the tale of the US–Russian space race. There was also a sci-fi film music prom with scores from cult space and sci-fi films, including Steve Price's *Gravity* and Mica Levi's *Under The Skin*. The Earth also featured in a second strand exploring our roles as guardians of our planet with works including John Luther Adams's *In The Name of the Earth*, a landscape-inspired choral work with four community choirs (over 600 singers), and the world premiere of Hans Zimmer's *Earth*. There was also a season-wide survey of well-loved and lesser-known violin concertos and in the bicentenary year of Queen Victoria's birth, a performance by Stephen Hough of Mendelssohn's *Piano Concerto No. 1* on Queen Victoria's very own piano in conjunction with songs written by Prince Albert. The proms also celebrated Sir James MacMillan in his 60th birthday year and other points of note included Karina Canellakis becoming the first woman to conduct the First Night of the Proms and the proms debut of the Shanghai Symphony Orchestra.

Sir James MacMillan celebrations also featured in the major festival of his native Scotland. The 2019 Edinburgh International Festival featured five concerts of MacMillan works including his organ concerto *A Scotch Bestiary*, his concerto for orchestra *Woman of the Apocalypse*, chamber work *Fourteen Little Pictures*, *Symphony No 2* conducted by MacMillan himself, his recent oratorio *All the Hills and Vales Along* and the world premiere of his fifth symphony *Le grand inconnu* – a major choral symphony performed by the Scottish Chamber Orchestra with The Sixteen, conducted by Harry Christophers. The Los Angeles Philharmonic, celebrating their centenary year, was the resident company at the festival with Music Director Gustavo Dudamel. The orchestra took part in a number of youth initiatives during its residency and gave performances including the European premiere of John Adams' new work *Must the Devil Have All the Good Tunes?* with pianist Yuja Wang and Mahler's *Symphony No. 2* with the Edinburgh Festival Chorus. The chorus also performed in MacMillan's *Quickening* with the Royal Scottish National Orchestra, Elgar's *The Kingdom* with the Hallé, and Britten's *War Requiem* with the Orchestre de Paris.

The Huddersfield Contemporary Music Festival packed more than 60 events and 50 premieres (including 26 world premieres) into its 10-day schedule. Building programmes around Swedish Composer-in-Residence Hanna Hartman, whose music is concerned with domestic minutiae, reinventing the household objects and collected clutter of our lives as music waiting to happen, the festival saw 'subtle, low-key innovations from many of modern music's most daring artists': a performance of Ann Cleare's music allowed audiences to become a part of the music's interactive spaces, Naomi Pinnock's work tied sound to where, when and how it was experienced, and the long-delayed festival performance of Frank Denyer's ambitious 1990s work *The Fish that became the Sun* for 37 musicians playing around 80 instruments across different tuning and intonation systems. Jenny Hval's new music theatre work *The Practice of Love* considered our intimate relationship with language while experimental musician and visual artist Christine Sun Kim contemplated what we can learn about sound from those who cannot hear it and how it may be held captive by capitalism. Improvisations were woven through the festival programme along with some unusual instruments. The most notable were Seth Parker Woods' ice cello, which honoured the legacy of its inventor, 1960s musical absurdist Charlotte Moorman, the cello melting as it was played, and an ondes Martenot performed by virtuoso Nadia Ratsimandresy, who customised this already rather singular

20th-century invention to incorporate real-time electronics. The festival also called for applications from young curators with a view to developing talent and leadership for music programmers, promoters and curators of the future.

In 2020, the Aldeburgh Festival was cancelled due to COVID-19 but presented an online celebration of past highlights and a series of podcasts, articles and social media projects, much of it sourced from a new interactive website project 'Festival Memories'. Here members of the public were encouraged to contribute their impressions and memories of the Aldeburgh Festival over its 72 years with a view to building a long-term archive.

Garsington Opera likewise had to cancel their festival but put on a late semi-staged performance of Beethoven's *Fidelio* as restrictions eased towards the end of the summer. Longborough Festival Opera likewise cancelled but would later put on a short run of performances of Leoncavallo's *I Pagliacci* in the winter. Grange Park Opera meanwhile broadcast 15 live performances to online audiences only, entitling them 'The Found Season', with themes they felt reflected the current situation such as 'Reflection' (with a performance of Schumann's *Liederkreis*), 'Anguish' (represented in Francis Poulenc's *La Voix Humaine* and Dominick Argento's *Miss Havisham's Wedding Night*) and 'Joy' (a recital by Wynne Evans), all building to a performance by 23 strings, safely distanced, of *Metamorphosen*, which Richard Strauss wrote while mourning the loss of culture during the Second World War. The Grange Festival opted to put on an outdoor in-person 'promenade' production – a sequence of performances by singers, players, actors and dancers – entitled 'Precipice', and Glyndebourne likewise staged several outdoor concerts and performances of Offenbach's *In the Market for Love*.

The Cheltenham Music Festival replaced its live performances with their 'Replay' celebration: an online series of videos (including films about premieres by the Ligeti quartet, past performances, and discussions on music careers and community work), podcasts (world premieres featuring Jonathan Dove, Judith Weir and John Tavener), playlists and Radio 3 recordings of past concerts.

In lieu of their usual festival, Buxton International Festival announced the 'BIF Digital 2020': a series of recorded interviews with special guests were released at 4pm each day of the festival including stage director Jacopo Spirei, composer Kate Whitley, librettist Laura Attridge, Buxton Opera House CEO Paul Kerryson and conductor Wyn Davies discussing a range of music topics such as the future of the arts post-COVID-19. The series also featured previously recorded performances including a selection from Dame Sarah Connolly and Mozart's *Piano Concerto No. 12* from Omer Meir Wellber and the BBC Philharmonic.

COVID-19 RESPONSE

In March 2020, all venues had to close and musicians were not able to perform publicly. A combination of great enterprise and partially eased restrictions did then lead to interesting alternatives, in a bid to keep spirits up, to connect people and music, where possible – with donations and ticket sales – to keep organisations and musicians financially afloat, and to preserve the arts. These ideas included: musicians recording parts on video at home which were then edited together to create complete performances, then streamed or broadcast to audiences; radio presenters broadcasting from home (including Radio 3's 'breakfast singalong' which encouraged the nation to sing songs to Anna Tilbrook's live accompaniment from their own homes); live-streamed performances – at the forefront of which were the Wigmore Hall and Radio 3 lunchtime solo recitals from the likes of Stephen Hough, Ailish Tynan and Roderick Williams who performed to the empty hall but were streamed and broadcast to a live audience; and new engaging

podcasts such as 'Choral Chihuahua' from *The Sixteen*'s Eamonn Dougan and Harry Christophers and *I Fagiolini*'s Robert Hollingworth. Interesting trends included more chamber music concerts (where social distancing was easier than larger groups), greater reach to audiences outside the concert hall and around the globe, more outdoor concerts and shorter programmes with no interval (reflecting both online concentration spans and an attempt to avoid audience mingling at intervals at live concerts when they restarted).

OBITUARIES

Jonathan Goldstein, who composed for the Royal Shakespeare Company, film, television and advertising campaigns, died aged 50 in a plane crash along with his wife, Hannah Marcinowicz, 36, a saxophonist who worked with many of the UK's leading orchestras. Italian operatic tenor Marcello Giordani, who sang in around 250 performances at the New York Met, particularly Verdi and Puccini, died aged 56. Composer Barrington Pheloung, remembered particularly for his scores to films *Truly, Madly, Deeply* and *Hilary and Jackie*, and series *Inspector Morse*, died aged 65.

Organist and conductor Stephen Cleobury, who was Music Director at King's College Cambridge for 37 years, leading the annually broadcast 'Nine Lessons and Carols' and who hugely influenced the choral world with his work, died aged 70. Neo-Romantic composer Christopher Rouse, who won the 1993 Pulitzer Prize for his Trombone Concerto, and Jane Parker-Smith, organist and campaigner for musicians' pay, also died aged 70. Composer Dmitri Smirnov, who co-founded Russia's Association for Contemporary Music then relocated to London after being blacklisted in his homeland for taking part in Western festivals, died aged 71. Peter Serkin, pianist and founder of the Tashi Quartet, died at 72. American operatic soprano Jessye Norman, who transcended race boundaries to sing roles from Purcell's Dido to Strauss's Salome with an almost elemental force, died aged 74. Roger Scruton, social thinker, moral commentator and author of several books on the philosophy of music, died aged 75. Organist Jennifer Bate, known best for her interpretations of Messiaen, died at 75. Conductor Mariss Jansons, particularly renowned for his Mahler, Tchaikovsky and Richard Strauss interpretations, died aged 76. American cellist Lynn Harrell died at 76. Harpsichordist, pianist and Baroque specialist Elizabeth de la Porte, who taught generations of juniors at the Royal College of Music for 55 years, died aged 78. American cellist and advocate of new music André Emelianoff died aged 78. Clifford Bartlett, prolific music editor and publisher in the 1980s and 1990s, died aged 79.

Mezzo-soprano Irina Bogacheva, one of the leading soloists at the Mariinksy Theatre, and pianist Hamish Milne, who made more than 200 recordings and championed several lesser-known composers, both died aged 80. Reinbert de Leeuw, the Dutch pianist, conductor and composer with a great passion for complex musical language, died aged 81. Charles Wuorinen, the youngest composer to receive the Pulitzer Prize (in 1962) and a man who was unafraid to push the boundaries of modern composition, also died at 81. Composer Nikolai Kapustin, championed by pianists Steven Osborne and Marc-André Hamelin, died aged 82. Mary Christie, devoted chatelaine of the Glyndebourne festival and daughter-in-law of the festival's founders, died aged 83. Peter Schreier, the East German tenor famous for his lieder interpretations, Mozart operas and Bach cantatas and oratorios, and later as a conductor specialising in Bach, Mozart and Haydn, died aged 84. Italian soprano Mirella Freni and Georgian composer Giya Kancheli also died aged 84. Likewise Harry Kupfer, who directed operas at the Bayreuth and Salzburg festivals and, for 20 years, at Berlin's Komische Oper. Herbert Chappell, composer and producer for television adverts and films, and opera director

Jonathan Miller, who created productions for ENO and Glyndebourne among others, died aged 85. Dutch cellist Anner Bylsma, a key member of the Dutch Baroque School, famous for his Bach cello suite recordings, also died aged 85. Polish composer Krzysztof Penderecki, whose 'modernist' music successfully attracted wider audiences and who later embraced a more Romantic style, died aged 86. John Poole, who conducted BBC Symphony Chorus before becoming Director of the BBC Singers for 17 years, also died at 86. French composer, conductor and pianist Roger Boutry, who worked at the Paris Conservatoire for 35 years, died aged 87. Anthony Hedges, composer and former chairman of the Composers' Guild of Great Britain, American operatic soprano Elinor Ross, and harpsichordist and organist Kenneth Gilbert, who produced new editions of François Couperin and Domenico Scarlatti, all died aged 88. Likewise Barry Tuckwell, the Australian horn player with a legacy of more than 50 solo recordings who commissioned works, now horn staples, from Oliver Knussen, Thea Musgrave and Richard Rodney Bennett among others. Mady Mesplé, one of the leading coloratura sopranos of her generation, died aged 89.

Rosalind Elias, the mezzo-soprano who originated the role of Erika in Barber's *Vanessa* at the New York Met, died at 90. Pianist Paul Badura-Skoda, known for his prolific recordings of Mozart, Beethoven and Schubert, and violinist Ida Haendel, whose career spanned seven decades and who played in 69 BBC Proms, both died aged 91. Composer Ennio Morricone, particularly famous for his film scores including the 'Spaghetti Westerns', also died at 91. Conductor, harpsichordist and composer, Raymond Leppard, a key figure in the revival of Italian Baroque opera, died aged 92. Hungarian pianist Márta Kurtág, known to the public most of all through her duo performances with husband György Kurtág for some 60 years, also died at 92.

American composer Ben Johnston, who developed microtonal music to create a large and varied set of compositions, and cellist Martin Lovett, the last surviving member of the Amadeus Quartet, both died aged 93. Joan Benson, American champion of the clavichord who played a major part in reviving CPE Bach, died aged 94. Rolando Panerai, one of Italy's most in-demand baritones, and Gabriel Bacquier, one of the great recitalists and opera baritones of the 20th century, both died aged 95. Likewise John Tooley, General Director at the Royal Opera House for 18 years who campaigned for arts funding, advocated affordable tickets and set up collaborative cost-saving initiatives between opera houses. Gerard Schurmann, composer and arranger of concert and film works, died at 96 and American pianist and teacher Abbey Simon died aged 99. Sid Ramin, composer and arranger of many Broadway shows including Bernstein and Sondheim, died aged 100.

NEW APPOINTMENTS AND HONOURS

2019–20 was Omer Meir Wellber's first season as the BBC Philharmonic's Chief Conductor and Maxim Emelyanychev's first as Principal Conductor of the Scottish Chamber Orchestra. Antony Hermus and Dalia Stasevska took up the role of Principal Guest Conductor at Opera North and the BBC Symphony Orchestra respectively. Anna-Maria Helsing was announced as new Principal Guest Conductor of the BBC Concert Orchestra. The Royal Liverpool Philharmonic announced the appointment of Domingo Hindoyan as Chief Conductor from September 2021 at which point Vasily Petrenko will become Conductor Laureate. The BBC National Orchestra of Wales announced the appointment of new Principal Guest Conductor Ryan Bancroft and new Director Lisa Tregale, and the Philharmonia announced the appointment of Alexander Van Ingen as Chief Executive. English National Opera announced the appointment of Annilese Miskimmon as Artistic Director and the Royal Philharmonic Orchestra announced a new five-year partnership with the Royal Albert Hall, becoming the venue's official Associate Orchestra.

In the New Year's and Queen's Birthday Honours (the latter delayed due to COVID-19), conductor Donald Runnicles and broadcaster Humphrey Burton were knighted. Timothy Walker, Chief Executive and Artistic Director of the London Philharmonic Orchestra, and composer Errollyn Wallen received CBEs. OBEs were awarded to composer Judith Bingham, oboist Nicholas Daniel, composer Sally Beamish, tenor John Mark Ainsley, conductor Jan Latham, and Cathryn Graham, Director of Music at the British Council. MBEs were awarded to cellist Sheku Kanneh-Mason, composer Helen Grime, violinist Jennifer Pike, conductor Stephen Layton, timpanist Paul Philbert and Martin McHale, conductor of the City of Cardiff Symphony Orchestra.

COMPETITIONS

In 2019, the Wigmore Hall/Independent Opera International Song Competition was won by Russian bass-baritone Mikhail Timoshenko while the other prizes were all claimed by British musicians: Second Prize was awarded to soprano Harriet Burns, Third Prize to mezzo-soprano Beth Taylor and Pianist's Prize to Michael Pandya.

Grange Festival's International Singing Competition was won by Kiandra Howarth and Second Prize was jointly awarded to soprano Samantha Clarke and mezzo-soprano Claire Barnett-Jones.

In 2020 many competitions were cancelled and postponed due to COVID-19. However, the end of 2020 saw the Handel Singing Competition resume with baritones Jerome Knox and Morgan Pearse taking First Prize and Second Prize respectively. Morgan Pearse also jointly won the Audience Prize with soprano Jessica Cale.

Jessica Cale also won the postponed Kathleen Ferrier Award, while sopranos Ella Taylor and Milly Forrest won the Second Prize and Song Prize respectively, and the Accompanist's Prize was awarded to Hamish Brown.

OPERA PRODUCTIONS

The list below summarises each opera company's activities. The date in parentheses indicates the year that the current production entered their repertory. 'CC' indicates where live performances were cancelled or postponed before the first performance due to COVID-19 restrictions.

ROYAL OPERA
Founded 1946
W www.roh.org.uk
REPERTORY: *Don Giovanni* (2014), *Werther* (2004), *Die Zauberflöte* (2003), *Otello* (2017), *La traviata* (1994), *La bohème* (2017).
NEW PRODUCTIONS: *Agrippina* (Handel). Conductor, Maxim Emelyanychev; director, Barrie Kosky. Joyce DiDonato (Agrippina), Gianluca Buratto (Claudio), Franco Fagioli (Nerone), Iestyn Davies (Ottone), Lucy Crowe (Poppea), Andrea Mastroni (Pallante), Eric Jurenas (Narciso), José Coca Loza (Lesbo).
Don Pasquale (Donizetti). Conductor, Evelino Pidò; director, Damiano Michieletto. Bryn Terfel (Don Pasquale), Mariusz Kwiecień (Docteur Malatesta), Ioan Hotea (Ernesto), Olga Peretyatko (Norina).
Death in Venice (Britten). Conductor, Mark Elder; director, David McVicar. Mark Padmore (Gustav von Aschenbach), Gerald Finley (Traveller/Elderly fop/Old gondolier/Hotel manager/Hotel barber/Leader of the players/Voice of Dionysus), Tim Mead (Voice of Apollo).

Alice's Adventures Under Ground (Gerald Barry). Conductor, Thomas Adès/Finnegan Downie Dear; director, Antony McDonald. Jennifer France/Claudia Boyle (Alice), Allison Cook/Clare Presland (Red Queen/Queen of Hearts), Hilary Summers/Carole Wilson (White Queen/Dormouse), Nicky Spence/Sam Furness (White King/Mad Hatter), Peter Tantsits/Robert Murray (March Hare/Tweedledee), Stephen Richardson/Mark Stone (White Knight/Cheshire Cat), Alan Ewing/Joshua Bloom (Red Knight/Humpty Dumpty).

Fidelio (Beethoven). Conductor, Antonio Pappano; director, Tobias Kratzer. Lise Davidsen (Leonore), Jonas Kaufmann/David Butt Philip (Florestan), Simon Neal (Don Pizarro), Georg Zeppenfeld (Rocco), Amanda Forsythe (Marzelline), Robin Tritschler (Jaquino), Egils Silins (Don Fernando).

CC: *Jenůfa* (Janáček), *The Turn of the Screw* (Britten), *Elektra* (Strauss), *Cavalleria rusticana* (Mascagni), *Pagliacci* (Leoncavallo), *Tristan und Isolde* (Wagner), *Lucia di Lammermoor* (Donizetti), *Madama Butterfly* (Puccini), *Don Carlo* (Verdi), *Tosca* (Puccini).

ENGLISH NATIONAL OPERA
Founded 1931
W www.eno.org
The English National Opera focused its season on the tale of Orpheus retold by different composers.
REPERTORY: *The Mikado* (1986), *Carmen* (2012), *Madam Butterfly* (2005).
NEW PRODUCTIONS: *Orpheus and Eurydice* (Gluck). Conductor, Harry Bicket; director, Wayne McGregor. Alice Coote (Orfeo/Orphée), Soraya Mafi (Amore/Amour), Sarah Tynan (Euridice/Eurydice).

Orpheus in the Underworld (Offenbach). Conductor, Sian Edwards/Valentina Peleggi; director, Emma Rice. Ed Lyon (Orphée), Mary Bevan (Eurydice), Alex Otterburn (Aristée/Pluton), Willard White/Robert Hayward (Jupiter), Lucia Lucas (L'Opinion Publique), Anne-Marie Owens (Junon), Keel Watson (Mars), Ellie Laugharne (Cupidon), Idunnu Münch (Diane), Alan Oke (John Styx).

The Mask of Orpheus (Harrison Birtwistle). Conductor, Martyn Brabbins; director, Daniel Kramer. Peter Hoare (Orpheus the Man), Daniel Norman (Orpheus the Myth/Hades), Yamoussa Bangoura (Orpheus the Hero), Marta Fontanals-Simmons (Eurydice the Woman), Susan Bickley (Eurydice the Myth/Persephone), Alfa Marks (Eurydice the Hero), James Cleverton (Aristaeus the Man), Simon Bailey (Aristaeus the Myth/Charon), Leo Hedman (Aristaeus the Hero), Claron McFadden (The Oracle of the Dead/Hecate), Robert Hayward (The Caller).

Orphée (Philip Glass). Conductor, Geoffrey Paterson; director, Netia Jones. Nicholas Lester (Orphée), Sarah Tynan (Eurydice), Jennifer France (Princess), Nicky Spence (Heurtebise), Anthony Gregory (Cégeste), Clive Bayley (Juge/Commissaire), Simon Shibambu (Poet), Rachael Lloyd (Algaonice), William Morgan (Reporter).

Luisa Miller (Verdi). Conductor, Alexander Joel; director, Barbora Horáková Joly. James Creswell (Il Conte di Walter), David Junghoon Kim (Rodolfo), Christine Rice (Federica), Solomon Howard (Wurm), Elizabeth Llewellyn/Olafur Sigurdarson (Luisa Miller), Nadine Benjamin (Laura).

The Marriage of Figaro (Mozart). Conductor, Kevin John Edusei/James Henshaw; director, Joe Hill-Gibbins. Bažidar Smiljanić (Figaro), Louise Alder (Susanna), Andrew Shore (Bartolo), Susan Bickley (Marcellina), Hanna Hipp (Cherubino), Johnathan McCullough (Count Almaviva), Colin Judson (Don Basilio/Don Curzio), Elizabeth Watts (Countess Almaviva), Clive Bayley (Antonio), Rowan Pearce (Barbarina).
CC: *Rusalka* (Dvořák).

OPERA NORTH
Founded 1978
W www.operanorth.co.uk
REPERTORY: *Giulio Cesare* (2012), *La bohème* (1993), *The Marriage of Figaro* (2015), *The Turn of the Screw* (2010).
NEW PRODUCTIONS: *The Greek Passion* (Martinů). Conductor, Garry Walker; director, Christopher Alden. Nicky Spence (Manolios), Magdalena Molendowska (Katerina), Paul Nilon (Yannakos), Jeffrey Lloyd-Roberts (Panait), Stephen Gadd (Priest Grigoris), John Savournin (Priest Fotis), Richard Mosley-Evans (Kostandis), Lorna James (Lenio), Steven Page (Captain), Jonathan Best (Archon), Rhodri Prys Jones (Michelis), Alex Banfield (Nikolio), Ivan Sharpe (Schoolmaster), Jeremy Peaker (Father Ladas).

Street Scene (Weill). Conductor, James Holmes; director, Matthew Eberhardt. Giselle Allen (Anna Maurrant), Robert Hayward (Frank Maurrant), Gillene Butterfield (Rose Maurrant), Alex Banfield (Sam Kaplan), Miranda Bevin (Greta Fiorentino), Christopher Turner (Lippo Fiorentino), Claire Pascoe (Emma Jones), Richard Mosley-Evans (George Jones), Michelle Andrews (Mae Jones), Rodney Vubya (Dick Mcgann), Amy J Payne (Olga Olsen), John Savournin (Carl Olsen), Byron Jackson/Jo Servi (Henry Davis), Quirijn De Lang (Harry Easter), Stuart Laing (Daniel Buchanan), Dean Robinson (Abraham Kaplan), Laura Kelly-Mcinroy (Jennie Hildebrand).

SCOTTISH OPERA
Founded 1962
W www.scottishopera.org.uk
REPERTORY: *Tosca* (1980).
NEW PRODUCTIONS: *Breaking the Waves* (Missy Mazzoli). Conductor, Stuart Stratford; director, Tom Morris. Sydney Mancasola (Bess McNeill), Duncan Rock (Jan Nyman), Wallis Giunta (Dodo McNeill), Susan Bullock (Mother), Elgan Llŷr Thomas (Dr Richardson), Byron Jackson (Terry), Freddie Tong (Councilman).

Nixon in China (John Adams). Conductor, Joana Carneiro; director, John Fulljames. Eric Greene (Richard Nixon), Mark Le Brocq (Mao Tse-tung), Nicholas Lester (Chou En-lai), Julia Sporsén (Pat Nixon), David Stout (Henry Kissinger), Hye-Youn Lee (Chiang Ch'ing – Madame Mao), Louise Callinan (First Secretary to Mao), Sioned Gwen Davies (Second Secretary to Mao), Emma Carrington (Third Secretary to Mao).
OPERA IN CONCERT: *Zanetto* (Mascagni), *Susanna's Secret* (Wolf-Ferrari), *Iris* (Mascagni).
CC: *A Midsummer Night's Dream* (Britten), *The Gondoliers* (Sullivan).

WELSH NATIONAL OPERA
Founded 1946
W www.wno.org.uk
REPERTORY: *Rigoletto* (2002), *The Cunning Little Vixen* (1980).
NEW PRODUCTIONS: *Carmen* (Bizet). Conductor, Harry Ogg/Tianyi Lu/Andrew Greenwood; director, Jo Davies. Julia Mintzer (Carmen), Ross Ramgobin (Morales), Elin Pritchard (Micaela), Peter Auty (Don Jose), Henry Waddington/John Savournin (Zuniga), Haegee Lee (Frasquita), Angela Simkin (Mercedes), Giorgio Caoduro (Escamillo), Howard Kirk (Dancaire), Joe Roche (Remendado).

Les vêpres siciliennes (Verdi). Conductor, Carlo Rizzi/Gareth Jones; director, David Pountney. Jung Soo Yun (Henri), Anush Hovhannisyan (La Duchesse Hélène), Giorgio Caoduro (Guy De Montfort), Wojtek Gierlach (Jean Procida), Wyn Pencarreg (Le Sire De Béthune), Christine Byrne (Ninette), Robyn Lyn Evans (Daniéli/Mainfroid), Gareth Brynmor John (Robert), Alexander Sprague (Thibault), Alastair Moore (Le Comte de Vaudemont).
CC: *Bluebeard's Castle* (Bartók), *The Nightingale* (Stravinsky).

AWARDS

GRAMOPHONE AWARDS 2019
Concerto – Saint-Saëns *Piano Concertos Nos. 2 and 5*; Solo piano works: Bertrand Chamayou (piano); French National Orchestra / Emmanuel Krivine
Chamber – Debussy 'Les Trois Sonates – The Late Works': Magali Mosnier (flute), Isabelle Faust (violin), Antoine Tamestit (viola), Xavier de Maistre (harp), Jean-Guihen Queyras (cello), Alexander Melnikov, Javier Perianes, Tanguy de Williencourt (piano)
Choral – Buxtehude 'Abendmusiken': Ensemble Masques / Olivier Fortin; Vox Luminis / Lionel Meunier
Contemporary – Dean *Hamlet*: Allan Clayton (Hamlet), Barbara Hannigan (Ophelia), Sarah Connolly (Gertrude), Rod Gilfry (Claudius), Kim Begley (Polonius), John Tomlinson (Ghost of Old Hamlet), David Butt Philip (Laertes); Glyndebourne Chorus; London Philharmonic Orchestra / Vladimir Jurowski
Early Music – Cardoso *Requiem*; *Lamentations*; *Magnificat*; Motets: Cupertinos / Luís Toscano
Instrumental – 'The Berlin Recital': Yuja Wang (piano)
Opera – Halévy *La reine de Chypre*: Véronique Gens (Catarina Cornaro), Cyrille Dubois (Gérard de Coucy), Étienne Dupuis (Jacques de Lusignan), Éric Huchet (Mocénigo), Christophoros Stamboglis (Andréa Cornaro); Flemish Radio Choir; Paris Chamber Orchestra / Hervé Niquet
Orchestral – Langgaard *Symphonies Nos 2 and 6*: Anu Komsi (soprano); Vienna Philharmonic Orchestra / Sakari Oramo
Recital – Cavalli 'Ombra mai fu': Philippe Jaroussky (countertenor) with Emőke Baráth (soprano), Marie-Nicole Lemieux (contralto); Ensemble Artaserse
Solo Vocal – Schumann 'Frage': Christian Gerhaher (baritone), Gerold Huber (piano)

SPECIAL AWARDS
Artist of the Year – Víkingur Ólafsson
Concept Album – softLOUD by Sean Shilbe
Label of the Year – Pentatone
Lifetime Achievement – Emma Kirkby
Orchestra of the Year – Hong Kong Philharmonic Orchestra
Special Achievement – Birgit Nilsson Foundation
Young Artist of the Year – Jakub Józef Orliński

BBC MUSIC MAGAZINE AWARDS 2019
Orchestral – Korngold *Symphony in F sharp*; *Theme and Variations*; *Straussiana*: Sinfonia of London / John Wilson
Concerto – Dvořák *Piano Concerto in G minor*; Martinů *Piano Concerto No. 4, 'Incantation'*: Ivo Kahánek (piano); Bamberg Symphony Orchestra / Jakub Hrůša
Opera (Recording of the Year) – Purcell *King Arthur*: Anna Dennis, Mhairi Lawson, Rowan Pierce, Carolyn Sampson (sopranos), Jeremy Budd (high tenor), James Way (tenor), Roderick Williams (baritone), Ashley Riches (bass-baritone). Gabrieli Players / Paul McCreesh
Chamber – Veress: *String Trio*; Bartók: *Piano Quintet in C major*: Barnabás Kelemen, Vilde Frang (violins), Katalin Kokas (viola), Nicolas Altstaedt (violoncello), Alexander Lonquich (piano)
Choral – Gabriel Jackson *The Passion of our Lord Jesus Christ*: Emma Tring (soprano), Guy Cutting (tenor); Choir of Merton College, Oxford, Oxford Contemporary Sinfonia / Benjamin Nicholas
Vocal – Janáček *The Diary of One Who Disappeared*; *Nursery rhymes*; *Moravian folk poetry in songs*: Nicky Spence (tenor), Julius Drake (piano); Václava Housková (mezzo) et al; Victoria Samek (clarinet)
Instrumental – Andrey Gugnin – Shostakovich *24 Preludes, Op. 34*; *Piano Sonatas Nos 1 & 2*: Andrey Gugnin (piano)
BBC Music Magazine Personality of the Year – Jamie Barton (mezzo-soprano)

JURY AWARDS
Premiere – Edmund Finnis *The Air, Turning*: Eloisa-Fleur Thorn (violin), Mark Simpson (clarinet), Víkingur Ólafsson (piano), Benjamin Bellman (violin); BBC Scottish Symphony Orchestra, Birmingham Contemporary Music Group, London Contemporary Orchestra, Britten Sinfonia / Ilan Volkov, Richard Baker, Andrew Gourlay
DVD – Barber *Vanessa*: Emma Bell, Virginie Verrez, Edgaras Montvidas, Rosalind Plowright, Donnie Ray Albert (voices); The Glyndebourne Chorus; London Philharmonic Orchestra / Jakub Hrůša; Dir. Keith Warner (Glyndebourne, 2018)
Newcomer – Elicia Silverstein 'The Dreams and Fables I Fashion – Works by Bach, Berio, Biber, Pandolfi and Sciarrino': Elicia Silverstein (violin), Michele Pasotti (lute), Mauro Valli (cello)

ROYAL PHILHARMONIC SOCIETY AWARDS 2019
RPS Gold Medal – Sofia Gubaidulina
Gamechanger – Chineke!
Chamber-Scale Composition – Tansy Davies Cave
Concert Series & Events – The Cumnock Tryst
Conductor – Mirga Gražinytė-Tyla
Ensemble – Aurora Orchestra
Impact – BSO Change Makers and Resound
Instrumentalist – Alina Ibragimova
Large-Scale Composition – Rebecca Saunders Yes
Opera & Music Theatre – *Lady Macbeth of Mtsensk* – Birmingham Opera Company
Singer – Nina Stemme
Storytelling – *Michael Tippett: The Biography* – Oliver Soden
Young Artists – Castalian String Quartet

CONSERVATION

NATURAL ENVIRONMENT

Peter Marren

NATURE UNDER LOCKDOWN

Travel restrictions meant that far fewer people travelled abroad in 2020. One outcome of the spring lockdown was that we grew to know our home patch perhaps better than ever before. In the absence of heavy traffic and overhead planes we could hear birdsong and the hum of bees and felt closer to nature than usual. 'There is no salve quite like nature for an anxious mind', noted the Director of Kew Gardens (though his gardens were unfortunately closed). There was also a big increase in the use of natural history webcams. Beaches and places such as the Lake District and the New Forest received even more visitors than usual. The downside was an increase in litter, especially when those normally employed to clean up our messes were furloughed. There were also heathland fires caused by portable barbecues, including a bad one at Wareham Forest in Dorset, and outbreaks of vandalism.

The quiet and weeks of sunshine brought unusual sightings such as the wild goats leaving their clifftop home to wander the streets of Llandudno. There were reports of birds nesting in empty car parks, and of the first cuckoo heard in west London for twenty years. People gathered at harbours to watch dolphins and porpoises undisturbed by boat traffic. It was, however, a difficult year for conservation charities whose income from visitors was curtailed after most properties were closed. Their incomes were already under strain after the withdrawal of European funds, and further stretched by emergencies such as the flooding of autumn 2019 and ash dieback. The National Trust had to dispense with its education officers as it sought to seal a £200m hole in its finances. Plantlife laid off nearly a quarter of its staff. Collectively the Wildlife Trusts lost £10m every month. Conservation projects were placed in abeyance after employees were furloughed. The knock-on effects on wildlife will be significant.

HIGH SPEED TWO

In February 2020, the government approved the HS2 high-speed railway, both for the immediate London- Birmingham phase and its later stages to Manchester and Leeds. After a delay forced by protestors on environmental grounds, construction began in September. Tunnelling through the Chilterns will commence early in 2021. The costs of the project, which in 2010 were estimated at £30–36bn, have already spiralled to £80–88bn and may eventually top £100bn. Even if the project runs on time, the Manchester stage will not be complete until 2040.

HS2 is to be a low-carbon enterprise, using electric trains powered by renewables. The developers are also committed to a policy of 'no net loss' in biodiversity. All the same, construction will damage or destroy a great many wildlife habitats along the route. The Wildlife Trusts claim that the line and its associated works will pass through, or close to, five sites of international importance, 31 Sites of Special Scientific Interest (SSSIs), 693 'local wildlife sites' and 108 ancient woods, not to mention 18 Wildlife Trust nature reserves. It will also require the removal of many old hedges and disrupt roosts and hunting territories of bats and owls. There are concerns that the tunnelling and other works will affect the groundwater and chalk aquifers. HS2 ltd disputes all these figures.

In mitigation, HS2 ltd plans to plant millions of trees and create new habitats such as ponds within what it refers to as a 'green corridor'. It will also salvage soil from wildlife habitats in its path. The line will be crossed by 16 'green bridges' and numerous underpasses. The broad idea is that natural habitats lost during construction will be replaced by planting and landscaping. HS2's full ecological report runs to 55,000 pages. Even so, the Wildlife Trusts are unimpressed and believe that the no-net-loss policy is in fact unachievable. As *The Guardian* journalist Patrick Barkham expressed it, this is a project where 'natural destruction is smoothed over with plenty of tree-planting, newt ponds and nice green talk.'

EVER MORE AMBITIOUS TREE PLANTING TARGETS

In the General Election of 2019, all the main political parties made extravagant pledges to expand Britain's forests. The Conservatives promised to plant thirty million trees each year. The Liberal Democrats and Scottish Nationalist Party proposed to double that. The Green Party wishes to plant 700 million trees over the next ten years. Right out in front was the Labour Party which proposed to plant two *billion* trees by 2040. Their enthusiasm is shared by many environmentalists. Friends of the Earth would like to double Britain's tree cover by planting up 3 million hectares – an area one-and-a-half times the size of Wales. The Woodland Trust heads a consortium aiming to plant 50 million trees over the next 25 years to create a 'Northern Forest', stretching across the Pennines from Liverpool to Hull. The National Trust pledged to plant 20 million trees on its own properties in England and Wales at a cost of about £5 per tree.

The aim of all this planting is not to satisfy Britain's timber needs so much as amenity and carbon storage. The National Trust, for example, hopes to achieve net-zero carbon emissions in this way. Like all green plants, trees reduce the impact of climate change by removing carbon dioxide – the main greenhouse gas – from the atmosphere and storing it as wood: trunks, roots, branches. At present the world's forests store roughly 45 per cent of all land carbon. Trees also filter out pollutants, prevent flooding, and of course they make people happy.

But there are nonetheless environmental drawbacks to a free-for-all planting policy. Firstly it seems to deny a tree's natural ability to regenerate by itself. Next, some of the trees will be planted on natural grassland and heathland, or boggy moors – habitats which are in much shorter supply than woodland. The wildlife benefits of dense plantations of young trees are strictly limited, and there are fears that planting will take the lion's share of government grants such as the £40m pledged for 'green spaces'.

Perhaps most significantly, young trees are not, in fact, very effective at storing carbon. They will become more so as they grow and mature, but whether many of these planted saplings will survive to become mature trees is open to doubt. Several recent academic studies have cast further doubt on whether mass planting is in fact a cost-effective, or even a sensible, policy. This debate is bound to run and run, since so many bodies are now committed to tree planting, strategically and financially.

THE STATE OF OUR BIRDS

Birds are considered to be a good indication of the broad state of wildlife in Britain. They are the only species for which good data is available and the determinants well understood. Regular health checks on breeding birds have revealed significant long-term changes, while short-term change tends to bounce up and down from year to year. Roughly speaking the winners and losers balance one another, and for about 40 per cent of our birds there has been little overall change. No one would be surprised to learn that jackdaws and wood pigeons have more than doubled their numbers since the 1970s, or that the turtle dove, tree sparrow and nightingale are no longer common everyday species.

Milder winters are boosting the numbers of wrens and blackcaps, while species like the nuthatch are extending their range northwards, probably in repose to climate change. Goldfinches have increased thanks to nut feeders but the greenfinch, which also enjoys feeders, has declined through disease and eating mouldy peanuts! Some of our migrant birds are suffering because of what is happening in other countries, including drought, habitat loss and shooting. Birdwatchers from the 1970s would be amazed by the numbers of avocets and black-tailed godwits along our muddy shores, but shocked by the scarcity of breeding curlews and lapwings in the lowlands, and wonder what has happened to the yellow wagtails that used to scuttle about under the feet of cattle. They would observe the growing number of little egrets with wonder, but be appalled to learn that the kittiwake is now an endangered species through its steep rate of decline. It seems to be a victim of the impact of climate change on the sea, which has diminished its food supply and hence its ability to feed its chicks.

Most raptors have increased their numbers. The red kite, introduced to England and Scotland in the 1990s, is now too numerous to count regularly, but there are certainly far more than the 'official' figure of 1,800 breeding pairs. The reintroduced white-tailed sea eagle is slowly expanding its range in Scotland, and has been introduced to the Isle of Wight. Peregrines are now nesting in many towns and cities. Even the hen harrier, which is persecuted illegally, managed 15 successfully breeding pairs in England, the highest total since 2006. Only the kestrel has bucked the trend and is in 'moderate decline'.

The RSPB believes there is room for optimism. Some of our rarer birds, such as corncrakes in the western isles and cirl buntings in Devon, have been saved by management for their needs, with the cooperation of farmers and crofters. Although many farm birds, migrant songbirds and seabirds have declined, government agri-environment schemes are having a positive effect, and current plans to replace EU farm subsidies for 'public goods', including wildlife, bode well.

THE STATE OF OUR INSECTS

A paper published in the journal *Biological Conservation* in February 2019 produced alarming evidence of insect decline across the world. In a review of the best 73 studies on the subject, the paper concluded that 40 per cent of the world's insects are declining and that one third are endangered. The rate of extinction appears to be eight times that of birds or mammals. Worse, the total mass of insects has fallen by 2.5 per cent per year for the last 25–30 years, a rate that would ensure the extinction of the world's insects within the coming half century, with catastrophic consequences to agriculture and ecosystems. The paper concluded gloomily that 'unless we change our ways of producing food, insects as a whole will go down the path of extinction'.

There is some confirmation of this in Germany, which found an alarming decrease in flying insects even on nature reserves, and in Britain where butterflies and moths are monitored by volunteers. One gauge of this is the much smaller number of insects that we find in our houses even on warm humid days in mid-summer. Another is the much lower number of moths coming to traps, and the near disappearance of some species, including the once well-known garden tiger moth. The rate of decline in Britain is higher than the European average. The causes of the crash are likely numerous, but systematic use of pesticides has been fingered as a likely contributor, as have chemical fertilisers that drift into nearby fields and freshwater.

One group that has suffered disproportionately is dung beetles. They provide a vital role as nature's dustmen, clearing up corpses and animal dung, and one of them, the scarab, was adopted by the ancient Egyptians as a symbol of resurrection and transformation. Unfortunately much of farmland dung is effectively toxic to beetles because the animals have been treated with insecticides to kill intestinal worms. Yet dung beetles are themselves useful to farmers by reducing the rate of nematode worm infections and reducing pest flies by rapidly breaking down the dung. By recycling nutrients into the soil they also aid the growth of grass. The loss of dung beetles has knock-on effects on the animals that feed on them, such as bats. Broadly speaking, our dependence on chemicals is having alarming effects on wildlife and natural food-chains.

BEAVERS EXPANDING THEIR RANGE

The Eurasian beaver (a different species from the better-known Canadian beaver) is a native animal which was hunted to extinction in Britain about 600 years ago. After long debate, a trial to see whether beavers could adapt to the modern British landscape began in 2009 in Knapdale, a remote forested area in western Scotland. That trial was deemed a success. At the same time, beavers escaping from captivity have established themselves on the River Tay catchment in Scotland and also the River Otter in Devon. In both places they are increasing their range naturally, and the Tay now has the largest number of wild-living beavers in Britain, estimated in 2018 at 114 active territories and upwards of 320 individual animals. Since then they have spread further into the Trossachs and the River Forth, and have even been spotted in the Glasgow area.

In November 2016 the Scottish government announced that the beaver could remain as a protected species. In 2019 it also agreed to allow the beavers to expand their range naturally without any need for further releases. Yet the success of the Scottish beavers has not been without friction. There is a mitigation scheme in place for removing the animals where they are causing trouble, but some 87 animals were shot by farmers in 2019.

On the River Otter the government has also accepted that the beavers can remain and expand their range, finding new areas to settle 'as they need'. Formal legal protection came into force in May 2019. On nearby Exmoor the National Trust's release of beavers on its Holnicote estate has already resulted in a dam and 'instant wetland'. Releases within fenced enclosures are much more numerous. Natural England has issued 13 such licenses since 2017, from Cumbria to Cornwall, and more are in the pipeline, including the 'wildland' at Knepp in Sussex, and the Exmoor estate owned by the Prime Minister's father. A breeding stock of beavers is to be Stanley Johnson's 80th birthday present. Some of these captive beavers will undoubtedly escape to form free-range wild colonies.

In time to come the beaver will probably be a familiar wild animal in Britain, with places where they can be watched without disturbing them. The beaver is regarded by ecologists as a keystone species that creates its own habitat of wet channels, deep pools and well-gnawed woodland, while improving water quality in the process. Other animals such as kingfishers and trout benefit from their activities. From being an endangered species not long ago, the Eurasian beaver has been nursed back to ecological health in most European countries, and Britain looks like being no exception.

CLIMATE CHANGE BENEFITS DRAGONFLIES – BUT NOT BUTTERFLIES

Books about dragonflies published before the present century will need to be rewritten. Previously Britain and Ireland had 38 resident species of dragonflies (including the smaller damselflies). Today we have at least 47 species, with more likely to cross the sea soon and join them. Moreover some of our hitherto rare species, such as the Norfolk Hawker and the Scarce Chaser, are increasing their range. Dragonflies, it seems, are very mobile species and able to take advantage of the warming climate. We can watch it happening in detail, year on year, because dragonfly-watching has become very popular. They are 'honorary birds', taken up by birders as an extra group to enjoy watching with binoculars.

The past two summers have been notable ones for dragonflies. Numbers of migratory Southern Migrant Hawkers, Vagrant Hawkers and Lesser Emperors have reached an all-time high, and newcomers such as Southern Emerald, Willow Damselfly and Small Red-eyed Damselfly are rapidly expanding their range northwards. The latest coloniser is the Dainty Damselfly, *Coenagrion scitulum*. Three-quarters of a century ago, this species briefly colonised the coast of Essex but disappeared after the floods of 1953. It has now returned and is breeding happily in a newly dug pond in Kent. The downside to our growing list of dragonflies is that some of the northern species may suffer, especially if hotter, drier summers become the norm.

Our butterflies, on the other hand, have remained much the same. The extinct Large Blue has been introduced successfully from Swedish stock, and the Chequered Skipper, extinct in England (but not Scotland) since 1976, was introduced into Rockingham Forest from Belgian stock in 2018. The one clear beneficiary of climate change is the Long-tailed Blue, formerly a very rare migrant with only a handful of British records. It is now a regular visitor to the south coast, and has established temporary breeding colonies here and there. Moreover in 2020 a former resident, the Large Tortoiseshell, bred successfully for the first time in half a century. European species, such as the Southern Small White and the Short-tailed Blue are moving northwards in response to climate change and have now reached the English Channel. They may be the next colonisers.

WORST YEAR YET FOR ASH

Ash die-back is a fungal disease which blocks the passages of the living tree and results in its death. Once a tree is infected, nothing other than the tree's natural defences can prevent the advance of the disease. It has already killed the majority of ash trees across northern Europe. The disease was first detected in Britain in 2012 on saplings in a tree nursery, and quickly spread into nearby woodland. It is now well-established throughout the UK and will have to take its course. Ash is the third commonest native tree with an estimated 126 million mature trees in woodland and 60 million more in hedgerows and open countryside. The death of the ash will have even greater impacts on the landscape than did Dutch elm disease in the 1970s.

Die-back has been making steady inroads into Britain's ash trees since its discovery, but 2020 has been the worst year yet. Disease may have been aided by the stresses caused by late winter flooding, late frosts and an abnormally hot, dry spring. The National Trust, which had been felling around 5,000 trees a year, had to fell at least 20,000 in 2020, especially in the Cotswolds and south-west England. Among the landscapes affected by the loss of this tree are those made famous by the paintings of John Constable, and the ashwoods of the Lake District that inspired Beatrix Potter. Some estates are now felling healthy trees too since felling the dead ones is more hazardous and expensive. Around 955 species of invertebrates,

mosses and lichens are associated with ash, and some of them depend on it. Ash die-back is estimated to cost the economy at least £15bn, including not only the removal costs but also the contribution the trees make to carbon storage and to air and water purification.

There are a few reasons for hope. It may well be that some trees are resistant to the disease, given that ash is genetically highly variable in Britain. There are also signs that the disease is slower in mature trees than younger ones, and that many isolated trees are escaping infection so far. The tree may also be more resistant in mixed woods than those dominated by ash. Given the rate at which ash saplings appear from seed, there is a possibility that the tree may self-select varieties that can resist the disease.

NO-GO ZONES FOR PHEASANTS

An estimated 60 million pheasants and red-legged partridges are released in England each year for shooting. This represents a considerable scaling-up from the 4 million or so birds released in the early 1970s, and in biomass terms it makes the pheasant the most abundant bird in England. However the pheasant is not a native species – their wild range is further east, in Asia and south-east Europe. Legally they are classed not as wild birds but as livestock. Most pheasants are raised in pens in woodland and released in late summer, ready for the winter shooting season. The impact of so many large omnivorous birds on native wildlife has not been investigated (perhaps no one is eager to sponsor research that may harm their interests). There is however anecdotal evidence that pheasants prey on young lizards, snakes and slow-worms. They also impact on woodland plants and invertebrates, while unwanted pheasant carcasses are routinely dumped in pits where they attract foxes and crows. This in turn increases predation on ground-nesting birds, many of which are in decline.

The campaign group Wild Justice argued successfully that the lack of regulation on pheasant releases contravenes EU wildlife protection rules. From February 2021 shooting interests will now require a license to release pheasants or red-legged partridges within 500 metres of a protected site, technically defined as either a SAC (Special Area of Conservation), or a SPA (Special Protection Area for birds). The RSPB (Royal Society for the Protection of Birds) welcomed the decision. Such licensing may reduce the current pheasant population by 7 million or so. The Environment Minister, George Eustice, noted judiciously that the move 'highlighted the need for a better understanding of how any localised impacts might be mitigated and existing arrangements strengthened'.

Shooting interests argue that the licensing is disproportionate, and that more evidence is needed to justify it. Moreover, they argue, pheasant shooting has preserved many small woods and encouraged management that benefits wildlife, such as the maintenance of broad open rides. Wild Justice, on the other hand, sees the 500-metre buffer area as a compromise, and will continue to campaign for a wider 1,000-metre zone around protected sites and a ban on the use of lead ammunition.

NATURAL HISTORY ON THE SCHOOL SYLLABUS

Natural history is to be taught in schools from 2022 as an optional GCSE subject. The growing 'disconnect' between young people and nature is widely recognised, and was demonstrated recently when only half the children asked could recognise a stinging nettle and only a fifth could recognise a bumblebee. Children spend more time indoors than earlier generations, and few of them are allowed to roam as in the past. Yet an awareness of nature is widely recognised as being good for us, benefitting mental health and tackling such social issues as depression and obesity. Of course it would also help the natural environment if more young people had some knowledge of it.

The campaign to teach natural history in schools was led by Mary Colwell, who four years ago launched a petition for a GCSE in the subject. Backed by the Green MP Caroline Lucas, and with encouragement from the then environment minister Michael Gove, the idea was taken forward by senior educationalists. Its advocates needed to convince civil servants and teachers that natural history is not the same thing as biology, and is a genuine educational gap. It is envisaged as a much broader subject embracing not only science but history, geography and the arts, as well as developing field skills. In May 2020 the proposal was formally approved and moved onto the consultation stage. It is expected that teachers will be assisted by nature experts, field centres and museums, particularly the Natural History Museum. Mary Colwell hopes that the GCSE will 'make nature part of British society again'.

NATURAL CAPITAL

The new buzzword in conservation is 'natural capital'. It is envisaged as the total stock of natural resources in any given area: rocks, soil, water, air and all living things. Fertile soil and clean water underwrite economies and make human life possible. Other natural assets provide what are termed ecosystem services, that is, goods and services based on the natural systems of the earth. Essentially, natural capital is an economist's way of viewing nature. It appeals to politicians and planners.

At the government's bidding, Natural England has spent much of the year producing Natural Capital 'atlases' for every English county and city region. These are now available online. They are seen as a framework 'to inform our understanding of the state of our natural assets'. To some this is a helpful way to value the natural world, including wildlife. To others it is a distortion of science by the cold arithmetic of money. The environmental critic George Monbiot, for instance, summed up Natural Capital as 'gibberish'.

BUILT HERITAGE

Matthew Saunders

COVID-19

Like everything in the United Kingdom in 2020, life in the world of historic buildings was dominated and diverted by the COVID-19 pandemic. For all those sites dependent on the visitor, the financial effect was potentially disastrous whilst fundraising campaigns were drastically limited by the ban on public gatherings. Westminster Abbey alone forecast a shortfall in 2020 of £12m. The Historic Houses Association, which brings together private country house owners, found, in a survey of members, that many had paused capital works, despite the fact that before COVID-19, there had already been an accumulated backlog of repairs of £1.4bn. Government came dramatically to the rescue, both indirectly through its furlough scheme for staff unable to work and directly through unprecedented cash injections, beginning with £1.57m in a Culture Recovery Fund, (including the Heritage Stimulus Fund) launched in the summer and disbursed in the autumn. This embraced £270m on loans, £880m in grants, £100m to national cultural institutions and £120m to the English Heritage Trust (the latter to keep it on course for the government's aim of financial self-sufficiency by 2023). Beneficiaries (given in full on **W** www.gov.uk/government/news) included national organisations such as Historic Royal Palaces, The Landmark Trust, English Heritage, The Churches Conservation Trust and The Friends of Friendless Churches, individual sites like the vast mansion at Wentworth

Woodhouse in Yorkshire, Waltham Abbey Gunpowder Mills and a goodly number of churches and cathedrals, and local bodies like The Great Yarmouth Preservation Trust, The Modernist Society in Manchester and conservation practitioners such as The Skillington Workshop. The National Lottery Heritage Fund, Historic England, Cadw (in Wales) and Historic Scotland were all channels for the distribution of much of this injection of funds but were also recast into fire-fighting mode when it came to disbursing their own grant monies. No new NLHF grants were offered in 2020–21 and the reopening to fresh applications from 2021–22 remains limited, as most funds were directed to the rescue and stabilization of existing projects and past customers.

As the physical retail unit, many of which are housed in historic town centres, became one of the most threatened of all building types, as Lockdowns hit hard, the pre-existing allocation by the Chancellor of some £95m to the Heritage Action Zones, nearly all of them in urban centres, became considerably more relevant. The grants, distributed by Historic England, were announced in early October. Amounts of £2m or thereabouts went to Tottenham, Hastings, Wednesbury, Plymouth, Gloucester, Kirkham, Sowerby Bridge and Huddersfield, with other appreciable beneficiaries at Bacup, Hexham, Tewkesbury, Bedford, Dunstable, Lincoln, Buxton, Gosport, Chatham and Kettering.

The principal proposal for constitutional change in the course of the year, indeed the most significant overhaul of the planning system for decades, was that laid out in *Planning for the Future,* published at the beginning of August. The system of heritage protection emerged with a clean bill of health, with no changes proposed in the listed building consent system. However, unintended indirect consequences are highly likely in the future, due to decision-making made less by discretionary judgment in individual cases and more by following a set rulebook. No decision has yet been made on a proposal in Wales, first recommended late in 2018, that the separate listed building consent regime in Wales be abolished and merged with planning permission.

Britain has more listed buildings, at 550,000 (400,000 in England) than any other country apart from Italy. The most effective form is statutory listing, in one of three grades, which requires a dedicated permission, known as listed building consent for works of demolition, alteration or extension. This is administered by Historic England through the Secretary of State for Digital, Culture, Media and Sport. Parallel to that is the system of Local Listing, operated by 45 per cent of local planning authorities. This is 'non-statutory' in that demolishing entries on such a list does not need express permission but becomes a material consideration when an associated planning application is lodged. Both regimes came under close attention in 2020 with the publication in November of the Saunders Report on The Future of the National Heritage List for England, commissioned by Historic England, and the announcement earlier in the year by the Ministry responsible for local listing, DCLG, that a budget of £700,000 was being set aside to stimulate the creation of further such Lists. Additions to the statutory lists in 2020 included the picturesque villa known as Eller How at Lindale in the Lake District, created by the renowned local practice known as 'Websters of Kendal', the former studio and workshop of Barbara Hepworth at St Ives and the BBC Recording Studio at Maida Vale with 24 additions from among post-war designed landscapes to the (non-statutory) Register of Parks and Gardens.

NEW ATTRACTIONS

2020 was a highly inauspicious year for the new venture but some did come on stream. A new rehearsal studio for the Halle Orchestra, in Manchester, based in the listed former church of

St Peter in Ancoats (1859) was opened in November 2019 as was The Fratry (new reception area for visitors) at Carlisle Cathedral, in July 2020, on the back of a £2m National Lottery grant. The most triumphant was undoubtedly the completion in the summer of the new Spa Hotel as the centrepiece of the Grade 1 listed 'The Crescent' at Buxton in Derbyshire. The Crescent has been at risk for forty years and it was only the determination of the developer, Trevor Osborne and the huge grants, totalling £24m from the National Lottery Heritage Fund (NLHF) that finally saw the project through. The new archives of the Church of England in the grounds of Lambeth Palace, paid for, without grant aid, by the Church Commissioners and containing some of the country's greatest treasures, is to admit the public (as it has done within the Palace itself since 1610) early in 2021. Openings projected for 2021 include the new visitor centre at Lincoln Cathedral, the new galleries at Northampton Museum and the Corinium Museum, Cirencester, a brand new museum for Petersfield in Hampshire and the new centre for Suffolk archives on Ipswich Waterfront to be termed 'The Hold'. 'Round Two' NLHF grants confirmed in 2020 promised vital kickstarts for major schemes to conserve and convert one of the greatest High Victorian buildings of the North, the Grade 1 listed Town Hall at Rochdale (NLHF grant £8.3m), that to repair and open up the 'Pitman's Parliament' at Redhill, Co.Durham (£400,000), the placing of the 'Coventry Tapestry' in, and associated repairs to, the Grade 1 listed St Mary's Guildhall in that city (£1,762,700), Exeter Cathedral (£4,290,500), Evesham Abbey Trust (£788,300) and St Peter's church Sudbury, Suffolk (£1.67m) to open this redundant church for wider community use. Further areas of Jewish history were opened up with the new museum in the cemetery of 1873 at Willesden in North West London whilst the future of one of the most memorable recent gardens, that known as The Laskett, at Much Birch in Herefordshire, created by Sir Roy Strong and his late wife, Julia Trevelyan Oman around a villa of 1830, is assured by its passing for preservation in perpetuity to the horticultural charity known as 'Perennial'. And in a similar act of philanthropy, Sir James and Lady Deirdre Dyson have announced plans for a brand new art gallery, open to the public, in the grounds of their Grade 1 listed house by James Wyatt, Dodington Park, Gloucestershire. But in such a traumatic year as 2020, there have steps back as well as forward. Kneller Hall, at Twickenham, the imposing listed home to Royal Military School of Music of 1848 is set to close

in 2021, the plans to create a centre for mental health in the former church of St Mary at Quay in Ipswich, owned by the Churches Conservation Trust have collapsed and the seventy-year-old Stamford-based organization known as 'Men of the Stones', set up to protect the masonry skills of the limestone belt has been closed down and its funds transferred. One of the most architecturally splendid of all Benedictine monasteries, Downside Abbey in Somerset, has announced that it is to shut (although the school is to survive) and the charming Museum of Mechanical Music based in a former church at Portfield near Chichester is no more. The Annual Report 2018–19 of the Methodist Church Conservation Section, published in 2020, highlighted the closure of four historic chapels – High House Church at Ireshopburn, Durham, Darlington Street Chapel, Wolverhampton and the major chapels at Redruth, Cornwall and Williton, Somerset.

ADVANCES IN KNOWLEDGE

Publications have suffered less than buildings. The year saw important additions in the Pevsner *Buildings of England* volumes with the revision of *Nottinghamshire* with that for *County Durham* promised for March 2021. There were significant new accounts of *Arts & Crafts Churches* by Alec Hamilton, porches on East Anglian medieval churches (by Helen Lunnon), additions (covering Derbyshire and Staffordshire) within the ongoing *Corpus of Anglo-Saxon Sculpture,* issued by the British Academy, the architecture of the Cooperative Movement (by Lynn Pearson) and Historic England's account of the development of Ramsgate. There were biographies of Sir Edward Maufe, architect, inter alia, of Guildford Cathedral (by Juliet Dunmur), of J.F.Bentley, the designer of Wesminster (RC) Cathedral (by Peter Howell) and of Edward L'Anson, and his son and grandson (by Peter Jefferson). *Somerset Architects and Surveyors: A Biographical Dictionary of Building Professionals, Artists and Craftsmen 1720-1939* by Russell Lillford, was published in 2020 on the website of the Somerset Building Preservation Trust. *Excellent Essex* by Gillian Darley, an episodic overview of the history, buildings and radicals of that county was a particular critical success.

Plans were announced to celebrate the tercentenary of the death of Sir Christopher Wren in 1723 (WREN300) and towards the end of the year a society to celebrate one of the country's greatest wood (and stone) carvers, Grinling Gibbons, received charitable status. It will launch formally in 2021 and events planned to celebrate his tercentenary include a major exhibition on the man and his work.

COVID-19

Jenni Reid

While a global pandemic has long been a concern of academics, governments and international organisations, few predicted that 2020 would be the year one emerged, or quite the extent of the socioeconomic impact one would have. Virtually no nation has escaped the effects of the novel coronavirus Covid-19 entirely, but the specific impacts – whether to public health, tourism, business or everyday life – have varied widely around the world.

THE SPREAD OF COVID-19

At the end of December 2019, the Wuhan Municipal Health Commission in China reported a cluster of pneumonia cases with an unknown cause. The World Health Organization (WHO) quickly began advising countries on detecting and managing a new coronavirus, based on its experiences with SARS and MERS. On 13 January, the first infection was reported outside of China, in Thailand. By the end of January, low numbers of cases had been detected in countries across Asia and Oceania, as well as in the Middle East, North America and Europe.

In February, the effects of the outbreak were largely being felt in Asia. Chinese cities restricted citizens' movements, countries began banning flights from China, and others introduced mandatory quarantine periods for people arriving from certain countries. Several cruise ships were prevented from docking by countries which feared passengers bringing the virus with them. By the end of the month, small numbers of deaths linked to the virus, now known as COVID-19 or severe acute respiratory syndrome coronavirus 2, were being reported around the world. On 25 February, the WHO announced there were more cases outside of China than within it: the virus had gone global. Italy appeared to be the European hotspot, with seven deaths reported by the end of February, and cases in nearby countries were traced back to it.

In March, it became clear that COVID-19 would cause disruption to many nations on a scale unprecedented in recent memory. On 11 March, the WHO assessed that due to the virus's 'alarming' levels of spread and severity, the situation could be characterised as a pandemic. The same day, the US barred entry to foreign nationals travelling from China, Iran and most European countries. Mass gatherings were banned, to varying degrees, around the world. States of emergency were declared. Schools, workplaces and hospitality venues closed. Flights were cancelled, and some countries closed their borders almost entirely. Countries or cities implemented what quickly became known as 'lockdowns', with citizens told to stay at home unless necessary. In some places this was backed up by fines or other punitive measures, in others it remained a recommendation. Events that were cancelled or postponed in 2020 ranged from the Tokyo Olympic and Paralympic games and the COP21 Climate Summit, to thousands of sporting events, music festivals, concerts, theatre productions and conferences.

While intergovernmental agencies like the WHO provided advice throughout the year, the world's response to its newest pandemic was marked by a fragmented approach. Even blocs like the European Union had little coordination in their responses, with different stances taken at different times on issues such as border restrictions, mask wearing, lockdowns and testing. The arrival of vaccines developed by several companies, which began to be rolled out in some countries in December, provided some much-needed hope for an end to the pandemic. Yet it also saw UN Secretary General Antonio

Guterres urge rich nations to make greater contributions to ensure it will be available around the world, and to warn against 'vaccine nationalism.'

On 31 December, one year after the first cases of what would later be identified as COVID-19 were reported, there had been over 83.9 million confirmed cases and over 1.8 million deaths linked to the virus worldwide. Europe and the Americas accounted for the lion's share of those cases, with Asia and Africa making up much smaller portions and Oceania barely any. The trend of cumulative cases and deaths worldwide was still moving up, and those figures pre-dated an expected rise in cases in many Western countries due to household mixing over Christmas and New Year's Eve. This data is imperfect, as countries carried out different levels of testing and disagreed on exactly how to measure deaths that followed infections. Still, it was apparent at the end of the year that several major economies in the Americas and Europe had taken the biggest hit both to their economies and their citizens' health, including the US and the UK.

COVID-19 IN THE UK

The first two cases of COVID-19 in the UK were reported on 30 January in York, England. The UK's official case tally did not begin to rise significantly until March, though it is likely the virus was spreading more rapidly than realised at the time. COVID-19 had its first major impact on UK public life on 16 March, when Prime Minister Boris Johnson held a press conference in which he urged people to work from home and avoid pubs, restaurants and other public spaces. The stated aim was to avoid overwhelming the National Health Service, due to an expected rise in hospitalisations.

On 18 March, schools in England, Wales and Scotland were shut down until further notice. On 20 March, a day after China reported zero local infections for the first time, the UK government ordered all pubs, restaurants, gyms and social venues to close. On 23 March, Johnson told all Britons they should only go outside to shop for essentials, to exercise for one hour each day, or to work if doing so at home was not possible. Those who did not comply were liable to pay a fine, and emergency legislation was passed to enable police enforcement. Several government figures were infected with the coronavirus during the succeeding weeks, including Johnson. The prime minister entered intensive care on 6 April due to the severity of his case. He recovered and was discharged on 14 April, and returned to work on 27 April.

The two months from 23 March were widely referred to as the UK's first 'lockdown'. The rules announced on that date largely remained in force until 15 June, when non-essential shops and places of worship were allowed to reopen. On 22 June, the public was given permission to meet outdoors in groups of up to six people, and to form a 'support bubble' with one other household to meet indoors. Pubs, restaurants and hotels began to reopen from 4 July. From 10 July, Britons were allowed to holiday without quarantining on their return in a list of countries from a 'travel corridor' list, where cases were judged sufficiently low, with the list updated weekly. Wedding receptions with limited numbers were allowed from 15 August.

The first lockdown largely succeeded in what government scientific advisors referred to as 'flattening the curve', by slowing the rate of new daily cases and eventually causing the number of cases to plateau. The NHS did not become overwhelmed (meaning COVID-19 patients being denied life-saving treatment due to a lack of resources), and a network of emergency hospitals that was established in venues such as conference centres and sports stadiums went largely unused. Cases went from over 4,000 per day throughout April to just over 1,400 per day at the end of May, to just over 600 per day at the end of June. However, the total death toll during this period was significant, rising from 1,172 at the start of lockdown on 27 March to 37,531 by the end of June.

Meanwhile, the daily case rate began to rise again as soon as society 'opened up' in July, hitting 800 cases by the end of the month and nearly 2,000 by the end of August. The summertime loosening of restrictions was tightened again in early September, when a UK-wide ban on gatherings of more than six people came into force. But at the same time, most children returned to school, many students arrived in university halls, leisure travel remained permitted and hospitality venues stayed open. New daily cases soared over the next two months, hitting a peak of 31,060 on 9 November (the number was substantially higher than at the peak of the first lockdown due to the wider availability of testing).

From September onwards, the UK nations began to take different approaches to tackling the pandemic, with decisions on covid-prevention measures taken by the devolved governments. Regional rules were also introduced: for example, areas of Leicestershire were placed back into lockdown on 29 June due to a surge in local infections, followed by parts of the north of England. On 12 October, England was placed into a 'three tier' system, with regions in the country placed under different restrictions based on their COVID-19 figures. On 14 October, Northern Ireland closed all pubs and restaurants. On 19 October, Wales entered a two-week 'firebreak' lockdown with only essential activities permitted. On 21 October, Scotland launched its own five-tier system.

Up to the year's end, the nations continued to move their regions into different levels of restrictions. The government was criticised for announcing that some household mixing would be allowed for a five-day period over Christmas in England, only to reverse this decision on 19 December. Following a dip in new daily cases due to lockdown measures through November, cases rose massively from 1 December to the end of the year, with 52,796 new cases on 31 December alone. By the end of the year, 73,512 Britons had died within 28 days of a positive coronavirus test.

THE ECONOMY

The pandemic had a dramatic impact on the UK economy in 2020. This was for a variety of reasons, most notably lockdown measures which included the instruction to stay at home unless necessary, and the resulting effect on businesses. The UK's GDP shrank by 19.8 per cent between April and June, the biggest slump since quarterly records began in 1955. In August, the ONS announced a cumulative 22.1 per cent fall in GDP in the first six months of 2020. This was among the highest drops in Europe, second only to the 22.7 per cent seen in Spain, and more than double the 10.6 per cent fall in the United States. A strong rebound was seen in the third quarter of the year, with a record 16 per cent expansion reported from July to September. But this news was tempered by the detail of a September slowdown, with experts predicting a weak fourth quarter. The Office for Budget Responsibility predicted the UK economy would shrink by 11.3 per cent overall in 2020.

The government rolled out numerous policies to attempt to counter the economic fallout. This began with the March 2020 budget, which brought with it the flagship Coronavirus Job Retention Scheme (CJRS), commonly referred to as the furlough scheme. The government initially covered 80 per cent of the wages of employees who were unable to work as a result of the pandemic, subject to a cap of £2,500 per month. These employees could not work for the company that had furloughed them, though they could volunteer or take on additional work that did not breach their contract. In May, when use of the scheme was at its highest, 30 per cent of the nation's workforce was furloughed. Gradual changes were made to the scheme from 1 July, when employers were able to bring back furloughed workers part-time. From 1 August, employers were asked to pay National Insurance and pension contributions for the hours employees were furloughed. From 1 September, the government's salary contribution was lowered to 70 per cent, and it dipped again to 60 per cent in October. Following several extensions, the CJRS was set to last until the end of April 2021, with further extension possible.

Financial support was also given to self-employed workers, who were able to claim through the Self-Employment Income Support Scheme (SEISS). This was open to people with annual profits of less than £50,000 who usually received at least half their income from self-employment, and whose work was adversely affected by the pandemic. Two grants were made available in 2020, in July and October, the first representing 80 per cent of average monthly trading profits, the second 70 per cent. Two more were set to be paid out in 2021.

By late 2020 it was difficult to say exactly how many jobs and livelihoods were preserved by the CJRS and SEISS, though it was likely in the thousands. However, the government was criticised for announcing one extension to the CJRS, from November to the end of March 2021, at very short notice, by which point some staff had already been laid off. Some also argued that jobs could have been saved had employers known the scheme would last for more than a year. Meanwhile, around 3 million people were estimated to have been ineligible for either scheme, including sole company directors, people who had been self-employed for less than a year, and people who normally moved between employment and self-employment.

While the CJRS and SEISS ran beyond the end of the year, the effects of the pandemic were already showing in employment figures. The UK unemployment rate rose to 4.9 per cent from July through September, 1.2 per cent higher than a year earlier and 0.7 per cent higher than in the previous quarter. Overall there were 819,000 fewer workers on UK company payrolls in November than in February. The biggest reductions over this period were in hospitality (297,000), retail and wholesale (160,000), manufacturing (115,000), culture and recreation (89,000) and admin and support services (58,000). In November, there were 2.7 million people claiming Jobseeker's Allowance or Universal Credit, 1.4 million more than in February. The OECD predicted UK unemployment would rise to an average of 7.4 per cent in 2021, up from 4 per cent pre-pandemic. The Bank of England expected unemployment to reach a high of 7.7 per cent in April to June 2021, though stated it could rise as high as 10 per cent, and further government support could alleviate this.

Many businesses were hit hard by the volatility of 2020, and policy measures to help them included Statutory Sick Pay refunds for coronavirus-related absences, a Coronavirus Business Interruption Loan Scheme for SMEs, Local Restrictions Support grants, and selected VAT cuts. Another was 'Eat Out To Help Out', a UK-wide scheme which saw the government subsidise a 50 per cent discount on food and soft drinks purchased in restaurants, cafes and pubs from Monday to Wednesday throughout August, in a bid to boost trade. By some measures the scheme was a success, with more than 49,000 businesses making a claim under the scheme and many calling for its continuation into the autumn. However, it was also criticised for its impact on the spread of the virus, with one study by the University of Warwick linking it to a sixth of new coronavirus case clusters over the summer.

The impact of COVID-19 on business could not be staved off entirely, and entire industries were pushed to crisis point, particularly hospitality, leisure, travel and tourism. Tens of thousands of pubs, restaurants, bars and hotels were put at risk of closure; pub groups including Marston's and Greene King cut jobs; and the airline Flybe and travel group Thomas Cook were pushed from precarious financial situations into collapse. The embattled British high street took a further blow, with big names including the Arcadia Group, Debenhams, Edinburgh Woollen Mill, Laura Ashley and Cath Kidston all entering administration. Nonetheless, the UK's company liquidation rate actually fell year-on-year in the 12 months ending in the third quarter of 2020, which the government attributed to financial support for businesses and the temporary prohibition of the use of statutory demands and certain winding-up petitions from 27 April to the end of the year.

Some businesses did well from the pandemic, including the major supermarket chains and web-only supermarket Ocado; Reckitt Benckiser, the producer of Dettol; and online gambling companies. The housing market was essentially suspended in late March, with the government telling people to delay home moves and preventing new viewings. But when it resumed in mid-May, with the government announcing a cut in stamp duty in England and Northern Ireland until 31 March and similar measures in place in Wales and Scotland, the market boomed. UK house prices increased by an average 7.6 per cent in the year to November, according to mortgage lender Halifax, and the end of June to the end of November saw the fastest five-month rise since 2004. Trends noted by housing websites included increased desires for gardens, as well as 'detached', 'rural' and 'secluded' homes, as lockdowns and the work-from-home lifestyle fuelled a desire for more space and fresh air.

The 2020 Autumn Budget was deferred to March 2021, when a full 'recovery plan' for the UK economy was set to be announced. As the year ended, cases of COVID-19 in the UK were soaring and most areas were under strict restrictions, raising the prospect of a grim remainder of the winter. In December, the Organisation for Economic Co-operation and Development (OECD) predicted that among major economies, the UK's would face the biggest hit from the pandemic second only to Argentina, and that it would be 6 per cent smaller than before the pandemic at the end of 2021. At this point it expects the overall global economy to be back to pre-pandemic levels. Also in December, the Office for Budget Responsibility (OBR) predicted the UK government would need to borrow £394bn to fund a tax shortfall and £280bn in public spending to tackle the pandemic, a cost that was over 80 per cent higher than the average among other G7 economies. It also estimated the UK was on course for a 90 per cent deeper decline in economic output in 2020, and almost 60 per cent more deaths. This was on top of the uncertainty posed by the UK's exit from the European Union, which was finally completed in 2020. While a trade deal was reached in December, it included additional barriers to trade, and the OBR forecasted a long-term loss of output of around 4 per cent compared with if the UK had remained in the EU.

SOCIETY

The pandemic had numerous effects on society and social issues, many of them negative. ONS figures published in August found that depression among British adults had doubled during the pandemic. Studies also showed an increase in rates of loneliness during lockdown periods. Women's Aid reported a significant rise in domestic violence linked to the pandemic. Meanwhile, hospitals were placed in the difficult position of having to restrict visitations, leading to thousands of people giving birth, undergoing serious treatments, or even dying with limited or no in-person contact with family or friends.

There were huge repercussions for non-covid-related healthcare during the pandemic. The NHS shut down or significantly reduced many areas of non-covid care during April, May and June. During this period, the British Medical Association estimated there were up to 286,000 fewer urgent cancer referrals, 25,900 fewer patients starting first cancer treatments following a decision to treat, and between 1.32 and 1.50 million fewer elective admissions than would usually be expected. NHS waiting times also reached a record high in England over the summer, according to a study published in the *British Medical Journal*.

The Social Care Institute for Excellence (SCIE) reported in September that the pandemic took a 'grim toll on social care in England'. Sector workers said many care homes had insufficient space to isolate people who had caught the virus. Others reported a lack of personal protective equipment, leaving staff as well as residents at risk. The same SCIE report stated that the pandemic exposed 'the deep levels of inequalities which exist in society, with evidence telling us that Black, Asian and minority ethnic (BAME) communities, adults with learning disabilities, and those on the lowest incomes, have been disproportionately affected.' A study by the University of Manchester in November estimated that 29,400 more care home residents died during the first 23 weeks of the pandemic than would be expected from historical trends, through causes directly and indirectly attributable to COVID-19.

Almost 700,000 people, including 120,000 children, fell into poverty as a result of the pandemic, according to analysis by thinktank The Legatum Institute. This took the number of people living in poverty in the UK to more than 15 million, or 23 per cent of the population. The Legatum Institute also found that an additional 700,000 people were prevented from falling into poverty by the temporary £20-a-week boost to universal credit which was introduced in April.

Homelessness was also impacted by COVID-19. Thousands of people were placed in temporary housing during the first lockdown, through what in England was called the 'Everyone In' scheme. Similar initiatives took place in Wales, Scotland and Northern Ireland. This saw local authorities find accommodation for all homeless people on their radar, regardless of factors such as perceived need, responsibility or immigration status. Chiefly using newly empty student accommodation and hotels, more than 29,000 people were housed in England alone, which medical journal *The Lancet* estimated avoided 1,164 covid-related hospital admissions and 266 deaths. Still, hundreds of people slipped through the cracks and continued to sleep rough throughout the year. This was especially due to the number of newly homeless people, exacerbated by the economic downturn and people in precarious housing situations being pushed into homelessness due to social distancing, restrictions on travel and other factors.

Significant disruption was caused to children's and higher education in 2020. Almost all schools in the UK closed on or around 20 March, except to the children of essential workers, and did not reopen until the new school year began in September. The Nuffield Trust described the result as an 'unprecedented disruption to the education of children and young people.' Teachers gave online lessons, and schools were tasked with both providing remote support for pupils and making sure they had a basic level of equipment. This included laptops, tablets and internet connectivity provided by the government, though some schools still reported an insufficient supply.

When children did return to school in September, the environment was still highly disrupted. Schools followed their own approaches for dividing children into 'bubbles': if one child in the bubble became ill, even with a cold, it sometimes led to dozens of children being sent home to isolate for two weeks. Teachers were leading lessons from behind masks and face shields. There was fierce debate between politicians, education authorities, teachers and others about whether to close schools early as cases soared in late autumn and winter. While the risk to children from COVID-19 appeared to be very low, schools were described as 'vectors for transmission', putting parents and teachers at greater risk. This came up against the strain put on parents from keeping children home, as well as the mental health and short- to long-term educational impact on children themselves.

All school leavers' exams, including A Levels, GCSEs, National Highers and Advanced Highers, were cancelled in 2020. Instead, exam boards calculated grades for students based on a combination of teacher assessments, class rankings and the past performance of their schools. The system was widely criticised as unfair, particularly for penalising students from disadvantaged backgrounds or who attended traditionally weaker-performing schools. Following a public outcry and student protests, by 17 August the administrations in England, Wales, Northern Ireland and Scotland all decided to allow students to receive teacher-assessed grades if they were higher than their standardised grades.

Students starting or returning to university in 2020 had a first term like no other. Those entering university accommodation were largely banned from socialising with people beyond their new flatmates, while the vast majority of teaching was done online. Where COVID-19 cases were discovered, some accommodation blocks were placed entirely into lockdown, with university administrators dropping off food and drink for students outside doors. The situation caused widespread anger and frustration among students, leading to the biggest wave of student rent strikes in 40 years.

TAKING STOCK

Describing the events of 2020 as 'unprecedented' became so commonplace that it turned into a running joke on social media. Yet the word is undoubtedly a fitting one for the wrenching societal and economic changes that took place, from a Conservative government embracing massive public sector borrowing and placing stringent limitations on public life, to the months-long closure of schools, offices, restaurants, pubs, hotels, theatres, cinemas and more. So many words shot to prominence that the *Oxford English Dictionary* team was unable to choose just one as its Word of the Year, instead highlighting several, including COVID-19, WFH (work from home), lockdown, circuit-breaker, support bubble, keyworker and furlough.

The pandemic's long-term effects are still to be revealed. Some believe it will lead many businesses to shift to a home-working model to save on costly city centre office space, for example, or turbocharge the dominance of online services like door-to-door delivery platforms. Mask-wearing on public transport, or when someone is sick, might become a common sight; or it might fade into memory. What is certain is that individuals will feel the impact in the years and decades to come: whether that's the adults to be hit by the predicted rise in unemployment; the children whose education has been unsettled; or the tens of thousands who have lost loved ones to COVID-19.

FILM

Trevor Johnston

STORM BEFORE THE QUIET

In any other year, a foreign-language title winning the Best Picture Oscar for the first time in history would come to be seen as a milestone. Yet when South Korea's *Parasite* took home no less than four statuettes from Hollywood's Dolby Theater on 9 February 2020 industry commentators were so busy taking in this unexpected triumph there was little thought given to the health crisis which would engulf the world in the months to follow. Two days later, the World Health Organisation gave a name to the mystery virus which had already begun to spread from its origins in China, officially designating it Covid-19. Devastating effects to film production, distribution and exhibition ensued as lockdown restrictions were subsequently imposed worldwide.

In the longer term however, the achievement of writer-director Bong Joon-ho will surely stand proud in the annals of the Academy Awards. His film *Parasite* was the first title ever to win both Best Picture and Best International Film (known prior to 2020 as the Best Foreign Language Film). Furthermore, Oscars for Best Director and Best Original Screenplay also meant Bong equalled Walt Disney's record 1954 personal tally of four wins in the same year – but is the only one to manage the feat for a single film. Among the best-reviewed films of the year prior to its Oscar coronation, *Parasite* begins like a light-hearted caper, following a cash-strapped but enterprising working-class family as they inveigle themselves into jobs in an upscale Seoul household, before a startling plot-twist proves the catalyst for a shocking yet somehow inevitable finale. It's certainly a story which peers accusingly at the social divide in South Korea, yet the film's blend of mischief and seriousness made it surprisingly accessible, relevant and indeed highly enjoyable, perhaps explaining how it broke through the traditional subtitles barrier for Academy voters and audiences worldwide. As such, it marked a watershed moment for South Korean cinema overall, which through a gifted generation of film-makers and acting talent had established itself in the previous decade as a powerhouse force on the global arthouse circuit. Bong and esteemed fellow directors like Park Chan-wook (famed for the outré gangster picture *Oldboy*) and Lee Chang-dong (a Cannes favourite, who also served as his country's Minister of Culture) were in the vanguard, with genre titles in the crime and horror categories also picking up an enthusiastic international following.

Prior to the Academy Awards ceremony itself, the talk was actually whether Martin Scorsese's epic gangster elegy *The Irishman* would bring streaming outfit Netflix their first Best Picture win, or if Britain's Sam Mendes might win the day for his seamlessly shot WWI drama *1917*. In the event, neither of them grabbed the major prizes, though Mendes had already triumphed at the BAFTA Awards, and elsewhere there was a not unfamiliar transatlantic consensus on the year's major awards, with same winners taking the four main acting gongs in Los Angeles and London. Hence, Joaquin Phoenix's tortured rendition of the title character in *Joker*, an abrasive and downbeat origin story for a regular villain in the Batman series won both Best Actor nods. Incidentally, this was the second occasion where the same role brought Academy Award acclaim for two actors in different films, as Phoenix followed the late Heath Ledger's Joker in 2008's somewhat more conventional superhero offering *The Dark Knight*, just as Marlon Brando (1972's *The Godfather*) and Robert De Niro (1974's *The Godfather: Part II*) were both rewarded for playing mafia kingpin Vito Corleone at different ages in Francis Ford Coppola's multi-part organised crime chronicle.

Renee Zellweger meanwhile took 2020's Best Actress for her full-on portrayal of fraying celluloid icon Judy Garland in the otherwise modest British-shot biographical portrait *Judy*, repeating an Oscar-BAFTA double-victory she'd also carried off for Best Supporting Actress as a zesty country lass in the 2003 adaptation of Civil War novel *Cold Mountain*. In turn, Laura Dern was 2020's dual-winner in the latter category for her lippy, domineering divorce lawyer in Noah Baumbach's serio-comic Netflix-backed break-up tale *Marriage Story*, while Brad Pitt won both key Best Supporting Actor awards for his seemingly easygoing yet astute and charismatic turn as the faithful stunt double for Leonardo DiCaprio's struggling TV star in Quentin Tarantino's fresco of 1969 Los Angeles *Once Upon a Time… in Hollywood* – a look back at a transitional moment for the film business from the vantage point of what might yet prove another time of industry change.

THE NUMBERS PEAK...

Such have been the debilitating effects of living through Covid-19 restrictions that the normal life we experienced before the onset of the virus, now seems like a halcyon era. The contrasts have proved stark indeed for the film industry, where the calendar year 2019 set new global box-office records, which will doubtless dwarf the totals when the 2020 figures are eventually tallied. In 2019 superhero epic *Avengers: Endgame*, which brought the 22 films of the interconnected Marvel Cinematic Universe to a crescendo, ousted James Cameron's *Avatar* as the all-time box office champion, a position the latter had held for a remarkable ten-year run. *Endgame*'s $858m take in the US still lags second overall to the $937m earned domestically by *Star Wars: The Force Awakens*, yet the $1.939bn *Endgame* collected internationally contributed to its overall $2.798bn worldwide gross, which eclipsed *Avatar*'s existing $2.789bn total and made it top of the heap.

That success fed into making 2019 the most lucrative year ever for global cinema takings, though again this was in part due to the strength of the international box office. The US figures of $11.4bn overall actually dropped 4.4 per cent from the previous year, but worldwide the $31.1bn figure – the first time that international receipts had topped $30bn – made the worldwide 2019 total of $42.5bn one for the record books. Not surprisingly, Hollywood studio product comprises the entire top ten films, all of which were sequels, remakes or part of an established franchise, though some original material did feature lower down the rankings. Running over a billion dollars behind *Endgame* in second place worldwide was *The Lion King* ($1.654bn), which, like the ninth placed *Aladdin* ($1.047bn), offered a vindication of Walt Disney's decision to proceed with a series of live-action remakes of past animated favourites, facilitated by the developments in computer-generated imagery which allowed the African wildlife in *The Lion King*, for instance, to be presented in photo-real visual quality… lip-synched talking animals notwithstanding.

In 2019's third place overall, *Frozen II* ($1.447bn) showed that Disney's long-established expertise in family-friendly traditional animated features still retained its lustre, and this was one of seven of the top ten worldwide grossing pictures to be produced by the Disney group of companies, which also include Marvel Studios (*Avengers: Endgame, Captain Marvel*), Pixar (*Toy Story 4*) and Lucasfilm (*Star Wars: The Rise of Skywalker*). Sony was the only other Hollywood major to manage two titles in the top ten (*Spider-Man: Far from Home*,

Jumanji: The Next Level), while Warner Bros. made up the numbers with *Joker*, another reminder that film adaptations from the DC Comics stable continued to lag behind material from their comic-book rivals Marvel in terms of commercial success. One also notes that *Spider-Man: Far From Home* was actually a co-production between Marvel Studios and Sony-owned Columbia Pictures, who have long controlled the distribution rights to this particular Marvel character. Hence, a percentage of the *Spider-Man* revenue stream found its way back to Marvel and their umbrella organisation Disney.

At the end of 2019, Disney therefore held a position of box-office dominance unparalleled in cinema history, pulling in a huge $11.1bn worldwide for the year, including a third of all US box-office revenues – closest competitor Warner Bros. pulled in just under 14 per cent by comparison. The 2019 figures also included grosses for rival studio 20th Century Fox (accounting for 5 per cent of US box-office returns), whose parent group 21st Century Fox had been acquired by Disney in March of that year, setting in motion a complex restructuring process which involved separating off Fox's considerable television interests into the newly formed Fox Corporation and paring away much of the film arm's production output and staff. Essentially, the number of established major film studios in Hollywood was thus reduced from six to five (Disney, Paramount, Sony, Universal, Warner Bros.), a process of consolidation occurring at a moment when the Covid-19 pandemic would be about to lay down an unprecedented challenge to their business model.

THE NUMBERS PLUMMET
In response to confirmation of the studio's global box-office dominance, Disney's co-chairmen released a celebratory statement to the effect that 2019 was "a year like no other!" Little did they know at the time that their words could be more properly applied to 2020, when the worldwide spread of Covid-19 brought film production mostly to a halt, and caused cinema closures which reduced the studios' income from distribution, yet more severely impacted on the financial fortunes of cinema owners in the exhibition sector. At the same time, captive audiences locked down at home brought a boom in online streaming, and whereas the likes of Netflix, Amazon Prime and Apple TV+ might previously have been seen as bitter rivals fighting for their share of the viewing audience, being able to shift release patterns from the physical to the online world, did at least offer the Hollywood majors some sort of revenue stream to help them through the crisis. Moreover, for Disney and Warner Bros. in particular, launching their own streaming services (Disney+ and HBO Max respectively) proved a potentially lucrative move in the straitened circumstances, while also looking forward to the post-Covid media landscape.

The earlier impact of the virus in China meant their cinemas had already faced closures in the early months of 2020, which hit particularly hard during the Lunar New Year holiday at the end of January, often a key period for the country's box-office income. The same pattern followed in the rest of the world from March onwards as waves of cinema closures and re-openings in various territories followed the series of tightening and loosening restrictions imposed by the scattershot international governmental response to the pandemic. The effect was that major film releases were postponed as audiences dwindled or dried up altogether, leaving some independent releases to fight for the scraps. *No Time to Die*, the twenty-fifth title in the James Bond franchise, originally slated for April 2020 was initially moved back to November, yet by October it was already clear that the market for a film skewed towards a slightly older demographic was unlikely to recover sufficiently, so the release was then pushed further back twice, to October 2021. In response, the Cineworld cinema chain,

who'd obviously been banking on 007 for a much-needed financial injection, decided to close its US and UK sites for the foreseeable future, causing lay-offs for 45,000 staff in the process.

In comparison, Warner Bros. had been less circumspect with the August international roll-out for Christopher Nolan's latest cerebral blockbuster *Tenet*, though neither the critical nor public response to the film was perhaps as warm as they might have hoped. Despite writer-director Nolan's sincere cheerleading for the primacy of the theatrical experience, with so much else on their minds viewers at that point appeared not to be willing to return to cinemas in their previous numbers. In fact, available box-office figures for the rest of 2020 bear out the extraordinary decline in revenues during this extraordinary moment. At the beginning of March, Pixar's *Onward*, a madcap comedy of fraternal bonding and reincarnation among faerie folk, took $39m over its opening weekend. Compare that with the very same slot in 2019 when the Marvel release *Captain Marvel* raked in $153m, and it's understandable that by 19 March, Disney had announced they would no longer report box-office figures. At the time of going to press, two Chinese releases, Sino-Japanese wartime spectacle *The Eight Hundred* and morale-raising portmanteau *My People, My Homeland* topped the worldwide box-office figures at $473m and $433m respectively (even though they'd only been on wide release in China), with Hollywood's most lucrative offerings, the buddy-cop sequel *Bad Boys for Life* and the aforementioned espionage thriller *Tenet*, coming in at $424m and $361m respectively. The final accounting will evidently show cinema box-office income reduced to a fraction of its 2019 high watermark.

THE AUDIENCE AT HOME
It won't go down as a critical favourite, but Universal's family-oriented digitally animated comedy *Trolls World Tour* was certainly a marker post in the changes affecting the film business in 2020. In early April the studio decided to make the film available to rent online on the same day it was released in the very few cinemas still open in the US, thus breaking established practice which gave cinemas a 90-day window before film titles moved to Video on Demand (VOD). US cinema chain AMC threatened a boycott of all future Universal releases, but when the studio announced that the film took $100m in its first three weeks of online release, more than its predecessor *Trolls* made in five months of US cinema release, it signalled a shift in the relationship between Hollywood and exhibitors – at least for the duration of the pandemic. More ructions were to come, when Disney announced that its live-action version of *Mulan*, expected to be one of the year's tentpole titles for struggling cinemas, would instead play as a Premium Video on Demand item on the studio's nascent Disney+ streaming service, occasioning a further payment on top of the existing monthly rental charge. While the film under-performed on its theatrical release in China, disappointing for its makers who had tried to make this version more culturally authentic than its admittedly popular knockabout forbear, the risky online strategy in the US boosted Disney+ downloads by 68 per cent on its opening weekend (compared to the previous weekend) and made $35m in rental fees during the same period, money which went directly into Disney coffers rather than sharing that income with the cinema chains as per familiar theatrical release arrangements.

If *Mulan* made it clear that viewers were prepared to pay over and above regular streaming fees for new movies they couldn't see in closed cinemas, Disney themselves chose to make other key releases, including the screen version of the Broadway smash *Hamilton* and the Afro-centric Pixar comedy *Soul*, part of the regular subscription, but the template was set, and Warner

Bros. followed suit by releasing their effects-heavy family frightener *Roald Dahl's The Witches* as a Premium Video on Demand release in time for Halloween on regular streaming platforms, before later startling the industry with a plan to issue all their major cinema releases for 2021 day and date in the US on HBO Max, their new streaming service – a WarnerMedia subsidiary out to challenge Netflix, Amazon Prime, Apple TV+ and Disney+. Just as the advent of DVD and Blu-Ray created a new revenue stream in the past, which has in good measure been succeeded by the VOD and streaming revolution as the technology makes it more viable, so the dividing line between cinema and home entertainment has become more blurred in 2020. That's significantly due to the pandemic causing cinema closures and VOD/streaming thus filling the viewer demand for film, yet as the major studios themselves play catch-up to offer streaming alternatives to Netflix and Amazon's existing offer, there's a sense that the Covid crisis has merely accelerated a process which would probably have happened anyway. Indeed, just as the Hollywood majors want to keep their profits rolling in through streaming, the streamers themselves have now become major players in supporting film production, building their own libraries of new releases to compete with the studios for prestige and critical acclaim and thus draw increasing numbers of new subscribers for their services. At present this is a media revolution in progress, but how the competition for eyeballs will impact on Hollywood, other key film producers, the streamers, and global broadcasters is something which will play out over the coming years.

AN ALTERED ECO-SYSTEM

The global health crisis had the effect of throwing world cinema's established eco-system out of balance, denying audiences their usual supply of summer blockbusters, while also affecting future releases of such potential money-spinners. Many finished films were held back in the meantime, and the production schedule was also slashed, though mega-productions like *The Batman* and *Mission: Impossible 7* found ways of battling, intermittently, through health and safety restrictions, and independent productions with a smaller footprint also found a way to continue. At the prestige end of the spectrum, the cancellation of the 2020 Cannes Film Festival, along with numerous other festival circuit events (though Venice did manage to hold a Covid-aware in-person edition), affected the regular channel for spotting arthouse achievement – *Parasite*, for instance, started its journey towards the Oscars by winning the Cannes Palme D'Or in 2019. At the same time, while a paucity of new Hollywood product left major cinema chains struggling even when screens were allowed to open, independent venues proved a resourceful alternative, opening myriad new specialty titles, supported by critical attention which might previously have been shared with more mainstream fare.

Moreover, the streaming and VOD sphere also presented an avenue of opportunity for independent film, not just from the array of prestige titles nestling among the broad cinematic spectrum on offer from the likes of Netflix and Amazon Prime, but also for arthouse-focused streaming entities like MUBI or the BFI Player in the UK, plus at a local level agile independent distributors (like Curzon or Modern Films in the UK) offering an additional online rental presence. In the circumstances, it was no surprise that the Oscars and the BAFTAs changed their eligibility requirements to allow films which had only had an online release to qualify for awards consideration (albeit with a slightly vague proviso that they would also have some future cinema distribution as well), nor indeed that streaming services

and VOD platforms also reported a significant uptake in subscriptions and rentals during lockdown periods in particular.

Hence, it was still possible during much of 2020 to keep a finger on the pulse of enterprising independent cinema without actually having to visit a cinema. A snapshot of the year then, might include *Time*, Garrett Bradley's documentary about a Louisiana wife and mother's decades-long campaign to free her husband serving a 60-year sentence for armed robbery. This was an empathetic and angry document redolent of the year of Black Lives Matter, as indeed was Spike Lee's *Da 5 Bloods*, which turns a latterday quest for buried Vietnam War loot into a mordant meditation on the conflict's destructive effect on a generation of African-American youth. Another genre hybrid flagging up issues of race, colonialism and oppression, *Bacurau*, from Brazilian co-directors Kleber Mendonça Filho and Juliano Dorneilles, contrived a striking blend of western and horror movie as a remote rural community drew on a history of resistance when under attack from both local politicians and unscrupulous gringos. The cultural currents of feminine empowerment also manifested themselves in a couple of powerful dramas from woman directors: Sarah Gavron's *Rocks* offered a touching story of friendship and resilience as an East London teen cared for her younger brother when their single mum leaves the nest, and Eliza Hittman's riveting *Never Rarely Sometimes Always* followed a Pennsylvania schoolgirl travels to New York for an abortion, unbeknown to her parents but with the support of her best friend. Some of those titles may yet be in contention when the year's awards are handed out, and though Rob Savage's micro-budget 56-minute horror featurette *Host* is less likely to figure, this convincingly mounted scarefest about unfolding mayhem during a séance held via video-calling application Zoom, was shot remotely during lockdown and encapsulates 2020's year of online communication, social distancing and mounting paranoia in a way which more prestigious cinematic offerings may find tough to match.

SIGNIFICANT FAREWELLS

In a year marked by an ever-mounting tally of heart-breaking Covid-related losses, the film community said farewell to four particular actors who departed due to natural causes, but whose footprint covered a huge swathe of cinema history. Leaving us at 103 and 104 years of age respectively, Kirk Douglas and Olivia de Havilland were surely the last survivors among the screen icons of Hollywood's golden age. He brought manly intensity and a famously dimpled chin to leading man roles from the 1950s onwards, while she found stardom in the 1930s, and subsequently won two Oscars after successful legal action to break free of her onerous studio contract. Sean Connery, who died aged 90, represented a different era of stardom, his combination of physique, charisma and beguiling Scots accent made a huge impression in his signature role as secret agent James Bond, yet his acting skills sustained a high-profile career spanning six decades from Macmillan's Britain to the era of digital effects-driven cinema. Chadwick Boseman, sadly, will never achieve the same longevity, having passed away at the age of 43, but will remain an icon of African-American cinema for a series of key performances, including the title role in Marvel's ground-breaking Afro-centric superhero picture *Black Panther* – much of which he delivered between bouts of surgery and chemotherapy for the ongoing colon cancer which ended his life. Powerful contributions to *Da 5 Bloods* and the posthumously released *Ma Rainey's Black Bottom* will keep his screen presence with us in the meantime, while his reputation will surely endure.

AWARDS

76TH VENICE INTERNATIONAL FILM FESTIVAL
Golden Lion – *Joker* (Todd Phillips)
Grand Jury Prize – *An Officer and a Spy* (Roman Polanski)

BRITISH ACADEMY FILM AWARDS 2020
Best Film – *1917* (Sam Mendes)
Director – Sam Mendes *(1917)*
Outstanding British Film – *1917* (Sam Mendes)
Outstanding Debut by a British Writer, Director or Producer
– *Bait* (Mark Jenkin)
Documentary – *For Sama* (Waad Al-Kateab, Edward Watts)
Original Screenplay – *Parasite* (Bong Joon-ho, Han Jin-won)
Adapted Screenplay – *Jojo Rabbit* (Taika Waititi)
Film Not in the English Language – *Parasite* (Bong Joon-ho)
Animated Film – *Klaus* (Sergio Pablos, Carlos Martinez
López)
Leading Actor – Joaquin Phoenix *(Joker)*
Leading Actress – Renée Zellweger *(Judy)*
Supporting Actor – Brad Pitt *(Once Upon a Time… In
Hollywood)*
Supporting Actress – Laura Dern *(Marriage Story)*
Fellowship – Kathleen Kennedy
Outstanding Contribution to British Cinema – Andy Serkis

92ND ACADEMY AWARDS
Best Picture – *Parasite* (Bong Joon-ho)
Director – Bong Joon-ho *(Parasite)*
Actor in a Leading Role – Joaquin Phoenix *(Joker)*
Actress in a Leading Role – Renée Zellweger *(Judy)*
Actor in a Supporting Role – Brad Pitt *(Once Upon a Time…
In Hollywood)*
Actress in a Supporting Role – Laura Dern *(Marriage Story)*
Animated Feature Film – *Toy Story 4* (Josh Cooley)
Writing (Original Screenplay) – *Parasite* (Bong Joon-ho, Han
Jin-won)
Writing (Adapted Screenplay) – *Jojo Rabbit* (Taika Waititi)
International Film – *Parasite* (Bong Joon-ho)
Documentary Feature – *American Factory* (Steven Bognar,
Julia Reichert)

70TH BERLIN INTERNATIONAL FILM FESTIVAL
Golden Bear – *There is No Evil* (Mohammad Rasoulof)
Grand Jury Prize – *Never Rarely Sometimes Always* (Eliza
Hittman)
Silver Bear for Best Director – Hong Sang-soo *(The Woman
who Ran)*

73RD CANNES FILM FESTIVAL
Event cancelled in its original form due to Covid-19: no prizes
awarded.

77TH VENICE INTERNATIONAL FILM FESTIVAL
Golden Lion – *Nomadland* (Chloé Zao)
Grand Jury Prize – *New Order* (Michael Franco)

LITERATURE

Nick Rennison

FICTION

It was not easy during 2020 to seek out silver linings amidst the dark clouds of the pandemic. If there was any consolation in the long periods of lockdown and disruption of our lives, it could possibly be found in the extra opportunities they provided for reading. And, although publication dates for many novels were either cancelled or postponed, there was still plenty of interesting fiction to attract attention.

There were new works from long-established writers. Set in 1977, Jonathan Coe's *Mr Wilder and Me* (Viking) followed the relationship between a young woman and the legendary film director Billy Wilder. Rose Tremain's *Islands of Mercy* (Chatto) was set in Bath in the 1860s, its central character torn between respectable marriage and an intense, illicit affair. Ali Smith's *Summer* (Hamish Hamilton) was the fourth volume of her 'Seasonal Quartet'. Martin Amis' *Inside Story* (Jonathan Cape) was a curious combination of fiction and semi-autobiography. Other novels by well-known names included William Boyd's *Trio* (Viking); Graham Swift's *Here We Are* (Scribner); Nick Hornby's *Just Like You* (Viking) and *The Autumn of the Ace* (Harvill Secker) by Louis de Bernières, the final novel in a trilogy.

The Mission House (Granta) by Carys Davies was a subtle story, set in what was once a hill station during the British Raj. Evie Wyld's *The Bass Rock* (Cape) conjured up the lives of three different women, separated by time, but linked by a connection to the forbidding Scottish island of the title. *The Liar's Dictionary* by Eley Williams (Heinemann), followed the parallel stories of two lexicographers, one in the 1890s and the other in the present day. David Mitchell's *Utopia Avenue* (Sceptre) was set in the music world of the late 1960s, as the 'Summer of Love' turned into something much darker.

DBC Pierre's *Meanwhile in Dopamine City* (Faber) was a first novel for six years by the winner of the 2003 Booker Prize; *Actress* (Cape) was a new work by another one-time Booker winner, Anne Enright; *Summerwater* (Picador) by Sarah Moss focused on 24 hours in the intertwined lives of a dozen people in the Scottish Highlands; and Victoria Hislop's *One August Night* (Headline) was a sequel to her bestselling novel *The Island*. Colum McCann's curiously titled *Apeirogon* (Bloomsbury), Andrew O'Hagan's *Mayflies* (Faber) and *The Midnight Library* (Canongate) by Matt Haig were other novels which were well received.

The Mirror and the Light (Fourth Estate) was the much-anticipated, concluding volume in Hilary Mantel's trilogy about Thomas Cromwell. Unlike its predecessors, it did not win the Man Booker Prize (it was not even shortlisted) but had all their storytelling energy and rich prose. Many other novelists turned to the past for their subjects. Stuart Turton's *The Devil and the Dark Water* (Raven) was a baroque adventure, set on board a 17th-century Dutch East India Company ship. Ian McGuire's *The Abstainer* (Scribner) examined the battle of wits between a policeman and an Irish-American assassin in 1860s Manchester. *A Room Made of Leaves* (Canongate) by the Australian novelist Kate Grenville retold the life of a pioneering woman in convict-era New South Wales. Other interesting historical novels included Kiran Millwood Hargrave's *The Mercies* (Picador); *V2* (Hutchinson) by Robert Harris; Matthew Kneale's *Pilgrims* (Atlantic); and Emma Donoghue's *The Pull of the Stars* (Picador) which echoed some of the strangeness of this year in its story of a Dublin nurse working through the 1918 flu pandemic.

Voices from America proved, as always, powerful and affecting. Colson Whitehead's *The Nickel Boys* (Fleet), first published in 2019, was the winner of the 2020 Pulitzer Prize for Fiction. *The Silence* (Picador) was a short but insightful work by the veteran novelist Don DeLillo; Marilynne Robinson's *Jack* (Virago) was the latest in her sequence of novels exploring the lives of one family from her fictional Midwestern town of Gilead; and *Rodham* (Doubleday) was an intriguing work of counterfactual fiction in which Curtis Sittenfeld imagined what might have happened if Hillary Clinton hadn't married Bill. Other notable works by American authors included Edmund White's *A Saint from Texas* (Bloomsbury); C. Pam Zhang's *How Much of These Hills is Gold* (Virago); Jenny Offill's *Weather* (Granta); and Brit Bennett's *A Vanishing Half* (Dialogue Books), a mesmerising exploration of racism in America through several decades.

Two major international prizes both went to Faber authors. The International Dublin Literary Award was won by Anna Burns' *Milkman*, first published in 2018, and Marieke Lucas Rijneveld was awarded the 2020 International Booker Prize for *The Discomfort of Evening*. Other translated fiction which received attention during the year included *The Lying Life of Adults* (Europa), the latest work by the reclusive Italian author Elena Ferrante; Daniel Kehlmann's *Tyll* (riverrun) which reimagined the German trickster figure of Tyll Eulenspiegel; Andres Neuman's *Fracture* (Granta) about an elderly Hiroshima survivor; and *The Wondrous and Tragic Life of Ivan and Ivana* (World Editions) by the Guadeloupe-born French novelist Maryse Condé.

Arguably the year's most illuminating volume of short fiction was Shirley Hazzard's *Collected Stories* (Virago), bringing together work from several decades by the much-admired Australian-American writer who died in 2016. John Lanchester's *Reality and Other Stories* (Faber) was a collection of tales in which the uncanny and modern technology met and mingled; and the stories in Kevin Barry's *That Old Country Music* (Canongate) were mostly set in the author's native Ireland.

In crime fiction, plenty of well-loved series characters featured in new stories. Ian Rankin's *A Song for the Dark Times* (Orion) provided another case for John Rebus, now retired from the Edinburgh police; *The Darkest Evening* (Macmillan) by Ann Cleeves was the latest of her novels about DCI Vera Stanhope; Val McDermid's *Still Life* (Little, Brown) was another excursion for DCI Karen Pirie; and *Troubled Blood* (Sphere) was a huge doorstop of a novel by J.K. Rowling, writing as Robert Galbraith, her fifth book about London private detective Cormoran Strike. Mark Billingham's *Cry Baby* (Little, Brown) gave a back story to his Detective Inspector Tom Thorne.

The most commercially successful debut in the crime genre was undoubtedly *The Thursday Murder Club* (Viking) by the quiz host Richard Osman, a 'cosy' tale told with much wit and sometimes unexpected bite. Far from cosy, John Banville's *Snow* (Faber) was a murder mystery set in the Irish countryside in the 1950s; Tana French's *The Searcher* (Viking) was an exceptionally powerful story of a child's disappearance; and *Little Disasters* (Simon & Schuster) by Sarah Vaughan was an ingenious new thriller by the author of the bestselling *Anatomy of a Scandal*.

Other interesting crime novels and thrillers included Jane Casey's *The Cutting Place* (HarperCollins); Sabine Durrant's *Finders, Keepers* (Hodder); *The Less Dead* (Harvill Secker) by Denise Mina; Lucy Foley's *The Guest List* (HarperCollins); and *Silver* (Wildfire), the latest example of what some critics have called 'outback noir' by the Australian writer Chris Hammer.

Peter May found the right year to publish *Lockdown* (Quercus), a dystopian thriller set during a flu pandemic. In a very different vein, Sophie Hannah served up a new Hercule Poirot mystery in *The Killings at Kingfisher Hill* (HarperCollins). Historical crime fiction of note included Andrew Taylor's *The Last Protector* (HarperCollins), his latest thriller set in Restoration England; *The Silver Collar* (Hodder) by Antonia Hodgson; and *Execution* (HarperCollins) by S. J. Parris, a further adventure for her Tudor-era secret agent Giordano Bruno.

Many of the big beasts of American crime fiction published new novels during the year. Michael Connelly's *The Law of Innocence* (Orion) was a courtroom thriller featuring his LA-based lawyer Mickey Haller; John Grisham returned to Jake Brigance, the hero of his very first book, *A Time to Kill*, in *A Time for Mercy* (Hodder); and *A Private Cathedral* (Orion) provided a new case for James Lee Burke's Louisiana detective Dave Robicheaux. Carl Hiaasen's *Squeeze Me* (Sphere) was another of his luridly over-the-top Florida-set crime stories. British writer Lee Child has long been resident in the USA and his character Jack Reacher is American. *The Sentinel* (Bantam), co-written with Andrew Child, was Reacher's twenty-fifth adventure.

In science fiction, the year began with the UK publication of a new novel by one of the most iconic names in the genre. William Gibson's *Agency* (Viking) was a typically inventive narrative set in both an alternative 2017 and a post-apocalyptic London of the future. Other well-known writers, with long and still productive careers, put their names to new work. These included Kim Stanley Robinson with *The Ministry for the Future* (Orbit), Paul McAuley with *War of the Maps* (Gollancz) and Peter F. Hamilton with *The Saints of Salvation* (Macmillan), the concluding volume of his 'Salvation' sequence. Christopher Priest's *The Evidence* (Gollancz) returned to the Dream Archipelago he created in earlier fiction.

Attack Surface (Head of Zeus) was the third title in Cory Doctorow's 'Little Brother' series; Adrian Tchaikovsky's *The Doors of Eden* (Tor) was a standalone work by the winner of last year's British Science Fiction Award for Best Novel; and Ken Liu's *The Hidden Girl* (Head of Zeus) was a volume of short stories by a much-praised practitioner of the format. Sarah Pinsker, already acclaimed for her shorter fiction, had her first novel, *A Song for a New Day* (Head of Zeus), published in the UK. In America, it had won the 2019 Nebula Award for Best Novel. Other notable titles included Christopher Paolini's *To Sleep in a Sea of Stars* (Tor); *The Vanished Birds* (Titan) by Simon Jimenez; and Micaiah Johnson's *The Space Between Worlds* (Hodder), an impressive debut work.

N. K. Jemisin, recipient this year of a so-called 'MacArthur Genius Grant', began a new series with *The City We Became* (Orbit). Jemisin's work often occupies that contested ground between science fiction and fantasy. More clearly falling into the latter category were Alix E. Harrow's *The Once and Future Witches* (Orbit); Andrea Stewart's *The Bone Shard Daughter* (Orbit); *Harrow the Ninth* (Tor), the second volume in Tamsyn Muir's 'The Locked Tomb' trilogy; and Silvia Moreno-Garcia's *Mexican Gothic* (Jo Fletcher). Alex Pheby's *Mordew* (Galley Beggar) was the first in a proposed trilogy; *Piranesi* (Bloomsbury) was a second novel by Susanna Clarke, the author of *Jonathan Strange and Mr Norrell*; and Natasha Pulley's *The Lost Future of Pepperharrow* (Bloomsbury) was set in a richly imagined alternative Japan. M. John Harrison's work is usually described as either science fiction or fantasy but, in truth, it defies easy definition. His latest novel was *The Sunken Land Begins to Rise Again* (Gollancz), winner of the year's Goldsmiths Prize for fiction, awarded for opening up 'new possibilities for the novel form'.

NON-FICTION

With the pandemic dominating the news, many people have taken comfort from the natural world. For a number of years,

some of the most inspiring works of non-fiction have been found amongst titles which can be broadly categorised as 'natural history', so it was little surprise that this continued to be true in 2020. Helen Macdonald's *Vesper Flights* (Cape) was her long-awaited follow-up to the bestselling *H is for Hawk*; *Diary of a Young Naturalist* (Little Toller), winner of the year's Wainwright Prize for Nature Writing, consisted of the astonishingly mature observations and thoughts of the teenage naturalist Dara McAnulty; *English Pastoral* (Allen Lane) was a new work by James Rebanks, author of *The Shepherd's Life*; and Raynor Winn's *The Wild Silence* (Michael Joseph) was a follow-up to her bestselling book *The Salt Path*.

This was also, of course, the year of the American presidential election, and books on politics, particularly across the other side of the Atlantic, unsurprisingly garnered attention. *Rage* (Simon & Schuster), by the near-legendary Watergate journalist Bob Woodward, was arguably the most authoritative *exposé* of the dysfunctionality of the Trump White House; and, for unflattering detail about the 45th President's character, nothing could match *Too Much and Never Enough* (Simon & Schuster), a devastating hatchet job by his niece Mary L. Trump. In sharp contrast, Barack Obama's *A Promised Land* (Viking), one of the year's most eagerly awaited works of non-fiction, proved a reminder of a very different era in American politics.

Compared to the more incendiary anti-Trump volumes, Tom Bower's *Boris Johnson: The Gambler* (WH Allen) was less of a character assassination than might have been expected but still revealed information the Prime Minister (and his father) might have hoped to keep hidden. Certainly David Cameron and many of those Tory politicians featured to their disadvantage in Sasha Swire's *Diary of an MP's Wife* (Little, Brown) would have wanted her to keep her gossipy indiscretions to herself.

The year's most original biography was undoubtedly Craig Brown's *One Two Three Four* (Fourth Estate), winner of the 2020 Baillie Gifford for Non-Fiction, which employed a dizzying array of techniques to offer new insights into the Beatles. Amongst other notable biographies were *Black Spartacus* (Allen Lane) by Sudhir Hazareesingh, about the Haitian revolutionary; Ben Macintyre's account of a Soviet spy's extraordinary life in *Agent Sonya* (Viking); and A.N. Wilson's idiosyncratic *The Mystery of Charles Dickens* (Atlantic). Hadley Freeman's *House of Glass* (Fourth Estate), about her Jewish family's experiences in the twentieth century, Pete Paphides's *Broken Greek* (Quercus) and *Motherwell* (Weidenfeld & Nicolson) by the journalist Deborah Orr, who died in 2019, were all, in very different ways, remarkable memoirs. Kate Summerscale's *The Haunting of Alma Fielding* (Bloomsbury) was a story of mediums and spiritualism in the shadow of war.

Amongst the year's most original works of history were Pen Vogler's *Scoff* (Atlantic), a fascinating account of food and class in Britain; *Conquistadores* (Allen Lane), an intriguing reassessment of the founders of the Spanish Empire, by Fernando Cervantes; *This Sporting Life* (Oxford University Press) by Robert Colls, a record of two centuries of sport in England; and Neil Price's *The Children of Ash and Elm* (Allen Lane) which was an epic new history of the Vikings. Charles Spencer's *The White Ship* (William Collins) was an account of a half-forgotten medieval disaster in which the heir to the English throne died; Peter Stothard's *The Last Assassin* (Weidenfeld & Nicolson) followed the hunt for the killers of Julius Caesar.

POETRY

This year's Nobel Prize for Literature went to a poet – the American Louise Glück who was cited for her 'unmistakable poetic voice that with austere beauty makes individual existence universal'. Other significant female voices were heard in the course of the year. The Irish poet Eavan Boland died in

April at the age of 75 but her posthumously published collection, *The Historians* (Carcanet), was a reminder of her exceptional gifts. Internationally renowned as a novelist, Margaret Atwood has always been a poet as well. *Dearly* (Chatto) was her first collection in more than a decade.

Randomly Moving Particles (Faber) by the former poet laureate Andrew Motion consisted of two long poems linked by three shorter pieces. The present Poet Laureate, Simon Armitage, gathered together poems, old and new, which were inspired by his home territory of West Yorkshire in *Magnetic Field: The Marsden Poems* (Faber). *The Late Sun* (Faber) was a new collection by Christopher Reid; and *Belongings* (Bloodaxe) was the latest volume by David Constantine, this year awarded the Queen's Gold Medal for Poetry. Other interesting collections included Natalie Diaz's *Postcolonial Love Poem* (Faber); *The Martian's Regress* (Cape) by J. O. Morgan; Sasha Dugdale's *Deformations* (Carcanet); Pascale Petit's *Tiger Girl* (Bloodaxe); and Glyn Maxwell's *How the Hell Are You* (Picador). *Zonal* (Faber) by the Scottish poet Don Paterson consisted of, in his own words, 'experiments in science-fictional or fantastic autobiography'.

Caroline Bird's *The Air Year* (Carcanet) won the 2020 Forward Prize for Best Poetry Collection. In *Rendang* (Granta), which took the Forward Prize for Best First Collection, Will Harris drew on his Anglo-Indonesian heritage to create potent poems about the complexities of personal and cultural identity. Notable amongst other debut collections were Rachel Long's *My Darling from the Lions* (Picador), Seán Hewitt's *Tongues of Fire* (Cape) and *Cannibal* (Picador) by Safiya Sinclair. In *Poor* (Penguin) Caleb Femi combined poetry and photography to create a memorable portrait of growing up black in south London. Jay Bernard, whose 2019 collection *Surge* (Chatto) commemorated those who lost their lives in the New Cross fire of 1981, was this year chosen as the winner of the Sunday Times Young Writer Award.

CHILDREN'S

Familiar and much-loved authors of children's fiction produced new work in 2020. Philip Pullman returned to the world of *His Dark Materials* with the novella *Serpentine* (Penguin). Michael Morpurgo's *The Puffin Keeper* (Puffin) was an enchanting tale of a man devoting his life to ensuring a lighthouse continued to shine. The ever-prolific David Walliams published *Slime* and *Code Name Bananas* (both HarperCollins). J.K. Rowling's *The Ickabog* (Little, Brown) was an original fairy tale. The former children's laureate and poet Michael Rosen, who survived a near-fatal encounter with the Covid virus, published *On the Move* (Walker), a collection of poems about experiences of migration.

The variety of books published for all age groups remained undiminished in 2020. Amongst picture books for younger children, *Where Snow Angels Go* (Walker) was written by the novelist Maggie O'Farrell and illustrated by Daniela Jaglenka Terrazzini, and Shirley Hughes revisited her much-loved character Dogger, first seen forty years ago, in *Dogger's Christmas* (Puffin). The Waterstones Children's Book Prize 2020 was won by a picture book first published the previous year – *Look Up!* (Puffin) by Nathan Bryon and Dapo Adeola.

Fiction for younger children included Kiran Millwood Hargrave's *A Secret of Birds & Bone* (Chicken House); David Almond's *Brand New Boy* (Walker); *The Monsters of Rookhaven* (Macmillan) by Pádraig Kenny; and Natasha Farrant's *Voyage of the Sparrowhawk* (Faber), an adventure story about a journey from England to France in the aftermath of World War One. *The Griffin Gate* (Barrington Stoke) was a steampunk fantasy by Vashti Hardy (her previous title *Wildspark* won a 2020 Blue Peter Book Award) and *The Beast and the Bethany* (Egmont) was an equally imaginative tale by Jack Meggitt-Phillips.

For older children and young adults, Holly Jackson's *Good Girl, Bad Blood* (Electric Monkey) was the sequel to the previous year's crime thriller *A Good Girl's Guide to Murder; Cane Warriors* (Andersen Press) by Alex Wheatle was a powerful tale of a slave uprising on a Jamaican sugar plantation in the 1760s; *The Great Godden* (Bloomsbury) was a finely crafted coming-of-age story by Meg Rosoff; and *The Ballad of Songbirds and Snakes* (Scholastic) was a new 'Hunger Games' novel by Suzanne Collins. Elle McNicoll's *A Kind of Spark* (Knights Of), *Burn* (Walker) by Patrick Ness, and Sally Nicholls's *The Silent Stars Go By* (Andersen) were among other titles that caught the eye.

NEWS

Like every other field of human endeavour, the book trade in 2020 was severely affected by the pandemic. Although bookshops petitioned to be classified as essential retailers, they were obliged to close for months at a time. Several very well-known shops faced the prospect of permanent closure. Shakespeare & Co., the legendary English-language bookshop in Paris, was forced to beg for help from its customers as its sales plummeted by 80 per cent over the summer. Travel and map specialist Stanfords, established in London in 1853, launched a crowdfunding project to keep it going. Throughout the year, the bigger publishing groups rejigged their publishing schedules. Many smaller firms, deprived of outlets for their books to be seen, saw revenues shrink. Writers' incomes were reduced. The Society of Authors, whose research showed 57 per cent of writers had suffered a substantial drop in earnings, dispensed more than £1m in emergency grants, and both Arts Council England and the TS Eliot Foundation provided assistance.

With the doors of bricks-and-mortar shops shut, Amazon's sales unsurprisingly soared. Independent bookshops fought back against the giant's ever-growing dominance with the arrival in the UK of an online retail platform which had already proved successful in the USA. Bookshop.org was launched in November to provide a means through which some of the nearly 900 independents in the country could reach new customers.

The news throughout the book trade was not all bad. There was much to celebrate. Lockdown created a new appetite for reading. The ebook had suffered a decline over the previous five years but sales grew by 17 per cent during the first six months of the year. At the same time purchases of audiobooks, already an increasing market, went up by 42 per cent. Worldwide sales of printed books unsurprisingly declined during lockdown but, when shops were able to open again, some titles had near-record sales on publication. *The Thursday Murder Club* by TV quiz presenter Richard Osman sold 45,000 copies in three days, becoming the fastest ever selling crime debut novel. The first week after reopening in June saw an increase of 31 per cent in the sales of printed books over the same week in the previous year. On what has been called 'Super Thursday', 3 September this year, nearly 600 hardbacks were published on one day. In that first week of September there were sales of books worth more than £33m, an 11 per cent increase on the corresponding week in 2019.

The future of literature and the book trade depends, of course, on today's children developing an enthusiasm for reading. Here the omens were mixed. Depressingly, a survey of nearly 60,000 children carried out by the National Literacy Trust found that a third do not see themselves in the books they read. Partly, the child's socioeconomic circumstances affected their ability to identify with the characters in books but, in a society in which only 5 per cent of children's books feature a black, Asian or minority ethnic main character, the biggest factor was ethnicity. Another study by the Centre for Literacy in Primary Education found that children's books were eight times as likely to include animals as main characters as BAME people. The one encouraging sign is that the percentage of children's books with BAME main characters has been steadily rising in the last few years. But there is still a long road to travel.

The often contentious Women's Prize for Fiction (known for many years as the Orange Prize for Fiction) marked its 25th anniversary with a public vote to decide the 'winner of winners' from all the novels awarded the prize. *Half of a Yellow Sun* by Chimamanda Ngozi Adichie emerged as the victor. In a year in which statues, for a variety of reasons, attracted much public debate, memorials to two celebrated women writers of the past were in the news. Maggi Hambling's sculpture to honour Mary Wollstonecraft, unveiled on Newington Green, London, was met with dismay by many critics who considered a silvery naked female form a poorly considered tribute to a famous feminist pioneer. And the campaign to install a life-size statue of Virginia Woolf on a terrace overlooking the Thames near Richmond Bridge was given an extra boost by a number of fundraising events.

And finally to the Literary Review's Bad Sex in Fiction award. Established in 1993 and given each year to the author judged to have written the worst, most embarrassing description of sex in a novel, it was cancelled in 2020. The judges announced that 'the public had been subjected to too many bad things this year to justify exposing it to bad sex as well'. It was difficult to disagree.

FAREWELLS

John le Carré, arguably the greatest of all writers of espionage fiction, died in December 2020 at the age of 89. Over a period of nearly sixty years, le Carré (real name David Cornwell) had produced a series of novels, including *The Spy Who Came in from the Cold*, *Tinker Tailor Soldier Spy* and *The Night Manager*, which explored the deceits and betrayals, first of the Cold War and then of global capitalism. In the figure of George Smiley, the self-effacing but brilliantly intelligent officer featured in many of his novels, he created one of the iconic characters of twentieth-century English literature. Jan Morris, who passed away a few weeks before le Carré, led one of the more extraordinary lives of the last hundred years. Born James Morris, she became a journalist under that name, reporting on the first ascent of Everest in 1953, and writing *Pax Britannica*, a three-volume history of the British Empire. *Conundrum*, published in 1974, was a bestselling account of her gender transition from James to Jan. Her travel writings included critically acclaimed works on Venice, Trieste and New York and her 1985 novel *Last Letters from Hav* was shortlisted for the Booker Prize.

Other writers who died during the year included the American novelists Alison Lurie, winner of the 1985 Pulitzer Prize for Fiction for her novel *Foreign Affairs*; Charles Portis, author of *True Grit*; and Charles Webb (*The Graduate*); the Swedish crime novelist Maj Sjöwall, co-creator with her partner Per Wahlöö of the detective Martin Beck; the travel writer Alexander Frater; the adventurer and writer Tim Severin; Luke Rhinehart (real name George Cockroft), author of the cult novel, *The Dice Man*; Elizabeth Wurtzel, the author of *Prozac Nation*; the philosopher Roger Scruton; Christopher Tolkien, who edited *The Silmarillion* and others of his father J.R.R. Tolkien's posthumously published works; the polymathic literary critic George Steiner; the Irish poets Eavan Boland and Derek Mahon; the biographer Fiona McCarthy; the American playwrights Mart Crowley (*The Boys in the Band*) and Larry Kramer (*The Normal Heart*); the often controversial German writer Rolf Hochhuth; the Spanish novelist Carlos Ruiz Zafón (*The Shadow of the Wind*); the thriller writer Clive Cussler (*Raise the Titanic!*); the children's writer Sam McBratney (*Guess How Much I Love You*); the American SF novelist Ben Bova; Albert Uderzo, co-creator of Asterix the Gaul; the Lancashire-born author of family sagas Josephine Cox; the American Beat poets Michael McClure and Ruth Weiss; the writer Charles Allen (*Tales from the Raj*); the Irish playwright and novelist Eugene McCabe; the feminist and sexologist Shere Hite (*The Hite Report*); the playwrights Ronald Harwood (*The Dresser*) and Mary O'Malley (*Once a Catholic*); the centenarian Welsh novelist Emyr Humphreys; the American crime novelist Mary Higgins Clark; the publisher Tom Maschler; the novelist and children's writer Jill Paton Walsh; and the much-admired, Irish short story writer Julia O'Faolain.

AWARDS

MAN BOOKER PRIZE 2020
Douglas Stuart - *Shuggie Bain* (Winner)

Shortlist
Diane Cook – *The New Wilderness*
Tsitsi Dangarembga – *This Mournable Body*
Avni Doshi – *Burnt Sugar*
Maaza Mengiste – *The Shadow King*
Brandon Taylor – *Real Life*

COSTA BOOK AWARDS 2020
Announced 4 January and 26 January 2021

WOMEN'S PRIZE FOR FICTION 2020
Maggie O'Farrell – *Hamnet* (Winner)

Shortlist
Angie Cruz – *Dominicana*
Bernardine Evaristo – *Girl, Woman, Other*
Natalie Haynes – *A Thousand Ships*
Hilary Mantel – *The Mirror and the Light*
Jenny Offill - *Weather*

CILIP CARNEGIE MEDAL IN CHILDREN'S LITERATURE 2020
Anthony McGowan – *Lark* (Winner)

Shortlist
Dean Atta – *The Black Flamingo*
Nick Lake – *Nowhere on Earth*
Randy Ribay – *Patron Saints of Nothing*
Annet Schaap – *Lampie*
Marcus & Julian Sedgwick – *Voyages in the Underworld of Orpheus Black*
Angie Thomas – *On the Come Up*
Chris Vick – *Girl. Boy. Sea.*

MEDIA

Steve Clarke

TELEVISION

The COVID-19 pandemic exerted a profound impact on television during the year under review. In the spring lockdown production was halted across TV. Flagship shows including the soaps were hit; for the first time in almost 60 years the *Coronation Street* set went dark; the veteran soap would celebrate its 60th anniversary in December. With people told to stay at home, other than to exercise, receive health care or to shop for food and medicine, TV ratings soared, especially for news programmes.

THE NATION TURNS TO THE BBC

In the short term, the clear winner was the BBC, which has seen support for its funding less secure under recent governments. Suddenly, the corporation went from being the subject of public criticism from the newly elected Boris Johnson-led government to serving as a vital conduit for ministers to communicate their messages to a deeply traumatised nation. A broadcast by the prime minster on 23 March announcing unprecedented peace-time restrictions on Briton's daily lives was watched by more than 27 million people, the majority – some 15.4 million – tuning into BBC One.

Government ministers, particularly health secretary Matt Hancock, were regularly seen – and heard – on BBC news and current affairs programmes. This represented an extraordinary volte-face as high-profile programmes like BBC Radio 4's *Today* had struggled in vain to get ministers to agree to appear. While political tensions were still evident between some government ministers and key parts of the broadcast media, especially the BBC, the effect of the pandemic tempered this public combativeness

With echoes of wartime radio bulletins, in the spring televised daily press conferences featuring the government's chief medical officer, Chris Witty, and chief scientific officer, Patrick Vallance, flanked by a member of Johnson's team, became a regular feature of life in lockdown.

PIERS MORGAN CAPTURES THE PUBLIC MOOD

As the COVID-19 death toll mounted amidst accusations of government incompetence (the shortage of personal protection equipment was highlighted by all parts of the media) ITV's daytime staple, *Good Morning Britain*, in the view of some commentators came into its own. Presenter Piers Morgan, once a supporter of the Conservative Party, became a vociferous and outspoken opponent of the Johnson administration's handling of the health crisis. In May, Morgan took to Twitter to describe Johnson's failure to sack Dominic Cummings for flouting lockdown rules as a 'disgrace.'

The Guardian's political sketch writer, John Crace, hailed Morgan for capturing the public mood. He was: "The everyman who isn't afraid to use what power he has to call out bullshit and incompetence for what it is. A kind of national group therapy for all those of us who feel powerless."

CHANNEL 4 FREEEZES OUT BORIS JOHNSON

The acrimony between some broadcasters and certain politicians was evident in December's especially fractious general election campaign. During a Channel 4 news party leaders' debate on climate change that Johnson had declined to appear on, he was replaced by a melting ice sculpture of the planet.

Such was the anger of some Conservative politicians at what they regarded as a cheap journalistic stunt, they said that privatising the broadcaster would be back on the agenda should Johnson be re-elected. In the event, he was returned to power with an impressive 80-seat majority.

Throughout much of 2020 the sight of TV news anchors and other presenters broadcasting from their homes became part of the 'new normal.' As the health crisis worsened Channel 4 quickly commissioned and broadcast several shows designed to cheer up the UK. *Grayson Perry's Art Club* invited audiences to discover their inner Van Gogh. 'Confined to his home studio, the artist surveils creative acts across the nation from a large computer screen, like a benign cultural security guard,' opined Hettie Judah in the *i*. In a similar mood, Jamie Oliver gave tips on how to prepare basic but nutritious meals in *Keep Cooking and Carry On*.

COVID-19 UPENDS TV BUDGETS

Channel 4 was putting on a brave face. In common with ITV, the economic firestorm of COVID-19 was forcing drastic budget cuts as advertising revenue vanished. The predominantly freelance workforce responsible for most TV production was hit particularly hard as overnight employment dried up.

In early lockdown, the BBC won widespread praise for its Bitesize home-schooling initiative. For mums and dads, the service was a game changer when schools and nurseries closed across the UK in late March. Not everyone was happy, however, as the *Daily Mail* reported one anonymous parent complaining: 'My son's school have decided this is what they'll do in terms of teaching... We don't have a TV licence as we have other online subscriptions. Will we be allowed to access the videos?'

With exquisite timing, on 24 March Disney's much anticipated video-on-demand service, Disney+, launched in the UK. Within a month the family-friendly film and TV online direct-to-consumer platform had acquired 4.3 million subscribers, making Disney+ arguably the most successful UK media debut of all time.

Throughout 2019–20 streaming platforms continued to gain ground at the expense of traditional broadcasters. BritBox, the joint BBC-ITV on-demand service, was launched in November 2019, and made a splash when it brought back *Spitting Image* in the autumn of 2020. In the summer it was revealed that YouTube was the UK's third most popular video service after the BBC and ITV. Ofcom reported that it was no longer only younger audiences watching on-demand services; in significant numbers, the over-55s were getting the Netflix habit too. Netflix *et al.* declines to publish regular viewing figures so accurate information regarding individual shows streamed by these companies is not available. But it was generally assumed that for those under 35 around half their viewing time was spent with streaming platforms. Shows like Netflix's *Tiger King*, *The Crown* and *The Queen's Gambit* were all ideal lockdown TV.

DRAMA CONTINUES TO OCCUPY CENTRE STAGE

Throughout 2019–20 the main networks continued to provide enough high-end drama series – and the occasional one-off – to remain competitive with the subscription video on demand platforms. BBC Three's adaptation of Sally Rooney's best-selling love story *Normal People* was widely admired. Also outstanding were BBC2's *The Windermere Children*, the story of Nazi concentration camp survivors brought to England as refugees, a feminist take on the Profumo scandal, BBC One's *The Trial of Christine Keeler* starring Sophie Cookson in the title role, and the sublime second series of *My Brilliant Friend* on Sky Atlantic. There was praise too for Sky Atlantic's uber-violent *The Gangs of London*.

Two retellings of recent history also stood out – ITV's *Quiz*, written by James Graham and based on the 'Coughing Major' *Who Wants To Be A Millionaire* incident, and BBC One's *The Salisbury Poisonings*, a three-part reconstruction of how the Wiltshire city reacted to the poisoning of Russian double agent, Sergei Skripal. The story was told from the perspective of local people, notably public health officer Tracy Daszkiewicz, played by Anne-Marie Duff. Screened in June, *The Salisbury Poisonings'* contemporary resonance as the coronavirus pandemic raged added to the programme's impact.

Mindful of the challenge presented by the popularity of its online rivals, the BBC put a lot of effort into promoting one of 2020's most original dramas, *I May Destroy You*, written by and starring Michaela Cole. In *The Guardian*, Lucy Mangan wondered if *I May Destroy You* was the year's best TV drama. 'It is an astonishing, beautiful, thrilling series – a sexual-consent drama if you want the one-line pitch, but so, so much more than that,' she wrote.

BLACK LIVES ON THE FRONT LINE
Another outstanding drama was *Small Axe*, a group of five films directed by the Oscar-winning Steve McQueen. It dealt with the experience of London's West Indian community in the 1960s, 1970s and early 1980s. Of the first film, *Mangrove*, *The Telegraph's* Anita Singh commented: 'Mangrove is a chronicle of racism and the black British experience, a gripping courtroom drama and a beautifully directed period piece. Watched in a packed cinema, I can imagine it is exhilarating. But as a television experience, it is pummelling.'

The murder of George Floyd in May in Minneapolis, USA reignited the Black Lives Matter movement and led to much soul searching by decision makers in British TV. Across the board, broadcasters announced new diversity schemes. In August, at the Edinburgh Television Festival, the historian, writer and broadcaster David Olusoga gave a blistering MacTaggart lecture in which he outlined how systemic racism had blighted his TV career and led to unrepresentative programmes that failed to reflect modern Britain.

Tim Davie, who took over as the BBC's new director general in September, appeared to be listening. He told the Royal Television Society that improving diversity among BBC staff, particularly those in senior jobs, was 'mission critical.' Davie pledged to create a '50-20-12 organisation', referring respectively to the proportion of staff from female, BAME and disabled backgrounds.

THE ROYAL SOAP OPERA REIGNITES
Television's relationship with the British royal family is symbiotic. In November 2019, BBC Two's *Newsnight* broadcasted an exclusive interview with Prince Andrew conducted by Emily Maitlis. He was grilled regarding his relationship with the billionaire paedophile Jeffrey Epstein. There was a consensus that the interview was a PR disaster for the prince but apparently the palace voiced few misgivings. Maitlis told *Radio Times*: 'we know that the palace was happy with the interview. We had plenty of engagement with them after it went out. I think their shock was not at the interview itself, but the reaction it caused in the days and weeks afterwards.' One immediate consequence of the programme was that Prince Andrew 'stepped back' from royal duties. He strenuously denied accusations that he had slept with a teenager at the home of Epstein's friend, Ghislaine Maxwell.

Another BBC royal interview caused ripples during 2019–20 –Martin Bashir's revealing interview with Princess Diana broadcast by *Panorama* in 1995 was placed centre stage. It was alleged by Diana's brother, Earl Spencer, that Bashir had used dirty tricks to secure the interview. The BBC announced a new inquiry to be conducted by Lord Dyson, a former Master of the Rolls, to examine the case.

Season four of *The Crown*, which was launched in the autumn, generated much controversy. Most of it concerned the unflattering light the series shone on Prince Charles' treatment of his young wife, Diana, played by Emma Corrin, who most critics agreed was exceptional in the role. Culture Secretary Oliver Dowden said *The Crown* should carry 'a health' warning to make it clear to audiences that the show was fiction. Opinion formers from both ends of the political spectrum criticised Dowden's idea. More tellingly, some columnists saw contemporary echoes in the depiction of the royal family's attitude to Diana. Writing in *The Guardian*, Rhiannon Lucy Cosslett opined: 'these days, many, many more young women identify as feminists, and as with the treatment of Monica Lewinsky, many of them are looking at the Diana story with horror. This is a generation raised in a celebrity culture obsessed with female pain and, now they are seeing the excoriation of the Duchess of Sussex in the press, they are wondering how much has really changed.'

COMFORT TV COMES TO THE FORE
The deep trauma of coronavirus led to record-breaking audiences in 2019–20 for some of British TV's most popular entertainment shows as people sought distraction from the health emergency. In the autumn the final of *The Great British Bake Off*, made in a so-called 'biosphere' to minimize social contact, was watched by a peak of 10.4 million on Channel 4; the first edition of the 20th season of ITV's *I'm A Celebrity...Get Me Out Of Here*, transferred from the Australian rainforest to a Welsh castle, was watched by a peak of 12 million viewers, the biggest overnight audience since *Gavin and Stacey's* Christmas special in 2019.

In December the final of BBC One's *Strictly Come Dancing*, the first to feature a same-sex couple, was seen by more than 13 million viewers. 'Strictly has provided much needed sparkle to our weekends this autumn,' said acting BBC One controller Kate Phillips. These shows had been made under new protocols designed to keep everybody involved in their production safe from the virus. The ingenuity of TV to adapt to the pandemic would be one of the legacies of a year that no one will ever forget.

RADIO

Radio's unique intimacy came into its own during the pandemic. Exactly how successful the medium was in informing and entertaining the UK during 2019–20 remains unknown because the body that measures radio audiences, RAJAR, suspended their work due to the difficulty of conducting face-to-face interviews with listeners. But there was no doubt that people stranded at home, especially those living alone, appreciated more than ever the special magic that is radio.

As Ofcom observed in its annual report on the BBC published in October: 'our research shows that around a third of adults tuned in to radio for up-to-date information about the pandemic at the start of lockdown and also indicates that listeners continued to turn to radio for companionship and music. Around a fifth of adults turned to BBC radio during the start of lockdown and the BBC's *Coronavirus Newscast* was the most popular podcast at that time.'

DOWNING STREET ENDS *TODAY* BOYCOTT
The spring lockdown had an immediate impact on radio listening. Levels of listening in cars and at workplaces, which typically accounts for around 40 per cent of all listening, fell. Radio was able to respond quickly to the crisis as home studios were set up apparently seamlessly. The BBC's director of audio James Purnell, interviewed by the Royal Television Society in

the summer, revealed that the BBC had considered shutting some of its radio stations. 'At one point, we were planning to close down various stations but, because of the flexibility and ingenuity of our technical staff, we suddenly found that a lot could be done from home,' explained Purnell. He indicated that Radio 4 was an immediate winner from the crisis as listeners turned to the service's news and current affairs coverage.

Number 10 had refused to allow ministers to appear on the flagship *Today* programme since the 2019 December general election. The prime minister's advisors were reportedly furious with the BBC for what they claimed were its anti-Brexit prejudices. The *PoliticsHome* website reported one as saying: 'the *Today* programme is irrelevant, it is not a serious programme anymore so we are not going to engage with it – it is far better for us to put people up on BBC *Breakfast* and *Five Live*." But at the end of February, Conservative MP Edward Argar, a health minister, became the first Government minister to appear on *Today* since the election. Subsequently, ministers regularly featured on the programme.

COMMERCIAL RADIO'S SUCCESS CONTINUES

Figures published for the first quarter of 2020 showed commercial stations such as Magic, Heart, Smooth and Kisstory continuing to put pressure on Radio 2, the UK's most popular station, with an audience of 14.4 million but 1 million fewer than the previous year. LBC reached a record 2.8 million listeners across the UK each week. Classic FM registered its highest audience for 13 years – some 5.5 million a week – while the number of listeners tuning into Radio 3 fell slightly to just under 2 million.

However, as the pandemic tightened its grip on the UK Radio 3 gained a new prominence in national life. With so much grim news, the service provided welcome relief. In May a *Guardian* leader opined: 'in this moment of lockdown, it is to BBC Radio 3 in particular that many are flocking, for it offers a very particular kind of shelter in the current storm. The network provides, above all, an escape: an escape from the news bulletins and speculation, an escape from the wranglings and bunglings, an escape from the sadness and anxiety.'

Listeners were discovering other types of music as well; Radio 1Xtra and Radio 6 Music both benefited from lockdown, and as Miranda Sawyer reported in the *Observer*: "No Signal's live soundclash show 10 v 10 has exploded into success, with hundreds of thousands tuning in worldwide to hear Vybz Kartel tracks played in competition against Wizkid's, or Ian Wright clash with Julie Adenuga with 80s v 90s tunes."

TIMES RADIO MAKES ITS DEBUT

The growing confidence in the commercial sector was evident when in June Times Radio, backed by the newspaper group, News UK, launched. A speech-based rival to Radio 4 had been a long time coming. Critics broadly approved of the new service which had successfully poached some former BBC presenters including Mariella Frostrup and John Pienaar. Writing in *The Sunday Times*, the doyenne of radio critics, Gillian Reynolds commented: 'Times Radio is unique. It is commercial, but doesn't carry commercials. It has acquired presenters and personnel from the BBC, but doesn't sound like a BBC network. It is sponsored by *The Times* and *The Sunday Times*, but will reach listeners who may not read either. As radio stations go, its first day was mostly charming but bland.' One of the first people to be heard on the new station was the unmistakable voice of the prime minister, interviewed by Aasmah Mir and Stig Abell on their breakfast show.

Later in the year there was outrage in Fleet Street and on social media when the BBC revealed that the host of Radio 2's breakfast show, Zoe Ball, was the second highest paid star on the corporation's pay roll – despite a dip in popularity for her show. 'Zoe Ball has lost a million listeners from the Radio 2

breakfast show since she took over from Chris Evans. On Tuesday we learnt that she has had a pay increase of a million pounds. A pound for every listener that she lost,' reckoned the *The Telegraph's* Charlotte Runcie, who was furious at Ball's £1.3m fee. 'How much more would they have paid her if she'd actually added listeners?' the columnist wanted to know. In November, *The Telegraph* told Radio 2 to 'up its game' when Graham Norton left the station to join Virgin.

EXIT MR BREXIT

Another radio presenter attracting controversy was the former UKIP leader, Nigel Farage, whose contract to present a five day a week show for LBC was abruptly terminated in June. A few days before his exit Farage had compared Black Lives Matters protestors to the Taliban for demolishing statues of slave traders. LBC's owner, Global Radio, was criticised by some presenters over its response to the protests, following the death of George Floyd. A Global Radio spokesperson told the BBC the company had taken 'several steps in recent days' to improve its inclusivity, 'including the formation of a BAME committee' adding: 'Global is committed to recruiting the highest level of expertise and experience, regardless of gender, race, sexual orientation or disability. Like a lot of businesses, we are honest enough to say that we are still finding our feet and learning fast.'

THE PRESS

The year 2019–20 was, to say the least, a challenging one for the press, both in terms of covering not only a general election but the biggest crisis to affect the UK since the Second World War. As with so many other areas of society, the pandemic accelerated trends that were present prior to coronavirus – in the newspaper sector falling sales and a still greater reliance on digital publication.

The December battle at the polls between Boris Johnson and Jeremy Corbyn once again brought into stark relief the support that most national papers gave to the Conservative Party. On election day *The Sun* carried a picture of Boris Johnson inside a glowing lightbulb and Jeremy Corbyn inside a dud. The front page read: 'if Boris wins today, a bright future begins tomorrow… but if Red Jez gets in, the lights will go out for good.' The *Daily Mail*, which during the period under review overtook *The Sun* to become Britain's biggest selling paper, emblazoned its front page with the word BORIS in huge type. Its readers were told that 'you MUST brave the deluge [a reference to the wintry weather] to back' the Tory leader.

FLEET STREET TURNS ON JOHNSON?

But as the health emergency began to take its toll and the prime minister's chief adviser, Dominic Cummings, was found to have broken lockdown rules, even the pro-Tory press turned on the government. In May, Cummings' failure to resign led to harsh criticism from the *Daily Mail*, which wanted to know apropos Johnson and Cummings, 'what planet are they on?', adding: 'neither man has displayed a scintilla of contrition for this breach of trust. Do they think we are fools?' Earlier in April *The Sunday Times*, another Conservative-supporting paper, had published an investigative piece headlined: 'Coronavirus: 38 days when Britain sleepwalked into disaster.' The article reported that the prime minister had skipped five meetings of the Cobra emergency committee devoted to the virus and suggested that the government's initial slow response to the pandemic may have costs thousands of lives.

As the second wave of COVID-19 began to surge in the autumn and many opinion formers again challenged the government's competence, *The Independent's* Sean O'Grady wrote: that 'the right-wing, traditionally Tory press in Britain, which is to say almost all of it, has turned a bit nasty.' *Mailonline* reported: 'in the week Boris told a battered Britain it was in for

994   The Year 2019–20

another six months of covid winter misery, his partner Carrie Symonds enjoys five-star Italian holiday at a £600-a-night Lake Como hotel.'

THE CHALLENGE OF REPORTING COVID-19

The ability of journalists to adequately cover what was in many ways a science story was raised by some commentors. Dorothy Byrne, editor at large at Channel 4, wondered if the majority of journalists lacked the necessary science backgrounds to understand the pandemic and therefore were equipped to ask tough questions of the ministers and health officials who at the first peak of the crisis gave televised daily press conference. By common consent, one journalist who undoubtedly became required reading was Tim Harford, a regular in *The Financial Times*, and Radio 4 broadcaster. His ability to make sense of the data deluge was invaluable.

The crisis sent newspaper circulations plummeting. ABC figures published in the autumn showed that only the *Observer's* sales were stable. With cities, particularly London, empty of commuters, free papers *Metro* and the *Evening Standard* registered huge declines, of 45 per cent and 39 per cent respectively. Sales of *The Financial Times* showed the biggest fall among paid-for titles, down 37 per cent.

Job cuts at newspapers loomed large. In the summer News UK, owners of *The Sun* and *The Sunday Times*, warned of a reduction in staff while *The Guardian* announced economies that could affect up to 180 jobs, with 70 in editorial. In August, it was reported that the *Evening Standard* was making a third of its staff redundant, with a 40 per cent reduction in newsroom staff. Reach, publishers of *The Daily Mirror*, *Daily Express* and *Daily Star* said it was axing 550 jobs, 12 per cent of its workforce. The move was designed to save £35m a year.

THE FT MAKES HISTORY

During the year under review Fleet Street announced the appointment of two new female editors. At the *Evening Standard*, former reporter Emily Sheffield succeeded George Osborne, who became editor-in-chief; Sheffield is the sister of David Cameron's wife, Samantha. More significantly *The Financial Times* appointed its first ever woman editor since the paper began publishing in 1888, Roula Khalaf, the paper's deputy editor. She succeeded Lionel Barber who was leaving following 14 years in charge.

Another female journalist who was the subject of media interest was the maverick *Guardian* columnist, Suzanne Moore. In November, she revealed she was leaving the paper after more than 300 members of staff accused her of writing a column that in their view was 'transphobic'. She tweeted: 'I have left *The Guardian*. I will very much miss SOME of the people there. For now that's all I can say.'

In a column she had written that a person's sex was a biological classification 'not a feeling.' She and her children were subjected to death and rape threats. They had contacted the police after 'being deemed transphobic by an invisible committee on social media,' she said.

MEGHAN MAULS THE *MAIL*

In the year under review Associated Newspapers, owners of the *Daily Mail*, were sued by the Duchess of Sussex, Meghan Markle, claiming it had unlawfully published one of her private letters, sent by Meghan to her father Thomas Markle. A statement published in October 2019 by the Duke of Sussex said he and Meghan were forced to act against 'relentless propaganda.' Prince Harry said: 'I lost my mother and now I watch my wife falling victim to the same powerful forces.'

In a year of unrelenting bad news, newspapers seized on the inspirational story of centenarian Captain Tom Moore, who incredibly raised over £30m for the NHS during the spring lockdown by walking laps of his garden. His heroic efforts won him a knighthood.

One of true giants of British journalism, Harold Evans died in September. He was 92. Evans was editor of *The Sunday Times* when it published its seminal investigation into the effects of thalidomide, which was subsequently banned. Opined the BBC's media editor, Amol Rajan: 'though he later fell out with Rupert Murdoch, and never forgave him, in his 14 years at the helm of *The Sunday Times* he redefined journalism itself.'"

THE INTERNET

The one clear winner from the pandemic was 'Big Tech'. Google, Amazon, Apple and Facebook all made a rapid recovery from a brief coronavirus-induced downturn in 2019–20 as staying and working from home, together with online shopping propelled these behemoths to new heights. 'Three months of lockdown has accelerated ecommerce by four years and households will spend more than ever before online, post-lockdown,' noted *Enders Analysis* in September.

JEFF BEZOS KEEPS GETTING RICHER

In October, *The Financial Times* reported that 'combined sales of the four big tech companies leapt 18 per cent year on year in the latest quarter, to $227bn, 4 per cent higher than expected, while their after-tax profits jumped by 31 per cent, to $39bn. The surge comes in a quarter when companies in the S&P 500 are expected to suffer an overall revenue decline of more than 2 per cent, with earnings down 17 per cent.'

The wealth of Amazon boss, Jeff Bezos, grew to an all-time high of $171.6bn. Prompted by the pandemic, some tech titans made considerable donations to charities – Microsoft's Melinda and Bill Gates gave $305m to COVID-19 causes while Twitter founder Jack Dorsey donated $1bn for pandemic relief.

Ofcom's annual report, *Online Nation*, published in June, showed just how much of our lives are lived online; it revealed that at the height of the spring lockdown, on average UK adults spent four hours and two minutes a day online, up from just under three-and-a-half hours in September 2019.

BOOM TIMES FOR ZOOM

As video conferences became a way of life, Zoom, hardly a household name before the virus struck, became ubiquitous. Between January to April UK Zoom users grew from 659,000 to 13 million, a rise of almost 2,000 per cent. Many believe that even when the pandemic ends online meetings are here to stay.

The service was such a vital part of many people's lockdown lives that Zoom was gold dust for comedians as people struggled with their mute buttons and camera connections. The BBC TV satire, *W1A*, posted a special episode online, *Initial Lockdown Meeting*, in which members of the cast discussed life after lockdown on a Zoom call. More seriously, a writer on the New Yorker, Jeffrey Toobin, was sacked after allegedly exposing himself on Zoom.

AMAZON SCORES AS IT TAKES PREMIER LEAGUE ONLINE – BUT *THE NEW YORK TIMES* CRIES FOUL

In 2019–20 the increasing part played by the tech giants in all our lives was evident prior to the pandemic. For the first time 20 Premier League matches were shown exclusively on Amazon Prime Video over the Christmas period, a move that broke Sky and BT's stranglehold on the game. Most reviewers agreed there was something reassuringly old-fashioned about Amazon's coverage, despite some teething problems affecting the quality of the video stream. 'This bold new world suddenly thrust upon us feels just like the old one. And yet – what took it so long?' observed *The Independent's* sportswriter Vithushan Ehantharajah.

At the retail end of the company's activities, it was estimated that Amazon had created 400,000 new jobs owing to the online shopping boom. However, not for the first time, pointed questions were asked of Amazon's working practices. More than 100 former and current Amazon employees were interviewed for a *New York Times* exposé of the company. It described working conditions devoid of empathy and which push employees to their limits in the name of productivity and efficiency. Bezos said the report was erroneous commenting: '[the article] claims that our intentional approach is to create a soulless, dystopian workplace where no fun is had and no laughter heard. I don't recognise this Amazon and I very much hope you don't, either.'

TIKTOK ENTERS THE MAINSTREAM
The Chinese social media service, TikTok, a favourite for children's home-made video clips, was another tech company on the rise during 2019–20. Ofcom estimated it had 12.9 million UK adult visitors in April, a huge increase from 5.4 million in January. As *Enders Analysis* observed: 'TikTok has confounded regulatory woes in India and the US, and renewed competition from US tech, to post dizzying user growth in every major internet region where it is available, casting off its image as a niche youth product and entering the mainstream.'

As the nation was trapped indoors the online world encouraged people to take more care of themselves. In the spring fitness instructor Joe Wicks became a YouTube phenomenon, thanks to his 20-minute exercise routines. It was estimated that more than 70 per cent of the nation joined in his workouts, which raised £580,000 for the NHS. 'He became the person, outside our nuclear family, who was most present in our lives during lockdown,' observed *The Guardian*.

IS SOCIAL MEDIA A THREAT TO OUR HEALTH?
During the year 2019–20 the pandemic and the US election re-enforced the view that the internet can be a place where conspiracy theories take root and fake news spreads noxiously. A peer-reviewed study published in the journal *Psychological Medicine* in June suggested that unregulated social media platforms like Facebook and YouTube may present a health risk because they spread conspiracy theories on coronavirus. People who obtain their news from social media were more likely to break lockdown rules, argued the study's authors, who concluded: 'one wonders how long this state of affairs can be allowed to persist while social media platforms continue to provide a worldwide distribution mechanism for medical misinformation.'

In the run-up to and during the November US presidential election, Facebook and Twitter doubled down on their efforts to stop fake news spreading on their sites. When President Donald Trump claimed the election was stolen from him, Facebook and Twitter immediately made it clear that his view was factually incorrect. Other, less well-known social media sites such as Parler were happy to feature posts from QAnon, the pro-Trump conspiracy theory that asserted that some top Democrats were satanic paedophiles.

REGULATORS WAIT IN THE WINGS
In December, the government announced more details of its long anticipated Online Harms Bill. Culture secretary Oliver Dowden told parliament the proposals involved 'decisive action' to protect both children and adults online. 'A 13-year-old should no longer be able to access pornographic images on Twitter, YouTube will not be allowed to recommend videos promoting terrorist ideologies and anti-Semitic hate crimes will need to be removed without delay.' He said that secondary legislation would be introduced to effect 'criminal sanctions for senior managers' if the social media companies failed to act. Critics, however, wondered if these plans would genuinely rid social media of damaging content and what impact lobbying by the tech giants was likely to have before the bill eventually became law. With so much money at their fingertips their powers of persuasion were likely to be considerable.

PARLIAMENT

By Patrick Robathan

Following his larger than expected election victory on 12 December 2019 (majority of 80), Prime Minister Boris Johnson promised that 2020 would be the year the UK finally 'got Brexit done' and that he would instigate his 'levelling up agenda.' What he could not have foreseen was COVID-19. Although he did secure a deal on the UK's exit from the EU at almost the last moment, Parliamentary business was disrupted and dominated by the pandemic. Parliament sat an exceptionally long time in 2020, for 40 weeks, which was the highest since 2010.

The Queen's Speech on 19 December set out plans to 'take us out of the EU, overhaul our immigration system, enshrine in law record investment for the NHS… it will take our country forward with an ambitious One Nation programme to unite and spread opportunity to every corner of our United Kingdom.' It included plans for some 36 Bills. Labour leader Jeremy Corbyn complained 'this Speech shows that what the Government are actually proposing is woefully inadequate for the scale of the problems.' Boris Johnson felt 'as we engage full tilt now in this mission of change, I am filled with invincible confidence in the ability of this nation, our United Kingdom, to renew itself in this generation as we have done so many times in the past. After the dither, after the delay, after the deadlock and after the paralysis and after the platitudes, the time has come for change and it is action that the British people will get.' Unusually instead of immediately debating the Queen's Speech on 20 December the House approved the second reading of European Union (Withdrawal Agreement) Bill by 358 votes to 234 and spent the first three days after the Christmas Recess (7/8/9 January) completing consideration of the Bill. On 7 January Defence Secretary Ben Wallace made a statement on the security situation in the Middle East. On 9 January Sports Minister Nigel Adams responded to an urgent question (UQ) from Labour's Carolyn Harris on the deal between the Football Association and Bet365 to screen live football matches. Foreign Office Minister Heather Wheeler made a statement on the Australian Bushfires.

On 13 January MPs returned to the debate on the Queen's Speech and after four days it was passed by 334 votes to 247 on 20 January. On 13 January Foreign Secretary Dominic Raab responded to UQ from Conservative Tobias Ellwood on Iran. On 14 January Transport Minister Paul Maynard replied to UQ from Conservative Caroline Nokes on support available to help Flybe, followed by a statement on the Iran nuclear agreement (Joint Comprehensive Plan of Action) by Dominic Raab. On 16 January Northern Ireland Secretary Julian Smith made a statement on formation of Northern Ireland Executive, followed by Housing, Communities and Local Government Secretary Robert Jenrick on a package of reforms to building safety. On 22 January Minister for Security Brandon Lewis responded to UQ from Shadow Home Secretary Diane Abbott on the Prevent programme. On 23 January Health and Social Care Secretary Matt Hancock made the first statement on the outbreak of a new coronavirus in Wuhan, China. On 27 January DCMS Minister Matt Warman replied to UQ from Conservative Tom Tugendhat on Huawei's involvement in the UK's 5G network, followed by Minister Policing Kit Malthouse responded to UQ from Lib Dem Sarah Olney on Automated Facial Recognition Surveillance. On 28 January Culture Secretary Lady Morgan of Coates made a statement in the Lords on the security of the telecoms supply chain, 'we will do three things simultaneously: seek to attract established vendors to our country who are not present in the UK; support the emergence of new, disruptive entrants to the supply chain; and promote the adoption of open, interoperable standards that will reduce barriers to entry.' On 30 January Foreign Office Minister Andrew Murrison replied to UQ from Shadow Foreign Secretary Emily Thornberry on President Trump's proposed Middle East peace plan.

On 3 February Dominic Raab made a statement on global Britain, 'now is the time to put our differences aside and come together, so together let us embrace a new chapter for our country, let us move forward united and unleash the enormous potential of the British people, and let us show the world that our finest achievements and our greatest contributions lie ahead.' This was followed by Matt Hancock with an update on the ongoing situation with the Wuhan coronavirus, 'close contacts will be given health advice about symptoms and emergency contact details to use, should they become unwell in the next 14 days. These tried and tested methods of infection control will ensure that we minimise the risk to the public.' Justice Secretary Robert Buckland made a statement about the terror attack in Streatham the previous day. On 4 February for Work and Pensions Minister Will Quince replied to UQ from SNP's Neil Gray on the delay to the full roll-out of Universal Credit, followed by Cabinet Office Minister Chloe Smith responding to UQ from Labour DCMS spokesperson Tracy Brabin on barring of certain journalists from official civil servant media briefings at the direction of special advisers and the arrangements for future lobby and media briefings, followed by a statement from Health Minister Nadine Dorries on the publication of the independent inquiry into disgraced surgeon, Ian Paterson. On 6 February Nigel Adams replied to UQ from Tracy Brabin on plans for BBC Licence Fee.

On 10 February Home Office Minister Kevin Foster responded to UQ from Labour's David Lammy on deportation flights to Jamaica, followed by a statement from Environment Secretary Theresa Villiers on flood response following Storm Ciara. On 11 February Boris Johnson made a statement on transport Infrastructure, 'a new anatomy of British transport— a revolution in the nation's public transport provision. It will be a sign to the world that, in the 21st century, this UK still has the vision to dream big dreams and the courage to bring those dreams about', followed by Matt Hancock updating the House on the Wuhan coronavirus. On 13 February Matt Warman replied to UQ from Conservative Julian Knight on plans for online harms legislation, followed by Nadine Dorries replying to UQ from Conservative Sir Roger Gale on provision and safety of maternity services in East Kent.

After the half-term recess on 24 February Foreign Office Minister James Cleverly replied to UQ from Tobias Ellwood on Syria, followed by a statement from Home Secretary Priti Patel on new points-based immigration system, followed by new Environment Secretary George Eustice on flooding caused by Storm Dennis. On 26 February former Home Secretary, Said Javid, made a personal statement following his resignation from the Government, followed by Matt Hancock with an update on COVID-19. On 27 February Chancellor of the Duchy of Lancaster Michael Gove made a statement on the future relationship with the EU, 'we got Brexit done, and we will use our recovered sovereignty to be a force for good in the world and a fairer nation at home. We want and we will always seek the best possible relationship with our friends and allies in Europe, but we will always put the welfare of the British people first. That means ensuring the British people exercise the democratic control over our destiny for which they voted so decisively.' This was followed by statements from Robert Jenrick on rough sleeping and Home Office Minister Victoria Atkins on child protection.

On 2 March Michael Gove replied to UQ from Jeremy Corbyn on apparent breaches of Ministerial Code following the resignation of Sir Philip Rutnam as Permanent Secretary at Home Office. This was followed by Transport Minister Kelly Tolhurst responding UQ from Labour Transport spokesperson Andy McDonald on airport expansion and then newly appointed Foreign Office Minister Nigel Adams to UQ from Labour's Tulip Siddiq on British citizens imprisoned abroad in countries where coronavirus was spreading rapidly. International Trade Secretary Liz Truss made a statement on UK-US Trade Deal. On 3 March Nigel Adams replied to UQ from Labour's Khalid Mahmood on violence in India and Matt Hancock made a statement about the Government's coronavirus action plan. On 4 March former Leader of the House Andrea Leadsom made a personal statement following her resignation from the Government. On 5 March Kelly Tolhurst made a statement on the collapse of Flybe.

On 9 March Matt Hancock responded to UQ from his Labour Shadow Jonathan Ashworth updating the House on the coronavirus, 'in the UK, as of this morning, there were 319 confirmed cases. Very sadly, this now includes four confirmed deaths. I entirely understand why people are worried and concerned.' On 10 March Nigel Adams replied to UQ from SNP spokesperson Joanna Cherry on refugees at Turkey-Greece border. On 11 March Chancellor of the Exchequer Rishi Sunak delivered his first Budget statement, 'from our national infrastructure strategy to social care and further devolution, this is the Budget of a Government that get things done—creating jobs, cutting taxes, keeping the cost of living low, investing in our NHS, investing in our public services, investing in ideas, backing business, protecting our environment, building roads, building railways, building colleges, building houses and building our Union.' He announced a £30bn package to boost the economy and get the country through the coronavirus outbreak; a suspension of business rates for many firms, extending sick pay and boosting NHS funding, with £12bn specifically targeted at coronavirus measures, including at least £5bn for the NHS and £7bn for business and workers across the UK.

Jeremy Corbyn did not agree. 'The reality is that this Budget is an admission of failure: an admission that austerity has been a failed experiment. It did not solve our economic problems but made them worse. It held back our own recovery and failed even in its own terms.' After four days of debate the Budget was approved on 18 March, The Finance Bill had its second reading on 24 March with third reading completed on 2 July and it gained Royal Assent on 22 July. Also on 11 March Matt Hancock updated the House on the day that the World Health Organisation declared coronavirus a global pandemic, 'we have resolved that we will keep Parliament open. Of course, in some ways this House may have to function differently, but the ability to hold the Government to account and to legislate are as vital in a time of emergency as in normal times.' On 12 March Robert Jenrick published Planning for the Future expanding on the housing measures set out in the Budget. Veterans Minister Johnny Mercer made a statement on veterans' mental health

On 16 March Matt Hancock was allowed to interrupt business to make a statement, 'having agreed a very significant step in the actions that we are taking from within that plan to control the spread of the disease… The measures that I have outlined are unprecedented in peacetime. We are in a war against an invisible killer and we have to do everything we can to stop it.' Speaker Sir Lindsey Hoyle made a statement on how Parliament would function under the new rules. On 17 March Dominic Raab made a statement advising British nationals

against non-essential travel globally, for an initial period of 30 days. On 18 March Education Secretary Gavin Williamson made a statement on changes to the operations of educational settings as a result of the pandemic. On 19 March Economic Secretary to the Treasury John Glen replied to UQ from Conservative Greg Clark on support for wages of employees. Priti Patel made a statement on the Windrush lessons learned review, 'the publication of this review is a small but vital step towards ensuring that the Home Office is trusted by all the people it serves. I encourage anyone who thinks that they have been affected by the Windrush scandal or who requires support or assistance to come forward.' It was agreed that there should be no sittings in Westminster Hall with effect from Friday 20 March until the House otherwise ordered.

On 23 March the Speaker updated MPs on plans for Parliament in lockdown. The Government introduced the Coronavirus Bill which received an unopposed Second Reading and completed all its Common's stages in one day. It was taken in the Lords on 24/25 March and received Royal Assent on 26 March. On 24 March Chief Secretary to the Treasury Steve Barclay responded to UQ from Lib Dem interim leader Sir Edward Davey on financial support for the self-employed in the light of the pandemic. Dominc Raab responded to UQ from Caroline Nokes on measures to assist British citizens abroad to return home. Matt Hancock gave an update, 'our instruction is simple: stay at home. People should only leave their home for one of four reasons: first, to shop for basic necessities, such as food, as infrequently as possible; secondly, to exercise once a day, for example a run, walk or cycle, alone or with members of the same household; thirdly, for any medical need, or to provide care or help to a vulnerable person; and fourthly, to travel to and from work, but only where it cannot be done from home, and employers should be taking every possible step to ensure that staff can work remotely.' On 25 March the Speaker allowed a longer than usual PMQs, 'to serve as an effective replacement for separate statements on the situation of coronavirus.' Friday sittings in the Commons were postponed by at least a month.

On 27 March Rishi Sunak updated the House on the economic response to coronavirus, 'right now, the most important thing for the health of our economy is the health of our people. Our strategy is to protect people and businesses through this crisis, by backing our public services and NHS with increased funding, strengthening our safety net to support those most in need, and supporting people to stay in work and keep their businesses going. Our response is comprehensive, coherent and co-ordinated.' The Finance Bill received an unopposed Second Reading. On 28 April the House observed one-minute's silence to reflect on the sacrifices being made by so many, Michael Gove made a statement on support for public services through the pandemic. On 29 April Nigel Adams made a statement on repatriation of UK Nationals in response to the pandemic.

Returning from the Easter Recess on 21 April MPs passed a motion to allow virtual participation in the House's proceedings and agreed to meet only on Mondays, Tuesdays and Wednesdays. On 22 April newly elected Labour leader Sir Keir Starmer had his first outing at PMQs but faced Dominic Raab as Boris Johnson was in hospital with COVID-19. Matt Hancock gave an update on coronavirus.

On 4 May Work and Pensions Secretary Thérèse Coffey made a statement on the work her Department were doing to provide help to those in need during the pandemic. On 5 May Matt Hancock updated Jonathan Ashworth on the Government's response, 'we have flattened the curve of this epidemic, ensured that the NHS is not overwhelmed and expanded testing capacity to over 100,000 tests a day… we have now built a national testing infrastructure of scale and will be delivering up to 30,000 tests a day to residents and staff in elderly care homes… and we are working to build the resilience of the NHS.' On 6 May the Speaker announced that remote voting would be introduced. Boris Johnson and Sir Keir Starmer had their first face to face PMQs. BEIS Minister Paul Scully responded to UQ from Andy McDonald on guidelines for workplace safety after the lifting of lockdown. International Development Secretary Anne-Marie Trevelyan updated the House on the UK's support for the global effort to tackle the pandemic.

On 11 May Boris Johnson made a statement about the next steps in the battle against coronavirus 'and how we can, with the utmost caution, gradually begin to rebuild our economy and reopen our society.' Conservative Greg Hands made a personal statement apologizing for his misuse of parliamentary stationery. MPs agreed to suspend Conservative Conor Burns from the House for a period of seven days following the recommendations of the Standards Committee into his conduct. On 12 May Rishi Sunak replied to an urgent question from Shadow Chancellor Anneliese Dodds on the Government's economic package in response to the outbreak, 'one of the most comprehensive anywhere in the world. We have provided billions of pounds of cash grants, tax cuts and loans for over 1 million businesses, tens of billions of pounds of deferred taxes, income protection for millions of the self-employed, and a strengthened safety net to protect millions of our most vulnerable people.' Business Secretary Alok Sharma updated the House on the Government's new COVID-19-secure workplace guidance. Transport Secretary Grant Shapps made a statement about the new transport guidance for passengers and operators. On 13 May Gavin Williamson replied to UQ from Lib Dem Education spokesperson Layla Moran on plans to reopen schools as part of the Government's recovery strategy. Robert Jenrick made a statement on COVID-19 and the housing market. The Speaker made a statement on the likely duration of hybrid proceedings and ensuring that those on the estate were safe while business is facilitated.

On 18 May Matt Hancock updated MPs, 'the number of people in hospital with coronavirus is half what it was at the peak…the number of patients in critical care is down by two thirds. Mercifully, the number of deaths across all settings is falling.' On 19 May the Speaker told the Government that it was unacceptable that answering written questions in a timely manner had not continued, 'the Government simply must do better.' Matt Hancock replied to UQ from Labour' Liz Kendall on coronavirus and care homes. Michael Gove responded to UQ from his Shadow Rachel Reeves on the third round of the negotiations on the UK's future relationship with the EU. On 20 May Leader of the House Jacob Rees-Mogg replied to UQ from Lib Dem Chief Whip Alistair Carmichael on conduct of business in the Commons after the Whitsun recess and the necessary motions to continue the online participation of Members. Michael Gove made a statement on the Government's approach to implementing the Northern Ireland protocol as part of the withdrawal agreement with the EU.

Returning from the Whitsun Recess on 2 June Dominic Raab updated the House on UK response to Hong Kong national security legislation. Matt Hancock updated MPs on coronavirus. MPs approved the rules for proceedings during the pandemic. On 3 June Kelly Tolhurst responded to UQ from Conservative Huw Merriman on COVID-19 and the economic impact on aviation. Priti Patel made a statement about the introduction of public health measures at the border in response to coronavirus. On 4 June Minister for Equalities Kemi Badenoch replied to UQ from Labour's Gill Furniss on Public Health England's review of disparities in risks and outcomes related to the COVID-19. Northern Ireland Minister Robin Walker replied to UQ from DUP Westminster leader Sir Jeffrey Donaldson on abortion regulations for Northern

Ireland and then to an urgent question from Labour Northern Ireland spokesperson Louise Haigh on the implementation of the payment scheme for victims of the troubles.

On 8 June Matt Hancock replied to UQ from Jonathan Ashworth on the R value and lockdown, 'thanks to the immense national effort on social distancing, as a country we have made real progress in reducing the number of new infections.' Priti Patel made a statement on public order following demonstrations in the UK after the death of George Floyd in the USA, 'I know that it is the sense of injustice that has driven people to take to the UK streets to protest.' Alistair Carmichael was granted an emergency debate on the conduct of House business during the pandemic. On 9 June Paymaster General Penny Mordaunt replied to UQ from Rachel Reeves on the fourth round of the negotiations on the UK's future relationship with the EU. Gavin Williamson made a statement regarding the wider opening of nurseries, schools and colleges in response to the pandemic. On 10 June Paul Scully replied to UQ from Labour spokesperson Chi Onwurah on support for sub-postmasters wrongly convicted in the Post Office Horizon scandal, 'we are committed to establishing an independent review to consider whether the Post Office has learned the necessary lessons from the Horizon dispute and court case, and to provide an independent and external assessment of its work to rebuild its relationship with its postmasters.' MPs then approved an extension to proxy voting. On 11 June Minister for Housing Christopher Pincher responded to UQ from his Labour Shadow Steve Reed on maintaining public confidence in the probity of the planning process. Robert Buckland made a statement on the Government's plans for the future of probation services in England and Wales.

On 15 June Minister for Health Edward Argar replied to UQ from Greg Clark on reviewing the 2 metre social distancing rule. Priti Patel made a statement on public order following demonstrations in London on a so-called mission to protect the statue of Sir Winston Churchill. On 16 June the Speaker set out the new Division procedure and proxy voting. Financial Secretary to the Treasury Jesse Norman replied to UQ from Anneliese Dodds on the economic outlook and the strategy to protect jobs and the economy in light of upcoming changes to the furlough scheme. Boris Johnson made a statement about the ambitions of a global Britain and the lessons of the pandemic, in particular the merging of the Foreign Office and the Department for International Development. Michael Gove updated MPs on the Government's negotiations on future relationship with the EU. On 17 June Matt Hancock responded to UQ from Jonathan Ashworth on the scientific effort on vaccines. Liz Truss made a statement on UK accession to Comprehensive and Progressive Agreement for Trans-Pacific Partnership. On 18 June Dominic Raab replied to UQ from Lib Dem Wendy Chamberlain on the merger of the Department for International Development with the Foreign and Commonwealth Office.

On 22 June Priti Patel made a statement on the terror attack in Reading at the weekend. Conservative Marcus Fysh made a personal statement on his failure to register unremunerated directorships. On 23 June Boris Johnson made a statement on next steps in the plan to rebuild the economy and reopen society, while waging the struggle against COVID-19. Priti Patel made a statement on the Windrush compensation scheme, 'nothing can ever undo the suffering experienced by members of the Windrush generation. No one should have suffered the uncertainty, complication and hardships brought on by the mistakes of successive Governments. Now is the time for more action to repay that debt of gratitude and to eliminate the challenges that still exist. Only then can we build a stronger, fairer and more successful country for the next generation.' On 25 June Work and Pensions Minister Will

Quince responded to UQ from Labour spokesperson Stephen Timms on the Court of Appeal decision on wronged Universal Credit claimants.

On 29 June Home Office Minister Chris Philp replied to UQ from SNP's Alison Thewliss on support and accommodation for asylum seekers during the pandemic following an incident in Glasgow at the weekend. Nigel Adams replied to UQ from Conservative Sir Iain Duncan Smith on the mistreatment by the Chinese Government of Uyghurs in Xinjiang. Later on Matt Hancock made a statement on local action to tackle coronavirus, with the number of recorded deaths at 25, so the Government had been able, carefully, to ease the national restrictions. On 30 June Michael Gove replied to UQ from Shadow Home Secretary Nick Thomas-Symonds on the appointment of the National Security Adviser. Justice Minister Alex Chalk answered UQ from David Lammy on the Government's implementation of the Lammy review, 'enormous progress has been made but… of course there is more to do.' On 1 July Dominic Raab made a statement on developments in Hong Kong, 'we want a positive relationship with China, but we will not look the other way when it comes to Hong Kong and we will not duck our historic responsibilities. We will continue to stand up for the people of Hong Kong, to call out the violations of their freedoms, and to hold China to its international obligations, freely assumed under international law.' On 2 July Gavin Williamson made a statement regarding the full opening of our schools and colleges to all pupils in September.

On 6 July Dominic Raab made a statement on global human rights sanctions regulations, with measures enacted to hold to account the perpetrators of the worst human rights abuses. On 7 July Matt Hancock responded to UQ from Jonathan Ashworth, 'we protected the NHS. We built the new Nightingale hospitals in 10 days. At all times, treatment was available for all. Our medical research has discovered the only drug known to work. We have built, almost from scratch, one of the biggest testing capabilities in the world. We are getting coronavirus cornered, but this is no time to lose our resolve. The virus exists only to spread, so we must all stay alert and enjoy summer safely.' DCMS Minister Caroline Dinenage replied to UQ from Labour Culture spokesperson Jo Stevens on support for arts, culture and heritage industries. On 8 July Rishi Sunak gave an economic update, 'it is a plan to turn our national recovery into millions of stories of personal renewal. It is our plan for jobs.' On 9 July Foreign Office Minister James Cleverly responded to UQ from Father of the House Sir Peter Bottomley on using the Government's relationship with Bahrain to raise the cases of two prisoners who had been sentenced to death. Nadine Dorries made a statement about the independent medicines and medical devices review.

On 13 July Minister for Trade Policy Greg Hands replied to UQ from Labour spokesperson Emily Thornberry on the resumption of the sale of arms to the Saudi-led coalition for use in the war in Yemen. Michael Gove made a statement on preparations for the end of the transition period. On 14 July Culture Secretary Oliver Dowden made a statement on UK telecommunications following the telecoms supply chain review to look at the long-term security of 5G and full-fibre networks. Matt Hancock then updated MPs, 'this deadly virus continues to diminish… for the third consecutive week, total deaths are lower than normal for this time of year.' On 16 July Johnny Mercer replied to UQ from Labour defence spokesperson John Healey on the Overseas Operations Bill's impact on the rights of British troops serving overseas to bring civil liability claims against the MOD and its implications for the Armed Forces Covenant. Alok Sharma published UK Internal Market White Paper. Late on Matt Hancock made a statement on action against coronavirus and the decisions

taken through the day to determine the future of the action needed in Leicester.

On 20 July Dominic Raab made a statement on the latest developments with respect to China and Hong Kong, 'we will stand up for our values, and we will hold China to its international obligations.' Matt Hancock made a further statement on action against coronavirus, which had allowed the Prime Minister to set out a conditional timetable for the further easings of the restrictions. On 21 July Culture Minister John Whittingdale replied to UQ from Lib Dem Daisy Cooper on changes to the licence fee exemptions, programming and job losses at the BBC, 'while the BBC remains operationally and editorially independent from the Government, we will continue to push it on these issues so that we can ensure that the BBC remains closer to the communities that it serves.' Priti Patel made a statement on the progress on the Windrush lessons learned review, 'we are determined to get this right… Home Office is working hard to be more diverse, more compassionate and worthy of the trust of the communities it serves.' On 22 July the Speaker announced an extension to virtual participation in Select Committee meetings. Minister for Security James Brokenshire responded to UQ from Nick Thomas-Symonds on the Intelligence and Security Committee's report into Russia. Christopher Pincher replied to UQ from Labour spokesperson Thangam Debbonaire on implications of the end of the evictions ban for people renting their home. Ben Wallace gave the regular counter-Daesh update.

Returning from the summer recess on 1 September the Speaker informed the House that a Member had been arrested in connection with an investigation into an allegation of a very serious criminal offence (no charges were subsequently made). Matt Hancock updated the House on developments over the summer, 'we will soon be launching a new campaign reminding people of how they can help to stop the spread of coronavirus: Hands, face, space and get a test if you have symptoms. As we learn more and more about this unprecedented virus, so we constantly seek to improve our response to protect the health of the nation and the things we hold dear.' Gavin Williamson made a statement about full opening of schools and colleges and updated the House on the current position regarding exam results for the year's GCSE and A-level students. On 2 September Chris Philp responded to UQ from Nick Thomas-Symonds on those crossing the English Channel in small boats, 'the majority of these crossings are facilitated by ruthless criminal gangs that make money from exploiting migrants who are desperate to come here.' Dominic Raab replied to UQ from his Labour shadow Lisa Nandy on the creation of the Foreign, Commonwealth and Development Office. On 3 September Thérèse Coffey answered UQ from Labour's Jonathan Reynolds on the implementation of the kickstart scheme.

On 7 September Grant Shapps made a statement about international travel corridors allowing people to return to the UK from low-risk countries without quarantine. Kit Malthouse made a statement on the Extinction Rebellion protests and on the incident in Birmingham over the weekend, a fatal stabbing in Lewisham and a serious shooting incident in Suffolk. On 8 September Northern Ireland Secretary Brandon Lewis responded to UQ from Louise Haigh on the UK's commitment to its legal obligations under the Northern Ireland protocol. Matt Hancock updated MPs, 'the threat posed by the virus has not gone away. Now, with winter on the horizon, we must all redouble our efforts and get this virus on the back foot.' On 10 September Matt Hancock made a further statement with a number of new measures that would help get the virus under control and to make the rules clearer, simpler and more enforceable.

On 14 September Liz Truss announced that the UK had reached agreement in principle on a free trade deal with Japan. The United Kingdom Internal Market Bill which Labour spokesperson Ed Milband felt contained 'provisions breaking international law and did not respect the devolution settlements.' received its Second Reading by 340 votes to 263. It was considered in Committee of the Whole House on 15/16/21/22 September and received a third reading on 29 September by 340 votes to 256. It was taken with second reading in the Lords 20 October, was amended in Committee between 26 October and 9 November and was given its Third reading on 2 December. The Bill 'ping-ponged' between the Houses between 8 and 16 December, before the Commons had their way and it received Royal Assent on 17 December. On 15 September Matt Hancock replied to UQ from Jonathan Ashworth, 'the challenges are serious. We must work to overcome them, optimistic in the face even of these huge challenges, and to keep this deadly virus under control.' On 16 September Robert Buckland published Sentencing White Paper. On 17 September Matt Hancock made a statement on plans to put the UK in the strongest possible position for this winter, 'we will soon be facing winter in this fight and, whether on our NHS emergency care wards or in our care homes, we will strain every sinew to give them what they need, so they are well equipped for this pandemic and, indeed, for the years ahead.'

On 21 September Matt Hancock made a further statement, 'the number of new cases in Europe is now higher than during the peak in March. The virus is spreading. We are at a tipping point. I set out today the measures the Government are taking so far. We are working right now on what further measures may be necessary.' On 22 September Boris Johnson made a statement on the response to the rising number of coronavirus cases, 'the Government will introduce new restrictions in England, carefully judged to achieve the maximum reduction in the R number with the minimum damage to lives and livelihoods.' On 23 September Christopher Pincher replied to UQ from Lib Dem Tim Farron on the end of the eviction moratorium. Michael Gove updated MPs on preparations for the end of the transition period that was just 100 days away. The House agreed to extend proxy voting. On 24 September Liz Truss (as Minister for Women and Equalities) replied to an urgent question from Conservative Crispin Blunt on the response to the consultation on the Gender Recognition Act 2004. Rishi Sunak set out the next phase of the planned economic response, 'plans that seek to strike a finely judged balance between managing the virus and protecting the jobs and livelihoods of millions.' Dominic Raab made a statement on the situation in Belarus following presidential elections in August. Conservative David Morris made a personal statement apologising for inadvertently breaching the paid advocacy rule.

On 29 September Gavin Williamson made a statement regarding the return of students to universities. On 30 September Sports Minister Nigel Huddleston replied to UQ from Conservative Tracey Crouch on support for professional and amateur sport. MPs passed Coronavirus Act 2020 (Review of Temporary Provisions) by 330 votes to 24. On 1 October Matt Hancock delivered an update and outlined a hospitality curfew, 'the second peak is highly localised, and in some parts of the country the virus is spreading fast. Our strategy is to suppress the virus, protecting the economy, education and the NHS, until a vaccine can make us safe.' Gavin Williamson made a statement regarding lifetime skills guarantee and post-16 education.

On 5 October Paul Scully responded to UQ from Labour's Kevan Jones on 44 Post Office prosecutions overturned by Criminal Cases Review Commission. Matt Hancock updated the House, 'now more than ever, with winter ahead, we must all remain vigilant and get the virus under control.' On 6 October Steve Barclay replied to UQ from Anneliese Dodds on economic support available in areas of the country subject to additional public health restrictions.

On 12 October Boris Johnson made a statement on how the Government intended to fulfil the simultaneous objectives of saving lives and protecting the NHS while keeping children in school and the economy running, 'the stark reality of the second wave of the virus is that the number of cases has quadrupled in the last three weeks…This is not how we want to live our lives, but this is the narrow path we have to tread between the social and economic trauma of a full lockdown and the massive human and, indeed, economic cost of an uncontained epidemic.' On 13 October Steve Barclay replied to UQ from Anneliese Dodds on economic support available in areas of the country subject to additional public health restrictions. The latest Coronavirus Regulations were passed by 299 votes to 82. On 15 October Matt Hancock made a further statement, 'the threat remains grave and serious. In Europe, positive cases are up 40 per cent from one week ago, and in Italy, Belgium and the Netherlands, they have doubled in the last fortnight. Here, we sadly saw the highest figure for daily deaths since early June… I know that those measures are not easy, but I also know that they are vital.'

On 19 October Michael Gove updated the House on the Government's negotiations with the EU on future trading relationships and the work of the UK/EU Joint Committee. Matt Hancock made a further statement, 'as winter draws in, the virus is on the offensive: 40 million coronavirus cases have now been recorded worldwide. Weekly deaths in Europe have increased by 33 per cent and here in the UK, deaths have tragically doubled in the last 12 days. The situation remains perilous.' On 20 October Matt Hancock made a late statement, 'it is the penetration of coronavirus into older age groups that gives the NHS the greatest cause for concern.' On 21 October Edward Argar made a statement on restrictions in South Yorkshire. On 22 October Rishi Sunak delivered an economic update, 'we have an economic plan that will protect the jobs and livelihoods of the British people, wherever they live and whatever their situation… we will listen and respond to people's concerns as the situation demands.' Kemi Badenoch made a statement on the disparate impact of COVID-19.

Returning from a short recess on 2 November Boris Johnson was told off by the Speaker for letting the main elements of his statement be announced over the weekend, welcoming the announcement of a leak inquiry. Boris Johnson made his statement on measures the UK must take to contain the autumn surge, protect the NHS and save lives, 'the R is still above one in every part of England—as it is across much of Europe—and the virus is spreading even faster than the reasonable worst-case scenario.' On 3 November Steve Barclay responded to UQ from Anneliese Dodds on economic support available during and after the recently announced lockdown. James Cleverly replied to UQ from Tulip Siddiq on Nazanin Zaghari-Ratcliffe. Labour's Dr Rosena Allin-Khan made a personal statement apologizing for the inappropriate use of House stationery for a third time. On 5 November Matt Hancock replied to an urgent question from Conservative Andrew Mitchell on the impact of new coronavirus regulations on terminally ill adults travelling abroad for an assisted death. Rishi Sunak gave an economic update, 'we are providing significant extra support to protect jobs and livelihoods in every region and nation of UK: an extension to the coronavirus job retention scheme; more generous support to the self-employed and paying that support more quickly; cash grants of up to £3,000 per month for businesses that are closed, worth over a billion pounds every month; £1.6 billion for English councils to support their local economy and local healthcare response; longer to apply for our loan schemes and the future fund; the chance to top up bounce back loans; and an extension to mortgage payment holidays. That is all on top of more than £200 billion of fiscal support since March.' James Brokenshire made a statement regarding the terrorism threat level, following recent events in France and Vienna.

On 9 November Foreign Office Minister Wendy Morton responded to UQ from Caroline Nokes on steps taken to secure the return of Jonathan Taylor to the UK in order to complete inquiries into corruption by SBM Offshore. Rishi Sunak updated the House on plans for financial services, 'they will be essential to our economic recovery from coronavirus, creating jobs and growth right across our country. As we leave the EU and start a new chapter in the history of financial services in this country, we want to renew the UK's position as the world's pre-eminent financial centre.' Thérèse Coffey made a statement on supporting disadvantaged families. On 10 November Defence Minister Jeremy Quin replied to UQ from John Healey on deployment of the armed forces to assist civilian authorities in dealing with the continuing pandemic. Matt Hancock updated the House, 'this is a disease that strikes at what it is to be human, at the social bonds that unite us. We must come together as one to defeat this latest threat to humanity. There are many hard days ahead, many hurdles to overcome, but our plan is working. I am more sure than ever that we will prevail together.' On 11 November now Housing Minister Kelly Tolhurst replied to UQ from Thangam Debbonaire on preventing homelessness and protecting rough sleepers during the second national lockdown. On 12 November Nigel Adams replied to UQ from Layla Moran on disqualification of pro-democracy lawmakers in Hong Kong, 'yesterday was another sad day for the people of Hong Kong.' Oliver Dowden outlined the Government's plans to mark HM the Queen's platinum jubilee in 2022.

On 16 November Jacob Rees-Mogg responded to UQ from Conservative John Baron on participation in debates, 'the clinically extremely vulnerable should not go into work, we should work with the House authorities to find a solution.' On 17 November Trade Minister Greg Hands replied to UQ from Emily Thornberry on parliamentary scrutiny of future Continuity Trade Agreements. On 18 November Robin Walker responded to UQ from Louise Haigh on preparations for implementation of the Northern Ireland Protocol. Robert Jenrick replied to UQ from Justin Madders on the towns fund. On 19 November Edward Argar replied to UQ from Conservative Sir Christopher Chope on his Department's poor performance in answering written questions. Boris Johnson updated the House on the Government's integrated review of foreign, defence, security and development policy, which would conclude 'early next year.' Nigel Huddleston made a statement on financial support for the sports sector.

On 23 November Boris Johnson made a statement on the winter plan, 'for the first time since this wretched virus took hold, we can see a route out of the pandemic.' On 24 November Christopher Pincher responded to UQ from Labour's Clive Betts on whether leaseholders were expected to pay for the removal of dangerous cladding from their homes. On 25 October Rishi Sunak outlined the Spending Review 2020. On 26 November Matt Hancock made a further statement, 'sadly, there is no quick fix... hope is on the horizon, but we still have further to go, so we must all dig deep. The end is in sight. We must not give up now. We must follow these new rules and make sure that our actions today will save lives in future and help get our country through this.' Dominic Raab made a statement on official development assistance, 'we have concluded after extensive consideration and with regret that we cannot for the moment meet our target of spending 0.7 per cent of gross national income on ODA, and we will move to a target of 0.5 per cent next year.'

On 30 November Chris Philp responded to UQ from Labour's Bell Ribeiro-Addy on the scheduled mass deportation by charter plane to Jamaica, 'they are all foreign national offenders who between them have served 228 years plus a life sentence in prison.' George Eustice made a statement on the agricultural transition plan. Brandon Lewis made a statement on the Supreme Court judgment in the case of Patrick Finucane. On 2 December Paul Scully replied to UQ from Edward Miliband on support for business and the retention of jobs on the high street in light of the announcement of Arcadia entering administration and Debenhams going into liquidation. Matt Hancock made a statement about vaccines, 'today marks a new chapter in our fight against this virus... I am delighted to inform the House that the MHRA has issued the clinical authorisation of the Pfizer/BioNTech vaccine.' On 3 December Gavin Williamson made a statement regarding testing and examinations in schools and colleges next year, 'we will not let covid damage the life chances of an entire year of students by cancelling next year's exams. We support Ofqual's decision that, in awarding next year's GCSEs, AS and A-levels, grading will be as generous and will maintain a similar profile as those grades awarded this year.' Robert Buckland made a statement on the recovery of courts and tribunals.

On 7 December Paymaster General Penny Mordaunt replied to UQ from Rachel Reeves on progress of the negotiations on the UK's future relationship with the EU and the end of the transition period. Nigel Adams responded to UQ from SNP's Alan Smyth on sentencing of three Hong Kong pro-democracy activists. On 8 December Matt Hancock replied to UQ from Jonathan Ashworth announcing the first person in the world to receive a clinically authorised vaccine, 'this marks the start of the NHS's Herculean task to deploy vaccine right across the UK... this simple act of vaccination is a tribute to scientific endeavour, human ingenuity and the hard work of so many people. Today marks the start of the fight back against our common enemy, coronavirus.' After a rebuke from the Speaker on the way the announcement had been handled Nigel Huddleston announced a review of the Gambling Act. On 9 December Michael Gove updated the House on the implementation of the Northern Ireland protocol as part of the withdrawal agreement with the EU. Defence Minister James Heappey made a statement on support for the UN stabilisation mission in Mali. The Taxation (Post-transition Period) Bill received its Second reading and Committee stage. On 10 December Penny Mordaunt replied to UQ from Rachel Reeves on the progress of negotiations on the UK's future relationship with the EU. Nadine Dorries made a statement on publication of the initial report from the Ockenden review into events at Shrewsbury and Telford Hospital NHS Trust.

On 14 December Matt Hancock announced that the NHS had begun vaccinations through GPs in England and in care homes in Scotland, 'day by day, we are giving hope to more people and making this country safer... it will take time for its benefits to be felt far and wide, so we must persevere because the virus remains as dangerous as it has always been.' Alok Sharma published the energy White Paper setting out immediate steps to achieve UK climate ambitions. On 15 December Labour's Chris Bryant made a personal statement apologising for his heckling during Prime Minister's questions and when he challenged the authority of the Chair. Oliver Dowden published the Government's response to the online harms consultation, 'we are proposing groundbreaking regulations that will make tech companies legally responsible for the online safety of their users... this will rebuild public trust and restore public confidence in the tech that has not only powered us through the pandemic, but will power us into the recovery.' On 16 December Chris Philp replied to UQ from Caroline Nokes on whether changes to the immigration rules would reduce the numbers of asylum seekers in supported accommodation. Nigel Adams replied to UQ from Sir Iain Duncan Smith on the overwhelming evidence of the Chinese Government's use of Uyghur slave labour in Xinjiang. The Trade (Disclosure of Information) Bill completed all its Commons stages in one day. On 17 December Matt Hancock gave an update confirming tougher restrictions, 'where they are necessary, we must put them in place to prevent the NHS from being overwhelmed and to protect life.' Robert Jenrick announced the provisional Local Government Finance Settlement. MPs then rose for the Christmas Recess.

On 23 December Parliament was recalled to approve the European Union (Future Relationship) Bill enacting the EU/ UK agreement on leaving the EU. Boris Johnson introduced the Bill by saying, 'having taken back control of our money, our borders, our laws and our waters by leaving the European Union on 31 January, we now seize this moment to forge a fantastic new relationship with our European neighbours based on free trade and friendly co-operation,' Sir Keir Starmer felt, 'a thin deal is better than no deal... I do hope that this will be a moment when our country can come together and look to a better future... The leave/remain argument is over— whichever side we were on, the divisions are over. We now have an opportunity to forge a new future: one outside the EU, but working closely with our great partners, friends and allies... We will always have shared values, experiences and history, and we can now also have a shared future.' Second reading was passed by 521 votes to 73. Whilst unhappy - especially Labour peer Lord Adonis, '"we have sustained a total and unmitigated defeat" - those were Winston Churchill's words on the Munich agreement 82 years ago. Alas, they apply word for word to the Brexit agreement we are being asked to rubber-stamp today', the Lords also passed the Bill unamended by 466 votes to 101. The Bill received Royal Assent at 12.30 am on 31 December, the last possible day. While the Lords debated the Bill, Matt Hancock made his final statement of the year, announcing approval had been granted for use of the Oxford University/AstraZeneca vaccine.

PUBLIC ACTS OF PARLIAMENT

Public acts included in this list are those which received royal assent between 31 July 2019 and 31 December 2020. The date stated after each act is the date on which it came into operation. For further information see **W** www.legislation.gov.uk

Kew Gardens (Leases) Act 2019 ch. 25 (9 September 2019) provides that the Secretary of State's powers in relation to the management of the Royal Botanic Gardens, Kew, include the power to grant a lease in respect of land for a period of up to 150 years.

European Union (Withdrawal) (No. 2) Act 2019 (repealed) ch. 26 (23 January 2020) Act repealed (23.1.2020) by European Union (Withdrawal Agreement) Act 2020

Parliamentary Buildings (Restoration and Renewal) Act 2019 ch. 27 (8 October 2019) makes provision in connection with works for or in connection with the restoration of the Palace of Westminster and other works relating to the Parliamentary Estate; and for connected purposes.

Census (Return Particulars and Removal of Penalties) Act 2019 ch. 28 (8 October 2019) amends the *Census Act 1920* and the *Census Act (Northern Ireland) 1969* in relation to the provision of particulars about sexual orientation and gender identity.

Early Parliamentary General Election Act 2019 ch. 29 (31 October 2019) makes provision for a parliamentary general election to be held on 12 December 2019.

Northern Ireland Budget Act 2019 ch. 30 (31 October) authorises the issue out of the Consolidated Fund of Northern Ireland of certain sums for the service of the year ending 31 March 2020; to appropriate those sums for specified purposes; to authorise the Department of Finance in Northern Ireland to borrow on the credit of the appropriated sums; and to authorise the use for the public service of certain resources (including accruing resources) for that year.

Historical Institutional Abuse (Northern Ireland) Act 2019 ch. 31 (5 November 2019) establishes the Historical Institutional Abuse Redress Board and to confer an entitlement to compensation in connection with children who were resident in certain institutions in Northern Ireland; and to establish the Commissioner for Survivors of Institutional Childhood Abuse.

European Union (Withdrawal Agreement) Act 2020 ch. 1 (23 January 2020) implements, and makes other provisions in connection with, the agreement between the United Kingdom and the EU under Article 50(2) of the Treaty on European Union which sets out the arrangements for the United Kingdom's withdrawal from the EU.

Direct Payments to Farmers (Legislative Continuity) Act 2020 ch. 2 (30 January 2020) makes provision for the incorporation of the Direct Payments Regulation into domestic law; for enabling an increase in the total maximum amount of direct payments under that Regulation; and for connected purposes.

Terrorist Offenders (Restriction of Early Release) Act 2020 ch. 3 (26 February 2020) make provision about the release on licence of offenders convicted of terrorist offences or offences with a terrorist connection; and for connected purposes.

Supply and Appropriation (Anticipation and Adjustments) Act 2020 ch. 4 (16 March 2020) authorises the use of resources for the years ending with 31 March 2020 and 31 March 2021; to authorise the issue of sums out of the Consolidated Fund for those years; and to appropriate the supply authorised by this Act for the year ending with 31 March 2020.

NHS Funding Act 2020 ch. 5 (16 March 2020) makes provision regarding the funding of the health service in England in respect of each financial year until the financial year that ends with 31 March 2024.

Contingencies Fund Act 2020 ch. 6 (25 March 2020) makes provision increasing the maximum capital of the Contingencies Fund for a temporary period.

Coronavirus Act 2020 ch. 7 (25 March 2020) makes provision in connection with coronavirus; and for connected purposes

Windrush Compensation Scheme (Expenditure) Act 2020 ch. 8 (8 June 2020) provides for the payment out of money provided by Parliament of expenditure incurred by the Secretary of State or a government department under, or in connection with, the Windrush Compensation Scheme.

Sentencing (Pre-consolidation Amendments) Act 2020 ch. 9 (8 June 2020) gives effect to Law Commission recommendations relating to commencement of enactments relating to sentencing law and to make provision for pre-consolidation amendments of sentencing law.

Birmingham Commonwealth Games Act 2020 ch. 10 (25 June 2020) makes provision about the Commonwealth Games that are to be held principally in Birmingham in 2022; and for connected purposes.

Divorce, Dissolution and Separation Act 2020 ch. 11 (25 June 2020) makes in relation to marriage and civil partnership in England and Wales provision about divorce, dissolution and separation; and for connected purposes.

Corporate Insolvency and Governance Act 2020 ch. 12 (25 June 2020) makes provision about companies and other entities in financial difficulty; and to make temporary changes to the law relating to the governance and regulation of companies and other entities.

Supply and Appropriation (Main Estimates) Act 2020 ch. 13 (22 July 2020) authorises the use of resources for the year ending with 31 March 2021; to authorise both the issue of sums out of the Consolidated Fund and the application of income for that year; and to appropriate the supply authorised for that year by this Act and by the Supply and Appropriation (Anticipation and Adjustments) Act 2020.

Finance Act 2020 ch. 14 (22 July 2020) grants certain duties, to alter other duties, and to amend the law relating to the national debt and the public revenue, and to make further provision in connection with finance.

Stamp Duty Land Tax (Temporary Relief) Act 2020 ch. 15 (22 July 2020) makes provision to reduce for a temporary period the amount of stamp duty land tax chargeable on the acquisition of residential property.

Business and Planning Act 2020 ch. 16 (22 July 2020) makes provision relating to the promotion of economic recovery and growth.

Sentencing Act 2020 ch. 17 (22 October 2020) consolidates certain enactments relating to sentencing.

Extradition (Provisional Arrest) Act 2020 ch. 18 (22 October 2020) creates a power of arrest, without warrant, for the purpose of extraditing people for serious offences.

Prisoners (Disclosure of Information About Victims) Act 2020 ch. 19 (4 November 2020) requires the Parole Board to take into account any failure by a prisoner serving a sentence for unlawful killing or for taking or making an indecent image of a child to disclose information about the victim.

Immigration and Social Security Co-ordination (EU Withdrawal) Act 2020 ch. 20 (11 November 2020) makes provision to end rights to free movement of persons under retained EU law and to repeal other retained EU law relating to immigration; to confer power to modify retained direct EU legislation relating to social security co-ordination; and for connected purposes.

Agriculture Act 2020 ch. 21 (11 November 2020) authorises expenditure for certain agricultural and other purposes; to makes provision about direct payments following the United Kingdom's departure from the European Union and about payments in response to exceptional market conditions affecting agricultural markets; confers power to modify retained direct EU legislation relating to agricultural and rural development payments and public market intervention and private storage aid; makes provision about reports on food security; makes provision about the acquisition and use of information connected with food supply chains; confers powers to make regulations about the imposition of obligations on business purchasers of agricultural products, marketing standards, organic products and the classification of carcasses; makes provision for reports relating to free trade agreements; makes provision for the recognition of associations of agricultural producers which may benefit from certain exemptions from competition law; makes provision about fertilisers; makes provision about the identification and traceability of animals; makes provision about red meat levy in Great Britain; makes provision about agricultural tenancies; confers power to make regulations about securing compliance with the WTO Agreement on Agriculture; and for connected purposes.

Fisheries Act 2020 ch. 22 (23 November 2020) makes provision in relation to fisheries, fishing, aquaculture and marine conservation; to make provision about the functions of the Marine Management Organisation; and for connected purposes.

Social Security (Up-rating of Benefits) Act 2020 ch. 23 (23 November 2020) makes provision relating to the up-rating of certain social security benefits.

Private International Law (Implementation of Agreements) Act 2020 ch. 24 (14 December 2020) implements the Hague Conventions of 1996, 2005 and 2007 and to provide for the implementation of other international agreements on private international law.

Parliamentary Constituencies Act 2020 ch. 25 (14 December 2020) makes provision about reports of the Boundary Commissions under the Parliamentary Constituencies Act 1986; to make provision about the number of parliamentary constituencies and other rules for the distribution of seats; and for connected purposes.

Taxation (Post-transition Period) Act 2020 ch. 26 (17 December 2020) makes provision (including the imposition and regulation of new duties of customs) in connection with goods in Northern Ireland and their movement into or out of Northern Ireland; to make provision amending certain enactments relating to value added tax, excise duty or insurance premium tax; to make provision in connection with the recovery of unlawful state aid in relation to controlled foreign companies; and for connected purposes.

United Kingdom Internal Market Act 2020 ch. 27 (17 December 2020) makes provision in connection with the internal market for goods and services in the United Kingdom (including provision about the recognition of professional and other qualifications); makes provision in connection with provisions of the Northern Ireland Protocol relating to trade and state aid; authorises the provision of financial assistance by Ministers of the Crown in connection with economic development, infrastructure, culture, sport and educational or training activities and exchanges; makes regulation of the provision of distortive or harmful subsidies a reserved or excepted matter; and for connected purposes.

Trade (Disclosure of Information) Act 2020 ch. 28 (17 December 2020) makes provision about the disclosure of information relating to trade.

European Union (Future Relationship) Act 2020 ch. 29 (31 December 2020) makes provision to implement, and make other provision in connection with, the Trade and Cooperation Agreement; to make further provision in connection with the United Kingdom's future relationship with the EU and its member States; makes related provision about passenger name record data, customs and privileges and immunities; and for connected purposes.

POP MUSIC

Piers Martin

CORONAVIRUS WIPES OUT LIVE SECTOR

This was a turbulent 12 months for the UK music industry, to say the least. The coronavirus pandemic had a devastating effect on the live music sector, forcing festivals, tours, concerts and club events to be postponed and cancelled as venues across the country closed in accordance with government regulations. Tough social distancing measures meant all venues, bars, pubs, theatres and clubs remained shut for most of 2020 and the first quarter of 2021, leading to businesses filing for bankruptcy and thousands of jobs being lost or placed on furlough. Those employed in the touring sector, such as tour managers, road crew and front of house production, were hit particularly hard as regular freelance work that was due to last all year dried up overnight. Professional musicians who would usually rely on income from touring the UK and Europe to survive also faced hardship when shows across the continent were cancelled, instantly wiping out, in many cases, a lucrative revenue stream.

Figures published in November by UK Music, the umbrella organisation representing the commercial music industry, showed that while the music industry grew in 2019 by 11 per cent, to be worth £5.8bn to the UK economy, that figure was predicted to collapse to £3bn in 2020. Worst hit was the live music sector which was valued at £1.3bn in 2019 – a record amount – and was predicted to fall by 85 per cent to around £300m in 2020, the report revealed. It also pointed out that while music creators – a broad term covering everyone from Ed Sheeran and Elton John to thousand of musicians, songwriters and producers – contributed some £2.7bn to the UK economy in 2019, most would see their income fall by 65 to 80 per cent in 2020 due to the absence of live events.

To help the sector deal with the impact of coronavirus, in October the government announced a £1.57bn Culture Recovery Fund that gave much-needed financial support to a wide range of venues, festivals, publishers, arts institutions and production companies. Grant recipients included more than 100 at-risk grassroots music venues and more established nightclubs such as Fabric and Corsica Studios in London, which otherwise had no viable means of securing income. The government said the grants were given to 'places that define culture in all corners of the country', while the culture secretary Oliver Dowden said: 'These places and organisations are irreplaceable parts of our heritage and what make us the cultural superpower we are.'

INDUSTRY GROWTH

On a brighter note, music consumption in the UK increased for the fifth year in a row, with 155m albums (or the equivalent) streamed or purchased in 2020, a rise of 8.2 per cent on 2019, according to figures released by the British Phonographic Industry (BPI). Listeners turned to music to lift their spirits during the months of lockdown, the figures suggest, accounting for 139bn audio streams – up by a fifth on 2019 – via platforms such as Spotify, Apple Music and Google Play. As an indicator of streaming's growth, this is a 3,000 per cent increase on the figures for 2012, the first year streaming data became available. Around 200 artists were streamed more than 100m times in the UK in 2020, led by the familiar likes of Lewis Capaldi, Dua Lipa, Adele, Stormzy, Harry Styles and Ed Sheeran. But a new generation of young British talent also racked up hundreds of millions of streams as fans propelled rappers J Hus, AJ Tracey, Aitch, KSI and Headie One, whose music variously blends grime, hip-hop, drill and African influences, to the top of the charts.

Sales of individual albums were down, however, and not one album released in 2020 was certified platinum (signifying 300,000 sales), the first time this has happened since records began in 1973.

Physical sales continued to thrive, with vinyl accounting for around a fifth (18 per cent) of all UK albums sold in 2020. The format's enduring appeal – sales increased by 11.5 per cent, up for the 13th consecutive year – was reflected in annual sales of 4.8m, up from 4.3m in 2019, which marked the best year for vinyl since 1990. Fans also bought twice as many cassettes this year as high-profile artists such as Lady Gaga, Yungblud, Dua Lipa and The 1975 all released new albums on tape. Some 156,542 cassettes were sold – the highest total since 2003, according to the BPI – an increase of 94.7 per cent on 2019's total and confirmation of sorts that listeners love to own a physical object to complement their streaming. Although sales of CDs continued their downward trend, 16m copies were still sold in 2020, representing 10.3 per cent of all music consumed. Sales of digital albums also fell – by 19 per cent – but still contributed 5.9m units in album equivalent sales.

The most streamed artist in the world this year was Bad Bunny, the Puerto Rican reggaeton star, who racked up 8.3bn streams of his songs across the various platforms. Popular in the Americas, he has yet to make a meaningful impact in the UK. Canadian singer-songwriter The Weeknd scored the biggest hit of 2020 with 'Blinding Lights', an infectious synth-pop cut with a 1980s sheen. Released in late November 2019, the track amassed 2.2m chart sales to become the top selling single in the UK this year, spending eight weeks at number one. The song was also Spotify's most streamed track of the year.

TOP SELLERS

For the second year in a row, the bestselling album of the year was Lewis Capaldi's 2019 debut *Divinely Uninspired to a Hellish Extent*. The self-deprecating Scottish singer's collection of big-hearted ballads sold 456,000 copies in the UK in 2020, according to the Official Charts Company, taking its sales total to more than 1m since it was released in May 2019. The album saw Capaldi, who was forced to reschedule a world tour, notch up a 77-week run in the UK Top 10, including ten at number one, which is a record by a solo artist. His unavoidable hit 'Someone You Loved' was named Song of the Year at the Brits.

Harry Styles, the former One Direction member, now firmly established as something of a fashion icon, had the second biggest-selling album of 2020 in the UK with *Fine Line*. His second solo set, which came out in December 2019, shifted 293,000 copies throughout the year, which rather pales to its first-week sales in the US, where the album sold 478,000 units to top the Billboard 200 chart, making it the largest sales week for an album by a solo British male artist for 30 years. Musically and sartorially, Styles, 26, takes cues from David Bowie, and though his middle of the road hits lack a certain edge, his progress from boy-band heartthrob to curious solo artist willing to explore new ideas has been one of the more diverting stories in pop. *Fine Line* also became 2020's top-selling new vinyl album, ranking fifth behind catalogue classics from Fleetwood Mac, Oasis, Amy Winehouse and Nirvana. Styles capped the year by gracing the cover of the December issue of the US edition of *Vogue* – the first solo man to do so – wearing a lace ball gown by Gucci and a black tuxedo jacket.

The bestselling album of the year that was actually released in 2020 was *Future Nostalgia* by Dua Lipa, the 25-year-old singer's second set of slick modernist pop. Released in March, this ended up selling 256,000 copies and was followed in September by a remix collection, *Club Future Nostalgia*, that would have lit up dancefloors had clubs been allowed to open. Unable to tour the album, Lipa instead broadcast a ticketed live event in November, called *Studio 2054*, that featured guests including Kyle Minogue, FKA Twigs and Elton John. Much like the ubiquity of Zoom calls, live streams have become an expedient way for acts to connect with fans around the world during the pandemic, though streaming technology and domestic broadband speeds mean the results are often far from adequate, while the events are difficult to monetise for all but the biggest acts. Lipa's *Studio 2054* event was one of the most successful of its kind, selling 284,000 tickets at £7.50, according to Rolling Stone, and attracting an audience of 5m globally, including 2m in China, where the event was shown for free.

LOCKDOWN ALBUMS

With tours cancelled and some scheduled album releases delayed, optimistically, until later in the year, the first lockdown in the spring provided many musicians with plenty of time to focus on their work. The first notable record made under these conditions was pop producer Charli XCX's *How I'm Feeling Now*, released in May. Produced in collaboration with her fans via Zoom, it turned out to be a lavish DIY affair full of cubist electro-pop that didn't diverge hugely in tone from her usual material.

In late July, the US star Taylor Swift surprised her colossal fanbase with an album called *Folklore*, a stripped-back indie-folk collection with intimate, contemplative lyrics that felt a world away from the bold commercial pop of her last album, 2019's *Lover*. Unable to tour that record due to the pandemic, Swift worked remotely with regular collaborator Jack Antonoff, Bon Iver and members of The National to fashion a rustic, nostalgic set that offered a sense of familiarity and comfort in a period of acute anxiety. *Folklore* entered the UK charts at number one and remained there for three weeks, the longest run at the top this year. Less than five months later, in December, Swift followed this with its companion piece *Evermore*, a similarly themed lockdown album of lush fireside folk that again topped the UK album chart.

The evergreen Australian star Kylie Minogue recorded much of her chart-topping *Disco* album while in lockdown and, upon its release in November, became the first female artist to have number one albums in the UK across five decades. As the title implies, *Disco* was a feel-good throwback to the bell-bottomed grooves and electronic pop of the 1970s and 80s, a style the chameleonic singer carried off with aplomb, just as she convinced as a country and western turn on 2018's *Golden*.

OLD-TIMERS RAVE ON

Paul McCartney made good use of his time while locked down on his Sussex estate, putting together a solo record that became *McCartney III*. The 78-year-old former Beatle, whose headline appearance at the 50th Glastonbury festival in June was shelved when the event was called off, sang, played and recorded all the parts on the album himself during the first half of the year. Well received, *McCartney III* became the 2020 Christmas number one album and his first solo number one since 1989's *Flowers In The Dirt*. The album is the third and final instalment of a solo trilogy that began with 1970's *McCartney* – made after The Beatles split – and followed ten years later with the experimental *McCartney II*, composed when his 1970s band Wings had folded.

McCartney's contemporary, Bob Dylan, made a strong comeback this year with *Rough and Rowdy Ways*, his 39th album, which topped charts around the world on its release in June and ended 2020 atop many critics' year-end lists. His first set of new material for eight years, the mercurial folk star, who

is 79, was on exceptional form, dishing up cryptic tales of magic and mystery and toying with his own mythology on the likes of 'I Contain Multitudes' and the 17-minute 'Murder Most Foul', which touches on the assassination of John F Kennedy, while 'Key West (Philosopher Pirate)' intrigued Dylanologists and critics with its allegorical twists and turns.

Dylan also made headlines in December when he sold his entire publishing catalogue to Universal Music for a figure rumoured to be north of $300m (£225m). One of the biggest publishing deals of the century, it included the rights to songs such as 'Blowin' in the Wind' and 'Knockin' on Heaven's Door' among the 600 compositions. Dylan became the latest music figure to sell his song rights for a sizeable sum, with stars including Neil Young, Shakira and Fleetwood Mac guitarist Lindsay Buckingham selling their catalogues to the private investment company Hipgnosis, a publicly listed company that views songs as a reliable investment. Merck Mercuriadis, CEO of Hipgnosis and a former manager of Elton John, has raised and then spent over $1bn across some 60 deals during the past two years, amassing a catalogue of 12,000 songs, including numbers such as Rihanna's 'Umbrella' and Eurythmics' 'Sweet Dreams (Are Made of This)'. His ulterior motive with Hipgnosis, he told *Music Business Worldwide*, was to gain enough market power in the music rights space to bring about a change in the recompense seen by songwriters in the streaming age.

THE STREAMING ECONOMY

The business models of the major streaming platforms came under scrutiny in November when MPs established a select committee to look into the impact streaming was having on musicians, labels and the sustainability of the industry. Although streaming in the UK brought in more than £1bn a year, it was widely believed that artists are not fairly paid for the use of their material on services such as Spotify and Apple Music. It was estimated Spotify pays between £0.002 and £0.0038 per stream, with Apple paying £0.0059. During the commons Digital, Culture, Music and Sport Select Committee into the economics of music streaming – which continued into 2021 – MPs heard from musicians including Nadine Shah, Guy Garvey of Elbow and Radiohead's Ed O'Brien. Garvey said the way artists are paid for streams was 'threatening the future of music.'

Deprived of the opportunity to tour and promote their work in 2020, artists found the year particularly tough. Labels also struggled to break new talent and saw their incomes dwindle. Album campaigns, that might have normally lasted six months to a year, were cut short without tours to extend the life of a record and bring in revenue. It proved difficult to launch new talent without showcases and the opportunity for acts to travel to different cities and even countries for promotional appearances. At the other end of the scale, one wonders how many major acts delayed releasing new material for fear it would not have the desired impact in these challenging conditions: perhaps Billie Eilish – Spotify's most streamed female artist of the year – or Adele, or Kendrick Lamar. As important as the internet has become to artists and the industry – and in 2020 it became essential – the tangible thrill of a concert was hugely missed.

Often positioned as the 'anti-Spotify', the music platform Bandcamp came to the rescue of many artists during the pandemic. Bandcamp allows any artist or label from anywhere in the world to sell their music – primarily downloads but also vinyl and cassettes – and merchandise through its platform and takes a 15 per cent cut of all sales, so the seller keeps 85 per cent of the fee, minus costs. From March, as the pandemic took hold, the site began an initiative called Bandcamp Fridays: on the first Friday of the month, it would waive its fees and the artist would receive 100 per cent of the profit. The initiative proved so popular that Bandcamp decided to keep it in place for the foreseeable future. After nine Bandcamp Fridays in 2020, $40m (£29m) had been raised for artists.

SOFT POWER

One of the few new acts to make headway in this odd year – perhaps because they refused to play the game – was the mysterious collective known as Sault. In 2019, they released two albums of streetwise funk and soul with a new-wave edge, called 5 and 7, which made waves without any fanfare, interviews or promotion. In 2020, they managed to remain anonymous – though some suspect the London producer and Michael Kiwanuka associate Inflo was involved – and released another two albums, this time of a more righteous and spiritual bent, but equally compelling. *Untitled (Black Is)* came out in June, a few weeks after George Floyd died in police custody in Minneapolis on 25 May, and seemed to chime with the issues raised by his killing which triggered the Black Lives Matter movement around the world. Sault followed this in September with *Untitled (Rise)* and by the end of the year, everyone knew their name but their identity was still unknown. In Coventry, meanwhile, a 23-year-old British-Gambian rapper called Pa Salieu capped a remarkable year when he was crowned the winner of the BBC Sound of 2021. His debut 'Frontline', a mix of Afrobeat, drill and grime, was the most played track on BBC 1Xtra in 2020, while his debut album *Send Them to Coventry* reached a respectable 36 in the album chart.

IN MEMORIAM

In a year when death was everywhere, there were a number of big losses in the music community. The British DJ and producer Andrew Weatherall (1963–2020) passed away unexpectedly in February at the age of 56. For three decades he was at the forefront of club culture, in his inimitable way, having produced, almost by accident, Primal Scream's 1991 groundbreaking album *Screamadelica*. He followed his nose in acts such as Sabres of Paradise and Two Lone Swordsmen, producing dozens of memorable remixes, and became something of a taslismanic figure for a generation who came of age after the second summer of love. One of his sayings was: 'If you're not living on the edge, you're taking up too much space.'

The co-founder of the pioneering German electronic group Kraftwerk, Florian Schneider (1947–2020), died in April aged 73, and the legendary US showman Little Richard (1932–2020) died in May at the age of 88. Coronavirus claimed the lives of the American musician Adam Schlesinger (1967–2020), 52, best known as the frontman of Fountains of Wayne, and the US country folk star John Prine(1946–2020), who was 73. The veteran reggae star Toots Hibbert (1942–2020), of

Toots and the Maytals, also passed away from COVID-19 in Kingston, Jamaica, at the age of 77.

Other notable musicians who passed this year includd:
Eddie Van Halen (1955–2020)
Simeon Coxe (Silver Apples) (1938–2020)
Tony Allen (1940–2020)
Peter Green (Fleetwood Mac) (1946–2020)
Tim Smith (Cardiacs) (1961–2020)
Vera Lynn (1917–2020)
Dave Greenfield (The Stranglers) (1949–2020)
Cristina (1956–2020)
Bill Withers (1938–2020)
Genesis P-Orridge (Throbbing Gristle, Psychic TV) (1950–2020)
Neil Peart (Rush) (1952–2020)
MF Doom (1971–2020)

AWARDS

MERCURY PRIZE 2019
Dave, *Psychodrama*

BRIT AWARDS 2020
British Male Solo Artist – Stormzy
British Female Solo Artist – Mabel
British Group – Foals
British Single – Lewis Capaldi, 'Someone You Loved'
British Album – Dave, *Psychodrama*
Rising Star – Celeste
International Male Solo Artist – Tyler, the Creator
International Female Solo Artist – Billie Eilish
British Breakthrough Act – Lewis Capaldi
British Producer – Fred Again

IVOR NOVELLO AWARDS 2020
PRS for Music Most Performed Work – Calvin Harris & Rag 'n' Bone Man, 'Giant'
Best Television Soundtrack – Labrinth, *Euphoria*
Best Original Film Score – Bobby Krlic, *Midsommar*
Best Contemporary Song – Dave, 'Black'
Best Video Game Score – Simon Poole, *Draugen*
Album Award – Little Simz, *Grey Area*
Best Song Musically and Lyrically – Jamie Cullum, 'Age of Anxiety'
Songwriter of the Year – Steve Mac
Academy Fellowship – Joan Armatrading
Rising Star – Mysie

MERCURY PRIZE 2020
Michael Kiwanuka, *Kiwanuka*

SCIENCE AND DISCOVERY

Storm Dunlop

CAN AXIONS SOLVE THREE PROBLEMS?

In March 2020, in *Physical Review Letters*, Raymond Co of the University of Michigan and Keisuke Harigaya of the Institute for Advanced Study suggested that an extremely light hypothetical particle known as the axion that hardly reacts with ordinary matter may solve three of the major questions that are not satisfactorily addressed by the Standard Model of particle physics. The axion was originally suggested in 1977 as a possible solution for a problem – known as the strong CP problem – with the properties of the neutron. Then in 1982 it was found to be capable of explaining the existence of dark matter. In the latest study, it is suggested that axions were present at the formation of the universe and that 'rotation' of axions could account for an imbalance between matter and antimatter, sufficient to account for the existence of just matter today.

HOW CAN MATTER EXIST?

In February 2020, an international team led by researchers at the University of Sussex, and including scientists from the Rutherford Appleton Laboratory and the Paul Scherrer Institute in Switzerland, reported in *Physical Review Letters* that they had finally succeeded in accurately measuring one specific property of the neutron. The particular property of interest is known as the 'electric dipole moment' (EDM): a slight difference in electrical charge at opposite sides of a neutron. This asymmetry is of fundamental importance in understanding the structural asymmetry that is thought to determine why matter exists in the universe. The current Standard Model of particle physics suggests that equal quantities of matter and antimatter were created at the origin of the universe (in the Big Bang), and that these would be expected to annihilate one another. EDM is a minute effect and the measurements required the use of highly sophisticated instrumentation and methods. The effect found is smaller than predicted, and rules out certain theories that attempt to explain the presence of matter in the universe.

CONFIRMATION OF THE EXISTENCE OF ANYONS

In our 3D space, there are two types of fundamental particles: fermions and bosons. Examples of each are, respectively an electron and a photon. In a 2D system, however, a third class of 'quasiparticle', known as an 'anyon' may exist. Anyons result from the collective motion of large numbers of electrons, which behave as a single particle. The quasiparticles are found in quantum effects. In June 2020 it was announced that experiments had revealed the existence of one property (known as 'braiding') of such quasiparticles. Braiding involves the change in the wave function of two anyons, preserving a history of their interaction, something impossible with fermions and bosons in a three-dimensional system. Knowledge of such 2D systems is considered to be important in the development of quantum computing.

THE EARLY CATACLYSMIC HISTORY OF THE SOLAR SYSTEM

In August 2019, a study by scientists at the University of Colorado at Boulder, aided by scientists at the University of Oslo, suggested that the Solar System was subjected to a series of cataclysmic collisions at a very early epoch – far earlier than previously thought. The bombardment by comets, asteroids, and proto-planets took place about 44,800 million years ago, shortly after the formation of the Sun, and was initiated by a period of 'giant planet migration'. This migration is necessary to account for the Solar System's current structure. Previous evidence from the Moon suggested that the heavy bombardment occurred much later, at around 3,900 million years ago. The earlier age has implications for the emergence of life on Earth, which would have been able to develop as long ago as 4,400 million years.

PLATE TECTONICS STARTED EARLIER THAN PREVIOUSLY THOUGHT

In early August 2019, a team, based at the University of Witwatersrand, revealed that plate tectonics had started earlier in the Earth's history than previously thought. The study showed that sea water had been transported by plate tectonics deep into the Earth's interior and subsequently trapped in ancient lavas. The research showed that plate tectonics was active 3,300 million years ago, about 600 million years earlier than previously believed. This date is approximately the same as the age when lifeforms first emerged on Earth.

GRAVITATIONAL WAVES BECOME ALMOST COMMONPLACE

The detection of gravitational waves has now become more-or-less routine, particularly since the VIRGO detector at Pisa in Italy entered service in August 2017 alongside the LIGO installations in the USA. Waves are now detected almost daily and the range of different masses of the objects that are merging is extremely wide. In August 2017 the first merger of two low-mass neutron stars (masses 1.46 and 1.27 solar masses) was observed. Detection of this exceptionally low-mass event is particularly significant for the study of neutron stars, and an indication of the potential for this method of observation (a second neutron-star merger has since been detected.) To date, observed black-hole mass pairs range from 10.9 and 7.6 solar masses to 85 and 66 solar masses. (The latter produced an extremely massive remnant at about 140 solar masses.) Events involving very unequal masses (eg 29.7 and 8.4 solar masses) have also been detected. There appears to be a 'mass gap' – a lack of intermediate-mass objects – but this has yet to be confirmed.

LOSS OF A MAJOR ASTRONOMICAL FACILITY

In August 2020, at the Arecibo Observatory in Puerto Rico, one of the main cables suspending the instrumentation platform some 450ft (137m) above the 1,000ft (305m) reflecting dish snapped. A second support cable snapped in November. It was decided that repair would be too dangerous and the instrument was due to be dismantled. On 1 December, yet another cable snapped, causing the instrument platform to fall and create catastrophic damage.

The radio telescope was originally completed in November 1963 and intended to study the upper atmosphere. It was soon employed in fundamental radio-astronomy studies, and had many improvements and additional equipment over the years. It remained the largest radio telescope in the world until July 2016, when the 500m Aperture Spherical Telescope (FAST) was completed in Guizhou, China. The newer telescope will not be fully commissioned for about three years, and, currently, does not have the radar capacity that was so successfully used at Arecibo. Astronomers have already revived a 'dormant' radio telescope in Argentina to see if it is able to continue the series of pulsar timings that was carried out so successfully at Arecibo. One casualty of the collapse is the radar study of minor planets, where the telescope had been particularly successful and uniquely placed to carry out such work.

WHAT HAVE WE FOUND?

In late 2019, an astronomer examining data from the Australian Square Kilometre Array Pathfinder (ASKAP) radio telescope array, detected a strange circular feature. Circular features are well-known in astronomy, and usually represent spherical shells produced by violent events. However, this was so large that if it originated in a central outburst, that must have occurred an extremely long time ago. Subsequent studies have revealed three (and possibly nine) more, similar objects, which are now known as 'Odd Radio Circles' (ORC). Despite numerous attempts to explain their occurrence, no process has been found to be suitable, so, for the present, they remain unexplained.

ANOTHER INTERSTELLAR INTERLOPER

After the detection of the first object ('Oumuamua) that originated outside the Solar System, on 30 August 2019, the amateur astronomer Gennady Borisov, from MARGO observatory in the Crimea, using a homemade 0.65-metre telescope, discovered another object arriving from interstellar space. (This is the eighth comet discovered by Borisov.) Given the initial provisional designation of C/2019 Q_4, the body (a comet) was formally named 2I/Borisov by the International Astronomical Union.

2I/Borisov reached perihelion (the closest point to the Sun) at a distance just outside the orbit of Mars on 7 December 2019. In March 2020, a large outburst with release of a major fragment occurred, although by April 2020 the fragment had disappeared. Unlike 1I/'Oumuamua, which was effectively inert and could have been an asteroidal body, 2I/Borisov is undoubtedly a comet, both dust and gases having been observed originating from the nucleus, the upper size of which is about 0.4km. The gases have been identified as revealing cyanide (CN), diatomic carbon (C_2), amine (NH_2) bands, atomic oxygen (suggesting the outgassing of water), and OH lines.

All this indicates that the way in which comets form is common to all stellar systems. It has been suggested that it would be possible to send a spaceprobe to fly by the comet in 2045, but this would require use of an (untried) major rocket and various gravity assists from the Sun and Jupiter, so is unlikely to go ahead. Estimates put the number of interstellar interlopers within the Solar System as hundreds, if not thousands, at any one time, although the majority are far too faint to be detectable.

SAMPLING MINOR PLANETS

In April 2019, the Japanese *Hayabusa 2* spaceprobe obtained a sample of the surface material from the minor planet (asteroid) 162173 Ryugu. Ryugu is a potentially hazardous body of the Apollo group and is a primitive body with characteristics of both what are known as B-type and C-type asteroids. On 11 July 2019, the spaceprobe touched down at the same site, extended a sampling tube, and fired a small tungsten projectile to break the surface. It collected some of the resulting debris, which should have originated from the interior of the body. It then returned to Earth and on 5 December 2020 dropped the sample capsule at the Woomera range in Australia, where both samples were successfully recovered. The spaceprobe itself has plenty of fuel and has been redirected to a flyby of another Apollo body, known provisionally as 2001 CC_{21} in July 2026 and then on to 1998 KY_{26}, which it will reach in July 2031.

On 20 October 2020, the Touch-And-Go Sample Acquisition Mechanisms (TAGSAM) on the NASA probe OSIRIS-Rex obtained samples from the primitive, carbonaceous chondritic, minor planet 01955 Bennu. It is expected to return its samples to Earth on 24 September 2023.

THE MYSTERIOUS FAST RADIO BURSTS AND MAGNETARS

The origins of the long-enigmatic fast radio bursts (FRBs), discovered in 2007, may have been found. These events are so transient, lasting just milliseconds, that they have been difficult to track down, even though a few of them are known to repeat. Now, at long last, a signal has been observed coming from a magnetar, a dense neutron star with an extremely strong magnetic field. This field is thought to be as high as one thousand trillion Gauss.

In May 2020, it was announced that the known magnetar, SGR 1935+2154, which is in our own galaxy, had emitted a pulse of radio waves with all the characteristics of an FRB. Magnetars are known to produce emit X-rays and gamma-rays, including bursts of such radiation.

In a separate development, in November 2020 a team, led by astrophysicists from Northwestern University in Evanston, Illinois, announced that they believed that they had observed the birth of a magnetar. On 22 May 2020, the light from a kilonova (a brilliant outburst some 1000 times brighter than a classical nova) arrived from a distant galaxy as a burst of gamma-rays. The amount of energy radiated in gamma-rays in just half a second was enormous. It amounted to more than the total energy output of the Sun over its whole lifetime of about 10,000 million years. The initial gamma-ray burst was detected by NASA's Swift space observatory. Many other telescopes then observed the object, including the Hubble Space Telescope, which detected anomalous near-infrared radiation.

It is believed that this event was the result of the merger of two neutron stars. Although such an event is thought to normally result in an object that immediately collapses into a black hole, in this instance it is believed that a supermassive neutron star (the magnetar) resulted from the merger. Rotating at some 1,000 times per second, the exceptionally strong magnetic field pumped energy into the ejecta left by the original explosion, giving rise to the large infra-red excess detected by the Hubble telescope.

GROUND-BASED ASTRONOMY UNDER THREAT

It has become obvious that commercial plans to launch thousands of satellites into orbit pose a very serious threat to certain astronomical studies. The SpaceX company has already launched many hundreds of small satellites, designed to provide fast broadband access anywhere on Earth. Other companies similarly intend to launch 'mega-constellations' of satellites, and a total of some 100,000 is likely if all plans go ahead. The threat to ground-based astronomy is extreme. Certain research activities are likely to be particularly affected. The search for near-Earth asteroids (the ones likely to pose a threat of impact) will be one of the worst affected. There are also concerns over the way in which radiation from the satellites will drown out faint radio signals from the cosmos. Certain surveys, such as that expected to be carried out by the Vera Rubin Telescope (formerly known as the Large Synoptic Survey Telescope) that is under construction in Chile, will be severely hampered and will lose up to 40 per cent of observing time at certain periods of the day. With no governmental restraints, commercial interests appear likely to prevent many serious scientific studies.

PLATE TECTONICS STARTED EARLIER THAN PREVIOUSLY THOUGHT

In early August 2019, a team, based at the University of Witwatersrand revealed that plate tectonics had started earlier in the Earth's history than previously thought. The study showed that sea water had been transported by plate tectonics deep into the Earth's interior and subsequently trapped in ancient lavas. The research showed that plate tectonics was active 3,300 million years ago, about 600 million years earlier than previously believed. This date is approximately the same as the age when lifeforms first emerged on Earth.

EXTREMELY EARLY BIPEDAL APES FROM EUROPE

In November 2019, it was announced by a team from the University of Tübingen in Germany that bones recovered from a site in Bavaria showed that the first apes to walk upright may have evolved in Europe, not Africa. The bones from the newly described species, *Danuvius guggenmosi*, are dated to an astonishing age of 11.6 million years. This is more than 5 million years earlier than the dates for *Sahelanthropus tchadensis* and *Orrorin tugenensis*, previously thought to be the earliest bipedal hominins. There are extreme implications for our view of human evolution and where this took place.

AN EARLY USE OF FIRE

In July 2019, evidence was presented that hominins in Kenya made use of fire as long ago as 1.5 million years. This extends evidence for the use of fire by several thousands of years and has re-opened debate about whether the consumption of more efficient food (ie, cooked meat) assisted the evolution of large-brained hominins.

The team, led by Sarah Hlubik of Rutgers University in New Jersey, found thousands of fragments of stone tools and burned bones at the site in the Kobe Fora region. In many cases the finds occurred around patches of burned ground, suggesting that tool-making (and perhaps cooking) were taking place close to open fires.

DID HOMININS ARISE IN EUROPE?

At a conference of the American Association of Physical Anthropologists in Cleveland, Ohio, in March 2019. David Begun of the University of Toronto presented evidence of a potential hominin ancestor found in southeastern Europe. The fragments of upper and lower jaw (initially assigned to the extinct ape *Ouranopithecus*), from Nikiti in northern Greece, are dated to 8 to 9 million years ago. They contained small, pointed canines (an attribute of hominins), and may belong to a formerly unrecognized species.

Previously the team had examined fossils of an ape known as *Graecopithecus*, that also lived in Greece, at 7.2 million years ago, and come to the tentative conclusion that they represented a hominin. These fossils also exhibited small canines, and additionally, the fused root to the premolars (another hominin attribute). It is therefore now suggested that the Nikiti form may have been the ancestor of the hominin, *Graecopithecus*, and that hominins migrated to Africa, where they evolved developed into several species and, eventually, into *Homo sapiens*.

WHO WAS OUR ANCESTOR?

In August 2019, the discovery by Professor Haile-Selassie (affiliated to the Cleveland Museum of Natural History in Ohio) was announced in Nature of a well-preserved and extremely old fossil of an ape-like species that may be the earliest human ancestor. The find was at Miro Dor, in the Mille District of Ethiopia's Afar Regional State. The fossil is of *Australopithecus anamensis*, which may have existed as long ago as 4.2 million years. *A. amanensis* was previously thought to be the direct ancestor of *Australopithecus afarensis*, (nicknamed 'Lucy'), believed to be a direct human ancestor. It is now obvious that the two species existed at the same time. This suggests that other advanced ape-like species may have co-existed, increasing the potential evolutionary routes to our eventual *Homo sapiens* species. This agrees with the recent acceptance that multiple hominin species existed at the same time and in the same locations.

THREE SPECIES OF HOMININS IN ONE PLACE

In April 2020, a team of 30 scientists from five countries revealed the discovery of *Homo erectus* remains at Drimolen, northwest of Johannesburg in South Africa. *H. erectus* is considered to be an ancestor of our species, *Homo sapiens*. The new remains are securely dated to 2 million years old. The same site also contained remains of a second ancestral species, *Paranthropus robustus*, also known from other local sites of the same geological age. A third species, *Australopithecus sebida*, occurs in nearby deposits of the same age. The existence of three hominin species in essentially the same place at the same time is highly significant and contradicts the conventional view of one species replacing another, more primitive, form.

WE ARE A MIXED LOT

In July 2019 it was announced in *Proceedings of the National Academy of Sciences* by researchers from the University of Adelaide's Australian Centre for Ancient DNA (ACAD), that genetic analysis has revealed that modern-day *Homo sapiens* has interbred with at least five different archaic groups of humans. We have known for some time that the human genome contains elements from Neanderthals and the species known as Denisovans, but the other (currently unnamed) species are detected only as traces of DNA. The diversity appears to increase towards the east. Interbreeding with Neanderthals appears to have occurred soon after humans left East Africa around 60,000 years ago and that probably happened in the Middle East (possibly around 50,000 to 55,000 years ago). As the ancestral humans travelled east, they seem to have interbred with at least four other distinct groups (one being the Denisovans). The islands of Southeast Asia appear to have harboured several distinct groups of ancient (now extinct) humans. It seems that these groups existed in isolation from one another until modern human ancestors arrived.

LATE SURVIVAL OF *HOMO ERECTUS*

The hominin species *Homo erectus* is believed to be a direct ancestor of our own species, *Homo sapiens*, and the first to walk fully upright. It has long been thought that *H. erectus* became extinct in eastern Asia about 400,000 years ago. In December 2019, a team from the University of Iowa announced a dating of between 117,000 and 108,000 years for numerous specimens of *H. erectus* from Ngandong on the Solo River in Java. The individuals are thought to have died at the same time, perhaps as a result of a lahar created by a nearby volcano. This dating raises the possibility that *H. erectus* may have been present when the ancestors of *H. sapiens* arrived on the island.

EARLIEST EUROPEAN BONE TOOLS DISCOVERED

In August 2020, researchers from University College London Institute of Archaeology and the London Natural History Museum announced the discovery of some of the earliest organic (ie, not stone) tools in the world and certainly the earliest known from Europe. They came from the Boxgrove site in Sussex and appear to have been used in the manufacture of the numerous flint tools found at the site. The hominins using the site (dated to 500,000 years ago) were members of *Homo heidelbergensis*, a possible *Homo sapiens* ancestor.

DENISOVAN ART?

In July 2019, bones were excavated at Lingjing in Henan Province, China, at a site where ancient hominins, believed to be Denisovans, lived. The site was occupied between 125,000 and 105,000 years ago. The bones bore engravings of lines, created with a sharp point and rubbed with red ochre to make them more visible. Although the marks are geometrically simple, there are profound implications for the cognitive skills of the hominins who produced them. Similarly, despite there being some doubt about who created these signs, because modern humans arrived in the area at about 100,000 years ago, there is a good probability that these were actually created by the mysterious Denisovans.

A MUCH EARLIER DATE FOR HUMANS IN THE AMERICAS

In July 2020, an international team from Universidad Autónoma de Zacatecas, Mexico, the University of Oxford, and others announced the discovery of artefacts from Chiquihuite Cave, a rock shelter in Zacatecas, Mexico. The stone tools are reliably dated to 33,000 years old by the Oxford Radiocarbon Accelerator Unit, using two, completely different, dating techniques. This date is more than twice the age of 11,500 years for the Clovis Culture, often regarded as the first inhabitants of the Americas, although in recent years discoveries at Mesa Verde in Chile and Buttermilk Creek in Texas, in particular, have thrown this into doubt.

The distribution of the stone tools (about 1,900 in number) suggests that the Chiquihuite Cave site was used for at least 2,000 years. Some archaeologists, however, have claimed that the finds are naturally shaped stones, not human artefacts. It was announced in August 2019 that a site at Coopers Ferry in western Idaho was occupied some 16,000 years ago, and this date is accepted by some as being the earliest settlement of the Americas by peoples using the coastal route from Siberia.

THE EARLIEST MODERN BIRD
In March 2020, the discovery was announced in the journal Nature of the remains of the earliest modern bird. The fossil was discovered in marine sedimentary rocks from Belgium, and has been named *Asteriornis maastrichtensis* (nicknamed 'Wonderchicken'). The skull, the most important part, was found by Daniel Field of the University of Cambridge and this team by the use of X-ray computed tomography. The extinct bird lived some 66.7 million years ago, thus well before the asteroidal impact that may have resulted in the extinction of the dinosaurs, which occurred 65 to 66 million years ago. The fossil displays features that relate it to the most common ancestor of modern birds. The skull exhibits features resembling those of modern chicken and also those of the duck family. The fragmentary limb bones suggest that the bird had long legs, which, together with the discovery site, suggest that it may have been a shorebird.

ENORMOUS PREHISTORIC CIRCLE DISCOVERED NEAR STONEHENGE
In late June 2020, archaeologists announced the discovery of an enormous circle of shafts, about 2km in overall diameter, enclosing the henge at Durrington Walls. The structure is larger than any other ever found in Britain. The discovery was made after a geophysical survey as part of the Stonehenge Hidden Landscape Project. The individual shafts are about 10m in diameter, and 5m deep. Archaeologists believe that the circle represents a boundary surrounding the religious site and thus warning people not to attempt to trespass on the sacred area but to use specific entrances.

DISCOVERY OF THE EARLIEST AND LARGEST MAYAN CONSTRUCTION
The largest Mayan complex was described in *Nature* in June 2020 by researchers from the University of Arizona. The previously unknown site in Mexico, called Aguada Fénix, was discovered by the use of airborne lidar instrumentation and reveals, amongst other features, a giant, raised ceremonial plaza, about 1,400m long and 400m wide. This enormous construction was built in the very early Mayan period, between 1,000 and 800 BC. No evidence has yet been found at Aguada Fénix of the existence of a powerful elite class that would oversee such a giant construction and other works in the surrounding area, suggesting that the works were carried out by the combined forces from small local settlements. Large Mayan cities and kingdoms did not develop in Southern Mexico and elsewhere in Central America until much later, around AD 250 to 900.

USA RETURNS TO MANNED SPACE FLIGHT
The United States returned to manned space flight in 2020, with the launch on 20 May 2020 by a Falcon 9 rocket of the SpaceX company's *Dragon 2* capsule (named *Endeavour*), with two astronauts, bound for the International Space Station (ISS).

The capsule later returned the astronauts safely to Earth on 2 August 2020. A second launch on 15 November carried four astronauts to the ISS. A test flight of Boeing's *Starliner* capsule in December 2019 failed to reach the ISS. A further flight is scheduled for 29 March 2021.

SPACEX COMPANY'S STARSHIP SPACECRAFT
In December 2020, the SpaceX company carried out the first major test of its reusable spacecraft design (known as *Starship*), in a sub-orbital flight from its Boca Chica facility in south Texas. *Starship* is a large vehicle (50m long), able to carry large numbers of passengers (with up to 40 individual cabins) or a heavy payload, to orbit and beyond. It uses its own, SpaceX-designed, Raptor engines and an unconventional horizontal attitude ('belly flop') method of atmospheric braking, before turning to the vertical for landing. In the first test, all stages were satisfactory, including the atmospheric braking, save that the vehicle landed too fast and suffered a catastrophic failure and explosion. The performance in all other stages were considered a great success.

In major missions, it would be teamed with the huge, reusable, SpaceX *Super Heavy* booster rocket, some 70m long, which has up to 28 Raptor engines and is actually more powerful than the *Saturn V* rocket used for the Apollo missions. It is capable of placing some 100,000kg of payload into low Earth orbit.

RETURN TO THE MOON
On 22 July 2019, the Indian Space Research Organisation launched the *Chandrayaan-2* spacecraft, which was inserted into lunar orbit on 20 August 2019. However, as a result of a software problem, the lunar lander (*Vikram*) crashed onto the lunar surface on 6 September 2019. A duplicate mission may be undertaken in 2021.

On 23 November 2020, the Chinese Lunar Exploration Programme launched the *Chang'e-5* lunar sample return spacecraft. This made a landing on the Mons Rümker area of Oceanus Procellarum, an area thought to be much younger than other regions of the Moon that have been sampled, most of which were affected by the giant Mare Imbrium impact at 3,900 million years ago. The probe rapidly obtained approximately 2kg of specimens, both scooped from the surface and drilled from a lower layer. The specimens were returned to Earth at a landing site in Inner Mongolie on 16 December 2020.

In November 2019 and December 2020, NASA designated six companies as potential suppliers of the Commercial Lunar Payload Services for various modules as part of its overall *Artemis* programme to return humans to the Moon. (Three contracts had previously been awarded to commercial companies for landers capable of delivering at least 10kg of scientific instrumentation by the end of 2021. Heavier payloads are being considered for delivery in 2023.) On 21 February 2019, NASA announced details of the first 12 payloads and on 1 July 2020 information on a further 12 payloads. The first of the small landers, *Peregrine Mission One*, is due for launch in July 2021.

MISSIONS TO MARS
Three missions to Mars were launched in July 2020 to take advantage of a favourable launch window. On 20 July, the United Arab Emirates launched the Emirates Mars Mission (named *Hope*) from Tanegashima Island in Japan. The spacecraft will be inserted into Mars orbit in February 2021 and then begin observations of the Martian atmosphere.

On 25 July 2020, China launched its *Tianwen-1* ('Questions to Heaven') Martian rover. The spacecraft was lifted off by a Long March 5 rocket from Wenchang spaceport on Hainan Island and is expected to enter Martian orbit in February 2021. The lander/rover is scheduled to reach the surface of Mars some two to three months later.

On 30 July 2020, NASA launched the spacecraft (*Mars 2020*) carrying the advanced *Perseverance* rover to Mars. This is scheduled to land at Jezero crater on 18 February 2021. The rover incorporates improvements made as a result of slight problems with NASA's highly successful *Curiosity* rover, and also includes more advanced instrumentation. The rover is accompanied by the simple helicopter *Ingenuity*, which, apart from being able to conduct scouting missions around the rover, has a primary objective of determining whether such drones can operate properly in the thin Martian atmosphere. The rover has a drill and can collect samples of rock, and store these in suitable containers. The overall aim is for a later mission to recover these containers and return them to Earth for study.

A CHANCE TO TACKLE PLASTIC POLLUTION
In September 2020, a team from the University of Portsmouth in the UK and the National Renewable Energy Laboratory (NREL) in the USA announced in *Proceedings of the National Academy of Sciences* that they had created a 'super-enzyme', by combining the PETase enzyme with another, called the MHETase enzyme, to obtain an enzyme that breaks down the PET plastic into its component parts, which can then be reused in other processes and materials. The original PETase enzyme, discovered at the Portsmouth Centre for Enzyme Innovation, broke down PET (the most ubiquitous plastic) at a rate far exceeding natural processes, but not fast enough for commercial use. The 'super-enzyme' acts six times faster, so that commercial applications and a solution to some of the problem of plastic pollution become practical.

MAJOR DEVELOPMENTS IN ELECTRON MICROSCOPY
In July 2019 it was announced that developments in cryo-electron microscopy (cryo-EM), giving exceptional increases in resolution was revolutionising biological research. The technique has been so refined that it has now been termed 'ultra-high-definition-3D-video-ology'. It is now possible to see the shape and structure of biological molecules in detail and the processes actually occurring inside cells. This is a major step forward in the development of drugs, especially for infectious diseases, and including problems such as those posed by Alzheimer's and Parkinson's diseases.

The technique involves freezing molecules (or viruses) within cells, and then making thousands of images from different angles and at different stages of a biological process. These images may then be used to create a video of the process in action.

EDITING DNA
In October 2019, the journal *Nature* carried details of a new method of editing DNA.

Although DNA may be edited with the Crispr-Cas9 technique, this depends on 'cutting' the strand of DNA and splicing in a suitable fragment. Unfortunately, the cuts are sometimes imperfect, occurring in the wrong place, so additional care needs to be taken to ensure that the final result is desirable.

In the new process, known as 'prime editing', the process allows one to search for a precise piece of the DNA sequence, and replace this with a known, required sequence. When used in combination with a specific enzyme, known as reverse transcriptase, the relevant 'edits' are incorporated into the DNA.

Prime editing has been used *in vitro* (in human cells) in the laboratory to reverse the effects of errors in various forms of disease, including one in the rare Tay-Sachs disease, and one in a form of sickle-cell anaemia.

It is estimated that prime editing has the potential to correct some 89 per cent of the approximately 75,000 mutations that may cause disease in people. As with all similar procedures much more work, likely to take years, is required before any benefit can be made available to individuals.

VACCINES AGAINST COVID-19
By mid-December 2020, as many as 57 vaccines against the COVID-19 coronavirus (coronavirus 2 or SARS-CoV-2) were in clinical trials, 40 in Phase I or II trials and 17 in Phase II to III trials. Those vaccines currently administered (except only the Russian Sputnik-5 vaccine) are known to have completed satisfactory Phase III trials.

The Oxford-AstraZeneca vaccine (AZD1222) is produced by what is known as a virus-vector method. In this, a virus, normally producing common-cold symptoms in chimpanzees, has been modified so that it will not reproduce in humans. In addition, changes cause the virus to produce 'spike' proteins like those by which the COVID-19 coronavirus infects human cells. With vaccination, the body recognises these foreign proteins and produces antibodies against them. It also activates special T-cells that destroy any cells with the 'spike' protein. The body is thus primed against any future infection, although at present it is not known how long (in terms of months or years) such resistance persists.

The Pfizer-Biontech vaccine (tozinameran) is of a new type known as an RNA vaccine. It uses a small fragment of the genetic code of the virus. When injected, this causes just a part of the virus to be produced within the body, which then recognises this as foreign and attacks it.

The Moderna vaccine (mRNA-1273) uses a similar method to that in the Pfizer-BioNTech vaccine.

No details are available of the Russian 'Sputnik-5' vaccine, administered before final trials had been concluded, and which is believed to be similar to the Oxford-AstraZeneca vaccine. Other vaccines are being developed in China by Wuhan Biological Products and Sinopharm (an inactivated virus vaccine) and in Russia by Gamaleya Research Institute (Gam-COVID-Vac, produced in a way similar to the Oxford-AstraZeneca method). All are in final trials. A trial in Brazil of an inactivated virus vaccine from the Chinese company, Sinovac, was halted after an unspecified adverse reaction.

WEATHER

In the text below, the 'average' refers to the average for the 30-year period 1981–2010, which is the standard reference period ('normal') for 2011–20. Values appearing in brackets after a quoted number represent the 30-year, long-term average. Daily rainfall totals are for 24-hour periods ending at 0900 GMT on the day indicated. The data was supplied by the Met Office and World Meteorological Organisation.

The UK's mean air temperature (July 2019–June 2020) was 9.61°C, the fifth warmest and highest since 2016/17 (9.73°C); the long-term average is 8.87°C. Only two months in this period, October and November, were below average and winter was exceptionally warm with January nearly 2°C above average. A warm spring followed with April 1.7°C above average, the joint fourth warmest (with 1943) and highest since 2014 (9.2°C). Scotland's mean temperature over the same period was 8.01°C (7.46°C), the 10th warmest in this period and highest since 2018/19 (8.05°C). January (2020) was very warm (4.8°C), over two degrees above average and joint fourth warmest (shared with 1932) and highest since 1989 (5.7°C). Overall, the winter (2019/20) ranked eighth warmest (4.01°C) and highest since 2016/17 (4.37°C). Wales' mean temperature was 9.93°C (9.16°C) over the 12-month period and was the fifth highest and warmest since 2016/17 (9.98°C). Most months were above average, and winter (2019/20) was particularly warm with 5.75°C (4.31°C), the joint 6th highest (shared with 1943), the previous winter was very slightly warmer (5.77°C). Spring was fifth warmest (9.11°C) and highest since 2017 (9.34°C). Northern Ireland's mean was 9.34°C (8.91°C), fourteenth warmest and highest since 2018/19 (9.46°C). Most months were above average, particularly April (9.0°C), was joint seventh warmest (shared with 2003) and the warmest since 2014 (9.6°C). England's 12-month mean was 10.56°C (9.66°C), fourth warmest and highest since 2016/17 (10.58°C). The winter 2019/20 was fourth warmest (5.98°C) and highest since 2015/16 (6.47°C). January was joint fifth warmest (6.2°C), shared with 1975 and 1990, and the highest since 2008 (6.3°C). Spring was fifth warmest (9.65°C) and highest since 2017 (10.01°C). April was joint third warmest (10.2°C), shared with 1943, and the warmest April since 2011 (11.5°C).

The UK total rainfall over the 12 months (July 2019–June 2020) was 1317.4 mm (1133.5mm), third wettest, and highest since 2015/16 (1332.7mm). February set a new record with 209.1 mm (87.2mm) and April and May were exceptionally dry with only 29.1mm (70.5mm) and 32.7mm (67.8mm) respectively, the lowest April since 2007 (26.6mm) and May 1991 (22.6mm) respectively. Scotland's rainfall totalled 1741.1mm (1521.8mm), the ninth wettest and highest since 2014/15 (1780.6mm). The winter 2019/20 was the fourth wettest with 674.7mm (465.8mm) and highest since 2015/16 (739.3mm). February, with 275.6mm (128.3mm) was its second wettest, the record being held by February 1990 (289.4mm). April was Scotland's third driest with 28.3mm (86.7mm) and lowest since 1980 (21.0mm). Wales' total was 1681.3mm (1412.4mm) over the 12-month period, its eleventh highest and wettest since 2015/16 (1767.1mm). February set a new record with 288.4mm (107.4mm), the previous highest was in 1923 (270.8mm). May was second driest with 14.3mm (83.2mm), its lowest since 1896 (7.3mm). Northern Ireland's 12-month total was 1218.0mm (1134.6mm), the wettest since 2017/18 (1255.7mm). February's rain set a new record with 222.7mm (83.1mm); the previous highest was set in 1990 (194.9mm). England's

rainfall total was 1014.1mm (845.8mm), the tenth wettest and highest since 2015/16 (1018.1mm). February set a new record with 154.9mm (59.6mm), the previous highest was in 1923 (134.4mm). May was record-breaking for dryness with 9.6mm (57.6mm), the previous lowest was 1896 (11.2mm).

UK sunshine (July 2019–June 2020) totalled 1574.5 hours (1368.6 hrs), a new record over this 12-month period. The previous sunniest was 1955/56 (1548.9 hrs). Both April and May set new records with 224.5 hours (147.9hours) and 265.5 hours (185.9 hrs) respectively; the previous highest were in 2015 (211.8 hrs) and 1989 (243.1 hrs) respectively. The spring, too, was record breaking with 626.2 hours (435.7 hrs), the previous highest was in 1948 (555.4 hrs). Scotland's sunshine total was 1277.2 hours (1170.5 hrs), seventh sunniest, although 2017/18 was higher (1310.8 hrs). April set a new record with 204.6 hours (134.0 hrs), replacing the previous sunniest set in 1942 (203.2 hours). The spring was also record-breaking with 518.4 hours (403.6 hrs), also set in 1942 (484.1 hrs). Wales, with 1565.4 hours (1384.5 hrs), was fifth sunniest and highest since 2014/15 (1579.1 hrs). April, with 217.1 hours (153.6 hrs) was second sunniest and highest since 2007 (221.5 hrs). May set a new record with 281.3 hours (186.3 hrs) replacing the previous highest of 262.5 hours (1948). Spring was also record-breaking with 640.7 hours (440.1 hrs), the previous highest was in 1948 (609.0 hrs). Northern Ireland, with 1395.4 hours (1228.2 hrs) was eighth sunniest and highest since 2014/15 (1411.3 hrs). April set a new record with 211.5 hours (143.6 hrs), the previous highest was in 2015 (209.3 hrs). Spring set a new record with 564.4 hours (419.2 hrs); the previous highest was in 1975 (541.5 hrs). England's sunshine total, over this 12-month period, was record-breaking with 1773.4 hours (1500.0 hrs), the previous highest was 2014/15 (1689.1 hrs). April and May set new records. April, with 239.0 hours (155.8 hrs) replaces 2015 (220.6 hrs) and May, with 299.4 hours (191.7 hrs), replaces 1989 (269.7 hrs). Spring also set a new record with 695.5 hours (456.0 hrs), the previous highest was in 1948 (594.4 hrs).

NEWSWORTHY EVENTS – UK AND THE WORLD

After a cool dry start across the UK July became unsettled. However, a very hot period developed later in the month giving rise to record-breaking temperatures and widespread thunderstorms, leading to some flooding, power outages and transport disruption.

Cars were buried in parts of Guadalajara city (Mexico) at the beginning of July by hail from thunderstorms of unprecedented severity. The threat of landslides from severe flooding on the island of Kyushu (Japan) led to more than one million people being ordered to evacuate their homes: severe rainfall and landslides later devastated parts of western Japan. Alaska (USA) experienced a record-breaking heatwave early in the month with temperatures reaching 32°C in Anchorage. Severe storms following a heatwave in Greece battered Halkidiki (10th) with cars overturned and casualties reported. Areas of Nepal, Bangladesh and India were severely affected by flooding from the ongoing Monsoon, causing the displacement of millions of people. Late in July Europe was engulfed in a heatwave with a record-high temperature of 42.6°C recorded on the 25th in Paris (France).

August's weather was mixed with periods of unsettled conditions and a hot spell in central and southern England later in the month. Accumulated heavy rainfall from late July and early August threatened to breach the Toddbrook reservoir at

Whaley Bridge (Derbyshire), leading to the evacuation of some residence in low-lying areas of the town.

Wind over 75 mph battered Australia's south-eastern states on the eighth, destroying part of Melbourne's Frankston pier and bringing down trees and powerlines. Originally a super typhoon, Lekima made landfall on the Zhejiang provence (China) on the 10th. Wind speeds of 116mph and heavy rainfall over several days caused flooding, landslides and power outages for over two million homes. At the same time, Typhoon Krosa brought heavy rain and strong winds to Guam and the Northern Mariana Islands, later moving on to Hiroshima (Japan). In late August, Hurricane Dorian tracked through the Caribbean, battering many islands. It grazed Puerto Rico (28th) as a developing hurricane and moved onto the Bahamas at the end of the month as a category 5 hurricane, the second most powerful on record, with wind gusts over 200mph and a seven metre storm-surge.

September began unsettled but high pressure soon brought settled weather. However, from the 20th it became very unsettled with heavy rain affecting a large part of the country causing flooding for some.

Hurricane Dorian continued its destructive path early in the month, moving from the Bahamas to the coasts of Florida and the Carolinas (USA), causing destruction from strong winds and storm-surge flooding. Typhoon Lingling struck North and South Korea on the 8th, before moving into China with wind gusts of 86mph. At this time, Typhoon Faxai made landfall near Tokyo (Japan) with 130mph winds, making it one of the strongest to hit the capital in a decade. Record-breaking torrential rain in southeastern Spain caused flash flooding in parts of Valencia, Murcia and eastern Andalucia. Just two weeks after the Bahamas was hit by Hurricane Dorian, Tropical Storm Humberto brought heavy rain and strong winds to parts of the islands on the 15th. On the 20th Hurricane Lorena passed over the southern tip of the Baja (Mexico), bringing 75mph winds and heavy rain to the peninsula. Over several days, from the 17th, a slow-moving Tropical Storm (Imelda) brought heavy rain and severe flooding to southeastern Texas (USA), with over a metre of rainfall recorded in parts of Jefferson County.

In general, October across the UK was unsettled with showers or longer spells of rain. Localised flooding caused some road closures and rail disruption in parts of the country.

On the 9th an intense area of cold affected the north-central USA with strong winds leading to blizzard conditions. Typhoon Hagibis made landfall on the Izu Peninsula, south-west of Tokyo (Japan) causing much flooding: Hakone recorded over a metre of rainfall in 48 hours. A rapidly deepening area of low pressure, known as a 'bomb cyclone', affected a large swathe of the eastern seaboard of the USA (16th/17th). Heavy rain and winds gusting to 90mph left over a million people without power. A hydro-electric dam in the region of Krasnoyarsk, Siberia (Russia), serving a gold mine community, collapsed after heavy rain (19th). Tropical Storm Nestor (19th) made landfall on Florida's St Vincent Island (USA) then moved across Florida's Panhandle. Despite the storm being a weakening system, it still produced severe flooding, gale-force winds and tornadoes as it moved inland. Heavy rain on the 23rd brought severe flooding to the south of France; north-east Spain, where the River Francoli burst its banks; and northern Italy, where the village of Castelletto d'Orba was badly flooded. At this time, a hurricane-like weather system, called a medicane, brought severe rain and damaging wind gusts to the eastern Mediterranean and unassociated thunderstorms battered Ibiza (Spain) with torrential rain and reports of a tornado. Another medicane, with 70mph winds, would badly affect Algeria in November. Several days later, in eastern and northeastern Japan, a months' worth of rain fell in only 12 hours causing landslides and severe flooding in some areas. In the Los Angeles region (USA)

74mph winds fanned wildfires and destroyed many homes late in October.

The first half of November was unsettled in the UK and mild before turning colder for a time with snow falling across high ground. Mild and wet conditions returned on the 21st. Heavy rain and high winds caused transport disruption to parts of England and Wales.

Storm Amelie (3rd) brought 100mph winds and heavy rain to parts of France and power outages to thousands of homes. Heavy rain across parts of New South Wales (Australia) on the 3rd brought some relief to the bushfires that had burned across the State since September. In South Africa, Zimbabwe's drought was said to be the worst in 100 years with Victoria Falls decreasing to a relative trickle. Further north rains heavier than usual brought severe flooding in Southern Sudan, Rwanda, Somalia, Tanzania, Uganda and Ethiopia; Kenya's usual period of 'short rains' were also heavier than usual. Cyclone Bulbul brought a two-metre storm surge and wind close to 100mph to coastal districts in Bangladesh and India on 10th, and the evacuation of over two million people.

December began settled and cold, but soon areas of low pressure brought a long, unsettled period of weather. Strong winds and flooding gave rise to transport and power disruption for parts of the country. Mid-month, snow made a stretch of the A59, near Harrogate, impassable to traffic. A tornado caused localised damage in Chertsey (Surrey) on the 21st.

Typhoon Kammuri (3rd) made landfall in the Sorsogon province, south of Manila (Philippines) with wind gusts in excess of 140mph and a three-metre storm surge. In Africa, heavy rain from Cyclone Pawan brought flooding to Somalia in early December. Storms Elsa and Fabien brought winds close to 100mph to Iberian Peninsula in quick succession (18th/21st) and on into France. Typhoon Phanfone passed over many islands of the central Philippines on Christmas Day bringing severe flooding and 118mph wind gusts, leaving a trail of devastation. At the end of the year, many bushfires continued to burn out of control in Australia amid a backdrop of a record-breaking average temperature of 41.9°C; in Delhi (India), the coldest day on record (9.4°C) was recorded, records began in 1901.

During January there was a good deal of dry and settled weather, although low-pressure systems did move in from the Atlantic at times bringing periods of wet and very windy weather. Strong winds close to mid-month caused travel chaos across the country bringing in some speed restrictions. Snow also hindered travel for some in Scotland (14th) and Wales (28th).

Heavy rain brought flooding and landslides to Jakarta (Indonesia) at the start of January with 377mm of rain being reported over 24 hours. Sunndalsora (Norway) recorded the country's highest ever January maximum air temperature of 19°C, over 25 degrees above average. In western Australia, Tropical Cyclone Blake brought gales and heavy rain to the Kimberley region (6th). Bushfires that had raged across eastern Australia since September were mostly dampened down by heavy rain on the 18th, but this brought the new threat of flooding. In Spain, Storm Gloria battered Valencia, the Balearic Islands and southern France on the 20th, bringing damaging wind gusts of 71mph and flooding.

February was largely very wet and windy with Storms Ciara, Dennis and Jorge bringing periods of exceptionally wet weather across the UK. Rainfall totals were record-breaking, leading to travel disruption, flooding and power outages.

A record-breaking temperature of 18.3°C was recorded on the northern tip of Antarctica (6th), beating the previous highest of 17.5°C set March 2015. Tropical Storm Damien brought heavy rain and damaging winds to western Australia (11th), damping down bushfires. Over several days, Saharan sandstorms whipped up by 75mph winds brought air travel to and from the Canary Islands (Spain) to a standstill (24th). At the same time Firefighters battled wildfires on the islands of Tenerife and Grand Canaria. An intense weather system brought heavy rain to the northern provinces of Argentina where widespread flooding forced the evacuation of hundreds of people. The weather system later affected Paraguay and Brazil, resulting in flooding and landslides.

March was cool and showery for the first half of the month but became milder. High pressure established later in the month, giving rise to dry and sunny conditions for a large part of the UK. There was localised flooding across the UK during the first half of the month which was compounded in some coastal areas of Wales by a tidal surge. Windy conditions close to mid-month led to reports of fallen trees and power outages in Northern Ireland.

Powerful tornadoes devastated parts of Nashville, Tennessee (USA) on 3rd. Winter across Europe was the warmest on record with the average temperature 1.4°C above the previous highest set 5 years earlier. Thunderstorms brought widespread severe flooding and high winds across Egypt (11th), where flood water demolished houses in the southern province of Qena. A few days earlier, parts of Southern California (USA) were hit by flash flooding and landslides.

April was mostly dominated by high pressure, giving rise to record-breaking amounts of sunshine.

In early April Cyclone Harold, a category 5 storm, hit the Solomon Islands, Vanuatu, Fiji and Tonga with winds up to 145mph causing widespread destruction. In the USA up to 60 tornadoes destroyed parts of Louisiana, Texas and Mississippi on the 12th, with some of these states affected again later in the month.

May was changeable with periods of cool showery weather, some wintry in nature. This was followed by warm, settled conditions with good amounts of sunshine. Weather impacts during the month varied from heath and grassland fires during dry periods, to periods of strong winds and heavy rain causing some power and transport disruption.

Super Cyclone Amphan made landfall along the western Bangladesh/eastern India coastline (20th) with destructive winds of 115mph and heavy rain which forced the evacuation of three million people. Ex-Tropical Storm Mangga, rejuvenated by a cold front in Western Australia, battered Perth and surrounding region with winds over 70mph and high rainfall totals. At the end of the month, Tropical Storm Amanda stuck El Salvador in South America bringing severe flash flooding and landslides.

June's weather was mixed with periods of settled conditions and showers, or longer spells of rain. A thundery episode close to mid-month gave rise to localised flooding in parts of the UK and fallen trees in the south-west, blocking some roads.

Cyclone Nisarga made landfall on India's west coast in the Raigad district (2nd), the worst of the winds narrowly missing the densely populated city of Mumbai. A massive Saharan dust cloud darkened the skies over parts of the Caribbean late in June. The islands of Guadeloupe and Martinique suffered their worse haze in a decade.

THE YEAR 2019

The UK's mean air temperature for 2019 was 9.39°C (8.88°C), twelfth highest and warmest since 2018 (9.45°C). Winter 2018/19, 5.05°C (3.83°C), highest since 2015/16 (5.47°C). Spring, 8.38°C (7.79°C), warmest since 2017 (9.12°C). England, 10.22°C (9.68°C), eleventh warmest year and highest since 2018 (10.43°C). Winter, 2018/19, 5.56°C (4.28°C), ninth warmest and highest since 2015/16 (6.47°C). Spring, 9.17°C (8.56°C), England's highest since 2017 (10.01°C). Summer, 16.27°C (15.53°C), eleventh warmest and highest since 2018 (17.10°C). Autumn, 10.08°C (10.32°C), the coolest since 2012 (9.56°C). Wales, 9.67°C (9.17°C), thirteenth warmest and highest since 2018 (9.71°C).

Winter 2018/19, 5.77°C (4.31°C), fifth warmest and highest since 2015/16 (6.37°C). Spring, 8.63°C (8.04°C), the sixteenth warmest and highest since 2017 (9.34°C). Summer, 15.06°C (14.48°C), the eighteenth highest and warmest since 2018 (15.89°C). Autumn, 9.57°C (9.86°C), the coolest since 2012 (8.96°C). Scotland, 7.93°C (7.47°C), eleventh warmest and warmest since 2017 (8.01°C). Winter 2018/19, 3.85°C (2.84°C), the fourteenth warmest and highest since 2016/17 (4.37°C). Spring, 7.01°C (6.42°C), its twenty-second highest and warmest since 2017 (7.58°C). Summer, 13.39°C (12.61°C), the eleventh warmest and highest since 2018 (13.62°C). Autumn, 7.37°C (7.99°C), the coolest since 2012 (6.94°C). Northern Ireland's 2019 mean was 9.35°C (8.92°C), the fourteenth warmest and highest since 2017 (9.48°C). Winter 2018/19, 5.97°C (4.41°C), the third warmest and highest since 1997/98 (5.98°C). Spring, 8.33°C (7.91°C), the warmest since 2017 (9.17°C). Summer, 14.44°C (13.94°C), the seventeenth highest and warmest since 2018 (14.95°C). Autumn, 8.97°C (9.40°C), the lowest since 2012 (8.39°C).

The global mean temperature for 2019 was 0.98°C above the 1950–1980 long term average (14.0°C). It was the second warmest year since records began in 1880, surpassed only by 2016 (+1.01°C).

UK rainfall totalled 1227.2mm (1131.5mm), the sixteenth wettest and highest since 2015 (1265.3mm). Winter 2018/19, 253.4mm (326.7mm), the driest since 2016/17 (246.6mm). Spring, 241.3mm (231.3mm), the wettest since 2015 (250.2mm). Regionally, Scotland with 1555.8mm (1516.7mm) was the wettest year since 2015 (1840.1mm). Winter 2018/19, 342.4mm (465.8mm) the driest since 2010 (275.3mm). Spring, 336.2mm (303.3mm), the wettest since 2015 (400.5mm). Summer, 436.2mm (290.2mm), the fourth wettest and highest since 1985 (478.8mm). Autumn, 382.7mm (462.6mm), the driest since 2016 (321.4mm). Wales, 1602.3mm (1412.1mm), the seventeenth wettest and highest since 2012 (1702.4mm). Winter, 2018/19, 358.7mm (423.3mm), the driest since 2017 (284.4mm). Spring, 322.2mm (283.1mm), the wettest since 2006 (407.0mm). Summer, 348.1mm (276.5mm), the wettest since 2017 (362.8mm). Autumn, 578.7mm (435.2mm), the wettest since 2000 (739.0mm). Northern Ireland, 1211.5mm (1140.7mm), the wettest year since 2015 (1319.4mm). Winter 2018/19, 242.6mm (315.4mm), the driest since 2017 (207.5mm). Spring, 293.8mm (243.4mm), the wettest since 2006 (329.7mm). Summer, 342.7mm (255.4mm), the wettest since 2017 (349.8mm). Autumn, 330.4mm (323.9mm), the wettest since 2017 (365.6mm). England, 971.9mm (842.3mm), the fifthteenth wettest and highest since 2014 (983.4mm). Winter 2018/19, 184.4mm (228.5mm), the driest since 2017 (160.2mm). Spring, 166.0mm (178.3mm), the driest since 2017 (144.7mm). Summer, 254.0mm (190.3mm), the wettest since 2012 (351.1mm). Autumn, 360.9mm (245.9mm), the fourth wettest and highest since 2000 (443.7mm).

UK sunshine totalled 1447.0 hours (1374.5 hrs), fourteenth highest, the sunniest since 2018 (1560.1 hrs). Winter 2018/19 with 186.1 hours (155.8 hrs) was sixth sunniest and highest since the previous winter (191.7 hrs). February was second sunniest with 99.1 hours (69.9 hrs), the highest since 2008 (101.3 hrs). Spring, 470.8 hours (435.7 hrs), the sunniest since 2017 (484.9 hrs). Within the four nations, Scotland, 1228.7 hours (1174.8 hrs), its nineteenth sunniest and highest since the previous year (1378.2 hrs). Winter 2018/19 with 143.9 hours (121.8 hrs) was eleventh sunniest and highest since the previous winter (163.1 hrs). January with 47.4 hours (32.9 hrs) was fifth sunniest and highest since 2001 (51.6 hrs). Spring, 425.9 hours (403.6 hrs), the sunniest since 2018 (460.6 hrs). Summer, 413.8 hours (425.7 hrs), the lowest since 2017 (374.1 hrs). Autumn, 247.2 hours (223.6 hrs), the fifteenth highest and sunniest since 2016 (254.7 hrs). Wales' annual

WEATHER STATISTICS 2019

	Mean Temp. °C	Diff. from normal °C*	Rainfall mm	Percentage of normal*	Sunshine hours	Percentage of normal*
England	10.22	+0.54	971.9	115%	1,607.4	107%
Wales	9.67	+0.50	1,602.3	113%	1,404.2	101%
Scotland	7.93	+0.46	1,555.8	103%	1,228.7	105%
Northern Ireland	9.35	+0.43	1,211.5	106%	1,221.7	99%
United Kingdom	9.39	+0.51	1,227.2	108%	1,447.0	105%

* The standard reference period ('normal') is the average for the 30-year period 1981–2010

sunshine was 1404.2 hours (1391.9 hrs), the sunniest since 2018 (1543.1 hrs). Winter 2018/19, 158.5 hours (156.6 hrs), the sunniest since 2017/18 (175.1 hrs). February with 104.7 hours (69.9 hrs) was second sunniest and highest since 2008 (107.2 hrs). Spring, 463.9 hours (440.1 hrs), the highest since 2017 (475.5 hrs). Summer, 484.4 hours (514.1 hrs), the lowest since 2016 (467.0 hrs). Autumn, 274.3 hours (275.9 hrs), the lowest since 2017 (229.9 hrs). Northern Ireland, 1221.7 hours (1231.4 hrs), slightly below average and the lowest since 2012 (1219.1 hrs). Winter 2018/19, 138.6 hours (142.8 hrs), the lowest since 2017 (134.1 hrs). Spring, 356.0 hours (419.2 hrs), the ninth dullest and lowest since 1998 (347.0 hrs). Summer, 430.6 hours (420.3 hrs), the highest since 2018 (511.0 hrs). Autumn, 276.8 hours (250.1 hrs), the highest since 2010 (298.2 hrs). October, with 106.6 hours, was seventh sunniest and highest since 1987 (111.4 hrs). England's total was 1607.4 hours (1504.7 hrs), thirteenth sunniest year and highest since 2018 (1691.7 hrs). The winter 2018/19 was third sunniest with 220.8 hours (177.5 hrs) and highest since 2014/15 (224.6 hrs). February set a new record with 120.1 hours (75.3 hrs) replacing the previous highest of 118.1 hours (2008). Spring, 510.6 hours (456.0 hrs), the highest since 2015 (530.9 hrs). Summer, 563.1 hours (561.3 hrs), the highest since 2018 (680.8 hrs). Autumn, 299.3 hours (306.5 hrs), the lowest since 2017 (286.4 hrs).

UK TEMPERATURE

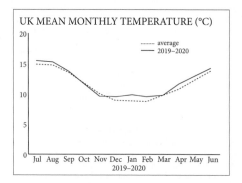

UK MEAN MONTHLY TEMPERATURE (°C)
.... average
—— 2019–2020
Jul Aug Sep Oct Nov Dec Jan Feb Mar Apr May Jun
2019–2020

Summer 2019, 15.14°C (14.41°C), was joint eleventh warmest, shared with 1911, and the warmest since 2018 (15.76°C). The highest site-specific maximum daytime air temperature over the season was 38.7°C (a new UK record) at Cambridge Botanic Gardens on 25 July. The lowest night-time minimum air temperature was −0.4°C at Altnaharra (Sutherland) on 8 July.

Autumn, 9.10°C (9.48°C), the coolest since 2012 (8.60°C). The highest site-specific maximum daytime air temperature was 27.7°C at Weybourne (Norfolk) on 22 September. The lowest night-time minimum air temperature of −9.9°C recorded at Braemar (Aberdeenshire) on 19 November.

Winter 2019/20, 5.28°C (3.83°C), the fifth warmest and highest since 2015/16 (5.47°C). The highest site-specific

maximum daytime air temperature was 18.7°C at Achfary (Sutherland) on 28 December. The lowest night-time air minimum was −10.3°C at Tulloch Bridge (Inverness-shire) on 1 December.

Spring, 8.66°C (7.79°C), the eighth warmest and highest since 2017 (9.12°C), the current record. The highest site-specific maximum daytime air temperature was 28.3°C at Cromdale (Morayshire) on 29 May. The lowest night-time air minimum was −7.6 °C at Aboyne (Aberdeenshire) on 16 March.

June's mean temperature was 14.0°C, nearly a degree above average. The highest site-specific daytime maximum air temperature was 33.4°C at Heathrow (Greater London) on the 25th. The lowest night-time minimum air temperature was −1.9°C at Tulloch Bridge (Inverness-shire) on the 8th.

UK RAINFALL

Summer 2019, 325.6mm (233.7mm), fourteenth wettest and highest since 2012 (378.7mm). The highest site-specific rainfall total occurred in the 24 hours ending at 0900 GMT on 11 July, 80.4mm of rain fell at Fettercairn (Kincardineshire).

Autumn, 385.0mm (336.5mm), the joint twenty-second wettest (shared with 1918) and highest since 2009 (386.2mm). The highest site-specific rainfall total occurred in the 24 hours ending at 0900 GMT on 26 October, 101.0mm of rain fell at Lebanus (Powys).

Winter 2019/20, 470.4mm (326.7mm) the fifth wettest and highest since 2016 (505.7mm). The highest site-specific rainfall total occurred in the 24 hours ending at 0900 GMT on 20 February, 180.4mm of rain fell at Honister Pass (Cumbria).

Spring, 139.7mm (231.3mm), the fifth driest and lowest since 1974 (123.1mm). The highest site-specific rainfall total occurred in the 24 hours ending at 0900 GMT on 8 March, 107.2mm of rain fell at Alltdearg House (Skye).

June 2020 totalled 105.7mm, 146 per cent of normal and wettest since the previous June (109.0mm). The highest site-specific rainfall total occurred in the 24 hours ending at 0900 GMT on 29th, 212.8mm of rain fell at Honister Pass (Cumbria).

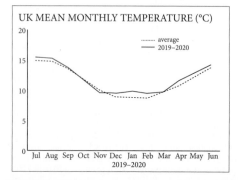

UK MEAN MONTHLY TEMPERATURE (°C)
.... average
—— 2019–2020
Jul Aug Sep Oct Nov Dec Jan Feb Mar Apr May Jun
2019–2020

UK SUNSHINE

Summer 2019 totalled 501.2 hours (505.6 hrs), slightly below average and the dullest since 2017 (478.8 hrs).

Autumn, 279.3 hours (273.9 hrs), slightly above average and the sunniest since the previous autumn (305.7 hrs).

Winter 2019/20, 163.4 hours (155.8 hrs), the nineteenth sunniest and highest since since winter 2018/19 (186.1 hrs).

Spring, 626.2 hours (435.7 hrs), a new record, replacing the previous highest of 555.4 hours set in 1948.

June's total sunshine was 164.2 hours, 97 per cent of average. The previous June was duller with 159.8 hours.

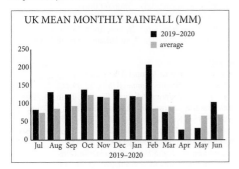

UK MEAN MONTHLY RAINFALL (MM)

SPORTS RESULTS

Due to the coronavirus pandemic, many sporting events were cancelled in 2020. Where these events did not take place, listed are the previous results and winners up to 31 October 2020.

ALPINE SKIING

WORLD CUP 2019–20

MEN
Downhill: Beat Feuz (Switzerland), 650pts
Slalom: Henrik Kristoffersen (Norway), 552pts
Giant Slalom: Mauro Caviezel (Switzerland), 365pts
Super G: Henrik Kristoffersen (Norway), 394pts
Combined: Alexis Pinturault (France), 280pts
Overall: Aleksander Kilde (Norway), 1,202pts

WOMEN
Downhill: Corinne Suter (Switzerland), 477pts
Slalom: Petra Vlhová (Slovakia), 460pts
Giant Slalom: Federica Brignone (Italy), 407pts
Super G: Corinne Suter (Switzerland), 360pts
Combined: Frederica Brignone (Italy), 200pts
Overall: Federica Brignone (Italy), 1378pts

AMERICAN FOOTBALL

AFC Championship 2019–20: Kansas City Chiefs beat Tennessee Titans 35–24
NFC Championship 2019–20: San Francisco 49ers beat Green Bay Packers 37–20
Super Bowl 54: Kansas City Chiefs beat San Francisco 49ers 31–20

ANGLING

NATIONAL CHAMPIONSHIPS 2020
Individual (ladies): Charlotte Gore
Team: Drennan Spotted Fin North West

AQUATICS

WORLD AQUATICS CHAMPIONSHIPS 2019
Gwangju, South Korea 12–28 July

SWIMMING

MEN
50m freestyle: Caeleb Dressel (USA), 21.04sec
100m freestyle: Caeleb Dressel (USA), 46.96sec
200m freestyle: Sun Yang (China), 1min 44.93sec
400m freestyle: Sun Yang (China), 3min 42.44sec
800m freestyle: Gregorio Paltrineri (Italy), 7min 39.27sec
1500m freestyle: Florian Wellbrock (Germany), 14min 36.54sec
50m backstroke: Zane Waddell (South Africa), 24.43sec
100m backstroke: Xu Jiayu (China), 52.43sec
200m backstroke: Evgeny Rylov (Russia), 1min 53.40sec
50m breaststroke: Adam Peaty (Great Britain), 26.06sec
100m breaststroke: Adam Peaty (Great Britain), 57.14sec

200m breaststroke: Anton Chupkov (Russia), 2min 06.12sec
50m butterfly: Caeleb Dressel (USA), 22.35sec
100m butterfly: Caeleb Dressel (USA), 49.66sec
200m butterfly: Kristof Milak (Hungary), 1min 50.73sec
200m medley: Daiya Seto (Japan), 1min 56.14sec
400m medley: Daiya Seto (Japan), 4min 08.95sec
4x100m freestyle relay: USA, 3min 09.06sec
4x200m freestyle relay: Australia, 7min 00.85sec
4x100m medley relay: Great Britain, 3min 28.10sec
4x100 mixed medley relay: Great Britain, 3min 28.10sec

WOMEN
50m freestyle: Simone Manuel (USA), 24.05sec
100m freestyle: Simone Manuel (USA), 52.04sec
200m freestyle: Federica Pellegrini (France), 1min 54.22sec
400m freestyle: Ariarne Titmus (Australia), 3min 58.76sec
800m freestyle: Katie Ledecky (USA), 8min 13.58sec
1500m freestyle: Simona Quadarella (Italy), 15min 40.89sec
50m backstroke: Olivia Smoliga (USA), 27.33sec
100m backstroke: Kylie Masse (Canada), 58.60sec
200m backstroke: Regan Smith (USA), 2min 03.69sec
50m breaststroke: Lilly King (USA), 29.84sec
100m breaststroke: Lilly King (USA), 1min 04.93sec
200m breaststroke: Yuliya Yefimova (Russia), 2min 20.17sec
50m butterfly: Sarah Sjostrom (Sweden), 25.02sec
100m butterfly: Maggie MacNeil (Canada), 55.83sec
200m butterfly: Boglarka Kapas (Hungary), 2min 06.78sec
200m medley: Katinka Hosszu (Hungary), 2min 07.53sec
400m medley: Katinka Hosszu (Hungary), 4min 30.39sec
4x100m freestyle relay: Australia, 3min 30.21sec
4x200m freestyle relay: Australia, 7min 41.50sec
4x100m medley relay: USA, 3min 50.40sec
4x100 mixed medley relay: Australia, 3min 39.08sec

DIVING

MEN
1m springboard: Wang Zongyuan (China), 440.25pts
3m springboard: Xie Siyi (China), 545.45pts
3m synchro springboard: Cao Yuan and Xie Siyi (China), 439.74pts
10m platform: Yang Jian (China), 598.65pts
10m synchro platform: Cao Yuan and Chen Aisen (China), 486.93pts

WOMEN
1m springboard: Chen Yiwen (China), 285.45pts
3m springboard: Shi Tingmao (China), 329.40pts
3m synchro springboard: Shi Tingmao and Wang Han (China), 342.00pts
10m platform: Chen Yuxi (China), 439.00pts
10m synchro platform: Lu Wei and Zhang Jiaqi (China), 345.24.24pts

MIXED
3m synchro springboard: Matthew Carter and Maddison Keeney (Australia), 304.86pts
10m synchro springboard: Lian Junjie and Si Yajie (China), 346.14pts
Team event: Yang Jian and Lin Shan (China), 416.65pts

ASSOCIATION FOOTBALL

LEAGUE COMPETITIONS 2019–20

ENGLAND AND WALES

Premier League
1. Liverpool, 99pts
2. Manchester City, 81pts
3. Manchester United, 66pts
4. Chelsea, 38pts
Relegated: Bournemouth, Watford, Norwich City

Championship
1. Leeds United, 93pts
2. West Brom, 83pts
Play-off winner and third promotion place: Fulham
Relegated: Charlton, Wigan Athletic, Hull City

League One
1. Coventry, 67pts
2. Rotherham, 62pts
*Play-off winner and third promotion place:*Wycombe
Relegated: AFC Wimbledon, Tranmere, Southend United, Bolton

League Two
1. Swindon Town, 69pts
2. Crewe Alexandria, 69pts
3. Plymouth Argyle, 68pts
Play-off winner and fourth promotion place: Northampton Town
Relegated: Macclesfield Town, Stevenage

National League
1. Barrow, 70pts
Play-off winner and second promotion place: Harrogate Town
*Relegated: Ebbsfleet United, ACF Fylde, Chorley
* Relegated teams go down to National League North or South dependent on location

Welsh Premier League
1. Connah's Quay Nomads, 56pts
2. The New Saints, 52pts
3. Bala Town, 49pts
Relegated: Carmarthen Town, Broughton

SCOTLAND

Scottish Premiership
1. Celtic, 70pts
2. Rangers, 67pts
Relegated: Hearts

Scottish Championship
1. Dundee United, 59pts
Relegated: Partick Thistle

Scottish League One
1. Raith, 53pts
Relegated: Stranraer

Scottish League Two
1. Cove Rangers, 79pts

NORTHERN IRELAND

NIFL Premiership
1. Linfield, 69pts
2. Coleraine, 65pts
3. Crusaders, 59pts

REPUBLIC OF IRELAND

League of Ireland Premier Division 2019: 1. Dundalk, 86pts; 2. Shamrock Rovers, 75pts; 3. Bohemians, 60pts

FRANCE
Ligue 1: 1. Paris Saint Germain, 68pts; 2. Marseille, 56pts; 3. Rennes, 50pts

GERMANY
Bundesliga: 1. Bayern Munich, 82pts; 2. Borussia Dortmund, 69pts; 3. RB Leipzig, 66pts

ITALY
Serie A: 1. Juventus, 83pts; 2. Inter Milan, 82pts; 3. Atlanta, 78pts

NETHERLANDS
Eredivisie: 1. Ajax, 56pts; 2. AZ Alkmaar, 56pts; 3. Feyenoord, 50pts

SPAIN
La Liga: 1. Real Madrid, 87pts; 2. Barcelona, 82pts; 3. Atlético Madrid, 70pts

CUP COMPETITIONS 2019–20

ENGLAND
FA Cup final 2020: Arsenal beat Chelsea 2–1
EFL Cup final 2020: Manchester City beat Aston Villa 2–1
EFL Trophy Final 2020: Portsmouth versus Salford City was postponed
FA Vase final 2020: Consett versus Hebburn Town was postponed
FA Trophy final 2020: Harrogate Town versus Concord Rangers was postponed
Community Shield 2020: Arsenal beat Liverpool 5–4 on penalties (1–1 aet)

WOMEN
FA Cup final 2020: Manchester City beat Everton 3–1
Women's Super League 2019–20: 1. Chelsea, 39pts; 2. Manchester City, 40pts; 3. Arsenal, 36pts
FA Women's National League Cup final 2020: Stoke City versus Sunderland was postponed

WALES
FAW Welsh Cup final 2019: New Saints FC beat Connah's Quay Nomads 3–0
Welsh League Cup final 2019: Cardiff Metropolitan University beat Cambrian and Clydach Vale 2–0

SCOTLAND
Scottish Cup final 2020: Celtic versus Hearts was postponed
League Cup final 2019: Celtic beat Rangers 1–0

NORTHERN IRELAND
Irish Cup final 2020: Glentoran beat Ballymena United 2–1 (aet)

EUROPE
UEFA Champions League final 2020: Bayern Munich beat Paris Saint Germain 1–0
UEFA Europa League final 2020: Sevilla beat Inter Milan 3–2
UEFA Women's Champions League final 2019: Lyon beat Barcelona 4–1

BALLON D'OR
2019 – Lionel Messi (Argentina)
2018 – Luka Modric (Croatia)
2017 – Cristiano Ronaldo (Portugal)
2016 – Cristiano Ronaldo (Portugal)
2015 – Lionel Messi (Argentina)
2014 – Cristiano Ronaldo (Portugal)
2013 – Cristiano Ronaldo (Portugal)
2012 – Lionel Messi (Argentina)

WOMEN'S BALLON D'OR
2019 – Megan Rapinoe (USA)
2018 – Ada Hegerberg (Norway)

ATHLETICS

EUROPEAN CROSS COUNTRY CHAMPIONSHIPS
Lisbon, Portugal, 8 December 2019

SENIOR MEN (10.3KM)
Individual: Robel Fsiha (Sweden), 29min 59sec
Team: Great Britain, 36pts

U23 MEN (8.3KM)
Individual: Jimmy Gressier (France), 24min 17sec
Team: France, 17pts

JUNIOR MEN (6.3KM)
Individual: Jakob Ingerbrigtsen (Norway), 18min 20sec
Team: Great Britain, 25pts

SENIOR WOMEN (8.3KM)
Individual: Yasemin Can (Turkey), 26min 52sec
Team: Great Britain, 26pts

U23 WOMEN (6.3KM)
Individual: Anna Emilie Moller (Denmark), 20min 30sec
Team: Netherlands, 17pts

JUNIOR WOMEN (4.3KM)
Individual: Nadia Battocletti (Italy), 13min 58sec
Team: Great Britain, 29pts

ENGLISH NATIONAL CROSS COUNTRY
CHAMPIONSHIPS
Nottingham, 22 February 2020

SENIOR MEN
Individual: Calum Johnson (Gateshead Harriers), 43min 36sec
Team: Tonbridge AC, 246pts

JUNIOR MEN
Individual: Zakariya Mahamed (Southampton AC), 36min
27sec
Team: Shaftesbury Barnet Harriets, 133pts

SENIOR WOMEN
Individual: Anna Holler (Aldershot Farnham and District),
32min 59sec
Team: Aldershot Farnham and District, 48ts

JUNIOR WOMEN
Individual: Amelia Quirk (Bracknell AC), 25min 33sec
Team: Bracknell AC, 55pts

LONDON MARATHON
London, 4 October 2020

Men: Shura Kitata (Ethiopia), 2hr 05min 41sec
Women: Brigid Kosgei (Kenya), 2hr 18min 58sec
Men's Wheelchair: Brent Lakatos (Canada), 1hr 36min 04sec
Women's Wheelchair: Nikita Den Boer (Netherlands), 1hr
40min 07sec

2019 EUROPEAN GAMES
Minsk, Belarus, 21–30 June

MEN
100m: Gold – Serhiy Smelyk (Ukraine); Silver – Zdenek
Stromsik (Czechia); Bronze – Jeremy Leroux (France)

110m Hurdles: Gold – Vitali Parakhonka (Belarus); Silver –
Maximilian Bayer (Germany); Bronze – Artem Shamatrin
(Ukraine)
High Jump: Gold – Maksim Nedasekau (Belarus); Silver –
Andriy Protsenko (Ukraine); Bronze –Falk Wendrich
(Germany)

WOMEN
100m: Gold – Krystsina Tsimanouskaya (Belarus); Silver –
Johanelis Herrera Abreu (Italy); Bronze – Hrystyna Stuy
(Ukraine)
100m Hurdles: Gold – Elvira Herman (Belarus); Silver –
Fanny Quenot (France); Bronze – Hanna Plotitsyna
(Ukraine)
High Jump: Gold – Maksim Nedasekau (Belarus); Silver –
Andriy Protsenko (Ukraine); Bronze –Falk Wendrich
(Germany)
Javelin: Gold – Tatsiana Khaladovich (Belarus); Silver –
Annika Fuchs (Germany); Bronze – Irena Sediva (Czechia)
Long Jump Gold – Maryna Bekh-Romanchuk (Ukraine);
Silver – Nastassia Mironchyk-Ivanova (Belarus); Bronze –
Roughi Sow (France)

MIXED
400m Relay: Gold - Czechia; Silver – Ukraine; Bronze –
France
Mixed Medley Relay: Gold – Ukraine; Silver – Belarus; Bronze
– Germany

17TH IAAF WORLD CHAMPIONSHIPS
Doha, Qatar 27 September – 6 October 2019

MEN
100m: Christian Coleman (USA), 9.76sec
200m: Noah Lyles (USA), 19.83sec
400m: Steven Gardiner (Bahamas), 43.48sec
*800m:*Donavan Brazier (USA), 1min 42.34sec
1500m: Timothy Cheruiyot (Kenya), 3min 29.26sec
5000m: Muktar Edris (Ethiopia), 12min 58.85sec
10,000m: Joshua Cheptegei (Uganda), 26min 48.36sec
Marathon: Lelisa Desisa (Ethiopia), 2hr 10. 40min.
110m Hurdles Grant Holloway (USA), 13.10sec
400m Hurdles: Karsten Warholm (Norway), 47.42sec
4x100m: USA, 37.10sec
4x400m: USA, 2min 56.69sec
High Jump: Mutaz Essa Barshim (Qatar), 2.37m
Pole Vault: Sam Kendricks (USA), 5.97m
Long Jump: Tajay Gayle (Jamaica), 8.69m
Triple Jump: Christian Taylor (USA), 17.92m
Shot Put: Joe Kovacs (USA), 22.91m
Discus: Daniel Stahl (Sweden), 67.59m
Hammer: Pawel Fajdek (Poland), 80.50m
Javelin: Anderson Peters (Grenada), 86.89m
Decathlon: Niklas Kaul (Germany), 8,691pts

WOMEN
100m: Shelly-Ann Fraser-Pryce (Jamaica), 10.71sec
200m: Dina Asher-Smith (Great Briain), 21.88sec
400m: Salwa Eid Naser (Bahrain), 48.14sec
800m: Halimah Nakaayi (Uganda), 1min 58.04sec
1500m: Sifan Hassan (Netherlands), 3min 51.95sec
5000m: Hellen Obiri (Kenya), 14min 26.72sec
10,000m: Sifan Hassan (Netherlands), 30min 17.62sec
Marathon: Ruth Chepngetich (Kenya), 2hr 32.43min
*100m Hurdles:*Nia Ali (USA), 12.34sec
400m Hurdles: Dalilah Muhammad (USA), 52.16sec
4x100m: Jamaica, 41.44sec
4x400m: USA, 3min 18.92sec
High Jump: Mariya Lasitskene (Authorised Neutral Athletes),
2.04m

Pole Volt: Anzhelika Sidorova (Authorised Neutral Athletes), 4.95m
Long Jump: Malaika Mihambo (Germany), 7.30m
Triple Jump: Yulimar Rojas (Venezuela), 15.37m
Shot Put: Gong Lijao (China), 19.55m
Discus: Yaime Perez (Cuba), 69.17m
Hammer: DeAnna Price (USA), 77.54m
Javelin: Kelsey-Lee Barber (Australia), 66.56m
Heptathlon: Katarina Johnson-Thompson (Great Britain), 6981pts

MIXED
400m Relay: USA, 3min 09.34sec

BADMINTON

EUROPEAN TEAM CHAMPIONSHIPS 2020
Lievin, France, 11–16 February 2020

Men's Team: Gold – Denmark; Silver – Netherlands; Bronze – Russia and France
Women's Team: Gold – Denmark; Silver – Germany; Bronze – France and Scotland

The 2020 European Championships were cancelled.

ENGLISH NATIONAL CHAMPIONSHIPS 2020
Winchester, 1–2 February

Men's Singles: Alex Lane beat Johnnie Torjussen 2–0
Women's Singles: Chloe Birch beat Freya Redfearn 2–0
Men's Doubles: Tom Wolfenden and Gregory Mairs beat Rory Easton and Ethan van Leeuwen 2–1
Women's Doubles: Chloe Birch and Lauren Smith beat Jenny Moore and Victorian Williams 2–1
Mixed Doubles: Max Flynn and Fee Teng Liew beat Tom Wolfenden and Jenny Moore 2–0

ALL ENGLAND CHAMPIONSHIPS 2020
Birmingham, 11–15 March

Men's Singles: Victor Axelsen (Denmark) beat Chou Tien-chen (Taiwan) 2–0
Women's Singles: Tai Tzu-ying (Taiwan) beat Chen Yufei (China) 2–0
Men's Doubles: Hiroyuki Endo and Yuta Watanabe (Japan) beat Marcus Gideon and Kevin Sukamuljo (Indonesia) 2–1
Women's Doubles: Yuki Fukushima and Sayaka Hirota (Japan) beat Du Yue and Li Yinhui (China) 2–0
Mixed Doubles: Praveen Jordan and Melati Oktavianti (Indonesia) beat Dechapol Puavaranukroh and Sapsiree Taerattanachai (Thailand) 2–1

SCOTTISH NATIONAL CHAMPIONSHIPS 2019
Perth, February

Men's Singles: Kieran Merrilees beat Ciar Pringle 2–0
Women's Singles: Kirsty Gilmour beat Holly Newall 2–0
Men's Doubles: Alex Dunn and Adam Hall beat Christopher Grimley and Matthew Grimley 2–0
Women's Doubles: Julie MacPherson and Holly Newall beat Ciara Torrance and Eleanor O'Donnell 2–1
Mixed Doubles: Adam Hall and Julie MacPherson beat Alex Dunn and Eleanor O'Donnell 2–0

WELSH NATIONAL CHAMPIONSHIPS 2020
Cardiff, February

Men's Singles: William Kitching beat Gareth Oates 2–0
Women's Singles: Jordan Hart beat Jessica Ding 2–0
Men's Doubles: Martyn Lewis and James Phillips beat Luke Bailey and Man Yin Leung 2–0

Women's Doubles: Jordan Hart and Lowri Hart beat Learna Herkes and Saffron Morris 2–0
Mixed Doubles: Phillip Eastwood and Sammy Hutt beat Hanna Pearce and Kevin Pearce 2–0

BASEBALL

American League Championship Series 2020: Tampa Bay Rays beat Houston Astros 4–3
National League Championship Series 2020: Los Angeles Dodgers beat Atlanta Braves 4–3
Major League Baseball World Series 2020: Los Angeles Dodgers beat Tampa Bay Rays 4–2

BASKETBALL

BRITISH

MEN
BBL Champions 2018–19: London Lions
BBL Play-off final 2018–19: Leicester Riders beat London City Royals 93–61
BBL Trophy final 2019–20: Newcastle Eagles beat Solent Kestrels 96–94
BBL Cup final 2019–20: Worcester Wolves beat Bristol Flyers 67–59

WOMEN
WBBL Champions 2018–19: Sevenoaks Suns
WBBL Play-off final 2018–19: Sevenoaks Suns beat Leicester Riders 60–55
WBBL Trophy 2018–19: Leicester Riders beat Durham Palatinates 76–74
WWBL Cup 2018–19: Sheffield Hatters beat Sevenoaks Suns 62–60

USA – NATIONAL BASKETBALL ASSOCIATION (NBA)
Eastern Conference final 2020: Miami Heat beat Boston Celtics 4–2
Western Conference final 2020: Los Angeles Lakers beat Denver Nuggets 4–1
NBA final 2020: Los Angeles Lakers beat Miami Heat 4–2

BOWLS — INDOOR

WORLD CHAMPIONSHIP 2020
Hopton-on-Sea, Norfolk, January

Men's Singles: Robert Paxton (England) beat Nick Brett (England) 2–1
Women's Singles: Julie Forrest (Scotland) beat Janice Gower (England) 2–0
Men's Pairs: Greg Harlow (England) and Nick Brett (England) beat Paul Foster (Scotland) and Alex Marshall (Scotland) 2–1
Mixed Pairs: Nick Brett (England) and Marion Purcell (Wales) beat Greg Harlow (England) and Alison Merrien (Guernsey) 2–0

BRITISH ISLES INDOOR BOWLS CHAMPIONSHIP 2020
Llanelli, Wales, 9–11 March

MEN
Singles: Andrew Walters (England) beat Connor Milne (Scotland) 21–15
Pairs: England beat Wales 20–18
Triples: Scotland beat England 22–8
Fours: Ireland beat England 20–12

WOMEN
Singles: Julie Forrest (Scotland) beat Alison Merrien (Channel Islands) 21–13
Pairs: England beat Ireland 23–16
Triples: Wales beat Scotland 21–13
Fours: Channel Islands beat Scotland 22–13

ENGLISH NATIONAL COMPETITION 2019
Nottingham IBC, March–April

MEN
Singles: A. Walters beat D. Bolt 21–8
Pairs: Whiteknights beat Norfolk 19–15
Triples: Bournemouth beat Exonia 19–17
Fours: Exonia beat Lincoln 19–16
Liberty Trophy (Inter-County Championship) final: Durham beat Berkshire 125–114
Champion of Champions: M. Puckett beat G. Smith 21–17

WOMEN
Singles: K. Rednall beat D. Cooper 21–8
Pairs: Westlecot beat Norfolk 14–12
Triples: Norfolk beat West Denton 19–9
Fours: Dolphin beat Swale 17–13
Atherley Trophy (Inter-County Championship) final: Cambridgeshire beat Sussex 144–102
Champion of Champions: K. Rednall beat J. Gower 21–20

SCOTTISH NATIONAL CHAMPIONSHIPS 2018–19
December 2018–March 2019

MEN
Singles: Prestwick beat Coatbridge 21–12
Pairs: Abbeyview beat West Lothian 23–15
Triples: East Kilbride beat East Fife 20–10
Fours: Galleon beat Tweedbank 21–18

WOMEN
Singles: Teviotdale beat East Fife 21–15
Pairs: Auchinleck beat Balbardie 18–17
Triples: Glasgow beat West of Scotland 25–5
Fours: Stonehaven beat East Fife 22–18

BOWLS — OUTDOOR

ENGLISH NATIONAL CHAMPIONSHIPS 2019
Royal Leamington Spa, August

Singles: Essex C beat Northamptonshire B 21–14
Pairs: Kent A beat Isle of Wight A 18–8
Triples: Berkshire B beat Cumbria A 16–13
Fours: Buckinghamshire A beat Berkshire A 23–22

SCOTTISH NATIONAL CHAMPIONSHIPS 2019
Ayr, July

Singles: Aberlady beat Dumfries 21–9
Pairs: Eddlewood beat Clackmannan 15–7
Triples: Townholm beat Melrose 20–8
Fours: Craigentinny beat Glencarse 19–12

WELSH NATIONAL CHAMPIONSHIPS 2019
Carmarthen, August

Singles: B. Thomas beat J. Davies 21–12
Pairs: L. Thomas and J. Thomlinson beat D. Weale and R. Weale 27–10
Triples: South Glamorgan beat Monmouthshire 26–6
Fours: Mid Wales beat South Glamorgan 28–6

BOXING

MEN'S WORLD CHAMPIONS
as at 2 November 2020

WORLD BOXING COUNCIL (WBC)
Heavy: Tyson Fury (Great Britain)
Cruiser: Junior Makabu (DRC)
Light-heavy: Artur Beterbiev (Russia)
Super-middle: vacant
Middle: Jermall Charlo (USA)
Super-welter: Jermall Charlo (USA)
Welter: Errol Spence Jr (USA)
Light-welter: José Carlos Ramirez (USA)
Light: Devin Haney (USA)
Super-feather: Miguel Berchelt (Mexico)
Feather: Gary Russell Jr (USA)
Super-bantam: Luis Nery (Mexico)
Bantam: Nordine Oubaali (France)
Super-fly: Juan Francisco Estrada (Mexico)
Fly: Julio Cesar Martinez (Mexico)
Light-fly: Ken Shiro (Japan)
Mini-fly: Wanheng Menayothin (Thailand)

WORLD BOXING ASSOCIATION (WBA)
Heavy: Anthony Joshua (Great Britain)
Cruiser: Arsen Goulamirian (France)
Light-heavy: Dmitry Bivol (Russia)
Super-middle: Callum Smith (Great Britain)
Middle: Canelo Alvarez (Mexico)
Super-welter: Jermall Charlo (USA)
Welter: Manny Pacquiao (Philippines)
Super-light: Josh Taylor (Great Britain)
Light: Teófimo López (USA)
Super-feather: Leo Santa Cruz (Mexico)
Feather: Leo Santa Cruz (Mexico)
Super-bantam: Murodjon Akhmadaliev (Uzbekistan)
Bantam: Naoya Inoue (Japan)
Super-fly: Román González (Nicaragua)
Fly: Artem Dalakian (Ukraine)
Light-fly: Hiroto Kyoguchi (Japan)
Mini-fly: Thammanoon Niyomtrong (Thailand)

WORLD BOXING ORGANISATION (WBO)
Heavy: Anthony Joshua (Great Britain)
Cruiser: vacant
Light-heavy: vacant
Super-middle: Billy Joe Saunders (Great Britain)
Middle: Demetrius Andrade (USA)
Junior-middle: Patrick Teixeira (Brazil)
Welter: Terence Crawford (USA)
Junior-welter: José Carlos Ramirez (USA)
Light: Teófimo López (USA)
Junior-light: Jamel Herring (USA)
Feather: Emanuel Navarrete (Mexico)
Super-bantam: Angelo Leo (USA)
Bantam: Johnriel Casimero (Philippines)
Super-flyweight: Kazuto Ioka (Japan)
Fly: vacant
Junior-fly: Elwin Soto (Mexico)
Mini-fly: Wilfredo Mendez (Puerto Rico)

INTERNATIONAL BOXING FEDERATION (IBF)
Heavy: Anthony Joshua (Great Britain)
Cruiser: Mairis Briedis (Latvia)
Light-heavy: Artur Beterbiev (Russia)
Super-middle: Caleb Plant (USA)
Middle: Gennady Golovkin (Kazakhstan)

Junior-middle: Jermall Charlo (USA)
Welter: Errol Spence Jr (USA)
Super-light: Josh Taylor (Great Britain)
Light: Teófimo López (USA)
Junior-lightweight: Joseph Diaz (USA)(
Feather: Josh Warrington (Great Britain)
Junior-feather: Murodjon Akhmadaliev (Uzbekistan)
Bantam: Naoya Inoue (Japan)
Junior-bantam: Jerwin Ancajas (Philippines)
Fly: Moruti Mthalane (South Africa)
Junior-fly: Felix Alvarado (Nicaragua)
Mini-fly: Pedro Taduran Jr (Philippines)

BRITISH CHAMPIONS
Heavy: Daniel Dubois
Cruiser: Richard Riakporhe
Light-heavy: Shakan Pitters
Super-middle: Lerrone Richards
Middle: Liam Williams
Super-welter: Scott Fitzgerald
Welter: Chris Jenkins
Super-light: Akeem Ennis-Brown
Light: James Tennyson
Super-feather: Anthony Carcace
Feather: Ryan Walsh
Super-bantam: Brad Foster
Bantam: Lee McGregor
Super-fly: Charlie Edwards
Fly: vacant

WOMEN'S WORLD CHAMPIONS
as at 2 November 2020

WORLD BOXING COUNCIL (WBC)
Heavy: vacant
Super-middle: Franchon Crews Dezurn (USA)
Middle: Claressa Shields (USA)
Light-middle: Claressa Shields (USA)
Welter: Jessica McGaskill (USA)
Light-welter: Chantelle Cameron (Great Britain)
Light: Katie Taylor (Ireland)
Super-feather: Terri Harper (Great Britain)
Feather: Jalena Mrdjenovich (Canada)
Super-bantam: Yamileth Mercado (Mexico)
Bantam: Mariana Juarez (Mexico)
Super-fly: Guadalupe Martínez Guzmán(Mexico)
Fly: Ibeth Zamora Silva (Mexico)
Light-fly: Yesenia Gòmez (Mexico)
Strawweight: Tina Rupprecht (Germany)
Light-straw: Fabiana Bytyqi (Czechia)

WORLD BOXING ASSOCIATION (WBA)
Heavy: vacant
Light-heavy: vacant
Super-middle: Elin Cederroos (Sweden)
Middle: Claressa Shields (USA)
Light-middle: Hanna Gabriels (Costa Rica)
Welter: Jessica McGaskill (USA)
Light-welter: vacant
Light: Katie Taylor (Ireland)
Super-feather: Hyun Mi Choi (South Korea)
Feather: Jalena Mrdjenovich (Canada)
Super-bantam: Mayerlin Rivas (Venezuela)
Bantam: vacant
Super-fly: Maribel Ramírez (Mexico)
Fly: Naoko Fujioka (Japan)
Light-fly: Yesica Bopp (Argentina)
Strawweight: Anabel Ortiz (Mexico)
Light-straw: Monserrat Alarcón (Mexico)

WORLD BOXING ORGANISATION (WBO)
Heavy: vacant
Cruiserweight: vacant
Light-heavy: Geovana Peres (Brazil)
Super-middle: Franchon Crews Dezurn (USA)
Middle: Claressa Shields (USA)
Light-middle: Claressa Shields (USA)
Welter: Jessica McGaskill (USA)
Light-welter: Christina Linardatou (Greece)
Light: Katie Taylor (Ireland)
Super-feather: Ewa Brodnicka (Poland)
Feather: Amanda Serrano (Puerto Rico)
Super-bantam: Dina Thorsland (Denmark)
Bantam: Daniela Romina Bermúdez (Argentina)
Super-fly: Miyo Yoshida (Japan)
Fly: Débora Anahi López (Argentina)
Light-fly: Tenkai Tsunami (Japan)
Strawweight: vacant
Light-straw: Mika Iwakawa (Japan)

INTERNATIONAL BOXING FEDERATION (IBF)
Heavy: vacant
Light-heavy: vacant
Super-middle: Elin Cederroos (Sweden)
Middle: Claressa Shields (USA)
Light-middle: Marie Dicaire (Canada)
Welter: Jessica McGaskill (USA)
Light-welter: Mary McGee (USA)
Light: Katie Taylor (Ireland)
Super-feather: Maiva Hamadouche (France)
Feather: Sarah Mahfoud (Faroe Islands)
Super-bantam: Marcela Acuña (Argentina)
Bantam: Maria Román (Argentina)
Super-fly: Jorgelina Guanini (Argentina)
Fly: Leonela Yúdica (Argentina)
Light-fly: Evelyn Nazarena Bermudez (Argentina)
Strawweight: Yokasta Valle (Costa Rica)
Light-straw: Saemi Hanagata (Japan)

CHESS

FIDE Chess World Cup 2019: Teimour Radjabov (Azerbaijan) beat Ding Liren (China) 6–4
FIDE Online Chess Olympiad 2020: India and Russia
Women's World Chess Championship 2020: Ju Wenjun (China) beat Aleksandra Goryachkina (Russia) 6(2½)–6(1½)
British Champion 2019: Michael Adams
British Women's Champion 2019: Jovanka Houska

CRICKET

TEST SERIES 2019–20

NEW ZEALAND V ENGLAND
Tauranga (20–25 November 2019): New Zealand won by an innings and 65 runs. New Zealand 615–9 dec; England 353 and 197
Hamilton (28 November–3 December 2019): Draw. New Zealand 375 and 241–2; England 476.

SOUTH AFRICA V ENGLAND
Centurion (26–30 December 2019): South Africa won by 107 runs. South Africa 284 and 272; England 181 and 268
Cape Town (3–7 January 2020): England won by 189 runs. England 269 and 391–8 dec; South Africa 223 and 248
Port Elizabeth (16–20 January 2020): England won by an innings and 53 runs. England 499–9 dec; South Africa 209 and 237

Johannesburg (24–28 January 2020): England won by 191 runs. England 400 and 248; South Africa 183 and 274

ENGLAND V WEST INDIES
Ageas Bowl (8–12 July 2020): West Indies won by 4 wickets. England 204 and 313; West Indies 318 and 200–6
Old Trafford (16–20 July 2020): England won by 113 runs. England 469–9 dec and 129–3 dec; West Indies 287 and 198
Old Trafford (24–28 July 2020): England won by 269 runs. England 369 and 226–2 dec; West Indies 197 and 129

ENGLAND V PAKISTAN
Old Trafford(5–9 August 2020): England won by 3 wickets. Pakistan 326 and 169; England 219 and 277–7
Ageas Bowl (13–17 August 2020): Draw. Pakistan 236; England 110–4
Ageas Bowl (21–25 August 2020): Draw. England 583–8 dec; Pakistan 273 and 187–4

ONE-DAY INTERNATIONALS 2020

SOUTH AFRICA V ENGLAND
Cape Town (4 February 2020): South Africa won by 7 wickets. England 258–8; South Africa 258–3
Durban (7 February 2020): No result
Johannesburg (9 February 2020): England won by 2 wickets. South Africa 256–7; England 257–8

ENGLAND V IRELAND
Ageas Bowl (30 July 2020): England won by 6 wickets. Ireland 172; England 174–4
Ageas Bowl (1 August 2020): England won by 4 wickets. Ireland 212–9; England 216–6
Ageas Bowl (4 August 2020): Ireland won by 7 wickets. England 328; Ireland 329–3

ENGLAND V AUSTRALIA
Old Trafford (11 September 2020): Australia won by 19 runs. Australia 294–9; England 275–9
Old Trafford (13 September 2020): England won by 24 runs. England 231–9; Australia 207
Old Trafford (16 September 2020): Australia won by 3 wickets. England 302–7; Australia 305–7

TWENTY20 INTERNATIONALS 2019–20

NEW ZEALAND V ENGLAND
Christchurch (1 November 2019): England won by 7 wickets. New Zealand 153–5; England 154–3
Wellington (3 November 2019): New Zealand won by 21 runs. New Zealand 176–8; England 155
Nelson (5 November 2019): New Zealand won by 14 runs. New Zealand 180–7; England 166–7
Napier (8 November 2019): England won by 76 runs. England 241–3; New Zealand 165
Auckland (10 November 2019): Match tied; England beat New Zealand in a Super Over. New Zealand 146–5 and 8–1; England 146–7 and 17

SOUTH AFRICA V ENGLAND
East London (12 February 2020): South Africa won by 1 run. South Africa 177–8; England 176–9
Durban (14 February 2020): England won by 2 runs. England 204–7; South Africa 202–7
Centurion (16 February 2020): England won by 5 wickets. South Africa 222–6; England 226–5

ENGLAND V PAKISTAN
Old Trafford (28 August 2020): No Result. England 131–6
Old Trafford (30 August 2020): England won by 5 wickets. Pakistan 195–4; England 199–5
Old Trafford (1 September 2020): Pakistan won by 5 runs. Pakistan 190–4; England 185–8

ENGLAND V AUSTRALIA
Ageas Bowl (4 September 2020): England won by 2 runs. Australia 160–6; England 162–7
Ageas Bowl (6 September 2020): England won by 6 wickets. Australia 157–7; England 158–4
Ageas Bowl (8 September 2020): Australia won by 5 wickets. Englang 145–6; Australia 146–5

ENGLAND AND WALES DOMESTIC COMPETITIONS 2019–20

Specsavers County Championship 2019, Division 1: Essex, 228; *Relegated* Nottinghamshire, 67pts; *Division 2: Promoted* Lancashire, 233 pts; Northamptonshire, 188pts; Gloucestershire, 182pts

Bob Willis Trophy 2020 final (replacing the County Championship, 23–27 September): Draw; Essex beat Somerset by scoring more in the first innings. Somerset 301 and 272–7 dec; Essex 337–8 dec and 179–6
Royal London One-Day Cup final 2019 (25 May): Somerset beat Hampshire by 6 wickets. Hampshire 244–8; Somerset 245–4
Vitality T20 Blast 2020 (4 October): Notts Outlaws beat Surrey by 6 wickets. Surrey 127–7; Notts Outlaws 129–4

WOMEN'S CRICKET
ICC Women's World Twenty20 2020 final, Melbourne (8 March): Australia beat India by 85 runs. Australia 184–4; India 99
Rachael Heyhoe Flint Trophy 2020 (27 September): Southern Vipers beat Northern Diamonds by 38 runs. Southern Vipers 231; Northern Diamonds 193

CURLING

MEN'S WORLD CHAMPIONSHIP 2019
Lethbridge, Canada, 30 March–7 April

Final: Sweden beat Canada 7–2

WOMEN'S WORLD CHAMPIONSHIP 2019
Silkeborg, Denmark, 16–24 March

Final: Switzerland beat Sweden 8–7

CYCLING

Vuelta a España 2020: Primoz Roglic (Slovenia)
Giro d'Italia 2020: Tao Geoghegan Hart (Great Britain)
Tour de France 2020: Tadej Pogacar (Slovenia)

BRITISH NATIONAL ROAD RACE CHAMPIONSHIPS 2019
Norwich, June

MEN
Road Race: Ben Smith

WOMEN
Road Race: Alice Barnes

UCI TRACK CYCLING WORLD CHAMPIONSHIPS 2020
Berlin, Germany, 26 February–1 March

MEN
Points Race: Corbin Strong (New Zealand)
Sprint: Harrie Lavreysen (Netherlands)
1km Time Trial: Sam Ligtlee (Netherlands)
Individual Pursuit: Filippo Ganna (Italy)
Scratch Race: Yauheni Karaliok (Belarus)
Keirin: Harrie Lavreysen (Netherlands)
Team Pursuit: Denmark
Madison: Lasse Norman Hanson and Michael Morkov (Denmark)
Team Sprint: Netherlands
Omnium: Benjamin Thomas (France)

WOMEN
Points Race: Elinor Barker (Great Britain)
Sprint: Emma Hinze (Germany)
500m Time Trial: Lea Friedrich (Germany)
Individual Pursuit: Chloé Dygert (USA)
Scratch Race: Kirsten Wild (Netherlands)
Keirin: Emma Hinze (Germany)
Team Pursuit: USA
Madison: Kirsten Wild and Amy Pieters (Netherlands)
Team Sprint: Germany
Omnium: Yumi Kajihara (Japan)

2019 EUROPEAN GAMES
Minsk, Belarus, June

ROAD
Men's Road Race: Gold – Davide Ballerini (Italy); Silver – Alo Jakin (Estonia); Bronze – Daniel Auer (Austria)
Women's Road Race: Gold – Lorena Wiebes (Netherlands); Silver – Marianne Vos (Netherlands); Bronze – Tatsiana Sharakova (Belarus)
Men's Time Trial: Gold – Vasil Kiryienka (Belarus); Silver – Nelson Oliveira (Portugal); Bronze – Jan Barta (Czechia)
Women's Time Trial: Gold – Marlen Reusser (Switzerland); Silver – Chantal Blaak (Netherlands); Bronze – Hayley Simmonds (Great Britain)

TRACK
Men's 1km Time Trial: Gold – Tomas Babek (Czechia); Silver – Francesco Lamon (Italy); Bronze – Krzysztof Maksel (Poland)
Women's 500m Time Trial: Gold – Daria Shmeleva (Russia); Silver – Olena Starikova (Ukraine); Bronze – Miriam Vece (Italy)
Men's Keirin: Gold –Harrie Lavreysen (Netherlands) ; Silver – Rayan Helal (France); Bronze – Denis Dmitriev (Russia)
Women's Keirin: Gold – Simona Krupeckaite (Lithuania); Silver – Shanne Braspennincx (Netherlands); Bronze – Daria Shmeleva (Russia)
Men's Madison: Gold – Switzerland; Silver – Netherlands; Bronze – Austria
Women's Madison: Gold – Great Britain; Silver – Netherlands; Bronze – Russia
Men's Omnium: Gold – Jan-Willem van Schip (Netherlands); Silver – Thery Schir (Switzerland); Bronze – Daniel Staniszewski (Poland)
Women's Omnium: Gold – Kirsten Wild (Netherlands); Silver – Evgeniia Augustinas (Russia); Bronze – Elisa Balsamo (Italy)
Men's Point Race: Gold – Christos Volikakis (Greece); Silver – Jan-Willem van Schip (Netherlands); Bronze – Dmitrii Mukhomediarov (Russia)

Women's Point Race: Gold – Ganna Solovei (Ukraine); Silver – Verena Eberhardt (Austria); Bronze – Jarmila Machavova (Czechia)
Men's Scratch: Gold – Christos Volikakis (Greece); Silver – Filip Prokopyszyn (Poland); Bronze – Yauheni Karaliok (Belarus)
Women's Scratch: Gold – Kirsten Wild (Netherlands); Silver – Martina Fidanza (Italy); Bronze – Hanna Tserakh (Belarus)
Men's Sprint: Gold – Jeffrey Hoogland (Netherlands); Silver – Harrie Lavreysen (Netherlands); Bronze – Denis Dmitriev (Russia)
Women's Sprint: Gold – Anastasiia Voinova (Russia); Silver – Mathilde Gros (France); Bronze – Daria Shmeleva (Russia)
Men's Team Sprint: Gold – Netherlands; Silver – France; Bronze – Great Britain
Women's Team Sprint: Gold – Russia; Silver – Lithuania; Bronze – Netherlands

DARTS

BDO World Championship 2020: Men: Wayne Warren (Wales) beat Jim Williams (Wales) 7–4; *Women:* Mikuru Suzuki (Japan) beat Lisa Ashton (England) 3–0
PDC World Championship 2020: Peter Wright (Scotland) beat Micahel van Gerwen (Netherlands) 7–3

EQUESTRIANISM

Burghley Horse Trials 2019: Pippa Funnell (Great Britain) on MGH Grafton Street
Badminton Horse Trials 2019: Piggy French (Great Britain) on Vanir Kamira
British Open Horse Trials 2019 (Gatcombe Park): Jonelle Price (New Zealand) on Classic Moet

ETON FIVES

Amateur Championship (Kinnaird Cup) final 2020: T. Dunbar and S. Cooley beat J. Troop and M. Wiseman 3–1
National Ladies' Championships 2020: K. Hird and C. Cooley beat A. Lumbard and E. Scoones 3–1
Alan Barber Cup final 2019: Old Harrovians beat Old Salopians – determined by arbitration committee
Schools' Championship 2019: Boys: Shrewsbury beat Eton 3–0; Girls: Shrewsbury 2 beat Shrewsbury 3 3–2
Preparatory Schools' Tournament 2019: Berkhamsted beat Ludgrove 2–0

FENCING

BRITISH CHAMPIONSHIPS 2019
London, April

MEN
Individual Foil: James-Andrew Davis
Individual Épée: James Frewin
Individual Sabre: William Deary

WOMEN
Individual Foil: Teagan Williams-Stewart
Individual Épée: Susan Maria Sica
Individual Sabre: Caitlin Maxwell

EUROPEAN CHAMPIONSHIPS 2019
Düsseldorf, Germany, June

MEN
Individual Foil: Alessio Foconi (Italy)
Individual Épée: Shalom Yuval Freilich (Israel)

Individual Sabre: Veniamin Reshetnikov (Russia)
Team Foil: France
Team Épée: Russia
Team Sabre: Germany

WOMEN
Individual Foil: Elisa Di Francisca (Italy)
Individual Épée: Coraline Vitalis (France)
Individual Sabre: Olga Kharlan (Ukraine)
Team Foil: Russia
Team Épée: Poland
Team Sabre: Russia

WORLD CHAMPIONSHIPS 2019
Budapest, Hungary, July

MEN
Individual Foil: Alessio Foconi (Italy)
Individual Épée: Gergely Siklosi (Hungary)
Individual Sabre: Oh Sang-uk (South Korea)
Team Foil: USA
Team Épée: France
Team Sabre: South Korea

WOMEN
Individual Foil: Inna Deriglazova (Russia)
Individual Épée: Nathalie Moellhausen (Brazil)
Individual Sabre: Olga Kherlan (Ukraine)
Team Foil: Russia
Team Épée: China
Team Sabre: Russia

FIGURE SKATING

BRITISH CHAMPIONSHIPS 2019
Sheffield, 26 November–1 December 2019
Men: Peter James Hallam
Women: Natasha McKay
Pairs: Zoe Jones and Christopher Boyadji
Ice Dance: Lilah Fear and Lewis Gibson

EUROPEAN CHAMPIONSHIPS 2020
Graz, Austria, 20–26 January 2020
Men: Dmitri Aliev (Russia)
Women: Alena Kostornaia (Russia)
Pairs: Aleksandra Boikova and Dmitrii Kozlovskii (Russia)
Ice Dance: Victoria Sinitsina and Nikita Katsalapov (Russia)

WORLD CHAMPIONSHIPS 2019
Saitama, Japan, 18–24 March
Men: Nathan Chen (USA)
Women: Alina Zagitova (Russia)
Pairs: Wenjing Sui and Cong Han (China)
Ice Dance: Gabriella Papadakis and Guillaume Cizeron (France)

GOLF (MEN)

THE MAJOR CHAMPIONSHIPS
US Masters 2020 (Augusta, 12–15 November): Dustin Johnson (USA), 268
US Open 2020 (Winged Foot Golf Club, 17–20 September): Bryson DeChambeau (USA), 274
The Open Championship 2019 (Royal Portrush GC, Northern Ireland, 18–21 July): Shane Lowry (Ireland), 269
US PGA Championship 2020 (Harding Park, 6–9 August): Collin Morikawa (USA), 267

WORLD RANKINGS *as at November 2020*

1. Dustin Johnson (USA); 2. Jon Rahm (Spain); 3. Justin Thomas (USA); 4. Rory McIlroy (Northern Island); 5. Collin Morikawa (USA)

PGA EUROPEAN TOUR 2019
Honma Hong Kong Open (Hong Kong GC): Aaron Rai (England), 263
Australian PGA Championship (Royal Pines Resort, Queensland): Cameron Smith (Australia), 272
Afrasia Bank Mauritius Open (Four Seasons GC, Mauritius): Kurt Kitayama (USA), 268
Joburg Open (Randpark GC, South Africa): Louis Oosthuizen (South Africa), 266
Alfred Dunhill Championship (Leopard Creed CC, South Africa): David Lipsky (USA), 274
Abu Dhabi HSBC Championship (Abu Dhabi GC, UAE): Shane Lowry (Ireland), 270
Omega Dubai Desert Classic (Emirates GC, UAE): Bryson DeChambeau (USA), 264
Saudi International (Royal Greens G&CC, Saudi Arabia): Dustin Johnson (USA), 261
ISPS Handa Vic Open (13th Beach GC, Australia): David Law (Scotland), 270
ISPS Handa World Super 6 (Lake Karrinyup CC, Australia): Ryan Fox (New Zealand), 208
WGC-Mexico Championship (Chapultepec GC, Mexico City): Dustin Johnson (USA), 263
Oman Open (Al Mouj Golf, Muscat): Kurt Kitayama (USA), 281
Commercial Bank Qatar Masters (Doha GC, Doha): Justin Harding (South Africa), 275
Magical Kenya Open (Karen CC, Nairobi): Guido Migliozzi (Italy), 268
Maybank Championship (Saujana G&CC, Malaysia): Scott Hend (Australia), 273
WGC-Dell Technologies Match Play (Austin CC, USA): Kevin Kisner (USA)
Hero Indian Open (DLF G&CC, New Delhi): Stephen Gallacher (Scotland), 279
Trophee Hassan II (Royal Golf Dar Es Salam, Morocco): Joge Campillo (Spain), 283
Volvo China Open (Genzon GC, Shenzhen): Mikko Korhonen (Finland), 268
Betfred British Masters (Hillside Golf Club, Southport): Marcus Kinhult (Sweden), 272
Made In Denmark (Himmerland G&SR, Farso): Bernd Wiesberger (Austria), 270
Belgian Knockout (Rinkven International GC, Antwerp): Guido Migliozzi (Italy), 136
BMW International Open (Golfclub München Eichenried, Germany): Andrea Pavan (Italy), 273
Estrella Damm Andalucía Masters (Real Club Valderrama, Spain): Christiaan Bezuidenhout (South Africa), 274
Dubai Duty Free Irish Open (Lahinch GC): Jon Rahm (Spain), 264
Aberdeen Standard Investments Scottish Open (The Renaissance Club, North Berwick): Bernd Wiesberger (Austria), 262
WGC-FedEx St Jude Invitational (TPC Southwind, USA): Brooks Koepka (USA), 264
D+D Real Czech Masters (Albatross GR, Prague): Thomas Pieters (Belgium), 269
Scandinavian Invitational (Hills G&SC, Gothenburg): Erik van Rooyen (South Africa), 264
Omega European Masters (Crans-sur-Sierre GC, Switzerland): Sebastian Soderberg (Sweden), 266
Porsche European Open (Green Eagle GC, Germany): Paul Casey (England), 274

KLM Open (The International, Netherlands): Sergio Garcia (Spain), 270

BMW PGA Championship (Virginia Water, England): Danny Willett (England), 268

Alfred Dunhill Links Championship (Kingsbarns, Scotland): Victor Perez (France), 266

Mutuactivos Open de España (Club de Campo Ville de Madrid): Jon Rahm, (Spain), 262

Italian Open (Olgiata GC, Rome): Bernd Weisberger (Austria), 268

Amundi Open de France (Le Gold National, Paris): Nicolas Colsaerts (Belgium), 272

Portugal Masters (Dom Pedro Victoria GC, Vilamoura): Steven Brown (England), 267

WGC-HSBC Champions (Sheshan International GC, China): Rory McIlroy (Northern Ireland), 269

Turkish Airlines Open (Montgomerie Maxx Royal, Antalya): Tyrrell Hatton (England), 268

Nedbank Golf Challenge (Gary Player CC, South Africa): Tommy Fleetwood (England), 276

DP World Tour Championship (Jumeirah Golf Estates, UAE): Jon Rahm (Spain), 269

PGA EUROPEAN TOUR 2020

Alfred Dunhill Championship (Leopard Creek CC, South Africa): Pablo Larrazábal, (Spain), 280

AFRASIA BANK Mauritius Open (Heritage GC): Rasmus Hojgaard (Denmark), 269

Australian Championship (Royal Pines Record, Queensland): Adam Scott (Australia), 275

South African Open (Randpark GC, Johannesburg): Brandon Grace (South Africa), 263

Abu Dhabi HSBC Championship (Abu Dhabi GC, UAE): Lee Westwood (England), 269

Omega Dubai Desert Classic (Emirates GC, UAE): Lucas Herbert, (Australia), 279

Saudi International (Royal Greens G&CC, King Abdullah Economic City): Graeme McDowell (Northern Ireland), 268

ISPS Handa Vic Open (13th Beach GC, Australia): Min Woo Lee (Australia), 269

WGC Mexico Championship (Chapultepec GC. Mexico City): Patrick Reed (USA), 266

Oman Open (Al Mouj Gold, Muscat): Sami Valimaki (Finland), 275

Commercial Bank Qatar Masters, (Education City GC, Doha): Jorge Campillo (Spain), 271

Austrian Open (Diamond CC, Atzenbrugg): Marc Warren (Scotland), 275

Euram Bank Open (GC Adamstal, Austria): Joel Stalter (France), 266

Betfred British Masters (Close House GC, Newcastle): Renato Paratore (Italy), 266

Hero Open (Forest of Arden CC, Birmingham): Sam Horsfield (England), 270

FedEx St Jude International (TPC Southwind, USA): Justin Thomas (USA), 267

English Championship (Hanbury Manor CC, Hertfordshire): Andy Sullivan (England), 257

Celtic Classic (Celtic Manor Resort, Wales): Sam Horsfield (England), 266

ISPS HANDA Wales Open (Celtic Manor Resort, Newport): Romain Langasque (France), 276

ISPS HANDA UK Championship (The Belfry, Sutton Coldfield): Rasmus Hojgaard (Denmark), 274

Estrella Damm N.A. Andalucia Masters (Real Club Valderrama, Spain): John Catlin (USA), 286

Portugal Masters (Dom Pedro Victoria GC, Vilamoura): George Coetzee (South Africa), 268

Open de Portugal (Royal Óbridos GR): Garrick Higgo (South Africa), 269

Dubai Irish Open (Galgorm Castle GC, Ballymena): John Catlin (USA), 270

Aberdeen Standard Investments Scottish Open (The Renaissance Club, North Berwick): Aaron Rai (England), 273

BMW PGA Championship (Wentworth GC, England): Tyrell Hatton (England), 269

Scottish Championship (Fairmont, St Andrews): Adrian Otaegui (Spain), 265

Italian Open (Chervo GC, Brescia): Ross McGowan (England), 268

Aphrodite Hills Cyprus Open (Aphrodite Hills, Paphos): Callum Shinkwin (England), 264

GOLF (WOMEN)

THE MAJOR CHAMPIONSHIPS

ANA Inspiration 2020 (Mission Hills CC, USA, 10–13 September): Mirim Lee (South Korea), 273

KPMG WPGA Championship 2020 (Aronimink GC, USA, 8–11 June): Kim Sei-young (South Korea), 266

US Women's Open 2019 (Country Club of Charleston, South Carolina): Jeonguen Lee6 (South Korea), 278

Women's British Open 2020 (Royal Troon Golf Club, Scotland, 20–23 August): Sophia Popov (Germany), 277

WORLD RANKINGS *as at November 2020*

1. Ko Jin-young (South Korea); 2. Kim Sei-young (South Korea); 3. Kelly Korda (USA); 4. Danielle Kang (USA); 5. Inbee Park (South Korea)

LADIES EUROPEAN TOUR 2019

Fatima Bint Mubarak Ladies Open (Saadiyat Beach GC, UAE): Charley Hull (England), 208

The Pacific Bay Resort Australian Ladies Classic (Bonville Golf Resort, New South Wales): Marianne Skarpnord (Norway), 280

ActewAGL Canberra Classic (Royal Canberra GC, Australia): Anne Van Dam (Netherlands), 196

Women's New South Wales Open (Queanbeyan GC, Australia): Meghan MacLaren (England), 272

Investec South African Women's Open (Westlake GC, Cape Town): Diksha Dagar (India), 211

Jordan Mixed Open (Ayla GC): Daan Huizing (Netherlands), 200

Lalla Meryem Cup (Royal Golf Dar Es Salam, Morrocco): Nuria Iturrios (Spain), 279

Omega Dubai Moonlight Classic (Emirates GC): Nuria Iturrios (Spain), 206

US Women's Open Qualifier (Buckinghamshire GC, England): Lucrezia Colombotto Rosso (Italy), 137

La Reserva de Sotogrande Invitational (La Reserva Club de Sotogrande, Spain): Celine Herbin (France), 282

Jabra Ladies Open (Evian Resort Golf Club, France): Annabel Dimmock (England), 206

Ladies European Thailand Championship (Pheonix G&CC): Atthaya Thitikul (Thailand), 266

Evian Championship (Evian Resort GC, France): Ko Jin-young (South Korea), 269

Aberdeen Standard Investments Scottish Open (The Renaissance Club): Mi Jung Hur (South Korea), 264

Tipsport Czech Open (GC Karlstejn): Carly Booth (Scotland), 207

Lacoste Ladies Open De France (Golf du Medoc): Kelly Korda (USA), 269

Estrella Damm Mediterranean Ladies Open (Golf de Terramar, Spain): Carlota Ciganda (Spain), 276

Hero Women's Indian Open (DLF G&CC): Christine Wolf (Austria), 277

Andalucia Costa Del Sol Open De Espana (Aloha GC): Ann Van Dam (Netherlands), 275

Magical Kenyan Ladies Open (Vipingo Ridge): Esther Henseleit (germany), 274

LADIES EUROPEAN TOUR 2020

Geoff King Motors Ladies Classic Bonville (Bonville GR, Australia): Stephanie Kyriacou (Australia), 266

Women's NSW Open (Dubbo GC, Australia): Julia Engstrom (Sweden), 274

Investec South African Women's Open (Westlake GC): Alice Hewson (England), 211

Aberdeen Standard Investments Ladies Scottish Open (The Renaissance Club): Stacey Lewis (USA), 279

Tipsport Czech Ladies Open (GC Beroun): Emily Kristine Pedersen (Denmark), 199

VP Bank Swiss Ladies Open (Golfpark Holzhäusen): Amy Boulden (Wales), 199

Lacoste Ladies Open de France (Gold Du Medoc, France): Julia Engstrom (Sweden), 206

GREYHOUND RACING

2019
Regency (Hove): Aayamza Breeze
Golden Jacket (Crayford): Stardom
Derby (Nottingham): Priceless Blake
Grand National (Sittingbourne): Caislean Fifi

2020
Regency (Hove): Zascandil
Golden Jacket (Crayford): Skilful Sandie
Derby (Nottingham): Deerjat Sydney
Grand National (Sittingbourne): Roxholme Biscuit

GYMNASTICS

BRITISH CHAMPIONSHIPS 2019
Liverpool, 14–17 March

MEN
All-Around: James Hall
Floor: Giarnni Regini-Moran
Pommel Horse: Max Whitlock
Rings: James Hall
Vault: Jake Jarman
Parallel Bars: Joe Fraser
Horizontal Bar: Joe Fraser

WOMEN
All-Around: Elissa Downie
Floor: Claudia Fragapane
Beam: Georgia-Mae Fenton
Vault: Elissa Downie
Uneven Bars: Elissa Downie

EUROPEAN CHAMPIONSHIPS 2019
Szczecin, Poland, 10–14 April

MEN
Team: Russia
All-Around: Nikita Nagornyy (Russia)
Floor: Artur Dalaloyan (Russia)

Pommel: Max Whitlock (Great Britain)
Rings: Denis Abliazin (Russia)
Vault: Denis Abliazin (Russia)
Parallel Bars: Nikita Nagornyy (Russia)
High Bar: Epke Zonderland (Netherlands)

WOMEN
Team: France
All-Around: Melanie De Jesus dos Santos (France)
Floor: Melanie De Jesus dos Santos (France)
Beam: Alice Kinsella (Great Britain)
Vault: Maria Paseka (Russia)
Uneven Bars: Anastasiia Ilankova (Russia)

2019 EUROPEAN GAMES
Minsk, Belarus, June

MEN
All-Around: Gold – David Belyavskiy (Russia); Silver – Oleg Verniaiev (Ukraine); Bronze – Vladislav Poliashov (Russia)
Floor: Gold – Emil Soravuo (Finland); Silver – Giarnni Regini-Moran (Great Britain); Bronze – Petro Pakhnuik (Ukraine)
Pommel Horse: Gold – David Belyavskiy (Russia); Silver – Oleg Verniaiev (Ukraine); Bronze – Andrey Likhovitskiy (Belarus)
Rings: Gold – Marco Lodadio (Italy); Silver – Vahagn Davtyan (Armenia); Bronze – Igor Radivilov (Ukraine)
Vault: Gold – Artur Davtyan (Armenia); Silver – Dmitrii Lankin (Russia); Bronze – Igor Radivilov (Ukraine)
Parallel Bars: Gold – Oleg Verniaiev (Ukraine); Silver – Marios Georgiou (Cyprus); Bronze – Ferhat Arican (Turkey)
Horizontal Bar: Gold – Robert Tvorogal (Lithuania); Silver – Ahmet Onder (Turkey); Bronze – David Vecsernyes (Hungary)

WOMEN
All-Around: Gold – Angelina Melnikova (Russia); Silver – Lorette Charpy (France); Bronze – Diana Varinska (Ukraine)
Floor: Gold – Anastasiia Bachynska (Ukraine); Silver – Aneta Holasova (Czechia); Bronze – Jessica Castles (Sweden)
Beam: Gold – Nina Derwael (Belgium); Silver – Angelina Melnikova (Russia); Bronze – Diana Varinska (Ukraine)
Vault: Gold – Teja Belak (Slovenia); Silver – Angelina Melnikova (Russia); Bronze – Sara Peter (Hungary)
Uneven Bars: Gold – Angelina Melnikova (Russia); Silver – Becky Downie (Great Britain); Bronze – Anastasiya Alistratava (Belarus)

HOCKEY

MEN
England Hockey League 2019–20: Premier Division: Surbiton, 47pts; *Division One North:* University of Durham, 46pts; *Division One South:* Oxted, 40pts
England Hockey League Championship Cup final 2020: Beeston beat Fareham 9–1

WOMEN
England Hockey League 2019–20: Premier Division: Surbiton, 46pts; *Division One North:* Swansea, 37pts; *Division One South:* Wimbledon, 51pts
England Hockey League Championship Cup final 2020: Beeston beat Clifton Robinsons 3–2

HORSE RACING

NATIONAL HUNT

LADBROKES TROPHY (FORMERLY HENNESSY GOLD CUP)
(1957) Newbury, 3 miles and about 2½ f
2015 Smad Place (8y), W. Hutchinson
2016 Native River (6y), R. Johnson
2017 Total Recall (8y), P. Townend
2018 Sizing Hennessee (10y), T. Scudamore
2019 De Rasher Counter (7y), B. Jones

TINGLE CREEK CHASE
(1957) Sandown, 2 miles
2015 Sire de Grugy (9y), J. Moore
2016 Un de Sceaux (8y), R. Walsh
2017 Politologue (6y), H. Cobden
2018 Altior (8y), N. de Boinville
2019 Defi Du Seuil (6y), B. Geraghty

KING GEORGE VI CHASE
(1937) Kempton, about 3 miles
2015 Cue Card (9y), P. Brennan
2016 Thistlecrack (8y), T. Scudamore
2017 Might Bite (8y), N. de Boinville
2018 Clan Des Obeaux (6y), H. Cobden
2019 Clan Des Obeaux (7y), S. Twiston-Davies

CHAMPION HURDLE
(1927) Cheltenham, 2 miles and about ½ f
2016 Annie Power (8y), R. Walsh
2017 Buveur d'Air (6y), N. Fehily
2018 Buveur D'Air (7y), B. Geraghty
2019 Espoir D'Allen (5y), M. Walsh
2020 Epatante (6y), B. Geraghty

QUEEN MOTHER CHAMPION CHASE
(1959) Cheltenham, about 2 miles
2016 Sprinter Sacre (10y), N. de Boinville
2017 Special Tiara (10y), N. Fehily
2018 Altior (8y), N. de Boinville
2019 Altoir (9y), N. de Boinville
2020 Politologue (9y), H. Skelton

CHELTENHAM GOLD CUP
(1924) 3 miles and about 2½ f
2016 Don Cossack (9y), B. Cooper

2017 Sizing John (7y), R. Power
2018 Native River (7y), R. Johnson
2019 Al Boum Photo (7y), P. Townend
2020 Al Boum Photo (8y), P. Townend

GRAND NATIONAL
(1837) Liverpool, 4 miles and about 4 f

2015 Many Clouds (8y), L. Aspell
2016 Rule The World (9y), D. Mullins
2017 One For Arthur (8y), D. Fox
2018 Tiger Roll (8y), D. Russell
2019 Tiger Roll (9y), D. Russell

BET365 GOLD CUP
(1957) Sandown, 3 miles and about 5 f
2015 Just A Par (8y), S. Bowen
2016 The Young Master (7y), S. Waley-Cohen
2017 Henllan Harri (9y), S. Bowen
2018 Step Back (8y), J. Moore
2019 Talkischeap (7y), W. Hutchinson

STATISTICS

WINNING NATIONAL HUNT TRAINERS 2018–19

P. Nicholls	£3,158,852
N. Henderson	2,836,312
D. Skelton	2,216,846
C. Tizzard	1,753,171
W. P. Mullins	1,336,423
G. Elliott	1,309,852
P. Hobbs	1,246,651
A. King	1,202,795
N. Twiston-Davies	1,134,609
T. George	803,454

WINNING NATIONAL HUNT JOCKEYS 2018–19

	1st	2nd	3rd	Unpl.	Total mts
R. Johnson	200	152	134	493	980
H. Skelton	178	122	102	343	745
B. Hughes	146	143	128	471	888
H. Cobden	109	93	55	261	518
S. Twiston-Davies	105	86	78	412	681
A. Coleman	95	68	90	329	582
S. Bowen	91	79	65	360	595
W. Hutchinson	88	64	48	213	413
N. de Boinville	86	56	32	207	381
T. Scudamore	82	83	75	445	685

The above statistics have been provided by *Timeform*, publishers of the *Racehorses* and *Chasers and Hurdlers* annuals. Data for 2019-20 was unavailable.

THE FLAT

THE CLASSICS

ONE THOUSAND GUINEAS

(1814) Rowley Mile, Newmarket, for three-year-old fillies

Year	Winner	Betting	Owner	Jockey	Trainer	Runners
2015	Legatissimo	13–2	J. Magnier, M. Tabor and D. Smith	R. Moore	D. Wachman	13
2016	Minding	11–10	J. Magnier, M. Tabor and D. Smith	R. Moore	A. O'Brien	16
2017	Winter	9–1	J. Magnier, M. Tabor and D. Smith	W. Lordon	A. O'Brien	14
2018	Billesdon Brook	66–1	Pall Mall Partners	S. Levey	R. Hannon	15
2019	Hermosa	14–1	J. Magnier, M. Tabor and D. Smith	W. Lordan	A. O'Brien	15
2020	Love	11–1	J. Magnier, M. Tabor and D. Smith	R. Moore	A. O'Brien	15

TWO THOUSAND GUINEAS

(1809) Rowley Mile, Newmarket, for three-year-olds

Year	Winner	Betting	Owner	Jockey	Trainer	Runners
2015	Gleneagles	4–1	D. Smith, J. Magnier and M. Tabor	R. Moore	A. O'Brien	18
2016	Galileo Gold	14–1	Al Shaqab Racing	F. Dettori	H. Palmer	13
2017	Churchill	6–4	D. Smith, J. Magnier and M. Tabor	R. Moore	A. O'Brien	10
2018	Saxon Warrior	3–1	D. Smith, J. Magnier and M. Tabor	D. O'Brien	A. O'Brien	14
2019	Magnia Grecia	11–2	D. Smith, J. Magnier and M. Tabor	D. O'Brien	A. O'Brien	19
2020	Kameko	10–1	Qatar Racing	O. Murphy	A. Balding	15

THE DERBY

(1780) Epsom, 1 mile and about 4 f, for three-year-olds

The first winner was Sir Charles Bunbury's Diomed in 1780. The owners with the record number of winners are co-owners Sue Magnier and Michael Tabor, who won in 2001 and 2002, and with Derrick Smith in 2011, 2012, 2013, 2014 (also with Teo Ah Khing), 2017, 2019 and 2020. Other winning owners include Lord Egremont (1782, 1804, 1805, 1807, 1826); Aga Khan III (1930, 1935, 1936, 1948, 1952); Duke of Grafton (1802, 1809, 1810, 1815); Mr J. Bowes (1835, 1843, 1852, 1853); Sir J. Hawley (1851, 1858, 1859, 1868); the 1st Duke of Westminster (1880, 1882, 1886, 1899); and Sir Victor Sassoon (1953, 1957, 1958, 1960).

The Derby was run at Newmarket in 1915–18 and 1940–5.

Year	Winner	Betting	Owner	Jockey	Trainer	Runners
2015	Golden Horn	13–2	Anthony Oppenheimer	F. Dettori	J. Gosden	12
2016	Harzand	13–2	A. Khan	P. Smullen	D. Weld	16
2017	Wings of Eagles	40–1	D. Smith, J. Magnier and M. Tabor	P. Beggy	A. O'Brien	19
2018	Masar	16–1	Godolphin	W. Buick	C. Appleby	9
2019	Anthony Van Dyck	13–2	D. Smith, S. Magnier, and M. Tabor	S. Heffernan	A. O'Brien	13
2020	Serpentine	25–1	D. Smith, S. Magnier, and M. Tabor	E. McNamara	A. O'Brien	16

THE OAKS

(1779) Epsom, 1 mile and about 4 f, for three-year-old fillies

Year	Winner	Betting	Owner	Jockey	Trainer	Runners
2015	Qualify	50–1	C. Regalado-Gonzalez	C. O'Donoghue	A. O'Brien	11
2016	Minding	10–11	J. Magnier, M. Tabor and D. Smith	R. Moore	A. O'Brien	9
2017	Enable	6–1	K. Abdullah	F. Dettori	J. Gosden	10
2018	Forever Together	7–1	Mr. M. Tabor, D. Smith and Mrs. J. Magnier	D. O'Brien	A. O'Brien	9
2019	Anapurna	8–1	Helena Springfield Ltd.	F. Dettori	J. Gosden	14
2020	Love	11–1	J. Magnier, M. Tabor and D. Smith	R. Moore	A. O'Brien	8

ST LEGER

(1776) Doncaster, 1 mile and about 6 f, for three-year-olds

Year	Winner	Betting	Owner	Jockey	Trainer	Runners
2015	Simple Verse	8–1	QRL, Sheikh Suhaim Al Thani and Al Kubais	A. Atzeni	R. Beckett	7
2016	Habour Law	22–1	J. Cornwell	G. Baker	L. Mongan	9
2017	Capri	3–1	D. Smith, J. Magnier and M. Tabor	R. Moore	A. O'Brien	11
2018	Kew Gardens	3–1	D. Smith, J. Magnier and M. Tabor	R. Moore	A. O'Brien	12
2019	Logician	5–6	Khalid Abdullah	F. Dettori	J. Gosden	8
2020	Galleo Chrome	6–1	Galileo Chrome Partnershi	T. Marquand	J. O'Brien	11

RESULTS

CAMBRIDGESHIRE HANDICAP
(1839) Newmarket, 1 mile and 1 f

2016 Spark Plug (5y), J. Fortune
2017 Dolphin Vista (4y), G. Wood
2018 Wissahickon (3y), F. Dettori
2019 Lord North (3y), F. Dettory
2020 Majestic Dawn (4y), P. Hannagan

PRIX DE L'ARC DE TRIOMPHE
(1920) Longchamp, Paris, 1½ miles

2016* Found (4y), R. Moore
2017* Enable (3y), F. Dettori
2018 Enable (4y), F. Detorri
2019 Waldgeist (5y), P. Boudot
2020 Sottsass (4y), C. Demuro
* Ran at Chantilly while Longchamp was closed for redevelopment

CESAREWITCH
(1839) Newmarket, 2 miles and about 2 f

2016 Sweet Selection (4y), S. De Sousa
2017 Withhold (3y), S. De Sousa
2018 Low Sun (5y), S. Herrernan
2019 Stratum (6y), J. Watson
2020 Great White Shark (6y), J Watson

CHAMPION STAKES
(1877) Newmarket, 1 mile and 2 f

2016 Almanzor (3y), C. Soumillon
2017 Cracksman (3y), F. Dettori
2018 Cracksman (4y), F. Dettori
2019 Magical (4y), D. O'Brien
2020 Addeybb (6y), T. Marquand

DUBAI WORLD CUP
(1996) Dubai, 1 mile and 2 f

2015 Prince Bishop (8y), W. Buick
2016 California Chrome (5y), V. Espinoza
2017 Arrogate (4y), M. E. Smith
2018 Thunder Snow (4y), C. Soumillon
2019 Thunder Snow (5y), C. Soumillon

LINCOLN HANDICAP
(1965) Doncaster, 1 mile

2015 Gabrial (6y), T. Hamilton
2016 Secret Brief (4y), W. Buick
2017 Bravery (4y), D. Tudhope
2018 Addeybb (4y), J. Doyle
2019 Auxerre (4y), J. Doyle

JOCKEY CLUB STAKES
(1894) Newmarket, 1½ miles

2015 Second Step (4y), A. Atzeni
2016 Exosphere (4y), R. Moore
2017 Seventh Heaven (4y), R. Moore
2018 Defoe (4y), A. Atzeni
2019 Communique (4y), S. de Sousa

PRIX DU JOCKEY CLUB
(1836) Chantilly, 1 mile and about 2½ f, for three-year-olds

2016 Almanzor, J. Eyquem
2017 Brametot, C. Demuro
2018 Study of Man, S. Pasquier
2019 Sottsass, C. Demuro
2020 Mishriff, I. Mendizebal

ASCOT GOLD CUP
(1807) Ascot, 2 miles and about 4 f

2016 Order of St George (4y), R. Moore
2017 Big Orange (6y), J. Doyle
2018 Stradivarius (4y), F. Dettori
2019 Stradivarius (5y), F. Dettori
2020 Stradivarius (6y), F. Dettori

IRISH DERBY
(1866) Curragh, 1½ miles, for three-year-olds

2016 Harzand, P. Smullen
2017 Capri. S. Heffernan
2018 Latrobe, D. O'Brien
2019 Sovereign, P. Beggy
2020 Santiago, S. Heffernan

ECLIPSE STAKES
(1886) Sandown, 1 mile and about 2 f

2016 Hawkbill (3), W. Buick
2017 Ulysses (4y), J. Crawley
2018 Roaring Lion (3y), O. Murphy
2019 Enable (5y), F. Dettori
2020 Ghaiyyath (5y), W. Bruick

KING GEORGE VI AND QUEEN ELIZABETH DIAMOND STAKES
(1952) Ascot, 1 mile and about 4 f

2016 Highland Reel (4y), R. Moore
2017 Enable (3y), F. Detorri
2018 Poets Word (5y), J. Doyle
2019 Enable (5y), F. Dettori
2020 Enable (67), F. Dettori

GOODWOOD CUP
(1812) Goodwood, about 2 miles

2016 Big Orange (5y), J. Spencer
2017 Stradivarius (3y), A. Atzeni
2018 Stradivarius (4y), A. Atzeni
2019 Stradivarius (5y), F. Dettori
2020 Stradivarius (6y), F. Dettori

STATISTICS

WINNING FLAT OWNERS 2018

Godolphin	£4,708,598
Qatar Racing Ltd	3,144,018
Mr Hamdan Al Maktoum	2,647,922
Mr. D. Smith, Mrs J. Magnier, Mr M. Tabor	2,616,575
Mr K. Abdullah	1,654,118
Mr Saeed Suhail	1,568,939
Cheveley Park Stud	1,344,705
Sheikh Hamdan Bin Mohammed Al Maktoum	1,342,207
Mr A. E. Oppenheimer	1,304,524
Mr B. E. Nielsen	1,183,727

WINNING FLAT TRAINERS 2018

J. Gosden	£8,288,597
A. O'Brien	5,461,634
Sir Michael Stoute	4,433,616
M. Johnston	3,970,316
C. Appleby	3,552,308
R. Fahey	3,097,749
W. Haggas	2,905,361
R. Hannon	2,855,956
A. Balding	2,329,863
R. Varian	1,894,302

WINNING FLAT SIRES 2018

	Races won	Stakes
Dubawi by Dubai Millennium	128	£3,573,742
Galileo by Sadler's Wells	43	3,058,599
Frankel by Galileo	70	2,977,256
Sea the Stars by Cape Cross	67	2,794,678
Kodiac by Danehill	180	2,486,230
Poet's Voice by Dubawi	97	2,358,344
Kitten's Joy by El Prado	20	2,221,258
Dark Angel by Acclamation	144	2,216,748
Invincible Spirit by Green Desert	110	1,857,549
Acclamation by Royal Applause	106	1,801,502

WINNING FLAT JOCKEYS 2018

	1st	2nd	3rd	Unpl.	Total mts
O. Murphy	198	179	155	598	1,130
S. De Sousa	176	133	109	517	935
J. Doyle	156	99	72	306	633
L. Morris	150	169	155	1,046	1,520
J. Fanning	137	140	105	553	935
J. Crowley	130	93	77	403	703
R. Havlin	127	97	99	356	678
A. Kirby	123	111	98	462	794
P. J. McDonald	120	112	101	558	891
D. Tudhope	116	101	86	394	697

The above statistics have been provided by *Timeform*, publishers of the *Racehorses* and *Chasers and Hurdlers* annuals. Data for 2019 was unavailable.

ICE HOCKEY

MEN'S WORLD CHAMPIONSHIP 2019
Slovakia, 10–26 May

Final: Finland beat Canada 3–1

WOMEN'S WORLD CHAMPIONSHIP 2019
Espoo, Finland, 4–14 April

Gold Medal Final: USA beat Finland 2–1

DOMESTIC COMPETITIONS
Elite League Champions 2018–19: Belfast Giants
Play-off Champions 2019: Cardiff Devils
Challenge Cup final 2019–20: Sheffield Steelers beat Cardiff Devils 4–3

NATIONAL HOCKEY LEAGUE
Stanley Cup final 2020: Tampa Bay Lightning beat Dallas Stars 4–2

JUDO

EUROPEAN CHAMPIONSHIPS 2019
Minsk, Belarus, 22–24 June

Mixed Team: Russia

MEN
Heavyweight (over 100kg): Guram Tushishvili (Georgia)
Light-heavyweight (100kg): Arman Adamian (Russia)
Middleweight (90kg): Mikhail Ozerler (Turkey)
Welterweight (81kg): Matthias Casse (Belgium)
Lightweight (73kg): Tommy Macais (Sweden)
Junior Lightweight (66kg): Georgii Zantaraia (Ukraine)
Bantamweight (60kg): Lukhumi Chkhivimiani (Georgia)

WOMEN
Heavyweight (over 78kg): Maryana Slutskaya (Belarus)
Light-heavyweight (78kg):Klara Apotekar (Slovenia)
Middleweight (70kg): Margaux Pinot (France)
Welterweight (63kg): Clarisse Agbegnenou (France)
Lightweight (57kg): Daria Mezhetskaia (Russia)
Junior Lightweight (52kg): Majlinda Kelmendi (Kosovo)
Bantamweight (48kg): Daria Bilodid (Ukraine)

BRITISH OPEN CHAMPIONSHIPS 2019
Sheffield, December

MEN
Heavyweight (over 100kg): Christopher Sherrington
Light-heavyweight (100kg): Cailin Calder
Middleweight (90kg): Jamal Petgrave
Welter (81kg): Stuart McWatt
Lightweight (73kg): Daniel Powell
Lightweight (66kg): Neil MacDonald
Bantamweight (60kg): Sam Hall

WOMEN
Heavyweight (over 78kg): Emily Ritchie
Light-heavyweight (78kg): Shelley Ludford
Middleweight (70kg): Kelly Petersen-Pollard
Welter (63kg): Bekky Livesey
Lightweight (57kg): Josie Steele
Lightweight (52kg): Yasmin Javadian
Bantamweight (48kg): Kimberley Renicks

MOTORCYCLING

MOTO 2019
Italy (Rimini): Marc Márquez (Spain), Honda
Spain (Aragón): Marc Márquez (Spain), Honda
Thailand (Chang International): Marc Márquez (Spain), Honda
Japan (Motegi): Marc Márquez (Spain), Honda
Australia (Phillip Island): Marc Márquez (Spain), Honda
Malaysia (Sepang): Maverick Viñales (Spain), Yamaha
Spain (Valencia): Marc Márquez (Spain), Honda
Riders' Championship 2019: 1. Marc Márquez (Spain), Honda, 420pts; 2. Andrea Dovizioso (Italy), Ducati, 269pts; 3. Maverick Viñales (Spain), Yamaha, 211pts

MOTOGP 2020
Spain (Jerez): Fabio Quartararo (France), Yamaha
Spain (Jerez): Fabio Quartararo (France), Yamaha
Czech Republic (Brno): Brad Binder (South Africa), KMT
Austria (Spielberg): Pol Espargaro (Spain), KMT
Austria (Spielberg): Joan Mir (Spain), Suzuki
Italy (Rimini): Franco Morbidelli (Italy), Yamaha
Italy (Rimini): Maverick Viñales (Spain), Yamaha
Spain (Catalonia): Fabio Quartararo (France), Yamaha
France (Le Mans): Danilo Petrucci (Italy), Ducati
Spain (Aragón): Alex Rins (Spain), Suzuki
Spain (Aragón): Franco Morbidelli (Italy), Yamaha

MOTO2 2019
Italy (Rimini): Augusto Fernandez (Spain), Kalex
Aragón (Spain): Brad Binder (South Africa), KMT
Thailand (Chang International): Luca Marini (Italy), Kalex
Japan (Motegi): Luca Marini (Italy), Kalex
Australia (Phillip Island): Brad Binder (South Africa), KMT
Malaysia (Sepang): Brad Binder (South Africa), KMT
Spain (Valencia): Brad Binder (South Africa), KMT
Riders' Championship 2019: 1. Alex Marquez (Spain), Kalex, 262pts; 2. Brad Binder (South Africa), KMT, 259pts; 3. Thomas Luthi (Switzerland), 250pts

MOTO2 2020
Qatar (Doha): Tetsuta Nagashima (Japan), Kalex
Spain (Jerez): Luca Marini (Italy), Kalex
Spain (Jerez): Enea Bastianini (Italy), Kalex
Czech Republic (Brno): Enea Bastianini (Italy), Kalex
Austria (Spielberg): Jorge Martin (Spain), Kalex
Austria (Spielberg): Marco Bezzecchi (Italy), Kalex
Italy (Rimini): Luca Marini (Italy), Kalex
Italy (Rimini): Enea Bastianini (Italy), Kalex
Spain (Catalonia): Luca Marini (Italy), Kalex
France (Le Mans): Sam Lowes (Great Britain), Kalex
Spain (Aragón): Sam Lowes (Great Britain), Kalex
Spain (Aragón): Sam Lowes (Great Britain), Kalex

MOTO3 2019
Italy (Rimini): Tatsuki Suzuki (Japanese), Honda
Aragón (Spain): Aron Canet (Spain), KMT
Thailand (Chang International): Albert Arenas (Spain), KMT
Japan (Motegi): Lorenzo Dalla Porta (Italy), Honda
Australia (Phillip Island): Lorenzo Dalla Porta (Italy), Honda
Malaysia (Sepang): Lorenzo Dalla Porta (Italy), Honda
Spain (Valencia): Sergio Garcia (Spain), Honda
*Riders' Championship 2019:*1. Lorenzo Dalla Porta (Italy),
    Honda, 279pts; 2. Aron Canet (Spain), KMT, 200pts; 3.
    Marco Ramirez (Spain), 183pts

MOTO3 2020
Qatar (Doha): Albert Arenas (Spain), KMT
Spain (Jerez): Albert Arenas (Spain), KMT
Spain (Jerez): Tatsuki Suzuki (Japanese), Honda
Czech Republic (Brno): Dennis Foggia (Italy), Honda
Austria (Spielberg): Albert Arenas (Spain), KMT
Austria (Spielberg): Celestino Vietti (Italy), KMT
Italy (Rimini): John McPhee (Great Britain), Honda
Italy (Rimini): Romano Fenati (Italy), Husqvarna
Spain (Catalonia): Darryn Binder (South Africa), KMT
France (Le Mans): Celestino Vietti (Italy), KMT
Spain (Aragón): Jaurne Masia (Spain), Honda
Spain (Aragón): Jaurne Masia (Spain), Honda

ISLE OF MAN TOURIST TROPHY 2019
Senior: Dean Harrison (England), Kawasaki
Supersport: Race 1 – Lee Johnston (Northern Ireland),
    Yamaha; Race 2 – Peter Hickman (England), Triumph

WORLD SUPERBIKES 2019
Final standings: 1. Jonathan Rea (Great Britain), Kawasaki,
    663pts; 2. Alvaro Bautista (Spain), Ducati, 498pts; 3. Alex
    Lowes (Great Britain), Yamaha, 341pts

WORLD SUPERBIKES 2020
Australia (Phillip Island): Race 1 – Toprak Razgatlioglu
    (Turkey), Yamaha; Race 2 – Alex Lowes, Kawasaki
Spain (Jerez): Race 1 – Scott Redding (Great Britain), Ducati;
    Race 2 – Jonathan Rea (Great Britain), Kawasaki
Portugal (Algarve): Race 1 – Jonathan Rea (Great Britain),
    Kawasaki; Race 2 – Jonathan Rea (Great Britain),
    Kawasaki
Spain (Aragón): Race 1 – Scott Redding (Great Britain),
    Ducati; Race 2 – Jonathan Rea (Great Britain), Kawasaki
Spain (Aragón): Race 1 – Michael Rinaldi (Italy), Ducati;
    Race 2 – Jonathan Rea (Great Britain), Kawasaki
Spain (Barcelona): Race 1 – Jonathan Rea (Great Britain),
    Kawasaki; Race 2 – Chaz Davies (Great Britain), Duacti
France (Magny-Cours): Race 1 – Jonathan Rea (Great
    Britain), Kawasaki; Race 2 – Scott Redding (Great
    Britain), Ducati
Portugal (Lisbon): Race 1 – Toprak Razgatlioglu (Turkey),
    Yamaha; Race 2 – Chaz Davies (Great Britain), Duacti

MOTOR RACING

FORMULA ONE GRAND PRIX 2019
Singapore (Marina Bay): Sebastian Vettel (Germany), Ferrari
Russia (Sochi): Lewis Hamilton (Great Britain), Mercedes
Japan (Suzuka): Valterri Bottas (Finland), Mercedes
Mexico (Mexico City): Lewis Hamilton (Great Britain),
    Mercedes
USA (Austin):Lewis Hamilton (Great Britain), Mercedes
Brazil (São Paulo): Max Verstappen (Netherlands), Red Bull
    Honda
Abu Dhabi (Yas Marina): Lewis Hamilton (Great Britain),
    Mercedes
Drivers' World Championship 2019: 1. Lewis Hamilton (Great
    Britain), Mercedes, 413pts; 2. Valtteri Bottas (Finland),
    Mercedes, 26pts; Max Verstappen (Netherlands), Red Bull
    Honda, 278pts
Constructors' World Championship 2019: 1. Mercedes, 739pts;
    2. Ferrari, 504pts; 3. Red Bull Honda, 417pts

FORMULA ONE GRAND PRIX 2020
Austria (Speilberg): Valtteri Bottas (Finland), Mercedes
Austria (Speilberg): Lewis Hamilton (Great Britain), Mercedes
Hungary (Budapest): Lewis Hamilton (Great Britain),
    Mercedes
Great Britain (Silverstone): Lewis Hamilton (Great Britain),
    Mercedes
Great Britain (Silverstone): Max Verstappen (Netherlands),
    Red Bull Honda
Spain (Barcelona): Lewis Hamilton (Great Britain), Mercedes
Belgium (Spa-Francorchamps): Lewis Hamilton (Great
    Britain), Mercedes
Italy (Monza): Pierre Gasly (France), Alphatauri Honda
Italy (Mugello): Lewis Hamilton (Great Britain), Mercedes
Russia (Sochi): Valtteri Bottas (Finland), Mercedes
Germany (Nürburgring): Lewis Hamilton (Great Britain),
    Mercedes
Portugal (Portimao): Lewis Hamilton (Great Britain),
    Mercedes
Italy (Imola): Lewis Hamilton (Great Britain), Mercedes

INDIANAPOLIS 500 2020
Indianapolis, USA, 23 August

Takumato Sato (Japan), Rahal Letterman Lanigan Racing

2020 24-HOURS OF LE MANS
Le Mans, France, 19–20 September

Sebastien Buemi (Switzerland), Kazuki Nakajima (Japan),
    Brendon Hartley (New Zealand), Toyota Gazoo Racing

MOTOR RALLYING

WORLD RALLY CHAMPIONSHIPS 2019
Turkey: Sébastien Ogier (France), Citroën
Great Britain: Ott Tänak (Estonia), Toyota
Spain: Thierry Neuville (Belgium), Hyundai

Drivers' World Championship 2019: 1. Ott Tänak (Estonia),
    Toyota, 263pts; 2. Thierry Neuville (Belgium), Hyundai,
    227pts; 3. Sébastien Ogier (France), Citroën, 217pts
Manufacturers' World Championship 2019: 1. Hyundai, 380pts;
    2. Toyota, 362pts; 3. Citroën, 284pts

WORLD RALLY CHAMPIONSHIPS 2020
Monte Carlo: Thierry Neuville (Belgium), Hyundai
Sweden: Elfyn Evans (Great Britain), Toyota
Mexico: Sébastien Ogier (France), Toyota
Estonia: Ott Tänak (Estonia), Hyundai
Turkey: Elfyn Evans (Great Britain), Toyota
Italy: Dani Sordo (Spain), Hyundai

DAKAR RALLY RAID 2020
Saudi Arabia, 5–17 January

Motorcycle: Ricky Brabec (USA), Honda
Quad: Ignascio Casale, (Chile), Casale Racing
Car: Carlos Sainz (Spain) and Lucas Cruz (Spain), Mini X-Raid
SSV: Emanuel Gyenes (Romania), Autonet
Truck: Andrey Karginov (Russia), Anrey Mokeev (Russia), Igor Leonov (Russia), Kamaz

NETBALL

Superleague Grand Final 2019: Manchester Thunder beat Wasps 57–52

NORDIC EVENTS

BIATHLON WORLD CUP 2019–20

MEN
Overall: Johannes Thingnes Boe (Norway), 913pts

WOMEN
Overall: Dorothea Wierer (Italy), 793pts

NORDIC COMBINED WORLD CUP 2019–20
World Cup: Jarl Magnus Riiber (Norway), 1,586pts
Nations' Cup: Norway, 5,660pts

POLO

Prince of Wales Trophy 2020: Park Place beat Les Lions 13–9
Queen's Cup final 2020: Les Lions/Great Oaks beat Park Place 9–8
Warwickshire Cup 2020: Lovelocks beat MT Vikings 11–8
Gold Cup (British Open) final 2020: Next Generation beat Les Lions/Great Oaks 14–12
Royal Windsor Cup final 2020: Four Quarters Orange beat White Crane 10–9

RACKETS

Noel Bruce Cup 2019: Winchester beat Cheltenham 4–1
World Singles 2019: T. Billings beat A. Duncliffe-Vines 5–0
Ladies Open Doubles Championship 2019: G. Willis and T. Lumley beat L. Gooding and I. Thorneycroft 3–2
UK Professional Singles Championship 2020: B. Crawston beat B. Bomford 2–1
Men's British Open Singles Championship 2020: T. Billings beat B. Cawston 4–0
Ladies British Open Singles Championship 2020: T. Lumley beat I. Deakin 3–2
Amateur Doubles Championship 2020: T. Billings and R. Owen beat J. Coyne and M. Farmiloe 3–1
Ladies World Doubles 2020: I. Deakin and T. Lumley beat L. Van der Zwalmen and L. Gengler-Saint 3–1

REAL TENNIS

MEN
British Open Singles final 2019: C. Riviere (USA) beat R. Fahey (Australia) 3–0
British Open Doubles final 2019: C. Riviere (USA) and J. Lumley (Great Britain) beat R. Fahey (Australia) and N. Howell (Australia) 3–0
Henry Leaf Cup final 2019 (public schools' old boys' doubles championship): Old Etonians beat Old Carthusians 2–0

Doubles World Championship 2019: T. Chisholm (USA) and C. Riviere (USA) beat R. Fahey (Australia) and N. Howell (Australia) 5–1
World Championship 2018: R. Fahey (Australia) beat C. Riviere (USA) 7–5

WOMEN
Ladies Open Singles Championship final 2019: C. Fahey (Great Britain) beat L. Van der Zwalmen (France) 2–0
World Single Championship 2019: C. Fahey (Great Britain) beat I. Candy (Great Britain) 2–0
World Doubles Championship 2019: J. Chan (Australia) and J. Edwards (Great Britain) beat P. Lumley (Great Britain) and T. Lumley (Great Britain) 2–1

ROWING

HENLEY ROYAL REGATTA 2019
King's Cup: United States Armed Forces (USA) beat Bundeswehr (Germany) by $\frac{3}{4}$ length
Grand Challenge Cup: Waiariki Rowing Club (New Zealand) beat Leander Club and Oxford Brookes University by 1 length
Stewards' Challenge Cup: Leander Club and Oxford Bookes University beat Leander Club by $2\frac{1}{2}$ lengths
Queen Mother Challenge Cup: Leander Club beat Frankfurter Rudergesellschaft Germania 1869 E.V. (Germany) easily
Silver Goblets and Nickalls' Challenge Cup: A. Diaz & A. Haack (Argentina) beat M.C. Oyen & M. Steenman (Netherlands) by $4\frac{3}{4}$ lengths
Double Sculls Challenge Cup: J.E. Collins & G.E. Thomas beat J. W. Storey & C. W. Harris (New Zealand) by 1 length
Diamond Challenge Sculls: O. Zeidler (Germany) beat G.G. Krommenhoek (Netherlands) by 5 lengths
Remenham Challenge Cup: Waiariki Rowing Club (New Zealand) beat Leander Club and Imperial College London by $1\frac{2}{3}$ lengths
Town Challenge Cup: Hollandia Roeiclub (Netherlands) beat Chinese National Rowing Team (China) by $4\frac{1}{2}$ lengths
Princess Grace Challenge Cup: Chinese National Rowing Team (China) beat Hollandia Roeiclub (Netherlands) by $1\frac{3}{4}$ lengths
Hambledon Pairs Challenge Cup: G.E. Prendergast & K.L. Gowler (New Zealand) beat X. Lin & R. Ju (China) easily
Stonor Challenge Cup: B.C. Donoghue & O.K. Loe (New Zealand) beat S. Lu & Y. Wang (China) by $3\frac{3}{4}$ lengths
Princess Royal Challenge Cup: E.K. Twigg (New Zealand) beat L.I. Scheenaard (Netherlands) by $2\frac{1}{2}$ lengths
Ladies' Challenge Plate: Oxford Brookes University A beat Hollandia Roeiclub (Netherlands) by 1 length
Visitors' Challenge Cup: Cambridge University and Leander Club beat Amsterdamsche Studenten Roeivereeniging Nereus and Delftsche Studenten Roeivereeniging Laga (Netherlands) easily
Prince of Wales Challenge Cup: Edinburgh University and Nottingham Rowing Club beat Algemene Amsterdamsche Studenten Roeivereniging Skoll and Algemene Utrechtse Studenten Roeivereniging Orca (Netherlands) by 1 length
Thames Challenge Cup: Roeivereniging Studenten Vrije Universiteit Okeanos (Netherlands) beat Thames Rowing Club A by 1 length
Wyfold Challenge Cup: Sydney Rowing Club (Australia) beat Norske Studenters Roklub (Norway) by 1 length
Britannia Challenge Cup: Molesey Boat Club beat Mercantile Rowing Club (Australia) by $\frac{1}{2}$ length
Temple Challenge Cup: Oxford Brookes University A beat Northeastern University A (USA) by $\frac{3}{4}$ length
Prince Albert Challenge Cup: Harvard University (USA) beat Durham University by $\frac{3}{4}$ length

Princess Elizabeth Challenge Cup: Eton College beat Scotch College, Melbourne (Australia) by $1\frac{1}{4}$ lengths
Fawley Challenge Cup: Leander Club A beat Henley Rowing Club A by $1\frac{1}{4}$ lengths
Diamond Jubilee Challenge Cup: Latymer Upper School A beat Headington School by $1\frac{3}{4}$ lengths

THE 165TH UNIVERSITY BOAT RACE
Putney–Mortlake, 4 miles, 1 f, 180 yd, 7 April 2019

MEN
Cambridge beat Oxford by 1 length; 16min 57sec

Cambridge have won 84 times, Oxford 80 and there has been one dead heat. The record time is 16min 19sec, rowed by Cambridge in 1998.

WOMEN
Cambridge beat Oxford by 5 lengths; 18min 47sec

Cambridge have won 44 times, Oxford 30

EUROPEAN ROWING CHAMPIONSHIPS 2020
Poznan, Poland, 9–11 October

MEN
Single Sculls: Sverri Sandberg Nielsen (Denmark)
Pair: Marius Cozimiuc and Ciprian Tudosa (Romania)
Double Sculls: Melvin Twellaar and Stef Broenink (Netherlands)
Four: Netherlands
Quadruple Sculls: Netherlands
Eight: Germany
Lightweight Single Sculls: Kristoffer Brun (Norway)
Lightweight Double Sculls: Stefano Oppo and Pietro Ruta (Italy)
Lightweight Four: Italy

WOMEN
Single Sculls: Sanita Puspure (Ireland)
Pair: Adriana Ailincai and Luliana Buhus (Romania)
Double Sculls: Nicoleta-Ancuta Bodnar and Simona Geanina Radis (Romania)
Fours: Netherlands
Quadruple Sculls: Netherlands
Eight: Romania
Lightweight Single Sculls: Martine Veldhuis (Netherlands)
Lightweight Double Sculls: Marieke Keijser and Ilse Paulis (Netherlands)
Lightweight Four: Italy

OTHER ROWING EVENTS
Wingfield Sculls 2020: Men, M. Haywood (Nottingham Rowing Club); *Women,* M. Hodgkins-Byrne (Reading Rowing Club)
Oxford Summer Eights 2019: Men, Oriel; *Women,* Wolfson
Torpid Races 2019: Men, Oriel; *Women,* Wadham
Head of the River 2019: Oxford Brookes University A

RUGBY FIVES

National Open Singles Championship final 2019: D. Tristao beat E. Kay 2–0
National Ladies' Singles Championship final 2020: S. Lundie beat E. Ware 15–9
National Ladies' Doubles Championship final 2020: L. Mathias and S. Zhang beat M. Nugent and K. Sumner 2–0
National Open Doubles Championship final 2019: E. Kay and D. Tristao beat C. Brooks and W. Ellison 2–1
National Mixed Doubles final 2019: H. Tunks and D. Law beat L. Mathias and D. Neale 2–1
National Club Championship final 2019: West of England beat Wessex 100–83

National Schools' Singles Championship final 2019: T. McGuire (Sedbergh) beat Wiseman 2–1
National Schools' Doubles Championship final 2019: Merchant Taylorss beat Alleyn's 2–1
Varsity Match 2020: Oxford beat Cambridge 356–145

RUGBY LEAGUE

Super League Grand Final 2019: St Helens beat Salford 23–6
Coral Challenge Cup final 2020: Leeds Rhinos beat Salford Red Devils 17–16
Betfred World Club Challenge 2020: Sydney Roosters beat St Helens 20–12

AMATEUR COMPETITIONS
National Conference League Premier Division Grand Final 2019: West Hull beat West Brow Hornets 24–16
Division One Champions 2019: Pilkington Recs
Division Two Champions 2019: West Bowling
BARLA National Cup final 2019: Thatto Heath Crusaders A beat West Hull 20–19
Varsity Match 2020: Oxford beat Cambridge 32–20

RUGBY UNION

SIX NATIONS CHAMPIONSHIP 2020

1 February	Cardiff	Wales beat Italy 42–0
	Dublin	Ireland beat Scotland 19–12
2 February	Paris	France beat England 24–17
8 February	Dublin	Ireland beat Wales 24–14
	Edinburgh	England beat Scotland 13–6
9 February	Paris	France beat Italy 35–22
22 February	Rome	Scotland beat Italy 10–0
	Cardiff	France beat Wales 27–23
	London	England beat Ireland 24–12
7 March	London	England beat Wales 33–30
8 March	Edinburgh	Scotland beat France 28–17
24 October	Dublin	Ireland beat Italy 50–17
31 October	Rome	England beat Italy 34–5
	Paris	France beat Ireland 35–27
3 November	Llanelli	Scotland beat Wales 14–10

Final standings: 1. England, 18pts; 2. France, 18pts; 3. Ireland, 14pts; 4. Scotland, 14pts; 5. Wales, 8pts; 6. Italy, 0pts

EUROPEAN CLUB COMPETITIONS 2019-20
European Rugby Challenge Cup: Bristol Bears beat Toulon 32–19
European Rugby Champions Cup: Exeter Chiefs beat Racing 92 31–27
Guinness Pro14 final: Leinster beat Ulster 27–5

DOMESTIC COMPETITIONS 2019–20

ENGLAND
English Premiership: Exeter Chiefs, 74pts
Aviva Premiership final: Exeter Chiefs beat Wasps 19–13
RFU Championship: Newcastle Falcons, 104pts
National League: Division 1, Richmond, 116pts; *Promotion from Division 2 (North):* Caldy, 119pts; *Promotion from Division 2 (South):* Taunton Titans, 101pts, Tonbridge Juddians, 98pts
County Championship final (Bill Beaumont Cup): Cornwall beat Cheshire 14–12
137th (2019) Varsity Match: Oxford beat Cambridge 38–16
Premiership Rugby Cup (formerly Anglo-Welsh Cup): Sale Sharks beat Harlequins 27–19

SCOTLAND (2018–19)
Premiership champions: Ayr
National League Division 1 champions: Marr RFC
Scottish Cup final: Ayr beat Heriot's 27–25

WALES (2018–19)
WRU Challenge Cup final: Cardiff beat Merthyr 25–19

IRELAND (2018–19)
All-Ireland League final: Cork Constitution beat Clontarf
  28–13

2019 RUGBY WORLD CUP
Japan, 20 September – 2 November 2019

GROUP A

	P	W	D	L	F	A	BP	PTS
Japan	4	4	0	0	115	62	3	19
Ireland	4	3	0	1	121	27	4	16
Scotland	4	2	0	2	119	55	3	11
Samoa	4	1	0	3	58	128	1	5
Russia	4	0	0	0	19	160	0	0

Japan beat Russia 30–10
Ireland beat Scotland 27–3
Samoa beat Russia 34–9
Japan beat Ireland 19–12
Scotland beat Samoa 34–0
Ireland beat Russia 35–0
Japan beat Samoa 38–19
Scotland beat Russia 61–0
Ireland beat Samoa 47–5
Japan beat Scotland 28–21

GROUP B

	P	W	D	L	F	A	BP	PTS
New Zealand	4	3	1	0	157	22	2	16
South Africa	4	3	0	1	185	36	3	15
Italy	4	2	1	1	98	78	2	12
Namibia	4	0	1	3	34	175	0	2
Canada	4	0	1	3	14	177	0	2

New Zealand beat South Africa 23–13
Italy beat Namibia 47–22
Italy beat Canada 48–7
South Africa beat Namibia 57–3
New Zealand beat Canada 63–0
South Africa beat Italy 49–3
New Zealand bet Namibia 71–9
South Africa beat Canada 66–7
New Zealand drew with Italy 0–0
Namibia drew with Canada 0–0

GROUP C

	P	W	D	L	F	A	BP	PTS
England	4	3	1	0	119	20	3	17
France	4	3	1	0	79	51	1	15
Argentina	4	2	0	2	106	91	3	11
Tonga	4	1	0	3	67	105	2	6
United States	4	0	0	4	52	156	0	0

France beat Argentina 23–21
England beat Tonga 35–3
England beat United States 45–7
Argentina beat Tonga 28–12
France beat United States 33–9
England beat Argentina 39–10
France beat Tonga 23–21
Argentina beat United States 47–17
England drew with France 0–0
Tonga beat United States 31–19

POOL D

	P	W	D	L	F	A	BP	PTS
Wales	4	4	0	0	136	69	3	19
Australia	4	3	0	1	136	68	4	16
Fiji	4	1	0	3	110	108	3	7
Georgia	4	1	0	3	65	122	1	5
Uruguay	4	1	0	3	60	140	0	4

Australia beat Fiji 39–21
Wales beat Georgia 43–14
Uruguay beat Fiji 30–27
Georgia beat Uruguay 33–7
Wales beat Australia 29–25
Fiji beat Georgia 45–10
Australia beat Uruguay 45–10
Wales beat Fiji 29–17
Australia beat Georgia 27–8
Wales beat Uruguay 35–13

QUARTER-FINALS
England beat Australia 40–16
New Zealand beat Ireland 46–14
Wales beat France 20–19
South Africa beat Japan 26–3

SEMI-FINALS
England beat New Zealand 19–7
South Africa beat Wales 19–16

BRONZE FINAL
New Zealand beat Wales 40–17

FINAL
South Africa beat England 32–12

WOMEN'S RUGBY

SIX NATIONS CHAMPIONSHIP 2019

1 February	Dublin	England beat Ireland 51–7
	Glasgow	Italy beat Scotland 28–7
2 February	Montpellier	France beat Wales 52–3
8 February	Glasgow	Ireland beat Scotland 22–5
9 February	Lecce	Italy drew with Wales 3–3
10 February	Doncaster	England beat France 41–26
23 February	Parma	Italy beat Ireland 29–27
	Lille	France beat Scotland 41–10
24 February	Cardiff	England beat Wales 51–12
8 March	Glasgow	Wales beat Scotland 17–15
9 March	Exeter	England beat Italy 55–0
	Dublin	France beat Ireland 47–17
16 March	London	England beat Scotland 80–0
17 March	Cardiff	Wales beat Ireland 24–5
	Padova	Italy beat France 31–12

Final standings: 1. England, 28pts; 2. Italy, 17pts; 3. France,
  16pts; 4. Wales, 11pts; 5. Ireland, 7pts; 6. Scotland, 1pts

WOMEN'S DOMESTIC COMPETITIONS 2018–19
Tyrrells Premier 15s final: Saracens Women beat Harlequins
  Ladies 33–17

SHOOTING

151TH NATIONAL RIFLE ASSOCIATION IMPERIAL
MEETING
Bisley, 11–19 September 2020

Queen's Prize: D.C. Luckman, 297.40 v-bulls
Grand Aggregate: P.M. Patel, 694.99 v-bulls
Prince of Wales Prize: P.M. Patel, 75.15 v-bulls
All Comers' Aggregate: T.J.D. Raincock, 373.46 v-bulls
Chancellor's Trophy: Cambridge University, 1024.125 v-bulls
Musketeers Cup: Durham University, 582.60 v-bulls

Mackinnon Challenge Cup: England, 1149.100 v-bulls
The Albert: C.N. Tremlett, 221.30 v-bulls
Hopton Challenge Cup: C.N. Tremlett, 1009.138 v-bulls

2019 EUROPEAN GAMES
Minsk, Belarus, June

MEN
10m Air Pistol: Gold – Artem Chernousov (Russia); Silver – Oleh Omelchuk (Ukraine); Bronze – Lauris Strautmanis (Latvia)
10m Air Rifle: Gold – Sergey Richter (Israel); Silver – Sergey Kamenskiy (Russia); Bronze – Filip Nepejchal (Czechia)
25m Rapid Fire Pistol: Gold – Oliver Geis (Germany); Silver – Jean Quiquampoix (France); Bronze – Clement Bessaguet (France)
50m Rifle 3 Positions: Gold – Sergey Kamenskiy (Russia); Silver – Yury Shcherbatsevich (Belarus); Bronze – Istvan Oeni (Hungary)
Shotgun Skeet: Gold – Stefan Nilsson (Sweden); Silver – Tomas Nydrle (Czechia); Bronze – Gabriele Rossetti (Italy)
Shotgun Trap: Gold – David Kostelecky (Czechia); Silver – Valerio Grazini (Italy); Bronze – Aaron Heading (Great Britain)

WOMEN
10m Air Pistol: Gold – Zorana Arunovic (Serbia); Silver – Anna Korakaki (Greece); Bronze – Antoaneta Boneva (Bulgaria)
10m Air Rifle: Gold – Laura Coman (Romania); Silver – Nina Christen (Switzerland); Bronze – Nikola Mazurova (Czechia)
25m Pistol: Gold – Anna Korakaki (Greece); Silver – Heidi Diethelm Gerber (Switzerland); Bronze – Antoaneta Boneva (Bulgaria)
50m Rifle 3 Positions: Gold – Yulia Zykova (Russia); Silver – Nikola Mazurova (Czechia); Bronze – Polina Khorosheva (Russia)
Shotgun Skeet: Gold – Diana Bacosi (Italy); Silver – Lucie Anastassiou (France); Bronze – Chiara Cainero (Italy)
Shotgun Trap: Gold – Silvana Stanco (Italy); Silver – Jessica Rossi (Italy); Bronze – Fatima Galvez (Spain)

MIXED
10m Air Pistol: Gold – Russia; Silver – Serbia; Bronze – Germany
10m Air Rifle: Gold – Russia; Silver – Russia; Bronze – Czechia
25m Standard Pistol: Gold – Germany; Silver – Germany; Bronze – Ukraine
50m Pistol: Gold – Russia; Silver – Latvia; Bronze – Georgia
50m Rifle Prone: Gold – Switzerland; Silver – Austria; Bronze – Russia
Shotgun Skeet: Gold – Italy; Silver – Italy; Bronze – Czechia
Shotgun Trap: Gold – Spain; Silver – Italy; Bronze – Russia

SNOOKER

2019–20
2019 Riga Masters: Yan Bingtao (China) beat Mark Joyce (England) 5–2
2019 International Championship (Daqing, China): Judd Trump (England) beat Mark Allen (Northern Island) 10–3
2019 China Championship (Guangzhou): Shaun Murphy (England) beat Mark Williams 10–9
2019 English Open (Crawley): Mark Selby (England) beat David Gilbert (England) 9–1
2019 World Open (Yushan, China): Judd Trump (England) beat Chepchaiya Un-Nooh (Thailand) 10–5

2019 Northern Ireland (Belfast): Judd Trump (England) beat Ronnie O'Sullivan (England) 9–7
2019 UK Championship (York): Ding Junhui (China) beat Stephen Maguire (Scotland) 10–6
2019 Scottish Open (Glasgow): Mark Selby (England) beat Jack Lisowski (England) 9–6
2020 European Masters (Dornbirn, Austria): Neil Robertson (Australia) beat Zhou Yuelong (China) 9–0
2020 German Masters (Berlin): Judd Trump (England) beat Neil Robertson (Australia) 9–6
2020 World Grand Prix (Cheltenham, England): Neil Roberson (Australia) beat Graeme Dott (Scotland) 10–8
2020 Welsh Open (Cardiff): Shaun Murphy (England) beat Kyren Wilson (England) 9–1
2020 Snooker Shootout (Watford): Michael Holt (England) beat Zhou Yuelong (China) 1–0
2020 Players Championship (Southport): Judd Trump (England) beat Yan Bingtao (China) 10–4
2020 Gibraltar Open: Judd Trump (England) beat Kyren Wilson (England) 4–3
2020 Tour Championship (Milton Keynes): Stephen Maguire (Scotland) beat Mark Allen (Northern Island) 10–6
World Snooker Championship (Sheffield): Ronnie O'Sullivan (England) beat Kyren Wilson (England) 18–8

SPEED SKATING

WORLD ALLROUND CHAMPIONSHIPS 2020
Hamar, Norway, 28 February–1 March

MEN
Gold: Patrick Roest (Netherlands); *Silver:* Sverre Lunde Pedersen (Norway); *Bronze:* Seitaro Ichinohe (Japan)
500m: Seitaro Ichinohe (Japan), 36.17sec
1500m: Patrick Roest (Netherlands), 1min 44.41sec
5000m: Patrick Roest (Netherlands), 6min 14.35sec
10,000m: Patrick Roest (Netherlands), 13min 02.45sec

WOMEN
Gold: Ireen Wust (Netherlands); *Silver:* Ivanie Blondin (Canada); *Bronze:* Antoinette de Jong (Netherlands)
500m: Karolina Bosiek (Poland), 38.76sec
1500m: Ireen Wust (Netherlands), 1min 53.89sec
3000m: Martina Sablikova (Czechia), 4min 01.89sec
5000m: Martina Sablikova (Czechia), 6min 53.94sec

EUROPEAN CHAMPIONSHIPS 2020
Heerenveen, Netherlands, 10–12 January

MEN
500m All-round: Pavel Kulizhnikov (Russia), 34.38sec
1000m All-round: Pavel Kulizhnikov (Russia), 1min 07.09sec
1500m All-round: Thomas Krol (Netherlands), 1min 43.67sec
5000m All-round: Patrick Roest (Netherlands), 6min 08.92sec
Team Pursuit: Netherlands, 3min 40.63sec
Team Sprint: Russia, 1min 18.92sec
Mass Start: Bart Swings (Belgium), 60pts

WOMEN
500m All-round: Olga Fatkulina (Russia), 37.40sec
1000m All-round: Jutta Leerdam (netherlands) 1min 13.67sec
1500m All-round: Ireen Wurst (Netherlands), 1min 54.88sec
3000m All-round: Esmee Visser (Netherlands), 3min 59.15sec
Team Pursuit: Netherlands, 2m 57.97sec
Team Sprint: Russia, 1min 26.17
Mass Start: Irene Schouten (Netherlands), 62pts

EUROPEAN SHORT TRACK CHAMPIONSHIPS 2020
Bedrecen, Hungry, 24–26 January

MEN
500m: Shaoang Liu (Hungary), 41.244sec
1000m: Shaoang Liu (Hungary), 1min 25.636sec
1500m: Shaolin Liu (Hungary), 2min 25.871sec
3000m: Semen Elistratov (Russia), 4min 57.674sec
5000m relay: Russia, 7min 06.884sec
Overall: Shaolin Liu (Hungary), 77pts

WOMEN
500m: Suzanne Schulting (Netherlands), 43.442sec
1000m: Suzanne Schulting (Netherlands), 1min 33.353sec
1500m: Suzanne Schulting (Netherlands), 2min 35.915sec
3000m: Ariana Fontana (Italy), 5min 46.150sec
3000m relay: Netherlands, 4min 12.877sec
Overall: Suzanne Schulting (Netherlands), 102pts

WORLD SHORT TRACK CHAMPIONSHIPS 2019
Sofia, Bulgaria, 8–10 March

MEN
500m: Hwang Dae Heon (South Korea), 42.490sec
1000m: Hyo Jun Lim (South Korea), 1min 26.468sec
1500m: Hyo Jun Lim (South Korea), 2min 31.632sec
3000m: Hyo Jun Lim (South Korea), 5min 00.998sec
5000m relay: South Korea, 7min 04.292sec
Overall: Hyo Jun Lim (South Korea), 102pts

WOMEN
500m: Lara van Ruijven (Netherlands), 43.267sec
1000m: Suzanne Schulting (Netherlands), 1min 28.986sec
1500m: Choi Min Jeong (South Korea), 2min 29.741sec
3000m: Suzanne Schulting (Netherlands), 5min 26.880sec
3000m relay: South Korea, 4min 13.904sec
Overall: Suzanne Schulting (Netherlands), 81pts

SQUASH

MEN
World Championships 2019–20: Tarek Momen (Egypt) beat
Paul Coll (New Zealand) 3–0
World Tour Finals 2019–20: Marwan El Shorbagy (Egypt)
beat Karim Abdel Gawad (Egypt) 3–0
European Individual Closed Championship 2019: Raphael Kandra
(Germany) beat Borja Golan (Spain) 3–2
British Open 2019: Mohamed El Shorbagy (Egypt) beat Ali
Farag (Egypt) 3–1
British National Championship 2020: James Willstrop (England)
beat Joel Makin (Wales) 3–1

WOMEN
World Championships 2019–20: Nour El Sherbini (Egypt) beat
Raneem El Weleily (Egypt) 3–1
World Tour Finals 2018–19: Raneem El Welily (Egypt) beat
Camille Serme (France) 3–2
European Individual Closed Championship 2019: Nele Gilis
(Belgium) beat Coline Aumard (France) 3–1
British Open 2019: Nour Gohar (Egypt) beat Camille Serme
(France) 3–0
British National Championship 2020: Sarah-Jane Perry
(England) beat Jasmine Hutton (England) 3–0

TABLE TENNIS

MEN'S WORLD CUP 2019
Chengdu, China, 29 November–1 December

Zhendong Fan (China) beat Tomokazu Harimoto (Japan)
4–2

WOMEN'S WORLD CUP 2019
Chengdu, China, 18–20 October

Liu Shiwen (China) beat Zhu Yuling (China) 4–2

WORLD CHAMPIONSHIPS 2019
Budapest, Hungary, 21–28 April
Men's Singles: Ma Long (China) beat Mattias Falk (Sweden)
4–1
Men's Doubles: Ma Long (China) and Wang Chuqin (China)
beat Ovidiu Ionescu (Romania) and Álvaro Robles (Spain)
4–1
Women's Singles: Ding Ning (China) beat Hyowon Suh (South
Korea) 4–1
Women's Doubles: Sun Yingsha (China) and Wang Manyu
(China) beat Hina Hayata (Japan) and Mima Ito (Japan)
4–2
Mixed Doubles: Xu Xin (China) and Liu Shiwen (China) beat
Maharu Yoshimura (Japan) and Kasumi Ishikawa (Japan)
4–1

ENGLISH NATIONAL CHAMPIONSHIPS 2020
Men's singles: Liam Pitchford beat Paul Drinkhall 4–2
Women's singles: Tin-Tin Ho beat Mari Baldwin 4–0

2019 EUROPEAN GAMES
Minsk, Belarus, June
Men's Singles: Gold – Timo Boll (Germany); Silver – Jonathan
Groth (Denmark); Bronze – Tomislav Pucar (Croatia)
Men's Team: Gold – Germany; Silver – Sweden; Bronze –
Portugal
Women's Singles: Gold – Yu Fu (Portugal); Silver – Han Ying
(Germany); Bronze – Ni Xialian (Luxembourg)
Women's Team: Gold – Germany; Silver – Romania; Bronze –
Poland
Mixed Doubles: Gold – Germany; Silver – Romania; Bronze –
France

TENNIS

WIMBLEDON CHAMPIONSHIPS 2019
Wimbledon, 24 June–14 July

Men's Singles: Novak Djokovic (Serbia) beat Roger Federer
(Switzerland) 7–6 (7–5), 1–6, 7–6 (7–4), 4–6, 13–12
(7–3)
Ladies' Singles: Sinoma Halep (Romania) beat Serena Williams
(USA) 6–2, 6–2
Men's Doubles: Juan Sebastián Cabal (Colombia) and Robert
Farah (Colombia) beat Nicolas Mahut (France) and
Édouard Roger-Vasselin (France) 6–7 (5–7), 7–6 (7–5),
7–6 (8–6), 6–7 (5–7), 6–3
Ladies' Doubles: Barbora Strycova (Czechia) and Su-wei Hsieh
(Taiwan) beat Gabriela Dabrowski (Canada) and Yifan Xu
(China) 6–2, 6–4
Mixed Doubles: Latisha Chan (Taiwan) and Ivan Dodig
(Croatia) beat Jalena Ostaoenko (Latvia) and Robert
Lindstedt (Sweden) 6–2, 6–3

AUSTRALIAN OPEN CHAMPIONSHIPS 2020
Melbourne, 14 January–2 February

Men's Singles: Novak Djokovic (Serbia) beat Dominic Thiem (Austria) 6–4, 4–6, 2–6, 6–3, 6–4

Women's Singles: Sofia Kenin (USA) beat Garbiñe Muguruza (Spain), 4–6, 6–2, 6–2

Men's Doubles: Joe Salisbury (Great Britain) and Rajeev Ram (USA) beat Luke Saville (Australia) and Max Purcell (Australia) 6–4, 6–2

Women's Doubles: Tímea Babos (Hungary) and Kristina Mladenovic (France) beat Hsieh Su-wei (Taiwan) and Barbora Strycova (Czechia) 6–2, 6–1

Mixed Doubles: Barbora Krejcikova (Czechia) and Nikola Mektic (Croatia) beat Bethanie Mattak-Sands (USA) and Jamie Murray (Great Britain) 5–7, 6–4 (10–1)

US OPEN CHAMPIONSHIPS 2020
New York, 31 August–13 September

Men's Singles: Dominic Thiem (Austria) beat Alexander Zverev (Germany) 4–6, 4–6, 6–4, 6–3, 7–6 (8–6)

Women's Singles: Naomi Osaka (Japan) beat Victoria Azarenka (Belarus) 1–6, 6–3, 6–3

Men's Doubles: Mate Pavic (Croatia) and Bruno Soares (Brazil) beat Nikola Mektic (Croatia) and Wesley Koolhof (Netherlands) 7–5, 6–3

Women's Doubles: Laura Siegemund (Germany) and Vera Zvonareva (Russia) beat Yifan Xu (China) and Nicole Melichar (USA) 6–4, 6–4

FRENCH OPEN CHAMPIONSHIPS 2020
Paris, 21 September–11 October

Men's Singles: Rafael Nadal (Spain) beat Novak Djokovic (Croatia) 6–0, 6–2, 7–5

Women's Singles: Igor Swiatek (Poland) beat Sofia Kenin (USA) 6–4, 6–1

Men's Doubles: Kevin Krawietz (Germany) and Andreas Mies (Germany) beat Mate Pavic (Croatia) and Bruno Soares (Brazil) 6–3, 7–5

Women's Doubles: Timea Babos (Hungary) and Kristina Mladenovic (France) beat Desirae Krawczyk (USA) and Alexa Guarachi (Chile) 6–4, 7–5

TEAM CHAMPIONSHIPS
Davis Cup final 2019: Spain beat Canada 2–0
Fed Cup final 2019: France beat Australia 3–2

SPORTS RECORDS

ATHLETICS WORLD RECORDS

As at November 2020

All the world records given below have been accepted by the International Amateur Athletic Federation. Fully automatic timing to 1/100th second is mandatory up to and including 400 metres. For distances up to and including 10,000 metres, records will be accepted to 1/100th second if timed automatically, and to 1/10th if hand timing is used.

MEN

TRACK EVENTS	hr	min	sec
100m			9.58
Usain Bolt (Jamaica), 2009			
200m			19.19
Usain Bolt (Jamaica), 2009			
400m			43.03
Wayde van Niekerk (South Africa), 2016			
800m		1	40.91
David Rudisha (Kenya), 2012			
1000m		2	11.96
Noah Ngeny (Kenya), 1999			
1500m		3	26.00
Hicham El Guerrouj (Morocco), 1998			
1 mile		3	43.13
Hicham El Guerrouj (Morocco), 1999			
2000m		4	44.79
Hicham El Guerrouj (Morocco), 1999			
3000m		7	20.67
Daniel Komen (Kenya), 1996			
5000m		12	35.36
Joshua Cheptegei (Uganda), 2020			
10,000m		26	17.53
Kenenisa Bekele (Ethiopia), 2005			
20,000m		56	26.00
Haile Gebrselassie (Ethiopia), 2007			
One Hour Race (21,330m)	1	0	0
Mo Farah (Great Britain), 2020			
25,000m	1	12	25.4
Moses Mosop (Kenya), 2011			
30,000m	1	26	47.4
Moses Mosop (Kenya), 2011			
Marathon	2	1	39
Eliud Kipchoge (Kenya), 2018			
110m Hurdles (0.84m)			12.80
Aries Merritt (USA), 2012			
400m Hurdles (0.76m)			46.78
Kevin Young (USA), 1992			
3000m Steeplechase		7	53.63
Saif Saaeed Shaheen (Qatar), 2004			

RELAYS		min	sec
4 x 100m			36.84
Jamaica, 2012			
4 x 200m		1	18.63
Jamaica, 2014			
4 x 400m		2	54.29
USA, 1993			
4 x 800m		7	2.43
Kenya, 2006			
4 x 1500m		14	22.22
Kenya, 2014			

FIELD EVENTS	m	ft	in
High Jump	2.45	8	0½
Javier Sotomayor (Cuba), 1993			
Pole Vault	6.18	20	3⅜
Armand Duplantis (Sweden), 2020			
Long Jump	8.95	29	4¼
Mike Powell (USA), 1991			
Triple Jump	18.29	60	0¼
Jonathan Edwards (Great Britain), 1995			
Shot	23.12	75	10¼
Randy Barnes (USA), 1990			
Discus	74.08	243	0
Jürgen Schult (GDR), 1986			
Hammer	86.74	284	7
Yuriy Sedykh (USSR), 1986			
Javelin	98.48	323	1
Jan Zelezny (Czechia), 1996			
Decathlon†			9,126pts
Kevin Mayer (France), 2018			

† Ten events comprising 100m, long jump, shot, high jump, 400m, 110m hurdles, discus, pole vault, javelin, 1500m

WALKING (TRACK)	hr	min	sec
20,000m	1	17	25.6
Bernardo Segura (Mexico), 1994			
30,000m	2	1	44.1
Maurizio Damilano (Italy), 1992			
50,000m	3	35	27.2
Yohann Diniz (France), 2011			

WOMEN

TRACK EVENTS	hr	min	sec
100m			10.49
Florence Griffith-Joyner (USA), 1988			
200m			21.34
Florence Griffith-Joyner (USA), 1988			
400m			47.6
Marita Koch (GDR), 1985			
800m		1	53.28
Jarmila Kratochvilova (Czechoslovakia), 1983			
1000m		2	28.98
Svetlana Masterkova (Russia), 1996			
1500m		3	50.07
Genzebe Dibaba (Ethiopia), 2015			
1 mile		4	12.33
Sifan Hassan (Netherlands), 2019			
2000m		5	23.75
Genzebe Dibaba (Ethiopia), 2017			
3000m		8	6.11
Wang Junxia (China), 1993			
5000m		14	6.62
Letesenbet Gidey (Ethiopia), 2020			
10,000m		29	17.45
Almaz Ayana (Ethiopia), 2016			
20,000m	1	5	26.6
Tegla Loroupe (Kenya), 2000			
One Hour Race (18,930m)	1	0	0
Sifan Hassan (Netherlands), 2020			
25,000m	1	27	5.9
Tegla Loroupe (Kenya), 2002			
30,000m	1	45	50
Tegla Loroupe (Kenya), 2003			
Marathon	2	14	4
Brigid Kosei (Kenya), 2019			
100m Hurdles (0.84m)			12.2
Kendra Harrison (USA), 2016			

400m Hurdles (0.76m)		52.16
Dalilah Muhammad (USA), 2020		
3000m Steeplechase	8	44.32
Beatrice Chepkoech (Kenya), 2018		

RELAYS	min	sec
4 x 100m		40.82
USA, 2012		
4 x 200m	1	27.46
USA, 2000		
4 x 400m	3	15.17
USSR, 1988		
4 x 800m	7	50.17
USSR, 1984		
4 x 1500m	16	33.58
Kenya, 2014		

FIELD EVENTS	m	ft	in
High Jump	2.09	6	10¼
Stefka Kostadinova (Bulgaria), 1987			
Pole Vault	5.06	16	7¼
Yelena Isinbaeva (Russia), 2009			
Long Jump	7.52	24	8¼
Galina Chistyakova (USSR), 1988			
Triple Jump	15.5	50	10¼
Inessa Kravets (Ukraine), 1995			
Shot	22.63	74	3
Natalya Lisovskaya (USSR), 1987			
Discus	76.8	252	0
Gabriele Reinsch (GDR), 1988			
Hammer	82.98	272	3
Anita Wlodarczyk (Poland), 2016			
Javelin	72.28	237	2
Barbora Spotakova (Czechia), 2008			
Decathlon†			8,358pts
Austra Skujyte (Lithuania), 2005			

† Ten events comprising 100m, long jump, shot, high jump, 400m, 110m hurdles, discus, pole vault, javelin, 1500m

WALKING (TRACK)	hr	min	sec
10,000m		41	56.23
Nadezhda Ryashkina (USSR), 1990			
20,000m	1	26	52.3
Olimpiada Ivanova (Russia), 2001			

ATHLETICS NATIONAL (UK) RECORDS

As at November 2020
Records set anywhere by athletes eligible to represent Great Britain and Northern Ireland.

MEN

TRACK EVENTS	hr	min	sec
100m			9.87
Linford Christie, 1993			
200m			19.87
John Regis, 1994			
400m			44.36
Iwan Thomas, 1997			
800m		1	41.73
Sebastian Coe, 1981			
1000m		2	12.18
Sebastian Coe, 1981			
1500m		3	28.81
Mo Farah, 2013			
1 mile		3	46.32
Steve Cram, 1985			
2000m		4	51.39
Steve Cram, 1985			
3000m		7	32.62
Mo Farah, 2016			
5000m		12	53.11

Mo Farah, 2011			
10,000m		26	46.57
Mo Farah, 2011			
20,000m		57	28.7
Carl Thackery, 1990			
One Hour Race (21,330m)	1	0	0
Mo Farah, 2020			
25,000m	1	15	22.6
Ron Hill, 1965			
30,000m	1	31	30.4
Jim Alder, 1970			
Marathon	2	7	13.0
Steve Jones, 1985			
3000m Steeplechase		8	7.96
Mark Rowland, 1988			
110m Hurdles			12.91
Colin Jackson, 1993			
400m Hurdles			47.82
Kriss Akabusi, 1992			

RELAYS	min	sec
4 x 100m		37.36
GB team, 2019		
4 x 200m	1	21.29
GB team, 1989		
4 x 400m	2	56.6
GB team, 1996		
4 x 800m	7	3.89
GB team, 1982		

FIELD EVENTS	m	ft	in
High Jump	2.37	7	9¼
Steve Smith, 1993			
Robbie Grabarz, 2012			
Pole Vault	5.85	19	2⅜
Harry Coppell, 2020			
Long Jump	8.51	27	11
Greg Rutherford, 2014			
Triple Jump	18.29	60	0¼
Jonathan Edwards, 1995			
Shot	21.92	71	11
Carl Myerscough, 2003			
Discus	68.24	223	10
Lawrence Okoye, 2012			
Hammer	80.26	263	3
Nick Miller, 2018			
Javelin	91.46	300	1
Steve Backley, 1992			
Decathlon			8,847pts
Daley Thompson, 1984			

WALKING (TRACK)	hr	min	sec
20,000m	1	23	26.5
Ian McCombie, 1990			
30,000m	2	11	54
Christopher Maddocks, 1989			
50,000m	4	5	44.6
Paul Blagg, 1990			
Two Hour Walk (27,262m)	2	0	0
Christopher Maddocks, 1989			

WOMEN

TRACK EVENTS	min	sec
100m		10.83
Dina Asher-Smith, 2019		
200m		21.88
Dina Asher-Smith, 2019		
400m		49.41
Christine Ohuruogu, 2013		
800m	1	56.21
Kelly Holmes, 1995		
1500m	3	55.22

		min	sec
1 mile Laura Muir, 2016		4	17.57
3000m Zola Budd, 1985		8	22.2
5000m Paula Radcliffe, 2002		14	29.11
10,000m Paula Radcliffe, 2004		30	1.09
Marathon Paula Radcliffe, 2002	2	15	25
100m Hurdles Paula Radcliffe, 2003			12.51
400m Hurdles Tiffany Porter, 2014			52.74
3000m Steeplechase Sally Gunnell, 1993		9	24.24
Barbara Parker, 2012			

RELAYS		min	sec
4 x 100m GB team, 2016			41.77
4 x 200m GB team, 2014		1	29.61
4 x 400m GB team, 2007		3	20.04
4 x 800m GB team, 2013		8	13.46

FIELD EVENTS	m	ft	in
High Jump Katarina Johnson-Thompson, 2016	1.98	6	6
Pole Vault Holly Bradshaw, 2017	4.81	00	6
Long Jump Shara Proctor, 2015	7.07	23	2
Triple Jump Ashia Hansen, 1997	15.15	49	8½
Shot Judy Oakes, 1988	19.36	63	6¼
Discus Margaret Ritchie, 1981	67.48	221	5
Hammer Sophie Hitchon, 2016	74.54	244	6½
Javelin Goldie Sayers, 2012	66.17	217	1
Heptathlon Katarina Johnson-Thompson, 2019	6,981pts		

SWIMMING WORLD RECORDS

50m-pool. As at November 2020

MEN

		min	sec
50m Freestyle Cesar Cielo Filho (Brazil), 2009			20.91
100m Freestyle Cesar Cielo Filho (Brazil), 2009			46.91
200m Freestyle Paul Biedermann (Germany), 2009		1	42.00
400m Freestyle Paul Biedermann (Germany), 2009		3	40.07
800m Freestyle Zhang Lin (China), 2009		7	32.12
1500m Freestyle Sun Yang (China), 2012		14	31.02
50m Breaststroke Adam Peaty (Great Britain), 2017			25.95
100m Breaststroke Adam Peaty (Great Britain), 2019			56.88
200m Breaststroke Anton Chupkov (Russia), 2019		2	6.12
50m Butterfly Andriy Govorov (Ukraine), 2018			22.27
100m Butterfly Caeleb Dressel (USA), 2019			49.50
200m Butterfly Kristof Milak (Hungary), 2019		1	50.73
50m Backstroke Kliment Kolesnikov (Russia), 2018			24.00
100m Backstroke Ryan Murphy (USA), 2016			51.85
200m Backstroke Aaron Peirsol (USA), 2009		1	51.92
200m Medley Ryan Lochte (USA), 2011		1	54.00
400m Medley Michael Phelps (USA), 2008		4	3.84
4 x 100m Freestyle relay USA, 2008		3	8.24
4 x 200m Freestyle relay USA, 2009		6	58.55
4 x 100m Medley relay USA, 2009		3	27.28

WOMEN

		min	sec
50m Freestyle Sarah Sjostrom (Sweden), 2017			23.67
100m Freestyle Sarah Sjostrom (Sweden), 2017			51.71
200m Freestyle Federica Pellegrini (Italy), 2009		1	52.98
400m Freestyle Katie Ledecky (USA), 2016		3	56.46
800m Freestyle Katie Ledecky (USA), 2016		8	4.79
1500m Freestyle Katie Ledecky (USA), 2018		15	20.48
50m Breaststroke Lilly King (USA), 2017			29.40
100m Breaststroke Lilly King (USA), 2017		1	4.13
200m Breaststroke Rikke Moeller-Pedersen (Denmark), 2013		2	19.11
50m Butterfly Sarah Sjostrom (Sweden), 2014			24.43
100m Butterfly Sarah Sjostrom (Sweden), 2016			55.48
200m Butterfly Liu Zige (China), 2009		2	1.81
50m Backstroke Liu Xiang (China), 2018			26.98
100m Backstroke Regan Smith (USA), 2019			57.57
200m Backstroke Regan Smith (USA), 2019		2	3.35
200m Medley Katinka Hosszu (Hungary), 2015		2	6.12
400m Medley Katinka Hosszu (Hungary), 2016		4	26.36
4 x 100m Freestyle relay Australia, 2018		3	30.05
4 x 200m Freestyle relay Australia, 2019		7	41.51
4 x 100m Medley relay USA, 2019		3	50.40

TIME AND SPACE

ASTRONOMY 2021

The following pages give astronomical data for each month of the year 2021. There are three pages of data for each month. All data are given for 0h Greenwich Mean Time (GMT), ie at the midnight at the beginning of the day named. This applies also to data for the months when British Summer Time is in operation (for dates, *see* below).

The astronomical data are given in a form suitable for observation with the naked eye, binoculars or with a small telescope. These data do not attempt to replace the *Astronomical Almanac* for professional astronomers. A fuller explanation of how to use the astronomical data is given after the data for the months.

CALENDAR FOR EACH MONTH

The calendar for each month comprises dates of general interest plus the dates of birth or death of well-known people. For key religious, civil and legal dates *see* page 9. For details of flag-flying days *see* page 23 and 24–5. For public The Year 2021.

Fuller explanations of the various calendars can be found under Time Measurement and Calendars.

The zodiacal signs through which the Sun is passing each month are illustrated.

JULIAN DATE

Julian dates are a continuous count of days since the beginning of the Julian Period and is used primarily by astronomers for calculating elapsed days between two events. Julian Day Number 0 is assigned to the day starting at noon on Monday, 1 January 4713 BCE as it precedes any dates in recorded history. The Julian date (JD) of any instant is the Julian day number plus the fraction of a day since the preceding noon in Universal Time. Julian dates are expressed as a Julian day number with a decimal fraction added.

The Julian date on 2021 January 0.0 is 2459214.5. To find the Julian date for any other date in 2021 (at 0h GMT), add the day of the year number on the extreme right of the calendar for each month to the Julian date for 0.0 given above.

BRITISH SUMMER TIME

British Summer Time is the legal time for general purposes during the period in which it is in operation (*see also* Time, British Summer Time). During this period, clocks are kept one hour ahead of Greenwich Mean Time. The hour of changeover is 01h Greenwich Mean Time. The duration of Summer Time in 2021 is from 28 March 01h GMT to 31 October 01h GMT.

SEASONS

The seasons are defined astronomically as follows:

Spring from the vernal equinox to the summer solstice
Summer from the summer solstice to the autumnal equinox
Autumn from the autumnal equinox to the winter solstice
Winter from the winter solstice to the vernal equinox

The times when the seasons start in 2021 (to the nearest hour) are:

Northern Hemisphere
Vernal Equinox	March 20d 10h GMT
Summer Solstice	June 21d 04h GMT
Autumnal Equinox	September 22d 19h GMT
Winter Solstice	December 21d 16h GMT

Southern Hemisphere
Autumnal Equinox	March 20d 10h GMT
Winter Solstice	June 21d 04h GMT
Vernal Equinox	September 22d 19h GMT
Summer Solstice	December 21d 16h GMT

The longest day of the year, measured from sunrise to sunset, is at the summer solstice. The longest day in the UK will fall on 21 June in 2021.

The shortest day of the year is at the winter solstice. The shortest day in the UK will fall on 21 December in 2021.

The equinox is the point at which day and night are of equal length all over the world.

In popular parlance, the seasons in the northern hemisphere comprise the following months:

Spring	March, April, May
Summer	June, July, August
Autumn	September, October, November
Winter	December, January, February

The March equinox can fall as early as 19 March but this has not happened since 1796 and it will not happen again until 2044. This equinox in 2007 was on 21 March, however in 2008 it occurred on 20 March and will not revert to 21 March again until 2102.

In 2008 the June solstice occurred on 20 June, the first time since 1897. The June solstice in 1975 was on 22 June, but it will not occur on this date again until 2203.

January 2021

FIRST MONTH, 31 DAYS. *Janus,* god of the portal, facing two ways, past and future

1	*Friday*	Euro notes and coins entered circulation in twelve European Union countries 2002	day 1
2	*Saturday*	In Paris, Louis Daguerre took the first photograph of the moon 1839	2
3	*Sunday*	General Washington's revolutionary forces defeated the British at the battle of Princeton 1777	3
4	*Monday*	Sir Isaac Newton, physicist and mathematician who discovered the law of gravitation *b.* 1642	week 1 day 4
5	*Tuesday*	The German Worker's Party, predecessor of the Nazi party, is founded in Munich 1919	5
6	*Wednesday*	Demonstration by Samuel Morse of the first electric telegraph system 1838	6
7	*Thursday*	The inventor Henry Mill obtains a patent for the first typewriter 1714	7
8	*Friday*	Stephen Hawking *b.* 1942. Galileo Galilei *d.* 1642	8
9	*Saturday*	280,000 coal miners began a seven-week strike against the government 1972	9
10	*Sunday*	The Metropolitan line, the world's first underground railway, opens to passengers in London 1863	10
11	*Monday*	Insulin was first administered to a diabetic patient in Canada 1922	week 2 day 11
12	*Tuesday*	The Royal Aeronautical Society of Great Britain was founded 1866	12
13	*Wednesday*	The National Geographic Society is founded in Washington DC 1888	13
14	*Thursday*	The American War of Independence ended 1784	14
15	*Friday*	The British Museum opened to the public in Montagu House, Bloomsbury, London 1759	15
16	*Saturday*	Prohibition, the attempt to ban alcohol sale and consumption, began in the USA 1920	16
17	*Sunday*	Benny Goodman and his orchestra performed the first jazz concert at Carnegie Hall 1938	17
18	*Monday*	Airbus' 840-passenger A380, the world's biggest passenger jet, was unveiled in France 2005	week 3 day 18
19	*Tuesday*	The US senate votes against participation in the League of Nations 1920	19
20	*Wednesday*	The House of Commons assembled for the first time 1265	20
21	*Thursday*	Concorde's first commercial flights take off simultaneously from London and Paris 1976	21
22	*Friday*	Roberta Bondar becomes the first Canadian woman in space 1992	22
23	*Saturday*	A disguised King Henry VIII jousts in Richmond and is applauded before revealing his identity 1510	23
24	*Sunday*	The Macintosh 128K, the first computer built by Apple Macintosh, was released 1984	24
25	*Monday*	Karel Capek's play R.U.R., which introduced the word 'robot', premiered in Prague 1921	week 4 day 25
26	*Tuesday*	The Republic of India was proclaimed with Rajendra Prasad as president 1950	26
27	*Wednesday*	Soviet troops liberated the Auschwitz concentration camp 1945	27
28	*Thursday*	Jane Austen's romantic novel Pride and Prejudice is published 1813	28
29	*Friday*	Edgar Allan Poe's poem 'The Raven' was published in the New York Evening Mirror 1845	29
30	*Saturday*	The Beatles gave their last public performance on top of their London recording studio 1969	30
31	*Sunday*	The 100th British soldier was killed in the Iraq conflict 2006	31

ASTRONOMICAL PHENOMENA

d	*h*	
2	14	Earth at perihelion (0.98326 AU)
2	22	Regulus 4.7°S of the Moon
3	15	Quadrantid meteor shower
6	10	Last Quarter Moon
10	05	Mercury 1.6°S of Saturn
11	11	Mercury 1.5°S of Jupiter
11	20	Venus 1.5°N of the Moon
13	05	New Moon
13	21	Saturn 3.2°N of the Moon
14	01	Jupiter 3.3°N of the Moon
14	08	Mercury 2.3°N of the Moon
14	-	Pluto solar conjunction
20	PM	Mars 1.6° from Uranus
20	21	First Quarter Moon
20	-	Sun crosses into Capricornus
21	05	Mars 5.0°N of the Moon
24	-	Mercury at greatest elongation (18° 34' E)
24	-	Saturn solar conjunction
28	19	Full Moon
28	-	Jupiter solar conjunction

CONSTELLATIONS

The following constellations are visible at midnight throughout the month:
Draco (below the Pole), Ursa Minor (below the Pole), Camelopardalis, Perseus, Auriga, Taurus, Orion, Eridanus and Lepus

PHASES OF THE MOON

Phase, Apsides and Node	*d*	*h*	*m*
◗ Last Quarter	6	9	37
● New Moon	13	5	0
◖ First Quarter	20	21	2
○ Full Moon	28	19	16
Perigee (367,387 km)	9	15	37
Apogee (404,360 km)	21	13	11

SUNRISE AND SUNSET

d	London 0° 05' / 51° 30'		Bristol 2° 35' / 51° 28'		Birmingham 1° 55' / 52° 28'		Manchester 2° 15' / 53° 28'		Newcastle 1° 37' / 54° 59'		Glasgow 4° 14' / 55° 52'		Belfast 5° 56' / 54° 35'	
	h m	h m	h m	h m	h m	h m	h m	h m	h m	h m	h m	h m	h m	h m
1	8 06	16 02	8 16	16 12	8 18	16 05	8 25	16 01	8 31	15 49	8 47	15 54	8 46	16 09
2	8 06	16 03	8 16	16 14	8 18	16 06	8 25	16 02	8 31	15 51	8 47	15 56	8 46	16 10
3	8 06	16 05	8 15	16 15	8 18	16 07	8 24	16 03	8 31	15 52	8 47	15 57	8 45	16 11
4	8 05	16 06	8 15	16 16	8 17	16 08	8 24	16 04	8 30	15 53	8 46	15 58	8 45	16 13
5	8 05	16 07	8 15	16 17	8 17	16 09	8 24	16 06	8 30	15 55	8 46	16 00	8 45	16 14
6	8 05	16 08	8 14	16 18	8 17	16 11	8 23	16 07	8 29	15 56	8 45	16 01	8 44	16 16
7	8 04	16 09	8 14	16 20	8 16	16 12	8 23	16 08	8 29	15 57	8 44	16 03	8 44	16 17
8	8 04	16 11	8 14	16 21	8 16	16 13	8 22	16 10	8 28	15 59	8 44	16 04	8 43	16 18
9	8 03	16 12	8 13	16 22	8 15	16 15	8 22	16 11	8 27	16 00	8 43	16 06	8 42	16 20
10	8 03	16 14	8 13	16 24	8 15	16 16	8 21	16 13	8 27	16 02	8 42	16 07	8 42	16 22
11	8 02	16 15	8 12	16 25	8 14	16 18	8 20	16 14	8 26	16 04	8 41	16 09	8 41	16 23
12	8 01	16 16	8 11	16 27	8 13	16 19	8 19	16 16	8 25	16 05	8 40	16 11	8 40	16 25
13	8 01	16 18	8 10	16 28	8 12	16 21	8 19	16 17	8 24	16 07	8 39	16 13	8 39	16 26
14	8 00	16 19	8 10	16 30	8 12	16 22	8 18	16 19	8 23	16 09	8 38	16 14	8 38	16 28
15	7 59	16 21	8 09	16 31	8 11	16 24	8 17	16 21	8 22	16 11	8 37	16 16	8 37	16 30
16	7 58	16 23	8 08	16 33	8 10	16 26	8 16	16 22	8 21	16 12	8 36	16 18	8 36	16 32
17	7 57	16 24	8 07	16 34	8 09	16 27	8 15	16 24	8 20	16 14	8 35	16 20	8 35	16 33
18	7 56	16 26	8 06	16 36	8 08	16 29	8 14	16 26	8 18	16 16	8 33	16 22	8 34	16 35
19	7 55	16 27	8 05	16 38	8 07	16 31	8 12	16 28	8 17	16 18	8 32	16 24	8 32	16 37
20	7 54	16 29	8 04	16 39	8 06	16 32	8 11	16 29	8 16	16 20	8 31	16 26	8 31	16 39
21	7 53	16 31	8 03	16 41	8 04	16 34	8 10	16 31	8 14	16 22	8 29	16 28	8 30	16 41
22	7 52	16 32	8 02	16 43	8 03	16 36	8 09	16 33	8 13	16 24	8 28	16 30	8 28	16 43
23	7 51	16 34	8 01	16 44	8 02	16 38	8 07	16 35	8 12	16 26	8 26	16 32	8 27	16 45
24	7 50	16 36	7 59	16 46	8 01	16 40	8 06	16 37	8 10	16 28	8 25	16 34	8 26	16 47
25	7 48	16 38	7 58	16 48	7 59	16 41	8 05	16 39	8 09	16 30	8 23	16 36	8 24	16 49
26	7 47	16 39	7 57	16 50	7 58	16 43	8 03	16 41	8 07	16 32	8 22	16 38	8 23	16 51
27	7 46	16 41	7 56	16 51	7 57	16 45	8 02	16 42	8 05	16 34	8 20	16 40	8 21	16 53
28	7 44	16 43	7 54	16 53	7 55	16 47	8 00	16 44	8 04	16 36	8 18	16 42	8 19	16 55
29	7 43	16 45	7 53	16 55	7 54	16 49	7 59	16 46	8 02	16 38	8 16	16 45	8 18	16 57
30	7 41	16 47	7 51	16 57	7 52	16 51	7 57	16 48	8 00	16 40	8 15	16 47	8 16	16 59
31	7 40	16 48	7 50	16 58	7 51	16 52	7 55	16 50	7 59	16 42	8 13	16 49	8 14	17 01

THE MOON

Day	Diam '	Phase %	Age d	Rise 52° h m	Rise 56° h m	Transit h m	Set 52° h m	Set 56° h m
1	31.0	96	16.8	18 21	18 0	1 44	10 7	10 31
2	31.2	91	17.8	19 39	19 22	2 37	10 37	10 54
3	31.4	84	18.8	21 0	20 48	3 29	10 59	11 13
4	31.6	76	19.8	22 20	22 14	4 18	11 19	11 27
5	31.8	66	20.8	23 41	23 41	5 7	11 37	11 39
6	32.0	55	21.8	-	-	5 55	11 53	11 51
7	32.2	43	22.8	1 3	1 8	6 44	12 11	12 4
8	32.4	32	23.8	2 27	2 38	7 36	12 31	12 19
9	32.6	22	24.8	3 52	4 9	8 30	12 57	12 38
10	32.6	13	25.8	5 18	5 41	9 27	13 29	13 6
11	32.4	6	26.8	6 38	7 5	10 27	14 14	13 45
12	32.2	2	27.8	7 46	8 16	11 29	15 12	14 42
13	32.0	0	28.8	8 40	9 7	12 28	16 21	15 55
14	31.6	1	0.3	9 19	9 42	13 25	17 38	17 16
15	31.2	4	1.3	9 48	10 5	14 17	18 56	18 40
16	30.8	9	2.3	10 10	10 23	15 5	20 12	20 2
17	30.4	16	3.3	10 28	10 35	15 50	21 25	21 19
18	30.2	24	4.3	10 43	10 46	16 32	22 35	22 34
19	29.8	33	5.3	10 57	10 56	17 13	23 44	23 47
20	29.6	42	6.3	11 11	11 5	17 54	-	-
21	29.6	51	7.3	11 25	11 16	18 35	0 52	1 0
22	29.6	61	8.3	11 42	11 28	19 19	2 1	2 14
23	29.6	70	9.3	12 4	11 45	20 5	3 11	3 29
24	29.8	78	10.3	12 30	12 7	20 53	4 20	4 43
25	30.0	85	11.3	13 6	12 38	21 45	5 28	5 54
26	30.4	92	12.3	13 53	13 23	22 39	6 30	6 58
27	30.8	96	13.3	14 53	14 24	23 34	7 23	7 51
28	31.0	99	14.3	16 5	15 39	-	8 5	8 31
29	31.4	100	15.3	17 22	17 4	0 29	8 38	8 57
30	31.6	98	16.3	18 44	18 31	1 22	9 3	9 19
31	32	94	17.3	20 7	20 0	2 14	9 25	9 34

THE PLANETS

MERCURY

Day	R.A.			Dec.	Mag.	Diam.	Phase	Rise			Transit			Set		
	h	m	s	°		"	%	h	m	s	h	m	s	h	m	s
1	19	18	2	-24.3	-1.0	4.8	98	9	1	59	12	34	34	16	7	25
6	19	53	18	-23.1	-0.9	5.0	95	9	7	16	12	50	3	16	33	19
11	20	27	41	-21.1	-0.9	5.3	90	9	7	20	13	4	31	17	2	22
16	20	59	55	-18.6	-0.9	5.8	82	9	2	0	13	16	37	17	32	1
21	21	27	43	-15.8	-0.8	6.4	68	8	50	43	13	23	50	17	57	40
26	21	47	1	-12.9	-0.3	7.4	47	8	32	20	13	21	53	18	11	45
31	21	52	22	-11.0	+0.8	8.6	23	8	5	36	13	5	20	18	4	34

VENUS

Day	R.A.			Dec.	Mag.	Diam.	Phase	Rise			Transit			Set		
	h	m	s	°		"	%	h	m	s	h	m	s	h	m	s
1	17	18	31	-22.4	-3.9	11.5	94	6	47	51	10	34	32	14	21	2
6	17	45	36	-22.9	-3.9	11.4	95	6	59	2	10	41	55	14	24	41
11	18	12	50	-23.2	-3.9	11.3	95	7	8	12	10	49	27	14	30	41
16	18	40	7	-23.1	-3.9	11.1	96	7	15	8	10	57	1	14	38	57
21	19	7	19	-22.7	-3.9	11.0	97	7	19	44	11	4	29	14	49	22
26	19	34	17	-22.1	-3.9	11.0	97	7	22	0	11	11	44	15	1	42
31	20	0	57	-21.1	-3.9	10.9	98	7	22	1	11	18	40	15	15	37

MARS

Day	R.A.			Dec.	Mag.	Diam.	Rise			Transit			Set		
	h	m	s	°		"	h	m	s	h	m	s	h	m	s
1	1	40	19	+11.3	-0.2	10.4	11	47	9	18	55	57	2	5	7
6	1	48	38	+12.2	-0.1	9.9	11	30	29	18	44	27	1	59	0
11	1	57	26	+13.1	0.0	9.5	11	14	8	18	33	27	1	53	31
16	2	6	40	+14.0	+0.1	9.0	10	58	7	18	22	54	1	48	36
21	2	16	19	+14.9	+0.2	8.6	10	42	25	18	12	46	1	44	11
26	2	26	20	+15.8	+0.3	8.3	10	27	2	18	3	0	1	40	11
31	2	36	41	+16.7	+0.4	7.9	10	11	59	17	53	36	1	36	32

JUPITER

Day	R.A.			Dec.	Mag.	Diam.	Rise			Transit			Set		
	h	m	s	°		"	h	m	s	h	m	s	h	m	s
1	20	20	47	-20.0	-2.0	32.9	9	31	17	13	35	15	17	39	22
6	20	25	32	-19.7	-1.9	32.7	9	14	32	13	20	19	17	26	16
11	20	30	20	-19.5	-1.9	32.6	8	57	46	13	5	27	17	13	16
16	20	35	10	-19.2	-1.9	32.5	8	40	58	12	50	36	17	0	22
21	20	40	0	-18.9	-1.9	32.5	8	24	8	12	35	46	16	47	31
26	20	44	51	-18.6	-1.9	32.5	8	7	16	12	20	56	16	34	43
31	20	49	41	-18.3	-2.0	32.5	7	50	21	12	6	6	16	21	57

Diam. = Equatorial. Polar Diam. is 94% of Equatorial Diam.

SATURN

Day	R.A.			Dec.	Mag.	Diam.	Rise			Transit			Set		
	h	m	s	°		"	h	m	s	h	m	s	h	m	s
1	20	15	53	-20.2	+0.6	15.2	9	27	29	13	30	15	17	33	9
6	20	18	16	-20.0	+0.6	15.2	9	9	21	13	12	58	17	16	44
11	20	20	42	-19.9	+0.6	15.2	8	51	12	12	55	44	17	0	23
16	20	23	9	-19.8	+0.6	15.2	8	33	4	12	38	31	16	44	4
21	20	25	36	-19.7	+0.6	15.2	8	14	56	12	21	18	16	27	47
26	20	28	4	-19.5	+0.6	15.2	7	56	47	12	4	6	16	11	31
31	20	30	31	-19.4	+0.6	15.2	7	38	37	11	46	53	15	55	15

Diam. = Equatorial. Polar Diam. is 90% of Equatorial Diam.
Rings – major axis 34", minor axis 12", Tilt 20°

URANUS

Day	R.A.			Dec.	Mag.	Diam.	Rise			Transit			Set		
	h	m	s	°		"	h	m	s	h	m	s	h	m	s
1	2	18	28	+13.4	+5.7	3.6	12	12	30	19	31	49	2	55	2
6	2	18	17	+13.3	+5.7	3.6	11	52	44	19	11	58	2	35	7
11	2	18	11	+13.3	+5.7	3.6	11	33	1	18	52	13	2	15	19
16	2	18	10	+13.3	+5.7	3.6	11	13	20	18	32	32	1	55	39
21	2	18	14	+13.3	+5.8	3.6	10	53	41	18	12	54	1	36	4
26	2	18	23	+13.4	+5.8	3.6	10	34	5	17	53	26	1	16	42
31	2	18	38	+13.4	+5.8	3.6	10	14	31	17	34	1	0	57	25

NEPTUNE

Day	R.A.			Dec.	Mag.	Diam.	Rise			Transit			Set		
	h	m	s	°		"	h	m	s	h	m	s	h	m	s
1	23	19	20	-5.6	+7.9	2.3	11	0	53	16	3	9	22	5	25
6	23	19	42	-5.5	+7.9	2.2	10	41	22	16	13	51	21	46	21
11	23	20	6	-5.5	+7.9	2.2	10	21	52	15	54	36	21	27	21
16	23	20	34	-5.4	+7.9	2.2	10	2	23	15	35	23	21	8	25
21	23	21	3	-5.4	+7.9	2.2	9	42	54	15	16	13	20	49	33
26	23	21	35	-5.3	+7.9	2.2	9	23	27	14	57	6	20	30	44
31	23	22	9	-5.2	+7.9	2.2	9	4	1	14	38	0	20	11	59

THE NIGHT SKY

Mercury moves into the evening sky following its superior conjunction last December but is not favourably placed for viewing until towards the end of the second week of January.

By the time it becomes visible, the innermost planet fits within a 5° circle with Jupiter and Saturn on the evening of the 9th. All are low in the southwest though, so find an unobstructed horizon in that direction.

Mercury closes to within 1½° of Saturn on the 10th and is the same distance from brighter Jupiter the next evening. The one-day old moon lies near the trio on the 14th and binoculars will help you follow the drama in the dusk.

Mercury's altitude then improves so that it does not set until nearly 1½ hours after the Sun mid-month. It reaches greatest elongation east on the 24th when Mercury climbs to almost 8° above the local horizon towards the end of civil twilight. Thereafter, it slides a little lower each evening, but remains reasonably easy pick out as a magnitude -0.7 spark.

Venus rises 1½ hours before the Sun at the beginning of January, but that interval rapidly diminishes, and we lose sight of the planet soon after the 21st as it is overwhelmed by the morning glow. We then do not see Venus again until April. The Moon is only two days before new when it is near the brilliant morning star on the 11th.

Mars continues to recede from Earth and dims from magnitude -0.2 to 0.4. The planet remains visible until the early hours though and does not set until the early hours all month. Mars crosses into Aries from Pisces on the 5th.

The Red Planet lies in the same binocular field as pea green *Uranus* (magnitude 5.7) during the second half of January, offering an ideal opportunity to spy the distant ice giant. The two are closest on the 20th when they are 1½° apart. The just past first quarter moon is in the area on the next night.

Jupiter (magnitude -1.9) is a bright evening object in Capricornus and can be found low in the southwest, setting about 100 minutes after the Sun at the beginning of the year.

Jupiter and Saturn are separated by 1° on January 1st following their recent Great Conjunction, but that gap widens daily due to Jupiter's more rapid motion on the celestial sphere. Both soon disappear into the Sun's glare, with Jupiter lost to view near the end of January as it reaches solar conjunction on the 29th.

Saturn (magnitude 0.6) can also be found in Capricornus but slips into the solar glare around mid-month and is at solar conjunction on the 24th.

The first of the major annual meteor showers are the Quadrantids that peak during the early hours of January 3rd. The light of the waning gibbous moon interferes somewhat this year.

February 2021

SECOND MONTH, 28 or 29 DAYS. *Februa*, Roman festival of Purification

1	*Monday*	The space shuttle *Columbia* breaks up as it re-enters the Earth's atmosphere 2003	week 5 day 32
2	*Tuesday*	The US supreme court convened for the first time 1790	33
3	*Wednesday*	Johannes Gutenberg, German publisher who invented movable type printing d. 1468	34
4	*Thursday*	Slavery was banned in the French Republic 1794	35
5	*Friday*	Sweet rationing ended in Great Britain 1953	36
6	*Saturday*	Alan Shepard became the first man to hit a golf ball on the Moon 1971	37
7	*Sunday*	The EU became official with the signing of the Maastricht Treaty 1991	38
8	*Monday*	The astronaut crew of the final Skylab mission returned to Earth 1974	week 6 day 39
9	*Tuesday*	Actor Joanne Woodward received the first star on the Hollywood Walk of Fame 1960	40
10	*Wednesday*	Wedding of Queen Victoria and Prince Albert at St James's Palace 1840	41
11	*Thursday*	Voltaire received 300 visitors in Paris the day after returning from 28 years in exile 1778	42
12	*Friday*	Lady Jane Grey was beheaded 1554	43
13	*Saturday*	The last 'Peanuts' comic strip appeared in newspapers, the day after Charles M. Schulz died 2000	44
14	*Sunday*	New York hosted the 'Boz' Ball, a lavish party in honour of Charles Dickens 1842	45
15	*Monday*	Galileo Galilei, mathematician and astronomer, the first man to use a telescope to study the skies b. 1564	week 7 day 46
16	*Tueday*	Fidel Castro became prime minister of Cuba 1959	47
17	*Wednesday*	The Blaine Act ends 13 years of prohibition in the USA 1933	48
18	*Thursday*	Mark Twain's *The Adventures of Huckleberry Finn* was first published 1885	49
19	*Friday*	The phonograph was patented by Thomas Edison 1878	50
20	*Saturday*	The New York Metropolitan Museum of Art opened 1872	51
21	*Sunday*	The Battle of Verdun, the longest battle of the First World War, began 1916	52
22	*Monday*	The American short story writer Raymond Chandler's *Will You Please Be Quiet, Please?* is published 1976	week 8 day 53
23	*Tuesday*	Passenger railway service linking Perth with Sydney (3,961km) opened 1970	54
24	*Wednesday*	Vladimir Putin dismissed the entire Russian government 2004	55
25	*Thursday*	Sylvia Plath and Ted Hughes first met at a party in Cambridge 1956	56
26	*Friday*	First factory for production of Volkswagen *Beetle*, the 'people's car', is opened by Adolf Hitler 1936	57
27	*Saturday*	Nigeria elected a civilian president, ending 15 years of military rule 1999	58
28	*Sunday*	James Watson and Francis Crick announced their discovery of the structure of DNA 1953	59

ASTRONOMICAL PHENOMENA

d	h	
1	-	Mars eastern quadrature
4	17	Last Quarter Moon
6	5	Venus 0.4°S of Saturn
8	-	Mercury inferior conjunction
10	21	Jupiter 3.7°N of the Moon
10	11	Saturn 3.5°N of the Moon
10	20	Venus 3.2°N of the Moon
11	12	Jupiter 0.4°N of Venus
11	19	New Moon
12	17	Mercury 4.8°N of Venus
13	19	Mercury 4.2°N of Jupiter
17	-	Sun crosses into Aquarius
18	23	Mars 3.7°N of the Moon
19	19	First Quarter Moon
20	-	Venus at aphelion
23	08	Mercury 4.0°N of Saturn
26	14	Regulus 4.6°S of the Moon
27	08	Full Moon
28	-	Mars 3°S of the Pleiades

CONSTELLATIONS

The following constellations are visible at midnight throughout the month:
Draco (below the Pole), Camelopardalis, Auriga, Taurus, Gemini, Orion, Canis Minor, Monoceros, Lepus, Canis Major and Puppis

PHASES OF THE MOON

Phase, Apsides and Node	d	h	m
☽ Last Quarter	4	17	37
● New Moon	11	19	6
☾ First Quarter	19	18	47
○ Full Moon	27	8	17
Perigee (370,116 km)	3	19	3
Apogee (404,467 km)	18	10	22

SUNRISE AND SUNSET

	London			Bristol			Birmingham			Manchester			Newcastle			Glasgow			Belfast		
	0^0	$05'$	51^0 $30'$	2^0	$35'$	51^0 $28'$	1^0	$55'$	52^0 $28'$	2^0	$15'$	53^0 $28'$	1^0	$37'$	54^0 $59'$	4^0	$14'$	55^0 $52'$	5^0	$56'$	54^0 $35'$
d	h	m	h m	h	m	h m	h	m	h m	h	m	h m	h	m	h m	h	m	h m	h	m	h m
1	7	38	16 50	7	48	17 00	7	49	16 54	7	54	16 52	7	57	16 44	8	11	16 51	8	13	17 03
2	7	37	16 52	7	47	17 02	7	47	16 56	7	52	16 54	7	55	16 46	8	09	16 53	8	11	17 05
3	7	35	16 54	7	45	17 04	7	46	16 58	7	50	16 56	7	53	16 48	8	07	16 55	8	09	17 07
4	7	34	16 56	7	43	17 06	7	44	17 00	7	49	16 58	7	51	16 50	8	05	16 57	8	07	17 09
5	7	32	16 57	7	42	17 08	7	42	17 02	7	47	17 00	7	49	16 52	8	03	17 00	8	05	17 11
6	7	30	16 59	7	40	17 09	7	40	17 04	7	45	17 02	7	47	16 54	8	01	17 02	8	03	17 13
7	7	29	17 01	7	38	17 11	7	39	17 06	7	43	17 04	7	45	16 57	7	59	17 04	8	01	17 15
8	7	27	17 03	7	37	17 13	7	37	17 08	7	41	17 06	7	43	16 59	7	57	17 06	7	59	17 17
9	7	25	17 05	7	35	17 15	7	35	17 09	7	39	17 08	7	41	17 01	7	55	17 08	7	57	17 19
10	7	23	17 07	7	33	17 17	7	33	17 11	7	37	17 10	7	39	17 03	7	53	17 11	7	55	17 21
11	7	21	17 08	7	31	17 19	7	31	17 13	7	35	17 12	7	37	17 05	7	50	17 13	7	53	17 23
12	7	20	17 10	7	29	17 20	7	29	17 15	7	33	17 14	7	35	17 07	7	48	17 15	7	51	17 26
13	7	18	17 12	7	28	17 22	7	27	17 17	7	31	17 16	7	33	17 09	7	46	17 17	7	49	17 28
14	7	16	17 14	7	26	17 24	7	25	17 19	7	29	17 18	7	31	17 11	7	44	17 19	7	47	17 30
15	7	14	17 16	7	24	17 26	7	23	17 21	7	27	17 20	7	29	17 13	7	41	17 21	7	45	17 32
16	7	12	17 18	7	22	17 28	7	21	17 23	7	25	17 22	7	26	17 15	7	39	17 24	7	43	17 34
17	7	10	17 19	7	20	17 29	7	19	17 25	7	23	17 24	7	24	17 18	7	37	17 26	7	40	17 36
18	7	08	17 21	7	18	17 31	7	17	17 27	7	21	17 26	7	22	17 20	7	35	17 28	7	38	17 38
19	7	06	17 23	7	16	17 33	7	15	17 28	7	19	17 28	7	20	17 22	7	32	17 30	7	36	17 40
20	7	04	17 25	7	14	17 35	7	13	17 30	7	17	17 30	7	17	17 24	7	30	17 32	7	34	17 42
21	7	02	17 27	7	12	17 37	7	11	17 32	7	14	17 32	7	15	17 26	7	27	17 35	7	31	17 44
22	7	00	17 28	7	10	17 38	7	09	17 34	7	12	17 34	7	13	17 28	7	25	17 37	7	29	17 46
23	6	58	17 30	7	08	17 40	7	07	17 36	7	10	17 35	7	10	17 30	7	23	17 39	7	27	17 48
24	6	56	17 32	7	06	17 42	7	05	17 38	7	08	17 37	7	08	17 32	7	20	17 41	7	25	17 50
25	6	54	17 34	7	04	17 44	7	03	17 40	7	06	17 39	7	06	17 34	7	18	17 43	7	22	17 52
26	6	52	17 36	7	02	17 46	7	00	17 42	7	03	17 41	7	03	17 36	7	15	17 45	7	20	17 54
27	6	50	17 37	6	59	17 47	6	58	17 43	7	01	17 43	7	01	17 38	7	13	17 47	7	17	17 56
28	6	47	17 39	6	57	17 49	6	56	17 45	6	59	17 45	6	59	17 40	7	10	17 50	7	15	17 58

THE MOON

Day	Diam	Phase	Age	Rise 52^0		Rise 56^0		Transit		Set 52^0		Set 56^0	
	'	%	d	h	m	h	m	h	m	h	m	h	m
1	32.0	88	18.3	21	29	21	28	3	4	9	43	9	47
2	32.2	80	19.3	22	52	22	55	3	53	10	0	9	59
3	32.2	70	20.3	-	-	-	-	4	42	10	17	10	11
4	32.2	59	21.3	0	15	0	25	5	32	10	36	10	25
5	32.2	47	22.3	1	39	1	54	6	25	11	0	10	42
6	32.2	36	23.3	3	2	3	25	7	20	11	28	11	7
7	32.0	25	24.3	4	23	4	49	8	18	12	7	11	40
8	32.0	16	25.3	5	34	6	3	9	17	12	59	12	28
9	31.8	9	26.3	6	32	6	59	10	16	14	3	13	34
10	31.6	4	27.3	7	16	7	41	11	13	15	16	14	52
11	31.2	1	28.3	7	48	8	7	12	6	16	33	16	15
12	31.0	0	29.3	8	12	8	27	12	56	17	50	17	37
13	30.6	2	0.7	8	31	8	41	13	42	19	5	18	57
14	30.4	5	1.7	8	47	8	52	14	26	20	17	20	14
15	30.0	10	2.7	9	2	9	2	15	8	21	28	21	29
16	29.8	17	3.7	9	15	9	12	15	48	22	37	22	43
17	29.6	25	4.7	9	30	9	22	16	30	23	46	23	56
18	29.6	34	5.7	9	46	9	33	17	12	-	-	-	-
19	29.6	43	6.7	10	5	9	48	17	57	0	55	1	11
20	29.6	52	7.7	10	28	10	7	18	43	2	4	2	25
21	29.8	62	8.7	11	0	10	33	19	33	3	12	3	38
22	30.2	71	9.7	11	40	11	12	20	26	4	16	4	45
23	30.4	79	10.7	12	34	12	6	21	21	5	13	5	43
24	31.0	87	11.7	13	41	13	14	22	16	5	59	6	27
25	31.4	93	12.7	14	58	14	35	23	10	6	36	6	58
26	31.8	98	13.7	16	19	16	4	-	-	7	4	7	22
27	32.2	100	14.7	17	44	17	34	0	3	7	28	7	39
28	32.4	99	15.7	19	9	19	5	0	55	7	47	7	53

THE PLANETS

MERCURY

Day	R.A. h	m	s	Dec. °	Mag.	Diam. "	Phase %	Rise h	m	s	Transit h	m	s	Set h	m	s
1	21	51	22	-10.8	+1.1	8.9	18	7	59	16	12	59	57	17	59	55
6	21	36	44	-10.7	+3.6	10.0	3	7	24	41	12	24	1	17	21	46
11	21	13	53	-12.2	+3.8	10.4	3	6	51	4	11	41	45	16	30	33
16	20	56	32	-14.0	+1.8	10.0	14	6	25	42	11	6	14	15	45	9
21	20	51	28	-15.3	+0.9	9.1	28	6	10	6	10	43	3	15	14	50
26	20	57	47	-16.0	+0.4	8.3	40	6	1	25	10	30	51	14	59	29

VENUS

Day	R.A. h	m	s	Dec. °	Mag.	Diam. "	Phase %	Rise h	m	s	Transit h	m	s	Set h	m	s
1	20	6	15	-20.9	-3.9	10.9	98	7	21	46	11	20	1	15	18	33
6	20	32	26	-19.7	-3.9	10.8	98	7	19	21	11	26	28	15	33	57
11	20	58	10	-18.2	-3.9	10.7	98	7	15	8	11	32	27	15	50	11
16	21	23	25	-16.5	-3.9	10.6	99	7	9	24	11	37	58	16	6	59
21	21	48	9	-14.6	-3.9	10.6	99	7	2	22	11	42	58	16	24	5
26	22	12	26	-12.5	-3.9	10.5	99	6	54	17	11	47	30	16	41	17

MARS

Day	R.A. h	m	s	Dec. °	Mag.	Diam. "	Rise h	m	s	Transit h	m	s	Set h	m	s
1	2	38	48	+16.8	+0.4	7.9	10	9	1	17	51	45	1	35	50
6	2	49	31	+17.7	+0.5	7.5	9	54	22	17	42	43	1	32	32
11	3	0	32	+18.5	+0.6	7.3	9	40	5	17	34	0	1	29	28
16	3	11	50	+19.3	+0.7	7.0	9	26	11	17	25	33	1	26	34
21	3	23	23	+20.0	+0.8	6.7	9	12	41	17	17	22	1	23	48
26	3	35	11	+20.8	+0.9	6.5	8	59	36	17	9	26	1	21	5

JUPITER

Day	R.A. h	m	s	Dec. °	Mag.	Diam. "	Rise h	m	s	Transit h	m	s	Set h	m	s
1	20	50	39	-18.2	-2.0	32.5	7	46	58	12	3	7	16	19	24
6	20	55	28	-17.9	-1.9	32.5	7	30	0	11	48	16	16	6	38
11	21	0	15	-17.6	-2.0	32.6	7	12	58	11	33	22	15	53	52
16	21	4	59	-17.3	-2.0	32.7	6	55	53	11	18	26	15	41	5
21	21	9	40	-16.9	-2.0	32.8	6	38	44	11	3	26	15	28	14
26	21	14	17	-16.6	-2.0	32.9	6	21	32	10	48	23	15	15	19

Diam. = Equatorial. Polar Diam. is 94% of Equatorial Diam.

SATURN

Day	R.A. h	m	s	Dec. °	Mag.	Diam. "	Rise h	m	s	Transit h	m	s	Set h	m	s
1	20	31	0	-19.4	+0.6	15.2	7	34	59	11	43	26	15	52	0
6	20	33	26	-19.2	+0.6	15.2	7	16	48	11	26	12	15	35	43
11	20	35	51	-19.1	+0.7	15.2	6	58	35	11	8	56	15	19	24
16	20	38	13	-18.9	+0.7	15.2	6	40	20	10	51	38	15	3	2
21	20	40	32	-18.8	+0.7	15.3	6	22	4	10	34	17	14	46	37
26	20	42	47	-18.7	+0.7	15.3	6	3	44	10	16	53	14	30	7

Diam. = Equatorial. Polar Diam. is 90% of Equatorial Diam.
Rings – major axis 34", minor axis 11", Tilt 19°

URANUS

Day	R.A. h	m	s	Dec. °	Mag.	Diam. "	Rise h	m	s	Transit h	m	s	Set h	m	s
1	2	18	41	+13.4	+5.8	3.6	10	10	37	17	30	8	0	53	34
6	2	19	1	+13.4	+5.8	3.5	9	51	6	17	10	49	0	34	26
11	2	19	26	+13.5	+5.8	3.5	9	31	37	16	51	34	0	15	26
16	2	19	56	+13.5	+5.8	3.5	9	12	11	16	32	24	23	52	41
21	2	20	30	+13.6	+5.8	3.5	8	52	47	16	13	19	23	33	54
26	2	21	9	+13.6	+5.8	3.5	8	33	25	15	54	18	23	15	14

NEPTUNE

Day	R.A. h	m	s	Dec. °	Mag.	Diam. "	Rise h	m	s	Transit h	m	s	Set h	m	s
1	23	22	16	-5.2	+7.9	2.2	9	0	8	14	34	11	20	8	14
6	23	22	52	-5.2	+8.0	2.2	8	40	43	14	15	7	19	49	32
11	23	23	29	-5.1	+8.0	2.2	8	21	18	13	56	5	19	30	53
16	23	24	8	-5.0	+8.0	2.2	8	1	54	13	37	4	19	12	15
21	23	24	48	-5.0	+8.0	2.2	7	42	31	13	18	5	18	53	39
26	23	25	29	-4.9	+8.0	2.2	7	23	8	12	59	6	18	35	5

THE NIGHT SKY

Mercury might be noticed very low in the south-western evening sky the first few days of the month but is getting a little fainter each day, which makes it more difficult to pick out of the twilight.

Mercury then switches to the morning sky for the second half of February following inferior conjunction on the 8th but struggles to only just 3° above the south-eastern horizon at the beginning of civil twilight on the 28th. The magnitude 0.5 planet is 4° from Saturn on the morning of the 23rd but they will be a challenge in a brightening sky.

Venus is too close to the Sun to be seen this month, but at more southerly latitudes it may be possible to glimpse it just 0.4° from Jupiter on the morning of February 11th. The pair only rise 20 minutes before the Sun from the UK that day, so any chance sighting is unlikely.

Mars continues its slow fade from magnitude 0.4 to 0.9 but is still not setting until just before 2am. The planet is at eastern quadrature on the 1st when the phase looks gibbous in a telescope. The Moon is then nearby on the evening of the 18th.

Mars moves into Taurus from Aries on the 24th and ends February close to the Pleiades star cluster. French astronomer Charles Messier (1730-1817) submitted the first draft of his famed catalogue of nebulous deep-sky objects 250 years ago this month, and the Pleiades were the last entry on that initial list, as number 45.

Missions from the United Arab Emirates, NASA, and the Chinese Space Agency all reach Mars this month. China's Tianwen-1 enters orbit on February 11th, from where it will study the Martian atmosphere and produce global maps. An onboard rover will land on the planet's surface two months later.

The UAE's Al-Amal ('Hope') arrives on the 15th, with the goal of investigating the Martian climate and atmosphere over a period of two years.

The last to make orbit is the US Mars 2020 from where it will release the Perseverance rover to land on February 18th in the 49 km diameter Jezero crater. The vehicle is designed for astrobiological and geological studies of the area and will cache material for a future Mars sample-return mission. Perseverance will also deploy the Ingenuity helicopter drone.

Jupiter (magnitude -2.0) emerges into the morning sky after conjunction with the Sun but is still a tough catch as it is only 1° up at the beginning of civil twilight at the end of the month.

Saturn (magnitude 0.7) also moves into the morning sky this month. It can be picked up low in the southeast during the last week of February when it rises an hour or so before the Sun. The northern aspect of its magnificent ring system is currently tilted a little more than 19° towards us.

March 2021

THIRD MONTH, 31 DAYS. *Mars,* Roman god of battle

1	*Monday*	The first recorded performance of Shakespeare's *Romeo and Juliet* occured at Lincoln's Inn Fields 1662	week 9 day 60
2	*Tuesday*	NASA launched *Pioneer 10*, which became the first space probe to exit the solar system 1972	61
3	*Wednesday*	The first edition of *Time* magazine was published, with Joseph G. Cannon on its cover 1923	62
4	*Thursday*	The Royal National Lifeboat Institution was founded 1824	63
5	*Friday*	Churchill claimed an 'iron curtain has descended across the continent' of Europe 1946	64
6	*Saturday*	German pharmaceutical company Friedrich Bayer & Co patented aspirin 1899	65
7	*Sunday*	Napoleon Bonaparte led France to victory against Prussian and Russian forces at Craonne 1814	66

8	*Monday*	BBC Radio 4 first broadcasts Douglas Adams' comic series *The Hitchhiker's Guide to the Galaxy* 1978	week 10 day 67
9	*Tuesday*	Northern Ireland votes to remain part of the UK in the sovereignty referendum 1973	68
10	*Wednesday*	The French Foreign Legion was established 1831	69
11	*Thursday*	Cai Lun, a Chinese eunuch, revolutionised papermaking, allowing it to be mass produced AD 105	70
12	*Friday*	Germany annexed Austria in the *Anshluss* 1938	71
13	*Saturday*	The German astronomer William Herschel discovers the planet Uranus 1781	72
14	*Sunday*	The first patient was successfully treated with penicillin 1942	73

15	*Monday*	Jesse Reno, an engineer, received a patent for the first escalator – the Reno Inclined Elevator 1892	week 11 day 74
16	*Tuesday*	The Lyttelton Theatre in London officially opened with Albert Finney as Hamlet 1976	75
17	*Wednesday*	A Van Gogh exhibition in Paris caused a sensation, 11 years after the artist's death 1901	76
18	*Thursday*	Cosmonaut Aleksey Leonov becomes the first person to walk in space 1965	77
19	*Friday*	Argentines hoisted a flag on South Georgia Island precipitating the Falklands War 1982	78
20	*Saturday*	Harriet Beecher Stowe's anti-slavery novel *Uncle Tom's Cabin* was published 1852	79
21	*Sunday*	The first driverless trains on the London Underground were demonstrated to the public 1963	80

22	*Monday*	The Football League was formed 1888	week 12 day 81
23	*Tuesday*	US President Ronald Reagan announced plans for a space-based defence system 1983	82
24	*Wednesday*	Union of English and Scottish crowns after Queen Elizabeth I's death 1603	83
25	*Thursday*	Christiaan Huygens discovered Saturn's largest moon, which was named Titan, 1655	84
26	*Friday*	Women were admitted to the London Stock Exchange 1973	85
27	*Saturday*	The European fighter jet made its maiden flight 1994	86
28	*Sunday*	Virginia Woolf commits suicide by filling her pockets with stones and walking into the River Ouse 1941	87

29	*Monday*	Queen Victoria opened the Royal Albert Hall 1871	week 13 day 88
30	*Tuesday*	Anaesthesia was used for the first time during an operation, in Georgia, USA 1842	89
31	*Wednesday*	The Greater London Council was abolished 1986	90

ASTRONOMICAL PHENOMENA

d	h	
4	-	Mars 2.6°S of Pleiades
5	07	Mercury 0.3°N of Jupiter
6	-	Mercury at greatest elongation (27° 16' W)
6	01	Last Quarter Moon
8	-	(4) Vesta at opposition
9	23	Saturn 3.7°N of the Moon
10	15	Jupiter 4.0°N of the Moon
11	01	Mercury 3.7°N of the Moon
11	-	Neptune solar conjunction
13	10	New Moon
13	-	Sun crosses into Pisces
13	00	Venus 3.9°N of the Moon
14	01	Venus 0.4°S of Neptune
19	18	Mars 1.9°N of the Moon
20	10	Vernal (Spring) equinox
21	15	First Quarter Moon
26	01	Regulus 4.7°S of the Moon
26	-	Venus at superior conjunction
28	19	Full Moon
30	19	Mercury 1.4°S of Neptune

CONSTELLATIONS

The following constellations are visible at midnight throughout the month:

Cepheus (below the Pole), Camelopardalis, Lynx, Gemini, Cancer, Leo, Canis Minor, Hydra, Monoceros, Canis Major and Puppis

PHASES OF THE MOON

Phase, Apsides and Node	d	h	m
◑ Last Quarter	6	1	30
● New Moon	13	10	21
◐ First Quarter	21	14	40
○ Full Moon	28	18	48
Perigee (365,423 km)	2	5	18
Apogee (405,253 km)	18	5	3
Perigee (360,309 km)	30	6	16

SUNRISE AND SUNSET

	London		Bristol		Birmingham		Manchester		Newcastle		Glasgow		Belfast	
	0^0	$05'$	51^0	$30'$	2^0	$35'$	51^0	$28'$	1^0	$55'$	52^0	$28'$	2^0	$15'$	53^0	$28'$	1^0	$37'$	54^0	$59'$	4^0	$14'$	55^0	$52'$	5^0	$56'$	54^0	$35'$
d	h	m	h	m	h	m	h	m	h	m	h	m	h	m	h	m	h	m	h	m	h	m	h	m	h	m	h	m
1	6	45	17	41	6	55	17	51	6	54	17	47	6	56	17	47	6	56	17	42	7	08	17	52	7	13	18	00
2	6	43	17	43	6	53	17	53	6	52	17	49	6	54	17	49	6	54	17	44	7	05	17	54	7	10	18	02
3	6	41	17	44	6	51	17	54	6	49	17	51	6	52	17	51	6	51	17	47	7	03	17	56	7	08	18	04
4	6	39	17	46	6	49	17	56	6	47	17	53	6	50	17	53	6	49	17	49	7	00	17	58	7	06	18	06
5	6	37	17	48	6	47	17	58	6	45	17	54	6	47	17	55	6	46	17	51	6	58	18	00	7	03	18	08
6	6	34	17	50	6	44	18	00	6	43	17	56	6	45	17	57	6	44	17	53	6	55	18	02	7	01	18	10
7	6	32	17	51	6	42	18	01	6	40	17	58	6	42	17	58	6	41	17	55	6	53	18	04	6	58	18	12
8	6	30	17	53	6	40	18	03	6	38	18	00	6	40	18	00	6	39	17	57	6	50	18	06	6	56	18	14
9	6	28	17	55	6	38	18	05	6	36	18	02	6	38	18	02	6	36	17	59	6	48	18	08	6	53	18	16
10	6	25	17	57	6	35	18	07	6	33	18	03	6	35	18	04	6	34	18	01	6	45	18	10	6	51	18	18
11	6	23	17	58	6	33	18	08	6	31	18	05	6	33	18	06	6	31	18	03	6	42	18	12	6	48	18	20
12	6	21	18	00	6	31	18	10	6	29	18	07	6	31	18	08	6	29	18	05	6	40	18	15	6	46	18	22
13	6	19	18	02	6	29	18	12	6	26	18	09	6	28	18	10	6	26	18	07	6	37	18	17	6	43	18	24
14	6	16	18	03	6	26	18	13	6	24	18	10	6	26	18	12	6	24	18	08	6	35	18	19	6	41	18	26
15	6	14	18	05	6	24	18	15	6	22	18	12	6	23	18	13	6	21	18	10	6	32	18	21	6	38	18	28
16	6	12	18	07	6	22	18	17	6	19	18	14	6	21	18	15	6	19	18	12	6	29	18	23	6	36	18	30
17	6	10	18	09	6	20	18	19	6	17	18	16	6	19	18	17	6	16	18	14	6	27	18	25	6	33	18	32
18	6	07	18	10	6	17	18	20	6	15	18	18	6	16	18	19	6	14	18	16	6	24	18	27	6	31	18	34
19	6	05	18	12	6	15	18	22	6	12	18	19	6	14	18	21	6	11	18	18	6	21	18	29	6	28	18	36
20	6	03	18	14	6	13	18	24	6	10	18	21	6	11	18	23	6	09	18	20	6	19	18	31	6	26	18	38
21	6	01	18	15	6	11	18	25	6	08	18	23	6	09	18	24	6	06	18	22	6	16	18	33	6	23	18	39
22	5	58	18	17	6	08	18	27	6	05	18	25	6	06	18	26	6	03	18	24	6	14	18	35	6	21	18	41
23	5	56	18	19	6	06	18	29	6	03	18	26	6	04	18	28	6	01	18	26	6	11	18	37	6	18	18	43
24	5	54	18	20	6	04	18	30	6	01	18	28	6	02	18	30	5	58	18	28	6	08	18	39	6	16	18	45
25	5	51	18	22	6	01	18	32	5	58	18	30	5	59	18	32	5	56	18	30	6	06	18	41	6	13	18	47
26	5	49	18	24	5	59	18	34	5	56	18	32	5	57	18	34	5	53	18	32	6	03	18	43	6	11	18	49
27	5	47	18	25	5	57	18	35	5	54	18	33	5	54	18	35	5	51	18	34	6	01	18	45	6	08	18	51
28	5	45	18	27	5	55	18	37	5	51	18	35	5	52	18	37	5	48	18	36	5	58	18	47	6	06	18	53
29	5	42	18	29	5	52	18	39	5	49	18	37	5	49	18	39	5	46	18	38	5	55	18	49	6	03	18	55
30	5	40	18	30	5	50	18	40	5	47	18	39	5	47	18	41	5	43	18	40	5	53	18	51	6	01	18	57
31	5	38	18	32	5	48	18	42	5	44	18	40	5	45	18	43	5	41	18	42	5	50	18	53	5	58	18	59

THE MOON

Day	Diam	Phase	Age	Rise		Rise		Transit		Set		Set	
	$'$	%	d	52^0	52^0	56^0	56^0			52^0	52^0	56^0	56^0
				h	m	h	m	h	m	h	m	h	m
1	32.6	96	16.7	20	34	20	36	1	46	8	5	8	6
2	32.6	91	17.7	22	0	22	8	2	36	8	22	8	18
3	32.6	83	18.7	23	27	23	40	3	28	8	40	8	31
4	32.6	73	19.7	-	-	-	-	4	20	9	3	8	47
5	32.4	62	20.7	0	52	1	12	5	16	9	29	9	9
6	32.2	51	21.7	2	14	2	40	6	13	10	6	9	38
7	31.8	40	22.7	3	29	3	57	7	11	10	52	10	22
8	31.6	29	23.7	4	30	4	58	8	10	11	52	11	22
9	31.4	20	24.7	5	16	5	43	9	6	13	2	12	35
10	31.0	12	25.7	5	51	6	13	10	0	14	17	13	57
11	30.8	6	26.7	6	17	6	33	10	50	15	33	15	18
12	30.6	2	27.7	6	37	6	48	11	37	16	48	16	38
13	30.2	0	28.7	6	53	7	0	12	21	18	1	17	56
14	30.0	0	0.2	7	7	7	10	13	3	19	12	19	12
15	29.8	2	1.2	7	21	7	19	13	44	20	22	20	27
16	29.6	6	2.2	7	35	7	28	14	25	21	32	21	41
17	29.6	12	3.2	7	50	7	39	15	7	22	41	22	55
18	29.4	18	4.2	8	7	7	52	15	51	23	50	-	-
19	29.6	26	5.2	8	28	8	8	16	36	-	-	0	10
20	29.6	35	6.2	8	56	8	30	17	25	0	58	1	24
21	29.8	44	7.2	9	31	9	4	18	16	2	4	2	33
22	30.2	54	8.2	10	19	9	49	19	8	3	3	3	34
23	30.4	64	9.2	11	19	10	50	20	2	3	53	4	23
24	31.0	73	10.2	12	30	12	6	20	55	4	34	4	58
25	31.4	82	11.2	13	49	13	30	21	48	5	4	5	25
26	32.0	90	12.2	15	12	15	0	22	41	5	29	5	44
27	32.4	96	13.2	16	38	16	31	23	32	5	50	5	58
28	32.8	99	14.2	18	5	18	4	-	-	6	8	6	11
29	33.0	100	15.2	19	33	19	38	0	24	6	25	6	23
30	33.2	98	16.2	21	2	21	14	1	16	6	43	6	36
31	33.2	93	17.2	22	33	22	50	2	10	7	4	6	51

THE PLANETS

MERCURY

Day	R.A. h	m	s	Dec. °	Mag.	Diam. "	Phase %	Rise h	m	s	Transit h	m	s	Set h	m	s
1	21	5	42	-16.1	+0.3	7.8	47	5	58	7	10	27	27	14	56	12
6	21	23	46	-15.7	+0.2	7.2	56	5	53	58	10	26	25	14	58	36
11	21	46	4	-14.7	+0.1	6.7	63	5	50	4	10	29	25	15	8	46
16	22	11	11	-13.0	0.0	6.2	69	5	45	33	10	35	8	15	24	59
21	22	38	20	-10.9	-0.1	5.9	75	5	40	2	10	42	47	15	46	3
26	23	7	4	-8.2	-0.2	5.6	80	5	33	31	10	52	0	16	11	15
31	23	37	16	-5.0	-0.4	5.4	85	5	26	8	11	2	40	16	40	14

VENUS

Day	R.A. h	m	s	Dec. °	Mag.	Diam. "	Phase %	Rise h	m	s	Transit h	m	s	Set h	m	s
1	22	26	47	-11.2	-3.9	10.5	99	6	49	0	11	50	1	16	51	36
6	22	50	24	-8.9	-3.9	10.5	100	6	39	39	11	53	54	17	8	46
11	23	13	41	-6.5	-3.9	10.5	100	6	29	43	11	57	27	17	25	51
16	23	36	43	-4.1	-3.9	10.4	100	6	19	21	12	0	45	17	42	50
21	23	59	34	-1.6	-3.9	10.4	100	6	8	42	12	3	52	17	59	46
26	0	22	18	0.0	-3.9	10.4	100	5	57	53	12	6	54	18	16	41
31	0	45	3	+3.4	-3.9	10.4	100	5	47	2	12	9	55	18	33	38

MARS

Day	R.A. h	m	s	Dec. °	Mag.	Diam. "	Rise h	m	s	Transit h	m	s	Set h	m	s
1	3	42	22	+21.2	+0.9	6.4	8	51	58	17	4	46	1	19	27
6	3	54	30	+21.8	+1.0	6.2	8	39	37	16	57	10	1	16	40
11	4	6	43	+22.3	+1.0	6.0	8	27	47	16	49	47	1	13	48
16	4	19	22	+22.9	+1.1	5.8	8	16	28	16	42	35	1	10	46
21	4	32	3	+23.4	+1.2	5.6	8	5	44	16	35	33	1	7	31
26	4	44	54	+23.8	+1.2	5.5	7	55	34	16	28	40	1	3	58
31	4	57	52	+24.2	+1.3	5.3	7	46	0	16	21	55	1	0	5

JUPITER

Day	R.A. h	m	s	Dec. °	Mag.	Diam. "	Rise h	m	s	Transit h	m	s	Set h	m	s
1	21	17	1	-16.4	-2.0	33.0	6	11	10	10	39	18	15	7	32
6	21	21	31	-16.1	-2.0	33.2	5	53	51	10	24	8	14	54	29
11	21	25	55	-15.7	-2.0	33.5	5	36	28	10	8	51	14	41	20
16	21	30	13	-15.3	-2.0	33.7	5	19	0	9	53	29	14	28	3
21	21	34	24	-15.1	-2.0	34.0	5	1	28	9	38	0	14	14	36
26	21	38	28	-14.8	-2.0	34.3	4	43	52	9	22	23	14	1	0
31	21	42	24	-14.4	-2.1	34.7	4	26	10	9	6	39	13	47	12

Diam. = Equatorial. Polar Diam. is 94% of Equatorial Diam.

SATURN

Day	R.A. h	m	s	Dec. °	Mag.	Diam. "	Rise h	m	s	Transit h	m	s	Set h	m	s
1	20	44	7	-18.6	+0.7	15.4	5	52	43	10	6	24	14	20	11
6	20	46	16	-18.5	+0.7	15.5	5	34	20	9	48	53	14	3	32
11	20	48	20	-18.3	+0.7	15.5	5	15	53	9	31	18	13	46	47
16	20	50	19	-18.2	+0.7	15.6	4	57	23	9	13	36	13	29	55
21	20	52	12	-18.1	+0.7	15.7	4	38	49	8	55	50	13	12	54
26	20	53	58	-18.0	+0.8	15.8	4	20	12	8	37	56	12	55	45
31	20	55	38	-17.9	+0.8	15.9	4	1	30	8	19	56	12	38	26

Diam. = Equatorial. Polar Diam. is 90% of Equatorial Diam.
Rings – major axis 35", minor axis 11", Tilt 18°

URANUS

Day	R.A. h	m	s	Dec. °	Mag.	Diam. "	Rise h	m	s	Transit h	m	s	Set h	m	s
1	2	21	34	+13.6	+5.8	3.5	8	21	48	15	42	55	23	4	4
6	2	22	19	+13.7	+5.8	3.5	8	2	29	15	24	0	22	45	34
11	2	23	7	+13.8	+5.8	3.5	7	43	12	15	5	9	22	27	8
16	2	23	59	+13.9	+5.8	3.4	7	23	57	14	46	21	22	8	48
21	2	24	54	+13.9	+5.9	3.4	7	4	43	14	27	36	21	50	32
26	2	25	52	+14.0	+5.9	3.4	6	45	31	14	8	54	21	32	20
31	2	26	52	+14.1	+5.9	3.4	6	26	20	13	50	15	21	14	12

NEPTUNE

Day	R.A. h	m	s	Dec. °	Mag.	Diam. "	Rise h	m	s	Transit h	m	s	Set h	m	s
1	23	25	54	-4.8	+8.0	2.2	7	11	30	12	47	43	18	23	56
6	23	26	36	-4.8	+8.0	2.2	6	52	7	12	28	45	18	5	23
11	23	27	18	-4.7	+8.0	2.2	6	32	45	12	9	48	17	46	50
16	23	27	60	-4.6	+8.0	2.2	6	13	23	11	50	50	17	28	17
21	23	28	42	-4.5	+8.0	2.2	5	54	1	11	31	52	17	9	44
26	23	29	23	-4.5	+8.0	2.2	5	34	38	11	12	54	16	51	10
31	23	30	4	-4.4	+8.0	2.2	5	15	16	10	53	55	16	32	34

THE NIGHT SKY

Mercury can be seen low in the southeast prior to sunrise up to the end of the first week of March, with the magnitude 0.2 sun-baked world rising 45 minutes before the Sun on the 1st. It reaches greatest western elongation on the 6th but morning apparitions at more northerly latitudes in the springtime are generally poor. Mercury quickly slips back into the solar glare soon after elongation and is lost to view for the rest of the month.

Venus is not visible during February as it will be on the far side of the Sun when it passes through superior conjunction on the 26th.

Mars makes its way across Taurus this month and remains on view until well after local midnight. The planet's disk continues to dwindle in size for telescope users though, and at $5\frac{1}{2}$ arc-seconds across, it is now only half as wide as it was at the start of the year.

Mars (magnitude 0.9) is closest to the Pleiades star cluster on the 4th when it is $2\frac{1}{2}°$ from the group's centre. They are one of the loveliest sights in the sky for binocular users, and any instrument reveals dozens of jewels scattered across the field. The cluster is roughly 115 million years old and lies about 445 light years away.

The Moon then passes by Mars on the 19th when they are less than 3° apart, while two days later, there is a chance contrast the tints of magnitude 1.2 Mars and the magnitude 0.8 orange-hued giant Aldebaran when the two are separated by 7°. As the month ends, Mars is in the same binocular field as the cluster NGC 1746.

Jupiter (magnitude -2.0) rises 45 minutes before the Sun at the beginning of March and heaves itself over the south-eastern skyline an hour beforehand by the 31st. Try to catch it close to magnitude 0.1 Mercury on the morning of the 5th when they are less than a half degree apart. The two are barely up at the start of civil twilight though for observers in the UK.

Saturn (magnitude 0.7) rises an hour before the Sun on March 1st but tacks an extra half hour onto that time by the end of the month.

For a few days either side of the new moon you can see the rest of the lunar disk faintly lit and nestling in the bright crescent. The phenomenon is known as earthshine and is due to sunlight bouncing off the day side of Earth on to the night side of the Moon, then back to the observer.

Leonardo da Vinci first correctly explained its cause, and spring evenings are a good opportunity to notice the glow. Look for an effect that is often called 'The Old Moon in the New Moon's arms' when the slender 32.5-hour old crescent lies in the western evening sky on the 14th.

April 2021

FOURTH MONTH, 30 DAYS. *Aperire*, to open; Earth opens to receive seed.

1	*Thursday*	VAT was introduced in the UK 1973	day 91
2	*Friday*	Charlie Chaplin returned to the USA for the first time in 20 years to collect an Oscar 1972	92
3	*Saturday*	The world's first mobile telephone call was placed in New York 1973	93
4	*Sunday*	NATO was established by 12 countries 1949	94

5	*Monday*	Julie Andrews won Best Actress at the Oscars for her role in *Mary Poppins* 1965	week 14 day 95
6	*Tuesday*	The modern Olympic Games were revived at Athens 1896	96
7	*Wednesday*	The unmanned *Mars Odyssey* spacecraft was launched from Cape Canaveral, Florida 1942	97
8	*Thursday*	The Venus de Milo was discovered on the Aegean island of Melos 1820	98
9	*Friday*	Captain Cook landed in Australia 1770	99
10	*Saturday*	The Titanic embarked on her maiden voyage 1912	100
11	*Sunday*	The *Ryan X-13 Vertijet*, the first jet to take off and land vertically, completed a full flight 1957	101

12	*Monday*	Yuri Gagarin became the first man to travel in space; the Soviet Union declared the space race won 1961	week 15 day 102
13	*Tuesday*	Ian Fleming's first James Bond novel, *Casino Royale*, adapted for cinema in 2006, was published 1953	103
14	*Wednesday*	The House of Lancaster won the Battle of Barnet in the War of the Roses 1471	104
15	*Thursday*	J. M. Barrie presents the copyright of his Peter Pan works to Great Ormond Street Hospital 1929	105
16	*Friday*	The Rolling Stones released their eponymous debut album 1964	106
17	*Saturday*	Geoffrey Chaucer first recited his Canterbury Tales 1397	107
18	*Sunday*	Over 60,000 people demonstrated against the hydrogen bomb in Trafalgar Square 1960	108

19	*Monday*	The American War of Independence began in Lexington, Mass. 1775	week 16 day 109
20	*Tuesday*	Edgar Allan Poe's 'The Murders in the Rue Morgue' was published 1841	110
21	*Wednesday*	Women in France received the right to vote 1944	111
22	*Thursday*	Germany first used poison gas against British troops 1915	112
23	*Friday*	The first decimal coins, 5p and 10p pieces, were issued 1968	113
24	*Saturday*	The Hubble space telescope was launched by the space shuttle Discovery 1990	114
25	*Sunday*	Scientists announced the discovery of the structure of DNA 1953	115

26	*Monday*	William Shakespeare was baptised at Holy Trinity Church, Stratford 1564	week 17 day 116
27	*Tuesday*	Betty Boothroyd became the first female Speaker of the House of Commons 1992	117
28	*Wendesday*	The League of Nations was founded 1919	118
29	*Thursday*	Women were admitted to Oxford University examinations 1885	119
30	*Friday*	New York opened its first World's Fair, attracting 44 million people over two seasons 1939	120

ASTRONOMICAL PHENOMENA

d	h	
4	10	Last Quarter Moon
6	08	Saturn 4.0°N of the Moon
7	07	Jupiter 4.4°N of the Moon
11	06	Mercury 3.0°N of the Moon
12	03	New Moon
12	10	Venus 2.9°N of the Moon
17	12	Mars 0.1°N of the Moon: Occultation
19	-	Sun crosses into Aries
20	07	First Quarter Moon
22	12	Lyrid meteor shower
22	10	Regulus 4.9°S of the Moon
22	23	Venus 0.25°S of Uranus
24	10	Mercury 0.8°N of Uranus
26	09	Mercury 1.3°N of Venus
26	PM	Mars very near M35
27	04	Full Moon
30	PM	Mercury 5° from the Pleiades

CONSTELLATIONS

The following constellations are visible at midnight throughout the month:
Cepheus (below the Pole), Cassiopeia (below the Pole), Ursa Major, Leo Minor, Leo., Sextans, Hydra and Crater

PHASES OF THE MOON

Phase, Apsides and Node	d	h	m
☽ Last Quarter	4	10	2
● New Moon	12	2	31
◑ First Quarter	20	6	59
○ Full Moon	27	3	32
Apogee (406,119 km)	14	17	46
Perigee (357,378 km)	27	15	22

SUNRISE AND SUNSET

	London				Bristol				Birmingham				Manchester				Newcastle				Glasgow				Belfast			
	0° 05'		51° 30'		2° 35'		51° 28'		1° 55'		52° 28'		2° 15'		53° 28'		1° 37'		54° 59'		4° 14'		55° 52'		5° 56'		54° 35'	
d	h	m	h	m	h	m	h	m	h	m	h	m	h	m	h	m	h	m	h	m	h	m	h	m	h	m	h	m
1	5	36	18	34	5	46	18	44	5	42	18	42	5	42	18	45	5	38	18	44	5	47	18	55	5	56	19	01
2	5	33	18	36	5	43	18	46	5	40	18	44	5	40	18	46	5	35	18	46	5	45	18	57	5	53	19	02
3	5	31	18	37	5	41	18	47	5	37	18	46	5	37	18	48	5	33	18	48	5	42	18	59	5	51	19	04
4	5	29	18	39	5	39	18	49	5	35	18	47	5	35	18	50	5	30	18	50	5	40	19	01	5	48	19	06
5	5	26	18	41	5	37	18	51	5	33	18	49	5	33	18	52	5	28	18	52	5	37	19	03	5	46	19	08
6	5	24	18	42	5	34	18	52	5	30	18	51	5	30	18	54	5	25	18	54	5	34	19	05	5	43	19	10
7	5	22	18	44	5	32	18	54	5	28	18	53	5	28	18	56	5	23	18	55	5	32	19	07	5	41	19	12
8	5	20	18	46	5	30	18	56	5	26	18	54	5	25	18	57	5	20	18	57	5	29	19	09	5	38	19	14
9	5	18	18	47	5	28	18	57	5	23	18	56	5	23	18	59	5	18	18	59	5	27	19	11	5	36	19	16
10	5	15	18	49	5	25	18	59	5	21	18	58	5	21	19	01	5	15	19	01	5	24	19	14	5	33	19	18
11	5	13	18	51	5	23	19	01	5	19	19	00	5	18	19	03	5	13	19	03	5	22	19	16	5	31	19	20
12	5	11	18	52	5	21	19	02	5	17	19	01	5	16	19	05	5	10	19	05	5	19	19	18	5	29	19	22
13	5	09	18	54	5	19	19	04	5	14	19	03	5	14	19	06	5	08	19	07	5	17	19	20	5	26	19	24
14	5	07	18	56	5	17	19	06	5	12	19	05	5	11	19	08	5	06	19	09	5	14	19	22	5	24	19	25
15	5	04	18	57	5	15	19	07	5	10	19	07	5	09	19	10	5	03	19	11	5	11	19	24	5	21	19	27
16	5	02	18	59	5	12	19	09	5	08	19	08	5	07	19	12	5	01	19	13	5	09	19	26	5	19	19	29
17	5	00	19	01	5	10	19	10	5	05	19	10	5	05	19	14	4	58	19	15	5	06	19	28	5	17	19	31
18	4	58	19	02	5	08	19	12	5	03	19	12	5	02	19	16	4	56	19	17	5	04	19	30	5	14	19	33
19	4	56	19	04	5	06	19	14	5	01	19	14	5	00	19	17	4	54	19	19	5	02	19	32	5	12	19	35
20	4	54	19	06	5	04	19	15	4	59	19	15	4	58	19	19	4	51	19	21	4	59	19	34	5	10	19	37
21	4	52	19	07	5	02	19	17	4	57	19	17	4	56	19	21	4	49	19	23	4	57	19	36	5	07	19	39
22	4	50	19	09	5	00	19	19	4	55	19	19	4	53	19	23	4	47	19	25	4	54	19	38	5	05	19	41
23	4	48	19	11	4	58	19	20	4	53	19	20	4	51	19	25	4	44	19	27	4	52	19	40	5	03	19	43
24	4	46	19	12	4	56	19	22	4	50	19	22	4	49	19	26	4	42	19	29	4	50	19	42	5	00	19	45
25	4	44	19	14	4	54	19	24	4	48	19	24	4	47	19	28	4	40	19	30	4	47	19	44	4	58	19	47
26	4	42	19	16	4	52	19	25	4	46	19	26	4	45	19	30	4	37	19	32	4	45	19	46	4	56	19	48
27	4	40	19	17	4	50	19	27	4	44	19	27	4	43	19	32	4	35	19	34	4	42	19	48	4	54	19	50
28	4	38	19	19	4	48	19	29	4	42	19	29	4	40	19	34	4	33	19	36	4	40	19	50	4	52	19	52
29	4	36	19	21	4	46	19	30	4	40	19	31	4	38	19	35	4	31	19	38	4	38	19	52	4	49	19	54
30	4	34	19	22	4	44	19	32	4	38	19	33	4	36	19	37	4	28	19	40	4	36	19	54	4	47	19	56

THE MOON

Day	Diam	Phase	Age	Rise		Rise		Transit		Set		Set	
				52°	52°	56°	56°			52°	52°	56°	56°
	'	%	d	h	m	h	m	h	m	h	m	h	m
1	33.0	86	18.2	23	59	-	-	3	6	7	29	7	10
2	32.6	76	19.2	-	-	0	25	4	5	8	3	7	37
3	32.2	66	20.2	1	20	1	49	5	5	8	46	8	17
4	31.8	55	21.2	2	27	2	57	6	5	9	43	9	13
5	31.6	44	22.2	3	18	3	47	7	2	10	51	10	23
6	31.2	33	23.2	3	55	4	20	7	57	12	6	11	42
7	30.8	24	24.2	4	24	4	42	8	48	13	21	13	5
8	30.4	16	25.2	4	44	4	57	9	35	14	36	14	25
9	30.2	9	26.2	5	1	5	9	10	19	15	49	15	43
10	30.0	4	27.2	5	15	5	19	11	1	17	0	16	58
11	29.8	1	28.2	5	29	5	28	11	42	18	10	18	13
12	29.6	0	29.2	5	42	5	37	12	23	19	20	19	27
13	29.6	1	0.7	5	56	5	47	13	5	20	29	20	42
14	29.4	3	1.7	6	12	5	59	13	47	21	39	21	56
15	29.4	7	2.7	6	31	6	13	14	32	22	48	23	11
16	29.4	13	3.7	6	56	6	32	15	20	23	55	-	-
17	29.6	20	4.7	7	28	7	1	16	9	-	-	0	23
18	29.8	28	5.7	8	11	7	39	17	0	0	56	1	28
19	30.0	37	6.7	9	5	8	33	17	52	1	49	2	20
20	30.4	47	7.7	10	10	9	42	18	44	2	32	2	59
21	30.8	57	8.7	11	23	11	3	19	36	3	5	3	29
22	31.4	68	9.7	12	43	12	27	20	28	3	32	3	49
23	31.8	77	10.7	14	6	13	56	21	18	3	53	4	4
24	32.4	86	11.7	15	31	15	27	22	9	4	11	4	18
25	32.8	93	12.7	16	58	17	0	23	0	4	28	4	29
26	33.2	98	13.7	18	28	18	36	23	53	4	45	4	41
27	33.4	100	14.7	19	59	20	14	-	-	5	4	4	54
28	33.4	99	15.7	21	32	21	53	0	50	5	27	5	11
29	33.2	95	16.7	22	59	23	28	1	49	5	57	5	34
30	33.0	88	17.7	-	-	-	-	2	51	6	37	6	9

THE PLANETS

MERCURY

Day	R.A. h	m	s	Dec. °	Mag.	Diam. "	Phase %	Rise h	m	s	Transit h	m	s	Set h	m	s
1	23	43	30	-4.3	-0.5	5.3	86	5	24	34	11	4	59	16	46	29
6	0	15	38	0.0	-0.8	5.2	91	5	16	29	11	17	35	17	20	6
11	0	49	42	+3.5	-1.2	5.1	96	5	8	9	11	32	9	17	57	52
16	1	26	2	+7.9	-1.8	5.0	99	4	59	59	11	49	0	18	40	4
21	2	4	45	+12.4	-2.0	5.1	100	4	52	29	12	8	10	19	26	10
26	2	45	10	+16.6	-1.6	5.3	95	4	46	14	12	28	54	20	13	51

VENUS

Day	R.A. h	m	s	Dec. °	Mag.	Diam. "	Phase %	Rise h	m	s	Transit h	m	s	Set h	m	s
1	0	49	36	+3.9	-3.9	10.4	100	5	44	52	12	10	32	18	37	2
6	1	12	27	+6.4	-3.9	10.4	100	5	34	7	12	13	40	18	54	6
11	1	35	29	+8.8	-3.9	10.4	100	5	23	35	12	17	0	19	11	18
16	1	58	47	+11.2	-3.9	10.4	100	5	13	26	12	20	36	19	28	40
21	2	22	24	+13.4	-3.9	10.5	99	5	3	49	12	24	31	19	46	9
26	2	46	24	+15.5	-3.9	10.5	99	4	54	55	12	28	50	20	3	41

MARS

Day	R.A. h	m	s	Dec. °	Mag.	Diam. "	Rise h	m	s	Transit h	m	s	Set h	m	s
1	5	0	28	+24.2	+1.3	5.3	7	44	10	16	20	34	0	59	15
6	5	13	34	+24.5	+1.3	5.2	7	35	21	16	13	57	0	54	53
11	5	26	46	+24.7	+1.4	5.1	7	27	11	16	7	26	0	50	3
16	5	40	3	+24.8	+1.4	4.9	7	19	39	16	0	59	0	44	44
21	5	53	22	+24.9	+1.5	4.8	7	12	46	15	54	35	0	38	53
26	6	6	44	+24.9	+1.5	4.7	7	6	31	15	48	14	0	32	29

JUPITER

Day	R.A. h	m	s	Dec. °	Mag.	Diam. "	Rise h	m	s	Transit h	m	s	Set h	m	s
1	21	43	10	-14.4	-2.1	34.7	4	22	37	9	3	29	13	44	26
6	21	46	56	-14.1	-2.1	35.0	3	58	59	8	47	34	13	30	23
11	21	50	32	-13.8	-2.1	35.5	3	46	58	8	31	30	13	16	8
16	21	53	58	-13.5	-2.1	35.9	3	29	0	8	15	16	13	1	37
21	21	57	13	-13.2	-2.2	36.4	3	10	57	7	58	51	12	46	50
26	22	0	17	-13.0	-2.2	36.9	2	52	48	7	42	14	12	31	46

Diam. = Equatorial. Polar Diam. is 94% of Equatorial Diam.

SATURN

Day	R.A. h	m	s	Dec. °	Mag.	Diam. "	Rise h	m	s	Transit h	m	s	Set h	m	s
1	20	55	57	-17.9	+0.8	15.9	3	57	46	8	16	19	12	34	57
6	20	57	28	-17.8	+0.7	16.0	3	38	59	7	58	11	12	17	26
11	20	58	52	-17.7	+0.7	16.2	3	20	9	7	39	54	11	59	43
16	21	0	7	-17.6	+0.7	16.3	3	1	14	7	21	30	11	41	49
21	21	1	14	-17.5	+0.7	16.4	2	42	15	7	2	57	11	23	42
26	21	2	12	-17.5	+0.7	16.6	2	23	10	6	44	15	11	5	23

Diam. = Equatorial. Polar Diam. is 90% of Equatorial Diam.
Rings – major axis 37", minor axis 11", Tilt 17°

URANUS

Day	R.A. h	m	s	Dec. °	Mag.	Diam. "	Rise h	m	s	Transit h	m	s	Set h	m	s
1	2	27	4	+14.1	+5.9	3.4	6	22	30	13	46	31	21	10	34
6	2	28	7	+14.2	+5.9	3.4	6	3	20	13	27	54	20	52	30
11	2	29	11	+14.3	+5.9	3.4	5	44	12	13	9	18	20	34	28
16	2	30	17	+14.4	+5.9	3.4	5	25	4	12	50	44	20	16	27
21	2	31	23	+14.5	+5.9	3.4	5	5	56	12	32	11	19	58	29
26	2	32	31	+14.6	+5.9	3.4	4	46	50	12	13	39	19	40	31

NEPTUNE

Day	R.A. h	m	s	Dec. °	Mag.	Diam. "	Rise h	m	s	Transit h	m	s	Set h	m	s
1	23	30	12	-4.4	+8.0	2.2	5	11	23	10	50	7	16	28	51
6	23	30	52	-4.3	+8.0	2.2	4	52	0	10	31	7	16	10	14
11	23	31	30	-4.3	+8.0	2.2	4	32	37	10	12	6	15	51	35
16	23	32	7	-4.2	+7.9	2.2	4	13	9	9	53	3	15	32	53
21	23	32	42	-4.1	+7.9	2.2	3	53	49	9	33	59	15	14	9
26	23	33	16	-4.1	+7.9	2.2	3	34	24	9	14	53	14	55	22

THE NIGHT SKY

Mercury emerges into the evening sky after superior conjunction on the 19th and may be seen hugging the west-northwest horizon during the last week or so of April. The planet's altitude improves daily though up to the end of the month when it is nearly 5° high at the end of civil twilight and setting more than an hour after the Sun. Look for Mercury's magnitude -1.1 glint about 5° below the Pleiades on the evening of the 30th.

Venus (magnitude -3.9) reappears this month and can be found low in the west-northwest from the second half of April. Venus and Mercury (magnitude -1.6) are less than one degree apart on the evening of the 25th but are sinking fast in the twilight. Once you find Venus, use binoculars to glimpse fainter Mercury nearby.

Mars hangs around until the early hours – especially with summertime now in effect. It has now faded a little more to magnitude 1.7 but is still a reasonably bright object as it charges through Taurus, before crossing into Gemini on the 25th.

A line drawn between Zeta and Beta Tauri, marking the horns of the celestial bull, is bisected by Mars on the night of the 13th. The Moon is then near the planet on the 17th, and Mars can be found very close to the open cluster M35 in the feet of Gemini on the 26th.

Jupiter (magnitude -2.1) rises just over an hour before the Sun at the beginning of April but appears nearly two hours beforehand by the end of the month. It can be found in the east-southeast at this time amongst the dim stars of Capricornus. The shallow angle the ecliptic makes with the morning horizon from northern temperate latitudes at this time of year means the planet will appear low, despite its early appearance.

Jupiter is extremely close to 44 Capricorni (magnitude 5.9) on the 2nd, when the star looks like an extra Jovian moon but is slightly outside their orbital plane. It will appear nearer to the planet's disk than some of the Galilean satellites that morning, but a predicted occultation of the star by Jupiter is after sunrise from the UK.

The waning Moon is close to Jupiter on the morning of April 7th and later in the month, on the 26th, the planet crosses into Aquarius. Beforehand though, on the 16th, Mu Capricorni (magnitude 5.0) also masquerades as an attendant of the gas giant as Jupiter drags his entourage of 79 moons across the sky.

Saturn (magnitude 0.7), in Capricornus, rises 1½ hours before the Sun on the 1st with that interval almost doubling by the end of April. Like Jupiter, it too remains rather poorly placed in the morning sky from the UK. The moon is a couple of days after last quarter when it is near Saturn on the 6th.

May 2021

FIFTH MONTH, 31 DAYS. *Maia*, goddess of growth and increase

1	*Saturday*	Queen Victoria opened the Great Exhibition at Hyde Park, celebrating the Industrial Revolution 1851	day 121
2	*Sunday*	The King James version of the Bible was published 1611	122

3	*Monday*	Lord Byron swam from Europe to Asia across the Hellespont Strait 1810	week 18 day 123
4	*Tuesday*	Margaret Thatcher became UK's first woman prime minister 1979	124
5	*Wendesday*	*The Examiner* published the Romantic poet John Keats' sonnet 'O Solitude' 1816	125
6	*Thursday*	Postage stamps were introduced 1840	126
7	*Friday*	Native Americans rebelled against British forces at Fort Detroit during Pontiac's War 1763	127
8	*Saturday*	The Irish Literary Theatre opened with a performance of Yeats' play *The Countess Cathleen* 1899	128
9	*Sunday*	*Sam and Friends*, Jim Henson's first puppet TV show, aired in Washington DC 1955	129

10	*Monday*	Nelson Mandela became South Africa's first black president 1994	week 19 day 130
11	*Tuesday*	The Academy of Motion Picture Arts and Sciences held its inaugural banquet 1927	131
12	*Wednesday*	The USSR lifted its blockade on Berlin 1949	132
13	*Thursday*	Marie Curie, Nobel prize winning physicist, became the first female professor at the Sorbonne 1906	133
14	*Friday*	The USA's first space station was launched; *Skylab* spent over six years orbiting Earth 1973	134
15	*Saturday*	The Royal Opera House in Covent Garden opened 1858	135
16	*Sunday*	Mao Zedong launched the Cultural Revolution in the People's Republic of China 1966	136

17	*Monday*	Compact discs were introduced by Phillips 1978	week 20 day 137
18	*Tuesday*	Napoleon Bonaparte was proclaimed emperor of France 1804	138
19	*Wednesday*	Balamurali Ambati, aged 17 years and 294 days, graduated to become the world's youngest doctor 1995	139
20	*Thursday*	Levi Strauss and Jacob Davis received a patent to create 'waist overalls', now known as blue jeans 1873	140
21	*Friday*	Daylight saving time was first used in Britain 1916	141
22	*Saturday*	Apollo 10's lunar module flew within 14 miles of the Moon's surface in a rehearsal for Apollo 11 1969	142
23	*Sunday*	The New York Public Library was dedicated by President Howard Taft 1911	143

24	*Monday*	Samuel Morse sent the first electric telegram from Washington DC to Baltimore 1844	week 21 day 144
25	*Tuesday*	Gilbert and Sullivan's comic opera *HMS Pinafore* opened in London 1878	145
26	*Wednesday*	The last Confederate army in the American Civil War surrendered near New Orleans 1865	146
27	*Thursday*	British and French troops began to evacuate from Dunkirk in Operation Dynamo 1940	147
28	*Friday*	Two monkeys, Able and Baker, became the first living creatures to survive space flight 1959	148
29	*Saturday*	Edmund Hillary and Tenzing Norgay reached the summit of Mount Everest 1953	149
30	*Sunday*	Joan of Arc was burnt at the stake 1431	150

31	*Monday*	John Harvey Kellogg applied for a patent for 'flaked cereal', now known as Corn Flakes 1884	week 22 day 151

ASTRONOMICAL PHENOMENA

d	h	
3	20	Last Quarter Moon
3	17	Saturn 4.2°N of the Moon
4	03	Mercury 2.1°S of Pleiades
4	21	Jupiter 4.6°N of the Moon
5	01	Eta-Aquarid meteor shower
11	19	New Moon
13	18	Mercury 2.1°N of the Moon
15	05	Mars 1.5°S of the Moon
15	-	Sun crosses into Taurus
17	-	Mercury at greatest elongation (22° 01' E)
19	19	First Quarter Moon
19	18	Regulus 5.0°S of the Moon
21	-	Jupiter at western quadrature
26	11	Total Lunar Eclipse; mag=1.009
26	11	Full Moon
28	06	Mercury 0.4°S of Venus
31	01	Saturn 4.2°N of the Moon

CONSTELLATIONS

The following constellations are visible at midnight throughout the month:

Cepheus (below the Pole), Cassiopeia (below the Pole), Ursa Minor, Ursa Major, Canes Venatici, Coma Berenices, Bootes, Leo, Virgo, Crater, Corvus and Hydra

PHASES OF THE MOON

Phase, Apsides and Node	d	h	m
◑ Last Quarter	3	19	50
● New Quarter	11	19	0
◐ First Moon	19	19	13
○ Full Quarter	26	11	14
Apogee (406,512 km)	11	21	53
Perigee (357,311 km)	26	1	50

SUNRISE AND SUNSET

	London				Bristol				Birmingham				Manchester				Newcastle				Glasgow				Belfast			
	0°	05'	51°	30'	2°	35'	51°	28'	1°	55'	52°	28'	2°	15'	53°	28'	1°	37'	54°	59'	4°	14'	55°	52'	5°	56'	54°	35'
d	h	m	h	m	h	m	h	m	h	m	h	m	h	m	h	m	h	m	h	m	h	m	h	m	h	m	h	m
1	4	32	19	24	4	42	19	34	4	36	19	34	4	34	19	39	4	26	19	42	4	33	19	56	4	45	19	56
2	4	30	19	25	4	40	19	35	4	34	19	36	4	32	19	41	4	24	19	44	4	31	19	58	4	43	20	00
3	4	28	19	27	4	39	19	37	4	32	19	38	4	30	19	43	4	22	19	46	4	29	20	00	4	41	20	02
4	4	27	19	29	4	37	19	39	4	31	19	39	4	28	19	44	4	20	19	48	4	27	20	02	4	39	20	03
5	4	25	19	30	4	35	19	40	4	29	19	41	4	26	19	46	4	18	19	50	4	25	20	04	4	37	20	05
6	4	23	19	32	4	33	19	42	4	27	19	43	4	24	19	48	4	16	19	52	4	22	20	06	4	35	20	07
7	4	21	19	34	4	31	19	43	4	25	19	44	4	23	19	50	4	14	19	53	4	20	20	08	4	33	20	09
8	4	20	19	35	4	30	19	45	4	23	19	46	4	21	19	51	4	12	19	55	4	18	20	10	4	31	20	11
9	4	18	19	37	4	28	19	47	4	22	19	48	4	19	19	53	4	10	19	57	4	16	20	12	4	29	20	13
10	4	16	19	38	4	26	19	48	4	20	19	49	4	17	19	55	4	08	19	59	4	14	20	14	4	27	20	14
11	4	15	19	40	4	25	19	50	4	18	19	51	4	15	19	57	4	06	20	01	4	12	20	16	4	25	20	16
12	4	13	19	41	4	23	19	51	4	16	19	53	4	14	19	58	4	04	20	03	4	10	20	18	4	23	20	18
13	4	11	19	43	4	22	19	53	4	15	19	54	4	12	20	00	4	02	20	04	4	08	20	19	4	21	20	20
14	4	10	19	44	4	20	19	54	4	13	19	56	4	10	20	02	4	01	20	06	4	06	20	21	4	20	20	22
15	4	08	19	46	4	19	19	56	4	12	19	57	4	09	20	03	3	59	20	08	4	05	20	23	4	18	20	23
16	4	07	19	47	4	17	19	57	4	10	19	59	4	07	20	05	3	57	20	10	4	03	20	25	4	16	20	25
17	4	06	19	49	4	16	19	59	4	09	20	00	4	05	20	06	3	55	20	12	4	01	20	27	4	15	20	27
18	4	04	19	50	4	14	20	00	4	07	20	02	4	04	20	08	3	54	20	13	3	59	20	29	4	13	20	28
19	4	03	19	52	4	13	20	02	4	06	20	03	4	02	20	10	3	52	20	15	3	58	20	30	4	11	20	30
20	4	01	19	53	4	12	20	03	4	04	20	05	4	01	20	11	3	51	20	17	3	56	20	32	4	10	20	32
21	4	00	19	55	4	10	20	04	4	03	20	06	4	00	20	13	3	49	20	18	3	54	20	34	4	08	20	33
22	3	59	19	56	4	09	20	06	4	02	20	08	3	58	20	14	3	47	20	20	3	53	20	36	4	07	20	35
23	3	58	19	57	4	08	20	07	4	00	20	09	3	57	20	16	3	46	20	21	3	51	20	37	4	06	20	36
24	3	57	19	59	4	07	20	08	3	59	20	11	3	56	20	17	3	45	20	23	3	50	20	39	4	04	20	38
25	3	55	20	00	4	06	20	10	3	58	20	12	3	54	20	19	3	43	20	25	3	48	20	40	4	03	20	39
26	3	54	20	01	4	05	20	11	3	57	20	13	3	53	20	20	3	42	20	26	3	47	20	42	4	02	20	41
27	3	53	20	02	4	04	20	12	3	56	20	15	3	52	20	21	3	41	20	28	3	46	20	44	4	00	20	42
28	3	52	20	04	4	03	20	13	3	55	20	16	3	51	20	23	3	39	20	29	3	44	20	45	3	59	20	44
29	3	51	20	05	4	02	20	15	3	54	20	17	3	50	20	24	3	38	20	30	3	43	20	47	3	58	20	45
30	3	51	20	06	4	01	20	16	3	53	20	18	3	49	20	25	3	37	20	32	3	42	20	48	3	57	20	47
31	3	50	20	07	4	00	20	17	3	52	20	20	3	48	20	26	3	36	20	33	3	41	20	49	3	56	20	48

THE MOON

Day	Diam	Phase %	Age d	Rise 52° h	Rise 52° m	Rise 56° h	Rise 56° m	Transit h	Transit m	Set 52° h	Set 52° m	Set 56° h	Set 56° m
1	32.6	80	18.7	0	16	0	47	3	54	7	30	7	0
2	32.0	70	19.7	1	15	1	45	4	55	8	37	8	8
3	31.6	59	20.7	1	58	2	25	5	52	9	52	9	26
4	31.2	48	21.7	2	30	2	49	6	45	11	10	10	50
5	30.6	38	22.7	2	52	3	7	7	33	12	25	12	12
6	30.4	28	23.7	3	10	3	20	8	18	13	39	13	31
7	30.0	20	24.7	3	25	3	30	9	1	14	50	14	47
8	29.8	13	25.7	3	38	3	39	9	42	16	0	16	1
9	29.6	7	26.7	3	50	3	47	10	22	17	9	17	15
10	29.4	3	27.7	4	4	3	56	11	3	18	19	18	30
11	29.4	1	28.7	4	19	4	7	11	45	19	29	19	45
12	29.4	0	0.1	4	37	4	20	12	30	20	39	20	59
13	29.4	1	1.1	5	0	4	37	13	16	21	47	22	13
14	29.6	4	2.1	5	28	5	3	14	5	22	50	23	21
15	29.6	9	3.1	6	7	5	36	14	55	23	46	-	-
16	29.8	15	4.1	6	57	6	25	15	47	-	-	0	18
17	30.0	23	5.1	7	58	7	28	16	39	0	32	1	0
18	30.4	32	6.1	9	8	8	43	17	30	1	8	1	33
19	30.8	42	7.1	10	23	10	6	18	20	1	36	1	55
20	31.2	52	8.1	11	42	11	30	19	9	1	57	2	12
21	31.8	63	9.1	13	4	12	57	19	57	2	16	2	25
22	32.2	73	10.1	14	27	14	26	20	46	2	33	2	36
23	32.6	83	11.1	15	53	15	58	21	37	2	49	2	47
24	33.0	91	12.1	17	23	17	34	22	31	3	6	2	59
25	33.4	97	13.1	18	54	19	13	23	29	3	26	3	13
26	33.4	100	14.1	20	27	20	51	-	-	3	52	3	32
27	33.4	100	15.1	21	51	22	22	0	30	4	26	4	1
28	33.2	96	16.1	23	1	23	34	1	34	5	14	4	43
29	32.8	91	17.1	23	54	-	-	2	38	6	16	5	45
30	32.2	83	18.1	-	-	0	23	3	40	7	31	7	4
31	31.8	74	19.1	0	31	0	53	4	37	8	51	8	29

THE PLANETS

MERCURY

Day	R.A.			Dec.	Mag.	Diam.	Phase	Rise			Transit			Set		
	h	m	s	°		"	%	h	m	s	h	m	s	h	m	s
1	3	25	32	+20.2	-1.1	5.7	83	4	41	56	12	49	16	20	58	30
6	4	3	22	+22.9	-0.7	6.2	68	4	40	3	13	6	46	21	34	46
11	4	36	30	+24.5	-0.2	6.9	53	4	40	22	13	19	18	21	58	54
16	5	3	23	+25.2	+0.3	7.8	40	4	41	38	13	25	24	22	9	15
21	5	22	54	+25.1	+0.9	8.9	28	4	41	56	13	23	57	22	5	37
26	5	34	11	+24.4	+1.7	10.0	18	4	39	3	13	14	12	21	48	34
31	5	36	51	+23.2	+2.6	11.0	9	4	31	9	12	55	58	21	19	32

VENUS

Day	R.A.			Dec.	Mag.	Diam.	Phase	Rise			Transit			Set		
	h	m	s	°		"	%	h	m	s	h	m	s	h	m	s
1	3	10	51	+17.4	-3.9	10.6	99	4	46	58	12	33	35	20	21	8
6	3	35	45	+19.2	-3.9	10.6	98	4	40	12	12	38	47	20	38	17
11	4	1	7	+20.7	-3.9	10.7	98	4	34	54	12	44	28	20	54	53
16	4	26	55	+22.0	-3.9	10.8	97	4	31	21	12	50	34	21	10	34
21	4	53	7	+23.0	-3.9	10.8	97	4	29	51	12	57	4	21	24	57
26	5	19	37	+23.8	-3.9	10.9	96	4	30	36	13	3	52	21	37	40
31	5	46	20	+24.3	-3.9	11.0	95	4	33	47	13	10	53	21	48	20

MARS

Day	R.A.			Dec.	Mag.	Diam.	Rise			Transit			Set		
	h	m	s	°		"	h	m	s	h	m	s	h	m	s
1	6	20	7	+24.8	+1.6	4.6	7	0	53	15	41	53	0	23	10
6	6	33	29	+24.7	+1.6	4.5	6	55	50	15	35	33	0	15	28
11	6	46	51	+24.4	+1.6	4.5	6	51	21	15	29	12	0	7	32
16	7	0	11	+24.1	+1.7	4.4	6	47	24	15	22	49	23	58	20
21	7	13	29	+23.8	+1.7	4.3	6	43	56	15	16	23	23	48	53
26	7	26	42	+23.3	+1.7	4.2	6	40	56	15	9	53	23	38	51
31	7	39	51	+22.8	+1.7	4.2	6	38	19	15	3	20	23	28	17

JUPITER

Day	R.A.			Dec.	Mag.	Diam.	Rise			Transit			Set		
	h	m	s	°		"	h	m	s	h	m	s	h	m	s
1	22	3	8	-12.7	-2.2	37.4	2	34	33	7	25	26	12	16	24
6	22	5	47	-12.5	-2.2	38.0	2	16	12	7	8	25	12	0	42
11	22	8	13	-12.3	-2.3	38.5	1	57	45	6	51	10	11	44	39
16	22	10	23	-12.1	-2.3	39.1	1	39	12	6	33	41	11	28	30
21	22	12	19	-12.0	-2.3	39.8	1	20	32	6	15	57	11	11	26
26	22	13	60	-11.9	-2.4	40.4	1	1	45	5	57	57	10	54	14
31	22	15	24	-11.7	-2.4	41.1	0	42	51	5	39	41	10	36	36

Diam. = Equatorial. Polar Diam. is 94% of Equatorial Diam.

SATURN

Day	R.A.			Dec.	Mag.	Diam.	Rise			Transit			Set		
	h	m	s	°		"	h	m	s	h	m	s	h	m	s
1	21	3	1	-17.4	+0.7	16.7	2	4	1	6	25	24	10	46	50
6	21	3	40	-17.4	+0.7	16.8	1	44	47	6	6	24	10	28	3
11	21	4	10	-17.4	+0.7	17.0	1	25	28	5	47	14	10	9	3
16	21	4	30	-17.4	+0.6	17.1	1	6	4	5	27	55	9	49	48
21	21	4	41	-17.4	+0.6	17.3	0	46	35	5	8	25	9	30	19
26	21	4	41	-17.4	+0.6	17.4	0	27	0	4	48	46	9	10	35
31	21	4	32	-17.4	+0.6	17.5	0	3	32	4	28	57	8	50	37

Diam. = Equatorial. Polar Diam. is 90% of Equatorial Diam.
Rings – major axis 39", minor axis 11", Tilt 17°

URANUS

Day	R.A.			Dec.	Mag.	Diam.	Rise			Transit			Set		
	h	m	s	°		"	h	m	s	h	m	s	h	m	s
1	2	33	39	+14.6	+5.9	3.4	4	27	43	11	55	7	19	22	33
6	2	34	47	+14.7	+5.9	3.4	4	8	37	11	36	35	19	4	36
11	2	35	54	+14.8	+5.9	3.4	3	49	31	11	18	3	18	46	38
16	2	37	1	+14.9	+5.9	3.4	3	30	25	10	59	30	18	28	38
21	2	38	7	+15.0	+5.9	3.4	3	11	18	10	40	57	18	10	38
26	2	39	12	+15.1	+5.9	3.4	2	52	11	10	22	22	17	52	35
31	2	40	15	+15.2	+5.9	3.4	2	33	3	10	3	45	17	34	30

NEPTUNE

Day	R.A.			Dec.	Mag.	Diam.	Rise			Transit			Set		
	h	m	s	°		"	h	m	s	h	m	s	h	m	s
1	23	33	48	-4.0	+7.9	2.2	3	14	58	8	55	45	14	36	32
6	23	34	17	-4.0	+7.9	2.2	2	55	38	8	36	35	14	17	38
11	23	34	45	-3.9	+7.9	2.2	2	36	5	8	17	23	13	58	41
16	23	35	10	-3.9	+7.9	2.2	2	16	47	7	58	8	13	39	40
21	23	35	32	-3.8	+7.9	2.3	1	57	7	7	38	51	13	20	35
26	23	35	52	-3.8	+7.9	2.3	1	37	37	7	19	31	13	1	25
31	23	36	9	-3.8	+7.9	2.3	1	18	5	7	0	8	12	42	11

THE NIGHT SKY

Mercury can be seen almost to the end of May in the evening sky and soars 10° above the northwest skyline on the 12th when the magnitude -0.2 world is setting around two hours after the Sun. Greatest elongation is reached on the 17th.

Mercury passes 2° from the Pleiades star cluster on May 4th, and is less than 3° from the two-day old moon on the evening of the 13th. Watch the fleet-footed world and Venus converge towards the end of the month - the two are closest on the 28th when they are a $\frac{1}{2}$° apart.

Venus (magnitude -3.9) remains quite low above the northwest horizon these evenings, but its brilliance catches the eye. It is setting $1\frac{1}{2}$ hours after the Sun at the end of the month. Venus passes about $4\frac{1}{2}$° from the Pleiades on the 9th but you will almost certainly need binoculars and a clear horizon to spot the cluster in the lingering twilight.

Mars (magnitude 1.6) continues to dwindle in size for telescope users and sets close to 1am summer time at the end of May. The planet dwells in the western sky presently and sits at the tip of an isosceles triangle with Castor and Pollux in Gemini on the 17th but is now dimmer than those two stars. Mars can be found to the upper left of the Moon on the evening of May 15th.

Jupiter (magnitude -2.3) rises two hours before the Sun at the beginning of May and three hours beforehand by the 31st. The Moon lies between Jupiter and Saturn on the morning of the 4th.

Saturn (magnitude 0.6) rises well before the Sun all month and telescope users can view the shadow of the planet's globe on the rings as it reaches western quadrature on the 3rd. The rings are currently tipped a little less than 17° earthward, their minimum for the year. On the morning of the 31st you will find Saturn to the upper left of the waning gibbous Moon as it rises.

Saturn is stationary on the 23rd and then begins to retrograde, travelling slowly westward across Capricornus to pass through opposition on August 2nd and then reaching its westernmost stationary point on October 11th.

A total lunar eclipse on May 26th is visible from Asia, Australia, New Zealand, Pacific countries, and the western parts of the Americas. The same night is also the biggest full moon of the year, and these are now popularly called supermoons.

May 26th's event is the shortest totality of the 21st century, as at maximum eclipse the northern limb of the Moon will touch the outer edge of Earth's umbra. The total phase will be just $14\frac{1}{2}$ minutes long, and the southern part of the Moon's disk will appear deeper coloured due to it being nearer the centre of Earth's shadow cast in space.

June 2021

SIXTH MONTH, 30 DAYS. *Junius,* Roman *gens* (family)

1	*Tueday*	Anne Boleyn, mother of Elizabeth I, was crowned Queen Consort of England 1533	152
2	*Wednesday*	Joan of Arc was burnt at the stake 1431	153
3	*Thursday*	The Tiananmen Square massacre took place in Peking (Beijing), China 1989	154
4	*Friday*	Allied forces completed their evacuation from Dunkirk 1940	155
5	*Saturday*	The Montgolfier Brothers demonstrated their hot air balloon in public for the first time 1783	156
6	*Sunday*	D-day: the Allied forces landed in Normandy 1944	157

7	*Monday*	Queen Elizabeth II's Silver Jubilee procession 1977	week 23 day 158
8	*Tuesday*	Margaret Bondfield became Britain's first woman cabinet minister 1929	159
9	*Wednesday*	A revamped Gatwick airport, costing £7.8m to build, was opened by Queen Elizabeth II 1958	160
10	*Thursday*	The first Oxford and Cambridge boat race took place 1829	161
11	*Friday*	The UN officially declared a famine in Sudan with over a million people facing starvation 1998	162
12	*Saturday*	Anne Frank was given a diary for her thirteenth birthday 1942	163
13	*Sunday*	The Beatles achieved their final US number one, 'The Long and Winding Road' 1970	164

14	*Monday*	English Civil War: parliamentarians defeated the royalists at the Battle of Naseby 1645	week 24 day 165
15	*Tuesday*	King John signed the Magna Carta at Runnymede in Surrey 1215	166
16	*Wednesday*	US aviation pioneer Henry Berliner conducted the first manned, controlled helicopter flight 1922	167
17	*Thursday*	The Statue of Liberty, a gift from France, arrived in New York 1885	168
18	*Friday*	The 1970 general election allowed people to vote from the age of 18 for the first time	169
19	*Saturday*	The first five-cent cinema, or 'nickelodeon', opened in Pittsburgh, USA 1905	170
20	*Sunday*	Queen Victoria became Queen of England at the age of 18 1837	171

21	*Monday*	The first stored-program computer, the Small-Scale Experimental Machine, ran its first program 1948	week 25 day 172
22	*Tuesday*	The Royal Greenwich Observatory, a centre for practical astronomy, was created by Royal Warrant 1675	173
23	*Wednesday*	Treatises attributed to John Frith were found in the belly of a cod at Cambridge market 1626	174
24	*Thursday*	Robert Bruce defeated Edward II at Bannockburn, securing Scottish independence 1314	175
25	*Friday*	Sioux Native Americans defeated General Custer and his men at the Battle of Little Bighorn 1876	176
26	*Saturday*	Representatives of 50 countries signed the United Nations Charter 1945	177
27	*Sunday*	The world's first atomic power station began producing electricity in Obninsk, Russia 1954	178

28	*Monday*	Archduke Franz Ferdinand of Austria was assassinated by Gavrilo Princip in Sarajevo 1914	week 26 day 179
29	*Tuesday*	The Globe Theatre burned down after fire broke out during a performance of Henry VIII 1613	180
30	*Wednesday*	Hitler ordered the assassination of hundreds of Nazis; now known as the Night of the Long Knives 1934	181

ASTRONOMICAL PHENOMENA

d	h	
1	09	Jupiter 4.6°N of the Moon
2	07	Last Quarter Moon
8	-	Juno at opposition
10	11	Annular solar eclipse; mag=0.943 (partial from the UK)
10	13	Mercury 4.0°S of the Moon
10	11	New Moon
11	-	Mercury at inferior conjunction
12	-	Venus at perihelion
12	07	Venus 1.5°S of the Moon
13	20	Mars 2.8°S of the Moon
15	23	Regulus 5.0°S of the Moon
18	04	First Quarter Moon
21	04	Summer solstice
21	-	Jupiter stationary, begins to retrograde
22	-	Sun crosses into Gemini
24	05	Mars 0.3°S of the Beehive star cluster in Cancer
24	19	Full Moon
26	09	Saturn 4.0°N of the Moon
28	18	Jupiter 4.5°N of the Moon

CONSTELLATIONS

The following constellations are visible at midnight throughout the month:
Cassiopeia (below the Pole), Ursa Minor, Draco, Ursa Major, Canes Venatici, Bootes, Corona, Serpens, Virgo and Libra

PHASES OF THE MOON

Phase, Apsides and Node	d	h	m
◑ Last Quarter	2	7	24
● New Moon	10	10	53
◐ First Quarter	18	3	54
○ Full Moon	24	18	40
Apogee (406,228 km)	8	2	27
Perigee (359,956 km)	23	9	55

SUNRISE AND SUNSET

	London				Bristol				Birmingham				Manchester				Newcastle				Glasgow				Belfast			
	0° 05'		51° 30'		2° 35'		51° 28'		1° 55'		52° 28'		2° 15'		53° 28'		1° 37'		54° 59'		4° 14'		55° 52'		5° 56'		54° 35'	
d	h	m	h	m	h	m	h	m	h	m	h	m	h	m	h	m	h	m	h	m	h	m	h	m	h	m	h	m
1	3	49	20	08	3	59	20	18	3	51	20	21	3	47	20	28	3	35	20	34	3	40	20	51	3	55	20	49
2	3	48	20	09	3	58	20	19	3	50	20	22	3	46	20	29	3	34	20	36	3	39	20	52	3	54	20	50
3	3	47	20	10	3	58	20	20	3	50	20	23	3	45	20	30	3	33	20	37	3	38	20	53	3	53	20	51
4	3	47	20	11	3	57	20	21	3	49	20	24	3	44	20	31	3	32	20	38	3	37	20	54	3	52	20	53
5	3	46	20	12	3	56	20	22	3	48	20	25	3	44	20	32	3	32	20	39	3	36	20	56	3	52	20	54
6	3	46	20	13	3	56	20	23	3	48	20	26	3	43	20	33	3	31	20	40	3	35	20	57	3	51	20	55
7	3	45	20	14	3	55	20	24	3	47	20	27	3	42	20	34	3	30	20	41	3	35	20	58	3	50	20	56
8	3	45	20	15	3	55	20	25	3	46	20	27	3	42	20	35	3	30	20	42	3	34	20	59	3	50	20	57
9	3	44	20	16	3	54	20	25	3	46	20	28	3	41	20	36	3	29	20	43	3	33	21	00	3	49	20	57
10	3	44	20	16	3	54	20	26	3	46	20	29	3	41	20	36	3	29	20	44	3	33	21	01	3	49	20	58
11	3	43	20	17	3	54	20	27	3	45	20	30	3	41	20	37	3	28	20	45	3	32	21	01	3	48	20	59
12	3	43	20	18	3	53	20	27	3	45	20	30	3	40	20	38	3	28	20	45	3	32	21	02	3	48	21	00
13	3	43	20	18	3	53	20	28	3	45	20	31	3	40	20	38	3	27	20	46	3	32	21	03	3	48	21	01
14	3	43	20	19	3	53	20	29	3	45	20	32	3	40	20	39	3	27	20	47	3	31	21	04	3	47	21	01
15	3	43	20	19	3	53	20	29	3	44	20	32	3	40	20	40	3	27	20	47	3	31	21	04	3	47	21	02
16	3	43	20	20	3	53	20	30	3	44	20	33	3	40	20	40	3	27	20	48	3	31	21	05	3	47	21	02
17	3	43	20	20	3	53	20	30	3	44	20	33	3	40	20	41	3	27	20	48	3	31	21	05	3	47	21	03
18	3	43	20	20	3	53	20	30	3	44	20	33	3	40	20	41	3	27	20	49	3	31	21	05	3	47	21	03
19	3	43	20	21	3	53	20	31	3	44	20	34	3	40	20	41	3	27	20	49	3	31	21	06	3	47	21	03
20	3	43	20	21	3	53	20	31	3	45	20	34	3	40	20	41	3	27	20	49	3	31	21	06	3	47	21	04
21	3	43	20	21	3	53	20	31	3	45	20	34	3	40	20	42	3	27	20	49	3	31	21	06	3	47	21	04
22	3	43	20	21	3	53	20	31	3	45	20	34	3	40	20	42	3	27	20	49	3	31	21	06	3	48	21	04
23	3	44	20	22	3	54	20	31	3	45	20	34	3	41	20	42	3	28	20	50	3	32	21	07	3	48	21	04
24	3	44	20	22	3	54	20	31	3	46	20	35	3	41	20	42	3	28	20	50	3	32	21	07	3	48	21	04
25	3	44	20	22	3	54	20	31	3	46	20	34	3	41	20	42	3	29	20	50	3	33	21	06	3	49	21	04
26	3	45	20	22	3	55	20	31	3	47	20	34	3	42	20	42	3	29	20	49	3	33	21	06	3	49	21	04
27	3	45	20	21	3	55	20	31	3	47	20	34	3	42	20	42	3	30	20	49	3	34	21	06	3	50	21	04
28	3	46	20	21	3	56	20	31	3	48	20	34	3	43	20	42	3	30	20	49	3	34	21	06	3	50	21	04
29	3	46	20	21	3	57	20	31	3	48	20	34	3	43	20	41	3	31	20	49	3	35	21	06	3	51	21	03
30	3	47	20	21	3	57	20	31	3	49	20	34	3	44	20	41	3	32	20	48	3	36	21	05	3	52	21	03

THE MOON

Day	Diam (')	Phase (%)	Age (d)	Rise 52° h	m	Rise 56° h	m	Transit h	m	Set 52° h	m	Set 56° h	m
1	31.2	64	20.1	0	57	1	14	5	28	10	10	9	55
2	30.8	53	21.1	1	17	1	29	6	16	11	26	11	16
3	30.4	43	22.1	1	33	1	40	7	0	12	39	12	34
4	30.0	33	23.1	1	46	1	49	7	41	13	50	13	50
5	29.8	25	24.1	1	59	1	57	8	22	14	59	15	4
6	29.6	17	25.1	2	12	2	6	9	3	16	8	16	18
7	29.4	10	26.1	2	26	2	16	9	44	17	18	17	33
8	29.4	5	27.1	2	43	2	27	10	28	18	28	18	48
9	29.4	2	28.1	3	4	2	43	11	13	19	38	20	1
10	29.6	0	29.1	3	30	3	6	12	2	20	43	21	12
11	29.6	0	0.6	4	7	3	36	12	52	21	42	22	14
12	29.8	2	1.6	4	53	4	21	13	43	22	32	23	0
13	30.0	6	2.6	5	50	5	20	14	35	23	10	23	37
14	30.2	12	3.6	6	59	6	32	15	27	23	40	-	-
15	30.6	19	4.6	8	12	7	52	16	17	-	-	0	1
16	30.8	28	5.6	9	29	9	14	17	5	0	3	0	19
17	31.2	37	6.6	10	47	10	38	17	52	0	23	0	33
18	31.6	48	7.6	12	7	12	4	18	39	0	39	0	44
19	32.0	59	8.6	13	29	13	31	19	28	0	54	0	55
20	32.4	70	9.6	14	54	15	2	20	18	1	10	1	6
21	32.8	80	10.6	16	22	16	36	21	12	1	28	1	18
22	33.0	89	11.6	17	52	18	14	22	11	1	50	1	34
23	33.2	95	12.6	19	21	19	48	23	13	2	19	1	57
24	33.2	99	13.6	20	40	21	10	-	-	3	0	2	30
25	33.0	100	14.6	21	42	22	11	0	17	3	55	3	22
26	32.6	98	15.6	22	27	22	51	1	21	5	5	4	34
27	32.2	93	16.6	22	57	23	17	2	22	6	24	6	1
28	31.8	86	17.6	23	21	23	35	3	17	7	47	7	29
29	31.2	78	18.6	23	38	23	47	4	8	9	7	8	55
30	30.8	69	19.6	23	53	23	57	4	54	10	23	10	17

THE PLANETS

MERCURY

Day	R.A.			Dec.	Mag.	Diam.	Phase	Rise			Transit			Set		
	h	m	s	°		"	%	h	m	s	h	m	s	h	m	s
1	5	36	24	+23.0	+2.9	11.2	8	4	28	53	12	51	22	21	12	31
6	5	29	58	+21.5	+4.3	12.0	2	4	14	6	12	24	33	20	33	21
11	5	19	10	+20.0	+5.4	12.2	0	3	54	35	11	54	4	19	51	59
16	5	8	30	+18.8	+4.1	11.9	3	3	32	35	11	24	26	19	15	11
21	5	2	18	+18.3	+2.7	11.0	8	3	10	39	10	59	38	18	48	12
26	5	3	12	+18.5	+1.7	9.9	17	2	50	55	10	42	1	18	33	23

VENUS

Day	R.A.			Dec.	Mag.	Diam.	Phase	Rise			Transit			Set		
	h	m	s	°		"	%	h	m	s	h	m	s	h	m	s
1	5	51	42	+24.3	-3.9	11.1	95	4	34	44	13	12	18	21	50	12
6	6	18	32	+24.4	-3.9	11.2	95	4	40	54	13	19	24	21	58	4
11	6	45	19	+24.3	-3.9	11.3	94	4	49	30	13	26	27	22	3	25
16	7	11	55	+23.8	-3.9	11.5	93	5	0	18	13	33	19	22	6	11
21	7	38	13	+23.0	-3.9	11.6	92	5	13	1	13	39	53	22	6	25
26	8	4	8	+22.0	-3.9	11.8	91	5	27	16	13	46	2	22	4	20

MARS

Day	R.A.			Dec.	Mag.	Diam.	Rise			Transit			Set		
	h	m	s	°		"	h	m	s	h	m	s	h	m	s
1	7	42	29	+22.7	+1.7	4.2	6	37	50	15	2	0	23	26	7
6	7	55	32	+22.2	+1.8	4.1	6	35	39	14	55	21	23	14	56
11	8	8	30	+21.5	+1.8	4.0	6	33	46	14	48	36	23	3	17
16	8	21	23	+20.8	+1.8	4.0	6	32	9	14	41	45	22	51	11
21	8	34	9	+20.1	+1.8	3.9	6	30	44	14	34	49	22	38	41
26	8	46	49	+19.2	+1.8	3.9	6	29	29	14	27	46	22	25	48

JUPITER

Day	R.A.			Dec.	Mag.	Diam.	Rise			Transit			Set		
	h	m	s	°		"	h	m	s	h	m	s	h	m	s
1	22	15	38	-11.7	-2.4	41.2	0	39	3	5	36	0	10	33	1
6	22	16	42	-11.7	-2.5	41.9	0	20	0	5	17	23	10	14	52
11	22	17	28	-11.6	-2.5	42.6	23	57	3	4	58	30	9	56	15
16	22	17	56	-11.6	-2.5	43.2	23	37	44	4	39	18	9	37	10
21	22	18	6	-11.6	-2.6	43.9	23	18	18	4	19	48	9	17	37
26	22	17	57	-11.6	-2.6	44.6	22	58	43	3	59	59	8	57	35

Diam. = Equatorial. Polar Diam. is 94% of Equatorial Diam.

SATURN

Day	R.A.			Dec.	Mag.	Diam.	Rise			Transit			Set		
	h	m	s	°		"	h	m	s	h	m	s	h	m	s
1	21	4	29	-17.4	+0.6	17.6	23	59	35	4	24	59	8	46	36
6	21	4	8	-17.4	+0.5	17.7	23	39	50	4	5	58	8	26	21
11	21	3	38	-17.5	+0.5	17.8	23	19	59	3	44	49	8	5	52
16	21	2	59	-17.5	+0.5	18.0	23	0	4	3	24	30	7	45	10
21	21	2	12	-17.6	+0.4	18.1	22	40	3	3	4	3	7	24	16
26	21	1	16	-17.7	+0.4	18.2	22	19	59	2	43	28	7	3	10

Diam. = Equatorial. Polar Diam. is 90% of Equatorial Diam.
Rings – major axis 40", minor axis 12", Tilt 17°

URANUS

Day	R.A.			Dec.	Mag.	Diam.	Rise			Transit			Set		
	h	m	s	°		"	h	m	s	h	m	s	h	m	s
1	2	40	28	+15.2	+5.9	3.4	2	29	13	10	0	2	17	30	52
6	2	41	29	+15.3	+5.9	3.4	2	10	5	9	41	23	17	12	43
11	2	42	27	+15.3	+5.9	3.4	1	50	55	9	22	42	16	54	31
16	2	43	23	+15.4	+5.8	3.4	1	31	44	9	3	58	16	36	15
21	2	44	17	+15.5	+5.8	3.4	1	12	32	8	45	12	16	17	54
26	2	45	7	+15.5	+5.8	3.5	0	53	18	8	26	22	15	59	29

NEPTUNE

Day	R.A.			Dec.	Mag.	Diam.	Rise			Transit			Set		
	h	m	s	°		"	h	m	s	h	m	s	h	m	s
1	23	36	12	-3.8	+7.9	2.3	1	14	11	6	56	15	12	38	20
6	23	36	25	-3.8	+7.9	2.3	0	54	38	6	36	49	12	19	0
11	23	36	36	-3.7	+7.9	2.3	0	35	4	6	17	20	11	59	36
16	23	36	43	-3.7	+7.9	2.3	0	15	29	5	57	48	11	40	7
21	23	36	48	-3.7	+7.9	2.3	23	51	57	5	38	13	11	20	34
26	23	36	50	-3.7	+7.9	2.3	23	32	19	5	18	35	11	0	55

THE NIGHT SKY

Mercury is not visible this month as it passes between us and the Sun when at inferior conjunction on the 11th.

Venus (magnitude -3.8) continues to dominate the evening sky despite its low altitude and does not set until 1½ hours after the Sun all month. Telescope users will note the planet's phase is presently almost full.

Venus is very close to the star cluster M35 in Gemini on the 3rd, but they are low at the time. The planet is then beautifully paired with the 35-hour old lunar crescent on the evening of the 11th, after which Venus makes rapid progress across the sky to end June not far from M44 in Cancer.

Mars is quite low in the dusk, but its eastward pace keeps it out of the solar glare a little longer. The ochre-hued world has now dimmed to magnitude 1.8 and is setting roughly three hours after the Sun for most of June.

Mars is near the Moon on the evening of the 13th, and it then passes directly in front of the Beehive star cluster (M44) in Cancer on the 23rd and 24th when binoculars reveal the swarm. About 7½° separate Mars and Venus when they lie either side of the Beehive on the 30th.

Jupiter (magnitude -2.5) rises in the early hours at the beginning of June and is up just after midnight at the end of the month. It easily dominates the southern sky during the brief night this time of year. Jupiter is near the Moon both on June 1st and 28th as it makes its appearance over the horizon.

Jupiter reaches its easternmost stationary point in Aquarius on June 21st and then begins to retrograde, moving southwest towards the constellation's border with Capricornus, which it will cross back into mid-August.

Saturn (magnitude 0.5), in Capricornus, rises not long after the witching hour on June 1st but is visible just before midnight by the end of June. Saturn is to the upper left of the Moon on the night of the 26th.

An annular solar eclipse visible across Arctic regions of Canada and Russia, as well as Greenland, on June 10th is partial that morning from the UK. It will take about an hour from the time you notice the first nick out of the Sun's edge until greatest eclipse.

The maximum obscuration of the solar disk ranges from almost 32% in Glasgow to 20% from London. The websites astro.ukho.gov.uk/eclipse/0232021/ or www.timeanddate.com/eclipse will give the local circumstances.

Great care should be taken if you try observing the event. The only suitable method for the general observer is to project the Sun's image with a telescope or binocular onto a piece of white card. Eclipse glasses will let you see it safely with the unaided eye but discard them if their filter material is damaged in any way.

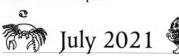

July 2021

SEVENTH MONTH, 31 DAYS. *Julius* Caesar, formerly *Quintilis*, fifth month of Roman pre-Julian calendar

1	*Thursday*	The Montgolfier Brothers demonstrated their hot air balloon in public for the first time 1783	day 182
2	*Friday*	Live 8 concerts were held around the globe to persuade political leaders to tackle poverty in Africa 2005	183
3	*Saturday*	After being stolen in 1296, the Stone of Scone is returned to Scotland by the British government 1996	184
4	*Sunday*	Marie Curie died, almost certainly due to her exposure to radiation 1934	185
5	*Monday*	The National Health Service Act came into effect 1948	week 27 day 186
6	*Tuesday*	Louis Pasteur began the modern era of immunisation by vaccinating a boy bitten by a rabid dog 1885	187
7	*Wednesday*	The Yardbirds broke up, leading to the creation of Led Zeppelin 1968	188
8	*Thursday*	The National Society for the Prevention of Cruelty to Children (NSPCC) was founded 1884	189
9	*Friday*	Michael Fagan breaks into Buckingham Palace and spends ten minutes talking to Queen Elizabeth II 1982	190
10	*Saturday*	*Telstar 1*, the first satellite to relay TV and telephone signals across the Atlantic, was launched 1962	191
11	*Sunday*	US space station *Skylab* re-entered Earth's atmosphere and disintegrated 1979	192
12	*Monday*	Ranjit Singh founds the Sikh Empire, based in the Punjab region 1799	week 28 day 193
13	*Tuesday*	Ruth Ellis, the last woman to be executed in Britain, was hanged 1955	194
14	*Wednesday*	*Mariner 4* takes the first up-close photos of another planet as it passes Mars 1965	195
15	*Thursday*	Emmeline Pankhurst, suffragette who helped women win the right to vote *b.* 1858	196
16	*Friday*	J. D. Salinger's seminal novel *The Catcher in the Rye* is published 1951	197
17	*Saturday*	Allied leaders held a conference in Potsdam to decide on the future of Germany 1945	198
18	*Sunday*	The Ballot Act 1872, requiring that elections are held by secret ballot, received royal assent	199
19	*Monday*	A French soldier uncovers the Rosetta Stone during Napoleon's Egyptian campaign 1799	week 29 day 200
20	*Tuesday*	US magazine *Billboard* published its first 'Music Popularity Chart' 1940	201
21	*Wednesday*	Neil Armstrong became the first man to walk on the Moon 1969	202
22	*Thursday*	The Tate Gallery opened 1897	203
23	*Friday*	Caravaggio received his first public commission, for the Contarelli Chapel in Rome 1599	204
24	*Saturday*	Amelia Earhart, who in 1932 became the first woman to fly solo over the Atlantic *b.* 1897	205
25	*Sunday*	Bob Dylan switched to an electric guitar at the Newport Folk Festival 1965	206
26	*Monday*	Apollo 15 launched, the first mission to the Moon which used the lunar rover 1971	week 30 day 207
27	*Tuesday*	Queen Elizabeth II declared the London 2012 Olympic Games open, after acting with James Bond 2012	208
28	*Wednesday*	Percy Bysshe Shelley and Mary Wollstonecraft eloped to France 1814	209
29	*Thursday*	The BBC Light Programme radio station began broadcasting 1945	210
30	*Friday*	US settlers and Shoshoni Native Americans signed the Treaty of Box Elder, Utah 1863	211
31	*Saturday*	Britain announced a total ban on the use of landmines 1998	212

ASTRONOMICAL PHENOMENA

d	h	
1	21	Last Quarter Moon
3	PM	Venus 0.1°N of Beehive
4	-	Mercury at greatest elongation (21° 33' W)
5	22	Earth is at aphelion
8	5	Moon 3°N of Mercury
10	1	New Moon
12	21	Moon 5°N of Mars and Venus
12	21	Venus 0.5°NW of Mars
13	-	Mars is at aphelion (1.66596 AU))
13	21	Venus 28' N of Mars
17	10	First Quarter Moon
17	-	Pluto at opposition (4.983 billion km distant)
21	-	Sun crosses into Cancer
21	PM	Venus 1°N of Regulus (daylight)
24	3	Full Moon
25	0	Jupiter, Saturn and Moon form a triangle
28	3	Delta-Aquarid meteor shower
29	PM	Mars 38'N of Regulus (daylight)
31	13	Last Quarter Moon

CONSTELLATIONS

The following constellations are visible at midnight throughout the month:

Ursa Minor, Draco, Corona, Hercules, Lyra, Serpens, Ophiuchus, Libra, Scorpius and Sagittarius

PHASES OF THE MOON

Phase, Apsides and Node	d	h	m
◑ Last Quarter	1	21	11
● New Moon	10	1	17
◐ First Quarter	17	10	11
○ Full Moon	24	2	37
	31	13	16
Apogee (405,341 km)	5	14	47
Perigee (364,520 km)	21	10	24

SUNRISE AND SUNSET

	London 0° 05'	51° 30'	Bristol 2° 35'	51° 28'	Birmingham 1° 55'	52° 28'	Manchester 2° 15'	53° 28'	Newcastle 1° 37'	54° 59'	Glasgow 4° 14'	55° 52'	Belfast 5° 56'	54° 35'
d	h m	h m	h m	h m	h m	h m	h m	h m	h m	h m	h m	h m	h m	h m
1	3 48	20 21	3 58	20 30	3 49	20 33	3 45	20 41	3 32	20 48	3 37	21 05	3 52	21 03
2	3 48	20 20	3 59	20 30	3 50	20 33	3 46	20 40	3 33	20 47	3 37	21 04	3 53	21 02
3	3 49	20 20	3 59	20 30	3 51	20 32	3 46	20 40	3 34	20 47	3 38	21 04	3 54	21 02
4	3 50	20 19	4 00	20 29	3 52	20 32	3 47	20 39	3 35	20 46	3 39	21 03	3 55	21 01
5	3 51	20 19	4 01	20 29	3 53	20 31	3 48	20 39	3 36	20 46	3 40	21 02	3 56	21 00
6	3 52	20 18	4 02	20 28	3 54	20 31	3 49	20 38	3 37	20 45	3 41	21 01	3 57	21 00
7	3 52	20 18	4 03	20 27	3 55	20 30	3 50	20 37	3 38	20 44	3 42	21 01	3 58	20 59
8	3 53	20 17	4 04	20 27	3 56	20 29	3 51	20 36	3 39	20 43	3 44	21 00	3 59	20 58
9	3 54	20 16	4 05	20 26	3 57	20 29	3 52	20 36	3 40	20 42	3 45	20 59	4 00	20 57
10	3 55	20 15	4 06	20 25	3 58	20 28	3 53	20 35	3 41	20 42	3 46	20 58	4 01	20 56
11	3 56	20 15	4 07	20 24	3 59	20 27	3 54	20 34	3 43	20 41	3 47	20 57	4 03	20 55
12	3 58	20 14	4 08	20 24	4 00	20 26	3 56	20 33	3 44	20 39	3 49	20 56	4 04	20 54
13	3 59	20 13	4 09	20 23	4 01	20 25	3 57	20 32	3 45	20 38	3 50	20 54	4 05	20 53
14	4 00	20 12	4 10	20 22	4 02	20 24	3 58	20 31	3 47	20 37	3 51	20 53	4 06	20 52
15	4 01	20 11	4 11	20 21	4 03	20 23	3 59	20 30	3 48	20 36	3 53	20 52	4 08	20 51
16	4 02	20 10	4 12	20 20	4 05	20 22	4 01	20 29	3 49	20 35	3 54	20 51	4 09	20 50
17	4 03	20 09	4 14	20 19	4 06	20 21	4 02	20 27	3 51	20 33	3 56	20 49	4 11	20 48
18	4 05	20 08	4 15	20 18	4 07	20 20	4 03	20 26	3 52	20 32	3 58	20 48	4 12	20 47
19	4 06	20 07	4 16	20 16	4 09	20 19	4 05	20 25	3 54	20 31	3 59	20 46	4 13	20 46
20	4 07	20 05	4 17	20 15	4 10	20 17	4 06	20 24	3 55	20 29	4 01	20 45	4 15	20 44
21	4 09	20 04	4 19	20 14	4 11	20 16	4 08	20 22	3 57	20 28	4 02	20 43	4 17	20 43
22	4 10	20 03	4 20	20 13	4 13	20 15	4 09	20 21	3 59	20 26	4 04	20 42	4 18	20 41
23	4 11	20 02	4 21	20 11	4 14	20 13	4 11	20 19	4 00	20 25	4 06	20 40	4 20	20 40
24	4 13	20 00	4 23	20 10	4 16	20 12	4 12	20 18	4 02	20 23	4 07	20 38	4 21	20 38
25	4 14	19 59	4 24	20 09	4 17	20 10	4 14	20 16	4 04	20 21	4 09	20 37	4 23	20 37
26	4 15	19 57	4 26	20 07	4 19	20 09	4 15	20 15	4 05	20 20	4 11	20 35	4 25	20 35
27	4 17	19 56	4 27	20 06	4 20	20 07	4 17	20 13	4 07	20 18	4 13	20 33	4 26	20 33
28	4 18	19 54	4 28	20 04	4 22	20 06	4 18	20 11	4 09	20 16	4 14	20 31	4 28	20 31
29	4 20	19 53	4 30	20 03	4 23	20 04	4 20	20 10	4 10	20 14	4 16	20 29	4 30	20 30
30	4 21	19 51	4 31	20 01	4 25	20 03	4 22	20 08	4 12	20 13	4 18	20 27	4 31	20 28
31	4 23	19 50	4 33	20 00	4 26	20 01	4 23	20 06	4 14	20 11	4 20	20 25	4 33	20 26

THE MOON

Day	Diam '	Phase %	Age d	Rise 52° h	Rise 52° m	Rise 56° h	Rise 56° m	Transit h	Transit m	Set 52° h	Set 52° m	Set 56° h	Set 56° m
1	30.4	59	20.6	-	-	-	-	5	38	11	36	11	34
2	30.0	49	21.6	0	6	0	6	6	19	12	47	12	50
3	29.8	39	22.6	0	19	0	15	7	0	13	57	14	4
4	29.6	30	23.6	0	33	0	24	7	42	15	6	15	19
5	29.4	22	24.6	0	49	0	35	8	25	16	16	16	34
6	29.4	15	25.6	1	8	0	50	9	10	17	26	17	49
7	29.6	9	26.6	1	32	1	9	9	57	18	34	19	0
8	29.6	4	27.6	2	6	1	36	10	46	19	36	20	6
9	29.8	1	28.6	2	48	2	17	11	38	20	29	20	58
10	30.0	0	0.1	3	42	3	12	12	31	21	11	21	39
11	30.2	1	1.1	4	48	4	21	13	23	21	44	22	6
12	30.6	4	2.1	6	2	5	39	14	14	22	9	22	26
13	30.8	9	3.1	7	18	7	3	15	3	22	29	22	41
14	31.0	16	4.1	8	37	8	26	15	50	22	46	22	53
15	31.4	24	5.1	9	56	9	51	16	37	23	1	23	3
16	31.6	34	6.1	11	15	11	16	17	24	23	17	23	14
17	32.0	45	7.1	12	37	12	43	18	12	23	33	23	25
18	32.2	57	8.1	14	1	14	13	19	3	23	52	23	38
19	32.4	68	9.1	15	28	15	47	19	58	-	-	23	58
20	32.6	78	10.1	16	55	17	20	20	57	0	17	-	-
21	32.8	87	11.1	18	17	18	47	21	59	0	51	0	24
22	32.8	94	12.1	19	26	19	56	23	2	1	37	1	8
23	32.6	98	13.1	20	18	20	46	-	-	2	40	2	10
24	32.4	100	14.1	20	54	21	17	0	4	3	57	3	29
25	32.0	99	15.1	21	22	21	38	1	3	5	19	4	59
26	31.6	95	16.1	21	42	21	52	1	56	6	42	6	27
27	31.2	90	17.1	21	58	22	4	2	45	8	2	7	53
28	30.8	83	18.1	22	12	22	13	3	31	9	18	9	14
29	30.4	74	19.1	22	25	22	22	4	14	10	31	10	32
30	30.0	65	20.1	22	39	22	31	4	56	11	42	11	48
31	29.8	55	21.1	22	54	22	41	5	37	12	52	13	3

THE PLANETS

MERCURY

Day	R.A.			Dec.	Mag.	Diam.	Phase	Rise			Transit			Set		
	h	m	s	°		"	%	h	m	s	h	m	s	h	m	s
1	5	12	14	+19.2	+1.0	8.8	27	2	35	3	10	32	26	18	30	40
6	5	29	31	+20.4	+0.3	7.8	40	2	24	31	10	30	58	18	38	38
11	5	54	53	+21.6	-0.2	6.1	54	2	21	13	10	37	30	18	55	4
16	6	27	60	+22.6	-0.7	6.1	69	2	27	35	10	51	42	19	16	44
21	7	7	45	+22.8	-1.2	5.6	84	2	45	50	11	12	22	19	39	3
26	7	51	38	+22.1	-1.6	5.2	95	3	16	5	11	36	53	19	56	55
31	8	36	7	+20.3	-2.0	5.0	100	3	54	44	12	1	39	20	7	9

VENUS

Day	R.A.			Dec.	Mag.	Diam.	Phase	Rise			Transit			Set		
	h	m	s	°		"	%	h	m	s	h	m	s	h	m	s
1	8	59	22	+20.7	-3.9	12.0	90	5	42	42	13	51	42	22	0	8
6	8	54	28	+19.2	-3.9	12.2	89	5	58	55	13	56	51	21	54	7
11	9	18	50	+17.4	-3.9	12.5	88	6	15	35	14	1	1	21	46	34
16	9	42	38	+15.5	-3.9	12.7	86	6	32	27	14	5	29	21	37	45
21	10	5	55	+13.4	-3.9	13.0	85	6	49	18	14	9	0	21	27	54
26	10	28	42	+11.1	-3.9	13.2	84	7	5	59	14	12	1	21	17	15
31	10	51	2	+8.8	-3.9	13.6	82	7	22	27	14	14	35	21	5	56

MARS

Day	R.A.			Dec.	Mag.	Diam.	Rise			Transit			Set		
	h	m	s	°		"	h	m	s	h	m	s	h	m	s
1	8	59	22	+18.4	+1.8	3.9	6	28	23	14	20	37	22	12	34
6	9	11	50	+17.5	+1.8	3.8	6	27	23	14	13	22	21	59	3
11	9	24	11	+16.5	+1.8	3.8	6	26	27	14	6	1	21	46	34
16	9	36	27	+15.5	+1.8	3.7	6	25	35	13	58	34	21	31	13
21	9	48	38	+14.4	+1.8	3.7	6	24	45	13	51	2	21	16	59
26	10	0	43	+13.4	+1.8	3.7	6	23	56	13	43	25	21	2	33
31	10	12	43	+12.2	+1.8	3.7	6	23	7	13	35	43	20	47	57

JUPITER

Day	R.A.			Dec.	Mag.	Diam.	Rise			Transit			Set		
	h	m	s	°		"	h	m	s	h	m	s	h	m	s
1	22	17	30	-11.7	-2.6	45.3	22	39	1	3	39	53	8	37	5
6	22	16	45	-11.8	-2.7	45.9	22	19	10	3	19	28	8	16	6
11	22	15	43	-11.9	-2.7	46.5	21	59	12	2	58	46	7	54	40
16	22	14	23	-12.1	-2.7	47.1	21	39	5	2	37	47	7	32	49
21	22	12	48	-12.2	-2.8	47.6	21	18	51	2	16	32	7	10	33
26	22	10	59	-12.4	-2.8	48.0	20	58	31	1	55	3	6	47	56
31	22	8	56	-12.6	-2.8	48.4	20	38	3	1	33	21	6	25	0

Diam. = Equatorial. Polar Diam. is 94% of Equatorial Diam.

SATURN

Day	R.A.			Dec.	Mag.	Diam.	Rise			Transit			Set		
	h	m	s	°		"	h	m	s	h	m	s	h	m	s
1	21	0	13	-17.8	+0.4	18.3	21	59	50	2	22	45	6	41	54
6	20	59	3	-17.9	+0.3	18.4	21	39	38	2	1	56	6	20	28
11	20	57	47	-18.0	+0.3	18.4	21	19	21	1	41	1	5	58	54
16	20	56	26	-18.1	+0.3	18.5	20	59	2	1	20	0	5	37	13
21	20	55	2	-18.2	+0.2	18.6	20	38	41	0	58	56	5	15	26
26	20	53	34	-18.3	+0.2	18.6	20	18	17	0	37	49	4	53	36
31	20	52	5	-18.4	+0.2	18.6	19	57	52	0	16	41	4	31	44

Diam. = Equatorial. Polar Diam. is 90% of Equatorial Diam.
Rings – major axis 42", minor axis 13", Tilt 17°

URANUS

Day	R.A.			Dec.	Mag.	Diam.	Rise			Transit			Set		
	h	m	s	°		"	h	m	s	h	m	s	h	m	s
1	2	45	54	+15.6	+5.8	3.5	0	34	2	8	7	29	15	40	59
6	2	46	37	+15.6	+5.8	3.5	0	14	45	7	48	33	15	22	23
11	2	47	16	+15.7	+5.8	3.5	23	55	26	7	29	32	15	3	41
16	2	47	52	+15.7	+5.8	3.5	23	36	5	7	10	28	14	44	53
21	2	48	22	+15.8	+5.8	3.5	23	16	42	6	51	19	14	25	59
26	2	48	49	+15.8	+5.8	3.5	22	57	16	6	32	6	14	6	58
31	2	49	11	+15.8	+5.8	3.6	22	37	49	6	12	49	13	47	51

NEPTUNE

Day	R.A.			Dec.	Mag.	Diam.	Rise			Transit			Set		
	h	m	s	°		"	h	m	s	h	m	s	h	m	s
1	23	36	48	-3.7	+7.9	2.3	23	12	41	4	58	54	10	41	12
6	23	36	44	-3.8	+7.9	2.3	22	53	1	4	39	10	10	21	24
11	23	36	37	-3.8	+7.9	2.3	22	33	19	4	19	23	10	1	32
16	23	36	26	-3.8	+7.9	2.3	22	13	37	3	59	34	9	41	35
21	23	36	14	-3.8	+7.8	2.3	21	53	54	3	39	42	9	21	34
26	23	35	58	-3.8	+7.8	2.3	21	34	9	3	19	47	9	1	28
31	23	35	40	-3.9	+7.8	2.3	21	14	24	2	59	49	8	41	19

THE NIGHT SKY

Mercury is low in the morning at the beginning of July and can be found just above the eastern horizon as the sky begins to lighten. The magnitude 0.6 planet reaches greatest elongation west on the 4th but is best picked up towards the end of the second week of the month as its altitude improves.

Mercury is to the lower right of the very old Moon on the morning of July 8th when the planet is also near the star Zeta Tauri. The innermost world remains on view up to the start of the last week of July but will have become difficult to see by then.

Venus is low in the evening twilight all month and sets 1½ hours after the Sun. Binoculars will show Venus skirting the edge of the Beehive star cluster (M44) on the 3rd.

Venus quickly catches up with Mars as the month progresses, and the two are closest on the 13th when they are a ½° apart. The young lunar crescent nearby adds to the scene on the evenings of the 11th and 12th. Venus then passes a degree from Regulus in Leo on the 21st, a star that is occasionally occulted by a planet due to its proximity to the ecliptic.

Mars (magnitude 1.8) is setting about an hour after the Sun this month and crosses into Leo on the 11th. It has a dramatic encounter with much brighter Venus mid-month, but also will pass close to Regulus on the 29th. The two are quite low at the time though above the west-northwest skyline.

Jupiter (magnitude -2.7) rises late evening and is visible throughout most of the night. An app like Gas Giants (iOS) or Moons of Jupiter (Android) will let you follow the changing aspect of the Galilean moons daily. You can find Jupiter to the upper left of the Moon on the evening of July 25th.

NASA's Juno spacecraft currently circling Jupiter is due to be de-orbited this month after a five year mission. As its manoeuvring fuel is exhausted, the probe will be commanded to burn up in the Jovian atmosphere to avoid the risk of it crashing uncontrollably into - and contaminating - a moon like Europa, which may have a sub-surface ocean.

Juno has returned a treasure trove of science from Jupiter and made significant studies of its atmosphere, and gravity and magnetic fields. The powerful radiation belts surrounding Jupiter meant Juno was placed in a highly elliptical polar orbit to limit exposure of its delicate instruments. ESA will launch the JUpiter ICy moons Explorer (JUICE) in 2022 and it reaches the gas giant in 2029 to study Ganymede, Callisto, and Europa.

Saturn (magnitude 0.3) rises slightly earlier than Jupiter these evenings and its slightly yellowish tint is unmistakable. Saturn is directly above the full moon as it rises on the 24th.

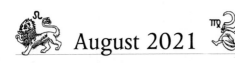

August 2021

EIGHTH MONTH, 31 DAYS. *Augustus*, formerly *Sextilis*, sixth month of Roman pre-Julian calendar

1 *Sunday*	MTV ('Music Television') began broadcasting with 'Video Killed the Radio Star' 1981		day 213

2 *Monday*	George Eliot began writing her masterpiece *Middlemarch* 1869	week 31 day 214
3 *Tuesday*	The Italian opera house La Scala opened 1778	215
4 *Wednesday*	President Woodrow Wilson proclaimed US neutrality from the war in Europe 1914	216
5 *Thursday*	The UK, USA and USSR signed the Nuclear Test Ban Treaty to prohibit above-ground nuclear tests 1963	217
6 *Friday*	The first atomic bomb was dropped by the USA on Hiroshima 1945	218
7 *Saturday*	An act was passed to make it illegal to employ anyone aged under 21 to sweep chimneys 1840	219
8 *Sunday*	President Nixon announced his resignation 1974	220

9 *Monday*	US writer Henry David Thoreau's book *Walden* was published 1854	week 32 day 221
10 *Tuesday*	The foundation stone was laid for the Royal Observatory at Greenwich 1675	222
11 *Wednesday*	The first Royal Ascot horse race took place 1711	223
12 *Thursday*	IBM introduced its personal computer for $1,600, which quickly came to dominate the market 1981	224
13 *Friday*	Barbed wire fences were put up overnight dividing East and West Berlin 1961	225
14 *Saturday*	Arthur Sullivan's *The Lost Chord* was used to demonstrate the newly perfected phonograph 1888	226
15 *Sunday*	The original Woodstock Music & Art Fair began in Bethel, New York 1969	227

16 *Monday*	The Peterloo Massacre takes place in Manchester, when cavalry charged a crowd 1819	week 33 day 228
17 *Tuesday*	Charles Blondin crossed the Niagara Falls on a tightrope 1859	229
18 *Wednesday*	Astronomer Pierre Janssen discovered helium in the solar spectrum 1868	230
19 *Thursday*	Mary Queen of Scots returned to Scotland aged 18 after spending 13 years in France 1561	231
20 *Friday*	The first round-the-world telegram was sent; it read 'This message sent around the world' 1911	232
21 *Saturday*	The *Mona Lisa* was stolen by Vincenzo Peruggia, a Louvre employee, who kept it for two years 1911	233
22 *Sunday*	The BBC performed its first experimental TV broadcast from Broadcasting House 1932	234

23 *Monday*	Film premiere of *The Big Sleep*, adapted from Raymond Chandler's novel 1946	week 32 day 235
24 *Tuesday*	Tom Stoppard's *Rosencrantz and Guildenstern are Dead* debuted 1966	236
25 *Wednesday*	The *Voyager 2* spacecraft reached Neptune after travelling for 12 years 1989	237
26 *Thursday*	US writer Ralph Waldo Emerson first met the influential writer Thomas Carlyle 1838	238
27 *Friday*	The first flight of a jet aircraft (*Heinkel He 178*) took place in Germany 1939	239
28 *Saturday*	Martin Luther King, Jr. delivered his 'I Have a Dream' speech, calling for an end to racism 1963	240
29 *Sunday*	Britain and China signed the Treaty of Nanking, ending the first Opium War 1842	241

30 *Monday*	Henry James returned to the USA after two decades in Europe 1904	week 35 day 242
31 *Tuesday*	Edvard Munch's *The Scream* was recovered by police, two years after its theft 2006	243

ASTRONOMICAL PHENOMENA

d	h	
2	-	Saturn at opposition
8	14	New Moon
9	12	Regulus 4.8°S of the Moon
9	03	Mercury 3.4°S of the Moon
10	00	Mars 4.3°S of the Moon
11	-	Sun crosses into Leo
11	07	Venus 4.3°S of the Moon
12	18	Mercury 1.2°N of Regulus
12	19	Perseid meteor shower
15	-	Jupiter without a visible Galilean moon
15	15	First Quarter Moon
16	18	Antares 4.5°S of the Moon
19	04	Mercury 0.1°S of Mars
20	-	Jupiter at opposition
20	22	Saturn 3.7°N of the Moon
21	05	Jupiter 4.0°N of the Moon
22	12	Full Moon
30	07	Last Quarter Moon

CONSTELLATIONS

The following constellations are visible at midnight throughout the month:
Draco, Hercules, Lyra, Cygnus, Sagitta, Ophiuchus, Serpens, Aquila and Sagittarius

PHASES OF THE MOON

Phase, Apsides and Node	d	h	m
● New Moon	8	13	50
◑ First Quarter	15	15	20
○ Full Moon	22	12	2
◐ Last Quarter	30	7	13
Apogee (404,410 km)	2	7	35
Perigee (369,124 km)	17	9	16
Apogee (404,100 km)	30	2	22

SUNRISE AND SUNSET

	London			Bristol			Birmingham			Manchester			Newcastle			Glasgow			Belfast		
	0° 05'	51° 30'		2° 35'	51° 28'		1° 55'	52° 28'		2° 15'	53° 28'		1° 37'	54° 59'		4° 14'	55° 52'		5° 56'	54° 35'	
d	h	m	h	m	h	m	h	m	h	m	h	m	h	m	h	m	h	m	h	m	h	m
1	4 24	19 48		4 34	19 58		4 28	19 59		4 25	20 05		4 16	20 09		4 22	20 23		4 35	20 24	
2	4 26	19 46		4 36	19 56		4 29	19 57		4 27	20 03		4 17	20 07		4 24	20 21		4 36	20 22	
3	4 27	19 45		4 37	19 55		4 31	19 56		4 28	20 01		4 19	20 05		4 26	20 19		4 38	20 20	
4	4 29	19 43		4 39	19 53		4 33	19 54		4 30	19 59		4 21	20 03		4 27	20 17		4 40	20 18	
5	4 30	19 41		4 41	19 51		4 34	19 52		4 32	19 57		4 23	20 01		4 29	20 15		4 42	20 16	
6	4 32	19 39		4 42	19 49		4 36	19 50		4 33	19 55		4 25	19 59		4 31	20 13		4 44	20 14	
7	4 33	19 38		4 44	19 48		4 37	19 48		4 35	19 53		4 26	19 57		4 33	20 11		4 45	20 12	
8	4 35	19 36		4 45	19 46		4 39	19 46		4 37	19 51		4 28	19 55		4 35	20 09		4 47	20 10	
9	4 37	19 34		4 47	19 44		4 41	19 45		4 38	19 49		4 30	19 53		4 37	20 07		4 49	20 08	
10	4 38	19 32		4 48	19 42		4 42	19 43		4 40	19 47		4 32	19 50		4 39	20 04		4 51	20 06	
11	4 40	19 30		4 50	19 40		4 44	19 41		4 42	19 45		4 34	19 48		4 41	20 02		4 53	20 04	
12	4 41	19 28		4 51	19 38		4 46	19 39		4 44	19 43		4 36	19 46		4 43	20 00		4 54	20 02	
13	4 43	19 26		4 53	19 36		4 47	19 37		4 45	19 41		4 38	19 44		4 45	19 57		4 56	20 00	
14	4 44	19 24		4 55	19 34		4 49	19 35		4 47	19 39		4 39	19 42		4 47	19 55		4 58	19 57	
15	4 46	19 22		4 56	19 32		4 51	19 33		4 49	19 37		4 41	19 39		4 49	19 53		5 00	19 55	
16	4 48	19 20		4 58	19 30		4 52	19 30		4 51	19 35		4 43	19 37		4 51	19 50		5 02	19 53	
17	4 49	19 18		4 59	19 28		4 54	19 28		4 52	19 33		4 45	19 35		4 53	19 48		5 04	19 51	
18	4 51	19 16		5 01	19 26		4 56	19 26		4 54	19 30		4 47	19 32		4 54	19 46		5 05	19 48	
19	4 52	19 14		5 02	19 24		4 57	19 24		4 56	19 28		4 49	19 30		4 56	19 43		5 07	19 46	
20	4 54	19 12		5 04	19 22		4 59	19 22		4 57	19 26		4 51	19 28		4 58	19 41		5 09	19 44	
21	4 56	19 10		5 06	19 20		5 00	19 20		4 59	19 24		4 52	19 25		5 00	19 38		5 11	19 42	
22	4 57	19 08		5 07	19 18		5 02	19 18		5 01	19 22		4 54	19 23		5 02	19 36		5 13	19 39	
23	4 59	19 06		5 09	19 16		5 04	19 15		5 03	19 19		4 56	19 21		5 04	19 33		5 15	19 37	
24	5 00	19 04		5 10	19 14		5 05	19 13		5 04	19 17		4 58	19 18		5 06	19 31		5 16	19 34	
25	5 02	19 02		5 12	19 12		5 07	19 11		5 06	19 15		5 00	19 16		5 08	19 29		5 18	19 32	
26	5 04	19 00		5 14	19 09		5 09	19 09		5 08	19 12		5 02	19 13		5 10	19 26		5 20	19 30	
27	5 05	18 57		5 15	19 07		5 10	19 07		5 10	19 10		5 04	19 11		5 12	19 23		5 22	19 27	
28	5 07	18 55		5 17	19 05		5 12	19 04		5 11	19 08		5 06	19 08		5 14	19 21		5 24	19 25	
29	5 08	18 53		5 18	19 03		5 14	19 02		5 13	19 05		5 07	19 06		5 16	19 18		5 26	19 22	
30	5 10	18 51		5 20	19 01		5 15	19 00		5 15	19 03		5 09	19 04		5 18	19 16		5 27	19 20	
31	5 11	18 49		5 22	18 59		5 17	18 58		5 17	19 01		5 11	19 01		5 20	19 13		5 29	19 17	

THE MOON

Day	Diam '	Phase %	Age d	Rise 52° h	Rise 52° m	Rise 56° h	Rise 56° m	Transit h	Transit m	Set 52° h	Set 52° m	Set 56° h	Set 56° m
1	29.6	46	22.1	23	12	22	55	6	20	14	2	14	19
2	29.6	37	23.1	23	33	23	12	7	4	15	13	15	34
3	29.6	28	24.1	-	-	23	36	7	50	16	22	16	48
4	29.6	20	25.1	0	4	-	-	8	39	17	26	17	55
5	29.8	13	26.1	0	41	0	11	9	31	18	23	18	53
6	30.0	7	27.1	1	32	1	2	10	23	19	8	19	38
7	30.4	3	28.1	2	34	2	7	11	16	19	45	20	9
8	30.6	0	29.1	3	47	3	23	12	8	20	13	20	32
9	31.0	0	0.5	5	4	4	46	12	58	20	35	20	48
10	31.2	2	1.5	6	24	6	12	13	47	20	52	21	0
11	31.4	7	2.5	7	44	7	37	14	35	21	8	21	12
12	31.8	13	3.5	9	4	9	4	15	22	21	23	21	22
13	32.0	22	4.5	10	26	10	31	16	10	21	39	21	32
14	32.0	32	5.5	11	49	11	59	17	0	21	57	21	45
15	32.2	43	6.5	13	14	13	31	17	52	22	19	22	2
16	32.4	54	7.5	14	40	15	2	18	48	22	49	22	24
17	32.4	66	8.5	16	1	16	31	19	48	23	29	23	1
18	32.4	76	9.5	17	14	17	45	20	49	-	-	23	53
19	32.2	85	10.5	18	10	18	41	21	50	0	24	-	-
20	32.2	92	11.5	18	52	19	18	22	49	1	34	1	6
21	32.0	97	12.5	19	23	19	42	23	44	2	54	2	30
22	31.6	100	13.5	19	45	19	57	-	-	4	17	4	0
23	31.4	100	14.5	20	2	20	10	0	35	5	38	5	26
24	31.0	97	15.5	20	17	20	20	1	22	6	56	6	50
25	30.6	93	16.5	20	30	20	29	2	7	8	12	8	11
26	30.2	87	17.5	20	44	20	38	2	50	9	24	9	28
27	30.0	80	18.5	20	58	20	47	3	32	10	36	10	45
28	29.8	71	19.5	21	14	21	0	4	14	11	47	12	1
29	29.6	62	20.5	21	34	21	14	4	58	12	58	13	18
30	29.6	53	21.5	22	1	21	35	5	43	14	7	14	33
31	29.6	43	22.5	22	34	22	6	6	31	15	14	15	43

THE PLANETS

MERCURY

Day	R.A. h	m	s	Dec. °	Mag.	Diam. "	Phase %	Rise h	m	s	Transit h	m	s	Set h	m	s
1	8	44	48	+19.8	-2.0	5.0	100	4	2	59	12	6	21	20	8	14
6	9	26	19	+16.9	-1.5	5.0	98	4	44	35	12	27	53	20	9	27
11	10	4	7	+13.6	-1.0	5.0	94	5	24	20	12	45	37	20	5	11
16	10	38	15	+9.9	-0.6	5.1	90	6	0	36	12	59	41	19	57	10
21	11	9	10	+6.2	-0.4	5.3	85	6	33	4	13	10	34	19	46	39
26	11	37	21	+2.5	-0.2	5.5	80	7	1	53	13	18	44	19	34	20
31	12	3	9	0.0	-0.1	5.8	75	7	27	16	13	24	30	19	20	41

VENUS

Day	R.A. h	m	s	Dec. °	Mag.	Diam. "	Phase %	Rise h	m	s	Transit h	m	s	Set h	m	s
1	10	55	28	+8.3	-3.9	13.6	82	7	25	43	14	15	4	21	3	37
6	11	17	22	+5.8	-4.0	14.0	81	7	41	55	14	17	12	20	51	43
11	11	38	59	+3.3	-4.0	14.3	79	7	57	54	14	19	3	20	39	28
16	12	0	23	0.0	-4.0	14.7	78	8	13	44	14	20	42	20	26	58
21	12	21	38	-1.8	-4.0	15.1	76	8	29	26	14	22	12	20	14	18
26	12	42	50	-4.4	-4.0	15.6	75	8	45	5	14	23	39	20	1	33
31	13	4	2	-6.9	-4.0	16.1	73	9	0	45	14	25	6	19	48	50

MARS

Day	R.A. h	m	s	Dec. °	Mag.	Diam. "	Rise h	m	s	Transit h	m	s	Set h	m	s
1	10	15	7	+12.0	+1.8	3.7	6	22	58	13	34	10	20	45	1
6	10	27	2	+10.8	+1.8	3.6	6	22	9	13	26	23	20	30	16
11	10	38	54	+9.7	+1.8	3.6	6	21	21	13	18	34	20	15	24
16	10	50	44	+8.4	+1.8	3.6	6	20	33	13	10	41	20	0	27
21	11	2	31	+7.2	+1.8	3.6	6	19	45	13	2	46	19	45	26
26	11	14	16	+5.9	+1.8	3.6	6	18	57	12	54	49	19	30	21
31	11	26	1	+4.7	+1.8	3.6	6	18	10	12	46	52	19	15	14

JUPITER

Day	R.A. h	m	s	Dec. °	Mag.	Diam. "	Rise h	m	s	Transit h	m	s	Set h	m	s
1	22	8	31	-12.7	-2.8	48.5	20	33	57	1	28	59	6	20	23
6	22	6	16	-12.9	-2.8	48.8	20	13	23	1	7	5	5	57	8
11	22	3	53	-13.1	-2.9	49.0	19	52	45	0	45	2	5	33	42
16	22	1	25	-13.4	-2.9	49.1	19	32	3	0	22	55	5	10	9
21	21	58	54	-13.6	-2.9	49.1	19	11	18	0	0	44	4	46	32
26	21	56	23	-13.8	-2.9	49.0	18	50	33	23	35	3	4	22	57
31	21	53	55	-14.0	-2.9	48.9	18	29	47	23	12	56	3	59	28

Diam. = Equatorial. Polar Diam. is 94% of Equatorial Diam.

SATURN

Day	R.A. h	m	s	Dec. °	Mag.	Diam. "	Rise h	m	s	Transit h	m	s	Set h	m	s
1	20	51	47	-18.4	+0.2	18.6	19	53	47	0	12	27	4	27	21
6	20	50	17	-18.5	+0.2	18.6	19	33	20	23	47	29	4	5	28
11	20	48	47	-18.6	+0.2	18.6	19	12	54	23	26	20	3	43	37
16	20	47	20	-18.7	+0.2	18.5	18	52	28	23	5	13	3	21	49
21	20	45	55	-18.8	+0.2	18.5	18	32	4	22	44	9	3	0	1
26	20	44	35	-18.9	+0.3	18.4	18	11	41	22	23	10	2	38	29
31	20	43	20	-19.0	+0.3	18.4	17	51	21	22	2	15	2	16	59

Diam. = Equatorial. Polar Diam. is 90% of Equatorial Diam.
Rings – major axis 42", minor axis 13", Tilt 18°

URANUS

Day	R.A. h	m	s	Dec. °	Mag.	Diam. "	Rise h	m	s	Transit h	m	s	Set h	m	s
1	2	49	15	+15.8	+5.8	3.6	22	33	55	6	8	56	13	44	0
6	2	49	31	+15.9	+5.8	3.6	22	14	24	5	49	33	13	24	44
11	2	49	42	+15.9	+5.8	3.6	21	54	51	5	30	5	13	5	21
16	2	49	49	+15.9	+5.7	3.6	21	35	15	5	10	32	12	45	50
21	2	49	50	+15.9	+5.7	3.6	21	15	36	4	50	54	12	26	13
26	2	49	47	+15.9	+5.7	3.6	20	55	56	4	31	11	12	6	27
31	2	49	39	+15.9	+5.7	3.6	20	36	12	4	11	23	11	46	35

NEPTUNE

Day	R.A. h	m	s	Dec. °	Mag.	Diam. "	Rise h	m	s	Transit h	m	s	Set h	m	s
1	23	35	37	-3.9	+7.8	2.3	21	10	26	2	55	50	8	37	17
6	23	35	16	-3.9	+7.8	2.3	20	50	39	2	35	49	8	17	4
11	23	34	53	-4.0	+7.8	2.3	20	30	52	2	15	47	7	56	47
16	23	34	29	-4.0	+7.8	2.4	20	11	3	1	55	43	7	36	28
21	23	34	3	-4.1	+7.8	2.4	19	51	14	1	35	38	7	16	6
26	23	33	35	-4.1	+7.8	2.4	19	31	24	1	15	31	6	55	42
31	23	33	6	-4.2	+7.8	2.4	19	11	33	0	55	22	6	35	16

THE NIGHT SKY

Mercury is at superior conjunction on the 1st but remains too deep in the bright twilight to be seen this month after it emerges into the evening sky.

Venus (magnitude -4.0) shines brightly low in the western sky these evenings and is presently setting an hour after the Sun. The young moon is nearby both on the 9th and 10th. Telescope users will notice Venus shows a gradually narrowing gibbous phase at present.

Mars (magnitude 1.8) is setting only 40 minutes after the Sun mid-month and so it will likely become lost to view for us around this time.

Jupiter (magnitude -2.9) is at opposition on the 20th in Capricornus when it rises around sunset and is visible throughout the night. The planet's annually improving position on the celestial sphere means better opportunities to come for northern hemisphere observers scrutinising detail in the gas giant's turbulent atmosphere through a telescope. Jupiter lies to the upper left of the almost full moon on the night of the 21st.

Jupiter is without a visible Galilean satellite on August 15th but they are absent during daylight from the UK. In the Americas, observers will see Io eclipsed and the shadows of the other three in transit – the next triple shadow crossing is not until December 2026 from the UK.

Saturn (magnitude 0.2) is also at opposition this month, but on the 2nd in Capricornus when the butterscotch-hued planet can be seen in the eastern sky as soon as twilight fades. Saturn does not show the same swirls and patterns in its atmosphere as Jupiter, but the magnificent ring system compensates. The nearly full moon is within 4° of Saturn on the 20th.

Saturn's largest moon Titan can be seen in steadily held binoculars, while a half dozen in total of its biggest satellites are within reach of most amateur telescopes. Note how much the ring system is tipped over the next few years as it slowly narrows until it becomes briefly edge-on from our perspective in 2025.

The four-day old Moon sets during the late evening on August 12th and so will not interfere with the maximum of the Perseid meteor shower. The radiant, or point of origin of the meteors when their paths are traced backward, lies in the constellation Perseus that is low in the northeast after dark. As the night progresses, rates improve as Perseus rises higher in the sky. Away from lit areas, you may see a meteor every couple of minutes.

Besides trying to glimpse the youngest moon, some observers like the challenge of sighting opposing crescents. This is where you can try for the shortest time between sightings of the Moon just before and after New. The Moon is 33 hours before New if spotted on the morning of the 7th, and less than 31 hours old on the evening of the 9th.

September 2021

NINTH MONTH, 30 DAYS. *Septem* (seven), seventh month of Roman pre-Julian calendar

1	*Wednesday*	A solar flare is observed for the first time by astronomer Richard Carrington 1859	day 244
2	*Thursday*	The original *Star Trek* was cancelled after its third season 1969	245
3	*Friday*	Oliver Cromwell's parliamentarians defeated Charles II's royalists at the second Battle of Worcester 1651	246
4	*Saturday*	Beatrix Potter wrote a letter containing the first incarnation of Peter Rabbit 1893	247
5	*Sunday*	James Glaisher and Henry Coxwell set a new altitude record when their balloon ascended 11km 1862	248
6	*Monday*	John Derry, piloting a de Havilland DH 108, became the first Briton to break the sound barrier 1948	week 36 day 249
7	*Tuesday*	The French poet Guillaume Apollinaire was mistakenly arrested for stealing the *Mona Lisa* 1911	250
8	*Wednesday*	Frank Sinatra, 19, appeared on the radio talent show *Major Bowes' Amateur Hour* 1935	251
9	*Thursday*	Scientists stated that the hole in the ozone layer had reached record size (28 million sq. km) 2000	252
10	*Friday*	Pablo Picasso's monumental painting, *Guernica*, was returned to Spain 1981	253
11	*Saturday*	The Siege of Drogheda ends with Oliver Cromwell's Roundheads massacring the defending Royalists 1649	254
12	*Sunday*	Four teenagers discovered paleolithic artwork on the walls of caves at Lascaux in south-west France 1940	255
13	*Monday*	A rail detector car which found faults in railroad tracks was demonstrated in New York, USA 1928	week 37 day 256
14	*Tuesday*	The Soviet Union's *Luna 2* became the first spacecraft to land on the Moon 1959	257
15	*Wednesday*	Allied nations celebrated Victory in Japan Day 1945	258
16	*Thursday*	The United Shakespeare Company bought the poet's childhood home in Stratford-upon-Avon 1847	259
17	*Friday*	*Lord of the Flies*, Nobel Prize winner William Golding's dystopian debut novel, was published 1954	260
18	*Saturday*	King George I sailed up the Thames to Greenwich, setting foot in England for the first time 1714	261
19	*Sunday*	Nikita Khrushchev was barred from visiting Disneyland 1959	262
20	*Monday*	The first Cannes film festival took place 1946	week 38 day 263
21	*Tuesday*	Great Britain abandoned the gold standard 1931	264
22	*Wednesday*	Charlotte Cooper, the first woman to win an Olympic gold medal, at the 1900 Olympic Games *b.* 1870	265
23	*Thursday*	Johan Galle discovered Neptune after using calculations predicting the planet's location 1846	266
24	*Friday*	Dougal Haston and Doug Scott became the first Britons to climb Everest 1975	267
25	*Saturday*	Diarist Samuel Pepys drank a cup of 'tee' for the first time 1660	268
26	*Sunday*	*West Side Story* premiered on Broadway 1957	269
27	*Monday*	*SMART-1*, the European Space Agency's first mission to the Moon, was launched from French Guiana 2003	week 39 day 270
28	*Tuesday*	William the Conqueror invaded England 1066	271
29	*Wednesday*	The Babi Yar massacre of nearly 34,000 Jews began in Nazi-occupied Ukraine 1941	272
30	*Thursday*	Neville Chamberlain declared 'peace for our time' after signing the Munich Agreement 1938	273

ASTRONOMICAL PHENOMENA

d	h	
4	04	Moon 2.9°N of the Beehive cluster
5	20	Regulus 4.8°S of the Moon
7	16	Mars 4.24°S of the Moon
7	00	New Moon
8	20	Mercury 6.5°S of the Moon
10	02	Venus 4.1°S of the Moon
13	21	First Quarter Moon
14	19	Mercury at greatest elongation (26° 46' E)
14	-	Neptune at opposition
17	02	Saturn 3.8°N of the Moon
17	-	Sun crosses into Virgo
18	07	Jupiter 4.0°N of the Moon
21	00	Full Moon (Harvest Moon)
21	02	Mercury 1.2°S of Spica
22	19	Autumnal equinox
29	02	Last Quarter Moon
30	15	Mercury 1.7°S of Spica

CONSTELLATIONS

The following constellations are visible at midnight throughout the month:

Draco, Cepheus, Lyra, Cygnus, Vulpecula, Sagitta, Delphinus, Equuleus, Aquila, Aquarius and Capricornus

PHASES OF THE MOON

Phase, Apsides and Node	d	h	m
● New Moon	7	0	52
◐ First Quarter	13	20	39
○ Full Moon	20	23	55
◑ Last Quarter	29	1	57
Perigee (368,461 km)	11	10	3
Apogee (404,640 km)	26	21	44

SUNRISE AND SUNSET

	London				Bristol				Birmingham				Manchester				Newcastle				Glasgow				Belfast			
	0°	05'	51°	30'	2°	35'	51°	28'	1°	55'	52°	28'	2°	15'	53°	28'	1°	37'	54°	59'	4°	14'	55°	52'	5°	56'	54°	35'
d	h	m	h	m	h	m	h	m	h	m	h	m	h	m	h	m	h	m	h	m	h	m	h	m	h	m	h	m
1	5	13	18	46	5	23	18	56	5	19	18	55	5	18	18	58	5	13	18	59	5	22	19	11	5	31	19	15
2	5	15	18	44	5	25	18	54	5	20	18	53	5	20	18	56	5	15	18	56	5	24	19	08	5	33	19	13
3	5	16	18	42	5	26	18	52	5	22	18	51	5	22	18	54	5	17	18	54	5	26	19	06	5	35	19	10
4	5	18	18	40	5	28	18	50	5	24	18	48	5	24	18	51	5	19	18	51	5	28	19	03	5	37	19	08
5	5	19	18	37	5	30	18	47	5	25	18	46	5	25	18	49	5	20	18	49	5	29	19	00	5	38	19	05
6	5	21	18	35	5	31	18	45	5	27	18	44	5	27	18	46	5	22	18	46	5	31	18	58	5	40	19	03
7	5	23	18	33	5	33	18	43	5	29	18	41	5	29	18	44	5	24	18	43	5	33	18	55	5	42	19	00
8	5	24	18	31	5	34	18	41	5	30	18	39	5	31	18	42	5	26	18	41	5	35	18	53	5	44	18	58
9	5	26	18	28	5	36	18	38	5	32	18	37	5	32	18	39	5	28	18	38	5	37	18	50	5	46	18	55
10	5	27	18	26	5	37	18	36	5	34	18	34	5	34	18	37	5	30	18	36	5	39	18	47	5	48	18	53
11	5	29	18	24	5	39	18	34	5	35	18	32	5	36	18	34	5	32	18	33	5	41	18	45	5	49	18	50
12	5	31	18	21	5	41	18	31	5	37	18	30	5	37	18	32	5	33	18	31	5	43	18	42	5	51	18	48
13	5	32	18	19	5	42	18	29	5	39	18	27	5	39	18	29	5	35	18	28	5	45	18	39	5	53	18	45
14	5	34	18	17	5	44	18	27	5	40	18	25	5	41	18	27	5	37	18	26	5	47	18	37	5	55	18	42
15	5	35	18	15	5	45	18	24	5	42	18	22	5	43	18	24	5	39	18	23	5	49	18	34	5	57	18	40
16	5	37	18	12	5	47	18	22	5	44	18	20	5	44	18	22	5	41	18	20	5	51	18	31	5	58	18	37
17	5	39	18	10	5	49	18	20	5	45	18	18	5	46	18	20	5	43	18	18	5	53	18	29	6	00	18	35
18	5	40	18	08	5	50	18	18	5	47	18	15	5	48	18	17	5	45	18	15	5	55	18	26	6	02	18	32
19	5	42	18	05	5	52	18	15	5	49	18	13	5	50	18	15	5	47	18	13	5	57	18	24	6	04	18	30
20	5	43	18	03	5	53	18	13	5	50	18	11	5	51	18	12	5	48	18	10	5	59	18	21	6	06	18	27
21	5	45	18	01	5	55	18	11	5	52	18	08	5	53	18	10	5	50	18	08	6	00	18	18	6	08	18	25
22	5	47	17	58	5	57	18	08	5	54	18	06	5	55	18	07	5	52	18	05	6	02	18	16	6	09	18	22
23	5	48	17	56	5	58	18	06	5	55	18	03	5	57	18	05	5	54	18	02	6	04	18	13	6	11	18	20
24	5	50	17	54	6	00	18	04	5	57	18	01	5	58	18	02	5	56	18	00	6	06	18	10	6	13	18	17
25	5	51	17	52	6	01	18	01	5	59	17	59	6	00	18	00	5	58	17	57	6	08	18	08	6	15	18	15
26	5	53	17	49	6	03	17	59	6	00	17	56	6	02	17	58	6	00	17	55	6	10	18	05	6	17	18	12
27	5	55	17	47	6	05	17	57	6	02	17	54	6	04	17	55	6	02	17	52	6	12	18	02	6	19	18	10
28	5	56	17	45	6	06	17	55	6	04	17	52	6	05	17	53	6	05	17	50	6	14	18	00	6	21	18	07
29	5	58	17	42	6	08	17	52	6	06	17	49	6	07	17	50	6	05	17	47	6	16	17	57	6	22	18	04
30	6	00	17	40	6	10	17	50	6	07	17	47	6	09	17	48	6	07	17	45	6	18	17	55	6	24	18	02

THE MOON

Day	Diam	Phase	Age	Rise 52°		Rise 56°		Transit		Set 52°		Set 56°	
	'	%	d	h	m	h	m	h	m	h	m	h	m
1	29.8	34	23.5	23	20	22	49	7	22	16	14	16	45
2	30.0	25	24.5	-	-	23	47	8	14	17	3	17	35
3	30.2	17	25.5	0	18	-	-	9	6	17	44	18	11
4	30.6	10	26.5	1	26	1	1	9	58	18	14	18	36
5	31.0	5	27.5	2	43	2	22	10	50	18	38	18	54
6	31.4	1	28.5	4	3	3	48	11	40	18	57	19	8
7	31.6	0	0.0	5	25	5	16	12	29	19	14	19	19
8	32.0	1	1.0	6	47	6	44	13	17	19	29	19	29
9	32.2	5	2.0	8	11	8	13	14	6	19	45	19	40
10	32.4	11	3.0	9	35	9	44	14	56	20	2	19	52
11	32.4	19	4.0	11	1	11	17	15	48	20	23	20	7
12	32.4	29	5.0	12	29	12	50	16	44	20	50	20	27
13	32.4	40	6.0	13	52	14	21	17	42	21	26	20	59
14	32.2	52	7.0	15	7	15	40	18	43	22	16	21	44
15	32.0	63	8.0	16	8	16	40	19	43	23	20	22	50
16	32.0	74	9.0	16	53	17	21	20	42	-	-	-	-
17	31.6	83	10.0	17	26	17	47	21	37	0	36	0	10
18	31.4	90	11.0	17	49	18	5	22	28	1	58	1	37
19	31.2	96	12.0	18	8	18	18	23	16	3	18	3	4
20	31.0	99	13.0	18	23	18	28	-	-	4	37	4	28
21	30.6	100	14.0	18	36	18	37	0	1	5	53	5	50
22	30.4	99	15.0	18	49	18	45	0	44	7	7	7	9
23	30.0	96	16.0	19	3	18	54	1	26	8	19	8	26
24	29.8	91	17.0	19	18	19	5	2	9	9	31	9	43
25	29.6	85	18.0	19	36	19	18	2	52	10	43	11	0
26	29.6	78	19.0	20	0	19	35	3	37	11	53	12	17
27	29.6	69	20.0	20	29	20	2	4	24	13	1	13	30
28	29.6	60	21.0	21	10	20	38	5	13	14	4	14	36
29	29.8	51	22.0	22	3	21	29	6	4	14	57	15	31
30	30.0	41	23.0	23	6	22	36	6	55	15	42	16	11

THE PLANETS

MERCURY

Day	R.A.			Dec.	Mag.	Diam.	Phase	Rise			Transit			Set		
	h	m	s	°		"	%	h	m	s	h	m	s	h	m	s
1	12	8	2	-1.7	0.0	5.9	74	7	31	56	13	25	22	19	17	49
6	12	31	7	-5.0	+0.1	6.2	68	7	53	6	13	28	23	19	2	52
11	12	51	42	-7.9	+0.1	6.7	62	8	10	9	13	28	48	18	46	55
16	13	9	8	-10.4	+0.2	7.2	54	8	21	44	13	25	56	18	29	54
21	13	22	8	-12.3	+0.4	7.9	44	8	25	18	13	18	23	18	11	42
26	13	28	35	-13.3	+0.7	8.7	32	8	16	42	13	3	59	17	52	13

VENUS

Day	R.A.			Dec.	Mag.	Diam.	Phase	Rise			Transit			Set		
	h	m	s	°		"	%	h	m	s	h	m	s	h	m	s
1	13	8	17	-7.4	-4.0	16.2	73	9	3	54	14	25	24	19	46	18
6	13	29	37	-9.9	-4.1	16.7	71	9	19	38	14	26	58	19	33	43
11	13	51	6	-12.3	-4.1	17.3	70	9	35	29	14	28	42	19	21	23
16	14	12	48	-14.6	-4.1	17.9	68	9	51	24	14	30	39	19	9	23
21	14	34	45	-16.8	-4.1	18.6	66	10	7	19	14	32	49	18	57	53
26	14	56	58	-18.8	-4.2	19.4	64	10	23	6	14	35	15	18	47	1

MARS

Day	R.A.			Dec.	Mag.	Diam.	Rise			Transit			Set		
	h	m	s	°		"	h	m	s	h	m	s	h	m	s
1	11	28	22	+4.4	+1.8	3.6	6	18	1	12	45	17	19	12	12
6	11	40	7	+3.1	+1.8	3.6	6	17	16	12	37	20	18	57	4
11	11	51	53	+1.8	+1.8	3.6	6	16	33	12	29	24	18	41	55
16	12	3	40	0.0	+1.8	3.6	6	15	53	12	21	30	18	26	47
21	12	15	30	0.0	+1.7	3.5	6	15	16	12	13	38	18	11	41
26	12	27	24	-2.2	+1.7	3.6	6	14	43	12	5	50	17	56	38

JUPITER

Day	R.A.			Dec.	Mag.	Diam.	Rise			Transit			Set		
	h	m	s	°		"	h	m	s	h	m	s	h	m	s
1	21	53	26	-14.1	-2.9	48.9	18	25	38	23	8	31	3	54	47
6	21	51	5	-14.3	-2.8	48.6	18	4	54	22	46	30	3	31	30
11	21	48	52	-14.5	-2.8	48.3	17	44	13	22	24	38	3	8	27
16	21	46	52	-14.7	-2.8	48.0	17	23	36	22	2	56	2	45	43
21	21	45	4	-14.8	-2.8	47.4	17	3	4	21	41	30	2	23	21
26	21	43	32	-14.9	-2.7	46.9	16	42	39	21	20	18	2	1	22

Diam. = Equatorial. Polar Diam. is 94% of Equatorial Diam.

SATURN

Day	R.A.			Dec.	Mag.	Diam.	Rise			Transit			Set		
	h	m	s	°		"	h	m	s	h	m	s	h	m	s
1	20	43	6	-19.0	+0.3	18.3	17	47	17	21	58	5	2	12	43
6	20	41	58	-19.1	+0.3	18.2	17	27	0	21	37	17	1	51	25
11	20	40	57	-19.2	+0.4	18.1	17	6	47	21	16	37	1	30	17
16	20	40	4	-19.2	+0.4	18.0	16	46	38	20	56	5	1	9	21
21	20	39	20	-19.3	+0.4	17.9	16	26	34	20	35	41	0	48	38
26	20	38	45	-19.3	+0.4	17.8	16	6	35	20	15	26	0	28	8

Diam. = Equatorial. Polar Diam. is 90% of Equatorial Diam.
Rings – major axis 41", minor axis 13", Tilt 19°

URANUS

Day	R.A.			Dec.	Mag.	Diam.	Rise			Transit			Set		
	h	m	s	°		"	h	m	s	h	m	s	h	m	s
1	2	49	36	+15.9	+5.7	3.7	20	32	15	4	7	25	11	42	36
6	2	49	22	+15.8	+5.7	3.7	20	12	29	3	47	31	11	22	35
11	2	49	3	+15.8	+5.7	3.7	19	52	40	3	27	33	11	2	27
16	2	48	40	+15.8	+5.7	3.7	19	32	48	3	7	30	10	42	13
21	2	48	13	+15.7	+5.7	3.7	19	9	3	2	47	23	10	21	52
26	2	47	41	+15.7	+5.7	3.7	18	49	8	2	27	12	10	1	26

NEPTUNE

Day	R.A.			Dec.	Mag.	Diam.	Rise			Transit			Set		
	h	m	s	°		"	h	m	s	h	m	s	h	m	s
1	23	33	1	-4.2	+7.8	2.4	19	7	35	0	51	21	6	31	10
6	23	32	31	-4.2	+7.8	2.4	18	47	44	0	31	12	6	10	43
11	23	32	1	-4.3	+7.8	2.4	18	27	53	0	11	2	5	50	15
16	23	31	30	-4.4	+7.8	2.4	18	8	1	23	46	57	5	29	47
21	23	31	0	-4.4	+7.8	2.4	17	48	10	23	26	47	5	9	19
26	23	30	30	-4.5	+7.8	2.4	17	28	18	23	6	38	4	48	52

THE NIGHT SKY

Mercury should be visible mid-month in the evening sky when it reaches greatest elongation east on the 14th. The elusive magnitude 0.1 planet is setting about 45 minutes after the Sun at this time. Mercury's spark will be low in the west-southwest though, and well to the lower right of Venus.

Venus (magnitude -4.1) hangs above the western skyline for about an hour after sunset. The disk is 68% illuminated mid-month for telescope users and is slowly growing less fat while also swelling in apparent size. The two-day old moon is close to Venus on the evening of the 9th but they will be low in the west-northwest.

Mars is too close to the Sun to be seen this month. However, it moves into Virgo from Leo on the 6th and then crosses the celestial equator, moving from north to south, on the 18th.

Jupiter (magnitude -2.8) can be seen in the eastern sky after sunset and is on view until the early hours. It can be found 8° to the upper right of the Moon on the 18th.

Saturn (magnitude 0.4) is similarly already up in the east as night falls but sets soon after 1am summertime at the end of the month. The waxing Moon is near Saturn on the evening of the 16th.

Neptune (magnitude 7.8) is at opposition on the 14th in eastern Aquarius and not far from magnitude 4.2 Phi Aquarii. Steadily held binoculars are sufficient to spot the distant world when used with a chart of the planet's location.

The full moon on September 20th is the Harvest Moon as it falls closest to the autumn equinox. On average, the Moon rises around one hour later each night. What marks out the Harvest Moon as special is that it appears to rise around sunset for several successive evenings due to the shallow angle the ecliptic makes with the horizon from temperate latitudes in the northern hemisphere.

In binoculars at time of full moon you can make out bright spoke-like features radiating from some lunar craters. One of the most prominent ray systems is that centred on the 90-kilometre-wide crater Tycho that lies towards the Moon's southern highlands. When the moon is full you can see its rays extending for hundreds of kilometres across the lunar maria.

Tycho is one of the youngest major craters with an estimated age of 110 million years and so its rays are relatively fresh. Two large craters on Oceanus Procellarum - the Ocean of Storms is the large 'sea' on the left side of the Moon's disk - are also major ray centres. Copernicus and the slightly smaller crater Kepler both have complex patterns of material splattered around them. Further north, you will see Aristarchus - the brightest feature on the Moon and the result of an ancient impact that excavated highly reflective material.

 October 2021

TENTH MONTH, 31 DAYS. *Octo* (eighth), eighth month of Roman pre-Julian calendar

1	*Friday*	The People's Republic of China was formally established 1949	day 274
2	*Saturday*	Charles Darwin returned from his momentous voyage to the Pacific aboard *HMS Beagle* 1836	275
3	*Sunday*	The reunification of East and West Germany was formerly completed and celebrated 1990	276
4	*Monday*	The Soviet Union launched *Sputnik 1*, the first man-made satellite, into orbit around the Earth 1957	week 40 day 277
5	*Tuesday*	*Monty Python's Flying Circus* first aired on BBC1 1969	278
6	*Wednesday*	The first feature-length 'talkie', *The Jazz Singer*, premiered in New York 1927	279
7	*Thursday*	The Soviet space probe *Luna 3* photographed the far side of the Moon for the first time 1959	280
8	*Friday*	The Post Office Tower, then the tallest building in London, was officially opened 1965	281
9	*Saturday*	Breathalyser tests came into force 1967	282
10	*Sunday*	William Lassell discovers Triton, Neptune's largest moon 1846	283
11	*Monday*	Kathryn D. Sullivan, a NASA astronaut, became the first woman to walk in space 1984	week 41 day 284
12	*Tuesday*	Oktoberfest took place in its original form: a celebration of a Bavarian royal wedding 1810	285
13	*Wednesday*	At the International Meridian Conference, Greenwich was adopted as the universal meridian 1884	286
14	*Thursday*	The first of A. A. Milne's *Winnie-the-Pooh* books was published 1926	287
15	*Friday*	The Black Panther Party, a black nationalist organisation, was formed in California 1966	288
16	*Saturday*	Samuel Franklin Cody completed the first aeroplane flight in the UK 1908	289
17	*Sunday*	British troops surrendered to American colonists at the Battle of Saratoga in New York 1777	290
18	*Monday*	The British Broadcasting Company, later the British Broadcasting Corporation, was founded 1922	week 42 day 291
19	*Tuesday*	The first battle of Ypres began marking the end of the 'Race to the Sea' 1914	292
20	*Wednesday*	Sydney Opera House was formally opened by Queen Elizabeth II 1973	293
21	*Thursday*	The Guggenheim museum opened in New York 1959	294
22	*Friday*	US president John F. Kennedy announced the discovery of Soviet nuclear weapons in Cuba 1962	295
23	*Saturday*	Edgehill, the first major battle of the English Civil War, ended indecisively 1642	296
24	*Sunday*	The United Nations formally came into existence 1945	297
25	*Monday*	The Charge of the Light Brigade, commemorated in Tennyson's famous poem, took place 1854	week 43 day 298
26	*Tuesday*	The leaders of Israel and Jordon signed a peace treaty, ending 46 years of war 1994	299
27	*Wednesday*	The Abortion Act was passed, allowing abortion for medical reasons 1967	300
28	*Thursday*	Jonathan Swift's classic novel *Gulliver's Travels* was published 1726	301
29	*Friday*	The US stock market collapsed, later known as the Wall Street Crash 1929	302
30	*Saturday*	Orson Welles' radio production of *War of the Worlds* first aired, inciting panic and complaints 1938	303
31	*Sunday*	The first collection of Arthur Conan Doyle's *The Adventures of Sherlock Holmes* was published 1892	304

ASTRONOMICAL PHENOMENA

2	-	Venus at aphelion
6	11	New Moon
8	-	Mars at solar conjunction
9	-	Mercury at inferior conjunction
9	08	Mercury 2.8°S of Mars
9	18	Venus 2.9°S of the Moon
13	03	First Quarter Moon
13	07	Saturn 3.9°N of the Moon
15	10	Jupiter 4.1°N of the Moon
16	14	Venus 1.4°N of Antares
18	-	Jupiter stationary, prograde motion resumes
20	15	Full Moon
21	11	Orionid meteor shower
25	-	Mercury at greatest elongation (18° 24' W)
28	20	Last Quarter Moon
28	-	Venus Dichotomy (half phase in a scope)
29	-	Venus at greatest elongation (47° 03' E)
30	-	Saturn at eastern quadrature

CONSTELLATIONS

The following constellations are visible at midnight throughout the month:
Ursa Major (below the Pole), Cepheus, Cassiopeia, Cygnus, Lacerta, Andromeda, Pegasus, Capricornus, Aquarius and Piscis Austrinus

PHASES OF THE MOON

Phase, Apsides and Node	d	h	m
● New Moon	6	11	5
◔ First Quarter	13	3	25
○ Full Moon	20	14	57
◑ Last Quarter	28	20	5
Perigee (363,386 km)	8	17	28
Apogee (405,615 km)	24	15	28

SUNRISE AND SUNSET

	London				Bristol				Birmingham				Manchester				Newcastle				Glasgow				Belfast			
	0° 05'		51° 30'		2° 35'		51° 28'		1° 55'		52° 28'		2° 15'		53° 28'		1° 37'		54° 59'		4° 14'		55° 52'		5° 56'		54° 35'	
d	h	m	h	m	h	m	h	m	h	m	h	m	h	m	h	m	h	m	h	m	h	m	h	m	h	m	h	m
1	6	01	17	38	6	11	17	48	6	09	17	45	6	11	17	45	6	09	17	42	6	20	17	52	6	26	17	59
2	6	03	17	36	6	13	17	46	6	11	17	42	6	13	17	43	6	11	17	39	6	22	17	49	6	28	17	57
3	6	04	17	33	6	14	17	43	6	12	17	40	6	14	17	41	6	13	17	37	6	24	17	47	6	30	17	54
4	6	06	17	31	6	16	17	41	6	14	17	38	6	16	17	38	6	15	17	34	6	26	17	44	6	32	17	52
5	6	08	17	29	6	18	17	39	6	16	17	35	6	18	17	36	6	17	17	32	6	28	17	42	6	34	17	50
6	6	09	17	26	6	19	17	37	6	18	17	33	6	20	17	33	6	19	17	29	6	30	17	39	6	36	17	47
7	6	11	17	24	6	21	17	34	6	19	17	31	6	22	17	31	6	21	17	27	6	32	17	36	6	37	17	45
8	6	13	17	22	6	23	17	32	6	21	17	28	6	23	17	29	6	22	17	24	6	34	17	34	6	39	17	42
9	6	14	17	20	6	24	17	30	6	23	17	26	6	25	17	26	6	24	17	22	6	36	17	31	6	41	17	40
10	6	16	17	18	6	26	17	28	6	24	17	24	6	27	17	24	6	26	17	19	6	38	17	29	6	43	17	37
11	6	18	17	15	6	28	17	25	6	26	17	22	6	29	17	22	6	28	17	17	6	40	17	26	6	45	17	35
12	6	19	17	13	6	29	17	23	6	28	17	19	6	31	17	19	6	30	17	15	6	42	17	24	6	47	17	32
13	6	21	17	11	6	31	17	21	6	30	17	17	6	32	17	17	6	32	17	12	6	44	17	21	6	49	17	30
14	6	23	17	09	6	33	17	19	6	32	17	15	6	34	17	15	6	34	17	10	6	46	17	19	6	51	17	28
15	6	24	17	07	6	34	17	17	6	33	17	13	6	36	17	12	6	36	17	07	6	48	17	16	6	53	17	25
16	6	26	17	05	6	36	17	15	6	35	17	10	6	38	17	10	6	38	17	05	6	50	17	14	6	55	17	23
17	6	28	17	03	6	38	17	13	6	37	17	08	6	40	17	08	6	40	17	03	6	52	17	11	6	57	17	21
18	6	30	17	00	6	40	17	11	6	39	17	06	6	42	17	06	6	42	17	00	6	54	17	09	6	59	17	18
19	6	31	16	58	6	41	17	08	6	40	17	04	6	44	17	03	6	44	16	58	6	56	17	06	7	01	17	16
20	6	33	16	56	6	43	17	06	6	42	17	02	6	46	17	01	6	46	16	55	6	59	17	04	7	03	17	14
21	6	35	16	54	6	45	17	04	6	44	17	00	6	47	16	59	6	48	16	53	7	01	17	02	7	04	17	11
22	6	37	16	52	6	46	17	02	6	46	16	58	6	49	16	57	6	50	16	51	7	03	16	59	7	06	17	09
23	6	38	16	50	6	48	17	00	6	48	16	56	6	51	16	55	6	52	16	49	7	05	16	57	7	08	17	07
24	6	40	16	48	6	50	16	58	6	49	16	53	6	53	16	53	6	54	16	46	7	07	16	54	7	10	17	05
25	6	42	16	46	6	52	16	56	6	51	16	51	6	55	16	50	6	56	16	44	7	09	16	52	7	12	17	02
26	6	44	16	44	6	53	16	54	6	53	16	49	6	57	16	48	6	58	16	42	7	11	16	50	7	14	17	00
27	6	45	16	42	6	55	16	52	6	55	16	47	6	59	16	46	7	00	16	40	7	13	16	48	7	16	16	58
28	6	47	16	41	6	57	16	51	6	57	16	45	7	01	16	44	7	02	16	37	7	15	16	45	7	18	16	56
29	6	49	16	39	6	59	16	49	6	59	16	43	7	03	16	42	7	04	16	35	7	17	16	43	7	20	16	54
30	6	51	16	37	7	00	16	47	7	00	16	42	7	04	16	40	7	06	16	33	7	19	16	41	7	22	16	52
31	6	52	16	35	7	02	16	45	7	02	16	40	7	06	16	38	7	08	16	31	7	22	16	39	7	24	16	50

THE MOON

Day	Diam	Phase	Age	Rise 52°		Rise 56°		Transit		Set 52°		Set 56°	
	'	%	d	h	m	h	m	h	m	h	m	h	m
2	30.6	23	25.0	0	18	-	-	8	38	16	41	16	59
3	31.2	15	26.0	1	36	1	19	9	28	17	1	17	15
4	31.6	8	27.0	2	58	2	46	10	18	17	19	17	26
5	32.0	3	28.0	4	20	4	15	11	7	17	34	17	37
6	32.4	0	29.0	5	45	5	45	11	56	17	50	17	47
7	32.6	0	0.5	7	11	7	18	12	46	18	6	17	58
8	32.8	3	1.5	8	40	8	52	13	40	18	25	18	11
9	32.8	9	2.5	10	10	10	30	14	36	18	50	18	29
10	32.8	17	3.5	11	39	12	5	15	35	19	24	18	57
11	32.6	26	4.5	12	59	13	32	16	36	20	10	19	37
12	32.4	37	5.5	14	6	14	39	17	38	21	11	20	38
13	32.0	49	6.5	14	55	15	25	18	37	22	24	21	56
14	31.8	60	7.5	15	31	15	54	19	33	23	44	23	21
15	31.4	70	8.5	15	56	16	14	20	25	-	-	-	-
16	31.0	79	9.5	16	15	16	28	21	13	1	4	0	48
17	30.8	87	10.5	16	31	16	38	21	58	2	22	2	12
18	30.6	93	11.5	16	44	16	46	22	40	3	38	3	33
19	30.2	97	12.5	16	57	16	54	23	23	4	52	4	52
20	30.0	100	13.5	17	10	17	3	-	-	6	4	6	9
21	29.8	100	14.5	17	24	17	12	0	5	7	16	7	27
22	29.6	98	15.5	17	40	17	23	0	47	8	29	8	44
23	29.6	95	16.5	18	2	17	39	1	32	9	40	10	0
24	29.4	90	17.5	18	28	18	2	2	18	10	50	11	17
25	29.4	84	18.5	19	5	18	32	3	6	11	54	12	27
26	29.6	76	19.5	19	51	19	18	3	56	12	52	13	26
27	29.6	68	20.5	20	49	20	18	4	47	13	39	14	10
28	30.0	58	21.5	21	58	21	30	5	38	14	16	14	43
29	30.2	49	22.5	23	12	22	51	6	28	14	44	15	5
30	30.6	39	23.5	-	-	-	-	7	18	15	5	15	21
31	31.2	29	24.5	0	30	0	15	8	6	15	23	15	34

THE PLANETS

MERCURY

Day	R.A.			Dec.	Mag.	Diam.	Phase	Rise			Transit			Set		
	h	m	s	°		"	%	h	m	s	h	m	s	h	m	s
1	13	25	46	-12.9	+1.5	9.5	17	7	50	31	12	40	9	17	31	43
6	13	12	24	-10.8	+3.3	10.2	4	7	3	53	12	6	12	17	11	28
11	12	53	14	-7.3	+4.7	10.0	1	6	5	21	11	27	46	16	53	31
16	12	39	58	-4.1	+1.7	9.1	13	5	16	16	10	56	32	16	39	16
21	12	41	23	-2.9	+0.1	7.8	36	4	53	2	10	40	4	16	28	9
26	12	56	42	-3.9	-0.6	6.7	59	4	55	4	10	36	54	16	18	39
31	13	20	35	-6.2	-0.8	6.0	76	5	13	2	10	41	44	16	9	45

VENUS

Day	R.A.			Dec.	Mag.	Diam.	Phase	Rise			Transit			Set		
	h	m	s	°		"	%	h	m	s	h	m	s	h	m	s
1	15	19	21	-20.6	-4.2	20.2	62	10	38	35	14	37	57	18	37	0
6	15	42	11	-22.3	-4.2	21.1	60	10	53	30	14	40	52	18	28	1
11	16	5	6	-23.7	-4.3	22.1	58	11	7	32	14	43	58	18	20	17
16	16	28	8	-24.9	-4.3	23.2	56	11	20	16	14	47	8	18	14	0
21	16	51	7	-25.9	-4.3	24.4	54	11	31	17	14	50	14	18	9	18
26	17	13	54	-26.6	-4.4	25.7	51	11	40	11	14	53	7	18	6	15
31	17	36	19	-27.0	-4.4	27.2	49	11	46	37	14	55	33	18	4	49

MARS

Day	R.A.			Dec.	Mag.	Diam.	Rise			Transit			Set		
	h	m	s	°		"	h	m	s	h	m	s	h	m	s
1	12	39	21	-3.5	+1.7	3.6	6	14	14	11	58	6	17	41	39
6	12	51	24	-4.8	+1.7	3.6	6	13	52	11	50	27	17	26	44
11	13	3	31	-6.1	+1.6	3.6	6	13	35	11	42	48	17	11	56
16	13	15	48	-7.4	+1.6	3.6	6	13	24	11	35	28	16	57	15
21	13	28	11	-8.6	+1.6	3.6	6	13	19	11	28	9	16	42	43
26	13	40	42	-9.9	+1.7	3.6	6	13	21	11	20	59	16	28	21
31	13	53	23	-11.1	+1.7	3.6	6	13	30	11	13	58	16	14	10

JUPITER

Day	R.A.			Dec.	Mag.	Diam.	Rise			Transit			Set		
	h	m	s	°		"	h	m	s	h	m	s	h	m	s
1	21	42	16	-15.0	-2.7	46.3	16	22	20	20	59	22	1	39	50
6	21	41	18	-15.1	-2.7	45.7	16	2	6	20	39	44	1	18	45
11	21	40	40	-15.1	-2.6	45.0	15	42	8	20	18	25	0	58	10
16	21	40	20	-15.2	-2.6	44.4	15	22	15	19	58	6	0	38	4
21	21	40	21	-15.1	-2.6	43.7	15	2	31	19	38	46	0	18	29
26	21	40	40	-15.1	-2.6	43.0	14	42	56	19	19	26	23	59	24
31	21	41	20	-15.0	-2.5	42.3	14	23	30	19	0	25	23	37	27

Diam. = Equatorial. Polar Diam. is 94% of Equatorial Diam.

SATURN

Day	R.A.			Dec.	Mag.	Diam.	Rise			Transit			Set		
	h	m	s	°		"	h	m	s	h	m	s	h	m	s
1	20	38	20	-19.3	+0.5	17.7	15	46	41	19	55	21	0	7	52
6	20	38	4	-19.3	+0.5	17.5	15	26	52	19	35	26	23	47	50
11	20	37	59	-19.3	+0.5	17.4	15	7	9	19	15	41	23	24	23
16	20	38	4	-19.3	+0.5	17.2	14	47	32	18	56	6	23	4	51
21	20	38	19	-19.3	+0.6	17.1	14	28	1	18	36	42	22	45	33
26	20	38	45	-19.3	+0.6	16.9	14	8	36	18	17	28	22	26	30
31	20	39	21	-19.3	+0.6	16.8	13	49	17	17	58	24	22	7	41

Diam. = Equatorial. Polar Diam. is 90% of Equatorial Diam.
Rings – major axis 39", minor axis 13", Tilt 19°

URANUS

Day	R.A.			Dec.	Mag.	Diam.	Rise			Transit			Set		
	h	m	s	°		"	h	m	s	h	m	s	h	m	s
1	2	47	6	+15.7	+5.7	3.7	18	29	10	2	6	58	9	40	54
6	2	46	28	+15.6	+5.7	3.7	18	9	11	1	46	40	9	20	17
11	2	45	47	+15.6	+5.7	3.7	17	49	10	1	26	19	8	59	36
16	2	45	3	+15.5	+5.7	3.7	17	29	8	1	5	56	8	38	52
21	2	44	17	+15.5	+5.7	3.8	17	9	5	0	45	30	8	18	4
26	2	43	30	+15.4	+5.7	3.8	16	49	2	0	25	3	7	57	14
31	2	42	41	+15.3	+5.6	3.8	16	28	57	0	4	36	7	36	23

NEPTUNE

Day	R.A.			Dec.	Mag.	Diam.	Rise			Transit			Set		
	h	m	s	°		"	h	m	s	h	m	s	h	m	s
1	23	30	1	-4.5	+7.8	2.4	17	8	27	22	46	29	4	28	26
6	23	29	32	-4.6	+7.8	2.4	16	48	35	22	26	21	4	8	1
11	23	29	5	-4.6	+7.8	2.4	16	28	45	22	6	14	3	47	39
16	23	28	40	-4.7	+7.8	2.3	16	8	54	21	46	9	3	27	19
21	23	28	16	-4.7	+7.8	2.3	15	49	5	21	26	6	3	7	2
26	23	27	54	-4.7	+7.8	2.3	15	29	16	21	6	5	2	46	48
31	23	27	34	-4.8	+7.8	2.3	15	9	28	20	46	5	2	26	38

THE NIGHT SKY

Mercury moves into the morning sky after inferior conjunction on the 9th and should be picked up around October 15th. However, your best chance of spotting the fleet-footed world is towards the end of the month as it gains in height daily and rapidly brightens then too.

Mercury is at greatest elongation west on the 25th and rises about an hour before the Sun. The magnitude -0.5 planet is then almost 10° above the eastern horizon at the beginning of civil twilight.

Venus is at greatest eastern elongation on the 29th and brightens a little in the evening sky. The main changes will require a scope though as the phase narrows from 62% illuminated on the 1st to 48% lit by Halloween.

Venus will be an exact half phase (dichotomy) on the 28th and reaches greatest elongation east a day later. Look for the glittering planet near the crescent moon on October 9th and close to Antares around the middle of the month.

Mars (magnitude 1.6) rises 50 minutes before the Sun at the end of October but is still too deep in the dawn glow to be visible. It passes through superior conjunction on the 8th.

Jupiter and Saturn both reach their stationary points this month and then go prograde, when their eastward motion on the celestial sphere resumes. Jupiter (magnitude -2.6) is setting at midnight by the end of October, but look for it near the Moon on the evening of the 15th.

NASA's Lucy mission to Jupiter's Trojan satellites is due to be launched this month. The targets are asteroids that cluster at a Lagrange point both ahead and behind Jupiter in its orbit by 60°. Lucy will use a series of complex manoeuvres to visit one Main Belt asteroid and seven Trojans over a 12 year mission.

Saturn (magnitude 0.5) slips from view even earlier than Jupiter and dips below the horizon by late-evening on the 31st. The Moon is a distant 9° from Saturn on the night of the 13th and the planet is at eastern quadrature on the 30th when telescope users again can see the globe's shadow cast on the rings.

The long awaited James Webb Space Telescope (JWST) is currently slated for launch on October 31st this year. Cost over-runs and technology challenges nearly scuppered the project, but JWST will be a worthy successor to the Hubble Space Telescope.

JWST has a 6.5-metre segmented primary mirror that will unfold as flower petals when it reaches its working orbit 1.2 million kilometres from Earth. Observations will largely be conducted in the infrared, allowing JWST to search for the first stars and infant galaxies, as well as study the evolution of proto-solar systems. The telescope will also be able to reveal more about the atmospheres of known extra-solar planets, maybe even finding they contain the building blocks of life.

November 2021

ELEVENTH MONTH, 30 DAYS. *Novem* (nine), ninth month of Roman pre-Julian calendar

1	*Monday*	Greenwich Mean Time was adopted as the standard against which the world's time zones were set 1884	week 44 day 305
2	*Tuesday*	Howard Hughes flew his eight-engine wooden aeroplane *Spruce Goose* for one minute 1947	306
3	*Wednesday*	The Soviet Union launched the first living creature into space, a dog named Laika 1957	307
4	*Thursday*	The entrance to Tutankhamun's tomb was discovered by the British archaeologist Howard Carter 1922	308
5	*Friday*	Guy Fawkes was found guarding explosives beneath the House of Lords during the Gunpowder Plot 1605	309
6	*Saturday*	George Eliot's first story, one of the *Scenes of Clerical Life*, was submitted for publication 1856	310
7	*Sunday*	Marie Curie, chemist and physicist who discovered radium and won two Nobel prizes *b.* 1867	311

8	*Monday*	The Bodleian library opened to scholars at Oxford University 1602	week 45 day 312
9	*Tuesday*	Physicist Gordon Gould wrote down the principles for the laser, but failed to patent his idea 1957	313
10	*Wednesday*	Fred Cohen presented his creation, the computer virus, to a security seminar in the USA 1983	314
11	*Thursday*	The signing of the Armistice at 11am marked the end of the First World War 1918	315
12	*Friday*	The Abbey Road recording studios in London were opened by Sir Edward Elgar 1931	316
13	*Saturday*	An aeroplane spread pellets of dry ice at 4,000m creating artificial snow for the first time 1946	317
14	*Sunday*	The Scottish Nationalist Party contested its first general election 1935	318

15	*Monday*	Brazil became a republic when the second and last emperor, Pedro II, was deposed in a military coup 1889	week 46 day 319
16	*Tuesday*	The discovery of Americium (atomic number 95) and curium (96), two new elements, was announced 1945	320
17	*Wednesday*	English-language bookshop and lending library Shakespeare and Company opened in Paris 1919	321
18	*Thursday*	Russia ratified the Kyoto Protocol on climate change 2004	322
19	*Friday*	The first National Lottery draw took place 1994	323
20	*Saturday*	Russia launched the first module of the International Space Station from Kazakhstan 1998	324
21	*Sunday*	Voltaire spent his 23rd birthday incarcerated in the Bastille 1717	325

22	*Monday*	Concorde began operating flights between New York and Europe with a flight time under 3.5 hours 1977	week 47 day 326
23	*Tuesday*	John Milton's *Areopagitica*, a pamphlet condemning pre-publication censorship, was published 1644	327
24	*Wednesday*	Charles Darwin's *On the Origin of Species* was published 1859	328
25	*Thursday*	Agatha Christie's murder mystery play *The Mousetrap* opens in London and is still running today 1952	329
26	*Friday*	The first Thanksgiving Day was celebrated nationally in America 1789	330
27	*Saturday*	US author Ken Kesey held his first all night 'acid test' party in California 1965	331
28	*Sunday*	The first female voters were allowed at a general election in New Zealand 1893	332

29	*Monday*	Rossini's *The Barber of Seville* became the first opera to be sung in Italian in the USA 1825	week 48 day 333
30	*Tuesday*	Production began on Alfred Hitchcock's film *Psycho* 1959	334

ASTRONOMICAL PHENOMENA

1	-	Sun crosses into Libra
3	19	Mercury 1.2°S of the Moon: Occultation
4	05	Mars 2.3°S of the Moon
4	21	New Moon
4	-	Uranus at opposition
8	05	Venus 1.1°S of the Moon: Occultation
10	04	Mercury 1.0°N of Mars
10	14	Saturn 4.1°N of the Moon
11	17	Jupiter 4.4°N of the Moon
11	13	First Quarter Moon
15	-	Jupiter is at eastern quadrature
17	18	Leonid meteor shower
19	09	Full Moon
19	09	Partial lunar eclipse; mag=0.974
24	-	Sun crosses into Scorpius
26	22	Regulus 5.2°S of the Moon
27	-	Ceres at opposition
27	12	Last Quarter Moon
29	-	Mercury at superior conjunction
30	-	Sun crosses into Ophiuchus

CONSTELLATIONS

The following constellations are visible at midnight throughout the month:
Ursa Major (below the Pole), Cepheus, Cassiopeia, Andromeda, Pegasus, Pisces, Aquarius and Cetus

PHASES OF THE MOON

Phase, Apsides and Node	*d*	*h*	*m*
● New Moon	4	21	15
◐ First Quarter	11	12	46
○ Full Moon	19	8	57
◑ Last Moon	27	12	28
Perigee (358,844 km)	5	22	18
Apogee (406,279 km)	21	2	13

SUNRISE AND SUNSET

d	London 0° 05' 51° 30'				Bristol 2° 35' 51° 28'				Birmingham 1° 55' 52° 28'				Manchester 2° 15' 53° 28'				Newcastle 1° 37' 54° 59'				Glasgow 4° 14' 55° 52'				Belfast 5° 56' 54° 35'			
	h	m	h	m	h	m	h	m	h	m	h	m	h	m	h	m	h	m	h	m	h	m	h	m	h	m	h	m
1	6	54	16	33	7	04	16	43	7	04	16	38	7	08	16	36	7	10	16	29	7	24	16	37	7	26	16	48
2	6	56	16	31	7	06	16	41	7	06	16	36	7	10	16	34	7	12	16	27	7	26	16	34	7	28	16	45
3	6	58	16	30	7	07	16	40	7	08	16	34	7	12	16	32	7	14	16	25	7	28	16	32	7	30	16	43
4	6	59	16	28	7	09	16	38	7	10	16	32	7	14	16	30	7	16	16	23	7	30	16	30	7	32	16	42
5	7	01	16	26	7	11	16	36	7	11	16	30	7	16	16	29	7	18	16	21	7	32	16	28	7	34	16	40
6	7	03	16	24	7	13	16	35	7	13	16	29	7	18	16	27	7	21	16	19	7	34	16	26	7	36	16	38
7	7	05	16	23	7	15	16	33	7	15	16	27	7	20	16	25	7	23	16	17	7	36	16	24	7	38	16	36
8	7	06	16	21	7	16	16	31	7	17	16	25	7	22	16	23	7	25	16	15	7	39	16	22	7	40	16	34
9	7	08	16	20	7	18	16	30	7	19	16	24	7	23	16	22	7	27	16	13	7	41	16	20	7	42	16	32
10	7	10	16	18	7	20	16	28	7	20	16	22	7	25	16	20	7	29	16	11	7	43	16	18	7	44	16	30
11	7	12	16	17	7	22	16	27	7	22	16	20	7	27	16	18	7	31	16	10	7	45	16	16	7	46	16	29
12	7	13	16	15	7	23	16	25	7	24	16	19	7	29	16	17	7	33	16	08	7	47	16	15	7	48	16	27
13	7	15	16	14	7	25	16	24	7	26	16	17	7	31	16	15	7	35	16	06	7	49	16	13	7	50	16	25
14	7	17	16	12	7	27	16	22	7	28	16	16	7	33	16	13	7	37	16	05	7	51	16	11	7	52	16	24
15	7	19	16	11	7	28	16	21	7	29	16	15	7	35	16	12	7	39	16	03	7	53	16	09	7	54	16	22
16	7	20	16	09	7	30	16	20	7	31	16	13	7	37	16	10	7	41	16	01	7	55	16	08	7	56	16	20
17	7	22	16	08	7	32	16	18	7	33	16	12	7	38	16	09	7	43	16	00	7	57	16	06	7	58	16	19
18	7	24	16	07	7	34	16	17	7	35	16	10	7	40	16	08	7	44	15	58	7	59	16	05	8	00	16	17
19	7	25	16	06	7	35	16	16	7	37	16	09	7	42	16	06	7	46	15	57	8	01	16	03	8	02	16	16
20	7	27	16	05	7	37	16	15	7	38	16	08	7	44	16	05	7	48	15	55	8	03	16	02	8	04	16	15
21	7	29	16	03	7	38	16	14	7	40	16	07	7	46	16	04	7	50	15	54	8	05	16	00	8	06	16	13
22	7	30	16	02	7	40	16	12	7	42	16	06	7	47	16	03	7	52	15	53	8	07	15	59	8	07	16	12
23	7	32	16	01	7	42	16	11	7	43	16	05	7	49	16	01	7	54	15	52	8	09	15	57	8	09	16	11
24	7	33	16	00	7	43	16	10	7	45	16	03	7	51	16	00	7	56	15	50	8	11	15	56	8	11	16	10
25	7	35	15	59	7	45	16	10	7	47	16	02	7	52	15	59	7	57	15	49	8	13	15	55	8	13	16	08
26	7	36	15	59	7	46	16	09	7	48	16	02	7	54	15	58	7	59	15	48	8	14	15	54	8	14	16	07
27	7	38	15	58	7	48	16	08	7	50	16	01	7	56	15	57	8	01	15	47	8	16	15	53	8	16	16	06
28	7	40	15	57	7	49	16	07	7	51	16	00	7	57	15	56	8	03	15	46	8	18	15	51	8	18	16	05
29	7	41	15	56	7	51	16	06	7	53	15	59	7	59	15	55	8	04	15	45	8	20	15	50	8	19	16	04
30	7	42	15	55	7	52	16	06	7	54	15	58	8	00	15	55	8	06	15	44	8	21	15	49	8	21	16	04

THE MOON

Day	Diam '	Phase %	Age d	Rise 52° h	Rise 52° m	Rise 56° h	Rise 56° m	Transit h	Transit m	Set 52° h	Set 52° m	Set 56° h	Set 56° m
1	31.6	20	25.5	1	50	1	42	8	54	15	39	15	44
2	32.2	11	26.5	3	13	3	10	9	42	15	54	15	54
3	32.6	5	27.5	4	38	4	41	10	32	16	9	16	4
4	33.0	1	28.5	6	6	6	16	11	24	16	27	16	16
5	33.2	0	29.5	7	38	7	54	12	20	16	49	16	31
6	33.2	2	0.9	9	11	9	35	13	20	17	19	16	55
7	33.2	6	1.9	10	40	11	10	14	23	18	1	17	29
8	33.0	14	2.9	11	55	12	30	15	27	18	59	18	24
9	32.6	23	3.9	12	53	13	25	16	30	20	10	19	38
10	32.2	33	4.9	13	35	13	59	17	28	21	29	21	6
11	31.8	44	5.9	14	2	14	23	18	22	22	52	22	33
12	31.4	55	6.9	14	24	14	37	19	11	-	-	23	59
13	31.0	66	7.9	14	40	14	48	19	57	0	11	-	-
14	30.6	75	8.9	14	53	14	57	20	40	1	27	1	21
15	30.2	83	9.9	15	6	15	5	21	22	2	41	2	39
16	30.0	90	10.9	15	18	15	13	22	3	3	53	3	56
17	29.8	95	11.9	15	31	15	21	22	45	5	4	5	13
18	29.6	98	12.9	15	47	15	31	23	29	6	16	6	30
19	29.6	100	13.9	16	6	15	45	-	-	7	28	7	47
20	29.4	100	14.9	16	30	16	5	0	14	8	39	9	2
21	29.4	98	15.9	17	3	16	32	1	2	9	46	10	16
22	29.4	94	16.9	17	45	17	13	1	51	10	46	11	20
23	29.6	89	17.9	18	39	18	8	2	41	11	37	12	9
24	29.6	82	18.9	19	43	19	15	3	32	12	17	12	45
25	29.8	74	19.9	20	55	20	32	4	23	12	47	13	10
26	30.2	65	20.9	22	10	21	53	5	11	13	10	13	28
27	30.6	56	21.9	23	27	23	16	5	58	13	29	13	41
28	31.0	45	22.9	-	-	-	-	6	45	13	44	13	52
29	31.4	35	23.9	0	46	0	40	7	31	13	59	14	1
30	32.0	25	24.9	2	7	2	7	8	18	14	13	14	10

THE PLANETS

MERCURY

Day	R.A. h	R.A. m	R.A. s	Dec. °	Mag.	Diam. "	Phase %	Rise h	Rise m	Rise s	Transit h	Transit m	Transit s	Set h	Set m	Set s
1	13	25	58	-6.8	-0.8	5.8	79	5	17	45	10	43	15	16	8	0
6	13	54	33	-9.9	-0.9	5.4	89	5	44	24	10	52	24	15	59	28
11	14	24	46	-13.0	-0.9	5.1	94	6	13	37	11	3	2	15	51	30
16	14	55	51	-16.0	-0.9	4.9	98	6	43	32	11	14	27	15	44	29
21	15	27	33	-18.6	-1.0	4.7	99	7	13	12	11	26	30	15	39	0
26	15	59	54	-21.0	-1.2	4.7	100	7	41	57	11	39	10	15	35	43

VENUS

Day	R.A. h	R.A. m	R.A. s	Dec. °	Mag.	Diam. "	Phase %	Rise h	Rise m	Rise s	Transit h	Transit m	Transit s	Set h	Set m	Set s
1	17	40	44	-27.1	-4.4	27.5	48	11	47	35	14	55	58	18	4	42
6	18	2	23	-27.2	-4.5	29.2	46	11	50	40	14	57	37	18	4	59
11	18	23	8	-27.2	-4.5	31.2	43	11	50	42	14	58	17	18	6	21
16	18	42	40	-26.8	-4.6	33.3	40	11	47	33	14	57	40	18	8	18
21	19	0	40	-26.3	-4.6	35.8	36	11	41	6	14	55	25	18	10	15
26	19	16	46	-25.6	-4.6	38.6	33	11	31	20	14	51	11	18	11	31

MARS

Day	R.A. h	R.A. m	R.A. s	Dec. °	Mag.	Diam. "	Rise h	Rise m	Rise s	Transit h	Transit m	Transit s	Set h	Set m	Set s
1	13	55	56	-11.4	+1.7	3.6	6	13	33	11	12	35	16	11	22
6	14	8	40	-12.6	+1.6	3.6	6	13	50	11	5	47	15	57	28
11	14	21	52	-13.7	+1.6	3.7	6	14	13	10	59	8	15	43	49
16	14	35	7	-14.8	+1.6	3.7	6	14	41	10	52	41	15	30	28
21	14	48	33	-15.9	+1.6	3.7	6	15	13	10	46	26	15	17	27
26	15	2	11	-16.9	+1.6	3.7	6	15	47	10	40	23	15	4	48

JUPITER

Day	R.A. h	R.A. m	R.A. s	Dec. °	Mag.	Diam. "	Rise h	Rise m	Rise s	Transit h	Transit m	Transit s	Set h	Set m	Set s
1	21	41	30	-15.0	-2.5	42.2	14	19	38	18	56	39	23	33	47
6	21	42	32	-14.9	-2.5	41.5	14	0	23	18	38	3	23	15	46
11	21	43	53	-14.8	-2.4	40.8	13	41	16	18	19	41	22	58	13
16	21	45	32	-14.6	-2.4	40.2	13	22	18	18	1	40	22	41	8
21	21	47	27	-14.5	-2.4	39.5	13	3	28	17	43	55	22	24	28
26	21	49	38	-14.3	-2.3	38.9	12	44	45	17	26	26	22	8	12

Diam. = Equatorial. Polar Diam. is 94% of Equatorial Diam.

SATURN

Day	R.A. h	R.A. m	R.A. s	Dec. °	Mag.	Diam. "	Rise h	Rise m	Rise s	Transit h	Transit m	Transit s	Set h	Set m	Set s
1	20	39	29	-19.2	+0.6	16.8	13	45	25	17	54	36	22	3	57
6	20	40	17	-19.2	+0.6	16.6	13	26	13	17	35	44	21	45	25
11	20	41	14	-19.1	+0.6	16.5	13	7	5	17	17	2	21	27	7
16	20	42	21	-19.1	+0.7	16.4	12	48	3	16	58	29	21	9	3
21	20	43	36	-19.0	+0.7	16.2	12	29	6	16	40	4	20	51	11
26	20	45	0	-18.9	+0.7	16.1	12	10	13	16	21	48	20	33	32

Diam. = Equatorial. Polar Diam. is 90% of Equatorial Diam.
Rings – major axis 37", minor axis 12", Tilt 19°

URANUS

Day	R.A. h	R.A. m	R.A. s	Dec. °	Mag.	Diam. "	Rise h	Rise m	Rise s	Transit h	Transit m	Transit s	Set h	Set m	Set s
1	2	42	31	+15.3	+5.6	3.8	16	24	56	0	0	30	7	32	12
6	2	41	42	+15.3	+5.6	3.8	16	4	52	23	36	8	7	11	20
11	2	40	53	+15.2	+5.7	3.8	15	44	47	23	15	39	6	50	28
16	2	40	5	+15.1	+5.7	3.8	15	24	43	22	55	12	6	29	37
21	2	39	18	+15.1	+5.7	3.8	15	4	39	22	34	45	6	8	47
26	2	38	33	+15.0	+5.7	3.7	14	44	36	22	14	20	5	48	1

NEPTUNE

Day	R.A. h	R.A. m	R.A. s	Dec. °	Mag.	Diam. "	Rise h	Rise m	Rise s	Transit h	Transit m	Transit s	Set h	Set m	Set s
1	23	27	31	-4.8	+7.8	2.3	15	5	30	20	42	6	2	22	36
6	23	27	14	-4.8	+7.8	2.3	14	45	43	20	22	10	2	2	31
11	23	26	60	-4.8	+7.9	2.3	14	25	57	20	2	16	1	42	30
16	23	26	49	-4.8	+7.9	2.3	14	6	12	19	42	25	1	22	32
21	23	26	41	-4.9	+7.9	2.3	13	46	29	19	22	38	1	2	42
26	23	26	35	-4.9	+7.9	2.3	13	26	46	19	2	53	0	42	55

THE NIGHT SKY

Mercury is visible in the morning sky up to around mid-month but is best seen in the first week when the planet rises nearly two hours before the Sun and glimmers at mag. -0.8.

Mercury passes about 4° from Spica in Virgo on November 2nd and the lunar crescent is 38 hours from New when 6° to the upper right of the planet on the 3rd. Mercury is then at superior conjunction with the Sun on the 29th when it will not be visible.

Venus (magnitude -4.9) is a brilliant 'star' in the southwest these evenings and sets 2½ hours after the Sun on the 30th. The planet passes below M8, the Lagoon Nebula, in Sagittarius on the 5th, and can be found to the lower right of the Moon on the 8th. The phase is now narrowing towards a plump crescent that can be seen towards the end of the month in a telescope.

Mars (magnitude 1.6) gradually pulls clear of the solar glare in the morning sky and rises 1½ hours before the Sun by the end of the month. On the morning of the 4th the Moon is only 14½ hours from New when it is 2° from Mars. It will be a challenge to see such a thin lunar crescent but it is possible given a clear east-southeast horizon.

Mars and magnitude -0.9 Mercury lie just 1° apart on the morning of the 10th, but separate quite quickly. The Red Planet then passes quite close to the magnitude 2.8 star Alpha Librae on the 22nd.

Jupiter (magnitude -2.4) is at eastern quadrature on the 15th when the planet's disk looks gibbous. It is an evening sky object setting at midnight on the 1st and 1½ hours earlier at the end of November. Jupiter is 5° above the first quarter moon on the 11th.

Saturn (magnitude 0.7) can also be found in Capricornus, and is on view until late evening. The Moon is near Saturn on the 10th.

Uranus (magnitude 5.6) is at opposition on November 5th in the southern part of Aries. That night, it is the rightmost 'star' of three-in-a-row similarly bright points of light comprising Sigma and Omicron Arietis, along with Uranus. All fit in the same low power field of view of standard binoculars. On a night of good clear skies, try spot Uranus with the unaided eye from a dark site.

A partial lunar eclipse on the morning of the 19th is in progress at moonset from the UK so we only see the initial stages of the event. The Moon passes south of Earth's shadow, so the northern part of the disk is more dimmed.

See **W** eclipsewise.com/lunar/lunar.html and **W** timeanddate.com for timings. The eclipsed Moon is about 6° below the Pleiades star cluster as they sink in the west, adding some drama to photographs of the event.

December 2021

TWELFTH MONTH, 31 DAYS. *Decem* (ten), tenth month of Roman pre-Julian calendar

1	*Wednesday*	British and French workers joined the two halves of the Channel tunnel 1990	day 335
2	*Thursday*	St Paul's Cathedral opened 1697	336
3	*Friday*	The Malta summit brought the Cold War to a close 1989	337
4	*Saturday*	Treaty of Paris, made by King Henry III and King Louis IX of France, ends 100 years of conflict 1259	338
5	*Sunday*	The *Mary Celeste* was found abandoned 1872	339
6	*Monday*	Johann Palisa, Austrian astronomer known for his discovery of 122 asteroids *b.* 1848	week 49 day 340
7	*Tuesday*	NASA launches *Apollo 17*, the sixth and last mission to land on the Moon 1972	341
8	*Wednesday*	The first female actor appeared in a Shakespeare production, as Desdemona in *Othello* 1660	342
9	*Thursday*	The *American Minerva*, New York City's first daily newspaper, was founded 1793	343
10	*Friday*	US president Woodrow Wilson won the Nobel Peace Prize 1920	344
11	*Saturday*	The first dental anaesthetic, nitrous oxide ('laughing gas'), was used for a tooth extraction 1844	345
12	*Sunday*	Kenya became independent from the United Kingdom 1963	346
13	*Monday*	Gordo, a monkey, was lost in the Atlantic due to a technical problem after a 482km space journey 1958	week 50 day 347
14	*Tuesday*	Max Planck presents his quantum theory to the German Physical Society in Berlin 1900	348
15	*Wednesday*	The Chernobyl nuclear plant in Ukraine was shut down, 14 years after the infamous disaster 2000	349
16	*Thursday*	The Boston Tea Party in protest against taxation brought in by the British parliament took place 1773	350
17	*Friday*	Orville Wright made the first powered flight 1903	351
18	*Saturday*	The first two volumes of Laurence Sterne's humorous novel *Tristram Shandy* were published 1759	352
19	*Sunday*	Charles Dickens' novella *A Christmas Carol*, featuring the miserly Ebenezer Scrooge, was published 1843	353
20	*Monday*	New York's Broadway became known as the 'Great White Way' after being lit by electricity 1880	week 51 day 354
21	*Tuesday*	The 11-member Commonwealth of Independent States was formed 1991	355
22	*Wednesday*	Electric lights were first used to decorate Christmas trees by Edward Johnson 1882	356
23	*Thursday*	Vincent Van Gogh cut off part of his right ear 1888	357
24	*Friday*	US General Dwight D. Eisenhower was appointed Supreme Allied Commander 1943	358
25	*Saturday*	King George V made the first royal Christmas day broadcast 1932	359
26	*Sunday*	Marie Curie, and her husband Pierre, announced the discovery of radium 1898	360
27	*Monday*	HMS *Beagle* set sail from Plymouth with a young Charles Darwin on board 1831	week 52 day 361
28	*Tuesday*	The first commercial movie screening, *Workers Leaving The Lumière Factory in Lyon*, took place 1895	362
29	*Wednesday*	London experienced its worst night of bombing in the Blitz 1940	363
30	*Thursday*	Percy Bysshe Shelley married writer Mary Wollstonecraft Godwin in London 1816	364
31	*Friday*	The farthing ceased to be legal tender 1960	365

ASTRONOMICAL PHENOMENA

3	00	Mars 0.7°S of the Moon
4	08	Total solar eclipse; mag=1.037
4	08	New Moon
7	01	Venus 1.9°N of the Moon
8	02	Saturn 4.2°N of the Moon
9	06	Jupiter 4.5°N of the Moon
9	18	Venus at greatest brilliancy
11	02	First Quarter Moon
11	18	Venus 0.08°N of Pluto
14	07	Geminid meteor shower
19	05	Full Moon
19	-	Sun crosses into Sagittarius
21	16	Winter solstice
22	15	Ursid meteor shower
24	05	Regulus 5.1°S of the Moon
27	09	Mars 4.5°N of Antares
27	02	Last Quarter Moon
29	01	Mercury 4.2°S of Venus
31	20	Mars 1.0°N of Moon: Occultation

CONSTELLATIONS

The following constellations are visible at midnight throughout the month:
Ursa Major (below the Pole), Ursa Minor (below the Pole), Cassiopeia, Andromeda, Perseus, Triangulum, Aries, Taurus, Cetus and Eridanus

PHASES OF THE MOON

Phase, Apsides and Node	*d*	*h*	*m*
● New Moon	4	7	43
◓ First Quarter	11	1	36
○ Full Moon	19	4	35
◑ Last Quarter	27	2	24
Perigee (356,794 km)	4	10	4
Apogee (406,320 km)	18	2	15

SUNRISE AND SUNSET

	London		Bristol		Birmingham		Manchester		Newcastle		Glasgow		Belfast	
	0° 05'	51° 30'	2° 35'	51° 28'	1° 55'	52° 28'	2° 15'	53° 28'	1° 37'	54° 59'	4° 14'	55° 52'	5° 56'	54° 35'
d	h m	h m	h m	h m	h m	h m	h m	h m	h m	h m	h m	h m	h m	h m
1	7 44	15 55	7 54	16 05	7 56	15 58	8 02	15 54	8 08	15 43	8 23	15 49	8 23	16 03
2	7 45	15 54	7 55	16 04	7 57	15 57	8 03	15 53	8 09	15 42	8 25	15 48	8 24	16 02
3	7 47	15 54	7 56	16 04	7 58	15 56	8 05	15 53	8 11	15 42	8 26	15 47	8 26	16 01
4	7 48	15 53	7 58	16 03	8 00	15 56	8 06	15 52	8 12	15 41	8 28	15 46	8 27	16 01
5	7 49	15 53	7 59	16 03	8 01	15 55	8 08	15 52	8 14	15 40	8 29	15 46	8 29	16 00
6	7 50	15 52	8 00	16 02	8 02	15 55	8 09	15 51	8 15	15 40	8 31	15 45	8 30	16 00
7	7 52	15 52	8 01	16 02	8 04	15 55	8 10	15 51	8 16	15 39	8 32	15 45	8 31	15 59
8	7 53	15 52	8 02	16 02	8 05	15 54	8 11	15 50	8 18	15 39	8 34	15 44	8 33	15 59
9	7 54	15 52	8 04	16 02	8 06	15 54	8 13	15 50	8 19	15 39	8 35	15 44	8 34	15 58
10	7 55	15 51	8 05	16 02	8 07	15 54	8 14	15 50	8 20	15 38	8 36	15 43	8 35	15 58
11	7 56	15 51	8 06	16 01	8 08	15 54	8 15	15 50	8 21	15 38	8 37	15 43	8 36	15 58
12	7 57	15 51	8 07	16 01	8 09	15 54	8 16	15 50	8 22	15 38	8 38	15 43	8 37	15 58
13	7 58	15 51	8 08	16 01	8 10	15 54	8 17	15 50	8 23	15 38	8 39	15 43	8 38	15 58
14	7 59	15 51	8 09	16 01	8 11	15 54	8 18	15 50	8 24	15 38	8 40	15 43	8 39	15 58
15	8 00	15 51	8 09	16 02	8 12	15 54	8 19	15 50	8 25	15 38	8 41	15 43	8 40	15 58
16	8 00	15 52	8 10	16 02	8 13	15 54	8 20	15 50	8 26	15 38	8 42	15 43	8 41	15 58
17	8 01	15 52	8 11	16 02	8 13	15 54	8 20	15 50	8 27	15 38	8 43	15 43	8 42	15 58
18	8 02	15 52	8 12	16 02	8 14	15 55	8 21	15 50	8 28	15 39	8 44	15 43	8 42	15 58
19	8 02	15 53	8 12	16 03	8 15	15 55	8 22	15 51	8 28	15 39	8 45	15 44	8 43	15 59
20	8 03	15 53	8 13	16 03	8 15	15 55	8 22	15 51	8 29	15 39	8 45	15 44	8 44	15 59
21	8 04	15 53	8 13	16 04	8 16	15 56	8 23	15 52	8 29	15 40	8 46	15 45	8 44	16 00
22	8 04	15 54	8 14	16 04	8 16	15 56	8 23	15 52	8 30	15 40	8 46	15 45	8 45	16 00
23	8 05	15 55	8 14	16 05	8 17	15 57	8 24	15 53	8 30	15 41	8 47	15 46	8 45	16 01
24	8 05	15 55	8 15	16 05	8 17	15 57	8 24	15 53	8 31	15 42	8 47	15 46	8 46	16 01
25	8 05	15 56	8 15	16 06	8 18	15 58	8 24	15 54	8 31	15 42	8 47	15 47	8 46	16 02
26	8 05	15 57	8 15	16 07	8 18	15 59	8 25	15 55	8 31	15 43	8 47	15 48	8 46	16 03
27	8 06	15 57	8 16	16 08	8 18	16 00	8 25	15 56	8 31	15 44	8 48	15 49	8 46	16 04
28	8 06	15 58	8 16	16 08	8 18	16 01	8 25	15 56	8 32	15 45	8 48	15 50	8 46	16 05
29	8 06	15 59	8 16	16 09	8 18	16 01	8 25	15 57	8 32	15 46	8 48	15 51	8 46	16 06
30	8 06	16 00	8 16	16 10	8 18	16 02	8 25	15 58	8 31	15 47	8 48	15 52	8 46	16 07
31	8 06	16 01	8 16	16 11	8 18	16 03	8 25	15 59	8 31	15 48	8 47	15 53	8 46	16 08

THE MOON

Day	Diam	Phase	Age	Rise 52°		Rise 56°		Transit		Set 52°		Set 56°	
	'	%	d	h	m	h	m	h	m	h	m	h	m
1	32.6	16	25.9	3	31	3	37	9	8	14	29	14	21
2	33.0	8	26.9	4	59	5	12	10	1	14	48	14	34
3	33.4	3	27.9	6	32	6	51	10	58	15	13	14	53
4	33.4	0	28.9	8	5	8	32	12	1	15	48	15	20
5	33.4	1	0.4	9	31	10	2	13	6	16	38	16	7
6	33.2	4	1.4	10	41	11	13	14	12	17	46	17	14
7	33.0	10	2.4	11	31	11	58	15	15	19	7	18	39
8	32.4	19	3.4	12	4	12	27	16	14	20	32	20	11
9	32.0	28	4.4	12	29	12	45	17	6	21	56	21	41
10	31.4	39	5.4	12	47	12	57	17	54	23	15	23	6
11	31.0	49	6.4	13	1	13	7	18	39	-	-	-	-
12	30.6	60	7.4	13	14	13	15	19	21	0	30	0	27
13	30.2	69	8.4	13	26	13	22	20	2	1	43	1	45
14	29.8	78	9.4	13	39	13	31	20	44	2	54	3	1
15	29.6	85	10.4	13	54	13	40	21	27	4	5	4	17
16	29.6	91	11.4	14	12	13	53	22	11	5	17	5	34
17	29.4	96	12.4	14	33	14	10	22	58	6	28	6	50
18	29.4	99	13.4	15	4	14	34	23	47	7	37	8	4
19	29.4	100	14.4	15	43	15	11	-	-	8	40	9	12
20	29.4	99	15.4	16	33	16	2	0	37	9	34	10	6
21	29.6	97	16.4	17	35	17	6	1	29	10	17	10	47
22	29.8	93	17.4	18	44	18	20	2	19	10	50	11	16
23	30.0	87	18.4	19	58	19	39	3	8	11	15	11	35
24	30.2	80	19.4	21	13	21	1	3	55	11	35	11	49
25	30.6	71	20.4	22	29	22	22	4	41	11	51	12	0
26	31.0	62	21.4	23	47	23	45	5	26	12	5	12	9
27	31.4	51	22.4	-	-	-	-	6	11	12	19	12	18
28	31.8	40	23.4	1	6	1	10	6	57	12	33	12	27
29	32.2	30	24.4	2	29	2	39	7	46	12	50	12	38
30	32.6	20	25.4	3	56	4	12	8	40	13	11	12	53
31	33.0	11	26.4	5	28	5	50	9	38	13	39	13	15

THE PLANETS

MERCURY

Day	R.A. h	m	s	Dec. °	Mag.	Diam. "	Phase %	Rise h	m	s	Transit h	m	s	Set h	m	s
1	16	32	56	-22.8	-1.2	4.6	100	8	9	7	11	52	32	15	35	23
6	17	6	40	-24.2	-1.0	4.7	99	8	33	55	12	6	34	15	38	49
11	17	40	60	-25.1	-0.8	4.7	98	8	55	27	12	21	13	15	46	44
16	18	15	44	-25.4	-0.8	4.9	96	9	12	48	12	36	13	15	59	36
21	18	50	50	-25.1	-0.7	5.1	93	9	25	8	12	51	11	16	17	24
26	19	24	34	-24.2	-0.7	5.4	88	9	31	43	13	5	21	16	39	22
31	19	56	43	-22.7	-0.7	5.8	80	9	31	52	13	17	22	17	3	26

VENUS

Day	R.A. h	m	s	Dec. °	Mag.	Diam. "	Phase %	Rise h	m	s	Transit h	m	s	Set h	m	s
1	19	30	35	-17.9	-4.7	41.7	29	11	18	11	14	44	34	18	11	21
6	19	41	43	-23.8	-4.7	45.2	25	11	1	36	14	35	7	18	8	58
11	19	49	38	-22.8	-4.7	49.0	20	10	41	23	14	22	20	18	3	29
16	19	53	48	-21.8	-4.6	53.2	16	10	17	22	14	5	43	17	54	7
21	19	53	45	-20.7	-4.6	57.5	11	9	49	23	13	44	51	17	40	16
26	19	49	17	-19.7	-4.5	61.6	7	9	17	31	13	19	41	17	21	42
31	19	40	41	-18.8	-4.3	65.0	3	8	42	23	12	50	43	16	58	51

MARS

Day	R.A. h	m	s	Dec. °	Mag.	Diam. "	Rise h	m	s	Transit h	m	s	Set h	m	s
1	15	19	3	-17.9	+1.6	3.8	6	16	22	10	34	33	14	52	34
6	15	30	7	-18.8	+1.6	3.8	6	16	55	10	28	56	14	40	48
11	15	44	24	-19.7	+1.6	3.8	6	17	23	10	23	32	14	29	34
16	15	58	54	-20.5	+1.6	3.9	6	17	42	10	18	20	14	18	52
21	16	13	37	-21.2	+1.6	3.9	6	17	49	10	13	21	14	8	48
26	16	28	31	-21.8	+1.6	3.9	6	17	41	10	8	34	13	59	24
31	16	43	38	-22.4	+1.5	4.0	6	17	13	10	3	59	13	50	44

JUPITER

Day	R.A. h	m	s	Dec. °	Mag.	Diam. "	Rise h	m	s	Transit h	m	s	Set h	m	s
1	21	52	5	-14.0	-2.3	38.4	12	26	9	17	9	12	21	52	21
6	21	54	46	-13.8	-2.3	37.8	12	7	40	16	52	12	21	36	51
11	21	57	40	-13.5	-2.2	37.3	11	49	16	16	35	26	21	21	42
16	22	0	47	-13.2	-2.2	36.8	11	30	58	16	18	52	21	6	52
21	22	4	4	-12.9	-2.2	36.3	11	12	45	16	2	29	20	52	19
26	22	7	32	-12.6	-2.2	35.9	10	54	36	15	46	17	20	38	4
31	22	11	10	-12.3	-2.1	35.5	10	36	30	15	30	14	20	24	3

Diam. = Equatorial. Polar Diam. is 94% of Equatorial Diam.

SATURN

Day	R.A. h	m	s	Dec. °	Mag.	Diam. "	Rise h	m	s	Transit h	m	s	Set h	m	s
1	20	46	32	-18.8	+0.7	16.0	11	51	25	16	3	40	20	16	4
6	20	48	12	-18.7	+0.7	15.9	11	32	41	15	45	40	19	58	47
11	20	49	58	-18.6	+0.7	15.8	11	14	0	15	27	46	19	41	40
16	20	51	51	-18.5	+0.7	15.7	10	55	23	15	9	59	19	24	43
21	20	53	49	-18.3	+0.7	15.6	10	36	48	14	52	17	19	7	54
26	20	55	53	-18.2	+0.7	15.5	10	18	16	14	34	41	18	51	13
31	20	58	1	-18.0	+0.7	15.5	9	59	46	14	17	9	18	34	39

Diam. = Equatorial. Polar Diam. is 90% of Equatorial Diam.
Rings – major axis 36", minor axis 11", Tilt 18°

URANUS

Day	R.A. h	m	s	Dec. °	Mag.	Diam. "	Rise h	m	s	Transit h	m	s	Set h	m	s
1	2	37	50	+15.0	+5.7	3.7	14	24	34	21	53	58	5	27	17
6	2	37	9	+14.9	+5.7	3.7	14	4	34	21	33	38	5	6	38
11	2	36	32	+14.9	+5.7	3.7	13	44	35	21	13	21	4	46	3
16	2	35	58	+14.8	+5.7	3.7	13	24	38	20	53	8	4	25	34
21	2	35	29	+14.8	+5.7	3.7	13	4	42	20	32	59	4	5	10
26	2	35	3	+14.8	+5.7	3.7	12	44	49	20	12	54	3	44	53
31	2	34	42	+14.7	+5.7	3.7	12	24	58	19	52	53	3	24	43

NEPTUNE

Day	R.A. h	m	s	Dec. °	Mag.	Diam. "	Rise h	m	s	Transit h	m	s	Set h	m	s
1	23	26	33	-4.9	+7.9	2.3	13	7	5	18	43	11	0	23	13
6	23	26	34	-4.9	+7.9	2.3	12	47	25	18	23	33	0	3	36
11	23	26	39	-4.8	+7.9	2.3	12	27	46	18	3	58	23	40	10
16	23	26	46	-4.8	+7.9	2.3	12	8	9	17	44	26	23	20	43
21	23	26	57	-4.8	+7.9	2.3	11	48	32	17	24	57	23	1	22
26	23	27	11	-4.8	+7.9	2.3	11	28	58	17	5	31	22	42	5
31	23	27	28	-4.7	+7.9	2.3	11	9	24	16	46	8	22	22	53

THE NIGHT SKY

Mercury may be spotted low in the southwest evening sky during the last few days of December when it sets about $1\frac{1}{2}$ hours after the Sun.

Venus climbs to greatest brilliancy (magnitude -4.9) in the evening sky this month as its phase slims to a thin crescent. It sets $2\frac{1}{2}$ hours after the Sun to begin with, but gradually slips from view earlier as the month progresses.

Venus is to the upper left of the crescent moon on the evening of December 6th and the planet - which has faded slightly to magnitude -4.3 at the time - is within $4\frac{1}{2}°$ of Mercury on the 28th.

Mars (magnitude 1.6) rises roughly an hour before the Sun all month but will be still somewhat low as twilight brightens. The disk currently measures less than four arc-seconds so is too small to make out any surface detail.

Mars crosses from Libra into Scorpius on the 16th, and then moves into Ophiuchus on Christmas Day. The planet is about $4\frac{1}{2}°$ from the red giant star Antares in Scorpius on the morning of the 27th.

The Moon is just $23\frac{1}{2}$ hours from New when it is near Mars on December 2nd. There is then another more distant encounter with the Moon on the morning of the 31st.

Jupiter (magnitude -2.2) and *Saturn* (magnitude 0.7) both set a few hours after the Sun these evenings and remain a fine sight through the telescope during December. Jupiter is near the Moon on the 9th and moves into Aquarius on the 15th. Saturn is about 8° from the Moon on the 7th.

The gibbous moon does not set until just after 3am on the night of the Geminids peak on December 13/14 and so will wash out all but the brighter meteors.

The Geminids are bright and leave persistent trails, possibly due to the nature of the material shed by the asteroid 3200 Phaethon, which is the shower's parent body. The object is sometimes dubbed a 'rock comet' and solar heating at perihelion cracks its surface, causing dust and other particles to be ejected. The composition of a Geminid meteor is therefore a little harder than the fluff from most comets.

The stream is inclined to Earth's orbit and we are presently fording its more dense regions. But that situation will not last as gravitational perturbations by Jupiter shifts the dust trail. In only a few hundred years our encounters with the Geminids will be no more.

Japan's space agency JAXA is developing a mission to be launched towards Phaethon in 2024. DESTINY+ will fly by a number of near-Earth objects, before an encounter with Phaethon in 2028.

The path of the total solar eclipse on December 4th crosses the Antarctic, eighteen years after one from the same saros (152) which was seen by a number of people on various chartered flights.

ECLIPSES 2021

During 2021 there will be four eclipses, two of the Sun and two of the Moon (all times are in GMT):

1. Total Lunar Eclipse on 26 May beginning 11h 19m will be visible from eastern Asia, Australia, Pacific, Americas. Not visible from the UK and Europe.
2. Annular Solar Eclipse on 10 June beginning at 10h 36m. This will be visible as an Annular Eclipse from parts of north Canada, Greenland, eastern Russia, and as a partial eclipse: north North America, UK, Europe, Asia. From the UK it will have a magnitude of 30 per cent in the south and 50 per cent in north Scotland. Member 23 of 80 of Saros 147. Maximum duration 3m 51s.
3. Partial Lunar Eclipse (97 per cent) on 19 November beginning at 9h 04m. Visible Americas, North Europe including UK, eastern Asia, Australia, Pacific. In the UK it is a morning eclipse maximum at 9h 03m, but Moon sets at 7h 30m.
4. Total Solar Eclipse on 4 December beginning at 7h 35m. Visible from the Antarctic peninsula, southern Atlantic and southern Pacific. Member 13 of 70 of Saros 152. Maximum duration 1m 54s.

EXPLANATION OF ASTRONOMICAL DATA

Positions of the heavenly bodies are given only to the degree of accuracy required by amateur astronomers for setting telescopes, or for plotting on celestial globes or star atlases. Where intermediate positions are required, linear interpolation may be employed.

Detailed definitions of the terms used cannot be given here. They must be sought in astronomical literature, the internet or textbooks.

For the Moon, two columns calculated for latitudes 52° and 56°, are devoted to risings and settings, so the range 50° to 58° can be covered by interpolation and extrapolation. The times given in these columns are Greenwich Mean Times for the meridian of Greenwich. An observer west of this meridian must add their longitude (in time) and vice versa.

In accordance with the usual convention in astronomy, + and − indicate respectively north and south latitudes or declinations.

All data are, unless otherwise stated, for 0h Greenwich Mean Time (GMT), ie at the midnight at the beginning of the day named. Allowance must be made for British Summer Time during the period that this is in operation.

PAGE ONE OF EACH MONTH

Under the heading *Astronomical Phenomena* will be found particulars of the more important conjunctions of the Sun, Moon and planets with each other, and also the dates of other astronomical phenomena of special interest.

The Constellations listed each month are those that are near the meridian at the beginning of the month at 22h local mean time. Allowance must be made for British Summer Time where appropriate. The fact that any star crosses the meridian 4m earlier each night or 2h earlier each month may be used, in conjunction with the lists given each month, to find which constellations are favourably placed at any moment.

The principal phases of *the Moon* are the GMTs when the difference between the longitude of the Moon and that of the Sun is 0°, 90°, 180° or 270°. T The times of perigee and apogee are those when the Moon is nearest to, and farthest from, the Earth, respectively. The nodes or points of intersection of the Moon's orbit and the ecliptic make a complete retrograde circuit of the ecliptic in about 19 years. From a knowledge of the longitude of the ascending node and the inclination, whose value does not vary much from 5°, the path of the Moon among the stars may be plotted on a celestial globe or star atlas.

PAGE TWO OF EACH MONTH

SUNRISE AND SUNSET

The GMTs of sunrise and sunset for seven cities, whose positions in longitude (W.) and latitude (N.) are given immediately below the name.

The times of sunrise and sunset are those when the Sun's upper limb, as affected by refraction, is on the true horizon of an observer at sea-level. Assuming the mean refraction to be 34', and the Sun's semi-diameter to be 16', the time given is that when the true zenith distance of the Sun's centre is 90°+34'+16' or 90° 50', or, in other words, when the depression of the Sun's centre below the true horizon is 50'. The upper limb is then 34' below the true horizon, but is brought there by refraction. An observer on a ship might see the Sun for a minute or so longer, because of the dip of the horizon, while another viewing the sunset over hills or mountains would record an earlier time. Nevertheless, the moment when the true zenith distance of the Sun's centre is 90° 50' is a precise time dependent only on the latitude and longitude of the place, and independent of its altitude above sea-level, the contour of its horizon, the vagaries of refraction or the small seasonal change in the Sun's diameter; this moment is suitable in every way as a definition of sunset (or sunrise) for all statutory purposes.

LIGHTING-UP TIME

The legal importance of sunrise and sunset is that the Road Vehicles Lighting Regulations 1989 (SI 1989 No. 1796) as amended, make the use of front and rear position lamps on vehicles compulsory during the period between sunset and sunrise. Headlamps on vehicles are required to be used during the hours of darkness on unlit roads, on lit roads with a speed limit exceeding 30mph, or whenever visibility is seriously reduced. The hours of darkness are defined in these regulations as the period between half an hour after sunset and half an hour before sunrise.

In all laws and regulations 'sunset' refers to the local sunset, ie the time at which the Sun sets at the place in question. This common-sense interpretation has been upheld by legal tribunals.

MEAN REFRACTION

Alt.	Ref.	Alt.	Ref.	Alt.	Ref.
° '	'	° '	'	° '	'
1 20	21	3 12	13	7 54	6
1 30	20	3 34	12	9 27	5
1 41	19	4 00	11	11 39	4
1 52	18	4 30	10	15 00	3
2 05	17	5 06	9	20 42	2
2 19	16	5 50	8	32 20	1
2 35	15	6 44	7	62 17	0
2 52	14	7 54		90 00	
3 12					

THE MOON

The GMT for moonrise, transit and moonset are given for each day. These times are independent of latitude but must be corrected for longitude. For places in the British Isles it suffices to add the longitude if west, and vice versa bearing in mind that 1° = 4m and 15' = 1m.

Diameter (Diam) indicates the apparent size of the Moon. The Moon's orbit around the Earth is an ellipse and this makes the Moon appear larger or smaller. In popular parlance Super Moons are when the Moon is full and also closest (perigee). The Moon's apparent size can vary from 29.4' to 33.5'. Note that the Sun's diameter can also vary from 31.4' in July to 32.5' in January. These values are important in determining whether a solar eclipse can be total or annular.

The Phase column shows the percentage of the area of the Moon's disk illuminated, this is also the illuminated percentage of the diameter at right angles to the line of cusps. The terminator is a semi-ellipse whose major axis is the line of cusps, and whose semi-minor axis is determined by the tabulated percentage, from New Moon to Full Moon the east limb is dark, and vice versa.

The Age of the Moon is the number of days elapsed since the last full Moon. There are 29.53 days between successive full Moons.

PAGE THREE OF EACH MONTH

THE PLANETS
Positions of Mercury are given for every second day, and those of Venus and Mars for every fifth day; linear interpolation can be used to give intermediate values to the same precision. The diameter (Diam.) is given in seconds of arc. The phase is the illuminated percentage of the disk. In the case of the inner planets this approaches 100 per cent at superior conjunction and zero at inferior conjunction. When the phase is less than 50 per cent the planet is crescent-shaped or horned; for greater phases it is gibbous. In the case of the exterior planet Mars, the phase approaches 100 per cent at conjunction and opposition, and is a minimum at the quadratures.

The particulars for the four outer planets resemble those for the planets Mercury and Venus, except that, because of the dimness of Uranus and Neptune, these two planets require an optical aid, such as binoculars or a small telescope, to be seen. The diameters given for the rings of Saturn are those of the major axis (in the plane of the planet's equator) and the minor axis respectively. The former has a small seasonal change due to the slightly varying distance of the Earth from Saturn, but the latter varies from zero when the Earth passes through the ring plane every 15 years to its maximum opening half-way between these periods. The rings were last open at their widest extent (and Saturn at its brightest) in 2017. The Earth passed through the ring plane in 2009.

The GMT at which planets transit the Greenwich meridian is also given. The times of transit may be corrected to local meridians, as described above. To determine if a planet is visible or not, the transit time should be examined. If the transit time coincides with hours of darkness the planet should be easy to find, provided it is bright enough. If the time of transit is between 00h and 12h the planet should be visible above the eastern horizon; if between 12h and 24h, above the western horizon. The closer the transit time to midnight (0h) the longer it will be visible. The inner planets - Mercury and Venus can never transit at midnight because they are, from Earth, seen to be too close to the Sun. If they transit close to noon (12h) then they will be too close to the Sun to be visible except during a total solar eclipse or if the planet passes in front of the Sun (known as a *transit*). The rise or set times should be examined to see if either is near sunrise or sunset. If this also coincides with a large positive declination (Dec.) then conditions are favourable for viewing in the northern hemisphere. A negative (southern) declination favours observations in the southern hemisphere.

Consulting *The Night Sky* paragraphs will also help determine observability. Under this heading will be found notes describing the position and visibility of the planets and other phenomena.

OTHER INFORMATION

MAGNITUDE
Magnitudes of astronomical objects are measured in what may be considered the reverse to the obvious. Magnitude +3 is brighter than +4, magnitude -2 is brighter than magnitude -1. So from brighter to dimmer: -4, -3, -2, -1, 0, +1, +2, +3

etc, with +6 being the dimmest considered visible with the naked eye in very dark skies. Each magnitude is roughly 2.5 times brighter than the next, so a magnitude +1 object is 100 times brighter than a magnitude +6 object.

TIME

From the earliest ages, the natural division of time into recurring periods of day and night has provided the practical time-scale for the everyday activities of the human race. Indeed, if any alternative means of time measurement is adopted, it must be capable of adjustment so as to remain in general agreement with the natural time-scale defined by the diurnal rotation of the Earth on its axis. Ideally the rotation should be measured against a fixed frame of reference; in practice it must be measured against the background provided by the celestial bodies. If the Sun is chosen as the reference point, we obtain Apparent Solar Time, which is the time indicated by a sundial. It is not a uniform time but is subject to variations which amount to as much as a quarter of an hour in each direction. Such wide variations cannot be tolerated in a practical time-scale, and this has led to the concept of Mean Solar Time in which all the days are exactly the same length and equal to the average length of the Apparent Solar Day. The positions of the stars in the sky are specified in relation to a reference point in the sky known as the First Point of Aries (or the Vernal Equinox). It is therefore convenient to adopt this same reference point when considering the rotation of the Earth against the background of the stars. The time-scale so obtained is known as Apparent Sidereal Time.

GREENWICH MEAN TIME
The daily rotation of the Earth on its axis causes the Sun and the other heavenly bodies, which are not circumpolar, to appear to cross the sky from east to west. Circumpolar objects (mostly stars) are close enough to the celestial pole that they never set. It is convenient to represent this relative motion as if the Sun really performed a daily circuit around a fixed Earth. Noon in Apparent Solar Time may then be defined as the time at which the Sun transits across the observer's meridian. In Mean Solar Time, noon is similarly defined by the meridian transit of a fictitious Mean Sun moving uniformly in the sky with the same average speed as the true Sun. Apparent Solar Time used to be observed on the meridian of the transit circle telescope of the Royal Observatory at Greenwich. Modern measurements are made from similar instruments across the world. Greenwich Mean Time (GMT) is derived from these observations. The mean solar day is divided into 24 hours and, for astronomical and other scientific purposes, these are numbered 0 to 23, commencing at midnight. Civil time is usually reckoned in two periods of 12 hours, designated am (*ante meridiem,* ie before noon) and pm (*post meridiem,* ie after noon), although the 24 hour clock is increasingly being used.

UNIVERSAL TIME
Before 1925 January 1, GMT was reckoned in 24 hours commencing at noon; since that date it has been reckoned from midnight. To avoid confusion in the use of the designation GMT before and after 1925, since 1928 astronomers have tended to use the term Universal Time (UT) or Weltzeit (WZ) to denote GMT measured from Greenwich Mean Midnight.

In precision work it is necessary to take account of small variations in Universal Time. These arise from small irregularities in the rotation of the Earth. Observed astronomical time is designated UT0. Observed time corrected for the effects of the motion of the poles (giving rise to a 'wandering' in longitude) is designated UT1. There is also a seasonal fluctuation in the rate of rotation of the Earth arising from meteorological causes, often called the annual fluctuation.

UT1 corrected for this effect is designated UT2 and provides a time-scale free from short-period fluctuations. It is still subject to small secular and irregular changes.

APPARENT SOLAR TIME
As mentioned above, the time shown by a sundial is called Apparent Solar Time. It differs from Mean Solar Time by an amount known as the Equation of Time, which is the total effect of two causes which make the length of the apparent solar day non-uniform. One cause of variation is that the orbit of the Earth is not a circle but an ellipse, having the Sun at one focus. As a consequence, the angular speed of the Earth in its orbit is not constant; it is greatest at the beginning of January when the Earth is nearest the Sun.

The other cause is due to the obliquity of the ecliptic; the plane of the equator (which is at right angles to the axis of rotation of the Earth) does not coincide with the ecliptic (the plane defined by the apparent annual motion of the Sun around the celestial sphere) but is inclined to it at an angle of about 23.4°. As a result, the apparent solar day is shorter than average at the equinoxes and longer at the solstices. From the combined effects of the components due to obliquity and eccentricity, the equation of time reaches its extreme values in February (-14 minutes) and early November (+16 minutes). It has a zero value on four dates during the year, and it is only on these dates (approximately April 15, June 14, September 1 and December 25) that a sundial shows Mean Solar Time.

SIDEREAL TIME
A sidereal day is the duration of a complete rotation of the Earth with reference to the First Point of Aries. The length of a sidereal day in mean time is 23h 56m 04s.09. The term sidereal (or 'star') time is a little misleading since the time-scale so defined is not exactly the same as that which would be defined by successive transits of a selected star, as there is a small progressive motion between the stars and the First Point of Aries due to the precession of the Earth's axis. This makes the length of the sidereal day shorter than the true period of rotation by 0.008 seconds. Superimposed on this steady precessional motion are small oscillations (nutation), giving rise to fluctuations in apparent sidereal time amounting to as much as 1.2 seconds. It is therefore customary to employ Mean Sidereal Time, from which these fluctuations have been removed.

EPHEMERIS TIME
An analysis of observations of the positions of the Sun, Moon and planets taken over an extended period is used in preparing ephemerides. (An ephemeris is a table giving the apparent position of a heavenly body at regular intervals of time, eg one day or ten days, and may be used to compare current observations with tabulated positions.) Discrepancies between the positions of heavenly bodies observed over a 300-year period and their predicted positions arose because the time-scale to which the observations were related was based on the assumption that the rate of rotation of the Earth is constant. It is now known that this rate of rotation is variable. A revised time-scale, Ephemeris Time (ET), was devised to bring the ephemerides into agreement with the observations.

The second of ET is defined in terms of the annual motion of the Earth in its orbit around the Sun (1/31556925.9747 of the tropical year for 1900 January 0d 12h ET). The precise determination of ET from astronomical observations is a lengthy process as the requisite standard of accuracy can only be achieved by averaging over a number of years.

In 1976 the International Astronomical Union adopted Terrestrial Dynamical Time (TDT), a new dynamical time-scale for general use whose scale unit is the SI second (see Atomic

Time, below). TDT was renamed Terrestrial Time (TT) in 1991. ET is now of little more than historical interest.

TERRESTRIAL TIME
The uniform time system used in computing the ephemerides of the solar system is Terrestrial Time (TT), which has replaced ET for this purpose. Except for the most rigorous astronomical calculations, it may be assumed to be the same as ET. In June 2021 the difference TT – UT is estimated to be 69.5 seconds. This is known as Delta T.

ATOMIC TIME
The fundamental standards of time and frequency must be defined in terms of a periodic motion which is adequately constant, enduring and measurable. Progress has made it possible to use natural standards, such as atomic or molecular oscillations. Continuous oscillations are generated in an electrical circuit, the frequency of which is then compared or brought into coincidence with the frequency characteristic of the absorption or emission by the atoms or molecules when they change between two selected energy levels. Since the 13th General Conference on Weights and Measures in October 1967, the unit of time, the second, has been defined in the International System of units (SI) as 'the duration of 9,192,631,770 periods of the radiation corresponding to the transition between the two hyperfine levels of the ground state of the caesium-133 atom'.

In the UK, the national time scale is maintained by the National Physical Laboratory (NPL), using an ensemble of atomic clocks based on either caesium or hydrogen atoms. In addition the NPL (along with several other national laboratories) has constructed and operates caesium fountain primary frequency standards, which utilise the cooling of caesium atoms by laser light to determine the duration of the SI second at the highest attainable level of accuracy. Caesium fountain primary standards typically achieve an accuracy of around 2 parts in 10,000,000,000,000,000, which is equivalent to one second in 158 million years.

Timekeeping worldwide is based on two closely related atomic time scales that are established through international collaboration. International Atomic Time (TAI) is formed by combining the readings of more than 400 atomic clocks located in more than 70 institutes and was set close to the astronomically based Universal Time (UT) near the beginning of 1958. It was formally recognised in 1971 and since 1988 January 1 has been maintained by the International Bureau of Weights and Measures (BIPM). Civil time in almost all countries is now based on Coordinated Universal Time (UTC), which differs from TAI by 37 seconds and was designed to make both atomic time and UT available with accuracy appropriate for most users. On 1 January 1972 UTC was set to be exactly 10 seconds behind TAI, and since then the UTC time-scale has been adjusted by the insertion (or, in principle, omission) of leap seconds in order to keep it within ±0.9s of UT. These leap seconds are introduced, when necessary, at the same instant throughout the world, either at the end of December or at the end of June. The last leap second occurred immediately prior to 0h UTC on 2017 January 1, and was the 27th leap second. All leap seconds so far have been positive, with 61 seconds in the final minute of the UTC month. The time 23h 59m 60s UTC is followed one second later by 0h 0m 00s of the first day of the following month. Notices concerning the insertion of leap seconds are issued by the International Earth Rotation and Reference Systems Service (IERS).

The computation of UTC is carried out monthly by the BIPM and takes place in three stages. First, a weighted average known as Echelle Atomique Libre (EAL) is calculated from all of the contributing atomic clocks. In the second stage, TAI is generated by applying small corrections, derived from the results contributed by primary frequency standards, to the scale interval of EAL to maintain its value close to that of the SI second. Finally, UTC is formed from TAI by the addition of an integer number of seconds. The results are published monthly in the BIPM Circular T in the form of offsets at 5-day intervals between UTC and the time scales of contributing organisations.

RADIO TIME-SIGNALS
UTC is made generally available through time-signals and standard frequency broadcasts such as MSF in the UK, CHU in Canada and WWV and WWVH in the USA. These are based on national time-scales that are maintained in close agreement with UTC and provide traceability to the national time-scale and to UTC. The markers of seconds in the UTC scale coincide with those of TAI.

To disseminate the national time-scale in the UK, special signals (call-sign MSF) are broadcast by the National Physical Laboratory. From April 1, 2007 the MSF service, previously broadcast from British Telecom's radio station at Rugby, has been transmitted from Anthorn radio station in Cumbria. The signals are controlled from a caesium beam atomic frequency standard and consist of a precise frequency carrier of 60 kHz which is switched off, after being on for at least half a second, to mark every second. The first second of the minute begins with a period of 500 ms with the carrier switched off, to serve as a minute marker. In the other seconds the carrier is always off for at least one tenth of a second at the start and then it carries an on-off code giving the British clock time and date, together with information identifying the start of the next minute. Changes to and from summer time are made following government announcements. Leap seconds are inserted as announced by the IERS and information provided by them on the difference between UTC and UT is also signalled. Other broadcast signals in the UK include the BBC six pips signal, the BT Timeline ('speaking clock'), the NPL telephone and internet time services for computers, and a coded time-signal on the BBC 198 kHz transmitters which is used for timing in the electricity supply industry. From 1972 January 1 the six pips on the BBC have consisted of five short pips from second 55 to second 59 (six pips in the case of a leap second) followed by one lengthened pip, the start of which indicates the exact minute. From 1990 February 5 these signals have been controlled by the BBC with seconds markers referenced to the satellite-based US navigation system GPS (Global Positioning System) and time and day referenced to the MSF transmitter. Formerly they were generated by the Royal Greenwich Observatory. The NPL telephone and internet time services are directly connected to the national time scale.

Due to digital latency, time pips received via Digital Audio Broadcasting (DAB) radio and internet streaming are received late by significant and variable amounts, rendering them inaccurate if received in this way.

Accurate timing may also be obtained from the signals of international navigation systems such as the ground-based eLORAN, or the satellite-based American GPS or Russian GLONASS systems.

STANDARD TIME
Since 1880 the standard time in Britain has been Greenwich Mean Time (GMT); a statute that year enacted that the word 'time' when used in any legal document relating to Britain meant, unless otherwise specifically stated, the mean time of the Greenwich meridian. Greenwich was adopted as the universal meridian on 13 October 1884. A system of standard time by zones is used worldwide, standard time in each zone differing from that of the Greenwich meridian by an integral number of hours or, exceptionally, half-hours or quarter-hours,

either fast or slow. The large territories of the USA and Canada are divided into zones approximately 7.5° on either side of central meridians.

Variations from the standard time of some countries occur during part of the year; they are decided annually and are usually referred to as Summer Time or Daylight Saving Time.

At the 180th meridian the time can be either 12 hours fast on Greenwich Mean Time or 12 hours slow, and a change of date occurs. The internationally recognised date or calendar line is a modification of the 180th meridian, drawn so as to include islands of any one group on the same side of the line, or for political reasons.

Lat.	Long	Lat.	Long
90° S.	180°	48° N.	180°
51° S.	180°	53° N.	170° E.
45° S.	172.5° W.	65.5° N.	169° W.
15° S.	172.5° W.	68° N.	169° W.
5° S.	180°	90° N.	180°

Changes to the date line require an international conference.

BRITISH SUMMER TIME
In 1916 an Act ordained that during a defined period of that year the legal time for general purposes in Great Britain should be one hour in advance of Greenwich Mean Time. The Summer Time Acts 1922 and 1925 defined the period during which Summer Time was to be in force, stabilising practice until the Second World War.

During the Second World War (1941–5) and in 1947 Double Summer Time (two hours in advance of Greenwich Mean Time) was used for the period in which ordinary Summer Time would have been in force. During these years clocks were also kept one hour in advance of Greenwich Mean Time in the winter. After the war, ordinary Summer Time was invoked each year from 1948–68.

Between 1968 October 27 and 1971 October 31 clocks were kept one hour ahead of Greenwich Mean Time throughout the year. This was known as British Standard Time.

The most recent legislation is the Summer Time Act 1972, which enacted that 'the period of summer time for the purposes of this Act is the period beginning at two o'clock, Greenwich Mean Time, in the morning of the day after the third Saturday in March or, if that day is Easter Day, the day after the second Saturday in March, and ending at two o'clock, Greenwich Mean Time, in the morning of the day after the fourth Saturday in October.'

The duration of Summer Time can be varied by Order in Council and in recent years alterations have been made to synchronise the period of Summer Time in Britain with that used in Europe. The rule for 1981–94 defined the period of Summer Time in the UK as from the last Sunday in March to the day following the fourth Saturday in October and the hour of changeover was altered to 01h GMT.

There was no rule for the dates of Summer Time between 1995–7. Since 1998 the 9th European Parliament and Council Directive on Summer Time has harmonised the dates on which Summer Time begins and ends across member states as the last Sundays in March and October respectively. Under the directive Summer Time begins and ends at 01hr Greenwich Mean Time in each member state. Amendments to the Summer Time Act to implement the directive came into force on 11 March 2002.

The duration of Summer Time in 2021 is:
March 28 01h GMT to October 31 01h GMT

ASTRONOMICAL CONSTANTS

Solar parallax	8.794″
Astronomical unit	149,597,870 km
Annual precession in longitude	50.288″
Precession in right ascension	3.075s
Precession in declination	20.043″
Constant of nutation	9.202″
Constant of aberration	20.496″
Mean obliquity of ecliptic (2018)	23° 26′ 13″
Moon's mean equatorial hor parallax	57′ 02.70″
Velocity of light in vacuo	299,792.5 km/s
Equatorial radius of the Earth	6,378 km
Polar radius of the Earth	6,356 km
North galactic pole	
(IAU standard)	RA 12h 51m Dec + 27.1° N.
Solar apex	RA 18h04m Dec.+30°
Solar motion	20.0 km/s

Length of year (in mean solar days)

Tropical	365.24217
Sidereal	365.25636
Anomalistic (perihelion to perihelion)	365.25964
Eclipse	346.62008

Length of month (mean values)	d	h	m	s
Synodic (new Moon to new Moon)	29	12	44	02.8
Sidereal	27	07	43	11.6
Anomalistic (perigee to perigee)	27	13	18	33.2

THE EARTH

The shape of the Earth is that of an oblate spheroid or solid of revolution whose meridian sections are ellipses not differing much from circles, while the sections at right angles are circles. The length of the equatorial axis is about 12,756 km, and that of the polar axis is 12,714 km. The mean density of the Earth is 5.5 times that of water. Density increases from about 3.3g/cc near to the surface to about 17g/cc at the centre. The Earth and Moon revolve about their common centre of gravity in a lunar month; this centre in turn revolves round the Sun in a plane known as the ecliptic, that passes through the Sun's centre. The Earth's equator is inclined to this plane at an angle of 23.4°. This tilt is the cause of the seasons. In mid-latitudes, and when the Sun is high above the Equator, not only does the high noon altitude make the days longer, but the Sun's rays fall more perpendicularly on the Earth's surface; these effects combine to produce summer. In equatorial regions the noon altitude is large throughout the year, and there is little variation in the length of the day. In higher latitudes the noon altitude is lower, and the days in summer are appreciably longer than those in winter.

The average velocity of the Earth in its orbit is 30km/s. It makes a complete rotation on its axis in about 23h 56m of mean time, which is the sidereal day. Because of its annual revolution round the Sun, the rotation with respect to the Sun, or the solar day, is more than this by about four minutes. The extremity of the axis of rotation, or the North Pole of the Earth, is not rigidly fixed, but wanders over an area roughly 20 metres in diameter.

Perihelion is when the Earth is closest to the Sun, and *aphelion* when the Earth is furthest from the Sun:

Perihelion January 2021 2d 13h 15m
  (147,093,162km, 0.983257060au)
Aphelion July 2021 5d 22h 27m
  (152,100,526km, 1.016729924au)

GEOMAGNETISM AND SPACE WEATHER

The geomagnetic field is generated in the Earth's partially molten core. The movement of molten iron creates electrical current, and this in turn generates magnetic field that reaches far out into space in a region called the magnetosphere. The field varies in strength and direction from place to place, but also with time. It is stronger at the poles, though not exactly at the geographic poles, and is weaker in the equatorial region, particularly in S. America. The strength of the magnetic field in 2021 in microTeslas ranges from a minimum of about 22 μT in N. Argentina to 67 μT at the S. magnetic dip-pole (see figure). Superimposed on the field from the core are local anomalies; these are due to the influence of mineral deposits in the Earth's crust.

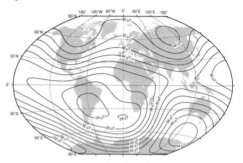

A small but highly dynamic proportion of the field is of external origin, associated with electrical current in the ionosphere and magnetosphere. The ionisation of the upper atmosphere depends on the incident particle and radiation flux, ultimately controlled by the Sun and the configuration of the internal magnetic field. There are short-term irregular storm events as well as regular daily, 27-day, seasonal and approximate 11-year variations in the external magnetic field. The term space weather refers to conditions on the Sun, in the solar wind and inside the magnetosphere that result in storm events which influence the performance and reliability of space-borne and ground-based technological systems.

A magnetic compass points along the horizontal component of a conceptual magnetic line of force. These lines of force converge on the magnetic dip-poles, the places where the Earth's magnetic field is vertical. These poles move with time, and their present (2021.0) approximate adopted mean positions are 86.4° N., 156.8° E. and 64.0° S., 135.7° E. It is important to realise that compasses do not point directly, ie via great circle routes, to the dip-poles.

There is also a 'magnetic equator', at all points of which the vertical component of the Earth's magnetic field is zero and a magnetised needle of a dip meter remains horizontal. This line, also called the dip equator, runs between 12° south and north of the geographical equator. North of the equator the dip meter needle points below the horizontal and south of the equator it points above the horizontal.

The following table indicates changes in magnetic declination (or variation of the compass relative to true north) at Greenwich over four centuries. Similar, though much smaller, changes have occurred in dip or magnetic inclination. These changes differ throughout the world.

London (Greenwich)

1580	11°	15′	E.	1873	19° 35′	W.
1665	01°	22′	W.	1925	13° 10′	W.
1730	13°	00′	W.	1950	09° 07′	W.
1773	21°	09′	W.	1975	06° 39′	W.
1823	24°	23′	W.(max)	1998	03° 32′	W.

In Great Britain, lines of equal declination (isogonics) now run approximately north–northeast to south–southwest. Though there are considerable local deviations due to geological causes, an approximate value of magnetic declination may be obtained by assuming that at 50° N. on the meridian of Greenwich (longitude 0°), the value in 2021 is 0° 44' east. Easterly declination is now being sensed for the first time in over 350 years as the zero isogonic line (the agonic line) passes westwards across the country. Allowing for 8' west for each degree of latitude northwards and one of 25' west for each degree of longitude westwards. For example, at 53° N., 5° W., declination will be about 0° 44' east + 24' west + 125' west, i.e. 1° 45' west. The average annual change at the present time is about 13' to the east. For navigation by compass using maps with the north lines from the British National Grid (as opposed to lines of equal longitude), account has to be taken of the difference between true north and grid north. This angle can be several degrees but does not vary with time.

Irregularly distributed around the world are about 160 magnetic observatories. A magnetic observatory measures the absolute magnetic field vector at a fixed location, typically for many decades. Due to the wide amplitude and frequency ranges of the natural field, highly sensitive and stable instruments are operated in an environment free from artificial magnetic disturbance. There are three in the UK, run by the British Geological Survey: at Hartland, north Devon; at Eskdalemuir, Dumfries and Galloway; and at Lerwick, Shetland Islands. Some recent annual mean values for Hartland:

Year	Declination West		Dip or inclination		Horizontal intensity	Vertical intensity
	°	'	°	'	nT	nT
1960	9	58.8	66	43.9	18.707	43.504
1970	9	06.5	66	26.1	19.033	43.636
1980	7	43.8	66	10.3	19.330	43.768
1990	6	15.0	66	09.7	19.539	43.896
2000	4	43.6	66	06.9	19.508	44.051
2019	1	31.9	65	58.5	19.809	44.438

nT = nanoTesla

The magnetic field is also observed by a series of specialised satellites, the current being a mission called Swarm. Three satellites launched by the European Space Agency in 2013, each equipped with magnetometers and star cameras for orientation, in 2020 continued to return accurate measurements of the Earth's magnetic field.

Reliance on the Earth's magnetic field for navigation by compass is not restricted to land, maritime or aeronautical navigation (in the latter two usually as a fail-safe back-up system). It also extends underground with the oil industry using magnetic survey tools when drilling well-bores. Very accurate estimates of the local magnetic field are required for this, taking into account the crustal and external fields. Modern smartphones include miniature magnetometers and tables of declination values for orientation of maps.

SPACE WEATHER

Occasionally, sometimes with great suddenness, the Earth's magnetic field is subject for several hours to marked disturbance. In many instances such storm events are accompanied by widespread displays of auroras, marked changes in the incidence of cosmic rays, an increase in the reception of 'noise' from the Sun at radio frequencies, and rapid changes in the ionosphere and induced electric currents within the Earth. These can adversely affect satellite operations, telecommunications and electric power transmission systems. The storm events are caused by changes in the solar wind, a stream of ionised particles which emanates from the Sun and through which the Earth is continuously passing. Some of these changes are associated with visible eruptions on the Sun, usually in the region of sun-spots for which there is an approximate 11-year cycle of occurrence. There is some tendency for storm events to recur after intervals of about 27 days, the period of rotation of the Sun on its axis as seen from the Earth but the sources of many events are shorter lived than this. Predicting such storm events with any useful accuracy remains challenging but the year 2021, at the start of the ascending phase of solar cycle 25, is generally expected to be quiet.

ELEMENTS OF THE SOLAR SYSTEM

Orb	Mean distance from Sun (Earth = 1)	km 10^6	Sidereal period days	Synodic period days	Incl. of orbit to ecliptic ° ′		Diameter km	Mass (Earth = 1)	Period of rotation on axis days
Sun	—	—	—	—	—		1,392,000	332,981	25–35*
Mercury	0.39	58	88.0	116	7	00	4,879	0.0553	58.646
Venus	0.72	108	224.7	584	3	24	12,104	0.8150	243.019r
Earth	1.00	150	365.3	—	—		12,756e	1.0000	0.997
Mars	1.52	228	687.0	780	1	51	6,794e	0.1074	1.026
Jupiter	5.20	778	4,331.0	399	1	18	142,984e 133,708p	317.83	0.410e
Saturn	9.58	1433	10,747	378	2	29	120,536e 108,728p	95.16	0.446e
Uranus	19.22	2875	30,589	370	0	46	51,118e	14.54	0.718r
Neptune	30.11	4504	56,800	367	1	46	49,528e	17.15	0.671
Pluto†	39.48	5906	90,560	367	17	10	2,390	0.002	6.387r

e equatorial, p polar, r retrograde, * depending on latitude, † reclassified as a dwarf planet since August 2006

THE SATELLITES

Name	Star mag.	Mean distance from primary km	Sidereal period of revolution d	Name	Star mag.	Mean distance from primary km	Sidereal period of revolution d
EARTH				**SATURN**			
I Moon	—	384,400	27.322	VII Hyperion	14	1,481,000	21.277
				VIII Iapetus	11	3,561,300	79.330
MARS				IX Phoebe	16	12,952,000	550.48r
I Phobos	11	9,378	0.319				
II Deimos	12	23,459	1.262	**URANUS**			
				VI Cordelia	24	49,770	0.335
JUPITER				VII Ophelia	24	53,790	0.376
XVI Metis	17	127,960	0.295	VIII Bianca	23	59,170	0.435
XV Adrastea	19	128,980	0.298	IX Cressida	22	61,780	0.464
V Amalthea	14	181,300	0.498	X Desdemona	22	62,680	0.474
XIV Thebe	16	221,900	0.675	XI Juliet	21	64,350	0.493
I Io	5	421,600	1.769	XII Portia	21	66,090	0.513
II Europa	5	670,900	3.551	XIII Rosalind	22	69,900	0.558
III Ganymede	5	1,070,000	7.155	XIV Belinda	22	75,260	0.624
IV Callisto	6	1,883,000	16.689	XV Puck	20	86,010	0.762
XIII Leda	20	11,165,000	240.92	V Miranda	16	129,960	1.413
VI Himalia	15	11,460,000	250.57	I Ariel	14	191,020	2.520
X Lysithea	18	11,717,000	259.22	II Umbriel	15	266,300	4.144
VII Elara	17	11,741,000	259.65	III Titania	14	435,910	8.706
XII Ananke	19	21,276,000	629.77r	IV Oberon	14	583,520	13.463
XI Carme	18	23,404,000	734.17r	XVI Caliban	22	7,230,000	579.5r
VIII Pasiphae	17	23,624,000	743.68r	XX Stephano	24	8,002,000	676.5r
IX Sinope	18	23,939,000	758.90r	XVII Sycorax	21	12,179,000	1,283.4r
				XVIII Prospero	23	16,256,000	1,977.3r
SATURN				XIX Setebos	23	17,418,000	2,234.8r
XVIII Pan	20	133,583	0.575				
XV Atlas	18	137,640	0.602	**NEPTUNE**			
XVI Prometheus	16	139,353	0.613	III Naiad	25	48,230	0.294
XVII Pandora	16	141,700	0.629	IV Thalassa	24	50,080	0.311
XI Epimetheus	15	151,422	0.694	V Despina	23	52,530	0.335
X Janus	14	151,472	0.695	VI Galatea	22	61,950	0.429
I Mimas	13	185,520	0.942	VII Larissa	22	73,550	0.555
II Enceladus	12	238,020	1.370	VIII Proteus	20	117,650	1.122
III Tethys	10	294,660	1.888	I Triton	13	354,760	5.877
XIII Telesto	19	294,660	1.888	II Nereid	19	5,513,400	360.136
XIV Calypso	19	294,660	1.888				
IV Dione	10	377,400	2.737	**PLUTO**			
XII Helene	18	377,400	2.737	I Charon	17	19,596	6.387
V Rhea	10	527,040	4.518				
VI Titan	8	1,221,850	15.945				

The total number of satellites known so far for the outer planets are: Jupiter 79, Saturn 62, Uranus 27, Neptune 14, Pluto 5.

ABBREVIATIONS AND ACRONYMS

A

ABA	Amateur Boxing Association
abr	abridged
ac	alternating current
AC	*ante Christum* before Christ
	Companion, Order of Australia
ADC	Aide-de-Camp
ADC (P)	Personal ADC to the Queen
Adj.	Adjutant
Adj. Gen.	Adjutant General
Adm.	Admiral
AE	Air Efficiency award
AEM	Air Efficiency Medal
aet	after extra time
AFC	Air Force Cross
AFM	Air Force Medal
AG	Attorney-General
AH	*anno Hegirae* in the year of the Hegira
AM	Assembly Member (Wales)
ANC	African National Congress
AO	Air Officer
	Officer, Order of Australia
AOC	Air Officer Commanding
apptd	appointed
APR	annual percentage rate
AUC	*ab urbe condita* from the foundation of Rome
	anno urbis conditae from the founding of the city

B

b.	born
	bowled (cricket)
BAFTA	British Academy of Film and Television Arts
BAS	Bachelor in Agricultural Science
	British Antarctic Survey
BBFC	British Board of Film Classification
BCE	Before the Common (or Christian) Era
BCH (D)	Bachelor of (Dental) Surgery
BCL	Bachelor of Civil Law
BCOM	Bachelor of Commerce
BD	Bachelor of Divinity
BDA	British Dental Association
BDS	Bachelor of Dental Surgery
BED	Bachelor of Education
BEM	British Empire Medal
BENG	Bachelor of Engineering
BFPO	British Forces Post Office
BLIT	Bachelor of Literature
BLITT	Bachelor of Letters
BM	Bachelor of Medicine
BMA	British Medical Association
BMUS	Bachelor of Music
Bp	Bishop
BPHARM	Bachelor of Pharmacy
BPHIL	Bachelor of Philosophy
BPS	British Psychological Society
Brig.	Brigadier
BSI	British Standards Institution
BST	British Summer Time
Bt.	Baronet
BTEC	Business and Technology Education Council
BVMS	Bachelor of Veterinary Medicine and Surgery

C

c.	*circa* about
C.	Conservative
Cantuar:	of Canterbury (Archbishop)
Capt.	Captain
Carliol:	of Carlisle (Bishop)
CB	Companion, Order of the Bath
CBE	Commander, Order of the British Empire

CC	Companion, Order of Canada
CCHEM	chartered chemist
CD	Civil Defence
	Corps Diplomatique
Cdr	Commander
Cdre	Commodore
CDS	Chief of the Defence Staff
CE	civil engineer
	Common (or Christian) Era
CENG	chartered engineer
Cestr:	of Chester (Bishop)
CET	Central European Time
cf	*confer* compare
CGC	Conspicuous Gallantry Cross
CGEOL	chartered geologist
CGM	Conspicuous Gallantry Medal
CGS	Chief of General Staff
CH	Companion of Honour
CHB/M	Bachelor/Master of Surgery
CI	Channel Islands
Cicestr:	of Chichester (Bishop)
C-in-C	Commander-in-Chief
CILIP	Chartered Institute of Library and Information Professionals
CIPFA	Chartered Institute of Public Finance and Accountancy
CIS	Commonwealth of Independent States
CLJ	Commander, Order of St Lazarus of Jerusalem
CM	*Chirurgiae Magister* Master of Surgery
CMG	Companion, Order of St Michael and St George
CO	Commanding Officer
C of E	Church of England
Col.	Colonel
cons.	consecrated
Cpl.	Corporal
CPS	Crown Prosecution Service
CVO	Commander, Royal Victorian Order

D

d	*denarius* penny
d.	died
DAB	Digital Audio Broadcasting
DBE	Dame Commander, Order of the British Empire
DCB	Dame Commander, Order of the Bath
D CH	*Doctor Chirurgiae* Doctor of Surgery
DCL	Doctor of Civil Law
DCM	Distinguished Conduct Medal
DCMG	Dame Commander, Order of St Michael and St George
DCVO	Dame Commander, Royal Victorian Order
DD	Doctor of Divinity
DDS	Doctor of Dental Surgery
DFC	Distinguished Flying Cross
DFM	Distinguished Flying Medal
DHL	*Doctor Humaniorum Literarum* Doctor of Humane Letters/Literature
DIP ED	Diploma in Education
DIP HE	Diploma in Higher Education
DL	Deputy Lieutenant
DLIT	Doctor of Literature
DLITT	Doctor of Letters
DLR	Docklands Light Railway
DLS	Duckworth–Lewis–Stern method (cricket)
DMUS	Doctor of Music
DNA	deoxyribonucleic acid
DPH *or*	Doctor of Philosophy
DPHIL	
DPP	Director of Public Prosecutions
DSC	Distinguished Service Cross
DSc	Doctor of Science
DSM	Distinguished Service Medal

DSO	Companion, Distinguished Service Order
Dunelm:	of Durham (Bishop)
DUP	Democratic Unionist Party

E

Ebor:	of York (Archbishop)
EC	Elizabeth Cross
	European Community
ECG	electrocardiogram
ED	Efficiency Decoration
EEA	European Economic Area
EEG	electroencephalogram
EIB	European Investment Bank
ER	*Elizabetha Regina* Queen Elizabeth
ERM	exchange rate mechanism
ESA	European Space Agency
et seq	*et sequentia* and the following
Exon:	of Exeter (Bishop)

F

FAQ	frequently asked questions
FBA	Fellow, British Academy
FBS	Fellow, Botanical Society
FBU	Fire Brigades Union
FCA	Fellow, Institute of Chartered Accountants in England and Wales
FCCA	Fellow, Chartered Association of Certified Accountants
FCIB	Fellow, Chartered Institute of Bankers
	Fellow, Corporation of Insurance Brokers
FCII	Fellow, Chartered Insurance Institute
FCIPS	Fellow, Chartered Institute of Purchasing and Supply
FCIS	Fellow, Institute of Chartered Secretaries and Administrators
FCIT	Fellow, Chartered Institute of Transport
FCMA	Fellow, Chartered Institute of Management Accountants
FCP	Fellow, College of Preceptors
FD	*Fidei Defensor* Defender of the Faith
FE	further education
FFA	Fellow, Faculty of Actuaries (Scotland)
	Fellow, Institute of Financial Accountants
FFAS	Fellow, Faculty of Architects and Surveyors
FFCM	Fellow, Faculty of Community Medicine
FFPHM	Fellow, Faculty of Public Health Medicine
FGS	Fellow, Geological Society
FHS	Fellow, Heraldry Society
FHSM	Fellow, Institute of Health Service Management
FIA	Fellow, Institute of Actuaries
FIBIOL	Fellow, Institute of Biology
FICE	Fellow, Institution of Civil Engineers
FICS	Fellow, Institution of Chartered Shipbrokers
FIEE	Fellow, Institution of Electrical Engineers
FIM	Fellow, Institute of Metals
FIMGT	Fellow, Institute of Management
FIMM	Fellow, Institution of Mining and Metallurgy
FLS	Fellow, Linnean Society
FMEDSCI	Fellow, Academy of Medical Sciences
fo	folio
FPHS	Fellow, Philosophical Society
FRAD	Fellow, Royal Academy of Dancing
FRAES	Fellow, Royal Aeronautical Society
FRAGS	Fellow, Royal Agricultural Societies
FRAM	Fellow, Royal Academy of Music
FRAS	Fellow, Royal Asiatic Society
	Fellow, Royal Astronomical Society
FRBS	Fellow, Royal Botanic Society
	Fellow, Royal Society of British Sculptors
FRCA	Fellow, Royal College of Anaesthetists
FRCGP	Fellow, Royal College of General Practitioners
FRCM	Fellow, Royal College of Music
FRCO	Fellow, Royal College of Organists
FRCOG	Fellow, Royal College of Obstetricians and Gynaecologists

FRCP	Fellow, Royal College of Physicians, London
FRCPATH	Fellow, Royal College of Pathologists
FRCPE *or* FRCPED	Fellow, Royal College of Physicians, Edinburgh
FRCPI	Fellow, Royal College of Physicians, Ireland
FRCPSYCH	Fellow, Royal College of Psychiatrists
FRCR	Fellow, Royal College of Radiologists
FRCS	Fellow, Royal College of Surgeons of England
FRCSE *or* FRCSED	Fellow, Royal College of Surgeons of Edinburgh
FRCSGLAS	Fellow, Royal College of Physicians and Surgeons of Glasgow
FRCSI	Fellow, Royal College of Surgeons in Ireland
FRCVS	Fellow, Royal College of Veterinary Surgeons
FRENG	Fellow, Royal Academy of Engineering
FRGS	Fellow, Royal Geographical Society
FRHISTS	Fellow, Royal Historical Society
FRHS	Fellow, Royal Horticultural Society
FRIBA	Fellow, Royal Institute of British Architects
FRICS	Fellow, Royal Institution of Chartered Surveyors
FRMETS	Fellow, Royal Meteorological Society
FRMS	Fellow, Royal Microscopical Society
FRNS	Fellow, Royal Numismatic Society
FRPHARMS	Fellow, Royal Pharmaceutical Society
FRPS	Fellow, Royal Photographic Society
FRS	Fellow, Royal Society
FRSA	Fellow, Royal Society of Arts
FRSC	Fellow, Royal Society of Chemistry
FRSE	Fellow, Royal Society of Edinburgh
FRSH	Fellow, Royal Society of Health
FRSL	Fellow, Royal Society of Literature
FSA	Fellow, Society of Antiquaries
FTII	Fellow, Chartered Institute of Taxation
FZS	Fellow, Zoological Society

G

GBE	Dame/Knight Grand Cross, Order of the British Empire
GC	George Cross
GCB	Dame/Knight Grand Cross, Order of the Bath
GCLJ	Knight Grand Cross, Order of St Lazarus of Jerusalem
GCMG	Dame/Knight Grand Cross, Order of St Michael and St George
GCVO	Dame/Knight Grand Cross, Royal Victorian Order
Gen.	General
GHQ	general headquarters
GLA	Greater London Authority
GM	George Medal
GMB	Britain's General Union
GMT	Greenwich Mean Time
GOC	General Officer Commanding
Gp Capt.	Group Captain
GPS	Global Positioning System
GRU	*Glavnoje Razvedgvatel'noje Upravlenijie* Russian military intelligence agency

H

HB	His Beatitude
HBM	Her/His Britannic Majesty('s)
HE	Her/His Excellency
	higher education
	His Eminence
HH	Her/His Highness
	Her/His Honour
	His Holiness
HIM	Her/His Imperial Majesty
HM	Her/His Majesty('s)
HMAS	Her/His Majesty's Australian Ship
HMC	Headmasters' and Headmistresses' Conference
HMI	Her/His Majesty's Inspector
HMS	Her/His Majesty's Ship
Hon.	Honorary
	Honourable
HRH	Her/His Royal Highness

HRT	hormone replacement therapy
HSE	*hic sepultus est* here is buried
HSH	Her/His Serene Highness

I

IB	International Baccalaureate
ICC	International Cricket Council
	International Criminal Court
ICJ	International Court of Justice
id	*idem* the same
IP	intellectual property
	internet protocol
IPSA	Independent Parliamentary Standards Authority
IRA	Irish Republican Army
IRC	International Rescue Committee
Is	Islands
IS	Islamic State
ISO	Imperial Service Order
	International Organisation for Standardisation
ISP	internet service provider
ISSN	International Standard Serial Number
ITU	International Telecommunication Union

J

JP	Justice of the Peace

K

KBE	Knight Commander, Order of the British Empire
KCB	Knight Commander, Order of the Bath
KCLJ	Knight Commander, Order of St Lazarus of Jerusalem
KCMG	Knight Commander, Order of St Michael and St George
KCVO	Knight Commander, Royal Victorian Order
KG	Knight of the Garter
KLJ	Knight, Order of St Lazarus of Jerusalem
KP	Knight, Order of St Patrick
KStJ	Knight, Order of St John of Jerusalem
Kt.	Knight
KT	Knight of the Thistle

L

Lab.	Labour
Lat.	Latitude
lbw	leg before wicket (cricket)
lc	lower case (printing)
LD	Liberal Democrat
LDS	Licentiate in Dental Surgery
LHD	*Literarum Humaniorum Doctor* Doctor of Humane Letters/Literature
Lib.	Liberal
LITT D	Doctor of Letters
LLB	Bachelor of Laws
LLD	Doctor of Laws
LLM	Master of Laws
loc cit	*loco citato* in the place cited
Londin:	of London (Bishop)
Long.	longitude
lsd	*librae, solidi, denarii* pounds, shillings and pence
Lt.	Lieutenant
LTA	Lawn Tennis Association
LVO	Lieutenant, Royal Victorian Order

M

m.	married
M	Monsieur
Maj.	Major
MB	*Medicinae Baccalaureus* Bachelor of Medicine
MBA	Master of Business Administration
MBE	Member, Order of the British Empire
MC	Master of Ceremonies
	Military Cross
MCB	Muslim Council of Britain
MCC	Marylebone Cricket Club

MCH(D)	Master of (Dental) Surgery
MDS	Master of Dental Surgery
ME	Middle English
	myalgic encephalomyelitis
MED	Master of Education
Mgr	Monsignor
MIT	Massachusetts Institute of Technology
MLA	Member of Legislative Assembly (NI)
MLITT	Master of Letters
Mlle	Mademoiselle
MM	Military Medal
Mme	Madame
MMR	measles, mumps and rubella (vaccine)
MN	Merchant Navy
MPHIL	Master of Philosophy
MR	Master of the Rolls
MRI	magnetic resonance imaging
MRSA	methicillin-resistant staphylococcus aureus
MS	manuscript (*pl* MSS)
	Master of Surgery
	multiple sclerosis
MSP	Member of Scottish Parliament
MUSB/D	Bachelor/Doctor of Music
MVO	Member, Royal Victorian Order

N

NAAFI	Navy, Army and Air Force Institutes
NAFTA	North American Free Trade Agreement
NAO	National Audit Office
NCO	non-commissioned officer
NDPB	non-departmental public body
NFU	National Farmers' Union
non seq	*non sequitur* it does not follow
Norvic:	of Norwich (Bishop)
NP	Notary Public
NSW	New South Wales (Australia)
NUJ	National Union of Journalists
NUS	National Union of Students
NUT	National Union of Teachers

O

Ob *or* obit	died
OBE	Officer, Order of the British Empire
OBR	Office for Budget Responsibility
OE	Old English
OED	*Oxford English Dictionary*
OHMS	On Her/His Majesty's Service
OM	Order of Merit
ono	or near(est) offer
op	*opus* work
op cit	*opere citato* in the work cited
OS	Ordnance Survey
OStJ	Officer, Order of St John of Jerusalem

P

PC	Plaid Cymru
	Police Constable
	Privy Counsellor
Petriburg:	of Peterborough (Bishop)
PG	parental guidance
	postgraduate
PHD	Doctor of Philosophy
pl	plural
PLO	Palestine Liberation Organisation
PM	post mortem
	Prime Minister
PO	Petty Officer
	Pilot Officer
	postal order
PPS	Parliamentary Private Secretary
PR	proportional representation
PRA	President of the Royal Academy
pro tem	*pro tempore* for the time being
prox	*proximo* next month
PRS	President of the Royal Society

PRSE	President of the Royal Society of Edinburgh
Pte.	Private

Q

QBD	Queen's Bench Division
QC	Queen's Counsel
QE	quantitative easing
QED	*quod erat demonstrandum* which was to be proved
QGM	Queen's Gallantry Medal
QHC	Queen's Honorary Chaplain
QHDS	Queen's Honorary Dental Surgeon
QHNS	Queen's Honorary Nursing Sister
QHP	Queen's Honorary Physician
QHS	Queen's Honorary Surgeon
QMG	Quartermaster-General
QPM	Queen's Police Medal
QSO	quasi-stellar object *(quasar)*
	Queen's Service Order
quango	quasi-autonomous non-governmental organisation
qv	*quod vide* which see

R

r.	*recto* on the right-hand page
R	*Regina* Queen
	Rex King
RA	Royal Academy/Academician
	Royal Artillery
RAC	Royal Armoured Corps
RADA	Royal Academy of Dramatic Art
RADC	Royal Army Dental Corps
RAEC	Royal Army Educational Corps
RAES	Royal Aeronautical Society
	Royal Academy of Music
RAMC	Royal Army Medical Corps
RAVC	Royal Army Veterinary Corps
RC	Red Cross
	Roman Catholic
RCN	Royal College of Nursing
RD	Royal Naval and Royal Marine Forces Reserve Decoration
REME	Royal Electrical and Mechanical Engineers
Rep	Republican
Rep.	Republic
Revd	Reverend
RGS	Royal Geographical Society
RHS	Royal Horticultural Society
RI	Royal Institute of Painters in Watercolours
	Royal Institution
RIR	Royal Irish Regiment
RM	Royal Marines
RMA	Royal Military Academy
RMT	National Union of Rail, Maritime and Transport Workers
RNIB	Royal National Institute of Blind People
RNID	Royal National Institute for Deaf People
RNR	Royal Naval Reserve
Roffen:	of Rochester (Bishop)
RPA	Rural Payments Agency
RSA	Royal Scottish Academician
	Royal Society of Arts
RSC	Royal Shakespeare Company
RSE	Royal Society of Edinburgh
Rt. Hon.	Right Honourable
RVS	Royal Voluntary Service

S

s	section (Public Acts)
	solidus shilling
Salop	Shropshire

Sarum:	of Salisbury (Bishop)
SCD	Doctor of Science
SDLP	Social Democratic and Labour Party
SEAQ	Stock Exchange Automated Quotations system
SEN	special educational needs
SF	Sinn Fein
SFO	Serious Fraud Office
SI	statutory instrument
	Système International d'Unités International System of Units
sic	*sic* so written
sig	signature
	Signor
SOE	Special Operations Executive
sp	*sine prole* without issue
Sr	Senior
	Sister (title)
SS	steamship
stet	*stet* let it stand (printing)
Sub Lt.	sub-lieutenant

T

TEFL	teaching English as a foreign language
TNT	trinitrotoluene (explosive)
trans.	translated
TRH	Their Royal Highnesses
trs	transpose (printing)

U

U	Unionist
uc	upper case (printing)
UDA	Ulster Defence Association
UG	undergraduate
UNESCO	United Nations Educational, Scientific, and Cultural Organization
USB	universal serial bus
USMCA	United States-Mexico-Canada Agreement
UTC	*Temps Universel Coordonné* coordinated universal time
UVF	Ulster Volunteer Force

V

v	*versus* against
v.	*verso* on the left-hand page
VC	Victoria Cross
Ven	Venerable
VR	Volunteer Reserves Service Medal
VSO	Voluntary Service Overseas

W

w.	widowed
WBC	World Boxing Council
WBO	World Boxing Organisation
WCC	World Council of Churches
WFTU	World Federation of Trade Unions
Winton:	of Winchester (Bishop)
WO	Warrant Officer
WRAC	Women's Royal Army Corps
WRAF	Women's Royal Air Force
WRNS	Women's Royal Naval Service
WS	Writer to the Signet

Y

YMCA	Young Men's Christian Association
YWCA	Young Women's Christian Association

Z

ZANU-PF	Zimbabwean African National Union-Patriotic Front

INDEX